REFERENCE ENCYCLOPEDIA

OF THE
AMERICAN INDIAN
4TH EDITION

BARRY T. KLEIN

Published by:
Todd Publications
P.O. Box 92
Lenox Hill Station
New York, New York 10021

REFERENCE ENCYCLOPEDIA OF THE AMERICAN INDIAN

Fourth Edition, Volume I

Copyright © 1986

TODD PUBLICATIONS

Library of Congress Catalog Card Number 86-050046

CONTENTS

INTRODUCTION

The course of U.S. Government relations with Indians began in colonial days and underwent several subsequent evolutions. The Continental Congress created the first Indian commissioners--among whom were Patrick Henry and Benjamin Franklin--to oversee trade with Indian tribes and cement military alliances. When the period of land purchases began shortly after the United States became an independent nation, there commenced the effort to exchange Indian lands in the East for lands in Indian Territory carved from the Louisiana Purchase. As the American population grew, and western lands also began to be coveted, U.S. Indian policy moved to one of military force. After the Indian wars came the treaty-making period and creation of reservations in the West. Then, later, came the effort to break up tribal Indian land holdings by allotting them to individual tribal members which caused the sale of much of the best Indian lands. Finally, in 1934, we entered a new era under the Indian Reorganization Act, which provided for restoration of tribal governments and launched a policy of Federal financial and technical aid to tribal groups. This is the basis for the trusteeship role played by the Bureau of Indian Affairs today over more than 50 million acres of Indian land.

Unintentionally, there evolved a "dependent" society among the tribal groups that emerged after 1934, and, although the situation today can be credited with making possible the survival of some Indian land areas and has slowed down the sale of these lands, it has also deprived the American community of possible contributions that the Indian people might have made to the shaping of contemporary society.

Most American Indians today are people in transition between two worlds. The problem facing Indians now is to adjust to contemporary life and not bury all Indian tradition and philosophy in the dust of history, which would be to deprive the American community of a heritage that is both timeless and timely. Also, today, emerging on the contemporary scene, is a new American Indian, still too often plagued by the poverty that stems from his physical isolation, but nonetheless a more vocal Indian, with a greater awareness of his place in American history and his role in contemporary society. This new group among the Indian people are newsmakers and trendsetters, as more and more of their number rise in the ranks of teachers and artists, public officials and businessmen.

According to figures released by the U.S. Census Bureau, there are approximately 1,750,000 American Indians, Eskimos and Aleuts in the United States. The most populous states in terms of Indians is California with approximately 225,000, Oklahoma, 175,000, Arizona, 160,000, and New Mexico, 115,000; Alaska has more than 65,000 Eskimos and Aleuts. Population figures have been increasing at a rate of more than 70% per decade since 1960. There is no one Federal or tribal definition that establishes a person's identity as Indian. Government Agencies use different criteria for determining who is an Indian. Similarly, tribal groups have varying requirements for determining tribal membership.

There are about 300 Federal Indian reservations and about 500 federally recognized tribes in the United States including 197 Alaska Native village groups. An Indian reservation is an area of land reserved for Indian use. The name comes from the early days of Indian-white relations when Indian tribes relinquished land through treaties, "reserving" a portion for their own use. Congressional acts, Executive orders, and agreements have also created reservations. Many reservations today, however, have some non-Indian residents and non-Indian landowners. "Tribe" among the North American Indians originally meant a body of

i

persons bound together by blood ties who were socially, politically, and religiously organized, and who lived together, occupying a definite territory and speaking a common language or dialect. With the relegation of Indians to reservations, the word "tribe" developed a number of different meanings. Today, it can be a distinct group within an Indian village or community, a large number of communities, several different groups or villages speaking different languages but sharing a common government, or a widely scatttered number of villages with a common language but no common government. According to a 1985 estimate of the Bureau of Indian Affairs, about 787,000 Indians live on or adjacent to Indian reservations. The remaining 1,000,000 American Indians reside in cities and suburbs across the country.

This Fourth Edition of *Reference Encyclopedia of the American Indian,* Volume I, is divided into two main parts. The first part contains source listings of organizations, associations, government agencies, reservations and tribal councils, museum and library collections, Indian health services, Indian schools, university and college course offerings, magazines and periodicals, and audio-visual material. Each listing gives address, phone number, chief personnel and, in most cases, a brief description of activities and pertinent information. Listings are arranged either alphabetically or alpha-geographically within categories. At the beginning of each section there is an explanatory note detailing the type of sources listed and the manner in which they are arranged. The length of each listing reflects the amount of material received from each source. Material has been researched directly from questionnaires or has been gathered from other reliable sources. For further information on any listed source, it is suggested that the reader write to the address or call the number given in the listing. The second part of the book is a bibliography of approximately 4,500 in-print books. Listed alphabetically, each book gives basic bibliographic information. The alphabetical section is broken down into a subject categories section with corresponding titles listed for each category. In many cases titles are repeated in two or more subject areas. A publishers index is provided at the end giving the publishers' addresses and phone numbers.

Much has been written about American Indians. Among their ranks are statesmen, scholars and artists. The magnitude of their role can be measured by the mass of material relating to Indians and Indian affairs that has been catalogued in this volume. It should serve the valued purposes of helping the Indian people to know more about themselves and helping their fellow Americans to understand better the contributions Indian people have made to the greatness of America.

Reference Encyclopedia of the American Indian, Volume II, Who's Who, a separate companion volume, contains approximately 1,500 biographical sketches of American Indians prominent in Indian Affairs, business, the arts and professions, as well as non-Indians active in Indian affairs, history, art, anthropology, archaeology, etc., and the many fields to which the subject of the American Indian is related.

Barry T. Klein
Editor

REFERENCE ENCYCLOPEDIA OF THE AMERICAN INDIAN

GOVERNMENT AGENCIES

This section is an alpha-geographical listing of government agencies—regional and state, mainly—concerned in various ways with the American Indian and his affairs. The principal federal agency in this area is the Bureau of Indian Affairs of the U.S. Department of the Interior. The following is a description of the activities of the Bureau, with a directory of its Central (Washington, D.C.) Office. The geographical listings follow.

BUREAU OF INDIAN AFFAIRS
1951 Constitution Ave., N.W.
WASHINGTON, D.C. 20245
  Ross O. Swimmer, Assistant Secretary
  Room 4160 N (202) 343-7163
  Carl Shaw, Director-Public Information Office
  Room 4627 N (202) 343-7445

Established in 1824, the Bureau of Indian Affairs is an agency of the U.S. Department of the Interior. Its original function was the trusteeship of Indian lands—which now number some fifty-three million acres of land held in trust by the U.S. for various Indian tribes and individuals. Though most trust land is reservation land, all reservation land is not trust land. The Secretary of the Interior functions on behalf of the U.S. as the trustee, with many of the more routine responsibilities delegated to the Bureau of Indian Affairs officials. The principal objectives of the Bureau are to actively encourage and train Indian and Alaskan Native people to manage their own affairs under the trust relationship to the Federal Government; to facilitate, with maximum involvement of Indian and Alaskan Native people, full development of their human and natural resource potentials; to mobilize all public and private aides to the advancement of Indian and Alaskan Native people for use by them; and to utilize the skill and capabilities of Indian and Alaskan Native people in the direction and management of programs for their benefit. *Today,* the Bureau provides a great many services and programs for Native Americans, some of which include:

Budget — The Bureau receives approximately one billion dollars per year for its programs and projects. This includes about $250 million for education; $250 million for Indian services which include law enforcement, social service programs and other local governmental programs; $100 million for natural resources development; $50 million for trust responsibilities; $100 million for facilities management; $75 million for general administration; and $75 million for construction. The B.I.A. receives an additional $100 million for reservation road construction through the Department of Transportation, under provisions of the Highway Improvement Act of 1982.

Education — There are approximately 250,000 Indian children of school age, two-thirds of whom are enrolled in public schools. *Legislation:* In recent years, two major laws have resulted in a restructuring of the entire Bureau education program. In 1975, the passage of P.L. 93-638, The Indian Self Determination and Education Assistance Act, greatly facilitated contracting for the operation of education programs by tribal groups. The passage of P.L. 95-561, The Indian Education Act, in 1978, mandated a major change in the operation of both Bureau-operated and tribally contracted schools. The implementation of P.L. 95-561 resulted in decision making powers for Indian school boards, local hiring of teachers and staff, direct funding to the schools, and increased authority for the Director of Indian Education Programs within the Bureau. *Federal Schools:* In 1986, the B.I.A. will fund a total of 182 education facilities. These include 57 day schools; 46 on-reservation boarding schools; seven off-reservation boarding schools; 58 tribally contracted schools; and 14 dormitories. Dormitories are operated by the Bureau to facilitate public school attendance for Indian students. *Indian Children in Federal Schools:* The estimated average daily membership in schools funded by the B.I.A. for 1986 is expected to be about 41,500, which includes 39,900 instructional and 1,600 dormitory students. *Public School Assistance (Johnson O'Malley Program);* The B.I.A. provides funds under the Johnson-O'Malley Act of 1934 to meet the special needs of Indian students in public schools. These funds, which are largely administered through contracts with tribal organizations, public school districts and state departments of education, enable the contractors to provide supplemental programs for Indian students. Approximately 180,000 Indian students in 26 states receive assistance from JOM funds. The Bureau has JOM contracts for administration and development of programs with about 230 tribal organizations, 76 public schools and six state departments of education. There are more than 800 Indian parent committees working with these contractors. *Indians in College:* Approximately 15,000 Indian students receive scholarship grants from the B.I.A. to enable them to attend colleges and universities. About 150 students receiving B.I.A. assistance are in law school and another 150 are in other graduate programs. The estimated number of college students is 30,000. Total appropriations provided through the B.I.A. for Indian higher education were about $27 million in 1985. *Tribally Controlled Colleges:* The B.I.A. provides grants for the operation of 19 tribally controlled community colleges. There are approximately 3,500 Indian students enrolled in these community colleges. Tribal colleges must pass a stringent feasibility study in order to be eligible for grants under the Tribally Controlled Community College Assistance Act of 1978. *B.I.A. Post-Secondary Schools:* The B.I.A. operates three post-secondary schools. They are Haskell Indian Junior College in Lawrence, Kansas with an enrollment of about 1,000 students; Institute of American Indian Arts at Santa Fe, New Mexico with about 200 students; and Southwestern Indian Polytechnic Institute at Albuquerque, New Mexico with about 700 students.

Health — *Indian Health Service:* An agency of the Department of Health and Human Services and the primary federal health resource for approximately one million eligible American Indians and Alaskan Natives.

Housing — In cooperation with the Department of Housing and Urban Development (HUD) tribes are treated as local government units with authority to establish local housing authorities, the instruments through which Indians may obtain low-income housing from the Federal Government. More than 150 tribes have established such housing authorities. In 1984 Housing inventory by the Bureau revealed that for approximately 185,000 Indian families, there are some 96,000 existing dwellings in standard condition and 54,300 substandard units, 30,700 of which are worth renovating. A total of about 59,000 new homes are required to replace existing substandard dwellings and to provide housing for families now living with other families in overcrowded conditions.

Financing for Indian Enterprises — Because of a lack of understanding of Indian matters, the American private banking industry has been slow to meet the financial requirements of individuals and tribal groups. The American Indian National Bank, established to meet these requirements, is not competitive with the private banking industry, but is rather a practical and educational procedure, both for Indians, and for the banking industry. The stock is owned by Native Americans.

Water Rights — The Office of Indian Water Rights, established in 1972, is designed to protect the water rights of reservation Indians. Since its formation, water allocation studies have been made on many reservations, and legal suits have been filed to protect Indian water.

Forestry — Established in 1910 to bring about order in the management of Indian owned forest property. Some objectives of management are to preserve the property in perpetuity by providing effective protection services, by applying sound silvicultural and economic principles to the harvesting of forest crops, and by making adequate provisions for the continuity in growth of forest crops.

Road Construction — The road construction program on Indian lands has been given increased funding, totalling $100 million as of 1986, which allows for the construction of hundreds of miles of road surfacing, grading and drainage, and for bridges.

Employment with the B.I.A. — The Bureau employs approximately 15,000 people. Native Americans make up more than 75% of that work force. (Preference in employment with the B.I.A. has been granted for some years to Indians who are members of Federally recognized tribes or are one-half or more degree Indian blood.) Native Americans hold most of the top management positions in the Bureau's Central and Area offices and constitutes most of the positions in the Bureau's federally operated schools of which many are teachers, teacher's aides, administrators and workmen.

*   *   *

The following is a directory of the Central (Washington, D.C.) Office (zip code 20245) of the Bureau of Indian Affairs and its various offices and divisions. Listings of B.I.A. area and field offices and agencies may be found under specific states in the geographical part of this section which follows *Independent Agencies.*

Personnel—Office of the Assistant Secretary for Indian Affairs: Ross O. Swimmer, Assistant Secretary; John W. Fritz, Deputy Assistant Secretary; Theodore Sudia, Senior Executive Assistant; Stewart Little, Executive Assistant; Carl F. Shaw, Director-Public Information Office; Richard J. Glynn, Executive Assistant; Leroy V. Clifford, Staff Assistant; Chizu Toda, Special Assistant; Bobby J. Railey, Special Assistant; Jay Gerst, Director-Management Improvement Program; Martha Chino, Staff Assistant-Communications; Carl Thorpe, Equal

Opportunity Officer; Frank Latta, Chief-Division of School Facilities (Box 2147, Albuquerque, N.M. 87103); Richard O. Power, Chief-Division of Facilities Engineering (Box 2147, Albuquerque, N.M. 87103); and Ralph Reeser, Congressional and Legislative Affairs Staff.

Personnel—Office of Trust Responsibilities: Sidney L. Mills, Director; Shirley M. Crosby, Program Coordination Staff; Charles P. Corke, Special Assistant to the Director; George P. Farris, Environmental Services Staff; John Vale, Head - Division of Trust Funds Management (Box 886, Albuquerque, N.M. 87103); William J. Bucholz, Acting Head - Division of Real Estate Services; Marshall M. Cutsforth, Head - Division of Forestry; Charles W. Tandy, Head - Fire Management (Boise Interagency Fire Center, 3905 Vista Ave., Boise, Idaho 83705); Robert W. Miller, Head - Branch of Forest Resources Planning (Box 3785, Portland, OR 97208); Joseph C. Johnston, Head - Division of Energy and Minerals Assistance (733 Simms St., Lakewood Office Plaza, Room 239, Golden, CO 80401); Edward H. Hall, Acting Head - Division of Transportation (Box 2185, Albuquerque, N.M. 87103); Vacant (at time of editing), Division of Water and Land Resources.

Personnel—Office of Indian Education Programs: Dr. Ken Ross, Acting Director; Nancy C. Garrett, Deputy Director; Dr. Dennis Fox, Assistant Director - Agencies; Dr. James Martin, Assistant Director - Areas and Post-Secondary Education; George Scott, Head - Planning, Oversight and Evaluation Staff; Kay Keely, Acting Chief - Branch of Financial Services; Leo Nolan, III, Chief, Branch of Management Information Systems; Samuel Johnson, Chief - Division of Education Programs; William Mehojah, Chief - Branch of Elementary and Secondary Education; Dr. Charles Cordova, Chief-Branch of Exceptional Education; Harvey Jacobs, Chief - Branch of Supplemental Support Services; Vacant, Chief - Branch of Administrative Services, and Chief - Branch of Post-Secondary Education.

Personnel—Office of Indian Services: Theodore Krenzke, Director; Hazel E. Elbert, Deputy Director and Acting Chief - Division of Tribal Government Services; John Geary, Head - Program and Budget; Joseph Weller, Chief Division of Financial Assistance; Ralph R. Pensoneau, Chief - Division of Law Enforcement Services; Mitchell Bush, Chief - Branch of Tribal Enrollment; John Shapard, Chief - Branch of Acknowledgement and Research; Ed Brown,

Chief - Division of Social Services; G. Ronald Peake, Chief - Division of Housing Services; Jay T. Suagee, Chief-Division of Self - Determination Services; and Robert Delaware, Chief - Division of Job Placement and Training.

Personnel—Office of Administration: Ronal D. Eden, Acting Director, and Deputy Director; Wilson C. Brady, Information Systems Specialist; Donald F. Asbra, Head - Contracting and Grants Administration Staff; Peter S. Markey, Head - Contracting and Grants Operations; Irene Fischer, Chief - Division of Personnel Management; and Sara Matte, Chief - Branch of Personnel Services.

Personnel—Financial Management: Charles B. Hughes, Assistant Director; Robert Walker, Chief - Division of Accounting Management; Salvador Nunez, Chief - Branch of Employee Data (Box 2026, Albuquerque, NM 87103); Don Gray, Chief - Branch of Finance and Accounting (Box 127, Albuquerque, NM 87103); Ike Eisenzimmer, Head - Financial Management Services (Box 127, Albuquerque, NM 87103); Thomas Stangl, Chief - Division of Program Development and Implementation; Glenda Brokeshoulder, Program Implementation Coordinator; and Geraldine Mitchell, Head - Budget and Finance Unit.

Personnel—Management Services: Charles Jaynes, Chief - Division of Safety Management (Field Safety Office, Box 2186, Albuquerque, NM 87103); James Dunn, Chief - Division of Management Research and Evaluation; Sam Adams, Chief - Branch of Organization and Evaluation; James Pinkerton, Acting Chief - Branch of Directives and Regulatory Management; Robert Parisien, Chief - Branch of Systems Control; Gilbert Robinson, Head - Files, Records, and Paper Work Services; Sara Hawkins, Records Supervisor; Charles E. Carter, Chief - Division of Property Management; James Harjo, Chief-Branch of Policy and Program Review; David Nephew, Chief - Branch of Property and Supply Operations; Nathaniel W. Lewis, Chief - Branch of Property Inventory Management; Ernest C. Bailey, Chief - Branch of Correspondence and Mail Distribution, and Notary Public; and Leon R. Leuppe, Chief - Branch of Correspondence-Telefax.

Personnel—Office of Data Systems: James S. Bregman, Acting Director.

Personnel—Indian Arts and Crafts Board: Robert Hart, General Manager (Room 4004)

* * *

The following are federal offices that direct special programs for Indians and related other federal and congressional offices.

EXECUTIVE BRANCH

The White House, 1600 Pennsylvania Ave., N.W., Washington, D.C. 20500 (202) 456-1414

Personnel: Robert Gleason, Jr., Special Assistant to the President for Intergovernment Affairs, Old Executive Office Bldg., Room 122, 17th and Pennsylvania Ave., N.W., Washington, D.C. 20500 (202) 456-7700; also, Hal Gordon, Senior Policy Analyst, Office of Policy Information (202) 456-6250; and Melvin Bradley, Minorities Special Assistant to the President, Public Liaison (202) 456-6560.

The Department of Agriculture, 14th and Independence Ave., S.W., Washington, D.C. 20250 (202) 447-2791

Personnel: Richard E. Lyng, Secretary - Room 200-A (202) 447-3631; Lawrence Bembry, Associate Director - Office of Equal Opportunity, Office of the Secretary, Room 102-W (202) 447-5681; Stuart Jamieson, Coordinator, Indian Affairs - Office of Intergovernmental Affairs, Room 102A, Administration Bldg., (202) 447-3805; Douglas V. Sellars, Liaison for Indian Assistance, Rural Development Staff, Soil Conservation Service, Room 6103, South Bldg., P.O. Box 2890, Washington, D.C. 20013 (202) 382-1855.

Department of Education, 400 Maryland Ave., S.W., Washington, D.C. 20201 (202) 245-3192

Personnel: William J. Bennett, Secretary-Room 4181 (202) 426-6420; Elizabeth Davis, Office of Bilingual Education and Minority Language Affairs, Room 422, Reporter's Bldg. (202) 245-2609; David Mack, Assistant Director - Regional Programs, National Institute of Education, Room 822 K, 1200 19th St., N.W., Washington, D.C. 20208 (202) 254-5654; Lincoln White, Executive Director — National Advisory Council on Indian Education (NACIE), 2000 L St., N.W., Suite 574, Washington, D.C. 20036 (202) 634-6160; and Frank Ryan, Director - Indian Education Programs, Room 2177, Federal Office Bldg. #6, Washington, D.C. 20202 (202) 732-1887.

Department of Energy, 1000 Independence Ave., S.W., Washington, D.C. 20585 (202) 252-5000

Personnel: John H. Herrington, Secretary, Room 7A257 (202) 6210; Marie A. Monsen, Chief of Local and Indian Affairs - Office of Intergovernmental Affairs, Room 8G045, Forrstal Bldg. (202) 252-5661.

Department of Health and Human Services, Humphrey Bldg., 200 Independence Ave., S.W., Washington, D.C. 20201 (202) 245-6296

Personnel: Margaret M. Heckler, Secretary, Room 615 F (202) 245-7000; Dr. Everett R. Rhoades, Director - Indian Health Service, Room 5A-55, Parklawn Bldg., 5600 Fishers Lane, Rockville, MD 20857 (301) 443-1083; Pecita Lonewolf, Director - Indian and Migrant Programs, Head Start Bureau, Room 5550, Donahoe Bldg., 400 6th St., S.W., Washington, D.C. 20201 (202) 755-7715; William Lynn Engels, Commissioner - Administration for Native Americans, Office of Human Development Services, Room 5300, North Bldg., 330 Independence Ave., S.W., Washington, D.C. 20201 (202) 245-7776; G. Sandra Fisher, Director - Division of Program Management and Regional Operations, Office of State and Tribal Programs - Administration on Aging, Room 4276, 330 Independence Ave., S.W., Washington, D.C. 20201 (202) 245-1826; and Sandra Spaulding, Executive Director - Intra-Departmental Council on Indian Affairs, Room 5300, North Bldg., 330 Independence Ave., S.W., Washington, D.C. 20201 (202) 245-6546.

Department of Housing and Urban Development (HUD), 451 7th St., S.W. Washington, D.C. 20410 (202) 755-5111

Personnel: Samuel R. Pierce, Jr., Secretary, Room 10000 (202) 755-6417; Raymond E. Combs, Special Assistant to the Secretary for Indian and Alaska Native Programs, Room 10222 (202) 755-6648; Warren T. Lindquist, Assistant Secretary for Public and Indian Housing, Room 4100 (202) 755-0950; John Meyers, Director Designate - Office of Indian Housing, Room 4232 (202) 755-6522; Patricia S.A. Arnado, Deputy Director - Office of Indian Housing, Room 4230; Alfred C. Moran, Special Assistant to the Secretary for Community Planning and Development, Room 7100 (202) 755-6270; and Marcia Brown, Assistant to the Director, Secretary's Fund, Indian Community Development Block Grant Program, Room 7134 (202) 755-6092.

Department of the Interior, 18th and C Sts, N.W., Washington, D.C. 20240 (202) 343-7220

Personnel: Donald P. Hodel, Secretary, Room 6151 (202) 343-7351; Tim Vollmann, Associate Solicitor - Division of Indian Affairs, Office of the Solicitor, Room 6458 (202) 343-9401; Ross O. Swimmer, Assistant Secretary for Indian Affairs, Room 4160 (202) 343-7163; Robert G. Hart, General Manager - Indian Arts and Crafts Board, Room 4004 (202) 343-2773; and Bernard V. Parrette, Chief Administrative Judge - Interior Board of Indian Appeals, 4015 Wilson Blvd., Room 1105, Arlington, VA 22203 (703) 235-3816.

Department of Justice, 10th and Constitution Ave., N.W., Washington, D.C. 20530 (202) 633-2000

Personnel: Edwin Meese, Attorney General, Room 5111 (202) 633-2001; James Brookshire, Chief - Indian Claims Section, Land and Natural Resources Division, Room 648, 550 11th St., N.W., Washington, D.C. 20530 (202) 724-7375; Hank Meshorer, Chief - Indian Resources Section, Land and Natural Resources Division, Room 624 (202) 724-7156; Gilbert G. Pompa, Director - Community Relations Service, Suite 330, 5550 Friendship Blvd., Chevy Chase, MD 20015 (301) 492-5929; and James M. Schermerhorn, Special Litigation Counsel - Civil Rights Division, Room 5704 (202) 633-4701.

Department of Labor, 200 Constitution Ave., N.W., Washington, D.C. 20210 (202) 523-6666

Personnel: Herbert Fellman, Chief - Division of Indian and Native American Programs, Employment and Training Administration, Room 6102, Patrick Henry Bldg., 601 D St., N.W., Washington, D.C. 20213 (202) 376-6442; and Mary Natani, Social Science Advisor - Division of Experimental Programs, Women's Bureau, Room S3319 (202) 523-6648.

Department of Transportation, 400 7th St., S.W., Washington, D.C. 20590 (202) 426-4000

Personnel: Elizabeth H. Dole, Secretary, Room 10200 (202) 426-1111; Sam Lubbert, Coordinator - American Indian Highway Safety, Office of State Program Assistance, National Highway Traffic Safety Administration, Room 7410 (202) 426-0837; and Michael Virts, Native American Program Coordinator - Office of Civil Rights, U.S. Urban Mass Transportation Administration, Room 7410 (202) 426-4018.

Department of the Treasury, 15th and Pennsylvania Ave., N.W., Washington, D.C. 20220 (202) 566-2111

Personnel: James A. Baker, III, Secretary, Room 3330 (202) 566-2533; and Fred Williams, Native Governments Coordinator - Office of Revenue Sharing, 2401 E St., N.W., Washington, D.C. 20226 (202) 634-5200.

LEGISLATIVE BRANCH
U.S. CONGRESS

SENATE

Select Committee on Indian Affairs, Room SH 838, Hart Senate Office Bldg., Washington, D.C. 20510

Personnel: Senator Mark Andrews (R-ND), Chairman (202) 224-2043; and Peter Taylor, Staff Director (202) 224-2251.

HOUSE OF REPRESENTATIVES

Committee on Interior and Insular Affairs, Room 1324, Longworth House Office Bldg., New Jersey and Independence Aves., S.E., Washington, D.C. 20515

Personnel: Congressman Morris K. Udall (D-AZ), Chairman (202) 225-4065; Franklin Ducheneaux, Counsel on Indian Affairs, Room 522, House Annex 1, C and New Jersey Ave., S.E., Washington, D.C. 20515 (202) 226-7393; and Michael D. Jackson, Republican Consultant on Indian Affairs, Room 501, House Annex 1 (202) 226-2311.

INDEPENDENT AGENCIES

Environmental Protection Agency, 401 M St., S.W., Washington, D.C. 20460 (202) 382-2090

Personnel: B. Leigh Price, Coordinator - Indian Work Group, Office of Federal Activities, Room 2119 (202) 382-5049.

Commission on Civil Rights, 1121 Vermont Ave., N.W., Washington, D.C. 20425

Personnel: John Hope, III, Deputy Staff Director for Regional Programs (202) 245-8130; and Caroline Davis Gleiter, Assistant Staff Director for Program and Policy Review (202) 376-8379.

Small Business Administration, 1441 L St., N.W., Washington, D.C. 20416 (202) 653-6601

Personnel: Maurine Fisher, General Business and Industry Specialist - Minority Small Business, Room 602 (202) 653-6851.

ALASKA

ANCHORAGE AGENCY
Bureau of Indian Affairs
P.O. Box 100120
ANCHORAGE 99501
(907) 271-4088
Albert Kahklen, Superintendent

Responsible for six Indian regional cooperative schools, and the maintenance of plant facilities for an additional 21 schools; active in numerous other projects and functions related to regional problems. *Tribes served:* Eskimo, Athapascan, Aleut. *Total population served:* 20,000. Under jurisdiction of Juneau Area Office.

BETHEL AGENCY
Bureau of Indian Affairs
P.O. Box 347
BETHEL 99559
(907) 543-2726
Anthony Vaska, Superintendent

Area served: Southwestern Alaska—Calista Region. *Tribe served:* Yup'ik Eskimo. *Total population served:* 20,000. *Programs:* All BIA programs—grants, natural resources, realty, social services, housing, etc. Under jurisdiction of Juneau Area Office.

FAIRBANKS AGENCY
Bureau of Indian Affairs
101 12th Ave., Box 16
FAIRBANKS 99707
(907) 456-0222
Perry Baker, Superintendent

Tribes served: Eskimo, Athapascan. *Total population served:* 12,000. Under jurisdiction of Juneau Area Office.

JUNEAU AREA OFFICE
Bureau of Indian Affairs
P.O. Box 3-8000
JUNEAU 99802
(907) 586-7177
Jacob Lestenkof, Area Director

Administers all BIA services within the State of Alaska. Responsible for the following agencies: Anchorage, Bethel, Fairbanks, Nome, Southeast, and the Seattle Support Center. *Tribes served:* Eskimo, Aleut, and Alaska Indians. *Total population served:* 70,000.

SOUTHEAST AGENCY
Bureau of Indian Affairs
P.O. Box 3-8000
JUNEAU 99802
(907) 586-7304
David A. Horton, Jr., Superintendent

Tribes served: Tlingit and Haida. *Total population served:* 12,000. Under jurisdiction of Juneau Area Office.

METLAKATLA FIELD STATION
Bureau of Indian Affairs
P.O. Box 560
METLAKATLA 99926
(907) 886-3791
Henry C. Alameda, Sr., Superintendent

Under jurisdiction of Portland Area Office.

NOME AGENCY
Bureau of Indian Affairs
P.O. Box 1108
NOME 99762
(907) 443-2284
George A. Walters, Superintendent

ARIZONA

CHINLE AGENCY
Bureau of Indian Affairs
P.O. Box 7H
CHINLE 86503
(602) 674-5211
Thomas H. Begay

Tribe served: Navajo. Under jurisdiction of Navajo Area Office.

SAN CARLOS IRRIGATION PROJECT
Bureau of Indian Affairs
COOLIDGE 85228
(602) 723-5439
Ralph Esquerra, Superintendent

Under jurisdiction of Phoenix Area Office.

FORT DEFIANCE AGENCY
Bureau of Indian Affairs
P.O. Box 619
FORT DEFIANCE 86504
(602) 729-5041
Wilfred Brown, Superintendent

Tribe served: Navajo. Under jurisdiction of Navajo Area Office.

HOPI AGENCY
Bureau of Indian Affairs
KEAMS CANYON 86034
(602) 738-2228
Alph Secakuku, Superintendent

Tribes served: Hopi and Paiute. *Total population served:* 7,500. Under jurisdiction of Phoenix Area Office.

COLORADO RIVER AGENCY
Bureau of Indian Affairs
Route 1, Box 9-C
PARKER 85344
(602) 669-2134
Walter R. Mills, Superintendent

Tribes served: Chemehuevi, Colorado River (in Arizona and California), Mohave (in Arizona, California and Nevada.) *Total population served:* 6,500. Under jurisdiction of Phoenix Area Office.

PHOENIX AREA OFFICE
Bureau of Indian Affairs
3030 N. Central, Box 7007
PHOENIX 85011
(602) 261-2305
James Stevens, Area Director

Administers BIA programs for regions of Arizona, California, Nevada and Utah. Responsible for the following agencies: Colorado River, Eastern Nevada, Fort Apache, Fort Yuma, Hopi, Papago, Pima, Salt River, San Carlos, San Carlos Irrigation Project, Truxton Canon, Uintah and Ouray, and Western Nevada.

PIMA AGENCY
Bureau of Indian Affairs
SACATON 85247
(602) 562-3326
Edmond Thompson, Superintendent

Tribes served: Papago, Pima, and Maricopa. *Total population served:* 10,000. Under jurisdiction of Phoenix Area Office.

SAN CARLOS AGENCY
Bureau of Indian Affairs
SAN CARLOS 85550
(602) 475-2321
George Keller, Superintendent

Tribe served: Apache. *Total population served:* 5,500. Under jurisdiction of Phoenix Area Office.

SALT RIVER AGENCY
Bureau of Indian Affairs
Route 1, Box 117
SCOTTSDALE 85256
(602) 241-2842
James Barber, Superintendent

Tribes served: Pima, Maricopa, Mohave, and Apache. *Total population served:* 3,500. Under jurisdiction of Phoenix Area Office.

PAPAGO AGENCY
Bureau of Indian Affairs
SELLS 85634
(602) 383-7286
Curtis Nordwall, Superintendent

Tribe served: Papago. *Total population served:* 11,000. Under jurisdiction of Phoenix Area Office.

WESTERN NAVAJO AGENCY
Bureau of Indian Affairs
P.O. Box 127
TUBA CITY 86045
(602) 283-6265
Irving Billy, Superintendent

Tribe served: Navajo. Under jurisdiction of Navajo Area Office.

TRUXTON CANON AGENCY
Bureau of Indian Affairs
P.O. Box 37
VALENTINE 86437
(602) 769-2241
C.L. Henson, Superintendent

Tribes served: Hualapai, Havasupai, Yavapai-Apache, Yavapai-Prescott, and Payson Tonto-Apache. *Total population served:* 3,000. Under jurisdiction of Phoenix Area Office.

FORT APACHE AGENCY
Bureau of Indian Affairs
WHITERIVER 85941
(602) 338-4364
Henry Dodge, Superintendent

Tribe served: Apache. *Total population served:* 7,000. Under jurisdiction of Phoenix Area Office.

NAVAJO AREA OFFICE
Bureau of Indian Affairs
P.O. Box M, Box 1
WINDOW ROCK 86515
(602) 871-5151
Wilson Barber, Area Director

Responsible for the following agencies: Navajo Area Office (Administration), Chinle, Eastern Navajo, Fort Defiance, Navajo Irrigation Project, Shiprock, and Western Navajo. *Tribe served:* Navajo (in Arizona, New Mexico and Utah.) *Total population served:* 165,000.

FORT YUMA AGENCY
Bureau of Indian Affairs
P.O. Box 1591
YUMA 85364
(714) 572-0248
Felix J. Montague, Superintendent

Tribes served: Cocopah, and Quechan (in California and Arizona.) *Total population served:* 1,800. Under jurisdiction of Phoenix Area Office.

CALIFORNIA

HOOPA AGENCY
Bureau of Indian Affairs
P.O. Box 367
HOOPA 95546
  (916) 625-4285
  Wilson Barber, Jr., Superintendent

Tribe served: Hoopa. *Total population served:*
2,500. Under jurisdiction of Sacramento Area
Office.

PALM SPRINGS FIELD OFFICE
Bureau of Indian Affairs
P.O. Box 2245
441 S. Calle Encilia, Suite 8
PALM SPRINGS 92262
  (619) 325-2086
  Richard S. McDermott

Under jurisdiction of Sacramento Area Office.

SOUTHERN CALIFORNIA AGENCY
Bureau of Indian Affairs
5750 Division St., Suite 201
RIVERSIDE 92506
  (714) 351-6624
  Tom Dowell, Superintendent

Serves the Mission area in southern California.
Under jurisdiction of Sacramento Area Office.

CENTRAL CALIFORNIA AGENCY
Bureau of Indian Affairs
1800 Tribute Rd.
P.O. Box 15740
SACRAMENTO 95813-0740
  (916) 484-4357
  Ronald Jaegar, Superintendent

Under jurisdiction of Sacramento Area Office.

SACRAMENTO AREA OFFICE
Bureau of Indian Affairs
Federal Office Bldg.
2800 Cottage Way
SACRAMENTO 95825
  (916) 484-4682
  Maurice W. Babby, Area Director

Administers BIA programs through the following
agencies: Central California, Hoopa, Southern
California, and Palm Springs Field Office. *Total
population served:* 45,000.

COLORADO

ALBUQUERQUE AREA OFFICE
Bureau of Indian Affairs
19th & Stout Sts.
DENVER 80202
  (303) 837-4281

District office of Albuquerque Area Office.

SOUTHERN UTE AGENCY
Bureau of Indian Affairs
P.O. Box 315
IGNACIO 81137
  (303) 563-4511
  Ralph Pensoneau, Superintendent

Tribe served: Ute. *Total population served:* 1,000.
Under jurisdiction of Albuquerque Area Office.

UTE MOUNTAIN UTE AGENCY
Bureau of Indian Affairs
TOWAOC 81334
  (303) 565-8471
  Michael H. Smith

Tribe served: Ute. *Total population served:* 1,750.
Under jurisdiction of Albuquerque Area Office.

DISTRICT OF COLUMBIA

BUREAU OF INDIAN AFFAIRS
1951 Constitution Ave., N.W.
WASHINGTON 20245

See *Central Office* listing at the beginning of this
section.

EASTERN AREA OFFICE
Bureau of Indian Affairs
1951 Constitution Ave., N.W.
WASHINGTON 20245
  (703) 235-2571
  William Ott, Area Director

Administers BIA programs through the following
agencies: Cherokee, Choctaw, Miccosukee,
Seminole, and New York Liaison Office.

INDIAN ARTS AND CRAFTS BOARD
Room 4004, U.S. Dept. of the Interior
WASHINGTON 20240
  (202) 343-2773
  Robert G. Hart, General Manager

Purpose: To promote the development of Indian
arts and crafts. *Activities:* Provides business and
personal professional advice, information, and
promotion to artists and craftsmen and their
organizations; operates three regional museums
located in reservation areas. *Publication: Indian,
Eskimo, Aleut Owned and Operated Arts
Businesses Source Directory.* Founded 1936.

FLORIDA

SEMINOLE AGENCY
Bureau of Indian Affairs
6075 Stirling Rd.
HOLLYWOOD 33024
(305) 581-7050
Harold L. LaRoche, Superintendent

Tribe served: Seminole. *Total population served:* 1,750. Under jurisdiction of Eastern Area Office.

MICCOSUKEE AGENCY
Bureau of Indian Affairs
P.O. Box 44021
TAMIAMI STATION 33144
(305) 323-8380
Buffalo Tiger, Superintendent

Tribe served: Miccosukee-Creek. *Total population served:* 600. Under jurisdiction of Eastern Area Office.

IDAHO

FORT HALL AGENCY
Bureau of Indian Affairs
FORT HALL 83203
(208) 237-0600
Duane Thompson, Superintendent

Tribes served: Shoshone and Bannock. *Total population served:* 4,000. Under jurisdiction of Portland Area Office.

NORTHERN IDAHO AGENCY
Bureau of Indian Affairs
LAPWAI 83540-0277
(208) 843-2267
Wyman J. McDonald, Superintendent

Tribes served: Coeur d'Alene, Kootenai, and Nez Perce. *Total population served:* 2,200. Under jurisdiction of Portland Area Office.

IOWA

SAC AND FOX AREA FIELD OFFICE
Bureau of Indian Affairs
TAMA 52339
(515) 484-4041
George Buffalo, Jr., Area Director

Tribe served: Sac and Fox. *Total population served:* 850. Under jurisdiction of Minneapolis Area Office.

KANSAS

HORTON AGENCY
Bureau of Indian Affairs
P.O. Box 31
HORTON 66439
(913) 486-2161
James Abeita, Superintendent

Tribes served: Iowa, Kickapoo, Sac and Fox, and Potawatomi. *Total population served:* 1,500. Under jurisdiction of Anadarko Area Office.

HASKELL INDIAN JUNIOR COLLEGE
Bureau of Indian Affairs
LAWRENCE 66044
(405) 841-2000
Gerald Gipp, Superintendent

Under jurisdiction of Anadarko Area Office.

MICHIGAN

MICHIGAN AGENCY
Bureau of Indian Affairs
Federal Square Office Plaza
P.O. Box 884
SAULT STE. MARIE 49783
(906) 632-6809
Alvin Picotta —

Under jurisdiction of Minneapolis Area Office.

MINNESOTA

MINNESOTA AGENCY
Bureau of Indian Affairs
RR 2, FC 200
CASS LAKE 56633
(218) 335-6913
Raymond Mayotta, Superintendent

Tribes served: Chippewa and Sioux. *Total population served:* 12,000. Under jurisdiction of Minneapolis Area Office.

MINNEAPOLIS AREA OFFICE
Bureau of Indian Affairs
15 South 5th St., 10th Floor
MINNEAPOLIS 55402
(612) 349-3390
Earl Barlow, Area Director

Administers BIA programs in the State of Iowa, Michigan, Minnesota, and Wisconsin. Responsible for the following agencies and field offices: Great Lakes, Michigan, Minnesota, Minnesota Sioux Area Field Office, Red Lake, and Sac and Fox Area Field Office. *Total population served: 22,000.*

MINNESOTA SIOUX AREA FIELD OFFICE
Bureau of Indian Affairs
2330 Sioux Trail, NW
PRIOR LAKE 55372
(612) 445-6565
Robert Jaeger, Area Director

Under jurisdiction of Minneapolis Field Office.

RED LAKE AGENCY
Bureau of Indian Affairs
RED LAKE 56671
(218) 679-3361
Dennis Whiteman, Superintendent

Tribe served: Chippewa (Red Lake Band.) *Total population served:* 4,500. Under jurisdiction of Minneapolis Area Office.

MISSISSIPPI

CHOCTAW AGENCY
Bureau of Indian Affairs
421 Powell
PHILADELPHIA 39350
(601) 656-1521
Robert C. Mann, Superintendent

Tribe served: Choctaw. *Total population served:* 18,000 (jurisdiction over 5,000.) Under jurisdiction of Eastern Area Office.

MONTANA

BILLINGS AREA OFFICE
Bureau of Indian Affairs
316 North 26th St.
BILLINGS 59101
(406) 657-6315
Richard Whitesell, Area Director

Administers BIA programs for the region of Montana and Wyoming. Responsible for the following agencies: Blackfeet, Crow, Fort Belknap, Fort Peck, Northern Cheyenne, Rocky Boy's, and Wind River. *Tribes served:* Blackeet, Crow, Gros-Ventre and Assiniboine, Sioux and Assiniboine, Northern Cheyenne, Chippewa Cree, and Shoshone and Arapahoe. *Total population served:* 48,000.

ROCKY BOY'S AGENCY
Bureau of Indian Affairs
BOX ELDER 59521
(406) 395-4476
John Pereau, Superintendent

Tribe served: Chippewa Cree. *Total population served:* 1,750. Under jurisdiction of Billings Area Office.

BLACKEET AGENCY
Bureau of Indian Affairs
BROWNING 59417
(406) 338-7544
Michael Fairbanks, Superintendent

Tribe served: Blackfeet. *Total population served:* 7,000. Under jurisdiction of Billings Area Office.

CROW AGENCY
Bureau of Indian Affairs
CROW AGENCY 59022
(406) 638-2671
Wyman Babby, Superintendent

Tribe served: Crow. *Total population served:* 5,000. Under jurisdiction of Billings Area Office.

FORT BELKNAP AGENCY
Bureau of Indian Affairs
P.O. Box 80
HARLEM 59526
(406) 353-2205
Elmer Main, Superintendent

Tribes served: Assiniboine and Gros Ventre. *Total population served:* 2,200. Under jurisdiction of Billings Area Office.

NORTHERN CHEYENNE AGENCY
Bureau of Indian Affairs
LAME DEER 59043
(406) 477-6211
Ernest T. Moran, Superintendent

Tribe served: Cheyenne. *Total population served:* 3,000. Under jurisdiction of Billings Area Office.

FORT PECK AGENCY
Bureau of Indian Affairs
P.O. Box 637
POPLAR 59255
(406) 768-5311
Tom Whitford, Superintendent

Tribes served: Sioux and Assiniboine. *Total population served:* 5,000. Under jurisdiction of Billings Area Office.

FLATHEAD AGENCY
Bureau of Indian Affairs
P.O. Box A
RONAN 59864
(406) 676-4700
Duane F. Thompson, Superintendent

Tribes served: Salish and Kootenai. *Total population served:* 6,000. Under jurisdiction of Billings Area Office.

NEBRASKA

WINNEBAGO AGENCY
Bureau of Indian Affairs
WINNEBAGO 68071
(402) 878-2200
Joe C. Christie, Superintendent

Tribes served: Omaha, Winnebago, and Santee Sioux. *Total population served:* 3,500. Under jurisdiction of Aberdeen Area Office.

NEVADA

EASTERN NEVADA AGENCY
Bureau of Indian Affairs
ELKO 89801
(702) 738-5165
Allen Core, Superintendent

Reservations served: Duck Valley, Te-Moak Bands—Western Shoshone, Battle Mountain Colony, Elko Colony, South Fork, Ruby Valley Allotments, Odgers Ranch, Goshute, Ely Colony, and Duck Water. *Total population served:* 3,500. Under jurisdiction of Phoenix Area Office.

WESTERN NEVADA AGENCY
Bureau of Indian Affairs
STEWART 89437
(702) 887-3500
Robert L. Hunter, Superintendent

Tribes served: Shoshone, Paiute, Washoe, and Goshute. *Total population served:* 6,500. Under jurisdiction of Phoenix Area Office.

NEW MEXICO

ALBUQUERQUE AREA OFFICE
Bureau of Indian Affairs
P.O. Box 8327
5301 Central East
ALBUQUERQUE 87198
(505) 766-3171
Vincent Little, Area Director

Administers BIA programs for regions of Colorado and New Mexico. Responsible for the following agencies: Jicarilla, Laguna, Mescalero, Northern Pueblos, Ramah-Navajo, Southern Pueblo, Southern Ute, Ute Mountain Ute, and Zuni. *Programs:* Full range of BIA land and human resource programs. *Total population served:* 55,000.

SOUTHERN PUEBLOS AGENCY
Bureau of Indian Affairs
P.O. Box 1667
ALBUQUERQUE 87103
(505) 766-3021
Samuel Montoya, Superintendent

Tribe served: Pueblo. *Total population served:* 17,500. Under jurisdiction of Albuquerque Area Office.

EASTERN NAVAJO AGENCY
Bureau of Indian Affairs
P.O. Box 328
CROWNPOINT 87313
(505) 786-5228
Edward O. Plummer, Superintendent

Tribe served: Navajo (in Arizona, New Mexico and Utah.) Under jurisdiction of Navajo Area Office.

JICARILLA AGENCY
Bureau of Indian Affairs
DULCE 87528
(505) 759-3651
Petry D. Parton, Superintendent

Tribe served: Jicarilla Apache. *Total population served:* 2,500. Under jurisdiction of Albuquerque Area Office.

NAVAJO IRRIGATION PROJECT
Bureau of Indian Affairs
3539 East 30th St.
NW Energy Bldg., Room 103
FARMINGTON 87401
(505) 325-1864
Albert L. Keller, Superintendent

Under jurisdiction of Navajo Area Office.

NAVAJO AREA OFFICE (ADMIN.)
Bureau of Indian Affairs
P.O. Box 1060
GALLUP 87301
(505) 863-9501
Wilfred G. Bowman, Area Director

Under jurisdiction of Navajo Area Office (Albuquerque.)

MESCALERO AGENCY
Bureau of Indian Affairs
MESCALERO 88340
(505) 671-4421

Tribe served: Mescalero Apache. *Total population served:* 2,500. Under jurisdiction of Albuquerque Area Office.

RAMAH-NAVAJO AGENCY
Bureau of Indian Affairs
RAMAH 87321
(505) 783-5731
Dotlanca Steele, Superintendent

Tribe served: Navajo (in Arizona, New Mexico and Utah.) *Total population served:* 1,750. Under jurisdiction of Albuquerque Area Office.

NORTHERN PUEBLOS AGENCY
Bureau of Indian Affairs
P.O. Box 849, Federal Office Bldg.
SANTA FE 87501
(505) 988-6431
Jose Carpio, Superintendent

Tribes served: Nambe Pueblo, Picuris Pueblo, Pojoaque Pueblo, San Ildefonso Pueblo, San Juan Pueblo, Santa Clara Pueblo, Taos and Tesuque Pueblo. *Programs:* All BIA programs; adult education and social services. *Total population served:* 6,500. Under jurisdiction of Albuquerque Area Office.

SHIPROCK AGENCY
Bureau of Indian Affairs
SHIPROCK 87420
(505) 368-4427
Edward McCabe, Jr., Superintendent

Tribe served: Navajo (in Arizona, New Mexico and Utah.) Under jurisdiction of Navajo Area Office.

ZUNI AGENCY
Bureau of Indian Affairs
P.O. Box 338
ZUNI 87327
(505) 782-4481
John Montgomery, Superintendent

Tribe served: Zuni. *Total population served:* 6,000. Under jurisdiction of Albuquerque Area Office.

NEW YORK

NEW YORK LIAISON OFFICE
Bureau of Indian Affairs
Federal Bldg., 100 S. Clinton St.
SYRACUSE 13202
(315) 423-5476
William Seneca, Superintendent

Administers BIA programs for reservations and tribes in New York State. *Tribes served:* Seneca, Cayuga, Mohawk, Onondaga, Poosepatuck, and Oneida. *Total population served:* 15,000. Under jurisdiction of Eastern Area Office.

NORTH CAROLINA

CHEROKEE AGENCY
Bureau of Indian Affairs
CHEROKEE 28719
(704) 497-9131
Jeff Muskrat, Superintendent

Tribe served: Cherokee. *Total population served:* 6,000. *Under jurisdiction of Eastern Area Office.*

NORTH DAKKOTA

TURTLE MOUNTAIN AGENCY
Bureau of Indian Affairs
BELCOURT 58316
(701) 477-3190
Russell Bradley, Superintendent

Tribe served: Chippewa. *Total population served:* 9,000. Under jurisdiction of Aberdeen Area Office.

FORT TOTTEN AGENCY
Bureau of Indian Affairs
FORT TOTTEN 58335
(701) 766-4545
William C. Gipp, Superintendent

Tribe served: Sioux. *Total population served:* 2,750. Under jurisdiction of Aberdeen Area Office.

STANDING ROCK AGENCY
Bureau of Indian Affairs
FORT YATES 58538
(701) 854-3430
Lionel Chase the Bear, Superintendent

Tribe served: Sioux (in North and South Dakota.) *Total population served:* 6,000. Under jurisdiction of Aberdeen Area Office.

FORT BERTHOLD AGENCY
Bureau of Indian Affairs
NEW TOWN 58763
(701) 627-4707
Leo Brockie, Superintendent

Tribes served: Arikara, Mandan, and Hidatsa. *Total population served:* 8,500. Under jurisdiction of Aberdeen Area Office.

WAHPETON SCHOOL
Bureau of Indian Affairs
WAHPETON 58075
(701) 642-3790
Leroy Chief, Principal

Under jurisdiction of Aberdeen Area Office.

OKLAHOMA

ANADARKO AGENCY
Bureau of Indian Affairs
P.O. Box 309
ANADARKO 73005
(405) 247-6673
Rupert Thompson, Superintendent

Tribes served: Apache, Kiowa, Comanche, Caddo, Delaware, and Wichita. *Total population served:* 22,000. Under jurisdiction of Anadarko Area Office.

ANADARKO AREA OFFICE
Bureau of Indian Affairs
WCD Office Complex, Box 368
ANADARKO 73005
(405) 247-6673
William P. Ragsdale, Area Director

Administers BIA programs for regions of Oklahoma, Kansas and Missouri. Responsible for the following agencies, schools, and offices: Anadarko, Concho, Horton, Pawnee, Shawnee, Concho Indian School, Riverside Indian School, Fort Sill Maintenance and Security Detachment, Chilocco Maintenance and Security Detachment, and Haskell Indian Junior College.

RIVERSIDE SCHOOL
Bureau of Indian Affairs
P.O. Box 489
ANADARKO 73005
(405) 247-6673
Ray Tahsuda, Principal

Under jurisdiction of Anadarko Area Office.

ARDMORE AGENCY
Bureau of Indian Affairs
P.O. Box 997
ARDMORE 73401
(405) 223-6767
Zane Browning, Superintendent

Tribe served: Chickasaw. *Total population served:* 7,000. Under jurisdiction of Muskogee Area Office.

CONCHO AGENCY
Bureau of Indian Affairs
CONCHO 73022
(405) 262-4855

Tribes served: Cheyenne, and Arapaho. *Total population served:* 7,000. Under jurisdiction of Anadarko Area Office.

CONCHO INDIAN SCHOOL
Bureau of Indian Affairs
P.O. Box 8
CONCHO 73022

(405) 262-0143
John Edwards, Principal

Under jurisdiction of Anadarko Area Office.

FORT SILL MAINTENANCE AND SECURITY DETACHMENT
Bureau of Indian Affairs
P.O. Box 885
LAWTON 73502
(405) 248-6301
Frank Kowena, Superintendent

Under jurisdiction of Anadarko Area Office.

MIAMI AGENCY
Bureau of Indian Affairs
P.O. Box 391
MIAMI 74354
(918) 542-3396
Jack Naylor, Superintendent

Tribes served: Shawnee, Miami, Seneca-Cayuga, and Quapaw. Under jurisdiction of Muskogee Area Office.

MUSKOGEE AREA OFFICE
Bureau of Indian Affairs
Old Federal Bldg.
MUSKOGEE 74401
(918) 687-2296
Donald Moon, Area Director

Administers BIA programs for regions of Oklahoma. Responsible for the following agencies: Ardmore, Okmulgee, Osage, Miami, Tahlequah, Talihina, and Wewoka. *Tribes served:* Cherokee, Chickasaw, Choctaw, Creek, Seminole, Osage, Seneca-Cayuga, Keetowah, Eastern Shawnee, Quapaw, Wyandotte, Miami, Peoria, Ottawa, Cherokee-Shawnee, and Modoc. *Total population served:* 75,000.

CHILOCCO MAINTENANCE AND SECURITY DETACHMENT
Bureau of Indian Affairs
P.O. Box 465
NEWKIRK 74647
(918) 448-3800
Willie James, Superintendent

Under jurisdiction of Anadarko Area Office.

OKMULGEE AGENCY
Bureau of Indian Affairs
P.O. Box 370
OKMULGEE 74447
(918) 756-3950
Harley Little, Superintendent

Tribe served: Creek. *Total population served:* 16,000. Under jurisdiction of Muskogee Area Office.

OSAGE AGENCY
Bureau of Indian Affairs
PAWHUSKA 74056
  (918) 287-2481
  Jack Shoemata, Superintendent

Tribe served: Osage. *Total population served:*
4,000. Under jurisdiction of Muskogee Area
Office.

PAWNEE AGENCY
Bureau of Indian Affairs
P.O. Box 440
PAWNEE 74058
  (918) 762-2585
  Robert D. Barracker, Superintendent

Tribes served: Kaw, Pawnee, Ponca, Otoe-
Missouria, and Tonkawa. Under jurisdiction of
Anadarko Area Office.

SHAWNEE AGENCY
Bureau of Indian Affairs
Federal Bldg.
SHAWNEE 74801
  (405) 273-0317
  Joe B. Walker, Superintendent

Tribes served: Iowa, Kickapoo, Citizen
Potawatomi, Sac and Fox, and Absentee
Shawnee. *Total population served:* 17,500. Under
jurisdiction of Anadarko Area Office.

TAHLEQUAH AGENCY
Bureau of Indian Affairs
P.O. Box 828
TAHLEQUAH 74465
  (918) 456-6146
  Joe Parker, Superintendent

Tribe served: Cherokee. *Total population served:*
14,000. Under jurisdiction of Muskogee Area
Office.

TALIHINA AGENCY
Bureau of Indian Affairs
P.O. Drawer H
TALIHINA 74571
  (918) 567-2207
  Loren Albright, Superintendent

Tribe served: Choctaw. *Total population served:*
12,000. Under jurisdiction of Muskogee Area
Office.

WEWOKA AGENCY
Bureau of Indian Affairs
P.O. Box 1060
WEWOKA 74884
  (405) 257-6257
  Cecil Shipp, Superintendent

Tribe served: Seminole. *Total population served:*
6,500. Under jurisdiction of Muskogee Area
Office.

OREGON

UMATILLA AGENCY
Bureau of Indian Affairs
P.O. Box 520
PENDLETON 97801
  (503) 276-3811
  William Sandoval, Superintendent

Tribes served: Cayuse, Umatilla, and Walla
Walla. *Total population served:* 2,000. Under
jurisdiction of Portland Area Office.

PORTLAND AREA OFFICE
Bureau of Indian Affairs
P.O. Box 3785
1425 N.E. Irving St.
PORTLAND 97208
  (503) 231-6702
  Stanley Speaks, Area Director

Administers BIA programs for regions of Oregon,
Washington, and Idaho. Responsible for the
following agencies, schools, and offices:
Chemawa School, Colville Agency, Fort Hall
Agency, Flathead Agency, Metlakatla Field
Station, Northern Idaho Agency, Spokane
Agency, Umatilla Agency, Wapato Irrigation
Project, Olympic Peninsula Agency, Siletz
Agency, Warm Springs Agency, Puget Sound
Agency, and Yakima Agency.

CHEMAWA SCHOOL
Bureau of Indian Affairs
3700 Hazel Green Rd., N.E.
SALEM 97203
  (503) 393-4511
  Gerald Gray, Principal

Under jurisdiction of Portland Area Office.

SILETZ AGENCY
Bureau of Indian Affairs
P.O. Box 539
SILETZ 97380
  (503) 444-1029
  Bernard Topash, Superintendent

Under the jurisdiction of Portland Area Office.

WARM SPRINGS AGENCY
Bureau of Indian Affairs
WARM SPRINGS 97761
  (503) 553-1121
  Kay Welch, Superintendent

Tribes served: Paiute, Walla Walla, Chinook,
Cayuse, and Wasco. *Total population served:*
2,750. Under jurisdiction of Portland Area Office.

SOUTH DAKOTA

ABERDEEN AREA OFFICE
Bureau of Indian Affairs
Federal Bldg.
115 4th Ave., S.E,
ABERDEEN 57401
(605) 225-0250
Jerry L. Jaeger, Ph.D., Area Director

Administers BIA programs for regions of North and South Dakota, and Nebraska. Responsible for the following agencies and schools: Cheyenne River Agency, Crow Creek Agency, Flandreau Indian School, Fort Berthold Agency, Fort Totten Agency, Lower Brule Agency, Pine Ridge Agency, Rosebud Agency, Sisseton Agency, Standing Rock Agency, Turtle Mountain Agency, Wahpeton Indian School, Winnebago Agency, and Yankton Agency.

CHEYENNE RIVER AGENCY
Bureau of Indian Affairs
P.O. Box 325
EAGLE BUTTE 57625
(605) 964-6611
Gordon Cannon, Superintendent

Tribe served: Sioux. *Total population served:* 5,000. Under jurisdiction of Aberdeen Area Office.

FLANDREAU INDIAN SCHOOL
Bureau of Indian School
FLANDREAU 57028
(605) 997-2451
Jack Belkham, Principal

Under jurisdiction of Aberdeen Area Office.

CROW CREEK AGENCY
Bureau of Indian Affairs
P.O. Box 616
FORT THOMPSON 57339
(605) 245-2311
Donald E. Whitener, Superintendent

Tribe served: Sioux. *Total population served:* 2,250. Under jurisdiction of Aberdeen Area Office.

LOWER BRULE AGENCY
Bureau of Indian Affairs
LOWER BRULE 57548
(605) 473-5512
Leo O'Connor, Superintendent

Tribe served: Sioux. *Total population served:* 1,200. Under jurisdiction of Aberdeen Area Office.

PINE RIDGE AGENCY
Bureau of Indian Affairs
PINE RIDGE 57770
(605) 867-5121
Anthony Whirlwind Horse, Superintendent

Tribe served: Oglala Sioux (in South Dakota and Nebraska.) *Total population served:* 13,500. Under jurisdiction of Aberdeen Area Office.

ROSEBUD AGENCY
Bureau of Indian Affairs
ROSEBUD 57570
(605) 747-2224
William C. Gipp, Superintendent

Tribe served: Rosebud Sioux. *Total population served:* 12,000. Under jurisdiction of Aberdeen Area Office.

SISSETON AGENCY
Bureau of Indian Affairs
SISSETON 57262
(605) 698-7676
Hargle Spencer, Superintendent

Tribe served: Sioux (in North and South Dakota.) *Total population served:* 3,000. Under jurisdiction of Aberdeen Area Office.

YANKTON AGENCY
Bureau of Indian Affairs
WAGNER 57380
(605) 384-3650
Herbert Hare, Superintendent

Tribe served: Sioux. *Total population served:* 1,250. Under jurisdiction of Aberdeen Area Office.

UTAH

UINTAH AND OURAY AGENCY
Bureau of Indian Affairs
FORT DUCHESNE 84026
(801) 722-2406
Lavern Collier, Superintendent

Tribes served: Ute and Goshute. *Total population served:* 2,000. *Publication: Ute Bulletin.* Under jurisdiction of Phoenix Area Office.

WASHINGTON

PUGET SOUND AGENCY
Bureau of Indian Affairs
3006 Colby Ave., Federal Bldg.
EVERETT 98201
(206) 258-2651
William A. Black, Superintendent

Under jurisdiction of Portland Area Office.

OLYMPIC PENNINSULA AGENCY
Bureau of Indian Affairs
P.O. Box 120, Post Office Bldg.
HOQUIAM 98550
(206) 538-1500
Raymond Maldonado, Superintendent

Under jurisdiction of Portland Area Office.

COLVILLE AGENCY
Bureau of Indian Affairs
P.O. Box 111-0111
NESPELEM 99155
(509) 634-4901
George Davis, Superintendent

Tribes served: Columbia, Colville, Lakes, Nespelem, and Nez Perce. *Total population served:* 3,500. Under jurisdiction of Portland Area Office.

SEATTLE SUPPORT CENTER
Bureau of Indian Affairs
P.O. Box 80947
SEATTLE 98108
(206) 764-3328
Gerald W. Taylor, Superintendent

Under jurisdiction of Juneau Area Office.

YAKIMA AGENCY
Bureau of Indian Affairs
P.O. Box 632
TOPPENISH 98948
(509) 865-2255
Hiram Olney, Superintendent

Tribe served: Yakima. *Total population served:* 9,000. Under jurisdiction of Portland Area Office.

WAPATO IRRIGATION PROJECT
Bureau of Indian Affairs
P.O. Box 220
WAPATO 98951
(509) 877-3155
Louis Hilderbrand, Superintendent

Under jurisdiction of Portland Area Office.

SPOKANE AGENCY
Bureau of Indian Affairs
P.O. Box 389
WELLPINIT 99040
(509) 258-4561
Gordon E. Cannon, Superintendent

Tribe served: Spokane. *Total population served:* 900. Under jurisdiction of Portland Area Office.

WISCONSIN

GREAT LAKES AGENCY
Bureau of Indian Affairs
ASHLAND 54806
(715) 682-4528
Robert St. Arnold, Superintendent

Tribes served: Chippewa, Oneida, Forest Potawatomi, Stockbridge-Munsee, Winnebago (in Minnesota and Wisconsin.) *Total population served:* 9,000. Under jurisdiction of Minneapolis Area Office.

WYOMING

WIND RIVER AGENCY
Bureau of Indian Affairs
FORT WASHAKIE 82514
(307) 255-8301
L.W. Collier, Superintendent

Tribes served: Arapaho and Shoshone. *Total population served:* 5,500. Under jurisdiction of Billings Area Office.

RESERVATIONS

Included in this section are reservations and communities, both recognized and unrecognized by the Bureau of Indian Affairs. Reservations and communities served by a Bureau of Indian Affairs agency or area office are noted, and where they are served by an agency or office in another state, listings appear in both states. Where possible, geographical location and mailing address is given. The existence of tribal councils (representative and policy-making bodies) has also been noted. The *In Residence* counts, in most cases have been approximated.

ALASKA

AKHIOK NATIVE VILLAGE
Akhiok, Alaska 99615

Tribe: Eskimo. *In residence:* 90.
Anchorage Agency.

AKIACHAK NATIVE VILLAGE
Akiachak, Alaska 99551

Tribe: Eskimo. *In residence:* 250.
Bethel Agency.

AKIAK NATIVE COMMUNITY
Akiak, Alaska 99552

Tribe: Eskimo. *In residence:* 225.
Bethel Agency.

AKUTAN VILLAGE
Akutan, Alaska 99553

Anchorage Agency.

ALAKANUK NATIVE VILLAGE
P.O. Box 84
Alakanuk, Alaska 99559

Bethel Agency.

ALATNA VILLAGE COUNCIL
Alatna, Alaska 99720

Fairbanks Agency.

ALEKNAGIK COMMUNITY
P.O. Box 123
Aleknagik, Alaska 99555

Tribe: Athapascan. *In residence:* 175.
Anchorage Agency.

**ALEUTIAN/PRIBILOF
ISLANDS ASSOCIATION**
1689 C St.
Anchorage, Alaska 99501

ALGAACIQ TRIBAL GOVERNMENT
P.O. Box 162
St. Mary's, Alaska 99658

ALLAKAKET COMMUNITY
Allakaket, Alaska 99720

Tribe: Athapascan. *In residence:* 120.
Fairbanks Agency.

AMBLER COMMUNITY COUNCIL
Ambler, Alaska 99786

Nome Agency.

ANAKTUVUK PASS VILLAGE COUNCIL
Anaktuvuk Pass, Alaska 99721

Tribe: Eskimo. *In residence:* 100.
Fairbanks Agency.

ANGOON COMMUNITY ASSOCIATION
Angoon, Alaska 99820

Southeast Agency.

ANIAK COMMUNITY COUNCIL
Aniak, Alaska 99557

Tribe: Eskimo. *In residence:* 150.
Bethel Agency.

ANVIK VILLAGE COUNCIL
Anvik, Alaska 99558

Tribe: Eskimo. *In residence:* 150.
Bethel Agency.

ATKA NATIVE VILLAGE
Atka, Alaska 99502

Anchorage Agency.

ATKASUK VILLAGE COUNCIL
Atkasuk, Alaska 99723

ATMAULTLUAK COMMUNITY
Atmaultluak, Alaska 99559

Bethel Agency.

BARROW COMMUNITY
Barrow, Alaska 99723

Tribe: Eskimo. *In residence:* 3,000.
Fairbanks Agency.

BEAVER COMMUNITY COUNCIL
Beaver, Alaska 99724

Tribes: Eskimo, Athapascan, Indian. *In residence:* 150. Fairbanks Agency.

BELKOFSKY NATIVE VILLAGE
Belkofsky, Alaska 99695

Tribe: Aleut. *In residence:* 200.
Anchorage Agency.

BETHEL NATIVE COUNCIL
P.O. Box 719
Bethel, Alaska 99559

Tribes: Eskimo and Indian. *In residence:* 150.
Bethel Agency.

BETTLES FIELD COMMUNITY
Bettles Field, Alaska 99726

Tribes: Eskimo and Indian. *In residence:* 65.
Fairbanks Agency.

BIRCH CREEK VILLAGE COUNCIL
Birch Creek, Alaska 99790

Nome Agency.

BREVIG MISSION COMMUNITY COUNCIL
Brevig Mission, Alaska 99785

Nome Agency.

BRISTOL BAY NATIVE ASSOCIATION
P.O. Box 189
Dillingham, Alaska 99756

Nome Agency.

BUCKLAND NATIVE VILLAGE
Buckland, Alaska 99727

Nome Agency.

CANTWELL NATIVE VILLAGE
P.O. Box 14
Cantwell, Alaska 99729

Tribe: Athapascan. Fairbanks Agency.

CHALKYITSIK COMMUNITY COUNCIL
Chalkyitsik, Alaska 99788

Nome Agency.

CHALOOHAWIK VILLAGE
c/o Emmonak, Alaska 99581

Bethel Agency.

CHEFORNAK COMMUNITY COUNCIL
Chefornak, Alaska 99561

Tribe: Eskimo. *In residence:* 175. Bethel Agency.

CHENEGA NATIVE VILLAGE
903 West North Lights Blvd., Suite 203
Anchorage, Alaska 99503

Anchorage Agency.

CHEVAK COMMUNITY COUNCIL
Chevak, Alaska 99563

Tribe: Eskimo. *In residence:* 400. Bethel Agency.

CHIGNIK NATIVE VILLAGE
Chignik, Alaska 99564

Tribe: Eskimo. *In residence:* 385. Bethel Agency.

CHIKALOON VILLAGE
2600 Fairbanks St.
Anchorage, Alaska 99503

Anchorage Agency.

CHILKAT INDIAN VILLAGE
P.O. Box 220
Haines, Alaska 99827

Southeast Agency.

CHILKOOT INDIAN ASSOCIATION
P.O. Box Q
Haines, Alaska 99827

Southeast Agency.

CHISTOCHINA NATIVE VILLAGE
P.O. Box 171
Gakona, Alaska 99586

Tribe: Athapascan. Bethel Agency.

CHITINA NATIVE VILLAGE
P.O. Box 3
Chitina, Alaska 99566

Bethel Agency.

CHUATHBALUK VILLAGE
Chuathbaluk, Alaska 99557

Bethel Agency.

CIRCLE VILLAGE COUNCIL
Circle, Alaska 99733

Tribe: Athapascan. *In residence:* 115.
Fairbanks Agency.

CLARK'S POINT VILLAGE
Clark's Point, Alaska 99569

Bethel Agency.

COOK INLET NATIVE ASSOCIATION
670 West Fireweed Lane
Anchorage, Alaska 99503

Anchorage Agency.

COPPER CENTER VILLAGE COUNCIL
P.O. Drawer G
Copper Center, Alaska 99573

Tribe: Athapascan. *In residence:* 115.
Bethel Agency.

COPPER RIVER NATIVE ASSOCIATION
P.O. Drawer H
Copper River, Alaska 99573

Bethel Agency.

CORDOVA COMMUNITY
Cordova, Alaska 99574

Tribes: Athapascan and Indian. *In residence:* 325.
Bethel Agency.

CRAIG COMMUNITY ASSOCIATION
P.O. Box 188
Craig, Alaska 99921

Southeast Agency.

CROOKED CREEK VILLAGE
Crooked Creek, Alaska 99757

Tribe: Athapascan. Bethel Agency.

DEERING NATIVE VILLAGE
Deering, Alaska 99736

Tribe: Eskimo. *In residence:* 250. Nome Agency

DILLINGHAM VILLAGE COUNCIL
P.O. Box 216
Dillingham, Alaska 99576

Tribes: Athapascan and Indian. *In residence:* 450.
Bethel Agency.

DIOMEDE NATIVE VILLAGE
Diomede, Alaska 99762

Nome Agency.

DOT LAKE NATIVE VILLAGE
P.O. Box 277
Dot Lake, Alaska 99739

Fairbanks Agency.

DOUGLAS COMMUNITY
Douglas, Alaska 99824

Southeast Agency.

EAGLE VILLAGE COUNCIL
Eagle, Alaska 99738

Tribes: Eskimo and Indian. Fairbanks Agency.

EEK NATIVE VILLAGE
Eek, Alaska 99578

Tribe: Eskimo. *In residence:* 190. Bethel Agency.

EGEGIK VILLAGE COUNCIL
Egegik, Alaska 99579

Tribes: Eskimo and Indian. *In residence:* 140.
Bethel Agency.

EKLUTNA COMMUNITY
Ikluat, Inc., P.O. Box 705
Chugiak, Alaska 99567

Tribe: Athapascan. Bethel Agency.

EKUK NATIVE VILLAGE
Ekuk, Alaska 99576

Bethel Agency.

EKWOK VILLAGE COUNCIL
Ekwok, Alaska 99580

Bethel Agency.

ELIM NATIVE VILLAGE
Elim, Alaska 99739

Tribe: Eskimo. *In residence:* 225. Nome Agency.

EMMONAK VILLAGE COUNCIL
Emmonak, Alaska 99581

Bethel Agency.

ENGLISH BAY VILLAGE COUNCIL
Homer, Alaska 99603

Tribe: Eskimo. *In residence:* 115. Anchorage
Agency.

EVANSVILLE VILLAGE COUNCIL
Bettles, Alaska 99726

Fairbanks Agency.

EYAK NATIVE VILLAGE
P.O. Box 878
Cordova, Alaska 99574

Bethel Agency.

FAIRBANKS NATIVE ASSOCIATION
950 Cowles St., Suite
Fairbanks, Alaska 99701

Anchorage Agency.

FALSE PASS NATIVE VILLAGE
False Pass, Alaska 99583

Bethel Agency.

FLAT COMMUNITY
Flat, Alaska 99584

Tribes: Athapscan and Eskimo. Bethel Agency.

FORT YUKON NATIVE VILLAGE
P.O. Box 126
Fort Yukon, Alaska 99740

Tribes: Athapascan and Indian.
In residence: 600. Nome Agency.

GAKONA NATIVE VILLAGE
P.O. Box 174
Gakona, Alaska 99586

Bethel Agency.

GALENA COMMUNITY
Galena, Alaska 99741

Tribe: Athapascan. *In residence:* 175. Nome
Agency.

GAMBELL NATIVE VILLAGE
P.O. Box 99
Gambell, Alaska 99742

Nome Agency.

GOLOVIN NATIVE VILLAGE
Golovin, Alaska 99762

Tribe: Eskimo; *In residence:* 140. Nome Agency.

GOODNEWS BAY NATIVE VILLAGE
Goodnews Bay, Alaska 99589

Bethel Agency.

GRAYLING NATIVE VILLAGE
Grayling, Alaska 99590

Bethel Agency.

GULKANA VILLAGE COUNCIL
P.O. Box 123
Gakona, Alaska 99586

Tribe: Athapascan. Bethel Agency.

HEALY LAKE VILLAGE COUNCIL
P.O. Box 667
Delta Junction, Alaska 99737

Fairbanks Agency.

HOLY CROSS VILLAGE COUNCIL
Holy Cross, Alaska 99602

Tribes: Eskimo and Athapascan. *In residence:*
220. Bethel Agency.

HOONAH INDIAN ASSOCIATION
P.O. Box 144
Hoonah, Alaska 99829

Southeast Agency.

HOOPER BAY NATIVE VILLAGE
Hooper Bay, Alaska 99604

Tribe: Eskimo. *In residence:* 450. Bethel Agency.

HUGHES VILLAGE COUNCIL
Hughes, Alaska 99745

Tribe: Athapascan. Fairbanks Agency.

HUSLIA VILLAGE COUNCIL
Huslia, Alaska 99746

Nome Agency.

**HYDABURG COOPERATIVE
ASSOCIATION**
P.O. Box 57
Hydaburg, Alaska 99922

Southeast Agency.

IGIUGIG VILLAGE COUNCIL
Iguigig, Alaska 99613

Bethel Agency.

ILAMNA VILLAGE
Ilamna, Alaska 99606

Tribes: Athapascan and Indian.
Anchorage Agency.

**INUPIAT COMMUNITY
OF THE ARCTIC SLOPE**
P.O. Box 437
Barrow, Alaska 99723

Fairbanks Agency.

IVANOFF BAY VILLAGE COUNCIL
Ivanoff Bay, Alaska 99695

Anchorage Agency.

**JUNEAU TLINGIT/HAIDA
CENTRAL COUNCIL**
320 West Willoughby Ave., #300
Juneau, Alaska 99801
  (312) 784-1050

Southeast Agency.

KAKE VILLAGE
P.O. Box 222
Kake, Alaska 99830

Southeast Agency.

KAKTOVIK VILLAGE COUNCIL
Kaktovik, Alaska 99747

Fairbanks Agency.

KALSKAG NATIVE VILLAGE
Kalskag, Alaska 99607

Tribe: Eskimo. *In residence:* 225. Bethel Agency.

KALTAG VILLAGE COUNCIL
Kaltag, Alaska 99748

Tribe: Athapascan. *In residence:* 190.
Fairbanks Agency.

KARLUK COMMUNITY
Karluk, Alaska 99608

Tribe: Aleut. *In residence:* 225.
Anchorage Agency.

KASAAN NATIVE VILLAGE
Kasaan, Alaska 99924

Southeast Agency.

KASIGLUK NATIVE VILLAGE
Kasigluk, Alaska 99609

Tribe: Eskimo. *In residence:* 175. Bethel Agency.

KAWERAK, INC.
P.O. Box 448
Nome, Alaska 99762

Nome Agency.

KENAITZE INDIANS OF ALASKA
P.O. Box 988
Kenai, Alaska 99611

Anchorage Agency.

KETCHIKAN INDIAN CORPORATION
P.O. Box 6855
Ketchikan, Alaska 99901

Southeast Agency.

KIANA COMMUNITY COUNCIL
Kiana, Alaska 99748

Tribe: Eskimo *In residence:* 220. Nome Agency.

KING COVE VILLAGE COUNCIL
P.O. Box 91
King Cove, Alaska 99612

Bethel Agency.

KING ISLAND NATIVE COMMUNITY
P.O. Box 992
Nome, Alaska 99762

Nome Agency.

KIPNUK NATIVE VILLAGE
Kipnuk, Alaska 99614

Bethel Agency.

KIVALINA NATIVE VILLAGE
Kivalina, Alaska 99750

Tribe: Eskimo. *In residence:* 175. Nome Agency.

KLAWOK COOPERATIVE ASSOCIATION
P.O. Box 112
Klawok, Alaska 99925

Southeast Agency.

KNIK VILLAGE COUNCIL
P.O. Box 2130
Wasilla, Alaska 99687

Bethel Agency.

KOBUK VILLAGE COUNCIL
Kobuk, Alaska 99751

Tribe: Eskimo. Nome Agency

KODIAK AREA NATIVE ASSOCIATION
402 Center Ave.
Kodiak, Alaska 99615

Bethel Agency.

KOKHANOK VILLAGE COUNCIL
Ilamna, Alaska 99606

Tribe: Aleut. Anchorage Agency.

KOLIGANEK VILLAGE COUNCIL
Koliganek, Alaska 99576

Tribes: Athapascan and Indian. *In residence:* 175.
Bethel Agency.

KONGIGANAK VILLAGE COUNCIL
Kongiganak, Alaska 99559

Bethel Agency.

KOTLIK NATIVE VILLAGE
Kotlik, Alaska 99620

Tribe: Eskimo. Bethel Agency.

KOTZEBUE NATIVE VILLAGE
P.O. Box 256
Kotzebue, Alaska 99752

Tribe: Eskimo. *In residence:* 850. Nome Agency.

KOYUK NATIVE VILLAGE
Koyuk, Alaska 99753

Tribe: Eskimo. *In residence:* 190. Nome Agency.

KOYUKUK VILLAGE COUNCIL
Koyukuk, Alaska 99754

Tribe: Athapascan. *In residence:* 115. Fairbanks
Agency.

KWETHLUK VILLAGE
Kwethluk, Alaska 99621

Tribe: Eskimo. *In residence:* 350. Bethel Agency.

KWIGILLINGOK NATIVE VILLAGE
Kwigillingok, Alaska 99622

Tribe: Eskimo. *In residence:* 350. Bethel Agency.

LARSEN BAY NATIVE VILLAGE
Larsen Bay, Alaska 99624

Tribe: Eskimo. Anchorage Agency.

LEVELOCK VILLAGE COUNCIL
Levelock, Alaska 99625

Tribe: Aleut. Anchorage Agency.

LIME VILLAGE COUNCIL
Lower Kalskag, Alaska 99626

Bethel Agency

LOUDON VILLAGE COUNCIL
Galena, Alaska 99741

Nome Agency.

LOWER KALSKAG VILLAGE
Lower Kalskag, Alaska 99626

Tribe: Eskimo. *In residence:* 175. Bethel Agency.

MANIILAQ ASSOCIATION
P.O. Box 256
Kotzebue, Alaska 99752

Nome Agency.

**MANLEY HOT SPRINGS
VILLAGE COUNCIL**
Manley Hot Springs, Alaska 99756

Nome Agency.

MANOKOTAK VILLAGE COUNCIL
Manokotak, Alaska 99628

Tribes: Eskimo and Indian. *In residence:* 190.
Anchorage Agency.

MARSHALL NATIVE VILLAGE
Marshall, Alaska 99585

Tribe: Eskimo. *In residence:* 115.
Anchorage Agency.

McGRATH NATIVE VILLAGE COUNCIL
McGrath, Alaska 99627

Tribes: Athapascan, Indian and Eskimo.
In residence: 125. Bethel Agency.

MEDFRA COMMUNITY
Medfra, Alaska 99629

Tribes: Athapascan and Indian. Bethel Agency.

MEKORYUK NATIVE VILLAGE
P.O. Box 66
Mekoryuk, Alaska 99630

Tribe: Eskimo. *In residence:* 220. Bethel Agency.

MENTASTA VILLAGE COUNCIL
Tok, Alaska 99780

Nome Agency.

METLAKATLA INDIAN COMMUNITY
Annette Island Reserve, P.O. Box 8
Metlakatla, Alaska 99926
  (907) 886-4441
  Harris Atkinson, Mayor

Portland Area Office.

MINTO NATIVE VILLAGE
Minto, Alaska 99758

Tribes: Athapascan and Indian. *In residence:* 225.
Nome Agency.

MOUNTAIN VILLAGE NATIVE VILLAGE
P.O. Box 204
Mountain Village, Alaska 99632

Tribe: Eskimo. *In residence:* 275. Bethel Agency.

NAKNEK NATIVE VILLAGE COUNCIL
P.O. Box 106
Naknek, Alaska 99633

Tribes: Aleut and Indian. Bethel Agency.

NAPAKIAK NATIVE VILLAGE
Napakiak, Alaska 99634

Tribe: Eskimo. *In residence:* 200. Bethel Agency.

NAPASKIAK VILLAGE COUNCIL
Napaskiak, Alaska 99559

Tribe: Eskimo. *In residence:* 175. Bethel Agency.

NELSON LAGOON NATIVE VILLAGE
via P. Miller, Alaska 99695

Anchorage Agency.

NENANA NATIVE ASSOCIATION
Nenana, Alaska 99760

Tribes: Athapascan and Indian. *In residence:*
175. Nome Agency.

NEW STUYAHOK VILLAGE
New Stuyahok, Alaska 99636

Tribe: Athapascan. *In residence:* 140.
Anchorage Agency.

NEWHALEN VILLAGE COUNCIL
via Iliamna, Alaska 99606

Tribes: Aleut and Indian. Anchorage Agency.

NEWTOK VILLAGE COUNCIL
Newtok, Alaska 99559

Bethel Agency.

NIGHTMUTE NATIVE VILLAGE
Nightmute, Alaska 99690

Tribe: Eskimo. Bethel Agency.

NIKOLAI VILLAGE COUNCIL
Nikolai, Alaska 99691

Tribes: Athapscans and Indian. *In residence:*
145. Bethel Agency.

NIKOLSKI NATIVE VILLAGE
Nikolski, Alaska 99638

Anchorage Agency.

NINILCHIK VILLAGE TRIBAL COUNCIL
P.O. Box 282
Ninilchik, Alaska 99689

Tribe: Kenaitse. *In residence:* 120.
Anchorage Agency.

NOATAK NATIVE VILLAGE
Noatak, Alaska 99761

Tribes: Eskimo and Indian. *In residence:* 550.
Nome Agency.

NOME ESKIMO COMMUNITY
P.O. Box 401
Nome, Alaska 99762

Tribes: Eskimo and Indian. *In residence:* 1,750.
Nome Agency.

NONDALTON VILLAGE COUNCIL
Nondalton, Alaska 99640

Tribe: Athapascan. *In residence:* 175.
Anchorage Agency.

NOORVIK NATIVE COMMUNITY
P.O. Box 71
Noorvik, Alaska 99763

Tribe: Eskimo. *In residence:* 450. Nome Agency.

NORTH PACIFIC RIM
903 West Northern Lights Blvd., Suite 203
Anchorage, Alaska 99503

Anchorage Agency.

NORTHWAY VILLAGE COUNCIL
Northway, Alaska 99764
Tribe: Athapascan. *In residence:* 150.
Fairbanks Agency.

NUIQSUT VILLAGE COUNCIL
Nuiqsut, Alaska 99723

Fairbanks Agency.

NULATO VILLAGE COUNCIL
Nulato, Alaska 99765

Tribe: Athapascan. *In residence:* 250.
Fairbanks Agency.

NUNAPITCHUK NATIVE VILLAGE
Nunapitchuk, Alaska 99641

Tribe: Eskimo. *In residence:* 200. Bethel Agency.

**OLD HARBOR VILLAGE
TRIBAL COUNCIL**
Old Harbor, Alaska 99643

Tribe: Eskimo. *In residence:* 200.
Anchorage Agency.

OSCARVILLE VILLAGE COUNCIL
Tribes: Indian and Eskimo. Bethel Agency.

OUZINKIE NATIVE VILLAGE
Ouzinkie, Alaska 99644

Anchorage Agency.

PALMER COMMUNITY
Palmer, Alaska 99645

Anchorage Agency.

PEDRO BAY VILLAGE COUNCIL
Pedro Bay, Alaska 99647

Tribe: Athapascan. Anchorage Agency.

**PELICAN TLINGIT
AND HAIDA INDIANS**
P.O. Box 727
Pelican, Alaska 99832

Southeast Agency.

PERRYVILLE NATIVE VILLAGE
P.O. Box 101
Perryville, Alaska 99648

Tribe: Eskimo. *In residence:* 175.
Anchorage Agency.

PETERSBURG INDIAN ASSOCIATION
P.O. Box 1128
Petersburg, Alaska 99833

Southeast Agency.

PILOT POINT NATIVE VILLAGE
Pilot Point, Alaska 99649

Bethel Agency.

PILOT STATION COMMUNITY COUNCIL
Pilot Station, Alaska 99650

Tribe: Eskimo. Bethel Agency.

PITKA'S POINT NATIVE VILLAGE
Pitka's Point, Alaska 99658

Tribe: Eskimo. Bethel Agency.

PLATINUM COMMUNITY COUNCIL
Platinum, Alaska 99651

Tribe: Eskimo. Bethel Agency.

POINT HOPE VILLAGE COUNCIL
Point Hope, Alaska 99766

Tribe: Eskimo. *In residence:* 385. Nome Agency.

POINT LAY VILLAGE COUNCIL
Point Lay, Alaska 99790

Tribe: Eskimo. *In residence:* 125. Nome Agency.

PORT GRAHAM VILLAGE COUNCIL
Via Homer, Alaska 99603

Tribe: Eskimo. *In residence:* 115.
Anchorage Agency.

PORT HEIDEN NATIVE COUNCIL
Port Heiden, Alaska 99549

Bethel Agency.

PORT LIONS NATIVE VILLAGE
Port Lions, Alaska 99550

Bethel Agency.

PORTAGE CREEK VILLAGE COUNCIL
Portage Creek, Alaska 99695

Anchorage Agency.

QUINHAGAK NATIVE VILLAGE
Quinhagak, Alaska 99655

Bethel Agency.

RAMPART VILLAGE COUNCIL
Rampart, Alaska 99767

Tribe: Athapascan. *In residence:* 140.
Nome Agency.

RED DEVIL NATIVE VILLAGE
Red Devil, Alaska 99656

Bethel Agency.

RUBY NATIVE COUNCIL
Ruby, Alaska 99768

Tribe: Athapascan. *In residence:* 150.
Nome Agency.

RUSSIAN MISSION NATIVE VILLAGE
Russian Mission, Alaska 99657

Tribe: Eskimo. Bethel Agency.

ST. GEORGE VILLAGE COUNCIL
St. George Island, Alaska 99660

Bethel Agency.

ST. MICHAEL NATIVE VILLAGE
St. Michael, Alaska 99659

Bethel Agency.

ST. PAUL ISLAND ALEUT COMMUNITY
St. Paul Island, Alaska 99660

Tribe: Aleut. Bethel Agency.

SALAMANTOFF NATIVE ASSOCIATION
P.O. Box 2682
Kenai, Alaska 99611

Bethel Agency.

SAND POINT NATIVE VILLAGE
Sand Point, Alaska 99661

Tribe: Aleut. Bethel Agency.

SAVOONGA NATIVE VILLAGE
P.O. Box 129
Savoonga, Alaska 99769

Tribe: Eskimo. *In residence:* 330. Nome Agency.

SAXMAN VILLAGE
P.O.Box 8558
Ketchikan, Alaska 99901

Portland Area Office.

SCAMMON BAY NATIVE VILLAGE
Scammon Bay, Alaska 99662

Bethel Agency.

SELAWIK NATIVE VILLAGE
Selawik, Alaska 99770

Nome Agency.

SELDOVIA NATIVE ASSOCIATION
P.O. Drawer L
Seldovia, Alaska 99663

Bethel Agency.

SHAGELUK NATIVE VILLAGE
Shageluk, Alaska 99665

Tribe: Athapascan. *In residence:* 150.
Bethel Agency.

SHAKTOOLIK NATIVE VILLAGE
Shaktoolik, Alaska 99771

Nome Agency.

SHELDON'S POINT NATIVE VILLAGE
Sheldon's Point, Alaska 99666

Bethel Agency.

SHISHMAREF NATIVE VILLAGE
Shishmaref, Alaska 99772

Tribe: Eskimo. *In residence:* 200. Nome Agency.

SHUNGNAK NATIVE VILLAGE
Shungnak, Alaska 99773

Tribe: Eskimo. *In residence:* 200. Nome Agency.

SITKA COMMUNITY ASSOCIATION
P.O. Box 4360
Mt. Edgecumbe, Alaska 99835

Southeast Agency.

SKAGWAY VILLAGE COUNCIL
P.O. Box 149
Skagway, Alaska 99840

SLEETMUTE NATIVE VILLAGE
Sleetmute, Alaska 99668

Tribes: Athapascan and Indian. *In residence:* 175.
Anchorage Agency.

SOUTH NAKNEK VILLAGE COUNCIL
South Naknek, Alaska 99670

Anchorage Agency.

STEBBINS COMUNITY ASSOCIATION
Stebbins, Alaska 99671

Tribe: Eskimo. *In residence:* 175. Anchorage
Agency.

STERLING COMMUNITY
Sterling, Alaska 99672

Anchorage Agency.

STEVENS VILLAGE COMMUNITY
Stevens Village, Alaska 99774

Tribe: Athapascan. *In residence:* 125. Nome
Agency.

STONY RIVER NATIVE VILLAGE
Stony River, Alaska 99557

Bethel Agency.

TAKOTNA VILLAGE COUNCIL
Takotna, Alaska 99675

Tribes: Eskimo and Indian. Anchorage Agency.

TANACROSS NATIVE VILLAGE
Tanacross, Alaska 99776

Tribe: Athapascan. *In residence:* 150. Nome
Agency.

TANANA NATIVE VILLAGE
P.O. Box 202
Tanana, Alaska 99777

Tribes: Athapascan and Indian. *In residence:* 225.
Nome Agency.

TATITLEK NATIVE VILLAGE
Tatitlek, Alaska 99677

Tribe: Aleut. *In residence:* 150. Anchorage
Agency.

TAZLINA NATIVE VILLAGE
P.O. Box 225
Glenallen, Alaska 99588

Bethel Agency.

TELIDA VILLAGE COUNCIL
Telida, Alaska 99627

Anchorage Agency.

TELLER VILLAGE COUNCIL
P.O. Box 548
Teller, Alaska 99778

Tribe: Eskimo. *In residence:* 200. Nome Agency.

TETLIN NATIVE VILLAGE
Tetlin, Alaska 99779

Tribe: Athapascan. *In residence:* 125. Nome
Agency.

TOGIAK VILLAGE
P.O. Box 99
Togiak, Alaska 99678

Tribe: Eskimo. *In residence:* 175. Bethel Agency.

TOK NATIVE ASSOCIATION
Tok, Alaska 99780

Nome Agency.

TOKSOOK BAY NATIVE VILLAGE
Toksook Bay, Alaska 99637

Bethel Agency.

TULUKSAK NATIVE COMMUNITY
Tuluksak, Alaska 99679

Tribe: Eskimo. *In residence:* 200. Bethel Agency.

TUNTUTULIAK NATIVE VILLAGE
Tuntutuliak, Alaska 99680

Tribe: Eskimo. *In residence:* 120. Bethel Agency.

TUNUNAK NATIVE VILLAGE
Tununak, Alaska 99681

Bethel Agency.

TWIN HILLS VILLAGE COUNCIL
via Togiak, Alaska 99678

Bethel Agency.

TYONEK NATIVE VILLAGE
Tyonek, Alaska 99682

Tribe: Athapascan. *In residence:* 200.
Anchorage Agency.

UGASHIK VILLAGE COUNCIL
Ugashik, Alaska 99683

Tribes: Eskimo and Indian. Anchorage Agency.

UNALAKLEET NATIVE VILLAGE
P.O. Box 70
Unalakleet, Alaska 99684

Tribes: Eskimo and Indian. *In residence:* 550.
Anchorage Agency.

UNALASKA VILLAGE COUNCIL
P.O. Box 134
Unalaska 99687

VALDEZ COMMUNITY
Valdez, Alaska 99686

Tribes: Aleut and Indian. *In residence:* 175.
Anchorage Agency.

VENETIE NATIVE VILLAGE
Venetie, Alaska 99781

Tribe: Athapascan. *In residence:* 125.
Nome Agency.

WAINWRIGHT VILLAGE COUNCIL
Wainwright, Alaska 99782

Tribe: Eskimo. *In residence:* 335. Nome Agency.

WALES NATIVE VILLAGE
Wales, Alaska 99783

Tribe: Eskimo. *In residence:* 225. Nome Agency.

WHITE MOUNTAIN NATIVE VILLAGE
White Mountain, Alaska 99784

Tribes: Eskimo and Indian. *In residence:* 200.
Nome Agency.

**WRANGELL COOPERATIVE
ASSOCIATION**
P.O. Box 868
Wrangell, Alaska 99929

Portland Area Office.

**YAKUTAT TLINGIT
AND HAIDA COUNCIL**
P.O. Box 171
Yakutat, Alaska 99689

Anchorage Agency.

ARIZONA

BECLABITO RESERVATION
c/o Shiprock Agency, P.O. Box 966
Shiprock, New Mexico 87420

Tribe: Navajo. Located in Arizona and New
Mexico. See listing under New Mexico.

BIRD SPRINGS RESERVATION
c/o Western Navajo Agency, P.O. Box 127
Tuba City, Arizona 86045

Tribe: Navajo.

BLUE GAP RESERVATION
c/o Chinle Agency, P.O. Box 7H
Chinle, Arizona 86503

Tribe: Navajo.

BROADWAY RESERVATION
c/o Western Navajo Agency, P.O. Box 127
Tuba City, Arizona 86045

Tribe: Navajo.

CAMERON RESERVATION
Cameron, Arizona 86020

Tribe: Navajo. Western Navajo Agency.

CAMP VERDE RESERVATION
P.O. Box 1188
Camp Verde, Arizona 86322
(602) 567-3649
Ned Russell, Chairman

Tribes: Yavapai and Apache. *In residence:* 550.
Area: 500 acres. Fort Apache Agency.

CHEMEHUEVI RESERVATION
c/o Colorado River Agency
Route 1, Box 9-C
Parker, Arizona 85344

Tribe: Chemehuevi. Located in California.
See listing under California.

CHILCHINBETO RESERVATION
c/o Western Navajo Reservation
P.O. Box 127
Tuba City, Arizona 86045

Tribe: Navajo. Located in Arizona and Utah.
See listing under Utah.

CHINLE RESERVATION
c/o Chinle Agency, P.O. Box 7H
Chinle, Arizona 86503.

Tribe: Navajo.

COALMINE RESERVATION
c/o Western Navajo Reservation
P.O. Box 127
Tuba City, Arizona 86045

Tribe: Navajo.

COCOPAH RESERVATION
P.O. Box Bin "G"
Somerton, Arizona 85350

(602) 627-2102
Fred Miller, Chief

Tribe: Cocopah. *In residence:* 550. Tribal council.

COLORADO RIVER INDIAN RESERVATION
Route 1, Box 23-B
Parker, Arizona 85344.
(602) 669-9211
Anthony Drennan, Sr., Chief

Tribes: Mohave, Chemehuevi, Hopi, Navajo. *In
residence:* 2,800. *Area:* 28,691 acres. *Local
attractions:* Colorado River; Old Mohave
Presbyterian Church, National Historic Site;
archaeological excavations and ruins of La Paz, a
former gold mining town; Tribal Museum and
Library. *Activities:* National Indian Day; rodeos.

COPPER MINE RESERVATION
c/o Western Navajo Agency
P.O. Box 127
Tuba City, Arizona 86045

Tribe: Navajo.

CORNFIELDS RESERVATION
c/o Fort Defiance Agency
P.O. Box 619
Fort Defiance, Arizona 86504

Tribe: Navajo.

COYOTE CANYON RESERVATION
c/o Fort Defiance Agency
P.O. Box 619
Fort Defiance, Arizona 86504

Tribe: Navajo.

CRYSTAL RESERVATION
c/o Fort Defiance Agency
P.O. Box 619
Fort Defiance, Arizona 86504

Tribe: Navajo. Located in Arizona and
New Mexico. See listing under New Mexico.

DENNEHOTSO RESERVATION
Dennehotso, Arizona 86535

Tribe: Navajo. Western Navajo Agency.

DILKON COMMUNITY
Winslow, Arizona 86047

Tribe: Navajo. *In residence:* 1,000.
Western Navajo Agency.

FOREST LAKE RESERVATION
Heber, Arizona 85928

Tribe: Navajo. Chinle Agency.

FORT APACHE INDIAN RESERVATION
P.O. Box 700
Whiteriver, Arizona 85941
(602) 338-4371
Ronnie Lupe, Chief

Tribe: White Mountain Apache. *In residence:*
8,500. *Area:* 1,664,872 acres. *Local attraction:*
Apache Cultural Center and Museum. Tribal
council. Western Navajo Agency.

FORT DEFIANCE RESERVATION
c/o Fort Defiance Agency
P.O. Box 619
Fort Defiance, Arizona 86504

Tribe: Navajo. Located in Arizona and
New Mexico. See listing under New Mexico.

FORT McDOWELL RESERVATION
P.O. Box 17779
Fountain Hills, Arizona 85269
(602) 990-0995
Benjamin Kill, Sr., Chief

Tribes: Mohave and Apache. *In residence:* 500.
Area: 24,680 acres; located twenty miles northeast
of Phoenix on the Verde River. *Local attractions:*
Roosevelt Dam and Reservoir; Bartlett
Reservoir. Tribal council. Salt River Agency.

FORT MOHAVE RESERVATION
Fort Mohave 86427

Tribe: Mohave. Located in Arizona, California
and Nevada. See listings under California and
Nevada. Colorado River Agency.

FORT YUMA RESERVATION
P.O. Box 1352
Yuma, Arizona 85364
(619) 572-0213
Elvin Kelly, Chief

Tribe: Quechan. Located in Arizona and
California. See listing under California.
Fort Yuma Agency.

GANADO RESERVATION
Ganado, Arizona 86505

Tribe: Navajo. Fort Defiance Agency.

GILA BEND RESERVATION
Gila Bend, Arizona 85337

Tribe: Papago. *In residence:* 300. *Area:* 10,000
acres. Located four miles north of Gila Bend.
Local attractions: Kitt Peak National
Observatory on San Xavier Reservation. Papago
Agency.

GILA RIVER RESERVATION
P.O. Box 97
Sacaton, Arizona 85247
(602) 562-3311
Donald R. Antone, Sr., Governor

Tribes: Pima and Maricopa. *In residence:* 9,750.
Area: 370,000 acres. Tribal council. Salt River
Agency.

GREASEWOOD RESERVATION
Greasewood, Arzizona 86505

Tribe: Navajo. Fort Defiance Agency.

HAVASUPAI RESERVATION
P.O. Box 10
Supai, Arizona 86435
(602) 448-2961
Wayne Sinyella, Chairman

Tribe: Havasupai. *In residence:* 500. *Area:* 3,058 acres. Located in Cataract Canyon, within the Grand Canyon. *Facilities:* Tribal lodge. Tribal council.

HOPI RESERVATION
P.O. Box 123
Oraibi, Arizona 86039
  (602) 734-2445
  Ivan Sidney, Chairman

Tribes: Hopi and Tewa. 2In residence: 8,500. *Area:* 1,565,376 acres. *Facilities:* Hopi Cultural Center; arts and crafts shops; tribal museum; motels and restaurants. Tribal council. Hopi Agency.

HOUCK RESERVATION
Houck, Arizona 86506

Tribe: Navajo. Fort Defiance Agency.

HUALAPAI RESERVATION
P.O. Box 168
Peach Springs, Arizona 86434
  (602) 769-2216
  Edgar Sinyella, Chairman

Tribe: Hualapai. *In residence:* 1,100. *Area:* 995,000 acres. Tribal council.

INSCRIPTION HOUSE RESERVATION
c/o Western Navajo Agency
P.O. Box 127
Tuba City, Arizona 86045

Tribe: Navajo.

JEDDITO RESERVATION
c/o Fort Defiance Agency
P.O. Box 619
Fort Defiance, Arizona 86504

Tribe: Navajo.

KAIBAB RESERVATION
Tribal Affairs Bldg.
Pipe Springs, Arizona 86022
  Delores Savala, Chairwoman

Tribe: Paiute. *In residence:* 250.
Located in Arizona and Utah. Tribal council.

KAIBITO RESERVATION
Kaibito, Arizona 86053

Tribe: Navajo. Western Navajo Agency.

KAYENTA RESERVATION
Kayenta, Arizona 86033

Tribe: Navajo. Western Navajo Agency.

KINLICHEE RESERVATION
c/o Fort Defiance Agency
P.O. Box 619
Fort Defiance, Arizona 86504

Tribe: Navajo.

KLAGETOH RESERVATION
c/o Fort Defiance Agency
P.O. Box 619
Fort Defiance, Arizona 86504

Tribe: Navajo.

LECHEE RESERVATION
c/o Western Navajo Agency
P.O. Box 127
Tuba City, Arizona 86045

Tribe: Navajo.

LEUPP RESERVATION
Leupp, Arizona 86035

Tribe: Navajo. Western Navajo Agency.

LOW MOUNTAIN RESERVATION
c/o Fort Defiance Agency
P.O. Box 619
Fort Defiance, Arizona 86504

Tribe: Navajo.

LUKACHUKAI RESERVATION
Lukachukai, Arizona 86507

Tribe: Navajo. Chinle Agency.

LUPTON RESERVATION
Lupton, Arizona 86508

Tribe: Navajo. Fort Defiance Agency.

MANY FARMS RESERVATION
Many Farms, Arizona 86538

Tribe: Navajo. Chinle Agency.

MARICOPA (AK CHIN) RESERVATION
Route 2, Box 27
Maricopa, Arizona 85239
  (602) 568-2227
  Leroy Narcia, Chairman

Tribes: Papago and Pima. *In residence:* 450. *Area:* 21,500 acres. Tribal council. Pima Agency.

MEXICAN SPRINGS RESERVATION
c/o Fort Defiance Agency
P.O. Box 619
Fort Defiance, Arizona 86504

Tribe: Navajo.

MEXICAN WATERS RESERVATION
c/o Shiprock Agency,
P.O. Box 966
Shiprock, New Mexico 87420

Tribe: Navajo. Located in Arizona, New Mexico and Utah. See listing under New Mexico and Utah.

NASCHITTI RESERVATION
c/o Fort Defiance Agency
P.O. Box 619
Fort Defiance, Arizona 86504

Tribe: Navajo.

NAVAJO MOUNTAIN RESERVATION
c/o Western Navajo Agency
P.O. Box 127
Tuba City, Arizona 86045

Tribe: Navajo. Located in Arizona and Utah.
See listing in Utah.

NAVAJO RESERVATION
P.O. Box 308
Window Rock, Arizona 86515
　(602) 871-4941
　Peterson Zah, Chairman

Tribe: Navajo. *In residence:* 167,000. *Area:* 16
million acres. Located in northern Arizona,
northwest New Mexico, and southern Utah.
Local attractions: Navajo Nation Fair
(September); summer and winter ceremonials
(each week); Museum. Library. Tribal council.
Navajo Area Office.

NAZLINI RESERVATION
c/o Chinle Agency, P.O. Box 7H
Chinle, Arizona 86503

Tribe: Navajo.

OAK SPRINGS RESERVATION
c/o Fort Defiance Agency
P.O. Box 619
Fort Defiance, Arizona 86504

Tribe: Navajo.

OLJATOH RESERVATION
c/o Western Navajo Agency
P.O. Box 127
Tuba City, Arizona 86045

Tribe: Navajo. Located in Arizona and Utah.
See listing under Utah.

PAPAGO (SELLS) RESERVATION
P.O. Box 837
Sells, Arizona 85634
　(602) 383-2236/2221
　Josiah N. Moore, Chairman

Tribe. Papago. *In residence:* 7,500. *Area:*
2,774,000 acres. Located 25 miles west of Tucson.
Tribal council. Papago Agency.

PASCUA YAQUI INDIAN COMMUNITY
4821 West Calley Vicam
Tucson, Arizona 85706
　(602) 883-2830
　David Ramirez, Chairman

PINON RESERVATION
Pinon, Arizona 86510

Tribe: Navajo. Chinle Agency.

RED LAKE RESERVATION
c/o Fort Defiance Agency
P.O. Box 619
Fort Defiance, Arizona 86504

Tribe: Navajo.

RED LAKE RSERVATION
c/o Western Navajo Agency
P.O. Box 127
Tuba City, Arizona 86045

Tribe: Navajo.

RED MESA RESERVATION
c/o Shiprock Agency
P.O. Box 966
Shiprock, New Mexico 87420

Tribe: Navajo. Located in Arizona, New Mexico
and Utah. See listings in New Mexico and Utah.

RED ROCK RESERVATION
c/o Shiprock Agency
P.O. Box 966
Shiprock, New Mexico 87420

Tribe: Navajo. Located in Arizona and
and New Mexico. See listing under New Mexico.

ROUGH ROCK RESERVATION
c/o Chinle Agency, P.O. Box 7H
Chinle, Arizona 86503

Tribe: Navajo.

ROUND ROCK RESERVATION
c/o Chinle Agency, P.O. Box 7H
Chinle, Arizona 86503

Tribe: Navajo.

ST. MICHAELS RESERVATION
c/o Fort Defiance Agency
P.O. Box 619
Fort Defiance, Arizona 86504

Tribe: Navajo.

SALT RIVER RESERVATION
Route 1, Box 216
Scottsdale, Arizona 85256
　(602) 941-7277
　Gerald Anton, Chairman

Tribes: Pima and Maricopa. *In residence:* 3,500.
Area: 46,619 acres. Located in Salt River Valley,
adjacent to Phoenix. Tribal council. Salt River
Agency.

SAN CARLOS APACHE RESERVATION
P.O. Box 0
San Carlos, Arizona 85550
  (602) 475-2361
  Ned Anderson, Chairman

Tribe: Apache. *In residence:* 6,000. *Area:*
1,877,216 acres. *Local attractions:* Coolidge Dam;
San Carlos Reservoir; Tonto National Forest.
Activities: Apache Tribal Fair (October); Indian
Round-up (May and November). Tribal council.
San Carlos Agency.

SAN XAVIER RESERVATION
San Xavier, Arizona 85640

Tribe: Papago. *In residence:* 1,000.
Area: 71,000 acres. Papago Agency.

SANOTSEE RESERVATION
c/o Shiprock Agency
P.O. Box 966
Shiprock, New Mexico 87420

Tribe: Navajo. Located in Arizona and
New Mexico. See listing under New Mexico.

SAWMILL RESERVATION
c/o Fort Defiance Agency
P.O. Box 619
Fort Defiance, Arizona 86504

Tribe: Navajo.

SHONTO RESERVATION
Shonto, Arizona 86054

Tribe: Navajo. Located in Arizona and Utah.
See listing under Utah. Western Navajo Agency.

STEAMBOAT RESERVATION
c/o Fort Defiance Agency
P.O. Box 619
Fort Defiance, Arizona 86504

Tribe: Navajo.

TEECNOSPOS RESERVATION
c/o Shiprock Agency
P.O. Box 966
Shiprock, New Mexico 87420

Tribe: Navajo. Located in Arizona, New Mexico
and Utah. See listings under New Mexico and
Utah.

TEESTO RESERVATION
c/o Fort Defiance Agency
P.O. Box 619
Fort Defiance, Arizona 86504

Tribe: Navajo.

TOHATCHI RESERVATION
c/o Fort Defiance Agency
P.O. Box 619
Fort Defiance, Arizona 86504

Tribe: Navajo.

TOLANI LAKE RESERVATION
c/o Western Navajo Agency
P.O. Box 127
Tuba City, Arizona 86045

Tribe: Navajo.

TONTO APACHE COMMUNITY
P.O. Box 1440
Payson, Arizona 85541
  (602) 474-5000
  Melton Campbell, Chairman

Tribe: Apache. San Carlos Agency.

TSAILE-WHEATFIELDS RESERVATION
Tsaile, Arizona 86556

Tribe: Navajo. Located in Arizona and
New Mexico. See listing under New Mexico.
Chinle Agency.

TSELANI RESERVATION
c/o Chinle Agency, P.O. Box 7H
Chinle, Arizona 86503

Tribe: Navajo.

TUBA CITY RESERVATION
Tuba City, Arizona 86045

Tribe: Navajo. Western Navajo Agency.

TWIN LAKES RESERVATION
c/o Fort Defiance Agency
P.O. Box 619
Fort Defiance, Arizona 86504

Tribe: Navajo.

WHITE CONE RESERVATION
c/o Fort Defiance Agency
P.O. Box 619
Fort Defiance, Arizona 86504

Tribe: Navajo.

WIDE RUINS RESERVATION
Wide Ruins, Arizona 86502

Tribe: Navajo. Fort Defiance Agency.

YAVAPAI-PRESCOTT RESERVATION
P.O. Box 348
Prescott, Arizona 86301
  (602) 445-8790
  Patricia McGee, Chairwoman

Tribe: Yavapai. *In residence:* 85.
Area: 1,500 acres. Fort Apache Agency.

CALIFORNIA

AGUA CALIENTE RESERVATION
441 South Calle Encilia, Suite 1
Palm Springs, California 92262
(619) 325-5673
Richard Milanovich, Chairman

Tribe: Cahuilla. *In residence:* 200. *Area:* 2,600 acres. Tribal council. Palm Springs Field Office.

ALTURAS RANCHERIA
P.O. Box 1035
Alturas, California 96101
Norma Jean Garcia, Chairwoman

Tribe: Pit River. In residence: 12. *Area:* 20 acres. General council. Central California Agency.

AUGUSTINE RESERVATION
Thermal, California 92274

Tribe: Cahuilla. Unoccupied. *Area:* 500 acres. Southern California Agency.

BARONA RESERVATION
1095 Barona Rd.
Lakeside, California 92040
(619) 433-6613
Edward L. Welch, Spokesman

Tribe: Diegueno (Barona Band of Mission Indians.) *In residence:* 300. *Area:* 5,000 acres. Tribal council. Southern California Agency

BENTON PAIUTE RESERVATION
Star Route 4, Box 56-A
Benton, California 93512
(619) 933-2321
Gladys Beauregard, Chairwoman

Tribe: Utu Utu Gwaitu Paiute. *In residence:* 68. *Area:* 160 acres. Located in Mono County, in Springs Valley about three miles from Benton Hot Springs. Tribal council. Central California Agency.

BERRY CREEK RANCHERIA
1956 B St.
Oroville, California 95965

Tribe: Yurok. *In residence:* 150. *Area:* 33 acres. Central California Agency.

BIG BEND RANCHERIA
P.O. Box 255
Big Bend, California 96001
(916) 337-6605
Kenneth Sisk, President

Tribe: Pit River. *In residence:* 110. *Area:* 40 acres. Hoopa Agency.

BIG LAGOON RANCHERIA
P.O. Box 795
Trinidad, California 95570
Dale Lara, Chairman

Tribes: Yurok and Tolowa. *In residence:* 10. *Area:* 9 acres. General council. Hoopa Agency.

BIG PINE RESERVATION
P.O. Box 384
Big Pine, California 93513
(619) 938-2121
Velma Jones, Chairwoman

Tribes: Paiute and Shoshone. *In residence:* 100. *Area:* 280 acres. General council. Central California Agency.

BIG SANDY INTERIM TRIBAL COUNCIL
P.O. Box 337
Auberry, California 93602
Donna Marvin, Chairwoman

Tribe: Mono. *In residence:* 50. *Area:* 8 acres. Tribal council. Central California Agency.

BISHOP INDIAN RESERVATION
P.O. Box 548
Bishop, California 93514
(619) 873-3584
Earl Frank, Chairman

Tribes: Paiute and Shoshone. *In residence:* 1,025. *Area:* 877 acres. *Facilities:* Culture Center. Tribal council. Central California Agency.

BRIDGEPORT INDIAN COLONY
P.O. Box 37
Bridgeport, California 93517
(619) 932-7083
Maurice Crawford, Chairman

Tribe: Paiute. *In residence:* 85. General council. Central California Agency.

CABAZON RESERVATION
84-245 Indio Spring Dr.
Indio, California 92201
(619) 342-2593
Art Welmas, Chairman

Tribe: Cahuilla. *In residence:* 25. General council. Southern California Agency.

CAHUILLA RESERVATION
Star Route, Box 185
Aguango, California 92302
(619) 658-2711
Eugene Madrigal, Spokesman

Tribe: Cahuilla. *In residence:* 165. *Area:* 18,270 acres. General council. Southern California Agency.

CAMPO RESERVATION
P.O. Box 1094
Boulevard, California 92005
(619) 766-4651
Valacia Thacker, Chairwoman

Tribe: Diegueno (Campo Band of Mission
Indians.) *In residence:* 215. *Area:* 15,000
acres. General council. Southern California
Agency.

CAPITAN GRANDE RESERVATION
Lakeside, California 92040

Tribe: Diegueno (Capitan Grande Band of
Mission Indians.) Southern California Agency.

CEDARVILLE RANCHERIA
P.O. Box 142
Cedarville, California 96104
Andrew Phoenix, Chairman

Tribe: Diegueno (Capitan Grande Band of
Mission Indians.) Southern California Agency.

CHEMEHUEVI RESERVATION
P.O. Box 1976
Chemehuevi Valley, California 92363
(619) 858-4531
Richard Alvarez, Chairman

Tribe: Chemehuevi. *In residence:* 125. Tribal
council. Located in California and Arizona.
Colorado River Agency.

COLD SPRINGS RANCHERIA
P.O. Box 209
Tollhouse, California 93667
(209) 855-2326
Dorothy Bill, Chairwoman

Tribe: Mono. *In residence:* 225. *Area:* 98 acres.
Tribal council. Central California Agency.

COLORADO RIVER RESERVATION
Route 1, Box 23-B
Parker, Arizona 85344
(602) 669-9211
Anthony Drennan, Sr., Chairman

Tribes: Mohave, Chemehuevi, Hopi, and Navajo.
In residence: 2,200. *Area:* 28,691 acres.
Tribal council. Colorado River Agency (See
listing under Arizona.) Located along the
Colorado River in southwest California.

COLUSA RANCHERIA
P.O. Box 8
Colusa, California 95932
(916) 458-8231
Michael E. Mitchum, Chairman

Tribe: Cachil DeHe Band of Wintun Indians.
In residence: 50. *Area:* 300 acres.
Community Council. Central California Agency.

CORTINA INDIAN RANCHERIA
P.O. Box 41113
Sacramento, California 95814
(916) 725-6104
Mary Norton, Chairwoman

Tribe: Wintun. *In residence:* 85. *Area:* 640 acres.
General council. Cental California Agency.

COYOTE VALLEY INDIAN COMMUNITY
P.O. Box 39
Redwood Valley, California 95470-0039
(707) 485-8723
Doris Renick, Chairwoman

CUYAPAIPE RESERVATION
P.O. Box 187
Campo, California 92006
(619) 478-5289
Tony J. Pinto, Chairman

Tribe: Diegueno (Campo Band of Mission
Indians.) *In residence:* 25. *Area:* 4,100
acres. General Council. Southern California
Agency.

DEATH VALLEY INDIAN COMMUNITY
P.O. Box 108
Death Valley, California 92325
Pauline Esteves, Chairwoman

Southern California Agency.

DRY CREEK RANCHERIA
P.O. Box 413
Geyserville, California 95441
(707) 433-1209
Amy Martin, Chairwoman

Tribe: Pomo. *In residence:* 25. *Area:* 75 acres.
General council. Central California Agency.

ENTERPRISE RANCHERIA
7470 Feather Falls, Star Route
Oroville, California 95965
(916) 589-0652
Glen Watson, Spokesman

Tribe: Maidu. *In residence:* 20. *Area:* 40 acres.
General council. Central California Agency.

FORT BIDWELL RESERVATION
P.O. Box 127
Fort Bidwell, California 96112
(916) 279-6310
Lucinda Lame Bull, Chairwoman

Tribe: Paiute. *In residence:* 175. *Area:* 3,335 acres.
Tribal council. Central California Agency.

FORT INDEPENDENCE RESERVATION
P.O. Box 67
Independence, California 93526
(619) 878-2126
Vernon Miller, Chairman

Tribes: Paiute and Shoshone. *In residence:* 100.
Area: 356 acres. Central California Agency.

FORT MOJAVE RESERVATION
500 Merriman Ave.
Needles, California 92363
(619) 326-4591
Nora Garcia, Chairwoman

Tribe: Mohave. *In residence:* 575.
Located in California and Arizona. Tribal
council. Colorado River Agency.

FORT YUMA RESERVATION
c/o Fort Yuma Agency
Yuma, Arizona 85364

Located in Arizona and California.
(See listing under Arizona.)

GRINDSTONE CREEK RANCHERIA
P.O. Box 63
Elk Creek, California 95939
(916) 968-5321
James Burrows, Chairman

Tribe: Wintun-Wailaki. *Area:* 80 acres.
General council. Central California Agency.

HOOPA EXTENSION RESERVATION
Weitchpec, California 95546

Tribe: Yurok. *In residence:* 300.
Area: 6,800 acres. Hoopa Agency.

HOOPA VALLEY RESERVATION
P.O. Box 1348
Hoopa, California 95546
(916) 625-4691
Elsie Ricklefs, Chairwoman

Tribe: Hoopa. *In residence:* 2,000.
Area: 86,042 acres. Located along the
Trinity River, 35 miles northeast of Eureka,
California. Business council. Hoopa Agency.

HOPLAND RANCHERIA
P.O. Box 610
Hopland, California 95449
(707) 744-1647
Ramon Billy, President

Tribe: Hopland Band of Pomo Indians.
In residence: 150. *Area:* 2,070 acres.
Tribal council. Central California Agency.

INAJA-COSMIT RESERVATION
P.O. Box 102
Santa Ysabel, California 92070
(619) 765-1993
Rebecca Contreras, Spokeswoman

Tribe: Diegueno. *In residence:* 12.
Area: 880 acres. Southern California Agency.

JACKSON RANCHERIA
12200 New York Ranch Rd.
Jackson, California 95642
(209) 223-1897
Margaret Dalton, Representative

Tribe: Me-Wuk (Miwok). *Area:* 330 acres.
Interim council. Central California Agency.

JAMUL DIEGUENO COMMUNITY
14191-A Highway 94
Jamul, California 92035
(619) 697-5041
Kenneth A. Meza, Chairman

Southern California Agency.

KAROK INDIAN COMMUNITY
P.O. Box 1098
Happy Camp, California 96039
(916) 493-2349
Paul Beck, Chairman

Tribe: Karok. Interim committee. Central
California Agency.

LA JOLLA BAND OF MISSION INDIANS
Star Route, Box 158
Valley Center, California 92082
(619) 742-3771
Doris J. Magante, Chairwoman

Tribe: Luiseno. *In residence:* 225.
General council. Southern California Agency.

LA POSTA RESERVATION
P.O. Box 894
Boulevard, California 92005
(619) 478-5523
Gwendolyn Sevella, Chairwoman

Tribe: Diegueno (La Posta Band of Mission
Indians). Unoccupied. *Area:* 3,600 acres. General
council. Southern California Agency.

LAYTONVILLE RANCHERIA
P.O. Box 1239
Laytonville, California 95454
(707) 984-6194
Gertrude Brown, Chairwoman

Tribe: Cahto-Pomo. *In residence:* 100. *Area:*
200 acres. General council. Central California
Agency.

LONE PINE RESERVATION
Star Route 1
1101 South Main St.
Lone Pine, California 93545
(619) 876-5414
Nedeen Naylor, Chairwoman

Tribes: Paiute and Shoshone. *In residence:* 150.
Area: 237 acres. Tribal council. Central California
Agency.

LOOKOUT RANCHERIA
P.O. Box 87
Lookout, California 96054
  Laura Craig, Representative

Tribe: Pit River. *Area:* 40 acres.
Central California Agency.

LOS COYOTES RESERVATION
P.O. Box 86
Warner Springs, California 92086
(619) 782-3269
  Banning Taylor, Spokesman

Tribe: Luiseno. *In residence:* 175. *Area:*
25,000 acres. General council. Southern
California Agency.

MANCHESTER RANCHERIA
P.O. Box 623
Point Arena, California
(707) 882-2788
  Kenneth Laiwa, Chairman

Tribe: Pomo. *In residence:* 90. *Area:* 364 acres.
Community council. Cental California Agency.

MANZANITA RESERVATION
P.O. Box 1302
Boulevard, California 92005
(619) 478-5028
  Frances Shaw, Chairman

Tribe: Diegueno (Manzanita Band of
Mission Indians.) *In residence:* 20.
Area: 3,579 acres. General council.
Southern California Agency.

MESA GRANDE RESERVATION
Mesa Grande Star Route
Santa Ysabel, California 92070
(619) 782-3521
  Brian Beresford, Chairman

Tribe: Diegueno (Mesa Grande Band of Mission
Indians). Unoccupied. *Area:* 120 acres. General
council. Southern California Agency.

MIDDLETOWN RANCHERIA
P.O. Box 292
Middletown, California 95461
  Larry Simon, President

Tribe: Pomo. *Area:* 109 acres. Interim council.
Central California Agency.

MONTGOMERY CREEK RANCHERIA
General Delivery
Montgomery Creek, California 96065
  Ross Montgomery, Spokesman

Tribe: Pit River. *Area:* 80 acres. Hoopa Agency.

MORONGO RESERVATION
11581 Potrero Rd.
Banning, California 92220

(714) 849-4697
  Robert Martin, Spokesman

Tribe: Cahuilla. *In residence:* 350. *Area:*
32,250 acres. General Council. Southern
California Agency.

PALA INDIAN RESERVATION
P.O. Box 43
Pala, California 92059
(619) 742-3784
  King Freeman, Chairman

Tribe: Luiseno (Pala Band). *In residence:* 375.
Area: 11,000 acres. Executive Committee.
Southern California Agency.

**PAUMA BAND OF MISSION
INDIANS RESERVATION**
P.O. Box 86
Pauma Reservation Rd., Highway 76
Pauma Valley, California 92061
(619) 742-1289
  Patricia A. Dixon, Chairwoman

Tribe: Luiseno. *In residence:* 35. *Area:* 5,750
acres. Tribal Council. Southern California
Agency.

PECHANGA RESERVATION
P.O. Box 181
Temecula, California 92390
(714) 676-6653
  Gabriel H. Pico, Spokesman

Tribe: Luiseno (Pechanga Band of Mission
Indians.) Tribal council. Southern
California Agency.

RESIGHINI RANCHERIA
P.O. Box 212
Klamath, California 95548
(707) 482-3371
  William John Scott, President

Tribe: Yurok. Unoccupied. *Area:* 230 acres.
Business Council. Central California Agency.

RINCON RESERVATION
P.O. Box 68
Valley Center, California 92082
(619) 749-1051
  Don Calac, Chairman

Tribe: Luiseno (Rincon Band of Mission Indians).
In residence: 150. Business Committee. Southern
California Agency.

ROBINSON CITIZENS BUSINESS COUNCIL
2000 Marconi Ave.
Sacramento, California 95821
(916) 922-4536
  Bernadine Tripp, Chairwoman

Tribe: Pomo. Central California Agency.

ROUND VALLEY RESERVATION
P.O. Box 448
Covelo, California 95428
(707) 983-6126
Daran Lincoln, President

Tribes: Wailaki, Yuki, Nomelacki, Mono, Pomo.
In residence: 450. *Area:* 18,706 acres.
Community Council. Central California Agency.

RUMSEY INDIAN RANCHERIA
P.O. Box 18
Brooks, California 95606
(916) 796-3182
Philip Knight, Chairman

Tribe: Wintun. *Area:* 67 acres. Community
Council. Central California Agency.

SAN MANUEL RESERVATION
5771 North Victoria Ave.
Highland, California 92346
(714) 862-2439
Henry Duro, Chairman

Tribe: Serrano (San Manual Band of Serrano
Mission Indians). *In residence:* 50. *Area:* 650
acres. General Council. Southern California
Agency.

SAN PASQUAL RESERVATION
P.O. Box 365
Valley Center, California 92082
(619) 749-3200
Robert L. Stewart, Spokesman

Tribe: Dieguino (San Pasqual Band of Mission
Indians.) *Area:* 1,380 acres. Tribal Council.
Southern California Agency.

SANTA ROSA RESERVATION
325 North Western St.
Hemet, California 92343
(714) 925-7190
Anthony Largo, Spokesman

Tribe: Cahuilla. *In residence:* 100. *Area:* 11,000
acres. General Council. Southern California
Agency.

SANTA ROSA RANCHERIA
16088 Alkalie Dr.
Lemoore, California 93245
(209) 924-1571
Clarence Atwell, Chairman

Tribe: Tache. *In residence:* 125. *Area:* 170 acres.
General council. Southern California Agency.

SANTA YNEZ RESERVATION
P.O. Box 517
Santa Ynez, California 93460
(805) 688-7997
James Pace, Chairman

*Tribe: Chumash (Santa Ynez Band of Chumash
Mission Indians). In residence:* 100. *Area:* 100
acres. General Council. Southern California
Agency.

SANTA YSABEL RESERVATION
P.O. Box 126
Santa Ysabel, California 92070
(619) 765-0845
Joan King, Chairwoman

Tribe: Dieguino (Santa Ysabel Band of Mission
Indians). *In residence:* 300. *Area:* 15,500 acres.
General Council. Southern California Agency.

SHEEP RANCH RANCHERIA
Sheep Ranch, California 95250

Tribe: Me-Wuk (Miwok). Central California
Agency.

SHERWOOD VALLEY RANCHERIA
2137 South State St.
Ukiah, California 95482
(707) 468-1337
Patricia Augustine, Chairwoman

Tribe: Pomo. General Council. Central California
Agency.

SHINGLE SPRINGS RANCHERIA
8024 Levering Way
Sacramento, California 95801
(916(421-7783
John Fenseca, Chairman

Tribe: Me-Wuk (Miwok). Unoccupied. *Area:* 160
acres. Central California Agency.

SOBOBA RESERVATION
P.O. Box 487
San Jacinto, California 92383
(714) 654-2765
Benny Helms, Sr., Spokesman

Tribe: Luiseno (Soboba Band of Mission
Indians). *In residence:* 300. *Area:* 5,000 acres.
General Council. Southern California Agency.

STEWARTS POINT RANCHERIA
1112 Mendocino Ave.
Santa Rosa, California 95401
(707) 528-1872
Langford Pinola, Chairman

Tribe: Kashia Pomo. *In residence:* 100. *Area:* 40
acres. Kashia Business Committee. Central
California Agency.

SULPHUR BANK RANCHERIA
P.O. Box 618
Clearlake Oaks, California 95423
(707) 998-1666
Raymond J. Brown, Chairman

Tribe: Elem Indian Colony of Pomo Indians. *In residence:* 50. *Area:* 50 acres. Elem General Council. Central California Agency.

SUSANVILLE INDIAN RANCHERIA
Drawer 'U'
Susanville, California 96130
(916) 257-6264
Nicolas J. Padilla, Chairman

Tribes: Paiute, Maidu, and Pit River. *In residence:* 350. *Area:* 140 acres. Business Council. Central California Agency.

SYCUAN RESERVATION
P.O. Box 2929
El Cajon, California 92021
(619) 445-4073
Anna Sandoval, Spokesman

Tribe: Diegueno (Sycan Band of Mission Indians.) *In residence:* 70. *Area:* 640 acres. General council. Southern California Agency.

TABLE BLUFF BOARD OF DIRECTORS
P.O. Box 519
Loleta, California 95551
(707) 733-5537
Robert Johnson, Chairman

Central California Agency.

TABLE MOUNTAIN RESERVATION
P.O. Box 243
Friant, California 93626
Lewis Barnes, Chairman

Southern California Agency.

TORRES-MARTINEZ RESERVATION
1866 East George
Banning, California 92220
(714) 849-2172
Ronald D. Cortez, Chairman

Tribe: Cahuilla. *In residence:* 85. *Area:* 25,000 acres. Business Committee. Southern California Agency.

TRINIDAD RANCHERIA
P.O. Box AA
Trinidad, California 95570
(707) 677-0211
Rose Joy Sundberg, Chairwoman

Tribe: Me-Wuk (Miwok), Cher-Ae Heights Indian Community. Community Council. Hoopa Agency.

TULE RIVER RESERVATION
P.O. Box 589
Porterville, California 93257
(209) 781-4271
Crispina Sierra, Chairwoman

Tribe: Tule River. *In residence:* 550. *Area:* 54,000 acres. Tribal Council. Central California Agency.

TUOLUMNE RANCHERIA
P.O. Box 696
Tuolumne, California 95379
(209) 928-4265
Stanley R. Cox, Jr., Chairman

Tribe: Me-Wuk (Miwok). *Area:* 325 acres. Community Council. Central California Agency.

TWENTY-NINE PALMS RESERVATION
Twenty-Nine Palms, California 92277

Tribe: Luiseno (Twenty-Nine Palms Band of Mission Indians). *Unoccupied. Area:* 160 acres. Southern California Agency.

VIEJAS (BARON LONG) RESERVATION
P.O. Box 908
Alpine, California 92001
(619) 445-3275
Anthony Pico, Spokesman

Tribe: Diegueno (Viejas Baron Long Capitan Grande Band of Mission Indians). *In residence:* 185. *Area:* 1,600 acres. Tribal Committee. Southern California Agency.

X-L (PIT RIVER) INDIAN RESERVATION
P.O. Box 763
Alturas, California 96101
(916) 335-3353
Leo Jones, Chairman

Tribe: Pit River. *Area:* 9,242 acres. Tribal Council. Central California Agency.

COLORADO

SOUTHERN UTE RESERVATION
P.O. Box 737
Ignacio, Colorado 81137
(303) 563-4525
Chris A. Baker, Chairman

Tribe: Southern Ute. *In residence:* 1,100. *Area:* 307,000 acres. Located along the Colorado—New Mexico border. *Activities:* Sun Dance, Bear Dance, and annual Ute Fair. Library. Tribal Council. Southern Ute Agency.

UTE MOUNTAIN RESERVATION
Tribal Office Bldg.
Towaoc, Colorado 81334
(303) 565-3751
Ernest House, Chairman

Tribe: Ute Mountain Ute. *In residence:* 1,500. *Area:* 590,000 acres. Located in Colorado, New Mexico, and Utah. Tribal Council. Ute Mountain Ute Agency.

CONNECTICUT

EASTERN PEQUOT RESERVATION
North Stonington, Connecticut 06359

Tribe: Pequot. *Area:* 220 acres. Eastern Area Office.

GOLDEN HILL RESERVATION
Trumbull, Connecticut 06611

Tribe: Pequot. Eastern Area Office.

MASHANTUCKET PEQUOT RESERVATION
P.O. Box 160
Ledyard, Connecticut 06339
(203) 536-2681
Richard Hayward, Chairman

Tribe: Pequot. *Area:* 184 acres. Eastern Area Office.

SCHAGHTICOKE INDIAN RESERVATION
Kent, Connecticut 06757

Tribe: Schaghticoke. *Area:* 400 acres. Eastern Area Office.

FLORIDA

BIG CYPRESS RESERVATION
c/o Seminole Agency
6075 Stirling Rd.
Hollywood, Florida 33024

Tribe: Miccosukee Seminole. *In residence:* 400. *Area:* 42,700. Located in southern Florida.

BRIGHTON RESERVATION
c/o Seminole Agency
6075 Stirling Rd.
Hollywood, Florida 33024

Tribe: Cow Creek. *In residence:* 400. *Area:* 35,800. Located in south-central Florida.

MICCOSUKEE RESERVATION
P.O. Box 44021, Tamiami Station
Miami, Florida 33144
(305) 223-8380/8383
Buffalo Tiger, Chairman

Tribe: Creek. *In residence:* 475. *Area:* 333 acres. Located on Tamiami Trail, forty miles west of Miami. Business Committee. Miccosukee Agency.

SEMINOLE RESERVATION
6073 Stirling Rd.
Hollywood, Florida 33024
(305) 583-7112
James Billie, Chairman

Tribe: Seminole. *In residence:* 500. *Area:* 480 acres. Located on U.S. 441, in the Fort Laurderdale—Miami area. *Local attractions:* Seminole Indian Village featuring typical village life and customs, native arts and crafts, native animal exhibits. *Activities:* Indian ceremonials held in mid-July. Tribal Council. Seminole Agency.

IDAHO

COEUR D'ALENE RESERVATION
Plummer, Idaho 83851
(208) 274-3101
Bernard J. Lasarte, Chairman

Tribe: Coeur D'Alene (Skitswish). *In residence:* 825. *Area:* 69,435 acres. Located 35 miles south of Coeur D'Alene, Idaho. Tribal Council. Northern Idaho Agency.

DUCK VALLEY RESERVATION
c/o Eastern Nevada Agency
Elko, Nevada 89801

Tribes: Shoshone and Paiute. Located in Idaho and Nevada.

FORT HALL RESERVATION
Fort Hall Tribal Office
Fort Hall, Idaho 83203
(208) 238-3700
Kelsey Edmo, Chairman

Tribes: Shoshone, Bannock, and Blackfeet. *In residence:* 3,900. *Area:* 523,917 acres. Located near Pocatello, Idaho, east and south of the Snake River. *Local attraction:* American Falls. Tribal Council. Fort Hall Agency.

KOOTENAI RESERVATION
P.O. Box 1002
Bonners Ferry, Idaho 83805
(208) 267-3519
Amelia C. Trice, Chairwoman

Tribe: Kootenai. *In residence:* 125. *Area:* 2,680 acres. Located in Boundary County, near Mirror Lake and the Canadian border. Tribal Council. Northern Idaho Agency.

NEZ PERCE RESERVATION
P.O. Box 305
Lapwai, Idaho 83540
(208) 843-2253
Allen V. Pinkham, Chairman

Tribe: Nez Perce. *In residence:* 2,000. *Area:* 92,685 acres. Located in Nez Perce, Lewis, Clearwater and Idaho Counties. Tribal Council. Northern Idaho Agency.

SUMMIT LAKE RESERVATION
P.O. Box 597
Fort Hall, Idaho 83203
(208) 237-6528
Murray Barr, Chairman

Tribe: Paiute. Tribal Council. Fort Hall Agency.

IOWA

OMAHA RESERVATION
Macy, Nebraska 68039
(402) 837-5391
Wallace W. Miller, Chairman

Tribe: Omaha. Located in Iowa and Nebraska. (See listing under Nebraska.) Tribal Council. Winnebago Agency.

SAC AND FOX RESERVATION
Route 2, Box 52C
Tama, Iowa 52339
(515) 484-4678
Louis Mitchell, Chairman

Tribe: Sac and Fox. *In residence:* 700. *Area:* Ten acres. Tribal Council. Sac and Fox Area Field Office.

WINNEBAGO RESERVATION
Winnebago, Nebraska 68071
(402) 878-2272
Reuben A. Snake, Jr., Chairman

Tribe: Winnebago. Located in Nebraska and Iowa (off-reservation lands in Iowa.) Tribal Council. (See listing under Nebraska.) Winnebago Agency.

KANSAS

IOWA RESERVATION
Route 1, Box 58A
White Cloud, Kansas 66094
(913) 595-3258
Leon Campbell, Chairman

Tribe: Iowa. *In residence:* 300. Located in Kansas and Nebraska. Tribal Council.(See listing under Nebraska.) Horton Agency.

KICKAPOO RESERVATION
Route 1, Box 157A
Horton, Kansas 66439
(913) 486-2131
Fred Thomas, Chairman

Tribe: Kickapoo. In residence: 600. Tribal Council. Horton Agency.

PRAIRIE POTAWATOMI RESERVATION
P.O. Box 97
Mayetta, Kansas 66509
(913) 966-2255/2771
George Wahquahboshkuk, Chairman

Tribe: Prairie Potawatomi. *In residence:* 1,250. Tribal Council. Horton Agency.

SAC AND FOX TRIBE OF THE MISSOURI RESERVATION
P.O. Box 38
Reserve, Kansas 66434
(913) 742-7471
Nancy Keller, Chairwoman

Tribe: Sac and Fox of the Missouri. Located in Kansas and Nebraska. Tribal Council. (See listing under Nebraska.) Horton Agency.

LOUISIANA

CHITIMACHA RESERVATION
P.O. Box 661
Charenton, Louisiana 70523
(318) 923-4973
Larry Burgess, Chairman

Tribe: Chitimacha. *In residence:* 300. *Area:* 283 acres. *Activities:* Chitimacha Tribal Fair (Fourth of July Weekend). Tribal Council. Choctaw Agency.

COUSHATTA RESERVATION
Coushatta, Louisiana 71019

Tribe: Coushatta. *In residence:* 275. Choctaw Agency.

HOUMA INDIAN COMMUNITIES

Tribe: Houma. *In residence:* 2,500 (six communities.) Located in southeast Louisiana, Terrebonne and Lafourche parishes. No coporate land base.

TUNICA-BILOXI INDIAN RESERVATION
P.O. BOX 331
Marksville, Louisiana 71351
(318) 253-9767
Earl Barbry, Sr., Chairman

Tribal Council. Choctaw Agency.

MAINE

HOULTON (MALISEET BAND) RESERVATION
P.O. Box 576
Houlton, Maine 04730

(207) 532-7339
Clair Sabattis, Chairwoman

Tribe: Maliseet. *In residence:* 250.
Tribal Council. New York Liaison Office.

INDIAN TOWNSHIP PASSAMAQUODDY RESERVATION
P.O. Box 301
Indian Township, Maine 04668
(207) 796-2301
John Stevens, Governor

Tribe: Passamaquoddy. *In residence:* 375. *Area:*
18,000 acres. Indian communities at Peter Dana
Point and "The Strip." Tribal Council. New York
Liaison Office.

PENOBSCOT RESERVATION
Six River Rd., Indian Island Reservation
Old Town, Maine 04468
(207) 827-7776
Timothy Love, Governor

Tribe: Penobscot. *In residence:* 1,050. *Area:*
4,400 acres. Located on Indian Island. Tribal
Council. New York Liaison Office.

PLEASANT POINT PASSAMAQUODDY RESERVATION
P.O. Box 343
Perry, Maine 04667
(207) 853-2551
Ralph F. Dana, Governor

Tribe: Passamaquoddy. *In residence:* 700. *Area:*
100 acres. Tribal Council. New York Liaison
Office.

MICHIGAN

BAY MILLS RESERVATION
Route 1, Box 313
Brimley, Michigan 49715
(906) 248-3241
Wade Teeple, President

Tribe: Chippewa (Bay Mills and Sault Ste.
Marie Bands.) *In residence:* 375. *Area:*
2,200 acres. Executive Council. Michigan
Agency.

GRAND TRAVERSE RESERVATION
Route 1, Box 118
Suttons Bay, Michigan 49682
(616) 271-3538
Joseph Raphael, Chairman

Tribe: Chippewa. Tribal Council. Michigan
Agency.

HANNAHVILLE INDIAN COMMUNITY
Route 1, Community Center
Wilson, Michigan 49896
(906) 466-2379
Henry Philemon, Sr., Chairman

Tribe: Potawatomi. *In residence:* 350. *Area:*
2,850 acres. Tribal Council. Michigan Agency.

ISABELLA RESERVATION
7070 East Broadway Rd.
Mount Pleasant, Michigan 48858
(517) 772-5700
Arnold Sowmick, Chief

Tribe: Saginaw Chippewa. *In residence:* 450.
Area: 1,125 acres. Tribal Council. Michigan
Agency.

L'ANSE (KEWEENAW BAY) RESERVATION
Tribal Center Bldg., Route 1
Baroga, Michigan 49908
(906) 353-6623
Myrtle Tolonen, President

Tribe: Chippewa (Keewanah Bay, L'Anse,
Lac Vieux Desert, and Ontonagan Bands.)
In residence: 900. *Area:* 10,000 acres.
Tribal council. Michigan Agency.

SAULT STE. MARIE TRIBE OF CHIPPEWA INDIANS RESERVATION
206 Greenough St.
Sault Ste. Marie, Michigan 49783
(906) 635-6050
Joseph Lumsden, President

Tribe: Sault Ste. Marie Chippewa. *In residence:*
2,500. *Area:* 242 acres. *Activities:* Tribal Pow-
Wows (two each summer.) Tribal Council.
Michigan Agency.

MINNESOTA

FOND DU LAC RESERVATION
105 University Rd.
Cloquet, Minnesota 55720
(218) 879-1251
Gary Donald, Chairman

Tribe: Chippewa. *In residence:* 1,000.
Area: 21,350 acres. Business Committee.
Minnesota Agency.

GRAND PORTAGE (PIGEON RIVER) RESERVATION
P.O. Box 428
Grand Portage, Minnesota 55605
(218) 475-2279/2277
Jim Hendrickson, Chairman

Tribe: Chippewa. *In residence:* 325. *Area:* 43,836 acres. Located near Lake Superior, adjacent to the Canadian border. Business Committee. Minnesota Agency.

LEECH LAKE RESERVATION
Route 3, Box 100
Cass Lake, Minnesota 56633
  (218) 335-2207
  Hartley White, Chairman

Tribe: Chippewa (Mississippi and Pillager Bands). *In residence:* 5,000. *Area:* 27,760 acres. *Activities:* Pow-Wows (five annually). Business Committee. Minnesota Agency.

LOWER SIOUX INDIAN COMMUNITY
Rural Route 1, Box 308
Morton, Minnesota 56270
  (507) 697-6185
  Michael Prescott, President

Tribe: Mdewakanton Sioux. *In residence:* 210. *Area:* 1,750 acres. Tribal Council. Minnesota Sioux Area Field Office.

MILLE LACS RESERVATION
Star Route
Onamia, Minnesota 56359
  (612) 532-4181
  Arthur Gahbow, Chairman

Tribe: Chippewa. *In residence:* 925. Area: 3,600 acres. Business Committee. Minnesota Agency.

NETT LAKE (BOIS FORT) RESERVATION
Nett Lake, Minnesota 55772
  (218) 757-3261
  Gary Donald, Chairman

Tribe: Chippewa (Deer Creek). *In residence:* 1,000. *Area:* 41,750 acres. Business Committee. Minnesota Agency.

PRAIRIE ISLAND RESERVATION
Route 2
Welch, Minnesota 55089
  (612) 388-8889
  Vine Wells, Presidence

Tribe: Mdewakanton Sioux. *In residence:* 125. *Area:* 534 acres. Tribal Council. Minnesota Sioux Area Field Office.

RED LAKE RESERVTION
Red Lake, Minnesota 56671
  (218) 679-3341
  Roger Jourdain, Chairman

Tribe: Chippewa. *In residence:* 4,500. *Area:* 564,364 acres. Located along lower Red Lake, 30 miles north of Bemidji, Minnesota. Tribal Council. Red Lake Agency.

SHAKOPEE MDEWAKANTON SIOUX COMMUNITY
c/o Minnesota Sioux Area Field Office
2330 Sioux Trail, NW
Prior Lake, Minnesota 55372

Tribe: Shakopee Mdewakanton Sioux. *In residence:* 100.

UPPER SIOUX INDIAN COMMUNITY
P.O. Box 147
Granite Falls, Minnesota 56241
  (612) 564-4504/4026
  Irene Howell, Chairwoman

Tribe: Santee Sioux. *In residence:* 135. *Area:* 750 acres. Board of Trustees. Minnesota Sioux Area Field Office.

WHITE EARTH RESERVATION
P.O. Box 418
White Earth, Minnesota 56591
  (218) 983-3285
  Darrell Wadena, Chairman

Tribe: Chippewa. *In residence:* 3,000. *Area:* 27,560 acres. Business Committee. Minnesota Agency.

MISSISSIPPI

MISSISSIPPI CHOCTAW RESERVATION
Route 7, Box 21
Philadelphia, Mississippi 39350
  (601) 656-5251
  Phillip Martin, Chief

Tribe: Mississippi Choctaw. *In residence:* 4,600. *Area:* 18,000 acres. Located in six east-central Mississippi counties centering on eight distinct Indian communities. *Activities:* Annual Choctaw Indian Fair (July). Tribal Council. Choctaw Agency.

MISSOURI

EASTERN SHAWNEE RESERVTION
P.O. Box 350
Seneca, Missouri 64865
  (918) 666-2435
  George Captain, Chief

Tribe: Shawnee. *In residence:* 350. Tribal Council. Miami Agency.

MONTANA

BLACKFEET RESERVATION
Browning, Montana 59417
(406) 338-7276
Earl Old Person, Chairman

Tribe: Blackfeet. *In residence:* 6,750.
Area: 955,241 acres. Located west of Glacier
National Park, south of the Canadian border.
Local attraction: Museum of the Plains Indians.
Activities: Annual Blackfeet Medicine Lodge
Ceremonial and Sun Dance (July.) Tribal
Council. Blackfeet Agency.

CROW INDIAN RESERVATION
Crow Agency, Montana 59022
(406) 638-2671
Donald Stewart, Sr., Chairman

Tribe: Crow. *In residence:* 5,000. *Area:*
1,575,326 acres. Located 15 miles southeast of
Hardin, Montana. *Local attraction:* Custer
Battlefield National Monument and Museum.
Tribal Council. Crow Agency.

FLATHEAD RESERVATION
P.O. Box 278
Pablo, Montana 59855
(406) 675-4600
Joseph Felsman, Chairman

Tribes: Salish and Kootenai. *In residence:* 3,500.
Area: 140,000 acres. Tribal Council. Flathead
Agency.

FORT BELKNAP RESERVATION
Harlem, Montana 59526
(406) 353-2205
Franklin (Randy) Perez, President

Tribes: Gros Ventre and Assiniboine-Sioux.
In residence: 2,100. *Area:* 622,644 acres.
Located 50 miles east of Havre, Montana.
Tribal Council. Fort Belknap Agency.

FORT PECK RESERVATION
Poplar, Montana 59255
(406) 768-5311
Norman Hollow, Chairman

Tribe: Assiniboine-Sioux. *In residence:* 5,000.
Area: 981,144 acres. Loctaed 20 miles south of
the Canadian border. Tribal Executive Board.
Fort Peck Agency.

NORTHERN CHEYENNE RESERVATION
Lame Deer, Montana 59043
(406) 477-6284
Allen Rowland, President

Tribe: Northern Cheyenne. *In residence:* 3,000.
Area: 425,000 acres. Tribal Council.
Northern Cheyenne Agency.

ROCKY BOY'S RESERVATION
P.O. Box 137
Box Elder, Montana 59521
(406) 395-4476
Rocky Stump, Sr., Chairman

Tribes: Chippewa and Cree. *In residence:* 1,000.
Area: 107,532 acres. Located in Bear Paw
Mountains, north-central Montana. Business
Committee. Rocky Boy's Agency.

NEBRASKA

IOWA RESERVATION
Route 1, Box 58A
White Cloud, Kansas 66094

Tribe: Iowa. Located in Kansas and Nebraska.
(See listing under Kansas.)

OMAHA RESERVATION
Macy, Nebraska 68039
(402) 837-5391
Wallace W. Miller, Chairman

Tribe: Omaha. *In residence:* 1,500. *Area:*
27,700 acres. Located in Nebraska and Iowa
Tribal Council. Winnebago Agency.

PINE RIDGE RESERVATION
Pine Ridge, South Dakota 57770

Tribe: Oglala Sioux. Located 60 miles east of
the Black Hills, extending into Nebraska.
(See listing under South Dakota.)

**SAC AND FOX TRIBE OF
THE MISSOURI RESERVATION**
P.O. Box 38
Reserve, Kansas 66434

Tribe: Sac and Fox of the Missouri. Located in
Nebraska and Kansas. (See listing under Kansas.)

SANTEE SIOUX RESERVATION
Route 2
Niobrara, Nebraska 68760
(402) 857-3302
Richard Kitto, Chairman

Tribe: Santee Sioux. *In residence:* 400.
Area: 3,600 acres. Tribal Council.
Winnebago Agency.

WINNEBAGO RESERVATION
Winnebago, Nebraska 68071
(402) 878-2272
Reuben A. Snake, Jr., Chairman

Tribe: Winnebago. *In residence:* 1,000.
Area: 27,000 acres. Located in Nebraska
and Iowa (off-reservation lands in Iowa.)
Tribal Council. Winnebago Agency.

NEVADA

BATTLE MOUNTAIN RESERVATION
Battle Mountain, Nevada 89820

Tribe: Te-Moak Band of Western Shoshone.
Area: 700 acres. Te-Moak Business Council
(Elko, Nevada.) Eastern Nevada Agency.

CARSON INDIAN COLONY
Carson City, Nevada 89701

Tribe: Washoe. *Area:* 150 acres.
Eastern Nevada Agency.

DRESSLERVILLE INDIAN COLONY
Gardnerville, Nevada 89401

Tribe: Washoe. *Area:* 40 acres.
Western Nevada Agency.

DUCK VALLEY RESERVATION
P.O. Box 219
Owyhee, Nevada 89832
(702) 756-3161
Whitney McKinney, Chairman

Tribes: Shoshone and Paiute. *In residence:*
1,100. *Area:* 145,000 acres. Located in
Nevada and Idaho. Business Council.
Eastern Nevada Agency

DUCKWATER RESERVATION
P.O. Box 68
Duckwater, Nevada 89314
(702) 863-0227
Jerry Millett, Chairman

Tribe: Shoshone. *In residence:* 140.
Area: 800 acres. Tribal Council.
Western Nevada Agency.

ELKO INDIAN COLONY
Elko, Nevada 89801

Tribe: Te-Moak Band of Western Shoshone.
Area: 200 acres. Te-Moak Business Council
(Elko, Nevada.) Eastern Nevada Agency.

ELY INDIAN COLONY
16 Shoshone Circle
Ely, Nevada 89301
(702) 289-6318
Sally Marques, Chairwoman

Tribe: Shoshone. *Population:* 235. *Area:* 111
acres. Tribal Council. Western Nevada Agency.

FALLON RESERVATION AND COLONY
Route 2, Box 232A
8955 Mission Rd.
Fallon, Nevada 89406
(702) 423-6075
Alvin Moyle, Chairman

Tribes: Paiute and Shoshone. *In residence:*
675. *Area:* 5,500 acres. Tribal Council.
Western Nevada Agency.

FORT McDERMITT RESERVATION
P.O. Box 457
McDermitt, Nevada 89421
(702) 532-8259
Glen Abel, Chairman

Tribes: Shoshone and Paiute. *In residence:* 650.
Area: 16,400 acres. Located in Nevada and
Oregon. Tribal Council. Western Nevada Agency.

FORT MOHAVE RESERVATION
Tribe: Mohave. Located in Arizona, California
and Nevada. (See listing under Arizona.)

LAS VEGAS INDIAN COLONY
1 Paiute Dr.
Las Vegas, Nevada 89106
(702) 386-3926
Billy J. Frye, Chairman

Tribe: Paiute. *In residence:* 125. *Area:* Ten
acres. Tribal Council. Western Nevada Agency.

LOVELOCK INDIAN COLONY
P.O. Box 878
Lovelock, Nevada 89419
(702) 273-7861
Dena J. Austin, Chairwoman

Tribe: Paiute. *In residence:* 175. *Area:* 20
acres. Tribal Council. Western Nevada Agency.

MOAPA RIVER INDIAN RESERVATION
P.O. Box 56
Las Vegas, Nevada 89025
(702) 865-2787
Clifton R. Surrett, Chairman

Tribe: Southern Paiute. *In residence:* 260.
Area: 73,258 acres. Business Council.
Western Nevada Agency.

PYRAMID LAKE RESERVATION
P.O. Box 256
Nixon, Nevada 89424
(702) 476-0140
Wilfred Shaw, Chairman

Tribe: Paiute. *In residence:* 750. *Area:*
1,195,000 acres. Tribal Council. Western
Nevada Agency.

RENO-SPARKS INDIAN COLONY
98 Colony Rd.
Reno, Nevada 89502
(702) 329-2936
Lawrence Astor, Chairman

Tribes: Washoe and Paiute. *In residence:* 600.
Tribal Council. Western Nevada Agency.

RUBY VALLEY
(TE-MOAK) RESERVATION
525 Sunset St.
Elko, Nevada 89801
(702) 738-9251
Felix Ike, Chairman

Tribe: Te-Moak Band of Western Shoshone.
Area: 15,000 acres. Business Council.
Eastern Nevada Agency.

SOUTH FORK INDIAN COLONY
Lee, Nevada 89829

Tribe: Te-Moak Band of Western Shoshone.
Area: 15,000 acres. Te-Moak Business Council
(Elko, Nevada). Eastern Nevada Agency.

SUMMIT LAKE RESERVATION
Stewart, Nevada 89437

Tribe: Paiute. *Area:* 10,500 acres.
Western Nevada Agency.

WALKER RIVER RESERVATION
P.O. Box 220
Schurz, Nevada 89427
(702) 773-2306
Elvin Willie, Jr., Chairman

Tribe: Paiute. *In residence:* 1,000. *Area:* 320,000
acres. Tribal Council. Western Nevada Agency.

WASHOE RESERVATION
Route 2, Box 68
Gardnerville, Nevada 89410
(702) 883-1446
Robert L. Frank, Chairman

Tribe: Washoe. *Area:* 900 acres.
Tribal Council. Western Nevada Agency.

WINNEMUCCA INDIAN COLONY
P.O. Box 1075
Winnemucca, Nevada 89445
(702) 623-3479
Robert Harney, Chairman

Tribe: Paiute. *In residence:* 100. *Area:*
340 acres. Tribal Council. Western Nevada
Agency.

YERRINGTON INDIAN COLONY
AND CAMPBELL RANCH
171 Campbell Lane
Yerington, Nevada 89447
(702) 463-3301
Kenneth M. Richardson, Chairman

Tribe: Paiute. *In residence:* 350. *Area:*
200 acres. Tribal Council. Western Nevada
Agency.

YOMBA RESERVATION
Route 1, Box 24A
Austin, Nevada 89310
(702) 964-2463
William Rosse, Sr., Chairman

Tribe: Shoshone. *In residence:* 120. *Area:*
4,700 acres. Tribal Council. Western Nevada
Agency.

NEW MEXICO

ACOMA PUEBLO
P.O. Box 309
Acomita, New Mexico 87034
(505) 552-6604
Merle Garcia, Governor

Tribe: Pueblo. *In residence:* 3,000. *Area:* 25,000
acres. Located 50 miles west of Albuquerque.
Tribal Council. Southern Pueblos Agency.

ANETH RESERVATION
c/o Shiprock Agency
P.O. Box 966
Shiprock, New Mexico 87420

Tribe: Navajo.

BACA RESERVATION
c/o Eastern Navajo Agency
P.O. Box 328
Crownpoint, New Mexico 87313

Tribe: Navajo.

BECENTI RESERVATION
Tribe: Navajo. c/o Eastern Navajo Agency.

BECALBITO RESERVATION
Tribe: Navajo. c/o Shiprock Agency.

BREAD SPRINGS RESERVATION
Tribe: Navajo. c/o Eastern Navajo Agency.

BURNHAM RESERVATION
Tribe: Navajo. c/o Shiprock Agency.

CANONCITO RESERVATION
Tribe: Navajo. c/o Eastern Navajo Agency.

CASAMERO LAKE RESERVATION
Tribe: Navajo. c/o Eastern Navajo Agency.

CHEECHILGEETHO RESERVATION
Tribe: Navajo. c/o Eastern Navajo Agency.

CHURCH ROCK RESERVATION
Tribe: Navajo. c/o Eastern Navajo Agency.

COCHITI PUEBLO
P.O. Box 70
Cochiti, New Mexico 87041
(505) 465-2244
Alvin Arquero, Governor

Tribe: Pueblo. *In residence:* 950. *Area:* 28,000 acres. Located in Sandoral County near U.S. 85 on the west bank of the Rio Grande River. Tribal Council. Southern Pueblos Agency.

CROWNPOINT RESERVATION
Tribe: Navajo. c/o Eastern Navajo Agency.

CRYSTAL RIVER RESERVATION
Tribe: Navajo. Located in Arizona and New Mexico.
(See listing under Arizona.)

DALTON PASS RESERVATION
Tribe: Navajo. c/o Eastern Navajo Agency.

FORT DEFIANCE RESERVATION
Tribe: Navajo. Located in Arizona and New Mexico.
(See listing under Arizona.)

HUERFANO RESERVATION
Tribe: Navajo. c/o Eastern Navajo Agency.

ISLETA PUEBLO
P.O. Box 317
Isleta, New Mexico 87022
(505) 869-3111
Alvino Lucero, Governor

Tribe: Pueblo. *In residence:* 3,200. *Area:* 209,000 acres. Tribal Council. Southern Pueblos Agency.

IYANBIT RESERVATION
Tribe: Navajo. c/o Eastern Navajo Agency.

JEMEZ PUEBLO
P.O. Box 78
Jemez Pueblo, New Mexico 87024
(505) 834-7359
Candido Armijo, Governor

Tribe: Pueblo. *In residence:* 1,900. *Area:* 88,500 acres. Located 44 miles north of Albuquerque. Tribal Council. Southern Pueblos Agency.

JICARILLA APACHE RESERVATION
P.O. Box 147
Dulce, New Mexico 87528
(505) 759-3242
Leonard Atole, President

Tribe: Jicarilla Apache. *In residence:* 2,400. *Area:* 742,303 acres. Located about two miles northwest of Albuquerque. Tribal Council. Jicarilla Agency.

LAGUNA PUEBLO
P.O. Box 194
Laguna, New Mexico 87026
(505) 552-6654
Chester T. Fernando, Governor

Tribe: Pueblo. *In residence:* 4,000. *Area:* 420,000 acres. Located 40 miles west of Albuquerque, on U.S. 66. Tribal Council. Southern Pueblos Agency.

LAKE VALLEY RESERVATION
Tribe: Navajo. c/o Eastern Navajo Agency.

LITTLE WATER RESERVATION
Tribe: Navajo. c/o Eastern Navajo Agency.

MANUELITO RESERVATION
Tribe: Navajo. c/o Eastern Navajo Agency.

MARIANO RESERVATION
Tribe: Navajo. c/o Eastern Navajo Agency.

MESCALERO APACHE RESERVATION
P.O. Box 176
Mescalero, New Mexico 88340
(505) 671-4495
Wendell Chino, President

Tribe: Mescalero Apache. *In residence:* 2,500. *Area:* 460,173 acres. Located 30 miles northeast of Alamagordo, New Mexico. Tribal Council. Mescalero Agency.

MEXICAN WATER RESERVATION
Tribe: Navajo. Located in Arizona and Utah. Shiprock Agency.

NAGEEZI RESERVATION
Tribe: Navajo. c/o Eastern Navajo Agency.

NAMBE PUEBLO
Route 1, Box 117-BB
Santa Fe, New Mexico 87501
(505) 455-7752
David Perez, Governor

Tribe: Pueblo. *In residence:* 370 acres. *Area:* 19,000 acres. Located five miles east of Pojoaque, New Mexico, on Highway 285. Tribal Council. Northern Pueblos Agency.

NENAHNEZAD RESERVATION
Tribe: Navajo. c/o Shiprock Agency.

OJO ENCINO RESERVATION
Tribe: Navajo. c/o Eastern Navajo Agency.

PICURIS PUEBLO
P.O. Box 127
Penasco, New Mexico 87553
(505) 587-2519
Gerald Nailor, Governor

Tribe: Pueblo. *In residence:* 175. *Area:* 1,500 acres. Located east of the Rio Grande River, 20 miles south of Taos, New Mexico. Tribal Council. Northern Pueblos Agency.

PINEDALE RESERVATION
Tribe: Navajo. c/o Eastern Navajo Agency.

PAJOAQUE PUEBLO
Route 11, Box 71
Santa Fe, New Mexico 87501
(505) 455-2278/2279
Jacob Viarrial, Governor

Tribe: Pueblo. *In residence:* 150. *Area:* 11,500 acres. *Activities:* Annual Feast Day (December). Tribal Council. Northern Pueblos Agency.

PUEBLO PLAINTADO RESERVATION
Tribe: Navajo. c/o Eastern Navajo Agency.

PUERTOCITO (ALAMO) RESERVATION
Tribe: Navajo. c/o Eastern Navajo Agency.

RAMAH RESERVATION
c/o Ramah-Navajo Agency
Ramah, New Mexico 87321

Tribe: Navajo.

RED LAKE RESERVATION
Tribe: Navajo. Located in Arizona and New Mexico.
(See listing under Arizona.)

RED MESA RESERVATION
Tribe: Navajo. Located in Arizona and Utah. c/o Shiprock Agency.

RED ROCK RESERVATION
Tribe: Navajo. c/o Eastern Navajo Agency.

RED ROCK RESERVATION

Tribe: Navajo. Located in Arizona and New Mexico. c/o Shiprock Agency.

ROCK POINT RESERVATION
Tribe: Navajo. c/o Shiprock Agency.

ROCK SPRINGS RESERVATION
Tribe: Navajo. c/o Eastern Navajo Agency.

SAN FELIPE PUEBLO
P.O. Box A
San Felipe Pueblo, New Mexico 87001
(505) 867-3381
Frank Tenorio, Governor

Tribe: Pueblo. *In residence:* 2,000. *Area:* 49,000 acres. Located ten miles north of Bernalillo, off U.S. 85. Tribal Council. Northern Pueblos Agency.

SAN ILDEFONSO PUEBLO
Route 5, Box 315A
Santa Fe, New Mexico 87501
(505) 455-2273
Gilbert Sanchez, Governor

Tribe: Pueblo. *In residence:* 450. *Area:* 26,000 acres. Located 20 miles northwest of Santa Fe, off Highway 285. Tribal Council. Northern Pueblos Agency.

SAN JUAN PUEBLO
P.O. Box 1099
San Juan Pueblo, New Mexico 87566
(505) 852-4400/4210
Jose Emelio Trujillo, Governor

Tribe: Pueblo. *In residence:* 1,000. *Area:* 12,000 acres. Located five miles north of Espanola, near Highway 64. Tribal Council. Northern Pueblos Agency.

SANDIA PUEBLO
P.O. Box 6008
Bernalillo, New Mexico 87004
(505) 867-2876
Esquipula Chaves, Governor

Tribe: Pueblo. *In residence:* 300. *Area:* 23,000 acres. Located 14 miles north of Albuquerque, on U.S. 85. Tribal Council. Northern Pueblos Agency.

SANOSTEE RESERVATION
Tribe: Navajo. c/o Shiprock Agency.

SANTA ANA PUEBLO
P.O. Box 37
Bernalillo, New Mexico 87004
(505) 867-3301
Eliseo Baton Sr. Governor

Tribe: Pueblo. *In residence:* 500. *Area:* 4,200 acres. Located near Jemez Creek, eight miles from Bernalillo. Tribal Council. Northern Pueblos Agency.

SANTA CLARA PUEBLO
P.O. Box 580
Espanola, New Mexico 87532
(505) 753-7330/7327
Lawrence Singer, Governor

Tribe: Pueblo. *In residence:* 1,200. *Area:* 45,744 acres. Located 25 miles northwest of Santa Fe. Tribal Council. Northern Pueblos Agency.

SANTO DOMINGO PUEBLO
P.O. Box 99
Santo Domingo, New Mexico 87052
(505) 465-2214
Alex Garcia, Governor

Tribe: Pueblo. *In residence:* 2,500. *Area:* 70,000 acres. Located in Sandoval County, ten miles east of the Rio Grande River. Tribal Council. Southern Pueblos Agency.

SHEEP SPRINGS RESERVATION
Tribe: Navajo. c/o Shiprock Agency.

SHIPROCK RESERVATION
Tribe: Navajo. c/o Shiprock Agency.

SMITH LAKE RESERVATION
Tribe: Navajo. c/o Eastern Navajo Agency.

STANDING ROCK RESERVATION
Tribe: Navajo. c/o Eastern Navajo Agency.

SWEETWATER RESERVATION
Tribe: Navajo. c/o Shiprock Agency.

TAOS PUEBLO
P.O. Box 1846
Taos, New Mexico 87571
(505) 758-8626
Joe C. Sandoval, Governor

Tribe: Pueblo. *In residence:* 1,250. *Area:* 75,000
acres. Tribal Council. Northern Pueblos Agency.

TEECNOSPOS RESERVATION
Tribe: Navajo. Located in Arizona, Utah and
New Mexico. c/o Shiprock Agency.

TESUQUE PUEBLO
Route 11, Box 1
Santa Fe, New Mexico 87501
(505) 983-2667
Joe A. Padilla, Governor

Tribe: Pueblo. *In residence:* 300. *Area:* 17,000
acres. Located ten miles north of Santa Fe. Tribal
Council. Northern Pueblos Agency.

THOREAU RESERVATION
Tribe: Navajo. c/o Eastern Navajo Agency.

**TORREON AND STAR LAKE
RESERVATION**
Tribe: Navajo. c/o Eastern Navajo Agency.

TSAYATOH RESERVATION
Tribe: Navajo. c/o Eastern Navajo Agency.

TSAILE-WHEATFIELDS RESERVATION
Tribe: Navajo. Located in Arizona and
New Mexico. (See listing under Arizona.)

TWO GREY HILLS RESERVATION
Tribe: Navajo. c/o Shiprock Agency.

UPPER FRUITLAND RESERVATION
Tribe: Navajo. c/o Shiprock Agency.

UTE MOUNTAIN RESERVATION
Tribe: Ute. Located in Colorado, Utah and
New Mexico. (See listing under Colorado.)

WHITE ROCK RESERVATION
Tribe: Navajo. c/o Eastern Navajo Agency.

WHITEHORSE LAKE RESERVATION
Tribe: Navajo. c/o Eastern Navajo Agency.

ZIA PUEBLO
General Delivery
San Ysidro, New Mexico 87053
(505) 867-3304
Augustin Pino, Governor

Tribe: Pueblo. *In residence:* 600. *Area:* 112,000
acres. Located 16 miles northwest of Bernalillo.
Tribal Council. Southern Pueblos Agency.

ZUNI RESERVATION
P.O. Box 737
Zuni, New Mexico 87327
(505) 782-4481
Chauncey Simplico, Governor

Tribe: Zuni Pueblo. *In residence:* 7,000. *Area:*
407,247 acres. Located 40 miles south of Gallup,
New Mexico, on the Arizona border. Tribal
Council. Zuni Agency.

NEW YORK

ABENAKI INDIAN VILLAGE
Lake George, New York 12845

Tribe: Abenaki.

ALLEGHENY RESERVATION
Salamanca, New York 14779

Tribes: Seneca and Cayuga. *In residence:* 700.
Area: 30,469 acres. Located along the Allegheny
River on Route 17. New York Liaison Office.

CATTARAUGUS RESERVATION
1490 Route 438
Irving, New York 14081
(716) 532-4900
Calvin E. Lay, President

Tribe: Seneca Nation. *In residence:* 5,500.
Area: 21,680 acres. Located along Route 438.
Tribal Council. New York Liaison Office.

CAYUGA NATION RESERVATION
P.O. Box 11,
Versailles, New York 14168
(716) 532-4847
Vernon Isaacs, Chief

Tribe: Cayuga. *In residence:* 100.
Tribal Council. New York Liaison Office.

OIL SPRING RESERVATION
Cuba Lake, New York 14727

Tribe: Seneca. *Area:* 640 acres. Located near
Cuba Lake in Allegheny County. New York
Liaison Office.

ONEIDA RESERVATION
Route 2, West Rd.
Oneida, New York 13424

Tribe: Oneida. New York Liaison Office.

ONONDAGA RESERVATION
P.O. Box 270A
Nedrow, New York 13120
(315) 469-8507
Leon Shenandoah, Chief

Tribes: Onondaga, Oneida and Cayuga. *In residence:* 1,500. *Area:* 7,300 acres. Located near Nedrow, six miles south of Syracuse. New York Liaison Office.

POOSPATUCK RESERVATION
Mastic, New York 11950

Tribe: Poospatuck. *In residence:* 100. *Area:* 60 acres. Located on Mastic River near Brookhaven, L.I., New York. Eastern Area Office.

ST. REGIS RESERVATION
Hogansburg, New York 13655
(518) 358-2272
Leonard Garrow, Head Chief

Tribe: Mohawk. *In residence:* 2,750. *Area:* 28,390 acres. Located in Franklin County on Route 37. Tribal Council. New York Liaison Office.

SHINNECOCK RESERVATION
Southampton, New York 11968

Tribe: Shinnecock. *In residence:* 330. *Area:* 400 acres. Located in Suffolk County, New York, near Southampton. Eastern Area Office.

TONAWANDA RESERVATION
7027 Meadville Rd.
Basom, New York 14013
(716) 542-4244
Emerson C. Webster, Chief

Tribe: Tonawanda Band of Seneca Indians. *In residence:* 625. *Area:* 7,550 acres. Located on Route 267, near Batavia, New York. Council of Chiefs. New York Liaison Office.

TUSCARORA RESERVATION
5616 Walmore Rd.
Lewiston, New York 14092
(716) 297-2053
Arnold Hewitt, Chief

Tribe: Tuscarora. *In residence:* 750. *Area:* 5,700 acres. Located in Niagara County near Sanborn and Lewiston on Upper Mountain Rd. Tribal Council. New York Liaison Office.

NORTH CAROLINA

CHEROKEE RESERVATION
P.O. Box 455
Cherokee, North Carolina 28719
(704) 497-2771
Robert Youngdeer, Principal Chief

Tribe: Eastern Cherokee. *In residence:* 5,750. *Area:* 56,572 acres. Located 50 miles west of Asheville, North Carolina. *Local attractions:* Replica of an Oconaluftee Indian Village; Museum of the Cherokee; Qualla Arts and Crafts Cooperative. Tribal Council. Cherokee Agency.

NORTH DAKOTA

DEVIL'S LAKE SIOUX RESERVATION
P.O. Box 300
Fort Totten, North Dakota 58335
(701) 766-4221
Carl McKay, Chairman

Tribe: Sisseton-Wahpeton Sioux. *In residence:* 3,125. *Area:* 185,045 acres. Located along the Cheyenne River. *Activities:* Annual Fort Totten Days Pow-Wow (July). Tribal Council. Fort Totten Agency.

FORT BERTHOLD RESERVATION
New Town, North Dakota 58763
(701) 627-4781
Alyce Spotted Bear, Chairman

Tribes: Gros Ventre, Arikara, Mandan and Hidatsa. *In residence:* 3,300. *Area:* 421,964 acres. Located above Garrison Dam on the Missouri River, southwest of Minot, North Dakota. Tribal Council. Fort Berthold Agency.

OJIBWA OF THE RED RIVER
Tribe: Ojibwa (Chippewa). *In residence:* 850. Located in northeast North Dakota.

STANDING ROCK RESERVATION
Fort Yates, North Dakota 58538
(701) 854-7231
Charles Murphy, Chairman

Tribe: Sioux. *In residence:* 8,000 (3,800 Yankton Sioux in North Dakota, and 4,200 Teton Sioux in South Dakota.) *Area:* 306,000 acres (ND); 540,000 acres (SD). Located 60 miles south of Bismarck, N.D., in North and South Dakota. Tribal Council. Standing Rock Agency.

TURTLE MOUNTAIN RESERVATION
Belcourt, North Dakota 58316
(701) 477-6451
Richard Lafromboise, Chairman

Tribe: Chippewa. *In residence:* 8,750. *Area:* 34,528 acres. Located west of the Canadian border. Tribal Council. Turtle Mountain Agency.

OKLAHOMA

NOTE: There are no "reservations" in Oklahoma. Rather, there are land holdings by the various Oklahoma Indian tribes.

ABSENTEE-SHAWNEE TRIBE
P.O. Box 1747
Shawnee, Oklahoma 74801
(405) 275-4030
Danny Little Axe, Governor

Tribe: Absentee-Shawnee. *Population:* 1,400. Tribal Executive Committee. Shawnee Agency.

ALABAMA-QUASSARTE TRIBAL TOWN
P.O. Box 284, Route 1
Gore, Oklahoma 74435
(918) 489-5543
Bill Beaver, Chief

Tribe: Creek. Tribal Council Okmulgee Agency.

APACHE TRIBE OF OKLAHOMA
P.O. Box 1220
Anadarko, Oklahoma 73005
(405) 247-9493
Leroy Nimsey, Chairman

Tribes: Apache and Kiowa. *Population:* 535.
Tribal Council. Anadarko Agency.

CADDO INDIAN TRIBE
P.O. Box 487
Binger, Oklahoma 73009
(405) 656-2344
Henry Shemayne, Chairman

Tribe: Caddo. *Population:* 1,250.
Tribal Council. Anadarko Agency.

CHEROKEE NATION OF OKLAHOMA
P.O. Box 948
Tahlequah, Oklahoma 74465
(918) 456-0671
Wilma P. Mankiller, Principal Chief

Tribe: Cherokee. *Population:* 43,000.
Tribal Council. Tahlequah Agency.

CHEYENNE-ARAPAHO TRIBE
P.O. Box 38
Concho, Oklahoma 73022
(405) 262-0345
Fred Hoffman, Chairman

Tribes: Cheyenne and Arapaho. *Population:*
7,000. Business Committee. Concho Agency.

CHICKASAW NATION OF OKLAHOMA
P.O. Box 1548
Ada, Oklahoma 74820
(405) 436-2603
Overton James, Governor

Tribe: Chickasaw. *Population:* 9,000.
Tribal Council. Wewoka Agency.

CHOCTAW NATION OF OKLAHOMA
1210 16th & Locust St.
Durant, Oklahoma 74701
(405) 924-8280
Hollis Roberts, Principal Chief

Tribe: Choctaw. *Population:* 20,000.
Tribal Council. Talahini Agency.

CITIZEN BAND POTAWATOMI TRIBE
Route 5, Box 151
Shawnee, Oklahoma 74801
(405) 275-3121
John A. Barrett, Jr., Chairman

Tribe: Citizen Band Potawatomi. *Population:*
11,500 (U.S.); 4,200 (Oklahoma). *Area:* 300 acres
(in trust). *Facilities:* Tribal Museum and Trading
Post. Business Committee. Shawnee Agency.

**COMANCHE INDIAN TRIBE
OF OKLAHOMA**
P.O. Box 908
Lawton, Oklahoma 73502
(405) 247-3444
Bernard Kahrahrah, Chairman

Tribe: Comanche. *Population:* 3,750.
Business Committee. Anadarko Agency.

**DELAWARE TRIBE OF
WESTERN OKLAHOMA**
P.O. Box 825
Anadarko, Oklahoma 73005
(405-247-2448
Edgar L. French, Jr., Chairman

Tribe: Delaware. *Population:* 1,050. *Area:* 2,400
acres held jointly with the Wichita and Caddo
Tribes. Executive Committee. Anadarko Agency.

**EASTERN SHAWNEE TRIBE
OF OKLAHOMA**

Tribe: Eastern Shawnee. c/o Miami Agency.

**FORT SILL APACHE TRIBE
OF OKLAHOMA**
Route 2, Box 121
Apache, Oklahoma 73006
(405) 588-2298
Mildred Cleghorn, Chairwoman

Tribe: Fort Sill Apache. *Population:* 350.
Business Committee. Anadarko Agency.

IOWA TRIBE OF OKLAHOMA
Iowa Veterans Hall, P.O. Box 190
Perkins, Oklahoma 74059
(405) 547-2403
Wallace C. Murray, Chairman

Tribe: Iowa. *Population:* 225. Business
Committee. Pawnee Agency.

KAW TRIBE OF OKLAHOMA
Drawer 50
Kaw City, Oklahoma 74641
(405) 269-2552
M.M. Chouteau, Chairman

Tribe: Kaw. *Population:* 1,100. Located at the
northeast section of Kay County, Oklahoma.
Activities: Tribal Pow-Wow (August). Business
Committee. Pawnee Agency.

**KIALEGEE TRIBAL TOWN
OF THE CREEK NATION**
928 Alex Noon Dr.
Wetumpka, Oklahoma 74883
James Wesley, Micco

Tribe: Creek. Business Committee.
Wewoka Agency.

KICKAPOO TRIBE OF OKLAHOMA
P.O. Box 58
McLoud, Oklahoma 74851
(405) 964-2075
Jim Wahpehah, Chairman

Tribe: Kickapoo. *Population:* 750.
Business Committee. Shawnee Agency.

KIOWA TRIBE OF OKLAHOMA
P.O. Box 369
Carnegie, Oklahoma 73015
(405) 654-2300
Billy Evans Horse, Chairman

Tribe: Kiowa. *Population:* 4,100.
Business Committee. Anadarko Agency.

MIAMI TRIBE OF OKLAHOMA
P.O. Box 636
Miami, Oklahoma 74355
(918) 542-1445
Louis Moore, Chief

Tribe: Miami. *Population:* 375.
Business Committee. Miami Agency.

MODOC TRIBE OF OKLAHOMA
P.O. Box 939
Miami, Oklahoma 74355
(918) 542-1190
Bill Follis, Chief

Tribe: Modoc. Tribal Council. Miami Agency.

**MUSCOGEE (CREEK) NATION
OF OKLAHOMA**
P.O. Box 580
Okmulgee, Oklahoma 74447
(918) 756-8700 ext. 200
Claude A. Cox, Principal Chief

Tribe: Muscogee Creek. *Population:* 30,000.
Area: 6,000 acres. Located in an eight county area
in northeastern Oklahoma—bounded on the
north at Admiral St. in the city of Tulsa, and on
the south by the Canadian River. *Activities:*
Green Corn, Creek Festival, and Creek Rodeo.
Tribal Council. Okmulgee Agency.

OSAGE TRIBE OF OKLAHOMA
Tribal Administration Bldg.
Pawhuska, Oklahoma 74056
(918) 287-4623
George Tallchief, Principal Chief

Tribe: Osage. *Population:* 5,800.
Tribal Council. Osage Agency.

OTOE-MISSOURIA TRIBE OF OKLAHOMA
P.O. Box 68
Red Rock, Oklahoma 74651
(405) 723-4334
C.O. Tillman, Chairman

Tribe: Otoe-Missouria. *Population:* 1,250.
Business Committee. Pawnee Agency.

OTTAWA TRIBE OF OKLAHOMA
P.O. Box 110
Miami, Oklahoma 74355
(918) 540-1536
Lewis H. Barlow, Chief

Tribe: Ottawa. Tribal Council. Miami Agency.

PAWNEE INDIAN TRIBE OF OKLAHOMA
P.O. Box 470
Pawnee, Oklahoma 74058
(918) 762-3624
Robert L. Chapman, President

Tribe: Pawnee. *Population:* 2,200.
Business Council. Pawnee Agency.

PEORIA TRIBE OF OKLAHOMA
P.O. Box 1527
Miami, Oklahoma 74355
(918) 540-2535
Rodney P. Arnette, Chief

Tribe: Peoria. Tribal Council. Miami Agency.

**PONCA TRIBE OF
INDIANS OF OKLAHOMA**
P.O. Box 2, White Eagle
Ponca City, Oklahoma 74601
(405) 762-8104
Oliver Littlecook, Chairman

Tribe: Ponca. *Population:* 2,200.
Business Committee. Shawnee Agency.

QUAPAW TRIBE OF OKLAHOMA
P.O. Box 765
Quapaw, Oklahoma 74363
(918) 542-1853
Jesse McKibben, Chairman

Tribe: Quapaw. *Population:* 1,250.
Business Committee. Miami Agency.

SAC AND FOX TRIBE OF OKLAHOMA
Route 2, Box 246
Stroud, Oklahoma 74079
  (918) 968-3526
  (405) 275-4270
  Alvin Falls, Principal Chief

Tribe: Sac and Fox. *Population:* 1,500.
Business Committee. Shawnee Agency.

SEMINOLE NATION OF OKLAHOMA
P.O. Box 745
Wewoka, Oklahoma 74884
  (405) 382-7913
  James Milam, Chief

Tribe: Seminole. *Population:* 3,850.
Tribal Council. Wewoka Agency.

SENECA-CAYUGA TRIBE OF OKLAHOMA
P.O. Box 1283
Miami, Oklahoma 74355
  (918) 542-6609
  James Allen, Chief

Tribes: Seneca and Cayuga. *Population:* 750.
Business Committee. Miami Agency.

THLOPTHLOCCO TRIBAL TOWN
8433 East 64th Place
Tulsa, Oklahoma 74135
  (918) 252-3195
  Elaine Branch, Town King

Tribe: Creek. Business Committee.
Okmulgee Agency.

TONKAWA TRIBE OF OKLAHOMA
P.O. Box 70
Tonkawa, Oklahoma 74653
  (405) 628-2561
  Henry L. Allen, President

Tribe: Tonkawa. *Population:* 1,350.
Business Committee. Pawnee Agency.

UNITED KEETOOWAH CHEROKEE TRIBE
P.O. Box 1329
Tahlequah, Oklahoma 74465
  (918) 234-3434
  John Hair, Chief

Tribe: United Keetoowah Cherokee.
Tribal council. Tahlequah Agency.

WICHITA TRIBE OF OKLAHOMA
Wichita Tribal Affairs Office
P.O. Box 729
Anadarko, Oklahoma 73005
  (405) 247-2425
  Newton Lamar, President

Tribe: Wichita. *Population:* 650.
Executive Committee. Anadarko Agency.

WYANDOTTE TRIBE OF OKLAHOMA
P.O. Box 470
Miami, Oklahoma 74355
  (918) 540-1541
  Leaford Bearskin, Chief

Tribe: Wyandotte. *Population:* 450.
Tribal Council. Miami Agency.

OREGON

BURNS PAIUTE INDIAN COLONY
P.O. Box 71
Burns, Oregon 97720
  (503) 573-2088
  Vernon Shake Spear, Chairman

Tribe: Paiute. *In residence:* 200. *Area:*
11,944 acres. Located in Harney Basin, Harney
County.Tribal Council. Warm Springs Agency.

**COW CREEK BAND
OF UMPQUA INDIANS**
1376 N.E. Walnut, Suite I
Roseburg, Oregon 97470
  (503) 672-9696
  Charles Jackson, Chairman

Tribe: Umpqua. Siletz Agency.

FORT McDERMITT RESERVATION
Tribes: Paiute and Shoshone. Located in Oregon
and Nevada. (See listing under Nevada.)

GRANDE RONDE INDIAN COMMUNITY
P.O. Box 94
Grande Ronde, Oregon 97347
  (503) 879-5253
  Katherine Harrison, Chairwoman

Tribes: Confederated Tribes. *In residence:* 600.
Located in northwest Oregon. Tribal Council.
Siletz Agency.

SILETZ RESERVATION
P.O. Box 540
Siletz, Oregon 97380
  (503) 444-2528
  Delores Piglsey, Chairwoman

Tribes: Confederated Tribes. *In residence:* 750.
Located on northwest Oregon coast. Tribal
Council. Siletz Agency.

UMATILLA RESERVATION
P.O. Bon 638
Pendleton, Oregon 97801
  (503) 276-3165
  Elwood Patawa, Chairman

Tribes: Umatilla, Cayuse, and Walla Walla. *In
residence:* 1,500. *Area:* 95,273 acres. Located in
Umatilla County, adjacent to Pendleton and west

of Umatilla National Forest. Board of Trustees. Umatilla Agency.

WARM SPRINGS RESERVATION
Warm Springs, Oregon 97761
(503) 553-1161
Zane Jackson, Sr., Chairman

Tribes: Warm Springs, Wasco, Paiute, Walla Walla, and Waco. *In residence:* 2,500. *Area:* 563,916 acres. Located in Jefferson and Wasco Counties, east of the Cascade Mountains. Tribal Council. Warm Springs Agency.

RHODE ISLAND

NARRAGANSETT INDIAN RESERVATION
RFD #2
Kenyon, Rhode Island 02836
(401) 364-6411
George Watson, Chief

Tribe: Narragansett. Tribal Council. Eastern Area Office.

SOUTH DAKOTA

CHEYENNE RIVER RESERVATION
P.O. Box 590
Eagle Butte, South Dakota 57625
(605) 964-4155
Morgan Garreau, Chairman

Tribe: Cheyenne River Sioux. *In residence:* 5,000. *Area:* 2,811,480 acres. Located in Dewey and Zeibach Counties. Tribal Council. Cheyenne River Agency.

CROW CREEK RESERVATION
P.O. Box 658
Fort Thompson, South Dakota 57339
(605) 245-2221/2222
Wallace Wells, Jr., Chairman

Tribe: Crow Creek Sioux. *In residence:* 2,100. *Area:* 125,000 acres. Tribal Council. Crow Creek Agency.

FLANDREAU SANTEE SIOUX RESERVATION
P.O. Box 292
Flandreau, South Dakota 57028
(605) 997-2924
Carolyn Sorensen, President

Tribe: Santee Sioux. *In residence:* 400. *Area:* 2,180 acres. Executive Committee. Flandreau School (Agency).

LOWER BRULE RESERVATION
Lower Brule, South Dakota 57548
(605) 473-5561
Patrick Spears, Chairman

Tribe: Lower Brule Sioux. *In residence:* 1,000. *Area:* 114,500 acres. Tribal Council. Lower Brule Agency.

PINE RIDGE RESERVATION
Pine Ridge, South Dakota 57770
(605) 867-5821
Newton Cummings, President

Tribe: Oglala Sioux. In residence: 13,500. *Area:* 1,560,196 acres (SD) and 90,000 acres (Nebraska). Located 60 miles east of the Black Hills, extending into Nebraska. *Local attractions:* Wounded Knee Battlefield (15 miles northeast of Pine Ridge); Badlands National Monument. *Activities:* Annual Oglala Sioux Sun Dance (August). Tribal Council. Pine Ridge Agency.

ROSEBUD RESERVATION
Rosebud, South Dakota 57570
(605) 747-2381
Webster Two Hawks, President

Tribe: Rosebud Sioux. *In residence:* 9,500. *Area: 964,778 acres. Located in south-central South Dakota, adjoining the Nebraska State line. Local attraction:* Crazy Horse Canyon Park (tribe-operated); St. Francis Mission; Sioux Indian Museum. Tribal Council. Rosebud Agency.

SISSETON-WAHPETON RESERVATION
Route 2
Agency Village, South Dakota 57262
(605) 698-3911
Russell Hawkins, Chairman

Tribe: Sisseton-Wahpeton Sioux. *In residence:* 3,850. *Area:* 105,000 acres. Located in North and South Dakota (only a minor portion in North Dakota.) Tribal Council. Sisseton Agency.

STANDING ROCK RESERVATION
Tribes: Teton Sioux (SD) and Yankton Sioux (ND). Located in North and South Dakota. (See listing under North Dakota.)

YANKTON SIOUX RESERVATION
Route 3, Box 248
Marty, South Dakota 57361
(605) 384-3641
Alvin Zephier, Chairman

Tribe: Yankton Sioux. *In residence:* 2,500. *Area:* 35,000 acres. Business and Claims Committee. Yankton Agency.

UTAH

CHILCHINBETO RESERVATION
Tribe: Navajo. Located in Utah and Arizona.
(See listing under Arizona.)

DENNEHOTSO RESERVATION
Tribe: Navajo. Located in Utah and Arizona.
(See listing under Arizona.)

GOSHUTE RESERVATION
Ibapah, Utah 87034
Chester Steele, Chairman

Tribe: Goshute. *In residence:* 215. *Area:*
76,500 acres. Located in Utah and Nevada.
Tribal Council. Eastern Nevada Agency.

KAYENTA RESERVATION
Tribe: Navajo. Located in Utah and Arizona.
(See listing under Arizona.)

MEXICAN WATER RESERVATION
Tribe: Navajo. Located in Utah and Arizona.
(See listing under New Mexico.)

NAVAJO MOUNTAIN RESERVATION
Tribe: Navajo. Located in Utah and Arizona.
(See listing under Arizona.)

OLJATOH RESERVATION
Tribe: Navajo. Located in Utah and Arizona.
(See listing under Arizona.)

PAIUTE INDIANS OF UTAH
600 North 100 East
Cedar City, Utah 84720
(801) 586-1111
General Anderson, Chairman

Tribe: Paiute. Communities of Cedar City, Indian
Peaks, Kanosh, Koosharen, and Shivwite. *In
residence:* 325. Tribal Council. Eastern Nevada
Agency.

RED MESA RESERVATION
Tribe: Navajo. Located in Utah and Arizona.
(See listing under New Mexico.)

SHONTO RESERVATION
Tribe: Navajo. Located in Utah and Arizona.
(See listing under Arizona.)

SKULL VALLEY INDIAN COMMUNITY
c/o Uintah and Ouray Agency
Fort Duchesne, Utah 84026
Bert Wash, Chairman

Tribe: Skull Valley Band of Goshute.
In residence: 75.

TEECNOSPOS RESERVATION
Tribe: Navajo. Located in Utah, Arizona and New
Mexico. (See listing under New Mexico.)

UINTAH AND OURAY RESERVATION
Fort Duchesne, Utah 84026
(801) 722-5141
Frank Wopsock, Chairman

Tribe: Ute. *In residence:* 1,900. *Area:* 852,411.
Located in the Uintah Basin in northeast Utah.
Business Council. Uintah and Ouray Agency.

UTE MOUNTAIN RESERVATION
Tribe: Ute. Located in Utah, New Mexico and
Colorado. (See listing under Colorado.)

WASHAKIE RESERVATION
Tribe: Northwest Band of Shoshone of Utah.
Located in Utah. (See listing under Idaho.)

WASHINGTON

CHEHALIS RESERVATION
P.O. Box 536
Oakville, Washington 98568
(206) 273-5911
Percy Youckton, Chairman

Tribe: Chehalis. *In residence:* 750. *Area:* 4,250
acres. Tribal Council. Olympic Peninsula Agency.

COLVILLE RESERVATION
P.O. Box 150
Nespelem, Washington 99155
(509) 634-4711
Al Aubertin, Chairman

Tribes: Confederated Tribes (Colville, Okanogan,
Lakes, San Poil, Methow, Nespelem, Entiat,
Wenatchee, Moses, Nez Perce, Palouse.) *In
residence:* 3,500 (Tribal rolls: 6,200). *Area:*
1,087,271 acres. Located in Okanogan and Ferry
Counties. *Local attractions:* Grand Coulee Dam;
Old Fort Okanogan; burial place of Nez Perce,
Chief Joseph. Business Council. Colville Agency.

HOH RESERVATION
Star Route 1, Box 917
Forks, Washington 98331
(206) 374-6582
Mary Leitka, Chairwoman

Tribe: Hoh. *In residence:* 65. *Area:* 443 acres.
Located at Cape Flattery in northwest Clallam
County. Business Council. Puget Sound Agency.

JAMESTOWN BAND
OF CLALLAM INDIANS
150 South 5th Ave.
Sequim, Washington 98382
(206) 683-1109
William Ron Allen, Chairman

Tribe: Clallam. Puget Sound Agency.

KALISPEL RESERVATION
P.O. Box 38
Usk, Washington 99180
(509) 445-1147
Glen Nenema, Chairman

Tribe: Kalispel. *In residence:* 225.
Spokane Agency.

**LOWER ELWHA
KLALLAM RESERVATION**
P.O. Box 1370
Port Angeles, Washington 98362
(206) 452-8471
Edward Sampson, Jr., Chairman

*Tribe: Lower Elwha Band of Klallam Indians.
In residence:* 450. *Area:* 430 acres.
Business Council. Olympic Peninsula Agency.

LUMMI RESERVATION
2616 Kwina Rd.
Bellingham, Washington 98225-9298
(206) 734-8180
Larry Kinley, Chairman

Tribe: Lummi. *In residence:* 2,300. *Area:*
8,338 acres. Business Council. Puget Sound
Agency.

MAKAH RESERVATION
P.O. Box 115
Neah Bay, Washington 98357
(206) 645-2205 ext. 36
George Bowechop, Chairman

Tribe: Makah. *In residence:* 1,000. *Area:* 27,012
acres. Located on the Pacific Ocean and Straits of
Juan De Fuca. Tribal Council. Puget Sound
Agency.

MUCKLESHOOT RESERVATION
39015 172nd S.E.
Auburn, Washington 98002
(206) 939-3311
Sonny Bargala, Chairman

Tribe: Muckleshoot. *In residence:* 2,300. *Area:*
1,959 acres. Tribal Council. Puget Sound Agency.

NISQUALLY INDIAN COMMUNITY
4820 She-Na-Num Dr., S.E.
Olympia, Washington 98503
(206) 456-5221
Richard Wells, Chairman

Tribe: Nisqually. *In residence:* 1,300. *Area:* 941
acres. Community Council. Olympic Peninsula
Agency.

NOOKSACK RESERVATION
P.O. Box 157
Deming, Washington 98244
(206) 592-5176
Harry E. Cooper, Chairman

Tribe: Nooksack. In residence: 700. *Area:*
2,906 acres. Tribal Council. Puget Sound Agency.

PORT GAMBLE INDIAN COMMUNITY
P.O. Box 280
Kingston, Washington 98346
(206) 297-2646
Ronald G. Charles, Chairman

Tribe: Port Gamble. *In residence:* 450. *Area:*
1,301 acres. Community Council. Puget Sound
Agency.

PORT MADISON RESERVATION
P.O. Box 498
Suquamish, Washington 98392
(206) 598-3311
Bennie J. Armstrong, Chairman

Tribe: Suquamish. *In residence:* 375. *Area:* 8,000
acres. *Activities:* Chief Seattle Day (annual
traditional tribal celebration, held in August).
Local attractions: Totem Poles throughout the
Reservation; Suquamish Museum. Tribal
Council. Puget Sound Agency.

PUYALLUP RESERVATION
2002 East 28th St.
Tacoma, Washington 98404
(206) 597-6200
Frank Wright, Jr., Chairman

Tribes: Puyallup, Nisqually, Muckleshoot,
Skwawksnamish, and Steilacoom. *Area:* 33 acres.
Tribal Council. Puget Sound Agency.

QUILEUTE RESERVATION
P.O. Box 279
La Push, Washington 98350
(206) 374-6163
Walter Jackson, Chairman

Tribe: Quileute. *In residence:* 390. *Area:*
900 acres. Located on the Pacific Ocean.
Activities: Quileute Days (August); Elders Week
Celebration (Spring). Tribal Council. Puget
Sound Agency.

QUINAULT RESERVATION
P.O. Box 189
Taholah, Washington 98587
(206) 276-8211
Joseph Delacruz, President

Tribe: Quinault. In residence: 2,000. *Area:
136,456 acres.* Located 40 miles north of
Hoquiam, on the Pacific Ocean. *Activities:*
Annual celebration in July. *Local attraction:*
Indian village. Business Committee. Olympic
Peninsula Agency.

SAUK-SUIATTLE INDIAN RESERVATION
5318 Chief Brown Lane
Darrington, Washington 98241
(206) 436-0131
David Moses, Sr., Chairman

Tribe: Sauk-Suiattle. *In residence:* 205. *Area:* 15
acres. *Activities:* Annual Huckleberry Festival
(September); Annual Yo-Buch Days (July).
Tribal Council. Puget Sound Agency.

SHOALWATER BAY RESERVATION
P.O. Box 579
Tokeland, Washington 98590
(206) 267-6766
Rachel Whitish, Chairwoman

Tribe: Shoalwater. *In residence:* 65. *Area:*
335 acres. Located in Pacific County, near
Tokeland. Tribal Council. Olympic Peninsula
Agency.

SKOKOMISH INDIAN RESERVATION
Route 5, Box 432
Shelton, Washington 98584
(206) 267-6766
Gary Peterson, Chairman

Tribe: Skokomish. *In residence:* 500. *Area:* 3,500
acres. Tribal Council. Olympic Peninsula Agency.

SPOKANE RESERVATION
P.O. Box 385
Wellpinit, Washington 99040
(509) 258-4581
James W. Hill, Chairman

Tribe: Spokane. *In residence:* 1,000 (tribal roll,
2,000). *Area:* 138,750 acres. Located in the
southwest corner of Stevens County. *Local
attractions:* Old Fort Spokane; Tsimshian
Mission (1838). Business Council. Spokane
Agency.

SQUAXIN ISLAND RESERVATION
West 81 - Highway 108
Shelton, Washington 98584
(206) 426-9781
David Whitener, Chairman

Tribes: Squaxin Island, Nisqually, Steilacoom,
and others. *In residence:* 950. Tribal Council.
Olympic Peninsula Agency.

STILLAGUAMISH RESERVATION
2704 State Rd., 530 N.E.
Arlington, Washington 98223
(206) 652-7362
Marie MacCurdy, Chairwoman

Tribe: Stillaguamish. Board of Directors.
Puget Sound Agency.

SWINOMISH RESERVATION
P.O. Box 817
La Conner, Washington 98257
(206) 466-3163
Robert Joe, Sr., Chairman

Tribes: Swinomish, Suiattle, Skagit, and
Kikiallus. *In residence:* 650. *Area:* 1,000
acres. Swinomish Indian Senate (tribal
council.) Puget Sound Agency.

TULALIP RESERVATION
6700 Totem Beach Rd.
Marysville, Washington 98270
(206) 653-4585
Stanley Jones, Sr., Chairman

Tribe: Tulalip (Snohomish, Snoqualmie, Skagit,
Suiattle, Samish, and allied bands). *In residence:*
850. *Area:* 22,000 acres. Board of Directors
(Tribal Council). Puget Sound Agency.

UPPER SKAGIT INDIAN RESERVATION
2284 Community Plaza
Sedro Wooley, Washington 98284
(206) 856-5501
Floyd Williams, Chairman

Tribe: Upper Skagit. *In residence:* 175. *Area:* 99
acres. Tribal Council. Puget Sound Agency.

YAKIMA RESERVATION
P.O. Box 151
Toppenish, Washington 98948
(509) 865-5121
Roger R. Jim, Sr., Chairman

Tribe: Yakima. *In residence:* 8,500. *Area:*
1,134,830 acres. *Activities:* All-Indian Rodeo
(June); Annual Pow-Wow (July); Huckleberry
Feast (August). Tribal Council. Yakima Agency.

WISCONSIN

BAD RIVER RESERVATION
Route 39
Ashland, Wisconsin 54806
(715) 682-4212
Robert Bender, Chairman

Tribe: Lake Superior Chippewa. *In residence:*
1,400. *Area:* 54,720 acres. Located on Lake
Superior, southeast of Duluth, Minnesota. Tribal
Council. Great Lakes Agency.

FOREST COUNTY
POTAWATOMI COMMUNITY
P.O. Box 346
Crandon, Wisconsin 54520
(715) 478-2903
Leroy Schotko, Chairman

Tribe: Potawatomi of Wisconsin. *In residence:* 400. *Area:* 10,000 acres. Tribal Council. Great Lakes Agency.

LAC COURTE OREILLES RESERVATION
Route 2
Hayward, Wisconsin 54843
(715) 634-8934
Odric Baker, Chairman

Tribe: Lake Superior Chippewa. *In residence:* 1,900. *Area:* 70,000 acres. Located within Sawyer County. Governing Board. Great Lakes Agency.

LAC DU FLAMBEAU RESERVATION
P.O. Box 67
Lac du Falmbeau, Wisconsin 54538
(715) 588-3306
Michael Allen, Sr., Chairman

Tribe: Lake Superior Chippewa. *In residence:* 1,500. *Area:* 44,400 acres. Tribal Council. Great Lakes Agency.

MENOMINEE RESERVATION
P.O. Box 397
Keshena, Wisconsin 54135
(715) 799-3341
Lynn Skenedore, Chairman

Tribe: Menominee. *In residence:* 3,500. *Area:* 233,800 acres. Tribal Legislature. Great Lake Agency.

ONEIDA RESERVATION
P.O. Box 365
Oneida, Wisconsin 54155
(414) 869-2771
Purcell Powless, Chairman

Tribe: Oneida. *In residence:* 2,500 (tribal roll: 3,500). *Area:* 2,600 acres. Executive Committee. Great Lakes Agency.

RED CLIFF RESERVATION
P.O. Box 529
Bayfield, Wisconsin 54814
(715) 779-5805
Richard Gurnoe, Chairman

Tribe: Lake Superior Chippewa. *In residence:* 1,400. *Area:* 7,311 acres. Extends over Lake Superior, approximately 25 miles northwest of Ashland, Wisconsin. Tribal Council. Great Lakes Agency.

ST. CROIX RESERVATION
Star Route
Webster, Wisconsin 54893
(715) 349-2295
Gene Taylor, Chairman

Tribe: Chippewa. *In residence:* 1,000. *Area:* 2,230 acres. Tribal Council. Great Lakes Agency.

SOKOAGON CHIPPEWA COMMUNITY
Route 1, Box 625
Crandon, Wisconsin 54520
(715) 478-3543
Arlyn Ackley, Chairman

Tribe: Mole Lake Chippewa. *In residence:* 250. *Area:* 1,700 acres. Tribal Council. Great Lakes Agency.

STOCKBRIDGE-MUNSEE COMMUNITY
RR 1
Bowler, Wisconsin 54416
(715) 793-4111
Leon Miller, Jr., Chairman

Tribe: Stockbridge-Munsee Mohican Indians of Wisconsin. *In residence:* 750 (tribal roll: 1,500). *Area:* 16,000 acres. Tribal Council. Great Lakes Agency.

WINNEBAGO RESERVATION
P.O. Box 311
Tomah, Wisconsin 54660
(715) 886-5010/5020
Kenneth Funmaker, Sr., Chairman

Tribe: Winnebago. *In residence:* 1,250. *Area:* 4,100 acres. Business Council. Great Lakes Agency.

WYOMING

NORTHWESTERN BAND OF SHOSHONE NATION
Star Route 2W
Rock Springs, Wyoming 82901
(307) 382-3943
Kenneth L. Neaman, Chairman

WIND RIVER RESERVATION
Fort Washakie, Wyoming 82514
(307) 255-8257 (Shoshone)
(307) 255-8394 (Arapahoe)
Robert N. Harris, Sr., Shoshone Chairman
Chester Armajo, Arapahoe Chairman

Tribes: Arapahoe and Shoshone. *In residence:* 5,000 (tribal roll: 6,000). *Area:* 1,887,372 acres. Located in east-central Wyoming. Business Councils. Wind River Agency.

TRIBAL COUNCILS

Listed in this section are reservation tribal councils, organizations, and governing bodies, which handle tribal and/or reservation affairs and which represent the tribes and create policy on land, enrollment, etc. Listings are arranged alphabetically within states. For further information refer to reservations.

ALASKA

The Alaska Native Claims Settlement Act of December 18, 1971, established regional village corporations and associations, both profit and non-profit. Listings are arranged alphabetically.

AHTNA, INCORPORATED
Drawer G
Copper Center, Alaska 99573
(907) 822-3476
Roy S. Ewan, President

A native for-profit regional corporation. *Activities:* Construction, real estate; student loans and scholarships, and loans to shareholders for business ventures. *Publications:* Annual reports; Shareholder's Handbook. Library.

ALASKA VILLAGE COUNCIL
P.O. Box 219
Bethel, Alaska 99559

A non-profit native association.

ALEUT CORPORATION
2550 Denali St.
Anchorage, Alaska 99501

A native for-profit regional corporation.

**ALEUTIAN PRIBILOFF
ISLAND ASSOCIATION**
1689 C St.
Anchorage, Alaska 99501
(907) 276-2700

A native non-profit association. Serves as a health clinic.

ARCTIC SLOPE NATIVE ASSOCIATION
P.O. Box 566
Barrow, Alaska 99723

A native non-profit association.

**ARCTIC SLOPE
REGIONAL CORPORATION**
P.O. Box 129
Barrow, Alaska 99723
(907) 852-8633/8533

A native for-profit regional corporation.

**BERING STRAITS
NATIVE CORPORATION**
P.O. Box 1008
Nome, Alaska 99762
(907) 443-5252

A native for-profit regional corporation.

**BRISTOL BAY AREA
HEALTH CORPORATION**
P.O. Box 10235
Dillingham, Alaska 99576
(907) 842-5266/5267
(907) 842-5201 (hospital)

Health clinic affiliated with Bristol Bay Native Association.

BRISTOL BAY NATIVE ASSOCIATION
P.O. Box 179
Dillingham, Alaska 99576
(907) 842-5257/5258

A native non-profit association.

BRISTOL BAY NATIVE CORPORATION
P.O. Box 198
Dillingham, Alaska 99576
(907) 842-5261

A native for-profit regional corporation.

CALISTA CORPORATION
516 Denali St.
Anchorage, Alaska 99501
(907) 279-5516/276-8837

A native for-profit regional corporation.

CHUGACH NATIVES, INCORPORATED
903 West Northern Lights #201
Anchorage, Alaska 99503
(907) 276-1080

A native for-profit regional corporation.

COOK INLET NATIVE ASSOCIATION
670 West Fireweed Lane
Anchorage, Alaska 99503
(907) 278-4641
Franklin L. Berry, Executive Director

A native non-profit association of approximately 1,500 Alaskan Natives and American Indians dedicated to nurturing pride in the heritage and traditions of Alaska Natives, and preserving the customs, folklore, and art of the people. Operates a health clinic, Alaska Native Community Center. *Publication: Trail Blazer,* quarterly newsletter.

COOK INLET REGION, INCORPORATED
P.O. Drawer 4-N
Anchorage, Alaska 99509
(907) 274-8638

A native for-profit regional corporation.

COPPER RIVER HEALTH AUTHORITY
P.O. Drawer H
Copper Center, Alaska 99573
(907) 822-3521

Health clinic of the Copper River Native Association.

COPPER RIVER NATIVE ASSOCIATION
P.O. Drawer G
Copper River, Alaska 99573
(907) 822-5241

A native non-profit association.

DOYON LIMITED
210 First Ave.
Fairbanks, Alaska 99701
(907) 452-4755

A native for-profit regional corporation.

KAWERAK, INCORPORATED
P.O. Box 505
Nome, Alaska 99762
(907) 443-5231

A native non-profit association.

KODIAK AREA NATIVE ASSOCIATION
402 Center Ave.
Kodiak, Alaska 99615
(907) 486-5725
Gordon L. Pullar, President

A native non-profit association promoting pride on the part of the natives of Alaska in their heritage and traditions; promotes the physical, economic, and social well-being of the natives of Alaska. *Activities:* Over 40 programs administered under the Department of Health; education and family services; community and economic development; health clinic. *Scholarships:* Higher education and adult vocational training scholarships funded by the Bureau of Indian Affairs; education and social work scholarships funded by the Department of Health and Human Services; *Skip Eaton Scholarship,* an independent local award. Library.

KONIAG, INCORPORATED
P.O. Box 746
Kodiak, Alaska 99615
(907) 486-4147

A native for-profit regional corporation.

MANIILAQ, INCORPORATED
P.O. Box 257
Kotzebue, Alaska 99752
(907) 442-3311
Marie N. Schwind, President

A native non-profit association which promotes the public health and social welfare in northwest Alaska; attempts to preserve and promote the Eskimo customs, arts and language, and advance education in all forms. Operates a health corporation comprising eleven Eskimo Villages, ranging from 60 to 2,400 in population. *Publications: Northwest Arctic Nuna,* monthly newsletter; *Nuna Regional Strategy Plan,* and *Nana Coastal Zone Management Plan.*

NANA REGIONAL CORPORATION
P.O. Box 49
Kotzebue, Alaska 99752
(907) 442-3301

A native for-profit regional corporation.

NORTH PACIFIC RIM NATIVE ASSOCIATION
903 West Northern Lights #203
Anchorage, Alaska 99503
(907) 276-2121

A native non-profit association. Operates a health clinic.

NORTH SLOPE BOROUGH HEALTH CORPORATION
P.O. Box 69
Barrow, Alaska 99723
(907) 852-3999

A health clinic.

NORTON SOUND HEALTH CORPORATION
P.O. Box 966
Nome, Alaska 99762
(907) 443-5411

A health clinic.

SEALASKA CORPORATION
One Sealaska Plaza, Suite 400
Juneau, Alaska 99801
(907) 586-1512
Byron I. Mallott, Chief Executive Officer

A regional native for-profit corporation, established by Congress under the Alaska Native Claims Settlement Act of 1971. *Activities:* Owns a forest products company, a seaford products company, and a building products company; conducts workshops for shareholders; political action committee, SEAPAC; Sealaska Heritage Foundation—an affiliate—preserves and promotes the cultural traditions of the Tlingit, Haida and Tsimpshian people; provides scholarships, and maintains archives. *Publications: The Sealaska Shareholder,* bimonthly newspaper; annual reports.

SOUTHEAST ALASKA
REGIONAL HEALTH CORPORATION
P.O. Box 2800
Juneau, Alaska 99801
    (907) 789-2131

A health clinic.

TANANA CHIEFS CONFERENCE
201 First Ave.
Fairbanks, Alaska 99701
    (907) 456-1275

A native non-profit association.

TANANA CHIEFS HEALTH AUTHORITY
First & Hall Sts., Doyon Bldg.
Fairbanks, Alaska 99701
    (907) 452-8251

A health clinic operated by the Tanana Chiefs Conference.

THIRTEENTH REGIONAL CORPORATION
4241 21st Ave., West, Suite 100
Seattle, Washington 98199
    (206) 281-5313

An Alaska Native non-profit association.

TLINGIT/HAIDA CENTRAL COUNCIL
320 West Willoughby Ave., Suite 300
Juneau, Alaska 99801
    (907) 586-1432
    Edward K. Thomas, President

A native non-profit association.

YUKON KUSKOKWIM
HEALTH CORPORATION
P.O. Box 528
Bethel, Alaska 99559
    (907) 543-3321

A health clinic.

The U.S. Department of the Interior, Bureau of Indian Affairs (BIA) is the agency that identifies and recognizes Indian tribal entities for establishing and maintaining federal government to government relations with Indians. Those tribes, bands and groups that have been recognized by the BIA are listed below, with the agency or area office (of the BIA) of jurisdiction indicated for each listing.

ALABAMA

POARCH BAND OF CREEKS
Route 3, Box 243-A
Atmore, Alabama 36502

ARIZONA

AK CHIN COMMUNITY COUNCIL
Route 2, Box 27
Maricopa, Arizona 85239
    (602) 568-2227
    Leroy Narcia, Chairman

Tribe served: Papago. Phoenix Area Office.

COCOPAH TRIBAL COUNCIL
P.O. Box Bin "G"
Somerton, Arizona 85350
    (602) 627-2102
    Fred Miller, Chairman

Tribe served: Cocopah. Phoenix Area Office.

COLORADO RIVER
INDIAN TRIBAL COUNCIL
Route 1, Box 23-B
Parker, Arizona 85344
    (602) 669-9211
    Anthony Drennan, Sr., Chairman

Tribes served: Mohave, Chemehuevi, Hopi, and Navajo. *Reservation served:* Colorado River Indian Reservation. *Tribal enrollment:* 2,800. *Tribal services:* Tribal police, courts, museum and library; also, departments: fish and game, education, health and social services, recreation, manpower, building and zoning, fire, housing. *Publication: Manataba Messenger,* monthly newsletter.

GILA RIVER COMMUNITY COUNCIL
P.O. Box 97
Sacaton, Arizona 85247
    (602) 562-3311
    Donald R. Antone, Sr., Governor

Tribes served: Pima and Maricopa. Phoenix Area Office.

HAVASUPAI TRIBAL COUNCIL
P.O. Box 10
Supai, Arizona 86435
(602) 448-2961
Wayne Sinyella, Chairman

Tribe served: Havasupai. Phoenix Area Office.

HOPI TRIBAL COUNCIL
P.O. Box 123
Oraibi, Arizona 86039
(602) 734-2445
Ivan Sidney, Chairman

Tribes served: Hopi and Tewa.
Phoenix Area Office.

HUALAPAI TRIBAL COUNCIL
P.O. Box 168
Peach Springs, Arizona 86434
(602) 769-2216
Edgar Sinyella, Chairman

Tribe served: Hualapai. Phoenix Area Office.

KAIBAB TRIBAL COUNCIL
Tribal Affairs Bldg.
Pipe Springs, Arizona 86022
Delores Savala, Chairwoman

Tribe served: Paiute. Phoenix Area Office.

**FORT McDOWELL MOHAVE-APACHE
COMMUNITY COUNCIL**
P.O. Box 17779
Fountain Hills, Arizona 85269
(602) 990-0995
Benjamin Kill, Sr., President

Tribes served: Mohave and Apache.
Phoenix Area Office.

NAVAJO TRIBAL COUNCIL
P.O. Box 308
Window Rock, Arizona 86515
(602) 871-4941
Peterson Zah, Chairman

Tribe served: Navajo of Arizona and New
Mexico. *Population served:* 167,000. Navajo Area
Office. *Special activities:* Navajo Nation Fair
(first weekend in September); summer and winter
ceremonials. Museum and library.

PAPAGO TRIBAL COUNCIL
P.O. Box 837
Sells, Arizona 85634
(602) 383-2236/2221
Josiah N. Moore, Chairman

Tribe served: Papago. *Reservations served:* Sells,
San Xavier, and Gila Bend. Phoenix Area Office.

PASCUA YAQUI TRIBAL COUNCIL
4821 West Calle Vicam
Tucson, Arizona 85706
(602) 883-2830
David Ramirez, Chairman

Tribe served: Pascua Yaqui. Phoenix Area Office.

QUECHAN TRIBAL COUNCIL
P.O. Box 1352
Yuma, Arizona 85364
(619) 572-0213
Elvin Kelly, President

Tribe served: Quechan. Phoenix Area Office.

**SALT RIVER PIMA-MARICOPA
COMMUNITY COLLEGE**
Route 1, Box 216
Scottsdale, Arizona 85256
(602) 941-7277
Gerald Anton, President

Tribes served: Pima and Maricopa. Phoenix
Area Office.

SAN CARLOS TRIBAL COUNCIL
P.O. Box 0
San Carlos, Arizona 85550
(602) 475-2361
Ned Anderson, Chairman

Tribe served: San Carlos Apache. Phoenix
Area Office.

TONTO APACHE TRIBAL COUNCIL
P.O. Box 1440
Payson, Arizona 85541
(602) 474-5000
Melton Campbell, Chairman

Tribe served: Tonto Apache. Phoenix
Area Office.

**WHITE MOUNTAIN APACHE
TRIBAL COUNCIL**
P.O. Box 700
Whiteriver, Arizona 85941
(602) 338-4371
Ronnie Lupe, Chairman

Tribe served: White Mountain Apache of the Fort
Apache Indian Reservation. Phoenix Area Office.

YAVAPAI-APACHE COMMUNITY
P.O. Box 1188
Camp Verde, Arizona 86322
(602) 567-3649
Ned Russell, Chairman

Tribe served: Yavapai-Apache.
Phoenix Area Office.

**YAVAPAI-PRESCOTT
BOARD OF DIRECTORS**
P.O. Box 348
Prescott, Arizona 86301
(602) 445-8790
Patricia McGee, Chairwoman

Tribe served: Yavapai. Phoenix Area Office.

CALIFORNIA

AGUA CALIENTE TRIBAL COUNCIL
441 South Calle Encilia, Suite 1
Palm Springs, California 92262
(619) 325-5673
Richard Milanovich, Chairman

Tribe served: Cahuilla. *Population served:* 200.
Sacramento Area Office.

BARONA BAND OF MISSION INDIANS
1095 Barona Rd.
Lakeside, California 92040
(619) 433-6613
Edward L. Welch, Spokesman

Tribe served: Diegueno. *Population served:* 300.
Sacramento Area Office.

BERRY CREEK TRIBAL COUNCIL
1956 B St.
Oroville, California 95965

Tribe served: Yurok. *Population
served:* 175. Sacramento Area Office.

BIG BEND GENERAL COUNCIL
P.O. Box 255
Big Bend, California 96001
(916) 337-6605
Kenneth Sisk, President

Tribe served: Pit River. *Population
served:* 115. Sacramento Area Office.

BIG LAGOON RANCHERIA
P.O. Box 795
Trinidad, California 95570
Dale Lara, Chairman

Tribes served: Yurok and Tolowa. Sacramento
Area Office.

BIG PINE GENERAL COUNCIL
P.O. Box 384
Big Pine, California 93513
(619) 938-2121
Velma Jones, Chairwoman

Tribes served: Paiute and Shoshone.
Population served: 450. Sacramento Area Office.

**BIG SANDY
INTERIM TRIBAL COUNCIL**
P.O. Box 337
Auberry, California 93602
Donna Marvin, Chairwoman

Sacramento Area Office.

BIG VALLEY RANCHERIA
921 El Camino Ave.
Sacramento, California 95815

Sacramento Area Office.

BISHOP INDIAN TRIBAL COUNCIL
P.O. Box 548
Bishop, California 93514
(619) 873-3584
Earl Frank, Chairman

Tribes served: Paiute and Shoshone. *Population
served:* 1,020. *Activities:* Toiyabe Indian health
project; career development; education center;
child care; elders program; culture center;
maintains museum. Sacramento Area Office.

BLUE LAKE RANCHERIA
P.O.Box 811
Blue Lake, California 95525

Sacramento Area Office.

BRIDGEPORT GENERAL COUNCIL
P.O. Box 37
Bridgeport, California 93517
(619) 932-7083
Maurice Crawford, Chairman

Tribe served: Paiute. *Population served:* 85.
Sacramento Area Office.

BUENA VISTA RANCHERIA
Route 1, Box 231
Ione, California 95640

Sacramento Area Office.

CABAZON GENERAL COUNCIL
84-245 Indio Spring Dr.
Indio, California 92201
(619) 342-2593
Art Welmas, Chairman

Tribe served: Cahuilla. *Population
served:* 25. Sacramento Area Office.

CAHUILLA GENERAL COUNCIL
Star Route, Box 185
Aguango, California 92302
(619) 658-2711
Eugene Madrigal, Spokesman

Tribe served: Cahuilla. Sacramento
Area Office.

CAMPO GENERAL COUNCIL
P.O. Box 1094
Boulevard, California 92005
(619) 766-4651
Valencia Thacker, Chairwoman

Tribe served: Diegueno. *Population served:* 210. Sacramento Area Office.

CEDARVILLE COMMUNITY COUNCIL
P.O. Box 142
Cedarville. California 96104
Andrew Phoenix, Chairman

Tribe served: Paiute. *Population served:* 20. Sacramento Area Office.

CHEMEHUEVI TRIBAL COUNCIL
P.O. Box 1976
Chemehuevi Valley, California 92363
(619) 858-4531
Richard Alvarez, Chairman

Tribe served: Chemehuevi. Population served: 130. Phoenix Area Office.

CHICKEN RANCH RANCHERIA
16929 Chicken Ranch Rd.
Jamestown, California 95327

Sacramento Area Office.

CLOVEDALE RANCHERIA
285 Santana Dr.
Cloverdale, California 95425

Sacramento Area Office.

COLD SPRINGS TRIBAL COUNCIL
P.O. Box 209
Tollhouse, California 93667
(209) 855-2326
Dorothy Bill, Chairwoman

Tribe served: Mono. *Population served:* 215. Sacramento Area Office.

COLUSA INDIAN COMMUNITY COUNCIL
P.O. Box 8
Colusa, California 95932
(916) 458-8231
Michael E. Mitchum, Chairman

Tribe served: Cachil DeHe Band of Wintun Indians. *Population served:* 50. Sacramento Area Office.

CORTINA GENERAL COUNCIL
P.O. Box 41113
Sacramento, California
(916) 725-6104
Mary Norton, Chairwoman

Tribe served: Wintun. *Population served:* 85. Sacramento Area Office.

COVELO COMMUNITY COUNCIL
Round Valley Reservation
P.O. Box 448
Covelo, California 95428
(707) 983-6126
Daran Lincoln, President

Tribe served: Maidu. *Population served:* 725. Sacramento Area Office.

**COYOTE VALLEY
INTERIM TRIBAL COUNCIL**
P.O. Box 39
Redwood Valley, California 95470-0039
(707) 485-8723
Doris Renick, Chairwoman

Tribe served: Pomo. Sacramento Area Office.

CUYAPAIPE GENERAL COUNCIL
P.O. Box 187
Campo, California 92006
(619) 478-5289
Tony J. Pinto, Chairman

Tribe served: Diegueno. *Population served:* 25. Sacramento Area Office.

DEATH VALLEY INDIAN COMMUNITY
P.O. Box 108
Death Valley, California 92325
Pauline Esteves, Chairwoman

Sacramento Area Office.

DRY CREEK TRIBAL COUNCIL
P.O. Box 413
Geyserville, California 95441
(707) 433-1209
Amy Martin, Chairwoman

Tribe served: Pomo. *Population served:* 135. Sacramento Area Office.

ELEM GENERAL COUNCIL
Sulphur Bank Rancheria
P.O. Box 618
Clearlake Oaks, California 95423
(707) 998-1666
Raymond J. Brown, Chairman

Tribe served: Pomo. *Population served:* 165. Sacramento Area Office.

ELK VALLEY RANCHERIA
P.O. Box 779
Crescent City, California 95531

Sacramento Area Office.

ENTERPRISE RANCHERIA
7470 Feather Falls Star Route
Oroville, California 95965
(916) 589-0652
Glen Watson, Spokesman

Tribe served: Maidu. *Population served:* 20. Sacramento Area Office.

FORT BIDWELL COMMUNITY COUNCIL
P.O. Box 127
Fort Bidwell, California 96112
(916) 279-6310
Lucinda Lame Bull, Chairwoman

Tribe served: Paiute. *Population served:* 175. Sacramento Area Office.

FORT INDEPENDENCE GENERAL COUNCIL
P.O. Box 67
Independence, California 93526
(619) 878-2126
Vernon Miller, Chairman

Tribe served: Paiute. *Population served:* 100. Sacramento Area Office.

FORT MOJAVE TRIBAL COUNCIL
500 Merriman Ave.
Needles, California 92363
(619) 326-4591
Nora Garcia, Chairwoman

Tribe served: Mojave. *Population served:* 550. Phoenix Area Office.

GREENVILLE RANCHERIA
Roundhouse Council, P.O. Box 217
Greenville, California 95947

Sacramento Area Office.

GRINDSTONE GENERAL COUNCIL
P.O. Box 63
Elk Creek, California 95939
(916) 968-5321
James Burrows, Chairman

Tribe served: Wintun. *Population served:* 185. Sacramento Area Office.

HOOPA VALLEY BUSINESS COUNCIL
P.O. Box 1348
Hoopa, California 95546
(916) 625-4691
Elsie Ricklefs, Chairwoman

Tribe served: Hoopa. *Population served:* 1,900. Sacramento Area Office.

HOPLAND INTERIM TRIBAL COUNCIL
P.O. Box 610
Hopland, California 95449
(707) 744-1647
Ramon Billy, President

Sacramento Area Office.

INAJA-COSMIT GENERAL COUNCIL
P.O. Box 102
Santa Ysabel, California 92070

(619) 765-1993
Rebecca Contreras, Spokesman

Tribe served: Diegueno. Sacramento Area Office.

JACKSON INTERIM COUNCIL
12200 New York Ranch Rd.
Jackson, California 95642
(209) 223-1897
Margaret Dalton, Representative

Tribe served: Miwok. Sacramento Area Office.

JAMUL GENERAL COUNCIL
14191-A Highway #94
Jamul, California 92035
(619) 697-5041
Kenneth A. Meza, Chairman

Sacramento Area Office.

KAPOK INTERIM COMMITTEE
P.O. Box 1098
Happy Camp, California 96039
(916) 493-2349
Paul Beck, Chairman

Sacramento Area Office.

KASHIA BUSINESS COMMITTEE
Stewarts Point Rancheria
1112 Mendocino Ave.
Santa Rosa, California 95401
(707) 528-1872
Langford Pinola, Chairman

Tribe served: Kashia-Pomo. *Population served:* 215. Sacramento Area Office.

LA JOLLA GENERAL COUNCIL
Star Route, Box 158
Valley Center, California 92082
(619) 742-3771
Doris J. Magante, Chairwoman

Tribe served: Luiseno. *Population served:* 235. Sacramento Area Office.

LA POSTA GENERAL COUNCIL
P.O. Box 894
Boulevard, California 92005
(619) 478-5523
Gwendolyn Sevella, Chairwoman

Tribe served: Luiseno. Sacramento Area Office.

LAYTONVILLE GENERAL COUNCIL
P.O. Box 1239
Laytonville, California 95454
(707) 984-6197
Gertrude Brown, Chairwoman

Tribe served: Cahto-Pomo. *Population served:* 190. Sacramento Area Office.

LONE PINE TRIBAL COUNCIL
Star Route 1, 1101 South Main St.
Lone Pine, California 93545
(619) 876-5414
Nedeen Naylor, Chairwoman

*Tribe served: Paiute-Shoshone. Population
served:* 225. Sacramento Area Office.

LOOKOUT RANCHERIA
P.O. Box 87
Lookout, California 96054
Laura Craig, Representative

Tribe served: Pit River. Sacramento Area Office.

LOS COYOTES GENERAL COUNCIL
P.O. Box 86
Warner Springs, California 92086
(619) 782-3269
Banning Taylor, Spokesman

*Tribe served: Luiseno. Population
served:* 175. Sacramento Area Office.

MANCHESTER COMMUNITY COUNCIL
P.O. Box 623
Point Arena, California 95468
(707) 882-2788
Kenneth Laiwa, Chairman

Tribe served: Pomo. *Population
served:* 100. Sacramento Area Office.

MANZANITA GENERAL COUNCIL
P.O. Box 1302
Boulevard, California 92005
(619) 478-5028
Frances Shaw, Chairman

Tribe served: Diegueno. *Population served:*
20. *Activities:* Economic Development Project.
Sacramento Area Office.

MESA GRANDE GENERAL COUNCIL
Mesa Grande Star Route
Santa Ysabel, California 92070
(619) 782-3521
Brian Beresford, Chairman

*Tribe served: Luiseno. Population
served:* 30. Sacramento Area Office.

MIDDLETOWN INTERIM COUNCIL
P.O. Box 292
Middletown, California 95461
Larry Simon, President

Tribe served: Pomo. *Population served:* 65.
Sacramento Area Office.

MONTGOMERY CREEK RANCHERIA
General Delivery
Montgomery Creek, California 96065
Ross Montgomery, Spokesman

Tribe served: Pit River. *Population
served:* 20. Sacramento Area Office.

MOORETOWN RANCHERIA
P.O. Box 7630 FF SR
Oroville, California 95965

Sacramento Area Office.

MORONGO GENERAL COUNCIL
11581 Potrero Rd.
Banning, California 92220
(714) 849-4697
Robert Martin, Spokesman

Tribe served: Serrano. *Population
served:* 750. Sacramento Area Office.

NORTH FORK RANCHERIA
P.O. Box 514
North Fork, California 93643

Sacramento Area Office.

PALA EXECUTIVE COMMITTEE
P.O. Box 43
Pala, California 92059
((619) 742-3785
King Freeman, Chairman

Tribe served: Cupa. *Population served:* 580.
Activities: Cupa Day (May); Museum.
Publication: Pala Mumalki, newsletter.
Sacramento Area Office.

PAUMA TRIBAL COUNCIL
P.O. Box 86
Pauma Valley, California 92061
(619) 742-1289
Patricia A. Dixon, Chairwoman

*Tribe served: Luiseno (Pauma Band of Mission
Indians.) Population served:* 35. *Activities:*
education center; memorial celebration.
Sacramento Area Office.

PECHANGA TRIBAL COUNCIL
P.O. Box 181
Temecula, California 92390
(714) 676-6653
Gabriel H. Pico, Spokesman

Tribe served: Luiseno. Population served: 450.
Sacramento Area Office.

PICAYUNE RANCHERIA
P.O. Box 426
Coorsegold, California 93614

Sacramento Area Office

PINOLEVILLE RANCHERIA
200 Pinoleville Dr.
Ukiah, California 95482

Sacramento Area Office.

PIT RIVER TRIBAL COUNCIL
P.O. Box 763
Alturas, California 96101
(619) 335-3353
Leo Jones, Chairman

Tribe served: Pit River. Sacramento Area Office.

POTTER VALLEY RANCHERIA
P.O. Box 94
Potter Valley, California 95469

Sacramento Area Office.

QUARTZ VALLEY RANCHERIA
10736 Quartz Valley Rd.
Fort Jones, California 96032

Sacramento Area Office.

REDDING RANCHERIA
2214 Rancheria Rd.
Redding, California 96001

Sacramento Area Office.

REDWOOD VALLEY RANCHERIA
P.O. Box 11
Redwood Valley, California 95470

Sacramento Area Office.

RESIGHINI BUSINESS COUNCIL
P.O. Box 212
Klamath, California 95548
(707) 482-3371
William John Scott, President

Tribe served: Yurok. *Population served:* 110.
Sacramento Area Office.

RINCON BUSINESS COMMITTEE
P.O. Box 68
Valley Center, California 92082
(619) 749-1051
Don Calac, Chairman

Tribe served: Luiseno. *Population:* 275.
Sacramento Area Office.

**ROBINSON CITIZENS
BUSINESS COUNCIL**
2000 Marconi Ave.
Sacramento, California 95821
(916) 922-4536
Bernadine Tripp, Chairwoman

Tribe served: Pomo. Sacramento Area Office.

ROHNERVILLE RANCHERIA
P.O. Box 483
Fortuna, California 95540

Sacramento Area Office.

RUMSEY COMMUNITY COUNCIL
P.O. Box 18
Brooks, California 95606
(916) 796-3182
Philip Knight, Chairman

Tribe served: Wintun. *Population served:* 50.
Sacramento Area Office.

SAN MANUEL GENERAL COUNCIL
5771 North Victoria Ave.
Highland, California 92346
(714) 862-2439
Henry Duro, Chairman

Tribe served: Serrano. *Population served:* 90.
Sacramento Area Office.

SAN PASQUAL GENERAL COUNCIL
P.O. Box 365
Valley Center, California 92082
(619) 749-3200
Robert L. Stewart, Spokesman

Tribe served: Luiseno (San Pasqual Band of
Mission Indians.) *Population served:* 350.
Sacramento Area Office.

SANTA ROSA GENERAL COUNCIL
325 North Western St.
Hemet, California 92343
(714) 925-7190
Anthony Largo, Spokesman

Tribe served: Cahuilla. *Population
served:* 275. Sacramento Area Office.

SANTA ROSA GENERAL COUNCIL
16088 Alkalie Dr.
Lemoore, California 93245
(209) 924-1571
Clarence Atwell, Chairman

Tribe served: Tache. *Population served:* 100.
Sacramento Area Office.

SANTA YNEZ GENERAL COUNCIL
P.O. Box 517
Santa Ynez, California 93460
(805) 688-7997
James Pace, Chairman

Tribe served: Chumash. *Population served:* 200.
Sacramento Area Office.

SANTA YSABEL GENERAL COUNCIL
P.O. Box 126
Santa Ysabel, California 92070
(619) 765-0845
Joan King, Chairwoman

Tribe served: Diegueno. *Population served:*
900. Sacramento Area Office.

**SHERWOOD VALLEY
GENERAL COUNCIL**
2137 South State St.
Ukiah, California 95482
(707) 468-1337
Patricia Augustine, Chairwoman

Tribe served: Pomo. *Population served:*
175. Sacramento Area Office.

SHINGLE SPRINGS RANCHERIA
8024 Levering Way
Sacramento, California 95801
(916) 421-7783
John Fenseca, Chairman

Tribe served: Miwok. Sacramento Area Office.

SMITH RIVER RANCHERIA
P.O. Box 23
Orick, California 95555

Sacramento Area Office.

SOBOBA GENERAL COUNCIL
P.O. Box 487
San Jacinto, California 92383
(714) 654-2765
Benny Helms, Sr., Spokesman

Tribe served: Luiseno (Soboba Band of Mission
Indians.) *Population served:* 460. Sacramento
Area Office.

**SUSANVILLE INDIAN RANCHERIA
BUSINESS COUNCIL**
Drawer 'U'
Susanville, California 96130
(916) 257-6264
Nicolas J. Padilla, Chairman

Tribes served: Paiute, Maidu, and Pit River.
Population served: 350. Sacramento Area Office.

SYCUAN GENERAL COUNCIL
P.O. Box 2929
El Cajon, California 92021
(619) 445-4073
Anna Sandoval, Spokeswoman

Tribe served: Diegueno. *Population served:*
70. Sacramento Area Office.

**TABLE BLUFF
BOARD OF DIRECTORS**
P.O. Box 519
Loleta, California 95551
(707) 733-5537
Robert Johnson, Chairman

Sacramento Area Office.

**TABLE MOUNTAIN
INTERIM TRIBAL COUNCIL**
P.O. Box 243
Friant, California 93626
Lewis Barnes, Chairman

Sacramento Area Office.

**TORRES-MARTINEZ
BUSINESS COUNCIL**
1866 East George
Banning, California 92220
(714) 849-2172
Ronald D. Cortez, Chairman

Tribe served: Cahuilla. *Population served:*
85. Sacramento Area Office.

TRINIDAD COMMUNITY COUNCIL
P.O. Box AA
Trinidad, California 95570
(707) 677-0211
Rose Joy Sundberg, Chairwoman

Tribe served: Yurok. *Population served:* 10.
Sacramento Area Office.

TULE RIVER TRIBAL COUNCIL
P.O. Box 589
Porterville, California 93257
(209) 781-4271
Crispina Sierra, Chairwoman

Tribe served: Tule River. *Population served:*
550. Sacramento Area Office.

TUOLUMNE COMMUNITY COUNCIL
P.O. Box 696
Tuolumne, California 95379
(209) 928-4265
Stanley R. Cox, Jr., Chairman

Tribe served: Miwok. *Population served:*
285. Sacramento Area Office.

**UPPER LAKE POMO
TRIBAL COUNCIL**
Upper Lake Rancheria
5738 Marconi Ave.
Carmichael, California 95608

Sacramento Area Office.

**UTU UTU GWAITU PAIUTE
TRIBAL COUNCIL**
Benton Paiute Reservation
Star Route 4, Box 56-A
Benton, California 93512
(619) 933-2321
Gladys Beauregard, Chairwoman

Tribe served: Paiute (Benton). *Population:* 70.
Activity: Annual Meeting. Sacramento Area
Office.

VIEJAS TRIBAL COMMITTEE
P.O. Box 908
Alpine, California 92001
  (619) 445-3275
  Anthony Pico, Spokesman

Tribe served: Diegueno. *Population served:*
190. Sacramento Area Office.

COLORADO

SOUTHERN UTE TRIBAL COUNCIL
P.O. Box 737
Ignacio, Colorado 81137
  (303) 563-4525
  Chris A. Baker, Chairman

Tribe served: Southern Ute. *Population served:*
1,100. *Activities: Sun Dance, Bear Dance, and
Ute Fair. Publication: Ute Drum,* newspaper.
Library. Albuquerque Area Office.

UTE MOUNTAIN TRIBAL COUNCIL
Tribal Office Bldg.
Towaoc, Colorado 81334
  (303) 565-3751
  Ernest House, Chairman

Tribe served: Ute Mountain. *Population
served:* 1,550. Albuquerque Area Office.

CONNECTICUT

MASHANTUCKET PEQUOT COUNCIL
P.O. Box 160
Ledyard, Connecticut 06339
  (203) 536-2681
  Richard Hayward, Chairman

Eastern Area Office.

FLORIDA

MICCOSUKEE BUSINESS COMMITTEE
P.O. Box 44021, Tamiami Station
Miami, Florida 33144
  (305) 223-8380/8383
  Buffalo Tiger, Chairman

Tribe served: Miccosukee-Creek. *Population
served:* 460. Eastern Area Office.

SEMINOLE TRIBAL COUNCIL
6073 Stirling Rd.
Hollywood, Florida 33024
  (305) 583-7112
  James Billie, Chairman

Tribe served: Seminole. *Population served:*
1,450. Museum and Library. Eastern Area Office.

IDAHO

COEUR D'ALENE TRIBAL COUNCIL
Plummer, Idaho 83851
  (208) 274-3101
  Bernard J. Lasarte, Chairman

Tribe served: Coeur d'Alene. *Population
served:* 850. Portland Area Office.

FORT HALL BUSINESS COUNCIL
Fort Hall Tribal Office
Fort Hall, Idaho 83203
  (208) 238-3700
  Kesley Edmo, Chairman

Tribe served: Shoshone-Bannock. *Population
served:* 3,900. Portland Area Office.

KOOTENAI TRIBAL COUNCIL
P.O. Box 1002
Bonners Ferry, Idaho 83805
  (208) 267-3519
  Amelia C. Trice, Chairwoman

Tribe served: Kootenai. *Population served:*
120. Portland Area Office.

**NEZ PERCE
TRIBAL EXECUTIVE COMMITTEE**
P.O. Box 305
Lapwai, Idaho 83540
  (208) 843-2253
  Allen V. Pinkham, Chairman

Tribe served: Nez Perce. *Population served:*
2,100. Portland Area Office.

SUMMIT LAKE PAIUTE COUNCIL
P.O. Box 597
Fort Hall, Idaho 83203
  (208) 237-6528
  Murray Barr, Chairman

Tribe served: Summit Lake Paiute.
Phoenix Area Office.

IOWA

SAC AND FOX TRIBAL COUNCIL
Route 2, Box 52C
Tama, Iowa 52339
  (515) 484-4678
  Louis Mitchell, Chairman

Tribe served: Sac and Fox. *Population
served:* 700. Minneapolis Area Office.

KANSAS

IOWA EXECUTIVE COMMITTEE
Route 1, Box 58A
White Cloud, Kansas 66094
(913) 595-3258
Leon Campbell, Chairman

Tribe served: Iowa of Kansas and Nebraska.
Population served: 285. Anadarko Area Office.

KICKAPOO TRIBAL COUNCIL
Route 1, Box 157A
Horton, Kansas 66439
(913) 486-2131
Fred Thomas, Chairman

Tribe served: Kickapoo. *Population served:*
600. Anadarko Area Office.

**PRAIRIE POTAWATOMI
TRIBAL COUNCIL**
P.O. Box 97
Mayetta, Kansas 66509
(913) 966-2255/2771
George Wahquahboshkuk, Chairman

Tribe served: Prairie Potawatomi.
Population: 1,350. Anadarko Area Office.

SAC AND FOX TRIBAL COUNCIL
P.O. Box 38
Reserve, Kansas 66434
(913) 742-7471
Nancy Keller, Chairwoman

Tribe served: Sac and Fox of Kansas and
Nebraska. Anadarko Area Office.

LOUISIANA

CHITIMACHA TRIBAL COUNCIL
P.O. Box 661
Charenton, Louisiana 70523
(318) 923-4973
Larry Burgess, Chairman

Tribe served: Chitimacha *Population served:*
300. *Activities:* Tribal fair (Fourth of July
weekend.) *Publication: The Chitimacha People,*
by Herbert T. Hoover (part of the tribal series.)
Museum and library. Eastern Area Office.

COUSHATTA TRIBAL COUNCIL
P.O. Box 988
Elton, Louisiana 70532
(318) 584-2242

Tribe served: Coushatta. *Population served:*
275. Eastern Area Office.

TUNICA-BILOXI INDIAN TRIBE
P.O. Box 331
Marksville, Louisiana 71351
(318) 253-9767
Earl Barbry, Sr., Chairman

Eastern Area Office.

MAINE

HOULTON MALISEET BAND COUNCIL
P.O. Box 576
Houlton, Maine 04730
(207) 532-7339
Clair Sabattis, Chairwoman

Tribe served: Maliseet. *Population served:*
250. Eastern Area Office.

**INDIAN TOWNSHIP
PASSAMAQUODDY TRIBAL COUNCIL**
P.O. Box 301
Indian Township 04668
(207) 796-2301
John Stevens, Governor

Tribe served: Passamaquoddy. *Population
served:* 385. Eastern Area Office.

PENOBSCOT TRIBAL COUNCIL
Six River Road Indian Island Reservation
Old Town, Maine 04468
(207) 827-7776
Timothy Love, Governor

Tribe served: Penobscot. *Population served:*
1,050. Eastern Area Office.

**PLEASANT POINT
PASSAMAQUODDY TRIBAL COUNCIL**
P.O. Box 343
Perry, Maine 04667
(207) 853-2551
Ralph F. Dana, Governor

Tribe served: Passamaquoddy. *Population
served:* 700. Eastern Area Office.

MICHIGAN

BAY MILLS EXECUTIVE COUNCIL
Route 1, Box 313
Brimley, Michigan 49715
(906) 248-3241
Wade Teeple, President

Tribe served: Chippewa. *Population served:*
475. Minneapolis Area Office.

GRAND TRAVERSE BAND
TRIBAL COUNCIL
Tribe served: Chippewa. Minneapolis Area
Office.

HANNAHVILLE INDIAN
COMMUNITY COUNCIL
Route 1, Community Center
Wilson, Michigan 49896
(906) 466-2379
Henry Philemon, Sr., Chairman

Tribe served: Potawatomi. *Population
served:* 350. Minneapolis Area Office.

KEWEENAW BAY TRIBAL COUNCIL
Tribal Center Bldg., Route 1
Baroga, Michigan 49908
(906) 353-6623
Myrtle Tolonen, President

Tribe served: Chippewa. *Population served:*
900. Minneapolis Area Office.

SAGINAW-CHIPPEWA
TRIBAL COUNCIL
7070 East Broadway Rd.
Mt. Pleasant, Michigan 48858
(517) 772-5700
Arnold Sowmick, Chief

Tribe served: Saginaw-Chippewa. Minneapolis
Area Office.

SAULT STE. MARIE
CHIPPEWA TRIBAL COUNCIL
206 Greenough St.
Sault Ste. Marie, Michigan 49783
(906) 635-6050
Joseph K. Lumsden, Chairman

Tribe served: Chippewa. *Reservations served:* St.
Ignace, Manistique, Munising, Michigan.
Activities: Tribal pow-wows (two each summer,
July 4th (Sault Ste. Marie), and first week in
August (St. Ignace.) *Publication: Nisasotowen,*
Tribal newspaper. Minneapolis Area Office.

MINNESOTA

FOND DU LAC RESERVATION
BUSINESS COMMITTEE
105 University Rd.
Cloquet, Minnesota 55720
(218) 879-1251
Gary Donald, Chairman

Tribe served: Chippewa. *Population served:*
1,450. Minneapolis Area Office.

GRAND PORTAGE RESERVATION
BUSINESS COMMITTEE
P.O. Box 428
Grand Portage, Minnesota 55605
(218) 475-2279/2277
Jim Hendrickson, Chairman

Tribe served: Chippewa. *Population served:*
325. Minneapolis Area Office.

LEECH LAKE RESERVATION
BUSINESS COMMITTEE
Route 3, Box 100
Cass Lake, Minnesota 56633
(218) 335-2207
Hartley White, Chairman

Tribe served: Chippewa (Mississippi and
Pillanger Bands.) *Population served:* 5,000.
Activities: Five annual pow-wows: Spring,
Fourth of July, Labor Day, Veterans Day, and
Winter. Minneapolis Area Office.

LOWER SIOUX
INDIAN COMMUNITY COUNCIL
Rural Route 1, Box 308
Morton, Minnesota 56270
(507) 697-6185
Michael Prescott, President

*Tribe served: Mdewakanton Sioux. Population
served:* 215. Minneapolis Area Office.

MILLE LACS RESERVATION
BUSINESS COMMITTEE
Star Route
Onamia, Minnesota 56359
(612) 532-4181
Arthur Gahbow, Chairman

Tribe served: Chippewa. *Population served:*
950. Minneapolis Area Office.

MINNESOTA CHIPPEWA
TRIBAL EXECUTIVE COMMITTEE
P.O. Box 217
Cass Lake, Minnesota 56633
(218) 335-2252
Darrell Wadena, President

Tribe served: Chippewa. *Reservations served:*
Nett Lake, Fond du Lac, Grand Portage,
Leech Lake, Mill Lac, and White Earth.
Minneapolis Area Office.

NETT LAKE RESERVATION (BOIS
FORTE TRIBE) BUSINESS COMMITTEE
Nett Lake, Minnesota 55772
(218) 757-3261
Gary Donald, Chairman

Tribe served: Chippewa. *Population served:*
1,000. Minneapolis Area Office.

**PRAIRIE ISLAND
COMMUNITY COUNCIL**
Route 2
Welch, Minnesota 55089
 (612) 388-8889
 Vine Wells, President

Tribe served: Mdewakanton Sioux. *Population
served:* 125. Minneapolis Area Office.

RED LAKE TRIBAL COUNCIL
Red Lake, Minnesota 56671
 (218) 679-3341
 Roger Jourdain, Chairman

Tribe served: Chippewa. *Population
served:* 4,500. Minneapolis Area Office.

SHAKOPEE BUSINESS COUNCIL
Box 150, Sioux Trail
Prior Lake, Minnesota 55372

Tribe served: Mdewakanton Sioux *Population
served:* 100. Minneapolis Area Office.

**UPPER SIOUX
BOARD OF TRUSTEES**
P.O. Box 147
Granite Falls, Minnesota 56241
 (612) 564-4504/4026
 Irene Howell, Chairwoman

Tribe served: Santee Sioux. *Population
served:* 135. Minneapolis Area Office.

**WHITE EARTH RESERVATION
BUSINESS COMMITTEE**
P.O. Box 418
White Earth, Minnesota 56591
 (218) 983-3285
 Darrell Wadena, Chairman

Tribe served: Chippewa. *Population
served:* 4,000. Minneapolis Area Office.

MISSISSIPPI

**TRIBAL COUNCIL OF THE
MISSISSIPPI BAND OF CHOCTAWS**
Route 7, Box 21
Philadelphia, Mississippi 39350
 (601) 656-5251
 Phillip Martin, Chief

Tribe served: Mississippi Band of Choctaws.
Population served: 4,600. *Activities:*
Annual Choctaw Indian Fair (July). Publications.
Museum. Library. Eastern Area Office.

MISSOURI

**EASTERN SHAWNEE
TRIBAL COUNCIL**
P.O. Box 350
Seneca, Missouri 64865
 (918) 666-2435
 George Captain, Chief

Tribe served: Eastern Shawnee of Oklahoma.
Population served: 350. Muskogee Area Office.

MONTANA

**BLACKFEET TRIBAL
BUSINESS COUNCIL**
Browning, Montana 59417
 (406) 338-7276
 Earl Old Person, Chairman

Tribe served: Blackfeet. *Population
served:* 6,750. Billings Area Office.

**CHIPPEWA CREE
BUSINESS COMMITTEE**
P.O. Box 137
Box Elder, Montana 59521
 (406) 395-4476
 Rocky Stump, Sr., Chairman

Tribes served: Chippewa and Cree.
Reservation served: Rocky Boy's Reservation.
Population served: 1,950. Billings Area Office.

**CONFEDERATED SALISH AND
KOOTENAI TRIBAL COUNCIL**
P.O. Box 278
Pablo, Montana 59855
 (406) 675-4600
 Joseph Felsman, Chairman

Tribe served: Salish & Kootenai.
Reservation served: Flathead. *Population
served:* 3,400. Portland Area Office.

CROW TRIBAL COUNCIL
Crow Agency, Montana 59002
 (406) 638-2671
 Donald Stewart, Sr., Chairman

Tribe served: Crow. *Population served:*
5,000. Billings Area Office.

**FORT BELKNAP
COMMUNITY COUNCIL**
Harlem, Montana 59526
 (406) 353-2205
 Franklin (Randy) Perez, President

Tribes served: Assiniboine Sioux and
Grosventre. *Population served:* 2,200.
Billings Area Office.

**FORT PECK
TRIBAL EXECUTIVE BOARD**
Poplar, Montana 59255
(406) 768-5311
Norman Hollow, Chairman

Tribe served: Assiniboine-Sioux.
Population served: 5,250.
Billings Area Office.

**NORTHERN CHEYENNE
TRIBAL COUNCIL**
Lame Deer, Montana 59043
(406) 477-6284
Allen Rowland, President

Tribe served: Northern Cheyenne.
Population served: 3,250.
Billings Area Office.

NEBRASKA

OMAHA TRIBAL COUNCIL
Macy, Nebraska 68039
(402) 837-5391
Wallace W. Miller, Chairman

Tribe served: Omaha. *Population served:*
1,500. Aberdeen Area Office.

SANTEE SIOUX TRIBAL COUNCIL
Route 2
Niobrara, Nebraska 68760
(402) 857-3302
Richard Kitto, Chairman

Tribe served: Santee Sioux. *Population
served:* 450. Aberdeen Area Office.

WINNEBAGO TRIBAL COUNCIL
Winnebago, Nebraska 68071
(402) 878-2272
Reuben A. Snake, Jr., Chairman

Tribe served: Winnebago. *Population
served:* 1,200. Aberdeen Area Office.

NEVADA

**DUCKWATER SHOSHONE
TRIBAL COUNCIL**
P.O. Box 68
Duckwater, Nevada 89314
(702) 863-0227
Jerry Millett, Chairman

Tribe served: Shoshone. *Population
served:* 145. Phoenix Area Office.

ELY COLONY COUNCIL
16 Shoshone Circle
Ely, Nevada 89301
(702) 289-6318
Sally Marques, Chairwoman

Tribe served: Shoshone. *Population served:* 235.
Phoenix Area Office.

**FALLON PAIUTE-SHOSHONE
BUSINESS COUNCIL**
Route 2, Box 232A
8955 Mission Rd.
Fallon, Nevada 89406
(702) 423-6075
Alvin Moyle, Chairman

Tribes served: Paiute-Shoshone. *Population
served:* 685. Phoenix Area Office.

**FORT McDERMITT
SHOSHONE-PAIUTE TRIBAL COUNCIL**
P.O. Box 457
McDermitt, Nevada
(702) 532-8259
Glen Abel, Chairman

Tribes served: Shoshone-Paiute. *Population
served:* 675. Phoenix Area Office.

LAS VEGAS COLONY COUNCIL
No. 1 Paiute Dr.
Las Vegas, Nevada 89106
(702) 386-3926
Billy J. Frye, Chairman

Tribe served: Paiute. *Population served:* 125.
Phoenix Area Office.

LOVELOCK TRIBAL COUNCIL
P.O. Box 878
Lovelock, Nevada 89419
(702) 273-7861
Dena J. Austin, Chairwoman

Tribe served: Paiute. *Population served:* 165.
Phoenix Area Office.

MOAPA BUSINESS COUNCIL
P.O. Box 56
Las Vegas, Nevada 89025
(702) 865-2787
Clifton R. Surrett, Chairman

Tribe served: Moapa Band of Paiute Indians
(Southern Paiute). *Population served:* 260.
Phoenix Area Office.

**PYRAMID LAKE PAIUTE
TRIBAL COUNCIL**
P.O. Box 256
Nixon, Nevada 89424
(702) 476-0140
Wilfred Shaw, Chairman

Tribe served: Paiute. *Population served:* 800.
Phoenix Area Office.

RENO-SPARKS INDIAN COUNCIL
98 Colony Rd.
Reno, Nevada 89502
(702) 329-2936
Lawrence Astor, Chairman

Tribes served: Washoe and Paiute. *Population served:* 625. Phoenix Area Office.

SHOSHONE-PAIUTE BUSINESS COUNCIL
P.O. Box 219
Owyhee, Nevada 89832
(702) 756-3161
Whitney McKinney, Chairman

Tribes served: Shoshone and Paiute. *Reservation served:* Duck Valley. Phoenix Area Office.

SUMMIT LAKE PAIUTE TRIBAL COUNCIL
444 Cheney St.
Reno, Nevada 89502

Tribe served: Paiute. Phoenix Area Office.

TE-MOAK BUSINESS COUNCIL
525 Sunset St.
Elko, Nevada 89801
(702) 738-9251
Felix Ike, Chief

Tribe served: Te-Moak Band of Western Shoshone. Phoenix Area Office.

WALKER RIVER PAIUTE TRIBAL COUNCIL
P.O. Box 220
Schurz, Nevada 89427
(702) 773-2306
Elvin Willie, Jr., Chairman

Tribe served: Paiute. *Population served:* 1,000.
Phoenix Area Office.

WASHOE TRIBAL COUNCIL
Route 2, Box 68
Gardnerville, Nevada 89410
(702) 883-1446
Robert L. Frank, Chairman

Tribe served: Washoe. *Population served:* 550.
Phoenix Area Office.

WINNEMUCCA COLONY COUNCIL
P.O. Box 1075
Winnemucca Nevada 89445
(702) 623-3479
Robert Harney, Chairman

Tribe served: Paiute. *Population served:* 85.
Phoenix Area Office.

YERINGTON TRIBAL COUNCIL
171 Campbell Lane
Yerington, Nevada 89447
(702) 463-3301
Kenneth M. Richardson, Chairman

Tribe served: Paiute. *Population served:* 350.
Phoenix Area Office.

YOMBA TRIBAL COUNCIL
Route 1, Box 24A
Austin, Nevada 89310
(702) 964-2463
William Rosse, Sr., Chairman

Tribe served: Shoshone. *Population served:* 115.
Phoenix Area Office.

NEW MEXICO

ACOMA PUEBLO TRIBAL COUNCIL
P.O. Box 309
Acomita, New Mexico 87034
(505) 552-6604
Merle Garcia, Governor

Tribe served: Pueblo. *Population served:* 3,000.
Albuquerque Area Office.

COCHITI PUEBLO TRIBAL COUNCIL
P.O. Box 70
Cochiti, New Mexico 87041
(505) 465-2244
Alvin Arquero, Governor

Tribe served: Pueblo. *Population served:* 925.
Albuquerque Area Office.

ISLETA PUEBLO TRIBAL COUNCIL
P.O. Box 317
Isleta, New Mexico 87022
(505) 869-3111
Alvino Lucero, Governor

Tribe served: Pueblo. *Population served:* 3,160.
Albuquerque Area Office.

JEMEZ PUEBLO TRIBAL COUNCIL
P.O. Box 78
Jemez, New Mexico 87024
(505) 834-7359
Candido Armijo, Governor

Tribe served: Pueblo. *Population served:* 1,900.
Albuquerque Area Office.

JICARILLA APACHE TRIBAL COUNCIL
P.O. Box 147
Dulce, New Mexico 87528
(505) 759-3242
Leonard Atole, President

Tribe served: Jicarilla Apache. *Population served:* 2,300. Albuquerque Area Office.

LAGUNA PUEBLO TRIBAL COUNCIL
P.O. Box 194
Laguna, New Mexico 87026
(505) 243-7616
Chester T. Fernando, Governor

Tribe served: Pueblo. *Population served:* 6,500.
Albuquerque Area Office.

**MESCALERO APACHE
TRIBAL COUNCIL**
P.O. Box 176
Mescalero, New Mexico 88340
(505) 671-4495
Wendell Chino, President

Tribe served: Mescalero Apache. *Population
served:* 2,450. Albuquerque Area Office.

NAMBE PUEBLO TRIBAL COUNCIL
Route 1, Box 117-BB
Santa Fe, New Mexico 87501
(505) 455-7752
David Perez, Governor

Tribe served: Pueblo. *Population served:* 385.
Albuquerque Area Office.

PICURIS PUEBLO TRIBAL COUNCIL
P.O. Box 127
Penasco, New Mexico 87553
(505) 587-2519
Gerald Nailor, Governor

Tribe served: Pueblo. *Population served:* 185.
Albuquerque Area Office.

POJOAQUE PUEBLO TRIBAL COUNCIL
Route 11, Box 71
Santa Fe, New Mexico 87501
(505) 455-2278/2279
Jacob Viarrial, Governor

Tribe served: Pueblo. *Population served:* 150.
Activity: Annual Feast Day (December).
Albuquerque Area Office.

**SAN FELIPE PUEBLO
TRIBAL COUNCIL**
P.O. Box A
San Felipe Pueblo, New Mexico 87001
(505) 867-3381
Frank Tenorio, Governor

Tribe served: Pueblo. *Population served:* 2,100.
Albuquerque Area Office.

**SAN ILDEFONSO PUEBLO
TRIBAL COUNCIL**
Route 5, Box 315A
Santa Fe, New Mexico 87501
(505) 455-2273
Gilbert Sanchez, Governor

Tribe served: Pueblo. *Population served:* 450.
Albuquerque Area Office.

SAN JUAN PUEBLO TRIBAL COUNCIL
P.O. Box 1099
San Juan Pueblo, New Mexico 87566
(505) 852-4400/4210
Jose Emelio Trujillo, Governor

Tribe served: Pueblo. *Population served:* 1,850.
Albuquerque Area Office.

SANDIA PUEBLO TRIBAL COUNCIL
P.O. Box 6008
Bernalillo, New Mexico 87004
(505) 867-2876
Esquipula Chaves, Governor

Tribe served: Pueblo. *Population served:* 300.
Albuquerque Area Office.

**SANTA ANA PUEBLO
TRIBAL COUNCIL**
P.O. Box 37
Bernalillo, New Mexico 87004
(505) 867-3301
Eliseo Raton, Sr., Governor

Tribe served: Pueblo. *Population served:* 510.
Albuquerque Area Office.

**SANTA CLARA PUEBLO
TRIBAL COUNCIL**
P.O. Box 580
Espanola, New Mexico 87532
(505) 753-7330/7327
Lawrence Singer, Governor

Tribe served: Pueblo. *Population served:* 2,350.
Albuquerque Area Office.

**SANTO DOMINGO PUEBLO
TRIBAL COUNCIL**
P.O. Box 99
Santo Domingo, New Mexico 87052
(505) 465-2214
Alex Garcia, Governor

Tribe served: Pueblo. *Population served:* 3,500.
Albuquerque Area Office.

TAOS PUEBLO TRIBAL COUNCIL
P.O. Box 1846
Taos, New Mexico 87571
(505) 758-8626
Joe C. Sandoval, Governor

Tribe served: Pueblo. *Population served:* 1,900.
Albuquerque Area Office.

TESUQUE PUEBLO TRIBAL COUNCIL
Route 11, Box 1
Santa Fe, New Mexico 87501
(505) 983-2667
Joe A. Padilla, Governor

Tribe served: Pueblo. *Population served:* 300.
Albuquerque Area Office.

ZIA PUEBLO TRIBAL COUNCIL
General Delivery
San Ysidro, New Mexico 87053
(505) 867-3304
Augustin Pino, Governor

Tribe served: Pueblo. *Population served:* 600.
Albuquerque Area Office.

ZUNI PUEBLO TRIBAL COUNCIL
P.O. Box 737
Zuni, New Mexico 87327
(505) 782-4481
Chauncey Simplico, Governor

Tribe served: Pueblo. *Population served:* 7,100.
Albuquerque Area Office.

NEW YORK

CAYUGA NATION TRIBAL COUNCIL
P.O. Box 11
Versailles, New York 14168
(716) 532-4847
Vernon Isaacs, Chief

Tribe served: Cayuga. Population served: 90.
Eastern Area Office.

ONEIDA NATION (NEW YORK)
TRIBAL COUNCIL
Route 2, West Rd.
Oneida, New York 13424

Tribe served: Oneida. *Population served:* 150.
Eastern Area Office.

ONONDAGA NATION TRIBAL COUNCIL
P.O. Box 270A
Nedrow, New York 13120
(315) 469-8507
Leon Shenandoah, Chief

Tribe served: Onondaga. Population served: 875.
Eastern Area Office.

ST. REGIS MOHAWK
COUNCIL CHIEFS
St. Regis Reservation
Hogansburg, New York 13655
(518) 358-2272
Leonard Garrow, Head Chief

Tribe served: Mohawk. *Population served:*
2,850. Eastern Area Office.

SENECA NATION TRIBAL COUNCIL
1490 Route 438
Irving, New York 14081
(716) 532-4900
Calvin E. Lay, President

Tribe served: Seneca. *Population served:* 5,500.
Eastern Area Office.

TONAWANDA BAND OF SENECAS
COUNCIL OF CHIEFS
7027 Meadville Rd.
Basom, New York 14013
(716) 542-4244
Emerson C. Webster, Chief

Tribe served: Seneca. *Population served:* 625.
Eastern Area Office.

TUSCARORA NATION TRIBAL COUNCIL
5616 Walmore Rd.
Lewiston, New York 14092
(716) 297-2053
Arnold Hewitt, Chief

Tribe served: Tuscarora. *Population served:* 750.
Eastern Area Office.

NORTH CAROLINA

CHEROKEE (EASTERN BAND)
TRIBAL COUNCIL
P.O. Box 455
Cherokee, North Carolina 28719
(704) 497-2771
Robert Youngdeer, Principal Chief

Tribe served: Eastern Band of Cherokees.
Population served: 5,750. Eastern Area Office.

NORTH DAKOTA

DEVILS LAKE SIOUX
TRIBAL COUNCIL
P.O. Box 300
Fort Totten, North Dakota 58335
(701) 766-4221
Carl McKay, Chairman

Tribe served: Sisseton-Wahpeton Sioux.
Population served: 3,110. *Activities:* Fort Totten
Days Pow-Wow (last weekend of July). Aberdeen
Area Office.

FORT BERTHOLD
TRIBAL BUSINESS COUNCIL
P.O. Box 220
New Town, North Dakota 58763
(701) 627-4781
Alyce Spotted Bear, Chairman

Tribes served: Three affiliated tribes: Gros Ventre,
Hidatsa and Mandan. *Population served:* 3,250.
Aberdeen Area Office.

**STANDING ROCK SIOUX
TRIBAL COUNCIL**
P.O. Box D
Fort Yates, North Dakota 58538
(701) 854-7231
Charles W. Murphy, Chairman

Tribe served: Standing Rock Sioux. *Population served:* 9,600. *Activities:* Pow-Wows. Aberdeen Area Office.

TURTLE MOUNTAIN TRIBAL COUNCIL
Belcourt, North Dakota 58316
(701) 477-6451
Richard Lafromboise, Chairman

Tribe served: Chippewa. *Population served:* 8,800. Aberdeen Area Office.

OKLAHOMA

**ABSENTEE-SHAWNEE
EXECUTIVE COMMITTEE**
P.O. Box 1747
Shawnee, Oklahoma 74801
(405) 275-4030
Danny Little Axe, Governor

Tribe served: Absentee-Shawnee. *Population served:* 1,400. Anadarko Area Office.

**ALABAMA-QUASSARTE
TRIBAL TOWN COUNCIL**
Route 1, Box 284
Gore, Oklahoma 74435
(918) 489-5543
Bill Beaver, Chief

Tribe served: Creek. Muskogee Area Office.

APACHE BUSINESS COMMITTEE
P.O. Box 1220
Anadarko, Oklahoma 73005
(405) 247-9493
Leroy Nimsey, Chairman

Tribe served: Apache. *Population served:* 550. Anadarko Area Office.

CADDO TRIBAL COUNCIL
P.O. Box 487
Binger, Oklahoma 73009
(405) 656-2344
Henry Shemayne, Chairman

Tribe served: Caddo. *Population served:* 1,250. Anadarko Area Office.

CHEROKEE TRIBAL COUNCIL
P.O. Box 948
Tahlequah, Oklahoma 74465
(918) 456-0671
Wilma P. Mankiller, Principal Chief

Tribe served: Cherokee. *Population served:* 45,000. Muskogee Area Office.

**CHEYENNE-ARAPAHO
BUSINESS COMMITTEE**
P.O. Box 38
Concho, Oklahoma 73022
(405) 262-0345
Fred Hoffman, Chairman

Tribes served: Cheyenne and Arapaho. Anadarko Area Office.

CHICKASAW NATION TRIBAL COUNCIL
P.O. Box 1548
Ada, Oklahoma 74820
(405) 436-2603
Overton James, Governor

Tribe served: Chickasaw. *Population served:* 8,600. Muskogee Area Office.

CHOCTAW TRIBAL COUNCIL
P.O. Drawer 1210
16th and Locust St.
Durant, Oklahoma 74701
(405) 924-8280
Hollis Roberts, Principal Chief

Tribe served: Choctaw. *Population served:* 20,000. Muskogee Area Office.

CITIZEN BAND BUSINESS COMMITTEE
Route 5, Box 151
Shawnee, Oklahoma 74801
(405) 275-3121
John A. Barrett, Jr., Chairman

Tribe served: Citizen Band Potawatomi. *Population served:* 4,200 in Oklahoma; 12,000 nationwide. Acts on behalf of the tribe on all matters except claims and treaties. Maintains Tribal Museum. *Publications: HowNikan,* tribal newsletter; *Grandfather, Tell Me A Story,* oral history book. Anadarko Area Office.

COMANCHE BUSINESS COMMITTEE
P.O. Box 908
Lawton, Oklahoma 73502
(405) 247-3444
Bernard Kahrahrah, Chairman

Tribe served: Comanche. *Population served:* 3,750. Anadarko Area Office.

DELAWARE EXECUTIVE COMMITTEE
P.O. Box 825
Anadarko, Oklahoma 73005
(405) 247-2448
Edgar L. French, Jr., President

Tribe served: Delaware. *Population served:* 550. *Publications: Cooley's Traditional Stories of the Delaware,* and *Turtle Tales: Oral Traditions of the Delaware of Western Oklahoma,* both edited by Duane Hale. Library. Anadarko Area Office.

**FORT SILL APACHE
BUSINESS COMMITTEE**
Route 2, Box 121
Apache, Oklahoma 73006
(405) 588-2298
Mildred Cleghorn, Chairwoman

Tribe served: Fort Sill Apache. *Population served:* 75. Anadarko Area Office.

IOWA BUSINESS COMMITTEE
Iowa Veterans Hall, P.O. Box 190
Perkins, Oklahoma 74059
(405) 547-2403
Wallace C. Murray, Chairman

Tribe served: Iowa. *Population served:* 220. Anadarko Area Office.

KAW BUSINESS COMMITTEE
Drawer 50
Kaw City, Oklahoma 74641
(405) 269-2552
M.M. Chouteau, Chairman

Tribe served: Kaw. *Population served:* 1,085. *Activities:* Tribal Pow-Wow (2nd Thursday of August). Anadarko Area Office.

KIALAGEE TRIBAL TOWN
928 Alex Noon Dr.
Wetumpka, Oklahoma 74883
James Wesley, Micco

Tribe served: Creek. Muskogee Area Office.

KICKAPOO BUSINESS COMMITTEE
P.O. Box 58
McLoud, Oklahoma 74851
(405) 964-2075
Jim Wahpehah, Chairman

Tribe served: Kickapoo. Anadarko Area Office.

KIOWA BUSINESS COMMITTEE
P.O. Box 369
Carnegie, Oklahoma 73015
(405) 654-2300
Billy Evans Horse, Chairman

Tribe served: Kiowa. *Population served:* 4,200. Anadarko Area Office.

MIAMI BUSINESS COMMITTEE
P.O. Box 636
Miami, Oklahoma 74355
(918) 542-1445
Louis Moore, Chief

Tribe served: Miami. *Population served:* 475. Muskogee Area Office.

MODOC TRIBAL COUNCIL
P.O. Box 939
Miami, Oklahoma 74355
(918) 542-1190
Bill Follis, Chairman

Tribe served: Modoc. Muskogee Area Office.

**MUSKOGEE (CREEK)
NATIONAL COUNCIL**
P.O. Box 580
Okmulgee, Oklahoma
(918) 756-8700 ext. 200
Claude A. Cox, Principal Chief

Tribe served: Muskogee Creek. *Population served:* 30,000. *Activities:* Green Corn, Creek Festival, Creek Rodeo. Museum Library. Muskogee Area Office.

OSAGE TRIBAL COUNCIL
Tribal Administration Bldg.
Pawhuska, Oklahoma 74056
(918) 287-4623
George Tallchief, Principal Chief

Tribe served: Osage. *Population served:* 5,750. Muskogee Area Office.

**OTOE-MISSOURIA
BUSINESS COMMITTEE**
P.O. Box 68
Red Rock, Oklahoma 74651
(405) 723-4334
C.O. Tillman, Chairman

Tribe served: Otoe-Missouria. *Population served:* 1,250. Anadarko Area Office.

OTTAWA COUNCIL
P.O. Box 110
Miami, Oklahoma 74355
(918) 540-1536
Lewis H. Barlow, Chief

Tribe served: Ottawa. Muskogee Area Office.

PAWNEE BUSINESS COUNCIL
P.O. Box 470
Pawnee, Oklahoma 74058
(918) 762-3624
Robert L. Chapman, President

Tribe served: Pawnee. *Population served:* 2,200. Anadarko Area Office.

PEORIA COUNCIL
P.O. 1527
Miami, Oklahoma 74355
(918) 540-2535
Rodney P. Arnette, Chief

Tribe served: Peoria. Muskogee Area Office.

PONCA BUSINESS COMMITTEE
P.O. Box 2, White Eagle
Ponca City, Oklahoma 74601
  (405) 762-8104
  Oliver Littlecook, Chairman

Tribe served: Ponca. *Population served:* 2,200.
Anadarko Area Office.

**QUAPAW TRIBAL
BUSINESS COMMITTEE**
P.O. Box 765
Quapaw, Oklahoma 74363
  (918) 542-1853
  Jesse McKibben, Chairman

Tribe served: Quapaw. *Population served:* 1,250.
Muskogee Area Office.

SAC AND FOX BUSINESS COMMITTEE
Route 2, Box 246
Stroud, Oklahoma 74079
  (918) 968-3526
  (405) 275-4270
  Alvin Falls, Principal Chief

Tribe served: Sac and Fox. *Population served:*
1,450. Anadarko Area Office.

SEMINOLE GENERAL COUNCIL
P.O. Box 745
Wewoka, Oklahoma 74884
  (405) 382-7913
  James Milam, Chief

Tribe served: Seminole. *Population served:* 3,850.
Muskogee Area Office.

**SENECA-CAYUGA
TRIBAL BUSINESS COMMITTEE**
P.O. Box 1283
Miami, Oklahoma 74355
  (918) 542-6609
  James Allen, Chief

Tribes served: Seneca and Cayuga. *Population
served:* 690. Muskogee Area Office.

**THLOPTHLOCCO TRIBAL TOWN
BUSINESS COMMITTEE**
8433 East 64th Place
Tulsa, Oklahoma 74135
  (918) 252-3195
  Elaine Branch, Town King

Tribe served: Creek. Muskogee Area Office.

TONKAWA BUSINESS COMMITTEE
P.O. Box 70
Tonkawa, Oklahoma 74653
  (405) 628-2561
  Henry L. Allen, President

Tribe served: Tonkawa. *Population served:* 1,300.
Anadarko Area Office.

**UNITED KEETOWAH
CHEROKEE COUNCIL**
P.O. Box 1329
Tahlequah, Oklahoma 74465
  (918) 234-3434
  John Hair, Chief

Tribe served: Cherokee. Muskogee Area Office.

WICHITA EXECUTIVE COMMITTEE
Wichita Tribal Affairs Office
P.O. Box 729
Anadarko, Oklahoma 73005
  (405) 247-2425
  Newton Lamar, President

Tribe served: Wichita. *Population served:* 625.
Anadarko Area Office.

WYANDOTTE COUNCIL
P.O. Box 470
Miami, Oklahoma 74355
  (918) 540-1541
  Leaford Bearskin, Chief

Tribe served: Wyandotte. *Population served:* 450.
Muskogee Area Office.

OREGON

BURNS-PAIUTE GENERAL COUNCIL
P.O. Box 71
Burns, Oregon 97720
  (503) 573-2088
  Vernon Shake Spear, Chairman

Tribe served: Burns Paiute. *Population served:*
200. Portland Area Office.

**CONFEDERATED TRIBES OF
THE GRANDE RONDE INDIAN
COMMUNITY COUNCIL**
P.O. Box 94
Grande Ronde, Oregon 97347
  (503) 879-5253
  Katherine Harrison, Chairwoman

Portland Area Office.

**CONFEDERATED TRIBES OF
SILETZ INDIANS TRIBAL COUNCIL**
P.O. Box 549
Siletz, Oregon 97380
  (503) 444-2528
  Delores Pigsley, Chairperson

Population served: 1,800. *Activities:*
Memorial Day and Restoration Day Celebrations in May and November respectively;
pow wow in August. Museum/Archive currently
being established. Portland Area Office.

COW CREEK BAND
OF UMPQUA INDIANS
COMMUNITY COUNCIL
1376 N.E. Walnut, Suite I
Roseburg, Oregon 97470
(503) 672-9696
Charles Jackson, Chairman

Portland Area Office.

UMATILLA BOARD OF TRUSTEES
P.O. Box 638
Pendleton, Oregon 97801
(503) 276-3165
Elwood Patawa, Chairman

Tribe served: Umatilla. *Population served:* 1,500.
Portland Area Office.

WARM SPRINGS TRIBAL COUNCIL
Warm Springs, Oregon 97761
(503) 553-1161
Zane Jackson, Sr., Chairman

Tribes served: Walla Walla and Cayuga.
Population served: 2,500. Portland Area Office.

RHODE ISLAND

NARRAGANSETT INDIAN
TRIBAL COUNCIL
RFD #2
Kenyon, Rhode Island 02836
(401) 364-6411
George Watson, Chief

Eastern Area Office.

SOUTH DAKOTA

CHEYENNE RIVER SIOUX
TRIBAL COUNCIL
P.O. Box 590
Eagle Butte, South Dakota 57625
(605) 964-4155
Morgan Garreau, Chairman

Tribe served: Cheyenne River Sioux. *Population
served:* 4,600. Aberdeen Area Office.

CROW CREEK SIOUX
TRIBAL COUNCIL
P.O. Box 658
Fort Thompson, South Dakota 57339
(605) 245-2221/2222
Wallace Wells, Jr., Chairman

Tribe served: Crow Creek Sioux. *Population
served:* 2,200. Aberdeen Area Office.

FLANDREAU SANTEE-SIOUX
EXECUTIVE COMMITTEE
P.O. Box 292
Flandreau, South Dakota 57028
(605) 997-2924
Carolyn Sorensen, President

Tribe served: Santee Sioux. *Population served:*
425. Aberdeen Area Office.

LOWER BRULE SIOUX
TRIBAL COUNCIL
Lower Brule, South Dakota 57548
(605) 473-5561
Patrick Spears, Chairman

Tribe served: Lower Brule Sioux. *Population
served:* 1,000. Aberdeen Area Office.

OGLALA SIOUX TRIBAL COUNCIL
Pine Ridge, South Dakota 57770
(605) 867-3821
Newton Cummings, President

Tribe served: Oglala Sioux. *Population served:*
14,000. Aberdeen Area Office.

ROSEBUD SIOUX TRIBAL COUNCIL
Rosebud, South Dakota 57570
(605) 747-2381
Webster Two Hawk, President

Tribe served: Rosebud Sioux. *Population served:*
10,000. Aberdeen Area Office.

SISSETON-WAHPETON SIOUX
TRIBAL COUNCIL
Route 2
Agency Village, South Dakota 57262
(605) 698-3911
Russell Hawkins, Chairman

Tribe served: Sisseton-Wahpeton Sioux.
Population served: 4,000. Aberdeen Area Office.

YANKTON SIOUX TRIBAL
BUSINESS AND CLAIMS COMMITTEE
Route 3, Box 248
Marty, South Dakota 57361
Alvin Zephier, Chairman

Tribe served: Yankton Sioux. *Population served:*
2,650. Aberdeen Area Office.

TEXAS

TEXAS BAND OF KICKAPOO INDIANS
311 North St., Calle-Victoria, Muzquiz
Coalhuila, Mexico

Tribe served: Kickapoo.

UTAH

GOSHUTE TRIBAL COUNCIL
Ibapah, Utah 87034
Chester Steele, Chairman

Tribe served: Goshute. *Population served:* 225.
Phoenix Area Office.

PAIUTE TRIBAL COUNCIL
600 North 100 East
Cedar City, Utah 84720
(801) 586-1111
General Anderson, Chairman

Tribe served: Paiute. *Population served:* 225.
Phoenix Area Office.

**SKULL VALLEY
COMMUNITY REPRESENTATIVE**
c/o Uintah and Ouray Agency
Bureau of Indian Affairs
Fort Duchesne, Utahj 84026
Bert Wash, Chairman

Tribe served: Goshute. *Population served:* 75.
Phoenix Area Office.

**UINTAH AND OURAY
TRIBAL BUSINESS COUNCIL**
Fort Duchesne, Utah 84026
(801) 722-5141
Frank Wopsock, Chairman

Tribe served: Ute. *Population served:* 2,000.
Phoenix Area Office.

WASHINGTON

CHEHALIS COMMUNITY COUNCIL
P.O. Box 536
Oakville, Washington 98568
(206) 273-5911
Percy Youckton, Chairman

Tribe served: Chehalis. *Population served:* 750.
Portland Area Office.

COLVILLE BUSINESS COUNCIL
P.O. Box 150
Nespelem, Washington 99155
(509) 634-4711
Al Aubertin, Chairman

Tribe served: Colville. *Population served:* 6,250.
Portland Area Office.

HOH TRIBAL BUSINESS COUNCIL
Star Route 1, Box 917
Forks, Washington 98331
(206) 374-6582
Mary Leitka, Chairwoman

Tribe served: Hoh. *Population served:* 65.
Portland Area Office.

**JAMESTOWN BAND OF KLALLEM
INDIANS BUSINESS COUNCIL**
150 South 5th Ave.
Sequim, Washington 98382
(206) 683-1109
William Ron Allen, Chairman

Tribe served: Jamestown Band of Klallem
Indians. Portland Area Office.

KALISPEL BUSINESS COMMITTEE
P.O. Box 38
Usk, Washington 99180
(509) 445-1641
Glen Nenema, Chairman

Tribe served: Kalispel. *Population served:* 215.
Portland Area Office.

LOWER ELWHA BUSINESS COMMITTEE
P.O. Box 1370
Port Angeles, Washington 98362
(206) 452-8471
Edward Sampson, Jr., Chairman
Lorna J. Mike, Vice-Chairman

Tribe served: Lower Elwha Band of Klallem
Indians (main membership). *Population served:*
450. *Activities:* substance abuse program; health
clinic; housing department; hatchery-fisheries
department; higher adult-vocational education
department. Portland Area Office.

LUMMI INDIAN BUSINESS COUNCIL
2616 Kwina Rd.
Bellingham, Washington 98226
(206) 734-8180
Larry G. Kinley, Chairman

Tribe served: Lummi. *Population served:*
1,500. *Activities:* Lummi Stommish Water
Carnival. Portland Area Office.

MAKAH INDIAN TRIBAL COUNCIL
P.O. Box 115
Neah Bay, Washington 98357
(206) 645-2205 ext. 36
George Bowechop, Chairman

Tribe served: Makah. *Population served:* 1,000.
Portland Area Office.

**MUCKLESHOOT INDIAN
TRIBAL COUNCIL**
39015 172nd S.E.
Auburn, Washington 98002
(206) 939-3311
Sonny Bargala, Chairman

Tribe served: Muckleshoot. Population served:
2,500. Portland Area Office.

**NISQUALLY INDIAN
COMMUNITY COUNCIL**
4820 She-Na-Num Dr., S.E.
Olympia, Washington 98503
(206) 456-5221
Richard Wells, Chairman

Tribe served: Nisqually. *Population served:*
1,350. Portland Area Office.

NOOKSACK TRIBAL COUNCIL
P.O. Box 157
Deming, Washington 98244
(206) 592-5176
Harry E. Cooper, Chairman

Tribe served: Nooksack. *Population served:* 750.
Portland Area Office.

PORT GAMBLE COMMUNITY COUNCIL
P.O. Box 280
Kingston, Washington 98346
(206) 297-2646
Ronald G. Charles, Chairman

Tribe served: Port Gamble Band of Klallam
Indians. *Population served:* 475. Portland Area
Office.

PUYALLUP TRIBAL COUNCIL
2002 East 28th St.
Tacoma, Washington 98404
(206) 597-6200
Frank Wright, Jr., Chairman

Tribe served: Puyallup. *Population served:* 5,900.
Portland Area Office.

QUILEUTE TRIBAL COUNCIL
P.O. Box 279
La Push, Washington 98350
(206) 374-6163
Walter Jackson, Chairman

Tribe served: Quileute. *Population served:* 390.
Activities: Quileute Days (August); Elders Week
Celebration (Spring). *Publiction: The Quileute of
La Push.* Portland Area Office.

QUINAULT BUSINESS COMMITTEE
P.O. Box 189
Taholah, Washington 98587
(206) 276-8211
Joseph Delacruz, President

Tribe served: Quinault. *Population served:* 2,200.
Portland Area Office.

SAUK-SUIATTLE TRIBAL COUNCIL
5318 Chief Brown Lane
Darrington, Washington 98241
(206) 436-0131
David Moses, Sr., Chairman

Tribe served: Sauk-Suiattle. *Population served:*
205. Activities. Huckleberry Festival

(September); Yo-Buch Days (July). Portland
Area Office.

SHOALWATER BAY TRIBAL COUNCIL
P.O. Box 579
Tokeland, Washington 98590
(206) 267-6766
Rachel Whitish, Chairwoman

Tribe served: Shoalwater. *Population served:* 70.
Portland Area Office.

SKOKOMISH TRIBAL COUNCIL
Route 5, Box 432
Shelton, Washington 98584
(206) 267-6766
Gary Peterson, Chairman

Tribe served: Skokomish. *Population served:*
1,050. Portland Area Office.

SPOKANE BUSINESS COUNCIL
P.O. Box 385
Wellpinit, Washington 99040
(509) 258-4581
James W. Hill, Chairman

Tribe served: Spokane. *Population served:* 2,000.
Portland Area Office.

SQUAXIN ISLAND TRIBAL COUNCIL
West 81 Highway 108
Shelton, Washington 98584
(206) 426-9781
David Whitener, Chairman

Tribe served: Squaxin Island. *Population served:*
1,000. Portland Area Office.

**STILLAGUAMISH
BOARD OF DIRECTORS**
2704 State Rd., 530 N.E.
Arlington, Washington 98223
(206) 652-7362
Marie MacCurdy, Chairwoman

Tribe served: Stillaguamish. Portland Area
Office.

SUQUAMISH TRIBAL COUNCIL
P.O. Box 498
Suquamish, Washington 98392
(206) 598-3311
Bennie J. Armstrong, Chairman

Tribe served: Suquamish. *Population served:* 620.
Activities: Chief Seattle Days (August).
*Publications: Dsub'Wub'Siatsub (Suquamish
News),* tribal newsletter; *A Guide to Oral History
in the Native American Community; Suquamish
Tribal Photographic Archives Project: A Case
Study; Suquamish Today;* and *The Eyes of Chief
Seattle* (exhibit catalog.) Museum. Photographic
Archives and Oral History Collection. Library.
Portland Area Office.

SWINOMISH INDIAN SENTATE
P.O. Box 817
La Connor, Washington 98257
(206) 466-3163
Robert Joe, Sr., Chairman

Tribe served: Swinomish. *Population served:* 675.
Portland Are Office.

THE TULALIP BOARD OF DIRECTORS
6700 Totem Beach Rd.
Marysville, Washington 98270
(206) 653-4585
Stanley Jones, Sr., Chairman

Tribe served: Tulalip. *Population served:* 900.
Portland Area Office.

UPPER SKAGIT TRIBAL COUNCIL
2284 Community Plaza
Sedro Wooley, Washington 98284
(206) 856-5501
Floyd Williams, Chairman

Tribe served: Skagit. *Population served:* 175.
Portland Area Office.

YAKIMA TRIBAL COUNCIL
P.O. Box 151
Toppenish, Washington 98948
(509) 865-5121
Roger R. Jim, Sr., Chairman

Tribe served: Yakima. *Population served:* 8,750.
Portland Area Office.

WISCONSIN

BAD RIVER TRIBAL COUNCIL
Route 39
Ashland, Wisconsin 54806
(715) 682-4212
Robert Bender, Chairman

Tribe served: Lake Superior Band of Chippewa.
Population served: 1,350. Minneapolis Area
Office.

FOREST COUNTY POTAWATOMI
GENERAL COUNCIL
P.O. Box 346
Crandon, Wisconsin 54520
(715) 478-2903
Leroy Schotko, Chairman

Tribe served: Forest County Potawatomi.
Population served: 400. Minneapolis Area Office.

LAC COURTE OREILLES
GOVERNING BOARD
Route 2
Hayward, Wisconsin 54843
(715) 634-8934
Odric Baker, Chairman

Tribe served: Lac Courte Oreilles Band of
Chippewa. *Population served:* 1,900.
Minneapolis Area Office.

LAC DU FLAMBEAU TRIBAL COUNCIL
P.O. Box 67
Lac du Flambeau, Wisconsin 54538
(715) 588-3306
Michael Allen, Sr., Chairman

Tribe served: Lac du Flambeau Band of
Chippewa. *Population served:* 1,550.
Minneapolis Area Office.

MENOMINEE TRIBAL LEGISLATURE
P.O. Box 397
Keshena, Wisconsin 54135
(715) 799-3341
Lynn Skenedore, Chairman

Tribe served: Menominee. *Population served:*
3,500. Minneapolis Area Office.

ONEIDA EXECUTIVE COMMITTEE
P.O. Box 365
Oneida, Wisconsin 54155
(414) 869-2771
Purcell Powless, Chairman

Tribe served: Oneida. *Population served:* 3,500.
Minneapolis Area Office.

RED CLIFF TRIBAL COUNCIL
P.O. Box 529
Bayfield, Wisconsin 54814
(715) 779-5805
Richard Gurnoe, Chairman

Tribe served: Red Cliff Band of Chippewa.
Population served: 1,500. Minneapolis Area
Office.

ST. CROIX COUNCIL
Star Route
Webster, Wisconsin 54893
(715) 349-2295
Gene Taylor, Chairman

*Tribe served: St. Croix Chippewa. Population
served:* 1,100. Minneapolis Area Office.

**SOKAOGON CHIPPEWA
TRIBAL COUNCIL**
Route 1, Box 625
Crandon, Wisconsin 54520
(715) 478-3543
Arlyn Ackley, Chairman

Tribe served: Mole Lake Band of Chippewa.
Minneapolis Area Office.

**STOCKBRIDGE-MUNSEE
TRIBAL COUNCIL**
RR 1
Bowler, Wisconsin 54416
(715) 793-4111
Leon Miller, Jr., Chairman

Tribe served: Stockbridge-Munsee Mohican
Indians of Wisconsin. *Population served:*
1,500. Library. Minneapolis Area Office.

**WISCONSIN WINNEBAGO
BUSINESS COUNCIL**
P.O. Box 311
Tomah, Wisconsin 54660
(715) 886-5010/5020
Kenneth Funmaker, Sr., Chairman

Tribe served: Wisconsin Winnebago. *Population
served:* 1,850. Minneapolis Area Office.

WYOMING

ARAPAHOE BUSINESS COUNCIL
P.O. Box 396
Fort Washakie, Wyoming 82514
(307) 255-8394
Chester Armajo, Chairman

Tribe served: Wind River Arapahoe.
Billings Area Office.

**NORTHWESTERN BAND OF SHOSHONI
BUSINESS COUNCIL**
Star Route 2 W
Rock Springs, Wyoming 82901
(307) 382-3943
Kenneth L. Neaman, Chairman

Tribe served: Northwestern Band of Shoshoni
Nation. Portland Area Office.

SHOSHONE BUSINESS COUNCIL
Fort Washakie, Wyoming 82514
(307) 255-8257
Robert N. Harris, Sr., Chairman

Tribe served: Wind River Shoshone. *Population
served:* 5,800. Billings Area Office.

OTHER INDIAN
TRIBES AND GROUPS

This section lists Indian tribes, groups, bands, and organizations who represent the interests of their members, or are recognized by various states and are now in the process of obtaining or reinstating their federal status. Information was provided by the Bureau of Indian Affairs. It is organized alphabetically by state and name of tribe or group.

ALABAMA

CHEROKEES OF JACKSON CITY
P.O. Box 41
Higdon, Alabama 35979

CHEROKEES OF NORTHEAST ALABAMA
3912 Cahaba Rd.
Birmingham, Alabama 34243

CHEROKEES OF SOUTHEAST ALABAMA
510 South Park Ave.
Dothan, Alabama 36301

ECHOTA CHEROKEE
TRIBE OF ALABAMA
Route 1, Box 122-A
Maylene, Alabama 35114

MACHIS LOWER
ALABAMA CREEK INDIAN TRIBE
708 South John St.
New Brockton, Alabama 36351

MOWA BAND OF CHOCTAW INDIANS
P.O. Box 268
McIntosh, Alabama 36553

MUSKOGEE CREEK INDIAN NATION
EAST OF THE MISSISSIPPI
P.O. Box 817
Perry, Alabama 32347

PRINCIPAL CREEK INDIAN NATION
EAST OF THE MISSISSIPPI
P.O. Box 201
Florala, Alabama 36442

STAR CLAN OF MUSKOGEE CREEK
TRIBE OF PIKE COUNTY
P.O. Box 126
Goshen, Alabama 36035

UNITED CHEROKEE
TRIBE OF ALABAMA
Route 2, Box 199
Midland City, Alabama 36350

ARIZONA

BARRIO PASCUA
San Ignacio Yaqui Council, Inc.
2256 North Calle Central
Tucson, Arizona 85705

GUADALUPE ORGANIZATIONS
8810 South 56th St.
Guadalupe, Arizona 85705

SAN JUAN NORTHERN PAIUTE
P.O. Box 2656
Tuba City, Arizona 86045

CALIFORNIA

AMERICAN INDIAN COUNCIL
OF MARIPOSA COUNTY
P.O. Box 1200
Mariposa, California 95318

ANTELOPE VALLEY
INDIAN COMMUNITY
P.O. Box 168
Coleville, California 96107

ATAHUN SHOSHONES
OF SAN JUAN CAPISTRANO
2352 Bahia Dr.
La Jolla, California 92037

BIG MEADOWS LODGE TRIBE
P.O. Box 362
Chester, California 96020

CALAVERAS COUNTY BAND
OF MIWOK INDIANS
Star Route #1
West Point, California 95255

CHOINUMNI TRIBE
2548 Cedar South
Fresno, California 93725

COASTAL BAND OF CHUMASH TRIBE
808 East Cota St.
Santa Barbara, California 93101

DUNLAP BAND OF MONO INDIANS
P.O. Box 126
Dunlap, California 93621

HOWNONQUET COMMUNITY
ASSOCIATION
P.O. Box 179
Smith River, California 95567

JAMUL BAND
P.O. Box 353
Jamul, California 92035

JUANENO BAND OF MISSION INDIANS
325 North Broadway #205
Santa Ana, California 92701

KERN VALLEY INDIAN COMMUNITY
P.O. Box 1438
Weldon, California 93283

**MAIDU HISTORICAL TRIBAL AND
CULTURAL ELDERS ORGANIZATION**
P.O. Box 333
Dobbins, California 95935

**MELOCHUNDUM BAND
OF TOLOWA INDIANS**
P.O. Box 388
Fort Dick, California 95538

MENDO LAKE POMO COUNCIL
564 South Dora St.
Ukiah, California 95538

MONO LAKE INDIAN COMMUNITY
P.O. Box 237
Lee Vining, California 93541

**NOR-EL-MUK BAND
OF WINTUN INDIANS**
P.O. Box 968
Hayfork, California 96041

NORTHERN MAIDU TRIBE
P.O. Box 217
Greenville, California 95947

SHASTA TRIBE
P.O. Box 1054
Yreka, California 96097

**SONOMA COUNTY
AMERICAN INDIAN COUNCIL**
930 Piner Rd.
Healdsburg, California 95401

TEHATCHAPI INDIAN TRIBE
219 East H St.
Tehatchapi, California 93561

TOLOWA-TUTUTNI TRIBE OF INDIANS
P.O. Box 388
Fort Dick, California 95538

**UNITED LUMBEE NATION OF
NORTH CAROLINA AND AMERICA**
P.O. Box 911
Exeter, California 93221

WINTU TRIBE
P.O. Box 669
Redding, California 96019

YOKAYO POMO RANCHERIA
1114 Helen Ave.
Unkiah, California 95482

CONNECTICUT

GOLDEN HILL PAUGUSSETT TRIBE
Reservation - Stanavage Rd.
Colchester, Connecticut 06415

MOHEGAN TRIBE
1814 Norwich-New London Turnpike
Uncasville, Connecticut 06832

PAUCATUCK PEQUOT TRIBE
939 Lantern Hill Rd.
Ledyard, Connecticut 06339

SCHAGTICOKE INDIAN TRIBE
P.O. Box 67
Kent, Connecticut 06757

DELAWARE

NANTICOKE TRIBE
RD #4, Box 268, Riverdale Park
Millsboro, Delaware 19966

FLORIDA

TOPACHULA INDIAN TRIBE
Pine Arbor Tribal Town
602 Gunther St.
Tallahassee, Florida 32308

**TUSCOLA UNITED CHEROKEE TRIBE
OF FLORIDA AND ALABAMA**
P.O. Box 5
Geneva, Florida 32732

GEORGIA

CHEROKEE INDIANS OF GEORGIA
1516 14th Ave.
Columbus, Georgia 31901

**GEORGIA TRIBE OF
EASTERN CHEROKEES**
Route 3
Dahlonega, Georgia 30533

**LOWER CREEK MUSKOGEE TRIBE
EAST OF THE MISSISSIPPI**
Route 1, Tama Reservation
Cairo, Georgia 31728

**SOUTHEASTERN
CHEROKEE CONFEDERACY**
Route 1, Box 111
Leesburg, Georgia 31763

IDAHO

DELAWARES OF IDAHO
3844 Sumter Way
Boise, Idaho 83709

INDIANA

**INDIANA MIAMI INDIAN
ORGANIZATIONAL COUNCIL**
641 Buchanan St.
Huntington, Indiana 46750

KANSAS

DELAWARE-MUNCIE TRIBE
P.O. Box 274
Pomona, Kansas 66076

**SWAN CREEK AND
BLACK RIVER CHIPPEWAS**
519 Willow St.
Ottawa, Kansas 66067

LOUISIANA

**APACHE-CHOCTAW INDIAN
COMMUNITY OF EBARB**
Route 1, Box 347
Zwolle, Louisiana 71486

CLIFTON-CHOCTAWS
Route 1, Box 61
Mora, Louisiana 71455

JENA BAND OF CHOCTAWS
P.O. Box 14
Jena, Louisiana 71342

LOUISIANA BAND OF CHOCTAWS
P.O. Box 547
Baker, Louisiana 70714

UNITED HOUMA NATION
Star Route, Box 95-A
Golden Meadows, Louisiana 70357

MAINE

**ASSOCIATION OF
AROOSTOOK INDIANS**
429 Main St.
Presque Island, Maine 04769

MARYLAND

PISCATAWAY INDIAN TRIBE
c/o Maryland Indian Heritage Society
P.O. Box 905
Waldorf, Maryland 20601

**PISCATAWAY INDIANS
PISCATAWAY-CONOY CONFEDRACY
AND SUB-TRIBE**
P.O. Box 48
Indian Head, Maryland 20640

MASSACHUSETTS

GAY HEAD WAMPANOAG TRIBE
State Rd., RFD Box 137
Gay Head, Massachusetts 02535

MASHPEE WAMPANOAG TRIBE
Route 130
Mashpee, Massachusetts 02649

**NEW ENGLAND COASTAL
SCHAGTICOKE INDIAN ASSOCIATION**
P.O. Box 551
Avon, Massachusetts 02322

**NIPMUC TRIBAL COUNCIL
OF MASSACHUSETTS**
Hassanamisco Reservation
Grafton, Massachusetts 01519

MICHIGAN

**CONSOLIDATED BAHWETIG
OJIBWAS AND MACKINAC TRIBE**
P.O. Box 697
Sault Ste. Marie, Michigan 49783

**GRAND RIVER BAND
OF THE OTTAWA NATION**
P.O. Box 54
Hart, Michigan 49420

HURON POTAWATOMI BAND
2221 1½ Mile Rd.
Fulton, Michigan 49052

**LAC VIEUX DESERT BAND OF LAKE
SUPERIOR CHIPPEWA INDIAN TRIBE**
P.O. Box 446
Watersmeet, Michigan 49969

NORTHERN MICHIGAN OTTAWA TRIBE
1391 Terrace St.
Muskegon, Michigan 49441

**POTAWATOMI INDIAN TRIBE
OF INDIANA AND MICHIGAN**
Route 6, Box 526
Dowagiac, Michigan 49047

MISSOURI

**NORTHERN CHEROKEE TRIBE
OF MISSOURI**
P.O. Box 1221
Columbia, Missouri 65205

MONTANA

**LITTLE SHELL TRIBE OF
CHIPPEWA INDIANS OF MONTANA**
426 West Quartz
Butte, Montana 59701

**SWAN CREEK AND
BLACK RIVER CHIPPEWA**
P.O. Box 197
Dixon, Montana 59831

NEW HAMPSHIRE

**PENNACOOK NEW HAMPSHIRE
INDIAN TRIBE**
83 Hanover St.
Manchester, New Hampshire 03101

NEW JERSEY

NANTICOKE-LENNI LENAPE TRIBE
28 Commerce St.
Bridgeton, New Jersey 08302
  (609) 451-9486

NATIVE DELAWARE INDIANS
c/o New Jersey Indian Office
300 Main St., Suite 3F
Orange, New Jersey 07050
  (201) 675-0694

POWHATTAN RENAPE NATION
P.O. Box 225
Rancocas, New Jersey 08073
  (609) 261-4747

RAMAPOUGH MOUNTAIN INDIANS
19 Mountain Rd.
Mahwah, New Jersey 07430
  (201) 529-5750

NEW MEXICO

**LOS COMANCHES
DE LA SERENA TRIBE**
P.O. Box 172
Ranchos de Taos, New Mexico 87557

**SAN JUAN DE GUADALUPE
TIWA TRIBE**
559 West Brown Rd.
Las Cruces, New Mexico 88001

NEW YORK

MONTAUK INDIAN TRIBE
Hempstead Dr.
Sag Harbor, New York 11963

POOSPATUCK TRIBE
Poospetuck Reservation
Mastic, New York 11950
  (516) 281-4791
  Sam Beeler, Chief

SHINNOECOCK TRIBE
P.O. Box 59
Southampton, New York 11968

NORTH CAROLINA

**CHEROKEE INDIAN TRIBE OF
ROBESON AND ADJOINING COUNTIES**
P.O. Box 25
Shannon, North Carolina 28386

CHEROKEE INDIANS OF HOKE CITY
Route 1, Box 129-C
Lumber Bridge, North Carolina 28357

COHAIRIE INTRA-TRIBAL COUNCIL
Route 3, Box 340-F
Clinton, North Carolina 28328

FAIRCLOTH INDIAN TRIBE
P.O. Box 161
Atlantic, North Carolina 28511

HALIWA-SAPONI INDIAN TRIBE
P.O. Box 66
Hollister, North Carolina 27844

HATTADARE INDIAN TRIBE
Route 1, Box 85-B
Bunnlevel, North Carolina 28323

HATTERAS TUSCARORA INDIAN TRIBE
Route 3, Box 47-A
Maxton, North Carolina 28364

LUMBEE TRIBE
East Main St., Box 68
Pembroke, North Carolina 28372

MEHERRIN INDIAN TRIBE
P.O. Box 508
Winton, North Carolina 27986

PERSON COUNTY INDIANS
Route 6, Box 104
Roxboro, North Carolina 27573

TUSCARORA INDIAN TRIBE
Drowning Creek Reservation
Route 2, Box 108
Maxton, North Carolina 28364

WACCAMAW SIOUAN TRIBE
P.O. Box 221
Bolton, North Carolina 28423

NORTH DAKOTA

**CHRISTIAN PEMBINA
CHIPPEWA TRIBE**
Belcourt, North Dakota 58316

**LITTLE SHELL BAND
OF THE NORTH DAKOTA TRIBE**
Dunseith, North Dakota 58329

OHIO

ALLEGANY NATION (OHIO BAND)
2239 Mahoning Rd., N.E.
Canton, Ohio 44705

**NORTHEASTERN UNITED STATES
MAIMI INTER-TRIBAL COUNCIL**
1535 Florencedale
Youngstown, Ohio 44505

**SHAWNEE NATION
UNITED REMNANT BAND**
P.O. Box 162
Dayton, Ohio 45401

OREGON

CHETCO TRIBE
P.O. Box 640
Brookings, Oregon 97415

CHINOOK TRIBE
P.O. Box 327
Oakland, Oregon 97462

**CONFEDERATED TRIBES
OF COOS, LOWER UMPQUAH
AND SIUSLAW INDIANS**
533 Buchanan
Coos Bay, Oregon 97420

COQUILLE INDIAN TRIBE
P.O. Box 4331
Eastside, Oregon 97420

KLAMATH TRIBE
P.O. Box 436
Chiloquin, Oregon 97624

**NORTHWEST CHEROKEE
WOLF BAND OF SOUTHEASTERN
CHEROKEE CONFEDERACY**
P.O. Box 592
Talent, Oregon 97549

TCHINOUK INDIANS
5621 Altamont Dr.
Klamath Falls, Oregon 97601

SOUTH CAROLINA

CATAWBA INDIAN TRIBE
Route 3, Box 324
Rock Hill, South Carolina 29730

**FOUR HOLES INDIAN ORGANIZATION
EDISTO TRIBE**
Route 3, Box 37-E
Ridgeville, South Carolina 29472

PEE DEE INDIAN ASSOCIATION
P.O. Box 6068
Clio, South Carolina 29525

SANTEE TRIBE
White Oak Indian Community
Route 1, Box 34-M
Holly Hill, South Carolina 29059

TENNESSEE

**RED CLAY INTER-TRIBAL
INDIAN BAND OF SOUTHEASTERN
CHEROKEE CONFEDERACY**
7703 Georgetown Rd.
Ooltewah, Tennessee 37363

TEXAS

**ALABAMA-COUSHATTA
TRIBES OF TEXAS**
Alabama-Coushatta Reservation
Route 3, Box 640
Livingston, Texas 77351

TIGUA (TIWA) TRIBE
P.O. Box 17579, Ysleta Station
El Paso, Texas 79917

UTAH

ALLEN CANYON UTE TRIBE
P.O. Box 916
Blanding, Utah 84511

**NORTHEASTERN BAND OF
SHOSHONE INDIANS**
660 South 200 West
Brigham City, Utah 84302

VERMONT

**ST. FRANCIS/SOKOKI BAND
OF ABENAKIS OF VERMONT**
P.O. Box 276
Swanton, Vermont 05488

VIRGINIA

CHICKAHOMINY INDIAN TRIBE
RFD 1, Box 226
Providence Forge, Virginia 23140

MATTAPONI INDIAN TRIBE
Mattaponi Indian Reservation
West Point, Virginia 23181

PAMUNKY INDIAN TRIBE
Pamunky Indian Reservation
Route 1, Box 218
King William, Virginia 23086

UNITED RAPPAHANNOCK TRIBE, INC.
Indian Neck, Virginia 23077

**UPPER MATTAPONI INDIAN
TRIBAL ASSOCIATION**
P.O. Box 12A
St. Stephens Church, Virginia 23148

WASHINGTON

ABORIGINAL SWINOMISH
P.O. Box 111
Friday Harbor, Washington 98250

CHINOOK INDIAN TRIBE
P.O. Box 228
Chinook, Washington 98614

COWLITZ TRIBE OF INDIANS
2815 Dale Lane East
Tacoma, Washington 98424

DUWAMISH TRIBE
15614 First Ave. South
Seattle, Washington 98148

**MARIETTA BAND OF
NOOKSACK INDIANS**
1927 Marine Dr.
Marietta, Washington 98268

MITCHELL BAY BAND
P.O. Box 4444
Friday Harbor, Washington 98250

NOO-WHA-HA BAND
1120 Huff Rd.
Burlington, Washington 98233

SAMISH INDIAN TRIBE
P.O. Box 217
Anacortes, Washington 98221

SNOHOMISH TRIBE OF INDIANS
119 Avenue B
Snohomish, Washington 98290

SNOQUALMIE TRIBE
18525 Novelty Hill Rd.
Redmond, Washington 98052

STEILACOOM TRIBE
19614 Mountain, Highway E
Spanaway, Washington 98387

WISCONSIN

**BROTHERTON INDIANS
OF WISCONSIN**
Route 4, Box 90-1
Arbor Vitae, Wisconsin 54510

FEDERALLY RECOGNIZED
TRIBES AND BANDS

ALASKAN NATIVES
Aleuts, Eskimos, and Indians (Athapascans)

APACHE
Apache Tribe of Oklahoma
Camp Verde Reservation, Arizona
Fort Apache Reservation (White
  Mountain), Arizona
Fort Sill Apache Tribe of Oklahoma
Fort McDowell Reservation, Arizona
Jicarilla Apache Reservation, New Mexico
Mescalero Apache Reservation, New Mexico
San Carlos Reservation, Arizona
Tonto Apache Tribe of Arizona

ARAPAHOE
Arapahoe Tribe of Oklahoma
Wind River Reservation, Wyoming

ASSINIBOINE-SIOUX
Fort Belknap Reservation, Montana
Fort Peck Reservation, Montana

BANNOCK (SHOSHONE-BANNOCK)
Fort Hall Reservation, Idaho

BLACKFEET
Blackfeet Reservation, Montana

CADDO
Caddo Indian Tribe of Oklahoma

CAHUILLA
Agua Calienta Reservation, Palm Springs,
  California
Augustine Reservation, California
Cabazon Reservation, California
Cahuilla Reservation, California
Los Coyotes Reservation, California
Morongo Reservation, California
Ramona Reservation, California
Santa Rosa Reservation, California
Torres Martinez Reservation, California

CAYUGA
Cayuga Nation of New York
Cayuga Tribe of Oklahoma

CHEHALIS
Confederated Tribes of the Chehalis
  Reservation, Washington

CHEMEHUEVI
Chemehuevi Reservation, California

CHEROKEE
Cherokee Nation of Oklahoma
Eastern Band of Cherokee, North Carolina
United Keetoowah Band of Cherokee Indians,
  Oklahoma

CHEYENNE
Cheyenne Tribe of Oklahoma
Northern Cheyenne Tribe of Montana

CHICKASAW
Chickasaw Nation of Oklahoma

CHIPPEWA
Bay Mills Reservation (Sault Ste. Marie Band),
  Michigan
Grande Traverse Band of Chippewa, Michigan
Isabella Reservation (Saginaw Chippewa),
  Michigan
L'Anse Reservation, Michigan
Lake Superior Band of Chippewa:
  Bad River Reservation, Wisconsin
  Lac Courte Oreilles Reservation, Wisconsin
  Lac du Flambeau Reservation, Wisconsin
  Red Cliff Reservation, Wisconsin
Minnesota Chippewa Tribe (six reservations):
  Nett Lake (Boise Forte) Reservation
  Fond du Lac Reservation
  Grand Portage Reservation
  Leech Lake Reservation
  Mill Lac Reservation
  White Earth Reservation
Red Lake Reservation, Minnesota
Rocky Boy's Reservation, Montana
Sault Ste. Marie Reservation, Michigan
St. Croix Reservation, Wisconsin
Sokoagon Chippewa Community
  (Mole Lake Band), Wisconsin
Turtle Mountain Reservation, North Dakota

CHITIMACHA
Chitimacha Tribe of Louisiana

CHOCTAW
Choctaw Nation of Oklahoma
Mississippi Band of Choctaw, Mississippi

CHUMASH (MISSION INDIANS)
Santa Ynez Reservation, California

COCOPAH
Cocopah Tribe of Arizona

COEUR D' ALENE
Coeur D' Alene Reservation, Idaho

COLORADO RIVER
Colorado River Reservation,
  Arizona and California

COLVILLE
Confederated Tribes of the Colville Reservation,
  Washington

COMANCHE
Comanche Indian Tribe of Oklahoma

COUSHATTA
Coushatta Tribe of Louisiana

CREE
Cree Indians of Rocky Boy's Reservation,
  Montana

CREEK
Alabama-Quassarte Tribal Town of the
  Creek Nation, Oklahoma
Creek Nation of Oklahoma
Kialegee Tribal Town of the Creek Nation,
  Oklahoma
Thlopthlocco Tribal Town of the Creek Nation,
  Oklahoma

CROW
Crow Tribe of Montana

DELAWARE
Delaware Tribes of Western Oklahoma

DIEGUENO (MISSION INDIANS)
Barona Reservation, California
Campo Reservation, California
Capitan Grande Reservation, California
Cuyapaipe Reservation, California
Inaga and Cosmit Reservations, California
LaPosta Reservation, California
Manzanita Reservation, California
Mesa Grande Reservation, California
San Pasqual Reservation, California
Santa Ysabel, Reservation, California
Sycuan Reservation, California
Viejas Reservtion, California

GOSHUTE
Confederated Tribes of the Goshute Reservation,
  Nevada and Utah
Skull Valley Band of the Goshute Indians of Utah

GROS VENTRE
Fort Belknap Reservation, Montana

HAVASUPAI
Havasupai Tribe of Arizona

HOH
Hoh Reservation, Washington

HOOPA
Hoopa Valley Reservation, California

HOPI
Hopi Tribe of Arizona

HUALAPAI
Hualapai Reservation, Arizona

IOWA
Iowa Tribe of Oklahoma
Iowa Reservation, Nebraska and Kansas

KALISPEL
Kalispel Reservation, Washington

KAROK
Karok Tribe of California

KAW
Kaw Indian Tribe of Oklahoma

KICKAPOO
Kickapoo Reservation, Kansas
Kickapoo Tribe of Oklahoma

KIOWA
Kiowa Tribe of Oklahoma

KLALLAM
Jamestown Band of Klallam Indians, Washington
Lower Elwha Reservation, Washington
Port Gamble Reservation, Washington

KOOTENAI
Kootenai Tribe of Idaho

LUISENO (MISSION INDIANS)
La Jolla Reservation, California
Pala Reservation, California
Pauma and Yuima Reservation, California
Pechanga Reservation, California
Rincon Reservation, California
Soboba Reservation, California
Twenty-Nine Palms Reservation, California

LUMMI
Lummi Reservation, Washington

MAIDU
Berry Creek Rancheria, California
Enterprise Rancheria, California
Round Valley Reservation (Covelo
  Indian Community), California

Susanville Indian Rancheria, California

MAKAH
Makah Reservation, Washington

MARICOPA
Gila River Reservation, Arizona
Salt River Reservation, Arizona

ME-WUK (MIWOK)
Jackson Rancheria, California
Sheep Ranch Rancheria, California
Shingle Springs Band of Me-Wuk
  Indians of California
Trinidad Rancheria (Cher-Ae Heights Indian
  Community), California
Tuolumne Band of Me-Wuk Indians of California

MENOMINEE
Menominee Reservation, Wisconsin

MIAMI
Miami Tribe of Oklahoma
Table Bluff Rancheria of California

MICCOSUKEE
Miccosukkee Tribe of Florida

MODOC
Modoc Tribe of Oklahoma

MOHAVE
Fort McDowell Reservation, Arizona

MOHAWK
St. Regis Band of Mohawk, New York

MONO
Cold Springs Rancheria, California

MUCKLESHOOT
Muckleshoot Reservation, Washington

NAVAJO
Navajo Reservation, Arizona, New Mexico and
Utah

NEZ PERCE
Nez Perce Reservation, Idaho

NISQUALLY
Nisqually Reservation, Washington

NOOKSACK
Nooksack Indian Tribe of Washington

OMAHA
Omaha Tribe of Nebraska

ONEIDA
Oneida Nation of New York
Oneida Tribe of Wisconsin

ONONDAGA
Onondaga Nation of New York

OSAGE
Osage Tribe of Oklahoma

OTOE-MISSOURIA
Otoe-Missouria of Oklahoma

OTTAWA
Grande Traverse Band, Michigan
Ottawa Tribe of Oklahoma

PAIUTE
Benton (Utu Utu Gwaitu) Paiute Reservation,
  California
Big Pine Reservation, California
Bishop Colony, California
Bridgeport Indian Colony, California
Burns Paiute Indian Colony, Oregon
Cedarville Rancheria, California
Duck Valley Reservation, Nevada
Fallon Reservation and Colony, Nevada
Fort Bidwell Reservation, California
Fort Independence Reservation, California
Fort McDermitt Reservation, Nevada
Kaibab Reservation, Arizona
Las Vegas Indian Colony, Nevada
Lone Pine Reservation, California
Lovelock Indian Colony, Nevada
Moapa River Reservation, Nevada

Pyramid Lake Reservation, Nevada
Reno-Sparks Indian Colony, Nevada
Summit Lake Reservation, Nevada
Utah: Cedar City, Indian Peaks, Kanosh,
  Koosharen and Shivwite
Walker River Reservation, Nevada
Winnemucca Indian Colony, Nevada
Yerington Colony and Campbell Ranch, Nevada

PAPAGO
Maricopa (Ak Chin) Reservation, Arizona
Gila Bend Reservation, Arizona
San Xavier Reservation, Arizona
Sells Reservation, Arizona

PASQUA YAQUI
Pascua Yaqui Tribe of Arizona

PASSAMAQUODDY
Passamaquoddy Tribe of Maine

PAWNEE
Pawnee Indian Tribe of Oklahoma

PENOBSCOT
Penobscot Tribe of Maine

PEORIA
Peoria Tribe of Oklahoma

PIMA
Gila River Reservation, Arizona
Salt River Reservation, Arizona

PIT RIVER
Alturas Indian Rancheria, California
Big Bend Rancheria, California
Lookout Rancheria, California
Montgomery Creek Rancheria, California
Roaring Creek Rancheria, California
Susanville Indian Rancheria, California
X-L Ranch Reservation, California

POMO
Coyote Valley Band, California
Dry Creek Rancheria, California
Hopland Rancheria (Hopland Band), California
Laytonville Rancheria (Cahto Indian Tribe),
  California
Manchester-Point Arena Rancheria
  (Manchester Band), California

Middletown Rancheria, California
Robinson Rancheria. California
Sherwood Valley Rancheria, California
Stewarts Point Rancheria (Kashia Band),
  California
Sulphur Bank Rancheria (Elem Indian Colony),
  California
Upper Lake Band, California

PONCA
Ponca Tribe of Indians of Oklahoma

POTAWATOMI
Citizen Band Potawatomi Indians of Oklahoma
Forest County Potawatomi Community of Wisconsin
Hannahville Indian Community of Michigan
Prairie Band of Potawatomi of Kansas

PUEBLO (NEW MEXICO)
Pueblo of Acoma
Pueblo of Cochiti
Pueblo of Jemez
Pueblo of Ildefonso
Pueblo of Isleta
Pueblo of Laguna
Pueblo of Nambe
Pueblo of Picuris
Pueblo of Pojoaque
Pueblo of San Felipe
Pueblo of San Juan
Pueblo of Sandia
Pueblo of Santa Ana
Pueblo of Santa Clara
Pueblo of Santo Domingo
Pueblo of Taos
Pueblo of Tesuque
Pueblo of Zia
Zuni Reservation (Zuni Tribe)

PUYALLUP
Puyallup Reservation, Washington

QUAPAW
Quapaw Tribe of Oklahoma

QUECHAN
Fort Yuma Reservation (Yuma), California

QUILEUTE
Quileute Reservation, Washington

QUINAULT
Quinault Reservation, Washington

SAC AND FOX
Sac and Fox Reservation (Sac and Fox of the Missouri), Kansas and Nebraska
Sac and Fox Tribe of the Mississippi, Iowa
Sac and Fox Tribe of Oklahoma

SALISH AND KOOTENAI
Flathead Reservation (Confederated Tribes), Montana

SAUK-SUIATTLE
Sauk-Suiattle Tribe of Washington

SEMINOLE
Seminole Nation of Oklahoma
Seminole Tribe of Florida

SENECA
Seneca-Cayuga Tribe of Oklahoma
Seneca Nation of New York
Tonawanda Band, New York

SERRANO
San Manual (Band) Reservation, California

SHAWNEE
Absentee Shawnee of Oklahoma
Eastern Shawnee Tribe of Oklahoma

SHOALWATER
Shoalwater Bay Reservation, Washington

SHOSHONE
Battle Mountain Colony
 (Te-Moak Band), Nevada
Big Pines Band (Owens Valley), California
Duck Valley Reservation, Nevada
Duckwater Reservation, Nevada
Elko Colony (Te-Moak Band), Nevada
Ely Indian Colony, Nevada
Fallon Reservation and Colony, Nevada
Fort McDermitt Reservation, Nevada
Lone Pine Reservation, California
Northwestern Band, Utah
South Fork Colony, Nevada
Wind River Reservation, Wyoming
Yomba Shoshone Tribe of Nevada

SILETZ
Confederated Tribes of the Siletz Reservation, Oregon

SIOUX
Cheyenne River Reservation, South Dakota
Crow Creek Reservation, South Dakota
Devils Lake Reservation, North Dakota
Flandreau Santee Sioux Reservation, South Dakota
Fort Peck Reservation (Assiniboine & Sioux), South Dakota
Lower Brule Sioux Reservation, South Dakota
Lower Sioux Community (Mdewakanton), Minnesota
Pine Ridge Reservation (Oglala), South Dakota
Prairie Island Reservation (Mdewakanton), Minnesota
Rosebud Reservation, South Dakota
Santee Sioux Reservation, Nebraksa
Shakopee Mdewakanton Sioux Community, Minnesota
Sisseton-Wahpeton Sioux Reservation, South Dakota
Standing Rock Reservation, North and South Dakota
Upper Sioux Reservation, Minnesota
Yankton Sioux Tribe of South Dakota

SKAGIT
Upper Skagit Indian Tribe of Washington

SKOKOMISH
Skokomish Reservation, Washington

SMITH RIVER
Big Lagoon Rancheria, California

SPOKANE
Spokane Tribe of Washington

SQUAXIN ISLAND
Squaxin Island Reservation, Washington

STILLAGUAMISH
Stillaguamish Tribe of Washington

STOCKBRIDGE-MUNSEE
Stockbridge-Munsee Community of Mohican Indians,
  Wisconsin

SWINOMISH
Swinomish Reservation, Washington

SUQUAMISH
Port Madison Reservation, Washington

TACHE
Santa Rosa Rancheria, California

**THREE AFFILIATED TRIBES
(GROSS VENTRE, HIDATSA, MANDAN)**
Three Affiliated Tribes of Fort Berthold,
  North Dakota

TOLOWA
Cher-Ae Heights Community,
  Trinidad Rancheria, California

TONKAWA
Tonawa Tribe of Oklahoma

TULALIP
Tule River Reservation, California

TUSCARORA
Tuscarora Nation of New York

UMATILLA
Confederated Tribes of the Umatilla Reservation,
  Oregon

UTE
Southern Ute Reservation, Colorado
Uintah and Ouray Reservation, Utah
Ute Mountain Reservation, Colorado,
  Utah and New Mexico

WYANDOTTE
Wyandotte Tribe of Oklahoma

WARM SPRINGS
Confederated Tribes of the Warm Springs
  Reservation (Walla Walla and Cayuga), Oregon

WASHOE
Carson Colony, Nevada
Dresslerville Rancheria, Nevada
Reno-Sparks Indian Colony, Nevada
Susanville Indian Rancheria, California
Washoe Rancheria, Nevada

WICHITA
Wichita Tribe of Oklahoma

WINNEBAGO
Winnebago Tribe of Nebraska
Winnebago Tribe of Wisconsin

WINTUN
Colusa Rancheria (Cachil DeHe Band),
  California
Cortina Indian Rancheria, California
Grindstone Indian Rancheria (Wintun-Wailaki),
  California
Rumsey Indian Rancheria, California

YAKIMA
Yakima Reservation (Confederated Tribes),
  Washington

YAVAPAI
Camp Verde Reservation, Arizona
Yavapai-Prescott Tribe of Arizona

YOKUT
Santa Rosa Rancheria, California
Table Mountain Rancheria, California

YUROK
Berry Creek Reservation, California
Hoopa Valley Reservation, California
Resighini Rancheria, California
Trinidad Rancheria (Cher-Ae Heights),
California

CANADIAN RESERVES
AND BANDS

This section contains a listing of Canadian Indian Reserves and Bands, with land areas of at least 1,000 acres. Many bands have more than one reserve in each province. In these cases, the land areas (indicated by an asterisk before the Reserve) are added together to provide a total for that Province. The Reserves are in bold type followed by the Bands and Acreage. Arranged alphabetically by Reserve and Province.

ALBERTA

Alexander—Alexander, 17,000 acres
Alexis—Alexis, 15,000 acres
Amber River—Slaves-Upper Hay River, 5,800 acres
Beaver Lake—Beaver Lake, 15,300 acres
Beaver Ranch—Fort Vermilion (Tallcree), 2,100 acres
Big Horn—Stony, 5,000 acres
Blackfoot—Blackfoot, 178,500 acres
*Blood—Blood, 346,500 acres
Boyer—Boyer River, 10,500 acres
Buck Lake—Paul, 2,500 acres
Bushe River—Slaves of Upper Hay River, 27,700 acres
Child Lake—Boyer River, 7,000 acres
*Chipewyan—Fort Chipewyan, 42,500 acres
Clear Hills—Beaver Band, 3,800 acres
Clearwater—Fort McMurray, 2,300 acres
*Cold Lake—Cold Lake, 46,500 acres
Drift Pile River—Drift Pile, 15,800 acres
*Eden Valley—Stony, 4,200 acres
Ermineskin—Ermineskin, 25,350 acres
Fox Lake—Little Red River, 25,800 acres
*Gregoire Lake—Fort McMurray, 6,000 acres
Hay Lake—Slaves of Upper Hay River, 30,500 acres
Heart Lake—Heart Lake, 11,000 acres
Horse Lakes—Beaver Band, 3,850 acres
Janvier—Janvier, 4,000 acres
John D'Or Prairie—Little Red River, 34,350 acres
Kehiwin—Kehiwin, 20,400 acres
Louis Bull—Louis Bull, 8,400 acres
*Makaoo—Onion Lake, 23,000 acres
Montana—Montana, 7,000 acres
*Namur Lake—Fort McKay, 13,200 acres
O'Chiese—O'Chiese, 38,150 acres
Pakashan—Grouard, 1,000 acres
Peace River Crossing—Duncan's, 5,100 acres
*Peigan—Peigan, 113,500 acres
Peigan Lake—Indians of Hobbema, 4,700 acres
Pushkiakiwenin—Frog Lake, 25,500 acres
Saddle Lake—Saddle Lake, 54,800 acres
*Samson—Samson, 32,700 acres
Sarcee—Sarcee, 70,000 acres
*Sawridge—Sawridge, 80,500 acres
Stony—Stony, 78,300 acres
Stony (Rabbit Lake)—Stony, 14,000 acres
Stony Plain—Enoch, 12,800 acres

*Sturgeon Lake—Sturgeon Lake, 22,150 acres
Sucker Creek—Sucker Creek, 15,000 acres
Sunchild—Sunchild Cree, 12,900 acres
Swan River—Swan River, 10,800 acres
*Tall Cree—Fort Vermilion (Tallcree), 7,000 acres
Unipouheos—Frog Lake, 21,000 acres
Upper Hay River—Slaves-Upper Hay River, 3,500 acres
*Utikoomak Lake—Whitefish Lake, 12,000 acres
*Wabamum—Paul, 15,200 acres
*Wabasca—Wabasca (Bigstone), 51,250 acres
White Fish Lake—Saddle Lake, 11,200 acres
Zama Lake—Slaves-Upper Hay River, 5,700 acres

BRITISH COLUMBIA

Aiyansk—Gitlakdamin, 3,100 acres
*Alexandria—Alexandria, 2,000 acres
*Alexis Creek—Alexis Creek, 5,500 acres
*Alkali Lake—Alkali Lake, 1,000 acres
*Anahim—Anaham, 3,500 acres
*Anahim's Flat—Anaham, 9,500 acres
*Anahim's Meadow—Anaham, 1,250 acres
Andimaul—Kitsequkla, 1,100 acres
*Ashnola—Lower Similkameen, 4,000 acres
*Babine—Lake Babine, 2,200 acres
Beaton River—Fort St. John, 2,850 acres
Bella Bella—Bella Bella, 1,600 acres
Bella Coola—Bella Coola, 3,350 acres
Blueberry River—Fort St. John, 2,850 acres
Boothanie—Lytton, 3,750 acres
*Boothroyd—Boothroyd, 1,200 acres
*Boston Bar—Boston Bar, 1,000 acres
*Bridge River—Bridge River, 1,700 acres
*Cahoose—Ulkatcho, 2,750 acres
*Camin Lake—Camin Lake, 5,000 acres
*Canoe Creek—Canoe Creek, 11,500 acres
Cape Mudge—Cape Mudge, 1,100 acres
Charley Boy's Cemetary—Alexis Creek, 1,100 acres
Chawuthen—Hope, 1,350 acres
Cheakanus—Squamish, 4,050 acres
*Chehalis—Chehalis, 1,500 acres
Chemainus—Chemainus, 2,700 acres
*Chilco Lake—Nemaiah Valley, 1,750 acres
*Chuchuwayha—Upper Similkameen, 5,500 acres

93

Cludolicum—Alkali Lake, 1,650 acres
Coldwater—Coldwater, 4,550 acres
Columbia Lake—Columbia Lake, 8,400 acres
*Cowichan—Cowichan, 5,800 acres
Creston—Creston, 1,800 acres
Deadman's Creek—Deadman's Creek, 19,500 acres
Deep Creek—Soda Creek, 4,050 acres
*Dog Creek—Canoe Creek, 1,350 acres
Dogfish Bay—Kincolith, 1,150 acres
Doig River—Fort St. John, 2,500 acres
Dolphin Island—Kitkala, 3,850 acres
Douglas—Douglas, 1,000 acres
Enderby—Spallumcheen, 5,600 acres
*Euchino Creek—Nazko, 1,500 acres
Fort George—Fort George, 1,300 acres
Fort Nelson—Fort Nelson, 23,450 acres
Fort Ware—Finley River, 1,000 acres
*Fountain—Fountain, 3,500 acres
Gelangle—Stuart-Trembleau Lake, 1,000 acres
Halfway River—Hudson Hope, 9,900 acres
*Hamilton Creek—Upper/Lower Nicola, 4,500 acres
Harwood Island—Sliammon, 2,100 acres
Hazelton—Hazelton, 2,600 acres
*High Bar—High Bar, 3,650 acres
Hope Island—Nuwitti, 8,500 acres
Hustalen—Adam's Lake, 2,200 acres

Kamloops—Kamloops, 32,500 acres
Katit—Oweekano, 1,600 acres
*Keremos Forks—Lower Similkammen, 3,700 acres
*Kincolith—Kincolith, 1,200 acres
Kisgegas—Hazelton, 2,400 acres
Kispaiox—Kispaiox, 2,850 acres
Kitselas—Kitselas, 1,075 acres
Kitsequecla—Kitsequkla, 2,350 acres
*Kitsumkaylum—Kitsumkaylum, 2,300 acres
*Kitwancool—Kitwancool, 2,100 acres
*Kitwanga—Kitwanga, 3,400 acres
Klahoose—Klahoose, 2,200 acres
*Kluskus—Kluskus, 1,275 acres
Kootenay—St. Mary's, 16,800 acres
Kuper Island—Chemainus, 2,150 acres
Lachkaltsap—Greenville, 4,000 acres
*Leon Creek—Pavilion, 1,600 acres
*Lillooet—Lillooet, 3,100 acres
*Little Springs—Alkali Lake, 1,200 acres
*Lower Kootenay—Lower Kootenay, 4,200 acres
Lyacksum—Syackson, 1,750 acres
*Lytton—Lytton, 3,000 acres
Moberly Lake—Saulteaun, 7,600 acres
Moricetown—Moricetown, 1,275 acres
Mosquito Creek—Liard River, 1,280 acres
Narcisse's Farm—Lower Similkameen, 1,850 acres
Nautley—Fraser Lake, 1,250 acres
*Nazco—Nazco, 1,250 acres
*Nedoats—Lake Babine, 1,500 acres

Nesikap—Lytton, 1,750 acres
Neskainlith—Neskainlith, 8,500 acres
Nicoelton—Cook's Ferry, 2,000 acres
Nicola Lake—Upper Nicola, 2,650 acres
Nicola Mameet—Lower Nicola, 11,200 acres
Nooaitch—Nooaitch, 2,200 acres
Nooaitch Grass—Nooaitch, 2,000 acres
North Thompson—North Thompson, 3,000 acres
Numukamis—Ohiet, 1,100 acres
Okanagan—Okanagan, 25,300 acres
105 Mile Point—Ashcrost, 3,350 acres
*Oregon Jack Creek—Oregon Jack Creek, 1,200 acres
*Osoyoos—Osoyoos, 32,200 acres
Pashilqua—Cayoosh Creek, 1,400 acres
Paul's Basin—Coldwater, 1,600 acres
*Pavilion—Pavilion, 3,000 acres
*Pemberton—Mount Currie, 5,500 acres
Pemynoos—Cook's Ferry, 4,400 acres
*Penticton—Penticton, 24,500 acres
Pete Suckers—Alkali Lake, 1,400 acres
*Pinchie Lake—Stuart—Trembleau Lake, 1,200 acres
Prophet River—Fort Nelson, 1,000 acres
Quaaout—Little Shuswap Lake, 4,250 acres
*Quesnel—Quesnel, 1,400 acres
Range—Lower Similkameen, 16,750 acres
*Redstone Flat—Alexis Creek, 1,500 acres
Salmon River—Spallumcheen, 3,800 acres
*Sampson's Meadow—Alkali Lake, 1,000 acres
Scotch Creek—Little Shuswap Lake, 2,050 acres
Seabird Island—Seabird Island, 4,350 acres
*Seaspunket—Fraser Lake, 1,000 acres
Shackan—Shackan, 6,400 acres
Shuswap—Shuswap, 2,700 acres
Sik-e-dakh—Glen Vowell, 1,600 acres
Skemeoskuankin—Lower Similkameen, 4,000 acres
*Skookumchuk—Skookum Chuck, 1,000 acres
Skumalaph—Dwaw-Kwaw-a-Pilt Skwah, Squila and Aitchelitz, 1,100 acres
*Slash—Seton Lake, 3,250 acres
Sliammon—Sliammon, 1,900 acres
Soda Creek—Soda Creek, 1,050 acres
Soldatquo—Shackan, 2,400 acres
Soowahlie—Soowahlie, 1,150 acres
*Spahomin Creek—Upper Nicola, 4,175 acres
Squianny—Nicomen, 1,500 acres
Squinas—Ulkatcho, 1,000 acres
Stellaquo—Stellaquo, 2,000 acres
*Stone—Stone, 4,800 acres
Stony Creek—Stony Creek, 6,370 acres
Switsemalph—Neskainlith, 1,250 acres
Tache—Stuart—Trembleau Lake, 2,100 acres
*Tahltan—Tahltan, 1,050 acres
Tobacco Plains—Tobacco Plains, 10,500 acres
*Toosey—Toosey, 5,800 acres
Tsimpsean—Port Simpson and Metlakatla, 33,700 acres
*Tsinstikeptum—West Bank, 2,300 acres

*Ulkatcho—Ulkatcho, 2,500 acres
Upper Hat Creek—Bonaparte, 2,000 acres
Williams Lake—Williams Lake, 4,000 acres
Whcott's Flat—Alkali Lake, 1,230 acres
*Zoht—Lower Nicola, 1,000 acres

MANITOBA

Berens River—Berens River, 6,350 acres
Birdtail Creek—Birdtail Sioux, 6,700 acres
Black River—Little Black River, 2,000 acres
Blood Vein River—Bloodview, 3,850 acres
Brochet—Barren Lands, 10,700 acres
Brokenhead—Brokenhead, 13,350 acres
Buffalo Point—Buffalo Point, 4,150 acres
*Chemahawin—Chemahawin, 5,000 acres
Crane River—Crane River, 8,750 acres
*Cross Lake—Cross Lake, 8,500 acres
*Dawson Bay—Shoal River, 3,300 acres
Dog Creek—Lake Manitoba, 9,400 acres
Ebb and Flow—Ebb and Flow, 11,500 acres
Fairford—Fairford, 12,750 acres
*Fischer River—Fischer River, 15,750 acres
Fort Alexander—Fort Alexander, 22,100 acres
God's Lake—God's Lake, 9,800 acres
Grand Rapids—Grand Rapids, 4,550 acres
Highrock—Mathias Colomb, 19,450 acres
Hollow Water—Hollow Water, 4,000 acres
*Island Lake—Island Lake, 18,000 acres
*Jackhead—Jackhead, 3,000 acres
Keeseekoowenin—Keeseekoowenin, 5,500 acres
Little Grand Rapids—Little Grand Rapids,
   5,600 acres
*Little Saskatchewan—Little Saskatchewan,
   3,500 acres
Lizard Point—Gambler and Waywayseecappo,
   24,950 acres
Long Plain—Long Plain, 7,000 acres
Long Plain Sioux—Long Plain Sioux,
   1,300 acres
*Moose Lake—Moose Lake, 4,000 acres
*Nelson House—Nelson House, 14,300 acres
Northwest Angle—Northwest Angle No. 37,
   1,450 acres
Norway House—Norway House, 37,300 acres
Oak Lake—Oak Lake, 2,700 acres
Oak River—Oak River Sioux, 9,700 acres
Oxford House—Oxford House, 12,050 acres
*Peguis—Peguis, 74,200 acres
Pine Creek—Pine Creek, 23,850 acres
Poplar River—Poplar River, 3,800 acres
Pukatawagan—Mathias Colomb, 3,800 acres
Reed River—Buffalo Point, 1,680 acres
Rolling River—Rolling River, 13,900 acres
*Roseau Rapids—Roseau River, 7,450 acres
Sandy Bay—Sandy Bay, 16,000 acres
*Shoal Lake—Northwest Angle No. 37-39-40,
   7,800 acres
*Split Lake—Split Lake, 11,300 acres
*Swan Lake—Swan Lake, 6,600 acres

*The Narrows—Lake St. Martin, 6,500 acres
*The Pas—The Pas, 7,800 acres
Valley River—Valley River, 11,500 acres
Waterhen—Waterhen, 4,600 acres

NEW BRUNSWICK

Big Hole Tract—Eel Ground and Red Back,
   5,850 acres
Burnt Church—Burnt Church, 2,050 acres
Eel Ground—Eel Ground, 2,680 acres
Kingsclear—Kingsclear, 1,000 acres
Papineau—Papineau, 1,000 acres
*Red Bank—Red Bank, 6,000 acres
Richibucto—Big Cove, 2,600 acres
Tabusintac—Burnt Church, 8,080 acres
Tobique—Tobique, 5,750 acres

NORTHWEST TERRITORY

Attawapiskat—Attawapiskat, 66,550 acres
Fort Albany—Albany, 89,750 acres
Fort Severn—Fort Severn, 9,600 acres
Winisk—Weenusk, 10,850 acres

NOVA SCOTIA

Bear River—Bear River, 1,600 acres
Chapel Island—Chapel Island, 1,275 acres
Cold River—Acadia, 1,000 acres
*Eskasoni—Eskasoni, 8,700 acres
Franklin Manor—Afton and Pictour Landing,
   1,000 acres
Malagawatch—Whycocomagh bands, 1,200
   acres
New Ross—Shubenacadie, 1,000 acres
*Shubenacadie—Shubenacadie, 4,000 acres
Whycocomagh—Whycocomagh, 1,500 acres
Wildcat—Acadia, 1,150 acres

ONTARIO

Abitibi—Abitibi Ontario & Dominion,
   19,250 acres
Alnwick (Alderville)—Alderville, 2,950 acres
*Big Trout Lake—Trout Lake, 54,400 acres
Big Grassy River—Assabaska, 8,900 acres
*Big Island—Big Island & Northwest Angle
   No. 37, 5,700 acres
Cape Crocker—Cape Crocker, 15,600 acres
Hunting Grounds—Crocker bands, 3,800 acres
Cardoc—Chippewas and Munceys of the
   Thames, 10,850 acres

Caribou Lake—Caribou Lake, 25,650 acres
*Chapleau—Chapleau Ojibway and Creek,
   2,700 acres

Chief's Point—Saugeen, 1,150 acres
*Christian Islands—Beausoleil, 13,300 acres.
Constance Lake—Constance Lake, 7,650 acres
Couchiching—Couchiching, 12,850 acres
Coulais Bay—Batchewana, 1,600 acres
Curve Lake—Curve Lake, 2,150 acres
Dokis—Dokis, 38,900 acres
Eagle Lake—Eagle Lake, 8,900 acres
*English River—Constance Lake & Grassy
  Narrows, 18,000 acres
Factory Island—Moose Factory, 14,700 acres
Flying Post—Flying Post, 14,275 acres
Fort Hope—Fort Hope, 64,000 acres
Fort William—Fort William, 14,275 acres
French River—Henvy Inlet, 6,300 acres
*Garden River—Garden River, 49,000 acres
Georgina Islands—Chippewas, 3,550 acres
Gibson—Gibson, 14,050 acres
Golden Lake—Golden Lake, 1,750 acres
*Gros Cap—Michipicoten, 9,000 acres
Gull River—Gull Bay, 9,800 acres
Henvy Inlet—Henvy Inlet, 23,750 acres
Hiawatha (Rice Lake)—Hiawatha, 1,925 acres
Islington—Islington, 21,000 acres
Kenora—Rat Portage & Dallas bands,
  8,000 acres
Kettle Point—Chippewas, 2,130 acres
Lac des Mille Lacs—Lac des Mille Lacs,
  3,750 acres
*Lake of the Woods—Big Island, Northwest
  Angle No. 37 and Assabaska — 9,000 acres
*Long Lake—Long Lake Nos. 58 & 77,
  17,800 acres
Magnetawan—Magnetawan, 11,600 acres
Manitou Rapids—Rainy River, 5,675 acres
Marten Falls—Marten Falls, 19,200 acres
Matachewan—Matachewan, 10,275 acres
Mattagami—Mattagami, 11,900 acres
Mississagi River—Mississagu, 4,285 acres
Moose Factory—Moose Factory, 42,240 acres
Moravian—Moravian of the Thames, 3,025 acres
Mountbatten—Brunswick House, 23,000 acres
Naiscoutaing—Shawanage, 2,650 acres
*Naongahing—Big Island and Assabaska,
  1,280 acres
Neguaguan Lake—Lac La Croix, 15,350 acres
New Credit—Mississaguas of the Credit,
  6,000 acres
New Post—New Post, 5,120 acres
Nipissing—Nipissing, 14,850 acres
*Northwest Angle—Northwest Angle
  Nos. 33 & 37, 4,800 acres
Obabikong Lakes—Assabaska, 1,750 acres
Oneida—Oneida of the Thomas, 5,275 acres
*Osnaburgh—Osnaburgh, 46,000 acres
Parry Island—Parry Island, 18,500 acres
Pikangikum—Pikangikum, 2,240 acres
Point Grondine—Wikwemikong, 10,100 acres
*Rainy Lake—Nicickousemenecaning,
  Stangecoming and Naicatchewenin, 20,000 acres
Rama—Chippewas, 2,240 acres

Rankin Location—Batchewana, 3,750 acres
Rat Portage—Rat Portage and Dallas bands,
  8,000 acres
*Sabaskong Bay—Sabaskong and White Fish,
  6,500 acres
Sachigo Lake—Trout Lake, 9,275 acres
Sandy Lake—Deer Lake, 10,500 acres
Sarnia—Chippewas, 4,150 acres
Saugeen—Saugeen, 8,050 acres
*Seine River—Seine River and Lac des
  Mille Lacs, 34,300 acres
*Shawanaga—Shawanaga, 17,000 acres
Sheguiandah—Shegiandah, 5,100 acres
Sheshegwaning—Sheshegwaning, 5,000 acres
*Shoal Lake—Big Island, Northwest Angle
  Nos. 37 & 39 and Shoal Lake Nos. 39 & 40,
  12,300 acres
Six Nations—Six Nations of the Grand River,
  45,000 acres
Spanish River—Spanish River, 27,850 acres
*St. Regis—Iroquois of the St. Regis,
  9,200 acres
Sturgeon Falls—Seine River, 6,150 acres
Sucker Creek—Sucker Creek, 1,575 acres
Swan Lake—Islington, 3,275 acres
The Dalles—Rat Portage and the Dallas bands,
  8,050 acres
Thessalon—Thessalon, 2,300 acres
Tyendinaga—Mohawks of the Bay of Quinte,
  17,450 acres
Wabauskang—Wabauskang, 8,050 acres
Wabigoon Lake—Wabigoon, 12,875 acres
Walpole Island—Walpole Island, 39,850 acres
Wanapitei—Wanapitei, 2,560 acres
West Bay—West Bay, 8,200 acres
Whitefish Bay—Whitefish Bay and Northwest
  Angle Nos. 33 & 37 — 4,600 acres
Whitefish Lake—Whitefish Lake, 43,750 acres
Whitefish River—Whitefish River, 9,750 acres
Wikwemikong—Wikwemikong, 105,300 acres
Winisk—Weenusk, 10,880 acres
Wunnumin Lake—Trout Lake, 17,300 acres
Yellow Girl Bay—Whitefish Bay, 4,450 acres

PRINCE EDWARD ISLAND

Lennox Island—Lennox Island, 2,400 acres

QUEBEC

Abitibi (Ontario)—Abitibi, 19,250 acres
Bersimis—Bersimis, 63,100 acres
Caughnawaga—Iroquois, 12,500 acres
Doncaster—Iroquois of Caughnawaga
  and Oka bands, 18,500 acres
Maniwaki—River Desert, 42,000 acres
Manuan—Manuan, 1,900 acres
Mistassini—Mistassini, 5,800 acres
Obedjiwan—Obedjiwan, 2,300 acres

Oka—Oka, 2,300 acres
Quiatchouan—Montagnais of Lake St. John, 3,800 acres
Pierreville (Odanak)—Odanak, 1,500 acres
Restigouche—Restigouche, 9,600 acres
*Seven Islands—Sept-Iles, 1,500 acres
Timiskaming—Timiskaming, 6,000 acres
Weymontachi—Weymontachi, 7,400 acres

SASKATCHEWAN

Amisk Lake—Peter Ballentyne, 5,100 acres
Assiniboine—Carry the Kettle, 41,000 acres
Atakakup—Sandy Lake, 43,000 acres
Beardy—Beardy's & Okemasis, 28,200 acres
Big Head—Joseph Bighead, 11,600 acres
*Big River—Big River, 28,600 acres
Birch Portage—Peter Ballentyne, 1,300 acres
*Canoe Lake—Canoe Lake, 9,500 acres
*Carrot River—Red Earth & The Pas, 5,250 acres
Chitek Lake—Pelican Lake, 8,600 acres
Cote—Cote, 22,900 acres
Cowessess—Cowessess, 29,000 acres
Cumberland—Cumberland House, 4,000 acres
Day Star—Day Star, 15,350 acres
*Fishing Lake—Fishing Lake, 9,500 acres
Gordon—Gordon, 35,400 acres
Grand Mother's Bay—Lac la Ronge, 11,100 acres
Grizzly Bear's Head and Lean Man— Mosquito-Grizzly and Bear's Head, 8,550 acres
James Smith—James Smith, 17,800 acres
Kahkewistahaw—Kahkewistahaw, 19,500 acres
*Keeseekoose—Keeseekoos, 11,000 acres
*Kinistino—Kinistino, 10,100 acres
La Loche—Portage La Loche, 14,200 acres
La Plonge—English River, 13,900 acres
Little Black Bear—Little Black Bear, 17,050 acres
*Little Hills—Lac la Ronge, 1,700 acres
Little Pine & Lucky Man—Little Pine & Lucky Man, 16,000 acres
*Little Red River—Lac la Ronge, 38,400 acres
Makaoo—Onion Lake (partly in Alberta), Alberta, 14,000 acres; Saskatchewan, 5,000 acres
*Makwa Lake—Loon Lake, 14,600 acres
*Maple Creek—Maple Creek, 4,000 acres
*Meadow Lake—Meadow Lake, 9,200 acres
Ministikwan—Island Lake, 18,000 acres
Minoahchak—Sakimay, 1,000 acres

Mirond Lake—Peter Ballentyne, 1,500 acres
Mistawasis—Mistawasis, 31,100 acres
*Montreal Lake—Montreal Lake, 20,600 acres
*Moosomin—Moosomin, 17,350 acres
Morin Lake—Lac la Ronge, 32,650 acres
Mosquito—Mosquito-Grizzly Bear's Head, 23,000 acres
Muscowpetung—Muscowpetung, 20,600 acres
Muskeg Lake—Muskeg Lake, 17,900 acres
Muskoday—John Smith, 24,000 acres
Muskowekwan—Muskowekwan, 16,350 acres
*New Thunderchild—Thunderchild, 15,600 acres
Nut Lake—Nut Lake, 14,600 acres
Ochapowace—Ochapowace, 34,600 acres
Okanese—Okanesel, 14,300 acres
Okemasis—Okemasis & Beandy's, 28,150 acres
One Arrow—One Arrow, 10,200 acres
Pasqua—Pasqua, 22,150 acres
Peepeekisis—Peepeekisis, 26,600 acres
Pelican Narrows—Peter Ballentyne, 1,300 acres
Peter Pond Lake—Peter Pond Lake, 26,450 acres
Piapot—Piapot, 20,150 acres
Poor Man—Poor Man, 18,900 acres
Potato River—Lac la Ronge, 1,000 acres
Poundmaker—Poundmaker, 19,150 acres
Red Earth—Red Earth, 3,600 acres
Red Pheasant—Red Pheasant, 24,300 acres
Sakimay—Sakimay, 21,700 acres
Sandy Narrows—Peter Ballentyne, 2,650 acres
*Saulteaux—Saulteaux, 14,300 acres
Seekaskootch—Onion Lake, 38,375 acres
Shesheep—Sakimay, 3,500 acres
Shoal Lake—Shoal Lake, 3,750 acres
Southend—Peter Ballentyne, 10,400 acres
Star Blanket—Star Blanket, 13,750 acres
*Sturgeon Lake—Sturgeon Lake, 21,850 acres
Sturgeon Weir—Peter Ballentyne, 5,750 acres
*Sweet Grass—Sweet Grass, 42,250 acres
The Key—Key, 15,000 acres
Thunderchild—Thunderchild, 1,280 acres
*Wahpeton—Sioux Wahpeton, 3,750 acres
Wapachewunak—English River, 1,000 acres
*Waterhen—Waterhen Lake, 19,775 acres
White Bear—White Bear, 29,900 acres
White Cap—Moose Woods, 4,700 acres
Witchekan Lake—Witchekan Lake, 4,250 acres
Wood Mountain—Wood Mountain, 5,900 acres
Woody Lake—Peter Ballentyne, 1,675 acres

NATIONAL ASSOCIATIONS

This section lists national associations, societies, and organizations active in Indian affairs; also, religious, charitable, and philanthropic associations. Listings are arranged alphabetically.

ALASKA FEDERATION OF NATIVES
411 W. Fourth Ave., Suite 301
Anchorage, Alaska 99501
(907) 274-3611
Janie Leask, President

Membership: 77,000 (Alaska Native-Aleut, Eskimo and Indian.) *Purpose:* To act as a lobbyist and advocate for the regional profit and non-profit corporations, and to provide technical assistance to these groups. Sponsors research programs and competitions. Maintains biographical archives and library of government reports and economic material. Publications. Founded 1966.

ALL INDIAN PUEBLO COUNCIL, INC.
2401 12th St., N.W.
Albuquerque, New Mexico 87197
(505) 247-0371
Gilbert M. Pena, Chairman

Membership: 20. *Purpose:* To advocate on behalf of 19 Pueblo Indian tribes on education, health, social and economic issues. *Activities:* Operates boarding school, and Indian Pueblo Cultural Center Museum. Maintains archival collection. *Project:* Indian Business Development Corporation. Founded 1968.

AMERICAN ACADEMY OF PEDIATRICS
Committee on Indian Health
P.O. Box 927
141 N.W. Point Rd.
Elk Grove Village, Illinois 60007
(312) 228-5005
M. Harry Jennison, M.D., Executive Director

Purpose: To provide leadership in the review and development of methods and procedures that will improve pediatric services to Indians and Alaskan natives. *Activities:* Provides advisory pediatric service to Indian and Alaskan natives through the Division of Indian Health, U.S. Public Health Service. Founded 1965.

AMERICAN ANTHROPOLOGICAL ASSOCIATION
1703 New Hampshire Ave., N.W.
Washington, D.C. 20009
(202) 232-8800
Edward J. Lehman, Executive Director

Membership: 10,000. Professional society of anthropologists, educators, students and others interested in the biological and cultural origin and development of mankind. *Publications: American Anthropologist,* quarterly; Newsletter; *Guide to Departments of Anthropology,* annual. Founded 1902.

AMERICAN ANTIQUARIAN SOCIETY
185 Salisbury St.
Worcester, Massachusetts 01609
(617) 755-5221
Marcus A. McCorrison, Director/Librarian

Membership: 450. *Purpose:* To collect, preserve and encourage serious study of the materials of American history and life through 1876. Library. Newsletter. Founded 1812.

AMERICAN ETHNOLOGICAL SOCIETY
1703 New Hampshire Ave., N.W.
Washington, D.C. 20009
(202) 232-8800
Judith Shapiro, President

Membership: 1,150. Anthropologists and others interested in the field of ethnology and social anthropology. *Publications: American Ethnologist,* quarterly; Proceedings, *The Development of Political Organization in Native North America.* Division of American Anthropological Association.

AMERICAN FOLFLORE SOCIETY
Maryland State Arts Council
15 W. Mulberry St.
Baltimore, Maryland 21201
(301) 685-6740
Charles Camp, Executive Secretary/Treasurer

Membership: 3,000. Individuals and institutes interested in the collection, discussion, and publication of folklore throughout the world, with emphasis on North America. *Publications: Journal of American Folklore,* quarterly; newsletter, 6/yr. Books for sale. Founded 1888.

AMERICAN FRIENDS SERVICE COMMITTEE
Native American Affairs
1501 Cherry St.
Philadelphia, Pennsylvania 19102
(215) 241-7000
Asia A. Bennett, Executive Secretary

One of the corporate expressions of Quaker faith and practice. *Purpose:* To conduct programs with U.S. communities on the problem of minority groups—housing, employment and denial of legal rights. Founded 1917.

AMERICAN HISTORICAL ASSOCIATION
400 A St., S.E.
Washington, D.C. 20003
(202) 544-2422
Samuel R. Gamnon, Executive Director

Membership: 13,000. Professional historians,

educators, and others interested in promoting historical studies and collecting and preserving historical manuscripts. *Publications: American Historical Review,* 5/yr. Library. Founded 1884.

AMERICAN INDIAN ADOPTION RESOURCE EXCHANGE
Council of Three Rivers American Indian Center, Inc.
200 Charles St.
Pittsburgh, Pennsylvania 15238
(412) 782-4457

AMERICAN INDIAN AND ALASKA NATIVE PERIODICALS RESEARCH CLEARINGHOUSE
Stabler Hall 502
University of Arkansas
33rd and University Ave.
Little Rock, Arkansas 72204

AMERICAN INDIAN BIBLE INSTITUTE
100020 N. 15th Ave.
Phoenix, Arizona 85021
(602) 944-3335
Carl Collins, President

Publication: The Thunderer, newsletter.

AMERICAN INDIAN CULTURE RESEARCH CENTER
P.O. Box 98
Blue Cloud Abbey
Marvin, South Dakota 57251
(605) 432-5528
Rev. Stanislaus Maudlin, O.S.B., Executive Director

Purpose: To support Indian leaders, and educators in their ambitions for rebuilding the Indian community; aids in teaching the non-Indian public of the culture and philosophy of the Indian. *Programs:* Compiled oral history and photographic collection; distributes films, records and tapes; provides assistance grants to Indian college students; conducts workshops and seminars; maintains speakers bureau. *Publication: Blue Cloud Quarterly.* Library. Founded 1967.

AMERICAN INDIAN DEVELOPMENT ASSOCIATION
P.O. Box 2793
Bellingham, Washington 98227
(206) 733-1336

Purpose: To assist American Indians and Indian organizations in developing resources in harmony with their culture. Founded 1973.

AMERICAN INDIAN EDUCATION POLICY CENTER
Pennsylvania State University
320 Rackley Bldg.
University Park, Pennsylvania 16803

(814) 865-1489
Dr. Grayson Noley, Director

Program: American Indian Leadership Program. Graduate degrees in education for American Indians. Fellowships. Library. Founded 1970.

AMERICAN INDIAN FILM INSTITUTE
5805 Uplander Way
Culver City, California 90230
Mike Smith, President

AMERICAN INDIAN HEALTH CARE ASSOCIATION
1625 I St., N.W., Suite 420
Washington, D.C. 20006
(202) 833-9282

AMERICAN INDIAN HERITAGE FOUNDATION
6051 Arlington Blvd.
Falls Church, Virginia 22044
(703) 237-7500
Princess Pale Moon, President

Membership. 110,000. Tribal members and individual donors. *Purpose:* To inform and educate non-Indians concerning the culture and heritage of the American Indian. *Programs:* Sponsors food and clothing distribution; bestows cash awards and medals to outstanding Indian youth; provides scholarships and camp grants; operates speakers bureau and museum; Inter-Tribal Advisory Council. *Publication: Pathfinder,* newsletter. Library.

AMERICAN INDIAN HISTORICAL SOCIETY
1451 Masonic Ave.
San Francisco, California 94117
(415) 626-5235
Jeanette Henry Costo, Executive Secretary

Sponsors classes, forums and lectures on the history of the American Indians. In the process of setting up the *Rupert Costo Chair in American Indian Affairs,* located at the University of California, Berkeley, California.

AMERICAN INDIAN HORSE REGISTRY
Route 1, Box 64
Lockhart, Texas 78644
(512) 398-6642
Nanci Falley, President

Membership: 1,200. Persons who own or desire to own American Indian horses. *Purpose:* To collect, record, and preserve the pedigrees of American Indian horses. Maintains Indian Horse Hall of Fame Museum. *Publications: American Indian Horse Studbook,* annual; quarterly newsletter. Library. Founded 1961.

AMERICAN INDIAN LAW CENTER
P.O. Box 4456, Station A
1117 Stanford, N.E.
Albuquerque, New Mexico 87196
(505) 277-5462
  Philip S. Deloria, Director

Staff of 12 Indian law graduates and attorneys; located at the University of New Mexico, School of Law. *Purpose:* To render services, primarily research and training, of a broad legal and governmental nature; and, to assist tribes in making legal decisions when assistance is necessary. *Programs:* Helped found and currently provides staff support to the Commission on State-Tribal Relations; provides individualized training for tribal judges and tribal prosecutors; administers the Special Scholarship Program in Law for American Indians through which students receive admission advice, financial assistance, tutorial aid, and job placement services; provides assistance to Alaskan natives; sponsors conferences and seminars. *Publications: American Indian Law Newsletter,* bimonthly; manuals for tribal judges and prosecutors, and on Indian criminal court procedures. Library. Founded 1967.

AMERICAN INDIAN LAW STUDENTS ASSOCIATION
American Indian Law Center
P.O. Box 4456, Station A
1117 Stanford, N.E.
Albuquerque, New Mexico 87196
(505) 277-5462
  Ronald Eagleye Johnny, President

Membership: 160. American Indian and native-Alaskan law students. *Purpose:* To promote unity, communication and cooperation among Indian law students. *Programs:* Research projects and curriculum development in Indian law; maintains speakers bureau of students in the field of Indian law. Newsletter. Founded 1970.

AMERICAN INDIAN LAWYER TRAINING PROGRAM, INC.
1712 N St., N.W., 3rd Floor
Washington, D.C. 20036
  Sharon Parker, Coordinator

AMERICAN INDIAN LIBERATION CRUSADE, INC.
4009 S. Halldale Ave.
Los Angeles, California 90062-1851
(213) 299-1810
  Dr. Henry E. Hedrick, Director

Purpose: To act as an information center, making known the needs of the American Indian; to help the Indians, both spiritually and materially. *Programs: The American Indian Hour*—the radio voice of the American Indian Liberation Crusade—broadcasts on 17 radio stations across the country. Located at P.O. Box 4187, Inglewood, California 90309-4187; relief ministry to Indian families on several major reservations; sending Indian children to summer Bible Camp; building Indian churches; supporting native pastors and missionaries. *Publication: Indian Crusader,* quarterly. Founded 1952.

AMERICAN INDIAN LIBRARY ASSOCIATION (AILA)
American Library Association
Office of Library Outreach Services (OLOS)
50 East Huron St.
Chicago, Illinois 60611
(312) 944-6780
  Rhonda Harris Taylor, President (AILA)
  Jean E. Coleman, Director, (OLOS)
  Janice M. Beaudin, Chairwoman, Committee on
  Library Services for American Indian People

AMERICAN INDIAN LORE ASSOCIATION
P.O. Box 9698
Anaheim, California 92802
  Stephen S. Jones, Director

Students and patrons of the Indian arts, crafts and history. *Purpose:* To study, interpret, and perpetuate the lore of the historical American Indian. *Award: Catlin Peace Pipe Award,* annual. *Publication: The Evanpaha,* bimonthly. Museum. Library. Founded 1957.

AMERICAN INDIAN MOVEMENT (AIM)
1209 Fourth St., S.E.
Minneapolis, Minnesota 55414
(612) 331-8862
  Clyde Howard Bellecourt, Director

Membership: 5,000. American Indians. *Purpose:* To encourage self-determination among American Indians; to establish international recognition of American Indian treaty rights. *Activities:* Founded Heart of the Earth Survival School which enrolls 600 Indian students in pre-school to adult programs; maintains historical archives; offers charitable, educational, and children's services; speakers bureau; conducts research. *Publication: Survival News,* quarterly. Founded 1968.

AMERICAN INDIAN NATIONAL BANK
1700 K St., N.W., Suite 2000
Washington, D.C. 20006
(202) 887-5252
  Alan Parker, President

Publishes newsletter.

AMERICAN INDIAN REGISTRY FOR THE PERFORMING ARTS
3390 Barham Blvd., Suite 208
Los Angeles, California 90068
(213) 851-9874

Publication: The American Indian Talent Directory.

AMERICAN INDIAN REFUGEES
P.O. Box 015368
Miami, Florida 33101
Alonzo M. Barker, President

Descendants of American Indian refugees; Indians who are non-reservation and non-tribal. *Purpose:* To acquire land for a tribal-communal way of life; attempts to help Indians gain economic self-sustenance through faith in self. Founded 1974.

AMERICAN INDIAN RESEARCH AND RESOURCE INSTITUTE
Gettysburg College
P.O. Box 576
Gettysburg, Pennsylvania 17325
(717) 337-6265
Dr. Frank W. Porter, III, Director

Purpose: To study the history and culture of American Indians, with emphasis on tribes residing in the eastern U.S.; to provide technical assistance to nonrecognized tribes seeking Federal acknowledgment from the B.I.A. Founded 1983.

AMERICAN INDIAN SCHOLARSHIPS
5106 Grand Ave., NE
Albuquerque, New Mexico 87108
(505) 265-8335
Lorraine P. Edmo, Director

Purpose: To provide scholarship assistance for Indian students at the graduate level; to encourage colleges and universities to cooperate in financial assistance to those Indian students receiving its grants. *Activities:* Bestows awards; maintains placement service. *Publication:* Quarterly newsletter. Founded 1969.

AMERICAN INDIAN SCIENCE AND ENGINEERING SOCIETY
1310 College Ave., Suite 1220
Boulder, Colorado 80302
(303) 492-8658
Norbert S. Hill, Jr., Executive Director

Membership: 425. American Indian and non-Indian students and professionals in science, technology, and engineering fields. *Purpose:* Seeks to motivate and encourage students to pursue graduate studies in science, engineering and technology. *Activities:* Bestows awards; maintains speakers bureau and placement service. *Publications: On the Way Up,* 3/yr.; newsletter

AMERICAN INDIAN TALENT SOCIETY
2225 Cavell Ave. North
Golden Valley, Minnesota 55427
Chris Spotted Eagle, Director

AMERICAN NATIVE PRESS RESEARCH ASSOCIATION
American Indian and Alaska Native Periodicals Research Clearinghouse
Stabler Hall 502, University of Arkansas
33rd and University Ave.
Little Rock, Arkansas 72204

AMERICAN SOCIETY FOR CONSERVATION ARCHAEOLOGY
Museum of New Mexico
P.O. Box 2087
Santa Fe, New Mexico 87503
(505) 827-8941
Curtis F. Schaafsma, President

Membership: 500. Promotes and coordinates activities, including public education which aid in the preservation and protection of historic and prehistoric archaeological resources. *Publications:* Bi-monthly report; directory; scholarly articles. Founded 1974.

AMERICAN SOCIETY FOR ETHNOHISTORY
Department of Anthropology
Texas Tech University
Lubbock, Texas 79409
(806) 742-2228
Philip A. Dennis, Secretary/Treasurer

Membership: 1,100. Anthropologists, historians, geographers, etc. *Purpose:* To promote and encourage original research relating to the cultural history of ethnic groups worldwide. *Awards:* Robert F. Heizer Award, annual for best article concerning ethnohistory; and Ermine Wheeler-Voegel Award, annual for best book-length work in ethnohistory. *Publication. Ethnohistory,* quarterly. Founded 1953.

AMERICAN STUDIES ASSOCIATION
307 College Hall/CO
University of Pennsylvania
Philadelphia, Pennsylvania 19104
(215) 898-5408
John F. Stephens, Executive Director

Membership: 2,200. Persons concerned with American culture. *Purpose:* To promote the interdisciplinary study of American culture. *Publication: American Quarterly; ASA Newsletter; American Studies: An Annotated Bibliography.* Founded 1951.

AMERICANS FOR INDIAN OPPORTUNITY
1010 Massachusetts Ave., N.W., Suite 200
Washington, D.C. 20001
(202) 371-1280
LaDonna Harris, Executive Director

Promotes economic self-sufficiency for American Indian tribes and individuals, and political self-government for members of American Indian tribes. *Purpose:* To help American Indians, Eskimos and Aleuts establish self-help programs at the local level; to improve communications among Native-Americans and with non-Indians; and to educate the public on the achievements and needs of Native-Americans today. *Activities:* Supports Indian action projects in education, health, housing, job development, and training and opportunities for Indian young people; conducts research; bestows awards; holds seminars and weekly meetings for Indian interest groups. *Publication: Red Alert,* irregular; *You Don't Have to Be Poor to Be Indian.* Founded 1970.

THE AMERIND FOUNDATION, INC.
Dragoon, Arizona 85609
(602) 586-3003
Anne I. Woosley, Ph.D., Director

Conducts research in anthropology and archaeology of the greater American Southwest and Northern Mexico, and in ethnology of the Western Hemisphere. Publishes monograph series in archaeology of the Southwest and Northern Mexico. Museum. Library. Founded 1937.

ANTHROPOLOGY FILM CENTER FOUNDATION
P.O. Box 493
Santa Fe, New Mexico 87594-0493
(505) 983-4127
Joan S. Williams, Director

Purpose: To further scholarship, research and practice in visual anthropology through consultation and research services, seminars, publications, teaching, equipment outfitting and specialized facilities. *Program:* Intensive 9 month filmmaking program stressing cultural factors in documentary film production. American Indian graduates: Larry Littlebird, Rain Parrish, George Burdeau, and Ron Sarracino, and others. *Publication: Filmography for American Indian Education.* Library-Archives. Founded 1971.

ANTHROPOLOGY RESOURCE CENTER
P.O. Box 15266
Washington, D.C. 20003
(703) 237-5376
Dr. Shelton H. Davis, Director

Membership: 8,000. Serves as a documentation and information center on land and economic issues involving Native-Americans and other indigenous peoples. *Publication: Global Reporter,* quarterly journal; books. Founded 1975.

ARCHAEOLOGICAL CONSERVANCY
415 Orchard Dr.
Santa Fe, New Mexico 87501
(505) 982-3278
Mark Michel, President

Membership: 2,000. People interested in preserving prehistoric and historic sites for interpretive or research purposes. *Purpose:* To acquire for permanent preservation the ruins of past American cultures, primarily those of American Indians. *Publication:* quarterly newsletter. Founded 1979.

ARCHAEOLOGICAL INSTITUTE OF AMERICA
P.O. Box 1901, Kensmore Station
Boston, Massachusetts 02215
(617) 353-9361
Raymond A. Liddell, Executive Director

Membership: 9,500. Educational and scientific society of archaeologists and others interested in archaeological study and research. *Publication: Archaeology,* bi-monthly; *American Journal of Archaeology,* quarterly. Founded 1879.

ARROW, INC.(AMERICANS FOR THE RESTITUTION AND RIGHTING OF OLD WRONGS)
1000 Connecticut Ave., N.W.
Washington, D.C. 20036
(202) 296-0685
Thomas Colosimo, Executive Director

Purpose: The betterment of American Indian health, education and justice. *Activities:* Undertakes constructive efforts at the reservation level embracing direct aid, education, health and training; recruits physicians and RN's from the private sector to help fill shortages at Indian hospitals; conducts training for Indian court and law enforcement personnel. *Committees:* American Indian Court System Improvement; and, National American Indian Youth. Founded 1949.

ASSOCIATED EXECUTIVE COMMITTEE OF FRIENDS OF INDIAN AFFAIRS
c/o Sterett L. Nash
612 Plum St.
Frankton, Indiana 46004
(317) 754-7977

Missionary project of the Religious Society of Friends (Quakers.) Work is concentrated in Indian Centers in Oklahoma and Alabama. *Publication: Indian Progress,* 3/yr. Founded 1869.

ASSOCIATED INDIGENOUS COMMUNICATIONS (AICom)
P.O. Box 71
Highland, Maryland 20777
(301) 854-0499
Dr. John Mohawk, President

Provides computer communication systems to Native American organizations, businesses, and individuals. Library. Founded 1985.

ASSOCIATION OF AMERICAN INDIAN AFFAIRS
95 Madison Ave.
New York, New York 10016
(212) 689-8720
Dr. Idrian N. Resnick, Executive Director

Membership: 50,000. *Purpose:* To assist Indian and Alaska Native communities in their efforts to achieve full economic, social, and civil equality, and to defend their rights. *Programs:* Conducts programs in Indian community and economic development, health, education, legal defense, and public education. Aids Indian tribes in mobilizing all available—federal, state and private—for a coordinated attack on the problems of poverty and injustice, and protects the constitutional and treaty rights of Native peoples, as well as their special aboriginal rights; the Emergency Aid Scholarship program provides grants of up to $300 to American Indian and Alaska Native college students. *Publications: Indian Affairs,* quarterly newsletter; *Indian Family Defense,* quarterly bulletin; *Indian Natural Resources,* quarterly; *Appointment Calendar; To Sing Our Own Songs: Cognition and Culture in Indian Education; The Destruction of American Indian Families.* Founded 1923.

ASSOCIATION OF AMERICAN INDIAN PHYSICIANS
6805 S. Western, Suite 504
Oklahoma City, Oklahoma 73139
(405) 631-0447
Terry Hunter, Executive Director

Membership: 80. Physicians (M.D. or D.O.) of 1/8 American Indian descent or more. *Purpose:* To encourage and recruit American Indians into the health professions; to provide a forum for the interchange of ideas and information of mutual interest between physicians; to make recommendations to government agencies regarding the health of American Indians and Alaska Natives; to enter into contracts with these agencies to provide consultation and other expert opinions regarding health care of American Indians and Alaska Natives. *Activities:* Seeks scholarship funds for Indian professional students; conducts seminars for students interested in health careers. *Publications:* Quarterly newsletter; *American Indian Health Careers Handbook.* Founded 1971.

ASSOCIATION OF CONTRACT TRIBAL SCHOOLS
c/o St. Francis Indian School
P.O. Box 155
St. Francis, South Dakota 57572
(605) 747-2296

Membership: 22. American Indian controlled schools organized under the Indian Self-Determination and Educational Assistance Act. *Purpose:* To provide technical assistance in making self-determination contracts. *Publication: ACTS Newsletter,* monthly; directory is planned. Founded 1982.

ATLATL
402 West Roosevelt
Phoenix, Arizona 85003
(602) 253-2731
Erin Younger, Executive Director

A non-profit Native American arts service organization founded as a national advocate for Native American art. *Activities:* Traveling Exhibit Service (circulate Native American art exhibits); offers technical assistance and consulting services; maintains resource files; slide packets of Native American arts. *Publications: Native Arts Update,* quarterly newsletter; periodic special reports *(Survey of State Arts Agency Support of Native Arts Programs); Women of Sweetgrass, Cedar and Sage* (exhibit catalog.) Founded 1977.

THE BEAR TRIBE
P.O. Box 9167
Spokane, Washington 99209
(509) 326-6561
Sun Bear, Founder; Wabun James, Executive Director

An educational organization. *Purpose:* "To teach people respect for the earth as the giver and sustainer of life. It uses the Native American ways of viewing the earth to help people find their connection with the earth so that people will begin to think about the effects of their actions on the earth." *Activities:* Educational workshops, lectures, tours, survival camps, visitor programs; operates a bookstore/mail order business; offers a barter or trade system for people who want to take their programs but cannot afford them—they offer their skills in return for the programs. *Publications: The Path of Power; The Medicine Wheel Book; Buffalo Hearts; The Self-Reliance Book.* Founded 1971.

**BUFFALO BILL
MEMORIAL ASSOCIATION**
Buffalo Bill Historical Center
P.O. Box 1000
Cody, Wyoming 82414
(307) 587-4771
(800) 533-3838
Peter H. Hassrick, Director

Purpose: The preservation and exhibition of
Western Americana pertaining to Rocky
Mountain and Northern Plains region. *Activities:*
Operates the Buffalo Bill Museum, Whitney
Gallery of Western Art, the Winchester Arms
Museum, and the Plains Indian Museum.
Publications: American West, 6/yr.; quarterly
newsletter. Library. Founded 1917.

**BUREAU OF CATHOLIC INDIAN
MISSIONS**
2021 H St., N.W.
Washington, D.C. 20002
(202) 331-8542
Rev. Msgr. Paul A. Lenz, Executive Director

Purpose: The support of Catholic Indian
missions, parishes, schools, centers, and activities;
the advocacy for national legislation for the
benefit of all American Indian tribes, pueblos,
nations. *Activities:* Participation in the
Tekakwitha Conference; testimony to
congressional committees on legislation affecting
Indian groups; presentations on Indian issues to
organizations; grants to Catholic Indian
organizations through the diocese in which they
are located. *Publication:* Monthly newsletter.
Archives—located in the library at Marquette
University, Milwaukee, Wisconsin. Founded
1874.

**CENTER FOR PACIFIC
NORTHWEST STUDIES**
Western Washington University
High St.
Bellingham, Washington 98225
(206) 676-3284/3125
Dr. James W. Scott

Purpose: To collect materials of every sort—
manuscripts, business records, maps,
photographs, tapes, etc.—of the people and
activities of the Pacific Northwest, past and
present. Publishes two series: *Occasional Papers*
(21 to-date) and *Informational Papers* (5 to-date.)
Archive-Library. Founded 1971.

CHEROKEE HISTORICAL ASSOCIATION
P.O. Box 398
Cherokee, North Carolina 28719
(704) 497-2111
Dr. Ed Hanson, Executive Director

Purpose: To preserve history and culture of the

Eastern Band of Cherokee Indians. *Exhibits:*
"Unto These Hills", an outdoor drama of the
Cherokee Indian; the Oconaluftee Indian Village,
a replica of a Cherokee community of the 1750
period; and the Cherokee Cyclorama Wax
Museum. *Scholarships:* Awards 8 to 10
scholarships each year in the amount of $500 each,
but the recipients must be an enrolled member of
the Eastern Band of Cherokee Indians, or the son
or daughter of an enrolled member. Founded
1948.

**CONFEDERATION OF AMERICAN
INDIANS**
P.O. Box 5474
New York, New York 10163
(212) 972-1020
Daniel McCord, Executive Director

Purpose: Seeks to promote the public image of
American Indians; to improve their social,
educational, cultural, health, and economic
opportunities; and to preserve their history and
heritage. *Activities:* Sponsors organizations
aimed at specific interest groups, including:
Council of American Indian Artists, American
Indian Economic Development, and Gay
American Indians; bestows honorary
memberships, and the *Sequoyah Award, for
projects in American Indian education. Library.
Founded 1982.*

**CONTINENTAL CONFEDERATION
OF ADOPTED INDIANS**
P.O. Box 9698
Anaheim, California 92802
Stephen S. Jones, Jr., Chief

Membership: 150. Non-Indians who have been
presented with honorary tribal chieftainship, an
official Indian name, or recipients of any other
Indian-oriented awards. Membership also open
to blooded Indians. *Activities:* Maintains Indian
Lore Hall of Fame; maintains speakers bureau;
bestows annual National Catlin Peace Pipe
Achievement Award. *Publication: The
Evanpaha,* bimonthly bulletin. Founded 1950.

**COUNCIL FOR NATIVE AMERICAN
INDIAN PROGRESS**
280 Broadway, Suite 316
New York, New York 10007
(212) 732-0485
Walter S. James, Jr., Executive Director

Membership: 900. Individuals interested in the
holistic philosophies and teachings of the earlier
indigenous groups of North and Central America.
Publications: Earth Walk and *Four Directions for
Peace and Medicine Lodge,* both newsletters.
Founded 1974.

COUNCIL FOR TRIBAL EMPLOYMENT RIGHTS (CTER)
19540 Pacific Highway South, Suite 102
Seattle, Washington 98188
(206) 878-3000

(Southwest Regional Office)
301 W. Indian School Rd., Suite 126
Phoenix, Arizona 85013
(602) 234-1871

COUNCIL OF AMERICAN INDIAN ARTISTS
P.O. Box 5474
New York, New York 10163
Adam Starchild, Chairman

Sponsored by the Confederation of American Indians. *Activities:* Promotes educational programs on American Indian art, including the Certified American Indian Design Program, which identifies authentic American Indian designs used in jewelry, clothing, fabric, etc.; presents grants to American Indian artists and offers apprenticeship and scholarship programs for American Indian students. Founded 1981.

COUNCIL OF ENERGY RESOURCE TRIBES (CERT)
1580 Logan St.
Denver, Colorado 80203
(303) 832-6600
David Lester, Executive Director

Membership: 40. American Indian tribes owning energy resources. *Purpose:* To promote the general welfare of members through the protection, conservation, control and prudent management of their oil, coal, natural gas, uranium, and other resources. *Activities:* Provides on-site, technical assistance to tribes in energy resource management; conducts programs to enhance tribal planning and management capacities; sponsors workshops. Founded 1975.

COUNCIL ON TRIBAL EMPLOYMENT
918 16th St., N.W., Suite 503
Washington, D.C. 20006

CRAZY HORSE FOUNDATION
Avenue of the Chiefs
The Black Hills
Crazy Horse, South Dakota 57730
(605) 673-4681
Ruth Ziolkowski, Chairwoman of the Board

Purpose: To carve a mountain (Thunderhead Mountain) into the memorial statue of the Sioux Chief Crazy Horse, astride his pony, pointing to the lands of his people (563' high and 641' long.) Begun by sculptor Korczak Ziolkowski, 1908-1982; and to build and maintain a university, museum, and medical center for the Indians.

Activities: Offers scholarships to Native-Americans. *Publications: Crazy Horse Progress,* quarterly newsletter; *Korczak: Storyteller in Stone* (biography); *Crazy Horse and Korczak.* Library. Founded 1948.

CREEK INDIAN MEMORIAL ASSOCIATION
Creek Council House Museum
Town Square
Okmulgee, Oklahoma 74447
(918) 756-2324
Mary Volturo, President

Membership: 120. *Activities:* Operates Museum of Creek Indian Culture; publishes booklets and leaflets on Creek history and legend. Founded 1914.

EARLY SITES RESEARCH SOCIETY
Long Hill
Rowley, Massachusetts 01969
(617) 940-2410
James P. Whittall, Director

Membership: 235. *Purpose:* To research and record unknown stonework, petroglyphs, artifacts, and other material in New England and related areas. *Activities:* Archaeological Field School; research awards, and art/archaeological grant; video material. *Publications:* Newsletter; bulletin; other occasional publications. Museum. Library. Founded 1973.

THE EDUCATIONAL FOUNDATION OF AMERICA
35 Church Lane
Westport, Connecticut 06880
(203) 226-6498

Provides educational grants—aid for American Indians. Grant application office: c/o Richard W. Hansen, 16250 Ventura Blvd., Suite 445, Encino, California 91436.

FIVE CIVILIZED TRIBES FOUNDATION
c/o Chickasaw Nation
P.O. Box 1548
Ada, Oklahoma 74820
(405) 436-2603
Overton James, Chairman

Comprised of the Cherokee, Choctaw, Chickasaw, Creek, and Seminole Nations of Oklahoma. *Purpose:* To provide coordination to tribal activities and programs including social programs, industrial development, and administrative activities; and provides representation for the tribes at the national level. Founded 1974.

FUTURES FOR CHILDREN
805 Tijeras, N.W.
Albuquerque, New Mexico 87102
(505) 247-4700
Ruth T. Frazier, President

Purpose: To promote American Indian community development through self-reliance. *Programs:* Community Self-Help Programs for Indian people. Currently working among Southwest American Indian tribes; maintains speakers bureau and children's services. Financial assistance to sponsored students from nine tribes in the Southwest. *Publication: Semiannual newsletter. Library. Founded 1961.*

GAY AMERICAN INDIANS
P.O. Box 5474
New York, New York 10163
(212) 972-1020
David McCord, Executive Director

Sponsored by the Confederation of American Indians. *Purpose:* To provide gay Indians with a sense of identity and to aid in establishing contact with other gay people at a national level through social and educational activities. Founded 1982.

GREAT COUNCIL OF U.S. IMPROVED ORDER OF RED MEN
P.O. Box 683
Waco, Texas 76703
(817) 756-1221
Robert E. Davus, National Secretary

Membership: 54,000. *Goals:* Freedom, friendship and charity. *Activities:* sponsors the education of approximately 200 American Indian children through Save the Children Federation; active in A.I.D., American Indians for Development. The Degree of Pocahontas—a degree of the Great Council for Red Men and their female relatives and friends. *Publications: Red Men Magazine,* 4/yr.; *History of Improved Order of Red Men.* Founded 1765.

GROTTO FOUNDATION, INC.
West - 2090 First National Bank Bldg.
St. Paul, Minnesota 55101
(612) 224-9431
A.A. Heckman, Executive Director

Provides grants for special projects relating to American Indians.

HAHN (PHILIP Y.) FOUNDATION
c/o California First Bank
P.O. Box B
Rancho Santa Fe, California 92067
(714) 294-4592
c/o Gilbert L. Brown, Jr., Manager
Alcala Park
San Diego, California 92110

Provides financial aid for needy American Indian children in the Southwest.

INDIAN ARTS AND CRAFTS ASSOCIATION
4215 Lead S.E.
Albuquerque, New Mexico 87108
(505) 265-9149
Dave Lewis, Executive Director

Purpose: To promote, preserve, and protect Indian arts and crafts. *Activities:* Semi-annual wholesale markets for retailers only; marketing information; Artist of the Year Prints. *Award:* Artist of the Year Award, annually, $200 and prints from limited edition. *Publications: Newsletter,* monthly; brochures for point-of-purchase distribution. Founded 1974.

INDIAN ARTS AND CRAFTS BOARD
Room 4004, U.S. Dept. of the Interior
Washington, D.C. 20240
(202) 343-2773
Robert G. Hart, General Manager

Purpose: To promote the development of Indian arts and crafts. *Activities:* Provides business and personal professional advice, information, and promotion to Native-American artists and craftsmen and their organizations; operates three regional museums: Museum of the Plains Indian and Crafts Center, Browning, Montana; Sioux Indian Museum and Cultural Center, Rapid City, South Dakota; and, Southern Plains Indian Museum and Cultural Center, Anadarko, Oklahoma. *Publication: Indian, Eskimo, Aleut Owned and Operated Arts Businesses Source Directory.* Founded 1936.

INDIAN EDUCATION INFORMATION SERVICE
ComTec, Inc.
1228 M St., N.W.
Washington, D.C. 20005

INDIAN HEALTH SERVICE
U.S. Department of Health and Human Services
5600 Fishers Lane, Parklawn Bldg.
Rockville, Maryland 20857
(301) 443-1083
Everett R. Rhoades, M.D., Director

Provides a full range of curative, preventive, and rehabilitative services for approximately one million eligible American Indians and Alaskan Natives. See Indian Health Service section for names and locations of facilities across the U.S.

INDIAN LAW RESOURCE CENTER
601 E St., S.E.
Washington, D.C. 20003
(202) 547-2800
Robert T. Coulter, Director

A legal, educational, counseling, and research service for American Indians and other Indians in the Western Hemisphere. *Purpose: Seeks to enable Indian people to survive as distinct peoples with unique living cultures; to combat discrimination and injustice in the law and in education. Activities:* Engages in human rights advocacy on behalf of Indians at the U.N.; offers free legal help; conducts research and educational programs. *Publications:* Articles, reports, and reprints. Founded 1978.

INDIAN RIGHTS ASSOCIATION
1505 Race St.
Philadelphia, Pennsylvania 19102
  (215) 563-8349
    Melanie Beth Oliviero, Ph.D., Executive Director

The oldest, continuous Indian advocacy organization in North America. *Purpose:* To assist Native-Americans in the full exercise of their social and legal rights. *Activities:* Education—informs both Indian and non Indian audiences on the nature of these rights; Technical Assistance—provides specific counsel for Indian individuals and tribes; Research—performs detailed investigations of timely policy issues; Advocacy— supports Indian people through presentations, testimony, and workshops. *Grants and awards:* Made on a discretionary basis— eligibility determined by the merit of the request, the proven management responsibility of the recipient, and the availability of funds. *Publication: Indian Truth,* bimonthly news journal; *The Aggressions of Civilization: Federal Indian Policy Since the 1880's.* Library. Founded 1882.

INDIAN YOUTH OF AMERICA
P.O. Box 2786
4509 Stone Ave.
Sioux City, Iowa 51106
  (712) 276-0794
    Patricia Trudell Gordon, Executive Director

Purpose: To improve the lives of Indian children; to inform families, social service agencies, and courts on the rights of Indian people under the Indian Child Welfare Act. *Program:* The American Indian Child Service Program— attempts to prevent the distressful effects brought on by the breakup of Indian families. *Facility:* Resource Center. *Publications:* Newsletter and brochure. Founded 1978.

INDIGENOUS PEOPLE'S NETWORK
P.O. Box 384
Rochester, Vermont 05767
  (802) 767-3324
    John Mohawk, Co-Director

Membership: 1,600. *Purpose:* To provide communications services and information to people in remote areas that have little access to public media; to disseminate information on threats to the existence of indigenous people. *Activities:* Maintains speakers bureau. *Publications: Native Peoples in Struggle* (book); weekly reports; emergency bulletins. Founded 1983.

INSTITUTE FOR THE DEVELOPMENT OF INDIAN LAW
1104 Glyndon St., S.E.
Vienna, Virginia 22180
  (703) 938-7822
    K. Kirke Kickingbird, Executive Director

Public interest law firm which functions as a research training center on federal Indian law, with emphasis on Indian sovereignty, encouragement of Indian self-confidence and self-government, and clarification of historical and legal foundations of modern Indian rights. *Activities:* Research and analysis; training and technical assistance; litigation; publication. *Programs:* American Indian Legal Studies; American Indian Life Coping Skills; and Indian Legal Curriculum and Training. *Publication: American Indian Journal,* monthly; books and films available. Founded 1971.

INSTITUTE FOR NATIVE AMERICAN DEVELOPMENT (INAD) NATIVE AMERICANN STUDIES (NAS)
1812 Las Lomas Dr., N.E.
University of New Mexico
Albuquerque, New Mexico 87131
  (505) 277-3917
    Ted Jojola, Director

Purpose: (INAD): To advocate and develop research for and with Native-Americans and their communities; (NAS): To develop and promote regional studies of Native-Americans, their concerns and their communities. *Activities:* Varies from year-to-year; sponsors lecture series, specialized seminars and conferences; regular course offerings. Publications. Library. Founded: (INAD) 1980; (NAS) 1971.

INSTITUTE OF AMERICAN INDIAN ARTS
College of Santa Fe Campus
Alexis Hall, St. Michaels Dr.
Santa Fe, New Mexico 87501
  (505) 988-6463
    Jon C. Wade, President

Administered by the Bureau of Indian Affairs. Offers learning opportunities in the arts and crafts to Native American youth (Indian, Eskimo and Aleut.) Emphasis is placed upon Indian traditions as the basis for creative expression in the fine arts.

Activities: Sponsors Indian arts-oriented Junior College offering Associate of Fine Arts degrees in various fields; biographical archives. *Publications: Coyote on the Turtle's Back,* annual; *Faculty Handbook and School Catalog,* annual; *Spawning the Medicine River,* annual. Museum and Library. Founded 1962.

INSTITUTE OF EARLY AMERICAN HISTORY AND CULTURE
P.O. Box 220
Williamsburg, Virginia 23187
(804) 229-2771
Thad W. Tate, Director

Purpose: To encourage study and research in American history before 1820, especially but not exclusively, through book and periodical publications, conferences, etc. *Programs:* Do not deal exclusively with American Indian history, but has been significantly represented in its recent activities; book publishing in conjunction with UNC Press. *Award:* Two-Year Postdoctoral Fellowships, annually—research topics on American Indian history, 1500-1820 are eligible. *Publications: The William and Mary Quarterly.* Library. Founded 1943.

INSTITUTE OF INDIAN STUDIES
University of South Dakota
Box 73, Dakota Hall, Room 12
Vermillion, South Dakota 57069

INSTITUTE OF THE GREAT PLAINS
Museum of the Great Plains
P.O. Box 68
601 Ferris, Elmer Thomas Park
Lawton, Oklahoma 73502
(405) 353-5675
Steve Wilson, Director

Membership: 825. *Purpose:* To further the study and understanding of the history, ecology, anthropology, archaeology, and sociology of the Great Plains of North America. *Activities:* Conducts research; maintains the Museum of the Great Plains, the Great Plains Archives, and Library. *Publications: Great Plains Journal,* annual; irregular newsletter; books for sale. Founded 1961.

INTER-AMERICAN INDIAN INSTITUTE
Av. Insurgentes Sur 1690
Col. Florida
Mexico D.F. 01030 MEXICO
(905) 660-0007/660-0132
Dr. Oscar Arze Quintanilla, Director

Activities: Conducts development programs for Indian communities in the Americas; trains technical personnel; investigates culture of extinct Indian groups; provides information services. *Publications: America Indigena;* quarterly journal; books. Library. Founded 1940.

INTER-TRIBAL INDIAN CEREMONIAL ASSOCIATION
P.O. Box 1
Church Rock, New Mexico 87311
(505) 863-3896
Laurence D. Linford, Executive Director

Membership: 375. Indian people, businessmen, dealers in Indian arts and crafts, and other individuals interested in the annual Inter-Tribal Indian Ceremonial, a four day Indian exposition of dances, sports, crafts, rituals and a rodeo, held each August at Gallup, New Mexico. *Activities:* Bestows awards; conducts specialized educational and children's services; maintains biographical archives, and a museum at Red Rock Park; plans a Hall of Fame; publishes educational material for teachers; slides of Ceremonial available. Library. Founded 1922.

INTERNATIONAL INDIAN TREATY COUNCIL
777 U.N. Plaza, Room 10F
New York, New York 10017
(212) 986-6000
William A. Means, Executive Director

An organization of 98 traditional Indian governments formed to draw attention to Indian problems and Indian rights, largely through the efforts of the American Indian Movement. *Activities:* Maintains NGO status with the U.N.; makes regular presentations to the U.N. Commission on Human Rights; maintains research and documentation center in South Dakota, and an American Indian Treaty Council Information Center in New York City. *Publication: Treaty Council News,* monthly. Founded 1974.

LITTLE BIG HORN ASSOCIATES
P.O. Box 633
Boaz, Alabama 35957
(205) 593-9701
W. Donald Horn, Chairman

Membership: 550. *Purpose:* Seeks to learn and preserve "the truth of the battle of the Little Big Horn," and Custer's life. *Activities:* Conducts research; annual conference. *Awards:* LBHA Literary Award; The Dr. Lawrence A. Frost Award. *Publications:* Newsletter, 8/yr.; Research Review, quarterly; books. Founded 1966.

MARQUETTE LEAGUE FOR CATHOLIC INDIAN MISSIONS
1011 First Ave.
New York, New York 10022
(212) 371-1000
Rev. Thomas A. Modugno, Director

Purpose: To provide financial support for the material welfare of Catholic Indian Missions in the U.S. Founded 1904.

McNICKLE (THE D'ARCY) CENTER FOR THE HISTORY OF THE AMERICAN INDIAN
Newberry Library
60 W. Walton St.
Chicago, Illinois 60610
Frederick E. Hoxie, Director
Helen Tanner, Acting Director
David Miller, Associate Director

See Library section for further information.

MIGIZI COMMUNICATIONS, INC.
2300 Cedar Ave. South
Minneapolis, Minnesota 55404
(612) 721-6631
Lori Mollenhoff, President—Board of Directors

Purpose: To provide a national Indian news service. *Goals:* To provide the best balanced coverage of Indian news and information to the American Indian and general public, and to train Indian journalists. *Activities:* Radio production— *First Person Radio,* Jackie Dionne, Producer—half-hour program of American Indian news, information and public affairs programming—the only weekly, nationally distributed American Indian radio program in the U.S.—goes out to over 50 stations in 23 states; produces the weekly local television public affairs program, *Madagimo,* for WUSA-TV, Gary D. Fife, Producer/Host; produces live radio programs, video documentaries, and publications; also produces public affairs announcements for Indian organizations and the City of Minneapolis. *Projects:* American Indian Women into Media, Gertrude Buckanaga, Director—trains high school girls and women in journalism, radio engineering, computer literacy and other skills; Achievement Through Communications, W. Roger Buffalohead, Director—after-school program for Indian high school students that introduces students to the expanding communications field; Media Access Project, Lesley Lilligren, Director—encourages more Indian people to enter media careers; Media Curriculum Project, Laura Waterman Wittstock, Director—to increase the reading skills of elementary students. *Publication: Communicator. ibrary. Founded 1977.*

NATIONAL ADVISORY COUNCIL ON INDIAN EDUCATION
2000 L St., N.W., Suite 574
Washington, D.C. 20036
(202) 634-6160
Lincoln C. White, Executive Director

Purpose: To assist the Secretary of Education in carrying out responsibilities under Section 441(a) of the Indian Education Act (Title IV of P.L. 92-318), through advising Congress, the Secretary of Education, the Under Secretary of Education, and the Assistant Secretary of Elementary and Secondary Education with regard to education programs benefiting Indian children and adults. *Activities:* Full Council/Subcommittee meetings in the field on or near Indian reservations to receive public testimony regarding Title IV monies. *Publications:* Newsletters and annual reports. Library. Founded 1972.

NATIONAL AMERICAN INDIAN CATTLEMAN'S ASSOCIATION
c/o Tim Foster, President
Route 2, Box 2492
Toppenish, Washington 98948
(509) 854-1329

Indian cattle producers. *Purpose:* To carry on all activities necessary for the betterment of the Indian cattle industry; and to serve as clearinghouse for the accumulation and dissemination of information. *Publication:* Monthly newsletter; yearbook. Founded 1974.

NATIONAL AMERICAN INDIAN COURT JUDGES
1000 Connecticut Ave., N.W., Suite 401
Washington, D.C. 20036
(202) 296-0685
E. Thomas Colosimo, Secretary

Membership: 260. Indian court judges. *Purpose:* To improve the American Indian court system throughout the U.S. by furthering knowledge and understanding of it, and maintaining its integrity in providing equal protection to all persons. *Activities:* Offers periodic training sessions on criminal law and family law/child welfare; conducts research and continuing education programs; annual meeting. *Publication: Indian Courts Newsletter,* quarterly. Founded 1968.

NATIONAL ASSOCIATION FOR ETHNIC STUDIES, INC.
1861 Rosemount Ave.
Claremont, California 91711
(714) 625-8070
Helen MacLam, President
Charles C. Irby, Editor of Publications

Purpose: To promote activities and scholarships in the field of ethnic studies. *Activities:* Sponsors Annual Conference on Ethnic and Minority Studies. *Publications: The Ethnic Reporter,* semiannual newsletter; *Explorations in Ethnic Studies,* semiannual; *Explorations in Sights and Sounds,* annual; occasional monographs. Founded 1975.

NATIONAL ASSOCIATION OF BLACKFEET INDIANS
Blackfeet Indian Reservation
Browning, Montana 59417

NATIONAL CENTER FOR AMERICAN INDIAN ALTERNATIVE EDUCATION
P.O. Box 18329, Capitol Hill Station
Denver, Colorado 80218
(303) 861-1052
David Nathan Friend, Executive Director

Purpose: To provide training and educational opportunities to American Indian college students and tribal leaders. *Activities:* Sponsors internships nationwide and specially designed workshops; conducts research and community programs; sponsors competitive scholarships for outstanding American Indian college students; annual meeting. *Publication:* Biennial journal. Library. Founded 1960.

NATIONAL CENTER FOR AMERICAN INDIAN MENTAL HEALTH RESEARCH
University of South Dakota
Julian Hall, Room 341
Vermillion, South Dakota 57069

NATIONAL COALITION TO SUPPORT INDIAN TREATIES
814 NE 41st St.
Seattle, Washington 98105
(206) 632-6496
Pamela Wojcik, Director

Local and national non-Indian organizations and individuals who have voiced support for the keeping of claims and treaties signed by the U.S. and Native-Americans. *Purpose:* To educate people to understand Native-American struggles for self-determination and the responsibility bequeathed to the non-native citizenry by the treaties. *Activities:* Maintains speakers bureau; workshops and teach-ins for members; legislative response network.

NATIONAL COMMITTEE ON INDIAN WORSHIP OF THE EPISCOPAL CHURCH
815 Second Ave.
New York, New York 10017

NATIONAL CONGRESS OF AMERICAN INDIANS
804 D St., N.E.
Washington, D.C. 20002
(202) 546-9404
Susan Shown Harjo, Executive Director

Membership: 2,200. Individuals and 155 tribes representing 750,000 Native-Americans. *Purpose:* To protect, conserve and develop Indian natural and human resources; to serve legislative interests of Indian tribes; to improve the health, education, and economic conditions of Native-Americans. *Activities:* Conducts research on Indian problems as service to Indian tribes; bestows congressional awards; administers NCAI fund for educational and charitable purposes; legal aid program;

maintains speakers bureau. *Publications:* *Sentinel,* quarterly newsletter; *Tribal Government Textbook;* annual conference report. Founded 1944.

NATIONAL COUNCIL OF THE BUREAU OF INDIAN AFFAIRS EDUCATORS
P.O. Box 5
Tuba City, Arizona 86045
Patrick J. Carr, President
(602) 283-4211 ext. 252

Purpose: To meet the unique needs and interests of education employees within the BIA's Office of Indian Education Programs. An affiliate of the National Education Association. *Activities:* The exclusive bargaining agent and representative for professional educators in schools within the Albuquerque and Navajo Area Offices; supports programs and projects that will improve the entire educational program in BIA schools. *Publication:* *Smoke Signals,* newsletter. Library. Founded 1966.

NATIONAL GEOGRAPHIC SOCIETY
17th & M Sts., N.W.
Washington, D.C. 20036
(202) 857-7000
Gilbert M. Grosvenor, President

Membership: 10,500,000. *Activities:* Sponsors expeditions and research in geography, archaeology, and ethnology of American Indians; disseminates knowledge through its magazine, maps, books, films, filmstrips, and information services for press, radio and network programs; maintains Explorer's Hall; produces Audiovisual materials for schools; awards gold medals for outstanding achievement. *Publications:* *National Geographic,* monthly magazine; *National Geographic World,* monthly; *National Geographic Research,* quarterly; *National Geographic Traveler,* quarterly. Library. Founded 1888.

NATIONAL INDIAN BUSINESS ASSOCIATION
P.O. Box 8716, Station C
Albuquerque, New Mexico 87108
(505) 299-9317

NATIONAL INDIAN BUSINESS COUNCIL
3575 S. Fox, P.O. Box 1263
Englewood, Colorado 80150-1263
(303) 692-6850
Delbert Militaire, Executive Director

Purpose: To promote the maximum use of Indian and Alaska Native owner businesses. *Activities:* Provides technical assistance and training to Indian and Alaska Native entities; management consultation; training for Indian and Alaska Natives; job marketing and placement assistance;

fund-raising; holds workshops and seminars; maintains a national computerized list of Indian businesses. *Grants:* Educational grants for college to qualified Native-American students. Founded 1983.

NATIONAL INDIAN COUNCIL ON AGING
P.O. Box 2088
Albuquerque, New Mexico 87103
(505) 766-2276
Alfred G. Elgin, Jr., Executive Director

Goal: To bring about improved comprehensive services to the Indians and Alaskan native elderly. *Purpose:* To act as a focal point for the articulation of the needs of Indian elderly. *Activities:* disseminates information on Indian aging programs; provides technical assistance and training to tribal governments and organizations in the development of their programs; conducts research on needs of Indian elderly. *Publication: Elder Voices,* monthly. Biennial conference. Founded 1976.

NATIONAL INDIAN COUNSELORS ASSOCIATION
Center for Counseling Service and Placement
San Diego State University
San Diego, California 92182

NATIONAL INDIAN EDUCATION ASSOCIATION
1115 Second Ave. South
Minneapolis, Minnesota 55403
(612) 333-5341
Karen Cornelius-Fenton, President

Membership: 2,000. *Purpose:* To evaluate and improve the delivery of state and local educational services; and to intercede and establish liaison with state and federal agencies. *Activities:* Conducts an annual National Conference on American Indian Education and holds workshops in conjunction with the conferences; assesses and coordinates existing technical assistance sources. *Scholarship:* John Rouillard Scholarship. Library. Founded 1970.

NATIONAL INDIAN EMPLOYMENT RESOURCE CENTER
2258 South Broadway
Denver, Colorado 80210
(303) 698-2911
Randolph J. Punley, Director

Activities: Promotes the employment of American Indians and Alaska Natives through educational, public relations and related efforts. Library. Founded 1982.

NATIONAL INDIAN HEALTH BOARD
1602 S. Parker Rd., Suite 200
Denver, Colorado 80231
(303) 752-0931
Jake L. Whitecrow, Executive Director

Purpose: To elevate the health status of American Indians and Alaska Natives equal to that of the rest of the U.S. population; to secure maximum tribal and consumer participation in the delivery of health services to Indian people; and, to enhance and promote education of Indian health issues. *Publications: NIHB Health Reporter,* newsletter; health conference report. Library. Founded 1972.

NATIONAL INDIAN LUTHERAN BOARD
35 E. Wacker Dr., Suite 1847
Chicago, Illinois 60641
(312) 726-3791
Eugene Crawford, Executive Director

Purpose: To advocate, on behalf of American Indians, on all areas of concern that Indian people bring before the board. *Activities:* Provides technical assistance; *Grants:* Small grants program to American Indian not-for-profit programs. No grants exceed $4,500. Founded 1970.

NATIONAL INDIAN SOCIAL WORKERS ASSOCIATION, INC.
1740 West 41st St.
Tulsa, Oklahoma 74107
(918) 446-8432
Ethel C. Krepps, President

Purpose: The development, support, and promotion of social services programs which adaquately meet the needs of Indian people and that are consistent with the desires, customs, and lifestyle and traditions of Indians. *Activities:* Annual conference; regional organizations. *Publication:* Quarterly newsletter. Founded 1970.

NATIONAL INDIAN TRADERS ASSOCIATION
3575 South Fox, P.O. Box 1263
Englewood, Colorado 80150-1263
(303) 692-6579
Gerald Smith, Director

Purpose: To provide a clearinghouse for Indian and Alaska Native arts and crafts wholesalers and retailers; promotes the purchase and utilization of Indian produced goods. *Publiction: National Indian Arts and Crafts Directory.* Founded 1985.

NATIONAL INDIAN TRAINING AND RESEARCH CENTER
2121 S. Mill Ave., Suite 216
Tempe, Arizona 85282
(602) 967-9484
Francis McKinley, Executive Director

Purpose: To involve American Indians in leadership and professional roles in training and research projects for the social and economic betterment of Indian people; to orient and train professionals working with American Indians.

Activities: Conduct training programs to educate; sponsors research and development to increase information and knowledge about American Indians. *Publication: Introducing Public School Finance to Native Americans.* Library. Founded 1969.

NATIONAL INDIAN YOUTH COUNCIL
318 Elm St., S.E.
Albuquerque, New Mexico 87102
(505) 266-7966
Gerald Wilkinson, Executive Director

Membership: 20,000. *Purpose:* To provide young Indian people with a working knowledge of serving and understanding their tribal communities and to implement educational resources through research, training and planning on local, regional and national levels. *Activities:* Operates Indian health, education, and employment programs; annual meeting. *Publication: Americans Before Columbus,* bimonthly. Founded 1961.

NATIONAL LEGAL AID AND DEFENDER ASSOCIATION
1625 K St., N.W., 8th Floor
Washington, D.C. 20006
(202) 452-0620
Clinton Lyons, Executive Director

Membership: 2,750. *Purpose:* To provide technical and management assistance to local organizations offering services to poor persons in civil or criminal cases. *Activities: Clearinghouse for information; sponsors research and educational training programs; presents awards. Committee:* Native American Committee. *Publications: Conerstone,* 10/yr.; *Directory of Legal Aid and Defender Offices in the U.S.,* semiannual. Founded 1911.

NATIONAL NATIVE AMERICAN CO-OPERATIVE
P.O. Box 5000
San Carlos, Arizona 85550
(602) 244-8244 ext. 1409
Fred Snyder, Director

Purpose: To provide incentives to Native-Americans for the preservation of their crafts, food, culture, and education. *Activities:* Multi-faceted marketing, barter and trade; information and consultant services; monthly Indian Market, Phoenix, Arizona; American Indian Crafts Cooperative; American Indian Chamber of Commerce. *Traveling Exhibits:* Basketry, beadwork/quillwork; Indian doll collection. *Publication: Native American Directory — Alaska, Canada, U.S.* Library. Founded 1969.

NATIONAL TRIBAL CHAIRMAN'S ASSOCIATION
818 18th St., N.W., Suite 420
Washington, D.C. 20006
(202) 293-0031
Elmer Savilla, Executive Director

Membership: 185. Federally recognized tribes and their leaders. *Purpose:* To provide a united front for elected Indian leaders to consult with government officials. *Activities:* Assists Indian groups in obtaining full rights from federal agencies; monitors federal programs that affect Indians. *Committees:* Education, Health,and Housing. *Publications: List of Tribes and Tribal Leaders,* quarterly; Newsbrief, irregular. Annual Conference. Founded. 1971.

NATIONAL URBAN INDIAN COUNCIL
2258 South Broadway
Denver, Colorado 80210
(303) 698-2911
Gregory W. Frazier, Chief Executive

Purpose: To promote the social and economic self-sufficiency of off-reservation American Indians and Alaska Natives. *Activities:* Community economic development; housing, employment and training; health, education, and advocacy for off-reservation Indian people. *Publication: Source Document of Urban American Indians and Alaska Natives.* Library. Founded 1977.

NATIONAL VIETNAM ERA VETERANS INTER-TRIBAL ASSOCIATION
Vet Center, 411 N. Lincoln Blvd.
Oklahoma City, Oklahoma 73105
(405) 270-5187
Marvin E. Stepson, Chairman of Board

Purpose: To promote the Indian Vietnam Veteran in a positive image; to remember those who gave their lives; to provide a way to express pride; to help and inform each other about problems related to Vietnam; to give Indian Veterans a united voice in veteran's affairs. *Activities:* The Annual National Vietnam Veterans Pow-Wow; a Vietnam Era Veteran's Gourd Clan; a Color Guard; Auxiliary for wives, mothers, daughters, etc. *Publication:* Quarterly newsletter. *Award:* National Honoree. Founded 1981.

NATIVE AMERICAN CONSULTANTS
725 Second St., N.E.
Washington, D.C. 20002
Louis R. Bruce, President

NATIONAL AMERICAN INDIAN HOUSING COUNCIL
P.O. BOX 776
Sells, Arizona 85634

**NATIVE AMERICAN INDIAN
MEDIA CORPORATION**
P.O. Box 59
Strawberry Plains, Tennessee 37871
(615) 933-6246
Frank Eastes, Jr., Executive Director

Purpose: To develop American Indian art and artists, and to develop Indian involvement in the media. *Programs:* Provides low-cost access to professional quality film and video equipment to independent filmmakers; provides equipment access grants; develops and sponsors Indian art projects. Maintains film, video and audio archives. Founded 1981.

NATIVE AMERICAN INDIANS IN MEDIA
P.O. Box 16115, UT Station
Knoxville, Tennessee 37916
Dr. MaCaki Peshewa, Director

**NATIVE AMERICAN MINISTRIES
UNITED PRESBYTERIAN CHURCH—USA**
475 Riverside Dr.
New York, New York 10027
Purpose: To advocate the rights of Native-Americans and to support their efforts in self-determination by making available all types of church resources. Library. Founded 1967.

NATIVE AMERICAN PRESS ASSOCIATION
Native American Rights Fund
1506 Broadway
Boulder, Colorado 80302

**NATIVE AMERICAN PUBLIC
BROADCASTING CONSORTIUM**
P.O. Box 83111
Lincoln, Nebraska 68501
(402) 472-3522
Frank Blythe, Executive Director

Purpose: To encourage the creation, production, promotion and distribution of quality programming by, for and about Native-Americans. *Activities:* New programs are screened and cataloged on a continuous basis from all available sources; bestows awards; makes available a job reference file listing qualified Native-Americans in the media; sponsors workshops. *Publications:* Newsletter, bimonthly; Library Catalog (all programs); *Native American Ascertainment,* three reports on serving Native-American broadcast needs. Library. Found 1977.

**NATIVE AMERICAN RESEARCH
INFORMATION SERVICE**
American Indian Institute
University of Oklahoma
Norman, Oklahoma 73069

NATIVE AMERICAN RIGHTS FUND
1506 Broadway
Boulder, Colorado 80302

(303) 447-8760
John Echohawk, Director

Purpose: The protection of Indian rights; the preservation of tribal existence; the protection of tribal natural resources; the promotion of human rights; the accountability of governments to Native-Americans; and the development of Indian law. *Activities:* Maintains the National Indian Law Library. *Publications: NARF Legal Review,* quarterly; annual report. Founded 1970.

**NATIVE AMERICAN SCIENCE
EDUCATION ASSOCIATION**
P.O. Box 6646, T Street Station
Washington, D.C. 20009-0246
(301) 262-0999 or (202) 638-7066
Gary G. Allen, Executive Director

Affiliated with the Phelps-Stokes Fund. *Purpose:* to nurture educational programs and activities which will increase the quality of education available to Indian students in science and mathematics; to bring together and support the exchange of information between local educators, tribal officials, colleges and universities, and others concerned about science and mathematics; and to explore and encourage careers in the sciences for Native-Americans. *Publication: Kui Tatk,* newsletter. Founded 1982.

**NATIVE CULTURE AND
ECOLOGY FOUNDATION**
2311 Mavis Circle
Tallahassee, Florida 32301

NAVAJO ARTS AND CRAFTS GUILD
P.O. Box 8
Window Rock, Arizona 86515
Purpose: The rehabilitation and better utilization of the resources of the Navajo and Hopi Tribes and reservations as (they) relate to the members of the Navajo Tribe. *Activities:* Maintains retail outlets; operates a mail order business and a wholesale business; crafts exhibit held at the Heard Museum. Founded 1941.

**NEW ENGLAND ANTIQUITIES
RESEARCH ASSOCIATION**
c/o Katherine M. Stannard, Executive Secretary
Three Whitney Dr.
Paxton, Massachusetts 01612
(617) 753-3992

**NORTH AMERICAN INDIAN
MUSEUMS ASSOCIATION**
c/o Seneca Iroquois National Museum
Allegany Indian Reservation
P.O. Box 442
Salamanca, New York 14779
(716) 945-1738
George H.J. Abrams, Chairman

Indian and Native-American cultural centers and tribal museums. *Purpose:* To preserve and perpetuate the traditional cultures, history and art of North American natives through museums. *Activities:* Assists tribal elders and religious leaders in the instruction of Indian children to respect traditional culture; coordinates development of member museums; provides technical assistance and training; sponsors national and regional workshops, internships and museum research. *Publication: Directory of Indian Museums,* annual; newsletter. Founded 1979.

**NORTH AMERICAN INDIAN
WOMEN'S ASSOCIATION**
1420 Mt. Paran Rd., N.W.
Atlanta, Georgia 30327
(404) 266-2848
Carmaleta Littlejohn Monteith, President

Women 18 years old and over who are members of federally recognized tribes. *Purpose:* To promote inter-tribal communications, awareness of the Native-American culture, betterment of family life, health and education. Annual meeting. Founded 1970.

ORDER OF THE INDIAN WARS
P.O. Box 7401
Little Rock, Arkansas 72217
(501) 225-3996
Jerry L. Russell, National Chairman

Membership: 500. Professionals and informal historians interested in the study of the frontier conflicts between the Indians and the white man, and among Indian tribes during the early settlement of the U.S. *Purpose:* Seeks to protect and preserve historic sites related to those wars. *Publications: Journal of the Order of the Indian Wars,* quarterly; *Communique,* monthly. Founded 1979.

**ORGANIZATION OF NORTH AMERICAN
INDIAN STUDENTS**
Four Lee Hall
Northern Michigan University
Marquette, Michigan 49855
(906) 227-1700
Nancie Hatch, Advisor

University students of American Indian ancestry and other interested students. *Purpose:* To encourage pride and identity in Indian culture and tradition; to establish communications among the native communities; to promote scholarships among Indian students attending institutes of higher learning; *Activities:* Sponsors basketweaving seminars; annual Indian Awareness Week. Library. Founded 1971.

PALEO-INDIAN INSTITUTE
Eastern New Mexico University
P.O. Box 2154
Portales, New Mexico 88130

PEOPLE OF THE EARTH
c/o Friends of the Earth
1045 Sansome St.
San Francisco, California 94111
(415) 433-7373
Randall L. Hayes, Director

Purpose: To produce an annual global directory of support groups and organizations cooperating with traditional native peoples who are dedicated to strengthening their sovereignty, self-reliance, and land base. Founded 1981.

**PHELPS-STOKES FUND
AMERICAN INDIAN PROGRAM**
1228 M St., N.W.
Washington, D.C. 20005
(202) 638-7066
Rose W. Robinson, V.P. and Director

Developed and staffed by Indians. *Purpose:* To develop linkages between Indian organizations and the philanthropic community through publications and personal contacts. *Activities:* Serves as a clearinghouse for information about private sector resources for Indian groups and organizations; provides technical assistance in proposal writing and fund-raising; research for foundations and corporations interested in defining their priorities in Indian affairs. *Affiliate:* Native American Science Education Association. *Publication: D.C. Directory of Native American Federal and Private Programs.* Founded 1911.

SAVE THE CHILDREN FEDERATION
54 Wilton Rd.
Westport, Connecticut 06880
(203) 226-7271
David L. Guyer, President

Purpose: To assist children, families and communities in the U.S. and abroad to achieve social and economic stability through community development and family self-help projects; and to aid victims of disaster. *Activities:* Conducts child sponsorship programs and community development projects, with emphasis on community self-help through grass roots organization as well as training and technical assistance; conducts programs on Indian reservations. *Scholarship: Ruth Bronson Memorial Scholarship for American Indian Graduate Students. Publications: Lifeline Magazine,* quarterly; annual reports, and papers on development issues. Library. Founded 1932.

SEALASKA HERITAGE FOUNDATION
Sealaska Corporation
One Sealaska Plaza, Suite 400
Juneau, Alaska 99801

Purpose: Preserves and promotes the cultural traditions of the Tlingit, Haida and Tsimpshian people. Maintains archives to preserve songs, stories, pictures, etc. of native people of southeast Alaska.

SEVENTH GENERATION FUND
FOR INDIAN DEVELOPMENT, INC.
P.O. Box 10
Forestville, California 95436
(707) 887-1559
John Mohawk, Chairman
Dagmar Thorpe, Acting Executive Director

Purpose: Committed to giving pragmatic political and economic reality to the concept of sovereignty. *Activities:* Provides private funding and technical assistance directly to local Indian communities for efforts to deal with their own problems; assists projects to generate and manage funds on their own behalf. *Program:* Operating Program in Economic Development—to develop new approaches to reservation economic development. *Grants:* Makes small seed grants averaging $3,000. *Publications: Native Self-Sufficiency,* quarterly newspaper; *Native Americans and Energy Development II* (book), in cooperation with the Akbar Fund, *American Indian Directions,* newsletter on Indian issues for the philanthropic community; *Field Notes on the Work of Native Women.* Library. Founded 1977.

SMOKI PEOPLE
P.O. Box 123
Prescott, Arizona 86302
(602) 778-5228
John Erickson, Chief

Membership: 1,750. Local business and professional people (non-Indian.) *Purpose:* To perpetuate by authentic artistic reproduction of the age-old ceremonials and dances of Indian tribes of North and South America. *Publication: Smoki Ceremonials and Snake Dance,* annual. Museum. Library. Annual meeting. Founded 1921.

SOCIETY FOR AMERICAN
ARCHAEOLOGY
1511 K St., N.W., Suite 716
Washington, D.C. 20005
(202) 638-6079
Jerome A. Miller, Executive Director

Membership: 4,500. *Purpose:* To stimulate scientific research in the archaeology of the New World by creating closer professional relations among archaeologists. *Publications: American Antiquity,* quarterly; monthly bulletin.

SOCIETY FOR ETHNOMUSICOLOGY
P.O. Box 2894
Ann Arbor, Michigan 48106
(313) 665-9400
William P. Malm, Director

Membership: 2,000. Ethnomusicologists, anthropologists, musicologists, and laymen interested in music as an aspect of culture. *Purpose:* Seeks to integrate the study of manifold facets of non-Western music with Western folk and art music. *Awards:* Seeger Prize and Jaap Kunst Prize. *Publications: Ethnomusicology,* 3/yr.; Directory, 3/yr.; Newsletter, 3/yr.; publishes monographs, bibliographies and pamphlets. Annual Conference. Founded 1955.

SOUTHWEST PARKS
AND MONUMENTS ASSOCIATION
221 N. Court Ave.
Tucson, Arizona 85701
(602) 622-1999
T.J. Priehs, Executive Director

Purpose. To aid in the preservation and interpretation of Southwestern features of outstanding national interests. *Activities:* Sponsors research projects; publishes authoritative literature, and books on Indians, archaeological ruins, and history. Founded 1937.

SURVIVAL OF AMERICAN
INDIAN ASSOCIATIONS
P.O. Box 719
Tacoma, Washington 98401
(206) 456-2567
Hank Adams, National Director

Membership: 500. *Activities:* Provides public education on Indian rights and tribal government reform action; supports independent Indian educational institutions; speakers bureau. *Publication: The Renegade: A Strategy Journal of Indian Opinion,* annual. Founded 1964.

THUNDERBIRD AMERICAN
INDIAN DANCERS
215 West 23rd St.
New York, New York 10011
(212) 741-9221
Louis Motsie, Director

Membership: 30. Indians and non-Indians who raise money for the Thunderbird Indian Scholarship Fund for Indian students. *Activities:* Offers cultural classes in crafts, singing, dancing, and language; sponsors Indian studies programs for Indian youth; monthly pow-wows in New York City—open to public. Founded 1956.

TRUSTEES OF RESERVATIONS
224 Adams St.
Milton, Massachusetts 02186

**UNITED INDIAN
DEVELOPMENT ASSOCIATION**
1541 Wilshire Blvd., Suite 418
Los Angeles, California 90017-2269
(213) 483-1460
Steven L.A. Stallings, President

Purpose: To promote business and economic development among American Indians. *Activities:* Provides management services and technical assistance; sponsors Management Institute— training for Indian managers; workshops and seminars. *Publication: Reporter,* quarterly voice of American Indian business. Library. Annual Indian Progress in Business Conference. Founded 1970.

UNITED INDIAN MISSIONS
P.O. Box U
2920 N. 3rd St.
Flagstaff, Arizona 86002

**UNITED INDIANS OF ALL
TRIBES FOUNDATION**
Day Break Star Arts Center
Discovery Park, Box C-99305
Seattle, Washington 98199
(206) 285-4425
Bernie Whitebear, Executive Director

Purpose: To advocate the interests of Native-Americans by helping to develop and expand Indian economic self-sufficiency, education, and the arts. *Activities:* Sponsors the National Indian Cultural-Educational Center—model education programs, community educational services, technical assistance, adult career education and employment assistance; maintains an Indian dinner theatre. *Publications: Daybreak Star,* monthly magazine; *Indian Educator,* monthly; Native-American curriculum materials for public schools. Museum. Media Center- Library. Founded 1970.

UNITED SOUTH AND EASTERN TRIBES
1101 Kermit Dr., Suite 800
Nashville, Tennessee 37217
(615) 361-8700
Rex Evans, Executive Director

Alliance of Indian tribes: Cherokees (NC), Choctaws (MS), Seminoles and Miccosukees (FL), Senecas (NY), Chitimacha and Coushatta (LA), St. Regis Mohawks (NY), Penobscot, Passamaquoddy and Maliseits (ME). *Activities:* Arranges and sponsors courses of special interest to Indian people; job training and placement; community development services and training; Indian Health Service. *Publication: The Calumet,* bimonthly newsletter. Semiannual meeting. Founded 1968.

**WENNER-GREN FOUNDATION
FOR ANTHROPOLOGICAL RESEARCH**
1865 Broadway
New York, New York 10023
(212) 957-8750
Lita Osmundsen, President

Activities: Provides grants-in-Aid to scholars for research and preparation of publications in all branches of anthropology and in related disciplines. *Publications: Current Anthropology,* bimonthly; issues Viking Fund Publications in Anthropology. Founded 1941.

**WESTERN AMERICA INSTITUTE
FOR EXPLORATION, INC.**
1821 East 9th St.
The Dalles, Oregon 97058
(503) 296-9414
Jay Ellis Ransom, Executive Director

Purpose: To disseminate new knowledge derived from research expeditions in fields of anthropology, archaeology, etc. Primarily concerned with the Aleutian Islands and Interior Alaska, along with the native populations of the Pacific Northwest (ethnography, linguistics, archaeology); currently involved with prehistoric rock structures in Western North America. *Publication: Archaeolinguistics and Paleoethnography of Ancient Rock Structures in Western North America.* Library. Founded 1954.

WINDFEATHER FOUNDATION
8306 Wilshire Blvd.
Beverly Hills, California 90211
Connie Stevens, Founder

WOMEN OF ALL RED NATIONS
P.O. Box 84905
1417 North Dr., No. 10
Sioux Falls, South Dakota 57118
(605) 332-5347
Madonna Thunderhawk, Field Coordinator

A grass roots organization of American Indian women seeking to advance the Native-American movement. *Activities:* Establish local chapters to work on issues like sterilization abuse and women's health, adoption and foster care abuse, community education, and problems caused by energy resource development; publishes reports on health problems of American Indian women. Founded 1978.

CANADA

ABORIGINAL INSTITUTE OF CANADA
4 Newgale St.
Ottawa, Ontario K2H 5R2

ANTHROPOLOGICAL ASSOCIATION OF CANADA
1575 Forlan Dr.
Ottawa, Ontario K2C 0R8
(613) 225-3405

ASSEMBLY OF FIRST NATIONS NATIONAL INDIAN BROTHERHOOD
47 Clarence St., Atrium Bldg., 3rd Floor
Ottawa, Ontario K1N 9K1
(613) 236-0673
Georges Erasmus, National Chief

Purpose: To represent the views and interests of Canada's First Nations in discussions with other levels of government on the issues; education, housing, economic development, health, and forestry; to inform other Canadians about the opportunities and issues relating to First Nation's self-government. *Scholarship: Omer Peters Award:* Educational scholarship. Library. Founded 1969.

CANADA — INDIAN AND NORTHERN AFFAIRS
400 Laurier Ave. West
Ottawa, Ontario K1A 0H4

CANADIAN ALLIANCE IN SOLIDARITY WITH THE NATIVE PEOPLES
16 Spadina Rd.
Toronto, Ontario M5R 2S7
(416) 964-0169
Mary Ann Clarke, President

Membership: 500. Native and non-native people working together to bring a better understanding to non-native people. *Purpose:* To bring awareness issues to the public as identified by native people. *Committees:* Aboriginal Rights, Child Welfare Native, Focus on the Canadian Constitution, Justice, Native Rights, and Prisons. *Publications: Phoenix,* quarterly newsletter; *Native Rights in Canada,* Third Edition. Maintains small resource center. Founded 1960.

CANADIAN HISTORICAL SOCIETY
395 Wellington St.
Ottawa, Ontario K1A 0N3

INDIAN RIGHTS FOR INDIAN WOMEN
19 Slackville St.
Toronto, Ontario M5A 3E1
(416) 368-3524

INSTITUTE FOR ENCYCLOPEDIA OF HUMAN IDEAS ON ULTIMATE REALITY AND MEANING
Regis College, 15 St. Mary St.
Toronto, Ontario M4Y 2R5
(416) 922-2476
Tibor Horvath, Director

Purpose: Interdisciplinary research on human effort to find meaning in our world; specifically how 63 North American and 72 South American Indian linguistic families with their 474 and 505 members respectively expressed the meaning of their lives and their concepts of ultimate reality and meaning. *Activities:* Biennial meetings and publications of essays in journal; scholars-experts in any of 979 American Indian groups listed in the Outline of the Research are welcome to submit essays following the guidelines of the Institute. *Publication: Ultimate Reality and Meaning;* newsletter. Library. Founded 1970.

INTERTRIBAL CHRISTIAN COMMUNICATIONS
P.O. Box 3765, Station B
Winnipeg, Manitoba R2W 3R6
(204) 661-9333

INUIT TAPIRISAT OF CANADA
176 Gloucester St., 3rd Floor
Ottawa, Ontario K2P 0A6
(613) 238-8181

National Inuit association.

NATIONAL ASSOCIATION OF FRIENDSHIP CENTRES
200 Cooper St., Suite 3
Ottawa, Ontario K2P 0G1
(613) 563-4844/5/6
Viola Thomas, President
Raymond Espaniel Hatfield, Executive Director

Purpose: To act in the capacity of social advocate for Canadian Native Peoples in an urban setting by qualifying or lobbying for special projects funding in the areas of Native self-sufficiency, alcohol, drug and solvent abuse counseling, courtwork representation, etc. *Activities:* Handles core support to new and satellite centres, as well as training support, capital constructions, and renovations of existing centres. *Publication:* Monthly nmewsletter. Library.

NATIONAL INDIAN ARTS AND CRAFTS CORPORATION
350 Slater St.
Ottawa, Ontario K1R 5B7

Publication: Canadian Indian Artcrafts, quarterly magazine.

**NATIONAL OFFICE FOR
THE DEVELOPMENT OF
INDIAN CULTURAL EDUCATION**
222 Queen St., 5th Floor
Ottawa, Ontario K1P 5V9
  (613) 232-5315

NATIVE COUNCIL OF CANADA
170 Laurier Ave. West, 5th Floor
Ottawa, Ontario K1P 5V5
  (613) 238-3511

NATIVE LAW CENTRE
University of Saskatchewan
150 Diefenbaker Centre
Saskatoon, Saskatchewan S7K 3S9
  (306) 966-6189
  Don Purich, Director

Purpose: To provide a "head start" program for
people of native ancestry who wish to enter law
school; to research problems related to native
legal rights, e.g. land claims; to provide a resource
to lawyers and researchers working in the area of
native law; and, to back up the courses in native
law taught in the College of Law, University of
Saskatchewan. *Activities:* Summer program of
legal study for native people; research. *Prizes:*
Harvey Bell Memorial Prize, $1,000 for a student
graduating from law school; Native Law Students
Association Writing Competition, $200 book
prize; book prize to student in summer program,
$150. *Publication: Canadian Native Law
Reporter,* quarterly journal; books for sale.
Library.

**NATIVE WOMEN'S ASSOCIATION
OF CANADA**
222 Queen St., 5th Floor
Ottawa, Ontario K1R 5V9
  (613) 236-6057

**NATIVE THEATRE SCHOOL
INDIGENOUS THEATRE CELEBRATION**
Association for Native Development
in the Performing and Visual Arts
27 Carlton St., Suite 208
Toronto, Ontario M5B 1L2
  (416) 977-2512

STATE AND REGIONAL
ASSOCIATIONS

This section is an alpha-geographical listing of state and regional agencies and organizations concerned mainly with Native-American affairs in their particular state and/or region of the U.S. and Canada.

ALABAMA

**ALABAMA INDIAN AFFAIRS
COMMISSION**
339 Dexter Ave., Suite 113
MONTGOMERY 36130

ALASKA

**INSTITUTE OF ALASKA
NATIVE ARTS**
P.O. Box 80583
FAIRBANKS 99708
(907) 456-7491
Jean Flanagan Carlo, Executive Director

Purpose: To provide opportunities for the continued development of the arts of Aleut, Eskimo and Indian people. *Activities:* Workshops and seminars; exhibitions; technical assistance; art study funds; materials inventory; educational material; Alaska Native Artists Resource Bank provides monthly information to native artists. *Scholarships:* The Art Study Funds program awards: "scholarships for academic study," "scholarships for short-term study," and, "fellowships." *Publications:* Bimonthly journal; *Earth Dyes; From Skins, Trees, Quills and Beads: The The Work of Nine Athabascans; Interwoven Expressions,* catalog. Library. Founded 1976.

**ASSISTANT FOR ALASKA
NATIVE AFFAIRS**
Office of the Governor
Pouch A
JUNEAU 99811

**SOUTHEAST ALAKSA
INDIAN CULTURAL CENTER**
P.O. Box 944
SITKA 99835-0944
(907) 747-8061
Jania Garcia, Chairperson

Provides a cultural awareness program about the Southeast Alaska Indians through interpretation, demonstration, and instruction of traditional arts and crafts at Sitka National Historical Park. A job source for Native artists, as well as a means of perpetuation of Southeast Alaskan Native art and culture. See Sitka National Historical Park under *Museums, Monuments and Parks* section.

ARIZONA

**ARIZONA COMMISSION
ON INDIAN AFFAIRS**
1645 W. Jefferson, Suite 433
PHOENIX 85007
Clinton M. Pattea, Chair

**INTER-TRIBAL COUNCIL
OF ARIZONA**
124 W. Thomas Rd., Suite 201
PHOENIX 85013

**ARIZONA ARCHAEOLOGICAL
AND HISTORICAL SOCIETY**
Arizona State Museum
University of Arizona
TUCSON 85721
(602) 621-4011

CALIFORNIA

**AMERICAN INDIAN COUNCIL
OF CENTRAL CALIFORNIA**
P.O. Box 3341
BAKERSFIELD 93385

**SOUTHERN INDIAN
HEALTH COUNCIL, INC.**
P.O. Box 20889
EL CAJON 92021
(619) 561-3700
Orin J. Tonemah, Executive Director

Purpose: To provide health care services to American Indians in the southern part of San Diego County. *Services:* Medical, dental, mental health, social, community health and outreach, environmental health. *Publication:* Newsletter, 6/yr. Founded 1982.

**CALIFORNIA INDIAN
EDUCATION ASSOCIATION**
P.O. Box 4095
MODESTO 95352

UNITED CALIFORNIA INDIANS
2290 Elgin St.
OROVILLE 95965

**CALIFORNIA NATIVE AMERICAN
HERITAGE COMMISSION**
915 Capitol Mall
SACRAMENTO 95814

COLORADO

**COLORADO COMMISSION
ON INDIAN AFFAIRS**
State Capitol Bldg., Room 144
DENVER 80203

**COLORADO INDIAN EMPLOYMENT
ASSISTANCE CENTER**
P.O. Box 10134, University Park Station
DENVER 80210-0134

CONNECTICUT

**CONNECTICUT INDIAN
AFFAIRS COUNCIL**
Department of Environmental Protection
165 Capitol Ave., Room 240
HARTFORD 06106

**AMERICAN INDIANS
FOR DEVELOPMENT, INC.**
P.O. Box 117
236 West Main St.
MERIDEN 06450
 (203) 238-4009
 Patricia Benedict, Executive Director

Purpose: To assist the native American
population in Connecticut through development
of education and employment opportunities, and
to act as a clearinghouse for social service
programs. *Activities:* Emergency food bank; pow-
wows and social events; educational material.
Publication: Bimonthly newsletter.

DELAWARE

OFFICE OF HUMAN RELATIONS
630 State College Rd.
DOVER 19901

FLORIDA

**FLORIDA GOVERNOR'S COUNCIL
ON INDIAN AFFAIRS**
521 E. College Ave.
TALLAHASSEE 32301

GEORGIA

OFFICE OF INDIAN HERITAGE
330 Capitol Ave., S.E.
ATLANTA 30334

HAWAII

**HAWAII COUNCIL
OF AMERICAN INDIAN NATIONS**
910 N. Vineyard Blvd.
HONOLULU 96817
 Joe Ide, Director

IDAHO

AMERICAN INDIAN COORDINATOR
State House
BOISE 83720

IOWA

OFFICE OF THE GOVERNOR
State Capitol
DES MOINES 50319

LOUISIANA

**GOVERNOR'S COMMISSION
ON INDIAN AFFAIRS**
P.O. Box 44455, Capitol Station
BATON ROUGE 70804

MAINE

**MAINE INDIAN AFFAIRS
COMMISSION**
State Health Station No. 38
AUGUSTA 04333

**CENTRAL MAINE
INDIAN ASSOCIATION, INC.**
352 Harlow St.
BANGOR 04401
 (207) 942-2926/2927
 Melvin L. Vicaire, Executive Director

Purpose: To develop and advance the health,
welfare, education, culture, leadership and
opportunity among Native-Americans in Maine.
Activities: Employment and training; substance
abuse counseling; Division of Business
Assistance; children, youth and family services;
food bank. *Publications: The Digest,* bimonthly
newspaper; pamphlets. Library. Founded 1975.

TRIBAL GOVERNORS
93 Maine St.
ORONO 04473

MARYLAND

**MARYLAND COMMISSION
ON INDIAN AFFAIRS**
45 Calvert St.
ANNAPOLIS 21401

MARYLAND INDIAN COUNCIL
P.O. Box 13161
BALTIMORE 21203

**MARYLAND INDIAN
HERITAGE SOCIETY**
P.O. Box 905
WALDORF 20601
(301) 888-1566
J. Hugh Proctor, President

MASSACHUSETTS

**MASSACHUSETTS COMMISSION
ON INDIAN AFFAIRS**
One Ashburton Place, Room 1004
BOSTON 02108
(617) 727-6394
John A. Peters, Executive Director

Consists of seven members of American Indian descent representing the major tribes of the Commonwealth of Massachusetts. Investigates problems common to Native-Americans residing in Massachusetts. *Program:* Native-American scholarship program. Library.

MICHIGAN

**MICHIGAN COMMISSION
FOR INDIAN AFFAIRS**
P.O. Box 30026
611 W. Ottawa St.
LANSING 48909

**INTER-TRIBAL COUNCIL
OF MICHIGAN**
405 E. Easterday Ave.
SAULT STE. MARIE 49783

**MICHIGAN INDIAN CHILD
WELFARE AGENCY**
P.O. Box 537
120 Ridge St.
SAULT STE. MARIE 49783
(906) 635-9400
Gloria McCullough, President
Dwight M. Teeple, Director

Preserves, protects and advances Indian culture and tradition by protecting Native-American families, clans, tribes, communities and groups.

Provides social services, foster care placement, foster home licensing, adoption placement and home studies. *Program:* Family Friend Program. *Publications: Family Friend Training Manual; Model Tribal Adoption Code.*

ABORIGINAL RESEARCH CLUB
c/o Ronald Covitz, President
7090 Valley Brook Rd.
WEST BLOOMFIELD 48033
(313) 626-2235

Professional and amateur archaeologists, historians and ethnologists interested in the archaeology of Michigan, Great Lakes region, and Indians of the area. Library.

MINNESOTA

**MINNESOTA DEPARTMENT
OF INDIAN WORK**
3045 Park Ave.
MINNEAPOLIS 55407

**ASSISTANT TO THE GOVERNOR
FOR INDIAN AFFAIRS**
State Capitol No. 122
ST. PAUL 55155

MINNESOTA HISTORICAL SOCIETY
690 Cedar St.
ST. PAUL 55101

MONTANA

**MONTANA INTER-TRIBAL
POLICY BOARD**
2303 Grand Ave., Suite 5
BILLINGS 59102
(406) 652-3113
Merle R. Lucas, Executive Director

Organized to represent, develop, protect, and advance the economic, cultural, social and political well-being of Indian people in the State of Montana. Provides training and technical assistance to seven Indian reservations in the areas of social services, economic development, law and order, natural resource development, and personnel management.

**MONTANA DEPARTMENT
OF COMMUNITY AFFAIRS**
Indian Affairs Division
1218 E. Sixth Ave.
HELENA 59620

**MONTANA UNITED INDIAN
ASSOCIATION**
436 N. Last Chance Gulch, No. 2
HELENA 59601

NEBRASKA

NEBRASKA INDIAN COMMISSION
P.O. Box 94914, State Capitol
LINCOLN 68509

**NEBRASKA INTER-TRIBAL
DEVELOPMENT CORPORATION**
Route 1, Box 66A
WINNEBAGO 68071

NEVADA

**INTER-TRIBAL COUNCIL
OF NEVADA**
650 S. Rock Blvd., Suite 11
RENO 89502

NEVADA INDIAN COMMISSION
472 Galleti Way
RENO 89431
  (702) 789-0347
  E. Mose, Executive Director

NEW JERSEY

NEW JERSEY INDIAN OFFICE
300 Main St., Suite 3F
ORANGE 07050
  (201) 675-0694
  James Lone Bear Revey, Chairman

Headquarters for the Delaware or Lenape Indians of New Jersey who can trace back to colonial times. Library of historical documents, genealogies; craft and ceremonial items; costume parts, etc. Publications on the Delaware or Lenape Indian are available.

NEW MEXICO

TEN SOUTHERN PUEBLOS COUNCIL
Pueblo of Acoma
P.O. Box 309
ACOMITA 87034

INDIAN ADVISORY COMMISSION
P.O. Box 1667
ALBUQUERQUE 87107

**NEW MEXICO INDIAN
BUSINESS ASSOCIATION**
P.O. Box 2247
ALBUQUERQUE 87103
  (505) 255-4537

**NEW MEXICO INDIAN
EDUCATION ASSOCIATION**
506 Lake St.
ALBUQUERQUE 87105

**STATE TRIBAL
RELATIONS COMMITTEE**
P.O. Box 4456, Station A
ALBUQUERQUE 87196
  (505) 277-5462

**HISTORICAL SOCIETY
OF NEW MEXICO**
Palace of the Governors
SANTA FE 87501

**NEW MEXICO OFFICE
ON INDIAN AFFAIRS**
La Villa Rivera Bldg.
SANTA FE 87501

NEW YORK

**NEW YORK STATE DEPARTMENT
OF INDIAN SERVICES**
General Donovan State Office Bldg.
125 Main St., Room 471
BUFFALO 14203

NORTH CAROLINA

**NORTH CAROLINA COMMISSION
ON INDIAN AFFAIRS**
P.O. Box 27228
227 E. Edenton St., Room 229
RALEIGH 27611

NORTH DAKOTA

**NORTH DAKOTA INDIAN
AFFAIRS COMMISSION**
State Capitol
BISMARCK 58505
  (701) 224-2428
  Juanita J. Helphrey, Executive Director

A liaison/referral agency. *Programs:* Indian Development Fund; Indian Scholarship Program; Native American Alcohol and Drug Abuse Education Program. *Publications: Update,* quarterly newsletter; *Fact Sheet on North Dakota Indian Reservations; Directory of Statewide Indian Programs.* Library.

**DAKOTA WOMEN
OF ALL RED NATIONS**
P.O. Box 516
FORT YATES 58538
(701) 854-7592
Mabel Ann Phillips, Chairperson

Advocacy for Native-American treaty rights.
Program: Health Education Program.
Newsletter.

OKLAHOMA

**OKLAHOMA INDIAN
ARTS AND CRAFTS COOPERATIVE**
P.O. Box 966
ANADARKO 73005
(405) 247-3486
Nettie Standing, Manager

Promotes the careers of contemporary Oklahoma
Indian artists and craftsmen by providing a sales
outlet for their works. Mail order price list
available.

**INTER-TRIBAL COUNCIL
OF NORTHEAST OKLAHOMA**
P.O. Box 1308
MIAMI 74354

**OKLAHOMA ANTHROPOLOGICAL
SOCIETY**
1000 Horn St.
MUSKOGEE 74403
(405) 364-2279
Alicia Jones Hughes, President

Encourages scientific collection, preservation,
classification and study of American Indian
ethnological and archaeological materials.
Newsletter; annual bulletin. Library (members
only.)

**OKLAHOMANS FOR INDIAN
OPPORTUNITY**
555 E. Constitution
NORMAN 73069

Purpose: To improve opportunities for
Oklahoma Indians and draw them more fully into
the Oklahoma economy and culture. *Programs:*
Indian education; job opportunity and training;
housing; health.

OKLAHOMA HISTORICAL SOCIETY
Wiley Post Bldg.
OKLAHOMA CITY 73105
(405) 521-2491
C. Earle Metcalf

Preservation microfilming of documents relating
to the Indian tribes of Oklahoma. An archives and
Manuscripts Division acts as a repository of a

large body of U.S. Government Indian records
and papers of missionaries to the tribes of
Oklahoma. *Publication: Chronicles of
Oklahoma,* quarterly. Library and museum.

**OKLAHOMA INDIAN
AFFAIRS COMMISSION**
4010 N. Lincoln Blvd.
OKLAHOMA CITY 73105

OREGON

**NATIVE AMERICAN REHABILITATION
ASSOCIATION OF THE NORTHWEST**
3020 S.E. Hawthorne
PORTLAND 97214
(503) 231-2641
Donald Graham. President

Operates an outpatient clinic and two residential
treatment centers, Totem Lodge—men and
women and Women's Support Center—women
and children, for the treatment of alcoholism and
alcohol/drug abuse in the Native-American
community with a specialist treatment approach
which embodies Indian cultural awareness and
the philosophy of Alcoholics Anonymous.

COMMISSION ON INDIAN AFFAIRS
454 State Capitol Bldg.
SALEM 97310

**OREGON INDIAN
EDUCATION ASSOCIATION**
1053 Koala North
SALEM 97303

RHODE ISLAND

RHODE ISLAND INDIAN COUNCIL
444 Friendship St.
PROVIDENCE 02907

SOUTH CAROLINA

ASSISTANT TO THE GOVERNOR
P.O. Box 11450
COLUMBIA 29211

**SOUTH CAROLINA COUNCIL
ON NATIVE AMERICANS**
P.O. Box 219221
COLUMBIA 29221

SOUTH DAKOTA

**SOUTH DAKOTA ARCHAEOLOGICAL
RESEARCH CENTER**
P.O. Box 152
FORT MEADE 57741

SOUTH DAKOTA HISTORICAL SOCIETY
Memorial Bldg.
PIERRE 57501

**SOUTH DAKOTA OFFICE
ON INDIAN AFFAIRS**
Kneip Bldg., 2nd Floor
PIERRE 57501

TEXAS

TEXAS INDIAN COMMISSION
P.O. Box 12030, Capitol Station
AUSTIN 78711
(512) 458-1203
Raymond D. Apodaca, Executive Director

Assists the Alabama-Coushatta Indian Tribe and the Tigua Tribe of Texas in the development of the human and economic resources of their respective Reservations; also assists the Texas Band of Kickapoo Indians in improving its health, educational, agricultural, business, and industrial capacities. Promotes unity and understanding among the American Indian people of Texas, and promotes and enhances increased understanding of American Indian and Texas Indian culture and history by the general public. Approximate Indian population is 65,000. *Publications: Americans Indians in Texas,* 1984; *Texas Indian Commission Profile and History,* 20 page report.

UTAH

**UTAH NAVAJO
DEVELOPMENT COUNCIL**
27 South 100 East
BLANDING 84511
(801) 678-2285
Herbert Clah, Executive Director

Works with the Navajos on the Utah Portion of the Navajo Reservation to provide services in health, education, natural resources, and housing. *Programs:* Operates clinics for medical services; adult education; vocational education; home rehabilitation; and construction. Scholarships. Artifacts exhibited.

UTAH DIVISION OF INDIAN AFFAIRS
6220 State Office Bldg.
SALT LAKE CITY 84114
(801) 533-5334
Travis N. Parashouts, Director

Assists tribes and Native-American organizations in Utah in solving problems, and serves as a liaison between the State and all tribes and Indian organizations.

VIRGINIA

INDIAN AFFAIRS COORDINATOR
Section of Human Resources
9th Street Office Bldg., Room 622
RICHMOND 23219

WASHINGTON

**WASHINGTON COMMISSION
FOR INDIAN AFFAIRS**
1057 Capitol Way
OLYMPIA 98504

**WASHINGTON STATE OFFICE
OF THE GOVERNOR—INDIAN DESK**
1515 S. Cherry KE-13
OLYMPIA 98504

WISCONSIN

**WISCONSIN GOVERNOR'S
INDIAN DESK**
P.O. Box 7863
MADISON 53701

**AMERICAN INDIAN COUNCIL
ON ALCOHOLISM**
2451 W. North Ave.
MILWAUKEE 53205

WYOMING

**WYOMING STATE
INDIAN COMMISSION**
2660 Peck Ave.
RIVERTON 82501

CANADA

ALBERTA

**CALGARY INDIAN
FRIENDSHIP CENTRE**
140 - 2nd Ave. S.W.
CALGARY T2P 0B9
(403) 482-6051

**ALBERTA NATIVE
COMMUNICATIONS SOCIETY**
11427 Jasper Ave.
EDMONTON

**ALBERTA NATIVE FRIENDSHIP
CENTRES ASSOCIATION**
10171 - 117 St.
EDMONTON T5K 1X3
(403) 488-5112

**ALBERTA NATIVE RIGHTS
FOR NATIVE WOMEN**
14211 - 130th Ave.
EDMONTON T5L 4K8
(403) 453-2808/454-8462

**CANADIAN NATIVE
FRIENDSHIP CENTRE**
10176 - 117th St.
EDMONTON T5K 1X3
(403) 482-6051

INDIAN ASSOCIATION OF ALBERTA
203 - 11710 Kingsway Ave.
EDMONTON T5G 0X5
(403) 452-7221

**THE METIS ASSOCIATION
OF ALBERTA**
12750 - 127th St.
EDMONTON T5L 1A5
(403) 452-9550

**VOICE OF ALBERTA
NATIVE WOMEN'S SOCIETY**
P.O. Box 87
STANDOFF T0L 1Y0
(403) 737-3753/3939

TREATY VOICE OF ALBERTA
WINTERBURN T0E 2N0
(403) 487-4141

Women's Indian Association.

BRITISH COLUMBIA

**BRITISH COLUMBIA NATIVE
WOMEN'S SOCIETY**
116 Seymour St.
KAMLOOPS V2C 2E1
(604) 573-3657/374-9412

**BRITISH COLUMBIA INDIAN RIGHTS
FOR INDIAN WOMEN**
1733 Highland Dr., North
KELOWNA V1Y 4K9
(604) 763-9718

**PACIFIC ASSOCIATION OF
COMMUNICATIONS IN FRIENDSHIP
INDIAN CENTRES**
Quesnel Tillicom Society
319 N. Fraser Dr.
QUESNEL V2Y 1Y9
(604) 522-0604

CANADIAN INDIAN VOICE SOCIETY
429 E. 6th St., North
VANCOUVER V7L 1P8

**INDIAN HOMEMAKERS ASSOCIATION
OF BRITISH COLUMBIA**
102 - 423 W. Broadway
VANCOUVER V5Y 1R4
(604) 876-4929

**NATIVE BROTHERHOOD
OF BRITISH COLUMBIA**
517 Ford Bldg.
193 E. Hastings St.
VANCOUVER V6A 1N7
(604) 685-2255

**UNION OF BRITISH COLUMBIA
INDIAN CHIEFS**
440 W. Hastings St.
VANCOUVER V6B 1L1
(604) 684-0231

UNITED NATIVE NATIONS
240 - 2609 Granville Ave.
VANCOUVER V6H 1N7
(604) 732-3726

VANCOUVER INDIAN CENTRE
1607 West Hastings St.
VANCOUVER V5L 1S7
(604) 736-8944

LABRADOR

LABRADOR FRIENDSHIP CENTRE
P.O. Box 767
HAPPY VALLEY A0P 1E0
  (709) 896-8302

LABRADOR INUIT ASSOCIATION
P.O. Box 70
NAIN A0P 1L0
  (709) 922-2942

MANITOBA

**NATIVE WOMEN'S ASSOCIATION
OF MANITOBA**
P.O. Box 177
RIVERTON R0C 2R0
  (204) 373-2396/378-2460

FOUR NATIONS CONFEDERACY
500 - 275 Portage Ave.
WINNIPEG R3B 2B3
  (204) 944-8245

Indian Association.

**INDIAN AND METIS
FRIENDSHIP CENTRE**
465 Alexander Ave.
WINNIPEG R3A 0N7
  (204 943-1501

**INTERTRIBAL CHRISTIAN
COMMUNICATIONS**
P.O. Box 3765, Station A
WINNIPEG R2W 3R6
  (204) 338-0311

**MANITOBA ASSOCIATION
OF FRIENDSHIP CENTRES**
503 Main St., Suite 1004
WINNIPEG R3B 1B8
  (204) 943-8082

MANITOBA METIS FEDERATION
211 Portage Ave., Room 100
WINNIPEG R3B 2A2
  (204) 956-2070

NATIVE WOMEN'S TRANSITION CENTRE
730 Alexander Ave.
WINNIPEG R3E 1H9
  (204) 783-5237

WINNIPEG INDIAN COUNCIL
650 Burrows Ave.
WINNIPEG R2W 2A8
  (204) 586-8561

NEW BRUNSWICK

**NATIVE WOMEN'S ASSOCIATION
OF NEW BRUNSWICK**
310 King St.
FREDERICTON E3B 1E3
  (506) 472-3479

**NEW BRUNSWICK METIS
AND NON-STATUS INDIAN ASSOCIATION**
390 King St.
FREDERICTON E3B 1E3
  (506) 455-4370

UNION OF NEW BRUNSWICK INDIANS
35 Dedam St.
FREDERICTON E3A 2V2
  (506) 472-6281/523-6144

NEWFOUNDLAND

**NEWFOUNDLAND INDIAN
GOVERNMENT**
P.O. Box 375
ST. GEORGE'S A0N 1Z0
  (709) 647-3733

Canadian Native Association.

**NATIVE PEOPLE'S SUPPORT GROUP
OF NEWFOUNDLAND AND LABRADOR**
P.O. Box 582, Station C
ST. JOHN'S A1C 5K8

NORTHWEST TERRITORY

INUIT CULTURAL INSTITUTE
ESKIMO POINT X0E 0EC
  (403) 857-2085

BAFFIN REGION INUIT ASSOCIATION
P.O. Box 219
FROBISHER BAY X0A 0H0
  (819) 979-5391

**COMMITTEE FOR ABORIGINAL
PEOPLE'S ENTITLEMENT (COPE)**
P.O. Box 2000
INUVIK X0E 0T0
  (403) 979-3510

Inuit Association.

**THE METIS ASSOCIATION
OF THE N.W.T.**
P.O. Box 1375
YELLOWKNIFE X0E 1H0
  (403) 873-3505

NATIVE WOMEN'S ASSOCIATION
OF THE N.W.T.
P.O. Box 2321
YELLOWKNIFE X0E 1H0
(403) 873-5509

N.W.T. ASSOCIATION
OF FRIENDSHIP CENTRES
P.O. Box 2859
YELLOWKNIFE X0E 1H0
(403) 920-2288

NOVA SCOTIA

MICMAC NATIVE FRIENDSHIP CENTRE
2281 Brunswick St.
HALIFAX B3K 2Y9
(902) 423-8247

NOVA SCOTIA NATIVE
WOMEN'S ASSOCIATION
RR 1, Brass Corner
LUNENBURG B0R 1A0
(902) 644-3398/543-5508

UNION OF NOVA SCOTIA INDIANS
P.O. Box 100
SHUBENACADIE B0N 2H0
(902) 758-2048/3856

MICMAC ASSOCIATION
OF CULTURAL STUDIES
P.O. Box 961
SYDNEY B1P 6J4
(902) 539-8037

NOVA SCOTIA NATIVE
COMMUNICATIONS SOCIETY
P.O. Box 344
SYDNEY B1P 6H2

NATIVE COUNCIL OF NOVA SCOTIA
P.O. Box 1320
TRYRO B2N 5N2
(902) 895-6579

ONTARIO

NORTHERN ONTARIO INDIAN
HOMEMAKERS ASSOCIATION
General Delivery
HERON BAY P0T 1R0
(807) 229-1486

Indian Women's Association.

GRAND COUNCIL TREATY No. 3
P.O. Box 1720
KENORA P9N 3X7
(807) 548-4214/4215

ASSOCIATION OF IROQUOIS
AND ALLIED NATIONS
908 - 77 Metcalfe St.
OTTAWA K1P 5L6
(613) 232-1719/1710

CONGRESS OF ALGONQUIN
INDIANS ASSOCIATION
347 Bell St. South
OTTAWA K1Y 3S9
(613) 722-1626

COUNCIL FOR YUKON INDIANS
151 Slater St., Suite 702
OTTAWA K1P 5H3
(613) 246-9844

Native and Indian Association.

INUIT DEVELOPMENT CORPORATION
280 Albert St., Suite 902
OTTAWA K1P 5G8
(613) 238-4981

ONTARIO NATIVE
WOMEN'S ASSOCIATION
278 Bay St.
THUNDER BAY P7B 1R8
(807) 345-9821

GRAND COUNCIL TREATY No. 9
71 - 3rd Ave.
TIMMONS P4N 1C2
(705) 267-7911

Indian Association.

JOINT INDIAN ASSOCIATION
COMMITTEE OF ONTARIO
22 College St., 2nd Floor
TORONTO M5G 1K2
(416) 924-2553

ONTARIO FEDERATION
OF INDIAN FRIENDSHIP CENTRES
234 Eglinton Ave. East, Suite 207
TORONTO M4P 1K5
(416) 484-1411
Sylvia Maracle, Executive Director

Assists and supports the 18 Indian Centres under its membership in Ontario. Promotes development of new centres, and provides programs and services to its member centres. Publications. Library.

ONTARIO INDIAN RIGHTS
FOR INDIAN WOMEN
100 Bain Ave., No. 2 Maples
TORONTO M4K 1E8

UNION OF ONTARIO INDIANS
27 Queen St. East
TORONTO M5C 1R2
(416) 366-3527
Joe Miskokomon, President
K. Gayle Mason, Executive Director

Represents 40 Indian bands and their 35,000
members. A political organization offering
technical and support services to member bands.
Library.

OJIBWE CULTURAL FOUNDATION
Excelsior Post Office
WEST BAY P0P 1G0
(705) 377-4902

**ONTARIO METIS AND NON-STATUS
INDIAN ASSOCIATION**
5385 Yonge St., Suite 30
PELLETIER-WILLOWDALE M2N 5R7
(416) 226-2890

PRINCE EDWARD ISLAND

**NATIVE COUNCIL
OF PRINCE EDWARD ISLAND**
P.O. Box 2170
129 Kent St.
CHARLOTTETOWN C1A 1N4
(902) 892-5314

QUEBEC

**LAURENTIAN ALLIANCE OF METIS
AND NON-STATUS INDIANS**
21 Brodeur Ave.
HULL J8Y 2P6
(613) 770-7763

**CONFEDERTION OF INDIANS
OF QUEBEC**
P.O. Box 729
KAHNAWAKE J0L 1B0
(514) 632-7321

**QUEBEC INDIAN RIGHTS
FOR INDIAN WOMEN**
P.O. Box 614
KAHNAWAKE J0L 1B0
(514) 632-6304

**ASSOCIATION DES FEMMES
AUTOCHTONES DU QUEBEC**
1410 Rue Stanley, 7 ieme etage
MONTREAL H3A 1P8
(514) 873-7029

**LE REGROUPEMENT DES CENTRES
D'AMITIE AUTOCHTONES DU QUEBEC**
5333 Sherbrooke est. Apt. 1009-B
MONTREAL H1T 3W2
(514) 254-2257

**ASSOCIATIONS DES METIS ET DES
INDIENS HORS RESERVES, INC.**
2023 Boulevard De'l'anse
ROBERVAL G8H 2N1
(418) 275-0198

GRAND COUNCIL OF THE CREES
1500 Sullivan Rd.
VAL D'OR J9P 1M1
(819) 825-3402

SASKATCHEWAN

**FEDERATION OF
SASKATCHEWAN INDIANS**
1114 Central Ave.
PRINCE ALBERT S6V 5T2
(306) 764-3411

**INDIAN AND METIS
FRIENDSHIP CENTRE**
14th St. & 1st Ave. East
PRINCE ALBERT S6V 0E6
(306) 764-3431

**ASSOCIATION OF METIS
AND NON-STATUS INDIANS
OF SASKATCHEWAN**
1170 - 8th Ave.
REGINA S4R 1C9
(306) 525-6721

**SASKATCHEWAN ASSOCIATION
OF FRIENDSHIP CENTRES**
1950 Broad St., 2nd Floor
REGINA S4P 1X9
(306) 352-4743

**SASKATCHEWAN NATIVE
WOMEN'S ASSOCIATION**
1401 Egbert Ave.
SASKATOON S7N 2L8
(306) 652-6564/373-1957

YUKON

COUNCIL OF YUKON INDIANS
22 Nisutlin Dr.
WHITEHORSE Y1A 3S5
(403) 667-7631

MUSEUMS, MONUMENTS
AND PARKS

This section is an alpha-geographical listing of museums, monuments and parks maintaining permanent exhibits or collections related to the Native-American. Where no annotation follows a listing, the museum failed to answer our questionnaire, but is known, from other sources, to display Indian artifacts.

ALABAMA

RUSSELL CAVE NATIONAL MONUMENT
Route 1, Box 175
BRIDGEPORT 35740
(205) 495-2672
Dorothy Marsh, Superintendent

Description: An excavated, 310-acre archaeological site which shows the life of the people Russell Cave sheltered for 8,000 years. From archaic man to Indians—Woodlands and Cherokee. Museum contains artifacts from the period. Library.

ALASKA

**ANCHORAGE HISTORICAL
AND FINE ARTS MUSEUM**
121 W. 7th Ave.
ANCHORAGE 99501
(907) 264-4326
Robert L. Shalkop, Director

Maintains permanent exhibits on Alaskan art and artifacts of all periods. Eskimo, Aleut, Tlingit and Athapaskan crafts. *Publications: An Introduction to the Native Art of Alaska;* monthly newsletter. Library. Museum shop.

ANGOON CULTURAL CENTER MUSEUM
ANGOON 99820

**INUPIAT UNIVERSITY
OF THE ARCTIC MUSEUM**
P.O. Box 429
BARROW 99723

YUGTARVIK REGIONAL MUSEUM
P.O. Box 388
BETHEL 99559
(907) 543-2098
Elizabeth A. Mayock, Curator

Eskimo history museum; Yup'ik Eskimo artifacts of southwest Alaska. *Publication:* Monthly newsletter.

UNIVERSITY OF ALASKA MUSEUM
P.O. Box 95351, 907 Yukon Dr.
COLLEGE 99708
(907) 474-7505
Basil C. Hedrick, Director

Collection of Eskimo artifacts by Otto Geist. Tlingit, Athapascan and Aleut material on exhibit.

BRISTOL BAY MUSEUM
DILLINGHAM 99576

DILLINGHAM HERITAGE MUSEUM
Pouch 202
DILLINGHAM 99576
(907) 842-5601/5221
Irma O'Brien, Coordinator
Norma Adkison, Chairwoman

Alaskan Indian museum with southwest Yup'ik Eskimo arts and crafts, and Siberian Yup'ik and Inupiak Eskimo artifacts.

**EAGLE HISTORICAL SOCIETY
AND MUSEUM**
EAGLE 99738

ALASKA NATIVE VILLAGE MUSEUM
P.O. Box 80583, Alaskaland Park
FAIRBANKS 99708

DINJII ZHUU ENJIT MUSEUM
P.O. Box 42
FORT YUKON 99740
(907) 622-2345
Audrey Fields, Coordinator

Exhibits artifacts of the Athapascan Indians of the Yukon region.

ALASKA INDIAN ARTS, INC.
P.O. Box 271, 23 Fort Seward Dr.
HAINES 99827
(907) 766-2160
Carl W. Heinmiller, Executive Director

Indian Living Village Museum, collection of Tlingit Indian costumes and art; Chilkat Indian dancing. Small reference library.

**SHELDON MUSEUM
AND CULTURAL CENTER**
P.O. Box 236, 25 Main St.
HAINES 99827
(907) 766-2366
Elisabeth S. Hakkinen, Curator

Historical and Tlingit art museum. *Publication: Journey to the Tlingits.* Library.

HOONAH CULTURAL CENTER
P.O. Box 218
HOONAH 99829

ALASKA STATE MUSEUM
Pouch FM
JUNEAU 99811
(907) 465-2901

Maintains a collection of more than 10,000 objects relating to the Eskimo, Northwest Coast, Athapascan, Aleut, and Haida. *Publications:* Newsletter; Northern Notebook Series; classroom materials for learning kits.

SEALASKA GALLERY CULTURAL MUSEUM
Sealaska Plaza Bldg.
JUNEAU 99801

**KENAI HISTORICAL SOCIETY
AND MUSEUM**
P.O. Box 1348
KENAI 99611

KETCHIKAN INDIAN MUSEUM
P.O. Box 5454
KETCHIKAN 99901

TONGASS HISTORICAL SOCIETY MUSEUM
629 Dock St.
KETCHIKAN 99901
(907) 225-5600
Virginia McGillvray, Director

Collections on Indian artifacts, objects and photos relating to the Tlingit, Haida and Tsimshian cultures. Totem Heritage Center— totem poles and fragments from Tlingit Villages of Village Island and Tongass Island, and from Haida Village. *Publications: Growth in Southeast Alaska Natives Look to the Future;* quarterly newsletter. Library.

**BARANOF MUSEUM
AND KODIAK HISTORICAL SOCIETY**
P.O. Box 61
KODIAK 99615

Maintains Aleut artifacts from pre-history to the present. Newsletter. Library.

KOTZEBUE MUSEUM, INC.
P.O. Box 46
KOTZEBUE 99752
(907) 442-3401
Gene Moore, Manager

Eskimo Museum.

NANA - MUSEUM OF THE ARCTIC
P.O. Box 49
KOTZEBUE 99752
(907) 442-3301

DUNCAN COTTAGE MUSEUM
P.O. Box 282, Duncan St.
Annette Island Reserve
METLAKATLA 99926
LaVerne Welcome, Director/Curator

Historic House, 1894—home of Father William Duncan, missionary teacher of the Tsimshian Indian people of Metlakatla.

BRISTOL BAY REGIONAL MUSEUM
P.O. Box 152
NAKNEK 99633

KUZHGIE CULTURAL CENTER MUSEUM
P.O. Box 949
NOME 99762

**McCLAIN MEMORIAL MUSEUM
AND ARCHIVES**
P.O. Box 53
200 Front St.
NOME 99762

SELDOVIA NATIVE ASSOCIATION
Fine Arts and Cultural Center Museum
P.O. Box 201
SELDOVIA 99663

SHELDON JACKSON MUSEUM
104 College Dr.
SITKA 99835
(907) 747-8981
Bette Hulbert, Director
Peter L. Corey, Curator

Features Alaskan Eskimo, Aleut, Athapascan, Tlingit, Haida and Tsimshian artifacts and Alaskan history collections. *Special collections:* Argillite carvings; 400 Eskimo dance masks. Publications. Library.

SOUTHEAST ALASKA INDIAN CULTURAL CENTER
Sitka National Historical Park
P.O.. Box 738, 106 Metlakatla St.
SITKA 99835
(907) 747-6281
Ernest J. Suazo, Superintendent

A collection of more than 4,000 artifacts; totem poles and Chilkat Robes; traditional native arts such as woodcarving, costume design, and metalworking. *Publication: Carved History: A Guide to the Totem Poles of Sitka National Historical Park.* Library.

TRIBAL HOUSE OF THE BEAR
Foot of Shakes St., Box 868
WRANGELL 99929
(907) 874-3505
Margaret Sturtevant, President

Indian Museum housed in Tribal House with exhibits of costumes, Tlingit totem poles, ancient wood carving. *Publication: Guide to Shakes Island.*

WRANGELL MUSEUM
Box 2050, 1126 Second St.
WRANGELL 99929
(907) 874-3770
Pat Green, Director/Curator

Displays Tlingit totem poles and artifacts; photo collection. *Publication: The History of Chief Shakes and His Clan;* newsletter.

ARIZONA

MONTEZUMA CASTLE
NATIONAL MONUMENT
P.O. Box 219
CAMP VERDE 86322
(602) 567-3322
Glen E. Henderson, Superintendent

Description: Prehistoric Pueblo Indian ruins. *Museum:* Indian artifacts obtained from the Monument excavations. Library.

CANYON DE CHELLY
NATIONAL MONUMENT
P.O. Box 588
CHINLE 86503
(602) 674-5436
Roger Siglin, Superintendent

Displays Anasazi and Navajo Indian artifacts from the area. Library. Bookstore.

TUZIGOOT NATIONAL MONUMENT
P.O. Box 68
CLARKDALE 86324
(602) 634-5564
Glen E. Henderson, Superintendent

Description: Remnants of prehistoric town built by the Sinagua Indians who farmed Arizona's Verde Valley between 1125-1400 A.D. *Museum:* Exhibits artifacts found during excavations. Library.

CASA GRANDE RUINS
NATIONAL MONUMENT
P.O. Box 518
COOLIDGE 85228
(602) 723-3172
Sam R. Henderson, Superintendent

Museum: Located on the Hohokam village site of 500-1450 A.D.; contains pre-Columbian Pueblo and Hohokam Indian artifacts; ehtnological material of the Pima and Papago Indians— basketry and pottery. Library.

THE AMERIND FOUNDATION, INC.
Dragoon Rd., Box 248
DRAGOON 85609
(602) 586-3003
William Duncan Fulton, President

Archaeology and Ethnology Museum: Maintains collections of archaeological specimans from the Southwest and Mexico; ethnological material from the Southwest, Great Plains, Eastern Woodlands, California, and the Arctic. Library.

MUSEUM OF NORTHERN ARIZONA
Route 4, Box 720
FLAGSTAFF 86001
(602) 774-5211
Philip M. Thompson, Director

Exhibits the arts and artifacts of the Indians of Northern Arizona, with specific reference to the Hopi and Navajo. *Publication: Plateau,* quarterly journal; bimonthly newsletter; Archaeological Research Papers; bulletins. Library.

WALNUT CANYON
NATIONAL MONUMENTT
Route 1, Box 25
FLAGSTAFF 86001
(602) 526-3367
T. Dwayne Collier, Superintendent

Located on the site of approximately 400 prehistoric Indian ruins of the Sinagua Indians dating back to 1100-1270 A.D. Displays artifacts excavated from the site. Library.

WUPATKI AND SUNSET CRATER
NATIONAL MONUMENT
HC 33, Box 444A
FLAGSTAFF 86001
(602) 527-7152
Henry L. Jones, Superintendent

Exhibits four sets of ruins: Lomaki, Nalakihu-Citadel, Wuwoki, and Wupatki. Displays artifacts excavated from the ruins. Library.

FORT APACHE CULTURAL CENTER
P.O. Box 507
FORT APACHE 85926

HUBBELL TRADING POST
NATIONAL HISTORIC SITE
P.O. Box 150
GANADO 86505
(602) 755-3475
    Charles B. Cooper, Superintendent

The oldest continually operating Indian trading
post, with extensive collections of Native-
American and Southwest art on display. *Special
programs:* Navajo rug weaving and silversmithing
demonstrations; buying and selling Navajo, Hopi,
Pueblo, Zuni and other tribal crafts. Library.

GILA COUNTY HISTORICAL MUSEUM
Box 2891, 1330 N. Broad St.
GLOBE 85502
(602) 425-7385
    Rayna Barela, Director

Maintains prehistoric Salado Indian artifacts
(1125-1400 A.D.) Library.

YAVAPAI MUSEUM
Grand Canyon National Park
P.O. Box 129
GRAND CANYON 86023
(602) 638-2411
    Richard Marks, Superintendent

Exhibits artifacts from the Tusayan prehistoric
ruins.

MOHAVE MUSEUM
OF HISTORY AND ARTS
400 W. Beale
KINGMAN 86401
(602) 753-3195
    Norma Hughs, Director

The Walapai Room: Houses a life size Indian
wickieup and figures; also Walapai, Mohave, and
prehistoric pottery. *Mohave Miniature:* A
miniature rendition of a typical Mohave Indian
Village. Research Library.

COLORADO RIVER INDIAN
TRIBES MUSEUM
Route 1, Box 23-B
PARKER 85344
(602) 669-9211
    Charles A. Lamb, Director

Indian Museum displaying Mohave,
Chemehuevi, Navajo and Hopi artifacts; also
prehistoric Mogollon, Anasazi, Hohokam and
Patayan collections. Old Presbyterian Indian
Church; Mohave and Chemehuevi Archives.
Library.

STRADLING MUSEUM OF THE HORSE
P.O. Box 413
PATAGONIA 85624
(602) 394-2264
    Anne C. Stradling, Director

Equine and Indian Museum. Library.

HUALAPAI TRIBAL MUSEUM
P.O. Box 68
PEACH SPRINGS 86434

THE HEARD MUSEUM
22 E. Monte Vista Rd.
PHOENIX 85004
(602) 252-8848
    Michael J. Fox, Director
    Robert Breunig, Ph.D., Chief Curator

Anthropology and art museum exhibiting works
by American Indians; Southwestern
archaeological and ethnological collection.
Special collections: Hopi Kachina dolls, and
Navajo rugs and blankets. Publications. Library.

PUEBLO GRANDE MUSEUM
4619 E. Washington St.
PHOENIX 85034
(602) 275-3452
    David E. Doyel, Ph.D., Director

Site museum containing exhibits of prehistoric
Hohokam cultural material, circa B.C. 300 to
A.D. 1450. *Special programs: Annual Indian
market; "how-to" workshops taught by Native-
Americans. Publications. Library.*

SMOKI MUSEUM
N. Arizona Ave., Box 123
PRESCOTT 86301

Indian Museum featuring artifacts of the
Tuzigoot, King and Fitzmaurice ruins. Paintings.
Annual Indian ceremonials.

TONTO NATIONAL MONUMENT
P.O. Box 707
ROOSEVELT 85545
(602) 467-2241

Description: Prehistoric Salado Indian Cliff
Dwellings in Sonoran Desert setting. *Museum:*
Collection of prehistoric Salado Indian
artifacts—pottery, cloth, tools, etc. Library.

GILA RIVER ARTS
AND CRAFTS MUSEUM
P.O. Box 45
SACATON 85247
(602) 963-3981

HOPI TRIBAL MUSEUM
P.O. Box 8
SECOND MESA 86035
(602) 734-2411

MUSEUM OF ANTHROPOLOGY
Eastern Arizona College
626 Church St.
THATCHER 85552
(602) 428-1133

Betty Graham Lee, Director

Displays artifacts from Mogollon, Anasazi and Hohokam material culture; ethnographics in Apache, Navajo and Hopi. Library.

NAVAJO NATIONAL MONUMENT
TONALEA 86044
(602) 672-2366
Stephen Miller, Superintendent

Exhibits materials of the Kayenta, Anasazi and Navajo cultures. On the site of three prehistoric Cliff Villages. Library. Arts and crafts for sale.

**THE NED A. HATATCHLI
CENTER MUSEUM**
Navajo Community College
TSAILE 86556

ARIZONA STATE MUSEUM
University of Arizona
TUCSON 85721
(602) 621 6281
Raymond H. Thompson, Ph.D., Director

Maintains a large collection of Hohokam items, artifacts of the Anasazi and Mogollon cultures. Library.

MISSION SAN XAVIER DEL BAC
Route 11, Box 645
TUCSON 85706
(602) 294-2624
Father Kieran McCarthy, Rector

Historic building and site of the Spanish-Colonial Indian Mission of 1783. Library.

**WESTERN ARCHAEOLOGICAL
AND CONSERVATION CENTER**
Box 41058, 1415 N. Sixth Ave.
TUCSON 85717
(602) 792-6501
Carol A. Martin, Chief

Displays Southwestern prehistoric and ethnographic artifacts. Publications. Library.

NAVAJO TRIBAL MUSEUM
P.O. Box 308, Highway 264
WINDOW ROCK 86515
(602) 871-6673
Russell P. Hartman, Director/Curator

Exhibits approximately 4,500 objects relating to the history and culture of the Navajo Indians and the prehistory and natural history of the Four-Corners area. Photo archive of about 35,000 negatives and prints, mostly from 1930-1960, relating to the Navajos. *Special programs:* Art exhibits/sales; Navajo information service; school and group tours. Publications.

ARKANSAS

THE UNIVERSITY MUSEUM
338 Hotz Hall
University of Arkansas
FAYETTEVILLE 72701
Johnnie L. Gentry, Jr., Director

Exhibits material relative to Arkansas Indians. Publications. Library.

HOT SPRINGS NATIONAL PARK
P.O. Box 1860
HOT SPRINGS 71901

Interpretive programs about the life of the Caddo Indians and their predescessors and explains the use of the thermal springs by the Indians. *Museum:* Exhibits Indian artifacts. *Publications: Indians of Tonico; The Valley of the Vapors.*

MUSEUM OF SCIENCE AND HISTORY
MacArthur Park
LITTLE ROCK 72202

Exhibits include material relating to Arkansas Mound Builders, Americn Plains Indians, and Southwestern Indians. Library.

KA-DO—HA INDIAN VILLAGE
P.O. Box 669, Route 1
MURFREESBORO 71958
(501) 285-3736
Sam Johnson, Director

Prehistoric Caddo Indian (Mound Builders) grounds with museum housing artifacts from the excavation of the site. Publications for sale. Library.

ARKANSAS STATE UNIVERSITY MUSEUM
P.O. Box 490
STATE UNIVERSITY 72467
(501) 972-2074
Charlott A. Jones, Ph.D., Director

Displays Native-American artifacts including Arkansas—Quapaw, Caddo, Osage, Cherokee, Choctaw and Chickasaw; Southwestern—Navajo, Hopi, Pueblo and Apache; and an exhibit of Indian baskets and Indian dolls. Newsletter. Library.

CALIFORNIA

MALKI MUSEUM, INC.
11-795 Fields Rd.
Morongo Indian Reservation
BANNING 92220
(714) 849-7289

Katherine Siva Saubel, President
Matt Pablo, Director/Curator

Maintains a collection of Cahuilla and other
California Indian tribe's artifacts. *Programs:*
College scholarship program for southern
California Indian students; research on California
Indians. *Publications:* Newsletter; brochures on
the Cahuilla, Serrans, Chemehuevi and Chumash;
Malki Museum Press publishes books on the
California Indians. Library.

ROBERT H. LOWIE MUSEUM
OF ANTHROPOLOGY
University of California
103 Kroeber Hall
BERKELEY 94720
(415) 642-3681
James J. Deetz, Curator

Research and study collections include California
archaeological and ethnographical items,
majority of which are basketry items representing
practically every tribe in California; also Eskimo
and Aleut material, and Plains Indian artifacts;
large collections of baskets and carvings from
Northwest Coast tribes, especially Haida, Tlingit
and Tsimshean. Library.

OWENS VALLEY PAIUTE-SHOSHONE
INDIAN CULTURAL CENTER MUSEUM
P.O. Box 1281
BISHOP 93514

CABOT'S OLD INDIAN
PUEBLO MUSEUM
67-616 E. Desert View Ave.
DESERT HOT SPRINGS 92240
(619) 329-7610
Colbert H. Eyraud, Chief Curator

A four story Hopi Indian style Pueblo built by
Cabot Yerxa as a tribute to the Indian cultures;
Peter Toth sculpture—monument 40' high, 20
tons from a Sequoia redwood; Pueblo Art
Gallery. *Exhibits:* Inuit collection; and Sioux
collection from the Battle of the Little Big Horn;
Chumash and Pueblo culture collections. *Special
programs:* Slide and lecture presentations to
schools and organizations; sculpting for the
handicapped; single artist exhibitions; arts
interview radio show. Library.

HOOPA TRIBAL MUSEUM
HOOPA 95546
(916) 626-4110

EASTERN CALIFORNIA MUSEUM
155 Grant St., Box 206
INDEPENDENCE 93526
(619) 878-2411
Dave Epley, Attendant

Collections of Paiute, Shoshone, Washoe and
Yokut Indian artifacts, including basketry,
beadwork and lithics. Library.

LOMPOC MUSEUM
200 South H St.
LOMPOC 93436
(805) 736-3888
Lucille E. Christie, Director

Clarence Ruth Collection: Chumash and western
Alaskan Indian artifacts. Newsletter. Library.

SOUTHWEST MUSEUM
234 Museum Dr.
LOS ANGELES 90042
(213) 221-2164
Patrick T. Houlihan, Ph.D., Director

Collections focus on native people of the
Americas including 100,000 artifacts pertaining to
the American Indian, Eskimo, and Aleut from
prehistoric, historic and modern times. *Special
program:* Annual Festival of Native American
Arts. *Publication: Masterkey,* quarterly journal.
Library.

MONTEREY STATE
HISTORICAL MONUMENT
210 Oliver St.
MONTEREY 93940

Holman Exhibit of American Indian Artifacts.

PRESIDIO (ARMY) MUSEUM
Presidio of Monterey
MONTEREY 93944-5006
(408) 242-8414
Margaret B. Adams, Curator

Exhibits artifacts of the Rumsen (Ohlone)
Indians. Library.

SIERRA MONO MUSEUM
Malum Ridge Rd. & Mammoth Pool Rd.
NORTH FORK 93643

MARIN MUSEUM
OF THE AMERICAN INDIAN
P.O. Box 864, 2200 Novato Blvd.
NOVATO 94947
(415) 897-4064
Mary Hilderman Smith, Executive Director

Collections oriented to Native-American cultures
of western North America, with particular
emphasis on Indian cultures of California,
especially local Coast Miwok people of Marin and
southern Sonoma Counties. *The Kettenhofen
Collection of Edward Curtis Photogravures.
Special program:* Educational classes, lectures,
and instruction. *Publications: Surface Scatter,*
quarterly newsletter. Library.

THE OAKLAND MUSEUM
1000 Oak St.
OAKLAND 94607

Exhibits present native Californians in pre-contact times.

WILL ROGERS STATE HISTORIC PARK
14253 Sunset Blvd.
PACIFIC PALISADES 90272
(213) 454-8212
Alice Karl, President

Description: Ranch belonged to the American humorist, Will Rogers (of Cherokee Indian descent), containing original buildings and furnishings; Indian artifacts, rugs and blankets. Bookstore.

CUPA CULTURAL CENTER
Temecula Rd., Box 1
PALA 92059

Located on the Pala Indian Reservation in San Diego County, the Cultural Center maintains a museum, library and work areas for crafts, and classroom space.

MUSEUM OF MISSION
SAN ANTONIO DE PALA
Highway 76, Box 66
PALA 92059

Historic Mission Building (Pala Indians.) Exhibits Indian artifacts—basketry, stone carvings, pottery and jewelry. Dance festivals.

REDDING MUSEUM AND ART CENTER
1911 Rio Dr., Box 427
REDDING 96099
(916) 243-4994
Carolyn Bond, Director

Exhibits Indian basketry and artifacts; also Pre-Columbian Art and Native-American Arts. Reference Library.

SAN BERNARDINO COUNTY MUSEUM
2024 Orange Tree Lane
REDLANDS 92373

Displays various artifacts and lithic tools of Indian occpuation of San Bernardino County; history and artifacts of remaining local tribes—Serrano, Cahuilla, Mojave, Chemehuevi, and others are being preserved. Publications. Library.

SHERMAN INDIAN MUSEUM
Sherman Institute
9010 Magnolia Ave.
RIVERSIDE 92503

CALIFORNIA STATE INDIAN MUSEUM
2618 K St.
SACRAMENTO 95816
(916) 324-0971
Mike Tucker, Area Manager

Collections pertain to the cultures of the Indians of California. Pomo feather baskets; artifacts from Ishi; northcoast redwood dugout. Emphasis is on lifestyle, spiritual and the continuing culture.

SAN DIEGO MUSEUM OF MAN
1350 El Prado, Balboa Park
SAN DIEGO 92101

Exhibits on Indians of three Americas—collections of material culture, Indian habitats. Library.

AMERICAN INDIAN HISTORICAL
SOCIETY, INC.
1451 Masonic Ave.
SAN FRANCISCO 94117

Jeanette Henry Costo, Director

Maintains a library and museum of Indian Arts. In the process of establishing the Rupert Costo Hall of American Indians at the University of California.

INDIAN CENTER OF SAN JOSE MUSEUM
3485 E. Hills Dr.
SAN JOSE 95127
(408) 259-9722

Exhibits artifacts and photos of tribal groups throughout the U.S.

JESSE PETER MEMORIAL MUSEUM
1501 Mendocino Ave.
SANTA ROSA 95401-4395
(707) 527-4479
Foley C. Benson, Director/Curator

Collections of traditional Native-American art, including Southwest pottery and Navajo rugs; and extensive North American basketry, especially of California. *Publications: Hopitu — A Collection of Kachina Dolls of the Hopi Indians; From Straw Into Gold (North American Basketry.)*

LAVA BEDS NATIONAL MONUMENT
P.O. Box 867
TULELAKE 96134
(916) 667-2282
Gary Hathaway, Curator

Description: Site of the Modoc Indian War (November 1872 to June 1873.) *Museum:* Modoc Indian artifacts; Indian rock art and pictographs on walls of caves.

RINCON TRIBAL EDUCATION CENTER
P.O. Box 1147
VALLEY CENTER 92082

SATWIWA CULTURAL CENTER PROJECT
c/o Santa Monica Mountains National
Recreation Area
National Park Service
WOODLAND HILLS 91364

YOSEMITE NATIONAL PARK
P.O. Box 577
YOSEMITE NATIONAL PARK 95389
(209) 372-4461 ext. 261
David M. Forgang, Curator

Indian Cultural Museum and Village: Depicts the
traditional culture of the Miwok and Paiute
people of the Yosemite region, from pre-contact
times through present day. *Special programs:*
Annual summer "Kaluga" dance celebration;
demonstrations of native crafts. Library.

SISKIYOU COUNTY MUSEUM
910 S. Main St.
YREKA 96097

Contains displays on Indians of Siskiyou
County—Modoc, Shasta, Yurok and Karak.
Maintains an extensive basket collection of the
Karak and Yurok tribes.

COLORADO

ADAMS STATE COLLEGE MUSEUM
ES Bldg.
ALAMOSA 81102
(303) 589-7011
Paul Reddin, Ph.D., Curator

Exhibits Pueblo Indian cultural artifacts,
primarily pottery; Navajo weaving.

THE TAYLOR MUSEUM
Colorado Springs Fine Arts Center
30 West Dale St.
COLORADO SPRINGS 80903
(303) 634-5581
Jonathan Batkin, Curator

Collections of Native-American arts of the Pacific
Northwest, Great Plains, Great Basin, and
California, including: Navajo rugs and blankets,
Pueblo woven textiles, baskets and pottery, Zuni
fetishes, Mimbres bowls, kachinas, and jewelry.
Special collection: John Frederick Huckel
Collection: Navajo sandpainting reproductions.
Publications. Library.

COLORADO STATE MUSEUM
Colorado Historical Society Museum
1300 Broadway
DENVER 80203
(303) 866-3682
Barbara Sudler, President

Extensive ethnological and photographic
collections of Plains and Southwest Indians;
source materials on the Indian Wars; materials
from the Rosebud Indian Agency, 1885 to 1890.
Publication: The Colorado Magazine. Library.

DENVER ART MUSEUM
100 W. 14th Ave. Parkway
DENVER 80204
(303) 575-2256
Richard Conn, Curator

Collection of North American Indian art; also, an
ethnographic collection of Indian women's
costumes, Navajo and Pueblo pottery, Hopi
kachina dolls, Blackfoot ceremonial equipment,
and wood carvings of the Northwest Coast.
Publications: Indian Leaflet Series; Material
Culture Notes. Library.

**DENVER MUSEUM
OF NATURAL HISTORY**
City Park
DENVER 80205

(303) 370-6357
Joyce L. Herold, Curator

Hall of Prehistoric People of the Americas:
Exhibits on early man, and collections of Paleo-
Indian specimens. *Special collection:* Crane
Collection of American Indian Materials.

**HISTORICAL MUSEUM AND INSTITUTE
OF WESTERN COLORAO**
4th and Ute
GRAND JUNCTION 81501

Special collections: Ute Indian Collection and
Teller Indian School Collection: Basketry,
artifacts, manuscripts and photographs of the Ute
Indians. Library.

KOSHARE INDIAN MUSEUM
115 W. 18th St.
LA JUNTA 81050
(303) 384-4801
J.F. Burshears, Executive Director

Indian arts and crafts museum. *Publication:*
Koshare News. Library. Indian arts and crafts for
sale.

**MESA VERDE
NATIONAL PARK MUSEUM**
MESA VERDE NATIONAL PARK 81330
(303) 529-4475
Donald C. Fiero, Chief of Interpretation

Description: A prehistoric Pueblo Indian community — pithouses, cliff dwellings, etc. *Museum:* Preserves Anasazi archaeological remains dating from 500-1330 A.D. Library.

UTE INDIAN MUSEUM
P.O. Box 1736, 17253 Chipeta Dr.
MONTROSE 81402
(303) 249-3098
Everlyn Casias, Curator

Indian History Museum located on the site of Chief Ouray's 400 acre farm. Depicts the history of the Utes through use of dioramas and objects which the Utes made and used; photographs and maps; portraits of some Ute leaders.

UTE MOUNTAIN TRIBAL PARK
General Delivery
TOWAOC 81334

CONNECTICUT

MUSEUM OF CONNECTICUT HISTORY
Connecticut State Library
231 Capitol Ave.
HARTFORD 06115

Special collection: George Mitchelson Collection: Contains pottery, tools, arrowheads, and other artifacts of Native-American culture of Connecticut. Library.

EELS-STOW HOUSE
Milford Historical Society
34 High St., Box 337
MILFORD 06460
(203) 874-2664
Virginia Hoagland, President

Special collection: Claude C. Coffin Indian Collection: Indian relics and artifacts primarily from the Milford-Stratford area of southern Connecticut. Library.

TANTAQUIDGEON INDIAN MUSEUM
1819 Norwich-New London Turnpike
UNCASVILLE 06382
(203) 848-9145
Harold and Gladys Tantaquidgeon,
Owners and Curators

Built in 1931 by the late John Tantaquidgeon and his son, Harold, direct descendents of Uncas, Chief of the once powerful Mohegan Nation.

Displays objects of stone, bone, and wood made by Mohegan and other New England Indian artists and craftsmen, past and present.

**AMERICAN INDIAN
ARCHAEOLOGICAL INSTITUTE**
P.O. Box 260
WASHINGTON 06793
(203) 868-0518
Susan F. Payne, Director

A research and education museum dedicated to discovering and interpreting our 10,000 year-old American Indian heritage—the history of Native-American people of the Northeast Woodlands. *Special Programs:* Field Trips/Assemblies; craft workshops; lectures; training sessions; exhibitions. *Publications: Artifacts,* quarterly magazine; research reports; books; and exhibition pamphlets. Library.

**HISTORICAL MUSEUM OF
THE GUNN MEMORIAL LIBRARY**
Wykeham Rd. at the Green
WASHINGTON 06793

Senator Orville Platt Memorial Indian Room: Contains Indian artifacts—including more than 100 baskets from many Western tribes.

DELAWARE

**NANTICOKE INDIAN
ASSOCIATION MUSEUM**
c/o Joan Harmon
Route 4, Box 170B
MILLSBORO 19966

DISTRICT OF COLUMBIA

**INDIAN ARTS AND CRAFTS BOARD
U.S. DEPT. OF INTERIOR ART MUSEUM**
Room 4004, U.S. Dept. of the Interior
18th & C Sts., N.W.
WASHINGTON 20240
(202) 343-2773
Robert G. Hart, General Manager
Myles Libhart, Director

Maintains collections of Native-American arts of the U.S. *Publications:* Source directory of Native-American owned and operated arts and crafts businesses; *Native American Art Series;* bibliography.

**NATIVE AMERICAN MUSEUMS
PROGRAM—SMITHSONIAN
INSTITUTION**
Office of Museum Programs
WASHINGTON 20560

(202) 357-3101
Nancy J. Fuller, Coordinator

Offers information services and specially designed educational opportunities to the personnel of Native-American urban and tribal museums and cultural centers for the advancement of museum practices.

NATIONAL ANTHROPOLOGICAL ARCHIVES
Natural History Building
WASHINGTON 20560
(202) 357-1976
Dr. Herman J. Viola, Director
Adrienne Kaeppler, Chair

Records and Manuscript Collections: Includes vocabularies, grammatical data, and texts relating to Native-Americans; also, ethnographic and archaeological field notes and drafts of reports, and transcripts of oral history and of music. *Photographs Collection:* A general file of black and white prints relating to the North American Indians. *Publication:* Monthly magazine. Library.

U.S. DEPT. OF THE INTERIOR MUSEUM
18th & C Sts., N.W.
WASHINGTON 20240
(202) 343-2743
Anne Madden, Director

Exhibits include dioramas, scientific specimens, and paintings. A collection of Native American pottery, baskets, and other artifacts such as kachinas and weavings. Library.

FLORIDA

LOWE ART MUSEUM
University of Miami
1301 Miller Dr.
CORAL GABLES 33146

Gallery's Barton Wing (Collection) contains 4,000 items — blankets, Pueblo pottery, Plains Indian baskets, kachina dolls, jewelry, costumes and ceramics, largely of Southwestern origin. Publications. Library.

CRYSTAL RIVER STATE ARCHAEOLOGICAL SITE
Route 3, Box 457-E
CRYSTAL RIVER 32629

Description: Pre-Columbian Indian ceremonial burial site. *Museum:* Indian artifacts—pottery, jewelry, tools; archaeological displays, Indian technical displays. *Publication: Florida Indians of Past and Present.*

MUSEUM OF ARCHAEOLOGY
100A South New River Rd.
FORT LAUDERDALE 33301
(305) 765-5964
Gypsy C. Graves, President

Exhibits archaeological artifacts—Tequesta Indian ceramics. *Research:* Tequesta Indian sites in Broward County. *Publication: Tequesta Talk,* monthly newsletter.

MUSEUM OF ART, INC.
426 E. Las Olas Blvd.
FORT LAUDERDALE 33301
(305) 463-5184
George S. Bolge, Executive Director

Displays Pre-Columbian and historic American Indian stone and wood carvings, ceramics, basketry, and textiles. Library.

ST. LUCIE COUNTY HISTORICAL MUSEUM
414 Seaway Dr.
FORT PIERCE 33450

Features Seminole Indian pictures, artifacts and records from the Brighton Seminole Indian Reservation. Indian-made handicrafts are sold.

INDIAN TEMPLE MOUND MUSEUM
P.O. Box 4009
139 Miracle Strip Parkway
FORT WALTON BEACH 32548
(904) 243-6521
Cynthia Moses NeSmith, Director

Exhibits prehistoric Indian artifacts found within a 40 mile radius of the museum are displayed interpreting 10,000 years of Gulf Coast living. The Temple Mound, a National Historic Landmark, is the largest Mississippian Temple Mound on the Gulf Coast. *Special programs:* Guided tours and slide shows. *Publications: Indians of the Florida Panhandle; Pottery of the Fort Walton Period; The Buck Burial Mound.* Library.

JACKSONVILLE CHILDREN'S MUSEUM
1025 Gulf Life Dr.
JACKSONVILLE 32207

Displays artifacts of the Florida Indians of the past and present, including the Seminole and Micosukee tribes. Research library.

MICCOUSUKEE CULTURAL CENTER
P.O. Box 44021, Tamiami Station
MIAMI 33144
(305) 223-8380

PENSACOLA HISTORICAL MUSEUM
405 S. Adams St.
PENSACOLA 32501

A collection of local Indian artifacts from the prehistoric period through the late 19th-century. A large collection relating to George Medhurst Wratten, interpreter for Geronimo and Apaches, and the Apaches as prisoners of war in Florida and Alabama (manuscript form.) Library.

SOUTHEAST ARCHAEOLOGICAL CENTER
P.O. Box 2416
TALLAHASSEE 32316
(904) 222-1167
Richard D. Faust, Chief

TALLAHASSEE JUNIOR MUSEUM, INC.
3945 Museum Dr.
TALLAHASSEE 32304

Special collection: Gundrum Collection: Displays reproductions of pre-Columbian Florida Indian pottery and weapons; Apalachee Indian Farm (Reconstructed.) *Publication: Apalachee Indian Farm Guide.*

SEMINOLE TRIBAL MUSEUM
5221 Orient Rd.
TAMPA 33610

GEORGIA

KOLOMOKI MOUNDS MUSEUM
Route 1
BLAKELY 31723
(912) 723-5296
Aubrey Jenkins, Superintendent

Description: Historic site—13th-century Indian burial mound and village—artifacts from the excavations are on display. *Publication: Report of the Excavations at Kolomoki.*

NEW ECHOTA
Route 3
CALHOUN 30701
(404) 629-8151
Edward Reed, Superintendent

A Preservation Project — 1825 Capitol town of the Cherokee Nation. *Research:* Cherokee genealogy; Trail of Tears.

ETOWAH MOUNDS ARCHAEOLOGICAL AREA
Route 1
CARTERSVILLE 30120
(404) 382-2704
Edwill Holcomb, Superintendent

Description: Large Indian site with seven mounds surrounded by a moat partially filled. Materials recovered from the excavations are on display.

INDIAN MUSEUM
Indian Springs State Park
INDIAN SPRINGS 30231
(404) 775-7241
Louis Taylor, Superintendent

Exhibits Creek Indian artifacts—items that reflect stages of Indian civilizations. *Research:* Creek Indians in Georgia.

OCMULGEE NATIONAL MONUMENT
1207 Emery Highway
MACON 31201
(912) 742-0447
Sibbald Smith, Superintendent

Description: Site of seven mounds constructed by a group of farming Indians one thousand years ago. *Archaeology Museum:* Collections explain the culture of the Indians who constructed the area mounds, and of five other Indian groups that have inhabited the area since. Publications. Creek Indian Trading Post. Library

CHIEFTAINS MUSEUM
80 Chatillon Rd.
ROME 30161
(404) 291-9494
Josephine Ransom, Director

History museum housed in a 1794 log cabin, and an 1820 plantation house belonging to Cherokee leader Major Ridge. Contains items from archaic Indian occupation to the present.

THE CHIEF JOHN ROSS HOUSE
P.O. Box 32
ROSSVILLE 30741
(404) 861-6342
Frances Jackson, President

Historic house of 1797 with displays of artifacts; Cherokee alphabet.

IDAHO

IDAHO STATE HISTORICAL MUSEUM
610 N. Julia Davis Dr.
BOISE 83702
(208) 334-2120

A collection of prehistoric and historic artifacts of the Shoshone, Nez Perce, Northern Paiute, with general Plains Indian material represented; a large collection of Northwest Coast and Alaskan material collected in the early 1900's. *Publications: Idaho Yesterdays,* quarterly magazine; newsletter. Library.

FORT HALL INDIAN MUSEUM
c/o Shoshone-Bannock Tribe
FORT HALL 83203

**NEZ PERCE NATIONAL
HISTORICAL PARK MUSEUM**
P.O. Box 93
SPALDING 83551
Stephen D. Shawley, Staff Curator

Located on an early mission site, this museum exhibits Nez Perce ethnological material; 3,000 photos of Nez Perce Indians. *Research:* Nez Perce Indians. Library.

ILLINOIS

**FIELD MUSEUM
NATURAL HISTORY**
Roosevelt Rd. at Lake Shore Dr.
CHICAGO 60605
(312) 922-9410
Dr. William Boyd, President
Dr. Glen Cole, Chairman-Anthropology

Seven exhibit halls devoted to the American Indian. Collections cover prehistoric and living Indians and Eskimos from Alaska to Cape Horn. Library.

**CAHOKIA MOUNDS
STATE HISTORIC SITE AND MUSEUM**
7850 Collinsville Rd.
EAST ST. LOUIS 62201
(618) 344-5268
Dr. Margaret Brown, Site Superintendent

Contains over 30 exhibits, including authentic and replica artifacts from site and region; dioramas, graphics, mostly dealing with prehistoric Cahokia Mounds site. Outdoor reconstruction of Late Woodland pithouses and Mississippian wall trench house, stockade, garden; Woodhenge reconstruction. *Special programs:* Slide/tape presentations; guided tours; Native-American craft classes; lecture series. *Publication: Cahokia,* newsletter; publishes books. Library.

**MADISON COUNTY
HISTORICAL MUSEUM**
715 N. Main St.
EDWARDSVILLE 62025

Special collection: John R. Sutter Collection—Contains more than 3,000 items of local and south central Illinois, as well as some from Southwest tribes. Library.

SCHOOL OF NATIONS MUSEUM
Principia College
ELSAH 62028
(618) 374-2131 ext. 312
Bonnie Gibbs, Director

Maintains a collection of American Indian crafts—baskets, clothing, dolls, pottery, textiles, etc. Library.

**KAMPSVILLE ARCHAEOLOGICAL
MUSEUM**
P.O. Box 1499, Highway 100 (Kampsville)
EVANSVILLE 60204
(618) 653-4614
Marguarite Schumann, Curator

Contains archaeological materials dating back to 8000 B.C.; a reconstructed Indian village. *Publication: Early Man,* quarterly magazine.

DICKSON MOUNDS MUSEUM
LEWISTON 61542
(309) 547-3721
Judith A. Franke, Director

Exhibits archaeological material from west central Illinois, Mississippian and Middle Woodland sites on grounds—Paleo-Indian to Mississippian cultures.

HAUBERG INDIAN MUSEUM
Black Hawk State Park
ROCK ISLAND 61201
(309) 788-9536
Elizabeth A. Carvey, Director

Artifacts on permanent display are of Sauk and Mesquakie origin; also other Eastern Woodland artifacts; includes many articles of Plains origin; large basket collection of the Northwest, West and Southwest; four dioramas depicting the daily life of the Sauk and Mesquakie about 1800. *Publication: Two Nations, One Land: A Cultural Summation of the Sauk and Mesquakie in Illinois.*

MUSEUM OF NATURAL HISTORY
University of Illinois
URBANA 61801

Maintains prehistoric and historic exhibits of Indians of North America, with emphasis on the prehistory of Illinois, the Navajo and Pueblo Indians, and the Eskimo of Greenland.

**STARVED ROCK STATE PARK
AND MUSEUM**
P.O. Box 116
UTICA 61373
(815) 667-4726
John Blume, Complex Superintendent

Located on the site of former Indian village of Illinois Indians, later occupied by Ottawa and Potawatomi Indians, 1673-1760.

INDIANA

INDIANA UNIVERSITY MUSEUM
Student Bldg.
BLOOMINGTON 47401

Exhibits approximtely 100,000 archaeological and ethnological specimens on American Indians from many areas of the New World. *Special collection:* Wanamaker Collectin of American Indian Photographs, taken by Joseph Dixon—includes about 15,000 items. Library.

WILLIAM HAMMOND MATHERS MUSEUM
601 E. 8th St.
Indiana University
BLOOMINGTON 47405
(812) 335-MUSE
Geoffrey W. Conrad, Director

Contains major ethnographic collections from North American Indians.

ANGEL MOUNDS STATE HISTORIC SITE
8215 Pollack Ave.
EVANSVILLE 47715
(812) 853-3956
Cary Floyd, Curator

Description: A 103 acre prehistoric Mississippian Indian archaeological site. Ten mounds, 1250-1450, inhabiting 1000 people; reconstructed structures: portion of a stockade house, and the temple. *Special program:* Native American Days Festival, annual in August. *Publication: Friends of Angel Mounds Newsletter,* quarterly. Library.

THE POTAWATOMI MUSEUM
P.O. Box 486, No. Wayne & City Limits
FREMONT 46737

Exhibits over 5,000 material cultural items of prehistoric and historic periods. Library.

CHILDREN'S MUSEUM OF INDIANAPOLIS
3010 N. Meridian St.
INDIANAPOLIS 46208

Collections consist of over 2,000 objects representing the tribes of Woodlands, Southeast, Plains, Plateau, Southwest, Northwest Coast, California and Canadian Indians. *Publication:* Newsletter. Library.

MUSEUM OF INDIAN HERITAGE
6040 De Long Rd.
INDIANAPOLIS 46254
(317) 293-4488
Vicki Cummings, Director

Maintains a Native-American archaeological and ethnographic collection, primarily from North America, with emphasis on the culture areas of the Northeast Woodlands, the Great Plains, and the Southwest. *Publication:* Quarterly newsletter. Library.

NORTHERN INDIANA HISTORICAL SOCIETY MUSEUM
112 S. Lafayette Blvd.
SOUTH BEND 46601

Exhibits on prehistoric Indians, the Mound Builders in Indiana; an historic Indian exhibit on the lifestyle of the Potawatomis and Miamis of northern Indiana. *Publication: The Old Courthouse News,* quarterly magazine.

SONOTABAC PREHISTORIC INDIAN MOUND AND MUSEUM
P.O. Box 1979, 2401 Wabash Ave.
VINCENNES 47591
(812) 885-4330/7679
John A. Ward, President

Description: Indian Museum and Historic Site located at the foot of the largest Ceremonial Mound in Indiana, containing exhibits covering 10,000 B.C. to the present. *Publication:* Monthly newsletter.

IOWA

UNIVERSITY OF NORTHERN IOWA MUSEUM
31st and Hudson Rd.
CEDAR FALLS 50613

Maintains a collection of approximately 8,000 Indian artifacts.

DAVENPORT MUSEUM
1717 W. 12th St.
DAVENPORT 52804

Maintains collections of prehistoric Indian artifacts from Mounds in central Mississippi River Valley; Southwestern basketry and pottery; and ethnological items from various tribes, primarily from the upper Great Lakes region and Plains. Library.

IOWA STATE HISTORICAL MUSEUM
East 12th and Grand Ave.
DES MOINES 50319
(515) 281-5111
Adrien D. Anderson, Director

Displays Indian beadwork; historic and prehistoric artifacts, photos, and relative written material. *Publication: The Annals of Iowa,* quarterly magazine. Library.

HAM HOUSE MUSEUM
P.O. Box 305, 1769 University Ave.
DUBUQUE 52001

Special collection: Herrmann Collection—
Contains artifacts from Midwest and Southwest
tribes: Zuni, Navajo, Sioux, Mesquakie, and
Winnebago. Library.

**AUDUBON COUNTY
HISTORICAL SOCIETY**
EXIRA 50076 (mail) AUDUBON 50025
(712) 563-3984
Fred Sievers, President

Indian Museum maintaining collections of Indian
artifacts.

**EFFIGY MOUNDS
NATIONAL MONUMENT**
P.O. Box K
McGREGOR 52157
(319) 873-2356
Thomas A. Munson, Superintendent

Consists of prehistoric Indian burial mounds with
an archaeological museum exhibiting artifacts
excavated from the mounds area. Library.

SIOUX CITY PUBLIC MUSEUM
2901 Jackson St.
SIOUX CITY 51104

Exhibits artifacts of the Plains and Eastern
Woodlands Indians. Library.

MUSEUM OF HISTORY AND SCIENCE
503 South St.
WATERLOO 50701

Contains six exhibit cases of Indian artifacts and
beadwork, and a rare book collection (53
volumes) of Indian history and lore.

KANSAS

KAW INDIAN MISSION
500 N. Mission
COUNCIL GROVE 66846
(316) 767-5410
Harriet Milligan, Curator

An historic house and museum featuring Kaw
Indian relics.

**IOWA, SAC AND FOX
PRESBYTERIAN MISSION MUSEUM**
Highway 136, Box 266
HIGHLAND 66035
(913) 442-3304
Art Snyder, Curator

Description: A three story stone house serving as a
mission to the Iowa, and Sac and Fox Indians.
Displays Iowa, and Sac and Fox Indian artifacts.

MUSEUM OF ANTHROPOLOGY
University of Kansas
LAWRENCE 66044
(913) 864-4245
Alfred E. Johnson, Director

Maintains a collection of Indian artifacts, with an
extensive skeletal collection of North American
Indians.

CORONADO-QUIVIRA MUSEUM
221 E Ave. South
LYONS 67554
(316) 257-3941
Clyde Ernst, Director/Curator

Exhibits Coronado and Quivira Indian artifacts,
and Papago Indian baskets, pre-1934.

RILEY COUNTY HISTORICAL MUSEUM
Memorial Auditorium Bldg.
11th and Poyntz Ave.
MANHATTAN 66502

Special collection: The Walter Collection—900
Indian relics and artifacts of northeast Kansas and
southwest Nebraska. *Publication:* Newsletter.
Library.

LAST INDIAN RAID MUSEUM
258 S. Penn Ave.
OBERLIN 67749
(913) 475-2712
Sandra Russell, Curator

History museum located on the site of the 1878
Last Indian Raid on Kansas soil. Displays Indian
artifacts.

OLD DEPOT MUSEUM
Tecumseh and Main
OTTAWA 66067

Special collection: Indians of Franklin County,
and Early Indian Clothing. Displays scrolls of
membership in the Chippewa Tribe, and maps
locating tribal lands.

PAWNEE INDIAN VILLAGE MUSEUM
Route 1
REPUBLIC 66964
(913) 361-2255
Edward Small, Curator

Archaeology museum located on the best
preserved Pawnee site on the Plains. Exhibits
artifacts to illustrate Pawnee life and customs.

EL QUARTELEJO KIVA
INDIAN MUSEUM
c/o News Chronicle Printing Co., Inc.
P.O. Box 218
SCOTT CITY 67871

Displays Cheyenne and Pueblo artifacts,
especially Taos; Indian War material.

SHAWNEE MISSION MUSEUM
3403 West 53rd
SHAWNEE MISSION 66205
(913) 262-0867
Lee Wright, Director

Description: Re-creation of Indian Manual Labor
School, operated 1830-1862, for Shawnee
children and other emigrant tribes. *Special
program:* Slide show of the history of the Mission.

KANSAS STATE
HISTORICAL SOCIETY MUSEUM
120 West 10th St.
TOPEKA 66612

Collection features Indian relics—tools, utensils
and clothing of Kansas Indian tribes.

THE MENNINGER FOUNDATION
MUSEUM AND ARCHIVES
5600 West 6th St.
TOPEKA 66601

Contains archaeological and anthropological
display rooms featuring American Indian history
and prehistory, focusing on Indian healing
ceremony artifacts, and emotional expression in
handicrafts. Library.

THE INDIAN MUSEUM
Mid-America All-Indian Center
650 N. Seneca
WICHITA 67203
William Jones, Executive Director

Description: Located on the site of old Indian
Council grounds. Maintains collections of Native-
American art and artifacts. *Research:* Native-
American life, art, and religion. *Publication:*
Gallery Notes, quarterly newsletter. Library.

KENTUCKY

MUSEUM OF ANTHROPOLOGY
Northern Kentucky University
University Dr.
HIGHLAND HEIGHTS 41076
(606) 572-5252
James F. Hopgood, Director

Displays Ohio Valley archaeological material;
artifacts from Southwest Indians, Southeast
Indians, and Huichol Indians.

MUSEUM OF ANTHROPOLOGY
University of Kentucky
Lafferty Hall
LEXINGTON 40506
(602) 258-4219
Dr. Lathel F. Duffield, Director

Exhibits archaeological material from sites
excavated in Kentucky, including Navajo and
Eskimo artifacts.

THE FILSON CLUB
118 W. Breckenridge St.
LOUISVILLE 40203

Contains prehistoric Indian relics from Ohio and
Mississippi Valleys; relics of Indian life in
Kentucky. Library.

J.B. SPEED ART MUSEUM
2035 S. Third St.
LOUISVILLE 40208

Maintains ethnological and archaeological
exhibits illustrating Indian life. *Special collection:*
Frederick Weygold Collection—Work in flint,
stone and bone from prehistoric Kentucky and
southern Indiana.

ANCIENT BURIED CITY
ARCHAEOLOGY MUSEUM
P.O. Box 155
WICKLIFFE 42087

Displays artifacts from the excavations of the
Mound Builders.

LOUISIANA

LOUISIANA ARTS
AND SCIENCE CENTER
100 S. River Rd.
BATON ROUGE 70801

Exhibits Eskimo soapstone carvings, artifacts and
lithographs; North American Indian crafts,
contemporary pottery and weaving.

LAFAYETTE NATURAL HISTORY
MUSEUM
637 Girard Park Dr.
LAFAYETTE 70503

Special collection: Contemporary Baskets of
Chitimacha and Koasati Indians of Louisiana—
Baskets and weaving of the Acadian culture and
Louisiana Indian cultures. Publications. Library.

GRINDSTONE BLUFF MUSEUM
P.O. Box 7965, 501 Jenkins Rd.
SHREVEPORT 71107
J. Ashley Sibley, President/Director

MAINE

ROBERT ABBE MUSEUM
P.O. Box 286
BAR HARBOR 04609
(207) 288-3519
Dr. Fay Lawson, Director
Diane Kopec, Curator

Displays Native-American prehistoric and ethnographic materials with emphasis on Maine and the Maritime provinces. Includes baskets and quillwork; Passamaquoddy and Penobscot birchbark. Publication. Library.

THE PEARY-MacMILLAN ARCTIC MUSEUM AND ARCTIC STUDIES CENTER
Hubbard Hall, Bowdoin College
BRUNSWICK 04011
(207) 725-8731 ext. 5416
Dr. Susan A. Kaplan, Director

An exhibition of Peary and MacMillan Arctic explorations — Labrador, Baffin and Greenland Inuit and Indian cultures; photographic archives. *Special programs:* Lecture series; tours. *Publication:* Newsletter. Library.

WILSON MUSEUM
Castine Scientific Society
Box 196, Perkins St.
CASTINE 04421
(207) 326-8753
E.W. Doudiet, Director

Contains Pueblo art and artifacts; Plains Indian ornamental beadwork; baskets of the Southwest and Northwest Coast; carvings of Northwest Coast Indians; Mississippi-Ohio area pottery; artifacts of Algonquian origin; tools and implements of Eskimos of Canada and of the Montagnais-Neskapi Indians of Labrador. *Publications: Wilson Museum Bulletin;* newsletter.

PENOBSCOT CULTURAL CENTER PROJECT
P.O. Box 561
OLD TOWN 04468

MAINE TRIBAL UNITY MUSEUM
Quaker Hill Rd.
UNITY 04988
(207) 948-3131
Christopher Marshall, Director

Indian Museum housed in 1880 Old Unity Town House, maintaining a collection of Northeast Indian basketry and artifacts. *Research:* Basket-making techniques. Library.

MARYLAND

PISCATAWAY MUSEUM PROJECT
c/o Mrs. Mervin Savoy
P.O. Box 48
INDIAN HEAD 20640

MASSACHUSETTS

ROBERT S. PEABODY FOUNDATION FOR ARCHAEOLOGY
P.O. Box 71, Phillips and Main Sts.
ANDOVER 01810
(617) 475-0248
Donald McNemar, Director

Exhibits cover archaeology of eastern North America from 7500 B.C. to the present—pottery and artifacts of Pecos Pueblo, New Mexico. Library.

CHILDREN'S MUSEUM
Museum Wharf, 300 Congress St.
BOSTON 02210
(617) 426-6500
Phyllis D. O'Connell, Acting Director
Joan Lester, Curator of Collections

Collection includes Penobscot, Passamaquoddy, Iroquois, Chippewa, Wampanoag and Narragansett materials from both past and present traditions. *Special exhibit:* We're Still Here—American Indians in New England Long Ago and Today. *Programs:* Workshops/courses. Museum Shop. Library. Open to public by appointment only to specially interested visitors, and classes studying Eastern cultures in depth (fee charged.)

PEABODY MUSEUM OF ARCHAEOLOGY AND ETHNOLOGY
11 Divinity Ave.
CAMBRIDGE 02138
(617) 495-2248
C.C. Lamberg-Karlowsky, Director

Contains large collections of archaeological, ethnological and somatological artifacts of North America. Newsletter. Library.

LONGHOUSE MUSEUM
Hassanamisco Reservation
GRAFTON 01519

Memorial to the Eastern Native-American: Artifacts of the Nipmuc Tribe (central Massachusetts); beadwork, utensils, baskets, paintings, and rugs. Publications. Library.

FRUITLANDS MUSEUM, INC.
102 Prospect Hill Rd.
HARVARD 01451
(617) 456-3924
Richard S. Reed, Director

American Indian Museum: Dioramas of local Indian scenes and specimens of historic Indian arts and industries. Publications. Library.

HOLYOKE MUSEUM—WISTARIAHURST
238 Cabot St.
HOLYOKE 01041

Maintains a collection of Northeast Indian artifacts—Iroquois masks and rattles; pottery of the Southeast and Southwest; basketry of the Southwest, Plains and Northwest Coast; Iroquois and Plains Indian beadwork.

WAMPANOAG INDIAN PROGRAM OF PLIMOTH PLANTATION
P.O. Box 1620
PLYMOUTH 02360
(617) 746-1622
David W. Chase, Director

An outdoor living history museum which displays Native-American artifacts from the colonial period.

MICHIGAN

MUSEUM OF ANTHROPOLOGY
University of Michigan
ANN ARBOR 48109-1079
(313) 764-0485
Dr. Jeffrey R. Parsons, Director

Contains extensive holdings in North American archaeology and ethnography. *Special collections:* Hinsdale Collection—Great Lakes Basketry; Greenland Eskimo Collection; Seri and Tarahumara Indian Collection. *Publications:* Papers, memoirs, and technical reports. Library.

CRANBROOK INSTITUTE OF SCIENCE
BLOOMFIELD HILLS 48013

Exhibits cover all major culture areas of North America, especially Woodlands and Plains. Publications.

GREAT LAKES INDIAN MUSEUM
CROSS VILLAGE 49723
Richard A. Pohrt, Owner

Historic Indian museum features material from the Great Lakes area and the western Plains.

CHILDREN'S MUSEUM
Detroit Public Schools
67 East Kirby
DETROIT 48202

Special collection: American Indian Collection—basketry, costumes, crafts, dolls, textiles, musical instruments, tools and weapons for various cultural areas of American Indians. Reference Library.

MUSEUM OF ANTHROPOLOGY
Department of Anthropology
Wayne State University
6001 Cass Ave.
DETROIT 48202
(313) 577-2552
Arnold Pilling, Ph.D., Director

Maintains a collection of Indian artifacts. Research.

MICHIGAN STATE UNIVERSITY MUSEUM
Division of Anthropology
EAST LANSING 48824
(517) 353-7861
Charles E. Cleland, Ph.D., Curator

Special collection: Indians of the Great Lakes—Contains 30 displays relating to the history, technology, religion, and social organization of the Indians of the Great Lakes area.

THE ANISHINABE AKI VILLAGE
Genessee Indian Center
124 West First St,
FLINT 48502
(313) 239-6621

Features Great Lakes Indian cultures, utilizing live demonstrations in authentic settings. *Museum for the Living Arts:* Maintains a collection of arts, crafts, and culture of various tribes. Special shows and cultural presentations are offered throughout the year.

GRAND RAPIDS PUBLIC MUSEUM
54 Jefferson
GRAND RAPIDS 49503
(616) 456-3977
Weldon D. Frankforter, Director

Exhibits Hopewell archaeological material; artifacts from the Historic Site—Norton Indian Mounds (Hopewell.)

ANDREW J. BLACKBIRD MUSEUM
349 East Main St.
HARBOR SPRINGS 49740
(616) 526-2104
Stephen B. Graham, Chairman

Indian Museum. 1855 Andrew J. Blackbird House displaying Indian artifacts and clothing of American Indians.

MICHIGAN HISTORICAL MUSEUM
Michigan History Division
Michigan Department of State
505 North Washington Ave.
LANSING 48918

Maintains Indian exhibits related to the history of Michigan and the old Northwest Territory.

MACKINAC ISLAND
STATE PARK MUSEUM
P.O. BOX 370
MACKINAC ISLAND 49757

Features Indian material from the upper Great Lakes; Chippewa Indian costumes. Publications. Library.

MARQUETTE COUNTY
HISTORICAL SOCIETY MUSEUM
213 North Front St.
MARQUETTE 49855

Displays Indian archaeological and historical material of the upper peninsula of Michigan. *Publications: Indians of Gitche Gumee; Harlow's Wooden Man,* quarterly magazine; books for sale. Library.

FORT ST. JOSEPH MUSEUM
508 East Main St.
NILES 49120
  (616) 683-4702
  D. Wayne Stiles, Director

Special collection: Plym/Quimby Collection of Sioux Indian artifacts—Drawings by Sitting Bull and Rain-in-the-Face, 1881-1883; Woodland Indian artifacts. *Research:* Sioux artifacts and art. Library.

FORT DE BUADE MUSEUM, INC.
334 N. State St.
Mail: 701 N. Logan, LANSING 48915
ST. IGNACE 49781
  (906) 643-8686
  Donald E. Benson, Director

Indian Museum located on the site of 1681, Fort de Buade, built by the French. Displays artifacts, beadwork, photos, lithos, and oils of Woodland Indians.

THE SCHOOLCRAFT
INDIAN AGENCY HOUSE
800 Cedar St.
SAULT STE. MARIE 49783

Historic house built by U.S. Indian agent Henry R. Schoolcraft, housing Indian artifacts.

LUCKHARD'S MUSEUM
THE INDIAN MISSION
821 E. Bay St.
SEBEWAING 48759

Exhibits Indian artifacts and pioneer relics of the 19th-century, housed in original Indian mission of the Chippewa Indians (1845.)

INDIAN DRUM LODGE MUSEUM
Camp Greilick, 4754 Scout Camp Rd.
Mail: 2308 North U.S. 31
TRAVERSE CITY 49684
  Martin A. Melkild, Curator

Indian Museum housed in 1850, Chief Peter Ringnose's log cabin, maintaining ceremonial artifacts, clothing, and wood crafts.

MINNESOTA

ST. LOUIS COUNTY
HISTORICAL SOCIETY MUSEUM
2228 East Superior St.
DULUTH 55812

Collections include paintings of Indians who resided in the County region (1856-1857); Indian artifacts; several volumes (testaments, dictionaries, hymn books) in the Chippewa language. Publications. Library.

MINNEAPOLIS AMERICAN INDIAN
CENTER MUSEUM
1530 East Franklin Ave.
MINNEAPOLIS 55404

PLAINS ART MUSEUM
Box 37, 521 Main Ave.
MOOREHEAD 56560
  (218) 236-7171
  Carol Rice, Curator

Exhibits North American Indian art and Eskimo sculpture.

LAC QUI PARLE
INDIAN MISSION CHURCH
RR 1, Box 125
MORTON 56270
  (507) 697-6321
  Tom Ellig, Director

An Historic Indian Mission—1835, restored in 1942; maintains history and archaeology collections.

PIPESTONE COUNTY
HISTORICAL MUSEUM
113 S. Hiawatha
PIPESTONE 56164
  (507) 825-2563
  Linda Lounsbury, Director

Contains artifacts from the Dakota and Ojibwa Tribes—Plains Indian saddle, and ceremonial pipes.

PIPESTONE NATIONAL MONUMENT
P.O. Box 727
PIPESTONE 56164
  Betty McSwain, Park Ranger

Description: Original pipestone (*catlinite*, named for noted painter of Indians, George Catlin) quarry from which the Dakota Sioux fashioned their ceremonial pipes. *Local History Museum and Upper Midwest Indian Cultural Center:* Exhibits Indian ceremonial pipes and pipestone objects; pipestone quarries. *Publications: Pipestone: A History; Pipes on the Plains;* booklets. Library.

**MINNESOTA HISTORICAL
SOCIETY MUSEUM**
1500 Mississippi St.
ST. PAUL 55101

Exhibits depicting prehistoric and contemporary Indian life in Minnesota. Major collecting areas include Dakota and Ojibwa material; photo collection. *Publication: Minnesota History,* quarterly magazine. Library.

MINNESOTA MUSEUM OF ART
30 E. 10th St.
ST. PAUL 55102

Maintains extensive displays of local Indian material, including Chippewa and Blackfeet Indian artifacts; dioramas and life-size habitat displays of Northwest, Southwest and Plains cultures.

WINNEBAGO AREA MUSEUM
WINNEBAGO 56098
  (506) 893-3692
  Marion Muir, President

An archaeological museum exhibiting Oneonta (900-1500 A.D.) artifacts, Woodland (1000-8000 B.C.) artifacts; beadwork of the Chippewa and Sioux. Library.

MISSISSIPPI

**WINTERVILLE INDIAN MOUNDS
STATE PARK**
Route 3, Box 600
GREENVILLE 38701

Museum: Collection of Indian artifacts, excavated from the Mounds area. Library.

JP MUSEUM OF INDIAN ARTIFACTS
Highway 49
Mail: Route 1, Box 715, SAUCIER 39574
LYMAN 39574
  John and Patricia Wright, Owner/Directors

Archaeology and Indian Museum housed in a

World War II barrack, containing more than 8,000 Indian artifacts from 14 States. *Research:* Indian artifacts and genealogy. Library.

COBB INSTITUTE OF ARCHAEOLOGY
Drawer AR
MISSISSIPPI STATE UNIVERSITY 39762
  (601) 325-3826
  E.J. Vardaman, Director

Exhibits Indian materials of Mississippi culture. *Publication: Indians of Mississippi.* Library.

**THE GRAND VILLAGE
OF THE NATCHEZ INDIANS**
400 Jefferson Davis Blvd.
NATCHEZ 39120
  (601) 446-6502
  James F. Barnett, Jr., Director

Description: A 128 acre National Historic Landmark site is the location of the ceremonial mound center for the Natchez tribe during the French colonization of the area (ca. 1682-1730.) *Museum:* Contains Indian and European artifacts gathered from the excavations and interpreted exhibits on the Natchez and Southeastern Indians. *Special progams:* Educational programs; slide lectures and guided tours. Library.

OLD SPANISH FORT AND MUSEUM
4602 Fort St.
PASCAGOULA 39567

Features Indian artifacts, tools and implements; and maps showing Indian settlements prior to 1700. Library.

**THE CHOCTAW MUSEUM
OF THE SOUTHERN INDIAN**
Mississippi Band of Choctaw Indians
Route 7, Box 21
PHILADELPHIA 39350
  (601) 656-5251

MISSOURI

MUSEUM OF ANTHROPOLOGY
University of Missouri
104 Swallow Hall
COLUMBIA 65211
  (314) 882-3764
  Dr. Lawrence H. Feldman, Director/Curator

Maintains collections of ethnographic material from the Plains and Southwest Indians; Eskimo and Mexican materials. Publications.

TOWOSAHGY STATE HISTORIC SITE
Big Oak Tree State Park
P.O. Box 35
EAST PRAIRIE 63845
  Ken Cole, Archaeologist

Exhibits Indian artifacts excavated from the site (1000-1400 A.D. Mississippian Culture Civic Ceremonial Center.)

MISSOURI STATE MUSEUM
State Capitol
JEFFERSON CITY 65101

Collections include Musquakie ceremonial material, Missouri pottery, Kema Cave artifacts, Indian burial mound material, stone artifacts and archaic Indian artifacts.

**KANSAS CITY MUSEUM
OF HISTORY AND SCIENCE**
3218 Gladstone Blvd.
KANSAS CITY 66208

Special collections: Osage Indians—Focuses on Woodlands village dwelling, hoe horticulture, Plains buffalo hunting, ceremonies, decorative arts, and straight dance; Daniel G. Crowley Collection—Plains Indian artifacts. *Publication: Frontier Gazette.* Library.

**WILLIAM ROCKHILL NELSON GALLERY
AND ATKINS MUSEUM OF FINE ARTS**
4525 Oak St.
KANSAS CITY 64111

Exhibits Native arts of the Americas, with emphasis on the Southwest, Mesoamerica, and South America. Publications. Library.

**LYMAN ARCHAEOLOGICAL
RESEARCH CENTER MUSEUM**
Route 1
MIAMI 65344

Contains 23 exhibits, including extensive research and study collection of Oneonta (protohistoric Missouri Indian tribe); Woodland and Archaic artifacts. *Publication: Missouri Indian Tribe in Archaeology and History.* Library.

**MUSEUM OF SCIENCE
AND NATURAL HISTORY**
Oak Knoll Park
ST. LOUIS 63105
(314) 726-2888
James G. Houser, Curator

Exhibits pre-Columbian North American Indian artifacts; collection on Missouri Indian archaeology. Library.

THE ST. LOUIS ART MUSEUM
Forest Park
ST. LOUIS 63110

Maintains a collection of artifacts, pottery, carvings, basketry and clothing of the Pueblo, Pueblo Mimbres, Plains, West Coast, and Mound Builder Indians. Bulletin. Library.

MONTANA

MUSEUM OF THE PLAINS INDIAN
P.O. Box 400, Highway 89
BROWNING 59417
(406) 338-2230
Rosemary Ellison, Curator

Administered by the Indian Arts and Crafts Board. Presents historic arts created by the tribal peoples of the Northern Plains, including the Blackfeet, Crow, Northern Cheyenne, Sioux, Assiniboine, Arapaho, Shoshone, Nez Perce, Flathead, Chippewa, and Cree. Displays the varied traditional costumes of Northern Plains men, women and children in complete detail on life-size figures. *Special programs:* Film, *Winds of Change*—about the evolution of Indian cultures on the Northern Plains, narrated by Vincent Price; series of one-person exhibitions; painted tipis on the grounds during summer; demonstrations of Native-American arts and crafts techniques; tours. *Publications:* Illustrated catalogs and brochures.

**CUSTER BATTLEFIELD
NATIONAL MONUMENT**
P.O. Box 39
CROW AGENCY 59022
(406) 638-2622
James V. Court, Superintendent

Description: Historic area commemorating the Battle of the Little Big Horn, where Lt. Col. George A. Custer and his troops of the 7th U.S. Cavalry were annihilated by Sioux and Cheyenne Indians. *Museum:* Contains historical documents authored by or associated with George A. Custer, the Battle of the Little Big Horn, and other events and persons associated with the Indian Wars on the Northern Plains (1865-1891.) Military and ethnographic specimens relating to the conflict, including items associated with the Sioux, Crow, and Northern Cheyenne Tribes. Publications.

**CROW TRIBE HISTORICAL
AND CULTURAL COMMISSION**
P.O. Box 173
CROW AGENCY 59022
(406) 638-2328

H. EARLE CLACK MUSEUM
P.O. Box 1675
HAVRE 59501
Duane Nabor, Director
Mrs. Louis Clack, Curator

Exhibit includes historic artifacts from the Chippewa and Cree Indians, excavated from site area; dioramas.

**MONTANA HISTORICAL
SOCIETY MUSEUM**
225 North Roberts
HELENA 59601

Special collection: Towe Ford Collection—
Features the chronological story of Montana's
frontier through dioramas and other displays.
C.M. Russell Gallery of Western Art.
Publications. Library.

**NORTHERN CHEYENNE
TRIBAL MUSEUM**
LAME DEER 59043

MONTANA STATE UNIVERSITY MUSEUM
Fine Arts Bldg.
MISSOULA 59801

Displays Indian art and artifacts of Montana.

FORT PECK TRIBAL MUSEUM
P.O. Box 115
POPLAR 59255

**CHIEF PLENTY COUPS
STATE MONUMENT**
P.O. Box 35
PRYOR 59066
  (406) 252-1289
  Jim Flynn, Director

Crow Indian Museum: Ethnographic material of
the Crow people; paintings, drawings; prehistoric
artifacts.

FLATHEAD INDIAN MUSEUM
Flathead Indian Reservation
P.O. Box 464
ST. IGNATIUS 59865
  Doug Allard, Director

BIG HOLE NATIONAL BATTLEFIELD
P.O. Box 237
WISDOM 59761
  (406) 689-2530
  Alfred W. Schulmeyer, Superintendent

Description: A 655 acre battlefield which
preserves the scene of a battle between Nez Perce
Indians and the Seventh U.S. Infantry, fought on
August 9 and 10, 1877. *Museum:* Exhibits
detailing Nez Perce culture and soldier life of the
1870's; audiovisual program. Library.

NEBRASKA

MUSEUM OF THE FUR TRADE
HC-74, Box 18
CHADRON 69337
  (308) 432-3843
  Charles E. Hanson, Jr., Director

Maintains a collection of material illustrating the
cultures of North American Indians, and the
influence of the fur trade on those cultures.
Restored and outfitted 1837 Indian trading post
and warehouse. Indian garden for crops obtained
from Mandan, Dakota, Assiniboine, Arikara,
Hidatsa and Omaha Indians. *Publication:*
Quarterly magazine. Library.

FORT ROBINSON MUSEUM
Nebraska State Historical Society
P.O. Box 304
CRAWFORD 69339

Exhibits archaeological and ethnological items.
Microfilm records of Red Cloud and Spotted Tail
Indian Agencies.

HASTINGS MUSEUM
1330 North Burlington
HASTINGS 68901

A collection of Indian artifacts; Sioux Indian
habitat group. Indian film. Publications.

FORT KEARNEY MUSEUM
311 South Central Ave.
KEARNEY 68847

Displays Indian art from the Rosebud Indian
Reservation.

**NEBRASKA STATE
HISTORICAL MUSEUM**
P.O. Box 82554, 131 N. Centennail Mall
LINCOLN 68501
  (402) 471-3279
  Marvin F. Kivett, Dirctor

Features collections in art, anthropology, and
archaeology; includes costumes and artifacts of
Indians of Nebraska and the central Plains.
Publication: Nebraska History, quarterly
magazine; monthly newsletter; books for sale.

NEVADA

NEVADA STATE MUSEUM
CARSON CITY 89701

Maintains study collections of Nevada Indian
artifacts. Publications. Library.

**STEWART INDIAN
MUSEUM ASSOCIATION**
5366 Snyder Ave.
CARSON CITY 89701

NORTHEASTERN NEVADA MUSEUM
P.O. Box 503, 1515 Idaho St.
ELKO 89801

Contains ten local Shoshone Indian exhibits.

NEW JERSEY

THE MONTCLAIR ART MUSEUM
3 S. Mountain Ave.
MONTCLAIR 07042

Exhibits feature costumes, jewelry, and artifacts of Eastern Woodlands, Desert Pueblo, Navajo, Apache, Plains, California and Northwest Indians and Eskimos. Publications. Library.

MORRIS MUSEUM OF ARTS AND SCIENCES
P.O. Box 125
Normandy Heights and Columbia Rds.
MORRISTOWN 07961

Woodland Indians Gallery: Shows the development of Woodland culture from the Paleo-Indian through Archaic to Woodland and historic periods. *North American Indian Gallery:* Exhibits on the Northwest Coast, the Southwest, and the Plains Indians. Library. Museum shop.

NEWARK MUSEUM
49 Washington St.
NEWARK 07101

Indian art and artifacts representative of the products of tribes in various parts of the country. Includes paintings on skin, totem poles, blankets, Hopi kachina dolls, pottery, silverwork, and basketry. Publications. Library.

PRINCETON UNIVERSITY MUSEUM OF NATURAL HISTORY
Guyot Hall
PRINCETON 08540

Exhibits Northwest Coast Indian art; also, artifacts, mainly Tlingit, of Yukatat and Sitka areas, Alaska, period 1876-1886. Publications. Library.

SETON HALL UNIVERSITY MUSEUM
South Orange Ave.
SOUTH ORANGE 07079
(201) 761-9543
Herbert C. Kraft, Director

An archaeology and Indian museum featuring Eastern Woodlands Indian artifacts, and material on New Jersey Indians of today. Library.

NEW JERSEY STATE MUSEUM
205 West State St.
TRENTON 08625

Maintains a collection of ethnographic artifacts of the Lenni Lenape; also, Plains Indian beadwork, and material from Southwest, Eskimo and Northeast Indians. Library.

NEW MEXICO

ACOMA MUSEUM
P.O. Box 309, Pueblo of Acoma
ACOMITA 87034
(505) 552-6606
Juan S. Juanico, Director

Indian history and culture museum with photo archives and documents relating to the history of Acoma; also artifacts. *Publication: One Thousand Years of Clay,* catalog. Library.

INDIAN PUEBLO CULTURAL CENTER
2401 12th St., N.W.
ALBUQUERQUE 87102
(505) 843-7270/7271

MAXWELL MUSEUM OF ANTHROPOLOGY
University and Ash, NE
ALBUQUERQUE 87131
(505) 277-4404
J.J. Brody, Director

Exhibits Navajo weaving, Mimbres and Pueblo pottery, Hopi kachinas, North American Indian basketry. *Publications: Seven Families in Pueblo Pottery; Anasazi Pottery,* et al. Library. Navajo and Pueblo silver jewelry for sale.

AZTEC RUINS NATIONAL MONUMENT
P.O. Box U
AZTEC 87410
(505) 334-6174
Clarence N. Gorman, Superintendent

Description: Prehistoric Pueblo Indian ruin. Two-(cultural) phase inhabitation, Chaco Canyon and Mesa Verde. *Archaeology Museum:* Materials gathered from excavations of area sites, and from sites in the Lower San Juan Basin. Library.

BENALLY BROTHERS MUSEUM OF INDIAN ART
1235 Aztec Blvd., NE
AZTEC 87410

CORONADO STATE MONUMENT
P.O. Box 95
BERNALILLO 87004

Description: Site of a partially reconstructed Pueblo Indian village ruin occupied circa 1300-1600. Includes a completely reconstructed underground ceremonial *kiva,* which was the first to be discovered bearing ceremonial murals. Exhibits material from the excavations and Pueblo Indian culture.

**CHACO CULTURE
NATIONAL HISTORICAL PARK**
Star Route 4, Box 6500
BLOOMFIELD 87413
(505) 786-5384
Tom Vaughan, Superintendent

Description: Thirteen major prehistoric Anasazi sites, and over 400 smaller village sites. *Museum:* Features 26 exhibits on prehistoric Pueblo Indians and Navajo people. Library.

RED ROCK MUSEUM
P.O. Box 328, Red Rock State Park
CHURCH ROCK 87311
(505) 722-5564
Belinda Casto-Landolt, Curator

Indian arts and crafts museum exhibiting crafts and artifacts of prehistoric Anasazi and Navajo, Hopi, Zuni, Rio Grande Pueblos, Apache and Plains Indians.

DEMING LUNA MIMBRES MUSEUM
P.O. Box 1617, 301 S. Silver
DEMING 88030
(505) 546-2382
Treva L. Mester, Coordinator

Exhibits Mimbrano Indian artifacts, and pottery.

JICARILLA ARTS AND CRAFTS MUSEUM
P.O. Box 147
DULCE 87528

**SAN JUAN COUNTY
ARCHAEOLOGICAL RESEARCH CENTER
AND LIBRARY AT SALMON RUIN**
No. 975 U.S. Highway 64
FARMINGTON 87401
(505) 632-2013
Jo Lynn Davenport Smith, Director

Contains exhibits of artifacts taken from the Anasazi ruin; extensive on-loan collection of Navajo legends, myths, chants, and religious ceremonies; slides of rock art; oral history tapes; maps. *Publications:* Newsletter; historical publications; technical reports. Research library.

**GALLUP MUSEUM
OF INDIAN ARTS AND CRAFTS**
P.O. Box 1395, 103 West 66th Ave.
GALLUP 87301

Exhibits Indian artifacts, arts and crafts of the Navajo, Hopi, and Zuni Indians of the Southwest; also material from other tribes of the Americas.

WOODARD'S INDIAN ARTS MUSEUM
224 W. Coal Ave.
GALLUP 87301
M.L. Woodard, Manager

Maintains original Indian paintings, including works by Beatien Yazz, Andy Tsinajinnie, and others. Also, kachina dolls, carvings, textiles, silver and ancient objects. Arts and crafts shop.

BANDELIER NATIONAL MONUMENT
LOS ALAMOS 87544
(505) 672-3861
John D. Hunter, Superintendent

Description: Approximately 29,000 acres of ruins of the Pueblo (Anasazi) culture, dating from about 1200-1600 A.D. Publications. Library.

**MESCALERO APACHE
CULTURAL CENTER MUSEUM**
P.O. Box 176
MESCALERO 88340
(505) 671-4495

SALINAS NATIONAL MONUMENT
Route 1, Box 496
MOUNTAINAIR 87036
(505) 847-2585
Thomas B. Carroll, Superintendent

Description: Located on the site of prehistoric pithouses, 800 A.D.; prehistoric Indian ruins 1100-1670 A.D.; four Spanish Mission ruins, 1627-1672. *Archaeology museum:* Maintains a collection of artifacts from the ruins. Library.

PECOS NATIONAL MONUMENT
P.O. Drawer 11
PECOS 87535
(505) 757-6414
John Bezy, Superintendent

Historic site located on prehistoric Pueblo ruins and ruins of four Spanish churches. Exhibits artifacts from kiva excavations.

PICURIS PUEBLO MUSEUM
P.O. Box 228
PENASCO 87553

PALEO-INDIAN INSTITUTE
P.O. Box 2154
Eastern New Mexico University
PORTALES 88130
Dr. George Agogino, Director

Maintains exhibits illustrating the life of the paleo-archaic and modern Indian. Library.

EL MORRO NATIONAL MONUMENT
RAMAH 87321
(505) 783-5132
Douglas Eury, Superintendent

Archaeological site of Inscription Rock, prehistoric Pueblo ruins. Library.

INSTITUTE OF AMERICAN INDIAN ARTS MUSEUM
1369 Cerrillos Rd.
SANTA FE 87501
(505) 988-6281
Charles A. Dailey, Director
Manuelita Lovato, Curator

Special collection: Student "Honors" Collection—Contains approximately 6,000 items—paintings, graphics, sculpture, ceramics, textiles, costumes, jewelry, and ethnological material of Native-American students' work. Also, more than 1,000 items of non-student work done by Indian artists throughout the U.S. *Special programs:* Art festival, lectures, workshops; arts and crafts for sale. *Publication: Spawing the Medicine River,* quarterly. Native-American Videotape Archives and Library.

MUSEUM OF INDIAN ARTS AND CULTURE — LABORATORY OF ANTHROPOLOGYLOGY
P.O. Box 2087, 708 Camino Lejo
SANTA FE 87504
(505) 827-8941
Dr. Mary Elizabeth King, Director

Consists of over 15,000 ethnographic objects and more than 26,000 archaeological objects, with emphasis on artifacts from the prehistoric, ethnographic, and present-day Indian Southwest. The *Museum of Indian Arts and Culture* is scheduled to open in the Spring of 1987, and will feature permanent exhibitions of Southwestern Indian culture. *Publications:* Papers in Anthropology; Research Records; Lab Notes; and Archaeological Surveys. Library.

MUSEUM OF NEW MEXICO FINE ARTS MUSEUM
P.O. Box 1727, 127 E. Palace Ave.
SANTA FE 87501

Special collection: Indian Arts Fund Collection—Contains pottery, jewelry, and costumes; art of the Southwest.

SAN ILDEFONSO PUEBLO MUSEUM
Route 5, Box 315-A
SANTA FE 87501
(505) 455-2424

THE WHEELWRIGHT MUSEUM OF THE AMERICAN INDIAN
P.O. Box 5153, 704 Camino Lejo
SANTA FE 87502
(505) 982-4636
Richard W. Lang, Director
LaRayne Parrish, Curator

Collections of Southwest ethnology—Navajo textiles and silver; Navajo, Apache, and Hopi basketry; Pueblo pottery; Navajo, Apache, and Pueblo cradleboards; Navajo sandpainting reproductions. *Special programs:* Lecture series; textile and basket-weaving workshops; craft demonstrations; Indian arts and crafts and books for sale. *Publication:* Quarterly newsletter. Library.

WESTERN NEW MEXICO UNIVERSITY MUSEUM
Campus Mail, WNMU
SILVER CITY 88062
(505) 538-6386
Douglas M. Dinwiddie, Director

Special collection: Eisele Collection of Ancient Mimbres Pottery. Also dozens of "picture bowls" depicting life and culture of the ancient Mimbres culture of circa 1100 A.D.; collection of Mogollon Culture artifacts, including lithics, pottery, and fiber.

THE HARWOOD FOUNDATION
University of New Mexico
Ledoux St.
TAOS 87571

Exhibits Indian artifacts pertaining to the Sioux, Zuni, Taos, Apache, Cheyenne, Ute, and Hopi Tribes. Library.

KIT CARSON MEMORIAL FOUNDATION
P.O. Drawer B, Old Kit Carson Rd.
TAOS 87571
(505) 758-4741
Jack Boyer, Director

Displays artifacts of prehistoric Indian culture of Taos and the Southwest. Library.

MILLICENT ROGERS MUSEUM
P.O. Box A
TAOS 87571
(505) 758-2462
Arthur H. Wolf, Director
Michael Stephens, Curator

Exhibits prehistoric and historic Southwest and Plains Native-American art and material culture.

ZUNI MUSEUM PROJECT
c/o Zuni Archaeological Program
P.O. Box 339
ZUNI 87327

NEW YORK

NEW YORK STATE MUSEUM
Cultural Education Center
Empire State Plaza
ALBANY 12224

Special collections: Morgan Collection—Mid 19th century Seneca ethnographic material; The Beauchamp Collection—Onondaga ethnographic material; The Parker Collection—Late 19th and 20th century Iroquois ethnological and general New York archaeological materials. Publications. Library.

SIX NATIONS INDIAN MUSEUM
ANCHIOTA 12968

OWASCO STOCKADED INDIAN VILLAGE
Emerson Park
Mail: 203 Genessee St.
AUBURN 13021
  (315) 253-8051
  Walter K. Long, Director

Indian History Museum: Maintains a collection of Indian artifacts. Crafts for sale. Library.

KATERI GALLERIES
The National Shrine of North American Martyrs
AURIESVILLE 12016
  (518) 853-3033
  Rec. Robert J. Boyle, S.J., Director
  Rev. John M. Dovlan, S.J., Curator

Located on the site of the martyrdom of Father Isaac Jogues, French Jesuit priest, and his companions who were killed by the Mohawk Indians in 1642. Also, the 1656 Birthplace of Kateri Tekakwitha. *Special collection:* Mohawk Indian Culture Collection—Indian artifacts and handicrafts; Indian longhouse dioramas. *Publication: Pilgrim,* quarterly magazine. Library.

TONAWANDA-SENECA MUSEUM
Tonawanda-Seneca Reservation
BASOM 14013

THE BROOKLYN CHILDREN'S MUSEUM
145 Brooklyn Ave.
BROOKLYN 11213

Exhibits Plains Indian material; also, Southwestern, Eastern Woodlands and Northwest Indian artifacts. Library.

BUFFALO AND ERIE COUNTY HISTORICAL SOCIETY MUSEUM
Humboldt Park
BUFFALO 14211

Maintains a collection of Niagara frontier Indian artifacts, including clothing, masks, and tools, mostly of Iroquois village life. Publications. Library.

MUSEUM OF THE HUDSON HIGHLANDS
The Boulevard
CORNWALL-ON-HUDSON 12520

Special collection: Eastern Woodlands Indians—Exhibits more than 80 stone artifacts; 40 modern reproductions made by a group of Iroquois. Library.

BLACK BEAR MUSEUM
ESOPUS 12429
  Roy Black Bear, Owner

THE MOHAWK-CAUGHNAWAGA MUSEUM
Route 5, Box 554
FONDA 12068
  (518) 853-3678
  Rev. Nicholas Weiss, Chairman
  Volkert Veeder, Curator

Located on the site of the 1666-1693 excavated Caughnawaga Indian Village. Displays North, South and Central American Indian artifacts, with emphasis on the Iroquois of central New York State. *Publication: Mohawk Indian-Mo and Their Valley. Library.*

TEKAKWITHA SHRINE
Route 5, Box 627, RD 1
FONDA 12068
  (518) 853-3646
  Rev. Nicholas Weiss, Director

Religious Shrine and Historic Archaeological Site, 1666-1693; Mohawk Indian Castle: residence of Kateri Tekakwitha.

AKWESASNE MUSEUM
Akwesasne Cultural Center
Route 37, Akwesasne Mohawk Nation
HOGANSBURG 13655
  (518) 358-2272 ext. 269

Showcases Mohawk culture by exhibiting contemporary Iroquoian art and historic artifacts. *Special programs:* Changing art exhibit; contemporary baskets by master basketmakers of Akwesasne; slide-tape shows on Iroquoian art; Native arts classes; produces movies, slide shows, and video; sells original handicrafts through *Sweetgrass Gift Shop. Publications: Akwesasne Notes; Indian Time; Akwekon Magazine; Kariwenhawi,* newsletter; Native-American art books for sale. Library.

SENECA INDIAN HISTORICAL SOCIETY
12199 Brant Reservation Rd.
IRVING 14081
   Twylah Nitsch, Director

STE. MARIE DE GANNENTAHA
P.O. Box 146, Onondaga Lake Park
LIVERPOOL 13088
(315) 457-2990
   Dennis Connors, Director

Description: A reconstruction of a 1656 French settlement among the Onondaga Iroquois. Maintains archaeological material from area sites—Onondaga cultural material. *Special programs:* Living History Program—interpretation of Onondaga Indian culture; lectures. *Publication: Onondaga Portrait of a Native People.* Library.

PLUME INDIAN MUSEUM
Route 208, Highland Mills Rd.
MONROE 10950

Exhibits ceremonial costumes, artifacts and relics, particularly of the Pueblo, Navajo, Iroquois and Sioux Indians. Indian Shop.

**AMERICAN INDIAN COMMUNITY
HOUSE GALLERY**
164 Mercer St.
NEW YORK 10003
(212) 226-7433

Displays art works by Native-Americans.

**AMERICAN MUSEUM
OF NATURAL HISTORY**
79th St. and Central Park West
NEW YORK 10024

(212) 873-1300 ext. 245/236
   Craig Morris, Ph.D., Chairman
   Stanley A. Freed, Ph.D., Curator

Special collections: Eskimo Exhibit, and Indians of the Northwest Coast—Artifacts of the Coast Salish, Nootka, Haida, Tsimpshean, Thompson, Bella Coola, Tlingit, and Kwakiutl; also, shamanistic regalia and ceremonial objects. *Publications: Natural History; Curator;* Bulletin; Anthropological Papers. Library and Reading Room.

MUSEUM OF THE AMERICAN INDIAN
Heye Foundation
Broadway at 155th St.
NEW YORK 10032
(212) 283-2420
   Dr. Roland W. Force, Director

"Acknowledged to be one of the largest and finest assemblage of artifacts representing the native cultures of North, Central, and South America,

the Museum (founded 1916) is a national treasury unsurpassed for its potential for education and research. Its areal and temporal scope is vast, ranging from Alaska to Chile and from the Paleo-Indian period to the present, encompassing societies as diverse as the 20th century hunting band societies of the Arctic and subarctic and the ancient agricultural civilizations of the Aztec and Inca. The artifacts in the collections range from precious ornaments to commonplace tools, from projectile points to abstract paintings by contemporary Indian artists. The Central and South American and the Caribbean collections include ancient ornaments of Mexican jade and turquoise, ancient gold, silver, basketry, fabrics, and pottery, stone, and shell scultpures from the Antilles. The North American collections include silver and turquoise jewelry, weavings, and pottery from the Southwest; painted wooden sculptures from the Northwest Coast; ancient carved shell artifacts from the Southeast; and carved ivory and stone from the Arctic." *Special programs:* Education Department offers guided tours, visiting Native-American artists and artisans, and a lecture series; The Film and Video Center researches and exhibits film and video productions concerned with Inuit and Indian peoples of the Americas; The Indian Information Center makes available to the public a wide variety of information concerning the native poeples of the Americas; The Museum Shop offers a wide variety of contemporary Indian crafts from many tribes, and books, slides, etc. *Publications: Indian Notes; MAI Newsletter,* quarterly; exhibition catalogs, archaeological reports, ethnological studies, bibliographies and biographies published by the Museum for sale; *Native American Film and Video Catalog. Photographic Archives:* Contains approximately 70,000 photographs documenting Native-American life in the Western Hemisphere. Slides and prints are available for purchase. Library.

**NATIVE AMERICAN CENTRE
FOR THE LIVING ARTS, INC.**
25 Rainbow Mall
NIAGARA FALLS 14303
(716) 284-2427
   Duffy Wilson, Executive Director
   Elwood Green, Curator

Maintains a collection of Native-American archaeological and ethnological artifacts; Native-American archives and iconography. *Publications: Turtle,* quarterly tabloid; *Art Catalogues,* book. Library.

SIX NATIONS INDIAN MUSEUM
ONCHIOTA 12968
(518) 891-0769
   Ray Fadden, Owner

Dedicated to preserving the culture of the Iroquois Confederacy (Mohawks, Senecas, Onondagas, Oneidas, Cayugas and Tuscaroras), the Museum exhibits pre-Columbian, historic, as well as contemporary items of Iroquois culture—clothing, tools, crafts, baskets, and objects of art; a collection of charts, posters, and written material; miniature Abenaki, Lakota, Delaware and Mohegan villages. *Special program:* Lectures on Native-American history and culture.

YAGER MUSEUM
Hartwick College
ONEONTA 13820
(607) 432-4200
Kathryn Flom, Curator

A collection of upper Susquehanna Indian artifacts, and Southwest basketry and pottery. Library.

ROCHESTER MUSEUM
AND SCIENCE CENTER
657 East Ave., Box 1480
ROCHESTER 14603
(716) 271-4320
Richard C. Shultz, President
Charles F. Hayes, III, Research Director

Exhibits Native-American material related to archaeology, ethnology, and physical anthropology, with emphasis on Iroquois and Algonkian cultures. Collection includes dioramas, Indian arts and artifacts; paintings by Ernest Smith. Publications. Library.

SENECA-IROQUOIS NATIONAL MUSEUM
Allegany Indian Reservation
P.O. Box 442, Broad St. Extension
SALAMANCA 14779
(716) 945-1738
George H.J. Abrams, Director

Devoted to the presentation of the prehistory, history, and contemporary culture of the Seneca Nation of Indians, and, in a wider sense, the Iroquois Indians. *Special program:* Living Artists Series—lectures. *Publication: 1981 Collections of the Seneca-Iroquois National Museum.* Library. Museum shop.

SCHOHARIE MUSEUM
OF THE IROQUOIS INDIAN
P.O. Box 158, North Main St.
SCHOHARIE 12157
(518) 295-8553/234-2276
Dr. Christina B. Johannsen, Director

Maintains an extensive collection of contemporary Iroquois fine art and craftwork; archaeological materials of the Northeast and Schoharie Valley occupations from the Archaic Period to the Contact Period (1700's);

photographic collections of contemporary Iroquois arts, ethnographic objects, events and people. *Special programs:* Educational programs; annual Iroquois Indian Festival (Labor Day Weekend) at SUNY, Cobleskill College. *Publications: Museum Notes,* irregular; *Stan Hill: Iroquois Art,* 1985 catalog; *Iroquois Arts: A Directory of a People and Their Work.* Library.

NORTH CAROLINA

CHEROKEE INDIAN CYCLORAMA
P.O. Box 398, Highway 19E
CHEROKEE 28719
(704) 497-4521 (April-October)
(704) 497-2111 (November-March)

Explains over 300 years of Cherokee history by the use of life-size wax figures depicting actual events. A large scale electronically lighted map of the Southeast shows the vast empire of the Cherokee Nation, covering over eight southern states, fade away to the present Qualla Indian Reservation. Displays portray the techniques in making Cherokee crafts and tools. Open April, May, September and October.

MUSEUM OF THE CHEROKEE INDIAN
U.S. Highway 441 North, Box 770-A
CHEROKEE 28719
(704-497-3481
Juanita Hughes, Curator
Maxine Hill, General Manager

Exhibits Cherokee Indian artifacts, relics and documents. *Publication: Journal of Cherokee Studies,* semiannual. Library.

SCHIELE MUSEUM REFERENCE
LIBRARY AND CENTER FOR
SOUTHEASTERN NATIVE
AMERICAN STUDIES
P.O. Box 953, 1500 E. Garrison Blvd.
GASTONIA 28053-0953
(704) 865-6131
Richard Alan Stout, Executive Director
Ms. M. Turner, Registrar and Librarian

Maintains extensive holdings of Native-American artifacts, clothing, utensils, rugs, pottery, jewelry, costumes, arts and crafts, etc. spanning known history; collections of 12 major cultural areas throughout the U.S. and Canada; specialized collections on Southeast Indians, especially pottery; also, lithic material from the Southeast with special sections relating to local areas of North Carolina. *The Catawba Village: A* replicated Southeastern Indian village, circa 1550, representing Catawba and Southeastern Indian architecture and lifestyles from the 16th through 19th centuries. *Special programs:* Catawba Village Study-Tour Program designed for grades 4 and up, where students explore the ways and means of aboriginal life; contract courses; workshops; The Southeastern Indian Culture Study Group; annual Native-American Fall Festival in September. Library.

INDIAN MUSEUM OF THE CAROLINAS
607 Turnpike Rd.
LAURINBURG 28352
  (919) 276-5880
  Dr. Margaret Houston, Director

Exhibits Indian ethnographic material and modern Native American art and artifacts of North and South Carolina, and the Southeast U.S. Comparative displays show artifacts from other georgaphic areas. *Special programs:* Evening speakers program; guided tours. Library.

INDIAN VILLAGE MUSEUM
Roanoke Island Historical Park
P.O. Box 906
MANTEO 27954

Located on the site selected for the first English colony attempt in America. Working exhibits of tools and methods of ancient inhabitants. Library.

TOWN CREEK INDIAN MOUND
STATE HISTORIC SITE
Route 3, Box 50
MT. GILEAD 27306
  (919) 439-6802
  Archie Smith, Manager

A reconstructed 16th-century Indian ceremonial center with mound, two temples, mortuary and palisade. *Museum:* Exhibits artifacts representing Indians of the Carolina Piedmont.

NATIVE AMERICAN RESOURCE CENTER
Pembroke State University
PEMBROKE 28372
  (919) 521-4214
  Linda E. Oxendine, Director

Displays authentic Indian artifacts, handicrafts, art, books, cassettes, record albums and filmstrips about Native-Americans with emphasis on the Lumbee Indians of Robeson County. *Publications: Good To Be An Indian: Proud and Free; North Carolina Indians: 65,000 Strong; The Early Americans.* Library.

NORTH CAROLINA DIVISION
OF ARCHIVES AND HISTORY MUSEUM
109 E. Jones St.
RALEIGH 27611

CATAWBA MUSEUM
OF ANTHROPOLOGY
2113 Brenner Ave., Heath Hill Forest
SALISBURY 28144
  (704) 637-4111/4447
  Dee Dee Joyce, Director/Curator

Exhibits on the prehistoric and historic culture of American Indians, primarily from the Mid-Atlantic and Southeast Plains.

MUSEUM OF MAN
Wake Forest University
WINSTON-SALEM 27106
  (919) 761-5282
  Linda B. Robertson, Director/Instructor

An anthropology museum exhibiting North and South American Indian artifacts.

NORTH DAKOTA

STATE HISTORICAL SOCIETY
OF NORTH DAKOTA
North Dakota Heritage Center
Capitol Grounds
BISMARCK 58505
  (701) 224-2666
  James E. Sperry, Superintendent

Collections include ethnological, ethnographical, and prehistory materials of all types dating throughout the eras of known occupation of the northern Great Plains by human beings (circa 10,000 B.C. to present.) *Publications: North Dakota History: Journal of the Northern Great Plains; Plains Talk,* Newsletter. Archives and Library.

BUFFALO TRAILS MUSEUM
EPPING 58843

Depicts Indian culture native to the region (Upper Missouri area.) Exhibits Plains Indian artifacts; dioramas: Assiniboine Village, Tree Burial, Hidatsa Fortified Site.

STANDING ROCK
RESERVATION MUSEUM
FORT YATES 58538

NORTH DAKOTA MUSEUM OF ART
P.O. Box 7305, University Station
GRAND FORKS 58202
  (701) 777-4195
  Laurel J. Reuter, Director

Displays American Indian art.

THREE AFFILIATED TRIBES MUSEUM
Fort Berthold Reservation
NEW TOWN 58763

OHIO

AKRON ART INSTITUTE
69 E. Market St.
AKRON 44308

Special collection: Dr. Edgar B. Foltz Collection—American Indian art and artifacts—kachinas, jewelry, musical instruments, blankets, beadwork, basketry, pottery. Library.

**MOUND CITY GROUP
NATIONAL MONUMENT**
16062 State Route 104
CHILLICOTHE 45601
(614) 774-1125
Kenneth Apschnikat, Superintendent

Description: A 67 acre park containing 23 burial mounds of the Hopewell Culture, circa 100 A.D. *Museum:* Exhibits of Hopewell artifacts. Library.

CINCINNATI ART MUSEUM
Eden Park
CINCINNATI 45202

Displays archaeological and ethnological specimens. Archaeological principally Mound Builder, also Adena, Hopewell, Fort Ancient cultures from Ohio; stone, bone, metal, shell, and pottery from Tennessee and Arkansas; Casas Grandes pottery. Ethnological material principally Plains and Northwest Coast. Library.

JOHNSON-HUMRICKHOUSE MUSEUM
Roscoe Village, 300 Whitewoman St.
COSHOCTON 43812
(614) 622-8710
Mary M. Shaw, Director

Indians of the Americas Gallery: Exhibits paleo to modern North American Indian and Eskimo arts, crafts, basketry and beadwork.

**RUTHERFORD B. HAYES
LIBRARY AND MUSEUM**
1337 Hayes Ave.
FREMONT 43420

A collection of artifacts, largely of the Plains Indians, the Sioux, and some Pueblo; prehistoric Ohio Indian artifacts. Library.

**SCHOENBRUNN VILLAGE
STATE MEMORIAL**
P.O. Box 129, East High Ave.
NEW PHILADELPHIA 44663
(216) 339-3636
Susan Colpetzer, Director

Description: Founded by David Zeisberger in 1772 as a Moravian mission to the Delaware Indians. Restored to appear as it did over 200 years ago. *Museum:* Tells the story of the Christian Delawares and the Moravian missionaries at Schoenbrunn. *Publication:* Schoenbrunn and the Moravian Missions in Ohio.

**MOUNDBUILDERS STATE MEMORIAL
AND MUSEUM**
99 Cooper Ave.
NEWARK 43055
(614) 344-1920
David Brockman, Manager

Prehistoric Indian Art Museum and Historic Site depicting *The Great Circle Earthworks*—ceremonial grounds of prehistoric Hopewell Indians, circa 1000 B.C. - 700 A.D. Exhibits art objects and other relics representing Adena and Hopewell cultures.

SERPENT MOUND MUSEUM
State Route 73, Box 234
PEEBLES 45660
(513) 587-2706
William E. Gustin, Manager

Indian Museum exhibiting material of Adena Indian culture.

PIQUA HISTORICAL AREA
9845 N. Hardin Rd.
PIQUA 45356
(513) 773-2522
Clinton P. Hosher, Site Manager

Indian historical museum, a restored 1809-1830 farmhouse, exhibiting artifacts excavated from the area—tools, weapons, costumes, art, canoes, etc.

OKLAHOMA

APACHE TRIBAL MUSEUM
P.O. Box 1220
ANADARKO 73005
(405) 247-9493

DELAWARE TRIBAL MUSEUM
c/o Delaware Executive Board
P.O. Box 369
ANADARKO 73005

INDIAN CITY, U.S.A.
Highway 8, Box 695
ANADARKO 73005
(405) 247-5661
George F. Moran, Director

Features reconstructed Plains Indian dwellings; also, Indian history museum located on site of 1887, *Tonkawa Massacre.* Exhibits Indian artifacts, pottery, dance costumes, and dolls.

THE NATIONAL HALL OF FAME
FOR FAMOUS AMERICAN INDIANS
Highway 62, Box 808
ANADARKO 73005
(405) 247-5795
Allie Reynolds, President
Paul T. Stonum, Executive V.P.

An outdoor museum containing sculptured bronze portraits of famous American Indians in a landscaped area. Includes portraits of Will Rogers, Jim Thorpe, Pocahontas, Chief Joseph, Sacajawea, Chief Quanah Parker, Charles Curtis, Osceola, Sequoyah, Pontiac, Hiawatha, et al. *Special programs:* Annual dedication ceremonies in August, when an honoree is inducted; educational seminars regarding inductee's history and contribution to the American way of life.

SOUTHERN PLAINS INDIAN MUSEUM
Highway 62 East, Box 749
ANADARKO 73005
(405) 247-6221
Rosemarie Ellison, Curator

Presents the "richness and diversity" of historic arts created by the tribal peoples of western Oklahoma, including the Kiowa, Comanche, Kiowa-Apache, Southern Cheyenne, Southern Arapaho, Wichita, Caddo, Delaware, and Fort Sill Apache. Highlighting the exhibit is a display of the varied traditional costumes of Southern Plains men, women and children, presented in complete detail on life-size figures; four dioramas and a mural illustrating historic Indian cultural subjects, created by artist and sculptor, Allan Houser, a Fort Sill Apache and native Oklahoman. *Special programs:* Annual series of one-person exhibitions; demonstrations of Native-American arts and crafts techniques; hosts events honoring Native-Americans; The American Indian Exposition, in August, features a week-long event of dance contests, arts and crafts; tours and Gallery discussions. *Publications:* Illustrated catalogs and brochures. Craft shop. Administered by the Indian Arts and Crafts Board.

WICHITA MEMORY EXHIBIT MUSEUM
Wichita Tribal Cultural Center
P.O. Box 729
ANADARKO 73005
(405) 247-2464

FORT SILL APACHE MUSEUM
Route 2, Box 121
APACHE 73006

WOOLAROC MUSEUM
Route 3, State Highway 123
BARTLESVILLE 74003
(918) 336-0307
Robert R. Lansdown, Director

Exhibits arts and crafts of the Southwest Indian tribes, as well as archaeological material from Oklahoma excavations. Publications. Library.

MEMORIAL INDIAN MUSEUM
P.O. Box 483
Second and Allen Sts.
BROKEN BOW 74728
(405) 584-6531
LaMarr Smith, Director

A collection of prehistoric Indian artifacts, Indian skeletal remains, early beadwork; displays modern textiles and basketry. *Research:* Prehistoric Caddo Indians and their pottery. Library.

COMANCHE CULTURAL
CENTER MUSEUM
P.O. Box 606
CACHE 73527

KIOWA TRIBAL MUSEUM
P.O. Box 369
CARNEGIE 73015

WILL ROGERS MEMORIAL
P.O. Box 157
CLAREMORE 74018
(918) 341-0719
Dr. Reba N. Collins, Director

Consists of four main galleries displaying the personal effects and memorabilia belonging to Will Rogers, his wife Betty, and infant son, Fred are buried in the tomb adjoining the Memorial building. *Special collection:* The original manuscripts and papers belonging to Will Rogers. An annual Will Rogers Day celebration is held on November 4, to commemorate his birthday. *Publication: Will Rogers Times,* irregular newsletter. Library.

NO MAN'S LAND HISTORICAL MUSEUM
P.O. Box 278, Sewell St.
GOODWELL 73939
(405) 349-2670
Dr. Harold S. Kachel, Curator

Special collections: William E. Baker Archaeology Collection, and W. Guy Clark Collection—Contains artifacts of the Plains Indians (buffalo hunters) and the Basketmaker Indian, all collected by local residents of the Oklahoma Panhandle on their land to preserve the Indian cultures that preceded them on the land. Library.

MUSEUM OF THE RED RIVER
812 S.E. Lincoln
IDABEL 74745
(405) 286-3616
Gregory Perino, Curator

Exhibits prehistoric Caddoan ceramics, stone tools; also, historical Choctaw items. Library.

COMANCHE CULTURAL CENTER
P.O. Box 908
LAWTON 73502
(405) 429-1990

MUSEUM OF THE GREAT PLAINS
P.O. Box 68, 601 Ferris Ave.
LAWTON 73502
Steve Wilson, Director
Dan Provo, Curator

Maintains exhibits and artifacts representing the Plains Indian material culture from prehistoric times to present. *Publications: Great Plains Journal;* Newsletter; books for sale. Library.

**BACONE COLLEGE MUSEUM
(ATALOA ART LODGE)**
East Shawnee
MUSKOGEE 74403
(918) 683-4581 ext. 212/229
Dr. Paul V. Moore, President

Displays American Indian stone artifacts, rugs, blankets, basketry, pottery, beadwork and quillwork. *Publications: Baconian and Smoke Signals,* booklets. Library.

FIVE CIVILIZED TRIBES MUSEUM
Agency Hill-Honor Heights Dr.
MUSKOGEE 74401
(918) 683-1701
Debra G. Synar, Director

Exhibits art, artifacts, books, documents, and letters pertaining to the history and culture of the Cherokees, Choctaws, Creeks, Chickasaws, and Seminoles. Housed in the Indian Agency Building built in 1875. Art Gallery of Traditional Indian Art, only by artists of Five Tribes heritage. Maintains an extensive art and sculpture collection, *Jerome Tiger Originals;* original carvings and sculptures of Willard Stone. *Special program:* Sponsors competitive arts and crafts shows. *Publications:* Quarterly newsletter; *Pow Wow Chow Cookbook; The Cherokees; The Muskogee Book;* Limited edition artist signed art prints. Library.

MUSEUM OF ART
University of Oklahoma
410 West Boyd St.
NORMAN 73069

Special collection: American Indian Painting Collection—Contains more than 200 original paintings by American Indian artists, some available for rental. Library.

**STOVALL MUSEUM
OF SCIENCE AND HISTORY**
University of Oklahoma
1335 Asp Ave.
NORMAN 73069
(405) 325-4712
Dr. Michael A. Mares, Director

Maintains a permanent exhibit on Oklahoma prehistory and historic Indian tribes; North American archaeological and ethnological specimens, depicting the development of Southern Plains, Southwest and Northwest Coast Indian cultures; also, material from the *Spiro Mounds. Special programs;* Educational; slide/tape programs: *Wichita Memories, The Plains Apache, Native American Games,* and *Spiro Mounds. Publications:* Newsletter; *Oklahoma Indian Artifacts.*

**THE STATE MUSEUM OF OKLAHOMA
OKLAHOMA HISTORICAL SOCIETY
MUSEUM**
2100 North Lincoln Blvd.
Wiley Post Historical Blvd.
OKLAHOMA CITY 73105
(405) 521-2491
Mac R. Harris, Director
John R. Hill, Curator

Indian and Regional History Museum: Exhibits Native-American art and artifacts. *Research:* U.S. Indian Policy. *Special collections:* Newspapers of Indian Territory; *Indian Archive Department—* contains more than three million documents pertaining to Indian history.

CREEK COUNCIL HOUSE MUSEUM
Creek Council House
OKMULGEE 74447
(918) 756-2324
Bruce M. Shackleford, Director

Creek Indian History Museum: Displays arts and artifacts of the Creek Indians. *Publications: History and Legends of the Creek; Indians of Oklahoma; Creek Nation Capitol.* Arts and crafts for sale.

OSAGE TRIBAL MUSEUM
Osage Agency Reserve
P.O. Box 178
PAWHUSKA 74056

Exhibits Osage artifacts, paintings, and pictures. Workshops. Library.

**PONCA CITY CULTURAL CENTER
AND MUSEUM**
1000 East Grand
PONCA CITY 74601
  (405) 765-5268
  La Wanda French, Director

Collections feature clothing, utensils, photographs, weapons, art, musical instruments, and ceremonial materials of the tribes of the Ponca City area: the Osage, Kaw, Ponca, and Otoe; also, Hopi pottery and kachinas; relics from the early French-Indian trading post in Oklahoma; Northwest Coast material, and Quileute and other northern tribes' material. Library.

SEQUOYAH HOME SITE
Route 1, Box 141
SALLISAW 74955
  (918) 775-2413
  Dillard Jordan, Curator

An Historic Building, 1829, Sequoyah log cabin containing artifacts of the life of Sequoyah and western Cherokees.

**POTAWATOMI INDIAN NATION
ARCHIVES AND MUSEUM**
Route 5, Box 151
SHAWNEE 74801

SHAWNEE INDIAN MISSION
SHAWNEE 74801

**SAC AND FOX TRIBAL RV PARK
AND MUSEUM/CULTURAL CENTER**
Route 2, Box 246
STROUD 74079
  (918) 968-3526/(405) 275-4270
  Jessica Patterson, Director/Curator

Special collections: The Frank Hanison Collection, and Jim Thorpe Collection— Contains displays of pictures, treaties and documents, old tribal rolls; exhibits paintings and artifacts by tribal members. *Special programs:* All-Indian Rodeo, and Arts and Crafts Show; annual Pow-Wow.

CHOCTAW CHIEF'S HOUSE
P.O. Box 165
SWINK 74761
  (405) 873-2492
  Gale Carter, Site Attendant

An Historic 1832 Old Chief's House with furniture and furnishings of the 1800's.

**CHEROKEE NATIONAL MUSEUM
(TSA-LA-GI)**
Cherokee Heritage Center
P.O. Box 515
TAHLEQUAH 74464
  (918) 456-6007
  Duane H. King, Director

Located on the site of the original 1851 Cherokee Female Seminary and Ancient Village. Collections on Cherokee history, heritage and culture. Library.

CHICKASAW COUNCIL HOUSE MUSEUM
P.O. Box 717
TISHOMINGO 73460
  (405) 371-3351
  Beverly J. Wyatt, Curator

Indian museum exhibiting items pertaining to the history and culture—government, education, religious and social life—of the Chickasaw Indians. Emphasis is placed on the Chickasaw Governors, their families and administrations, from 1855 to the present day. Library.

TONKAWA TRIBAL MUSEUM
P.O. Box 40
TONKAWA 74653

PHILBROOK ART CENTER
P.O. Box 52510, 2727 S. Rockford Rd.
TULSA 74152
  (918) 749-7941
  Jesse G. Wright, Jr., President/Director

Special collections: Clark Field Collection— American Indian basketry and pottery; Roberta Campbell Lawson Collection—American Indian costumes and artifacts; Philbrook Collection— American Indian paintings; The Butler Museum of American Indian Art Collection; The Elizabeth Cole Butler Collection of Native American Art. Library.

**THOMAS GILCREASE INSTITUTE
OF AMERICAN HISTORY AND ART**
1400 North 25 West Ave.
TULSA 74127
  (918) 581-5311
  Fred A. Myers, Director

Exhibits artifacts relating to the culture of the Five Civilized Tribes. *Publications: Gilcrease Magazine,* quarterly; *Catlin Catalogue.* Library.

YELLOW BULL MUSEUM
Northern Oklahoma College
1220 E. Grand
TONKAWA 74653

**CHOCTAW NATION
HISTORICAL MUSEUM**
General Delivery
TUSKAHOMA 74574

SEMINOLE NATION MUSEUM
524 South Wewoka, Box 1532
WEWOKA 74884
(405) 257-5580
Margaret Jane Norman, Curator

Maintains exhibits and artifacts relating to the history of the Oklahoma Seminoles, the Freedmen, early pioneers and oil boom history of the area. *Special exhibits:* Dioramas depicting the Indian Stick Ball Game, The Seminole Whipping Tree, a life-size replica of the Florida Seminole home (Chickee), and exhibits depicting the Florida Seminoles, The Seminole Hunter Warrior, Law-Man (Lighthorseman), and Medicine Man. *Publication: Este Cate,* a history of the Seminoles written by Museum Director, Tuskahoma B. Miller. Library.

**PLAINS INDIANS
AND PIONEERS MUSEUM**
P.O. Box 1167, 2009 Williams Ave.
WOODWARD 73802
(405) 256-6136
Sarah Taylor, Director

Collection consists of archival materials, agricultural equipment, items from early settlers, and local Plains Indian items, including beadwork, tools and clothing. *Special programs:* Monthly lectures; slide program, *Plains Indian Heritage of Northwestern Oklahoma,* for local and statewide use. Publications.

JIM THORPE'S HOME
YALE 74085

OREGON

JACKSONVILLE MUSEUM
206 North 5th St.
JACKSONVILLE 97530

Exhibits feature Takelma, Klamath and northern California artifacts; also, Navajo blankets, tools, weapons and implements. Library.

**COLLIER STATE PARK
LOGGING MUSEUM**
P.O. Box 428
KLAMATH FALLS 97601

Located on the Klamath Indian Reservation, the museum exhibits Indian stone utensils and unexcavated pit houses. Library.

**FAVELL MUSEUM OF WESTERN ART
AND INDIAN ARTIFACTS**
125 West Main
KLAMATH FALLS 97601
(503) 882-9996
Gene Favell, Owner

Exhibits of contemporary original Western and wildlife art; 60,000 arrowheads; pictographs, baskets, pottery, and mortors.

PORTLAND ART MUSEUM
1219 S.W. Park
PORTLAND 97205

Special collection: Axel Rasmussen Collection of Northwest Indian Art—Contains approximately 500 objects—items of dress, tools and equipment used in hunting and fishing; also, Eskimo pieces. *Publication: Art in the Life of the Northwest Coast Indian.* Library.

PENNSYLVANIA

**LENNI LENAPE HISTORICAL
SOCIETY OF PENNSYLVANIA**
c/o Carla Messinger
RD 2, Fish Hatchery Rd.
ALLENTOWN 18103

E.M. PARKER MUSEUM
247 Main St.
BROOKVILLE 15825
E.M. Parker, Owner

Exhibits Indian artifacts from Pennsylvania, eastern Ohio region, and New York. Library.

**CUMBERLAND COUNTY
HISTORICAL SOCIETY MUSEUM**
21 North Pitt St.
CARLISLE 17013

Special collection: Carlisle Indian School Collection— Contains photographs, publications, and memorabilia. *Publications: An Account of Illustrated Talks to Indian Chiefs,* by Charles F. Himes; and *The Indian Industrial School at Carlisle: Its Origin, Purpose, Progress and Difficulties,* by Richard H. Pratt. Library.

HERSHEY MUSEUM OF AMERICAN LIFE
One Chocolate Ave.
HERSHEY 17033

North American Indian and Eskimo exhibits containing collections from the Southwestern, North Pacific Coast, and Great Plains cultural areas; also, exhibits 19th century Indian lifestyles and artifacts representative of the archaic, woodland, and colonial periods.

BUSHY RUN BATTLEFIELD PARK
Bushy Run Rd.
JEANNETTE 15644

Description: Located on the site of Chief Pontiac's rebellion of 1763. *Museum:* Contains copies of maps and letters relating to the Campaign of 1763, Pontiac's War; exhibits Indian artifacts.

**READING PUBLIC MUSEUM
AND ART GALLERY**
500 Museum Rd.
READING 19611
(215) 371-5850
  Bruce L. Dietrich, Director

Exhibit includes examples of cultural materials, pottery, clothing, tools, toys, ceremonial objects of the following cultural areas: Woodland, Plains, Southwest Desert, California, Northwest Coast, and Inuit. *Special collections:* Study collection of southeastern Pennsylvania lithic objects, approximately 10,000 pieces; study collection of mound pottery; Speck Colletion—Delaware material collected during Speck's research of Oklahoma and Canadian dwellings of Delaware peoples. *Special program:* A Museum-School Native-American Studies Project—Elementary education programs for local schools using exhibit areas and Museum classroom lessons. Publications. Library.

EVERHART MUSEUM OF NATURAL HISTORY, SCIENCE AND ART
Nay Aug Park
SCRANTON 18510

American Indian Gallery: Survey of American Indian art covering five major regions of the U.S. Library.

RHODE ISLAND

**HAFFENREFFER MUSEUM
OF ANTHROPOLOGY**
Brown University, Mt. Hope Grant
BRISTOL 02809
(401) 253-8388
  Barbara A. Hail, Director/Curator

Collections of Native-Americans of the Northeast, Plains, Southwest, Northwest Coast, as well as Eskimo and Mesoamerican and Andean. Exhibits tribal arts from around the world. *Special programs:* Education programs for school children; Gallery Talks. *Publications: A 17th Century Wampanoag Burial Ground in Warren, Rhode Island; Hau, Kola! The Plains Indian Collection of the Haffenreffer Museum of Anthropology.* Library.

**TOMAQUAG INDIAN
MEMORIAL MUSEUM**
Dovecrest Indian Cultural Center
Summit Rd.
EXETER 02822
(401) 539-7795

Archaeology, ethnology, and natural history exhibits related to southern New England Indian cultures. *Publications: Indians of Southern New England,* by Princess Red Wing; *Musical Expressions of Early Indians of Rhode Island; Indian Communications.* Library.

MUSEUM OF PRIMITIVE CULTURE
604 Kingstown Rd.
PEACE DALE 02883
(401) 783-5711
  Sarah Peabody Turnbaugh, Associate Curator

An archaeoogical and ethnology museum exhibiting artifacts of northeast North America. *Publication: Rhode Island's Prehistoric Past,* catalog.

**RHODE ISLAND
HISTORICAL SOCIETY MUSEUM**
52 Power St.
PROVIDENCE 02906
(401) 331-8575
  Nina Zannieri, Curator

Maintains a collection of 11,000 objects and artifacts pertaining to Rhode Island history; displays Narragansett and Wampanoag Tribes' artifacts—stone bowls, baskets, metal combs, jewelry, hair ornaments. *Publication: Rhode Island History,* journal. Library.

ROGER WILLIAMS PARK MUSEUM
PROVIDENCE 02891

Exhibits feature Woodland Indian culture—model village; canoe; model Pueblo; Plains and Northwest Coast Indian artifacts; Eskimo material; American Indian plants; and maps.

SOUTH CAROLINA

THE CHARLESTON MUSEUM
121 Rutledge Ave.
CHARLESTON 29401

Indian relics included in extensive collections of South Carolina archaeological material, plus material from other areas of North America. Library.

**CHESTER COUNTY
HISTORICAL SOCIETY MUSEUM**
124 Saluda St.
CHESTER 29706
  Louis Warmoth, President

Special collection: The Gatlin Catawba Indian
Collection— Displays more than 30,000 artifacts.

McKISSICK MUSEUM
University of South Carolina
COLUMBIA 29208
  (803) 777-7251
  George D. Terry, Director
  Catherine W. Horne, Curator

Exhibits more than 200 Catawba Indian pottery
and baskets from the 19th and 20th centuries;
Folk Art Resource Center with primary and
secondary sources on South Carolina Indians.

SOUTH DAKOTA

DACOTAH PRAIRIE MUSEUM
21 South Main St., Box 395
ABERDEEN 57401

Exhibits Sioux Indian artifacts—beadwork,
quillwork, decorated ceremonial and functional
leather items, pictographs, ghost dress, and
pictures. Library. Sales Shop features
contemporary Sioux handicrafts.

AGRICULTURAL HERITAGE MUSEUM
South Dakota State University
BROOKINGS 57007

Special collection: Indian Agricultural Heritage
Collection of South Dakota. Reference Library.

INDIAN MUSEUM OF NORTH AMERICA
Crazy Horse Memorial Foundation
Avenue of the Chiefs-The Black Hills
CRAZY HORSE 57730-9998
  (605) 673-4681

Exhibits Indian art and artifacts. *Publication:*
Crazy Horse Progress, 3/yr. Library.

**HARVEY V. JOHNSON AMERICAN
INDIAN CULTURAL CENTER MUSEUM**
Cheyenne River Reservation
P.O. Box 857
EAGLE BUTTE 57625

**AMERICAN INDIAN CULTURE
RESEARCH CENTER**
Blue Cloud Abbey
MARVIN 57251
  (605) 432-5528
  Rev. Stanislaus Maudlin, Director

Maintains a collection of Maria Pottery; artifacts.
Research Library: 2,500 Native-American books.

OSCAR HOWE CULTURAL CENTER
119 West Third
MITCHELL 57301

A collection of twelve paintings by Oscar Howe,
Sioux artist.

ROBINSON MUSEUM
500 E. Capitol, Memorial Bldg.
PIERRE 57501
  (605) 773-3797
  David B. Hartley, Director

Special collection: Plains Indian Collection—
Contains primarily Sioux Indian artifacts.
Publication: South Dakota History, quarterly.
Library.

THE HERITAGE CENTER
P.O. Box 100
PINE RIDGE 57770
  (605) 867-5491
  Bro. C.M. Simon, S.J., Director

Indian Art Museum: Housed in 1888 Holy Rosary
Mission, scene of Battle day after the Wounded
Knee Massacre; maintains a collection of
paintings by American Indian artists, mainly
Oglala Sioux; also, star quilt, beadwork,
quillwork and pottery collections; graphics,
Eskimo prints, and Northwest Coast prints.
Special program: Red Cloud Indian Art Show
held every summer. Library.

SIOUX INDIAN MUSEUM
P.O. Box 1504
RAPID CITY 57709
  (605) 348-0557

Administered by the Indian Arts and Crafts
Board. Exhibits historic Sioux arts and other
Native-American arts and crafts of the U.S.
Special program: One-person exhibition series.
Publications. Museum Sales Shop.

**WINONA CLUB SIOUX
CULTURAL CENTER MUSEUM**
P.O. Box 775
RAPID CITY 57709

BUECHEL MEMORIAL LAKOTA MUSEUM
St. Francis Indian Mission
350 South Oak St., Box 149
ST. FRANCIS 57572
  (605) 747-2828
  Victor Douville, Chairman
  Paul J. Whiting, Director

Sioux Indian Museum: Exhibits ethnographic
material of the reservation period of the Rosebud
and Pine Ridge Sioux. *Publications: A Grammar
of Lakota; Everyday Lakota; Dictionary; Bible
History in Lakota; Lakota Prayer Book; Lakota
Names and Traditional Uses of Native Plants by*

Sigangu People; Crying for a Vision; A Rosebud Sioux Trilogy. Indian arts and crafts for sale. Library.

CENTER FOR WESTERN STUDIES
Augustana College, P.O. Box 727
SIOUX FALLS 57197
(605) 336-4007
Dr. Sven G. Froiland, Director

An Historical Research and Archival Agency which maintains a collection of Native-American art work and artifacts. *Research:* Native-Americans. *Publication: Sundancing at Rosebud and Pine Ridge.* Library.

SIOUXLAND HERITAGE MUSEUM
THE PETTIGREW MUSEUM
131 North Duluth
SIOUX FALLS 57104

Special collections: The Pettigrew-Drady Indian Collection: Chief emphasis is on Dakota (Sioux) Indian artifacts, circa 1870-1920, including: clothing, tools, pipes, weapons, tepee, Ghost Dance shirt; and a Photograph Collection covering 1870-1900. Library.

BEAR BUTTE STATE PARK
2209 Thompson St.
STURGIS 57785
(605) 347-3176
William A. Gullet, Park Manager

Description: Located on a Native-American traditional religious site. *Museum:* Exhibits archaeological site materials; Native-American clothing and religious artifacts. *Research:* Native-American Indian religion, anthropology, archaeology and geography.

W.H. OVER STATE MUSEUM
414 E. Clark
VERMILLION 57069
(605) 677-5228
Julia R. Vodicka, Director

Displays Sioux artifacts from the late 19th century to the present. *Special collection:* Morrow Photographs, 1869-1883. *Publication: Over Museum News, 1939-1972.* Library.

DAKOTA TERRITORIAL MUSEUM
Westside Park, Box 412
YANKTON 57078

Exhibits Indian artifacts from the Dakota Territory, and the history of Yankton.

TENNESSEE

RED CLAY STATE HISTORICAL PARK
Route 6, Box 733
CLEVELAND 37311
(615) 472-2626
Jennings W. Bunn, Jr., Supervisor

Description: The 1832-1838 seat of the Cherokee Government, and site of 11 General Councils on national affairs. *Collection:* Paleo, Archaic, Mississippian, Woodland, and historical period artifacts. *Research:* Cherokee Removal Story, 1832-1838. Research Library of Cherokee history.

C.H. NASH MUSEUM — CHUCALISSA
1987 Indian Village Dr.
MEMPHIS 38109
(901) 785-3160
Gerald P. Smith, Curator

An archaeological museum with a collection of Indian artifacts from the site in western Tennessee and adjacent areas. *Facility:* Reconstructed Mississippian Period Village. Library.

CUMBERLAND MUSEUM
AND SCIENCE CENTER
800 Ridley Blvd.
NASHVILLE 37203
(615) 259-6099
Bill Bradshaw, Director

Maintains approximately 4,000 objects on Native-Americans; small exhibit on Native-Americans in their environment. *Special program:* School programs on Native-Americans and archaeology. *Publication: Museum Notes,* monthly newsletter.

TENNESSEE STATE MUSEUM
7th and Union, War Memorial Bldg.
NASHVILLE 37219

Exhibits artifacts of prehistoric Indian life and culture, including stone implements, ceremonial objects and pottery.

PINSON MOUNDS
STATE ARCHAEOLOGICAL AREA
Ozier Rd., Route 1, Box 316
PINSON 38366
(901) 988-5614
Mary L. Kwas, Area Supervisor

Description: A Middle Woodland Period ceremonial site with mounds and earthworks. *Collection:* Historic and prehistoric material from throughout Tennessee and on-site fieldwork. *Special program:* Indian Culture Festival. Library.

TEXAS

CADDOAN MOUNDS STATE HISTORIC SITE
Route 2, Box 85C
ALTO 75925
(409) 858-3218
Erwin Roemer, Superintendent

Description: An archaeological site of prehistoric Caddoan village and ceremonial center, with three earthen mounds occupied 750-1300 A.D. *Collection:* Dioramas and prehistoric artifacts of early Caddoan culture excavated at the site—ceramic vessels, stone tools, etc.; replicated Caddo house on site. *Publication: Caddoan Mounds, Temples and Tombs of an Ancient People.*

TEXAS MEMORIAL MUSEUM
University of Texas
24th and Trinity
AUSTIN 78705

A collection on American Indian anthropology, with emphasis on Indians of North America and Texas. Library.

PANHANDLE PLAINS HISTORICAL MUSEUM
P.O. Box 967, W.T. Station
2401 Fourth Ave.
CANYON 79016
(806) 655-7194
Byron Price, Director

Hall of the Southern Plains: Exhibit of artifacts of the Southern Plains Indians—Comanche, Kiowa, Cheyenne, Arapaho, Apache; material on the Indian wars; trade goods. *Publication: Panhandle Plains Historical Review,* newsletter. Library.

NATIVE AMERICAN CULTURAL HERITAGE CENTER
Dallas Independent School District
DALLAS 75204

TIGUA PUEBLO MUSEUM
Tigua Arts and Crafts Center
Texas Indian Reservation
EL PASO 79907
(915) 859-7913

YSLETA DEL SUR PUEBLO MUSEUM
P.O. Box 17579, 119 S. Old Pueblo Rd.
Tigua Indian Reservation
EL PASO 79917
(915) 859-7913/3916
Johnny R. Hisa, Tribal Governor
Raymond Ramiriz, Superintendent

Historic House, 1700-1850 Alderite/Candelaria House; on grounds of 1680 Ysleta and Sur Pueblos and Mission Church. Maintains a collection of art of the Pueblos.

ALABAMA-COUSHATTA INDIAN MUSEUM
Route 3, Box 640, U.S. Highway 190
LIVINGSTON 77351
(713) 563-4391
Tony Byars, Superintendent

Located on the Alabama-Coushatta Indian Reservation, the museum contains a dioramic historical display of tribes, and a Living Indian Village. Indian arts and crafts for sale.

INDIAN HORSE HALL OF FAME
American Indian Horse Registry
Route 1, Box 64
LOCKHART 78644
(512) 398-6642
Nanci Falley, President

Museum: A collection of saddle, bridal and art representing 19th century Southwest U.S.

CADDO INDIAN MUSEUM
701 Hardy St.
LONGVIEW 75604
(214) 759-5739
Mrs. James L. Jones, Director

Collection includes approximately 30,000 artifacts pertaining to the prehistoric and historic Indian cultures who inhabited east Texas, primarily tribes of the Kad had acho, Hasinai, and Natchitoches confederacies of the Caddo Indians; extensive ceramic and stone pre-Columbian burial artifacts belonging to the prehistoric Indians of east Texas.

THE MUSEUM OF TEXAS TECH UNIVERSITY
P.O. Box 4499
LUBBOCK 79409

Exhibits Yaqui, Comanche and other Indian artifacts. Publications. Library.

STONE FORT MUSEUM
P.O. Box 607, S.F.A. Station
NACOGDOCHES 75962

Special collection: Caddo Indian Artifacts Collection—beads, pottery, arrow points, pipes, etc. from the site of new Lake Nacogdoches, as well as from various Indian sites across the County. Library.

CROCKETT COUNTY MUSEUM
404 11th St., Box 667
OZONA 76943

Special collection: Frank Mills Indian Collection—ornaments, jewelry, pottery, weapons, utensils, implements and ceremonial costumes. Cave exhibits. Library.

WITT MEMORIAL MUSEUM
3801 Broadway
SAN ANTONIO 78209

Displays artifacts of the Plains Indian, Apache, Navajo, California Indians, Comanche-Kiowa, Eastern Woodlands, Northwest Coast, and Eskimo and Arctic Indians, including basketry, pottery, blankets and costumes. Library.

SUNSET TRADING POST
OLD WEST MUSEUM
Route 1
SUNSET 76270
  (817) 872-2027
  Jack N. Glover, Owner/Curator

Exhibits Indian artifacts. *Publication: Sex Life of American Indians.* Library.

UTAH

EDGE OF THE CEDARS STATE
HISTORICAL MONUMENT AND MUSEUM
P.O. Box 788, 660 West, 400 North
BLANDING 84511
  (801) 678-2238
  John Knudson, Park Superintendent
  Sloan Emery, Curator

Description: Located on the remains of 700-1200 A.D. structures, ancient dwellings of the Anasazi Indian culture. *Collection:* Maintains artifacts of prehistoric Anasazi Indian Tribe; Anasazi pottery; also, Navajo, Ute and Paiute Indian artifacts. Indian arts and crafts for sale. Library.

UTAH NAVAJO MUSEUM
Broken Arrow Center
P.O. Box 827
BLANDING 84511

ANASAZI INDIAN VILLAGE
STATE HISTORICAL MONUMENT
P.O. Box 393
BOULDER 84716
  (801) 335-7308
  Larry Davis, Ranger-in-Charge
  Dee Hardy, Curator

Description: Located on a 1050-1200 A.D. excavated Anasazi Indian Village. *Museum:* Maintains a collection of artifacts representative of the Kayenta Anasazi culture; diorama of Combs Village burial display.

UTE TRIBAL MUSEUM
P.O. Box 190, Highway 40
FORT DUCHESNE 84026
  (801) 722- 4992
  Clifford Duncan, Director

Located on the site of U.S. Cavalry and Old Fort Duchesne. Maintains Indian produced artwork in various media artifacts. *Research:* Ute history archives; personal interviews with elderly to document verbal Indian history. *Publication: A History of Northern Ute People.* Library.

PREHISTORIC MUSEUM OF
THE COLLEGE OF EASTERN UTAH
PRICE 84501

Utah archaeological exhibits, including 9th century Indian material of the Fremont culture.

MUSEUM OF PEOPLES AND CULTURES
Brigham Young University
710 No. 100 East, Allen Bldg.
PROVO 84602
  (801) 378-6112
  Dr. Joel C. Janetski, Director

An archaeology and ethnology museum exhibiting artifacts of prehistoric and historic Indian cultures. Publications. Library.

JACOB HAMBLIN HOME
U.S. Highway 91, 444 S. 300 East
SANTA CLARA (ST. GEORGE) 84770
  (801) 673-2161

Description: The headquarters of Church Missionary work among Southwest Indians (1850's and 1860's); and focal point of Anglo-Indian relations.

NATURAL HISTORY STATE MUSEUM
P.O. Box 396, 235 E. Main St.
VERNAL 84116

Ute Indian Hall: Exhibits Ute Indian artifacts. Library.

VIRGINIA

SOUTHWEST VIRGINIA MUSEUM
10 W. First St.
BIG STONE GAP 24219

Maintains artifacts representing the culture of the southern Appalachians, including artifacts of the Cherokee and Shawnee Nations. Library.

SYMS-EATON MUSEUM
418 W. Mercury Blvd.
HAMPTON 23666
  (804) 727-6248
  Charles E. Smith, Manager

Historic Kecoughtan Indian Village; exhibits artifacts from Village area. *Publication: Indian Recipe.*

**PAMUNKEY CULTURAL
CENTER MUSEUM**
Pamunkey Research Center/Indian Village
Route 1, Box 217-AA
KING WILLIAM 23806
(804) 843-3648

**ARCHAEOLOGICAL SOCIETY
OF VIRGINIA**
4414 Park Ave.
RICHMOND 23221
(804) 359-0442
William Thompson, President

Maintains collections on Virginia archaeological
and Indian artifacts. Library.

THE VALENTINE MUSEUM
1015 E. Clay St.
RICHMOND 23219

Exhibits Indian artifacts and local material of
historical interest, including skeletal remains from
Virginia and North Carolina mounds. Library.

HISTORIC CRAB ORCHARD MUSEUM
P.O. Box 12, Route 19 and 460
TAZEWELL 24651
(703) 988-6755
Nellie White Bundy, Director

Located on Big Crab Orchard Archaeological and
Historic Site, exhibiting prehistoric Woodlands
Indian artifacts. *Publication:* Quarterly
newsletter. Library.

JAMESTOWN FOUNDATION MUSEUM
James Festival Park
P.O. Box JF
WILLIAMSBURG 23185

Exhibits Virginia Indian artifacts and pioneer
items; reconstruction of Powhatan's Indian
Lodge. Publications. Library.

WASHINGTON

LELOOSKA FAMILY MUSEUM
5618 Lewis River Rd.
ARIEL 98603

**FORT OKANOGAN
INTERPRETIVE CENTER**
Bridgeport State Park
P.O. Box 846
BRIDGEPORT 98813
(509) 686-7231
Jan Tveten, Director
Richard J. Clifton, Chief-Interpretive Services

Indian History Museum: Exhibits fur trade items,
and Indian and pioneer artifacts—basketry,
weapons, etc.

LEWIS COUNTY HISTORICAL MUSEUM
599 N.W. Front St.
CHEHALIS 98532
(206) 748-0831
James Buckman, President

Maintains a collection of Chehalis Indian
artifacts. Indian archive collection in library.

ALPOWAI INTERPRETIVE CENTER
Highway 12
CLARKSTON 99403
(509) 758-9580
Jan Tveten, Director

An ethnology and Indian msueum exhibiting Nez
Perce Indian artifacts from 1880-1920; Nez Perce
canoe. *Research:* Nez Perce Indians.

**COLVILLE CONFEDERATED
TRIBES MUSEUM**
Star Route
COULEE DAM 99116

MAKAH CULTURAL RESEARCH CENTER
P.O. Box 95
NEAH 98357
(206) 645-2711

SACAJAWEA INTERPRETIVE CENTER
Sacajawea State Park
PASCO 99301
(509) 545-2361
Jan Tveten, Director

Indian Museum honoring Sacajawea of the Lewis
and Clark Expedition. Exhibits artifacts of
southeast Washington Indians; photo-essay of
culture and lifestyle. *Special programs:* Photo-
essay and slide show of Lewis and Clark
Expedition; summer interpretive programs
related to area Indians and the Lewis and Clark
Expedition. Library.

DAYBREAK STAR ARTS CENTER
P.O. Box 99253
SEATTLE 98199
(206) 285-4425

WASHINGTON STATE MUSEUM
Thomas Burke Memorial
University of Washington
SEATTLE 98195
(206) 543-5590
Patrick V. Kirch, Director
Dr. James D. Nason, Chair-Anthropology
Division
Bill Holm, Curator-Northwest Coast Indian Art

Exhibits Northwest Coast Indian art and
artifacts; maintains ethnological and
archaeological collections of the Pacific Rim and
Islands. Publications.

CHENEY COWLES MEMORIAL MUSEUM
Eastern Washington State Historical Society
West 2316 First Ave.
SPOKANE 99204
(509) 456-3931
Glenn Mason, Director

Special collection: The Chap C. Dunning
Collection—An exhibit of material culture of the
Plateau Indians. Also, collections from the
Northwest Coast, California, and Plains culture
groups. *Publications: Cornhusk Bags of the
Plateau Indian;* Text/fiche of 170 cornhusk bags
(both sides illustrated.) Exhibition poster on sale,
Native American Collection. Library.

**MUSEUM OF NATIVE
AMERICAN CULTURES**
E. 200 Cataldo
SPOKANE 99220
(509) 324-4550
Dr. J.E. Mauger

Maintains collections of Native-American
historic, ethnographic, and archaeological
materials from North, Central, and South
America; 19th and 20th century Western art.
Special collection: Largest trade bead collection
in the U.S. Library.

SUQUAMISH MUSEUM
P.O. Box 498
SUQUAMISH 98392
(206) 598-3311

Exhibit: The Eyes of Chief Seattle—The history
and culture of the Puget Sound Indians.

PUYALLUP TRIBE MUSEUM
2215 E. 22nd St.
TACOMA 98404
(206) 597-6479

**WASHINGTON STATE
HISTORICAL SOCIETY MUSEUM**
315 N. Stadium Way
TACOMA 98403
(206) 593-2830
Anthony King, Director

Exhibits collections of Northwest history and
Indian artifacts; 200,000 rare pictures and maps.
*Publications: The Indian Woodcarvings of
Harvey Kyllonen; Northwest Indian Basketry;
They Walked Before: The Indians of Washington
State.* Library.

TOPPENISH MUSEUM
1 South Elm
TOPPENISH 98945
(509) 865-4510
Tish Cooper, Director

Historic Museum housed in 1923 first Agency

Building for the Yakima Indian Nation. Exhibits
artifacts and Indian baskets. Library.

YAKIMA NATION MUSEUM
Yakima Nation Cultural Center
P.O. Box 151
TOPPENISH 98948
(509) 865-2800
Vivian M. Adams, Curator

Collection reflects traditional crafts of the
Yakima people, including utility and ceremonial
items; also, items from Southwest and Plains
tribes, but mainly items important to Yakima (or
Columbia Basin Plateau area) tribes and bands
culture and history. Includes baskets, parfleches,
beaded clothing, stones, pipes; Navajo blankets,
kachinas, clothing and jewelry; several large oil
paintings of Columbia Plateau family elders.
Publications. Library.

WEST VIRGINIA

**WEST VIRGINIA STATE GOVERNMENT
ARCHIVES AND HISTORY MUSEUM**
Dept. of Archives and History
Capitol Complex-Science and Cultural Center
CHARLESTON 25305

MOUND MUSEUM
Tenth St. and Tomlinson Ave.
MOUNDSVILLE 26041

WISCONSIN

RED CLIFF TRIBAL MUSEUM
Arts and Crafts Cultural Center
P.O. Box 529
BAYFIELD 54814
(715) 779-5609/5805
Francis Montano, Director

LOGAN MUSEUM OF ANTHROPOLOGY
Beloit College
BELOIT 53511
(608) 365-3391 ext. 305
J. Edson Way, Ph.D., Director
Jane K. Troszack, Curator

Exhibits material of North American Indian
ethnology (Great Lakes, Plains, and Southwest),
Arikara-Mandan archaeology, Archaic and
Woodland archaeology, and northern Wisconsin.
Publications.

**STOCKBRIDGE-MUNSEE
HISTORICAL LIBRARY AND MUSEUM**
Route 1, Box 300
BOWLER 54416
(715) 793-4270

CHIPPEWA VALLEY MUSEUM
P.O. Box 1204, Carson Park
EAU CLAIRE 54701

Maintains a collection of artifacts and photographs of the Chippewa, Menominee and Winnebago Indians. Library.

CHIEF OSHKOSH MUSEUM
EGG HARBOR 54209
(414) 868-3240
  Mrs. Roy Oshkosh, Director

Indian Museum exhibiting Indian artifacts, craftwork and possessions belonging to the late Chief Oshkosh, last Chief of the Menominees.

HISTORYLAND
HAYWARD 54843

"The museum is geared toward the Indian people with the hope that they will continue to identify themselves as Indians and preserve their cultural arts." Exhibits Ojibwa crafts and artifacts.

OJIBWA NATION MUSEUM
HAYWARD 54843

LAC DU FLAMBEAU INDIAN MUSEUM
LAC DU FLAMBEAU 54538

**STATE HISTORICAL SOCIETY
OF WISCONSIN MUSEUM**
816 State St.
MADISON 53706

Special collections: H.P. Hamilton Collection— Contains old copper implements of the Wiscosnin and Plains Indians; The Titus Collection— Features Southwest pottery. Ethnological collections are from all Wisconsin tribes, Plains Indians, Northwest Coast, and Eskimo. Maintains photograph, manuscript and tape collections. Publications. Library.

THE RAHR PUBLIC MUSEUM
610 N. 8th St.
MANITOWOC 54220

Special collection: Manitowoc County Indian Artifacts Collection—Indian archaeological material from Old Copper artifacts to Upper Mississippi group; dioramas. Library.

MILWAUKEE PUBLIC MUSEUM
800 W. Wells St.
MILWAUKEE 53233
(414) 278-2752
  Kenneth Starr, Ph.D., Director
  Nancy Oestreich Lurie, Ph.D., Head Curator-Anthropology

Maintains a collection of more than 100,000 North American Indian artifacts from all major culture areas, including Arctic. *Special collection:*

Dioramas, including Crow Indian Bison Hunt. *Special programs:* Study collections; tours of American Indian areas for school and other groups; also, "suit case exhibits" which travel to schools in the Milwaukee area. *Publications: Lore,* quarterly; *North American Indian Lives; Building a Chippewa Indian Birchbark Canoe; Prehistoric Indians of Wiscosnin;* et al. Reference Library.

ONEIDA NATION MUSEUM
P.O. Box 365
ONEIDA 54155
  Bob Smith, Director

Located on the site of one of the last parcels of the original Reservation lands. Exhibits artifacts, clothing, tools and ceremonial garments of the Oneida Indians.

OSHKOSH PUBLIC MUSEUM
1331 Algoma Blvd.
OSHKOSH 54901
(414) 424-0452
  Robert Hruska, Director/Curator

Maintains a collection of Wisconsin Indian archaeological and ethnographical artifacts. Library.

JOHN MICHAEL KOHLER ARTS CENTER
P.O. Box 489, 608 New York Ave.
SHEBOYGAN 53081
(414) 458-6144
  Ruth DeYoung Kohler, Director

Special collection: Kuehne Collection of Prehistoric Wisconsin Indian Artifacts—6,000 pieces, including pottery, projectiles, copper, celts, grooved axes, etc. Library. Facilities available to researchers only.

FAIRLAWN HISTORICAL MUSEUM
906 East 2nd St.
SUPERIOR 54880
(715) 394-5712
  Thomas C. Hendrickson, Jr., Director

Special collections: David F. Barry Collection of Sioux Indian Portraits; and, Catlin Lithographs of Indians of the Plains. Exhibits Indian artifacts. Library.

**WAUKESHA COUNTY
HISTORICAL MUSEUM**
101 W. Main St.
WAUKESHA 53186
(414) 544-8430
  Jean Penn Loerke, Director

Located on *Mound of the Turtle,* prehistoric Indian burial mound. Exhibits Indian artifacts from site.

WISCONSIN PUBLIC INDIAN MUSEUM
P.O. Box 441
WISCONSIN DELLS 53965
(608) 254-2268
Roxanne Little Eagle, Director

WYOMING

**BRADFORD BRINTON
MEMORIAL MUSEUM**
P.O. Box 23
BIG HORN 82833
(307) 672-3173
James T. Forrest, Director

Exhibits American Indian costumes, bead and quill work, tools, baskets, blankets, weapons, and interpretive materials; mostly Plains tribes, but also some from the Southwest and Northwest Coast. Library.

WYOMING STATE MUSEUM
Barrett Bldg., AMH Dept.
22nd and Central Ave.
CHEYENNE 82002
(307) 777-7510
Dr. Robert D. Bush, Director

Displays Sioux, Arapaho, Cheyenne, Blackfeet, Shoshone, and Flathead Indian artifacts.

PLAINS INDIAN MUSEUM
Buffalo Bill Historical Center
P.O. Box 1000, 720 Sheridan Ave.
CODY 82414
(307) 587-4771
George P. Horse Capture, Curator

Contains collections of ethnographical and archaeological material; Indian artifacts. *Research:* Native-American studies. Library.

ARAPAHOE CULTURAL MUSEUM
Wind River Reservation
P.O. Box 127
ETHETE 82520

**UNIVERSITY OF WYOMING
ANTHROPOLOGY MUSEUM**
Anthropology Building
LARAMIE 82071
(307) 766-5136
George W. Gill, Curator

Maintains a collection of American Indian artifacts.

GRAND TETON NATIONAL PARK
MOOSE 83013

Colter Bay Indian Art Museum: Displays approximately 1,500 items of American Indian art (collected by David Vernon) from most culture

areas, with emphasis on Northern Plains and Eastern Woodlands, 1875-1925. *Special programs:* Native-American culture films, guided tours, and Native-American crafts demonstrations. Programs conducted during summer months.

CANADA

ALBERTA

LUXTON MUSEUM
BANFF

Western Canadian Indian museum.

OLDMAN RIVER CULTURAL CENTRE
P.O. Box 70
BROCKET T0K 0H0
(403) 965-3939

**GLENBOW-ALBERTA
INSTITUTE MUSEUM**
Glenbow Centre
9th Ave. and First St., S.E.
CALGARY

PROVINCIAL MUSEUM OF ALBERTA
12845 - 102 Ave.
EDMONTON T5N 0M6
(403) 427-1730
John Fortier, Director
Dr. Patricia A. McCormack, Curator-Ethnology

Collections focus on the material culture and lifeways of indigenous peoples of Alberta (Beaver, Slavey, Chipewyan, Northern and Plains Cree, Blackfoot, Blood, Peigan, Sarsi, Assiniboine, Kutenai, Sauteaux, Metis) and other groups relevant to the histories of indigenous peoples in Alberta (e.g. Iroquois.) Contains approximately 12,000 items, strong in both functional and religious Plains materials; tipis and moccasins are extensive; Inuit clothing and other items from the Canadian Arctic. *Special programs:* Research and collecting projects—Native lifeways and material cultures in Alberta, focusing on 20th century items. *Publications: Storyteller,* monthly; books for sale. Library.

BRITISH COLUMBIA

ALERT BAY MUSEUM
Fir St., Box 208
ALERT BAY

Indian museum displaying Salish Indian relics.

ATLIN MUSEUM
Fourth and Trainor Sts.
ATLIN

Exhibits Tlingit Indian artifacts.

CAMPBELL RIVER MUSEUM
P.O. Box 101, 1235 Island Highway
CAMPBELL RIVER

Indian museum displaying Northwest Coast material.

KSAN INDIAN MUSEUM
P.O. Box 333
HAZELTON

Maintains a collection of Northwest Coast Indian artifacts.

KAMLOOPS MUSEUM
207 Seymour
KAMLOOPS

Exhibits Indian artifacts, mostly Shuswap Indians, with some material relevant to other tribes of the Interior Salish. Archives and library.

MUSEUM OF NORTHERN
BRITISH COLUMBIA
P.O. Box 669
PRINCE RUPERT V8J 3S1
 (604) 624-3207
 Elaine Moore, Curator/Director

Exhibits a collection of ethnographic artifacts representing Tsimshian native people (coast, Gitksan and Nisgha) and Haida and Tlingit to a lesser extent; Northwest Coast Indian artifacts, and other cultural remains relating to regional history. *Publication: The Curator's Log,* quarterly. Library.

ED JONES HAIDA MUSEUM
Second Beach Skidgate
QUEEN CHARLOTTE CITY V0T 1S0
 (604) 559-4643

CENTENNIAL MUSEUM
1100 Chestnut
VANCOUVER

UNIVERSITY OF BRITISH COLUMBIA
MUSEUM OF ANTHROPOLOGY
6393 N.W. Marine Dr.
VANCOUVER V6T 1W5
 (604) 228-5087

Major research and study collections include Northwest Coast archaeology and ethnology, and ethnological specimens from other North American Indian cultures. *Publications: Anthropology at the Academy,* newsletter; *The Elkus Collection of Southwestern Indian Art; Hopi Kachina: Spirit of Life.* Library.

BRITISH COLUMBIA
PROVINCIAL MUSEUM
Heritage Court, 601 Belleville St.
VICTORIA

PROVINCIAL ARCHIVES
OF BRITISH COLUMBIA
Parliament Bldg.
VICTORIA

MANITOBA

ESKIMO MUSEUM
James St.
CHURCHILL R0B 0E0

CROSS LAKE
CULTURAL/EDUCATION CENTRE
Cross Lake Indian Reserve
CROSS LAKE R0B 0J0
 (204) 676-2268/2218

CULTURAL CENTER
Fort Alexander Band
P.O. Box 1610
PINE FALLS R0E 1M0
 (204) 367-8740

MANITOBA INDIAN CULTURAL
EDUCATION CENTRE
119 Sutherland Ave.
WINNIPEG R2W 3C9
 (204) 942-0228

MANITOBA MUSEUM
OF MAN AND NATURE
190 Rupert Ave.
WINNIPEG

NEW BRUNSWICK

PAPINEAU INDIAN CULTURAL CENTRE
P.O. Box 8, Site 22
BATHURST E2A 3Y8
 (506) 548-9211

BIG COVE CULTURAL CENTRE
Big Cove Reserve, RR 1
REXTON E0A 2L0
 (506) 523-6384

THE NEW BRUNSWICK MUSEUM
277 Douglas Ave.
SAINT JOHN

NORTHWEST TERRITORIES

INUIT CULTURAL INSTITUTE
ESKIMO POINT X0C 0E0
 (819) 857-2803

NOVA SCOTIA

NOVA SCOTIA MUSEUM
1747 Summer St.
HALIFAX B3H 3A6
(902) 429-4610
Candace Stevenson, Director

Contains an extensive collection and exhibit of Micmac material culture—stone tools, basketry, birchbark objects, quill boxes, and bone implements. *Publications: Micmac Quillwork; Elitekey; Red Earth; Withe Baskets, Traps and Brooms.* Library.

ONTARIO

**WOODLAND INDIAN
CULTURAL EDUCATIONAL CENTRE**
P.O. Box 1506
BRANTFORD N3T 5V6
(519) 759-2653

JOSEPH BRANT MUSEUM
1240 North Shore Blvd.
BURLINGTON

A collection of Joseph Brant (Iroquois) memorabilia; general material on the Iroquois culture. Library.

ALGONQUIN MUSEUM
Via Algonquin Park
GOLDEN LAKE

**LAKE OF THE WOODS
OJIBWAY CULTURAL CENTRE**
P.O. Box 1720
KENORA P9N 3X7
(807) 548-5744

**THE McMICHAEL CANADIAN
COLLECTION—ART MUSEUM**
KLEINBERG

Exhibits of Eskimo sculpture and prints; works of art by West Coast and Woodlands Indians.

MUSEUM OF INDIAN ARCHAEOLOGY
University of Western Ontario
Lawson-Jury Bldg.
LONDON N6G 3M6
(519) 473-1360
    William D. Finlayson, Ph.D., Executive Director
    Debra Bodner, Curator

Large (over one-half million specimens) archaeological collections from throughout southern Ontario; small ethnographic collection from Ontario, Canadian Plains, and the Arctic.

Lawson Prehistoric Indian Village: An open-air facility featuring excavation, reconstruction and interpretation of a prehistoric Neutral village. *Programs:* Exhibition Gallery; study and layout space; tours and lectures; Research Associate Program; Archaeological Contracting and Consulting Services; archaeological field schools and courses. *Publications:* Newsletter; Bulletin; Research Reports. Library.

**SAINTE-MARIE
AMONG THE HURONS MUSEUM**
R.R. 1
MIDLAND

**NATIONAL MUSEUM OF MAN
NATIONAL MUSEUMS OF CANADA**
OTTAWA K1A 0M8
    (819) 994-6113 (Archaeological Survey of Canada)
    (613) 996-4540 (Canadian Ethnological Service)
    Ian G. Dyck, Ph.D., Chief-Archaeology
    A. McFadyen Clark, Chief Ethnologist

Archaeological Collection: Contains approximately 2,500,000 specimens from Canada and Alaska; collections from the Eastern Woodlands (Ontario eastward to the Atlantic Provinces) and the Eskimo (Arctic) areas; the Arctic Coast, Northwest Coast, Plateau, western Boreal forest, and Plains. *Ethnological Collection:* Approximately 50,000 artifacts, 90% of which are Canadian Indian and Inuit material (including modern works of Indian and Inuit art) with emphasis on Inuit and Pacific Coast Indian traditional material culture. *Programs:* Responsible for the survey and rescue of Canada's prehistoric sites; to record the languages and cultures of Canadian Indians, Inuit and Metis. Publications. Library.

**LAURENTIAN UNIVERSITY
MUSEUM AND ARTS CENTRE**
John St.
SUDBURY P3E 2C6
    (705) 675-1151 ext. 400/401
    Pamela Krueger, Director

Collection areas relate to contemporary native and Inuit artists of Canada, and native and Indian artists of Northern Ontario; also, approximately 600 Canadian artists, historical and contemporary. *Publications: Communique,* published every six weeks; exhibition catalogues. Library.

**OJIBWAY AND CREE
CULTURAL CENTRE**
59 - 71 Third Ave.
TIMMINS P4N 1C2
(705) 267-7911

ROYAL ONTARIO MUSEUM
100 Queens Park
TORONTO M5S 2C6
(416) 978-3654 (Ethnology)
(416) 978-3668 (Archaeology)
Edward S. Rogers, Ph.D., Curator-Ethnology
Peter L. Storck, Ph.D., Curator-Archaeology

Ethnology: Collections of material for the following geographical areas and tribes: Arctic—Eastern Canadian Eskimo, Netsilik Eskimo, Copper Eskimo, Western Canadian Eskimo; Northwest Coast—Kwakiutl, Tsimshian, Haida, Gitskan, Bella Bella; Northeast Coast—Iroquois, Cree Ojibwa, Montagnais-Naskapi; Plains—Blackfoot, Cree and Saulteaux, Canadian Plains. *Archaeology:* Provincial collections of Ontario archaeological material; and material from the rest of Canada; material from the U.S., including the Southwest and Mississippi Valley cultures. *Publications: Arcaheological Newsletter; Rotunda,* quarterly magazine; Monographs and Papers; *Round Lake Ojibwa* (monograph); contemporary native arts catalogs; *Native People of Canada* (7 booklets); books for sale. Library.

PRINCE EDWARD ISLAND

**PRINCE EDWARD ISLAND
HERITAGE FOUNDATION MUSEUM**
P.O. Box 922
CHARLOTTETOWN

QUEBEC

KANIEN'KEHA...RAOTITOHKWA
P.O. Box 750
KAHNAWAKE J01 1B0
(514) 638-0880

**RIVER DESERT
CULTURAL EDUCATION CENTRE**
River Desert Band, P.O. Box 309
MANIWAKI J9E 3B3
(819) 449-4575

OKA CULTURAL CENTRE
P.O. Box 640
OKA J0N 1L0
(514) 479-8373

**INSTITUT CULTUREL ET EDUCATIF
ATTIKAMEK-MONTAGNAIS**
Boulevard Bastien
VILLAGE HURON G0A 4V0
(418) 842-0277

SASKATCHEWAN

**BATTLEFORD NATIONAL
HISTORIC PARK MUSEUM**
P.O. Box 70
BATTLEFORD

PRAIRIE PIONEER MUSEUM
P.O. Box 273
CARIK

MOOSE JAW ART MUSEUM
Crescent Park
MOOSE JAW

**THE SASKATOON GALLERY
AND CONSERVATORY CORP. MUSEUM**
Mendel Art Gallery
950 Spadina Crescent East
SASKATOON

VIGFUSSON MUSEUM
University of Saskatchewan
Room 69, Arts Bldg.
SASKATOON

LIBRARIES

These alpha-geographically arranged listings, like those in the *Museums* section, include libraries with both large and small holdings, pertaining, in whole or in part, to the subject of the North American Indian.

ALASKA

ANCHORAGE HISTORICAL AND FINE ARTS MUSEUM LIBRARY
121 West Seventh Ave.
ANCHORAGE 99501
(907) 264-4326

Collection includes more than 500 volumes on the Tlingit, Haida, Northwest Coast, Athapaskan, Aleut, and Eskimo, especially as pertains to Alaskan groups; photograph collection; slides.

AHTNA, INC. LIBRARY
Drawer G
COPPER CENTER 99573
(907) 822-3476

Contains mostly publications dealing with land and resources in interior Alaska, with some on native culture (Athabascan.)

ALASKA'S MOTION PICTURE FILM ARCHIVE CENTER
P.O. Box 95203, University of Alaska
FAIRBANKS 99701
(907) 479-7296
Reg Emmert, Director

A repository of Alaskan archival film. Catalog of available films is available.

INSTITUTE OF ALASKA NATIVE ARTS LIBRARY
P.O. Box 80583
FAIRBANKS 99708
(907) 456-7491

ELMER E. RASMUSON LIBRARY
University of Alaska
FAIRBANKS 99701

Special collections: Skinner Collection— Contains material regarding Alaska and the Polar regions (Arctic and Antarctic); more than 4,000 volumes on the Athapaskan, Haida, Tlingit, Tsimshean, and Eskimo. University Archives and Manuscript Collections (Alaskana only)— Consists of journals, records, historic photos, tape recordings *(Alaska Native Stories);* 4,000 historic photos of Alaska natives.

ALASKA STATE DIVISION OF STATE LIBRARIES HISTORICAL LIBRARY
Pouch G
JUNEAU 99801

ROBBIE BATHOLOMEW MEMORIAL LIBRARY
Tongass Historical Society
629 Dock St.
KETCHIKAN 99901
(907) 225-5600

TOTEM HERITAGE CENTER LIBRARY
629 Dock St.
KETCHIKAN 99901
(907) 225-5900

KODIAK AREA NATIVE ASSOCIATION LIBRARY
402 Center Ave.
KODIAK 99615
(907) 486-5725

General book collection. Museum/Cultural Center and Research Library in planning stages.

SITKA NATIONAL HISTORICAL PARK LIBRARY
P.O. Box 738
SITKA 99835
(907) 747-6281

ARIZONA

CANYON DE CHELLY NATIONAL MONUMENT LIBRARY
P.O. Box 588
CHINLE 86503
(602) 674-5436

TUZIGOOT NATIONAL MONUMENT LIBRARY
P.O. Box 68
CLARKDALE 86324
(602) 634-5564

**CASA GRANDE RUINS
NATIONAL MONUMENT LIBRARY**
P.O. Box 518
COOLIDGE 85228
(602) 723-3172

Contains a collection of 1,500 volumes on Hohokam archaeology and culture; Indians of area.

**THE AMERIND FOUNDATION
RESEARCH LIBRARY**
P.O. Box 248
DRAGOON 85609
(602) 586-3003
Anne I. Woosley, Director

Maintains a collection of 20,000 volumes focusing on American archaeology, ethnology, history and art; many on the American Indian.

**HAROLD S. COLTON
MEMORIAL LIBRARY**
Museum of Northern Arizona
P.O. Box 1389
FLAGSTAFF 86002

Collection contains more than 10,000 books, including the subjects of Hopi and Navajo Indians, and archaeology of the Southwestern U.S.

**WUPATKI NATIONAL
MONUMENT LIBRARY**
HC 33, Box 444A
FLAGSTAFF 86001
(602) 527-7152

**HUBBELL TRADING POST
NATIONAL HISTORIC SITE LIBRARY**
P.O. Box 150
GANADO 86505
(602) 755-3475

Contains materials relevant to Navajo culture, Indian arts and crafts, history of native Americas, oral interviews, and trading information.

**COLORADO RIVER INDIAN TRIBES
PUBLIC LIBRARY**
Route 1, Box 23-B
PARKER 85344
(602) 669-9211
Amelia Aspa, Librarian

Holdings include 25,000 volumes: documents, photographs, microfilms, and magazines related to the history and culture of the four tribes of Colorado River Indian Reservation, the Mohave, Chemehuevi, Navajo and Hopi. *Archives:* 780 volumes of information on the subjects of dreams, myths, personal accounts of early reservation life, census reports, agent's letters and reports, arts and crafts, and social events of the four tribes; archival photograph collection.

**STRADLING MUSEUM
OF THE HORSE LIBRARY**
P.O. Box 413
PATAGONIA 85624
(602) 394-2264

Maintains a collection of 1,000 volumes on Indian history; Indian rugs.

THE HEARD MUSEUM LIBRARY
22 E. Monte Vista Rd.
PHOENIX 85004
(602) 252-8840
Mary Graham, Librarian

Research collection of approximately 35,000 volumes. An anthropology library with emphasis on the greater Southwest, Native-American art and the art of Africa and the South Pacific; also, a small original collection of films and video cassettes concerned with American Indian arts and artists, including demonstrations of techniques, dance festivals and museum exhibits.

PHOENIX INDIAN CENTER LIBRARY
1337 North First St.
PHOENIX 85004
(602) 256-2000

A collection of Indian resource books.

**PHOENIX INDIAN MEDICAL CENTER
HEALTH SCIENCES LIBRARY**
4212 North 16th St.
PHOENIX 85016
(602) 263-1200
Thomas Mead, Librarian

Basic professional and medical collection with special collection on Indian health concerns.

PUEBLO GRANDE MUSEUM LIBRARY
4619 East Washington St.
PHOENIX 85034
(602) 275-3452

Collection primarily on Southwest archaeology with volumes pertaining to the American Indian. Open to scholars on appointment basis only.

**STATE OF ARIZONA — DEPARTMENT
OF LIBRARY AND ARCHIVES**
Third Floor Capitol
PHOENIX 85007

Contains over 500,000 volumes, including much material on Southwestern Indians. Numerous exhibits supplement library research and consists primarily of artifacts, pottery, basketry, paintings, pictures, and odd items.

SMOKI PEOPLE LIBRARY
P.O. Box 123
PRESCOTT 86302
(602) 778-5228

A collection of 600 volumes on North and South American Indian dance and ceremonials.

**NATIONAL INDIAN TRAINING
AND RESEARCH CENTER LIBRARY**
2121 South Mill Ave., Suite 216
TEMPE 85282
   (602) 967-9484

Contains 1,000 volumes relating to Indian education.

**NAVAJO NATIONAL
MONUMENT LIBRARY**
TONALEA 86044
   (602) 672-2366

A collection of approximately 600 volumes on Navajo history and archaeology.

**NAVAJO COMMUNITY
COLLEGE LIBRARY**
Rural Post Office
TSAILE 86556
   (602) 724-3311

Special collection: Moses Donner Indian Collection—An extensive collection of publications on Indians.

**ARIZONA HISTORICAL
ASSOCIATION LIBRARY**
949 East Second St.
TUCSON 85719

Holdings include 35,000 volumes related to Arizona and the Southwest. Manuscript Division contains 500 collections of historical documents.

ARIZONA STATE MUSEUM LIBRARY
University of Arizona
TUCSON 85721
   (602) 621-6281

Contains approximately 32,000 volumes of published materials as well as archives of unpublished documents, field notes, diaries, primarily related to Southwest archaeology and ethnology, many of which are on the subject of the American Indian; extensive microfilm collection.

**MISSION SAN XAVIER
DEL BAC LIBRARY**
Route 11, Box 645
TUCSON 85706
   (602) 294-2624

A collection of about 5,000 volumes pertaining to Aztec and Native-American ethnography and anthropology.

SOUTHWEST FOLKLORE CENTER
University of Arizona
TUCSON 85706
   (602) 626-3392

Contains four videotaped conversations: Navajo singer Andrew Natonabah, writers Leslie Marmon Silko and N. Scott Momaday, and Papago storyteller Ted Rios. Available on 2" videotape.

**UNIVERSITY OF ARIZONA
COLLEGE OF LAW LIBRARY**
TUCSON 85721

Maintains a special collection on law relating to the American Indian.

**WESTERN ARCHAEOLOGICAL AND
CONSERVATION CENTER LIBRARY**
P.O. Box 41058, 1415 N. Sixth Ave.
TUCSON 85717
   (602) 792-6501

Collection includes 15,000 volumes on archaeology, anthropology, history of the Southwest, California and Hawaii; 1,000 volumes pertain to the American Indian.

NATIVE AMERICAN RESEARCH LIBRARY
Navajo Nation Library System
Window Rock Public Library
WINDOW ROCK 86515
   Richard G. Heyser, Director —
   Cultural Resources Dept. (Navajo Nation)

Holdings include more than 2,000 volumes; 1,000 manuscripts, films, tapes, and microfilm on the Navajo Indians; Southwest archaeology, Indians of America, and Arizona history.

ARKANSAS

**ARKANSAS STATE UNIVERSITY
MUSEUM LIBRARY**
P.O. Box 490
STATE UNIVERSITY 72467
   (501) 972-2074

Contains 1,200 books, documents and reference materials on Indian history and culture.

CALIFORNIA

**AMERICAN INDIAN LORE
ASSOCIATION LIBRARY**
P.O. Box 9698
ANAHEIM 92802

A collection of 1,000 volumes on North American Indian lore, ethnology, anthropology, and folklore.

MALKI MUSEUM LIBRARY
11-795 Fields Rd.
Morongo Indian Reservation
BANNING 92220
(714) 849-7289

Collection consists of 500 volumes on southern California Indians.

UNIVERSITY OF CALIFORNIA
ANTHROPOLOGY LIBRARY
230 Kroeber Hall
BERKELEY 94720

UNIVERSITY OF CALIFORNIA
NATIVE AMERICAN STUDIES LIBRARY
343 Dwinelle Hall
BERKELEY 94720

A collection of 2,000 books on Native-Americans, anthropology, and sociology; microfilm, records, tapes, videotapes; journals and newspapers.

CABOT'S OLD INDIAN PUEBLO
MUSEUM LIBRARY
67-616 East Desert View Ave.
DESERT HOT SPRINGS 92240
(619) 329-7610

LOMPOC MUSEUM LIBRARY
200 South H St.
LOMPOC 93431
(805) 736-3888

Contains over 1,000 volumes on Chumash Indians, Indians of southern California, and Lompoc history and archaeology.

AMERICAN INDIAN STUDIES
CENTER LIBRARY
3220 Campbell Hall
University of California
LOS ANGELES 90024
(213) 825-4591
Velma Salabiye, Librarian

Approximately 6,000 volumes comprise the Library's core collection, covering the subject of the Indians of North America, with a strong emphasis on California and the Southwest. The primary focus is on American Indian life, culture, and state-of-affairs in historical and contemporary perspectives. Augmenting the circulating and reference collections are dissertations, audio-visual materials, serials/periodicals, and a vertical file.

LOS ANGELES PUBLIC LIBRARY
History Department
630 West Fifth St.
LOS ANGELES 90071

Maintains a special collection on the American Indian.

SOUTHWEST MUSEUM
BRAUN RESEARCH LIBRARY
P.O. Box 128, 234 Museum Dr.
LOS ANGELES 90042
(213) 221-2164
Daniela Moneta, Librarian

Collection consists of 50,000 volumes including monographs and serials on ethnography and archaeology of the Western Hemisphere and Native-American studies; manuscript collections and sound archives; and 150,000 photographs. There is a strong emphasis on Southwestern tribes but material is available concerning all native people in the Western Hemisphere. *Special collections:* The Papers of Frederick Webb Hodge, Frank Hamilton Cushing, George Bird Grinnell, Charle F. Lummis, and George Wharton James.

MARIN MUSEUM OF
THE AMERICAN INDIAN LIBRARY
P.O. Box 864, 2200 Novato Blvd.
NOVATO 94948
(415) 897-4064
Mary Hilderman Smith, Executive Director

A reference library of approximately 1,000 volumes/periodicals oriented heavily to California Indians, especially Coast Miwok.

INDIAN CENTER
OF SAN JOSE LIBRARY
3485 East Hills Dr.
SAN JOSE 95127
(408) 259-9722
Gerald L. Casimere, Director

Contains 4,000 books on Indian history, culture, tribal groups, and literature. *Special collection:* The Indian Tribal Series: Consists of tribal newsletters, periodicals, films, filmstrips, and records. *Publication:* Newsletter.

PALOMAR COMMUNITY
COLLEGE LIBRARY
West Mission Rd.
SAN MARCOS 92069

A collection of 2,000 volumes pertaining to American Indian culture, history, arts and crafts, and social problems; Bureau of Ethnology Reports.

HELD-POAGE RESEARCH LIBRARY
603 West Perkins St.
UKIAH 95482
(707) 462-6969
Mrs. Robert J. (Lila J.) Lee, Director

A history research library with a collection of over 1,200 volumes on American Indians, and 3,000 on U.S. history; photographic negative collection; artifacts, maps.

UNIVERSAL CITY STUDIOS
RESEARCH DEPARTMENT LIBRARY
UNIVERSAL CITY 91608

A special collection of 7,500 books dealing with
Western Americana and the American Indian.

COLORADO

NATIONAL INDIAN LAW LIBRARY
Native American Rights Fund
1506 Broadway
BOULDER 80302-6296
(303) 447-8760
Deana J. Harragarra Waters, Director

Serves as a clearinghouse for all legal materials
pertinent to Federal Indian Law. Includes all
cases, briefs, pleadings, orders, legal opinions,
rulings, memoranda, treatises, studies, books,
articles, reports, and legislative histories pertinent
to Federal Indian Law. *Publications: National
Indian Law Catalogue, An Index to Indian Legal
Materials and Resources; Bibliography on Indian
Economic Development,* Second Edition; *Indian
Claims Commission Decisions and Index.*

COLORADO SPRINGS
FINE ARTS CENTER LIBRARY
30 West Dale St.
COLORADO SPRINGS 80903
(303) 634-5581
Roderick Dew, Director

A collection of approximately 8,000 volumes on
Indians of the Southwest, Mexico and
Guatemala, with emphasis on art, textiles and
pottery. Contains a large collection of periodicals,
some from the late 19th century.

COLORADO HISTORICAL
SOCIETY LIBRARY
1300 Broadway
DENVER 80203
(303) 866-3682

Contains extensive ethnological collections on
Plains and Southwest Indians; Mesa Verde Plains
and Mountain Indian materials; source materials
on the history of the Indian wars; materials from
the Rosebud Indian Agency, 1885-1890; and
photograph collection.

FREDERIC H. DOUGLAS
MEMORIAL LIBRARY
Denver Art Museum
100 West 14th Ave. Parkway
DENVER 80204
(303) 575-2256

Holdings include more than 50,000 volumes; 80
journals; and a special collection on the American
Indians.

NATIONAL CENTER
FOR AMERICAN INDIAN
ALTERNATIVE EDUCATION LIBRARY
P.O. Box 18329, Capitol Hill Station
DENVER 80218
(301) 861-1052

Contains a collection of over 1,500 volumes on
Indian related issues and education.

NATIONAL URBAN INDIAN COUNCIL
AND NATIONAL INDIAN EMPLOYMENT
RESOURCE CENTER LIBRARY
2258 South Broadway
DENVER 80210
(303) 698-2911

Contains publications on employment-related
subjects; extensive listings of employment
opportunities and other books concerning Indian
people, law, foundations and population.

KOSHARE INDIAN LIBRARY
Koshare Indian Museum
115 West 18th St.
LA JUNTA 81050

Collection contains 2,000 volumes on Indian
history, religion, legends, art, handicrafts, etc.
Reference use only.

MESA VERDE NATIONAL PARK LIBRARY
MESA VERDE NATIONAL PARK 81330
(303) 529-4475

Maintains more than 4,000 volumes on
archaeology and ethnography, with many on the
Indians of the Mesa Verde area, and North
America.

CONNECTICUT

CONNECTICUT STATE LIBRARY
231 Capitol Ave.
HARTFORD 06115

Maintains an American Indian collection
emphasizing languages and history; its core
deriving from the library of J. Hammond
Trumball.

AMERICAN INDIAN ARCHAEOLOGICAL
INSTITUTE RESEARCH LIBRARY
Route 199, Box 260
WASHINGTON 06793
(203) 868-0518

Collection contains 2,000 volumes, periodicals
and maps. For use by members, scholars and
students with letters from professors. By
appointment only.

DISTRICT OF COLUMBIA

AMERICAN HISTORICAL ASSOCIATION LIBRARY
400 A St., S.E.
WASHINGTON 20003
(202) 544-2422

LIBRARY OF CONGRESS
1st and Independence, S.E.
WASHINGTON 20540
(202) 287-5522
Daniel J. Boorstin, Librarian

GENERAL REFERENCE AND BIBLIOG-RAPHYY DIVISION: A collection of approximately 16,000 volumes covering virtually all subjects relating to North American tribes. Includes various bibliographies, catalogs, and guides to other collections containing material on Indians, such as *Dictionary Catalog of the Edward E. Ayer Collection of Americana and American Indians,* the *Dictionary Catalog of the American Indian Collection,* Huntington Free Library and Reading Room, New York, and the *Biographical and Historical Index of American Indians and Persons Involved in Indian Affairs.* *MICROFORM READING ROOM:* Contains much Indian-related material from a variety of print and nonprint sources. For example: *North American Indians: Photographs from the National Anthropological Archives, Smithsonian Institution,* compiled by Herman Viola—contains approximately 4,700 photographs on microfiche of Indians and Indian artifacts; individual and group portraits; *Doctoral Dissertation Series.* University Microfilms has published *North American Indians: Dissertation Index,* written between 1904-1976 at North American universities; *Early State Records*—The study of colonial relations with Indians; also includes public and private collections noted for Indian-related material, such as: *The Connecticut Archives Indian Volumes, 1647-1820; The Henry O'Reilly Papers, 1744-1825*—Relating to the Six Nations and Indians of the Old Northwest; *Records of the Five Civilized Tribes, 1840-1905; The Penn Manuscripts, 1687-1801,* and, *The Timothy Horsfield Papers, 1733-1771*—The last two collections involving Indians in Pennsylvania and surrounding areas; *Pamphlets in American History*—Microfiche collection of rare pamphlets includes many dealings with American Indians; *British Manuscripts Project*—contains abundant source material on Indians especially for the period of the French and Indian War. *MANUSCRIPT DIVISION:* The Papers of the President, military officers, agents in Indian affairs, and other public and private individuals who dealt with Indians at various periods, such as those of Thomas A. Jesup, Henry L. Dawes,

Edward S. Godfrey, Henry Rowe Schoolcraft, Philip Sheridan, Samuel P. Heintzelman, and John M. Schofield. Important collections available on microfilm include the papers of the American Missionary Society, the American Indian Correspondence Collection, and the Moravian Archives, as well as the papers of Timothy Pickering, Henry Knox, and Lyman C. Draper. Transcripts and photocopies of collections in foreign archives and libraries, such as the Indian records in the Public Archives of Canada. *SERIAL AND GOVERNMENT PUBLICATIONS DIVISION:* The Senate Confidential Executive Documents and Reports: Dating from the 17th Congress (1821)—comprised of formerly confidential documents which relate primarily to treaties. Patrons who wish to use this material should write to the Chief of this Division of the Library of Congress, or phone (202) 287-5647. *PRINTS AND PHOTOGRAPHS DIVISION:* Maintains holdings of nearly 4,000 prints, photographs, and engravings. *The Edward S. Curtis Collection*—Contains more than 1,600 photographs of Indians of the Plains, the Central Plateau, the Northwest Coast, the Southwest, and California; *The Heyn-Matzen Collection*—Contains approximately 550 photographs, mostly of Sioux, Crow and other Plains tribes; *The John Grabill Collection*—Consists mainly of photographs of Western frontier life, but includes many of Indians; also more than 200 stereo views of Indians, and a miscellaneous collection of uncataloged and unsorted prints and photographs. Copies of the division's material not covered by copyright may be purchased from the Library's Photoduplication Service. *ARCHIVE OF FOLK CULTURE:* Joseph C. Hickerson, Head. *The Smithsonian-Densmore Collection*—Contains more than 3,500 cylinder recordings of songs of 35 tribal groups, compiled from 1907-1932; *Peabody Museum Collection*—Compiled in the 1890's by anthropologist Jesse Walter Fewkes, this collection contains more than 50 recordings reproducing the music and language of tribes like the Passamaquoddy, Hopi, Zuni, and Kwakiutl; *The Willard Rhodes Collection*—Contains the music of 50 Indian tribes, recorded on disc and tape from 1940-1952, when Rhodes worked for the B.I.A. 19 long-playing records of selections from these and other collections are available for purchase. For information and descriptive literature write the Archive, or phone (202) 287-5510. *MOTION PICTURE, BROADCASTING AND RECORDED SOUND DIVISION:* Contains films of ceremonial dances and of everyday Indian life; maintains several filmographies and guides to titles of films about Indians. For information regarding viewing films and video tapes write Division.

NATIONAL ARCHIVES
AND RECORDS ADMINISTRATION
8th and Pennsylvania Ave., N.W.
WASHINGTON 20408
(202) 523-3238
Robert M. Kvasnicka, Assistant Chief

*Scientific, Economic and Natural Resources
Branch:* Contains records of the Bureau of Indian
Affairs, and tribal enrollment records for the
period prior to 1940; *Motion Picture Branch:*
Consists of films showing Indian life-ways in the
1930's, and Plains Indian sign language.

NATIONAL GEOGRAPHIC
SOCIETY LIBRARY
17th and M Sts., N.W.
WASHINGTON 20036
(202) 857-7000

SMITHSONIAN INSTITUTION
NATIONAL ANTHROPOLOGICAL
ARCHIVES
Natural History Bldg., Room 60-A
10th and Constitution Ave., N.W.
WASHINGTON 20560
(202) 357-1986
Dr. Herman Viola, Director

Conatins over 53,000 volumes on all branches of
anthropology. Maintains the *Bureau of
Ethnology Collection* and *Hrdlicka Collection:*
Extensive collection of manuscripts,
photographs, books, periodicals and journals
relating to North American Indians,
anthropological institutions, and history of
anthropology.

U.S. DEPARTMENT OF
THE INTERIOR LIBRARY
18th and C Sts., N.W.
WASHINGTON 20240
(202) 343-5810
Robert Uskavitch, Chief-Information Services

Maintains a large collection of Indian reference
material.

U.S. DEPARTMENT OF
JUSTICE LIBRARY
Land and Natural Resources Division
550 11th St., N.W.
WASHINGTON 20530
James Brookshire, Chief-Indian Claims Section
(202) 724-7375
Hank Meshorer, Chief-Indian Resources Section
(202) 724-7156

Maintains library holdings of more than 600,000
volumes, many of which are on Indian claims and
natural resources as it relates to Indian
reservation land.

WILKINSON, CRAGUN
AND BARKER LIBRARY
1735 New York Ave., N.W.
WASHINGTON 20006

Maintains a special collection of American
Indian-Federal Government legal material.

FLORIDA

TEMPLE MOUND MUSEUM LIBRARY
P.O. Box 4009, 139 Miraclestrip Parkway S.E.
FORT WALTON BEACH 32548
(904) 243-6521

Collection consists of 1,200 volumes on the
archaeology of the site, and Indians of the region.

SEMINOLE TRIBE LIBRARY
6073 Stirling Rd.
HOLLYWOOD 33024
(305) 583-7112 ext. 263/264

Contains books, manuscripts, periodicals,
photographs and microfilm on the history and
culture of the Seminole Indian Tribe of Florida.

HISTORICAL ASSOCIATION
OF SOUTHERN FLORIDA
LIBRARY
3280 South Miami Ave., Bldg. B
MIAMI 33129

Holdings include the *Claud C. Matlack
Collection* of early Seminole society photographs;
Indian wars and Florida history.

FLORIDA HISTORICAL
SOCIETY LIBRARY
University of South Florida
TAMPA 33620

Holdings are mainly of Seminole Indian material.

GEORGIA

OCMULGEE NATIONAL
MONUMENT LIBRARY
1207 Emery Highway
MACON 31201
(912) 742-0447

A collection of over 1,000 volumes on
anthropology, archaeology, and prehistoric and
historic Indians of the area; history of the
Southeast U.S.

IDAHO

**IDAHO STATE
HISTORICAL SOCIETY LIBRARY**
610 North Julia Davis Dr.
BOISE 83702
(208) 334-3356
Arthur A. Hart, Director

Collections include more than 200 volumes of Lapwai Agency records of 1871-1883; diaries and private papers. *The Alice Fletcher-Jane Gay Nez Perce Allotment Photograph Collection, 1882-1892;* Idaho Superintendency and other Indian records (National Archives microfilm); Indian files in the territorial section of State Archives; Nez Perce and Shoshone literature.

**UNIVERSITY OF IDAHO — ARCHIVE
OF PACIFIC NORTHWEST
ARCHAEOLOGY**
Department of Sociology/Anthropology
MOSCOW 83843

Holdings include 2,000 complete photocopies of all material relating to the archaeology and physical anthropology of the Pacific Northwest.

**NEZ PERCE
NATIONAL HISTORICAL PARK LIBRARY**
P.O. Box 93
SPALDING 83551

Collection consists of more than 600 volumes on Nez Perce Indian history and culture.

ILLINOIS

THE NEWBERRY LIBRARY
60 West Walton
CHICAGO 60610
Frederick E. Hoxie, Director

D'Arcy McNickel Center for the History of the American Indian: A collection of scholarly information on Indian history. *E.E. Ayer Collection:* Consists of thousands of volumes, manuscripts, prints and photographs on the American Indian; Indian-White contact and response; Native-American linguistics; Government-Indian relations prior to the New Deal; and maps.

**CAHOKIA MOUNDS
STATE HISTORIC SITE LIBRARY**
7850 Collinsville Rd.
EAST ST. LOUIS 62201
(618) 344-5268

Contains research data on the excavations at Cahokia Mounds Site; and generally related Mississippian Site; volumes on Illinois and Midwestern archaeology.

INDIANA

**INDIANA UNIVERSITY
MUSEUM LIBRARY**
Student Bldg. 107
BLOOMINGTON 47401

A collection of 2,000 volumes on the American Indian.

THE POTAWATOMI MUSEUM LIBRARY
P.O. Box 486, No. Wayne & City Limits
FREMONT 46737

Holdings include 1,000 reference books on the American Indian. By appointment only.

**MUSEUM OF INDIAN HERITAGE
REFERENCE LIBRARY**
6040 De Long Rd.
INDIANAPOLIS 46254
(317) 293-4488
Vicki Cummings, Director

Collections consist of approximately 2,000 volumes on Native American ethnology, archaeology, art, and language; also, periodicals; Bureau of American Ethnology annual reports; historical accounts of early contact; treaties; and literature. Tribal works emphasize Northwest Coast, Eskimo, Southwest, California, Great Plains, Eastern Woodlands, and works on Central and South American tribes.

IOWA

**IOWA STATE
HISTORICAL MUSEUM LIBRARY**
East 12th & Grand Ave.
DES MOINES 50319
(515) 281-5111

**IOWA STATE
HISTORICAL SOCIETY LIBRARY**
402 Iowa Ave.
IOWA CITY 52240
(319) 338-5471
David Crosson, Director

A collection of 120,000 books and bound periodicals, microforms, newspapers, maps, etc. of which there is a small collection of books relating to tribes that lived in Iowa, census data, public records, documents from Indian Claims Commission court cases, theses, manuscripts, maps, paintings and drawings, and several hundred Mesquakie Indian photographs.

**EFFIGY MOUNDS
NATIONAL MONUMENT LIBRARY**
P.O. Box K
McGREGOR 52157
(319) 873-2356

A collection of 500 volumes on the archaeology and ethnography of Effigy Mounds region.

MORNINGSIDE COLLEGE LIBRARY
SIOUX CITY 51106

Contains a special collection on the American Indian.

MUSEUM OF HISTORY AND SCIENCE
503 South St.
WATERLOO 50701

KANSAS

**CULTURAL HERITAGE
AND ARTS CENTER LIBRARY**
P.O. Box 1275
DODGE CITY 67801

Consists of more than 2,000 books, films, and records on North American Indians, with emphasis on Indians of the Southwest.

**KANSAS STATE
HISTORICAL SOCIETY LIBRARY**
Memorial Bldg., 120 West 10th St.
TOPEKA 66612

Holdings include a special collection of approximately 3,500 books on the American Indians and the West; also Kansas State public records and documents; microfilm, maps, paintings and drawings, photographs, etc.

**MID-AMERICA ALL INDIAN
CENTER LIBRARY**
650 North Seneca
WICHITA 67203

Contains a collection of over 400 volumes on the American Indian.

LOUISIANA

GRINDSTONE BLUFF MUSEUM LIBRARY
P.O. Box 7965, 501 Jenkins Rd.
SHREVEPORT 71107

Collection consists of approximately 3,600 volumes, with emphasis on Caddo and other area Indians.

MAINE

**MAINE TRIBAL UNITY
MUSEUM LIBRARY**
Quaker Hill Rd.
UNITY 04988
(207) 948-3131

MASSACHUSETTS

**ROBERT S. PEABODY FOUNDATION
FOR ARCHAEOLOGY LIBRARY**
P.O. Box 71, Phillip & Main Sts.
ANDOVER 01810
(617) 475-0248

Collection contains more than 5,000 volumes on the archaeology, anthropology and ethnology of the American Indian.

**CHILDREN'S MUSEUM
RESOURCE CENTER**
300 Congress St.
BOSTON 02210
(617) 426-6500

Holdings include 10,000 cultural materials relating to the American Indian.

TOZZER LIBRARY
21 Divinity Ave.
CAMBRIDGE 02138
(617) 495-2253
G. Edward Evans, Librarian

Collection consists of over 150,000 volumes relating to all aspects of anthropology, archaeology and biological anthropology; strong collection on Maya archaeology.

BOSTON INDIAN COUNCIL LIBRARY
105 S. Huntington
JAMAICA PLAIN 02130
(617) 232-0343

A collection of various materials related to Indian programs, history and culture.

PEABODY MUSEUM OF SALEM LIBRARY
East Indian Square
SALEM 01970

Collection contains 1,000 books, plus periodicals and pamphlets on the history and culture of North American Indians, with emphasis on the Northeastern section of the U.S.

CHAPIN LIBRARY OF RARE BOOKS
Williams College
WILLIAMSTOWN 01267

Contains 16th to 18th century documents relating to Indians of North and South America.

**AMERICAN ANTIQUARIAN
SOCIETY LIBRARY**
185 Salisbury St.
WORCESTER 01609
(617) 755-5221

A collection of five million books, prints, maps, and periodicals on American history, archaeology, and life through 1876.

MICHIGAN

UNIVERSITY OF MICHIGAN
WILLIAM L. CLEMENTS LIBRARY
South University St.
ANN ARBOR 48104

Collection consists of over 40,000 books and bound periodicals on Americana to 1830, including Indian relations.

GENESEE INDIAN CENTER LIBRARY
124 West First St.
FLINT 48502-1311
(313) 239-6621

Contains a collection of reference books and records on American Indian history and culture.

CHIPPEWA NATURE CENTER LIBRARY
400 South Badour, Route 9
MIDLAND 48640
(517) 631-0830

Contains 1,200 volumes on the American Indian.

LAKE SUPERIOR STATE COLLEGE
MICHIGAN COLLECTION
SAULT STE. MARIE 49783

Collection of 1,000 volumes on the history of Michigan's Upper Peninsula, including Indians and local history.

MINNESOTA

BECKER COUNTY
HISTORICAL SOCIETY LIBRARY
915 Lake Ave.
DETROIT LAKES 56501

Holdings include 1,500 volumes pertaining to the White Earth Indian Reservation, covering twelve townships of Becker County, Minnesota.

MINNEAPOLIS COLLEGE OF ART AND
DESIGN—LEARNING RESOURCE
CENTER
200 East 25th St.
MINNEAPOLIS 55404

Special collection: The American Indian Book Collection.

MINNEAPOLIS PUBLIC LIBRARY
AND INFORMATION CENTER
MINNEAPOLIS ATHENAEUM LIBRARY
300 Nicollet Mall
MINNEAPOLIS 55404

NATIONAL INDIAN EDUCATION
ASSOCIATION LIBRARY
1115 Second Ave. South
Ivory Tower Bldg., 2nd Floor
MINNEAPOLIS 55403

Library of material written by, about, and for American Indians and Alaskan natives. Holdings include approximately 5,000 books, 1,000 films and filmstrips, microfiche, tapes, cassettes, journals and newspapers on Native-Americans.

UPPER MIDWEST INDIAN
CULTURE CENTER LIBRARY
P.O. Box 727, Pipestone National Monument
PIPESTONE 56164

Collection of 500 volumes on Indian history of the northern Plains.

MINNESOTA HISTORICAL SOCIETY
AUDIO-VISUAL LIBRARY
690 Cedar St.
ST. PAUL 55101
(612) 296-2489
This collection of over 30 films from the 1930's to the 1950's, includes recent additions on Ojibwa, Blackfeet and other Minnesota Indian people.

MINNESOTA HISTORICAL SOCIETY
Division of Archives and Manuscripts
1500 Mississippi St.
ST. PAUL 55101
(612) 296-6980
Sue E. Holbert, State Archivist

Maintains a collection of material on the Ojibwe and Dakota tribes, plus a small amount on Winnebago; includes information on Indian education, state census schedules with listings of Indian people, and correspondence on Indian matters in the Governor's papers.

WINNEBAGO AREA MUSEUM LIBRARY
WINNEBAGO 56098
(506) 893-3692

MISSISSIPPI

JP MUSEUM OF INDIAN
ARTIFACTS LIBRARY
Route 1, Box 715
Highway 49 (LYMAN)
SAUCIER 39574

Contains a collection on Indian history and culture; artifact reference.

**THE GRAND VILLAGE OF
THE NATCHEZ INDIANS—LIBRARY**
400 Jefferson Davis Blvd.
NATCHEZ 39120
  (601) 446-6502
  James F. Barnett, Jr., Director

Reference library. Researchers with legitimate
research needs may apply for use of the library.

NATCHEZ TRACE PARKWAY LIBRARY
R.R. 1, NT 143
TUPELO 38801

Maintains a special collection of 200 items of
papers and letters relating to Choctaw and
Chickasaw Indians.

MISSOURI

**SOUTHEAST MISSOURI STATE
UNIVERSITY LIBRARY**
CAPE GIRARDEAU 63701

Extensive collection on North American
archaeology and Indians.

**NATIONAL ARCHIVES
KANSAS CITY BRANCH**
2312 East Bannister Rd.
KANSAS CITY 64131
  (816) 926-7271
  R. Reed Whitaker, Director

Collection consists of Federal Indian records
created on Indian reservations and schools in
North and South Dakota, Minnesota, Kansas and
Nebraska. The tribes included on these
reservations include the Chippewa and the
various tribes of the Sioux Confederation, as well
as the Iowa, Kickapoo, Omaha, Potawatomi,
Ponca, Sac and Fox, Winnebago and Munsee;
also, records of the Bismarck, Flandreau, Haskell,
Pierre, Pipestone, Rapid City, and Wahpeton
Indian schools; some records relate to tribes and
reservations in Wisconsin, primarily the
Menominee. Information contained are:
censuses, tribal enrollment rosters, annuity
payrolls, individual Indian bank account ledgers,
land allotment rolls, employee payrolls and
student case files; also extensive series of
superintendent's (agent's) correspondence files.

**UNIVERSITY OF MISSOURI, K.C.
GENERAL LIBRARY**
5100 Rockhill Rd.
KANSAS CITY 64110

Special collection: Snyder Collection of
Americana—25,000 volumes—historical and
Indian-related works.

**UNIVERSITY OF MISSOURI—LYMAN
ARCHAEOLOGICAL RESEARCH CENTER
MUSEUM—LIBRARY AND ARCHIVES**
Route 1
MIAMI 65344

**MISSOURI HISTORICAL
SOCIETY LIBRARY**
Jefferson Memorial Bldg.
ST. LOUIS 63112

Holdings include more than 2,000 volumes on the
American Indian.

MONTANA

**MUSEUM OF THE PLAINS INDIAN
LIBRARY AND ARCHIVES**
P.O. Box 400, Highway 89
BROWNING 59417
  (406) 338-2230

Collection consists of volumes on Plains
ethnology and archaeology; Montana ethnology
and history; and Blackfeet life and history.

**CUSTER BATTLEFIELD
NATIONAL MONUMENT LIBRARY**
P.O. Box 39
CROW AGENCY 59022
  (406) 638-2622

**CROW INDIAN HOSPITAL
MEDICAL LIBRARY**
U.S. Public Health Service
CROW AGENCY 59022

**HISTORICAL SOCIETY OF MONTANA
LIBRARY AND ARCHIVES**
225 North Roberts
HELENA 59601

Holdings include 50,000 volumes on Montana
history, frontier life, Indians and Indian affairs,
Lewis and Clark Expedition, and other related
subjects.

**UNIVERSITY OF MONTANA
SCHOOL OF LAW LIBRARY**
MISSOULA 59801

Maintains a special collection on Indian law; 120
treaties.

**BIG HOLE NATIONAL
BATTLEFIELD SITE LIBRARY**
P.O. Box 237
WISDOM 59761
  (406) 689-2530

A collection of 100 books on the Nez Perce Indian
War of 1877.

NEBRASKA

CENTER FOR GREAT PLAINS STUDIES
University of Nebraska
Oldfather Hall, 12th Floor
LINCOLN 68588

A collection of videotapes on several Nebraska tribes for use as elementary and secondary school curriculum material. Ten one-hour tapes concentrate on oral tradition and include storytelling, history, and elders' reminiscences by members of the Lakota, Brule Sioux, Santee Sioux, Omaha, Pawnee and Winnebago tribes. Videotapes in ¾ inch cassette and ½ inch reel-to-reel formats are available at the cost of duplication and cassette.

NATIVE AMERICAN PUBLIC BROADCASTING CONSORTIUM LIBRARY
P.O. Box 83111
LINCOLN 68501
(402) 472-3522

A collection of videotapes and films include Native-American programs which have been screened and evaluated by the Consortium for technical quality and accuracy of portrayal and content. Topics include: history, culture, education, economic development, current events and the arts.

NEBRASKA STATE HISTORICAL SOCIETY LIBRARY
1500 R St.
LINCOLN 68508

Holdings include more than 70,000 volumes on Nebraska history, Indians of the Great Plains, genealogy; 465 photographs in the *John A. Anderson Photograph Collection of Brule Sioux*.

NEW JERSEY

NEWARK MUSEUM LIBRARY
43-49 Washington St.
NEWARK 07101

Colection covers American Indian art, crafts, life, ethnology, etc.

HERBERT LEWIS TAYLOR ARCHAEOLOGICAL ASSOCIATION LIBRARY
739 West 8th St.
PLAINFIELD 07060

Collection contains more than 20,000 volumes on anthropology, archaeology and history, many of which are on the subject of the American Indian.

SETON HALL UNIVERSITY MUSEUM LIBRARY
South Orange Ave.
SOUTH ORANGE 07079
(201) 761-9543

Contains a collection of 1,000 volumes on prehistoric Indians of New Jersey.

NEW MEXICO

MAXWELL MUSEUM OF ANTHROPOLOGY CLARK FIELD ARCHIVES
University of New Mexico
University and Ash N.E.
ALBUQUERQUE 87131
(505) 277-4404
Garth L. Bawden, Director

Collection of 2,500 volumes on archaeology, anthropology and ethnology, with emphasis on the Southwestern U.S.

AMERICAN INDIAN LAW CENTER LIBRARY
University of New Mexico-School of Law
P.O. Box 4456, Station A, 1117 Stanford N.E.
ABUQUERQUE 87196
(505) 277-5462

Maintains a special collection on American Indian law.

ACOMA MUSEUM LIBRARY AND ARCHIVES
P.O. Box 309, Pueblo of Acoma
ACOMITA 87034
(505) 552-6606

Contains photographs and documents relating to the history of Acoma Pueblo.

AZTEC RUINS NATIONAL MONUMENT LIBRARY
P.O. Box U
AZTEC 87410
(505) 334-6174

A collection of 300 volumes on the ethnography and archaeology of Southwestern Indians and prehistoric Pueblo Indians.

CHACO CULTURE NATIONAL HISTORICAL PARK LIBRARY
Star Route 4, Box 6500
BLOOMFIELD 87413
(505) 786-5384

Study library housing hundreds of volumes on prehistory and history of Chaco area, Southwestern archaeology, ethnology, including journals, photographs, and records of historic period.

**SAN JUAN COUNTY
ARCHAEOLOGICAL RESEARCH CENTER
AND LIBRARY AT SALMON RUIN**
No. 975, U.S. Highway 64
FARMINGTON 87401
  (505) 632-2013
  Ouida Steward, Librarian

Research library of prehistory and history of the
Four Corners area, including 800 books, 1,100
pamphlets, 1,100 technical reports, 20 slide shows,
35 oral history tapes and transcriptions; on loan
collection of Navajo material and rock art slides.

**GALLUP INDIAN
MEDICAL CENTER LIBRARY**
PHS — Indian Health Service
P.O. Box 1337, East Nizhoni Blvd.
GALLUP 84301

Maintains a special collection on the Navajo
Indians.

GALLUP PUBLIC LIBRARY
115 West Hill
GALLUP 87301

A collection of rare, out-of-print and
contemporary titles on Southwestern tribes:
Navajo, Hopi and Zuni.

**ERIC CLEARINGHOUSE ON RURAL
EDUCATION AND SMALL SCHOOLS**
P.O. Box 3AP, New Mexico State University
LAS CRUCES 88003

**BANDELIER NATIONAL
MONUMENT LIBRARY**
LOS ALAMOS 87544
  (505) 672-3861

Contains a collection of 2,000 volumes on the
archaeology of the area, and Pueblo Indians.

**SALINAS NATIONAL
MONUMENT LIBRARY**
Route 1, Box 496
MOUNTAINAIRE 87036
  (505) 847-2585

PALEO-INDIAN INSTITUTE LIBRARY
Eastern New Mexico University
Campus Box 2154
PORTALES 88130

**EL MORRO NATIONAL
MONUMENT LIBRARY**
RAMAH 87321
  (505) 783-5132

A collection of 400 volumes on the archaeology of
the prehistoric site and historic Pueblos.

**ANTHROPOLOGY FILM CENTER
FOUNDATION LIBRARY**
P.O. Box 493
SANTA FE 87594-0493
  (505) 983-4127

A study collection of films, especially those
produced by graduates of the Film Center training
program.

**INSTITUTE OF AMERICAN INDIAN
ARTS LIBRARY—NATIVE AMERICAN
VIDEOTAPES ARCHIVES**
Learning Resource Center, College of Santa Fe
Alexis Hall - St. Michael's Dr.
SANTA FE 87501
  (505) 988-6670
  Karen Highfill, Librarian

Collection consists of more than 12,000 volumes
on North American Indian art, history and
culture; 800 videotapes, recording tribal and
reservation history, tribal projects and activities,
such as the reservation medical center or tribal
government—catalogue available for $3.00;
30,000 Smithsonian photographs of Native-
American culture; 911 recordings of Native-
American music; 9,000 slides of art of all types and
Native-American art objects; 15 linear feet of
school archives.

MUSEUM OF NEW MEXICO LIBRARY
Museum of Indian Arts and Laboratory of
Anthropology
P.O. Box 2087, 708 Camino Lejo
SANTA FE 87504
  (505) 827-8941

Maintains a collection of 16,000 volumes
including journal holdings, concentrating on
Southwestern anthropology, as well as the
personal library of Sylvanus G. Morley with many
rare Mesoamerican titles.

NEW MEXICO STATE LIBRARY
123 North Federal Place
SANTA FE 87501

Holdings include a special collection on
Southwestern U.S. history.

**WHEELWRIGHT MUSEUM OF THE
AMERICAN INDIAN — MARY CABOT
WHEELWRIGHT RESEARCH LIBRARY**
P.O. Box 5153, 704 Camino Lejo
SANTA FE 87501

Maintains over 10,000 volumes on the art, history,
and religions of the Navajo and other tribes;
archives contain 1,000 examples of Navajo
ceremonial art, 3,000 Navajo ceremonial music
recordings, 100 Navajo myth texts, 1,000 Navajo
sandpaintings on slides, and 100 music and prayer
tapes.

**GILA CLIFF DWELLINGS NATIONAL
MONUMENT — VISITOR
CENTER LIBRARY**
Route 11, Box 100
SILVER CITY 88061

A collection of books on prehistoric Mogollon
Indians, archaeology and natural history.

**KIT CARSON MEMORIAL
FOUNDATION LIBRARY**
P.O. Drawer B, Old Kit Carson Rd.
TAOS 87571
(505) 758-4741

Contains a collection of 5,500 volumes on the
prehistoric Indian culture of Taos and the
Southwest.

NEW YORK

**TONAWANDA INDIAN
COMMUNITY LIBRARY**
P.O. Box 326, 372 Bloomingdale Rd.
AKRON 14001-0326
(716) 542-5618
Ramona Charles, Director

**CAYUGA MUSEUM OF HISTORY
AND ART—LIBRARY AND ARCHIVES**
203 Genessee St.
AUBURN 13021

NATIONAL KATERI CENTER LIBRARY
The National Shrine of N.A. Martyrs
AURIESVILLE 12016
(518) 853-3033
Rec. Robert J. Boyle, S.J., Director

**MUSEUM OF THE AMERICAN INDIAN
HUNTINGTON FREE LIBRARY**
9 Westchester Square
BRONX 10461
(212) 829-7770
Mary B. Davis, Librarian

One of the leading research sources on Indians of
the Western Hemisphere, this non-circulating
collection contains more than 40,000 volumes on
the archaeology, ethnology, and history of the
native peoples of the Americas, as well as
exceptional selections in Indian languages,
codices, current Native American affairs, and
Indian biography and related ephemera;
maintains a large collection of Indian newspapers,
manuscripts and field notes, and microform and
audio-visual material.

**BUFFALO AND ERIE COUNTY
HISTORICAL SOCIETY LIBRARY**
5 Nottingham Court
BUFFALO 14216

Holdings include books and manuscripts related
to the Seneca Indians and other Indians of the
Niagara frontier.

**THE MOHAWK-CAUGHNAWAGA
MUSEUM LIBRARY**
Route 5, Box 554
FONDA 12068
(518) 853-3678

A collection of 4,500 volumes on American
Indians and American history.

AKWESASNE LIBRARY
Akwesasne Mohawk Nation, Route 37
HOGANSBURG 13655
(518) 358-2240

General public library with a large selection of
publications on the North American Indian.

SENECA NATION LIBRARY
1490 Route 438
IRVING 14081

**AMERICAN MUSEUM
OF NATURAL HISTORY
DEPARTMENT OF LIBRARY SERVICES**
Central Park West at 79th St.
NEW YORK 10024
(212) 873-1300
Nina J. Root, Librarian

Contains approximately 50,000 volumes,
primarily on the anthropology of North American
Indian tribes (ethnology and archaeology), along
with accounts and descriptions of explorers;
125,000 photographs, primarily black-and-white
of the early 20th century and some recent color
photographs of artifacts. Maintains a special film
collection with a limited number of films on
Indians.

**CONFEDERATION OF AMERICAN
INDIANS LIBRARY**
P.O. Box 5474
NEW YORK 10163
(212) 972-1020

Maintains a collection of over 500 volumes on
American Indian history, culture and affairs.

THE NEW YORK PUBLIC LIBRARY
42nd St. and Fifth Ave.
NEW YORK 10018
(212) 930-0826
Timothy Troy, Bibliographer of
American Indian Material

Maintains one of the largest collections of Indian bibliographical material in the world. Includes material from all cultural areas and time periods, from pre-Columbian eras to the present. The collections range through the disciplines of anthropology, archaeology, history, linguistics, and literature. Contains writings by Indians, runs of related periodicals and serials, pictures (photographs and engravings), works on Indian place names, and a collection of Indian captivity journals. Collects contemporary Native-American literature (in English or Indian languages.) The Library has materials in all written Indian languages from throughout the Western Hemisphere. Many items concerning the Indians of the Americas, particularly 16th and 17th century material in Spanish and English, are located in various special collections.

WENNER-GREN FOUNDATION FOR ANTHROPOLOGICAL RESEARCH LIBRARY
1865 Broadway
NEW YORK 10023
(212) 957-8750

NATIVE AMERICAN CENTRE FOR THE LIVING ARTS LIBRARY
25 Rainbow Mall
NIAGARA FALLS 14303
(716) 284-2427

A collection of 3,000 volumes on Native-American history, art, culture and crafts. Interlibrary loan.

SIX NATIONS INDIAN MUSEUM
ONCHIOTA 12968
(518) 891-0769

Collection includes charts, posters, and other written material concerning many aspects of Iroquois history and culture.

THE MUSEUM AT HARTWICK LIBRARY
Hartwick College
ONEONTA 13820
(607) 432-4200

A collection of over 800 volumes on American Indian history.

NEW YORK STATE ARCHAEOLOGICAL ASSOCIATION LIBRARY
Rochester Museum and Science Center
P.O. Box 1480, 657 East Ave.
ROCHESTER 14603
(716) 271-4320

Contains more than 8,500 volumes: books, manuscripts and emphemera on the history and technology of the Genesee Valley region.

SENECA-IROQUOIS NATIONAL MUSEUM LIBRARY
Allegany Indian Reservation
P.O. Box 442, Broad St. Ext.
SLAMANCA 14779
(716) 945-1738

A collection of books and periodicals on the Seneca and Iroquois Indians; museum administration, conservation and law.

SCHOHARIE MUSEUM OF THE IROQUOIS INDIAN LIBRARY
P.O. Box 158
SCHOHARIE 12157
(518) 295-8553/234-2276

Contains 400 volumes on Iroquois and other Native-American groups. Available for research upon request.

NORTH CAROLINA

MUSEUM OF THE CHEROKEE INDIAN LIBRARY
P.O. Box 770-A, U.S. Highway 441 North
CHEROKEE 28719
(704) 497-3481

Collection contains more than 3,000 volumes on Cherokee Indian history and culture. Reference use only.

SCHIELE MUSEUM REFERENCE LIBRARY
Center for Southeastern Native American Studies
P.O. Box 953, 1500 East Garrison Blvd.
GASTONIA 28053-0953
(704) 865-6131
Ms. M. Turner, Registrar/Librarian

Contains a collection of more than 6,000 volumes, serving the Reference Centers for the Library of Congress. 20% of holdings, including subject index files, graduate papers, monographs, as well as bound volumes, are on broad areas of Native-American topics representing all major Indian groups in U.S. and Canada with special emphasis on Indians of the Southeast. *Special collections:* Lilly Hobbs Schiele Collection; W.M. Modisette Collection; The Red Dawn Collection; and, The McCuen Collection. Open to the public by appointment only.

INDIAN MUSEUM OF THE CAROLINAS LIBRARY
607 Turnpike Rd.
LAURINBURG 28352
(919) 276-5880

Maintains a collection of 500 volumes on Indian literature, archaeology, and history. Reference.

ROANOKE ISLAND
HISTORICAL PARK LIBRARY
P.O. Box 906
MANTEO 27954

A special collection of approximately 500 volumes on American Indians of Virginia and North Carolina.

NATIVE AMERICAN LIBRARY
Lumbee Indian Education
Lumbee Regional Development Association
P.O. Box 637, East Main St.
PEMBROKE 28372

NATIVE AMERICAN
RESOURCE CENTER LIBRARY
Pembroke State University
College Rd.
PEMBROKE 28372
(919) 521-4214
Dr. Robert C. Heisoh, Librarian

A collection of 500 volumes with emphasis on Lumbee Indians of North Carolina; audio-visual material; archival documents.

NORTH DAKOTA

STATE HISTORICAL SOCIETY
OF NORTH DAKOTA LIBRARY
North Dakota Heritage Center
Capitol Grounds
BISMARCK 58505
(701) 224-2666

Holdings include 20,000 volumes on North Dakota history and the history of the American Indian; extensive photographs archive; government documents; genealogical collections; sound and visual recordings, including Native-American music.

CHESTER FRITZ LIBRARY
University of North Dakota
GRAND FORKS 58202

MINOT STATE COLLEGE
MEMORIAL LIBRARY
MINOT 58701

Maintains a special collection on Indians of the North Central States.

OHIO

AKRON ART INSTITUTE LIBRARY
69 East Market St.
AKRON 44308

MOUND CITY GROUP
NATIONAL MONUMENT LIBRARY
16062 State Route 104
CHILLICOTHE 45601
(614) 774-1125

A collection of 1,500 volumes on Hopewell and Adena Indian culture, and other Indian culture of Ohio; archaeological research on Hopewell and Adena cultures is conducted at Monument.

CINCINNATI ART MUSEUM LIBRARY
Eden Park
CINCINNATI 45202

RUTHERFORD B. HAYES
LIBRARY AND MUSEUM
1337 Hayes Ave.
FREMONT 43420

Contains a collection of 2,000 books and pamphlets on Plains Indians, the Sioux, and some Pueblo prehistoric Indians of Ohio.

OKLAHOMA

WOOLAROC MUSEUM LIBRARY
State Highway 123, Route 3
BARTLESVILLE 74003
(918) 336-0307

A collection of 1,000 volumes on American Indians and Oklahoma history.

MEMORIAL INDIAN MUSEUM LIBRARY
P.O. Box 483, Second and Allen Sts.
BROKEN BOW 74728
(405) 584-6531

Maintains a collection of 3,000 volumes on American Indian history and culture.

WILL ROGERS MEMORIAL LIBRARY
P.O. Box 157
CLAREMORE 74018
(918) 341-0719
Patricia Lowe, Librarian

Contains the original papers of Will Rogers; also, 2,500 volumes concerning Will Rogers and his times; 6,000 photos of Roger's family and others; and Will Rogers memoirs.

MUSEUM OF THE RED RIVER LIBRARY
812 S.E. Lincoln
IDABEL 74745
(405) 286-3616

Maintains more than 1,000 volumes, with emphasis on Choctaw Indians.

**INSTITUTE OF THE GREAT PLAINS
LIBRARY AND ARCHIVES**
P.O. Box 68, 601 Ferris, Elmer Thomas Park
LAWTON 73502
(405) 353-5675

Collection consists of a special collection of
approximately 10,000 volumes on Plains Indian
history and prehistory; documents and photos.

**BACONE COLLEGE
RESEARCH LIBRARY**
East Shawnee
MUSKOGEE 74402
(918) 683-4581

Maintains a special collection of 3,500 books on
the North American Indian.

**OKLAHOMA ANTHROPOLOGICAL
SOCIETY LIBRARY**
1000 Horn St.
MUSKOGEE 74403
(405) 364-2279

Holdings of more than 35,000 volumes; archives
contain over three million documents of the Five
Civilized Tribes; newspaper library of thirty
million pages.

**UNIVERSITY OF OKLAHOMA
LAW LIBRARY**
NORMAN 73069

Maintains a collection on Indian law and Indian
land titles.

**UNIVERSITY OF OKLAHOMA
WESTERN HISTORY COLLECTION
DIVISION OF MANUSCRIPTS AND
LIBRARY**
401 West Brooks St.
NORMAN 73069

Contains a collection of 40,000 books and
pamphlets; 200,000 historic photos; four million
manuscripts; principally regional; Indian,
Oklahoma, and Southwest history.

COOKSON INSTITUTE LIBRARY
623 Culbertson Dr.
OKLAHOMA CITY 73105

A collection of 1,000 volumes on American Indian
thought with emphasis on Cherokee, Arawak,
Maya, and Caddo Indians Available to research
scholars associated with the Institute.

**OKLAHOMA HISTORICAL SOCIETY
INDIAN ARCHIVES DIVISION**
2100 North Lincoln Blvd.
OKLAHOMA CITY 73105
(405) 521-2481
Jack Wettengel, Public Information Director

Collection of 40,000 volumes; holdings include
approximately 6,000 books covering the subject
areas of the Creek Nation, and Indian and pioneer
history; three million documents on American
Indian history; and newspapers of Indian
territories.

**CREEK INDIAN
MEMORIAL ASSOCIATION LIBRARY**
Creek Council House
OKMULGEE 74447
(918) 756-2324

Contains a collection of 250 volumes on Creek
Indian readers, dictionaries; documents and
newspapers; Oklahoma and Indian history.

**OKLAHOMA STATE
UNIVERSITY LIBRARY**
Curriculum Materials Laboratory
STILLWATER 74074

Maintains a children's collection of books on the
Indians of North America.

CHEROKEE HERITAGE CENTER LIBRARY
P.O. Box 515, TSA-LA-GI
TAHLEQUAH 74464

A collection of 2,500 volumes on Cherokee
heritage, including manuscripts and photographs.

JOHN VAUGHN LIBRARY
Northeastern State University
TAHLEQUAH 74464
(918) 456-5511 ext. 3252
Delores T. Sumner, Special Collections
Librarian

Consists of a collection of approximately 8,000
books on Cherokee history; tribes of Oklahoma;
Native-American mythology and religion;
Oklahoma history; Indian Territory history;
Native-American history, culture, social
structures, and conditions; local towns, counties,
city histories; Oklahoma tribal rolls. *Special
collections:* John Ross Letters; Indian Affairs
Miscellaneous Letters; Ballenger Miscellaneous
Letters; Ballenger Manuscripts Relating to
Cherokee History; Andrew Nave Collections
(Business Accounts and Letters); Letters To and
From Stand Watie. All bound volumes typed
from the originals. Originals are housed in
Archives.

CHICKASAW COUNCIL HOUSE LIBRARY
P.O. Box 717
TISHOMINGO 73460
(405) 371-3351

Contains about 150 volumes on Chickasaw
Indian history, geography and geneaology.

PHILBROOK ART CENTER LIBRARY
ROBERTA CAMPBELL LAWSON
INDIAN LIBRARY
P.O. Box 52510, 2727 S. Rockford Rd.
TULSA 74152
(918) 749-7941

A collection of approximately 2,000 volumes on
Indian art and history. Reference only.

THOMAS GILCREASE INSTITUTE
OF AMERICAN HISTORY
AND ART LIBRARY
1400 Gilcrease Museum Rd.
TULSA 74127
(918) 582-3122
Sarah Erwin, Librarian

Contains a collection of about 7,500 volumes
relating to most American Indian tribes with
emphasis on the Five Civilized Tribes. *Special
collections:* John Ross Papers (Cherokee); Peter
Pitchlynn Papers (Choctaw); John Drew Papers
(Cherokee); Cherokee Papers; Chickasaw Papers;
Choctaw Papers; Creek Papers; and Seminole
Papers.

UNIVERSITY OF TULSA
THE McFARLAND LIBRARY
TULSA 74104
(918) 592-6000

The repository for many unique primary
documents and published works pertinent to
Native-Americans and governmental relations of
the historic period in eastern Oklahoma and
adjacent areas.

UNIVERSITY OF TULSA
COLLEGE OF LAW LIBRARY
3120 East Fourth Place
TULSA 74104
(918) 592-6000

A collection of 750 volumes on Indian law.

SEMINOLE NATION LIBRARY
P.O. Box 1532, 524 South Wewoka
WEWOKA 74884
(405) 257-5580

Contains books, and documents on the history of
the Seminoles, the history of Wewoka, and the
history of oil in Oklahoma; *Special exhibit:*
Cultural Continuities in Seminole County,
Oklahoma—provides detailed information on the
clans, bands, churches, and homes of the
Seminoles; and the Dawes rolls for reference into
Seminole genealogy

OREGON

ALEUTIAN-BERING SEA
EXPEDITIONS RESEARCH LIBRARY
1821 East 9th St.
THE DALLES 97058
(503) 296-9414
Jay Ellis Ransom, Librarian

Consists primarily of research field notes and
manuscripts currently archived in the Suzzallo
Library, University of Washington, Seattle. Basic
coverage is linguistic (with some ethnology) on the
Fox Island Aleut people of Unalaska and
Nikolski, Alaska; Kalispel (Flathead) Indians of
western Montana; Duwamish of the
Muckleshoots Reservation, Washington; Haida
and Tlingit villagers of southeast Alaska. Also,
basic archaeological researches since 1924 of
ancient rock structures of Western North America
relating to the Bighorn Medicine Wheel
cosmological complex, including a major
published monograph concerning the origins and
interpretations of the Uto-Aztecan thought-world
and complex. *Special collections:* Photographic
negatives of Aleutian Islands and native Indian
villages of central Alaska, 1936-1940; linguistic
material of numerous Native-American and
Siberian languages.

PENNSYLVANIA

CUMBERLAND COUNTY HISTORICAL
SOCIETY — HAMILTON LIBRARY
21 North Pitt St.
CARLISLE 17013

Maintains a special collection of magazines and
journals published by the Carlisle Indian School.

LIBRARY OF AMERICAN
INDIAN LANGUAGES
American Philosophical Society
104 South 5th St.
PHILADELPHIA 19106
(215) 627-0706

Collection of books on American Indian
linguistics; Franz Boas collection of 18th and 19th
century Indian vocabularies.

FREE LIBRARY OF PHILADELPHIA
Social Science and History Department
Logan Square
PHILADELPHIA 19103

Special collection: The Wilberforce Eames
Collection on American Indians.

**INDIAN RIGHTS
ASSOCIATION LIBRARY**
1505 Race St.
PHILADELPHIA 19102
  (215) 563-8349

Contains a collection of 500 texts on assorted subjects ranging from Indian history and political analysis to tribally specific accounts; extensive periodical and federal Indian law files.

**UNIVERSITY OF PENNSYLVANIA
MUSEUM LIBRARY**
33rd & Spruce Sts.
PHILADELPHIA 19104

A collection of 50,000 volumes on world archaeology, anthropology and ethnology. *Special collection:* Brinton Collection— Aboriginal American linguistics and ethnology.

**COUNCIL OF THREE RIVERS
AMERICAN INDIAN CENTER LIBRARY**
200 Charles St.
PITTSBURGH 15238
  (412) 782-4457

Cultural library on Indian tribes, cultures, customs and traditions. Maintains the Indian Child Welfare Resource Library.

**AMERICAN INDIAN EDUCATION
POLICY CENTER LIBRARY**
Pennsylvania State University
320 Rackley Bldg.
UNIVERSITY PARK 16803
  (814) 865-1489

Maintains a collection of 1,000 volumes on American Indian education.

RHODE ISLAND

**HAFFENREFFER MUSEUM
OF ANTHROPOLOGY LIBRARY**
Brown University, Mt. Hope Grant
BRISTOL 02809
  (401) 253-8388
  Barbara A. Hail, Associate Director

Contains a collection of 2,500 volumes in the field of anthropology, with material on American Indian culture and history.

**TOMAQUAG INDIAN MEMORIAL
MUSEUM LIBRARY**
Summit Rd.
EXETER 02822
  (401) 539-7795

**RHODE ISLAND
HISTORICAL SOCIETY LIBRARY**
52 Power St.
PROVIDENCE 02906

SOUTH CAROLINA

THE CHARLESTON MUSEUM LIBRARY
121 Rutledge Ave.
CHARLESTON 29401

**SOUTH CAROLINA DEPARTMENT
OF ARCHIVES AND HISTORY**
P.O. Box 11669, 1430 Senate St.
COLUMBIA 29211

FLORENCE MUSEUM LIBRARY
558 Spruce St.
FLORENCE 29501

SOUTH DAKOTA

**CRAZY HORSE MEMORIAL
FOUNDATION LIBRARY**
Ave. of the Chiefs, The Black Hills
CRAZY HORSE 57730-9998
  (605) 673-4681

A collection of 15,000 volumes on art, Indian culture and history.

**BADLANDS NATIONAL
MONUMENT LIBRARY**
P.O. Box 72
INTERIOR 57750

Maintains a collection of 1,000 books and 500 bound periodicals on the Badlands and Indians of South Dakota.

**THE OGLALA LAKOTA
HISTORICAL CENTER LIBRARY**
P.O. Box 490, Oglala Lakota College
KYLE 57752
  (605) 455-2321

Holdings include tribal college and government records; personal papers of Dr. Valentine T. McGillycuddy; photographs and oral histories, and other historical material.

**AMERICAN INDIAN CULTURE
RESEARCH CENTER LIBRARY**
P.O. Box 98, Blue Cloud Abbey
MARVIN 57251
  (605) 432-5528

Collection of more than 8,000 books on American Indian culture.

**SOUTH DAKOTA
HISTORICAL RESOURCE CENTER**
Memorial Bldg.
PIERRE 57501

Contains 1,000 books concerning Indian history and culture, with emphasis on the Sioux Indians.

THE HERITAGE CENTER LIBRARY
Red Cloud Indian School
PINE RIDGE 57770
(605) 867-5491

Collection of 1,000 volumes on Indian history and culture.

LAKOTA ARCHIVES AND
HISTORICAL RESEARCH CENTER
P.O. Box 490, Sinte Gleska College
ROSEBUD 57570
(605) 747-2263/2264

Maintains a collection of books and periodicals on the Lakota language and Sioux Indians, as well as material on other Indian tribes of North America.

THE CENTER FOR
WESTERN STUDIES LIBRARY
Augustana College, 29th & S. Summit
SIOUX FALLS 57197
(605) 336-4007

A collection of 30,000 volumes of Trans-Mississippi West and Upper Great Lakes archaeology, anthropology and ethnology.

INSTITUTE OF INDIAN
STUDIES LIBRARY
University of South Dakota
VERMILLION 57069

Contains a collection of about 1,000 books on ethnology and contemporary affairs of the northwest Plains Indians.

W.H. OVER STATE MUSEUM LIBRARY
414 East Clark
VERMILLION 57069
(605) 677-5228

Collection on northern Plains ethnography and history.

TENNESSEE

RED CLAY STATE
HISTORICAL PARK LIBRARY
Route 6, Box 733
CLEVELAND 37311
(615) 472-2626

A collection on Cherokee history and Removal.

C.H. NASH MUSEUM
CHUCALISSA—LIBRARY
1987 Indian Village Dr.
MEMPHIS 38109
(901) 785-3160

Contains a collection of 2,000 volumes on Indian history and culture.

TENNESSEE STATE
LIBRARY AND ARCHIVES
State Library Division, Seventh Ave. North
NASHVILLE 37203

A collection of books on the American Indian with emphasis on Indian wars.

PINSON MOUNDS STATE
ARCHAEOLOGICAL AREA LIBRARY
Route 1, Box 316, Ozier Rd.
PINSON 38366
(901) 988-5614

Consists of 400 volumes on the archaeology of Pinson Mounds area.

TEXAS

PANHANDLE-PLAINS HISTORICAL
MUSEUM—LIBRARY AND ARCHIVES
P.O. Box 967, W.T. Station
2401 Fourth Ave.
CANYON 79016
(806) 655-7194

Contains a collection of books on the Indians of the Great Plains; and archaeology of the Texas Panhandle.

AMON CARTER MUSEUM
OF WESTERN ART LIBRARY
3501 Camp Bowie Blvd.
FORT WORTH 76101

SUNSET TRADING POST
OLD WEST MUSEUM—LIBRARY
Route 1
SUNSET 76270
(817) 872-2027

A collection of 500 volumes on American Indians, and the frontier.

UTAH

UTE TRIBAL MUSEUM LIBRARY
Ute Tribe, P.O. Box 190, Highway 40
FORT DUCHESNE 84026
(801) 722-4992

Maintains a collection of books on the Ute Indians; American Indian history and culture; and early Western American history.

MUSEUM OF PEOPLES
AND CULTURE LIBRARY
Brigham Young University
710 North 100 East, Allen Bldg.
PROVO 84601
(801) 378-6112

A collection of 2,500 volumes including many on Native-American history and culture.

**UNIVERSITY OF UTAH
MARRIOTT LIBRARY**
Ethnic Reading Room
SALT LAKE CITY 84112

**UTAH STATE
HISTORICAL SOCIETY LIBRARY**
300 Rio Grande
SALT LAKE CITY 84101
(801) 533-5755
Melvin T. Smith, Director

A collection of books and periodicals on the history of Utah, Mormons, Indians, and the West.

VIRGINIA

**ARCHAEOLOGICAL SOCIETY
OF VIRGINIA LIBRARY**
4414 Park Ave.
RICHMOND 23221
(804) 359-0442

Contains 1,200 volumes on archaeology and American Indians.

WASHINGTON

**LEWIS COUNTY
HISTORICAL LIBRARY**
599 N.W. Front St.
CHEHALIS 98532
(206) 748-0831

Holdings of about 1,600 volumes in the Indian archive collection.

**WASHINGTON ARCHAEOLOGICAL
RESEARCH CENTER LIBRARY**
Washington State University, Commons Hall 326
PULLMAN 99161

**UNIVERITY OF WASHINGTON
PACIFIC NORTHWEST COLLECTION**
Special Collections Division
SEATTLE 98195

Holdings include extensive collections of materials on Indians of the Pacific Northwest.

**OREGON PROVINCE ARCHIVES
CROSBY LIBRARY**
Gonzaga University
SPOKANE 99258
(509) 328-4220
Fr. Neill R. Meany, S.J., Archivist

Special collections: Jesuit Missions Collection—150 volumes of Jesuit missionaries among Indians

of Northwest—Blackfeet, Coeur d' Alenes, Yakimas, Cheyennes. Northwest Mission Papers—500 boxes, 45,000 items—correspondence, diaries, photos, microfilm, relating to Jesuit Missionary activity in Alaska, and the Northwest States, including the Athapaskans and Eskimos to the previous tribes mentioned. The Indian Language Collection—50,600 pages—manuscript dictionaries, grammars, catechisms, gospels, prayer books, sermons in the Indian languages of the Rocky Mountains, and the Eskimo languages of Alaska. Among the languages are: Assiniboine, Blackfoot, Crow, Chinook, Columbia, Colville, Gros Ventre, Inuit, Kalispel, Nez Perce, Okanagan, Sioux, Tlingit, and Yakima. Most are contained on microfilm.

**WASHINGTON STATE
HISTORICAL SOCIETY LIBRARY**
315 North Stadium Way
TACOMA 98403
(206) 593-2830
Anthony G. King, Director
Frank L. Green, Librarian

A collection of books, pamphlets, manuscripts and photographs dealing with the Pacific Northwest Indians in general and Washington tribes in particular. Complete set of Edward Curtis with folios; and a file of newspaper clippings.

TOPPENISH MUSEUM LIBRARY
1 South Elm
TOPPENISH 98945
(509) 865-4510

Maintains a collection of 18,500 volumes including many on the Indians of the Northwest, and Native-American history and culture.

YAKIMA NATION LIBRARY
P.O. Box 151, Yakima Nation Cultural Center
TOPPENISH 98948
(509) 865-2800
Sherry Hokansen, Librarian

Colection contains 500 volumes on Native-Americans and Yakima history; also, older books from Yakima Agency—reports, periodicals, magazines and photo collection.

WISCONSIN

**STOCKBRIDGE MUNSEE
HISTORICAL LIBRARY**
Route 1, Box 300
BOWLER 54416
(715) 793-4270
Bernice Miller Pigeon, Director

HOARD HISTORICAL MUSEUM LIBRARY
407 Merchant Ave.
FORT ATKINSON 53538

Maintains a special collection of rare books on the Black Hawk War, 1800-1840.

**STATE HISTORICAL SOCIETY
OF WISCONSIN LIBRARY**
816 State St.
MADISON 53706

MILWAUKEE PUBLIC MUSEUM LIBRARY
800 West Wells St.
MILWAUKEE 53233
  (414) 278-2752

Reference library maintaining classic studies and contemporary journals and other publications relating to American Indians.

OSHKOSH PUBLIC MUSEUM LIBRARY
1331 Algoma Blvd.
OSHKOSH 54901
  (414) 424-0452

WYOMING

**BRADFORD BRINTON
MEMORIAL MUSEUM LIBRARY**
P.O. Box 23
BIG HORN 82833
  (307) 672-3173

**WYOMING STATE ARCHIVES
AND HISTORICAL DEPARTMENT**
State Office Bldg. E
CHEYENNE 82002

WYOMING STATE LIBRARY
Supreme Court & State Library Bldg.
CHEYENNE 82002

**HAROLD McCRACKEN
RESEARCH LIBRARY**
Buffalo Bill Historical Center
P.O. Box 1000, 720 Sheridan Ave.
CODY 82414
  (307) 587-4771
  Albert C. Minnick, Librarian

A collection of 1,500 volumes on the Plains Indians; some material on the Sheepeaters; vertical files on specific tribes, e.g. Blackfeet; photographs—The Cheyenne Sun Dance, Crow Indians, 19th to 20th century. *Special collections:* Yellowstone National Park-Indians; Photographs by Anne Black, D.H. Barry, J.H. Sharp, L.A. Huffman; Bureau of American Ethnology Annual Reports, 1880's to 1940's.

CANADA

ALBERTA

**GLENBOW-ALBERTA
INSTITUTE LIBRARY**
902 - 11th Ave., S.W.
CALGARY T2R 0E7

Holdings include more than 25,000 books pertaining to Western Canadiana, Indian and Eskimo peoples of the Arctic and the Northwest U.S.

**ALBERTA NATIVE COMMUNICATIONS
SOCIETY LIBRARY**
9311 60th Ave.
EDMONTON T6E 0C2
  (403) 437-0580

A collection of approximately 160 films and videotapes covering a wide range of topics—health, life of the Inuit, economic development, Indian education, dance and song performances, elders talking on Canadian tribal culture. Available for rental and duplicates for purchase.

PROVINCIAL ARCHIVES OF ALBERTA
12845 102 Ave.
EDMONTON T5N 0M6

A collection of 20,000 volumes on local history (Alberta), western Canadian history, archaeology and ethnology.

**UNIVERSITY OF ALBERTA
BOREAL INSTITUTE FOR
NORTHERN STUDIES LIBRARY**
EDMONTON T6G 2E9

**UNIVERSITY OF ALBERTA
COLLEGE OF ST. JEAN LIBRARY**
8406 91st St.
EDMONTON T6C 4G9

Maintains a collection of 50,000 volumes, many of which are on the anthropology and ethnology of North American Indians.

BRITISH COLUMBIA

**UNIVERSITY OF BRITISH
COLUMBIA LIBRARY**
Social Science Division
VANCOUVER V6T 1W5

Contains a special collection on Canadian Indians and Eskimos.

**UNIVERSITY OF BRITISH COLUMBIA
MUSEUM OF ANTHROPOLOGY LIBRARY**
6393 N.W. Marine Dr.
VANCOUVER V6T 1W5
  (604) 228-5087

MANITOBA

ESKIMO MUSEUM LIBRARY
242 La Verendrye St.
CHURCHILL R0B 0E0
  (204) 675-2541

A collection of ethnographic material on the Eskimos.

**DEPARTMENT OF CULTURAL AFFAIRS
AND HISTORICAL RESOURCES
PROVINCIAL ARCHIVES**
200 Vaughan St.
WINNIPEG R3C 0V8

Focus Program: A collection of master tapes and duplicates made with Indian people in Manitoba.

HUDSON'S BAY COMPANY LIBRARY
77 Main St.
WINNIPEG R3C 2R1

NOVA SCOTIA

**DALHOUSIE UNIVERSITY MARITIME
SCHOOL OF SOCIAL WORK LIBRARY**
6420 Coburg Rd.
HALIFAX B3H 3J5

Special collection: Native Peoples Collection—books and journals on Indians, Eskimos and Metis.

NOVA SCOTIA MUSEUM LIBRARY
1747 Summer St.
HALIFAX B3H 3A6

Contains a collection of books on Micmac material culture and ethnography.

ONTARIO

**ASSEMBLY OF FIRST NATIONS
NATIONAL INDIAN
BROTHERHOOD LIBRARY**
47 Clarence St., Atrium Bldg., 3rd Floor
OTTAWA K1N 9K1
  (613) 236-0673

Maintains a collection of 10,000 volumes; books and monographs (unpublished reports); 100 Native-American periodicals; and law cases.

**CANADA—DEPT. OF INDIAN AFFAIRS
NORTHERN DEVELOPMENTAL LIBRARY**
400 Laurier Ave. West, Room 823
OTTAWA K1A 0H4

Holdings include over 50,000 books on North American Indians and Eskimos.

**NATIONAL ASSOCIATION OF
FRIENDSHIP CENTRES LIBRARY**
200 Cooper St., Suite 3
OTTAWA K2P 0G1
  (613) 563-4844

Contents include documents recording the history of the Native Friendship Centre Movement in Canada, as well as pamphlets, books and magazines about Native or supportive organizations.

**THE NATIONAL MUSEUMS
OF CANADA LIBRARY**
360 Lisgar St.
OTTAWA K1A 0M8

Maintains a collection of 35,000 volumes on anthropology, including many on the Indians and native peoples of Canada. *Museocinematography: Ethnographic Film Programs.*

**LAURENTIAN UNIVERSITY MUSEUM
AND ARTS CENTRE LIBRARY**
John St.
SUDBURY P3E 2C6

A collection of books covering all areas of art with special sections on native and Inuit peoples.

ROYAL ONTARIO MUSEUM LIBRARY
100 Queen's Park
TORONTO M5S 2C6

A collection of 50,000 volumes, and 20 journals of anthropological interest; many books on the Indians and native peoples of Canada.

SASKATCHEWAN

NATIVE LAW LIBRARY
Native Law Centre
University of Saskatchewan
150 Diefenbaker Centre
SASKATOON S7N 0W0
  (306) 966-6189
  Linda Fritz, Native Law Librarian

A collection of 6,000 volumes referring to law as it applies to Canadian Indians; archival collection of materials from the Mackenzie Valley Pipeline Inquiry; and a complete collection of native law cases.

NATIVE AMERICAN CENTERS

This section lists Indian centers initiated and developed by Native Americans to provide services for Indian communities in cities where there are substantial Indian populations. Entries are arranged alpha-geographically.

ALASKA

**ALEUTIAN PRIBILOFF
ISLAND ASSOCIATION**
1689 C St.
ANCHORAGE 99501
(907) 276-2700

Health Clinic.

ALASKA NATIVE COMMUNITY CENTER
670 West Fireweed Lane
ANCHORAGE 99503
(907) 278-4641

Health Center of the Cook Inlet Native Association.

**NORTH PACIFIC RIM
NATIVE ASSOCIATION**
903 West Northern Lights No. 203
ANCHORAGE 99503
(907) 276-2121

Health Clinic.

**NORTH SLOPE BOROUGH
HEALTH CORPORATION**
P.O. Box 69
BARROW 99723
(907) 852-3999

Health Clinic.

**YUKON-KUSKOKWIM
HEALTH CORPORATION**
P.O. Box 528
BETHEL 99559
(907) 543-3321

Health Clinic.

COPPER RIVER HEALTH AUTHORITY
P.O. Drawer H
COPPER CENTER 99573
(907) 822-3521

Health Clinic.

**BRISTOL BAY AREA
HEALTH CORPORATION**
P.O. Box 10235
DILLINGHAM 99576
(907) 842-5266/7
(907) 842-5201 (Hospital)

Health Clinic.

TANANA CHIEFS HEALTH AUTHORITY
First and Hall Sts., Doyon Bldg.
FAIRBANKS 99701
(907) 452-8251

Health Clinic.

**SOUTHEAST ALASKA
REGIONAL HEALTH CORPORATION**
P.O. Box 2800
JUNEAU 99801
(907) 789-2131

Health Clinic.

KODIAK AREA NATIVE ASSOCIATION
P.O. Box 172, 402 Center Ave.
KODIAK 99615
(907) 486-5725/6
Gordon L. Pullar, President

Health Clinic.

MAUNELUK ASSOCIATION
P.O. Box 256
KOTZEBUE 99752
(907) 442-3311
Marie N. Schwind, President

Health corporation comprising 11 Alaskan Eskimo villages. Promotes public health and social welfare in northwest Alaska.

**NORTON SOUND
HEALTH CORPORATION**
P.O. Box 966
NOME 99762
(907) 443-5411

Health Clinic.

ARIZONA

**NATIVE AMERICANS FOR
COMMUNITY ACTION, INC.**
Flagstaff Indian Center
P.O. Box 572, 15 North San Francisco
FLAGSTAFF 86001
(602) 774-6613
Steve Darden, Executive Director
Joe Washington, Planner

PHOENIX INDIAN CENTER
1337 North First St.
PHOENIX 85004
  (602) 256-2000
  Phyllis J. Bigpond, Executive Director

Develops and maintains a wide range of service program opportunitie. *Programs:* Economic Development; Social Services; Aging and Behavioral Services; Child Welfare; Individual and Family Services; Urban Indian Law Project. *Publication: Eagle Free Press,* newspaper. Library.

URBAN INDIAN HEALTH PROJECT
4143 North 16th St.
PHOENIX 85016
  (602) 263-8094

TRADITIONAL INDIAN ALLIANCE
2925 South 12th Ave.
TUCSON 85713
  (602) 882-0555

TUCSON AMERICAN INDIAN ASSOCIATION
P.O. Box 7246
TUCSON 85725

TUCSON INDIAN CENTER
92 West Simpson St.
TUCSON 85701
  (602) 884-7131
  Floyd Brown, Executive Director

WINSLOW INDIAN CENTER
110 East Second St.
WINSLOW 86047
  (602) 289-4525
  Cheryl Sorrell, Executive Director

Alcoholism Project.

ARKANSAS

THE AMERICAN INDIAN CENTER OF ARKANSAS
2 Van Circle, Suite 7
LITTLE ROCK 72207
  (501) 666-9032
  Paul S. Austin, Director

Serves Native-Americans living in Arkansas through job training, and promotes Indian culture to both Indians and non-Indians. *Program:* Job training and partnership grant.

CALIFORNIA

AMERICAN INDIAN COUNCIL OF CENTRAL CALIFORNIA
201 California Ave.
BAKERSFIELD 93304
  (805) 327-7429

FEDERATED INDIAN TRIBES
9831 East Arkansas
BELLFLOWER 90706

MANY TRAIL INDIAN CLUB
367 West Spazier Ave.
BURBANK 91501

INDIAN CENTER
6279 East Clauson
COMMERCE 90040

Satellite of Los Angeles Indian Center.

AMERICAN INDIAN FREE CLINIC
1330 South Long Beach Blvd.
COMPTON 90221
  (213) 537-0103

INDIAN CENTER WEST
4840 Sepulveda Blvd.
CULVER CITY 90230

Satellite of Los Angeles Indian Center.

TECUMSEH CENTER
University of California
DAVIS 95616
  (916) 752-3237
  Dave Risling, Coordinator

UNITED NATIVE AMERICANS
7787 Earl St.
EL CERRITO 94530

INDIAN ACTION COUNCIL OF NORTHWESTERN CALIFORNIA
P.O. Box 1287, 2725 Myrtle Ave.
EUREKA 95502-1287
  (707) 443-8401
  June Chilton, Director

UNITED INDIAN LODGE
1116 9th St.
EUREKA 95501

ASSOCIATED INDIAN SERVICES
1279 North Wishon
FRESNO 93728
  (209) 268-7037

COMPREHENSIVE INDIAN REHABILITATION PROGRAM
3621 North Parkway Dr.
FRESNO 93711

FRESNO AMERICAN INDIAN COUNCIL
North 5150 6th Ave., No. 169
FRESNO 93721
(209) 222-7741

ORANGE COUNTY INDIAN CENTER
12511 Brookhurts St.
GARDEN GROVE 92643

MENDOCINO COUNTY INDIAN CENTER
Native-American Education Center
P.O. Box 495, Highway 101 South
HOPLAND 95449

INDIAN FREE CLINIC
7300 South Santa Fe Ave.
HUNTINGTON PARK 90225

MI-PI-SHO DEVELOPMENT CENTER
P.O. Box 297, 210 Clay St.
INDEPENDENCE 93526

LOS ANGELLES
AMERICAN INDIAN CENTER
1610 West Seventh St., 3rd Floor
LOS ANGELES 90017
(213) 413-3156
Lymon Pierce, Director

Programs: Health Care (medical and dental); Day Care centers for small children; High School program for Indians; Emergency Housing and Welfare Assistance; Employment Assistance; among others. *Publication: Talking Leaf,* monthly American Indian newspaper with national news.

LOS ANGELES INDIAN
HEALTH CENTER
1525 Pizarro St.
LOS ANGELES 90026

UNITED AMERICAN
INDIAN INVOLVEMENT
118 Winston St.
LOS ANGELES 90013

CALIFORNIA URBAN INDIAN
HEALTH COUNCIL, INC.
1615 Broadway, Suite 210
OAKLAND 94612
(415) 763-3430

INTERTRIBAL FRIENDSHIP HOUSE
523 East 14th St.
OAKLAND 94606
(415) 452-1235
Thomas Brown, Executive Director

NATIVE AMERICAN ALCOHOLISM
AND DRUG ABUSE PROGRAM
1815 39th Ave. No. A
OAKLAND 94601

URBAN INDIAN CHILD
RESOURCE CENTER
390 Euclid Ave.
OAKLAND 94610
(415) 832-2386
Carol Marquez-Baines, M.P.H., Director

Serves the American Indian people residing in the San Francisco Bay area. *Programs:* Indian Child Welfare Act Advocacy; Mental Health Services; Foster Care Recruitment and Certification; Social Services; Cultural Awareness; Treatment Seminars; In-Service Training to public and private agencies; continuing education. Library.

CHRISTIAN HOPE INDIAN-ESKIMO
FELLOWSHIP (CHIEF)
P.O. Box 2600
ORANGE 92669

AMERICAN INDIAN
EDUCATION CENTER
P.O. Box 10
PALA 92059
(619) 742-1121

JURUPA MOUNTAINS
CULTURAL CENTER
7621 Highway 60
RIVERSIDE 92509

SACRAMENTO INDIAN CENTER
Alcoholism Awareness Program
1409 32nd St.
SACRAMENTO 95816

SACRAMENTO URBAN INDIAN
HEALTH PROJECT
801 Broadway, Suite B
SACRAMENTO 95818

UNITED AMERICAN INDIAN
EDUCATION CENTER
2100 28th St.
SACRAMENTO 95818
(916) 731-5300
Deborah Lovely, Executive Director

AMERICAN INDIAN MEDICAL CLINIC
2561 First Ave.
SAN DIEGO 92103
(714) 234-2158

AMERICAN INDIAN
FRIENDSHIP HOUSE
80 Julian Ave.
SAN FRANCISCO 94103

FRIENDSHIP HOUSE
FOR THE AMERICAN INDIAN
1340 Golden Gate Ave.
SAN FRANCISCO 94115

NATIVE AMERICAN HEALTH CENTER
56 Julian Ave.
SAN FRANCSICO 94103
 (415) 621-8051

SAN FRANCISCO INDIAN CENTER
225 Valencia St.
SAN FRANCISCO 94103
 (415) 552-1070
Allene Cottier, Executive Director

FOUR WINDS LODGE
1565 East Santa Clara St.
SAN JOSE 95116

INDIAN CENTER OF SAN JOSE, INC.
3485 East Hills Dr.
SAN JOSE 95127
 (408) 259-9722
Julian P. Armour, Executive Director

Promotes the social, educational and economic welfare, and secures justice and equal opportunity for persons of American Indian descent. *Programs:* Adult Employment and Training; Youth Education (K-12); Adult Education (G.E.D.); Alcohol Rehabilitation; Summer Youth Employment; Indian Child Welfare and Advocacy; Indian Elders Program; Youth Alcohol Abuse Prevention Program. *Publication: Monthly newsletter. Museum. Library.*

URBAN INDIAN HEALTH PROJECT
616 North Milpas St.
SANTA BARBARA 93101
 (805) 965-0718

ANTELOPE INDIAN CIRCLE
P.O. Box 790
SUSANVILLE 96130

MENDOCINO COUNTY INDIAN CENTER
1621 Talmadge Rd.
UKIAH 95482

AMERICAN INDIAN CULTURAL GROUP
P.O. Box 2000
VACAVILLE 95688

COLORADO

CRUSADE FOR JUSTICE
1567 Downing St.
DENVER 80218

DENVER INDIAN HEALTH BOARD
2035 East 18th St., Suite 8
DENVER 80206
 (303) 320-3974

DENVER NATIVE AMERICANS
UNITED, INC.
4407 Morrison Rd.
DENVER 80219
 (303) 937-0401

EAGLE LODGE—AMERICAN INDIAN
ALCOHOLISM REHABILITATION
PROGRAM
1264 Race St.
DENVER 80206

INTER-TRIBAL HERITAGE PROJECT
3401 Pecos St.
DENVER 80211

WHITE BUFFALO COUNCIL
OF AMERICAN INDIANS
P.O. Box 4131, Santa Fe Station
DENVER 80204

CONNECTICUT

AMERICAN INDIANS
FOR DEVELOPMENT
P.O. Box 117
MERIDAN 06450

DISTRICT OF COLUMBIA

AMERICAN INDIAN CENTER
519 5th St., S.E.
WASHINGTON 20003
 (202) 343-3592

AMERICAN INDIAN CENTER
OF HONOLULU
810 North Vineyard Blvd.
HONOLULU 96817
 (808) 847-3544
John H. Ide, Contact

Provides a meeting place for and services to American Indians and Native Alaskans in Hawaii. *Programs:* American Indian Service Corporation; alcoholism counseling and referral service; Hawaii Council of American Indian Nations; American Indian Pow-Wow Association; social and cultural programs; Indian education programs. *Publication: Honolulu Drum Newsletter. Library.*

ILLINOIS

AMERICAN INDIAN CENTER
1630 West Wilson
CHICAGO 60640
 (312) 275-5871/561-8183
Hank Bonga, Director

AMERICAN INDIAN HEALTH SERVICE
838 West Irving Park Rd.
CHICAGO 60613
(312) 883-9100

NATIVE AMERICAN COMMITTEE
1628 West Belmont
CHICAGO 60657

ST. AUGUSTINE'S CENTER
4512 North Sheridan Rd.
CHICAGO 60640
(312) 784-1050
Elmira McClure, Director

IOWA

**NATIVE AMERICAN
ALCOHOLISM TREATMENT PROGRAM**
P.O. Box 790-A
2720 Larpenteau Ave., Bldg. 544
SARGEANT BLUFF 51054

INDIAN YOUTH OF AMERICA
P.O. Box 2786
SIOUX CITY 51106

**SIOUX CITY
AMERICAN INDIAN CENTER**
304 Pearl St.
SIOUX CITY 51101
(712) 255-8957

KANSAS

**HASKELL INDIAN ALCOHOL
AND PREVENTION PROGRAM**
P.O. Box 3015, Jayhawk Station
LAWRENCE 66044

THE INDIAN CENTER OF LAWRENCE
P.O. Box 1016, 2326 Louisiana St.
LAWRENCE 66044
(913) 841-7202
Bertha K. Lieb, Executive Director

I CARE RECOVERY HOME
P.O. Box 1307, 1012 North Jackson
TOPEKA 66601

MID-AMERICAN ALL-INDIAN CENTER
650 North Seneca
WICHITA 67203
(316) 262-5221
Bill M. Jones, Director

WICHITA INDIAN HEALTH CENTER
2318 East Central
WICHITA 67214
(316) 262-2415

MAINE

**CENTRAL MAINE
INDIAN ASSOCIATION**
95 Main St.
ORONO 04473

MARYLAND

**BALTIMORE AMERICAN
INDIAN CENTER**
113 South Broadway
BALTIMORE 21231
(301) 675-3535
Barry Richardson, Executive Director

Helps American Indians with their cultural, social, economic, housing and educational needs. *Programs:* BAIC Scholarship Fund; Rev. James Dial Memorial Fund; housing; business development; job placement; community services; alcoholism; youth program; Brantley Blue Awards; Annual Pow-Wow. *Publiction: Smoke Signals,* newsletter.

**MARYLAND INDIAN
HERITAGE SOCIETY, INC.**
P.O. Box 905
WALDORF 20601
(301) 888-1566
Hugh Proctor, President

MASSACHUSETTS

BOSTON INDIAN COUNCIL, INC.
105 South Huntington
Jamaica Plain 02130
(617) 232-0343
Jimmy L. Sam, Executive Director

A multi-service social delivery system for the American Indian community of the Greater Boston area, and provides a mechanism for cultural activities. *Programs:* Employment and training; adult education; Head Start; day care; elderly; crafts; Indian Health Service; battered women; housing assistance; alcoholic treatment with halfway house; and speakers bureau. *Publication: The Circle,* monthly newsletter. Library.

MICHIGAN

AMERICAN INDIANS UNLIMITED
515 East Jefferson
ANN ARBOR 48104

SOUTH EASTERN MICHIGAN INDIANS
8830 Ten Mile Rd.
CENTERLINE 48015
(313) 756-1350

AMERICAN INDIAN SERVICES
13340 Michigan Ave.
DEARBORN 48126

AMERICAN INDIAN HEALTH CENTER
3750 Woodward Ave., Suite LL21
DETROIT 48201
(313) 832-3281

ASSOCIATED INDIANS OF DETROIT
3901 Cass
DETROIT 48201

**NORTH AMERICAN INDIAN
ASSOCIATION OF DETROIT, INC.**
360 John R.
DETROIT 48209
(313) 963-1710
Irene Lowry, Director

Promotes economic development and self-sufficiency for American Indian people through human services. *Programs:* Employment and educational services; senior center offers nutrition, social and educational services; Indian child welfare provides protective services for Indian children and families; Arts and Crafts Gallery business. *Russ Wright Scholarship Fund*—assists students with the expense of educational supplies. *Publication: Native Sun Newsletter,* monthly. Library.

GENESSEE INDIAN CENTER
124 West First St.
FLINT 48502-1311
(313) 239-6621
Jennifer A. Smith, Executive Director

Provides social and economic development opportunities to the 6,000 Native-Americans living in the following Michigan Counties: Genessee, Lapeer, Shiawassee, Huron, Sanilac and Tuscola. *Programs:* Outreach services (housing, education, health, etc.); cultural and recreational activities; craft classes; Native-American art shows; Indian crafts store. *Publication: GVIA Grapevine,* monthly newsletter. Museum. Library.

**GRAND RAPIDS
INTER-TRIBAL COUNCIL**
45 Lexington N.W.
GRAND RAPIDS 49504
(616) 774-8331

ALL TRIBES INDIAN CENTER
118 West Pine St.
IRONWOOD 39938

**LANSING NORTH AMERICAN
INDIAN CENTER**
820 West Saginaw
LANSING 48912

NORTH AMERICAN INDIAN CLUB
8760 Troy Rd.
OAK PARK 48237

**SAGINAW INTER-TRIBAL
ASSOCIATION, INC.**
3239 Christy Way
SAGINAW 48603
(517) 792-4610
Victoria G. Miller, Executive Director

Services the socio-economic needs of American Indians in the Saginaw-Bay area. *Programs:* Cultural enrichment and awareness classes; community health and health referrals; substance abuse referrals; genealogy referrals; information. *Publication: Bear Talk,* monthly newsletter. Exhibits artifacts. Library.

MICHIGAN INDIAN CHILD WELFARE
P.O. Box 537, 120 Ridge St.
SAULT STE. MARIE 49783

SOUTHEASTERN MICHIGAN INDIANS
P.O. Box 861
WARREN 48909

MINNESOTA

INDIAN CENTER
5633 Regent Ave. North
MINNEAPOLIS 55440

INDIAN FAMILY SERVICES, INC.
1315 Penn Ave. North
MINNEAPOLIS 55411
(612) 348-5788
Betty Greene, Executive Director

Helps the Indian elderly and disabled become more independent through social and recreational activities.

**INDIAN HEALTH BOARD
OF MINNEAPOLIS**
1315 East 24th St.
MINNEAPOLIS 55404
(612) 721-7425
Noreen Smith, Director of
Indian Family Services.

**MINNEAPOLIS REGIONAL
NATIVE AMERICAN CENTER**
1530 Franklin Ave. East
MINNEAPOLIS 55404

UPPER MIDWEST
AMERICAN INDIAN CENTER
1113 West Broadway
MINNEAPOLIS 55411
  (612) 522-4436
  Dennis Morrison, Executive Director

AMERICAN INDIAN
HEALTH CARE ASSOCIATION
245 East Sixth St., Suite 815
ST. PAUL 55101
  (612) 293-0233

IRA HAYES FRIENDSHIP HOUSE
1671 Summit Ave.
ST. PAUL 55105

JUEL FAIRBANKS
CHEMICAL DEPENDENCY SERVICES
804 North Albert St.
ST. PAUL 55104

ST. PAUL AMERICAN INDIAN CENTER
506 Kenny Rd.
ST. PAUL 55101
  (612) 776-8592
  Gene Stacy, Director

SOUTH ST. PAUL
INDIAN EDUCATION
125 Sixth Ave. North
SOUTH ST. PAUL 55075

TWIN CITIES CHIPPEWA COUNCIL
1592 Hoyt Ave. East
ST. PAUL 55105

MISSOURI

INDIAN PEOPLES MINISTRY
The Auditorium
INDEPENDENCE 64051

HEART OF AMERICA INDIAN CENTER
1340 East Admiral Blvd.
KANSAS CITY 64124
  (816) 421-7608

AMERICAN INDIAN CULTURAL
CENTER OF MID-AMERICA
4648 Gravois St.
ST. LOUIS 63110
  (314) 353-4517

SOUTHEAST MISSOURI
INDIAN CENTER
322 East Pershing, Suite A
SPRINGFIELD 65806

MONTANA

ANACONDA INDIAN ALLIANCE
HEALTH PROGRAM
P.O. Box 1108, 506 East Park
ANACONDA 59711
  (406) 563-3459

BILLINGS AMERICAN INDIAN COUNCIL
P.O. Box 853
BILLINGS 59103
  (406) 248-1648

INDIAN HEALTH BOARD OF BILLINGS
P.O. Box 203, 721 North 29th
BILLINGS 59101

BUTTE INDIAN ALCOHOL PROGRAM
Metal Banks Bldg., Suite 309
BUTTE 59701

NORTH AMERICAN INDIAN ALLIANCE
P.O. Box 286, 12 East Galena
BUTTE 59701
  (406) 723-4361

GREAT FALLS
INDIAN EDUCATION CENTER
P.O. Box 2531
GREAT FALLS 59403
  (406) 761-3165

NATIVE AMERICAN CENTER
HEALTH PROGRAM
P.O. Box 2612, 700 Tenth St. South
GREAT FALLS 59403

HELENA INDIAN ALLIANCE
Leo Pocha Memorial Health Clinic
436 North Jackson
HELENA 59601
  (406) 442-9334

INDIAN DEVELOPMENT
AND EDUCATION ALLIANCE
P.O. Box 726
MILES CITY 59301
  (406) 232-6112

MISSOULA QUA QUI CORPORATION
401 East Railroad
MISSOULA 59801
  (406) 728-0340

NATIVE AMERICAN SERVICES AGENCY
URBAN INDIAN HEALTH CLINIC
508 Toole Ave.
MISSOULA 59802

NEBRASKA

INDIAN CENTER, INC.
1100 Military Rd.
LINCOLN 68508
  (402) 474-5231
  Sidney Beane, Executive Director

**AMERICAN INDIAN CENTER
OF OMAHA, INC.**
613 South 16th St.
OMAHA 68102
  (402) 344-0111
  Wayne Tyndell, Executive Director

FOUR WINDS ALCOHOL PROGRAM
3483 Larimore Ave., Suite 2
OMAHA 68111

UNITED INDIANS OF NEBRASKA
1402 South 78th St.
OMAHA 68144
  (402) 397-2820

NEVADA

NATIVE AMERICAN ELDERS UNITED
808 Ivy St.
CARSON 89701

INTER-TRIBAL FRIENDSHIP HOUSE
1050 Graham Lane
FALLON 89406

LAS VEGAS INDIAN CENTER
418 Hoover Ave., Suite One
LAS VEGAS 89101
  (702) 385-0211

INTER-TRIBAL COUNCIL OF NEVADA
650 South Rock Blvd.
RENO 89502
  (702) 786-3128

**NEVADA URBAN INDIANS
HEALTH PROGRAM**
917 East Sixth St.
RENO 89512
  (702) 329-2573

NEW JERSEY

**NEW JERSEY
AMERICAN INDIAN CENTER**
503 Wellington Place
ABERDEEN 07747

NEW MEXICO

ALBUQUERQUE INDIAN CENTER
1114 7th St., NW
ALBUQUERQUE 87102
  (505) 243-2253
  (505) 243 2296 (Health section)

**ALBUQUERQUE URBAN INDIAN
HEALTH CLINIC**
304 San Pablo, SE, Suite C
ALBUQUERQUE 87108

SIPI ALCOHOLISM PROGRAM
P.O. Box 10146, 9169 Coors Rd., NW
ALBUQUERQUE 87114

**FARMINGTON INTERTRIBAL
INDIAN ORGANIZATION**
P.O. Box 2322, 100 West Elm
FARMINGTON 87401
  (505) 327-6296

GALLUP FRIENDSHIP HOUSE
301 East Aztec Ave.
GALLUP 87301

GALLUP INDIAN COMMUNITY CENTER
200 West Maxwell
GALLUP 87017
  (505) 722-4388

INDIAN YOUTH COUNCIL
P.O. Box 892
GALLUP 87301

CENTRAL CLEARING HOUSE
107 Cienega St.
SANTA FE 87501

NEW YORK

**TONAWANDA INDIAN
COMMUNITY LIBRARY**
P.O. Box 326, 372 Bloomingdale Rd.
AKRON 14001-0326
  (716) 542-5618
  Ramona Charles, Director

**AMERICAN INDIAN
INFORMATION CENTER**
139-11 87th Ave.
BRIARWOOD 11435
  (718) 291-7732
  Mifaunwy Shuntona Hines, Director

**BUFFALO NORTH AMERICAN
INDIAN CULTURE CENTER**
1047 Grant St.
BUFFALO 14207

AMERICAN INDIAN COMMUNITY HOUSE
842 Broadway, 8th Floor
NEW YORK 10003
(212) 598-0100
Michael A. Bush, Executive Director

Attempts to further the status of the American
Indian through education, social services, media
promotion, and business sponsorships.
Programs: Job training and placement;
alcoholism and substance abuse; Indian health
services; community development; social services;
art gallery, and theatre ensemble. *Publication:*
Man-Ah-Atn, newsletter.

AMERICAN INDIAN CLUB
OF ROCHESTER, INC.
P.O. Box 272
ROCHESTER 14601
(716) 244-7353

NATIVE AMERICAN CULTURAL CENTER
2115 East Main St.
ROCHESTER 14609

NORTH AMERICAN INDIAN CLUB
P.O. Box 851
SYRACUSE 13201
(315) 476-7425

NORTH CAROLINA

METROLINA NATIVE
AMERICAN ASSOCIATION
800 Briar Creek Rd., Suite CC-13
CHARLOTTE 28205
(704) 333-0135

CUMBERLAND COUNTY
ASSOCIATION OF INDIAN PEOPLE
102 Indian Dr.
FAYETTEVILLE 28301

GUILFORD NATIVE
AMERICAN ASSOCIATION
P.O. Box 5623, 400 Prescott
GREENSBORO 27403
(919) 273-8686

NORTH DAKOTA

DAKOTA ASSOCIATION
OF NATIVE AMERICANS, INC.
P.O. Box 696, 201 East Front Ave.
BISMARCK 58501
(701) 258-0040

FARGO-MOORHEAD INDIAN CENTER
P.O. Box 42, 1444 - 4th Ave. North
FARGO 58107
(701) 293-6863
Sheron Brown Konecki, Executive Director

OHIO

CLEVELAND AMERICAN
INDIAN CENTER
5500-02 Loraine Ave.
CLEVELAND 44102
(216) 961-3490

NATIVE AMERICAN INDIAN CENTER
1535 South High St.
COLUMBUS 43207

OHIO INDIAN CENTER
c/o R. Smith, 3949 Dryden Dr.
NORTH OLMSTED 44070

OKLAHOMA

INDIAN OPPORTUNITY CENTER
555 Constitution Ave.
NORMAN 73069

AMERICAN INDIAN CENTER
1608 N.W. 35th
OKLAHOMA CITY 73117

AMERICAN INDIAN TRAINING
AND EMPLOYMENT PROGRAM
2900 South Harvey
OKLAHOMA CITY 73109
(405) 272-0651
Bob Giago, Director

NATIVE AMERICAN CENTER
2900 South Harvey
OKLAHOMA CITY 73109
(405) 232-2512
Millie Giago, Director

OKLAHOMA CITY
INDIAN HEALTH PROJECT
1214 North Hudson
OKLAHOMA CITY 73103
(405) 232-1526

AMERICAN INDIAN
REFERRAL CENTER
R.R. 6, Box 241
PONCA CITY 74601

INDIAN HEALTH CARE
RESOURCE CENTER
P.O. Box 184, 915 South Cincinnati
TULSA 74119
(918) 582-7225

**NATIVE AMERICAN COALITION
OF TULSA, INC.**
1740 West 41st St.
TULSA 74107
  (918) 446-8432
  John McClelland, Chairman
  Pam Chibitty Tyner, Executive Director

Serves more than 100 tribes and 38,000 Native-Americans. *Programs:* Transportation service for the elderly; nutrition; Headstart; Indian child welfare attorney; clothing and food donations for families; referrals. *Publication:* Semiannual paper.

**TULSA INDIAN COUNCIL
ON ALCOHOL AND DRUG ABUSE**
304 South Trenton
TULSA 74120

TULSA INDIAN YOUTH COUNCIL
716 South Troost
TULSA 74120

OREGON

SWEATHOUSE LODGE
Cascadia School Bldg.
48085 Santium Highway
FOSTER 97345

KLAMATH ALCOHOL AND DRUG ABUSE
1435 Esplanade
KLAMATH FALLS 97601

**ORGANIZATION OF
THE FORGOTTEN AMERICAN**
1020 Pine St.
KLAMATH FALLS 97601
  (503) 882-4441/2
  Leonard Norris, Director

INDIAN ARTS FESTIVAL
P.O. Box 193
LA GRANDE 97850

URBAN INDIAN COUNCIL
1115 S.E. Morrison
PORTLAND 97214
  (503) 235-2311
  Lowell McGraw, Director

URBAN INDIAN PROGRAM
1634 S.W. Alder
PORTLAND 97210
  (503) 248-4562

**CHEMAWA ALCOHOLISM
EDUCATION CENTER**
3760 Hazelgreen Rd., NE
SALEM 97202

PENNSYLVANIA

**NATIVE AMERICAN
CULTURAL CENTER**
927 North Sixth St.
PHILADELPHIA 19123

**UNITED AMERICAN INDIANS
OF THE DELAWARE VALLEY**
225 Chestnut St.
PHILADELPHIA 19106
  (215) 574-9020
  Tom Carrgian, Director

**COUNCIL OF THREE RIVERS
AMERICAN INDIAN CENTER, INC.**
200 Charles St.
PITTSBURGH 15238
  (412) 782-4457
  Russell Sims, Executive Director

Addresses the needs and secures services for the Native-American community. *Programs:* Indian manpower employment and training; Native-American elders program; Native-American cultural programs; Native-American family and child services; Native-American Adoption Resource Exchange, and Indian Adoption Awareness Project (national); Singing Winds Head Start; Rainbow Project—adoption agency for western Pennsylvania. Financial assistance for education and training is provided through the Job Training Partnership Act Program. *Publication: The Singing Winds Newsletter,* monthly; Pow-Wow Booklet, annual. Library.

SOUTH DAKOTA

HAN-PA-O-YE
P.O. Box 624, Northern State College
ABERDEEN 57401

ALL INDIAN ASSOCIATION
EAGLE BUTTE 57570

**SOUTH DAKOTA
URBAN INDIAN HEALTH, INC.**
423 South Pierre St.
PIERRE 57501
  (605) 224-8841

**RAPID CITY
INDIAN SERVICE COUNCIL**
Mother Butler Indian Center
P.O. Box 7038
RAPID CITY 57709
  (605) 342-4772
  Karen Means, Executive Director

SIOUX SAN ALCOHOLISM PROGRAM
3200 Canyon Lake Dr.
RAPID CITY 57701

AMERICAN INDIAN SERVICE CENTER
100 West 6th St.
SIOUX FALLS 57102

MINNEHAHA INDIAN CLUB
1413 Thompson Dr.
SIOUX FALLS 57105

LAKOTA AOMICIYE
Black Hills State College
SPEARFISH 57783

TEXAS

**AMERICAN INDIAN CENTER
OF DALLAS, INC.**
1314 Munger Blvd.
DALLAS 75206
(214) 826-8856
Larry Grospe, Executive Director

**DALLAS INTER-TRIBAL
CENTER, INC.**
209E Jefferson
DALLAS 75203
(214) 941-1050 (Community/ Health Services)
(214) 941-6535 (Employment/ Training Services)
Richard Lucero, Executive Director

Provides health care and other social services to
Indian families residing in the Dallas/ Fort Worth
area. *Programs:* Community services such as:
emergency food assistance, transportation, crisis
intervention services, information and referral;
Indian child welfare; medical-dental clinic; WIC
Program; nutrition education services; health
education; screening. *Publication: DIC Smoke
Signals,* monthly newsletter.

**COUNCIL HOUSE
ALCOHOLISM PROGRAM**
818 East Davis
GRAND PRAIRIE 75050

UTAH

**INDIAN ALCOHOLISM COUNSELING
AND RECOVERY HOUSE PROGRAM**
P.O. Box 1500, 538 South West
SALT LAKE CITY 84101

INDIAN CENTER OF SALT LAKE
21 East Kelsey
SALT LAKE CITY 84111

**SALT LAKE CITY
INDIAN HEALTH CENTER**
508 East South Temple, No. 219
SALT LAKE CITY 84102
(801) 532-2034

VERMONT

ABENAKI SELF-HELP ASSOCIATION
P.O. Box 276
SWANTON 05488

WASHINGTON

KITSAP COUNTY INDIAN CENTER
1200 Fairgrounds Rd.
BREMERTON 98310

**TULALIP TRIBES
ENTERTAINMENT CENTER**
MARYSVILLE 98270
(206) 653-5551

**AMERICAN INDIAN
WOMEN'S SERVICE LEAGUE**
617 2nd Ave.
SEATTLE 98104

**SEATTLE INDIAN
ALCOHOLISM PROGRAM**
1912 Minor Ave.
SEATTLE 98101

SEATTLE INDIAN CENTER
121 Stewart St.
SEATTLE 98101
(206) 624-8700
Camille Monzon-Khamsei, Executive Director

SEATTLE INDIAN HEALTH BOARD
P.O. Box 3364, 1122 12th Ave. S.
SEATTLE 98114
(206) 324-9360

KITSAP COUNTY INDIAN CENTER
3337 N.W. Byron St.
SILVERDALE 98383
(206) 692-7460
Larry Dixon, Director

**AMERICAN INDIAN
COMMUNITY CENTER**
East 801 Second Ave.
SPOKANE 99202
(509) 489-2370
Leonard Hendricks, Executive Director

**PACIFIC NORTHWEST
INDIAN CENTER, INC.**
East 200 Cataldo
SPOKANE 99202
  (509) 326-4550
  B.T. Arfenault, Executive Director

**SPOKANE URBAN INDIAN
HEALTH SERVICES**
North 2002 Atlantic
SPOKANE 99205

**UNITED INDIAN ASSOCIATION
OF CENTRAL WASHINGTON**
106 South 4th St.
YAKIMA 98093
  (509) 575-0835

WISCONSIN

INDIAN DEVELOPMENT CENTER
P.O. Box 11064, 1183 West Mason St.
GREEN BAY 54307
  (414) 494-2961

UNITED AMERINDIAN HEALTH CENTER
401 Ninth St.
GREEN BAY 54304
  (414) 435-6773

**AMERICAN INDIAN
COUNCIL ON ALCOHOLISM**
2240 West National Ave.
MILWAUKEE 53204

**MILWAUKEE INDIAN
HEALTH BOARD AND CENTER**
930 North 27th St.
MILWAUKEE 53208
  (414) 931-8111

WYOMING

THUNDERCHILD
VA Hospital, Bldg. 24
SHERIDAN 82801

INDIAN HEALTH SERVICES

The Indian Health Service, an agency of the Department of Health and Human Services, is the primary federal health resource for more than one million American Indians and Alaskan Natives. This section lists hospitals, medical and health centers under the jurisdiction of the Indian Health Service. Listings are arranged alpha-geographically.

**INDIAN HEALTH SERVICE
(HEADQUARTERS)**
Parklawn Bldg., Room 5A-55
5600 Fishers Lane
ROCKVILLE 20857
(301) 443-1083
Dr. Everett R. Rhoades, Director
Dr. Joseph N. Exendine, Deputy Director
Dr. John G. Todd, Chief of Staff
Dr. James D. Felsen, Chief Medical Officer

ALASKA

**ALASKA AREA NATIVE
HEALTH SERVICE OFFICE**
Indian Health Service
P.O. Box 7-741
ANCHORAGE 99510
(907) 279-6661

Responsible for six health centers and six hospitals in Alaska.

**ALASKA NATIVE
MEDICAL CENTER (HOSPITAL)**
P.O. Box 7-741
ANCHORAGE 99510
(907) 265-3252

Affiliated with Alaska Area Native Health Service.

ALASKA NATIVE HOSPITAL
BARROW 99723
(907) 852-4611

Affiliated with Alaska Area Native Health Service.

**YUKON-KUSKOKWIM DELTA
ALASKA NATIVE HOSPITAL**
BETHEL 99559
(907) 543-3711

Affiliated with Alaska Area Native Health Service.

ALASKA NATIVE HEALTH CENTER
1638 Cowles St.
FAIRBANKS 99701
(907) 452-2131

Affiliated with Alaska Area Native Health Service.

ALASKA NATIVE HEALTH CENTER
P.O. Box 890
JUNEAU 99801
(907) 586-1600/6663

Affiliated with Alaska Area Native Health Service.

ALASKA NATIVE HEALTH CENTER
3289 Tongass Ave.
KETCHIKAN 99901
(907) 225-4156

Affiliated with Alaska Area Native Health Service.

ALASKA NATIVE HOSPITAL
KOTZEBUE 99752
(907) 442-3321

Affiliated with Alaska Area Native Health Service.

ALASKA NATIVE HEALTH CENTER
P.O. Box 428
METLAKATLA 99926
(907) 886-4741

Affiliated with Alaska Area Native Health Service.

ALASKA NATIVE HOSPITAL
P.O. Box 4577
MT. EDGECUMBE 99835
(907) 966-2411/8333

Affiliated with Alaska Area Native Health Service.

ALASKA NATIVE HEALTH CENTER
ST. GEORGE ISLAND 99660

Affiliated with Alaska Area Native Health Service.

ALASKA NATIVE HEALTH CENTER
ST. PAUL ISLAND 99660

Affiliated with Alaska Area Native Health Service.

ALASKA NATIVE HOSPITAL
TANANA 99777
(907) 366-7200

Affiliated with Alaska Area Native Health Service.

ARIZONA

CHINLE INDIAN HOSPITAL
CHINLE 86503
(602) 674-5282

Affiliated with Navajo Area Indian Health
Service.

CIBECUE INDIAN HEALTH CENTER
CIBECUE 85911
(602) 338-4911

Affiliated with Phoenix Area Indian Health
Service.

FORT DEFIANCE INDIAN HOSPITAL
FORT DEFIANCE 86504
(602) 729-5741

Affiliated with Navajo Area Indian Health
Service.

TOYEI INDIAN HEALTH CLINIC
FORT DEFIANCE 86504
(602) 736-2436

Affiliated with Navajo Area Indian Health
Service.

KAYENTA INDIAN HEALTH CENTER
KAYENTA 86033
(602) 697-3211

Affiliated with Phoenix Area Indian Health
Service.

KEAMS CANYON INDIAN HOSPITAL
P.O. Box 98
KEAMS CANYON 86034
(602) 738-2211

Affiliated with Navajo Area Indian Health
Service.

OWYHEE INDIAN HOSPITAL
P.O. Box 212
OWYHEE 89832
(702) 757-2415

Affiliated with Navajo Area Indian Health
Service.

PARKER INDIAN HOSPITAL
Route 1, Box 12
PARKER 85344
(602) 669-2137

Affiliated with Navajo Area Indian Health
Service.

**PEACH SPRINGS
INDIAN HEALTH CENTER**
PEACH SPRINGS 86434
(602) 769-2321

Affiliated with Navajo Area Indian Health
Service.

**PHOENIX AREA
INDIAN HEALTH SERVICE**
3738 North 16th St., Suite A
PHOENIX 85016
(602) 241-2052
George Blue Spruce, Jr., D.D.S.
Assistant Surgeon General

Consists of one medical center, eight hospitals,
four health centers, and two school health clinics.
Serves 47 separate tribes (Papago, Apache, Pima,
Maricopa, Hopi, Paiute, Navajo, Ute, Goshute,
Shoshone, Washoe, Hualapai, Havasupai,
Mojave, Cocopah, Quechan, and urban tribes in
the metropolitan area.) *Number of professionals
on staff:* 772. *Number of beds:* 424. *Numbers
served annually (1985):* In-patient, 12,900; Out-
patient, 424,500. *Services:* All primary medical
services are provided. *Programs:* Accredited
residency programs in obstetrics, pediatrics,
family practice, dental, general practice, and
public health nursing; continuing education;
research (sponsored by the National Institutes of
Health) at several facilities; Health Education
Program—comprised of 15 professional staff who
provide a coordinated program of health
education throughout the Phoenix area; Indian
Health Service Training Committee; instrumental
in implementing the Health Emphasis Campaign,
a seven year program to develop disease
prevention and health promotion practices
among Indian community residents.
Scholarships: Participates in the National Health
Service Corps and the Indian Health Care
Improvement Scholarship Programs. Library.

PHOENIX INDIAN MEDICAL CENTER
4212 North 16th St.
PHOENIX 85016-5981
(602) 263-1200

Affiliated with Phoenix Area Indian Health
Service.

SACATON INDIAN HOSPITAL
SACATON 85247
(602) 562-3321

Affiliated with Phoenix Area Indian Health
Service.

SAN CARLOS INDIAN SERVICE
P.O. Box 208
SAN CARLOS 85550
(602) 475-2381

Affiliated with Phoenix Area Indian Health
Service.

**SECOND MESA
INDIAN HEALTH CENTER**
General Delivery
SECOND MESA 86043
(602) 734-2496

Affiliated with Phoenix Area Indian Health
Service.

**SANTA ROSA
INDIAN HEALTH CENTER**
Star Route, Box 71
SELLS 85634
(602) 261-7611

Affiliated with Tucson Program Office.

SELLS INDIAN HOSPITAL
SELLS 85634
(602) 261-7251

Affiliated with Tucson Program Office.

SUPAI INDIAN HEALTH CLINIC
SUPAI 86435
(602) 488-2131

Affiliated with Phoenix Area Indian Health
Service.

**KAIBETO INDIAN SCHOOL
HEALTH CLINIC**
TUBA CITY 86045
(602) 673-3497

Affiliated with Navajo Area Indian Health
Service.

TUBA CITY INDIAN HOSPITAL
TUBA CITY 86045
(602) 283-6211

Affiliated with Navajo Area Indian Health
Service.

**SAN XAVIER
INDIAN HEALTH CENTER**
TUCSON 85734
(602) 792-6192

Affiliated with Tucson Program Office.

TUCSON PROGRAM OFFICE
Indian Health Service
Office of Research and Development
P.O. Box 11340
TUCSON 85734
(602) 629-5010

WHITERIVER INDIAN HOSPITAL
WHITERIVER 85941
(602) 338-4911

Affiliated with Phoenix Area Indian Health
Service.

**NAVAJO AREA OFFICE
INDIAN HEALTH SERVICE**
P.O. Box G
WINDOW ROCK 86515
(602) 871-5811

**WINSLOW COMPREHENSIVE
HEALTH CENTER**
WINSLOW 86047
(602) 289-4646

Affiliated with Navajo Area Indian Health
Service.

FORT YUMA INDIAN HOSPITAL
P.O. Box 1368
YUMA 85364
(602) 572-0217

Affiliated with Phoenix Area Indian Health
Service.

CALIFORNIA

**AMERICAN INDIAN
FREE CLINIC, INC.**
1330 South Long Beach Blvd.
COMPTON 90221
(213) 537-0103
Joan Freeman, Executive Director

Supplies quality low-cost medical, psychological,
dental, social and related services to American
Indians and others in Los Angeles county.

**THE LOS ANGELES
INDIAN HEALTH CENTER**
1525 West Pizarro St.
LOS ANGELES 90026
(213) 484-2212 (clinic)
(213) 484-9898 (administration)

Provides general medical and dental services.
Special program: Family Life Information and
Education Program; psychological services—
counseling.

**RIVERSIDE INDIAN SCHOOL
HEALTH CENTER**
8934 Magnolia
RIVERSIDE 92503
(714) 787-1622

Affiliated with Phoenix Area Indian Health
Service.

CALIFORNIA PROGRAM OFFICE
Indian Health Service
2999 Fulton Ave.
SACRAMENTO 95821
(916) 484-4836

COLORADO

INDIAN HEALTH CENTER
IGNACIO 81137
  (303) 563-4584

Affiliated with Albuquerque Area Indian Health
Service.

**SOUTHERN COLORADO
UTE INDIAN HOSPITAL**
P.O. Box 778
IGNACIO 81137
  (303) 563-9443

Affiliated with Albuquerque Area Indian Health
Service.

INDIAN HEALTH CENTER
TOWAOC 81334
  (303) 565-4441

Affiliated with Albuquerque Area Indian Health
Service.

IDAHO

**FORT HALL
INDIAN HEALTH CENTER**
P.O. Box 317
FORT HALL 83203
  (208) 238-3958

Affiliated with Portland Area Indian Health
Service.

**NORTHERN IDAHO
INDIAN HEALTH CENTER**
P.O. Drawer 367
LAPWAI 83540
  (208) 843-2271

Affiliated with Portland Area Indian Health
Service.

KANSAS

HOLTON INDIAN HEALTH CENTER
HOLTON 66436
  (913) 364-2177

Affiliated with Oklahoma City Area Indian
Health Service.

**HASKELL INDIAN JUNIOR COLLEGE
PHS INDIAN CENTER**
LAWRENCE 66044
  (913) 843-3750

Affiliated with Oklahoma City Area Indian
Health Service.

MICHIGAN

**KINCHELOE INDIAN
HEALTH CENTER**
Indian Health Facility
KINCHELOE 49788
  (906) 495-5615

Affiliated with Bemidji Program Office.

MINNESOTA

BEMIDJI PROGRAM OFFICE
Indian Health Service
P.O. Box 489, 203 Federal Bldg.
BEMIDJI 56601
  (218) 751-7701

**GREATER LEECH LAKE
INDIAN HOSPITAL**
CASS LAKE 56633
  (218) 335-2293

Affiliated with Bemidji Program Office.

RED LAKE INDIAN HOSPITAL
RED LAKE 56671
  (218) 679-3912

Affiliated with Bemidji Program Office.

**WHITE EARTH
INDIAN HEALTH CENTER**
WHITE EARTH 56591
  (218) 983-3221

Affiliated with Bemidji Program Office.

MISSISSIPPI

PHILADELPHIA INDIAN HOSPITAL
Route 7, Box 50-R
PHILADELPHIA 39350
  (601) 656-2211

Affiliated with United Southeast Tribal Program.

MONTANA

**BILLINGS AREA OFFICE
INDIAN HEALTH SERVICE**
P.O. Box 2143, 2727 Central Ave.
BILLINGS 59103
  (406) 657-6403

**ROCKY BOY'S
INDIAN HEALTH CENTER**
BOX ELDER 59521
  (406) 395-4486

Affiliated with Billings Area Indian Health
Service.

**BROWNING (BLACKFEET)
INDIAN HOSPITAL**
BROWNING 59417
(406) 338-7283

Affiliated with Billings Area Indian Health
Service.

CROW AGENCY INDIAN HOSPITAL
CROW AGENCY 59022
(406) 638-2626

Affiliated with Billings Area Indian Health
Service.

FORT BELKNAP INDIAN HOSPITAL
HARLEM 59526
(406) 353-2278

Affiliated with Billings Area Indian Health
Service.

**NORTHERN CHEYENNE
INDIAN HEALTH CENTER**
LAME DEER 59043
(406) 477-6201

Affiliated with Billings Area Indian Health
Service

**LODGE GRASS
INDIAN HEALTH CENTER**
LODGE GRASS 59040
(406) 639-2317

Affiliated with Billings Area Indian Health
Service.

**FORT PECK
INDIAN HEALTH CENTER**
POPLAR 59255
(406) 768-3491

Affiliated with Billings Area Indian Health
Service.

FLATHEAD INDIAN HEALTH CENTER
ST. IGNATIUS 59865
(406) 745-2422

Affiliated with Billings Area Indian Health
Service.

**WOLF POINT (FORT PECK)
INDIAN HEALTH CENTER**
WOLF POINT 59201
(406) 653-1641

Affiliated with Billings Area Indian Health
Service.

NEBRASKA

**OMAHA-WINNEBAGO
INDIAN HOSPITAL**
WINNEBAGO 68071
(402) 878-2231

Affiliated with Aberdeen Area Indian Health
Service.

NEVADA

**STEWART INDIAN SCHOOL
HEALTH CENTER**
CARSON CITY 89437
(702) 470-5911

Affiliated with Phoenix Area Indian Health
Service.

SCHURZ INDIAN HOSPITAL
SCHURZ 89427
(702) 470-5541

Affiliated with Phoenix Area Indian Health
Service.

SPARKS INDIAN HEALTH CENTER
206 B Cal Lane
SPARKS 89431
(702) 784-5327

Affiliated with Phoenix Area Indian Health
Service.

NEW MEXICO

**ALBUQUERQUE AREA OFFICE
INDIAN HEALTH SERVICE**
Federal Bldg., 500 Gold Ave., SW
ALBUQUERQUE 87101
(505) 766-2151

ALBUQUERQUE INDIAN HOSPITAL
801 Vassar Dr., NE
ALBUQUERQUE 87106
(505) 766-2117

Affiliated with Albuquerque Area Indian Health
Service.

**SOUTHWESTERN INDIAN
POLYTECHNIC INSTITUTE
INDIAN SCHOOL HEALTH CENTER
INDIAN TRAINING CENTER
DENTAL TRAINING CENTER (SIPI)**
P.O. Box 25927, 9168 Coors Rd., NW
ALBUQUERQUE 87125
(505) 766-2755

Affiliated with Albuquerque Area Indian Health
Service.

INDIAN TRAINING CENTER
NURSING EDUCATION CENTER
P.O. Box 849
ALBUQUERQUE 87103
(505) 766-1234

Affiliated with Albuquerque Area Indian Health
Service.

CANONCITO INDIAN
HEALTH CENTER
CANONCITO 87026
(505) 831-6152

Affiliated with Albuquerque Area Indian Health
Service.

CROWNPOINT INDIAN HOSPITAL
CROWNPOINT 87313
(505) 786-5291

Affiliated with Navajo Area Indian Health
Service.

DULCE INDIAN HEALTH CENTER
DULCE 87528
(505) 759-3291

Affiliated with Albuquerque Area Indian Health
Service.

FORT WINGATE INDIAN SCHOOL
HEALTH CENTER
GALLUP 87301
(505) 488-5481

Affiliated with Navajo Area Indian Health
Service.

GALLUP INDIAN HOSPITAL
GALLUP 87301
(505) 722-1000

Affiliated with Navajo Area Indian Health
Service.

TOHATCHI INDIAN HEALTH CLINIC
GALLUP 87301
(505) 733-2244

Affiliated with Navajo Area Indian Health
Service.

ISLETA INDIAN HEALTH CENTER
ISLETA 87022
(505) 869-3200

Affiliated with Albuquerque Area Indian Health
Service.

JEMEZ INDIAN HEALTH CENTER
JEMEZ 87024
(505) 834-7413

Affiliated with Albuquerque Indian Health
Service.

MESCALERO INDIAN HOSPITAL
MESCALERO 88340
(505) 671-4441

Affiliated with Albuquerque Area Indian Health
Service.

LAGUNA INDIAN HEALTH CENTER
P.O. Box 199
NEW LAGUNA 87038
(505) 552-6641

Affiliated with Albuquerque Area Indian Health
Service.

ACOMA-CANONCITO LAGUNA
INDIAN HOSPITAL
P.O. Box 130
SAN FIDEL 87049
(505) 552-6634

Affiliated with Albuquerque Area Indian Health
Service.

SANTA FE INDIAN HOSPITAL
Cerrillos Rd.
SANTA FE 87501
(505) 988-9821

Affiliated with Albuquerque Area Indian Health
Service.

SANOSTEE INDIAN HEALTH CLINIC
SHIPROCK 87420
(505) 723-2484

Affiliated with Navajo Area Indian Health
Service.

SHIPROCK INDIAN HOSPITAL
SHIPROCK 87420
(505) 368-4971

Affiliated with Navajo Area Indian Health
Service.

TAOS INDIAN HEALTH CENTER
TAOS 87571
(505) 758-4224

Affiliated with Albuquerque Area Indian Health
Service.

ZUNI INDIAN HOSPITAL
ZUNI 87327
(505) 782-4431

Affiliated with Albuquerque Area Indian Health
Service.

NORTH CAROLINA

CHEROKEE INDIAN HOSPITAL
CHEROKEE 28719
(704) 497-9163

NORTH DAKOTA

**TURTLE MOUNTAIN
INDIAN HOSPITAL**
BELCOURT 58316
  (701) 447-6111

Affiliated with Aberdeen Area Indian Health
Service.

STANDING ROCK INDIAN HOSPITAL
FORT YATES 58538
  (701) 854-3831

Affiliated with Aberdeen Area Indian Health
Service.

**MINNE-TOHE
INDIAN HEALTH CENTER**
NEW TOWN 58763
  (701) 627-4701

Affiliated with Aberdeen Area Indian Health
Service.

OKLAHOMA

CARL ALBERT INDIAN HOSPITAL
1001 North Country Club Rd.
ADA 74820
  (405) 436-3980
  Jeannie Lunsford, Director

Offers general out-patient medical services;
workshops and in-service training. *Professionals
on staff:* 4. *Numbers served:* 200,000 annually.
Affiliated with Oklahoma City Area Indian
Health Service.

ANADARKO INDIAN HEALTH CENTER
ANADARKO 73005
  (405) 247-6673

Affiliated with Oklahoma City Area Indian
Health Service.

CHICKASAW NATION HEALTH CLINIC
2400 Chickasaw Blvd.
ARDMORE 73401
  (405) 226 8181
  Jeannie Lunsford, Director

Offers general out-patient medical services;
workshops and in-service training. *Professionals
on staff:* 7. *Numbers served:* 5,400 annually.
Library.

**JOHN ANDERSON
MEMORIAL HEALTH CENTER**
BROKEN BOW 74728
  (405) 584-2740

Affiliated with Oklahoma City Area Indian
Health Service.

CLINTON INDIAN HOSPITAL
CLINTON 73601
  (405) 323-2884

Affiliated with Oklahoma City Area Indian
Health Service.

CLAREMORE INDIAN HOSPITAL
CLAREMORE 74017
  (918) 341-8430

Affiliated with Oklahoma City Area Indian
Health Service.

**CONCHO INDIAN SCHOOL
HEALTH CENTER**
CONCHO 73022
  (405) 262-7631

Affiliated with Oklahoma City Area Indian
Health Service.

EUFAULA INDIAN HEALTH CENTER
800 Forest Ave.
EUFAULA 74432
  (918) 689-2547

Affiliated with Oklahoma City Area Indian
Health Service.

HUGO INDIAN HEALTH CENTER
109 East Main
HUGO 74742
  (405) 326-7561

Affiliated with Oklahoma City Area Indian
Health Service.

LAWTON INDIAN HOSPITAL
LAWTON 73501
  (405) 353-0350

Affiliated with Oklahoma City Area Indian
Health Service.

McALESTER INDIAN HEALTH CENTER
McALESTER 74501
  (918) 423-8440

Affiliated with Oklahoma City Area Indian
Health Service.

MIAMI INDIAN HEALTH CENTER
P.O. Box 1498
MIAMI 74355
  (918) 542-1655
  John Daugherty, Jr., Director

Tribes served: Seneca-Cayuga, Eastern Shawnee,
Miami, Modoc, Ottawa, Quapaw, Peoria,
Wyandott and Cherokee. *Professionals on staff:*
15; *Numbers served:* Out-patients, 35,000
annually. *Medical services:* Medical, pharmacy,
dental, optometry, mental health, public health
nursing and laboratory. *Community programs:*
Educational activities in the schools and tribal
communities. Small medical library.

OKEMAH INDIAN HEALTH CENTER
OKEMAH 74859
(918) 623-0555

Affiliated with Oklahoma City Area Indian
Health Service.

OKLAHOMA CITY AREA OFFICE
INDIAN HEALTH SERVICE
215 Dean A. McGee St., N.W.
OKLAHOMA CITY 73102
(405) 231-4796

OKMULGEE INDIAN HEALTH CENTER
OKMULGEE 74447
(918) 756-8874

Affiliated with Oklahoma City Area Indian
Health Service.

PAWHUSKA INDIAN HEALTH CENTER
PAWHUSKA 74056
(918) 287-2489

Affiliated with Oklahoma City Area Indian
Health Service.

WHITE EAGLE
INDIAN HEALTH CENTER
PONCA CITY 74058
(405) 765-2501

Affiliated with Oklahoma City Area Indian
Health Service.

SAPULPA INDIAN HEALTH CENTER
SAPULPA 74066
(918) 224-6402

Affiliated with Oklahoma City Area Indian
Health Service.

SHAWNEE INDIAN HEALTH CENTER
SHAWNEE 74801
(405) 275-6930

Affiliated with Oklahoma City Area Indian
Health Service.

TAHLEQUAH INDIAN HOSPITAL
1120 Grand
TAHLEQUAH 74464
(918) 456-5571

Affiliated with Oklahoma City Area Indian
Health Service.

TALIHINA INDIAN HOSPITAL
TALIHINA 74571
(918) 567-2211

Affiliated with Oklahoma City Area Indian
Health Service.

CHICKASAW NATION HEALTH CENTER
P.O. Box 430, 815 East 6th St.
TISHOMINGO 73460
(405) 371-2392
Jeannie Lunsford, Director

Offers general out-patient medical services;
workshops and in-service training. *Professionals
on staff:* 8. *Numbers served:* 8,000 annually.
Library. Affiliated with Oklahoma City Area
Indian Health Service.

WATONGA INDIAN HEALTH CENTER
P.O. Box 878, Highway 281
WATONGA 73772
(405) 623-4991
Dr. Michael J. Alpert, Facility Director

Tribes served: Primarily Cheyenne and Arapaho;
members of all local tribes. *Professionals on staff:*
10. *Numbers served annually:* Out-patient, 1,200
plus. *Medical services:* General out-patient
medical and dental services. *Community
programs:* Weekly diabetic and prenatal clinics;
headstart dental prevention and nursing bottle
caries prevention. Small medical library.
Affiliated with Oklahoma City Area Indian
Health Service.

WEWOKA INDIAN HEALTH CENTER
WEWOKA 74884
(405) 257-6282

Affiliated with Oklahoma City Area Indian
Health Service.

OREGON

YELLOWHAWK INDIAN
HEALTH CENTER
P.O. Box 159
PENDLETON 97801
(503) 276-3811 ext. 279

Affiliated with Portland Area Indian Health
Service.

PORTLAND AREA OFFICE
INDIAN HEALTH SERVICE
Federal Bldg., Room 476
1220 S.W. 3rd Ave.
PORTLAND 97204
(503) 221-2020

WESTERN OREGON
CHEMAWA INDIAN HEALTH CENTER
3750 Hazelgreen Rd., NE
SALEM 97303
(503) 370-4200

Affiliated with Portland Area Indian Health
Service.

**WARM SPRINGS
INDIAN HEALTH CENTER**
P.O. Box H
WARM SPRINGS 97761
(503) 553-1196

Affiliated with Portland Area Indian Health
Service.

SOUTH DAKOTA

**ABERDEEN AREA OFFICE
INDIAN HEALTH SERVICE**
Federal Bldg., 115 4th Ave., S.E.
ABERDEEN 57401
(605) 225-0250

CHEYENNE RIVER INDIAN HOSPITAL
EAGLE BUTTE 57625
(605) 964-2811

Affiliated with Aberdeen Area Indian Health
Service.

**FORT THOMPSON
INDIAN HEALTH CENTER**
P.O. Box 597
FORT THOMPSON 57339
(605) 245-2383

Affiliated with Aberdeen Area Indian Health
Service.

**FORT TOTTEN
INDIAN HEALTH CENTER**
FORT TOTTEN 58335
(701) 766-4291

Affiliated with Aberdeen Area Indian Health
Service.

McLAUGHLIN INDIAN HEALTH CENTER
McLAUGHLIN 57642
(605) 832-4459

Affiliated with Aberdeen Area Indian Health
Service.

PINE RIDGE INDIAN HOSPITAL
PINE RIDGE 57770
(605) 867-5131

Affiliated with Aberdeen Area Indian Health
Service.

RAPID CITY INDIAN HOSPITAL
RAPID CITY 57701
(605) 348-1900

Affiliated with Aberdeen Area Indian Health
Service.

ROSEBUD INDIAN HOSPITAL
ROSEBUD 57570
(605) 474-2231

Affiliated with Aberdeen Area Indian Health
Service.

**SISSETON-WAHPETON
INDIAN HOSPITAL**
SISSETON 57262
(605) 698-7606

Affiliated with Aberdeen Area Indian Health
Service.

YANKTON-WAGNER INDIAN HOSPITAL
WAGNER 57380
(605) 384-3621
George E. Howell, MSW, Director

Tribes served: Yankton Sioux and Santee Sioux.
Professionals on staff: 30; *Number of Beds:* 26.
Medical services: In-patient; medical and surgical.
Library. Affiliated with Aberdeen Area Indian
Health Service.

WANBLEE INDIAN HEALTH CENTER
WANBLEE 57577
(605) 462-6155

Affiliated with Aberdeen Area Indian Health
Service.

TENNESSEE

NASHVILLE PROGRAM OFFICE
Indian Health Service
Oaks Tower Bldg., Suite 810
1101 Kermit Dr.
NASHVILLE 37217-2191
(615) 251-5104

UTAH

**INTERMOUNTAIN INDIAN SCHOOL
HEALTH CENTER**
P.O. Box 602
BRIGHAM CITY 84302
(801) 723-4332

Affiliated with Billings Area Indian Health
Service.

**UINTAH-OURAY
INDIAN HEALTH CENTER**
P.O. Box 967
ROOSEVELT 84066
(801) 722-2241

Affiliated with Phoenix Area Indian Health
Service.

WASHINGTON

**NORTHWEST WASHINGTON
LUMMI INDIAN HEALTH CENTER**
2592 Kwina Rd.
BELLINGHAM 98226-9297
(206) 676-8373

Affiliated with Portland Area Indian Health
Service.

NEAH BAY INDIAN HEALTH CENTER
P.O. Box 418
NEAH BAY 98357
(206) 654-2233

Affiliated with Portland Area Indian Health
Service.

COLVILLE INDIAN HEALTH CENTER
NESPELEM 99155
(509) 634-4723

Affiliated with Portland Area Indian Health
Service.

**PUGET SOUND
INDIAN HEALTH CENTER**
Federal Center South, Room 1470
4735 East Margina Way South
SEATTLE 98134-2381
(206) 764-6552

Affiliated with Portland Area Indian Health
Service.

TAHOLAH INDIAN HEALTH CENTER
P.O. Box 219
TAHOLAH 98587
(206) 276-4405

Affiliated with Portland Area Indian Health
Service.

YAKIMA INDIAN HEALTH CENTER
Route 1, Box 1104
TOPPENISH 98948
(509) 865-2102

Affiliated with Portland Area Indian Health
Service.

WELLPINIT INDIAN HEALTH CENTER
P.O. Box 391
WELLPINIT 99040
(509) 258-4517

Affiliated with Portland Area Indian Health
Service.

WISCONSIN

**RHINELANDER INDIAN HEALTH
SERVICE FIELD OFFICE**
P.O. Box 537
9A South Brown St., Debyle Bldg.
RHINELANDER 54501
(715) 362-5145

Affiliated with Bemidji Program Office.

WYOMING

**ARAPAHOE INDIAN
HEALTH CENTER**
ARAPAHOE 82510
(306) 255-8233

Affiliated with Billings Area Indian Health
Service.

**WIND RIVER
INDIAN HEALTH CENTER**
FORT WASHAKIE 82514
(306) 255-8220

Affiliated with Billings Area Indian Health
Service.

SCHOOLS

Indian children attend Federal, public, private and mission schools. There are approximately 250,000 Indian students, age 5 to 18 years inclusive, enrolled in these schools in the U.S. Education of Indian children residing in the States of California, Idaho, Michigan, Minnesota, Nebraska, Oregon, Texas, Washington, and Wisconsin is the responsibility of the State concerned.

Listed here are elementary and high schools operated by the Bureau of Indian Affairs, as well as other Indian schools; arranged by type of school (i.e., day and boarding schools), and by geographic location.

ALASKA

AKIACHAK IRA CONTRACT SCHOOL
General Delivery
AKIACHAK 99551
(907) 825-4428
Gil Gutierrez, Principal
Willie Kasayulie, Chair

Day School; Grades K-8. Under jurisdiction of Bethel Agency.

AKIAK IRA CONTRACT SCHOOL
AKIAK 99552
(907) 543-2002
Ed Graf, Principal
Owen Ivan, Chair

Day School; Grades K-8. Under jurisdiction of Bethel Agency.

CHEFORNAK IRA CONTRACT SCHOOL
General Delivery
CHEFORNAK 99561
(907) 867-8707
Jerry Twitchell, Principal
Peter Panruk, Chair

Day School; Grades K-8. Under jurisdiction of Bethel Agency.

CHEVAK IRA CONTRACT SCHOOL
CHEVAK 99563
(907) 858-7713
Alex Tatem, Principal
Xiver Atcherian, Chair

Day School; Grades K-12. Under jursidiction of Bethel Agency.

KASIGLUK DAY SCHOOL
KASIGLUK 99609
(907) 477-6714
Karen A. Rhoades, Principal
Yeako Slim, Chair

Day School; Grades K-8. Under jurisdiction of Bethel Agency.

KIPNUK DAY SCHOOL
KIPNUK 99614
(907) 896-5513
Leslie Smith, Principal/Teacher
Peter J. Paul, Chair

Day School; Grades K-8. Under jurisdiction of Bethel Agency.

NEWTOK DAY SCHOOL
General Delivery
NEWTOK 99559
(907) 237-2328
Rodney Sehorn, Principal
Joseph Tommy, Chair

Day School; Grades 1-8. Under jurisdiction of Bethel Agency.

NUNAPITCHUK DAY SCHOOL
NUNAPITCHUK 99641
(907) 527-5711
Karen K. Waters, Principal/Teacher
Jimmy Stevens, Chair

Day School; Grades K-8. Under jurisdiction of Bethel Agency.

MT. EDGECUMBE HIGH SCHOOL
P.O. Box 2628
SITKA 99835
(907) 966-2201
Bill Denkinger, Principal
Larrae Rocheleau, Superintendent

Boarding School; Grades 9-12; Enrollment: 300. *Special courses:* Pacific Rim Cultures; Alaska Native History.

TOKSOOK BAY DAY SCHOOL
TOKSOOK 99637
(907) 543-2746
Wilma M. Moore, Principal/Teacher
Joseph Henry, Chair

Day School; Grades 1-6. Under jurisdiction of Bethel Agency.

TULUKSAK IRA CONTRACT SCHOOL
TULUKSAK 99679
(907) 695-6212
Howard Diamond, Principal
Andrew Alexie, Chair

Day School; Grades K-8. Under jurisdiction of
Bethel Agency.

ARIZONA

CASA BLANCA DAY SCHOOL
P.O. Box 1112
BAPCHULE 85221
(602) 562-3489
Paul J. Robinson, Principal
Garold Charles, Chair

Day School; Grades K-4. Under jurisdiction of
Pima Agency.

WIDE RUINS BOARDING SCHOOL
CHAMBERS 86502
(602) 652-3251
Lena May Jim, Principal
Johnnie E. Hale, Chair

Boarding School; Grades K-5. Under jurisdiction
of Fort Defiance Agency.

COTTONWOOD DAY SCHOOL
CHINLE 86503
(602) 725-3256
Peter P. Sandoval, Principal
Billy Nez, Chair

Day School; Grades K-6. Under jurisdiction of
Chinle Agency.

LOW MOUNTAIN BOARDING SCHOOL
CHINLE 86503
(602) 674-3619
Richard D. Simpson, Principal
Marlene Hoskie, Chair

Boarding School; Grades K-4. Under jurisdiction
of Chinle Agency.

ROCK POINT COMMUNITY SCHOOL
CHINLE 86503
(602) 659-4224
Benjamin Barney, Director
Kim L. Nih, Chair

Day School; Grades K-12. Contract-
Independent.

CIBECUE COMMUNITY SCHOOL
CIBECUE 85911
(602) 332-4480
Dr. Gerald Knowles, Chief Administrator

Day School; Grades K-9; Enrollment: 200.
Special courses: Enrichment, Bilingual (Apache).
Instructors: Dr. John Reyhner, Academic
Coordinator; Ruth Hunsinger, Media Center
Director; Diana Campbell, Title IV Enrichment
Director; Sue Zann Jordan, Chapter I
Coordinator; Donna Craft, Special Ed.
Coordinator. *Special programs:* American Indian
Day Pageant, in Sept.; Arts and Crafts Fair/ Pow-
Wow, in May. *Publication: Bizhii* (student
magazine), 4/yr. Under jurisdiction of Fort
Apache Agency.

BLACKWATER COMMUNITY SCHOOL
P.O. Box 1137
COOLIDGE 85228
(602) 723-5859
S. Jo Lewis, Principal
Drake Lewis, Chair

Day School. Grades K-1. Under jurisdiction of
Pima Agency.

DENNEHOTSO BOARDING SCHOOL
P.O. Box LL
DENNEHOTSO 86535
(602) 658-3201
Dr. Irving Jones, Principal
Thomas Redhouse, Chair

Boarding School; Grades K-8. Under jurisdiction
of Westrern Navajo Agency.

FLAGSTAFF DORMITORY
P.O. Box 609
FLAGSTAFF 86002
(602) 774-5270
James Kimery, Supvisor/ Guidance Counselor
Roger Wilson, Chair

Dormitory School; Grades 9-12. Under
jurisdiction of Western Navajo Agency.

THEODORE ROOSEVELT SCHOOL
P.O. Box 567
FORT APACHE 85926
(602) 338-4464/4486
Leon W. Ben, Principal
Reno Johnson, Chair

Day and Boarding School; Grades 4,5,9-12
(Boarding only), 6-8 (Day). Under jurisdiction of
Fort Apache Agency.

GREASEWOOD BOARDING SCHOOL
GANADO 86505
(602) 654-3331
James K. Byrnes, Principal
Ronald Gishey, Chair

Boarding School; Grades K-8. Under jurisdiction
of Fort Defiance Agency.

KINLICHEE BOARDING SCHOOL
GANADO 86505
(602) 755-3439
Vincent C. Beach, Principal
Dr. Samuel Billison, Chair

Boarding School; Grades K-6. Under jurisdiction
of Fort Defiance Agency.

NAZLINI BOARDING SCHOOL
GANADO 86505
(602) 755-6125
Lorraine Etsitty, Principal
Calvin Yazzie, Chair

Boarding School; Grades K-5. Under jurisdiction
of Chinle Agency.

TOYEI BOARDING SCHOOL
GANADO 86505
(602) 736-2401
Jill Lorah, Principal
Eugene Lewis, Chair

Boarding School; Grades K-8. Under jurisdiction
of Fort Defiance Agency.

HOLBROOK DORMITORY
P.O. Box 758
HOLBROOK 86025
(602) 524-6222
Grace P. Yazzie, Principal
Maye Bigboy, Chair

Dormitory School; Grades 9-12. Under
jurisdiction of Fort Defiance Agency.

**HOTEVILLA BACAVI
COMMUNITY SCHOOL**
P.O. Box 48
HOTEVILLA 86030
(602) 734-2462
Louis Barajas, Chief Administrator
Clifford Balenquah, Chair

Day School; Grades K-8. Under jurisdiction of
Hopi Agency.

PINE SPRINGS BOARDING SCHOOL
P.O. Box 198
HOUCK 86506
(602) 871-4311
Lena R. Wilson, Principal
Ernest Hubbell, Chair

Boarding School; Grades K-3. Under jurisdiction
of Fort Defiance Agency.

KAIBETO BOARDING SCHOOL
KAIBETO 86053
(602) 673-3480
Roland E. Smith, Principal
Tullie Mann, Chair

Boarding School; Grades K-8. Under jurisdiction
of Western Navajo Agency.

CHILCHINBETO DAY SCHOOL
P.O. Box 547
KAYENTA 86033
(602) 697-3448
George Mitchell, Principal
Carl Sharkey, Chair

Day School; Grades K-6. Under jurisdiction of
Western Navajo Agency.

KAYENTA BOARDING SCHOOL
P.O. Box 188
KAYENTA 86033
(602) 697-3439
Robert B. Leflore, Principal
Keith H. Smith, Chair

Boarding School; Grades K-8. Under jurisdiction
of Western Navajo Agency.

KEAMS CANYON BOARDING SCHOOL
P.O. Box 397
KEAMS CANYON 86034
(602) 738-2385
Newton F. Carl, Chair

Boarding School; Grades K-8. Under jurisdiction
of Hopi Agency.

HOPI DAY SCHOOL
P.O. Box 42
KYAKOTSMOVI 86039
(602) 734-2468
Martin A. Green, Principal
Wilma Laban, Chair

Day School; Grades K-8. Under jurisdiction of
Hopi Agency.

GILA CROSSING DAY SCHOOL
Route 1, Box 770
LAVEEN 85339
(602) 237-4834
Stanley Parker, Chair

Day School; Grades K-5. Under jurisdiction of
Pima Agency.

LUKACHUKAI BOARDING SCHOOL
LUKACHUKAI 86507
(602) 787-2301
Larry Tsosie, Principal
Addie Sarracino, Chair

Boarding School; Grades K-8. Under jurisdiction
of Chinle Agency.

CHINLE BOARDING SCHOOL
P.O. Box 70
MANY FARMS 86503
  (602) 781-6221
  Roland E. Kimbrough, Principal
  Addie Sarracino, Chair

Boarding School; Grades K-8. Under jurisdiction
of Chinle Agency.

MANY FARMS HIGH SCHOOL
MANY FARMS 86538
  (602) 781-6227
  Dr. Phillip Hardy, Principal
  Teddy Begay, Chair

Boarding School; Grades 9-12. Under jurisdiction
of Chinle Agency.

PHOENIX INDIAN HIGH SCHOOL
P.O. Box 7188
PHOENIX 85011
  (602) 241-2126
  Richard T. Christman, Principal
  Wesley Bonito, Chair

Boarding School; Grades 9-12. Under jurisdiction
of Phoenix Area Office.

PINON BOARDING SCHOOL
P.O. Box 66
PINON 86510
  (602) 725-3250
  William H. Draper, Principal
  Victor Beck, Chair

Boarding School; Grades K-4. Under jurisdiction
of Chinle Agency.

POLACCA DAY SCHOOL
POLACCA 86042
  (602) 737-2581/2681
  Thomas E. Goff, Principal
  Waylon F. Pahona, Chair

Day School; Grades K-6. Under jurisdiction of
Hopi Agency.

RED ROCK DAY SCHOOL
P.O. Drawer 10
RED VALLEY 86544
  (602) 653-4456
  Johnny C. Begay, Supervisor
  Harry V. Lee, Chair

Day School; Grades K-8. Under jurisdiction of
Shiprock Agency.

BLACK MESA COMMUNITY SCHOOL
Star Route 1, Box 215
ROUGH ROCK 86510
  (602) 674-3632
  Dorothy R. Yazzie, Director
  Jones Begay, Chair

Day School; Grades K-8. Under jurisdiction of
Chinle Agency.

**ROUGH ROCK DEMONSTRATION
SCHOOL**
Star Route 1
ROUGH ROCK 86510
  (602) 728-3311
  Jimmy C. Begay, Director
  Emmett Bia, Chair

Day School; Grades K-12. Under jurisdiction of
Chinle Agency.

HUNTERS POINT BOARDING SCHOOL
P.O. Box Drawer N
ST. MICHAELS 86511
  (602) 871-4439
  Roy H. Chase, Principal
  Katherine Keeto, Chair

Boarding School; Grades 1-5. Under jurisdiction
of Fort Defiance Agency.

SALT RIVER DAY SCHOOL
Route 1, Box 117
SCOTTSDALE 85256
  (602) 241-2810
  Farrell B. Whitey, Principal
  Brian Antone, Chair

Day School; Grades K-6. Under jurisdiction of
Phoenix Area Office.

SECOND MESA DAY SCHOOL
P.O. Box 728
SECOND MESA 86043
  (602) 737-2571
  Donald Covington, Principal
  Emilio Reynosa, Chair

Day School; Grades K-6. Under jurisdiction of
Hopi Agency.

SAN SIMON SCHOOL
Star Route 1, Box 92
SELLS 85634
  (602) 383-2231
  Della R. Williams, Principal
  Roy Calabaza, Chair

Boarding School; Grades K-8. Under jurisdiction
of Papago Agency.

SANTA ROSA BOARDING SCHOOL
SELLS 85634
  (602) 383-2330
  Clyde V. Peacock, Principal
  Willard Juan, Chair

Boarding School; Grades K-9. Under jurisdiction
of Papago Agency.

SHONTO BOARDING SCHOOL
SHONTO 86054
(602) 672-2340
Lyle G. Elton, Principal
Alfred Nelson, Chair

Boarding School; Grades K-8. Under jurisdiction
of Western Navajo Agency.

SNOWFLAKE DORMITORY
P.O. Box 370
SNOWFLAKE 85937
(602) 536-4532
Leonard Smith, Principal
Maye Bigboy, Chair

Dormitory School; Grades 9-12. Under
jurisdiction of Fort Defiance Agency.

HAVASUPAI SCHOOL
P.O. Box 40
SUPAI 86435
(602) 448-2901
John Reyhner, Principal
Bernadine Siyuja, Chair

Day School; Grades K-8. Under jurisdiction of
Phoenix Area Office.

TEECNOSPOS BOARDING SCHOOL
TEECNOSPOS 86514
(602) 656-3252
Jerry Walker, Supervisor
Charley Francis, Chair

Boarding School; Grades K-8. Under jurisdiction
of Shiprock Agency.

COOK CHRISTIAN TRAINING SCHOOL
708 South Lindon Lane
TEMPE 85281

RED LAKE DAY SCHOOL
P.O. Box 62
TONALEA 86044
(602) 283-5324
Ray L. Interpreter, Principal
Grey Farrell, Chair

Day School; Grades K-6. Under jurisdiction of
Western Navajo Agency.

MOENCOPI DAY SCHOOL
P.O. Box 185
TUBA CITY 86045
(602) 283-5361
Elvira J. Pasena, Principal
Leonard Dallas, Chair

Day School; Grades K-6. Under jurisdiction of
Hopi Agency.

NAVAJO MOUNTAIN BOARDING SCHOOL
P.O. Box 787
TUBA CITY 86045

(602) 283-5320
Blanche M. Barrows, Principal
Gilmore Grey Mountain, Chair

Boarding School; Grades K-6. Under jurisdiction
of Western Navajo Agency.

ROCKY RIDGE BOARDING SCHOOL
P.O. Box 235
TUBA CITY 86045
(602) 674-3686
Frederick M. Johnson, Principal
Melvin K. Bedonie, Chair

Boarding School; Grades K-7. Under jurisdiction
of Western Navajo Agency.

TUBA CITY BOARDING SCHOOL
P.O. Box 187
TUBA CITY 86045
(602) 283-4531
Jerry E. Diebel, Principal
Chester Yellowhair, Chair

Boarding School; Grades K-8. Under jurisdiction
of Western Navajo Agency.

TUBA CITY HIGH SCHOOL
P.O. Box 15E
TUBA CITY 86045
(602) 283-4531
Andrew M. Tah, Principal
Lee F. Johnson, Chair

Boarding School; Grades 9-12. Under jurisdiction
of Western Navajo Agency.

SANTA ROSA RANCH SCHOOL
Sells Star Route, Box 230
TUCSON 85735
(602) 383-2359
Jean Tyson, Principal
Frances Francisco, Chair

Boarding School; Grades K-8. Under jurisdiction
of Papago Agency.

J.F. KENNEDY DAY SCHOOL
P.O. Box 130
WHITERIVER 85941
(602) 338-4593
Patricia L. Banashley, Principal
Davis Susan, Sr., Chair

Day School; Grades K-8. Under jurisdiction of
Fort Apache Agency.

DILCON BOARDING SCHOOL
Star Route
WINSLOW 86047
(602) 657-3211
Berlyn R. Yazzie, Principal
Jerry Freddie, Chair

Boarding School; Grades K-8. Under jurisdiction
of Fort Defiance Agency.

LEUPP BOARDING SCHOOL
Star Route H-C61
WINSLOW 86047
(602) 686-6211
Mark W. Sorensen, Principal
Jimmie Store, Chair

Boarding School; Grades K-9. Under jurisdiction
of Western Navajo Agency.

LITTLE SINGER COMMUNITY SCHOOL
Star Route, Box 239
WINSLOW 86047
(602) 774-7456
Dr. Lloyd House, Director
Benny Y. Singer, Chair

Boarding School; Grades 1-8. Under jurisdiction
of Western Navajo Agency.

SEBA DALKAI BOARDING SCHOOL
Star Route 1
WINSLOW 86047
(602) 657-3209
Lulu M. Stago, Principal
Marlin Scott, Chair

Boarding School; Grades K-6. Under jurisdiction
of Fort Defiance Agency.

WINSLOW DORMITORY
P.O. Box 610
WINSLOW 86047
(602) 289-3242
Ernest Rivera, Principal
Walter Shurley, Chair

Dormitory School; Grades 7-12. Under
jurisdiction of Fort Defiance Agency.

CALIFORNIA

SHERMAN INDIAN HIGH SCHOOL
9010 Magnolia Ave.
RIVERSIDE 92503
(714) 351-6328
Mahlon I. Marshall, Principal
Billy Kane, Chair

Boarding School; Grades 9-12. Under jurisdiction
of Phoenix Area Office.

FLORIDA

AHFACHKEE DAY SCHOOL
Star Route, Box 40
CLEWISTON 33440
(813) 983-6348
Rondell Clay, Principal
Lydia Cypress, Chair

Day School; Grades K-5. Under jurisdiction of
Eastern Area Office.

MICCOSUKEE INDIAN SCHOOL
P.O. Box 440021, Tamiami Station
MIAMI 33943
(305) 223-8380
Maria Osceola-Branch, Principal
Andrew Buster, Chair

Day School; Grades K-12. Under jurisdiction of
Eastern Area Office.

IDAHO

COEUR d'ALENE TRIBAL SCHOOL
P.O. Box A
DeSMET 83824
(208) 274-6921
Don Beach, Superintendent
Rose Goddard, Chair

Day School; Grades K-8. Under jurisdiction of
Portland Area Office.

**SHOSHONE-BANNOCK
ALTERNATIVE SCHOOL**
P.O. Box 449
FORT HALL 83203
(208) 238-3975
John Haas, Director
Maxine Edmo, Chair

Day School; Grades 7-12. Under jurisdiction of
Portland Area Office.

IOWA

SAC AND FOX SETTLEMENT SCHOOL
Route 2
TAMA 52339
(515) 484-4990
George D. Dorazil, Director
Louis Mitchell, Chair

Day School; Grades K-5. Under jurisdiction of
Minneapolis Area Office.

KANSAS

HASKELL INDIAN JUNIOR COLLEGE
P.O. Box H1305
LAWRENCE 66044
(913) 749-8472
Dr. Gerald E. Gipp, President
Mary Mae Norton, Chair

Administered by the Bureau of Indian Affairs,
under the jurisdiction of the Horton Agency.

KICKAPOO NATION SCHOOL
P.O. Box 106
POWHATTAN 66527
(913) 474-3364
James H. Kennedy, Superintendent
Len Belle Smith, Chair

Day School; Grades K-12. Under jurisdiction of
Anadarko Area Office.

LOUISIANA

CHITIMACHA DAY SCHOOL
Route 2, Box 222
JEANERETTE 70544
(318) 923-4921
John E. Singleton, Principal
Ralph Darden, Chair

Day School; Grades K-8. Under jursidiction of
Choctaw Agency.

MAINE

INDIAN TOWNSHIP SCHOOL
Peter Dana Point
INDIAN TOWNSHIP 04668
(207) 796-5483
James H. Sanborn, Principal
Edward DiCensa, Superintendent

Day School; Grades K-8; Enrollment: 100.
Special course: Passamaquoddy Language/
Culture. *Instructor:* Karen Sabbattus.

INDIAN ISLAND SCHOOL
P.O. Box 566
OLD TOWN 04468
(207) 827-4285
Sr. Helen McKeough, Principal
L. Kenneth Paul, Chair

Day School; Grades K-6. Under jurisdiction of
Eastern Area Office.

BEATRICE RAFFERTY SCHOOL
Pleasant Point Reservation
PERRY 04667
(207) 853-4811
Sr. Maureen Wallace, Principal
Grace Roderick, Chair

Day School; Grades K-8. Under jurisdiction of
Eastern Area Office.

MICHIGAN

HANNAHVILLE INDIAN SCHOOL
Route 1
WILSON 49896
(906) 466-2556
Thomas G. Miller, Administrator
Henry Philemon, Sr., Chair

Day School; Grades K-8. Under jurisdiction of
Minneapolis Area Office.

MINNESOTA

CHIEF BUG-O-NAY-GE SHIG SCHOOL
P.O. Box 308
CASS LAKE 56633
(218) 665-2282
Dr. Kenneth Litzau, Director
Hartley White, Chair

Day School; Grades K-12. Under jurisdiction of
Minneapolis Area Office.

FOND DU LAC OJIBWAY SCHOOL
105 University Rd.
CLOQUET 55720
(218) 879-4593
Donald Wiesen, Director
William J. Houe, Chair

Day School; Grades 7-12. Under jurisdiction of
Minneapolis Area Office.

NAY AH SHING SCHOOL
Star Route
ONAMIA 56359
(612) 532-4181 ext. 53
Lindy S. Grell, Commissioner of Education

Day School; Grades 7-12. *Enrollment:* 35. *Special
courses:* Native American Studies; Cultural
Crafts; Reservation History Curriculum; Native
Ojibwe Language Curriculum; basic core
curriculum. *Instructors:* Millie Benjamin, Lynn
Fischer, Kathy Morrow, Natalie Weyaus, and
Jade Racelo. *Publications: Mille Lacs Nay Ah
Shing School Newsletter; Broken Windows* (book
of poetry, 1980) Under jurisdiction of
Minneapolis Area Office.

CIRCLE OF LIFE SURVIVAL SCHOOL
P.O. Box 447
WHITE EARTH 56591
(218) 983-3285 ext. 269
Karen Brown, Director
Darrell Wadena, Chair

Under jurisdiction of Minneapolis Area Office.

MISSISSIPPI

RED WATER DAY SCHOOL
Route 4, Box 30
CARTHAGE 39051
(601) 267-7447
William F. Bell, Principal

Day School; Grades K-8. Under jurisdiction of
Choctaw Agency.

CONEHATTA DAY SCHOOL
Route 1, Box 331
CONEHATTA 39057
(601) 775-3503
Bruce Marlin, Principal

Day School; Grades K-8. Under jurisdiction of
Choctaw Agency.

BOGUE CHITTO DAY SCHOOL
Route 2, Box 274
PHILADELPHIA 39350
(601) 656-1419
Dr. Dianne Cuchens, Principal

Day School; Grades K-8. Under jurisdiction of
Choctaw Agency.

CHOCTAW CENTRAL SCHOOL
Route 7, Box 72
PHILADELPHIA 39350
(601) 656-7841
Calvin J. Isaac, Principal

Day School; Grades K-12. Under jurisdiction of
Choctaw Agency.

STANDING PINE DAY SCHOOL
Route 2, Box 236
PHILADELPHIA 39350

Day School; Grades K-6. Under jurisdiction of
Choctaw Agency.

TUCKER DAY SCHOOL
Route 4, Box 351
PHILADELPHIA 39350
(601) 656-2619
John W. Brewer, Principal

Day School; Grades K-8. Under jurisdiction of
Choctaw Agency.

MONTANA

LABRE INDIAN SCHOOL
P.O. Box 406
ASHLAND 59003
(406) 784-2347
William D. Walker, Superintendent
Nellie Speelman, Chair

Day School; Grades K-12. Under jurisdiction of
Billings Area Office.

ROCKY BOY'S TRIBAL HIGH SCHOOL
Rocky Boy's Route
BOX ELDER 59521
(406) 395-4270
Edward Parisian, Superintendent
Dorothy Small, Chair

Day School; Grades 9-12. Under jurisdiction of
Billings Area Office.

BLACKFEET DORMITORY
Blackfeet Agency
BROWNING 59417
(406) 338-7441
Leonard L. Guardipee, Supervisor/Guidance

Dormitory School; Grades 1-12. Under
jurisdiction of Billings Area Office.

BUSBY SCHOOL
P.O. Box 38
BUSBY 59016
(406) 592-3646
Robert Bailey, Superintendent
Johnny Russell, Chair

Day School; Grades K-12. Under jurisdiction of
Billings Area Office.

TWO EAGLE RIVER SCHOOL
Star Route, Box 11
DIXON 59831
(406) 246-3598
Richard E. Barber, Principal
Lorena Lawson, Chair

Day School; Grades 9-12. Under jurisdiction of
Portland Area Office.

NEVADA

**DUCKWATER SHOSHONE
ELEMENTARY SCHOOL**
P.O. Box 38
DUCKWATER 89314
(702) 863-0242
Roberta Thompson, Administrator
Kathleen Millett, Chair

Day School; Grades K-8. Under jurisdiction of
Phoenix Area Office.

PYRAMID LAKE HIGH SCHOOL
P.O. Box 241
NIXON 89424
(702) 476-0183
Gordon V. Ruff, Superintendent
Anita Phoenix, Chair

Day School; Grades 9-12. Under jurisdiction of
Phoenix Area Office.

NEW MEXICO

SOUTHWESTERN INDIAN POLYTECHNIC INSTITUTE
P.O. Box 10146, 9169 Coors Rd., NW
ALBUQUERQUE 87184
(505) 766-3197 (Freshman)
(505) 474-3197 (Sophomore)
Robert G. Martin, President
Virgil Wyaco, Chair

Administered by the Bureau of Indian Affairs, under the jurisdiction of Albuquerque Area Office.

AZTEC DORMITORY
P.O. Box W
AZTEC 87410
(505) 334-2711
Jack Nolan, Supervisor
Charley Francis, Chair

Dormitory School; Grades 9-12. Under jurisdiction of Shiprock Agency.

DZILTH-NA-0-DITH-HLE COMMUNITY SCHOOL
P.O. Box 5003
BLOOMFIELD 87413
(505) 632-1697/3674
D. Duane Robinson, Principal
Eugene Guerito, Chair

Boarding School; Grades K-8. Under jurisdiction Eastern Navajo Agency.

HUERFANO DORMITORY
P.O. Box 639
BLOOMFIELD 87413
(505) 325-3007
Daniel W. Fox, Principal
Harry Jack, Chair

Dormitory School; Grades K-12. Under jurisdiction
of Eastern Navajo Agency.

CROWNPOINT COMMUNITY SCHOOL
P.O. Box 178
CROWNPOINT 87313
(505) 786-5342
Joe E. Frazier, Principal
Bobbie Willeto, Chair

Boarding School; Grades K-8. Under jurisdiction
of Eastern Navajo Agency.

DIBE YAZHI HABITIIN OLTA, INC. BORREGO PASS SCHOOL
P.O. Drawer A
CROWNPOINT 87313
(505) 786-5237

Donald D. Creamer, Executive Director
George S. Jim, Chair

Boarding School; Grades K-8. Under jurisdiction
of Eastern Navajo Agency.

LAKE VALLEY NAVAJO SCHOOL
P.O. Drawer E
CROWNPOINT 87313
(505) 786-5392
David J. Atanasoff, Principal
Hoskie Juan, Chair

Boarding School; Grades K-8. Under jurisdiction
of Eastern Navajo Agency.

MARIANO LAKE COMMUNITY SCHOOL
P.O. Box 498
CROWNPOINT 87313
(505) 786-5256
Stanton D. Curtis, Principal
Louise Nez, Chair

Boarding School; Grades K-5. Under jurisdiction
of Eastern Navajo Agency.

STANDING ROCK COMMUNITY SCHOOL
Drawer H
CROWNPOINT 87313
(505) 786-5389
Tito Maryinez, Principal
Jennie Bradley, Chair

Boarding School; Grades K-2. Under jurisdiction
of Eastern Navajo Agency.

NA'NEELZHIIN JI' OLTA[2]
Star Route
CUBA 87013
(505) 731-2272
Harvey Dale Allison, Principal
Charlie Toledo, Chair

Boarding School; Grades K-8. Under jurisdiction
of Eastern Navajo Agency.

OJO ENCINO DAY SCHOOL
P.O. Box 57
CUBA 87013
(505) 731-2333
Richard Toledo, Principal
Jimmy Wellito, Chair

Day School; Grades K-8. Under jurisdiction of
Eastern Navajo Agency.

PUEBLO PINTADO COMMUNITY SCHOOL
Star Rouite 2
CUBA 87013
(505) 655-3341
Clyde David Kannon, Principal
Frank C. Wellito, Chair

Boarding School; Grades K-8. Under jurisdiction
of Eastern Navajo Agency.

JICARILLA DORMITORY
P.O. Box 167
DULCE 87528
(505) 759-3649
Emilio Cordova, Supervisor/Guidance

Dormitory School; Grades K-12. Under jurisdiction of Albuquerque Area Office.

SANTA CLARA DAY SCHOOL
P.O. Box HHH
ESPANOLA 87532
(505) 753-4406
Solomon Padilla, Jr., Principal
Herbert Martinez, Chair

Day School; Grades K-6. Under jurisdiction of Northern Pueblos Agency.

NAVAJO MISSION ACADEMY
1200 West Apache
FARMINGTON 87401
(505) 326-6571
Dillon Platero, Headmaster
Samuel Billison, Chair

Boarding School; Grades 9-12. Under jurisdiction of Shiprock Agency.

WINGATE ELEMENTARY SCHOOL
P.O. Box 1
FORT WINGATE 87316
(505) 488-5466
Beverly J. Crawford, Principal
Leis H. Begay, Chair

Boarding School; Grades 1-8. Under jurisdiction of Eastern Navajo Agency.

WINGATE HIGH SCHOOL
P.O. Box 2
FORT WINGATE 87316
(505) 488-5402/5403
Jay Bruce Hoover, Principal
Raymond Morgan, Chair

Boarding School; Grades 9-12. Under jurisdiction of Eastern Navajo Agency.

NENAHNEZAD BOARDING SCHOOL
P.O. Box 337
FRUITLAND 87416
(505) 598-6922
Kenneth L. Benally, Supervisor
Jay Vazzie, Sr., Chair

Boarding School; Grades K-6. Under jurisdiction of Shiprock Agency.

BREAD SPRINGS DAY SCHOOL
P.O. Box 1117
GALLUP 87301
(505) 778-5665
Jerry V. Collins, Principal
Gilbert Morgan, Chair

Day School; Grades K-3. Under jurisdiction of Eastern Navajo Agency.

ISLETA ELEMENTARY SCHOOL
P.O. Box 312
ISLETA 87022
(505) 869-2321
Mary McBride, Principal
Mike Jiron, Chair

Day School; Grades K-6. *Enrollment:* 254. *Instructors:* Joyce Flournoy, Sofia Sanchez, Ethel Trujillo, Pauline Gallegos, and Mike Jojola. *Publication: Isleta Eagle Pride,* newspaper. Under jurisdiction of Southern Pueblos Agency.

JEMEZ DAY SCHOOL
P.O. Box 238
JEMEZ PUEBLO 87024
(505) 834-7304
Dr. Juanita Complo, Principal
Gloria Fragua, Chair

Day School; Grades K-6. Under jurisdiction of Southern Pueblos Agency.

LAGUNA ELEMENTARY SCHOOL
P.O. Box 191
LAGUNA 87026
(505) 552-9200
Robert Pacheco, Principal
Malcomb Pedro, Chair

Day School; Grades K-6. Under jurisdiction of Laguna Agency.

TO'HAJIILEE-HE[3]
P.O. Box 438
LAGUNA 87026
(505) 831-6426
John D. Wahnee, Principal
Art Platero, Chair

Boarding School; Grades K-12. Under jurisdiction of Eastern Navajo Agency.

ALAMAO NAVAJO SCHOOL
P.O. Box 907
MAGDALENA 87825
(505) 854-2543
Dr. William O. Berlin, Executive Director
Walter Apachito, Chair

Day School; Grades K-12. Under jurisdiction of Eastern Navajo Agency.

MAGDALENA DORMITORY
P.O. Box 385
MAGDALENA 87825
(505) 854-2503
John A. Blomquist, Principal
Loli Gonadanegro, Chair

Dormitory School; Grades 1-12. Under jurisdiction of Eastern Navajo Agency.

CRYSTAL BOARDING SCHOOL
NAVAJO 87328
(505) 777-2385
David S. Jones, Principal
Mary Stevens, Chair

Boarding School; Grades K-6. Under jurisdiction of Fort Defiance Agency.

PINE HILL SCHOOLS
CPO Drawer H
PINE HILL 87321
(505) 755-3241
Anna Mae Pino, Director of Education
Chavez Coho, Chair

Boarding School; Grades K-12. Under jurisdiction of Albuquerque Area Office,

BACA COMMUNITY SCHOOL
P.O. Box 509
PREWITT 87045
(505) 876-2969
Beatrice L. Charlie, Principal
Hoskie Largo, Chair

Boarding School; Grades K-1. Under jurisdiction of Eastern Navajo Agency.

SAN FELIPE DAY SCHOOL
P.O. Box E
SAN FELIPE PUEBLO 87001
(505) 867-3364
Edward Doler, Principal
Henry Esquibel, Chair

Day School; Grades K-6. Under jurisdiction of Southern Pueblos Agency.

SKY CITY COMMUNITY SCHOOL
P.O. Box 97
SAN FIDEL 87049
(505) 552-6671
Cyrus J. Chino, Principal
Carl Valley, Chair

Day School; Grades K-8. Under jurisdiction of Southern Pueblos Agency.

SAN JUAN DAY SCHOOL
P.O. Box 1077
SAN JUAN PUEBLO 87566
(505) 582-2154
Malinda M. Pekarchik, Principal
Pauline Antoine, Chair

Day School; Grades K-6. Under jurisdiction of Northern Pueblos Agency.

ZIA DAY SCHOOL
SAN YSIDRO 87053
(505) 867-3553
Gilbert Lucero, Principal
Celestino Gachupin, Chair

Day School; Grades K-6. Under jurisdiction of Southern Pueblos Agency.

SANOSTEE DAY SCHOOL
SANOSTEE 87461
(505) 723-2476
James Mosher, Supervisor
Eddie Mike, Chair

Day School; Grades K-1. Under jurisdiction of Shiprock Agency.

SAN ILDEFONSO DAY SCHOOL
Route 5, Box 308
SANTA FE 87501
(505) 455-2366
Kathleen M. Sanchez, Principal
Gov. Jay Mountain, Chair

Day School; Grades 1-6. Under jurisdiction of Northern Pueblos Agency.

SANTA FE INDIAN SCHOOL
1300 Cerrillos Rd.
SANTA FE 87501
(505) 988-6291
Joseph Abeyta, Sr., Superintendent
Herbert Yates, Chair

Boarding School; Grades 7-12. Under jurisdiction of Albuquerque Area Office.

TESUQUE DAY SCHOOL
Route 11, Box 2
SANTA FE 87501
(505) 982-1516
Dolly Smith, Principal
Tony Dorame, Chair

Day School; Grades 1-6. Under jurisdiction of Northern Pueblos Agency.

BECLABITO DAY SCHOOL
P.O. Box 1146
SHIPROCK 87420
(602) 656-3215
Heber C. Black, Supervisor
Bruce Billy, Chair

Day School; Grades K-4. Under jurisdiction of Shiprock Agency.

COVE DAY SCHOOL
P.O. Box 190
SHIPROCK 87420
(602) 653-4457
Lucy Mae Roanhorse, Supervisor
Ruby Tsosie, Chair

Day School; Grades K-6. Under jurisdiction of Shiprock Agency.

CHARLES RENK ELEMENTARY SCHOOL
c/o Shiprock Alternative High School
P.O. Box 1799
SHIPROCK 87420
(505) 368-4904/5145
Kenneth Nabahe, Director
Lucy Keeswood, Chair

Day School; Grade K. Under jurisdiction
of Shiprock Agency.

**SHIPROCK ALTERNATIVE
HIGH SCHOOL**
P.O. Box 1799
SHIPROCK 87420
(505) 368-5144
Kenneth Nabahe, Director
Lucy Keeswood, Chair

Boarding School; Grades 9-12. Under jurisdiction
of Shiprock Agency.

SHIPROCK RESERVATION DORMITORY
P.O. Box 1180
SHIPROCK 87420
(505) 368-5114
Betty Yabeny, Supervisor
Virgil L. Kirk, Sr., Chair

Dormitory School; Grades K-12. Under
jurisdiction of Shiprock Agency.

TAOS DAY SCHOOL
P.O. Box Drawer X
TAOS 87571
(505) 758-3652
Roy French, Principal
Janice Mirabel, Chair

Day School; Grades K-8. Under jurisdiction
of Northern Pueblos Agency.

DLO'AY AZHI COMMUNITY SCHOOL
P.O. Box 789
THOREAU 87323
(505) 862-7525
Amy W. Mathis, Principal
Lena Miller, Chair

Boarding School; Grades K-5. Under jurisdiction
of Eastern Navajo Agency.

TOADLENA BOARDING SCHOOL
TOADLENA 87324
(505) 789-3205
Jeanne Haskie, Supervisor
Leonard Begaye, Chair

Boarding School; Grades K-8. Under jurisdiction
of Shiprock Agency.

**CHUSKA/TOHATCHI
CONSOLIDATED SCHOOL**
P.O. Box 321
TOHATCHI 87325

(505) 733-2280
Dr. Helen Zongolowicz, Principal
Richard Bowman, Chair

Boarding School; Grades K-8. Under jurisdiction
of Fort Defiance Agency.

CHI-CH'IL TAH COMMUNITY SCHOOL
P.O. Box 365
VANDERWAGEN 87326
(505) 778-5591
John L. Taylor, Principal
Margie Willie, Chair

Day School; Grades K-4. Under jurisdiction
of Eastern Navajo Agency.

JONES RANCH DAY SCHOOL
Zuni Route
VANDERWAGEN 87326
(505) 778-5573
John L. Taylor, Principal
Kee Houston, Chair

Day School; Grades K-4. Under jurisdiction
of Eastern Navajo Agency.

NORTH CAROLINA

CHEROKEE CENTRAL SCHOOL
CHEROKEE 28719
(704) 497-9131/5511 ext. 274
Richard Sneed, Chair

Day School; Grades K-12. *Enrollment:*
Approximately 1,500. Under jurisdiction of
Eastern Area Office.

NORTH DAKOTA

OJIBWA INDIAN SCHOOL
P.O. Box A-3
BELCOURT 58316
(701) 477-3108
Sr. Judith Emge, Executive Director
Marilyn Delorme, Chair

Boarding School; Grades K-8. Under jurisdiction
of Turtle Mountain Agency.

**TURTLE MOUNTAIN COMMUNITY
ELEMENTARY AND MIDDLE SCHOOL**
BELCOURT 58316
(701) 477-6471 ext. 270
Elner C. Monson, Elementary Principal
Louis Dauphinais, Middle Principal
Daniel F. Jerome, Superintendent

Day School; Grades K-8. Under jurisdiction of
Turtle Mountain Agency.

**TURTLE MOUNTAIN
COMMUNITY HIGH SCHOOL**
BELCOURT 58316
(701) 477-6471 ext. 222
Dr. Duane Schindler, Principal
Daniel F. Jerome, Superintendent

Day School; Grades 9-12. *Enrollment:* 405.
Special courses: Vocational (building, welding,
health, distributive education); special education
(speech and emotionally disturbed.) *Instructors:*
Verlin Allery, Robert Marion, Marilyn Dionne,
Frank Bercier, Tilmer Ruff, Louise Fraser, Marie
Hanson, Kristi Ammerman, Sharon Rance, Mary
Glover, and Tom Glover. Library.

**THEODORE JAMERSON
ELEMENTARY SCHOOL**
3315 South Airport Rd.
BISMARCK 58501
(701) 255-3285 ext. 305
Joan R. Estes, Principal
Melvin White Eagle, Chair

Boarding School; Grades K-8. Under jurisdiction
of Aberdeen Area Office.

DUNSEITH DAY SCHOOL
P.O. Box 310
DUNSEITH 58371
(701) 263-4636
Karen J. Gillis, Principal
Joyce Fandrick, Chair

Day School; Grades K-6. Under jurisdiction of
Turtle Mountain Agency.

FOUR WINDS COMMUNITY SCHOOL
P.O. Box 199
FORT TOTTEN 58335
(701) 766-4161
Terry Yellow Fat, Principal
Paul Yankton, Chair

Day School; Grades K-6. Under jurisdiction of
Fort Totten Agency.

STANDING ROCK COMMUNITY SCHOOL
P.O. Box 377
FORT YATES 58538
(701) 854-3865 (K-6)
(701) 854-3461 (7-12)
Linda Lawrence, Elementary Principal
Roman Weiler, High School Principal

Boarding School; Grades K-12. *Enrollment:*
approximately 800. Under jurisdiction of
Standing Rock Agency.

TWIN BUTTES DAY SCHOOL
HALLIDAY 58636
(701) 938-4396
Barbara Thronson, Administrator
Eugene Holen, Chair

Day School; Grades K-8. Under jurisdiction of
Fort Berthold Agency.

MANDAREE DAY SCHOOL
MANDAREE 58757
(701) 759-3311
Frank Taylor, Superintendent
Leroy Young Bird, Chair

Day School; Grades K-12. Under jurisdiction
of Fort Berthold Agency.

WHITE SHIELD SCHOOL
ROSEGLEN 58775
(701) 743-4350
Ron Hauf, Principal
Edmund White Bear, Chair

Day School; Grades K-12. Under jurisdiction
of Fort Berthold Agency.

WAHPETON INDIAN BOARDING SCHOOL
WAHPETON 58075
(701) 642-3796
Leroy W. Chief, Superintendent
Willard Yellow Bird, Sr., Chair

Boarding School; Grades 4-8. Under jurisdiction
of Aberdeen Area Office.

OKLAHOMA

RIVERSIDE INDIAN SCHOOL
P.O. Box 489
ANADARKO 73005
(405) 247-6673 ext. 323
Ray Tahsuda, Principal
Jack McLane, Chair

Boarding School; Grades 2-12. Under jurisdiction
of Anadarko Area Office.

CARTER SEMINARY
P.O. Box 1268
ARDMORE 73401
(405) 223-8547
Dalton Henry, Administrator
Pat Woods, Chair

Dormitory School; Grades 1-12. Under
jurisdiction of Muskogee Area Office.

EUFAULA DORMITORY
P.O. Box 466
EUFAULA 74432
(918) 689-2522
Van McIntosh, Administrator
Mark Downing, Chair

Dormitory School; Grades 1-12. Under
jurisdiction of Muskogee Area Office.

JONES ACADEMY
Route 1
HARTSHORNE 74547
(918) 297-2518
Delton Cox, Home Living Specialist
Ramona Allen, Chair

Dormitory School; Grades 1-12. Under jurisdiction of Muskogee Area Office.

SEQUOYAH HIGH SCHOOL
P.O. Box 558
TAHLEQUAH 74464
(918) 456-0631
Nadine Givens, Principal
Don Crittenden, Chair

Boarding School; Grades 9-12. Under jurisdiction of Muskogee Area Office.

OREGON

CHEMAWA INDIAN SCHOOL
3700 Chemawa Rd., N.E.
SALEM 97303
(503) 393-4511
Gerald J. Gray, Principal
V. Mae Taylor, Chair

Boarding School; Grades 9-12. Under jurisdiction of Portland Area Office.

SOUTH DAKOTA

AMERICAN HORSE SCHOOL
P.O. Box 448
ALLEN 57714
(605) 455-2480
Ronald L. Riggs, Principal
Raymond Whirlwind Horse, Chair

Day School; Grades K-8. Under jurisdiction of Pine Ridge Agency.

BULLHEAD DAY SCHOOL
BULLHEAD 57621
(605) 823-4971
Michael Downer, Principal
Charles Red Bear, Chair

Day School; Grades K-8. Under jurisdiction of Standing Rock Agency.

CHERRY CREEK DAY SCHOOL
CHERRY CREEK 57622
(605) 538-4238
Faye Longbrake, Principal
Roland Roach, Chair

Day School; Grades K-6. Under jurisdiction of Cheyenne River Agency.

CHEYENNE-EAGLE BUTTE SCHOOL
EAGLE BUTTE 57625
(605) 964-8744
Jerry Smith, Principal
Jerry Farlee, Chair

Boarding School; Grades K-12. *Enrollment:* 900. Under jurisdiction of Cheyenne River Agency.

RED SCAFFOLD SCHOOL
Star Route 97
FAITH 57626
(605) 538-4315
Dr. Cherie Farlee, Executive Director
Brian Charging Cloud, Chair

Day School; Grades 1-8. Under jurisdiction of Cheyenne River Agency.

FLANDREAU INDIAN SCHOOL
FLANDREAU 57028
(605) 997-2451
Jack Belkham, Principal
Berle Johnson, Home Living Director
Cynthia Kipp, Chair

Boarding School; Grades 9-12. *Enrollment:* 750. Under jurisdiction of Aberdeen Area Office.

FORT THOMPSON ELEMENTARY SCHOOL
FORT THOMPSON 57339
(605) 245-2372
Dan Shroyer, Principal
Rose Sazue, Chair

Day School; Grades K-6. *Enrollment:* 200. Under jurisdiction of Crow Creek Agency.

SWIFT BIRD DAY SCHOOL
Route 3
GETTYSBURG 57442
(605) 733-2143
Dr. Asad Khan, Principal
Ellsworth Brown, Jr., Chair

Day School; Grades 1-6. Under jurisdiction of Cheyenne River Agency.

BRIDGER DAY SCHOOL
HOWES 57748
(605) 538-4313
Faye Longbrake, Principal
Ted Buffalo, Chair

Day School; Grades 1-6. Under jurisdiction of Cheyenne River Agency.

LITTLE WOUND DAY SCHOOL
KYLE 57752
(605) 455-2461
Dr. Ray Phipps, Director
Delano Featherman, Chair

Day School; Grades K-12. *Enrollment:* 500. Under jurisdiction of Pine Ridge Agency.

LITTLE EAGLE DAY SCHOOL
LITTLE EAGLE 57639
(605) 823-4235
Adele F. Little Dog, Principal
Magdelena Red Legs, Chair

Day School; Grades 1-8. *Enrollment:* 100.
Under jurisdiction of Standing Rock Agency.

LOWER BRULE DAY SCHOOL
P.O. Box 315
LOWER BRULE 57548
(605) 473-5658 (Elementary)
(605) 473-5510 (Secondary)
Dan Yost, Elementary Principal
Jerry Johnson, Secondary Principal

Day School; Grades K-12. *Enrollment:* 225.
Under jurisdiction of Lower Brule Agency.

MANDERSON DAY SCHOOL
MANDERSON 57756
(605) 867-5433
Donald R. Wince, Principal
John Her Many Horses, Chair

Day School; Grades K-8. *Enrollment:* 225.
Under jurisdiction of Pine Ridge Agency.

MARTY INDIAN SCHOOL
P.O. Box A
MARTY 57361
(605) 384-5431
Richard Christensen, Superintendent
Lynda Cooke, Chair

Boarding School; Grades K-12. Under
jurisdiction of Aberdeen Area Office.

ROSEBUD DORMITORIES
P.O. Box 669
MISSION 57555
(605) 856-4486
Leland M. Bordeaux, Home Living Specialist
Sylvia Konop, Chair

Dormitory School; Grades 1-12. *Enrollment:* 250.
Under jurisdiction of Rosebud Agency.

PROMISE DAY SCHOOL
MOBRIDGE 57601
(605) 733-2148
Dr. Asad Khan, Principal
Tony Rivers, Jr., Chair

Day School; Grades 1-6. Under jurisdiction of
Cheyenne River Agency.

LONEMAN DAY SCHOOL
OGLALA 57764
(605) 867-5633
Duane Ross, Principal
Stanley Starr, Chair

Day School; Grades K-8. Under jurisdiction
of Pine Ridge Agency.

PIERRE INDIAN LEARNING CENTER
Star Route 3
PIERRE 57501
(605) 224-8661
A. Gay Kingman, Superintendent
Al Zephier, Chair

Boarding School; Grades 1-8. *Enrollment:* 100.
Special courses: Special education school for
children with learning disabilities or emotional
problems. Contract school serving 15 reservations
in North and South Dakota, and Nebraska.
Under the jurisdiction of Aberdeen Area Office.

PINE RIDGE SCHOOL
PINE RIDGE 57770
(605) 867-5198
Benjamin R. Tyon, Principal
Crystal Eagle Elk, Chair

Boarding School; Grades K-12. *Enrollment:*
1,000. Under jurisdiction of Pine Ridge Agency.

RED CLOUD INDIAN SCHOOL
Holy Rosary Mission
PINE RIDGE 57770
(605) 867-5491
Rev. E.J. Kurth, S.J., Superintendent

Boarding School; Grades K-12. *Special program:*
Montessori pre-school (ages 3 and up, including
some first graders.)

PORCUPINE DAY SCHOOL
P.O. Box 180
PORCUPINE 57772
(605) 867-5336
Marvin W. Waldner, Principal
Orland Big Owl, Chair

Day School; Grades K-8. Under jurisdiction
of Pine Ridge Agency

ST. FRANCIS INDIAN SCHOOL
P.O. Box 155
ST. FRANCIS 57572
(605) 747-2296
Roger C. Bordeaux, Executive Director
Manley Night Pipe, Chair

Boarding School; Grades K-12. Under
jurisdiction of Rosebud Agency.

**CROW CREEK RESERVATION
HIGH SCHOOL**
STEPHAN 57346
(605) 852-2455
Dr. Donald Ross, Superintendent
Wally Wells, Chair

Boarding School; Grades 7-12. Under jurisdiction
of Crow Creek Agency.

CRAZY HORSE SCHOOL
P.O. Box 296
WANBLEE 57577
  (605) 462-6511
  Charles Maxon, Director
  Ward J. Williams, Chair

Day School; Grades K-12. Under jurisdiction
of Pine Ridge Agency.

ENEMY SWIM DAY SCHOOL
RR 2
WAUBAU 57442
  (605) 947-4605
  Cecil Phillips, Principal
  Donna O'Riley, Chair

Day School; Grades K-3. Under jurisdiction
of Sisseton Agency.

WHITE HORSE DAY SCHOOL
WHITE HORSE 57661
  (605) 733-2383
  Dr. Asad Khan, Principal
  Francis Rousseau, Chair

Day School; Grades 1-8. Under jurisdiction
of Cheyenne River Agency.

UTAH

ANETH COMMUNITY SCHOOL
ANETH 84510
  (801) 651-3271
  Eva M. Benally, Supervisor
  Eugene Etsitty, Chair

Boarding School; Grades K-6. Under jurisdiction
of Shiprock Agency.

RICHFIELD DORMITORY
P.O. Box 664
RICHFIELD 84701
  (801) 896-5101
  Kevin Skenandore, Supervisor
  Anna Kelly, Chair

Dormitory School; Grades 9-12. Under
jurisdiction of Western Navajo Agency.

WASHINGTON

LUMMI TRIBAL SCHOOL
1790 Bayon Rd.
BELLINGHAM 98225
  (206) 733-7211
  Russell Alway, Principal
  Earl Thomas, Chair

Day School; Grades K, 7-8. Under jurisdiction
of Portland Area Office.

QUILEUTE TRIBAL SCHOOL
P.O. Box 279
LaPUSH 98350
  (206) 374-6163
  Stephen F. Vause, Superintendent
  Helen Harrison, Chair

Day School; Grades K-8. Under jurisdiction
of Portland Area Office.

WA-HE-LUT INDIAN SCHOOL
11110 Conine Ave., S.E.
OLYMPIA 98503
  (206) 456-1311
  Angela A. Begay, Pricnipal

Day School; Grades K-8. *Enrollment:* 36.
Instructors: Clayton Conway, Susan
Schumacher, and Evelyn Ren. *Special program:*
Cultural Enrichment Program. Under
jurisdiction of Portland Area Office.

PASCHAL SHERMAN INDIAN SCHOOL
Omak Lake Rd.
OMAK 98841
  (509) 826-2097
  Jerry Bergloff, Superintendent
  Lottie Hanway, Chair

Boarding School; Grades K-9. Under jurisdiction
of Portland Area Office.

**PUYALLUP NATION
EDUCATION SYSTEM**
2002 East 28th St.
TACOMA 98404
  (206) 597-6210
  Sasha Soboleff, Supoerintendent
  Frank Wright, Jr., Chair

Day School; Grades K-12. Under jurisdiction
of Portland Area Office.

YAKIMA TRIBAL SCHOOL
P.O. Box 151
TOPPENISH 98948
(509) 865-5121
  Martha B. Yallup, Chief School Supt.
  Melvin Sampson, Chair

Day School; Grades K, 7-12. Under jurisdiction
of Portland Area Office.

WISCONSIN

**LAC COURTE OREILLES
OJIBWA SCHOOL**
Route 2
HAYWARD 54843
(715) 634-8924
  Mike Gross, Administrator
  Gordon Thayer, Chair

Day School; Grades K-12. Under jurisdiction
of Minneapolis Area Office.

ONEIDA TRIBAL SCHOOL
P.O. Box 365
ONEIDA 54155-0365
(414) 869-2795
  William Gollnick, Administrator
  Gary Metoxen, Chair

Day School; Grades K-8. Under jurisdiction
of Minneapolis Area Office.

WYOMING

WYOMING INDIAN HIGH SCHOOL
ETHETE 82520

ST. STEPHENS INDIAN SCHOOL
P.O. Box 345
ST. STEPHEN 82524
(307) 856-4147
  Louis Headley, Superintendent
  John A. Warren, Sr., Chair

Boarding School; Grades K-12. Under
jurisdiction of Billings Area Office.

COLLEGE COURSES

This section, alpha-geographically arranged, lists departments and personnel of various institutions of higher learning which offer courses on the American Indian. Includes both Indian colleges, and universities with Native Studies Departments, departments of anthropology, and other departments offering related courses.

ALASKA

ANCHORAGE COMMUNITY COLLEGE
2533 Providence Ave.
ANCHORAGE 99504
(907) 263-1653/1536

Department: Anthropology; *Instructors:* Douglas W. Veltre, Ph.D., John E. Lobdell, Ph.D., and Robert A. Mack.

UNIVERSITY OF ALASKA
3211 Providence Dr.
ANCHORAGE 99508
(907) 786-1375

Department: Anthropology; *Instructors:* William B. Workman, Ph.D., Chair; Steve Conn, J.D.; and Arthur E. Hippler, Ph.D., Institute of Social and Economic Research.

UNIVERSITY OF ALASKA
College of Liberal Arts
FAIRBANKS 99701
(907) 474-7288

Departments: Department of Anthropology; and Department of Alaskan Native Studies. *Courses:* Native Cultures of North America, South America, and Alaska; Arctic and New World Prehistory; Biology of Arctic Peoples; seminars on specialized aspects of Eskimo, Aleut, and Athapaskan groups. *Instructors:* Jean S. Aigner, Ph.D., Lydia Black, Ph.D., Joseph J. Gross, Ph.D., W. Rogers Powers, Ph.D., Ann D. Shinkwin, Ph.D., Dean of College, G. Richard Scott, Ph.D., Head of Department. *Programs:* Graduate and faculty research is primarily directed to the study of Eskimo-Aleuts and North American Indians (their prehistory, cultural variability, and human biology); teaching assistantships to graduate students. *Affiliated facilities:* University of Alaska Museum; Alaska Native Language Center. *Publications:* Anthropological Papers of the University of Alaska.

ISLAND COMMUNITY COLLEGE
1101 Sawmill Creek Blvd.
SITKA 99835

Department: Alaska Native History. *Instructor:* Frank O. Williams.

SHELDON JACKSON COLEGE
SITKA 99835

Native Studies Program.

ARIZONA

NORTHERN ARIZONA UNIVERSITY
FLAGSTAFF 86011
(602) 523-4521

Departments: Native American Indian Studies Program; and Anthropology. Courses: Native American Indian History; Contemporary U.S. Indians; Southwest Ethnology: Pueblo and non-Pueblo; Tribal Law and Government; Financing Tribal Government and Administration; Tribal Planning and Management; Current Issues in Tribal Administration. *Instructors: Reed D. Riner, Ph.D., Advisor to Program; Joanne W. Kealiinohomoku, Ph.D., P. David Seaman, Ph.D., David R. Wilcox, Ph.D., Ross L. Wooduff, Ph.D. Special program:* Native American United Club. *Affiliated facilities:* Museum of Northern Arizona; Native Americans for Community Action, Flagstaff.

COLLEGE OF GANADO
GANADO 86505
(602) 755-3442
Daniel Honahni, President

Departments: Anthropology/Archaeology-Donna Rosh, Head; Humanities-Marvin Jacobs, Head. *Courses:* Indians of North America; Contemporary Native American Issues and Affairs; Field Courses in Archaeology (Navajo, Hopi, and Tewa tribes); Navajo Studies. *Scholarships:* Title IV funding programs; and institutional grants and scholarships.

AMERICAN INDIAN BIBLE COLLEGE
100020 North 25th Ave.
PHOENIX 85021
(602) 944-3335
Carl Collins, President

ARIZONA STATE UNIVERSITY
TEMPE 85287
(602) 965-6213

Department: Anthropology. *Division:* Indian Education; American Indian Linguistics; and

Center for Indian Affairs. *Instructors (partial):* Elizabeth A. Brandt, Ph.D., Robert F. Bruenig, Ph.D., Kathleen M. Sands, Ph.D. (Dept. of English). *Facilities:* Heard Museum; Pueblo Grande Museum; A.A. Dahlberg Memorial Colection of 9,000 Pima Indian dental casts and genealogies.

EASTERN ARIZONA COLLEGE
626 Church St.
THATCHER 85552

NAVAJO COMMUNITY COLLEGE
Rural Post Office
TSAILE 86556
(602) 724-3311
Dean Jackson, President

Department: Navajo and Indian Studies Program. Offers many courses in the broad area of Navajo studies; some are directly related to the Navajo, and others are related to Indians in general. *Courses (partial):* Navajo History and Culture; Navajo Language; American Indian Economic Development; The Urban Indians; Navajo Crafts courses. *Instructors (partial):* Wilson Aronilth, Jr., and Lorraine C. Begay, *Programs:* Special Services Program for academically unprepared students; Learning Center provides tutorial services for students. *Scholarships:* For information, contact the Financial Aide Office, ext. 223/224. *Facility:* College Library houses the Moses Donner Indian Collection. *Branch:* Shiprock Branch, P.O. Box 580, Shiprock 87420.

UNIVERSITY OF ARIZONA
TUCSON 85721
(602) 621-2585/2966

Departments: Anthropology-American Indian Studies; Linguistics—special programs in American Indian languages; Bureau of Applied Research in Anthropology. *Instructors:* Jane E. Hill, Ph.D.; Earl W. Jernigan, Ph.D.; James E. Officer, Ph.D.; Susan U. Philips, Ph.D.; Daniel S. Matson, M.A.; Clara Lee Tanner, M.A.; Keith H. Basso, Ph.D.; Raymond H. Thompson, Ph.D., Director of Arizona State Museum; Gordon V. Krutz, M.A.; Thomas R. McGuire, Ph.D.; Emory Sekaquaptewa, J.D. *Programs:* Archaeological Field School. *Facilities:* Western Archaeologicl Center; Arizona State Museum.

ARIZONA WESTERN COLLEGE
YUMA 85364

ARKANSAS

UNIVERSITY OF ARKANSAS
FAYETTEVILLE 72701
(501) 575-2508

Department: Anthropology. *Courses:* American Indians Today; Indians of Arkansas and the South; North American Prehistory. *Instructors:* Michael P. Hoffman, Ph.D.; Marvin Kay, Ph.D. *Program:* Archaeological Field School. *Scholarships:* Arkansas residency for tuition purposes to tribes which once lived in the State (Caddo, Cherokee, Choctaw, Osage, and Quapaw. *Facility:* University of Arkansas Museum.

CALIFORNIA

HUMBOLDT STATE UNIVERSITY
THE CENTER FOR COMMUNITY
DEVELOPMENT
ARCATA 95521
(707) 826-3711
Tom Parsons, Director

American Indian Languages and Literature Program: The program first adapted an internationally acknowledged, easy-to-learn, uniphonetic alphabet to write Indian languages precisely, and then schooled fluent local speakers in its use and dissemination. The program has enabled four northwestern California tribes to salvage their venerable literatures; publish them in tribally compiled textbooks; document their (pre-history); and, record and compile their traditional music. The Program has produced five internationally acclaimed documentary films explicating this complex cultural regenerative process; and organize these elements into curricula for use in preschool, elementary and secondary schools, and in college and unversity classrooms. A scholarly curriculum was created in an intertribal network of American Indian community development projects. The California Department of Education recognized the program, and the most eminent (generally elderly) Indian graduates were given credentials to teach in the public schools and colleges. *Special program:* Special project/lectureship stipends and bilingual teacher training internships. Publications. Library (primarily own publications, such as Indian language and literature texts, and American Indian bilingual teacher training instructional materials.)

UNIVERSITY OF CALIFORNIA
BERKELEY 94720
(415) 642-3391

Departments: Anthropology-William S. Simmons, Ph.D., Secrectary, Executive Committee; Linguistics-Mary Haas, Ph.D.; Ethnic/Native American Studies—*Instructors (partial):* Terry P. Wilson, Ph.D., Clara Sue Kidwell, Ph.D., and Marcia A. Herndon, Ph.D. *Publications:* Papers of the Kroeber Anthropological Association. *Facility:* Lowie Museum of Anthropology.

D.Q. UNIVERSITY
P.O. Box 409
DAVIS 95616
(916) 758-0470
Carlos Cordero, President

A University dedicated to the progress of the Native-American and Chicano people.

UNIVERSITY OF CALIFORNIA
DAVIS 95616

Department: Native American Studies. *Instructors (partial):* Jack D. Forbes, Ph.D., Sarah H. Hutchison, Ph.D., and George C. Longfish, Ph.D.

CALIFORNIA STATE UNIVERSITY
HAYWARD 94542

Department: Native American Studies.

CALIFORNIA STATE UNIVERSITY
1250 Bellflower Blvd.
LONG BEACH 90840
(213) 498-5171

Department: Anthropology. *Special program:* Certificates in American Indian Studies. *Instructors (partial):* Dorothy Libby, Ph.D., and R. Clyde McCone, Ph.D.

AMERICAN INDIAN STUDIES CENTER
UNIVERSITY OF CALIFORNIA
3220 Campbell Hall
LOS ANGELES 90024
(213) 825-7315
Dr. Charlotte Heth, Director

Coordinates educational, research, and action-oriented programs designed to meet the needs of American Indian students at UCLA and the American Indian communities in general. *Activities:* Encourages the development of new courses; promotes hiring of Native American faculty; sponsors research on American Indians; publishes journals, books, monographs, and other media reflecting contemporary Indian research and issues. *Staff:* Dr. Anthony D. Brown, Assistant Director; Marie Shepherd, Administrative Assistant; Donna Kuyiyesva,

Secretary; Judy Takata, Conference Coordinator; Earl Dean Sisto, Coordinator of Student/Community Relations; Velma Salabiye; Librarian; William Oandasan, Coordinator of Publications; Dr. Lenore A. Stiffarm-Noriega, Coordinator of Research Development and Extramural Funding. *Program:* Administers an Interdepartmental M.A. Program in American Indian Studies. *Instructors:* Duane Champagne (Sociology); Jennie Joe (Anthropology); Charlotte Heth (Music). *Fellowships:* Postdoctoral Fellowships in American Indian Studies. *Facilities:* The Museum of Cultural History; Library.

CALIFORNIA STATE UNIVERSITY
18111 Nordhoff St.
NORTHRIDGE 91330
(818) 885-3331

Department: Anthropology. *Program:* American Indian Studies Program. *Instructor:* Beatrice Medicine, Ph.D.

SONOMA STATE UNIVERSITY
1801 East Cotati Ave.
ROHNERT PARK 94928
(707) 664-2312

Departments: Anthropology; Native American Studies; American Multi-Cultural Studies. *Courses:* Indians of California, North America, and Southwest; Native American Philosophic Systems; Archaeology of California; Seminar of California Indian Communities. *Instructors:* David A. Frederickson, Ph.D., Shirley K. Silver, Ph.D., Albert L. Wahrhaftig, Ph.D., and David W. Peri, B.A. *Facilities:* Archaeology and ethnography labs and archives.

CALIFORNIA STATE UNIVERSITY
6000 Jay St.
SACRAMENTO 95819
(916) 454-6452

Department: Anthropology. *Special program:* California Indian Studies. *Instructors:* Warren A. Snyder, Ph.D., Dorothea J. Theodoratus, Ph.D., and Valerie Wheeler, Ph.D.

SAN DIEGO STATE UNIVERSITY
SAN DIEGO 92182

Department: Native American Studies.

SAN FRANCISCO STATE UNIVERSITY
1600 Holloway Ave.
SAN FRANCISCO 94132
(415) 469-2046

Departments: American Indian Studies; Anthropology. *Instructors: John Adair, Ph.D., Luis S. Kemnitzer, Ph.D., and Mary Shepardson, Ph.D. Program:* On-going research project in physical anthropology of California Indians.

Facility: The Adan E. Treganza Anthropology Museum.

PALOMAR COLLEGE
1140 West Mission
SAN MARCOS 92069

Department: American Indian Studies.

COLORADO

ADAMS STATE COLLEGE
ALAMOSA 81102

COLORADO COLLEGE
COLORADO SPRINGS 80903
(303) 473-2233 ext. 358

Department: Anthropology. *Instructors:* Paul Kutsche, Ph.D., Marianne L. Stoller, Ph.D., Pauline Turner Strong, M.A., Barrik Van Winkle, M.A., Laurel J. Watkins, Ph.D., H. Marie Wormington, Ph.D., and Linda J. Goodman, Ph.D. (Music). *Facility:* Alice Bemis Taylor Museum.

FORT LEWIS COLLEGE—DIVISION OF INTERCULTURAL STUDIES
120 Miller Student Center
DURANGO 81301
    Mary Jean Mosely, Director

Courses: Native American and Southwest Studies. *Activities:* Hozhoni Days—a celebration sponsored by the Indian Club for sharing Native-American culture with students and faculty on campus. *Scholarships:* Tuition waiver for Native-American students certified by their respective tribes. *Facility:* The Center for Southwest Studies—a research oriented center holding collections of documents focused on various regional topics including the American Indian. *Publication: Wamidiota Newsletter.*

COLORADO STATE UNIVERSITY NATIVE AMERICAN STUDENT SERVICES
317 Student Services Bldg.
FORT COLLINS 80523
    (303) 491-1332
    Mr. Francis D. Becenti, Director

Provides support services for Native-American students of Colorado State University. *Programs:* Recruiting; orientation; skill development workshops; tutorial assistance; employment opportunity advisement; financial aid assistance; peer counseling; social and cultural activities.

CONNECTICUT

WESLEYAN UNIVERSITY
MIDDLETOWN 06457
(203) 347-9411

Department: Anthropology. *Courses:* Ethnography of Southeastern, Southwestern and Northeastern U.S.; Native American Music. *Instructors:* Willard Walker, Ph.D., and David McAllester, Ph.D. (Music).

DISTRICT OF COLUMBIA

THE AMERICAN UNIVERSITY
4400 Massachusetts Ave., N.W.
WASHINGTON 20016
(202) 885-1830
William L. Leap, Ph.D., Chair

Department. Anthropology *Courses;* North American Indians; Bilingual Eduction (heavy Indian emphasis); American Indian Languages. A graduate (MA) degree in applied anthropology, emphasizing language and education, cultural resource management, and the process of rural community development is available throughout the department. Doctoral students often concentrate on American Indian related cultural and/or linguistic questions. *Instructors:* John J. Bodine, Ph.D., and William L. Leap, Ph.D. *Special program:* Summer training program operated on Northern Ute reservation providing instruction in language analysis, language awareness, curriculum development, and language instruction techniques to teachers of Uto-Aztecan languages and cultures in public and tribally controlled schools. *Financial assistance:* Students of American Indian background are eligible for special opportunity funds from several sources. *Facilities:* Library of Congress and Smithsonian Institution (among others.)

ILLINOIS

NAES COLLEGE
2838 West Peterson Ave.
CHICAGO 60659

INDIANA

BALL STATE UNIVERSITY
MUNCIE 47306
(317) 285-1575

Department: Anthropology. Native American Studies Minor. *Instructor:* James L. Coffin, Ph.D. *Special program:* An Interdisciplinary Native American Studies Program. *Facility:* Archaeology Laboratory.

PURDUE UNIVERSITY
WEST LAFAYETTE 47907
(317) 494-4672

Department: Sociology and Anthropology. *Courses:* Indians of North America; Indians of the Greater Southwest and Great Basin; Archaeology of North America; Native American Religions and World Views; Peoples of Middle America. *Instructors: Richard E. Blanton, Ph.D., Chair of Anthropology, and Jack O. Waddell, Ph.D.*

IOWA

MORNINGSIDE COLLEGE
SIOUX CITY 51106

Department: Indian Studies Program-Robert J. Conley, Ph.D., Director. *Courses:* The Indian in American History; Native American Arts and Crafts, Literature, Education, Contemporary Issues, and Religions; Federal Indian Law; Dakota Language. *Programs:* Major in Indian Studies and Tribal Management; Minor in Indian Studies. *Facility:* College Library with special Indian studies collection.

KANSAS

HASKELL INDIAN JUNIOR COLLEGE
P.O. Box H1305
LAWRENCE 66044
(913) 749-8472
Gerald E. Gipp, Ph.D., President
Mary Mae Norton, Chair

Operated by the Bureau of Indian Affairs.

UNIVERSITY OF KANSAS
LAWRENCE 66045
(913) 864-4103

Department: Anthropology. *Courses:* North American Indians; Contemporary North American Indians; North Americn Archaeology; Archaeology of the Great Plains; Ancient American Civilizations; Indians of South America; Physical Anthropology of American Indians; North American Indian Languages. *Instructors:* Alfred E. Johnson, Ph.D., Chair of Anthropology; Donald D. Stull, Ph.D., Robert J. Squier, Ph.D., Michael J. Crawford, Ph.D., Akira Y. Yamamoto, Ph.D., and Robert J. Smith, Ph.D. *Special programs:* Dr. Yamamoto works

closely with the Hualapai; Dr. Stull works closely with the Kansas Kickapoo; research, technical assistance, and employment opportunities are available in the areas of applied linguistics, applied anthropology, planning and development, tribal studies, and curriculum development. *Scholarships:* Graduate fellowships and teaching and research assistantships. *Facility:* Museum of Anthropology.

KANSAS STATE UNIVERSITY
204 Waters Hall
MANHATTAN 66506
(913) 532-6865

Department: Sociology, Anthropology, and Social Work. *Courses:* North American Indians; Indians of Kansas; Plains Indians; North American Indian Archaeology. *Instructors:* Robert B. Taylor, Ph.D., and Patricia J. O'Brien. *Special program:* Kansas Archaeological Field School during summer with the University of Kansas.

KENTUCKY

NORTHERN KENTUCKY UNIVERSITY
University Drive
HIGHLAND HEIGHTS 41076
(606) 572-5259

Department: Anthropology Program. *Courses:* North American Indians; Modern American Indians; Indians of Mexico and Guatemala; North American Archaeology. *Instructors: James F. Hopgood, Ph.D., Head; Sharlotte Neely, Ph.D., and Barbara Thiel, Ph.D. Facility:* Museum of Anthropology.

MASSACHUSETTS

UNIVERSITY OF MASSACHUSETTS
Harbor Campus
BOSTON 02125
(617) 929-8150/8151

Department: Anthropology. *Courses:* North American Indians; Cultures and History of Native New England; Language in Culture; Anthropology of Religion; New World Archaeology; Prehistory of Eastern North America; Meso-America: Peoples and Cultures, Prehistory and Ethnohistory. *Instructors:* Thomas Buckley, Ph.D., Barbara E. Luedtke, Ph.D., Lucy Kaplan, M.A., David Landy, Ph.D., R. Timothy Sieber, Ph.D., Michiko Takaki, Ph.D., and Alan Harwood, Ph.D. *Special programs:* Field seminar in archaeology;

Independent Research in Native-American Cultures and History; programs in urban anthropology and in contemporary ethnicity in the U.S.; Native American Support Group (student organization.) *Facilities:* Boston Museum of Fine Arts; Boston Library Consortium.

MICHIGAN

UNIVERSITY OF MICHIGAN
ANN ARBOR
(313) 764-7275

Department: Anthropology. *Instructors:* Sergei Kan, Ph.D., Richard I. Ford, Ph.D., James B. Griffin, Ph.D., John O'Shea, Ph.D., John D. Speth, Ph.D., and Harriet Whitehead, Ph.D. *Facility:* Museum of Anthropology.

MINNESOTA

BEMIDJI STATE UNIVERSITY
BEMIDJI 56601

Department: American Indian Studies.

COLLEGE OF ST. SCHOLASTICA
1200 Kenwood Ave.
DULUTH 55811

Department: Indian Studies.

UNIVERSITY OF MINNESOTA
2400 Oakland Ave.
DULUTH 55812

Department: American Indian Studies.

MINNESOTA COMMUNITY COLLEGE
1501 Hennepin Ave.
MINNEAPOLIS 55403

Department: Social Sciences/American Indians.

UNIVERSITY OF MINNESOTA
MINNEAPOLIS 55455

Departments: American Indian Studies; Anthropology.

MOORHEAD STATE UNIVERSITY
11th St. South
MOORHEAD 56560

Department: Indian Studies.

MISSOURI

UNIVERSITY OF MISSOURI
210 Switzler Hall
COLUMBIA 65211
(314) 882-4731

Department: Anthropology. *Courses:* Cultures of Native America; Ancient American Civilization; North American Archaeology; North American Indian Culture. *Instructors:* Carl H. Chapman, Ph.D., H. Clyde Wilson, Ph.D., W. Raymond Wood, Ph.D., and Robert F.G. Spier, Ph.D. *Special facility:* The Missouri Cultural Heritage Center—provides research opportunities in historical archaeology, history and ethnography of Missouri and surrounding states.

MONTANA

EASTERN MONTANA COLLEGE
1500 North 30th St.
BILLINGS 59101

Department: Native American Studies.

MONTANA STATE UNIVERSITY
BOZEMAN 59717
(406) 994-4200

Center for Native American Studies.

BLACKFEET COMMUNITY COLLEGE
P.O. Box 55
BROWNING 59417
(406) 338-7755
Donald Pepion, President

LITTLE BIG HORN COLLEGE
P.O. Box 370, Crow Center
Education Commission
CROW AGENCY 59022
(406) 638-2228
Janine Pease-Windy Boy, President

FORT BELKNAP COLLEGE
P.O. Box 39
HARLEM 59526
(406) 353-2205 ext. 241
Maria Lavigna, President

DULL KNIFE MEMORIAL COLLEGE
P.O. Box 206
LAME DEER 59043
(406) 477-8273
Darius Rowland, President

UNIVERSITY OF MONTANA
MISSOULA 59812
(406) 243-2693

Department: Anthropology. *Instructors:* Dee C. Taylor, Ph.D., Chair of Department; Carling I. Malouf, Ph.D., Anthony Mattina, Ph.D., and Katherine M. Weist, Ph.D. *Special resources:* Extensive study collections of northwest plains ethnological and archaeological materials; Northern Plains Ethnohistory Project; Salish Linguistic Studies. *Special program:* Ethnological and archaeological field courses. *Publications:* Papers in anthropology and linguistics.

SALISH—KOOTENAI COLLEGE
P.O. Box 278
PABLO 59855
 (406) 675-4800
 Joseph McDonald, Ph.D., President

FORT PECK COMMUNITY COLLEGE
P.O. Box 575
POPLAR 59255
 (406) 768-5105
 Marilyn Ridenhower, President

NEBRASKA

**NEBRASKA INDIAN
COMMUNITY COLLEGE**
P.O. Box 752
WINNEBAGO 68071
 (402) 878-2414
 Milton Holtz, Ph.D., President

NEW HAMPSHIRE

DARTMOUTH COLLEGE
HANOVER 03755
 (603) 646-3256

Department: Native American Studies. *Instructors:* Elaine A. Jahner, Michael A. Dorris, M.Phil., and Elmer Harp, Jr., Ph.D. *Facility:* Hood Museum of Art.

NEW JERSEY

UPSALA COLLEGE
EAST ORANGE 07019
 (201) 266-7282

Department: Sociology, Anthropology, and Social Work. *Instructor:* Sylvia MacColl Rudy, Ph.D., Chair. *Special facilities:* North American Indian Library collection; ethnographic film collection.

**RAMAPO COLLEGE
SCHOOL OF INTERCULTURAL STUDIES**
P.O. Box 542
MAHWAH 07430

NEW MEXICO

**SOUTHWESTERN INDIAN
POLYTECHNIC INSTITUTE**
P.O. Box 10146, 9169 Coors Rd., NW
ALBUQUERQUE 87184
 (505) 766-3197 (Freshman)
 (505) 474-3197 (Sophomore)
 Robert G. Martin, President
 Virgil Wyaco, Chairman

Administered by the Bureau of Indian Affairs.

UNIVERSITY OF NEW MEXICO
ALBUQUERQUE 87131
 (505) 277-4524

Departments: Native American Studies; Anthropology. *Facility:* Maxwell Museum of Anthropology. *Publication: Journal of Anthropological Research.* Library.

NEW MEXICO STATE UNIVERSITY
Box 3BV
LAS CRUCES 88003
 (505) 646-3821

Department: Sociology and Anthropology. *Instructors:* Bradley A. Blake, Ph.D., Pamela A. Bunte, Ph.D., Malcolm D. Holmes, Ph.D., and Steadman Upham, Ph.D. *Special program:* Cultural Resources Management Division—specializing in New Mexico; summer field school in archaeology (Mogollon), Southwest studies. *Facilities:* University Museum; laboratories for research.

**NEW MEXICO
HIGHLANDS UNIVERSITY**
LAS VEGAS 87701

Native American Studies: Provides an opportunity for Indians and non-Indians to study Indian cultures and their significant contributions to contemporary U.S. culture. It is a compenent of the Behavioral Sciences Department and has the concentration of study in sociology/anthropology; provided in combination with courses containing Indian content offered in other University divisions. *Instructors:* Margaret Vasquez, Ph.D. (anthropolgy), Michael L. Olsen, Ph.D. (history), William Lux, Ph.D. (history), and Wallace Johnson (art.) *Special program:* Kat-Zi-Ma-To-Wah—Native American students club. Scholarships available. Write to financial aids director.

EASTERN NEW MEXICO UNIVERSITY
PORTALES 88130
 (505) 562-2438/2583

Department: Social and Behavioral Science-

Anthropology Program. *Instructors:* George Agogino, Ph.D., John L. Montgomery, Ph.D., and Hayward H. Franklin, Ph.D. *Special facilities:* Peleo-Indian Institute and Museum; ceramic and lithic anaylsis laboratories; University Library.

INSTITUTE OF AMERICAN INDIAN ARTS
College of Santa Fe Campus
St. Michael's Dr.
SANTA FE 87501-9990

SCHOOL OF AMERICAN RESEARCH
P.O. Box 2188
SANTA FE 87504-2188
(505) 982-3583

Courses: American Indian art and archaeology; Southwest archaeology and anthropology; Pueblo pottery. *Instructors:* Jonathan Haas, Ph.D., Michael J. Hering, M.A., Jane Kepp, M.A., Shelby J. Tisdale, M.A., Winifred Creamer, Ph.D., Harriet Kimbro, B.A., and David G. Noble, B.A. *Special programs:* Resident Scholar Programs; Anthropology Program; Fellowships in Native American Art and Education Program; lectures and exhibitions. *Special resources:* Large collection of Southwest Indian art; archaeology laboratory. *Publications:* Advanced Seminar Series; American Indian Art Series; Grand Canyon Archaeology Series; Arroyo Hondo Archaeological Series. Library.

NAVAJO COMMUNITY COLLEGE
P.O. Box 580
SHIPROCK 87420
(505) 368-5291

See Navajo Community College (Tsaile, Arizona) listing.

NEW YORK

STATE UNIVERSITY OF NEW YORK
ALBANY 12222
(518) 442-3300

Department: Anthropology. *Institutes:* Mesoamerican Studies; Native Northeastern Studies. *Instructors:* William N. Fenton, Ph.D., Peter T. Furst, Ph.D., Robert W. Jarvenpa, Ph.D., Gail H. Landsman, Ph.D., Marianne Mithun, Ph.D., Lawrence M. Schell, Ph.D., Gary A. Wright, Ph.D., and Jill Leslie Furst, Ph.D. *Research:* Sponsors research projects in archaeology, ethnohistory and ethnology. *Publications:* Monograph series.

STATE UNIVERSITY OF NEW YORK
4242 Ridge Lea Rd.
BUFFALO 14261
(716) 636-2414

Department: Anthropology. *Programs:* Linguistics; American Studies. *Instructors:* Frederick Gearing, Ph.D., Ann P. McElroy, Ph.D., Ben A. Nelson, Ph.D., Ezra B. W. Zubrow, Ph.D., Paul L. Garvin, Ph.D., William Engelbrecht, Ph.D., Charles M. Keil, Ph.D., and Madeleine Mathiot, Ph.D. *Special program:* Contemporary North American Indians and Eskimos; Northeast U.S. prehistory. Museum. Library.

COLGATE UNIVERSITY
HAMILTON 13346
(315) 824-1000

Department: Sociology and Anthropology. *Instructors:* John M. Longyear, III, Ph.D., Kathleen S. Ryan, Ph.D., Gary Urton, Ph.D., and Anthony F. Aveni, Ph.D. *Special program:* Interdisciplinary topical concentration in Amerindian Studies, embracing the fields of Native-American religion, astronomy, art, and archaeology. *Special facility:* Longyear Museum of Anthropology and laboratory—features large collections of local Oneida Iroquois and Mesoamerican archaeological materials.

CORNELL UNIVERSITY
ITHACA 14853

Department: American Indian Studies.

STATE UNIVERSITY OF NEW YORK COLLEGE
NEW PALTZ 12561
(914) 257-2272

Department: Anthropology. *Programs:* Native American Studies Minor; summer Archaeology Field School: Northeast Woodlands.

STATE UNIVERSITY OF NEW YORK COLLEGE
OSWEGO 13126
(315) 341-4190

Department: Anthropology and Sociology. *Program:* Native American Studies.

STATE UNIVERSITY OF NEW YORK COLLEGE
POTSDAM 13676
(315) 267-2053

Department: Anthropology. *Program:* Native American Studies minor.

NORTH CAROLINA

PEMBROKE STATE UNIVERSITY
PEMBROKE 28372

Native American Resource Center.

NORTH DAKOTA

TURTLE MOUNTAIN COLLEGE
P.O. Box 340
BELCOURT 58316
(701) 477-5605
Gerald Monette, President

**UNITED TRIBES
EDUCATIONAL AND TECHNICAL
CENTER**
3315 South Airport Rd.
BISMARCK 58501

LITTLE HOOP COMMUNITY COLEGE
P.O. Box 147
FORT TOTTEN 58335
(701) 766-4415 ext. 4205
Myrna DeMarce, President

**STANDING ROCK
COMMUNITY COLLEGE**
P.O. Box 450
FORT YATES 58538
Wayne Stein, President

Department: Native American Studies.

UNIVERSITY OF NORTH DAKOTA
GRAND FORKS 58202
(701) 777-3008

Departments: Indian Studies; Anthropology.
Instructors: Joseph DeFlyer, Ph.D., John Salter,
Ph.D., Mary Jane Schneider, Ph.D., Janet G.
Ahler, Ph.D.(Center for Teaching and Learning),
John Crawford, Ph.D. (English), Fred Schneider,
Ph.D., Chair (Anthropology), Larry Loendorf,
Ph.D., Stanley A. Ahler, Ph.D., and William R.
Fowler, Jr., Ph.D. *Special programs:* Specializes
in the archaeology and anthropology of the
Northern Plains; summer Field School in
Archaeology; Archaeology programs at Knife
River Indian Villages and Knife River Flint
Quarries.

**FORT BERTHOLD
COMMUNITY COLLEGE**
P.O. Box 490
NEW TOWN 58763
(701) 627-4738
Bennett Yellow Bird, President

OKLAHOMA

UNIVERSITY OF OKLAHOMA
455 Lindsey
NORMAN 73069
(405) 325-3261/3262

Department: Anthropology. *Instructors:* Robert
E. Bell, Ph.D., William E. Bittle, Ph.D., Emanuel
J. Drechsel, Ph.D., John A. Dunn, Ph.D., Paul E.
Minnis, Ph.D., John H. Moore, Ph.D., Morris E.
Opler, Ph.D., Susan C. Vehik, Ph.D., Joseph
Whitecotton, Ph.D., Patricia A. Gilman, Ph.D.,
Timothy G. Baugh (Oklahoma Archaeological
Survey), Rain Vehik, Ph.D. (Archaeology
Research and Management Center), and Don G.
Wyckoff, Ph.D. (Oklahoma Archaeological
Survey.) The Department specializes in the study
of the American Indian with emphasis on the
Indians of Oklahoma, the Plains, the
southwestern U.S. and Mexico. *Facilities:* The
university is within easy access to representatives
of more than 60 Indian tribes; the presence of an
active Salvage archaeology program for the State
of Oklahoma; the resources of the Stovall
Museum, and an extensive library collection on
the American Indian offer special opportunities
for the study of the archaeology, linguistics,
ethnohistory and ethnology of the American
Indian.

NORTHEASTERN STATE UNIVERSITY
TAHLEQUAH 74464

PENNSYLVANIA

**THE PENNSYLVANIA STATE
UNIVERSITY—AMERICAN INDIAN
EDUCATION POLICY CENTER**
320 Rackley Bldg.
UNIVERSITY PARK 16803
(814) 865-1489
Grayson Noley, Ph.D., Director

American Indian Leadership Program: Provides
graduate degrees in education for American
Indians. Fellowships available. Publications.
Library.

SOUTH DAKOTA

**CHEYENNE RIVER
COMMUNITY COLLEGE**
P.O. Box 707
EAGLE BUTTE 57625
(605) 964-6044
Ellsworth Lebeau, Ph.D., President

OGLALA LAKOTA COLLEGE
P.O. Box 351
KYLE 57752
(605) 455-2321
Elgin Bad Wound, President

SINTE GLESKA COLLEGE
P.O. Box 8
MISSION 57555
Victor Douville, Department Head

Department: Lakota Studies/Creative Writing Program. *Instructors:* Charlene Lowry and Simon J. Ortiz. *Special activities:* Annual creative writing and storytelling festival; poetry reading series and residences, and performances and lectures by writers, scholars, and oral tradition masters; awards for creative writing (fiction and poetry.) *Publication: Wanbli Ho Journal,* by creative writing program.

OGLALA SIOUX COMMUNITY COLLEGE
PINE RIDGE 57770

SINTE GLESKA COLLEGE
P.O. Box 490, Rosebud Sioux Reservation
ROSEBUD 57570-0490
Gloria Dyc, Head (General Studies)
Rodger Hornby, Head (Human Services)

Departments: General Studies and Human Services. *General Studies courses:* Contemporary/traditional Indian painting; Plains Indian design composition; quiltmaking (traditional Lakota star quilts); traditional Lakota arts I and II; hide tanning and painting; Lakota carving and sculpture; featherwork; The Indian in western thought; Native-American children's literature; Lakota music and dance; contemporary Indian literature; Indian art history. *Human Services courses:* Anthropology; Lakota medicine; reservation legal system; alcohol and drug abuse among American Indians; reservation analysis; tribal law, treaties and government; reservation/American Indian health care; American Indian criminal justice and corrections. *Human Services special program:* A Health Careers Opportunity Program (Oyate Kin Zanipi Ktelo-Health for the People) designed to increase the number of American Indians entering health professions—health careers financial aid information is available directly from the Health Careers Program. *Financial Aid:* Available through the College's Financial Aid Office. *Special facility:* Lakota Archives and Historical Center.

SIOUX FALLS COLLEGE
1501 South Prairie Ave.
SIOUX FALLS 57101

Department: Native American Studies.

SISSETON-WAHPETON COLLEGE
P.O. Box 262
SISSETON 57262
(605) 698-3966
Schuyler Houser, President

UNIVERSITY OF SOUTH DAKOTA INSTITUTE OF INDIAN STUDIES
VERMILLION 57069
(605) 677-5400

YANKTON COLLEGE
YANKTON 57078

TEXAS

UNIVERSITY OF TEXAS
AUSTIN 78712
(512) 471-4206

Department: Anthropology. *Instructors:* Richard Bauman, Ph.D., Thomas N. Campbell, Ph.D., E. Mott Davis, Ph.D., J. Gilbert McAllister, Ph.D., James A. Neely, Ph.D., William W. Newcomb, Jr., Ph.D., Joel Sherzer, Ph.D., Greg P. Urban, Ph.D., M. Jane Young, Ph.D., Anthony C. Woodbury (Linguistics Dept.) *Special programs:* MA and PhD in Folklore. *Special facility:* Texas Archaeological Research Laboratory; Texas Memorial Museum; Linguistic Research Center; A.A. Hill Linguistics Library.

TEXAS TECH UNIVERSITY
LUBBOCK 79409
(806) 742-2228

Department: Anthropology. *Program:* Ethnic Studies, James A. Goss, Ph.D., Director.

INCARNATE WORD COLLEGE
4301 Broadway
SAN ANTONIO 78209
(512) 828-1261 ext. 247

Department: Anthropology. *Program:* Native American Studies. *Instructors:* Donald L. McKain, Ph.D., and Eloise Stoker, M.A. *Special program: Interdisciplinary Program in Native American Studies.*

UTAH

BRIGHAM YOUNG UNIVERSITY
PROVO 84602
(801) 378-3058

Departments: Indian Education; Anthropology. *Indian Education instructors:* Willis M. Banks, Owen C. Bennion, Hall L. Black, Janice White Clemmer, Arturo DeHoyos, William Fox,

Frederick R. Gowans, Rondo S. Harmon, Kenneth Rush Sumpter, Victor R. Westover, Darlene Herndon, Charlotte D. Lofgreen, John R. Maestas, Vergus C. Osborn, and W. Dean Rigby. *Anthropology instructors:* Dale L. Berge, Ph.D., Donald W. Forsyth, Ph.D., Ray T. Matheny, Ph.D., Merlin G. Myers, Ph.D., Bruce W. Warren, Ph.D., Joel C. Janetski, Ph.D., Asa S. Nielson, M.A., John S. Robertson, Ph.D., and Larry R. Stucki, Ph.D. *Special programs:* Field Schools, historic and prehistoric site, Utah; Nancy Patterson Village Project, southeastern Utah. *Special facilities:* Museum of Peoples and Cultures; archaeological laboratories; Gates Collection on Middle American Languages. Library.

WASHINGTON

LUMMI COMMUNITY COLLEGE
P.O. Box 11, 2522 Kwina Rd.
BELLINGHAM 98226
(206) 734-8180 ext. 251
Robert Lorence, Ph.D., President

WESTERN WASHINGTON UNIVERSITY
BELLINGHAM 98225
(206) 676-3613

Department: Anthropology. *Instructors:* Garland F. Grabert, Ph.D., Howard L. Harris, M.A., Herbert C. Taylor, Jr., Ph.D., Colin E. Tweddell, Ph.D., and Lynn A. Robbins, Ph.D. *Special program:* Archaeological Field School. *Special facilities:* Archaeological laboratory; Northwest Archival Center (research on culture change and American Indian ethnohistory.)

CENTRAL WASHINGTON UNIVERSITY
ELLENSBURG 98926
(509) 963-3201

Departments: Anthropology and Museum; Indian Studies. *Instructors:* James M. Alexander, III, Ph.D., Clayton C. Denman, Ph.D., Catherine J. Sands, M.A., William C. Smith, Ph.D., and John A. Alsoszatai-Petheo, M.A. *Special program:* Ethnic Studies Program. *Special facilities:* Central Washington Archaeological Survey; Museum artifacts collection.

WASHINGTON STATE UNIVERSITY
PULLMAN 99164-4901
(509) 335-3441

Departments: Anthropology; Comparative American Studies. *Instructors:* Robert E. Ackerman, Ph.D., Mark S. Fleisher, Ph.D., Geoffrey L. Gamble, Ph.D., Timothy A. Kohler, Ph.D., William D. Lipe, Ph.D., Richard D. Daugherty, Ph.D., John J. Flenniken, Ph.D., Allan H. Smith, Ph.D., Lillian A. Ackerman,

Ph.D., Dale R. Croes, Ph.D., Kennth C. Reid, Ph.D., and William Willard, Ph.D. (Comparative American Studies.) *Special programs:* Archaeology and ethnography of the western U.S., with emphasis on American Indian, Pacific and Asian cultural, anthropology, linguistics and archaeology. *Special facilities:* Research laboratories; Washington Archaeological Research Center; extensive research and reference collections in western U.S. archaeology, botany, and ethnographic basketry.

UNIVERSITY OF WASHINGTON
SEATTLE 98195
(206) 543-5240

Department: Anthropology. *The American Indian Studies Center,* which offers some instruction in North American Indian languages, is an integral part of the Department. *Instructors:* Marilyn G. Bentz, Ph.D., Carol M. Eastman, Ph.D., Donald K. Grayson, Ph.D., Eric Alden Smith, Ph.D., Julie K. Stein, Ph.D., Elizabeth A. Edwards, Ph.D., Bill Holm, MFA, Joan Megan Jones, Ph.D., Barbara Lane, Ph.D., James D. Nason, Ph.D., Marshall T. Newman, Ph.D., George I. Quimby, M.A., Diana Ryesky, Ph.D., and Gail Thompson, Ph.D. *Special facilities:* Specialized library collection on the American Indian; Thomas Burke Memorial Museum (extensive collections of Northwest Coast Indians and Eskimos artifacts.)

WISCONSIN

NORTHLAND COLLEGE
1411 Ellis Ave.
ASHLAND 54806

Department: Native American Studies.

LAC COURTE OREILLES
OJIBWA COLLEGE
R.R. 2
HAYWARD 54843
(715) 634-4790
John Anderson, President

MARQUETTE UNIVERSITY
MILWAUKEE 53233
(414)224-6838

Department: Social and Cultural Sciences. *Instructors:* Claude E. Stipe, Ph.D., Chair; Alice B. Kehoe, Ph.D. *Special program:* American Indian Counselor. Financial aid available.

UNIVERSITY OF WISCONSIN
P.O. Box 413
MILWAUKEE 53201

College of Letters and Science: Native American Studies Program, John Boatman, Coordinator. *Courses:* Great Lakes American Indian ethnobotany; anthropology (courses on American Indians of Northeast, Wisconsin, general American Indian societies and cultures, religions, and the southwest); ethnic studies (western Great Lakes American Indian community life of the past); history (courses on American Indian history); philosophy (Great Lakes American Indian philosophy); dreams and visions in American Indian metaphysics. *Instructors:* John Boatman, Ph.D., Coordinator of Program; Jo Allyn Archambault, Ph.D.; Keewaydinoquay, and Fixico. *Special programs:* American Indian Art Festival; Wisconsin Woodland American Indian Summer Field Institute. *Financial aid:* Minority Achievement Scholarship for high school seniors; Undergraduate Minority Retention Grant for 2nd, 3rd and 4th year college students; Bureau of Indian Affairs and Wisconsin Indian grants. *Special facility:* Milwaukee Public Museum.

CANADA

ALBERTA

OLD SUN COMMUNITY COLLEGE
P.O. Box 339
GLEICHEN T0J 1N0
(403) 734-3862

BRITISH COLUMBIA

UNIVERSITY OF BRITISH COLUMBIA
6303 N.W. Marine Dr.
VANCOUVER V6T 2B2
(604) 228-2878

Department: Anthropology. *Instructors:* David F. Aberle, Ph.D., Harry B. Hawthorn, Ph.D., J.E. Michael Kew, Ph.D., William Robin Ridington, Ph.D., and Wolfgang George Jilek, *M.D. Special program:* Summer Field School in Archaeology. *Special facilities:* Research laboratories in archaeology, ethnomethodology and socio-linguistics, and ethnography; Museum of Anthropology.

UNIVERSITY OF VICTORIA
VICTORIA V8W 2Y2
(604) 721-7046

Department: Anthropology. *Instructors:* Leland H. Donald, Ph.D., Chair; N. Ross Crumrine, Ph.D., Kathleen A. Mooney, Ph.D., Eric A. Roth, Ph.D., and Charles R. Wicke, Ph.D. *Special facilities:* Provincial Archives and Museum; archaeological, ethnological and linguistic (especially in Coast Salish languages through the Lingistics Department) field training; Pacific Studies; and Interdisciplinary Studies Program.

MANITOBA

UNIVERSITY OF BRANDON
BRANDON

Department of Native Studies.

UNIVERSITY OF MANITOBA
WINNIPEG R3T 2N2
(204) 474-9361

Department: Anthropology. *Instructors:* Louis Allaire, Ph.D., Richard T. Carter, Jr., Ph.D., Joan B. Townsend, Ph.D., H. Christoph Wolfart, Ph.D., E. Leigh Syms, Ph.D., Paul H. Voorhis, Ph.D., William W. Koolage, Ph.D., Gregory Monks, Ph.D., Dwight A. Rokala, Ph.D., and David H. Stymeist, Ph.D. *Special programs:* Population biology and medical anthropology of North American Indians; indigenous languages of Canada, especially Siouan and Algonquian (Cree Language Project.) *Special facilities:* Anthropology Laboratories; The Provincial Archives.

UNIVERSITY OF WINNIPEG
515 Portage Ave.
WINNIPEG R3B 2E9
(204) 786-9875

Department: Anthropology. *Instructors:* William H. Morgan, Ph.D., Chair; Wing Sam Chow, Ph.D., Gary R. Granzberg, Ph.D., and John H. Steinbring, Ph.D. *Special program:* Archaeological Field School. *Special facilities:* Algonkian ethnological collections; Hudson's Bay Company Archives Research Centre; ethnology, archaeology, and physical anthropology laboratories.

NEW BRUNSWICK

UNIVERSITY OF NEW BRUNSWICK
FREDERICTON E3B 5A3
(506) 453-4975

Department: Anthropology. *Instructors:* Charles Ackerman, Ph.D., Vincent O. Erickson, Ph.D., Peter R. Lovell, Ph.D., and Gail R. Pool, Ph.D.

Special resources: Local fieldwork opportunities (Maliseet-Micmac Indian communities); archaeology-anthropology laboratory. Archives. Library.

NEWFOUNDLAND

MEMORIAL UNIVERSITY OF NEWFOUNDLAND
ST. JOHN'S A1C 5S7
(709) 737-8870/8871

Department: Anthropology. *Instructors:* Gordon Inglis, Ph.D., Joan C. Kennedy, Ph.D., Thomas F. Nemec, Ph.D., Adrian Tanner, Ph.D., and James A. Tuck, Ph.D. *Special foci:* Field research programs—Arctic, Subarctic, and circumpolar (especially Lapps, Algonquin, Inuit and white settlers); northern North Atlantic (Newfoundland, Labrador, Baffin, Iceland.) *Special facility:* Killam Arctic Library.

ONTARIO

NORTH AMERICAN INDIAN TRAVELLING COLLEGE
Onake Corporation, R.R. 3
CORNWALL ISLAND K6H 5R7
(613) 932-9452

YORK UNIVERSITY
4700 Keele St.
DOWNSVIEW M3J 1P3

Graduate program in Native Canadian Relations in the faculty of Environmental Studies.

UNIVERSITY OF WESTERN ONTARIO
LONDON N6A 5C2
(519) 679-3430

Department: Anthropology. *Center for Research and Teaching of Native Languages,* administered within the Department, offers research funds and facilities for faculty and students working on Canadian native languages. *Instructors:* Chet Creider, Ph.D., Chair; Margaret Seguin, Ph.D., Michael W. Spence, Ph.D., William R. Thurston, Ph.D., and David G. Smith, M.A. *Special facility:* Museum of Indian Archaeology.

TRENT UNIVERSITY
PETERBOROUGH K9J 7B8
(705) 748-1325

Department: Anthropology. *Special Program:* Native Studies. *Instructors:* Charles Hamori-Torok, Ph.D., Evelyn M. Todd, Ph.D., and Joan M. Vastokas, Ph.D. *Special facility:* Archaeological Centre.

LAURENTIAN UNIVERSITY
Ramsey Lake Rd.
SUDBURY P3E 2C6

Department: Native Studies.

LAKEHEAD UNIVERSITY
THUNDER BAY P7B 5E1
(807) 345-2121 ext. 632/568

Department: Anthropology. *Special programs:* Native Studies; Boreal Studies. *Instructors:* Paul Driben, Ph.D., Chair; Kenneth C.A. Dawson, M.A., and Joe D. Stewart, Ph.D.

UNIVERSITY OF TORONTO
Sidney Smith Hall
TORONTO M5S 1A1
(416) 978-5416

Department: Anthropology. *Instructors:* Ivan Kalmer, Ph.D., Martha A. Latta, Ph.D., Richard B. Lee, Ph.D., Albert Mohr, Ph.D., Stuart Piddock, Ph.D., Joseph C. Sawchuck, Ph.D., Kyrstyna Siesiechowicz, Ph.D., Rosamund Vanderburgh, M.A., and William D. Finlayson, *Ph.D. Special program:* Northern Yukon Research Project; excavations at historic and prehistoric Huron villages and older sites in Ontario; research among Canadian Indians, rural and urban.

UNIVERSITY OF WATERLOO
WATERLOO N2L 3G1
(519) 885-1211 ext. 2520

Department: Anthropology. *Courses:* Prehistoric man in America/Great Lakes area - A survey; Inuit and Eskimo cultures; the contemporary Canadian Indian scene; comparative policies on native minorities; early man in the new world. *Instructors:* Thomas S. Abler, Ph.D., Chair; William B. Roosa, Ph.D., and Sally M. Weaver, Ph.D. *Award:* Graham Goddard Anthropology Medal—silver medal awarded annually to a 3rd and 4th year anthropology major or honours student who has demonstrated an interest in native peoples of North America.

QUEBEC

McGILL UNIVERSITY
855 Sherbrooke West, Leacock Bldg.
MONTREAL H3A 2T7
(514) 392-5176

Departments: Anthropology; Linguistics. *Special program:* A cohesive group of Iroquoian archaeologists forms a core of an intimate group in archaeology. *Instructors:* Carmen Lamber, Ph.D., and C.D. Ellis, Ph.D. (Linguistics).

UNIVERSITY OF MONTREAL
CP 6128, Succursale 'A'
MONTREAL H3C 3J7
(514) 343-6560

Department: Anthropology. *Instructors:*
Franklin Auger, Asen Balikci, Ph.D., Norman
Clermont, Ph.D., Remi Savard, Gilles Lefebvre,
Ph.D. (Linguistics), and Marcel Rioux, M.A.
(Sociology). *Special programs:* Northeast
archaeology; Summer Field Programs (Inuit and
Canadian Indian areas—ethnology.)

UNIVERSITE LAVAL
Cite Universitaire
STE-FOY G1K 7P4
(418)656-5867

Department: Anthropologie. *Courses:* ethnologie
des Amerindiens; ethnologie des Inuit; dossiers
autochtones contemporains. *Instructors:* Paul
Charest, M.A., Gerry McNulty, M.A., Bernard
Saladin d'Anglure, Francois Trudel, Ph.D.,
Louis-Jacques Dorais, Pierre Miranda, and Yvan
Simonis. *Special programs:* North American
Indian; Canadian Inuit. *Special facility:* Centre
d'etudes nordiques. *Publications: Etudes Inuit
Studies; Anthropologie et Societes.*

SASKATCHEWAN

UNIVERSITY OF REGINA
REGINA S4S 0A2
(306) 584-4189

Department: Anthropology. *Instructors:* George
W. Arthur, Ph.D., Head; J.J. McHugh, Ph.D.,
R.K. Pope, M.A., and C.R. Watrall, Ph.D.
Special facilities: Canadian Plains Research
Centre; Saskatchewan Archives; Saskatchewan
Indian Federated College. Publications.

**SASKATCHEWAN INDIAN
CULTURAL COLLEGE**
University of Saskatchewan Campus
P.O. Box 3085
SASKATOON S7K 3S9
(306) 244-1146

UNIVERSITY OF SASKATCHEWAN
SASKATOON S7K 3S9
(306) 966-4176

Departments: Anthropology and Archaeology;
Native Studies. *Instructors:* Alexander M. Ervin,
Ph.D., Head; Urve Linnamae, Ph.D., Mary C.
Marino, Ph.D., James F.V. Miller, Ph.D., Zenon
S. Pohorecky, Ph.D., Ernest G. Walker, Ph.D.,
Robert G. Williamson, Ph.D., and James B.
Waldram, Ph.D. *Special programs:* Emphasis is
given to research in the Prairie Provinces of
western Canada, Arctic, Subarctic and Northwest
Territories of Canada; summer fieldwork in
archaeology and ethnology in Saskatchewan
and/or NWT. *Special facilities:* Indian and
Northern Curriculum Resources Centre, College
of Education, with a specialized collection in
North American Indian and crosscultural
education; Saskatchewan Provincial Archives;
Shortt Reference Library.

UNIVERSITY OF SASKATCHEWAN
SASKATOON S7N 0W0

Native Law Centre. Instructors: Linda Fritz, J.D.,
Norman K. Zlotkin, J.D., Donald J. Purich, J.D.,
Fergus J. O'Connor, J.D., and Zandra
MacEachern, J.D.

COMMUNICATIONS

This section lists radio and television stations, programs, and projects throughout the U.S. and Canada. Listings are arranged alpha-geographically.

ALASKA

ASRC COMMUNICATIONS, INC.
P.O. Box 129
BARROW 99723
(907) 852-8633

BARROW CABLE TV
P.O. Box 129
BARROW 99723

KUAC RADIO
FAIRBANKS 99701
(907) 474-7491

KTOO - FM
224 4th St.
JUNEAU 99801
(907) 586-1670

KRBD - FM / KTKN - AM
P.O. Box 6855
KETCHIKAN 99901

KOTZ RADIO
P.O. Box 78
KOTZEBUE 99752
(907) 442-3434

KCAW - RAVEN RADIO
P.O. Box 1766
SITKA 99835
(907) 747-5877

ARIZONA

KTVK CHANNNEL 3 (ABC)
3435 North 16th St.
PHOENIX 85016
(602) 266-5691

21st Century Native-American: Roy Track, Host; Sunday, 12:00 PM.

KNCC - FM
Navajo Community College
TSAILE 85445
(602) 724-3311

KUAT 1550 AM
University of Arizona
TUCSON 85721

Desert Visions: Native-American Radio Program.

KNNB - FM
P.O. Box 310
WHITERIVER 85941
(602) 338-4371

Native-American Radio Program.

CALIFORNIA

ROUND VALLEY RADIO PROJECT
P.O. Box 8
COVELO 95428

Native-American Radio Project.

KIDE - FM
P.O. Box 1220
HOOPA 95546
(916) 625-4245

THE AMERICAN INDIAN HOUR
P.O. Box 4187
INGLEWOOD 90309
(213) 299-1810

The radio voice of the American Indian Liberation Crusade (see National Associations section.) Broadcasts on 17 radio stations across the country.

KPOO - 88 FM
P.O. Box 11008
SAN FRANCISCO 94101
(415) 346-5373

Red Voices: Tuesday, 7:00 PM.

COLORADO

KGNU - PUBLIC RADIO
2049 N. Broadway
BOULDER 80302
(303) 449-4885

Native-American Radio News Program.

KSUT - FM
P.O. Box 737
IGNACIO 81137
(303) 563-4507

MINNESOTA

MIGIZI COMMUNICATIONS
2300 Cedar Ave. South
MINNEAPOLIS 55404
 (612) 721-6631
 Lori Mollenhoff, President

See National Associations section.

RED LAKE CHIPPEWA RADIO PROJECT
RED LAKE 56671

Native-American Radio Project.

KTCA - CHANNEL 2
1640 Como Ave.
ST. PAUL 65108
 (612) 646-4611

Native-American TV Program: Chris Spotted Eagle, Host.

MONTANA

BLACKFEET MEDIA
Blackfeet Tribe
P.O. Box 850
BROWNING 59417

Native-American Radio Project.

KFBB CHANNEL 5
P.O. Box 1139
GREAT FALLS 59403
 (406) 453-4377

Native-American TV Program. On the Air 4th Sunday of each month at 11:30 AM.

DULL KNIFE PUBLIC TV
Dull Knife Memorial College
P.O. Box 98
LAME DEER 59043
 Ron Holt, Director

KZIN - 96.8 FM / KSEN - 1150 AM
830 Oilfield Ave.
SHELBY 59425

On the Air Monday, Wednesday, and Friday at 9:10 AM.

NEW MEXICO

KTDB - FM
P.O. Box 18
RAMAH 87121
 (505) 783-5456

KSHI - FM
P.O. Box 339
ZUNI 87327
 (505) 782-4811

NEW YORK

WBAI - 99.5 FM
505 Eighth Ave.
NEW YORK 10016
 (212) 279-0707

Drumbeats: 6:00 PM, Saturday.

AKWESASNE FREE RADIO
c/o Ray Cook
ROOSEVELTOWN 13683

NORTH DAKOTA

KEYA - FM
P.O. Box 190
BELCOURT 58316
 (701) 477-5686

FORT BERTHOLD COMMUNICATIONS
P.O. Box 220
NEW TOWN 58763

Native-American Radio Project.

KMHA - FM
P.O. Box 220
NEW TOWN 58763
 (701) 627-3686

OKLAHOMA

KIOWA TRIBAL RADIO STATION
P.O. Box 361
CARNEGIE 73015
 (405) 654-2300

OREGON

CONFEDERATED TRIBES TELECOMMUNICATION PROJECT
P.O. Box 584
WARM SPRINGS 97761

Native-American Radio Project.

SOUTH DAKOTA

KILI - FM
Lakota Communications
P.O. Box 378
PINE RIDGE 57770
(605) 867-5002

Native-American Radio Project.

KINI - FM
Rosebud Education Association
ST. FRANCIS 57572
(605) 747-2291

WASHINGTON

KRNB - FM
P.O. Box 96
NEAH BAY 98357

Native-American Radio Program.

QUINALT INDIAN NATION
P.O. Box 189
TAHOLAH 98587

Native-American Radio Project.

WISCONSIN

WOJB - FM
Route 2, Box 2788
HAYWARD 54843
(715) 634-2100

WIRC - FM
University of Wisconsin
216 College of Professional Studies
STEVENS POINT 54481
(715) 346-2746

WYOMING

KIEA - FM
Wind River Indian Education Association
Wyoming Indian High School
ETHETE 82520
(307) 332-2793

Native-American Radio Project.

CANADA

ALBERTA

CKUA - AM/FM
Native Voice of Alberta. On the Air 4:30 PM,
Sunday, in the following cities: Edmonton, Grand
Prairie, Medicine Hat, Lethbridge, Red Deer, and
Peace River.

'YR' RADIO
Native Voice of Alberta. On the Air 9:30 AM,
Sunday, in the following cities: Hinton,
Whitecourt, Edson, Jasper, Grand Cache.

CFAC - FM
Treaty No. 7 Radio Program
CALGARY

News Information Program. On the Air 10:30 to
10:45 AM, Sunday.

CJOK - FM
FORT McMURRAY

Native Voice of Alberta. On the Air 7:30 PM,
Sunday.

CILA - FM
Red Rock Radio
LETHBRIDGE

Native Rock Program. On the Air 1:00 to 2:00
PM, Sunday.

CJOC - FM
LETHBRIDGE

Native-American Radio Program catering to
tribes of southern Alberta. On the Air 11:30 AM
to 12:00 PM, Sunday.

CIOK - FM
ST. PAUL

Native Voice of Alberta. On the Air 8:00 PM,
Sunday.

CKTA - FM
TABOR

Native-American Elders Program. On the Air
10:30 to 11:00 AM, Sunday.

MANITOBA

OUR NATIVE LAND TV
CBC Radio, P.O. Box 160
WINNIPEG

ONTARIO

KENOMADIWIN RADIO
P.O. Box 609, Longlac No. 58 Reserve
LONG LAKE P0T 2A0
 (807) 876-2865

CHMD - 1450 RADIO
P.O. Box 400, James Bay Broadcasting Corp.
MOOSONEE P0L 1Y0
 (705) 335-2701

TV NAKINA
Centre St.
NAKINA P0T 2H0

SASKATCHEWAN

CJUS - FM
SASKATOON

Native Voice of Alberta. On the Air 4:30 PM,
Sunday.

MOCCASIN TELEGRAPH
c/o Saskatchewan Indian
1630 Idylwyld Dr.
SASKATOON S7K 3S9

AUDIO-VISUAL AIDS

This section lists Indian-related films, videos, recordings, filmstrips, picture-sets, and maps. Films and videos are color/sound unless otherwise stated in the listing. Entries are arranged alphabetically by title. At the end of each entry there are code letters which correspond to the distributor and address listed at the end of the section.

FILMS AND VIDEOS

ABORIGINAL RIGHTS:
I CAN GET IT FOR YOU WHOLESALE
TV Ontario, Producer
Historical photos and on-sight footage trace the history of aboriginal rights in North America from Mexico to Canada. 1976. 60 minutes. 2" quad; 1" & ¾" video. Rental: $80/week. NAPBC.

ACORNS: STAPLE FOOD
OF CALIFORNIA INDIANS
Clyde B. Smith, Producer
A film on the gathering, storing and processing of acorns, a staple food of the Pomo Indians. Includes scenes showing original primitive methods. 1962. 28 minutes. Purchase: 16mm, $390; video, $270. Rental. UC and PSU.

AGUEDA MARTINEZ:
OUR PEOPLE, OUR COUNTRY
Explores the history, life, and values of Agueda Martinez, a 77 year-old woman of Navajo-Mexican descent. 1977. 17 minutes. Rental. PSU.

ALASKAN ESKIMO
Dramatizes the daily struggle for survival of an Eskimo family living in northern Alaska. 1957. 27 minutes. Rental, $16.55. MM.

ALASKAN SLED DOG
The story of the puppy Nan-Nook and his young Eskimo master. Illustrates the training and use of the Alaskan sled dog. 1967. 18 minutes. All ages. Rental, $13.50. MM.

ALICE ELLICOTT
Richard Lair, Director
A look at the life and work of one of the few remaining Pomo Indian basketmakers. 1975. 11 minutes. Purchase: 16mm, $210. Rental. UC.

THE AMERICAN AS ARTIST:
A PORTRAIT OF BOB PENN
SD ETV, Producer
Penn offers his insights into the essence of being an artist and a Native-American in the U.S. 1976. 30 minutes. 2"quad; 1" and ¾" video. Rental, $40. NAPBC.

THE AMERICAN INDIAN
AFTER THE WHITE MAN CAME
Examines the profound impact white expansion had upon the many tribes of Native-Americans. The formation of U.S. governmental policies as well as contemporary social issues are discussed. Narrated by Iron Eyes Cody. 27 minutes. 16mm and ¾" beta. Purchase: $410. HF.

AMERICAN INDIAN ARTISTS
PARTS I & II
Tony Schmitz and Don Cirillo, Directors
Part I: Six programs, profiling seven contemporary Native American artists: Grace Medicine Flower and Joseph Lonewolf, potters; Fritz Scholder, R.C. Gorman, and Helen Hardin, painters; Allen Houser, sculptor; and Charles Loloma, jeweler. 1976. Part II: Three programs—Larry Golsh's artistry in gold and precious stones, 1982; James Quick-To-See Smith, painter, 1982; and Dan Namingha, artist, 1984. 30 minutes each. 16mm; 2"quad; 1" and ¾" video. Rental: $40 each. NAPBC.

THE AMERICAN INDIAN
BEFORE THE WHITE MAN
Presents a study of the American Indian from early migration routes to the development of the main tribes of North America. Narrated by Iron Eyes Cody. 19 minutes. 16mm; ¾" beta video. Purchase: $335. HF.

THE AMERICAN INDIAN
INFLUENCE ON THE U.S.
Albert Saparoff, Producer
Narrated by Barry Sullivan, this film depicts how life in the U.S. today has been influenced by the American Indian. 20 minutes. 8mm, 16mm, and video. Purchase, $475.00; rental, $50.00. DANA. Rental only, UK and UM.

AMERICAN INDIAN OF TODAY (LOS
INDIOS NORTAMERICANOS DE HOY)
Examines current trends that are shaping the future of American Indians in their adjustment to new ways of making their living. 1957. 16 minutes. Spanish edition. 16mm. UA.

THE AMERICAN INDIAN SPEAKS
Visits three tribes—the Muskogee Creek, the Rosebud Sioux, and the Nisqually—to emphasize the injustices done to the American Indian by the white man. 1973. 23 minutes. Rental. MM, IU and UM.

AMERICAN INDIANS
AS SEEN BY D.H. LAWRENCE
Walter P. Leisohn, Producer
D.H. Lawrence's wife discusses the novelist's beliefs and thoughts. Aldous Huxley presents selections from Lawrence, revealing his deep insights into Indian culture. 14 minutes. Rental. UM.

AMERICAN INDIANS
BEFORE EUROPEAN SETTLEMENT
David Baerreis, Ph.D.
Where they came from, how they lived, and unique aspects of their cultures as related to their environment are examined. 1959. 11 minutes. Grades 4 to 12. Purchase: 16mm, $255; video, $180. Rental. COR and UA.

AMERICAN INDIANS:
YESTERDAY AND TODAY
Don Klugman
Shows that various Indian tribes have different histories and ways of life. A young Shoshone-Paiute man from the Owens Valley in California, an elderly Northern Cheyenne man from Lame Deer, Montana, and a young Seneca woman from New York State tell about their history and modern lifestyles of their tribes. 1982. Grades K-8. 19 minutes. 16mm. Purchase: $375; rental: $40. FF.

AMIOTTE
Bruce Baird, KUSD-TV, Producer
Explores Sioux painter Arthur Amiotte's art and the reasons for returning to his native culture and religion. 1976. 30 minutes. 2" quad; 1" and ¾" video. Rental: $40. NAPBC.

AMISK
Alanis Obomsawin, Director/Producer
The traditional lands of the Cree of Misstassini in northern Quebec are being threatened by a Hydro-Electric Power project. Shows a festival, with Cree music and dance, to raise money to fight against this project. 1977. 38 minutes. 16mm. NFBC.

AN ANCIENT GIFT
Illustrates the central role that sheep traditionally play in Navajo nourishment, culture, and social life. Scenes of daily life show the interdependence. 18 minutes. Purchase: 16mm, $315; video, $240. Rental, $32. UC.

...AND THE MEEK
SHALL INHERIT THE EARTH
Examines the American Indians of Menominee County, Wisconsin. 1972. 59 minutes. Rental. IU and UM.

ANGOON ONE HUNDRED YEARS LATER
KTOO-TV Juneau, Alaska, Producer
Provides the history and culture of the Tlingit Indians while telling of the 1882 destruction of the Tlingit Indian village of Angoon, Alaska, by U.S. Naval forces. 1982. 30 minutes. 2" quad; 14 and ¾" video. Rental, $40. NAPBC.

ANGOTEE: STORY OF AN ESKIMO BOY
Douglas Wilkinson, Director
A documentary account of an Indian boy's life from infancy to maturity. 1953. 31 minutes. Grades 6 and up. 16mm. In English or French. Rental. IFB, CRM, UC, PSU.

ANIMATION FROM CAPE DORSET
A collection of short animated sequences produced by Eskimos of the Cape Dorset (Baffin Island.) 19 minutes. Grades 7-adult. Rental, $17.95. MM.

ANNIE AND THE OLD ONE
Miska Miles, Writer
A dramatized film for young people with non-professional Navajo actors, about the relationship between a ten-year-old girl and her grandmother (the Old One.) 1976. 15 minutes. Grades 1-8. Rental. BFA, UA, IU.

ANNIE MAE—BRAVE HEARTED WOMAN
Lan Brooke Ritz, Writer/Producer/Director
A documentary portrait of Annie Mae Pictou Aquash, a young Native American woman and activist for human rights, found dead on the prairie in South Dakota in 1974, a year after the Wounded Knee uprising. Explores the events leading up to her death and investigates her unsolved murder. 1982. 79 minutes. 16mm; 2" quad; 1" and ¾" video. Rental: $120/week. BBP and NAPBC.

ANOTHER WIND IS MOVING:
THE OFF-RESERVATION
INDIAN BOARDING SCHOOL
A documentary film. 1985. 16mm STULL.

THE APACHE INDIAN
Shows the life of Apache Indians on their reservation in the White Mountains of Wyoming; their ancient ceremonies, and contemporary education, work, and the role of the tribal council in determining the direction of tribal affairs. Revised 1973 edition. Ten minutes. Grades K-6. Purchase: 16mm, $250; video, $175. COR. Rental. UA.

ARCHAEOLOGY:
PURSUIT OF MAN'S PAST
15 minutes. 16mm. Rental. UA.

ARROW TO THE SUN
Gerald McDermott
From the Acoma Pueblo in New Mexico comes
this classic tale of a boy's search for his father: the
universal search for identity, purpose, and
continuity. 1973. 12 minutes. Grades K-8. 16mm
and ¾" video. TF and MM.

THE ART OF BEING INDIAN:
FILMED ASPECTS OF THE
CULTURE OF THE SIOUX
SD-ETV, Producer
Presents an overview of the cultural heritage of
the Sioux from their early days in the Northeast to
the Dakotas. Illustrates with paintings and
sketches by George Catlin, Seth Eastman, and
Karl Bochner; photography by Edward S. Curtis,
Stanley Morrow, and the St. Francis Mission; and
contemporary paintings by Sioux artist Bob
Penn. 1976. 30 minutes. 2" quad; 1" and ¾" video.
Rental, $40. NAPBC.

AS LONG AS THE GRASS SHALL GROW
Lynn Brown, Writer/Producer
A series of eight programs designed for classroom
use with pre-school age children. Combines
elements of Seneca life to teach children to count
to ten in Seneca, and at the same time helps build
positive self-images. 1978. 15 minutes each. ¾"
videotape. The SN.

AT THE TIME OF WHALING
Leonard Kamerling and Sarah Elder
Depicts an Eskimo whale hunt at Gambell,
Alaska, a Yup'ik-speaking community on St.
Lawrence Island in the Bering Sea. 1974. 38
minutes. Purchase: 16mm, $650; rental, $60.
DER.

AUGUSTA
Anne Wheeler, Director
Portrait of Augusta Evans, an 88 year-old
granddaughter of a Shuswap chief, who lives
alone in a cabin in the caribou country of British
Columbia, Canada. She discusses her past and
present. 1978. 17 minutes. 16mm. PHOENIX and
NFBC.

THE BALLAD OF CROWFOOT
Willie Dunn, Director
Graphic history of the Canadian West created by
a film crew of Canadian Indians who reflect on the
traditions, attitudes, and problems of their
people. 1968. 11 minutes; bxw. Grades 5-12.
CRM, PSU, MM and UC.

BASKETRY OF THE POMO
Clyde B. Smith, Producer
A series of three films. An introductory film shows
Indians gathering raw materials for baskets, and
demonstrates, in slow motion and animation, the
ten Pomo basketmaking techniques. 30 minutes.
Purchase: 16mm, $410; video, $290. *Techniques:*
A more detailed film on Pomo basketry
techniques, showing precisely how the various
weaves were executed. 33 minutes. Purchase:
16mm, $455; video, $310. *Forms and
Ornamentation:* Illustrates the great variety of
shapes, sizes, and design elements of Pomo
baskets. 21 minutes. Purchase: 16mm, $300;
video, $210. 1962. Also available for rental. UC
and PSU.

BEAUTIFUL TREE—CHISHKALE
Clyde B. Smith, Producer
The Southwestern Pomo called the tan oak
chishkale (the beautiful tree.) Cooking methods
and processing techniques used in making acorn
bread are demonstrated. 1965. 20 minutes.
Purchase: 16mm, $285; video, $200. Rental. UC
and PSU.

BEFORE THE WHITE MAN CAME
John E. Maple
A feature film made in the Big Horn Mountains of
Montana and Wyoming in the early 1920's with
the cooperation of the Crow. An all-Indian cast
presents authentic rites and ceremonies. 50
minutes. bxw. FCE.

BE-TA-TA-KIN
A cliff-dwelling of the Indians who lived in
Arizona at the time of the Crusades. Shows the
canyons and mesas of these early Indians; their
lives, agriculture, and industry. 11 minutes.
Rental. NYU and PSU.

THE BELL THAT RANG
TO AN EMPTY SKY
William Farley
A film essay using animation techniques and
suggestive cutting to make a comment on the
relationship between the expansion of white
society onto Indian territories and the increase of
wealth in the Federal Treasury. Commentary by
Russell Means. 1977. Five minutes. 16mm. SB.

BETWEEN TWO RIVERS
Tells the story of the Indians' continuing battle for
identity. The tragedy of Thomas Whitehawk
caught between the world of the white man and
the Indian. 1970. 26 minutes. Rental. UM.

BILL REID
Jack Long, Director
Haida carver and jewelry-maker, Bill Reid, speaks
of his work and what his Haida heritage has meant
for him as an artist. 1979. 28 minutes. 16mm.
NFBC.

BLACK COAL, RED POWER
Shelly Grossman, Producer
Examines the effects coal strip-mining has had on the Navajo and Hopi reservations in Arizona. 1972. 41 minutes. 16mm. Rental. IU, UC, UA.

THE BLACK HILLS ARE NOT FOR SALE
Sandra Osawa, Producer
Taped at the 1980, International Survival Gathering in South Dakota, Sioux people tell why "the Black Hills are not for sale." Provides historical background on the Laramie Treaty of 1868 which guaranteed the Sioux ownership of their lands. 1980. 28 minutes. ¾" video. UP.

BLUNDEN HARBOR
Shows a group of Pacific Northwest Kwakiutl Indians living in Blunden Harbor and sustaining themselves by the sea. Includes the Legend of Killer Whale, and a dance ceremony. 1951. 20 minutes/bxw. Rental, $11.50. PSU and UMI.

BORN TO BE A NATION
Documents the proceedings of the 1976, International American Indian Treaty Conference on the Yankton Sioux Reservation. Native American leaders speak of the history of treaties recognizing Indian sovereignty and of the attempts by non-Indian interests to ignore those treaties because of resources found on Indian lands. 1976. 15 minutes. bxw. ½" (reel) and ¾" video. UCV.

BOX OF TREASURES
Chuck Olin and U'mista Cultural Society
In 1921 the Kwakiutl people of Alert Bay, British Columbia, Canada, held their last secret potlatch. Fifty years later, the masks, blankets, and copper heirlooms that had been confiscated by the Canadian government were returned. The Kwakiutl built a cultural center to house these treasures and named it U'Mista "something of great value that has come back." 28 minutes. Purchase: 16mm, $480; ¾" video, $350. Rental. DER.

BOY OF THE NAVAJOS
Depicts life among the Navajos as seen through the eyes of Tony, a present day Navajo Indian boy. Revised 1974 edition. Grades K-6. 11 minutes. Purchase: 16mm, $255; video, $180. Rental. Coronet, UA, IU, and UM.

BOY OF THE SEMINOLES (INDIANS OF THE EVERGLADES)
Wendell W, Wright, Ph.D.
A visit to the Seminole tribe in the Everglades of Florida. 1956. Grades K-6. 11 minutes. Purchase: 16mm, $255; video, $180. Rental. COR and UM.

BROKEN TREATY AT BATTLE MOUNTAIN
Joel Freedman, Director
Shows the dramatic story of the traditional Western Shoshone Indians of Nevada and their struggle to regain 24 million acres of land stolen from them by the U.S. Government. Also, a portrait of the traditional Indian way of life. Narrated by Robert Redford. 1974. 60 minutes. Purchase: 16mm, $795; video, $595. Rental. CG, UNI, UN, MM.

BUCKEYES: FOOD OF CALIFORNIA INDIANS
Clyde B. Smith, Producer
Shows harvesting, stone boiling, and leaching of buckeyes (horse chestnuts) by Niseanan Indians, a centuries-old method of changing poisonous nuts into edible mush or soup. 1961. 13 minutes. Purchase: 16mm, $240; video, $180. Rental. UC and PSU.

BUFFALO: AN ECOLOGICAL SUCCESS STORY
How Indian tribes depended on the buffalo for food, clothing, shelter, weapons and fuel. Also, the life story of the buffalo. 1972. 14 minutes. Grades 6-12. Rental. UMI.

BUFFALO, BLOOD, SALMON AND ROOTS
George Burdeau, Writer/Director
Filmed at the Flathead, Kalispel and Coeur d' Alene Reservations in western Montana, the Idaho panhandle and eastern Washington, this film shows the old tribal ways of gathering and preserving food. 1976. 28 minutes. 16mm and video. GPN, NAPBC and PBS.

4-BUTTE-1: A LESSON IN ARCHAEOLOGY
Clyde B. Smith and Tony Gorsline
Shows the excavations and analyzes the artifacts of a Maidu Indian village in California Sacramento Valley. 33 minutes. Purchase: 16mm, $455; video, $320. Rental. $38. UC

BY NO MEANS CONQUERED PEOPLE
Verity Lund and John Moore;
Richard Erdoes, photography
Presents issues that the Longest Walk, 1978, was organized around. The Walk was made across the U.S. to demonstrate their concern about proposed legislation: eleven bills, one of which would abrogate all treaties between the U.S. and Indian tribes. Dick Gregory and Clyde Bellacourt were speakers at the gathering. 1979. 26 minutes. ¾" video. bxw. VL.

BY THE WORK OF OUR HANDS
Designed to be used with the text of the same name. However, it can be used independently. Focuses on drum making, and both oak and cane basket making. Teacher's guide. 30 minutes. Grades 3-8. Purchase: ¾" video, $85. Rental, $10/two weeks. CHP.

BY THIS SONG I WALK: NAVAJO SONG
Larry Evers with Andrew Natonabah
Natonabah sings as he travels through Canyon de Chelly where the Navajo believe the songs were originally created and he discusses the songs and their origin. In Navajo with English subtitles. 1978. 25 minutes. Purchase: video, $175. CLEAR.

CALUMET, PIPE OF PEACE
Describes Indian use of pipes and tobacco, and shows traditional Indian methods of fashioning, decorating and consecrating pipe bowl and stem. 1964. 23 minutes. Purchase: 16mm, $320; video, $225. Rental. UC and PSU.

CANADA'S ORIGINAL PEOPLES: THEN AND NOW
TV Ontario, Producer
Contrasts the life of native Canadians before the arrival of Europeans with contemporary native life in Canada. In two parts: part 1, Then; part 2, Now. 1977. 20 minutes. 2" quad, 1" and ¾" video. Rental, $40. NAPBC.

CARIBOU HUNTERS
Studies the nomadic life of the Cree and Chippewa Indians of northern Manitoba, Canada. 1950. 18 minutes. Grades 6-adult. Rental. MM and UMI.

CATLIN AND THE INDIANS
The biography of George Catlin. Shows how his works captured the forms and rituals of Indian society during the 1800's. 1967. 24 minutes. Rental. UM.

CEREMONIAL PIPES
A dramatized re-enactment and explanation of former Plains Indian customs. Focuses on the symbolic and religious place of ceremonial pipes and the importance of tobacco, pipes, and other smoking agents in the world of the Plains Indians. 1955. 16 minutes. 16mm. Rental, $13.50. PSU.

CESAR'S BARK CANOE
Bernard Gosselin, Director
Cesar Newashish, a Cree Indian, peels the bark from a birch tree and with his pocket knife and axe, constructs a canoe. Subtitles in Cree, French and English. 1971. 58 minutes. Grades 7-adult. EDC

THE CHACO LEGACY
Graham Chedd, Director
Explores the excavations of the first monumental stone ruins discovered in North America, the Pueblo Bonito community in Chaco Canyon, New Mexico. Teachers guide. 1980. 59 minutes. Purchase: 16mm, $600. Rental, $60. DER.

CHARLES KILLS ENEMY, MEDICINE MAN
This film shows Kills Enemy in a Sweat Lodge Ceremony and a Lowanpi Ceremony. 16mm. BCA.

CHARLEY SQUASH GOES TO TOWN
An animated, imaginative simplification of the acculturation-identity crisis of an Indian. 1969. Five minutes. Grades 6-adult. 16mm. Rental. MM, UM and UA.

CHECK IT OUT
Johnny, a Hopi Indian boy from northern Arizona comes to live in the neighborhood. 1976. 13 minutes. Grades K-9. Rental, UM.

CHEROKEE
Philip Hobel, Executive Producer
Examines the modern Cherokee's efforts to preserve native traditions. Cherokees are shown performing ceremonies and activities of the past, and discusses their heritage and hopes for the future. 1972. 26 minutes. Purchase: 16mm, $400; video, $340. Rental. CG.

CHEYENNE AUTUMN
Based on an actual incident, this film tells of the valiant efforts of the Cheyenne Indians to escape to their Wyoming homeland from their wretched Oklahoma reservation. 1965. 156 minutes. Rental. UM.

CHILDREN OF THE LONG-BEAKED BIRD
Peter Davis and Swedish TV
Portrait of Dominic Old Elk, a 12 year old Crow Indian, exploring his life and interests; a view of Native American life and history. Seeks to erase many stereotypes. 1976. 30 minutes. 2" quad; 1" and ¾" video; 16mm. Rental. BULL and NILB.

CHILDREN OF THE PLAINS INDIANS
Through the daily activities of Red Cloud, an Indian youth in training to become a brave, this film portrays the life of the Plains Indians in about 1750. 1962. 20 minutes. Rental. UA and UM. Purchase and rental. CRM.

CHOCTAW TRIBAL GOVERNMENT
Designed to be used with text *Tribal Government: A New Era*, but can be used independently. Introduces Choctaw tribal government and what is happening on the reservation today. 17 minutes. Grades 5-adult. ¾" VHS, $85; rental, $10 (two weeks.) CHP.

CIRCLE OF SONG
Cliff Sijohn and George Burdeau
Presents the Indian concept of the "Circle of Life" on which important life events and the songs and dances associated with them are point. In two parts. 1976. 28 minutes each. 16mm and video. GPN, NAPBC, and PBS.

CIRCLE OF THE SUN
Colin Low, Director
Documents the life and ceremonial customs of the Blood Indians of Alberta, Canada, and contrasts their present existence on the reservation. 1961. 30 minutes. Grades 7-adult. Purchase: 16mm, $550; video, $350; rent, $60. NFBC. Rental. MM, UA, IU, UM.

CIVILIZED TRIBES
Philip Hobel, Executive Producer
Life is reconstructed at the Seminole Reservation in Florida to simulate that of their Seminole ancestors. Also focuses on their present conditions. 1972. 26 minutes. Purchase: 16mm, $400; video, $340. Rental. CG and IU.

CLASH OF CULTURES
Scott Nielsen and Dick Blofson
Four elders from the Lakota tribe, drawing on the oral tradition of Indian life in the late 19th-century, explain the cultural attitudes of the Indians and the clash of attitudes with white settlers. 1978. 28 minutes. 16mm and video. UMA.

COLLIDING WORLDS
Orie Sherman
A documentary film made by a Mono woman about the Western Mono located in the Sierra Nevada mountains of California. 1980. 30 minutes. 16mm and video. HP.

COLOURS OF PRIDE
Henning Jacobson
Four Indian artists of Canada are interviewed in their home studios by Tom Hill, a Seneca from the Six Nations Reserve in Ontario. 1974. 24 minutes. 16mm. NFBC.

COME FORTH LAUGHING:
VOICES OF THE SUQUAMISH PEOPLE
Provides an account of the life of the Suquamish over the past one hundred years. 16mm and video. SM.

CONCERNS OF AMERICAN
INDIAN WOMEN
Will George, Director
Interviews with Marie Sanchez, North Cheyenne judge, and Dr. Connie Uri, Choctaw-Cherokee physician and law student. 1977. 30 minutes. ¾" video. PBS.

THE CONQUERED DREAM
Features sequences on Eskimo art and folklore, traditional hunting methods, health problems and education of today's Eskimo. 51 minutes. CEN.

CONSONANTS WITH COYOTE
Animated Navajo language film. Consonents with common sounds to both Navajo and English. Nine minutes. All grades. 16mm and video. SAN.

A CONVERSATION WITH
VINE DELORIA, JR.
Larry Evers, University of Arizona
The writer discusses the gulf between Indian and non-Indian culture and the "schizophrenia" of white expectations for the Indian. 1978. 29 minutes. Purchase: Video, ¾" VHS, ½" beta, $175. CLEAR.

CORN IS LIFE
This film depicts the traditional activities associated with corn that are still an important part of Hopi family and community life. Includes scenes of daily Hopi life. 19 minutes. Purchase: 16mm, $330; video, $250. Rental. UC.

CORN AND THE ORIGINS OF
SETTLED LIFE IN MESO-AMERICA
Jack Churchill, Director
Presents the work of three scholars, Michael Coe, Paul Mangelsdorf, and Richard MacNeish. 1964. 40 minutes. 16mm. EDC.

COYOTE STORIES
Animated Navajo language films. Six legendary coyote stories. All grades. 16mm and video. SAN.

A CREE HEALER
Consists of interviews with the healer and shows segments where he prepares for the sweatlodge ceremony. The interview concerns the issues and controversies encountered by this native healer in openly discussing the subject. 22 minutes. Video. UADA

CREE HUNTERS OF MISTASSINI
Tony Ianzelo and Boyce Richardson, Directors
The setting up of a winter camp by 16 Cree Indians. Indian life is observed in the bush. 1974. 58 minutes. Grades 7-adult. 16mm and video. NFBC, DEC, MM, UC, and PSU.

CREE WAY
Tony Ianzelo and Boyce Richardson, Director
Provides a view of a successful bilingual education project which connects Cree children to their past and future. 1977. 28 minutes. 16mm. NFBC.

CROOKED BEAK OF HEAVEN
David Attenborough, Writer/Narrator
A Haida chief bestows lavish gifts on his tribesmen and then smashes his most valuable possessions, a *potlatch* ceremony. Contrasted

with footage made of the Kwakiutl by Edward S. Curtis in 1912. 1976. 52 minutes. 16mm. TIME, UC, MM and UI.

CROW DOG
Mike Cuesta and David Baxter, Directors
Documentary portrait of Sioux medicine man, Leonard Crow Dog, the spiritual leader of 89 American Indian tribes and the spokesman for the traditionalists. 1979. 57 minutes. Purchase: 16mm, $795; video, $595; rental, $95. CG and UNI.

CROW DOG'S PARADISE
Portrays the values, beliefs and rituals of a modern Dakota Sioux medicine man. 1982. 28 minutes. Purchase: 16mm, $675; video, $450. TC.

CULTURAL CHANGES
The pre-reservation life of the buffalo hunting Indians of the southern Plains is told through the use of pictographic drawings made by Kiowa and Cheyenne young men imprisoned in Fort Marion, Florida, in 1875. 1970. 17 minutes. 16mm. Rental. UM.

CUSTER: THE AMERICAN SURGE WESTWARD
Documents one of the most famous battles in U.S. history, "The Battle of the Little Bighorn." 1966. 33 minutes. Grades 6-adult. Rental. MM and UMI.

THE DAWN RIDERS: NATIVE AMERICAN ARTISTS
Robert and Dona DeWeese
Three prominent Indian painters, Woody Crumbo (Potawatomi), Blackbear Bosin (Kiowa-Comanche) and Dick West (Cheyenne), talk about their work and influences on their art. 1969. 27 minutes. 16mm. LF.

DE GRAZIA
Ted De Grazia, well-known Arizona artist, discusses how his life among the Indians and Mexicans of the Southwest is reflected in his work. 1967. 29 minutes. 16mm. Rental. UA.

DESERT PEOPLE (PAPAGO)
1949. 25 minutes. Rental. UA.

A DIFFERENT DRUM
The story of a young Comanche boy who is torn between his family's desire for him to attend college and his own natural aptitude for auto mechanics. 1974. 21 minutes. Rental. UK.

DINEH: THE PEOPLE
Jonathan Reinis and Stephen Hornick
Documentary focusing on the impending relocation of several thousand Navajo from a joint-use land area surrounding the Hopi Reservation which is located in the midst of the Navajo Reservation. Portrays the cultural and economic conditions under which the Navajo attempt to survive while striving to preserve their traditional values. 1976. 77 minutes. 2" quad, 1" and ¾" video. Rental, $120/week. NAPBC. 16mm, UC.

DISCOVERING AMERICAN INDIAN MUSIC
Bernard Wilets
Songs and dances of tribes from various parts of the country performed in authentic costumes. All ages. 24 minutes. $480. BARR. Rental. MM, IU, UM and UK.

THE DISPOSSESSED
A statement about the dominating institutions of American society and their destructive effects on the lives and resources of the American Indian. 1970. 33 minutes. 16mm. Rental. MM and UMI.

THE DIVIDED TRAIL
Jerry Aronson and Michael Goldman
Follows the lives of three Chippewa as they moved from various stages of activism and discontent into vocational alternatives. 1978. 33 minutes. 16mm. PHOENIX.

DREAM DANCES OF THE KASHIA POMO
Clyde B. Smith, Producer
Pomo women dance the Bole Maru nearly a century after it first evolved, blending the native Kaksu cult with the Maru or dream religion. Five dances are shown. The shaman expresses her religious beliefs in her own words. 1964. 30 minutes. Purchase: 16mm, $410; video, $290. Rental. UC, IU and PSU.

DREAMSPEAKER
An emotionally disturbed boy runs away from an institution and is "adopted" by an old Indian shaman. The Indian vision of life and death are reviewed. 1977. 75 minutes. Rental, $45.30. MM.

THE DRUM IS THE HEART
Randy Croce, Producer
Narrated entirely by Indian participants, ranging from children to elders, this film focuses on the Blackfeet, Blackfoot, Blood and Peigan tribes that make up the Blackfoot Nation at their celebrations, speaking about their contemporary lives and traditional values. 1982. 29 minutes. Video. Purchase: $100; rental, $40. UCV and BM.

THE DRUMMAKER
Presents an Ojibwa Indian, William Bineshi Baker, Sr., on the Lac Court Oreilles Reservation in northern Wisconsin, one of the last of his people to continue the art of drummaking. Step-by-step he constructs a dance drum, and expresses his beliefs about tradition, as well as frustrations. 1978. 37 minutes/bxw. Purchase: 16mm, $390; video, $175. Rental, $19.50. PSU.

THE DRUMMER
Thomas Vennum, Jr.
William Bineshi Baker, Jr., an Ojibwa, living on the Lac Courte Oreilles Reservation in northern Wisconsin constructs a drum step-by-step. 1978. 38 minutes. 16mm/bxw. PSU.

THE EAGLE AND THE CONDOR
KBYU-TV, Provo Utah, Producer
Examines the interaction between the Native American cultures of North and South America. Native American entertainers of BYU's Laminite Generation tour South America performing and discussing differences and similarities in cultures. 1975. 30 minutes. 2" quad; 1" and ¾" video. Rental, $40/reel. NAPBC.

THE EAGLE AND THE MOON
Wango Weng, Director
An animated Haida story presenting elements of Haida culture such as the class and their totem poles. 1971. Ten minutes. 16mm. WALL.

THE EARLY AMERICANS
Traces the rise of man from his arrival in North America as an ice age wanderer, to builder of complex societies more than 2,000 years before Columbus. 1976. 42 minutes. UA.

EMERGENCE: A GRASS ROOTS ACCOUNT OF INDIAN ACTIVISM
Walter Verbanie
Documents how the Potawatomi in Kansas lost lands through disadvantageous treaties and divisions in the tribe between members of the Mission and Prairie bands. 1977. 35 minutes. 16mm. CF.

THE EMERGING ESKIMO
Deals with the impact of the white man upon the native Eskimos. 15 minutes. Grades 1-8. Rental. UK.

END OF THE TRAIL:
THE AMERICAN PLAINS INDIANS
Surveys the westward movement in America during the last century and the tragic impact of that movement on the American Indians. 1966. 53 minutes/b&w. Grades 6-adult. MM, UA and UM.

AN END TO ISOLATION
Urban Indians and the Phoenix Indian Center capture some of the unique problems faced by Indian people as they move to a large urban area. 30 minutes. ½" VHS. Rental, $10. NILB.

ESKIMO ARTIST - KENOJUAK
John Geeney, Director
Inuit artist Kenojuak shows the sources of her inspiration and methods used to transfer her carvings to stone. 1964. 20 minutes. Grades 7-adult. Purchase: 16mm, $410; and video, $300. Rental, $50. NFBC, UK and PSU.

ESKIMO ARTS AND CRAFTS
Laura Boulton, Director
The activities of Eskimos of Baffin Island are filmed by a noted ethnomusicologist. Emphasis is on the significance of the role of women in Eskimo life. 1944. 20 minutes. 16mm. IFB and PSU.

ESKIMO CHILDREN
Portrays the activities of a typical Eskimo family living on Nunivak Island off the Alaskan coast. 1941. 11 minutes. Grades 4-adult. In English and Spanish. Rental. UA,UM and UK.

ESKIMO FAMILY
Pictures an Eskimo family during its journey to and its life in a spring hunting and camp site; its summer visit to a trading post. Emphasizes acculturation of the Eskimos. 1960. 17 minutes/b&w. Grades 4-12. Rental, $10.25. MM.

ESKIMO: FIGHT FOR LIFE
Asen Balikci, Advisor and Narrator
Shows the careful division of tasks among the different members of a group of Netsilek Eskimos camped together during the winter seal hunting season. 1970. 51 minutes. Grades 7-adult. 16mm. EDC, MM and UW.

ESKIMO HUNTERS
Presents the life of the Eskimos who live in the cold areas of Alaska. 1949. 22 minutes/bxw. Rental. UK.

THE ESKIMO IN LIFE AND LEGEND
Shows how the Inuit's way of life, his legends, and his art of stone carving are interrelated. 1960. 22 minutes. Grades 7-adult. Rental. EB, UA, UM.

THE ESKIMO SEA HUNTERS
How Eskimo people live in regions where the weather is always cold. 1949. 20 minutes/bxw. Rental. UK.

ESKIMO SUMMER
Portrays the importance of group activity to the survival of those bands which live away from the Canadian and American settlements. 1949. 15 minutes/bxw. Rental. UM.

ESKIMOS: A CHANGING CULTURE
Wayne Mitchell
Examines the lives of two generations of Inuit Eskimos who live on Nunivak Island in the Bering Sea off the coast of Alaska. 1971. 17 minutes. Grades 4-adult. 16mm. BFA, IU and BYU.

ESKIMOS: WINTER IN WESTERN ALASKA
Life among present-day Eskimos along the Bering Straits. 1950. 11 mintues/bxw. Grades 4-adult. Rental. UMI.

THE EXILES
Kent Mackenzie, Producer
Classic depiction of one anguished but typical night in the lives of three young American Indians who have left the reservation and come to live in downtown Los Angeles. 1961. 72 minutes/bxw. Purchase: 16mm, $790; video, $615. Rental. UC, UA, UM, UK, IU and PSU.

EXPEDITION ARIZONA:
MISSIONS OF OLD ARIZONA
Reviews the buildings of San Xavier del Bac which is still used by the Papago people after 260 years, and the contributions of Father Kino to Indian culture. 1960. 27 minutes/bxw. Rental. UA.

EXPEDITION ARIZONA:
SHARDS OF THE AGES
Shows three ancient cultures: the Hohokam of the desert, the Mogollon of the mountains, and the Anasazi of the plateau regions of Arizona. 1960. 27 minutes/bxw. Rental. UA.

EXPRESSIONS OF ESKIMO CULTURE:
INUIT PRINTMAKING AND CARVING
Two Inuit artists demonstrate the art of Inuit printmaking and carving. 1980. 51 minutes. Purchase: video, $175.00; rental, $20.00. MM.

FAMILY LIFE OF
THE NAVAJO INDIANS
Highlights some of the ways in which the Navajo child develops into adulthood. 31 minutes. 16mm/bxw. Rental. NYU and UT.

FEAST
University of Michigan anthropologist Napoleon Chagnon discusses and shows excerpts from his award-winning film "The Feast." 1971. 30 minutes/b&w. Purchase: video, $175.00; rental, $20.00. MM.

FEATHERS
Larry Littlebird, Writer;
Frank Marrero (WGBH), Producer
Dramatizes personal and social problems encountered by teenagers over how far they, as Indians, should go in joining the mainstream of American life. Emphasizes the closeness of family and community life. 1980. 30 minutes. Video. WGBH and GPN.

FEDERAL INDIAN LAW
Joel Freedman; Joan Kaehl, Writer
Traces the development of federal Indian law through treaties, statutes, and court decisions. By using real life examples, it illustrates the impact that federal Indian law can have on tribal economics and community lifestyles, and how law can be made to work for your tribe. Narrated by Kirke Kickingbird, Kiowa attorney and founder of the Institute for the Development of Indian Law. 1980. 19 minutes. 16mm. IDIL.

THE FIGHTING CHEYENNE
Depicts the Cheyenne Indians' battles with white travelers on the trail. Relates the historic tale of Dull Knife and his Cheyenne band. 30 minutes. 16mm. Rental. UT.

FIRES OF SPRING
Henry T. Lewis, Ph.D., Writer/Producer
Shows how, among the Slavey and Beaver tribes of northern Alberta, Canada, fire was used to carefully maintain and improve selected habitats of plants, game and furbearing animals. 1978. 33 minutes. Purchase: 16mm, $300 (Canadian); and, ¾" video, $125. BINS and PSU.

THE FIRST AMERICANS
In two parts. Part I: *And Their Gods*—The migration of people into the Americas and the eventual setting and differentiating of these people into tribes. 11 minutes. Part II: *Some Indians of the Southlands*—Depicts customs and beliefs of certain Indians in the southern half of U.S.: Natchez, the "Moundbuilders," the Hopi, Zuni and Navajo. 17 minutes. 1969. Grades 7-adult. 16mm. IFF and UT.

THE FIRST NORTHWESTERNERS:
THE ARCHAEOLOGY OF EARLY MAN
Louis and Ruth Kirk, Producers
Examines the first northwest environment of more than 10,000 years ago and the first humans known to have lived there. 1979. 29 minutes. Purchase: 16mm, $425; ¾" beta, $225; ½" VHS, $215. UW.

A FISHING PEOPLE:
THE TUTLALIP TRIBE
Heather Oakson
Tells the story of their history as a fishing people and provides an overview of the tribe's current involvement with fishing as an industry. 1980. 17 minutes. The TT.

FOLKLORE OF THE
MUSCOGEE (CREEK) PEOPLE
Gary Robinson, Creek Nation
and KOED-TV, Tulsa, Oklahoma
Host Dr. Ruth Arrington (Creek Nation) describes the nature of folklore within Creek culture, and explains the breakdown of folklore into three categories: legends, myths and fables. 1983. 30 minutes. Grades 3-12. 2" quad, 1" and ¾" video. Rental, $40. NAPBC.

FOREST SPIRITS
NEWIST, Producer
A series of seven half-hour programs on the Oneida and Menominee tribes of Wisconsin. #1: *To Keep a Heritage Alive*—Oneida children learn their native tongue, religious code and moral ethic. #2: *The Learning Path*—The educational system and the Native American. #3: *Land Is Life*—Documents Oneida's troubles over land.

#4: *Ancestors Of Those Yet Unborn*—
Menominee lifestyle. #5: *Living With Tradition*—
Menominee traditions and reaffirmation of
heritage. #6 & 7: *Dreamers With Power*—Part 1:
Explores stereotypes and truths about
Menominee Reservation life; and Part 2:
Menominee's history. Grades 4-adult. 2" quad, 1"
and ¾" video; rental, $40/week. NAPBC.
Purchase: ½ and ¾" video, $65; rental, $25 (five
days). Teacher's guide, 30¢. GPN.

THE FORGOTTEN AMERICAN
A documentary filmed in the Southwest and in the
urban Indian communities of Los Angeles and
Chicago. Shows the impoverishment of the
American Indian, his loss of identity and self-
respect. 1968. 25 minutes. Purchase and rental.
CF, PSU, MM and UA.

FORGOTTEN FRONTIER
    KAET-TV Phoenix, Producer
Documents Spanish mission settlements of
southern Arizona, and the conversion and
teaching of skills to Indians. 1976. 30 minutes.
2"quad, 1" and ¾" video. Rental, $40/week.
NAPBC.

FORTY-SEVEN CENTS
    Lee Callister and Wendy Carrel, Producers
Focuses on the land claims of the Pit River
Indians in northern California and the processes
by which Indians are unfairly treated. 1973. 25
minutes. 16mm/bxw. UC and UNI.

FRANZ BOAS, 1852-1942
    T.W. Timreck
A profile of Franz Boas, his work with Northwest
American Indian tribes and his teaching of
anthropology. 1980. 60 minutes. Purchase: ¾"
beta or VHS, $250; rental, $90/week. PBS.
Purchase: 16mm, $600; rental, $60. Educator's
guide. DER.

FROM THE FIRST PEOPLE
    Leonard Kamerling and Sarah Elder
Shows change and contemporary life in
Shungnak, a village on the Kobuk River in
northwestern Alaska. An old man shares his
feelings about the changes he has seen. 1976. 45
minutes. Purchase: 16mm, $650; rental, $60.
DER.

GAME OF STAVES
    Clyde B. Smith, Producer
Pomo boys demonstrate the game of staves, a
variation of the dice game using six staves and 12
counters, played by most of the Indian tribes of
North America. Explains the individualized
pyrographic ornamentation of the staves and
counters. 1962. 15 minutes. 16mm and video. UC
and PSU.

**GATECLIFF: AMERICAN INDIAN
ROCK-SHELTER**
Led by Dr. David Hurst Thomas, amateur
archaeologists attempt to discover the identity of
ancient inhabitants of this shallow rock-shelter in
Monitor Valley, Nevada. Teacher's guide. 1974.
24 minutes. Purchase: 16mm, $345; video, $315.
NGS.

GERONIMO JONES
A young American Indian of Apache and Papago
descent, living on a reservation with his mother
and grandfather, explores the conflicts he faces,
torn between pride in his heritage and his future in
modern American society. 1970. 21 minutes. All
ages. Purchase: 16mm, $295; rental, $30. LCA,
MM, UA, UI.

GIRL OF THE NAVAJOS
    Norman Nelson
A story about two Navajo girls who become
friends. 1977. 15 minutes. Grades K-6. Purchase:
16mm, $335; video, $235. Rental, $40. COR.

GONE WEST
In Two Parts: Part I - The Lewis and Clark
Expedition; Part II - The gold rush begins a mass
migration west. Both parts show the affect of
white migrations on Indian nations. 1972. 26
minutes each. Rental. UK.

GOOD MEDICINE
    Chris Gaul, Writer/Producer
Documentary on Native American medicine,
narrated by John Bolindo, Kiowa-Navajo who
was at the time of the film the executive director of
the National Indian Health Board. Emphasizes
the holistic nature of Indian medicine. Settings
include the Rosebud and Navajo Reservations.
1979. 59 minutes. ¾" video, WQED; 16mm, LU.

THE GOOD MIND
    Robert Stiles and United Methodist
    Publishing House
Narrated by Steve Charleston, a Choctaw Indian,
this film explores the similarities between
Christian beliefs and Native American beliefs.
Free viewer's guide available. 1983. 30 minutes. 2"
quad, 1" and ¾" video. Rental, $40/week. NILB.

GRAND CANYON
Dr. Joseph Wood Krutch journeys on mule down
the canyon to the Colorado River. The Havasupai
Indian settlement at Bright Angel Creek is
compared with the outside world. 1966. 26
minutes. Rental. UA.

GREAT SPIRIT WITHIN THE HOLE
Chris Spotted Eagle, KTCA, Producer
A narrative around the words of Indian people in our nation's prisons. The movie demonstrates how freedom of Indian religious practice aids in rehabilitation. Narrated by Will Sampson, with original soundtrack by Buffy Sainte-Marie. 1983. 60 minutes. 16mm and video. Purchase: 16mm, $495; video, $200. Rental, $90. UCV.

HAA SHAGOON
Joe Kawaky, Producer
Documents a day of Tlingit Indian ceremony held along the Chilkoot River, ancestral home of the Chilkoot Tlingit of Alaska. Ceremony consists of time-honored prayers, songs and dances. 29 minutes. Purchase: 16mm, $460; video, $345. Rental, $38. UC.

HAIDA CARVER
Richard Gilbert, Director
Shows a young Haida Indian artist on the Pacific coast of Canada shaping miniature totems from argillite, a soft dark slate. 1964. 12 minutes. Grades 9-adult. IFB, UA.

HANDS OF MARIA
A pictorial study of Maria Martinez, an Indian potter, and of her work which has brought fame to her and to her pueblo. 1968. 17 minutes. Rental. UA.

HASKIE
Jack L. Crowder
The story of a young Navajo Indian boy, who wants to become a medicine man but instead attends a boarding school to meet the requirements of compulsory education. 1970. 25 minutes. 16mm. Rental. IU.

HEALTH CARE CRISIS AT ROSEBUD
SD ETV, Producer
Explores and offers some possible solutions to a serious shortage of physicians on the Rosebud Sioux Reservation in South Dakota. 1973. 20 minutes. 2" quad, 1" and ¾" video. Rental, $40/week. NAPBC.

HERITAGE IN CEDAR:
NORTHWEST COAST: INDIAN
WOODWORKING, PAST AND PRESENT
Louis and Ruth Kirk
From Oregon to Alaska, tribesmen lived in houses built of cedar planks and traveled in canoes hollowed from cedar logs. This film explores the Northwest Coast Indian legacy by going to abandoned villages and to living villages, to archaeological digs and to museums. 1979. 29 minutes. Purchase: 16mm, $425; ¾" or ½" VHS, $215. UW.

HERITAGE OF THE SEA:
MAKAH INDIAN TREATY RIGHTS
Louis and Ruth Kirk
Examines fishing as the Makahs presently practice it, regard it, and view it historically. In two parts: Part I - Makah reminiscences about the past and comments on the future of their tribal salmon management programs. Part II - Represents comments by Makah fisherman and elders. 29 minutes each. Purchase: 16mm, $425 each; ¾" beta, $225, or ½" VHS, $215 each. UW.

HERMAN RED ELK:
A SIOUX INDIAN ARTIST
SD ETV, Producer;
Bill Hopkins, Project Director
Red Elk speaks of his lifelong interest in art and of the influences of his grandfather's teachings. Points out the role of skin painting in Plains Indian history. 1975. 29 minutes. 2" quad, 1" and ¾" video. Rental, $40/week. NAPBC.

HISTORY OF SOUTHERN CALIFORNIA
In two parts: Part I, *From Prehistoric Times to the Founding of Los Angeles* - major sequences include, prehistoric life, Indian economy, European explorations, and establishment of pueblos, missions and presidios; Part II, *Rise and Fall of the Spanish and Mexican Influences.* 1967. 17 minutes each. Grades 4-9. Rental. UA.

HOHOKAM: AT PEACE WITH THE LAND
Bill Land
The archaeologist Emil Haury discusses his excavations at the earliest Hohokam site, Snaketown, which dates from approximately 2,000 years ago, and their descendants, the Pima and Papago, who still live in the region near Phoenix, Arizona. 1976. 20 minutes. 16mm. UA.

HOME OF THE BRAVE
A capsulized history of the Western Indian, documenting the five hundred year story of a people. 1970. Three minutes. Grades 4-adult. Rental, $10.00. MM.

HOME OF THE BRAVE
Helena Solberg-Ladd, Director
This documentary examines the contemporary plight of Indian peoples of North and South America, and the impact of development on Native people. Includs interviews with numerous Indian leaders. 1984. 53 minutes. Purchase: 16mm, $850; video, $595. Rental, $90. CG.

HOPEWELL HERITAGE
A study of the excavations and recreation of the Hopewell Indian culture, a highly organized society which became extinct almost 1,000 years before the discovery of America. 1964. 29 minutes/b&w. Purchase: 16mm and video, $175.00; rental, $20.00. MM.

HOPI
Wayne Ewing
Consists of interviews with several elders who recall their experiences as young people forced to conform to white culture. They describe their concerns with the land, harmony with nature, growing corn, and continuing the Hopi way. Also includes the history of Hopi-white cntacts using archival photos. 1981. 60 minutes. 16mm and ¾" beta. EWING.

THE HOPI INDIAN
Observes Hopi men and women in daily routines and in special celebrations, such as the secret Hopi wedding ceremony. 11 minutes. Revised. Grades K-6. Purchase: 16mm, $255; video, $180. Rental, $40. COR, UA, UM, and IU.

HOPI INDIAN ARTS AND CRAFTS
Shows traditional skills as the Hopi work at weaving, basket-making, silversmithing and ceramics. 11 minutes. Grades K-6. Purchase: 16mm, $250; video, $175. Rental, $40. COR and UA.

HOPI INDIAN VILLAGE LIFE
J. Lawrence Walkup, Ed.D.
A portrayal of the Hopi Indians and their mode of living as it exists today. 11 minutes/bxw. Grades 1-6. Rental. UM.

HOPI KACHINAS
Shows an artisan in the complete process of carving, assembling and painting a doll; also, Hopi life and dance. 1960. Ten minutes. 16mm. UA.

HOPI: SONGS OF THE FOURTH WORLD
The study of the Hopi that captures their deep spirituality and reveals their integration of art and daily life. In two parts: Part I - Story of emergence into 4th world; explanation of corn (color and directions) and planting; Hopi courtship and marriage ceremonies; Hopi kachinas. Part II - Hopi religion; interviews with Hopi painter and potter; women's roles; child-raising and traditional education; games, clowns and Hopi humor. A study guide/resource book. 30 minutes each. 16mm and all video formats. Purchase: $425 each. Rental, 16mm (58 minute, full-length only), $100. FF.

THE HOPI WAY
Shelly Grossman; Mary Louise Grossman, Writer
The history of the Hopi is briefly discusses by David Mongnongyi who shows pictographs made by Hopi ancestors. Presents a concise picture of Hopi traditionalism and current threats to that way of life. 1972. 23 minutes. Grades 4-adult. 16mm. Purchase. FILMS. Rental, $16.20. UA and MM.

HOPIS—GUARDIANS OF THE LAND
Dennis Burns, Producer
Explores the traditional Hopi way of life and the threat of men's desecration of the land and life they have known. 1972. Ten minutes. Purchase: 16mm, $150; rental, $10. UC and FF.

HOW BEAVER STOLE FIRE
Caroline Leaf
A retelling, through animation, of a Northwest American Indian legend of how the Animal People all worked together to capture fire from the Sky People. 1972. 12 minutes. 16mm. AIMS, BYU, UI.

HOW INDIANS BUILD CANOES
An Algonquin chief and his wife fashion a watertight canoe, using ancient Indian secrets. 1948. 11 minutes/b&w. Grades 7-adult. Rental, $10.50. MM.

**HOW MAN ADAPTS
TO HIS PHYSICAL ENVIRONMENT**
The film uses as examples the Pueblo Indians, Navahos, and the early Caucasians. 1970. 20 minutes. Rental. UA and IU.

HOW TO BUILD AN IGLOO
Douglas Wilkinson, Director
Two Inuit Eskimos give a step-by-step demonstration of Igloo construction. 1950. 11 minutes. Grades K-8. 16mm/bxw. MM and SEF.

**HOW THE WEST WAS WON
...AND HONOR LOST**
Ross Devenish, Producer
A re-enactment, using photographs, paintings and newspaper accounts, telling the story of the white man's treatment of American Indians in the westward push for land. Broken treaties, railroad building, decimation of the buffalo, and the massacre at Wounded Knee. 1970. 25 minutes. 16mm. CRM, PSU and IU.

HOW THE WEST WAS LOST
Document Associates and BBC, Co-Producers
Highlights the prime of Plains Indian civilization and focuses upon the temporary Indian effort to maintain a sense of their own identity. 1972. 26 minutes. Purchase: 16mm, $400; video, $340. Rental, $55. CG.

**HUPA INDIAN
WHITE DEESKIN DANCE**
Shows a dance of the Hupa Indians of northwestern California. 1958. 11 minutes. Grades 4-adult. Rental. BARR.

I AM DIFFERENT FROM MY BROTHER: DAKOTA NAME-GIVING

A real-life docu-drama depicting the Name-Giving Ceremony of three young Flandreau Dakota Sioux Indian children. 1981. 20 minutes. 2" quad, 1" and ¾" video. Rental, $40/week. NAPBC.

I HEARD THE OWL CALL MY NAME

Roger Gimbel, Producer

A story about how an Anglican priest, who with a short time to live learns acceptance of death from the Indians. 1974. 78 minutes. 16mm. Rental. UA, MM and UM.

I WILL FIGHT NO MORE FOREVER

Richard T. Efron, Director
Stan Margulies, Producer

A dramatization of the struggle of the Nez Perce Indians and their leader Chief Joseph, who attempted to take his people to Canada to avoid being placed on a reservation. 1976. 106 minutes. 16mm. FILMS and UA.

ICE PEOPLE

An anthropological study showing that the modern Eskimo must adapt again. 1970. 23 minutes. Grades 6-adult. 16mm. Rental. MM, UM, UA and UMI.

IHANBLA WAKTOGLAG WACIPI

Henry Smith

A dance showcasing Solaris, a modern dance theatre company, and Sioux Indian dancers drawn from the nine reservations of the Lakota Nation in South Dakota. 1981. 60 minutes. ¾" video. SO.

I'TSAW: HOPI COYOTE STORIES

Larry Evers, University of Arizona

With Helen Sekaquaptewa. In Hopi with English subtitles. 1978. 18 minutes. Purchase: video, $150. CLEAR.

THE IMAGE MAKER AND THE INDIANS

George I. Quimby, Bill Holm and David Gerth

Shows how the famous pioneer cinematographer, Edward S. Curtis, made the first full-length documentary film of Native Americans among the Northwest Coast Indians of 1914. Edited and restored in 1973. 17 minutes; color/bxw. Purchase: 16mm, $275; ¾" and ½" VHS, $165. UW.

IMAGES OF INDIANS

Robert Hagopian and Phil Lucas, KCTS 9, KCTS 9, Seattle

A five-part series, narrated by Will Sampson, examines the stereotypes drawn by the movies and questions what the effect of the Hollywood image has been on the Indian's own self-image. 1) *The Great Movie Massacre* - Indian's warrior image. 2) *Heathen Injuns and the Hollywood Gospel* - The distortion and misrepresentation of Indian religion and values in Hollywood movies. 3) *How Hollywood Wins the West* - Deals with the one-sided presentation of Indian history despite the frequent use of Indian culture in Hollywood films. 4) *The Movie Reel Indians* - The image of Indians as savage murderers is commented on by Dennis Banks and Vine Deloria. 5) *Warpaint and Wigs* - Examines how the movie, *Nobel Savage* and the *Savage-Savage,* has affected the Native American self-image. 1980 30 minutes each. 16mm. VCA.

IN THE LAND OF THE WAR CANOES: KWAKIUTL INDIAN LIFE ON THE NORTHWEST COAST

Edward S. Curtis; Edited and Restored by George Quimby and Bill Holm

A saga of Kwakiutl Indian life filmed in 1914 in Vancouver Island, British Columbia, Canada. 47 minutes. Sound/bxw. Purchase: 16mm, $650; ¾" beta, $425, ½" VHS, $400. UW. Rental. UA and PSU.

IN SEARCH OF THE LOST WORLD

Tells the story of Indian cultures: complex, urbane and ancient. 1972. 52 minutes. 16mm. Rental. UA.

INDIAN AMERICA

The story of the American Indian and his desparate struggle against extinction. Indian activists, tribal leaders, and poor sheep herders tell about themselves and their heritage. 52 minutes. Grades 4-adult. Purchase: 16mm, $600; video, $350. SEF. Rental. UA.

INDIAN ART OF THE PUEBLOS

Bert Van Bork

An introductory survey of traditional art forms being produced by contemporary Pueblo artists of Arizona and New Mexico, including artists Blue Corn and Lucy Lewis. The film stresses that Pueblo artists and craftsmen are preserving their culture. 1976. 13 minutes. 16mm. EB.

INDIAN ARTIFACTS OF THE SOUTHWEST

Examines the arts and crafts of several Southwestern tribes, including: Zuni, Hopi and Navajo. Stresses the history and tradition which are apparent in the objects. 1972. 15 minutes. 16mm. Rental. IU.

INDIAN ARTISTS OF THE SOUTHWEST

Deals with the history of American Indian paintings and its rich heritage from petroglyphs to the modern artists. Shows techniques, symbolism and style. 1972. 15 minutes. Grades 4- adult. 16mm. Rental. MM and UA.

INDIAN ARTS AT THE
PHOENIX HEARD MUSEUM
KAET-TV Phoenix, Producer
Dick Peterson, Director
Explores six major areas of Native American Art:
#1: Basketry - Naomi White, guest; #2: Painting -
Larry Golsh and "Pop" Chalee, guests; #3: Pottery
- Mabel Sunn, guest; #4: Textiles - Martha Began
and Lillian Dineyazhe; #5: Jewelry - John E.
Salaby; and #6: Katchinas. 1975. 30 minutes each.
2" quad, 1" and ¾" video. Rental, $40/week.
NAPBC.

INDIAN BOY IN TODAY'S WORLD
Presents a picture of life on the Makah
Reservation and shows how the way of life on the
Reservation is changing as a result of interaction
with the outside world—the conflict of Indian and
non-Indian cultures. 1971. 14 minutes. Grades 4-
adult. Rental. UA and IU.

INDIAN BOY OF THE SOUTHWEST
Toboya, a Hopi Indian boy, tells of his life and his
home on a high mesa in the Southwestern desert
of the U.S. 1963. 15 minutes. Grades 4-9. 16mm.
Rental. UA and UM.

INDIAN CANOES ALONG
THE WASHINGTON COAST
Louis and Ruth Kirk
This film demonstrates how and with what tools a
canoe is carved; also, river and salt water races are
shown. 1971. 18 minutes. Purchase: 16mm, $250;
¾" beta, $175; and ½" VHS, $165. UW.

INDIAN CONVERSATION
Portrays two Indians, one raised in an urban
environment, the other on a reservation. Both are
college graduates and explore their identities as
Indians. 1974. 13 minutes. 16mm. Rental. UK.

INDIAN COUNTRY?
Document Associates and BBC
Indian journalist, Richard LaCourse, discusses
the revolution of attitudes within the younger
American Indians creating a new mood of
militancy. Also, interviews with Indian educators
discussing the efforts to preserve the integrity of
the Native American culture. 1972. 26 minutes.
Purchase: 16mm, $400; video, $340; rental, $55.
CG.

INDIAN FAMILY OF LONG AGO:
BUFFALO HUNTERS OF THE PLAINS
Tells the story of the Sioux Indian buffalo hunters
who roamed the great western plains of the U.S.
more than 200 years ago. 1957. 14 minutes.
Grades 4-9. 16mm. UA, MM and UM.

INDIAN FAMILY OF
THE CALIFORNIA DESERT
A woman from the Cahuilla Indian Tribe from the
desert of Palm Springs recalls her primitive life
and illustrates her tribe's culture. 1967. 16
minutes. Grades 4-9. 16mm. UA and UM.

INDIAN HERITAGE—THE TREASURE
Two young Indian brothers want to modernize
their father's fishing methods. 1970. 14 minutes.
Grades 4-12. 16mm. Rental. MM.

INDIAN HOUSE:
THE FIRST AMERICAN HOME
Remnants of the dwellings of Indians in the
Southwest represent the oldest homes in America.
1950. 11 minutes/bxw. 16mm. Rental. UA.

INDIAN HUNTER-GATHERERS
OF THE DESERT: KILIWA
Focuses on subsistence activities of Baja
California Indians. 1975. 14 minutes. 16mm.
Rental. PSU.

INDIAN INFLUENCES IN THE U.S.
David A. Baerreis, Ph.D.
Presents many aspects of Indian heritage in the
mainstream of American society today, in music,
art and the foods we eat. 1964. 11 minutes. Grades
4-9. 16mm. UM, UA and UK.

INDIAN LAND:
THE NATIVE AMERICAN ECOLOGIST
Herbert McCoy, Jr., Director/Producer
American Indians discuss their traditional
veneration for the Earth. 21 minutes; color/bxw.
FILMS.

INDIAN LEGENDS OF CANADA
Daniel Bertolino, Director
This series of 15 films provides an authentic
backdrop against which to study the first native
peoples of Canada. *The Winter Wife* (Ojibwa);
The Windigo (Montagnais); *Megmuwesug*
(MicMac); *The Path of Souls* (3 films, Ojibwa);
Moowis, Where Area You Moowis, and *The
Return of the Child* (Algonguian); *Mandamin, Or
the Legend of Corn* (Ojibwa); *Pitchie the Robin*
and *The Path Without End* (Ojibwa); *The Spirit
of the Dead Chief* (Chippewa); *Glooscap,* and *The
Invisible Man* (MicMac). 1981-1982. Available in
English and French. Purchase: 16mm, $675 each;
¾" and ½" VHS, $450 each. Rent, $65 each; series,
$8,450. TC.

INDIAN MAINSTREAM
Emphasizes rediscovery of language and rituals
which have been suppressed over the last three
generations, and the need to pass on the Indian
heritage to the young before it is forgotten.
Sponsored by the Dept. of Labor to regenerate the
Indian culture of the tribes in northern California,
specifically the Hupa, Karok, Tocowa, and Yurok
tribes. 1971. 25 minutes. 16mm. Rental. PSU.

INDIAN MUSICAL INSTRUMENTS
Construction and use of Plains Indian musical instruments in dances and songs: drums, mariachi, rattles, whistles and flute. 1955. 13 minutes. 16mm. Rental, $12.50. PSU.

INDIAN POTTERY OF SAN ILDEFONSO
Rick Krepela
Documentary of renowned Pueblo artist Maria Martinez making hand fired black pottery using techniques redeveloped after they had fallen from use. Maria, in her mid-eighties at the time, works closely with her son Popovi Da at San Ildefonso Pueblo, New Mexico. 1972. 27 minutes. 16mm. NAC.

INDIAN RIGHTS, INDIAN LAW
Joseph and Sandra Consentino, Directors
Film documentary focusing on the Native American Rights Fund, its staff and certain casework. 1978. 60 minutes. Grades 10-adult. 16mm. Rental. AF, IRA, FILMS.

INDIAN SELF-RULE:
A PROBLEM OF HISTORY
Selma Thomas
Traces the history of white-Indian relations from 19th century treaties through the present, as tribal leaders, historians, teachers, and other Indians gather at a 1983 conference organized to reevaluate the significance of the Indian Reorganization Act of 1934. The experience of the Flathead Nation of Montana, the Navajo Nation of the Southwest, and the Quinault people of the Olympic Peninsula, Washington, illustrates some of the ways Indians have dealt with shifting demands upon them. 1984. 58 minutes. Purchase: video, $400. Rental, $60. DER.

INDIAN TRIBAL GOVERNMENT
Filmed at the Gila River Indian Reservation, this film shows how effective tribal governments operate and what tribal members should expect from their governments. 1980. 16 minutes. 16mm. IDIL.

THE INDIANS
The story of the conflict between the Indian and the white man in the Colorado Territory during the time when white traders, trappers and settlers moved into the Great Plains. 1969. 31 minutes. Grades 4-12. Rental. UA.

INDIANS AND CHIEFS
Judith MacDougall
Unnarrated documentary in cinema verite style which shows the problems of Indians in maintaining their own identity while learning to master the white man's world. Records one summer's events at the Los Angeles Indian Center. 1972. 40 minutes. 16mm/bxw. UC.

INDIANS IN THE AMERICAS
Surveys (using panoramas, still photos, and paintings) the development of the American Indian civilizations from the first nomadic hunter to the European explorers. 1971. 15 minutes. Rental. IU.

INDIANS OF CALIFORNIA
Tells the story of a primitive people as they lived before the white man came to the Pacific Coast. In two parts: Part 1, *Village Life* - includes trading, house building, basket-making, use of a tule boat, the sweat house, songs and dances. 15 minutes. Part 2, *Food* - includes bow and arrow making, a deer hunt, gathering and preparing acorns, a family meal, and the story teller. 14 minutes. 1955. Also, a LP record, *California Indian Songs,* $5.00. BARR, MM and UA.

INDIANS OF EARLY AMERICA
Classifies all of the Indians of early America according to four general geographic regions, and represents each region by one dominant and characteristic tribe. 1957. 22 minutes. Grades 4-adult. In English and Spanish. UA, PSU, MM and UM.

INDIANS OF THE PLAINS:
LIFE IN THE PAST
This film describes how the Plains Indians depended on the buffalo for almost all the necessities of life. Also, quillwork, beadwork and painting are presented. 11 minutes. 16mm. Rental. UT an PSU.

INDIANS OF THE PLAINS:
PRESENT DAY LIFE
Life and activites on a Blackfeet Indian reservation in Montana. Interviews with some of the Indians. 1954. 11 minutes. Grades 4-adult. Rental. UMI.

INDIANS OF THE PLAINS:
SUN DANCE CEREMONY
Pictures erection of the tepee or tent for lodging. Features the "Sweat Lodge," "Sun Dance Ceremony" and "Grass Dance." 11 minutes. Grades 4-adult. 16mm. Rental. UT, MM and PSU.

INDIANS OF THE SOUTHWEST
Focuses on the history and culture of the Indians of the Southwest; their descendants, the Pueblos, and other tribes that settled in the Southwest, including the Navajos, Hopi and Zuni. 16 minutes. Grades 4-9. 16mm. FILMS.

**INSTITUTE FOR THE
DEVELOPMENT OF INDIAN LAW**
A series of five seven minute films providing a review of vital areas of federal Indian law and their effect on tribal government. They include: *A Question of Indian Sovereignty, Indian Treaties, Indians and the U.S. Government, Indian Jurisdiction,* and *The Federal-Indian Trust Relationship.* Purchase: 16mm, $550/set. IDIL.

INUIT
Bo Boudart, Director
Documents the first Inuit Circumpolar Conference of 1977. Provides an overview of the issues that concern Native peoples in the Arctic. 1978. 28 minutes. 16mm. BO and PI.

IROQUOIS SOCIAL DANCE
Nick Manning
Presents, in two parts, social dances of the Mohawk Indians, filmed on the Reserve at St. Regis, Canada. Part I, 15 minutes; part II, 11 minutes. Teacher's guide. RM and GREEN.

Manning and Green.

ISHI IN TWO WORLDS
The story of the Yahi Indians of California. Ishi, the last of the Yahi, was the last person in North America known to have lived a totally aboriginal existence. 1967. 19 minutes. Grades 6-adult. 16 mm. Rental. UT, MM, PSU and UA.

ITS NOT JUST A TIME FOR FUN
Looks at the annual "Choctaw Fair" held every June on the Choctaw Reservation. Introduces all the activities of the Fair. All grades. 15 minutes. Purchase: ¼" VHS, $85; rental, $10 (two weeks). CHP.

**IYAIIKIMIX, BLACKFEET
BEAVER BUNDLE CEREMONY**
Sacred bundles are collections of artifacts and sacred natural objects belonging to clan ancestors and passed on to their descendants. The ritual consists of dancing with the chanting to the bundle's individual parts. Presents the religion's ritual in its entirety. 58 minutes. 16mm. UAB.

JOE KILLS RIGHT—OGLALA SIOUX
Jon Alpert (DTC-IV)
Portrait of a young Sioux man living in New York City. Scenes of Joe living in one of New York City's worst neighborhoods. He loses his job, begins drinking and using drugs, then enters a treatment center. After, he returns to the reservation. Includes dialogue of educational and health services on the reservation. 1980. 25 minutes. ¾" beta and ½" VHS. DTC.

JOHNNY FROM FORT APACHE
Records the readjustments in lifestyle the Russells, an Indian family, experience when they move from the reservation to San Francisco.

1971. 15 minutes. Grades 4-adult. 16mm. Rental. UA and IU.

JOSHUA'S SOAPSTONE CARVING
Joshua Qumaluk, an Eskimo, helps his Uncle Levi hunt, fish and trap. He learns to carve soapstone sculptures to sell. 23 minutes. Grades 4-adult. Purchase: 16mm, $495; video, $290; rental, $60. COR.

**JOURNEY TO THE SKY:
A HISTORY OF THE ALABAMA
COUSHATTA INDIANS**
Robert Cozens; KUHT Film Productions
Alabama Chief, Fulton Battise relates in his native dialect the fantasy tale of three youths traveling to the ends of the earth and beyond. Describes the struggle of a people to preserve their way of life. 1980. 53 minutes. 2" quad, 1" and ¾" video. Rental, $80/week. NAPBC.

KAINAI
Raoul Fox, Director
On the Blood Indian Reserve, near Cardston, Alberta, Canada, a pre-fab factory has been built to employ the residents. 27 minutes. 16mm. NFBC.

**KASHIA MEN'S DANCES:
SOUTHWESTERN POMO INDIANS**
Clyde B. Smith, Producer
Preserves four authentic Pomo dances as performed in full costume on the Kashia Reservation on the northern California coast. 1969. 40 minutes. Purchase: 16mm, $540; video, $380. Rental. UC and PSU.

KEEPER OF THE WESTERN DOOR
Eight short films made on the Cattaraugus and Allegany Reservations in western New York. Each program investigates Seneca life. *The Music and Dance of the Senecas,* 11 minutes; *A Seneca Language Class,* 11 minutes; *Preparing Seneca Food,* 18 minutes; *The Seneca People— Past and Present,* 13 minutes; *A Visit to the Basketmaker,* 12 minutes; *A Visit to the Beader,* 15 minutes; *A Visit to the Seneca Museum,* 15 minutes; *A Visit With a Seneca Artist,* 17 minutes. 1980. ¾" video. SN.

KENOJUAK
Eskimo artist, her drawings, and her thoughts. 1964. 20 minutes. Grades 6-adult. Rental. MM.

KEVIN ALEC
Beverly Shaffer, Director
Kevin, an 11 year-old Indian boy from the Fountain Indian Reserve in British Columbia, Canada, whose parents are dead, lives with his grandmother. He leaves, participates and builds pride in the value of tribal life. 1976. 16½ minutes. Grades 1-8. Purchase: 16mm, $290; video, $145; rental, $28. MG.

THE KWAKIUTL
OF BRITISH COLUMBIA
Franz Boas; Bill Holm, Editor
A documentary film made by noted anthropologist Dr. Franz Boas, in 1930 at Fort Rupert on Vancouver Island. Includes scenes depicting traditional Kwakiutl dances, crafts, games, oratory and actions of a shaman. 1950. 55 minutes. Silent/bxw. Purchase: 16mm, $500; ¾" beta, $350; ½" VHS, $340. UW. Rental. IU.

LA CROSSE STICK MAKER
Jack Ofield, Director/Producer
Onondaga craftsmen of the sovereign Onondaga Nation, located in New York State, demonstrate the ancient craft of steaming and binding wood to make lacrosse sticks.They discusses tools and techniques, play a game and reflect on their cultural heritage and lifestyle. 1974. Nine minutes. 16mm. OFIELD and BGF.

THE LAKOTA:
ONE NATION ON THE PLAINS
Fran Cantor
Narrated by N. Scott Momaday, this film opens by evoking traditional Lakota philosophy, and conveys history as it is understood in the Lakota tradition. 1976. 29 minutes. 16mm and ¾" beta-video. UMA.

LAMENT OF THE RESERVATION
Discusses the living conditions of the 600,000 Indians on barren reservations, pointing out high infant mortality and suicide rates. 23 minutes. 16mm. Rental, $25. UT.

THE LAND IS THE CULTURE
Fred Cawsey
The pursuit of land claims by Indian tribes of British Columbia, Canada. Narrated by Philip Paul, the Union of British Columbia India Chiefs land claims director. 1975. 30 minutes. 16mm. PC.

LAND OF THE LONG DAY
Depicts the life of the Eskimos on Baffin Island. 1952. 36 minutes/bxw. Rental. UM.

LAST SALMON FEAST
OF THE CELILO INDIANS
Produced prior to the Dalles Dam inundation of the last major salmon fishery of the Wy-am Pum, a branch of lower Deschute Indians, the Yakimas and the Warm Springs, and other central Oregon tribes. 1955. 18 minutes/bxw. Purchase: 16mm, $150; rental, $10. OHS.

LEGEND
A story based on a west Canadian Indian legend in which a youth must perform certain feats to win a fair maiden. 1970. 15 minutes. 16mm. Rental. UM.

LEGEND OF THE BOY
AND THE EAGLE
The Hopi legend of Tutevina, the young Indian boy who is banished from his tribe for freeing the sacrificial bird. 21 minutes. 16mm. WD.

LEGEND OF THE MAGIC KNIVES
A totem village in the Pacific Northwest provides the setting for this portrayal of an ancient Indian legend, recountered by means of figures on a totem pole and authentic Indian masks. 1970. 11 minutes. Grades 4-12. 16mm. Rental. UA, MM and PSU.

LEGENDS OF THE SIOUX
Filmed in South Dakota, this film relates many of the legends of the Sioux Indians. 27 minutes. 16mm. Rental. UK.

LIKE THE TREES
Rose, a Metis Indian from northern Alberta, leaves the city to find her roots among the Woodland Cree. 15 minutes. 16mm. NFBC.

LITTLE DIOMEDE
Portrays the life of Eskimos on Diomede Island in the Bering Straits. 1957. 16 minutes. Grades 4-9. 16mm. Rental. UMI.

LITTLE WHITE SALMON INDIAN SETTLEMENT
Harry Dawson, Director; Leo Alexander, Advisor
Cooks Landing, the site of one of the oldest Indian fishing villages in North America, is the subject of this documentary produced in cooperation with members of the Yakima Indian Tribe. 1972. 31 minutes. 16mm. Purchase or rental. UNI and PSU.

LIVE AN REMEMBER
Using some footage of *Vision Dance,* as well as new interviews and footage shot on Rosebud Reservation in South Dakota, this film examines the role and sacred nature of dance, music and oral tradition in Lakota culture and what it means to be Indian living in America today. 1986. SOLARIS.

THE LIVING STONE
John Freeney, Director
Contemporary Inuit Eskimos of Cape Dorset on Baffin Island continue an ageless tradition of creative craftsmenship carving stone into evocative portrayals of Inuit life. 1958. 32 minutes. Grades 7-adult. Purchase: 16mm, $550; video, $350. Rental, $60. NFBC. Rental only, MM.

LIVING TRADITION:
FIVE INDIAN WOMEN ARTISTS
Denise Mayotte, Kathee Prokop
and Fran Belvin
The relationship between traditional Indian values and the handiwork of five Indian women artists from Minnesota is examined. Shows the role of culture handed down from generation to generation. 1983. Video. Purchase: $150; rental, $75. UCV.

THE LONG WALK
KQED-TV San Francisco
Explores the contemporary life of the Navajo and describes their history. 1970. 60 minutes. 16mm. FW and UC.

THE LONG WALK OF FRED YOUNG
Michael Barnes
The story of a child, Fred Young, who only spoke the Ute and Navajo languages, went to a medicine man when he was sick. Today, he is Dr. Frederick Young a nuclear physicist. 1979. 16mm. 49 minutes; ¾" video, 58 minutes. WGBH.

THE LONGEST WALK:
S.F. TO D.C. 1978
A documentary of the spiritual and political walk across the nation from Alcatraz Island to Washington, D.C. to protest anti-Indian legislation and inform local communities about eleven bills then currently before Congress. 60 minutes. Also available are three 20 minute videotapes which are supplemental reference information: *John Trudell—Pueblo Rally Speech; A Look Behind Indian Legislation;* and, *Dennis Banks—AIM Leader in Exile.* Video only. Purchase: $170 (Documentary), $75 (each supplement.) Rental: $50 (Documentary), $35 (each supplement.) CLP.

THE LONGEST WAR
Diane Orr, Director
An interview with Dennis Banks, founder of the American Indian Movement (AIM). Shows scenes of the occupation of Wounded Knee and the burning of the Courthouse at Custer, South Dakota in 1973. Interviews with participants at Wounded Knee. 1974. 30 minutes. 16mm and ¾" video. BF.

THE LONGHOUSE PEOPLE
Tom Daly, Producer
The life and religion of the Iroquois today. Shows a rain dance, a healing ceremony, and a celebration of a new chief. 1951. 23 minutes. Grades 7-adult. Purchase: 16mm, $500; video, $300. Rental, $50. NFBC.

THE LOON'S NECKLACE
Crawley Films, Producer
A Spanish language film recreating a Salish legend which tells how the loon came to receive his distinguished neckband. Authentic ceremonial masks establish the characters of the story. 1949. 11 minutes. Grades 4-adult. 16mm. EB, UC, MM, PSA and UT.

LOS INDIOS NAVAJOS
A Spanish language film which shows the Navajo people in their own environment. 1939. 11 minutes; bxw. Grades 4-8. UA.

LUCY COVINGTON:
NATIVE AMERICAN INDIAN
Steve Heiser, Director
Filmed on the Colville Reservation in eastern Washington, Lucy Covington, chairperson of the Colville tribe and granddaughter of Chief Moses, gives an account of her part in the effort to prevent federal termination of the tribe. She talks about the Indian heritage and Indian identity, and how the land is central to these. 1978. 16mm. EB.

LUCY SWAN
An Indian woman born on the Rosebud Reservation at the turn of the century remembers the old ways but does not entirely discount the new. 16mm. BCA.

LUMAAQ - AN ESKIMO LEGEND
Co Hoedeman, Director
Lumaaq tells the story of a legend widely believed by the Povungnituk Inuit. 1975. Eight minutes. Grades 7-adult. Purchase: 16mm, $200; video, $150; rental, $35. NFBC.

MAGIC IN THE SKY
An examination of the impact of TV on Eskimos and their efforts to establish their own network. Mirrors the struggle of any culture to preserve its unique identity. 57 minutes. Grades 7-adult. Purchase: 16mm, $775; video, $450. Rental, $80. NFBC.

THE MAN AND THE GIANT:
AN ESKIMO LEGEND
Co Hoedeman, Director
An Inuit legend acted out by the Inuit people themselves. They use their traditional form of singing, "katadjak," or throat singing. 1975. Eight minutes. All ages. PHOENIX.

MAN OF LIGHTNING
Gary Moss, Producer
Based on two Cherokee Indian legends, this film is a drama of the long-vanished world of the Cherokee years before European contact. 1982. 29 minutes. 2"quad, 1" and ¾" video. Rental, $40/week. NAPBC.

THE MAN, THE SNAKE AND THE FOX
Portrays an Ojibway Indian legend through the traditional story-telling framework. 1978. 12 minutes. Grades 1-8. MOKIN.

MAN'S ROLE IN THE COMMUNITY
Pictographic drawings and live scenes are combined to present daily life as seen through Indian eyes. 1970. 15 minutes. Rental. UM.

MAN'S ROLE IN THE FAMILY
Courtship customs and the man's responsibility in protecting and providing for his family are told by a Kiowa man who describes details of this aspect of the Indian life to the Kiowa boy. 1970. 15 minutes. Rental. UM.

MARIA AND JULIAN'S BLACK POTTERY
  Arthur Baggs
Shows famous potters Maria and Julian Martinez in the step-by-step process of creating the famed "black-on-black" pottery that revivied at San Ildefonso Pueblo, New Mexico. 1938/1977. 11 minutes. 16mm/silent. Purchase, $190; Rental, $11.50. MM and PSU.

MARIA OF THE PUEBLOS
The life of the famous Pueblo potter, Maria Martinez. Provides an understanding of the culture, philosophy, art and economic condition of the Pueblo Indians of San Ildefonso, New Mexico. 15 minutes. Grades 4-adult. Purchase: 16mm, $345; video, $240. Rental, $50. COR.

THE MARMES ARCHAEOLOGICAL DIG
  Louis and Ruth Kirk, Producers
Presents the oldest fully documented discovery of early man in the Western Hemisphere. 1971. 18 minutes. Purchase: 16mm, $250; ¾" beta, $175; ½" VHS, $165. UW.

MATTHEW ALIUK:
ESKIMO IN TWO WORLDS
  Bert Sulzman, Writer/Director
The relationship of an Eskimo boy assimilated into the city life of Anchorage. Tells the story of a proud people's struggle for cultural survival in a changing world. 1973. 18 miutes. All ages. Purchase: 16mm, $270. Rental, $25. LCA.

MEDOONAK, THE STORMMAKER
  Les Krizsan, Director
A MicMac Indian legend. 1975. 13 minutes. Grades 7-12. Rental. IFB and UA.

MEET THE SIOUX INDIAN
Shows the transient life of the Sioux Indians. 1949. Ten minutes. Grades 4-adult. Rental. UM and UMI.

MENOMINEE
This documentary examines the historical development of the many social and political problems faced by the Menominee Indians of northwestern Wisconsin. 1974. 59 minutes. 2" quad, 1" and ¾" video. Rental $80/week. NAPBC.

MESA VERDE: MYSTERY OF
THE SILENT CITIES
Views (using extensive aerial photography) the ruined cities and multiply family cliff dwellings of the 13th century Indians of the Mesa Verde. 1975. 14 minutes. 16mm. Rental. IU.

MESQUAKIE
  Alan Weber and Michael Bartell
Looks at the Mesquakie Indian settlement at Tama, Iowa, where carious activities of the traditional days are shown through old photographs and present-day film footage. 1976. Ten minutes. ISU.

MIGHTY WARRIORS
During the mass migration west, the white man encountered the Plains Indians. Familiar battles are depicted in the light of the true facts. 1964. 30 minutes. Grades 6-adult. 16mm. UA and UM.

MI'KMAQ
A series of five programs recreating, in dramatized form, the seasonal round of Micmac life in Nova Scotia, Canada, before European contact as it might have been experienced by a single, extended Micmac family. Performed by Native people in the Micmac language. Available in French and English. Teacher's guide. Grades 6-adult. NS.

MINORITIES IN AGRICULTURE:
THE WINNEBAGO
  Ralph A. Swain, Briar Cliff College
Highlights the economic development programs of the Winnebago Tribe of Nebraska. 1984. 29 minutes. 2" quad, 1" and ¾" video. Rental, $40/week. NAPBC.

MINORITY YOUTH: ADAM
The narration of a teenage American Indian's view of himself, his race, and his cultural heritage that is in danger of being lost. 1971. Ten minutes. 16mm. Rental. IU.

MISS INDIAN AMERICA
  KBYU-TV, Provo, Utah
Covers the 20th annual Miss Indian America Pageant in 1973 at Sheridan, Wyoming. Contest represents 30 American Indian tribes from all over the U.S. 59 minutes. 2" quad, 1" and ¾" video. Rental, $80/week. NAPBC.

MISSION LIFE:
ALTA CALIFORNIA 1776
22 minutes. 16mm. Rental. UA.

MISSION OF FEAR
Fernand Dansereau, Director
The story of the Jesuit martyrs who lived with their Huron converts, Indians of Midland, Ontario. 79 minutes/bxw. NFBC.

MISSION SAN XAVIER DEL BAC
33 minutes. 16mm. Rental. UA.

MISSIONS OF CALIFORNIA:
NEW WAYS IN NEW WORLD
21 minutes. 16mm. Rental. UA.

MISSIONS OF THE SOUTHWEST
15 minutes. 16mm. Rental. UA.

MODOC
Peter Winograd
By the use of archival photos by Edward S. Curtis and news clippings, this film tells the story of the Modoc Indians of California and their struggle to remain on their own lands. 1979. 15 minutes. bxw. 16mm and ¾" beta. EM.

MOHAWK BASKETMAKING:
A CULTURAL PROFILE
Frank Semmens
Features a sensitive and personal look at the life and work of master basketmaker Mary Adams. 1980. 28 minutes. Purchase: 16mm, $385; rental, $19.50. PSU. Rental: 16mm, $95/3 days. AM. ¾" Video. IF.

MONUMENT VALLEY:
LAND OF THE NAVAJOS
Shows the life of the Navajo Indians in the four-corner area where Arizona, New Mexico, Colorado and Utah meet. 1959. 17 minutes. Grades 6-adult. 16mm. UA.

MORE BOWS AND ARROWS
Roy Williams, Director
Shows the Impact Native Americans have had on the development of the U.S. Narrated by N. Scott Momaday, a prominenet Kiowa Indian writer and educator. 1977. 58 minutes. Grades 5-adult. Purchase and rental. COP, NILB, IRA, PSU.

MOTHER CORN
KBYU-TV, Provo, Utah
Examines the historical significance of various types of corn among Native American cultures. 1977. 29 minutes. 2" quad, 1" and ¾" video. Rental, $40/week. NAPBC.

MOTHER OF MANY CHILDREN
Alanis Obomsawin, Director
Agatha Marie Goodine, 108 year-old member of the Hobbema tribe, contrasts her memories with the conflicts that most Indian and Inuit woman face today. 1977. 58 minutes. Grades 9-adult. Purchase: 16mm, $775; videp, $450. Rental, $80. NFBC.

MUSIC AND DANCE OF THE MOHAWK
Traces the origin, development and meaning behind Iroquois social songs; and the making of Iroquois musical instruments. 16mm. Rental, $95/3 days. AM.

MY FATHER CALLS ME SON:
RACISM AND NATIVE AMERICANS
David Fanning, Executive Producer for KOCE-TV
Examines the problem of discrimination and some of the parallel pressures against Indian people to give up their uniqueness and become more like whites. 1975. 29 minutes. ¾" video. PBS.

MY HANDS ARE TOOLS OF MY SOUL:
ART AND POETRY OF THE
AMERICAN INDIAN
Arthur Barron and Zina Voynoz
A survey of American Indian achievements in poetry, music, sculpture, philosophy and history. Dialogue in tribal language as well as English. 1975. 54 minutes. 16mm and video. TF, MM and PSU.

THE MYSTERY OF THE ANASAZI
Russ Morash, Director; WGBH, Producer
A study of the ruins of the "Anasazi," the builders, ancestors of the Navajo. 1976. 59 minutes. 16mm and video. TIME, PSU, MM and ISU.

MYTHS AND THE MOUNDBUILDERS
Graham Chedd, WGBH, Producer
Archaeologists probe mysterious mounds in the Eastern U.S. uncovering clues about a lost Indian civilization. Educator's guide. 1980. 60 minutes. 16mm and video. PBS and DER.

NANOOK OF THE NORTH
Robert Flaherty
A documentary studying the life of an Eskimo hunter and his constant struggle for survival against the menaces of nature. 1922. 16mm/bxw/silent. Original silent version, MMA; silent version with text, PSU and MM; restored version with musical score, FILMS.

NATIVE AMERICAN ARTS
Indian Arts and Crafts Board
The development of Native American arts in the U.S. Shows that contemporary artists and craftsmen (Indian Eskimo and Aleut) are making unique and significant contributions to the cultural life of our nation. 20 minutes. Purchase: 16mm, $116. Rental, $15/3 days. NAC.

NATIVE AMERICAN MYTHS
An animated film introduced by Native American narrator Ned Romero, who briefly explains the relevant background information for each of five authentic myths: *Sky Woman,* a Seneca myth; *How Raven Gave Daylight to the World,* Haida myth; *The First Strawberry,* Cherokee myth; *The People Came Out of the Underworld,* Hopi myth. 1977. 24 minutes. 16mm. Rental. EB and UT.

NATWANIWA: A HOPI PHILOSOPHICAL STATEMENT
Larry Evers, University of Arizona
With George Nasoftie, a ceremonial leader, talks of cultivation of the land—how every crop and action has significance for his future life. In Hopi with English subtitles. 27 minutes. Video. CLEAR.

NAVAJO
KBYU, Provo, Utah
Teaching children the way and heritage of the Navajo people. 1979. 29 minutes. 2" quad, 1" and ¾" video. Rental, $40/week. NAPBC.

NAVAJO
The Navajos of the Grand Canyon. 16 minutes. Grades 7-12. 16mm. FILMS.

THE NAVAJO
A visit to the Navajo Reservation in northeastern Arizona to discover the values held by this indigenous community. Navajo medical practices, religious rituals and beliefs are compared to modern practices, with a discussion of the problems of reconciling traditional Navajo ways with modern technology. 1969. 58 minutes/bxw. Grades 9-adult. Rental. UA.

THE NAVAJO
The history, customs, and life of the Navajo Indian Nation (15 million acres within the Southwestern part of the U.S.) are described in this film. 1972. 21 minutes. 16mm. Rental. IU.

NAVAJO CANYON COUNTRY
Depicts the way of life of the Navajos and provides some of the historical background of Indian life in Arizona and New Mexico. 1954. 13 minutes. 16mm. Rental. IU, UM and PSU.

NAVAJO CHILDREN
Deals with the semiannual migration of a Navajo family to its summer home. 1938. 11 minutes/bxw. 16mm. Rental. UK, UM, UMI.

NAVAJO CODE TALKERS
Tom McCarthy
Documentary using interviews and archival footage to show the vital role a small group of Navajo Marines played in the South Pacific during World War II. Interviews with Peter McDonald, Navajo Chairman; Carl Gorman, artist and scholar; and R.C. Gorman, Taos artist. 28 minutes. 16mm and video. NMFV and OW.

NAVAJO COUNTRY
Shows the nomadic life of the Navajo Indian in northwestern Arizona. 1951. Ten minutes. Grades 1-6. 16m. Rental. UA, UM, IU.

NAVAJO COYOTE TALES: LEGEND TO FILM
Animate in English and Navajo. Shows how coyote films were animated on computer. 18 minutes. Grades 6-adult. Purchase: 16mm, $260. Video. Rental, $11/week. SAN.

NAVAJO FILM THEMSELVES
Sol Worth and John Adair
Concerned with seeing how Navajo Indians, taught the technology of filmmaking might show a definite Navajo perspective in their films. Five films are descriptive of processes; two are concerned with man's relationship to nature. *A Navajo Weaver,* by Susie Benally; *A Navajo Silversmith,* by Johnny Nelson; *Old Antelope Lake,* by Mike Anderson; *The Shallow Well Project,* by Johnny Nelson; *Second Weaver,* by Alta Kahn; and, *The Spirit of the Navajo,* by Maxine and Mary Jane Tsosie.1966. 16mm/bxw. MMA.

NAVAJO GIRL
Life on an Indian reservation in northeast Arizona. Focuses on the life of a ten year old girl and her family. 1973. 20 minutes. Grades 3-12. Rental, $17.50. MM.

THE NAVAJO INDIAN
Provides a picture of the changing life styles of the Navajos who live on an Arizona reservation. 1975 revised edition. Ten minutes. Grades K-6. Purchase: 16mm, $250; video, $175; rental, $40. COR and UA.

NAVAJO INDIANS
Portrays the Navajos in their native environment. 1939. 11 minutes. Grades 4-9. 16mm/bxw. Rental. UA, PSU, UK, UM and IU.

NAVAJO LIFE
Shows the National Monument of Canyon de Chelly, describing the life of the Navajo Indians living in the canyon. 1961. Nine minutes. 16mm. Rental. IU.

THE NAVAJO MOVES INTO THE ELECTRONIC AGE
Briefly describes the background of the Navajo before World War II. Then points out how the tribal council invested income from oil discoveries into projects to benefit the entire tribe. 19 minutes. 16mm. Rental. UK and UA.

NAVAJO NIGHT DANCES
Walter P. Lewisohn, Producer
Deals with a Navajo family at the Nine Day Healing Chant, a feast, and the Arrow, Feather and Fire Dance rituals. 1957. 12 minutes. 16mm. Rental. UM, UK and UA.

NAVAJO - A PEOPLE BETWEEN TWO WORLDS

Francis R. Line

Effects of modern culture upon the largest remaining Indian tribe on a reservation in Arizona. 1958. 18 minutes. 16mm. Rental, $14. PSU.

NAVAJO, RACE FOR PROSPERITY

Document ASssociates & BBC

Offers a contemporary view of life on the Navajo reservation and focuses upon the development of industries on the reservation. 1972. 26 minutes. Purchase: 16mm, $400; video, $340. CG.

NAVAJO: SHEPHERDS OF THE DESERT

Describes a day in the life of a typical Navajo family. 1970. Nine minutes. Grades 4-adult. 16mm. Rental. UA.

NAVAJO SILVERSMITHING

Focuses on a Navajo craftsman, Tom Burnside, on an Arizona reservation, who has come to grips with modern technology while still maintaining the values of his own culture. 1960. 11 minutes. Grades 4-adult. Rental. UM, MM, PSU and UA.

NAVAJO: A STUDY IN CULTURAL CONTRAST

Portrays the culture, social organization, and physical environment of the Navajo Indian. 1968. 16 minutes. Grades 6-12. 16mm. Rental. UA, PSU and IU.

NAVAJO: THE LAST RED INDIANS

Michael Baines

Contains scenes of Navajo ceremonies including diagnosing illnesses by trance-like "hand trembling" and a "sing" or healing ceremony. The integration of traditional healing practices with those of white doctors is shown. 1972. 35 minutes. 16mm and video. TIME, UC and UA.

THE NAVAJO WAY

Robert Northshield, Director

Survival as a tribe within American society is said to come from the involvement with tradition, the Navajo way. Reflects the spiritual life of the traditional community. 1975. 52 minutes. 16mm. (Sales only). FILMS.

THE NAVAJOS AND ANNIE WAUNEKA

Annie Wauneka, awarded the Freedom Medal by President Kennedy for her achievements in public health education among her fellow Navajo Indian, visits the homes of her people instructing them in simple health measures. 1965. 26 minutes. Grades 9-adult. 16mm. Rental. UA.

NAVAJOS, CHILDREN OF THE GODS

Explores the traditions and lifestyles of the Navajos. 1967. 20 minutes. Grades 5-adult. 16mm. Rental. UM and MM.

NAVAJOS OF THE 70's

Deals with the customs, history, economics, current problems and future prospects of the Navajo Indians. 15 minutes. Grades 1-8. 16mm. Rental. UM and UK.

NEHI CHEII TOAD COUNTS HIS CORN

Math concept of place value taught using coyote and toad. Available in English and Navajo version. Animated. Ten minutes. Grades 2-8. 16mm and video. Rental, $10/week. SAN.

NESHNABEK: THE PEOPLE

Gene Bernofsky; Donald Stull, Project Director

Based on footage of the Prairie Band Potawatomi of Kansas by amatuer anthropologist Floyd Schultz between 1927-1941, this film was edited and suppied with a soundtrack based on recent interviews with elderly Potawatomi. Covers reservation life, culture and the people. 1979. 30 minutes. STULL and UK.

NETSILIK ESKIMO SERIES

Quenten Brown, Ph.D., Director

At The Autumn River Camp: Two Parts: Part 1, In late autumn, the Inuit travel through soft snow and build karmaks in the river valley. Fishing through ice. 26 minutes. Part 2, The men build an igloo, make a seligh; women work on parka; children play. 33 minutes. *At The Caribou Crossing Place:* Two Parts: Part 1, Early autumn; caribou hunting and skins. 30 minutes. Part 2, Caribou hunting. 29 minutes. *At The Spring Sea Ice Camp:* Three Parts: Part 1, Two Inuit families travel across the wide sea ice; build small igloos. 27 minutes. Part 2, The men hunt seal through ice, then skin it. 27 minutes. Part 3, Hunting and fishing; women sewing; breaking camp moving ashore to tents for summer. 27 minutes. *At The Winter Sea Ice Camp:* Four Parts: Part 1, Seal hunting; making camp for winter. 36 minutes. Part 2, Women with furs; men hunting; children play; games. 36 minutes. Part 3, Comunity igloos; games; hunting and fishing. 30 minutes. Part 4, Family activities; games and music. 35 minutes. *Building A Kayak:* Two Parts: Part 1, Summer, ice melts, time to build a kayak. 33 minutes. Part 2, Building a kayak. 33 minutes. *Stalking Seal On The Spring Ice:* Two Parts. Part 1, Seal hunt and skinning; use of fur and meat. 25 minutes. Part 2, Seal hunt. 34 minutes. *The Eskimo: Fight For Life; People of the Seal: Eskimo Summer/Winter; Yesterday, Today: The Netsilik Eskimo.* 1969. Grades 7-adult. 16mm. EDC, UEVA, PSU and UA.

THE NEW CAPITALISTS: ECONOMICS IN INDIAN COUNTRY

Portrays developments on some 30 reservations from Alaska to Florida. Examines the quantum leap into the 20th century being made by Native Americans. Provides insight into Native

American culture, Narrated by Eric Sevareid. Adult. 30 minutes. 16mm and video. Free loan. Odyssey. Rental, 60 minute ½″ VHS, $10. NILB.

THE NEW INDIANS
Shows a young Creek woman as she attends an intertribal conference; a Kwakiutl chief; a Navajo woman attorney; etc. 1977. 59 minutes. Purchase: 16mm, $595; video, $545. NGS.

NINOS NAVAJOS
Spanish language film. 11 minutes. 16mm/bxw. Rental. UA.

THE NORTH AMERICAN INDIAN
In three parts: Part 1: *Treaties Made, Treaties Broken*—presents the conflict between the Nisqually and Washington State over fishing rights. 17 minutes. Part 2: *How the West Was Won, And Honor Lost*—presents a chronology of Indian-white relations from the landing of Columbus to the defeat of Geronimo in 1866. 25 minutes. Part 3: *Lament of the Reservation*—presents the living conditions of the Sioux Indians on Pine Ridge Reservation in the Badlands of South Dakota. Also looks at another reservation in Washington State where suicide is above the national average. 23 minutes. 1971. Narrated by Marlon Brando; music by Buffy St. Marie. 16mm. Rental. UM, MM, IU and PSU.

NORTH AMERICAN INDIAN ARTS AND CRAFTS SERIES
  Geoff Voyce
Commissioned by the Canadian National Indian Arts and Crafts Corporation, this film shows individual artists in their local setting and their artistic processes examined. The following films are available in English, French and Indian languages: *Beads and Leather of Manitoba* - ten minutes, Cecilia Ross (Cree); *Birch Bar Biting* - six minutes, Angelique Mirasty (Cree); *A Ceremonial Pipe* - ten minutes, Guy Suvi (Abenaki); *A Corn Husk Doll* - Deanna Skye (Cayuga); *Fort Albany Carver* - 14 minutes, Lawrence Mark (Cree); *Fort Albany Carver* - 14 minutes, Lawrence Mark (Cree); *Iroquoian Pottery* - 18 minutes, Bill Parker (Iroquois); *Joe Jacobs-Stone Carver* - ten minutes, (Cayuga); *A Malecite Fancy Basket* - 12 minutes, Veronica and Jim Atwin (Malecite); *A Micmac Scale Basket* - 12 minutes, Rita and Noel Michae (Micmac); *A Noon Mask* - Freda Deising (Haida); *A Pair of Moccasins* - Mary Thomas (Shuswap); *Porcupine Quill Work* - ten minutes, Bernadette Pangawish (Odawa); *Robert Bellegarde, A Prairie Artist* - 12 minutes, (Cree); *Sara Smith, Mohawk Potter* - 18 minutes; *A Silver Choice* - ten minutes, Joseph Gabriel (Mohawk); *Tony Hunt, Kwakiutl Artist* - ten minutes; *A Willow Basket* - 11 minutes, Florence Hotomani (Assiniboine); *Wood Flowers of Nova Scotia* - Matilda Paul (Micmac.) 1977-1979. 16mm. NAIF.

NORTH AMERICAN INDIAN LEGENDS
Dramatizes several Indian legends with special effects photography to emphasize their mythical quality. 1973. 21 minutes. Grades 1-8. 16mm. Rental. IU and UA.

NORTH AMERICAN INDIAN TODAY
Covers contemporary attitudes of Indians as well as their cultural past. 1977. 25 minutes. Purchase: 16mm, $395; video, $360. NGS.

NORTH OF 60°: DESTINY UNCERTAIN
  TV Ontario, Producer
Five 30 minute programs exploring areas of Canada's Northwest Territories, the Yukon and Alaska. Depicts the reality of life in the far north, and the future of this land and the culture of its original inhabitants. See NAPBC for titles and prices.

THE NORTHERN PLAINS
An examination of the history of legendary plains warriors (the Sioux and Crow tribes) who fought against the U.S. for their lands and means of survival. 1966. 30 minutes/b&w. Purchase: video, $175; rental, $20. MM.

NORTHWEST COAST INDIANS: A SEARCH FOR THE PAST
  Louis and Ruth Kirk
Archaeologists and students reconstruct the Ozette Indian Village at Cape Alava, Washington, an abandoned seafaring hunter's village site. 1973. 26 minutes. Purchase: 16mm, $340; ¾″ VHS, $200; ½″ VHS, $200. UW.

NORTHWEST INDIAN ART
  Walter P. Lewisohn, Producer
Shows material collected from six different museums, including double-faced mechanical masks. 1966. Ten minutes. 16mm. Rental. UM and UK.

NORTHWESTERN AMERICAN INDIAN WAR DANCE CONTEST
Covers an annual contest portraying The War Dance, The Feather Dance, The Fancy Dance, and The Hoop Dance. 1971. 12 minutes. Purchase: 16mm, $200; ¾″ VHS, $150; ½″ VHS, $140. UW.

NOUISE KENE SERIES
  Simon Brascoupe, Executive Producer
Nouise Kene means "our children" in Dene; four films about child care in remote Native American regions, focusing on basic care in pregnancy and for newborn and pre-school children. *Preparing For Parenting*, 15 minutes; *Infant Care*, 12 minutes; *The Early Years*, 12 minutes; *Our Children, Our Future*, 14 minutes. 1980. 16mm. NAIF.

NOW AND FOREVER
Shows scenes of Oregon Indians from 1915 to 1945. 80 minutes/bxw. Rental. OHS.

NOW THE BUFFALO'S GONE
 Ross Deveish, Director
Analyzes the history of massacres, broken promises, worthless treaties, and land-grabbing that the Indian nations as a whole have suffered. Narrated by Marlon Brando. 1969. 75 minutes. Purchase: 16mm, $995; video, 225. Rental, $80/3 days. MG

OBSIDIAN POINT-MAKING
 Clyde B. Smith, Producer
A Tolowa Indian demonstrates an ancient method of fashioning an arrow point from obsidian. Describes various tribes' folklore customs connected with obsidian-chipping and explains the significance, history, and uses of obsidian points. 1964. 13 minutes. Purchase: 16mm, $240; video, $180. Rental. UC and PSU.

OLD CHIEF'S DANCE
Portrays the life of a Sioux Indian chief told in dance. 1951. Nine minutes. Grades 6-adult. Rental. UM.

OMAHA TRIBE FILMS
 David Conger, Director
Documentary of Native American life on a reservation presented through portraits of several Omaha people of different ages. *The Land, The People, and The Family.* 1978. 30 minutes each. 16mm and video. NETCHE.

ON THE PATH TO SELF-RELIANCE
 Peter J. Barton Productions
Narrated by James Billie, Chairman of the Seminole Tribe of Florida, this film provides an overview of tribal history and current tribal economic development. 1982. 45 minutes. 2" quad, 1" and ¾" video. Rental, $80/week. NAPBC.

ON THE SPRING ICE
Walrus as well as whales are hunted by the Eskimos of Gambell on St. Lawrence Island. 45 minutes. Purchase: 16mm, $700. Rental, $60. DER.

**1,000 YEARS OF
MUSCOGEE (CREEK) ART**
 Gary Robinson, Producer
Traces the development of Creek Indian art forms from the prehistoric period of the mound-builders to the present. Examines over 175 examples of Creek art. 1982. 28 minutes. 2" quad, 1" videotape, and ¾"video. Rental, $40/week. NAPBC.

ONENHAKENRA: WHITE SEED
Explores the development of Iroquois culture because of corn. Features local people of Akwasasne. 1984. 16mm and video. AM.

**THE ORIGIN OF THE CROWN
DANCE: AN APACHE NARRATIVE
AND BA'TS'OOSEE: AN APACHE
TRICKSTER CYCLE**
 Larry Evers, University of Arizona
With Rudoplh Kane. Apache and English subtitles. 40 minutes. Purchase: Video, $220. CLEAR.

OSCAR HOWE: THE SIOUX PAINTER
 KUSD-TV, Producer
Vincent Price adds his narrative to the personal commentary of Oscar Howe, focusing on his art, philosophy and cultural heritage, as he designs and paints the brilliant "Sioux Eagle Dancer." 1973. 27 minutes. Grades 9-adult. 16mm and video. COR and NAPBC.

**THE OTHER SIDE OF THE LEDGER:
AN INDIAN VIEW OF THE
HUDSON'S BAY COMPANY**
 Martin Defalco and Willie Dunn, Directors
Presents the view of spokesmen for Canadian Indian and Metis groups. With archival materials and contemporary examples, this film includes scenes from a conference in which Hudson's Bay Co. officials respond to Native people's objections. 1972. 43 minutes. 16mm. NFBC.

OUR LAND IS OUR LIFE
The Cree Indian people of the Mistassini area in northern Quebec meet to discuss their long-term future. 1975. 58 minutes. Rental, $27.60. MM.

OUR PROUD LAND
Written and narrated from the Navajo point of view, this film presents a number of sequences of modern day life of the Navajo Indians. 30 minutes. 16mm. Rental. UK.

OUR TOTEM IS THE RAVEN
Features Chief Dan George in a contemporary tale of a young Indian boy's initiation into manhood and his acceptance of his Indian heritage. 1971. 21 minutes. 16mm. Rental. IU.

**THE OWL AND THE LEMMING:
AN ESKIMO LEGEND**
 Co. Hoedeman, Director
An example of the Inuit art and folklore. 1971. Six minutes. All ages. Purchase: 16mm, $150; video, $150. Rental, $35. NFBC.

**THE OWL AND THE RAVEN:
AN ESKIMO LEGEND**
 Co Hoedeman, Director
An Inuit legend is retold using puppets of sealskin in traditional Inuit design and accompanied by a music track of Inuit songs. 1974. Seven minutes. Grades 1-6. All ages. Purchase: 16mm, $200; video, $150. Rental, $35. NFBC.

THE OWL WHO MARRIED A GOOSE: AN ESKIMO LEGEND
Caroline Leaf, Director
An example of commitment and love. 1974. Eight minutes. All ages. 16mm and video. CF and MM.

PAGES ON THE PAST
A series of four films which tell the story of the peoples of the Pacific Northwest from the time of the Ice Age to the coming of Lewis and Clark. *An Age of Ice:* How the peoples of the Northwest adapted and endured; *After the Flood:* Floods 13,000 years ago signalling the end of the Ice Age; *Landmarks In Time:* The time of the eruption of Mt. Mazama about 7,000 years ago; and, *History In the Making:* Portrays the expansion of Native American civilization throughout the region up to the coming of Lewis and Clark. Study guide and maps. 30 minutes each. Grades 9-adult. Purchase: 16mm, $550 each (1,990/series); video, $450 each ($1,590/series). Rental: 16mm and video, $50/week. TBM and COP.

PAINTING WITH SAND: A NAVAJO CEREMONY
Portrays the traditional sand painting healing rite as performed by a Navajo medicine man for his ailing son. 1950. Eleven minutes. Grades 4-12. Rental, $10.50. MM.

PARALEGAL FILM SERIES
In four parts; one part demonstrates how Native Americans can protect themselves against consumer fraus, employment discrimination, etc. 16mm and video. ICVT.

PAUL KANE GOES WEST
Gerald Budner, Director
Artist Paul Kane traveled Canada in the mid-19th century depicting the Indians through his skecthes and paintings. 1972. 15 minutes. Grades 4-12. 16mm and video. EB and MM.

PEACEFUL ONES
Shows life and customs of the Hopi in the painted desert, including cultivating the land, harvesting crops, weaving, kachinas, and snake dance. 1953. 12 minutes. Grades 4-adult. 16mm. Rental. UT, PSU and UA.

PEOPLE OF THE BUFFALO
Austin Campbell
Dramatic contemporary paintings of life on the Western Plains, portray the unique relationship between the Indians and buffalo. 1968 revised edition. 14 minutes. Grades 5-adult. Rental. PSU, MM, EB and UA.

PEOPLE OF THE FIRST LIGHT
WGBY-TV Springfield, Mass.
Seven, 30 minute films about Native Americans living in Rhode Island, Massachusetts and Connecticut: The Narragansetts, Pequots, Wampanoags, Mohegans, Nipnucs and Paugausetts, descendents of the original Eastern Woodland Algonquin Indians. *Indians In Southern New England* (The Survivors); *The Wampanoags of Gay Head* (Community Spirit and Islnd Life); *The Boston Indian Community* (Change and Identity); *The Narragansett* (Tradition); *Indians of Connecticut* (The Importance of Land); *The Indian Experience: Urban and Rural* (Survival); *The Mashpee Wampanoags* (Tribal Identity.) 1979. GPN and NAPBC.

PEOPLE OF THE SEAL
Michael McKennirey and George Pearson, Producers
Part I: *Eskimo Summer* - Documents the summer activities of th Netsilik Inuit, which take place on the land. Part II: *Eskimo Winter* - Search for seal holes; building igloos; seal hunting. 1971. 52 minutes each. Grades 7-adult. 16mm and video. EDC.

PIKI: THE HOPI WAY
Pat Ferrero, Director/Producer
A view of the Hopi, particularly Hopi women. "Piki" is the sustenance for everyday, for ceremonials and for the very sick. By the presentation of piki for the religious societies, women contribute to the success of ritual celebrations. 1980. Seven minutes. ¾" video. FF-NDF.

PINE NUTS
Clyde B. Smith, Producer
Members of the Paviotso and Paiute tribes demonstrate how the pine nut, from the pinon tree, were harvested and prepared as food, using ancient techniques. 1961. 13 minutes. Purchase: 16mm, $240; video, $180. Rental. UC and PSU.

PLAY AND CULTURAL CONTINUITY: Part 4, MONTANA INDIAN CHILDREN
On the Flathead Indian Reservation and surrounding countryside, the play of Indian children ranges from the universal domestic activities and "monster" play themes of those mirroring individualistic cultural elements, such as wrapping of babies, drumming, singing, and hunting. 1975. 29 minutes. Rental, $15. PSU.

POMO SHAMAN
A shortened version of the complete research documentary, *Sucking Doctor.* 1963. 20 minutes. 16mm/bxw. Purchase, $275. Rental. PSU and UC.

PORTRAIT OF LUCY SWAN
Elderly Lucy Swan, Cheyenne River Sioux, reminisces about family and tribal history. Illustrates past/present living conditions on the reservation. Adult. 30 minutes. 16mm. Rental, $15. NILB.

POTLATCH PEOPLE
Document Associates & BBC
Presents the Indians of the Pacific Northwest and the ceremonial potlatch feast. 1972. 26 minutes. Purchase: 16mm, $400; video, $340. Rental, $55. CG.

POTLATCH: A STRICT
LAW BIDS US DANCE
Dennis Wheeler, Director
Features the outlawed Kwakiutl Potlatch ceremony. The confiscation of an enormous and valuable collection of dancing masks and costumes. Shows a Potlatch given by the Cranmer family. Narrated by Gloria Cranmer Webster. 1975. 55 minutes. 16mm. PC.

POW-WOW!
Displays North American Indian dances at a gathering of more than 20 tribes. Chiricahua Apaches perform their ancient sacred Fire Dance; Comanches execute the Gourd Dance; the Intertribal Dance; and, the War Dance. Indians speak of their traditions, ceremonies and heritage. All ages. Purchase: 16mm, $355; video, $245. Rental, $40. COR.

POWERLESS POLITICS
Sandra Orawa—KNBC-TV, Producer
Provides an overview of the legal relationship between the U.S. and Indian tribes showing how shifts and emphasis in the government "Indian policy" have had far reaching effects on Indian life. 1975. 28 minutes. ¾" video. BYU-N.

PREHISTORIC MAN
Traces the development of the Indians in the American West. 1970. 17 minutes. Grades 4-12. Rental. UA.

THE PRIDE AND THE SHAME
Focuses on the Sioux Indians of the Black Hills of North Dakota. 30 minutes/bxw. Rental. UM.

PRIDE, PURPOSE AND PROMISE:
PAIUTES OF THE SOUTHWEST
KLUX-TV, Channel 10 Las Vegas, Nevada
Interviews with tribal leaders and members of the Kaibab Reservation in Arizona, the Shivwits Reservation in Utah, and the Moapa Reservation in Nevada. Discusses tribal lands, history, education and economic development, and the present day Indian reservation life. 1982. 28 minutes. 2" quad, 1" and ¾" video. Rental, $40/reel. NAPBC.

THE PRIMAL MIND
Jamake Highwater, Writer/Host
Explores the basic differences between Native American and Western cultures, while examining two cultures' contrasting views of nature, time, space, art, archaeology, dance and language. 1981. 58 minutes. Purchase: 16mm, $895; video, $595. Rental, $100. CG.

THE PROBABLE PASSING
OF ELK CREEK
Rob Wilson, Producer
Documentary focusing on the controversy between a little town, Elk Creek, and the Grindstone Indian Reservation over a government planned resevoir. 60 minutes. Purchase: 16mm, $900; video, $750. Rental, $90. CG.

PROTEIN FROM THE SEA
13th Regional Corporation of Alaska Natives
A look into the seafood industry and what Natives are doing to keep their heritage of the sea alive. The film follows the construction of the ship *Al-Ind-Esk-A Sea*, the scenic voyage up the Inside Passage to Alaska, and crab processing aboard the ship; rare World War II footage is included to cover the history of Cold Bay as a strategic location in the Aleutian campaign and the role Alaska Natives played in winning back their homeland from the Japanese. 1981. 26 minutes. 16mm. Purchase, $395; rental, $39/three days. COP.

PUEBLO BOY
Tells the story of a young Indian boy being instructed in the ancient and modern ways and traditions of his people, the Pueblos of the Southwest. 24 minutes. 16mm. Rental. UK.

THE PUEBLO PRESENCE
Hugh and Suzanne Johnston, WNET-13
Examines the continuity of ancient Pueblo civilization into the present. Zuni historian Andrew Napetcha discusses the ancestry of Pueblo peoples. Art, religion, ceremonials, language, architecture, and daily activities and relationship to the natural world. 1981. 58 minutes. 16mm and ¾" VHS. JOHNSTON.

PUEBLO RENAISSANCE
Philip Hobel, Executive Producer
Provides an authentic view of the sacred traditions, ancient religious and agricultural ceremonies of the Pueblo people. 1972. 26 minutes. Purchase: 16mm, $400; video, $340. Rental, $55. CG and IU.

THE PUEBLO EXPERIENCE:
MAKING A NEW WORLD
Richard Marquand, Director/Producer
The story of a 17 year-old girl, Charity, in Puritan Massachusetts in 1640. Captured by the Indians then returned, Charity rebells against the Puritan doctrine and treatment of the Indians. 1975. 31 minutes. All ages. Purchase: 16mm, $425; rental, $40. LCA.

QUILLAYUTE STORY

Documentary on the transition of the Northwest Indian from primitive culture to the present-day culture of the whites. Rare interior scenes of the Shaker Indian religion. 1951. 24 minutes. Grades 9-adult. Rental, $15. MM.

THE RAINBOW OF STONE

When drought threatens the grazing lands of the Navajos, an old chief tells his grandson the tribal legend of a wonderful country beyond "The Rainbow of Stone." 22 minutes. 16mm. Rental, $15. UT.

THE REAL PEOPLE

KSPS-TV Spokane, Washington

Nine, 30 minute programs on Indian tribes of Northwest. The Colville, the Flathead, the Couer d' Alene, the Kalispel, the Kootenai, the Nez Perce and the Spokane. Examines the lifestyles, culture and lore of these seven tribes. Teacher's guide. 1976. Grades 5-adult. 16mm and video. GPN and NAPBC.

THE RED DRESS

Michael Scott, Director

Tells the story of conflicting loyalties to the past, the demands of the present day, traditional values and family affections. 1978. 28 minutes. Grades 7-adult. Purchase: 16mm, $500; video, $300. Rental, $50. NFBC.

REPORT FROM WOUNDED KNEE

A short history of the official attitudes and postures towards the American Indian that led to the infamous massacre of the Sioux at Wounded Knee, 11 minutes. Grades 7-12. Purchase: 16mm, $225; video, $130. SEF.

RETURN TO SOVEREIGNTY: SELF-DETERMINATION AND THE KANSAS KICKAPOO

A documentary film about the Kickapoo Indians of Kansas and their struggle to regain control of their future. 1982. Purchase and rental. STULL.

RICHARD'S TOTEM POLE

Richard Harris, 16, is a Gitskan Indians living in British Columbia, Canada, while helping his father a master totem pole carver, he begins to take an interest in his heritage. Through his carving he discovers his roots, culture and family traditions. 25 minutes. Grades 4-adult. Purchase: 16mm, $495; video, $290. Rental, $60. COR.

RIVER PEOPLE

The Pima Indians reconstruct their old ways of life for this film. 1949. 25 minutes. Grades 4-adult. Rental. UA.

ROCK PAINTINGS OF BAJA CALIFORNIA

Examines the rock paintings at a recently discovered site. Shows in great detail the paintings and explains how they were painted, their age, and their significance to the Indian who painted them. 17 minutes. Purchase: 16mm, $245; video, $170. Rental, $27. UC.

RONNIE

A sketch of a young Canadian Indian. Ronnie describes his life on the reserve and his belief in the need for greater educational opportunities and self-initiative for his people. 1968. 26 minutes/bxw. Rental. UM.

ROSEBUD TO DALLAS

Jed Riffe and Robert Rouse

Tells the story of five families who come to Dallas from the Rosebud Sioux Reservation in South Dakota to make a better life through vocational education and on the job training. 1977. 60 minutes. ¾" video. THRC.

ROUND DANCE

A group of dancers perform a round dance. Three minutes. All grades. Purchase: 16mm, $110. Rental, $10/week. Also available in video. SAN.

RUNNING ON THE EDGE OF THE RAINBOW: LAGUNA STORIES AND POEMS

Larry Evers, University of Arizona

With Leslie Marmon Silko—reflects on the nature of Laguna storytelling, its functions and the problems she has faced as an Indian poet. 28 minutes. Purchase: ¾" & ½" VHS and ½" beta, $175. CLEAR.

THE SACRED CIRCLE

In two parts: Part I: Invites the viewer through a bold series of symbolic imagery to participate in the mystical harmony of the Native world. Culminates in the ritual expression of the Sun Dance. The film combines animation, documentary photographs, paintings and on location realism, augmented by lyrical narrative. Part II: *Recovery*—moves from the frontal assault on Native culture by missionaries and others in the last century to a series of vignettes reflecting its contemporary face, while conveying the tragedy of cultural loss. 29 minutes each. Purchase: 16mm, $700 (both parts); video, $500. Rental, $110. SC.

SACRED GROUND

The story of the North American Indian's relationship to the land. Their intimate involvement and reverence for places throughout the land that hold a special religious and traditional significance for their race. Provides a detailed look at the specific geographic places all over America that are and always were sacred to the American Indian. Narrated and hosted by Cliff Robertson. A two-part (25 minutes each) series or combined 50 minute 16mm film. NV.

SANANGUAGAT: INUIT MASTERWORKS
Derek May, Director

An exhibition of Inuit carvings from public and private collections. Views of daily life in the Iglootik settlement of the Northwest Territories. 1974. 25 minutes. Grades 7-adult. Purchase: 16mm, $500; video, $300. Rental, $50. NFBC.

THE SEA IS OUR LIFE
Bo Boudart

Inuit speak out about the effects of offshore drilling. Shows the growing political awareness and their efforts to organize. 1979. 16 minutes. 16mm. BO and PI.

SEEKING THE FIRST AMERICANS
Graham Chedd

Archaeologists from Texas and Arkansas search for clues to the identity of the first North Americans. 60 minutes. Adult. Purchase: 16mm, $600; rental, $60. Educator's guide. DER. Purchase: ¾" beta/VHS, $250; rental, $90/week. PBS.

SEMINOLE INDIANS
A study of Seminole life on the hummocks of the Everglades in Florida. 1951. 11 minutes. Rental. UM.

THE SENECAS
Ron Hagell

Through interviews and narration, this film views the contemporary Seneca Indian of New York State and their history. 1980. 29 minutes. ¾" VHS. WXXI.

SEQUOYAH
The story of the Cherokee Indian who developed the first written American Indian language. 15 minutes. 16mm. WD.

SEYEWAILO: THE FLOWER WORLD
Larry Evers, University of Arizona

Yaqui Deer Songs as they are sung and danced to at a fiesta, the "pahko." Yaqui with English subtitles. 51 minutes. Purchase: ¾" & ½" VHS, and ½" beta, $290. CLEAR.

THE SHADOW CATCHER:
EDWARD S. CURTIS AND
THE NORTH AMERICAN INDIAN
T.C. McLuhan, Director/Producer

A film about Edward S. Curtis, photographer, anthropologist and filmmaker. Features marked Kwakiutl dancers, a Navajo Yebechai Ceremony, and Curtis' own initiation into the Hopi Snake Fraternity. Soundtrack features original Indian music and contemporary Comanche variations. 1975. 88 minutes. Grades 10-adult. 16mm. Rental. IRA, PHOENIX, MM, PSU, UC, UK and UA.

THE SILENT ENEMY
H.P. Carver

Chief Yellow Robe, a noted Sioux, who acts in the film, points out the usefulness of the film in preserving an authentic image of the old days. Documents a band of Ojibwa in winter. 1930. 88 minutes. 16mm/bxw. FCE and BL.

SINEW-BACKED BOW AND ITS ARROWS
Clyde B. Smith, Producer

Follows the construction of a sinew-backed bow, by a Yurok craftsman. Also demonstrates the making of arrows. 1961. 24 minutes. Purchase: 16mm, $330; video, $230. Rental. UC and PSU.

SIOUX LEGENDS
Charles and Jane Nauman

Recreates some of the legends closest to the philosophy and religion of the Sioux culture. Demonstrates the Indian feeling of identification with the forces of nature. 1973. 20 minutes. Grades 4-adult. Purchase: 16mm, $415; video, $100; rental, $30. AIMS.

SISIBAKWAT:
THE OJIBWAY MAPLE HARVEST
Presents the springtime story of the forest Indians who dwelt along the rivers and lakes. 18 minutes. Rental. UM.

SITTING BULL:
A PROFILE IN POWER
The tragic but heroic saga of Indian/U.S. relations in this interview with Sitting Bull, portrayed by August Schellenberg. 1977. 26 minutes. All ages. Purchase: 16mm, $325; rental, $30. LCA.

THE SIX NATIONS
Nick Gosling, Director

The President of the Seneca Nation and the Mayor of the town of Salamanca discuss the various aspects of Indian and white coexistence. 1972. 26 minutes. Purchase: 16mm, $400; video, $340. Rental, $55. CG.

SKOKOMISH INDIAN BASKETS:
THEIR MATERIALS AND TECHNIQUES
Documents the varied techniques of basket-making by the Skokomish Indians from the Puget Sound region in western Washington State. 1977. 28 minutes/bxw/silent. Super 8mm and video. Rental. UW.

SNAKETOWN
This study of the Snaketown archaeological excavation in southern Arizona, explores the Hohokam Indian culture, 40 minutes. Purchase: 16mm, $540. Rental, $42. UC.

SOMETIMES WE FEEL
William Maheras, Director
Brad Stanley, Writer/Producer

A young Indian tells of a life of sorrow, poverty,

neglect, and isolation on an Arizona reservation.
Ten minutes. 16mm. Rental. UA.

A SONG FOR THE DEAD WARRIORS

Examines the reasons for the Wounded Knee
occupation in the Spring of 1973 by Oglala Sioux
Indians. 1973. 25 minutes. 16mm. Rental. UNI
and UC.

SONGS OF MY HUNTER HEART: LAGUNA SONGS AND POEMS

Larry Evers, University of Arizona
Harold Littlebird continues the oral tradition of
his people by incorporating contemporary themes
into his work which retains the Pueblo reverence
for the Spoken word. 1978. 34 minutes. Purchase:
¾" & ½" VHS, and ½" beta, $220. CLEAR.

SOUTHWEST INDIAN ARTS AND CRAFTS

Shows techniques in Navajo rug-making; San
Ildefonso and Acoma pottery; Hopi and Zuni
jewelry and kachina dolls; and Pima and Papago
basket-making. 1973. 14 minutes. Grades K-12.
Purchase: 16mm, $320; video, $225; Rental, $40.
COR. Rental. IU and UK.

SOUTHWEST INDIAN OF EARLY AMERICA

Uses Indian actors, dioramas, and narration to
help recreate what life might have been like about
600 years ago for the Hohokam and Anasazi
Indians of northern Arizona and New Mexico.
1973. 14 minutes. Grades 4-8. Purchase: 16mm,
$330; video, $230. Rental, $40. COR. Rental. IU
and UK.

SPIRIT IN THE EARTH

The legend of a Western Indian tribe, describing
the phenomenon of "Old Faithful" in terms of the
Plains' Indians concept of original sin. 22 minutes.
Rental. UK.

SPIRIT OF THE HUNT

Narrated by Will Sampson, this film features a
spiritual search for the essential elements of what
the Buffalo meant historically and in the present
to people of the Chippewa, Cree and Dogrib
tribes. Historical footage combined with a
modern hunt, illustrates the central concept. 1982.
29 minutes. Purchase: 16mm, $675; video, $450.
TC.

SPIRIT OF THE WHITE MOUNTAINS

Documents the activities of the White Mountain
Apaches, and how they support themselves by
developing the natural resources of their
reservation. 1959. 13 minutes. Grades 4-9. 16mm.
Rental. UMI, IU, and UA.

STEVE CHARGING EAGLE

A film about an American Indian man from Red
Scaffold, South Dakota. Quiet, proud, a man of
responsibility, he performs in a War Dance
competition. Rental. BCA.

STICKS AND STONES WILL BUILD A HOUSE

Traces the development of Indian architecture in
the Southwestern U.S. 1970. 30 minutes. Rental.
IU.

STONE AGE AMERICANS

Jules Powers and Daniel Wilson, Producers
Discovery Series, NBC
Introduces the vanished Indians of the Mesa
Verde in Colorado. The film presents the history
of these farmer Indians by examining the cliff
dwellings and artifacts discovered in 1888. 21
minutes. 16mm. Rental. UA.

STOP RUINING AMERICA'S PAST

Covers the problem of the destruction of
archaeological sites by urban and industrial
expansion, as illustrated by the case histories of
two prehistoric Indian communities in Illinois -
Cahokia Mounds and Hopewell Mounds. 1968.
22 minutes. 16mm/bxw. Rental. UA and UM.

THE STORY OF TUKTU SERIES

Lawrence Hyde, Director
A children's adventure series, starring Tuktu, an
Inuit boy, in 13 film adventures. 1966-1968.
Approximately 14 minutes each. Grades 1-8.
FILMS.

SUCKING DOCTOR

William Heick, Prodcuer
A documentary presenting the final night of a
curing ceremony held by the Kashia group of
Southwestern Pomo Indians. The Indian
"Sucking Door" is a prophet of the Bole Maru
religion, spiritual head of the Kashia community.
1963. 45 minutes. bxw. Purchase: 16mm, $550.
Rental. UC and PSU.

THE SUMMER OF JOHNSON HOLIDAY - NAVAJO BOY

Johnson Holiday lives in Monument Valley.
During the summer he herds the family sheep and
goats; during the winter he attends the white
man's school. 12 minutes. Grades 1-8. Rental.
UK.

THE SUN DAGGER

The Solstice Project
Tells the story of Anna Sofaer, A Washington,
D.C. artist who having climbed to the top of a
high butte in Chaco Canyon, New Mexico, saw a
dagger of light pierce an ancient spiral rock
carving. After careful study, she found that the
dagger marks solstices, equinoxes, and the 19-
year lunar cycle. Narrated by Robert Redford,
this film explores the Anasazi culture that
produced this calendar and thrived over 1,000
years ago in the Chaco Canyon environment.
1983. 29 minutes. 16mm and video. NAPBC and
UT.

**TAHTONKA: PLAINS
INDIANS BUFFALO CULTURE**
Charles and Jane Nauman, Producers
A re-enactment of the Plains Indian's culture from the pre-horse era to the time of the Wounded Knee massacre. 1966. 30 minutes. Grades 4-adult. 16mm and video. AIMS and NILB.

TALES OF HIAWATHA
An animated puppet film based on the poem. It relates the classic Indian legend of Hiawatha. 1967. 20 minutes. Grades 3-8. Rental. MM and UM.

TALKING HANDS
Demonstrates the sign language of the Plains Indians. Tells the story of the Battle of the Washita in sign language with background narration. 20 minutes. 16mm. Rental, $15. UT.

**TEN THOUSAND BEADS
FOR NAVAJO SAM**
Focuses on Sam Begay, a full-blooded Navajo, who has left the reservation to make a new alien, but secure, life for himself and his family in Chicago. 1971. 25 minutes. 16mm. Rental. IU and MM.

**THAT ONE GOOD SPIRIT -
AN INDIAN CHRISTMAS STORY**
Larry Cesspooch, Writer/ Director
A clay animated tale of a young Ute Indian boy. 1981. 16 minutes. Grades K-3. 2" quad, 1" videotape, ¾" VHS. Rental, $40/week. NAPBC.

THEY PROMISED TO TAKE OUR LAND
Document Associates & BBC
Discusses the misunderstanding by the white man of the value of land to the Indian. 1972. 26 mintues. Purchase: 16mm, $400; video, $340. Rental, $55. CG.

THIEVES OF TIME
Gerald Richman
Describes the problems of pot hunters looting valuable archaeological sites in Arizona. 1978. 28 minutes. ¾" video. PBS.

THIS SIDE
Monona Wali
Focuses on concerns of Onondaga Indians of New York State. Discusses social problems and political awareness. 1978. 30 minutes. ¾" and ½" VHS; bxw. SVC.

THIS WAS THE TIME
Eugene Boyko and William Brind, Directors
A recreation of Haida Indian life in a village in the Queen Charlotte Islands. Portrays the potlatch and totems which existed. 16 minutes. 16mm. NFBC.

**THOSE BORN AT MASSET:
A HAIDA STONEMOVING AND FEAST**
Covers the Haida ritual, the modern equivalent of the traditional memorial potlatch. 1976. 70 minutes/ bxw. 16mm and video. UW.

THREE STONE BLADES
Valerie L. Smith, Director
A dramatization of an Inuit legend from the Bering Strait reconstructing aboriginal Eskimo customs and values. 1971. 16 minutes. 16mm. Rental. IFB, UC, UA, and MM.

THREE WARRIORS
Keith Merrill, Director
Portrays the problems encountered by a 13 year-old on the Warm Springs Indian Reservation in Oregon, and his coming to terms with his heritage. 1977. 105 minutes. 35mm & 16mm. ZAENTZ.

TIME OF THE CREE
Bob Rodgers and Gail Singer
Records a "salvage" archaeological dig near Southern Indian Lake on the Churchill River in northern Manitoba, Canada. Shows a Cree family in the area living a trditional way of life. 1974. 26 minutes. 16mm. RODGERS.

**TOM SAVAGE:
BOY OF EARLY VIRGINIA**
Dramatizes the story of a boy given to the Indians. Depicts his new life, and his learning of their language, skills and tribal customs. 1958. 22 minutes. Grades 4-9. Rental. UA and UM.

TOMORROW'S YESTERDAY
KBYU-TV Provo, Utah, Producer
Shows how the Pueblo people adapt to the challenges of modern civilization while maintaining their identity and culture. 1971. 29 minutes. 2" quad, 1" videotape and ¾" VHS. Rental, $40/week. NAPBC.

TOTEM POLE
Clyde B. Smith, Producer
Illustrates the seven types of totem poles and relates each to a social system and mythology that laid great stress on kinship, rank, and ostentatious displays of wealth. The carving of a pole by Mungo Martin, a famous carver and chief of the Kwakiutl is shown. 27 minutes. Purchase: 16mm, $380; video, $265. Rental. UC and PSU.

TRAIL OF BROKEN TREATIES
Document Associates & BBC, Producer
Examines the past and present injustices and focuses on the attempt of Indian leaders to improve the situation. 1972. 26 minutes. Purchase: 16mm, $400; video, $340. Rental, $55. CG.

TRAIL OF THE BUFFALO
Eight minutes. 16mm. Rental. UA.

TRAIL OF TEARS
WETA-TV Washington, D.C.
Focuses on the forced removal of the Cherokees from their homelands and their exodus to the West, and the Cherokee's struggle to maintain their identity and their heritage. 20 minutes. Grades 7-12. 16-page teacher's guide, $1.95. Purchase: 16mm, $300; video, $150. AIT.

TREATIES
Sandra Osawa, Writer/Producer
Julian Finkelstein, Director
Retraces Indian treaty history from Colonial times to the present. Discusses the treaty as a legal concept and historical reality. 1975. 28 minutes. ¾" VHS. BYU-N.

TREATIES MADE—TREATIES BROKEN
Discusses the land grabbing, broken promises and treaties made by the white man with the Nisqually Indian tribe of Washington State. 18 minutes. 16mm. Rental, $21. UT.

THE TREE IS DEAD
Describes one of the last Indian reservations in the State of Minnesota, Red Lake, and the disintegration of their own culture. 11 minutes/bxw. Rental. UM.

THE TRIAL OF LEONARD PELTIER
Paul Burtness, et al
The U.S. Government's murder case against American Indian Movement leader Leonar Peltier. Voices criticism of Native American's experiences with the Federal government, both on their reservations and with the proceedings of Peltier's case. 1977. 16 minutes/b&w. Video. Purchase: $75; rental, $35. UCV.

THE TRIBE AND THE PROFESSOR:
OZETTE ARCHAEOLOGY
Louis and Ruth Kirk, Producers
Professor Richard Daugherty and his students from Washington State University returned to Ozette Indian Village to resume archaeological investigation begun in 1966. Results in the reconstruction of the Makah's past. Revised 1978 edition. 44 minutes. Purchase: 16mm, $550; ¾" beta, $425; ½" VHS, $400. UW.

TRIBE OF THE TURQUOISE WATERS
Records the life of the Havasupai Indians in Arizona, and how their lives are shaped by their environment. 1952. 13 minutes. Grades 6-adult. Rental. UA.

TUKTU STORIES
Lawrence Hyde, Writer/Editor
A series of 13 stories on Inuit culture. 1969. 14 minutes each. 16mm. Grades 3-9. See FILMS and MM for titles and prices.

TULE TECHNOLOGY: NORTHERN
PAIUTE USES OF MARSH RESOURCES
IN WESTERN NEVADA
A film about Northern Paiute Indian people who have lived near the Stillwater marshes of western Nevada for generation. Focuses on Wuzzie George and members of her family constructing a duck egg bag, cattail house, duck decoy, and tule boat. 1983. 42 minutes. Purchase: 16mm, $420; video, $185. Rental, $20.50. PSU.

TUNUNEREMIUT:
THE PEOPLE OF TUNUNAK
Portrays aspects of the lives of the people (Eskimos) of Tununak, a village on the southwestern coast of Alaska. 1973. 35 minutes. Purchase: 16mm, $550. Rental, $50. DER.

TWO INDIANS -
RED REFLECTIONS OF LIFE
Documentary study of two North American Indian high school students and their classmates. 1973. 26 minutes. 16mm. Rental. UK.

UMEALIT: THE WHALE HUNTERS
John Angier (WGBH)
The Inuit and the controversy of whale hunting for subsistence versus the international effort to save the whales. 1980. 58 minutes. ¾" video. WGBH.

UNIVERSITY OF CALIFORNIA:
AMERICAN INDIAN FILM SERIES
Samuel A. Barrett and Clyde Smith
Each of 12 films uses the memories and oral traditions of contemporary Indians as well as anthropological records to document their cultural skills. Tribes filmed include: Southwestern Pomo, Kwakiutl, Yurok, Paviotso, Washo, Tolowa, Nisenan, and Brule Sioux. See UC for titles and prices.

URBAN FRONTIER
Seattle Indian Center, Producer
Narrated by Dr. John Fuller and Will Sampson, this film provides an insight into the historical problems that have confronted Indian culture, and that have set the stage for the difficulties of adaptation in today's fast-paced society. A story which is told by Indians themselves, and illustrates how Indians have banded together in cities to form urban Indian centers; how they are putting their traditional values to work to help solve their problems. Two versions, 26 minutes and 17 minutes. Purchase: 16mm—27 minute version, $390; video, $290; 16mm—17 minute version, $260; video, $160. Rental (16mm only): 26 minute version, $35; 17 minute version, $25. COP.

VALLEY OF THE STANDING ROCKS
Portrays the life of the Navajo Indians on their reservations in Arizona and Utah. 1957. 24 minutes. Grades 4-adult. 16mm. Rental. MM and UM.

VANISHING PRAIRIE:
BUFFALO: MAJESTIC SYMBOL
OF THE AMERICAN PLAINS
Explains how the American Indian civilization depended on the 60 million buffalo which roamed the prairie a century ago. 1963. 12 minutes. Grades 4-adult. Rental, $11.25. MM.

VILLAGE OF NO RIVER
Barbara Lipton, Writer/Director/Producer
Yup'ik Eskimo film, 1935-1940 and 1979-1980, illustrating change and continuity in the culture. Discusses present problems and concerns. 1981. 58 minutes. 16mm/bxw. In English and Yup'ik with English subtitles. NM.

VILLAGES IN THE SKY
Shows life in the high mesa villages of the Hopi. Women are shown making baskets and pottery, and baking; also, dances. 1952. 12 minutes. Grades 6-adult. 16mm. Rental, $15. UT and UA.

VISION DANCE
Henry Smith and Skip Sweeney, Directors
Showcases the talents of SOLARIS Dance Theatre and Lakota Sioux Indian Dancers drawn from nine reservations of the Lakota Nation in South Dakota. Lakota legends, myths and spirit qualities are juxtaposed with modern dance interpretations. 1982. 58½ minutes. Purchase: ¾" or ½" Video, $300; rental, $75. SOLARIS.

VISION QUEST
Dramatization of the spiritual experience required of 14 year old Western Indian boy before his acceptance as a man and a warrior. Shows phases of Indian life. 1961. 30 minutes. 16mm. Color/bxw. Rental. PSU.

WALKING IN A SACRED MANNER
Stephen Cross; Joseph Epes Brown, Consultant
Opens with photography by Edward S. Curtis and the words of many Native American orators, this film conveys the respect felt by Native Americans for the natural world. 1980. 30 minutes. 16mm. IFB and UA.

WANAGI IS GONE
Bruce Baird
The uncovering of a massive ancient grave site raises questions about the excavations of such sites and examines Indian traditional views as well as scientific significance. 1978. 30 minutes. 2" quad, 1" videotape, ¾" VHS. KUSD.

WARRIORS AT PEACE
Depicts the life of the Apache Indians in eastern Arizona with emphasis on their customs and traditions. 1953. 11 minutes. Grades 4-adult. Rental. UA and UK.

WASHOE
Veronika Pataky
Depicts the transition of the Washoe Tribe in Nevada from traditional customs to the 20th century. 1968. 54 minutes. 16mm/bxw. In Washoe with English narration. UW, UK, IU and UM.

THE WATER IS SO CLEAR
THAT A BLIND MAN COULD SEE
New Mexico's Taos Indians believe that all life (plant and animal) is sacred and live without disturbing their environment. Lumber companies are trying to get permission from the Federal Government to lumber the Taos Indian area. 1970. 30 minutes. 16mm. Rental, $16.50. PSU.

THE WAY
Sandra Osawa (KNBC-TV)
A sketch of Native American religion and its place in contemporary Indian life. Focuses on the Cherokee, Cheyenne and Ojibwa religious practices, and Indian spirituality. 1975. 28 minutes. ¾" VHS. BYU-N.

A WAY OF LIFE
CBC Northern Services, Producer
The lifestyle of Henry Evaluarjuk, Inuit carver, who, with his family and two other families, chose to live on an uninhabited and secluded inlet on Baffin Island. 1983. 28 minutes. 2" quad, 1" videotape, and ¾" VHS. Rental, $40/week, NAPBC.

WAY OF OUR FATHERS
Members of several northern California Indian tribes depict unique elements of a way of life as it flourished before the imposition of European culture. 33 minutes. Purchase: 16mm, $455; video, $310. Rental. UC and PSU.

WE REMEMBER
Raymond Yakeleya
Yakeleya, a Slavey Indian, traveled to five communities to talk with some of the elders of the Slavey and Loucheau tribes of Canada about their past, present and thoughts for the future. 1979. In two parts. 30 minutes each. 16mm. CFMDC.

WEAVERS OF THE WEST
A film which shows the Navajo's process of rug-making. 1954. 13 minutes. Rental. UM.

WEDDING OF PALO
F. Dalsheim and Knud Rasmussen
Rasmussen, the Danish Inuit anthropologist and explorer directed this film based on a traditional Inuit tale about the courtship and marriage of a young man and woman. 1937. 72 minutes. 35mm/16mm/bxw. In Inuit with English subtitles. MMA.

WELCOME TO NAVAHO LAND
Paul Auguston
Navajo children's drawings are animated with the children telling the stories their work illustrates. Navajo songs. In two parts: Part I, 12 minutes; Part 2, 20 minutes. ¾" video. UMC.

WESTWARD EXPANSION
Traces the westward growth of the U.S. from the first colonial rumbles to the disappearance of the "Old West." 1969. 25 minutes. Rental. IU. Purchase and rental. CRM.

WHERE HAS THE WARRIOR GONE?
Explores the life of Ted Cly, a typical Navajo father living on a reservation in Utah. 13 minutes. Grades 1-8. Rental. UK.

WHY DID GLORIA DIE?
Depicts the tragic life of Gloria Curtis, a Chippewa woman who died of hepatitis at age 17. Deals with the adjustments one must make from reservation to urban life. 1973. 27 minutes. Rental. IU and UM.

WINDWALKER
Keith Merrill, Director
Feature film providing an unusual authentic treatment of Native American culture. Spoken language is Crow or Cheyenne. Trevor Howard as Windwalker, an old dying Cheyenne man. All other actors are Indian. 1980. 108 minutes. 35mm/16mm. English subtitles. PI.

WINTER IN ESKIMO LAND
Father Hubbard explains to Lowell Thomas the life and recreation of the Eskimo people during the winter months. 1941. Grades 6-12. 11 minutes/bxw. Rental. UM.

WOODEN BOX:
MADE BY STEAMING AND BENDING
Clyde B. Smith, Producer
The Indians of the Northwest Pacific Coast developed woodworking; a specialty was steaming and bending of a single wooden slab to form a box. This film follows, carefully, every stage of making the Kwakiutl box. 1962. 33 minutes. Purchase: 16mm, $455; video, $320. Rental. UC and PSU.

WOODLAND INDIANS
OF EARLY AMERICA
Roy A. Price, Ed.D.
Authentic reconstructions and scenes in the eastern and Great Lakes regions provide settings for this study of Woodland Indian life (Chippewa) prior to European influence. 1958. 11 minutes. Grades K-6. Purchase: 16mm, $250; video, $175. Rental, $40. COR. Rental, $10.50, MM.

WOONSPE (EDUCATION AND THE SIOUX)
SD ETV
Explores the problems of Native American education. 1974. 28 minutes. 2" quad, 1" videotape and ¾" VHS. Rental, $40/week. NAPBC.

WORDS AND PLACE:
NATIVE LITERATURE FROM
THE AMERICAN SOUTHWEST
Denny Carr, Director; Larry Evers, Producer
Series of videotapes focus on traditional and modern Native American literature as told or written by individuals of various Southwestern tribes: Apache, Yaqui and Hopi people speak of their traditional philosophy, rituals and songs. ¾" video. See CLEAR for titles and prices.

YAQUI
Arizona artist Ted De Grazia narrates this filmic story of his paintings that depict the Yaqui Indian Ceremony. 1973. 19 minutes. Grades 4-adult. 16mm. Rental. UA.

YESTERDAY'S CHILDREN
Skokomish youth interview two elders on the Skokomish Reservation on Hood Canal in western Washington State. The elders talk about their lives and changes they have experienced. Teacher's guide and lesson plans. 30 minutes. Grades 9-adult. Purchase: ½" beta, and ¾" VHS, $110. Rental, $25. DSP.

YESTERDAY, TODAY:
THE NETSILIK ESKIMO
Gilles Blais
Traces the adaptation of the Netsilik from a migratory people to settlers in a government village. Filmed ten years after the documentary film, *The Eskimo: Fight for Life. 1974. 58 minutes. Grades 7-adult. 16mm. EDC, MM and UA.*

YOU ARE ON INDIAN LAND
Mort Ransen, Director; Mike Mitchel, Project Director
Report of a protest demonstration by Mohawk Indians of the St. Regis Reservation on the international Bridge between Canada and U.S. 1969. 37 mintues. 16mm/bxw. CRM, UC and PSU.

FILMSTRIPS AND SLIDES

**AKWASASNE RESERVATION
SLIDE SHOW**
A complete package of slide carousel, tape and script. Includes Iroquois legends, corn husk doll-making, Mohawk basketmaking, Iroquois Wampum and Cradleboards. 1984. Ten minutes long. Rental, $15/three days. AM.

AMERICA'S 19th CENTURY WARS
Covers the Indian Wars. Includes guide. Grades 7-12. Six filmstrips/cassettes. $141. LL.

AMERICAN INDIAN FOLK LEGENDS
Myths and legends of the American Indian. The White Buffalo; The First Tom-Tom; First Winter, First Summer; The Four Thunders, two parts; How Fire Came to Earth. Six filmstrips; records or cassettes. $130. RH.

AMERICAN INDIAN LEGENDS
Adventure stories showing many customs and rituals of American Indians. Aids vocabulary growth. Grades 3-5. Six filmstrips / cassettes, $119.00; six filmstrips (captioned), $55. RH.

AMERICAN INDIAN LIFE
Nine color filmstrips comparing and contrasting the ways of life of Indians in different sections of the U.S. Grades 1-6. CMC.

**THE AMERICAN INDIAN:
A STUDY IN DEPTH**
Dr. Ethel J. Alpenfeis traces the history and development of the American Indians over the past 400 centuries. Six color filmstrips/cassettes. PHM.

**AMERICAN INDIANS OF
THE NORTH PACIFIC COAST**
Their history, arts and crafts, myths and ceremonies. Grades 4-6. Six filmstrips/cassettes. $119. COR.

**AMERICAN INDIANS OF
THE NORTHEAST**
A study of the rise and fall of the Algonquin and Iroquois Indian empires, migrants from Asia to the Northeastern U.S. and southern Canada. Who they are, their history, religion, handicrafts. Grades 4-6. Six filmstrips/cassettes. $119. COR.

AMERICAN INDIANS OF THE PLAINS
Presents the history, tribes, culture, arts and crafts, and religion of the Plains Indians. Grades 4-9. Six filmstrips/cassettes. $119. COR.

**AMERICAN INDIANS
OF THE SOUTHEAST**
A full-blooded Cherokee explains their life today. Reveals the life of the Southeastern Indian tribes from prehistoric times to the present. Grades 4-9. Six filmstrips/cassettes. $119. COR.

**AMERICAN INDIANS
OF THE SOUTHWEST**
A history-oriented presentation of the Pueblo tribes, examining their customs and languages. Grades 4-9. Six filmstrips/cassettes. $119. COR.

**AMERICAN MUSEUM OF NATURAL
HISTORY—PHOTOGRAPHIC AND
FILM COLLECTION**
Contains thousands of bxw photographs, color slides, and color transparencies of Native Americans; may be rented for reproduction, or purchased. For films, short footage segments may be available for reproduction upon payment of film/video duplication costs and use fees. AM.

THE BATTLE OF THE LITTLE BIGHORN
A detailed study of the impact of Custer's defeat by the Sioux and Cheyenne. Grades 7-12. Filmstrip/cassette. $26. LL.

BATTLE OF THE LITTLE BIG HORN
A series of 80 slides depicting the Battle which took place in 1876. Includes a map and reading list. SI.

CAHOKIA SLIDE PACKAGE
A set of 77 slides with a cassette tape and written text, illustrating the history of Indian culture at Cahokia, as well as the archaeological techniques used to explore and study the site. Three week loan. Fee is the return first class postage. CMM.

CLIMBING THE HILL
A specialized filmstrip developed for men and women who are interested in following the kind of leadership demonstrated by the old Dakota Holy Men. AICRC.

**CONTEMPORARY INDIAN AND
ESKIMO CRAFTS OF THE U.S.**
74 full-color, 35mm slides with lecture text booklet illustrating the great variety of distinctive craft forms created by numerous contemporary Native American craftsmen. $50. TIPI.

CONTEMPORARY SIOUX PAINTING
77 full-color and bxw, 35mm slides with lecture text booklet. Illustrates the historic development of expressive forms of painting created by Sioux artists during the past 200 years. $50. TIPI.

THE CORPS OF DISCOVERY:
THE LEWIS AND CLARK EXPEDITION
An exploration that had a significant impact on opening up Western America. Grades 7-12. Two filmstrips; cassette. $31. LL.

THE DRUM IS THE HEART
Randy Croce, Producer

Focuses on the Blackfeet, Blackfoot, Blood and Peigan tribes that make up the Blackfoot Nation at their celebrations, speaking about their contemporary lives and traditional values. Filmstrip and slide set. Purchase and rental. UCV and BM.

THE EARTH KNOWERS:
THE NATIVE AMERICANS SPEAK
Statements of Indian wise men who relied on religious and cultural experience to deal with technological and social reorganization. Guide. Grades 7-12. Filmstrip/cassette. $26. LL.

ESKIMOS OF ALASKA (ARCTIC LIFE)
Four color filmstrips providing a picture of the life of Eskimos in Alaska. Emphasis is placed on activities of children. Grades 4-8. CMC.

FAMOUS INDIAN CHIEFS
Examines eight famous Indian chiefs: Pontiac (Ottawa), Joseph Brant (Mohawk), Tecumseh (Shawnee), Black Hawk (Sauk), Osceola (Seminole), Chief Joseph (Nez Perce), Sitting Bull (Sioux), and Geronimo (Apache). Grades 4-6. Eight filmstrips; cassettes. $149. COR.

THE FAR NORTH
Deals with the art and culture of the Alaskan Eskimo Aleuts and the Athapascan and Tlingit Indians, focusing on the art and ways of life. 1975. 48 color slides. Free rental. NGA.

THE FIRST PEOPLE OF NORTH
AMERICA: INDIANS AND INUIT
Presents an historical overview of the various native cultures existing in North America. The distinctive lifestyles of native peoples of differing geographic regions are examined with an emphasis on environmmental factors. One filmstrip is devoted to the study of the Inuit of the Arctic. Six filmstrips; cassettes; one sound filmstrip guide with discussion questions; one script booklet. $160. UL.

FOLKTALES OF ETHNIC AMERICA
Includes *The Brahman, The Tiger,* and *The Six Judges* (Indian); and *The Blind Boy and the Loon* (Alaskan.) Grades 3-6. Six filmstrips/cassettes. $119. RH.

THE FRENCH AND INDIAN WARS:
ROAD TO THE AMERICAN REVOLUTION?
Reviews the outstanding developments which lead to independence, including the French and Indian War 1689-1762. Grades 7-12. Two filmstrips/cassettes. $31. LL.

HOMES OF ANCIENT PEOPLE
A color filmstrip showing the ruins of ancient Indian homes at Mesa Verde, Canyon de Chelly, and Walnut Canyon. Grades 4-8. CMC.

HOW THE INDIANS
DISCOVERED A NEW WORLD
Paleo-Indian transition from hunting to farming, trade and communications. Grades 6-12. Two filmstrips; cassettes. $33. RH.

HUNGER WALKS AMONG INDIANS
Indian Ministries Task Force on some of the work they have done to alleviate hunger problems of Native Americans. 85 slides; cassette. Rental, $5. NILB.

INDIAN AMERICANS:
STORIES OF ACHIEVEMENT
A four filmstrip set which portrays, in illustrations and soundtracks, the contributions of four great Indian Americans: Hiawatha, Ely S. Parker, Washakie, and Pocahontas. Four records or cassettes; teacher's guide. WD.

INDIAN ART IN AMERICA:
THE ARTS AND CRAFTS OF THE
NORTH AMERICAN INDIANS
51 slides. MAI.

AN INDIAN JESUS
Richard West, a Cheyenne Indian, is a Christian and an artist. Through his paintings, he helps us see Jesus through Native American eyes. 42 frames; color. Reading script and guide. Grades 3-12. $10. FP.

INDIAN PAINTING
63 subjects (slide sets.) See MAI for ordering information.

INDIAN ROCK ART
Portrays one of the most ancient art forms in New Mexico, illustrating the timeless images of a mysterious art. 12 minute slide-tape program. Available for loan or purchase. MNM.

INDIAN SOVEREIGNTY—INDIAN
TREATIES—INDIANS AND THE U.S.
GOVERNMENT—INDIAN JURISDICTION
FEDERAL INDIAN TRUST RELATIONSHIP
A series of five instructional programs of four filmstrips each explaining the legal concepts and the history behind many of the present areas of controversy involving Indian tribes. Researched by the Institute for the Development of Indian Law, Inc. Includes a response sheet master for practice quizzes; and trainer's guide for each. Pre/post tests available. $6 per topic. $120 each; $480 per set. COOK.

INDIAN VILLAGE ARCHAEOLOGY
Documents the rediscovery of ancient Ozette by archaeologists. 1972. 88 color frames; teacher's guide and cassette. UW.

INDIANS OF HISTORIC TIMES
Slide sets on the following areas: Eskimo and Arctic (33 subjects); Northwest Coast (221 subjects); Woodlands and Northeast (118 subjects); Southeast (38 subjects); Plains and Plateau (446 subjects); Southwest (184 subjects); and, Far West (73 subjects). See MAI for ordering information.

INDIANS OF NORTH AMERICA
North America's native peoples from ancient to modern times. A series of five sound filmstrips: *The First Americans; The Eastern Woodlands; The Plains; West of the Shining Mountains;* and, *Indians Today.* 13-14 minutes each. Grades 5-12. $99.50. NGS.

**INDIANS: THE SOUTHWEST
AND THE PLAINS INDIANS**
The history of the American Indian poeple and how they live today. *The Southwest Indians* and *The Sundance People.* Two filmstrips, cassettes each, $48 each. Grades 6-8. RH.

**INSIDE THE CIGAR STORE:
IMAGES OF THE AMERICAN INDIAN**
Focuses on the contradictory stereotypes of the American Indian which have been perpetuated by mass media and textbooks, and pleads for the replacement of the inacurate images with the knowledge about contemporary American Indian people. Filmstrip/cassette. MRC.

LEGENDS OF THE MICMAC
The use of puppetry and mask-making in providing an instructive introduction to one of the earliest tribes to settle in North America. Grades 2-5. Four filmstrips, cassettes; teacher's guide. $95. RH.

THE LIFE OF THE AMERICAN INDIAN
Two sound filmstrips: *The Eastern Woodlands and the Plains* - explains how eastern tribes utilize their environment; and *The Northwest Coast and the Southwest* - Southwestern Indians farm arid lands and dance for rain, while Northwest Coast Indians fish and hold potlatches. 1977. 13-14 minutes each. Grades K-4. $50. NGS.

**THE MAKE-BELIEVE INDIAN:
NATIVE AMERICANS IN THE MOVIES**
  Gretchen Bataille and Charles L.P. Silet
Demonstrates the influence of early travel narratives, literature, the visual arts, and the wild west shows on the Native American image in the movies. Examples are drawn from silent films, serials, and contemporary feature films. 140 slides and carousel tray; audio-cassette; bibliography;

script; suggestions. Purchase: $99; rental, $15/3 days. MRC.

**THE MAN FROM DEER CREEK,
THE STORY OF ISHI**
A Yahi Indian in 1911, the last of his tribe, and the last to grow up without contact with American civilization. Grades 7-12. Two filmstrips, cassette. $41. LL.

THE "MARMES MAN" DIG
  Louis and Ruth Kirk, Producer
An account of an archaeologicl discovery in eastern Washington State. The remains of early man in the Western Hemisphere. A graphic exposition of the techniques of archaeology. 1968. 61 color frames. $10. UW.

**MICMAC: THE PEOPLE
AND THEIR CULTURE**
A kit of nine filmstrips provide an overview of Micmac culture—structures, transportation, hunting and fishing, recretion and domestic crafts. Grade 6. NOVA.

**NAKED CLAY: 3,000 YEARS
OF UNADORNED POTTERY OF
THE AMERICAN INDIAN**
Features American Indian artistry in modelled ceramics. Includes a 72-page catalog. 90 slides. MAI.

**NAVAJO CULTURAL
FILMSTRIPS AND SLIDES**
Contains 23 filmstrips with cassettes ranging in time from five minutes to 20 minutes. All grades. See SAN for titles and prices.

**NORTHWEST COAST INDIAN
TRADITIONS TODAY:
A CONTEMPORARY
LOOK AT REMNANTS OF A HERITAGE**
  Louis and Ruth Kirk, Producers
Features dugout canoes hollowed from cedar logs, the netting and prparation of fish, baskets made from swamp and saltwater marsh grasses, etc. 1972. 90 color/sound frames. 15 minutes. Cassette/booklet. $25. UW.

OUR HEARTS BEAT AS ONE
Provides an historical view of tribes in Oregon. Two carousel slide trays; 160 slides. Grades 6-adult. Rental, $15. NILB.

OZETTE ARCHAEOLOGY
  Louis and Ruth Kirk, Producers
Tells the story of the past and the present as it is being continually uncovered at the Ozette Archaeological Dig, Cape Alava, Washington State. Sumarizes the resources available to the Makah Indians living on the Northwest Coast of the Olympic Peninsula. 1979. 153 color; sound frames. 21 minutes. Cassette - booklet. $25. UW.

A POINT OF PARTNERSHIP
Depicts some of the work of the National Indian Lutheran Board. All ages. 12 minutes. Filmstrip/cassette. NILB.

PRE-COLUMBIAN CULTURES
A series of slide sets. United States (231 subjects); Canada (three subjects). All archaeological specimens are of pottery. MAI.

PUEBLO INDIANS OF NEW MEXICO
Examines the history and culture of the Pueblo Indians. Includes images of the people, ancient and modern villages, crafts and ways of life many of which are drawn from the Museum of New Mexico's collection of historic photographs and rare old hand-tinted glass slides. 17 minute slide-tape program. Available for loan or purchase. MNM.

THE PURITAN EXPERIENCE:
MAKING A NEW WORLD
Life in Massachusetts—the Higgin's family daughter, a captive of the Indians for a while, resents the Puritans' treatment of the Indians, and challenges strict Puritan authority. Grades 7-12. Two filmstrips, cassettes. $60. LL.

READ ALONG
AMERICAN INDIAN LEGENDS
Stimulates reading interest with tales of Indian lore. Vocabulary-building captions. Program guide. Grades 2-5. Six filmstrips, cassettes. $119. RH.

THE SACRED PIPE
A filmstrip of the Sacred Pipe, the central instrument of the Dakota religion. Gives the proper understanding of the origin and use of the Pipe. AICRC.

SANDSTONE COUNTRY: THE CANYONS AND INDIANS OF THE SOUTHWEST
  Louis and Ruth Kirk, Producers
Arizona and Utah apartment-dwelling Indians before Columbus, reveals the ancient cities and the geological history. Teacher's guide. 1970. 70 color frames. $10. UW.

SICA HOLLOW
An historical and religious filmstrip. One of the old story of the flood—localized on the Sisseton-Wahpeton Reservation. AICRC.

THE SIOUX
Black Elk's words from a broken treaty. Study of the Sioux, past and present, are analyzed to show the Indian in confrontation with cultural crisis and identity loss. Includes a script. Grades 7-12. Filmstrip/cassette. $30. LL.

THE SOUTHWEST: EARLY INDIAN CULTURES: THE SPANISH HERITAGE: THE EARLY ANGLO PERIOD: THE MODERN SOUTHWEST
The influence of the desert environment on the culture and lifestyle of the Indians. Four sound filmstrips, two cassettes. Script/guide. $90. UL.

SOUTHWEST INDIAN FAMILIES
A day in the lives of four real families from four different tribes: Navajo, Zuni, Apache and Hopi. Grades 1-3. Four filmstrips, four cassettes; four filmstrips/captioned. $40. COR.

SURVIVAL: A HISTORY OF NORTHWEST INDIAN TREATY FISHING RIGHTS
A slide presentation produced by the Point No Point Treaty Council. Recounts the history of Indian fishing before the arrival of white people in the Northwest, and of treaties and legal decisions culminating in the 1974 "Boldt Decision." Techer's guide and student handouts and worksheets. 20 minutes. Grades 4-adult. Purchase: $195; rental, $30. DSP.

TALES OF THE PLAINS INDIANS
Gives insight into the religion, culture, and relationship to nature of the Blackfeet, Sioux, Pawnee and Cheyeen tribes. Grades 3-5. Six filmstrips, cassettes. $119. RH.

TRIBAL ARCHIVES
In two parts: Part 1: *An Introduction* - Discusses what an archives is, what you need to establish one, and how you will benefit from an archives program. Slide/tape program; 110 slides; 1983, 13½ minutes. Part 2: *Getting Started* - A slide/tape program. Includes a booklet containing script, a bibliography, a glossary, and a list of resources. 1986. Purchase: $80 each; rental, $17 each. SI-OMP.

TWO EAGLES LEGEND
This filmstrip is a morality story; a young man, betrayed by his friend, is saved by two young eagles. (In Dakota tradition, the Eagle is always a symbol of God's presence.) AICRC.

UNLEARNING INDIAN STEREOTYPES
Works with myths and images from books and television. 15 minutes. Grades 3-6. Filmstrip, cassette. Rental, $5. NILB.

A VISIT TO THE FATHER
Authentic Navajo origin legend in four filmstrip episodes. Translated and illustrated by Navajo artist Auska Kee. All ages. $67.50 with cassettes. CEN.

VOICES FROM THE CRADLEBOARD
Slide presentation of traditional child rearing practices, such as the use of legends and the cradleboard, which emphasizes the importance of children in past and present Indian societies. 30 minutes. Grades 9-adult. Purchase, $185; rental, $30. DSP.

WHITE MAN AND INDIAN:
THE FIRST CONTACTS
Depicts the first explorers and their halting, initial contacts with the Indians of Eastern America. Grades 7-12. Two filmstrips, cassettes. $31. LL.

WOLF GIRL
This filmstrip is a morality story. In non-Indian myth, the Wolf is always an evil animal. Indian people, however, have discovered the wolf to be a friend and a helpful animal. AICRC.

RECORDINGS

ALASKAN ESKIMO
SONGS AND STORIES
Lorraine D. Koranda; illustrated by Robert Mayokok
42 stories and songs on one LP. Sung in Eskimo and told in English. 1971. 50 page booklet. UW.

AMERICAN INDIAN DANCES
Recordings of the following Indian dances: Rabbit Dance, Sun Dance and Omaha Dance (Sioux); Devil Dance (Apache); Eagle Dance (San Ildefonso); Harvest Dance and Rain Dance (Zuni); Squaw Dance (Navajo); War Dance and Dog Dance (Plains); Snake Dance and Pow-Wow Dance (Flathead). 12". $9.98. FR.

AMERICAN INDIAN MEDICINE
Rolling Thunder, a Medicine Man, describes the difficulties Indians have had in preserving their philosophy and culture, while being captives in the white man's society. 60 minutes. cassette. BSR.

THE AMERICAN INDIAN
ORAL HISTORY COLLECTION
Dr. Joseph H. Cash, General Editor
Contains 15 interviews on audiocassette conducted by historians and anthropologists for students and scholars: *The Sundance* (Crow); *Medicine Men and Women I & II* (Cheyenne River Sioux, Crow and Rosebud Sioux); *The Buffalo Hunt I & II* (Crow); *Kinship, I, II & III* (Crow); *Legends* (Chipewa); *The Drum Society* (Mille Lacs Chippewa); *Little Bighorn; The BIA* (Oglala Sioux); *The BIA* (Rosebud Sioux); *Indian Students* (Oglala Sioux); *Life in 1900* (Cheyenne River Sioux). 30 minutes each. $15 each; $350 per set. CLEAR.

AMERICAN INDIANS
IN FACT AND SYMBOL
In two parts by Dr. Joseph Henderson: Part 1: *The American Indian and the Jungian Orientation* —Dr. Henderson offers an historical sketch of the white man's attitudes and actions toward American Indians. Part 2: *The American Indian—A Sioux Shaman* — Dr. Henderson speaks of Black Elk, who at the age of nine had a vision which later evolved into the seven secret rites of the soul. Three hours, two tapes. BSR.

AN HISTORICAL ALBUM
OF BLACKFOOT INDIAN MUSIC
12". $10.98. FR.

ANAPAO
Indian tales. Spoken and written by Jamake Highwater. Cassette. $10.98. FR.

THE ANGRY INDIANS
Documentary on American Indian Conference at the University of Chicago in 1961, whose objectives were to get Indians from all parts of the U.S. together so that they could discuss their common problems and determine what they want from the U.S. Government and people. 26 minutes. Cassette. AUDIO.

ANTHOLOGY OF NORTH AMERICAN
INDIAN & ESKIMO MUSIC
A two-record set, compiled by Michael I. Asch, of the music of many of the tribes of North America. Two 12". $21.96. FR.

THE ARCHIVE OF FOLK CULTURE
NATIVE AMERICAN RECORDINGS
Contains the following material: 1) The Jesse Walter Fewkes' 1890 cylinders of Passamaquaddy Indians—earliest field recordings made anywhere in the world; 2) More than 3,500 cylinders assembled between 1907 and 1940 by Francis Densmore and others for the Smithsonian Institution, Bureau of American Ethnology; 3) Several hundred discs and tapes 1940 to 1952 by Willard Rhodes for the Bureau of Indian Affairs. The following recordings were edited by William N. Fenton: *Songs From the Iroquois Longhouse; Seneca Songs From Coldspring Longhouse; Songs of the Chippewa; Songs of the Sioux; Songs of the Yuma, Cocopa, and Yuqui, Songs of the Pawnee and Northern Ute; Songs of the Papago; Songs of the Nootka and Quileute; Songs of the Menominee, Mandan and Hidatsa.* The following songs were recorded and edited by Willard Rhodes: *Northwest (Puget Sound); Kiowa; Indian Songs of Today; Delaware, Cherokee, Choctaw and Creek; Great Basin: Paiute, Washo, Ute, Bannock, Shoshone; Plains: Comanche, Cheyenne, Kiowa, Caddo, Wichita, Pawnee; Sioux; Navaho; Apache; Pueblo: Taos,*

San Ildefonso, Zuni, Hopi. Copies of most of the Archive's recorded collections can be purchased from: Recording Laboratory, Archive of Folk Culture, Library of Congress, Washington, D.C. 20540. (202) 287-5510. Photocopies of folklore and ethnomusicology material which are not protected by copyright or other restrictions may be ordered from: Photoduplication Service, Library of Congress, Washington, D.C. 20540.

AS LONG AS THE GRASS SHALL GROW
Peter LaFarge sings 13 of his own songs. A 12-page brochure includes words and transcriptions of songs. 12". $10.98. FR.

THE BADLAND SINGERS
Two cassettes. Volume 1: *Assiniboine-Sioux Grass Dance* — Ten grass dance songs; Volume 2: *Live at United Tribes* - Recorded live at at the 10th Anniversary United Tribes Days International Championship Dancing and Singing Contest, Bismarck, North Dakota. Cassettes. NSS.

BLACKFOOT A-1 CLUB SINGERS
Includes four war dance songs, and two chicken dance songs. Cassette. NSS.

CHEYENNE PEYOTE SONGS
Two cassettes. NSS.

CHIPPEWA SONGS, 1
12". $10.98. FR.

CRY FROM THE EARTH
Music of North American Indians. 12". $10.98. FR.

CULTURAL PLURALISM AND THE RECOVERY OF THE CLASSIC
Uses poetry of the American Indian and reservation treaties of the 19th century to reveal the wisdom and philosophy of Indian leaders. 1972. 59 minute cassette. NCTE.

DELAWARE, CHEROKEE, CHOCTAW & CREEK SONGS
Songs of the Delaware Big House, Peyote Song, and War Dance Song; Cherokee Lullaby, Stomp Dance Song, Christian Hymn, Horse Dance Song, Quail Dance Song, Pumpkin Dance Song; Choctaw Hymn; and Creek Ball Game Song, Lullaby, etc. Recorded and edited by Willard Rhodes. 12" LP. LC.

ENGLISH AND AMERICAN INDIAN STUDIES
Robert Lewis sets forth dos and donts for English teachers who plan to use Native American materials. 1972. 35 minutes. NCTE.

ESKIMO MUSIC OF ALASKA AND THE HUDSON BAY
Record and notes by Laura Boulton. 12". $10.98. FR.

ESKIMO SONGS FROM ALASKA
Twenty contemporary and ancient songs recorded by Miriam C. Stryker on St. Lawrence Island. Edited by Charles Hoffman. Includes an illustrated brochure. 12". $10.98. FR.

GREAT AMERICAN INDIAN SPEECHES
Narrated by Vine Deloria, Jr. and Arthur S. Junaluska. Includes speeches of Geronimo, Standing Bear, Cochise, Black Elk and others. Grades 7-12. Two cassettes. $19.95. LL.

GREAT BASIN: PAIUTE, WASHO, UTE, BANNOCK, AND SHOSHONE
Northwest tribe's dances, games, parade songs, and lullabies. Recorded and edited by Willard Rhodes. 12" LP. LC.

HEALING SONGS OF THE AMERICAN INDIANS
Healing songs of the Chippewa, Sioux, Yuman, Northern Ute, Papago, Makah and Menominee Indians.Text included. 12". $10.98. FR.

HO HWO SJU LAKOTA SINGERS TRADITIONAL SONGS BY THE SIOUX
Includes the Sioux National Anthem, among other traditional songs of the Sioux. Cassette. NSS.

HOPI KATCHINA SONGS AND SIX SONGS BY HOPI CHANTERS
Recorded in Arizona in 1924. Text included. 12". $10.98. FR.

HOPI TALES
Four legends of the Hopi people, read by Jack Moyles, from Harold Coulander's book *People of the Short Blue Corn*. Includes the following legends: "Journey to the Land of the Dead","The Sun Caller", "Coyote's Needle and Honwyma and the Bear", and "Fathers of Tokoanave." 12". $10.98. FR.

INDIAN HOUSE RECORDS & TAPES
Includes the following records and cassettes: *Round Dance Songs of Taos Pueblo,* Two volumes; *Taos Round Dance,* Two parts; *Taos Pueblo Round Dance; Ditch-Cleaning & Picnic Songs of Picuris Pueblo; Turtle Dance Songs of San Juan Pueblo; Cloud Dance Songs of San Juan Pueblo; Zuni Fair-Live; Navajo Sway Songs; Night & Daylight Yeibichei; Navajo Skip Dance & Two Step Songs; Navajo Round Dance; Navajo Gift Songs & Round Dance; Navajo Corn Grindings & Shoe Game Songs; Klagetoh Maiden Singers; Navajo Songs About Love* - The Klagetoh Swingers, Six volumes; The San Juan Singers - *Navajo Skip Dance Songs; Navajo Skip Dance & Two-Step Songs* - The Rock Point Singers, Two volumes; *Navajo Peyote*

Ceremonial Songs, Four volumes; War Dance Songs of the Ponca, Two volumes; Ponca Peyote Songs, Three volumes; Cheyenne Peyote Songs, Two volumes; Comanche Peyote Songs, Two volumes; Handgame of the Kiowa, Kiowa Apache, & Comanche, Two volumes; Kiowa Gourd Dance, Two volumes; Kiowa 49 - War Expedition Songs; Kiowa Church Songs, Two Volumes; War Dance Songs of the Kiowa—O-ho-mah Lodge Singers, Two volumes; Flute Songs of the Kiowa & Comanche - Tom Mauchahty-Ware; Songs of the Muskogee Creek, Two parts; Stomp Dance - Muskogee, Seminole, Yuchi, Two volumes; Blackfoot A-1 Club Singers, Two volumes; Old Agency Singers of the Blood Reserve, Two parts; The Badland Singers - Live at Bismarck; The Badland Singers at Home; Kahoini Songs - The Badland Singers; The Badland Singers, Live at United Tribes, Two volumes; Ashland Singers - North Cheyenne War Dance; Ho Hwo Sju Lakota Singers - Traditional Songs of the Sioux; Love Songs of the Lakota, performed on Flute by Kevin Locke; Ironwood Singers - Songs of the Sioux, Live at Rosebud Fair; Yankton Sioux Peyote Songs, Eight volumes; Songs of the Native American Church - Sung by Rev. Joseph M. Shields; Red Earth Singers, Live at Bismarck, Two volumes; Sounds of Indian America - Plains & Southwest; Pueblo Songs of the Southwest. Cassette or LP recordings available for most selections. $8 each cassette or LP. See IH for further information.

INDIAN MUSIC OF THE CANADIAN PLAINS
Recordings of the Blood, Cree, Blackfoot and Assiniboine Indians made on the reservation. Includes war songs, greeting songs, stick games, Dance songs, etc. 12" LP, $10.98. FR.

INDIAN MUSIC OF THE PACIFIC NORTHWEST COAST
A two-record set containing 27 songs and dances recorded by Dr. Ida Halpern, mostly from the Kwakiutl Tribe with Nootka and Tlingit songs and dances included. 12" LP. $21.96. FR.

INDIAN MUSIC OF THE SOUTHWEST
Includes Hopi, Zuni, Navajo, Taos, San Ildefonso, Santa Ana, Mohave, Papago, Pima and Apache music. Record and notes by Dr. Laura Boulton. 12" LP. $10.98. FR.

INDIAN SONGS OF TODAY
Seminole, Creek, Potawatomi, Sioux, Navajo, Tlingit and Kiowa songs sung by Indian youths. Recorded and edited by Willard Rhodes. LC.

KIOWA
Dance and war songs of the Kiowa Indians. 12" LP. LC and FR.

KIOWA GOURD DANCE
Includes 12 Kiowa gourd dance songs. Cassette. NSS.

KIOWA PEYOTE MEETING
Documents the vision-producing peyote ritual. Three record set. Edited by Harry E. Smith. 12" LP. $10.98. FR.

KWAKIUTL, NORTHWEST INDIANS
Two record set. 12". $25. FR.

MUSIC OF THE ALASKAN KUTCHIN INDIANS
12" LP. $10.98. FR.

MUSIC OF THE ALGONKIANS, NORTHEAST INDIANS
12" LP. $10.98. FR.

MUSIC OF THE AMERICAN INDIANS OF THE SOUTHWEST
Includes the Navajo, Zuni, Hopi, San Ildefonso, Taos, Apache, Yuma, Papago, Walapai and Havasupai tribal music. Recorded by Willard Rhodes in cooperation with the Bureau of Indian Affairs. Notes by Harry Tschopik, Jr. and Willard Rhodes. 12" LP. $10.98. FR.

MUSIC OF THE PAWNEE
Contains 45 Pawnee Indian songs sung by Mark Evarts and recorded in 1935 by Dr. Gene Weltfish. Reflects all aspects of Pawnee life. 12" LP. $10.98. FR.

MUSIC OF THE PLAINS APACHE
15 songs recorded and edited by Dr. John Beatty. Includes children's songs, lullabies, church songs, dance songs, hand game songs, and peyote songs. Notes and background of songs included. 12" LP. $10.98. FR.

MUSIC OF THE PUEBLOS, APACHE, AND NAVAJOS
Recorded by David P. MacAllester and Donald N. Brown. 12" LP. TM.

MUSIC OF THE SIOUX AND THE NAVAJO
Sioux recordings include, among others, Rabbit Dance, Sun Dance, love songs; Navajo recordings include: Squaw Dance, Night Chant, riding song, etc. Notes included. Recorded by Willard Rhodes in cooperation with the Bureau of Indian Affairs. 12" LP. $10.98. FR.

MY LIFE IN RECORDING CANADIAN—INDIAN FOLKLORE
Canadian ethnomusicologist Dr. Marcus C. Barbeau relates his experiences and sings a wide variety of Huron, Algonquin, Lillooet, Shusways and Tsimsyan tribal songs. 12" LP. $10.98. FR.

NAVAHO
Navaho chants, game, love and peyote songs. Recorded and edited by Willard Rhodes. 12" LP. LC.

NAVAJO AND ENGLISH CASSETTES
19 audiocassettes. Grades 1-6. See SAN for titles and prices. **NAVAJO DEDICATIONS-MODERN MUSIC**
Based on Navajo ceremonies by David Cope Vortex. Rituals, parallax, Teec Nos Pos. 12" LP. $10.98. FR.

NAVAJO ROUND DANCE
Contains 50 Navajo gift songs and 29 Navajo round dance songs from the Enemy Way Ceremony recorded at Klagetoh, Arizona. Cassette. NSS.

**NOOTKA MUSIC—INDIANS
OF THE PACIFIC NORTHWEST,
BRITISH COLUMBIA, CANADA**
Two record set. 12" LP. $21.96. FR.

NORTHWEST (PUGET SOUND)
Includes Skagit, Lummi, Chinook, Klallam, Quinault and Tsalyak songs. Recorded and edited by Willard Rhodes. 12" LP. LC.

PETER LA FARGE—ON THE WARPATH
Includes 14 contemporary protest songs by Peter La Farge, accompanied by Nick Navarro, Indian drums. 12" LP. $10.98. FR.

**PLAINS: COMANCHE, CHEYENNE,
KIOWA, CADDO, WICHITA, PAWNEE**
Selections include recordings of raid, war, love, rain, flag and hunting songs. Recorded and edited by Willard Rhodes. 12" LP. LC.

**PUEBLOS: TAOS,
SAN ILDEFONSO, ZUNI, HOPI**
Songs, dances, lullabies and chants recorded and edited by Willard Rhodes. 12" LP. LC.

**RED EARTH SINGERS,
LIVE AT BISMARCK**
Includes Grand Entry Song, eight war dance songs, and one trick contest song. Cassette. NSS.

**THE RENAISSANCE OF
THE AMERICAN INDIAN**
Describes the social barriers the American Indian has had to face; his experiences in various careers, and the anachronistic traditions of Indian culture that confuses his progress. 1968. Cassette. AUDIO.

**ROUND DANCE SONGS
OF TAOS PUEBLO**
Includes 16 round dance songs. Cassette. NSS.

**SELF-DETERMINATION FOR AMERICAN
INDIANS: 1) DEVELOPMENT OF THEIR
LANDS; 2) CULTURES IN CONFLICT**
Recorded and edited by Henry W. Hough: 1) Traces the history of reservations and discusses the present development of resources on Indian reservations. 2) Why Indians cling to their way of life although proud of their American citizenship. 1968. Cassettes, 25 minutes each. AUDIO.

SENECA SOCIAL DANCE MUSIC
Recorded by M.F. Reimer. 12" LP. $10.98. FR.

**SENECA SONGS FROM
COLDSPRING LONGHOUSE**
Songs include the Drum Dance, Bear Society, Fish Dance, and others. Recorded and edited in 1941-1945 by Willard N. Fenton. 12" LP. LC.

SIOUX
Contains Sioux love, death, dance and peyote songs recorded and edited by Willard Rhodes. 12" LP. LC.

**SONGS AND DANCES OF
THE FLATHEAD INDIANS**
A complete musical culture of the Salish people. Illustrated notes included. 12" LP. $10.98. FR.

**SONG AND DANCES OF
THE GREAT LAKES INDIANS**
Music of the Algonquins and Iroquois. Recordfed in Iowa, Wisconsin, Michigan and New York State by Gertrude P. Kurath. Text included. 12" LP. $10.98. FR.

**SONGS FROM
THE IROQUOIS LONGHOUSE**
Selections include: Creator's Songs; Midwinter Festival Chants; Medicine Men's Celebration (Onondaga.) Recorded and edited by William N. Fenton in cooperation with the Smithsonian Institution. 12" LP. LC.

SONGS OF THE CHIPPEWA
Chippewa dream songs, war songs, love songs, songs of the treatment of the sick, and dancing songs. Recorded and edited by Frances Densmore. 12" LP. LC.

**SONGS OF THE MENOMINEE,
MANDAN AND HIDATSA**
Includes hunting, war, dream and legendary songs and chants, recorded and edited by Frances Densmore. 12" LP. LC.

SONGS OF THE MUSKOGEE CREEK
In two parts: Part 1: Includes the buffalo dance song, the long dance song and five stomp dance songs. Part 2: A stomp dance song, a friendship dance song, a stomp dance song, a gar dance song, guinea dance song, and morning dance song. Cassettes. NSS.

**SONGS OF THE
NOOTKA AND QUILEUTE**
Potlatch, dancing, game, dream, Klokali songs, and others. Recorded and edited by Frances Densmore. 12" FR.

SONGS OF THE PAPAGO
Recorded and edited by Frances Densmore. 12" LP. LC.

**SONGS OF THE PAWNEE
AND NORTHERN UTE**
Recorded and edited by Frances Densmore. 12" LP. LC.

**SONGS OF THE SEMINOLE
INDIANS OF FLORIDA**
33 songs recorded by Frances Densmore. Includes songs concerning the removal of the Seminole to Oklahoma. 12" LP. $10.98. FR.

SONGS OF THE SIOUX
Recorded and edited by Frances Densmore. 12" LP. LC.

SONGS OF THE WIGWAM
Contains more than a dozen songs portraying native life and thought in the forest around the Great Lakes. 24 pages. 95¢ each; 65¢ each, 15 or more. WAS.

**SONGS OF THE YUMA,
COCOPA, AND YAQUI**
Recorded and edited by Frances Densmore. 12" LP. LC.

**SOUNDS OF INDIAN AMERICA —
PLAINS 7 SOUTHWEST RECORDED
"LIVE" AT THE GALLUP CEREMONIALS**
Includes the Buffalo Dance, Jemez Eagle Dance, Ute Bear Dance, San Juan Butterfly Dance, Zuni Rain Song Dance by the Olla Maidens, Navajo Feather Dance, Taos Belt Dance, Pawnee Ghost Dance, Zuni Doll Dance, Crow Sun Dance, Kiowa Attack Dance. Cassettes. NSS.

**STOMP DANCE—MUSKOGEE,
SEMINOLE AND YUCHI**
Two cassettes. NSS.

**SYMBOLIC SHAMANISM: A STUDY
OF NAVAJO MEDICINE MEN**
Dr. Donald Sandner describes the healing process of medicine men and attempts to explain the sandpaintings, how they are made, how images are evoked for each patient, and how cures are performed. Two hours/two cassettes. BSR.

TURTLE MOUNTAIN MUSIC
Recorded and issued by the North Dakota Council of the Arts. Two record set. 12" LP. $25. FR.

A VOICE FOR THE AMERICAN INDIAN
A program on Indian culture and history, and the current struggles for political rights and power. Produced by Pacifica, KPFA. 1971. 54 minutes. AUDIO.

WAR WHOOPS AND MEDICINE SONGS
33 songs collected at the Upper Dells of the Wisconsin River where more than 200 American Indians from five different tribes assembled for the annual Star Rock Indian Ceremonial. Includes an illustrated brochure. Edited by Charles Hoffman. 12". $10.98. FR.

**WASHO PEYOTE SONGS:
SONGS OF THE AMERICAN
INDIAN NATIVE CHURCH**
Recorded by Dr. Warren d'Azevedo. 12" LP. $10.98. FR.

YANKTON SIOUX PEYOTE SONGS
Contains 24 peyote songs. Cassette. NSS.

PHOTOGRAPHS, PICTURE SETS
POSTERS AND KITS

**BOSTON CHILDREN'S MUSEUM
BORROW A KIT**
The Indians Who Met the Pilgrims: Presents the Wampanoag people of Massachusetts past and present; *Hopi Culture:* Describes a public kachina dance and its connection to contemporary Hopi culture. These two kits may be used as curriculum units, include cultural objects, oral history, texts and guides, A-V materials, and classroom activities; prepared with the participation of Native American people. Two other kits, *The Navajo* and *Northwest Coast Indians,* contain cultural objects and related labels for classroom exhibit. CMB.

EDUCATIONAL AID KITS
Children's touchable exhibits contained in a large footlocker-type trunk. Artifacts are compiled from the Museum of New Mexico's collections and various other sources in Santa Fe. Includes: Anglo Pioneer Family; Apache Family; Navajo Family; Pueblo Indian Family; and Spanish Frontier Family. Grades 1-6. Available for loan in the State of New Mexico only. Free one month rental. MNM.

**INDIAN PHOTOGRAPHS
FROM THE SMITHSONIAN**
There are four sets of five prints each. Set 1) Selected portraits: Kicking Bear, Geronimo, Chief Joseph, Quanah Parker, and Wolf Robe; Set 2-4) Lifestyles, Northwestern Indians - Southwestern Indians - Plains Indians. 11" x 14". SI.

THE INDIANS OF THE PLAINS

Contains 46, 11" x 14" photographs explaining the Plains Indians culture, government, society and habits; and how they were discovered in 1805. $43.50. DPA.

MUSEUM OF THE AMERICAN INDIAN PHOTOGRAPHIC ARCHIVES

Covers all areas and aspects of Native American life in the Western Hemisphere. Includes photographs by Curtis, Matteson and Jackson; Pepper, Wildschut and Verrill. 42,000 negatives, 28,000 bxw prints, and 5,000 color transparancies and slides; bxw prints, 5x7" or 8x10" format; 35mm color slides; and 4x5" coor transparencies. A slide list is available for a modest fee. MAI.

MUSEUM OF NEW MEXICO PHOTOGRAPHIC PORTFOLIOS

Includes three Native American photographic portfolios: *Pueblo Indians of New Mexico; Apache Indians of New Mexico;* and, *Navajo Indians of New Mexico.* Each set contains 16 photographs illustrating important aspects of the subject group's life and history during the late 19th and early 20th centuries. Large bxw photographs printed on heavy glossy paper. Each portfolio also contains a brief history of the group plus a vocabulary list, bibliography, and descriptive captions for the photographs. $6.95 each. MNM.

NAVAJO INDIAN CULTURAL CARD SETS & POSTERS

Contains 16 in all. All grades. See SAN for titles and prices.

NAVAJO INSTRUCTIONAL PROGRAMS, KITS AND PACKETS

See SAN for titles and prices.

SLECTED PORTRAITS OF PROMINENT NORTH AMERICAN INDIANS

8x10" glossy or matte prints. SI.

MAPS

COLOR MAP

Shows the distribution of Indian tribes in New York City and vicinity during the 17th century. $1.50. MAI.

DISTRIBUTION OF INDIAN TRIBES OF NORTH AMERICA

Map by Dr. A.L. Kroeber. 21x28" map of the time of first contact with white men. SM.

THE GABRIELINO INDIANS AT THE TIME OF THE PORTOLA EXPEDITION

Map by Allen M. Welts. 22x15" map showing locations of ancient Indian villages in southern California. SM.

HISTORICAL MAP, WARM SPRINGS INDIAN RESERVATION

Map by Ralph M. Shane and Ruby D. Leno, showing historical trails, sites and modern Kah-Nee-Ta. 15x18" color. OHS.

INDIAN LAND AREAS—GENERAL

A multicolor map that indicates the location and size of Federal Indian reservations, Indian groups, etc. SD.

INDIAN RESERVATIONS MAP

Black and white map of the U.S. showing where the Indian tribes, reservations, and settlements are located. IRA.

INDIAN TRIBES AND LANGUAGES OF OLD OREGON TERRITORY

22x33" color map. OHS.

INDIANS OF NORTH AMERICA

An archaeological and ethnological map. 32½x37½" with ethnological descriptive notes and illustrations. 1979. NGS.

MAP'N'FACTS: NATIVE PEOPLES OF NORTH AMERICA

Two full-color maps show—before Columbus—and today. 23x35". Two bxw maps on reverse set forth population and language groups. $4.50. FP.

NAVAJOLAND

A full-color illustrated map of the Southwestern U.S. where the Navajos live. Covers four states and 16 million acres. KC.

THREE MAPS OF INDIAN COUNTRY

Haskell Indian Junior College, Lawrence Kansas 66044. No charge.

MICROFICHE

AMERICAN INDIAN PERIODICALS

From the *State Historical Society of Wisconsin.* Tribal news, political issues, humor, commuity services, scholarly research. Silver halide film; 12 reels (approximate) 5mm silver halide microfilm. $585. From the *Princeton University Library on Microfiche.* Part 1, 96 titles: 2,068 fiche and two reels 35mm film, $5,000; Part 2, 34 titles: 401 fiche and two reels 35mm film, $1,000. See CLEAR for individual titles and prices.

TRAVELING EXHIBITS

INDIAN CULTURE AND HISTORY
A new microform index to Wisconsin Native American periodicals, 1879-1981. Edited by James P. Danky. Six computer-output microfiche; 42:1 reduction ratio. 1984. $30. GP.

THE LAKE MOHONK CONFERENCE OF FRIENDS OF THE INDIAN
From 1883 to 1916 the center of the movement to reform federal Indian policy was the annual Lake Mohonk Conference, and its significance on Indian-white relations in the U.S. Details the opinions and programs of a distinguished group of American reformers. Microfiche (80 fiche), $200. Index volume, $25. CLEAR.

RECORDS OF THE U.S. INDIAN CLAIMS COMMISSION
Includes 550,000 pages—6,140 silver halide microfiche, $12,000. Historical, anthropological and economic reports of the American Indian. *The Decisions,* Volumes 1-47 & Appeals, 355 fiche, $750; *Expert Testimony,* 400 volumes, 100,000 pages, 1,270 fiche, $2,500/Supplement #1: 48 titles on 125 fiche, $250;#2: 97 titles on 209 fiche, $400. *Transcripts of Oral Expert Testimony,* 400 volumes, 100,000 pages, 1,398 fiche, $2,800/Supplement; 77 titles, 420 fiche, $850. *The Briefs,* 3,000 volumes, 125,000 pages, 1,536 fiche, $3,000. *GAO Reports,* 80 volumes, 25,000 pages, 300 fiche, $600/Supplement; 11 titles, 34 fiche, $75. Index to Decisions, $25. Index to Expert Testimony, $25. Legislative History of the Indian Claims Commission Act, 12 fiche, $35. Docket Books, 41 fiche, $80. Journal, 32 fiche, $60. CLEAR.

AKWESASNE TRAVELLING EXHIBITS
Teionkwahontasen Basketmakers of Akwesasne: Ten panel, color and bxw photo display detailing the history of basketry. *Tsinikaiatotenne Ne Akwesasne - A Portrait of Akwesasne:* Ten panel bxw historical photo display of Akwesasne family, religion, sports and lifestyles of the Mohawk of Akwesasne. *Our Strength Our Spirit:* Art exhibit by contemporary artists of Akwesasne. Catalog available. Cost negotiable. AM.

CAHOKIA TRAVELING DISPLAYS
A large free-standing exhibit on Cahokia with texts, photos and artifacts. Depicts the phases of Illinois prehistory. A booklet, *Illinois Archaeology,* is included. Two weeks, no charge. Must be picked up by the borrower. CMM.

MUSEUM OF NEW MEXICO TRAVELING EXHIBITS
Maintains the following traveling exhibits: Art of the Rainmakers: Prehistoric Indian Art and Architecture; Crystal to Burnt Water: Navajo Regional Style Textiles; People of the Sun: Photographs by Buddy Mays; The Portrait: Historic Photographs of New Mexicans; Sacred Paths: Aspects of the Native American and Hispanic Religious Experience in the Southwest; Traditions in Transition: Contemporary Basket Weaving of the Southwestern Indians; and, Turquoise and Tobacco: Trade Systems in the Southwest. The exhibits include historical and contemporary artifacts, drawings, prints, photographs, and paintings which have been assembled for exhibition in museums, libraries, community and art centers, and any other public space with controlled access. Pieces in the exhibitions are framed and matted with descriptive or interpretive labels printed directly on the mats and faced with plexiglass. In addition, each exhibition contains a title and statement panel. The exhibitions are offered free of charge and are transported in sturdy, custom-built crates. MNM.

(ACA) Art Council Aids, P.O. Box 641, Beverly Hills, California 90213

(AF) Association Films, Ford Foundation Film, 866 Third Ave., New York, New York 10022 (212) 935-4210

(AICRC) American Indian Culture Research Center, Blue Cloud Abbey, Marvin, South Dakota 57251

(AIMS) AIMS Media, 6901 Woodley Ave., Van Nuys, California 91406-4878 (800) 367-2467 / (818) 785-4111 (for those in California, Alaska and Hawaii)

(AIT) Agency for Instructional Technology, Box A, Bloomington, Indiana 47402 (812) 339-2203

(AITC) American Indian Treaty Council, 777 United Nations Plaza, 10F, New York, New York 10017 (212) 986-6000

(AM) Akwesasne Museum, Route 37, Hogansburg, New York 13655 (518) 358-2272 ext. 269

(AMNH) American Museum of Natural History, Department of Library Services, Central Park West at 79th St., New York, New York 10024 (212) 873-1300 ext. 346/347

(AUDIO) Audio-Forum, Jeffrey Norton Publishers, Inc., 96 Broad St., Guilford, Connecticut 06437 (203) 453-9794

(BARR) Barr Films, 3490 East Foothill Blvd., P.O. Box 5667, Pasadena, California 91107 (213) 681-6978

(BBP) Brown Bird Productions, Inc., 1971 North Curson Ave., Hollywood, California (213) 851-8928

(BCA) Blue Cloud Abbey, Film Department, Marvin, South Dakota 57251

(BF) Beecher Films, 219 Edison St., Salt Lake City, Utah 84111 (801) 328-1401

(BFA) BFA Educational Media (See **PHOENIX**)

(BGF) Bowling Green Films, P.O. Box 12792, San Diego, California 92112 (619) 462-6494

(BH) Billip-Harris, 626 East 20th St., #3A, New York New York 10003 (212) 982-7131

(BINS) Boreal Institute for Northern Studies, University of Alberta, Edmonton, Alberta, Canada T6G 2E9

(BL) Blackhawk, P.O. Box 3990, 1235 West Fifth St., Davenport, Iowa 52808 (319) 323-9735

(BM) Blackfeet Media, P.O. Box 850, Browning, Montana 59417 (406) 338-7179 ext. 268

(BO) Bo Boudart Films, P.O. Box 10-101, Anchorage, Alaska 99511 (907) 345-2240

(BSR) Big Sur Recordings, 2015 Bridgeway, Sausalito, California 94965

(BYU) Brigham Young University, Eductional Media Center, 290 Herald R. Clark Bldg., Provo, Utah 84602 (801) 378-2713

(BYU-N) Brigham Young University—Native American Series, Multi-Cultural Education Department, 115 BRMB, Provo, Utah 84602

(BULL) Bullfrog Films, Oley, Pennsylvania 19547 (215) 779-8226

(CA) Cinema Associates. 3000 First Ave., Seattle, Washington 98121 (206) 622-7378

(CEN) Centron Films, 1621 West Ninth St., Lawrence, Kansas 66044

CF) Carousel Films, 1501 Broadway, New York, New York 10036 (212) 354-0315

(CFI) Churchill Films, Inc., 662 North Robertson Blvd. Los Angeles, California 90069 (800) 334-7830 / (213) 657-5110 (for those in California)

(CFMDC) Canadian Filmmakers Distribution Center, 144 Front St., West, Suite 430, Toronto, Ontario, Canada (416) 593-1808

(CG) The Cinema Guild, 1697 Broadway, New York, New York 10019 (212) 246-5522

(CHP) Choctaw Heritage Press, Mississippi Band of Choctaw Indians, Route 7, Box 21, Philadelphia, Mississippi (601) 656-5251

(CLEAR) Clearwater Publishing Co., Inc., 1995 Broadway, New York, New York 10023 (800) 231-2266

(CLP) Creative Light Productions, P.O. Box 537, San Anselmo, California 94960 (707) 795-0388

(CMB) The Children's Museum, Boston, Museum Wharf, 300 Congress St., Boston, Massachusetts (617) 426-6500

(CMC) Curriculum Materials Corporation, 1319 Vine St., Philadelphia, Pennsylvania 19107

(CMM) Cahokia Mounds Museum, Educational Programs, 7850 Collinsville Rd., East St. Louis, Missouri 62201

(COOK) Cook School, 708 South Lindon Lane, Tempe, Arizona 85281

(COP) Camera One Productions, 8024 11th Ave., N.E., Seattle, Washington 98115 (206) 524-5326

(COR) Coronet Films & Video, 108 Wilmot Rd., Deerfield, Illinois 60015 (800) 621-2131 / (312) 940-1260 (for those in Illinois, Hawaii and Alaska)

(CRM) CRM/McGraw-Hill Films, P.O. Box 641, Del Mar, California 92014 (619) 453-5000

(DANA) Dana Productions, 6249 Babcock Ave., North Hollywood, California 91606 (213) 877-9246.

(DER) Documentary Educational Resources, 5 Bridge St., Watertown, Massachusetts 02172 (617) 926-0491

(DPA) Documentary Photo Aids, P.O. Box 956, Mt Dora, Florida 32757 (904) 383-8435

(DSP) Daybreak Star Press Film & Video, United Indians of All Tribes Foundation, Daybreak Star Cultural/Educational Center, Discovery Park, P.O. Box 99253, Seattle, Washington (206) 285-4425

(DTC) DTC-TV Downtown Community Television, 87 Lafayette St., New York, Ne York 10013 (212) 966-4510

(EB) Encyclopedia Britannica, Educational Corporation, 425 North Michigan Ave., Chicago, Illinois 60611 (800) 558-6968 / (312) 347-7400 (for those in Illinois)

(EDC) Education Development Center, 55 Chapel St., Newton, Massachusette 02160 (800) 225-4276 / (617) 969-7100 (for those in Massachusetts)

(EM) Eductional Mcdia Corporation, 6930½ Tujunga Ave., North Hollywood, California 91605 (213) 985-3921

(EWING) Wayne Ewing, P.O. Box 32269, Washington, D.C. 20007 (202) 462-1037

(FCE) Film Classic Exchange, 1914 South Vermont Ave., Los Angeles, California 90007 (213) 731-3854

(FF) FilmFair Comunications, 10900 Ventura Blvd., Studio City, California 91604 (213) 985-0244

(FF-NDF) Ferrero Films/New Day Films, 1259A Folsom St., San Francisco, California 94103 (415) 626-FILM

(FILMS) Films, Inc., 733 Green Bay Rd., Wilmette, Illinois 60091 (800) 323-4222 / (312) 256-3200 (for those in Illinois)

(FP) Friendship Press Distribution Office, P.O. Box 37844, Cincinnati, Ohio 45237 (513) 761-2100

(FW) Film Wright, 4530 18th St., San Francisco, California 94114 (415) 863-6100

(GAUL) Chris Gaul, 825 South Braddock Ave., Pittsburgh, Pennsylvania 15221 (412) 371-1381

(GP) Greenwood Press, 88 Post Rd. West, Box 5007, Westport, Connecticut 06881

(GPN) GPN, P.O. Box 80669, Lincoln, Nebraska 68501 (800) 228-4630

(GREEN) Green Mountain Cine Works, 53 Hamilton Ave., Staten Island, New York 10301 (212) 981-0120

(HF) Handel Film Corporation, 8730 Sunset Blvd., West Hollywood, California 90069 (213) 657-8990

(HP) Hugaitha Productions, 1626 North Wilcox, Hollywood, California 90028

(ICVT) Institute for Career and Vocational Training, 5819 Uplander Way, Culver City, California (213) 204-2080

(IDIL) Institute for the Development of Indian Law, 1104 Glyndon St., S.E., Vienna, Virginia 22180 (703) 938-7822

(IF) Image Film, 37 Burkhard Place, Rochester, New York, New York 14620 (716) 473-8070

(IH) Indian House, P.O. Box 472, Taos, New Mexico 87571 (800) 545-8152 / (505) 776-2953 (for those in New Mexico)

(IRA) Indian Rights Association, Film Rental Program, 1505 Race St., Philadelphia, Pennsylvania 19102 (215) 563-8349

(IU) Indiana University, Audio-Visual Center, Bloomington, Indiana 47405 (812) 335-8087

(IFB) International Film Bureau, 332 South Michigan Ave., Chicago, Illinois 60604 (312) 427-4545

(IFF) International Film Foundation, 155 West 72nd St., Room 306, New York, New York 10023 (212) 580-1111

(ISU) Iowa State University, Media Resources Center, 121 Pearson Hall, Ames Iowa 50010 (515) 294-1540

(JOHNSTON) Hugh and Suzanne Johnston, 16 Valley Rd., Princeton, New Jersey 08540 (609) 924-7505

(KC) KC Publications, Box 14883, Las Vegas, Nevada 89114 (703) 731-3123

(KM) Kraus Microform, Route 100, Millwood, New York 10546 (914) 762-2200

(KUSD) KUSD-TV, 310 East Clark St., Vermillion, South Dakota 57069 (605) 677-5277

(LC) Library of Congress, Music Division - Recorded Sound Section, Washington, D.C. 20540

(LCA) Learning Corporation of America, 1350 Ave. of the Americas, New York, New York 10019 (212) 397-9330

(LF) Lodestar Films, 42-28 East 103rd St., Tulsa, Oklahoma 74136 (918) 299-7711

(LL) Listening Library, Inc., P.O. Box L, Old Greenwich, Connecticut 06870 (800) 243-4504

(LU) Lumiere, 826 Savanah Ave., Pittsburgh, Pennsylvania 15221 (412) 241-1127

MAI) Museum of the American Indian, Photographic Archives, Broadway at 155th St., New York, New York 10032 (212) 283-2420

(MANNING) Robert N. Manning, 53 Hamilton Ave., Staten Island, New York 10301

(MG) The Media Guild, 11562 Sorrento Valley Rd., Suite J, San Diego, California 92121 (619) 755-9191

(MM) Michigan Media, 400 Fourth St., Ann Arbor, Michigan 48109 (313) 764-5360

(MMA) Museum of Modern Art, 11 West 53rd St., New York, New York 10019 (212) 956-4204

(MNM) Museum of New Mexico, Programs and Education A-V Specialist, Santa Fe, New Mexico 87503 (505) 827-2070

(MOKIN) Arthur Mokin Productions, 2900 McBride Lane, Santa Rosa, California 95401 (707) 542-4868

(MRC) Media Resources Center, 121 Pearson Hall, Iowa State University, Ames, Iowa 50011 (515) 294-1540

(NAC) National Audiovisual Center, General Services Administration, Order Section NA/REF SECT EC, Washington, D.C. 20409 (202) 763-1896

(NAIF) North American Indian Films, 177 Nepean St., Ottawa, Ontario, Canada K2P 0B4 (613) 238-7713

(NAPBC) Native American Public Broadcasting Consortium, P.O. Box 83111, Lincoln, Nebraska 68501 (402) 472-3522

(NCTE) National Council of Teachers of English, 1111 Kenyon Rd., Urbana, Illinois 60640

(NETCHE) NETCHE, Box 83111, Lincoln, Nebraska 68501 (402) 472-3611

(NFBC) National Film Board of Canada (*Rent:*) Film Library, 22 Riverside Dr., Wayne, New Jersey 07470-3191 (201) 628-9111; (*Purchase:*) 1251 Ave. of the Americas, 16th Floor, New York, New York 10020 (212) 586-5131

(NGA) National Gallery of Art, Extension Services, Washington, D.C. 20565

(NGS) National Geographic Society, Educational Services, Department 82, Washington, D.C. 20036 (301) 948-5926

(NILB) National Indian Lutheran Board, 35 East Wacker Dr., Suite 1847, Chicago, Illinois 60601 (312) 726-3791

(NM) The Newark Museum, 49 Washington St., Newark, New Jersey 07101 (201) 733-6600

(NMFV) New Mexico Film & Video, Box 272, Tesuque, New Mexico 87574 (505) 983-3094

(NOVA) Nova Scotia Department of Education, Education Media Services, 6955 Bayers Rd., Halifax, Nova Scotia, Canada B3L 4S4 (902) 453-2810

(NSS) Native Self-Sufficiency, P.O. Box 10, Forestville, California 95436

(NV) New Visions, P.O. Box 599, Aspen, Colorado 81612 (303) 925-2640

(NYU) New York University Film Library, 26 Washington Pl., New York, New York 10003

(OFIELD) Jack Ofield, P.O. Box 12792, San Diego, California 92112 (619) 462-8266

(OHS) Oregon Historical Society, Education Department, 1230 S.W. Park Ave., Portland, Oregon 97205 (503) 222-1741 ext. 36

(OP) Odyssey Productions, 122 N.W. Third Ave., Portland, Oregon 97209 (503) 223-3480

(OW) One West, 535 Cordova Rd., Suite 410, Santa Fe, New Mexico 87501 (505) 983-8685

(PC) Pacific Cinematheque, 1616 West Third Ave, Vancouver, British Columbia, Canada V6J 1K2 (604) 732-5322

(PBS) PBS Video, 475 L'Enfant Plaza, S.W., Washington, D.C. 20024 (800) 344-3777

(PHOENIX) Phoenix/BFA Films, Inc., 468 Park Ave. South, New York, New York 10016 (800) 221-1274 / (212) 684-5910 (for those in New York State)

(PHM) Prentice Hall-Media, SerCode HB, 150 White Plains Rd., Tarrytown, New York 10591

(PI) Pictures, Inc., 81 West 8th Ave., Anchorage, Alaska 99501

(PIE) Pacific International Enterprises, 1133 South Riverside, Suite 1, Medford, Oregon 97501 (503) 779-0990

(PSU) The Pennsylvania State University, Audio-Visual Services, Special Services Bldg., University Park, Pennsylvania 16802 (800) 826-0132 / (814) 865-6314 (for those in Pennsylvania, Hawaii and Alaska)

(RH) Random House—School Division, Dept. 9020, 400 Hahn Rd., Westminster, Maryland 21157 (800) 638-6460 / (800) 492-0782 (for those in Maryland) / (301) 876-2286 (for those in Alaska and Hawaii)

(RITZ) Lan Brook Ritz, Brown Bird Productions, 1971 North Curson Ave., Hollywood, California 90046 (213) 851-8928

(RODGERS) Bob Rodgers, Media Centre, University of Toronto, 121 St. George St., Toronto, Ontario, Canada M5S 1A1

(SAN) San Juan District Media Center, Curriculum Division, 28 West 200 North, P.O. Box 804, Blanding, Utah 84511 (801) 678-2281

(SB) Serious Business Co., 1145 Mandana Blvd., Oakland, California 94610 (415) 832-5600

(SC) Sacred Circle, Department of Radio & Television, CW 005 Biological Sciences Centre, University of Alberta, Edmonton, Alberta, Canada T6G 2E9

(SEF) Sterling Educational Films, 241 East 34th St., New York, New York 10016 (212) 683-6300

(SHSW) State Historical Society of Wisconsin, 816 State St., Madison, Wisconsin 53706

(SI) Smithsonian Institution, Photographic Services, Washington, D.C. 20560

(SI-OMB) Smithsonian Institution, Office of Museum Programs, A-V Loan Program, Washington, D.C. 20560 (202) 357-3101

(SM) Southwest Museum, Highland Park, Los Angeles, California 90042

(SN) Seneca Nation of Indians, P.O. Box 442, Salamanca, New York 14779 (716) 945-1790

(SO) Solaris, 264 West 19th St., New York, New York 10011 (212) 741-0778

(STULL) Donald D. Stull, 2900 Westdale Rd., Lawrence, Kansas 66044 (913) 842-8055

(SUPT) Superintendent of Documents, Government Printing Office, Washington, D.C. 20402

(SUQ) Suquamish Museum, P.O. Box 498, Suquamish, Washington 98392 (206) 598-3311

(SVC) Synapse Video Center, Syracuse University, 103 College Place, Syracuse, New York 13210 (315) 423-3100

(TM) Taylor Museum, Colorado Springs Fine Arts Center, 30 West Dale, Colorado Springs, Colorado 80903

(TBM) Thomas Burke Memorial, Washington State Museum, DB-10, University of Washington, Seattle, Washington 98195 (206) 543-5884

(TC) Telefilm Canada, 1-1226 Homer St., Vancouver, British Columbia, Canada V6B 2Y8 (604) 687-4215; or, Unit 12, 1770 Albion Rd., Rexdale, Ontario, Canada M9V 1C2 (416) 745-0708

(TF) Texture Films, P.O. Box 1337, Skokie, Illinois 60076 (312) 256-4436

(THRC) Texas Human Resources Center, University of Texas, Arlington, Library, P.O. Box 19497, Arlington, Texas 76019 (817) 273-2767

(TIME) Time-Life Video, 100 Eisenhower Dr., Paramus, New Jersey 07652 (201) 843-4545

(TIPI) Tipi Shop, Inc., P.O. Box 1542, Rapid City, South Dakota 57709

(TT) Tulalip Tribe, 6700 Totem Beach Rd., Marysville, Washington 98270 (206) 653-4585

(UA) University of Arizona, Media Services-Film Library, Tucson, Arizona 85706 (602) 626-3282

(UAB) University of Alberta, Motion Picture Division, Edmonton, Alberta, Canada (403) 432-3302

(UADA) University of Alberta, Department of Anthropology, 13-15 HM Tory Bldg., Edmonton, Ontario T6G 2H4 Canada (403) 432-3879

(UC) University of California, Extension Media Center, 2223 Fulton St., Berkeley, California 94720 (415) 642-5578 - Purchase) (415) 642-0460 - Preview or Rent)

(UCV) University Community Video, 425 Ontario, S.E., Minneapolis, Minnesota 55414 (612) 376-3333

(UEVA) Universal Education and Visual Arts, 100 Universal City Plaza, Universal City, California 91608 (213) 985-4321

(UI) University of Illinois Film Center, 1325 S. Oak St., Champaign, Illinois 61820 (217) 333-1360

(UK) University of Kansas, Audio Visual Center, 746 Massachusetts St., Lawrence, Kansas 66044 (913) 864-3352

(UL) United Learning, 6633 West Howard St., P.O. Box 718, Niles, Illinois 60648 (800) 323-9468

(UM) University of Minnesota, Audiovisual Library Services, 3300 University Ave., S.E., Minneapolis, Minnesota 55414 (612) 373-3810

(UMA) University of Mid-America (See GPN)

(UMC) Utah Media Center, 20 South West Temple, Salt Lake City, Utah 84101

(UMI) University of Michigan, Audio Visual Education Center, 416 Fourth St., Ann Arbor, Michigan 48103 (313) 764-5360

(UN) University of Nevada Film Library, Getchell Library, Reno, Nevada 89557 (702) 784-6037

(UNI) Unifilm, 419 Park Ave. South, 19th Floor, New York, New York 10016 (212) 686-9890

(UP) Upstream Productions, 921 N.E. Boat, Seattle, Washington 98105 (206) 547-7799

(UT) University of Texas Film Library, Drawer W, University Station, Austin, Texas 78712-7448 (512) 471-3572

(UW) University of Washington, Instructional Media Services, Booking Office—Kane Hall, DG-10, Seattle, Washington 98195 (206) 543-9909

(VCA) Video Communications of America, 610 N.W. 44th St., Seattle, Washington 98107 (206) 789-8333

(VL) Verity Lund, Henry Street Settlement, 265 Henry St., New York, New York 10002 (212) 766-9200

(WALL) Alfred Wallace, 420 Riverside Dr., New York, New York 10025 (212) 865-8817

(WD) Walt Disney Educational Media Co., 500 South Buena Vista, Burbank, California 91521

(WGBH) WGBH Distribution Office, 125 Western Ave., Boston, Massachusetts 02134 (617) 492-2777

(WQED) WQED-TV, Distribution Department, 4802 Fifth Ave., Pittsburgh, Pennsylvania 15213 (412) 622-1356

(WRS) World Around Songs, 5790 Highway 80S, Burnsville, North Carolina 28714

(WXXI) WXXI-TV, 280 State St., P.O. Box 21, Rochester, New York 14601 (716) 325-7500

(ZAENTZ) The Saul Zaentz Productions Co., 2600 Tenth St., Berkeley, California 94710 (800) 227-0602

MAGAZINES AND PERIODICALS

Arranged alphabetically by publication title, this section lists those periodicals which deal directly or indirectly with the history, culture, and contemporary issues of the North American Indian and Eskimo.

ABSARAKA
Crow Indian Agency
Crow Agency, Montana 59022

ACCESS
Office of Minority Business Enterprise
Department of Commerce
Washington, D.C. 20230

THE ACTION NEWS
P.O. Box 605
New Town, North Dakota 58763

AHTNA KANAS
Ahtna, Inc.
P.O. Drawer G
Copper Center, Alaska 99573
(907) 822-3476

Bi-monthly shareholder newsletter of Ahtna, Inc., the Copper River Native Association.

AKWEKON LITERARY JOURNAL
Akwesasne Notes
P.O. Box 223, The Mohawk Nation
Hogansburg, New York 13655
(518) 358-9531
  Alex Jacobs, Peter Blue Cloud,
  Dan Thompson and Salli Benedict, Editors

A national Native American quarterly on literature and the arts. 76 pages; color cover; perfect bound.

AKWESASNE NOTES
P.O. Box 196, The Mohawk Nation
Rooseveltown, New York 13683-0196
(518) 358-9531/9535
  Peter Blue Cloud and Alex
  (Karoniaktatie) Jacobs, Editors

A journal for Native and natural peoples. Focus is on Native North Americans and Central and South American Indians. Subjects covered are: land and treaty rights; economic development; environmental issues; human rights; art and culture. Book reviews; announcements; no ads. 32 pages. Published six times per year. *Subscription:* $10 (regular mail); $15 (first class); foreign, $20 (regular), $35 (air). Sample copy, $1. Catalog of books, posters, crafts, $1 tabloid. Microfilm/fiche available.

ALABAMA INDIAN ADVOCATE
Perry Hill Office Park 211
3815 Interstate Court
Montgomery, Alabama 36109

ALASKA FEDERATION OF NATIVES (AFN) NEWS
411 West Fourth Ave.
Anchorage, Alaska 99501

ALASKA NATIVE BROTHERHOOD NEWSLETTER
P.O. Box 112
Juneau, Alaska 99801

ALASKA STATE MUSEUM NEWSLETTER
Pouch FM
Juneau, Alaska 99811
(907) 465-2901

ALLIGATOR TIMES
Seminole Tribe
6073 Stirling Rd.
Hollywood, Florida 33024

Monthly Seminole news.

AMERICAN ANTHROPOLOGICAL ASSOCIATION NEWSLETTER
1703 New Hampshire Ave., N.W.
Washington, D.C. 20009
(202) 232-8800

Published ten times per year.

AMERICAN ANTHROPOLOGIST
American Anthropological Association
1703 New Hampshire Ave., N.W.
Washington, D.C. 20009
(202) 232-8800

Quarterly journal.

AMERICAN ANTIQUARIAN SOCIETY NEWSLETTER
185 Salisbury
Worcester, Massachusetts 01609
(617) 755-5221

AMERICAN ANTIQUITY
Society for American Archaeology
1511 K St., N.W., Suite 716
Washington, D.C. 20005
(202) 638-6079

Quarterly journal.

AMERICAN ETHNOLOGICAL ASSOCIATION MONOGRAPHS
1703 New Hampshire Ave., N.W.
Washington, D.C. 20009

AMERICAN ETHNOLOGIST
American Ethnologcal Society
c/o Alvin W. Wolfe
University of South Florida
Tampa, Florida 33620
(813) 974-2150

Quarterly journal.

AMERICAN HERITAGE
American Heritage Publishing Co.
10 Rockefeller Plaza
New York, New York 10020
(212) 399-8900
Alvin M. Josephy, Jr., Editor

Covers all aspects and periods of American history, with frequent articles on American Indian personalities, events associated with the American Indian, and interaction between the American Indian and white communities and their individual members. Hardbound. Published bimonthly with an annual index.

THE AMERICAN HISTORICAL REVIEW
American Historical Association
400 A St., S.E.
Washington, D.C. 20003
(202) 544-2422

Published five times per year.

THE AMERICAN INDIAN
225 Valencia St.
San Francisco, California 94103

AMERICAN INDIAN ART MAGAZINE
7314 East Osborn Dr.
Scottsdale, Arizona 85251
(602) 994-5445

Published quarterly.

AMERICAN INDIAN BASKETRY
AND OTHER NATIVE ARTS
John M. Gogol, Publisher
P.O. Box 66124
Portland, Oregon 97266
(503) 233-8131
John M. Gogol et al, Editors

Contains articles, book reviews, and lists of new exhibits; advertising. Published four times per year. *Subscription:* $30 per year. Sample copy, $7.95.

AMERICAN INDIAN CLUB NEWSLETTER
P.O. Box 7, Gonzaga University
Spokane, Washington 99202

AMERICAN INDIAN COMMUNITY
SERVICES — DIRECTORY
NAES College Press
2838 West Peterson
Chicago, Illinois 60659

AMERICAN INDIAN CULTURE
AND RESEARCH CENTER NEWSLETTER
Marvin, South Dakota 57251

AMERICAN INDIAN CULTURE
AND RESEARCH JOURNAL
American Indian Studies Center
Room 3220 Campbell Hall, UCLA
405 Hilgard Ave.
Los Angeles, California 90024
(213) 206-1433
William Oandasan and Zoila Cruz, Editors

A quarterly interdisciplinary research forum for scholars and innovators in the areas of historical and contemporary American Indian life and culture. Book reviews; essays and suitable poems; advertising. *Subscription:* $20/individuals; $30/institutions. No complimentary copies.

AMERICAN INDIAN DIRECTIONS
The Seventh Generation Fund
P.O. Box 10
Forestville, California 95436
(707) 887-1559

Newsletter on Indian issues for the philanthropic community.

AMERICAN INDIAN EDUCATION
CENTER NEWSLETTER
P.O. Box 40
Pala, California 92059

AMERICAN INDIAN FELLOWSHIP
ASSOCIATION NEWSLETTER
2 East Second St.
Duluth, Minnesota 55802

AMERICAN INDIAN HORSE NEWS
American Indian Horse Registry
Route 1, Box 64
Lockhart, Texas 78644
(512) 398-6642

Published quarterly. Annual *Studbook.*

AMERICAN INDIAN JOURNAL
Institute for the Development of Indian Law
1104 Glyndon St., S.E.
Vienna, Virginia 22180
(703) 938-7822
Kirk Kickingbird, Editor

Contains scholarly articles on Indian history and Indian law, as well as articles of current interest in Indian affairs. Book reviews. Published monthly. *Subscription:* $25/individuals; $35/organizations.

AMERICAN INDIAN LAW NEWSLETTER
American Indian Law Center
P.O. Box 4456, Station A
Albuquerque, New Mexico 87196
(505) 277-5462

Includes articles on American Indian law, Indian-related policy issues, service programs, legislation at the national, regional, state, local and tribal government levels; also provides information on projects impacting the political, administrative, and leadership capabilities of tribal government. No advertising. *Subscription:* General public— $20/year, $36/2 years, $48/3 years; American Indians—$15/year, $27/2 years, $36/3 years. Complimentary copy available upon request for subscription information. Open to exchanges with other publications.

AMERICAN INDIAN LAW REVIEW
University of Oklahoma
College of Law, 300 Timberdell Rd.
Norman, Oklahoma 73019
(405) 325-2840

A scholarly journal covering topics of interest in American Indian law. Includes articles by legal professionals and scholars, notes written by students, and recent developments in the federal courts on American Indian issues. Book reviews. Advertising. *Contest:* The American Indian Law Writing Competition. Published twice per year. *Subscription:* $10/year. Back copies available from William S. Hein & Co., 1285 Main St., Buffalo, New York 14209. $12 (two issues).

AMERICAN INDIAN LAW STUDENTS ASSOCIATION NEWSLETTER
American Indian Law Center
University of New Mexico-School of Law
1117 Stanford Dr., NE
Albuquerque, New Mexico 87196
(505) 277-5462

Published irregularly.

AMERICAN INDIAN LAWYER TRAINING PROGRAM NEWSLETTER
1712 N St., N.W.
Washington, D.C. 20036

AMERICAN INDIAN LIBRARIES NEWSLETTER
American Indian Library Association
Office of Library Outreach Services (OLOS)
c/o American Library Association
50 East Huron St.
Chicago, Illinois 60611
(312) 944-6780
Jean E. Coleman, Director (OLOS)
Thomas J. Blumer, Editor

Contains information of interest to American Indian librarians. Includes short papers, programs, and activities and events of American Indian libraries. Editorial office: European Law Division, Law Library, Library of Congress, Washington, D.C. 20540. Published quarterly. *Subscription:* $5/individuals; $7/libraries, institutions and agencies; $10/foreign; back issues, $2 each.

AMERICAN INDIAN NATIONAL BANK — BANKNOTES
1700 K St., N.W., Suite 2000
Washington, D.C. 20006
(202) 887-5252

AMERICAN INDIAN NEWS
Office of Native American Programs
P.O. Box 217
Fort Washakie, Wyoming 82514

AMERICAN INDIAN NEWS
Thunderbird American Indian Dancers
215 West 23rd St.
New York, NY 10011
(212) 741-9221

AMERICAN INDIAN PROGRAM NEWSLETTER
Washington State University
Pullman, Washington 99164

AMERICAN INDIAN SCHOLARSHIPS, INC. NEWSLETTER
5106 Grand Ave., NE
Albuquerque, New Mexico 87108
(505) 265-8335

Published quarterly.

AMERICAN INDIAN SCIENCE AND ENGINNERING SOCIETY—NEWSLETTER
1310 College Ave., Suite 1220
Boulder, Colorado 80302
(303) 492-8658

Published four times per year.

AMERICAN INDIAN SOCIETY NEWSLETTER
519 4th St., S.E.
Washington, D.C. 20003

AMERICAN INDIAN STUDIES NEWSLETTER
University of Minnesota
1314 Social Sciences Bldg.
Minneapolis, Minnesota 55455

AMERICAN INDIAN STUDY CENTER—NEWSLETTER
211 South Broadway
Baltimore, Maryland 21231

AMERICAN INDIANS FOR DEVELOPMENT—NEWSLETTER
P.O. Box 117, 236 West Main St.
Meriden, Connecticut 06450
(203) 238-4009
Jose E. Rodriguez-Sellas, Erin Lamb,
and Patricia Benedict, Editors

Contains job information for American Indians; general news about Indian people, tribes and cultural activities. Published bimonthly. Donations accepted. Complimentary copies available upon request.

AMERICAN INDIANS UNLIMITED—NEWSLETTER
240 Michigan Union, 530 South St.
Ann Arbor, Michigan 48104

AMERICAN JOURNAL OF ARCHAEOLOGY
Archaeological Institute of America
P.O. Box 1901, Kensmore Station
Boston, Massachusetts 02215
(617) 353-9361

Professional archaeological journal with book reviews on New World archaeology. Published quarterly.

AMERICAN QUARTERLY
American Studies Association
307 College Hall, University of Pennsylvania
Philadelphia, Pennsylvania 19104-6303
(215) 898-6252
Janice Radway, Editor

Contains scholarly articles on various aspects of American culture. Advertising. Published six times per year; last issue of year contains book reviews. *Subscription:* $30/year (libraries).

AMERICAN WEST
Buffalo Bill Memorial Association
Buffalo Bill Historical Center
P.O. Box 1000
Cody, Wyoming 82414
(307) 587-4771

Published six times per year.

AMERICANA
Americana Magazine, Inc.
29 West 38th St.
New York, New York 10018
(212) 398-1550

AMERICANS BEFORE COLUMBUS
National Indian Youth Council
318 Elm St., SE
Albuquerque, New Mexico 87102

Bimonthly newsletter.

ANISHINABE DEE-BAH-GEE-MO-WIN
White Earth Reservation Tribal Council
P.O. Box 418
White Earth, Minnesota 56591
(218) 983-3285
Norma L. Felty, Editor

ANTHROPOLOGICAL PAPERS UNIVERSITY OF ALASKA
Department of Anthropology
Fairbanks, Alaska 99775
(907) 474-7288
Anne Shinkwin, Ph.D. and
Linda J. Ellana, Ph.D., Editors

Articles dealing with northern socio-cultural anthropology and archaeology. Published twice annually. $8/issue.

ANTHROPOLOGICAL PAPERS THE AMERICAN MUSEUM OF NATURAL HISTORY
Central Park West at 79th St.
New York, New York 10024

Contains the current reports of the Museum's Department of Anthropology.

AN CHI MO WIN
Rocky Boy's Reservation
Chippewa Cree Tribe
Box Elder, Montana 59521

ANISHNABE NEWS
P.O. Box 55
Stillwater, Minnesota 55082

THE APACHE SCOUT
Mescalero Reservation
Mescalero, New Mexico 88340

APACHE SENTINEL
P.O. Box 809
Apache Junction, Arizona 85205

ARAPAHOE AGENCY COURIER
Arapahoe Agency, Wyoming 82510

ARCHAEOLOGICAL CONSERVANCY NEWSLETTER
415 Orchard Dr.
Santa Fe, New Mexico 87501
(505) 982-3278

Published quarterly.

ARCHAEOLOGY MAGAZINE
Phyllis Pollak Katz, Publisher
15 Park Row
New York, New York 10038
(212) 732-5154
Bea Riem Schneider, Editor

Bimonthly newsletter of the Archaeological

Institute of America; provides consistent treatment of the archaeology of North and South American Indians; book reviews on the art and archaeology of the Americas.

**ARCHAEOLOGY OF
EASTERN NORTH AMERICA**
Archeological Society of Connecicut
P.O. Box 260, Curtis Rd.
Washington, Connecticut 06793

ARCTIC VILLAGE ECHOES
Arctic Village School
Arctic Village, Alaska 99722

ARIZONA HISTORY
949 East 2nd St.
Tucson, Arizona 85719

ARIZONA TRIBAL DIRECTORY
Arizona Commission on Indian Affairs
1645 West Jefferson
Phoenix, Arizona 85007

ARROW
St. Labre Indian School
Ashland, Montana 59003

ARTIFACTS
American Indian Archaeological Institute
P.O.Box 260
Washington, Connecticut 06793
  (203) 868-0518

Quarterly membership magazine.

ARTIFACTS
The Artifact Society
Tiffin, Ohio 44883

Published quarterly. *Subscription:* $12/year.

ARTS AND CULTURE OF THE NORTH
Box 1333, Gracie Square Station
New York, New York 10028
  (212) 879-9019

Newsletter devoted to Eskimo art and culture. Back issues available. Publication ceased end of 1984.

**ASSOCIATION OF AMERICAN INDIAN
PHYSICIANS—NEWSLETTER**
6805 South Western, Suite 504
Oklahoma City, Oklahoma 73139
  (405) 631-0447

Published quarterly.

**ASSOCIATION OF CONTRACT TRIBAL
SCHOOLS (ACTS) NEWSLETTER**
c/o St. Francis Indian School
P.O. Box 155
St. Francis, South Dakota 57572
  (605) 747-2296

Published monthly.

ATOKA INDIAN CITIZEN
P.O. Box 160
Atoka, Oklahoma 74525

ATOME—NORTHERN CHEYENNE NEWS
P.O.Box 401
Lame Deer, Montana 59043

AU-AUTHM ACTION NEWS
Route 1, Box 216
Scottsdale, Arizona 85251

AWATTIM AWAHAN
c/o Salt River Tribal Office
Route 1, Box 700
Scottsdale, Arizona 85251

B

BACONE COLLEGE—SMOKE SIGNALS
Muskogee, Oklahoma 74401

BANKNOTES
American Indian National Bank
1700 K St., N.W., Suite 2000
Washington, D.C. 20006
  (202) 887-5252

BEAR FACTS NEWSLETTER
Room 18, Eshelman Hall, 3rd Floor
University of California
Berkeley, California 94720

BERING STRAITS AGLUKTUK
Bering Straits Native Corporation
P.O. Box 1008
Nome, Alaska 99762

**BILLINGS INDIAN CENTER
NEWSLETTER**
P.O. Box 853
Billings, Montana 59103

BISHINIK
Choctaw Nation
P.O. Drawer 1210
Durant, Oklahoma 74701

BIZHII
Cibecue Community School
Cibecue, Arizona 85911
  (602) 332-4480

Student magazine. Published four times per year.

BALCKFEET INDIAN NEWS BULLETIN
National Association of Blackfeet Indians
P.O. Box 340
Browning, Montana 59417

BLACKFEET TRIBAL NEWS
Blackfeet Media
P.O. Box 850
Browning, Montana 59417

BLUE CLOUD QUARTERLY
Blue Cloud Abbey
P.O. Box 98
Marvin, South Dakota 57251
(605) 432-5528

Features creative writing by and/or about
American Indians.

**BOSTON INDIAN MULTISERVICE
CENTER NEWSLETTER**
105 South Huntington Ave.
Jamaica Plain, Massachusetts 02130

BRONCOS MONTHLY NEWS
Sanostee Rural Station
Shiprock, New Mexico 87420

BROWNING SENTINEL
National Association of Blackfeet Indians
P.O. Box 340
Browning, Montana 59417

BTIR
Tribal Newsletter
P.O. Box 71
Burns, Oregon 97720

THE BUCKSKIN
Route 3
Eaufaula, Oklahoma 74432

BUFFALO CHIPS
Center for Western Studies
Augustana College, P.O. Box 727
Sioux Falls, South Dakota 57197
(605) 336-4007

Semiannual newsletter. $15/year, membership.

BUFFALO GRASS NEWSLETTER
Missoula Indian Center
508 Toole
Missoula, Montana 59801

**BUREAU OF CATHOLIC INDIAN
MISSIONS—JOURNAL
AND NEWSLETTER**
2021 H St., N.W.
Washington, D.C. 20006
(202) 331-8542

Quarterly journal; monthly newsletter.

**BUREAU OF INDIAN AFFAIRS
RESEARCH BULLETIN**
Indian Education Center
Albuquerque, New Mexico 87103

**BUREAU OF INDIAN AFFAIRS
TRIBAL NEWSLETTER**
Phoenix Area Office
P.O. Box 7007, 3030 North Central
Phoenix, Arizona 85011

BURNS-PAIUTE TRIBAL NEWSLETTER
P.O. Box 71
Burns, Oregon 97720

**BUYERS GUIDE TO PRODUCTS
MANUFACTURED ON AMERICAN
INDIAN RESERVATIONS**
U.S. Government Printing Office
Washington, D.C. 20402
(202) 275-3314

C

**CAOS; NEW MEXICO
ARCHAEOLOGY AND HISTORY**
CAOS Publishing and Research
P.O. Box 3 CP
Las Cruces, New Mexico 88003

CAHOKIAN
Cahokia Mounds Museum Society, Publisher
7850 Collinsville Rd.
East St. Louis, Missouri 62201
(618) 344-5268

Newsletter.

CALIFORNIA NEWSDRUM
225 Valencia St.
San Francisco, California 94103

CALISTEM ERINI
Calista Corporation
516 Denali St.
Anchorage, Alaska 99501

THE CALUMET
United Southern and Eastern Tribes
1101 Kermit Dr., Suite 800
Nashville, Tennessee 37217
(615) 361-8700

Bimonthly newsletter.

CANYON SHADOWS
General Delivery
Supai, Arizona 86435

CAP NEWSLETTER
Rosebud Sioux Tribe
Rosebud, South Dakota 57570

CAPITAL NEWS
Santo Domingo, New Mexico 87052

**CAREER DEVELOPMENT
OPPORTUNITIES FOR
NATIVE AMERICANS**
Bureau of Indian Affairs
Bureau of Higher Education
P.O. Box 1788
Albuquerque, New Mexico 87103

THE CAROLINA INDIAN VOICE
P.O. Box 1075
Pembroke, North Carolina 28372

CAVO TRANSPORTER
Chey-Arap Veterans Organization
P.O. Box 34
Concho, Oklahoma 73022

**CENTER FOR THE STUDY OF
EARLY MAN — CURRENT RESEARCH**
University of Maine
495 College Ave.
Orono, Maine 04473

**CENTRAL STATES
ARCHAEOLOGICAL JOURNAL**
1757 West Adams
St. Louis, Missouri 63122

Published quarterly. $12/year, membership.

CHAHTA ANUMPH
The Choctaw Times
P.O. Box 12392
Nashville, Tennessee 37212

CHAR-KOOSTA
Confederated Salish and Kostensi Tribes
P.O. Box 278
Pablo, Montana 59855
  (406) 675-2000 ext. 555
  P.S. Blomquist, Editor

Biweekly magazine format featuring news of interest to Native Americans with emphasis on Flathead Reservation Indian affairs. Advertising. *Subscription:* $22/year. Special rates for tribal members; regular advertisers are entitled to free subscription for duration of their ads.

CHEHALIS NEWSLETTER
P.O. Box 536
Oakvilke, Washington 98568

CHEMAWA AMERICAN
Chemawa Indian School
5495 Chugach St., N.E.
Chemawa, Oregon 97303

CHEROKEE ADVOCATE
Cherokee Nation of Oklahoma
P.O. Box 948
Tahlequah, Oklahoma 74465

CHEROKEE NATION NEWS
P.O. Box 119
Tahlequah, Oklahoma 74465

CHEROKEE ONE FEATHER
Eastern Band of Cherokee Indians
P.O. Box 501
Cherokee, North Carolina 28719
  (704) 497-2771

CHEROKEE TIMES
P.O. Box 105
Cherokee, North Carolina 28719

THE CHESOPIEAN JOURNAL
The Chesopiean
7507 Pennington Rd.
Norfolk, Virginia 23505

Published three to six times per year. *Subscription:* $10/year.

CHEYENNE-ARAPAHO BULLETIN
Cheyenne-Arapaho Business Committee
P.O. Box 38
Concho, Oklahoma 73022
  (405) 262-0345

**CHEYENNE RIVER AGENCY
NEWS BULLETIN**
Eagle Butte, South Dakota 57625

THE CHICKASAW TIMES
Chickasaw Nation Tribal Government
P.O. Box 1548
Ada, Oklahoma 74820

CHINOOK
215 Viking Union
Western Washington College
Bellingham, Washington 98225

CHOCTAW COMMUNITY NEWS
Mississippi Band of Choctaw Indians
Route 7, Box 21
Philadelphia, Mississippi 39350
  (601) 656-5251
  Julie Kelsey, Editor

Monthly tribal newspaper containing articles; primarily concerned with local events which involve Mississippi Choctaws. Book reviews. Limited advertising. Free subscription by request, donations accepted.

THE CIRCLE
Boston Indian Council
105 South Huntington Ave.
Jamaica Plain, Massachusetts 02130

Contains information on urban Indians, particularly in the Boston area, as well as significant events involving Native peoples in New England and throughout the U.S. and Canada. Published monthly. Single copies free.

THE CIRCLE NEWSPAPER
Minneapolis Native American Center
1530 East Franklin Ave.
Minneapolis, Minnesota 55404

CITY SMOKE SIGNALS
304 Pearl
Sioux City, Iowa 51101

CLAN DESTINY
Seneca Indian History Society
Irving, New York 14081

COCOPAH NEWSLETTER
P.O. Box G
Somerton, Arizona 85350

COEUR D'ALENE COUNCIL FIRES
Coeur D'Alene Tribal Council
Plummer, Idaho 83851

COKTV TVLEME
Seminole Nation of Oklahoma
P.O. Box 745
Wewoka, Oklahoma 74884

COLUMBIA RIVER INDIAN NEWS
P.O. Box 5
Cooks, Washington 98605

THE COLUMNS NEWSLETTER
Cherokee National Museum
P.O. Box 515
Tahlequah, Oklahoma 74464
  (918) 456-6007

Published quarterly.

COMANCHE
Comanche Tribe of Oklahoma
P.O. Box 908
Lawton, Oklahoma 73502

**COMMITTEE OF CONCERN FOR
TRADITIONAL INDIAN NEWSLETTER**
P.O. Box 5167
San Francisco, California 94101

COMMUNICATOR
Migizi Communications, Inc.
2300 Cedar Ave. South
Minneapolis, Minnesota 55404
  (612) 721-6631

COMMUNIQUE
Order of the Indian Wars
P.O. Box 7401
Little Rock, Arkansas 72217
  (501) 225-3996
  Jerry L. Russell, Editor

Monthly newsletter.

**CoMTec INDIAN EDUCATION
INFORMATION SERVICE**
1228 M St., N.W.
Washington, D.C. 20005
  (202) 638-7066

Monthly subscription service providing coverage
on issues affecting only Indian education. It
synopsizes pending legislation, appropriations
issues, national reports, federal and private

funding opportunities, and other information for
those involved in Indian education. *Subscription:*
$45 per six months; $65 per nine months.

CONFEDERATED INDIAN TRIBES
Washington State Penitentiary
P.O. Box 520
Walla Walla, Washington 99362

CONFEDERATED UMATILLA JOURNAL
P.O. Box 638
Pendleton, Oregon 97801

CONTEMPORARY INDIAN AFFAIRS
Navajo Community College
Tsaile, Arizona 86556

COUNCIL FIRES
Coeur D'Alene Tribal Council
Plummer, Idaho 83851

**COUNCIL FOR MINORITY
EDUCATION NEWS**
470 Oregon Hall, University of Oregon
Eugene, Oregon 97403

**COUNCIL OF ENERGY RESOURCE
TRIBES (CERT) REPORT**
1580 Logan St.
Denver, Colorado 80203
  (303) 832-6600

**COUNCIL OF THREE
RIVERS NEWSLETTER**
803 North Homewood Ave.
Pittsburgh, Pennsylvania 15208

COYOTE ON THE TURTLE'S BACK
Institute of American Indian Arts
College of Santa Fe Campus
Alexis Hall, St. Michael's Dr.
Santa Fe, New Mexico 87501
  (505) 988-6463

Published annually.

CRAZY HORSE PROGRESS
Crazy Horse Memorial Foundation
Avenue of the Chiefs—The Black Hills
Crazy Horse, South Dakota 57730-9988
  (605) 673-4681
  Robb DeWall, Editor

Published three times per year. Free.

CREEK NATION NEWS
P.O. Box 1114
Okmulgee, Oklahoma 74447

CROWNDANCER
San Carlos Apache Tribe
P.O. Box 0
San Carlos, Arizona 85550

CURRENT ANTHROPOLOGY
Wenner-Gren Foundation for
Anthropological Research
1865 Broadway
New York, New York 10023
(212) 957-8750

Bimonthly journal.

CURTIS (CARL T.)
HEALTH CENTER NEWS
Omaha Indian Reservation
Macy, Nebraska 68039

CUSTER BATTLEFIELD
NATIONAL MONUMENT NEWSLETTER
P.O. Box 39
Crow Agency, Montana 59022
(406) 638-2622

Published quarterly.

D

DALLAS INTER-TRIBAL CENTER
(DIC) SMOKE SIGNALS
209 East Jefferson Blvd.
Dallas, Texas 75203
(214) 941-1050

Monthly newsletter.

DAYBREAK STAR INDIAN READER
United Indians of All Tribes Foundation
P.O. Box C-99305
Seattle, Washington 98199
(206) 285-4425

A 24-page children's learning resource featuring
culturally focused articles of interest to students in
grades 4-6. Includes creative writing exercises,
games and puzzles, legends, math and science
activities, book and movie reviews. Publishes
eight monthly issues per year, October through
May. See publisher for multiple copy rates.

DE-BAH-JI-MON
P.O. box 308
Cass Lake, Minnesota 56633

DENVER INDIAN HEALTH
BOARD NEWSLETTER
2035 East 18th Ave. #5
Denver, Colorado 80206

DENVER NATIVE AMERICANS
UNITED NEWSLETTER
4407 Morrison Rd.
Denver, Colorado 80219
(303) 937-0401

DEPARTMENT OF AMERICAN
STUDIES NEWSLETTER
University of Minnesota
West Bank Campus, 1314 Social Science Bldg.
Minneapolis, Minnesota 55455

THE DESERT BREEZE
P.O. Box 256
Nixon, Nevada 89424

DEVILS LAKE SIOUX
TRIBE NEWSLETTER
Public Information Office
Fort Totten, North Dakota 58335

THE DIC SMOKE SIGNALS
Dallas Inter-Tribal Center
209 East Jefferson Blvd.
Dallas, Texas 75203
(214) 941-1050

Monthly newsletter.

DIRECTORY OF AMERICAN
INDIAN BUSINESSES
United Indian Development Association
1541 Wilshire Blvd., Suite 418
Los Angeles, Callifornia 90017-2269
(213) 483-1460

Published annually.

DIRECTORY OF INDIAN MUSEUMS
North American Indian Museums Association
c/o Seneca Iroquois National Museum
Allegany Indian Reservation, P.O. Box 442
Salamanca, New York 14779
(716) 945-1738

Published annually.

DISTANT VISIONS
Institute of American Indian Art
College of Santa Fe
Santa Fe, New Mexico 87503

DISTRICT OF COLUMBIA (D.C.)
DIRECTORY OF NATIVE AMERICAN
FEDERAL AND PRIVATE PROGRAMS
American Indian Education Program
The Phelps-Stokes Fund
1228 M St., N.W.
Washington, D.C. 20005
(202) 638-7066

250 entries. Published annually. $5.00;
$25/year for updates.

DNA IN ACTION
P.O. Box 36
Window Rock, Arizona 86515

DRUMBEAT
U.S. Penitentiary
Leavenworth, Kansas 66048

THE DRUMBEAT
Crow Creek Reservation High School
Stephan, South Dakota 57346

DSUQ' WUB' SIATSUB
Suquamish Tribe
P.O. Box 556
Suquamish, Washington 98392

DUCK VALLEY ROUNDUP
P.O. Box 219
Owynee, Nevada 89832

DXWHIIDA
National Coalition to Support Indian Treaties
814 N.E. 40th St.
Seattle, Washington 98105

E

EAGLE BUTTE NEWS
Eagle Butte, South Dakota 57625

EAGLE FREE PRESS
Phoenix Indian Center, Inc.
1337 North 1st St.
Phoenix, Arizona 85004
  (602) 256-2000

EAGLE VIEWS
Intermountain Indian School
Brigham City, Utah 84302

EAGLE WING PRESS, INC.
P.O. Box 579MO
Naugatuck, Connecticut 06770
  (203) 274-6058
  Jim Roaix, Managing Editor
  Barrie Kavasch, Book Review Editor

American Indian newspaper presenting positive American Indian press to non-Indian public. Funds generated beyond publication costs are comitted to a scholarship fund which provides monies to American Indian/Alaskan Native post high school students studying education or journalism. Published six times per year.

EAGLE'S EYE
Tribe of Many Feathers
360A Brimhall Bldg.
Brigham Young University
Provo, Utah 84601

EARLY MAN
Center for American Archaeology
1911 Ridge Ave.
Evanston, Illinois 60201

EARLY SITES RESEARCH SOCIETY NEWSLETTER
c/o James Whittall, Archaeology Director
Long Hill
Rowley, Massachusetts 01969
  (617) 948-2410

Published bimonthly.

EARTH WALK
Council for Native American Indian Progress
280 Broadway, Suite 316
New York, New York 10007
  (212) 732-0485

Newsletter.

ECH-KA-NAV-CHA
P.O. Box 888
Needles, California 92363

ECHO—TOWAOC COMMUNITY NEWSPAPER
Ute Mountain Tribe
Towaoc, Colorado 81334

EIGHT NORTHERN PUEBLOS NEWS
P.O. Box 927
San Juan Pueblos, New Mexico 87566

ELDER VOICES
National Indian Council on Aging
P.O. Box 2088
Albuquerque, New Mexico 87103
  (505) 766-2276

Published monthly.

ELKO COMMUNITY NEWS
Nevada Intertribal Council
Elko, Nevada 89801

EOP NEWSLETTER
350 Waldo Hall, Oregon State University
Corvallis, Oregon 97331

ETHNIC DIRECTORY OF CALIFORNIA NORTHWEST COAST OF U.S.
Western Publishers
P.O. Box 30193, Station B
Calgary, Alberta, Canada

ETHNOHISTORY
American Society for Ethnohistory
Dept. of Anthropology, Texas Tech University
Lubbock, Texas 79409
  (806) 742-2228

Published quarterly.

ETHNOMUSICOLOGY
Society for Ethnomusicology
P.O. Box 2894
Ann Arbor, Michigan 48106
  (313) 665-9400

THE EVANPAHA
American Indian Lore Association
P.O. Box 9698
Anaheim, California 92802

Published bimonthly.

THE EXCHANGE/ROUNDUP
Phelps-Stokes Fund
1228 M St., N.W.
Washington, D.C. 20005
(202) 638-7066

EXPLORATIONS IN ETHNIC STUDIES
National Association for Ethnic Studies
1861 Rosemont Ave.
Claremont, California 91711
(714) 625-8070
Charles C. Irby, Editor

An interdisciplinary journal devoted to the study of ethnicity, ethnic groups, intergroup relations, and the cultural life of ethnic minorities. *Sights and Sounds,* annual supplement to the journal; includes reviews of books and non-print media. *Subscription:* $25/year (membership); also *The Ethnic Reporter,* semiannual newsletter for members.

EYAPIOAYE
Assiniboine and Sioux Tribes
Poplar, Montana 59255

F

**FIVE CIVILIZED TRIBES
MUSEUM NEWSLETTER**
Agency Hill on Honor Heights
Muskogee, Oklahoma 74401
(918) 683-1701

FIVE FEATHERS NEWS
Tribe of Five Feathers
P.O. Box W
Lompoc, California 93436

FIVE TRIBES JOURNAL
Five Civilized Tribes Foundation
c/o Chickasaw Nation, P.O. Box 1548
Ada, Oklahoma 74820

**FLAGSTAFF INDIAN
CENTER NEWSLETTER**
P.O. Box 572
Flagstaff, Arizona 86002

FLANDREAU SPIRIT
Flandreau Indian School
Flandreau, South Dakota 57028

FOCUS: INDIAN EDUCATION
Minnesota Department of Education
Capitol Square Bldg.
St. Paul, Minnesota 55101

FOLKLIFE CENTER NEWS
American Folklife Center
The Library of Congress
Washington, D.C. 20540
(202) 287-6590

Quarterly newsletter providing information about current projects; and lists current publications.

FOND DU LAC RESERVATION NEWS
105 University Dr.
Cloquet, Minnesota 55720

FORT APACHE SCOUT
P.O. Box 898
Whiteriver, Arizona 85941

FORT HALL NEWSLETTER
Bureau of Indian Affairs
Fort Hall, Idaho 83203

FORT McDOWELL NEWSLETTER
P.O. Box 17779
Fountain Hills, Arizona 85268

FORT YUMA NEWSLETTER
P.O. Box 890
Yuma, Arizona 85364

FOUR DIRECTIONS
Kiva Club
1812 Las Lomas, NE
Albuquerque, New Mexico 87131

**FOUR DIRECTIONS FOR PEACE
AND MEDICINE LODGE**
Council for Native American Indian Progress
280 Broadway, Suite 316
New York, New York 10007
(212) 732-0485

Newsletter.

FOUR WINDS
Hundred Arrows Press
P.O. Box 156
Austin, Texas 78767
(512) 472-8877/956-7048

Published quarterly.

FOUR WINDS
Washington State Penitentiary
P.O. Box 520
Walla Walla, Washington 99362

**FUTURES FOR CHILDREN
AMERICAN INDIAN NEWSLETTER**
805 Tijeras, NW
Albuquerque, New Mexico 87102
(505) 247-4700

Published semiannually.

G

GALLERY NOTES
The Indian Museum
Mid-America All Indian Center
650 North Seneca
Wichita, Kansas 67203

Quarterly newsletter.

THE GANADO STORY
College of Ganada
Ganado, Arizona 86505

GANADO TODAY
Ganado Mission
Ganado, Arizona 86505

**GENESEE INDIAN CENTER
GVIA GRAPEVINE**
124 West First St.
Flint, Michigan 48502-1311
(313) 239-6621

Monthly newsletter. *Subscription:* $4.00/year.

GILA RIVER NEWS
P.O. Box 97
Sacaton, Arizona 85247

GILCREASE MAGAZINE
Thomas Gilcrease Institute of
American History and Art
1400 North 25 West Ave.
Tulsa, Oklahoma 74127
(918) 581-5311

Published quarterly.

GLACIER REPORTER
P.O. Box R
Browning, Montana 59417

**GRAND RAPIDS
INTERTRIBAL NEWSLETTER**
45 Lexington, N.W.
Grand Rapids, Michigan 49504

GREAT LAKES AGENCY NEWS
Great Lakes Indian Agency
Ashland, Wisconsin 54806

GREAT LAKES INDIAN NEWS BUREAU
Route 5, Box 5355
Hayward, Wisconsin 54843

GREAT LAKES PATHFINDER
460 Spruce St.
Sault Ste. Marie, Michigan 49783

GREAT PLAINS JOURNAL
Institute of the Great Plains
Museum of the Great Plains
P.O. Box 68, 601 Ferris
Elmer Thomas Park
Lawton, Oklahoma 73502
(405) 353-5675

Contains articles concerning the history, archaeology, ecology or natural history of the ten-state Great Plains region. Published annually.

GREAT PLAINS OBSERVER
218 South Egan
Madison, South Dakota 57042

GREAT PLAINS QUARTERLY
Center for Great Plains Studies
University of Nebraska, 1214 Oldfather Hall
Lincoln, Nebraska 68588-0313
(402) 472-6058
Frances W. Kaye, Editor

A scholarly, interdisciplinary journal which publishes refereed articles in the geography, history, literature, anthropology, ethnology, folklore, fine arts, sociology, political science, economics, and agriculture of the Great Plains region. Book reviews. Advertising. *Subscription:* U.S. - $15/year, $28/two years; Canada - $18/year; $34/two years; Overseas - $21/year, $40/two years. $5 (single issue). Complimentary copies available.

GREATER LOWELL INDIAN CULTURAL ASSOCIATION—NEWSLETTER
551 Textile Ave.
Dracut, Massachusetts 01826

GUM-U
P.O. Box 168
Peach Springs, Arizona 86425

H

HARVARD INDIAN NEWSLETTER
Native American Program
Graduate School of Education
Harvard University
Cambridge, Massachusetts 02138

HEALTH REPORTER
National Indian Health Board
1602 South Parker Rd, Suite 200
Denver, Colorado 80231
(303) 752-0931

Published ten times per year.

**HEART OF AMERICA
INDIAN CENTER NEWSLETTER**
1340 East Admiral
Kansas City, Missouri 64106

HELLO CHOCTAW
P.O. Box 59
Durant, Oklahoma 74701

HISTORICAL ARCHAEOLOGY
The Society for Historical Archaeology
P.O. Box 241
Glassboro, New Jersey 08028

Semiannual journal. *Subscription:*
$20/individuals; $40/institutions, annual
membership dues.

THE HO CHUNK
P.O. Box 311
Tomah, Wisconsin 54660

HONGA
American Indian Center of Omaha
613 South 16th
Omaha, Nebraska 68102

HOPI ACTION NEWS
Winslow Mail
Winslow, Arizona 86047

HOPI CRIER
Hopi Day School
Oraibi, Arizona 86039

HOPI TRIBAL NEWS
P.O. Box 123
Oraibi, Arizona 86039

HOW NI KAN
Citizen Band Potawatomi Tribe
Route 5, Box 151
Shawnee, Oklahoma 74801
(405) 275-3121
Patricia Sulcer, Editor

Monthly tribal newsletter. *Subscription:*
$6/year.

**HUMAN DEVELOPMENT NEWS
(NATIVE AMERICAN NEWS INSERT)**
HHH Bldg., Room 350G
200 Indepedence Ave., S.W.
Washington, D.C. 20201

HUNTER QUARTERLY
North American Indian Center
P.O. Box 7
Deer Lodge, Montana 59722

I

INDIAN AFFAIRS
Association of American Indian Affairs
95 Madison Ave.
New York, New York 10016
(212) 689-8720

Covers current news about and of interest to
American Indians and to those interested in
Indian affairs. Published quarterly with
occasional special issues.

INDIAN AFFAIRS NEWS
Brigham Young University
Provo, Utah 84601

INDIAN AFFAIRS NEWSLETTER
Bureau of Indian Affairs
1951 Constitution Ave., N.W.
Washington, D.C. 20245

INDIAN AMERICAN QUARTERLY
P.O. Box 443
Hurst, Texas 76053

INDIAN ARCHIVES
Antelope Indian Circle
P.O. Box 790
Susanville, California 96130

INDIAN ARIZONA TODAY
IDDA
1777 West Camelback Rd. #A108
Phoenix, Arizona 85015

INDIAN ARTIFACT MAGAZINE
Fogelman Publishing Co.
RD 1, Box 240
Turbotville, Pennsylvania 17772
(717) 437-3698
Gary L. Fogelman, Editor/Publisher

Contains articles and book reviews on Indian
artifacts and lifestyle. Published quarterly.
Advertising. *Subscription:* $15/year. Sample
copy, $4.

**INDIAN ARTS AND CRAFTS
ASSOCIATION (IACA) NEWSLETTER**
4215 Lead, SE
Albuquerque, New Mexico 87108
(505) 265-9149
Dave Lewis, Editor

Contains information on markets, meetings, new
members, applications, and other news of interest
to those in the industry; helps in the education of
consumers. Advertising accepted from members
only. Published monthly for IACA members and
a limited "press" list.

**INDIAN CENTER OF
SAN JOSE, INC. NEWSLETTER**
3485 East Hills Dr.
San Jose, California 95127
(408) 259-9722

Published monthly.

INDIAN COMMUNICTIONS
Dovecrest Indian Cultural Center
Summit Rd.
Exeter, Rhode Island 02822

Monthly newsletter.

INDIAN COURTS
National American Indian Court Judges
1000 Connecticut Ave., N.W., Suite 401
Washington, D.C. 20036
(202) 296-0685

Quarterly newsletter.

THE INDIAN CRUSADER
American Indian Liberation Crusade, Inc.
4009 South Halldale Ave.
Los Angeles, California 90062-1851
(213) 299-1810
Basil M. Gaynor and Henry E. Hedrick, Editors

Published quarterly. No charge (tax deductible
donations accepted.)

**INDIAN CULTURAL
EDUCATION NEWSLETTER**
3602 West Government Way
Seattle, Washington 98199

INDIAN EDUCATION
National Indian Education Association
1115 South Second Ave.
Minneapolis, Minnesota 55404

INDIAN EDUCATION NEWSLETTER
United Tribes of South Dakota
P.O. Box 1193
Pierre, South Dakota 57501

**INDIAN EDUCATION
RECORD OF OKLAHOMA**
Tulsa Indian Youth Council
716 South Troost
Tulsa, Oklahoma 74114

INDIAN EDUCATOR
United Indians of All Tribes Foundation
Day Break Star Arts Center
Discovery Park, Box C-99305
Seattle, Washington 98199
(206) 285-4425

Monthly newsletter.

**INDIAN, ESKIMO, ALEUT OWNED
AND OPERATED ARTS BUSINESS
SOURCE DIRECTORY**
Indian Arts and Crafts Board
Room 4004, U.S. Department of the Interior
Washington, D.C. 20240
(202) 343-2773

Published annually.

INDIAN EXTENSION NEWS
New Mexico State University
Box 3AP
Las Cruces, New Mexico 88003

INDIAN FAMILY DEFENSE
Association of American Indian Affairs
95 Madison Ave.
New York, New York 10016
(212) 689-8720

Concerned with Indian child-welfare issues, and
in particular with the large numbers of Indian
children removed from their families to be placed
in adoptive homes, foster care, special
institutions, and federal boarding schools; reports
on actions by the state and federal governments
and the courts, Indian tribes and urban Indian
groups, and Congress. Published quarterly. No
charge.

INDIAN FINANCE DIGEST
American Indian National Bank (AINB)
Scholarship Fund
1029 Vermont Ave., N.W., Suite 1100
Washington, D.C. 20005

INDIAN FORERUNNER
Eight Northern Pueblos
P.O. Box 927
San Juan Pueblo, New Mexico 87566

INDIAN HEALTH NEWSLETTER
Indian Unit-Fhss, 714-744 P St.
Sacramento, California 95814

**INDIAN HEALTH UNIT
BMCH NEWSLETTER**
2151 Berkeley Way
Berkeley, California 94704

INDIAN HERITAGE NEWSLETTER
Ranier Beach High School
8815 Seward Park Ave. South
Seattle, Washington 98109

INDIAN HIGHWAYS
Cook Christian Training School
708 South Lindon Lane
Tempe, Arizona 85281

THE INDIAN HISTORIAN
American Indian Historical Society
1451 Masonic Ave.
San Francisco, California 94117
  (415) 626-5235
  Jeanette Henry, Editor

Back issues are available.

THE INDIAN JOURNAL
Indian Journal Printing Co.
Eufaula, Oklahoma 74432

INDIAN LAW PROJECT NEWSLETTER
Connecticut Legal Services
114 East Main St.
Meriden, Connecticut 06450

INDIAN LAW REPORTER
319 MacArthur Blvd.
Oakland, California 94610

INDIAN LAW RESOURCE
601 E St., S.E.
Washington, D.C. 20004

INDIAN LEADER
Haskell Indian Junior College
Lawrence, Kansas 66044

INDIAN NATURAL RESOURCES
Association on American Indian Affairs
95 Madison Ave.
New York, New York 10016
  Steven Unger, Editor

Exclusively concerned with Indian natural
resource issues, and the options available to
Indian tribes as they formulate their own
programs for resource protection, conservation,
and development; reports on important federal,
state, tribal, and corporate actions. Published
quarterly. No charge.

INDIAN NEWS
Indian Employment Program
630 West 7th St.
Tulsa, Oklahoma 74101

INDIAN NEWS NOTES
Bureau of Indian Affairs
1951 Constitution Ave., N.W.
Washington, D.C. 20245

INDIAN NOTES
Museum of the American Indian
Heye Foundation, Broadway at 155th St.
New York, New York 10032
  (212) 283-2420

Presents the currrent activities of the Museum.
Published quarterly.

INDIAN NOTES
P.O. Box 66
Wellpinit, Washington 99040

INDIAN PROGRAMS
University of Arizona
Tucson, Arizona 85721

INDIAN PROGRESS
Associated Executive Committee of
Friends on Indian Affairs
P.O. Box 161, 612 Plum St.
Frankton, Indiana 46004
  (317) 754-7977

Published three times per year.

THE INDIAN RELIC TRADER
P.O. Box 88
Sunbury, Ohio 43074
  Janie Jinks-Weidner, Editor

Features articles on prehistoric relics, current
archaeological findings and research; calendar of
events and meetings; sources for books and
supplies. Advertising. *Subscription:* $8/year;
sample copies available, $1.00 each.

INDIAN RECORD
Bureau of Indian Affairs
1951 Constitution Ave., N.W.
Washington, D.C. 20245

INDIAN REPORTER
3254 Orange St.
Riverside, California 92501

INDIAN SCHOOL JOURNAL
Chilocco Indian School
Bureau of Indian Affairs
Chilocco, Oklahoma 74635

INDIAN SIGNS
Blackfeet Tribal Business Center
Browning, Montana 59417

INDIAN STUDIES QUARTERLY
400 Caldwell Hall
Cornell University
Ithaca, New York 14853
  (607) 256-8402
  Ray Fougnier, Director
  Jose Barreiro, Editor

Contains articles, national tribal news, media
notes, poetry, and book reviews. Published
quarterly. *Subscription:* $12/year, U.S.;
$18/year, Canada; $28/year, Europe.

INDIAN TIME
Akwesasne Notes
P.O. Box 196, Mohawk Nation
Rooseveltown, New York 13683-0196
  (518) 358-9535/9531

An eight page weekly newspaper of the St. Regis
Mohawk Reservation (New York-Quebec-
Ontario.) Promotes unity for all Mohawk groups
through communicating information on the

environment, health, women, youth and Iroquois history; also Native American and Canadian news. Advertising. *Subscription:* $33/year, U.S.; $40/year, Canada. Sample copies, $1.00 each.

INDIAN TIME
North Carolina Commission on Indian Affairs
P.O. Box 2722
Raleigh, North Carolina 27611

INDIAN TIMES
P.O. Box 4121, Santa Fe Station
Denver, Colorado 80204

INDIAN TOWNSHIP NEWSLETTER
Princeton, Maine 04668

INDIAN TRADER
P.O. Box 1421
Gallup, New Mexico 87301
 (505) 722-6694

Monthly newspaper of American Indian arts, crafts, and culture. *Subscription:* $15/year, $27/two years, $40/three years; $26/year, foreign.

INDIAN TRUTH
Indian Rights Association
1505 Race St.
Philadelphia, Pennsylvania 19102
 (215) 563-8349
 Suzy Glazer, Editor

Bimonthly news journal highlighting news events from throughout Indian country with feature articles on current, and critical topics; coverage of major Indian news from Congress, the Courts, and Indian country. Book reviews. *Subscription:* $20/year. Complimentary copies on exchange basis only.

INDIAN VOICE
American Indian Folklore Group
P.O. Box 55
Stillwater, Minnesota 55082

INDIAN VOICE, STOWW
P.O. Box 578
Sumner, Washington 98390

**INDIAN YOUTH
OF AMERICA NEWSLETTER**
P.O. Box 2786, 4509 Stone Ave.
Sioux City, Iowa 51106
 (712) 276-0796

INDIANS OF ALL TRIBES CLUB
P.O. Box 777
Monroe, Washington 98272

INI-MI-KWA-ZOO-MIN
Minnesota Chippewa Tribe
P.O. Box 217
Cass Lake, Minnesota 56633
 Betty Blue, Editor

**INSTITUTE OF EARLY AMERICAN
HISTORY AND CULTURE—NEWSLETTER**
P.O. Box 220
Williamsburg, Virginia 23187

**INSTITUTE OF INDIAN STUDIES
NEWS REPORT AND BULLETIN**
P.O. Box 133, Room 18, Dakota Hall
University of South Dakota
Vermillion, South Dakota 57069

INUPIAT KATITUAT
Norton Sound Health Corporation
Nome, Alaska 99762

THE IOWA INDIAN
Sioux City Public Library
6th & Jackson Sts.
Sioux City, Iowa 51105

ISLETA EAGLE PRIDE
Isleta Elementary School
P.O. Box 312
Isleta, New Mexico 87022
 (505) 869-2321

School newspaper.

J

JICARILLA CHIEFTAIN
Jicarilla Apache Tribe
P.O. Box 507
Dulce, New Mexico 87528
 (505) 759-3242
 Mary F. Polanco, Editor
 Vida L. Vigil, Co-Editor

Contains information of general importance to tribal members, as well as national and state news pertaining to other tribes and Indian affairs. Advertising. Published biweekly. *Subscription:* $12/year, U.S.; $18/year, Canada and Mexico; $24/year, foreign.

JOURNAL OF ALASKA NATIVE ARTS
Institute of Alaska Native Arts
P.O. Box 80583
Fairbanks, Alaska 99708
 (907) 456-7491
 Jan Steinbright, Editor

A twelve page bimonthly journal containing interviews with Alaskan Native artists; news of opportunities of interest to artists; and photographs, poetry and issues affecting Alaskan Native artists.

JOURNAL OF AMERICAN FOLKLORE
American Folklore Society
Maryland State Arts Council
15 Wersst Mulberry St.
Baltimore, Maryland 21201
 (301) 685-6740

JOURNAL OF AMERICAN INDIAN EDUCATION

Center for Indian Education
Farmer Bldg., Room 302
Arizona State University
Tempe, Arizona 85287
(602) 965-6292
John Red Horse, Ph.D., Director

Publishes papers directly related to the education of North American Indians and Alaskan Natives. Emphasis is on research: experimental, historical, and field study reports. Published three times per year (October, January, and May.) Submits four complimentary copies of the Journal to authors of accepted manuscripts. *Subscription:* $12/year, U.S.; $14.50/year, Canada. Available on microfilm from Xerox University Microfilms, 300 North Zeeb Rd., Ann Arbor, Michigan 48106.

JOURNAL OF AMERICAN INDIAN FAMILY RESEARCH

Histree 23011 Moulton Parkway FGA
Laguna Hills, California 92653

JOURNAL OF ANTHROPOLOGICAL RESEARCH

University of New Mexico
Albuquerque, New Mexico 87131

JOURNAL OF ARIZONA HISTORY

Arizona Historical Society
949 East Second St.
Tucson, Arizona 85719

Contains articles, critical essays, and book reviews on the history of Arizona and the Southwest, and northern Mexico when appropriate. Articles often include appraisals of American Indian life and lore, the Indian wars and Anglo-Indian relations. Published quarterly.

JOURNAL OF CALIFORNIA AND GREAT BASIN ANTHROPOLOGY

Department of Anthropology
University of California
Riverside, California 92521
 Matthew Hall, Michael Lerch
 and Mark Sutton, Editors

The journal of Malki Museum publishes original manuscripts on the ethnography, languages, arts, archaeology, and prehistory of ther Native peoples of Alta and Baja California and the Great Basin. Published twice yearly. *Subscription:* $14/year, individuals; $17/year, institutions. Back issues may be obtained from Coyote Press, P.O. Box 3377, Salinas, California 93912.

JOURNAL OF CHEROKEE STUDIES

Museum of the Cherokee Indian
P.O. Box 770-A
Cherokee, North Carolina 28719
(704) 497-3481

Published semiannually.

JOURNAL OF NEW WORLD ARCHAEOLOGY

Institute of Archaeology
405 Hilgard Ave.
Los Angeles, California 90024
(213) 825-4711

Dr. Ernestine S. Elster

Contains contributions on original research throughout America. Published infrequently. $20 per issue.

JOURNAL OF THE ORDER OF THE INDIAN WARS

Order of the Indian Wars
P.O. Box 7401
Little Rock, Arkansas 72217
(501) 225-3996

Published quarterly.

JOURNAL OF THE WEST

P.O. Box 1009, 1531 Yuma
Manhattan, Kansas 66502

KAHEE NEWSLETTER

P.O. Box 433
Crow Agency, Montana 59022

KALIHUI SAKS

P.O. Box 365
Oneida, Wisconsin 54155

KARIWEHAWI NEWSLETTER

Akwesasne Museum
Route 3, St. Regis Reservation
Hogansburg, New York 13655

KEE-YOKA

Swinomish Tribal Community
P.O. Box 338
La Connor, Washington 98257

KEYAPI NEWS

Fort Thompson, South Dakota 57339

KINZUA PLANNING NEWSLETTER

Seneca Nation, P.O. Box 231
Salamanca, New York 14779

KIOWA INDIAN NEWS

P.O. Box 361
Carnegie, Oklahoma 73015

THE KIVA
Arizona Archaeological and Historical Society
Arizona State Museum, University of Arizona
Tucson, Arizona 85721

KLALLAM NEWSLETTER
Port Gamble-Klallam Nation Tribal Council
P.O. Box 28
Kingston, Washington 98346

KLAH'CHE'MIN
Squaxin Tribal Center
Route 1, Box 257
Shelton, Washington 98584

**KROEBER ANTHROPOLOGY
SOCIETY PAPERS**
Department of Anthropology
University of California
Berkeley, California 94720

KUI TATK
Native American Science Education Association
P.O. Box 6646,T Street Station
Washington, D.C. 20009-0246
(202) 638-7066
(301) 262-0999
Gary G. Allen, Director

Newsletter of current information on local
programs, its activities and other information on
science and mathematics education relative to
Native-Americans.

L

LAC COURTE OREILLES JOURNAL
LCO Graphic Arts, Route 2
Hayward, Wisconsin 54843
(715) 634-8934

LAC DU FLAMBEAU UPDATE
LDF Tribal Office
Lac du Flambeau, Wisconsin 54538

LAKOTA OYATE-KO
Oregon State Penitentiary
2605 State St.
Salem, Orgon 97310

THE LAKOTA TIMES
P.O. Box 189
Martin, South Dakota 57551
  Tim Giago, Editor/Publisher

LAKOTA TIMES WEEKLY
P.O. Box 1051
Pine Ridge, South Dakota 57770

**LAKOTA WOMEN'S
ORGANIZATION NEWSLETTER**
Lantry, South Dakota 57636

LIFELINE MAGAZINE
Save the Children Federation
54 Wilton Rd.
Westport, Connecticut 06880
(203) 226-7271

Published quarterly.

**LIST OF TRIBES
AND TRIBAL LEADERS**
National Tribal Chairman's Association
818 18th St., N.W., Suite 420
Washington, D.C. 20006
(202) 293-0031

Published quarterly.

**LITTLE BIG HORN ASSOCIATES
RESEARCH REVIEW AND NEWSLETTER**
P.O. Box 633
Boaz, Alabama 35959
(205) 593-9701

Research Review: Published quarterly;
Newsletter: Published eight times per year.

LITTLE SIOUX
Rosebud Education Society
St. Francis, South Dakota 57572

LORE
Friends of the Museum, Inc.
Milwaukee Public Museum
800 West Wells St.
Milwaukee, Wisconsin 53233
(414) 278-2752

Published quarterly.

THE LUMBEE OUTREACH
Lumbee Regional Development Association
P.O. Box 68
Pembroke, North Carolina 28372

LUMMI SQUOL QUOL
2616 Kquina Rd.
Bellingham, Washington 98225

M

MAINE INDIAN NEWSLETTER
Pine St.
Freeport, Maine 04032

MAKAH DAKAH
P.O. Box 547
Neah Bay, Washington 98357

MAKAH VIEWERS
P.O. Box 115
Neah Bay, Washington 98357

MAMMOTH TRUMPETS
Center for the Study of Early Man
University of Maine
Orono, Maine 04473
(207) 581-2197
Dr. M. Sorg, Editor

Contains articles, interviews, news of new and significant discoveries about Pleistocene populations and their environments in the Western Hemisphere; announcements of recent relevant publications and conferences. Published quarterly. *Subscription:* $5/year. Complimentary copies available upon request.

MAN-AH-ATN
American Indian Community House
842 Broadway
New York, New York 10003
(212) 598-0100
Alexander Ewen, Editor

Provides a forum for the introduction of issues and the expressions of viewpoints on Indian affairs in a fair and truthful way, and in a way that will bring some measure of unity to Indian people. Published bimonthly. No charge (donations accepted.)

MANATABA MESSENGER
P.O. Box 810
Parker, Arizona 85344

MANELUK REPORT
P.O. Box 256
Kotzebue, Alaska 99752

MANY SMOKES METIS/EARTH
Awareness Magazine
Bear Tribe Medicine Society
P.O. Box 9167
Spokane, Washington 99206

MARIN MUSEUM OF THE AMERICAN INDIAN—MUSEUM QUARTERLY
P.O. Box 864, 2200 Novato Blvd.
NOVATO 94948
(415) 897-4064

THE MARYLAND INDIAN
P.O. Box 13161
Baltimore, Maryland 21203

MASTERKEY
Southwest Museum
P.O. Box 128, Highland Park Station
234 Museum Dr.
Los Angeles, California 90065
(213) 221-2164
Steven Le Blanc, Editor
Susan Kenagy, Associate Editor

Devoted to the anthropology and archaeology of the Americas; contains articles, book reviews, and a conservation column. Published quarterly. *Subscription:* $12/year.

MAWIW-KILUN
Tribal Governors, Inc.
Indian Township
Princeton, Maine 04668

Contains community news, tribal activities, health and social service articles. Published bimonthly.

THE MEDICINE BAG
SLC Indian Health Center
508 East South Temple #319
Salt Lake City, Utah 84115

MEDICINE BUNDLE
Montana United Scholarship Services
510 1st Ave. North, Suite 103
Great Falls, Montana 59401

MEETING GROUND
D'Arcy McNickle Center for the
History of the American Indian
Newberry Library
60 West Walton St.
Chicago, Illinois 60610
(312) 943-9090
Colin G. Calloway, Editor

Semiannual newsletter containing information on Center activities, fellowships. No charge.

MENOMINEE TRIBAL NEWS
P.O. Box 397
Keshena, Wisconsin 54135
(715) 799-3341

THE MESSINGER
San Fidel, New Mexico 87049

MICCOSUKEE EVERGLADES NEWS
Miccosukee Tribe of Florida
Box 440021, Tamiami Station
Miami, Florida 33144

THE MICHIGAN INDIAN
Baker Olen Bldg. West, Room 313
Lansing, Michigan 48926

MID-AMERICA ALL INDIAN CENTER NEWSLETTER
650 North Seneca
Wichita, Kansas 67203

MIGIZI COMMUNICATIONS
2300 Cedar Ave. South
Minneapolis, Minnesota 55404
(612) 721-6631

MILLE LAC NEWS
Onamia, Minnesota 56395

**MINNESOTA ARCHAEOLOGICAL
SERIES REPORT**
Minnesota Historical Society
690 Cedar St.
St. Paul, Minnesota 55101

MINNESOTA ARCHAEOLOGIST
Minnesota Archaeological Society
Fort Snelling History Center
St. Paul, Minnesota 55111
    (218) 236-2633
    Michael G. Michlovic, Editor

Contains articles on archaeology and ethnology
of Minnesota. Book reviews. Published twice
yearly. *Subscription:* $15/year.

MINNESOTA HISTORY
Minnesota Historical Society
690 Cedar St.
St. Paul, Minnesota 55101

Deals with events, places, and personalities in
Minnesota history, often touching upon events
related to Minnesota's Indian tribes. Published
quarterly.

MINNESOTA WINNEBAGO NEWSLETTER
St. Paul Urban League
401 Selby Ave.
St. Paul, Minnesota 55103

MISKWEEWA PINAYWIN
Lakes Publishing Co.
Detroit Lakes, Minnesota 56501

MITTARK, WAMPANOAG INDIANS
P.O. Box 1048
Mashpee, Massachusetts 02649

MOCCASIN TELEGRAPH
Community Action Program
Grand Portage, Minnesota 55605

**MONTANA INTER-TRIBAL
POLICY BOARD NEWSLETTER**
Department of Indian Affairs
6301 Grand Ave.
Billings, Montana 59103

**MONTANA, THE MAGAZINE
OF WESTERN HISTORY**
Montana Historical Society
Roberts and Sixth Ave.
Helena, Montana 59601

Deals with Western history, often touching upon
the Indian's involvement. Published quarterly.

THE MORNING STAR PEOPLE
St. Labre Indian School
Ashland, Montana 59003

MUKLUKS HEMCUNGA
Organization of the Forgotten American
P.O. Box 1257
Klamath Falls, Oregon 97601

**MUSEUM OF THE AMERICAN INDIAN
QUARTERLY NEWSLETTER**
Museum of the American Indian
Broadway at 155th St.
New York, New York 10032
    (212) 283-2420

**MUSEUM OF THE FUR
TRADE QUARTERLY**
HC 74, Box 18
Chadron, Nebraska 69337

**MUSEUM OF THE GREAT
PLAINS NEWSLETTER**
P.O. Box 68
Lawton, Oklahoma 73502
    (405) 353-5675

**MUSEUM OF INDIAN
HERITAGE NEWSLETTER**
6040 De Long Rd.
Indianapolis, Indiana 46254
    (317) 293-4488

Published quarterly.

MUSKOGEE NATION NEWS
P.O. Box 580
Okmulgee, Oklahoma 74447
    (918) 756-8700
    Gary Breshears, Executive Director
    Helen Chalakee, Managing Editor

Published monthly.

MUSTANG NEWS
Little Wound School Board
Kyle, South Dakota 57752.

N

NAN ITCH TENAS
Indian Education Program
P.O. Box 1367
Tacoma, Washington 98401

NAS-NW NEWSLETTER
University of Idaho
Moscow, Idaho 83843

NATION NOTES
Penobscot Nation Newsletter
Old Town, Maine 04468

**NATIONAL ADVISORY COUNCIL
ON INDIAN AFFAIRS**
2000 L St., N.W., Suite 574
Washington, D.C. 20036
  (202) 634-6160

**NATIONAL AMERICAN INDIAN
CATTLEMAN'S ASSOCIATION
NEWSLETTER AND YEARBOOK**
c/o Tim Foster, President
Route 2, Box 2492
Toppenish, Washington 98948
  (509) 854-1329

Monthly newsletter.

**NATIONAL AMERICAN INDIAN COURT
JUDGES ASSOCIATION NEWSLETTER**
1000 Connecticut Ave., N.W., #501
Washington, D.C. 20036

**NATIONAL CENTER
FOR AMERICAN INDIAN
ALTERNATIVE EDUCATION JOURNAL**
P.O. Box 18329, Capitol Hill Station
Denver, Colorado 80218
  (303) 861-1052

Published biennially.

**NATIONAL COALITION TO SUPPORT
INDIAN TREATIES NEWSLETTER**
814 N.E. 40th St.
Seattle, Washington 98105

NATIONAL GEOGRAPHIC
National Geographical Society
17th & M Sts., N.W.
Washington, D.C. 20036
  (202) 857-7000

Monthly magazine.

**NATIONAL INDIAN ARTS
AND CRAFTS DIRECTORY**
National Indian Traders Association
P.O. Box 1263, 3575 South Fox
Englewood, Colorado 80150-1263
  (303) 692-6579

Published annually

**NATIONAL INDIAN COUNCIL
ON AGING UPDATE/QUARTERLY**
P.O. Box 2088
Albuquerque, New Mexico 87103

**NATIONAL INDIAN
EDUCATION NEWSLETTER**
Ivy Tower Bldg.
1115 Second Ave. South
Minneapolis, Minnesota 55403
  (612) 333-5341

Published bimonthly.

**NATIONAL INDIAN HEALTH BOARD
(NIHB) HEALTH REPORTER**
1602 South Parker Rd., Suite 200
Denver, Colorado 80231

**NATIONAL INDIAN SOCIAL WORKERS
ASSOCIATION NEWSLETTER**
1740 West 41st St.
Tulsa, Oklahoma 74107
  (918) 446-8432

**NATIONAL TRIBAL CHAIRMAN'S
ASSOCIATION NEWSBRIEF**
818 18th St., N.W., Suite 420
Washington, D.C. 20006
  (202) 293-0031

**NATIONAL VIETNAM ERA VETERANS
INTER-TRIBAL ASSOCIATION
NEWSLETTER**
Veterans Center, 4111 N. Lincoln Blvd.
Oklahoma City, Oklahoma 73105
  (405) 270 5187

Published quarterly.

**NATIONAL WOMEN'S PROGRAM
DEVELOPMENT, INC. NEWSLETTER**
Oyoho Resource Center
2301 Midwestern Parkway, S-214
Wichita Falls, Texas 76308

**NATIONS: THE NATIVE
AMERICAN MAGAZINE**
P.O. Box 30510
Seattle, Washington 98103

Published quarterly.

NATIVE AMERICAN ANNUAL
Native American Publishing Co., Inc.
P.O. Box 6338, 760 Mays Blvd., Suite 6
Incline Village, Nevada 89450
  (702) 831-7726
  Margaret Clark-Price, Editor

A non-political media created as a communicative
tool to assist in cultural awareness profiling tribal
history, location and present day activities
throughout the U.S. $8.95. Quarterly
supplements planned.

NATIVE AMERICAN COUNCIL
204 Hagestad Student Center
University of Wisconsin
River Falls, Wisconsin 54022

**NATIVE AMERICAN
EDUCATION COUNCIL FOR
INDIAN EDUCATION NEWSLETTER**
517 Rimrock Rd.
Billings, Montana 59102
  (406) 252-1800

Published quarterly.

NATIVE AMERICAN NEWSLETTER
Intercultural Center, Fort Lewis College
Durango, Colorado 81301

**NATIVE AMERICAN PUBLIC BROAD-
CASTING CONSORTIUM NEWSLETTER**
P.O. Box 83111
Lincoln, Nebraska 68501
 (402) 472-3522

Published bimonthly.

**NATIVE AMERICAN RIGHTS FUND
LEGAL REVIEW**
1506 Broadway
Boulder, Colorado 80302
 (303) 447-8760
 Anita Austin, Editor

Published semiannually. No charge.

NATIVE AMERICAN SCHOLAR
Bureau of Indian Affairs
Higher Education Program
P.O. Box 1788
Albuquerque, New Mexico 87103

**NATIVE AMERICAN
STUDENTS BULLETIN**
University of California
Riverside, California 92507

**NATIVE ARTS UPDATE
AND NEWSLETTER**
ATLATL
402 West Roosevelt
Phoenix, Arizona 85003
 (602) 253-2731

Published quarterly.

**NATIVE CALIFORNIAN
INDIAN NEWSLETTER**
Office Planning/Research
1400 10th St., #109
Sacramento, California 95814

THE NATIVE NEVADAN
Nevada Intertribal Council
650 South Rock 11
Reno, Nevada 89502

NATIVE NEWS
Eugene Public News
200 North Monroe
Eugene, Oregon 97402

**NATIVE NEWS AND BUREAU OF
INDIAN AFFAIRS BULLETIN**
P.O. Box 3-8000
Juneau, Alaska 99801

NATIVE NORTHWEST
802 East First St.
Toppenish, Washington 98948

NATIVE SELF-SUFFICIENCY
Seventh Generation Fund for
Indian Development, Inc.
P.O. Box 10
Forestville, California 95436
 (707) 887-1559

Quarterly newspaper focusing on practical
information for increasing community self-
reliance. Emphasis is on appropriate technologies
and how they can and are being used as alternative
tools for economic development on Indian land.
Subscription: $6/year, individual; $15/year,
institution/foreign.

NATIVE SUN
Detroit Indian Center
360 John R
Detroit, Michigan 48226
 (313) 963-1710

Monthly newsletter.

NAVAJO AREA NEWSLETTER
Bureau of Indian Affairs
P.O. Box 269
Window Rock, Arizona 86515

Contains information of interest to Navajo Area,
B.I.A.'s employees on education, personnel
actions, Bureau policy, etc. Published monthly.
No charge.

**NAVAJO COMMUNITY
COLLEGE NEWSLETTER**
Publications Department
Tsaile, Arizona 86556

NAVAJO EDUCATION NEWSLETTER
Navajo Area Office
Bureau of Indian Affairs
Window Rock, Arizona 86515

THE NAVAJO NATION TIMES
Navajo Times Company
P.O. Box 310
Window Rock, Arizona 86515

A newspaper which covers Navajo tribal interests;
also, other tribes, local, state, and federal
government news. Published weekly.

NAVAJO TIMES TODAY
Navajo Times Company
P.O. Box 310
Window Rock, Arizona 86515

NAVAJOLAND PUBLICATIONS
Navajo Tribal Museum
Window Rock, Arizona 86515

NEE-ME-POC TUM TYNE
Lapwai, Idaho 83540

NETT LAKE NEWS
Nett Lake, Minnesota 55772

**THE NEW ENGLAND ANTIQUITIES
RESEARCH ASSOCIATION JOURNAL**
3 Whitney Dr.
Paxton, Massachusetts 01612

Published quarterly. *Subscription:* $20/year
membership.

**NEW MEXICO ASSOCIATION ON
INDIAN AFFAIRS NEWSLETTER**
Santa Fe, New Mexico 87501

NEW MEXICO HISTORICAL REVIEW
University of New Mexico Press
Mesa Vista 1013
Albuquerque, New Mexico 87112

Concerned with events, places and personalities in
New Mexico history, often touching upon events
related to the American Indian. Published
quarterly.

NEWS BEAT
405 East Easterday Ave.
Sault Ste. Marie, Michigan 49783

NEZ PERCE TRIBAL NEWSPAPER
P.O. Box 305
Lapwai, Idaho 85341

NI-MI-KWA-ZOO-MIN
Minnesota Chippewa Tribe
P.O. Box 217
Cass Lake, Minnesota 56633

NISH-NA-BA
American Indian Culture Group
P.O. Box 2
Lansing, Kansas 66043

NISHNAWBE NEWS
Organization of North American Indian Students
Northern Michigan University
140 University Center
Marquette, Michigan 49855

NOOKSACK NEWSLETTER
P.O. Box 157
Deming, Washington 98244

NORTH AMERICAN ARCHAEOLOGIST
Baywood Publishing Co., Inc.
120 Marine St., Box D
Farmingdale, New York 11735

NORTH AMERICAN INDIAN
2370 Esplanade
Chico, California 95926

**NORTH AMERICAN INDIAN MUSEUMS
ASSOCIATION NEWSLETTER**
c/o Seneca Iroquois National Museum
Allegany Indian Reservation
P.O. Box 442
Salamanca, New York 14779
(716) 945-1738

**NORTH CAROLINA
HISTORICAL REVIEW**
North Carolina Division of
Archaeology and History
109 East Jones St.
Raleigh, North Carolina 27601

**NORTH DAKOTA HISTORY:
JOURNAL OF THE NORTHERN PLAINS**
State Historical Society of North Dakota
North Dakota Heritage Center
Capitol Grounds
Bismarck, North Dakota 58505
(701) 224-2666

Published quarterly. *Subscription:* $10/year,
U.S.; $15/year, foreign.

NORTH DAKOTA QUARTERLY
University of North Dakota Press
Grand Forks, North Dakota 58201

NORTHERN CHEYENNE NEWS
P.O. Box 401
Lame Deer, Montana 59043

**NORTHERN PUEBLOS
AGENCY NEWS DIGEST**
P.O. Box 580
Santa Fe, New Mexico 87501

NORTHWEST ARCTIC NUNA
Maniilaq, Inc.
P.O. Box 256
Kotzebue, Alaska 99752
(907) 442-3311

Monthly newsletter.

NORTHWEST INDIAN NEWS
Seattle Indian Center
121 Stewart St.
Seattle, Washington 98101

NORTHWEST INDIAN TIMES
Gonzaga University
Spokane, Washington 99202

NUGGUAM
Quinault Tribal Affairs
P.O. Box 1118
Taholah, Washington 98587

O

O-HE-YOY NOH
Seneca Nation of Indians
Museum Annex Bldg., Route 1
Allegany Indian Reservation
Salamanca, New York 14779

OGALALA NATION NEWS
P.O. Box 320
Pine Ridge, South Dakota 57770

**OKLAHOMA ANTHROPOLOGICAL
SOCIETY NEWSLETTER**
c/o Rose King, 1000 Horn St.
Muskogee, Oklahoma 74403

Published nine times per year (September-May).
Subscription: $12/year. individuals; $15/year,
institutions; $17/year, foreign.

**OKLAHOMANS FOR INDIAN
OPPORTUNITY NEWSLETTER**
555 Constitution
Norman, Oklahoma 73069

**OLD NORTHWEST
CORPORATION NEWSLETTER**
Sonotabac Prehistoric Indian Mounds and
Museum
2401 Wabash Ave.
Vincennes, Indiana 47591
 (812) 885-4330/7679

Published monthly.

ON THE WAY UP
American Indian Science and Engineering
Society
1310 College Ave., Suite 1220
Boulder, Colorado 80302
 (303) 492-8658

Published three times per year.

ORDER OF THE INDIAN WARS JOURNAL
P.O. Box 7401
Little Rock, Arkansas 72217
 (501) 225-3996
 Jerry L. Russell, Editor/Publisher

Contains reprinted articles on the history of the
Indian wars. Published quarterly.

OSAGE NATION NEWS
P.O. Box 1346
Pawhuska, Oklahoma 74056

OSHKABEWIS
Indian Studies Program
Bemidji State University
Bemidji, Minnesota 56601

**OWENS VALLEY INDIAN
EDUCATION CENTER NEWSLETTER**
P.O. Box 1648
Bishop, California 93514

OYATE NAT E NATA YAZADI PHEZUTA
University of Colorado
Campus Box 135
Boulder, Colorado 80309

P

**PACIFIC COAST
ARCHAEOLOGICAL SOCIETY
QUARTERLY**
P.O. Box 10926
Costa Mesa, California 92627

THE PADRE'S TRAIL
St. Michael's, Arizona 86511

PAHA SAPA WAHOSE
c/o Student Special Services
Black Hills State College
Spearhead, South Dakota 57783

PAN-AMERICAN INDIANS NEWSLETTER
League of Nations
1139 Lehman Place
Johnston, Pennsylvania 15902

**PANHANDLE-PLAINS
HISTORICAL REVIEW**
Panhandle-Plains Historical Museum
P.O. Box 967, W.T. Station
2401 Fourth Ave.
Canyon, Texas 79016
 (806) 655-7194

PAPAGO BULLETIN
P.O. Box 364
Sells, Arizona 85634

PAPAGO RUNNER
P.O. Box 837
Sells, Arizona 85634

PASCUA PUEBLO NEWS
4821 West Calle Vicam
Tucson, Arizona 85706

PATHFINDER NEWSLETTER
American Indian Heritage Foundation
6051 Arlington Blvd.
Falls Church, Virginia 22044
 (703) 237-7500

Published quarterly.

**PHOENIX INDIAN
CENTER NEWSLETTER**
3302 North 7th St.
Phoenix, Arizona 85014

PIERRE CHIEFTAIN
Pierre Indian School
Pierre, South Dakota 57501

**PIERRE INDIAN
LEARNING CENTER (PILC) NEWS**
Star Route 3
Pierre, South Dakota 57501

PILGRIM
Kateri Galleries—National Kateri Center
The National Shrine of N.A. Martyrs
Auriesville, New York 12016
  (518) 853-3033

PIMA-MARICOPA ECHO
Gila River Indian Community
P.O. Box 338
Sacaton, Arizona 85247

PLAINS ANTHROPOLOGIST
410 Wedgewood Dr.
Lincoln, Nebraska 68510
  Joseph Tiffany, Editor

Contains articles and book reviews. Published
quarterly. Complimentary copies available upon
request.

PLAINS TALK
State Historical Society of North Dakota
North Dakota Heritage Center, Capitol Grounds
Bismarck, North Dakota 58505
  (701) 224-2666

Quarterly newsletter. No charge.

POINT HOPE NEWS
Point Hope, Alaska 99766

**POINT NO POINT
TREATY COUNCIL NEWSLETTER**
P.O. Box 746
Kingston, Washington 98346

PORTLAND INDIAN NEWS
5353 S.E. 89th
Portland, Oregon 97204

PREHISTORIC ARTIFACTS
Genuine Indian Relic Society
3335 Junaluska
Columbus, Georgia 31907

PUEBLO HORIZON
Indian Pueblo Cultural Center, Inc.
2401 12th St., N.W.
Albuquerque, New Mexico 87102

PUEBLO NEWS
P.O. Box 6507
1015 Indian School Rd., NW
Albuquerque, New Mexico 87107

**PYRAMID LAKE
INDIAN RESERVATION NEWSLETTER**
P.O. Box 256
Nixon, Nevada 89424

Q

QUA-TOQTI
Hopi Publishers
P.O. Box 266
Kykotsmovi, Arizona 86039

QUALLA RESERVATION NEWS
Cherokee Agency
Cherokee, North Carolina 28719

QUECHAN NEWS
Fort Yuma Indian Reservation
P.O. Box 1169
Yuma, Arizona 85364

QUILEUTE NEWSLETTER
Quileute Tribal Council
P.O. Box 1587
LaPush, Washington 98359

R

THE RAVEN SPEAKS
3061 Cridelle
Dallas, Texas 75220

THE RAWHIDE PRESS
The Spokane Tribe
P.O. Box 393
Wellpinit, Washington 99040
  (509) 258-4581

RED ALERT
Americans for Indian Opportunity
1010 Massachusetts Ave., N.W., Suite 200
Washington, D.C. 20001
  (202) 371-1280

RED CLIFF TRIBAL NEWS
P.O. Box 529
Bayfield, Wisconsin 54814

RED CLOUD COUNTRY
Red Cloud Indian School
Pine Ridge, South Dakota 57770
  (605) 867-5491
  Rev. E.J. Kurth, S.J., Editor

Contains information about Red Cloud School. Sent to donors, friends and benefactors of the school. Published quarterly.

RED EARTH NEWS
37 East Indian School Rd.
Phoenix, Arizona 85012

RED HILLS NEWSLETTER
Kaibab Tribal Council
Tribal Affairs Bldg.
Pipe Springs, Arizona 86002

RED LAKE NEWSLETTER
Red Lake Reservation
Red Lake, Minnesota 56671

RED MEN MAGAZINE
Great Council of U.S. Improved Order of Red Men
P.O. Box 683
Waco, Texas 76703
  (817) 756-1221

Published three times per year.

RED PAGES:
BUSINESS ACROSS INDIAN AMERICA
LaCourse Communications Corporation
P.O. Box 431
Toppenish, Washington 98948
  Richard LaCourse, Editor

A nationwide listing of tribally owned and individually owned Indian businesses in the U.S. with over 5,000 entries. SIC coded names, addresses, phone numbers, and contact people. Published annually. $65.00.

RED TIMES
P.O. Box 46
Laguna, New Mexico 87026

REDSKIN
Phoenix Indian High School
Phoenix, Arizona 85012

THE RENEGADE: A STRATEGY JOURNAL OF INDIAN OPINION
P.O. Box 719
Tacoma, Washington 98401
  (206) 456-2567

Published annually.

REPORTER
United Indian Development Association
1541 Wilshire Blvd., Suite 418
Los Angeles, California 90017-2269
  (213) 483-1460

The journal of American Indian business. Published quarterly.

RISING UP
Indian Awareness Group
P.O. Box 1000
Englewood, Colorado 80110

RIVER TRIBES REVIEW
Colorado River Agency
Parker, Arizona 85344

ROCKY BOY'S NATIVE VOICE
Rocky Boy's Health Board
Box Elder, Montana 59521

ROCKY BOY'S NEWS
Rocky Boy's Route
Box Elder, Montana 59521

WILL ROGERS TIMES
Will Rogers Memorial
P.O. Box 157
Claremore, Oklahoma 74018
  (918) 341-0719

ROSEBUD SIOUX HERALD
P.O. Box 65
Rosebud, South Dakota 57570

ROUGH ROCK NEWS
Dine'Biolta'Daahani
Rough Rock Demonstration School
Rough Rock, Arizona 86503

Provides a view of the life-style and attitudes of a desert community that is determined to control its own destiny. Published monthly during academic year.

S

SAC AND FOX NEWS
Route 2, Box 246
Stroud, Oklahoma 74079

ST. CHRISTOPHER'S MISSION
News Center
Bluff, Utah 84512

SAN JUAN COUNTY ARCHAEOLOGICAL RESEARCH CENTER MUSEUM NEWSLETTER
#975 U.S. Highway 64
Farmington, New Mexico 87401
  (505) 632-2013

SANDPAINTER
P.O. Box 791
Chinle, Arizona 86503

**SCHOHARIE MUSEUM OF THE
IROQUOIS INDIAN—MUSEUM NOTES**
P.O. Box 158
Schoharie, New York 12157
(518) 295-8553/234-2276
Dr. John P. Ferguson, Editor

A newsletter reporting on the Museum's activities;
scholarly articles on the Iroquois. *Subscription:*
$10/year. Complimentary copies available upon
request.

THE SCOUT
Episcopal Church
Lower Brule, South Dakota 57548

SCREAMING EAGLE
P.O. Box 715
San Mateo, California 94401

SEALASKA SHAREHOLDER
Sealaska Corporation
One Sealaska Plaza, #400
Juneau, Alaska 99801
Ross Soboleff, Editor

SEE YAHTSUB
Maryville, Washington 98270

THE SEMINOLE TRIBUNE
Seminole Tribe
6333 N.W. 30th St.
Hollywood, Florida 33024
(305) 583-7112 ext. 346
Twila Perkins and Barbara Billie, Editors

Provides news about the Seminole Tribe; also,
news about other tribes across the country.
Advertising. Published biweekly. *Subscription:*
$15/year.

THE SENTINEL
National Congress of American Indians
804 D St., N.E.
Washington, D.C. 20002
(202) 546-9704

A quarterly newsletter which reports on the
activities of the Congress.

SHENANDOAH NEWSLETTER
133 East Wisconsin Ave.
Appleton, Wisconsin 54911
(414) 734-6189
Paul A. Skenandore (Scandoa),
Editor/Reporter

A 21-page monthly on Native American history.
"To show the legal arguments to be used against
the U.S.A." *Subscription:* $10/year, individuals;
$15/year, institutions.

SHO-BAN NEWS
Shoshone-Bannock Tribal Council
P.O. Box 306
Fort Hall, Idaho 83203
(208) 238-3887/3888
Laverne Sheppard, Editor

Weekly tribal newspaper. Classified advertising,
Subscription: $10/year; 25¢ each.
Complimentary copies available upon request.

SILETZ NEWSLETTER
Confederated Tribes of Siletz Indians
P.O. Box 549
Siletz, Oregon 97380

THE SINGING SANDS
Ramah Navajo High School
Ramah, New Mexico 87351

THE SINGING WINDS NEWSLETTER
Council of Three Rivers
American Indian Center, Inc.
200 Charles St.
Pittsburgh, Pennsylvania 15238
(412) 782-4457
Russell Simms, Executive Director

Published monthly.

**SINTE GLESKA
COLLEGE NEWSLETTER**
Rosebud, South Dakota 57570

SIOUX JOURNAL
Cheyenne River Sioux Tribal Council
P.O. Box 590
Eagle Butte, South Dakota 57625

SIOUX MESSENGER
Yankton Sioux Tribe
Route 3
Wagner, South Dakota 57380

SIOUX SAN SUN
PHS Indian Hospital
Rapid City, South Dakota 57701

SISSETON AGENCY NEWS
Bureau of Indian Affairs
Sisseton, South Dakota 57262

SLEEPING RED GIANT
Community Services
Sacaton, Arizona 85347

SMOKE DREAMS
Riverside High School
Anadarko, Oklahoma 73005

SMOKE SIGNALS
Baltimore Indian Center
113 South Broadway
Baltimore, Maryland 21231

SMOKE SIGNALS
Bacone College
Muskogee, Oklahoma 74401

SMOKE SIGNALS
National Council of Bureau of
Indian Affairs Educators
P.O. Box 5
Tuba City, Arizona 86045
(602) 283-4211/5968 ext. 252

SMOKE SIGNALS
Colorado River Indian Tribes
Route 1, Box 23-B
Parker, Arizona 85344

SMOKE SIGNALS
Confederated Tribes of the Grande Ronde
Indian Community
P.O. Box 94
Grand Ronde, Oregon 97347
(503) 879-5253

SMOKE SIGNALS
Route 2, Box 400
Odanah, Wisconsin 54806

SMOKE TALK
Brotherhood of American Indians
P.O. Box 500
Steilacoom, Washington 98388

**SMOKI CEREMONIALS
AND SNAKE DANCE**
Smoki People, P.O.Box 123
Prescott, Arizona 86302
(602) 778-5228

Published annually.

SOTA-EYE-YE-YAPI
P.O. Box 241
Sisseton, South Dakota 57262

SOUTH DAKOTA HISTORY
South Dakota State Historical Society
800 North Illinois
Pierre, South Dakota 57501-2294
(605) 773-3615
Nancy Tystad Koupal, Editor

A scholarly journal inviting scholarly articles,
edited documents, and other annotated,
unpublished primary materials that contribute to
the knowledge of the history of South Dakota and
the surrounding region. Book reviews. Published
quarterly. *Subscription:* $10/year, membership.

**SOUTHEASTERN CHEROKEE
CONFEDERACY, INC. NEWS**
National Tribal Office
Route 1, Box 111
Leesburg, Georgia 31763
(912) 436-9040

A four-page bimonthly newsletter.

**THE SOUTHERN INDIAN HEALTH
COUNCIL, INC. NEWSLETTER**
P.O. Box 20889
El Cajon, California 92021
(619) 561-3700

Published six times per year.

**SOUTHERN PUEBLOS
AGENCY BULLETIN**
Bureau of Indian Affairs
1000 Indian School Rd., NW
Albuquerque, New Mexico 87103

SOUTHERN UTE DRUM
P.O. Box 737, Tribal Affairs Bldg.
Ignacio, Colorado 81137

**SOUTHWEST ASSOCIATION ON
INDIAN AFFAIRS NEWSLETTER**
P.O. Box 1964
Santa Fe, New Mexico 87501

**SOUTHWEST RESOURCE AND
EVALUATION NEWSLETTER**
National Indian Training Research Center
2121 South Mill Ave., Suite 218
Tempe, Arizona 85282

**SOUTHWESTERN ASSOCIATION OF
INDIAN AFFAIRS, INC. QUARTERLY**
Roswell Printing Company
110 North Pennsylvania
Roswell, New Mexico 88201

SOUTHWESTERN LORE
Colorado Archaeological Society, Inc.
P.O. Box 36217
Denver, Colorado 80236
(303) 236-8675
Ann M. Johnson, Ph.D., Editor
Oayson D. Sheets, Ph.D., Book Review Editor

A scientific journal covering the Rocky Mountain
and high Plains region research on archaeological
sites and related subjects. Published quarterly.
Subscription: Annual membership,
$10/individuals; $15/institutions.

SPAWING THE MEDICINE RIVER
Institute of American Indian Arts Museum
1369 Cerrillos Rd.
Santa Fe, New Mexico 87501
(505) 988-6281

Published quarterly.

SPEAKING LEAVES
American Indian Cultural Group
P.O. Box 2000
Vacaville, California 95688

SPEAKING OF OURSELVES
NI-MI-KWA-ZOO-MIN
Minnesota Chippewa Tribe
P.O. Box 217
Cass Lake, Minnesota 56633

SPECTRUM PRESS
Anchorage Community College
2533 Providence Ave.
Anchorage, Alaska 99504

SPILYAY RYMOO
P.O. Box 735
Warm Springs, Oregon 97761

THE SQUAW'S MESSAGE
Sisterhood of American Indians
P.O. Box 17
Big Harbor, Washington 98335

SQUOL - QUOL
Lummi Tribal Office
P.O. Box 309
Marietta, Washington 98268

STANDING ROCK STAR
P.O. Box 483
Fort Yates, North Dakota 58538

STEALING OF CALIFORNIA
Native American Training Association Institute
P.O. Box 1505
Sacramento, California 95807

STOCKBRIDGE MUNSEE
TRIBAL NEWSLETTER
RR 1
Bowler, Wisconsin 54416

STOWW INDIAN VOICE
P.O. Box 578
Sumner, Washington 98390

THE SUN CHILD
Missoula Qua Qui Corporation
401 East Railroad
Missoula, Montana 59801
(406) 721-4494

The only national Indian children's magazine. Published weekly during the school year (30 weeks.)

SUNDEVIL ROUNDUP
Rough Rock Comunity High School
Star Route 1
Rough Rock, Arizona 85021

SURFACE SCATTER
Marin Museum of the American Indian
P.O. Box 864, 2200 Novato Blvd.
Novato, California 94947
(415) 897-4064

Qaurterly newsletter.

SURVIVAL NEWS
American Indian Movement (AIM)
1209 Fourth St., S.E.
Minneapolis, Minnesota 55414
(612) 331-8862

Published quarterly.

T

TA NEWSLETTER OF UIATF
Daybreak Star Press
P.O. Box 99253
Seattle, Washington 98199

TALKING LEAF NEWSPAPER
3460 East Olympic Blvd.
Los Angeles, California 90023
(213) 265-0769
Mike Burgess, Managing Editor
George Howell, Operations Editor
Robert Melson, Circulation Manager

Monthly American Indian newspaper providing news of North American Indian people written for, by and about Native Americans; also, news of Los Angeles County area. Microfilm. *Subscription:* $10/year, $15/two years; foreign, $13/year, $20/two years.

TALKING PEACEPIPE
Southeast Michigan Indians, Inc.
P.O. Box 861
Warren, Michigan 48090
(313) 756-1350

Monthly newsletter. Advertising.
Subscription: $3/year.

TEEPEE TALK
P.O. Box 501
Portersville, California 93258

TEMIPITE TOPICS
P.O. Box 5396
Fresno, California 93755

TEQUESTA TALK
Museum of Archaeology
100A South New River Dr.
Fort Lauderdale, Florida 33301
(305) 765-5964

Monthly newsletter.

THEATA
Cross Cultural Communications Department
University of Alaska, Alaskan Native Program
Fairbanks, Alaska 99708
(907) 474-7181
Pat Kwachka, Editor

Alaskan Native college students writing on
traditional and contemporary topics.

THE THUNDERER
American Indian Bible Institute
100020 North 15th Ave.
Phoenix, Arizona 85021

TI SWANNI ITST
Skokomish Indian Tribal Center
Route 5, Box 432
Shelton, Washington 98584

THE TIMES
P.O. Box 450
Farmington, Minnesota 87401

TLIN TSIM HAI
Ketchikan Indian Corporation
P.O. Box 6855
Ketchikan, Alaska 99901

TLINGIT/HAIDA TRIBAL NEWS
Tlingit/Haida Central Council
320 West Willoughby Ave. #300
Juneau, Alaska 99801
(312) 784-1050

TODD COUNTY TRIBUNE AND EYAPAH
Mission, South Dakota 57555

TOMAHAWK
Oregon State University
P.O. Box 428
Warm Springs, Oregon 97761

TONAWANDA INDIAN NEWS
P.O. Box 64, Bloomingdale Rd.
Akron, New York 14001

TRAIL BLAZER
Cook Inlet Native Association
670 West Fireweed Lane
Anchorage, Alaska 99503
(907) 278-4641

Quarterly newsletter.

TREATY COUNCIL NEWS
International Indian Treaty Council
777 UN Plaza, Room 10F
New York, New York 10017
(212) 986-6000

Published monthly.

TRIBAL DIRECTORY
Arizona Commission on Indian Affairs
1645 West Jefferson
Phoenix, Arizona 85007

**TRIBAL PEOPLES
SURVIVAL NEWSLETTER**
P.O. Box 7082
Albuquerque, New Mexico 87194

TRIBAL SPOKESMAN
Inter-Tribal Council of California
1314 H St. #100
Sacramento, California 95814-1999

TRIBAL TRAILES
911 Franklin St.
Petosky, Michigan 49770

TRIBAL TRIBUNE
Colville Tribe, P.O. Box 150
Nespelem, Washington 99155

**TSA' ASZI'
MAGAZINE OF NAVAJO CULTURE**
Tsa'Aszi Graphics Center
Ramah Navajo School Board
CPO Box 12, Pine Hill
Pine Hill, New Mexico 87321

TSISTSISTAS PRESS
P.O. Box 552
Birney, Montana 59012

TUMBLEWOOD CONNECTION
The College of Ganada
Ganado, Arizona 86505

TUNDRA DRUMS
P.O. Box 468
Bethel, Alaska 99559

THE TUNDRA TIMES
P.O. Box 104480
Anchorage, Alaska 99510-4480

TURTLE
Native American Center for Living Arts
25 Rainbow Mall
Niagara Falls, Ne York 14801

TURTLE MOUNTAIN ECHOES
P.O. Box 432
Belcourt, North Dakota 58516

TURTLE TALK
45 Lexington, N.W.
Grand Rapids, Michigan 49504

U

UMATILLA AGENCY NEWSLETTER
Bureau of Indian Affairs
P.O. Box 520
Pendleton, Oregon 97801

**UNISHENABIG ENWAYWON
INDIAN NEWS**
3202 Oswego Ave.
Fort Wayne, Indiana 46805

**UNITED INDIAN DEVELOPMENT
ASSOCIATION REPORTER**
1541 Wilshire Blvd., Suite 418
Los Angeles, California 90017-2269
   (213) 483-1460

The voice of American Indian business. Quarterly
journal.

**UNITED INDIANS OF ALL TRIBES
FOUNDATION—TA NEWSLETTER**
Daybreak Star Press
P.O. Box 99253
Seattle, Washington 98199

UNITED LUMBEE NATION TIMES
United Lumbee Nation of
North Carolina and America
P.O. Box 512
Fall River Mills, California 96028
   (916) 336-6701
   Silver Star Reed, Editor

Tribal newspaper with articles and information
concerning members of the Lumbee Nation of
Indians. Published quarterly. Advertising.
Subscription: $4/year; $1.00 each.
Complimentary copies available upon request.

UNITED SIOUX TRIBES NEWS
P.O. Box 1193
Pierre, South Dakota 57501

**UNITED TRIBES OF
NORTH DAKOTA NEWSLETTER**
3315 South Airport Rd.
Bismarck, North Dakota 58501

**UNITED TRIBES OF
SOUTH DAKOTA NEWSLETTER**
P.O. Box 1193
Pierre, South Dakota 57501

**UNIVERSITY OF MINNESOTA
DEPARTMENT OF AMERICAN INDIAN
STUDIES NEWSLETTER**
West Bank Campus, 1314 Social Sciences Bldg.
Minneapolis, Minnesota 55455

**UNIVERSITY OF SOUTH
DAKOTA BULLETIN**
Institute of Indian Studies
Vermillion, South Dakota 57069

THE USET CALUMET
1101 Kermit Dr., Suite 800
Nashville, Tennessee 37212

UTAH INDIAN JOURNAL
Division of Indian Affairs
University of Utah
Salt Lake City, Utah 84112

UTAH INDIAN NEWS
21 East Kelsey
Salt Lake City, Utah 84111

UTE BULLETIN
Ute Indian Tribe
Fort Duchesne, Utah 84026

UTKEGVIK NATCHIK
Barrow Junior High School
Barrow, Alaska 99723

V

VALLEY ROUND UP
Shoshone-Paiute Business Council
P.O. Box 219
Owyhee, Nevada 89832

THE VOICE OF BROTHERHOOD
423 Seward St.
Juneau, Alaska 99801

VOICE OF THUNDER
Amerine Enterprises
P.O. Box 238
Carlin, Nevada 89822

W

WABANAKI ALLIANCE
Indian Resource Center
95 Main St.
Orono, Maine 04473

WAMIDIOTA NEWSLETTER
Fort Lewis College
Division of Intercultural Studies
120 Miller Student Center
Durango, Colorado 81301

**WANBLI HO:
A LITERARY ARTS JOURNAL**
Lakota Studies/Creative Writing Program
Sinte Gleska College, P.O. Box 8
Mission, South Dakota 57555
   Victor Douville, Editor

Features short fiction, poetry, literary articles,
oral tradition texts, and artwork. Focuses on
contemporary and traditional Native-American
literature and art. Published twice a year.
Subscription: $7.50/year; $4.50 each issue.

WARPATH
7787 Earl Court
El Cerrito, California 94530

THE WARRIOR
American Indian Center
1630 West Wilson
Chicago, Illinois 60640

THE WASHINGTON NEWSPAPER
3833 Stone Way, North
Seattle, Washington 98103

WASSO-GEE-WAD-NEE
Council—Marquette Branch Prison
P.O. Box 779
Marquette, Michigan 49855

WE SA MI DONG
Route 2
Hayward, Wisconsin 54843

WHISPERING WINDS
Tule River Tribal Council
Porterville, California 93258

WHITE EARTH RESERVATION NEWS
P.O. Box 274
White Earth, Minnesota 56591

**WHITE MOUNTAIN
APACHE NEWSPAPER**
P.O. Box 700
White River, Arizona 85941

WHITE MOUNTAIN EAGLE
P.O. Box 678
Show Low, Arizona 85901

WI GUABA
Havasupai Tribal Council
P.O. Box 10
Supai, Arizona 86435

WIG-I-WAM
Department of Indian Work
Minnesota Council of Churches
3045 Park Ave. South
Minneapolis, Minnesota 55407

WIGWAM CLUB MONTHLY
Greater Minneapolis Council of Churches
122 West Franklin Ave.
Minneapolis, Minnesota 55404

WIN-A-WAENEN-NISITOTUNG
Saulte Ste. Marie Tribe of Chippewa Indians
206 Greenough
Sault Ste. Marie, Michigan 49783
  (906) 635-6050
  Susan Matrious and Leslie Eger, Editors

Monthly newspaper containing local and some
national news; photographs and written features.
Advertising. *Subscription:* $7/year.
Complimentary copies available upon request.

WIND RIVER JOURNAL
Shoshone Tribe, P.O. Box 157
Fort Washakie, Wyoming 82514

WIND RIVER RENDEZVOUS
St. Stephan's Mission
St. Stephan, Wyoming 82524

WINNEBAGO INDIAN NEWS
Winnebago Tribal Council
Winnebago, Nebraska 68071

WINNEBAGO NEWS
Creamery News, Route 1
Nekossa, Wisconsin 54457

WOPEEDAM
Immaculate Conception Mission
Stephan, South Dakota 57346

WOTANIN-WOWAPI
Williston Herald
P.O. Box 1447
Williston, North Dakota 58802

WONTANIN WOWAPI
P.O. Box 493
Poplar, Montana 59255

**WYOMING INDIAN
HIGH SCHOOL NEWSLETTER**
P.O. Box 145
Ethete, Wyoming 82520

Y

YAKIMA DRUMBEAT
P.O. Box 31
Toppenish, Washington 98948

YAKIMA NATION REVIEW
Yakima Indian Nation
P.O. Box 386
Toppenish, Washington 98948-0386
  (509) 865-5121
  Ronn L. Washines, Editor

Contains articles pertaining to and affecting
Indian people, human interest articles involving
Indian population, governmental action on
national, state and local levels relevant to the
Yakima Tribal Government structure.
Advertising. Published biweekly. *Subscription:*
$15/year. Complimentary copies available upon
request.

YAQUI BULLETIN
4730 West Calle Tetakusin
Tucson, Arizona 85910

YOIDA NAVA
Indian Club, Arizona Western College
Yuma, Arizona 85364

YUGTARVIK REGIONAL
MUSEUM NEWSLETTER
P.O. Box 338
Bethel, Alaska 99559

Published monthly.

Z

ZUNI CARRIER
Zuni Pueblo
Zuni, New Mexico 87327

ZUNI LEGAL AID NEWSLETTER
Zuni, New Mexico 87327

ZUNI TRIBAL NEWSLETTER
Box 339, Zuni Tribal Office
Zuni, New Mexico 87327

CANADA

THE ALLIANCE JOURNAL
838 - 3rd Ave.
Val D'or, Quebec J9P 1T1
  (819) 825-5753

ANTHROPOLOGICAL JOURNAL
OF CANADA
Anthropological Association of Canada
1575 Forlan Dr.
Ottawa, Ontario K2C 0R8

ASSOCIATION FOR NATIVE
DEVELOPMENT IN THE PERFORMING
AND VISUAL ARTS NEWSLETTER
27 Carlton St., Suite 208
Toronto, Ontario M5B 1L2

BRITISH COLUMBIA AND
YUKON NEWSLETTER
303 - 325 Granville St.
Vancouver 2, British Columbia

BROTHER OF TIME
Native Brotherhood of Millhaven
P.O. Box 280
Bath, Ontario K0H 1G0

CANADIAN HISTORICAL ASSOCIATION
NEWSLETTER/BULLETIN
395 Wellington St.
Ottawa, Ontario K1A 0N3

CANADIAN INDIAN ARTCRAFTS
National Indian Arts and Crafts Corporation
350 Slater St.
Ottawa, Ontario K1R 5B7

Published quarterly.

CANADIAN JOURNAL
OF ANTHROPOLOGY
Department of Anthropology
University of Alberta
Edmonton, Alberta T6G 2H4

CANADIAN JOURNAL

Department of Anthropology
University of Victoria
Victoria, British Columbia V8W 2Y2

CANADIAN JOURNAL
OF NATIVE EDUCATION
University of Alberta—
Publications Services
4 - 116 Education North
Edmonton, Alberta T6G 2G5

CANADIAN JOURNAL
OF NATIVE STUDIES
1229 Lorne Ave.
Brandon, Manitoba R7A 0V3

CANADIAN NATIVE FRIENDSHIP
CENTER NEWSLETTER
EDMONTON NATIVE NEWS
10176 - 177 St.
Edmonton, Alberta T5T 0P1

CANADIAN NATIVE LAW REPORTER
Native Law Centre
University of Saskatchewan
Room 141, Diefenbaker Centre
Saskatoon, Saskatchewan S7N 0W0
  (306) 966-6189
  Zandra MacEachern, Editor

A specialized law report series, providing full,
comprehensive coverage of native law judgements
in Canada. Research features: subject index,
statutes judicially considered; year end
cumulative indexes; articles and case comments.
Advertising. Published quarterly (March, June,
September and December.) *Subscription:*
$45/year (1986). Back issues: 1984-1985,
$45/year; 1979-1983, $30/year.

ELBOW DRUMS
Calgary Indian Friendship Society
140 - 2nd Ave., S.W.
Calgary 1, Alberta

ESKIMO
P.O. Box 10
Churchill, Manitoba R0B E0E

ETHNIC DIRECTORY OF CANADA
Western Publishers
P.O. Box 30193, Station "B"
Calgary, Alberta
  (403) 289-3301
  Vladimir Markotic, Editor

ETUDES/INUIT/STUDIES
Inuksiutiit Katimajiit Association
Department of Anthropology, Laval University
Quebec, Quebec G1K 7P4
  (418) 656-2353
  Francois Therien, Editor

Contains articles in French and English on the
Inuit culture, language and history of Siberia,
Greenland, and Canada. Book reviews.
Advertising. Published twice annually.
Subscription: $8/year, students; $14/year,
individuals; $20/year, institutions. Back issues
available, $8 each.

THE FIRST CITIZEN
P.O. Box 760, Station A
Vancouver, British Columbia

THE FORGOTTEN PEOPLE
170 Laurier West, 5th Floor
Ottawa, Ontario K1P 5V5
  (613) 238-3511

HA-SHILTH-SA
P.O. Box 1225
Port Alberni, British Columbia V9Y 7M1
  (604) 724-2822

HOLMAN ESKIMO PRINTS
Canadian Arctic Producers Limited
P.O. Box 4132. Postal Station E
Ottawa, Ontario K1S 5S2

INDIAN BROTHERHOOD NEWS
615 Blundell Rd.
Richmond, British Columbia V7C 1H6

INDIAN ECHO
Canadian Department of Justice
Penitentiary Branch
Ottawa, Ontario

INDIAN—ESKIMO
ASSOCIATION BULLETIN
277 Victoria St.
Toronto 2, Ontario

INDIAN FREE PRESS N'AMERIND
London's Indian Friendship Centre
613 Wellington St.
London, Ontario

INDIAN LIFE
Intertribal Christian Communications
P.O. Box 3765, Station B
Winnipeg, Manitoba R2W 3R6
  (204) 661-9333
  George McPeek, Editor

Contains first person stories, legends with
Christian applications; general interest stories
written by Native people from a Christian
perspective. Published bimonthly. $5/year.

INDIAN AND INUIT
GRADUATE REGISTER
Canada Department of Indian Affairs
and Northern Affairs
400 Laurier Ave. West
Ottawa, Ontario K1A 0H4

INDIAN MAGAZINE NEWSLETTER
Canadian Broadcasting Company, Publishers
P.O. Box 500, Station A
Toronto 116, Ontario

INDIAN NEWS
Canada Department of Indian Affairs
and Northern Development
400 Laurier Ave. West
Ottawa, Ontario K1A 0H4

INDIAN OUTLOOK
Federation of Saskatchewan Indians
P.O. Box 886
Regina, Saskatchewan

INDIAN RECORD
480 Aulneau St.
Winnipeg, Manitoba R2H 2V2
  (204) 233-6430
  Rev. G. Laviolette, OMI, Editor

Contains articles on the Canadian Indians from
coast to coast. Published four times per year.
Advertising. *Subscription:* $4/year, $7/two years,
$10/three years.

THE INDIAN VOICE
Canadian Indian Voice Society
429 East 6th St. North
Vancouver, British Columbia V7L 1P8
  (604) 876-0944

INDIAN WORLD MAGAZINE
Union of British Columbia Indian Chiefs
440 West Hastings, 3rd Floor
Vancouver, British Columbia V6B 1L1
  (604) 684-0231

INDIANS OF QUEBEC
c/o Coalition of Nations
P.O. Box 810
Caughnawaga, Quebec J0L 1B0
  (514) 632-7321

INUIT TODAY
176 Gloucester St., Third Floor
Ottawa, Ontario K2P 0A6
  (613) 238-8181

INUKTITUT
Canada Department of Indian Affairs
and Northern Development
400 Laurier Ave. West
Ottawa, Ontario K1A 0H4

INUVIALUIT
Committee for Original People's Entitlement
P.O. Box 200
Inuvik, Northwest Territory X0E 0T0

KAINAI NEWS
P.O. Box 58
Standoff, Alberta T0L 1Y0
(403) 737-3784/3785

KATERI-EDITION-FRANCAISE
C.P. 70
Caughnawaga, Quebec J0L 1B0

LE METIS
Manitoba Metis Federation
301 - 374 Donald St.
Winnipeg, Manitoba R3B 2J2

LONGHOUSE NEWS
P.O. Box 1
Kanonsonnionwe Ksahnawake Branch of Six
Nations
Caughnawaga, Quebec J0L 1B0

MANITOBA INDIAN NEWS
807 - 191 Lombard Ave.
Winnipeg 2, Manitoba

METIS NEWSLETTER
12750 - 127 St.
Edmonton, Alberta T5L 1A5

MICMAC NEWS
Nova Scotia Native Communications Society
P.O. Box 344
Sydney, Nova Scotia B1P 6H2

THE MIDDEN
Archaeological Society of British Columbia
P.O. Box 520, Station A
Vancouver, British Columbia V6C 2N3

  Kathryn Bernick, Editor

Contains articles, book reviews, news items
related to British Columbia archaeology—
prehistoric and historic periods. Published five
times per year. *Subscription:* $10/year; $12/year,
overseas.

MIDNIGHT SUN
c/o Settlement Council
Igloolik, Northwest Territory X0E 0L0

MIRAMICHI NEWS
Miramichi Indian Agency
P.O. Box 509
Chatham, New Brunswick

MOCCASIN TELEGRAPH
c/o Saskatchewan Indians
1030 Idylwyld Dr.
Saskatoon, Saskatchewan S7K 3S9

THE NATIONAL INDIAN
102 Bank St., Bankal Bldg., 1st Floor
Ottawa, Ontario K1P 5N4
(613) 236-0673

NATIONAL INDIAN BROTHERHOOD
Varette Bldg., Suite 1610
130 Albert St.
Ottawa, Ontario K1P 5G4

NATIVE ALLIANCE FOR RED POWER
P.O. Box 6152
Vancouver, British Columbia

NATIVE BROTHERHOOD NEWS
P.O. Box 60
Mission, British Columbia V2Y 4L1

NATIVE BROTHERHOOD NEWSCALL
Saskatchewan Pentitentiary
P.O. Box 160
Prince Albert, Saskatchewan S6V 5R6

NATIVE ISSUES
Native Peoples Support Group
of Newfoundland and Labrador
P.O. Box 582, Station C
St. John's, Newfoundland A1C 5K8

THE NATIVE PEOPLE
Alberta Native Communications Society
9331 - 60 Ave.
Edmonton, Alberta T6E 0C2
(403) 437-0580

THE NATIVE PERSPECTIVE
200 Cooper St., Suite 2
Ottawa, Ontario K2P 9Z9

NATIVE PRESS
Indian Brotherhood of the Northwest Territory
P.O. Box 2338
Yellowknife, Northwest Territory X0E 1H0
(403) 873-2661/2662

THE NATIVE SISTERHOOD
P.O. Box 515
Kingston, Ontario K7L 4W7

NATIVE TIMES
Canadian Indian Center of Toronto
210 Beverly St.
Toronto 130, Ontario

NESIKA
United Native Nations
1451 Broadway, #201
Vancouver, British Columbia V6H 1H6

THE NEW NATION
P.O. Box 5
Thompson, Manitoba R8N 1M9
(204) 778-7279/8385

NEWS AND VIEWS
Canada Department of Indian Affairs
and Northern Development
10 Wellington
Ottawa, Ontario K1A 0H4

NICOLA INDIAN
Nicola Valley Indian Administration
P.O. Box 188
Merritt, British Columbia V0K 2B0
  (604) 378-6441/4235

THE NORTHIAN
University of Saskatchewan
Saskatoon, Saskatchewan S7N 0W0

ONTARIO ARCHAEOLOGIST
Ontario Archaeological Society
P.O. Box 241, Station P
Toronto, Ontario M5S 2S8

ONTARIO INDIAN
Union of Ontario Indians
27 Queen St. East
Toronto, Ontario M5C 1R5
  (416) 366-3527

Published monthly.

ONTARIO NATIVE EXAMINER
United Indians of Ontario
145 Yonge St., 19th Floor
Toronto 1, Ontario

ONTARIO NATIVE EXPERIENCE
Ontario Federation of Friendship Centres
234 Eglington Ave., East, Suite 203
Toronto, Ontario M4P 1K5

**ONTARIO NATIVE WOMEN'S
ASSOCIATION NEWSLETTER**
278 Bay St.
Thunder Bay, Ontario

PHOENIX NEWSLETTER
Canadian Alliance in Solidarity
With the Native Peoples
16 Spadina Rd.
Toronto, Ontario M5R 2S7
  (416) 964-0169

Published quarterly.

**SASKATCHEWAN ARCHAEOLOGICAL
SOCIETY NEWSLETTER**
c/o Saskatchewan Museum
Wascona Park, Saskatchewan S4S 0B3

SASKATCHEWAN INDIAN
P.O. Box 1644
Prince Albert, Saskatchewan S6V 4V6

SASKATCHEWAN INDIAN
P.O. Box 3085
Saskatoon, Saskatchewan S7K 3SP
  (306) 244-1146

THE SCOUT
Indian-Metis Friendship Centre
Brandon Friendship Centre
836 Lorne Ave.
Brandon, Manitoba R7A 0TB

TAQRALIK
Northern Quebec Inuit Association
P.O. Box 179
Fort Chimo, Quebec J0M 1C0

THE TALKING LEAVES
Native Brotherhood Association
P.O. Box 880
Kingston, Ontario

TAWOW
Canada Department of Indian Affairs
and Northern Development
400 Laurier Ave. West #802
Ottawa, Ontario K1A 0H4

**TEKAWENMAKE SIX NATIONS
NEW CREDIT REPORTER**
Woodland Indian Cultural Education Center
184 Mohawk St., Box 1506
Brantford, Ontario N3T 5V6
  (519) 753-5531

TORONTO NATIVE TIMES
16 Spadina Rd.
Toronto, Ontario M5R 2S8
  (416) 964-9087

TREATY No. 3 COUNCIL FIRE
37 Main St. South
Kenora, Ontario P9N 1S8

TRENT NATIVE NEWS
Department of Native Studies
Trent University
Petersborough, Ontario K9J 7B7

TRIBAL INDIAN NEWS N'AMERIND
London's Indian Friendship Centre
613 Wellington St.
London, Ontario

UNION OF ONTARIO INDIANS
3028 Danforth Ave., 2nd Floor
Toronto, Ontario M4C 1N2

WAWATAY NEWS
P.O. Box 1180, 34 Front St.
Sioux Lookout, Ontario P0V 2T0
  (807) 737-2951

WINNIPEG INDIAN TIMES
Indian and Metis Friendship Centre
73 Princess St.
Winnipeg 3, Manitoba

YUKON INDIAN NEWS
Yeja To Communications Society
22 Nisutlin Dr.
Whitehorse, Yukon Territory Y1A 1C5

BIBLIOGRAPHY

This section contains an alphabetical listing of approximately 3,500 in-print books about or relating to Indians of North America. In each listing, the reader will find—where sufficient material has been provided—the title, author or editor, information on pagination, whether illustrated, indexed, etc., name of publisher, the year of publications, and price. The address of the publishers are contained in the *Publishers Index*. An asterisk (*) preceding a title indicates it is of primarily juvenile or young adult interest; the specific age group for which such titles are intended has been noted, if available. If you require material on a particular subject or interest area, refer to the subject listings in the *Subject Classifications* section, located at the end of this section.

A

THE ABNAKIS AND THEIR HISTORY
E. Vetromile
Reprint of 1866 edition. AMS, $22.50.

ABORIGINAL CHIPPED STONE IMPLEMENTS OF NEW YORK
William M. Beauchamp
Reprint of 1897 edition. AMS, $14.50.

ABORIGINAL AND HISTORIC GROUPS OF THE UTE INDIANS OF UTAH: AN ANALYSIS
Julian H. Steward
121 pp. Clearwater, 1973. $39.00.

ABORIGINAL INDIAN BASKETRY
Otis T. Mason
Reprint of 1973 edition. Illus. 640 pp. Rio Grande, $32.50.

ABORIGINAL LAND USE AND OCCUPANCY OF THE PIMA-MARICOPA INDIANS
Robert A. Hackenberg
Two volumes. 634 pp. Clearwater, 1973. $177.00 per set.

ABORIGINAL LOCATION OF THE KADOHADCHO AND RELATED INDIAN TRIBES IN ARKANSAS AND LOUISIANA, 1542-1954
Stephen Williams
60 pp. Clearwater, 1974. $27.00.

ABORIGINAL MONUMENTS OF THE STATE OF NEW YORK
E.B. Squier
Reprint of 1849 edition. Illus. 200 pp. Sourcebook, $18.95.

ABORIGINAL OCCUPATION OF NEW YORK
William M. Beauchamp
Reprint of 1900 edition. AMS, $22.00.

ABORIGINAL PREHISTORY IN NEW ENGLAND: AN ARCHAEOLOGICAL SURVEY OF NORTHEASTERN NEW SOUTH WALES
Isabel McBryde
Illus. 400 pp. International Specialized Books, 1974. $45.00.

ABORIGINAL REMAINS OF TENNESSEE
J. Jones
Reprint of 1880 edition. Illus. 186 pp. Sourcebook, $16.95.

ABORIGINAL SOCIETY IN SOUTHERN CALIFORNIA
W.D. Strong
Reprint of 1929 edition. Paper. Kraus, $51.00.

ABORIGINAL SUBSISTENCE TECHNOLOGY ON THE SOUTHEASTERN COASTAL PLAIN
Lewis H. Larson
University Presses of Florida.

ABORIGINAL TERRITORY OF THE KALISPEL
Stuart A. Chalfant
61 pp. Clearwater, 1974. $27.00.

ABORIGINAL TERRITORY OF THE NEZ PERCE INDIANS
Stuart A. Chalfant
135 pp. Clearwater, 1973. $43.50.

ABORIGINAL USE AND OCCUPANCY OF LANDS WEST OF THE MISSISSIPPI RIVER BY THE OSAGE INDIAN TRIBE: VILLAGE LOCATIONS AND HUNTING TERRITORIES UP TO 1808
Carl H. Chapman
70 pp. Clearwater, 1973. $26.00.

ABORIGINAL USE OF WOOD IN NEW YORK
William M. Beauchamp
Reprint of 1905 edition. AMS, $27.50.

**ABORIGINAL WOMEN,
SACRED AND PROFANE**
Phyllis M. Kaberry
Gordon Press, $69.95.

THE ABORIGINES OF SOUTH DAKOTA
Charles E. Deland
Reprint of 1906 edition. AMS, $30.00.

**ABSALOKA:
CROW CHILDREN'S WRITING**
Paper. Council for Indian Education, 1971. 75¢.

ABSARAKA: HOME OF THE CROWS
Margaret I. Carrington
Illus. 285 pp. University of Nebraska Press, 1983.
$21.50; paper, $6.95.

AB-SA-RA-KA; OR, WYOMING OPENED
M.I. Carrington
The experience of an officer's wife on the Plains
with an Outline of Indian Operations and
Conferences Since 1865. Reprint of 1896 edition.
Kraus, $28.00.

**ABSENTEE DELAWARE TRIBE OF
OKLAHOMA AND DELAWARE TRIBE,
1856-1857: APPRAISAL OF LAND
IN NORTHEASTERN KANSAS:
A PART OF ROYCE AREA 316**
Richard B. Hall
140 pp. Clearwater, 1973. $45.00.

**ACCOUNT OF AN EXPEDITION FROM
PITTSBURGH TO THE ROCKY
MOUNTAINS, PERFORMED IN
THE YEARS 1819 & 1820**
Edwin James
Reprint of 1823 edition. Two volumes.
Greenwood, $21.75 per set.

**ACCULTURATION AND PERSONALITY
AMONG THE WISCONSIN CHIPPEWA**
Victor Barnouw
Reprint of 1950 edition. Paper. AMS, $19.50.
Kraus, $20.00.

**ACCULTURATION IN
SEVEN INDIAN TRIBES**
Ralph Linton
Reprint. Peter Smith, $10.00.

**ACHEII BAHANE
GRANDFATHER STORIES, Volume II**
Marvin Yellowhair
46 pp. Paper. Navajo Curriculum Press, 1984.
$8.00.

ACOMA
Peter Neill
Paper. Leetes Island Books, 1978. $3.95.

ACOMA
Tryntje V. Seymour
Lime Rock Press. Portfolio, $295.00.

ACOMA GRAMMAR AND TEXTS
W.R. Miller
Reprint of 1965 edition. Paper. University of
California Press, $8.00. Kraus, $15.00.

THE ACOMA INDIANS OF NEW MEXICO
Leslie A. White
Reprint of 1934 edition. Illus. 240 pp.
Rio Grande Press, $20.00.

**ACOMA INDIANS: PAPER FROM THE
BUREAU OF AMERICAN ETHNOLOGY
ANNUAL REPORT FOR 1929-1930**
Leslie White
Reprint of 1934 edition. Illus. 238 pp. Rio Grande
Press, $17.50.

ACOMA-LAGUNA LAND CLAIMS
Florence H. Ellis
318 pp. Clearwater, 1973. $91.50.

**ACOMA LAND UTILIZATION:
AN ETHNOHISTORICAL REPORT**
Robert L. Rands
189 pp. Clearwater, 1973. $57.00.

ACOMA: PUEBLO IN THE SKY
Ward Minge
Illus. 176 pp. Paper. University of New Mexico
Press, 1976. $8.95.

**ACOMA PUEBLO LAND, NEW MEXICO:
APPRAISAL REPORT, 1901-1936**
R.H. Sears
246 pp. Clearwater, 1973. $75.00.

*ACROSS THE TUNDRA
Marjorie Vandervelde
Grades 4-12. Council for Indian Education, 1972.
$5.95; paper, $1.95.

**THE ACT OF UNION BETWEEN THE
EASTERN AND WESTERN CHEROKEES,
THE CONSTITUTION AND AMENDMENTS
AND LAWS OF THE CHEROKEE NATION**
Reprint of 1870 edition. Scholarly Resources,
$12.00.

**ACTS AND RESOLUTIONS OF
INDIAN NATIONS-TRIBAL COUNCILS**
A series of books on laws, treaties and unions
among Indians of certain nations. See Scholarly
Resources for titles and prices.

ACTIONS WITH INDIANS
Dale R. Floyd
Paper. Old Army, 1983. $4.95.

ADAIR'S HISTORY OF THE INDIANS
Samuel Cole Williams, Editor
A source book of the southern Indians: Catawbas,
Cherokees, Creeks, Choctaws, and Chickasaws.
508 pp. Johnson (NC), $20.00.

THE ADENA PEOPLE
William S. Webb and Charles E. Snow
Illus. 390 pp. University of Tennessee Press, 1974. $19.95.

ADVANCING THE FRONTIER, 1830-1860
Grant Foreman
Reprint of 1933 edition. Illus. University of Oklahoma Press, $16.95.

AESTHETICS OF INDIAN FOLK DANCE
P. Baneji
Illus. Humanities Press, 1983. $33.50.

AFRICANS AND CREEKS: FROM THE COLONIAL PERIOD TO THE CIVIL WAR
Daniel F. Littlefield, Jr.
Illus. Greenwood Press, 1979. $29.50.

AFRICANS AND SEMINOLES: FROM REMOVAL TO EMANCIPATION
Daniel F. Littlefield, Jr.
Illus. Greenwood Press, 1977. $19.95.

*AGALIHA': INDIAN SELF-ESTEEM CURRICULUM ACTIVITY BOOK
Indian Developed Curriculum & Publishing Corp.
Encourages Indian students to feel pride in their heritage. Grades 1-8. 62 pp. Daybreak Star Press, $12.95.

THE AGATE BASIN SITE: A RECORD OF THE PALEOINDIAN OCCUPATION OF THE NORTHWESTERN HIGH PLAINS
George Frisom and Dennis Stanford
440 pp. Academic Press, 1982. $74.50.

AGREEMENT WITH YAKIMA NATION OF INDIANS AND A DRAFT OF A BILL TO RATIFY SAME
Secretary of Interior letter to U.S. Senate. Reprint of 1894 edition. 41 pp. Paper. Shorey Publications, $4.00.

THE AGGRESSIONS OF CIVILIZATION: FEDERAL INDIAN POLICY SINCE THE 1880s
Sandra L. Cadwalader and Vine Deloria, Jr., Editors
Illus. 272 pp. Temple University Press, 1984. $29.95.

THE AGRICULTURAL AND HUNTING METHODS OF THE NAVAHO INDIANS
Willard W. Will
Reprint of 1938 edition. AMS, $19.50.

AGRICULTURAL TERRACING IN THE ABORIGINAL NEW WORLD
Robin Donkin
Illus. University of Arizona Press, 1979. $8.50.

AGRICULTURE OF THE HIDATSA INDIANS: AN INDIAN INTERPRETATION
Gilbert L. Wilson
Reprint of 1917 edition. AMS, $24.50.

AK CHIN RESERVATION, PINAL COUNTY, ARIZONA: DECLINE OF GROUND WATER LEVELS
Leonard Halpenny
73 pp. Clearwater, 1973. $44.50.

AKICITA: EARLY PLAINS AND WOODLANDS INDIAN ART FROM THE COLLECTION PF ALEXANDER ACEVEDO
Introduction by Peter Welsh. 51 pp. Southwest Museum, 1983. $9.95.

AKWESASNE HISTORICAL POSTCARDS; PEACEMAKER AND HIAWATHA POSTERS
Akwesasne Museum, 50¢/postcard; 75¢/poster.

ALAAWICH
Judy Arvidson
Malki Museum Press, 1978. $2.00.

ALABADO, A STORY OF OLD CALIFORNIA
Paul Kocher
Franciscan Herald, 1978. $6.95.

ALABAMA AND THE BORDERLANDS: FROM PREHISTORY TO STATEHOOD
Laurence A. Clayton and R. Reid Badger
Illus. 240 pp. University of Alabama Press, 1985. $27.50.

ALABAMA—COUSHATTA (CREEK) INDIANS
Includes other texts. Illus. Garland, $52.00.

ALABAMA—COUSHATTA INDIANS OF TEXAS AND THE COUSHATTA INDIANS OF LOUISIANA, 1540-1855
Daniel Jacobson
150 pp. Clearwater, 1974. $48.00.

ALABAMA AND COUSHATTA TRIBES OF TEXAS: ETHNOHISTORICAL ANALYSIS OF DOCUMENTS
Howard N. Martin
66 pp. Clearwater, 1973. $24.00.

ALABAMA: HISTORICAL REPORT ON THE SALE OF PUBLIC LANDS, 1806-1820
James F. Doster
36 pp. Clearwater, 1974. $21.00.

*ALASKA IN THE DAYS THAT WERE BEFORE
Tanya Hardgrove
Grades 2-10. Paper. Council for Indian Education, 1985. $2.45.

ALASKA NATIVE PREFERENCE IN EMPLOYMENT AND CONTRACTING
Daniel S. Press
Council for Tribal Employment Rights, $33.00.

ALASKA NATIVES AND AMERICAN LAWS
David S. Case
608 pp. University of Alaska Press, 1984. $25.00; paper, $15.00.

ALASKA'S NATIVE PEOPLE
Lael Morgan, Editor
Illus. Paper. Alaska Northwest, 1979. Album style, $24.95.

*ALBUM OF THE AMERICAN INDIAN
Rose Yellow Robe
Grades 4-6. Illus. Paper. Franklin Watts, 1969. $5.90.

ALEUT AND ESKIMO ART: TRADITION AND INNOVATION IN SOUTH ALASKA AND NORTH ALASKA
Dorothy J. Ray
Two volumes. Illus. North, 350 pp.; South, 250 pp. University of Washington Press, $35.00 each.

ALEUT LANGUAGE
R. Geoghgen
Facsimile edition. 169 pp. Shorey, $9.95

ALEUTIAN INDIAN AND ENGLISH DICTIONARY
Charles Lee
Facsimile edition. 23 pp. Shorey Publications.

*ALFORD WATERS
Emanuel Skolnick
Grades 5-adult. Illus. 64 pp. Paper. Dillon Press, 1980. $6.95.

ALGIC RESEARCHERS: COMPRISING INQUIRIES RESPECTING THE MENTAL CHARACTERISTICS OF THE NORTH AMERICAN INDIANS
Henry Schoolcraft
Reprint. Garland Publishing, $80.00.

*ALGONQUIAN INDIANS: AT SUMMER CAMP
June Behrens and Pauline Brower
Grades K-3. Illus. Childrens Press, 1977. $8.65.

*ALGONKIANS OF THE EASTERN WOODLANDS
Claudine Goller
Grades 2-4. Franklin Watts, 1984. $8.90.

THE ALGONQUIANS, THE INDIANS OF THAT PART OF THE NEW WORLD FIRST VISITED BY THE ENGLISH
F. Roy Johnson

In two volumes: Volume 1: *Pre-History and Culture,* 112 pp., 1968. $7.50. Volume 2: *History—Traditions,* 240 pp., 1972. $9.50. Illus. Johnson (NC).

ALLIANCE IN ESKIMO SOCIETY
D.L. Guemple, Editor
University of Washington Press, 1972. $16.50.

*ALMOST BROTHERS
Edna Walker Chandler
Present day life on an Indian reservation. Illus. 128 pp. Grades 3-6. Albert Whitman & Co., 1971.

ALMOST WHITE
Brewton Berry
Illus. Paper. Macmillan, 1969. $1.25.

ALTERNATIVE TO EXTINCTION: FEDERAL INDIAN POLICY AND THE BEGINNINGS OF THE RESERVATION SYSTEM, 1846-1851
Robert A. Trennert, Jr.
Temple University Press, 1975. $16.00.

AMERICAN INDIAN GESTURAL CODE BASED ON UNIVERSAL AMERICAN INDIAN HAND TALK
M. Skelly, Editor
528 pp. Elsevier, 1979. $51.50; paper, $27.50.

AMERICA'S FASCINATING INDIAN HERITAGE
Reaers Digest Editors
Illus. W.W. Norton & Co., Inc., 1979. $17.95.

AMERICAN ANTHROPOLOGICAL ASSOCIATION — MEMOIRS
Deals primarily with North American cultures, scholarly monographs describing the ethnology and archaeology of native peoples. Reprint. Nos. 1-96, 1905-1963. Kraus, $1,426.00; paper, $1,201.00.

AMERICAN EPIC: THE STORY OF THE AMERICAN INDIAN
Alice Marriott and Carol K. Rachlin
Illus. Paper. New American Library, 1970. $1.50.

AMERICAN FOLKLORE SOCIETY MEMOIRS
Monographs recording the beliefs, practices, legends and tales of various peoples throughout the world. Reprint. Volumes 1-51, 1894-1960. Kraus, $1,379.00.

AMERICAN GENESIS: THE AMERICAN INDIAN AND THE ORIGINS OF MODERN MAN
Jeffrey Goodman
Illus. 288 pp. Summit Books, 1981. $11.95.

THE AMERICAN HERITAGE BOOK OF INDIANS
William Brandon
Illus. 424 pp. American Indian Books, $12.98.

THE AMERICAN HERITAGE HISTORY OF THE GREAT WEST
D. Lavender
Westward expansion; Indian wars. Illus. 416 pp. Maps. American Indian Books, $12.98.

THE AMERICAN HERITAGE HISTORY OF THE INDIAN WARS
Robert M. Utley and Wilcomb Washburn
Illus. 352 pp. American Heritage, 1977. $12.95.

*AMERICAN INDIAN
Grades 4-6. Paper. Wonder-Treasure Books, $1.00.

THE AMERICAN INDIAN
Raymond F. Locke, Editor
Paper. Mankind, 1976. $1.75.

AMERICAN INDIAN
Lee F. Harkins, Editor
Reprint. Liveright, 1970. Slipcased, $99.99.

AMERICAN INDIAN AND ALASKA NATIVE NEWSPAPERS AND PERIODICALS, 1826-1924
Daniel Littlefield, Jr. and James Parins
496 pp. Greenwood, 1984. $45.00.

THE AMERICAN INDIAN: THE AMERICAN FLAG
Richard A. Pohrt
Illus. 152 pp. Flint Institute of Arts, $12.50; paper, $7.50

AMERICAN INDIAN ARCHERY
Reginald and Gladys Laubin
Illus. 179 pp. University of Oklahoma Press and American Indian Books, 1980. $16.50.

AMERICAN INDIAN ARCHIVAL MATERIAL: A GUIDE TO HOLDINGS IN THE SOUTHEAST
R. Chepesiuk and A. Shankman, Editors
323 pp. Greenwood, 1982. $45.00.

AMERICAN INDIAN AREAS AND ALASKA NATIVE VILLAGES, 1980
38 pp. Supt. of Documents, 1984. $2.75.

AMERICAN INDIAN ARTIFACT PRICE GUIDES: NORTHWEST COAST
Dennis Eros
Paper. Wallace-Homestead Book Co., $5.00.

AMERICAN INDIAN ARTIFACT WITH JEWELRY PRICE GUIDE
Dennis Eros
Paper. Wallace-Homestead, $5.00.

THE AMERICAN INDIAN AS PARTICIPANT IN THE CIVIL WAR
Annie H. Abel
Reprint of 1919 edition. Johnson Reprint, $22.00.

THE AMERICAN INDIAN, 1492-1976: A CHRONOLOGY AND FACT BOOK
Henry C. Dennis
Second edition. 177 pp. Oceana Publications, 1977. $8.50.

AMERICAN INDIAN COLLECTIONS IN EUROPEAN MUSEUMS AND ARCHIVES
Office of Museum Programs, 1985.

AMERICAN INDIAN COOKING AND HERB CARE
J. Ed Sharpe and Thomas Underwood
Contains dozens of recipes. Illus. 32 pp. Paper. American Indian Books, $3.50.

THE AMERICAN INDIAN CRAFT BOOK
Marz Minor and Nono Minor
Illus. 416 pp. Paper. University of Nebraska Press, 1978. $7.95.

$22.50; paper, $5.50.

AMERICAN INDIAN CRAFT INSPIRATIONS
Alex and Janet D'Amato
Illus. 224 pp. M. Evans & Co., 1972. $7.95.

AMERICAN INDIAN DESIGN AND DECORATION
Leroy H. Appleton
Reprint. Illus. Peter Smith, $16.75.

AMERICAN INDIAN ECOLOGY
Donald J. Hughes
Illus. 228 pp. Texas Western, 1983. $20.00.

AMERICAN INDIAN ECONOMIC DEVELOPMENT
Sam Stanley, Editor
Beresford Book Service, 1978. $44.00.

AMERICAN INDIAN EDUCATION: GOVERNMENT SCHOOLS AND ECONOMIC PROGRESS
Evelyn C. Adams
Reprint of 1964 edition. Ayer Co. Publishers, $14.00.

AMERICAN INDIAN ENERGY RESOURCES AND DEVELOPMENT
Roxanne D. Ortiz, Editor
Includes *Transnational Energy Corporations and American Indian Development*, by Richard Nafziger, and *The Role of Policy in American Indian Mineral Development*, by Lorraine Turner Ruffing. 80 pp. Paper. University of New Mexico, Native American Studies, 1980. $5.00.

AMERICAN INDIAN ENVIRONMENTS: ECOLOGICAL ISSUES IN NATIVE AMERICAN HISTORY
C. Vecsy and R.W. Venables, Editors
Illus. 236 pp. Syracuse University Press, 1980.
$19.50; paper, $9.95.

AMERICAN INDIAN AND ESKIMO AUTHORS
Arlene Hirschfelder, Editor
Lists 389 titles by American Indian and Eskimo authors from 106 tribes. 112 pp. Paper. Interbook, Inc., 1974. $5.00.

AMERICAN INDIAN ETHNOHISTORY
David A. Horr
118 volumes. Illus. Garland, $38.00 each.
$2,400.00 per set.

AMERICAN INDIAN FICTION
Charles R. Larson
208 pp. University of New Mexico Press, 1978.
$14.95.

AMERICAN INDIAN FOOD AND LORE
Carolyn Neithammer
Illus. 195 pp. Paper. Macmillan, 1974. $9.95.

AMERICAN INDIAN FOODS AND VEGETABLES
Harriet L. Smith
Illus. Paper. SSS Publishing, 1982. $3.50.

THE AMERICAN INDIAN FRONTIER
W.C. MacLeod
Reprint of 1928 edition. Dawson & Co., $18.50.

AMERICAN INDIAN HEALTH CAREERS HANDBOOK
Association of American Indian Physicians.

AMERICAN INDIAN HISTORY: A READER IN EARLY CULTURE CONTACT, 1492-1760
Kenneth M. Morrison
American Indian Studies Center.

*THE AMERICAN INDIAN IN AMERICA
Jayne C. Jones
Illus. Grades 5-11. Two volumes: Volume 1, 96 pp.; Volume 2, 104 pp. Lerner Publications, 1973.
$5.95 each.

AMERICAN INDIAN IN ENGLISH LITERATURE OF THE 18th CENTURY
Benjamin H. Bissell
Reprint of 1925 edition. Illus. 225 pp. Shoe String Press, $21.00.

THE AMERICAN INDIAN IN GRADUATE STUDIES: A BIBLIOGRAPHY OF THESES AND DISSERTATIONS
Frederick J. Dockstader

Two volumes. Paper. Museum of the American Indian, 1973. $10.00 each; $18.00 per set.

THE AMERICAN INDIAN IN SHORT FICTION: AN ANNOTATED BIBLIOGRAPHY
Peter G. Beidler and Marion F. Egge
215 pp. Scarecrow Press, 1979. $16.50.

AMERICAN INDIAN IN THE UNITED STATES, PERIOD 1850-1914
Warren K. Moorehead
Facsimile of 1914 edition. Bibliographies Reprint Series. Ayer Co., Publishers, $35.00.

THE AMERICAN INDIAN IN URBAN SOCIETY
J.O. Waddell and O.M. Watson, Editors
Reprint of 1971 edition. Illus. 425 pp. Paper. University Press of America, $15.00.

AMERICAN INDIAN INDEX
Contains more than 6,000 addresses and contacts for American Indian and Alaska Native groups. 325 pp. Arrowstar Publishing, $19.95.

AMERICAN INDIAN AND INDO-EUROPEAN STUDIES: PAPERS IN HONOR OF MADISON S. BELLER
Kathryn Klar, et al, Editors
495 pp. Mouton, 1980. $84.50.

AMERICAN INDIAN INTELLECTUALS: 1976 PROCEEDINGS
Margot Liberty, Editor
Illus. Paper. West Publishing, 1978. $18.95.

AMERICAN INDIAN ISSUES IN HIGHER EDUCATION
206 pp. American Indian Studies Center, 1981.
$14.00.

AMERICAN INDIAN: LANGUAGE AND LITERATURE
Jack W. Marken
Paper. Harlan Davidson, 1978. $14.95.

AMERICAN INDIAN LANGUAGE SERIES
Includes: *Mayan Linguistics,* 267 pp., $5.00; *Hualapai Reference Grammar,* 575 pp., $17.50; and *Chem'ivillu' (Let's Speak Cahuilla),* 316 pp., $17.50. The American Indian Studies Center.

AMERICAN INDIAN LANGUAGES AND AMERICAN LINGUISTICS
Wallace Chafe, Editor
Paper. Humanities Press, 1976. $9.00.

AMERICAN INDIAN LAW IN A NUTSHELL
William C. Canby, Jr.
300 pp. Paper. West Publishing, 1981. $7.95.

THE AMERICAN INDIAN LAW SERIES
A series of seven pamphlets: *Indian Sovereignty; Indian Treaties; Indians and the U.S. Government; Indian Jurisdiction; The Federal Indian Trust Relationship; Indian Water Rights;* and *Introduction to Oil and Gas.* Institute for the Development of Indian Law. $7.00 each; $30.00 per set.

AMERICAN INDIAN LEADERS: STUDIES IN DIVERSITY
R. David Edmunds, Editor
Illus. 271 pp. University of Nebraska Press, 1980. $19.50; paper, $5.95.

AMERICAN INDIAN LEGAL MATERIALS: A UNION LIST
Laura N. Gasaway, et al
E.M. Coleman, 1980. $49.50.

AMERICAN INDIAN LIFE
Elsie C. Parsons, Editor
Illus. University of Nebraska Press, 1967. $28.95; paper, $6.95.

AMERICAN INDIAN LINGUISTICS
Ten volumes. See Garland Publishing for title names and prices.

AMERICAN INDIAN LITERATURE: AN ANTHOLOGY
Alan R. Velie
Illus. University of Oklahoma Press, 1979. $21.95; paper, $10.95.

AMERICAN INDIAN MEDICINE
Virgil J. Vogel
Illus. 583 pp. University of Oklahoma and American Indian Books, 1977. $28.95.

AMERICAN INDIAN MONOGRAPH SERIES
Includes: *The Yuchi Green Corn Ceremonial: Form and Meaning,* 81 pp., $7.50; and *Kashaya Pomo Plants, 171 pp., $15.00. The American Indian Studies Center.*

*AMERICAN INDIAN MUSIC AND MUSICAL INSTRUMENTS
George S. Fichter
Grades 5-10. David McKay, 1978. $7.95.

AMERICAN INDIAN MYTHOLOGY
Alice Marriott and Carol K. Rachlin
Illus. 210 pp. Paper. T.Y. Crowell, 1972. $3.95. New American Library, $1.95.

AMERICAN INDIAN MYTHS AND LEGENDS
Richard Erdoes and Alfonso Ortiz
Illus. 504 pp. Pantheon, 1984. $19.95.

AMERICAN INDIAN MYTHS AND MYSTERIES
Vincent H. Gaddis

Chilton Book Co., 1977. $8.95. Paper. New Americn Library, $1.95.

AMERICAN INDIAN NEEDLEPOINT DESIGNS, FOR PILLOWS, BELTS, HANDBAGS, AND OTHER PROJECTS
Roslyn Epstein
Illus. 38 pp. Paper. American Indian Books, $2.95.

AMERICAN INDIAN NEEDLEPOINT WORKBOOK
Margaret Boyles
Illus. 96 pp. Paper. Macmillan, 1976. $4.95.

THE AMERICAN INDIAN: NORTH, SOUTH AND CENTRAL AMERICA
A. Hyatt Verrill
Gordon Press, 1977. $59.95.

AMERICAN INDIAN PAINTERS: A BIOGRAPHICAL DIRECTORY
Jeanne O. Snodgrass
269 pp. Paper. Museum of the American Indian, 1968. $7.50.

AMERICAN INDIAN PAINTING AND SCULPTURE
Patricia J. Broder
Illus. 165 pp. Abbeville Press, 1981. $35.00.

THE AMERICAN INDIAN: PAST AND PRESENT
Roger L. Nichols
Third edition. 280 pp. Alfred A. Knopf, $12.95.

AMERICAN INDIAN PERIODICALS IN THE PRINCETON UNIVERSITY LIBRARY: GUIDE TO THE COLLECTION
Alfred L. Bush
List of over 500 titles in microfiche. See Clearwater Publishing for titles and prices.

THE AMERICAN INDIAN: PERSPECTIVES FOR THE STUDY OF SOCIAL CHANGE
Fred Eggan
192 pp. Cambridge University Press, 1981. $34.50; paper, $9.95.

AMERICAN INDIAN POETRY
Sharon Wirt
Illus. 32 pp. Paper. Hancock House, 1984. $3.95.

AMERICAN INDIAN POETRY: AN ANTHOLOGY OF SONGS AND CHANTS
George W. Cronyn, Editor
Liveright Publishing, 1970.

AMERICAN INDIAN POLICY
Theodore W. Taylor
Illus. 230 pp. Lomond, 1983. $14.95.
Microfilm, $12.95.

**AMERICAN INDIAN POLICY IN
CRISIS: CHRISTIAN REFORMERS
AND THE INDIAN, 1865-1900**
Francis P. Prucha
Illus. 468 pp. Maps. University of Oklahoma
Press, 1976. $24.95.

**AMERICAN INDIAN POLICY
IN THE FORMATIVE YEARS:
THE INDIAN TRADE AND
INTERCOURSE ACTS, 1790-1834**
Francis P. Prucha
292 pp. Paper. University of Nebraska Press,
$3.25.

**AMERICAN INDIAN POLICY
IN THE JACKSONIAN ERA**
Ronald N. Satz
Illus. 343 pp. University of Nebraska Press,
1975. $14.95; paper, $4.25.

**AMERICAN INDIAN POLICY
IN THE TWENTIETH CENTURY**
Vine Deloria, Jr., Editor
272 pp. University of Oklahoma Press, 1985.
$16.95.

**AMERICAN INDIAN POTTERY:
AN IDENTIFICATION AND
VALUE GUIDE**
John M. Barry
Second Edition. Illus. 213 pp. Books Americana
and American Indian Books, 1984. $29.95.

**THE AMERICAN INDIAN:
PREHISTORY TO THE PRESENT**
Arrell Gibson
618 pp. Paper. D.C. Heath & Co., 1981. $15.95.

**AMERICAN INDIAN PROSE AND
POETRY: WE WAIT IN THE DARKNESS**
Putnam Publishing Group, 1974.

**THE AMERICAN INDIAN
READER SERIES**
Jeannette Henry, Editor
Five volumes covering separate subject areas:
Anthropology, 174 pp.; Education, 300 pp.;
Literature, 248 pp.; History, 149 pp.; and Current
Affairs, 248 pp. Paper. The Indian Historian,
1974. $6.75 each; $32.95 per set.

AMERICAN INDIAN RELIGIONS
John M. Hurdy
Sherbourne, $2.50.

**THE AMERICAN INDIAN:
A RISING ETHNIC FORCE**
Herbert L. Marx, Editor
H.W. Wilson, 1973. $7.00.

**AMERICAN INDIAN SCULPTURE:
A STUDY OF THE NORTHWEST COAST**
Paul S. Wingert

Reprint of 1949 edition. AMS, $27.50;
Hacker Art Books, $30.00.

*AMERICAN INDIAN SONGS
Charles Hofmann
Grades 3-6. Illus. John Day Co., 1967. $12.49.

**AMERICAN INDIAN SPEAKS:
POETRY, FICTION AND ART
BY THE AMERICAN INDIAN**
John R. Milton, Editor
Illus. 191 pp. Paper. Dakota Press, 1969. $5.00.

***AMERICAN INDIAN STEREOTYPES
IN THE WORLD OF CHILDREN:
A READER AND BIBLIOGRAPHY**
Arlene B. Hirschfelder
312 pp. Scarecrow Press, 1982. $19.00.

AMERICAN INDIAN TODAY
Stuart Levine and Nancy O. Laurie, Editors
Illus. 358 pp. Everett/Edwards, $15.00.

***AMERICAN INDIAN
TOOLS AND ORNAMENTS**
David MacKay Co., 1980. $8.95.

**AMERICAN INDIAN TREATIES
PUBLICATIONS SERIES**
Includes: *Public Law 280: State Jurisdiction Over
Reservation Indians*, 27 pp., $5.00; *An Inventory
of the Paca Indian Agency Records*, 87 pp. $5.00;
*An Inventory of the Mission Indian Agency
Records*, 66 pp. $5.00; and *An Introduction to the
Bureau of Indian Affairs*, 27 pp. $2.00. American
Indian Studies Center.

**THE AMERICAN INDIAN
TREATY SERIES**
Compiles treaties and agreements made between
the U.S. Government and Indian Tribes. Nine
volumes. Separate books for treaties and
agreements of the Sioux Nation, the Pacific
Northwest, the Northern Plains, eastern
Oklahoma, the Southwest (western Oklahoma),
the Five Civilized Tribes, the Chippewa, and the
Great Lakes region. 102-278 pp each. Institute for
the Development of Indian Law, 1973-1975. $7.00
each; $55.00 per set.

*AMERICAN INDIAN TRIBES
Marion E. Gridley
Grades 5-adult. Illus. Maps. Dodd, Mead & Co.,
1974. $7.95.

**THE AMERICAN INDIAN
UNDER RECONSTRUCTION**
Annie H. Abel
Reprint of 1925 edition. Johnson Reprint, $19.50.

**THE AMERICAN INDIAN AND THE
U.S.: A DOCUMENTARY HISTORY**
Wilcomb E. Washburn, Editor
Four volumes. Greenwood Press, 1973. $175.00
per set. Random House, $135.00 per set.

AMERICAN INDIAN UTENSILS: HOW
TO MAKE BASKETS, POTTERY AND
WOODENWARE WITH NATURAL
MATERIALS
Evelyn Wolfson
Illus. David McKay Co., 1979. $8.95.

*AMERICAN INDIAN WAYS OF LIFE
Thorne Deuel
Grades 6-adult. 80 pp. Paper. American
Indian Books, $2.00.

AMERICAN INDIAN AND WHITE
CHILDREN: A SOCIOPSYCHOLOGICAL
INVESTIGATION
R.J. Havighurst and B.L. Neugarten
Reprint of 1969 edition. University of
Chicago Press, $17.00.

AMERICAN INDIAN AND
WHITE RELATIONS TO 1830
William N. Fenton
Reprint of 1957 edition. Russell & Russell, $10.00.

AMERICAN INDIAN WOMEN:
TELLING THEIR LIVES
Gretchen M. Bataille and Kathleen M. Sands
210 pp. University of Nebraska Press, 1984.
$18.95.

AMERICAN INDIANS
Describes the Federal Government's economic
policy affecting Indian tribes and Alaska natives.
45 pp. Paper. Supt. of Documents, 1984. $2.50.

*AMERICAN INDIANS
Bearl Brooks
Grades 3-6. 24 pp. ESP, 1977. Workbook, $5.00.

AMERICAN INDIANS
F. Starr
Reprint. of 1899 edition. AMS Press, $21.50.

AMERICAN INDIANS
William T. Hagan
A history of the relationship between the white
man and the Indian. Illus. 190 pp. University of
Chicago Press, 1961. $15.00; paper, $4.95.

THE AMERICAN INDIANS
Edward H. Spicer
176 pp. Paper. Howard University Press, 1982.
$5.95.

AMERICAN INDIANS,
AMERICAN JUSTICE
Vine Deloria, Jr. and Clifford M. Lytle
278 pp. University of Texas Press, 1983.
$19.95; paper, $9.95.

AMERICAN INDIANS
AND AMERICAN LIFE
G. Simpson and M.J. Yinger, Editors
Reprint of 1957 edition. 236 pp. Russell
& Russell, $15.00. Kraus, $21.00.

AMERICAN INDIANS AND
CHRISTIAN MISSIONS:
STUDIES IN CULTURAL CONFLICT
Henry W. Bowden
256 pp. University of Chicago Press, 1981.
$14.95; paper, $7.95.

AMERICAN INDIANS DISPOSSESSED:
FRAUD IN LAND CESSIONS
FORCED UPON THE TRIBES
Walter H. Blumenthal
Facsimile of 1955 edition. Arno Press, $13.00.

AMERICAN INDIANS: FACTS—FUTURE
TOWARD ECONOMIC DEVELOPMENT
FOR NATIVE AMERICAN COMMUNITIES
Subcommittee on Economy in Government
Reprint of 1969 edition. Arno Press, $10.00.

AMERICAN INDIANS
AND FEDERAL AID
Alan L. Sorkin
231 pp. Brookings Institution, 1971. $9.95.

AMERICAN INDIANS IN COLORADO
J. Donald Hughes
Illus. 152 pp. Paper. Pruett, 1977. $5.95.

AMERICAN INDIANS
AND OUR WAY OF LIFE
Sylvester M. Morey, Editor
A discussion of the Iroquois to American
democracy and the uniting of our original
colonists into States. Paper. The Myrin Institute.
$1.00.

AMERICAN INDIANS
AND THEIR MUSIC
Frances Densmore
Reprint of 1926 edition. Johnson Reprint, $11.00.

AMERICAN INDIANS
OF THE SOUTHWEST
Bertha P. Dutton
Revised edition. Illus. 320 pp. Paper.
University of New Mexico Press, 1983. $14.95.

AMERICAN INDIANS: A SELECT
CATALOG OF NATIONAL ARCHIVES
MICROFILM PUBLICATIONS
103 pp. National Archives, 1984. $2.00.

*AMERICAN INDIANS TODAY
Olga Hoyt
Material on the Navajo, Hopis, Pueblos,
Apaches, Zunis, Shoshones, Utes, Chinooks,
Crees, Arapahoes, Paiutes, Cherokees, Omahas,
Seminoles, Mohawks and Senecas. Grades 7-
adult. Illus. 192 pp. Abelard-Schuman, 1972.
$6.95.

***AMERICAN INDIANS:
YESTERDAY AND TODAY**
  Bruce Grant; L.F. Bjorklund, Illustrator
An encyclopedia designed as a reference work as
well as a history of the American Indian. Includes
biographies of great Indian chiefs and leaders.
Grades 7-adult. Illus. 352 pp. E.P. Dutton, 1960.
$9.95.

**AMERICAN MEDICAL ETHNOBOTANY:
A REFERENCE DICTIONARY**
  Daniel E. Moerman
Garland Publishing, 1977. $51.00.

**AMERICAN PROTESTANTISM AND
U.S. INDIAN POLICY, 1869-1882**
  Robert H. Keller, Jr.
Illus. 400 pp. University of Nebraska Press,
1983. $27.95.

**AMERICAN SOCIETY FOR PROMOTING
THE CIVILIZATION AND GENERAL
IMPROVEMENT OF THE INDIAN
TRIBES WITHIN THE U.S.**
Reprint of 1824 edition. Kraus, $20.00.

**AMERICAN TABLEAUX No. 1:
SKETCHES OF ABORIGINAL LIFE**
  V.V. Vide
Reprint of 1846 edition. Garland, $40.00.

**AN AMERICAN URPHILOSOPHIE:
AN AMERICAN PHILOSOPHY -
BP (BEFORE PRAGMATISM)**
  Robert Bunge
218 pp. University Presses of America, 1984.
$22.00; paper, $10.75.

**AMERICANIZING OF THE AMERICAN
INDIANS: WRITINGS BY THE
"FRIENDS OF THE INDIAN", 1880-1900**
  Francis P. Prucha, Editor
Harvard University Press, 1973. $20.00.

AMERICA'S ANCIENT TREASURES
  Folsom & Folsom
A travel guide to U.S. and Canadian
archaeological sites and museums of
prehistoric Indian life. 420 pp. Paper.
American Indian Books, $16.95.

**AMERICAS ON THE
EVE OF DISCOVERY**
  Harold E. Driver, Editor
Reprint of 1964 edition. Greenwood, $18.75.

AMERIND FOUNDATION PUBLICATIONS
Monographs on Native Americans. Reprint.
Volumes 1-8, 1940-1958. Kraus, $433.00 per set.

**AMERINDIANS AND THEIR PALEO-
ENVIRONMENTS IN NORTHEASTERN
NORTH AMERICA, Volume 288**
  Walter Newman and Bert Salwen
New York Academy of Science, 1977. $35.00.

AMONG THE APACHES
  Frederick Schwatka
Reprint of the 1887 articles. Collected
observations of several visits to the Apache Indian
agencies. Tells of life as it was. Illus. 30 pp. Filter
Press, 1974. $7.00; paper, $1.50.

**AMONG THE INDIANS: FOUR YEARS
ON THE UPPER MISSOURI, 1858-1862**
  Henry Boller; Milo M. Quaife, Editor
Reprint. Narrative of fur-trading among the
Plains Indians of the Upper Missouri. Illus. 386
pp. Paper. University of Nebraska Press, 1972.
$6.95.

*AMONG THE PLAINS INDIANS
  Lorenz Engel
Based upon the journals of the German explorer
Maximilian, as well as upon the records of George
Catlin furing the early 1830's. Grades 5-12. Illus.
112 pp. Lerner, 1972. $7.95.

AMONG THE SHOSHONES
  Elijah N. Wilson
A true story of a white man (the author), who at 12
years of age chose to live with the Shoshones for
two years. Facsimile of 1910 edition. Illus. 224 pp.
Pine Cone, $9.00.

**AN ANALYSIS OF COASTAL
ALGONQUIAN CULTURE**
  Regina Flannery
Reprint of 1939 edition. AMS, $22.50.

**AN ANALYSIS OF
COEUR D'ALENE INDIAN MYTHS**
  Gladys A. Reichard
Reprint of 1947 edition. Kraus, $23.00.

**ANALYSIS OF INDIAN VILLAGE
SITE COLLECTIONS FROM
LOUISIANA AND MISSISSIPPI**
  J.A. Ford
Reprint of 1937 edition. Kraus, $31.00.

**AN ANALYSIS OF
NAVAJO TEMPORALITY**
  Douglas R. Givens
Paper. University Press of America, 1977. $6.50.

THE ANASAZI
  Richard J. Ambler
Illus. Paper. Museum of Northern Arizona, $4.95.

**ANASAZI PAINTED POTTERY
IN THE FIELD MUSEUM
OF NATURAL HISTORY**
  Paul Martin and Elizabeth Willis
Reprint of 1940 edition. Kraus, $40.00.

**ANASAZI: PIONEER EXPLORER
OF SOUTHWESTERN RUINS**
  Parker McKenzie and Richard Wetherill
Reprint of 1957 edition. Illus. Maps. 370 pp.
Paper. University of New Mexico Press, $5.50.

ANASAZI SUBSISTENCE AND
SETTLEMENT ON WHITE MESA,
SAN JUAN COUNTY, UTAH
William S. Davis, et al, Editors
Illus. 645 pp. University Press of America,
$36.50; paper, $24.75.

ANCESTOR'S FOOTSTEPS
Moore
Council for Indian Education, 1978. $1.95.

THE ANCESTORS: NATIVE AMERICAN
ARTISANS OF THE AMERICAS
Anna C. Roosevelt and J.G. Smith, Editors
Illus. 197 pp. Paper. Museum of the American
Indian, 1979. $9.95.

ANCESTRAL LANDS, ALIEN LAWS:
JUDICIAL PERSPECTIVES
ON ABORIGINAL TITLE
49 pp. Native Law Centre Publications, $9.00.

ANCIENT ART OF THE
AMERICAN WOODLAND INDIAN
David S. Brose
Illus. 240 pp. Harry N. Abrams, 1985. $35.00.

ANCIENT CULTURE OF THE
FREMONT RIVER IN UTAH
Noel Morss
Reprint of 1931 edition. Paper. Kraus, $26.00.

ANCIENT INDIAN MEDICINE
P. Kutembiash
288 pp. State Mutual Book, 1979. $10.00.

*ANCIENT INDIANS
OF THE SOUTHWEST
Alfred Tamarin and Shirley Glubok
Grades 4-7. Illus. 96 pp. Paper. Doubleday,
1975. $5.95.

ANCIENT LIFE IN
THE AMERICAN SOUTHWEST
Edgar Hewett
Reprint of 1930 edition. Illus.
Biblo & Tannen, 1968. $15.00.

ANCIENT MEN OF THE ARCTIC
James L. Giddings
Illus. Alfred A. Knopf, 1967. $14.50.

ANCIENT MIMBRENOS
P.H. Nesbitt
Reprint of 1931 edition. Paper. Kraus, $32.00.

ANCIENT MODOCS OF
CALIFORNIA AND OREGON
Carrol Howe
Illus. Paper. Binford & Mort, 1979. $6.50.

ANCIENT MONUMENTS
OF THE MISSISSIPPI VALLEY
Ephraim G. Squier and E.H. Davis
Reprint of 1948 edition. Illus. AMS, $37.50.

ANCIENT NORTH AMERICANS
Jesse Jennings, Editor
Illus. 642 pp. W.H. Freeman, 1983. $27.95.

ANCIENT ROCK CARVINGS
OF THE CENTRAL SIERRA: THE
NORTH FOLK INDIAN PETROGLYPHS
Willis A. Gortner
Illus. Portola Press, 1984. $14.50.

ANCIENT TRIBES OF
THE KLAMATH COUNTRY
Carol B. Howe
Illus. Paper. Binford and Mort, 1968. $6.95.

AND EAGLES SWEEP ACROSS
THE SKY: INDIAN TEXTILES
OF THE NORTH AMERICAN WEST
Dena S. Katzenberg
Illus. Baltimore Museum, 1977. $12.00.

*AND IT IS STILL THAT WAY
Byrd Baylor, Editor
Grades 1-4. 128 pp. Charles Scribner's Sons, 1976.
$7.95.

AND STILL THE WATERS RUN:
THE BETRAYAL OF THE FIVE
CIVILIZED TRIBES
Angie Debo
Reprint of 1940 edition. Illus. 448 pp. Paper.
University of Oklahoma Press, $12.95.

ANDELE, OR THE MEXICAN—KIOWA
CAPTIVE, A STORY OF REAL LIFE
AMONG THE INDIANS
John J. Methvin
Reprint of 1899 edition, et al. Bound with
other captivity stories. Garland, $40.00.

*ANGELS AND INDIANS
Joan Hodgson
Grades 2-7. Illus. DeVorss, 1974. $5.95.

ANGELS TO WISH BY
Joseph Juknialis
Paper. Resource Publications, 1984. $7.95.

*ANIMAL PEOPLE
A coloring book of the animal people which figure
in many Indian legends. Teacher's guide. Grades
Preschool-2. 14 pp. Daybreak Star Press, $3.50.

ANISHNABE: SIX STUDIES
OF MODERN CHIPPEWA
J. Paredes
Illus. 447 pp. University Presses of Florida, 1980.
$27.50.

THE ANNALS OF THE CAKCHIQUELS
Adrian Recinos and Delia Goetz, Translators
Rerint of 1953 edition. Bound with Title of the
Lords of Totonicapan. Paper. University of
Oklahoma Press, $4.95.

**ANNALS OF SHAWNEE METHODIST
MISSION AND INDIAN MANUAL
LABOR SCHOOL**
Martha B. Caldwell
Second edition. Illus. Paper. Kansas State
Historical Society, 1977. $2.95.

*ANNIE WAUNEKA
Mary C. Nelson
A biography of the Navajo leader. Grades 5-9.
Ilus. 75 pp. Dillon Press, 1973. $7.95.

**AN ANNOTATED BIBLIOGRAPHY
OF AMERICAN INDIAN AND
ESKIMO AUTOBIOGRAPHIES**
H. David Brumble, III
182 pp. University of Nebraska Press, 1981.
$15.50.

**AN ANNOTATED BIBLIOGRAPHY OF
AMERICAN INDIAN PAINTING**
Doris O. Dawdy
50 pp. Paper. Museum of the American Indian,
1968. $2.50.

**ANNOTATED STATUTES OF
THE INDIAN TERRITORY**
Reprint of 1899 edition. AMS, $98.50.

***ANPAO: AN AMERICAN
INDIAN ODYSSEY**
Jamake Highwater
Grades 5-9. J.B. Lippincott, 1977. $13.50; paper,
$3.95..

ANTELOPE BILL
Parker I. Pierce
Facsimile of 1898 edition. A participant's account
of the Sioux uprising of 1862. Limited edition.
Roos & Haines, $12.50.

**ANTHOLOGY: OBSERVATIONS ON
MISSISSIPPI VALLEY AND
TRANS-MISSISSIPPI INDIANS**
Jean A. Delanglez; Mildred M. Wedel, Editor
399 pp. Garland Publishing, 1985. $50.00.

**ANTHROPOLOGIA ANTHROPOLOGICA:
THE NATIVE RACES OF AMERICA**
James G. Frazier and Robert A. Downie, Editors
Reprint of 1939 edition. Illus. AMS, $47.50.

**ANTHROPOLOGICAL OBSERVATIONS
ON THE CENTRAL ESKIMOS**
Kaj Birket-Smith; W.E. Calvert, Translator
Reprint of 1928 edition. Illus. AMS, $45.00.

**ANTHROPOLOGICAL REPORT ON
THE INDIAN OCCUPANCY OF
ROYCE AREA 243**
Harold Hickerson
273 pp. Clearwater, 1973. $81.00.

**ANTHROPOLOGICAL REPORT ON
INDIAN OCCUPANCY OF CERTAIN
TERRITORY CLAIMED BY THE DAKOTA
SIOUX INDIANS AND BY RIVAL
TRIBAL CLAIMANTS**
Wesley R. Hurt
250 pp. Clearwater, 1973. $75.00.

**ANTHROPOLOGICAL REPORT ON
INDIAN OCCUPANCY OF THAT PORTION
OF ROYCE AREA 148 EAST OF THE
FOX RIVER IN ILLINOIS**
David A. Berreis, et al
190 pp. Clearwater, 1973. $72.00.

**ANTHROPOLOGICAL REPORT ON
INDIAN OCCUPANCY OF ROYCE
AREAS 149, 174 & 245**
J.A. Jones
193 pp. Clearwater, 1973. $58.00.

**ANTHROPOLOGICAL REPORT ON
THE INDIAN OCCUPANCY OF
ROYCE AREA 262 IN IOWA**
David B. Stout
40 pp. Clearwater, 1974. $23.00.

**ANTHROPOLOGICAL REPORT ON
THE INDIANS OCCUPYING AN AREA
BOUNDED ROUGHLY BY THE KANKAKEE
ILLINOIS, MISSISSIPPI, OHIO,
WABASH, AND TIPPECANOE RIVERS**
David B. Stout
32 pp. Clearwater, 1973. $18.00.

**ANTHROPOLOGICAL REPORT ON
INDIAN USE AND OCCUPANCY OF
ROYCE AREAS 69 & 120 IN IOWA
AND MISSOURI**
Zachary Gussow
90 pp. Clearwater, 1974. $34.00.

**ANTHROPOLGICAL REPORT ON THE
INDIAN USE AND OCCUPANCY OF
ROYCE AREA 332, CEDED BY THE
CHIPPEWA INDIANS OF LAKE
SUPERIOR AND THE MISSISSIPPI
UNDER THE TREATY OF SEPT. 30, 1854**
Harold Hickerson
151 pp. Clearwater, 1973. $48.00.

**ANTHROPOLOGICAL REPORT ON
THE NAVAJO INDIANS**
Frank D. Reeve
99 pp. Clearwater, 1973. $33.00.

**ANTHROPOLOGICAL STUDIES
RELATED TO HEALTH PROBLEMS
OF NORTH AMERICAN INDIANS**
Robert S. Corruccini, et al , Editors
148 pp. Irvington Publishers, 1974. $19.50.

**ANTHROPOLOGICAL STUDY OF
INDIAN TRIBES IN ROYCE AREAS 48,
96-A, 110, 177 & 98, ILLINOIS
AND INDIANA, 1640-1832**
Joseph Jablow
Two volumes. 398 pp. Clearwater, 1973. $160.00
per set.

**ANTHROPOLOGY AND THE
AMERICAN INDIAN**
Report of a symposium held in 1970 by the
American Anthropological Association on the
issues raised by Vine Deloria's book, *Custer Died
for Your Sins.* Among the distinguished scholars
participating were: Nancy O. Lurie, Phileo Nas,
Omer C. Stewart, Margaret Mead, Bea Medicine,
and Alfonso Ortiz. 125 pp. Paper. Indian
Historian Press, $5.50.

**ANTHROPOLOGY OF FRANZ BOAS:
ESSAYS ON THE CENTENNIAL
OF HIS BIRTH**
Walter Goldschmidt, Editor
Reprint of 1959 edition. Paper. Kraus, $20.00.

**THE ANTHROPOLOGY
OF KODIAK ISLAND**
Alex Hrdlicka
Reprint of 1944 edition. Illus. AMS, $60.50.

ANTHROPOLOGY ON THE GREAT PLAINS
W. Raymond Wood and Margot Liberty,
Editors
Illus. 301 pp. University of Nebraska Press, 1980.
$25.00.

**ANTHROPOMETRIC OBSERVATIONS
ON THE ESKIMOS AND INDIANS
OF LABRADOR**
Thomas D. Stewart
Reprint of 1939 edition. Paper. AMS, $17.75.
Paper. Kraus, $20.00.

**ANTIQUITIES OF NEW ENGLAND
INDIANS**
C.C. Willoughby
Reprint of 1935 edition. AMS Press, $34.00.

**ANTIQUITIES OF THE SOUTHERN
INDIANS, PARTICULARLY OF THE
GEORGIA TRIBES**
C.C. Jones, Jr.
Reprint of 1873 edition. Illus. 548 pp.
Reprint Co., $27.50.

**ANTIQUITIES OF THE MESA VERDE
NATIONAL PARK, CLIFF PALACE**
Jesse W. Fewkes
Reprint of 1911 edition. Kraus, $15.00.

**ANTIQUITIES OF THE
NEW ENGLAND INDIANS**
Charles C. Willoughby

Reprint of 1935 edition. Illus. AMS, $20.00;
paper, 17.50.

**ANTIQUITIES OF THE SOUTHERN
INDIANS PARTICULARLY OF THE
GEORGIA TRIBES**
C.C. Jones, Jr.
Reprint of 1987 edition. Illus. AMS Press, $57.50.

**THE ANTIQUITY AND ORIGIN
OF NATIVE AMERICANS**
Clark S. Larseon
171 pp. Garland Publishing, 1985. $25.00.

*THE APACHE
Patricia McKissack
Illus. 48 pp. Grades K-4. Childrens Press,
$10.60; paper, $3.95.

**APACHE AGENT:
THE STORY OF JOHN P. CLUM**
W. Clum
Illus. 300 pp. Gordon Press, 1977. $59.95 (library
binding.) University of Nebraska, 1978. $13.95;
paper, $5.95.

APACHE COUNTRY
Paper. W.W. Norton, 1978. $1.50.

**THE APACHE FRONTIER: JACOBO
U GARTE AND SPANISH-INDIAN
RELATIONS IN NORTHERN NEW
SPAIN, 1769-1791**
Max Moorhead
Illus. University of Oklahoma Press, 1968.
$17.95; paper, $9.95.

APACHE GOLD AND YAQUI SILVER
J. Dobie
Illus. 384 pp. Paper. University of New Mexico
Press, $5.95.

APACHE INDIAN BASKETS
Clara L. Tanner
Illus. 204 pp. University of Arizona Press, 1982.
$39.95.

APACHE INDIANS
David A. Horr, Editor
A study of the Apache Indians. 12 Volumes.
Garland, 1978. $51.00 each volume. See publisher
for titles and prices.

**APACHE INDIANS IN TEXAS,
NEW MEXICO AND ARIZONA**
Albert H. Schroeder
Clearwater, $99.00.

**APACHE INDIANS OF TEXAS: ETHNO-
HISTORICAL ANALYSIS OF DOCUMENTS**
Verne F. Ray
265 pp. Clearwater, 1973. $78.00.

*APACHE INDIANS:
RAIDERS OF THE SOUTHWEST
Sonia Bleeker; Althea Karr, Illustrator
Describes the life and customs of the Apache
Indians. Grades 4-7. Illus. 160 pp. William
Morrow & Co., 1951. $8.75.

*APACHE INDIANS:
RAIDERS OF THE SOUTHWEST
Gordon C. Baldwin
Grades 7-adult. Illus. School Book Service, 1978.
$9.95.

APACHE JIM: STORIES FROM HIS
PRIVATE FILES ON TREASURES
Apache Jim
Illus. 107 pp. Paper. H.G. Carson, 1973. $4.00.

APACHE, KIOWA AND COMANCHE
INDIAN RESERVATIONS IN
SOUTHWESTERN OKLAHOMA
Richard B. Hall
Clearwater, 1976. $78.00.

APACHE LANDS
Albert H. Schroeder
573 pp. Clearwater, 1973. $159.00.

AN APACHE LIFE-WAY:
THE ECONOMIC, SOCIAL, AND
RELIGIOUS INSTITUTIONS OF
THE CHIRICAHUA INDIANS
Morris E. Opler
Reprint of 1941 edition. Based on the author's two
years of field work. Illus. Maps. 500 pp. Cooper
Square Publishers, $23.50.

APACHE LIGHTNING:
THE LAST GREAT BATTLES
OF THE AJO CALIENTES
Joseph A. Stout, Jr.
Concentrates on the final years of Victorio, 1877-
1880, the last great leader of the Warm Springs
Apaches. 222 pp. Oxford University Press, 1974.
$12.95.

APACHE ODYSSEY:
A JOURNEY BETWEEN TWO WORLDS
Morris E. Opler; G. and L. Spindler, Editors
A biographical narrative of a Mescalero Apache.
A study of an incipient shaman, and of
shamanism. Reprint of 1969 edition. Illus. 320 pp.
Paper. Irvington, $12.95.

APACHE, NAVAHO AND SPANIARD
Jack D. Forbes
Illus. Maps. Biblio. Index. 304 pp. Paper.
University of Oklahoma Press, 1960. $8.95.

APACHEAN CULTURE
HISTORY AND ETHNOLOGY
Keith H. Basso; Morris E. Opler, Editor
Illus. 172 pp. Paper. University of Arizona, 1971.
$7.95.

THE APACHES:
A CRITICAL BIBLIOGRAPHY
Michael Melody
96 pp. Paper. Indiana University, 1977. $6.95.

THE APACHES:
EAGLES OF THE SOUTHWEST
Donald Worcester
Illus. University of Oklahoma, 1979. $21.95.

APACHES: A HISTORY AND
CULTURE PORTRAIT
James L. Haley
Illus. 504 pp. Doubleday, 1981. $17.95.

APACHES AND LONGHORNS
Will C. Barnes
214 pp. University of Arizona Press, $17.50;
paper, $8.50.

APOLOGIES TO THE IROQUOIS
Edmund Wilson
Concerns the present situation of the Indians of
the Six Great Nations Confederacy in the U.S.
and Canada. Paper. Random House, 1966. $2.95.

APOLOGIES TO THE IROQUOIS:
WITH A STUDY OF THE MOHAWKS
IN HIGH STREET
Edmund Wilson and Joseph Mitchell
Reprint of 1959 edition. Octagon, $15.50.

APPALACHIAN INDIAN FRONTIER:
THE EDMOND ATKIN REPORT AND
PLAN OF 1755
Edmond Atkin; Wilbur R. Jacobs, Editor
Illus. 125 pp. Paper. University of Nebraska
Press, 1967. $3.95.

APPRAISAL OF THE BLACK HILLS
AREA OF SOUTH DAKOTA, 1877
Harry R. Fenton
190 pp. Clearwater, 1973. $57.00.

APPRAISAL OF THE BLACK HILLS
LANDS OF THE SIOUX NATION, 1877
Donald D. Myers and Frank R. Kleinman
150 pp. Clearwater, 1973. $48.00.

APPRAISAL OF THE
CREEK CESSION, 1856
H.J. Garrett and Roscoe H. Sears
110 pp. Clearwater, 1973. $37.50.

APPRAISAL OF THE FORMER MALHEUR
RESERVATION IN EASTERN OREGON
M.A. Palmer
95 pp. Clearwater, 1974. $43.50.

APPRAISAL OF LAND INCLUDED IN
THE AGREEMENT OF SEPT. 26, 1872
BETWEEN THE U.S. AND EASTERN
SHOSHONE INDIANS
E.O. Fuller
320 pp. Clearwater, 1973. $92.00.

**APPRAISAL OF THE LANDS CEDED
BY THE CREEK NATION FOR THE
SEMINOLES, AUGUST 7, 1856**
Elbridge A. Tucker
115 pp. Clearwater, 1973. $39.00.

**APPRAISAL OF LANDS IN ILLINOIS
AND WISCONSIN, CEDED BY THE
WINNEBAGO INDIANS IN ROYCE AREAS**
Walter R. Kuehnle
570 pp. Clearwater, 1973. $158.00.

**APPRAISAL OF LANDS IN NORTHERN
OKLAHOMA CHEROKEE OUTLET, 1893**
Richard B. Hall
96 pp. Clearwater, 1974. $39.00.

**APPRAISAL OF THE LANDS OF
THE BAY MILLS INDIAN COMMUNITY**
Gordon E. Elmquist
90 pp. Clearwater, 1973. $31.50.

**APPRAISAL OF THE LANDS OF THE
FORT McDOWELL MOHAVE-APACHE
THE YAVAPAI-APACHE COMMUNITIES
IN ARIZONA**
Donald D. Myers, et al
Two volumes. 394 pp. Clearwater, 1974. $106.50
per set.

**APPRAISAL OF THE LANDS OF
THE FORT SILL APACHE TRIBE
OF OKLAHOMA, 1886**
Donald Myers and Frank Kleinman, Jr.
383 pp. Clearwater, 1973. $109.50.

**APPRAISAL OF THE LANDS OF THE
GOSHUTE TRIBE OR IDENTIFIABLE
GROUP REPRESENTED BY THE CONFED-
ERATED TRIBES OF THE GOSHUTE
RESERVATION IN UT AND NV, 1875**
Idaho Land and Appraisal Service
190 pp. Clearwater, 1973. $60.50.

**APPRAISAL OF THE LANDS OF THE
HUALAPAI RESERVATION, ARIZONA**
Donald D. Myers
400 pp. Clearwater, 1973. $112.50.

**APPRAISAL OF THE LANDS OF THE
LOWER SIOUX COMMUNITY IN MINN.**
Gordon E. Elmquist
142 pp. Clearwater, 1974. $46.00.

**APPRAISAL OF MINERAL RESOURCES
IN THE LANDS OF THE CONFEDERATED
TRIBES OF THE GOSHUTE RESERVATION**
Roy P. Full
Four volumes. 1,572 pp. Clearwater, 1973.
$420/set.

**APPRAISAL OF MINERAL RESOURCES
IN THE LANDS OF THE SIOUX NATION
ACQUIRED UNDER TREATY OF
APRIL 26, 1868**
P.J. Shenon and Roy P. Full
Four volumes. 1,860 pp. Clearwater, 1973.
$500/set.

**APPRAISAL OF NOOKSACK TRACT,
WASHINGTON, 1859**
Vern A. Englehorn
350 pp. Clearwater, 1973. $100.00.

**APPRAISAL OF OIL AND GAS LANDS
OF THE PORTION OF WIND RIVER
BASIN, WYOMING, CEDED BY THE
BRUNOT AGREEMENT-SEPT. 26, 1872.**

T.S. and J.W. Harrison
84 pp. Clearwater, 1974. $32.00.

**APPRAISAL OF THE PAPAGO TRIBE
OF ARIZONA, 1916, AND THE LOUIS
MARIA BACA GRANT, Float #3, 1906**
Idaho Land and Appraisal Service
260 pp. Clearwater, 1973. $101.50.

**APPRAISAL OF THE RENTAL VALUE
OF THE FORT SILL APACHE TRIBE
OF OKLAHOMA IN ARIZONA AND
NEW MEXICO: FROM 1848 to 1886**
Idaho Land and Appraisal Service
190 pp. Clearwater, 1973. $57.00.

**APPRAISAL REPORT OF LANDS IN
CENTRAL INDIANA: PURCHASED FROM
THE MIAMI TRIBE OF INDIANS, 1818**
Paul Starrett
170 pp. Clearwater, 1973. $52.50.

**APPRAISAL REPORT-WARM SPRINGS
RESERVATION IN OREGON, 1859**
M.J. Holbrook et al
Three volumes. 682 pp. Clearwater, 1974. $197.00
per set.

**APPRAISAL REPORT-BRUNOT LAND,
WYOMING, SOLD BY SHOSHONE TRIBE**
Vern A. Englehorn
199 pp. Clearwater, 1974. $60.00.

**APPRAISAL REPORT-LAND EXCLUDED
FROM THE RED LAKE RESERVATION
BY ERRONEOUS SURVEY**
William H. Muske
125 pp. Clearwater, 1973. $40.50.

THE ARAPAHO
Alfred L. Kroeber
How the Arapaho of the Great Plains lived and
worked before white culture arrived. Reprint. Ye
Galleon Press, $14.95.

ARAPAHO—CHEYENNE INDIANS
Illus. Map. 342 pp. Garland, $42.00.

ARAPAHO—CHEYENNE LAND AREA:
HISTORICAL BACKGROUND
AND DEVELOPMENT
Leroy Hafen
69 pp. Clearwater, 1974. $28.50.

THE ARAPAHO SUN DANCE, THE
CEREMONY OF THE OFFERINGS LODGE
G.A. Dorsey
Reprint of 1903 edition. Kraus, $88.00.

THE ARAPAHOE
Alfred L. Kroeber
Illus. 480 pp. University of Nebraska Press, 1983.
$24.95; paper, $8.95.

ARAPAHOE POLITICS, 1851-1978:
SYMBOLS IN CRISES OF AUTHORITY
Loretta Fowler
Illus. 375 pp. University of Nebraska Press, 1982.
$26.50.

THE ARAPAHOES, OUR PEOPLE
Virginia Trenholm
Illus. University of Oakhoma Press, 1970. $17.95.

ARCHAEOLINGUISTICS AND PALEO-
ETHNOGRAPHY OF ANCIENT ROCK
STRUCTURES IN WEST NORTH AMERICA
Western American Institute for Explorations,
Inc.

ARCHAEOLOGICAL EXPLORATIONS
ON THE MIDDLE CHINLE
Noel Morss
Reprint of 1927 edition. Paper. Kraus, $16.00.

ARCHAEOLOGICAL COLLECTIONS
FROM THE WESTERN ESKIMOS
Therkel Mathiassen
Reprint of 1930 edition. Illus. AMS, $42.00.

ARCHAEOLOGICAL EXCAVATIONS AT
KUKULIK, ST LAWRENCE ISLAND, AK
Otto W. Geist and Froelich G. Rainey
Reprint of 1936 edition. AMS, $35.00.

ARCHAEOLOGICAL EXPLORATIONS
ON THE MIDDLE CHINLE, 1925
Noel Morss
Reprint of 1927 edition. Kraus, $16.00.

ARCHAEOLOGICAL HISTORY
OF NEW YORK
Arthur C. Parker
Reprint of 1922 edition. AMS, $57.50.

ARCHAEOLOGICAL INSTITUTE
OF AMERICA, PAPERS
Adolph F. Bandelier
Reprint of 1942 edition. Six volumes.
AMS, $150.00 per set.

ARCHAEOLOGICAL INVESTIGATIONS
IN THE ALEUTIAN ISLANDS
Vladimir I. Iokhelson
Reprint of 1925 edition. AMS, $42.00.

ARCHAEOLOGICAL INVESTIGATIONS
OF THE KIOWA AND COMANCHE
INDIAN AGENCY COMMISSARIES
Daniel J. Crouch
Illus. Paper. Museum of the Great Plains, 1978.
$11.30.

ARCHAEOLOGICAL RECONNAISSANCE
OF FORT SILL, OKLAHOMA
C.R. Ferring
Illus. Paper. Museum of the Great Plains, 1978.
$22.00.

ARCHAEOLOGICAL SITE NEAR
GLEESON, ARIZONA
William S. Fulton and Carr Tuthill
Reprint of 1940 edition. Kraus, $28.00.

AN ARCHAEOLOGICAL STUDY OF
THE MISSISSIPPI CHOCTAW INDIANS
John H. Blitz
Illus. 120 pp. Paper. Mississippi Department of
Archives and History, 1985. $7.50.

ARCHAEOLOGICAL SURVEY IN THE
LOWER MISSISSIPPI ALLUVIAL
VALLEY, 1940-1947
P. Phillips, J.A. Ford, and J.B. Griffin
Reprint of 1951 edition. Paper. Kraus, $93.00.

ARCHAEOLOGICAL SURVEY OF
THE PUEBLO PLATEAU
R.G. Fisher
Reprint of 1930 edition. Paper. Kraus, $15.00.

ARCHAEOLOGICAL SURVEY OF
WEST CENTRAL NEW MEXICO AND
EAST CENTRAL ARIZONA
Edward B. Danson
Reprint of 1957 edition. Paper. Kraus, $26.00.

ARCHAEOLOGICAL SURVEY ON
THE NORTHERN NORTHWEST COAST
Phiilip Drucker
Extract from 1943 edition. Illus. Map. 133 pp.
Paper. Shorey, $10.00.

ARCHAEOLOGY AS ANTHROPOLOGY:
A CASE STUDY
William Longacre
Focuses on organizational and behavioral aspects
of societies which emerged approximately 1500
B.C. through 1350 AD. 57 pp. Paper. University
of Arizona Press, 1970. $3.95.

ARCHAEOLOGY IN WASHINGTON
Bruce Stallard
Reprint of 1958 edition. 64 pp. Paper. Shorey,
$4.00

ARCHAEOLOGY OF ALKALI RIDGE, SOUTHEASTERN UTAH
J.O. Brew
Reprint of 1946 edition. Paper. Kraus, $79.00.

ARCHAEOLOGY OF COOK INLET, ALASKA
Frederick De Laguna
Reprint of 1934 edition, AMS, $59.50.

THE ARCHAEOLOGY OF MICHIGAN: A GUIDE TO THE PREHISTORY OF THE GREAT LAKES REGION
James E. Fitting
Illus. 274 pp. Paper. Cranbrook, 1975. $7.50.

ARCHAEOLOGY OF MISSISSIPPI
Calvin S. Brown
Reprint of 1926 edition. Illus. AMS Press, $49.50.

THE ARCHAEOLOGY OF MISSOURI
Carl H. Chapman
Examines the cultural adaptation of Missouri's first inhabitants. 320 pp. University of Missouri Press, 1975. $26.00.

ARCHAEOLOGY OF NEW YORK STATE
William A. Ritchie
Reprint of 1969 revised edition. Illus. Harbor Hill Books, 1980. $22.50.

THE ARCHAEOLOGY OF NORTH AMERICA: AMERICAN INDIANS AND THEIR ORIGINS
Dean Snow; Werner Forman, Illustrator
Illus. 272 pp. Paper. Thames Hudson, 1980. $12.95.

ARCHAEOLOGY OF THE BERING SEA REGION: EXTRACTS
Henry B. Collins
Facsimile of 1933 edition. 27 pp. Paper. Shorey, $3.00.

ARCHAEOLOGY OF THE CENTRAL ESKIMO
Therkel Mathiassen
Reprint of 1927 edition. Two parts in one. Illus. AMS, $150.00.

ARCHAEOLOGY OF THE DELAWARE VALLEY
Ernest Volk
Reprint of 1911 edition. Paper. Kraus, $47.00.

THE ARCHAEOLOGY OF THE EASTERN UNITED STATES
James B. Griffin, Editor
28 archaeologists present a survey of the area east of the Rocky Mountains. Illus. 598 pp. University of Chicago Press, 1952. $20.00.

ARCHAEOLOGY OF THE FLORIDA GULF COAST
G.R. Willey
Reprint of 1949 edition. Illus. AMS Press, $72.50.

ARCHAEOLOGY OF THE ONEIDA IROQUOIS, Volume 1
Peter Pratt
Pierce College, 1976. $12.50.

ARCHAEOLOGY OF THE U.S.
Samuel F. Haven
Reprint of 1856 edition. AMS Press, $37.50.

THE ARCHAEOLOGY OF THE YAKIMA VALLEY
Harlan I. Smith
Reprint of 1910 edition. AMS Press.

ARCHAEOLOGY OF THE YAKUTAT BAY AREA, ALASKA
Frederick De Laguna, et al
Reprint of 1964 edition. Scholarly Press.

ARCHAEOLOGY: SUPPLEMENT TO THE HANDBOOK OF MIDDLE AMERICAN INDIANS, Volume 1
Jeremy A. Sabloff, Editor
Illus. 480 pp. University of Texas Press, 1981. $55.00.

ARCHAIC HUNTERS AND GATHERERS IN THE AMERICAN MIDWEST
James A. Brown; James L. Phillips, Editor
Academic Press, 1983. $45.00.

ARCHITECT OF AMERICA'S EARLY INDIAN POLICY: 1816-1830
Herman J. Viola and Thomas L. McKenney
Swallow Press, 1974. $20.00.

ARCTIC ARCHAEOLOGY: AN ANNOTATED BIBLIOGRAPHY AND HISTORY
Albert A. Dekin, Jr.
Includes books, articles, unpublished papers, dissertations, museums with Arctic colletions, libraries, etc., all on Arctic studies. 280 pp. Garland, 1975. $33.00.

ARCTIC ART: ESKIMO IVORY
James G. Smith
Examples of Eskimo art from the Museum's collection. The text discusses the people of the Arctic. 127 pp. Paper. Museum of the American Indian, $19.95.

ARCTIC ESKIMO
C. Whittaker
Reprint of 1937 edition. A record of fifty years experience and observations among the Eskimo. Illus. Map. AMS Press.

ARCTIC LIFE:
CHALLENGE TO SURVIVE
  M. Jacobs and J. Richardson, III, Editors
Illus. 208 pp. Paper. University of Washington
Press, 1982. $17.50.

AN AREAL-TYPOLOGICAL STUDY
OF AMERICAN INDIAN LANGUAGES
NORTH OF MEXICO
  J. Sherzer
Paper. Elsevier-Nelson, 1976. $25.75.

ARGILLITE: ART OF THE
HAIDA NATIVE CULTURE
  Leslie Drew and Douglas Wilson
Illus. 350 pp. Hancock House, 1980. $35.00.
Universe Books, $40.00.

*ARILLA SUN DOWN
  Virginia Hamilton
Part Black, part Indian, Arilla Sun Down
struggles to find her own sense of self. Grades 7-
12. 248 pp. Greenwillow Books, 1976. $10.95.

ARISTOTLE AND THE AMERICAN
INDIAN: A STUDY IN RACE
PREJUDICE IN THE MODERN WORLD
  Lewis Hanke
Paper. Indiana University Press, 1970.

ARK OF EMPIRE:
THE AMERICAN FRONTIER
  Dale Van Every
Reprint of 1963 edition. Ayer Co. Publishers,
$15.00.

THE ARMY AND THE NAVAJO:
THE BOSQUE REDONDO RESERVATION
EXPERIMENT, 1863-1868
  Gerald Thompson
Chronicles the federal government's attempt to
find solutions to problems of raids by Navajo
and Apache Indians. 196 pp. Paper. University
of Arizona Press, 1976. $7.50.

THE ARROW AND THE CROSS
  John U. Terrell
Capra Press, 1979. $14.95.

ARROW-MAKER
  Mary H. Austin
Revised 1915 edition. AMS Press, $12.50.

ARROWS FOUR: PROSE AND POETRY
BY YOUNG AMERICAN INDIANS
  Terry D. Allen, Editor
Paper. Pocket Books, Inc., $1.95.

ART AND ARTIFACTS OF THE
PACIFIC, AFRICA AND
THE AMERICAS
  Steven Phelps
Illus. Rowman & Littlefield, 1976. $52.50.

ART AND ENVIRONMENT
IN NATIVE AMERICA
  M.E. King and I.R. Traylor, Jr. Editors
Illus. 169 pp. Paper. Texas Tech Press, 1974.
$8.00.

ART AND INDIAN CHILDREN OF
THE DAKOTAS...AN INTRODUCTION
TO ART AND OTHER IDEAS
Three volumes: Book 2, 167 pp., paper, $6.50;
Book 4, 81 pp., paper, $5.00; Book 5, 206 pp.,
cloth, $10.00. Supt. of Documents.

ART AND INDIAN INDIVIDUALISTS
  Guy and Doris Monthan
The lives and works of 17 Indian artists. Illus.
168 pp. Northland Press, 1975. $40.00.

ART IN THE LIFE OF THE
NORTHWEST COAST INDIANS
  Erna Gunther
Illus. 275 pp. Paper. International Specialized
Books, 1966. $12.95.

ART OF THE AMERICAN INDIAN
  Levin, et al: Vandervelde, Editor
Paper. Council for Indian Education, 1973. $1.95.

THE ART OF AMERICAN
INDIAN COOKING
  Yeffe Kimball and Jean Anderson
Presents nearly 200 American Indian historic
recipes. 216 pp. Doubleday, 1965. $8.95.

THE ART OF NORVAL MORRISSEAU
  Lister Sinclair and Jack Pollack
Illus. Methuen, Inc., 1979. $50.00.

ART OF THE EASTERN
PLAINS INDIANS: THE NATHAN
STURGIS COLLECTION
  Norman Feder
Illus. 72 pp. Paper. Brooklyn Museum, 1964.
$2.50.

*ART OF THE ESKIMO
  Shirley Glubok
Grades 2-6. Illus. Harper & Row, 1964. $8.95.

ART OF THE FIRST AMERICANS
  Cincinnati Art Museum
Illus. 104 pp. Paper. University of Washington
Press, 1976. $15.00.

*ART OF THE NORTH
AMERICAN INDIAN
  Shirley Glubok
Grades 2-6. Illus. Harper & Row, 1964. $8.95.

ART OF THE NORTHERN TLINGIT
  Aldona Jonaitis
Illus. 232 pp. University of Washington Press,
1985. $30.00.

ART OF THE NORTHWEST
COAST INDIANS
Robert B. Inverarity
Second edition. Illus. 244 pp. Paper. University
of California Press, 1967. $12.95.

*THE ART OF THE
NORTHWEST COAST INDIANS
Shirley Glubok
Grades 4-12. Illus. 48 pp. Macmillan, 1975. $8.95

*THE ART OF THE PLAINS INDIANS
Shirley Glubok
Grades 4-12. Illus. 48 pp. Macmillan, 1975, $8.95.

THE ART OF PRECOLUMBIAN GOLD:
THE JAN MITCHELL COLLECTION
Julie Jones, et al
Illus. 256 pp. New York Graphic Society, 1985.
$39.00.

*THE ART OF THE
SOUTHEASTERN INDIANS
Shirley Glubok
Grades 4-12. Illus. Macmillan, 1978. $10.95.

*THE ART OF
THE SOUTHWEST INDIANS
Shirley Glubok
Grades 4-12. Illus. Macmillan, 1971. $6.95.

ART OF THE TOTEM
Maurice Barbeau
Illus. 64 pp. Hancock House, 1984. $5.95.

*THE ART OF THE
WOODLAND INDIANS
Shirley Glubok
Grades 4-12. Illus. 48 pp. Macmillan,
1976. $10.95.

ARTIFACTS OF
PREHISTORIC AMERICA
Louis A. Brennan
Illus. Stackpole Books, 1975. $17.95.

ARTIST WANDERING
AMONG CHEYENNES
Frederic Remington
Reprint of 1889 edition. Illus. 11 pp. Paper.
Shorey, $3.00.

ARTS AND CRAFTS
OF THE CHEROKEE
Rodney Leftwich
Appalachian Consortium, $8.95.

ARTS OF THE INDIAN AMERICAS:
NORTH, CENTRAL AND SOUTH:
LEAVES FROM THE SACRED TREE
Jamake Highwater
Illus. 320 pp. Harper & Row, 1983. $35.00.

ARTS OF THE RAVEN: MASTERWORKS
BY THE NORTHWEST COAST INDIAN
Wilson Duff
Illus. 112 pp. Paper. University of Washington
Press, 1967. $12.50.

AN ASIAN ANTHROPOLOGIST IN THE
SOUTH: FIELD EXPERIENCES WITH
BLACKS, INDIANS AND WHITES
Choong S. Kim
University of Tennessee, 1977. $10.00; paper,
$5.95.

*AS GRANDFATHER TOLD ME
Ugadali
Grades 5-9. Council for Indian Education, $6.45;
paper, $1.95.

AS IN A VISION: MASTERWORKS
OF AMERICAN INDIAN ART
Edwin L. Wade, et al
Illus. 144 pp. Paper. University of Oklahoma
Press, 1983. $19.95.

AS LONG AS THE RIVER SHALL RUN:
AN ETHNOHISTORY OF PYRAMID
LAKE INDIAN RESERVATION
Marta Knack and Omer C. Stewart
416 pp. University of California Press, 1984.
$35.00.

AS LONG AS THE SUN SHINES
AND WATER FLOWS: A READER IN
CANADIAN NATIVE STUDIES
Ian A. Getty and Antoine S. Lussier
384 pp. International Specialized Book Service,
1983. $29.95; paper, $12.50.

ASIATIC INFLUENCES IN
PRE-COLUMBIAN AMERICAN INDIAN
Paul Shao
Illus. Iowa State University Press, 1976. $25.00.

ASPECTS OF INDIAN HISTORY
AND CIVILIZATION
B. Prakash
Lawrence Verry, Inc., 1965. $8.50.

ASPECTS OF UPPER GREAT LAKES
ANTHROPOLOGY: PAPERS IN HONOR
OF LLOYD A. WILFORD
Elden Johnson, Editor
Illus. 190 pp. Paper. Minnesota Historical
Society, 1974. $10.50.

THE ASSAULT ON INDIAN
TRIBALISM: THE GENERAL ALLOTMENT
LAW (DAWES ACT) OF 1887
Wilcomb E. Washburn
79 pp. Paper. J.B. Lippincott and Robert E.
Krieger, 1975. $2.95.

THE ASSAULT ON ASSIMILATION: JOHN COLLIER AND THE ORIGINS OF INDIAN POLICY REFORM
Laurence C. Kelly
Illus. 432 pp. University of New Mexico Press, 1983. $24.50.

THE ASSINIBOINE
R.H. Lowie
Reprint of 1909 edition. Illus. AMS Press, $22.45.

ASSOCIATION ON AMERICAN INDIAN AFFAIRS: APPOINTMENT CALENDAR
Indian history and portraits of today's Indian people by Indian photographers. Association on American Indian Affairs, $11.00 each.

ASSOMPION SASH
Marius Barbeau
Describes various garters and sashes made by French Canadians, Indians and Norwegians. Illus. 52 pp. Paper. National Museum of Canada, $3.25.

*AT THE CENTER OF THE WORLD
Betty Baker
An adaptation of Pima and Papago Indian creation of myths into a continuous flowing tale. Grades 3-6. Illus. 64 pp. Macmillan, 1973. $4.95.

ATHAPASKAN ADAPTATIONS: HUNTERS AND FISHERMEN OF THE SUBARCTIC FORESTS
James W. Van Stone
176 pp. Paper. Harlan Davidson, 1974. $8.95.

THE ATHAPASKANS: STRANGERS OF THE NORTH
A. McFadyen Clark
Illus. Paper. University of Chicago Press, 1974. $9.95.

ATTITUDES OF COLONIAL POWERS TOWARD THE AMERICAN INDIAN
Howard Peckham and Charles Gibson, Editors
University of Utah Press, 1976. $8.00.

ATNATATNAS NATIVES OF COPPER RIVER, ALASKA
Lt. Henry T. Allen
Extracted from 1886 edition. Paper. Shorey, $2.00.

AUDIOVISUAL PRODUCTIONS FOR AND ABOUT NATIVE AMERICAN MUSEUMS AND CULTURAL CENTER
Office of Museum Programs, 1985.

*A'UNA
Traditional Indian athletic activities, and recipes productive of good health are described. Grades 4-12. 40 pp. Daybreak Star Press, $5.00.

AUTHENTIC AMERICAN INDIAN BEADWORK AND HOW TO DO IT: WITH 50 CHARTS FOR BEAD-WEAVING AND 21 FULL SIZE PATTERNS FOR APPLIQUE
Pamela Stanley-Millner
48 pp. Paper. Dover, 1985. $2.75.

AUTHENTIC AND COMPREHENSIVE HISTORY OF BUFFALO, 1864-1865
W. Ketchum
Two volumes. Scholarly Press, $35.00 per set.

AUTHENTIC INDIAN DESIGNS
Maria Naylor, Editor
2,500 illustrations from reports of the Bureau of American Ethnology. Illus. 256 pp. Peter Smith, $16.75. Paper, Dover, $7.95.

THE AUTOBIOGRAPHY OF DELFINA CUERO: A DIEGUENO WOMAN
Delfina Cuero
Paper. Malki Museum Press, 1970. $4.50.

AUTOBIOGRAPHY OF A PAPAGO WOMAN
Ruth Underhill
Reprint of 1936 edition. Paper. Kraus, $12.00.

AUTOBIOGRAPHY OF A WINNEBAGO INDIANS
Paul Radin
Reprint of 1920 edition. 91 pp. Peter Smith, $8.00. Paper. Dover, $2.25.

AUTOBIOGRAPHY OF A YAQUI POET
Refugio Savala
Edited with background and interpretation by Kathleen Sands, and with an introduction by Edward H. Spicer
Illus. 225 pp. University of Arizona Press, 1980. $18.50; paper, $8.95.

AWAKENING MINORITIES: CONTINUITY AND CHANGE
John R. Howard, Editor
Second edition. Includes: *American Indians; Goodbye to Tonto,* and *Iowa's Indians Come of Age.* 130 pp. Transaction Books, 1982. $15.95; paper, $7.95.

. B

BACKGROUND HISTORY OF THE COEUR D'ALENE INDIAN RESERVATION
Jerome Peltier
100 pp. Ye Galleon Press.

BACKWARD: AN ESSAY ON INDIANS, TIME AND PHOTOGRAPHY
Will Baker
Illus. 420 pp. North Atlantic, 1983. $24.95; paper, $12.95.

BAD MEDICINE AND GOOD:
TALES OF THE KIOWAS
W.S. Nye; Nick Eggenhofer, Illustrator
Reprint of 1962 edition. Illus. Maps. Index. 291 pp.
Paper. University of Oklahoma Press, $9.95.

*A BAG OF BONES: LEGENDS
OF THE WINTU INDIANS OF
NORTHERN CALIFORNIA
Marcelle Masson
Grades 4-12. Naturegraph, 1966. $10.95; paper, $4.95.

THE BARK CANOES AND
SKIN BOATS OF NORTH AMERICA
Edwin Adney and Howard Chapelle
Reprint of 1964 second edition. Illus. 242 pp.
Smithsonian, Institution Press, $19.95.

BASKETMAKER CAVES IN
THE PRAYER ROCK DISTRICT,
NORTHEASTERN ARIZONA
Elizabeth A. Morris
Paper. University of Arizona Press, 1980. $8.50.

BASKETMAKER CAVES OF
NORTHEASTERN ARIZONA
S.J. Guernsey and A.V. Kidder
Reprint of 1921 edition. Illus. Paper. Kraus, $20.00.

BASKETRY DESIGNS OF
THE SALISH INDIANS
Livingston Farrand
Reprint of 1900 edition. AMS, $15.00.

BASKETRY OF THE PAPAGO
AND PIMA INDIANS
Mary Lois Kissell
A study of the art and handicraft of basket-weaving by Indians of Arizona. Reissue of 1916 edition. Revised publisher's preface, and new introduction. Illus. 158 pp. Rio Grande Press, 1982. $12.00.

BASKETRY OF THE SAN CARLOS
APACHE INDIANS
Helen H. Roberts
Illus. 220 pp. Paper. Rio Grande Press, 1985. $12.00.

BATTLE OF HORSESHOE BEND
W.H. Brantley, Jr.
Illus. Paper. Southern University Press, 1955, $3.75.

THE BATTLE OF WASHITA:
THE SHERIDAN-CUSTER INDIAN
CAMPAIGN OF 1867-1869
Stan Hoig
300 pp. University of Nebraska Press, $21.50; paper, $6.95.

THE BATTLE OF WISCONSIN HEIGHTS
Crawford B. Thayer, Editor
Illus. 416 pp. Paper. Thayer Associates, 1983. $10.95.

BAYOU SALADO
Virginia M. Simmons
Illus. 280 pp. Paper. Century One, 1982. $8.95.

BEADS AND BEADWORK OF
THE AMERICAN INDIAN
William C. Orchard
Revised 1929 second edition. 184 pp. Paper.
Museum of the American Indian, $9.95.

BEAR CHIEF'S WAR SHIRT
James W. Schultz and Wilbur Betts
Illus. 240 pp. Mountain Press, 1984. $14.95; paper, $8.95.

THE BEAR RIVER MASSACRE
Newell Hart
Illus. 300 pp. Cache Valley, 1982. $35.00.

*BEAR'S HEART: SCENES FROM
THE LIFE OF A CHEYENNE ARTIST
OF ONE HUNDRED YEARS AGO
WITH PICTURES OF HIMSELF
Burton Supree and Ann Ross
Grades 7-adult. Illus. 64 pp. J.B. Lippincott, 1977. $13.95.

*BEAUTIFUL INDIAN PEOPLE
"The Weewish Tree" Editors
Biographies. Illus. Paper. The Indian Historian Press, 1981. $9.95.

BEFORE COLUMBUS: LINKS BETWEEN
THE OLD WORLD AND ANCIENT
AMERICA
Cyrus H. Gordon
Crown Publishers, 1971. $9.95.

*BEFORE THE WHITE MAN CAME
Meldred Jenkins
How the Pacific Coast Indians lived. Grades 4-9.
Illus. 182 pp. Binford & Mort, 1951.

BEGINNING CHEROKEE
Ruth B. Holmes and Betty S. Smith
Revised edition. Illus. 364 pp. University of Oklahoma Press, 1978. $18.50; paper, $9.95.

BEHIND THE TRAIL OF
BROKEN TREATIES
Vine Deloria, Jr.
Historical review of Indian political recognition and land title with respect to other nations. 296 pp.
Paper. University of Texas Press, 1974. $9.95.
Institute for the Development of Indian Law, $3.45.

BEHIND THE TREE OF PEACE:
A SOCIOLOGICAL ANALYSIS
OF IROQUOIS WARFARE
George Snyderman
Reprint of 1948 edition. AMS, $17.00.

THE BELCHER MOUND:
A STRATIFIED CADDOAN SITE
IN CADDO PARISH, LOUISIANA
C.H. Webb
Reprint of 1959 edition. Paper. Kraus, $40.00.

BELDEN, THE WHITE CHIEF:
OR, TWELVE YEARS AMONG THE WILD
INDIANS OF THE PLAINS FROM THE
DIARY AND MANUSCRIPTS OF
GEORGE BELDEN
James Brisbin, Editor
Facsimile of the 1870 edition. Illus. 535 pp.
Ohio University Press, $10.95.

BELIEF AND WORSHIP
IN NATIVE NORTH AMERICA
Ake Hultkrantz; Christopher Vecsey, Editor
358 pp. Syracuse University Press, 1981. $30.00.

BELLA BELLA TALES
Franz Boas
Reprint of 1932 edition. Kraus, $16.00.

*BELLE HIGHWALKING: THE NARRA-
TIVE OF A NORTHERN CHEYENNE
WOMAN
Katheryne Weist, Editor
Grades 5-12. 66 pp. Council for Indian Education,
1979. $6.95; paper, $2.95.

*BENEATH THE SINGING PINES
Louise J. Walker
Grades 6-10. Hillsdale Educational, 1967. $8.50.

*ROBERT BENNETT
Mary C. Nelson
Grades 5-12. Illus. Dillon Press, 1976. $7.95.

BEOTHUK AND MICMAC
Frank G. Speck
Reprint of 1922 edition. AMS Press, $41.00.

THE BEOTHUCKS, OR RED INDIANS,
THE ABORIGINAL INHABITANTS
OF NEWFOUNDLAND
James P. Howley
Reprint of 1915 edition. AMS Press, $49.50.

O.E. BERNINGHAUS - TAOS, N.M.
MASTER PAINTER OF AMERICAN
INDIANS AND FRONTIER WEST
Gordon E. Sanders
Illus. 152 pp. Taos Heritage Press, 1985. $40.00.

*BETRAYED
Virginia D. Sneve
Grades 7-12. 128 pp. Holiday House, 1974. $6.95.

A BETTER KIND OF HATCHET:
LAW, TRADE, DIPLOMACY IN
THE CHEROKEE NATION
John P. Reid
262 pp. Penn State University Press, 1975. $27.50.

*BETWEEN SACRED MOUNTAINS:
NAVAJO STORIES AND LESSONS
FROM THE LAND
Sam and Janet Bingham, Editors
Grades 4-12. Illus. 290 pp. University of Arizona
Press, $35.00; paper, $19.95.

BEYOND THE RIVER AND THE BAY:
THE CANADIAN NORTHWEST IN 1811
Eric Ross
Illus. Paper. University of Toronto Press, 1970.
$6.95.

A BIBLIOGRAPHICAL GUIDE TO
THE HISTORY OF INDIAN-WHITE
RELATIONS IN THE UNITED STATES
Francis P. Prucha
Lists and discusses more than 9,000 items
including materials in the National Archives.
University of Chicago Press, 1977. $25.00; paper,
$9.95.

BIBLIOGRAPHIES OF THE LANGUAGES
OF THE NORTH AMERICAN INDIANS
James C. Pilling
Reprint of 1894 edition. Consists of nine parts in
three volumes. AMS Press, $125.00 per set.

BIBLIOGRAPHY: NATIVE AMERICAN
ARTS AND CRAFTS OF THE U.S.
A selection of books and pamphlets chosen and
annotated for their pertinence to the field of
contemporary Native American arts and crafts of
the U.S. 8 pp. Indian Arts and Crafts Board. No
charge.

BIBLIOGRAPHY OF
THE ALGONQUIAN LANGUAGES
James C. Pilling
Reprint of 1891 edition. Scholarly Press.

BIBLIOGRAPHY OF ARTICLES
AND PAPERS ON NORTH AMERICAN
INDIAN ART
Anne D. Harding and Patricia Bolling
Reprint of 1938 edition. Gordon Press, 1980.
Library binding, $75.00.

A BIBLIOGRAPHY OF
THE ATHAPASKAN LANGUAGES
Richard T. Parr
Paper. National Museum of Canada, $3.95.

A BIBLIOGRAPHY OF CALIFORNIA INDIANS: ARCHAEOLOGY, ETHNOGRAPHY, INDIAN HISTORY
Robert F. Heizer and Albert B. Elsasser
Covers the prehistoric archaeology of California and the history of California Indians from the mid-16th century to the present. 280 pp. Garland, 1976. $41.00.

A BIBLIOGRAPHY OF CONTEMPORARY NORTH AMERICAN INDIANS: SELECTED AND PARTIALLY ANNOTATED WITH STUDY GUIDES
William H. Hodge; intro. by Paul Prucha
320 pp. Interland Publishing, 1976. $27.50.

BIBLIOGRAPHY OF NON-PRINT INSTRUCTIONAL MATERIALS ON THE AMERICAN INDIAN
R. Irwin Goodwin
221 pp. Paper. Brigham Young University Press, 1972. $3.95.

BIBLIOGRAPHY OF THE CHINOOKAN LANGUAGE
James C. Pilling
Extracted from 1893 edition. Illus. 81 pp. Paper. Shorey Publications, $8.00.

BIBLIOGRAPHY OF THE CHUMASH AND THEIR PREDECESSORS
Eugene N. Anderson, Jr.
Paper. Ballena Press, 1978. $.6.95.

BIBLIOGRAPHY OF THE CONSTITUTIONS AND LAWS OF THE AMERICAN INDIANS
Lester Hargrett
Reprint of 1947 edition. Illus. Paper. Kraus, $14.00. Also available on microfilm.

A BIBLIOGRAPHY OF CURRENT AMERICAN INDIAN POLICY
Jim Buchanan and Fran Burkert
Paper. Vance Bibliographies, 1979. $8.00.

BIBLIOGRAPHY OF THE DIEGUENO INDIANS
Ruth F. Almstedt
Lists more than 400 titles from the days of the earliest explorers of the 16th century to the present. Map. 52 pp. Paper. Ballena Press, 1974. $3.95.

BIBLIOGRAPHY OF THE ENGLISH COLONIAL TREATIES WITH THE AMERICAN INDIAN
H. De Puy
Reprint of 1917 edition. Paper. Scholarly Press, $10.00.

BIBLIOGRAPHY OF THE ESKIMO LANGUAGE
James C. Pilling
Reprint of 1887 edition. Shorey Publications and Scholarly Press.

BIBLIOGRAPHY OF LANGUAGE ARTS MATERIALS FOR NATIVE NORTH AMERICANS, 1965-1974 & 1975-1976
G. Edward Evans, Karin Abbey and Dennis Reed
Paper. American Indian Studies Center, 1977. (1965-1974), 283 pp. $5.00; (1975-1976), 153 pp., $4.00.

BIBLIOGRAPHY OF LANGUAGES OF NATIVE CALIFORNIA: INCLUDING CLOSELY RELATED LANGUAGES OF ADJACENT AREAS
William Bright
234 pp. Scarecrow Press, 1982. $17.50.

BIBLIOGRAPHY OF THE LUISENO INDIANS
Carol Walker, Compiler
Paper. Acoma Books, 1976.

BIBLIOGRAPHY OF THE NAVAHO INDIANS
Clyde Kluckhohn and K. Spencer
Reprint of 1940 edition. AMS Press, $16.00.

A BIBLIOGRAPHY OF NAVAJO AND NATIVE AMERICAN TEACHING MATERIAL
T.L. McCarthy and Regina Lynch
Revised edition. 165 pp. Navajo Curriculum, 1983. $8.50.

BIBLIOGRAPHY OF NORTH AMERICAN FOLKLORE AND FOLKSONG
Charles Haywood
Two volumes. Lists all available information on the myths and rituals of more than 250 tribes of American and Canadian Indians and Eskimos. Reprint of 1951 edition. Illus. Index. Biblio. Dover Publications, $20.00.

BIBLIOGRAPHY OF NORTH AMERICAN INDIAN MENTAL HEALTH
Dianne Kelso and Carolyn Attneave, Editors
Illus. 404 pp. Greenwood Press, 1981. $45.00.

BIBLIOGRAPHY OF THE OSAGE
Terry P. Wilson
172 pp. Scarecrow Press, 1985. $15.00.

BIBLIOGRAPHY OF THE SIOUX
Jack W. Marken and Herbert T. Hoover
388 pp. Scarecrow Press, 1980. $20.00.

BIG BEAD MESA: AN ARCHAEOLOGICAL STUDY OF NAVAHO ACCULTURATIONS
D.L. Keur
Reprint of 1941 edition. Paper. AMS Press and Kraus Reprint, $15.00.

BIG BEAR: THE END OF FREEDOM
Hugh A. Dempsey
Illus. 227 pp. University of Nebraska Press, 1985. $22.95.

BIG BROTHER'S INDIAN PROGRAMS: WITH RESERVATIONS
Sar A. Levitan and Barbara Hetrick
256 pp. McGraw-Hill, 1971., $11.95.

BIG CYPRESS: A CHANGING SEMINOLE COMMUNITY
M. Garbarino; Spindler, Editors
Paper. Holt Rinehart & Winston, 1972. $7.95.

*BIG ENOUGH
Penny Nearing, et al
Grades 2-5. Paper. Council for Indian Education, 1974. $1.95.

BIG FALLING SNOW: A TEWA-HOPI INDIANS LIFE AND TIMES AND THE HISTORY AND TRADITIONS OF HIS PEOPLE
Albert Yava; Harold Courlander, Editor
Illus. 190 pp. Paper. University of New Mexico Press, 1982. $9.95.

THE BIG MISSOURI WINTER COUNT
Roberta C. Cheney
Illus. 48 pp. Naturegraph, 1979. $9.95; paper, $3.95.

BILINGUAL EDUCATION FOR AMERICAN INDIANS
U.S. Bureau of Indian Affairs
Francesco Cordasco, Editor
Reprint of 1971 edition. Ayer Co. Publishers, $22.00.

BILINGUALISM IN THE SOUTHWEST
Paul Turner, Editor
Includes a separate section on the American Indians.
352 pp. Paper. University of Arizona Press, 1973. $7.95.

*BILL RED COYOTE IS A NUT
Hap Gilliland
Grades K-3. Paper. Council for Indian Education, 1981. $1.95.

A BIOBIBLIOGRAPHY OF NATIVE AMERICAN WRITERS, 1772-1924: SUPPLEMENT
Daniel F. Littlefield, Jr. and
James W. Parsons
350 pp. Scarecrow Press, 1985. $27.50.

BIOCULTURAL ADAPTATION IN PREHISTORIC AMERICA
Robert L. Blakely, Editor
144 pp. Paper. University of Georgia Press, 1977. $7.50.

BIOGRAPHICAL AND HISTORICAL INDEX OF AMERICAN INDIANS AND PERSONS INVOLVED IN INDIAN AFFAIRS
U.S. Bureau of Indian Affairs
Lists the biography, history and social conditions of American Indians from the latter half of the 19th century to about 1920. Eight volumes. 6,600 pp. Biblio. G.K. Hall, 1966. $855.00.

BIOGRAPHICAL DICTIONARY OF INDIANS OF THE AMERICAS
Contains over 1,200 detailed biographies of significant Indians past and present, and 300 portraits. Two volumes. 300 photos. 570 pp. American Indian Publishers, 1984. $145.00 per set.

BIOGRAPHY OF FRANCIS SLOCUM, THE LOST SISTER OF WYOMING: A COMPLETE NARRATIVE OF HER CAPTIVITY AND WANDERINGS AMONG THE INDIANS
John F. Meginness
Reprint of 1891 edition. 260 pp. Ayer Co. Publishers, $21.00.

*BLACK ELK SPEAKS
John Neihardt
Grades 10-12. 272 pp. Paper. Washington Square Press, $3.95.

BLACK HAWK: AN AUTOBIOGRAPHY
Donald Jackson
Reprint of 1955 edition. Maps. 177 pp. Paper. University of Illinois Press, $3.95

*BLACK HAWK AND JIM THORPE: SUPER HEROES
Betty Greison, Sam Bloom and Hap Gilliland
Biographies of two Sauk heroes. Grades 5-12. Council for Indian Education, $9.95; paper, $4.95.

BLACK HAWK SONGS, POEMS
Michael Borich
86 pp. University of Illinois Press.

THE BLACK HILLS; OR, THE LAST HUNTING GROUND OF THE DACOTAHS
Annie Tallent
Reprint of 1899 edition. 594 pp. Brevit Press, $14.95; limited leather edition, $50.00. Facsimile edition. Illus. Ayer Co. Publishers, $62.00.

BLACK MOUNTAIN BOY
Vada Carlson and Gary Witherspoon
Illus. 81 pp. Paper. Navajo Curriculum, 1982. $4.50.

**BLACK SAND: PREHISTORY
IN NORTHERN ARIZONA**
Harold S. Colton
Reprint of 1960 edition. Illus. 132 pp. Greenwood,
$22.50.

BLACKFEET AND BUFFALO
James W. Schultz; Keith C. Seele, Editor
Reprint of 1962 edition. Illus. Glossary. Index.
Map. 384 pp. University of Olahoma Press.

**BLACKFEET AND GROS VENTRE
TRIBES OF INDIANS, APPRAISAL OF
LANDS IN NORTHERN MONTANA, 1888**
Darwin Harbin
402 pp. Clearwater, 1973. $114.00.

**BLACKFEET AND GROS VENTRE
TRIBES OF INDIANS, LANDS
IN NORTHERN MONTANA, 1888**
John C. Ewers
180 pp. Clearwater, 1973. $55.50.

**BLACKFEET AND GROS VENTRE
TRIBES IN MONTANA IN THE AGREE-
MENT OF MAY 1, 1888: HISTORICAL
REPORT ON LANDS CEDED**
Merrill Burlingame
Illus. 80 pp. Clearwater, 1974. $31.50.

**THE BLACKFEET INDIAN
RESERVATION IN MONTANA:
HISTORICAL REPORT**
Thomas R. Wessell
Clearwater Publishing, $95.00.

BLACKFEET INDIANS
John C. Ewers
Reprint. Illus. Map. 312 pp. Garland Publishing,
$42.00.

BLACKFEET INDIANS
W. Reiss and F.B. Linderman
Reprint. Gordon Press, 1977. $75.95.

**THE BLACKFEET: RAIDERS ON
THE NORTHWESTERN PLAINS**
John C. Ewers
Reprint of 1958 edition. Illus. 377 pp. University
of Oklahoma Press, 1983. $22.95.

BLACKFEET: THEIR ART AND CULTURE
John C. Ewers
Illus. 96 pp. Paper, Hancock House, 1985. $6.95.

BLACKFEET: THEIR HISTORY
John C. Ewers
Reprint. 96 pp. Paper. Hancock House, $6.95.

**BLACKFEET TRIBE CEDED LANDS
IN MONTANA, AGREEMENT OF
MAY 1, 1888: VALUATION**
Mont H. Saunderson
Illus. 100 pp. Clearwater, 1974. $36.00.

A BLACKFOOT-ENGLISH VOCABULARY
C.C. Uhlenbeck and R.H. Van Gulik
Reprint of 1934 edition. AMS Press, $45.00.

**BLACKFOOT LODGE TALES:
THE STORY OF A PRAIRIE PEOPLE**
George B. Grinnell
Reprint of 1892 edition. 310 pp. Corner House,
$10.00. Paper. University of Nebraska Press,
$6.95.

A BLACKFOOT SOURCEBOOK
Clark Wisler
Reprint. 510 pp. Garland Publishing, $60.00.

BLESSINGWAY
Leland C. Wyman
The central rite of Navajo religion. Prsents
Navajo origin myths and ritual poetry. Illus. 660
pp. University of Arizona Press, 1970. $19.95.

**BLOOD OF THE LANDS: THE GOVERN-
MENT AND CORPORATE WAR AGAINST
THE AMERICAN INDIAN MOVEMENT**
Rex Weyler
Illus. 302 pp. Paper. Random House, 1984. $8.95.

THE BLOOD PEOPLE
Adolf Hungry Wolf
Harper & Row, 1977. $12.95.

BLOODY KNIFE
Ben Innis
Illus. Old Army Press, 1973. $9.95.

***BLUE JACKET:
WAR CHIEF OF SHAWNEES**
Allen W. Eckert
Grades 7-adult. 177 pp. Paper. Landfall Press,
1983. $5.95.

*BLUE THUNDER
Richard Throssel
Grades 6-12. 32 pp. Paper. Council for Indian
Education, 1976. $1.95.

FRANZ BOAS, 1858-1942
A.L. Kroeber
Reprint of 1943 edition. Paper. Kraus, $12.00.

**"BO'JOU, NEEJEE!":
PROFILES OF CANADIAN INDIAN ART**
Ted J. Brasser
Source of ethnographic information on central
Indian artifacts. Illus. 204 pp. Paper. National
Museums of Canada and University of Chicago
Press, 1976. $16.95.

**BOOK OF AUTHENTIC INDIAN
LIFE CRAFTS**
Oscar E. Norbeck
Revised edition. Illus. 260 pp. Galloway, 1974.
$9.95.

**BOOK OF THE GODS AND RITES
AND THE ANCIENT CALENDAR**
Fr. Diego Duran; Fernando Horcasitas and
Doris Heyden, Translators
Illus. University of Oklahoma Press, 1970. $19.95;
paper, $9.95.

BOOK OF THE HOPI
Frank Waters
Reveals the Hopi view of life, kept secret for
generations. Illus. 448 pp. Paper. Viking-Penguin,
1977. $4.95.

**THE BOOK OF INDIAN
CRAFTS AND COSTUMES**
Bernard S. Mason
Describes the crafts and customs of the Indians of
the Woodlands and Plains. Illus. 118 pp. John
Wiley & Sons, 1946. $14.95.

**THE BOOK OF INDIAN
CRAFTS AND INDIAN LORE**
Julian H. Salomon
A general discussion of the Indians of the U.S.
Reprint. Illus. Biblio. Index. 418 pp. Gordon
Press, $69.95.

***THE BOOK OF INDIAN
CRAFTS AND INDIAN LORE**
Julian H. Salomon
Reprint. Grades 5-adult. Illus. 418 pp. Harper &
Row, $16.00.

THE BOOK OF INDIANS
S.G. Drake
Reprint of 1841 edition. AMS Press, $49.00.

BOOK OF THE NAVAJO
Raymond F. Locke
Revised edition. Illus. Paper. Mankind, 1979.
$4.95.

**A BOOK OF TALES, BEING MYTHS
OF THE NORTH AMERICAN INDIANS**
Charles E. Woods
Reprint. Gordon Press, $59.95.

**BOOKS ON AMERICAN INDIANS
AND ESKIMOS**
Mary J. Lass-Woodfin
American Library Association, 1977. Text
edition, $25.00.

**BORDER TOWNS OF
THE NAVAJO NATION**
Aaron Yava
Second edition. Illus. 80 pp. Paper. Holmgangers,
1975. $4.00.

**BOSQUE REDONDO: A STUDY
OF CULTURAL STRESS AT THE
NAVAJO RESERVATION**
Lynn R. Bailey
Illus. 275 pp. Westernlore, $8.50.

**THE BOX OF DAYLIGHT:
NORTHWEST COAST INDIAN ART**
Bill Holm
Illus. 160 pp. University of Washington Press,
1983. $40.00; paper, $19.95.

**THE BOY CAPTIVES, BEING THE
TRUE STORY OF THE EXPERIENCES
AND HARDSHIPS OF CLINTON L.
SMITH AND JEFF D. SMITH, AMONG
THE COMANCHE AND APACHE INDIANS
DURING THE EARLY DAYS**
Clinton Smith
Reprint of 1927 edition. Garland Publishing,
$42.00.

**THE BOY GEORGE WASHINGTON
AGED SIXTEEN: HIS OWN ACCOUNT
OF AN IROQUOIS INDIAN DANCE**
Albert C. Myers
Reprint of 1932 edition. Norwood Editions,
$15.00.

**THE BOYS SITE AND THE EARLY
ONTARIO IROQUOIS TRADITION**
C.S. Reid
Paper. National Museums of Canada, $3.95.

A BRANCH OF CALIFORNIA REDWOOD
William Oandasan
62 pp. Paper. American Indian Studies Center,
1980. $3.00.

**A BRIEF HISTORY
OF THE PEQUOT WAR**
J. Mason
Facsimile of 1736 edition. Ayer Co. Publishers,
$10.00.

**A BRIEF AND TRUE REPORT OF
THE NEW FOUND LAND IN VIRGINIA**
Thomas Harriot
Reprint of 1588 edition. 48 pp. Walter J. Johnson,
$7.00.

**THE BRIGHT EDGE: A GUIDE
TO THE NATIONAL PARKS OF
THE COLORADO PLATEAU**
Stephen Trimble
Illus. Paper. Museum of Northern Arizona, 1979.
$4.95.

**BRINGING HOME ANIMALS:
RELIGIOUS IDEOLOGY AND MODE OF
PRODUCTION OF THE MISTASSINI
CREE HUNTERS**
Adrian Tanner
St. Martin's Press, 1979. $25.00.

**BRITISH ADMINISTRATION OF THE
SOUTHERN INDIANS,** 1756-1783
Helen Shaw
Reprint of 1931 edition. AMS Press, $24.50.

BRITISH TRAVELERS AMONG THE
SOUTHERN INDIANS, 1660-1763
J. Ralph Randolph
350 pp. University of Oklahoma Press, 1973.
$14.50.

*BROKEN ICE
Hap Gilliland
Grades 1-8. Paper. Council for Indian Education,
1972. $1.95.

BROKEN K PUEBLO: PREHISTORIC
SOCIAL ORGANIZATION IN THE
AMERICAN SOUTHWEST
James N. Hill
149 pp. Paper. University of Arizona Press, 1970.
$6.95.

BROKEN PATTERN SUNLIGHT AND
SHADOWS OF HOPI HISTORY
Vada Carlson
The coming of the Spanish broke the ancient
pattern life of the Hopis. Illus. by Joe Rodriguez.
Naturegraph Publishers.

BROKEN PEACE PIPES:
A FOUR-HUNDRED YEAR HISTORY
OF THE AMERICAN INDIAN
Irvin M. Peithmann
320 pp. Charles C. Thomas, 1964. $9.75.

THE BROKEN RING: THE DESTRUC-
TION OF THE CALIFORNIA INDIANS
Van H. Sarner
Illus. Westernlore, 1981. $9.50.

*BROTHER OF THE WOLVES
Jean Thompson; illus. by Steve Marchesi
An orphaned Indian whose first year of life is
spent among a lupine family. Grades 3-6. 160 pp.
William Morrow, 1978. $9.75.

*JOSEPH BROWN: OR, THE YOUNG
TENNESSEAN WHOSE LIFE WAS SAVED
BY THE POWER OF PRAYER,
AN INDIAN TALE
Thomas O. Summers
Reprint of 1856 edition. Garland Publishing,
$42.00.

BRUCHKO
Olson
Paper. Creation House, 1977. $1.95.

BUCKSKIN AND BLANKET DAYS:
MEMOIRS OF A FRIEND OF
THE INDIANS
Thomas Tribbles
336 pp. Paper. University of Nebraska Press,
1969. $5.95.

BUFFALO BILL AND THE WILD WEST
A picture book; analyzes the phenomenon of

Buffalo Bill—from the perspective of the 1980's.
Illus. 96 pp. University of Pittsburgh Press, 1981.
$12.95.

BUFFALO HEARTS
Sun Bear
Paper. Bear Tribe, 1976. $3.50.

*BUFFALO MOON
G. Wisler
Grades 5-9. 144 pp. Lodestar Books, 1984. $10.95.

THE BUFFALO WAR: THE HISTORY OF
THE RED RIVER UPRISING OF 1874
James L. Haley
Illus. Doubleday, 1976. $9.95

*BUFFALO WOMAN
Dorothy M. Johnson
The story of a Sioux Indian woman. Grades 10-
adult. Dodd, Mead & Co., 1977. $7.95.

BUILDING A CHIPPEWA INDIAN
BIRCHBARK CANOE
Robert E. Ritzenhaler
Second revised edition. 42 pp. Milwaukee Public
Museum, 1984. $4.00.

BULL CREEK
Jesse D. Jennings and Dorothy Sammons-Lohse
Paper. University of Utah Press, 1982. $15.00.

BURNT COPPER
Wendy Rose
Malki Museum Press, 1980. $9.95.

BURIAL MOUNDS OF CENTRAL
MINNESOTA: EXCAVATION REPORTS
Lloyd A. Wilford
Illus. Paper. Minnesota Historical Society, 1969.
$3.50.

BURIAL MOUNDS OF THE
RED RIVER HEADWATERS
Lloyd A. Wilford
Illus. 36 pp. Paper. Minnesota Historical Society,
1970. $2.00.

BURIALS OF THE ALGONQUIAN,
SIOUIAN AND CADDOAN TRIBES
WEST OF THE MISSISSIPPI
David I. Bushnell
Reprint of 1927 edition. Scholarly Press, $10.50.

BURNT-OUT FIRES:
CALIFORNIA'S MODOC INDIAN WAR
Richard N. Dillon
Illus. 384 pp. Prentice-Hall, 1973. $9.95.

**BURY MY HEART AT WOUNDED KNEE:
AN INDIAN HISTORY OF THE
AMERICAN WEST**
Dee Brown
Illus. Holt, Rinehart & Winston, 1971. $16.95.
Paper. Washington Square Press, $4.95.

***BURY MY HEART AT WOUNDED KNEE:
AN INDIAN HISTORY OF THE
AMERICAN WEST**
Dee Brown
Grades 6-adult. Illus. 225 pp. Paper. Holt,
Rinehart, 1974. $6.95.

BY CHEYENNE CAMPFIRES
George B. Grinnell
A collection of war stories, mystery stories, tales
of creation. Illus. Paper. University of Nebraska
Press, 1971. $7.50.

**BY THE PROPHET OF THE EARTH:
ETHNOBOTANY OF THE PIMA**
L.S. Curtin
Illus. 156 pp. Paper. University of Arizona Press,
1984. $7.95.

***BY THE WORK OF OUR HANDS:
CHOCTAW MATERIALS CULTURE**
Looks at several aspects of Choctaw material
culture. Grades 7-12. 84 pp. Choctaw Heritage
Press, $8.00. Teacher's guide, $5.00.

C

CADDO INDIAN POTTERY
Sam Johnson
Illus. Paper. American Indian Books, $5.95.

A CADDO SOURCEBOOK
H.F. Gregory and D.H. Thomas, Editors
Reprint. 550 pp. Garland Publishing, $65.00.

**CADDO INDIAN TRACT SITUATED IN
SOUTHWESTERN ARKANSAS AND
NORTHWESTERN LOUISIANA, 1835:
APPRAISAL**
175 pp. Clearwater, 1973. $54.00.

**THE CADDO INDIANS IN
LOUISIANA AND TEXAS**
Stuart O. Landry
60 pp. Clearwater, 1974. $27.00.

**CADDO TREATY OF JULY 1, 1835:
HISTORICAL AND ANTHROPOLOGICAL
BACKGROUND**
Charles H. Lange
165 pp. Clearwater, 1974. $52.00.

**CADDO TRIBE OF OKLAHOMA,
1541-1859**
Helen Tanner
130 pp. Clearwater, 1974. $45.00.

**CADDO TRIBE OF OKLAHOMA,
REBUTTAL STATEMENT**
Helen Tanner
144 pp. Clearwater, 1973. $46.50.

**THE CADDOAN CULTURAL AREA:
AN ARCHAEOLOGICAL PERSPECTIVE**
Don G. Wyckoff
250 pp. Clearwater, 1973. $75.00.

CADDOAN INDIANS
David Horr, Editor
Four volumes. Volume 1, Stephen Williams;
Volume 2, Robert Neuman; Volume 3, Jack
Hughes; Volume 4, Helen Tanner. Garland
Publishing, 1978. $42.00 each.

**THE CADDOAN, IROQUOIAN
AND SIOUIAN LANGUAGES**
Wallace L. Chafe
Paper. Mouton Publishers, 1976. $20.75.

**CADDOAN TEXTS, PAWNEE,
SOUTH BAND DIALECT**
Gene Weltfish
Reprint of 1937 edition. AMS Press, $32.00.

**CADDOAN TRIBES: DATA RELATIVE
TO THEIR HISTORIC LOCATIONS**
Robert W. Neuman
150 pp. Clearwater, 1973. $48.00.

**THE CAHOKIA AND SURROUNDING
MOUND GROUPS**
David I. Bushnell, Jr.
Reprint of 1904 edition. Paper. Kraus, $14.00.

CAHOKIA BROUGHT TO LIFE
Reprint. Illus. 100 pp. Paper. American Indian
Books, $3.00.

THE CAHOKIA MOUND GROUP
P.F. Titterington
Reprint of 1938 edition. Illus. 40 pp. Paper.
American Indian Books, $3.00.

CAHUILLA DICTIONARY
Hansjakob Seiler and Kojiro Hioki
Paper. Malki Museum Press, 1979. $15.00.

**THE CAHUILLA INDIANS OF THE
COLORADO DESERT: ETHNOHISTORY
AND PREHISTORY**
P.J. Wilke, et al; Lowell J. Bean, Editor
Early observations on the cultural geography of
Coachella Valley. Illus. 73 pp. Paper. Ballena
Press, 1975. $7.95.

**THE CAHUILLA INDIANS
OF SOUTHERN CALIFORNIA**
John L. Bean and Harry W. Lawton
Paper. Malki Museum Press, 1965. $1.00.

**CAHUILLA TEXT WITH
AN INTRODUCTION**
Hans J. Seiler
Paper. Research Center for Language, 1970.
$8.50.

**CALENDAR HISTORY OF THE KIOWA
INDIANS**
James Mooney
Reprint. Illus. 460 pp. Paper. Smithsonian,
$15.00.

CALIFORNIA
Robert F. Heizer, Editor
Illus. 800 pp. Smithsonian, $25.00

CALIFORNIA ARCHAEOLOGY
Michael J. Moratto
Paper. Academic Press, 1984. $68.00; paper,
$37.50.

**CALIFORNIA INDIAN
NIGHTS ENTERTAINMENT**
E. Gifford and G. Block, Compilers
Reprint of 1930 edition. AMS Press, $32.50.

**CALIFORNIA INDIANS:
AN ANNOTATED BIBLIOGRAPHY**
Robert Heizer and Albert Elsasser
Garland Publishing, 1977. $28.00.

CALIFORNIA INDIANS
David Horr, Editor
Eight volumes. Illus. Maps. Garland Publishing,
1978. $51.00 each. See publisher for titles and
descriptions.

**CALIFORNIA INDIANS: PRIMARY
RESOURCES—A GUIDE TO
MANUSCRIPTS,
ARTIFACTS, DOCUMENTS, SERIALS,
MUSIC AND ILLUSTRATIONS**
Lowell J. Bean and Sylvia B. Vane
227 pp. Paper. Ballena Press, 1972. $9.50.

**THE CALIFORNIA INDIANS:
A SOURCE BOOK**
Robert F. Heizer and M.A. Whipple. Editors
A collection of writings. Second revised edition.
University of California Press, 1971. $33.00;
paper, $11.95.

**CALIFORNIA UNIVERSITY
PUBLICATIONS IN LINGUISTICS**
40 volumes. Berkeley, 1943-1965. Explores
languages and dialects and the evolutionary
nature of language. A number of these studies
focus on Native American languages. Kraus,
$1,182.00 per set; paper, $1.047.00 per set.

CALIFORNIA'S GABRIELINO INDIANS
Bernice Johnston
Illus. 198 pp. Southwest Museum, 1962. $12.50;
paper, $6.00.

**CAMERON CREEK VILLAGE, A SITE
IN THE MIMBRES AREA IN GRANT
COUNTY, NEW MEXICO (Santa Fe, NM)**
Wesley Bradfield
Reprint of 1929 edition. Illus. 244 pp. Kraus,
$30.00.

**CAMP BEALE'S SPRINGS
AND THE HUALAPAI INDIANS**
Dennis G. Casebier
Illus. 240 pp. Tales Mojave Rd., 1980. $19.50.

**CAMP, CLAN AND KIN AMONG THE
COW CREEK SEMINOLES OF FLORIDA**
Alexander Spoehr
Reprint of 1941, 1942, 1944, and 1947 editions.
Illus. Paper. Kraus, $20.00.

CAMPAIGNING WITH CROOK
Charles King
Reprint of 1964 edition. Illus. Map. 166 pp.
University of Oklahoma Press, $5.95.

**CAN THE RED MAN
HELP THE WHITE MAN?**
Sylvester M. Morey, Editor
130 pp. Illus. Paper. Myrin Institute, 1970. $3.50.

CANADA: THE WAR OF CONQUEST
Guy Fregault; Margaret Cameron, Translator
A study of the causes, events and results of the
Seven Years' War in North America. Reprint of
1955 edition. 446 pp. Oxford University Press,
$14.50.

CANADA'S INDIANS
James Wilson
Paper. Interbook, 1974. $2.50.

**CANADA'S INDIANS:
CONTEMPORARY CONFLICTS**
J. Frideres
Paper. Prentice-Hall, 1974. $11.25.

THE CANADIAN DAKOTA
Wilson D. Wallis
Reprint of 1947 edition. AMS Press, $35.00.

A CANADIAN INDIAN BIBLIOGRAPHY
Tom Abler, et al Editors
University of Toronto Press, 1974. $35.00.

**CANADIAN INDIAN POLICY:
A CRITICAL BIBLIOGRAPHY**
Robert J. Surtees
Illus. 120 pp. Paper. Indiana University Press,
1982. $4.95.

CANADIAN NATIVE LAW CASES
Brian Slattery and Linda Charlton
Three volumes. Volume 1, 1763-1869, 478 pp,
1980, $50.00; Volume 2, 1870-1890, 634 pp., 1981,
$65.00; Volume 3, 1891-1910, 663 pp., 1985,
$65.00. Native Law Centre Publications.

CANADIAN PREHISTORY SERIES
Each book includes time charts, graphs, maps, photos and drawings which picture the life of native peoples of Canada before the arrival of Jacques Cartier. The titles are: *Canadian Arctic Prehistory,* by Robert McGhee, the prehistoric ancestors of the Inuit. 136 pp., $8.50; *The Dig,* by George MacDonald and Richard Inglis, the story of the Coast Tsimshian people. 102 pp., $7.50; *Maritime Provinces Prehistory,* by James A. Tuck, the story of the Micmacs nd Malecites. 112 pp., $12.95; *Newfoundland and Labrador Prehistory,* by James A. Tuck. 135 pp. $5.50; *Six Chapters of Canada's Prehistory,* by J.V. Wright. 118 pp. $5.50; *Quebec Prehistory,* by J.V. Wright. 128 pp. $5.50; *Ontario Prehistory,* by J.V. Wright. 132 pp. Paper. $5.50. Paper. National Museums of Canada.

THE CANADIAN SIOUX
James H. Howard
210 pp. University of Nebraska Press, 1984. $17.95.

A CANNNONEER IN NAVAJO COUNTRY: JOURNAL OF PRIVATE JOSIAH M. RICE, 1851
Richard H. Dillon, Editor
Illus. Old West, 1970. $16.50.

CANOEING WITH THE CREE
Eric Sevareid
Reprint of 1935 edition. Illus. 206 pp. Paper. Minnesota Historical Society, $4.95.

CANYON DE CHELLY: ITS PEOPLE AND ROCK ART
Campbell Grant
290 pp. University of Arizona Press, 1978. $25.00; paper, $12.50.

*CANYON SUMMER
Jack and Mike Couffer
Grades 6-9. Illus. G.P. Putnam's Sons, 1977. $7.95.

CAPTAIN JACK, MODOC RENEGADE
Doris P. Payne
Illus. Paper. Binford & Mort, 1979. $6.95.

THE CAPTIVITY OF JAMES KIMBALL
James Kimball
Ye Galleon Press.

CAPTIVITY OF MARY SCWANDT
Mary Schwandt
Paper. Ye Galleon Press, $3.50.

CAPTIVITY OF THE OATMAN GIRLS: AMONG THE APACHES AND MOJAVE INDIANS
Royal B. Stratton
Reprint of 1857 edition. Illus. 300 pp. Paper. University of Nebraska Press, $7.95.

THE CAPTIVITY AND SUFFERINGS OF GEN. FREEGIFT PATCHIN... AMONG THE INDIAN..DURING THE BORDER WARFARE IN THE TIME OF THE AMERICAN REVOLUTION
Reprint of 1933 edition. Garland, 1977. $44.00.

CAPTIVITY OF FATHER PETER MILET: AMONG THE ONEIDA INDIANS
Pierre Miller
His own narrative with supplementary documents. Bound with other captivity stories. Reprint of 1888 edition, et al. Garland, $42.00.

CAPTIVITY TALES: AN ORGINIAL ANTHOLOGY
Reprint of 1974 edition. Illus. Ayer Co. Publishers, $15.00.

THE CAPTURE AND ESCAPE: OR, LIFE AMONG THE SIOUX
Sarah L. Larimer
Reprint of 1870 edition. Garland, $42.00.

CAPTURED BY THE INDIANS: 15 FIRSTHAND ACCOUNTS, 1750-1870
Frederick Drimmer, Editor
384 pp. Paper. Dover, 1985. $6.95.

CAPTURED BY THE INDIANS: REMINISCENCES OF PIONEER LIFE IN MINNESOTA: THE FOUNDING OF HARMAN'S STATION WITH AN ACCOUNT OF THE INDIAN CAPTIVITY OF MRS. JENNIE WILEY
M.B. Carrigan; William E. Connelley, Editor
Reprint of 1907 and 1910 editions. Garland, $42.00.

CAPTURED HERITAGE: THE SCRAMBLE FOR NORTHWEST COAST ARTIFACTS
Douglas Cole
Illus. University of Washington Press, 1985. $17.50.

CAROLINA INDIAN FRONTIER
David Corkran
Paper. University fo South Carolina Press, 1970. $3.00.

A CASE STUDY OF A NORTHERN CALIFORNIA INDIAN TRIBE: CULTURAL CHANGE TO 1860
Robert M. Peterson
R & E Research Associates, 1977. $11.00.

THE CASE OF THE SENECA INDIANS IN THE STATE OF NEW YORK
Reprint. E.M. Coleman Enterprise, $32.50.

CASES AND MATERIALS ON FEDERAL INDIAN LAW
David H. Getches, et al
West Publishing, 1979. $18.95.

CASPER COLLINS: THE LIFE AND
EXPLOITS OF AN INDIAN FIGHTER
OF THE SIXTIES
Agnes Spring
Reprint of 1927 edition. AMS Press, 16.00.

CATAWBA INDIANS:
THE PEOPLE OF THE RIVER
Douglas S. Brown
Illus. University of South Carolina Press, 1966.
$15.95.

CATAWBA NATION
Charles Hudson, Jr.
152 pp. Paper. University of Georgia Press, 1970.
$6.50.

CATAWBA TEXTS
Frank G. Speck
Reprint of 1934 edition. AMS Press, $18.00.

CATHLAMET ON THE COLUMBIA
Thomas N. Strong
New edition. Illus. Paper. Binford & Mort, 1981.
$6.95.

THE CATHOLIC INDIAN MISSIONS
IN MAINE (1611-1820)
Sr. Mary Leger
Reprint of 1929 edition. AMS Press, $26.00.

THE CATLIN (GEORGE) BOOK
OF AMERICAN INDIAN
Royal Hassrick
168 paintings. Character and costumes of more
than 40 tribes are reproduced. A & W Publishers,
$15.00.

CATLIN COLLECTION OF
INDIAN PAINTINGS
Mathew Matthews
Facsimile of 1890 edition. Illus. 17 pp. Paper.
Shorey, $3.00.

GEORGE CATLIN: EPISODES FROM
"LIFE AMONG THE INDIANS"
AND "LAST RAMBLES
George Catlin; Marvin Ross, Editor
University of Oklahoma Press, 1979. $25.00;
paper, $12.50.

CATLIN'S NORTH AMERICAN INDIAN
PORTFOLIO: A REPRODUCTION
George Catlin
Reprint of 1845 edition. Swallow Press, $200.00.

CAUSES OF THE MARYLAND
REVOLUTION OF 1689
F.E. Sparks
Reprint of 1896 edition. Johnson Reprint, $12.00.

CAUTANTOWWIT'S HOUSE: AN INDIAN
BURIAL GROUND ON THE ISLAND OF
CONANICUT IN NARRAGANSETT BAY
William Simmons
Illus. 198 pp. University Presses of New England,
1970. $12.00.

CAVALRY WIFE: THE DIARY OF
EVELINE M. ALEXANDER, 1866-1867
Eveline Alexander; S. Myers, Editor
Illus. 186 pp. Texas A&M University Press, 1977.
$14.50.

THE CAYUSE INDIANS: IMPERIAL
TRIBESMEN OF OLD OREGON
Robert H. Rubie and John A. Brown
Illus. 320 pp. University of Oklahoma Press, 1972.
$18.95; paper, $9.95.

CAVALRY WIFE: THE DIARY OF
EVELINE M. ALEXANDER, 1866-1867
Eveline M. Alexander
Illus. 186 pp. Texas A&M University Press, 1977.
$12.50.

CENTENNIAL CAMPAIGN:
THE SIOUX WAR OF 1876
John S. Gray
Reprint of 1977 edition. Paper. Old Army, $11.95.

THE CENTRAL CONCEPTS OF
NAVAJO WORLD VIEW
Gary Witherspoon
22 pp. Paper. Humanities Press, 1977. $2.00.

THE CENTRAL ESKIMO
Franz Boas
A record of Eskimo life in the 1880s. Reprint of
1884 edition. Illus. 280 pp. Scholarly Press,
University of Nebraska Press, Shorey and Peter
Smith.

CENTRAL SIERRA MIWOK
DICTIONARY WITH TEXTS
L.S. Freeland and S.M. Broadbent
Reprint of 1960 edition. Paper. Kraus, $10.00.

CENTURY OF DISHONOR: THE EARLY
CRUSADE FOR INDIAN REFORM
Helen H. Jackson; Rolle, Editor
Reprint of 1888 edition. Paper. Peter Smith,
$11.25.

A CENTURY OF DISHONOR: A SKETCH
OF THE U.S. GOVERNMENT'S DEALING
WITH SOME OF THE INDIAN TRIBES
Helen Jackson
Reprint of 1888 edition. 514 pp. Scholarly Press,
$59.00.

CERAMIC DECORATION SEQUENCE
AT AN OLD INDIAN VILLAGE SITE
NEAR SICILY ISLAND, LOUISIANA
James A. Ford
Reprint of 1935 edition. Kraus, $16.00.

A CEREMONIAL CAVE IN THE
WINCHESTER MOUNTAINS, ARIZONA
William S. Fulton
Reprint of 1941 edition. Kraus, $28.00.

CEREMONIAL SONGS OF THE
CREEK AND YUCHI INDIANS
Frank G. Speck
Reprint of 1911 edition. AMS Press, $20.00.

CEREMONIES OF THE PAWNEE
Two parts. Illus. 509 pp. Supt. of Documents,
$13.00.

THE CERRO COLORADO SITE AND
PITHOUSE ARCHITECTURE IN THE
SOUTHWESTERN U.S. PRIOR
TO A.D. 900
William R. Bullard, Jr.
Reprint of 1962 edition. Paper. Kraus, $45.00.

CERTAIN CADDO SITES IN ARKANSAS
Mark R. Harrington
Reprint of 1920 edition. AMS Press, $40.00.

CHACO CANYON RUINS: ANCIENT
SPIRITS WERE OUR NEIGHBORS
Ramona Rollins-Griffin
104 pp. Illus. Northland Press, $10.00.

CHAHTA HAPIA HOKE:
WE ARE CHOCTAW
Provides basic information about the Choctaw
Tribe from oral tradition through the annual
Choctaw Fair to economic development and
education. Illus. 52 pp. Choctaw Museum, $5.00.

CHANGE FOR CONTINUITY:
THE PEOPLE OF A THOUSAND LAKES
Vivian J. Rohrl
269 pp. University Press of America, 1981. $25.00;
paper, $13.00.

CHANGING CONFIGURATIONS IN THE
SOCIAL ORGANIZATION OF A
BLACKFOOT TRIBE DURING
THE RESERVE PERIOD
E.S. Goldfrank; L.M. Hanks and J. Richardson
Bound with *Observations on Northern Blackfoot
Kinship. Illus. 81 pp. University of Washington
Press, 1945. $15.00*

CHANGING CULTURE OF
AN INDIAN TRIBE
Margaret Mead
Reprint of 1932 edition. AMS Press, $32.50.

CHANGING NAVAJO RELIGIOUS
VALUES: A STUDY OF CHRISTIAN
MISSIONS TO THE RIMROCK NAVAHOS
R.N. Rappoport
Reprint of 1954 edition. Paper. Kraus, $29.00.

THE CHANGING PATTERN OF
HOPI AGRICULTURE
R. Bradfield
State Mutual Book, 1971. $40.00.

CHANGING PHYSICAL ENVIRONMENT
OF THE HOPI INDIANS OF ARIZONA
John Hack
Reprint of 1942 edition. Paper. Kraus, $26.00.

*CHANT OF THE RED MAN
Hap Gilliland
Grades 7-adult. Illus. Council for Indian
Education,
1976. $8.95; paper, $4.95.

CHANTS OF THE HOKAPAT CLAN
Elihu Blotnick
Illus. Paper. Charles C. Thomas, Publisher, 1980.
$4.00.

CHAPTERS ON THE ETHNOLOGY OF
THE POWHATAN TRIBES OF VIRGINIA
Frank G. Speck
Reprint of 1928 edition. AMS Press, $29.50.

CHARACTER AND DERIVATION OF
THE JICARILLA HOLINESS RITE
Morris E. Opler
Reprint of 1943 edition. Paper. Kraus, $12.00.

CHARACTER AND INFLUENCE OF
INDIAN TRADE IN WISCONSIN:
A STUDY OF THE TRADING POST
AS AN INSTITUTION
F.J. Turner; David and Harry Miller, Editors
Reprint of 1891 edition. Burt Franklin, $17.50.
Paper. Johnson Reprint, $10.00. University of
Oklahoma Press, $11.95. AMS Press, $11.50.

CHARLO'S PEOPLE
Adolf Hungry Wolf
Illus. Paper. Good Medicine Books, 1974. $5.00.

CHASING GERONIMO: THE JOURNAL
OF LEONARD WOOD, MAY-SEPT., 1886
Leonard Wood; Jack C. Lane, Editor
Illus. 160 pp. University of New Mexico Press,
1970. $7.95.

CHEHALIS: ANTHROPOLOGICAL
INVESTIGATION RELATIVE TO
TRIBAL IDENTITY AND ABORIGINAL
POSSESSION OF LANDS
Herbert Taylor
34 pp. Clearwater, 1974. $20.00.

CHEHALIS AND CHINOOK TERRITORIAL DISTRIBUTION OF SOME OF THE ABORIGINAL POPULATION OF WESTERN WASHINGTON
Jacob Fried
45 pp. Clearwater, 1974. $25.00.

CHEHALIS: HISTORICAL, ETHNOGRAPHICAL AND ARCHAEO-LOGICAL REPORT
Herbert Taylor
35 pp. Clearwater, 1974. $22.00.

CHEM'IVILLU: LET'S SPEAK CAHUILLA
316 pp. Paper. American Indian Studies Center, 1982. $20.00.

THE CHEMEHUEVI INDIANS OF SOUTHERN CALIFORNIA
Ron Miller and Peggy Jean Miller
Paper. Malki Museum Press, 1973. $1.00.

THE CHEMEHUEVIS
Carobeth Laird
Paper. Malki Museum Press, 1976. $15.00.

*THE CHEROKEE
Emilie U. Lepthien
Illus. 48 pp. Grades K-4. Paper. Childrens Press, 1985. $3.95.

CHEROKEE AND CREEK INDIANS
Illus. Map. 639 pp. Garland Publishing, $42.00.

CHEROKEE ARCHAEOLOGY: A STUDY OF THE APPALACHIAN SUMMIT
Bennie C. Keel
Illus. 312 pp. University of Tennessee Press, 1975. $21.95.

THE CHEROKEE BAND OF INDIANS: ANTHROPOLOGICAL REPORT ON THE INDIAN OCCUPANCY OF ROYCE AREA 79, CEDED ON SEPT. 14, 1816
246 pp. Clearwater, 1973. $75.00.

CHEROKEE CAVALIERS: FORTY YEARS OF CHEROKEE HISTORY AS TOLD IN THE CORRESPONDENCE OF THE RIDGE-WATIE-BOUDINOT FAMILY
E.E. Dale and Gaston Litton
Reprint of 1939 edition. Illus. University of Oklahoma Press, $10.00.

THE CHEROKEE CROWN OF TANNASSY
William O. Steele
John F. Blair, 1977. $8.95.

CHEROKEE DANCE AND DRAMA
Frank G. Speck and Leonard Broom
Reprint of 1951 edition. Illus. 160 pp. University of Oklahoma Press, $14.95.

CHEROKEE-ENGLISH INTERLINER, FIRST EPISTLE OF JOHN OF THE NEW TESTIMENT
Ralph E. Dawson, III and Shirley Dawson
25 pp. Indian University Press of Oklhoma, 1982. Spiral binding, $2.50.

THE CHEROKEE EXCAVATIONS: HOLOCENE ECOLOGY AND HUMAN ADAPTATIONS IN NORTHEASTERN IOWA
Duane C. Anderson and Holmes Semken, Editors
Academic Press, 1980. $25.00.

THE CHEROKEE FREEDMEN: FROM EMANCIPATION TO AMERICAN CITIZENSHIP
Daniel F. Littlefield, Jr.
Greenwood Press, 1978. $19.95.

THE CHEROKEE FRONTIER: CONFLICT AND SURVIVAL, 1740-1762
David H. Corkran
Reprint of 1962 edition. Illus. Maps, Index. 300 pp. University of Oklahoma Press, $12.95.

*CHEROKEE FUN AND LEARN BOOK
Ed Sharpe
Educational book for children; word games, etc. Illus. 38 pp. Paper. American Indian Books, $3.00.

THE CHEROKEE GHOST DANCE
William G. McLoughlin
425 pp. Mercer University Press, 1984. $35.00.

THE CHEROKEE INDIAN NATION: A TROUBLED HISTORY
Duane H. King
Illus. 276 pp. Univerity of Tennessee Press, 1979. $13.50.

*THE CHEROKEE: INDIANS OF THE MOUNTAINS
Sonia Bleeker
Describes the daily life of the Cherokee Indians of the past. Tells the story of Sequoyah (who invented an alphabet.) Grades 3-6. Illus. William Morrow, 1952. $9.00.

CHEROKEE LAND LOTTERY OF GEORGIA, 1832
James F. Smith
Reprint of 1838 edition. Illus. Genealogical Publishing, $20.00.

CHEROKEE MESSINGER: A LIFE OF SAMUEL AUSTIN WORCESTER
Althea Bass
Reprint of 1936 edition. Illus. University of Oklahoma Press, $17.50.

CHEROKEE NATION
Marion I. Starkey
Reprint of 1946 edition. Illus. Russell & Russell,
$22.00.

**CHEROKEE NATION INDIAN
RESERVATIONS IN THE INDIAN
TERRITORY, OKLAHOMA: APPRAISAL**
Roscoe H. Sears
73 pp. Clearwater, 1973. $27.00.

**CHEROKEE NATION: LAND CESSIONS
IN TENNESSEE, MISSISSIPPI,
NORTH CAROLINA, GEORGIA,
ALABAMA, 1785-1835**
James H. Goff
278 pp. Clearwater, 1974. $80.00.

THE CHEROKEE NATION OF INDIANS
Charles Royce; Herman Viola, Editor
288 pp. Beresford Book Service, 1975. $12.50.

**CHEROKEE OUTLET IN THE INDIAN
TERRITORY, STATE OF OKLAHOMA:
APPRAISAL**
Oscar Monrad and Roscoe H. Sears
92 pp. Clearwater, 1973. $35.00.

**CHEROKEE OUTLET IN OKLAHOMA,
APPRAISAL, 1893**
Elbridge A. Tucker
128 pp. Clearwater, 1973. $42.00.

**CHEROKEE OUTLET LANDS DEEDED
BY THE CHEROKEE NATION TO THE
U.S. IN TRUST ON JUNE 14, 1883:
APPRAISAL**
Elbridge A. Tucker
113 pp. Clearwater, 1973. $40.00.

**CHEROKEE PREHISTORY: THE PASGAH
PHASE IN THE APPALACHIAN
SUMMIT REGION**
Roy S. Dickens, Jr.
Illus. 260 pp. University of Tennessee Press, 1976.
$19.95.

THE CHEROKEE PERSPECTIVE
Laurence French and Jim Hornbuckle, Editors
Appalachian Consortium, 1981. $7.95.

A CHEROKEE PRAYERBOOK
Howard Meredith and Adeline Smith
44 pp. Paper. Indian University Press, 1981.
$1.50.

CHEROKEE RECOLLECTIONS
Maude W. DuPriest, et al
Indian Woman's Pocahontas Club, 1976. $10.00.

***CHEROKEE REMOVAL 1838:
AN ENTIRE INDIAN NATION IS
FORCED OUT OF ITS HOMELAND**
Glen H. Fleischmann
Grades 7-adult. Illus. Franklin Watts, 1971.
$4.90; paper, $1.50.

**CHEROKEE REMOVAL: THE "WILLIAM
PENN" ESSAYS AND OTHER WRITINGS
BY JEREMIAH EVARTS**
Francis P. Prucha, Editor
320 pp. University of Tennessee Press, 1981.
$20.00.

**CHEROKEE SUNSET —
NATION BETRAYED**
Samuel Carter, III
Illus. Doubleday, 1976. $12.95.

*THE CHEROKEE TALE—TELLER
Maggi Cunningham
Grades 5-12. Illus. Dillon Press, 1978. $9.95.

CHEROKEE TRAGEDY
Thurman Wilkins
Macmillan, 1970. $10.00.

CHEROKEE VISION OF ELOH'
Howard Meredith and Virginia E. Milan
Wesley Proctor, Translator
37 pp. Paper. Indian University Press, 1981.
$8.00.

CHEROKEE WOMAN
Francis M. Daves
Branden Press, 1973. $9.95.

CHEROKEES
Grace Woodward
Reprint of 1963 edition. Illus. 359 pp. Paper.
University of Oklahoma Press, $11.95.

CHEROKEES AT THE CROSSROADS
John Gulik
With a new chapter by Sharlotte N. Williams. The
cultural patterns of the Eastern Cherokees during
1956-1958. 222 pp. Institute for Research in Social
Science, 1973. $8.00.

**THE CHEROKEES:
A CRITICAL BIBLIOGRAPHY**
Raymond J. Fogelson
112 pp. Paper. Indiana University Press, 1978.
$4.95.

**THE CHEROKEES IN
PRE-COLUMBIAN TIMES**
Cyrus Thomas
Reprint of 1890 edition. AMS Press, $17.50.

CHEROKEES IN TRANSITION:
A STUDY OF CHANGING CULTURE
AND ENVIRONMENT PRIOR TO 1775
Gary C. Goodwin
Illus. Paper. University of Chicago, Dept. of
Geography, 1977. $8.00.

CHEROKEES AND MISSIONARIES,
1789-1839
William G. McLoughlin
375 pp. Yale University Press, 1984. $33.50.

CHEROKEES OF THE OLD SOUTH:
A PEOPLE IN TRANSISITION
Henry T. Malone
Illus. Maps. Biblio. 238 pp. University of Georgia
Press, 1956. $9.50.

THE CHERRY VALLEY MOUNDS
AND MOUND No. 3
Gregory Perino
Describes an Indian culture from eastern
Arkansas area. Illus. 88 pp. Paper. American
Indian Books, $3.00.

CHEYENNE
George A. Dorsey
How the Cheyenne lived and worked before the
white man arrived. In two parts: *The Ceremonial
Organization,* and *The Sun Dance.* Reprint of
1905 edition. Illus. 72 pp. Kraus, $34.00. Paper. Ye
Galleon Press, $10.95.

CHEYENNE AND ARAPAHOE
ABORIGINAL OCCUPATION
Zachery Gussow
64 pp. Clearwater, 1973. $24.00.

CHEYENNE AND ARAPAHO:
HISTORICAL BACKGROUND
Arthur Ekirch
45 pp. Clearwater, 1974. $22.50.

CHEYENNE-ARAPAHO INDIAN LANDS:
MINERAL EVALUATION COVERING
PARTS OF COLORADO, KANSAS,
NEBRASKA AND WYOMING
Stoddard Barton and Milhollin Co.
140 pp. Clearwater, 1973. $45.00.

CHEYENNE AND ARAPAHO INDIAN
RESERVATION IN THE INDIAN
TERRITORY, STATE OF OKLAHOMA,
1869 & 1891: APPRAISAL
Roscoe H. Sears
Two separate volumes. 51 and 89 pp. respectively.
Clearwater, 1973. $20.00 and $31.00.

CHEYENNE AND ARAPAHO LANDS
IN COLORADO, KANSAS, WYOMING,
AND NEBRASKA, 1865: APPRAISAL
Homer Hoyt
358 pp. Clearwater, 1974. $100.00.

CHEYENNE-ARAPAHO LANDS IN
EASTERN COLORADO, WESTERN
KANSAS, SOUTHWESTERN NEBRASKA
AND SOUTHWESTERN WYOMING:
APPRAISAL
Jeffrey Holbrook
109 pp. Clearwater, 1974. $37.00.

CHEYENNE AND ARAPAHO MUSIC
Frances Densmore
Reprint of 1936 edition. 111 pp. Southwest
Museum, $5.00.

THE CHEYENNE AND ARAPAHO
ORDEAL: RESERVATION AND
AGENCY LIFE
Donald J. Berthrong
Illus. Maps. Biblio. 418 pp. University of
Oklahoma Press, 1976. $19.95.

CHEYENNE AND ARAPAHO TRIBES IN
NORTHERN AND WESTERN OKLAHOMA,
1891: APPRAISAL OF CERTAIN LANDS
Edward A. Rambo
145 pp. Clearwater, 1973. $46.00.

CHEYENNE-ARAPAHO TRIBES OF
INDIANS: MINERAL EVALUATION
OF CEDED LANDS
Charles C. O'Boyle
45 pp. Clearwater, 1973. $18.00.

CHEYENNE AND SIOUX: THE
REMINISCENCES OF FOUR INDIANS
AND A WHITE SOLDIER
Ronald H. Limbaugh and Thomas B. Marquis
Illus. 79 pp. Holt-Atherton, 1973. $5.50.

CHEYENNE ARTIST:
THE STORY OF RICHARD WEST
Charles A. Waugaman
Paper. Friendship Press, 1970. $1.25.

CHEYENNE AUTUMN
Mari Sandoz
The story of the Northern Cheyennes, who fled
the reservation in 1878 to return to their ancestral
hunting grounds. Illus. 288 pp. Paper. Avon,
$4.95.

*CHEYENNE FIRE FIGHTERS:
MODERN INDIANS FIGHTING
FOREST FIRES
Henry Tall Bull and Tom Weist
Grades 4-12. Council for Indian Education, 1973.
$5.95; paper, $1.95.

THE CHEYENNE IN PLAINS INDIAN
TRADE RELATIONS, 1795-1840
Joseph Jablow
A study of the effects of the fur trade and diffusion
of the horse upon the Cheyenne. Illus. Maps.
Biblio. 110 pp. University of Washington Press,
1951. $6.00.

THE CHEYENNE INDIANS:
SKETCH OF THE CHEYENNE GRAMMAR
J. Mooney and R.C. Petter
Reprint of 1907 edition. Paper. Kraus, $15.00.

THE CHEYENNE INDIANS:
THE SUN DANCE
George A. Dorsey
A study of the famed ceremonial. Reissue of 1905 edition. Illus. 286 pp. Rio Grande Press, $22.00.

CHEYENNE INDIANS, THEIR
HISTORY AND WAYS OF LIFE
George B. Grinell
Reprint of 1923 edition. Two volumes: Volume 1, 368 pp.; Volume 2, 438 pp. Illus. Cooper Square, $30.00 per set. Paper. University of Nebraska Press, Volume 1, $7.95; Volume 2, $8.95.

*CHEYENNE LEGENDS OF CREATION
Henry Tall Bull and Tom Weist
Grades 4-9. Paper. Council for Indian Education, 1972. $1.95.

CHEYENNE MEMORIES
John and Liberty Stands in Timber
Illus. 350 pp. Paper. University of Nebraska Press, 1972. $7.95.

*CHEYENNE SHORT STORIES: A
COLLECTION OF TEN TRADITIONAL
STORIES OF THE CHEYENNES
Grades 2-12. Council for Indian Education, 1977. $1.95.

*CHEYENNE WARRIORS
Henry Tall Bull and Tom Weist
Grades 2-12. Council for Indian Education, 1976. $5.95; paper, $1.95.

THE CHEYENNE WAY:
CONFLICT AND CASE LAW
IN PRIMITIVE JURISPRUDENCE
Karl Llewellen and E. Adamson Hoebel
Reprint of 1941 edition. Illus. 375 pp. University of Oklahoma Press, $17.95; paper, $11.95.

THE CHEYENNES:
INDIANS OF THE GREAT PLAINS
E. Adamson Hoebel
A portrait of the Cheyenne Indians. Second edition. 125 pp. Paper. Holt, Rinehart, 1978. $9.95.

THE CHEYENNES, MA HEO O'S
PEOPLE: A CRITICAL BIOGRAPHY
Peter J. Powell
128 pp. Paper. Indiana University Press, 1980. $5.95.

THE CHEYENNES OF MONTANA
Thomas Marquis; Tom Weist, Editor
Reference Publications, 1978. $19.50.

*CHI—WEE
Grace Moon
Grades 4-6. Doubleday, 1925. $4.50.

THE CHICKASAWS
Arrell M. Gibson
Illus. 320 pp. Paper. University of Oklahoma Press, 1971. $10.95.

CHICKASAWS AND CHOCTAWS
Reprint. Comprises the treaties of 1855 and 1866; the history, education and inter-tribal relations. Scholarly Resources.

CHIEF BOWLES AND
THE TEXAS CHEROKEES
Mary W. Clarke
Illus. University of Oklahoma Press, 1971. $9.95.

*CHIEF JOSEPH
R.P. Johnson
A biography of the famous Nez Perce leader. Grades 5-9. Illus. 75 pp. Dillon Press, 1975. $7.95.

CHIEF JOSEPH COUNTRY:
LAND OF THE NEZ PERCE
Bill Gulick
Illus. 450 pp. Caxton, 1981. $29.95.

*CHIEF JOSEPH OF THE NEZ PERCE
Dean Pollock
Grades 5-12. Illus. Binford & Mort, 1950. $5.95.

*CHIEF JOSEPH'S OWN STORY AS
TOLD BY CHIEF JOSEPH IN 1879
Grades 4-12. 32 pp. Council for Indian Education, 1972. $5.95; paper, $1.95.

CHIEF LAWYER OF THE NEZ PERCE
INDIANS, 1796-1876
Clifford M. Drury
Illus. Arthur H. Clark, 1979. $22.75.

CHIEF LEFT HAND:
SOUTHERN ARAPAHO
Margaret Coel
Illus. 352 pp. University of Oklahoma Press, 1981. $17.95.

*CHIEF PLENTY COUPS:
LIFE OF THE CROW INDIAN CHIEF
Flora Hatheway
Grades 4-12. 32 pp. Council for Indian Eduction, 1971. $5.95; paper, $1.95.

*CHIEF RED HORSE
TELLS ABOUT CUSTER
Jessie B. McGaw
Grades 4-12. Illus. 64 pp. Elsevier-Nelson, 1981. $9.25.

CHIEF SARAH: SARAH WINNEMUCCA'S
FIGHT FOR INDIAN RIGHTS
Dorothy N. Morrison
Illus. 170 pp. Atheneum, 1980. $9.95.

CHIEF SEATTLE'S
UNANSWERED CHALLENGE
John M. Rich
61 pp. Paper. Ye Galleon Press, 1970. $3.95.

*CHIEF SEALTH AND HIS PEOPLE
The life of Chief Sealth of the Suquamish on
Puget Sound. Grades 1-3. Illus. 36 pp. Daybreak
Star Press, $3.75.

CHIEF WASHAKIE
Mae Urbanek
Illus. 150 pp. Urbanek, $5.00.

CHIEFS AND CHALLENGERS: INDIAN
RESISTANCE AND COOPERATION
IN SOUTHERN CALIFORNIA
George H. Phillips
An historical and ethnographic study of the
California Indians. University of California
Press, 1975. $14.50.

*CHII-LA-PE AND
THE WHITE BUFFALO
John Nicholson
Grades 2-9. Council for Indian Education, $6.95;
paper, $2.95.

THE CHILD CAPTIVES: A TRUE
TALE OF LIFE AMONG THE
INDIANS OF THE WEST
Margaret K. Hosmer
Reprint of 1870 edition. Garland, $42.00.

CHILD OF THE HOGAN
Ray B. Louis
Illus. Brigham Young University Press, 1975.
$7.95; paper, $4.95.

*CHILD OF THE NAVAJOS
Seymour Reit
Grades 2-5. Illus. Dodd, Mead & Co., 1971. $5.95.

THE CHILD AND THE SERPENT:
REFLECTIONS ON POPULAR
INDIAN SYMBOLS
Jyoti Sahi
Illus. 192 pp. Paper. Routledge & Kegan, 1980.
$12.50.

*A CHILD'S HISTORY OF
THE AMERICAN INDIAN
"The Weewish Tree", Editors
Illus. Paper. The Indian Historian Press, 1981.
$9.95.

*ACHILD'S WORLD
Exhibit catalog of the Museum. Grades 3-7.
16 pp. Paper. Museum of the American Indian,
1983. $2.25.

CHILDHOOD AND FOLKLORE:
A PSYCHOANALYTIC STUDY OF
APACHE PERSONALITY
L. Bryce Boyer
Psychohistory Press, 1979. $17.95; paper, $9.95.

CHILDHOOD AND YOUTH IN
JICARILLA APACHE SOCIETY
Morris E. Opler
Reprint of 1946 edition. Illus. 180 pp. AMS Press,
$21.00. Paper. Southwest Museum, $6.00.

CHILDREN AT RISK:
MAKING A DIFFERENCE THROUGH
THE COURT APPOINTED SPECIAL
ADVOCATE PROJECT
Michael Blady
Illus. 318 pp. NCJW, 1982. Workbook, $7.50.

CHILDREN INDIAN CAPTIVES
Roy D. Holt
Eakin Publications, 1980. $5.95.

THE CHILDREN OF AATAENTSIC:
A HISTORY OF THE HURON
PEOPLE TO 1660
Bruce G. Trigger
Illus. McGill-Queens University Press, 1976.
$60.00 per set.

CHILDREN OF THE ANCIENT ONES
Little Pigeon, Pseud.
Paper. Herald House, 1982. $12.00.

CHILDREN OF THE PEOPLE:
THE NAVAHO INDIVIDUAL
AND HIS DEVELOPMENT
D.C. Leighton and C. Kluckhohn
Reprint of 1947 edition. Octagon, $17.50.

CHILDREN OF THE RAVEN:
THE SEVEN INDIAN NATIONS
OF THE NORTHWEST COAST
H.R. Hays
Illus. 352 pp. McGraw-Hill, 1975. $12.95.

CHILDREN OF THE SALT RIVER
Mary R. Miller
Paper. Resource Center for Language Semiotic,
1977. $12.00.

CHILDREN OF THE SUN
William E. Curtis
Reprint of 1883 edition. AMS Press, $15.00.

***CHILDREN OF THE SUN:
THE PUEBLOS, NAVAJOS, AND
APACHES OF NEW MEXICO**
Maudie Robinson
Grades 4-12. Illus. 96 pp. Julian Messner, 1973.
$7.95.

**CHILDREN OF THE TWILIGHT:
FOLKTALES OF INDIAN TRIBES**
Emma-Lindsay Squier
Gordon Press, 1977. $34.95.

THE CHILKAT DANCING BLANKET
Cheryl Samuel
Illus. 248 pp. Pacific Search, 1982. $29.95.

CHINIGCHINICH
Geronimo Boscana
Malki Museum Press, 1978. $25.00.

**CHINIGCHINIX, AN INDIGENOUS
CALIFORNIA INDIAN RELIGION**
James R. Moriarty
Illus. Maps. 70 pp. Southwest Museum, 1969.
$7.50.

*CHINOOK
Jessie Marsh
Grades K-9. 32 pp. Paper. Council for Indian
Education, 1976. $1.95.

**CHINOOK: A HISTORY
AND DICTIONARY**
Edward Thomas
185 pp. Binford & Mort, $7.50.

**CHINOOK INDIAN LANDS IN
WASHINGTON AND OREGON,
1851: APPRAISAL**
Gifford P. Owen and John F. Lietz
Two volumes. 330 pp. Clearwater, 1973. $95.00
per set.

THE CHINOOK INDIAN LANGUAGE
Franz Boas
Extracted from 1911 edition. 78 pp. Paper.
Shorey, $6.00.

**CHINOOK INDIANS:
ANTHROPOLOGICAL IDENTITY AND
ABORIGINAL POSSESSION OF LANDS**
H.C. Taylor
Clearwater, $27.00.

**THE CHINOOK INDIANS: TRADERS
OF THE LOWER COLUMBIA RIVER**
Robert H. Rubie and John A. Brown
Illus. Maps. 380 pp. University of Oklahoma,
1976. $22.95.

**CHINOOK TRIBE AND BANDS TRIBAL
ISLANDS, 1851: APPRAISAL**
Leroy D. Draper
180 pp. Clearwater, 1973. $56.00.

CHIPPEWA AND DAKOTA INDIANS
Subject catalog of books, pamphlets, periodical
articles and manuscripts in the Minnesota
Historical Society. Paper. Minnesota Historical
Society, 1970. $7.50.

**CHIPPEWA AND THEIR NEIGHBORS:
A STUDY IN ETHNOHISTORY**
Harold Hickerson; G. and L. Spindler, Editors
Paper. Irvington Publishers, 1970. $7.95.

**CHIPPEWA CHILD LIFE AND
ITS CULTURAL BACKGROUND**
Inez Hilger
Reprint of 1951 edition. Scholarly Press, $29.00.

**CHIPPEWA CREE TRIBE OF
ROCKY BOY, MONTANA, AND THE
LITTLE BAND OF INDIANS, 1888**
John C. Ewers
170 pp. Clearwater, 1973. $52.50.

*CHIPPEWA CUSTOMS
Francis Densmore
Reprint of 1929 edition. Illus. 204 pp. Johnson
Reprint, $24.00. Paper. Minnesota Historical
Society, $7.95.

CHIPPEWA INDIANS
David A. Horr, Editor
Seven volumes. Illus. Maps. Garland Publishing,
$51.00 each. See publisher for titles and
descriptions.

**CHIPPEWA INDIANS AS RECORDED BY
REV. FREDERICK BARAGA IN 1847**
Rev. Frederick Baraga, Editor
82 pp. Studia Slovenica, 1976. $5.00.

**CHIPPEWA INDIANS OF LAKE
SUPERIOR: ECONOMIC AND
HISTORICAL BACKGROUND OF
NORTHEASTERN MINNESOTA LANDS,
SEPT. 30, 1854, ROYCE AREA 332**
Helen E. Knuth
100 pp. Clearwater, 1973. $34.50.

***THE CHIPPEWA INDIANS: RICE
GATHERERS OF THE GREAT LAKES**
Sonia Bleeker; illus by Patricia Boodell
Grades 3-6. Illus. 160 pp. William Morrow, 1955.
$9.00.

CHIPPEWA MUSIC
Francis Densmore
Reprint of 1911 and 1913 editions. Two volumes
110 pp. Ross & Haines, Scholarly Press, Da Capo
Press.

**THE CHIPPEWA NATION OF INDIANS:
ANTHROPOLOGICAL REPORT ON THE
INDIAN OCCUPANCY OF AREA 242,
CEDED UNDER TREATY OF JULY 1837**

Harold Hickerson
292 pp. Clearwater, 1973. $85.00.

CHIPPEWA OF EASTERN LOWER MICHIGAN, 1785-1837
Helen Tanner
25 pp. Clearwater, 1974. $18.00.

THE CHIPPEWA OF THE MISSISSIPPI AND LAKE SUPERIOR: ANTHROPOLOGICAL REPORT ON THE INDIAN OCCUPANCY OF ROYCE AREAS CEDED BY THE PILLAGER BAND OF CHIPPEWA
Harold Hickerson
190 pp. Clearwater, 1974. $58.00.

CHIPPEWA, OTTAWA AND POTAWATOMI LANDS IN ILLINOIS AND WISCONSIN: VALUATION AS OF 1835
Roger K. Chisholm
Clearwater, 1976. $67.00.

CHIPPEWA TRACT IN MINNESOTA, APRIL 26, 1866: APPRAISAL
Bernard C. Meltzer and Roland J. Schaar
345 pp. Clearwater, 1973. $100.00.

CHIPPEWA TRIBE: APPRAISAL OF LANDS IN MINNESOTA, ROYCE AREA 332, 1855
Dewey Newcombe and Howard Lawrence
292 pp. Clearwater, 1973. $86.00.

THE CHIPPEWAS OF LAKE SUPERIOR
Edmund J. Danziger, Jr.
Illus. University of Oklahoma, 1979. $19.95.

CHIRICAHUA APACHE LANDS: ANALYSIS OF THE MINERAL PRODUCTION PRIOR TO SEPT. 4, 1866
Roy P. Full
64 pp. Clearwater, 1973. $24.00.

CHIRICAHUA APACHE TRIBE: APPRAISAL OF MINERAL RESOURCES IN THE LANDS
Four volumes. 1,782 pp. Clearwater, 1973. $500.00 per set.

CHIRICAHUA AND MESCALERO APACHE TEXTS
Harry Hoijer and Morris E. Opler
Reprint of 1838 edition. AMS Press, $36.50.

*A CHOCTAW ANTHOLOGY, I & II
Papers written by Choctaw high school and college prep students on Choctaw history, culture and current events. Grades 7-12. Choctaw Heritage Press, I—$2.75; II—$7.00. $8.50/set.

THE CHOCTAW BEFORE REMOVAL
Carolyn K. Reeves, Editor
University Press of Mississippi, 1985. $25.00.

CHOCTAW HYMN BOOK
John Swanton
Reprint. Choctaw Museum of the Southern Indian.

CHOCTAW MUSIC
Francis Densmore
Reprint of 1943 edition. Illus. 110 pp. Da Capo Press, $19.50.

THE CHOCTAW OF BAYOU LACOMB, ST. TAMMANY PARISH, LOUISIANA
D. Bushnell, Jr.
Reprint of 1909 edition. Scholarly Press, $17.00.

A CHOCTAW SOURCEBOOK
John H. Peterson, Editor
Reprint. 257 pp. Garland Publishing, $30.00.

*THE CHOCTAWS BEFORE DANCING RABBIT CREEK
A collection of scholarly papers on the history of the Choctaws from pre-contact through the "Removal Treaty" in 1830. Grades 7-12. University Press of Mississippi.

THE CHOCTAWS: A CRITICAL BIBLIOGRAPHY
Clara S. Kidwell and Charles Roberts
128 pp. Paper. Indiana University Press, 1981. $4.95.

THE CHOCTAWS: CULTURAL EVOLUTION OF A NATIVE AMERICAN TRIBE
Jesse O. McKee and Jon A. Schlenker
University Press of Mississippi, 1980. $17.50.

*THE CHOCTAWS IN THE 19th AND 20th CENTURY
A collection of scholarly papers on the history of the Mississippi Band of Choctaw Indians from 1830 to the present. Focuses on the several removal attempts and their effects on the tribe. Grades 7-12. University Press of Mississippi.

CHRISTIAN INDIANS AND INDIAN NATIONALISM, 1855-1950: AN INTERPRETATION IN HISTORICAL AND THEOLOGICAL PERSPECTIVES
George Thomas
271 pp. Peter Lang Publishing, 1979. $25.00.

CHRISTIAN LEADERSHIP IN INDIAN AMERICA
Tom Claus and Dale Kietzman, Editors
Paper. Moody Press, 1977. $3.00.

CHRONICLES OF BORDER WARFARE: HISTORY OF THE SETTLEMENTS BY WHITES OF NORTHWESTERN VIRGINIA
Alexander S. Withers
Reprint of 1895 edition. Ayer Co. Publishers, $30.00. Reprint of 1931 edition. McClain, $15.00.

CHRONOLOGICAL ANALYSIS OF TSEGI PHASE SITES IN NORTHEASTERN AZ
Jeffrey S. Dean
Reports on 13 Pueblo III sites. 207 pp. Paper. University of Arizona Press, $10.00.

CHRONOLOGICAL HISTORY OF THE ALEUTIAN ISLANDS
Vasilii N. Berkh; Richard A. Price, Editor
Illus. Limestone Press, 1974. $7.00.

CHRONOLOGICAL LIST OF ENGAGEMENTS BETWEEN THE REGULAR ARMY OF THE U.S. AND VARIOUS TRIBES OF HOSTILE INDIANS...1790-1898
George W. Webb
Reprint of 1939 edition. AMS Press, $17.50.

CHRONOLOGY OF THE PUEBLO DE LA YSLETA DEL SUR IN COLORADO, NEW MEXICO AND TEXAS, 10,000 B.C. to 1969
Rash Diamond and Scwartz, Inc.
86 pp. Clearwater, 1974. $33.00.

CHULO: A YEAR AMONG THE COATIMUNDIS
Bill Gilbert
Illus. 297 pp. Paper. University of Arizona Press, 1984. $9.50.

THE CHUMASH INDIANS OF SOUTHERN CALIFORNIA
Eugene Anderson
Paper. Malki Museum Press, 1973. $1.00.

CHURCHMEN AND THE WESTERN INDIANS, 1820-1920
Clyde Milner, II, and Floyd O'Neil
Illus. 272 pp. University of Oklahoma Press, 1985. $19.95.

THE CIBECUE APACHE
Keith H. Basso
Paper. Holt, Rinehart & Winston, 1970. $6.95.

*CIRCLE OF LIFE: THE MICCOSUKEE WAY
Nancy Henderson and Jane Dewey
The history, religion and persent-day life of this Florida tribe. Grades 3-12. Illus. Julian Messner, 1974.$6.00.

THE CIRCLE WITHOUT END: A SOURCEBOOK OF AMERICAN INDIAN ETHICS
Gerald and Francis Lombardi
Illus. 212 pp. Naturegraph, 1980. $12.95; paper, $6.95.

CIRCLES, CONSCIOUSNESS AND CULTURE
James A. Mischke
Paper. Navajo College Press, 1984. $1.50.

CIRCLES OF THE WORLD: TRADITIONAL ART OF THE PLAINS INDIANS
Richard Conn
Illus. 152 pp. Paper. Denver Art Museum, 1982. $14.95.

CIRCUMPOLAR HEALTH: PROCEEDINGS
Roy J. Shephard and S. Itoh, Editors
Third International Symposium, Yellowknife, Northwest Territory. Illus. University of Toronto Press, 1976. $27.50.

CIRCUMPOLAR PEOPLES: AN ANTHROPOLOGICAL PERSPECTIVE
N. Grayburn and B. Strong
Goodyear Publishing, 1973. $9.95; paper, $6.95.

CIVIL SERVICE EXAMINATION PASSBOOK: INDIAN EDUCATION
Jack Rudman
Three volumes: *Elementary Teacher, Secondary Teacher,* and *Guidance Counselor.* National Learning Corp.

CIVILIZATION AND THE STORY OF THE ABSENTEE SHAWNEES: AS TOLD TO FLORENCE DRAKE
Thomas W. Alford
Reprint of 1936 edition. Illus. 203 pp. University of Oklahoma Press, $14.95; paper, $7.95.

CIVILIZATION OF THE INDIAN NATIVES
H. Jackson
Reprint of 1830 edition. Scholarly Press, $25.00.

CIVILIZATIONS OF ANCIENT AMERICA
Sol Tax, Editor
29th Congress of Americanists. Reprint. Illus. Cooper Square Publishers, 1967. $17.50.

CLAIMS FOR DEPREDATIONS BY SIOUX INDIANS
38th U.S. Congress
Material on the Sioux Indian War of 1962. 25 pp. Paper. Ye Galleon Press, 1975. $3.00.

WILLIAM CLARK: JEFFERSONIAN MAN ON THE FRONTIER
Jerome O. Steffen
Reprint of 1977 edition. Illus. University of Oklahoma Press, $9.95.

CLASH OF CULTURES: FORT BOWIE AND THE CHIRICAHUA APACHES
Describes the Chiricahua Apaches of the Great Plains, and the historical relationship of Fort Bowie, Arizona in the Indian Wars of the 1880's. Reprint of 1977 edition. Illus. 88 pp. Paper. Supt. of Documents, $3.00.

THE CLASSIC SOUTHWEST: READINGS IN ARCHAEOLOGY, ETHNOHISTORY AND ETHNOLOGY
Basil C. Hedrick, et al
206 pp. Southern Illinois University Press, 1973. $10.00.

CLASSIFICATION AND DEVELOPMENT OF NORTH AMERICAN INDIAN CULTURES: A STATISTICAL ANALYSIS OF THE DRIVER-MASSEY SAMPLE
Harold E. Driver and James L. Coffin
Illus. Paper. American Philosophical Society, 1975. $7.00.

THE CLASSIFICATION AND DISTRIBUTION OF THE PIT RIVER INDIAN TRIBES OF CALIFORNIA
Clinton H. Merriam
Reprint of 1926 edition. AMS Press, $15.00.

CLASSIFIED ENGLISH-SHUSWAP WORD LIST
A.H.A. Kuipers
Humanities Press, 1975. $3.50.

CLAY FIGURINES OF THE AMERICAN SOUTHWEST
N. Morss
Reprint of 1954 edition. Paper. Kraus, $31.00.

*THE CLIFF DWELLERS
Rebecca B. Marcus
The story of the cliff-dwelling Indians of the southwestern U.S. and their culture. Grades 4-6. Franklin Watts, 1968. $5.00.

CLIFF DWELLERS OF THE MESA VERDE
Gustaf Nordenskiold
Reprint. Illus. Map. 382 pp. Rio Grande Press, $20.00.

*CLIFF DWELLINGS: ANCIENT RUINS FROM AMERICA'S PAST
Carroll B. Colby
Photographs and discussions of the ruins and artifacts of the Pueblo Indians of the Southwest. Grades 4-6. Illus. Maps. Coward-McCann, 1965. $5.00.

*CLIMBING SUN: THE STORY OF A HOPI INDIAN BOY
Marjorie Thayer and Elizabeth Emanuel
Grades 5-12. Illus. 96 pp. Dodd, Mead & Co., 1983. $7.95.

CLOTHED-IN-FUR AND OTHER TALES: AN INTRODUCTION TO AN OJIBWA WORLD VIEW
Thomas W. Overholt and J. Biard Callicott
198 pp. University Presses of America, 1982. $26.00; paper, $12.00.

COACOOCHEE, MADE FROM THE SANDS OF FLORIDA: AN ACCOUNT OF A ONCE FREE SEMINOLE CHIEF PRESENTED IN FREE VERSE
Arthur E. Francke
Illus. 60 pp. Paper. St. Johns Oklawaha, 1982. $5.95.

THE COAST INDIANS OF SOUTHERN ALASKA AND NORTHERN BRITISH COLUMBIA
Albert P. Niblack
Reprint of 1890 edition. Johnson Reprint, $25.00.

THE COAST SALISH OF BRITISH COLUMBIA
Homer Barnett
Reprint of 1955 edition. Illus. 320 pp. Greenwood, $25.00.

COAST SALISH: THEIR ART, CULTURE AND LEGENDS
Reg Ashwell
Illus. Paper. Universe Books, 1978. $5.00.

COAST SALISH AND WESTERN WASHINGTON INDIANS
Five volumes. Illus. Maps. Garland Publishing, $42.00 each. See publisher for titles and descriptions.

THE COCHISE CULTURAL SEQUENCE IN SOUTHEASTERN ARIZONA
E.B. Sayles, et al
192 pp. Paper. University of Arizona Press, 1983. $12.95.

COCHITI: NEW MEXICO PUEBLO, PAST AND PRESENT
Charles H. Lange
Illus. 642 pp. Southern Illinois University Press, 1968. $14.95; paper, $11.95.

COCOPA ETHNOGRAPHY
William H. Kelly
A study of the Cocopa Tribe of the Colorado River Delta during the late 1880s. Paper. University of Arizona Press, 1977. $7.95.

CODE OF FEDERAL REGULATIONS, TITLE 25, INDIANS, REVISED APRIL 1, 1985
Also available in nine microfiche. 844 pp. Supt. of Documents, 1985. $18.00. Microfiche, $3.75.

COEUR D'ALENE INDIAN ABORIGINAL DISTRIBUTION: ETHNOLOGICAL FIELD INVESTIGATION AND ANALYSIS OF HISTORICAL MATERIAL
Stuart A. Chalfant
155 pp. Clearwater, 1974. $50.00.

THE COEUR D'ALENE RESERVATION
Lawrence Palladino
Bound with *Our Friends the Coeur D'Alene Indians*. Paper. Ye Galleon Press, 1967. $3.00.

THE COEUR D'ALENE INDIANS
Teit and Boas
175 pp. Paper. Shorey, $10.00.

COEUR D'ALENE TRACT, IDAHO AND WASHINGTON, 1873, 1887, 1891: APPRAISAL
C. Marc Miller
210 pp. Clearwater, 1973. $65.00.

COEUR D'ALENE TRIBE OF NORTHERN IDAHO: APPRAISAL OF ABORIGINAL LANDS
Henry T. Murray
92 pp. Clearwater, 1974. $36.00.

FELIX S. COHEN'S HANDBOOK OF FEDERAL INDIAN LAW
Felix S. Cohen
Facsimile of 1942 edition. University of New Mexico Press, $25.00. 950 pp. Michie Co., 1982. $80.00.

MICHAEL COLEMAN
Illus. Paper. University of Nebraska Press, 1979. $12.95.

COLLECTING SHAWNEE POTTERY: A PICTORIAL REFERENCE AND PRICE GUIDE
Mark Supnick
Illus. 64 pp. Paper. M. Supnick, 1983. $9.95.

COLLECTING SOUTHWESTERN NATIVE AMERICAN JEWELRY
Mark Bahti
Illus. David McKay, 1980. $12.95; paper, $8.95.

A COLLECTION OF ETHNOGRAPHICAL ARTICLES ON CALIFORNIA INDIANS
Robert Heizer
Illus. Map. 103 pp. Paper. Ballena Press, 1976. $5.95.

A COLLECTION OF SOME OF THE MOST INTERESTING NARRATIVES OF INDIAN WARFARE IN THE WEST
S. Metcalf
Reprint of 1821 edition. Garland Publishing, $44.00.

JOHN COLLIER'S CRUSADE FOR INDIAN REFORM, 1920-1954
Kenneth R. Philp
Commissioner of Indian Affairs under FDR, Collier rejected the idea of "Americanizing" Indians in favor of preserving their traditions. 304 pp. Paper. University of Arizona Press, 1977. $8.95.

A COLONY ON THE MOVE: GASPAR CASTANO DE SOSA'S JOURNAL, 1590-1591
A.H. Schroeder and Dan Matson
Illus. University of New Mexico Press, 1965. $8.95.

COLOR AND SHAPE IN AMERICAN INDIAN ART
Z. Mathews; M. Aspinwall and A. Hobar, Editors
Illus. 24 pp. Paper. Metro Museum of Art, 1983. $2.95.

COLUMBIA SALISH OF CENTRAL WASHINGTON: ABORIGINAL LAND-USE AND OCCUPANCY
Stuart A. Chalfant
78 pp. Clearwater, 1973. $29.00.

COLVILLE TRACTS, STATE OF WASHINGTON, 1872: APPRAISAL
C. Marc Miller
210 pp. Clearwater, 1973. $64.50.

THE COLVILLE TRIBE, SAN POIL AND NESPELEM TRIBES, THE LEKES, OKANOGANS, METHOWS: APPRAISAL OF THE TRIBAL LANDS, STATE OF WASHINGTON, 1872
Ralph W. Watson
291 pp. Clearwater, 1973. $84.00 per set.

COMANCHE
David Dary
Illus. 19 pp. Paper. University of Kansas, Museum of Natural History, 1976. $1.00.

THE COMANCHE, APACHE AND KIOWA INDIANS BEFORE 1867: HABITAT AND RANGE
Ernest Wallace
Clearwater, 1976. $99.00.

THE COMANCHE BARRIER TO SOUTH PLAINS SETTLEMENT
Rupert N. Richardson
Reprint of 1933 edition. 424 pp. Kraus, $42.00.

COMANCHE DAYS
Albert S. Gilles, Sr.
Author recalls father's trading post in Comanche country. 144 pp. Paper. Southern Methodist University Press, 1974. $7.95.

COMANCHE TEXTS
Elliott Canonge
Paper. Summer Institute of Linguistics, 1958. $5.00.

COMANCHES
T.R. Fehrenbach
Alfred A. Knopf, 1974. $22.50.

THE COMANCHES:
LORDS OF THE SOUTH PLAINS
Ernest Wallace and E. Adamson Hoebel
Illus. Map. 400 pp. University of Oklahoma Press,
$19.95.

*COME TO OUR SALMON FEAST
Martha F. McKeown
Grades 4-9. Illus. 80 pp. Binford & Mort, 1959.
$6.95.

COMMERCE OF THE PRAIRIES
Josiah Gregg; Max Moorhead, Editor
Illus. Maps. 475 pp. University of Oklahoma
Press, 1974. $19.95; paper, $8.95. Reprint.
Peter Smith, $10.00.

COMMON EDIBLE AND USEFUL
PLANTS OF THE EAST AND MIDWEST
Muriel Sweet
Illus. 64 pp. Naturegraph, 1975. $6.95;
paper, $2.95.

COMMUNITY-BASED RESEARCH: A
HANDBOOK FOR NATIVE AMERICANS
Susan Guyette
358 pp. Paper. American Indian Studies Center,
$15.00.

COMMUNITY HEALTH AND MENTAL
HEALTH CARE DELIVERY FOR
NORTH AMERICAN INDIANS
E. Fuller Torry, et al
Irvington Publishers, 1974. $21.00.

COMPANION ISSUE
Adolph Hungry Wolf
Illus. Paper. Good Medicine Books, 1971. $2.00.

A COMPANY OF HEROES: THE
AMERICAN FRONTIER, 1775-1783
D. Van Every
Reprint of 1962 edition. Ayer Co. Publishers,
$15.00.

COMPARATIVE HOKAN-
COAHUILTECAN STUDIES
Margaret Langdon
Illus. 114 pp. Paper. Mouton, 1974. $20.75.

A COMPARATIVE RACIAL STUDY
OF THE PAPAGO
N.E. Gabel
Reprint of 1949 edition. Paper. Kraus, $13.00.

COMPARATIVE STUDIES IN
AMERINDIAN LANGUAGES
Esther Matteson, et al
251 pp. Paper. Summer Institute of Linguistics,
1972. $31.00.

COMPARATIVE STUDIES OF
NORTH AMERICAN INDIANS
Harold E. Driver and William C. Massey
Illus. 164 maps. 292 pp. Paper. American

Philosophical Society, 1957. $10.00.

COMPARATIVE VOCABULARIES AND
PARALLEL TEXTS IN TWO YUMAN
LANGUAGES OF ARIZONA
Leslie Spier
Reprint of 1946 edition. Paper. Kraus and
AMS Press, $15.00.

COMPARATIVE VOCABULARIES OF THE
TRIBES OF WESTERN WASHINGTON
AND NORTHWESTERN OREGON
George Gibbs, et al
Reprint of 1877 edition. Illus. Map. 40 pp.
Shorey, $5.00.

*COMPETING FOR GLORY:
THE INDIAN WORLD OF SPORTS
"The Weewish Tree", Editors
Grades 4-12. Illus. Paper. The Indian Historian
Press, 1981. $9.95.

COMPILED LAWS OF
THE CHEROKEE NATION
Reprint of 1881 edition. Scholarly Resources,
$35.00.

*THE COMPLETE HOW-TO BOOK
OF INDIAN CRAFT
W. Ben Hunt
Grades 7-adult. 80 pp. Paper. Macmillan, 1973.
$4.95.

CONCEPT OF THE GUARDIAN
SPIRIT IN NORTH AMERICA
Ruth Benedict
Reprint of 1923 edition. Paper. Kraus, $12.00.

A CONCISE BLACKFOOT GRAMMAR
Christianus C. Uhlenbeck
Reprint of 1938 edition, AMS Press, $29.50.

A CONCISE DICTIONARY OF
INDIAN TRIBES OF NORTH AMERICA
Barbara Leitch; Kendall LePoer, Editor
Reference Publications, 1980. $59.95.

A CONDENSED HISTORY OF THE
APACHE AND COMANCHE INDIAN
TRIBES
Jonathan H. Jones
Reprint of 1899 edition. Garland, $42.00.

THE CONDITION OF AFFAIRS IN
INDIAN TERRITORY AND CALIFORNIA
Charles C. Painter
Reprint of 1888 edition. AMS Press, $14.00.

CONDITION OF THE INDIAN TRADE
IN NORTH AMERICA, 1767: AS
DESCRIBED IN A LETTER TO
SIR WILLIAM JOHNSON
Guy C. Dorchester
Reprint of 1890 edition. 16 pp. Paper.
Burt Franklin, $12.00.

**CONFEDERATED BANDS OF UTE
INDIANS: APPRAISAL OF MINERAL
RESOURCES IN LANDS**
Ben H. Parker and John W. Vanderwilt
Five volumes. 873 pp. Clearwater, 1973.
$250.00 per set.

**CONFEDERATED SALISH AND
KOOTENAI TRIBE LANDS OF THE
FLATHEAD INDIAN RESERVATION,
1859: VALUATION**
Mont H. Saunderson
100 pp. Clearwater, 1973. $35.00.

**CONFEDERATED SALISH AND
KOOTENAI TRIBES, APPRAISAL
OF THE LANDS IN MONTANA, 1859**
Harry R. Fenton
175 pp. Clearwater, 1973. $54.00.

**CONFEDERATED SALISH AND
KOOTENAI TRIBE OF THE
FLATHEAD RESERVATION: A HISTORY**
Clearwater, 1976. $30.00.

**CONFEDERATED UTE INDIAN LANDS
IN SOUTHWESTERN COLORADO, CEDED
SEPT. 13, 1873: APPRAISAL**
Gerald T. Hart
315 pp. Clearwater, 1973. $91.00.

**THE CONFLICT BETWEEN THE
CALIFORNIA INDIAN AND
WHITE CIVILIZATION**
Sherburne F. Cook
Reprint of 1888 edition. Four volumes in one.
University of California Press, $48.50.

**CONFLICT AND SCHISM IN
NEZ PERCE ACCULTURATION**
Deward Walker
Illus. Paper. University Press of Idaho, 1968.
$9.95.

**THE CONFLICT OF EUROPEAN AND
EASTERN ALGONKIAN CULTURES,
1504-1700: A STUDY IN
CANADIAN CIVILIZATION**
Alfred Bailey
Second edition. Paper. University of Toronto
Press, 1969. $8.50.

**CONFLICTING PERCEPTIONS:
WESTERN ECONOMICS AND
THE GREAT WHALE CREE**
Richard H. Wills
96 pp. Tutorial, Illinois, 1985. $12.95.

CONQUERING HORSE
Frederick Manfred
370 pp. Paper. University of Nebraska Press,
1983. $9.95.

CONQUEST OF APACHERIA
Dan Thrapp
Illus. University of Oklahoma Press, 1967.
$19.95; paper, $9.95.

**THE CONQUEST OF THE COEUR
D'ALENES, SPOKANES AND PALOUSES**
Benjamin F. Manring
280 pp. Ye Galleon Press, 1975. $14.95.

**CONSIDERATIONS ON THE PRESENT
STATE OF THE INDIANS AND THEIR
REMOVAL TO THE WEST OF
THE MISSISSIPPI**
Lewis Cass
Reprint of 1828 edition. Ayer Co. Publishers,
$13.50.

**THE CONSTITUTIONS AND LAWS
OF THE AMERICAN INDIAN TRIBES**
This program presents the complete collection of
the written constitutions and laws of the
American Indian tribes to 1906 when tribal
governments in Indian territory were abolished.
The constitutions for the following tribes are
included: The Chickasaw, Osage, Cherokee,
Choctaw, Muskogee, Creek, and Sac and Fox.
Two series. 53 volumes. See Scholarly Resources
for titles, descriptions and prices.

**CONSTITUTION OF THE
STATE OF SEQUOYAH**
Reprint of 1906 edition. Three volumes in one.
AMS Press, $18.00.

**A CONSTITUTIONAL ANALYSIS OF
THE CRIMINAL JURISDICTION AND
PROCEDURAL GUARANTEES OF
THE AMERICAN INDIAN**
Brent H. Gubler
Reprint of 1963 edition. Paper. R & E Research,
$10.00.

**CONTEMPORARY INDIAN ARTISTS:
MONTANA, WYOMING AND IDAHO**
Catalog of an exhibition presented at the Museum
of the Plains Indian in Browning, Montana.
Reviews the diversity of painting by
contemporary Indian artists representing major
tribes of the northwestern plains and adjacent
northern Rocky Mountain area. An introductory
text traces developments of 19th and 20th century
American Indian art. Illus. Map. 80 pp. Northern
Plains Indian Crafts Association, $4.50.

**CONTEMPORARY IROQUOIS AND
THE STRUGGLE FOR SURVIVAL:
FROM WORLD WAR II TO THE
EMERGENCE OF RED POWER**
Lawrence Hauptman
Illus. 385 pp. Syracuse University Press, 1985.
$37.50; paper, $15.95.

CONTEMPORARY NAVAJO AFFAIRS
Norman Eck
243 pp. Navajo Curriculum, 1982. $15.00.

CONTEMPORARY PUEBLO
INDIAN POTTERY
Harlow and Young
Illus. Paper. Museum of New Mexico Press, 1974.
$2.25.

CONTEMPORARY SIOUX PAINTING
Catalog to an exhibition presented at the Sioux
Indian Museum, Rapid City, South Dakota.
Presents an historic survey of painting by
contemporary Sioux artists. Includes a text
tracing the development of Sioux art from the
19th century. Illus. Map. 80 pp. Tipi Shop, Inc.,
1970. $3.25.

CONTEMPORARY SOUTHERN PLAINS
INDIAN METALWORK
Catalog to an exhibition presented at the
Southern Plains Indian Museum in Anadarko,
Oklahoma. Explores an important tradition of
distinctive jewelry and ornamentation created of
nickel-silver by modern tribal craftsmen of the
Southern Plains region. Illus. Map. 80 pp.
Oklahoma Indian Arts and Crafts Cooperative,
$5.75.

CONTEMPORARY SOUTHERN PLAINS
INDIAN PAINTING
Catalog to an exhibition presented at the
Southern Plains Indian Museum, Anadarko,
Oklahoma. An historic survey of contemporary
painting by Indian artists of the Southern Plains
region. Photo portraits, along with biographical
information on the artists. Illus. Map. 80 pp.
Oklahoma Indian Arts and Crafts Cooperative,
1972. $4.25.

CONTENT AND STYLE OF AN ORAL
LITERATURE: CLACKAMAS CHINOOK
MYTHS AND TALES
Melville Jacobs
285 pp. University of Chicago Press, 1959. $17.50.

CONTINENT LOST-A CIVILIZATION
WON: INDIAN LAND TENURE
IN AMERICA
J.P. Kinney; Dan C. McCurry and
Richard E. Rubinstein, Editors
Reprint of 1937 edition. Illus. 336 pp. Ayer Co.
Publishers, $27.00. Octagon Books, $19.00.

CONTINENTS IN COLLISION:
THE IMPACT OF EUROPE ON THE
NORTH AMERICAN INDIAN SOCIETIES
Robert A. Hecht
337 pp. University Press of America, 1980.
$25.25; paper, $14.00.

CONTINUITIES OF HOPI
CULTURE CHANGE
Richard O. Clemmer
Paper. Acoma Books, 1978. $9.50.

CONTRACTS BETWEEN IROQUOIS
HERBALISM AND COLONIAL MEDICINE
William N. Fenton
Reprint of 1941 edition. Illus. 28 pp. Paper.
Shorey, $2.50.

CONTRIBUTIONS AND ACHIEVEMENTS
OF THE AMERICAN INDIAN
Rupert Costo
Illus. The Indian Historian, 1976. $12.50.

CONTRIBUTIONS TO ANTHROPOLOGY:
SELECTED PAPERS OF A.
IRVING HALLOWELL
A. Irving Hallowell
University of Chicago Press, 1976. $40.00.

CONTRIBUTIONS TO CANADIAN
ETHNOLOGY, 1975
David Brez Carlisle, Editor
Paper. National Museums of Canada, $3.95.

CONTRIBUTIONS TO
CHIPEWYAN ETHNOLOGY
Kaj Birket-Smith
Reprint of 1930 edition. AMS Press, $38.50.

CONTRIBUTIONS TO THE
ETHNOGRAPHY OF THE KUTCHIN
Cornelius Osgood
Reprint of 1936 edition. 190 pp. Paper. HRAFP,
$15.00.

CONTRIBUTIONS TO FOX ETHNOLOGY
T. Michelson
Reprint of 1927 edition. Scholarly Press, $19.00.

COPPER: ITS MINING AND USE
BY THE ABORIGINES OF THE
LAKE SUPERIOR REGION
George A. West
Reprint of 1929 edition. Greenwood Press,
$13.00.

COPPER PALADIN:
THE MODOC TRAGEDY
Walter Palmberg
208 pp. Dorrance, 1982. $12.00.

THE COQUILLE INDIANS:
YESTERDAY, TODAY AND TOMORROW
Roberta L. Hall
Illus. 250 pp. Paper. SSS Publishing, 1984. $9.95.

CORN AMONG THE INDIANS
OF THE UPPER MISSOURI
George F. Will and George E. Hyde
323 pp. University of Nebraska Press, 1964.
$23.95; paper, 5.95.

**CORN GODDESS AND OTHER TALES
FROM INDIAN CANADA**
Diamond Jenness
Illus. 120 pp. Paper. University of Chicago Press,
1980. $3.50.

**CORNHUSK BAGS OF
THE PLATEAU INDIANS**
Cheney Cowles Memorial Museum
Microfiche. Illus. University of Chicago Press,
1976. $30.00.

**THE CORPORATION AND THE INDIAN:
TRIBAL SOVEREIGNTY AND
INDUSTRIAL CIVILIZATION IN
INDIAN TERRITORY, 1865-1907**
H. Craig Minor
256 pp. University of Missouri Press, 1976.
$15.00.

**THE CORRECT LANGUAGE,
TOJOLABAL: A GRAMMAR
WITH ETHNOGRAPHIC NOTES**
Louanna Furbee-Losee
Garland Publishing, 1976. $38.00.

**COSTUMES OF THE PLAINS INDIANS
AND STRUCTURAL BASIS TO THE
DECORATION OF COSTUMES AMONG
THE PLAINS INDIANS**
Clark Wissler
Reprint of 1915 edition. Illus. 88 pp. AMS Press,
$17.00.

*COU-YAN-NAI
Weechees
Grades 4-9. Council for Indian Education, $5.95;
paper, $1.95.

*COULD IT BE OLD HIARI
Marjorie Vandervelde
Grades 5-9. Council for Indian Education, 1975.
$1.95.

COUNCIL FIRES ON THE UPPER OHIO
Randolph C. Downs
Illus. Paper. University of Pittsburgh Press,
1969. $6.95.

**THE COVENANT CHAIN: INDIAN
CEREMONIAL AND TRADE SILVER**
Jaye Frederickson and Sandra Gibb
Illus. 168 pp. National Museums of Canada, 1980.
$12.50; paper, $9.00. University of Chicago Press,
$24.95; paper, $17.95.

**COWBOYS, INDIANS AND
OTHER CHARACTERS**
Larry Fotine
Paper. Poly Tone, 1981. $7.50.

*COYOTE AND KOOTENAI
Louie Gingras and Jo Rainboldt
Grades 2-6. Council for Indian Education, 1977.
$1.95.

*COYOTE STORIES
Robert Roessel, Jr. and Dillon Platero
Grades 3-12. Illus. 141 pp. Paper, Navajo
Curriculum Center Press, 1975. $5.75.

COYOTE STORIES
Mourning Dove (Okinagan Indian)
Heister D. Guil, Editor
Reprint of 1933 edition. Illus. AMS Press, $27.50.

COYOTE STORIES
Martha B. Kendall
Paper. University Microfilms, 1981. $12.00.

**COYOTE TALES OF
THE MONTANA SALISH**
Pierre Pichette; H. Miller
and E. Harrison, Editors
Contains 13 folk tales of folk hero Coyote. An
introductory text outlines the history of the Salish
tribes. Illus. Maps. 80 pp. Northern Plains Indian
Crafts Association, $4.50

**COYOTE WAS GOING THERE:
INDIAN LITERATURE OF
THE OREGON COUNTRY**
Jarold Ramsey
Illus. 336 pp. Paper. University of Washington
Press, 1977. $9.95; paper, $7.95.

*COYOTE'S POW-WOW
Hap Gilliland
Grades 1-6. Paper. Council for Indian Education,
1972. $1.95.

**COYOTEWAY: A NAVAJO HOLYWAY
HEALING CEREMONIAL**
Karl W. Luckert
Includes more than 100 photos, plus song and
prayer texts. Illus. 243 pp. Paper. University of
Arizona Press, 1979. $14.95.

**CRAFTS FROM NORTH AMERICAN
INDIAN ARTS: TECHNIQUES, DESIGNS
AND CONTEMPORARY APPLICATIONS**
Mary Lous Stribling
Illus. 288 pp. Crown Publishers, 1975. $14.95;
paper, $7.95.

***CRAFTS OF THE NORTH AMERICAN
INDIANS: A CRAFTSMAN'S MANUAL**
Richard C. Schneider
Grades 9-12. Illus. 325 pp. Paper. R. Schneider
Publishers, 1981. $15.95.

**CRASHING THUNDER: THE AUTO-
BIOGRAPHY OF AN AMERICAN INDIAN**
Paul Radin, Editor
250 pp. University of Nebraska Press, 1983.
$19.95; paper, $7.95.

*CRAZY HORSE
Mary Carroll Nelson
A biography. Grades 5-9. Illus. 75 pp. Dillon
Press, 1975. $5.95.

CRAZY HORSE: THE STRANGE
MAN OF THE OGLALAS
Mari Sandoz
Illus. 428 pp. Hastings House, 1961. $12.95.
Paper. University of Nebraska Press. $5.95.

*CREATION TALES FROM THE SALISH
W.H. McDonald
Grades 3-9. Paper. Council for Indian Education,
1973. $1.95.

CREATIVE WEST:
TAOS AND NORTHERN NEW MEXICO
Philip Bareiss; James Parsons, Editor
Illus. Gallery West, 1983. $1.50.

THE CREEK FRONTIER, 1540-1783
David H. Corkran
A history of the Creek Tribe during the colonial
period. Illus. Biblio. 360 pp. University of
Oklahoma Press, 1967. $12.95.

CREEK INDIAN LANDS IN
OKLAHOMA: APPRAISAL OF
LAND VALUES AS OF 1907
Samuel L. Stores
Clearwater, 1976. $100.00.

CREEK INDIAN TERRITORIAL
EXPANSION: THE HUDSON BAY AREA
TO INTERIOR SASKATCHEWAN
AND MISSOURI PLAINS
Floyd W. Sharrock and Susan R. Sharrock
200 pp. Clearwater, 1973. $60.00.

*THE CREEK INDIANS
Grant Lyons
Grades 4-12. Illus. 96 pp. Julian Messner, 1978.
$8.00.

CREEK INDIANS
James F. Doster; David A. Horr, Editor
Two volumes. 652 pp. Map. Garland, 1978.
$42.00 each.

CREEK INDIANS: INFORMATION
RELATIVE TO THE CLAIMS OF
THE CREEKS AGAINST THE U.S.
FOR FLORIDA LANDS TAKEN BY
THE U.S. UNDER THE TREATY
OF MOULTRIE CREEK, 1823
James F. Doster
376 pp. Clearwater, 1974. $102.00.

CREEK INDIANS OF TASKIGI TOWN
Frank G. Speck
Reprint of 1907 edition. Paper. Kraus, $15.00.

CREEK INDIANS AND THEIR
FLORIDA LANDS, 1740-1805
James F. Doster
Illus. 268 pp. Clearwater, 1974. $76.50.

CREEK NATION: APPRAISAL OF
CEDED LANDS IN SOUTHERN
GEORGIA AND SOUTHEASTERN
ALABAMA
Paul Starrett
21 pp. Clearwater, 1973. $15.00.

CREEK NATION EAST OF THE
MISSISSIPPI: APPRAISAL OF
LANDS IN GEORGIA AND ALABAMA
AS OF AUGUST 9, 1814
M.J. Williamson
21 pp. Clearwater, 1974. $17.00.

CREEK NATION LANDS IN ALABAMA:
LAND APPRAISAL AS OF 1832
Ernest G. Booth
Clearwater, 1976. $45.00.

CREEK NATION LANDS IN OKLAHOMA:
APPRAISAL OF OIL, GAS, COAL
AND MINERALS
Josef Faust and John Hassler
Clearwater, 1976. $225.00.

THE CREEK NATION AND PRIVATE
LAND SALES IN ALABAMA, AND AN
APPRAISAL OF CREEK NATION LANDS
M.J. Williamson
Clearwater, 1976. $99.00.

CREEK (MUSKOGEE)
NEW TESTAMENT CONCORDANCE
Lee Chupco and Ward Coachman
167 pp. Indian University Press, 1982. $12.50.

A CREEK SOURCEBOOK
William C. Sturtevant, Editor
Reprint. Garland Publishing, $90.00.

THE CREEK VERB
Henry O. Harwell and Deloris T. Harwell
57 pp. Indian University Press, 1981. $6.00.

CREEK WAR OF 1813 and 1814
H.S. Halbert and T.H. Ball;
Frank Owsley, Jr., Editor
Reprint of 1895 edition. 366 pp. University
of Alabama Press, $19.95.

THE CREEKS:
A CRITICAL BIBLIOGRAPHY
Michael D. Green
Paper. Indiana University Press, 1979. $4.95.

THE CRESCENT HILLS
PRHISTORIC QUARRYING AREA
David J. Ives
Paper. Museum of Anthropology, University of
Missouri, 1975. $2.00.

CRIME AGAINST THE YAKIMAS
Lucullus V. McWhorter
Facsimile reprint. 57 pp. Paper. Shorey, $6.95.

**CRIMINAL JURISDICTION
ALLOCATION IN INDIAN COUNTRY**
Ronald B. Flowers
Associate Faculty Press, 1983. $14.50.

**CRIMSON DESERT: INDIAN WARS
OF THE AMERICAN SOUTHWEST**
Odie B. Faulk
Illus. Maps. 250 pp. Oxford University Press,
1974.$12.95.

**CRIMSONED PRAIRIE:
THE INDIAN WARS**
S.L. Marshall
Reprint of 1972 edition. Illus. 285 pp. Charles
Scribner's Sons, $20.00; Paper. Da Capo Press,
$9.95.

**CROOKED BEAK OF HEAVEN:
MASKS AND OTHER CEREMONIAL
ART OF THE NORTHWEST COAST**
Bill Holm
Illus. 96 pp. University of Washington Press,
1972.

**CROOKS SITE, A MARKSVILLE
PERIOD BURIAL MOUND IN THE
LA SALLE PARISH, LOUISIANA**
J.A. Ford and G. Willey
Reprint of 1940 edition. Kraus, $20.00.

**CROSSCURRENTS ALONG THE
COLORADO: THE IMPACT OF
GOVERNMENT POLICY ON
THE QUECHEN INDIANS**
Robert Bee
184 pp. Paper. University of Arizona Press, 1981.
$7.50.

**CROSSING THE CULTURAL DIVIDE:
INDIANS AND NEW ENGLANDERS,
1605-1763**
Alden T. Vaughan and Daniel K. Richter
76 pp. Paper. American Antiquarian, 1980. $5.00.

CROW CREEK SITE: 39 BF 11, # 7
Marvin F. Kivett and Richard Jensen
Ilus. Paper. Nebraska Historical Society, $6.00.

**CROW INDIAN ART: PAPERS
PRESENTED AT THE CROW INDIAN
ART SYMPOSIUM SPONSORED BY
THE CHANDLER INSTITUTE**
R. Pohrt, Jr. and B. Lanford;
F. Dennis Lessurd, Editor
Illus. 68 pp. Paper. Chandler Institute, 1984.
$12.00.

**CROW INDIAN BEADWORK: A DE-
SCRIPTIVE AND HISTORICAL STUDY**
William Wildschut and John C. Ewers
Second edition. Illus. 108 pp. Eagles View,
$14.95; paper, $8.95.

**CROW INDIAN LANDS CEDED IN
THE FORT LARAMIE TREATY
OF 1868: APPRAISAL**
Mont H. Saunderson
80 pp. Clearwater, 1973. $29.00.

CROW INDIAN MEDICINE BUNDLES
William Wildschut; John C. Ewers, Editor
Reprint of 1960 edition. Illus. 187 pp. Paper.
Museum of the American Indian, 1975. $10.00.

THE CROW INDIANS
Robert H. Lowie
Reprint of 1935 edition. 350 pp. Paper. University
of Nebraska Press, $9.95. Irvington, $10.50.

CROW INDIANS
Norman B. Plummer
Illus. Map. 317 pp. Garland Publishing, $51.00.

**CROW LANDS IN MONTANA AND
WYOMING, 1868: APPRAISAL**
Norman B. Plummer
201 pp. Clearwater, 1973. $60.00.

**CROW MAN'S PEOPLE:
THREE SEASONS WITH THE NAVAJO**
Nigel Pride
Illus. 222 pp. Universe Books, 1985. $15.00.

CROW TEXTS
Dorothea V. Kaschube, Editor
Paper. University Microfilms, 1978. $12.00.

CROWFOOT: CHIEF OF THE BLACKFEET
Hugh Dempsey
Illus. 230 pp. University of Oklahoma Press, 1972.
$12.95; paper, $6.95. Paper. Hutig, $6.95.

***A CRY FROM THE EARTH: MUSIC
OF THE NORTH AMERICAN INDIANS**
J. Bierhorst
Grades 5-12. Illus. Scholarly Book Service, 1979.
$9.95.

**CRY OF THE THUNDERBIRD: THE
AMERICAN INDIAN'S OWN STORY**
Charles Hamilton, Editor
Illus. 283 pp. University of Oklahoma Press, 1972.
$18.95; paper, $8.95.

**CRYING FOR A VISION: ROSEBUD
SIOUX TRILOGY, 1886-1976**
J.A. Anderson and E. Buechel;
J. Alinder and D.Doll, Editors
Illus. Paper. Morgan & Morgan, 1976. $10.95.

**CRYSTALS IN THE SKY: AN
INTELLECTUAL ODYSSEY INVOLVING
CHUMASH ASTRONOMY, COALMOLOGY,
AND ROCK ART**
Travis Hudson and Ernest Underhay
Paper. Ballena Press, 1978. $8.95.

**CULTURAL CHANGE AND
CONTINUITY ON CHAPIN MESA**
Arthur H. Rohn
Illus. University Press of Kansas, 1977. $27.50.

**CULTURAL AND ENVIRONMENTAL
HISTORY OF CIENEGA VALLEY,
SOUTHEASTERN ARIZONA**
Frank W. Eddy and Maurice E. Cooley
62 pp. University of Arizona Press, 1983. $7.95.

**CULTURE IN CRISIS:
A STUDY OF THE HOPI INDIANS**
Laura Thompson
Reprint of 1950 edition. Illus. 221 pp. Russell &
Russell, $22.00.

CULTURE OF THE LUISENO INDIANS
Philip Sparkman
Reprint of 1908 edition. A study of southern
California Indians. Paper. Ballena Press, $4.95.

**CULTURES IN CONTACT: THE EURO-
PEAN IMPACT ON NATIVE CULTURAL
INSTITUTIONS IN EASTERN NORTH
AMERICA A.D. 1000-1800**
William W. Fitzhugh, Editor
Illus. 360 pp. Smithsonian, 1985. $29.95.

**CULTURES OF THE
NORTH PACIFIC COAST**
Philip Drucker
Illus. Paper. Harper & Row, 1965. $13.50.

**EDWARD S. CURTIS: PHOTOGRAPHER
OF THE NORTH AMERICAN INDIANS**
Victor Boesen and Florence C. Graybill
Grades 7-12. Dodd, Mead & Co., 1977. $6.95.

**CURTIS' WESTERN INDIANS: LIFE
AND WORKS OF EDWARD C. CURTIS**
R.W. Andrews
Encore edition. Illus. Superior, 1962. $9.50.

*CUSTER COUNTRY
Ralph E. Scudder
The story of the Custer massacre at the Little Big
Horn. Grades 7-9. 64 pp. Illus. Binford & Mort,
1963. $7.50.

**THE CUSTER TRAIL: A NARRATIVE
OF THE LINE OF MARCH OF TROOPS
SERVING IN THE CAMPAIGN AGAINST
HOSTILE SIOUX, 1876 FORT ABRAHAM
LINCOLN TO THE MONTANA LINE**
Frank L. Anders
Illus. 148 pp. Arthur H. Clark, 1983. $55.00.

**CUSTER'S FALL: THE INDIAN
SIDE OF THE STORY**
David H. Miller
Illus. 275 pp. University of Nebraska Press, 1985.
$7.95.

CUSTER'S LAST
Don Russell
Illus. Amon Carter Museum of Western Art,
1968. $7.95.

*CUSTER'S LAST STAND
Quenten Reynolds
The story of the Battle of the Little Big Horn,
including a biography of General Custer. Grades
4-6. Illus. 185 pp. Random House, 1951. $4.95.

CUSTER'S LUCK
Edgar I. Stewart
Reprint of 1955 edition. Illus. 520 pp. University
of Oklahoma Press, $9.95.

**CUSTOMS AND LEGENDS OF THE
TLINGIT INDIANS OF ALASKA**
O.M. Salisbury
Reprint. Superior Publishing.

CUT-OUTS: NATIVE AMERICAN ART
James H. Howard
Illus. 32 pp. Milwaukee Public Museum, 1982.
$4.95.

**CYCLES OF CONQUEST: THE IMPACT
OF SPAIN, MEXICO AND THE U.S.
ON INDIANS OF THE SOUTHWEST,
1533-1960**
Edward H. Spicer
More than 400 years of cultural history of some
25 Southwestern tribes. Illus. 609 pp. Paper.
University of Arizona Press, 1962. $12.50.

D

**DAHCOTAH: OR, LIFE AND
LEGENDS OF THE SIOUX AROUND
FORT SNELLING**
Mary Eastman
Facsimile of 1849 edition. Illus. Ayer Co.
Publishers, $18.00.

*DAISY HOOEE NAMPEYO
Carol Fowler
Grades 5-12. Illus. Dillon Press, 1977. $6.95.

DAKOTA GRAMMAR
Ella C. Deloria; Agnes Picotte, Editor
Paper. Dakota Press, 1979. $6.95.

***DAKOTA AND OJIBWE
PEOPLE IN MINNESOTA**
Frances Densmore
Grades 7-9. Illus. Paper. Minnesota Historical
Society, 1977. $3.00.

DAKOTA TEXTS
Ella C. Deloria
Reprint of 1932 edition. AMS Press, $23.00.
Paper. Dakota Press, $6.95.

**DAKOTA TWILIGHT: THE
STANDING ROCK SIOUX, 1874-1890**
Edward Milligan
Exposition Press, 1976. $8.50.

**DAKOTA VISIONS:
A COUNTRY APPROACH**
David J. Holden
Examines Dakota Indian heritage. Illus. 392 pp.
Paper. Center for Western Studies, 1982. $14.95.

DAKOTA WAR WHOOP
H.E. McConkey
Reprint of 1864 edition. Ross & Haines, $15.00.

**DAKOTA WAR WHOOP; OR, INDIAN
MASSACRES AND WAR IN MINNESOTA**
H.E. Bishop; Wilcomb Washburn, Editor
Reprint of 1863 edition. Garland Publishing,
$44.00.

**DAMMED INDIANS: THE PICK-SLOAN
PLAN AND THE MISSOURI
RIVER SIOUX, 1944-1980**
Michael L. Lawson
Illus. 288 pp. University of Oklahoma Press,
1982. $19.95.

**DANCE AND SONG RITUALS OF
SIX NATIONS RESERVE, ONTARIO**
Gertrude Prokosch Kurath
Illus. 205 pp. National Museums of Canada,
$8.50;   paper, $4.95.

**DANCE AROUND THE SUN: THE
LIFE OF MARY LITTLE BEARY
INKANISH: CHEYENNE**
Alice Marriott and Carol K. Rachlin
Illus. Thomas Y. Crowell, 1977. $12.95.

**DANCE DOWN THE RAIN, SING
UP THE CORN: AMERICAN INDIAN
CHANTS AND GAMES FOR CHILDREN**
Millie Burnett
R & E Research Associates, 1975. $5.00.

**DANCE AND SONG RITUALS OF
SIX NATIONS RESERVE, ONTARIO**
Gertrude P. Kurath
Illus. 205 pp. Paper. University of Chicago Press,
1968. $5.00.

**DANCES OF THE TEWA PUEBLO
INDIANS: EXPRESSIONS OF LIFE**
Jill D. Sweet
Illus. 100 pp. Paper. School of American
Research, $8.95.

**DANCING GODS: INDIAN CEREMO-
NIALS OF NEW MEXICO AND ARIZONA**
Erna Fergusson
Illus. 286 pp. Paper. University of New Mexico
Press, 1970. $6.95.

DANCING WITH CREATION
Martha Kirk
Paper. Resource Publications, 1983. $6.95.

**DARING DONALD McKAY: OR, THE
LAST WAR TRIAL OF THE MODOCS**
Keith and Donna Clark, Editors
Illus. Paper. Oregon Historical Society, 1971.
$2.95.

*THE DARK SIDE OF THE MOON
Tom Kovach
Grades 4-12. 32 pp. Council for Indian Education,
1984. $6.95; paper, $2.45.

DAUGHTERS OF THE EARTH
Carolyn Niethammer
Paper. Macmillan, 1977. $10.95.

***DAVID, YOUNG CHIEF OF THE
QUILEUTES: AN AMERICAN
INDIAN TODAY**
Ruth Kirk
Grades 3-5. Illus. Harcourt Brace, 1967. $5.95.

**THE DAWES ACT AND THE
ALLOTMENT OF INDIAN LAND**
D.S. Otis
215 pp. University of Oklahoma Press, 1973.
$9.95.

DAWN IN ARCTIC ALASKA
Diamond Jenness
Illus. 225 pp. Paper. University of Chicago Press,
1985. $8.95.

**DAWN OF THE WORLD, STORIES
OF THE COAST MIWOK INDIANS**
Bonnie Peterson, Editor
Illus. Paper. Timal Land, 1976. $3.00.

***DAYBREAK STAR PRESCHOOL
ACTIVITIES BOOK**
Grades Preschool-2. 60 pp. Daybreak Star Press,
$5.75.

THE DAYS OF THE HERCULES
John Fahey
Illus. University Press of Idaho, 1978. $10.95.

**DE GRAZIA PAINTS CABEZA
DE VACA: THE FIRST NON-INDIAN
IN TEXAS, NEW MEXICO AND
ARIZONA, 1527-1536**
Ted De Grazia
University of Arizona Press, 1973. $19.50.

**DE GRAZIA PAINTS
THE YAQUI EASTER**
Ted Grazia
Collection of Yaqui Lenten ceremonies, the full
40 day observance in as many full-page paintings.
Illus. 92 pp. University of Arizona Press, 1968.
$19.50.

DEAD TOWNS OF ALABAMA
W. Stuart Harris
176 pp. Ilus. University of Arizona Press, 1977.
$9.95.

THE DEATH AND REBIRTH
OF THE SENECA
Anthony F. Wallace
416 pp. Paper. Random House, 1972. $5.95.

THE DEATH OF JIMMY LITTLEWOLF:
AN INDIAN BOY AT BOYS RANCH
R.L. Templeton
Eakin Publications, 1980. $6.95.

THE DEATH OF THE GREAT SPIRIT
Earl Shorris
208 pp. Paper. New American Library, 1974.
$2.00.

DEATH, TOO, FOR THE
HEAVY-RUNNER
Ben Bennett
Illus. 192 pp. Mountain Press, 1982. $14.95;
paper, $7.95.

DECEMBER'S CHILD: A BOOK
OF CHUMASH ORAL NARRATIVES
Thomas Blackburb, Editor
360 pp. Univerity of California Press, 1976.
$22.50; paper, $9.95.

THE DECORATIVE ART OF
THE INDIANS OF THE NORTH
PACIFIC COAST
Franz Boas
Reprint of 1897 edition. Illus. AMS Press, $14.00.

DECORATIVE ART OF
THE SOUTHWESTERN INDIANS
Dorothy Sides
Reprint of 1962 edition. Illus. Peter Smith,
$12.00. Paper. Dover, $2.95.

A DELAWARE INDIAN SYMPOSIUM
Herbert C. Kraft, Editor
Illus. 160 pp. Pennsylvania Historical and
Museum Commission, 1974. $9.95.

THE DELAWARE INDIAN
WESTWARD MIGRATION
C.A. Weslager
Illus. Middle-Atlantic Press, 1978. $16.00.

*THE DELAWARE INDIANS:
EASTERN FISHERMEN AND FARMERS
Sonia Bleeker
Grades 3-6. Illus. 160 pp. William Morrow & Co.,
1953. $9.00.

THE DELAWARE INDIANS:
A HISTORY
C.A. Weslager
Illus. 576 pp. Rutgers University Press, 1972.
$35.00.

DELAWARE OUTLET IN NORTH-
EASTERN KANSAS, 1854: APPRAISAL
Richard B. Hall
120 pp. Clearwater, 1973. $39.00.

DELAWARE'S BURIED PAST:
A STORY OF ARCHAEOLOGICAL
ADVENTURE
C.A. Weslager
Illus. Paper. Rutgers University Press, 1968.
$2.95.

THE DELAWARES:
A CRITICAL BIBLIOGRAPHY
C.A. Weslager
Paper. Indiana University Press, 1978. $4.95.

DELIGHT MAKERS
Adolph F. Bandelier
A fictional reconstruction of prehistoric Indian
culture in the American Southwest by a 19th
century archaeologist. Illus. 490 pp. Paper.
Harcourt Brace, 1971. $8.95.

DENE NATION. THE COLONY WITHIN
Mel Watkins
University of Toronto Press, 1977. $17.50; paper,
$6.95.

DENETSOSIE
B. Johnson and S.M. Callaway, Editors
Revised edition. Illus. 51 pp. Navajo Curriculum,
1974. $4.50.

FRANCES DENSMORE AND
AMERICAN INDIAN MUSIC
Charles Hofmann
127 pp. Paper. Museum of the American Indian,
1968. $5.00.

DEPRADATIONS AND MASSACRE
BY THE SNAKE RIVER INDIANS
Edward Geary
A report on Indian trouble in southern Idaho.
Reprint of 1966 edition. Paper. Ye Galleon, 1966.
$2.50.

THE DEPTH OF THE GREAT SPIRIT
Earl Shorris
208 pp. Paper. New American Library, 1974.
$1.50.

DESCRIPTION — NATURAL HISTORY
OF THE COASTS OF NORTH AMERICA
N. Denys; W.F. Ganong, Editor
Reprint of 1908 edition. Greenwood Press,
$42.00.

DESCRIPTION OF A JOURNEY AND
VISIT TO THE PAWNEE INDIANS
Dottlieb Oehler and David Smith
32 pp. Ye Galleon Press, $4.95; paper, $3.00.

**DESCRIPTION OF THE
NEW NETHERLANDS**
A. Van Der Donch; Thomas F. O'Donnell,
Editor
Syracuse University Press, 1968. $10.00.

**DESERT DRUMS: THE PUEBLO
INDIANS, NEW MEXICO, 1540-1928**
Leo Crane
Reprint of 1928 edition. Illus. 490 pp. Paper.
Rio Grande Press, $12.00.

**DESERT FORAGERS AND HUNTERS:
INDIANS OF THE DEATH
VALLEY REGION**
William J. and Edith Wallace
Illus. Paper. Acoma Books, 1979. $3.50.

**THE DESERT PEOPLE: A STUDY
OF THE PAPAGO INDIANS**
Alice Joseph and R. Spicer
Reprint of 1947 edition. Illus. 288 pp. University
of Chicago Press, $11.00.

**DESERT IMMIGRANTS: THE
MEXICAN OF EL PASO, 1880-1920**
Mario T. Garcia
Illus. 328 pp. Yale University Press, 1981. $23.00.

**THE DESERT SMELLS LIKE RAIN:
A NATURALIST IN PAPAGO
INDIAN COUNTRY**
Gary P. Nabhan
Illus. 192 pp. North Point Press, 1982. $15.00.

**DESIGNS FROM THE ANCIENT
MIMBRENOS WITH HOPI
INTERPRETATION**
Fred Kabotie
Illus. 100 pp. Northland Press, 1982. $40.00.

**DESIGNS ON PREHISTORIC
HOPI POTTERY**
Jesse W. Fewkes
Illus. Paper. Dover, 1973. $4.00.

**THE DESTRUCTION OF
AMERICAN INDIAN FAMILIES**
Steven Unger, Editor
Paper. Association on American Indian Affairs,
1977. $4.25.

**DETAILED REPORT ON THE
SALBURGER EMIGRANTS WHO
SETTLED IN AMERICA: 1734-1735**
Samuel Urlsperger; George F. Jones, Editor
253 pp. University of Georgia Press, 1969. $12.00.

**THE DEVELOPMENT OF CAPITALISM
IN THE NAVAJO NATION: A
POLITICAL-ECONOMIC HISTORY**
Lawrence D. Weiss
180 pp. MEP Publications, 1984. $29.95.

**DIAGNOSIS AND TREATMENT OF
PREVALENT DISEASES OF NORTH
AMERICAN INDIAN POPULATIONS**
M. Lee, Max Miller, et al, Contributors
A collection of articles and papers providing an
introduction to the more commonly diagnosed
ailments among North American Indians. Two
volumes. 302 pp. and 250 pp. Irvington
Publishers, 1974. $24.50 each.

**DICTIONARY CATALOG OF THE
AMERICAN INDIAN COLLECTION**
Huntington Free Library and Reading Room
G.K. Hall & Co., 1977. $350.00.

**DICTIONARY OF THE EDWARD E.
AYER COLLECTION OF AMERICANS
AND AMERICAN INDIANS**
16 volumes. G.K. Hall, 1961. $1,165.00 per set.

**A DICTIONARY OF THE ATAKAPA
LANGUAGE ACCOMPANIED BY
TEXT MATERIAL**
A. Catschett and J. Swanton
Reprint of 1932 edition. Scholarly Press, $9.50.

DICTIONARY OF CHINOOK JARGON
Reprint. 42 pp. Paper. Shorey, $4.95.

**A DICTIONARY OF THE CHOCTAW
LANGUAGE**
C. Byington
Reprint of 1915 edition. Scholarly Press, $39.00

**DICTIONARY OF DAILY LIFE OF
INDIANS OF THE AMERICAS, A-Z**
Two volumes. 2,000 pp. American Indian
Publishers, 1982. $165.00 per set.

**DICTIONARY OF INDIAN TRIBES
OF THE AMERICAS**
Second edition. Four volumes. Illus. 2,000 pp.
American Indian Publishers, 1981. $285.00.

**DICTIONARY OF INDIANS
OF NORTH AMERICA**
Harry Waldman, Editor
Three volumes. Scholarly Press, 1978. $145/set.

**DICTIONARY OF THE LANGUAGES
OF THE MICMAC INDIANS, WHO
RESIDE IN NOVA SCOTIA, NEW
BRUNSWICK, PRINCE EDWARD
ISLAND, CAPE BRETON AND
NEWFOUNDLAND**
Silas T. Rand
Reprint of 1888 edition. Johnson Reprint, $40.00.

**A DICTINARY OF THE
OSAGE LANGUAGE**
F. LaFleche
Reprint of 1932 edition. Scholarly Press, $35.00.

DICTIONARY OF PREHISTORIC INDIAN ARIFACTS OF THE AMERICAN SOUTHWEST
Franklin Barnett
Illus. 128 pp. Paper. Northland Press, 1973. $8.95.

DICTIONARY OF PUGET SALISH
Thom Hess
dialects. Illus. Maps. 766 pp. University of Washington Press, 1976. $19.50.

A DICTIONARY OF THE CHOCTAW LANGUAGE
Cyrus Byington
Reprint of 1915 edition. Scholarly Press.

DICTIONARY OF THE NISQUALLY INDIAN LANGUAGE
George Gibbs
Extracted from 1877 edition. 76 pp. Paper. Shorey, $12.00.

A DICTIONARY OF THE OSAGE LANGUAGE
Francis LaFleche
Reprint of 1932 edition. Scholarly Press.

A DICTIONARY OF THE OTCHIPWE LANGUAGE-EXPLAINED IN ENGLISH
Friedrick Baraga
Reprint of 1853 edition. Scholarly Press.

THE DIEGUENO INDIANS
Albert L. Kroeber, and J.P. Harrington
Reprint of 1976 edition. Paper. Acoma Books, $2.00.

DIGEST OF DECISIONS RELATING TO INDIAN AFFAIRS
U.S. Burau of Indian Affairs
Reprint of 1901 edition. Kraus, $29.00.

THE DINE: ORIGIN MYTHS OF THE NAVAHO INDIANS
Aileen O'Brien
Reprint of 1956 edition. Scholarly Press, $19.00.

DINE BAHANE: THE NAVAJO CREATION STORY
Paul G. Zolbrod
368 pp. University of New Mexico Press, 1984. $22.50.

DINETAH: NAVAJO HISTORY
Robert A. Roessel; T.L. McCarty, Editor
Volume III. Illus. 180 pp. Navajo Curriculum, 1983. $15.00.

DIRTY BOY: A JICARILLA TALE OF RAID AND WAR
Morris E. Opler
Reprint of 1938 edition. Kraus, $15.00.

DISCOVERIES OF THE TRUTH
Diane E. Wirth
Illus. Paper. D.E.Wirth, 1978. $4.95.

DISCOVERY OF THE YOSEMITE AND THE INDIAN WAR OF 1851
L.H. Bunnell
Facsimile of 1880 edition. Ayer Co. Publishers, $21.00.

DISCOVERY, SETTLEMENT AND PRESENT STATE OF KENTUCKE
John Filson
Reprint. Peter Smith, $8.00.

DISINHERITED: THE LOST BIRTH-RIGHT OF THE AMERICAN INDIAN
Dale Van Every
The story of the events preceding the Removal Act. Maps. 304 pp. Paper. Avon, 1967. $2.95.

DISPOSSESSING THE AMERICAN INDIAN: INDIAN AND WHITES ON THE COLONIAL FRONTIER
Wilbur R. Jacobs
Illus. 256 pp. Paper. University of Oklahoma Press, 1972. $9.95.

DISTRICT OF COLUMBIA (D.C.) DIRECTORY OF NATIVE AMERICAN FEDERAL AND PRIVATE PROGRAMS
Lists 250 programs; various resources, points of interest and gathering spots. Annual. Paper. American Indian Education Program, Phelps-Stokes
Fund. $5.00.

DIVING FOR NORTHWEST RELICS
James S. White
Illus. Binfort & Mort, 1979. $8.95; paper, $6.50.

DIVISIVENESS AND SOCIAL CONFLICT: AN ANTHROPOLOGICAL APPROACH
Alan R. Beals and Bernard J. Siegel
Stanford University Press, 1966. $17.50.

DIX-HUNT ANS CHEZ LES SAUVAGES: VOYAGES ET MISSIONS DE MONSEIGNEUR HENRY FARAUD
Henry Faraud
Reprint of 1866 edition. Johnson Reprint, $28.00.

A DOCUMENTARY HISTORY OF RELIGION IN AMERICA
Edwin S. Gaustad, Editor
Volume I includes Native-American religion. 540 Paper. William B. Eerdmans Publishing, 1982. $15.95.

DOCUMENTATION OF AMERICAN INDIAN MUSIC AND MUSICIANS
Charlotte Heth
American Indian Studies Center.

DOCUMENTS OF U.S. INDIAN POLICY
Francis P. Prucha, Editor
278 pp. Paper. University of Nebraska Press,
1975. $6.50.

**DOCUMENTS RELATING TO
INDIAN AFFAIRS, 1750-1754**
W.L. McDowell, Jr., Editor
University of South Carolina Press, 1958. $27.50.

**DOING FIELDWORK:
WARNINGS AND ADVICE**
Rosalie H. Wax
Paper. University of Chicago Press, 1971. $8.50.

**DRAMATIC ELEMENTS IN
AMERICAN INDIAN CEREMONIALS**
Virginia S. Heath
Paper. Haskell House, 1970. $19.95.

**THE DREAM DANCE OF THE
CHIPPEWA AND MENOMINEE
INDIANS OF NORTHERN WISCONSIN**
Samuel A. Barrett
Reprint of 1911 edition. AMS Press and Garland
Publishing, $26.00.

**THE DREAM HELPER IN
SOUTH-CENTRAL CALIFORNIA**
Richard Applegate
Paper. Ballena Press, 1979. $5.95.

**DREAM TRACKS: THE RAILROAD
AND THE AMERICAN INDIAN**
T.C. McLuhan
Illus. 210 pp. Harry N. Abrams, 1985. $37.50.

**DREAMERS WITH POWER:
THE MENOINEE**
George and Louise Spindler
Reprint of 1971 edition. Illus. 208 pp. Paper.
Waveland Press, 1984. $7.95.

**DRESS CLOTHING OF
THE PLAINS INDIANS**
Ronald P. Koch
Illus. 238 pp. University of Oklahoma Press, 1977.
$17.95.

**DRINKING BEHAVIOR AMONG
SOUTHWESTERN INDIANS: AN
ANTHROPOLOGICAL PERSEPCTIVE**
Jack Waddell and Michael Everett, Editors
Examines the drinking behavior of four tribes:
Papago, Taos Pueblo, Navajo and White
Mountain
Apache. 245 pp. University of Arizona Press,
1980. $16.50; paper, $9.50.

**GABRIEL DUMONT: THE METIS
CHIEF AND HIS LOST WORLD**
George Woodcock
A biography of this legendary plainsman. Illus.
Hurtig Publishers, $8.95; paper, $6.95.

**THE DUNBAR-ALLIS
LETTERS ON THE PAWNEE**
John Dunbar and Samuel Allis
Reprint. 214 pp. Garland Publishing, $30.00.

**DURING MY TIME: FLORENCE
EDENSHAW DAVIDSON, A HAIDA
WOMAN**
Margaret B. Blackman
Illus. 192 pp. University of Washington Press,
1982. $19.95; paper, $8.95.

**DUWAMISH, SNOHOMISH AND
SUQUAMISH TRACTS: APPRAISAL**
C. Marc Miller
210 pp. Clearwater, 1973. $65.00.

**THE DYNAMICS OF GOVERNMENT
PROGRAMS FOR URBAN INDIANS
IN THE PRAIRIE PROVINCES**
Raymond Breton and Gail Grant
628 pp. Paper. Brookfield Publishing Co., 1984.
$19.95.

E

**EARLY ACCOUNT OF
THE CHOCTAW INDIANS**
John Swanton
Reprint of 1918 edition. Paper. $15.00.

**EARLY AMERICAN INDIAN DOCUMENTS
TREATIES AND LAWS, 1607-1789**
Alden T. Vaughan
20 volumes. University Publications, 1983.
$1,100.00 per set.

**EARLY DAYS AMONG THE CHEYENNE
AND ARAPAHOE INDIANS**
John Seger; Stanley Vestal, Editor
Reprint of 1934 edition. Illus. Paper. University
of Oklahoma Press, $5.95.

**EARLY HISTORY OF THE CREEK
INDIANS AND THEIR NEIGHBORS**
John Swanton
Reprint of 1922 edition. Scholarly Press, $46.00.

AN EARLY INDIAN MISSION
Louis Baroux
Reprint of 1913 edition. Hardscrabble Books,
$4.50.

EARLY INDIAN TRADE GUNS:
1625-1775
T.M. Hamilton
Illus. Paper. Museum of the Great Plains, 1968.
$2.50.

THE EARLY PREHISTORIC
SOUTHEAST: A SOURCEBOOK
Jerald T. Milanich, Editor
400 pp. Garland Publishing, 1985. $50.00.

EARLY PUEBLOAN OCCUPATIONS:
TESUQUE BY-PASS AND UPPER
RIO GRANDE VALLEY
Charles McNutt
Illus. Paper. University of Michigan, Museum of
Anthropology, 1969. $3.00.

EARTH DYES
Rita Blumenstein
General information and recipes for making dyes
from natural materials the Yup'ik Eskimo way.
Illus. 24 pp. Institute of Alaska Native Arts,
$5.00.

EARTH, FATHER SKY AND ECONOMIC
DEVELOPMENT: NAVAJO RESOURCES
AND THEIR USE
Philip Reno
Illus. 200 pp. University of New Mexico Press,
1981. $12.50.

*THE EARTH IS SORE:
NATIVE AMERICANS ON NATURE
Aline Amon
Grades 5-12. Illus. 96 pp. Atheneum, 1981. $9.95.

EARTH MEDICINE—EARTH FOODS:
PLANT REMEDIES, DRUGS, AND
NATURAL FOODS OF THE NORTH
AMERICAN INDIANS
Michael A. Weiner
Second edition. Macmillan, 1980. $15.95; paper,
$8.95.

EARTHDIVERS: TRIBAL NARRATIVES
ON MIXED DESCENT
Ruth Benedict
Illus. 195 pp. University of New Mexico Press,
1981. $14.95.

THE EASTERN BAND OF
CHEROKEES, 1819-1900
John R. Finger
Illus. 268 pp. University of Tennessee Press, 1984.
$24.95; paper, $12.50.

THE EASTERN CHEROKEES
William H. Gilbert
Reprint of 1943 edition. AMS Press, $27.50.

*CHARLES EASTMAN
Betsy Lee
Grades 5-12 Illus. Dillon Press, 1979. $6.95.

*EASY TO MAKE NORTH
AMERICAN INDIAN CRAFTS
Frieda Gates
Grades 3-6. Illus. 48 pp. Harvey House, 1981.
$6.79.

ECHOES OF OUR BEING
Robert J. Conley, Editor
Illus. 76 pp. Paper. Indian University Press, 1982.
$5.00.

THE ECONOMIC BOTANY OF
THE KIOWA INDIANS
Paul A. Vestal and Richard E. Schultes
Reprint of 1939 edition. AMS Press, $21.50.

ECONOMIC DEVELOPMENT ON
AMERICAN INDIAN RESERVATIONS
Roxanne D. Ortiz, Editor
157 pp. Paper. University of New Mexico, Native
American Studies, 1979. $8.95.

ECONOMICS FOR ADMINISTRATORS
J.N. Mongia
600 pp. Advent Books, 1982. $40.00.

ECONOMICS OF MINORITIES:
A GUIDE TO INFORMATION SOURCES
Kenneth Gazala
339 pp. Gale Research Co., 1976. $60.00.

ECONOMICS OF THE IROQUOIS
Sara Stites
Reprint of 1905 edition. AMS Press, $18.00.

THE ECONOMICS OF SAINTHOOD:
RELIGIOUS CHANGE AMONG
THE RIMROCK NAVAJOS
Kendall Blanchard
Illus. 244 pp. Fairleigh Dickinson, 1976. $22.50.

EDUCATION AND THE AMERICAN
INDIAN: THE ROAD TO SELF-
DETERMINATION SINCE 1928
Margaret C. Szasz
Second edition. Illus. 252 pp. Paper. University
of New Mexico Press, 1974. $10.95.

EDUCATION: THE DILEMMA OF
THE INDIAN AMERICAN
George L. Farmer
Sun Dance Books, 1969. $15.00.

EL GRINGO: OR, NEW MEXICO
AND HER PEOPLE
William W. Davis
Reprint of 1857 edition. Illus. 436 pp. Ayer Co.
Publishers, $24.00.

THE ELDER AMERICAN INDIAN
Frank Dukepoo
South Dakota State University Press, 1978. $3.50.

ELDERBERRY FLUTE SONGS:
CONTEMPORARY COYOTE TALES
Peter Blue Cloud; Illus. by Bill Cosby
More than 50 stories from Peter Blue Cloud,
Mohawk poet. 142 pp. The Crossing Press,
$17.95; paper, $8.95.

ELEMENTARY FORMS OF
THE RELIGIOUS LIFE
E. Durkheim; J.W. Swain, Translator
Totems. Paper. Free Press, 1965. $14.95.

JOHN ELIOT'S INDIAN DIALOGUES:
A STUDY IN CULTURAL INTERACTION
J. Eliot; H.W. Bowden and J. Rhonda, Editors
Illus. 173 pp. Greenwood Press, 1980. $29.95.

THE ELKUS COLLECTION:
SOUTHWESTERN INDIAN ART
California Academy of Sciences
Illus. 244 pp. Paper. University of Washington
Press, $19.95.

ELUSIVE TREASURE
Brian Fagan
Illus. Charles Scribner's Sons, 1977. $7.95.

THE EMBATTLED NORTHEAST: THE
ELUSIVE IDEAL OF ALLIANCE IN
ABENAKI-EUROAMERICAN RELATIONS
Kenneth Morison
University of California Press, 1984. $24.95.

THE EMIGRANT INDIANS OF KANSAS:
A CRITICAL BIBLIOGRAPHY
William E. Unrau
96 pp. Paper. Indiana University Press, 1979.
$4.95.

ENCHANTED MOCCASINS AND OTHER
LEGENDS OF THE AMERICAN INDIANS
Cornelius Mathews, Editor
Reprint of 1877 edition. AMS Press, $24.75.

THE END OF INDIAN KANSAS:
A STUDY OF CULTURAL REVOLUTION,
1854-1871
H. Craig Miner and William E. Unrau
Illus. University Presses of Kansas, 1977. $17.95.

THE ENDURING NAVAHO
Laura Gilpin
Illus. 277 pp. University of Texas Press, 1968.
$37.50.

THE ENDURING STRUGGLE
George H. Phillips, Jr.; N. Hundley
and John Schutz, Editors
Illus. 110 pp. Paper. Boyd & Fraser, 1981. $6.95.

ENDURING VISIONS: ONE THOUSAND
YEARS OF SOUTHWESTERN INDIAN ART
D. Erdman and P.M. Hortstein, Editors
Illus. Paper. Aspen Center for Visual Arts, 1979.
$12.95.

ENEMY WAY MUSIC: A STUDY OF
SOCIAL AND AESTHETIC VALUES
AS SEEN IN NAVAHO MUSIC
D.P. McAllester
Reprint of 1954 edition. Paper. Kraus, $26.00.

AN ENGLISH—BLACKFOOT
VOCABULARY
C.C. Uhlenbeck and R.H. Van Gulik
Reprint of 1930 edition. AMS Press, $27.50.

ENGLISH—CHEYENNE DICTIONARY
Paper. Council for Indian Education, 1976. $4.95.

ENGLISH—ESKIMO,
ESKIMO—ENGLISH DICTIONARY
P. Shalom Publications, $12.50; thumb-index
edition, $14.50.

ENGLISH—ESKIMO, AND
ESKIMO—ENGLISH VOCABULARIES
R. Wells, Compiler; John Kelley, Translator
Reprint of 1890 edition. AMS Press, $12.50

ENGLISH INSTITUTIONS AND
THE AMERICAN INDIAN
James A. James
Reprint of 1894 edition. Paper. Johnson Reprint,
$11.50.

ENGLISH TO CHOCTAW AND
CHOCTAW TO ENGLISH DICTIONARIES
Cyrus Byingtons
Choctaw Museum.

ENGLISH-ESKIMO AND
ESKIMO-ENGLISH VOCABULARIES
R. Wells, Compiler; John Kelly, Translator
72 pp. Paper. Charles E. Tuttle, 1982. $6.95.

ENJU: THE LIFE AND STRUGGLE
OF AN APACHE CHIEF FROM THE
LITTLE RUNNING WATER
Sinclair Browning
Illus. 160 pp. Northland Press, 1982. $15.95;
paper, $9.95.

ENQUIRY INTO THE CAUSES OF
THE ALIENTATION OF THE
DELAWARE AND SHAWNEE INDIANS
FROM BRITISH INTERESTS
C. Thompson
Reprint of 1759 edition. Scholarly Press, $19.00.

THE ENSLAVEMENT OF
THE AMERICAN INDIAN
Barbara Olexer
Illus. 280 pp. Library Research Associates, 1982.
$19.95.

EROTICA IN INDIAN DANCE
P. Baneji
171 pp. Humanities Press, 1983. $44.50.

THE ESKIMO ABOUT BERING STRAIT
Edward W. Nelson
Reprint of 1899 edition. Examines many aspects of dwindling Eskimo group. Illus. 520 pp. Paper. Smithsonian Institution Press, $25.00.

THE ESKIMO AND HIS ART
Carson I. Ritchie
St. Martin's Press, 1974. $14.50.

*THE ESKIMO: ARCTIC HUNTERS AND TRAPPERS
Sonia Bleeker; Patricia Boodell, Illustrator
A study of the nomadic life of the Eskimo. Grades 3-6. 160 pp. William Morrow, 1959. $9.00.

ESKIMO ART: TRADITION AND INNOVATION IN NORTH ALASKA
Dorothy J. Ray
Illus. University of Washington Press, 1976.

*ESKIMO BOY TODAY
Byron Fish, et al
Grades 7-adult. Illus. 64 pp. Alaska Northwest Publishing, 1971. $7.95.

ESKIMO BOYHOOD: AN AUTO-BIOGRAPHY IN PSYCHOSOCIAL PERSPECTIVE
Charles C. Hughes
University Press of Kentucky, 1974. $14.50.

ESKIMO CAPITALISTS: OIL, POLITICS AND ALCOHOL
Samuel Z. Klausner and Edward A. Foulks
Illus. 360 pp. Allanheld, 1982. $39.50.

ESKIMO CHILDHOOD AND INTER-PERSONAL RELATIONSHIPS: NUNIVAK BIOGRAPHIES AND GENEALOGIES
Margaret Lantis
A collection of life stories of 18 Eskimos. Illus. Map. 326 pp. University of Washington Press, 1960.

ESKIMO—ENGLISH, ENGLISH-ESKIMO VOCABULARIES
R. Wells, Compiler; John W. Kelly, Translator
Reprint. 72 pp. Paper. Charles E. Tuttle, 1982. $6.95.

*AN ESKIMO FAMILY
Bryan and Cherry Alexander
Grades 2-5. Illus. 39 pp. Lerner Publications, 1985. $8.95.

ESKIMO MASKS: ART AND CEREMONY
Dorothy J. Ray
Discusses the forms, meanings, and uses of masks in the context of 19th century aboriginal Eskimo culture. Illus. 272 pp. Paper. University of Washington Press, 1975. $14.50.

ESKIMO MEDICINE MAN
Otto George
Illus. 324 pp. Paper. Oregon Historical Society, 1979. $7.95.

ESKIMO POEMS FROM CANADA AND GREENLAND
Tom Lowenstein, Translator
University of Pittsburgh Press, 1973. $14.95.

ESKIMO PRINTS
James Houston
Prints and stencils executed by a group of Kingnaimuit Eskimos on West Baffin Island, with a text by James Houston. Illus. 112 pp. Barre Publishers, 1971.

ESKIMO SCHOOL ON THE ANDREAFSKY: A STUDY OF EFFECTIVE BICULTURAL EDUCATION
Judith S. Kleinfeld
209 pp. Praeger Publishers, 1979. $34.95.

THE ESKIMO STORYTELLER: FOLKTALES FROM NOATAK, ALASKA
Edwin S. Hall, Jr.
Illus. 510 pp. University of Tennessee Press, 1975. $25.00.

THE ESKIMO TRIBES
Hinrich J. Rink
Reprint of 1891 edition. Covers their distribution and characteristics, especially in regard to language. Map. Two volumes in one. AMS Press, $37.50.

*ESKIMOS
Mary Bringle
Accents the Eskimo of today and dispels some common stereotypes. Grades 4-7. Illus. Maps. 87 pp. Franklin Watts, 1973.

*ESKIMOS
Wally Herbert
Details the author's life among the Eskimos. Grades 7-adult. Illus. Map's. Biblio. 128 pp. Franklin Watts, 1977.

*ESKIMOS
Susan Purdy and Cass R. Sandak
Grades 4-6. Illus. 32 pp. Franklin Watts, 1982. $7.90.

ESKIMOS AND ALEUTS
Don E. Dumond
Illus. Thames Hudson, 1977. $19.95.

ESKIMOS AND EXPLORERS
Wendall H. Oswald
Illus. 368 pp. Chandler and Sharp, 1979. $15.00.

ESKIMOS, CHICANOS, INDIANS
Robert Coles
Children of Crisis Series, Volume 4. Little, Brown & Co., 1978. $15.00.

**ESKIMOS OF NORTHEAST LABRADOR:
A HISTORY OF ESKIMO—WHITE
RELATIONS, 1771-1955**
Helge Kleivan
Paper. Universitetsforlaget, 1966. $10.00.

**THE ESKIMOS OF THE BERING
STRAIT, 1650-1898**
Dorothy J. Ray
Illus. Maps. 332 pp. University of Washington
Press, 1976. $19.95.

**THE ESKIMOS OF THE NUSHAGAK
RIVER: AN ETHNOGRAPHIC HISTORY**
James W. Van Stone
An archaeological and ethnographic investigation
into the Eskimos of southeastern Alaska. Illus.
Maps. 216 pp. University of Washington Press,
1967. $14.50.

*ESKIMOS OF THE WORLD
Paul M. Elliott
People caught between two different worlds.
Grades 4-6. Illus. 128 pp. Julian Messner, 1976.
$8.95.

*THE ESKIMOS: PEOPLE OF ALASKA
Patricia M. Martin
Grades 1-4. Illus. Parents Magazine, 1970. $5.95.

ESKIMOS, REVISED
Jill Hughes
Illus. 32 pp. Franklin Watts, 1984. $9.40.

**THE ESKIMOS: THEIR
ENVIRONMENT AND FOLKWAYS**
Edward M. Weyer, Jr.
Maps. Biblio. 505 pp. The Shoe String Press,
1962. $25.00.

**ETHNIC AMERICAN MINORITIES:
A GUIDE TO MEDIA AND MATERIALS**
Harry A. Johnson, Editor & Compiler
Includes one section on American Indians.
304 pp. R.R. Bowker Co., 1976.

**ETHNIC DIRECTORY OF ALASKA,
HAWAII, OREGON AND WASHINGTON**
Vladimir Markotic
81 pp. Western Publishers, 1977.

**ETHNIC IDENTITY AND THE
BOARDING SCHOOL EXPERIENCE OF
WEST-CENTRAL OKLAHOMA
AMERICAN INDIANS**
Sally J. McBeth
Illus. 184 pp. University Press of America, 1983.
$24.75; paper, $11.25.

**ETHNIC MEDICINE IN
THE SOUTHWEST**
Edward H. Spicer et al, Editor
A four-part study of medical beliefs among

Indians, Mexican-Americans, Blacks and Anglos.
291 pp. Paper. University of Arizona Press,
1977. $7.95.

**ETHNIC SERIALS AT SELECTED UNI-
VERSITY OF CALIFORNIA LIBRARIES**
368 pp. Paper. American Indian Studies Center,
1977. $6.50.

**THE ETHNICS IN AMERICAN
POLITICS: AMERICAN INDIANS**
Frances Svensson
Paper. Burgess Publishing, 1973. $2.95.

**ETHNOBIOLOGY OF THE
PAPAGO INDIANS**
Edward F. Castetter and Ruth Underhill
Reprint of 1935 edition. AMS Press, $15.00.

**THE ETHNOBOTANY OF THE
COAHUILLA INDIANS OF
SOUTHERN CALIFORNIA**
David P. Barrows
Reprint of 1900 edtition. AMS Press, $15.00.
Paper. Malki Museum Press, $6.95.

**ETHNOBOTANY OF THE
FOREST POTAWATOMI INDIANS**
Huron H. Smith
Reprint of 1933 edition. AMS Press, $29.00.

**ETHNOBOTANY OF THE
GOSIUTE INDIANS OF UTAH**
Ralph V. Chamberlin
Reprint of 1911 edition. Paper. Kraus, $11.00.

ETHNOBOTANY OF THE HOPI
Alfred F. Whiting
Reprint of 1939 edition. AMS Press, $16.00.

**ETHNOBOTANY OF THE
MENOMINEE INDIANS**
Huron H. Smith
Reprint of 1923 edition. Greenwood Press,
$22.50.

**ETHNOBOTANY OF THE
MESKWAKI INDIANS**
Huron H. Smith
Reprint of 1928 edition. Bound with *Ethnobotany
of the Menomini Indians*. AMS Press, $40.50.

ETHNOBOTANY OF THE NAVAJO
Francis H. Elmore
Reprint of 1944 edition. AMS Press, $22.50.

**ETHNOBOTANY OF THE RAMAH
NAVAHO**
Paul A. Vestal
Reprint of 1952 edition. Kraus, $20.00.

ETHNOBOTANY OF THE TEWA INDIANS
W.W. Robbins
Scholarly Press, $19.00.

**ETHNOBOTANY OF THOMPSON
INDIANS OF BRITISH COLUMBIA**
Elsie V. Steedman
Reprint. 81 pp. Paper. Shorey Publications,
$4.95.

**ETHNOGRAPHIC BIBLIOGRAPHY
OF NORTH AMERICA**
Five volumes. HRAFP, 1975. $40.00 per volume.

**ETHNOGRAPHIC SKETCH OF
THE KLAMATH INDIANS OF
SOUTHWEST OREGON**
A. Gatschet
Facsimile reprint. 120 pp. Paper. Shorey, $8.95.

**ETHNOGRAPHY AND PHILOLOGY
OF THE HIDATSA INDIANS**
Washington Matthews
U.S. Geoological Survey of the Territories. Pubn.
#7.
Reprint of 1897 edition. Johnson Reprint, $20.00.

**ETHNOGRAPHY OF FRANZ BOAS;
LETTERS AND DIARIES OF FRANZ
BOAS WRITTEN ON THE NORTHWEST
COAST FROM 1886-1931**
Franz Boas; Ronald P. Rohner, Editor
Reprint. Illus. University of Chicago Press,
$16.00.

ETHNOGRAPHY OF THE FOX INDIANS
William Jones
Reprint of 1939 edition. Scholarly Press, $15.00.

**AN ETHNOGRAPHY OF
THE HURON INDIANS**
Elizabeth Tooker
Reprint of 1964 edition. Scholarly Press, $39.00.

ETHNOGRAPHY OF THE KUTENAI
H.H. Turney-High
Reprint of 1941 edition. Paper. Kraus, $23.00.

**ETHNOGRAPHY OF THE
NORTHERN UTES**
Anne M. Smith
Illus. Paper. Museum of New Mexico Press, 1974.
$11.95.

**ETHNOGRAPHY OF
SANTA CLARA PUEBLO**
W.W. Hill; Charles H. Lange, Editor
Illus. 550 pp. University of New Mexico Press,
1982. $35.00.

ETHNOGRAPHY OF THE TANAINA
Cornelius Osgood
A study of the Tanaina of Cook Inlet, Alaska.
Reprint of 1937 edition. Illus. 229 pp. Paper.
HRAFP, $10.00.

**ETHNOHISTORICAL REPORTS ON
INDIAN USE AND OCCUPANCY IN
OHIO, MICHIGAN AND INDIANA**
Erminie Wheeler-Voegelin
Six volumes. Clearwater, 1974. See publisher for
titles and prices.

**ETHNOHISTORY IN THE ARCTIC:
THE BERING STRAITS ESKIMO**
Dorothy J. Ray; Richard A. Pierce, Editor
Illus. 280 pp. Limestone Press, 1983. $27.00.

**AN ETHNOHISTORY OF
THE WESTERN ALEUTIANS**
Lydia T. Black
Illus. 291 pp. Limestone Press, 1984. $26.00.

**ETHNOLOGICAL FIELD INVESTIGA-
TION AND ANALYSIS OF HISTORICAL
MATERIAL RELATIVE TO GROUP DIS-
TRIBUTION AND UTILIZATION OF
NATURAL RESOURCES AMONG PUGET
SOUND INDIANS IN WASHINGTON**
Carroll L. Riley
59 pp. Clearwater, 1974. $27.50.

**ETHNOLOGICAL RESULTS OF
THE POINT BARROW EXPEDITION**
John Murdock
Illus. 450 pp. Paper. Smithsonian Institution
Press, 1986. $17.50.

**ETHNOLOGY AND LINGUISTICS
OF BAJA CALIFORNIA**
Miguel del Barco
A Baja California Travels Series book. 113 pp.
Dawson's Book Shop, 1981. $30.00.

ETHNOLOGY OF THE GROS VENTRE
Alfred L. Kroeber
Reprint of 1908 edition. AMS Press, $17.50.

ETHNOLOGY OF THE YUCHI INDIANS
Frank G. Speck
Reprint of 1909 edition. Illus. AMS Press, $28.00.

ETOWAH PAPERS
Warren K. Moorehead
The Etowah site in Georgia is examined. Illus.
177 pp. American Indian Books, $14.95.

**THE EUROPEAN AND THE INDIAN:
ESSAYS IN THE ETHNOHISTORY
OF COLONIAL NORTH AMERICA**
James Axtell
Illus. 256 pp. Oxford University Press, 1982.
$25.00; paper, $9.95.

EVA: AN ARCHAIC SITE
Thomas Lewis and Madeline Lewis
Illus. Paper. University of Tennessee Press,
1961. $8.50.

**EVALUATING AMERICAN INDIAN
BILINGUAL PROGRAMS: A
TOPICAL BIBLIOGRAPHY**
Douglas Knox, et al
60 pp. National Clearinghouse of Bilingual
Education, 1982. $5.65.

**EVALUATION OF THE MINERAL
LANDS IN INDIAN CESSION 175
OF EASTERN IOWA**
W.A. Broughton
58 pp. Clearwater, 1973. $22.50.

**AN EVALUATIVE ETHNOHISTORICAL
BIBLIOGRAPHY OF THE
MALECITE INDIANS**
Michel R.P. Herisson
Paper. National Museums of Canada, $3.95.

EVERETT MASSACRE
Walker C. Smith
Reprint of 1916 edition. Paper. Shorey, $8.00.

**EVERYDAY LIFE OF THE
NORTH AMERICAN INDIAN**
Jon M. White
Illus. 256 pp. Holmes & Meier, 1979. $22.50.
David & Charles, $22.50.

**THE EVOLUTION OF
THE AMERICAN INDIAN**
Arnold M. Mathews
Two volumes. Illus. 369 pp. Foundation for
Classical Reprints, 1984. $237.50.

**EXCAVATIONS AT HELLS MIDDEN,
DINOSAUR NATIONAL MONUMENT**
R.H. Lister
Reprint of 1951 edition. Paper. Kraus, $16.00.

EXCAVATIONS AT MAGIC MOUNTAIN
Cynthia Irwin-Williams
Paper. Denver Museum of Natural History, 1966.
$4.95.

**EXCAVATION OF MAIN PUEBLO
AT FITZMAURICE RUIN**
Franklin Barnett
Illus. Paper. Museum of Northern Arizona, 1974.
$7.50.

**EXCAVATIONS OF LOS MUERTOS AND
NEIGHBORING RUINS IN THE SALT
RIVER VALLEY, SOUTHERN ARIZONA**
Emil W. Haury
Reprint of 1945 edition. Paper. Kraus, $40.00.

**EXCAVATIONS AT SNAKETOWN:
MATERIAL CULTURE**
Harold S. Gladwin, et al
Reconstructs a building at a Hohokam site.
Reprint of 1965 edition. 305 pp. University
of Arizona Press, $19.95.

**EXCAVATIONS, 1940,
AT UNIVERSITY INDIAN RUIN**
Julian Hayden
Illus. Maps. 234 pp. Paper. Southwest Parks and
Monuments, 1957. $3.00.

**EXECUTIVE ORDERS RELATING TO
INDIAN RESERVATIONS FROM 1855-
1912; AND FROM 1912-1922**
Reprint of 1922 edition. Two volumes in one.
Scholarly Resources, $45.00.

EXILES OF FLORIDA
Joshua R. Giddings
Facsimile of 1858 edition. Illus. University
Presses of Florida and Ayer Co. Publishers,
$15.00.

**EXPEDITION AGAINST THE
SAUK AND FOX INDIANS, 1832**
Henry Smith
Reprint of 1833 edition. 19 pp. Paper. Ye Galleon
Press, $2.50.

**EXPEDITION INTO MEXICO,
MADE BY ANTONIO DE ESPEJO**
D.P. De Luxan; George P. Hammond, Editor
Reprint of 1929 edition. Ayer Co. Publishers,
$12.00.

**EXPEDITION TO THE PAWNEE
PICT VILLAGE IN 1834**
Thompson Wheelock
Reprint. Paper. Ye Galleon Press, $3.95.

**EXPERIENCES OF A
SPECIAL INDIAN AGENT**
E.E. White
Revised edition. Illus. University of Oklahoma
Press, 1966. $6.95.

**EXPERT TESTIMONY BEFORE
THE INDIAN CLAIMS COMMISSION**
400 volumes. Illus. Maps. Photos. Biblios.
Indexes. See Clearwater for titles, descriptions
and prices.

**EXPLORATION OF MOUNDS
COAHOMA COUNTY, MISSISSIPPI**
Charles Peabody
Reprint of 1904 edition. Paper. Kraus, $14.00.

EXPLORATIONS IN THE FAR NORTH
F. Russell
Reprint of 1898 edition. AMS Press, $25.00.

**EXPLORATIONS IN THE INTERIOR
OF THE LABRADOR PENINSULA,
THE COUNTRY OF THE MONTAGNAIS
AND NASQUAPEE INDIANS**
H.Y. Hind
Reprint of 1863 edition. Kraus, $55.00.

**EXPLORATIONS IN
NORTHEASTERN ARIZONA**
Samuel J. Guernsey
Reprint fo 1931 edition. Paper. Kraus, $24.00.

**EXPLORATIONS INTO
CAHOKIA ARCHAEOLOGY**
Illus. 175 pp. Paper. American Indian Books,
$3.50.

**EXPLORATIONS OF KEY
DWELLERS' REMAINS ON THE
GULF COAST OF FLORIDA**
F.H. Cushing
Reprint of 1896 edition. AMS Press, $22.00.

**EXPLORING IOWA'S PAST: A GUIDE
TO PREHISTORIC ARCHAEOLOGY**
Lynn M. Alex
Illus. 180 pp. Paper, University of Iowa Press,
1980. $7.95.

**EXPLORING THE OUTDOORS
WITH INDIAN SECRETS**
Allan A. Macfarlan
Illus. 224 pp. Paper. Stackpole, 1982. $9.95.

**EXTENDING THE BENEFITS OF
VOCATIONAL EDUCATION TO INDIAN
POPULATIONS: INTEGRATED
PLANNING PACKAGE**
Carol J. Minugh and Miller R. Tiger
175 pp. National Center of Research for Vocational Education, 1980. $15.00.

**EXTENDING THE RAFTERS:
INTERDISCIPLINARY APPROACHES
TO IROQUOIS STUDIES**
Michael K. Foster, et al, Editors
396 pp. State University of New York Press, 1984.
$48.50; paper, $16.95.

**AN EXTRACT FROM THE KLAMATH
INDIANS OF SOUTHEASTERN OREGON**
Albert Gatschet
Reprint of 1890 edition. Paper. Shorey Publications, $4.50.

**THE EYAK INDIANS OF THE
COPPER RIVER DELTA, ALASKA**
Kaj Birket-Smith and F. De Laguna
Reprint of 1938 edition. Illus. AMS Press, $42.50.

**THE EYE OF THE FLUTE: CHUMASH
TRADITIONAL HISTORY AND RITUAL**
F. Librado
141 pp. Paper. Malki Museum Press, 1981. $8.95.

F

**FACE MASKS IN NAVAHO
CEREMONIALISM**
B. Haile
Reprint of 1947 edition. AMS Press, $17.50.

**FACIAL PAINTINGS OF
THE INDIANS OF NORTHERN
BRITISH COLUMBIA**
Franz Boas
Reprint of 1898 edition. AMS Press, $20.00.

**FACING WEST: THE META-
PHYSICS OF INDIAN-HATING
AND EMPIRE BUILDING**
Richard Drinnon
Illus. 544 pp. Paper. New American Library,
$9.95.

FAITH, FLOWERS AND FIESTAS
Muriel T. Painter
A guide to tribal ceremonies featuring drawings
by Yaqui children, photos, and a calendar of
Yaqui religious events. Illus. 24 pp. Paper.
University of Arizona Press, 1962. $2.00.

FAITHFUL MOHAWKS
John W. Lydekker
Reprint of 1938 edition. Illus. Ira J. Friedman,
$8.50.

**FAMILY HUNTING TERRITORIES IN
NORTHEASTERN NORTH AMERICA**
D.S. Davidson
Reprint of 1928 edition. Illus. Map. 46 pp.
Paper. Museum of the American Indian, $1.00.

*FAMINE WINTER
John W. Schultz
Grades 4-10. Paper. Council for Indian
Education, 1984. $1.00.

*FAMOUS AMERICAN INDIAN LEADERS
Bearl Brooks
Grades 4-6. 24 pp. ESP. Workbook, $5.00.

*FAMOUS INDIAN TRIBES
David C. Cooke and William Moyers
Grades 1-4. Illus. Random House, 1954. $4.39.

**THE FAR NORTH: TWO THOUSAND
YEARS OF AMERICAN ESKIMO
AND INDIAN ART**
Henry B. Collins, et al
Illus. Indiana University Press, 1977. $22.50;
paper, $14.95.

FATHERS AND CHILDREN: ANDREW JACKSON AND THE SUBJUGATION OF THE AMERICAN INDIAN
Michael P. Rogin
Paper. Random House, 1976. $4.95.

THE FAUNEL REMAINS FROM ORROYO HONDO, NEW MEXICO
Richard W. Lang and Arthur Harris
Illus. 150 pp. Paper. Scholarly American Research, 1984. $8.00.

FEASTING WITH CANNIBLAS: AN ESSAY ON KWAKIUTL COSMOLOGY
Stanley Walens
Illus. 236 pp. Princeton University Press, 1981. $17.50.

THE FEDERAL BUY INDIAN PROGRAM: PROMISE VERSUS PERFORMANCE
Moses Lukaczer
126 pp. Mojave Books, 1976. $9.00; paper, $7.00.

FEDERAL CONCERN ABOUT CONDITIONS OF CALIFORNIA INDIANS 1853-1913: EIGHT DOCUMENTS
Robert Heizer
Paper. Ballena Press, 1979. $9.95.

FEDERAL INDIAN LAW CASES AND MATERIALS
David H. Getches, et al
Richard West, 1979. $24.95; paper, 7.95.

FEDERAL INDIAN RELATIONS, 1774-1788
Walter H. Mohr
Reprint of 1933 edition. AMS Press, $19.45.

FEDERAL POLICY AND AMERICAN INDIAN HEALTH NEEDS
Everett R. Rhoades, M.D.
32 pp. Paper. Interbook, Inc., 1974. $1.00.

FETISHES AND CARVINGS OF THE SOUTHWEST
Oscar T. Branson
Illus. Paper. Treasure Chest, 1976. $7.95.

A FEW SUMMER CEREMONIALS AT THE TUSAYON PUEBLOS: NATAL CEREMONIES OF THE HOPI INDIANS AND A REPORT ON THE PRESENT CONDITION OF A RUIN IN ARZIONA CALLED CASA GRANDE
J. Fewkes and J. Owens
Reprint of 1892 edition. AMS Press, $30.00.

A FEW SUMMER CEREMONIALS AT ZUNI PUEBLO: ZUNI MELODIES, RECONNAISANCE OF RUINS IN OR NEAR THE ZUNI RESERVATION
J. Fewkes and B. Gilman
Reprint of 1891 edition. AMS Press, $25.00.

A FIELD GUIDE TO CONSERVATION ARCHAEOLOGY IN NORTH AMERICA
Georgess McHargue and Michael Roberts
J.B. Lippincott Co., 1977. $9.50; paper, $4.95.

FIELD GUIDE TO INDIAN POINT TYPES OF THE STATE OF FLORIDA
Anderson and Puckett
Shows 50 Indian point types. Illus. 20 pp. Paper. American Indian Books, $5.00.

FIELD MANUAL OF PREHISTORIC SOUTHWESTERN POTTERY TYPES
F.M. Hawley
Reprint of 1936 edition. Paper. Kraus, $13.00.

FIFTH ANNUAL INDIAN LAW SEMINAR
Federal Bar Association Conference of 1980.
100 pp. Federal Bar Association, $15.00.

FIFTH ANNUAL PLAINS INDIAN SEMINAR IN HONOR OF DR. JOHN C. EWERS
George Horse Capture and Gene Ball
Buffalo Bill Historical Center, 1984.

FIFTY YEARS ON THE TRAIL, A TRUE STORY OF WESTERN LIFE: THE ADVENTURES OF JOHN YOUNG NELSON, AS DESCRIBED TO HARRINGTON O'REILLY
John Y. Nelson
Reprint of 1963 edition. Illus. University of Oklahoma Press, $7.95.

FIG TREE JOHN: AN INDIAN IN FACT AND FICTION
Peter G. Beidler
152 pp. Paper. University of Arizona Press, 1977. $5.95.

*THE FIGHT FOR FREEDOM, 1750-1783
N. Farr and D. Postert; L. Block, Editor
Grades 4-12. Illus. Pendulum, 1976. $1.95; paper, $1.25.

FIGHT WITH FRANCE FOR NORTH AMERICA
A.G. Bradley
Reprint of 1900 edition. Illus. Ayer Co. Publishers, $25.50.

FIGHTBACK: FOR THE SAKE OF THE PEOPLE, FOR THE SAKE OF THE LAND
Simon J. Ortiz
Paper. University of New Mexico, Native American Studies, 1980. $6.95.

THE FIGHTING CHEYENNES
George F. Grinnell
Reprint of 1956 edition. Illus. 450 pp. University of Oklahoma Press, $24.95; paper, $14.95.

FIGHTING RED CLOUD'S WARRIORS: TRUE TALES OF INDIAN DAYS WHEN THE WEST WAS YOUNG
E.A. Brinninstool
Reprint of 1926 edition. Illus. 241 pp. Cooper Square Publishers, $20.00.

FIGHTING TUISCARORA: THE AUTOBIOGRAPHY OF CHIEF CLANTON RICHARD
Barbara Graymont, Editor
Reprint of 1973 edition. Illus. 212 pp. Paper. Syracuse University Press, $14.95.

FILMOGRAPHY FOR AMERICAN INDIAN EDUCATION
Carroll Williams and Gloria Bird, Editors
A bibliography of approximately 400 films for American Indian education. Anthropology Film Center Foundation.

A FINAL PROMISE: THE CAMPAIGN TO ASSIMILATE THE INDIANS, 1880-1920
Frederick E. Hoxie
365 pp. University of Nebraska Press, 1984. $25.95.

FINAL REPORT OF INVESTIGATIONS AMONG THE INDIANS OF THE SOUTHWESTERN U.S.
A.F. Bandelier
Reprint of 1890-1892 edition. Two volumes in one. Kraus, $100.00.

*FIRE PLUME: LEGENDS OF THE AMERICAN INDIAN
J. Bierhorst and H.R. Schoolcraft
Grades 4-6. Illus. Dial Press, 1969. $5.00.

FIRE AND THE SPIRITS: CHEROKEE LAW FROM THE CLAN TO COURT
Rennard Strickland
Illus. 350 pp. University of Oklahoma Press, 1975. $14.95.

THE FIRST AMERICANS
Robert Claiborn
Detailed account of the discoveries of our continent. Illus. 160 pp. American Indian Books, $9.98.

THE FIRST AMERICANS GET TO WASHINGTON: THE POLITICS OF AMERICAN INDIAN POLICY
Robert Bee
284 pp. Schenkman, 1981. $17.95; paper, $8.95.

*THE FIRST AMERICANS: TRIBES OF NORTH AMERICA
Jane W. Watson
Grades 1-4. Illus. Pantheon, 1980. $7.95.

*FIRST BOOK OF THE INDIAN WARS
Richard B. Morris
Grades 4-6. Illus. Paper. Franklin Watts, 1959. $5.00.

THE FIRST CALIFORNIANS
M.A. Whipple and N.E. Heizer
Peek Publications, 1971. $6.95; paper, $4.95.

*FIRST CAME THE INDIANS
M.J. Wheeler
Grades 1-5. Illus. 32 pp. Atheneum Publishers, 1983. $9.95.

FIRST ESTABLISHMENT OF THE FAITH IN NEW FRANCE
C. Le Clereq
Reprint of 1881 edition. Two volumes. AMS Press, $67.50/set.

FIRST MAN WEST
A. Mackenzie; W. Sheppe, Editor
Reprint of 1962 edition. Illus. 366 pp. Greenwood, $25.00.

FIRST ON THE LAND: THE NORTH CAROLINA INDIANS
Ruth Y. Wetmore
Illus. John F. Blair, 1977. $10.95.

FIRST PENTHOUSE DWELLERS OF AMERICA
Ruth Underhill
Illus. William Gannon, 1976. $15.00; paper, $4.95.

FIRST SCALP FOR CUSTER: THE SKIRMISH AT WARBONNET CREEK, NEBRASKA, JULY 17, 1876
Paul L. Hedrin
Illus. 106 pp. Arthur H. Clark, 1981. $38.00.

*FISHERMAN ON THE PUYALLUP
A fictional account of a young Puyallup boy, Seeyap, learning to fish from his grandfather. Teacher's guide. Grades 4-6. Illus. 29 pp. Daybreak Star Press, $3.75.

FIVE CIVILIZED TRIBES
Grant Foreman
Illus. Paper. University of Oklahoma Press, 1971. $9.95.

FIVE INDIAN TRIBES OF THE UPPER MISSOURI: SIOUX, ARICKARAS, ASSINIBOINES, CREES AND CROWS
Edwin Denig
Illus. University of Oklahoma Press, 1961. $12.95; paper, $6.95.

FIVE KIDNAPPED INDIANS
Anne Molloy
Illus. Grades 6-9. Hastings House, 1968. $7.95.

**FIVE PREHISTORIC ARCHAEOLOGICAL
SITES IN LOS ANGELES COUNTY,
CALIFORNIA**
E.F. Walker
Reprint of 1951 edition. Illus. 116 pp. Southwest
Museum, $5.00.

**FIVE YEARS A CAPTIVE AMONG
THE BLACKFEET INDIANS**
S. Crakes
Reprint of 1858 edition. Garland Publishing,
$44.00.

THE FLATHEAD INDIANS OF MONTANA
H.H. Turney-High
Reprint of 1937 edition. Paper. Kraus, $13.00.

**FLATHEAD, PEN D'OREILLE AND
KUTENAI INDIANS CEDED LANDS:
HISTORICAL REPORT**
Merrill Burlingame
105 pp. Clearwater, 1974. $37.50.

THE FLIGHT OF THE NEZ PERCE
Mark H. Brown
Illus. 408 pp. Paper. University of Nebraska
Press, 1982. $9.95.

**FLIGHT OF THE SEVENTH MOON:
THE TEACHING OF THE SHIELDS**
Lynn F. Andrews
Illus. 208 pp. Harper & Row, 1984. $13.50.

**FLINT QUARRIES: THE SOURCES
OF TOOLS AND THE FACTORIES
OF THE AMERICAN INDIANS**
K. Bryan
Reprint of 1950 edition. Paper. Kraus, $14.00.

*THE FLOOD
Grades 3-12. Council for Indian Education, 1976.
$5.95; paper, $1.95.

**FLORIDA ANTHROPOLOGICAL
SOCIETY PUBLICATIONS**
Reprint. Volumes 1-5. Johnson Reprint, $27.00.

THE FLORIDA INDIANS
Charles H. Fairbanks
286 pp. Clearwater, 1973. $85.00.

FLORIDA INDIANS
David A. Horr, Editor
Three volumes. Garland Publishing, 1978.
$42.00 each.

**FLORIDA PLACE-NAMES OF
INDIAN ORIGIN AND SEMINOLE
PERSONAL NAMES**
William A. Reed
Paper. Books on Demand. $22.30.

THE FLORIDA WARS
Virginia Peters

Illus. Maps. Biblio. Index. 331 pp. The Shoe
String Press, 1979. $25.00.

**FLORIDA'S PREHISTORIC STONE
TECHNOLOGY: A STUDY OF THE
FLINTWORKING TECHNIQUES OF
EARLY FLORIDA STONE
IMPLEMENT-MAKERS**
Barbara Purdy
Illus. 175 pp. University Presses of Florida,
1981. $25.00.

FLORIDA'S SEMINOLE INDIANS
Wilfred Neill and E. Ross Allen
Illus. Paper. Great Outdoors, 1965. $3.95.

FODOR'S INDIAN AMERICA
Jamake Highwater
A cultural guide to America's Indians. Illus.
430 pp. David McKay Co., 1975. $12.95.

**FOLK-LORE OF THE MESQUAKIE
INDIANS OF NORTH AMERICA**
May A. Owen
Includes a catalogue of beadwork and other
objects in the collection of the folklore society.
Paper. Kraus, $12.00.

**FOLK MEDICINE OF THE DELAWARE
AND RELATED ALGONKIAN INDIANS**
Gladys Tantaquidgeon
Illus. 145 pp. Pennsylvania Historical & Museum
Commission, 1972. $6.50; paper, $4.75.

FOLK-TALES OF THE COAST SALISH
E.T. Adamson, Editor
Reprint of 1934 edition. Kraus, $40.00.

**FOLK-TALES OF THE SALISHAN
AND SAHAPTIN TRIBES**
Franz Boas, Editor
Reprint of 1917 edition. Kraus, $21.00.

**FOLKLORE OF THE
MENOMINI INDIANS**
Alanson B. Skinner and John V. Satterlee
Reprint of 1915 edition. AMS Press, $22.00.

FOLLOWING THE GUIDON
Elizabeth Custer
A view of Custer and military life in the old
West. Illus. 340 pp. Paper. University of Okla-
homa Press, $7.95.

FOOLS CROW
Thomas E. Mails
Illus. Doubleday, 1979. $12.95.

**FORGOTTEN FOUNDERS: BENJAMIN
FRANKLIN, THE IROQUOIS AND THE
RATIONALE FOR AMERICAN
REVOLUTION**
Bruce E. Johansen
167 pp. Harvard Common Press, 1982. $10.95.

**FORGOTTEN FRONTIERS: A STUDY OF
THE SPANISH INDIAN POLICY OF DON
JUAN BAUTISTA DE ANZA, GOVERNOR
OF NEW MEXICO, 1777-1778**
Alfred B. Thomas, Editor
Reprint of 1932 edition. University of Oklahoma
Press, $19.95.

**THE FORGOTTEN PEOPLE:
THE WOODLAND ERIE**
Harry F. Lupold
Exposition Press, 1975. $6.75; paper, 4.50.

**THE FORGOTTEN SIOUX: AN
ETHNOHISTORY OF THE LOWER
BRULE RESERVATION**
Ernest L. Schusky
Illus. 272 pp. Nelson-Hall, 1975. $18.95; paper,
$9.95.

**FORKED TONGUES AND
BROKEN TREATIES**
Donald Worcester, Editor
Illus. 449 pp. Caxton Printers, 1975. $9.95.

**FORLORN HOPE: THE BATTLE OF
WHITEBIRD CANYON AND THE
BEGINNING OF THE NEZ PERCE WAR**
John D. McDermott
Illus. 230 pp. Idaho State Historical Society,
1978. $9.95; paper, $4.95.

**FORM AND FREEDOM: A DIALOGUE
ON NORTHWEST COAST INDIAN ART**
Bill Holm and William Reid;
Edmund Carpenter, Editor
Institute for the Arts, 1975. $12.95.

**THE FORMATIVE CULTURES OF
THE CAROLINA PIEDMONT**
J.L. Coe
Reprint of 1964 edition. American Philosophical
Society, $10.00.

**FORMS OF PLAY OF NATIVE
NORTH AMERICANS: PROCEEDINGS**
Edward Norbeck and Claire Ferrer, Editors
Illus. Paper. West Publishing, 1979. $14.95.

FORT ANCIENT ASPECT
James B. Griffin
Illus. Paper. University of Michigan, Museum of
Anthropology, 1966. $6.00.

**THE FORT BELKNAP ASSINIBOINE
OF MONTANA: A STUDY IN
CULTURE CHANGE**
David Rodnick
Reprint of 1938 edition. AMS Press, $24.50.

**THE FORT BELKNAP AND BLACKFEET
INDIAN RESERVATION IN MONTANA: A
HISTORY OF ECONOMIC INFLUENCES**
Paul W. Gates
Clearwater Publishing, $54.00.

**THE FORT BELKNAP RESERVATION
IN MONTANA: HISTORICAL REPORT,
1878-1946**
Edward Barry
Clearwater Publishing, $89.00.

**THE FORT BERTHOLD INDIANS:
APPRAISAL OF LAND IN
NORTH DAKOTA, 1891**
Darwin Harbin
159 pp. Clearwater Publishing, 1973. $50.00.

FORT DEFIANCE AND THE NAVAJOS
Maurice Frink
Illus. 150 pp. Paper. Pruett Publishing, 1968.
$5.95.

FORT LARAMIE AND THE SIOUX
Remi Nadeau
Illus. 375 pp. Paper. University of Nebraska
Press, 1982. $9.95.

**FORT MELLON: MICROCOSM OF THE
SECOND SEMINOLE WAR, 1837-1842**
Arthur E. Francke, Jr.
Illus. Banyon Books, 1977. $9.95.

**FORT MOHAVE INDIAN RESERVATION
LANDS: PLANNING REPORT AND
GROSS APPRAISAL**
Albert L. Johnson
157 pp. Clearwater Publishing, 1973. $50.00.

**FORT SILL APACHE TRACT:
MINERAL APPRAISAL, 1886**
Ernest Oberbilling
171 pp. Clearwater Publishing, 1973. $52.50.

**FORT SILL APACHE TRIBE OF
OKLAHOMA: LAND APPRAISAL**
Two volumes. Clearwater, 1973.

**FORTH TO THE WILDERNESS: THE
FIRST AMERICAN FRONTIER,
1754-1774**
D. Van Every
Reprint of 1961 edition. Ayer Co. Publishers,
$15.00.

**FORTY MILES A DAY ON BEANS
AND HAY: THE ENLISTED SOLDIER
FIGHTING THE INDIAN WARS**
Don Rickey, Jr.
Illus. Paper. University of Oklahoma Press, 1977.
$8.50.

**FOUR CENTURIES OF
SOUTHERN INDIANS**
Charles M. Hudson, Editor
183 pp. University of Georgia Press, 1975. $10.00.

THE FOUR CHURCHES OF PECOS
Alden C. Hayes
Illus. 96 pp. Paper. University of New Mexico
Press, 1974. $4.95.

FOUR DAYS IN A MEDICINE LODGE
Walter McClintock
Facsimile of 1900 edition. 14 pp. Paper. Shorey, $1.50.

FOUR MASTERWORKS OF AMERICAN INDIAN LITERATURE
John Bierhorst, Editor
416 pp. Farrar, Straus & Giroux, 1974. $12.95; paper, $6.95.

"THE FOURTH WORLD" AN INDIAN REALITY
George Manuel and Michael Posluns
Illus. Free Press, 1974. $7.95.

FOX MISCELLANY
T. Michelson
Reprint of 1936 edition. Scholarly Press, $19.00.

FOX TEXTS
William Jones
Reprint of 1907 edition. AMS Press, $42.00.

FRANCISCAN AWATOVI: THE EXCAVATION AND CONJECTURAL RE-CONSTRUCTION OF A 17th CENTURY SPANISH MISSION ESTABLISHMENT AT A HOPI INDIAN TOWN IN NORTHEASTERN ARIZONA
R.G. Montgomery, et al
Reprint of 1949 edition. Paper. Kraus, $26.00.

THE FREMONT CULTURE: A STUDY IN CULTURE DYNAMICS ON THE NORTHERN ANASAZI FRONTIER
James H. Gunnerson
Paper. Peabody Museum, 1969. $15.00.

FRENCH AND INDIAN CRUELTY
Bound with various narratives of captivity. Reprint of 1757 edition. Garland, $44.00.

FRIEND AND FOE: ASPECTS OF FRENCH-AMERICAN CULTURAL CONTACT IN THE 16th & 17th CENTURIES
Cornelius J. Jaenen
Illus. Columbia University Press, 1976. $21.50.

FRIENDS OF THUNDER: FOLKTALES OF THE OKLAHOMA CHEROKEES
Jack and Anna Kilpatrick
Reprint of 1964 edition. 216 pp. Paper. Southern Methodist University Press. $7.95.

FROM THE CENTER: A FOLIO OF NATIVE AMERICAN ART AND POETRY
Maurice Kenny, Editor
Illus. 30 pp. Paper. Strawberry Press, 1981. $8.50.

FROM THE DEEP WOODS TO CIVILIZATION: CHAPTERS IN THE

AUTOBIOGRAPHY OF AN INDIAN
Charles A. Eastman
Illus. Paper. University of Nebraska Press, 1977. $6.50.

*FROM FREE RANGE TO RESERVA-TION: SOCIAL CHANGE AMONG THE COLVILLE, QUINAULT, AND LUMMI IN WASHINGTON STATE, 1855-1960
A series of interviews of Indian elders. Teacher's guide. Grades 7-12. Illus. Daybreak Star Press, $7.00.

FROM HELL TO BREAKFAST
Mody C. Boatright an Donald Day, Editors
Reprint of 1944 edition. Illus. 226 pp. Southern Methodist University Press, $9.95.

FROM ICE MOUNTAINS: INDIAN SETTLEMENT OF THE AMERICAS
Don Perceval
Illus. Northland Press, 1979. $16.00.

FROM INDIANS TO CHICANOS: THE DYNAMICS OF MEXICAN-AMERICAN CULTURE
James D. Virgil
Illus. 245 pp. Paper. Waveland Press, $9.95.

FROM RIVER BANKS AND SACRED PLACES: ANCIENT INDIAN TERRACOTTAS
Paper. Museum of Fine Arts of Boston, $3.00.

FROM SKINS, TREES, QUILLS AND BEADS: THE WORK OF NINE ATHAPASCANS
Documents the arts and crafts of nine Athapascan communities. Illus. Institute of Alaska Native Arts, $12.50.

FROM THE EARTH TO BEYOND THE SKY: AN ETHNOGRAPHIC APPROACH TO FOUR LONGHOUSE IROQUOIS SPEECH EVENTS
Michael K. Foster
Paper. National Museums of Canada, $3.95.

FRONTIER PATROL: THE ARMY AND THE INDIANS IN NORTHEASTERN CALIFORNIA, 1861
L. White
28 pp. Association for Northern California Records and Reserch, 1974. $4.00.

THE FRONTIER PEOPLE: THE GREATER SOUTHWEST IN PROTOHISTORIC PERIOD
Carroll L. Riley
Illus. 182 pp. Paper. Center for Archaeologicl Studies, 1982. $15.00.

**FRONTIER REGULARS: THE U.S.
ARMY AND THE INDIAN, 1866-1891**
Robert M. Utley
Reprint of 1977 edition. Illus. 475 pp. Paper.
University of Nebraska Press, $12.95.

THE FRONTIERSMEN
Allan Eckert
Little, Brown & Co., 1967. $17.50.

**FULL COLOR AMERICAN INDIAN
DESIGNS FOR NEEDLEPOINT RUGS**
Dorothy Sides
32 pp. Paper. Dover, 1975. $3.50.

**FUNCTIONS OF WAMPUM AMONG
THE EASTERN ALGONKIAN**
Frank G. Speck
Reprint of 1919 edition. Paper. Kraus, $12.00.

**FUNDAMENTALS OF
AGE-GROUP SYSTEMS**
Frank H. Stewart
Academic Press, 1977. $58.00.

*THE FUR TRADER AND THE INDIAN
Lewis O. Saum
Illus. 336 pp. Grades 9 and up. University of
Washington Press, 1965. $18.00; paper, $9.95.

***FUR TRAPPERS AND TRADERS:
THE INDIANS, THE PILGRIMS,
AND THE BEAVER**
Beatrice Siegel
Grades 3-7. Illus. 64 pp. Walker & Co., 1981.
$9.50.

G

**GABRIELINO INDIANS OF
SOUTHERN CALIF.: AN ANNOTATED
ETHNO-HISTORIC BIBLIOGRAPHY**
Mary LaLone
72 pp. Paper. UCLA Archaeology, 1980. $5.00.

**GALENA AND ABORIGINAL TRADE
IN EASTERN NORTH AMERICA**
John A. Walthall
Illus. 66 pp. Paper. Illinois State Museum, 1981.
$3.00.

**GAMBLING MUSIC OF THE
COAST SALISH INDIANS**
Wendy Bross Stuart
Paper. National Museums of Canada, $3.95.

**GAMES OF THE NORTH
AMERICAN INDIANS**
Stewart Culin
Illus. 846 pp. Paper. American Indian Books,
$14.50.

**GAMES OF THE NORTH
AMERICAN INDIANS**
Robert S. Culin
Reprint of 1907 edition. Illus. AMS Press,$85.00.
Paper. Dover Press, $10.00.

**HALIN GARLAND'S OBSERVATIONS
ON THE AMERICAN INDIAN,
1895-1905**
L.E. Underhill and D.F. Littlefield, Editors
24 pp. University of Arizona Press, 1976. $9.95;
paper, $5.95.

**GARMENTS OF BRIGHTNESS:
THE NAVAJO WEAVING TRADITION**
Alice Kaufman and Christopher Selser
Illus. 160 pp. E.P. Dutton, 1985. $35.95; paper,
$24.95.

**GATHERED SKETCHES FROM THE
EARLY HISTORY OF NEW HAMPSHIRE
AND VERMONT**
Francis Chase
Reprint of 1856 edition. Garland Publishing,
$42.00.

**A GATHERING OF SPIRIT:
WRITING AND ART BY NORTH
AMERICAN INDIAN WOMEN**
Beth Brant, Editor
Illus. 240 pp. Paper. Sinister Wisdom Books,
1984. $7.95.

*THE GATHERERS
Daniel Jacobson
Grades 7-12. Illus. 96 pp. Paper. Franklin Watts,
1977. $5.00.

**GATHERING WHAT THE GREAT
NATURE PROVIDED: FODD
TRADITIONS OF THE KITKSAN**
People of 'Ksan
Illus. 160 pp. University of Washington Press,
1980. $17.95.

**GENERAL CROOK AND THE
SIERRA MADRE ADVENTURE**
Dan L. Thrapp
Illus. Paper. University of Oklahoma Press, 1977.
$6.95.

**GENERAL CUSTER AND THE BATTLE
OF THE LITTLE BIG HORN:
THE FEDERAL VIEW**
John M. Carroll, Editor
Amereon Ltd., 1985. $25.00; paper, $10.00.

**GENERAL HENRY ATKINSON:
A WESTERN MILITARY CAREER**
Roger Nichols
Illus. University of Oklahoma Press, 1965.
$10.95; paper, $6.95.

**GENERAL ORDERS OF 1757 ISSUED
BY THE EARL OF LOUDON AND
PHINEAS LYMAN IN THE CAMPAIGN
AGAINST THE FRENCH**
Loudon and Lyman
Facsimile of 1899 edition. Ayer Co. Publishers,
$14.00.

**GENERAL POPE AND
U.S. INDIAN POLICY**
Richard Ellis
287 pp. University of New Mexico Press, 1970.
$10.00.

**GENERAL VIEW OF THE ARCHAE-
OLOGY OF THE PUEBLO REGION:
EXTRACTS**
Edgar Hewett
Facsimile of 1904 edition. Paper. Shorey, $4.00.

GENOCIDE AGAINST THE INDIANS
George Novak
Paper. Pathfinder Press, $1.00.

**GENOCIDE IN NORTH-
WESTERN CALIFORNIA**
Jack Norton
Genocide against the Hupa, Yurok, Karok,
Mattole, and Wintun Indians. Illus. Maps. Paper.
The Indian Historian Press, $12.00.

**GEOGRAPHICAL NAMES OF
THE KWAKIUTL INDIANS**
Franz Boas
Reprint of 1934 edition. AMS Press, $25.00.

**GERANIUMS FOR THE IROQUOIS:
A FIELD GUIDE TO AMERICAN
INDIAN MEDICINAL PLANTS**
Daniel E. Moerman; Keith Irvine, Editor
Illus. Reference Publications, 1982. $19.95;
paper, $9.95.

**GERMAN ARTIST ON THE TEXAS FRON-
TIER: FRIEDRICH RICHARD PETRI**
William K. Newcomb, Jr.
Illus. University of Texas Press, 1978. $20.00.

*GERONIMO CHINO
Paula Paul
Grades 4-10. Council for Indian Education, $8.45;
paper, $4.45.

*GERONIMO: THE FIGHTING APACHE
Ronald Syme
A biography which dispels his image as a ruthless
savage. Grades 3-7. Illus. Biblio. 96 pp. William
Morrow, 1975. $8.95.

GERONIMO'S STORY OF HIS LIFE
S.M. Barrett, Editor
Autobiography. Geronimo talks of the Apache
Indians while being held prisoner. Reprint of 1906
edition. Illus. 216 pp. Paper. Irvington Publishers,
$9.95.

GHOST DANCE
David H. Miller
Illus. 325 pp. University of Nebraska Press, 1985.
$23.95; paper, $8.95.

**GHOST DANCE MESSIAH:
THE JACK WILSON STORY**
Paul Bailey
Westernlore, $8.50.

**GHOST-DANCE RELIGION AND
THE SIOUX OUTBREAK OF 1890**
James Mooney; Anthony Wallace, Editor
Paper. University of Chicago Press, 1965. $11.00.

*THE GHOSTS THE INDIANS FEARED
Sigmund A. Levine
Grades 5-12. Illus. 64 pp. Dodd, Mead & Co.,
1975. $5.95.

GIFT IS RICH
F. Russell Carter
Revised edition. Illus. Paper. Friendship Press,
1955. $3.50.

**GIFTS OF THE EARTH:
AMERICAN INDIAN COOKBOOK**
Juli S. Trapp
Illus. 44 pp. Paper. Stonehenge Books, 1981.
$9.95.

THE GIFT OF THE SACRED PIPE
Vera L. Drysdale and Joseph E. Brown
Illus. 128 pp. University of Oklahoma Press, 1982.
$29.95.

**THE GIFT OF SPIDERWOMAN:
SOUTHWESTERN TEXTILES,
THE NAVAJO TRADITION**
Joe B. Wheat
Illus. 48 pp. Paper. University of Pennsylvania,
1984. $10.00.

**THE GILA RIVER
INDIAN RESERVATION**
George A. Morrison
50 pp. Clearwater, 1973. $23.50.

**GILA RIVER RESERVATION IN
ARIZONA, 1936-1961: APPRAISAL**
Walter D. Armer
105 pp. Clearwater, 1973. $36.00.

**GILA RIVER RESERVATION LEASED
LAND IN ARIZONA, 1916-1937:
HISTORICAL REPORTS**
Joseph L. Diddock
29 pp. Clearwater Publishing, 1973. $18.00.

GIRL CAPTIVES OF THE CHEYENNES
Grace E. Meredith
Bound with other captivity narratives. Reprint of
1927 edition. Garland, $42.00.

GIVE OR TAKE A CENTURY:
AN ESKIMO CHRONICLE
Joseph E. Senungetuk
The first professional, full length work to be
published by an Eskimo author. Illus. Map.
206 pp. Paper. The Indian Historian Press,
1971. $12.50.

THE GONDS OF ANDHRA PRADESH:
TRADITION AND CHANGE IN
AN INDIAN TRIBE
Christoph Von Fuer Haimendorf
Illus. 569 pp. Advent Books, 1981. $40.00.

THE GOOD MESSAGE OF
HANDSOME LAKE
Joseph Bruchac
Handsom Lake was an early 19th century Seneca
prophet. Paper. Unicorn, $5.00.

*GOOD STONES
Anne M. Epstein
Grades 5-9. Houghton Mifflin, 1977. $6.95.

GOODBIRD THE INDIAN
Gilbert L. Wilson
Illus. 112 pp. Paper. Minnesota Historical
Society, 1985. $5.95.

CARL GORMAN'S WORLD
Henry and Georgia Greenberg
Illus. 200 pp. University of New Mexico Press,
1984. $35.00.

GOSHUTE SHOSHONE INDIANS:
APPRAISAL OF LANDS, 1875
Mont H. Saunderson
115 pp. Clearwater, 1973. $39.00.

GOSHUTE TRACT IN NEVADA AND
UTAH: MINERAL VALUATION
AS OF 1875
Ernest Oberbilling
155 pp. Clearwater Publishing, 1973. $40.50.

GOVERNMENT AND RELIGION
OF THE VIRGINIA INDIANS
S.R. Hendren
Reprint of 1895 edition. Paper. AMS Press,
$11.50.

GRAMMAR AND DICTIONARY OF
THE LANGUAGE OF THE HIDATSA
Washington Matthews
Reprint of 1873 edition. AMS Press, $27.50.

A GRAMMAR OF DIEGUENO NOMINALS
Larry P. Gorbet
Garland Publishing, 1976. $51.00.

A GRAMMAR DISCOVERY PROCEDURE
FOR THE STUDY OF A DAKOTA
HEALING RITUAL
L.S. Kemnitzer
Paper. Humanities Press, 1975. $1.00.

A GRAMMAR OF AKWESASNE MOHAWK
Nancy Bonvillain
Paper. National Museums of Canada, $3.95.

A GRAMMAR OF BILOXI
Paula F. Einaudi
Garland Publishing, 1976. $51.00.

GRAMMAR OF THE LANGUAGE OF THE
LENNI LENAPE OR DELAWARE INDIANS
D. Zeisberger; trans. by Peter S. Du Ponceau
Reprint of 1827 edition. AMS Press, $29.50.

GRAMMAR OF THE MIKMAQUE
LANGUAGE OF NOVA SCOTIA
A. S. Maillard; Joseph M. Bellenger, Editor
Reprint of 1864 edition. AMS Press, $28.50.

A GRAMMAR OF PAWNEE
Douglas R. Parks
Garland Publishing, 1976. $51.00.

A GRAMMAR OF SOUTHWESTERN POMO
Julius A. Moshinsky
Paper. University of California Press, 1974.
$18.50.

A GRAMMAR OF TUSCARORA
Marianne M. Williams
Garland Publishing, 1976. $46.00.

A GRAMMAR OF THE WAPPO LANGUAGE
P.A. Radin
Reprint of 1929 edition. Kraus, $51.00.

THE GRAND VILLAGE OF THE
NATCHEZ INDIANS REVISITED
Robert Neitzel; Patricia Galloway, Editor
215 pp. Paper. Mississippi Dept. of Archaeology,
1983. $15.00.

*GRANDFATHER AND THE
POPPING MACHINE
Henry Tall Bull and Tom Weist
Grades 2012. Council for Indian Education, 1970.
$5.95; paper, $1.95.

GREAT BASIN ATLAS STUDIES
T.R. Hester; R.F. Heizer, Editor
Illus. 60 pp. Paper. Ballena Press, 1974. $6.95.

GREAT BLACK ROBE
Jean Pitrone
Illus. Daughters of St. Paul, 1965. $4.00; paper,
$3.00.

*THE GREAT CHIEFS
B. Capps
Grades 5-12. Illus. Silver Burdette, 1975. $17.27.

THE GREAT FATHER: THE U.S.
GOVERNMENT AND AMERICAN INDIANS
Francis Prucha
Two volumes. Illus. 1.250 pp. University of
Nebraska Press, 1984. $60.00.

GREAT INDIAN CHIEFS
Albert Britt
Facsimile of 1938 edition. Ayer Co. Publishers, $21.50.

*GREAT INDIANS OF CALIFORNIA
Maurice Vallejo, et al
Grade 6. Illus. 48 pp. Paper. Bellerophon Books, 1981. $2.95.

GREAT NORTH AMERICAN INDIANS: PROFILES IN LIFE AND LEADERSHIP
Frederick J. Dockstader
Illus. Van Nostrand Reinhold, 1977. $17.95.

GREAT PLAINS COMMAND: WILLIAM B. HAZEN IN THE FRONTIER WEST
Marvin E. Kroeker
Illus. 200 pp. University of Oklahoma Press, 1976. $12.95.

GREAT SALT LAKE TRAIL
H. Inman and W.F. Cody
Reprint of 1897 edition. Illus. Ross & Haines, $12.50.

THE GREAT SIOUX NATION
Roxanne D. Ortiz
Paper. University of New Mexico, Native American Studies, $7.95.

THE GREAT SIOUX TRAIL
Joseph Altsheler
Amereon Ltd., $18.95.

GREAT WESTERN INDIAN FIGHTS
Potomac Coral of the Westerners
Illus. Paper. University of Nebraska Press, 1966. $4.00.

GREENER FIELDS: EXPERIENCES AMONG THE AMERICAN INDIANS
Alice L. Marriott
Reprint of 1953 edition. Greenwood Press, $15.00.

GREENVILLE GOODWIN AMONG THE WESTERN APACHE: LETTERS FROM THE FIELD
Morris E. Opler, Editor
Apache beliefs and customs; anthropological field work. 103 pp. University of Arizona Press, 1973. $5.00.

THE GREENVILLE TREATY, 1795
Helen H. Tanner
70 pp. Clearwater Publishing, 1973. $40.00.

GREGORIO, THE HANDTREMBLER: A PSYCHOBIOLOGICAL PERSONALITY STUDY OF A NAVAHO INDIAN
A.H. and D.C. Leighton
Reprint of 1949 edition. Paper. Kraus, $29.00.

GROS VENTRE OF MONTANA
Regina Flannery
Reprint of 1956 edition. Two volumes: Volume 1: *Social Life;* Volume 2: *Religion and Ritual.* Illus. Gros Ventre Treaty, $21.00 per set.

GROWING STRAIGHT: THE FITNESS SECRET OF THE AMERICAN INDIAN
Maud S. Williams
200 pp. Paper. Newcastle Publishing, 1981. $6.95.

*GROWING UP WITH NORTH AMERICAN INDIANS
Pat Hodgson
Grades 6-10. Illus. 72 pp. David & Charles, 1980. $14.95.

*GUARDIAN SPIRIT QUEST
Ella Clark
Grades 5-10. Paper. Council for Indian Education, 1974. $1.95.

GUESTS NEVER LEAVE HUNGRY: THE AUTOBIOGRAPHY OF JAMES SEWID, A KWAKIUTL INDIAN
James Sewid; James P. Spradley, Editor
Illus. Yale University Press, 1969. $20.00.

GUIDE TO AMERICAN INDIAN DOCUMENTS IN THE CONGRESSIONAL SERIAL SET: 1817-1899
Steven L. Johnson
Clearwater Publishing, 1977. $35.00.

A GUIDE TO AMERICA'S INDIANS: CEREMONIALS, RESERVATIONS AND MUSEUMS
Arnold Marquis
Illus. 400 pp. University of Oklahoma Press, 1974. $21.95; paper, $12.95.

A GUIDE TO CASE LAW ON THE INDIAN ACTS OF CANADA
David Knoll
100 pp. University of Saskatchewan, College of Law, 1981. $20.00.

A GUIDE TO CHEROKEE DOCU- MENTS IN FOREIGN ARCHIVES
William L. Anderson and James A. Lewis
770 pp. Scarecrow Press, 1983. $37.50.

GUIDE TO DECISIONS OF THE INTERIOR DEPARTMENT OF INDIAN LANDS
James R. Young, Editor
Two volumes. 1,055 pp. Paper. American Indian Studies Center, 1980. $10.00 per set. Also available on microfiche.

**GUIDE TO THE IDENTIFICATION
OF CERTAIN AMERICAN INDIAN
PROJECTILE POINTS**
Four volumes. Illus. 105 pp. Paper. American
Indian Books, $10.00 each; $40.00 per set.

**GUIDE TO INDIAN ARTIFACTS
OF THE NORTHEAST**
Roger W. Moeller
Illus. 32 pp. Paper. Hancock House, 1984. $3.95.

GUIDE TO INDIAN HERBS
Ray Stark; Margaret Campbell
Illus. 48 pp. Paper. Hancock House, 1984. $4.95.

**GUIDE TO INDIAN ROCK CARVINGS
OF THE PACIFIC NORTHWEST COAST**
Beth Hill
Illus. Paper. Hancock House, 1979. $3.50.

**A GUIDE TO THE INDIAN
TRIBES OF OKLAHOMA**
Muriel H. Wright
Reprint of 1951 edition. Illus. University of
Oklahoma Press, $12.50.

**A GUIDE TO ISSUES IN
INDIAN LANGUAGE RETENTION**
James J. Bauman
70 pp. Paper. Center for Applied Linguistics,
1980. $6.95.

**GUIDE TO RECORDS IN THE
NATIONAL ARCHIVES RELATING
TO AMERICAN INDIANS**
476 pp. National Archives, 1981. $15.00.

**GUIDE TO RESEARCH ON
NORTH AMERICAN INDIANS**
Arlene B. Hirschfelder
340 pp. American Library Association, 1983.
$75.00.

**A GUIDE TO SUPPLEMENT A GUIDE
TO MANUSCRIPTS RELATING TO
THE AMERICAN INDIAN IN THE
LIBRARY OF THE AMERICAN
PHILOSOPHICAL SOCIETY**
Daythal Kendall
American Philosophical Society, 1981. $15.00.

**A GUIDE WITHOUT END: A
SOURCEBOOK OF AMERICAN ETHICS**
Gerald S. and Francis G. Lombardi
208 pp. Naturegraph, 1982. $12.95; paper, $7.95.

**GUNBOAT FRONTIER: BRITISH
MARITIME AUTHORITY AND NORTH-
WEST COAST INDIANS, 1846-1890**
Barry M. Gough
Illus. 256 pp. International Specialty Books,
1984. $27.95.

**GUNS ON THE EARLY FRONTIERS:
A HISTORY OF FIREARMS FROM
COLONIAL TIMES THROUGH THE
YEARS OF THE WESTERN FUR TRADE**
Carl P. Russell
395 pp. University of Nebraska Press, 1980.
$19.50; paper, $6.95.

H

**HABOO: NATIVE AMERICAN
STORIES FROM PUGET SOUND**
Vi Hilbert, Editor and Translator
Illus. 227 pp. Paper. University of Washington
Press, 1985. $9.95.

*HAH—NEE
Mary and Conrad Buff
Grades 4-6. Houghton Mifflin, 1965. $5.95.

HAIDA INDIAN LANGUAGE
John R. Swanton
Reprint of 1911 edition. 77 pp. Paper. Shorey,
$6.95.

**HAIDA MONUMENTAL ART: VILLAGES
OF THE QUEEN CHARLOTTE ISLANDS**
George F. MacDonald
Illus. 240 pp. Internatinal Specialty Books,
1983. $140.00.

HAIDA POTLATCH
Ulli Steltzer
Illus. 128 pp. University of Washington Press,
1984. $14.95.

HAIDA SONGS AND TSIMSHIAN TEXTS
John Swanton and Franz Boas
Reprint of 1912 edition. AMS Press, $34.00.

**HAIDA TEXTS AND MYTHS: SKIDGATE
DIALECT**
John R. Swanton
Reprint of 1905 edition. Paper. Johnson Reprint,
$34.00.

**HAIDAH INDIANS OF
QUEEN CHARLOTTE ISLANDS**
John G. Swanton
Reprint of 1874 edition. 17 pp. Paper. Shorey,
$7.95.

THE HAIDAS
George Dawson
Facsimile of 1882 edition. 10 pp. Paper. Shorey,
95¢.

**HALF—SUN ON THE COLUMBIA:
A BIOGRAPHY OF CHIEF MOSES**
Robert H. Ruby and John A. Brown
Reprint of 1965 edition. Illus. University of
Oklahoma Press, $19.95.

THE HAN INDIANS: A COMPILATION OF ETHNOGRAPHIC AND HISTORICAL DATA ON THE ALASKA—YUKON BOUNDARY AREA
Cornelius Osgood
Paper. Yale University, Anthropology, 1971. $7.50.

HANDBOOK OF AMERICAN INDIAN GAMES
Allan and Paulette Macfarlan
288 pp. Paper. Dover, 1985. $5.95.

HANDBOOK OF THE AMERICAN INDIAN LANGUAGES
Franz Boas
Reprint. Four volumes. Scholarly Press, $159.00 per set.

HANDBOOK OF AMERICAN INDIANS NORTH OF MEXICO, 1907-1910
F.W. Hodge
Reprint of 1910 edition. Two volumes, Illus. Greenwood, $90.25. Paper. Rowman & Littlefield, $45.00.

HANDBOOK OF FEDERAL INDIAN LAW
Felix S. Cohen, Editor
Reprint of 1942 edition. AMS Press, $25.00.

HANDBOOK OF THE INDIANS OF CALIFORNIA
Alfred L. Kroeber
Reprint of 1925 edition. Illus. 1,025 pp. Scholarly Press, $79.00. Paper. William Gannon, $18.00; Dover, $10.00.

THE HANDBOOK OF MIDDLE AMERICAN INDIANS: VOLUME 1 ARCHAEOLOGY—SUPPLEMENT
Victoria R. Bricker and
Jeremy A. Sabloff, Editors
Illus. 475 pp. University of Texas Press, 1981. $55.00.

HANDBOOK OF NORTH AMERICAN INDIANS
Six handbooks discussing the culture, history, and language of North American Indians. Vol. 5: *Arctic,* 861 pp., 1984, $29.00; Vol. 6: *Subarctic,* 853 pp., 1981, $25.00; Vol. 8: *California,* 800 pp., 1978, $25.00; Vol. 9: *Southwest - Puebloan Peoples,* 701 pp., 1979, $23.00; Vol. 10: *Southwest - Non-Puebloan People,* 884 pp., 1983, $25.00; Vol. 15: *Northeast,* 924 pp., 1978, $27.00. Illus. Supt of Documents. Smithsonian, Vol. 5 only, $29.00.

HANDBOOK OF NORTHERN ARIZONA POTTERY WARES
Harold S. Colton and Lyndon L. Hargrave
Reprint of 1937 edition. AMS Press, $32.50.

HANDBOOK OF THE CREEK LANGUAGE
Anna Bosch
35 pp. Paper. Indian University Press, 1984. $5.00.

HANDBOOK OF THE YOKUTS INDIANS
Frank F. Lotta
Illus. Bear State, 1979. $24.95.

HANO: A TEWA INDIAN COMMUNITY IN ARIZONA
Edward P. Dozier
Paper. Holt, Rinehart & Winston, 1966. $5.00.

HANTA YO: AN AMERICAN SAGA
Ruth B. Hill
112 pp. Paper. Warner Books, 1980. $5.95.

HAPPY HUNTING GROUNDS
Stanley Vestal
Illus. 228 pp. University of Oklahoma Press, $9.95; paper, $5.95.

*HARDY RACE OF MEN: AMERICA'S EARLY INDIANS
Eileen T. Callan
Grades 7-12. Illus. Harcourt Brace, 1970. $4.95.

THE HARROWING OF EDEN: WHITE ATTITUDES TOWARD NATIVE AMERICANS
J.E. Chamberlin
Continuum, 1975. $8.95.

HART'S PREHISTORIC PIPE RACK
Gordon Hart
Illus. 272 pp. Hart Publishers, $44.50.

HAVASUPAI ETHNOGRAPHY
Leslie Spier
Reprint of 1928 edition. AMS Press, $57.50.

HAVASUPAI HABITAT: A.F. WHITING'S ETHNOGRAPHY OF A TRADITIONAL INDIAN CULTURE
Steven A. Weber and David P. Seaman, Editors
288 pp. University of Arizona Press, 1985. $21.95.

HAVASUPAI INDIANS
R.A. Manners, et al; David A. Horr, Editor
Garland Publishing, 1974. $42.00.

HAVASUPAI INDIANS, 1150-1890
Robert C. Euler
50 pp. Clearwater Publishing, 1974. $25.00.

HAVASUPAI INDIANS: AN ETHNOHISTORICAL REPORT
Robert A. Manners
151 pp. Clearwater Publishing, 1973. $48.00.

HAVASUPAI RELIGION AND MYTHOLOGY
Carma Smithson and Robert Euler
Reprint of 1964 edition. 120 pp. Johnson Reprint, $19.00. AMS Press, $15.00.

HAVASUPAI SONGS: A LINGUISTIC PERSPECTIVE
Leanne Hinton
357 pp. Paper. John Benjamins North America, 1984. $46.00.

THE HAVASUPAI WOMAN
Carma Smithson
Reprint of 1959 edition. Illus. 178 pp. AMS Press, $16.75.

HE WHO HUNTED BIRDS IN HIS FATHER'S VILLAGE: THE DIMEN-SIONS OF A HAIDA MYTH
Gary Snyder
154 pp. Paper. Grey Fox, 1979. $5.95.

HEAD AND FACE MASKS IN NAVAHO CEREMONIALISM
Bernard Haile
Reprint of 1947 edition. AMS Press, $17.50.

HEALTH AND DISEASES OF AMERICAN INDIANS NORTH OF MEXICO: A BIBLIOGRAPHY, 1800-1969
Mark V. Barrow, et al
University Presses of Florida, 1972. $8.00.

HEAR ME MY CHIEFS: NEZ PERCE LEGEND AND HISTORY
Lucullus V. McWhorter
Reprint. Illus. 640 pp. Caxton Printers, $24.95; paper. $17.95.

HEARING BEFORE THE JOINT COMMISSION OF THE CONGRESS OF THE U.S., 63 rd CONGRESS, TO INVESTIGATE INDIAN AFFAIRS, SEPT. 1913 — DEC. 1914
Reprint of 1914 edition. Two volumes. AMS Press, $63.50.

*HEART BUTTE: A BLACKFEET INDIAN
John Reyhner
Grades 4-12. 24 pp. Paper. Council for Indian Education, 1984. $1.95.

HELD CAPTIVE BY INDIANS: SELECTED NARRATIVES, 1642-1836
Richard VanDerBeets, Editor
Illus. 378 pp. University of Tennessee Press, 1973. $19.95.

HERE COMES THE NAVAJO
Ruth Underhill
288 pp. Paper. Treasure Chest, 1983. $12.95.

*THE HERITAGE
Nancy Armstrong et al
Grades 3-6. Council for Indian Education, 1977. $1.95.

THE HERITAGE OF KLICKITAT BASKETRY: A HISTORY AND ART PRESERVED
Nettie Kuneki and Marie Teo
Illus. 40 pp. Paper. Oregon Historical Society, 1982. $5.95.

HERITAGE OF RAVEN
John A. Warner; M. Campbell, Editor
Reprint of 1981 edition. Illus. 200 pp. Hancock House, $25.00.

HEROES OF THE AMERICAN INDIAN
Sol Stember
Grades 8-12. Illus. Paper. Fleet Press, 1971. $6.95.

HEROIC WOMEN OF THE WEST
John Frost
Reprint of 1854 edition. Garland, $40.00.

HIDATSA EAGLE TRAPPING
Gilbert L. Wilson
Reprint of 1928 edition. AMS Press, $15.00.

THE HIDATSA EARTHLODGE
Gilbert L. Wilson; Bella Weitzner, Editor
Reprint of 1934 edition. AMS Press, $29.00.

HIDATSA SHRINE AND THE BELIEFS RESPECTING IT
G.H. Pepper and G.L. Wilson
Reprint of 1908 edition. Kraus, $15.00.

THE HIDDEN AGENDA: INDIAN POLICY AND THE TRUDEAU GOVERNMENT
Sally Weaver
University of Toronto Press, 1980. $25.00; paper, 10.00.

THE HIDDEN HALF: STUDIES OF PLAINS INDIAN WOMEN
Patricia Albers and Beatrice Medicine
286 pp. University Presses of Ameica, 1983. $25.50; paper, $13.25.

THE HILL CREEK HOMESTEAD AND THE LATE MISSISSIPPIAN SETTLEMENT IN THE LOWER ILLINOIS VALLEY
Michael D. Connor, Editor
Illus. 239 pp. Paper. Center for American Archaeology, 1985. $9.95.

THE HISPANIC ACCULTURATION OF THE GILA RIVER PIMAS
P.H. Ezell
Reprint of 1961 edition. Paper. Kraus, $23.00.

HISTOIRE DES ABENAKIS: A BIBLIOGRAPHY OF CANADIANA
J. Maurault
Reprint of 1866 edition. Johnson Reprint, $38.50.

HISTORIC BAKERVILLE
Lorraine Harris
Illus. 52 pp. Hancock House, 1984. $5.95.

**HISTORIC AND ETHNOGRAPHIC
STUDY OF THE SNOHOMISH,
SPECIFICALLY CONCERNING
THEIR ABORIGINAL AND
CONTINUED EXISTENCE**
Colin Tweddell
237 pp. Clearwater Publishing, 1974. $69.00.

**HISTORIC HOPI CERAMICS: THE
THOMAS V. KEARN COLLECTION
OF THE PEABODY MUSEUM OF
ARCHAEOLOGY AND ETHNOLOGY,
HARVARD UNIVERSITY**
Edwin L. Wade and Lea S. McChesney
Illus. 550 pp. Paper. Peabody-Harvard, 1981.
$30.00.

HISTORIC PUEBLO INDIAN POTTERY
Francis Harlow
Illus. 50 pp. Paper. University of New Mexico
Press and American Indian Books, 1967. $3.00.

**HISTORICAL ACCOUNT OF THE DOINGS
AND SUFFERINGS OF THE CHRISTIAN
INDIANS IN NEW ENGLAND IN
THE YEARS 1675, 1676, 1677**
Daniel Gookin
Reprint of 1836 edition. Ayer Co. Publishers,
$21.00.

**HISTORICAL AND STATISTICAL
INFORMATION RESPECTING THE
HISTORY, CONDITION AND PROS-
PECTS OF THE INDIAN TRIBES
OF THE U.S.**
H.R. Schoolcraft; Francis Nichols, Editor
Reprint of 1857 edition. Seven volumes. Illus.
AMS Press, $1.500.00 per set.

A HISTORICAL ATLAS OF TEXAS
William C. Pool
100 detailed maps of Texas geography and
history. The Encino Press, $17.50.

**HISTORICAL COLLECTIONS OF
THE INDIANS OF NEW ENGLAND**
Daniel Gookin
Reprint of 1792 edition. Ayer Co. Publishers,
$17.00.

**HISTORICAL INTRODUCTIONS TO
STUDIES AMONG THE SEDENTARY
INDIANS OF NEW MEXICO AND A
REPORT ON THE RUINS OF
THE PUEBLO AT PECOS**
Adolf F. Bandelier
Reprint of 1881 edition. Kraus, $23.00. Paper.
AMS Press, $15.00.

**AN HISTORICAL JOURNAL OF
THE CAMPAIGNS IN NORTH AMERICA
IN THE YEARS 1757-1760**
A.G. Doughty
Facsimile of 1916 edition. Two volumes. Ayer Co.
Publishers and Greenwood Press, $125.00/set.

**HISTORICAL MEMOIRS, RELATING
TO THE HOUSATONIC INDIANS**
Samuel Hopkins
Reprint of 1911 edition. Johnson Reprint, $17.00.

**HISTORICAL SKETCH OF
THE CHEROKEE**
James Mooney
272 pp. Beresford Book Service, 1975. $12.50;
paper, $4.95.

**HISTORICAL SKETCH OF
THE FLATHEAD NATION**
Peter Ronan
Reprint of 1890 edition. Ross & Haines, $6.95.

**HISTORICAL SKETCHES OF
TOMO-CHI-CHI, MICO OF
THE YAMACRAWS**
C.C. Jones
Reprint of 1868 edition. Kraus, $20.00.

**HISTORY, MANNERS AND CUSTOMS
OF THE INDIAN NATIONS WHO ONCE
INHABITED PENNSYLVANIA AND
NEIGHBORING STATES**
John Heckewelder
Reprint of 1819 edition. Illus. Ayer Co.
Publishers, $23.00.

**HISTORY OF ALABAMA,
AND INCIDENTALLY OF GEORGIA
AND MISSISSIPPI, FROM THE
EARLIEST PERIOD**
Albert J. Pickett
Reprint of 1851 edition. Illus. Ayer Co.
Publishers, $47.00.

A HISTORY OF ALBERTA
James G. MacGregor
Covers the nomadic lifestyles of the Cree,
Assiniboine, and Blackfoot tribes. Illus. Maps.
368 pp. Paper. Hurtig Publishers, 1981. $15.95.

HISTORY OF THE AMERICAN INDIANS
James Adair
Reprint of 1775 edition. Johnson Reprint, $31.00.

**HISTORY OF BAPTIST
INDIAN MISSIONS**
Isaac McCoy
Reprint of 1840 edition. Johnson Reprint, $36.00.

**A HISTORY OF THE BUREAU OF
INDIAN AFFAIRS AND ITS
ACTIVITIES AMONG INDIANS**
Curtis E. Jackson and Marcia J. Galli
Paper. R & E Research Associates, 1977. $14.00.

HISTORY OF CANADA,
OR NEW FRANCE
F. Du Creaux; J.B. Conacher, Editor
Reprint of 1951 edition. Two volumes.
Greenwood Press, $30.00 each.

HISTORY OF THE CATHOLIC
MISSIONS AMONG THE INDIAN
TRIBES OF THE U.S., 1529-1854
John D. Shea
Reprint of 1855 edition. Ayer Co. Publishers,
$26.50; AMS Press, $28.50.

HISTORY OF THE CHEROKEE
INDIANS AND THEIR LEGENDS
AND FOLKLORE
Emmet Starr
Reprint of 1921 edition. Kraus, $52.00.

*A HISTORY OF THE
CHEYENNE PEOPLE
Tom Weist
Grades 6-12. Illus. 227 pp. Paper. Council for
Indian Education, 1977. $7.95.

HISTORY OF THE CHOCTAW,
CHICKASAW AND NATCHEZ INDIANS
Horatio B. Cushman; Angie Debo, Editor
Reprint of 1899 edition. Russell & Russell, $23.00.

HISTORY OF THE DAKOTA OR SIOUX
INDIANS
D. Robinson
Reprint of 1967 edition. Ross & Haines, $15.00.

HISTORY OF THE EARLY SETTLE-
MENT AND INDIAN WARS OF
WESTERN VIRGINIA
Willis De Hass
Reprint of 1851 edition. McClain Printing,
$15.00.

HISTORY OF EVENTS RESULTING
IN INDIAN CONSOLIDATION WEST
OF THE MISSISSIPPI
Annie H. Abel
Reprint of 1908 edition. AMS Press, $14.50.

*HISTORY OF THE FIVE INDIAN
NATIONS OF CANADA
Cadwallader Colden
Reprint of 1922 edition. Grades 7-12. 250 pp.
AMS Press, $55.00. Paper. Cornell University
Press, $6.95.

HISTORY OF INDIAN EDUCATION
P.L. Rawat
Seventh edition. International Publications
Service, 1973. $6.00.

HISTORY OF INDIAN MISSIONS
ON THE PACIFIC COAST
M. Eells
Reprint of 1882 edition. Paper. Shorey, $2.50.

A HISTORY OF INDIAN
POLICY: SYLLABUS
Judith Bachman
Paper. National Book, $6.00; cassette recording,
$150.00.

HISTORY OF THE INDIAN
TRIBES OF HUDSON'S RIVER
E. Ruttenber
Reprint of 1872 edition. Illus. Scholarly Press,
$29.00.

HISTORY OF THE INDIAN WARS
Samuel Penhallow
Reprint of 1726 edition. 208 pp. Corner House,
$15.00.

HISTORY OF THE INDIAN WARS
IN NEW ENGLAND, FROM THE FIRST
SETTLEMENT TO THE TERMINATION
OF THE WAR WITH KING PHILIP
IN 1677
William Hubbard
Reprint of 1865 edition. Burt Franklin, $32.50.

HISTORY OF THE INDIANS
OF THE UNITED STATES
Angie Debo
University of Oklahoma Press, 1974. $21.95;
paper, $12.95.

A HISTORY OF THE NEW YORK
IROQUOIS, NOW COMMONLY CALLED
THE SIX NATIONS
William M. Beauchamp
Reprint of 1905 edition. Illus. AMS Press, $27.50.

HISTORY OF THE LEGAL STATUS
OF THE AMERICAN INDIAN WITH
PARTICULAR REFERENCE TO
CALIFORNIA: THESIS
Donald R. Beatty
Paper. R & E Research Associates, 1974. $8.00.

THE HISTORY OF THE LIFE AND
ADVENTURES OF MR. ANDERSON
E. Kimber; Wilcomb E. Washburn, Editor
Garland Publishing, 1975. $40.00.

HISTORY OF THE MICHIGAN
COMMISSION ON INDIAN AFFAIRS
James Hillman
Hillman Publications.

HISTORY OF THE MINGO INDIANS
William Cobb and Andrew Price
Reprint of 1921 edition. McClain Printing, $4.00.

HISTORY OF THE MISSION OF THE
UNITED BRETHREN AMONG THE
INDIANS IN NORTH AMERICA
G.H. Loskiel; C. Latrobe, Translator
Reprint of 1794 edition. Scholarly Press, $25.00.

HISTORY OF NEW FRANCE
Marc Lescarbot
Reprint of 1907 edition. Three volumes.
Greenwood Press.

HISTORY OF NEW MEXICAN—LATINS INDIAN RELATIONS
Charles Kenner
Illus. University of Oklahoma Press, 1969. $14.95.

HISTORY OF THE NEW YORK INDIANS AND INDIANS OF THE PRINTUP FAMILY
A.D. Printup
Illus. 89 pp. DeWitt & Sheppard, 1985. $42.60.

HISTORY OF THE OJIBWAY INDIANS
Peter Jones
Reprint of 1861 edition. Ayer Co., $24.50.

HISTORY OF THE OJIBWAY PEOPLE
William W. Warren
Illus. 387 pp. Paper. Minnesota Historical Society, 1984. $11.95.

HISTORY OF THE SANTEE SIOUX: U.S. INDIAN POLICY ON TRIAL
Roy W. Meyer
452 pp. Paper. University of Nebraska Press, 1967. $7.95.

HISTORY OF THE SECOND SEMINOLE WAR
John K. Mahon
Illus. University Presses of Florida, 1967. $10.00.

A HISTORY OF THE SHOSHONE—PAIUTES OF THE DUCK VALLEY INDIAN RESERVATION
Whitney McKinney
Illus. 176 pp. Howe Brothers, 1982. $15.95.

HISTORY OF THE SPIRIT LAKE MASSACRE AND OF MISS ABIGAIL GARDINER'S THREE MONTH CAPTIVITY AMONG THE INDIANS
L.P. Lee
Reprint of 1857 edition. Ye Galleon Press, $5.50.

HISTORY OF TEXAS, 1673-1779
Fray Morfi; Carlos Casteneda, Editor
Reprint of 1935 edition. Two parts. Ayer Co. Publishers, $34.00.

HISTORY AND PRESENT DEVELOPMENT OF INDIAN SCHOOLS IN THE U.S.
Solomon R. Ammon
Reprint of 1935 edition. Paper. R & E Associates, $10.95.

THE HISTORY AND PRESENT STATE OF VIRGINIA
R. Beverley; Louis B. Wright, Editor
Reprint of 1947 edition. Illus. 366 pp. Paper. Books on Demand, $76.40.

HIWASSEE ISLAND: AN ARCHAEOLOGICAL ACCOUNT OF FOUR TENNESSEE INDIAN PEOPLES
Thomas N. Lewis and Madeline Kneberg
Illus. 328 pp. University of Tennessee Press, 1984. $28.50; paper, $14.95.

THE HOE AND THE HORSE ON THE PLAINS: A STUDY OF CULTURAL DEVELOPMENT AMONG NORTH AMERICAN INDIANS
Preston Holder
Illus. 192 pp. University of Nebraska Press, 1970. $14.50; paper, $4.75.

HOGANS: NAVAJO HOUSES AND HOUSE SONGS
David and Susan McAllester
Illus. 115 pp. Wesleyan University Press, $19.50.

THE HOHOKAM: DESERT FARMERS AND CRAFTSMEN: EXCAVATIONS AT SNAKETOWN, 1964-1965
Emil W. Haury
412 pp. University of Arizona Press, 1976. $25.00.

THE HOHOKAM INDIANS OF THE TUCSON BASIN
Linda Gregonis and Karl J. Reinhard
A layman's guide to Hohokam lifeways. 48 pp. Paper. University of Arizona Press, 1979. $4.95.

HOHOKAM AND PATAYAN: PREHISTORY OF SOUTHWESTERN ARIZONA
R. McGuire and M. Schiffer, Editors
Academic Press, 1982. $47.50.

THE HOLLYWOOD INDIAN: STEREOTYPES OF NATIVE AMERICANS IN FILMS
Illus. 80 pp. New Jersey State Museum, 1981. $5.95.

HOLY WIND IN NAVAJO PHILOSOPHY
James K. McNeley
120 pp. Paper. University of Arizona Press, 1981. $6.95.

*HOMER LITTLE BIRD'S RABBIT
Limana Kachel
Grades K-2. Council for Indian Education, $5.95; paper, $1.95.

HONOR DANCE: NATIVE AMERICAN PHOTOGRAPHS
John Running and William A. Allard
Illus. 168 pp. University of Nevada Press, 1985. $40.00

THE HOPEWELL MOUND GROUP OF OHIO
Warren and Moorhead
Reprint of 1922 edition. Illus. AMS Press, $42.50.

HOPEWELL VILLAGE: A SOCIAL
AND ECONOMIC HISTORY OF AN
IRON-MAKING COMMUNITY
  J.E. Walker
University of Pennsylvania Press, 1966. $25.00;
paper, $11.95.

HOPEWELLIAN STUDIES
  Joseph Caldwell and Robert Hall, Editors
Facsimile edition. Illus. 156 pp. Illinois State
Museum, 1977. $4.00.

HOPI
  Susanne and Jake Page
Illus. 240 pp. Harry N. Abrams, 1982. $50.00.

HOPI AND HOPI-TEWA POTTERY
32 pp. Paper. Museum of Northern Arizona,
1982. $4.00.

HOPI BIBLIOGRAPHY:
COMPRHENSIVE AND ANNOTATED
  W. David Laird
3,000 sources. 735 pp. Paper. University of
Arizona Press, 1977. $8.95.

THE HOPI CHILD
  Wayne Dennis
Reprint of 1940 edition. Illus. 232 pp. Ayer Co.
Publishers, $16.00.

HOPI COOKERY
  Juanita Tiger Kavena
Includes over 100 authentic Hopi recipes. 115 pp.
Paper. University of Arizona Press, 1980. $8.50.

HOPI COYOTE TALES:
ISTUTUWUTSI
  Ekkehart Malotki and Michael Lomatuway'ma
350 pp. University of Nebraska Press, 1984.
$19.95; paper, $12.95.

HOPI DAYS
  Mary-Russell F. Colton
Second edition. Illus. Paper. Museum of
Northern Arizona, 1978. $5.95.

HOPI DREAM
  Adolf Hungry Wolf
Illus. 32 pp. Paper. Good Medicine Books, 1974.
$2.00.

HOPI DYES
  Mary-Russell Colton
Second edition. Illus. Paper. Museum of
Northern Arizona, $4.95.

HOPI INDIANS
  W. Hough
Reprint of 1915 edition. Illus. 265 pp. Paper.
Shorey, $13.95.

HOPI INDIANS
Illus. Garland Publishing, $42.00.

HOPI JOURNALS
  A.M. Stephen; Elsie C. Parsons, Editor
Reprint of 1936 edition. Two volumes. AMS
Press, $47.50 each.

HOPI KACHINA DOLLS WITH A
KEY TO THEIR IDENTIFICATION
  Harold S. Colton
Revised edition. Illus. 150 pp. Paper. University
of New Mexico Press, 1971. $8.95.

HOPI KACHINA: SPIRIT OF LIFE
  Dorothy Washburn, Editor
Illus. 160 pp. Paper. University of Washington
Press and California Academy of Sciences, 1980.
$14.95.

HOPI KACHINAS
  Edwin Earle and Edward A. Kennard
Second edition. Illus. 50 pp. Museum of the
American Indian, 1971. $12.50. Portfolio
of 28 color plates from the book, $3.50.

HOPI KACHINAS DRAWN
BY NATIVE ARTISTS
  Jesse W. Fewkes
Reprint of 1903 edition. Illus. 190 pp.
Rio Grande Press, $25.00.

*HOPI MYSTERIES
  Jack Woolgar and Barbara J. Rudnicki
Grades 5-9. Council for Indian Education, 1974.
$5.95; paper, $1.95.

HOPI OF THE SECOND MESA
  Ernest and Pearl Beaglehole
Reprint of 1935 edition. Paper. Kraus, $15.00.

HOPI PAINTING: THE
WORLD OF THE HOPIS
  Patricia J. Broden
E.P. Dutton, 1978. $25.00.

HOPI PHOTOGRAPHERS—HOPI IMAGES
  Victor Masayesva and Erin Younger, Editors
Illus. 111 pp. University of Arizona Press, 1983.
$25.00; paper, $14.95.

HOPI SONGS
  B. Gilman
Reprint of 1908 edition. AMS Press, $35.00.

HOPI TALES
  Ekkehart Malotki, et al
Illus. Paper. Museum of Northern Arizona, 1978.
$8.00.

**THE HOPI: THEIR HISTORY AND
USE OF LANDS IN NEW MEXICO
AND ARIZONA, 1200s TO 1900s**
Florence H. Ellis
250 pp. Clearwater Publishing, 1973. $75.00.

**THE HOPI VILLAGES (THE ANCIENT
PROVINCE OF TUSAYAN)**
John W. Powell
Illus. 48 pp. Filter Press, 1972. $7.00; paper,
$1.50.

**HOPI VOICES: RECOLLECTIONS,
TRADITIONS AND NARRATIVES
OF THE HOPI INDIANS**
Harold Courlander, Editor
224 pp. University of New Mexico Press, 1982.
$17.50.

HOPI VOICES AND VISIONS
Michael Kabotie, et al, Editors
80 pp. Paper. Street Press, 1984. $7.50.

HOPI WAY
Laura Thompson and Alice Joseph
Reprint of 1944 edition. Illus. Russell &
Russell, $14.00.

*THE HOPI WAY
Mary Elting
Grades 4-6. Illus. 64 pp. M. Evans & Co., 1969.
$3.95.

HOPI AND ZUNI CEREMONIALISM
Elsie C. Parsons
Reprint of 1933 edition. Paper. Kraus, $12.00.

**HOPIS: PORTRAIT OF
A DESERT PEOPLE**
Walter C. O'Kane
Reprint of 1953 edition. Illus. University of
Oklahoma Press, $14.50.

**HOPITUTUWUTSI—HOPI TALES:
A BILINGUAL COLLECTION OF
HOPI INDIAN STORIES**
H. Talashoma and E. Malotki, Editors
213 pp. University of Arizona Press, 1983. $24.50;
paper, $14.50.

**HORN AND BONE IMPLEMENTS
OF THE NEW YORK INDIANS**
W.M. Beauchamp
Reprint of 1902 edition. AMS Press, $19.50.

**TOM HORN, GOVERNMENT SCOUT
AND INDIAN INTERPRETER**
Tom Horn
Autobiography. An account of the Apache Indian
Wars. Reprint of 1904 edition. Illus. 318 pp.
Rio Grande Press, $15.00.

**THE HORSE AND THE DOG
IN HIDATSA CULTURE**
Gilbert L. Wilson
Reprint of 1924 edition. AMS Press, $23.00.

**THE HORSE IN BLACKFOOT
INDIAN CULTURE**
John C. Ewers
Bound with comparative material from other
western tribes. Reprint of 1955 edition.
Scholarly Press, $59.00.

**THE HORSEMEN OF THE AMERICAS:
AN EXHIBITION FROM THE HALL OF
THE HORSEMEN OF THE AMERICAS**
Sheila Ohlendorf and William D. Wittliff
Illus. Paper. University of Texas, Humanities,
1968. $5.00.

**HOSTEEN KLAH: NAVAHO MEDICINE
MAN AND SAND PAINTER**
Franc J. Newcomb
Illus. 227 pp. Paper. University of Oklahoma
Press, 1971. $7.95.

**HOUSES AND HOUSE LIFE OF
THE AMERICAN ABORIGINES**
Lewis H. Morgan
Illus. University of Chicago Press, 1966. $12.95;
paper, $3.95.

*THE HOUSES THE INDIAN BUILT
Sigmund A. Levine
Grades 5-12. Dodd, Mead & Co., 1975. $5.95.

***HOW THE DOGS SAVED
THE CHEYENNES**
Hap Gilliland
Grades 1-4. Paper, Council for Indian Education,
1972. $1.95.

**HOW GEORGE ROGERS CLARK WON
THE NORTHWEST AND OTHER ESSAYS
IN WESTERN HISTORY**
R.G. Thwaites
Facsimile of 1903 edition. Ayer Co. Publishers,
$19.50.

*HOW THE INDIANS REALLY LIVED
Gordon C. Baldwin
Grades 5-9. Illus. Berkley, 1967. $6.00.

**HOW INDIANS USE WILD PLANTS
FOR FOOD, MEDICINE AND CRAFTS**
Frances Densmore

Formerly *Uses of Plants by the Chippewa
Indians.* Reprint. Illus. 162 pp. Peter Smith,
$10.00. Paper. Americn Indian Books, $4.95;
Dover, $3.95.

*HOW THE FLOWERS CAME TO BE
Choctaw story that reinforces many traditional Choctaw values. Grades Preschool-3. 14 pp. Choctaw Heritage Press, $3.50.

*HOW THE PLAINS INDIANS LIVED
George Fichter
Grades 6-12. David McKay, 1980. $8.95.

HOW TO COLLECT NORTH AMERICAN INDIAN ARTIFACTS
Robert F. Brand
Illus. 151 pp. Robert F. Brand and American Indian Books, $12.95.

HOW WE LIVED: REMINISCENCES, STORIES, SPEECHES, AND SONGS OF CALIFORNIA INDIANS
Malcolm Margolin
Heyday Books, 1981. $10.95; paper, $5.95.

HOWARD'S CAMPAIGN AGAINST THE NEZ PERCE INDIANS, 1878
Thomas A. Sutherland
Ye Galleon Press, 1982. $14.95.

HUALAPAI INDIANS
Four volumes. Illus. Maps. Garland, $42.00 each.

HUALAPAI INDIANS OF ARIZONA
Robert A. Manners
194 pp. Clearwater Publishing, 1973. $58.50.

HUALAPAI INDIANS OF ARIZONA: EVALUATION STUDY OF MINERAL RESOURCES
P.J. Shenon and Roy P. Full
Four volumes. 1,670 pp. Clearwater, 1973. $450.00 per set.

HUALAPAI REFERENCE GRAMMAR
575 pp. Paper. American Indian Studies Center, 1982. $17.50.

HUALAPAI TRIBAL LANDS: ESTIMATE OF THE VALUE OF MINERALS AS OF 1833
Still & Still, Engineers
324 pp. Clearwater Publishing, 1974. $68.00.

HUALAPAI TRIBAL LANDS IN NORTHEASTERN ARIZONA: APPRAISAL
William S. Winter
180 pp. Clearwater Publishing, 1973. $56.00.

*THE HUNT
Samuel Stanley and Pearl Oberg
Grades 5-9. 32 pp. Paper. Council for Indian Education, 1976. $1.95.

*HUNTED LIKE A WOLF: THE STORY OF THE SEMINOLE WAR
Milton Meltzer
Grades 7-12. Illus. 224 pp. Farrar, Straus & Giroux, 1972, $6.95.

*THE HUNTER AND THE RAVENS
Mary Holthaus
Grades 1-6. 32 pp. Council for Indian Education, 1976. $2.00.

*THE HUNTERS
Daniel Jacobson
Grades 4-7. 96 pp. Paper. Franklin Watts, 1974. $4.90.

HUNTERS OF THE BUFFALO
R. Stephen Irwin
Illus. 52 pp. Paper. Hancock House, 1984. $3.95.

HUNTERS OF THE EASTERN FOREST
52 pp. Paper. Hancock House, 1984. $3.95.

HUNTERS OF THE ICE
R. Stephen Irwin
Illus. 84 pp. Paper. Hancock House, 1984. $5.95.

HUNTERS OF THE NORTHERN FOREST
R. Stephen Irwin
Illus. 52 pp. Paper. Hancock House, 1984. $3.95.

HUNTERS OF THE SEA
Steven Irwin
Illus. 52 pp. Hancock House, 1984. $3.95.

HURON: FARMERS OF THE NORTH
B.G. Trigger
Paper. Holt, Rinehart & Winston, 1969. $9.95.

I

I AM THE FIRE OF TIME: THE VOICES OF NATIVE AMERICAN WOMEN
Jane B. Katz, Editor
Paper. E.P. Dutton, 1977. $7.95.

*I CAN READ ABOUT THE INDIANS
Elizabeth I. Warren
Grades 2-4. Illus. Paper. Troll Associates, 1974. $1.50.

I HAVE SPOKEN: AMERICAN HISTORY THROUGH THE VOICES OF THE INDIANS
Virginia I. Armstrong, Editor
Paper. Swallow Press, 1971. $5.95.

I SEND A VOICE
Evelyn Eaton
A first person account of what actually transpires inside of an Amerindian Sweat Lodge. Illus. 180 pp. Theosophical Publishing House, 1978. $10.95; paper, $4.95.

I'ISHIYATAM
K.S. Saubel and A. Galloway
Malki Museum Press, 1978. $3.00.

I WILL DIE AN INDIAN
E. Richard Hart, Editor
116 pp. Paper. Howe Brothers, $5.95.

**I WILL FIGHT NO MORE FOREVER:
CHIEF JOSEPH AND NEZ PERCE WAR**
Merrill D. Beal
Illus. 384 pp. Paper. University of Washington
Press, 1963. $7.95.

**THE IDEAL OF FERTILIZATION
IN THE CULTURE OF THE
PUEBLO INDIANS**
Herman K. Haeberlin
Reprint of 1916 edition. Paper. Kraus, $15.00.

**IDENTIFICATION OF UNIQUE
FEATURES IN EDUCATION AT
AMERICAN INDIAN SCHOOLS**
Curtis E. Jackson
Reprint of 1965 edition. Paper. R & E Research
Associates, $8.00.

***IF YOU LIVED WITH
THE SIOUX INDIANS**
Ann McGovern
Grades 2-4. Illus. 96 pp. School Book Service,
1974. $6.95; paper, $1.50.

**IF YOU TAKE MY SHEEP...THE
EVOLUTION AND CONFLICTS OF
NAVAJO PASTORALISM, 1630-1868**
Lynn R. Bailey
Illus. 304 pp. Westernlore, $12.00.

IGLOO LIFE
62 pp. Paper. Albert Saifer, Publisher, $15.00.

**THE ILLINOIS AND
INDIANA INDIANS**
H.W. Beckwith
Facsimile of 1884 edition. Ayer Co., $10.00.

**THE ILLUSTRATED BIOGRAPHICAL
ENCYCLOPEDIA OF ARTISTS OF
THE AMERICAN WEST**
Peggy and Harold Samuels
Doubleday, 1976. $30.00.

**ILLUSTRATED HISTORY OF
INDIAN BASKETS AND PLATES**
Viola Roseberry
Illus. Paper. Ten Speed Press, 1974. $2.50.

IMAGES OF AMERICAN INDIAN ART
Robert Ashton and Jozefa Stuart
Walker & Co., 1977. $12.95; paper, $7.95.

**IMAGES OF AMERICAN INDIANS IN
FILM: AN ANNOTATED BIBLIOGRAPHY**
Gretchen M. Bataille
Garland Publishing, 1985.

IMAGES: STONE: B.C.
Wilson Duff and Hilary Stewart

Illus. Universe Books, 1975. $17.95. Hancock
House, $14.95; paper, $7.95.

**THE IMPERIAL OSAGES: SPANISH—
INDIAN DIPLOMACY IN THE
MISSISSIPPI VALLEY**
Gilbert Din and Abraham P. Nasatir
Illus. 432 pp. University of Oklahoma Press,
1983. $39.95.

*IN THE BEGINNING
Ella Clark, Editor
Grades 5-12. Council for Indian Education,
1977. $1.95.

**IN THE BEGINNING:
THE NAVAHO CREATION MYTH**
Stanley Fishler
Reprint of 1953 edition. AMS Press, $26.50.

**IN THE COUNTRY OF
THE WALKING DEAD**
Walter O'Meara
256 pp. Paper. Charter Books, 1980. $1.95.

**IN THE DAYS OF VICTORIO:
RECOLLECTIONS OF A WARM
SPRINGS APACHE**
Eve Ball
Records an Apache's own account of their history
from 1878-1886. 222 pp. Paper. University of
Arizona Press, 1970. $7.95.

**IN THE LAND OF THE GRASSHOPPER
SONG: TWO WOMEN IN THE KLAMATH
RIVER INDIAN COUNTRY 1908-1909**
Mary Arnold and Mabel Reed
Illus. 313 pp. University of Nebraska Press, 1980.
$17.95; paper, $5.95.

***IN OUR HOGAN: ADVENTURE
STORIES OF NAVAJO CHILDREN**
Jean Wood and Nancy Armstrong
Grades 4-8. Paper. Council for Indian Education,
1976. $1.95.

IN RED MAN'S LAND
Francis E. Leupp
A study of red/white confrontation over
government policies. Reprint of 1914 edition.
Biblio. 170 pp. Rio Grande, $10.00.

IN A SACRED MANNER WE LIVE
Edward S. Curtis
Reprint. Illus. 149 pp. American Indian Books,
$10.00.

**IN A SACRED MANNER WE LIVE:
PHOTOGRAPHS OF THE AMERICAN
INDIAN AT THE BEGINNING OF
THE TWENTIETH CENTURY**
Don D. Fowler
Illus. 196 pp. Paper. Barre, 1972. $6.95.

IN THE MIDDLE: THE ESKIMO TODAY
Stephen G. Williams
Illus. 112 pp. Godine Publishing, 1983. $20.00;
paper, $9.95.

IN THE SPIRIT OF CRAZY HORSE
Peter Matthiessen
Illus. 704 pp. Viking Press, 1983. $20.95.

**IN THE TIME THAT WAS:
BEING LEGENDS OF THE KLINGITS**
J. Frederic Thorne
Reprint of 1909 edition. Paper. Shorey, $2.50.

**IN VAIN I TRIED TO TELL YOU:
ESSAYS IN NATIVE AMERICAN
ETHNOPOETICS**
Dell Hymes
416 pp. University of Pennsylvania Press, 1981.
$35.00; paper, $12.95.

**INCONSTANT SAVAGE: ENGLAND
AND THE NORTH AMERICAN
INDIANS, 1500-1660**
H.C. Porter
588 pp. Biblio Distribution Centre, 1979. $34.95.

*INDEH: AN APACHE ODYSSEY
Eve Ball
Illus. Brigham Young University Press, 1980.
$19.95.

**INDEX TO THE BRIEFS, TRAN-
SCRIPTS AND GAO REPORTS BEFORE
THE INDIAN CLAIMS COMMISSION**
Norman A. Ross
192 pp. Clearwater Publishing, 1973. $15.00.

**INDEX TO THE DECISIONS OF
THE INDIAN CLAIMS COMMISSION**
Norman A. Ross
168 pp. Clearwater Publishing, 1973. $15.00.

**INDEX TO THE EXPERT TESTIMONY
PRESENTED BEFORE THE INDIAN
CLAIMS COMMISSION**
Norman A. Ross
112 pp. Clearwater Publishing, 1973. $15.00.

**INDEX TO THE FRANZ BOAS
COLLECTION OF MATERIALS FOR
AMERICAN LINGUISTICS**
C.F. Voegelin and Z.S. Harris
Reprint of 1945 edition. Paper. Kraus, $16.00.

**INDEX TO LITERATURE ON
THE AMERICAN INDIAN**
Indian Historian Press Editors
Four volumes. Paper. The Indian Historian Press,
1970-1973. $15.00 each volume.

**INDEX TO THE RECORDS OF THE
MORAVIAN MISSION AMONG THE
INDIANS OF NORTH AMERICA**
Carl J. Fliegel, Compiler
Two volumes. Research Publications, 1970.
$375.00 per set.

**INDEX TO SCHOOLCRAFT'S
"INDIAN TRIBES OF THE U.S."**
F.S. Nichols
Reprint of 1954 edition. Scholarly Press, $39.00.

THE INDIAN ACT OF CANADA
Richard Bartlett
36 pp. University of Saskatchewan, 1980. $6.50.

**INDIAN ACTS AND AMENDMENTS,
1868-1975, INDEXED COLLECTION**
Sharon Venne
Canada. 528 pp. University of Saskatchewan,
1981. $45.00

THE INDIAN AFFAIR
Vine Deloria, Jr.
The responsibility of the Christian churches
toward American Indians. Paper. Friendship
Press, 1974. $5.00.

**INDIAN AFFAIRS IN GEORGIA,
1732-1756**
John P. Corry
Reprint of 1936 edition. AMS Press, $21.50.

**INDIAN AFFAIRS IN TERRITORIES
OF OREGON AND WASHINGTON: FIRST
SESSION, 35th CONGRESS, 1858**
J. Ross Brown
Ye Galleon Press, 1973. $4.95.

**INDIAN AFFAIRS:
LAWS AND TREATIES**
Charles J. Kappler, Editor
Reprint of 1941 edition. Five volumes. 4,667 pp.
Supt. of Documents, $90.00; AMS Press, $475.00.

**INDIAN AFFAIRS PAPERS:
AMERICAN REVOLUTION**
Maryly Penrose
Illus. 400 pp. Liberty Bell Associates, 1981.
$25.00.

**INDIAN AFFAIRS AND THEIR
ADMINISTRATION, WITH SPECIAL
REFERENCE TO THE FAR WEST,
1849-1860**
A.W. Hoopes
Reprint of 1932 edition. Kraus, $26.00.

**INDIAN AGENTS OF
THE OLD FRONTIER**
Flora W. Seymour
Reprint of 1941 edition. Octagon Books, 1973.
$27.50. Kraus, $30.00.

**INDIAN AMERICA: A GEOGRAPHY
OF NORTH AMERICAN INDIANS**
M. Wallace Ney
Illus. 56 pp. Paper. American Indian Books,
$5.00.

**THE INDIAN: AMERICA'S
UNFINISHED BUSINESS**
William A. Brophy and Sophie D. Aberle
Illus. Paper. University of Oklahoma Press, 1978.
$6.95.

**INDIAN ANTIQUITIES OF
THE KENNEBEC VALLEY**
Charles Willoughby; Arthur E. Spiess, Editor
Illus. 160 pp. Maine State Museum, 1980. $22.00.

INDIAN ART AND CULTURE
Della Kew and P.E. Goddard
Reprint of 1978 second edition. 96 pp. Paper.
Hancock House, $7.95.

**INDIAN ART AND HISTORY: THE
TESTIMONY OF PREHISTORIC
ROCK PAINTINGS**
Clement Meighan
Dawson's Book Shop, $36.00.

**INDIAN ART IN PIPESTONE:
GEORGE CATLIN'S PORTFOLIO
IN THE BRITISH MUSEUM**
John C. Ewers
Illus. 80 pp. Smithsonian, 1979. $15.00.

INDIAN ART OF THE AMERICAS
Frederick J. Dockstader
Exhibit catalog of Native-American art from
3000 B.C. to the present. 304 pp. Museum of the
American Indian, 1973. $5.00.

**INDIAN ART OF THE NORTHWEST
COAST: A DIALOGUE ON CRAFTS-
MANSHIP AND ATHLETICS**
Bill Holm and Bill Reid
Illus. Paper. University of Washington Press,
1978. $15.95.

INDIAN ART OF THE U.S.
F.H. Douglas and R. D'Harmoncourt
Reprint of 19451 edition. Illus. Ayer Co., $20.00.

**INDIAN ART TRADITIONS
ON THE NORTHWEST COAST**
Roy L. Carlson, Editor
Illus. 214 pp. Paper. University of Washington
Press, 1984. $15.00.

INDIAN ARTIFACTS
Virgil Russell
Illus. 167 pp. Paper. American Indian Books,
$7.95.

**INDIAN ARTIFACTS OF
THE EAST AND SOUTH**
Robert Swope, Jr.
Illus. 150 pp. Paper. American Indian Books,
$12.00.

**INDIAN ARTIFACTS OF
THE NORTHWEST COAST**
Hilary Stewart
Illus. 172 pp. University of Washington Press,
1976. $20.00.

INDIAN ARTISTS AT WORK
Ulli Steltzer
Illus. 144 pp. University of Washington Press,
1977. $30.00; paper, $14.95.

**THE INDIAN ARTS AND CRAFTS
BOARD: AN ASPECT OF THE
NEW DEAL POLICY**
Robert F. Schrader
Illus. 384 pp. University of New Mexico Press,
1983. $19.95.

INDIAN ARTS IN NORTH AMERICA
G.C. Vaillant
Reprint of 1939 edition. Illus. 63 pp. Cooper
Square, $30.00.

***THE INDIAN AS A SOLDIER AT
FORT CUSTER, MONTANA, 1890-1895:
LT. SAMUEL C. ROBERTSON'S FIRST
CAVALRY CROW INDIAN CONTINGENT**
Richard Upton
Grades 7-12. Illus. 147 pp. Upton Sons, 1985.
$27.50.

INDIAN ATROCITIES
Bound with other narratives. Reprint of 1846
edition. Garland, $42.00.

INDIAN BASKET WEAVING
Navajo School of Indian Basketry
Illus. Paper. Dover, 1971. $2.50.

INDIAN BASKETRY
George W. James
Reprint. Illus. 271 pp. Peter Smith, $14.75.
Paper. Dover, $5.95.

**INDIAN BASKETRY, AND
HOW TO MAKE BASKETS**
George W. James
Enlarged 1903 edition. Two volumes in one. Illus.
Biblio. 424 pp. Rio Grande Press, $22.50.

INDIAN BASKETS AND CURIOS
Illus. Paper. Binford & Mort, $3.50.

**INDIAN BASKETS OF
THE NORTHWEST COAST**
Art Wolfe, Photographer
Illus. 128 pp. Graphic Arts Center, 1978. $19.50;
Limited edition, $30.00.

INDIAN BASKETS OF THE SOUTHWEST
Clara L. Tanner
Illus. 256 pp. University of Arizona Press, 1983.
$39.95.

**INDIAN BATTLES ALONG THE ROGUE
RIVER: ONE OF AMERICA'S WILD
AND SCENIC RIVERS**
Frank K. Walsh
Illus. 32 pp. Paper. Te-Cum-Tom, 1972. $1.95.

**INDIAN BATTLES AND SKIRMISHES
ON THE AMERICAN FRONTIER,
1790-1898**
Joseph P. Peters
Reprint of 1966 edition. 256 pp. Ayer Co., $30.50.

***INDIAN BEAD—WEAVING PATTERNS:
CHAIN WEAVING DESIGNS AND BEAD
LOOM WEAVING—AN ILLUSTRATED
"HOW—TO" GUIDE**
Horace R. Goodhue
Grades 3-12. Illus. 64 pp. Paper. Bead Craft,
1984. $4.95.

**INDIAN BIOGRAPHIES: NORTH
AMERICAN NATIVES DISTINGUISHED
AS ORATORS, WARRIORS, STATESMEN**
Benjamin B. Thatcher
Reprint of 1832 edition. Illus. 668 pp. Rio Grande,
$30.00.

**INDIAN BLANKETS
AND THEIR MAKERS**
George W. James
Enlarged 1892 edition. Illus. Biblio. 352 pp.
Rio Grande, $27.50. Paper. Dover, $6.95.

INDIAN BLOOD
Evelyn Olsen
Illus. McClain Printing, 1967. $10.00.

*THE INDIAN BOOK
Merwyn Garbarino and World Book Staff
Grades K-6. Illus. 304 pp. World Book-Childcraft
International, 1980.

*INDIAN BOYHOOD
Charles Eastman (Ohiyesa)
A Santee Sioux recalls his boyhood among the
Sioux Indians of the Plains. Grades 3-7. Illus.
330 pp. Peter Smith, $14.00. Paper. Dover, $4.00.

**THE INDIAN BOY'S DAYS: THE
INDIAN THEN AND NOW - HIS
PRSENCE AND INFLUENCE ON
OUR LIFE STYLE**
Allan Hulsizer
Illus. 64 pp. Exposition Press, 1983. $6.00.

*THE INDIAN AND THE BUFFALO
Robert Hofsinde
Grades 3-7. Illus. Paper. William Morrow, 1961.
$7.00.

**INDIAN BURIAL PLACE AT
WINTHROP, MASSACHUSETTS**
C.C. Willoughby
Reprint of 1924 edition. Paper. Kraus, $16.00.

***THE INDIAN AND THE
CALIFORNIA MISSION**
Linda Lyngheim; Brian Skipper, Editor
Grades 4-6. 128 pp. Paper. Langtry Publications,
1984. $9.95.

INDIAN CAMPAIGNS
Charles King
Illus. Old Army, 1984. $37.50.

**AN INDIAN CANAAN: ISAAC McCOY
THE VISION OF AN INDIAN STATE**
George A. Schultz
Illus. 350 pp. University of Oklahoma Press, 1972.
$17.95; paper, $8.95.

*INDIAN CANOEING
Pierre Pulling
Grades 6-12. Illus. Council for Indian Education,
1976. $5.95; paper, $1.95.

**THE INDIAN CAPTIVE: A NARRA-
TIVE OF THE ADVENTURES AND
SUFFERINGS OF MATTHEW BRAYTON,
IN HIS 34 YEARS OF CAPTIVITY
AMONG INDIANS OF NORTHWEST U.S.**
John H. Bone
Reprint. 65 pp. Paper. Ye Galleon Press, $10.95.

**THE INDIAN CAPTIVE: OR, A
NARRATIVE OF THE CAPTIVITY AND
SUFFERINGS OF ZADOCK STEELE**
Zadeck Steele
Reprint of 1908 edition. Ayer Co., $14.00.

INDIAN CAPTIVITIES
A series of Indian captivity narratives.
See Garland Publishing for titles and prices.

**INDIAN CAPTIVITIES: OR,
LIFE IN THE WIGWAM**
S.G. Drake
Reprint of 1851 edition. AMS Press, $27.50.

**INDIAN CHIEFS OF
SOUTHERN MINNESOTA**
Thomas Hughes
Reprint. Ross & Haines, $8.75.

INDIAN CHILDREN'S BOOKS
Hap Gilliland
An annotated list of 1,650 children's books with
evaluations. 230 pp. Council for Indian
Education, $12.95; paper, $7.95.

INDIAN CLOTHING BEFORE CORTES: MESOAMERICAN COSTUMES FROM THE CODICES
Patricia R. Anawalt
Illus. 400 pp. University of Oklahoma Press, 1981. $45.00.

*INDIAN COSTUMES
Robert Hofsinde (Gray-Wolf)
Grades 3-7. Illus. 96 pp. William Morrow, 1968. $9.00.

INDIAN COUNCIL AT WALLA WALLA, WASHINGTON
Lawrence Kip
Reprint of 1897 edition. Paper. Shorey, $2.95.

INDIAN COUNTRY
Peter Matthiessen
320 pp. Viking Press, 1984. $17.95.

INDIAN COUNTRY OF THE TUBATULABAL: FIRST RESIDENTS OF KERN RIVER VALLEY
Bob Powers
Illus. Westernlore, 1981. $18.00.

*INDIAN CRAFTS
K. Brandt
Grades 2-6. Illus. 32 pp. Troll Associates, 1985. $7.95; paper, $2.50.

*INDIAN CRAFTS
Janet and Alex D'Amato
Grades 1-4. Illus. Lion Press, $8.95.

INDIAN CRAFTS AND LORE
Ben Hunt
Western Publishing, $10.95; paper, $2.95.

INDIAN CRISIS: THE BACKGROUND
J.S. Hoyland
Reprint of 1943 edition. Ayer Co., $17.00.

INDIAN CULTURE AND EUROPEAN TRADE GOODS: THE ARCHAEOLOGY OF THE HISTORIC PERIOD IN THE WESTERN GREAT LAKES REGION
George I. Quimby
Reprint of 1966 edition. Greenwood Press, 1978. $22.50.

INDIAN DANCES OF NORTH AMERICA: THEIR IMPORTANCE TO INDIAN LIFE
Reginald and Gladys Laubin
Illus. University of Oklahoma Press, 1977. $29.95.

INDIAN DAYS OF LONG AGO
Edward S. Curtis
Reprint. Illus. 221 pp. Ten Speed Press, $9.95; paper, $5.95.

INDIAN DESIGNS
David and Jean Villasenor
Shows quilt patterns, applique, needlepoint, stitchery, fabric painting, etc. Illus. 48 pp. Paper. Naturegraph, and American Indian Books, 1983. $4.95.

INDIAN DRINKING: NAVAJO PRACTICES AND ANGLO-AMERICAN THEORIES
Jerold E. Levy and Stephen J. Kunitz
Reprint of 1974 edition. Books on Demand, $67.30.

INDIAN EDUCATION
Jack Rudman
Three volumes. Elementary, Secondary and Guidance.
Paper. National Learning Corp., $10.00 each.

INDIAN EDUCATION ACT: INDIAN STUDENTS HAVE THE RIGHTS TO EXCELLENCE IN EDUCATION, 10th ANNUAL REPORT TO CONGRESS OF THE U.S., 1983
47 pp. Supt. of Documents, 1984. $2.25.

INDIAN EDUCATION AND CIVILIZATION
A. Fletcher, U.S. Bureau of Education
Reprint of 1888 edition. Kraus, $36.00.

INDIAN, ESKIMO, ALEUT OWNED AND OPERATED ARTS BUSINESSES SOURCE DIRECTORY
Indian Arts and Crafts Board.

INDIAN AND ESKIMO ARTIFACTS OF NORTH AMERICA
Reginald P. Bolton
Crown Publishers, 1981. $8.95.

INDIAN AND ESKIMO BASKETRY: A KEY TO IDENTIFICATION
M. Wallace Ney
Illus. 144 pp. Paper. American Indian Books, $5.00.

INDIAN EXODUS: TEXAS INDIAN AFFAIRS
Kenneth Neighbors
Eakin Publications, 1972. $6.95.

INDIAN FAMILIES OF THE NORTHWEST COAST: THE IMPACT OF CHANGE
Claudia Lewis
University of Chicago Press, 1970. $12.00.

*INDIAN FESTIVALS
Keith Brandt
Grades 2-6. Illus. 32 pp. Troll Associates, 1985. $8.00; paper, $2.50.

*INDIAN FESTIVALS
Paul Showers
Grades K-3. Illus. Paper. T.Y. Crowell, 1969.
$6.95.

INDIAN FIGHTS AND FIGHTERS
Cyrus Brady
Illus. 495 pp. University of Nebraska Press,
1971. $29.50; paper, $8.95.

INDIAN FISHING: EARLY METHODS
ON THE NORTHWEST COAST
Hilary Stewart
University of Washington Press, 1977. $19.95.

*INDIAN FOE, INDIAN FRIEND
Jules Archer
Grades 7-12. Illus. Macmillan, 1970. $4.95.

*INDIAN FOLK TALES
FROM COAST TO COAST
Jessie Marsh
Grades 3-6. Illus. Council for Indian Education,
1978. $1.95.

INDIAN AND FREE: A CONTEM-
PORARY PORTRAIT OF LIFE ON
A CHIPPEWA RESERVATION
Charles Brill
Illus. 140 pp. University of Minnesota Press,
1974. $12.95.

THE INDIAN FRONTIER OF THE
AMERICAN WEST, 1846-1890
Robert M. Utley
Illus. 320 pp. University of New Mexico Press,
1984. $19.95; paper, $10.95.

*INDIAN GAMES AND CRAFTS
Robert Hofsinde
Grades 5-9. Illus. William Morrow, 1957. $7.00.

INDIAN GAMES AND DANCES
WITH NATIVE SONGS
Alice C. Fletcher
Reprint of 1915 edition. AMS Press, $14.50.

INDIAN GEOGRAPHIC NAMES
OF WASHINGTON
Edmund Meany
20 pp. Paper. Shorey, $3.95.

INDIAN GIVER
Peter Toth
Third Edition. Illus. 236 pp. Tribal Press, 1983.
$11.95.

*INDIAN HARVESTS
William Grimm
Grades 5-12. Illus. 128 pp. McGraw-Hill, 1977.
$7.95.

INDIAN HEALING: SHAMANISM
CEREMONIALISM IN THE
PACIFIC NORTHWEST TODAY

Wolfgang G. Jilek
Revised edition. 184 pp. Paper. Universe Books,
1981. $7.95.

INDIAN HEALTH TRENDS
AND SERVICES
Presents current and trend information about
the demographic characteristics and health
status of Indians and Alaska Natives. Illus.
89 pp. Supt. of Documents, 1978. $5.50.

INDIAN HERBS
Raymond Stark; Margaret Campbell, Editor
Illus. 50 pp. Paper. Hancock House, 1984. $4.95.

INDIAN HERITAGE, INDIAN PRIDE:
STORIES THAT TOUCHED MY LIFE
Jimalee Burton
Illus. 160 pp. Paper. University of Oklahoma
Press, 1974. $14.95.

THE INDIAN HERITAGE
OF AMERICANS
John Frank Phillips
The tools of the American Indians are examined;
some achievements of the American Indians. 54
pp. Paper. American Indian Books, $2.95.

*THE INDIAN AND HIS HORSE
Robert Hofsinde
Grades 3-7. Illus. Paper. William Morrow, 1960.
$7.00.

INDIAN AND HIS PROBLEM
Francis E. Leupp
Reprint of 1910 edition. Johnson Reprint, $24.00;
Ayer Co., $24.50.

THE INDIAN HISTORY
OF THE MODOC WAR
Jeff C. Riddle
Illus. 292 pp. Urion Press, 1975. $10.95; paper,
$6.95. Pine Cone, $10.00.

*INDIAN HOMES
Keith Brandt
Grades 2-6. Illus. 32 pp. Troll Associates, 1985.
$7.59; paper, $1.95.

THE INDIAN AND THE HORSE
Frank G. Roe
Reprint of 1955 edition. Illus. 465 pp. Univer-
sity of Oklahoma Press, $17.95; paper, $9.95.

THE INDIAN HOW BOOK
Arthur C. Parker
Reprint. Illus. 335 pp. Paper. Peter Smith,
$13.50. Paper. Dover, $4.95.

*INDIAN HUNTING
Robert Hofsinde
Grades 4-7. Illus. William Morrow, 1962. $6.00.

**INDIAN HUNTING, TRAPPING AND
FISHING RIGHTS IN THE PRAIRIE
PROVINCES OF CANADA**
Kent McNeil
64 pp. University of Saskatchewan, 1983. $20.00.

THE INDIAN IN AMERICA
Wilcomb Washburn
Illus. 330 pp. Harper & Row, 1975. $19.18; paper,
$6.95.

THE INDIAN IN AMERICAN HISTORY
William T. Hagan
Paper. American Historical Association, 1971.
$1.50.

INDIAN IN AMERICAN HISTORY
Francis P. Prucha
Paper. Holt, Rinehart & Winston, 1971. $7.95.

THE INDIAN IN AMERICAN LIFE
Gustavus E. Lindquist
Reprint of 1944 edition. AMS Press, $17.50.

**THE INDIAN IN HIS WIGWAM: OR,
CHARACTERISTICS OF THE
RED RACE IN AMERICA**
Henry R. Schoolcraft
Reprint of 1848 edition. AMS Press, $29.00.

**INDIAN AND JESUIT:
A 17th CENTURY ENCOUNTER**
James Moore
Loyola University Press, 1982. $12.95.

INDIAN JEWELRY MAKING
Oscar T. Branson
Illus. Paper. Wallace-Homestead, $7.95.

**INDIAN JEWELRY OF THE
PREHISTORIC SOUTHWEST**
Jerry D. Jacka and Nancy S. Hammack
Illus. Paper. University of Arizona Press, 1975.
$4.95.

**INDIAN JUSTICE: A
RESEARCH BIBLIOGRAPHY**
Vincent J. Webb
CPL Biblios, 1976. $6.50.

**INDIAN LAND CESSIONS
IN THE UNITED STATES**
Charles C. Royce
Reprint of 1900 edition. Illus. Ayer Co., $42.00.

**INDIAN LAND TENURE:
BIBLIOGRAPHICAL ESSAYS AND
A GUIDE TO THE LITERATURE**
Irme Sutton
Illus. Clearwater, 1975. $25.00; paper, $12.95.

INDIAN LEADERSHIP IN THE WEST
Walter Williams, Editor
Paper. Sunflower University Press, 1984. $9.95.

***INDIAN LEGACY: NATIVE
AMERICAN INFLUENCES ON
WORLD LIFE AND CULTURE**
Hermina Poatgieter
Grades 7-12. Illus. 192 pp. Julian Messner, 1981.
$10.79.

**INDIAN LEGACY OF
CHARLES BIRD KING**
Herman J. Viola
Illus. 152 pp. Smithsonian, 1976. $25.00.

INDIAN LEGENDS
Iron Eyes and Birdie Parker Cody
35 pp. Paper. American Indian Books, $4.50.

**INDIAN LEGENDS OF
THE NORTHERN ROCKIES**
Ella E. Clark
Reprint of 1966 edition. Illus. 416 pp. University
of Oklahoma Press, $17.95.

***INDIAN LEGENDS OF
THE PACIFIC NORTHWEST**
Ella E. Clark
Grades 9-12. Illus. Paper. University of California
Press, 1953. $5.95.

INDIAN LIFE AT THE OLD MISSIONS
Edith B. Webb
Reprint of 1952 edition. Illus. 385 pp. University
of Nebraska Press, $35.00.

**INDIAN LIFE ON THE NORTHWEST
COAST OF NORTH AMERICA AS SEEN
BY THE EARLY EXPLORERS AND FUR
TRADERS DURING THE LAST
DECADES OF THE 18th CENTURY**
Erna Gunther
Illus. 296 pp. Paper. University of Chicago Press,
1975. $6.95.

**INDIAN LIFE ON THE UPPER GREAT
LAKES: 11,000 BC TO 1800 AD**
George I. Quimby
Paper. University of Chicago Press, 1971. $4.95.

**INDIAN LIFE ON THE
UPPER MISSOURI**
John C. Ewers
Illus. University of Oklahoma Press, 1968. $15.95.

**INDIAN LIFE: TRANSFORMING
AN AMERICAN MYTH**
William Savage, Editor
Illus. 300 pp. University of Oklahoma Press,
1978. $16.95.

**INDIAN MISSIONS:
A CRITICAL BIBLIOGRAPHY**
James P. Rhonda and James Axtell
Paper. Indiana University Press, 1978. $4.95.

INDIAN MONEY AS A FACTOR IN NEW ENGLAND CIVILIZATION
W.B. Weeden
Reprint of 1884 edition. AMS Press, $11.50.
Paper. Johnson Reprint, $8.00.

*INDIAN MUSIC MAKERS
Robert Hofsinde
Grades 3-7. Illus. William Morrow, 1967. $7.00.

*INDIAN MUSIC AND MUSICAL INSTRUMENTS
George S. Fichter
Grades 5-10. David McKay Co., 1978. $7.95.

INDIAN MYTHS
Ellen Emerson
Gordon Press, $59.95.

*INDIAN MYTHS FROM THE SOUTHEST
Beatrice Levin
Grades 4-12. Council for Indian Education, 1974.
$1.95.

INDIAN NAMES FOR PLANTS AND ANIMALS AMONG CALIFORNIAN AND OTHER WESTERN NORTH AMERICAN TRIBES
C. Hart Merriam, Editor
Paper. Ballena Press, 1979. $12.95.

INDIAN NAMES IN CONNECTICUT
J. Hammond Trumbull
Facsimile of 1881 edition. 105 pp. Shoe String Press, $12.50.

INDIAN NAMES IN MICHIGAN
Virgil J. Vogel
Illus. University of Michigan Press, 1985.
$22.00; paper, $13.95.

THE INDIAN NATIONS OF AMERICA
P. Jacquin
Illus. Gordon Cremonesi, 1980. $14.95.
Atheneum Publishers, $14.95.

INDIAN NEW ENGLAND BEFORE THE MAYFLOWER
Howard S. Russell
Illus 300 pp. University Press of New England,
1980. $25.00; paper, $11.95.

INDIAN NULLIFICATION OF THE UNCONSTITUTIONAL LAWS OF MASSACHUSETTS, RELATIVE TO THE MARSHPEE TRIBE: OR, THE PRETENDED RIOT EXPLAINED
William Apes
Reprint of 1835 edition. E.M. Coleman, $17.50.

THE INDIAN OF WESTERN MONTANA: ECONOMY AND LAND USE
Carling Malouf
Clearwater Publishing, $28.00.

THE INDIAN OFFICE: GROWTH AND DEVELOPMENT OF AN AMERICAN INSTITUTION, 1865-1900
Paul Stuart
University Microfilms, 1980. $44.95.

INDIAN ORATORY: A COLLECTION OF FAMOUS SPEECHES BY NOTED INDIAN CHIEFTAINS
W.C. Vanderwerth
Reprint of 1971 edition. Illus. 291 pp. Paper.
University of Oklahoma Press, and American Indian
Books, $8.95.

INDIAN OUTBREAKS
Daniel Buck
Reprint of 1965 edition. Ross & Haines, $9.95.

*INDIAN PATRIOTS OF THE EASTERN WOODLANDS
Bennett Wayne, Editor
Grades 5-12. Illus. 168 pp. Paper. Garrard, 1976.
$7.00.

INDIAN PATRIOTS OF THE GREAT WEST
Bennett Wayne, Editor
Grades 5-12. Illus. 168 pp. Garrard, 1974. $8.88.

INDIAN PEACE MEDALS IN AMERICAN HISTORY
Francis P. Prucha
Illus. 200 pp. University of Nebraska Press,
1976. $15.00.

THE INDIAN PEOPLES OF EASTERN AMERICA: A DOCUMENTARY HISTORY OF THE SEXES
James Axtell, Editor
Illus. 256 pp. Paper. Oxford University Press,
1981. $9.95.

INDIAN PETROGLYPHS OF THE PACIFIC NORTHWEST
Beth and Ray Hill
Illus. 314 pp. University of Washington Press,
1975. $21.50.

*INDIAN PICTURE WRITING
Robert Hofsinde (Gray-Wolf)
Text and 248 pictures explain how to write the Indian way and provide a secret method of writing letters. Grades 3-7. Illus. 96 pp. William Morrow,
1959. $9.00.

INDIAN PLACE NAMES IN ALABAMA
William A. Read
Illus. 128 pp. University of Alabama Press, 1984.
$20.00; paper, $8.95.

INDIAN PLACE NAMES IN ILLINOIS
Virgil J. Vogel
Paper. Illinois State Historical Society, 1963.
$2.00.

INDIAN PLACE-NAMES IN NORTH AMERICA
N. Holmer, et al
Reprint. Two volumes. Paper. Kraus, $15.00/set.

INDIAN PLACE NAMES OF NEW ENGLAND
John C. Huden
408 pp. Paper. Museum of the American Indian, 1962. $7.50.

INDIAN PLACE—NAMES: THEIR ORIGIN, EVOLUTION AND MEANING, COLLECTED IN KANSAS FROM THE SIOUAN, ALGONQUIAN, SHOSHONEAN, CADDOAN, IROQUOIAN, AND OTHER TONGUES
John Rydjord
Illus. 380 pp. University of Oklahoma Press, 1981. $19.95.

INDIAN POINTS, VALUE AND IDENTIFICATION GUIDE
Illus. Wallace-Homestead, $2.95.

INDIAN POLICE AND JUDGES: EXPERIMENTS IN ACCULTURATION AND CONTROL
William T. Hagan
220 pp. University of Nebraska Press, 1980. $17.50; paper, $4.95.

INDIAN POLICY IN U.S. HISTORICAL ESSAYS
Francis P. Prucha
Illus. 272 pp. University of Nebraska Press, 1981. $19.95.

INDIAN POPULATION IN THE U.S. AND ALASKA, 1910, 1937
U.S. Bureau of the Census
Reprint of 1915 and 1937 editions. Kraus, $51.00 and $21.00 respectively.

INDIAN PORTRAITS OF THE PACIFIC NORTHWEST
George M. Cochran
Second edition. Illus. Paper. Binford & Mort, 1977. $2.50.

INDIAN POTTERY
Sharon West
Illus. Paper. Hancock House, 1984. $3.95.

INDIAN PREFERENCE - A GUIDE TO TRIBAL ACTION
Daniel S. Press
Council for Tribal Employment Rights, $28.00.

INDIAN PREFERENCE IN CONSTRUCTION CONTRACTING
Daniel S. Press
Council for Tribal Employment Rights, $28.00.

THE INDIAN PRIEST: PHILIP B. GORDON
Paula Delfeld
Franciscan Herald, 1977. $6.95.

INDIAN PROJECTILE POINT TYPES FROM VIRGINIA AND THE CAROLINAS
Rodney M. Peck
Illus. 45 pp. Paper. American Indian Books, $4.00.

INDIAN PUEBLO COLOR BOOK
O.T. Branson
32 pp. Paper. Treasure Chest, 1984. $1.95.

INDIAN RAWHIDE: AN AMERICAN FOLK ART
Mable Morrow
Illus. 240 pp. University of Oklahoma Press, 1975. $27.50; paper, $14.50.

INDIAN READING SERIES: STORIES AND LEGENDS OF THE NORTHWEST
See Supt. of Documents for titles and prices.

THE INDIAN RELIC COLLECTOR'S GUIDE
Moore
Illus. 36 pp. Paper. American Indian Books, $2.00.

INDIAN RELICS OF NORTHEAST ARKANSAS AND SOUTHEAST MISSOURI
James M. Dethrow
Shows flint, pottery, axes, celts, plummets, bead and shell artifacts. Illus. 151 pp. American Indian Books, $20.00.

INDIAN RELICS OF THE PACIFIC NORTHWEST
N.G. Seaman
Enlarged second edition. Illus. Paper. Binford & Mort, 1967. $12.50.

INDIAN REMOVAL: THE EMIGRATION OF FIVE CIVILIZED TRIBES OF INDIANS
Grant Foreman
Illus. 424 pp. University of Oklahoma Press, 1976. $19.95; paper, $10.95.

INDIAN RIGHTS ASSOCIATION, 1885-1901
Historical Society of Pennsylvania
Association's papers include records of its activities. Microfilm—26 rolls. Scholarly Resources, $800.00.

THE INDIAN RIGHTS ASSOCIATION: THE HERBERT WELSH YEARS, 1882-1904
William T. Hagan
301 pp. University of Arizona Press, 1985. $21.95.

INDIAN RIGHTS ASSOCIATION PAPERS: A GUIDE TO THE MICRO-FILM EDITION, 1864-1973
Jack T. Erickson, Editor
233 pp. Paper. Microfilming Corp., 1975. $50.00.

INDIAN RIGHTS MANUALS
A Manual for Protecting Indian Natural Resources, 151 pp., $25.00; *A Self-Help Manual for Indian Economic Development,* 300 pp., $35.00; *A Manual on Tribal Regulatory Systems,* 110 pp., $25.00; and *Handbook of Federal Indian Laws,* 130 pp., $15.00. Native American Rights Fund.

INDIAN RIGHTS TO THE SUBSOIL UNDER SPANISH AND MEXICAN LAW, 1387-1783
Marvin D. Bernstein
Clearwater Publishing, $34.00.

INDIAN ROCK ART OF THE SOUTHWEST
Polly Schaafsma
Illus. 379 pp. University of New Mexico Press, 1980. $40.00.

INDIAN ROCK PAINTINGS OF THE GREAT LAKES
S. Dewdney and K.E. Kidd
Revised edition. Illus. University of Toronto Press, 1967. $15.00.

INDIAN RUNNING
Peter Nabokov
Illus. 208 pp. Paper. Capra Press, 1981. $9.95.

*INDIAN SCOUT CRAFT AND LORE
C. Eastman
Grades 6-12. Illus. 190 pp. Paper. American Indian Books, $4.00.

INDIAN SELF-RULE: FIRST-HAND ACCOUNTS OF INDIAN-WHITE RELATIONS - ROOSEVELT TO REAGAN
Kenneth R. Philp
350 pp. Howe Brothers, 1985. $21.50; paper, $12.50.

INDIAN SHAKERS: A MESSIANIC CULT OF THE PACIFIC NORTHWEST
Homer Barnett
Illus. 383 pp. Paper. Southern Illinois University Press, 1972. $7.95.

INDIAN SIDE OF THE WHITMAN MASSACRE
T.E. Jessett
Reprint. 45 pp. Paper. Ye Galleon Press, $3.00.

THE INDIAN SIGN LANGUAGE
W.P. Clark

450 pp. University of Nebraska Press, 1982. $26.95; paper, $8.50.

*INDIAN SIGN LANGUAGE
Robert Hofsinde (Gray-Wolf)
Shows how to form more than 500 words in Indian sign language; 200 drawings. Grades 3-7. 96 pp. William Morrow, 1956. $10.88.

INDIAN SIGN LANGUAGE
W. Tompkins
Original title: *Universal Sign Language of the Plains Indians of North America.* Reprint of 1969 edition. Illus. Paper. Dover, $2.75.

INDIAN SILVER JEWELRY OF THE SOUTHWEST, 1868-1930
L. Frank and M.J. Holbrook
Illus. New York Graphic Society, 1979. $29.95.

INDIAN SILVER: NAVAJO AND PUEBLO JEWELERS
M. Bedinger
Paper. University of New Mexico Press, 1976 $9.95.

INDIAN SLAVERY IN COLONIAL TIMES WITHIN THE PRESENT LIMITS OF THE U.S.
A.W. Lauber
Reprint of 1913. AMS Press, $11.50.

INDIAN, SOLDIER AND SETTLER: EXPERIENCES IN THE STRUGGLE FOR THE AMERICAN WEST
Robert M. Utley
Illus. 86 pp. Paper. University of Washington Press, 1977. $3.95.

*INDIAN SONGS AND LEGENDS
Guy C. Earl
Grades 4-12. 80 pp. Arthur H. Clark, 1980. $10.00.

INDIAN STORIES AND LEGENDS OF THE STILLAGUAMISH, SAUKS, AND ALLIED TRIBES
Nels Bruseth
Upper Puget Sound Indian material. 35 pp. Paper. Ye Galleon Press, 1972. $3.95.

INDIAN STORIES FROM THE PUEBLOS: TALES OF NEW MEXICO AND ARIZONA
F.G. Applegate
Reprint of 1929 edition. Illus. 198 pp. Rio Grande, 1977. $10.00.

INDIAN STORY AND SONG FROM NORTH AMERICA
A. Fletcher
Reprint of 1900 edition. AMS Press, $9.50; Johnson Reprint, $16.00.

INDIAN STUDENTS AND GUIDANCE
J.F. Bryde
Paper. Houghton Mifflin, 1971. $2.50.

*INDIAN TALES
J. De Angulo
Grades 5-12. Illus. Paper. Hill & Wang, 1962.
$4.00.

**INDIAN TALES OF NORTH AMERICA:
AN ANTHOLOGY OF THE ADULT READER**
T.P. Coffin, Editor
45 tales for the general reader. 150 pp. Paper.
University of Texas Press, 1961. $6.95.

***INDIAN TALES OF
THE NORTHERN PLAINS**
Sally Old Coyote and Joy Yellow Tail Toineeta
Grades 2-5. Council for Indian Education, 1972.
$1.95.

***INDIAN TALK: HAND SIGNALS OF
THE NORTH AMERICAN INDIANS**
Iron Eyes Cody
Grades 1-12. Illus. 112 pp. Naturgraph, 1970.
$10.95; paper, $4.95.

THE INDIAN TESTIONY
Amiya Chakravarty
Paper. Pendle Hill, 1983. $5.00.

**INDIAN THOUGHTS:
THE CHILDREN OF GOD**
Norman H. Russell
38 pp. Paper. American Indian Studies Center,
1975. $2.00.

INDIAN THOUGHTS: I AM OLD
Norman Russell
San Marcos Press, $2.00.

**THE INDIAN TIPI: ITS HISTORY,
CONSTRUCTION AND USE**
Reginald and Gladys Laubin
Second edition. Illus. 288 pp. University of Okla-
homa Press, 1977. $21.95. Paper. Ballantine,
$2.95.

THE INDIAN TODAY
C. Eastman
Reprint of 1915 edition. AMS Press, $17.50.

INDIAN TRADE GOODS
Arthur Woodward
Trade goods used in exchange with Indians of the
Pacific Northwest, and the way natives adapted
these to their own use. Second edition. Illus.
40 pp. Paper. American Indian Books, and
Binford & Mort, $2.50.

INDIAN TRADE GUNS: 1625-1775
T.M. Hamilton
Illus. Paper. Museum of the Great Plains, 1968.
$4.00.

THE INDIAN TRADERS
Frank McNitt
393 pp. University of Oklahoma Press, 1972.
$16.95.

**INDIAN TRADERS ON THE MIDDLE
BORDER: THE HOUSE OF EWING,
1827-1854**
Robert A. Trennert, Jr.
Illus. 280 pp. University of Nebraska Press,
1981. $19.95.

**INDIAN TRADERS OF THE SOUTH-
WESTERN SPANISH BORDER LANDS:
PANTON AND FORBES CO. 1783-1847**
W.S. Coker and T.D. Watson
Illus. 450 pp. University Presses of Florida,
1985. $35.00.

INDIAN TREATIES, 1778-1883
C.J. Kappler, Editor
Contains a listing of every treaty and agreement
made between the U.S. and Native Americans.
Reprint of 1904 edition. Illus. Map. 1,100 pp.
Interland, $75.00.

**INDIAN TREATIES:
AMERICAN NIGHTMARE**
C. Herb Williams and Walt Neubrech
Illus. Outdoor Empire, 1977. $3.95; paper, $1.95.

**INDIAN TREATIES:
TWO CENTURIES OF DISHONOR**
R. Costo and J. Henry
A concise response to the continuing attack on
the Indian tribes. The Indian Historian Press,
$9.95.

**INDIAN TRIBAL COURTS IN THE
U.S.: A MODEL FOR CANADA?**
Bradford Morse
41 pp. University of Saskatchewan, 1980. $5.50.

**INDIAN TRIBES: A CONTINUING
QUEST FOR SURVIVAL, A REPORT**
Illus. 204 pp. Supt. of Documents, 1981. $7.50.

**INDIAN TRIBES IN SOUTHEASTERN
MICHIGAN AND NORTHERN OHIO:
A HISTORY**
Helen H. Tanner
55 pp. Clearwater Publishing, 1973. $21.00.

**INDIAN TRIBES OF
ALASKA AND CANADA**
J. Swanton
Facsimile of 1952 edition. 80 pp. Paper. Shorey,
$6.95.

*INDIAN TRIBES OF AMERICA
M. Gridley
Reprint of 1940 edition. Illus. Random House,
$4.95.

**INDIAN TRIBES OF THE LOWER
MISSISSIPPI VALLEY AND ADJACENT
COAST OF THE GULF OF MEXICO**
J. Swanton
Reprint of 1911 edition. Johnson Reprint, $33.00.

INDIAN TRIBES OF NORTH AMERICA
J. Swanton
Reprint of 1952 edition. Illus. 726 pp. Scholarly
Press, $89.00. Paper. Smithsonian, $35.00.

**INDIAN TRIBES OF NORTH AMERICA:
WITH BIOGRAPHICAL SKETCHES
AND ANECDOTES OF THE
PRINCIPAL CHIEFS**
McKenney and Hall
Three volumes. Scholarly Press, 1974.
$250.00/set.

INDIAN TRIBES OF THE NORTHWEST
Reg Ashwell
74 pp. Paper. Universe Books, 1977. $4.00.

**THE INDIAN TRIBES OF OHIO:
HISTORICALLY CONSIDERED,
A PRELIMINARY PAPER**
W.K. Moorehead
Reprint of 1899 edition. AMS Press, $18.50.

INDIAN TRIBES OF TEXAS
Illus. Texian, 1971. $15.95.

**INDIAN TRIBES OF
THE UPPER MISSOURI**
Edwin Denig
Facsimile of 1930 edition. Paper. Shorey, $16.00.

**INDIAN TRIBES OF WASHINGTON,
OREGON AND IDAHO**
John R. Swanton
Reprint. Ye Galleon Press, $6.00.

**INDIAN TRIBES OF
WASHINGTON TERRITORY**
George Gibbs
56 pp. Ye Galleon, 1978. $7.95; paper, $4.95.

**INDIAN UPRISING IN LOWER
CALIFORNIA, 1734-1737**
S. Taraval
Reprint of 1931 edition. AMS Press, $24.00.

**INDIAN VILLAGE SITE AND
CEMETARY NEAR MADISONVILLE, OH**
E.A. Hooten
Reprint of 1920 edition. Paper. Kraus, $20.00.

**INDIAN VILLAGES OF THE
ILLINOIS COUNTRY: HISTORIC
TRIBES. AND SUPPLEMENT**
Wayne C. Temple
Facsimile edition. Illus. 218 pp. Paper. Illinois State Museum, 1977. $5.00. Supplement,
4 pp. 39 maps. $5.00.

**INDIAN VILLAGES OF
SOUTHEAST ALASKA**
Herbert Krieger
Facsimile edition. 46 pp. Paper. Shorey, $4.95.

**INDIAN VOICES: THE
NATIVE AMERICAN TODAY**
Jeanette Henry, Editor
The Second Convocation of Indian Scholars,
1971, discussing the education, health and
medicine, communications, etc. of American
Indians. 250 pp. Paper. The Indian Historian
Press, 1974. $8.50.

INDIAN WAR OF 1864
E.F. Ware; Clyde Walton, Editor
Tells of the Indian war against the Cheyennes
and Sioux in the Dakotas, Coorado, Wyoming,
Kansas and Nebraska. Illus. Paper. University
of Nebraska Press, 1963. $4.95.

***INDIAN WARRIORS AND
THEIR WEAPONS**
Robert Hofsinde (Gray-Wolf)
Grades 3-6. Illus. 96 pp. William Morrow, 1965.
$9.00.

INDIAN WARS
Robert Utley and W. Washburn
Illus. 362 pp. Paper. Houghton Mifflin, 1985.
$8.95.

**INDIAN WARS IN NORTH CAROLINA,
1663-1763**
E. Lawrence Lee
Illus. Paper. North Carolina Office of Archives
and History, 1968. $2.00.

INDIAN WARS OF NEW ENGLAND
H.M. Sylvester; R.H. Kohn, Editor
Reprint of 1910 edition. Three volumes. AMS,
$106.00/set. Ayer Co., $121.50/set.

INDIAN WARS OF THE NORTHWEST
A.J. Bledsoe
Reprint of 1885 edition. Sullivan Books, $20.00.

**INDIAN WARS OF THE
PACIFIC NORTHWEST**
Ray Glassley
Second edition. Illus. 274 pp. Binford & Mort,
1972. $9.50.

INDIAN WARS OF PENNSYLVANIA
C. Hale Sipe
Reprint of 1929 edition. Illus. Ayer Co., $54.00.

INDIAN WARS OF THE WEST
Timothy Flint
Reprint of 1833 edition. Ayer Co., $20.00.

INDIAN WATER RIGHTS
Richard L. Foreman
233 pp. Paper. Interstate, 1980. $8.95.

**INDIAN WEAVING, KNITTING, AND
BASKETRY OF THE NORTHWEST COAST**
Elizabeth Hawkins
Illus. 32 pp. Paper. Hancock House, 1978. $3.00.

**INDIAN—WHITE RELATIONS IN
THE U.S.: A BIBLIOGRAPHY OF
WORKS PUBLISHED, 1975-1980**
Francis P. Prucha
180 pp. University of Nebraska Press, 1982.
$15.95; paper, $7.95.

**INDIAN—WHITE RELATIONSHIPS IN
NORTHERN CALIFORNIA, 1849-1920**
Norris Bleyhl
109 pp. Association of Northern California
Records, 1978. $12.00.

**INDIAN AND WHITE: SELF—IMAGE
AND INTERACTION IN A CANADIAN
PLAINS COMMUNITY**
Niels W. Braroe
Illus. Stanford University Press, 1975. $17.50;
paper, $5.95.

**INDIAN AND THE WHITEMAN
IN CONNECTICUT**
Chandler Whipple
Illus. 95 pp. Paper. The Berkshire Traveller,
1972. $3.50.

**THE INDIAN AND WHITEMAN IN
MASSACHUSETTS AND RHODE ISLAND**
Chandler Whipple
Illus. 156 pp. Paper. The Berkshire Traveller,
1973. $4.50.

**THE INDIAN AND WHITEMAN
IN NEW ENGLAND**
Chandler Whipple
Illus. The Berkshire Traveller, 1976. $12.00;
paper, $8.00.

INDIAN WOMEN CHIEFS
Carolyn T. Foreman
Reprint of 1954 edition. Zenger, $8.50.

*INDIANS
Teri Martini
Grades K-4. Illus. 48 pp. Childrens Press, 1982.
$10.60; paper, $3.95.

*THE INDIANS
Ben Capps
Grades 7 and up. Illus. Silver Burdette, 1973.
$17.27.

*INDIANS
Edwin Tunis
Revised 1959 edition. Grades 5-12. Illus.
T.Y. Crowell, $12.95.

**INDIANS, ANIMALS, AND THE
FUR TRADE: A CRITIQUE OF
KEEPERS OF THE GAME**
Shepard Krech, Editor
214 pp. University of Georgia Press, 1981. $14.00.

**INDIANS AND ARCHAEOLOGY
OF MISSOURI**
Carl H. and Eleanor F. Chapman
Revised edition. Illus. 168 pp. Paper. University
of Missouri Press, and American Indian Books,
1983. $9.95.

**INDIANS AND ARTIFACTS
OF THE SOUTHEAST**
Dr. Bert W. Bierer
Illus. 478 pp. Paper. American Indian Books,
$20.00.

THE INDIANS AND THEIR CAPTIVES
James Levermier and Henry Cohen, Editors
Greenwood Press, 1977. $29.95.

**INDIANS AS THE WESTERNER
SAW THEM**
Ralph Andrews
Encore edition. Superior, 1963. $9.95.

*INDIANS AT HOME
Robert Hofsinde (Gray-Wolf)
Grades 3-7. Illus. Paper. William Morrow, 1964.
$10.88.

INDIANS' BOOK
N. Curtis
Illus. Paper. Dover, 1968. $6.95.

**INDIANS AND BUREAUCRATS:
ADMINISTERING THE RESERVATION
POLICY DURING THE CIVIL WAR**
Edmund J. Danziger, Jr.
250 pp. University of Illinois Press, 1974. $12.50.

**INDIANS, BUREAUCRATS AND LAND:
THE DAWES ACT AND THE DECLINE
OF INDIAN FARMING**
Leonard A. Carlson
231 pp. Greenwood Press, 1981. $29.95.

**INDIANS: THE CAMERA REVEALS
THE REALITY OF NORTH AMERICAN
INDIAN LIFE: 1847-1929**
Joanna C. Scherer
Illus. Crown Publishers, 1974. $12.95.

INDIANS AND CRIMINAL JUSTICE
Laurence French, Editor
224 pp. Biblio Distribution and Allanheld, 1982.
$23.95.

*INDIANS, THE FIRST AMERICANS
Kathryn F. Ernst
Grades 2-4. Illus. Franklin Watts, 1979. $6.00.

INDIANS: GREAT PHOTOGRAPHS THAT REVEAL NORTH AMERICAN INDIAN LIFE, 1847-1929, FROM THE UNIQUE COLLECTIONS OF THE SMITHSONIAN INSTITUTION
J.C. Scherer and J.B. Walker
Over 140 photos view the customs, rituals, dress and daily tribal life of Native Americans. Illus. 190 pp. American Indian Books, and Publishers Central Bureau, $12.00.

THE INDIANS IN AMERICAN SOCIETY
Francis P. Prucha
University of California Press, 1985. $15.95.

INDIANS IN CALIFORNIA HISTORY
George H. Phillips, Jr.; Norris Hundley and John A. Schutz, Editors
Illus. 110 pp. Paper. Boyd & Fraser, 1981. $4.95.

*INDIANS IN CAREERS
A series of in-depth interviews with Indians in different careers. Grades 7-12. Illus. 67 pp. Daybreak Star Press, $6.00.

INDIANS IN MARYLAND AND DELA-WARE: A CRITICAL BIBLIOGRAPHY
Frank W. Porter
128 pp. Paper. Indiana University Press, 1979. $4.95.

INDIANS IN MINNESOTA
E. Ebbot; Judith Rosenblatt, Editor
University of Minnesota Press, 1985. $25.00; paper, $12.95.

THE INDIANS IN OKLAHOMA
Rennard Strickland
Illus. University of Oklahoma Press, 1980. $12.95; paper, $5.95.

INDIANS IN PENNSYLVANIA
Paul A. Wallace
Illus. 200 pp. Pennsylvania Historical and Museum
Commission, 1981. $8.95; paper, $5.00.

INDIANS IN 17th CENTURY VIRGINIA
Ben C. McCary
Reprint of 1957 edition. 93 pp. Paper. University Presses of Virginia, $2.95.

*INDIANS KNEW
Tillie S. Pine and Joseph Levine
Grades 1-4. Illus. Paper. McGraw-Hill, 1957. $7.95.

THE INDIANS' LAND TITLE IN CALIFORNIA: A CASE IN FEDERAL EQUITY, 1851-1942
Ruth C. Dyer
Paper. R & E Research Associates, 1975. $10.95.

INDIANS LAST FIGHT OR THE DULL KNIFE RAID
Dennis Collins
Reprint of 1915 edition. AMS Press, $25.00.

INDIANS OF THE AMERICAN SOUTHWEST
Bertha P. Dutton
336 pp. University of New Mexico Press, 1981. $17.50; paper, $8.95.

INDIANS OF ARIZONA: A CONTEMPORRY PERSPECTIVE
Thomas Weaver, Editor
Focuses on the Indian's role in society. Paper. University of Arizona Press, 1974. $4.95.

INDIANS OF CALIFORNIA: THE CHANGING IMAGE
James J. Rawls
Illus. 293 pp. University of Oklahoma Press, 1984. $19.95.

THE INDIANS OF CALIFORNIA: A CRITICAL BIBLIOGRAPHY
Robert F. Heizer
Paper. 80 pp. Indiana University Press, 1976. $4.95.

THE INDIANS OF CANADA
Diamond Jenness
Sixth Edition. Paper. University of Toronto Press, 1963. $13.50.

INDIANS OF CANADA: CULTURAL DYNAMICS
J. Price
Paper. Prentice-Hall, 1979. $8.95.

INDIANS OF CAPE FLATTERY
James G. Swan
Facsimile edition. 108 pp. Paper. Shorey, $8.95.

*INDIANS OF THE EASTERN WOODLANDS
Rae Bains
Grades 2-6. Illus. 32 pp. Troll Associates, 1985. $6.95; paper, $1.95.

*INDIANS OF THE EASTERN WOODLANDS
Sally Sheppard
Grades 5-12. Illus. 96 pp. Paper. Franklin Watts, 1975. $4.00.

INDIANS OF THE FORT BELKNAP RESERVATION, MONTANA: ANTHRO-POLOGICAL CONSIDERATIONS
Verne Ray
Clearwater Publishing, $36.00.

**INDIANS OF THE GREAT BASIN:
A CRITICAL BIBLIOGRAPHY**
Omer C. Stewart
152 pp. Paper. Indiana University Press, 1982.
$5.95.

THE INDIANS OF THE GREAT PLAINS
Norman Bancroft-Hunt and Foreman Werner
Illus. 128 pp. William Morrow, 1982. $25.00.

**THE INDIANS OF GREATER NEW YORK
AND THE LOWER HUDSON**
Clark Wissler
Reprint of 1909 edition. AMS Press, $24.50.

**INDIANS OF THE HIGH PLAINS:
FROM THE PREHISTORIC PERIOD
TO THE COMING OF EUROPEANS**
George E. Hyde
Illus. University of Oklahoma Press, 1976. $17.95;
paper, $8.95.

INDIANS OF IDAHO
Deward E. Walker
University Press of Idaho, 1978. $10.95.

**INDIANS OF ILLINOIS AND
INDIANA: ILLINOIS KICKAPOO
AND POTAWATOMI INDIANS**
Joseph Jablow; David A. Horr, Editor
Garland Publishing, 1974. $42.00.

**INDIANS OF ILLINOIS AND
NORTHEASTERN INDIANA**
Illus. Garland Publishing, $42.00.

**INDIANS OF THE
LAKE MEAD COUNTRY**
Maxon
Authoritative handbook, popularly written. Illus.
64 pp. Paper. Southwest Parks and Monuments,
50¢.

***INDIANS OF THE LONGHOUSE**
Sonia Bleeker; illus. by Althea Karr
Grades 3-6. Illus. 160 pp. William Morrow, 1950.
$10.00.

***THE INDIANS OF LOUISIANA**
Fred Kniffen
Traces the journey of the first Indians to arrive
in Louisiana; Indian legends and tales. Reprint
of 1945 edition. Grades 6-12. Illus. 110 pp.
Pelican, $12.50.

**INDIANS OF THE LOWER
HUDSON REGION: THE MUNSEE**
Julian Harris-Salomon
Illus. 95 pp. Rockland County Historical Society,
1983. $18.95; paper, $14.95.

**INDIANS OF THE LOWER SOUTH:
PAST AND PRESENT: PROCEEDINGS**
John K. Mahon, Editor

Paper. University of Western Florida and
Historic
Pensicola, 1974. $7.95.

**THE INDIANS OF MAINE AND
THE ATLANTIC PROVINCES:
A BIBLIOGRAPHIC GUIDE**
Roger B. Ray
Paper. Maine Historical Society, 1972. $5.00.

**INDIANS OF MANHATTAN ISLAND
AND VICINITY**
Alanson B. Skinner
Reprint of 1915 edition. AMS Press, $21.00.

**THE INDIANS OF NEW ENGLAND:
A CRITICAL BIBLIOGRAPHY**
Neal Salisbury
128 pp. Paper. Indiana University Press, 1982.
$4.95.

***THE INDIANS OF NEW JERSEY:
DICKON AMONG THE LENAPE**
M.R. Harrington
Grades 4-6. Illus. Paper. Rutgers University
Press, 1963. $7.95.

INDIANS OF NORTH AMERICA
Geoffrey Turner
Illus. 261 pp. Paper. Sterling Publishing, 1979.
$6.95.

***INDIANS OF NORTH AMERICA**
Daniel Jacobson
Grades 4-12. Illus. 96 pp. Franklin Watts, $8.90.

INDIANS OF NORTH AMERICA
Harold E. Driver
Second revised edition. Illus. University of
Chicago Press, 1969. $25.00; paper, $15.95.

**INDIANS OF NORTH AMERICA:
METHODS AND SOURCES FOR
LIBRARY RESEARCH**
Marilyn Haas
160 pp. Shoe String Press, 1984. $21.50.

**INDIANS OF NORTH AMERICA:
SURVEY OF TRIBES THAT
INHABIT THE CONTINENT**
Paula Franklin
Illus. David McKay, 1979. $9.95.

***INDIANS OF THE NORTH
AMERICAN PLAINS**
Virginia Luling
Grades 6 and up. 64 pp. Silver Burdette, $12.68.

**INDIANS OF THE
NORTH PACIFIC COAST**
Tom McFeat, Editor
286 pp. Paper. University of Washington Press,
1967. $7.95.

INDIANS OF NORTH AND SOUTH
AMERICA: BIBLIOGRAPHY BASED
ON THE COLLECTION AT THE
WILLARD E. YAGER LIBRARY -
MUSEUM, HARTWICK COLLEGE,
ONEONTA, N.Y.
Carolyn E. Wolf and Karen R. Folk
Scarecrow Press, 1977. $25.00.

INDIANS OF THE NORTHEAST:
A CRITICAL BIBLIOGRAPHY
Elisabeth Tooker
Paper. Indiana University Press, 1978. $4.95.

INDIANS OF NORTH-
EASTERN ILLINOIS
Illus. Garland Publishing, $42.00.

INDIANS OF NORTHERN INDIANA
AND SOUTHWESTERN MICHIGAN:
AN HISTORICAL REPORT ON
INDIAN USE AND OCCUPANCY
Donald J. Berthrong
Garland Publishing, 1974. $38.00.

INDIANS OF NORTHERN OHIO AND
SOUTHEASTERN MICHIGAN
Illus. Garland Publishing, $42.00.

INDIANS OF THE NORTHWEST COAST
Philip Drucker
Illus. Paper. Natural History Press, $4.95.

INDIANS OF THE NORTHWEST COAST
Pliny Goddard
Reprint of 1934 edition. Illus. 175 pp. Cooper
Square Publishers, $25.00.

INDIANS OF NORTHEST OHIO: AN
ETHNOHISTORICAL REPORT ON THE
WYANDOT, POTAWATOMI, OTTAWA
AND CHIPPEWA OF NORTHWEST OHIO
E. Wheeler-Voegelin; David A. Horr, Editor
Garland Publishing, 1974. $42.00.

INDIANS OF OHIO, INDIANA,
ILLINOIS, SOUTHERN MICHIGAN
AND SOUTHERN WISCONSIN:
FINDINGS OF FACT AND OPINION
David A. Horr, Editor
Three volumes. Garland Publishing, 1974. $99.00.

INDIANS OF OHIO AND
INDIANA PRIOR TO 1795
E. Wheeler-Voegelin and Helen H. Tanner
Two volumes. Illus. Garland Publishing, 1976.
$76.00 per set; $42.00 each.

INDIANS OF OHIO AND
WYANDOT COUNTY
John Vogel
Vantage Press, $4.95.

*INDIANS OF THE
PACIFIC NORTHWEST
Vine Deloria, Jr.
Grades 6-9. Doubleday, 1977. $7.95.

INDIANS OF THE
PACIFIC NORTHWEST
Ruth Underhill
Reprint of 1945 edition. AMS Press, $29.50.

INDIANS OF THE PACIFIC
NORTHWEST: A HISTORY
Robert H. Rubie and John A. Brown
Illus. 300 pp. University of Oklahoma Press,
1981. $28.95.

INDIANS OF PECOS PUEBLO
Ernest A. Hooton
Elliots Books, 1930. $200.00.

INDIANS OF THE
PIKE'S PEAK REGION
Irvin Howbert
An account of the Sand Creek massacre of 1864,
with material on the Ute Indians of the area
east of the Rockies. Reprint of 1914 edition.
Illus. Maps. 262 pp. Rio Grande Press, $12.50.

*INDIANS OF THE PLAINS
Rae Bains
Grades 2-6. Illus. 32 pp. Troll Associates, 1985.
$6.89; paper, $1.95.

INDIANS OF THE PLAINS
Robert H. Lowie
Reprint. 250 pp. University of Nebraska Press,
$19.50; paper, $7.95.

*INDIANS OF THE PLAINS
Sally Sheppard
Grades 5-12. Illus. 72 pp. Paper. Franklin Watts,
1976. $5.00.

*INDIANS OF THE PLAINS
Eugene Rachlis and John C. Ewers
Grades 5-12. Illus. 153 pp. American Heritage,
1960. $9.95.

THE INDIANS OF POINT OF PINES,
ARIZONA: A COMPARATIVE STUDY OF
THEIR PHYSICAL CHARACTERISTICS
Kenneth A. Bennett
Reprint of 1973 edition. Books on Demand,
$20.80. Paper. University of Arizona Press,
$4.95.

INDIANS OF THE PUGET SOUND
H. Haeberlin and E. Gunther
Reprint of 1930 edition. Illus. 84 pp. Paper.
University of Washington Press, $4.95.

THE INDIANS OF PUGET SOUND: THE NOTEBOOKS OF MYRON EELS
Myron Eels; George Castile, Editor
Illus. 440 pp. University of Washington Press, $40.00.

INDIANS OF THE RIO GRANDE VALLEY
A.F. Bandelier and E. Hewett
Reprint of 1937 edition. AMS Press, $33.00.
Reprint of 1939 edition. Illus. 274 pp.
Cooper Square Publishers, $17.50.

INDIANS OF THE SOUTH
Maxine Alexander, Editor
Illus. 120 pp. Paper. Institute of Southern Studies, 1985. $4.00.

INDIANS OF THE SOUTH CAROLINA LOW COUNTRY, 1562-1751
Gene Waddell
484 pp. Reprint Co., 1980. $30.00.

INDIANS OF THE SOUTHEASTERN U.S.
John Swanton
Reprint of 1943 edition. Illus. 943 pp.
Scholarly Press, $49.00; Greenwood Press, $53.25. Paper. Smithsonian, $25.00.

INDIANS OF SOUTHERN CALIFORNIA
Ruth Underhill
Reprint of 1941 edition. AMS Press, $15.00.

INDIANS OF SOUTHERN ILLINOIS
Irvin Peithman
Photocopy spiral edition. Illus. 172 pp.
Charles C. Thomas, 1964. $12.50.

INDIANS OF THE SOUTHWEST
George A. Dorsey
Reprint of 1903 edition. Illus. AMS Press, $19.50.

INDIANS OF THE SOUTHWEST
Pliny E. Goddard
Reprint of 1913 edition. 248 pp. Rio Grande Press, $15.00. Reprint of 1931 edition. 205 pp. Cooper Square Publishers, $25.00.

INDIANS OF THE SOUTHWEST: A CENTURY OF DEVELOPMENT UNDER THE U.S.
Edward E. Dale
Illus. Paper. University of Oklahoma Press, 1976. $9.95.

INDIANS OF THE SOUTHWEST: A CRITICAL BIBLIOGRAPHY
Henry Dobyns and Robert Euler
176 pp. Paper. Indiana University Press, 1981. $4.95.

THE INDIANS OF THE SUBARCTIC: A CRITICAL BIBLIOGRAPHY
June Helm
104 pp. Paper. Indiana Unviersity Press, 1976. $6.95.

INDIANS OF THE TERRACED HOUSES: THE PUEBLO INDIANS OF NEW MEXICO AND ARIZONA, 1902-1910
Charles F. Saunders
Reprint of 1912 edition. Illus. 430 pp.
Rio Grande Press, $15.00.

THE INDIANS OF TEXAS: FROM PREHISTORIC TO MODERN TIMES
W.W. Newcomb, Jr.
Illus. 422 pp. University of Texas Press, 1961. $20.00; paper, $9.95.

THE INDIANS OF TODAY
G.B. Grinnell
Reprint of 1911 edition. Illus. AMS Press, $34.50.

INDIANS OF THE UNITED STATES AND CANADA: A BIBLIOGRAPHY
Dwight L. Smith
Volume II. 345 pp. ABC-Clio, 1983. $64.00.

INDIANS OF THE U.S.: FOUR CENTURIES OF THEIR HISTORY AND CULTURE
Clark Wissler
Paper. Doubleday, 1966. $6.50.

INDIANS OF THE UPPER TEXAS COAST
Laurence Aten
338 pp. Academic Press, 1983. $39.50.

INDIANS OF THE URBAN NORTHWEST
Marian W. Smith
Reprint of 1949 edition. AMS Press, $37.50.

THE INDIANS OF WASHTENAW COUNTY, MICHIGAN
Wilbert B. Hinsdale
Reprint of 1927 edition. Paper. George Wahr, $1.95.

*INDIANS OF THE WEST
Rae Bains
Grades 2-6. Illus. 32 pp. Troll Associates, 1985. $7.59; paper, $1.95.

INDIANS OF THE WESTERN GREAT LAKES, 1615-1760
W. Vernon Kinietz
440 pp. Paper. University of Michigan Press, 1965. $9.95.

INDIANS OF WESTERN ILLINOIS AND SOUTHERN WISCONSIN
Illus. Garland Publishing, $42.00.

INDIANS OF THE WOODLANDS:
FROM PREHISTORIC TIMES TO 1725
George E. Hyde
Illus. Paper. University of Oklahoma Press, 1975.
$7.95.

INDIANS: OR, NARRATIVES OF
MASSACRES AND DEPREDATIONS ON
THE FRONTIER IN WAWASINK AND
ITS VICINITY DURING THE
AMERICAN REVOLUTION
Abraham G. Bevier
Reprint of 1846 edition. 90 pp. Paper. Library
Research Associates, $3.95.

*INDIANS ON THE MOVE
Robert Hofsinde (Gray-Wolf)
How the Indian traveled and their equipment they
devised for their trips. Grades 3-7. Illus.
Paper. William Morrow, 1970. $8.95.

INDIANS OVERSEAS IN BRITISH
TERRITORIES, 1834-1854
I.M. Cumpston
Reprint of 1953 edition. Dawson & Co., 1969.
$15.00.

INDIANS AND PIONEERS:
THE STORY OF THE AMERICAN
SOUTHWEST BEFORE 1830
Grant Foreman
Reprint of 1936 edition. Illus. University of
Oklahoma Press, $15.95; paper, $7.95.

THE INDIAN'S SIDE OF
THE INDIAN QUESTION
W. Barrows
Reprint of 1887 edition. Ayer Co., $13.00.

INDIANS AND TAXATION IN CANADA
Richard Bartlett
80 pp. University of Saskatchewan, 1980. $7.50.

*INDIANS WHO LIVED IN TEXAS
Betsy Warren
Reprint of 1970 edition. Grades 2-12. Illus.
48 pp. Hendrick-Long, $8.95.

INGALIK MATERIAL CULTURE
C. Osgood
Reprint of 1940 edition. Illus. Biblio. 500 pp.
Paper. HRAFP, $25.00.

INICA: SPIRIT WORLD OF
THE BERING SEA ESKIMOS
William Fitzhugh and Susan Kaplan
Illus. 296 pp. Smithsonian Institution Press,
1982. $35.00; paper, $15.00.

INLAND CHUMASH ARCHAEOLOGY:
AN ANNOTATED BIBLIOGRAPHY
Helen F. Wells and William C. Clemlow, Jr.
Illus. 35 pp. UCLA Archaeology, 1979. $3.00.

THE INLAND WHALE:
NINE STORIES RETOLD FROM
CALIFORNIA INDIAN LEGENDS
Theodora Kroeber
Illus. Paper. University of California Press,
1959. $3.95.

THE INSTITUTE OF AMERICAN
INDIAN ARTS, ALUMNI EXHIBITION
Intro. by Lloyd K. New
Illus. 72 pp. Paper. Amon Carter Museum, 1974.
$3.95.

INTERIOR SALISH AND EASTERN
WASHINGTON INDIANS
Four volumes. Illus. Garland Publishing,
$42.00 each.

INTERPRETING THE INDIAN:
20th CENTURY POETS AND
THE NATIVE AMERICAN
Michael Castro
224 pp. University of New Mexico Press, 1983.
$22.50.

INTERWOVEN EXPRESSIONS: WORKS
BY CONTEMPORARY ALASKA NATIVE
BASKET MAKERS ORGANIZED BY THE
INSTITUTE OF ALASKA NATIVE ARTS
AND UNIVERSITY OF ALASKA MUSEUM
Illus. Institute of Alaska Native Arts.
Catalog, $6.50; poster, $6.50.

INTERWOVEN: A PIONEER CHRONICLE
Sallie R. Matthews
Reprint of 1936 edition. Illus. 264 pp. Texas
A&M University Press, $14.95.

INTRODUCING WESTERN
INDIAN BASKETRY
Joan M. Jones
Illus. 64 pp. Paper. Universe Books, 1981.

INTRODUCTION TO AMERICAN
INDIAN ART
O. LaFarge, et al
Reprint of 1932 edition. Two volumes. Illus.
200 pp. Paper. Rio Grande Press, $20.00.

AN INTRODUCTION TO THE BUREAU
OF INDIAN AFFAIRS RECORDS
Jack Allen and Dennis Moristp
27 pp. Paper. American Indian Studies Center,
1971. $2.00.

AN INTRODUCTION TO THE ECOLOGY
OF EARLY HISTORIC COMMUNAL
BISON HUNTING AMONG THE
NORTHERN PLAINS INDIANS
George W. Arthur
Paper. National Museums of Canada, $3.95.

INTRODUCTION TO THE HANDBOOK
OF AMERICAN INDIAN LANGUAGES
Franz Boas; Preston Holder, Editor
Bound with *Indian Linguistic Families of
America North of Mexico*, by W.J. Powell.
Reprint. 221 pp. Paper. University of
Nebraska Press, $5.50.

INTRODUCTION TO THE HANDBOOK
OF AMERICAN INDIAN LANGUAGES
Franz Boas
Reprint of 1911 edition. Illus. 70 p. Paper.
Shorey, $7.95. Georgetown University Press,
$3.95.

INTRODUCTION TO HOPI KACHINAS
Museum of Northern Arizona Editors
Illus. Paper. Museum of Northern Arizona, 1977.
$1.50.

INTRODUCTION TO HOPI POTTERY
Francis H. Harlow
Illus. Paper. Museum of Northern Arizona, 1978.
$2.50.

INTRODUCTION TO THE
KICKAPOO LANGUAGE
Paul H. Voorhis
120 pp. Paper. Research Center for Language,
1974. $7.50.

INTRODUCTION TO NAVAHO
CHANT PRACTICE
C. Kluckhohn and L.C. Wyman
Reprint of 1940 edition. Paper. Kraus, $23.00.

INTRODUCTION TO THE STUDY OF
INDIAN LANGUAGES WITH WORDS,
PHRASES, AND SENTENCES
TO BE COLLECTED
J.W. Powell
Gordon Press, 1977. $69.95.

INTRODUCTION TO THE STUDY OF
MORTUARY CUSTOMS OF THE NORTH
AMERICAN INDIANS; WITH A
FURTHER CONTRIBUTION TO THE
STUDY OF THE MORTUARY CUSTOMS
OF NORTH AMERICAN INDIANS
H.C. Yarrow
Reprint of 1881 edition. AMS Press, $33.00.

INTRODUCTION TO THE STUDY
OF SOUTHWESTERN ARCHAEOLOGY
Alfred V. Kidder
Illus. Paper. Yale University Press, 1962.
$14.95.

INUIT ARTISTS PRINT WORKBOOK
Sandra B. Barz, Editor
Illus. 324 pp. Paper. Arts and Culture of the
North, 1981. $58.00.

THE INUIT LIFE AS IT WAS
Richard Harrington
150 portraits conveying the spirit of the culture
of the Inuit as the author observed it. Illus.
144 pp. Paper. Hurtig Publishers, 1981. $14.95.

INUIT: THE NORTH IN TRANSITION
Ulli Steltzer
Illus. 224 pp. University of Washington Press,
1983. $29.95. Paper. University of Chicago Press,
$22.50.

THE INUIT PRINT, L'ESTAMPE INUIT
Helga Goetz
The art of the Canadian Inuit. Illus. 267 pp.
University of Chicago Press, 1977. $24.95; paper,
$17.95.

THE INVASION WITHIN: THE
CONTEST OF CULTURES IN
COLONIAL NORTH AMERICA
James Axtell
Illus. 355 pp. Oxford University Press, 1985.
$29.95.

AN INVENTORY OF THE MISSION
INDIAN AGENCY RECORDS
James Young, Dennis Moristo
and G. David Tanenbaum
66 pp. Paper. American Indian Studies Center,
1976. $5.00.

AN INVENTORY OF THE PALA
INDIAN AGENCY RECORDS
James Young, Dennis Moristo
and G. David Tanenbaum
87 pp. Paper. American Indian Studies Center.
1976. $5.00.

IOWA TRIBE: APPRAISAL OF LANDS
IN KANSAS AND NEBRASKA, 1857
Richard B. Hall
110 pp. Clearwater Publishing, 1973. $38.00.

THE IOWAY INDIANS
Martha R. Blaine
Illus. University of Oklahoma Press, 1979.
$29.95.

IROQUOIAN COSMOLOGY
John H. Hewitt
Reprint of 1928 edition. AMS Press, $60.00.

IROQUOIS
Frank G. Speck
Second edition. Illus. 95 pp. Paper. Cranbrook
Institute, 1955. $4.50.

IROQUOIS BOOK OF RITES
Horatio Hale, Editor
Reprint of 1883 edition. AMS Press, $30.00.
University of Toronto Press, $25.00.

**IROQUOIS CEREMONIAL
OF MIDWINTER**
Elisabeth Tooker
Illus. Syracuse University Press, 1970. $18.95.

IROQUOIS CRAFTS
Carrie A. Lyford
Illus. 100 pp. Paper. R. Schneider Publishers,
1982. $5.95.

**THE IROQUOIS EAGLE DANCE, AN
OFFSHOOT OF THE CALUMET DANCE**
W.N. Fenton
Reprint of 1953 edition. Scholarly Press, $25.00.

IROQUOIS FOLK LORE
William M. Beauchamp
Reprint of 1922 edition. AMS Press, $21.00.

**IROQUOIS IN THE
AMERICAN REVOLUTION**
Barbara Graymont
Illus. Maps. 359 pp. Syracuse University Press,
1972. $17.95; paper, $9.95.

**THE IROQUOIS IN THE FOUNDING
OF THE AMERICAN INDIAN**
Donald A. Grinde, Jr.
The interplay and struggle between tribes of the
colonies. Illus. Paper. The Indian Historian
Press, $9.95.

IROQUOIS INDIANS
Donald Kent
Two volumes. Illus. Garland Publishing,
$51.00 each.

**IROQUOIS INDIANS: A DOCU-
MENTARY HISTORY - GUIDE TO
THE MICROFILM COLLECTION**
Mary Druke, Editor
718 pp. Research Publications, $180.00.

**IROQUOIS MUSIC AND DANCE:
CEREMONIAL ARTS OF TWO
SENECA LONGHOUSES**
Gertrude P. Kurath
Reprint of 1964 edition. Scholarly Press, $39.00.

THE IROQUOIS AND THE NEW DEAL
Laurence Hauptman
Illus. 288 pp. Syracuse University Press, 1984.
$20.00.

**THE IROQUOIS RESTORATION:
IROQUOIS DIPLOMACY ON THE
COLONIAL FRONTIER, 1701-1754**
Richard Aguila
Illus. 286 pp. Wayne State University Press,
1982. $18.95.

AN IROQUOIS SOURCEBOOK
Elisabeth Tooker, Editor
Reprint. Three volumes. Vol. 1, *Political and
Social Organization,* 400 pp., $50.00; *Calendric
Rituals,* 292 pp., $35.00; and *Medicine Society
Rituals,* 360 pp., $45.00. Garland Publishing.

***IROQUOIS STORIES: HEROES AND
HEROINES, MONSTERS AND MAGIC**
Retold by Joseph Bruchac
A collection of 30 tales told in the Longhouses
of the Iroquois Indians. Grades 3-7. Illus.
208 pp. The Crossing Press, $16.95.

**IROQUOIS - THEIR ART,
CULTURE AND CRAFTS**
Carie Lyford
Illus. 100 pp. Paper. Hancock House, 1985. $5.95.

THE IROQUOIS TRAIL
W. Beauchamp
Reprin tof 1892 edition. AMS Press, $15.00.

IROQUOIS WATERCRAFT
Eugene Van Voorhis
Illus. Paper. Freshwater Logistics, 1976. $2.00.

*ISHI
Kathleen A. Meyer
Grades 5-12. Illus. Dillon Press, 1980. $7.95.

**ISHI IN TWO WORLDS:
A BIOGRAPHY OF THE LAST
WILD INDIAN IN NORTH AMERICA**
T. Kroeber
Reprint of 1961 edition. Illus. University of
California Press, $14.95; paper, $5.95.

*ISHI, LAST OF HIS TRIBE
Theodora Kroeber
Grades 4-12. Illus. Parnassus, 1964. $7.95.
Paper. Bantam, $2.95.

ISHI MEANS MAN
Thomas Merton
Five essays about Native American Indians. Illus.
Paper. Unicorn, 1976. $5.00.

ISLETA PAINTINGS
E.C. Parsons
Reprint of 1962 edition. Scholarly Press, $59.00.

***ISSIWIN: BOXELDER AND
HIS SACRED LANCE**
Father Powell
Grades 3-12. Illus. Council for Indian Education,
1976. $2.00.

**ISSUES FOR THE FUTURE OF AMERICAN
INDIAN STUDIES**
Susan Guyette
American Indian Studies Center.

J

WILLIAM JACKSON, INDIAN SCOUT
James W. Schultz
Reprint of 1976 edition. 200 pp. Borgo Press,
$19.95.

***JAMES AT WORK**
Looks at reservation life through the eyes of
a Choctaw Indian boy. Grades Preschool-3. 14
14 pp. Choctaw Heritage Press, $2.75.

***MARY JAMISON: SENECA CAPTIVE**
Jeanne L. Gardner
Grades 5-7. Illus. Harcourt Brace, 1966. $6.50.

**JEDDITO 264: A BASKET-MAKER III
PUEBLO I SITE, NORTHEASTERN AZ**
H. Diafuku
Reprint of 1961 edition. Paper. Kraus, $13.00.

**JESUITS AND THE INDIAN WARS
OF THE NORTHWEST**
Robert I. Burns
Reprint of 1966 edition. Illus. 550 pp. University Press of Idaho, $10.95.

**JICARILLA APACHE AREA OF
NORTHEASTERN NEW MEXICO**
Donald C. Cutter
35 pp. Clearwater Publishing, 1974. $21.00.

**JICARILLA APACHE CLAIM AREA:
ENVIRONMENT, SETTLEMENT,
AND LAND USE**
B.L. Gordon, et al
364 pp. Clearwater Publishing, 1973. $103.50.

**JICARILLA APACHE IN NEW MEXICO
AND OKLAHOMA: ANTHROPOLOGICAL
REPORT, 1540-1898**
Charles C. DiPeso
430 pp. Clearwater Publishing, 1974. $115.00.

**JICARILLA APACHE INDIANS,
1848-1887**
Averam B. Bender
185 pp. Clearwater Publishing, 1974. $57.00.

**THE JICARILLA APACHE INDIANS,
A HISTORY, 1598-1888**
Alfred B. Thomas
152 pp. Clearwater Publishing, 1973. $32.00.

**JICARILLA-APACHE RESERVATION,
1887 and 1907: APPRAISAL**
105 pp. Clearwater Publishing, 1973. $36.00.

**JICARILLA APACHE TRIBAL LANDS
ACQUIRED BY THE U.S. ON
AUGUST 20, 1883: VALUATION**
Allan L. McMullen
160 pp. Clearwater Publishing, 1973. $50.00.

**JICARILLA APACHE TRIBE,
1883: APPRAISAL**
250 pp. Clearwater Publishing, 1973. $75.00.

**THE JICARILLA APACHE TRIBE:
A HISTORY, 1846-1870**
Veronica E. Tiller
Illus. 285 pp. University of Nebraska Press,
1983. $23.95.

**JICARILLA APACHE TRIBE OF THE
JICARILLA INDIAN RESERVATION IN
NEW MEXICO, 1849-1870: HISTOR-
ICAL AND DOCUMENTARY EVIDENCE**
Stanford Research Institute
108 pp. Clearwater Publishing, 1974. $37.50.

**THE JICARILLA APACHES:
A STUDY IN SURVIVAL**
Dolores Gunnerson
Illus. 348 pp. Northern Illinois University
Press, 1973. $17.50.

***PAULINE JOHNSON**
Lucie K. Hartley
Grades 5-12. Illus. Dillon Press, 1978. $7.95.

JOHNSON OF THE MOHAWKS
Arthur Pound and Richard E. Day
Reprint of 1930 edition. Ayer Co., $44.00.
Gordon Press, $59.95.

**EASTMAN JOHNSON'S
LAKE SUPERIOR INDIANS**
Patricia C. Johnston
Illus. 72 pp. Johnston Publishing, 1983. $12.95.

***PHILIP JOHNSTON AND THE
NAVAJO CODE TALKERS**
Syble Lagerquist
Grades 4-12. 31 pp. Paper. Council for Indian
Education, 1975. $2.45.

**THE JOSEPH BAND OF NEZ PERCE
INDIANS, 1805-1905**
Verne F. Ray
108 pp. Clearwater Publishing, 1973. $37.50.

***JOSEPH, CHIEF OF THE NEZ PERCE**
Dean Pollock
Grades 5-12. Illus. Binford & Mort, 1950. $5.95.

**JOURNAL OF THE ADVENTURES
OF MATTHEW BUNN**
Matthew Bunn
Facsimile of the 1962 edition. Paper. Newberry
Library Center, $1.75.

**A JOURNAL OF SIBLEY'S INDIAN
EXPOSITION DURING THE SUMMER
OF 1863 AND RECORD OF THE
TROOPS EMPLOYED**
Arthur M. Daniels
Reprint. Illus. 154 pp. Thueson, $30.00.

JOURNAL OF THE SOUTHERN INDIAN MISSION: DIARY OF THOMAS D. BROWN
Juanita Brooks, Editor
Paper. Utah State Univerity Press, 1972. $5.00.

JOURNAL OF A TWO MONTHS TOUR, WITH A VIEW TO PROMOTING RELIGION
C. Beatty
Reprint of 1768 edition. Scholarly Press, $25.00.

JOURNALS OF THE COMMISSIONER OF THE INDIAN TRADE, SEPT. 1718
W.L. McDowell, Jr.
Reprint of 1955 edition. University of South Carolina Press, $34.95.

JOURNALS OF JOSEPH N. NICOLLET: 1836-1837
Martha Bray; Andre Fertey, Translator
288 pp. Minnesota Historical Society, 1970. $16.50.

JOURNALS OF THE MILITARY EXPEDITION OF MAJOR GENERAL JOHN SULLIVAN AGAINST SIX NATIONS OF INDIANS IN 1779
J. Sullivan and F. Cook
Reprint of 1887 edition. Ayer Co. Publishers, $39.00.

JOURNEY FROM PRINCE OF WALES' FORT IN HUDSON'S BAY TO THE NORTHERN OCEAN, 1769-1772
Samuel Hearne
Reprint of 1795 edition. Illus. Maps. 437 pp. Charles E. Tuttle, $20.00; Greenwood Press, $32.75.

JOURNEY INTO WILDERNESS: AN ARMY SURGEON'S ACCOUNT OF LIFE IN CAMP AND FIELD DURING CREEK AND SEMINOLE WARS, 1836-1838
Jacob R. Motte
Illus. University Presses of Florida, 1953. $10.00.

JOURNEY TO ALASKA IN 1868
E. Teichmann
Reprint of 1925 edition. Argosy, $17.50. Delux edition, $50.00.

JUST BEFORE SUNSET
Lora L. Cline
Revised edition. Illus. 162 pp. Paper. J & L Enterprises, 1984. $11.95.

K

FRED KABOTIE: HOPI INDIAN ARTIST
Fred Kabotie and Bill Belknap
Illus. Northland Press, 1977. $35.00.

KACHINA CEREMONIES AND KACHINA DOLLS
Martina M. Jacobs
Illus. 72 pp. Paper. Carnegie Board, 1980. $3.00.

KACHINAS: A HOPI ARTIST'S DOCUMENTARY
Barton Wright
237 color plates. Illus. 272 pp. Northland Press, 1973. $45.00.

KACHINAS — PAONE
Ann O.W. Robinson
Photographs of kachina dolls plus reproductions of Peter Paone's paintings inspired by kachinas and Hopi mythology. The Encino Press, $7.50.

KACHINAS: A SELECTED BIBLIOGRAPHY
Marcia Muth
32 pp. Paper. Sunstone Press, 1984. $4.95.

KAHBE NAGWIWENS - THE MAN WHO LIVED IN THREE CENTURIES
Carl A. Zapffe
Illus. 100 pp. Paper. Historical Heart Associates, 1975. $5.95.

KALISPEL COUNTRY IN WASHINGTON, 1809-1903
W.N. Bischoff
80 pp. Clearwater Publishing, 1974. $32.50.

KALISPEL: HISTORICAL REPORT
Nancy O. Lurie
25 pp. Clearwater Publishing, 1974. $16.25.

PAUL KANE, THE COLUMBIA WANDERER: SKETCHES, PAINTINGS AND COMMENT, 1846-1847
Thomas Vaughn, Editor
Illus. 80 pp. Paper. Oregon Historical Society, 1971. $3.95.

KANSAS INDIANS: A HISTORY OF THE WIND PEOPLE, 1673-1873
William E. Unrau
Illus. University of Oklahoma Press, 1971. $15.95.

THE KANSAS INDIANS, PREHISTORIC AND HISTORIC HABITAT
Waldo R. Wedel
Clearwater Publishing, $20.00.

**THE KARANKARA INDIANS,
THE COAST PEOPLE OF TEXAS**
A.S. Gatschet
Reprint of 1891 edition. Paper. Kraus, $15.00.

THE KAROK LANGUAGE
W. Bright
Reprint of 1957 edition. Paper. Kraus, $60.00.

KARUK INDIAN MYTHS
J. Harrington
Reprint of 1932 edition. Scholarly Press, $19.00.

KASHAYA POMO PLANTS
Jennie Goodrich, Claudia Lawson,
and Vana P. Lawson
171 pp. Paper. American Indian Studies Center,
1981. $15.00.

**KASKA INDIANS: AN ETHNO-
GRAPHIC RECONSTRUCTION**
John J. Honigmann
163 pp. Paper. HRAFP, 1964. $15.00.

KATE CORY
Museum of Northern Arizona, 1978. $30.00.

**KAWAIISU MYTHOLOGY: AN ORAL
TRADITION OF SOUTH-CENTRAL
CALIFORNIA**
Maurice L. Zigmond
Illus. 252 pp. Paper. Ballena Press, 1980.
$12.95.

*KEEPER OF FIRE
James Magorian
Grades 4-12. Illus. 78 pp. Council for Indian
Education, 1984. $9.45; paper, $4.95.

**KEEPERS OF THE GAME:
INDIAN-ANIMAL RELATIONSHIP
OF THE FUR TRADE**
Calvin Martin
Illus. Paper. University of California Press,
1978. $6.95.

**KERESAN BRIDGE: A PROBLEM
IN PUEBLO ETHNOLOGY**
Robin Fox
Humanities Press, 1967. $20.75.

KERESAN TEXTS
Franz Boas
Reprint of 1928 edition. Two volumes.
AMS Press, $60.00 per set.

**A KEY INTO THE LANGUAGE
OF AMERICA**
Roger Williams
Includes the fourth edition, J. Hammond
Trumbull, editor, *The Narragansett Edition,*
(1866), and the fifth edition, edited
with an introduction.

The first book on the Indian language in English.
Reprint of 1936 edition. Two volumes in one.
230 pp. Gale, $31.00. Reprint of 1866 edition.
Russell & Russell, $18.00. Wayne State Univer-
sity Press. Reprint edition. 264 pp., $14.95.

**KICKAPOO, ILLINOIS AND
POTAWATOMI INDIANS: ANTHRO-
POLOGICAL REPORTS**
David B. Stout
122 pp. Clearwater Publishing, 1973. $40.00.

**KICKAPOO INDIANS IN ILLINOIS
AND MISSOURI: AN APPRAISAL**
D.R. Kaltreider, et al
Clearwater Publishing, 1976. $35.00.

**KICKAPOO LANDS IN KANSAS
1863: APPRAISAL**
William Murray
89 pp. Clearwater Publishing, 1973. $31.00.

KICKAPOO TALES
William Jones; trans. by T. Michelson
Reprint of 1915 edition. AMS Press, $24.00.

**KICKAPOO TRACTS IN MISSOURI
AND KANSAS, 1835: APPRAISAL**
William G. Murray
150 pp. Clearwater Publishing, 1973. $48.00.

**KICKAPOO TRIBAL LANDS IN
ILLINOIS AND INDIANA: AN
APPRAISAL AS OF 1820**
Harry R. and Everett W. Fenton
Clearwater Publishing, 1976. $225.00.

**KICKAPOOS: LORDS OF
THE MIDDLE BORDER**
Arrell M. Gibson
Illus. Paper. University of Oklahoma Press,
1976. $7.95.

KIIKAAPOU: THE KANSAS KICKAPOO
Donald D. Stull
Illus. 214 pp. Paper. Kickapoo Tribal Press,
1984. $12.00.

**KILIWA TEXTS: "WHEN I HAVE
DONNED MY CREST OF STARS"**
Mauricio J. Mixco
Illus. 250 pp. Paper. University of Utah Press,
1983. $25.00.

*KILLER-OF-DEATH
Betty Baker
Grades 7-12. Harper & Row, 1963. $9.00.

KILLING THE HIDDEN WATERS
Charles Bowden
Illus. 186 pp. University of Texas Press, 1977.
$9.95.

**KINAALADA: A NAVAJO
PUBERTY CEREMONY**
Shirley M. Begay and Verna Clinton-Tullie
Illus. 171 pp. Paper. Navajo Curriculum, 1983.
$15.00.

**KING OF THE DELAWARES:
TEEDYUSCUNG, 1700-1763**
Anthony Wallace
Facsimile of 1949 edition. Ayer Co., $19.00.

KINNAN MASSACRE
Boyd B. Stutler
Reprint of 1969 edition. McClain Printing, $3.50.

**KINO'S HISTORICAL MEMOIR
OF PRIMERIA ALTA**
Eusebio F. Kino
Reprint of 1919 edition. Two volumes in one.
AMS Press, $52.50.

**KINSMEN OF ANOTHER KIND:
DAKOTA—WHITE RELATIONS IN THE
UPPER MISSISSIPPI VALLEY,
1650-1862**
Gary C. Anderson
400 pp. University of Nebraska Press, 1984.
$25.00.

**KIOWA, COMANCHE AND APACHE
LANDS IN OKLAHOMA AND TEXAS:
VALUATION STUDY AS OF 1900**
Clearwater Publishing, 1976. $250.00.

KIOWA—COMANCHE INDIANS
David A. Horr, Editor
Two volumes. Garland Publishing, 1976. $76.00
per set; $42.00 each.

KIOWA TALES
Elsie Parsons
Reprint of 1929 edition. Kraus, $16.00.

***KIOWA VOICES: CEREMONIAL
DANCE, RITUAL AND SONG**
Maurice Boyd
Grades 3-12. Illus. 165 pp. Paper. Texas
Christian University Press, 1981. $29.95.

**KIOWA VOICES: MYTHS,
LEGENDS AND FOLKTALES**
Maurice Boyd
Volume II/ Illus. 356 pp. Texas Christian
Unviersity Press, 1983. $39.95.

THE KIOWAS
Mildred P. Mayhall
Revised 1972 edition. Illus. University of
Oklahoma Press, $17.95; paper, $9.95.

THE KIT CARSON CAMPAIGN
Clifford E. Trafzer
An account of the bloody events of Col. Kit
Carson's campaign against the Navajos in the
1860's. 277 pp. Paper. American Indian Books,
$14.95.

**KITCHI-GAMI: LIFE AMONG
THE LAKE SUPERIOR OJIBWAY**
Johann G. Kohl; trans. by L. Wraxall
Paper. Minnesota Historical Society, 1985.
$11.95.

**KIVA MURAL DECORATIONS AT
AWATOVI AND KAWAIKA-A**
W. Smith
Includes a survey of other wall paintings in the
Pueblo of the Southwest. Paper. Kraus, $34.00.

**KLAMATH CONCESSION:
TIMBER VALUES, JUNE 26, 1906**
Bruce Mason and Girard Co. et al
30 pp. Clearwater Publishing, 1973. $21.00.

KLAMATH DICTIONARY
M.A.R. Barker
Reprint of 1963 edition. Kraus, $68.00.

KLAMATH GRAMMAR
M.A.R. Barker
Reprint of 1964 edition. Kraus, $47.00.

**THE KLAMATH INDIANS AND THEIR
FOREST RESOURCES, OREGON,
1864-1961**
Verne F. Ray
Clearwater Publishing, $44.00.

**KLAMATH AND MODOC TRIBES AND
THE YAHOOSKIN BAND OF SNAKE
INDIANS: APPRAISALS**
Two volumes. Clearwater Publishing, 1973-4.

**THE KLAMATH RESERVATION,
APPRAISAL**
C. Marc Miller
190 pp. Clearwater Publishing, 1973. $57.00.

KLAMATH TEXTS
M.A.R. Barker
Reprint of 1963 edition. Kraus, $42.00.

**THE KLAMATH TRIBE AND FEDERAL
MANAGEMENT OF THE TRIBAL FOREST**
Norman A. Ross, Editor
Three volumes. Clearwater, 1976. $200.00 per set.

*KOMANTCIA
Harold Keith
Grades 7-12. Thomas Y. Crowell, 1965. $8.95.

**KOOTENAI TRIBE IN IDAHO:
APPRAISAL**
Henry T. Murray
220 pp. Clearwater Publishing, 1974. $64.50.

**KOOTENAI TRIBE LANDS IN
NORTHERN IDAHO AND MONTANA,
1859: APPRAISAL**
Homer Hoyt
73 pp. Clearwater Publishing, 1973. $27.00.

**KOPET: CHIEF JOSEPH'S LAST
YEARS, A DOCUMENTARY NARRATIVE**
Mick Gidley
Illus. 200 pp. University of Washington Press,
1981. Paper. Contemporary Books, $9.95.

KORCZAK: STORYTELLER IN STONE
The biography of Korczak Ziolkowski, the sculp-
ture of "Crazy Horse" from Thunderhead
Mountain. Crazy Horse Memorial Foundation.

THE KORYAK
V.I. Iokhel'Son
Reprint of 1908 edition. AMS Press, $82.50.

**KUMEYAAY POTTERY:
PADDLE-AND-ANVIL TECHNIQUES
OF SOUTHERN CALIFORNIA**
Gena R. Van Camp
Illus. Paper. Ballena Press, 1979. $7.95.

KUTENAI TALES
Boaz and Chamberlain
Reprint of 1918 edition. Scholarly Press, $32.00.

KWAKIUTL ART
Audrey Hawthorn
Illus. 292 pp. University of Washington Press,
1979. $35.00.

**KWAKIUTL CULTURE AS
REFLECTED IN MYTHOLOGY**
Franz Boas
Reprint of 1935 edition. Kraus, $21.00.

KWAKIUTL ETHNOGRAPHY
Franz Boas; Helen Codere, Editor
Illus. University of Chicago Press, 1967. $30.00.

**KWAKIUTL: INDIANS OF
BRITISH COLUMBIA**
R.P. Rohner and E. Rohner
Paper. Holt, Rinehart & Winston, 1970. $5.95.

KWAKIUTL LEGENDS
James Wallas and Pamela Whitaker
150 pp. Universe Books, 1981. $17.95.

**THE KWAKIUTL OF
VANCOUVER ISLAND**
Franz Boas
Reprint of 1909 edition. AMS Press, $58.00.

KWAKIUTL TALES
Franz Boas
Reprint of 1910 edition. AMS Press, $42.50.

KWAKIUTL TALES: NEW SERIES
Franz Boas
Reprint of 1943 edition. Two volumes. AMS
Press, $20.00 each.

KWAKIUTL TEXTS
Franz Boas and George Hunt
Reprint of 1905 edition. AMS Press, $49.50.
Second series reprint of 1906 edition. AMS Press,
$30.00.

A KWAKIUTL VILLAGE AND SCHOOL
Harry F. Wolcott
Reprint of 1967 edition. Illus. 132 pp.
Paper. Waveland Press, 1984. $6.95.

L

**LABOR LAW, UNIONS, AND
INDIAN SELF-DETERMINATION**
Daniel S. Press
Council for Tribal Employment Rights, $28.00.

THE LAGUNA CALENDAR
B.P. Dutton
Reprint of 1936 edition. Paper. Kraus, $14.00.

**LAGUNA LAND UTILIZATION:
AN ETHNOHISTORICAL REPORT**
Robert L. Rands
102 pp. Clearwater Publishing, 1973. $24.00.

**LAGUNA PUEBLO LAND CLAIMS,
1598-1935**
Myra E. Jenkins
195 pp. Clearwater Publishing, 1973. $58.50.

**LAGUNA PUEBLO LAND CLAIMS:
ANTHROPOLOGY**
Florence H. Ellis
106 pp. Clearwater Publishing, 1973. $36.00.

**LAGUNA PUEBLO LAND IN NEW
MEXICO: APPRAISAL REPORT,
1908-1936**
R.H. Sears
206 pp. Clearwater Publishing, 1973. $63.00.

**THE LAKE MOHONK CONFERENCE OF
FRIENDS OF THE INDIAN: GUIDE
TO THE ANNUAL REPORTS**
Larry E. Burgess and Laurence M. Hauptman
Illus. 200 pp. Clearwater Publishing, 1975.
$15.00.

LAKE OF THE SKY
George W. James
Reprint of 1928 edition. Charles T. Powner,
$7.95.

LAKOTA BELIEF AND RITUAL
James R. Walker
Illus. 329 pp. University of Nebraska Press,
1980. $21.50.

LAKOTA MYTH
James R. Walker; Elaine A. Jahner, Editor
428 pp. University of Nebraska Press, 1983.
$27.95; paper, $14.95.

LAKOTA SOCIETY
James R. Walker; Raymond J. DeMallie, Editor
Illus. 250 pp. University of Nebraska Press,
1982. $19.95.

**LAMBSHEAD BEFORE INTERWOVEN:
A TEXAS RANGE CHRONICLE**
Frances M. Holden
Illus. Maps. Biblio. 292 pp. Texas A&M
University Press, 1981. $15.95.

**LAME DEER: SEEKER OF VISIONS:
THE LIFE OF A SIOUX MEDICINE MAN**
John Fire/Lame Deer and Richard Erdoes
Chief Lame Deer, the chief medicine man for the
western Sioux tribes, tells of the modern Indian
experience. Paper. Simon & Schuster, 1972.
$3.95.

LAMP OF THE ESKIMO
Walter Hough
Illus. 88 pp. Paper. Shorey, $6.95.

THE LAND OF THE CLIFF—DWELLERS
Frederick H. Chapin
Reprint of 1892 edition. AMS Press, $25.00.

THE LAND OF THE DACOTAHS
Bruce Nelson
Illus. Paper. University of Nebraska Press, 1963.
$4.95.

**LAND OF THE NORTH UMPQUAS:
PEACEFUL INDIANS OF THE WEST**
Lavolla J. Bakken
Illus. 32 pp. Paper. Te-Cum-Tom, 1973. $1.95.

LAND OF THE POCO TIEMPO
Charles F. Lummis
Illus. Paper. University of Ne Mexico Press,
1981. $6.95.

LAND OF THE SPOTTED EAGLE
Luther Standing Bear
Illus. 275 pp. Paper. University of Nebraska
Press, 1978. $6.95.

**LAND RIGHTS OF INDIGENOUS
CANADIAN PEOPLES**
Brian Slattery
478 pp. University of Saskatchewan, 1979. $70.00.

**LANGUAGE AND ART IN
THE NAVAJO UNIVERSE**
Gary Witherspoon
Illus. 234 pp. University of Michigan Press,
1977. $16.00; paper, $8.95.

**LANGUAGE, CULTURE AND HISTORY:
ESSAYS BY MARY R. HAAS**
Mary R. Haas; Anwar S. Dil, Editor
398 pp. Stanford University Press, 1978. $27.50.

**LANGUAGE, CULTURE AND
PERSONALITY: ESSAYS IN
MEMORY OF EDWARD SAPIR**
Leslie Spier, et al
Reprint of 1941 edition. Illus. Paper. Unversity
of Utah Press, $9.00.

**LANGUAGE OF THE
PAPAGO OF ARIZONA**
John A. Hason
Paper. Books on Demand, $22.00.

**LANGUAGE RENEWAL AMONG
AMERICAN INDIAN TRIBES**
Robert N. St. Clair and William L. Leap
176 pp. Paper. National Clearinghouse Bilingual
Education, 1982. $9.95.

**LANGUAGES AND LORE OF
THE LONG ISLAND INDIANS**
Gaynell Levine and Nancy Bonvillain, Editors
Illus. 320 pp. Paper. Ginn Custom, 1981. $15.00.

**LANGUAGES OF NATIVE AMERICA:
HISTORICAL AND COMPARATIVE
ASSESSMENT**
Lyle Campbell and Marianne Mithun, Editors
1,040 pp. University of Texas Press, 1979. $35.00.

**LANGUAGES OF THE TRIBES OF
THE EXTREME NORTHWEST: ALASKA,
THE ALEUTIANS AND ADJACENT
TERRITORIES**
George Gibb, et al
Reprint of 1877 edition. Illus. Paper. Shorey,
$7.00.

THE LAST ALGONQUIN
Theodore L. Kazimiroff
224 pp. Paper. Dell, 1983. $3.95.

***THE LAST BUFFALO: CULTURAL
VIEWS OF THE SIOUX OR
DAKOTA NATION**
Willard Rosenfelt
Grades 4-12. Illus. T.S. Dennison, $6.95.

THE LAST CAPTIVE
A.C. Greene
Uncensored story of Herman Lehmann's capture
in 1870 by Comanche tribes, and his subsequent
readjustment to living in a white world. The
Encino Press, 1982. $15.00.

*THE LAST CHEROKEE WARRIORS
Phillip Steele
Grades 6-12. Second edition. Illus. 111 pp.
Pelican Publishing, 1978. $7.95; paper, $5.95.

THE LAST AND FIRST ESKIMOS
Robert Coles
Illus. New York Graphic Society, 1978. $24.95.

LAST DAYS OF THE SIOUX NATION
Robert M. Utley
Illus. Maps. Biblio. 314 pp. Yale University
Press, 1963. $25.00; paper, $8.95.

*THE LAST FIGHTING INDIANS
OF THE AMERICAN WEST
B.W. Bancroft; Marjorie Reeves, Editor
Grades 7-12. Illus. 96 pp. Paper. Longman, 1976.
$3.75

THE LAST FREE MAN: THE TRUE
STORY OF THE MASSACRE OF
SHOSHONE MIKE AND HIS BAND
OF INDIANS IN 1911
Dayton O. Hyde
Illus. 288 pp. Dial Press, 1973. $7.95.

THE LAST RUNNING
John Graves
Story about Plains Indians' way of life meeting
the 20th century. The Encino Press, $12.50.

LAST TREK OF THE INDIANS
Grant Foreman
Reprint of 1946 edition. Illus. Russell & Russell,
$26.00.

THE LAST WAR TRIAL: THE UTES
AND THE SETTLEMENT OF COLORADO
Robert Emmitt
Illus. 352 pp. University of Oklahoma Press,
1954. $14.95; paper, $5.95.

THE LATE PREHISTORIC SOUTHEAST:
A SOURCEBOOK
Chester B. DePratter, Editor
Reprint. 548 pp. Garland Publishing. $65.00.

AUGUSTINE LAURE, S.J.
MISSIONARY TO THE YAKIMAS
Victor Garrard
Ye Galleon Press, 1977. $7.50; paper, $4.95.

THE LAUREL CULTURE IN MINNESOTA
James B. Stoltman
Illus. 146 pp. Paper. Minnesota Historical
Society, 1973. $5.50.

LAW AND THE AMERICAN INDIAN:
READINGS, NOTES AND CASES
Monroe E. Price and Robert Clinton
Second edition. 800 pp. Michie Co., 1983. $28.50.

LAW AND GOVERNMENT OF
THE GRAND RIVER IROQUOIS
John A. Noon
Reprint of 1949 edition. Paper. Johnson Reprint,
$15.50.

LAW AND IDENTITY: LAWYERS,
NATIVE AMERICANS AND
LEGAL PRACTICE
Linda Medcalf
Paper. Books on Demand, 1978. $37.00.

A LAW OF BLOOD: THE PRIMITIVE
LAW OF THE CHEROKEE NATION
John Phillip Reid
New York Univerity Press, 1970. $12.50.

THE LAW ON INDIAN PREFERENCE
IN EMPLOYMENT AND CONTRACTING
Daniel S. Press
Council for Tribal Employment Rights, $33.00.

LAWS OF THE COLONIAL AND STATE
GOVERNMENTS RLATING TO INDIANS
AND INDIAN AFFAIRS, 1633-1831
Reprint of 1832 edition. E.M. Coleman, $27.50.

A LAYMAN'S GUIDE TO INDIAN
HUNTING, TRAPPING AND FISHING
RIGHTS IN MANITOBA
K. Young and A. Skarsgard
25 pp. University of Saskatchewan, 1983. $5.00.

LEAGUE OF THE HO-DE-NO-SAU-NEE
OR IROQUOIS
L.H. Morgan; Henry Lloyd, Editor/Annotator
Reprint of 1904 edition. Two volumes. Illus.
Burt Franklin, $49.50 per set.

LEAGUE OF THE IROQUOIS
L.H. Morgan
Reprint of 1904 edition. 477 pp. Peter Smith.
$15.25. Paper. Citadel Press, $7.95.

LEGAL CONSCIENCE,
SELECTED PAPERS
Felix S. Cohen; Lucy K. Cohen, Editor
Reprint of 1960 edition. 505 pp. Shoe String
Press, $30.00.

LEGAL INFORMATION SERVICE
32 volumes on Canadian Indian legal affairs.
See University of Saskatchewan for titles and
prices.

LEGAL ISSUES IN
INDIAN JURISDICTION
63 pp. National Attorney's General, 1976.
$3.50.

LEGAL PROCESS AND THE
RESOLUTION OF INDIAN CLAIMS
Eric Golvin
Studies in Canadian aboriginal rights. 29 pp.
University of Saskatchewan, 1981. $6.50.

THE LEGAL STATUS OF THE INDIAN
Robert Weil
Reprint of 1888 edition. 76 pp. AMS Press,
$12.50.

**LEGAL STRUCTURES FOR INDIAN
BUSINESS DEVELOPMENT ON RESER-
VATIONS - A TRIBAL SOVEREIGNTY
APPROACH**
Daniel S. Press
Council for Tribal Employment Rights, $33.00.

LEGEND OF THE DOUBLE FACE WOMAN
Explains how the Dakota Sioux Indians
developed the skill of decorating with
porcupine quills. Poster, 24 x 20".
Supt. of Documents, 1982. $2.25.

LEGEND OF THE GHOSTWAY RITUAL
Berard Haile
Reprint of 1950 edition. AMS Press, $25.00.

**LEGEND OF THE PIPE AND THE
WHITE BUFFALO CALF WOMAN**
Includes a sketch and text explaining this
Indian legend. Poster, 24x20". Supt. of Docu-
ments, 1982. $2.25.

THE LEGENDARY ARTISTS OF TAOS
Mary C. Nelson
Illus. 176 pp. Watson-Guptill, 1980. $25.00.

**LEGENDS AND LORE OF THE
PAPAGO AND PIMA INDIANS**
Dean and Lucille Saxton
441 pp. Paper. University of Arizona Press, 1973.
$6.95.

*LEGENDS OF CHIEF BALD EAGLE
Harry B. Shows and Hap Gilliland
Grades 2-10. Paper. Council for Indian
Education, 1977. $1.95.

**LEGENDS OF THE DELAWARE
INDIANS AND PICTURE WRITINGS**
R.C. Adams
Reprint of 1905 edition. Scholarly Press, $30.00.

*LEGENDS OF THE GREAT CHIEFS
Emerson Matson
Grades 8-12. Illus. 144 pp. Paper. Storypole,
$5.95.

LEGENDS OF THE IROQUOIS
William W. Canfield
Reprint of 1902 edition. Kennikat Press, $12.00.

LEGENDS OF THE LAKOTA
James LaPointe; illus. by Louis Amiotte
Illus. 184 pp. The Indian Historian Press, 1975.
$11.00; paper, $6.00.

LEGENDS OF THE LONGHOUSE
J.J. Cornplanter
Reprint of 1938 edition. Ira J. Friedman, $12.50.

LEGENDS OF THE MICMACS
Silas Rand
Reprint of 1894 edition. Johnson Reprint, $42.00.

LEGENDS OF THE MIGHTY SIOUX
Federal Writers' Project, South Dakota
Reprint of 1941 edition. AMS Press, $15.00.

**LEGENDS, TRADITIONS AND LAWS OF
THE IROQUOIS: OR, SIX NATIONS,
HISTORY OF THE TUSCARORA INDIANS**
Elias Johnson
Reprint of 1881 edition. AMS Press, $24.50.

THE LEMHI: SACAJAWEA'S PEOPLE
Brigham Madsen
Illus. Paper. Caxton Printers, 1980. $4.95.

THE LENAPE AND THEIR LEGENDS
W. Olum; Daniel G. Brinton, Editor
Reprint of 1884 edition. Scholarly Press, $29.00.

LESSONS IN HOPI
Milo Kalectaca; Ronald W. Langacker, Editor
30 grammar lessons, ten exemplary dialogs, and
Hopi—English, English—Hopi lexicons. 234 pp.
Paper. University of Arizona Press, 1978. $11.95.

**LET MY PEOPLE KNOW: AMERICAN
INDIAN JOURNALISM, 1828-1978**
James E. and Sharon M. Murphy
300 pp. The Indian Historian Press and University of Oklahoma Press, 1979. $16.95.

*LET'S BE INDIANS
Peggy Parish
Grades 1-5. Illus. Paper. Harper & Row, 1962.
$8.00.

LET'S FIND OUT ABOUT INDIANS
Charles and Martha Shapp
Grades K-3. Illus. Paper. Franklin Watts, 1962.
$5.00.

***LET'S REMEMBER...
INDIANS OF TEXAS**
Betsy Warren
Grades 3-8. Illus. 32 pp. Paper. Hendrick-Long,
$4.50.

**LET'S TALK 'LIPAY AA:
AN INTRODUCTION TO THE
MESA GRANDE DIEGUEÑO LANGUAGE**
Ted Couro and Margaret Langdon
Illus. 262 pp. Paper. Malki Museum Press and
Ballena Press., 1975. $7.50.

LETTERS FROM FORT SILL
Marion T. Brown
Letters of a young woman from an outpost in
Indian territory. The Encino Press, $10.00.

**LETTERS AND NOTES ON THE
MANNERS, CUSTOMS AND CONDITIONS
OF THE NORTH AMERICAN INDIANS**
George Catlin
Two volumes. Illus. 264 pp. Paper. Dover, 1973.
$6.95 each.

**THE LETTERS OF JACOB BAEGERT,
1749-1761: JESUIT MISSIONARY
IN BAJA CALIFORNIA**
Doyce B. Nunis, Jr.
Illus 238 pp. Dawson's Book Shop, 1982. $36.00.

**THE LETTERS OF GEORGE CATLIN
AND HIS FAMILY: A CHRONICLE
OF THE AMERICAN WEST**
Marjorie C. Roehm, Editor
University of California Press, 1966. $32.50.

**LETTERS OF ELEAZAR
WHEELOCK'S INDIANS**
James D. McCallum, Editor
Reprint of 1932 edition. Illus. 327 pp. Paper.
University Press of New England, $5.00.

*LEWIS & CLARK
Francene Sabin
Grades 2-6. Illus. 32 pp. Troll Associates, 1985.
$7.59; paper, 1.95.

LEWIS & CLARK AMONG THE INDIANS
James P. Ronda
Illus. 325 pp. University of Nebraska Press,
1984. $24.95.

***THE LEWIS & CLARK EXPEDITION,
1804-1806**
Dan Lacy
Grades 7-adult. Illus. Maps. Biblio. 72 pp.
Franklin Watts, 1974. $6.00.

THE LEWIS & CLARK EXPEDITION
Patrick McGrath
Illus. 64 pp. Silver Burdette, 1985. $14.00.

**LEWIS & CLARK'S AMERICA -
VOYAGE OF DISCOVERY**
Seattle Art Museum
Two volumes. Paper. University of Washington
Press, $15.00.

LEXICAL RECONSTRUCTION
D. Dyen and D. Aberle
Illus. 484 pp. Cambridge University Press, 1974.
$59.50.

**LIBRARY OF ABORIGINAL
AMERICAN LITERATURE**
Daniel G. Brinton, Editor
Reprint of 1890 edition. Eight volumes. AMS
Press.

LIBRARY OF AMERICAN LINGUISTICS
John Shea, Editor
Reprint of 1860-1864 editions. 13 volumes. AMS
Press, $370.00 per set; $28.50 each.

**LICENSE FOR EMPIRE: COLONIALISM
BY TREATY IN EARLY AMERICA**
Dorothy V. Jones
University of Chicago Press, 1982. $25.00.

**LIETENANT ZAGASKIN'S TRAVELS
IN RUSSIAN AMERICA, 1842-1844:
THE FIRST ETHNOGRAPHIC AND
GEOGRAPHIC INVESTIGATIONS IN
THE YUKON AND KUSKOKWIM
VALLEYS OF ALASKA**
Henry N. Michael, Editor
Illus. University of Toronto Press, 1967. $22.50.

**LIFE AND ADVENTURES OF JAMES P.
BECKWOURTH, MOUNTAINEER, SCOUT
AND PIONEER, AND CHIEF OF THE
CROW NATION OF INDIANS**
J. Beckwourth; T.D. Bonner, Editor
Reprint of 1856 edition. 650 pp. Paper.
University of Nebraska Press, $10.95.

**LIFE AGAINST THE LAND: A SHORT
HISTORY OF THE PUEBLO INDIANS**
Mary Wood
Paper. Timberline Books, 1978. $1.00.

LIFE AMONG THE APACHES
John C. Cremony
322 pp. Paper. University of Nebraska Press,
1983. $6.00.

**LIFE AMONG THE CHOCTAW INDIANS
AND SKETCHES OF THE SOUTHWEST**
Henry C. Benson
Reprint of 1860 edition. Johnson Reprint, $15.50.

LIFE AMONG THE INDIANS
George Catlin
Reprint. Scholarly Press, $39.00.

**LIFE AMONG THE INDIANS: BEING
AN INTERESTING NARRATIVE OF THE
CAPTIVITY OF THE OATMAN GIRLS,
AMONG THE APACHE AND
MOHAVE INDIANS**
Royal Stratton
Reprint of 1857 edition. Garland, $42.00.

**LIFE AMONG THE MODOCS:
UNWRITTEN HISTORY**
Joaquin Miller
Reprint of 1873 edition. 440 pp. Paper. Urion
Press, 1982. $7.95.

**LIFE AMONG THE PAIUTES:
THEIR WRONGS AND CLAIMS**
Sarah Hopkins
Reprint of 1883 edition. Chalfant Press, 1971.
$12.95; paper, $8.95.

LIFE AMONG THE QALLUNAAT
Minnie Aodla Freeman
A young Inuit girl goes to Ottawa and finds the customs of the natives bizarre. Hurtig Publishers, $9.95.

THE LIFE AND ART OF JEROME TIGER: WAR TO PEACE, DEATH TO LIFE
Peggy Tiger and Molly Babcock
Illus. 350 pp. University of Oklahoma Press, 1980. $35.00.

LIFE AND JOURNALS OF KAH-KE-WA-QUO-NA
Peter Jones
Reprint of 1860 edition. AMS Press, $26.00.

LIFE IN CUSTER'S CAVALRY: DIARIES AND LETTERS OF ALBERT AND JENNIE BARNITZ, 1867-1868
Robert M. Utley, Editor
Illus. Yale University Press, 1977. $26.50.

LIFE IS WITH PEOPLE: HOUSEHOLD ORGANIZATION OF THE CONTEMPORARY PAIUTE INDIANS
Martha C. Knack
106 pp. Paper. Ballena Press, 1981. $6.95.

LIFE OF GEORGE BENT: WRITTEN FROM HIS LETTERS
George E. Hyde; Savoie Lottinville, Editor
Illus. 389 pp. Paper. University of Oklahoma Press, 1983. $14.95.

THE LIFE OF BLACKHAWK DICTATED BY HIMSELF
J.B. Patterson
Enlarged edition. Ye Galleon Press, 1975. $9.95.

LIFE OF JOSEPH BRANT (THAYENDANEGEA)
W.L. Stone
Includes the border wars of the American Revolution and sketches of Indian campaigns, 1783-1795. Reprint of 1838 edition. Two volumes. Kraus and Scholarly Press, $56.00/set.

LIFE OF TECUMSEH AND HIS BROTHER THE PROPHET: WITH AN HISTORICAL SKETCH OF THE SHAWANOE INDIANS
B. Drake
Reprint of 1841 edition. Ayer Co., $14.00.

LIFE OF TOM HORN, GOVERNMENT SCOUT AND INTERPRETER, WRITTEN BY HIMSELF, TOGETHER WITH HIS LETTERS AND STATEMENTS BY HIS FRIENDS: A VINDICATION
Tom Horn
Paper. University of Oklahoma Press, 1964. $4.95.

LIFE AND TIMES OF DAVID ZEISBERGER: THE WESTERN PIONEER AND APOSTLE OF THE INDIANS
Edmund De Schweinitz
Reprint of 1870 edition. Johnson Reprint, $42.50.

THE LILLOOET INDIANS
James A. Teit
Reprint of 1906 edition. AMS Press, $20.00.

LINCOLN AND THE INDIANS: CIVIL WAR POLICY AND POLITICS
David A. Nichols
256 pp. University of Missouri Press, 1978. $20.00.

*LINDA'S INDIAN HOME
Grades 3-7. Illus. Binford & Mort, 1969. $5.95.

LINGUISTIC CONVERGENCE: AN ETHNOGRAPHY OF SPEAKING AT FORT CHIPEWYAN
Ronald and Suzanne B. Scollon
Academic Press, 1979. $39.50.

LINGUISTIC MATERIAL FROM THE TRIBES OF SOUTHERN TEXAS AND NORTHEASTERN MEXICO
J. Swanton
Reprint of 1940 edition. Scholarly Press, $25.00.

LINGUISTIC STRUCTURES OF NATIVE AMERICA
H. Hoijer, et al; Cornelius Osgood, Editor
A series of papers on linguistics. Reprint of 1946 edition. Paper. Johnson Reprint, $29.00.

THE LIPAN APACHE AND MESCALERO APACHE TRIBES
Kenneth F. Neighbours
75 pp. Clearwater Publishing, 1973. $27.00.

THE LIPAN AND MESCALERO APACHE IN TEXAS
Morris E. Opler
165 pp. Clearwater, 1973. $51.00.

LITERARY ASPECTS OF NORTH AMERICAN MYTHOLOGY
Paul Radin
Norwood Editions, $15.00.

LITERARY VOYAGER OR MUZZENIEGUN
H.R. Schoolcraft; Philip P. Mason, Editor
Reprint of 1962 edition. Illus. 193 pp. Greenwood, $12.75.

LITERATURE BY AND ABOUT THE AMERICAN INDIAN: AN ANNOTATED BIBLIOGRAPHY
Anna L. Stensland, Compiler
Lists 775 books. Second edition. 382 pp. Paper. National Council of Teachers of English, 1979. $9.75; members, $7.50.

LITERATURE OF THE AMERICAN INDIAN
Thomas E. Sanders
Abridged edition. Paper. Macmillan.

LITTLE BIG HORN DIARY: CHRONICLE OF THE 1876 INDIAN WAR
James Willert
Second Edition. Illus. 520 pp. J. Willert, 1982. $60.00.

*LITTLE JOE: A HOPI INDIAN BOY LEARNS A HOPI INDIAN STORY
Tery Latterman
Kachinas in a Hopi Kiva is the setting for the Powamu ceremony. Grades 4-8. 32 pp. Pussywillow Publishing, 1985. $12.95.

*THE LITTLE PEOPLE
Flora Hathaway
Grades 2-9. Paper. Council for Indian Education, 1971. $1.95.

*LITTLE TURTLE
Maggi Cunningham
Grades 5-12. Illus. Dillon Press, 1978. $6.95.

LIVING ARCHITECTURE: INDIAN
Andreas Wolwahsen
Illus. Hennessey & Ingalls, 1969. $12.95.

LIVING THE SKY: THE COSMOS OF THE AMERICAN INDIAN
Ray A. Williamson
Illus. 300 pp. Houghton Miflin, 1984. $19.95.

THE LIVINGSTON INDIAN RECORDS, 1666-1723
Lawrence H. Leder, Editor
Reprint of 1956 edition. E.M. Coleman, $25.00.

LO, THE POOR INDIAN: A SAGA OF THE SUISUN INDIANS OF CALIFORNIA
Ethel M. Read
580 pp. Panorama West, 1980. $20.00; paper, $12.00.

*LODGE STORIES
Edward and M.P. Dolch
Tales of the Cherokee, the Natchez and the Seminole Indians. 176 pp. Grades 1-6. Garrard Publishing, 1957. $7.29.

LOGAN, THE LAST OF THE RACE OF SHIKELLEMUS, CHIEF OF THE CAYUGA NATION
Reprint of 1868 edition. McClain Printing, $5.00.

LOGS OF THE CONQUEST OF CANADA
W. Wood, Editor
Reprint of 1909 edition. Greenwood Press, $29.00.

LONG DISTANCE: THE TRUE STORY OF AN IMPOSTER
Donald B. Smith
Illus. 325 pp. Paper. University of Nebraska Press, 1983. $8.95.

LONG DEATH
Ralph Andrist
Ilus. Paper. Macmillan, 1969. $4.95.

LONG DIVISION: A TRIBAL HISTORY
Wendy Rose
Second Edition. Illus. Paper. Strawberry Press, 1981. $2.50.

THE LONG HOUSE OF THE IROQUOIS
Spencer Adams
Reprint of 1944 edition. Illus. AMS Press, $27.50.

LONG JOURNEY TO THE COUNTRY OF THE HURONS
G. Sagard-Theodat; George M. Wrong, Editor
Reprint of 1939 edition. Greenwood Press, $29.95.

LONG LANCE: THE TRUE STORY OF AN IMPOSTER
Donald B. Smith
Illus. 325 pp. Paper. University of Nebraska Press, 1983. $8.95.

*THE LONG SEARCH
Richard A. Boning
Grades 5-11. Illus. 48 pp. B. Loft, 1972. $7.50.

*LONG SHADOWS: INDIAN LEADERS STANDING IN THE PATH OF MANIFEST DESTINY 1600-1900
Jack Jackson
Grades 3-8. Illus. 128 pp. Paramount, 1985. $17.95.

THE LONG WALK: HISTORY OF THE NAVAJO WARS, 1846-1868
Lynn R. Bailey
Illus. 300 pp. Westernlore, $9.50.

LOOKING AT INDIAN ART OF THE NORTHWEST COAST
Hilary Stewart
Illus. 112 pp. Paper. University of Washington Press, 1979. $8.95.

LORD OF THE MOHAWKS: A BIOGRAPHY OF SIR WILLIAM JOHNSON
James T. Flexner
Revised edition. Arthur C. Little, 1979. $16.95.

LORE OF THE GREAT TURTLE: INDIAN LEGENDS OF MACKINAC RETOLD
Dirk Gringhuis
Illus. 96 pp. Paper. Mackinac Island State Park, 1970. $2.50.

**LOS ANGELES FROM THE
DAYS OF THE PUEBLO**
W.W. Robinson; Doyce B. Nunis, Jr., Editor
Paper. Chronicle Books, 1982. $7.95.

**LOS PRIMEROS POBLADORES:
HISPANIC AMERICANS OF
THE UTE FRONTIER**
Frances L. Swadesh
288 pp. University of Notre Dame Press, 1974.
$6.95.

LOST COPPER
Wendy Rose
Malki Museum Press, 1980. $8.95.

**LOST MINES OF THE
GREAT SOUTHWEST**
John D. Mitchell
Legends of the hidden treasures of the Indians
and Spaniards. Reprint of 1933 edition. Illus.
Maps. 202 pp. Rio Grande Press, $10.00.

**THE LOST UNIVERSE:
PAWNEE LIFE AND CULTURE**
Gene Weltfish
Illus. University of Nebraska Press, 1977.
$21.50; paper, $6.95.

**LOUIE NO ONE: A BIOGRAPHY
OF LOUIS ST. GERMAINE:
AMERICAN INDIAN**
Thomas Hollatz
Illus. 192 pp. Laranmark, 1984. $10.95; paper,
$5.95.

**LOVE-MAGIC AND BUTTERFLY PEOPLE:
THE SLIM CURLY VERSION OF THE
AJJEE AND MOTHWAY MYTHS**
Berard Haile
Reprint. Illus. 184 pp. Paper. University of
Nebraska Press and Museum of Northern
Arizona, $14.95.

**LOWER PEN D'OREILLE OR KALISPEL
INDIAN LANDS: NORTHEAST WASH-
INGTON, NORTHERN IDAHO AND
WESTERN MONTANA**
Harold C. Starkey and Roy C. Carlson
197 pp. Clearwater Publishing, 1973. $60.00.

**LOWRY RUIN IN SOUTHWESTERN
COLORADO—ARCHAEOLOGICAL WORK
IN THE ACKMAN-LOWRY AREA,
1936-1938**
P.S. Martin
Reprint of 1938 edition. Paper. Kraus, $66.00.

**LOWER UMPQUA TEXTS AND NOTES
ON THE KUSAN DIALECTS**
Leo J. Frachtenberg
Reprint of 1914 edition. AMS Press, $24.00.

***LUCY LEARNS TO WEAVE:
GATHERING PLANTS**
Virginia Hoffman
Grades 1-4. Illus. 46 pp. Paper. Navajo Curricu-
lum Center Press, 1974. $2.75.

THE LUMBEE PROBLEM
Karen Blu
Illus. Cambridge University Press, 1980. $34.50;
paper, $10.95.

**LUMMI INDIANS OF
NORTHWEST WASHINGTON**
Bernhard J. Stern
Reprint of 1934 edition. AMS Press, $22.00.

*LUSHOOTSEED
Vi Hilbert and Thom Hess
Grammars for teaching the Salish language.
Grades 6-12. 233 pp. Daybreak Star Press,
$7.00 each; $11.00 per set. $12.00 for tapes.

M

**MACKINAC ISLAND AND
SAULTE STE. MARIE**
Stanley D. Newton
Illus. Paper. Black Letter, 1976. $8.00.

MADAM DORIAN
Jerome Peltier
44 pp. Ye Galleon Press, $7.50; paper, $4.95.

**A MAGIC DWELLS: A POETIC
AND PSYCHOLOGICAL STUDY OF
THE NAVAHO EMERGENCE MYTH**
Sheila Moon
Paper. Wesleyan University Press, 1970. $6.95.

**MAGIC IMAGES: CONTEMPORARY
NATIVE AMERICAN ART**
Edwin Wade and Rennard Strickland
Illus. 125 pp. Paper. Southwestern Art Associa-
tion and University of Oklahoma Press, 1982.
$15.95.

MAIDU TEXTS AND DICTIONARY
W.F. Shipley
Reprint of 1963 edition. Paper. Kraus, $52.00.

**THE MAIN STALK: A SYNTHESIS
OF NAVAJO PHILOSOPHY**
John R. Farella
221 pp. University of Arizona Press, 1984.
$19.95.

THE MAKAH INDIANS
Elizabeth Colson
Reprint of 1953 edition. Illus. 308 pp. Greenwood,
21.00.

MAKAH INDIANS: ANTHROPOLOGICAL INVESTIGATION RELATIVE TO TRIBAL IDENTITY AND ABORIGINAL POSSESSION OF LANDS
H.C. Taylor, Jr.
61 pp. Clearwater Publishing, 1973. $23.00.

MAKAH INDIANS OF WESTERN WASHINGTON: A STUDY OF GROUP DISTRIBUTION, POLITICAL ORGANIZATION AND CONCEPTS OF LAND USE
Carroll L. Riley
Clearwater Publishing, 1976. $20.00.

THE MAKAH—QUILEUTE TRIBAL BOUNDARY
Verne F. Ray
85 pp. Clearwater Publishing, 1974. $33.00.

*THE MAMOOK BOOK
Students learn about past and present Northwest Coast Indian culture through a series of activities. *O Wakaga,* a companion book, teaching about Plains Indian cultures in particular about Lakota life. Grades 4-6. Illus. 40 pp. each. Daybreak Star Press, $6.00 each.

MAN IN NORTHEASTERN NORTH AMERICA
Frederick Johnson, Editor
Reprint of 1946 edition. AMS Press, $42.50.

MAN OF THE PLAINS: RECOLLECTIONS OF LUTHER NORTH, 1856-1882
Luther North; Donald Danker, Editor
Illus. 350 pp. University of Nebraska Press, 1961. $18.50.

MAN WHO KILLED THE DEER
Frank Waters
Reprint. 266 pp. Paper. Ohio University Press, $6.95.

THE MAN WHO MARRIED THE MOON AND OTHER PUEBLO INDIAN FOLK-STORIES
Charles Lummis
Reprint of 1894 edition. Illus. AMS Press, $20.00.

MAN'S KNIFE AMONG THE NORTH AMERICAN INDIANS: A STUDY IN THE COLLECTIONS OF THE U.S. NATIONAL MUSEUM
Otis T. Mason
24 pp. Amereon Ltd., $9.95. Paper. Shorey, $1.95.

MAN'S RISE TO CIVILIZATION: THE CULTURAL ASCENT OF THE INDIANS OF NORTH AMERICA
Peter Farb
Second revised edition. E.P. Dutton, 1978. $15.00. Paper. Bantam, $3.00.

MANDAN AND HIDATSA MUSIC
F. Densmore
Reprint of 1923 edition. Illus. 236 pp. Da Capo Press, $25.00.

MANDAN—HIDATSA MYTHS AND CEREMONIES
M.W. Beckwith, Editor
Reprint of 1938 edition. Kraus, $32.00.

MANDANS, A STUDY OF THEIR CULTURE, ARCHAEOLOGY AND LANGUAGE
George Will and H.J. Spinden
Reprint of 1906 edition. Illus. Paper. Kraus, $15.00.

RAY MANLEY'S COLLECTING SOUTHWESTERN INDIAN ARTS AND CRAFTS
Clara L. Tanner, et al
Third revised edition. Illus. Paper. Ray Manley, 1979. $5.00.

RAY MANLEY'S HOPI KACHINA
Clara L. Tanner
Illus. Paper. Ray Manley, 1980. $4.00.

RAY MANLEY'S INDIAN LANDS
Clara L. Tanner
Illus. Ray Manley, 1979. $10.00; paper, $6.00.

RAY MANLEY'S PORTRAITS AND TURQUOISE OF SOUTHWEST INDIANS
Clara L. Tanner
Ray Manley, 1975. $6.00; paper, $3.00.

MANNERS AND CUSTOMS OF SEVERAL INDIAN TRIBES LOCATED WEST OF THE MISSISSIPPI
John D. Hunter
Reprint of 1823 edition. Garland, $42.00.

A MANUAL OF NAVAHO GRAMMAR
Berard Haile
Reprint of 1926 edition. AMS Press, $26.00.

MANY—FORKED BRANCH
Ewan Clarkson
Illus. E.P. Dutton, 1980. $10.95.

MANY TRAILS: INDIANS OF THE LOWER HUDSON VALLEY
Catherine C. Brawer, Editor
Illus. 112 pp. Paper. Katonah Gallery, 1983. $12.50.

*MANY WINTERS
Nancy Winters
Grades 6-12. 80 pp. Doubleday, 1974. $7.95.

MAP OF NORTH AMERICAN INDIAN LANGUAGES
C.F. Voegelin and F.M. Voegelin
Revised edition. Univerity of Washington Press, 1967. $3.00.

A MAP OF VIRGINIA: THE PROCEED-INGS OF THE ENGLISH COLONIE IN VIRGINIA
John Smith
Reprint of 1612 edition. 164 pp. Walter J. Johnson, $18.50.

THE MARICOPA INDIAN WAR 1850-1851: DIARIES OF ROBERT ECCLESTON—THE CALIFORNIA GOLD RUSH, YOSEMITE AND THE HIGH SIERRA
C. Gregory Crampton, Editor
Reprint of 1957 edition. 175 pp. University of Utah Press, $15.00.

*MARK OF OUR MOCCASINS
Colleen Reece
Grades 5-12. Council for Indian Education, 1982. $6.95; paper, $2.95.

MARIA
Richard L. Spivey
Illus. Northland Press, 1979. $35.00.

*MARIA MARTINEZ
Mary C. Nelson
Biography of the woman who revived clasic Indian pottery of San Ildefonso Pueblo in the 20th century. Grades 5-9. Illus. 75 pp. Dillon Press, $7.95.

MARTYRS OF THE OBLONG AND LITTLE NINE
Defost Smith
Reprint of 1948 edition. Brown Book Co., $6.00.

THE MARU CULT OF POMO INDIANS: A CALIFORNIA GHOST DANCE SURVIVAL
Clement W. Meighan and Francis A. Riddele
134 pp. Southwest Museum, 1972. $12.50.

MARVELOUS COUNTRY
Samuel Cozzens
Reprint of 1967 edition. Ross & Haines, $12.50.

MARY AND I: FORTY YEARS WITH THE SIOUX
Stephen Riggs
Reprint. Ross & Haines, $15.00.

MARYLAND INDIANS YESTERDAY AND TODAY
Frank W. Porter, III
Illus. 32 pp. Paper. Maryland Historical Society, 1983. $4.95.

MARYLAND'S ATTITUDE IN THE STRUGGLE FOR CANADA
J. Black
Reprint. Paper. Johnson Reprint, $9.00.

MARXISM AND NATIVE AMERICANS
Ward Churchill, Editor
250 pp. South End Press, 1984. $20.00; paper, $7.50.

THE MASCOUTENS: AN ANTHROPOLOGICAL REPORT
David A. Barreis, et al
96 pp. Clearwater Publishing, 1973. $33.00.

MASCOUTENS OR PRAIRIE POTAWATOMI INDIANS: SOCIAL LIFE AND CEREMONIES
Alanson Skinner
Reprint of 1924 edition. Greenwood Press, $15.00.

MASINAIGANS: THE LITTLE BOOK
Sr. Bernard Coleman and Sr. Verona LaBud
Illus. 368 pp. St. Scholastica Priory, 1972. $8.00.

MASKED GODS: NAVAHO AND PUEBLO CEREMONIALISM
Frank Waters
Reprint of 1950 edition. 438 pp. Paper. Ohio University Press, $10.95.

MASKS, LABRETS AND CERTAIN ABORIGINAL CUSTOMS
William Dall
Facsimile of 1884 edition. 138 pp. Paper. Shorey, $6.50.

MASSACRE!
Frank Laumer
Illus. Paper. University Presses of Florida, 1968. $5.00.

MASSACRE AT FORT BULL: THE DELERY EXPEDITION AGAINST ONEIDA CARRY, 1756
Gilbert Hagerty
Illus. Mowbray, 1971. $8.00.

THE MASSACRE OF LT. GRATTAN AND HIS COMMAND BY INDIANS
Paul L. Hedren
Arthur H. Clark, 1983. $95.00.

MASSACRE: A SURVEY OF TODAY'S AMERICAN INDIAN
Robert Gessner
Reprint of 1931 edition. 418 pp. Da Capo Press, $45.00.

MASSACRE: THE TRAGEDY AT WHITE RIVER
Marshall Sprague
Illus. 365 pp. University of Nebraska Press, 1980. $25.95; paper, $6.95.

*MASSASOIT: FRIEND OF THE PILGRIMS
Virginia Voight

Grades 2-5. Illus. Paper. Garrard Publishing, 1971. $7.47.

MATERIAL ASPECTS OF POMO CULTURE
Samuel Barrett
Reprint of 1952 edition. AMS Press, $57.50.

**MATERIAL CULTURE OF
THE BLACKFOOT INDIANS**
Clark Wissler
Reprint of 1910 edition. AMS Press, $20.00.

**THE MATERIAL CULTURE
OF THE CROW INDIANS**
Robert H. Lowie
Reprint of 1922 edition. AMS Press, $12.50.

**MATERIAL CULTURE AND THE
STUDY OF AMERICAN LIFE**
Ian M. Quimby
Illus. W.W. Norton & Co., 1978. $12.95; paper,
$5.95.

**THOMAS MAYHEW, PATRIARCH
TO THE INDIANS, 1593-1682**
L.C. Hare
Reprint of 1932 edition. Illus. AMS Press, $20.00.

R. BROWNELL McGRAW
R. Brownell McGraw
Illus. Lowell Press, 1978. $25.00.

**THOMAS L. McKENNEY: ARCHITECT
OF AMERICA'S EARLY INDIAN
POLICY, 1816-1830**
Herman J. Viola
Illus. 365 pp. Ohio University Press, 1974.
$15.00; paper, $8.95.

**JOHN McMURTRY AND THE
AMERICAN INDIAN: A FRONTIERS-
MAN IN THE STRUGGLE FOR
THE OHIO VALLEY**
Richard K. McMurtry
Illus. Paper. Current Issues, 1980. $14.95.

**ME AND MINE: THE LIFE
OF HELEN SEKAQUAPTEWA**
Louise Udall
The story of a girl raised in the Hopi tradition
yet educated in the white man's schools. 262 pp.
Paper. University of Arizona Press, 1969. $7.50.

***ME RUN FAST GOOD: BIOGRAPHIES
OF TEWANIMA (HOPI), CARLOS
MONTEZUMA (APACHE) AND
JOHN HORSE (SEMINOLE)**
Beatrice Levin and Marjorie Vanderveld
Grades 4-12. 32 pp. Paper. Council for Indian
Education, 1983. $1.95.

**MEDICINAL USES OF PLANTS
BY INDIAN TRIBES OF NEVADA**
Percy Train, et al
Reprint of 1957 edition. Quarterman, $25.00.

**MEDICINE AMONG THE
AMERICAN INDIANS**
Eric Stone
Reprint of 1932 edition. Illus. AMS Press,
$18.00.

**MEDICINE AMONG THE AMERICAN
INDIANS: CIBA SYMPOSIA, 1939**
William Krogman, et al
Paper. Acoma Books, $4.95.

**MEDICINE CEREMONY OF THE
MENOMINI, IOWA, AND WAHPETON
DAKOTA: WITH NOTES OF THE
CEREMONY AMONG THE PONCA,
BUNGI, OJIBWA AND POTAWATOMI**
Alanson Skinner
Reprint of 1920 edition. AMS Press, $28.00.

**THE MEDICINE-MAN OF THE
AMERICAN INDIAN AND HIS
CULTURAL BACKGROUND**
W. Corlett
Reprint of 1935 edition. AMS Press, $35.00.

**THE MEDICINE—MAN: A SOCIO-
LOGICAL STUDY OF THE CHARACTER
AND EVOLUTION OF SHAMANISM**
J.L. Maddox
Reprint of 1923 edition. Gordon Press, $59.95.
Paper. AMS Press, $28.00.

THE MEDICINE MAN OF THE APACHE
John Bourke
Reprint of 1887 edition. Westernlore, $10.00.

**MEDICINE AND POLITICS AMONG
THE GRAND RIVER IROQUOIS: A
STUDY OF THE NON-CONSERVATIVES**
Sally Weaver
Illus. 182 pp. Paper. National Museums of
Canada, and University of Chicago Press,
1972. $7.95.

**MEDICINE TALK: A GUIDE TO
WALKING IN BALANCE AND
SURVIVING ON THE EARTH MOTHER**
Brad Steiger
216 pp. Paper. Doubleday, 1976. $3.95.

MEDICINE WOMAN
Lynn V. Andrews
Illus. 288 pp. Harper & Row, 1981. $12.95.

**MEDITATION WITH NATIVE
AMERICANS: LAKOTA SPIRITUALITY**
Paul Steinmetz
Illus. 144 pp. Paper. Bear & Co., 1984. $7.95.

**MEET CREE: A GUIDE TO
THE CREE LANGUAGE**
C.H. Wolfart and J.F. Carroll
120 pp. University of Nebraska Press, 1981.
$12.50.

*MEET THE NORTH AMERICAN INDIANS
Elizabeth Paine
Grades 2-6. Illus. Paper. Random House, 1965.
$3.95.

**MEMOIR OF INDIAN WARS AND
OTHER OCCURENCES BY THE LATE
COLONEL STUART OF GREENBRIER**
John Stuart; Charles Stuart, Editor
Reprint of 1833 edition. McClain Printing, $9.50.

**MEMOIRE JUSTIFICATIF OF THE
CHEVALIER MONTAULT
DE MONBERAUT:
INDIAN DIPLOMACY IN BRITISH
WEST FLORIDA, 1763-1765**
M.B. Howard, Jr. and Roberta Rea, Editors
University of Alabama Press, 1965. $12.95.

**MEMOIRS OF A CAPTIVITY AMONG
THE INDIANS OF NORTH AMERICA,
FROM CHILDHOOD TO THE AGE
OF NINETEEN**
John Hunter
Reprint of 1823 edition. Johnson Reprint, $28.00.

MEMOIRS OF LT. HENRY TIMBERLAKE
H. Timberlake
Reprint of 1927 edition. Ayer Co. Publishers,
$18.00.

**MEMOIRS OF THE REVEREND DAVID
BRAINARD: MISSIONARY TO THE
INDIANS ON THE BORDER OF
NEW YORK, NEW JERSEY
AND PENNSYLVANIA**
David Brainard, et al
Reprint of 1822 edition. Scholarly Press, $49.00.

MEMOIRS OF A WHITE CROW INDIAN
Thomas Leforge; Thomas Marquis, Narrator
380 pp. University of Nebraska Press, 1974.
$25.95; paper, $6.50.

MEMOIRS, OFFICIAL AND PERSONAL
Thomas L. McKenney; Herman J. Viola, Editor
Insight into Indian affairs by Thomas McKenney,
Director of Indian Affairs, 1816-1830. 340 pp.
Paper. University of Nebraska Press, 1973. $5.95.

**MEMORANDUM ON LEGISLATIVE
HISTORY, CONGRESSIONAL ACTS
PERTAINING TO INDIAN TRUST
FUNDS: TEMOAK BANDS AND
MESCALERO APACHE**
Charles A. Hobbs, et al
96 pp. Clearwater Publishing, 1973. $34.50.

MENOMINEE DRUMS: A HISTORY
Patricia K. Ouranda
Illus. 300 pp. University of Oklahoma Press,
1979. $19.95.

**MENOMINEE DRUMS: TRIBAL
TERMINATION AND RESTORATION,
1954-1974**
Nicholas C. Peroff
Illus. 304 pp. University of Oklahoma Press,
1982. $19.95.

MENOMINEE INDIANS: A HISTORY
Patricia K. Ourada
Illus. University of Oklahoma Press, 1979. $14.95.

MENOMINEE MUSIC
Francis Densmore
Reprint of 1932 edition. Illus. 286 pp. Scholarly
Press, $15.00. Da Capo Press, $19.50.

**MENOMINI INDIANS OF WISCONSIN:
A STUDY OF THREE CENTURIES OF
CULTURAL CONTACT AND CHANGES**
F.M. Keesing
Reprint of 1939 edition. Johnson Reprint, $32.00.

MENOMINI INDIANS
Walter J. Hoffman
Reprint of 1896 edition. Johnson Reprint, $46.00.

MENOMINI TEXTS
L. Bloonfield
Reprint of 1928 edition. AMS Press, $58.00.

**MENOMINI WOMEN
AND CULTURAL CHANGE**
L.S. Spindler
Reprint of 1962 edition. Paper. Kraus, $20.00.

THE MESCALERO APACHE, 1653-1874
Alfred B. Thomas
47 pp. Clearwater Publishing, 1973. $22.50.

**MESCALERO APACHE INDIANS IN NEW
MEXICO AND ARIZONA, 1846-1880**
A.B. Bender
238 pp. Clearwater Publishing, 1974. $69.00.

**MESCALERO APACHE SUBSISTENCE
PATTERNS AND SOCIO-POLITICAL
ORGANIZATION, NEW MEXICO,
1796-1875**
Harry W. Basehart
166 pp. Clearwater Publishing, 1974. $52.00.

THE MESCALERO APACHES
C.L. Sonnichsen
Illus. 300 pp. Paper. University of Oklahoma
Press, 1980. $9.95.

**MESSAGE OF AN INDIAN RELIC:
SEATTLE'S OWN TOTEM POLES**
J.P. Lloyd
Facsimile of 1909 edition. Illus. 29 pp. Paper.
Shorey, $1.95.

METAL WEAPONS, TOOLS AND ORNAMENTS OF THE TETON DAKOTA INDIANS
James A. Hanson
Illus. 118 pp. University of Nebraska Press, 1975. $16.50.

METALLIC ORNAMENTS OF THE NEW YORK INDIANS
W.M. Beauchamp
Reprint of 1930 edition. 160 pp. AMS Press, $16.00.

METATES AND MANOS
Frank W. Eddy
Illus. Paper. Museum of New Mexico Press, 1964. $1.00.

METHOD AND THEORY IN HISTORICAL ARCHAEOLOGY
Stanley South
Academic Press, 1977. $30.00.

METLAKATLA: MISSION TO TSIMSHIAN INDIANS
G.T. Davis
Reprint of 1904 edition. Illus. 128 pp. Paper. Shorey, $10.95.

MEXICAN MASKS
Donald Cordry
Illus. 36 pp. Paper. Amon Carter Museum, 1973. $2.00.

MEXICAN AND PUEBLO INDIANS IN NEW MEXICO: LAND OCCUPATION AND USE
Harold H. Dunham
Clearwater Publishing, $59.00.

MEXICAN KICKAPOO INDIANS
R. Ritzenthaler
Reprint of 1956 edition. Greenwood Press, $15.00.

MIAMI INDIANS
Bert Anson
Reprint of 1970 edition. Illus. Books on Demand, $90.80.

MIAMI INDIANS 1805 & 1809: APPRAISAL OF LANDS IN SOUTHERN INDIANA
Richard B. Hall
325 pp. Clearwater Publishing, 1973. $93.00.

MIAMI TRACT IN KANSAS, 1854: APPRAISAL
William G. Murray
107 pp. Clearwater Publishing, 1973. $36.00.

MIAMI TRIBE: APPRAISAL OF LANDS IN NORTH CENTRAL INDIANA
Homer Hoyt
294 pp. Clearwater Publishing, 1974. $82.50.

MIAMI, WEA AND EL-RIVER INDIANS OF SOUTHERN INDIANA
E. Wheeler-Voegelin; David Horr, Editor
Garland Publishing, 1974. $42.00.

MIAMI, WEA AND POTAWATOMI: HISTORICAL REPORT ON INDIAN USE AND OCCUPANCY OF AREAS IN NORTHERN INDIANA AND SOUTHWESTERN MICHIGAN
Donald Berthrong
330 pp. Clearwater Publishing, 1973. $94.50.

THE MIDDLE FIVE: INDIAN SCHOOLBOYS OF THE OMAHA TRIBES
Francis La Flesche
Illus. 152 pp. University of Nebraska Press, 1978. $14.50; paper, $4.50.

THE MIDDLE GROUND: SOCIAL CHANGE IN AN ARCTIC COMMUNITY, 1967-1971
Joel S. Savishinsky and Susan B. Frimmer
Illus. 60 pp. Paper. University of Chicago Press, 1973. $2.00.

MIGRATION LEGEND OF THE CREEK INDIANS
A.S. Gatschet
Reprint of 1884 edition. AMS Press, $30.00; Kraus, $34.00.

THE MILES EXPEDITION OF 1874-1875
Scout J.T. Marshall
A factual account of Miles' last large-scale campaign against the Southern Cheyenne, Comanche and Kiowa tribes. The Encino Press, $15.00.

THE MILITARY CONQUEST OF THE SOUTHERN PLAINS
William H. Leckie
Reprint of 1963 edition. Illus. Books on Demand, $56.10.

MILITARY EDGED WEAPONS OF THE SECOND SEMINOLE WAR: 1835-1842
Ron G. Hickox
Illus. 70 pp. Paper. Ron G. Hickox, 1984. $19.95.

MIMBRES PAINTED POTTERY
J.J. Brody
Illus. 253 pp. University of New Mexico Press, 1977. $40.00.

THE MIMBRES PEOPLE: ANCIENT PUEBLO PAINTERS OF THE AMERICAN SOUTHWEST
Steven A. LeBlanc
Illus. Thames Hudson, 1983. $29.95.

MINKAPEE
Anna Malakoff and Francis Powdrell
Illus. 88 pp. GWP, 1983. $11.95.

**MINNESOTA CHIPPEWA INDIANS,
1838: APPRAISAL OF ROYCE AREA
242 IN WISCONSIN AND MINNESOTA**
Walter R. Kuehnle
230 pp. Clearwater Publishing, 1973. $69.00.

**MINNESOTA CHIPPEWA TRIBE:
APPRAISAL OF LANDS IN
NORTHWESTERN MICHIGAN
AND NORTHERN WISCONSIN**
Three volumes. 557 pp. Clearwater Publishing,
1973. $155.00 per set.

**MINNESOTA CHIPPEWA TRIBE:
MINERAL APPRAISAL OF 1843**
Ernest Oberbilling
135 pp. Clearwater Publishing, 1973. $43.50.

**MINNESOTA CHIPPEWA TRIBE:
VALUATION OF CEDED LANDS
AS OF 1865 and 1867**
W.D. Davis
225 pp. Clearwater Publishing, 1973. $94.00.

**MINNESOTA'S BROWNS VALLEY MAN
AND ASSOCIATED BURIAL ARTIFACTS**
Albert E. Jenks
Reprint fo 1937 edition. Paper. Kraus, $15.00.

MINNETONKA STORY
Blanche N. Wilson
Reprint. Ross & Haines, $8.75.

**MINORITY ORGANIZATIONS:
A NATIONAL DIRECTORY**
Katherine W. Cole, Editor
Lists minority membership organizations or programs developed by other groups to serve minority group members. Includes over 100 Alaska Native-oriented and 1,500 American Indian-oriented organizations. Second edition. 814 pp. Garrett Park Press, $30.00.

**MINORITY WITHOUT A CHAMPION:
KANAKAS ON THE PACIFIC COAST,
1788-1850**
Janice K. Duncan
Illus. 24 pp. Paper. Oregon Historical Society,
1972. $1.00.

MIRACLE AT METLAKATLA
Margaret Poynter
Illus. Concordia Publishing House, 1978. $4.95;
paper. $2.95.

**MIRACLE HILL: THE
STORY OF A NAVAHO BOY**
Emerson Mitchell and T.D. Allen
230 pp. Paper. University of Oklahoma Press,
1967. $6.95.

MISSION AMONG THE BLACKFEET
Howard L. Harrod
Illus. University of Oklahoma Press, 1971. $10.95.

MISSION AT SAN Y SYDRO
Michael R. Conroy
Yellow Jacket Press, 1975. $12.95.

**MISSION OF SORROWS:
JESUIT GUEVAVE AND THE
PIMAS, 1691-1767**
John L. Kessell
Paper. Books on Demand, $60.00.

**MISSION SAN XAVIER DEL BAC:
A.PHOTOGRAPHIC ESSAY ON THE
DESERT PEOPLE AND THEIR CHURCH**
Bernard Fontana; Helga Teiwes, Photographer
Illus. 32 pp. Paper. University of Arizona Press,
1973. $3.50.

***MISSION TALES: STORIES OF THE
HISTORIC CALIFORNIA MISSIONS**
Helen M. Roberts
Grades 3-6. Seven volumes, Illus. Pacific Books,
1962. Set, text edition, $20.00.

**MISSIONARIES, MINERS, AND
INDIANS: SPANISH CONTACT WITH
THE YAQUI NATION OF NORTH-
EASTERN NEW SPAIN, 1533-1820**
Evelyn Hu-DeHart
160 pp. University of Arizona Press, 1981.
$19.95; paper, $9.95.

**MISSIONS AND PUEBLOS
OF THE OLD SOUTHWEST**
Earle R. Forrest
Reprint of 1929 edition. Illus. 398 pp.
Rio Grande Press, $15.00.

**MISSISSIPPI CHOCTAWS AT PLAY:
THE SERIOUS SIDE OF LEISURE**
Kendall Blanchard
248 pp. University of Illinois Press, 1981.
$15.95.

**THE MISSISSIPPI, PILAGER
AND WINNIBIGOSHISH BANDS OF
CHIPPEWA INDIANS: ANTHROPO-
LOGICAL REPORT ON THE INDIAN
OCCUPANCY OF ROYCE AREA 357
IN MINNESOTA**
Harold Hickerson
301 pp. Clearwater Publishing, 1974. $84.00.

**MISSISSIPPIAN STONE
IMAGES IN ILLINOIS**
Thomas E. Emerson
Illus. 50 pp. Paper. Univerity of Illinois
Archaeology, 1982.

*MISTA
Henry Tall Bull and Tom Weist
Grades 2-12. Paper. Council for Indian
Education. 1971. $1.95.

MIWOK MATERIAL CULTURE
S.A. Barrett and E.W. Gifford
Illus. 257 pp. Paper. Yosemite, $6.95.

THE MOBILE INDIANS
Jay Higginbotham
Paper. Rockwell Publications, 1966. $5.96.

**MOBILITY AND ADAPTATION: THE
ANASAZI OF BLACK MESA, ARIZONA**
Shirley Powell
304 pp. Southern Illinois University Press, 1983.
$25.00.

**MOCCASINS AND THEIR
RELATION TO ARCTIC FOOTWEAR**
G. Hatt
Reprint of 1916 edition. Paper. Kraus, $12.00.

**MOCCASINS ON PAVEMENT: THE
URBAN INDIAN EXPERIENCE,
A DENVER PORTRAIT**
Michael Taylor, et al
Illus. Paper. Denver Museum of Natural History,
1978. $2.50.

**THE MODAL PERSONALITY STRUC-
TURES OF THE TUSCARORA INDIANS**
A.F. Wallace
Reprint of 1952 edition. Scholarly Press, $19.00.

**MODERN BLACKFEET:
MONTANANS ON A RESERVATION**
Malcolm McFee
Illus. 134 pp. Paper. Waveland Press, 1984. $6.95.

**MODERN GROWTH OF THE TOTEM
POLE ON THE NORTHWEST COAST**
Marius Barbeau
Facsimile of 1939 edition. 16 pp. Paper. Shorey,
$1.00.

MODERN INDIAN PSYCHOLOGY
John F. Bryde
Paper. Dakota Press, 1971. $8.00.

**MODERN PRIMITIVE ARTS OF
MEXICO, GUATEMALA AND
THE SOUTHWEST**
C. Oglesby
Facsimile of 1939 edition. Ayer Co., $16.00.

**THE MODERN SIOUX: SOCIAL
SYSTEMS AND RESERVATION CULTURE**
Ethel Nurge, Editor
Illus. 350 pp. University of Nebraska Press,
1970. $24.95.

**MODERN TRANSFORMATIONS
OF MOENKOPI PUEBLO**
Shuichi Nagata
Illus. 350 pp. Paper. University of Illinois
Press, 1970. $10.95.

MODOCS AND THEIR WAR
Keith A. Murray
Reprint of 1959 edition. Illus. 358 pp. Paper.
University of Oklahoma Press, $8.95.

**MOGOLLON ARCHAEOLOGY:
PROCEEDINGS**
P. Beckett and K. Silverbird, Editors
The Mogollon Conference, 1980, Las Cruces,
N.M.
Illus. 386 pp. Paper. Acoma Books, 1982. $19.95.

**MOGOLLON CULTURE IN
THE FORESTDALE VALLEY,
EAST-CENTRAL ARIZONA**
Emil W. Haury
Reprint. 454 pp. University of Arizona Press,
$27.50.

**MOGOLLON CULTURE
PRIOR TO 1000 A.D.**
J.B. Wheat
Reprint of 1955 edition. Paper. Kraus, $23.00.

**MOHAVE ETHNOPSYCHIATRY AND
SUICIDE: THE PSYCHIATRIC KNOW-
LEDGE AND THE PSYCHIC DISTUR-
BANCES OF AN INDIAN TRIBE**
George Devereux
Reprint of 1961 edition. Scholarly Press, $59.00.

MOHAVE INDIANS
A. Kroeber; David A. Horr, Editor
Reprint. Map. 177 pp. Garland Publishing,
$42.00.

**MOHAVE INDIANS: APPRAISAL
OF LANDS, 1853, 1865**
Donald D. Myers and Frank R. Kleinman
175 pp. Clearwater Publishing, 1973. $54.00.

**THE MOHAVE TRIBE IN ARIZONA:
AN APPRAISAL OF LAND VALUES**
Mervin Christensen and R.G. Hill
Clearwater Publishing, 1976. $50.00.

**MOHAVE TRIBE OF INDIANS OF
ARIZONA, CALIFORNIA AND NEVADA:
AND THE MOHAVE INDIANS OF THE
COLORADO RIVER INDIAN TRIBES:
EVALUATION STUDY OF
MINERAL RESOURCES**
P.J. Shenon and Roy P. Full
78 pp. Clearwater Publishing, 1973. $28.50.

**MOHAVE TRIBE: REPORT OF
ABORIGINAL TERRITORY AND
OCCUPANCY**
Alfred L. Kroeber
98 pp. Clearwater Publishing, 1973. $34.50.

MOHAWK INDIANS AND THEIR VALLEY
Thomas Grassman
Illus. Magi Books, 1969. $25.00.

**THE MOHAWK THAT REFUSED
TO ABDICATE**
David P. Morgan
Kalmbach Publishing, 1975. $25.00.

**THE MOJAVES: HISTORIC INDIANS OF
SAN BERNARDINO COUNTY**
Gerald A. Smith
Illus. San Bernardino, 1977. $5.50; paper, $3.50.

*THE MONEY GOD
Dolly Hildreth, et al
Grade 6. Paper. Council for Indian Education,
1972. $1.95

***MONSTER ROLLING SKULL AND
OTHER NATIVE AMERICAN TALES**
Anita Gustafson and Marilyn Kriney
Grades 4-6. Illus. T.Y. Crowell, 1980. $8.95.

**THE MONTAGNAIS "HUNTING
TERRITORY" AND THE FUR TRADE**
E. Leacock
Reprint of 1954 edition. Paper. Kraus, $12.00.

**THE MONTANA CREE: A
STUDY IN RELIGIOUS RESISTENCE**
Verne Dusenberry
280 pp. Paper. Humanities Press, 1962. $27.50.

MONTCALM AND WOLFE
F. Parkman
Reprint. Illus. 640 pp. Peter Smith and
Atheneum, $19.95.

MONUMENTS IN CEDAR
L. Keithan, Editor
Encore edition. Superior Publishing, 1963. $9.95.

*MOONSONG LULLABY
Jamake Highwater; photos by Marcia Keegan
The author turns several themes into a poem.
Grades K-3. 32 pp. Lothrop, Lee & Shepard,
1981. $9.95.

**MORAL EDUCATION AMONG
THE NORTH AMERICAN INDIANS**
Claude A. Nichols
Reprint of 1930 edition, AMS Press, $22.50.

*MORNING ARROW
Nanabah Chee Dodge; J. Lunge, Illustrator
The relationship between a ten-year-old Navajo
boy and his blind grandmother. Grades 3-7. 48 pp.
Lothrop, Lee & Shepard, 1975. $9.00.

***MORNING STAR, BLACK SUN:
THE NORTHERN CHEYENNE INDIANS
AND AMERICA'S ENERGY CRISIS**
Brent Ashabranner
Grades 7-12. Illus. 160 pp. Dodd, Mead & Co.,
1982. $10.95.

**MORPHOLOGY OF THE
HUPA LANGUAGE**
P.E. Goddard
Reprint of 1905 edition. Kraus Reprint, $51.00.

**EARL MORRIS AND
SOUTHWESTERN ARCHAEOLOGY**
Florence and Robert H. Lister
Illus. Paper. University of New Mexico Press,
1977. $6.95.

*GEORGE MORRISON
Dragos Kostich
Grades 5 and up. Illus. Dillon Press, 1976. $7.95.

**MORTUARY CUSTOMS OF THE
SHAWNEE
AND OTHER EASTERN TRIBES**
Ermine W. Voegelin
Reprint of 1944 edition. AMS Press, $26.00.

**MOTHER EARTH, FATHER SKY,
AND ECONOMIC DEVELOPMENT:
NAVAJO RESOURCES AND THEIR USE**
Philip Reno
Illus. 183 pp. University of New Mexico,
Native American Studies, 1981. $12.75.

**MOTHER EARTH, FATHER SKY:
PUEBLO AND NAVAJO INDIANS
OF THE SOUTHWEST**
Marcia Keegan
Illus. 128 pp. Viking-Penguin, 1974. $16.95.

**MOUNTAIN WOLF WOMAN, SISTER
OF CRASHING THUNDER: THE AUTO-
BIOGRAPHY OF A WINNEBAGO INDIAN**
Nancy O. Lurie, Editor
Illus. 164 pp. Paper. University of Michigan
Press, 1961. $5.95.

THE MOUNTAINWAY OF THE NAVAJO
Leland Wyman
The examination of a Navajo song ceremonial
and various branches, phases and ritual. Illus.
271 pp. University of Arizona Press, 1975. $14.50.

**THE MOUTH OF HEAVEN: AN
INTRODUCTION TO KWAKIUTL
RELIGIOUS THOUGHT**
Irving Goldman
Reprint of 1975 edition. 284 pp. Robert E.
Krieger, $19.50. John Wiley & Sons, $22.50.

**MOVEMENT FOR INDIAN
ASSIMILATION, 1860-1890**
Henry E. Fritz
Reprint of 1963 edition. Illus. 244 pp.
Greenwood Press, $23.50.

**MUKAT'S PEOPLE: THE CAHUILLA
INDIANS OF SOUTHERN CALIFORNIA**
Lowell J. Bean
Illus. 300 pp. University of California Press,
1972. $16.95; paper, $6.75.

MULTICULTURAL CURRICULUM
A manual developed from workshops conducted
by United Indians of All Tribes Foundation,
discussing the concept of culture. 20 pp.
Daybreak Star Press, $5.00.

**MULTICULTURAL EDUCATION
AND THE AMERICAN INDIAN**
170 pp. Paper. American Indian Studies Center,
1980. $10.00.

**MULTIDISCIPLINARY RESEARCH
AT GRASSHOPPER PUEBLO, ARIZONA**
W.A. Longacre and S.J. Holbrook, Editors
138 pp. Paper. University of Arizona Press, 1982.
$12.95.

*JIM MUSCO
Dorothy Hamilton; J.J. Ponter, Illustrator
Real-life story of a 12-year old Delaware Indian
boy who chose to stay with his mother in Indiana
after it become a state instead of moving west
with his tribe. Grades 7-12. Illus. 95 pp. Paper.
Herald Press, 1972.

***MARY MUSGRAVE:
GEORGIA INDIAN PRINCESS**
Helen Todd
Grades 6-12. 152 pp. Paper. Cherokee, 1981.
$4.95.

**MUSHROOM STONES OF MESO-
AMERICA**
Karl H. Meyer
Illus. Paper. Acoma Books, 1977. $4.95.

**MUSIC AND DANCE
OF THE TEWA PUEBLOS**
Gertrude P. Kurath
Illus. Paper. Museum of New Mexico Press, 1968.
$7.95.

**MUSIC AND DANCE RESEARCH
ON THE SOUTHWESTERN INDIANS**
Charlotte Frisbie
Information Coordinators, 1977. $9.75.

**MUSIC OF ACOMA, ISLETA,
COCHITI AND ZUNI PUEBLOS**
Francis Densmore
Reprint of 1957 edition. Illus. 142 pp.
Da Capo Press, $19.50.

**MUSIC OF THE INDIANS
OF BRITISH COLUMBIA**
Francis Densmore
Reprint of 1943 edition. Illus. 118 pp.
Da Capo Press, $19.50.

MUSIC OF THE MAIDU INDIANS
Francis Densmore
Reprint of 1958 edition. 67 pp. 53 songs.
Southwest Museum, $7.50; paper, $5.00.

**THE MUSIC OF THE
NORTH AMERICAN INDIAN**
Francis Densmore
13 volumes. Da Capo Press, 1972. $295.00 per set.

MY ADVENTURES IN ZUNI
Frank H. Cushing
Illus. Filter Press, 1967. $8.00; paper, $2.50.

**MY GRANDFATHER'S HOUSE:
TLINGIT SONGS OF DEATH
AND SORROW**
David Cloutier
Illus. 40 pp. Paper. Holmgangers, 1980. $3.00.

MY HORSE AND A JUKEBOX
Barney Bush
The author works toward an Indian
consciousness
of tribes and places that would bind Native Americans together. 44 pp. Paper. American Indian
Studies Center, 1979. $2.00.

MY LIFE AS AN INDIAN
James W. Schultz
328 pp. Beaufort Books, 1981. $17.95; paper,
$9.95.

MY LIFE ON THE PLAINS
George A. Custer; Milo M. Quaife, Editor
Illus. Paper. University of Nebraska Press, 1966.
$6.95.

MY LUISENO NEIGHBORS
Eleanor Beemer
Illus. 91 pp. Acoma Books, 1980. $9.95.

**MY OLD PEOPLE SAY: AN ETHNO-
GRAPHIC SURVEY OF SOUTHERN
YUKON TERRITORY**
Catharine McClelland
Two volumes. 677 pp. Paper. National Museums
of Canada, $18.00.

MY PEOPLE THE SIOUX
L. Standing Bear; E.A. Brininstool, Editor
Reprint of 1928 edition. Illus. University of
Nebraska Press, $22.95; paper, $5.50.

MY WORK AMONG THE
FLORIDA SEMINOLES
James Glenn; Harry Kersey, Jr., Editor
Illus. 125 pp. University Presses of Florida,
1982. $12.00.

MYRON EELS AND THE
PUGET SOUND INDIANS
Robert W. Ruby and John A. Brown
Illus. Biblio. 128 pp. Superior Publishing,
$18.95.

THE MYSTIC LAKE SIOUX:
SOCIOLOGY OF THE
MDEWAKANTONWAN SANTEE
Ruth Landes
Illus. Map. 234 pp. University of Wisconsin
Press, 1969. $21.50.

MYSTIC WARRIORS OF THE PLAINS
Thomas E. Mails
Illus. 608 pp. Doubleday, 1972. $50.00.

THE MYTH AND PRAYERS OF
THE GREAT STAR CHANT AND
THE MYTH OF THE COYOTE CHANT
Mary C. Wheelwright
Illus. 190 pp. Paper. Navajo College Press, 1985.

MYTH OF HIAWATHA, AND OTHER
ORAL LEGENDS, MYTHOLOGIC AND
ALLERGORIC, OF THE NORTH
AMERICAN INDIAN
H.R. Schoolcraft
Reprint of 1856 edition. Kraus Reprint, $28.00.

MYTHOLOGICAL TALES AND THE
ALLEGANY SENECA: A STUDY OF
THE SOCIO-RLIGIOUS CONTEXT OF
TRADITIONAL ORAL PHENOMENA
IN AN IROQUOIS COMMUNITY
Thomas McElwain
Paper. Humanities Press, 1978. $18.25.

THE MYTHOLOGY OF THE
BELLA COOLA INDIANS
Franz Boas
Reprint of 1898 edition. AMS Press, $20.00.

MYTHOLOGY OF THE
BLACKFOOT INDIANS
C. Wissler and D. Duvall
Reprin tof 1909 edition. Illus. 88 pp. AMS Press,
$17.00.

MYTHOLOGY OF THE THOMPSON
INDIANS
J. Teit
Reprint of 1912 edition. AMS Press, $27.50.

MYTHOLOGY AND VALUES:
AN ANALYSIS OF NAVAHO
CHANTWAY MYTHS
Katherine Spencer
Reprint of 1957 edition. 248 pp. Paper.
University of Texas Press, 1957. $6.95.

MYTHS AND FOLKTALES OF THE
ALABAMA-COUSHATTA INDIANS
Howard N. Martin
45 stories. The Encino Press, 1982. $10.95.

MYTHS AND HUNTING STORIES OF
THE MANDAN AND HIDATSA SIOUX
M.W. Beckwith
Reprint of 1930 edition. AMS Press, $16.00.

MYTHS AND LEGENDS OF
THE INDIAN SOUTHWEST
Bertha Dutton and Caroline Olin
Illus. Paper. Bellerophon Books, 1978. $2.95.

MYTHS AND LEGENDS OF
THE LIPAN APACHE INDIANS
M. Opler
Reprint of 1940 edition. Kraus Reprint, $23.00.

MYTHS AND LEGENDS OF
THE NORTH AMERICAN INDIAN
Lewis Spence
Illus. Biblio. 396 pp. Paper. Multimedia
Publishing, $7.50.

MYTHS AND TALES FROM
THE SAN CARLOS APACHE
P.E. Goddard
Reprint of 1918 edition. AMS Press, $17.50.

MYTHS AND TALES OF THE
CHIRICAHUA APACHE INDIANS
M. Opler
Reprint of 1942 edition. Kraus Reprint, $16.00.

MYTHS AND TALES OF THE
JICARILLA APACHE INDIANS
M. Opler
Reprint of 1938 edition. Kraus Reprint, $40.00.

MYTHS AND TALES OF
THE SOUTHEASTERN INDIANS
John Swanton
Reprint of 1929 edition. Scholarly Press, and
AMS Press, $20.00

MYTHS AND TALES OF THE
WHITE MOUNTAINS APACHE
G. Goodwin, Editor
Reprint of 1939 edition. Kraus Reprint, $32.00.

MYTHS OF THE CHEROKEE
James Mooney
Reprint of 1900 edition. Scholarly Press, $89.00.

**MYTHS OF THE CHEROKEE
AND SACRED FORMULAS
OF THE CHEROKEES**
James Mooney
Reprint. Illus. Charles and Randy Elder,
Publishers, $20.00; paper, $14.00.

MYTHS OF IDAHO INDIANS
Deward E. Walker, Jr.
Revised edition. Illus. 188 pp. Paper.
University Press of Idaho, 1980. $7.50.

**MYTHS OF THE MODOCS: INDIAN
LEGENDS FROM THE NORTHWEST**
J. Curtin
Reprint of 1912 edition. Ayer Co., $20.00.

**MYTHS OF THE NEW WORLD INDIANS:
A TREATISE ON THE SYMBOLISM
AND MYTHOLOGY OF THE RED
RACE OF AMERICA**
D.G. Brinton
Reprint of 1896 edition. Illus. 360 pp. Gale
Research, $30.00. Paper. Garber Communications, $8.50.

MYTHS OF PRE-COLUMBIAN AMERICA
D.A. MacKenzie
Reprint of 1923 edition. Longwood Press, 1978.
$40.00.

N

*NA YO PISA
A noun recognition book for young readers.
Includes three scenes from reservation life
are shown, home-school-town. Grades K-3. 7 pp.
Choctaw Heritage Press, $3.00.

THE NAKED MAN
Claude Levi-Strauss
Translated by John and Doreen Weightman.
Illus.
440 pp. Harper & Row, 1981, $35.00.

**NAMBE PUEBLOS: ANTHROPOLOGICAL
DATA PERTAINING TO LAND CLAIMS**
Florence Ellis
Illus. Clearwater Publishing, 1976. $50.00.

**THE NANTICOKE COMMUNITY
OF DELAWARE**
F.G. Speck
Reprint of 1915 edition. Illus. 88 pp. AMS Press,
$20.00.

**THE NANTICOKE AND
CONOY INDIANS**
F.G. Speck
Reprint of 1927 edition. AMS Press, $11.00.

THE NANTICOKE INDIANS
C.A. Weslager
Reprint of 1948 edition. 350 pp. AMS Press,
$20.00. University of Delaware Press, $28.50.

**THE NAOMIKONG SITE AND THE
DIMENSIONS OF LAUREL IN THE
LAKE SUPERIOR REGION**
Donald Janzen
Illus. Paper. University of Michigan, Museum of
Anthropology, 1968. $3.00.

**NARRATIVE OF THE CAPTIVITY
OF EBENEZER FLETCHER**
Ebenezer Fletcher
Reprint. 28 pp. Paper. Ye Galleon, $3.00.

**A NARRATIVE OF THE CAPITIVITY
AND REMOVES OF MARY ROWLANDSON**
Mary Rowlandson
Reprint. 122 pp. Ye Galleon Press, $9.95.

**A NARRATIVE OF THE EARLY
DAYS AND REMEMBRANCES OF
OCEOLA NIKKANOCHEE, PRINCE
OF ECONCHATTI**
A. Welch
Reprint of 1841 edition. University Presses
of Florida, $12.00.

**NARRATIVE OF THE EXPEDITION TO
THE SOURCE OF ST. PETER'S RIVER**
W.H. Keating
Facsimile of 1825 edition. Illus. Ross & Haines,
$12.50.

**NARRATIVE OF THE LIFE
OF MRS. MARY JAMISON**
James E. Seaver
The life of Mary Jamison, who was taken by the
Indians at age 12, lived among them, and married
into the tribe. Reprint. Peter Smith, $12.00.

**NARRATIVE OF THE MANNER IN
WHICH THE CAMPAIGN AGAINST THE
INDIANS IN THE YEAR 1791 WAS
CONDUCTED UNDER THE COMMAND
OF MAJOR GENERAL ST. CLAIR**
A. St. Clair
Reprint of 1812 edition. Ayer Co., $18.00.

NARRATIVE OF MATTHEW BUNN
Matthew Bunn
60 pp. Ye Galleon Press.

**NARRATIVE OF THE MISSION OF THE
BRETHREN AMONG THE DELAWARE
AND MOHEGAN INDIANS**
J. Heckewelder
Reprint of 1820 edition. Ayer Co., $29.00.

**NARRATIVE OF OCCURENCES
IN THE INDIAN COUNTRIES
OF NORTH AMERICA**
S.H. Wilcocke
Reprint of 1817 edition. Beekman Publishers,
$16.50.

**NARRATIVES OF CAPITIVITY AMONG
THE INDIANS OF NORTH AMERICA: A
LIST OF BOOKS AND MANUSCRIPTS
ON THE SUBJECT IN THE EDWARD A.
AYER COLLECTION OF THE
NEWBERRY LIBRARY**
Lists 339 narratives. Supplement of the 1928
edition, with 143 narratives, contains different
editions of some of the narratives of the first
list, plus 78 new narratives. Reprint of 1912
edition. 185 pp. Gale Research Co., $35.00.

**NARRATIVES OF THE
INDIAN WARS, 1675-1699**
Charles Lincoln, Editor
Reprint of 1913 edition. 312 pp. Barnes and
Noble Imports, $21.50.

**NARRATIVES OF NORTH AMERICAN
INDIAN CAPTIVITY: A SELECTIVE
BIBLIOGRAPHY**
Alden T. Vaughan
100 pp. Garland Publishing, 1983. $18.00.

**NASKAPI: THE SAVAGE HUNTERS
OF THE LABRADOR PENINSULA**
F.G. Speck
Reprint of 1935 edition. Illus. University
of Oklahoma Press, $12.50; paper, $5.95.

**NATIONAL INDIAN ARTS
AND CRAFTS DIRECTORY**
National Indian Traders Association.
**NATIONS REMEMBERED: AN ORAL
HISTORY OF THE FIVE CIVILIZED
TRIBES, 1865-1907**
T. Perdue
230 pp. Greenwood Press, 1980. $29.95.

**THE NATIONS WITHIN:
THE PAST AND FUTURE OF
AMERICAN INDIAN SOVEREIGNTY**
Vine Deloria, Jr. and Clifford Lytle
336 pp. Paper. Pantheon, 1984. $11.95.

**NATIVE ACCOUNTS OF
NOOTKA ETHNOGRAPHY**
E. Sapir and M. Swadesh
Reprint of 1955 edition. AMS Press, $34.50.

**NATIVE AMERICAN ART
AT PHILBROOK**
Philbrook Art Center
Paper. Southwest Art Association, 1980. $9.95.
Philbrook Art Center, $8.00.

NATIVE AMERICAN BOWS
T.M. Hamilton and Bill Holm
Indian archery is examined. Revised Second
Edition. 163 pp. Paper. American Indian Books,
$10.00.

**NATIVE AMERICAN CHRISTIAN
COMMUNITY**
365 pp. World Vision International, $7.30.

**NATIVE AMERICAN DIRECTORY:
ALASKA, U.S. AND CANADA**
Fred Snyder, Editor
First edition. 366 pp. Paper. National Native
American Cooperative, 1982. $21.95.

**NATIVE AMERICAN IN AMERICAN
LITERATURE: A SELECTIVELY
ANNOTATED BIBLIOGRAPHY**
Roger O. Rock
225 pp. Greenwood Press, 1985. $35.00.

**NATIVE AMERICAN OF NORTH
AMERICA: A BIBLIOGRAPHY BASED
ON COLLECTIONS IN LIBRARIES OF
CALIFORNIA STATE UNIVERSITY,
NORTHRIDGE**
D. Perkins and N. Tanis
Illus. Scarecrow Press, 1975. $20.00.

**NATIVE AMERICAN MUSEUMS:
DEVELOPMENT AND RELATED
ISSUES—A BIBLIOGRAPHY**
Office of Museum Programs-Smithsonian, 1984.

**NATIVE AMERICAN PAINTING:
SELECTIONS FROM THE MUSEUM
OF THE AMERICAN INDIAN**
David M. Fawcett and Lee A. Callander
Illus. 96 pp. Paper. Museum of the American
Indian, 1982. $15.95.

***THE NATIVE AMERICAN
PEOPLE OF THE WEST**
P. Richard Metcalf, Editor
Grades 9-12. 159 pp. Paper. Pendulum, 1973.
$7.95.

**NATIVE AMERICAN PERIODICALS
AND NEWSPAPERS, 1828-1982:
BIBLIOGRAPHY, PUBLISHING
RECORD AND HOLDINGS**
James P. Danky, Editor
Maureen E. Hady, Compiler
Lists 1,200 Native American periodicals in 146
libraries in North America. Illus. 625 pp.
Greenwood Press, 1983. $49.95.

**NATIVE AMERICAN PREHISTORY:
A CRITICAL BIBLIOGRAPHY**
Dean Snow
96 pp. Paper. Indiana University Press, 1980.
$3.95.

NATIVE AMERICAN PRESS IN WISCONSIN AND THE NATION: PROCEEDINGS OF THE CONFERENCE ON THE NATIVE AMERICAN PRESS IN WISCONSIN AND THE NATION, APRIL, 1982
James P. Danky and Maureen B. Hady
197 pp. Paper. University of Wisconsin Library School, 1982. $7.50.

NATIVE AMERICAN RELIGIONS
Sam Gill
208 pp. Wadsworth, 1981.

NATIVE AMERICAN RENAISSANCE
Kenneth Lincoln
320 pp. University of California Press, 1983. $22.50.

NATIVE AMERICAN RESEARCH INFORMATION SERVICE
William Carmack, et al
275 pp. Paper. American Indian Studies Center, 1983. $15.00.

*NATIVE AMERICAN TESTIMONY: AN ANTHOLOGY OF INDIAN AND WHITE RELATIONS, FIRST ENCOUNTER TO DISPOSSESSION
Peter Nabakov, Editor
Grades 7-and up. Illus. Paper. Harper & Row, 1978 $4.95.

NATIVE AMERICAN TRIBALISM: INDIAN SURVIVALS AND RENEWALS
D'Arcy McNickle
Illus. 120 pp. Paper. Oxford University Press, 1973. $6.95.

NATIVE AMERICAN TRADITIONS
Sam Gill
200 pp. Paper. Wadsworth Publishing, 1983. $10.95.

NATIVE AMERICAN WOMEN: A CONTEXTUAL BIBLIOGRAPHY
Rayna Green
128 pp. Indiana University Press, 1983. $19.50.

*THE NATIVE AMERICANS
Polly and John Zane
Grades 1-12. Teacher's edition. Proof Press, 1976. $32.00.

NATIVE AMERICANS AND ENERGY DEVELOPMENT II
Joseph G. Jorgensen, Editor
An analysis of the effects of energy development on Indian reservations in the American West. foreword by Daniel Bomberry, and afterword by John Mohawk. Illus. 250 pp. Paper. Anthropology Research Center, and The Seventh Generation Fund, 1984. $6.95.

NATIVE AMERICANS: ETHNOLOGY AND BACKGROUNDS OF THE NORTH AMERICAN INDIANS
Robert Spencer
Second edition. Illus. Harper & Row, $28.95.

NATIVE AMERICANS: 23 INDIAN BIOGRAPHIES
Roger W. Axford
128 pp. Illus. Paper. Halldin Publishing, $4.50.

*THE NATIVE AMERICANS: NAVAJOS
Richard Erdoes
Grades 5-12. Illus. Sterling Publishing, 1978. $14.95; paper, $13.29.

NATIVE AMERICANS: THE NEW INDIAN RESISTANCE
William Meyer
Paper. Books on Demand, 1971. $24.00.

NATIVE AMERICANS AND NIXON: PRESIDENTIAL POLITICS AND MINORITY SELF—DETERMINATION, 1969-1972
Jack D. Forbes
148 pp. Paper. American Indian Studies Center, 1982. $12.00.

NATIVE AMERICANS OF THE NORTHWEST COAST: A CRITICAL BIBLIOGRAPHY
Robert S. Grumet
128 pp. Paper. Indiana University Press, 1979. $5.95.

NATIVE AMERICANS OF THE PACIFIC COAST
Vinson Brown
Illus. 272 pp. Naturegraph.

NATIVE AMERICANS OF TEXAS
Sandra L. Myers
Illus. 46 pp. American Press, 1981. $1.95.

*NATIVE AMERICANS OF WASHINGTON STATE: A CURRICULUM GUIDE FOR THE ELEMENTARY GRADES
A guide to aid the elementary classroom teacher in implementing Native American curriculum in the classroom. Grades 1-6.
40 pp. Daybreak Star Press, $5.50.

NATIVE AMERICANS ON FILM AND VIDEO
Elizabeth Weatherford, with Emilia Seubert, Editors
Detailed descriptions of approximately 400 films and videotapes about Indians and Inuit of the Americas. 151 pp. Paper. Museum of the American Indian, 1981. $5.00.

*NATIVE AMERICANS: THE PUEBLOS
Richard Erdoes
Grades 4-12. Illus. 96 pp. Sterling Publishing, 1983. $16.95.

*NATIVE AMERICANS: THE SIOUX
Richard Erdoes
Grades K-12. Illus. 96 pp. Sterling Publishing, 1982. $16.95; library edition, $19.99.

NATIVE AMERICANS TODAY: SOCIOLOGICAL PERSPECTIVES
Howard M. Bahr
Illus. Paper. Harper & Row, 1971. $14.95.

NATIVE ARTS OF NORTH AMERICA
Christian F. Feest
Illus. 220 pp. Thames Hudson, 1980. $19.95; paper, $9.95.

THE NATIVE ARTS OF NORTH AMERICAN INDIANS: AN EVOLVING TRADITION
Marvin Cahodes, et al
Illus. 320 pp. Paper. Hudson Hills, $50.00.

THE NATIVE BROTHERHOODS: MODERN INTER-TRIBAL ORGANIZATIONS ON THE NORTHWEST COAST
P. Drucker
Reprint of 1958 edition. Scholarly Press, $29.00.

NATIVE FACES
P. Trenton and P.T. Houlihan
Illus. 116 pp. Southwest Museum, 1984. $15.95.

NATIVE HARVESTS: RECIPES AND BOTANICALS OF THE AMERICAN INDIAN
Barrie Kavasch
Illus. Random House, 1979. $10.00; paper, $5.95.

NATIVE LANGUAGES OF THE AMERICAS
Thomas Sebeok, Editor
Two volumes. Volume 1: 630 pp., 1976; Volume 2: 535 pp, 1977. Plenum Publishing, $65.00 each.

NATIVE LAW BIBLIOGRAPHY
Linda Fritz
100 pp. University of Saskatchewan, 1984. $20.00.

NATIVE NORTH AMERICAN ART HISTORY—SELECTED READINGS
Zena Mathews and Adona Jonaitis
Illus. 500 pp. Paper. Peek Publications, 1982. $16.95.

NATIVE NORTH AMERICAN CULTURES: FOUR CASES
George and Louis Spindler
Paper. Holt, Rinehart & Winston, 1977. $8.95.

NATIVE NORTH AMERICAN MUSIC AND ORAL DATA: A CATALOGUE OF SOUND RECORDINGS, 1893-1976
Dorothy S. Lee
480 pp. Indian University Press, 1979. $25.00.

NATIVE NORTH AMERICAN SPIRITUALITY OF THE EASTERN WOODLANDS: SACRED MYTHS, DREAMS, VISION SPEECHES, HEALING FORMULAS, RITUALS AND CEREMONIES
Elisabteh Tooker, Editor
302 pp. Paper. Paulist Press, 1979. $9.95.

NATIVE NORTH AMERICANS IN DOCTORAL DISSERTATIONS, 1971-1975: A CLASSIFIED AND INDEXED RESEARCH BIBLIOGRAPHY
S. Gifford Nickerson
CPL Biblios, 1977. $7.50.

NATIVE PEOPLE IN CANADA: CONTEMPORARY CONFLICTS
James Frideres
Second Edition. 350 pp. Prentice-Hall, 1983.

NATIVE PEOPLES IN STRUGGLE: RUSSELL TRIBUNE AND OTHER INTERNATIONAL FORUMS
Jose Barreiro and Robin M. Wright, Editors
Illus. 166 pp. Paper. Native American Studies Center, and Anthropology Resource Center, 1982. $12.00.

THE NATIVE RACES
H.H. Bancroft
Reprint of 1888 edition. Five volumes. Bancroft Press, $150.00 per set.

NATIVE STUDIES: AMERICAN AND CANADIAN INDIANS
John A. Price
Paper. McGraw-Hill, 1978. $30.95.

NATIVE TRIBES MAP
Alfred L. Kroeber
Paper. University of California Press, $2.50.

NATIVE VILLAGES AND VILLAGE SITES EAST OF THE MISSISSIPPI
D.I. Bushnell, Jr.
Reprint of 1919 edition. Scholarly Press, $17.00.

NATIVES OF THE GOLDEN STATE: THE CALIFORNIA INDIANS
Rupert Costo
The history and culture of the Indians of California. Illus. Maps. The Indian Historian Press, 1982. $17.50; paper, $15.00.

THE NATURAL MAN OBSERVED:
A STUDY OF CATLIN'S
INDIAN GALLERY
William Truettner
Illus. 323 pp. Smithsonian Institution Press,
1979. $45.00.

THE NATURAL WORLD OF
THE CALIFORNIA INDIANS
Robert Heizer and Albert Elsasser
Illus. University of California Press, 1980.
$14.95; paper, $7.95.

THE NAVAHO
Clyde Kluckhohn and Dorothea Leighton
Revised 1973 edition. Illus. 365 pp. Harvard
University Press, $16.50; paper, $6.95.

THE NAVAJO
James F. Downs
Illus. 136 pp. Paper. Waveland Press, 1984.
$6.95.

NAVAHO ACTIVITIES AFFECTING
THE ACOMA-LAGUNA AREA,
1746-1910
Myra E. Jenkins and Ward A. Minge
220 pp. Clearwater Publishing, 1973. $66.00.

NAVAHO ACQUISITIVE VALUES
R. Hobson
Reprint of 1954 edition. Paper. Kraus, $16.00.

NAVAJO ARCHITECTURE: FORMS
HISTORY, DISTRIBUTIONS
Stephen C. Jett and Virginia E. Spencer
Illus. 312 pp. University of Arizona Press,
1981. $37.50; paper, $14.95.

NAVAHO ART AND CULTURE
George T. Mills
Reprint of 1959 edition. Illus. 273 pp.
Greenwood Press, $39.75.

NAVAJO BIOGRAPHIES
Virginia Hoffman and Broderick Johnson
New edition-volume 2. Navajo Curriculum
Center Press, 1978. $10.00.

NAVAJO BLESSINGWAY SINGER:
THE AUTOBIOGRAPHY OF FRANK
MITCHELL, 1881-1967
Charlotte Frisbie and
David McAllester, Editors
446 pp. Paper. University of Arizona Press,
1978. $14.95.

A NAVAJO BRINGING-HOME CERE-
MONY: THE CLAUS CHEE SONNY
VERSION OF DEERWAY AJILEE
Karl W. Luckert
Illus. 224 pp. paper. University of Nebraska
Press and Museum of Northern Arizona, 1980.
$14.95.

NAVAJO CHANGES: A HISTORY
OF THE NAVAJO PEOPLE
Teresa McCarty and staff, Editors
107 pp. Navajo Curriculum Center Press, 1983.
$10.00.

*NAVAJO CHILDREN
Nancy Armstrong
Grades 2-6. Paper. Council for Indian Education,
1975. $1.95.

NAVAHO CLASSIFICATION
OF THEIR SONG CEREMONIALS
L.C. Wyman and C. Kluckhohn
Reprint of 1938 edition. Paper. Kraus, $15.00.

THE NAVAJO CODE TALKERS
Doris A. Paul
Illus. 160 pp. Dorrance, 1973. $10.00.

NAVAJO COLOR BOOK
O.T. Branson
32 pp. Paper. Treasure Chest, 1983. $1.95.

NAVAJO COYOTE TALES: THE
CURLY TO AHEEDLIINII VERSION
Berard Haile
Reprint. Illus. 150 pp. University of Nebraska
Press, $17.95; paper, $8.95.

NAVAJO CREATION MYTH:
THE STORY OF EMERGENCE
H. Klah
Reprint of 1942 edition. AMS Press, $24.50.

NAVAJO CULTURAL GUIDES,
EXPERIENCE STORIES, AND
CULTURAL READERS
See San Juan District Media Center for titles,
prices and grade levels.

THE NAVAJO DESIGN BOOK
Paper. Fun Publications, 1975. $3.95.

NAVAJO EDUCATION IN ACTION: THE
ROUGH ROCK DEMONSTRATION
SCHOOL
Robert A. Roessel, Jr.
149 pp. Navajo Community College Press, 1977.
$10.00.

NAVAJO EDUCATION, 1948-1978:
ITS PROGRESS AND PROBLEMS
Robert A. Roessel, Jr.
Illus. 339 pp. Navajo Community College Press,
1979. $14.95.

NAVAJO ENERGY RESOURCES
Ken D. Williamson
Paper. Navajo Community College Press, 1984.
$1.50.

NAVAHO ESCHATOLOGY
L.C. Wyman, W.W. & I. Osanai
Reprint of 1942 edition. Paper. Kraus, $15.00.

THE NAVAHO (OR CORRAL) FIRE DANCE
B. Haile
Reprint of 1946-7 editions. Three volumes in one. AMS Press, $15.00. Paper. St. Michaels, $5.00.

NAVAJO FOREIGN AFFAIRS: 1795-1846
Frank D. Reeve
Paper. Navajo Community College Press, 1983. $3.00.

NAVAHO GRAMMAR
G.A. Reichard
Reprint of 1951 edition. AMS Press, $47.00.

*THE NAVAJO: HERDERS, WEAVERS AND SILVERSMITHS
Sonia Bleeker; Patricia Boodell, Illustrator
Describes life on a modern reservation; Navajo customs, belief and special ceremonies. Grades 3-6. Illus. William Morrow, 1958. $9.00.

THE NAVAJO AND HIS BLANKET
U.S. Hollister
An illustrated presentation of primitive textile weaving. Reprint of 1903 edition. Illus. 176 pp. Rio Grande Press, $15.00.

NAVAJO HISTORY
Ethelou Yazi, Editor
Revised edition. Volume I. Illus. 100 pp. Paper. Navajo Curriculum Center Press, 1982. $11.00.

NAVAJO AND HOPI WEAVING TECHNIQUES
Mary Pendleton
Illus. 224 pp. Paper. Macmillan, 1974. $8.95.

THE NAVAJO HUNTER TRADITION
Karl W. Luckert
Hunter myths and rituals are examined in conjunction with other deities and the rise of shamanism. 239 pp. Paper. University of Arizona Press, 1975. $9.50.

THE NAVAJO INDIAN BOOK
Paper. Fun Publications, 1975. $2.50

NAVAJO INDIAN ETHNOENTOMOLOGY
L.C. Wyman and F.L. Bailey
Reprint of 1964 edition. Paper. Kraus, $16.00

NAVAJO INDIAN MEDICAL ETHNOBOTANY
L. Wyman and S. Harris
Reprint of 1941 edition. Paper. Kraus and AMS Press, $16.00.

THE NAVAJO INDIANS
D. and M. Coolidge
Reprint of 1930 edition. AMS Press, $28.50.

THE NAVAJO INDIANS: AN ANTHROPOLOGICAL STUDY
Florence H. Ellis
Clearwater Publishing, 1976. $125.00

NAVAJO INDIANS
Three volumes. Illus. Maps. Garland, $42.00 each.

NAVAJO INDIANS AND FEDERAL INDIAN POLICY, 1900-1935
Laurence C. Kelly
Paper. Books on Demand, $57.80.

THE NAVAJO INDIANS IN NEW MEXICO, TO 1870
Frank D. Reeve
98 pp. Clearwater Publishing, 1973. $34.50.

NAVAJO INFANCY: AN ETHNOLOGICAL STUDY OF CHILDREN DEVELOPMENT
James S. Chisholm
267 pp. Aldine Publishing, 1983. $29.95.

NAVAJO KINSHIP AND MARRIAGE
Gary Witherspoon
Illus. 150 pp. Paper. University of Chicago Press, 1975. $6.00.

NAVAJO LAND USE: AN ETHNOARCHAEOLOGICAL STUDY
Klara B. Kelley
Academic Press.

NAVAJO LEADERSHIP AND GOVERNMENT
Title IV Materials Development Staff
149 pp. Navajo Curriculum Center Press, 1977. $7.50.

NAVAJO LEGENDS
W. Matthews
Reprint of 1897 edition. Kraus Reprint, $26.00.

NAVAJO LIVESTOCK REDUCTION: A NATIONAL DISGRACE
B. Johnson and R. Russell, Editors
Illus. Navajo Community College Press, 1974. $9.95.

*NAVAJO LONG WALK
Nancy Armstrong
Grades 4-9. Council for Indian Education, $9.95; paper, $4.95.

NAVAJO MATERIALS CULTURE
C. Kluckhohn, et al
Illus. Harvard University Press, 1971. $25.00.

NAVAJO MEDICINE MAN SAND PAINTINGS
Gladys Reichard
Reprint. Illus. Peter Smith, $16.50. Paper. Dover, $8.95.

THE NAVAJO MOUNTAIN COMMUNITY: SOCIAL ORGANIZATION AND KINSHIP TERMINOLOGY
Mary Shepardson and Blodwen Hammond
University of California Press, 1970. $25.00.

NAVAJO MOUNTAIN AND RAINBOW BRIDGE RELIGION
Karl W. Luckert
Translated by I.W. Goosen and H. Bilagody, Jr.
Illus. 164 pp. University of Nebraska Press, 1977. $9.95. Paper. Museum of Northern Arizona, $6.95.

THE NAVAJO NATION
Peter Iverson
Illus. 275 pp. Greenwood Press, 1981. $29.95. Paper. University of New Mexico Press, $9.95.

NAVAJO NATIVE DYES: THEIR PREPARATION AND USE
Nonobah Bryan and Stella Young
Reprint of 1940 edition. Illus. AMS Press, $11.50.

NAVAHO NEIGHBORS
Franc J. Newcomb
Illus. University of Oklahoma Press, 1966. $12.95; paper, $5.95.

NAVAJO ORAL HISTORY
Alfred W. Yazzie
Gene and Isaac Johnson, Editors
Illus. 56 pp. Paper. Rough Rock Demonstration School, 1984.

NAVAJO ORAL TRADITIONS
Alfred W. Yazzie; Jeri Eck, Editor
Illus. 72 pp. Paper. Navajo Curriculum Center Press, 1984.

NAVAJO PAINTING
Katherin Chase
Paper. Museum of Northern Arizona, 1982. $4.00.

NAVAHO PHONOLOGY
H. Hoijer
Reprint of 1945 edition. Paper. Kraus, $15.00.

NAVAJO POLICE
Alfred Yazzie
144 pp. Paper. Navajo Curriculum Center Press, 1980. $8.95.

NAVAHO POTTERY MAKING
H. Tschopik
Reprint of 1941 edition. Illus. Paper. Kraus, $13.00.

NAVAJO POTTERY MANUFACTURE
W.W. Hill
Reprint of 1937 edition. Paper. Kraus, $14.00.

NAVAHO RELIGION: A STUDY OF SYMBOLISM
Gladys A. Reichard
Reprint of 1963 edition. 804 pp. Paper.
Books on Demand, $120.00.

NAVAJO RESOURCES AND ECONOMIC DEVELOPMENT
Philip Reno
Formerly, *Mother Earth, Father Sky and Economic Development; Navajo Resources and Their Use.* Illus. 183 pp. Paper. University of New Mexico Press, and Native American Studies Center, 1981. $6.50.

NAVAJO SALT GATHERING
W.W. Hill
Reprint of 1940 edition. Paper. Kraus, $14.00.

NAVAJO SANDPAINTING ART
Eugene B. Joe, et al
Illus. 32 pp. Paper. Treasure Chest, 1978. $4.95.

NAVAJO SANDPAINTING: FROM RELIGIOUS ACT TO COMMERCIAL ART
Nancy J. Parejo
251 pp. University of Arizona Press, 1983. $29.95.

NAVAJO SANDPAINTING: THE HUCKEL COLLECTION
Leland C. Wyman
Illus. Paper. Taylor Museum, 1971. $5.00.

NAVAJO SHEPARD AND WEAVER
Gladys Reichard
Reprint of 1936 edition. 280 pp. Paper.
Rio Grande Press. $11.00.

*NAVAJO SLAVE
Lynne Gessner
A dramatic story, set in the 1860's, of a young Navajo's ordeal. Grades 5-9. Harvey House, $8.00.

*NAVAHO STORIES
Edward and M.P. Dolch
Reprint of 1957 edition. Grades 1-6. Illus. Garrard Publishing, $7.29.

NAVAJO STORIES OF THE LONG WALK PERIOD
Broderick H. Johnson, Editor
Navajo Community College Press, 1975. $15.30.

NAVAHO SYMBOLS OF HEALING
Donald Sandner
Paper. Harcourt Brace Jovanovich, 1979. $8.95.

NAVAJO SYNTAX
H.J. Lander
Reprint of 1963 edition. Paper. Kraus, $16.00.

**NAVAJO TECHNIQUES
FOR TODAY'S WEAVER**
Joanne Mattera
Illus. 160 pp. Watson-Guptill, 1975. $15.95.

**NAVAHO TERRITORY AND
ITS BOUNDARIES IN ARIZONA,
COLORADO AND NEW MEXICO:
BIOGRAPHICAL REFERENCES**
Lucy Wales
275 pp. Clearwater Publishing, 1974. $78.00.

**NAVAJO TEXTILES FROM
THE RED MULLAN COLLECTION**
Jon T. Erickson and H. Thomas Cain
Illus. 80 pp. Paper. University of Washington
Press, 1981. $12.95.

NAVAJO TEXTS
P. Goddard
Reprint of 1933 edition. AMS Press, $16.00.

THE NAVAJO TREATY, 1868
KC Publications, 1968. $3.50; paper, $1.00.

**NAVAJO UPWARD—REACHING WAY:
OBJECTIVE BEHAVIOR, RATIONALE,
AND SANCTION**
L.C. Wyman and F.L. Bailey
Reprint of 1943 edition. Paper. Kraus, $15.00.

**NAVAJO AND UTE PEYOTISM:
A CHRONOLOGICAL AND
DISTRIBUTIONAL STUDY**
D.F. Aberle
Reprint of 1957 edition. Paper. Kraus, $13.00.

**NAVAJO VETERANS:
A STUDY OF CHANGING VALUES**
E.Z. Vogt
Reprint of 1951 edition. Paper. Kraus, $40.00.

***NAVAJO VICTORY —
BEING A NATIVE AMERICAN**
Jane Claypool Miner
Howard Schroeder, Editor
Grades 4-5. Illus. 64 pp. Crestwood House,
1982. $7.95.

NAVAJO WAR DANCE
B. Haile
Reprint of 1946 edition. Paper. St. Michaels,
$5.00.

**NAVAJO WAYS IN GOVERNMENT:
A STUDY IN POLITICAL PROCESS**
M. Shepardson
Reprint of 1963 edition. Paper. Kraus, $20.00.

NAVAJO WEAVERS
W. Matthews
Facsimile reprint edition. Illus. 32 pp.
Paper. Shorey, $3.95.

NAVAJO WEAVERS AND SILVERSMITHS
W. Matthews
Illus. Filter Press, 1968. $8.00; paper, $1.50.

NAVAJO WEAVING HANDBOOK
Revised edition. Illus. Paper. Museum
of New Mexico Press, 1977. $5.95.

**A NAVAHO WEAVING,
ITS TECHNIC AND HISTORY**
C.A. Amsden
A comprehensive study of primitive textile
weaving. Reprint of 1934 edition. Illus. 460 pp.
Rio Grande Press, and Southwest Museum,
$20.00.

**NAVAJO WEAVING:
THREE CENTURIES OF CHANGE**
Kate P. Kent
Illus. 152 pp. School of American Research,
and University of Washington Press, 1985.
$30.00; paper, $14.95.

NAVAHO WITCHCRAFT
C. Kluckhohn
Reprint of 1944 edition. Paper. Kraus, $32.00.

THE NAVAJOS
R. Underhill
Reprint of 1956 edition. Illus. 288 pp.
University of Oklahoma Press, $14.95;
paper, $9.95.

THE NAVAJOS ARE COMING TO JESUS
Thomas Dolaghan and David Scates
Illus. Paper. William Carey Library, 1978.
$4.95.

NAVAJOS CALL IT HARD GOODS
Gloria Frazier
The art of making jewelry with silver and
turquoise. Illus. 66 pp. Paper. American
Indian Books, $2.00.

NAVAJOS HAVE FIVE FINGERS
T.D. Allen
Illus. 249 pp. University of Oklahoma Press,
1982. $17.95; paper, $8.95.

**NAVAJOS IN THE CATHOLIC CHURCH
RECORDS OF NEW MEXICO, 1694-1875**
David M. Brugge
Navajo Community College Press, 1984. $10.99.

**THE NAVAJOS LONG
WALK FOR EDUCATION**
H. Thompson; Broderick Johnson, Editor
Illus. 248 pp. Navajo Community College Press,
1975. $15.30.

THE NAVAJOS AND THE NEW DEAL
Donald L. Parman
Illus. 320 pp. Yale University Press, 1976.
$25.00.

NAVAJOS AND WORLD WAR II
  Broderick H. Johnson, Editor
Translated by Laura Begay and Henry Brown.
Illus. Paper. Navajo Community College Press,
1977. $5.50.

**NEGRO—INDIAN RELATIONSHIPS
IN THE SOUTHEAST**
  L. Foster
Reprint of 1935 edition. AMS Press, $15.00.

NEHALEM TILLAMOOK TALES
  Elizabeth and Melville Jacobs
Paper. University of Oregon Books, 1959. $3.00.

**THE NEUTRAL INDIANS:
A SOURCE BOOK**
  G.K. Wright
Reprint of 1963 edition. Paper. Kraus, $21.00.

**THE NEW AMERICAN STATE PAPERS:
INDIAN AFFAIRS, 1789-1860,
SUBJECT SET, 13 Volumes**
  Loring B. Priest, Editor
  Thomas C. Cochran, General Editor
Contains reports of the commissioners of Indian
Affairs, personal accounts of Indian life and
culture, etc. Facsimile reprint. Illus.
Scholarly Resources, $750.00 per set.

**THE NEW DEAL AND AMERICAN
INDIAN TRIBALISM: THE ADMIN-
ISTRATION OF THE INDIAN
REORGANIZATION ACT, 1934-1945**
  Graham D. Taylor
210 pp. University of Nebraska Press, 1980.
$16.95.

**NEW DIRECTIONS IN FEDERAL
INDIAN POLICY: A REVIEW OF
AMERICAN INDIAN POLICY
REVIEW COMMISSION**
Collection of articles presented as papers
at a 1978 conference sponsored by the American
Indian Studies Center, UCLA. 150 pp. Paper.
American Indian Studies Center, 1979. $10.00.

**NEW ECHOTA LETTERS:
CONTRIBUTIONS OF SAMUEL
L. WORCESTER TO THE
CHEROKEE PHOENIX**
  Jack and Anna Kilpatrick, Editors
The *Phoenix* was the first newspaper
printed in part in an American Indian
language. A white missionary, Worcester,
writes of a crucial period in Cherokee
history. 136 pp. SMU Press, 1968. $14.95.

THE NEW ENGLAND COMPANY
  W. Kellaway
Reprint of 1961 edition. Illus. 303 pp.
Greenwood Press, $22.50.

THE NEW ENGLAND INDIANS
  C. Keith Wilbur
Illus. Paper. Globe Piquot, 1978. $8.95.

NEW ENGLAND'S PROSPECT
  W. Wood; Alden T. Vaughan, Editor
Reprint of 1634 edition. Illus. 104 pp.
University of Massachusetts Press, $12.50.
Walter J. Johnson, $16.00.

**NEW ENGLISH CANAAN OR
NEW CANAAN, CONTAINING AN
ABSTRACT OF NEW ENGLAND**
  T. Morton
Reprint of 1637 edition. 192 pp.
Walter J. Johnson, $28.00.

**THE NEW FOUND WORLDE,
OR ANTARCTIKE**
  Andre Thevet
Reprint of 1568 edition. 296 pp.
Walter J. Johnson, 1971. $28.00.

NEW INDIAN SKETCHES
  P.J. DeSmet
Reprint of 1904 edition. Paper. Shorey, $8.50.

NEW INDIANS
  Stan Steiner
Illus. Harper & Row, 1968. $14.37.
Paper. Dell, $2.75.

**NEW MEXICO UNIVERSITY
PUBLICATIONS IN ANTHROPOLOGY**
Concentrate mainly on the southwestern U.S.
Indian tribes, including the Navajo, Pueblo
and Papago. Vols. 1-14, 1945-1965. Kraus,
$165.00 per set; paper, $129.00 per set.

**NEW NATIVE AMERICAN DRAMA:
THREE PLAYS**
  Hanay Geiogamah, Editor
Illus. University of Oklahoma Press, 1980.
$12.95; paper, $6.95.

**THE NEW PEOPLES: BEING
AND BECOMING METIS IN
NORTH AMERICA**
  Jacqueline Peterson and
  Jennifer S. Brown, Editors
Illus. 225 pp. University of Nebraska Press,
1984. $22.50.

NEW PERSPECTIVES ON THE PUEBLOS
  A. Ortiz, Editor
Illus. 340 pp. Paper. University of New Mexico
Press, 1970. $10.95.

**NEW RELATION TO GASPESIA:
WITH THE CUSTOMS AND RELIGION
OF THE GASPESIAN INDIAN**
  C. Le Clercq
Reprint of 1910 edition. Greenwood Press,
$33.75.

**A NEW SERIES OF
BLACKFOOT TEXTS**
C.C. Uhlenbeck
Reprint of 1912 edition. AMS Press, $38.50.

**NEW TRADITIONS: AN EXHIBITION
OF ALASKA NATIVE SCULPTURE**
Illus. Paper. Institute of Alaska Native
Arts, $2.00.

**NEW TRAILS IN MEXICO:
TRAVELS AMONG THE PAPAGO,
PIMA AND COCOPA INDIANS**
Carl Lumholtz
A study of the Sonora Desert and its aboriginal
peoples. Reprin tof 1912 edition. Illus. Biblio.
576 pp. Rio Grande Press, $20.00.

**NEW VIEWPOINTS ON THE SPANISH
COLONIALIZATION OF AMERICA**
Silvio Zavala
Translated by Joan Coync. Reprint of 1943
edition. Russell & Russell, $7.50.

**NEW VIEWS OF THE ORIGIN
OF THE TRIBES AND NATIONS
OF AMERICA**
B.S. Barton
Reprint of 1798 edition. Kraus Reprint, $29.00.

NEW VOYAGE TO CAROLINA
John Lawson; Hugh T. Lefler, Editor
University of North Carolina Press, 1967.
$14.95.

NEW VOYAGES TO NORTH AMERICA
L. Lahontan
Reprint of 1905 edition. Two volumes.
Burt Franklin, $55.50.

**NEW YORK CITY IN
INDIAN POSSESSION**
Reginald P. Bolton
Second Edition. Illus. 170 pp. Paper. Museum
of the American Indian, 1975. $6.00.

**NEWE NATEKWINAPPEH: SHOSHONI
STORIES AND DICTIONARY**
W. Miller
Reprint of 1972 edition. AMS Press, $24.00.

**NEZ PERCE CEDED TRACT,
OREGON, WASHINGTON AND IDAHO,
1867: APPRAISAL**
C. Marc Miller
217 pp. Clearwater Publishing, 1973. $66.00.

NEZ PERCE GRAMMAR
Harro Aoki
University of California Press, 1974. $34.50.

**NEZ PERCE INDIAN RESERVATION:
REPORT OF GOLD PRODUCTION,
1860-1866**

Stodard Barton, et al
70 pp. Clearwater Publishing, 1973. $25.50.

**NEZ PERCE INDIAN RESERVATION:
REPORT ON POSSIBILITY OR
IMPOSSIBILITY OF DETERMINING
GOLD REMOVED, TO 1867**
Stoddard Barton, et al
105 pp. Clearwater Publishing, 1973. $36.00.

NEZ PERCE INDIANS
H.J. Spinden
Reprint of 1908 edition. Paper. Kraus, $13.00.

NEZ PERCE INDIANS
Illus. Garland Publishing, $42.00.

**THE NEZ PERCE INDIANS AND
THE OPENING OF THE NORTHWEST**
Alvin M. Josephy, Jr.
Abridged edition. Illus. 683 pp. University of
Nebraska Press, 1979. $29.50; paper, $9.95.

NEZ PERCE JOSEPH
O. Howard
Reprint of 1881 edition. Illus. 274 pp.
Da Capo Press, 1972. $32.50.

**NEZ PERCE RESERVATION:
EVALUATION OF THE GOLD
MINED BEFORE APRIL 17, 1867**
P.J. Shenon and Roy P. Full
Four volumes. 1,350 pp. Clearwater Publishing,
1974. $372.00 per set.

**NEZ PERCE RESERVATION LAND:
APPRAISAL**
William C. Brown
402 pp. Clearwater Publishing, 1973. $114.00.

NEZ PERCE TEXTS
Haruo Aoki
University of California Press, 1979. $14.00.

NEZ PERCE TEXTS
A. Phinney
Reprint of 1934 edition. AMS Press, $34.50.

**NEZ PERCE TRIBAL LANDS IN
NORTHERN IDAHO, 1894: APPRAISAL**
Homer Hoyt
116 pp. Clearwater Publishing, 1973. $39.00.

**NEZ PERCE TRIBE OF INDIANS:
EVALUATION STUDY OF THE
MINERAL RESOURCES, 1867**
P.J. Shenon and Roy P. Full
Four volumes. 1,100 pp. Clearwater, 1973.
$300.00 per set.

**NEZ PERCES: TRIBESMEN
OF THE COLUMBIA PLATEAU**
Francis Haines
Reprint of 1955 edition. Illus. Paper.
University of Oklahoma Press, $12.95.

THE NIGHT CHANT:
A NAVAHO CEREMONIAL
W. Matthews
Reprint of 1902 edition. AMS Press, $70.00.

NIGHT FLYING WOMAN:
AN OJIBWAY NARRATIVE
Ignatia Broker
135 pp. Minesota Historical Society, 1983.
$12.95; paper, $7.95.

*NIGHTWALKER AND THE BUFFALO
Althea Bass
Grades 4-9. Paper. Council for Indian
Education, 1972. $1.95.

NIHI HAHOODZOODOO-DUJJIDIDOO
ADAADAA: OUR COMMUNITY—
TODAY AND YESTERDAY
Fred Bia and R. Lynch
Illus. 98 pp. Navajo Curriculum Center Press,
1982. $12.00.

NINE YEARS WITH SPOKANE
INDIANS: DIARY OF
ELKANAH WALKER
Clifford Drury
Illus. Arthur H. Clark Co., Publishers,
1976. $26.50.

NINSTINTS: HAIDA WORLD
HERITAGE SITE
George F. MacDonald
Illus. 64 pp. Paper. International Specialized
Book Service, 1983. $8.95.

NISQUALLY, STEILACOOM AND
SQUAXIN LANDS, STATE OF
WASHINGTON, 1855: APPRAISAL
John D.Van Wick
30 pp. Clearwater Publishing, 1973. $19.00.

NO MORE BUFFALO
Bob Scriver
Illus. 150 pp. Lowell Press, 1982. $35.00.

NO MORE BUFFALOS
Charles R. Penoi
Second edition. 115 pp. Paper. Pueblo
Publishing Press, 1982. $4.75.

*NO ONE LIKE A BROTHER
Hap Gilliland
Grades 4-12. Council for Indian Education,
1970. $5.95; paper, $1.95.

NO TURNING BACK: A HOPI
INDIAN WOMAN'S STRUGGLE
TO LIVE IN TWO WORLDS
Polingaysi Qoyawayma
180 pp. Paper. University of New Mexico
Press, 1977. $7.95.

THE NOME LACKEE INDIAN
RESERVATION, 1854-1870

Donald L. Hislop
99 pp. Association for Northern California
Records, 1978. $7.00.

NOOTKA AND QUILEUTE MUSIC
F. Densmore
Reprint of 1939 edition. Illus. 416 pp.
Da Capo Press, $29.50.

*NORTH AMERICAN INDIAN
Grades 4-6. Paper. Wonder-Treasure, $1.25

THE NORTH AMERICAN INDIAN
Edward S. Curtis
A series of 20 volumes describing the Indians
of the U.S. and Alaska. Reprint of 1907-1930
editions. Illus. Johnson Reprint, $40.00 each.
Supplement/four volumes, $50.00 each.

NORTH AMERICAN INDIAN ART
Peter T. and Jill L. Furst
Illus. 265 pp. Rizzoli International, 1982.
$45.00. Paper. American Indian Books, $19.95.

NORTH AMERICAN INDIAN ARTIFACTS
Lar Hothem
Contains 2,300 listings and their prices.
Illus. 472 pp. Paper. Books Americana,
and American Indian Books, 1984. $10.95.

THE NORTH AMERICAN
INDIAN CAPTIVITY
Wilcomb E. Washburn and John Aubrey
Illus. Garland Publishing, 1977. $24.00.

NORTH AMERICAN INDIAN
LANGUAGE MATERIALS, 1890-1965
G. Edward Evans and Jeffrey Clark
An annotated bibliography of monographic
works
providing an update of James C. Pilling's nine
American Indian linguistic bibliographies pub-
lished for the U.S. Bureau of Ethnology. 187
entries. 153 pp. Paper. American Indian Studies
Center, 1979. $3.00.

NORTH AMERICAN INDIAN LIVES
Nancy O. Lurie
Illus. 80 pp. Paper. Milwaukee Public Museum,
1985. $7.95.

*NORTH AMERICAN INDIAN MASKS
Frieda Gates
Illus. 64 pp. Walker & Co., 1982. $8.95.

NORTH AMERICAN INDIAN
MUSICAL STYLES
Bruno Nettle
Paper. University of Texas Press, 1954. $2.95.

NORTH AMERICAN INDIAN POINTS
Books Americana
Illus. 208 pp. Paper. Books Americana, and
American Indian Books, 1984. $7.95.

NORTH AMERICAN INDIAN WARS
Richard Dillon
Illus. 256 pp. Facts-on-File, $29.95.

NORTH AMERICAN INDIANS
George Catlin
Reprint. Two volumes. Illus. 264 and 266 pp.
Paper. American Indian Books, $6.95 each.

*NORTH AMERICAN INDIANS
Marigold Coleman
Grades 7-12. Viking-Penguin, Inc., 1977. $5.95.

*NORTH AMERICAN INDIANS
Marie Gorsline and Douglas Gorsline
Grades Preschool-2. Random House, 1978. $4.99.

*NORTH AMERICAN INDIANS
Susan Purdy and Cass R. Sandek
Grades 4-6. Illus. Franklin Watts, 1982. $7.90.

*NORTH AMERICAN INDIANS
Ralph Taylor and B. Brooks
Grades 4-6. Workbooks Press, 1979. $5.00.

**NORTH AMERICAN INDIANS
COLORING ALBUM**
Rite Warner, Illustrator
Illus. 32 pp. Paper. Troubador Press, 1978.
$3.95.

**NORTH AMERICAN INDIANS:
A COMPREHENSIVE ACCOUNT**
Alice B. Kehoe
Illus. 564 pp. Paper. Prentice-Hall, 1981.
$20.95.

**NORTH AMERICAN INDIANS:
A DISSERTATION INDEX**
University Microfilms International, 1976.
$28.00.

**NORTH AMERICAN INDIANS
IN HISTORICAL PERSPECTIVE**
Eleanor B. Leacock and Nancy O. Lurie
512 pp. Random House, 1971. $14.95.

**NORTH AMERICAN INDIANS
IN TOWNS AND CITIES:
A BIBLIOGRAPHY**
Wayne Bramstedt
Paper. Vance Bibliographies, 1979. $7.50.

**NORTH AMERICAN INDIANS: AN
INTRODUCTION TO THE CHITIMECA**
George Castile
Illus. McGraw-Hill, 1978. $13.95.

**NORTH AMERICAN INDIANS
OF THE PLAINS**
C. Wissler
Reprint fo 1934 edition. Burt Franklin, $23.50.

**THE NORTH AMERICAN INDIANS:
PHOTOGRAPHS BY EDWARD S. CURTIS**

Edward S. Curtis
Illus. Aperture, 1972. $20.00; paper, $12.95.

NORTH AMERICAN MYTHOLOGY
H.B. Alexander
Reprint of 1932 edition. Illus. Cooper Square,
$30.00.

**THE NORTH AMERICANS
OF YESTERDAY**
F.S. Dellenbaugh
A comparative study of North American Indian
life, customs and products, on the theory of
the ethnic unity of the race. Reprint of 1901
edition. Gordon Press, $69.95.

**NORTH CAROLINA INDIAN
LEGENDS AND MYTHS**
F. Roy Johnson
Illus. 112 pp. Johnson Publishing (NC),
1981. $8.50.

**FRANK J. NORTH: PAWNEE SCOUT,
COMMANDER AND PIONEER**
Ruby F. Wilson
Illus. 335 pp. Ohio University Press, 1982.
$19.95.

NORTHEAST
Bruce G. Trigger
Illus. 942 pp. Smithsonian, 1979. $27.00.

**NORTHEAST CAPTIVES CARRIED
TO CANADA BETWEEN 1677-1760
DURING FRENCH AND INDIAN WARS**
Reprint. Ayer Co. Publishers, $44.00.

**A NORTHEASTERN ALGONQUIAN
SOURCEBOOK**
Edward S. Rogers, Editor
364 pp. Garland Publishing, 1985. $45.00.

**THE NORTHERN ALGONQUIAN
SUPREME BEING**
J.M. Cooper
Reprint of 1934 edition. AMS Press, $14.00.

NORTHERN IROQUOIAN TEXTS
Marianne Mithun and Hanna Woodbury,
Editors
168 pp. Paper. University Microfilms, 1980.
$13.25.

THE NORTHERN MAIDU
Marie Potts
Illus. Naturegraph, 1977. $9.95; paper, $3.95.

THE NORTHERN MAIDU
R. Dixon
Reprint of 1905 edition. AMS Press, $31.50.

**NORTHERN PAIUTE INDIANS:
ANTHROPOLOGICAL REPORT**
Julian Steward and Ermine Wheeler-Voegelin
312 pp. Clearwater Publishing, 1973. $90.00.

**THE NORTHERN PAIUTE INDIANS
OF CALIFORNIA AND NEVADA**
R. Underhill
Reprint of 1941 edition. AMS Press, $14.00.

**NORTHERN PAIUTE NATION:
APPRAISAL OF LANDS IN NEVADA
AND CALIFORNIA, 1853-1863**
Homer Hoyt
Three volumes. 540 pp. Clearwater Publishing,
1973. $150.00 per set.

**NORTHERN PAIUTE NATION:
EVALUATION STUDY OF
MINERAL RESOURCES**
P.J. Shenon, et al
Three volumes 1,185 pp. Clearwater Publishing,
1973. $330.00 per set.

THE NORTHERN SHOSHONE
R. Lowie
Reprint of 1909 edition. AMS Press, $16.00.

THE NORTHERN SHOSHONI
Brigham D. Madsen
Illus. 262 pp. Caxton Printers, 1980. $17.95;
paper, $12.95.

**NORTHERN TONTO CLAIM AREA:
ENVIRONMENT AND ECOLOGY**
Homer Aschermann
54 pp. Clearwater Publishing, 1973. $21.00.

NORTHERN UTE MUSIC
F. Densmore
Reprint of 1922 edition. Illus. 236 pp.
Da Capo Press, $25.00.

**NORTHWEST COAST INDIAN ART:
AN ANALYSIS OF FORM**
Bill Holm
Illus. 133 pp. University of Washington
Press, 1965. $17.95; paper, $8.95.

**NORTHWEST COAST INDIAN
GRAPHICS: AN INTRODUCTION
TO SILK SCREEN PRINTS**
Edwin S. Hall, Jr., et al
Illus. 144 pp. University of Washington
Press, 1981. $35.00.

NORTHWEST INDIAN BASKETRY
Genevieve Baird
Paper. Washington State Historical Society,
1976. $3.75.

**NOT FOR INNOCENT EARS:
SPIRITUAL TRADITIONS OF A
DESERT CAHUILLA MEDICINE WOMAN**
Ruby Modesto and Guy Mount
Illus. 128 pp. Paper. Sweetlight, 1980. $6.95.

N. Morss
Reprint of 1931 edition. Paper. Kraus,
$10.00.

**NOTES ON THE BUFFALO-HEAD
DANCE OF THE BEAR GENS
OF THE FOX INDIANS**
T. Michelson
Reprint of 1928 edition. Scholarly Press,
$29.00.

NOTES ON THE CADDO
E. Parsons
Reprint of 1941 edition. Paper. Kraus, $20.00.

NOTES ON COCHITI, NEW MEXICO
Noel Dumarest
Reprint of 1919 edition. Paper. Kraus, $12.00.

**NOTES ON COLONIAL INDIANS
(SEMINOLE) AND COMMUNITIES
IN FLORIDA, 1700-1821**
Howard F. Cline
220 pp. Clearwater Publishing, 1974. $75.50.

**NOTES ON THE CUSTOMS
OF THE DAKOTAS**
Paul Beckwith
Reprint. 16 pp. Paper. Shorey, $1.95.

**NOTES ON THE EASTERN CREE
AND NORTHERN SALTEAUX**
A.B. Skinner
Reprint of 1911 edition. AMS Press, $15.50.

**NOTES ON THE ETHNOLOGY OF
THE INDIANS OF PUGET SOUND**
T.T. Waterman
Illus. 96 pp. Paper. Museum of the American
Indian, 1973. $3.50.

**NOTES ON THE GYNECOLOGY AND
OBSTETRICS OF THE ARIKARA
TRIBE OF INDIANS**
Melvin Gilmore
Paper. Acoma Books, 1980. $2.50.

NOTES ON HOPI ECONOMIC LIFE
E. Beaglehle
Reprin tof 1937 edition. AMS Press, $18.50.

NOTES ON IROQUOIS ARCHAEOLOGY
A.B. Skinner
Reprint of 1921 edition. AMS Press, $26.00.

**NOTES ON THE IROQUOIS: OR,
CONTRIBUTIONS TO THE STATISTICS,
ABORIGINAL HISTORY, ANTIQUITIES
AND GENERAL ETHNOLOGY OF
WESTERN NEW YORK**
H. Schoolcraft
Reprint of 1846 edition. Kraus, $32.00.
AMS Press, $31.00.

NOTES AND OBSERVATIONS ON THE
KWAKIOOL PEOPLE OF THE NORTHERN
PART OF THE VANCOUVER ISLAND
AND ADJACENT COASTS, MADE
DURING THE SUMMER OF 1885:
WITH A VOCABULARY OF
ABOUT 700 WORDS
George M. Dawson
37 pp. Paper. Ye Galleon Press, $3.50.

NOTES OF A TWENTY-FIVE
YEARS' SERVICE IN THE
HUDSON'S BAY TERRITORY
John McLean; W.S. Wallace, Editor
Reprint of 1932 edition. Greenwood Press,
$29.50.

NOTES ON THE ARCHAEOLOGY OF
THE KAIBETO AND RAINBOW
PLATEAUS IN ARIZONA

NOTES ON THE SETTLEMENT
AND INDIAN WARS
J. Doddridge
Reprint of 1824 edition. McClain Printing,
$15.00.

NOTES ON THE SETTLEMENT
AND INDIAN WARS OF THE WESTERN
PARTS OF VIRGINIA AND PENNSYL-
VANIA FROM THE YEAR 1763 UNTIL
THE YEAR 1783 INCLUSIVE
J. Doddridge
Reprint of 1824 edition. Garland Publishing,
$44.00.

NOTES ON THE SKIDI
PAWNEE SOCIETY
G.A. Dorsey and A. Spoehr
Reprint of 1940 edition. Paper. Kraus, $12.00.

NOTES ON THE SOCIAL ORGANIZA-
TION AND CUSTOMS OF THE MANDAN,
HIDATSA AND CROW INDIANS
R.H. Lowie
Reprint of 1917 edition. AMS Press, $13.45.

NOTES ON ZUNI
E.C. Parsons
Reprint of 1917 edition. Two volumes. Paper.
Kraus, $12.00 each.

NOTICES OF EAST FLORIDA:
WITH AN ACCOUNT OF THE
SEMINOLE NATION OF INDIANS
W. Simmons; George Buker, Editor
Reprint of 1822 edition. University Presses
of Florida, $6.00.

NOTICES OF FLORIDA
AND THE CAMPAIGNS
M. Cohen; O.Z. Taylor, Jr., Editor
Facsimile of 1836 edition. University Presses
of Florida, $10.75.

NOTICES OF SULLIVAN'S CAMPAIGN
H. O'Reilly
Reprint of 1842 edition. Associate Faculty
Press, $21.50.

NOW THAT THE BUFFALO'S
GONE: A STUDY OF TODAYS
AMERICAN INDIANS
Alvin M. Josephy
Illus. 334 pp. Paper. University of Oklahoma,
1984. $9.95.

O

O-KEE-PA: A RELIGIOUS
CEREMONY AND OTHER CUSTOMS
OF THE MANDANS
George Catlin; John Ewers, Editor
Illus. 116 pp. Paper. University of Nebraska
Press, 1976. $7.95.

OBJECTS OF A BRIGHT PRIDE:
NORTHWEST COAST INDIAN ART
FROM THE AMERICAN MUSEUM
OF NATURAL HISTORY
Allen Wardell
Illus. 128 pp. University of Washington Press,
1977. $19.95. Paper. American Federation of
Arts, $10.95..

OBSERVATIONS OF THE ETHNOLOGY
OF THE SAUK INDIANS
A.B. Skinner
Reprint of 1923-1925 edition. Illus. 180 pp.
Greenwood Press, $15.00.

OCCUPATION OF WOUNDED KNEE
Robert Hecht; Siguid C. Rahmas, Editor
32 pp. SamHar Press, 1982. $3.50; paper,
$1.95.

OF THE CROW NATION
E. Denig; John Ewers, Editor
Reprint of 1953 edition. AMS Press, $15.00.

OF EARTH AND LITTLE RAIN:
THE PAPAGO INDIAN
Bernard L. Fontana
Illus. 145 pp. Northland Press, 1981. $27.50.

OF MOTHER EARTH AND FATHER SKY
Fred Bia and T.L. McCarthy
Illus. 69 pp. Paper. Navajo Curriculum
Center Press, 1983. $17.00.

OF SKY AND EARTH: ART OF
THE SOUTHEASTERN INDIANS
Roy S. Dickens, Jr., Editor
Illus. 96 pp. Paper. Georgia Department of
Archives and University of Tennessee Press,
1983. $9.95.

**OFFICE OF INDIAN AFFAIRS,
1824-1880: HISTORICAL SKETCHES**
Edward E. Hill
Clearwater Publishing, 1974. $25.00.

**OFFICE OF INDIAN AFFAIRS:
ITS HISTORY, ACTIVITIES
AND ORGANIZATIONS**
L.F. Schmeckebier
Reprint of 1927 edition. AMS Press, $37.50.

**OGLALA LAKOTA CRAZY HORSE:
A PRELIMINARY GENEALOGICAL
STUDY AND AN ANNOTATED
LISTING OF PRIMARY SOURCES**
Richard G. Hardorff
Illus. Amereon Ltd. $15.95; paper, $9.95.

OGLALA RELIGION
William Powers
Illus. 250 pp. Paper. University of Nebraska
Press, 1977. $5.95.

**OHIYESA: CHARLES EASTMAN,
SANTEE SIOUX**
Raymond Wilson
Illus. University of Illinois Press, 1983.
$16.95.

**THE OHLONE WAY: INDIAN LIFE
IN THE SAN FRANCISCO AND
MONTEREY BAY AREAS**
Malcolm Margolin
Illus. Heyday Books, 1978. $8.95; paper,
$5.95.

OJIBWA CRAFTS
Carrie A. Lyford
Illus. 216 pp. Paper. R. Schneider
Publishers, 1982. $7.95.

**THE OJIBWA DANCE DRUMS:
ITS HISTORY AND CONSTRUCTION**
Thomas Vennum, Jr.
Illus. 320 pp. Paper. Smithsonian, 1982.
$12.50; Supt. of Documents, $7.50.

OJIBWA INDIAN LEGENDS
Wah-Be-Gwo-Nese, pseud.
Illus. Northern Michigan University Press,
1972. $2.95.

OJIBWA SOCIOLOGY
R. Landes
Reprint of 1937 edition. AMS Press, $22.00.

OJIBWA SUMMER
Black Ice, 1972. $20.00; paper, $10.00.

OJIBWA TEXTS
W. Jones and T. Michelson, Editors
Reprint of 1917 edition. Two volumes. AMS
Press, $96.50.

OJIBWA WOMAN
R. Landes
Reprint of 1938 edition. AMS Press, $27.50.
Paper. W.W. Norton & Co., $4.95.

**THE OJIBWAS: A
CRITICAL BIBLIOGRAPHY**
Helen H. Tanner
88 pp. Paper. Indiana Univerity Press, 1976.
$4.95.

OJIBWAY HERITAGE
Basil Johnston
Illus. Columbia University Press, 1976.
$15.00.

**THE OJIBWAY OF WALPOLE ISLAND,
ONTARIO: A LINGUISTIC STUDY**
Nils M. Holmer
Reprint of 1953 edition. AMS Press, $18.00.

***OKEMOS: STORY OF A
FOX INDIAN OF HIS YOUTH**
George Fox and Lela Puffer
Grades 3-9. Paper. Council for Indian
Education, 1976. $1.95.

***OKLA APILACI:
COMMUNITY HELPERS**
Text in Choctaw with English translation.
All participants are Choctaw. Different pro-
fessions on reservation are featured. Grades
Preschool-3. 14 pp. Choctaw Heritage Press,
$3.50.

**OKLAHOMA DELAWARE CEREMONIES:
FEASTS AND DANCES**
F.G. Speck
Reprint of 1937 edition. AMS Press, $21.50.

OKLAHOMA INDIAN ARTIFACTS
Robert E. Bell
Illus. 114 pp. Paper. American Indian Books,
$3.75.

**OKLAHOMA SEMINOLES:
MEDICINES, MAGIC AND RELIGION**
James H. Howard and Willie Lena
Illus. 300 pp. University of Olahoma Press,
1984. $19.95.

**OLD CROW WING:
HISTORY OF A VILLAGE**
Sr. Bernard Coleman, et al
Illus. Paper. St. Scholastica, 1967. $2.00.

OLD FATHER'S LONG JOURNEY
Beulah Karney
Illus. 192 pp. CLC Press, 1985. $19.95;
paper, $7.95.

**OLD FRONTIERS: THE STORY OF
THE CHEROKEE INDIANS FROM THE
EARLIEST TIMES TO THE DATE OF
THEIR REMOVAL TO THE WEST, 1838**
J.P. Brown
Reprint of 1838 edition. Illus. Ayer Co.,
$38.50.

**OLD INDIAN TEMPLES,
IDOLS AND WORSHIP**
E. Herrick
Reprint of 1882 edition. Illus. 154 pp.
Foundation for Classical Reprints, $91.45.

**OLD JOHN NEPTUNE AND OTHER
MAINE INDIAN SHAMANS**
Fannie H. Eckstorm
209 pp. Paper. University of Maine Press,
1980. $5.95.

**OLD LIGHT ON SEPARATE WAYS:
THE NARRAGANSETT DIARY OF
JOSEPH FISH, 1765-1776**
Wiliam and Cheryl Simmons
Illus. 187 pp. University Press of
New England, 1982. $16.00.

*OLD MAN COYOTE
Flora Hathaway
Grades 2-9. Paper. Council for Indian
Education, 1970. $1.95.

**OLD MEXICAN, NAVAHO INDIANS:
A NAVAHO AUTOBIOGRAPHY**
Walter Dyk, Editor
Reprint of 1947 edition. Paper. Johnson
Reprint, $19.00.

**OLD NAVAJO RUGS: THEIR
DEVELOPMENT FROM 1900-1940**
Marian E. Rodee
Illus. 96 pp. Paper. University of New
Mexico Press, 1981. $15.95.

**THE OLD NORTH TRAIL: OR,
LIFE, LEGENDS AND RELIGION
OF THE BLACKFEET INDIANS**
Walter McClintock
Illus. 550 pp. Paper. University of Nebraska
Press, 1968. $11.50.

OLD ORAIBI
M. Titiev
A study of the Hopi Indians of Third Mesa.
Reprint of 1944 edition. Illus. Paper.
Kraus, $48.00.

OLD PROBLEMS—PRESENT ISSUES
A collection of nine essays on American
Indian law, discussing the urgent concerns
of American Indians. 25 pp. Paper. Institute
for the Development of Indian Law, 1979. $2.00.

**OMAHA INDIAN MYTHS
AND TRICKSTER TALES**
Roger Welsch
350 pp. Ohio University Press, 1980. $15.95.

OMAHA INDIANS
G. Hubert Smith; David Horr, Editor
Garland Publishing, 1974. $42.00.

OMAHA SECRET SOCIETIES
R. Fortune
Reprint of 1932 edition. AMS Press, $27.50.

OMAHA SOCIOLOGY
J. Dorsey
Reprint of 1884 edition. Johnson Reprint,
$18.00.

**OMAHA TRACT IN NEBRASKA,
1854: APPRAISAL**
William G. Murray
143 pp. Clearwater Publishing, 1974. $46.50.

OMAHA TRIBE
A. Fletcher and F. LaFlesche
Reprint of 1911 edition. Two volumes. Illus.
Volume 1, 312 pp.; Volume 2, 355 pp. Johnson
Reprint, $50.00 per set. Paper. University of
Nebraska Press, $7.95 per set.

**OMAHA TRIBE OF INDIANS:
VALUATION STUDY OF THE
AREA CEDED, 1854**
Three volumes. 1,660 pp. Clearwater
Publishing, 1973. $450.00 per set.

ON THE BORDER WITH CROOK
John Bourke
Paper. University of Nebraska Press, 1971.
$8.50.

**ON THE GLEAMING WAY: NAVAJOS,
EASTERN PUEBLOS, ZUNIS, HOPIS,
APACHES AND THEIR LAND, AND
THEIR MEANING TO THE WORLD**
John Collier
Illus. 163 pp. Paper. Swallow Press, 1962.
$5.95.

**ON THE MUSIC OF THE
NORTH AMERICAN INDIANS**
Theodore Baker; Ann Buckley, Translator
Da Capo Press, 1977. $22.50.

*ONCE MORE UPON A TOTEM
Christie Harris
Grades 4-7. 208 pp. Atheneum, 1973. $5.95.

ONE OF THE KEYS: 1676-1776-1976: WAMPANOAG INDIAN CONTRIBUTION
Milton A. Travers
A list of words and definitions from the language of the historical Indians of southeastern Massachusetts. Illus. 64 pp. Christopher Publishing, 1975. $4.95.

ONE THOUSAND YEARS ON MOUND KEY
R. Schell
Revised 1968 edition. Illus. Island Press, $3.95; paper, $1.50.

THE ONEIDA AND STOCKBRIDGE TRIBES: AN ANALYSIS OF THE AWARENESS OF THE CONTINENTAL CONGRESS AND THE U.S. GOVERNMENT OF RELATIONS AND TREATIES WITH NEW YORK STATE
M. Kline, et al
Clearwater Publishing, 1976. $50.00.

ONEIDA VERB MORPHOLOGY
Floyd G. Lounsbury
111 pp. Paper. HRAFP, 1976. $15.00.

ONEONTA STUDIES
Guy E. Gibbon and
Robert F. Spencer, Editors
122 pp. Paper. University of Minnesota, Department of Anthropology, 1983. $7.50.

THE ONLY GOOD INDIAN... THE HOLLYWOOD GOSPEL
Ralph and Natasha Friar
Reprint of 1972 edition. Native American Studies Center.

THE ONLY LAND I KNOW: A HISTORY OF THE LUMBEE INDIANS OF NORTH CAROLINA
Adolph Dial and David Eliades
Illus. 240 pp. The Indian Historian Press, 1974. $9.75; paper, $6.00.

ONLY LAND THEY KNEW: THE TRAGIC STORY OF THE AMERICAN INDIANS IN THE OLD SOUTH
J. Leitch Wright, Jr.
Illus. 372 pp. Macmillan, 1981. $19.95.

*ONLY THE NAMES REMAIN: THE CHEROKEES AND THE TRAIL OF TEARS
Alex Bealer
Grades 1-3. Little, Brown & Co., 1972. $10.45.

ONONDAGA IROQUOIS PREHISTORY: A STUDY IN SETTLEMENT ARCHAEOLOGY
James A. Tuck
Syracuse University Press, 1971. $14.95.

ONONDAGA: PORTRAIT OF A NATIVE PEOPLE
Dennis Connors, Editor
Illus. 120 pp. Paper. Syracuse University Press, 1985. $12.50.

THE ONTARIO IROQUOIS TRADITION
J.V. Wright
Paper. National Museums of Canada, $3.95.

*OOTI
Richard Simpson
Grades 6-12. Paper. Celestial Arts, 1977. $6.95.

ORAIBI MARAU CEREMONY - BRIEF MISCELLANEOUS HOPI PAPERS
H.R. Voth
Reprint of 1912 edition. Paper. Kraus, $48.00.

ORAIBI SOYAL CEREMONY AND ORAIBI POWAMU CEREMONY, AND MISHONGNOVI CEREMONIES OF THE SNAKE AND ANTELOPE FRATERNITIES AND ORAIBI SUMMER SNAKE CEREMONY
G.A. Dorsey and H.R. Voth
Reprint of 1901-1903 editions. Four volumes in one. Paper. Kraus Reprint, $77.00.

*OREGON COUNTRY INDIAN LEGENDS
Mike Helm
Grades 8-12. 300 pp. Paper. Rainy Day Press, 1981. $8.95.

OREGON INDIANS
Two volumes. Illus. Garland Publishing, $42.00 each.

OREGON INDIANS: CULTURE, HISTORY AND CURRENT AFFAIRS
Jeff Zucker and Kay Hummel
Illus. 192 pp. Paper. Oregon Historical Society, 1983. $15.95.

OREGON TRAIL
F. Parkman; E.N. Feltskog, Editor
Illus. 854 pp. University of Wisconsin Press, 1964. $30.00.

THE OREGON TRAIL
F. Parkman; David Levin, Editor
Reprint. Paper. Penguin, $4.95.

*OREGON TRAIL
F. Parkman
Grades 6-12. Paper. Airmont, 1964. $1.50; New American Library, $2.95.

ORIGIN LEGEND OF THE NAVAJO ENEMY WAY
B. Haile
Reprint of 1938 edition. 328 pp. AMS Press, $37.50.

ORIGIN LEGEND OF
THE NAVAJO FLINTWAY
G.B. Grinnell
Reprint of 1943 edition. AMS Press, $49.50.

ORIGIN MYTH OF ACOMA,
AND OTHER RECORDS
M.W. Stirling
Reprint of 1942 edition. Scholarly Press,
$19.00.

THE ORIGIN OF TABLE MANNERS
Claude Levi-Strauss
Illus. Harper & Row, 1979. $30.00.

OSAGE ANTHROPOLOGICAL REPORT
Fred W. Voget
420 pp. Clearwater Publishing, 1973. $117.00.

OSAGE CEDED LANDS, 1865:
APPRAISAL
H.C. Brady
120 pp. Clearwater Publishing, 1973. $52.00.

OSAGE CEDED LANDS: VALUATION
STUDY AS OF SEPT. 29, 1865
W.W. Davis
240 pp. Clearwater Publishing, 1974. $87.00.

OSAGE INDIAN CUSTOMS AND MYTHS
Louis F. Burns
Illus. 240 pp. Ciga Press, 1984. $20.00.

THE OSAGE INDIAN TRIBE:
AN ETHNOGRAPHICAL, HISTORICAL
AND ARCHAEOLOGICAL STUDY
Carl H. Chapman
315 pp. Clearwater Publishing, 1973. $91.50.

OSAGE INDIAN VILLAGE SITES
AND HUNTING TERRITORY IN KANSAS,
MISSOURI AND OKLAHOMA
Carl Chapman
Clearwater Publishing, $22.00.

OSAGE INDIANS: BANDS AND CLANS
Louis F. Burns
196 pp. Ciga Press, 1984. $20.00.

OSAGE INDIANS
Five volumes. Illus. Maps. Garland Publishing,
$51.00 each. See publisher for titles and prices.

OSAGE INDIANS:
ANTHROPOLOGICAL STUDY
Alice Marriott
215 pp. Clearwater Publishing, 1973. $66.00.

THE OSAGE NATION IN EASTERN
OKLAHOMA AND NORTHWEST
ARKANSAS, 1775-1818
Dale Henning
Clearwater Publishing, $20.00.

OSAGE NATION: INVESTIGATION
OF LANDS OF TREATY OF
JUNE 21, 1867
Thomas LeDuc
99 pp. Clearwater Publishing, 1974. $45.00.

OSAGE NATION LAND CESSION
IN MISSOURI AND ARKANSAS,
1810: APPRAISAL
William Murray
196 pp. Clearwater Publishing, 1974. $59.00.

OSAGE TRIBAL COUNCIL,
1810: APRAISAL OF LANDS
IN MISSOURI AND ARKANSAS
M.J. Williamson
250 pp. Clearwater Publishing, 1973. $75.00.

OSAGES: CHILDREN OF
THE MIDDLE WATERS
J. Mathews
Reprint of 1961 edition. Illus. 848 pp. Paper.
University of Oklahoma Press, $18.95.

OTHER MEN'S SKIES
Robert M. Bunker
Reprint of 1956 edition. Kraus, $26.00.

OTO
W. Whitman
Reprint of 1937 edition. AMS Press, $16.00.

OTO AND MISSOURI INDIANS
Berlin Chapman; David Horr, Editor
Garland Publishing, 1978. $42.00.

OTOE AND MISSOURIA LANDS
Berlin Chapman
150 pp. Clearwater Publishing, 1974. $60.00.

OTOE AND MISSOURIA LANDS
Thoms H. LeDuc
183 pp. Clearwater Publishing, 1974. $70.00.

OTOE AND MISSOURIE TRIBES,
IOWA, OMAHA, AND SAC AND FOX
TRIBES: APPRAISAL
William Murray
363 pp. Clearwater Publishing, 1973. $127.00.

OTTAWA AND CHIPPEWA LANDS
IN MICHIGAN: ECONOMIC AND
HISTORICAL BACKGROUND FOR
A VALUATION AS OF 1836
Helen Knuth
Clearwater Publishing, 1976. $67.00.

OTTAWA AND POTAWATOMI LANDS:
ECONOMIC AND HISTORICAL BACK-
GROUND FOR VALUATION AS OF
AUGUST 29, 1821
Helen Knuth
137 pp. Clearwater Publishing, 1974. $45.00.

OTTAWA, CHIPPEWA AND
POTAWATOMI NATIONS OF
INDIANS: APPRAISAL
Paul Stewart
250 pp. Clearwater Publishing, 1973. $75.00.

OTTAWA TRIBE OF INDIANS:
APPRAISAL OF LANDS IN
NORTHWESTERN OHIO AND
SOUTHESTERN MICHIGAN
Richard Hall
139 pp. Clearwater Publishing, 1973. $45.00.

*OUR AMERICAN INDIANS
Monroe Heath
Grades 9-12. Paper. Pacific Coast, 1961. $1.95.

OUR ANCIENT PEOPLE
William W. McAfee
Paper. Vantage Press, 1978. $7.50.

OUR BROTHER'S KEEPER:
THE INDIAN IN WHITE AMERICA
Edgar Cahn, Editor
Paper. New American Library, $8.95.

OUR FRIENDS: THE NAVAJOS
Broderick Johnson, Editor
Illus. Paper. Navajo Community College
Press, 1976. $4.95.

OUR INDIAN WARDS
G.W. Manypenny
Reprint of 1880 edition. Da Capo Press,
$35.00.

*OUR MOTHER CORN
Discusses the meaning of corn to Indian
people. Teacher's guide. Grades 7-12. Illus.
79 pp. Daybreak Star Press, $7.00.

OUR RED BROTHERS AND THE
PEACE POLICY OF PRESIDENT
ULYSSES S. GRANT
Lawrie Tatum
Illus. 375 pp. University of Nebraska Press,
1970. $26.50.

OUR WESTERN BORDER, ITS LIFE,
COMBATS, ADVENTURES, FORAYS,
MASSCRES, CAPTIVITIES, SCOUTS,
RED CHIEFS, PIONEERS, WOMEN:
100 YEARS AGO, CAREFULLY
WRITTEN AND COMPILED
C. Knight
Reprint of 1876 edition. Illus. Johnson
Reprint, $50.00.

OUR WILD INDIANS: 33 YEARS
PERSONAL EXPERIENCE AMONG THE
RED MEN OF THE GREAT WEST
R.I. Dodge
Reprint of 1883 edition. Corner House, $24.95.

AN OUTLINE OF THE DOCUMENTARY
HISTORY OF THE ZUNI TRIBE:
SOMATOLOGICAL OBSERVATIONS
OF INDIANS OF THE SOUTHWEST
A.F. Bandelier and H.F. Ten Kate
Reprint of 1892 edition. AMS Press, $25.00.

*OX'ZEM: BOXELDER
AND HIS SACRED LANCE
Father Powell
Grades 2-6. Paper. Council for Indian
Education, $1.95.

OZARK BLUFF-DWELLERS
Mark R. Harrington
Reprint of 1960 edition.Illus. 185 pp. Paper.
Museum of the American Indian, $5.00.

P

*PACHEE GOYO: HISTORY AND
LEGENDS FROM THE SHOSHONE
Rupert Weeks
Paper. Jelm Mountain Publications, 1981.
$6.00.

*PACIFIC COAST INDIANS
OF NORTH AMERICA
Grant Lyons
Grades 4-6. Illus. 96 pp. Julian Messner,
1983. $9.29.

PACIFYING THE PLAINS: GENERAL
ALFRED TERRY AND THE DECLINE
OF THE SIOUX, 1866-1890
John Bailey
Greenwood Press, 1979. $18.95.

PAGES FROM HOPI HISTORY
Harry C. James
An authentic account of the Hopi way of life.
258 pp. Paper. University of Arizona Press,
1974. $6.50.

PAINTED CAVE,
NORTHEASTERN ARIZONA
E.W. Haury
Reprint of 1945 edition. Kraus Reprint, $50.00.

PAINTED CERAMICS OF THE
WESTERN MOUND AT AWATOVI
W. Smith
Paper. Kraus Reprint, 1971. $56.00.

PAIUTE ARCHAEOLOGY IN
NEVADA AND CALIFORNIA
Gordon Grosscup
Clearwater Publishing, $24.00.

**PAIUTE INDIAN LANDS IN
CALIFORNIA AND NEVADA: MINERAL
VALUATION AS OF 1853-1863**
Ernest Oberbilling
294 pp. Clearwater Publishing, 1973. $85.50.

PAIUTE INDIANS
Five volumes. Garland Publishing, $42.00 each.
See publisher for titles and prices.

PAIUTE SORCERY
B. Whiting
Reprint of 1950 edition. Paper. Johnson
Reprint, $15.50.

PALEO POINTS
G. Bradford
Chronological coverage of the more important
Paleo Indian projectile points. Illus. 48 pp.
Paper. American Indian Books, $4.95.

**PALUS IDNIANS: ETHNOHISTORICAL
REPORT ON ABORIGINAL LAND
OCCUPANCY AND UTILIZATION**
Stuart Chalfant
49 pp. Clearwater Publishing, 1974. $24.00.

**THE PALUS TRIBE: A NARRATIVE
STATEMENT AND MEMORANDUM**
Verne Ray
Clearwater Publishing, $33.00.

**THE PAMUNKEY INDIANS
OF VIRGINIA**
G. Pollard
Reprint of 1894 edition. Scholarly Press,
$25.00.

A PAPAGO CALENDAR RECORD
Ruth Underhill
Reprint of 1938 edition. Paper. Kraus,
and AMS Press, $16.00.

PAPAGO INDIAN RELIGION
Ruth Underhill
Reprint of 1946 edition. AMS Press, $37.50.

PAPAGO INDIANS
Three volumes. Illus. Garland Publishing,
$51.00 each.

**PAPAGO INDIANS: APPRAISAL OF
MINERAL RESOURCES IN LANDS
ACQUIRED BY U.S. IN ARIZONA**
Roy P. Full
Three volumes. 1.380 pp. Clearwater, 1973.
$337.50 per set.

PAPAGO INDIANS AT WORK
Jack Waddell
Illus. 160 pp. Paper. University of Arizona
Press, 1969. $4.95.

**PAPAGO INDIANS IN ARIZONA:
ABORIGINAL LAND USE
AND OCCUPANCY**
Robert A. Hackenberg
Clearwater Publishing, $89.00.

**THE PAPAGO INDIANS OF ARIZONA
AND THEIR RELATIVES THE PIMA**
Ruth Underhill
Reprint of 1940 edition. AMS Press, $16.50.

PAPAGO MUSIC
F. Densmore
Reprint of 1929 edition. Illus. 276 pp.
Da Capo Press, $25.00.

PAPAGO MUSIC AND DANCE
Richard J. Haefer
37 pp. Paper. Navajo Community College
Press, 1977. $1.50.

**THE PAPAGO AND PIMA
INDIANS OF ARIZONA**
Ruth Underhill
Illus. Filter Press, 1979. $7.00; paper. $2.00.

PAPAGO POPULATION STUDY
William S. King
Clearwater Publishing, $103.00.

**PAPAGO TRACT, ARIZONA:
MINERAL APPRAISAL**
Ernest Oberbilling
433 pp. Clearwater Publishing, 1973. $121.50.

**THE PAPAGO TRIBE OF ARIZONA:
ANTHROPOLOGICAL REPORT**
Bernard L. Fontana
70 pp. Clearwater Publishing, 1973. $25.50.

**PAPAGO TRIBE OF ARIZONA:
APPRAISAL OF LANDS,
1906 & 1916**
Donald Myers and Frank Kleinman
Three volumes. Clearwater Publishing, 1973.
$247.50 per set.

**PAPER STAYS PUT: A COLLECTION
OF INUIT WRITING**
Robin Gedalof, Editor
An anthology of Inuit literature. Illus.
176 pp. University of Washington Press,
and Hurtig Publishers, 1980. $12.95.

**PAPERS IN LINGUISTICS FROM
THE 1972 CONFERENCE ON
IROQUOIAN RESEARCH**
Michael K. Foster
Paper. National Museums of Canada, $3.95.

**THE PAPERS OF THE ORDER
OF THE INDIAN WARS**
John Carroll, Editor
Illus. Old Army, 1975. $27.50.

**PAPERS OF THE SIXTH
ALGONQUIAN CONFERENCE 1974**
William Cowan, Editor
Paper. National Museums of Canada, $3.95.

**CYNTHIA ANN PARKER:
INDIAN CAPTIVE**
Catherine T. Gonzales
Eakin Publications, 1980. $5.95.

PARKER ON THE IROQUOIS
Arthur Parker; William Fenton, Editor
Bound with *The Code of Handsome Lake, the
Seneca prophet; The Constitution of the Five
Nations;* and, *Iroquois Uses of Maize and
Other Food Plants.* Illus. 530 pp. Paper.
Syracuse University Press, 1968. $14.95.

**A PARTICULAR HISTORY OF
THE FIVE YEARS FRENCH
AND INDIAN WAR**
S.G. Drake
312 pp. Heritage Books, 1984. $25.00.

**THE PASCAGOULA, BILOXI AND
MOBILIAN CONSOLIDATED BAND**
Charles Fairbanks
205 pp. Clearwater Publishing, 1974. $72.00.

THE PASCAGOULA INDIANS
Jay Higginbotham
Illus. Paper. Rockwell Publications, 1967.
$3.00.

**PASCUA: A YAQUI
VILLAGE IN ARIZONA**
Edward Spicer
Illus. 325 pp. Paper. University of Arizona
Press, 1984. $9.95.

PASSAMAQUODDY TEXTS
J.D. Price
Reprint of 1921 edition. AMS Press, $19.00.

**THE PATH ON THE RAINBOW:
AN ANTHOLOGY OF SONGS AND
CHANTS FROM THE INDIANS
OF NORTH AMERICA**
George W. Cronyn
Reprint of 1918 edition. Century One Press,
$20.00. Arden, $25.00.

**PATHWAYS TO SELF-DETERMINATION:
CANADIAN INDIANS AND THE
CANADIAN STATE**
Leroy Little Bear, et al, Editors
192 pp. University of Toronto Press, 1984.
$25.00; paper, $9.95.

**PATRIOT CHIEFS: A CHRONICLE
OF AMERICAN INDIAN RESISTANCE**
Alvin M. Josephy, Jr.
Illus. Paper. Penguin, 1969. $5.95.

**THE PATTERN OF AMERINDIAN
IDENTITY: PROCEEDINGS OF THE
SYMPOSIUM ON AMERINDIANS,
ROYAL SOCIETY OF CANADA**
Marc-Adelard Tremblay, Editor
Illus. Paper. International Scholarly Book
Service, 1977. $20.00.

PATTERNS OF CULTURE
Ruth Benedict
Houghton-Mifflin, 1961. $10.95; paper, $4.95.

**PATTERNS AND SOURCES
OF NAVAJO WEAVING**
W.D. Harmsen
Revised edition. Illus. Harmsen Publishing,
1978.

**PAWNEE—MONO TRACTS OF
THE NORTHERN PAIUTE NATION**
Robert Nathan
Four volumes. 1,000 pp. Clearwater Publishing,
1973. $247.50 per set.

**THE PAWNEE GHOST DANCE HAND
GAME: GHOST DANCE REVIVAL
AND ETHNIC IDENTITY**
A. Lesser
Reprint of 1933 edition. Illus. AMS Press,
$37.00.

**PAWNEE HERO STORIES AND
FOLKTALES WITH NOTES ON THE
ORIGIN, CUSTOMS AND CHARACTER
OF THE PAWNEE PEOPLE**
George Grinnell
Reprint of 1961 edition. Illus. 425 pp. Univer-
sity of Nebraska Press, $29.95; paper, $7.95.

**THE PAWNEE: HISTORICAL AND
ECONOMIC GEOGRAPHY OF THE LANDS**
Thomas Griffiths
Clearwater Publishing, $38.00.

**THE PAWNEE IN OKLAHOMA:
ANTHROPOLOGY NOTES**
Franklin Fenenga and John Champe
129 pp. Clearwater Publishing, 1973. $56.00.

THE PAWNEE INDIANS
George E. Hyde
Illus. 310 pp. University of Oklahoma Press,
1974. $18.95.

PAWNEE AND KANSA (KAW) INDIANS
Illus. Garland Publishing, $42.00.

PAWNEE AND LOWER LOUP POTTERY
Rogert Grange, Jr.
Volume 3. Paper. Nebraska State Historical
Society, 1968. $6.00.

PAWNEE MUSIC
F. Densmore
Reprint of 1929 edition. 160 pp. Da Capo
Press, $19.50.

**PAWNEE TRACTS IN NEBRASKA
AND IN KANSAS: APPRAISAL**
William Murray
Two volumes. 480 pp. Clearwater Publishing,
1974. $159.00 per set.

PAWNEES: A CRITICAL BIBLIOGRAPHY
Martha P. Blaine
Illus. 128 pp. Paper. Indiana University Press,
1981. $3.95.

**THE PEACE CHIEFS
OF THE CHEYENNES**
Stan Hoig
Illus. University of Oklahoma Press, 1980.
$16.95.

**PEACE WITH THE APACHES
OF NEW MEXICO AND ARIZONA**
V. Colyer
Facsimile of 1872 edition. Ayer Co., $12.00.

**PELTS, PLUMES AND HIDES:
WHITE TRADERS AMONG THE
SEMINOLE INDIANS, 1870-1930**
Harry Kersey, Jr.
Illus. 169 pp. University Presses of Florida,
1980. $5.95.

PENHALLOW'S INDIAN WARS
E. Wheelock, Editor
Facsimile of 1924 edition. Ayer Co. Publishers.

**PENNSYLVANIA'S INDIAN
RELATIONS TO 1754**
S.P. Uhler
Reprint of 1951 edition. AMS Press, $22.50.

**PENOBSCOT MAN: THE LIFE HISTORY
OF A FOREST TRIBE IN MAINE**
F.G. Speck
Reprint. Octagon Books, $17.50.

PENOBSCOT SHAMANISM
F.G. Speck
Reprint of 1919 edition. Paper. Kraus, $15.00.

**PEOPLE FROM OUR SIDE: AN INUIT
RECORD OF SEEKOOSEELAK - THE
LAND OF THE PEOPLE OF CAPE
DORSET, BAFFIN ISLAND**
Peter Pitseolak and Dorothy Eber
Describes Eskimo camp life as it existed until
the mid-sixties. 125 photographs. Paper. Hurtig
Publishers, $5.95.

**THE PEOPLE NAMED THE CHIPPEWA:
NARRATIVE HISTORIES**
Gerald Vizenor

Illus. 175 pp. University of Minnesota Press,
1984. $22.50; paper, $12.95.

PEOPLE OF THE BLUE WATER
Flora G. Iliff
Paper. University of Arizona Press, 1985. $8.95.

PEOPLE OF THE BUFFALO
Maria Campbell
International Scholarly Book Service, $8.50.

**PEOPLE OF THE CENTER:
AMERICAN INDIAN RELIGIONS
AND CHRISTIANITY**
Carl Starkloff
Continuum Publishing, 1974. $5.95.

**PEOPLE OF THE DESERT AND SEA:
ETHNOBOTANY OF THE SERI INDIANS**
Richard Felger and Mary Moser
435 pp. University of Arizona Press, 1984.
$65.00.

**PEOPLE OF THE HIGH COUNTRY:
JACKSON HOLE BEFORE THE SETTLERS**
Gary Wright
Illus. 191 pp. Paper. Peter Lang Publishing,
1984. $20.00.

**PEOPLE OF THE ICE WHALE:
ESKIMOS, WHITE MEN
AND THE WHALE**
David Boeri
Illus. 300 pp. E.P. Dutton, 1984. $19.95.
Paper. Harcourt Brace Jovanovich, $7.95.

THE PEOPLE OF THE LAND OF FLINT
Richard D. Campbell
University Press of America, 1985. $19.75;
paper, $9.25.

**PEOPLE OF THE MAGIC WATERS:
THE CAHUILLA INDIAN
OF PALM SPRINGS**
John Brumgardt and Larry Bowles
Illus. ETC Publications, 1981. $9.95.

**PEOPLE OF THE MIDDLE PLACE:
A STUDY OF THE ZUNI INDIANS**
Dorothea Leighton and John Adair
189 pp. Paper. HRAFP, 1966. $15.00.

**PEOPLE OF THE MOUNTAIN PLACE:
PICURIS PUEBLO, NEW MEXICO**
Donald Brown
University of Arizona Press.

**PEOPLE OF THE SACRED MOUNTAIN:
A HISTORY OF THE NORTHERN
CHEYENNE CHIEFS AND WARRIOR
SOCIETIES, 1830-1879**
Peter Powell
Two volumes. Illus. 1,376 pp. Harper & Row,
1981. $125.00 per set.

THE PEOPLE OF THE SAINTS
George Mills
Illus. Paper. Taylor Museum, 1967. $3.75.

**PEOPLE OF THE SHINING
MOUNTAINS: THE UTE INDIANS
OF COLORADO**
Charles S. Marsh
Illus. 200 pp. Pruett Publishing, 1984. $14.95;
paper, $7.95.

**PEOPLE OF THE TOTEM:
THE INDIANS OF THE
PACIFIC NORTHWEST**
Norman Bancroft-Hunt and Werner Forman
Reprint of 1979 edition. Illus. 128 pp.
Merrimack Publishers Circle, $20.00.

**PEOPLE OF THE VALLEY:
THE CONCOW MAIDU**
Don Chase
Illus. 47 pp. Paper. Don M. Chase, 1973. $3.00.

**A PEOPLE'S ARMY: MASSACHUSETTS
SOLDIERS AND SOCIETY IN
THE SEVEN YEAR'S WAR**
Fred Anderson
Illus. 292 pp. University of North Carolina
Press, 1984. $28.00.

**THE PEOPLE'S LAND: ESKIMOS AND
WHITES IN THE EASTERN ARCTIC**
Brody
Paper. Viking-Penguin, Inc., $3.95.

**PEOPLES OF THE COAST: THE
INDIANS OF THE PACIFIC NORTHWEST**
George Woodcock
Reprint of 1977. Illus. 208 pp. Indian
University Press, $18.95.

PEOPLES OF THE SEA WIND
Vinson Brown
Paper. Macmillan, 1977. $7.95.

**PEORIA IN OKLAHOMA:
VALUE OF LAND**
Roger Chisholm
148 pp. Clearwater Publishing, 1974. $47.50.

**PEORIA TRIBE: GEOGRAPHICAL
AND HISTORICAL ANALYSIS OF
ROYCE AREAS 63, 73 & 74**
John Long
30 pp. Clearwater Publishing, 1973. $18.50.

**THE PEORIA TRIBE AND KASKASIA
NATION: AN APPRAISAL OF LANDS
IN ILLINOIS, 1803-1820**
Roger Chisholm
Clearwater Publishing, $95.00.

**PEORIA TRIBE OF OKLAHOMA,
ABSENTEE DELAWARE TRIBES OF**

**OKLAHOMA, AND THE DELAWARE
NATION: ANALYSIS OF THE LAND
IN SOUTHWESTERN INDIANA**
John Long and Richard Hall
Two separate volumes. Long, 39 pp., $20.00;
Hall, 190 pp., $57.00. Clearwater, 1973.

**PEORIA TRIBE OF OKLAHOMA,
1807: APPRAISAL OF LAND IN
SOUTHEASTERN ILLINOIS**
Richard Hall
246 pp. Clearwater Publishing, 1973. $75.00.

**PERSISTENT PEOPLES: CULTURAL
ENCLAVES IN PERSPECTIVE**
George Castile and
Gilbert Kushner, Editors
290 pp. University of Arizona Press, 1981.
$24.00; paper, $10.50.

**PERSONAL MEMOIRS OF A RESIDENCE
OF 30 YEARS WITH THE INDIAN
TRIBES ON THE AMERICAN
FRONTIERS, 1812-1842**
H.R. Schoolcraft
Reprint of 1851 edition. AMS Press, $37.50;
Ayer Co. Publishers, $54.00.

**PERSONAL RECOLLECTIONS AND
OBSERVATIONS OF GENERAL
NELSON A. MILES**
N.A. Miles
Revised 1896 edition. Illus. Da Capo Press,
$69.50.

**PERSPECTIVES IN AMERICAN
INDIAN CULTURE CHANGE**
Edward Spicer
Paper. University of Chicago Press, 1975.
$17.00.

PETROGLYPHS OF OHIO
James Swauger
Illus. 350 pp. Ohio University Press, 1984.
$49.95.

THE PEYOTE CULT
Weston LaBarre
Fourth Edition. Illus. 296 pp. Shoe String
Press, 1975. $20.00.

PEYOTE: THE DEVINE CACTUS
Edward F. Anderson
Questions the use of peyote in Native American
religious ceremonies, with a firsthand account
of a peyote ceremony. Illus. 248 pp. University
of Arizona Press, 1980. $14.95; paper, $6.95.

**PEYOTE HUNT: THE SACRED
JOURNEY OF HUICHOL INDIANS**
Barbara Myerhoff
Illus. 288 pp. Paper. Cornell University
Press, 1974. $9.95.

PEYOTE MUSIC
D. McAllester
Reprint of 1949 edition. Paper. Johnson
Reprint, $19.00.

THE PEYOTE RELIGION
J.S. Slotkin
Reprint of 1956 edition. 195 pp. Octagon
Books, $17.00.

**PEYOTISM IN THE WEST:
A HISTORICAL AND CUL-
TURAL PERSPECTIVE**
Omer Stewart, Editor
Illus. 168 pp. Paper. University of Utah
Press, 1984. $17.50.

***PHANTOM HORSE OF
COLLISTER'S FIELDS**
Gail Johnson
Grades 4-12. Council for Indian Education,
1974. $5.95; paper, $1.95.

**PHOENIX; THE DECLINE AND
REBIRTH OF THE INDIAN PEOPLE**
William E. Coffer
Illus. 272 pp. Van Nostrand Reinhold, 1979.
$14.95; paper, $9.95.

**THE PHOENIX FROM THE FLAME:
THE AMERICAN INDIAN TODAY**
Paper. Family Services, 1980. $4.75.

**THE PHOENIX OF THE WESTERN
WORLD: QUETZALCOATL AND
THE SKY RELIGION**
Burr C. Brundage
Illus. 320 pp. University of Oklahoma Press,
1982. $22.50.

**PHYSIOLOGICAL AND MEDICAL
OBSERVATIONS AMONG THE INDIANS
OF SOUTHWESTERN U.S. AND
NORTHERN MEXICO**
A. Hrdlicka
Reprint of 1908 edition. Scholarly Press, $27.00.

**PIANKASHAW INDIANS:
ANTHROPOLOGICAL REPORT**
Dorothy Libby
280 pp. Clearwater Publishing, 1973. $83.00.

**PIANKASHAW LANDS IN ROYCE
AREA 63, LAND VALUES OF 1805**
Roger Chisholm
110 pp. Clearwater Publishing, 1973. $37.50.

**THE PICK-SLOAN PLAN AND
THE MISSOURI RIVER SIOUX,
1944-1980**
Michael L. Lawson
Illus. 350 pp. University of Oklahoma, 1982.
$19.95.

**PICTOGRAPHIC HISTORY
OF THE OGLALA SIOUX**
Amos Brad Heart Bull and Helen Blish
Illus. 552 pp. University of Nebraska Press,
1968. $31.50.

**A PICTORIAL HISTORY
OF THE AMERICAN INDIAN**
Oliver LaFarge
Revised edition. Illus. 288 pp. Crown, 1984.
$10.98; American Indian Books, $15.00.

**PICTORIAL HISTORY OF
THE NAVAJO FROM 1860-1910**
Robert A. Roessel, Jr.
Illus. 240 pp. Navajo Curriculum Center Press,
1980. $14.95.

**PICTURE-WRITING OF
THE AMERICAN INDIANS**
Garrick Mallery
Reprint. Two volumes. Illus. 822 pp. Peter
Smith, $32.50/set. Dover, $9.95 each.

***PIECES OF WHITE SHELL:
A JOURNEY TO NAVAJOLAND**
Terry T. William
Grades 7-12. Illus. 160 pp. Charles Scribners
Sons, 1984. $14.95.

**A PILLAR OF FIRE TO FOLLOW:
AMERICAN INDIAN DRAMAS,
1808-1859**
Priscilla F. Sears
149 pp. Bowling Green University Press, 1982.
$12.95; paper, $6.95.

PIMA INDIAN LEGENDS
Anna Shaw
Illus. 112 pp. Paper. University of Arizona
Press, 1968. $4.95.

THE PIMA INDIANS
Frank Russell
A turn-of-the-century study of the Gila River
Pimas and their cousing the Papagos of southern
Arizona. Revised 1975 edition. Illus. 479 pp.
Paper. University of Arizona Pres, $9.95.

PIMA-MARICOPA INDIANS
Two volumes. Illus. Garland Publishing,
$42.00 each.

**PIMA AND PAPAGO
INDIAN AGRIXULTURE**
E.F. Castetter and W. Bell
Reprint of 1942 edition. AMS Press, $21.00.

PIMA AND PAPAGO RITUAL ORATORY
Donald M. Bahr
The author's personal relationship with the
Pima and Papago. Illus. Paper. The Indian
Historian Press, 1975. $6.00.

A PIMA PAST
Anna Shaw
Pima traditions and stories of family history
at the turn-of-the-century. 263 pp. Paper.
University of Arizona Press, 1974. $4.95.

A PIMA REMEMBERS
George Webb
Reprint of 1959 edition. Illus. Paper.
University of Arizona Press, $3.95.

**PIMAN SHAMANISM AND STAYING
SICKNESS: KA: CIM MUMKIDAG**
Donald Bahr, Juan Gregorio, David Lopez
Describes and analyzes a non-Western system of
medicine. 332 pp. Paper. University of Arizona
Press, 1974. $9.95.

**PIONEER MISSIONARY TO
THE BERING STRAIT ESKIMOS**
Louis Renner, et al
Illus. Binford and Mort, 1979. $12.50.

**PIONEERING IN MONTANA: THE
MAKING OF A STATE, 1864-1887**
Stuart Granville; Paul Phillips, Editor
Original title: *Forty Years on the Frontier.*
Reprint of 1977 edition. Illus. 265 pp. University of Nebraska Press, $18.95; paper, $5.25.

**THE PIONEERS OF NEW
FRANCE IN NEW ENGLAND**
J.P. Baxter
Reprint of 1894 edition. 450 pp. Heritage
Books, $25.00.

PIPES ON THE PLAINS
Discusses smoking in the Plains Indian culture,
as well as legends of the pipe. Illus. 40 pp.
Paper. American Indian Books, $2.00.

PITSEOLAK: A CANADIAN TRAGEDY
David Raine
Reveals the conflicts created by the meeting
of the ancient Eskimo culture with modern
society. 176 pp. Hurtig Publishers, $12.95.

**A PLACE OF REFUGE FOR
ALL TIME: MIGRATION OF THE
AMERICAN POTAWATOMI INTO
UPPER CANADA, 1830-1850**
James A. Clifton
Paper. National Museums of Canada, $3.95.

**A PLAINS ARCHAEOLOGY
SOURCEBOOK: SELECTED PAPERS
OF THE NEBRASKA STATE
HISTORICAL SOCIETY**
Wald R. Wedie, Editor
314 pp. Garland Publishing, 1985. $40.00.

THE PLAINS CREE
D.G. Mandelbaum
Reprint of 1940 edition. AMS Press, $21.00.

PLAINS CREE: GRAMMATICAL STUDY
Hans Wolfart
Paper. American Philosophical Society, 1973.
$2.50.

PLAINS CREE TEXTS
L. Bloomfield
Reprint of 1934 edition. AMS Press, $36.00.

**PLAINS INDIAN ART
FROM FOR MARION**
Karen D. Petersen
Illus. 360 pp. University of Oklahoma Press,
1971. $24.95.

THE PLAINS INDIAN BOOK
Paper. Fun Publishing, 1974. $2.50.

PLAINS INDIAN DESIGNS
Caren Caraway
Illus. 48 pp. Stemmer House, 1984. $3.50.

PLAINS INDIAN MYTHOLOGY
Alice Marriott and Carol Rachlin
Illus. 224 pp. T.Y. Crowell, 1975. $14.37.

**PLAINS INDIAN PAINTING: A
DESCRIPTION OF ABORIGINAL
AMERICAN ART**
John Ewers
Reprint of 1939 edition. AMS Press, $24.50.

**PLAINS INDIAN RAIDERS: THE
FINAL PHASES OF WARFARE FROM
THE ARKANSAS TO THE RED RIVER**
Wilbur S. Nye
Illus. 438 pp. Paper. University of Oklahoma
Press, 1974. $10.95.

*PLAINS INDIANS
Christopher Davis
Grades 4-12. Illus. 32 pp. Franklin Watts,
1978. $9.40.

**PLAINS INDIANS: A
CRITICAL BIBLIOGRAPHY**
E. Hoebel
88 pp. Paper. Indian University Press, 1977.
$4.95.

**PLAINS INDIANS: AN
EDUCATIONAL COLORING BOOK**
Grades 1-8. Illus. 32 pp. Paper. Spizzirri
Publishing, 1981. $1.50.

**THE PLAINS INDIANS
OF THE 20th CENTURY**
Peter Iverson, Editor
Illus. 288 pp. University of Oklahoma Press,
1985. $21.95; paper, $9.95

**PLAINS INDIANS: THEIR
ORIGINS, MIGRATIONS AND
CULTURAL DEVELOPMENT**
F. Haines

Illus. 225 pp. T.Y. Crowell, 1976. $12.45.

**PLANNING PROCESS ON THE
PINE RIDGE AND ROSEBUD
INDIAN RESERVATION**
Richard E. Brown
University of South Dakota, Government
Research Bureau, 1969.

**PLANTS USED AS CURATIVES BY
CERTAIN SOUTHEASTERN TRIBES**
Lyda Taylor
Reprint of 1940 edition. AMS Press, $14.50.

**PLANTS USED IN BASKETRY
BY THE CALIFORNIA INDIANS**
Ruth Merrill
Reprint. Illus. Acoma Books, $2.95.

A PLEA FOR THE INDIANS
John Beeson
184 pp. Ye Galleon Press, 1981. $12.00.

**PLENTY-COUPS, CHIEF
OF THE CROWS**
F. Linderman
Reprint of 1962 edition. Illus. 325 pp. Paper.
University of Nebraska Press, $7.95.

**RACHEL PLUMMER'S NARRATIVE
OF 21 MONTHS SERVITUDE AS
A PRISONER AMONG THE
COMANCHE INDIANS**
Rachel Plummer
Reprint of 1838 edition. Jenkins Publishing,
$19.50.

**PO PAI MO: THE SEARCH
FOR WHITE BUFFALO WOMAN**
Robert Boissiere
Illus. 96 pp. Paper. Sunstone Press, 1983.
$8.95.

A POCKET OF PROSE AND VERSE
A. Kellet; W. Washburn, Editor
Garland Publishing, 1975. $42.00.

THE POKAGONS
C.B. Buechner
Reprint of 1933 edition. Hardscrabble Books,
$5.00.

**THE POKAGONS, 1683-1983:
CATHOLIC POTAWATOMI INDIANS OF
THE ST. JOSEPH RIVER VALLEY**
James A. Clifton
Illus. 182 pp. University Press of American,
1985. $22.75; paper, $11.50.

**POLISHED STONE ARTICLES
USED BY THE NEW YORK
ABORIGINES BEFORE AND
DURING EUROPEAN OCCUPATION**
W.M. Beauchamp
Reprint of 1905 edition. AMS Press, $27.50.

**A POLITICAL HISTORY OF THE
CHEROKEE NATION, 1838-1907**
M.L. Wardell
Reprint of 1938 edition. Illus. 383 pp. Paper.
University of Oklahoma Press, $10.95.

**A POLITICAL HISTORY
OF THE NAVAJO TRIBE**
Robert W. Young; Broderick Johnson, Editor
Illus. Navajo Community College Press, 1978.
$12.60.

**POLITICAL ORGANIZATIONS
AND LAW-WAYS OF THE
COMANCHE INDIANS**
E.A. Hoebel
Reprint of 1940 edition. Kraus Reprint, $12.00.

**POLITICAL ORGANIZATIONS
OF NATIVE NORTH AMERICANS**
Ernest L. Shusky
University Press of America, 1980. $23.50;
paper, $13.75.

**POLITICAL ORGANIZATION OF THE
PLAINS INDIANS: WITH SPECIAL
REFERENCE TO THE COUNCIL**
M.G. Smith
Reprin tof 1924 edition. AMS Press, $15.00.

**THE POLITICAL OUTSIDERS:
BLACKS AND INDIANS IN A
RURAL OKLAHOMA COUNTY**
Brian F. Rader
Paper. R & E Research Associates, 1978. $13.00.

**THE POLITICS OF AMERICAN
INDIAN POLICY**
Robert Bee
250 pp. Schenkman Books, 1982. $17.95;
paper, $9.95.

**THE POLITICS OF INDIAN REMOVAL:
CREEK GOVERNMENT AND
SOCIETY IN CRISES**
Michael D. Green
Illus. 250 pp. University of Nebraska Press,
1982. $18.95; paper, $5.95.

**POLITICS AND POWER:
AN ECONOMIC AND POLITICAL
HISTORY OF THE WESTERN PUEBLO**
Steadman Upham
Academic Press, 1982. $29.50.

**THE POLLEN PATH: A
COLLECTION OF NAVAJO MYTHS**
Retold by M.S. Link
Reprint of 1956 edition. Illus. Stanford
University Press, $15.00.

POMO INDIAN BASKETRY
S.A. Barrett
Second Edition. An anthropological study and
dissertation on a rare art form. Reprint of
1908 edition. Illus. 288 pp. Paper. Rio
Grande Press, $10.00.

***POMO INDIANS OF CALIFORNIA
AND THEIR NEIGHBORS**
Vinson Brown; Albert Alsasser, Editor
Grades 4-12. Illus. Naturegraph, 1969. $10.95;
paper, $4.50.

**THE PONCA CHIEFS: AN ACCOUNT
OF THE TRIAL OF STANDING BEAR**
Thomas Tibbles; Kay Graber, Editor
150 pp. University of Nebraska Press, 1972.
$12.95; paper, $3.50.

PONCA INDIANS
Joseph Jablow; David A. Horr, Editor
Illus. Map. 424 pp. Garland Publishing, 1974.
$42.00.

**PONCA INDIANS: APPRAISAL OF
LAND IN NORTHERN NEBRASKA AND
SOUTHERN SOUTH DAKOTA, SOUTH
AND WEST OF THE MISSOURI
RIVER ON BOTH SIDES OF
THE NIOBARA RIVER**
Richard Hall
182 pp. Clearwater Publishing, 1973. $55.50.

**PONCA INDIANS WITH REFERENCE
TO THEIR CLAIM TO CERTAIN LANDS**
Joseph Jablow
356 pp. Clearwater Publishing, 1973. $102.00.

**PONCA RESERVATION, 1877:
APPRAISAL OF LAND IN
NORTHEASTERN NEBRASKA**
Richard Hall
86 pp. Clearwater Publishing, 1973. $31.50.

*PONTIAC, CHIEF OF THE OTTAWA
Jane Fleischer
Grades 4-6. Illus. 48 pp. Troll Associates,
$8.00; paper, $2.00. Cassette available.

PONY TRACKS
F. Remington
Reprint of 1961 edition. Illus. Paper.
University of Oklahoma Press, 1977. $6.95.

**THE POOL AND IRVING VILLAGES:
A STUDY OF HOPEWELL OCCUPATION**
John McGregor
Reprint of 1958 edition. Illus. Books on
Demand, $61.00.

**THE POPULATION OF CALIFORNIA
INDIANS, 1769-1970**
Sherburne F. Cook
Includes six essays on the native California
population at the time of initial settlement
in 1769. 239 pp. University of California
Press, 1976. $32.00.

**THE PORTABLE COSMOS: EFFIGIES,
ORNAMENTS AND INCISED STONE
FROM THE CHUMASH AREA**
Georgia Lee
Illus. 114 pp. Paper. Ballena Press, 1981.
$6.95.

**THE PORTABLE NORTH
AMERICAN INDIAN READER**
Frederick W. Turner, III
Third Edition. A collection of myths, tales,
poetry, speeches, and passages from Indian
autobiographies, and recent writings.
Viking-Penguin, 1977. $7.95.

**PORTRAIT MASKS OF THE
NORTHWEST AMERICAN COAST**
Jonathan King
Illus. Paper. Thames Hudson, 1979. $6.95.

**PORTRAITS FROM NORTH
AMERICAN INDIAN LIFE**
Edward S. Curtis
A collection of photographs documenting the
vanished culture of the North American Indian.
192 p. Paper. A & W Publishers, 1975. $12.98.

PORTRAITS OF THE WHITEMAN
Keith Basso
Cambridge University Press, 1979. $21.95;
paper, $7.95.

POSTS AND RUGS
H.L. James; Earl Jackson, Editor
The story of Navajo rugs and their homes. Illus.
73 full-color photos; maps. 136 pp. Southwest
Parks and Monuments, 1976. $10.00; paper,
$8.00.

**POTAWATOMI CEDED LANDS
AND AN INDIAN HISTORY OF
NORTHEASTERN ILLINOIS**
Helen H. Tanner
Clearwater, 1976. $29.00.

**POTAWATOMI KANSAS CESSION:
GOVERNMENT SALES OF LANDS**
Ida Fox
38 pp. Clearwater, 1973. $20.00.

**POTAWATOMI LANDS IN IOWA AND
KANSAS: VALUE OF FARMLAND
IMPROVEMENTS AND OTHER NATURAL
RESOURCES, 1840-1850**
John L. Coulter
77 pp. Clearwater, 1974. $38.00.

POTAWATOMI LANDS IN THE INDIAN TERRITORY, 1890: APPRAISAL
Harry James and William Winter
152 pp. Clearwater, 1973. $48.00.

POTAWATOMI TRACTS IN IOWA AND KANSAS, 1846: APPRAISAL
William Murray
239 pp. Clearwater, 1973. $97.00.

POTAWATOMI TRIBE OF INDIANS: NATURAL RESOURCE, AGRICULTURAL AND ECONOMIC SURVEY FROM 1795-1846 OF CERTAIN LANDS CEDED BY THE PRAIRIE BAND
John Coulter
96 pp. Clearwater, 1973. $46.00.

POTAWATOMI TRIBE: TRANSCRIPTION OF TREATY OF FEBRARY 22, 1855, AT WASHINGTON, D.C.
George W. Manypenny
120 pp. Clearwater, 1973. $39.00.

POTAWATOMI RESERVE LANDS IN KANSAS, SOLD BY THE PRAIRIE BAND
37 pp. Clearwater, 1973. $32.00.

POTAWATOMIS: KEEPERS OF THE FIRE
R. David Edmunds
Illus. University of Oklahoma Press, 1978. $19.95.

POTLATCH
George Clutesi
188 pp. Paper. Superior Publishing, 1969. $2.95.

POTTERY OF THE ANCIENT PUEBLOS
W.H. Holmes
Reprint of 1886 edition. Illus. 103 pp. Paper. Shorey, $8.95.

POTTERY OF THE PAJARITO PLATEAU AND OF SOME ADJACENT REGIONS IN NEW MEXICO
A.V. Kidder
Reprint of 1915 edition. Paper. Kraus, $12.00.

POTTERY TECHNIQUES OF NATIVE NORTH AMERICA: AN INTRODUCTION TO TRADITIONAL TECHNOLOGY
John K. White
University of Chicago Press, 1976. $38.00. Includes four-color fiches.

THE POWER OF SYMBOLS: MASKS AND MASQUERADE IN THE AMERICAS
N. Ross Crumrine and
Marjorie M. Halpin, Editors
Illus. 256 pp. International Specialized Books, 1983. $40.00.

*POWWOW
June Behrens
Grades K-4. Illus. 32 pp. Childrens Press, 1983. $10.60.

*POW-WOW
Mimi Chenfeld and Marjorie Vandervelds
Grades 5-12. Paper. Council for Indian Education, 1972. $1.95.

*PRAIRIE LEGENDS
M. Earring, et al
Grades 6-9. Paper. Council for Indian Education, 1978. $1.95.

PRAIRIE SMOKE
M. Gilmore
Reprint of 1929 edition. Illus. AMS Press, $18.00.

PRE-COLUMBIAN ARCHITECTURE, ART AND ARTIFACTS SLIDE CATALOG
H.L. Murvin
40 pp. Paper. H.L. Murvin, 1983. $3.95.

PREHISTORIC AGRICULTURE AT POINT OF PINES, ARIZONA
R.B. Woodbury
Reprint of 1961 edition. Paper. Kraus, $15.00.

PREHISTORIC BIOLOGICAL RELATIONSHIP IN THE GREAT LAKES REGION
Richard Wilkinson
Illus. Paper. University of Michigan, Museum of Anthropology, 1971. $3.50.

PREHISTORIC BURIAL PLACES IN MAINE
C.C. Willoughby
Reprint of 1898 edition. Paper. Kraus, $10.00.

PREHISTORIC COAL MINING IN THE JEDDITO VALLEY, ARIZONA
J.T. Hack
Reprint of 1942 edition. Paper. Kraus, $10.00.

PREHISTORIC IMPLEMENTS
Warren Moorehead
Ornaments, utensils and other tools used by the prehistoric Indian in North America. Illus. 437 pp. Paper. American Indian Books, $15.00.

PREHISTORIC INDIANS OF THE SOUTHEAST: ARCHAEOLOGY OF ALABAMA AND THE MIDDLE SOUTH
John Walthall
Illus. 288 pp. University of Alabama Press, 1980. $25.00.

PREHISTORIC INDIANS OF THE SOUTHWEST
H.M. Wormington
192 pp. Illus. Paper. Denver Museum of Natural History, 1947. $4.75.

**PREHISTORIC INDIANS
OF WISCONSIN**
Robert Ritzenthaler
Third revised edition. Illus. 62 pp. Paper.
American Indian Books, and Milwaukee Public
Museum, $4.95.

**PREHISTORIC KIVAS OF ANTELOPE
MESA, NORTH EASTERN ARIZONA**
W. Smith
Reprint. Kraus, 1971. $18.00.

**PREHISTORIC MAN ON
THE GREAT PLAINS**
Waldo Wedel
Illus. University of Oklahoma, 1961. $22.95.

**PREHISTORIC MAN OF
THE SANTA BARBARA COAST**
David Rogers
Reprint of 1929 edition. AMS Press, $57.50.

PREHISTORIC PIPES
Ahlstrom
Study of the Reeve Village Site, Lake County,
Ohio. Shows dozens of pipes. Illus. 147 pp.
Paper. American Indian Books, $7.95.

PREHISTORIC RELICS
Warren Moorehead
Facsimile edition. Illus. 165 pp. Paper.
Shorey, $10.95.

**A PREHISTORIC SEQUENCE IN THE
MIDDLE PECOS VALLEY, NEW MEXICO**
A. Jelinek
Paper. University of Michigan, Museum of
Anthropology, 1967. $3.00.

**PREHISTORIC SOUTHWESTERN
CRAFT ARTS**
Clara L. Tanner
Discusses baskets, pottery, textiles, ornaments,
and other crafts of the Southwest's prehistoric
peoples. Illus. 226 pp. University of Arizona
Press, 1976. $20.00; paper, $9.95.

**PREHISTORIC SOUTHWESTERNERS
FROM BASKETMAKER TO PUEBLO**
C.A. Amsden
Reprint of 1949 edition. Illus. Maps. 177 pp.
Southwest Museum, $5.00.

**PREHISTORIC STONE IMPLEMENTS
OF NORTHEASTERN ARIZONA**
R.B. Woodbury
Reprint of 1954 edition. Illus. Kraus, $32.00.

**PREHISTORIC TEXTILES
OF THE SOUTHWEST**
Kate P. Kent
Illus. 416 pp. University of New Mexico Press,
1982. $50.00.

**PREHISTORIC WEAPONS
IN THE SOUTHWEST**
Stewart Peckham
Illus. Paper. Museum of New Mexico Press,
1965. $1.50.

**PREHISTORY IN THE NAVAJO
RESERVOIR DISTRICT**
Frank W. Eddy
Illus. Paper. Museum of New Mexico Press,
1966. Two parts, $7.95 each.

**THE PREHISTORY OF INDIANS
OF WESTERN CONNECTICUT**
Edmund K. Swigart
49 pp. Paper. American Indian Archaeological
Institute.

**THE PREHISTORY OF NORTHERN
NORTH AMERICA AS SEEN
FROM THE YUKON**
F. De Laguna
Reprint of 1947 edition. Paper. Kraus, $63.00.

**A PRELIMINARY STUDY OF THE
PUEBLO OF TAOS, NEW MEXICO**
M.L. Miller
Reprint of 1898 edition. AMS Press, $10.00.

**PRELIMINARY STUDY OF TRADITIONAL
KUTCHIN CLOTHING IN MUSEUMS**
Judy Thompson
Paper. National Museums of Canada, $3.95.

PRELUDE TO GLORY
Herbert Krause and Gary Olson
A collection of primary sources on the viola-
tion of 1868 treaty; white views of Indians
and civilization. 279 pp. Paper. The Center
for Western Studies, $7.95.

**PRESBYTERIAN MISSIONARY
ATTITUDES TOWARD
AMERICAN INDIANS**
Michael C. Coleman
Illus. University Press of Mississippi, 1985.
$25.00.

PRESENT STATE OF NEW ENGLAND
Co Mather
Reprint of 1690 edition. Haskell House, $49.95.

**PRESIDENT WASHINGTON'S INDIAN
WAR: THE STRUGGLE FOR THE
OLD NORTHWEST, 1790-1795**
Wiley Sword
Illus. 432 pp. University of Oklahoma Press,
1985. $24.95.

**PRETTY-SHIELD, MEDICINE
WOMAN OF THE CROWS**
F. Linderman
An Indian woman's side of life. Reprint of 1932

edition. Illus. 256 pp. Paper. University of Nebraska Press, 1974. $6.95.

PRIESTS AND WARRIORS: SOCIAL STRUCTURES FOR CHEROKEE POLITICS IN THE 18th CENTURY
F.O. Gearing
Reprint of 1962 edition. Paper. Kraus, $20.00.

THE PRIMAL MIND: VISION AND REALITY IN INDIAN AMERICA
Jamake Highwater
256 pp. Harper & Row, 1981. $16.00. Paper. New American Library, $7.95.

PRIMITIVE MAN IN OHIO
W.K. Moorehead
Reprint of 1892 edition. AMS Press, $19.00.

PRIMITIVE PRAGMATISTS: THE MODOC INDIANS OF NORTHERN CALIFORNIA
Verne V. Ray
Illus. University of Washington Press, 1963. $11.50.

THE PROBLEM OF INDIAN ADMINISTRATION
Brookings Institution
Reprint of 1928 edition. Johnson Reprint, $70.00.

PROCEEDINGS: NORTHERN ATHAPASKAN CONFERENCE, 1971
A. McFadyen-Clark, Editor
Two volumes. Paper. National Museums of Canada,
$3.95.

PROCEEDINGS OF THE COMMISSIONER OF INDIAN AFFAIRS
F.B. Hough
Reprint. Scholarly Press, $59.00.

PROCEEDINGS OF THE GREAT PEACE COMISSION
A commission authorized to negotiate peace treaties with the Indian tribes of the Great Plains. 176 pp. Paper. Institute for the Development of Indian Law, 1975. $7.00.

PROPERTY CONCEPTS OF THE NAVAHO INDIANS
B. Haile
Reprint of 1954 edition. AMS Press, $12.50. Paper. St. Michaels, $6.00.

THE PROPHET DANCE OF THE NORTHWEST AND ITS DERIVATIVES: THE SOURCE OF THE GHOST DANCE
L. Spier
Reprint of 1935 edition. AMS Press, $18.00.

PROPHETIC WORLDS: INDIANS AND WHITES ON THE COLUMBIA PLATEAU
Christopher C. Miller
180 pp. Rutgers University Press, 1985. $27.00.

A PROTO—ALGONQUIAN DICTIONARY
George F. Augin
Paper. National Museums of Canada, $3.95.

THE PROVIDERS
Stephen Irwin
Illus. 296 pp. Hancock House, 1984. $19.95; paper, $12.95.

PSYCHOLOGICAL RESEARCH ON AMERICAN INDIAN AND ALASKA NATIVE YOUTH: AN INDEXED GUIDE TO DISSERTATIONS
Spero M. Manson, et al, Editors
Illus. 230 pp. Greenwood Press, 1984. $35.00.

THE PSYCHOSOCIAL ANALYSIS OF A HOPI LIFE—HISTORY
D.F. Aberle
Reprint of 1951 edition. Paper. Kraus, $13.00.

PUBLIC LAW 280: STATE JURISDICTION OVER RESERVATION INDIANS
Carole Goldberg
27 pp. Paper. American Indian Studies Center, 1975. $5.00.

PUEBLO ANIMALS AND MYTH
Hamilton Tyler
300 pp. University of Oklahoma Press, 1975. $13.95.

PUEBLO BIRDS AND MYTHS
Hamilton Tyler
Illus. Univerity of Oklahoma Press, 1979. $13.95.

PUEBLO CRAFTS
R. Underhill; Willard Beatty, Editor
Reprint of 1945 edition. Illus. 147 pp. AMS Press, $32.50. Paper. R. Schneider Publishers, and Filter Press, $7.95.

PUEBLO DESIGNS: 176 ILLUSTRATIONS OF THE RAIN BIRD
H.R. Mera; drawings by Tom Lea
Reprint. Illus. Peter Smith, $9.00. Paper. Dover, $4.95.

A PUEBLO GOD AND MYTHS
Hamilton Tyler
Illus. 336 pp. Paper. University of Oklahoma Press, 1984. $8.95.

PUEBLO INDIAN EMBROIDERY
N.R. Mera
Illus. 80 pp. William Gannon, 1975. $15.00; paper, $7.95.

PUEBLO INDIAN JOURNAL
E.C. Parsons
Reprint of 1925 edition. Paper. Kraus, $12.00.

PUEBLO INDIAN LAND GRANTS OF THE "RIO ABAJO" NEW MEXICO
H.O. Brayer
Reprint of 1938 edition. Ayer Co., $12.00.

PUEBLO INDIAN POTTERY: MATERIALS, TOOLS AND TECHNIQUES
Marjorie F. Lambert
Illus. Paper. Museum of New Mexico Press, 1966. $1.50.

PUEBLO INDIAN TEXTILES: A LIVING TRADITION
Kate P. Kent
Illus. 136 pp. Scholarly Resources and University of Washington Press, 1983. $30.00; paper, $14.95.

PUEBLO INDIAN WATER RIGHTS: STRUGGLE FOR A PRECIOUS RESOURCE
Charles T. DuMars, et al, Editors
183 pp. University of Arizona Press, 1984. $22.50.

THE PUEBLO INDIAN WORLD
E. Hewett and B. Dutton;
John Harrington, Editor
Reprint of 1945 edition. AMS Press, $37.50.

THE PUEBLO INDIANS
Joe Sando
The history of the Pueblos; includes the constitution of the All Indian Pueblo Council. Illus. 246 pp. Paper. The Indian Historian Press, 1976. $8.50.

PUEBLO INDIANS
Five volumes. Illus. Garland Publishing, $51.00 each. See publisher for titles and descriptions.

THE PUEBLO INDIANS OF NEW MEXICO: THEIR LAND ECONOMY AND CIVIL ORGANIZATION
S.B. de Aberle
Reprint of 1948 edition. Paper. Kraus, $12.00.

THE PUEBLO INDIANS OF NORTH AMERICA
E. Dozier
Reprint. 224 pp. Paper. Waveland Press, $7.95.

PUEBLO INDIANS OF SAN ILDEFONSO
W. Whitman
Reprint of 1947 edition. AMS Press, $16.50.

PUEBLO MATERIAL CULTURE IN WESTERN UTAH
J.H. Steward
Reprint of 1936 edition. Paper. Kraus, $12.00.

PUEBLO OF ACOMA: HISTORICAL TREATISE IN DEFENSE OF THE LAND CLAIM
Ward Minge
86 pp. Clearwater Publishing, 1973. $32.50.

THE PUEBLO OF JEMEZ
E.C. Parsons
Reprint of 1925 edition. AMS Press, $47.50.

PUEBLO OF SAN FELIPE
L. White
Reprint of 1932 edition. Paper. Kraus, $12.00.

PUEBLO OF SANTA ANA, NEW MEXICO
L. White
Reprint of 1942 edition. Paper. Kraus, $34.00.

PUEBLO OF SANTO DOMINGO, NEW MEXICO
L. White
Reprint of 1935 edition. Paper. Kraus, $23.00.

THE PUEBLO POTTER: A STUDY OF CREATIVE IMAGINATION IN PRIMITIVE ART
Ruth L. Bunzel
Reprint of 1926 edition. Illus. 160 pp. AMS Press, $55.00. Paper. Peter Smith, $14.00; Dover, $5.95.

PUEBLO POTTERY MAKING: A STUDY OF THE VILLAGE OF SAN ILDEFONSO
C.E. Guthe
Reprint of 1925 edition. AMS Press, $30.00.

PUEBLO POTTERY OF THE NEW MEXICO INDIANS
Betty Toulouse
Illus. Paper. Museum of New Mexico Press, 1977. $6.95.

*PUEBLO STORIES
E. Dolch and MP.P. Dolch
Reprint of 1956 edition. Grade 1-6. Garrard Publishing, 1956. $7.29.

*A PUEBLO VILAGE
Hilda Aragon, Illustrator
Preschool-7. Illus. 8 pp. Paper. Pueblo of Acoma Press, $1982. $4.00.

PUEBLO WEAVING AND TEXTILE ARTS
Nancy Fox
Paper. Museum of New Mexico Press, 1979. $6.00.

THE PUEBLOS OF ZIA, SANTA ANA
AND JEMEZ: ANTHROPOLOGICAL
EVIDENCE IN SUPPORT OF
LAND CLAIMS
Florence H. Ellis
Clearwater Publishing, 1976. $30.00.

PUMPKIN SEED POINT:
BEING WITHIN THE HOPI
Frank Waters
175 pp. Ohio University Press, 1973. $9.95;
paper, $6.95.

PURITAN JUSTICE AND THE
INDIAN: WHITE MAN'S LAW IN
MASSACHUSETTS, 1630-1763
Yasuhide Kawashima
The Puritans' use of the law as a tool of
imperialism and social control over Native
Americans. Illus. Map. Biblio. 288 pp.
Wesleyan University Press, 1984. $35.00.

PURITANS AMONG THE INDIANS:
ACCOUNTS OF CAPITIVITY AND
REDEMPTIONS 1676-1724
Alden Vaughan and Edward Clark
Illus. 352 pp. Harvard University Press, 1981.
$20.00.

PUYALLUP-NISQUALLY
M.W. Smith
Reprint of 1940 edition. AMS Press, $34.50.

Q

QUANAH: A PICTORIAL HISTORY
OF THE LAST COMANCHE CHIEF
Pauline D. Robertson and R.D. Robertson
Illus. 192 pp. Paramount, 1985. $19.95.

QUANAH, THE SERPENT EAGLE
Paul Foreman
Illus. 160 pp. Paper. Northland Press, 1982.
$8.95.

THE QUAPAW AND THEIR POTTERY,
1650-1750 A.D.
Roy Hathcock
Illus. 176 pp. American Indian Books, $50.00.

THE QUAPAW INDIANS: A HISTORY
OF THE DOWNSTREAM PEOPLE
W. David Baird
Illus. University of Oklahoma Press, 1980.
$21.95.

THE QUEST FOR FOOD AND FURS:
THE MISTASSINI CREE, 1953-1954
Edward S. Rogers
Paper. National Museums of Canada, $3.95.

QUILEUTE: AN INTRODUCTION
TO THE INDIANS OF LA PUSH
Jay Powell and Vickie Jensen
Illus. 80 pp. University of Washington
Press, 1976. $15.00; paper, $6.95.

QUILL AND BEADWORK
OF THE WESTERN SIOUX
Carrie Lyford
Reprint of 1979 edition. Illus. 116 pp.
Paper. Johnson Books, $5.95.

R

RACE, LANGUAGE AND CULTURE
Franz Boas
Reprint. Illus. 650 pp. Paper. University
of Chicago Press, $15.00.

RACE RELATIONS IN BRITISH
NORTH AMERICA 1607-1783
Bruce Glasrud and Alan Smith
368 pp. Nelson-Hall, Inc., 1982. $24.95.

RACIAL PREHISTORY IN THE SOUTH-
WEST AND THE HAWIKUH ZUNIS
C.C. Seltzer
Reprint of 1944 edition. Paper. Kraus, $16.00.

RAIN ON THE DESERT
Gordon Fraser
160 pp. Paper. Moody Press, 1975. $1.50.

RAINHOUSE AND OCEAN:
SPEECHES FOR THE PAPAGO YEAR
Ruth Underhill, et al
Illus. 160 pp. Paper. Museum of Northern
Arizona and University of Nebraska Press,
1980. $12.95.

THE RAIN—MAKERS: INDIANS
OF ARIZONA AND NEW MEXICO
M. Coolidge
Reprint of 1929 edition. AMS Press, $35.00.

THE RANCHERIA, UTE AND
SOUTHERN PAIOTE PEOPLE
Bertha Dutton
Paper. Prentice-Hall, 1976. $3.95.

THE RAPE OF THE INDIAN
LANDS: AN ORIGINAL ANTHOLOGY
Paul Gates and Stuart Bruchey, Editors
Ayer Co. Publishers, 1978. $23.00.

READINGS IN THE HISTORY
OF THE AMERICAN INDIAN
M.W. Roe
Paper. Irvington Publishers, 1971. $7.95.

**READJUSTMENT OF INDIAN
AFFAIRS: HEARINGS**
U.S. Congress, Committee on Indian Affairs
Reprint of 1934 edition. AMS Press, $36.00.

**THE RE-ESTABLISHMENT OF THE
INDIANS IN THEIR PUEBLO LIFE
THROUGH THE REVIVAL OF THEIR
TRADITIONAL CRAFTS**
H. Burton
A study in home extension education. Reprint
of 1936 edition. Kraus, $18.00; AMS Press,
$20.00.

**REALITY AND DREAM: PSYCHO-
THERAPY OF A PLAINS INDIAN**
G. Devereaux
Revised and updated. Illus. New York
University Press, 1969. $17.50.

**THE REBIRTH OF
CANADA'S INDIANS**
Harold Cardinel
An affirmation of the Indian culture.
Hurtig Publishers, $9.95; paper, $4.95.

**RECOLLECTIONS OF
THE FLATHEAD MISSION**
Fr. G. Mengarini; Gloria Lothrop, Editor
A source document by Father Mengarini; an
ethnohistory of the Flathead Indians. Illus.
The Arthur H. Clark Co., 1977. $16.95.

**RECONNAISSANCE AND EXCAVATION
IN SOUTHEASTERN NEW MEXICO**
H.P. Mera
Reprint of 1938 edition. Paper. Kraus, $12.00.

**RECONSTRUCTING REPHISTORIC
PUEBLO SOCIETIES**
W. Longacre, Editor
247 pp. Paper. Univerity of New Mexico Press,
1970. $6.95.

**RECONSTRUCTION IN
INDIAN TERRITORY**
M. Thomas Bailey
A story of avarice, discrimination, and
opportunism. Associated Faculty Press,
1972. $18.50.

**RECONSTRUCTION OF BASIC JEMEZ
PATTERN OF SOCIAL ORGANIZATION**
F.H. Ellis
Reprint of 1964 edition. Paper. Kraus, $16.00.

**RECURRENT THEMES AND
SEQUENCES IN NORTH AMERICAN
INDIAN — EUROPEAN
CULTURE CONTACT**
Edward Larrabee
Illus. Paper. American Philosophical Society,
1976. $6.00.

*RED BROTHER
R. Ray Baker
Reprint of 1927 edition. Paper. George Wahr
Publishing, $2.95.

**RED CAPITALISM: AN ANALYSIS
OF THE NAVAJO ECONOMY**
Larry Galbreath
150 pp. Paper. Books on Deamnd, 1973. $39.30.

RED CAROLINIANS
C.J. Milling
460 pp. University of South Carolina Press,
1969. $19.95.

RED CHILDREN IN WHITE AMERICA
Ann H. Beuf
168 pp. University of Pennsylvania Press, 1977.
$16.00.

RED CLOUD AND THE SIOUX PROBLEM
James Olson
Illus. 388 pp. University of Nebraska Press,
1965. $26.95; paper, $8.50.

**RED CLOUD'S FOLK: A HISTORY
OF THE OGLALA SIOUX INDIANS**
George E. Hyde
Reprint of 1937 edition. Illus. 350 pp. Univer-
sity of Oklahoma Press, $15.95; paper, $7.95.

RED CROW: WARRIOR CHIEF
Hugh A. Dempsey
Illus. 256 pp. University of Nebraska Press,
1980. $18.95.

**RED EAGLE AND THE WARS WITH
THE CREEK INDIANS OF ALABAMA**
G.C. Eggleston
Reprint of 1878 edition. AMS Press, $22.50.

**RED EAGLES OF THE NORTHWEST:
THE STORY OF CHIEF JOSEPH
AND HIS PEOPLE**
F. Haines
Reprint of 1939 edition. Illus. 376 pp.
AMS Press, $32.50.

***RED HORSE AND THE
BUFFALO ROBE MAN**
Dygert
Grades 4-8. Council for Indian Education,
$5.95; paper, $1.95.

**RED HUNTERS AND
THE ANIMAL PEOPLE**
C. Eastman
Reprint of 1904 edition. Illus. AMS Press,
$21.00.

**RED LAKE BAND OF CHIPPEWA
INDIANS: APPRAISAL OF
LANDS IN MINNESOTA**
96 pp. Clearwater Publishing, 1973. $34.50.

RED LAKE AND PEMBINA BANDS OF CHIPPEWA INDIANS: VALUATION STUDY OF THE RED RIVER VALLEY OF THE NORTH AREA IN NORTH DAKOTA AND MINNESOTA, CEDED OCTOBER 3, 1863.
John Coulter
410 pp. Clearwater Publishing, 1973. $147.50.

RED LAKE AND PEMBINA CHIPPEWA: ANTHROPOLOGICAL REPORT
Ermine Wheeler-Voegelin
200 pp. Clearwater Publishing, 1973. $60.00.

*RED MAN IN ART
Rena Coen
Grades 5-12. Illus. 72 pp. Lerner Publications, 1972. $5.95.

RED MAN IN THE U.S.
G. Lindquist
Reprint of 1923 edition. Illus. Augustus M. Kelley, $39.50.

RED MAN'S AMERICA: A HISTORY OF INDIANS IN THE U.S.
Ruth Underhill
Revised edition. Illus. 398 pp. University of Chicago Press, 1971. $25.00; paper, $10.95.

RED MAN'S RELIGION: BELIEFS AND PRACTICES OF THE INDIANS NORTH OF MEXICO
Ruth Underhill
Illus. 350 pp. Paper. University of Chicago Press, 1965. $10.00.

RED MEN AND HAT-WEAVERS: VIEWPOINTS IN INDIAN HISTORY
Daniel Tyler, Editor
Illus. 160 pp. Paper. Pruett Publishing, 1976. $5.95.

RED MEN OF FIRE: A HISTORY OF THE CHEROKEE INDIANS
Irvin M. Peithmann
Illus. 172 pp. Charles C. Thomas, 1969. $11.75.

THE RED OCHRE PEOPLE: HOW NEWFOUNDLAND'S BEOTHUK INDIANS LIVED
Ingeborg Marshall
International Scholarly Book Service, $8.50.

RED OVER BLACK: BLACK SLAVERY AMONG THE CHEROKEE INDIANS
R. Halliburton, Jr.
Illus. Greenwood Press, 1977. $15.95.

RED PATRIOTS: THE STORY OF THE SEMINOLES
C. Coe
Facsimile of 1898 edition. 347 pp. University Presses of Florida, $12.00.

RED POWER: THE AMERICAN INDIANS' FIGHT FOR FREEDOM
Alvin M. Josephy, Jr.
Excerpts from key speeches, articles, declarations, studies and other documents which have led the Federal Government toward a long overdue policy of self-determination for Native Americans. 352 pp. Paper. McGraw-Hill, 1971. $3.95.

RED RAIDERS RETALIATE: THE STORY OF LONE WOLF (THE ELDER GUIPAGHO) FAMOUS KIOWA INDIAN CHIEF
J. Lee Jones, Editor
Illus. 96 pp. Pioneer Book Co., 1980. $8.95.

*RED RIBBONS FOR EMMA
Grades 3-12. Illus. 48 pp. New Seed, 1981. $5.00.

RED AND WHITE: INDIAN VIEWS OF THE WHITE MAN, 1492-1982
Annette Rosentiel
Illus. 192 pp. Universe Books, 1983. $14.95.

THE RED RECORD OF THE SIOUX
W. Johnson
Reprint of 1891 edition. AMS Press, $44.50.

THE RED SWAN: MYTHS AND TALES OF THE AMERICAN INDIANS
John Bierhorst, Translator
Reprint of 1976 edition. 386 pp. Octagon, $31.50.

RED, WHITE AND BLACK: SYMPOSIUM ON INDIANS IN THE OLD SOUTH
Charles Hudson
Paper. University of Georgia Press, 1971. $6.00.

RED AND WHITE: INDIAN VIEWS OF THE WHITE MAN, 1492-1982
Annette Rosensteil
Illus. 192 pp. Universe Books, 1983. $14.95.

RED WORLD AND WHITE: MEMORIES OF A CHIPPEWA BOYHOOD
John Rogers
150 pp. University of Olahoma Press, 1974. $11.95.

THE REDEEMED CAPTIVE
John Williams; Edward W. Clark, Editor
Reprint. Illus. University of Massachusetts Press, $10.00.

THE REDEEMED CAPTIVE RETURNING TO ZION
John Williams
The captivity and deliverance of Rev. John

Williams of Deerfield, Mass. Reprint of 1908 edition. Kraus, $23.00; facsimile of 1853 edition. Ayer Co., $19.00.

REDISCOVERED LINKS IN THE COVENANT CHAIN: PREVIOUSLY UNPUBLISHED TRANSCRIPTS OF NEW YORK INDIANS TREATY MINUTES, 1677-1691
Daniel K. Richter
41 pp. Paper. American Antiquarian and University Press of Virginia, 1982. $4.50.

REDSKINS, RUFFLESHIRTS AND REDNECKS: INDIAN ALLOTMENTS IN ALABAMA AND MISSISSIPPI, 1830-1860
Mary Young
Reprint of 1961 edition. Illus. Books on Demand, $58.30.

THE RE-ESTABLISHMENT OF THE INDIANS IN THEIR PUEBLO LIFE THROUGH THE REVIVAL OF THEIR TRADITIONAL CRAFTS: A STUDY IN HOME EXTENSION EDUCATION
H. Burton
Reprint of 1936 edition. Kraus, $18.00; AMS, $22.50.

REFLECTIONS OF SOCIAL LIFE IN THE NAVAHO ORIGIN MYTH
K. Spencer
Reprint of 1947 edition. AMS Press, $20.00. Paper. Kraus, $15.00.

REGENERATION THROUGH VIOLENCE: THE MYTHOLOGY OF THE AMERICAN FRONTIER, 1600-1860
Richard Slotkin
The white-Indian encounter. Paper. Columbia University Press, $27.50; paper, $8.95.

REGISTER OF THE DEPARTMENT OF STATE
U.S. Dept. of State
Reprint of 1874 edition. Johnson Reprint, $10.00.

RELATIONS OF NATURE TO MAN IN ABORIGINAL AMERICA
C. Wissler
Reprint of 1926 edition. AMS Press, $22.00.

THE RELATION OF SENECA FALSE FACE MASKS TO SENECA AND ONTARIO ARCHAEOLOGY
Zena P. Mathews
Garland Publishing, 1978. $44.00.

THE RELATIONSHIP SYSTEMS OF THE TLINGIT, HAIDA AND TSIMSHIAN
T. Durlach
Reprint of 1928 edition. AMS Press, $27.50.

RELIGION AND CEREMONIES OF THE LENAPE
M.R. Harrington
Reprint of 1921 edition. AMS Press, $31.50.

THE RELIGION OF THE CROW INDIANS
R.H. Lowie
Reprint of 1922 edition. AMS Press, $15.00.

RELIGION OF THE KWAKIUTL INDIANS
Franz Boas
Two volumes. Reprint of 1930 edition. AMS Press, $60.00/set; $30.00 each.

THE RELIGIONS OF THE AMERICAN INDIANS
Ake Hultkrantz
University of California Press, 1979. $18.95; paper, $7.95.

THE REMEMBERED EARTH: AN ANTHOLOGY OF CONTEMPORARY NATIVE AMERICAN LITERATURE
Geary Hobson, Editor
Reprint of 1981 edition. 440 pp. Paper. University of New Mexico Press, $9.95.

REMINGTON'S FRONTIER SKETCHES
F. Remington
Reprint of 1898 edition. Illus. Burt Franklin, $25.50.

REMINISCENCE OF THE INDIANS
C. Washburn
Reprint of 1869 edition. Johnson Reprint, $27.00.

REMINISCENCES OF SEATTLE, WASHINGTON TERRITORY AND THE U.S. SLOOP-OF-WAR DECATUR DURING THE INDIAN WAR OF 1855-1856
Thomas Phelps
Reprint. Ye Galleon Press, $5.50.

REMOVAL OF THE CHEROKEE INDIANS FROM GEORGIA
W. Lumpkin
Reprint of 1907 edition. Ayer Co., $32.00.

THE REMOVAL OF THE CHEROKEE NATION: MANIFEST DESTINY OF NATIOAL DISHONOR
Louis Filler and Allen Guttman, Editors
128 pp. Paper. Robert E. Krieger Publishing, 1977. $5.50.

REMOVAL OF THE CHOCTAW INDIANS
Arthur DeRosier, Jr.
Illus. 224 pp. University of Tennessee Press, 1970. $14.95; paper, $6.95.

REOPENING THE MOJAVE ROAD
Dennis G. Lasebier
128 pp. Tales Mojave Rd., 1983. $17.50.

**REPORT OF CHARLES A. WETMORE,
SPECIAL U.S. COMMISSIONER
OF MISSION INDIANS OF
SOUTHERN CALIFORNIA**
Norman Tanis, Editor
Paper. California State University,
Northridge, 1977. $10.00.

**REPORT OF THE COMMISSIONER
OF INDIAN AFFAIRS FOR THE
TERRITORIES OF WASHINGTON,
IDAHO AND OREGON, 1870**
75 pp. Ye Galleon, 1981. $10.95.

**REPORT OF THE COMMISSIONER
OF INDIAN AFFAIRS: REPORTS
FOR THE YEARS 1824-1899**
U.S. Office of Indian Affairs
65 volumes. Reprint of 1899 edition. AMS
Press, $2,330.50 per set.

**REPORT OF A VISIT TO SOME
OF THE TRIBES OF INDIANS,
LOCATED WEST OF THE
MISSISSIPPI RIVER**
John Long and Samuel Taylor
34 pp. Ye Galleon Press, 1973. $5.50.

**REPORT ON THE MOUND
EXPLORATIONS OF THE BUREAU**
Cyrus Thomas; Bruce Smith, Intro.
Revised edition. Illus. 758 pp. Paper.
Smithsonian Institution Press, 1985. $25.00.

**REPORT TO THE SECRETARY OF WAR
OF THE U.S., ON INDIAN AFFAIRS**
J. Morse
Reprint of 1822 edition. Illus. 400 pp.
Scholarly Press, $25.00; Augustus M.
Kelley, $39.50.

**REQUIEM FOR A PEOPLE: THE ROGUE
INDIANS AND THE FRONTIERSMEN**
Stephen D. Beckham
Illus. University of Oklahoma Press, 1975.
$14.95; paper, $7.95.

THE RESERVATION
Ted Williams
Tales of life on the Tuscarora Indian Reservation in New York State, from the late 1930's
to the 1950's. Illus. 260 pp. Paper. Syracuse
University Press, 1976. $9.95.

**THE RESERVATION BLACKFEET,
1885-1945: A PHOTOGRAPHIC
HISTORY OF CULTURAL SURVIVAL**
William E. Farr
240 pp. University of Washington Press, 1984.
$24.95.

**RESERVATION TO CITY:
INDIAN URBANIZATION AND
FEDERAL RELOCATION**
Elaine M. Neils
200 pp. Paper. University of Chicago,
Department of Geography, 1971. $10.00.

**RESPECT FOR LIFE: THE
TRADITIONAL UPBRINGING OF
AMERICAN INDIAN CHILDREN**
S.M. Morey and O.L. Gilliam, Editors
Illus. 202 pp. Paper. Myrin Institute, 1974.
$4.95.

**RESTITUTION: THE LAND
CLAIM CASES OF THE MASHPEE,
PASSAMAQUODDY AND PENOBSCOT
INDIANS OF NEW ENGLAND**
Paul Brodeur
Illus. 160 pp. New England University Press,
1985. $19.95.

THE RETURN OF CHIEF BLACK FOOT
Victoria Mauricio
Illus. 140 pp. Paper. Donnling Co., 1981. $5.95

**REVOLT OF THE PUEBLO INDIANS
OF NEW MEXICO AND OTERMIN'S
ATTEMPTED RECONQUEST, 1680-1682**
C.W. Hackett
Two volumes. Reprint of 1942 edition. University of New Mexico Press, $30.00 per set.

**RIDING ON THE FRONTIER'S
CREST: MAHICAN INDIAN CULTURE
AND CULTURAL CHANGE**
Ted J. Brasser
Paper. National Museums of Canada, $3.95.

THE RIGHT TO BE INDIAN
Ernest Schusky
Considers the great differences betwen the
current civil rights issue, and the special
position of the American Indian. Biblio.
67 pp. Paper. The Indian Historian Press,
1970. $5.00.

***THE RINGS ON WOOT-KEW'S TAIL:
INDIAN LEGENDS OF THE ORIGIN
OF THE SUN, MOON AND STARS**
Will Gerber, et al
Grades 3-9. Paper. Council for Indian
Education, 1973. $1.95.

**RISE AND FALL OF
THE CHOCTAW REPUBLIC**
Angie Debo
Reprint of 1934 edition. Second Edition.
Illus. Maps. Biblio. 317 pp. Paper. University of Oklahoma Press, 1967. $9.95.

**RITUAL IN PUEBLO ART:
HOPI LIFE IN HOPI PAINTING**
Byron Harvey, III

Illus. 265 pp. Paper. Museum of the American Indian, 1970. $10.00.

RITUAL OF THE WIND:
NORTH AMERICAN INDIAN
CEREMONIES, MUSIC AND DANCE
  Jamake Highwater
Revised edition. Illus. 196 pp. Paper. Harper & Row, and Van der Marck, 1984. $14.95.

THE ROAD: INDIAN TRIBES
AND POLITICAL LIBERTY
  Russell Barsh and J. Youngblood Henderson
University of California Press, 1980. $22.50; paper, $7.95.

THE ROAD OF LIFE AND DEATH
  Paul Radin
A presentation of th most sacred ritual of the Winnebago Indians of Wisconsin. Reprint of 1945 edition. Princeton University Press, $33.00.

THE ROAD TO DISAPPEARANCE: A
HISTORY OF THE CREEK INDIANS
  Angie Debo
Reprint of 1941 edition. Illus. Paper. University of Oklahoma Press, $12.95.

ROBES OF WHITE SHELL
AND SUNRISE
  Richard Conn
Illus. Paper. Denver Art Museum, 1974. $7.50.

ROCK ART IN THE COCHITI
RESERVOIR DISTRICT
  Polly Schaafsma
Illus. Paper. Museum of New Mexico Press, 1975. $8.95.

ROCK ART OF THE
AMERICAN INDIAN
  Campbell Grant
Illus. 192 pp. Outbooks, 1972. $9.95.

THE ROCK ART OF UTAH
  Polly Schaafsma
Illus. Paper. Peabody Museum, 1976. $18.50.

THE ROCK POINT EXPERIENCE:
A LONGITUDINAL STUDY OF A
NAVAJO SCHOOL PROGRAM
(SAAD NAAKI BEE NA'NITIN)
  Paul Rosier and Wayne Holm
95 pp. Paper. Center for Applied Linguistics, 1980. $8.50.

THE ROCKS BEGIN TO SPEAK
  LaVan Martineau
Illus. K C Publications, 1973. $10.95.

ROCKY MOUNTAIN WEST IN 1867
  Louis Simonin; translated by Wilson Clough
Illus. University of Nebraska Press, 1966. $12.95.

ROLE OF CONJURING
IN SAULTEAN SOCIETY
  A.I. Hallowell
Reprint. Octagon Books, $10.50.

THE ROLES OF MEN AND
WOMEN IN ESKIMO CULTURE
  N.M. Giffen
Reprint of 1930 edition. AMS Press, $14.00.

THE ROLL CALL OF THE
IROQUOIS CHIEFS: A STUDY
OF A MNEMONIC CANE FROM
THE SIX NATIONS RESERVE
  W.N. Fenton
Reprint of 1950 edition. AMS Press, $20.00.

*THE ROLLING HEAD:
CHEYENNE TALES
  Henry Tall Bull and Tom Weist
Grades 3-9. Paper. Council for Indian Education, 1971. $1.95.

ROLLING THUNDER: A PERSONAL
EXPLORATION INTO THE SECRET
HEALING POWER OF AN AMERICAN
INDIAN MEDICINE MAN
  Doug Boyd
288 pp. Paper. Dell, 1974. $8.95.

THE ROOTS OF THE
AMERICAN INDIAN
  Edward P. Kellogg
Explores ancient mysteries and origins of the American Indians. EHUD, 1980. $14.95; paper, $8.95.

THE ROOTS OF DEPENDENCY:
SUBSISTENCE, ENVIRONMENT AND
SOCIAL CHANGE AMONG THE
CHOCTAWS, PAWNEES AND NAVAJOS
  Richard White
Illus. 425 pp. University of Nebraska Press, 1983. $26.50.

ROOTS OF OPPRESSION: THE
AMERICAN INDIAN QUESTION
  Steve Talbot
240 pp. International Publishing Co., 1981. $14.00; paper, $5.00.

ROOTS OF RESISTANCE:
LAND TENURE IN NEW MEXICO
(1680-1980)
  Roxine Dunbar Ortiz
202 p. American Indian Studies Center, 1981. $14.94; paper, $9.95.

THE ROOTS OF TICASUK:
AN ESKIMO WOMAN'S STORY
  Emily I. Brown
120 pp. Paper. Alaska Northwest Publishing, 1981. $4.95.

**JOHN ROSS AND THE
CHEROKEE INDIANS**
R.C. Eaton
Reprint of 1921 edition. AMS Press, $24.50.

**THE ROUND VALLEY INDIANS OF
CALIFORNIA: AN UNPUBLISHED
CHAPTER IN ACCULTURATION IN
SEVEN AMERICAN INDIAN TRIBES**
Paper. Books on Demand, $35.30.

**RUN TOWARD THE NIGHTLAND:
MAGIC OF THE OKLAHOMA CHEROKEES**
  Jack and Anna Kilpatrick
Secrets of Indian witchcraft and a wide variety
of magical incantations are translated. Illus.
212 pp. Paper. Southern Methodist University
Press, 1967. $9.95.

RUXTON OF THE ROCKIES
  George F. Ruxton; R. LeRoy, Editor
Illus. 34 pp. Paper. University of Olahoma
Press, 1984. $8.95.

S

**SAAD AHAAH SINIL:
DUAL LANGUAGE**
  Martha Austin and Regina Lynch
41 pp. Navajo Curriculum Center Press, 1983.
$5.00.

**SAC AND FOX CESSION
IN IOWA: APPRAISAL**
  William Murray
Two volumes. 148 pp. and 380 pp. Clearwater,
1973. $48.00 and $108.00 respectively.

**SAC AND FOX INDIAN LANDS
IN MISSOURI 1824: APPRAISAL**
  Arthur S. Kirk
160 pp. Clearwater Publishing, 1973. $50.00.

THE SAC AND FOX INDIANS
  W.T. Hagan
Reprint of 1958 edition. Illus. 320 pp.
University of Oklahoma Press, $18.95.

**SAC AND FOX LANDS IN ROYCE AREA
50 IN ILLINOIS AND WISCONSIN:
SOILS AND SOIL FORMING FACTORS**
  A.J. Beaver
50 pp. Clearwater Publishing, 1974. $24.00.

**SAC AND FOX AND IOWA INDIAN
LAND CESSIONS IN EASTERN
IOWA: APPRAISAL**
  William Murray
328 pp. Clearwater Publishing, 1973. $94.50.

SAC, FOX AND IOWA INDIANS
Three volumes. Illus. Garland Publishing,
1978. $42.00 each. See publisher for titles
and descriptions.

**SAC, SOX AND IOWA LANDS IN
SOUTH CENTRAL IOWA, 1839-1843,
ROYCE AREA 262: VALUATION**
  Conrad H. Hammar
194 pp. Clearwater Publishing, 1974. $58.50.

**SAC, FOX AND IOWA TRIBES:
VALUATION F LANDS IN EASTERN
IOWA, 1833-1839**
  R. Barlowe and C. Hammar
243 pp. Clearwater Publishing, 1973. $73.50.

**SAC AND FOX LANDS: APPRAISAL
PORTIONS IN ROYCE AREA 50 IN
WISCONSIN, ILLINOIS AND MISSOURI**
  R. Barlowe
70 pp. Clearwater Publishing, 1974. $28.50.

**SAC AND FOX LANDS IN ROYCE
AREA 262 IN IOWA: SOILS AND
RELATED PHYSICAL FEATURES,
1856-1874**
  F.F. Riecken
262 pp. Clearwater Publishing, 1975. $75.00.

**SAC AND FOX MINERAL LANDS IN
NORTHWESTERN ILLINOIS AND
SOUTHWESTERN WISCONSIN:
GEOLOGICAL STUDY**
  Harris Plamer
75 pp. Clearwater Publishing, 1974. $30.00.

**SAC, FOX AND MISSISSIPI
TRACTS IN KANSAS, 1854
AND 1860-1867 & 1868**
  William Murray
Two volumes. 147 pp. and 108 pp. Clearwater,
Publishing 1973. $48.00 and $37.50 respectively.

**SAC AND FOX TRACT INDIAN
TERRITORY: APPRAISAL**
  Roscoe Sears and H.J. Garret
160 pp. Clearwater Publishing, 1974. $50.00.

*SACAGEWEA
  Betty W. Skold
Grades 5-12. Illus. Paper. Dillon Press, 1977.
$7.95.

*SACAJAWEA
  Olive Burt
Grades 6-12. Illus. Franklin Watts, 1978.
$6.90.

SACAJAWEA
  Harold P. Howard
The saga of a Shoshoni Indian woman with
the Lewis and Clark Expedition. Illus.
Paper. American Indian Books, $6.95.

SACRED BUNDLES OF THE SAC AND FOX INDIANS
M.R. Harrington
Reprint of 1914 edition. Illus. 192 pp.
University Museum of Utah, $10.50;
AMS Press, $30.00.

SACRED CIRCLES: TWO THOUSAND YEARS OF NORTH AMERICAN INDIAN ART
Ralph Coe
Illus. 260 pp. Paper. Nelson Atkins, $12.95.
University of Washington Press, 1977. $15.00.

THE SACRED MOUNTAINS OF THE NAVAJO
Leland Wyman
Illus. Paper. Museum of Northern Arizona,
1976. $1.00.

THE SACRED PATH: SPELLS, PRAYERS AND POWER SONGS OF THE AMERICAN INDIAN
John Bierhorst, Editor
Illus. 192 pp. Paper. William Morrow, 1984.
$6.95.

THE SACRED PIPE: BLACK ELK'S ACCOUNT OF THE SEVEN RITES OF OGLALA SIOUX
Joseph Brown, Editor
Reprint of 1953 edition. Illus. University
of Oklahoma Press, $15.95.

SACRED SCROLLS OF THE SOUTHERN OJIBWAY
Selwyn Dewdney
University of Toronto Press, 1974. $27.50.

SACRED STORIES OF THE SWEET GRASS CREE
L. Bloomfield
Reprint of 1930 edition. AMS Press, $34.50.

THE SACRED: WAYS OF KNOWLEDGE, SOURCES OF LIFE
Peggy Beck and Anna Walters
Illus. 384 pp. Navajo Community College
Press, 1977. $14.40.

SACRED WORDS: A STUDY OF NAVAJO RELIGION AND PRAYER
Sam Gill
Illus. 283 pp. Greenwood Press, 1981. $29.95.

THE SAGA OF CHIEF CRAZY HORSE
Garrett Springer
The story of the battle of Custer versus
the Sioux Indians, written in rhyme. The
Battle of the Little Big Horn is described.
Illus. Paper. Indian Publications, $5.00.

SAGINAW CHIPPEWA: APPRAISAL OF LANDS IN MICHIGAN
Four volumes. Illus. Clearwater Publishing,
1973. See publisher for titles and prices.

SAINT CLAIR PAPERS: THE LIFE AND PUBLIC SERVICES OF ARTHUR ST. CLAIR, WITH HIS CORRESPONDENCE AND OTHER PAPERS
W.H. Smith
Facsimile of 1881 edition. Two volumes.
Illus. Ayer Co., $62.00 per set.

SALINAN INDIANS OF CALIFORNIA AND THEIR NEIGHBORS
Betty Brusa
Illus. 96 pp. Naturegraph, 1975. $8.50;
paper, $4.50.

SALISH AND CHIMAKUAM-SPEAKING INDIANS OF THE PUGET SOUND BASIN OF WASHINGTON
Caroll Riley
60 pp. Clearwater Publishing, 1973. $22.50.

*SALISH FOLK TALES
Katheryn Law
Grades 2-8. Paper. Council for Indian
Education, 1972. $1.95.

SALISH AND KOOTENAI TRIBES: ANTHROPOLOGY AND TRIBAL HISTORY
E.O. Fuller
Two volumes. Clearwater Publishing, $102/set.

SALISH SONGS AND RITUALS
Carl Carey
Paper. Goliards Press, 1969. $2.00.
Delux edition, $15.00.

SALISH WEAVING
Paul Gustafson
Illus. 132 pp. University of Washington
Press, 1980. $27.50.

SALISHAN TRIBES OF WESTERN PLATEAUS
James Teit and Franz Boas
Reprint of 1930 edition. Shorey, $40.00.

THE SALSBURY STORY: A MEDICAL MISSIONARY'S LIFETIME OF PUBLIC SERVICE
Clarence G. Salsbury and Paul Hughes
275 pp. University of Arizona Press, 1969.
$12.50.

SALVATION AND THE SAVAGE: AN ANALYSIS OF PROTESTANT MISSIONS AND AMERICAN INDIAN RESPONSE, 1787-1862
R.F. Berkhofer
Reprint of 1965 edition. Greenwood Press,
$22.50. Paper. Atheneum Publishers, $4.95.

*SAM AND THE GOLDEN PEOPLE
Marjorie Vandervelde
Grades 4-9. Paper. Council for Indian
Education, 1972. $1.95.

**SAMISH TRIBAL LANDS:
APPRAISAL, 1859**
H.B. Nelson
80 pp. Clearwater Publishing, 1973. $36.00.

**SAN CARLOS AND NORTHERN TONTO
APACHE TRACTS IN ARIZONA:
MINERAL APPRAISAL AS OF
VARIOUS DATES, 1863-1960**
Ernest Oberbilling
78 pp. Clearwater Publishing, 1973. $28.50.

**SAN DIEGO COUNTY INDIANS
AS FARMERS AND WAGE EARNERS**
Teo Couro
Paper. Acoma Books, $1.00.

**SANAPIA: COMANCHE
MEDICINE WOMAN**
David E. Jones
Reprint of 1972 edition. 107 pp. Paper.
Waveland Press, $6.95.

THE SAND CREEK MASSACRE
Stan Hoig
Illus. Paper. University of Oklahoma Press,
$6.95.

**SAND IN A WHIRLWIND:
THE PAIUTE INDIAN WAR, 1860**
Ferol Egan
Illus. 316 pp. Paper. University of Nevada
Press, 1985. $11.25.

**THE SANDAL AND THE CAVE:
THE INDIANS OF OREGON**
Luther S. Cressman
Illus. 96 pp. Paper. Oregon State University
Press, 1981. $5.00.

**SANDPAINTING OF THE
NAVAJO SHOOTING CHANT**
F. Newcomb and G. Reichard
Reprint. Illus. Peter Smith, $11.50. Paper.
Dover, $7.95.

**THE SANDPAINTINGS OF
THE KAYENTA NAVAHO**
L.C. Wyman
Reprint of 1952 edition. Paper. Kraus, $13.00.

**THE SANPOIL AND NESPELEM:
SALISHAN PEOPLES OF NORTH-
EASTERN WASHINGTON**
Verne F. Ray
Reprint of 1933 edition. AMS Press, $24.50.

**SANTO DOMINGO PUEBLO: HISTORY
OF THE ABORIGINAL TITLE AREA**
Albert Schroeder

Clearwater Publishing, $41.00.

SARAH WINNEMUCCA
Katherine Gehm
185 pp. O'Sullivan Woodside, 1975. $8.95.

*SARAH WINNEMUCCA
Doris Kloss
Grades 5-12. Illus. Dillon Press, 1981. $6.95.

**SARAH WINNEMUCCA OF
THE NORTHERN PAIUTES**
Gae W. Canfield
Illus. 336 pp. University of Oklahoma Press,
1983. $19.95.

**SATANTA, THE GREAT CHIEF OF
THE KIOWAS AND HIS PEOPLE**
C. Wharton
Reprint of 1935 edition. AMS Press, $18.00.

**SAUK, FOX AND IOWA INDIANS:
ETHNOLOGICAL REPORT ON THEIR
HISTORIC HABITAT**
Zachary Gussow
62 pp. Clearwater Publishing, 1973. $24.00.

**SAUK AND FOX NATIONS OF
THE INDIANS: APPRAISAL**
Walter R. Kuehnle
300 pp. Clearwater Publishing, 1973. $87.00.

**THE SAUKS AND THE
BLACK HAWK WAR**
P.A. Armstrong
Reprint of 1887 edition. Illus. AMS Press,
$47.50.

**THE SAULTE STE. MARIE AREA:
HISTORICAL REPORT**
Robert Warner and Lois Grossbeck
21 pp. Clearwater Publishing, 1973. $16.00.

THE SAVAGE AND HIS TOTEM
P. Hadfield
Reprint of 1938 edition. AMS Press, $16.00.

**SAVAGE SCENE: THE LIFE
AND TIMES OF JAMES KIRKER,
FRONTIER KING**
William McGaw
Illus. 288 pp. Hastings House Publishers, 1972.
$10.95.

SAVAGISM AND CIVILITY
Bernard Sheehan
Cambridge University Press, 1980. $39.50;
paper, $10.95.

**SAVAGISM AND CIVILIZATION:
A STUDY OF THE INDIAN AND
THE AMERICAN MIND**
R.H. Pearce and J.H. Miller, Editors
272 pp. Paper. Johns Hopkins Press, 1967.
$7.95.

**SAYNDAY'S PEOPLE: THE
KIOWA INDIANS AND THE
STORIES THEY TOLD**
Alice Marriott
A collection of Kiowa folktales. Illus.
226 pp. Paper. University of Nebraska
Press, 1963. $2.95.

SCALP CEREMONIAL OF ZUNI
E.C. Parsons
Reprint of 1924 edition. Paper. Kraus, $15.00.

SCARLET PLUME
Frederick Manfred
365 pp. Paper. University of Nebraska Press,
1983. $8.95.

**SCHAT-CHEN: HISTORY, TRADITIONS
AND NARRATIVES OF THE QUERES
INDIANS OF LAGUNA AND ACOMA**
John Gunn
Reprint of 1917 edition. AMS Press, $22.00.

**SCHOLARS AND THE INDIAN
EXPERIENCE: CRITICAL REVIEWS
OF RECENT WRITINGS IN THE
SOCIAL SCIENCES**
W.R. Swagerty
280 pp. Indiana University Press, 1984.
$22.50; paper, $9.95.

**THE SCHOOL AT MOPASS:
A PROBLEM OF IDENTITY**
A. Richard King
Describes the educational process in a residen-
tial school for Indian children in the Yukon
Territory of Northwest Canada. Reprint of 1967
edition. 96 pp. Paper. Irvington, $7.95.

SCHOOLCRAFT: LITERARY VOYAGER
Philip Mason, Editor
208 pp. Michigan State University Press, 1962.
$5.00.

**SCHOOLCRAFT'S EXPEDITION TO
LAKE ITASCA: THE DISCOVERY OF
THE SOURCE OF THE MISSISSIPPI**
Philip Mason, Editor
406 pp. Michigan State University Press, 1958.
$10.00

**SCHOOLCRAFT'S INDIAN LEGENDS
FROM ALGIC RESEARCHES**
H.R. Schoolcraft; M. Williams, Editor
Reprint of 1956 edition. Greenwood Press,
$21.00.

**SCOORWA: JAMES SMITH'S
INDIAN CAPTIVITY NARRATIVE**
James Smith
Reprint. Illus. 176 pp. Paper. Ohio Historical
Society, $5.95.

SCOUT AND RANGER
James Pike

Reprint of 1932 edition. Illus. 164 pp. Da Capo
Press, $19.50.

SCULPTURING TOTEM POLES
Walt Way; Jack Ekstrom, Editor
Illus. 26 pp. Paper. Vestal, 1985. $5.00.

**SEA AND CEDAR: HOW THE
NORTHWEST COAST INDIANS LIVED**
Lois McConkey
Illus. Paper. Madrona Publishers, 1973. $6.95.

***THE SEA HUNTERS: INDIANS
OF THE NORTHWESTERN COAST**
Sonia Bleeker
Grades 3-6. Illus. William Morrow, 1951. $8.00.

**SEA IN THE PRE-COLUMBIAN WORLD:
CONFERENCE AT DUMBARTON OAKS,
OCTOBER 26-27, 1974**
Elizabeth P. Benson, Editor
Illus. Center for Pre-Columbian Studies, 1977.
$15.00.

THE SEA PEOPLE OF OZETTE
Allan May
Illus. 112 pp. Paper. B & E Enterprises, 1975.
$3.95.

SEAHB SIWASH
Leon L. Stock
Illus. 352 pp. Todd & Honeywell, 1981.
$15.00.

*SEAL FOR A PAL
Paul E. Layman
Grades 4-9. Paper. Council for Indian
Education, 1972. $1.95.

**THE SEARCH FOR AN AMERICAN
INDIAN IDENTITY: MODERN
PAN-AMERICAN MOVEMENTS**
Hazel W. Hertzberg
Illus. 362 pp. Syracuse University Press,
1971. $18.95; paper, $10.95.

SEASONAL WOMAN
Luci Tapahonso
Drawings by R.C. Gorman. 55 pp. Native
American Studies Center, 1982. $5.00.

**SECOND LANGUAGE LEARNING
FOR AMERICAN INDIANS: A
TOPICAL BIBLIOGRAPHY**
Douglas Knox, et al
43 pp. National Clearinghouse for Bilingual
Education, 1982. $5.65.

**THE SECOND LONG WALK:
THE NAVAJO-HOPI LAND DISPUTE**
Jerry Kammer
Paper. University of New Mexico Press, 1980.
$14.95.

SECRET OF THE TOTEM
Andrew Lang
Reprint of 1905 edition. AMS Pres, $16.75

THE SECRET SAGA OF FIVE-SACK
Henry L. Reimers
25 pp. Paper. Ye Galleon Press, 1975. $3.00.

SECRETS OF THE MIGHTY SIOUX
F. Edward Butterworth
Paper. Indian Univerity Press, 1982. $11.00.

SEEDS OF EXTINCTION:
JEFFERSONIAN PHILANTHROPY
AND THE AMERICAN INDIAN
Bernard Sheehan
320 pp. University of North Carolina Press,
1973. $25.00. Paper. W.W. Norton, $5.95.

SEEING WITH THE NATIVE EYE:
CONTRIBUTIONS TO THE STUDY OF
NATIVE AMERICAN RELIGION
Walter H. Capps
Paper. Harper & Row, 1976 $6.95.

SELECTED PREFORMS, POINTS
AND KNIVES OF THE NORTH
AMERICAN INDIANS, VOL. 1
Gregory Perino
Illus. 404 pp. Gregory Perino, $42.00.

SELECTED PROBLEMS IN YAVAPAI
SYNTAX: THE VERDE VALLEY DIALECT
Martha Kendall
Garland Publishing, 1976. $51.00.

THE SELECTED WRITING
OF EDWARD S. CURTIS
Barry Gifford, Editor
Two comprehensive selections from Curtis'
legendary 24-volume, *The North American*
Indian. A selection of Curtis' writings
from his studies of more than 80 tribes west
of the Mississippi. Illus. 200 pp. Paper.
Creative Arts Book Co., 1981. $5.95.

SELECTED WRITINGS OF EDWARD
SAPIR IN LANGUAGE, CULTURE
AND PERSONALITY
E. Sapir; David G. Mandelbaum, Editor
Reprint of 1949 edition. University of
California Press, $38.50; paper, $14.95.

SELECTION OF SOME OF THE
MOST INTERESTING NARRATIVES
OF OUTRAGES COMMITTED BY THE
INDIANS IN THEIR WARS WITH
THE WHITE PEOPLE
Archibald Loudon
Reprint of 1808 edition. Two volume in one.
Ayer Co., $36.00.

*THE SEMINOLE
Emilie U. Lepthien

Grades K-4. Illus. 48 pp. Children's Press,
1985. $3.95.

THE SEMINOLE
T. Pratt
Reprint of 1954 edition. Great Outdoors.

SEMINOLE LANDS IN FLORIDA:
APPRAISAL
William Murray
220 pp. Clearwater, 1974. $64.50.

SEMINOLE LANDS: MINERAL
INTERESTS IN OKLAHOMA
Josef Faust and Martin Lee
184 pp. Clearwater, 1973. $57.00.

SEMINOLE MUSIC
F. Densmore
Reprint of 1956 edition. Illus. 276 pp.
Da Capo Press, $25.00.

SEMINOLE NATION: APPRAISAL
OF TRACTS OF LAND CEDED
IN 1823 and 1832
William Edgemon
140 pp. Clearwater, 1973. $45.00.

THE SEMINOLE NATION: AN
ETHNO-HISTORICAL REPORT OF THE
FLORIDA INDIANS AS OF 1823
Charles Fairbanks
Clearwater, 1976. $84.00.

THE SEMINOLE OF
FLORIDA TO 1823
Charles Fairbanks
292 pp. Clearwater, 1974. $82.50.

SEMINOLE PATCHWORK BOOK
Cheryl G. Bradkin
Illus. 48 pp. Paper. Yours Truly, 1980. $7.50.

SEMINOLE SAGA:
THE JESUP REPORT
Thomas Jesup; Byron Troyer, Editor
Illus. 28 pp. Paper. Island Press, 1973. $1.00.

THE SEMINOLE SEED
Robert N. Peck
420 pp. Pineapple Press, 1983. $14.95.

A SEMINOLE SOURCEBOOK
W.C. Sturtevant, Editor
856 pp. Garland Publishing, 1985. $90.00.

SEMINOLES
Edwin McReynolds
Reprint of 1957 edition. Illus. Paper.
University of Oklahoma Press, $10.95.

*A SENECA GARDEN
Geri Guidetti
Grades 2-8. Illus. 26 pp. Paper. KMG
Publications, 1981. $3.95.

SENECA MYTHS AND FOLK TALES
A. Parker
Reprint of 1923 edition. AMS Press, $35.00.

**SENECA NATIONS AND TONAWANDA
BAND OF SENECA INDIANS,
APPRAISAL OF LANDS IN
WESTERN NEW YORK STATE**
Walter Kuehnle
410 pp. Clearwater, 1973. $115.50.

SENECA THANKSGIVING RITUALS
W. Chafe
Reprint of 1961 edition. Scholarly Press,
$36.00.

**SENECAS AND SANDUSKY:
APPRAISAL OF LANDS IN
NORTHWESTERN OHIO, 1831**
Richard Hall
140 pp. Clearwater, 1973. $45.00.

*SEQUOYAH AND HIS MIRACLE
William L. Roper
Grades 6-12. Paper. Council for Indian
Education, 1972. $1.95.

**A SERPENT FOR A DOVE:
THE SUPPRESSION OF THE
AMERICAN INDIAN**
Noel Grisham
Illus. 168 pp. Jenkins Publishing, $7.50.

**THE SERPENT SYMBOL, AND
THE WORSHIP OF THE RECIPROCAL
PRINCIPLES OF NATURE IN AMERICA**
E.G. Squier
Reprint of 1851 edition. Kraus, $21.00.

**THE SERRANO INDIANS OF
SOUTHERN CALIFORNIA**
Frank Johnston
Malki Museum Press, 1967. $1.00.

**SETTLEMENT PATTERNS IN
LATE ZUNI PREHISTORY**
Keith W. Kintigh
Paper. University of Arizona Press, 1984.
$14.95.

**SETTLEMENT, SUBSISTENCE, AND
SOCIETY IN LATE ZUNI PREHISTORY**
Keith W. Kintigh
132 pp. Paper. University of Arizona Press,
1985. $14.95.

***SETTLERS AND STRANGERS:
NATIVE AMERICANS OF THE
DESERT SOUTHWEST AND
HISTORY AS THEY SAW IT**
Betty Baker
Grades 3-6. Illus. 96 pp. Macmillan, 1977.
$9.95.

**SETTLING WITH THE INDIANS: THE
MEETING OF ENGLISH AND INDIAN
CULTURES IN AMERICA, 1580-1640**
Karen Kupperman
Rowman & Litlefield, 1980. $24.50.

**SEVEN FAMILIES IN
PUEBLO POTTERY**
Maxwell Museum of Anthropology
Illus. 116 pp. University of New Mexico
Press, 1974. $7.95.

**SEVEN AND NINE YEARS AMONG
THE COMANCHES AND APACHES:
AN AUTOBIOGRAPHY**
Edwin Eastman
Reprint of 1873 edition. Garland, $42.00.

**SEX BELIEFS AND PRACTICES
IN A NAVAHO COMMUNITY WITH
COMPARATIVE MATERIAL FROM
OTHER NAVAJO AREAS**
Flora Bailey
Reprint of 1950. Paper. Peabody Museum,
$10.00.

SHADOW COUNTRY
Paula G. Allen
49 pp. Paper. American Indian Studies Center,
1982. $7.50.

**SHADOW OF THE HUNTER:
STORIES OF ESKIMO LIFE**
Richard K. Nelson
Illus. 282 pp. University of Chicago Press,
1980. $12.50; paper, $8.95.

**THE SHADOW OF SEQUOYAH:
SOCIAL DOCUMENTS OF THE
CHEROKEES, 1862-1964**
Jack and Anna Kilpatrick, Editors
143 pp. University of Oklahoma Press, 1965.
$11.95; paper, $4.95.

**SHADOWS OF THE BUFFALO: A
FAMILY ODYSSEY AMONG THE INDIANS**
Adolf and Beverly Hungry Wolf
Pat Golbitz, Editor
Illus. 288 pp. Paper. William Morrow, 1985.
$6.95.

**SHADOWS OF THE INDIAN: STEREO-
TYPES IN AMERICAN CULTURE**
Raymond Stedman
Illus. 300 pp. University of Oklahoma Press,
1982. $24.95.

**THE SHAMAN AND THE
MEDICINE WHEEL**
Evelyn Eaton
Illus. 206 pp. Theosophical Publishing, 1982.
$13.95; paper, $7.50.

SHAMANISM IN WESTERN NORTH AMERICA
W.Z. Park
Reprint of 1938 edition. 166 pp. Cooper Square Publishers, $20.00.

THE SHAMANS HEALING WAY
Spencer Rogers
Paper. Acoma Books, 1976. $4.95.

A SHANADITTI: THE LAST OF THE BEOTHUCKS
Keith Winter
Paper. International Scholarly Book Service, $7.50.

SHAPES OF THEIR THOUGHTS: REFLECTIONS OF CULTURAL CONTACT IN NORTHWEST COAST INDIAN ART
Victoria Wyatt
Illus. 80 pp. University of Oklahoma Press, and American Indian Books, 1984. $9.95.

SHARING A HERITAGE: AMERICAN INDIAN ARTS
Charlotte Heth
American Indian Studies Center.
SHARING OUR WORLDS
A photographic documentary of children from three families sharing their multi-cultural experiences. Grades 2-6. Illus. 32 pp. Daybreak Star Press, $4.75.

THE SHASTA
R. Dixon
Reprint of 1907 edition. 256 pp. AMS Press, $26.50.

THE SHAWNEE
Jerry Clark
Illus. 112 pp. University Press of Kentucky, 1977. $6.95.

SHAWNEE: THE CEREMONIALISM OF A NATIVE AMERICAN TRIBE AND ITS CULTURAL BACKGROUND
James Howard
Illus. 460 pp. Ohio University Press, 1981. $28.95; paper, $14.95.

SHAWNEE HOME LIFE: THE PAINTING OF ERNEST SPYBUCK
Lee Callander and Ruth Slivka
Illus. 32 pp. Paper. Museum of the American Indian, 1984. $8.95.

THE SHAWNEE PROPHET
R. David Edmunds
Illus. 275 pp. University of Nebraska Press, 1983. $16.95; paper, $7.95.

SHAWNEE TRACT IN KANSAS, APPRAISAL, 1854
William Murray
170 pp. Clearwater, 1973. $52.50.

SHAWNEES TRADITIONS
C.C. Trowbridge;
V. Kinietz and E. Voegelin, Editors
Reprint of 1939 edition. AMS Press, $17.00.

THE SHE-WOLF OF TSLA-A-WAT: INDIAN STORIES FROM BRITISH COLUMBIA
Anne Simeon
International Scholarly Book Service, $7.50.

THE SHEFFIELD SITE: AN ONEONTA SITE ON THE ST. CROIX RIVER
Guy E. Gibbon
Illus. 62 pp. Paper. Minnesota Historical Society, 1973. $4.00.

SHERIDAN'S TROOPERS ON THE BORDERS: A WINTER CAMPAIGN ON THE PLAINS
B. Randolph Keim
A participant's account. Reissue of 1870 edition. Illus. 366 pp. Rio Grande Press, 1977. $15.00.

THE SHINNECOCK INDIANS: A CULTURE HISTORY
Gaynell Stone, et al, Editors
Illus. 404 pp. Paper. Ginn Press, 1984. $28.00.

SHIRLEY: THE WAY: AN ANTHOLOGY OF AMERICAN INDIAN LITERATURE
Stan Steiner and Shirley Witt
Alfred A. Knopf, 1972. $10.00.

SHONTO: STUDY OF THE ROLE OF THE TRADER IN A MODERN NAVAJO COMMUNITY
W.Y. Adams
Reprint of 1963 edition. Scholarly Press, $49.00.

A SHORT BIOGRAPHY OF JOHN LEETH; WITH AN ACCOUNT OF HIS LIFE AMONG THE INDIANS
E. Jeffries; R.G. Thwaites, Editor
Ayer Co., Publishers, $18.00.

A SHORT HISTORY OF THE INDIANS OF THE U.S.
Edward H. Spicer
Reprint of 1969 edition. 320 pp. Paper. Robert E. Krieger, $9.50.

SHOSHONE INDIANS
Illus. Garland Publishing, $42.00.

SHOSHONE LANDS MINERAL VALUATION, NEVADA, 1872, AND CALIFORNIA, 1853
Ernest Oberbilling
208 pp. Clearwater, 1973. $64.50.

SHOSHONE TRIBAL LANDS, CALIFORNIA, 1853, AND NEVADA, 1872: APPRAISAL
John Vaughan, Jr.
91 pp. Clearwater, 1973. $31.50.

A SHOSHONEAN SOURCEBOOK
David H. Thomas, Editor
779 pp. Garland Publishing, 1985. $9.00.

THE SHOSHONI-CROW SUN DANCE
Fred W. Voget
Illus. 368 pp. University of Oklahoma, 1984. $19.95.

THE SHOSHONI FRONTIER AND THE BEAR RIVER MASSACRE
Brigham D. Madsen
Illus. 336 pp. University of Utah Press, 1985. $19.95.

THE SHOSHONI INDIANS OF INYO COUNTY, CALIFORNIA
Charles N. Irwin
Illus. 114 pp. Paper. Ballena Pres, 1980. $6.95.

THE SHOSHONIS: SENTINELS OF THE ROCKIES
V. Trenholm and M. Carley
Illus. Paper. University of Oklahoma Press, 1964. $11.95.

THE SHUSWAP
J. Teit
Reprint of 1909 edition. AMS Press, $37.50.

THE SHUSWAP LANGUAGE
A.H. Kuipers
297 pp. Paper. Mouton Publishers, 1974. $42.40.

SIGN LANGUAGE AMONG NORTH AMERICAN INDIANS COMPARED WITH THAT AMONG OTHER PEOPLES AND DEAF MUTES
D. Garrick Mallery
Reprint of 1881 edition. Illus. 552 pp. Mouton Publishers, $40.80.

*SILAS AND THE MAD-SAD PEOPLE
Grades 1-5. Paper. New Seed Press, 1981. $3.50.

SILENT ARROWS: INDIAN LORE AND ARTIFACT HUNTING
Earl F. Moore
Third Edition. Illus. Tremaine Graphic and Publishing, 1973.

SILETZ INDIAN RESERVATION, APPRAISAL REPORT OF LANDS CEDED UNDER AGREEMENT OF OCTOBER 31, 1892, BY THE TILLAMOOK TRIBE OF INDIANS
Norman Plummer
158 pp. Clearwater, 1973. $50.00.

THE SILVER ARROW AND OTHER INDIAN ROMANCES OF THE DUNE COUNTRY
E.H. Reed
Gordon Press, 1977. $59.95.

SIMIKAMEEN COUNTRY
N.L. Barlee
Revised edition. Illus. 96 pp. Hancock House, 1985. $7.95.

SINGING FOR POWER: THE SONG MAGIC OF THE PAPAGO INDIANS OF SOUTHERN ARIZONA
Ruth Underhill
University of California Press, 1977. $19.50; paper, $3.95.

*SINOPAH, THE INDIAN BOY
James W. Schultz
Grades 4-7. Illus. 104 pp. Beaufort Books, 1983. $15.95; paper, $7.95. Paper. Confluence Press, $6.95.

SIOUAN (TETON AND SANTEE DIALECTS) DAKOTA
Franz Boas and John Swanton
Reprint of 1911 edition. 94 pp. Paper. Shorey, $7.95.

THE SIOUAN TRIBES OF THE EAST
James Mooney
Reprint of 1894 edition. Illus. Johnson Reprint, $39.00.

*THE SIOUX
Alice Osinski
Grades K-4. Illus. 48 pp. Children's Press, 1984. $10.60; paper, $3.95.

SIOUX CESSION IN IOWA AND MINNESOTA, APPRAISAL
William Murray
165 pp. Clearwater Publishing, 1973. $51.00.

A SIOUX CHRONICLE
G. Hyde
Reprint of 1956 edition. 334 pp. University of Oklahoma Press, $15.95.

SIOUX COLLECTIONS
T. Emogene Paulson
245 pp. Dakota Press, 1982. $17.50.

THE SIOUX: A CRITICAL BIBLIOGRAPHY
Herbert Hoover
96 pp. Paper. Indiana University Press, 1979. $4.95.

SIOUX INDIAN LEGENDS
Mildred Fielder
Illus. 160 pp. American Indian Books, $12.95.

**SIOUX INDIAN TRIBE: APPRAISAL
OF LANDS IN NORTH DAKOTA, SOUTH
DAKOTA, NEBRASKA, WYOMING, AND
MONTANA - 1869**
William Murray
442 pp. Clearwater Publishing, 1973. $124.50.

SIOUX INDIANS
Four volumes. Illus. Garland Publishing,
$42.00 each.

***THE SIOUX INDIANS: HUNTERS
AND WARRIORS OF THE PLAINS**
Sonia Bleeker
Grades 3-6. Illus. Wiliam Morrow, 1962.
$10.88.

**SIOUX LANDS IN THE BLACK
HILLS, SOUTH DAKOTA: MINERAL
VALUE AS OF 1877**
Ernest Oberbilling
130 pp. Clearwater Publishing, 1973. $42.00.

**SIOUX: LIFE AND CUSTOMS
OF A WARRIOR SOCIETY**
R.B. Hassrick, et al
Reprint of 1964 edition. Illus. University
of Oklahoma Press, $19.95.

SIOUX MUSIC
William N. Fenton
Scholarly Press, $29.00.

**SIOUX NATION LANDS ACQUIRED
BY THE U.S. UNDER TREAY OF
APRIL 29, 1868: APPRAISAL**
Frank Kleinman and Donald Myers
317 pp. Clearwater Publishing, 1973. $91.50.

**SIOUX OCCUPATION OF MISSOURI
TERRITORY, 1640-1868**
Harry Anderson
Clearwater Publishing, $24.00.

**THE SIOUX OF THE ROSEBUD:
A HISTORY IN PICTURES**
Henry and Jean Hamilton
Illus. 320 pp. Paper. University of Oklahoma
Press, and American Indian Books, 1971. $16.50.

SIOUX QUILLWORK TECHNIQUES
Illus. Poster, 24x20". Supt. of Documents,
1982. $2.25.

THE SIOUX UPRISING OF 1862
Kenneth Carley
Revised edition. Illus. 102 pp. Minnesota
Historical Society, 1976. $7.95; paper, $4.95.

**SIPAPU: THE STORY OF
THE INDIANS OF ARIZONA
AND NEW MEXICO**
William E. Coffer
Illus. 144 pp. Van Nostrand Reinhold, 1982.
$15.95.

**SIR WALTER RALEIGH AND
HIS COLONY IN AMERICA**
I.N. Tarbox, Editor
Burt Franklin, Publisher, 1966. $24.00.

**SISSETON AND WAHPETON BANDS:
APPRAISAL OF LANDS IN MINNESOTA,
WISCONSIN, SOUTH DAKOTA AND IOWA**
Dewey Newcombe and Howard Lawrence
320 pp. Clearwater Publishing, 1973. $92.00.

**THE SISSETON AND WAHPETON
TRIBES IN NORTH DAKOTA AND
SOUTH DAKOTA AND THE TREATY
OF 1867 AND AGREEMENT OF 1872**
Helen H. Tanner
134 pp. Clearwater Publishing, 1974. $44.50.

**SISSETON AND WAHPETON
TRIBES OF NORTH DAKOTA:
APPRAISAL OF LANDS**
William Muske
100 pp. Clearwater Publishing, 1974. $36.00.

**SISTER TO THE SIOUX: THE
MEMOIRS OF ELAINE GOODALE
EASTMAN, 1885-1891**
Elaine Eastman; Kay Graber, Editor
Illus. University of Nebraska Press, 1978.
$10.95.

**SITANKA: THE FULL
STORY OF WOUNDED KNEE**
Forrest W. Seymour
A fresh account of the major events preced-
ing, during and immediately after the battle
of 1890 at Wounded Knee. The Christopher
Publishing House, 1981. $10.75.

*SITTING BULL
Faith Knoop
A biography. Grades 5-9. Illus. 75 pp. Dillon
Press, 1974. $7.95.

**SITTING BULL, CHAMPION
OF THE SIOUX: A BIOGRAPHY**
S. Vestal
Reprint of 1957 edition. Illus. University
of Oklahoma Press, $19.95.

***SITTING BULL:
GREAT SIOUX CHIEF**
L. Anderson
Grades 2-5. Illus. Garrard Publishing, 1970.
$7.00.

SITTING BULL:
THE YEARS IN CANADA
Grant MacEwan
An account of the Sioux chief's four-year
asylum in the Canadian West. Illus. Paper.
Hurtig Publishers, $4.95.

*SITTING BULL:
WARRIOR OF THE SIOUX
Jane Fleischer
New edition. Grades 4-6. Illus. 48 pp. Troll
Associates, 1979. $8.00; paper, $2.00.

*SITTING ON THE BLU-EYED BEAR:
NAVAJO MYTHS AND LEGENDS
Gerald Hausman
Grades 7-12. Illus. Lawrence Hill, 1976.
$10.00.

SIX MONTHS AMONG THE INDIANS
Darius B. Cook
Reprint of 1889 edition. Illus. 101 pp.
Avery Color, $5.95.

SIX NATIONS, WYANDOT AND
DELAWARE: HISTORICAL REPORT
ON PENNSYLVANIA'S PURCHASES
FROM THE INDIANS, 1784, 1785
& 1789: INDIAN OCCUPANCY
OF AREAS PURCHSED
Donald Kent
270 pp. Clearwater Publishing, 1973. $79.50.

SIX WEEKS IN THE SIOUX TEPEES:
A NARRATIVE OF INDIAN CAPTIVITY
Sarah Wakefield
Bound with other captivity narratives.
Reprint of 1863 edition, et al. Ye Galleon
Press, $13.00.

SIXTY YEARS OF INDIAN AFFAIRS:
POLITICAL, ECONOMIC AND DIPLO-
MATIC, 1789-1850, CHAPEL HILL,
NORTH CAROLINA
G.D. Harmon
Reprint of 1941 edition. Kraus, 29.00.

SKAGIT TRACT, WASHINGTON,
SUPPLEMENTING APPRAISALS OF
THE DUWAMISH, SNOHOMISH
AND SUQUAMISH TRACTS
C. Marc Miller
59 pp. Clearwater Publishing, 1973. $22.50.

SKETCHES OF AMERICAN INDIAN
TRIBES: 1841-1843
Edward Goodall
Farrar Straus & Giroux, 1978. $12.00.

SKETCHES OF INDIAN LIFE
IN THE PACIFIC NORTHWEST
Alexander Diomedi
Ye Galleon Press, 1978. $12.00.

SKETCHES OF MISSION LIFE
AMONG THE INDIANS OF OREGON
Zachariah Mudge
Ye Galleon Press, 1983. $12.00.

SKETCHES OF A TOUR TO THE LAKES
T. McKenney
A sourcebook of early Indian life among the
Chippewa and the Sioux. Reprint. Illus.
Ross & Haines, $12.50.

SKETCHES OF WESTERN ADVENTURE
John McClung
Reprint of 1832 edition. Ayer Co., $13.00.

S'KLALLAM TRACT: APPRAISAL
C. Marc Miller
196 pp. Clearwater Publishing, 1973. $60.00.

SKOKOMISH TRACT: APPRAISAL
C. Marc Miller
188 pp. Clearwater Publishing, 1973. $57.00.

*SKUNNY WUNDY SENECA
INDIAN TALES
Arthur C. Parker
Grades 3-8. Illus. Albert Whitman, 1970.
$5.95.

THE SKY IS MY TIPI
Mody Boatright, Editor
Reprint of 1949 edition. Illus. 254 pp.
Southern Methodist University Press, $6.95.

*SKY MAN ON THE TOTEM POLE
Christie Harris
Grades 4-7. Illus. 176 pp. Atheneum, 1975.
$7.95.

*SKY WATCHERS OF AGES PAST
Malcolm E. Weiss
Grades 5-9. Houghton Mifflin, 1982. $7.95.

SLAVEHOLDING INDIANS
A.H. Abel
Reprint of 1919 edition. Three volumes.
Scholarly Press, $49.00 each; $125.00/set.

SLAVERY AND THE EVOLUTION OF
CHEROKEE SOCIETY, 1540-1866
Maps. 222 pp. University of Tennessee
Press, 1979. $17.95.

SLEEPING GIANTS
William Coffer and Koi Hosh
Paper. University Press of America, 1979.
$9.25.

SMALL BONES, LITTLE EYES
Nila Northsun: Kirk Robertson, Editor
72 pp. Paper. Duck Down, 1981. $5.00.

*SMALL WORLD OF PLAINS INDIANS
Pluckrose, Editor
Grades K-3. Franklin Watts, 1980. $6.95.

JOHN SIMPSON SMITH, 1810-1871
Stan Hoig
Reprint of 1974 edition. Illus. 30 pp. Paper.
Pueblo County Historical Society, $3.50.

**SLIM BUTTES, 1876: AN EPISODE
OF THE GREAT SIOUX WAR**
Jerome A. Greene
Illus. 208 pp. Univerity of Oklahoma Press,
1982. $16.95.

**SMILING DAN: STRUCTURE
AND FUNCTION AT A MIDDLE
WOODLAND SETTLEMENT IN
THE ILLINOIS VALLEY**
Barbara Stafford and Mark Sant, Editors
Illus. 513 pp. Paper. Center for American
Archaeology, 1985. $12.95.

**SMOKE FROM THEIR FIRES:
THE LIFE OF KWAKIUTL CHIEF**
C.S. Ford
Reprint of 1941 edition. Illus. 248 pp.
Shoe String Press, $20.00.

**SMOKING TECHNOOGY OF THE
ABORIGINES OF THE IROQUOIS
AREA OF NEW YORK STATE**
Edward S. Rutsch
252 pp. Fairleigh Dickinson University Press,
1972. $25.00.

**SMOKY-TOP: THE ART AND
TIMES OF WILLIE SEAWEED**
Bill Holm
Illus. 160 pp. University of Washington Press,
1983. $24.95.

THE SNAKE CEREMONIALS AT WALPI
J.W. Fewkes, et al
Reprint of 1894 edition. AMS Press, $25.00.

**THE SNAKE COUNTRY EXPEDITION
OF 1830-1831: JOHN WORK'S
FIELD JOURNAL**
John Work; Francis D. Haines, Editor
Illus. 224 pp. University of Oklahoma Press,
1971. $11.95.

**THE SNAKE DANCE OF
THE HOPI INDIANS**
Earle Forrest
Reprint of 1961 edition. Illus. Westernlore,
$8.95.

**THE SNAKE DANCE OF
THE MOQUIS OF ARIZONA**
John G. Bourke
Illus. 371 pp. Paper. University of Arizona
Press, 1984. $10.95.

**SNAKE-PAIUTE TRACT IN OREGON,
APPRAISAL, JANUARY 1879**
C. Marc Miller
107 pp. Clearwater Publishing, 1973. $50.00.

**SNARES, DEADFALLS AND OTHER
TRAPS OF THE NORTHERN ALGON-
QUIAN AND NORTHERN ATHAPASKANS**
J.M. Cooper
Reprint of 1934 edition. AMS Press, $14.00.

**A SNUG LITTLE PURCHASE:
HOW RICHARD HENDERSON
BOUGHT KAINTUCKEE FROM
THE CHEROKEES IN 1775**
Charles Brashers
Illus. Associated Creative Writers, 1979.
$7.95; paper, $4.95.

**THE SOBAIPURI INDIANS OF THE
UPPER SAN PEDRO RIVER VALLEY,
SOUTHEASTERN ARIZONA**
Charles DiPeso
Reprint of 1953 edition. Kraus, $71.00.

**SOCIAL ANTHROPOLOGY OF
NORTH AMERICAN INDIAN TRIBES**
Fred Eggan, et al
Enlarged edition. 574 pp. Paper. University
of Chicago Press, 1972. $3.95.

**SOCIAL AND CEREMONIAL
ORGANIZATION OF COCHITI**
E. Goldfrank
Reprint of 1927 edition. Paper. Kraus, $15.00.

**SOCIAL CONDITIONS, BELIEFS
AND LINGUISTIC RELATIONSHIP
OF THE TLINGIT INDIANS**
John Swanton
Reprint of 1908 edition. Johnson Reprint,
$19.00.

**SOCIAL AND ECONOMIC CHANGE
AMONG THE NORTHERN OJIBWA**
R.W. Dunning
Paper. University of Toronto Press, 1959.
$6.95.

**THE SOCIAL ECONOMY OF
THE TLINGIT INDIANS**
Kalervo Oberg
Ilus. 144 pp. Paper. University of Washington
Press, 1980. $7.50.

SOCIAL LIFE OF THE CROW INDIANS
R. Lowie
Reprint of 1912 edition. AMS Press, $12.50.

**SOCIAL LIFE OF
THE NAVAJO INDIANS**
G. Reichard
Reprint of 1928 edition. AMS Press, $31.00.

**SOCIAL ORGANIZATION
OF THE PAPAGO INDIANS**
R. Underhill
Reprint of 1939 edition. AMS Press, $32.50.

**SOCIAL ORGANIZATION OF
THE TEWA OF NEW MEXICO**
E.C. Parsons
Reprint of 1929 edition. Paper. Kraus, $34.00.

**SOCIAL ORGANIZATION
OF THE WESTERN PUEBLOS**
Fred Eggan
Paper. University of Chicago Press, 1973.
$2.95.

**SOCIAL ORGANIZATION AND
RITUALISTIC CEREMONIES OF
THE BLACKFOOT INDIANS**
C. Wissler
Reprint of 1912 edition. Illus. 312 pp.
AMS Press, $24.00.

**SOCIAL ORGANIZATION AND
THE SECRET SOCIETIES OF
THE KWAKIUTL INDIANS**
Franz Boas
Reprint of 1897 edition. Johnson Reprint,
$60.00.

**SOCIAL ORGANIZATION AND
SOCIAL USAGES OF THE INDIANS
OF THE CREEEK CONFEDERACY**
John Swanton
Reprint of 1928 edition. Johnson Reprint,
$37.00.

**A SOCIAL STUDY OF 150 CHIPPEWA
INDIAN FAMILIES OF THE WHITE
EARTH RESERVATION OF MINNESOTA**
Inez Hilger
Reprint of 1939 edition. AMS Press, $26.00.

SOCIETIES OF THE PLAINS INDIANS
C. Wissler
Reprint of 1916 edition. 13 parts in one.
Illus. 1,034 pp. AMS Press, $70.00.

SOCIETY AGAINST THE STATE
Pierre Clastres; trans. by Robert Hurley
Urizen Books, 1977. $12.95; paper, $6.95.

**SOCIOLOGY OF AMERICAN INDIANS:
A CRITICAL BIBLIOGRAPHY**
Russell Thornton and Mary Grasmick
128 pp. Paper. Indiana University Press, 1981.
$4.95.

*SOKOSI ALIHA
Vehicle for learning important skills and
knowledge; language development in Choctaw
and
English. Emphasis is on Mississippi Choctaw
communities. Teacher's guide. Grades Pre-
school-3. 7 pp. Choctaw Heritage Press, $2.75.

**SOLDIER AND BRAVE: HISTORIC
PLACES ASSOCIATED WITH INDIAN
AFFAIRS AND INDIAN WARS IN
TRANS-MISSISSIPPI WEST**
Illus. 453 pp. Supt. of Documents, 1971.
$13.00.

**SOLDIERING IN DAKOTA: AMONG
THE INDIANS IN 1863-1865**
F. Myers
Reprint of 1888 edition. Ayer Co., $12.00.
Facsimile. 50 pp. Ye Galleon Press, $4.95.

SOLDIERS OF THE CROSS
J.B. Salpointe
Reprint of 1898 edition. Documentary
Publications, $24.95.

**SOME KIND OF POWER:
NAVAJO CHILDREN'S SKIN-
WALKER NARRATIVES**
Margaret K. Brady
224 pp. University of Utah Press, 1984.
$14.95.

**SOME NEWSPAPER REFERENCES
CONCERNING INDIAN—WHITE RE-
LATIONSHIPS IN NORTHEASTERN
CALIFORNIA, 1850-1920**
Norris Bleyhl
209 pp. Association of Northern California
Records, 1979. $9.00.

**SOME SEX BELIEFS AND PRACTICES
IN A NAVAHO COMMUNITY**
F.L. Bailey
Reprint of 1950 edition. Paper. Peabody
Museum, $5.00; Kraus, $12.00.

**SOME WARMER TONE: ALASKA
ATHAPASKAN BEAD EMBROIDERY**
Kate Duncan
Illus. University of Alaska Museum, $17.50.

*SON OF THE DINE'
J. Walter Wood
Grades 5-9. Paper. Council for Indian
Education, 1972. $1.95.

**SON OF THE MORNING STAR:
CUSTER AND THE LITTLE BIG HORN**
Evan S. Connell
Illus. 464 pp. North Point Press, 1984.
$20.00.

**SON OF OLD MAN HAT:
A NAVAHO AUTOBIOGRAPHY**
Walter Dyk, Editor
385 pp. Paper. University of Nebraska Press,
1967. $7.95.

SON OF OLD MAN HAT II:
MARRIAG AND ADULT LIFE
Walter and Ruth Dyk
Illus. 624 pp. Columbia University Press,
1980. $27.50.

SONG FROM THE EARTH:
AMERICAN INDIAN PAINTING
Jamake Highwater
Illus. Paper. New York Graphic Society, 1980.
$16.95.

SONG OF THE EARTH SPIRIT
Susanne Anderson
Illus. 128 pp. Friends of the Earth. 1974.
$14.95.

SONG OF THE PACIFIC NORTHWEST
Phil J. Thomas
Illus. Hancock House, 1979. $14.95.

*SONG TO THE CEDAR TREE
A board game in which players work in cooperation to fill the Longhouse with food and
cedar products. Grades 4-12. Daybreak Star
Press, $10.75.

SONGS OF THE TETON SIOUX
Harry Paige
Illus. Westernlore, 1969. $9.50.

SONGS OF THE TEWA
H.J. Spinden, Editor/Translator
Reprint of 1933 edition. AMS Press, $15.00.

THE SOUL OF THE INDIAN:
AN INTERPRETATION
Charles A. Eastman
175 pp. Paper. University of Nebraska Press,
1980. $4.95.

SOURCE MATERIAL FOR THE
SOCIAL AND CEREMONIAL LIFE
OF THE CHOCTAW INDIANS
John Swanton
Reprint of 1931 edition. Choctaw Museum,
and Scholarly Press, $25.00.

SOURCE MATERIAL ON THE
HISTORY AND ETHNOLOGY
OF THE CADDO INDIANS
John Swanton
Reprint of 1942 edition. Scholarly Press,
$25.00.

THE SOUTH CORNER OF TIME:
HOPI, NAVAJO, PAPAGO, AND
YAQUI TRIBAL LITERATURE
Larry Evers, Editor
A collection of outstanding prose and poetry,
and photographs reflecting the four tribes'
literary traditions. 240 pp. University of
Arizona Press, $35.00; paper, $14.95.

SOUTH FLORIDA'S VANISHED
PEOPLE: TRAVELS IN THE
HOMELAND OF ANCIENT CALUSA
Byron Voegelin
Island Press, 1977. $5.95; paper, $2.95.

SOUTHEAST INDIANS: AN
EDUCATIONAL COLORING BOOK
Linda Spizzirri & Staff
Grades K-5. Illus. 32 pp. Paper. Spizzirri
Publishing, 1985. $1.49.

THE SOUTHEASTERN CEREMONIAL
COMPLEX AND ITS INTERPRETATION
J.H. Howard and C.H. Chapman
Illus. 169 pp. Paper. Missouri Archaeological
Society, 1968. $4.00.

SOUTHEASTERN FRONTIERS:
EUROPEAN, AFRICANS, AND THE
AMERICAN INDIANS, 1513-1840:
A CRITICAL BIBLIOGRAPHY
James H. O'Donnell, III
136 pp. Paper. Indiana University Press, 1984.
$4.95.

THE SOUTHEASTERN INDIANS
Charles Hudson
Illus. 596 pp. University of Tennessee Press,
1976. $29.95; paper, $12.95. Paper. American
Indian Books, $14.50.

SOUTHEASTERN INDIANS
SINCE THE REMOVAL ERA
Walter Williams, Editor
Illus. 270 pp. Paper. University of Georgia
Press, 1979. $10.00.

SOUTHEASTERN WOODLAND
INDIAN DESIGNS
Caren Caraway
Illus. 48 pp. Paper. Stemmer House, 1985.
$3.95.

THE SOUTHERN CHEYENNES
Donald Berthrong
Illus. Maps. Biblio. 456 pp. Paper. Uni-
versity of Oklahoma Press, 1963. $12.95.

THE SOUTHERN FRONTIER, 1670-1732
Verner Crane
Reprint of 1956 edition. Greenwood Press,
$22.50.

SOUTHERN INDIANS IN
THE AMERICAN REVOLUTION
James O'Donnell, III
Reprint of 1973 edition. 188 pp. Paper.
Books on Demand. $46.30.

THE SOUTHERN INDIANS:
THE STORY OF THE CIVILIZED
TRIBES BEFORE REMOVAL
R.S. Cotterill

259 pp. University of Oklahoma Press, 1954.
$17.95; paper, $9.95.

SOUTHERN PAIUTE
E. Sapir
Bound with *Texts of the Kaibab Paiutes
and Uintah Utes; Southern Paiute Dictionary.*
Reprint of 1931 edition. AMS Press, $72.00.

**SOUTHERN PAIUTE AND CHEMEHUEVI:
AN ETHNOHISTORICAL REPORT**
Robert Manners
188 pp. Clearwater Publishing, 1973. $57.00.

**SOUTHERN PAIUTE ETHNOGRAPHY:
THE EASTERN BANDS**
Isabel T. Kelly
188 pp. Clearwater Publishing, 1973. $57.00.

SOUTHERN PAIUTE ETHNOHISTORY
Robert Euler
Reprint of 1966 edition. Illus. 176 pp.
AMS Press, $24.00. Paper. University of
Utah Press, $15.00.

SOUTHERN PAIUTE ETHNOLOGY
I.T. Kelly
Reprint of 1964 edition. AMS Press, $17.50.

**THE SOUTHERN SIERRA
MIWOK LANGUAGE**
S.M. Broadbent
Reprint of 1964 edition. Paper. Kraus, $47.00.

**SOUTHERN UTE INDIANS
OF EARLY COLORADO**
Verner Z. Reed; William Jones, Editor
Illus. Paper. Outbooks, 1980. $2.00.

SOUTHWEST
Alfonso Ortiz, Editor
Illus. 701 pp. Smithsonian, 1980. $23.00.

**SOUTHWEST: HANDBOOK OF
NORTH AMERICAN INDIANS**
Illus. 868 pp. Smithsonian, 1983. $25.00.

**SOUTHWEST INDIAN ARTS
AND CRAFTS**
Mark Bahti
Illus. 48 pp. KC Publications, 1983. $8.95;
paper, $3.95.

SOUTHWEST INDIAN CRAFT ARTS
Clara L. Tanner
Covers baskets, jewelry, textiles, silver,
pottery, carving and minor crafts of recent
and contemporary tribes. Illus. 206 pp.
University of Arizona Press, 1968. $27.50.

SOUTHWEST INDIAN DRYPAINTING
Leland C. Wyman
Illus. 432 pp. University of New Mexico Press,
1983. $55.00.

**SOUTHWEST INDIAN PAINTING:
A CHANGING ART**
Clara L. Tanner
Represents Indian easel art from 200 artists
from Arizona and New Mexico; 300 illustrations.
Revised edition. 477 pp. University of Arizona
Press, 1980. $50.00.

**SOUTHWEST INDIAN SILVER
FROM THE DONEGHY COLLECTION**
Louise Lincoln, Editor
Illus. 189 pp. University of Texas Press,
1982. $29.95; paper, $15.95.

SOUTHWESTERN ARCHAEOLOGY
John C. McGregor
Second Edition. Contains data and inven-
tories of material traits concerning the
prehistory of the Southwest. Illus. University of Illinois Press, 1965. $20.00.

**SOUTHWESTERN ARCHAEOLOGY:
A BIBLIOGRAPHY**
Frank Anderson
Covers 1850-1978. 5,400 items, scholarly
books and articles. 650 pp. Garland Pub-
lishing, 1981. $75.00.

**THE SOUTHWESTERN CHIPPEWA:
AN ETHNOLOGICAL STUDY**
H. Hickerson
Reprint of 1962 edition. Paper. Kraus, $20.00.

**SOUTHWESTERN COOKERY: INDIAN
AND SPANISH INFLUENCES**
Reprint of 1973 edition. Ayer Co., $12.00.

**SOUTHWESTERN INDIAN
ARTS AND CRAFTS**
Mark Bahti
Second Edition. Illus. 48 pp. KC Publications,
1983. $8.95; paper, $3.75.

**SOUTHWESTERN INDIAN
ARTS AND CRAFTS**
Tom Bahti
First Edition. Illus. KC Publications, 1966.
$7.50; paper, $2.00.

**SOUTHWESTERN INDIAN
CEREMONIALS**
Tom Bahti
Illus. KC Publications, 1970. $8.95; paper,
$3.75.

**THE SOUTHWESTERN
INDIAN DETOURS**
D.H. Thomas
Illus. Hunter Publishing, 1978. $8.95; paper,
$5.95.

SOUTHWESTERN INDIAN DRYPAINTING
Leland C. Wyman
Illus. 432 pp. University of New Mexico Press, 1985. $55.00.

SOUTHWESTERN INDIAN RITUAL DRAMA
Charlotte Frisbie, Editor
Illus. 384 pp. University of New Mexico, 1980. $30.00.

SOUTHWESTERN INDIAN TRIBES
Tom Bahti
Illus. KC Publications, 1968. $7.95; paper, $3.75.

SOUTHWESTERN WEAVING: THE COLLECTION OF THE MAXWELL MUSEUM
Marian E. Rodee
Second revised edition. Illus. 318 pp. Paper. University of Ne Mexico Press, 1981. $14.95.

SPANDA-KARIKAS: THE DIVINE CREATIVE IMPULSE
Jaideva Singh
209 pp. Lawrence Verry, 1981. $15.00.

SPANISH AND INDIAN PLACE NAMES OF CALIFORNIA: THEIR MEANING AND THEIR ROMANCE
Nellie Sanchez; Carlos Cortes, Editor
Reprint of 1930 edition. Illus. Ayer Co., $23.00.

*SPARROW HAWK
Meridel Le Sueur
The story of a white boy and his Sauk Indian friend. Grades 3-7. 164 pp. Holy Cow! Press, 1986. $10.95.

SPEAKING OF INDIANS; WITH AN ACCENT ON THE SOUTHWEST
Bernice Johnston
Answers hundreds of questions about Indians. Reprint of 1970 edition. Illus. 112 pp. Paper. Books on Demand, $28.00.

SPEAKING OF INDIANS
Ella Deloria; Agnes Picotte and Paul Pavich, Editors
Paper. Dakota Press, 1979. $5.95.

SPEECH VARIATION IN ACOMA KERESAN
Joel Maring
Paper. Humanities Press, 1975. $1.00.

SPEECHES ON THE PASSAGE OF THE BILL FOR THE REMOVAL OF THE INDIANS
U.S. 21st Congress
Reprint of 1830 edition. Kraus, $29.00.

SPIDER WOMAN STORIES: LEGENDS OF THE HOPI INDIANS
G.M. Mullet, Editor
11 tales of the Hopi gods, drawn from oral tradition, in a turn of the century interpretation. 142 pp. Unviersity of Arizona Press, 1979. $12.95; paper, $4.95.

SPIDER WOMAN: A STORY OF NAVAJO WEAVERS AND CHANTERS
G. Reichard
How a white woman living among the Navajo learned to weave as only the Navajo women can. Reprint of 1934 edition. Illus. Map. 344 pp. Rio Grande Press, $12.00.

SPIRIT KEEPERS OF THE NORTH: ESKIMOS OF WESTERN ALASKA
Susan Kaplan
Illus. 32 pp. Paper. University of Pennsylvania Press, 1983. $5.00.

SPIRIT MOUNTAIN: AN ANTHOLOGY OF YUMAN STORY AND SONG
Leanne Hinton and Lucille Watahomigie, Editors
344 pp. University of Arizona Press, 1984. $37.50; paper, $19.95.

THE SPIRIT OF THE ALBERTA INDIAN TREATIES
Richard Price
202 pp. Paper. Renouf, 1979. $8.95.

SPIRIT WOMAN
Stan Steiner
Illus. 256 pp. Harper & Row, 1980. $12.95.

SPIRITS OF THE SACRED MOUNTAINS: CREATION STORIES OF THE AMERICAN INDIAN
William E. Coffer
Van Nostrand Reinhold, 1978. $8.95.

SPIRITUAL LEGACY OF THE AMERICAN INDIAN
Joseph E. Brown
Reprint of 1964 edition. Illus. 175 pp. Paper. Pendle Hill, $2.50.

THE SPOKAN INDIANS IN WASHINGTON: ETHNOHISTORICAL REPORT ON LAND USE AND OCCUPANCY
S. Chalfant
Clearwater Publishing, $41.00.

SPOON
J. Christgau
Viking-Penguin, Inc., 1978. $10.95.

*SPORTS AND GAMES THE INDIANS GAVE US
Alex Whitney
Grades 7 and up. David McKay, 1977. $7.95.

*THE SPOTTED HORSE
Henry Tall Bull
Grades 2-10. Council for Indian Education,
1970. $5.95; paper, $1.95.

**SPOTTED TAIL'S FOLK: A
HISTORY OF THE BRULE SIOUX**
George E. Hyde
Revised 1974 edition. Illus. 361 pp. Paper.
University of Oklahoma Press, $8.95.

**STALLING'S ISLAND MOUND,
COLUMBIA COUNTY, GEORGIA**
W.H. Claflin, Jr.
Reprint of 1931 edition. Paper. Kraus, $15.00.

**THE STAR LAKE ARCHAEOLOGICAL
PROJECT: ANTHROPOLOGY OF A
HEADWATERS AREA OF CHACO
WASH, NEW MEXICO**
Walter Wait and Ben Nelson, Editors
Illus. 480 pp. Southern Illinois University
Press, 1983. $18.95.

STAR QUILT
Roberta Hill Whiteman
Poems by an Oneida woman. 79 pp. Holy Cow!
Press, 1983. $13.00; paper, $6.95.

**STAR WOMAN AND OTHER
SHAWNEE TALES**
James A. Clifton
94 pp. University Press of America, 1984.
$17.75; paper, $5.75.

**STARKWEATHER RUIN: A MOGOLLON
PUEBLO SITE IN THE UPPER
GILA AREA OF NEW MEXICO**
P.H. Nesbitt
Reprint of 1938 edition. Paper. Kraus, $48.00.

THE STARSHIP AND THE CANOE
K. Brower
Paper. Holt, Rinehart & Winston, 1978. $8.95.

*STARTING AN INDIAN TEEN CLUB
A pamphlet to help Indian teens establish
Indian teen clubs. Grades 7-12. 30 pp.
Daybreak Star Press, $1.75.

STATEMENT ON AMERICAN INDIANS
Paper. U.S. Catholic Conference, 95¢.

**STATISTICS OF INDIAN TRIBES,
AGENCIES AND SCHOOLS**
U.S. Bureau of Indian Affairs
Reprint of 1903 edition. Kraus, $24.00.

**STEILACOOM, NISQUALLY AND
SQUAXIN TRACTS IN WESTERN
WASHINGTON: APPRAISAL
AS OF MARCH 3, 1855**
Frank and Chase Raney
176 pp. Clearwater Publishing, 1974. $54.00.

***STOLEN PRINCESS: A
NORTHWEST INDIAN LEGEND**
Willard N. Morss and Janet M. Herren
Grades 4-8. Illus. 44 pp. Paper. J.M. Herren,
1983. $9.95.

STONE AGE OF THE COLUMBIA RIVER
Emory Strong
An account of the prehistoric Indian culture
along the Columbia River. Illus. Photos and
maps. 256 pp. Binford & Mort, 1967. $8.95.

**STONE ORNAMENTS USED BY
INDIANS IN THE U.S. AND CANADA**
Warren Moorhead
Reprint of 1917 edition. AMS Press, $55.00.

**STONE TOOLS AND RELICS
OF THE AMERICAN INDIAN**
Moore
Illus. 19 pp. Paper. American Indian Books,
$2.00.

**STONES, BONES AND SKIN:
RITUAL AND SHAMANTIC ART**
Artscanada
Illus. 200 pp. University of Washington
Press, 1981. $14.95.

***STORIES CALIFORNIA
INDIANS TOLD**
Anne B. Fisher
Grades 3-7. Illus. 110 pp. Parnassus Press,
1957. $6.95.

**STORIES FROM INDIAN WIGWAMS
AND NORTHERN CAMPFIRES**
E.R. Young
Reprint. Gordon Press, 1977. $59.95.

STORIES FROM THE LAND
32 pp. Paper. Museum of Northern Arizona,
1981. $3.00.

STORIES FROM PANGNIRTUNG
Illus. by Germaine Arnaktauyok
A collection of reminiscences about the
Inuit way of life before the arrival of
the Europeans. Illus. Jurtig Publishers,
$3.95.

*STORIES FROM UGADALI
Ugadali
Grades 2-8. Council for Indian Education,
$5.95; paper, $1.95.

***STORIES OF THE OLD
CHEROKEES: A COLLECTION**
F. Roy Johnson
Grades 4-8. Illus. 112 pp. Johnson
Publishing (NC), 1975. $7.50.

*STORIES OF OUR BLACKFEET GRANDMOTHERS
Mary C. Boss-Ribs
and Jenny Running-Crane
Grades 1-6. Paper. Council for Indian Education, 1984. $1.45.

STORIES OF TRADITIONAL NAVAJO LIFE AND CULTURE
Broderick H. Johnson, Editor
Illus. 335 pp. Paper. Navajo Community College Press, 1977. $15.00.

STORMS BREWED IN OTHER MEN'S WORLDS: THE CONFRONTATION OF INDIANS, SPANISH, AND FRENCH IN THE SOUTHWEST, 1540-1795
Elizabeth A.H. John
A view of Indian peoples and European intruders in the early Southwest. The worlds of the Comanche, Apache, Navajo, Hopi and other Pueblo, Caddo, Wichita, Tonkawas, and Utes were irrevocably altered. Illus. Maps. 840 pp. Texas A&M University Press, 1975. $24.50.

THE STORY OF CAPTAIN JASPER PARRISH, CAPTIVE, INTERPRETER AND U.S. SUB—AGENT TO THE SIX NATIONS INDIANS
Bound with other captivities. Reprint of 1903 edition. Garland Publishing, $44.00.

THE STORY OF INDIAN MUSIC: ITS GROWTH AND SYNTHESIS
O. Gosvami
Reprint of 1961 edition. 332 pp. Scholarly Press, $59.00.

THE STORY OF THE INDIANS
George B. Grinnell
Reprint of 1909 edition. Richard West, $12.50.

*THE STORY OF LITTLE BIG HORN
R.C. Stern
Grades 3-6. Childrens Press, 1983. $9.50.

THE STORY OF PUEBLO POTTERY
H.M. Wormington and Arminta Neal
Fourth Edition. Paper. Denver Museum of Natural History, 1974. $1.50.

STORY OF THE RED MAN
Flora W. Seymour
Facsimile of 1929 edition. Ayer Co., $27.50.

STORY OF A TLINGIT COMMUNITY: PROBLEM IN THE RELATIONSHIP BETWEEN ARCHAEOLOGICAL, ETHNOLOGICAL AND HISTORICAL METHODS
Frederica De Laguna
Reprint of 1960 edition. Scholarly Press, $39.00.

*STORY OF THE TOTEM POLE
Ruth Brindze; illus. by Yefee Kimball
The story of the totem pole's origin, its uses, and how to read its colorful decorations. Reprint of 1951 edition. Grades 4-8. Illus. 64 pp. Vanguard, $9.95.

*THE STORY OF WOUNDED KNEE
R.C. Stein
Grades 3-6. Illus. 32 pp. Childrens Press, 1983. $9.25.

STRAIGHT TONGUE: MINNESOTA INDIAN ART FROM THE BISHOP WHIPPLE COLLECTIONS
Louise Casagrande and Melissa Ringheim
Illus. 94 pp. Paper. University of Washington Press, 1980. $9.95.

STRAIGHT WITH THE MEDICINE: NARRATIVES OF WASHOE FOLLOWERS OF THE TIPI WAY
Warren L. D'Azevedo. Illus. 64 pp. Paper. Heyday Books, 1985. $5.95.

STRIP PATCHWORK: QUICK AND EASY PATCHWORK USING THE SEMINOLE TECHNIQUE
Taimi Dudley
112 pp. Van Nostrand Reinhold, 1980. $16.95.

A STRUCTURAL AND LEXICAL COMPARISON OF THE TUNICA, CHITIMACHA, AND ATAKAPA LANGUAGES
John Swanton
Reprint of 1919 edition. Scholarly Press, $19.00.

STRUGGLE FOR EMPIRE: A BIBLIOGRAPHY OF THE FRENCH AND INDIAN WARS
James G. Lydon
275 pp. Garland Publishing, 1985. $35.00.

JOHN STUART AND THE SOUTHERN COLONIAL FRONTIER: A STUDY OF INDIAN RELATIONS, WAR, TRADE, LAND PROBLEMS IN THE SOUTHERN WILDERNESS, 1754-1775
J. Alden
Reprint of 1944 edition. Illus. Gordian Press, $17.50.

STUDIES IN AMERICAN INDIAN LANGUAGES
Jesse Sawyer
University of California Press, 1974. $36.50.

STUDIES IN CALIFORNIA LINGUISTICS
W. Bright
Reprint of 1964 edition. Paper. Kraus, $31.00.

**STUDIES IN SOUTHEASTERN
INDIAN LANGUAGES**
James Crawford, Editor
463 pp. University of Georgia Press, 1975.
$25.00.

**STUDIES IN THE
ATHAPASKAN LANGUAGES**
H. Hoijer, et al
Reprint of 1963 edition. Paper. Kraus, $23.00.

**A STUDY IN CULTURE CONTACT
AND CULTURE CHANGE: THE
WHITEROCK UTES IN TRANSITION**
G.O. Lang
Reprint of 1953 edition. AMS Press, $10.50.

**A STUDY IN THE ETYMOLOGY
OF THE INDIAN PLACE NAME**
G.A. McAleer
Reprint. Gordon Press, 1977. $59.50.

**THE STUDY OF AMERICAN
INDIAN RELIGIONS**
Ake Hultkrantz
Illus. 142 pp. Scholars Press, 1983. $12.95.

**A STUDY OF THE DELAWARE
INDIAN BIG HOUSE CEREMONY:
IN NATIVE TEXT DICTATED
BY WITAPANOXWE**
F.G. Speck
Reprint of 1931 edition. AMS Press, $24.00.

**A STUDY OF DELAWARE
INDIAN MEDICINE PRACTICE
AND FOLK BELIEFS**
Gladys Tantiquidgeon
Reprint of 1942 edition. AMS Press, $18.00.

**STUDY OF THE ESKIMO BOWS
IN THE U.S. NATIONAL MUSEUM**
J. Murdoch
Facsimile edition. Illus. 24 pp. Shorey, $1.95.

STUDY OF INDIAN MUSIC
F. Densmore
Facsimile edition. 32 pp. Paper. Shorey, $3.95.

STUDY OF NAVAJO SYMBOLISM
Reprint of 1956 edition. Three parts in one.
Part I: *Navago Symbols in Sandpaintings
and Ritual Objects,* F.J. Newcomb; Part II:
Navajo Picture Writing, S.A. Fishler;
Part III: *Notes on Corresponding Symbols
in Various Parts of the World,* M.C. Wheel-
wright. Paper. Kraus, $23.00.

STUDY OF OMAHA INDIAN MUSIC
A.C. Fletcher
Includes transcriptions of 92 songs, words
and music. Reprint of 1893 edition. Paper.
Kraus, $20.00.

A STUDY OF PREHISTORIC CHANGE
Fred Plog
Academic Press, 1974. $21.00.

**A STUDY OF THE ROLE OF
THE FEDERAL GOVERNMENT
IN THE EDUCATION OF THE
AMERICAN INDIAN**
T. Fischbacher
Reprint of 1967 edition. Paper. R & E
Research Associates, $10.00.

STUDY OF THE SIOUAN CULTS
J.O. Dorsey
Reprint of 1894 edition. Illus. 208 pp.
Paper. Shorey, $11.95.

**SU SITE: EXCAVATIONS AT A
MOGOLLON VILLAGE, WESTERN
NEW MEXICO, 1st to 3rd SEASONS**
Paul Martin
Reprint of 1940-1947 editions. Paper. Kraus,
$34.00.

**THE SUBARCTIC ATHAPASCANS: A
SELECTED, ANNOTATED BIBLIOGRAPHY**
Arthur E. Hippler and John R. Wood
380 pp. Paper. University of Alaska Institute
of Social Sciences, 1974. $15.00.

**SUBJUGATION AND DISHONOR: A
BRIEF HISTORY OF THE TRAVAIL
OF THE NATIVE AMERICANS**
Philip Weeks and James B. Gidney
Paper. Robert E. Krieger, 1980. $5.95.

**SUBSTANCE OF A JOURNAL
DURING A RESIDENCE AT
THE RED RIVER COLONY**
John West
Reprint of 1824 edition. Johnson Reprint,
$19.00.

SUN BEAR: THE PATH OF POWER
Sun Bear, et al
Illus. 272 pp. Paper. Bear Tribe, 1983. $8.95.

**THE SUN CAME DOWN: THE
HISTORY OF THE WORLD AS MY
BLACKFEET ELDERS TOLD IT**
P. Bullchild
384 pp. Harper & Row, 1985. $22.95.

**SUN CHIEF: THE AUTOBIOGRAPHY
OF A HOPI INDIAN**
Leo W. Simmons, Editor
Revised 1963 edition. Illus. Paper. Yale
University Press, $8.95.

**SUN CIRCLES AND HUMAN HANDS:
THE SOUTHEASTERN INDIANS,
ART AND INDUSTRIES**
E.L. Fundaburk and M.D. Forman, Editors
Illus. Emma Lilla Fundaburk, $12.00.

THE SUN DANCE OF
THE CROW INDIANS
R. Lowie
Reprint of 1915 edition. AMS Press, $12.50.

THE SUN DANCE AND OTHER
CEREMONIES OF THE OGLALA
DIVISION OF THE TETON DAKOTA
J.R. Walker
Reprint of 1917 edition. AMS Press, $21.50.

THE SUN DANCE PEOPLE
Richard Erdoes
Illus. 241 pp. Paper. Random House, 1982.
$1.95.

*THE SUN DANCE PEOLE:
THE PLAINS INDIANS,
THEIR PAST AND PRESENT
Richard Erdoes
Grades 5-8. Illus. 224 pp. Alfred A. Knopf,
1972. $6.95.

THE SUN DANCE RELIGION:
POWER FOR THE POWERLESS
Joseph G. Jorgensen
Illus. 372 pp. Paper. University of Chicago
Press, 1972. $12.50.

THE SUN GIRL
E. White, pseud.
Reprint of 1941 edition. Illus. Museum of
Northern Arizona. $5.00.

SUN IN THE SKY
Walter O'Kane
Reprint of 1950 edition. Illus. Books on
Demand, $68.50.

SUN MEN OF THE AMERICAS
Grace Cooke
De Vorss & Co., $5.95.

SUNDANCING AT ROSEBUD
AND PINE RIDGE
Thomas Mails
Describes the Sun Dance Ceremony of the Sioux
Indians. Illus. 400 pp. Center for Western
Studies, and University of Nebraska Press,
1978. $36.50.

A SUPPLEMENT GUIDE TO MANU-
SCRIPTS: RELATING TO THE
AMERICAN INDIANS IN THE
LIBRARY OF THE AMERICAN
PHILOSOPHICAL SOCIETY
Daythal Kendall
American Philosophical Society, 1983. $15.00.

SUPPLEMENT TO THE HANDBOOK
OF MIDDLE AMERICAN INDIANS,
Vol. 1: ARCHAEOLOGY
Victoria R. Bricker and
Jeremy A. Sabloff, Editor

Illus. 475 pp. University of Texas Press,
1981. $55.00.

SUPPLEMENT TO THE HANDBOOK
OF MIDDLE AMERICAN INDIANS,
Vol. 2: LINGUISTICS
Victoria Bricker and
Munro Edmonson, Editors
224 pp. University of Texas Press, 1984.
$35.00.

*SUQUAMISH TODAY
A documentary on the Suquamish of Port
Madison Reservation, Washington. Teacher's
guide. Grades 4-8. Illus. 21 pp. Daybreak
Star Press, $4.50.

A SURPRISING ACCOUNT OF THE
CAPTIVITY AND ESCAPE OF PHILIP
McDONALD AND ALEXANDER McLEOD,
FROM THE CHIKKAMAUGGA INDIANS
McDonald and McLeod
Reprint. 23 pp. Ye Galleon Press, $7.50.

SURVEY AND EXCAVATION OF
CAVES IN HIDALGO COUNTY,
NEW MEXICO
M.F. Lambert and J.R. Ambler
Reprint of 1961 edition. Illus. Paper.
Museum of New Mexico Press, $2.50.

SURVIVAL ARTS OF THE
PRIMITIVE PAIUTES
Margaret Wheat
Illus. 120 pp. Paper. University of Nevada
Press, 1977. $7.50.

SURVIVAL: LIFE AND ART
OF THE ALASKAN ESKIMO
The Newark Museum; Text by Barbara Lipton
Text and photographs of Alaska and objects:
tools, utensils, dress, art created by the
Eskimo. Illus. 96 pp. Paper. Museum
Publications, 1977. $9.00.

THE SURVIVAL OF THE BARK CANOE
John McPhee
Farrar, Straus & Grioux, 1975. $7.95.

SURVIVAL OF A NOBLE RACE
August Nylander
Carlton Press, 1983. $12.00.

SURVIVAL SKILLS OF THE
NORTH AMERICAN INDIANS
Peter Goodchild
Illus. 224 pp. Chicago Review Press, 1985.
$16.95; paper, $9.95.

SUSQUEHANNA'S INDIANS
Barry C. Kent
Illus. 438 pp. Pennsylvania Historical
and Museum Commission, 1984. $15.95.

SWAMP SAILORS: RIVERLINE
WARFARE IN THE EVERGLADES,
1835-1842
George Buker
152 pp. University Presses of Florida, 1975.
$6.50.

SWARTS RUIN: A TYPICAL
MIMBRES SITE IN SOUTHWESTERN
NEW MEXICO
H.S. and C.B. Cosgrove
Reprint of 1932 edition. Paper. Kraus,
$54.00.

THE SWEET GRASS LIVES ON:
FIFTY CONTEMPORARY NORTH
AMERICAN INDIAN ARTISTS
Jamake Highwater
Illus. 192 pp. Harper & Row, 1980. $35.00.

SWEET MEDICINE: THE CONTINUING
ROLE OF THE SACRED ARROWS,
THE SUN DANCE, AND THE SACRED
BUFFALO HAT IN NORTHERN
CHEYENNE HISTORY
Peter J. Powell
Illus. 986 pp. University of Oklahoma Press,
1969. $55.00.

SYMBOL AND SUBSTANCE
IN AMERICAN INDIAN ART
Zena Mathews; Amy Hobar, Editor
24 pp. Paper. Metropolitan Museum of Art,
1984. $4.95.

SYMPOSIUM ON AMERICAN
INDIAN LINGUISTICS
Papers from the Symposium held at Berkeley,
California in 1951. Reprint of 1954 edition.
Paper. Kraus, $12.00.

SYMPOSIUM ON CHEROKEE
AND IROQUOIS CULTURE
William Fenton and John Gulick
Reprint of 1961 edition. Scholarly Press,
$21.00.

SYMPOSIUM ON LOCAL DIVERSITY
IN IROQUOIS CULTURE
William Fenton
Reprint of 1951 edition. Scholarly Press,
$21.00.

SYNTAX AND SEMANTICS:
THE SYNTAX OF NATIVE
AMERICAN LANGUAGES
Eung-Do Cook and Donna B. Gerdts
Volume 16 of Syntax and Semantics. Academic
Press, 1984. $59.00.

T

TABLEAU'S NARRATIVE OF
LOISEL'S EXPEDITION TO
THE UPPER MISSOURI
P. Tabeau
Reprint of 1939 edition. Illus. University
of Oklahoma Press, $14.95.

TACACHALE: ESSAYS ON THE
INDIANS OF FLORIDA AND SOUTH-
EASTERN GEORGIA DURING THE
HISTORIC PERIOD
J.T. Milanich and
Samuel Proctor, Editors
Illus. University Presses of Florida, 1978.
$12.50.

TAH-KOO WAH-KAN: OR, THE
GOSPEL AMONG THE DAKOTAS
S. Riggs
Reprint of 1869 edition. 534 pp. Ayer Co.,
$33.00.

THE TAHLTAN INDIANS
G.T. Emmons
Reprint of 1911 edition. Humanities Press,
$17.25.

*TAKEN BY THE INDIANS:
TRUE TALES OF CAPTIVITY
Alice Dickinson
Grades 7-12. Illus. 192 pp. Franklin Watts,
1976. $7.00.

*THE TALE OF THE POSSUM
A popular Choctaw story told by elders to
children. Grades Preschool-3. 9 pp. Choctaw
Heritage Press, $2.75.

*TALES FROM THE
BITTERFOOT VALLEY
Katheryn Law
Grades 1-4. Paper. Council for Indian
Education, 1971. $1.95.

TALES FROM THE IGLOO
Maurice Metayer
A collection of Eskimo legends for all ages.
Illus. Hurtig Publishers, $4.95.

TALES FROM THE MOHAVES
Herman Grey
96 pp. Paper. University of Oklahoma Press,
1980. $4.95.

TALES FROM THE SMOKEHOUSE
Hebert Schwartz, Editor
A collection of erotic Indian legends.
Illus. by Daphne Odjig. Paper. Hurtig
Publishers, $6.95.

TALES OF THE BIG BEND
Elton Miles
Stories of scalphunter John Glanton. Illus.
Biblio. 200 pp. Texas A&M University Press,
1976. $10.00.

TALES OF THE COCHITI INDIANS
Ruth Benedict
256 pp. Gordon Press, $59.50. Paper.
University of New Mexico Press, $12.95.

TALES OF KANKAKEE LAND
C.H. Bartlett
Reprint of 1907 edition. Hardscrabble Books,
$7.50.

TALES OF THE NEZ PERCE
Donald M. Hines
232 pp. Ye Galleon, 1984. $19.95.

**TALES OF THE NORTH
AMERICAN INDIAN**
Stith Thompson, Editor
Illus. 416 pp. Paper. Indiana University
Press, 1900. $9.95.

**TALES OF THE NORTHWEST:
ON SKETCHES OF INDIAN
LIFE AND CHARACTER**
W.J. Snelling
Reprint of 1830 edition. Ross & Haines,
$10.00.

TALES OF THE OKANOGANS
Donald Hines, Editors
Ye Galleon Press, 1976. $12.50.

***TALKING BONES: SECRETS
OF INDIAN MOUND BUILDERS**
Wiluam O. Steele
Grades 2-5. Illus. Paper. Harcourt Brace
Jovanovich, and Harper & Row, 1978. $6.95.

***TALKING HANDS:
INDIAN SIGN LANGUAGE**
Aline Amon
Grades 4-7. Doubleday, 1968. $7.95.

***THE TALKING STONE: AN
ANTHOLOGY OF NATIVE AMERICAN
TALES AND LEGENDS**
Dorothy deWit, Editor; Illus. by D. Crews
27 tales divided by region of origin. Grades
7-12. Illus. 192 pp. Greenwillow Books, 1979.
$10.75.

*TALKING TOTEM POLE
Lurline Mayol
Legends and stories of the North Pacific
Indians. Grades 4-9. Illus. 140 pp.
Binford & Mort, 1964. $13.95.

TANAINA TALES FROM ALASKA
Bill Vaudrin

133 pp. Paper. University of Oklahoma Press,
1981. $4.95.

TAOS ADOBES
Bunting, et al
Paper. Museum of New Mexico Press, 1975.
$7.95.

THE TAOS INDIANS
Blanche C. Grant
Reissue of 1925 edition. Illus. 198 pp.
Paper. Rio Grande Press, $7.50.

**TAOS INDIANS' PUEBLO LAND
GRANT: HISTORICAL STUDY OF
LAND USE PRIOR TO 1848**
Harold Dunham
29 pp. Clearwater Publishing, 1973. $17.25.

***THE TAOS INDIANS AND
THEIR SACRED BLUE LAKE**
Marcia Keegan
Grades 3-6. Illus. 64 pp. Julian Messner,
1972. $6.00.

**TAOS LAND CLAIM:
ANTHROPOLOGICAL DATA**
Florence Ellis
115 pp. Clearwater Publishing, 1973. $39.00.

**TAOS: 1847: THE REVOLT
IN CONTEMPORARY ACCOUNTS**
Michael McNierney, Editor
Paper. Johnson Books, 1980. $4.95.

TAOS TALES
E. Parsons
Reprint of 1940 edition. Kraus, $26.00.

**THE TAOS TRAPPERS: THE FUR
TRADE IN THE FAR SOUTHWEST**
David J. Webber
Illus. 280 pp. Paper. University of Oklahoma
Press, 1980. $7.95.

**TATANGA MANI: WALKING
BUFFALO OF THE STONIES**
J.W. Grant MacEwan
Biography of the legendary Stoney chieftain.
Reprint. Paper. Hurtig Publishers, $4.50.

**TATTOOING AND FACE AND BODY
PAINT OF THE THOMPSON INDIANS
OF BRITISH COLUMBIA**
James A. Teit
Illus. 60 pp. Shorey, $6.95.

TAXING THOSE THEY FOUND HERE
Resource document designed to give an
historical overview of taxation and the
American Indian. Covers major cases in
federal court. 191 pp. Paper. Institute
for the Development of Indian Law, 1972.
$2.00.

THE TCHEFUNCTE CULTURE,
AN EARLY OCCUPATION OF THE
LOWER MISSISSIPPI VALLEY
J.A. Ford and G.I. Quimby
Reprint of 1945 edition. Paper. Kraus,
$23.00.

TEACHING ABOUT AMERICAN
INDIANS IN CONNECTICUT
17 pp. University of Connecticut
Education, 1982. $1.00.

TEACHING AMERICAN INDIAN
HISTORY: AN INTERDISCI-
PLINARY APPROACH
Larry L. Vantine
Paper. R & E Research Associates, 1978.
$11.95.

TEACHING OF NATURE
Adolf Hungry Wolf
Paper. Good Medicine Books, 1975. $3.50.

TEACHINGS FROM THE AMERICAN
EARTH: INDIAN RELIGION
AND PHILOSOPHY
Dennis and Barbara Tedlock, Editors
Illus. 280 pp. Paper. Liveright Publishing,
1975. $7.95.

THE TECHNIQUE OF PORCUPINE
QUILL DECORTION AMONG THE
INDIANS OF NORTH AMERICA
William C. Orchard; Monte Smith, Editor
Illus. 88 pp. Paper. Eagles View Publishing,
1982. $8.95.

TECUMSEH AND THE QUEST
FOR INDIAN LEADERSHIP
R. David Edmunds
Paper. Little, Brown & Co., 1984. $5.95.

TEEPEE NEIGHBORS
Grace Coolidge
200 pp. Paper. University of Oklahoma Press,
1984. $7.95.

TEMALPAKH: CAHUILLA INDIAN
KNOWLEDGE AND USAGE OF PLANTS
Lowell Bean and Katherine Saubel
Malki Museum Press, 1972. $10.00; paper,
$6.50.

THE TEN GRANDMOTHERS
A. Marriott
Reprint of 1945 edition. Illus. 300 pp.
Paper. University of Oklahoma Press, $9.95.

TEN YEARS OF MISSIONARY WORK
AMONG THE INDIANS AT SKOKOMISH
M. Eells
Illus. 271 pp. Paper. Shorey, $19.95.

TEN YEARS OF UPPER CANADA
IN PEACE AND WAR, 1805-1815

M.R. Edgar
Reprint of 1890 edition. Garland Publishing,
$38.00.

*TENDOY, CHIEF OF THE LEMHIS
David Crowder
Grades 5-9. Illus. Paper. Caxton, 1969. $3.00.

TENNESSEE'S INDIAN PEOPLES:
FROM WHITE CONTACT TO REMOVAL,
1540-1840
Ronald N. Satz
Illus. 110 pp. University of Tennessee Press,
1979. $8.50; paper, $3.50.

TENTING ON THE PLAINS
Elizabeth B. Custer
Reprint of 1887 edition. 403 pp. Corner House,
$9.50.

TEODORA DE CROIX AND THE
NORTHERN FRONTIER OF
NEW SPAIN, 1776-1783
A.B. Thomas
Reprint of 1941 edition. University of
Oklahoma Press, $16.95.

*TEPEE STORIES
Edward and M.P. Dolch
Grades 1-6. Garrard Publishing, 1956. $6.00.

*TEPEE TALES OF
THE AMERICAN INDIAN
Dee Brown
Grades 5-12. Illus. Holt, Rinehart & Winston,
1979. $7.95.

TERRITORIAL SUBDIVISIONS AND
BOUNDARIES OF THE WAMPANOAG,
MASSACHUSETT AND NAUSET INDIANS
F.G. Speck
Reprint of 1928 edition. AMS Press, $15.00.

TETON SIOUX MUSIC
F. Densmore
Reprint of 1918 edition. Illus. 722 pp.
Da Capo Press, $49.50.

TEWA TALES
E. Parsons
Reprint of 1926 edition. Kraus, $26.00.

TEWA WORLD: SPACE, TIME,
BEING, AND BECOMING IN
A PUEBLO SOCIETY
Alfonso Ortiz
Paper. University of Chicago Press, 1969.
$8.75; paper, 7.00.

THE TEXAS CANNIBALS: OR,
WHY FATHER SERRA CAME
TO CALIFORNIA
S. Morrill
28 pp. Holmes Book Co., 1964. $5.00.

TEXAS' LAST FRONTIER: FORT STOCKTON AND THE TRANS-PECOS, 1861-1895
Clayton Williams; Ernest Wallace, Editor
Settlements and battles with the Indians.
Illus. Maps. Biblio. 496 pp. Texas A&M University Press, 1981. $19.50.

TEXTBOOKS AND THE AMERICAN INDIAN
Jeanette Henry and
Rupert Costo, Editors
Educators use this book as a model in evaluating historical accounts in the textbooks. 269 pp. Paper. The Indian Historian Press, 1969. $9.50.

TEXTILES OF THE PREHISTORIC SOUTHWEST
Kate P. Kent
Illus. 416 pp. University of New Mexico Press, 1982. $45.00.

THEIR NUMBER BECOME THINNED: NATIVE AMERICAN POPULATION DYNAMICS IN EASTERN NORTH AMERICA
Henry F. Dobyns
Illus. 382 pp. University of Tennessee Press, 1983. $29.95; paper, $14.95.

THERE IS MY PEOPLE SLEEPING
Sarain Stump
Illus. 200 pp. Paper. Superior, 1970. $2.95.

THESE ARE MY CHILDREN
A. Murray
Ye Galleon Press, 1977. $9.95.

*THESE WERE THE SIOUX
Marie Sandoz
The philosophy and practical wisdom of the Sioux Indians, including their beliefs and customs. Reprint of 1961 edition. Grades 6-12. Illus. 118 pp. Paper. University of Nebraska Press, $4.95.

*THEY CAME HERE FIRST: THE EPIC OF THE AMERICAN INDIAN
D'Arcy McNickle
Grades 9-12. Octagon Books, 1975. $17.50. Paper. Harper & Row, $3.95.

THEY HAVE NO RIGHTS
Walter Ehlich
266 pp. Paper. Jefferson National, 1979. $7.95.

*THEY PUT ON MASKS
Byrd Baylor
Grades 1-4. Illus. 48 pp. Charles Scribner's Sons, 1974. $7.95.

THEY SANG FOR THE HORSES: THE IMPACT OF THE HORSE ON NAVAJO AND APACHE FOLKLORE
LaVerne Clark; illus. by Ted DFeGrazier
The weaving of the horse into existent mythology of the Navajo and Apache tribes. Illus. 225 pp. Paper. University of Arizona Press, 1966. $14.95.

THEY WALKED BEFORE: THE INDIAN OF WASHINGTON STATE
Cecilia S. Carpenter
Illus. 71 pp. Paper. Washington State Historical Society, 1977. $6.00.

THIRTY INDIAN LEGENDS OF CANADA
Margaret Bemister
Illus. 154 pp. Paper. Merrimack Publishers Circle, 1983. $8.95.

THIS COUNTY WAS OURS: A DOCUMENTARY HISTORY OF THE AMERICAN INDIAN
Virgil J. Vogel
512 pp. Harper & Row, 1972. $13.95; paper, $5.95.

THIS IS OUR LAND
Val J. McClellan
Illus. Western Publishers, 1978. $12.50.

THIS LAND WAS THEIRS: A STUDY OF THE NORTH AMERICAN INDIAN
Wendell H. Oswait
Third edition. 569 pp. Paper. Random House, 1978. $29.95.

*THIS SONG REMEMBERS: SELF—PORTRAITS OF NATIVE AMERICANS IN THE ARTS
Jane Katz
Grades 7-12. Houghton Mifflin, 1980. $8.95.

THE THOMPSON INDIANS OF BRITISH COLUMBIA
J. Teit; Franz Boas, Editor
Reprint of 1900 edition. AMS Press, $32.50.

THOREAU AND THE AMERICAN INDIANS
Robert F. Sayre
Princeton University Press, 1977. $16.00.

THOSE TREMENDOUS MOUNTAINS: THE STORY OF THE LEWIS AND CLARK EXPEDITION
David F. Hawke
Illus. 290 pp. W.W. Norton, 1980. $12.95; paper, $6.95.

A THOUSAND WORDS OF MOHAWK
Michael Jones
Paper. National Museums of Canada, $3.95.

***A THOUSAND YEARS OF
AMERICAN INDIAN STORYTELLING**
"The Weewish Tree", Editors
Illus. Paper. The Indian Historian Press,
1981. $9.95.

**THREE AFFILIATED TRIBES OF
THE FORT BERTHOLD RESERVATION:
APPRAISAL OF LANDS**
Gordon Elmquist
210 pp. Clearwater Publishing, 1973. $64.50.

**THREE AFFILIATED TRIBES OF
FORT BERTHOLD RESERVATION,
MARCH 3, 1891: VALUATION
OF CEDED LANDS**
Mont Saunderson
74 pp. Clearwater Publishing, 1973. $27.00.

THREE INDIAN CAMPAIGNS
W. Merritt
Reprint of 1890 edition. 19 pp. Paper. Shorey,
$3.95.

**THREE NAVAHO HOUSEHOLDS:
A COMPREHENSIVE STUDY IN
SMALL GROUP CULTURE**
J.M. Roberts
Reprint of 1951 edition. Paper. Kraus, $23.00.

**THREE YEARS AMONG THE
COMANCHES, THE NARRATIVE
OF NELSON LEE, TEXAS RANGER**
Reprint of 1859 edition. Garland Publishing,
$44.00.

**A THRILLING NARRATIVE OF THE
SUFFERINGS OF JANE ADELINE
WILSON DURING HER CAPTIVITY
AMONG THE COMANCHE INDIANS**
Jane A. Wilson
Reprint. 28 pp. Ye Galleon Press, $5.50;
paper, $3.95.

**THROUGH NAVAJO EYES: AN
EXPLORATION IN FILM COMMUN-
ICATION AND ANTHROPOLOGY**
Sol Worth and John Adair
Illus. 320 pp. Indiana University Press,
1973. $20.00; paper, $7.95.

***THUNDER IN THE MOUNTAINS:
LEGENDS OF CANADA**
Hilda M. Hooke
Grades 5-7. Illus. Oxford University Press,
1947. $10.50.

**THUNDER—ROOT: TRADITIONAL
AND CONTEMPORARY NATIVE
AMERICAN VERSE**
J. Ivaloo Volborth
51 pp. Paper. American Indian Studies Center,
1978. $2.00.

***THUNDER WATERS: EXPERIENCES
OF GROWING UP IN DIFFERENT
INDIAN TRIBES**
Frances Snow, et al
Grades 3-8. Council for Indian Education,
1975. $4.75; paper, $1.95.

**THE TIGUA SUMA AND MANSO
INDIANS OF WESTERN TEXAS AND
NEW MEXICO: FROM ABORIGINAL
TIMES TO THE LATE 1880s**
Rex E. Gerald
116 pp. Clearwater Publishing, 1974. $26.50.

***THE TIGUAS: THE LOST
TRIBE OF CITY INDIANS**
Stan Steiner
Grades 5-12. Illus. Paper. Macmillan, 1972.
$4.95.

**TILLAMOOK BAND OF TILLAMOOKS
AND NEHALEM BAND OF TILLAMOOKS
TRIBAL LANDS: APPRAISAL**
Leroy Draper
338 pp. Clearwater Publishing, 1973. $97.50.

**TILLAMOOK INDIANS: ANTHROPOLO-
LOGICAL IDENTITY AND ABORIGINAL
POSSESSION OF LANDS**
H.C. Taylor
Clearwater Publishing, $31.00.

**TILLAMOOK INDIANS
OF THE OREGON COAST**
John Sauter and Bruce Johnson
Illus. Binford & Mort, 1974. $8.95; paper,
$5.95.

TILLAMOOK-NEHALEM LANDS
James Hatfield
142 pp. Clearwater Publishing, 1974. $46.00.

**TILLAMOOK: REPORT ON 1894
VALUES OF LANDS AND RESOURCES
IN WASHINGTON**
E.O. Fuller
196 pp. Clearwater Publishing, 1974. $60.00.

**TIME: SPACE AND TRANSITION
IN ANASAZI PREHISTORY**
Michael S. Berry
112 pp. University of Utah Press, 1982. $20.00.

**TIMOTHY: NEZ PERCE CHIEF,
LIFE AND TIMES, 1800-1891**
Rowena Alcorn
Ye Galleon Press.

***THE TIPI: A CENTER
OF NATIVE AMERICAN LIFE**
Charlotte Yue
Grades 4-7. Illus. 96 pp. Paper. Alfred
A. Knopf, 1983. $10.95.

TIXIER'S TRAVELS ON THE OSAGE PRAIRIES
Victor Tixier; J. McDermott, Editor
Reprint of 1940 edition. Illus. University of Oklahoma Press, $16.95.

TLINGIT DESIGNS AND CARVING MANUAL
Aan-Ta-T'Loot and Raymond Pack
Illus. Paper. Superior Publishing, 1978. $7.95.

THE TLINGIT INDIANS: RESULTS OF A TRIP TO THE NORTHWEST COAST OF AMERICA AND THE BERING STRAITS
Aurel Krause
Illus. 320 pp. Paper. University of Washington Press, 1970. $8.95.

TLINGIT MYTHS AND TEXTS
John Swanton
Reprint of 1909 edition. Johnson Reprint, $34.00. Scholarly Press, $49.00.

TLINGIT TALES: POTLATCH AND TOTEM POLES
Lorie Harris
Illus. 64 pp. Naturegraph, $10.95; paper, $4.95.

TLINGIT: THEIR ART, CULTURE AND LEGENDS
Daniel and N. Kaiper
Illus. Paper. Universe Books, 1978. $4.00.

TO BE AN INDIAN
J. Cash
251 pp. Paper. Robert E. Krieger, 1971. $7.50.

TO THE DELAWARE INDIANS
R.C. Adams
Reprint of 1904 edition. Scholarly Press, $19.00.

TO THE FOOT OF THE RAINBOW
C. Kluckhohn
Three months of travel on horseback through the Southwest Indian country in 1925. Reprint of 1927 edition. Illus. 427 pp. Rio Grande Press, $25.00; paper, $15.00.

*TO LIVE IN TWO WORLD: AMERICAN INDIAN YOUTH TODAY
Brent Ashabranner
Grades 7 and up. Illus. 160 pp. Dodd, Mead & Co., 1984. $12.95.

TO LIVE ON THIS EARTH: AMERICAN INDIAN EDUCATION
Estelle Fuchs and Robert Havighurst
Revised 1983 edition. 408 pp. Paper. University of New Mexico Press, $1.95.

TO PRESERVE A CULTURE: THE TWENTIETH-CENTURY FIGHT OVER INDIAN REORGANIZATION
Jon F. Rice, Jr.
Illus. 60 pp. The Committee, 1981. $2.00.

TO RUN AFTER THEM: CULTURAL AND SOCIAL BASES OF COOPERATION IN A NAVAJO COMMUNITY
Louise Lamphere
A field study examining the cultural system, structure, and economic, ritual and cooperative activities of the Navajos. 230 pp. University of Arizona Press, 1977. $12.50; paper, $6.50.

TOBACCO, PEACEPIPES AND INDIANS
Louis Seig
Ilus. Filter Press, 1971. $8.00; paper, $2.50.

TOBACCO, PIPES AND SMOKING CUSTOMS OF THE AMERICAN INDIANS
G.A. West
Reprint of 1934 edition. Greenwood Press, $57.50.

TOBACCO PIPES OF THE MISSOURI INDIANS
Henry Hamilton; Carl H. Chapman, Editor
Illus. 49 pp. Paper. Missouri Archaeolgical Society, 1967. $2.00.

THE TOBACCO SOCIETY OF THE CROW INDIANS
R.H Lowie
Reprint of 1919 edition. AMS Press, $15.00.

TOBIAS
Patrick Ross
Paper. Tyndale House Publishers, 1977. $1.95.

*TOMAHAWKS AND TROMBONES
Barbara Mitchell
Grades 1-4. Illus. 56 pp. Carolrhoda Books, 1982. $8.95.

*TOMO-CHI-CHI
Sara G. Harrell
Grades 5-12. Illus. Dillon Press, 1977. $7.95.

TOMOCHICHI: INDIAN FRIEND OF THE GEORGIA COLONY
Helen Todd
Illus. Cherokee Publishing, 1977. $7.95.

TOMOL: CHUMASH WATERCRAFT
Travis Hudson, et al
Illus. Paper. Ballena Press, 1978. $8.95.

TONGUES AND TOTEMS: COMPARATIVE ARTS OF THE PACIFIC BASIN
Starr and Richard Davis
Paper. Alaska International Art, 1974. $8.95.

**TONKAWA, AN INDIAN
LANGUAGE OF TEXAS**
Harry Hoijer
Paper. J.J. Augustin, Inc., Publisher, $5.00.

***TONWEYA AND THE EAGLES AND
OTHER LAKOTA INDIAN TALES**
Rosebud Y. Robe
Grades 2-6. Illus. Dial Press, 1979. $7.95.

TOPICS IN MOJAVE SYNTAX
Pamela E. Munro
Garland Publishing, 1976. $51.00.

**TOPOGRAPHICAL DESCRIPTION OF
THE STATE OF OHIO, INDIANA
TERRITORY AND LOUISIANA**
Jervis Cutler
Reprint of 1812 edition. Illus. Ayer Co.,
$17.00.

**THE TORTURE OF CAPTIVES
BY INDIANS OF EASTERN
NORTH AMERICA**
Nathaniel Knowles
Bound with other captivity narratives.
Reprint of 1940 edition, et al. Garland
Publishing, $35.00.

**THE TOTEM CARVERS:
CHARLIE JAMES, ELLEN NEEL,
AND MUNGO MARTIN**
Phil Nuytten
Illus. 132 pp. University of Washington
Press, 1983. $32.00.

**TOTEM POLES: AN
ILLUSTRATIVE GUIDE**
Marjorie M. Halpin
Illus. 64 pp. International Specialized Books,
1982. $19.95. Paper. University of Washington
Press, $8.95.

**TOTEM POLES OF THE
GITKSAN, UPPER SKEENA
RIVER, BRITISH COLUMBIA**
Marius Barbeau
Illus. Paper. University of Chicago Press,
1973. $4.00.

*TOTEM POLES AND TRIBES
Nancy Lyon
Grades 4-6. Illus. Paper. Raintree Press,
1977. $14.25.

TOTEM TALES
W.E. Crane
Reprint of 1922 edition. Paper. Shorey, $7.95.

TOTEM TALES OF OLD SEATTLE
Gordon Newell and Don Sherwood
Paper. Comstock Editions, 1974. $1.50.

TOTEMISM
C. Levi-Strauss
Paper. Beacon Press, 1963. $6.95.

**TOUCH THE EARTH: A SELF
PORTRAIT OF INDIAN EXISTENCE**
T.C. McLuhan
Paper. Simon & Schuster, 1976. $8.95.

**TOUR OF THE AMERICAN LAKES
AND AMONG THE INDIANS OF THE
NORTHWEST TERRITORY, IN 1830**
C. Colton
Reprint of 1833 edition. Two volumes. Kennikat
Press, $47.00 per set.

TOUR ON THE PRAIRIES
W. Irving; John McDermott, Editor
Reprint of 1956 edition. University of Oklahoma
Press, $9.95.

TOVANGER
Anne Galloway
Paper. Malki Museum Press, 1978. $2.00.

**TRADERS OF THE WESTERN
MORNING: ABORIGINAL COMMERCE
IN PRCOLUMBIAN NORTH AMERICA**
John U. Terrell
Illus. Maps. 145 pp. Southwest Museum, 1967.
$12.50.

**TRADERS TO THE NAVAJOS:
THE STORY OF THE WETHERILLS
OF KAYENTA**
F. Gillmor and L. Wetherill
The story of John Wetherill, who discovered
the ruins of Mesa Verde, Betatakin, Keet Seel,
and others. Reprint of 1953 edition. 265 pp.
Paper. University of New Mexico Press, $6.95.

**TRADITION, CHANGE AND CONFLICT
IN INDIAN FAMILY BUSINESS**
Allan R. Cohen
347 pp. Paper. Mouton Publishers, 1974. $26.75.

**TRADITIONAL LITERATURES OF
THE AMERICAN INDIAN: TEXTS
AND INTERPRETATIONS**
Ruth Benedict
162 pp. University of Nebraska Press, 1981.
$16.50; paper, $5.95.

**TRADITIONAL OJIBWA RELIGION
AND ITS HISTORICAL CHANGES**
Christopher Vecsey
American Philosophical Society, 1983. $12.00.

**TRADITIONS IN TRANSITION:
CONTEMPORARY BASKET WEAVING
OF THE SOUTHWESTERN INDIANS**
Barbara Maudlin
Illus. 60 pp. Paper. Museum of New Mexico
Press, 1984. $5.95.

TRADITIONS AND LAWS OF THE IROQUOIS: OR, SIX NATIONS, AND HISTORY OF THE TUSCARORA INDIANS
Elias Johnson
Reprint of 1881 edition. AMS Press, $20.00.

TRADITIONS OF THE ARAPAHO
G.A. Dorsey and A.L. Kroeber
Reprint of 1903 edition. Paper. Kraus, $48.00.

TRADITIONS OF THE CADDO
G.A. Dorsey
Reprint of 1905 edition. AMS Press, $16.50.

TRADITIONS OF THE CHILCOTIN INDIANS
L. Farand
Reprint of 1900 edition. AMS Press, $17.50.

THE TRADITIONS OF THE HOPI: THE STANLEY McCORMIC HOPI EXPEDITION
H.R. Voth, Translator
Reprint of 1905 edition. Paper. AMS Press, and Kraus, $39.00.

TRADITIONS OF THE NORTH AMERICAN INDIANS
J.A. Jones
Three volumes. Gordon Press, $300.00 per set.

TRADITIONS OF THE OSAGE
G. Dorsey
Reprint of 1904 edition. AMS Press, $12.50.

TRADITIONS OF THE QUINAULT INDIANS
L. Farrand and W.S. Kahnweiler
Reprint of 1902 edition. AMS Press, $17.50.

TRADITIONS OF THE SKIDI PAWNEE
G.A. Dorsey
Reprint of 1904 edition. Illus. Kraus, $34.00.

TRADITIONS OF THE THOMPSON RIVER INDIANS OF BRITISH COLUMBIA
J.A. Teit
Reprint of 1898 edition. Kraus, $16.00.

THE TRAGEDY OF THE BLACKFOOT
W. McCluntock
Reprint of 1930 edition. Illus. 53 pp. Southwest Museum, $5.00.

*TRAGEDY OF TENAYA
Allan Shields
Grades 6-12. Council for Indian Education, 1974. $5.95; paper, $1.95.

TRAGEDY OF THE WAHK-SHUM
L. McWhorter
Prelude to the Yakima Indian War of 1855-1856. Reprint of 1968 edition. 44 pp. Paper. Ye Galleon Press, $5.50.

TRAGEDY STRIKES AT WOUNDED KNEE
Will H. Spindler
Covers the tragic battle of 1890. Revised edition. Illus. 138 pp. Paper. Dakota Press, 1972. $1.95.

THE TRAIL OF LEWIS AND CLARK: 1804-1904
O. Wheeler
Reprint of 1904 edition. Two volumes. AMS Press, $57.50 per set.

TRAITS OF AMERICAN INDIAN LIFE AND CHARACTER
P. Ogden
Reprint of 1933 second edition. AMS Press, $17.50.

TRANSRACIAL ADOPTION
Rita Simon and Howard Altstein
John Wiley & Sons, 1977. $20.00.

TRAPS OF THE AMERICAN INDIANS
Otis T. Mason
Facsimile of 1901 edition. Illus. 18 pp. Paper. Shorey, $2.95.

TRAVELS
W. Bantram; Mark Van Doren, Editor
Contains descriptions of the Cherokee, Creek and Seminoles from 1773-1778. Reprint. Illus. Peter Smith, $9.00. Paper. Dover, $4.50.

TRAVELS AND ADVENTURES IN CANADA AND THE INDIAN TERRITORIES, 1760 & 1776
A. Henry; James Bain, Editor
Reprint of 1809 edition. Garland, $44.00.

TRAVELS IN THE GREAT WESTERN PRAIRIES
T.J. Farnham
Reprint of 1843 edition. Two volumes in one. 612 pp. Da Capo Press, $75.00.

TRAVELS IN NORTH AMERICA, INCLUDING A SUMMER WITH THE PAWNEES
C. Murray
Reprint of 1839 Second Edition. 878 pp. Da Capo Press, $85.00.

TRAVELS IN THE REPUBLIC OF TEXAS, 1842
Francis Latham
Texas frontier society. The Encino Press, $15.00.

**TREATIES ON TRIAL: THE
CONTINUING CONTROVERSY OVER
NORTHWEST INDIAN FISHING RIGHTS**
Fay G. Cohen, et al
Illus. 280 pp. University of Washington
Press, 1985. $20.00; paper, $9.95.

**TREATIES WITH THE CREEK AND
SEMINOLE INDIANS, 1763-1815**
Howard Cline and Timothy King
Clearwater Publishing, $23.00.

**TREATY BETWEEN THE U.S.
AND THE DWAMISH, SUQUAMISH
AND OTHER ALLIED AND SUBOR-
DINATE TRIBES OF INDIANS
IN WASHINGTON TERRITORY**
Isaac Stevens
Facsimile of 1855 edition. 7 pp. Paper.
Shorey, $3.00.

**TREATY BETWEEN THE U.S.
AND THE INDIANS OF THE
WILLAMETTE VALLEY**
I.I. Stevens
Facsimile of 1855 edition. 8 pp. Paper.
Shore, $3.00.

**TREATY BETWEEN THE U.S.
AND THE MAKAH TRIBE**
Isaac Stevens
Facsimile of 1855 edition. 8 pp. Paper.
Shorey, $3.00.

**TREATY BETWEEN THE U.S.
AND THE NISQUALLY AND
OTHER BANDS OF INDIANS**
Isaac Stevens
Facsimile of 1855 edition. 8 pp. Paper.
Shorey, $3.00.

**TREATY BETWEEN THE U.S. AND
THE YAKIMA NATION OF INDIANS**
Isaac Stevens
Facsimile of 1855 edition. 8 pp. Paper.
Shorey, $3.00.

TREATY OF MEDICINE LODGE
Douglas Jones
Illus. 237 pp. University of Oklahoma Press,
1974. $12.95; paper, $5.95.

**TREND AND TRADITION IN THE
PREHISTORY OF THE EASTERN U.S.**
J.R. Caldwell
Reprint of 1958 edition. Paper. Kraus, $12.00.

**TRIBAL APPRENTICESHIP
TRAINING PROGRAM MANUAL**
Lorentino Lalio
Council for Training and Employment Rights,
$33.00.

**TRIBAL DESIGNS FOR NEEDLE-
POINT: 30 ORIGINAL DESIGNS
ADAPTED FROM ESKIMO, POLY-
NESIAN AND INDIAN ART**
Gay Ann Rogers
Paper. Doubleday, 1977. $5.95.

**TRIBAL DISPOSSESSION AND OTHER
OTTAWA INDIAN UNIVERSITY FRAUD**
William E. Unrau and H. Craig Miner
Illus. 224 pp. University of Oklahoma Press,
1985. $17.95.

TRIBAL DISTRIBUTION IN OREGON
J.V. Berreman
Reprint of 1937 edition. Paper. Kraus, $15.00.

TRIBAL GOVERNMENT: A NEW ERA
A collection of papers follows Choctaw Tribal
Government from precontact through the Treaty
of ancing Rabbit Creek right up till today.
Includes Choctaw Tribal constitution and all
Choctaw treaties with U.S. Government.
Choctaw Heritage Press, $6.00.

TRIBAL GOVERNMENT TEXTBOOK
National Congress of American Indians.

***TRIBAL SOVEREIGNTY: INDIAN
TRIBES IN U.S. HISTORY**
Four scholarly papers which consider the
issue of tribal sovereignty. Papers by: Dr.
Fay Cohen, Dr. D'Arcy McNickle, Dr. Roger
Buffalohead, and Dr. Mary Young. Studies the
impact of non-Indian settlement and U.S.
Government policy. Teacher's guide. Grades
7-12. Illus. 60 pp. Daybreak Star Press, $5.50.

TRIBES OF CALIFORNIA
S. Powers
American Indian ethnography of California.
Reprint of 1877 edition. Illus. 482 pp. Univer-
sity of California Press, $40.00; paper, $10.95.

**TRIBES OF THE COLUMBIA
VALLEY AND THE COAST OF
WASHINGTON AND OREGON**
A.B. Lewis
Reprint of 1906 edition. Paper. Kraus, $15.00.

**TRIBES OF THE EXTREME NORTH-
WEST, ALASKA, THE ALEUTIANS
AND ADJACENT TERRITORIES**
G. Gibbs, et al
Reprint of 1877 edition. Illus. Paper. Shorey,
$9.95.

**TRIBES OF WESTERN WASHINGTON
AND NORTHWEST OREGON**
George Gibbs, et al
200 pp. Paper. Shorey, $16.95.

TRIBES THAT SLUMBER: INDIANS OF THE TENNESSEE REGION
T. Lewis and M. Kneberg
Reprint of 1958 edition. Illus. 208 pp. University of Tennessee Press, $17.95; paper, $7.95.
Paper. American Indian Books, $7.95.

TRICKSTER: STUDY IN AMERICAN INDIAN MYTHOLOGY
Paul Radin
Reprint of 1956 edition. 223 pp. Greenwood Press, $22.50. New edition. 223 pp. Paper. Shocken Books, 1972. $6.95.

A TRIP TO NEW ENGLAND: WITH A CHARACTER OF THE COUNTRY AND PEOPLE
E. Ward
Reprint of 1905 edition. Burt Franklin, $19.00.

A TRUE DISCOURSE OF THE PRESENT ESTATE OF VIRGINIA
R.A. Hamor
Reprint of 1615 edition. 70 pp. Walter J. Johnson, $13.00.

A TRUE HISTORY OF THE CAPTIVITY AND RESTORATION OF MRS. ROWLANDSON
Bound with other Indian captivities. Reprint of 1682 edition, et al. Garland, $33.00.

TRUE STORIES OF NEW ENGLAND CAPTIVES CARRIED TO CANADA DURING THE OLD FRENCH AND INDIAN WARS
Charlotte A. Baker
Reprint of 1897 edition. Garland, $33.00.

THE TRUTH ABOUT GERONIMO
Britton Davis; M.M. Quaife, Editor
Illus. 293 pp. University of Nebraska Press, 1976. $16.95; paper, $5.25.

TRUTH OF THE HOPI
E. Nequatewa
Illus. 112 pp. Paper. Northland, 1973. $8.95.

TSALI
Denton R. Bedford
Tsali, a hero of the Cherokee people, he survived the Georgia Army bandits in 1838, the year of the infamous Cherokee Removal. Illus. 256 pp. The Indian Historian Press, $15.00; paper, $11.00.

TSEE-MA'HEONE-NEMEOTOTSE: CHEYENNE SPIRITUAL SONGS
David Graber, Editor
227 pp. Faith & Life, 1982. $29.95.

THE TSIMSHIAN: IMAGES OF THE PAST, VIEWS FROM THE PRESENT
Margaret Seguin, Editor
Illus. 210 pp. International Specialized Book Service, 1984. $26.95.

TSIMSHIAN INDIAN AND THEIR ARTS
Viola Garfield and Paul Wingert
Illus. 108 pp. Paper. University of Washington Press, 1966. $4.95.

TSIMSHIAN INDIANS AND THEIR ARTS
Viola Garfield and Paul Wingert
Illus. 108 pp. Paper. University of Washington Press, 1966. $4.95.

THE TSIMSHIAN AND OTHER PEOPLES OF THE NORTHWEST COAST
Jay Miller and Carol Eastman, Editors
University of Washington Press, 1982.

THE TSIMSHIAN AND THEIR NEIGHBORS OF THE NORTH PACIFIC COAST
Jay Miller and Carol Eastman, Editors
Illus. 366 pp. University of Washington Press, 1985. $35.00.

TUBERCULOSIS AMONG CERTAIN INDIAN TRIBES OF THE U.S.
A. Hrdlicka
Reprint of 1909 edition. 96 pp. Scholarly Press, $29.00.

TULAPAI TO TOKAY: A BIBLIOGRAPHY OF ALCOHOL USE AND ABUSE AMONG NATIVE AMERICANS OF NORTH AMERICA
David R. McDonald
372 pp. HRAFP, 1981, $25.00.

TUNICA TEXTS, TUNICA DICTIONARY
M.R. Haas, Editor
Reprint of 1950 and 1953 editions. Paper. Kraus, $44.00.

TURQUOISE AND THE NAVAJO
Lee Hammons and Gertrude Hill
Illus. 36 pp. Paper. Arizona Maps and Books, 1975. $1.95.

TUSCARORA LANGUAGE
Elton Green
Johnson Publishing (NC) $4.95.

*THE TUSCARORAS
Shirley H. Witt
Grades 5-12. Illus. Paper. Macmillan, 1972. $4.95.

TUSCARORAS
F. Roy Johnson
Two volumes. Volume 1: *Mythology, Medicine and Culture;* Volume 2: *History, Tradition and Cultural Modifications. Illus. Johnson Publishing (NC), 1968. $7.50 and $9.50.*

TWANA GAMES
A handbook of games played by Twana people of the Skokomish Reservation in western Washington State. Illus. 20 pp. Daybreak Star Press, $3.50.

THE TWO BATTLES OF THE LITTLE BIG HORN
John M. Carroll
Paper. Amereon Ltd., 1985. $12.95.

TWO CROWS DENIES IT: A HISTORY OF CONTROVERSY IN OMAHA SOCIOLOGY
R.H. Barnes
Illus. 288 pp. University of Nebraska Press, 1984. $24.95.

TWO LEGGINGS: THE MAKING OF A CROW WARRIOR
Peter Nabakov
Illus. 250 pp. Paper. Thomas Y. Crowell, 1970. $4.95; University of Nebraska Press, $6.95.

TWO STRATIFIED SITES ON THE DOOR PENINSULA OF WISCONSIN
R.I. Mason
Paper. University of Michigan, Museum of Anthropology, 1966. $3.00.

TWO WORLDS OF THE WASHO: AN INDIAN TRIBE OF CALIFORNIA AND NEVADA
James F. Downs
Paper. Holt, Rinehart & Winston, 1966. $9.96.

U

UINTAH UTE TRACT: PRELIMINARY APPRAISAL REPORT
C. Marc Miller
50 pp. Clearwater Publishing, 1973. $19.50.

UINTAH VALLEY INDIAN RESERVATION LANDS IN UTAH, APPRAISAL OF 1881
Werner Kiepe
212 pp. Clearwater Publishing, 1973. $64.50.

UKOMNO'M: THE YUKI INDIANS OF NORTHERN CALIFORNIA
Virginia P. Miller
Illus. Paper. Ballena Press, 1979. $8.95.

THE UMATILLA, WALLA WALLA AND CAYUSE INDIANS RELATIVE TO SOCIO-POLITICAL ORGANIZATION AND LAND USE
Robert J. Suphan
90 pp. Clearwater Publishing, 1973. $32.50.

UNCLE SAM'S STEPCHILDREN: THE REFORMATION OF U.S.

INDIAN POLICY, 1865-1887
L.B. Priest
Reprint of 1942 edition. 310 pp. Paper. University of Nebraska Press, $6.95.

UNCOMMON CONTROVERSY: FISHING RIGHTS OF THE MUCKLESHOOT, PUYALLUP AND NISQUALLY INDIANS
American Friends Service Committee
Illus. 264 pp. University of Washington Press, 1970. $7.50.

UNCONQUERED SEMINOLE INDIANS
Irvin Peithman
Illus. Paper. Great Outdoors Publishing, 1956. $2.95.

UNDER THE INDIAN TURQUOISE SKY
Rosemary Davey
Ye Galleon Press, 1985. $9.95.

THE UNDERGROUND RESERVATION: OSAGE OIL
Terry P. Wilson
Illus. 172 pp. University of Nebraska Press, 1985. $22.95.

UNITED NATION OF CHIPPEWA, OTTAWA AND POTAWATOMIE INDIANS: ANTHROPOLOGICAL REPORT ON THE INDIAN OCCUPANCY IN ILLINOIS AND WISCONSIN, CEDED UNDER THE TREATY OF SEPT. 26, 1833
J.A. Jones
80 pp. Clearwater Publishing, 1973. $48.00.

UNITED SENECAS AND SHAWNEES, 1833: APPRAISAL OF LANDS IN NORTHEASTERN OKLAHOMA
Richard Hall
45 pp. Clearwater Publishing, 1973. $18.00.

UNITED STATES—COMANCHE RELATIONS: THE RESERVATION YEARS
William Hagan
Yale University Press, 1976. $22.50.

U.S. CONGRESS: REPORT... WASHINGTON, 1813
Wilcomb E. Washburn, Editor
Reprint of 1813 edition. Garland, $35.00.

UNITED STATES INDIAN POLICY: A CRITICAL BIBLIOGRAPHY
Francis P. Prucha
64 pp. Paper. Indiana University Press, 1977. $4.95.

U.S. MILITARY EDGED WEAPONS OF THE SECOND SEMINOLE WAR: 1835-1842
Ron G. Hickox
Illus. 102 pp. Paper. Ron G. Hickox, 1984. $15.95.

UNITED TRIBES OF OTTAWAS,
CHIPPEWAS AND POTAWATOMIES:
ANTHROPOLOGICAL REPORT ON THE
INDIAN OCCUPANCY OF ROYCE
AREAS 77 AND 78
E. Wheeler-Voegelin and E.J. Blasingham
217 pp. Clearwater Publishing, 1973. $66.00.

UNITED TRIBES OF SAC AND FOX
INDIANS: ANTHROPOLOGICAL REPORT
ON THE INDIAN OCCUPANCY OF
ROYCE AREA 50, CEDED UNDER
THE TREATY OF NOVEMBER 3, 1804
E. Wheeler-Voegelin, et al
310 pp. Clearwater Publishing, 1973. $90.00.

THE UNKNOWN INDIAN
G.B. Brown
Gordon Press, 1977. $59.95.

UNLEARNING "INDIAN" STEREOTYPES
56 pp. Paper. Council for Interracial
Books for Children, $3.95.

UNWILLING URBANITES: THE
LIFE OF CANADIAN INDIANS
IN A PRAIRIE CITY
James Kerri
Paper. University Press of America, 1978.
$8.50.

THE UNWRITTEN LITERATURE
ON THE HOPI
H.G. Lockett
Reprint of 1933 edition. AMS Press, $18.00.

UPPER MISSISSIPPI: OR,
HISTORICAL SKETCHES OF THE
MOUND-BUILDERS, THE INDIAN
TRIBES, AND THE PROGRESS OF
CIVILIZATION IN THE NORTH-
WEST; FROM 1600-1867
G. Gale
Reprint of 1867 edition. Kraus, $32.00.

THE UPPER PIMA OF SAN
CAYETANO DEL TUMACACORI
C. DiPeso
Reprint of 1956 edition. Kraus, $111.00.

THE URBAN AMERICAN INDIAN
Alan Sorkin
Illus. 176 pp. Lexington Books, 1978. $21.50.

URBAN INDIANS OF ARIZONA:
PHOENIX, TUCSON AND FLAGSTAFF
Joyotpaul Chaudhuri
Paper. University of Arizona Press, 1974.
$1.95.

URBAN INDIANS: THE STRANGERS
IN CANADA'S CITIES
Larry Krotz; photos by John Paskievich
Examines the problems faced by thousands of

Canadian natives who are moving from rural
areas to the cities. Illus. 176 pp. Paper.
Hurtig Publishers, $9.95.

URBAN INSTITUTIONS AND
PEOPLE OF INDIAN ANCESTRY
Raymond Breton and Gail Akian
52 pp. Paper. Brookfield Publishing, 1978.
$3.00.

URBAN RENEGADES: THE CULTURAL
STRATEGY OF AMERICAN INDIANS
Jeanne Guillemin
336 pp. Columbia University Press, 1975.
$29.00.

URBANIZATION OF AMERICAN
INDIANS: A CRITICAL
BIBLIOGRAPHY
Russell Thornton, et al
96 pp. Paper. Indiana University Press, 1982.
$4.95.

USES OF PLANTS BY THE INDIANS
OF THE MISSOURI RIVER REGION
Melvin Gilmore
Illus. University of Nebraska Press, 1977.
$13.95; paper, $5.95.

UTE CEDED TRATC, COLORADO,
1873-1874
C. Marc Miller
316 pp. Clearwater Publishing, 1973. $91.50.

UTE INDIANS
Two volumes. Illus. Maps. Garland, $42.00.

UTE INDIANS AND THE
SAN JUAN MINING REGION:
HISTORICAL SUMMARY
Leroy Hafen
54 pp. Clearwater Publishing, 1974. $25.00.

UTE PEYOTISM: A STUDY
OF A CULTURAL COMPLEX
O.C. Stewart
Reprint of 1948 edition. Paper. Kraus,
$16.00.

THE UTE WAR: A HISTORY OF
THE WHITE RIVER MASSACRE
Thomas Dawson and F.J. Skiff
64 pp. Paper. Vic Press and Johnson Books,
1975. $6.95.

V

THE VAIL SITE: A PALEO-
INDIAN ENCAMPMENT IN MAINE
Richard M. Gramley
Ilus. 183 pp. Paper. Buffalo Museum of
Science, $12.95.

VALLEY OF THE MISSISSIPPI
Henry Lewis; Bertha Heilbron, Editor
Illus. 423 pp. Minnesota Historical Society,
1967. $39.75; uncut edition, $50.00.

**VALLEY OF THE SIX NATIONS:
A COLLECTION OF DOCUMENTS
OF THE INDIAN LANDS OF
THE GRAND RIVER**
Charles Johnston
Illus. University of Toronto Press, 1965.
$17.50.

**VALLEY OF THE SPIRITS:
THE UPPER SKAGIT INDIANS
OF WESTERN WASHINGTON**
June Collins
Illus. 282 pp. University of Washington
Press, 1974. $20.00; paper, $9.95.

**VANISHED ARIZONA: RECOL-
LECTIONS OF THE ARMY LIFE
OF A NEW ENGLAND WOMAN**
Martha Summerhayes
Reissue of 1908 edition. Illus. Map. 392 pp.
Rio Grande Press, $12.00.

**THE VANISHING AMERICAN:
THE EPIC OF THE INDIAN**
Zane Grey
Paper. Pocket Books, 1982. $3.50.

**THE VANISHING AMERICAN:
WHITE ATTITUDES AND U.S.
INDIAN POLICY**
Brian W. Dipple
Illus. 432 pp. Wesleyan University Press,
1982. $27.95.

**THE VANISHING RACE: THE LAST
GREAT INDIAN COUNCIL, 1909,
GEN. CUSTER'S INDIAN SCOUTS'
ACCOUNT OF LITTLE BIG HORN**
Dr. Joseph Dixon
Photos of famous Indians and places. Reprint
of 1913 edition. Illus. 325 pp. Rio Grande
Press, $20.00.

**THE VANISHING RACE AND
OTHER ILLUSIONS: PHOTOGRAPHS
OF INDIANS BY EDWARD S. CURTIS**
Christopher M. Lymans
Illus. 158 pp. Smithsonian Institution Press,
1982. $22.50.

**THE VANISHING RACE: SELEC-
TIONS FROM EDWARD S. CURTIS'**
THE NORTH AMERICAN INDIAN
Mick Gidley, Editor
Illus. Taplinger Publishing, 1977. $9.95.

THE VANISHING WHITE MAN
Stan Steiner
Paper. Harper & Row, 1976. $3.95.

**VARIATIONS IN VALUE
ORIENTATIONS**
K. Kluckhohn and F. Strodtbeck
Reprint of 1961 edition. Illus. 437 pp.
Greenwood Press, $31.00; paper, $7.95.

VAST DOMAIN OF BLOOD
Don Schellie
289 pp. Westernlore, 1968. $9.50.

*VEHO
Henry Tall Bull and Tom Weist
Grades 2-6. Paper. Council for Indian
Education, 1971. $1.95.

**VICTORIO AND THE
MIMBRES APACHES**
Dan L. Thrapp
Illus. 420 pp. Paper. University of Oklahoma
Press, 1980. $12.95.

**A VIEW OF THE AMERICAN
INDIANS: GENERAL CHARACTER,
CUSTOMS, LANGUAGE, PUBLIC
FESTIVALS, RELIGIOUS RITES
AND TRADITIONS**
I. Worsley; Moshe Davis, Editor
Reprint of 1828 edition. Ayer Co., $19.00.

VIEWS OF A VANISHING FRONTIER
John C. Ewers, et al
Illus. 103 pp. Univerity of Nebraska Press,
1984. $29.95. Joslyn Art, $29.95; paper,
$14.95.

**THE VILLAGE INDIANS OF THE
UPPER MISSOURI: THE MANDANS,
HIDATSAS AND ARIKARAS**
Roy W. Meyer
Illus. 355 pp. University of Nebraska Press,
1977. $21.50.

**THE VILLAGE OF THE GREAT
KIVAS ON THE ZUNI RESERVATION,
NEW MEXICO**
Frank Roberts, Jr.
Reprint of 1932 edition. Scholarly Press,
$19.00.

VILLAGERS
Claire Fejas
Random House, 1981. $14.95.

**VILLAGES OF THE ALGONQUIAN,
SIOUAN AND CADDOAN TRIBES
WEST OF THE MISSISSIPPI**
D. Bushnell, Jr.
Reprint of 1922 edition. Scholarly Press,
$21.00.

**VISUAL METAPHORS: A FORMAL
ANALYSIS OF NAVAJO ART**
Evelyn Hatcher
West Publishing, 1975. $25.95.

**VITALS SOULS: BORORO COS-
MOLOGY, NATURAL SYMBOLISM
AND SHAMANISM**
J. Christopher Crocker
University of Arizona Press, 1985. $29.95.

**VOCABULARY OF THE
KIOWA LANGUAGE**
J.P. Harrington
Reprint of 1928 edition. Scholarly Press,
$19.00.

**A VOICE IN HER TRIBE:
A NAVAJO WOMAN'S OWN STORY**
Irene Stewart
Illus. Paper. Ballena Press, 1980. $8.95.

VOICES IN THE CANYON
Viele
The story of a Navajo National Monument's
amazing cliff dwellings written for laymen
and reviewed by professionals. Illus. 50
color photos. Maps. 76 pp. Paper. Southwest
Parks and Monuments, $6.00.

VOICES OF EARTH AND SKY
Vinson Brown
Illus. 177 pp. Paper. Naturegraph, 1976.
$5.95.

**VOLCANO TALES: INDIAN LEGENDS
OF THE CASCADE MOUNTAINS**
Mike Helm; Jery Keuter, Editor
200 pp. Rainey Day Press, 1980.

***VOSTAAS: THE STORY OF
MONTANA'S INDIAN NATIONS**
Maxine Ruppel
Grades 3-10. 68 pp. Council for Indian
Education, 1970. $6.95; paper, $2.95.

VOYAGE OF ALEXANDER MACKENZIE
Facsimile reprint. Paper. Shorey, $5.75.

**VOYAGES FROM MONTREAL THROUGH
THE CONTINENT OF NORTH AMERICA
TO THE FROZEN AND PACIFIC
OCEANS IN 1789 & 1793, WITH
AN ACCOUNT OF THE RISE AND
STATE OF THE FUR TRADE**
A. Mackenzie
Reprint of 1922 edition. Two volumes. AMS
Press, $47.50.

**VOYAGES OF PETER ESPRIT
RADISSON: BEING AN ACCOUNT OF
HIS TRAVELS AND EXPERIENCES
AMONG THE NORTH AMERICAN
INDIANS, 1652-1684**
P.E. Radisson
Reprint of 1885 edition. Illus. Burt Franklin,
$26.50.

**VOYAGES OF SAMUEL DE
CHAMPLAIN, 1604-1618**
W.L. Grant, Editor
Reprint of 1907 edition. Barnes and Noble,
$18.50.

**VOYAGES AND TRAVELS OF AN
INDIAN INTERPRETER AND TRADER
DESCRIBING THE MANNERS AND
CUSTOMS OF THE NORTH
AMERICAN INDIANS**
John Long
Reprint of 1791 edition. Johnson Reprint,
$18.00.

W

**WAHEENEE: AN INDIAN
GIRL'S STORY**
Gilbert L. Wilson
Illus. 190 pp. University of Nebraska Press,
1981. $15.95; paper, $4.95.

**WAH'KON-TAH: THE OSAGE
AND THE WHITE MAN'S ROAD**
John Mathews
Illus. 359 pp. Paper. University of Oklahoma
Press, $10.95.

WALAPAI ETHNOGRAPHY
A. Kroeber
Reprint of 1935 edition. Paper. Kraus, $34.00.

**WALK IN BEAUTY: THE NAVAJO
AND THEIR BLANKETS**
Anthony Berland and Mary Kahlenberg
Illus. New York Graphic Society, 1977. $37.50.

**WALK IN YOUR SOUL:
LOVE INCANTATIONS OF
THE OKLAHOMA CHEROKEES**
Jack and Anna Kilpatrick
An annotated rendering in English of erotic
charms from the manuscripts collected by the
author. Reprint of 1965 edition. Illus. 174 pp.
Paper. Southern Methodist University Press,
$9.95.

**WAMPUM AND SHELL ARTICLES
USED BY THE NEW YORK INDIANS**
W.M. Beauchamp
Reprint of 1901 edition. AMS Press, $21.50.

**WAMPUM, WAR AND TRADE
GOODS WEST OF THE HUDSON**
Gilbert W. Hagerty
Illus. 310 pp. Heart of the Lakes, 1985.
$50.00.

**WANGKA: AUSTRONESIAN
CANOE ORIGINS**
Edwin Doran, Jr.
Illus. 121 pp. Texas A & M University Press,
1981. $15.00.

THE WAPPO: A REPORT
Yolande S. Beard
Paper. Malki Museum Press, 1979. $5.25.

***WAR CLOUDS IN THE WEST:
INDIANS AND CAVALRYMEN,
1860-1890**
Albert Martin
Grades 5-12. Illus. 192 pp. Atheneum, 1984.
$14.95.

**WAR EAGLE: A LIFE OF
GENERAL EUGENE A. CARR**
James T. King
Illus. 325 pp. University of Nebraska Press,
1964. $24.50.

*WAR PONY
D. E. Worcester
Reprint of 1961 edition. Grades 3-6. Illus.
95 pp. Texas Christian University Press,
$10.95.

**WAR-PATH AND BIVOUAC:
THE BIG HORN AND YELLOW-
STONE EXPEDITION**
John Finerty; Milo M. Quaife, Editor
Reprint of 1966 edition. Illus. Paper. Uni-
versity of Nebraska Press, and University
of Oklahoma Press, $7.95.

**WAR-PATH AND BIVOUAC: OR,
THE CONQUEST OF THE SIOUX**
John Finerty
Illus. Paper. University of Oklahoma Press,
1977. $7.95.

**WARBONNET, A SYMBOL
OF GOOD DEEDS**
Includes sketch and caption on the Indian
war bonnet. Poster, 24x20". Supt. of Documents,
1982. $2.00.

**THE WARDELL BUFFALO TRAP FORTY
EIGHT SU THREE HUNDRED AND ONE:
COMMUNAL PROCUREMENT IN THE
UPPER GREEN RIVER BASIN, WY**
George C. Frison
Paper. University of Michigan, Museum of
Anthropology, 1973. $3.00.

**THE WARING PAPERS:
THE COLLECTED WORKS OF
ANTONIO J. WARING**
Stephen Williams
Paper. Peabody Museum, 1977. $20.00.

THE WARREN WAGONTRAIN RAID
B. Capps
Illus. Dial Pres, 1974. $8.95.

**WARRIORS OF THE COLORADO:
THE YUMAS OF THE QUENCHAN
NATION AND THEIR NEIGHBORS**
Jack Forbes
Illus. University of Oklahoma, 1965. $19.95.

***WARRIORS OF THE RAINBOW:
STRANGE AND PROPHETIC DREAMS
OF THE INDIAN PEOPLES**
William Willoya and Vinson Brown
Grades 4-12. Illus.104 pp. Naturegraph, 1962.
$11.95; paper, $5.95.

**WARRIORS WITHOUT WEAPONS:
A STUDY OF THE SOCIETY AND
PERSONALITY DEVELOPMENT OF
THE PINE RIDGE SIOUX**
Gordon Macgregor, et al
Illus. 228 pp. Paper. University of Chicago
Press, 1975. $9.00.

**THE WARS OF THE IROQUOIS:
A STUDY IN INTERTRIBAL
TRADE RELATIONS**
George T. Hunt
Reprint of 1940 edition. Map. 218 pp. Paper.
University of Wisconsin Press, $11.75.

WAS IT MURDER
W. C. Smith
Reprint of 1922 edition. 48 pp. Paper. Shorey,
$3.95.

**THE WASCO AND TENINO INDIANS:
POLITICAL ORGANIZATION
AND LAND USE**
Robert J. Suphan
72 pp. Clearwater Publishing, 1973. $27.00.

**WASHAKI: AN ACCOUNT OF INDIAN
RESISTANCE OF THE COVERED WAGON
AND UNION PACIFIC RAILROAD
INVASION OF THEIR TERRITORY**
Grace Hebard
Reprint of 1940 edition. AMS Press, $29.00.

THE WASHO INDIANS
S.A. Barrett
Reprint of 1917 edition. AMS Press, $14.00.

**WASHO INDIANS OF CALIFORNIA
AND NEVADA**
W. Azevedo, Editor
Reprint of 1963 edition. AMS Press, $22.50.

**WASHO SHAMANS AND PEYOTISTS:
RELIGIOUS CONFLICT IN AN
AMERICAN INDIAN TRIBE**
Edgar E. Siskin
Illus. 300 pp. University of Utah Press,
1983. $25.00.

**WASHOE INDIAN LANDS:
MINERAL VALUATION STUDY**
Ernest Oberbilling
238 pp. Clearwater Publishing, 1973. $72.00.

**WASHOE INDIANS OF CALIFORNIA
AND NEVADA: TIMBERLAND
VALUATION STUDY**
Myron Wall
93 pp. Clearwater Publishing, 1973. $33.00.

**WASHOE TRIBE: EVALUATION
OF MINERAL RESOURCES**
P.J. Shenon and Roy P. Full
Five volumes. 1,570 pp. Clearwater, 1973.
$420.00 per set.

**WASHOE TRIBE:
FISHERY EVALUATION**
Arthur Reber
26 pp. Clearwater Publishing, 1973. $19.50.

**WASHOE TRIBE OF INDIANS:
APPRAISAL OF LANDS IN NEVADA,
1862, AND IN CALIFORNIA, 1853**
Homer Hoyt
Two volumes. 259 pp. Clearwater Publishing,
1973. $76.50 per set.

**WASHOE TRIBE OF NEVADA AND
CALIFORNIA: APPRAISAL OF LANDS**
Noble T. Murray
266 pp. Clearwater Publishing, 1973. $103.00.

**WASI-CHII: THE CONTINUING
INDIAN WARS**
Bruce Johansen and Roberto Maestas
Illus. 268 pp. Paper. Monthly Review, 1979.
$6.95.

WATER ON THE PLATEAU
Paper. Museum of Northern Arizona, 1981.
$3.00.

*WATERLESS MOUNTAIN
Laura A. Armer
Reprint of 1931 edition. Grades 5-8. Illus.
David McKay Co., $10.95.

*ALFRED WATERS
Emanuel Skolnick
Grades 5 and up. Illus. 64 pp. Dillon Press,
1980. $7.95.

WATERWAY
B. Haile
Reprint. Illus. 155 pp. Paper. University
of Nebraska Press, $12.95.

THE WAY TO RAINY MOUNTAIN
N. Scott Momaday
An account of the historic trek of the Kiowa
Indians to Oklahoma. Illus. 90 pp. Paper.
University of New Mexico Press, 1976. $4.95.

**THE WAY WE LIVED: CALIFORNIA
INDIAN REMINISCENCES,
STORIES AND SONG**
Malcolm Margolin, Editor
Heyday Books, 1981. $12.95; paper, $6.95.

ANTHONY WAYNE, A NAME IN ARMS
Anthony Wayne; R.C. Knopf, Editor
Reprint of 1960 edition. Illus. 556 pp.
Greenwood Press, $37.50.

**WAYS OF EFFECTIVELY ADDRESSING
CULTURAL RESPONSIBILITIES, PRO-
CEEDINGS OF THE 1983 NATIVE
AMERICAN DIRECTORS WORKSHOP**
Office of Museums Programs, Smithsonian,
1985.

WAYS OF INDIAN MAGIC
Teresa VanEtten
96 pp. Paper. Sunstone Press, 1985. $8.95.

THE WAYS OF MY GRANDMOTHERS
Beverly H. Wolf
224 pp. William Morrow & Co., 1980. $12.95;
paper, $6.95.

***WAYS OF THE LUSHOOTSEED
PEOPLE: CEREMONIES AND TRADI-
TIONS OF THE NORTHERN PUGET
SOUND INDIANS**
Readings. Written in English and Lushoot-
seed. Grades 7-12. Illus. 56 pp. Daybreak
Star Press, $6.00.

**WE ARE METIS: THE ETHNOGRAPHY
OF A HALFBREED COMMUNITY IN
NORTHERN ALBERTA**
Paul Driben
Reprint. Illus. 190 pp. AMS Press, $32.50.

***WE HAVE NOT VANISHED:
EASTERN INDIANS OF THE U.S.**
Alfred Tamarin
Grades 3-6. Illus. 128 pp. Paper. Follett,
1974. $6.00.

*WE LIVE ON INDIAN RESERVATION
Hap Gilliland
Grades 1-6. Paper. Council for Indian
Education, 1981. $1.95.

***WE RODE THE WIND:
RECOLLECTIONS OF THE
19th-CENTURY TRIBAL LIFE**
Jane B. Katz, Editor
Grades 7-12. Illus. 112 pp. Paper. Lerner
Publications, 1975. $6.95.

WE WERE NOT SUMMER SOLDIERS:
THE INDIAN WAR DIARY OF
PLYMPTON J. KELLY, 1855-1856
W.N. Bischoff, Introduction
Reprint. 191 pp. Washington State Historical
Society, $8.75.

WEAVING ARTS OF THE
NORTH AMERICAN INDIANS
Freerick J. Dockstader
Illus. T.Y. Crowell, Publisher, 1978. $25.00.

WEAVING A NAVAJO BLANKET
G. Reichard
Reprint of 1936 edition. Illus. 256 pp.
Dover, $4.50.

CONRAD WEISER, 1696-1760;
FRIEND OF COLONIST AND MOHAWK
P.A. Wallace
Reprint of 1945 edition. Illus. Russell &
Russell, $27.50; Ayer Co., $24.00.

*WELCOME TO CHOCTAW FAIR
A cultural incentive to reading for pre-
school children. Positive self-concept and
self-expression are encouraged. Teacher's
guide. Grades Preschool-3. 12 pp. Choctaw
Heritage Press, $2.75.

WENATCHI SALISH OF CENTRAL
WASHINGTON: REPORT ON ANTHRO-
POLOGICAL AND ETHNOGRAPHIC
MATERIAL RELATIVE TO ABORI-
GINAL LAND USE AND OCCUPANCY
Stuart Chalfant
51 pp. Clearwater Publishing, 1974. $24.00.

THE WENATCHIE INDIANS:
GUARDIAN OF THE VALLEY
Richard D. Scheuerman
200 pp. Ye Galleon Press, 1983. $12.00.

WESTERN AMERICAN INDIAN:
CASE STUDIES IN TRIBAL HISTORY
Richard N. Ellis, Editor
203 pp. University of Nebraska Press, 1972.
$16.95; paper, $4.95.

THE WESTERN APACHE CLAN SYSTEM:
ORIGINS AND DEVELOPMENT
C.R. Kaut
Reprint of 1957 edition. Paper. Kraus, $12.00.

WESTERN APACHE RAIDING
AND WARFARE
Grenville Goodwin; Keith H. Basso, Editor
Personal narratives of six Apaches complement
the ethnographer's notes on weapons, war dances,
scalping, etc. Illus. Maps. Photos. 330 pp.
Paper. University of Arizona Press, 1971.
$11.95.

THE WESTERN APACHE RANGE:
TERRAIN AND ECOLOGICAL
CONDITIONS
Homer Aschmann
54 pp. Clearwater Publishing, 1973. $21.00.

WESTERN APACHE WITCHCRAFT
Keith H. Basso, Editor
Reprint. Paper. Books on Demand, $20.30.

WESTERN BAND OF SHOSHONE:
APPRAISAL OF LANDS IN
NEVADA AND CALIFORNIA
Donald Myers and Frank Kleinman
Two volumes. Clearwater Publishing, 1974.
$151.50 per set.

WESTERN BANDS OF SHOSHONE
INDIANS: EVALUATION STUDY
OF MINERAL RESOURCES
P.J. Shenon and Roy P. Full
12 volumes. 5,000 pp. Clearwater Publishing,
1973. $1,300.00 per set.

WESTERN EXPANSION AND
INDIGE NOUS PEOPLES: THE
HERITAGE OF LAS CASAS
Elias Sevilla-Casas, Editor
Beresford Book Service, 1977. $26.00.

WESTERN INDIANS: COMPARATIVE
ENVIRONMENTS, LANGUAGES AND
CULTURES OF 172 WESTERN
AMERICAN INDIAN TRIBES
Joseph G. Jorgensen
Illus. 673 pp. W.H. Freeman, 1980. $39.95.

WESTERN MILITARY FRONTIER,
1815-1846
H.P. Beers
Reprint of 1935 edition. Illus. 230 pp.
Porcupine Press, $19.50.

WESTERN MISSIONS AND
MISSIONARIES
P.J. DeSmet
Reprint of 1863 edition. 562 pp. Rowman &
Littlefield, $37.50.

WESTERN NORTH AMERICAN INDIAN
BASKETS FROM THE COLLECTION
OF CLAY P. BEDFORD
Clay P. Bedford, Editor
Illus. 68 pp. Paper. California Academy of
Sciences, 1980. $10.00.

*WESTWARD ADVENTURE: THE
TRUE STORIES OF SIX PIONEERS
William O. Steele
Grades 4-6. Illus. Paper. Harcourt Brace
Jovanovich, 1962. $5.95.

LEWIS WETZEL, INDIAN FIGHTER
C.B. Allman
Illus. Devin-Adair, 1961. $7.50.

**THE WEYMONTACHING
BIRCHBARK CANOE**
Camil Guy
Illus. Paper. University of Chicago Press,
1974. $3.50.

***WHEN BUFFALO FREE THE MOUN-
TAINS: A UTE INDIAN JOURNEY**
Nancy Wood
Grades 10-12. Illus. 256 pp. Doubleday, 1980.
$14.95.

WHEN BUFFALO RAN
George Grinnell
Illus. Paper. University of Oklahoma Press,
1966. $4.95.

*WHEN CLAY SINGS
Byrd Baylor
Grades 1-5. Illus. 32 pp. Paper. Atheneum,
$2.95.

**WHEN DID THE SHOSHONI BEGIN TO
OCCUPY SOUTHERN IDAHO: ESSAYS
ON LATE PREHISTORIC CULTURAL
REMAINS FROM THE UPPER SNAKE
AND SALMON RIVER COUNTIES**
B. Robert Butler
30 pp. Paper. Idaho Museum of Natural History,
1981. $5.00.

WHEN THE EARTH WAS YOUNG
David Yeadon
Paper. Doubleday, 1978. $5.95.

***WHEN GRANDFATHER JOURNEYS
INTO WINTER**
Craig Kee Strete; Illus. by Hal Frenck
The story of a Native American grandfather and
his grandson. Grades 7-12. 96 pp. Greenwillow
Books, 1979. $9.00.

**WHEN IT RAINS: PAPAGO
AND PIMA POETRY**
Ofelia Zepeda, Editor
In Native language and English translation.
90 pp. University of Arizona Press, 1982.
$8.95; paper, $4.50.

*WHEN THE MOON IS NEW
Laura Bannon
Grades 3-5. Illus. Albert Whitman & Co., 1953.
$5.95.

**WHEN NAVAJOS HAD TOO
MANY SHEEP: THE 1940's**
George A. Boyce; Jeanette Henry, Editor
Stock overgrazing led to rapidly eroding farm-
land. Illus. Map. 288 pp. Paper. The Indian
Historian Press, 1974. $11.00.

***WHEN SHALL THEY REST?
THE CHEROKEES LONG STRUGGLE
WITH AMERICA**
Peter Collier
Grades 7-12. Illus. 192 pp. Holt, Rinehart
& Winston, 1973. $6.95.

**WHEN YOU AND I WERE
YOUNG, WHITEFISH**
Dorothy M. Johnson
192 pp. Mountain Press, 1982. $13.95.

WHERE IS THE EAGLE?
William E. Coffer
A colection of tales. Illus. 288 pp. Van
Nostrand Reinhold, 1981. $16.95.

**WHERE THE WEST BEGINS:
ESSAYS ON MIDDLE BORDER
AND SIOUXLAND WRITING**
Arthur Huseboe and William Geyer, Editors
Illus. Paper. Center for Western Studies,
1978. $3.95.

**THE WHITE CANOE AND OTHER
LEGENDS OF THE OJIBWAYS**
E. Monckton
Gordon Press, 1977. $59.95.

*WHITE CAPITVES
Evelyn S. Lampman
Grades 4-7. 192 pp. Atheneum Publishers, 1975.
$6.95.

***THE WHITE DOE: THE FATE OF
VIRGINIA DARE, AN INDIAN LEGEND**
S.S. Cotten
Reprint of 1901 edition. Grades 8-12. Illus.
94 pp. Johnson Publishing (NC), $6.50.

**WHITE INTO RED: A STUDY OF
THE ASSIMILATION OF WHITE
PERSONS CAPTURED BY INDIANS**
Norman Heard
Illus. Scarecrow Press, 1973. $8.00.

**THE WHITE MAN'S INDIAN:
IMAGES OF THE AMERICAN INDIAN
FROM COLUMBUS TO THE PRESENT**
Robert Berkhofer, Jr.
Illus. Alfred A. Knopf, 1978. $15.00. Paper.
Random House, $5.95.

**WHITE ON RED: IMAGES
OF THE AMERICAN INDIAN**
Nancy B. Black and
Bette S. Weidman, Editors
Associated Facultu Press, 1976. $24.50.

**WHITE RIVER UTE INDIANS:
NATIVE COMPONENTS**
Julian H. Steward
50 pp. Clearwater, 1974. $24.00.

WHITE SETTLERS AND NATIVE
PEOPLES: AN HISTORICAL STUDY
OF RACIAL CONTACTS BETWEEN
ENGLISH-SPEAKING WHITES AND
ABORIGINAL PEOPLES IN THE
U.S., CANADA, AUSTRALIA
AND NEW ZEALAND
A.G. Price
Reprint of 1950 edition. Illus. 232 pp.
Greenwood, $19.75.

WHITE SHADOWS AMONG
THE MIGHTY SIOUX
F. Edward Butterworth
Independence Press, $10.00.

WHITE SIOUX
Iris Allan
Superior Publishing, 1969. $9.95.

WHITEHALL AND THE WILDERNESS:
THE MIDDLE WEST IN BRITISH
COLONIAL POLICY, 1760-1775
Jack Sosin
Reprint of 1961 edition. Illus. 318 pp.
Greenwood Press, $35.00.

JIM WHITEWOLF: THE
LIFE OF A KIOWA APACHE
Charles Brant
144 pp. Paper. Dover, 1969. $3.75.

WHO'S WHO AMONG NATIVE
AMERICANS, 1982: FORTY FIVE
HUNDRED BRIEF BIOGRAPHIES
Beacon Press Staff, Editors
293 pp. Gormezano Reference Publications,
1982. $979.95.

WHO'S WHO IN INDIAN RELICS
Ben W. Thompson
Volumes 1, 4, 5 and 6 are available. Illus.
96 pp. each. American Indian Books, $25.00
each.

WHY GONE THOSE TIMES?
BLACKFOOT TALES
J.W. Schultz (Apikuni);
L. Silliman, Editor
Illus. 271 pp. Paper. University of Oklahoma
Press, and American Indian Books, 1974. $8.95.

WHY THE NORTH STAR
STANDS STILL
William Palmer
Illus. 118 pp. Paper. Zion Natural History
Museum, 1978. $2.50.

*WHY THE POSSUM'S TAIL IS
BARE: AND OTHER NORTH AMERICAN
INDIAN NATURE TALES
James E. Connolly, Editor
Grades 3-12. Illus. 56 pp. Stemmer House,
1985. $12.95.

WI-NE-MA, THE WOMAN-CHIEF
AND HER PEOPLE
A.B. Meacham
Reprint of 1876 edition. AMS Press, $17.50.

THE WICHITA AND AFFILIATED
TRIBES: USE AND OCCUPANCY
OF THEIR LANDS
W.W. Newcomb
Clearwater Publishing, $27.00.

WICHITA GRAMMAR
David Rood
Garland Publishing, 1976. $51.00.

WICHITA INDIAN ARCHAEOLOGY
AND ETHNOHISTORY: A PILOT STUDY
Robert Bell et al, Editors
340 pp. Clearwater Publishing, 1973. $97.50.

*WIGWAM STORIES
Edward and M.P. Dolch
Reprint of 1956 edition. Grades 1-6. Garrard
Publishing, $7.29.

WIGWAM STORIES
M.C. Judd
Gordon Press, 1977. $59.95.

WIKCHAMNI GRAMMAR
Geoffrey Gamble
University of California Press, 1978. $17.00.

*WILD BROTHERS OF THE
INDIANS: AS PICTURED BY
THE ANCIENT AMERICANS
Alice Wesche
Grades 3-8. Illus. Paper. Treasure Chest,
1977. $4.95.

WILD LIFE ON THE PLAINS AND
HORRORS OF INDIAN WARFARE
George A. Custer
Reprint of 1891 edition. Ayer Co., $22.50.

WILDERNESS CHRISTIANS:
THE MORAVIAN MISSION TO
THE DELAWARE INDIANS
E. & L. Gray
Reprint of 1956 edition. Illus. 368 pp.
Russell & Russell, $22.00.

WILDERNESS EMPIRE
Allan Eckert
Illus. Arthur C. Little, 1969. $22.00.

WILDERNESS POLITICS AND
INDIAN GIFTS: THE NORTHERN
COLONIAL FRONTIER, 1748-1763
WIlbur Jacobs
Reprint. Illus. 208 pp. Peter Smith, $10.75.
Paper. University of Nebraska Press, $4.95.

THE WILDERNESS TRAIL
C.A. Hanna
Reprint of 1911 edition. Two volumes. Illus.
AMS Press, $74.50 per set.

THE WILLIAMS SITE: A FRONTIER MOGOLLON VILLAGE IN WEST CENTRAL NEW MEXICO
W. Smith
Paper. Kraus, 1973. $15.00.

JOHN P. WILLIAMSON: A BROTHER TO THE SIOUX
W.W. Barton
Reprint of 1919 edition. Illus. 308 pp.
Sunnycrest, $16.00.

THE WINDING TRAIL: THE ALABAMA—COUSHATTA INDIANS
Vivien Fox
Illus. Eakin Publications, 1983. $7.95.

THE WINDWAYS OF THE NAVAJO
Leland Wyman
Paper. Taylor Museum, 1962. $4.00.

WINNEBAGO INDIANS
Illus. Garland Publishing, $42.00.

WINNEBAGO INDIANS: ECONOMIC AND HISTORICAL BACKGROUND FOR ROYCE AREAS 149, 174, 245
Alice Smith and Vernon Carstensen
223 pp. Clearwater Publishing, 1973. $67.50.

WINNEBAGO LANDS IN IOWA AND MINNESOTA
William Murray
273 pp. Clearwater Publishing, 1973. $81.00.

WINNEBAGO LANDS IN MINNESOTA, 1846, 1855, 1863
D. Newcombe and H. Lawrence
27 pp. Clearwater Publishing, 1974. $20.00.

THE WINNEBAGO TRIBE
Paul Radin
Reprint of 1915 edition. Illus. Johnson
Reprint, $50.00.

WINNEBAGO TRIBE: VALUATION REPORT ON ROYCE AREA 267, 1847
Robert Nathan
100 pp. Clearwater Publishing, 1973. $34.50.

SARAH WINNEMUCCA
Katherine Gehm
185 pp. O'Sullivan Woodside, 1975. $8.95.

*SARAH WINNEMUCCA
Doris Kloss
Grades 5-12. Illus. Dillon Press, 1981. $6.95.

SARAH WINNEMUCCA OF THE NORTHERN PAIUTES
Gae W. Canfield
Illus. 336 pp. University of Oklahoma Press, 1983. $19.95.

WINNERS OF THE WEST: A CAMPAIGN PAPER PUBLISHED IN THE INTERESTS OF THE VETERANS OF ALL INDIAN WARS, THEIR WIDOWS AND ORPHAN CHILDREN
Reprint of 1944 edition. 2,040 pp. Amereon
Ltd. Microfiche only, $195.00.

*THE WINTER HUNT
Henry Tall Bull and Tom Weist
Grades 3-9. Council for Indian Education, 1971. $5.95; paper, $1.95.

*WINTER TELLING STORIES
A. Marriott
Grades 3-7. Illus. T.Y. Crowell, 1969. $8.00.

THE WINTUN INDIANS OF CALIFORNIA AND THEIR NEIGHBORS
Peter Knudtson
Illus. Naturegraph, 1977. $10.95; paper, $4.95.

WISCONSIN CHIPPEWA MYTHS AND TALES AND THEIR RELATION TO CHIPPEWA LIFE
Victor Barnouw
Illus. Maps. 304 pp. University of Wisconsin
Press, 1977. $25.00; paper, $8.95.

WISCONSIN INDIANS: LIVES AND LANDS
Nancy Lurie
Illus. 66 pp. State Historical Society of Wisconsin, 1970. $2.00.

WISHRAM TEXTS: TOGETHER WITH WASCO TALES AND MYTHS
E. Sapir, Editor
Reprint of 1909 edition. AMS Press, $38.00.

WITCHCRAFT IN THE SOUTHWEST: SPANISH AND INDIAN SUPERNATURALISM ON THE RIO GRANDE
Marc Simmons
Illus. 185 pp. Paper. University of Nebraska
Press, 1980. $5.50.

WITH A CAMERA IN OLD NAVAHOLAND
Earle Forrest
Illus. University of Oklahoma Press, 1970. $8.95.

WITH EAGLE GLANCE: AMERICAN INDIAN PHOTOGRAPHIC IMAGES, 1868-1931
N. Scott Momaday
Includes 50 portraits and scenes of Indian life and land. Illus. 63 pp. Paper. Museum of the American Indian, 1982. $6.95.

WITH THE NEZ PERCES: ALICE FLETCHER IN THE FIELD, 1889-1892
E. Jane Gay; Frederick E. Hoxie and Joan T. Mark, Editors
Illus. 226 pp. University of Nebraska Press, 1981. $19.95.

WITH ONE SKY ABOVE US: LIFE ON AN INDIAN RESERVATION AT THE TURN OF THE CENTURY
Marion Gidley
G.P. Putnam's Sons, 1979. $14.95.

WITHIN THE UNDERWORLD SKY: MIMBRES ART IN CONTEXT
Barbara Moulard
190 pp. Twelvetrees Press, 1984. $40.00.

WITHOUT SURRENDER, WITHOUT CONSENT: A HISTORY OF THE NISHAGA LAND CLAIMS
Danies Raunet
244 pp. Paper. Merrimack, 1985. $10.95.

THE WIYOT LANGUAGES
K.V. Teeter
Reprint of 1964 edition. Paper. Kraus, $15.00.

WIZARD OF THE FOUR WINDS: A SHAMAN'S STORY
Douglas Sharon
Illus. Free Press, 1978. $19.95.

WO'WAKITA (RESERVATION RECOLLECTIONS)
Lewis
249 pp. Paper. Center for Western Studies, $10.95.

WOLF AND THE RAVEN: TOTEM POLES OF SOUTHEASTERN ALASKA
Viola Garfield and Linn Forrest
Second Edition. Illus. 161 pp. Paper. University of Washington Press, 1961. $8.95.

WOLF THAT I AM: IN SEARCH OF THE RED EARTH PEOPLE
Fred McTaggart
Paper. University of Oklahoma Press, 1984. $7.95.

WOLVES FOR THE BLUE SOLDIERS: INDIAN SCOUTS AND AUXILIARIES WITH THE U.S. ARMY, 1860-1890
Thomas W. Dunlay
Illus. 325 pp. University of Nebraska Press, 1982. $23.95.

WOMEN AND INDIANS ON THE FRONTIER, 1825-1915
Glenda Riley
Illus. 320 pp. University of New Mexico Press, 1984. $24.95; paper, $12.95.

WOMEN IN NAVAJO SOCIETY
Ruth Roessel
Illus. 184 pp. Navajo Curriculum Center Press, 1981. $15.00.

WOOD'S NEW ENGLAND PROSPECT
W. Wood; Jeremiah Colburn, Editor
Burt Franklin, Publisher, 1966. $20.00.

WOODEN LEG: A WARRIOR WHO FOUGHT CUSTER
Thomas Marquis, Translator
Illus. 390 pp. Paper. University of Nebraska Press, 1962. $6.50.

WOODLAND CULTURES OF SOUTHERN ILLINOIS
M.S. Maxwell
Reprint of 1951 edition. Paper. Kraus, $56.00.

WOODLAND INDIANS OF THE WESTERN GREAT LAKES
Robert and Pat Ritzenthaler
Second Edition. Illus. 154 pp. Paper. Milwaukee Public Museum, and American Indian Books 1983. $7.95.

WOODLAND SITES IN NEBRASKA
M.F. Kivett
102 pp. Paper. Nebraska State Historical Society, 1970. $6.00.

WOODWARD'S REMINISCENCES OF THE CREEK OR MUSKOGEE INDIANS: ALABAMA, GEORGIA AND MISSISSIPPI
Thomas Woodward
Revised edition. Paper. Southern University Press, 1970. $10.00.

WORDARROWS: INDIANS AND WHITE IN THE NEW FUR TRADE
Gerald Vizenor
Contemporary American Indian experience presented with wry humor in a series of sketches and narratives. 175 pp. University of Minnesota Press, 1978. $7.95.

WORDS IN THE BLOOD: CONTEMPORARY INDIAN WRITERS OF NORTH AND SOUTH AMERICA
Jamake Highwater
416 pp. Paper. New American Library, 1984. $8.95.

WORK A DAY LIFE OF THE PUEBLOS
R. Underhill; W.W. Beatty, Editor
Reprint of 1946 edition. AMS Press, $32.50.

THE WORLD OF THE AMERICAN INDIAN
Illus. 400 pp. National Geographic Society, 1974. $9.95.

A WORLD OF FACES: MASKS OF THE NORTHWEST COAST INDIANS
Edward Malin
Illus. 158 pp. Paper. Timberline, 1978.

*WORLD OF THE SOUTHERN INDIANS
Virginia Brown and Laurella Owens
Grades 6-9. Illus. 176 pp. Beechwood Books, 1983. $15.95.

WORLD'S RIM: GREAT MYSTERIES OF THE NORTH AMERICAN INDIANS
Hartley Alexander
Illus. 260 pp. Paper. University of Nebraska Press, 1967. $4.95.

THE WORLDS BETWEEN TWO RIVERS: PERSPECTIVES ON AMERICAN INDIANS IN IOWA
Gretchen M. Bataille, et al, Editors
Illus. Iowa State University Press, 1978. $8.50.

*WOUNDED KNEE: HISTORY OF THE AMERICAN WEST
Dee Brown; Amy Ehrlich, Editor
Grades 6-12. Illus. 224 pp. Holt, Rinehart & Winston, 1974. $6.95.

*WOUNDED KNEE: AN INDIAN HISTORY OF THE AMERICAN WEST
Dee Brown
Grades 7 and up. Paper. Dell, 1974. $1.75.

WOUNDED KNEE: THE MEANING AND SIGNIFICANCE OF THE SECOND INCIDENT
Rolling Dewing
417 pp. Irvington, 1984. $39.50; paper, $19.95.

*WOVOKA
Mel Boring
Grades 5-12. Illus. 64 pp. Dillon Press, 1981. $7.95.

WRITINGS OF GENERAL JOHN FORBES RELATING TO HIS SERVICE IN NORTH AMERICA
John Forbes
Reprin tof 1938 edition. Ayer Co., $22.00.

WYANDOT RESERVATIONS IN MICHIGAN AND OHIO: AN HISTOR-ICAL REPORT FOR APPRAISING LAND VALUES
Helen Tanner, et al; Norman Ross, Editor
Clearwater Publishing, 1976. $75.00.

Y

YAKIMA INDIAN RESERVATION: APPRAISAL OF PATENTED LANDS,

STATE OF WASHINGTON
C. Marc Miller
160 pp. Clearwater Publishing, 1973. $49.50.

THE YAKIMAS: A CRITICAL BIBLIOGRAPHY
Helen H. Schuster
168 pp. Paper. Indiana University Press, 1982. $5.95.

YANA DICTIONARY
E. Sapir and M. Swadesh
Reprint of 1960 edition. Paper. Kraus, $15.00.

YANKTON SIOUX: ETHNOHISTORICAL REPORT ON THE INDIAN OCCUPANCY OF ROYCE ARE 410
Alan R. Woolworth
224 pp. Clearwater Publishing, 1973. $67.50.

YANKTON SIOUX TRIBE: APPRAISAL OF LANDS IN NEBRASKA, IOWA, MINNESOTA, SOUTH DAKOTA, AND NORTH DAKOTA, AS OF 1858
Thomas M. Griffiths
Clearwater Publishing, 1976. $150.00.

YANKTON AND TETON SIOUX, 1851: USE AND OCCUPANCY OF FORT LARAMIE LANDS
Fred Nichlason and John Champe
Clearwater Publishing, $43.00.

YANKTON TRIBAL LANDS: AN HISTORICAL ANALYSIS OF THE OPENING AND DEVELOPMENT FROM 1849 TO 1869
Michael F. Foley
Clearwater Publishing, 1976. $75.00.

A YAQUI EASTER
Muriel Painter
The rituals observed by these people are affectionately described. 40 pp. Paper. University of Arizona, 1971. $2.00.

A YAQUI LIFE: THE PERSONAL CHRONICLE OF A YAQUI INDIAN
Rosalio Moises, et al
Illus. 251 pp. University of Nebraska Press, 1977. $22.95; paper, $5.95.

YAQUI MYTHS AND LEGENDS
Ruth Giddings
61 tales narrated by Yaquis reflect the tribe's sense of the sacred and material value of their territory. 180 pp. Paper. University of Arizona Press, 1968. $3.95.

YAQUI WOMEN: CONTEMPORARY LIFE HISTORIES
Jane Holden Kelley
Illus. 265 pp. University of Nebraska Press, 1978. $19.95.

THE YAQUIS: A CULTURAL HISTORY
Edward H. Spicer
Illus. 385 pp. University of Arizona Press,
1980. $28.50; paper, $14.50.

YAVAPAI HISTORY
Albert Schroeder
310 pp. Clearwater Publishing, 1973. $90.00.

YAVAPAI INDIANS
Ilus. Garland Publishing, $33.00.

YAVAPAI MINERAL REPORT
E. Oberbilling
136 pp. Clearwater Publishing, 1973. $43.50.

**YAVAPAI TRIBE: APPRAISAL
OF LANDS, 1873**
John Vaughan, Jr.
114 pp. Clearwater Publishing, 1973. $39.00.

**YAVAPAI TRIBE: EVALUATION
STUDY OF MINERAL RESOURCES, 1873**
Roy P. Full and Richard F. Harty
Three volumes. 1,340 pp. Clearwater Publishing,
1974. $357.00.

YAZZ: NAVAJO PAINTER
Sallie Wagner and J.J. Broady
Illus. 78 pp. Northland Press, 1983. $24.50;
paper, $17.95.

THE YEAR OF THE HOPI
Tyrone Stewart, et al
Illus. 96 pp. Paper. Rizzoli International,
1982. $14.95.

YEARS WITH THE OSAGE
Viahnett St. Martin
Illus. 184 pp. Paper. Edgemoor Publishing,
1975. $3.00.

YELLOW WOLF: HIS OWN STORY
L. McWhorter
Reprint. Illus. 325 pp. Caxton Printers,
$17.95; paper, $12.95.

THE YEMASSEE
Wiliam Simms; Joseph Ridgely, Editor
Paper. College and University Press, 1964.
$4.95.

YER DAILEGE! KUNA WOMEN'S ART
Mari L. Salvador
103 pp. Illus. Paper. University of New Mexico
Press, 1978. $10.95.

YOSEMITE INDIANS
Elizabeth Godfrey
Illus. 36 pp. Paper. Yosemite, 1971. $2.50.

**THE YUCHI GREEN CORN
CEREMONIAL: FORM AND MEANING**
W.L. Ballard
81 pp. Paper. American Indian Studies Center,
1978. $7.50.

YUCHI TALES
G. Wagner
Reprint of 1931 edition. AMS Press, $27.00.

**THE YUKAGHIR AND THE
YUKAGHIRIZED TUNGUS**
V.I. Iokhel'Son
Reprint of 1926 edition. AMS Press, $52.50.

**THE YUMA RESERVATION:
LAND USE AND OCCUPANCY**
Herbert Harvey
Clearwater Publishing, $40.00.

YUMAN AND YAQUI MUSIC
F. Densmore
Reprint of 1932 edition. Illus. 272 pp.
Da Capo Press, $25.00.

**YUMAN COMPLEX: PREHISTORIC
INDIAN OCCUPATION WITHIN
THE EASTERN AREA OF THE
YUMAN COMPLEX: A STUDY
IN APPLIED ARCHAEOLOGY**
Henry Dobyns
Three volumes. 700 pp. Clearwater Publishing,
1973. $130.00 per set.

YUMAN TRIBES OF THE GILA RIVER
L. Spier
Reprint of 1933 edition. Illus. Cooper Square
Publishers, $25.00. Paper. Dover, $7.95.

**YUNINI'S STORY OF
THE TRAIL OF TEARS**
Ada Barry
Reprint of 1932 edition. Illus. AMS Press,
$34.50.

**YUROK LANGUAGE: GRAMMAR,
TEXTS, AND LEXICON**
R.H. Robins
Reprint of 1958 edition. Paper. Kraus, $40.00.

YUROK MYTHS
A.L. Kroeber
A study of the Yurok Indians. Reprint. 460 pp.
University of California, $28.50; paper, $6.95.

**YUWIPI: VISION AND EXPERIENCE
IN OGLALA RITUAL**
William K. Powers
Illus. 113 pp. Paper. University of Nebraska
Press, 1982. $4.95.

Z

**ZEISBERGER'S INDIAN DIC-
TIONARY: ENGLISH, GERMAN
IROQUOIS, ONONDAGA AND
ALGONQUIN—THE DELAWARE**
David Zeisberger
Reprint of 1887 edition. 248 pp. AMS Press,
$42.50.

**ZIA, JEMEZ AND SANTA ANA
PUEBLO LANDS, NEW MEXICO**
R.H. Sears & Co.
215 pp. Clearwater Publishing, 1973. $66.00.

A ZUNI ATLAS
T.J. Ferguson and E. Richard Hart
Illus. 160 pp. University of Oklahoma Press,
1985. $24.95.

ZUNI BREADSTUFF
F.H. Cushing
Reprint of 1920 edition. 736 pp. AMS Press,
$48.50. Paper. Museum of the American Indian,
$10.00.

ZUNI FETISHES
F.H. Cushing
Illus. Paper. KC Publications, 1966. $3.00.

ZUNI FOLK TALES
F.H. Cushing
Reprint of 1901 edition. AMS Press, $35.50.

ZUNI GRAMMAR
S. Newman
Reprint of 1965 edition. Paper. Kraus, $10.00.

**THE ZUNI INDIANS: THEIR
MYTHOLOGY, ESOTERIC FRATER-
NITIES AND CEREMONIES**
M.C. Stevenson
Reprint of 1904 edition. Illus. 748 pp. Rio
Grande Press, $45.00.

ZUNI KATCHINAS
Ruth Bunzel
Illus. 358 pp. Rio Grande Press, 1984. $30.00.

ZUNI KIN AND CLAN
A. Kroeber
Reprint of 1917 edition. AMS Press, $32.50.

ZUNI LAW: A FIELD OF VALUES
W. Smith and J.M. Roberts
Includes an appendix: A Practical Zuni
Orthography, by Stanley Newman. Reprint
of 1954 edition. Paper. Kraus, $35.00.

ZUNI MYTHOLOGY
Ruth Benedict
Reprint of 1935 edition. Two volumes. AMS
Press, $30.00 each.

**ZUNI: SELECTED WRITINGS
OF FRANK HAMILTON CUSHING**
F.H. Cushing; Jesse Green, Editor
Illus. 450 pp. University of Nebraska Press,
1979. $26.50; paper, $8.50.

ZUNI TEXTS
Ruth Bunzel
Reprint of 1933 edition. AMS Press, $34.50.

THE ZUNIS OF CIBOLA
C. Gregory Crampton
Illus. University of Utah Press, 1977. $20.00.

SUBJECT CLASSIFICATIONS

In this section, titles annotated in the alphabetically arranged bibliography are grouped under one or more subjet headings.

AGRICULTURE AND FARMING

The Agricultural and Hunting Methods of the Navaho Indians

Agricultural Terracing in the Aboriginal New World

Agriculture of the Hidatsa Indians

American Indian Foods and Vegetables

The Changing Pattern of Hopi Agriculture

*The Delaware Indians: Eastern Fishermen and Farmers

Indians, Bureaucrats and Land: The Dawes Act and the Decline of Indian Farming

*Our Mother Corn

ALASKA NATIVES

*Alaska in the Days That Were Before

Alaska Native Preference in Employment

Alaska Natives and American Laws

Alaska's Native People

Aleut and Eskimo Art: Tradition and Innovation

Aleut Language

Aleutian Indian and English Dictionary

Alliance in Eskimo Society

American Indian and Alaskan Native Newspapers and Periodicals, 1826-1924

American Indian and Eskimo Music

An Annotated Bibliography of American Indian and Eskimo Autobiographies

Arctic Archaeology: An Annotated Bibliography and History

Arctic Art: Eskimo Ivory

Arctic Life: Challenge to Survive

Books on American Indians and Eskimos

The Coast Indians of Southern Alaska and Northern British Columbia

Dawn in Arctic Alaska

Earth Dyes

English-Eskimo and Eskimo-English Vocabularies

*The Eskimo: Arctic Hunters and Trappers

Eskimo Capitalists

An Eskimo Family

Eskimo Medicine Man

Eskimo School on the Andreafsky: A Study of Effective Bicultural Education

The Eskimo Tribes

*Eskimos

Eskimos and Aleuts

Eskimos, Chicanos, Indians

Eskimos and Explorers

Eskimos, Revised

The Eskimos: Their Environment and Folkways

Ethnography of the Tanaina

Ethnohistory in the Arctic: The Bering Strait Eskimos

An Ethnohistory of the Western Aleutians

Ethnological Results of the Point Barrow Expedition

The Eyak Indians of the Copper River Delta

The Far North: Two Thousand Years of American Eskimo and Indian Art

From Skins, Trees, Quills, Quills and Beads: The Work of Nine Athabascans

Give or Take a Century: An Eskimo Chronicle

The Han Indians: A Compilation of Ethnographic and Historical Data on the Alaska-Yukon Boundary Area

Handbook of North American Indians: Arctic

Igloo Life

In the Middle: The Eskimo Today

Indian and Eskimo Artifacts of North America

Indian and Eskimo Basketry: A Key to ID

Indian Tribes of Alaska and Canada

The Indians of the Subarctic: A Critical Bibliography

Ingalik Material Culture

Inica: Spirit World of the Bering Sea Eskimos

Interwoven Expression: Works By Contemporary Alaska Native Basket Makers Organized By the Institute of Alaska Native Arts and University of Alaska Museum

Inuit Artists Print Workbook

The Inuit Life As It Was

Inuit: The North in Transition

The Inuit Print, L'Estampe Inuit

Journey to Alaska in 1868

Lamp of the Eskimo

The Last and First Eskimos

Miracle at Metlakatla

Modern Growth of the Totem Pole on the Northwest Coast

My Grandfather's House: Tlingit Songs of Death and Sorrow

Native Accounts of Nootka Ethnography

New Traditions: AN Exhibition of Alaska Native Scultpure

Paper Stays Put: A Collection of Inuit Writings

People of the Ice Whale: Eskimos, White Men and the Whale

The People's Land: Eskimos and Whites in the Eastern Arctic

Pioneer Missionary to the Bering Strait Eskimos

Proceedings: Northern Athapaskan Conference

Psychosocial Research on American Indian and Alaska Native Youth: An Indexed Guide to Recent Dissertations

The Roles of Men and Women in Eskimo Culture

The Roots of Ticasuk: An Eskimo Woman's Family Story

Shadow of the Hunter: Stories of Eskimo Life

Social Conditions, Beliefs and Linguistics Relationship of the Tlingit Indians

The Social Economy of the Tlingit Indians

Some Warmer Tone: Alaska Athabaskan Bead Embroidery

Spirit Keepers of the North: Eskimos of Western Alaska

Studies in the Athapaskan Languages

Study of the Eskimo Bows in the U.S. National Museum

The Subarctic Athabascans: A Selected, Annotated Bibliography

Survival: Life and Art of the Alaskan Eskimo

Tanaina Tales from Alaska

Tlingit Designs and Carving Manual

The Tlingit Indians: Results of a Trip to the Northwest Coast of America and the Bering Straits

Tlingit Myths and Texts

Tlingit: Their Art, Culture and Legends

Tribes of the Extreme Northwest, Alaska, the Aleutians and Adjacent Territories

ALABAMA-COUSHATTA INDIANS

Alabama-Coushatta Indians of Texas and the Coushatta Indains of Louisiana, 1540-1855

Alabama and Coushatta Tribes of Texas

Myths and Folktales of the Alabama-Coushatta Indians

The Winding Trail: The Alabama-Coushatta Indians

ALGONQUIAN INDIANS

*Algonkians of the Eastern Woodlands

*Algonquian Indians: At Summer Camp

The Algonquians, The Indians of that Part of the New World First Visited by the English

An Analysis of Coastal Algonquian Culture

The Conflict of European and Eastern Algonkian Cultures, 1504-1700

Functions of Wampum Among the Eastern Algonkian

The Last Algonquian

A Northeastern Algonquian Sourcebook

The Northern Algonquian Supreme Being

A Proto-Algonquian Dictionary

Villages of the Algonquian, Siouan and Caddoan Tribes West of the Mississippi

ANTIQUITIES

Aboriginal Chipped Stone Implements of New York

Aboriginal Land Use and Occupancy of the Pima-Maricopa Indians

Aboriginal Location of the Kadohadcho and Related Indian Tribes in Arkansas and Louisiana, 1542-1954

Aboriginal Monuments of the State of New York

Aboriginal Occupation of New York

Aboriginal Prehistory in New England: An Archaeological Survey of Northeastern New South Wales

Aboriginal Remains of Tennessee

Aboriginal Subsistence Technology on the Southeastern Coastal Plain

Aboriginal Territory of the Kalispel

Aboriginal Territory of the Nez Perce Indians

Aboriginal Use and Occupancy of Lands West of the Mississippi River by the Osage Indian Tribe

Indian Days of Long Ago

Indian Thoughts: I Am Old

Indians and Archaeology of Missouri

Indians of the Upper Texas Coast

Inland Chumash Archaeology: An Annotated
Bibliography

Introduction to the Study of Southwestern
Archaeology

The Ioway Indians

Jeddito 264: A Basket Maker III Pueblo I Site
in Northeastern Arizona

Method and Theory in Historical Archaeology

Mississippian Stone Images in Illinois

Mobility and Adaptation: The Anasazi of
Black Mesa, Arizona

Mogollon Archaeology: Proceedings

Mogollon Culture Prior to 1000 A.D.

Native American Prehistory: A Critical
Bibliography

Notes on the Archaeology of the Kaibeto and
Rainbow Plateaus in Arizona

Oneonta Studies

Onondaga Iroquois Prehistory: A Study in
Settlement Archaeology

People of the High Country: Jackson Hole
Before the Settlers

Petroglyphs of Ohio

Pre-Columbian Architecture, Art and Artifacts
Slide Catalog

Prehistoric Indians of the Southeast: Archaeology of Alabama and the Middle South

Prehistoric Indians of the Southwest

Prehistoric Indians of Wisconsin

Prehistoric Pipes

Prehistoric Southwestern Craft Arts

Prehistoric Southwesterners from Basketmaker
to Pueblo

The Prehistory of Indians of Western
Connecticut

Reconnaissance and Excavation in Southeastern
New Mexico

Smiling Dan: Structure and Function at a Middle
Woodland Settlement in the Illinois Valley

The Sobaipuri Indians of the Upper San Pedro
River Valley, Southeast Arizona

Southwestern Archaeology

Southwestern Archaeology: A Bibliography

The Star Lake Archaeological Project: Anthropology of a Headwaters Area of Chaco Wash,
New Mexico

Starkweather Ruin: A Mogollon Pueblo Site in
the Upper Gila River Area of New Mexico

The Tchefuncte Culture, An Early Occupation
of the Lower Mississippi Valley

Time: Space and Transition in Anasazi
Prehistory

Trend and Tradition in the Prehistory of the
Eastern U.S.

The Vail Site: A Paleo-Indian Encampment in
Maine

The Waring Papers: The Collected Works of
Antonio J. Waring

APACHE INDIANS

Among the Apaches

*The Apache

Apache Agent: The Story of John P. Clum

Apache Country

Apache Gold and Yaqui Silver

Apache Indians I-XII

The Apache Indians in Texas, New Mexico
and Arizona

Apache Indians of Texas

*The Apache Indians: Raiders of
the Southwest

Apache Jim: Stories from His Private
Files on Treasures

Apache, Kiowa and Comanche Indian
Reservation in Southeastern Oklahoma

Apache Lands

Apache Life-Way

Apache Lightning: The Last Great
Battles of the Ajo Calientes

Apache, Navaho and Spaniard

The Apaches: A Critical Bibliography

Apachean Culture History and Ethnology

The Apaches: Eagles of the Southwest

Apaches: A History and Culture Portrait

Apaches and Longhorns

Appraisal of the Lands of the Fort McDowell
Mohave-Apache and the Yavapai-Apache
Communities in Arizona

Appraisal of the Lands of the Fort Sill
Apache Tribe of Oklahoma, 1886

Appraisal of the Rental Value of the
Fort Sill Apache Tribe of Oklahoma
in Arizona and New Mexico

Basketry of the San Carlos Apache Indians

Childhood and Folklore: A Psychoanalytic
Study of Apache Personality

Childhood and Youth in Jicarilla
Apache Society

Chiricahua Apache Lands

Chiricahua Apache Tract

Chiricahua Apache Tribe

Chiricahua and Mescalero Apache Texts

The Cibecue Apache

The Comanche, Apache and Kiowa Indians
Before 1867: Habitat and Range

A Condensed History of the Apache and
Comanche Indian Tribes

Dirty Boy: A Jicarilla Tale of Raid and War

Enju: The Life and Struggle of an Apache
Chief from the Little Running Water

Fort Sill Apache Tract

Fort Sill Apache Tribe of Oklahoma

Grenville Goodwin Among the Western Apache:
Letters from the Field

In the Days of Victorio: Recollections
of a Warm Springs Apache

Indeh: An Apache Odyssey

Jicarilla Apache Area of Northeastern
New Mexico

Jicarilla Apache Claim Area

Jicarilla Apache in Ne Mexico and Oklahoma

Jicarilla Apache Indians, 1848-1887

The Jicarilla Apache Indians, A History,
1598-1888

Jicarilla-Apache Reservation, 1887 and 1907

Jicarilla Apache Tribal Lands Acquired by
the U.S. on August 20, 1883: Valuation

Jicarilla Apache Tribe, 1883: Appraisal

Jicarilla Apache Tribe: A History, 1846-1870

Jicarilla Apache Tribe of the Jicarilla Indian
Reservation in New Mexico, 1849-1870

The Jicarilla Apaches: A Study in Survival

The Lipan Apache Tribe and the Mescalero
Apache Tribe

The Lipan and Mescalero Apache in Texas

The Medicine Man of the Apache

Memorandum on Legislative History, Congressional Acts Pertaining to Indian Trust
Funds: Temoak Bands and Mescalero Apache

The Mescalero Apache, 1653-1874

Mescalero Apache Indians in New Mexico
and Arizona, 1846-1880

Mescalero Apache Subsistence Patterns
and Socio-Political Organization,
New Mexico, 1796-1875

The Mescalero Apaches

Mimbres Painted Pottery

Myths and Legends of the Lipan
Apache Indians

Myths and Tales from the San
Carlos Apache

Myths and Tales of the Chiricahua
Apache Indians

Myths and Tales of the Jicarilla
Apache Indians

Peace With the Apaches of New Mexico
and Arizona

San Carlos and Northern Tonto Apache
Tracts in Arizona

Seven and Nine Years Among the Comanches
and Apaches: An Autobiography

The Truth About Geronimo

Victorio and the Mimbres Apaches

The Western Apache Clan System:
Origins and Development

Western Apache Raiding and Warfare

The Western Apache Range

Jim Whitewolf: The Life of a Kiowa Apache

ARCHITECTURE-DWELLINGS

Cliff Dwellers of the Mesa Verde

*Indian Homes

The Indian Tipi: Its History, Construction,
and Use

Houses and House Life of the American
Aborigines

The Hidatsa Earthlodge

Hogans: Navajo Houses and House Songs

*The Houses the Indian Built

*Indian Homes

The Indian In His Wigwam: Or, Characteristics
of the Red Race in America

Living Architecture: Indian

Navajo Architecture: Forms, History,
Distributions

Pre-Columbian Architecture, Art and
Artifacts Slide Catalog

*The Tipi: A Center of Native American Life

Voices in the Canyon

ARMS AND ARMOR

American Indian Archery

Frontier Patrol: The Army and the Indians in
Northeastern California, 1861

Guns on the Early Frontiers: A History of
Firearms from Colonial Times Through the
Years of the Western Fur Trade

Indian Trade Guns: 1625-1775

*Indian Warriors and Their Weapons

Metal Weapons, Tools and Ornaments
of the Teton Dakota Indians

Native American Bows

Prehistoric Weapons in the Southwest

ART

Akicita: Early Plains and Woodlands Indian
Art From the Collection of Alexander Acevedo

Aleut and Eskimo Art: Tradition and Innovation
in South Alaska and North Alaska

American Indian Painting and Sculpture

American Indian Sculpture: A Study
of the Northwest Coast

American Indian Speaks: Poetry, Fiction
and Art by the American Indian

The Ancestors: Native American Artisans
of the Americas

Ancient Art of the American Woodland Indians

Arctic Art: Eskimo Ivory

Argillite: Art of the Haida Native Culture

Art and Artifacts of the Pacific, Africa and
the Americas

Art and Environment in Native America

Art in the Life of the Northwest Coast Indians

Art of the American Indian

Art of the Eastern Plains Indians:
The Nathan Sturges Jarvis Collection

Art of the First Americans

*Art of the North American Indian

Art of the Northwest Coast Indians

The Art of Norval Morrisseau

*The Art of the Plains Indians

The Art of Precolumbian Gold:
The Jan Mitchell Collection

*The Art of the Southeastern Indians

*The Art of the Southwest Indians

Art of the Totem

*Art of the Woodland Indians

Arts of the Indian Americas: North, Central
and South: Leaves from the Sacred Tree

Arts of the Raven: Masterworks by the
Northwest Coast Indian

As in a Vision: Masterworks of
American Indian Art

Bibliography of Articles and Papers
on North American Indian Art

Bo'Jou, Neejee: Profiles of Canadian Indian Art

The Box of Daylight: Northwest Coast Indian Art

Burnt Copper

Circles of the World: Traditional Art
of the Plains Indians

Color and Shape in American Indian Art

The Covenant Chain: Indian Ceremonial
and Trade Silver

Creative West: Taos and Northern New Mexico

Crow Indian Art

Cut-Outs: Native American Art

The Elkus Collection: Southwestern Indian Art

Enduring Visions: One Thousand Years
of Southwestern Indian Art

The Far North: Two Thousand Years
of American Eskimo and Indian Art

Fetishes and Carvings of the Southwest

From River Banks and Sacred Places:
Ancient Indian Terracottas

From Skins, Trees, Quills and Beads:
The Work of Nine Athabascans

From the Center: A Folio of Native
American Art and Poetry

A Gathering of Spirit: Writing and Art
by North American Indian Women

Guide to Indian Rock Carvings of
the Pacific Northwest Coast

Heritage of Raven

Historic Hopi Ceramics

Hopi Kachinas Drawn by Native Artists

Hopi Painting; The World of the Hopis

Images of American Indian Art

Images: Stone: B.C.

Indian Art and Culture

Indian Art and History: The Testimony
of Prehistoric Rock Paintings

Indian Art in Pipestone: George Catlin's
Portfolio in the British Museum

Indian Art of the Northwest Coast: A
Dialogue on Craftsmanship and Athletics

Indian Art Traditions of the Northwest Coast

Indian Art of the U.S.

Indian Artists at Work

Indian Arts in North America

*Indian Crafts

ARTIFACTS

American Indian Artifact Price Guides

American Indian Artifact With Jewelry Price Guide

Captured Heritage: The Scramble for Northwest Coast Artifacts

Dictionary of Prehistoric Indian Artifacts of the American Southwest

Diving for Northwest Relics

Guide to the Identification of Certain American Indian Projectile Points

Guide to Indian Artifacts of the Northwest

How to Collect North American Indian Artifacts

Indian Artifacts

Indian Artifacts of the East and South

Indian Artifacts of the Northwest Coast

Indian and Eskimo Artifacts of North America

Indian Points, Value and Identification Guide

Indian Projectile Point Types from Virginia and the Carolinas

The Indian Relic Collector's Guide

Indian Relics of Norhteast Arkansas and Southeast Missouri

Indians and Artifacts of the Southeast

North American Indian Artifacts: A Collector's Identification and Value Guide

North American Indian Points

Oklahoma Indian Artifacts

Paleo Points

Pre-Columbian Architecture, Art and Artifacts Slide Catalog

Prehistoric Relics

BIBLIOGRAPHIES

American Indian and Eskimo Music: A Selected Bibliography through 1981

The American Indian in Graduate Studies: A Bibliography of Theses and Dissertations

The American Indian in Short Fiction: An Annotated Bibliography

American Indians: A Select Catalog of National Archives Microfilm Publications

An Annotated Bibliography of American Indian and Eskimo Autobiographies

The Apaches: A Critical Bibliography

A Bibliographical Guide to the History of Indian-White Relations in the U.S.

Bibliographies of the Languages of the North American Indians

Bibliography of Articles and Papers on North American Indian Art

A Bibliography of the Athapaskan Languages

A Bibliography of California Indians

Bibliography of the Chumash and Their Predecessors

Bibliography of the Constitutions and Laws of the American Indian

A Bibliography of Contemporary North American Indians

A Bibliography of Current American Indian Policy

Bibliography of the English Colonial Treaties with the American Indians

Bibliography of Language Arts Materials for Native North Americans

Bibliography of the Languages of Native California

Bibliography of the Navaho Indians

A Bibliography of Navajo and Native American Teaching Material

Bibliography of North American Indian Mental Health

Bibliography of the Osage

Bibliography of the Sioux

Books on American Indians and Eskimos

California Indians: An Annotated Bibliography

Canadian Indian Policy: A Critical Bibliography

The Cherokees: A Critical Bibliography

The Cheyennes, Ma heo o's People: A Critical Bibliography

Chippewa and Dakota Indians: A Subject Catalog

The Choctaws: A Critical Bibliography

The Creeks: A Critical Bibliography

The Delawares: A Critical Bibliography

Dictionary Catalog of the American Indian Collection — Huntington Free Library

Dictionary Catalog of the Edward E. Ayer Collection of Americans and American Indians

The Emigrant Indians of Kansas: A Critical Bibliography

Ethnic Serials at Selected University of California Libraries

Evaluating American Indian Bilingual Programs: A Topical Bibliography

An Evaluative Ethnohistorical Bibliography
of the Malecite Indians

Filmography for American Indian Education

A Guide to Cherokee Documents in Foreign
Archives

A Guide to Supplement a Guide to Manuscripts
Relating to the American Indian in Library
of the American Philosophical Society

Health and Diseases of American Indians North
of Mexico: A Bibliography, 1800-1969

Hopi Bibliography

Images of American Indians in Film:
An Annotated Bibliography

Index to Literature on the American Indian

Index to Schoolcraft's "Indian Tribes
of the U.S."

Indian Children's Books

Indian Land Tenure: Bibliographical Essays

Indian Missions: A Critical Bibliography

Indian-White Relations in the U.S.

Indians in Maryland and Delaware:
A Critical Bibliography

The Indians of California: A Critical
Bibliography

Indians of the Great Basin: A Critical
Bibliography

The Indians of Maine and the Atlantic
Provinces: A Bibliographic Guide

The Indians of New England: A Critical
Bibliography

Indians of North and South America:
Bibliography

Indians of the Northeast: A Critical
Bibliography

Indians of the Southwest: A Critical
Bibliography

The Indians of the Subarctic: A Critical
Bibliography

Indians of the U.S. and Canada:
A Bibliography

Inland Chumash Archaeology: An Annotated
Bibliography

Kachinas: A Selected Bibliography

Language, Culture and Personality:
Essays in Memory of Edward Sapir

Literature By and About the American Indian:
An Annotated Bibliography

Narratives of North American Indian
Captivity: A Selective Bibliography

Native American Museums Program:
Publications and Resources

Native American Women: A Contextual
Bibliography

Native Americans of the Northwest Coast:
A Critical Bibliography

North American Indian Language Materials,
1890-1965

North American Indians in Towns and Cities:
A Bibliography

The Ojibwas: A Critical Bibliography

Pawnees: A Critical Bibliography

Second Language Learning for American
Indians: A Topical Bibliography

The Selected Writings of Edward S. Curtis

The Sioux: A Critical Bibliography

Sociology of American Indians: A Critical
Bibliography

Southwestern Archaeology: A Bibliography

The Subarctic Athapascans: A Selected,
Annotated Bibliography

Tulapai to Tokay: A Bibliography
of Alcohol Use and Abuse Among
Native Americans of North America

U.S. Indian Policy: A Critical Bibliography

The Yakimas: A Critical Bibliography

BIOGRAPHIES

American Indian Intellectuals

An Annotated Bibliography of American Indian
and Eskimo Autobiographies

Apache Agent: The Story of John P. Clum

Autobiography of a Papago Woman

*Beautiful Indian People

Big Bear: The End of Freedom

A Biobibliography of Native American Writers,
1772-1924: A Supplement

Biographical Dictionary of Indians of the
Americas

Biographical and Historical Index of
American Indians and Persons Involved
in Indian Affairs

*Black Hawk and Jim Thorpe: Super Heroes

Black Mountain Boy

*Chief Joseph's Own Story As Told by
Chief Joseph in 1879

Chief Left Hand: Southern Arapaho

*Chief Plenty Coups: Life of the Crow
Indian Chief

*Chief Sealth and His People

Chief Seattle's Unanswered Challenge

Chief Washakie

William Clark: Jeffersonian Man on the Frontier

Crashing Thunder: The Autobiography of an American Indian

Crowfoot: Chief of the Blackfeet

Dance Around the Sun: The Life of Mary Little Bear Inkanish: Cheyenne

Gabriel Dumont: The Metis Chief and His Lost World

During My Time: Florence Edenshaw Davidson, A Haida Woman

*Charles Eastman

Enju: The Life and Struggle of an Apache Chief From the Little Running Water

*Famous American Indian Leaders

Fighting Tuscarora: The Autobiography of Chief Clanton Richard

Five Kidnapped Indians

From the Deep Woods to Civilization

*Geronimo: The Fighting Apache

Geronimo's Story of His Life

Goodbird the Indian

Carl Gorman's World

*The Great Chiefs

Great Indian Chiefs

Great North American Indians

Half-Sun on the Columbia: A Biography of Chief Moses

*Heroes of the American Indian

I Will Die an Indian

The Illustrated Biographical Encyclopedia of Artists of the American West

Indian Biographies: North American Natives Distinguished as Orators, Warriors, and Statesmen

Indian Patriots of the Great West

The Indian Priest: Philip B. Gordon

Indian Tribes of North America with Biographical Sketches and Anecdotes of the Principal Chiefs

Indian Women Chiefs

*Ishi

Ishi in Two Worlds: A Biography of the Last Wild Indian in North America

Ishi, Last of His Tribe

William Jackson, Indian Scout

*Pauline Johnson

*Joseph, Chief of the Nez Perce

Kitchi-Gami: Life Among the Lake Superior Ojibway

Kopet: Chief Joseph's Last Years, A Documentary Narrative

Korczak: Storyteller in Stone

The Life and Art of Jerome Tiger

Life of Joseph Brant (Thayendanegea)

Life and Times of David Zeisberger

*Little Turtle

Long Lance: The True Story of an Imposter

Lord of the Mohawks: A Biography of Sir William Johnson

Louie No One: A Biography of Louis St. Germaine: American Indian

*Massasoit: Friend of the Pilgrims

Thomas Mayhew, Patriarch to the Indians, 1593-1682

Me and Mine: The Life Story of Helen Sekaquaptewa

*Me Run Fast Good: Biographies of Tewanima (Hopi), Carlos Montezuma (Apache), and John Horse (Seminole)

*Mary Musgrave: Georgia Indian Princess

My Life As An Indian

Native Americans: 23 Indian Biographies

Navajo Biographies

Navajo Blessingway Singer: The Autobiography of Frank Mitchell, 1881-1967

Ohiyesa: Charles Eastman, Santee Sioux

The Pokagons

*Pontiac, Chief of the Ottawa

Pretty Shield, Medicine Woman of the Crows

Quanah, The Serpent Eagle

Red Crow, Warrior Chief

Red Raiders Retaliate: The Story of Lone Wolf, Famous Kiowa Indian Chief

Ruxton of the Rockies

*Sacajawea

Sacajawea

The Saga of Chief Crazy Horse

Sanapia: Comanche Medicine Woman

Satanta, The Great Chief of the Kiowas and His People

A Shananditti: The Last of the Beothucks

Sioux Indian Leaders

Sitting Bull: The Years in Canada

Tatanga Mani: Walking Buffalo of the Stonies

*Tendoy, Chief of the Lemhis

Tobias

The Totem Carvers: Charlie James, Ellen Neel,
  Mungo Martin

Tsali

Who's Who in Indian Relics

*Sarah Winnemucca

Sarah Winnemucca of the Northern Paiutes

Timothy: Nez Perce Chief, Life and Times,
  1800-1891

*Tomo-Chi-Chi

Who's Who Among Native Americans

Yazz: Navajo Painter

BLACKFEET INDIANS

Blackfeet and Gros Ventre Tribes
  in Montana

Blackfeet Tribe Ceded Lands in Montana

Blackfeet and Gros Ventre Tribes of Indians

The Blackfeet Indian Reservation in Montana

Blackfeet Indians

The Blackfeet: Raiders on the Northwestern Plains

Blackfeet: Their Art and Culture

Blackfeet: Their History

Crowfoot: Chief of the Blackfeet

The Fort Belknap and Blackfeet Indian
  Reservation in Montana

The Fort Belknap Reservation in Montana

*Heart Butte: A Blackfeet Indian

Mission Among the Blackfeet

Modern Blackfeet: Montanans on a Reservation

The Old North Trail: Or, Life, Legends and
  Religion of the Blackfeet Indians

The Reservation Blackfeet, 1885-1945: A Photographic History of Cultural Survival

BLACKFOOT INDIANS

A Blackfoot-English Vocabulary

Blackfoot Lodge Tales

A Blackfoot Sourcebook

A Concise Blackfoot Grammar

An English-Blackfoot Vocabulary

Material Culture of the Blackfoot Indians

Mythology of the Blackfoot Indians

A New Series of Blackfoot Texts

The Return of Chief Black Foot

Social Organization and Ritualistic
  Ceremonies of the Blackfoot Indians

Why Gone Those Times? Blackfoot Tales

BOATS AND CANOES

The Bark Canoes and Skin Boats of North
  America

Building a Chippewa Indian Birchbark
  Canoe

Canoeing With the Cree

*Indian Canoeing

The Starship and the Canoe

The Survival of the Bark Canoe

Tomol: Chumash Watercraft

Wangka: Austronesian Canoe Origins

The Weymontaching Birchbark Canoe

CADDO INDIANS

Caddo Indian Pottery

Caddo Indian Tract

The Caddo Indians in Louisiana and Texas

A Caddo Sourcebook

Caddo Treaty of July 1, 1835

Caddo Tribe of Oklahoma, 1541-1859

Caddo Tribe of Oklahoma, Rebuttal Statement

The Caddoan Cultural Area: An Archaeological
  Perspective

Caddoan Indians I-IV

The Caddoan, Iroquoian and Siouan Languages

Caddoan Texts, Pawnee, South Band Dialect

Caddoan Tribes

Notes on the Caddo

Source Material on the History and
  Ethnology of the Caddo Indians

Traditions of the Caddo

CANADIAN INDIANS

The Abnakis and Their History

The Algonquians, the Indians of That Part of
  the New World First Visited by the English

An Analysis of Coastal Algonquian Culture

As Long As the Sun Shines and Water Flows:
  A Reader in Canadian Native Studies

Assompion Sash

Native Peoples in Canada:
Contemporary Conflicts

Native Rights in Canada

The New Peoples: Being and Becoming Metis in
North America

New Relations of Gaspesia: With the Customs
and Religion of the Gaspesian Indians

New Voyages to North America

Ninstints: Haida World Heritage Site

A Northeastern Algonquian Sourcebook

The Northern Algonquian Supreme Being

The Ojibway on Walpole Island, Ontario:
A Linguistic Study

The Ontario Iroquois Tradition

Paper Stays Put: A Collection
of Inuit Writing

Papers of the Sixth Algonquian
Conference, 1974

Pathways to Self-Determination: Canadian
Indians and the Canadian State

People From Our Side: An Inuit Record
of Seekooseelak - The Land of the
People of Cape Dorset, Baffin Island

People of the Buffalo

Pitseolak: A Canadian Tragedy

A Place of Refuge for All Time

Preliminary Study of Traditional
Kutchin Clothing in Museums

A Proto-Algonquian Dictionary

The Quest for Food and Furs: The
Mistassini Cree, 1953-1954

The Rebirth of Canada's Indians

Red Earth: Tales of the Micmac

The Red Ochre People: How Newfoundland's
Beothuck Indians Lived

The Relation f Seneca False Face Masks to
Seneca and Ontario Archaeology

Riding on the Frontier's Crest: Mahican
Indian Culture and Cultural Change

The School at Mopass: A Problem of Identity

A Shananditti: The Last of the Beothucks

The Shuswap

Sitting Bull: The Years in Canada

Snares, Deadfalls and Other Traps
of the Northern Algonquian and
Northern Athapaskans

Social and Economic Change Among
the Northern Ojibwa

Stone Ornaments Used by Indians
in the U.S. and Canada

Stories From Pangnirtung

Substance of a Journal During a Residence
at the Red River Colony

Ten Years of Upper Canada in Peace and War,
1805-1815

Thirty Indian Legends of Canada

The Thompson Indians of British Columbia

A Thousand Words of Mohawk

*Thunder in the Mountains: Legends of Canada

Totem Poles of the Gitksan, Upper Skeena River,
British Columbia

Traditions of the Thompson River Indians of
British Columbia

Travels and Adventures in Canada and the Indian
Territories Between 1760 and 1776

Unwilling Urbanites: The Life of Canadian
Indians in a Prairie City

Urban Indians: The Strangers in Canada's Cities

Valley of the Six Nations

Voyage of Alexander Mackenzie

Voyages from Montreal through the
Continent of North America to
the Frozen and Pacific Oceans

Voyages of Samuel de Champlain, 1604-1618

CAPTIVITIES

Andele, Or the Mexican-Kiowa Captive,
A Story of Real Life Among the Indians

Biography of Francis Slocum, The Lost
Sister of Wyoming

The Boy Captives

*Joseph Brown: Or, The Young Tennessean
Whose Life Was Saved by the Power of Prayer

Captivity of Father Peter Milet:
Among the Oneida Indians

The Captivity of James Kimball

Captivity of the Oatman Girls

Captivity of Mary Schwandt

The Captivity and Sufferings of
Gen. Freegift Patchin

Captivity Tales: An Original Anthology

The Capture and Escape

Captured by the Indians: 15 Firsthand
Accounts, 1750-1870

Captured by the Indians: Reminiscences of
Pioneer Life in Minnesota

The Child Captives: A True Tale of Life
Among the Indians of the West

Children Indian Captives

A Collection of Some of the Most Interesting Narratives of Indian Warefare in the West

Five Years a Captive Among the Blackfeet Indians

Gathered Sketches from the Early History of New Hampshire and Vermont

Girl Captives of the Cheyennes: A True Story of the Capture and Rescue of Four Pioneer Girls, 1874

Held Captive by Indians; Selected Narratives, 1642-1836

Heroic Women of the West

The History of the Life and Adventures of Mr. Anderson

The History of Maria Kittle

History of the Spirit Lake Massacre and of Miss Abigail Gardiner's Three Month's Captivity Among the Indians

In the Country of the Walking Dead

Indian Attrocities

The Indian Captive: A Narrative of the Adventures and Sufferings of Matthew Brayton

The Indian Captive: Or, A Narrative of the Captivity and Sufferings of Zadock Steele

Indian Captivities: Or, Life In the Wigwam

Indians: Or Narratives of Massacres and Depredations

The Indians and Their Captives

*Mary Jemison: Seneca Captive

Journal of the Adventures of Matthew Bunn

Kinnan Massacre

The Last Captive

Life Among the Indians: Being an Interesting Narrative of the Captivity of the Oatman Girls Among the Apache and Mohave Indians

Manners and Customs of Several Indian Tribes Located West of the Mississippi...

Memoirs of a Captivity Among the Indians of North America, from Childhood to the Age of Nineteen

Narrative of the Captivity of Ebenezer Fletcher

A Narrative of the Captivity and Removes of Mrs. Mary Rowlandson

Narrative of the Life of Mrs. Mary Jamison

Narrative of Matthew Bunn

Narratives of Captivity Among the Indian of North America

North American Indian Captivity

Rachel Plummer's Narrative of 21 Months Servitude As a Prisoner Among the Comanche Indians

Puritans Among the Indians: Accounts of Captivity and Redemptions 1676-1724

The Redeemed Captive, Returning to Zion

Scoorwa: James Smith's Indian Captivity Narrative

Selection of Some of the Most Intersting Narratives of Outrages Committed by the Indians in Their Wars with the White People

Seven and Nine Years Among the Comanches and Apaches: An Autobiography

Six Weeks in the Sioux Tepees

The Story of Captain Jasper Parrish, Captive, Interpreter and U.S. Sub-Agent to the Six Nations Indians

*Taken by the Indians: True Tales of Captivity

Tales of the Northwest: On Sketches of Indian Life and Character

Three Years Among the Comanches, The Narrative of Nelson Lee, the Texas Ranger

A Thrilling Narrative of the Sufferings of Mrs. Jane Adeline Wilson During Her Captivity Among the Comanche Indians

The Torture of Captives by Indians of Eastern North America

A True History of the Captivity and Restoration of Mrs. Mary Rowlandson

True Stories of New England Captives Carried to Canada During the Old French and Indian Wars

U.S. Congress: Report...Washington, 1813

*White Captives

White Into Red: A Study of the Assimilation of White Persons Captured by Indians

CATLIN, GEORGE (PAINTER OF INDIANS) 1796-1872

The George Catlin Book of American Indians

Catlin Collection of Indian Paintings

George Catlin: Episodes from "Life Among the Indians" and "Last Rambles"

Catlin's North American Indian Portfolio: A Reproduction

Indian Art in Pipestone: George Catlin's Portfolio in the British Museum

The Letters of George Catlin and His Family

Life Among the Indians

The Natural Man Observed: A Study of Catlin's Indian Gallery

North American Indians

CHEROKEE INDIANS

The Act of Union Between the Eastern
and Western Cherokees

Arts and Crafts of the Cherokee

Beginning Cherokee

A Better Kind of Hatchet: Law, Trade,
Diplomacy in the Cherokee Nation

*The Cherokee

Cherokee Archaeology: A Study of the
Appalachian Summit

The Cherokee Band of Indians

Cherokee and Creek Indians

Cherokee Dance and Drama

Cherokee-English Interliner

The Cherokee Excavations

The Cherokee Freedmen: From Emancipation
to American Citizenship

*Cherokee Fun and Learn Book

The Cherokee Ghost Dance

The Cherokee Indian Nation: A Troubled History

*The Cherokee: Indians of the Mountains

Cherokee Land Lottery of Georgia, 1832

Cherokee Messenger

Cherokee Nation

Cherokee Nation Indian Reservation in the
Indian Territory, Oklahoma

Cherokee Nation: Land Cessions in Tennessee,
Mississippi, North Carolina, Georgia,
Alabama, 1785-1835

The Cherokee Nation of Indians

Cherokee Outlet in the Indian Territory,
State of Oklahoma

The Cherokee Perspective

A Cherokee Prayerbook

Cherokee Prehistory: The Pisgah Phase
in the Appalachian Summit Region

Cherokee Recollections

*Cherokee Removal, 1838

Cherokee Removal: The "William Penn" Essays

*Cherokee Tale-Teller

Cherokee Tragedy

Cherokee Vision of Eloh'

Cherokee Woman

Cherokees

The Cherokees: A Critical Bibliography

Cherokees at the Crossroads

The Cherokees in Pre-Columbian Times

Cherokees in Transition

Cherokees and Missionaries, 1789-1839

Constitution of the State of Sequoyah

The Eastern Band of Cherokees, 1819-1900

The Eastern Cherokees

Fire and the Spirits: Cherokee Law from
Clan to Court

Friends of Thunder: Folktales of the
Oklahoma Cherokees

A Guide to Cherokee Documents in Foreign
Archives

Historical Sketch of the Cherokee

History of the Cherokee Indians and Their
Legends and Folklore

*The Last Cherokee Warriors

A Law of Blood: The Primitive Law of the
Cherokee Nation

Myths of the Cherokee

Myths of the Cherokee and Sacred Formulas
of the Cherokees

New Echota Letters: Contributions of Samuel
A. Worcester to the Cherokee Phoenix

*Only the Names Remain: The Cherokees and
the Trail of Tears

A Political History of the Cherokee Nation

Red Over Black: Black Slavery Among
the Cherokee Indians

Removal of the Cherokee Indians from Georgia

The Removal of the Cherokee Nation:
Manifest Destiny or National Dishonor

John Ross and the Cherokee Indians

Run Toward the Nightland: Magic of the
Oklahoma Cherokees

The Shadow of Sequoyah: Social Documents
of the Cherokees, 1862-1964

Slavery and the Evolution of Cherokee
Society, 1540-1866

A Snug Little Purchase: How Richard Henderson
Bought Kaintuckee from the Cherokees in 1775

*Stories of the Old Cherokees: A Collection

Symposium on Cherokee and Iroquois Culture

Tsali

Walk in Your Soul: Love Incantations of
the Oklahoma Cherokees

*When Shall They Rest? The Cherokees Long
Struggle With America

Yunini's Story of the Trail of Tears

CHEYENNE AND ARAPAHOE INDIANS

The Arapaho

The Arapahoe

Arapaho-Cheyenne Indians

Arapaho-Cheyenne Land Area: Historical Background and Development

Arapahoe Politics, 1851-1978: Symbols in Crises of Authority

The Arapaho Sun Dance, The Ceremony of the Offerings Lodge

The Arapahoes, Our People

Artist Wandering Among Cheyennes

*Bear's Heart: Scenes from the Life of a Cheyenne Artist

*Belle Highwalking: The Narrative of a Northern Cheyenne Woman

By Cheyenne Campfires

Cheyenne

The Cheyenne

Cheyenne and Arapahoe Aboriginal Occupation

Cheyenne and Arapaho: Historicl Background

Cheyenne-Arapaho Indian Lands

Cheyenne and Arapaho Indian Reservations

Cheyenne and Arapaho Music

The Cheyenne and Arapaho Ordeal: Reservation and Agency Life

Cheyenne and Arapaho Tribes

Cheyenne Autumn

*Cheyenne Fire Fighters: Modern Indians Fighting Forest Fires

Cheyenne Indians: Sketch of the Cheyenne Grammar

The Cheyenne Indians: The Sun Dance

Cheyenne Indians, Their History and Ways of Life

*Cheyenne Legends of Creation

Cheyenne Memories

*Cheyenne Short Stories

Cheyenne and Sioux: The Reminiscences of Four Indian and a White Soldier

*Cheyenne Warriors

The Cheyenne Way: Conflict and Case Law in Primitive Jurisprudence

The Cheyennes, Indians of the Great Plains

The Cheyennes of Montana

Dance Around the Sun

Early Days Among the Cheyenne and Arapahoe Indians

English-Cheyenne Dictionary

The Fighting Cheyennes

*A History of the Cheyenne People

*How the Dogs Saved the Cheyennes

The Miles Expedition of 1874-1875

*Morning Star, Black Sun: The Northern Cheyenne Indians and America's Energy Crisis

The Peace Chiefs of the Cheyennes

People of the Sacred Mountain: A History of the Northern Cheyenne Chiefs and Warrior Societies, 1830-1879

*The Rolling Head: Cheyenne Tales

The Southern Cheyennes

Sweet Medicine: The Continuing Role of the Sacred Arrows, The Sun Dance, and the Sacred Buffalo Hat in Northern Cheyenne History

Traditions of the Arapaho

Tsee-Ma'Heone-Nemeototse: Cheyenne Spiritual Songs

CHIEF JOSEPH

*Chief Joseph of the Nez Perce

*Chief Joseph's Own Story as Told by Chief Joseph in 1879

I Will Fight No More Forever: Chief Joseph and the Nez Perce War

*Joseph, Chief of the Nez Perce

Nez Perce Joseph

Red Eagles of the Northwest: The Story of Chief Joseph and His People

CHILDREN

Absaloka: Crow Children's Writing

American Indian and White Children: A Sociopsychological Investigation

*Cherokee Fun and Learn Book

*Child of the Navajos

Childhooh and Folklore: A Psychoanalytic Study of Apache Personality

Childhood and Youth in Jicarilla Apache Society

Children at Risk: Making a Difference Through the Court Appointed Special Advocate Project

Children of the People

Children of the Salt River

Chippewa Child Life and Its Cultural
Background

*Crickets and Corn

Dance Down the Rain, Sing Up the Corn:
American Indian Chants and Games
for Children

The Death of Jimmy Littlewolf:
An Indian Boy at Boys Ranch

The Hopi Child

*Indian Boyhood

*Mista

*Jim Musco

Navajo Infancy: An Ethological Study
of Child Development

Respect for Life: The Traditional
Upbringing of American Indian Children

*Thunder Waters: Experiences of Growing
Up in Different Indian Tribes

*To Live in Two Worlds: American Indian
Youth Today

Transracial Adoption

CHIPPEWA INDIANS

Acculturation and Personality Among
the Wisconsin Chippewa

Anishnabe: Six Studies of Modern Chippewa

Building a Chippewa Indian Birchbark Canoe

Chippewa Child Life and Its Cultural
Background

Chippewa Cree Tribe of Rocky Boy, Montana

Chippewa Customs

Chippewa and Dakota Indians: A Subject
Catalog of Books, Pamphlets, Periodical
Articles and Manuscripts

Chippewa Indians I-VII

Chippewa Indians as Recorded by
Rev. Frederick Baraga in 1847

Chippewa Indians of Lake Superior

*The Chippewa Indians: Rice Gatherers
of the Great Lakes

Chippewa Music

The Chippewa Nation of Indians

Chippewa of Eastern Lower Michigan,
1785-1837

Chippewa, Ottawa and Potawatomie
Lands in Illinois and Wisconsin

The Chippewas of Lake Superior

The Chippewa of the Mississippi and
Lake Superior

The Chippewa and Their Neighbors

Chippewa Tracts in Minnesota

Chippewa Tribe

The Dream Dance of the Chippewa and
Menominee Indians of Northern Wisconsin

How Indians Use Wild Plants for Food,
Medicine and Crafts

Minnesota Chippewa Indians, 1838

Minnesota Chippewa Tribe

The Mississippi, Pilager and Winnibigoshish
Bands of Chippewa Indians

The People Named the Chippewa:
Narrative Histories

Red Lake Band of Chippewa Indians

Red Lake and Pembina Bands of
Chippewa Indians

Red World and White: Memories of
a Chippewa Boyhood

Saginaw Chippewa

Saginaw Chippewa Indian Tribe of Michigan

A Social Study of One Hundred Fifty
Chippewa Indian Families of the
White Earth Reservation of Minnesota

The Southwestern Chippewa: An Ethnohistorical Study

Wisconsin Chippewa Myths and Tales and
Their Relation to Chippewa Life

CHOCTAW INDIANS

*By the Work of Our Hands: Choctaw
Materials Culture

Chahta Hapia Hoke: We Are Choctaw

*A Choctaw Anthology, I and II

The Choctaw Before Removal

Choctaw Hymn Book

Choctaw Music

The Choctaw of Bayou Lacomb

A Choctaw Sourcebook

*The Choctaws Before Dancing Rabbit Creek

The Choctaws: A Critical Bibliography

The Choctaws: Cultural Evolution
of a Native American Tribe

*The Choctaws in the 19th and 20th Century

Early Account of the Choctaw Indians

History of the Choctaw, Chickasaw
and Natchez Indians

Life Among the Choctaw Indians and
Sketches of the Southwest

Mississippi Choctaws at Play:
The Serious Side of Leisure

*Okla Apilaci: Community Helpers

Removal of the Choctaw Indians

Rise and Fall of the Choctaw Republic

The Roots of Dependency

*Sokosi Aliha

Source Material for the Social and
Ceremonial Life of the Choctaw Indians

*The Tale of the Possum

Tribal Government: A New Era

CLIFF DWELLERS

Cliff Dwellers of the Mesa Verde

The Land of the Cliff-Dwellers

Voices in the Canyon

COMANCHE INDIANS

Comanche

The Comanche Barrier to South Plains
Settlement

Comanche Days

Comanches

The Comanches, Lords of the South Plains

Kiowa, Comanches and Apche Lands
in Oklahoma and Texas

Kiowa-Comanche Indians

Political Organizations and Law-Ways
of the Comanche Indians

Sanapia: Comanche Medicine Woman

Three Years Among the Comanches

United States-Comanche Relations:
The Reservation Years

COMMERCE

American Indian Policy in the Formative
Years: The Indian Trade and Intercourse
Acts, 1790-1834

Character and Influence of the Indian
Trade In Wisconsin: A Study of the
Trading Post as an Institution

Condition of the Indian Trade in North
America, 1767: As Described in a
Letter to Sir William Johnson

*The Fur Trader and the Indian

Indian Trade Goods

Indian Trade Guns: 1625-1775

The Indian Traders

Indian Traders of the Southwestern Spanish
Border Lands: Panton and Forbes Co. 1783-1847

Indian Traders on the Middle Border: The House
of Ewing, 1827-1854

Indian, Animals, and the Fur Trade: A Critique
of "Keepers of the Game"

Journals of the Commissioner of the Indian
Trade, Sept. 20, 1718

Metal Weapons, Tools and Ornaments
of the Teton Dakota Indians

The Montagnais "Hunting Territory"
and the Fur Trade

Navaho Neighbors

Pelts, Plumes and Hides: White Traders
Among the Seminole Indians, 1870-1930

Shonto: Study of the Role of the Trader
in a Modern Navajo Community

The Southern Frontier, 1670-1732

Traders of the Western Morning: Aboriginal
Commerce in Precolumbian North America

The Wars of the Iroquois: A Study in
Intertribal Trade Relations

COSTUME AND ADORNMENT

American Indian Crafts Inspirations

American Indian Design and Decoration

*American Indian Tools and Ornaments

Authentic American Indian Beadwork and
How To Do It

Beads and Beadwork of the American Indian

*Beneath the Singing Pines

Costume of the Plains Indians and Structural
Basis to the Decoration of Costumes Among
the Plains Indians

Crow Indian Beadwork: A Descriptive and
Historical Study

Dress Clothing of the Plains Indians

Head and Face Masks in Navaho Ceremonialism

Indian Clothing Before Cortes: Mesoamerican
Costumes from the Codices

*Indian Costumes

Ray Manley's Portraits and Turquois
of Southwest Indians

Metallic Ornaments of the New York Indians

Pueblo Indian Embroidery

Robes of White Shell and Sunrise

Stone Ornaments Used by Indians in the U.S. and Canada

CREE INDIANS

Chippewa Cree Tribe of Rocky Boy, Montana

Meet Cree: A Guide to the Cree Language

The Montana Cree: A Study in Religious Persistence

Notes on the Eastern Cree and Northern Salteaux

The Plains Cree

Plains Cree: Grammatical Study

Plains Cree Texts

Sacred Stories of the Sweet Grass Cree

CREEK INDIANS

Africans and Creeks: From the Colonial Period to the Civil War

Alabama-Coushata (Creek) Indians

Appraisal of the Creek Cession, 1856

Appraisal of the Lands Ceded by the Creek Nation for the Seminoles, August 7, 1857

Cherokee and Creek Indians

Creek Indian Lands in Oklahoma

Creek Indian Territorial Expansion

Creek Indians

*The Creek Indians

Creek Indians: Information Relative to the Claims of the Creeks Against the U.S. for Florida Lands Taken by the U.S. Under the Treaty of Moultrie Creek, 1823

Creek Indians of Taskigi Town

Creek Indians and Their Florida Lands, 1740-1805

Creek Nation: Appraisal of Ceded Lands in Southern Georgia and Southeastern Alabama

Creek Nation East of the Mississippi

Creek Nation Lands in Alabama: Land Appraisal As of 1832

Creek Nation Lands in Oklahoma

The Creek Nation and Private Land Sales in Alabama, and an Appraisal of Creek Nation Lands

Creek (Muskogee) New Testament Concordance

A Creek Sourcebook

The Creek Verb

Creek War of 1813 and 1814

The Creeks: A Critical Bibliography

Early History of the Creek Indians and Their Neighbors

Handbook of the Creek Langauge

Journey Into Wilderness

Migration Legend of the Creek Indians

Myths and Folktales of the Alabama-Coushatta Indians

The Politics of Indian Removal: Creek Government and Society in Crises

Red Eagle and the Wars With the Creek Indians of Alabama

The Road to Disappearance: A History of the Creek Indians

Social Organizations and Social Usages of the Indians of the Creek Confederacy

Treaties With the Creek and Seminole Indians, 1763-1815

Woodward's Reminiscences of the Creek or Muscogee Indians: Alabama, Georgia and Mississippi

CROW INDIANS

Absaloka: Crow Children's Writing

Absaraka: Home of the Crows

*Chief Plenty Coups: Life of the Crow Indian Chief

Crow Creek Site

Crow Indian Art

Crow Indian Beadwork

Crow Indian Lands

Crow Indian Medicine Bundles

Crow Indians

The Crow Indians

Crow Lands in Montana and Wyoming, 1868

Crow Texts

Fools Crow

*The Indian as a Soldier at Fort Custer, Montana, 1890-1895

Life and Adventures of James P. Beckwourth

The Material Culture of the Crow Indians

Memoirs of a White Crow Indian

Notes on the Social Organization and Customs of the Mandan, Hidatsa, and Crow Indians

Of the Crow Nation

Old Crow Wing: History of a Village

Plenty-Coups, Chief of the Crows

Pretty-Shield, Medicine Woman of the Crows

The Religion of the Crow Indians

The Shoshini-Crow Sun Dance

Social Life of the Crow Indians

The Sun Dance of the Crow Indians

The Tobacco Society of the Crow Indians

Two Crows Denies It: A History of
Controversy in Omaha Sociology

Two Leggings: The Making of a Crow Warrior

CULTURAL ASSIMILATION

Acculturation in Seven Indian Tribes

Almost White

The Assault on Assimilation: John Collier
and the Origins of Indian Policy Reform

Changing Culture of an Indian Tribe

Cherokees and Missionaries, 1789-1839

Cultures in Contact: The European Impact on
Native Cultural Institutions in Eastern
North America, 1000-1800 A.D.

A Final Promise: The Campaign to Assimilate
the Indians, 1880-1920

Hamlin Garland's Observations on the
American Indian, 1895-1905

The Hispanic Acculturation of the
Gila River Pimas

An Indian Canaan: isaac McCoy and
the Vision of an Indian State

Indian Police and Judges: Experiments
in Acculturation and Control

The Indians in American Society

The Last Running

Me and Mine: The Life Story of Helen
Sekaquaptewa

Navajo Infancy: An Ethological Study
of Child Development

North American Indian Lives

The Right to Be Indian

Savagism and Civilization: A Study
of the Indian and the American Mind

Settling With the Indians: The Meeting
of English and Indian Cultures in
America, 1580-1640

A Study in Culture Contact and Culture
Change: The Whiterock Utes in Transition

Unwilling Urbanites: The Life of Canadian
Indians in a Prairie City

The Vanishing American: White Attitudes
and U.S. Indian Policy

Wasi-Chii: The Continuing Indian Wars

CULTURE

American Indian Speaks: Poetry, Fiction
and Art by the American Indian

American Indians and American Life

American Society for Promoting the
Civilization and General Improvement
for the Indian Tribes Within the U.S.

Ancestor's Footsteps

Angels to Wish By

Art and Environment in Native America

Aspects of Indian History and Civilization

Belden, the White Chief: Or, Twelve Years
Among the Wild Indians of the Plains

Between Sacred Mountains: Navajo Stories
and Lessons from the Land

*By the Work of Our Hands: Choctaw
Materials Culture

Can the Red Man Help the White Man

Changing Culture of an Indian Tribe

The Covenent Chain: Indian Ceremonial
and Trade Silver

Companion Issue

Crossing the Cultural Divide: Indians
and New Englanders, 1605-1763

Cultures in Contact: The European Impact
on Native Cultural Institutions in
Eastern North America 1000-1800 A.D.

Cycles of Conquest: The Impact of Spain,
Mexico and the U.S. on Indians of
the Southwest, 1533-1960

Dance Down the Rain, Sing Up the Corn:
American Indian Chants and Games
for Children

Dancing With Creation

John Eliot's Indian Dialogues:
A Study in Cultural Interaction

Erotica in Indian Dance

The Fighting Cheyennes

The Fremont Culture: A Study in Culture
Dynamics on the Northern Anasazi Frontier

From Hell to Breakfast

Gift Is Rich

Greener Fields: Experiences Among
the American Indians

Happy Hunting Grounds

Hogans: Navajo Houses and House Songs

The Horse and Dog in Hidatsa Culture

The Horse in Blackfoot Indian Culture; With
Comparative Material from Other Tribes

The Idea of Fertilization in the Culture
of the Pueblo Indians

Indian Art and Culture

Indian Dances of North America:
Their Importance to Indian Life

Indian Education and Civilization

Indian Games and Dances With Native Songs

Indian Heritage, Indian Pride: Stories
that Touched My Life

The Indian and the Horse

The Indian In His Wigwam: Or, Characteristics of the Red Race in America

Indian Life on the Northwest Coast of
North America As Seen by the Early
Explorers and Fur Traders During the
Last Decades of the 18th Century

The Indian Nations of America

Iroquois Music and Dance: Ceremonial
Arts of Two Seneca Longhouses

Just Before Sunset

Kinaalada: A Navajo Puberty Ceremony

The Kiowas

Lame Deer: Seeker of Visions

The Lillooet Indians

*The Mamook Book

Moral Education Among the North
American Indians

Multi-Cultural Curriculum

Music and Dance Research of
the Southwestern Indians

Navajo Cultural Guides, Experience
Stories, and Cultural Readers

The Navajos

Notes on the Ethnology of the Indians
of Puget Sound

Of Mother Earth and Father Sky

Ojibway Heritage

Oklahoma Delaware Ceremonies,
Feasts and Dances

Oregon Indians: Culture, History
and Current Affairs

*Our Mother Corn

Patterns of Culture

The People of the Saints

Peoples of the Coast: The Indians
of the Pacific Northwest

*Pieces of White Shell: A Journey
to Navajoland

Puyallup-Nisqually

Race, Language and Culture

Ritual of the Wind: North American Indian
Ceremonies, Music and Dance

Rolling Thunder: A personal Exploration
Into the Secret Healing Power of an
American Indian Medicine Man

The Sacred Path: Spells, Prayers and
Power Songs of the American Indian

The Sioux of the Rosebud: A History
in Pictures

Statement on American Indians

A Study in Culture Contact and Culture
Change: The Whiterock Utes in Transition

The Sun Dance and Other Ceremonies of the
Oglala Division of the Teton Dakota

Sun in the Sky

Symposium on Cherokee and Iroquois Culture

Symposium on Local Diversity in
Iroquois Culture

Tales from the Mohaves

Teachings from the American Earth:
Indian Religion and Philosophy

The Ten Grandmothers

Three Navaho Households: A Comprehensive
Study in Small Group Culture

Touch the Earth: A Self-Portrait
of Indian Existence

The Vanishing American:
The Epic of the Indian

The Western Apache Clan System:
Origins and Development

Why Gone Those Times? Blackfoot Tales

The Yaquis: A Cultural History

CURTIS, EDWARD S.

*Edward S. Curtis: Photographer of
the North American Indian

Curtis' Western Indians: Life and Works
of Edward S. Curtis

In a Sacred Manner We Live

The North Ameriacn Indian

The North American Indians: Photographs
by Edward S. Curtis

Portraits from North American Indian Life

The Vanishing Race and Other Illusions:
Photographs of Indians by Edward S. Curtis

The Vanishing Race: Selections from Edward
S. Curtis' "The North American Indian"

DANCES

Aesthetics of Indian Folk Dance

The Arapaho Sun Dance, The Ceremony of the Offerings Lodge

Cherokee Dance and Drama

The Cherokee Ghost Dance

The Cheyenne Indians: The Sun Dance

Dance Down the Rain, Sing Up the Corn: American Indian Chants and Games for Children

Dance and Song Rituals of Six Nations Reserve, Ontario

Dances of the Tewa Pueblo Indians: Expressions of Life

Dancing Gods: Indian Ceremonials of New Mexico and Arizona

Dancing With Creation

Erotica In Indian Dance

Indian Dances of North America. Their Importance to Indian Life

*Indian Games and Crafts

Indian Games and Dances With Native Songs

The Iroquois Eagle Dance, An Offshoot of the Calumet Dance

Iroquois Music and Dance: Ceremonial Arts of Two Seneca Longhouses

Music and Dance Research of the Southwestern Indians

The Navaho (Or Corral) Fire Dance

Notes on the Buffalo-Head Dance of the Bear Gens of the Fox Indians

Oklahoma Delaware Ceremonies, Feasts and Dances

The Pawnee Ghost Dance Hand Game: Ghost Dance Revival and Ethnic Identity

The Prophet Dance of the Northwest and Its Derivatives: The Source of the Ghost Dance

Ritual of the Wind: North American Indian Ceremonies, Music and Dance

The Shoshoni-Crow Sun Dance

The Snake Dance of the Hopi Indians

The Snake Dance of the Moquis of Arizona

The Sun Dance and Other Ceremonies of the Oglala Division of the Teton Dakota

The Sun Dance of the Crow Indians

Sundancing at Rosebud and Pine Ridge

DELAWARE INDIANS

Absentee Delaware Tribe of Oklahoma and Delaware Tribe, 1856-1857

A Delaware Indian Symposium

The Delaware Indian Westward Migration

*The Delaware Indians: Eastern Fishermen and Farmers

The Delaware Indians: A History

The Delawares: A Critical Bibliography

Enquiry Into the Causes of the Alienation of the Delaware and Shawnee Indians from British Interests

Folk Medicine of the Delaware and Related Algonkian Indians

Grammar of the Language of the Lenni Lenape or Delaware Indians

*The Indians of New Jersey: Dickon Among the Lenapes

King of the Delawares. Teedyuscung, 1700-1763

Legends of the Delaware Indians and Picture Writings

The Lenape and Their Legends

Oklahoma Delaware Ceremonies, Feasts and Dances

Religion and Ceremonies of the Lenape

A Study of the Delaware Indian Big House Ceremony: In Native Text Dictated by Witapanoxwe

A Study of Delaware Indian Medicine Practice and Folk Beliefs

To the Delaware Indians

Wilderness Christians: The Moravian Mission to the Delaware Indians

DRAMA

Arrow-Maker

Dramatic Elements in American Indian Ceremonials

New Native American Drama: Three Plays

A Pillar of Fire To Follow: American Indian Dramas, 1808-1859

Road of Life and Death

ECONOMIC CONDITIONS

Alaska Native Preference in
Employment and Contracting

American Indian Economic Development

American Indian Education: Government
Schools and Economic Progress

American Indian Energy Resources
and Development

American Indians: Facts — Future Toward
Economic Development for Native
American Communities

American Indians and Federal Aid

Awakening Minorities: Continuity and Change

Conflicting Perceptions: Western Economics
and the Great Whale Cree

The Development of Capitalism in the
Navajo Nation: Political-Economic History

Economic Development on American Indian
Reservations

Economics for Administrators

Economics for Minorities: A Guide
to Information Sources

Economics of the Iroquois

The Federal Buy Indian Program:
Promise Versus Performance

Indian Preference in Construction
Contracting

Mother Earth, Father Sky, and Economic
Development: Navajo Resources and Their Use

Native Americans and Energy Development II

Navajo Energy Resources

Navajo Resources and Economic Development

Notes on Hopi Economic Life

Property Concepts of the Navaho Indians

The Re-Establishment of the Indians in
Their Pueblo Life Through the Revival
of Their Traditional Crafts: A Study
in Home Extension Education

Red Capitalism: An Analysis
of the Navajo Economy

The Roots of Dependency: Subsistence,
Environment and Social Change Among
the Choctaws, Pawnees and Navajos

The Roots of Oppression: The American
Indian Question

San Diego County Indians As Farmers
and Wage Earners

Tribal Apprenticeship Training
Program Manual

The Underground Reservation: Osage Oil

EDUCATION

American Indian Education: Government
Schools and Economic Progress

American Indian Issues in Higher Education

The American Indian Reader

Annals of Shawnee Methodist Mission
and Indian Manual Labor

Bilingual Education for American Indians

*Daybreak Star Preschool Activities Book

Education and the American Indian: The Road
to Self-Determination Since 1928

Education: The Dilemma of the Indian-American

Ethnic Identity and Boarding School Experience
of West-Central Oklahoma American Indians

Filmography for American Indian Education

History of Indian Education

History and Present Development of Indian
Schools in the U.S.

Identification of Unique Features in
Education at American Indian Schools

Indian Education and Civilization

Indian Education - Guidance Counselor

Indian Education - Elementary Teacher

Indian Education - Secondary Teacher

Letters of Eleazar Wheelock's Indians

Moral Education Among the North American
Indians

Multicultural Education and the American
Indian

*Na Yo Pisa

*Native Americans of Washington State: A
Curriculum Guide for the Elementary Grades

The Navajos Long Walk for Education

No Turning Back: A Hopi Indian Woman's
Struggle to Live in Two Worlds

The Re-Establishment of the Indians in Their
Pueblo Life Through the Revival of Their
Traditional Crafts: A Study in Home
Extension Education

Respect for Life: The Traditional Upbringing
of American Indian Children

The Rock Point Experience: A Longitudinal
Study of a Navajo School Program
(Saad Naaki Bee Na' Nitin)

Sleeping Giants

A Study of the Role of the Federal Government
in the Education of the American Indian

To Live on This Earth: American Indian
Education

To Sing Our Own Songs: Cognition and Culture in Indian Education

*Welcome to Choctaw Fair

ESKIMOS

Alaska Natives and American Laws

Aleut and Eskimo Art: Tradition and Innovation in South Alaska and North Alaska

Alliance in Eskimo Society

American Indian and Alaska Native Newspapers and Periodicals, 1826-1924

American Indian and Eskimo Music: A Selected Bibliography Through 1981

An Annotated Bibliography of American Indian and Eskimo Autobiographies

Arctic Art: Eskimo Ivory

Arctic Life

Arts and Culture of the North

Books on American Indians and Eskimos

English-Eskimo and Eskimo-English Vocabularies

*An Eskimo Family

Eskimo Medicine Man

Eskimo Poems from Canada and Greenland

Eskimo School on the Andreafsky: A Study of Effective Bicultural Education

The Eskimo Tribes

*Eskimos

Eskimos and Aleuts

Eskimos and Explorers

Eskimos, Revised

Ethnohistory in the Arctic: The Bering Strait Eskimo

Ethnological Results of the Point Barrow Expedition

Igloo Life

In the Middle: The Eskimo Today

Inuit Artists Print Workbook

Inuit Life As It Was

Inuit: The North in Transition

The Inuit Print, L'Estampe Inuit

Lamp of the Eskimos

The Last and First Eskimos

Native American Women: A Contextual Bibliography

Paper Stays Put: A Collection of Inuit Writings

People of the Ice Whale: Eskimos, White Men and the Whale

The Roles of Men and Women in Eskimo Culture

The Roots of Ticasuk: An Eskimo Woman's Family Story

Shadow of the Hunter: Stories of Eskimo Life

Stories from Pangnirtung

Study of the Eskimo Bows in the U.S. National Museum

Tales from the Igloo

ETHICS

The Circle Without End: A Sourcebook of American Indian Ethics

The Guide Without End: A Sourcebook of American Indian Ethics

Moral Education Among the North American Indians

FICTION

The American Indian in Short Fiction: An Annotated Bibliography

American Indian Life

Arrows Four: Prose and Poetry by Young American Indians

Daring Donald McKay: Or, The Last War Trial of the Modocs

Four Masterworks of American Indian Literature

Happy Hunting Grounds

Ishi Means Man

Man Who Killed the Deer

The Portable North American Indian Reader

The Yemassee

FICTION, JUVENILE

*Betrayed

*Chi-Wee

*Climbing Sun: The Story of a Hopi Indian Boy

*Fisherman on the Puyallup

*Good Stones

*Hah-Nee

*Iroquois Stories: Heroes and Heroines, Monsters and Magic

*Killer-of-Death

*Komantcia

*Mission Tales: Stories of the
Historic California Missions

*Red Brother

*Waterless Mountain

*When the Moon Is New

FIVE CIVILIZED TRIBES

The Act of Union Between the Eastern and
Western Cherokees, the Constitution and
Amendments and Laws of the Cherokee Nation

And Still the Waters Run: The Betrayal
of the Five Civilized Tribes

Antiquities of the Southern Indians
Particularly of the Georgia Tribes

The Chickasaws

Constitution and Laws of the Cherokee Nation:
Passed at Tah-Le-Quah, Cherokee Nation, 1839

Five Civilized Tribes

Indian Removal: The Emigration of Five
Civilized Tribes of Indians

Laws and Joint Resolutions of
the Cherokee Nation

Nations Remembered: An Oral History of
the Five Civilized Tribes, 1865-1907

Notices of East Florida; With An Account
of the Seminole Nation of Indians

Reconstruction in Indian Territory

The Southern Indians: The Story of the
Civilized Tribes Before Removal

FOOD—COOKING

American Indian Cooking and Herb Care

American Indian Food and Lore

Art of American Indian Cooking

Common Edible and Useful Plants of the East
and Midwest

Earth Medicine - Earth Foods: Plant Remedies,
Drugs, and Natural Foods of the North
American Indian

Gathering What the Great Nature Provided:
Food Traditions of the Kitksan

Gifts of the Earth: American Indian Cookbook

Hopi Cookery

*Indian Harvests

Indian Herbs

Kashaya Pomo Plants

Native Harvests: Recipes and Botanicals
of the American Indian

Zuni Breadstuff

FRENCH AND INDIAN
WAR, 1755-1763

Empire and Liberty: American Resistance
to British Authority, 1755-1763

Fawn

*The Fight for Freedom, 1750-1783

Fight With France for North America

French and Indian Cruelty

General Orders of 1757, Issued by the
Earl of Loudoun and Phineas Lyman
in the Campaign Against the French

An Historical Journal of the Campaigns in
North America for the Years 1757-1760

Logs of the Conquest of Canada

Lord of the Mohawks: A Biography of Sir
William Johnson

Maryland's Attitude in the Struggle
for Canada

Massacre at Fort Bull: The Delery
Expedition Against Oneida Carry, 1756

Memoirs of Lt. Henry Timberlake

Montcalm and Wolfe

New England Captives Carried to Canada
Between 1677-1760, During French
and Indian Wars

Northeast Captives Carried to Canada Between
1677-1760 During the French and Indian Wars

A Particular History of the Five Years
French and Indian War

A People's Army: Massachusetts Soldiers
and Society in the Seven Year's War

Pioneers of New France in New England

Struggle for Empire: A Bibliography
of the French and Indian Wars

Wilderness Empire

Wilderness Politics and Indian Gifts: The
Northern Colonial Frontier, 1748-1763

Writings of General John Forbes Relating
to His Service in North America

GAMES

*Cherokee Fun and Learn Book

*Competing for Glory: The Indian
World of Sports

GHOST DANCE

GOVERNMENT RELATIONS

HAIDA INDIANS

Haida Monumental Art: Villages of
the Queen Charlotte Islands

Haida Potlatch

Haida Songs and Tsimshian Texts

Haida Texts and Myths: Skidgate Dialect

Haidah Indians of Queen Charlotte Islands

The Haidas

He Who Hunted Birds in His Father's Village:
The Dimensions of a Haida Myth

The Relationship Systems of the Tlingit,
Haida and Tsimshian

HAVASUPAI INDIANS

Havasupai Ethnography

Havasupai Habitat

Havasupai Indians

Havasupai Indians, 1150-1890

Havasupai Indians: An Ethnohistorical Report

Havasupai Religion and Mythology

Havasupai Songs: A Linguistic Perspective

The Havasupai Woman

HEALTH AND MEDICINE

American Indian Medicine

American Medical Ethnobotany:
A Reference Dictionary

Ancient Indian Medicine

Anthropological Studies Related to Health
Problems of North American Indians

*A'Una

Bibliography of North American Indian
Mental Health

Circumpolar Health: Proceedings

Community Health and Mental Health Care
Delivery for North American Indians

Contacts Between Iroquois Herbalism
and Colonial Medicine

Crow Indian Medicine Bundles

Diagnosis and Treatment of Prevalent
Diseases of North American Indian
Populations, I and II

Earth Medicine - Earth Foods: Plant
Remedies, Drugs, and Natural Foods
of the North American Indian

Ethnic Medicine in the Southwest

Federal Policy and American Indian
Health Needs

Folk Medicine of the Delaware and
Related Algonkian Indians

Geraniums for the Iroquois: A Field Guide
to American Indian Medicinal Plants

Growing Straight: The Fitness Secret
of the American Indian

Guide to Indian Herbs

Health and Diseases of American Indians
North of Mexico: A Bibliography, 1800-1969

Indian Drinking: Navajo Practices
and Anglo-American Theories

Indian Herbs

Introduction to Navaho Chant Practice

Lakota Belief and Ritual

Medicinal Uses of Plants by Indian
Tribes of Nevada

Medicine Among the American Indians

Medicine Among the American Indians:
CIBA Symposia, 1939

The Medicine Man of the American Indian
and His Cultural Background

The Medicine Man of the Apache

Medicine and Politics Among the Grand River
Iroquois: A Study of the Non-Conservatives

Medicine Talk: A Guide to Walking in Balance
and Surviving on the Earth Mother

Mohave Ethnopsychiatry and Suicide: The
Psychiatric Knowledge and the Psychic
Disturbances of an Indian Tribe

Navaho Classification of Their
Song Ceremonials

Navajo Indian Medical Ethnobotany

Navajo Medicine Man Sand Paintings

Navaho Symbols of Healing

Notes on the Gynecology and Obstetrics
of the Arikara Tribe of Indians

Physiological and Medical Observations
Among the Indians of Southwestern
U.S. and Northern Mexico

Piman Shamanism and Staying Sickness:
Ka: Cim Mumkidag

Plants Used as Curatives by Certain
Southeastern Tribes

Pretty-Shield, Medicine Woman of the Crows

Rolling Thunder: A personal Exploration Into
the Secret Healing Power of an American
Indian Medicine Man

Sanapia: Comanche Medicine Woman

The Shaman and the Medicine Wheel

A Study of Delaware Indian Medicine
Practice and Folk Beliefs

HISTORY

Actions With Indians

America's Fascinating Indian Heritage

American Epic: The Story of the
American Indian

American Genesis: The American Indian
and the Origins of Modern Man

The American Heritage Book of Indians

The American Heritage History
of the Great West

The American Heritage History
of the Indian Wars

The American Indian

American Indian Ethnohistory

The American Indian Frontier

American Indian History: A Reader
in Early Culture Contact, 1492-1760

The American Indian: Past and Present

American Indian Policy

American Indian Policy in Crisis:
Christian Reformers and the Indian,
1865-1900

The American Indian Reader

The American Indian Under Reconstruction

American Indian and the U.S.

American Indian and White Relations to 1830

American Indians

Americas on the Eve of Discovery

Among the Apaches

Ancient North Americans

As Long As the River Shall Run:
An Ethnohistory of Pyramid Lake
Indian Reservation

Aspects of Indian History and Civilization

Attitudes of Colonial Powers Toward the
American Indian

Bear Chief's War Shirt

*Between Sacred Mountains: Navajo Stories
and Lessons from the Land

Bibliography of the English Colonial
Treaties with the American Indians

Blood of the Land: The Government
and Corporate War Against the
American Indian Movement

Bloody Knife

Broken Peace Pipes: A Four-Hundred
Year History of the American Indian

The Broken Ring: The Destruction
of the California Indians

Buffalo Hearts

*Bury My Heart at Wounded Knee: An
Indian History of the American West

Centennial Campaign: The Sioux War of 1876

The Cherokee Freedmen: From Emancipation
to American Citizenship

The Cherokee Indian Nation:
A Troubled History

Cherokee Recollections

Cherokee Removal: The "William Penn" Essays
and Other Writings by Jeremiah Evarts

The Cherokees in Pre-Columbian Times

Cherokees in Transition: A Study of Changing
Culture and Environment Prior to 1775

Chief Lawyer of the Nez Perce Indians,
1796-1876

Chiefs and Challengers

*A Child's History of the American Indian

Chinigchinich

The Chipewa and Their Neighbors:
A Study in Ethnohistory

A Condensed History of the Apache
and Comanche Indian Tribes

Cry of the Thunderbird: The American
Indian's Own Story

*Dakota and Ojibwe People in Minnesota

The Days of the Hercules

The Delaware Indians: A History

The Depth of the Great Spirit

Dinetah: Navajo History

Disinherited: The Lost Birthright
of the American Indian

Dreamers With Power: The Menominee

Early Days Among the Cheyenne and
Arapaho Indians

Early History of the Creek Indians
and Their Neighbors

Education and the American Indian: The
Road to Self-Determination Since 1928

The End of Indian Kansas: A Study
of Cultural Revolution, 1854-1871

The Enduring Struggle

Enquiry Into the Cause of the Alienation
of the Delaware and Shawnee Indians
from British Interests

The Enslavement of the American Indian

The European and the Indian: Essays in the
Ethnohistory of Colonial North America

Everett Massacre

From Ice Mountains: Indian Settlement
of the Americas

Frontier Regulars: The U.S. Army
and the Indian, 1866-1891

Genocide Against the Indians

Genocide in Northwestern California

Great Indian Chiefs

Hanta Yo: An American Saga

Havasupai Indians, 1150-1890

*The Heritage

Historic Bakerville

Historical Account of the Doings and
Sufferings of the Christian Indians
in New England in the Years 1675-1677

Historical Sketch of the Cherokee

A History of Alberta

History of the American Indians

History of the Cherokee Indians and
Their Legends and Folklore

History of the Choctaw, Chickasaw
and Natchez Indians

*History of the Five Indian Nations
of Canada

History of Indian Education

A History of Indian Policy: Syllabus

History of the Indian Wars

History of the Indians of the U.S.

History of the Ojibway People

History of Texas, 1673-1779

I Have Spoken: American History
Through the Voices of the Indians

Indian Affairs Papers: American Revolution

The Indian: America's Unfinished Business

Indian Country

Indian Country of the Tubatulabal: First
Residents of the Kern River Valley

The Indian Frontier of the American
West, 1846-1890

The Indian History of the Modoc War

Indian in American History

The Indian in American History

The Indian in American Life

The Indian Nations of America

Indian New England Before the Mayflower

Indian Side of the Whiteman Massacre

Indian Women Chiefs

The Indians in Oklahoma

Indians in California History

Indians of California: The Changing Image

Indians of the High Plains: From the

Prehistoric Period to the Coming
of Europeans

Indians of the Lower Hudson Region:
The Munsee

Indians of the South Carolina Lowcountry,
1562-1751

Indians of the U.S.: Four Centuries
of Their History and Culture

Indians of the Woodlands: From
Prehistoric Times to 1725

The Iroquois in the Founding of
the American Indian

Ishi, Last of His Tribe

The Jicarilla Apache Tribe:
A History, 1846-1870

Kalispel: Historical Report

Kansas Indians: A History of the
Wind People, 1673-1873

The Lake Mohonk Conference of Friends of
the Indian: Guide to the Annual Reports

The Last Free Man: The True Story of the
Massacre of Shoshone Mike and His
Band of Indians in 1911

Last Trek of the Indians

A Law of Blood: The Primitive Law
of the Cherokee Nation

The Lemhi: Sacajawea's People

Life Among the Modocs: Unwritten History

Logan, The Last of the Race of Shikellemus,
Chief of the Cayuga Nation

Long Division: A Tribal History

Maryland Indians Yesterday and Today

Massacre: The Tragedy at White River

Memoris, Official and Personal

The Mescalero Apaches

The Middle Five: Indian Schoolboys
of the Omaha Tribes

Minkapee

Narratives of North American Indian
Captivity: A Selective Bibliography

Native American Renaissance

Native American Tribalism: Indian
Survivals and Renewals

Natives of the Golden State:
The California Indians

Navajo Changes: A History of
the Navajo People

Navajo Oral History and Traditions

North American Indians in
Historical Perspective

The Northern Shoshoni

HISTORY, SOURCES

The Sun Came Down: The History of the
World as My Blackfeet Elders Told It

The Country Was Ours: A Documentary History
of the American Indian

Writings of Gen. John Forbes Relating
to His Service in North America

HOPEWELL CULTURE

The Hopewell Mound Group of Ohio

Hopewell Village: A Social and Economic
History of an Iron Making Community

Hopewellian Studies

The Pool and Irving Villages: A Study
of Hopewell Occupation in the
Illinois River Valley

HOPI INDIANS

Big Falling Snow: A Tewa-Hopi Indians
Life and Times and the History and
Traditions of His People

Book of the Hopi

Broken Pattern Sunlight Shadows
of Hopi History

The Changing Pattern of Hopi Agriculture

Changing Physical Environment of the Hopi
Indians of Arizona

*Climbing Sun: The Story of a Hopi
Indian Boy

Continuities of Hopi Culture Change

Culture in Crisis: A Study of
the Hopi Indians

Designs from the Ancient Mimbrenos
with Hopi Interpretation

Designs on Prehistoric Hopi Pottery

Ethnobotany of the Hopi

Historic Hopi Ceramics

Hopi

Hopi Bibliography

The Hopi Child

Hopi Cookery

Hopi Coyote Tales: Istutuwutsi

Hopi Days

Hopi Dream

Hopi Dyes

Hopi and Hopi-Tewa Pottery

Hopi Indians

Hopi Journals

Hopi Kachina Dolls with a Key
to Their Identification

Hopi Kachina: Spirit of Life

Hopi Kachinas

Hopi Kachinas Drawn by Native Artists

*Hopi Mysteries

Hopi of the Second Mesa

Hopi Painting: The World of the Hopis

Hopi Photographers - Hopi Images

The Hopi: Their History and Use of Lands in
New Mexico and Arizona, 1200's to 1900's

Hopis: Portrait of a Desert People

Hopi Songs

Hopi Tales

The Hopi Villages

Hopi Voices: Recollections, Traditions
and Narratives of the Hopi Indians

Hopi Voices and Visions

Hopi Way

*The Hopi Way

Hopi and Zuni Ceremonialism

Hopitutuwutsi-Hopi Tales: A Bilingual
Collection of Hopi Indian Stories

Introduction to Hopi Pottery

Kachinas: A Selected Bibliography

Lessons in Hopi

*Little Joe: A Hopi Indian Boy Learns
a Hopi Indian Story

No Turning Back: A Hopi Indian Woman's
Struggle to Live in Two Worlds

Notes on Hopi Economic Life

Old Oraibi

Oraibu Maru Ceremony

Pages From Hopi History

Pumpkin Seed Point: Being Within the Hopi

Ritual in Pueblo Art: Hopi Life in Hopi
Painting

The Snake Dance of the Hopi Indians

The South Corner of Time

Spider Woman Stories: Legends of the
Hopi Indians

Sun Chief: The Autobiography of
a Hopi Indian

The Traditions of the Hopi

The Unwritten Literature on the Hopi

The Year of the Hopi

HUALAPAI INDIANS

Appraisal of the Lands of the Hualapai
Reservation, Arizona

Camp Beale's Springs and the
Hualapai Indians

Hualapai Indians

Hualapai Indians of Arizona

Hualapai Reference Grammar

Hualapai Tribal Lands

HUNTING AND FISHING

The Agricultural and Hunting Methods
of the Navaho Indians

Bringing Home Animals: Religious Ideology
and Mode of Production of the Mistassini
Cree Hunters

*Fur Trappers and Traders: The Indians,
The Pilgrims, and the Beaver

Hidatsa Eagle Trapping

*The Hunt

Hunter of the Sea

*The Hunters

Hunters of the Buffalo

Hunters of the Eastern Forest

Hunters of the Ice

Hunters of the Northern Forest

Hunters of the Sea

Indian Fishing: Early Methods
of the Northwest Coast

*Indian Hunting

An Introduction to the Ecology of Early
Historic Communal Bison Hunting Among
the Northern Plains Indians

The Montagnais "Hunting Territory"
and the Fur Trade

Snares, Deadfalls and Other Traps
of the Northern Algonquian and
Northern Athapaskans

Traps of the American Indians

Uncommon Controversy: Fishing Rights
of the Muckleshoot, Puyallup and
Nisqually Indians

IMPLEMENTS

Aboriginal Chipped Stone Implements
of New York

*American Indian Tools and Ornaments

Florida's Prehistoric Stone Technology:
A Study of the Flintworking Techniques
of Early Florida Stone Implement-Makers

Metates and Manos

Minnesota's Browns Valley Man and
Associated Burial Artifacts

North American Indian Points

Prehistoric Implements

Prehistoric Stone Implements of
Northeastern Arizona

Stone Tools and Relics of the American Indian

INDIANS OF CALIFORNIA

Aboriginal Society in Southern
California

Alabado, A Story of Old California

Bibliography of the Languages
of Native California

A Branch of California Redwood

The Broken Ring: The Destruction
of the California Indians

Cahuilla Dictionary

The Cahuilla Indians of Southern
California

Cahuilla Text With an Introduction

California

California Indian Nights Entertainment

California Indians, I-VI

California Indians: An
Annotated Bibliography

The California Indians: A Source Book

California's Gabrielino Indians

A Case Study of a Northern California
Indian Tribe: Cultural Change to 1860

Central Sierra Miwok Dictionary With Texts

The Chemehuevi Indians of
Southern California

The Chemehuevis

Chem'ivillu: Let's Speak Cahuilla

Chinigchinix, An Indigenous California
Indian Religion

The Chumash Indians of Southern California

A Collection of Ethnographical Articles
on the California Indians

The Condition of Affairs in Indian
Territory and California

The Conflict Between the California
Indian and White Civilization

Crystals in the Sky: An Intellectual
Odyssey Involving Chumash Astronomy,
Coamology, and Rock Art

Dawn on the World, Stories
of the Coast Miwok Indians

December's Child: A Book of
Chumash Oral Narratives

Dictionary of Mesa Grande Diegueno

The Diegueno Indians

The Dream Helper in South-Central
California

The Ethno-Botany of the Coahuilla
Indians of Southern California

The Eye of the Flute: Chumash
Traditional History and Ritual

Federal Concern About Conditions
of California Indians, 1853-1913:
Eight Documents

The First Californians

Gabrielino Indians of Southern California

Genocide in Northwestern California

A Grammar of Diegueno Nominals

*Great Indians of California

Handbook of the Indians of California

How We Lived: Reminiscences,
Stories, Speeches, and Songs
of California Indians

*The Indian and the California Mission

Indian Names for Plants and Animals
Among Californian and Other Western
North American Tribes

Indian-White Relationships in
Northern California, 1849-1920

Indians in California History

Indians of California: The Changing Image

Indians of Southern California

The Inland Whale: Nine Stories Retold
from California Indian Legends

Kawaiisu Mythology: An Oral Tradition
of South-Central California

Let's Talk 'Lipay AA: An Introduction
to the Mesa Grande Diegueno Language

Lo, the Poor Indian: A Saga of
the Suisun Indians of California

Material Aspects of Pomo Culture

Mukat's People: The Cahuilla Indians
of Southern California

Music of the Maidu Indians

My Luiseno Neighbors

Natives of the Golden State:
The California Indians

The Natural World of the
California Indians

The Nome Lackee Indian Reservation,
1854-1870

The Northern Maidu

Not for Innocent Ears: Spiritual
Traditions of a Desert Cahuilla
Medicine Woman

The Ohlone Way: Indian Life in the San
Francisco and Monterey Bay Areas

People of the Magic Waters: The Cahuilla
Indians of Plam Springs

People of the Valley: The Concow Maidu

Pomo Indian Basketry

*Pomo Indians of California
and Their Neighbors

The Population of the California
Indians, 1769-1970

Prehistoric Man of the Santa Barbara Coast

Report of Chas. A. Wetmore, Special U.S.
Commissioner of Mission Indians
of Southern California

Salinan Indians of California
and Their Neighbors

The Serrano Indians of Southern
California

The Southern Sierra Miwok Language

Spanish and Indian Place Names
of California

*Stories California Indians Told

Temalpakh: Cahuilla Indian Knowledge
and Usage of Plants

The Texas Cannibals, Or, Why Father
Serra Came to California

Tribes of California

Ukomno'm: The Yuki Indians of
Northern California

The Wappo: A Report

The Way We Lived: California Indian
Reminiscences, Stories and Songs

The Wintun Indians of California and
Their Neighbors

INDIANS OF NORTH
AMERICA—GENERAL

*Album of the American Indian

*American Indian

The American Indian: The American Flag

American Indian Archival Material: A
Guide to Holdings in the Southeast

The American Indian, 1492-1976:
A Chronology and Fact Book

American Indian Ecology

American Indian Energy Resources
and Development

American Indian Fiction

*The American Indian in America

American Indian and Indoeuropean Studies

American Indian Leaders: Studies
in Diversity

American Indian Literature:
An Anthology

American Indian Myths and Mysteries

The American Indian: North, South
and Central America

The American Indian: Prehistory
to the Present

The American Indian: A Rising
Ethnic Force

American Indians

*American Indians

The American Indians

American Indians in Colorado

*American Indians Today

*Angels and Indians

Anthropology and the American Indian

Anthropology on the Great Plains

Backward: An Essay on Indians,
Time and Photography

Belief and Worship in Native
North America

The Book of Indians

California

The California Indians: A Sourcebook

A Concise Dictionary of Indian
Tribes of North America

Conquering Horse

Contemporary American Indian Issues Series

Dictionary of Indian Tribes of the Americas

Dictionary of Indians of North America

Directory of Financial Aids for Minorities

D.C. (District of Columbia) Directory
of Native American Federal and
Private Programs

Echoes of Our Being

The Elder American Indian

The Evolution of the American Indian

Extending the Benefits of Vocational
Education to Indian Populations

*Famous Indian Tribes

Fightback: For the Sake of the People,
for the Sake of the Land

*The First Americans: Tribes
of North America

*First Came the Indians

Five Indian Tribes of the Upper Missouri

The Florida Indians

Four Centuries of Southern Indians

*Growing Up With North American Indians

A Guide to America's Indians: Ceremonies,
Reservations and Museums

A Guide to the Indian Tribes of Oklahoma

Guide to Records in the National Archives
Relating to American Indians

Guide to Research on North American Indians

Handbook of American Indians North of Mexico

Hear the Creator's Song

Historical and Statistical Information
Respecting the History, Condition and
Prospects of the Indian Tribes of the U.S.

The Hoe and the Horse on the Plains:
A Study of Cultural Development Among
North American Indians

The Illinois and Indiana Indians

Inconstant Savage: England and the
North American Indian, 1500-1660

The Indian Affair

Indian America: A Geography of North
American Indians

The Indian Boy's Days: The Indian
Then and Now

Indian, Eskimo, Aleut Owned and Operated
Arts Businesses Source Directory

*Indian Festivals

The Indian Heritage of Americans

Indian Crisis: The Background

Indian Exodus: Texas Indian Affairs

The Indian in America

Indian Leadership

*Indian Legacy: Native American Influences
on World Life and Culture

Indian Life: Transforming an American Myth

Indian Oratory: Famous Speeches
by Noted Indian Chieftains

Indian Peace Medals in American History

The Indian Peoples of Eastern America:
A Documentary History of the Sexes

Indian Population in the U.S.
and Alaska, 1910, 1930

Indian Preference - A Guide
  to Tribal Action

Indian Slavery in Colonial Times

The Indian Today

*Indian Tribes of America

Indian Tribes of North America

Indian Tribes of Texas

The Indian's Side of the Indian Question

*Indians

*The Indians

*Indians, The First Americans

*Indians in Careers

Indians in Minnesota

The Indians in Oklahoma

Indians of the Great Basin

Indians of the Great Plains

*The Indians of Louisiana

Indians of the Lower South

Indians of North America

Indians of North America: Methods
  and Sources for Library Research

Indians of North America: Survey of
  Tribes That Inhabit the Continent

Indians of Ohio, Indiana, Illinois,
  Southern Michigan and Southern Wisconsin

Indians of Ohio and Indiana Prior to 1795

Indians of the Plains

*Indians of the Plains

Indians of the South

Indians of Texas

The Indians of Today

Indians of the Western Great Lakes,
  1615-1760

Indians Overseas in British
  Territories, 1834-1854

*Indians Who Lived in Texas

Interpreting the Indians: 20th Century
  Poets and the Native American

The Invasion Within: The Contest of
  Cultures in Colonial North America

Letters and Notes on the Manners,
  Customs and Conditions of the
  North American Indians

Man's Rise to Civilization: The Cultural
  Ascent of the Indians of North America

*Meet the North American Indians

The Mobile Indians

National Indian Arts and
  Crafts Directory

Native American Directory:
  Alaska, U.S. and Canada

Native American Periodicals
  and Newspapers, 1828-1982

Native American Press in Wisconsin
  and the Nation

Native American Research
  Information Service

*The Native Americans

Native Americans and Broadcasting

Native Americans of Texas

Native Peoples in Struggle

The Native Races

Native Studies: American
  and Canadian Indians

Native Tribes Map

The Neutral Indians: A Sourcebook

The North American Indian

*North American Indians

North American Indians:
  A Comprehensive Account

North American Indians:
  A Dissertation Index

North American Indians: An
  Introduction to the Chichimeca

North American Indians of the Plains

The North Americans of Yesterday

Now That the Buffalo's Gone: A Study
  of Today's American Indians

*Our American Indians

Our Brother's Keeper: The Indian
  in White America

Our Wild Indians, Etc.

The Phoenix From the Flame:
  The American Indian Today

Pioneering in Montana: The Making
  of a State, 1864-1887

The Primal Mind: Vision and Reality
  in Indian America

Red Children in White America

A Serpent for a Dove: The Suppression
  of the American Indian

Six Months Among the Indians

Small Bones, Little Eyes

Society Against the State

The Southeastern Indians

Southeastern Indians Since
  the Removal Era

Speaking of Indians

*Starting an Indian Teen Club

Stories of Survival

The Story of the Indian

*The Sun Dance People: The Plains
Indians, Their Past and Present

Survival of a Noble Race

Tennessee's Indian Peoples: From White
Contact to Removal, 1540-1840

Tribes of California

Tribes That Slumber: Indians
of the Tennessee Region

Tulapai to Tokay: A Bibliography of
Alcochol Use and Abuse Among Native
Americans of North America

The Unknown Indian

The Urban American Indian

Urbanization of American Indians:
A Critical Bibliography

The Vanishing Race: Selections
from Edward S. Curtis' the
North American Indian

Views of a Vanishing Frontier

*We Live on Indian Reservation

The White Man's Indian

Wisconsin Indians

Wordarrows: Indians and Whites
in the New Fur Trade

Words in the Blood: Contemporary Indian
Writers of North and South America

INDIANS OF THE
GREAT LAKES REGION

Aspects of Upper Great Lakes
Anthropology

Council Fires on the Upper Ohio

The Forgotten People: The Woodland Erie

Indian Life on the Upper Great Lakes:
11,000 B.C. to A.D. 1800

Indian Rock Paintings of the Great Lakes

Indians of the Western Great Lakes,
1615-1760

Eastman Johnson's Lake Superior Indians

Lore of the Great Turtle: Indian Legends
of Mackinac Retold

Mackinac Island and Sault Ste. Marie

Monuments in Cedar

The Naomikong Site and the Dimensions
of Laurel in the Lake Superior Region

Prehistoric Biological Relationship
in the Great Lakes Region

The Sault Ste Marie Area

Sketches of a Tour to the Lakes

Woodland Indians of the Western
Great Lakes

INDIANS OF THE
GREAT PLAINS

Anthropology on the Great Plains

*The Art of the Plains Indians

Circles of the World: Traditional Art
of the Plains Indians

Costumes of the Plains Indians and
Structural Basis to the Decoration
of Costumes Among the In Plains Indians

Dress Clothing of the Plains Indians

Fifth Annual Plains Indian Seminar
in Honor of John C. Ewers

Great Plains Command

The Hidden Half: Studies of
Plains Indian Women

History of New Mexico-Plains
Indian Relations

*How the Plains Indians Lived

Indian Chiefs of Southern Minnesota

*Indian Tales of the Northern Plains

The Indians of the Great Plains

Indians of the Plains

*Indians of the Plains

The Mystic Warriors of the Plains

No More Buffalos

North American Indians of the Plains

Pipes of the Plains

The Plains Indian Book

Plains Indian Mythology

Plains Indian Raiders

*Plains Indians

*Plains Indians: An Educational
Coloring Book

Political Organization of the
Plains Indians

Prehistoric Man on the Great Plains

Reality and Dream: Psychotherapy
of a Plains Indian

Sheridan's Troopers on the Borders

*Small World of Plains Indians

Societies of the Plains Indians

*The Sun Dance People: The Plains
Indians, Their Past and Present

When Buffalo Ran

INDIANS OF THE NORTHEAST

Akwasane Historical Postcards

Akwesasne Peacemaker and Hiawatha Posters

American Indians and Our Way of Life

Amerinds and Their Paleoenvironments
in Northeastern North America

The Catholic Indian Missions in Maine,
1611-1820

Cautantowwit's Hoise: An Indian Burial
Ground on the Island of Conanicut
in Narragansett Bay

Civilization of the Indian Natives

Description of the New Netherlands

The Embattled Northeast

An Ethnography of the Huron Indians

Ethnology of the Yuchi Indians

Fighting Tuscarora: The Autobiography
of Chief Clanton Richard

Guide to Indian Artifacts of the Northeast

History, Manners and Customs of the Indian
Nations Who Once Inhabited Pennsylvania
and the Neighboring States

History of the Indian Tribes
of Hudson's River

History of the Mingo Indians

History of New York Indians and Indians
and Indians and the Printup Family

Horn and Bone Implements of the
New York Indians

Huron: Farmers of the North

Indian Blood

Indian Money as a Factor in
New England Civilization

Indian Names in Connecticut

Indian Patriots of the Eastern Woodlands

Indian Place Names of New England

Indian Wars of New England

Indian and the Whiteman in Connecticut

The Indian and the Whiteman in
Massachusetts and Rhode Island

The Indian and the Whiteman in New England

Indians in Maryland and Delaware:
A Critical Bibliography

*Indians of the Eastern Woodlands

*Indians of Greater New York
and the Lower Hudson

Indians of the Lower Hudson Region:
The Munsee

The Indians of Maine and the Atlantic
Provinces: A Bibliographic Guide

The Indians of Manhattan Island
and Vicinity

The Indians of New England:
A Critical Bibliography

*The Indians of New Jersey:
Dickon Among the Lenapes

Indians of the Northeast:
A Critical Bibliography

Indians in Pennsylvania

Languages and Lore of the Long
Island Indians

Logan, The Last of the Race of Shikellemus,
Chief of the Cayuga Nation

Man in Northeastern North America

Many Trails: Indians of the
Lower Hudson Valley

Martyrs of the Oblong and Little Nine

Maryland Indians Yesterday and Today

Metallic Ornaments of the New York Indians

The Modal Personality Structure
of the Tuscarora Indians

The Nanticoke Community of Delaware

The Nanticoke and Conoy Indians

The Nanticoke Indians

Native North American Spirituality
of the Eastern Woodlands

The New England Indians

New England's Prospect

New England Canaan or New Canaan

New York City in Indian Possession

Old Light on Separate Ways

Old John Neptune and Other Maine
Indian Shamans

One Thousand Years on Mound Key

The Oneida and Stockbridge Tribes

Palus Indians

Passamaquoddy Texts

Penobscot Man

Penobscot Shamanism

The People of the Land of Flint

A Pocket of Prose and Verse

Portrait of Akwesasne

Rediscovered Links in the Covenant Chain

Register of the Department of State

The Reservation

Susquehanna's Indians

Teaching About American Indians
in Connecticut

Territorial Subdivisions and Boundaries
of the Wampanoag, Massachusett
and Nauset Indians

Their Number Become Thinned

*Tomahawks and Trombones

Travels

A Trip to New England

Tuscaroras

Wampum and Shell Articles Used
by the New York Indians

Wood's New England Prospect

INDIANS OF THE NORTHWEST

Aboriginal Territory of the Kalispel

American Indian Sculpture: A Study
of the Northwest Coast

Analysis of Coeur D'Alene Indian Myths

Ancient Tribes of the Klamath Country

Art in the Life of the Northwest
Coast Indians

Art of the Northwest Coast Indians

Arts of the Raven: Masterworks
by the Northwest Coast Indian

The Assiniboine

Background History of the Coeur D'Alene
Indian Reservation

The Box of Daylight: Northwest Coast
Indian Art

Captured Heritage: The Scramble
for Northwest Coast Artifacts

The Cayuse Indians

Children of the Raven

The Chinook Indians

The Coast Indians of Southern Alaska
and Northern British Columbia

The Coeur D'Alene Reservation

The Conquest of the Coeur D'Alenes,
Spokanes and Palouses

Content and Style of an Oral Literature:
Clackamas Chinook Myths and Tales

Contributions to the Ethnography
of the Kutchin

*Coyote and Kootenai

Crime Against the Yakimas

Cultures of the North Pacific Coast

The Decorative Art of the Indians
of North Pacific Coast

Diving for Northwest Relics

Ethnographic Sketch of the Klamath
Indians of Southwestern Oregon

Ethnography of Franz Boas

Ethnography of the Kutenai

Ethnological Field Investigation
and Analysis

An Extract from the Klamath Indians
of Southwestern Oregon

The Eyak Indians of the Copper
River Delta, Alaska

Facial Paintings of the Indians
of Northern British Columbia

The Flathead Indians of Montana

The Fort Belknap Assiniboine of Montana

*From Free Range to Reservation

Guid to Indian Rock Carvings of
the Pacific Northwest Coast

Historic and Ethnographic Study
of the Snohomish

Historical Sketch of the Flathead Nation

History of Indian Missions
on the Pacific Coast

Images: StoneL B.C.

In the Land of the Grasshopper Songs

Indian Affairs in Territories of Oregon
and Washington

Indian Art of the Northwest Coast

Indian Art Traditions of
the Northwest Coast

Indian Artifacts of the Northwest Coast

Indian Baskets of the Northwest Coast

Indian Council at Walla Walla, Washington

Indian Families of the Northwest Coast

Indian Fishing: Early Methods
on the Northwest Coast

Indian Healing: Shamanic Ceremonialism
in the Pacific Northwest Today

Indian Legends of the Northern Rockies

*Indian Legends of the Pacific Northwest

Indian Life on the Northwest Coast
of North America

Indian Petroglyphs of the Pacific Northwest

Indian Portraits of the Pacific Northwest

Indian Relics of the Pacific Northwest

Indian Shakers: A Messianic Cult
of the Pacific Northwest

Indian Tribes of the Northwest

Indian Tribes of Washington,
Oregon and Idaho

Twana Games

Uncommon Controversy: Fishing Rights of the Muckleshoot, Puyallup and Nisqually Indians

Valley of the Spirits: The Upper Skagit Indians of Western Washington

Volcano Tales: Indian Legends of the Cascade Mountains

*Vostaas: The Story of Montana's Indian Nation

The Ways of My Grandmothers

Wolf of the Raven: Totem Poles of Southeastern Alaska

A World of Faces: Masks of the Northwest Coast Indians

The Yakimas: A Critical Bibliography

INDIANS OF THE SOUTH

Alabama and the Borderlands

American Indian Archival Material

Antiquities of the Southern Indians

*The Art of the Southeastern Indians

An Asian Anthropologist in the South

British Administration of the Southern Indians, 1756-1783

British Travelers Among the Southern Indians, 1660-1763

Carolina Indian Frontier

Catawba Indians

Catawba Nation

Chapters of the Ethnology of the Powhatan Tribes of Virginia

Documents Relating to Indian Affairs

The Early Prehistoric Southeast: A Sourcebook

Exiles of Florida

Field Guide to Indian Point Types of the State of Florida

First on the Land: The North Carolina Indians

Florida Anthropological Society Publications

The Florida Indians

Florida Place Names of Indian Origin

The Florida Wars

The Formative Cultures of the Carolina Piedmont

Four Centuries of Southern Indians

Government and Religion of the Virginia Indians

The Grand Village of the Natchez Indians Revisited

History of Alabama, and Incidentally of Georgia and Mississippi, from the Earliest Period

The History and Present State of Virginia

Indian Affairs in Georgia, 1732-1756

*Indian Myths from the Southeast

Indian Place Names in Alabama

Indian Tribes of the Lower Mississippi Valley and Adjacent Coast of the Gulf of Mexico

Indians in Seventeenth Century Virginia

*The Indians of Louisiana

Indians of the Lower South

Indians of the Rio Grande Valley

Indians of the South

Indians of the South Carolina Lowcountry, 1526-1751

Indians of the Southeastern U.S.

Journal of the Southern Indian Mission

The Karankara Indians, The Coast People of Texas

The Late Prehistoric Southeast: A Sourcebook

The Lumbee Problem

A Map of Virginia

Memoire Justicatif of the Chevalier Montault de Monberaut: Indian Diplomacy in British West Florida, 1763-1765

Myths and Tales of the Southeastern Indians

A Narrative of the Early Days and Remembrances of Oceaola Nikkanochee

Negro-Indian Relationships in the Southeast

New Voyages to Carolina

North Carolina Indian Legends and Myths

Notices of East Florida

Notices of Florida and the Campaigns

Of Sky and Earth: Art of the Southeastern Indians

The Only Land I Know: A History of the Lumbee Indian of North Carolina

Only Land They Knew: The Tragic Story of the American Indians in the Old South

The Pamunkey Indians of Virginia

The Pascagoula, Biloxi and Mobilian Consolidated Band

Plants Used as Curatives by Certain Southeastern Tribes

Prehistoric Indians of the Southeast

Red Carolinians

Redskins, Ruffleshirts and Rednecks

South Florida's Vanished People

The Southestern Ceremonial Complex and
Its Interpretation

The Southeastern Indians

Southeastern Indians Since the Removal Era

Southeastern Woodland Indian Designs

Southern Indians in the American Revolution

The Southern Indians: The Story of
the Civilized Tribes Before Removal

Stalling's Island Mound, Columbia
County, Georgia

John Stuart and the Southern
Colonial Frontier

Studies in Southeastern Indian Languages

Sun Circles and Human Hands:
The Southeastern Indians,
Art and Industries

Tacachale: Essays on the Indians
of Florida and Southeastern Georgia
During the Historical Period

Tomochichi: India Friend of
the Georgia Colony

A True Discourse of the Present Estate
of Virginia

*World of the Southern Indians

INDIANS OF THE SOUTHWEST

American Indians of the Southwest

*Ancient Indians of the Southwest

Ancient Life in the American Southwest

Archaeological Explorations on the
Middle Chinlee

Archaeology of Alkali Ridge,
Southeastern Utah

*The Art of the Southwest Indians

Basketmaker Caves in the Prayer Rock
District, Northeastern Arizona

Basketmaker Caves of Northeastern Arizona

Black Sand: Prehistory in Northern Arizona

Circles, Consciousness and Culture

The Classic Southwest

Clay Figurines of the American Southwest

Cliff Dwellings of the Mesa Verde

Cocopa Ethnography

The Cochise Cultural Sequence in
Southeastern Arizona

Cultural and Environmental History of
Cienega Valley, Southeastern Arizona

Cycles of Conquest

Decorative Art of the Southwestern Indians

Desert Foragers and Hunters

Dictionary of Prehistoric Indian
Artifacts of the Amerian Southwest

Drinking Behavior Among Southwestern Indians

The Elkus Collection: Southwestern Indian Art

Enduring Visions: One Thousand Years
of Southwestern Indian Art

Ethnic Medicine in the Southwest

Ethno-Botany of the Gosiute Indians of Utah

Excavations of Los Muertos and Neighboring Ruins in the Salt River
Valley, Southern Arizona

Expeditions Into New Mexico

Explorations in Northeastern Arizona

Fetishes and Carvings of the Southwest

Final Report of Investigations Among
the Indians of the Southwestern U.S.

First Penthouse Dwellers of America

Forgotten Frontiers

The Frontier People

Grand Circle Adventure

Handbook of Northern Arizona Pottery Wares

Historical Introduction to Studies Among
Sedentary Indian sof New Mexico

The Hohokam Indians of the Tucson Basin

Indian Baskets of the Southwest

Indian Jewelry of the Prehistoric Southwest

Indian Rock Art of the Southwest

Indian Silver Jewelry of the Southwest,
1868-1930

Indians of the American Southwest

Indians of Arizona

Indian sof the Lake Mead Country

Indians of the Pike's Peak Region

The Indians of Point of Pines, Arizona

Indians of teh Southwest

Indians of the Southwest: A Century
of Development Under the U.S.

Indians of the Southwest: A
Critical Bibliography

Ray Manley-s Indian Lands

Ray Manley's Portraits and Turquois
of Southwest Indians

Earl Morris and Southwestern Archaeology

Music and Dance Research of the
Southwestern Indians

Myths and Legends of the Indian Southwest

On the Gleaming Way: Navajos, Eastern
Pueblos, Zunis, Hopis, Apaches and Their
Land, and Their Meanings to the World

People of the Blue Water

People of the Desert and Sea

Physiological and Medical Observations
Among the Indians of Southwestern U.S.
and Northern Mexico

Pottery of the Pajarito Plateau and of
Some Adjacent Regions in New Mexico

Prehistoric Indians of the Southwest

Prehistoric Southwestern Craft Arts

Prehistoric Southwesterners from
Basketmaker to Pueblo

Prehistoric Textiles of the Southwest

Prehistoric Weapons in the Southwest

The Rain-Makers: Indians of Arizona
and New Mexico

Rain on the Desert

*Settlers and Strangers: Native Americans
of the Desert Southwest and History
As They Saw It

Sipapu: The Story of the Indians
of Arizona and New Mexico

Southwest: Handbook of North
American Indians

Southwest Indian Craft Arts

Southwest Indian Drypainting

Southwest Indian Painting: A Changing Art

Southwest Indian Silver from the Doneghy
Collection

Southwestern Archaeology

Southwestern Archaeology: A Bibliography

Southwestern Arts and Crafts

Southwestern Indian Arts and Crafts

Southwestern Indian Ceremonials

The Southwestern Indian Detours

Southwestern Indian Ritual Drama

Southwestern Indian Tribes

Southwestern Weaving

Speaking of Indians: With an Accent
on the Southwest

Storms Brewed in Other Men's Worlds

Swarts Ruin

Textiles of the Prehistoric Southwest

The Tigua Suma and Manso Indians of
Western Texas and New Mexico

To the Foot of the Rainbow

Traditions in Transition: Contemporary
Basket Weaving of the Southwestern Indians

Urban Indians of Arizona

Witchcraft in the Southwest

INDUSTRIES

Aboriginal Indian Basketry

American Indian Craft Book

American Indian Craft Inspirations

American Indian Needlepoint Designs
for Pillows, Belts, Handbags,
and Other Projects

American Indian Utensils: How to Make
Baksets, Pottery and Woodenware
with Natural Materials

The Ancestors: Native American Artisans
of the Americas

Apache Indian Baskets

Arts and Crafts of the Cherokees

Authentic Indian Designs

Basketmaker Caves of Northeastern Arizona

Basketry Designs of the Salish Indians

Basketry of the Papago and Pima Indians

Basketry of the San Carlos Apache Indians

Book of Authentic Indian Life Crafts

The Book of Indian Crafts and Costumes

The Book of Indian Crafts and Indian Lore

The Complete How-To Book of Indian Craft

Copper: Its Mining and Use by the Aborigines
of the Lake Superior Region

Cornhusk Bags of the Plateau Indians

Crafts from North American Indian Arts:
Techniques, Designs and Contemporary
Applications

*Crafts of the North American Indians:
A Craftsman's Manual

The Crescent Hills Prehistoric Quarrying Area

Designs from the Ancient Mimbrenos
with Hopi Interpretation

*Easy to Make North American Indian Crafts

The Heritage of Klickitat Basketry:
A History and Art Preserved

Hopi Kachina Dolls with a Key
to Their Identification

Illustrated History of Indian Baskets
and Plates

The Indian Arts and Crafts Board:
An Aspect of the New Deal Policy

Indian Basket Weaving

Indian Basketry

Indian Basketry and How to Make Baskets

Indian Baskets of the Northwest Coast

Indian Baskets of the Southwest

*Indian Crafts

Indian Crafts and Lore

Indian Designs

Indian and Eskimo Basketry: A key to ID

The Indian How Book

Indian Weaving, Knitting, and Basketry
of the Northwest Coast

Interwoven Expression: Works by Contemporary Alaska Native Basket Makers

Introducing Western Indian Basketry

Introduction to Hopi Kachinas

Iroquois Crafts

Iroquois Watercrafts

Ray Manley's Collecting Southwestern
Indian Arts and Crafts

Ray Manley's Hopi Kachina

Metallic Ornaments of the New York Indians

Navajo Weavers and Silversmiths

Quill and Beadwork of the Western Sioux

Northwest Indian Basketry

Ojibwa Crafts

Plants Used in Basketry by the
California Indians

Pomo Indian Basketry

Pueblo Crafts

Pueblo Designs: 176 Illustrations
of the Rain Bird

The Re-Establishment of the Indians
in Their Pueblo Life Through the
Revival of Their Traditional Crafts:
A Study in Home Extension Education

Southwest Indian Craft Arts

Southwestern Indian Arts and Crafts

Sun Circles and Human Hands: The Southestern Indians, Art and Industries

Traditions in Transition: Contemporary
Basket Weaving of the Southwestern Indians

Western North American Indian Baskets from
the the Collection of Clay P. Bedford

Work a Day Life of the Pueblos

IROQUOIS INDIANS

Apologies to the Iroquois

Archaeology of the Oneida Iroquois

Behind the Tree of Peace: A Sociological
Analysis of Iroquois Warfare

The Boy George Washington Aged Sixteen: His
Own Account of an Iroquois Indian Dance

The Boys Site and the Early Ontario
Iroquois Tradition

The Caddoan, Iroquoian and Siouan Languages

Contacts Between Iroquois Herbalism and
Colonial Medicine

Contemporary Iroquois and the Struggle
for Survival

Economics of the Iroquois

Extending the Rafters: Interdisciplinary
Approaches to Iroquois Studies

Forgotten Founders: Benjamin Franklin,
The Iroquois and the Rationionale
for American Revolution

A History of the Iroquois

Iroquoian Cosmology

Iroquois

Iroquois Book of Rites

Iroquois Ceremonial of Midwinter

Iroquois Crafts

The Iroquois Eagle Dance

Iroquois Folk Lore

Iroquois in the American Revolution

The Iroquois in the Founding of the
American Indian

Iroquois Indians

Iroquois Music and Dance

The Iroquois and the New Deal

The Iroquois Restoration: Iroquois
Diplomacy on the Colonial Frontier,
1701-1754

An Iroquois Sourcebook

*Iroquois Stories

Iroquois - Their Art, Culture and Crafts

The Iroquois Trail

Iroquois Watercrafts

Law and Government of the Grand
River Iroquois

League of the Ho-De-No-Sau-Nee
or Iroquois

League of the Iroquois

Legends of the Iroquois

Legends, Traditions and Laws
of the Iroquois

The Long House of the Iroquois

Medicine and Politics Among the
Grand River Iroquois

Northern Iroquoian Texts

Notes on Iroquois Archaeology

Notes on the Iroquois

Oneida Verb Morphology

Onondaga Iroquois Prehistory

Onondaga: Portrait of a Native People

The Ontario Iroquois Tradition

Papers in Linguistics from the 1972
Conference on Iroquoian Research

Parker on the Iroquois

The Roll Call of the Iroquois Chiefs

Smoking Technology of the Aborigines of
the Iroquois Area of New York State

Symposium on Cherokee and Iroquois Culture

Symposium on Local Diversity in
Iroquois Culture

Traditions and Laws of the Iroquois

JEWELRY

American Indian Artifact With Jewelry
Price Guide

Collecting Southwestern Native
American Jewelry

Indian Jewelry Making

Indian Jewelry of the Prehistoric Southwest

Indian Silver Jewelry of the Southwest,
1868-1930

Indian Silver: Navajo and Pueblo Jewelers

Navajo Weavers and Silversmiths

Navajos Call It Hard Goods

Turquoise and the Navajo

JOURNALISM

Let My People Know: American Indian
Journalism, 1828-1978

Native American Press in Wisconsin
and the Nation

JUVENILE LITERATURE

*Across the Tundra

*Album of the American Indian

*Algonkians of the Eastern Woodlands

*Algonquian Indians: At Summer Camp

*American Indian

*The American Indian in America

*American Indian Music and
Musical Instruments

*American Indian Tools and Ornaments

*Ancient Indians of the Southwest

*American Indians Today

*The Apache Indians: Raiders of the Southwest

*Arilla Sun Down

*Art of the North American Indian

*The Art of the Plains Indians

*The Art of the Southwest Indians

*As Grandfather Told Me

*Bear's Heart: Scenes from the Life of a
Cheyenne Artist of One Hundred Years Ago
With Pictures of Himself

*Big Enough

*Bill Red Coyote Is a Nut

*Blue Jacket: War Chief of the Shawnees

*Blue Thunder

*Broken Ice

*Brother of the Wolves

*Buffalo Moon

*Chant of the Red Man

*The Cherokee: Indians of the Mountains

*Cherokee Removal 1838: An Entire Indian
Nation Is Forced Out Of Its Homeland

*Cheyenne Legends of Creation

*Cheyenne Warriors

*Chief Joseph's Own Story As Told By
Chief Joseph in 1879

*Chief Red Horse Tells About Custer

*Chii-La-Pe and the White Buffalo

*A Child's History of the American Indian

*Chinook

*The Chippewa Indians: Rice Gatherers
of the Great Lakes

*Come to Our Salmon Feast

*Cou-Yan-Nai

*Could It Be Old Hiari

*Coyote's Pow-Wow

*Creation Tales from the Salish

*Crickets and Corn

*Daisy Hooee Nampeyo

*The Dark Side of the Moon

*David, Young Chief of the Quileutes:
An American Indian Today

*The Delaware Indians: Eastern Fishermen
and Farmers

*The Earth Is Sore: Native Americans
on Nature

*Famine Winter

*Famous Indian Tribes

*First Book of the Indian Wars

*The Flood

*Fur Trappers and Traders: The Indians,
The Pilgrims, and the Beaver

*The Gatherers

*Geronimo Chino

*The Ghosts the Indians Feared

*Grandfather and the Popping Machine

*Great Indians of California

*Growing Up With North American Indians

*hardy Race of Men: America's Early Indians

*Heart Butte: A Blackfeet Indian

*Heroes of the American Indian

*Homer Little Bird's Rabbit

*Hopi Mysteries

*The Hopi Way

*How the Flowers Came To Be

*How the Indians Really Lived

*How the Plains Indians Lived

*The Hunt

*The Hunters

*I Can Read About the Indians

*If You Lived With the Sioux Indians

*The Indian Book

*Indian Boyhood

*The Indian and the Buffalo

*Indian Canoeing

Indian Children's Books

*Indian Crafts

*Indian Festivals

*Indian Foe, Indian Friend

*The Indian and His Horse

*Indian Hunting

*Indian Legacy: Native American Influences
on World Life and Culture

*Indian Patriots of the Eastern Woodlands

*Indian Tribes of America

*Indians

*Indians at Home

*Indians, The First Americans

*Indians Knew

*Indians of the Longhouse

*Indians of the Pacific Northwest

*Indians of the Plains

*Indians on the Move

*Philip Johnston and the Navajo Code Talkers

*Joseph, Chief of the Nez Perce

*Keeper of Fire

*Kiowa Voices: Ceremonial Dance,
Ritual and Song

*Mary Jemison: Seneca Captive

*Let's Be Indians

*Let's Find Out About Indians

*Linda's Indian Home

*Little Joe: A Hopi Indian Boy
Learns A Hopi Story

*The Little People

*Little Turtle

*The Long Search

*Lucy Learns to Weave: Gathering Plants

*Mark of Our Moccasins

*Massasoit: Friend of the Pilgrims

*Me Run Fast Good: Biographies of Tewanima
(Hopi), Carlos Montezuma (Apache), and
John Horse (Seminole)

*Meet the North American Indians

*The Money God

*Moonsung Lullaby

*Morning Arrow

*Morning Star, Black Sun: The Northern
Cheyenne Indians and America's
Energy Crisis

*Jim Musco

*Native Americans: The Sioux

*Navajo Children

The Navajo: Herders, Weavers
and Silversmiths

*Navajo Long Walk

*Navajo Slave

*Navajo Victory—Being a Native American

*No One Like a Brother

*North American Indian Masks

*North American Indians

*Okemos: Story of a Fox Indian In His Youth

*Old Man Coyote

*Only the Name Remains the Same: The Cherokees and the Trail of Tears

*Our American Indians

*Pacific Coast Indians of North America

*Phantom Horse of Collister's Fields

*Plains Indians

*Plains Indians: An Educational Coloring Book

*Pow Wow

*A Pueblo Village

*Red Horse and the Buffalo Robe Man

*The Rings of Woot-Kew's Tail: Indian Legends of the Origin of the Sun, Moon and Stars

*Sacagawea

*Sam and the Golden People

*The Sea Hunters: Indians of the Northwestern Coast

*Seal for a Pal

*Seneca Garden

*The Sioux Indians: Hunters and Warriors of the Plains

*Sky Watchers of Ages Past

*Son of the Dine'

*The Spotted Horse

*Stories from Ugadali

*The Story of Wounded Knee

*The Tale of the Possum

*Talking Bones: Secrets of Indian Mound Builders

*Talking Hands: Indian Sign Language

*These Were the Sioux

*They Put On Masks

*A Thousand Years of American Indian Storytelling

*The Tiguas: The Lost Tribe of City Indians

*The Tipi: A Center of Native American Life

*To Live In Two Worlds: American Indian Youth Today

*Tomo-Chi-Chi

*Totem Poles and Tribes

*tragedy of Tenaya

*The Tuscaroras

*Veho

*War Clouds in the West: Indians and Cavalrymen, 1860-1890

*War Pony

*Alford Waters

*we Have Not Vanished: Eastern Indians of the U.S.

*We Rode the Wind: Recolletions of the 19th Century Tribal Life

*Westward Adventure: The True Stories of Six Pioneers

*When Buffalo Free the Mountains: A Ute Indian Journey

*When Clay Sings

*When Grandfather Journeys Into Winter

*Sara Winnemucca

*The Winter Hunt

*Wovoka

KACHINAS

Hopi Kachina Dolls With a Key to Their Identification

Hopi Kachinas

Hopi Katchinas Drawn by Native Artists

Introduction to Hopi Kachinas

Kachinas-Paone

Kachinas: A Selected Bibliography

Ray Manley's Hopi Kachina

KICKAPOO INDIANS

Indians of Illinois and Indiana: Illinois Kickapoo and Potawatomi Indians

Kickapoo, Illinois and Potawatomi Indians

Kickapoo Indians in Illinois and Missouri

Kickapoo Lands in Kansas, 1863

Kickapoo Tales

Kickapoo Tracts in Missouri and Kansas, 1835

Kickapoo Tribal Lands in Illinois and Indiana

Kickapoos: Lords of the Middle Border

Mexican Kickapoo Indians

KIOWA INDIANS

Apache, Kiowa and Comanche Indian Reservation in Southwestern Oklahoma

Bad Medicine and Good: Tales of the Kiowas

Calendar History of the Kiowa Indians

The Economic Botany of the Kiowa Indians

Kiowa, Comanche and Apache Lands in Oklahoma and Texas

Kiowa Tales

*Kiowa Voices: Ceremonial Dance, Ritual and Song

Kiowa Voices: Myths, Legends and Folktales

The Kiowas

Satanta, The Great Chief of the Kiowas
and His People

Saynday's People: The Kiowa Indians and
the Stories They Told

Vocabulary of the Kiowa Language

KWAKIUTL INDIANS

Feasting With Cannibals: An Essay on
Kwakiutl Cosmology

Geographical Names of the Kwakiutl Indians

Guests Never Leave Hungry: The Autobiography
of James Sewid, A Kwakiutl Indian

Kwakiutl Art

Kwakiutl Culture as Reflected in Mythology

Kwakiutl Ethnography

Kwakiutl: Indians of British Columbia

Kwakiutl Legends

The Kwakiutl of Vancouver Island

Kwakiutl Tales

Kwakiutl Tales

Kwakiutl Texts

The Mouth of Heaven: An Introduction
to Kwakiutl Religious Thought

Notes and Observations on the Kwakiutl
People of the Northern Part of the
Vancouver Island Adjacent Coasts

Religion of the Kwakiutl Indians

Smoke From Their Fires: The Life of
a Kwakiutl Chief

LAND CESSIONS, TENURES
REMOVALS AND DISPUTES

American Indians Dispossessed: Fraud in
Land Cessions Forced Upon the Tribes

Cherokee Nation: Land Cessions in Tennessee
Mississippi, North Carolina, Georgia,
Alabama, 1785-1835

*Cherokee Removal 1838: An Entire Indian
Nation Is Forced Out of Its Homeland

Cherokee Removal: The "William Penn" Essays
and Other Writings by Jeremiah Evarts

The Choctaw Before Removal

Considerations on the Present State of the
Indians and Their Removal to the West of
the Mississippi

Continent Lost—A Civilization Won:
Indian Land Tenure in America

Creek Indians: Information Relative to the
Claims of the Creeks Against the U.S. for
Florida Lands Taken by the U.S. Under the
Treaty of Moultrie Creek, 1823

The Dawes Act and the Allotment Indian Land

Dispossessing the American Indian: Indian and
Whites on the Colonial Frontier

Fathers and Children: Andrew Jackson and
the Subjugation of the American Indian

Guide to Decisions of the Interior
on Indian Lands

Indian Land Tenure: Bibliographic Essays
and a Guide to the Literature

Indian Removal: The Emigration of Five
Civilized Tribes of Indians

Indians, Bureaucrats and Land: The Dawes
Act and the Decline of Indian Farming

*Only the Names Remain: The Cherokees and
the Trail of Tears

The Rape of the Indian Lands: An Original
Anthology

Reconstruction in Indian Territory

Removal of the Cherokee Indians from Georgia

The Removal of the Cherokee Nation: Manifest
Destiny or National Dishonor

Removal of the Choctaw Indians

Reservation to City: Indian Urbanization
and Federal Relocation

Roots of Resistance: Land Tenure in New Mexico

The Second Long Walk: Navajo-Hopi Land
Dispute

Speeches on the Passage of the Bill for the
Removal of the Indians

Taos Land Claim: Anthropological Data

LANGUAGES, DICTIONARIES
GLOSSARIES, ETC.

Acheii Bahane' Grandfather Stories

Alaawich

Aleut Language

Aleutian Indian and English Dictionary

American Indian: Language and Literature

American Indian Language Series

American Indian Languages and American
Linguistics

An Areal-Typological Study of American
Indian Languages North of Mexico

Beginning Cherokee

Bibliographies of the Languages of
the North American Indians

*Lushootseed

A Manual of Navaho Grammar

Map of North American Indian Languages

Meet Cree: A Guide to the Cree Language

Menomini Lexicon

*Na Yo Pisa

Native Languages of the Americas

Navaho Grammar

Navajo Texts

A New Series of Blackfoot Texts

Newe Natekwinappeh: Shoshoni Stories
and Dictionary

Nez Perce Grammar

North American Indian Language Materials,
1890-1965

Notes of a Twenty-Five Years' Service
in the Hudson's Bay Territory

One of the Keys: 1676-1776-1976:
The Wampanoag Indian Contribution

Oneida Verb Morphology

Papers in Linguistics from the 1972
Conference on Iroquoian Research

Plains Cree: Grammatical Study

A Proto-Algonquian Dictionary

Race, Language and Culture

Saad Ahaah Sinil: Dual Language

Second Language Learning for American
Indians: A Topical Bibliography

Selected Problems in Yavapai Syntax:
The Verde Valley Dialect

The Shuswap Language

The Siouan Indian Language
(Teton and Santee Dialects) Dakota

*Sokosi Aliha

The Southern Sierra Miwok Language

Speaking of Indians

Speech Variation i Acoma Keresan

A Structural and Lexical Comparison of the
Tunica, Chitimacha, and Atakapa Languages

Studies in American Indian Languages

Studies in the Athapaskan Languages

Studies in Southeastern Indian Languages

Supplement to the Handbook of Middle
American Indians: Linguistics

Symposium on American Indian Linguistics

Syntax and Semantics: The Syntax
of Native American Languages

Tonkawa, An Indian Language of Texas

Topics in Mojave Syntax

Tovangar

Tunica Texts; With Tunica Dictionary

Tuscarora Language

Vocabulary of the Kiowa Language

Voyages and Travels of an Indian
Interpreter and Trader

Western Indians: Comparative Environments,
Languages and Cultures of 172 Western
American Indian Tribes

Where the West Begins: Essays on
Middle Border and Siouxland Writing

Wichita Grammar

Wikchamni Grammar

Wishram Texts: Together With Wasco
Tales and Myths

Zeisberger's Indian Dictionary

LEGAL, LAWS, ETC.

Acts and Resolutions (of National
Tribal Councils)

The Aggressions of Civilization: Federal
Indian Policy Since the 1880's

Alaska Natives and American Laws

American Indian Law In a Nutshell

The American Indian Law Series

American Indian Legal Materials:
A Union List

American Indians, American Justice

Annotated Statutes of the Indian Territory

Behind the Trail of Broken Treaties

Cases and Materials on Federal Indian Law

The Cheyenne Way: Conflict and Case Law
in Primitive Jurisprudence

The Constitution and Laws of the American
Indian Tribes

A Constitutional Analaysis of the Criminal
Jursidiction and Procedural Guarantees of
the American Indian

Felix S. Cohen's Handbook of
Federal Indian Law

Constitution of the State of Sequoyah

Criminal Jurisdiction Allocation in
Indian Country

Documents of U.S. Indian Policy

Early American Indian Documents:
Treaties and Laws, 1607-1789

English Institutions and the
American Indian

Facing West: The Metaphysics of
Indian-Hating and Empire Building

Fifth Annual Indian Law Seminar

Guide to American Indian Documents in the
Congressional Serial Set: 1817-1899

Guide to Decisions of the Interior
Department on Indian Lands

Handbook of Federal Indian Law

History of the Legal Status of the
American Indian With Particular
Reference to California: Thesis

Indian Nullification of the Unconstitutional Laws of Massachusetts, Relative
to the Marshpee Tribe: Or, the
Pretended Riot Explained

Indian Police and Judges: Experiments
in Acculturation and Control

The Indian Rights Association: The
Herbert Welsh Years, 1882-1904

Indian Rights Association Papers: A Guide
to the Microfilm Edition, 1864-1973

Indian Rights Manual

Indians and Criminal Justice

Labor Laws, Union, and Indian
Self-Determination

Law and the American Indian:
Readings, Notes and Cases

Law and Identity: Lawyers, Native
Americans and Legal Practice

The Law on Indian Preference in
Employment and Contracting

Laws of the Colonial and State Governments
Relating to Indians and Indian Affairs,
From 1633-1831

Legal Conscience, Selected Papers

The Legal Status of the Indian

Legal Structures for Indian Business
Development on Reservations - A Tribal
Sovereignty Approach

Legends, Traditions and Laws of the
Iroquois: Or, Six Nations, and History
of the Tuscarora Indians

The Livingston Indian Records, 1666-1723

Native American Politics Series

Native Americans and Nixon: Presidential
Politics and Minority Self-Determination,
1969-1972

Native People in Canada: Contemporary
Conflicts

The New Deal and American Indian
Tribalism: The Administration of the
Indian Reorganization Act, 1934-1945

Old Problems—Present Issues

Puritan Justice and the Indian: White
Man's Law in Massachusetts, 1630-1763

Taxing Those They Found Here

LEGENDS

American Indian Myth and Legends

American Indian Mythology

Blackfeet Lodge Tales

Caddoan Texts, Pawnee, South Band Dialect

Catawba Texts

Cheyenne Memories

The Child and the Serpent: Reflections
on Popular Indian Symbols

Children of the Twilight: Folktales
of Indian Tribes

Clothed-in-Fur and Other Tales: An Introduction to an Ojibwa World View

Current and Style of an Oral Literature:
Clackamas Chinook Myths and Tales

Corn Goddess and Other Tales
from Indian Canada

Coyote Stories

Coyote Was Going There: Indian Literature
of the Oregon Country

Dakota Texts

Dine Bahane' The Navajo Creation Story

Dirty Boy: A Jicarilla Tale of Raid and War

Enchanted Moccasins and Other Legends
of the American Indian

Folk-Tales of the Salishan and
the Sahaptin Tribes

Fox Texts

Haboo: Native American Stories
from Puget Sound

Haida Texts and Myths: Skidgate Dialect

Hear Me My Chief: Nez Perce Legend
and History

Hopi Coyote Tales: Istutuwutsi

Hopitutuwutsi - Hopi Tales: A Bilingual
Collection of Hopi Indian Stories

In the Time That Was: Being Legends
of the Tlingits

Indian Legends

Indian Legends of the Northern Rockies

Indian Stories from the Pueblos: Tales of
New Mexico and Arizona

Indian Stories and Legends

Indian Story and Song from North America

Indian Tales

Indian Tales of North America: An
Anthology of the Adult Reader

The Inland Whale: Nine Stories Retold
from California Indian Legends

Karuk Indian Myths

Keresan Texts

Kickapoo Tales

Kiowa Tales

Kiowa Voices: Myths, Legends and Folktales

Kutenai Tales

Kwakiutl Tales

Kwakiutl Tales: New Series

Legend of the Ghostway Ritual

Legends and Lore of the Papago
and Pima Indians

Legends of the Delaware Indians
and Picture Writings

Legends of the Iroquois

Legends of the Lakota

Legends of the Longhouse

Legends of the Micmacs

Legends of the Mighty Sioux

The Lenape and Their Legends

Literary Aspects of North American Mythology

Lore of the Great Turtle: Indian Legends
of Mackinac Retold

Lost Mines of the Great Southwest

Lower Umpqua Texts and Notes on
the Kusan Dialects

Lummi Indians of Northwest Washington

The Man Who Married the Moon and
Other Pueblo Indian Folk-Stories

Mandan-Hidatsa Myths and Ceremonies

Masked Gods: Navaho and
Pueblo Ceremonialism

Minnetonka Story

Myths and Hunting Stories of the Mandan
and Hidatsa Sioux

Myth of Hiawatha, and Other Oral Legends,
Mythologic and Allegoric, of the North
American Indians

The Mythology of the Bella Coola Indians

Myths and Folktales of the Alabama-Coushatta
Indians

Myths and Legends of the Indian Southwest

Myths and Legends of the Lipan Apache Indians

Myths and Legends of the North American
Indians

Myths and Tales from the San Carlos Apache

Myths and Tales of the Chiricahua Apache
Indians

Myths and Tales of the Jicarilla Apache Indians

Myths and Tales of the White Mountain Apache

Myths of the Modocs: Indian Legends from the
Northwest

Navajo Coyote Tales

Navaho Legends

Navajo Stories of the Long Walk Period

Nehalen Tillamook Tales

Newe Natekwinappeh: Shoshoni Stories and
Dictionary

Nez Perce Texts

North Carolina Indian Legends and Myths

Ojibwa Indian Legends

Ojibway Heritage

Omaha Indian Myths and Trickster Tales

Origin Legend of the Navajo Enemy Way

Origin Legend of the Navajo Flintway

The Origin of Table Manners

Pawnee Hero, Stories and Folktales
with Notes on the Origin, Customs
and Character of the Pawnee People

Plains Cree Texts

Plains Indian Mythology

The Pollen Path: A Collection
of Navajo Myths

The Portable North American Indian Reader

Prairie Smoke

The Red Swan: Myths and Tales
of the American Indians

The Sacred Path: Spells, Prayers and
Power Songs of the American Indian

Sacred Stories of the Sweet Grass Cree

Saynday's People: The Kiowa Indians
and the Stories They Told

The She-Wolf of Tsla-A-Wat:
Indian Stories from British Columbia

The Sky Is My Tipi

Spider Woman Stories: Legends
of the Hopi Indians

Spirit Mountain: An Anthology
of Yuman Story and Song

Star Woman and Other Shawnee Tales

Schoolcraft's Indian Legends
from Algic Researches

The Silver Arrow and Other Indian
Romances of the Dune Country

Stories from the Indian Wigwams
and Northern Campfires

Tales from the Igloo

Tales from the Smokehouse

Tales of the Big Bend

Tales of Kankakee Land

Tales of the North American Indian

Tales of the Okanogans

Taos Tales

The Ten Grandmothers

Tewa Tales

Thirty Indian Legends of Canada

Tlingit Tales: Potlatch and Totem Poles

Totem Tales

Totem Tales of Old Seattle

Traditions of the Caddo

Traditions of the Quinault Indians

The Unwritten Literature of the Hopi

Volcano Tales Indian Legends of the Cascade
Mountains

The Way to Rainy Mountain

Where Is the Eagle?

The White Canoe and Other Legends
of the Ojibways

Why Gone Those Times? Blackfoot Tales

Why the North Star Stands Still

Wigwam Stories

Wisconsin Chippewa Muths and Tales
of Their Relation to Chippewa Life

Zuni Folk Tales

Zuni Mythology

Yaqui Myths and Legends

Yuchi Tales

LEGENDS, JUVENILE
LITERATURE

*And It Is Still That Way

*Animal People

*Anpao: An American Indian Odyssey

*At the Center of the World

*A Bag of Bones

*The Cherokee Tale-Teller

*Cheyenne Legends of Creation

*Cheyenne Short Stories

*Coyote and Kootenai

*Coyote Stories

*Creation Tales from the Salish

*Fire Plume: Legends of the American Indian

*How the Dogs Saved the Cheyennes

*The Hunter and the Ravens

*In the Beginning

*In Our Hogan: Adventure Stories
of Navajo Children

*Indian Folk Tales from Coast to Coast

*Indian Legends of the Pacific Northwest

*Indian Songs and Legends

*Indian Tales of the Northern Plains

*Issiwin: Boxelder and His Sacred Lance

*Lodge Stories

*Monster Rolling Skull and Other Native
American Tales

*Navaho Stories

*Nightwalker and the Buffalo

*Legends of Chief Bald Eagle

*Once More Upon a Totem

*Ox'Zem: Boxelder and His Sacred Lance

*Pachee Goyo: History and Legends
from the Shoshone

Pima India Legends

*Prairie Legends

*Pueblo Stories

*The Ring on Woot-Kew's Tail: Indian Legends
of the Origin of the Sun, Moon and Stars

*The Rolling Head: Cheyenne Tales

*Salish Folk Tales

*Sequoyah and His Miracle

*Sitting on the Blue-Eyed Bear:
Navajo Myths and Legends

*Skunny Wundy Seneca Indian Tales

*Sky Man on the Totem Pole

*Stolen Princess: A Northwest Indian Legend

*Stories California Indians Told

*The Tale of the Possum

*Tales from the Bitterfoot Valley

*The Talking Stone: An Anthology of
Native American Tales and Legends

*Talking Totem Pole

*Tepee Stories

*Tepee Tales of the American Indian

*Tonweya and the Eagles and Other
Lakota Indian Tales

*The White Doe: The Fate of Virginia Dare,
An Indian Legend

*Wigwam Stories

*Winter Telling Stories

LEWIS AND CLARK EXPEDITION

Lewis and Clark Among the Indians

How George Rogers Clark Won the West

*Lewis and Clark

The Lewis and Clark Expedition

Those Tremendous Mountains: The Story of
the Lewis and Clark Expedition

The Trail of Lewis and Clark: 1804-1904

MAGIC

Navaho Witchcraft

Paiute Sorcery

Role of Conjuring in Saultean Society

Run Toward the Nightland: Magic of the
Oklahoma Cherokees

Sacred Bundles of the Sac and Fox Indians

Witchcraft in the Southwest: Spanish and
Indian Supernaturalism on the Rio Grande

THE MAKAH INDIANS

The Makah Indians

Makah Indians: Anthropological Investigation
Relative to Tribal Identity and Aboriginal
Possession of Lands

Makah Indians of Western Washington

The Makah-Quileute Tribal Boundary

MANDAN AND HIDATSA INDIANS

Agriculture of the Hidatsa Indians

Ethnography and Philology of the
Hidatsa Indians

Grammar and Dictionary of the Languages
of the Hidatsa

Hidatsa Eagle Trapping

The Hidatsa Earthlodge

Hidatsa Shrine and the Beliefs Respecting It

The Horse and the Dog in Hidatsa Culture

Mandan and Hidatsa Music

Mandan-Hidatsa Myths and Ceremonies

Mandans, A Study of Their Culture,
Archaeology and Language

Myths and Hunting Stories of the Mandan
and Hidatsa Sioux

O-Kee-Pa: A Religious Ceremony and Other
Customs of the Mandans

The Village Indians of the Upper Missouri:
The Mandans, Hidatsas and Arikaras

MASKS

Head and Face Masks in Navaho
Ceremonialism

Masks, Labrets, and Certain
Aboriginal Customs

Mexican Masks

*North American Indian Masks

Portrait Masks of the Northwest
American Coast

The Power of Symbols: Masks and
Masquerade in the Americas

The Relation of Seneca and Seneca False Face
Masks to Seneca and Ontario Archaeology

*They Put on Masks

A World of Faces: Masks of the Northwest
Coast Indians

MEDICINE MAN

The Medicine Man of the American Indian
and His Cultural Background

The Medicine Man of the Apache

The Medicine-Man: A Sociological Study of
the Character and Evolution of Shamanism

Medicine Woman

Navajo Medicine Man Sandpaintings

Pretty Shield, Medicine Woman of the Crows

Rolling Thunder: A personal Exploration Into
the Secret Healing Power of an American
Indian Medicine Man

Sanapia: Comanche Medicine Woman

MENOMINEE INDIANS

Dreamers With Power: The Menominee

Ethnobotany of the Menomini Indians

Folklore of the Menomini Indians

Menominee Drums: Tribal Termination
and Restoration, 1854-1974

Menominee Indians: A History

Menomini Indians of Wisconsin

Menomini Lexicon

Menominee Music

Menomini Texts

Menomini Women and Cultural Change

MISSIONS

Alabado, A Story of Old California

American Indian Policy in Crisis: Christian Reformers and the Indian, 1865-1900

American Indians and Christian Missions: Studies in Cultural Conflict

Annals of Shawnee Methodist Mission and Indian Manual Labor School

Bruchko

Cherokee Messenger: A Life of Samuel Austin Worcester

Cherokees and Missionaries, 1789-1839

Christian Leadership in Indian America

Churchmen and the Western Indians, 1820-1920

Detailed Report on the Salburger Emigrants Who Settled in America

An Early Indian Mission

The Four Churches of Pecos

Great Black Robe

Historical Memoirs, Relating to the Housatonic Indians

History of Baptist Indian Missions

History of the Catholic Missions Among the Indian Tribes of the U.S., 1529-1854

History of Indian Missions on the Pacific Coast

History of the Mission of the United Brethren Among the Indians in North America

History of Texas, 1673-1779

Index to the Records of the Moravian Mission Among the Indians of North America

*The Indian and the California Mission

The Indian in American Life

Indian and Jesuit: A 17th Century Encounter

Indian Life at the Old Missions

Indian Missions: A Critical Bibliogrphy

An Inventory of the Mission Indian Agency Records

Jesuits and the Indian Wars of the Northwest

Journal of the Southern Indian Mission: Diary of Thomas D. Brown

Journal of a Two Months Tour, With a View to Promoting Religion

Kino's Historical Memoir of Primeria Alta

Augustine Laure, S.J., Missionary to the Yakimas

The Letters of Jacob Baegert, 1749-1761: Jesuit Missionary in Baja California

Letters of Eleazar Wheelock's Indians

Mary and I: Forty Years With the Sioux

Masinaigans: The Little Book

Memoirs of the Reverend David Brainard: Missionary to the Indians on the Border of New York, New Jersey and Pennsylvania

Metlakatla: Mission to Tsimshian Indians

Mission Amon the Blackfeet

Mission San Xavier Del Bac: A Photographic Essay on the Desert People and Their Church

*Mission Tales: Stories of the Historic California Missions

Missionaries, Miners, and Indians: Spanish Contact With the Yaqui Nation of Northwestern New Spain, 1533-1820

Missions and Pueblos of the Old Southwest

The New England Company

Old Frontiers: The Story of the Cherokee Indians From the Earliest Times to the Date of Their Removal to the West, 1838

People of the Center: American Indian Religions and Christianity

Rain on the Desert

Recollections of the Flathead Mission

Red Man in the U.S.

Reminiscence of the Indians

The Salsbury Story: A Medical Missionary's Lifetime of Public Service

Salvation and the Savage: An Analysis of Protestant Missions and American Indian Response, 1787-1862

Sketches of Mission Life Among the Indians of Oregon

Teepee Neighbors

Western Missions and Missionaries

Wilderness Christians: The Moravian Mission to the Delaware Indians

MODOC INDIANS

Ancient Modocs of California and Oregon

Burnt-Out Fires: California's Modoc Indian War

Captain Jack, Modoc Renegade

Copper Paladin: The Modoc Tragedy

The Indian History of the Modoc War

Klamath and Modoc Tribes and Yoahooskin Band of Snake Indians

Life Among the Modocs: Unwritten History

Modocs and Their War

Myths of the Modocs: Indian Legends from the Northwest

MOHAVE INDIANS

The Mojaves: Historic Indians
  of San Bernardino Indians
Mohave Ethnopsychiatry and Suicide
Mohave Indians
Mohave Indians: Appraisal of Lands
The Mohave Tribe in Arizona
Mohave Tribe of Indian of Arizona,
  California and Nevada
Mohave Tribe: Report on Aboriginal
  Territory and Occupancy
Reopening the Mojave Road
Tales from the Mohaves
Topics in Mojave Syntax

MOHAWK INDIANS

Faithful Mohawks
A Grammar of Akwesasne Mohawk
Johnson of the Mohawks
Mohawk Directory
Mohawk Indians and Their Valley
The Mohawk That Refused to Abdicate
A Thousand Words of Mohawk

MOUNDS, MOUND-BUILDERS

Aboriginal Monuments of the State of
  New York
Burial Mounds of the Red River Headwaters
Cahokia Brought to Life
The Cahokia Mound Group
Cahokia Mounds Museum Society Publications
The Cherry Valley Mounds and Mound No. 3
Crooks Site, A Marksville Period Burial
  Mound in the LaSalle Parish, Louisiana
Explorations Into Cahokia Archaeology
Guidebook to Cahokia Mounds
The Hopewell Mound Group of Ohio
Indian City on the Mississippi
Report on the Mound Explorations of
  the Bureau of Ethnology
*Talking Bones: Secrets of Indian
  Mound Builders

MUSIC

American Indian and Eskimo Music: A
  Selected Bibliography Through 1981
*American Indian Music and Musical
Instruments
*American Indian Songs
American Indians and Their Music
Cheyenne and Arapaho Music
Chippewa Music
Choctaw Hymn Book
Choctaw Music
*A Cry from the Earth: Music of
  the North American Indians
Dance and Song Rituals of Six Nations
  Reserve, Ontario
Dance Down the Rain, Sing Up the Corn:
  American Indian Chants and Games
  for Children
Frances Densmore and American Indian Music
Documentation of American Indian Music
  and Musicians
Enemy Way Music: A Study of Social and
  Aesthetic Values As Seen in Navaho Music
Gambling Music of the Coast Salish Indians
Haida Songs and Tsimshian Texts
Havasupai Songs: A Linguistic Perspective
Hopi Songs
In Vain I Tried to Tell You: Essays
  in Native American Ethnopoetics
Indian Games and Dances With Native Songs
*Indian Music Makers
*Indians Music and Musical Instruments
*Indian Songs and Legends
Indian Story and Song From North America
Indians' Book
Introduction to Navaho Chant Practice
Iroquois Music and Dance: Ceremonial Arts
  of Two Seneca Longhouses
Mandan and Hidatsa Music
Menominee Music
Music and Dance of the Tewa Pueblos
Music and Dance Research of the
  Southwestern Indians
Music of Acoma, Isleta, Cochiti
  and Zuni Pueblos
Music of the Indians of British Columbia
Music of the Maidu Indians
The Music of the North American Indian

Native North American Music and
Oral Data: A Catalogue of Sound
Recordings, 1893-1976

Navaho Classification of Their
Song Ceremonials

Nootka and Quileute Music

North American Indian Musical Styles

Northern Ute Music

The Ojibwa Dance Drums: Its History
and Construction

On the Music of the North American Indians

Papago Music

The Path on the Rainbow: An Anthology
of Songs and Chants from the Indians
of North America

Pawnee Music

Peyote Music

Rituals of the Wind: North American Indian
Ceremonies, Music and Dance

The Sacred Path: Spells, Prayers and
Power Songs of the American Indian

Salish Songs and Rituals

Singing for Power: The Song Magic of the
Papago Indians of Southern Arizona

Sioux Music

Songs of the Pacific Northwest

Songs of the Teton Sioux

Songs of the Tewa

Spirit Mountain: An Anthology of Yuman
Story and Song

The Story of Indian Music: Its Growth
and Synthesis

Study of Omaha Indian Music With a Report
of the Structural Peculiarities of the
Music by J.C. Fillmore

Teton Sioux Music

Tsee-Ma'Heone-Nemeototse: Cheyenne
Spiritual Songs

Yuman and Yaqui Music

NAVAJO INDIANS

The Agricultural and Hunting Methods
of the Navaho Indians

An Analysis of Navajo Temporality

Anthropological Report on the Navajo Indians

Apache, Navaho and Spaniard

The Army and the Navajo

*Between Sacred Mountains: Navajo Stories
and Lessons from the Land

Bibliography of the Navaho Indians

Big Bead Mesa: An Archaeological Study of
Navaho Acculturation

Blessingway

Book of the Navajo

Border Towns of the Navajo Nation

Bosque Redondo: A Study of Cultural Stress
at the Navajo Reservation

A Cannoneer in Navajo Country

The Central Concepts of Navajo World View

*Child of the Navajos

Circles, Consciousness and Culture

Contemporary Navajo Affairs

Coyoteway: A Navajo Holyway Healing
Ceremonial

Crow Man's People: Three Seasons
with the Navajo

Denetsosie

The Development of Capitalism in the Navajo
Nation: A Political-Economic History

Dine Bahane', The Navajo Creation Story

The Dine: Origin Myths of the Navaho Indians

Dinetah: Navajo History

The Economics of Sainthood: Religious
Change Among the Rimrock Navajos

The Enduring Navaho

Enemy Way Music

Ethnobotany of the Navajo

Fort Defiance and the Navajos

Garments of Brightness: The Navajo
Weaving Tradition

The Gift of Spiderwoman: Southwestern
Textiles, The Navajo Traditions

Gregorio, The Handtrembler: A Psychobiological Personality Study of
a Navaho Indian

Head and Face Masks in Navaho Ceremonialism

Here Comes the Navajo

Hogans: Navajo Houses and House Songs

Holy Wind in Navajo Philosophy

Hosteen Klah: Navaho Medicine Man and
Sand Painter

If You Take My Sheep...The Evolution and
Conflicts of Navajo Pastoralism, 1630-1868

In the Beginning: The Navaho Creation Myth

*In Our Hogan: Adventure Stories
of Navajo Children

Indian Drinking: Navajo Practices
and Anglo-American Theories

Indian Silver: Navajo and Pueblo Jewelers

Introduction to Navaho Chant Practice

*Philip Johnston and the Navajo Code Talkers

Kinaalada: A Navajo Puberty Ceremony

Language and Art in the Navajo Universe

The Long Walk: A History of the Navajo Wars

A Magic Dwells: A Poetic and Psychological
Study of the Navaho Emergence Myth

The Main Stalk: A Synthesis of Navajo
Philosophy

A Manual of Navaho Grammar

Masked Gods: Navaho and Pueblo
Ceremonialism

Miracle Hill: The Story of a Navaho Boy

Mother Earth, Father Sky, and Economic
Development: Navajo Resoures and Their Use

Mother Earth, Father Sky: Pueblo and Navajo
Indians of the Southwest

The Mountainway of the Navajo

Mythology and Values: An Analysis
of Navaho Chantway Myths

*The Native Americans: Navajos

The Navaho

Navajo Activities Affecting the Acoma-
Laguna Area, 1746-1910

Navajo Architecture

Navaho Art and Culture

Navajo Biographies

Navajo Blessingway Singer

A Navajo Bringing-Home Ceremony

Navajo Changes: A History of
the Navajo People

*Navajo Children

Navaho Classification of
Their Song Ceremonials

The Navajo Code Talkers

Navajo Color Book

Navajo Creation Myth: The
Story of Emergence

Navajo Cultural Guides, Experience
Stories, and Cultural Readers

The Navajo Design Book

Navajo Education, 1948-1978:
Its Progress and Problems

Navajo Energy Resources

The Navaho (Or Corral) Fire Dance

Navaho Grammar

Navajo Foreign Affairs: 1795-1846

*The Navajo: Herders, Weavers
and Silversmiths

The Navajo and His Blanket

Navajo History

Navajo and Hopi Weaving Techniques

The Navajo Hunter Tradition

The Navajo Indian Book

Navajo Indian Medical Ethnobotany

The Navajo Indians

Navajo Indians

The Navajo Indians: An Anthropological Study

The Navajo Indians in New Mexico, to 1870

Navajo Infancy: An Ethological Study
of Child Development

Navajo Kinship and Marriage

Navaho Legends

Navajo Livestock Reduction:
A National Disgrace

*Navajo Long Walk

Navaho Material Culture

Navajo Medicien Man Sand Paintings

The Navajo Mountain Community

Navajo Mountain and Rainbow Bridge Religion

The Navajo Nation

Navajo Native Dyes

Navaho Neighbors

Navajo Oral Traditions

Navajo Oral History and Traditions

Navajo Police

Navaho Pottery Making

Navaho Religion: A Study of Symbolism

Navajo Resources and Economic Development

Navajo Sandpainting Art

Navajo Sandpainting from Religious
Act to Commercial Art

Navajo Shepherd and Weaver

*Navajo Slave

*Navaho Stories

Navajo Stories of the Long Walk Period

Navaho Symbols of Healing

Navajo Techniques for Today's Weaver

Navaho Territory and Its Boundaries
in Arizona, Colorado and New Mexico

Navajo Textiles from the Red Mulan
Collection

Navajo Texts

The Navajo Treaty, 1868

*Navajo Victory-Being a Native American

Navajo Weavers

Navajo Weavers and Silversmiths

Navajo Weaving Handbook

A Navaho Weaving, Its Technic and History

Navajo Weaving: Three Centuries of Change

Navaho Witchcraft

The Navajos

The Navajos Are Coming to Jesus

Navajos Call It Hard Goods

Navahos Have Five Fingers

Navajos in the Catholic Church Records

The Navajos Long Walk for Education

The Navajos and the New Deal

Navajos and World War II

The Night Chant: A Navaho Ceremonial

Of Mother Earth and Father Sky

Old Mexican, Navaho Indian: A Navaho
  Autobiography

Old Navajo Rugs: Their Development
  from 1900 to 1940

Origin Legend of the Navajo Enemy Way

Origin Legend of the Navajo Flintway

Our Friends: The Navajos

Patterns and Sources of Navajo Weaving

Pictorial History of the Navajo
  from 1860-1910

*Pieces of White Shell: A Journey
  to Navajoland

A Political History of the Navajo Tribe

The Pollen Path: A Collection
  of Navajo Myths

Posts and Rugs

Prehistory in the Navajo Reservoir District

Property Concepts of the Navaho Indians

Red Capitalism: An Analysis of the
  Navajo Economy

Reflections of Social Life in the
  Navaho Origin Myth

The Roots of Dependency: Subsistence,
  Environment and Social Change Among
  the Choctaws, Pawnees and Navajos

Saad Ahaah Sinil: Dual Language

The Sacred Mountains of the Navajo

Sacred Words: A Study of Navajo Religion
  and Prayer

Sandpaintings of the Navajo Shooting Chant

Sex Beliefs and Practices in a Navaho
  Community

Shonto: Study of the Role of the Trader
  in a Modern Navajo Community

*Sitting on the Blue-Eyed Bear

Social Life of the Navajo Indians

Son of Old Man Hat

The South Corner of Time

Spider Woman

Stories of Traditional Navajo
  Life and Culture

Study of Navajo Symbolism

Three Navaho Households

Through Navajo Eyes

To Run After Them: Cultural and Social Bases
  of Cooperation in a Navajo Community

Traders to the Navajos

Turquoise and the Navajo

Visual Metaphors: A Formal Analysis
  of Navajo Art

A Voice in Her Tribe: A Navajo Woman's
  Own Story

Voices in the Canyon

Walk in Beauty: The Navajo and
  Their Blankets

Weaving a Navajo Blanket

When Navajos Had Too Many Sheep:
  The 1940's

The Windways of the Navaho

With a Camera in Old Navaholand

Yazz: Navajo Painter

NEZ PERCE INDIANS

Aboriginal Territory of the Nez Perce
  Indians

Chief Joseph Country; Land of the Nez Perce

*Chief Joseph of the Nez Perce

*Chief Joseph's Own Story as Told
  by Chief Joseph in 1879

Chief Lawyer of the Nez Perce Indian,
  1796-1876

Conflict and Schism in Nez Perce
  Acculturation

The Flight of the Nez Perce

Forlorn Hope

Hear Me My Chiefs: Nez Perce Legend
  and History

Howard's Campaign Against the Nez Perce
  Indians, 1878

I Will Fight No More Forever: Chief
  Joseph and the Nez Perce War

The Joseph Band of Nez Perce Indians,
  1805-1905

*Joseph, Chief of the Nez Perce

Nez Perce Ceded Tract, Oregon,
Washington and Idaho, 1867

Nez Perce Grammar

Nez Perce Indian Reservation

Nez Perce Indians

The Nez Perce Indians and the Opening
of the Northwest

Nez Perce Joseph

Nez Perce Reservation

Nez Perce Reservation Land

Nez Perce Texts

Nez Perce Tribe Lands in Northern
Idaho, 1894

Nez Perce Tribe of Indians

Nez Perces: Tribesmen of the
Columbia Plateau

Red Eagles of the Northwest: The Story
of Chief Joseph and His People

With the Nez Perces: Alice Fletcher
in the Field, 1889-1992

OJIBWA INDIANS

Clothed-in-Fur and Other Tales: An
Introduction to an Ojibwa World View

History of the Ojibwa Indians

Ojibwa Crafts

The Ojibwa Dance Drums

Ojibwa Indian Legends

Ojibwa Sociology

Ojibwa Texts

Ojibwa Woman

The Ojibwas: A Critical Bibliography

Ojibway Heritage

Sacred Scrolls of the Southern Ojibway

Traditional Ojibwa Religion and Its
Historical Changes

The White Canoe and Other Legends
of the Ojibways

OMAHA INDIANS

Omaha Indian Myths and Trickster Tales

Omaha Indians

Omaha Secret Societies

Omaha Sociology

Omaha Tribe

Study of Omaha Indian Music

ORIGIN

Discoveries of the Truth

The First Americans

My Horse and a Jukebox

New Views of the Origin of the Tribes
and Nations of America

Roots of the American Indian

OSAGE INDIANS

Bibliography of the Osage

A Dictionary of the Osage Language

The Imperial Osages

Osage Anthropological Report

Osage Ceded Lands

The Osage Indian Tribe

Osage Indian Village Sites and Hunting
Territory in Kansas, Missouri and Oklahoma

Osage Indians

Osage Indians: Anthropological Study

Osage Indians: Bands and Clans

The Osage Nation in Eastern Oklahoma
and Northwest Arkansas, 1775-1818

Osage Nation: Investigation of Lands

Osage Nation Land Cession in Missouri
and Arkansas, 1810

Osage Tribal Council, 1810

Osages: Children of the Middle Waters

Tixier's Travels on the Osage Prairies

Traditions of the Osage

Wah-Kon-Tah: The Osage and the White
Man's Road

Years With the Osage

PAIUTE INDIANS

Life Among the Paiutes

Life Is With Poeple

Northern Paiute Indians

The Northern Paiute Indians of California

Northern Paiute Nation

Paiute Archaeology in Nevada and California

Paiute Indian Lands in California and Nevada

Paiute Indians

Paiute Sorcery

Paviotso-Mono Tracts of the Northern
Paiute Nation

The Rancheria, Ute and Southern
  Paiute Peoples

Snake-Paiute Tract in Oregon

Southern Paiute

Southern Paiute and Chemehuevi

Southern Paiute Ethnography

Southern Paiute Ethnohistory

Southern paiute Ethnology

Survival Arts of the Primitive Paiutes

Sarah Winnemucca of the Northern Paiutes

PAPAGO AND PIMA INDIANS

Appraisal of the Papago Tribe of
  Arizona, 1916

Autobiography of a Papago Woman

Basketry of the Papago and Pima Indians

By the Prophet of the Earth: Ethnobotany
  of the Pima

A Comparative Racial Study of the Papago

The Desert People: A Study of the Papago
  Indians

The Desert Smells Like Rain

The Ethnobiology of the Papago Indians

The Gila River Indian Reservation

Gila River Reservation

The Hispanic Acculturation of the
  Gila River Pimas

Legends and Lore of the Papago and
  Pima Indians

New Trails in Mexico: Travels Among
  the Papago, Pima and Cocopa Indians

A Papago Calendar Record

Pima Indian Legends

Papago Indian Religion

Papago Indians

Papago Indians at Work

Papago Indians in Arizona

The Papago Indians of Arizona and
  Their Relatives the Pima

Papago Music

The Papago and Pima Indians of Arizona

Papago Population Study

Papago Tract, Arizona

The Papago Tribe of Arizona

The Pima Indians

Pima-Maricopa Indians

Pima and Papago Indian Agriculture

Pima and Papago Ritual Oratory

A Pima Past

A Pima Remembers

Piman Shamanism and Staying Sickness

Rainhouse and Ocean: Speeches
  for the Papago Year

Singing for Power: The Song Magic of the
  Papago Indians of Southern Arizona

Social Organization of the Papagp Indians

The South Corner of Time

When It Rains: Papago and Pima Poetry

PAWNEE INDIANS

Description of a Journey and Visit
  to the Pawnee Indians

The Dubar-Allis Letters on the Pawnee

Expedition to the Pawnee Pict
  Village in 1834

The Lost Universe: Pawnee Life
  and Culture

Frank J. North: Pawnee Scout,
  Commander and Pioneer

Notes on the Skidi Pawnee Society

Pawnee Hero Stories and Folktales

The Pawnee

The Pawnee in Oklahoma

The Pawnee Indians

Pawnee and Kansa (Kaw) Indians

Pawnee and Lower Loup Pottary

Pawnee Tracts in Nebraska and in Kansas

Pawnees: A Critical Bibliography

The Roots of Dependency

Traditions of the Skidi Pawnee

Travels in North America, Including
  a Summer with the Pawnees

PERIODICALS

American Indian

American Indian and Alaska Native Newspapers
  and Periodicals, 1826-1924

American Indian Periodicals in the Princeton
  University Library: Guide to the Collection

Schoolcraft: Literary Voyager

PEYOTE, PEYOTISM

The Peyote Cult

Peyote: The Divine Cactus

Peyote Hunt: The Sacred Journey
of Huichol Indians

Peyote Music

The Peyote Religion

Peyotism in the West: A Historical
and Cultural Perspective

Ute Peyotism: A Study of a Cultural Complex

Washo Shaman and Peyotists: Religious
Conflict in an American Indian Tribe

PHILOSOPHY

An American Urphilosophie: An American
Philosophy-BP (Before Pragmatism)

The Central Concepts of Navajo World View

Classification and Development of North
American Indian Cultures: A Statistical
Analysis of the Driver-Massey Sample

Holy Wind in Navajo Philosophy

The Indian Testimony

Indian Thoughts: The Children of God

The Main Stalk: A Synthesis of
Navajo Philosophy

Spanda-Karikas: The Divine Creative Impulse

Teaching of Nature

Teachings from the American Earth:
Indian Religion and Philosophy

PICTURE-WRITING

*Indian Picture Writing

Picture-Writing of the American Indians

PICTURES, PHOTOGRAPHS
AND PORTRAITS

American Indians—Photographic Notecards

*Among the Plains Indians

Association on American Indian Affairs:
Appointment Calendar

O.E. Berninghaus - Taos, New Mexico:
Master Painter of American Indians
and Frontier West

The Big Missouri Winter Count

Buffalo Bill and the Wild West

Catlin Collection of Indian Paintings

Catlin's North American Indian Portfolio

Children of the First People:
A Photographic Essay

Michael Coleman

Crying for a Vision: Rosebud Sioux Trilogy,
1886-1976

*Edward S. Curtis: Photographer of
the North American Indian

Curtis' Western Indians: Life and Works
of Edward C. Curtis

De Grazia Paints Cabeza de Vaca: The First
Non-Indian in Texas, New Mexico and
Arizona, 1527-1536

German Artist on the Texas Frontier:
Friedrich Richard Petri

Honor Dance: Native American Photographs

Hopi Photographers—Hopi Images

Hopis: Portrait of a Desert People

The Horsemen of the Americas: An
Exhibition from the Hall of the
Horsemen of the Americas

In a Sacred Manner We Live

Indian Portraits of the Pacific Northwest

Indians: The Camera Reveals the Reality of
North American Indian Life: 1847-1929

Indians: Great Photographs that Reveal
North American Indian Life, 1847-1929,
from the Unique Collection of the
Smithsonian Institution

New Indian Sketches

North American Indians Coloring Album

The North American Indians: Photographs by
Edward S. Curtis

Pictographic History of the Oglala Sioux

A Pictorial History of the American Indian

Picture-Writing of the American Indians

Plains Indian Raiders: The Final Phases of
Warfare from the Arkansas to the Red River

Portraits from North American Indian Life

*Red Man in Art

Remington's Frontier Sketches

The Reservation Blackfeet, 1885-1945: A
Photographic History of Cultural Survival

*Sharing Our Worlds

Sketches of American Indian Tribes: 1841-1843

The Vanishing Race and Other Illusions:
Photographs of Indians by Edward S. Curtis

When the Earth Was Young

With Eagle Glance: American Indian
Photographic Images, 1868-1931

PLACE NAMES

Florida Place-Names of Indian Origin
and Seminole Personal Names

Geographical Names of the Kwakiutl Indians

Indian Place Names in Alabama

Indian Names in Connecticut

Indian Place Names in Illinois

Indian Place Names of New England

Indian Place-Names: Their Origin, Evolution
and Meaning, Collected in Kansas from the
Siouan, Algonquian, Shoshonean, Caddoan,
Iroquoian, and Other Tongues

Spanish and Indian Place Names of California:
Their Meaning and Their Romance

A Study in the Etymology of the Indian
Place Name

POETRY

American Indian Speaks: Poetry, Fiction
and Art by the American Indian

Arrows Four: prose and Poetry by Young
American Indians

Autobiography of a Yaqui Poet

Elderberry Flute Songs

From the Center: A Folio of Native
American Art and Poetry

The Good Message of Handsome Lake

A Magic Dwells: A Poetic and Psychological
Study of the Navaho Emergence Myth

The South Corner of Time: Hopi, Navajo,
Papago, Yaqui Tribal Literature

Thunder-Root: Traditional and Contemporary
Native American Verse

When It Rains: Papago and Pima Poetry

PONCA INDIANS

The Ponca Chiefs

Ponca Indians

Ponca Indians: Appraisal of Land

The Ponca Indians With Reference to
Their Claim to Certain Lands

Ponca Reservation, 1877

POTAWATOMI INDIANS

Chippewa, Ottawa and Potawatomi Lands
in Illinois and Wisconsin

Ethnobotany of the Forst Potawatomi Indians

Indian of Illinois and Indiana: Illinois,
Kickapoo and Potawatomi Indians

Kickapoo, Illinois and Potawatomi Indians:
Anthropological Reports

Mascoutens of Prairie Potawatomi Indians

Potawatomi Ceded Lands and an Indian
History of Northeastern Illinois

Potawatomi Kansas Cession

Potawatomi Lands in the Indian
Territory, 1890

Potawatomi Lands in Iowa and Kansas

Potawatomi Tracts in Iowa and Kansas, 1846

Potawtomi Tribe of Indians

Potawatomi Reserve Lands in Kansas

Potawatomi Tribe

The Potawatomis: Keepers of the Fire

United Nations of Chippewa, Ottawa and
Potawatomi Indians

POTLATCH

Haida Potlatch

Tlingit Tales: Potlatch and Totem Poles

POTTERY

American Indian Pottery: An Identification
and Value Guide

Anasazi Painted Pottery in the Field Museum
of Natural History

Caddo Indian Pottery

Ceramic Decoration Sequence at an Old Indian
Village Site Near Siciliy Island, Louisiana

Collecting Shawnee Pottery: A Pictorial
Reference and Price Guide

Contemporary Pueblo Indian Pottery

Designs on Prehistoric Hopi Pottery

Field Manual of Prehistoric Southwest
Pottery Types

Handbook of Northern Arizona Pottery Wares

Historic Pueblo Indian Pottery

Hopi and Hopi-Tewa Pottery

Indian Pottery

Introduction to Hopi Pottery

Kumeyaay Pottery: Paddle-and-Anvil
Techniques of Southern California

Mimbres Painted Pottery

Navaho Pottery Making

Pottery of Ancient Pueblos

Pottery of the Pajarito Plateau and of
Some Adjacent Regions in New Mexico

Pottery Techniques of Native North America:
An Introduction to Traditional Technology

Pueblo Indian Pottery: Materials, Tools
and Techniques

The Pueblo Potter: A Study of Creative
Imagination in Primitive Art

Pueblo Pottery Making: A Study of
the Village of San Ildefonso

Pueblo Pottery of the New Mexico Indians

The Quapaw and Their Pottery, 1650-1750 A.D.

Seven Families in Pueblo Pottery

The Story of Pueblo Pottery

Swarts Ruin: A Typical Mimbres Site in
Southwestern New Mexico

Within the Underworld Sky: Mimbres Art
in Context

*When Clay Sings

PSYCHOLOGY

Algic Researches: Comprising Inquiries
Respecting the Mental Characteristics
of the North American Indians

American Indian and White Children:
A Sociopsychological Investigation

Bibliography of North American Indian
Mental Health

Gregorio, the Handtrembler: A Psychobiological Personality Study of a
Navaho Indian

Indian Students and Guidance

The Modal Personality Structure of the
Tuscarora Indians

Mohave Ethnopsychiatry and Suicide: The
Psychiatric Knowledge and the Psychic
Disturbances of an Indian Tribe

Modern Indian Psychology

The Pattern of Amerindian Identity:
Proceedings

Psychosocial Research on American Indian
and Alaska Native Youth: An Indexed
Guide to Recent Dissertations

Reality and Dream: Psychotherapy
of a Plains Indian

Warriors Without Weapons: A Study of the
Society and Personality Development
of the Pine Ridge Sioux

PUEBLO INDIANS

Acoma

Acoma Grammar and Texts

The Acoma Indians

Acoma Indians of New Mexico

Acoma-Laguna Land Claims

Acoma Land Utilization

Acoma Pueblo Land, New Mexico

Broken K Pueblo

Cochiti: New Mexico Pueblo,
Past and Present

Chronology of the Pueblo de La Ysleta del
Sur in Colorado, New Mexico and Texas

Contemporary Pueblo Indian Pottery

Dances of the Tewa Pueblo Indians

Desert Drums: The Pueblo Indians,
New Mexico

Ethnobotany of the Tewa Indians

Excavation of Main Pueblo at
Fitzmaurice Ruin

A Few Summer Ceremonials at Zuni Pueblo

General View of the Archaeology of the
Pueblo Region

Hano: A Tewa Indian Commuity in Arizona

Historic Pueblo Indian Pottery

Historical Introduction to Studies Among
the Sedentary Indians of New Mexico

The Idea of Fertilization in the Culture
of the Pueblo Indians

Indian Silver: Navajo and Pueblo Jewelers

Indian Stories from the Pueblos

Indians of Pecos Pueblos

Indians of the Terraced Houses

Keresian Bridge: A Problem in
Pueblo Ethnology

The Laguna Calendar

Laguna Land Utilization

Laguna Pueblo Land Claims, 1598-1935

Laguna Pueblo Land Claims: Anthropology

Laguna Pueblo Land in New Mexico

Life Against the Land: A Short History
of Pueblo Indians

Los Angeles from the Days of the Pueblo

The Man Who Married the Moon and Other
Pueblo Indian Folk-Stories

Masked Gods: Navaho and Pueblo
Ceremonialism

Zuni Kin and Clan

Zuni Mythology

Zuni: Selected Writings of Frank
  Hamilton Cushing

Zuni Texts

The Zunis of Cibola

RELIGION AND MYTHOLOGY

American Indian Mythology

The Arrow and the Cross

Blessingway

Book of the Gods and Rites and
  the Ancient Calendar

A Book of Tales, Being Myths of
  the North American Indians

A Cherokee Prayerbook

American Indian Religions

Analysis of Coeur D'Alene Indian Myths

The Cherokee Ghost Dance

Cherokee Vision of Eloh'

Chinigchinix, An Indigenous California
  Indian Religion

Christian Indians and Indian Nationalism,
  1855-1950

Concept of the Guardian Spirit
  in North America

Creek (Muskogee) New Testiment Concordance

The Creek Verb

The Death of the Great Spirit

A Documentary History of Religion in America

The Dine: Origin Myths of the Navaho Indians

The Economics of Sainthood: Religious Change
  Among the Rimrock Navajos

Elementary Forms of the Religious Life

A Few Summer Ceremonials at the Tusayon
  Pueblos: Natal Ceremonies of the
  Hopi Indians

Flight of the Seventh Moon: The Teaching
  of the Shields

Ghost Dance

Ghost Dance Messiah: The Jack Wilson Story

Ghost-Dance Religion and the Sioux Outbreak
  of 1890

*Guardian Spirit Quest

He Who Hunted in His Father's Village:
  The Dimensions of a Haida Myth

Hopi Dream

Hopi Kachina Dolls With a Key to
  Their Identification

Hopi Kachinas

Hopi and Zuni Ceremonialism

The Idea of Fertilization in the Culture
  of the Pueblo Indians

In the Beginning: The Navaho Creation Myth

Indian Myths

Indian Shakers: A Messianic Cult of the
  Pacific Northwest

Iroquoian Cosmology

Kawaiisu Mythology: An Oral Tradition
  of South-Central California

Kwakiutl Culture as Reflected in Mythology

Lakota Belief and Ritual

Lakota Myth

Literary Aspects of North American Mythology

Living the Sky: The Cosmos of the American
  Indian

Love-Magic and Butterfly People: The Slim
  Curly Version of the Ajjee and Mothway Myths

Medicine Talk: A Guide to Walking in Balance
  and Surviving on the Earth Mother

Meditation With Native Americans:
  Lakota Spirituality

The Montana Cree: A Study in Religious
  Persistence

The Mouth of Heaven: An Introduction
  to Kwakiutl Religious Thought

The Myth and Prayers of the Great Star
  Chant and the Myth of the Coyote Chant

Mythological Tales and the Allegany Seneca

Mythology of the Blackfoot Indians

Mythology and Values: An Analysis
  of Navaho Chantway Myths

Myths of the Cherokees and Sacred
  Formulas of the Cherokees

Myths of Idaho Indians

Myths of the New World Indians

Myths of the New World: A Treatise
  on the Symbolism and Mythology of
  the Red Race of America

Myths and Tales of the Southeastern Indians

The Naked Man

Native North American Spirituality of the
  Eastern Woodlands

A Navaho Bringing-Home Ceremony: The Claus
  Chee Sonny Version of Deerway Ajilee

Navajo Creation MythL The Story of Emergence

Navajo Mountain and Rainbow Bridge Religion

Navaho Religion: A Study of Symbolism

The Navajos Are Coming to Jesus

North American Mythology

The Northern Algonquian Supreme Being

Not For Innocent Ears: Spiritual Traditions of a Desert Cahuilla Medicine Woman

Oglala Religion

O-Kee-Pa: A Religious Ceremony and Other Customs of the Mandans

Old Indian Temples, Idols and Worship

The Old North Trail: Or, Life, Legends and Religion of the Blackfeet Indians

Papago Indian Religion

The Peyote Cult

Peyote Hunt: The Sacred Journey of Huichol Indians

The Phoenix of the Western World: Quetzalcoatl and the Sky Religion

Plains Indian Mythology

The Pollen Path: A Collection of Navajo Myths

A Pueblo God and Myths

Rainhouse and Ocean: Speeches for the Papago Year

Red Man's Religion: Beliefs and Practices of the Indians of North of Mexico

Reflections of Social Life in the Navaho Origin Myth

Religion and Ceremonies of the Lenape

The Religion of the Crow Indians

Religion of the Kwakiutl Indians

The Religions of the American Indians

The Sacred Mountains of the Navajo

Sacred Scrolls of the Southern Ojibway

Sacred Stories of the Sweet Grass Cree

The Sacred: Ways of Knowledge, Sources of Life

Sacred Words: A Study of Navajo Religion and Prayer

Scalp Ceremonial of Zuni

Seeing With the Native Eye: Contributions to the Study of Native American Religion

The Soul of the Indian: An Interpretation

Spirits of the Sacred Mountains: Creation Stories of the American Indian

Spiritual Legacy of the American Indian

The Study of American Indian Religions

The Sun Dance Religion: Power for the Powerless

Sun Men of the Americas

Tah-Koo Wah-Kan: Or, The Gospel Among the Dakotas

Teachings from the American Earth: Indian Religion and Philosophy

Tlingit Myths and Texts

Traditional Ojibwa Religion and Its Historical Changes

Trickster: Study in American Indian Mythology

Voices of Earth and Sky

*Warriors of the Rainbow: Strange and Prophetic Dreams of the Indian Peoples

Washo Shamans and Peyotists: Religious Conflict in an American Indian Tribe

Waterway

Yurok Myths

Zuni Fetishes

RITES AND CEREMONIES

Book of the Gods and Rites and the Ancient Calendar

Chants of the Hokapat Clan

Coyoteway: A Navajo Holyway Healing Ceremonial

Dancing Gods: Indian Ceremonials of New Mexico and Arizona

DeGrazia: paints the Yaqui Easter

Dramatic Elements in American Indian Ceremonials

The Dream Helper in South-Central California

The Eye of the Flute: Chumash Traditional History and Ritual

Four Days ina Medicine Lodge

A Grammar Discovery Procedure for the Study of a Dakota Healing Ritual

*Guardian Spirit Quest

Head and Face Masks in Navaho Ceremonialism

Hogans: Navajo Houses and House Songs

I Send a Voice

Iroquois Ceremonial of Midwinter

An Iroquois Sourcebook: Medicine Society Rituals

Kinaalada: A Navajo Puberty Ceremony

*Kiowa Voices: Ceremonial Dance, Ritual and Songs

Love-Magic and Butterfly People: The Slim Curly Version of the Ajjee and Mothway Myths

Medicine Cermony of the Menomini, Iowa and Wahpeton Dakota

The Mountainway of the Navaho

Native North American Spirituality
of the Eastern Woodlands

A Navajo Bringing-Home Ceremony

Navajo Mountain and Rainbow Bridge Religion

The Night Chant: A Navaho Ceremonial

Oklahoma Delaware Ceremonies,
Feasts and Dances

On the Gleaming Way

Oraibi Soyal Ceremony and Oraibi Powamu
Ceremony, and Mishongnovi Ceremonies of
the Snake and Antelope Fraternities and
Oraibi Summer Snake Ceremony

Oraibu Marau Ceremony

Rainhouse and Ocean: Speeches
for the Papago Year

Religion and Ceremonies of the Lenape

Ritual of the Wind: North American Indian
Ceremonies, Music and Dance

Road of Life and Death

Rolling Thunder: A personal Explortion
Into the Secret Healing Power of an
Amerian Indian Medicine Man

The Sacred Pipe: Black Elk's Account
of the Seven Rites of Oglala Sioux

Sandpaintings of the Navajo Shooting Chant

Scalp Ceremonials of Zuni

Seneca Thanksgiving Rituals

The Serpent Symbol, and the Worship of the
Reciprocal Principles of Nature in America

The Snake Ceremonials at Walpi

Social Organization and Ritualistic
Ceremonies of the Blackfoot Indians

Southwestern Indian Ceremonials

A Study of the Delaware Indian Big House
Ceremony

The Sun Dance and Other Ceremonies of the
Oglala Division of the Teton Dakota

*Ways of the Lushootsed People:
Ceremonies and Traditions of the
Northern Puget Sound Indians

World's Rim: Great Mysteries of the
North American Indians

A Yaqui Easter

The Yuchi Green Corn Ceremonial

Yuwipi: Vision and Experience
in Oglala Ritual

ROCK ART—PETROGLYPHS

Ancient Rock Carvings of the Central
Sierra The North Folk Indian Petroglyphs

Archaeolinguistics and Paleoethnography
of Ancient Rock Structures in Western
North America

Canyon de Chelly: Its People and Rock Art

Crystals in the Sky: An Intellectual Odyssey
Involving Chumash Astronomy, Coamology,
and Rock Art

Guide to Indian Rock Carvings of
the Pacific Northwest Coast

Indian Art and History: The Testimony
of Prehistoric Rock Paintings

Indian Petroglyphs of the Pacific Northwest

Indian Rock Art of the Southwest

Indian Rock Paintings of the Great Lakes

Painted Cave, Northeastern Arizona

Petroglyphs of Ohio

The Rocks Begin to Speak

SAC, FOX AND
IOWA INDIANS

Contributions to Fox Ethnology

Expedition Against the Sauk and Fox
Indians, 1832

Fox Miscellany

Fox Texts

Observations of the Ethnology of
the Sauk Indians

Sac and Fox Cession in Iowa

Sac and Fox Indian Lands

The Sac and Fox Indians

Sac and Fox and Iowa Indian Cessions
in Eastern Iowa

Sac, Fox and Iowa Indians

Sac, Fox and Iowa Lands in South Central
Iowa, 1839-1843

Sac, Fox and Iowa Tribes

Sac and Fox Lands: Appraisal

Sac and Fox Mineral Lands

Sac, Fox and Mississippi Tracts in Kansas

Sacred Bundles of the Sac and Fox Indians

Sac and Fox of Missouri Tract in Kansas

Sac and Fox Tract Indian Territory

Sauk and Fox Nations of the Indians

The Sauks and the Black Hawk War

United Tribes of Sac and Fox Indians

SALISH AND
KOOTENAI INDIANS

Basketry Designs of the Salish Indians

The Coast Salish of British Columbia

Coast Salish: Their Art, Culture
and Legends

Coast Salish and Western Washington Indians

Confederated Salish and Kootenai Tribe

*Creation Tales from the Salish

Columbia Salish of Central Washington

Folk-Tales of the Coast Salish

Folk-Tales of the Salishan and
Sahaptin Tribes

Gambling Music of the Coast
Salish Indians

Interior Salish and Eastern
Washington Indians

†Lushootseed

Salish and Chimakuam-Speaking Indians
of the Puget Sound Basin of Washington

*Salish Folk Tales

Salish and Kootenai Tribes

Salish Songs and Rituals

Salishan Tribes of the Western Plateaus

Salish Weaving

The Sanpoil and Nespelem: Salishan Peoples
of Northeastern Washington

Wenatchi Salish of Central Washington

SANDPAINTING

Hosteen Klah: Navaho Medicine Man
and Sand Painter

Navajo Medicine Man Sandpaintings

Navajo Painting

Navajo Sandpainting Art

Navajo Sandpainting From Religious Act
to Commercial Art

Navajo Sandpainting: The Huckel Collection

Sandpainting of the Navajo Shooting Chant

Song from the Earth: American Indian Painting

SECRET SOCIETIES

The Native Brotherhoods: Modern Inter-
Tribal Organizations on the Northwest Coast

Omaha Secret Societies

Social Organization and the Secret
Societies of the Kwakiutl Indians

Societies of the Plains Indians

The Tobacco Society of the Crow Indians

SEMINOLE INDIANS

Africans and Seminoles: From
Removal to Emancipation

Big Cypress: A Changing Seminole Community

Coacoochee, Made from the Sands of Florida

Este Cate

Florida's Seminole Indians

Fort Mellon: Microcosm of the Second
Seminole War, 1837-1842

History of the Second Seminole War

*Hunted Like a Wolf: The Story of
the Seminole War

Journey Into Wilderness

Military Edged Weapons of the Second
Seminole War: 1835-1842

My Work Among the Florida Seminole

Notes on Colonial Indians (Seminole)
and Communities in Florida

Oklahoma Seminoles: Medicines, Magic
and Religion

Pelts, Plumes and Hides

Red Patriots: The Story of the Seminoles

The Seminole

Seminole Lands in Florida

Seminole Lands: Mineral Interests
in Oklahoma

Seminole Music

Seminole Nation: Appraisal of Land

The Seminole Nation: An Ethno-
Historical Report

The Seminole of Florida to 1823

Seminole Saga: The Jesup Report

The Seminole Seed

Seminoles

Strip Patchwork

Unconquered Seminole Indians

SENECA INDIANS

The Case of the Seneca Indians in
the State of New York

The Death and Rebirth of the Seneca

Mythological Tales and the Allegany Seneca

The Relation of Seneca False Face Masks
to Seneca and Ontario Archaeology

Seneca Myths and Folk Tales

Seneca Nations and Tonawanda Band
of Seneca Indains

Seneca Thanksgiving Rituals

Senecas of Sandusky

*Skunny Wundy Seneca Indian Tales

United Senecas and Shawnees, 1833

SHAMANISM

Indian Healing: Shamanic Ceremonialism
in the Pacific Northwest Today

The Medicine-Man: A Sociological Study of
the Character and Evolution of Shamanism

Old John Neptune and Other Maine
Indian Shamans

Penobscot Shamanism

Piman Shamanism and Staying Sickness:
Ka: Cim Mumkidag

The Shaman and the Medicine Wheel

Shamanism in Western North America

The Shamans Healing Way

Stones, Bones and Skin: Ritual
and Shamanic Art

Washo Shamans and Peyotists: Religious
Conflict in an American Indian Tribe

Wizard of Four Winds: A Shaman's Story

SHAWNEE INDIANS

*Blue Jacket: War Chief of Shawnees

Civilization and the Story of the Absentee
Shawnees

Mortuary Customs of the Shawnee and Other
Eastern Tribes

The Shawnee

Shawnee: The Ceremonialism of a Native
American Tribe and Its Cultural Background

Shawnee Home Life: The Painting of
Ernest Spybuck

The Shawnee Prophet

Shawnee Tract in Kansas: Appraisal, 1854

Shawnee Traditions

Star Woman and Other Shawnee Tales

United Senecas and Shawnees, 1833

SHOSHONI INDIANS

Appraisal of Land Included in the
Agreement of Sept. 26, 1872 Between
the U.S. and Eastern Shoshone Indians

Among the Shoshones

Goshute Shoshone Indians: Appraisal
of Lands, 1875

A History of the Shoshone-Paiutes of
the Duck Valley Indian Reservation

Newe Natekwinappeh: Shoshoni Stories
and Dictionary

The Northern Shoshoni

*Pachee Goyo: History and Legends
from the Shoshone

Shoshone Indians

The Shoshoni-Crow Sun Dance

The Shoshoni Indians of Inyo County,
California

Shoshone Lands Mineral Valuation

Shoshone Tribal Lands, California
and Nevada

The Shoshonis: Sentinels of the Rockies

Western Band of Shoshone

When Did the Shoshoni Begin to Occupy
Southern Idaho?

SIGN LANGUAGE

American Indian Gestural Code Based on
Universal American Indian Hand Talk

The Indian Sign Language

*Indian Sign Language

Indian Talk: Hand Signals of the North
American Indians

Sign Language Among North American Indians
Compared With That Among Other Peoples
and Deaf Mutes

*Talking Hands: Indian Sign Language

SIOUX INDIANS

Anthropological Report on Indian
Occupancy of Certain Territory Claimed
by the Dakota Sioux Indians and by
Rival Tribal Claimants

Appraisal of the Black Hills Lands
of the Sioux Nation, 1877

Appriasal of the Lands of the Lower Sioux
Unity in Minnesota

Sitting Bull: The Years in Canada

Slim Buttes, 1876. An Episode of the Great Sioux War

Songs of the Teton Sioux

*The Story of Little Bighorn

Study of the Siouan Cults

The Sun Dance and Other Ceremonies of the Oglala Division of the Teton Dakota

Sundancing at Rosebud and Pine Ridge

Teton Sioux Music

*These Were the Sioux

*Tonweya and the Eagles and Other Lakota Indian Tales

Tragedy Strikes at Wounded Knee

Warriors Without Weapons: A Study of the Society and Personality Development of the Pine Ridge Sioux

Where the West Begins: Essays on Middle Border and Siouxland Writing

White Shadows Among the Mighty Sioux

White Sioux

Yankton Sioux

Yankton Sioux Tribe

Yankton and Teton Sioux, 1851: Use and Occupancy of Fort laramie Lands

Yuwipi: Vision and Experience in Oglala Ritual

SITTING BULL
DAKOTA CHIEF, 1834-1890

*Sitting Bull

Sitting Bull: Champion of the Sioux: A Biography

*Sitting Bull: Great Sioux Chief

*Sitting Bull: Warrior of the Sioux

Sitting Bull: The Years in Canada

*The Story of Little Bighorn

SOCIAL CONDITIONS

Algic Researches: Comprising Inquiries Respecting the Mental Characteristics of the North American Indians

The American Indian in Urban Society

American Indians: Facts - Future Toward Economic Development for Native American Communities

Changing Configurations in the Social Organization of a Blackfoot Tribe During the Reserve Period

Conflicting Perceptions: Western Economics and the Great Whale Cree

The Destruction of American Indian Families

Dictionary of Daily Life of Indians of the Americas, A to Z

Disinherited: The Lost Birthright of the American Indian

Economic Development on American Indian Reservations

Everyday Life of the North American Indian

From Indians to Chicanos: The Dynamics of Mexican American Culture

The Havasupai Woman

Indian Police and Judges: Experiments in Acculturation and Control

Indian-White Relations in the U.S.: A Bibliography of Works Published, 1975-1980

Indians and Criminal Justice

Life Is With People: Household Organization of the Contemporary Paiute Indians

Marxism and Native Americans

Moccasins on Pavement: The Urban Indian Experience, A Denver Portrait

Native Americans Today: Sociological Perspectives

North American Indians in Historical Perspective

Political Organization of the Plains Indians

The Re-Establishment of the Indians in Their Pueblo Life Through the Revival of Their Traditional Crafts

The Roots of Dependency: Subsistence, Environment and Social Change Among the Choctaws, Pawnees and Navajos

Roots of Oppression: The American Indian Question

Statistics of Indian Tribes, Agencies and Schools

Subjugation and Dishonor: A Brief History of the Travail of the Native Americans

To Be an Indian

Tradition, Change and Conflict in Indian Family Business

The Underground Reservation: Osage Oil

Urban Renegades   The Cultural Strategy of American Indians

Villages of the Algonquian, Siouan and Caddoan Tribes West of the Mississippi

Wasi-Chii: The Continuing Indian Wars

SOCIAL LIFE AND CUSTOMS

The American Indian: Perspectives
for the Study of Social Change

*American Indian Ways of Life

American Indians and American Life

American Indians and Their Music

Among the Shoshones

Arapahoe Politics, 1851-1978: Symbols
in the Crisis of Authority

Autobiography of a Winnebago Indians

*Beneath the Singing Pines

*Between Sacred Mountains: Navajo Stories
and Lessons fromthe Land

Broken K Pueblo: Prehistoric Social
Organization in the American Southwest

California Indian Nights Entertainment

Camp, Clan and Kin Among the
Cow Creek Seminole

Changing Culture of an Indian Tribe

Chippewa Customs

*Come to Our Salmon Feast

Corn Among the Indians of the Upper Missouri

Cry to the Thinderbird: The American
Indian's Own Story

Daughters of the Earth

Depredations and Masscre by
the Snake River Indians

The Destruction of American Indian Families

Everyday Life of the North American Indian

Facial Paintings of the Indians
of Northern British Columbia

Forms of Play of Native North Americans

Friends of Thunder: Folktales of
the Oklahoma Cherokees

*From Free Range to Reservation

Fundamentals of Age-Group Systems

The Gonds of Andhra Pradesh: Tradition
and Change in an Indian Tribe

The Grand Village of the Natchez
Indians Revisited

Hogans: Navajo Houses and House Songs

The Hollywood Indian: Stereotypes
of Native American in Films

Houses and House Life of the American Indian

How We Lived: Reminiscences, Stories,
Speeches and Songs of California Indians

I am the Fire of Time: The Voices
of Native American Women In the Land of

Grasshopper Song:
Two Women in the Klamath River
Indian Country in 1908-1909

*Indian Games and Crafts

Indian Life on the Upper Missouri

Indian Running

Indians: Great Photographs That Reveal
North American Indian Life, 1847-1929

The Indians of the Great Plains

The Indians of Puget Sound: The
Notebooks of Myron Eells

Indians of the U.S.: Four Centuries
of Their History and Culture

Introductory to the Study of Mortuary
Customs of the North American Indians

*James At Work

Keresan Bridge: A Problem in
Pueblo Ethnology

Letters from Fort Sill

Lexical Reconstruction

The Makah Indians

Menominee Music

Moccasins and Their Relation
to Arctic Footwear

Modern Blackfeet: Montanans
on a Reservation

The Modern Sioux: Social Systems
and Reservation Culture

Montezuma's Dinner

Native American Traditions

Native North American Spirituality
of the Eastern Woodlands

The Natural World of the California Indians

The Navajo Hunter Tradition

Navajo Kinship Marriage

Notes on the Buffalo-Head Dance of
the Bear Gens of the Fox Indians

Notes on the Social Organization and Customs
of the Mandan, Hidatsa and Crow Indians

Oglala Religion

Ojibwa Woman

The Old North Trail: Or, Life, Legends
and Religion of the Blackfeet Indians

Omaha Sociology

Osages: Children of the Middle Waters

Persistent Peoples: Cultural Enclaves
in Perspective

Pima and Papago Ritual Oratory

Political Organizations and Law-Ways
of the Comanche Indians

Portraits of the Whiteman

Reconstruction of Basic Jemez Pattern

Red Hunters and the Animal People

Reflections of Social Life in the Navaho
Origin Myth

The Relationship Systems of the Tlingit,
Haida and Tsimshian

Respect for Life: The Traditional Upbringing of American Indian Children

The Search for an American Indian Identity

Shadows of the Indian: Stereotypes
in American Culture

Shamanism in Western North America

Silent Arrows

Social Life of the Crow Indians

Social Anthropology of North American Tribes

Social and Ceremonial Organization of Cochiti

Social Life of the Navajo Indians

Social Organization of the Papago Indians

Social Organization and Ritualistic
Ceremonies of the Blackfoot Indians

Social Organization and the Secret
Societies of the Kwakiutl Indians

Social Organizations and Social Usages
of the Indians of the Creek Confederacy

A Social Study of One Hundred Fifty
Chippewa Indian Families of the
White Earth Reservation of Minnesota

Son of Old Hat: A Navaho Autobiography

Source Material for the Social and
Ceremonial Life of the Choctaw Indians

Southwestern Indian Ceremonials

Tobacco, Peacepipes and Indians

Tobacco, Pipes and Smoking Customs
of the American Indians

Traditions of the Chilcotin Indians

The Traditions of the Hopi: The Stanley
McCormic Hopi Expedition

Traditions of the North American Indians

Traditions of the Osage

Traditions of the Quinault Indians

Traits of American Indian Life and Character

Travels in North America, Including
a Summer with the Pawnees

Two Crows Denies It: A History
of Controversy in Omaha Sociology

Two Leggings: The Making of a Crow Warrior

Urban Institutions and People of Indian
Ancestry

Valley of the Spirits: The Upper Skagit
Indian of Western Washington

Walk in Your Soul: Love Incantations
of the Oklahoma Cherokees

The Way We Live: California Indian
Reminiscences, Stories and Songs

With One Sky Above Us: Life on an Indian
Reservation at the Turn of the Century

Woodland Indians of the Western Great Lakes

SPORTS AND FITNESS

*A'Una

*Competing for Glory: The Indian World
of Sports

Growing Straight: The Fitness Secret
of the American Indian

*Sports and Games the Indians Gave Us

STUDY AND TEACHING

Community-Based Research: A Handbook
for Native Americans

Guide to Records in the National Archives
Relating to American Indians

Guide to Research on North American Indians

Indians of North America: Methods and
Sources for Library Research

Issues for the Future of American
Indian Studies

Native American Directory: Alaska,
U.S. and Canada

Native American Periodicals and Newspapers,
1828-1982: Bibliography, Publishing Record
and Holdings

Native American Research Information Service

Native Studies: American and Canadian Indians

Teaching American Indian History: An
Interdisciplinary Approach

SUN DANCE

The Arapaho Sun Dance, The Ceremony
of the Offering Lodge

The Cheyenne Indians: The Sun Dance

Shoshoni-Crow Sun Dance

The Sun Dance of the Crow Indians

The Sun Dance Religion: Power for the
Powerless

Sundancing at Rosebud and Pine Ridge

TEXTILE INDUSTRY
AND FABRICS

American Indian Needlepoint Workbook

And Eagles Sweep Across the Sky: Indian Textiles of the North American West

The Chilkat Dancing Blanket

Folk-Lore of the Mesquakie Indians of North America and Catalogue of Beadwork and Other Objects in the Collection of the Folk Lore Society

Full Color American Indian Designs for Needlepoint Rugs

Garments of Brightness: The Navajo Weaving Tradition

The Gift of Spiderwoman: Southwestern Textiles, the Navajo Tradition

Hopi Dyes

*Indian Bead-Weaving Patterns: Chain Weaving Designs and Bead Loom Weaving An Illustrated "How-to" Guide

Indian Blankets and Their Makers

Indian Designs

The Navajo Design Book

The Navajo and His Blanket

Navajo and Hopi Weaving Techniques

Navajo Native Dyes: Their Preparation and Use

Navajo Shepherd and Weaver

Navajo Techniques for Today's Weaver

Navajo Textiles from the Red Mullan Collection

Navajo Weavers

Navajo Weavers and Silversmiths

Navajo Weaving Handbook

A Navaho Weaving, Its Technic and History

Navajo Weaving: Three Centuries of Change

Old Navajo Rugs: Their Development from 1900 to 1940

Patterns and Sources of Navajo Weaving

Posts and Rugs

Prehistoric Textiles of the Southwest

Pueblo Indian Textiles: A Living Tradition

Pueblo Weaving and Textile Arts

Salish Weaving

Southwestern Weaving: The Collection of Maxwell Museum

Spider Woman: A Story of Navajo Weavers and Chanters

Strip Patchwork: Quick and Easy Patchwork Using the Seminole Technique

Textiles of the Prehistoric Southwest

Walk in Beauty: The Navajo and Their Blankets

Weaving Arts of the North American Indians

Weaving a Navajo Blanket

TLINGIT INDIANS

The Relationship Systems of the Tlingit, Haida and Tsimshian

The Tlingit Indians: Results of a Trip to the Northwest Coast of America and the Bering Straits

Tlingit Myths and Texts

Tlingit Tales: Potlatch and Totem Poles

Tlingit: Their Art, Culture and Legends

TOTEMS, TOTEMISM

Art of the Totem

Elementary Forms of the Religious Life

Message of an Indian Relic: Seattle's Own Totem Pole

Modern Growth of the Totem Pole on the Northwest Coast

*Once More Upon a Totem

People of the Totem: Indians of the Pacific Northwest

The Savage and His Totem

Sculpturing Totem Poles

*Sky Man on the Totem Pole

*Story of the Totem Pole

*Talking Totem Pole

Tlingit Tales: Potlatch and Totem Poles

Tongues and Totems: Comparative Arts of the Pacific Basin

The Totem Carvers: Charlie James, Ellen Neel, and Mungo Martin

Totem Poles: An Illustrative Guide

Totem Poles of the Gitksan, Upper Skeena River, British Columbia

*Totem Poles and Tribes

Totem Tales

Totem Tales of Old Seattle

Totemism

Wolf of the Raven: Totem Poles of Southeastern Alaska

TREATIES

American Indian Treaties Publications
Series

The American Indian Treaty Series

Behind the Trail of Broken Treaties

Bibliography of the English Colonial
Treaties with the American Indians

Early American Indian Documents:
Treaties and Laws, 1607-1789

The Greenville Treaty, 1795

Indian Treaties: American Nightmare

Indian Treaties: Two Centuries of Dishonor

License for Empire: Colonialism by Treaty
in Early America

The Navajo Treaty, 1868

Proceedings of the Great Peace Commission

Rediscovered Links in the Covenant Chain:
Previously Unpublished Transcripts of New
York Indian Treaty Minutes, 1677-1691

The Spirit of the Alberta Indian Treaties

Treaties with the Creek and Seminole
Indians, 1763-1815

Treaty Between the U.S. and the Dwamish,
Suquamish and Other Allied and Subordinate
Tribes of Indians in Washington Territory

Treaty Between the U.S. and the Makah Tribe

Treaty Between the U.S. and the Nisqually and
Other Bands of Indians

Treaty Between the U.S. and the
Yakima Nation of Indians

Treaty of Medicine Lodge

TRIBAL GOVERNMENT

A Bibliography of Current American
Indian Policy

The Nations Within: The Past and Future
of American Indian Sovereignty

Political Organizations of Native Americans

The Politics of Indian Removal: Creek
Government and Society in Crisis

The Road: Indian Tribes and Political Liberty

Tribal Government: A New Era

Tribal Government Textbook

Tribal Sovereignty: Indian Tribes
in U.S. History

TSIMSHIAN INDIANS

Haida Songs and Tsimshian Texts

Metlakatla: Mission to Tsimshian Indians

The Relationship Systems of the Tlingit,
Haida and Tsimshian

The Tsimshian: Images of the Past, Views
from the Present

Tsimshian Indians and Their Arts

The Tsimshian and Their Neighbors of the
Northwest Coast

UTE INDIANS

Aboriginal and Historic Groups of the
Ute Indians of Utah: An Analysis

Bull Creek

Confederated Bands of Ute Indians

Confederated Ute Indian Lands in
Southwestern Colorado

Ethnography of the Northern Utes

The Last War Trail: The Utes and the
Settlement of Colorado

Northern Ute Music

People of the Shining Mountains:
The Ute Indians of Colorado

The Rancheria, Ute and Southern
Paiute Peoples

Southern Ute Indians of Early Colorado

A Study in Culture Contact and Culture
Change: The Whiterock Utes in Transition

Uintah Ute Tract

Ute Ceded Tract, Colorado, 1873-1874

Ute Indians

Ute Indians and the San Juan Mining Region:
Historical Summary

Ute Peyotism: A Study of a Cultural Complex

The Ute War

*When Buffalo Free the Mountains:
A Ute Indian Journey

White River Ute Indians: Native Components

WARS — GENERAL

The American Heritage History of
the Indian Wars

Bury My Heart at Wounded Knee: An
Indian History of the American West

Crimsoned Prairie: The Indian Wars

Chronological List of Engagements Between
the Regular Army of the U.S. and Various
Tribes of Hostile Indians...1790-1898

The Conflict Between the California
Indian and White Civilization

Dakota War Whoop; Or, Indian Masscres
and War in Minnesota

Fighting Red Cloud's Warriors: True Tales
of Indian Days When the West Was Young

*First Book of the Indian Wars

*The Great Chiefs

Great Western Indian Fights

History of the Indian Wars

Indian Battles Along the Rogue River:
One of America's Wild and Scenic Rivers

Indian Wars

Indian Wars of the Northwest

Indian Wars of the Pacific Northwest

*The Last Cherokee Warriors

Long Death

Memoirs of Indian Wars and Other
Occurrences by the Late Colonial
Stuart of Greenbrier

Our Indian Wards

The Papers of the Order of the Indian Wars

Red Eagle and the Wars With the
Creek Indians of Alabama

Seminole Saga: The Jesup Report

Three Indian Campaigns

The Wars of the Iroquois: A Study
in Intertribal Trade Relations

*Wounded Knee: History of the American West

WARS, 1600-1800

The Apache Frontier: Jacobo U Garte
and Spanish-Indian Relations in
Northern New Spain

Ark of Empire: The American Frontier,
1784-1803

A Brief of the Pequot War

The Captivity and Sufferings of Gen.
Freegift Patchin...Among the Indians
During the Border Warfare in the
Time of the American Revolution

Causes of the Maryland Revolution of 1689

Chronicle of Border Warfare; Or, A
History of the Settlements by the
Whites of Northwestern Virginia

A Company of Heroes: The American
Frontier, 1775-1783

Continents in Collision: The Impact
of Europe on the North American
Indian Societies

Discovery, Settlement and Present
State of Kentucke

*The Fight for Freedom, 1750-1783

First Establishment of the Faith
in New France

Forth to the Wilderness: The First
American Frontier, 1754-1774

The Frontiersmen

Historical Collections of the
Indians of New England

History of the Early Settlement and
Indian Wars of Western Virginia

History of the Indian Wars in New England
from the First Settlement to the Termination of the War with King Philip in 1677

Indian Wars in North Carolina, 1663-1763

Journal of the Adventures of Mathew Bunn

Journals of the Military Expedition of
Major General John Sullivan Against
Six Nations of Indians in 1779

Life of Joseph Brant (Thayendanegea)

John McMurtry and the American Indian

Narrative of the Manner in Which the
Campaign Against the Indians in the
Year 1791 Was Conducted Under the
Command of Major General St. Clair

Narratives of the Indian Wars, 1675-1699

Notes on the Settlement and Indian Wars
of the Western Parts of Virginia and
Pennsylvania, 1763-1783

Notices of Sullivan's Campaign

Our Western Border, Its Life, Combats,
Adventures, Forays, Massacres, Captivities,
Scouts, Red Chiefs, Pioneers, Woman...

Particular History of the Five Years
French and Indian War, 1744-1748

Penhallow's Indian Wars

*Pontiac, Chief of the Ottawas
Present State of New England

President Washington's Indian War: The
Struggle for the Old Northwest, 1790-1795

Redeemed Captive Returning to Zion

Saint Clair Papers

The Southern Frontier, 1670-1732

Southern Indians in the American Revolution

Tecumseh and the Quest for Indian Leadership

Anthony Wayne, A Name in Arms

Lewis Wetzel, Indian Fighter

Wilderness Empire

WARS, 1800-1900

Advancing the Frontier, 1830-1860

The American Indian as Participant
in the Civil War

Antelope Bill

The Battle of Horseshoe Bend

The Battle of Washita: The Sherman-Custer
Indian Campaign of 1867-1869

The Battle of Wisconsin Heights

The Bear River Massacre

Burnt-Out Fires: California's Modoc
Indian War

Bury My Heart at Wounded Knee: An Indian
History of the American West

Campaigning With Crook

A Cannoneer in Navajo Country: Journey
of Private Josiah M. Rice, 1851

The Kit Carson Campaign

Casper Collins: The Life and Exploits
of an Indian Fighter of the Sixties

Cavalry Wife: The Diary of Eveline
M. Alexander, 1866-1867

Centennial Campaign: The Sioux War of 1876

*Chief Joseph of the Nez Perce

Conquest of Apacheria

Copper Paladin: The Modoc Tragedy

Creek War of 1813 and 1814

The Custer Trail: A Narrative of the Line
of March of Troops Serving in the Campaign
Against Hostile Sioux, 1876, Fort Abraham
Lincoln to the Montana Line

Custer's Fall: The Indian Side of the Story

Dakota War Whoop

Death, Too, For the Heavy-Runner

Discovery of the Yosemite and the
Indian War of 1851

Exiles of Florida

The Fighting Cheyennes

First Scalp for Custer

The Florida Wars

Following the Guidon

Forlorn Hope: The Battle of Whitebird Canyon
and the Beginning of the Nez Perce War

Fort Mellon: Microcosm of the Second
Seminole War, 1837-1842

Forty Miles a Day on Beans and Hay: The
Enlisted Soldier Fighting the Indian Wars

Frontier Regulars: The U.S. Army
and the Indian, 1866-1891

General Henry Atkinson: A Western
Military Career

General Crook and the Sierra Madre Adventure

General Custer and the Battle of the Little
Big Horn: The Federal View

History of the Second Seminole War

General Pope and U.S. Indian Policy

Tom Horn, Government Scout and Indian
Interpreter

*Hunted Like a Wolf: The Story of the
Seminole War

I Will Fight No More Forever:
Chief Joseph and the Nez Perce War

*The Indian as a Soldier at Fort Custer,
Montana, 1890-1895

Indian Fights and Fighters

The Indian History of the Modoc War

Indian Outbreaks

Indian War of 1864

Indians Last Fight or the Dull Knife Raid

Journey Into Wilderness

Last Days of the Sioux Nation

The Last War Trail: The Utes and the
Settlement of Colorado

Life in Custer's Cavalry

Life of George Bent

Life of Tom Horn

Little Big Horn Diary: Chronicle
of the 1876 Indian War

The Long Walk: A History of the
Navajo Wars, 1846-1868

Man of the Plains: Recollections
of Luther North, 1856-1882

The Mariposa Indian War, 1850-1851

Massacre!

The Massacre of Lt. Grattan and
His Command by Indians

The Military Conquest of the
Southern Plains

Military Edged Weapons of the
Second Seminole War, 1835-1842

Modocs and Their War

My Life on the Plains

On the Border With Crook

Personal Recollection and Observations
of General Nelson A. Miles

Plains Inian Raiders

Pony Tracks

Reminiscences of Seattle, Washington
Territory and the U.S. Sloop-of-War
Decatur During the Indian War of 1855-6

The Sand Creek Massacre

Scarlet Plume

Scout and Ranger

Secrets of the Mighty Sioux

The Sioux Uprising of 1862

Sitanka: The Full Story of Wounded Knee

Slim Buttes, 1876; An Episode
of the Great Sioux War

Soldiering in Dakota: Among the
Indians in 1863-1865

Son of the Morning Star: Custer
and the Little Big Horn

*The Story of Little Big Horn

Swamp Sailors: Riverine Warfare
in the Everglades, 1835-1842

Taos, 1847: The Revolt in Contemporary
Accounts

Two Battles of the Little Big Horn

The Ute War

Vanished Arizona

The Vanishing Race: The Last Great Indian
Council, 1909, General Custer's Indian
Scouts' Account of Little Big Horn

Vast Domain of Blood

*War Clouds in the West, Indians
and Cavalrymen, 1860-1890

War Eagle: A Life of General Eugene A. Carr

War-Path and Bivouac: The Big Horn
and Yellowstone Expedition

War-Path and Bivouac: Or, The Conquest
of the Sioux

The Warren Wagontrain Raid

We Were Not Summer Soldiers

Wooden Leg: A Warrior Who Fought Custer

*Wounded Knee: History of the American West

WASHO INDIANS

Two Worlds of the Washo: An Indian
Tribe of California and Nevada

The Washo Indians

Washoe Indian Lands

Washo Indians of California and Nevada

Washo Shamans and Peyotists: Religious
Conflict in an American Indian Tribe

Washoe Tribe: Fishery Evaluation

Washoe Tribe: Evaluation of Mineral Resources

Washoe Tribe of Indians: Appraisal of Lands

Washoe Tribe of Nevada and California:
Appraisal of Lands

WINNEBAGO INDIANS

Appraisal of Lands in Illinois and
Wisconsin Ceded by the Winnebago Indians

Autobiography of a Winnebago Indians

Mountain Wolf Woman, Sister of Crashing
Thunder: The Autobiography of a
Winnebago Indian

Winnebago Indians

Winnebago Indians: Economic and
Historical Background

Winnebago Lands in Iowa and Minesota

Winnebago Lands in Minnesota

The Winnebago Tribe

WOMEN

American Indian Women:
Telling Their Lives

The Autobiography of Delfina Cuero:
A Diegueno Woman

Cherokee Woman

During My Time: Florence Edenshaw
Davidson, A Haida Woman

A Gathering of Spirit: Writing and Art
by North American Indian Women

The Hidden Half: Studies of Plains
Indian Women

I Am the Fire of Time: The Voices
of Native American Women

Indian Women Chiefs

Medicine Woman

Menomini Women and Cultural Change

Native American Women: A Contextual
Bibliography

No Turning Back: A Hopi Indian Woman's
Struggle to Live in Two Worlds

Po Pai Mo: The Search for
White Buffalo Woman

Pretty Shield, Medicine Woman
of the Crows

Sacajawea

Sanapia: Comanche Medicine Woman

Spirit Woman

A Voice in Her Tribe: A Navajo
Woman's Own Story

PUBLISHERS INDEX

The following is a list of publishers whose
books appear in the bibliography. Entries
are arranged alphabetically, with complete
zip-coded addresses and phone numbers.

ABC-Clio, P.O. Box 4397, 2040 A.P.S.,
Santa Barbara, California 93140-4397
(805) 963-4221

AMS Press, 56 East 13th St., New York,
New York 10003 (212) 777-4700

A & W Visual Library, 95 Madison Ave.,
New York, New York 10016 (212) 725-4970

Abbeville Press, 505 Park Ave.,
New York, New York 10022 (212) 888-1969

Abingdon Press, 201 Eighth Ave. South,
Nashville, Tennessee 37202 (615) 749-6301

Harry N. Abrams, 100 Fifth Ave.,
New York, New York 10011 (212) 206-7715

Academic Press, Orlando, Florida 32887
(305) 345-4100

Ace Books, Distributed by ICD,
250 West 55th St. New York, New York 10019
(212) 262-7444

Acoma Books, P.O. Box 4, Ramona,
California 92065 (619) 789-1288

Adler's Foreign Books, 28 West 25th St.
New York, New York 10010 (212) 691-5151

Advent Books, 141 East 44th St., Suite 511
New York, New York 10017 (212) 697-0887

Airmont Publishing, 401 Lafayette St.,
New York, New York 10003

Alaska Federation of Natives, 411 W. Fourth
Ave., Suite 301, Anchorage, Alaska 99501
(907) 274-3611

Alaska International Art Institute,
26241 Foxgrove Ave., Sun City,
California 92381

Alaska Northwest Publishing, 130 Second
Ave. So., Edmonds, Washington 98020
(206) 774-4111

Alaska Travel Publications, P.O. Box 4-2031,
Anchorage Alaska 99509 (907) 274-2869

Aldine Publishing, 200 Saw Mill River Rd.,
Hawthorne, New York 10532 (914) 747-0110

Allenheld, Osmun & Co., Publishers,
81 Adams Dr., Totowa, New Jersey 07512
(201) 256-8600

Allyn & Bacon, Inc., College Division,
1 Pond Rd. Rockleigh, New Jersey 07647
(800) 526-4799

Amereon Ltd., P.O. Box 1200, Mattituck,
New York 11952 (516) 298-4247

American Academy of Political and Social
Science; Distributed by Sage Publications

American Antiquarian Society; Distributed
by University Press of Virginia

American Federation of Arts, 41 East 65th St.,
New York, New York 10021 (212) 988-7700

American Heritage Publishing, 10 Rockefeller
Plaza, New York, New York 10020
(212) 399-8900

American Historical Association, 400 "A" St.,
S.E., Washington, D.C. 20003 (202) 544-2422

American Historical Publishers, Inc.,
177F Riverside Dr., Newport Beach,
California 92663

American Indian Archaeological Institute,
Box 260, Washington, Connecticut 06793

American Indian Books, Joe Thompson,
533 Summit, Webster Groves, Missouri 63119
(314) 962-8250

American Indian Education Program,
The Phelps-Stokes Fund, 1228 M St., N.W.,
Washington, D.C. 20005 (202) 638-7066

American Indian Publishers, 177F Riverside
Dr., Newport Beach, California 92663

American Indian Studies Center, University
of California, 3220 Campbell Hall,
405 Hilgard Ave., Los Angeles,
California 90024 (213) 825-7315

American Library Association, 50 East
Huron St., Chicago, Illinois 60611
(312) 944-6780

American Philosophical Society, 104 S.
Fifth St., Philadelphia, Pennsylvania
19106 (215) 627-0706

American Press, 520 Commonwealth Ave.,
No. 416, Boston, Massachusetts 02215
(617) 247-0022

Amherst Press, P.O. Box 296, Amherst,
Wisconsin 54406 (715) 824-5890

Amon Carter Museum of Western Art;
Distributed by University of Texas Press

Anchor Books; Division of Doubleday & Co.

The Anchorage Historical and Fine Arts
Museum,
121 West 7th Ave., Anchorage, Alaska 99501

Anthropology Film Center Foundation, Box 493,
Santa Fe, New Mexico 87594-0493
(505) 983-4127

Anthropology Resource Center; Distributed
by Cultural Survival, 11 Divinity Ave.,
Cambridge, Massachusetts 02138

Aperture; Distributed by Viking-Penguin

Apollo Editions; Distributed by Harper & Row

Appalachian Consortium, University Hall,
Appalachian State University, Boone,
North Carolina 28608

Appleton-Century-Crofts;
Division of Prentice-Hall

Archive of Folk Culture, American Folklife
Center, Library of Congress, 10 First St.,
S.E., Washington, D.C. 20540

Arden Library, Mill & Main Sts., Darby,
Pennsylvania 19023 (215) 726-5505

Argosy-Antiquarian, 116 East 59th St.,
New York, New York 10022 (212) 753-4455

Arizona Maps and Books, Box 1133,
Sedona, Arizona 86336

Arrowstar Publishing, 10134 University
Park Station, Denver, Colorado 80210

Arts and Culture of the North, P.O. Box 1333,
Gracie Square Station, New York, New York
10028 (212) 879-9019

Aspen Center for Visual Arts; Distributed by
Publishing Center for Cultural Resources,
625 Broadway, New York, New York 10012

Associated Booksellers, P.O. Box 6361,
Bridgeport, Connecticut 06606
(203) 366-5494

Associated Creative Writers, 9231 Molly
Woods Ave., La Mesa, California 92041

Associated Faculty Press, Route 100,
Milwood, New York 10546 (914) 762-2200

Association for Northern California Records
and Research, P.O. Box 3024, Chico,
California 95927 (916) 895-5710

Association of American Indian Physicians,
6805 S. Western, Suite 504, Oklahoma City,
Oklahoma 73139 (405) 631-0447

Association on American Indian Affairs,
95 Madison Ave., New York, New York 10016
(212) 689-8720

Association Press; Division of Follett
Publishing Co., Box 0, Wilton, Connecticut
06897 (203) 762-0393

Atheneum Publishers, Riverside Distribution
Center, Front and Brown Sts., Riverside,
New Jersey 08075

J.J. Augustin, Publisher, Locust Valley,
New York 11560 (516) 676-1510

Avery Color Studios, Star Route, Box 275,
Au Train, Michigan 49806 (906) 892-8251

Avon Books, 1790 Broadway, New York,
New York 10019 (212) 399-4500

Ayer Co. Publishers, Inc., 382 Main St.,
P.O. Box 958, Salem, New Hampshire 03079
(603) 898-1200

B

B & E Enterprises, Publishers,
P.O. Box 984, Everett, Washington 98206

Baker Book House, P.O. Box 6287, 6030 E.
Fulton, Grand Rapids, Michigan 49506
(616) 9186

Balcom Books, 320 Bawden St., Apt. 401,
Ketchikan, Alaska 99901 (907) 225-2496

Ballantine Books; Division of Random House

Ballena Press, Publishers Service,
P.O. Box 2510, Novato, California
94948 (415) 323-9261

Baltimore Museum of Art, The Museum Shop,
Art Museum Dr., Baltimore, Maryland 21218
(301) 396-6338

Bancroft Press, 27 McNear Dr., San Rafael,
California 94901 (415) 454-7094

Bantam Books, 414 East Golf Rd., Des Plains,
Illinois 60016 (212) 765-6500

Banyon Books, P.O. Box 431160, Miami,
Florida 33243 (305) 665-6011

A.S. Barnes & Co., 9601 Aero Dr., San Diego,
California 92123 (619) 560-5163

Barre Publishing Co.; Distributed
by Crown Publishers

William L. Bauhan, Inc., Old Country Rd.,
Dublin, New Hampshire 03444 (603) 563-8020

Beacon Press; Distributed by Harper & Row

Bead Craft, 1549 Ashland Ave., St. Paul,
Minnesota 55104 (612) 645-1216

Bear & Co., P.O. Box 2860, Santa Fe,
New Mexico 87504 (505) 983-5968 (NM)
(800) 932-3277

Bear State Books, 304 High St., Santa Cruz,
California 95060 (408) 426-3272

Bear Tribe Publishing Co., P.O. Box 9167,
Spokane, Washington 99209 (509) 326-6561

Beaufort Books, 9 East 40th St.,
New York, New York 10016

Beechwood Books, P.O. Box 20484,
Birmingham, Alabama 35216 (205) 823-2376

Beckman Publishers, P.O. Box 888,
Woodstock, New York 12498 (914) 679-2300

Bellerophon Books, 36 Anacapa St.,
Santa Barbara, California 93101
(805) 965-7034

John Benjamins North America, 1 Buttonwood
Square #202, Philadelphia, Pennsylvania
19130 (215) 564-6379

Beresford Book Service, 1525 East 53 St.,
Suite 431, Chicago, Illinois 60615

Berkshire Traveller Press, Pine St.,
Stockbridge, Massachusetts 02162
(413) 298-3636

Biblio Distribution Centre, 81 Adams Dr.,
P.O. Box 327, Totowa, New Jersey 07511
(201) 256 8600

Biblio & Tannen Booksellers & Publishers,
321 Sandbank Rd., P.O. Box 302, Cheshire,
Connecticut 06410 (203) 272-2308

Binford & Mort Publishing, 1202 N.W.
17th Ave., Portland, Oregon 97209
(503) 221-0866

Black Ice Publications, 100 Prescott St.,
Worcester, Massachusetts 01605
(617) 755-1525

Black Letter Press, 601 Bridge St.,
N.W., Grand Rapids, Michigan 49504
(616) 538-2516

John F. Blair, Publisher, 1406 Plaza Dr.,
Winston-Salem, North Carolina 27103
(919) 768-1374

Clark Boardman Co., 435 Hudson St.,
New York, New York 10014 (212) 929-7500

Bobbs-Merrill Co., 630 Third Ave.,
New York, New York 10017 (212) 697-7050

Bookpeople, 2929 Fifth St., Berkeley,
California 94710 (415) 549-3030

Books, Americana, P.O. Box 2326,
Florence, Alabama 35630 (205) 757-9966

Books on Demand, 300 N. Zeeb Rd.,
Ann Arbor, Michigan 48106 (313) 761-4700

Borgo Press, P.O. Box 2845, San Bernardino,
California 92406 (714) 884-5813

R.R. Bowker Co., P.O. Box 1807, Ann Arbor,
Michigan 48106 (212) 916-1600

Boyd & Fraser Publishing, 286 Congress St.,
Boston, Massachusetts 02210 (617) 426-2292

Bradbury Press; Affiliate of
Macmillan Publishing Co.

Branch-Smith, P.O. Box 1868,
120 St. Louis Ave., Fort Worth,
Texas 76101 (817) 332-6377

Robert F. Brand, 1029 Lake Lane,
Pennsburg, Pennsylvania 18073

Branden Press, P.O. Box 843, 17 Station St.,
Brookline Village, Massachusetts 02147
(617) 734-2045

George Braziller, One Park Ave.,
New York, New York 10016 (212) 889-0909

Brevet Press, Box 1404, Sioux Falls,
South Dakota 57101 (605) 361-6121

Brigham Young University Press,
205 University Press Bldg.,
Provo, Utah 84602 (801) 378-2809

Brookfield Publishing Co., Old Post Rd.,
Brookfield, Vermont 05036 (802) 276-3162

Brookings Institution, 1775 Massachusetts
Ave., N.W., Washington, D.C. 20036-2188
(202) 797-6000

Brooklyn Museum, Publications-Marketing
Service, 188 Eastern Parkway, Brooklyn,
New York 11238 (718) 638-5000

Brown Book Co., 2130 N.E. 206th St.,
N. Miami Beach, Florida 33179
(305) 932-0707

Brown University Press, Alumnae Hall,
194 Meeting St., Providence,
Rhode Island 02912 (401) 863-2455

Buffalo Bill Historical Center,
P.O. Box 1000, Cody, Wyoming 82414
(800) 533-3838

Buffalo Museum of Science, Publications
Office, Humboldt Parkway,
Buffalo, New York, 14211

Bureau of Indian Affairs, Publications
Dept., 1951 Constitution Ave., N.W.,
Washington, D.C. 20242 (202) 343-7445

Burgess Publishing, 7108 Ohms Lane,
Minneapolis, Minnesota 55435
(612) 831-1344

C

CLC Press, P.O. Box 478, San Andreas,
California 95249 (209) 745-3457

CPL Bibliographies, 1313 East 60 St.,
Merriam Center, Chicago, Illinois 60637
(312) 947-2007

Cache Valley Newsletter Publishing Co.,
Route 3, Box 273, Preston, Idaho 83263
(208) 852-3167

Cahokia Mounds Museum Society,
P.O. Box 382, Collinsville, Illinois
62234 (618) 344-9221

Cahokia Mounds State Historic Site
and Museum, 7850 Collinsville Rd.,
East St. Louis, Illinois 62201
(618) 344-5268

California Academy of Sciences Publications,
Golden State Park, San Francisco,
California 94118 (415) 221-5100

California State University, Northridge
Library, 18111 Nordhoff St., Northridge,
California 91330 (818) 885-2271

Cambridge University Press, 510 North Ave.,
New Rochelle, New York 10801
(914) 235-0300

Campanile Press, The San Diego State
University, 5189 College Ave., San Diego,
California 92182 (619) 265-6220

Canadian Alliance in Solidarity With
the Native Peoples, 16 Spadina Rd.,
Toronto, Ontario M5R 2S7 (416) 964-0169

Capra Press, P.O. Box 2068, Santa Barbara,
California 93120 (805) 966-4590

William Carey Library Publishers,
1705 N. Sierra Bonita Ave., P.O. Box 128-C,
Pasadena, California 91104 (213) 798-0819

Carlton Press, 11 West 32 St., New York,
New York 10001 (212) 714-0300

Carolrhoda Books, 241 First Ave., N.,
Minneapolis, Minnesota 55401
(612) 332-3344

Caxton Printers, Ltd., P.O. Box 700,
Caldwell, Idaho 83605 (208) 459-7421

Celestial Arts Publishing Co., P.O. Box 7327,
Berkeley, California 94704 (415) 524-1801

Center for Applied Ling iistics; Distributed
by Harcourt Brace Jovanovich, Orlando,
Florida 32887 (305) 345-3800

Center for Archaeological Investigations,
Southern Illinois University, Carbondale,
Illinois 62901 (618) 536-5529

Center for Pre-Columbian Studies,
Dumbarton Oaks, 1703 32 St., N.W.,
Washington, D.C. 20007 (202) 232-3101

Center for Western Studies, Augustana
College, Box 727, Sioux Falls,
South Dakota 57197 (605) 336-4007

Century Bookbindery, P.O. Box 6471,
Philadelphia, Pennsylvania 19145

Century One Press, 2325 E. Platte Ave.,
Colorado Springs, Colorado 80909
(303) 471-1322

Chalfant Press, 312 Park St.,
Huron, Ohio 44835 (419) 433-6266

Chandler and Sharp Publishers,
11A Commercial Blvd., Novato,
California 94947 (415) 883-2353

Charter Books, ICD, 250 West 55 St.,
New York, New York 10019 (212) 262-7444

Don M. Chase, 8569 Lawrence Lane,
Sebastopol, California (707) 823-7670

Cherokee Publishing, P.O. Box 1523,
Marietta, Georgia 30061 (404) 424-6241

Chicago Review Press, 213 W. Institute,
Chicago, Illinois 60610 (312) 337-0747

Childrens Press, 1224 W. Van Buren St.,
Chicago, Illinois 60607 (312) 666-4200

Chilton Book Co., School Library Services,
Chilton Way, Radnor, Pennsylvania 19089
(215) 964-4729

Choctaw Heritage Press, Route 7, Box 21,
Philadelphia, Mississippi 39350
(601) 656-5251

Choctaw Museum of the Southern Indian,
Mississippi Band of Choctaw Indians,
Route 7, Box 21, Philadelphia, Mississippi
39350 (601) 656-5251

Exposition Press of Florida, 1701 Blount Rd.,
Suite C, Pompano Beach, Florida, 33069
(305) 979-3200

F

Fairleigh Dickinson University Press,
440 Forsgate Dr., Cranbury, New Jersey
08512 (609) 655-4770

Faith and Life Press, 718 Main St.,
Boc 347, Newton, Kansas 67114
(316) 283-5100

Family Service of America. 44 East 23 St.,
New York, New York 10010 (212) 674-6100

Farrar, Straus & Giroux, 19 Union Square
West, New York, New York 10003
(212) 741-6900

Fawcett Book Group, 201 East 50 St.,
New York, New York 10022 (212) 751 2600

Federal Bar Association, 1815 H St., N.W.,
Washington, D.C. 20006 (202) 638-0252

Filter Press, P.O. Box 5, Palmer Lake,
Colorado 80133 (303) 481-2523

Fleet Press, 160 Fifth Ave., New York,
New York 10010 (212) 243-6100

Follett Publishing, 1010 W. Washington
Blvd., Chicago, Illinois 60607
(312) 666-5858

The Foundation for Classical Reprints,
607 McNight St., N.W., Albuquerque,
New Mexico 87102

Four Winds Press, Box 126,
Bristol, Florida 32321

Franciscan Herald Press, 1434 West 51 St.,
Chicago, Illinois 60609 (312) 254-4462

Burt Franklin, Publisher; Distributed
by Lenox Hill Publishing, 235 East
44 St., New York, New York 10017
(212) 687- 5250

Free Press, Front and Brown Sts.,
Riverside, New Jersey 08370
(609) 461-6500

Franklin Pierce College, Department of
Anthropology, Rindge, New Hampshire 03461

W.H. Freeman & Co., 4419 West 1980 South,
Salt lake City, Utah 84104 (212) 532-7660

Freshwater Press, P.O. Box 14009,
Cleveland, Ohio 44114 (216) 241-0373

Ira J. Friedman, Route 100, Millwood,
New York 10546 (914) 767-2200

Friends of the Earth, 1045 Sansome,
San Francisco, California 94111
(415) 433-7373

Friendship Press, Distribution Office,
P.O. Box 37844, Cincinnati, Ohio 45237
(513) 761-2100

The Frontier Press Co., P.O. Box 1098,
Columbus, Ohio 43216 (614) 864-3737

Fun Publishing, P.O. Box 2049, Scottsdale,
Arizona 85252 (602) 946-2093

Emma Lila Fundaburk, Publisher,
P.O. Box 231, Luverne, Alabama 36049

G

GWP, National Literary Guild,
210 N. Pass Ave., Suite 204, Durbank,
California 91505 (818) 845-2687

Gale Research Co., Book Tower, Detroit,
Michigan 48226 (313) 961-2242

Gallery West, P.O. Box 1598, Taos,
New Mexico 87571 (505) 758-0100

Galloway Publications, 2940 N.W. Circle
Blvd., Corvallis, Oregon 97330-3999
(503) 754-7464

Gambit, Publishers, 27 N. Main St.,
Ipswich, Massachusetts 01938
(617) 356-2956

William Gannon, Publisher, 205 E.
Palace Ave., Santa Fe, New Mexico
87501 (505) 983-1579

Garland Publishing, 136 Madison Ave.,
New York, New York 10016 (212) 686-7492

Garrard Publishing, 1607 N. Market St.,
Champaign, Illinois 61820 (217) 352-7685

Garrett Park Press, P.O. Box 190F,
Garrett Park, Maryland 20896

Genealogical Publishing, 1001 N. Calvert
St., Baltimore, Maryland 21202
(301) 837-8271

Georgetown University Press, International
Center, Room 111, Washington, D.C. 10057
(202) 625-8041

Georgia Department of Archives and History,
330 Capitol Ave., Atlanta, Georgia 30334
(404) 656-2393

Ginn Custom, Ginn Press, 191 Spring St.,
Lexington, Massachusetts 02173
(617) 861-1670

Glencoe Publishing, 17337 Ventura Blvd.,
Encino, California 91316 (818) 990-3080

Globe Pequot Press, Old Chester Rd.,
Box Q, Chester, Connecticut 06412
(203) 526-9572

David R. Godine Publishing, 306 Dartmouth
Boston, Massachusetts 02116 (617) 536-0761

Golden Bell Press, 2403 Champa St.,
Denver, Colorado 80205 (303) 572-1777

Goliards Press, 3515 18th St.,
Bellingham, Washington 98225

Good Medicine Books;
Distributed by Bookpeople

Goodyear Publishing, 4700 South 5400 West,
Box 18486, Salt Lake City, Utah 84118
(801) 966-1411

Gordian Press, 85 Tompkins St.,
P.O. Box 304, Staten Island,
New York, 10304 (718) 273-4700

Gordon & Breach Science Publishers,
50 West 23 St., Ne York, New York 10010
(212) 206-8900

Gordon Press Publishers, P.O. Box 459,
Bowling Green Station, New York, New York
10004 (212) 668-8819

Gormezano Reference Publications, 2921 E.
Madison St., Suite 7 BIP, Seattle,
Washington, 98112 (206) 322-1431

Graphic Impressions, 1939 West 32nd Ave,
Denver, Colorado 80211 (303) 458-7475

Great Outdoors Publishing, 4747 28th St.,
North, St. Petersburg, Florida 33714
(813) 525-6609

Stephen Greene Press, P.O. Box 1000,
Brattleboro, Vermont 05301
(802) 257-7757

Greenwillow Books, Wilmor Warehouse,
6 Henderson Dr., W. Caldwell,
New Jersey 07006 (212) 889-3050

Greenwood Press, 88 Post Rd., West,
P.O. Box 5007, Westport, Connecticut
06881 (203) 226-3571

Gregg Press; Division of G.K. Hall & Co.

Grey Fox Press; Distributed by
Subterranean Co., P.O. Box 10233,
Eugene, Oregon 97440 (503) 343-6324

Gros Ventre Treaty Committee, Fort
Belknap Agency, Harlem, Montana 59526

H

Hacker Art Books, 54 West 57 St.,
New York, New York 10019 (212) 757-1450

Hafner Press; Division of
Macmillan Publishing

G.K. Hall & Co., 70 Lincoln St., Boston,
Massachusetts 02111 (800) 343-2806

A.G. Halldin Publishing, P.O. Box 667,
Indiana, Pennsylvania 15701
(412) 463-8450

Halsted Press; Division of
John Wiley & Sons

Hancock House Publishers, 1431 Harrison
Ave., Blaine, Washington 98230

Harbor Hill Books, Inc., P.O. Box 407,
Harrison, New York 10528 (914) 698-3495

Harcourt Brace Jovanovich, 1250 Sixth Ave.,
San Diego, California 92101 (619) 231-6616

Hardscrabble Books, Route 2, Box 285,
Berrien Springs, Michigan 49103
(616) 473-5570

Harlan Davidson, 3110 N. Arlington
Heights Rd., Arlington Heights,
Illinois 60004 (312) 253-9720

Harlo Press, 50 Victor Ave., Detroit,
Michigan 48203 (313) 883-3600

Harmsen Publishing, 1331 E. Alameda
Ave., Denver, Colorado 80209

Harper & Row Publishers, Keystone Industrial
Park, Scranton Pennsylvania 18512

Hart Publishers, P.O. Box 422,
Bluffton, Indiana 46714

Harvard Common Press; Distributed by
Kampmann & Co., 9 East 40 St., New York,
New York 10016 (212) 685-2928

Harvard University Press, Customer Service,
79 Garden St., Cambridge, Massachusetts
02138 (617) 495-2600

Harvey House, Publishers, 128 W. River St.,
Chippewa Falls, Wisconsin 54729
(715) 723-2814

Haskell Booksellers, P.O. Box FF,
Blythebourne Station, Brooklyn,
New York 11219 (718) 435-0500

Hastings House Publishers, 10 East 40 St.,
New York, New York 10016 (212) 689-5400

Hawthorne Books; Division of E.P. Dutton

Hayden Book Co., 10 Mulholland Dr.,
Hasbrouck Heights, New Jersey 07604
(201) 393-6300

Heart of the Lakes Publishing,
2989 Lodi Rd., Interlaken, New York
14848 (607) 532-4997

D.C. Heath & Co., Distribution Center,
2700 Richardt Ave., Indianapolis,
Indiana 46219 (317) 359-5585

William S. Heinman, Imported Books,
P.O. Box 926, Ansonia Station,
New York, New York 10019
(212) 757-7628

T. Emmett Henderson, 130 W. Main St.,
Middletown, New York 10940
(914) 343-1038

Hendrick-Long Publishing, 4811 W. Lovers
Lane, P.O. Box 12311, Dallas, Texas 75225

Hennessey & Ingalls, 8325 Campion Dr.,
Los Angeles, California 90045
(213) 458-9074

Herald Press; Division of Mennonite
Publishing House, Inc., 616 Walnut Ave.,
Scottsdale, Pennsylvania 15683
(412) 887-8500

Janet M. Herren, 4750 Crystal Springs Dr.,
Bainbridge Island, Washington 98110
(206) 842-3484

Heyday Books, P.O. Box 9145, Berkeley,
California 94709 (415) 549-3564

Ron G. Hickox, c/o Antique Arms and
Military Research, P.O. Box 36006,
Tampa, Florida 33673-0006
(813) 237-0764

Highlights for Children, 2300 W.
Fifth Ave., P.O. Box 269, Columbus,
Ohio 43216 (614) 486-0631

Lawrence Hill & Co., 520 Riverside Ave.,
Westport, Connecticut 06880
(203) 226-9392

Hill & Wang; Division of
Farrar, Straus & Giroux

Hillman Publications, 7152 S.
Cleve-Massilion Rd., Clinton,
Ohio 44216 (216) 374-6973

Hillsdale Educational Publishers, Inc.,
39 North St., Box 245, Hillsdale,
Michigan 49242 (517) 437-3179

Historic Pensacola Preservation Board;
Distributed by John C. Pace Library,
University of West Florida, Pensacola,
Florida 32504 (904) 476-9500

Holiday House, 18 East 53 St.,
New York, New York 10022
(212) 688-0085

Holloway House Publishing, 8060 Melrose
Ave., Los Angeles, California 90046
(213) 653-8060

Holmes Book Co., 274 14th St., Oakland,
California 94612 (415) 893-6860

Holmgangers Press, 95 Carson Court
Shelter Cove, Whitehorn, California
95489 (707) 986-7700

Holt-Atherton Pacific Center for Western
Studies, University of the Pacific,
Stockton, California 95211 (209) 946-2404

Holt, Rinehart & Winston, 383 Madison Ave.,
New York, New York 10017 (212) 872-2000

Holy Cow! Press, P.O. Box 2692,
Iowa City, Iowa 52244

Houghton Mifflin Co., Wayside Rd.,
Burlington, Massachusetts 01803
(617) 272-1500

Howard University Press, 2900 Van Ness
St., N.W., Washington, D.C. 20008
(202) 686-6696

Howe Brothers, P.O. Box 6394,
Salt Lake City, Utah 84106

Hudson Hills Press; Distributed
by Viking-Penguin

HRAF Press, Human Relations Area Files
Press, P.O. Box 2015, Yale Station,
New Haven, Connecticut 06520
(203) 777-2334

Humanities Press International,
Atlantic Highlands, New Jersey 07716
(201) 872-1441

Hunter Publishing, P.O. Box 9533,
Phoenix, Arizona 85068 (602) 944-1022

Hurtig Publishers, 10560 - 105 St.,
Edmonton, Alberta T5H 2W7 Canada
(403) 426-2359; (800) 661-6464

I

Idaho Museum of Natural History,
Campus Box 8096, Idaho State University,
Pocatello, Idaho 83209 (208) 236-3168

Illinois State Museum Society, Spring
& Edwards, Springfield, Illinois 62706
(217) 782-7386

Independence Press, P.O. Box HH, 3225 S.
Noland Rd., Independence, Missouri 64055
(816) 252-5010

Indian Arts and Crafts Association
4215 Lead S.E., Albuquerque, New Mexico
87108 (505) 265-9149

Indian Arts and Crafts Board, Room 4004,
U.S. Department of the Interior,
Washington, D.C. 20240 (202) 343-2773

Indian Feather Publishing, 7218 S.W. Oak,
Portland, Oregon 97223

Indian Historian Press, 1451 Masonic Ave.,
San Francisco, California 94117
(415) 626-5235

Indian Publications, 1868 Second Ave.,
New York, New York 10029 (212) 370-2187

Indian Rights Association, 1505 Race St.,
Philadelphia, Pennsylvania 19102
(215) 563-8349

Indian University Press, Bacone College,
Muskogee, Oklahoma 74403 (918) 683-4581

Indiana University Press, Tenth and
Morton Sts., Bloomington, Indiana 47403
(812) 335-8287

Information Coordinators, 1435-37 Randolph
St., Detroit, Michigan 48226
(313) 962-9720

Institute for the Arts, Rice University,
P.O. Box 1892, Houston, Texas 77001
(713) 527-8101

Institute for the Development of Indian Law,
1104 Glyndon St., S.E., Vienna, Virginia
22180 (703) 938-7822

Institute for Research in Social Sciences,
University of North Carolina, Manning Hall,
026A, Chapel Hill, North Carolina 27514
(919) 962-3204

Institute for Southern Studies, 604 Chapel
Hill St., Durham, North Carolina 27701
(919) 688-8167

Institute of Alaska Native Arts, Inc.,
P.O. Box 80583, Fairbanks, Alaska 99708
(907) 456-7491

Integrated Education Associates,
University of Massachusetts, School
of Education, Amherst, Massachusetts
01003 (413) 545-0327

Interbook, 611 Broadway, Room 227,
New York, New York 10012 (212) 677-9201

International Publications Service;
Division of Taylor & Francis,
242 Cherry St., Philadelphia,
Pennsylvania (800) 821-8312

International Publishers, 381 Park Ave.
South, Suite 1301, New York, New York
10016 (212) 685-2864

International Scholarly Book Services
P.O. Box 1632, Beaverton, Oregon 97075
(503) 292-2606

International Specialized Book Service,
P.O. Box 1632, Beaverton, Oregon 97075
(503) 292-2606

Interstate, 19-27 N. Jackson St., Danville,
Illinois 61832-0594 (217) 446-0500

Iowa State University Press, 2121 S. State
Ave., Ames, Iowa 50010 (515) 294-5280

Irvington Publishers, 740 Broadway,
New York, New York 10003 (212) 777-4100

Island Press; Division of Round Valley
Agrarian Institute, Star Route 1,
Box 38, Covelo, California 95428
(707) 983-6432

Island Press, 175 Bahia Via, Fort Myers
Beach, Florida 33931 (813) 463-9482

J

J & L Enterprises, 2485 Riverside Dr.,
Laramie, Wyoming 82070

Jefferson National Expansion Historical
Association, 11 N. 4th St., St. Louis,
Missouri 63102

Jelm Mountain Publications, c/o Green
Mountain Book Co., P.O. Box 338,
Marklesville, California 96120
(916) 694-2141

Jenkins Publishing, P.O. Box 2085,
Austin, Texas 78767 (512) 444-6616

Little, Brown & Co., 200 West St., Waltham, Masschusetts 02154 (617) 890-0250

Liveright Publishing, 500 Fifth Ave., New York, New York 10110 (212) 354-5500

Lodestar Books, 2 Park Ave., New York, New York 10016 (212) 725-1818

Loft-Barnell, 958 Church St., Baldwin, New York 11510 (516) 868-6064

Lomond Publications, P.O. Box 88, Mt. Airy, Maryland 21771 (301) 829-1496

Longman, Inc., 95 Church St., White Plains, New York 10601 (914) 993-5000

Longwood Publishing Group, 51 Washington St. Dover, New Hampshire 03820 (603) 749-5038

Lothrop, Lee & Shepard Books, Wilmor Warehouse, 6 Henderson Dr., W. Caldwell, New Jersey 07006 (212) 899-3050

Louisiana State University Press, Baton Rouge, Louisiana 70893 (504) 388-6666

Lowell Press, 115 E. 31 St., P.O. Box 1877, Kansas City, Missouri 64141 (816) 753-4545

Loyola University Press, 3441 N. Ashland Ave., Chicago, Illinois 60657 (312) 1818

M

Mackinac Island State Park Commission, Box 370, Mackinac Island, Michigan 49757 (906) 847-3328

Macmillan Publishing, Front & Brown Sts., Riverside, New Jersey 08370 (212) 935-2000

Madrona Publishers; Distributed by Kampmann & Co., 9 East 40 St., New York, New York 10016 (212) 685-2928

Magi Books, 33 Buckingham Dr., Albany, New York 12208 (518) 482-7781

Maine Historical Society, 485 Congress St., Portland, Maine 04111 (207) 774-1822

Maine State Museum Publications, State House Sta. 83, Augusta, Maine 04333 (207) 289-2301

Maine Studies Committee, University of Maine, PICS Bldg., Orono, Maine 04469 (207) 581-1700

Malki Museum Press, 11-795 Fields Rd., Morongo Indian Reservation, Banning, California 92220 (714) 849-7289

Manitoba Museum of Man and Nature, Education Office, 190 Ruper Ave., Winnipeg, Manitoba R3B 0N2 Canada

Mankind Publishing, 8060 Melrose Ave., Los Angeles, California 90046 (213) 653-8060

Ray Manley Commercial Photography, 238 S. Tucson Blvd., Tucson, Arizona 85716 (602) 623-0307

Maryland Historical Press, 9205 Tuckerman St., Lanham, Maryland 20706 (301) 577-5308

Mason/Charter, VNR Order Processing, 7625 Empire Dr., Florence, Kentucky 41042 (212) 265-8700

McClain Printing Co., 212 Main St., Parsons, West Virginia 26287 (304) 478-2881

McGill-Queens Unviversity Press, c/o University of Toronto Press

McGraw-Hill Book Co., Princeton Rd., Hightstown, New Jersey 08520 (609) 426-5254; Or, 8171 Redwood Highway, Novato, California 94947 (415) 897-5201

David McKay Co., Inc., Fodor's/McKay, O'Neill Highway, Dunsmore, Pennsylvania 18512 (717) 344-2614

MEP Publications, University of Minnesota, c/o Anthropology Dept., 215 Ford Hall, 224 Church St., S.E., Minneapolis, Minnesota 55455 (612) 922-7993

Merrimack Publishers Circle, 47 Pelham Rd., Salem, New Hampshire 03079 (617) 887-2440

Julian Mesner; Division of Gulf & Western Corp., 1230 Ave. of the Americas, New York, New York 10020 (212) 245-6400

Methuen, Inc., 29 West 35 St., New York, New York 10001 (212) 244-3336

Metropolitan Museum of Art, Fifth Ave. and 82 St., New York, New York 10028 (212) 879-5500

The Michie Co., P.O. Box 7587, Charlottesville, Virginia 22906 (804) 295-6171

Michigan State University Press, 1405 S. Harrison Rd., 25 Manly Miles Bldg., East Lansing, Michigan 48824 (517) 355-9543

Microfilming Corp. of America, 200 Park Ave., New York, New York 10166 (212) 972-1070

Middle Atlantic Press, P.O. Box 263, Wallingford, Pennsylvania 19086 (215) 565-2445

Milwaukee Public Museum, 800 W. Wells St., Milwaukee, Wisconsin 53233 (414) 278-2787

Minnesota Historical Society, 1500 Mississippi St., St. Paul, Minnesota 55101 (612) 297-3243

Mississippi Department of Archives and History, P.O. Box 571, Jackson, Mississippi 39205 (601) 359-1424

Mojave Books, 7118 Canby Ave., Reseda, California 91335 (818) 342-3403

Montana Historical Society Press, 225 N. Roberts St., Helena, Montana 59620 (406) 444-4708

Monthly Review Press, 155 West 23 St., New York, New York 10011 (212) 691-2555

Moody Press, 820 N. LaSalle Dr., Chicago, Illinois 60610 (312) 973-7800

Morgan & Morgan, 145 Palisades St., Dobbs Ferry, New York 10522 (914) 693-0023

William Morrow & Co., Wilmor Warehouse, 6 Henderson Dr., West Caldwell, New Jersey 07006 (212) 889-3050

Mountain Press Publishing, P.O. Box 2399, Missoula, Montana 59806 (406) 728-1900

Mouton Publishers; Division of Walter De Gruyter, 200 Sw Mill River Rd., Hawthorne, New York 10532 (914) 747-0111

H.L. Murvin Publisher, 500 Vernon St., Oakland, California 94610 (415) 658-7517

Museum of the American Indian, Broadway at 155 St., New York, New York 10032 (212) 283-2420

Museum of Fine Arts, 465 Huntington Ave., Boston, Massachusetts 02115 (617) 267-9300

Museum of the Great Plains, Publications Dept., 601 Ferris, Box 68, Lawton, Oklahoma 73502 (405) 353-5675

Museum of New Mexico Press, P.O. Box 2087, Santa Fe, New Mexico 87503 (505) 827-6455

Museum of Northern Arizona, Route 4, Box 720, Flagstaff, Arizona 86001 (602) 774-5211

Museum of the Plains Indian, P.O. Box 400, Browning, Montana 59417

Museum Publications, P.O. Box 376, Southampton, New York 11968 (516) 283-7450

Myrin Institute, 136 East 64 St., New York, New York 10021 (212) 758-6475

N

NCJW, Inc., 15 East 26 St., New York, New York 10010 (212) 532-1740

National Academy Press, Publications Sales Office, 2101 Constitution Ave., Washington, D.C. 20418 (202) 334-3313

National Archives and Records Administration, Publications Division, Washington, D.C. 20408

National Book Co.; Division of Educational Research Associates, 333 S.W. Park Ave., Portland, Oregon 97205-3784 (503) 228-6345

National Clearinghouse for Bilingual Education, 1555 Wilson Blvd., Suite 605, Roslyn, Virginia 22209 (800) 336-4560

National Congress of American Indians, 804 D St., N.E., Washington, D.C. 20002 (202) 546-9404

National Council of Teachers of English, Public Information Office, 1111 Kenyon Rd., Urbana, Illinois 61801 (217) 328-3870

National Geographic Society, 17th & M Sts., N.W., Washington, D.C. 20036 (202) 857-7000

National Indian Traders Association, 3575 S. Fox, Box 1263, Englewood, Colorado 80150-1263 (303) 692-6579

National Learning Corp., 212 Michael Dr., Syosset, New York 11791 (516) 921-8888

National Museums of Canada; Distributed by The University of Chicago Press

National Native American Cooperative, P.O. Box 5000, San Carlos, Arizona 85550-0301 (602) 244-8244

Native American Studies Center, University of New Mexico, 1812 Las Lomas N.E., Albuquerque, New Mexico 87131 (505) 277-3917

Natural History Press;
Distributed by Doubleday

Naturegraph Publishers, P.O. Box 1075,
Happy Camp, California 96039
(916) 493-5353

Navajo Community College Press,
Navajo Community College, Tsaile,
Arizona 86556 (602) 724-3311

Navajo Curriculum Center Press,
Rough Rock Demonstration School,
Star Route 1, Rough Rock, Arizona 86503

Nebraska State Historical Society,
1500 R St., P.O. Box 82554, Lincoln,
Nebraska 68501 (402) 471-4745

Nelson-Atkins Museum of Art,
4525 Oak St., Kansas City, Missouri
64111 (816) 561-4000

Nelson-Hall, 111 N. Canal St., Chicago,
Illinois (312) 930-9446

Thomas Nelson, Publishers, P.O. Box 14100,
Nelson Place at Elm Hill Pike, Nashville,
Tennessee 37214 (615) 889-9000

New Age Press, P.O. Box 1216,
Black Mountain, North Carolina 28711
(704) 669-6214

New American Library, 1633 Broadway,
New York, New York 10019 (212) 397-8000

New Jersey State Museum, 205 W. State St.,
Trenton, New Jersey 08625

New Mexico Department of Development,
Tourist Division, 113 Washington Ave.,
Santa Fe, New Mexico 87503

New Seed Press; Distributed by Bookpeople;
Or, Inland Book Co., 22 Hemingway Ave.,
E. Haven, Connecticut 06512

New York Academy of Sciences,
Publications Dept., 2 East 63 St.,
New York, New York 10021 (212) 838-0230

New York Graphic Society; Distributed
by Little, Brown & Co. (617) 227-0730

New York Labor News, 914 Industrial Ave.,
Palo Alto, California 94303 (415) 494-1532

New York University Press; Distributed by
Columbia University Press (212) 316-7100

Newberry Library, 60 W. Walton St.,
Chicago, Illinois 60610 (312) 943-9090

Newcastle Publishing; Orders to
Borgo Press, (818) 873-3191

North Atlantic Books, 2320 Blake St.,
Berkeley, California 94704

North Carolina Division of Archives and
History, 109 E. Jones St., Raleigh,
North Carolina 27611 (919) 733-7442

North Point Press; Distributed by Farrar,
Straus & Grioux (212) 741-6900

North Star Press, P.O. Box 451, St. Cloud,
Minnesota 56301 (612) 253-1636

Northern Illinois University Press, DeKalb,
Illinois 60115 (815) 753-1826

Northern Michigan University Press,
607 Cohodas Administration Center,
Marquette, Michigan 49855 (906) 227-2720

Northland Press, P.O. Box N, Flagstaff,
Arizona 86002 (602) 774-5251

Northwestern Publishing House, 3624 W.
North Ave., Milwaukee, Wisconsin 53208
(414) 442-1810

W.W. Norton & Co., Inc., 500 Fifth Ave.,
New York, New York 10110 (212) 354-5500

Norwood Editions, P.O. Box 38, Norwood,
Pennsylvania 19074 (215) 583-4550

Nova Scotia Museum Publications,
P.O. Box 637, Halifax, Nova Scotia
B3S 2T3 Canada

Noyes Data Corp., Mill Rd. at Grand
Ave., Park Ridge, New Jersey 07656
(201) 391-8484

O

Oceana Publications, 75 Main St.,
Dobbs Ferry, New York 10522
(914) 693-1733

Octagon Books, 19 Union Square
West, New York, New York 10003
(212) 741-6961

Ohio Historical Society, 1985 Velma Ave.,
Columbus, Ohio 43211 (614) 466-1500

Ohio University Press; Orders to
Harper & Row

Old Army Press, P.O. Box 2243,
Fort Collins, Colorado 80521
(303) 484-5535

Old West Publishing, 1228 E. Colfax Ave.,
Denver, Colorado 80218 (303) 832-7190

Oregon Historical Society, 1230 S.W.
Park Ave., Portland, Oregon, 97205-2483
(503) 222-1741

Oregon State University Press, 101 Waldo
Hall, Oregon State University, Corvallis,
Oregon 97331 (503) 754-3166

O'Sullivan, Woodside & Co.; Distributed
by Caroline House Publishers, 236 Forest
Park Place, Ottawa, Illinois 61350
(815) 434-7905

Outbooks, 217 Kimball Ave., Golden,
Colorado 80401

Oxford University Press, 16-00 Pollitt
Dr., Fair Lawn, New Jersey 07410
(201) 796-8000

P

Pacific Books, P.O. Box 558,
Palo Alto, California 94302
(415) 856-0550

Pacific Search Press, 222 Dexter Ave.,
N., Seattle, Washington 98109
(206) 682-5044

Panjandrum Books; Distributed by Publishers
Group West, 5855 Beaudry, Emeryville,
California 94608 (415) 549-3033;
Or, Inland Book, 22 Hemingway Ave.,
E. Haven, Connecticut 06618

Panorama West Books, 2002 N. Gateway,
Suite 102, Fresno, California 93728
(209) 251-7801

Pantheon Books, 400 Hahn Rd.,
Westminster, Maryland 21157
(212) 751-2600

Parents Magazine Press; Distributed
by E.P. Dutton & Co.

Parnassus Imprints, 21 Canal Rd., Box 335,
Orleans, Massachusetts 02653
(617) 225-2932

Pathfinder Press, 410 West St.,
New York, New York 10014
(212) 741-0690

Pathfinder Publications, 4704 Wilford Way,
Minneapolis, Minnesota 55435
(612) 835-1128

Paulist Press, 997 MacArthur Blvd.,
Mahwah, New Jersey 07430 (201) 825-7300

Peabody Museum of Archaeology
and Ethnology; Distributed by
Harvard University Press

Peek Publications, P.O. Box 50123,
Palo Alto, California 94303
(415) 962-1010

Pelican Publishing, 1101 Monroe St.,
P.O. Box 189, Gretna, Louisiana 70053
(504) 368-1175

Pendle Hill Publications, 338 Plush Mill
Rd., Wallingford, Pennsylvania 19086
(215) 566-4507

Pendulum Press, Academic Bldg., Saw Mill
Rd., West Haven, Connecticut 06516
(203) 933-2551

Penguin Books, 40 West 23 St., New York,
New York 10010 (212) 807-7300

Pennsylvania Historical & Museum
Commission, Publications Sales Office,
Box 1026, Harrisburg, Pennsylvania
17108-1026 (717) 783-2618

Pennsylvania State University Press,
215 Wagner Bldg., University Park,
Pennsylvania 16802 (814) 865-1327

Gregory Perino, 1509 Cleveland,
Idabel, Oklahoma 74745

Philbrook Art Center, 2727 S. Rockford Rd.,
P.O. Box 52510, Tulsa, Oklahoma 74152
(918) 749-7941

Pineapple Press, 202 Pineapple St.,
P.O. Box 314, Englewood, Florida 33533
(813) 475-2238

Pioneer Book Publishers, Box 426,
Seagraves, Texas 79359 (806) 546-2498

Pocket Books, 1230 Ave. of the Americas,
New York, New York 10020 (212) 246-2121

Poly Tone Press, 16027 Sunburst St.,
Sepulveda, California 91343
(818) 892-0044

Porcupine Press, 1926 Arch St., 3rd Floor,
Philadelphia, Pennsylvania 19103-1444
(215) 563-2288

Portola Press, P.O. Box 1225,
Santa Barbara, California 93102
(805) 682-7974

Charles T. Powner Co., 7056 W. Higgins Rd.,
Chicago, Illinois 60656 (312) 939-7360

Praeger Publishers, 521 Fifth Ave.,
New York, New York 10175 (212) 599-8413

S

SSS Publishing, 17515 S.W. Blue Heron Rd., Lake Oswego, Oregon 97034 (503) 636-2979

Sage Publications, 275 S. Beverly Dr., Beverly Hills, California 90212 (212) 274-8003

Albert Saifer Publisher, Box 239 W.O.B., West Orange, New Jersey 07052

St. Johns-Oklawaha Rivers Trading Co., 110 S. Woodland Blvd. #130, Deland, Florida 32720 (904) 738-1210

St. Martin's Press, 175 Fifth Ave., New York, New York 10010 (212) 674-5151

St. Michaels Historical Museum, St. Michaels Mission, Drawer D, St. Michaels, Arizona 86511 (602) 871-4172

St. Scholastica Priory, Duluth, Minnesota 55811 (218) 728-1817

SamHar Press, Charlottesville, New York 12036 (607) 397-8725

San Bernardino County Museum Association, 2024 Orange Tree Lane, Redlands, California 92373 (714) 792-1334

San Juan District Media Center, Curriculum Division, 28 W. 200 North, Box 804, Blanding, Utah 84511 (801) 678-2281

San Marcos Press, 4705 Marquette N.E., Albuquerque, New Mexico 87108 (505)266-4412

Scarecrow Press, 52 Liberty St., Box 656, Metuchen, New Jersey 08840 (201) 548-8600

Schenkman Books, 190 Concord Ave., Cambridge, Massachusetts 02138 (617) 492-4952

R. Schneider Publishers, 312 Linwood Ave., Stevens Point, Wisconsin 54481 (715) 341-0020

Schocken Books, 62 Cooper Square, New York, New York 10003 (212) 475-4900

Scholarly Press, P.O. Box 160, Saint Clair Shores, Michigan 48080 (313) 884-0400

Scholarly Resources, 104 Greenhill Ave., Wilmington, Delaware 19805 (302) 654-7713

Scholars Press, Customer Service, P.O. Box 4869, Hampton Station, Baltimore, Maryland 21211 (404) 329-6950

Scholastic, Inc., P.O. Box 7502, 2931 E. McCurty St., Jefferson City, Missouri 65102 (212) 505-3000

School of American Research Press, P.O. Box 2188, Santa Fe, New Mexico 87504 (505) 984-0741

Scott, Foresman & Co., 1900 E. Lake Ave., Glenview, Illinois 60025 (312) 729-3000

Charles Scribner's Sons, Front & Brown Sts., Riverside, New Jersey 08075 (800) 257-5755

Seminole Nation Museum, P.O. Box 1532, Wewoka, Oklahoma 74884

Seven Oaks Press, 405 S. 7th St., Charles, Illinois 60174 (312) 584-0187

Seventh Generation Fund, P.O. Box 10, Forestville, California 95436 (707) 887-1559

P. Shalom Publications, 5409 18th Ave., Brooklyn, New York 11204

Shoe String Press, P.O. Box 4327, 995 Sherman Ave., Hamden, Connecticut 06514 (203) 248-6307

Shorey Publications, 110 Union St., Seattle, Washington 98101 (206) 624-0221

Silver Burdett Co., 250 James St., CN 1918, Morristown, New Jersey 07960-1918

Simon & Schuster, 1230 Ave. of the Americas, New York, New York 10020 (212) 245-6400

Peter Smith, Publisher, 6 Lexington Ave., Magnolia, Massachusetts 01930 (617) 525-3562

Smithsonian Institution A & I 2235, Office of Museum Publications, Washington, D.C. 20560 (202) 357-3101

Smithsonian Institution Press, P.O. Box 1579, Washington, D.C. 20013 (202) 357-1793

Social Sciences and Sociological Resources, P.O. Box 241, Aurora, Illinois 60507

Somerset Publishers, 200 Park Ave., Suite 303E, New York, New York 10017 (313) 884-0400

The Sourcebook Project, P.O. Box 107, Glen Arm, Maryland 21057 (301) 668-6047

South End Press, 300 Raritan Center Parkway CN-3137, Edison, New Jersey 08818 (617) 266-0629

Southern Illinois University Press,
P.O. Box 3697, Carbondale, Illinois 62901
(618) 453-2281

Southern Methodist University Press,
P.O. Box 415, Dallas, Texas 75275
(214) 692-2263

Southern University Press, 130 S. 19th St.,
Birmingham, Alabama 35233 (205) 251-5113

Southwest Book Services, 4951 Top Line Dr.,
Dallas, Texas 75247 (214) 688-1591

Southwest Museum, P.O. Box 42128,
Highland Park Station, Los Angeles,
California 90042 (213) 221-2164

Southwest Parks and Monuments Association,
221 N. Court, Tucson, Arizona 85701
(602) 622-1999

Southwestern Art Association,
P.O. Box 52510, Tulsa, Oklahoma 74152

Southwestern Cooperative Educational
Laboratory, 229 Truman N.E.,
Albuquerque, New Mexico 87108

Spizzirri Publishing, P.O. Box 664,
Medinah, Illinois 60157 (312) 529-1181

Springer Publishing, 536 Broadway,
New York, New York 10012 (212) 431-4370

Stackpole Books, P.O. Box 1831, Cameron &
Keller Sts., Harrisburg, Pennsylvania
17105 (717) 234-5041

Stanford University Press, Stanford,
California 94305 (415) 497-9434

State Historical Society of Wisconsin,
816 State St., Madison, Wisconsin 53706
(608) 262-1368

State Mutual Book & Periodical Service,
521 Fifth Ave., 17th Floor, New York,
New York 10017 (212) 682-5844

State University of New York Press,
P.O. Box 6525, Ithaca, New York 14850
(518) 472-5000

Stein & Day, Scarborough House, Briarcliff
House, Briarcliff Manor, New York 10510
(914) 762-2151

Stemmer House Publishing, 2627 Canes Rd.,
Owing Mills, Maryland 21117 (301) 363-3690

Stonehenge Books, 12375 E. Cornell Ave.,
Unit No. 7, Aurora, Colorado 80014
(303) 695-4710

Storypole Press, 11015 Bingham Ave., E.,
Tacoma, Washington 98446 (206) 531-2032

Strawberry Press, P.O. Box 451, Bowling
Green Station, New York, New York 10004

Street Press, P.O. Box 555, Port Jefferson,
New York 11777 (516) 928-4958

Studia Slovenica, P.O. Box 232,
New York, New York 10032

Summer Institute of Linguistics, Academic
Publications, 7500 W. Camp Wisdom Rd.,
Dallas, Texas 75236 (214) 298-3331

Sun Dance Books, 1520 N. Crescent Hgts.,
Hollywood, California 90046
(213) 654-2383

Sun Publishing, P.O. Box 5588, Santa Fe,
New Mexico 87502-5588 (505) 988-2033

Sun Tracks, Dept. of English, University
of Arizona, Tucson, Arizona 85721

Sunflower University Press, 1531 Yuma,
Box 1009, Manhattan, Kansas 66502
(913) 532-6733

Sunnycrest Publishing, Route 1, Box 1,
Clements, Minnesota 56224
(507) 692-2246

The Sunstone Press, P.O. Box 2321,
Santa Fe, New Mexico 87504-2321
(505) 988-4418

Superior Publishing, 708 Sixth Ave., N.,
P.O. Box 1710, Seattle, Washington 98111
(206) 282-4310

Mark Supnick, 8524 N.W. Second St.,
Coral Springs, Florida 33065
(305) 755-3448

Sweetlight Books, P.O. Box 307,
Arcata, California 95521 (707) 839-3973

Syracuse University Press, 1600 Jamesville
Syracuse, New York 13210 (315) 423-2596

T

Tales of the Mojave Road Publishing,
P.O. Box 307, Norco, California 91760
(714) 737-3150

Tamal Land Press, 39 Merwin Ave.,
Fairfax, California 94930
(415) 456-4705

Taylor Museum, The Library, Colorado
Springs Fine Arts Center, 30 W. Dale St.,
Colorado Springs, Colorado 80903
(303) 634-5581

Te-Cum-Tom Enterprises, 1725 Shorepines Dr., Coos Bay, Oregon 97420 (503) 888-6363

Temple University Press, Philadelphia, Pennsylvania 19122 (215) 787-8787

Ten Speed Press, P.O. Box 7123, Berkeley, California 94707 (415) 845-8414

Texas A & M University Press, Drawer "C", College Station, Texas 77843 (713) 845-1436

Texas Christian University Press, Box 30783, Fort Worth, Texas 76129 (817) 921-7822

Texas Tech Press, Sales Office, Texas Tech University, Room 4240, Lubbock, Texas 79409 (806) 742-1569

Texas Western Press, Univerity of Texas, El Paso, Texas 79968 (915) 747-5688

Texian Press, P.O. Box 1684, Waco, Texas 76703 (817) 754-5636

Thames Hudson; Distributed by W.W. Norton & Co.

Thayer & Associates, 522 Wilcox St., Fort Atkinson, Wisconsin 53538

Theosophical Publishing House, 306 W. Geneva Rd., Wheaton, Illinois 60189-0270 (312) 665-0123

Charles C. Thomas, Publisher, 2600 S. First St., Springfield, Illinois 62717 (217) 789-8980

Timber Press, 9999 S.W. Wilshire, Portland, Oregon 97225 (503) 292-0745

Timberline Books, 25890 Weld Rd. 53, Kersey, Colorado 80644 (303) 353-3785

Time-Life Books; Orders to Silver Burdett Co.

Todd & Honeywell, 10 Cuttermill Rd., Great Neck, New York 11021 (516) 487-9777

Trans-Anglo Books, P.O. Box 38, Corona Del Mar, California 92625 (714) 645-7393

Transaction Books, Rutgers University, Box C16, New Brunswick, New Jersey 08903 (201) 932-2280

Treasure Chest Publications, P.O. Box 5250, Tucson, Arizona 85703 (602) 623-9558

Tremaine Graphic and Publishing, 2727 Front St. Klamath Falls, Oregon 97601 (503) 884- 4193

Tribal Press, c/o Lowell Jensen, Route 2, Box 599, Cable, Wisconsin, 54821 (715) 794-2247

Troll Associates 320 State Highway 17, Mahwah, New Jersey 07430 (201) 529-4000

Troubador Press; Distributed by Price/Stern/Sloan Publishers, 410 N. La Cienega Blvd., Los Angeles, California 90048 (213) 657-6100

Tutorial Press, 323 S. Franklin Bldg., Suite &-206, Chicago, Illinois 60606

Charles E. Tuttle Co., Inc., P.O. Box 410, 28 S. Main St., Rutland, Vermont 05701-0410 (802) 773-8229

Twelve Trees Press, P.O. Box 188, Pasadena, California 91102 (818) 798-5207

Tyndale House Publishers, 336 Gunderson Dr., Box 80, Wheaton, Illinois 60189 (312) 668-8300

U

Frederick Unger Publishing, 36 Cooper Square, New York, New York 10003 (212) 473-7885

Unicorn Press, P.O. Box 3307, Greensboro, North Carolina 27402 (919) 852-0281

U.S. Catholic Conference, Publications Office, 1312 Massachusetts Ave., N.W., Washington, D.C. 20008 (202) 659-6640

Universe Books, 381 Park Ave. South, New York, New York 10016 (212) 685-7400

Universitetsforlaget; Distributed by Columbia University Press

University Microfilms International, 300 N. Zeeb Rd., Ann Arbor, Michgian 48106 (313) 761-4700

University of Alabama Press, P.O. Box 2877, University, Alabama 35486 (205) 348-5180

University of Arizona Press, 1615 E. Speedway, Tucson, Arizona 85719 (602) 621-1441

University of California Press, 2120 Berkeley Way, Berkeley, California 94720 (714) 642-6683

University of Chicago, Dept. of Geography, Research Paper, 5828 S. University Ave., Chicago, Illinois 60637 (312) 962-8314

University of Chicago Press,
11030 S. Langley Ave., Chicago,
Illinois 60628 (312) 568-1550

University of Connecticut Education,
The Thut World Education Center,
School of Education, Storrs,
Connecticut 06268 (203) 486-3321

University of Georgia Press, Terrell Hall,
Athens, Georgia 30602 (404) 542-2830

University of Illinois Archaeology,
109 Davenport Hall, 607 S. Mathews Ave.,
Urbana, Illinois 61801

University of Illinois Press, 54 E.
Gregory Dr. Champaign, Illinois 61820
(217) 333-0950

University of Iowa Press, Graphic
Services Bldg., Iowa City, Iowa 52242
(319) 353-4171

University of Kansas, Museum of Natural
History, Lawrence, Kansas 66045
(913) 864-4540

University of Massachusetts Press,
P.O. Box 429, Amherst, Massachusetts 01004
(413) 545-2217

University of Michigan, Museum of
Anthropology, Publications Dept.,
4009 Museum Bldg., 1109 Geddes,
Ann Arbor, Michigan 48109 (313) 764-6867

University of Michigan Press, 839 Greene St.,
Ann Arbor, Michigan 48106 (313) 764-4392

University of Minnesota, Bell Museum of
Pathology, P.O. Box 302, Mayo Memorial Bldg.
Minneapolis, Minnesota 55455

University of Minnesota, Department of
Anthropology, 215 Ford Hall, 224 Church
St., S.E., Minneapolis, Minnesota 55455
(612) 373-4614

University of Minnesota Press,
2037 University Ave., S.E., Minneapolis,
Minnesota 55414 (612) 373-3266

University of Missouri, Museum of
Anthropology, 104 Swallow Hall, Columbia,
Missouri 65211 (314) 882-3764

University of Missouri Press, 200 Lewis,
Columbia, Missouri 65211 (314) 882-7641

University of Nebraska Press, 901 N.
17th St. Lincoln, Nebraska 68588
(402) 472-3581

University of Nevada Press, Reno,
Nevada 89557 (702) 784-6573

University of New Mexico, Native American
Studies Department, 1812 Las Lomas, N.E.
Albuquerque, Ne Mexico (505) 277-3917

University of New Mexico Press,
Albuquerque, New Mexico 87131
(505) 277-2346

University of North Carolina Press,
P.O. Box 2288, Chapel Hill, North Carolina
27514 (919) 966-3561

University of Oklahoma Press,
P.O. Box 1657, Hagerstown, Maryland
21741 (800) 638-3030

University of Oregon Books, University
Publications, 101 Chapman Hall, Eugene,
Oregon 97403 (503) 686-5396

University of Pennsylvania, University
Museum, 33rd & Spruce Sts., Philadelphia,
Pennsylvania 19174 (215) 243-4119

University of Pittsburgh Press;
Distributed by Harper & Row

University of South Carolina Press,
Columbia, South Carolina 29208
(803) 777-5243

University of South Dakota, Government
Research Bureau, Vermillion, South Dakota
57069 (605) 677-5242

University of Tennessee Press,
293 Communications Bldg., Knoxville,
Tennessee 37996-0325 (615) 974-3321

University of Texas, Harry Ransom,
Humanities Research Center, P.O. Box 7219,
Austin, Texas 78713 (512) 471-9113

University of Texas, Institute of Texas
Cultures, P.O. Box 1226, San Antonio,
Texas 78294 (512) 226-7651

University of Texas Press, P.O. Box 7819,
Austin, Texas 78713 (512) 471-4032

University of Toronto Press, 33 E.
Tupper St., Buffalo, New York 14203
(416) 978-6817

University of Utah Press, Salt Lake City,
Utah 84112 (801) 581-6771

University of Washington Press,
P.O. Box C50096, Seattle, Washington
98145 (206) 543-8870

University of Wisconsin Library School,
Publications Committee, 600 N. Park St.
Madison, Wisconsin 53706

Franklin Watts, Sherman Turnpike,
Danbury, Connecticut 06816
(800) 672-6672

Waveland Press, P.O. Box 400, Prospect
Heights, Illinois 60070 (312) 634-0081

Wayne State University Press, Leonard
N. Simons Bldg., 5959 Woodward Ave.,
Detroit, Michigan 48202 (313) 577-4603

Wesleyan University Press;
Orders to Harper & Row

Richard West, P.O. Box 6404,
Philadelphia, Pennsylvania 19145

Western America Institute for Exploration,
1821 E. 9th St., The Dalles, Oregon 97058
(503) 296-9414

Western Publishers, 1711 S. Lakeside Dr.,
Lake Worth, Florida 33460 (305) 588-6848

Western Publishing, Dept. M, P.O. Box 700,
Racine, Wisconsin 53401 (414) 633-2431

Westernlore Publications, P.O. Box 35305,
Tucson, Arizona 85740 (602) 297-5491

Westminster Press, P.O. Box 718,
William Penn Annex, Philadelphia,
Pennsylvania 19105 (215) 928-2700

Albert Whitman & Co., 5747 W. Howard St.,
Niles, Illinois 60648 (312) 647-1355

John Wiley & Sons, 605 Third Ave.,
New York, New York 10158 (212) 850-6418

James Willert, 12804 S. Graff Dr.,
La Mirada, California 90638

H.W. Wilson Co., 950 University Ave.,
Bronx, New York 10452 (212) 588-8400

Diane E. Wirth, 16804 E. Peakview Ave.,
Aurora, Colorado 80016

Wonder-Treasure Books, 410 N. La Cienega
Blvd., Los Angeles, California 90048

Workbooks Press, P.O. Box 8504, Atlanta,
Georgia 30306 (404) 874-1044

World Book, Merchandise Mart Plaza,
Room 510, Chicago, Illinois 60654
(312) 245-3456

World Vision International, 919 W.
Huntington Dr., Monrovia, California 91016

Y

Yale University Press, 92A Yale Station,
New Haven, Connecticut 06520
(203) 436-7582

Yale University Publications in Anthropology
P.O. Box 2114, Yale Station, New Haven,
Connecticut 06520 (203) 436-7807

Ye Galleon Press, P.O. Box 25, Fairfield,
Washington 99012 (509) 283-2422

Yellow Jacket Press, 901 Alspaugh Lane,
Grand Prairie, Texas 75052

Yosemite National History Association,
Box 545, Yosemite National Park,
California 95389 (209) 372-4532

Yours Truly, Inc., 5502 Peachtree Rd.,
Atlanta, Georgia 30341 (800) 241-9488

Z

Zenger Publishing, P.O. Box 42026,
Washington, D.C. 20015 (301) 881-1470

Zia Cine, Inc., P.O. Box 493,
Santa Fe, New Mexico 87501

Zion Natural History Association,
Zion National Park, Springdale,
Utah 84767 (801) 772-3256

REFERENCE ENCYCLOPEDIA

OF THE
AMERICAN INDIAN
4TH EDITION

BARRY T. KLEIN

Published by:
Todd Publications
P.O. Box 92
Lenox Hill Station
New York, New York 10021

REFERENCE ENCYCLOPEDIA OF THE AMERICAN INDIAN

Fourth Edition, Volume II

Copyright © 1986

TODD PUBLICATIONS

Library of Congress Catalog Card Number 86-050046

Contents

Introduction

The following is an alphabetically arranged listing of American Indians prominent in Indian affairs, business, the arts and professions, as well as non-Indians active in Indian affairs, history, art, anthropology, archaeology, and the many fields to which the subject of the American Indian is related. Included are the biographical sketches of individuals named in Volume I—authors of books listed in the *Bibliography,* curators listed under *Museums,* tribal chiefs listed under *Tribal Councils,* etc. In this issue, for the first time, we have added a *Geographical Index.* This will allow the reader to see, at a glance, all listees in a particular state or city.

Format and style: The reader will note that these biographical sketches concentrate primarily on professional achievement; therefore, the usual personal data—name of spouse, date of marriage, and names of children, etc.—have not been included. The greater bulk of information has been culled from research questionnaires completed by the individuals themselves; however, in the case of a hastily written or otherwise incomplete questionnaire, I have consulted other reliable published sources. Whenever possible, direct quotations have been employed to give the reader greater insight into the life and work of each biographee than mere facts can supply. The length of each listing reflects the quantity of material received; no judgement is intended. Home and/or business addresses have been included when available.

The names and addresses of individuals who merit inclusion in future editions should be forwarded to The Editors, *Reference Encyclopedia of the American Indian,* Todd Publications, P.O. Box 92, Lenox Hill Station, New York, N.Y. 10021.

Barry T. Klein
Editor

REFERENCE ENCYCLOPEDIA OF THE AMERICAN INDIAN

AASBY, LEROY H. 1926-
(teacher, principal)

Born March 28, 1926, Hyde County, S.D. *Education:* Dakota State College, B.S., 1955; University of North Dakota, University of South Dakota, Augustana College, 1958-1972. *Principal occupation:* Teacher, principal. *Affiliations:* Teacher, South Dakota rural schools, 1947-1951; teacher and principal, B.I.A., Bridger Day School, Howes, S.D., 1955-. *Military service:* U.S. Army, 1951-1953 (several decorations). *Community activities:* TriCommunity Development Association (advisor, 1966-; Black Hills Girl Scout Council and Board, 1968-1975; president, 1972-1975); Boy Scout Committeeman, 1971-; Operation Friendship, 1972. *Memberships:* Phi Delta Kappa. *Awards, honors:* Outstanding Teacher Award, 1972; Service Award, Girl Scouts. *Interests:* Mr. Aasby is considered by others to be an expert in Indian culture (Lakota).

ABERLE, DAVID FRIEND 1918-
(anthropologist, educator)

Born November 23, 1918, St. Paul, Minn. *Education:* Harvard University, B.A., 1940; University of New Mexico, 1938-1940; Columbia University, Ph.D., 1950. *Principal occupation:* Professor of anthropology. *Affiliations:* Instructor, Harvard University, 1947-1950; visiting associate professor, Johns Hopkins University, 1950-1952; associate professor and professor, University of Michigan, 1952-1960; visiting professor and honorable research associate, Manchester University, 1960-1961; professor, Brandeis University, 1961-1963; professor of anthropology, University of Oregon, 1963-. *Military service:* U.S. Army, 1942-1946 (Army Commendation Ribbon). *Community activities:* Faculty-Student Committee to Stop the War in Vietnam, University of Oregon (chairman, 1965). *Memberships:* American Anthropological Association (Fellow); American Sociological Association; Royal Anthropological Institute of Great Britain and Ireland; American Ethnological Society; Society of Applied Anthropology. *Awards, honors:* Sohier Prize for B.A. thesis, Center for Advanced Study in the Behavioral Sciences, 1955-1956. *Interests:* Navaho Indians; Native American Church

and other religious movements; Mongol culture. *Published works: Psychological Analysis of a Hopi Life-History* (Comp. Psych. Monog. Series, 1951); *Kinship System of the Kalmuk Mongols* (University of New Mexico Publications in Anthropology, 1953); *Navaho and Ute Peyotism: A Chronological and Distributional Study,* with Omer C. Stewart (University of Colorado Series in Anthropology, 1957); *The Peyote Religion Among the Navaho* (Aldine Press, 1966).

ABEYTA, NARCISO *(Ha-Sodeh)*
(Navajo) 1918-
(interpreter)

Born December 18, 1918, Canyoncito, N.M. *Education:* Santa Fe Indian School, 1939; University of New Mexico, B.A. (Fine Arts, Economics). *Principal occupation:* Interviewer, interpreter, New Mexico State Employment Commission, 1952-. *Military service:* U.S. Army, 1941-1945. *Community activities:* American Legion. *Memberships:* International Association of Personnel in Employment Security, 1953-1965. *Awards, honors:* Second Prize, Advertising Poster, San Francisco Exposition, 1939. *Published works:* (as illustrator): *Aychee, Son of the Desert* (Hoffman Birney Penn Publishing Co., 1935).

ABRAMS, GEORGE H.J. (Seneca) 1939-
(museum director)

Born May 4, 1939, Allegany Indian Reservation, Salamanca, N.Y. *Education:* State University of New York, Buffalo, B.A., 1965, M.A., 1967; University of Arizona, Ph.D. program, 1968-1971. *Principal occupation:* Museum director. *Home address:* Salamanca, N.Y. 14779. *Affiliations:* Chairman, North American Indian Museums Association, Salamanca, N.Y., 1978-. *Other professional posts:* Trustee, Museum of the American Indian-Heye Foundation, New York, New York, 1977-; member, advisory board, Center for the History of the American Indian, The Newberry Library, Chicago, 1980-; member, Commission on Museums for a New Century, American Association of Museums, Washington, D.C., 1981-; member, National Advisory and Coordinating Council on Bilingual

Education, Washington, D.C., 1984-. *Community activities:* Seneca Nation Library, N.Y. (member, board of trustees, 1978-); Mohawk-Caughnawaga Museum, Fonda, N.Y. (member, board of advisors, 1980-); Gannagaro Archaeological Site, New York State Division of Historic Preservation, Parks and Recreation (member, advisory group.) *Membership:* American Association of University Professors. *Awards, honors:* John Hay Whitney Fellow, 1968-1969; American Indian Graduate Scholarship Program Grant, School of Law, University of New Mexico, 1971. *Interests:* Contemporary American Indian anthropology; American Indian education; applied anthropology; ethnohistory, museology, Iroquois Indians. *Published works:* "The Cornplanter Cemetary" (*Pennsylvania Archaeologist,* 1965); "Moving of the Fire: A Case of Iroquois Ritual Innovation" *(Iroquois Culture, History and Prehistory,* 1967); "Red Jacket" *(The World Book Encyclopedia,* 1976); *The Seneca People* (Indian Tribal Series, Phoenix, 1976).

ACKERMAN, LILLIAN A. 1928-
(anthropologist)

Born April 14, 1928, Detroit, Mich. *Education:* University of Michigan, B.A., 1950, M.A., 1951; Washington State University, Ph.D., 1982. *Principal occupation:* Anthropologist. *Home address:* Route 2, Box 559, Pullman, Wash. 99163. *Affiliations:* Researcher (courtesy faculty), Washington State University, Pullman, Wash. *Other professional posts:* Ethnographic consultant. · *Community activities:* Development Services Board (for developing and overseeing programs for the mentally retarded; served as chairperson several times); American Civil Liberties Union (board member). *Memberships:* American Anthropological Association, 1950-; American Ethnological Society, 1980-; Sigma Xi, 1982-. *Awards, honors:* Woodrow Wilson Fellowship; American Association of University Women - Dissertation Fellowship. *Interests:* "Primary areas of research interests are in the Indians of the Plateau Culture Area, and the Yupik Eskimos of Alaska. I studied sexual equality on the Colville Indian Reservation for six months and did a short study of Nez Perce socialization of children. I have made several short visits to the Colville Reservation since 1982. Spent three seasons doing research in Alaska, and made several trips there for the purpose of contract research." *Published works:* "Sexual Equality in the Plateau Culture Area" (Ph.D. dissertation, Washington State University, 1982); several shorter articles.

ACKERMAN, ROBERT E. 1928-
(professor of anthropology)

Born May 21, 1928, Grand Rapids, Mich. *Education:* University of Michigan, A.B., 1950, M.A., 1951; University of Pennsylvania, Ph.D., 1961. *Principal occupation:* Professor of anthropology. *Home address:* Route 2, Box 559, Pullman, Wash. 99163. *Affiliations:* Instructor to professor in anthropology, Washington State University, Pullman, Wash., 1961-. *Military service:* Airman first class, U.S. Air Force, 1952-1956. *Memberships:* American Anthropological Association (Fellow), 1951-; Society for American Archaeology, 1951-; American Association for the Advancement of Science (Fellow), 1960-; Arctic Institute of North America (Fellow, 1969; American University of University Professors, 1962-; Sigma Xi, 1968-. *Awards, honors:* Research grants from the Arctic Institute of North America for archaeological studies in southwest and southeast Alaska, 1962; National Science Foundation, 1966, 1967, 1971. Fellowships in the American Anthropological Association, the American Association for the Advancement of Science, and the Arctic Institute of North America, for contributions to the discipline of anthropology and arctic research. *Interests:* Archaeological research and surveys throughout Alaska and Canada. *Biographical sources:* Who's Who in the West; American Men of Science; International Scholars Directory; Contemporary Authors. *Published works:* Various articles and reports.

ADAMS, MARGARET B. (Navajo) 1936-
(anthropologist-museologist, art historian)

Born April 29, 1936, Toronto, Ontario, Can.

Education: Monterey Peninsula College, A.A., 1969; San Jose State University, B.A. (Anthropology and Art History), 1971; University of Utah, M.A. (Anthropology), 1973. *Principal occupation:* Anthropologist, museologist, art historian. *Home address:* 363 Hillcrest Ave., Pacific Grove, Calif. 93950. *Affiliations:* Chief of Museum Branch, Fort Ord Military Complex; and, Head Curator of Fort Ord and Presidio of Monterey Museums, 1974-. *Other professional posts:* Panel member (Indians in Science) for American Association for the Advancement of Science, 1972-; reviewer, "Project Media" of American Indian Education Association. *Community activities:* American Indian Information Center of Monterey Peninsula (volunteer executive director); member of Monterey Speaker's Bureau. *Memberships:* National Indian Education Association; California Indian Education Association; American Anthropological Association; American Association of Museums; Monterey History & Art Association. *Interests:* "Higher education for Native Americans, particularly in the sciences; media presentations concerning Native Americans; review of media on Native Americans and advertising of bad publications; observations and reporting of improper excavation of Native American ceremonial and burial sites; preservation of Native American ceremonial, burial, and historical sites." *Biographical sources:* *Who's Who in America; World's Who Who of Women; The Science Teacher* (Journal); *Women in the Social Sciences.* Published works: *Indian Tribes of North America and a Brief Chronology of Ancient Pueblo Indian and Old World Events* (Monterey Museum of Art, 1975); *History of Navajo and Apache Painting* (Indian America, Tulsa, 1976); *Historic Old Monterey* (DeAnza College History Center, 1977); *Silver & Sheen—Southwestern Indian Jewelry* (Indian America, Tulsa, 1977).

ADAMS, RICHARD EDWARD WOOD (Osage) 1931-
(archaeologist)

Born July 17, 1931, Kansas City, Mo. *Education:* University of New Mexico, B.A., 1953; Harvard University, M.A., 1960, Ph.D., 1963. *Principal occupation:* Archaeologist. *Home address:* 208 Village Circle, San Antonio, Texas 78232. *Affiliations:* Professor of anthropology, University of Minnesota, 1963-1972; dean of humanities and social sciences, University of Texas, San Antonio, 1972-. *Other professional posts:* Professor of anthropology, U.T.S.A., Guerrero Project, Mexico. *Military service:* U.S. Marine Corps, 1954-1957. *Memberships:* American Anthropological Association; Society for American Archaeology; Seminario de Cultura Maya; Sociedad Mexicana de Antropologia; American Association for the Advancement of Science (Fellow); Royal Anthropological Society of Great Britain and Ireland (Fellow). *Interests:* Middle American anthropology, especially prehistory; world archaeology. *Travels, expeditions:* Archaeologist, Tikal Project, Guatemala, 1958; archaeologist, Altar de Sacrificios Project, Guatemala, 1961-1963; project director, Cotzal Project, Guatemala, 1965-1966; field director, National Geographic Society, Becan Project, 1970; director, Rio Bee Project, 1973. *Published works: The Ceramics of Altar de Sacrificios* (Peabody Museum, Harvard University, 1971); *Prehistoric Mesoamerica* (Little, Brown & Co., 1977); editor, *The Origins of Maya Civilization* (University of New Mexico Press, 1977); various papers.

ADAMS, VIVIAN M. (Yakima, Puyallup, Suquamish, Quinault) 1943-
(museum curator)

Born March 21, 1943, Toppenish, Wash. *Education:* Institute of American Indian Art, Santa Fe, N.M., AFA (Museology), 1981. Principal occupation: Museum curator. *Affiliation:* Yakima Nation Cultural Center, P.O. Box 151, Toppenish, Wash. 98948. *Community activities:* Yakima Agency Employees Club (secretary-treasurer); IAIA Student Senate Representative; Yakima Women's Investor's Club. *Memberships:* Washington State Folklife Council; American Association of State & Local History; Toppenish Chamber of Commerce; Yakima Chamber of Commerce; Washington Museum Association; Yakima Valley Visitors and Convention Bureau; National Trust for Historic Preservation; Native American Task Force, Washington State Centennial; Washington State Native American Task Force, Native American Consortium; Washington State Centennial Heritage Subcommittee of Lasting Legacy. *Awards, honors:* Outstanding Artistic and Academic Achievement, 1980-1981; Institute of American Indian Art President's Award; Who's Who Among Students, American Junior Colleges, 1981; Scholastic Achievement Award, Yakima Nation Education, 1982. *Interests:* "My main interest is two-dimensional art (sketching, pen and ink). I love to work with Indian artifacts—those items which are hand made of natural materials. Plus, it is a joy to design ways to display these items which teach a lesson in an aesthetic manner. It is important to present our cultural history and traditions from our (Native American) point of view to promote a better understanding by other cultures--and to learn from them. Oral history and elders input into telling our ways is extremely important to accomplishing those goals of the museum. Therefore, museology is my second interest, my financial base to a sporadic art career! But being a curator allows me the time to work with objects of art—my main love. My third interest is pursuing conservation techniques: recognizing and maintaining basket weaving, textile weaving, restoration techniques, time allowing I hope to accomplish conservator's training." *Biographical sources:* Yakima Herald Republic news article; Girl Scouts of America; *Who's Who Among Students in American Junior Colleges.*

AGOGINO, GEORGE A. 1920-
(distinguished professor of
anthropology, museum director)

Born November 18, 1920, West Palm Beach, Fla. *Education:* University of New Mexico, B.A., 1949, M.A., 1951; Syracuse University, Ph.D., 1958; Harvard University, Wenner-Gren Foundation Post Doctoral Fellowship in Anthropology, 1961-1962. *Principal occupation:* Distinguished professor of anthropology, museum director. *Home address:* 1600 S. Main, Portales, N.M. 88130. *Affiliations:* Instructor in anthropology, Syracuse University, 1956-1958; museum director and assistant profes-

sor, University of South Dakota, 1958-1959; assistant professor of anthropology, University of Wyoming, 1959-1962; associate professor of anthropology, Baylor University, 1962-1963; professor of anthropology and museum director, Eastern New Mexico University, 1963-; director of Paleo-Indian Institute, 1968-. *Other professional posts:* Founding director, Blackwater Draw, Miles Museum and Anthropology Museum of Eastern New Mexico University, Potales, N.M. *Military service:* U.S. Army Signal Corps, 1943-1946. *Community activities:* Eastern New Mexico University, Local National Educational Association (president and vice-president, 1976-). *Memberships:* American Anthropological Association (Fellow); American Association for the Advancement of Science (Fellow); Royal Anthropological Institute of Great Britain and Ireland (Fellow); Institute Inter-American (Fellow); Current Anthropology (Associate); Explorers' Club (Fellow); Senato Academico (regent) Accademmia Romania de Science ed Arti. *Awards, honors:* Ph.D. Rome (Italy) Institute of Arts and Sciences; multiple grants from Wenner-Gren Foundation for Anthropology, American Philosophical Society, Sigma Xi; twice Eastern New Mexico University Outstanding Educator, 1972, 1974-1975; fourth distinguished professor in 70-year history of Eastern New Mexico University. *Interests:* Indian religion and culture; North America and Mexico Paleo Indian; Indian physical anthropology, pictoglyphs. "Have worked with and published on Navajo, Kickapoo, Seminole, Seri, Yaqui, Sioux, Mayo, Maya, Huastica and Otomi Indians." *Travels, expeditions:* Anthropological research in Canada, Mexico, New Guinea and Australia. *Biographical sources: Who's Who Among Authors and Journalists; Directory of International Biography; Who's Who in the Southwest; Who's Who in the West; Who's Who in American Education; Dirctory of International Biography; Contemporary Authors; Outstanding Educators in America; American Men of Science.* Published works: Over 225 articles and monographs, including: *Sandia Cave,* 1973; and *Ceremonialism of the Tepecano,* 1972 (Eastern New Mexico University Press).

AHSHAPANEK, DON COLESTO
(Delaware-Nanticoke) 1932-
(professor of biological sciences)

Born April 29, 1932, Milton, Del. *Education:* Indiana University, 1949-1950; University of Kansas, 1951; Haskell Institute (Business Certificate), 1953; Central (Okla.) State University, B.S. (Biology), 1956; University of Oklahoma, M.S. (Botany), 1960, Ph.D. (Botany), 1962. *Home address:* 1845 W. 28th Terrace, Lawrence, Kansas 66044. *Affiliations:* Clerk, stenographer, Bureau of Indian Affairs, Anadarko, Okla., 1953-1954, 1957, 1959; assistant professor of biology, 1962-1967, associate professor of biology, 1967-1971, Kansas State Teachers College, Emporia, Kansas; instructor of biological sciences, 1971-1973, chairman, Native American Culture Division, 1973-1976, instructor of biological sciences and program director—Haskell Minority Biomedical Sciences Program (NIH), Haskell Indian Junior College, Lawrence, Kan. *Other professional posts:* Taught biology in the Indian Health Careers Program at Mackinaw City, Mich. (summers, 1975-1977); taught courses, "The Native American in Contemporary Society," for the Master of Liberal Arts Program, Baker University, Bladwin, Kan. (summer, 1975). *Memberships:* National Indian Education Association; National Congress of American Indians; The Ecological Society of America; Southwestern Association of Naturalists; Kansas Academy of Sciences.

AGUILAR, ALFRED *(Sa wa pin)*
(San Ildefonso Pueblo) 1933-
(artist, teacher)

Born July 1, 1933, San Ildefonso Pueblo, N.M. *Education:* Santa Fe Indian School; Pojoaque High School; University, Albuquerque, N.M. *Principal occupation:* Artist, teacher (Chapter I, 1967-). *Home address:* Route 5, Box 318C, Santa Fe, N.M. 87501. *Military service:* U.S. Air Force, 1952-1956 (Good Service Award). *Community activities:* Pueblo official council member. *Memberships:* Eight Northern Pueblo Art Council; The Indian Pueblo Cultural Center. *Awards, honors:* For painting, pottery, and sculptures from the New Mexico State Fair, Inter-Tribal Ceremonial, Jemez Pueblo, Heard Museum, and New Mexico Fine Arts Museum. *Interests:* Education, art-travel expeditions. Mr. Aguilar "specializes in black and red pottery, and is well known by many people around the world with his nativity set and story teller. He sculptures black on black buffalos, and animal and dancing figures on pottery. He has gained versatility in water color, and is adept in depicting Indian dances and in preserving ancient design and symbols on his work."

AGUILAR, JOSE V. *(Suwu-Peen)*
(Tewa Pueblo) 1924-
(technical graphic artist)

Born January 8, 1924, San Ildefonso, N.M. *Education:* Otis Art Institute, Certificate, 1949; Hill and Canyon School of Art, 1950. *Principal occupation:* Technical graphic artist. *Home address:* 9682 Mt. Darnard Dr., Buena Park, Calif. 90620. *Affiliation:* Project Coordinator, Rockwell International, Downey, Calif., 1954-. *Military service:* U.S. Army, 1944-1946 (European Theatre Medal; Purple Heart). *Memberships:* National Congress of American Indians, 1954-. *Awards, honors:* Certificate of Merit, Inter-Tribal Indian Ceremonial Association, 1949; First Purchase Award, Philbrook Art Center, 1953; Denver Art Museum Purchase Award; Mary Wartrous Award, 1954; Honorable Mention, Philbrook Art Center, 1959; Lippencott and Wellington Award; Museum of New Mexico Award for Collection of Museum of Contemporary Art; paintings in permanent collections of Philbrook Art Center, Museum of New Mexico, and Museum of the American Indian. *Private collections include:* Millard Sheet, artist and educator; Vincent Price, actor and art collector; and Darwin Goody, educator.

ALFONSI, JOHN 1961-
(archaeologist, cultural resources management)

Born January 16, 1961, New York, N.Y. *Education:* University of Alaska, Fairbanks (degree in progress). *Principal occupation:* Archaeologist, cultural resources management. *Home address:* Mile 1403.5 Alaska

Hiway, Delta Junction, Alaska 99737. *Affiliation:* Ahtna, Inc., Fairbanks, Alaska. *Membership:* Alaska Anthropological Association, 1984-. *Awards, honors:* Outstanding Senator and Outstanding Student—USUA, University of Alaska, Fairbanks Student Government, 1984 and 1985, respectively. *Interests:* Hunting, trapping, fishing, building; cultural resource assessments throughout Alaska. *Published works:* (In progress) Ahtna Cultural Resources throughout the region. Work includes mainly archaeological fieldwork and intensive investigation, e.g. on-the-ground archaeological survey of the Copper River Basin. "First of its kind."

ALLARD, L. DOUG (Flathead-Confederated Salish and Kootenai) 1931-
(museum founder and owner)

Born August 30, 1931, St. Ignatius, Mont. *Education:* Montana State University, B.S., 1956. *Principal occupation: Founder and owner of the Flathead Indian Museum and Allard Auctions. Home address:* P.O. Box 460, St. Ignatius, Mont. 59865. *Military service:* U.S. Marine Corps, 1950-1953 (Korean War Ribbon, U.N. Medal, two Battle Stars, Good Conduct Medal). *Memberships:* Indian Arts and Crafts Association (charter member, board of directors); International Society of Appraisers; Big Brothers and Sisters (director). *Awards, honors:* Million Dollar Round Table — National Association of Life Underwriters. *Interests:* Tribal culture; avid collector of Indian artifacts. *Biographical source: Who's Who in the West.*

AMBLER, J. RICHARD 1934-
(professor of anthropology, university archaeologist)

Born January 23, 1934, Denver, Colo. *Education:* University of Colorado, B.A., 1958, Ph.D. (Anthropology), 1966; University of Arizona, M.A. (Anthropology), 1961. *Principal occupation:* Professor of anthropology, university archaeologist. *Address:* Department of Anthropology, Box 15200, Northern Arizona University, Flagstaff, Arizona 86011. *Affiliations:* Field foreman and research assistant to director, University of Colorado Museum, 1956-1957; ranger, archaeologist, Mesa Verde National Park and Great Sand Dunes National Monument, 1957-1958; foreman, University of Colorado Field School, 1958; archaeology field assistant, University of Utah, 1958; museum assistant, Arizona State Museum, 1958-1959; field foreman and research archaeologist, University of Utah, 1959-1960; field foreman, archaeologist, Museum of New Mexico, 1960-1961; archaeologist, Glen Canyon Project, Museum of Northern Arizona, 1961-1963; teaching assistant, University of Colorado, 1963-1965; archaeologist, University of Utah, 1964-1965; instructor in anthropology, University of Colorado, Denver Center, 1965; executive director, Texas Archaeological Salvage Project, University of Texas, 1965-1967; assistant professor of anthropology, University of Texas, 1966-1967; associate professor of anthropology, 1967-1984, professor of anthropology, 1984-, and university archaeologist, 1968-, Northern Arizona University. *Memberships:* Society for American Archaeology, 1957-; Sigma Xi, 1965-. *Biographical source: American Men of Science. Published works:* Various articles, papers and reports on anthropology and archaeology.

AMES, MICHAEL M. 1933-
(professor of anthropology, museum director)

Born June 19, 1933, Vancouver, Can. *Education:* University of British Columbia, B.A., 1956; Harvard University, Ph.D., 1961. *Principal occupation:* professor of anthropology, museum director. *Home address:* 6393 N.W. Marine Dr., Vancouver, B.C. V6T 1W5. *Affiliation:* Museum of Anthropology, University of British Columbia, Vancouver, B.C. *Memberships:* Canadian Ethnology Society; American Anthropological Association; Canadian Museum Association; American Association of Asian Studies. *Awards, honors:* Guggenheim Fellowship; Fellow of the Royal Society of Canada. *Interests:* Research in Northwest Coast of North America and South Asia. *Published works: Manlike Monsters on Trial,* co-edited with M. Halpin (UBC Press, 1980; *Museums, The Public and Anthropology* (Concept and UBC Press, 1985.)

AMIOTTE, ARTHUR DOUGLAS
(Oglala-Teton Sioux) 1942-
(artist, teacher)

Born March 25, 1942, Pine Ridge, S.D. *Education:* Northern State College, B.S. (Art Education), 1964. *Principal occupation:* Artist, teacher. *Affiliations:* Iowa State Education Association and Sioux City Education Association, 1964-. *Community activities:* Community speakers panel on promoting minority and ethnic group awareness; lecturer on American Indians. *Memberships:* Northern Art Education Association. *Awards, honors:* South Dakota Indian Scholarship, 1960-1964; inclusion in Who's Who in American Universities and Colleges, 1964; various awards in art education and sculpture from Gallery of American Indian Art, the Philbrook Art Center, the Institute of American Indian Art, 1963-; nominated for Outstanding Teacher of Year, Sioux City, 1966. *Interests:* Art education, Plains Indian culture.

AMYLEE (Iroquois) 1952-
(director of Indian organization)

Born January 3, 1952, Ohio. *Education:* State University of New York, 1976-1979; Kent State University, 1970-1980 (concurrent). *Principal occupation:* Director of Indian organization. *Home address:* Hawk Hollow Private Nature Preserve, Tippecanoe, Ohio 44699. *Affiliations:* Founder and director, American Indian Rights Association, Kent State University, 1970-1983; director, Native American Indian Resource Center, Inc.; Licensed Raptor (Bird of Prey) Rehabilitator (ongoing); Medicine Woman Initiate (ongoing). *Other professional posts:* Professional lecturer and artist for NAIRC, Inc. *Memberships:* National Wildlife Rehabilitators Association; Earthwalker Learning Lodge. *Awards, honors:* Numerous awards for artistic achievement. *Interests:* AmyLee has appeared with Native American leaders and dignitaries including Sakokwenonkwas of Akwesasne, Mad Bear, Rolling Thunder, Sun Bear, Grandfather Sky Eagle and Vernon Bellecourt. She has also had the opportunity to serve as a script consultant for the Smithsonian Institution and a character actress in the Public Broadcast System's film, *Americas Ethnic Sym-*

phony. Published works: The Pathfinder Directory: A Guide to Native Americans in the Ohiyo Country (Indian House, 1982).

ANTIQUIA, CLARENCE (Tlingit) 1940-
(federal government administrator)

Born April 16, 1940, Sitka, Alaska. *Education:* Sheldon Jackson Junior College, Sitka, Alaska, 1958-1959. *Principal occupation:* Federal government administrator. *Home address:* Box 1111, Juneau, Alaska 99802. *Affiliations:* Area director, Bureau of Indian Affairs, Juneau, Alaska, 1965-1975. *Awards, honors:* Outstanding Performance Awards, B.I.A., 1965, 1967, 1970. *Interests:* Public administration, government, personnel management, race relations, Indian affairs.

APODACA, RAYMOND D. (Ysleta del Sur Pueblo) (Tigua Indian Tribe of Texas) 1946-
(administrator)

Born October 15, 1946, Las Cruces, N.M. *Education:* New Mexico State University, B.A., 1969, M.A. (Public Administration), 1976. *Principal occupation:* Administrator. *Home address:* 8220 Research, Apt. 116B, Austin, Texas 78758. *Affiliation:* Executive director, Texas Indian Commission (State of Texas), Austin, Texas, 1983-. *Military service:* U.S. Air Force, 1969-1972. *Memberships:* National Indian Education Association, 1973-1980; National Congress of American Indians, 1973-; Governors' Interstate Indian Council, 1977- (national president, 1985-1986); Texas American Indian Sesquicentennial Association (executive board member, 1985-); Texas State Agency Business Administrators Association, 1982-; North Amerian Indian Museums Association, 1977-1980; New Mexico State University All-Indian Adult Advisory Board, 1976-; Citizens' Advisory Board, ETCOM Public Radio (El Paso, Texas), 1980-1985; OPM—Intergovernmental Committee on Indian Affairs, Southwest Region, 1982-; University of Texas, Austin, El Paso, Master of Science in Social Work Program, Advisory Council, 1984-; Texas State Committee on the Protection of Human Remains and Sacred Objects (American Indian) (co-chairman, 1984-). *Awards, honors:* Colonel Aide-de-Camp, Governor, State of New Mexico, 1977. *Interests:* History, government, theology, education. *Biographical source: To Live in Two Worlds,* by Brent Ashabrenner (Dodd, Mead & Co., 1984.) *Published work: Directory of Information on Health Careers for American Indians* (ERIC/CRESS, National Education Laboratory Publishers, Inc., 1977.)

ARAGON, ARNOLD (Crow-Pueblo) 1953-
(artist)

Born July 9, 1953, Crow Agency, Mont. *Education:* American Indian Art Institute, Santa Fe, N.M. (Art/Sculpture), 1979 graduate; University of Nevada, Reno, 1980-1984. *Principal occupation:* Professional artist. *Home address:* P.O. Box 64, Walker River Reservation, Schurz, Nev. 89427. *Affiliation:* Rites of Passage Wilderness Camp, Schurz, Nevada. *Other professional posts:* Art consultant, board member, Nevada Urban Indians—Earth Window. *Interests:* Sculpturing using hand tools. His art includes water colors, pastels and pencil drawings. Arnold's sculptures are in various galleries and museums throughout the West as well as private collections throughout the country. He enjoys travel and the outdoors.

ARMAGOST, JAMES GRAYHAWK (Mohican) 1945-
(silversmith and lapidary)

Born July 8, 1945, Johnstown, Penn. *Education:* Accredited G E D two year college. *Principal occupation:* Silversmith and lapidary. *Address:* c/o The Silver Phoenix, 2946-D Chain Bridge Rd., Oakton, Virginia 22124. *Affiliation:* Owner, The Silver Phoenix, Oakton, Virginia. The Silver Phoenix has been promoting Native American crafts for over ten years. *Military service:* U.S. Army Special Forces. *Community activities:* American Indian Inter-Tribal Cultural Organization (member, board of directors.) *Awards, honors:* Numerous first place and Best of Show Awards for his jewelry in assorted regional competitions (Native American and non-Native American). *Art*

form: "His Navajo leafwork and multi-level chizeled boarders are some of the cleanest to be found. The geometrics in his overlay styles are crisp and exact, and his animals, plants and people are nearly animated. He has also produced breathtaking pieces blending inlaid stone and highly polished metal with flawless skill. He has walked away with top prizes in every competition he has ever entered."

ARTICHOKER, JOHN HOBART, Jr. (Sioux) 1930-
(government administrator)

Born January 17, 1930, Pine Ridge, S.D. *Education:* State University of South Dakota, B.S. (Education), 1951, M.A., 1957. *Principal occupation: Government administrator. Home address:* 4722 W. State Ave., Glendale, Ariz. *Affiliations:* Director of Indian education, State of South Dakota, 1951-1961; tribal operations officer, B.I.A., Billings, Mont., 1961-1962; superintendent, Northern Cheyenne Reservation, 1963-1968; superintendent, Papago Agency, Sells, Ariz., 1968-1969; superintendent, Colorado River Agency, Parker, Ariz., 1969-1972; area director, B.I.A., Phoenix Area Office, 1972-. *Community activities:* Division of Indian Services, University of Montana (advisory council); Tongue River Jacees (board of directors); National Advisory Committee on Indian Work, National Council of Episcopal Church. *Awards, honors:* Ten Outstanding Young Men Award. U.S.J.C.'s, 1965; Indian Achievement Award, 1965. *Published works: Indians of South Dakota* (South Dakota Dept. of Public Instruction, 1956); *The Sioux Indian Goes to College,* master's thesis, with Neil Palmer (Institute of Indian Studies, Vermillion, S.D.)

ATKINSON, LA VERNE D. (Navajo) 1934-
(teacher)

Born July 3, 1934, Ganado, Ariz. *Education:* University of Minnesota, B.S., 1960. *Principal occupation:* Teacher. *Home address:* 404 Shonto Blvd., Window Rock, Ariz. 86515. *Affiliation:* Program specialist, Cultural Awareness Center Trilingual Institute,

Albuquerque, N.M., 1976-. *Other professional posts:* Steering committee, Native American Bilingual Education Association. *Memberships:* New Mexico Association for Bilingual Education; Arizona Bilingual Association; Native American Bilingual Education Association. *Interests:* "Mainly interested in bilingual, bicultural education for the Native Americans."

AUSTIN, FRANK *(Bahah-Zhonie)* (Navajo) 1938-
(artist)

Born April 10, 1938, Tsegi Canyon, Ariz. *Education:* Phoenix Indian School; University of Arizona; Tempe College, 1959. *Principal occupation:* Textile artist and painter. *Home address:* 710 Memorial Dr., Cortez, Colo. 81321. *Affiliation:* President, Nizhonie, Inc., Cortez, Colo., 1970- *Memberships:* American Craftsmen's Council, 1961-; American Institute of Interior Designers; Arizona Arts and Crafts. *Awards, honors:* American Institute of Interior Designers Award; Walter Brimson Grand Award; Catherine J. McWhirter Grand Award; Scottsdale National Exhibit Award. *Biographical source:* Contemporary Craftsmen of the Far West.

B

BAERREIS, DAVID A. 1916-
(professor of anthropology)

Born November 2, 1916, New York, N.Y. *Education:* University of Oklahoma, B.A., 1941, M.A., 1943; Columbia University, Ph.D., 1948. *Principal occupation:* Professor of anthropology. *Home address:* 4715 Sheboygan Ave., Apt. 106, Madison, Wis. 53705. *Affiliation:* Professor of anthropology, University of Wisconsin, 1947-; chairman, Department of Sociology and Anthropology, 1956-1958, 1959-1960; chairman, Department of Anthropology, 1971-1973. *Military service:* U.S. Army. *Memberships:* American Ethnohistoric Conference (president, 1957); American Folklore Society (vice-president, 1958, executive committee, 1959-1961); Society for American Archaeology (secretary, 1959-1965; president, 1962); American Association for the Advancement of Science (chairman, secretary, vice-president, 1963); American Anthropological Association (Fellow); Royal Anthropological Institute. *Awards, honors:* Lapham Research Medal, Wisconsin Archaeological Society. *Interests:* Prehistory and ethnohistory of North and South American Indians; field trips to Wisconsin, Oklahoma, New Mexico, South Dakota, Iowa, Brazil. *Published works: The Preceramic Horizons of Northeastern Oklahoma* (Anthropological Paper, Museum of Michigan, No. 6, 1951); editor, *The Indian in Modern America* (State Historical Society of Wisconsin, 1956); articles in various journals.

BAHTI, MARK 1950-
(shop owner)

Born September 28, 1950, Tucson, Ariz. *Education:* Prescott College, 1968-1969, University of Arizona, 1969-1970. *Principal occupation:* Owner of Tom Bahti Indian Arts and Crafts, 1972-. *Home address:* 1708 East Speedway, Tucson, Ariz. 85719. *Affiliation:* Coordinator, 'Indian Advocacy Program,' 1976-. *Community activities:* Society of Professional Anthropologists, Tucson (senior advisor); Tucson Chapter of American Indian Affairs (charter member.) *Memberships:* Association of American Indian Affairs; Inter-Tribal Ceremonial Association; Indian Arts and Crafts Association (charter member, past president, board of directors). *Awards, honors:* Established award for Outstanding Indian Graduate Student at the University of Arizona, 1975; studied jewelry under Charles Loloma, 1965. *Published works: Consumer's Guide to Southwestern Indian Arts and Crafts,* 1975; *Navaho Sandpainting Art,* with Eugene Baatsolani Joe (Treasure Chest Publications, 1978).

BAINES, RAYMOND GEORGE (Tlingit-Tsimpshean) 1926-
(pastor)

Born September 26, 1926, Ketchikan, Alaska. *Education:* Phillips University, B.A., 1959; Pacific School of Religion, B.D., 1963. *Principal occupation:* Pastor. *Affiliations:* Executive director, United Church

Committee on Indian Work; pastor of churches, El Cerrito and Berkeley, California, Gardiner, Oregon, and Metlakatla and Sitka, Alaska. *Military service:* U.S. Army Infantry, 1944-1945. *Community activities:* School board, P.T.A., Metlakatla, Alaska (vice-president); Central Council, Tlingit and Haida Indians of Alaska (executive treasurer). *Memberships:* Minnesota, Minneapolis, St. Paul Councils of Churches; Governor's Advisory Committee on Children and the Young; Minnesota Fair Employment Practices Commission; Minnesota Council on Religion and Race.

BAKER, ANSON A. (Mandan-Hidatsa) 1927-
(government administrator)

Born May 26, 1927, Elbowoods, N.D. *Education:* North Dakota Agricultural College, 1946-1947; Minot Business College, 1947-1948, 1949-1950. *Principal occupation:* Government administrator. *Home address:* Box 237, Browning, Mont. 59417. *Affiliations:* Clerk, Aberdeen Area Office, B.I.A., Aberdeen, S.D., 1953-1955; credit officer, Rosebud Indian Reservation, Aberdeen, S.D., 1953-1954; property and supply assistant, loan examiner, Pine Ridge Indian Reservation, Pine Ridge, S.D., 1955-1960; supervisory finance specialist, Fort Belknap Indian Reservation, Harlem, Mont., 1960-1964; administrative manager, Blackfeet Indian Reservation, Browning, Mont., 1964-1967; superintendent, Fort Peck Indian Reservation, 1967-1971; superintendent, Crow Indian Reservation, Crow Agency, Mont., 1971-1973; superintendent, Fort Berthold Reservation, New Town, N.D., 1973-1976; superintendent, Blackfeet Indian Reservation, Browning, Mont., 1976-1979. *Military service:* Seaman First Class, U.S. Navy, 1945-1946. *Community activities:* American Legion, Pine Ridge, S.D. (Post Commander, 1958); American Legion Post 300, New Town, N.D. (Post Commander, 1976); Little Shell Pow-wow, New Town, N.D. (president, 1976.) *Awards, honors:* Certificate of Superior Performance, B.I.A., 1964; Boss of Year Award, Browning, Mont., 1966; Boss of Year Award, Poplar Jaycees, Poplar, Mont., 1968; Certificate of Appreciation, Fort Peck

Tribal Industries, 1969, 1970; Fort Berthold Person Award, Fort Berthold Reservation, N.D., 1974. *Interests:* "My interest is working with people, attempting to bring about a better understanding of Indian people and their tribal government." *Biographical source: Indians of Today,* Fourth Edition (Marion E. Gridley).

BAKER, ARLENE ROBERTA *(Cata)* (Seneca-Cayuga-Pueblo) 1938-
(English instructor)

Born April 13, 1938, Albuquerque, N.M. *Education:* Northeast Oklahoma A & M Jr. College, A.A., 1969; Missouri Southern State College, B.S. (Education), 1972. *Principal occupations:* English instructor (secondary). *Home address:* Route 2, Box 1C, Fairland, Okla 74343. *Affiliation:* Fairland, Okla, 1972-. *Memberships:* Oklahoma Council of Teachers of English, 1977-; Oklahoma Education Association.

BAKER, BETTY 1928-
(writer)

Born June 20, 1928, Bloomsburg, Penn. *Principal occupation:* Writer. *Memberships:* Western Writers of America, 1963-. *Awards, honors:* Western Heritage Awards for *Killer-of-Death,* 1963, and for *And One Was a Wooden Indian,* 1971. *Interests:* The American Indian. Miss Baker proposes that the non-Indian recognize the differing cultural traits of the many American tribes, instead of lumping them together in one mass. Miss Baker writes, "I detest authors who portray Indians as one's next-door neighbors in costume. Tribes differed as much as Indian and white-eye. The tribal beliefs, codes, and even the geography of their lands, formed thought, action and reaction. Apaches didn't think like Papagos, nor did Hopi react like Iroquois, but few authors take the trouble of slipping inside the Indian's mind. The view is entirely different from back of the eyes." *Published works: Little Runner of the Longhouse* (Harper, 1962); *The Shaman's Last Raid* (Harper, 1963); *Killer-of-Death* (Harper, 1963); *The Treasure of the Padres* (Harper, 1964); *Walk the World's Rim* (Harper, 1965); *Blood of the Brave* (Harper, 1966); *The Dunder Head War* (Harper, 1967); *Great Ghost Stories of the Old West* (Four Winds, 1968); *Do Not Annoy the Indians* (Macmillan, 1968); *Arizona* (Coward-McCann, 1969); *The Pig War* (Harper, 1969); *And One Was a Wooden Indian* (Macmillan, 1970); *The Big Push* (Coward-McCann, 1972); *A Stranger and Afraid* (Macmillan, 1972); *At the Center of the World* (Macmillan, 1973).

BAKER, ODRIC (RICK) (Lac Courte Oreilles Chippewa, Wisconsin) 1931-
(tribal council chairman)

Born May 26, 1931, Lac Courte Oreilles Indian Reservation, Wisconsin. *Principal occupation:* Tribal council chairman. *Home address:* Route 5, Hayward, Wis. 54843. *Affiliations: Tribal chairman, Lac Courte Oreilles Tribe, 1973- Other professional posts:* Past-president, Great Lakes Intertribal Council, Wisconsin; past-treasurer, National Tribal Chairman's Association, Washington, D.C.; consultant, O.M.B., Washington, D.C. *Membership:* Loyal Order of Moose (legionnaire degree.) *Interests:* "Indian affairs—advocate of Indian sovereignty, pursuit of recognition, dignity, and peace for Indian people; defense of Indian treaties and agreements with the U.S. Government.

BALES, JEAN ELAINE MYERS
(Iowa Tribe) 1946-
(artist)

Born December 25, 1946, Pawnee, Okla. *Education:* Oklahoma College of Liberal Arts, B.A. (Professional Art), 1969. *Principal occupation:* Artist. *Home address:* Box 274, Washita, Okla. 73094. *Community activities:* National Wildlife Federation (member). *Memberships:* Oklahoma Indian Art League, 1973-1974; Indian Arts and Crafts Association (member-board of directors, 1978-1981, 1976-.) *Awards, honors:* Governor's Oklahoma Cup for Outstanding Indian Artist of the Year, 1973; awards and exhibitions at the following shows: 1973 Annual Festival of Arts, Altus Air Force Base; Shepherd Mall Indian Show; American Indian Exhibition; Ward Mall Indian Art Show; Heard Museum Indian Art Exhi-

bition; works displayed at the Oklahoma Historical Society Museum. Red Cloud National Indian Art Show, 1974; Scottsdale National Indian Art Show, 1974; Philbrook Art Center Annual Indian Exhibition, 1974; 43rd Annual American Indian Exposition; one woman show at the Southern Plains Indian Museum, Anadarko, Oklahoma; one woman show at the Museum of the Western Prairie; works displayed at the Oklahoma Historical Society Museum; Eight Northern Pueblos Art Show, 1975; Gallup Intertribal Ceremonial, 1975; Gallup Intertribal Ceremonial, 1976; selected as one of the Oklahomans for Indian Opportunity (OIO) calendar artist for the painting "Oklahoma Open Drum." 33rd Annual American Indian Artists Exhibition, Philbrook Art Center, 1977; New Mexico State Fair, 1977; Comanche Cultural Center, Indian Art Exhibition, 1977. *Interests:* Mrs. Bales writes, "I have done and still do lectures and seminars for groups and colleges throughout the U.S. I am very active with school systems throughout Oklahoma. By taking the Indian art forms into the classroom we help students (whether they are Indian or non-Indian) to appreciate the rich American Indian culture we have in Oklahoma. I have worked with the schools planning counselors to plan curriculum to include Indian studies. My works are represented in many private and public collections throughout the U.S., Canada and Europe.

BALL, EVE
(teacher, writer)

Born in Clarksville, Tenn. *Education:* Kansas State Teachers College, B.S.; Kansas State University, M.S. *Principal occupation:* Teacher (retired), writer. *Home address:* Box 3215, Ruidoso, N.M. *Affiliations:* Various teaching appointments until retirement; presently operates own business. *Memberships:* Pi Lamda Theta; Delta Kappa Gamma; Kappa Kappa Iota; New Mexico Folklore Society; New Mexico Historical Society; Western Writers of America. *Awards, honors:* Elected to Hall of Fame, New Mexico Folklore Society, 1970. *Interests:* Mrs. Ball writes, "My major interest is in the field of Southwestern history, and particularly that of the Apaches. I have done twenty years of intensive research from accounts given me by sons or grandsons of the famous Chiricahua and Warm Springs chiefs; but I have not neglected to do the conventional research through publications." *Published works: Ruidoso, the Last Frontier* (Naylor, 1963); *Bob Crosby, World Champion Cowboy,* with Thelma Crosby (Clarendon Press, 1966); *Ma'am Jones of the Pecos* (Arizona University Press, 1969); *In the Days of Victorio* (Arizona University Press, 1970); more than 50 magazine articles in *Arizona and the West, New Mexico Magazine, Frontier Heritage Press,* and *Western Publications.*

BALLARD, JOHN K. (Cherokee) 1920-
(teacher, principal)

Born September 20, 1920, Bernice, Okla. *Education:* Arizona State College, B.S., 1949; Northern State College, M.S., 1957. *Principal occupation:* Elementary school principal. *Affiliations:* Teacher, Santa Fe Indian School, 1949-1953; teacher, Mt. Edgecumbe Indian School, 1953-1956; teacher, Cheyenne River Boarding School, 1956-1960; Chemawa Indian School, 1960-1965; principal, Porcupine Day School, Porcupine, S.D. *Military service:* U.S. Navy, 1941-1945 (Purple Heart).

BALLARD, LOUIS WAYNE (Quapaw-Cherokee) 1931-
(composer, educator)

Born July 8, 1931, Miami, Okla. *Education:* Northeast Oklahoma A & M, A.A., 1951; University of Oklahoma, 1949-1950; University of Tulsa, B.A., B.M.E., 1954, M.M., 1962; College of Santa Fe, Doctor of Music, Honoris Causa. *Principal occupation:* Composer, educator. *Home address:* 3956 Old Santa Fe Trail, Santa Fe, N.M. 87501. *Affiliations:* Chairman, Music Department, Institute of American Indian Arts, Santa Fe, N.M., 1962-1964; chairman, Performing Arts Department, Institute of American Indian Arts, 1964-1969; music curriculum specialist, Central Office-Education, B.I.A., Washington, D.C., 1969-1979; chairman, Minority Awareness Committee for New Mexico Education Association; project director and composer, First National All

Indian Honor Band, Santa Fe, N.M., 1979-. *Other professional posts:* Music consultant and lecturer; president, First American Indian Films, Inc. *Memberships:* ASCAP; American Music Center; American Symphony Orchestra League; National Music Educator's Association; Minority Concerns Commission, MENC (member); Society for Ethnomusicology. *Awards, honors:* Composer's Assistance Grants, Select Composer's Bicentennial Grant, National Endowment for the Arts; New Mexico American Revolution Bicentennial Commission Grant, 1967-1976; First Marion Nevins MacDowell Award, Chamber Music, 1969; Ford Foundation Grant, American Indian Music and Music Education, 1970; Outstanding Indian of the Year, Tulsa Council of the American Indian, 1970; National Indian Achievement Award, Indian Council Fire, 1972; Distinguished Alumnus Award, Tulsa University, 1972; Outstanding Indian of the Year, American Indian Exposition, Anadarko, Oklahoma, 1973; Certificate of Special Achievement, Department of the Interior, 1974; Catlin Peace Pipe Award, National Indian Lore Association, 1976; Annual ASCAP Awards, 1966-1976. *Interests:* Mr. Ballard has traveled extensively throughout the U.S. as music consultant for Volt Technical Corp. headstart programs, to B.I.A. area offices and workshops establishing bicultural music programs from kindergarten to college level. He has lectured at U.C.L.A., Northern Arizona University, 1970, and at the M.E.N.C. Regional Music Conference, Albuquerque, N.M., on a variety of subjects relating to American Indian art and music; Mr. Ballard has been a guest composer and conductor at numerous events across the country. *Published works: The American Indian Sings,* Book 1, 1970; Composed: (ballets) *Ji-Jo Gweh, Koshare, The Four Moons;* (orchestral music) *Scenes From Indian Life, Why the Duck Has a Short Tail, Devil's Promenade, Incident at Wounded Knee, Fantasy Aborigine, Nos. I, II and III;* (chamber music) *Ritmo Indio, Desert Trilogy, Kacina Dances, Rio Grande Sonata, String Trio 1, Rhapsody for Four Bassoons;* (choral cantatas) *Portrait of Will Rogers, The Gods Will Hear, Thus Spake Abraham;* (band works) *Siouxiana, Scenes From Indian Life, Ocotillo Festival Overture, Nighthawk Kee-*

towa; (percussion) *Cecega Ayuwipi;* numerous others. Sheet music of Mr. Ballard's are available from the following publishers: Bourne Music Co., 1212 Ave. of the Americas, New York, N.Y. 10019; and Belwin-Mills Publishing Corp., 25 Deshon Dr., Melville, N.Y. 11747.

BALLARD, W.L. 1936-
(professor)

Born April 5, 1936, Fargo, N.D. *Education:* Tufts University, B.A. (summa cum laude), 1958; University of Calfiornia, Berkeley, Ph.D., 1969. *Principal occupation: University professor. Home address:* 132 Aidai Shukushya, 1375 Yokogaward, Shigenobo-Cho, Onsen gun, Ehime, Japan 791-02. *Affiliations:* Professor, Georgia State University, Atlanta, 1969-1985; professor, Ehime University, Matsuyama, Japan, 1985-. *Military service:* U.S. Navy, 1958-1963. *Memberships:* Linguistic Society of America, 1969-; Society for the Study of the Indigenous Languages of the Americas; Chinese Linguistic Society of Japan, 1985-. *Awards, honors:* Sigma Xi, Phi Beta Kappa; Distringuished Alumni Professor, Georgia State University, 1985. *Interests:* Chinese dialects, dialectology, phonology theory; history of chinese; languages and cultures of the American Southeast, especially Yuchi. *Published works:* Monograph: *The Yuchi Green Corn Ceremonial: Form and Meaning,* (American Indian Studies Center, University of California, Los Angeles, 1978); articles: "Aspects of Yuchi Morphonology, Studies in Southeastern Indian Languages," edited by James Crawford (University of Georgia Press, 1975); "More on Yuchi Pronouns," (IJAL, 1978); "Lexical Borrowing Among Southeastern Native American Languages, Proceedings of the 17th MALC," (University of Kansas, 1982).

BANK, THEODORE P., III 1923-
(cultural anthropologist)

Born August 31, 1923, Patterson, La. *Education:* Harvard University, 1941-1943; University of Michigan, B.S., 1946, M.S., 1950, plus four years advanced research and study. *Principal occupation:* Cultural anthropologist. *Home address:* 1809 Nichols Rd., Kalamazoo, Michigan 49007. *Affiliations:* Associate professor of anthropology and chairman of the World Explorations Program, Western Michigan University, 1973-; assistant professor and director of the Aleutian-Bering Sea Institutes, Western Michigan University, 1967-. *Other professional post:* Executive director, American Institute for Exploration, Inc. *Military service:* U.S. Navy Air Corps, Aerology, 1944-1946, North Pacific campaign. *Community activities:* Subcommittee on ethnobotany, Pacific Science Association (chairman, 1954-1958). *Memberships:* American Anthropological Association (Fellow); Society for American Archaeology (Fellow); American Association for the Advancement of Science (Fellow); Polar Society; Current Anthropology; The Explorers Club (Fellow); contributing editor, *The Explorers Journal. Awards, honors:* Fulbright Research Fellow in Anthropology, Japan, 1955-1956; research grants from various organizations. *Travels, expeditions:* Leader, Interdisciplinary (anthropology, bio-ecology, archaeology—expeditions to Alaska and the Aleutian Isles, Bering Sea region (1948-1954, 1958, 1962, 1966, 1969-; leader, joint Japanese-American expeditions to the Aleutian Islands, 1975-; leader, joint British-American Expedition to Bering Sea, 1977-1978; leader, expeditions to Canadian Arctic, and elsewhere; filming expeditions in the Arctic, Aleutians, Japan and around the world. Major fieldwork among the Aleut-Eskimos. *Biographical sources: Who's Who in America; Who's Who in the Midwest; Who's Who in California; World Who's Who in Science and Industry; American Men of Science; The Blue Book (England); International Directory of Educational Specialists; Contemporary Authors; Who's Who Among Authors and Journalists;* and others. *Published works: Birthplace of the Winds* (Thomas Y. Crowell, 1956); *Student Manual for Cultural Anthropology* (Quest, 1966); *People of the Bering Sea* (MSS, 1971); *Aleut-Eskimo,* 1973; *Ethnobotany as an Adjunct to Archaeology,* 1977; (script and narration) *Canoeing Into the Past,* 1979; associate editor, *Current Field Reports* (Anthropology), 1968-; various articles.

BARRETT, JOHN ADAMS (ROCKY), Jr. (Citizen Band Potawatomi) 1944- (corporate president)

Born March 25, 1944, Shawnee, Okla. *Education:* Princeton University, 1962-1964; University of Oklahoma, 1964-1965; Oklahoma City University, B.S. (Business), 1968, M.S. (Business), 1986. *Principal occupation:* Corporate president. *Home address:* 4002 N. Market St., Shawnee, Okla. 74801. *Affiliations:* Warehouseman and salesman, U.S. Plywood Corp., Oklahoma City, Okla.,1966-1969; promotion and supervisor of construction, Greenbriar Development Co., Memphis, Tenn., 1969-1970; Barrett Construction Co., Southaven, Miss., 1970-1971; director, C.T.S.A. Enterprise, Shawnee, Okla., 1971-1974 (intertribal organization, under Indian Action Team Training Contract from B.I.A., whose objective was to trade hard-core unemployed adult Indians in construction trades); Barrett Drilling Co. (family owned business in contract drilling and oil production), 1974-1982; self employed, J. Barrett Co., 1982-1983; tribal administrator, Citizen Band Potawatomi Tribe, 1983-1985, chairman, 1985-; president, Barrett Refining, Shawnee, Okla., 1985-. In the Fall of 1985, Barrett Refining was awarded a $52 million jet fuel contract from the U.S. Department of Defense—the only Defense contract to go to an Indian. *Other Professional posts:* Paid lobbyist for Oklahoma Home Builders Association in the Oklahoma Legislature; Citizen Band Potawatomi Tribe (business committee member, tribal administrator (1983-1985), vice-chairman, and chairman (1985-). *Other tribal activities:* Member, board of directors, United Western Tribes (representing 32 tribes in Oklahoma and Kansas); chairman and director, Shawnee Service United Indian Health Service Advisory Board; director, Oklahoma Indian Health Service Advisory Board; president, National Indian Action Contractors Association; delegate to National Tribal Chairman's Association and National Congress of American Indians. *Community activities:* Member, Emanuel Episcopal Church (ordained lay reader); member, board of directors, Shawnee Quaterback Club; Elks (B.P.O.E.); member, Shawnee Citizens Advisory Council, Lions Club, and Boy Scouts of America as troop leader.

BARSE, HAROLD G. (Kiowa, Wichita, Sioux) 1947- (readjustment counseling specialist)

Born June 30, 1947, Riverside, Calif. *Education:* Black Hills State College, Spearfish, S.D., B.S. (Secondary Education), 1973; University of Oklahoma, Norman, Okla., M.Ed. (Guidance and Counseling), 1979. *Principal occupation:* Readjustment counseling specialist. *Home address:* 1814 Windsor Way, Norman, Oklahoma 73069. *Affiliations:* Director, Adult Education Program, Lake Traverse Sisseton-Wahpeton Sioux Tribe, Sisseton, S.D., 1973-1975; instructor, Sinte Gleska Community College, Rosebud Sioux Reservation, S.D., 1975; director, Inhalent Abuse Treatment Project, Oklahoma City Native American Center, 1977-1980; outreach specialist, Veterans Administration's Vietnam Veteran Outreach Program, 1980-; founder, Vietnam Era Veterans Inter-Tribal Association, 1981-; planned and organized first National Vietnam Veterans Pow-Wow, 1982. *Other professional post:* Co-chairman, Vet Center's American Indian Working Group. *Military service:* U.S. Army, 1969-1971 (secialist 4th class E-4). *Memberships:* Kiowa Blacklegging Society (Kiowa Veterans Association), 1983-; Native American Veterans Association. *Interests:* "Working with Vietnam veterans; primary program development specialist for video *Shadow of the Warrior: American Indian Counseling Perspectives.*

BARZ, SANDRA 1930- (editor, publisher)

Born August 4, 1930, Chicago, Ill. *Education:* Skidmore College, B.A., 1952. *Principal occupation:* Editor, publisher. *Home address:* 162 East 80 St., New York, N.Y. 10021. *Affiliation: Editor, publisher, Arts and Culture of the North* (newsletter, journal), 1976-. *Community activities:* Yorkville Civic Council (member of board). *Interests:* "Eskimo art—circumpolar; traveled to Alaska, Canada (Arctic) and Greenland, and have lead tours to Arctic Canada and Greenland; run conferences at major museums in Canada and the U.S. since 1978, where Eskimo art-related activities are taking place." *Published works: Inuit Artists*

Print Workbook (Arts and Culture of the North, 1981); newsletter/journal *Arts and Culture of the North (seven volumes, 1976-1981; 1983-1984).*

BATAILLE, GRETCHEN M. 1944-
(professor)

Born September 28, 1944, Mishawaka, Ind. *Education:* Purdue University, 1962-1965; California State Polytechnic University, B.S., 1966, M.A., 1967; Drake University, D.A., 1977. *Principal occupation:* Professor. *Home address:* 1861 Rosemount Ave., Claremont, Calif. 91711. *Affiliation:* Iowa State University, Ames, Iowa, 1967-. *Community activities:* Iowa Civil Rights Commission, 1975-1979 (chairman, 1977-1979); Iowa Humanities Board, 1981- (president, 1984-1985.) *Memberships:* National Association for Ethnic Studies (executive council, 1980-; treasurer, 1982-); Association for the Study of American Indian Literature (executive board, 1978-1981; Modern Language Association. *Interests:* "I am interested in American Indian literature in the academic sense as well as the literature as a reflection of the culture, history, and world view of diverse peoples. As a collector of popular culture artifacts representing American Indians, I find the popular view in sharp contrast to the image presented in both the oral tradition and contemporary literary expressions." *Published works: The Worlds Between Two Rivers: Perspectives on American Indians in Iowa* (Iowa State University Press, 1978); *The Pretend Indians: Images of Native Americans in the Movies* (Iowa State University Press, 1980); *American Indian Literature: A Selected Bibliography for Schools and Libraries* (NAIES, Inc., 1981); *American Indian Women Telling Their Lives* (University of Nebraska Press, 1984); *Images of American Indians in Film: An Annotated Bibliography* (Garland Publishing, 1985).

BEALER, ALEX W., III 1921-
(writer)

Born March 6, 1921, Valdosta, Georgia. *Education:* Emory University, B.A., 1942; Northwestern University, 1946. *Principal occupation:* Writer. *Home address:* 5180 Riverview Rd., Atlanta, Ga. 30327. *Affiliation:* Alex W. Bealer & Associates, Atlanta, Ga. *Military service:* U.S. Marine Corps Reserves, 1942-1961. *Community activities:* Trustee, Atlanta Historical Society, Westville Handicrafts, Inc.; Georgia Republican Party (state, district and county executive committees; press secretary; assistant state chairman, 1960-1969); Pocket Theatre, Atlanta, Georgia (former president, board of directors, 1958-1962); Honorary Royal Swedish Consul, 1969-. *Memberships:* Commerce Club, Atlanta, 1960-; Artist Blacksmiths Associaiton of North America (president, 1973-1974; director.) *Awards, honors:* Eagle Scout, B.S.A. *Interests:* Advertising, writing (published articles in various journals since 1936); wrote and helped produce a 30 minute television documentary on the Cherokee Removal, shown on WSB TV, Atlanta in December, 1965; historical research; painting; study of the American Indian; blacksmithing; general crafts. Mr. Bealer has lived with the Teton Sioux, Rosebud Reservation, S.D. in 1941, and the Eastern Cherokees of North Carolina at different times between 1939 and 1942; and others. *Published works: The Picture-Skin Story* (Holiday House, 1957); *Only the Names Remain; The Cherokees and the Trail of Tears* (Little, Brown, 1972); and others.

BEAN, LOWELL JOHN 1931-
(anthropologist, ethnologist)

Born April 26, 1931, St. James, Minn. *Education:* Los Angeles City College, 1954-1955; University of California, Los Angeles, B.A., 1958, M.A., 1961, Ph.D., 1970. *Principal occupation:* Anthropologist, ethnologist. *Home address:* 1555 Lakeside Dr. #64, Oakland, Calif. 94612. *Affiliations:* Reading and teaching assistant, U.C.L.A., 1958-1960; instructor, Pasadena Junior College, 1962-1965; curator of ethnology, Palm Springs Desert Museum, 1962-1964; instructor and professor of anthropology (chairman, 1973-), Department of Anthropology, California State University at Hayward, 1965-; research fellow, R.H. Lowie Museum of Anthropology, University of California, Berkeley, 1971-1973; curator, Clarence E. Smith Museum of Anthropology, CSUH, 1974-1978. *Other professional posts:* Consultant on ethnographic films, North American Films, 1963-1964; contributing editor, *American Indian Historian,* 1968-1972; consultant, American Indian Scholars Conference, American Historical Society, 1969; consultant, Rincon Reservation Water Case, 1971; member, California State Board of Education Task Force on Social Studies Textbooks, 1972. *Military service:* U.S. Marine Corps, 1951-1953. *Community activities:* American Friends Service, Southwest Indian Committee (member, advisory Indian committee, 1961-1963); Teaching Institute, American Indian Historical Society (participant, 1968); American Indian Studies Curriculum Committee, San Francisco State College (consultant); Planning Committee for Gabrileno Cultural Center, Rancho Los Alamitos, 1972; Malki Museum (member, board of trustees); *Journal of California Anthropology* (associate editor); editor, Ballena Press *Anthropolical Papers. Memberships:* American Anthropological Association (Fellow); Society for California Archaeology; Southwestern Anthropological Association (president, 1974-1975). *Awards, honors:* George Barker Memorial Grant-in-Aid for research among American Indian, 1960; National Science Foundation Faculty Research Grant-in-Aid, California State University, Hayward, 1967-1972; Postdoctoral Museum Fellowship, Wenner-Gren Foundation for Anthropological Research, 1971; Smithsonian Institute (Center for the Study of Man) Grant to research the history of economic development at Morongo Indian Reservation, Banning, California, 1972-1974; Grant-in-Aid, American Philosophical Society, 1972; Outstanding Educators of America Award, 1972; National Geographic Society (grantee, 1975; California State University at Hayward (minigrantee, 1977). *Interests:* California Indians; Ethnographic research; directed field studies among Miwok, Wintun, Tubatulabal and Chemehuevi Indians of California. *Published works: The Romero Expeditions in California and Arizona, 1823-1826,* with William Mason (Palm Springs Desert Museum, 1962); *Cahuilla Indian Cultural Ecology,* Ph.D. dissertation (University Microfilms, 1970); *Temalpah: Cahuilla Knowledge and Uses of Plants* (Malki Museum, 1972); *Mukat's People: The*

Cahuilla Indians of Southern California (University of California, Berkeley Press, 1972); *Antap: California Indian Policy and Economic Organization,* with T. King (Ballena Press, 1974); *Native American California: Essays on Culture and History,* with T. Blackburn (Ballena Press, 1975); *California Indians: Primary Resources,* with Sylvia Vane (Ballena Press, 1976); *A Comparative Ethnobotany of Twelve Southern California Tribes,* with Charles Smith; *Ethnography and Culture History of the Southwestern Kashia Pomo Indians; The Native Californian: A Regional Ethnology;* and *Madman or Philosopher: Essays on Shamanism,* with Rex Jones.

BEARTUSK, KEITH LOWELL (Northern Cheyenne) 1947- (forest manager)

Born December 21, 1947, Crow Agency, Mont. Education: Eastern Montana College (two years); University of Montana, B.S. (Forestry), 1971. *Principal occupation:* Forest manager. *Home address:* P.O. Box 445, Lame Deer, Mont. 59043. Military service: Montana National Guard, 1971-1977 (American Spirit Honor Medal).

BEATTY, JOHN J. (Mohawk) 1939- (anthropologist)

Born September 5, 1939, Brooklyn, N.Y. *Education:* Brooklyn College, B.A., 1964; University of Oklahoma, M.A., 1966; City Univerity of New York, Ph.D. (Anthropology), 1972. *Principal occupation:* Anthropologist. *Home address:* 2983 Bedford Ave., Brooklyn, N.Y. 11210. *Affiliations:* Teaching assistant, University of Oklahoma, 1964-1965; instructor, Long Island University, 1966-1967; professor of anthropology, Brooklyn College, CUNY, 1966-. *Other professional post:* Private investigator, Phoenix Investigative Associates, 1982-. *Military service:* New York Guard (captain.) *Major research work:* Ethnographic and linguistic: American Indians in Urban Areas (major U.S. cities) 1963-; Tlingit Language and Culture (in New York and Alaska) 1964-1967; Totonac Language and Culture (in New York and Mexico) 1964-1967; Kiowa-Apache Language and Culture (Anadarko,

Oklahoma) 1965-; Mohawk Language and Culture (New York City and various Mohawk Reserves) 1964-; Japanese and Japanese Americans: Language and Culture, 1973-; Scots and Scottish Americans, 1974-; Cross Cultural Perspectives on Police, 1978-. *Memberships:* American Anthropological Association (Fellow); New York Academy of Sciences (Fellow); American Indian Community House. *Awards, honors:* National Science Foundation Training Grant, University of Oklahoma, 1965 (for research with the Kiowa-Apache); City University of New York and National Science Foundation Dissertation Year Fellowships, 1971 (for research with Mohawk languages); National Science Foundation Grant (U.S. - Japanese Co-operative Program, 1973); Brooklyn College Faculty Award, 1973, for research with Japanese macaques; Faculty Research Award Program, CUNY, 1974 and 1975, for research with chimpanzees and for research on sexual behavior; Department of Health, Education and Welfare: Office of Native American Programs, 1975 grant to work with urban American Indians in New York State; National Endowment for the Arts, 1977, for filming Iroquois social dances; Rikkyoo University (Japan) Research Fellowship, 1986-1987, for research on solidarity; Certificate of Appreciation, New York Academy of Sciences; Sigma Xi. *Interests:* Anthropology; linguistics, symbolic anthropology - American Indians; Asia; theatre; forensics; lecture series on American Indians and Japanese culture, 1969-. *Published works:* Kiowa-Apache Music and Dance (Museum of Anthropology, University of Northern Colorado, 1974); *Mohawk Morphology* (Museum of Anthropology, University of Northern Colorado, 1974); *A Guide to New York for Japanese: An Ethnographic Approach* (Gloview Press, Tokyo, 1985); numerous articles. Recording: *Music of the Plains Apache* (Folkways Records). Films: *Iroquois Social Dances,* Two parts, with Nick Manning, 1979; and others. Videotapes: *The American Indian Art Center,* 1978; *American Indians at Brooklyn College,* 1978; Scottish Highland Dances, 1979; *Custer Revisited,* 1980. Books being developed: *Intercultural Communications; The Anthropology of Sexual Behavior; The Nature of Language and Culture;* and Cross *Cultural Perspectives on Police.*

BEATTY, PATRICIA 1922-
(writer)

Born August 26, 1922, Portland, Oregon. *Education:* Reed College, B.A., 1944. *Principal occupation:* Writer. Home address: 5085 Rockledge Dr., Riverside, Calif. 92506. *Affiliations:* Teacher, Coeur D'Alene (Idaho) High School, 1947-1950; librarian, Riverside (Calif.) Public Library, 1953-1957; teacher, creative writing, University of Califorinia, Riverside, 1967-1968, U.C.L.A., 1968-1969. *Memberships:* Riverside Roundtable Women's Organization (secretary, president); Society of Children's Book Writers. *Awards, honors:* Honorary member, Quileute Tribe. *Interests:* Travel for book research. *Biographical sources: Contemporary Authors; Dictionary of International Biography; Third Book of Junior Authors; Who's Who in California. Published works: Indian Canoemaker* (Caxton); *Squaw Dog* (William Morrow); *The Lady from Black Hawk* (McGraw-Hill); *At the Seven Stars,* 1965; *Campion Towers,* 1966; *Hail Columbia,* 1970; *A Long Way to Whiskey Creek,* 1971; *Who Comes to King's Mountain,* 1975; *Lupita Manana,* 1981; among others.

BEAUDIN, JOHN A. (Lac Courte Oreilles Chippewa Band of Great Lakes Ojibwe) 1946-
(attorney)

Born June 28, 1946, Chicoutimi, Quebec, Can. *Education:* University of Wisconsin, Green Bay, B.S.; University of Wisconsin, Madison, J.D. *Principal occupation:* Attorney. *Home address: 1317 Reetz Rd., Madison, Wisc. 53711. Affiliation:* Partner (four years), Dewa, Beaudin & Kelly, 217 S. Hamilton St., Madison, Wisc. *Other professional post:* President, Native Horizons, Inc. *Military service:* U.S. Army, 1966-1969 (rank SP/5-E5; Bronze Star with clusters, Army Commendation Medal, Viet Nam Combat and Campaign Medals). *Community activities:* Director, American Indian Peace & Justice League; board of directors, Madison Indian Parents, School Superintendent's Human Relations Advisory Committee; lobbying. *Membership:* American Indian Lawyer's League. *Interests:* Advocate of Indian rights, human rights and educational needs and issues, and general practice. *Published works: American Indian Rights* (Madison Metro School District, 1981); many articles dealing with Indian or legal affairs. "Major work in development for Wisconsin judges and attorneys dealing with Indian Child Welfare Act."

BEAUVAIS, ARCHIE BRYAN (Rosebud Sioux) 1948- (education administrator and instructor)

Born December 30, 1948, Rosebud, S.D. *Education:* Northern Arizona University, Flagstaff, B.A., 1970, M.A. (Education), 1976; Harvard University, Ed.D., 1982. *Principal occupation:* Education administrator and instructor. *Home address:* P.O. Box 426, Mission, S.D. 57555. *Affiliation:* Department chair, Education Department, Sinte Gleska College, Rosebud, S.D., 1984-. *Military service:* U.S. Army, 1967-1970 (Vietnam, 1968-1969, Specialist Fifth Class, Army Commendation Medal.) *Community activities:* Doctoral student representative to Student Association Cabinet, Harvard Graduate School of Education. *Memberships:* School Administrators of S.D.; Ducks Unlimited; Harvard Chapter of Phi Delta Kappa; S.D. Indian Education Association. *Interests:* "Primary vocational interest is furthering the cause of education on the Rosebud Sioux Reservation by making some impact as a higher education administrator and instructor. Also, to act as a positive role-model for young people and convey the fact that with education comes the right to make the right choices that effect a person's destiny."

BEAVER, FRED (Creek) 1911- (artist)

Born July 2, 1911, Eufaula, Okla. *Education:* Haskell Institute, 1933-1935; Bacone Junior College, 1931-1932. *Principal occupation:* Freelance artist. *Home address:* 437 Locust St., N.W., Ardmore, Okla. 73401. *Affiliations:* Clerk, Bureau of Indian Affairs, Okmulgee and Ardmore, Okla.,

1935-1960; freelance artist, 1960-. *Military service:* P.F.C., U.S. Army Air Force, 1942-1945. *Community activities:* Postal Employees Credit Union (supervisor); Federal Employees Union, B.I.A. (president). *Awards, honors:* Waite Phillips Trophy Award, Philbrook Art Center, Tulsa, Okla., 1963; Outstanding Contribution in Religious Activities, Bacone College; various art prizes in shows throughout the U.S. *Interests:* Painting and exhibiting professionally; has performed as baritone soloist; painting reproductions for books: *Songs from the Earth; Southeastern Indians;* also in Dorothy Dunn's *American Indian Arts,* exhibited personally in 36 states; illustrated book, *Creek-Seminole Legends,* by Strickland and Gregory.

BECENTI, FRANCIS D. (Navajo) 1952- (higher education administrator)

Born May 18, 1952, Fort Defiance, Ariz. *Education:* Navajo Community College, A.A., 1973; University of California, Berkeley, B.A., 1975. *Principal occupation:* Higher education administrator. *Home address:* 1624 E. Pitkin, Fort Collins, Colo. 86504. *Affiliations:* Director of financial aid, Navajo Community College, 1975-1979; director of financial aid, University of Albuquerque, 1980-1981; director of student services, College of Ganado, 1981-1984; director, Native American Student Services, Colorado State University, Fort Collins, 1984-.

BECK, SAMUEL (Catawba) 1916- (electrician, tribal secretary-treasurer)

Born February 12, 1916, Rock Hill, S.C. *Principal occupation:* Electrician. *Home address:* Route 3, Box 324, Rock Hill, S.C. 29730. Affiliation: Rock Hill Printing and Finishing Co., Rock Hill, S.C., 1946-. *Other professional post:* Secretary and treasurer, Catawba Nation. *Military service:* U.S. Army, 1943-1946 (T-4 Sergeant).

BEELER, SAMUEL W., Jr.
(Cherokee) 1950-
(tribal executive director, planner)

Born January 29, 1950, Paterson, N.J. *Education:* Passaic County School of Nursing, Wayne, N.J., Nursing Degree; American Indian School on Alcohol and Drug Abuse, Reno, Nev., Certified Counselor. *Principal occupation:* Executive director and tribal planner. *Home address:* Poospatuck Indian Reservation, Mastic, N.Y. 11950. *Affiliations:* Executive director, Paumanok Algonquian, Poospatuck Indian Reservation, Mastic, N.Y. *Other professional post:* Tribal planner, Poospatuck Tribal Council, Poospatuck Indian Reservation. *Military service:* U.S. Air Force, 1968-1970. *Community activities:* Executive director, New Jersey American Indian Center, Hillside, N.J. *Memberships:* American Indian Nurses Association; American Indian Medicine Society; National Congress of American Indians; Association of American Indian Social Workers, Vietnam Era Veterans Inter-Tribal Association; Cherokee National Historical Society.

BEGAY, D.Y. (Navajo) 1953-
(weaver, textile consultant)

Born September 3, 1953, Ganado, Ariz. *Education:* Rocky Mountain College, 1974; Arizona State University, B.A., 1978. *Principal occupation:* Weaver, textile consultant. *Home address:* 10 Fairview Ave., Woodcliff Lake, N.J. 07675. *Affiliation:* Owner, Navajo Textiles & Arts, Woodcliff Lake, N.J., 1984-. *Other professional posts:* Textile instructor, lecturer. *Memberships:* Palisades Guild; Indian Education; Museum of Natural History, Museum of the American Indian; Handweavers Guild of America. *Interests:* "Have done extensive traveling (Canada, Mexico, Europe and U.S.) All my interest is in the field of textiles (Navajo weaving). *Biographical sources:* "A Navajo Weaver" (*N.Y. Times*); "Navajo Weaving" (*Bergen Record*). *Published works:* Co-editor, *The Sheep* (documentary film), 1982.

BEGAY, EUGENE A., Sr. (Lac Courte Oreilles Chippewa, Wisc.) 1933-
(business administration, Indian affairs, mechanical engineer)

Born June 6, 1933, Hayward, Wis. *Education:* North Park College, 1952-1954 (Pre-Medicine); Illinois Institute of Technology, 1955-1959 (Mechanical Engineering). *Principal occupation:* Business administration, Indian affairs, mechanical engineer. *Home address:* 765 Hartwell St., Teaneck, N.J. 07666. *Affiliations:* Executive director, United Southeastern Tribes, Inc., Nashville, Tenn., 1972-1976; Associate Native American Ministry, United Presbyterian Church-USA, New York, N.Y., 1976-. *Other professional posts:* Consultant, B.I.A. and Indian Health Service, U.S. Government. *Military service:* Illinois National Guard, 1950-1952. *Community activities:* Chicago American Indian Center (board of directors); National Indian Review Board (NIAAA/HEW) (chairman); National Indian Board on Mental Health (chairman); National Indian Council Fire (member). *Memberships:* National Congress of American Indians; Research Committee on Mental Health (NIMH/HEW). *Interests:* "Active originally in Indian affairs in the area of developing priority by the Federal Government in mental health and alcoholism programs and services. I have lobbied in Congress and advocated amongst tribes and tribal organizations in the area of economic development, education, nutrition, housing, and health services. I am currently active in Indian rights, treaty rights, jurisdiction, and land issues. I provided White House testimony on these issues at the request of the Vice President."

BEGAY, JIMMIE C. (Navajo) 1948-
(Indian educator)

Born September 4, 1948, Rough Rock, Ariz. *Education:* New Mexico Highlands University, A.S., 1969, B.A., 1972, M.A., 1974. *Principal occupation:* Indian educator. *Home address:* Box 656, Rough Rock, Ariz. 86503. *Affiliations:* Teacher, principal, executive director, Rough Rock Demonstration School. *Other professional posts:* Native American Studies teacher; coordinator,

Black Mesa Day School. *Community activities:* Navaho Culture Organization (chairman); originator of Navaho psychology classes; sponsor of Black Mesa five mile run. *Memberships:* National Association of Secondary School Principals; Smithsonian Institution; Harvard Education Review; Dine Biolta Association. *Award:" "Outstanding Accomplishments," Rough Rock School Board. Interests:* Betterment in education programs, especially for Indians; travel. "(I) would like to pursue higher educational goals." *Biographical sources: "Principals and Views About Indian Education," (Rough Rock News);* "Candidate for NACIE" *(Navajo Times); History of Rough Rock,* by Robert Roessell. *Published works: Navajo Culture Outline,* and *Navajo Philosophy of Education.*

BEGAY, RUTH TRACY (Navajo) 1940-
(family nurse practitioner)

Born May 14, 1940, Ganado, Ariz. *Education:* Loretto Heights College, School of Nursing, Denver, Colo., B.S.N., 1978. *Principal occupation:* Family nurse practitioner, director, Navajo Community College Health Center, 1978-. *Address:* P.O. Box 193, Navajo Community College, Tsaile, Ariz. 86556. *Other professional posts:* Member, Navajo Health Authority, Office of Nursing Education Board; member, Navajo Community College Nursing Program Board. *Memberships:* Arizona Nurses Association (council on practice); Arizona Public Health Association; Pacific Coast College Health Association; *Awards, honors:* Two documentary films on Nurse Practitioner on Navajo Reservation by NBC and University of Arizona, School of Medicine, 1973; Navajo Community College 1978 Student Service Employee of the Year Award; Outstanding Young Woman of the Year, 1977. *Interests:* "Involvement in local community health-social work among the Navajo people. Travel locally, regionally in college health service and nurses association. Interested in continual growth and development in cross-cultural aspects of a different society integrated with our own Navajo Society." *Biographical sources:* Articles: Arizona Nurses Association *Newsletter,* 1973; *The Navajo Times,* 1973; *Gallup Independent,* 1977.

BELGARDE, HAROLD (Turtle Mountain Chippewa) 1939-
(teacher, media specialist)

Born October 1, 1939, Belcourt, N.D. *Education:* Utah State University, M.Ed., 1975. *Principal occupation:* Teacher, media specialist. *Home address:* 1408 Como St., #4, Carson City, Nev. 89701. *Affiliation:* Teacher (library usage), Bureau of Indian Affairs, Stewart, Nev., 1975-. *Community activities:* Stewart Booster Club (president). *Published works: Resource Materials on American Indians* (Harry Belgarde, 1975).

BELINDO, DENNIS WAYNE
(A un-So-Te) (Kiowa-Navajo) 1938-
(artist)

Born December 12, 1938, Phoenix, Ariz. *Education:* Bacone College, Diploma, 1958; University of Oklahoma, B.F.A., 1962. *Principal occupation:* Art teacher. *Affiliation:* Central High, Oklahoma City, Okla., 1963-. *Other professional post:* Freelance commercial artist. *Military service:* U.S. National Guard, 1955-1957. *Memberships:* Artists of Oklahoma. *Awards, honors:* Honorable Mention, Philbrook Art Center Indian Annual, 1956, 1961; First Award, Poster Division and Plains Division, Gallup Inter-Tribal Ceremonials.

BELINDO, JOHN (Kiowa-Navajo) 1935-
(organization executive)

Born November 3, 1935, Phoenix, Ariz. *Education:* Central State College, Edmond, Okla., B.S., 1966. *Principal occupation:* Organization executive. *Affiliations:* Staff announcer, KOCY-AM and -FM, and KFNB-FM, radio stations, Oklahoma City, Okla; columnist, *Oklahoma Journal,* Oklahoma City, Okla., 1965-; director, Washington Office, National Congress of American Indians. *Military service:* U.S. Marine Corps Reserves, 1954-1960.

BELL, AMELIA RECTOR
(anthropologist)

Born in Oak Ridge, Tenn. *Education:* Georgia State University, Atlanta, B.A., 1977;

University of Chicago, M.A., 1979, Ph.D., 1984. *Principal occupation:* Anthropologist. *Home address:* 950 East Ave., Rochester, N.Y. 14607. *Affiliations:* Research assistant, Department of Anthropology, and Department of Linguistics, University of Chicago, 1977-1982; instructor, Field Museum of Natural History, Chicago, 1979; assistant professor, Department of Anthropology, University of Rochester, N.Y., 1983-. *Memberships:* American Anthropological Association; American Society for Ethnohistory; Central States Anthropological Society; Mid-America Linguistics Conference; Oklahoma Historical Society; Northeastern Anthropological Association; Rochester Academy of Sciences; Royal Anthropological Institute of Great Britain and Ireland; Society for Linguistic Anthropology; Society for the Study of the Indigenous Languages of the Americas; Southern Anthropological Society. *Research and teaching specialization:* Linguistic anthropology, sociocultural anthropology, Native North Americans, and West Africa. *Awards, honors:* Research grants from: Georgia State University (for B.A. thesis, 1977, *Instant Indians: An Analysis of Cultural Identity in the Southeastern U.S.);* Whatcom Museum of History and Art; American Philosophical Society, National Science Foundation, Wenner-Gren Foundation for Anthropological Research, University of Rochester, Archival Research Grant. *Dissertation and theses: M.A. thesis, 1979, Coming from the Sun: The Kashita Legend;* Ph.D. dissertation, 1984, *Creek Ritual: The Path to Peace. Interests:* Field research: Creek Indians, Oklahoma and Georgia; Seminole Indians, Oklahoma and Florida; Mississippi Band of Choctaw Indians; Cherokee Indians, North Carolina and Oklahoma; and Yuchi Indians of Oklahoma. Linguistics: Algonquian, Shawnee linguistic analysis, and Muskogean (Creek, Seminole and Choctaw); archival research. *Published works:* Numerous papers and articles on the Creek Indians, 1977-; forthcoming, *The White Path to Peace: Creek Ritual, Politics, and Language (book); Creek Women: The Ideology of Gender and Social Reproduction,* (paper); "Language and the Poetics of Politics: The Logic of Conflict and a Creek Stikinni" (article).

BELL, WILLIAM F. (Mississippi Choctaw) 1932-
(elementary principal)

Born December 27, 1932, Philadelphia, Miss. *Education:* Meridian Jr. College, A.A., 1955; Univerity of Southern Mississippi, B.S., 1957; University of Mississippi, M.Ed., 1964, Ed. Sp., 1976. *Principal occupation:* Elementary principal. *Home address:* P.O. Box 15, Carthage, Miss. 39051. *Affiliation:* School system, Carthage, Miss., 1976-. *Other professional posts:* Teacher, guidance counselor; administrative assistant, Governor's Office of Education and Training; director, Off-Reservation Indian Manpower Programs; planning specialist, National Indian Management Service, Inc. *Community activities:* Governor's Council on Manpower Planning, 1973-1975; Governor's Council on Adult Basic Education, 1973-1975. *Memberships:* Kappa Delta Pi, 1956-; Phi Delta Kappa, 1977. *Awards, honors:* Appointed by Governor of Miss. as liaison officer between State government and tribal government. *Interests:* "Research and writing are my primary interests. I have written several articles about Indian education for college classes."

BENEDICT, PATRICIA (Abenaki) 1956-
(executive director-Indian organization)

Born August 11, 1956, Waterbury, Conn. *Education:* Mattatuck Community College, Waterbury, Conn., A.S. (Alcohol and Drug Counseling), 1980. *Principal occupation:* Executive director, Indian organization. *Home address:* 53 Green St., Waterbury, Conn. 06708. *Affiliation:* American Indians for Development, Meriden, Conn. (social worker, 1975-1981; executive director, 1981- *Other professional post:* Co-editor of American Indians for Development *Newsletter. Community activities:* American Indians for Development (past chairman, board of directors); member, Energy Assistance Program Policy Making Board, Meriden, Conn.; member, Federal Regional Support Center, American Indian Committee, New Haven, Conn.; organized Waterbury Indian community into an organization. *Membership:* Title IV Indian Education Committee, Waterbury, Conn.

(chairperson). *Interests:* "Personal interests include: furthering my education in the field of social work, attending and participating in Native American cultural activities, and with the assistance from my staff and Indians in Connecticut, American Indians for Development will once again become a multi-service agency."

BENHAM, WILLIAM JOSEPHUS, Jr.
(Creek) 1928-
(B.I.A. administrator)

Born June 4, 1928, Lamar, Okla. *Education:* East Central State University, Okla., B.A., 1950; Univerity of Oklahoma, Ed.M., 1956, Ed.D., 1965. *Principal occupation:* B.I.A. administrator. *Home address:* 8790 Lagrima De Oro, NE, Albuquerque, N.M. 87111. *Affiliations:* Junior management assistant, Dept. of the Interior, Management Training Program, 1950-1951; principal, teacher, Leupp School, B.I.A., Leupp, Ariz., 1951-1953; principal, Tuba City Boarding School, B.I.A., Ariz., 1953-1954; assistant to director of schools, B.I.A., Window Rock, Ariz., 1954-1955; education specialist, adult education, assistant area director, B.I.A., Gallup Area, N.M., 1957-1963; area director of schools, B.I.A., Gallup Area, N.M., 1963-1966; acting commissioner of education and programs, B.I.A., Washington, D.C., 1970; director of schools, Navajo Area Office, B.I.A., Window Rock, Ariz., 1966-1972; acting director, Office of Indian Education Programs, B.I.A., Washington, D.C., 1973-1974; administrator, Indian Education Resources, B.I.A., Albuquerque, N.M., 1974-. *Community activities:* National Council, Boy Scouts of America (member, Interrelationships Committee and executive board, 1957-); American Association of School Administrators (panel discussions, 1957-); Southern Baptist Churches (superintendent, teacher, 1957-); Annual National Tribal Leaders' Conference on Scouting (member, Steering Committee, 1958-); worked with Navajo Tribe in getting boards of education established for all Navajo schools operated by B.I.A., 1966-1970; *Journal of American Indian Education* (member, editorial board, 1966-1970); Southwest Cooperative Educational Laboratory, Albuquerque (member, board of directors, 1966-1970); Ganado Presbyterian

Mission (member, advisory board to president, 1968-1969); *Indian Ed,* University of Alberta, Can. (member, editorial board.) *Memberships:* American Association of School Administrators; National Indian Education Association (charter member). *Awards, honors:* Silver Beaver Award, Boy Scouts of America, 1969; Distinguished Alumnus Award, East Central Oklahoma University, 1975; Meritorious Service Award, Department of the Interior, 1977. *Biographical sources: Who's Who in Government,* Second Edition, 1975-1976; *Indians of Today,* Fourth Edition, 1971; *Who's Who in American Education,* Volume XVIII, 1957-1958. *Published works:* Numerous articles in the *Journal of American Indian Education,* among others.

BENN, ROBERT C. (Choctaw) 1934-
(printer)

Born September 10, 1934, Philadelphia, Miss. *Education:* Clarke Memorial College; Mississippi College, B.A., 1956. *Principal occupation:* Printer. *Home address:* R.F.D., Box 9-A, Carthage, Miss. 39051. *Military service:* U.S. Navy, 1957-1962. *Interests:* "Promoting and encouraging younger Choctaws to prepare themselves and become better citizens of America."

BENNETT, KAY C. (Navajo) 1922-
(writer, doll maker)

Born July 15, 1922, Sheepsprings, N.M. *Education:* "Acquired, for the most part, as a teacher-interpreter at the Phoenix, Arizona Indian Boarding School." *Principal occupation:* Writer, doll maker. *Home address:* 6 Aida Ct., Gallup, N.M. 87301. *Community activities:* New Mexico Human Rights Commissioner, 1969-1971; Inter-Tribal Indian Ceremonial (director); McKinley County Hospital (advisory board). *Memberships:* Heard Museum, Gallup, N.M. (Navajo central committee); City of Gallup Citizens Committee. *Awards, honors:* Appointed Colonel-Aide-de Camp, staff of the Governor of New Mexico; elected New Mexico Mother of the Year, 1968; "have received many awards at state fairs and ceremonials for dolls and dresses I have created." *Interests:* Doll making, dress designing; entertaining as a singer; "have published two albums of Navajo songs. I'm especially interested in Navajo culture, and serve on a school advisory board as a lecturer at schools in New Mexico and Arizona;" travel. *Published works: Kaibah: Recollections of a Navajo Girlhood* (Westernlore Press, 1965; paperback, Kay Bennett, 1976); *A Navajo Saga* (Naylor Co., 1969).

BENNETT, NOEL KIRKISH 1939-
(organization director, author, artist, teacher)

Born December 23, 1939, San Jose, Calif. *Education:* Stanford University, B.A. (Art), 1961, M.A., 1962; Navajo Reservation Weaving Apprenticeship, 1968-1976. *Principal occupation:* Organization director, author, artist, teacher. *Home address:* P.O. Box 1175, Corrales, N.M. 87048. *Affiliations:* Lecturer, College of Notre Dame, Belmont, Calif., 1963-1967; lecturer, University of New Mexico, 1971-1976; lecturer, International College, Los Angeles, 1979-1981; founder, Navajo Weaver Restoration Center, 1978-; Director, Shared Horizons, Corrales, N.M. (non-profit, educational, perpetuating the Navajo, Southwest textile art tradition. *Other professional post:* Navajo weaving workshops, lectures, demonstrations to museums, universities, and guilds across the nation, 1971-. *Awards, honors:* Cum Laude graduate and recipient of the Mortimer C. Levintritt Award for outstanding work in Departments of Art and Architecture, Stanford University, 1961; Weatherhead Foundation Grant, 1975; Communication Arts Award, "Three Looms, One Land: Shared Horizons" poster award for concept, copy, photo, 1982. *Interests:* Painting, tapestry weaving, restoration of Navajo rugs, philosophy. "Though intensely involved in my own painting, weaving and writing, the area of Navajo life and weaving continues to provide inspiration and satisfaction. With the nine years that I lived and wove on the Navajo Reservation as a basis, my core goals have been to seek out, internalize and share the beauty of traditional Navajo weaving in three main areas: the pure symetry and balance of designs, refined through generations of use; the rhythm of effortless techniques, a oneness of self and loom evolving over time; and the underlying sustaining beliefs, legends and taboos that give meaning not only to the activity but beyond, to life itself." *Biographical sources: Contemporary Authors; World Who's Who of Authors; Dictionary of International Biography; World Who's Who of Women; The Directory of Distinguished Americans; International Book of Honor; Personalities of America; Personalities of the West and Midwest; 5,000 Personalities of the World; International Directory of Distinguished Leadership; International Authors' and Writers' Who's Who. Published works: Working With the Wool -- How to Weave a Navajo Rug,* with Tiana Bighorse (Northland Press, 1971); *Genuine Navajo Rug -- Are You Sure?* (Museum of Navajo Ceremonial Art - Wheelwright Museum - and the Navajo Tribe, 1973); *The Weaver's Pathway -- A Clarification of the "Spirit Trail" in Navajo Weaving* (Northland Press, 1974); "How to Tell a Genuine Navajo Rug" (final chapter) *Navajo Weaving Handbook* (Museum of New Mexico Press, 1974, 1977); *Designing With the Wool -- Advanced Navajo Weaving Techniques* (Northland Press, 1979); *Shared Horizons/Navajo Textiles,* (catalog of exhibition) with Susan McGreevy and Mark Winter (Wheelwright Museum, 1981).

BENNETT, ROBERT L. (Oneida) 1912-
(former commissioner of Indian Affairs)

Born November 16, 1912, Oneida, Wisc. *Education:* Haskell Institute; Southeastern University, LL.B., 1941. *Home address: 604 Wagon Train, S.E., Albuquerque, N.M. 87123. Affiliations:* Former area director, Bureau of Indian Affairs; former commissioner of Indian Affairs, Bureau of Indian Affairs, Washington, D.C., 1965-1968. *Military service:* U.S. Marine Corps, 1944-1945. *Memberships:* American Society for Public Administration; Society for Applied Anthropology; American Academy of Political and Social Science, 1960-. *Awards, honors:* Indian Achievement Award, Indian Council Fire, 1962. *Biographical sources: Indians of Today* (Indian Council Fire, 1960).

BENNETT, RUTH (Shawnee) 1942-
(assistant director of
Indian organization)

Born December 12, 1942. *Education:* Indiana University, B.A., 1964; University of Washington, M.A. (English), 1968; California State University, San Francisco, Standard Secondary Teaching Credential (Multi-Cultural Education), 1973; University of California, Berkeley, Ph.D. (language and reading development with a specialization in bilingual education), 1979. *Principal occupation:* Assistant director of Indian organization. *Home address:* P.O. Box 883, Hoopa, Calif. 95546. *Affiliations:* Teaching assistant, University of Washington, 1964-1966; pre-school teacher, Inner Sunset Neighborhood Cooperative, San Francisco, 1971-1972; teaching assistant, University of California, Berkeley, 1973-1974; children's literature instructor, School of the Arts, Berkeley High School, Calif., 1973-1974; enrichment program instructor, Washington Laboratory School, Berkeley, 1975-1978; resource teacher, Hoopa Elementary School, 1976-; field director, Native Language and Culture Program, 1978-1979, assistant director, 1980-, Center for Community Development; director, Title VII, Institute of Higher Education Training Grant, Bilingual Emphasis Program, Center for Community Development, 1981-; teacher, Department of Education, Humboldt State University, 1981-. *Memberships:* Phi Delta Kappa, Phi Beta Kappa, Alpha Lambda Delta, Alpha Omicron Pi; University of California and Indiana University Alumni Associations. *Interests:* Dr. Ruth Bennett has conducted innovative curriculum work for 15 years, leading to computer uses for curriculum. *Published works: Downriver Indians' Legends,* 1983; *Let's Go Now,* 1983; *1983 Hupa Calendar,* 1982; *Karuk Fishing,* 1983; *Look Inside and Read,* 1982; *Unifon Update,* 1983; *1983-1984 Yurok Unifon Calendar,* 1983; *Origin of Fire; Songs of a Medicine Woman; Hupa Spelling Book; Legends and Personal Experiences; Ceremonial Dances; Yurok Spelling Book; What Is An Indian?; Karuk Vocabulary Book; Karuk Fishing; Basket Weaving Among the Karuk; Tolowa Legends; Tolowa/English Lesson Units; and others (all published by The Center for Community*

Development, Humboldt State University; numerous articles, including Ph.D. dissertation, *"Hoopa Children's Storytelling,"* University of California, Berkeley.

BERRIGAN, TED (Choctaw) 1934-
(poet)

Born November 15, 1934, Providence, R.I. *Education:* University of Tulsa, B.A., M.A. (English Literature.) *Principal occupation:* Poet. *Affiliations:* Editor, *"C," A Journal of Poetry,* 1963-; New York editor, *Long Hair* magazine, London; editorial assistant, *Art News* magazine; instructor, Poetry Workshop, University of Iowa. *Military service:* U.S. Army, 1954-1957 (Good Conduct Medal; U.N. Service Medal; Korean Service Medal). *Published works: The Sonnets* (C Press, 1964, Grove Press); *Many Happy Returns* (Corinth); *In the Early Morning Rain* (Goliard, Grossman); *Bean Spasms,* with Ron Padgett Kulchur).

BERTHRONG, DONALD J. 1922-
(professor of history)

Born October 2, 1922, La Crosse, Wisc. *Education:* University of Wisconsin, B.S., 1947, M.S., 1948, Ph.D., 1952. *Principal occupation:* Professor of history. *Address:* Department of History, Purdue University, Lafayette, Ind. 49707. *Affiliations:* Instructor, University of Kansas City; assistant professor, associate professor, professor of history, University of Oklahoma; professor and head, Department of History, Purdue University. *Military service:* U.S. Army and Air Force, 1942-1946. *Memberships:* American Historical Association; Association of American History; Olahoma Historical Society; Western Historical Society. *Awards, honors:* Fellowship, Social Science Research Council; Fellowship, Americn Philosophical Society; Award of Merit, Society for State and Local History, for *The Southern Cheyennes. Interests:* Western U.S. history; expert witness before the Indian Claims Commission; Fulbright lecturer in American history at the University of Hong Kong and Chinese University (Hong Kong, B.C.C.) *Published works:* Co-editor, *Joseph Redford Walker and the Arizona Adventure* (University of Oklahoma Press, 1956); *The Southern Cheyennes* (University of Oklahoma Press, 1963); *A Confederate in the Colorado Gold Fields* (University of Oklahoma Press, 1970); *Indians of Northern Indiana and Southwestern Michigan* (Garland, 1974); *The Cheyenne and Arapaho Ordeal: Reservation and Agency Life in the Indian Territory, 1875-1907* (University of Oklahoma Press, 1976.

BETTELYOUN, LULU F. (JANIS)
(Oglala Sioux) 1947-
(teacher, social welfare/caseworker)

Born April 10, 1947, Pine Ridge, S.D. *Education:* Northern State College, Aberdeen, S.D., 1965-1968; Black Hills State College, Spearfish, S.D., B.S. (Education), 1972. *Principal occupation:* Teacher, social welfare/caseworker. *Home address:* P.O. Box 66, Pine Ridge, S.D. 57770.

BIGSPRING, WILLIAM F., Sr.
(Blackfeet) 1919-
(rancher, artist)

Born January 3, 1919, East Glacier Park, Mont. *Principal occupation:* Rancher, artist. *Home address:* Box 531, East Glacier Park, Mont. 59434. *Military service:* U.S. Army Infantry, 1944-1945. *Commuity activities:* Art Exhibition, Glacier Park, Mont. (chairman). *Memberships:* Blackfeet Artists Group (president, 1964); Montana Institute of Arts, 1962-.

BITSIE, OSCAR (Navajo) 1935-
(teacher)

Born October 30, 1935, Tohatchi, N.M. *Education:* Fort Lewis College, B.A., 1964; Northern Arizona University, M.A., 1973, Post Graduate work in School Administration, 1974-1975. *Principal occupation:* Teacher. *Home address:* P.O. Box 1496, Tohatchi, N.M. 87325-1496. *Affiliations:* Gallup-McKinley County Schools, Gallup, N.M.; teacher of social studies, Tohatchi Middle School, Tohatchi, N.M. (21 years).

Other professional posts: Coordinated Title 7 - Bilingual Education, Johnson-O'Malley Indian Education, Title IV - home/school liaison coordinator. *Military service:* U.S. Army 1958-1960 (Expert Rifle; Good Conduct Medal). *Community activities:* Tohatchi Chapter President, 1970-1974, Vice President, 1978-1982; Public Health Service, Gallup, N.M. (board member, 1970-1980); Public Health Service, Gallup Indian Medical Center (health board president, 1980-); Friendship Service for Alcoholic Recovery Center (board of directors, vice-president, 1982-1985). *Memberships:* Christian Reformed Church (delegate to Calvin College in Michigan, 1976); Navajo Tribe. *Awards, honors:* Community service award by Tohatchi Chapter for Community Leadership. *Interests:* Reading books in social studies; travel throughout the Rockies for historical information; political activities in Navajo Tribe, county and state.

BLUE SPRUCE, BERYL
(Laguna/San Juan Pueblo) 1934-
(obstetrician)

Born November 24, 1934, Santa Fe, N.M. *Education:* Stanford University, B.S., 1960; University of Southern California, M.D., 1964. *Principal occupation:* Obstetrician. *Community activities:* Indian Rights Association, American Friends Service Committee (board of directors); National Indian Youth Council. *Memberships:* American College of Obstetrics and Gynecology (Fellow); Phi Rho Sigma. *Awards, honors:* John Hay Whitney Fellow, 1961-1962.

BLUE SPRUCE, GEORGE, Jr.
(Laguna/San Juan Pueblo) 1931-
(health systems director)

Born January 16, 1931, Santa Fe, N.M. *Education:* Creighton University, D.D.S., 1956; University of California School of Public Health, M.P.H., 1967; Feeral Executive Institute, Certificate, 1973. *Principal occupation:* Health systems director. *Home address:* 3834 E. Yale, Phoenix, Ariz. 85008. *Affiliations:* Dental officer, U.S. Navy Dental Clinic, 1956-1958; dental officer, U.S.P.H.S. Indian Hospital, Fort Belknap,

Mont., 1958-1960; U.S.P.H.S. Outpatient Clinic, New York, N.Y. (resident, 1960-1961; deputy dental director, 1961-1963); resident in dental public health, Dental Health Center, San Francisco, Calif., 1967-1968; consultant in dental health (special assignment), Pan American Health Organization, World Health Organization, Washington, D.C., 1968-1970; Education Development Branch, Division of Dental Health, National Institutes of Health, Bethesda, Md. - chief, Auxiliary Utilization Section, 1971, special assistant to the director for American Indian Affairs, 1971, director, Office of Health Manpower Opportunity, 1971-1973; liaison officer for Indian concerns, Health Resources Administration, U.S.P.H.S., Department of HEW, 1973-1974; director, Office of Native American Programs, Office of Human Development, Dept. of HEW, 1976-1978; director, Indian Health Manpower Development, Indian Health Service, DHEW, 1978-1979; director, Phoenix Area Indian Health Service, DHEW, 1979-. *Other professional posts:* Chairman, Intra-Departmental Council on Indian Affairs (DHEW); chairman, Health Manpower Opportunity Advisory Committee; chairman, Feasibility Study Team for Project: Center for Health Professions Education (Navajo Reservation, Arizona); special consultant, Special Committee for the Socio-economically Disadvantaged, American Dental Hygienist's Association. *Memberships:* National Indian Education Association (board of directors); Health Education Media Association (board of directors, Minority Affairs); American Indian Bank (board of directors); American Fund for Dental Education (member, Selection Committee); Task Force for Medical Academic Achievement Program; Students American Veterinary Medicine Association (member, Selection Committee); Health Manpower Study for American Indians (member, Advisory Committee); Navajo Health Authority (member, board of commissioners, Kellog Scholarship Committee, Dean Selection Committee, Health Professions Education Committee); American Indian School of Medicine - Feasibility Study (member, Advisory Council); Health Professions Education System,

Rockville, Md. (board of directors); U.S.P.H.S. Commissioned Officers' Association ; American Public Health Association; American Indian Physicians' Association; American Dental Association; American Association of Dental Schools; New Mexico State Dental Society; North Americn Indian Tennis Association; U.S. Lawn Tennis Association. *Awards, honors:* Outstanding American Indian for 1972, American Indian Exposition, Inc., Anadarko, Okla.; Outstanding American Indian Achievement Award, 1974, American Indian Council Fire, Inc., Washington, D.C.; "Award of Merit", presented by the Association of American Indian Physicians for: "Significant Contributions Towards Raising the Level of Health Care of the American Indian and Alaskan Native," August 1980; "Alumni of the Year," presented by Creighton University, Omaha, Neb. in May 1984, for "his distinguished service to his fellow man and his alma mater while keeping with the finest traditions of the University. *Biographical sources: American Indians of Today; Contemporary American Indian Leaders; Who's Who in the Federal Government,* Second Edition; *National Indian Directory* (National Congress of American Indians); *Dictionary of International Biography; Men of Achievement,* 1974. *Interests:* Recruitment of minority students into health professions; health manpower development for American Indians; American Indian education; public health administration. *Published works:* Articles: "Toward More Minorities in Health Professions" (National Medical Association Journal, Sept. 1972); "Needed: Indian Health Professionals" (Harvard Medical Alumni Bulletin, Jan.-Feb. 1972); "Health Manpower Grants Open New Opportunities for American Indians" (Official Newsletter of the Association of American Indian Physicians, Vol. 1, No. 1, Nov. 1972); "The American Indian as a Dental Patient" (Public Health Reports, Dec. 1961); *The Fabrication of Simplified Dental Equipment - A Manual* (Pan American Health Organization Publication, pending publication); *The Development and Testing of a Mobile Dental Care Unit* (Public Health Residency Report).

BLUMER, THOMAS J. 1937-
(senior editor, Library of Congress)

Born July 7, 1937, Freeport, N.Y. *Education:* University of Mississippi, B.A., 1967, M.A., 1968; University of South Carolina, Ph.D. (English Literature), 1976. *Principal occupation:* Senior editor, Library of Congress (Law Library). *Home address:* 642 A St., N.E., Washington, D.C. 20002. *Affiliations:* Assistant professor, Tidewater Community College, Portsmouth, Va., 1968-1972; Teaching assistant, University of South Carolina, Columbia, S.C., 1972-1976; lecturer in English, Winthrop College, Rock Hill, S.C., 1976-1977; Data Analyst, Planning Research Corp., McLean, Va., 1977-1978; senior editor, European Law Division, Law Library, Library of Congress, 1978-; consultant, Native American Rights Fund, Boulder, Colo., 1980-; consultant, McKissick Museums, University of South Carolina, 1984-; consultant, Pamunkey Indian Museum, King William, Va., 1985; editor, American Indian Libraries Newsletter, American Library Association, Chicago, Ill., 1984-. *Military service:* U.S. Navy, 1956-1960. *Memberships:* American Library Association; American Indian Library Association, 1982-; American Folklore Association; Mid-Atlantic Folklife Association, 1982-; Library of Congress Professional Association. *Interests:* Southeastern Indians, Catawba Indian history, Pamunkey Indian history, Southern Indian pottery traditions (Catawba, Cherokee, Pamunkey); lectures. *Published works: Catawba Indian Pottery: An Exhibition* (Winthrop College, 1977); *Catawba Indian Bibliography* (Scarecrow Press, 1985); numerous articles. *Works in Progress: Catawba Indian Folk History Project; Pamunkey Indian Folklife Project; "The Pamunkey Indians in the War Between the States."*

BOISSEVAIN, ETHEL 1913-
(professor of anthropology and archaeology)

Born February 5, 1913, New York, N.Y. Education: Vassar College, B.A., 1934; University of Prague, Prague, Czechoslovakia, Ph.D., 1936. *Principal occupation:* Professor of anthropology and archaeology. *Home address:* 1350 - 15th St., Apt. 12-O, Fort Lee,

N.J. 07024. *Affiliations:* Professor of anthropology, Hunter College, 1937-1944, 1959-1967; professor of anthropology, Drew University, 1967-1968; professor of anthropology, Lehman College, CUNY, 1968-1979. *Community activities:* American Civil Liberties Union (member, American Indian committee, 1956-1959.) *Memberships:* Americn Anthropological Association (Fellow); American Society for Ethnohistory, 1954-; Society for Historical Archaeology, 1968-; Archaeological Society of New Jersey, 1943-. *Awards, honors:* Grants from the Rhode Island Historical Preservation Commission: For surveying and mapping the historic village of the Narragansett Indians in Charlestown, R.I., 1969; Lehman College Grant for Faculty Research (George N. Shuster Fellowship Fund); from the Research Center of C.U.N.Y., a grant in support of research on the ethnohistory of the Indians of Southern New England and Eastern Long Island, for writing a chapter on this subject for the Smithsonian Institution's, *Handbook of the North American Indians,* 1971. *Interests:* New England ethnohistory and ethnoarchaeology; travel to central and eastern Europe. Dr. Boissevain writes, "My major areas of vocational interest are teaching and researching American Indian cultures." *Published works: The Narragansett People* (Indian Tribal Series, Phoenix, Ariz., 1975); *Hidden Minorities* (University Press of America, 1981); numerous articles and papers published in journals and as chapters of professional anthropological texts.

BOISSIERE, ROBERT 1914-
(retired, writer)

Born December 23, 1914, France. *Education:* Law School, Paris (three years). *Principal occupation:* Retired, writer. *Home address:* Route 11, Box 6B, Santa Fe, N.M. 87501. Military service: World War II, Frnce (two decorations). Memberships: Western Writers of America. *Biographical sources: Contemporary Authors. Published works: Po-Pai-Mo - The Search for White Buffalo Woman* (Sunstone Press, 1983); *The Hopi Way - An Odyssey* (Sunstone Press, 1985); *Meditations With the Hopi* (Bear and Co., 1986).

BOMBERRY, DANIEL RICHARD
(Cayuga) 1945-
(organizer, educational administrator)

Born March 24, 1945, North Vancouver, British Columbia, Can. *Education:* California State University, A.B. (Political Science), 1970. *Principal occupation:* Organizer, educational administrator. *Affiliations:* Coordinator, American Indian Center, California State University, Long Beach, 1969-1970; associate director, Educational Opportunity Program, California State University, 1970-1971; director, Owens Valley Indian Education Center, Bishop Reservation, California, 1971-. *Community activities:* American Indian Culture Program Board, U.C.L.A., 1969-1970; American Indian Education Council, California State Department of Education; Native American Alliance of California (organizer, 1969-1971); Coalition of Indian Controlled School Boards, Denver, Colorado (executive board, 1972-1973); D.Q. University, Davis, Calif. (board, 1972-1973). *Memberships:* California Indian Education Association (1969-; nominating committee, 1973); Nationl Indian Education Association, 1971-; Indian Fair Association, 1972-; Bishop Indian Athletic Association, 1972-. *Awards, honors:* Robert F. Kennedy Memorial Fellowship for 1973 to organize a statewide network of Indian controlled educational programs throughout rural California. *Interests:* "Organizing Indian communities or groups to assume control of their own educational programs."

BONNEY, RACHEL A. 1939-
(professor of anthropology)

Born March 28, 1939, St. Paul, Minn. *Education:* University of Minnesota, B.A., 1961, M.A., 1963; University of Arizona, Ph.D., 1975. *Principal occupation:* Professor of anthropology. *Home address:* Route 1, Box 395, Mooresville, N.C. 28115. *Affiliations:* Assistant professor, Tarkio College, Mo., 1965-1967; instructor, University of South Florida, 1967-1970; graduate teaching associate, University of Arizona, 1971-1973;

instructor and professor, University of North Carolina at Charlotte, 1973-. *Other professional posts:* Teacher, guidance, B.I.A., Teec Nos Pos Boarding School, Ariz. (Navajo), 1964. *Community activities:* Charlotte-Mecklenburg Title IV (Indian Education Act) Indian Parent Committee (ex-officio member, 1975-1977); Metrolina Native American Association, Charlotte, N.C.; UNCC Phoenix Society (American Indian Student Organization) and Phoenix Dancer (Indian dance team), (advisor). *Memberships:* American Anthropological Association (Fellow) 1963-; American Ethnological Society, 1967-1971, 1977-; Southern Anthropological Association, 1973-; National Congress of American Indians, 1972-1973; Anthropological Council on Education, 1977-; National Indian Education Association, 1977-; Southeastern Indian Cultural Association, 1977-. *Awards, honors:* HEW Title IX (ethnic heritage studies) Project Grant, 1977-1978. *Interests:* Indian studies; multi-ethnic studies; culture change (Catawba land claims case); Indian powwows; powwows with Phoenix Dancers; archaeological projects in Minnesota, New York, New Mexico, and Austria. *Biographical sources: Who's Who in America - The South* (Marquis). *Published works: "American Indian Studies in the Social Studies Curriculum" (Proceedings,* North Carolina Association for Research in Education, May, 1975); *"The Role of Women in Indian Activism" (The Western Canadian Journal of Anthropology,* Vol. VI, No. 3, 1976); *"The Role of AIM Leaders in Indian Nationalism" (American Indian Quarterly,* Vol. 3, No. 3, 1977); *"Indians of the Americas, Courtship Customs" (Encyclopedia of Indians of the Americas,* Scholarly Press, 1978); among others.

BORMAN, LEONARD D. 1927-
(anthropologist, research associate)

Born May 24, 1927, Toledo, Ohio. *Education:* University of Toledo, 1946-1948; University of Chicago, M.A. (Thesis: *Work Camp Among the Penobscot Indians*), 1952, Ph.D., 1965. *Principal occupation:* Anthropologist, research associate. *Home address:* 2405 Lawndale, Evanston, Ill. 60201. *Affiliations:* Director of program development, Stone Brandel Center, Chicago, 1966-1970; program director, W. Clement & Jessie V. Stone Foundation, Chicago, 1970-1974; research associate and director, Self-Help Institute, Center for Urban Affairs, Northwestern University, 1974-; research associate, Department of Behavioral Science (Human Development), University of Chicago, 1976- . *Other professional posts:* Chief, Anthropological Section, V.A. Hospital, Downey, Ill., 1958-1965; consultant, North American Indian Foundation, Norman, Okla., 1973-1975. *Field work:* Penobscot and Passamaquoddy Indians, Maine (financed by grant from the American Friends Service Committee, Philadelphia, Pa.). *Community activities:* American Indian Center, Chicago (member, board of directors, 1956-1968); Grand Council of the American Indian Center, Chicago (member, 1968-; chairman, 1968-1970); Self-Help Development Institute, Evanston (president, 1975); Council for the Study of Mankind (member, board of directors, 1977); *Memberships:* American Anthropological Association (Fellow); Society of Sigma Xi; Society for Applied Anthropology (Fellow); National Association of Social Workers; Current Anthropology (Associate, Fellow); Council on Anthropology and Education; Council on Medical Anthropology; American Association for the Advancement of Science; Royal Anthropological Institute of Great Britain and Ireland (Fellow). *Biographical sources: Who's Who in the Midwest; Dictionary of International Biography; Royal Blue Book; Two Thousand Men of Achievement; Roster of Prominent Americans; Community Leaders of America; International Who's Who in Community Service. Published works:* "Indian Citizenry: A Bridge or a Sawdust Trail" (*Down East* magazine, Nov., 1954); "An Indian Chief Retires" (*Down East* magazine, June 1957); "American Indian Tribal Support Systems and Economic Development" (*The Diverse Society: Implications for Social Policy,* National Association of Social Workers, 1976) "American Indian: The Reluctant Urbanites" (*The Center Magazine,* Center for the Study of Democratic Institutions, March-April, 1977); among others.

BOSIN, BLACKBEAR (Kiowa-Comanche) 1921-
(artist, muralist, designer)

Born June 15, 1921, Anadarko, Okla. *Principal occupation:* Artist, muralist, designer. *Affiliation:* Artist, president, Blackbear's Ltd., Great Plains Studio, Wichita, Kansas. *Other professional posts:* Advisor, Wichita Art Museum, Mobil Gallery; board, acquisitions committee, Mid-America All Indian Center, Kansas. *Military service:* U.S. Marines, 1943-1945. *Memberships:* Advertising Club of Wichita; Wichita Artists Guild, 1948-; International Arts & Letters, Switzerland. *Awards, honors:* Invited to the Festival of Arts, The White House, 1965; delivered a paper on "Traditional Indian Arts" at the Convocation of American Indian Scholars, Princeton University, 1970; commissioned to design a 44' Indian figure made of Corten steel given to the City of Wichita, Bicentennial Commission for Kansas; medallic designer for the Historical Indian series for the Franklin Mint; recipient of the National American Indian Achievements Award for Visual Arts, Traditional Painter; Kansas Art Commission appointed Governor's artist, 1977. *Biographical sources: Who's Who in American Art. Exhibits:* The Smithsonian Institute; Eisenhower Museum, Abilene, Kansas; Albany Institute of History and Art; Currier Gallery of Art; Miami Beach Art Center; Wichita Art Association; George Walter Vincent Smith Art Museum; Museum of the Great Plains; Los Angeles County Museum; Palace of the Legion of Honor; Denver Art Museum; Heard Museum; Philbrook Museum; Chicago Indian Center; Oklahoma City Art Center; The National Gallery; Whitney Museum; The White House. *Lectures:* Wichita State University; Princeton University; Mid-America All Indian Center, Wichita; and Philbrook Art Center, Tulsa, Okla.

BOURGEAU, DEAN (Colville) 1928-
(musician)

Born July 14, 1928, Inchelium, Wash. *Principal occupation:* Musician. *Home address:* Inchelium, Was. 99137. *Affiliations:* Colville Business Council; Indian police. *Mil-*

itary service: U.S. Army, 1950-1952, 1956-1957 (U.N. Service Medal, Combat Medal.) *Community activities:* American Legion; Eagles.

BOUWENS, WILLIAM CLAYTON, Jr. (Aleut, Tanaina-Kenaitze) 1947-
(president, Alaska Cultural Services)

Born November 23, 1947, Anchorage, Alaska. *Education:* Univerity of Alaska at Fairbanks, Anchorage, and Soldotna, 1966-1972. *Principal occupation:* President, Alaska Cultural Services, 1976-. *Home address:* Box 173, Ninilichik, Alaska. *Other professional posts:* Shareholder, Cook Inlet Region, Inc.; secretary-treasurer, Ninilichik Native Association. *Military service:* Air National Guard, 1971-1976. *Memberships:* American Legion; Cook Inlet Native Association; Alaska Federation of Natives; American Indian Education Association, Project Media Evaluation, 1977-1978.

BOVIS, PIERRE G. 1943-
(shop owner)

Born February 3, 1943, Nice, France. *Education:* Beaux Arts, France, B.A. equivalent. *Principal occupation:* Shop owner. *Home address:* P.O. Box 324, Santa Fe, N.M. 87501. *Affiliation:* Owner, Winona Trading Post, Santa Fe, N.M., 1968-. *Military service:* French Army (two years). *Community activities:* Loaned Indian artifacts for local and national traveling exhibits. *Memberships:* Appraisers Association of America; Indian Arts and Crafts Association; Genuine Indian Relic Society; English Westerners, London. *Awards, honors:* "Have won several first, second and third place cups and trophies for my displays of Indian artifacts at Indian shows." *Biographical sources: Who's Who in Indian Relics,* Vol. III: *International Who's Who in Art & Antiques,* Vol. XI. *Interests:* "Interests lie in anthropology and primitive art, and I travel through Europe and Far East, etc." *Published works: American Indian and Eskimo Basketry: A Key to Identification,* with Charles Miles, 1970; *Pine Ridge, 1890: Eye Witness Account of the Events Surrounding Wounded Knee,* 1972. Both published by Mr. Bovis.

BOWLAN, LORI A. 1964-
(tribal rolls director)

Born June 25, 1964, Danbury, Conn. *Education:* Oklahoma State University, Stillwater, (four years, degree pending). *Principal occupation:* Tribal rolls director. *Home address:* P.O. Box 746, Tecumseh, Oklahoma 74873. *Other professional posts:* Scholarship committee director.

BOY, CALVIN J. *(Warring Shield)* (Blackfoot) 1923-
(artist)

Born September 18, 1923, Browning, Mont. *Education:* High school. *Principal occupation:* Artist. *Home address:* General Delivery, Browning, Mont. 59417. *Affiliations:* Machine shop apprentice (three years); railroad foreman (ten years); worked with John C. Ewers as an illustrator.

BOYD, ROSE MARIE (Chippewa-Oneida) 1958-
(administrative assistant)

Born March 2, 1958, Detroit, Mich. *Education:* Schoolcraft College, Livonia, Mich., 1975-1978. *Home address:* 16739 Beaverland, Detroit, Mich. 48219. *Affiliations:* Administrative assistant, South Eastern Michigan Indians, Inc., Warren, Mich., 1985-.

BOYER, MOMMA QUAIL (United Lumbee-Cherokee) 1925-
(homemaker)

Born October 16, 1925, Oklahoma. *Education:* High school. *Principal occupation:* Homemaker. *Home address:* P.O. Box 512, Fall River Mills, Calif. 96028. *Other professional post:* National secretary, United Lumbee Nation of N.C. and America. *Affiliations:* United Lumbee Nation of N.C. and America (Grand Council, national secretary); Title IV and Johnson O'Malley Indian Education Program in Tulare, Kings Counties, Calif. (parent committee & chairperson, five years); *Memberships:* Native American Wolf Clan (1977-1982; chief, 1982-); Chapel of Our Lord Jesus (treasurer, vice-chief).

BRADLEY, RUSSELL (Kickapoo) 1942-
(B.I.A. agency superintendent)

Born July 25, 1942, St. Joseph, Mo. *Education:* Haskell Institute (Business), 1962; Metropolitan Junior College, Kansas City (Business Admininistration), 1966. *Principal occupation:* B.I.A. agency superintendent. *Home address:* Box 2075, Whiteriver, Arizona 85941. *Affiliations:* Assistant director, United Tribes of North Dakota Training Center, Bismarck, N.D., 1972; employment director, United Sioux Tribes, Pierre, S.D., 1973; superintendent, Winnebago Agency, Winnebago, Neb. (four years); superintendent, Turtle Mountain Agency, Belcourt, N.D. (two years); superintendent, Fort Apache Agency, Whiteriver, Ariz. (two years). *Military service:* U.S. Army, 1964-1966 (Specialist 5th Class, Good Conduct Medal.) *Community activities:* Requires alignment with most all community services and functions, such as: education, law enforcement, social services, economic development and planning, road and judicial services. *Memberships:* Younghawk/Bear American Legion Post (Albuquerque chapter, 11 years); Haskell Alumni Association; National Indian Contractors Association; National Intertribal Timber Council. *Awards, honors:* B.I.A. Outstanding Achievement Award, 1982; Community Service Award, 1984, Turtle Mountain Chippewa Tribe. *Interests:* Minority employment development; reservation economic development; Indian education; traditional preservation and enhancement of recreation and athletics on reservations. "Enhancing tribal governments in serving its members provides the greatest challenge and satisfaction." *Biographical sources: Who's Who in North Dakota,* 1984.

BRANDON, WILLIAM 1914-
(writer)

Born September 21, 1914, Kokomo, Ind. *Principal occupation:* Writer. *Affiliations:* Visiting lecturer, University of Massachusetts, 1967, California State College (Los Angeles, 1970, Long Beach, 1970). *Military service:* U.S. Air Force, 1944-1945. *Awards, honors:* Western Heritage Award for *The American Heritage Book of Indians,* 1961.

Interests: Mr. Brandon writes, "I have been interested in introducing experimental courses in American Indian literature, and in American Indians and American history, at various colleges and universities. My essay, 'American Indians and American History,' published in *The American West,* Journal of the Western History Association in 1965, has been used as the basis of these courses. Most of 1969 was spent traveling over the country, preparing a series of articles on current Indian matters, titles, 'American Indians: The Alien Americans,' published in *The Progressive* from December, 1969 to February, 1970 (and) reprinted in various publications, including the *Congressional Record.* I attended as an invited observer the First Convocation of Americn Indian Scholars, held at Princeton (University) in March, 1970." *Published works: The Men and the Mountain* (William Morrow, 1955); *The Amerian Heritage Book of Indians* (American Heritage Publishing Co., 1961; Dell, 1964); *The Magic World: American Indian Songs and Poems* (William Morrow, 1971).

BRAUKER, SHIRLEY M. (Ottawa) 1950
(potter)

Born August 11, 1950, Angola, Ind. *Education:* Mid-Michigan Community College, Harrison, A.A., 1980; Central Michigan University, Mt. Pleasant, B.A., 1982, M.A., 1983. *Principal occupation:* Potter. *Home address:* 1044 Silver Rd., Coldwater, Mich. 49036. *Affiliation:* Secretary, Central Michigan University, 1982-1984. *Memberships:* National Collegiate Education of Ceramics; National Honor Society. *Art Exhibitions:* Bachelor of Fine Arts, Central Michigan University, 1981; Great Lakes Traveling Indian Art Exhibition, Dept. of the Interior, Washington, D.C., 1983; Ethnic Art Show, Lansing Art Gallery, 1983; Sacred Circle Gallery, Seattle, Wash., "American Indian Ceramic Art; Yesterday, Today and Tomorrow" exhibit, 1984; Midland Christmas Arts Festival, 1984; Museum of the Plains Indian, Browning, Mont., "Contemporary Clay Indian Art" exhibit, 1985; Larson

Gallery, Grand Rapids, Mich. *Community activities:* Demonstrates pottery techniques aboard the Traveling Art Train, 1983; worked on a documentary film depicting Indian artists in Michigan, 1983; illustrates pamphlets and handouts for community service. *Awards, honors:* Outstanding Community College Student Scholarship Award, 1980; Mae Beck Indian Artist Scholarship Award, 1982; Potter of the Month, Lansing Art Gallery, 1983. *Interests:* Indian history, culture and art work; craft work, doll making, quilting, painting, beadwork, stained glass; travel and camping. *Biographical sources:* Documentary film: *Woodland Traditions: The Art of Three Native Americans; American Indian Index.*

BRENNAN, LOUIS ARTHUR 1911-
(writer, archaeologist)

Born February 5, 1911. *Education:* University of Notre Dame, A.B., 1932. *Principal occupation:* Writer, archaeologist. *Home address:* 39 Hamilton Ave., Ossining, N.Y. 10562. *Affiliations:* Assistant professor, Pace University; director, Museum and Laboratory for Archaeology at Muscoot Farm (Westchester County Parks Dept.) *Other professional posts:* Editor, *Archaeology of Eastern North America;* editor, New York State Archaeological Association journal of archaeology, *The Bulletin. Military service:* U.S. Naval Reserve, 1943-1945 (Bronze Star for gallantry). *Memberships:* Society for Professional Archaeologists; Society for American Archaeology. *Awards, honors:* Achievement Award, NYSAA: fellow, NYSAA. *Interests:* American archaeology and prehistory; field of specialty, historical and prehistoric archaeology of Lower Hudson Valley. *Published works: The Long Knife,* (Dell, 1957) and *Tree of Arrows,* (Macmillan, 1964) both historical novels; *No Stone Unturned: An Almanac of North American Prehistory* (Random House, 1959); *The Buried Treasure of Archaeology* (Random House, 1964); *American Dawn: A New Model of American Prehistory* (Macmillan, 1970); Beginner's Guide to Archaeology (Stackpole, 1974; Dell, 1975); *Artifacts of Prehistoric America* (Stackpole, 1975); numerous articles.

BRESCIA, WILLIAM, Jr.
(Mississippi Choctaw) 1947-
(director, research and curriculum development)

Born November 4, 1947, Chicago, Ill. *Education:* Wartburg College, Waverly, Iowa, B.A. (Drama), 1970; University of Wisconsin, Madison, M.S. (Curriculum and Instruction), 1973. *Principal occupation:* Director, research and curriculum development. *Home address:* Route 5, Box 364, Union, Miss. 39365. *Affiliation:* Editor, *Daybreak Star Magazine* (Daybreak Star Press, 1976-1981; Curriculum coordinator, 1976-1978, director, Community Educational Services, 1978-1981, United Indians of All Tribes Foundation, Seattle, Wash.; director, Curriculum Developer, Ethnic Heritage Program, 1981-1982, director, Division of Research and Curriculum Development, Mississippi Band of Choctaw Indians, Philadelphia, Miss., 1982-. *Other professional posts:* Computer education consultant, Mississippi State Department of Education, 1984-. *Community activities:* D'Arcy McNickle Center, Newberry Library, Chicago, Ill. (advisor, 1985-); ERIC/CRESS National Advisory Board (American Indian educational specialist, 1984-); *The Native American* (advisory committee member, 1984-); Indian representative, Washington Urban Rural Racial Disadvantaged Advisory Committee, 1979-1980; Indian representative, *New Voice* Advisory committee, WGBH-TV, Boston, Mass, 1977-1980; Scientists and Citizens Organized on Policy Issues, Seattle, Wash., 1980-1981; Seattle Museum of History and Industry, 1979-1981. *Memberships:* American Education Research Association; International Reading Association; National Indian Education Association; National Association for Bilingual Education; Mid-South Educational Research Association; Association for Supervision and Curriculum Development. *Awards, honors:* American Indian Heritage High School (special recognition for work in support of that school and Indian education); Northwest American Indian Womens Circle (special recognition for work in support of National Conference, 1979); Northwest Regional Folklife Festival (for administration of Seattle Pow-Wow, 1978); Ethnic Heritage

Employee of the Year, 1981; Choctaw Department of Education (Employee of the Year, 1982). *Interests:* Computers in education; curriculum development; learning styles and brain functions; economic education; organic gardening; Choctaw literacy. *Published works:* Co-author, *Reeves-Brescia, Developmental Checklist,* (Mississippi Band of Choctaw Indians, 1975); *script advisor, Yesterdays Children: Indian Elder Oral History,* 30 minute video (Daybreak Star Press, 1980); co-author, *Development of Native American Curriculum,* workbook (Daybreak Star Press, 1979); editor, *Ways of the Lushootseed People: Ceremonies and Traditions of the Northern Puget Sound Indians* (Daybreak Star Press, 1980); editor, *Sharing Our Worlds* (Daybreak Star Press, 1980); script advisor, *Voices from the Cradleboard,* 30 minute slide presentation (Daybreak Star Press, 1980); editor, *Indians in Careers* (Daybreak Star Press, 1980); editor, *Starting an Indian Teen Club* (Daybreak Star Press, 1980); co-author, *Fisherman on the Puyallup & Teachers Guide* (Daybreak Star Press, 1980); co-author, *Suquamish Today & Teachers Guide* (Daybreak Star Press, 1980); executive editor, *Tribal Sovereignty, Indian Tribes in U.S. History* (Daybreak Star Press, 1981); editor, *Free Range to Reservation: Social Change on Selected Washington Reservations* (Daybreak Star Press, 1981); editor, *Outdoor Education for Indian Youth* (Daybreak Star Press, 1981); *Getting Control of Your Money* (Daybreak Star Press, 1981); *Knowing Your Legal Rights* (Daybreak Star Press, 1981); editor, *"Daybreak Star Pre-School Activities Book* (Daybreak Star Press, 1979); editor, *Twana Games* (Daybreak Star Press, 1981); editor, *Our Mother Corn* (Daybreak Star Press, 1981); *A'una* (Daybreak Star Press, 1981); editor, *Washington State Indian History for Grades 4-6, A Techer's Guide* Daybreak Star Press, 1981); editor, *O'Wakaga* (Daybreak Star Press, 1981); editor, *By the Work of Our Hands,* co-editor, *"Teacher's Guide* (Choctaw Heritage Press, 1982); editor, *Choctaw Tribal Government* (Choctaw Heritage Press, 1982); co-author, *Looking Around, Na Yo Pisa* (Choctaw Heritage Press, 1982); editor, *Okla Apilachi* (Choctaw Heritage Press, 1982); editor, *How the Flowers Came to Be* (Choctaw Heritage Press, 1982); executive editor, *Choctaw Anthology I, II, and III* (Choctaw Heritage Press, 1984); *Lowak Mosoli* (Choctaw Heritage Press, 1984); editor, *Little Pigs - Shokoshi Althiha* (Choctaw Heritage Press, 1984); editor, *The Tale of the Possum* (Choctaw Heritage Press, 1984); editor, *Welcome to the Choctaw Fair!* (Choctaw Heritage Press, 1984); *James at Work* (Choctaw Heritage Press, 1984); "The Choctaw Oral Traditions Relating to Their Origin," chapter from *The Choctaw Before Removal* (University of Mississippi Press, 1985).

BRESHEARS, GARY
(executive director)

Affiliation: Executive director, Creek Nation, P.O. Box 580, Okmulgee, Okla. 74447.

BRIGHT, WILLIAM 1928-
(professor)

Born August 13, 1928, Oxnard, Calif. *Education:* University of California at Berkeley, A.B., 1949, Ph.D., 1955. *Principal occupation:* Professor. *Affiliation:* Professor of linguistics and anthropology, University of California at Los Angeles, 1959-. *Military service:* U.S. Army, 1954-1955 (captain). *Memberships:* Linguistic Society of America (editor, *Language*); American Anthropological Association. *Awards, honors:* Fellowship, American Council of Learned Societies, 1964-1965: Guggenheim Fellowship, 1972. *Interests:* Field work in languages of California Indians, and languages of India. *Published works: The Karok Language* (University of California Press, 1957); editor, *Studies in California Linguistics* (University of California Press, 1964); editor, *Sociolinguistics* (Monton, 1966); *A Luiseno Dictionary* (University of California Press, 1968).

BROCKIE, LEO
(B.I.A. superintendent)

Affiliation: Superintendent, Fort Berthold Agency, Bureau of Indian Affairs, New Town, N.D. 58763.

BRODY, J.J. 1929-
(professor)

Born April 24, 1929, Brooklyn, N.Y. *Education:* The Cooper Union, New York, N.Y. (Certificate of Fine Arts), 1950; University of New Mexico, B.A., 1956, M.A., 1964, Ph.D., 1970. *Principal occupation:* Professor. *Home address:* 1824 Luthy Dr. N.E., Albuquerque, N.M. 87112. *Affiliations:* Curator of art, Everhart Museum, Scranton, Penna., 1957-1958; curator, Isaac Delago Museum of Art, New Orleans, 1958-1960; curator, Museum of International Folk Art, Santa Fe, 1960-1961; curator and director, Maxwell Museum of Anthropology, University of New Mexico, 1962-; professor of anthropology and art history, University of New Mexico, 1964-. *Other professional post:* Research curator, Maxwell Museum of Anthropology. *Military service:* U.S. Army, 1952-1954 (sergeant). *Community activities:* City of Albuquerque (art advisory board, 1970-1974); Seton Museum and Library, Ghost Ranch Museum, Mimbres Valley Museum (board member); Governor of New Mexico Task Force Paleontological Resources, 1978-1979. *Memberships:* American Association of Museums; International Commission on Museums; Society for American Archaeology; Mountain Plains Museum Conference; New Mexico Museum Association; New Mexico Cactus and Succulent Society. *Awards, honors:* Popejoy Prize, University of New Mexico best dissertation, 1971; non-fiction award for *Indian Painters and White Patrons,* Border Regional Library Conference, 1971; 1977 Art Book Award for *Mimbres Painted Pottery; Award of Honor, New Mexico Historic Preservation Commission, 1978; resident scholar, School of American Research, 1980-1981. Interests:* Indian art, especially of the Southwest; museology; rock art; education; museum exhibitions. *Biographical sources: Who's Who in America; Who's Who in the West; Who's Who in American Art. Published works: Indian Panters and White Patrons* (UNM Press, 1971); *Between Traditions* (UNM Press, 1976; *Mimbres Painted Pottery* (School of American Research and UNM Press, 1977); *Beatien Yazz: Indian Painter,* with Sallie Wagner and B. Yazz (School of American Research, 1983); *Mimbres Pottery,* with

Catherine Scott and Steve LeBlanc (Hudson Hills Press, 1983.)

BROSE, DAVID S. 1939-
(professor)

Born February 20, 1939, Detroit, Mich. *Education:* University of Michigan, B.A. (cum laude), 1960; University of Rome (Italy), graduate studies, 1960-1961; University of Michigan, M.A., 1966, Ph.D., 1968. *Principal occupation:* Professor. *Affiliations:* Director, Archaeological Field School, Ann Arbor, Mich., 1967; research assistant, University of Michigan, Museum of Anthropology, 1964-1968; assistant professor of anthropology, Case Western Reserve University, 1971-. *Other professional posts:* Docent, University of Michigan Exhibits Museum, 1950-1960; associate curator of anthropology, Cleveland Museum of Natural Science, 1969-; archaeologist, Western Reserve Historical Society, 1970-. *Military service:* U.S. Army, 1962-1964. *Memberships:* American Anthropological Association (Fellow); American Association for the Advancement of Science; Archaeological Institute of America; American Ethnological Society; Central States Anthropological Society; Council on Michigan Archaeology; Current Anthropology (Associate); Michigan Academy of Science, Arts and Letters; Michigan Archaeological Society; Michigan Historical Society; Ohio Academy of Science; Great Lake Prehistory Foundation (board member); Ohio Archaeological Society; Society for American Archaeology; Society for Pennsylvania Archaeology; The Wiliam Clements Library (Associate); The Society for Historical Archaeology. *Awards, honors:* National Science Foundation: U.S.E.P. participant, 1964; University of Michigan, Rackham Research Grant, 1966, Graduate Fellow, 1966; Kettering Foundation Grant, 1968-1969; National Science Foundation Grant, 1970-1971—for analysis of the late prehistoric period in northeast Ohio; N.E.H. grant for research on pioneer settlement in the Western Reserve, 1971-1972. *Interests:* Prehistoric archaeology, paleo-ecology, prehistoric social organization; prehistory and protohistory of the Great Lakes and Central Sub-Arctic; ethnohistory and acculturation of North American Indians; historic sites archaeology; problems and procedures in archaeological research. *Field work:* Michigan, Wisconsin, 1964-1966; Michigan, Ontario, 1967; Ohio, 1968-1970, 1970-1971; Florida, 1970. *Published works: The Archaeology of Summer Island: Changing Settlement Systems in Northern Lake Michigan* (Anthropological Papers, Museum of Anthropology, University of Michigan, No. 41, 1970) *Prehistoric Cultural Ecology and Social Organization in the Northern Lake Michigan Area* (CWRU Studies in Anthropology, No. 1, 1970); many articles and papers published in professional journals.

BROWMAN, DAVID L. 1941-
(professor, consultant)

Born December 9, 1941, Missoula, Mont. *Education:* University of Washington, A.M., 1966; Harvard University, Ph.D., 1970. *Principal occupation:* Professor, consultant. *Home address:* 429 Treetop Lane, St. Louis, Mo. 63122. *Affiliation:* Professor and consultant, Department of Anthropology, Washington University, St. Louis, Mo., 1970-. *Other professional posts:* Consulting survey archaeologist; pastoral development consultant for Andean arid lands. *Community activities:* Advisory Council on Historic Preservation (historic archaeologist). *Memberships:* American Anthropological Association; Society of Professional Archaeologists (assistant secretary treasurer, secretary treasurer, board of directors); Missouri Association of Professional Archaeologists (board of directors); Academia Nacional de Ciencas, Bolivia; Archaeological Institute of America; Society for American Archaeology; International Union of Anthropological and Ethnological Sciences (Commission on Nomadic Peoples; Association for Field Archaeology; Institute for Andean Studies. *Awards, honors:* National Science Foundation Fellowship and Research Grants; Latin American Studies Research Grant. *Interests:* "Special focus on Andes; worked several years in Peru and Bolivia; also worked/visited several other Latin American countries, conducting anthropological research; current interest focus on camelid and ovicaprid pastoralism in the semi-arid Andes; previous

work includes several archaeological excavation projects in Peru, Bolivia, and the U.S. states of New Mexico, Washington, Idaho, Montanma, Illinois, and Missouri." *Biographical source: Who's Who in the Midwest. Published works: The Central Peruvian Prehistoric Interaction Sphere* (R.S. Peabody, Andover, 1975); *Advances in Andean Archaeology* (Mouton, The Hague, 1978); *Cultural Continuity in Mesoamerica* (Mouton, The Hague, 1979); *Peasants, Primitives and Proeletariates* (Mouton, The Hague, 1979); *Spirits, Shamans and Stars* (Mouton, The Hague, 1979); *Early Native Americans* (Mouton, The Hague, 1980); *Social and Economic Organization in the Prehispanic Andes* (BAR International, Oxford, 1984.)

BROWN, CHARLES ASA *(Fus Elle Haco)*(Muskogee) *(Gos Quillen)*(Shawnee) *(Eagle Star)*(Cherokee) 1912-
(attorney, farm owner, lecturer)

Born October 17, 1912, Woodsfield, Ohio. *Education:* Virginia Military Institute, A.B., 1935; University of Michigan Law School, 1935-1937; Western Reserve University Law School, J.D., 1938. *Principal occupation:* Attorney, farm owner, lecturer. *Home address:* 721 Washington St., Portsmouth, Ohio 45662. *Affiliations:* Self-employed lawyer and farmer, Portsmouth, Ohio, 1938-; Municipal Prosecuting Attorney, Portsmouth, Ohio, 1946; Assistant Attorney General, State of Ohio, 1963. *Military service:* U.S. Army (active duty, 1941-1946; reserve service, 1931-1972) (Lt. Colonel; American Defense; European Theater Medal with three battle stars; Purple Heart; Bronz Star with oak leaf cluster; Victory Medal; German Occupation Medal; Distinguished Unit Presidential Citation; Army Reserve Longevity Medal). *Community activities:* Scioto Area Council (executive board); Boy Scouts of America, Portsmouth, Ohio (merit badge counselor, 1946-, commissioner); co-founder, Jaycees, Portsmouth, 1938; Chamber of Commerce, Portsmouth; Bentonville, Ohio, Anti-Horse Thief Society. *Indian activities:* Member, Cedar River Tulsa Band, Muskogee Indian Tribe, Holdinville, Okla.; honorary councilman, Creek Indian Nation, Tulsa, Okla., 1962-1969; councilman, Western Black Elk Keetowah, Cherokee Nation; councilman,

Feerated Indian Tribes. *Memberships:* Scioto County Bar Association (trustee); Ohio State Bar Association; American Indian Bar Association; Phi Delta Phi Legal Fraternity; American Legion; Retired Officers Association and Reserve Officers Association, Washington, D.C. (life member); U.S. Horse Cavalry Association (life member); Masonic Lodge. *Awards, honors:* Silver Beaver Award, Boy Scouts of America; Vigil Honor, Order of the Arrows; President's Award for Distinguished Service, 1982, Boy Scouts of America; Advisory Chief of Indian Tribes, 1961-1980); Master Mason, 1944-; Chief's liaison to visiting persons at ceremonials; *"Tecumseh was my great-great grandfather." Interests:* Lecturer on Indian lore throughout the U.S.; writer on many Indian subjects; writer on various Masonic subjects; speaker at many public gatherings of all kinds continually. *Biographical sources: Who's Who in Freemasonry; Who's Who in the Midwest; Who's Who in the World; Who's Who in Ohio; Distinguished Americans. Published works:* Numerous articles in various publications.

BROWN, DEE ALEXANDER 1908-
(librarian, educator, author)

Born in 1908, Louisiana. *Education:* George Washington University, B.S., 1937; University of Illinois, M.S., 1951. *Principal occupation:* Librarian, educator, author. *Home address:* 7 Overlook Dr., Little Rock, Ark. 72207. *Affiliations:* Librarian, Department of Agriculture, Washington, D.C. 1934-1942; librarian, Aberdeen Proving Ground, Md., 1945-1948; agricultural librarian, 1948-1972, professor, 1962-1975, University of Illinois, Urbana. *Military service:* U.S. Army, 1942-1945. *Memberships:* Authors Guild; Society of American Historians; Western Writers of America; Beta Phi Mu. *Published works: Wave High the Banner,* 1942; *Grierson's Raid,* 1954; *Yellowhorse,* 1956; *Cavalry Scout,* 1957; *The Gentle Tamers: Women of the Old Wild West,* 1958; *The Bold Cavaliers,* 1959; *They Went Thataway,* 1960; *Fighting Indian of the West,* with M.F. Schmitt, 1948; *Trail Driving Days,* with M.F. Schmitt; *The Settler's West,* with M.F. Schmitt; *Fort Phil Kearny,* 1962; *The Galvanized Yankees,* 1963; *Show-down at Little Bighorn,* 1964; *The Girl From Fort Wicked,* 1964; *The Year of the Century,* 1966; *Bury of My Heart at Wounded Knee,* 1971; *The Westerners,* 1974; *Hear That Lonesome Whistle Blow,* 1977; *Tepee Tales,* 1979; *Creek Mary's Blood,* 1980; editor: *Agricultural History,* 1956-1958; *Pawnee, Blackfoot and Cheyenne,* 1961.

BROWN, DONALD NELSON 1937-
(professor, researcher)

Born February 1, 1937, Colorado Springs, Colo. *Education:* Harvard College, B.A., 1959; University of Arizona, M.A., 1967, Ph.D., 1973. *Principal occupation: Professor and researcher in anthropology. Affiliations:* Assistant professor of anthropology, Oklahoma State University, 1971-. *Other professional posts:* Editor of recordings of Indian music for the Taylor Museum, Colorado Springs Fine Arts Center and Taos Recordings and Publications, Taos, N.M. *Memberships:* American Anthropological Association; Society for Ethnomusicology; Society for Applied Anthropology; American Ethnological Society; Committee on Research in Dance (board). *Awards, honors:* Jaap Kunst Prize, Society for Ethnomusicology. *Interests:* Research on contemporary Native Americans; Native American music and dance; prehistoric music and dance in North America; ethnography of the Rio Grande Pueblos. *Published works: Masks, Mantas, and Moccasins: Dance Costumes of the Pueblo Indians* (Taylor Museum, 1962); *A Study of Heavy Drinking at Taos Pueblo, N.M.* (mimeographed for restricted distribution, 1965); *Archaeological investigations at the Hermitage* (Ladies Hermitage Association, 1972); *Inventory of Archaeological Sites* (Sargent and Lundy Engineers, 1973).

BROWN, JOHN (Seminole) 1914-
(tribal official)

Born February 20, 1914, Sasakwa, Okla. *Education:* Elementary school. *Principal occupation:* Tribal official. *Home address:* P.O. Box 24, Sasakwa, Okla. 74867. *Affiliation:* Past chairman, general council, Seminole Nation of Oklahoma. *Memberships:*

Five Civilized Tribes Inter-Tribal Council; S.E.E., Inc. (board of directors); Five Civilized Tribes Foundation, Inc.; Inter-Tribal Counci (secretary, treasurer); Five Tribes Museum (board of directors).

BROWN, JOSEPH (Blackfeet)
(clergyman)

Education: Loyola University, M.A., 1942; Alma College, M.A., 1949. *Principal occupation:* Clergyman. *Home address:* Box 95, Spokane, Wash. 99107. *Affiliation:* Member, Society of Jesus, Portland, Oreg., 1935-. *Other professional posts:* Teaching grade school, high school, college; administration—mission grade schools, pastoral ministry. *Community activities:* Spokane Urban Indian Health Board; Kona Lodge (chairman of board). *Memberships:* American Indian Historical Association; National Congress of American Indians. *Interests:* "The promotion of studies for and about Indians." *Biographical source: Indians of Today* (Marion E. Gridley). *Published work: Louise Sinxuim, Coeur de Alene Tribe,* 1977.

BROWN, JOSEPH EPES 1920-
(professor, writer)

Born September 9, 1920, Ridgefield, Conn. *Education:* Bowdoin College, 1940-1942; Haverford College, B.A. (Anthropology), 1947; University of New Mexico (graduate studies in anthropology), 1954-1956; Stanford University, M.A. (Anthropology), 1966; University of Stockholm (Doctorate, Anthropology and History of Religions, 1970. *Principal occupation:* Professor, writer. *Home address:* Kootenai Creek Ranch, 363 Kootenai Creek, Stevensville, Mont. 59870. *Affiliations:* Teacher, Verde Valley School, Sedona, Ariz., 1952-1953, 1956-1960, 1961-1965; assistant professor, Prescott College, 1966-1969; associate professor, Department of Religious Studies, Indiana University, 1970-1972; University of Montana, Department of Religious Studies (associate professor, 1972-1976; professor, 1977-.) *Editorial work:* Consulting editor, *Parabola: The Magazine of Myth and Tradition;* advisor, "The Zuni Pueblo Film Project," Byron Earhart, Western Michigan

University; editor for Vol. V, *American Indian Traditions,* for Crossroad Press, 25 Vols., World Spirituality Series. *Memberships:* American Anthropological Association; Museum of Northern Arizona; Foundation of North American Indian Culture (advisory board.) *Awards, honors:* Smith-Mundt Grant to teach in Morocco, 1960-1961; The Joseph E. Brown American Indian Scholarship Fund established in Mr. Brown's honor at Verde Valley School, Sedona, Ariz. *Interests:* Research among the Plains Indians; has traveled extensively and has done research in Morocco, North Africa. Major interest within anthropology is the study of diverse cultures. *Published works: The Sacred Pipe* (University of Oklahoma Press, 1953; Penguin Books, with new introduction, 1971; Swedish, Spanish and Japanese translation); *The Spiritual Legacy of the American Indian* (Pendle Hill, 1964, 8th edition, 1976); *The North American Indians: The Photographs of Edward S. Curtis, Aperture,* (Vol. 16, no. 4, Philadelphia Museum of Art, 1972); The Spiritual Legacy of the American Indian, a collection of articles by Mr. Brown (Crossroad Publishing, 1980); *The Gift of the Sacred Pipe* (University of Oklahoma Press, 1982); *chapters in books:* "The Spiritual Legacy of the American Indian, *Sources,* Theodore Roszak, 1972; "The Question of 'Mysticism' with Native American Traditions,*" Mystics and Scholars,* Harold Coward and Terence Penelhum, editors (Ross-Erickson Publishers, 1979); "The Roots of Renewal," *Seeing with a Native Eye,* Walter Capps, Editor (Harper & Row, 1977); "Relationship and Unity in American Indian Experience," *The Unanimous Tradition* (Sri Lanka Institute of Traditional Studies, 1982); "Americn Indian Living Religions," *Handbook of Living Religions,* edited by John Hinnells (Penguin Books, 1983); numerous articles, papers and lectures.

BROWN, VINSON 1912-
(writer, naturalist, publisher)

Born December 7, 1912, Reno, Nev. *Education:* University of California at Berkeley, A.B., 1939; Stanford University, M.A., 1947. *Principal occupation:* Writer, naturalist, publisher. *Home address:* Happy Camp,

Calif. 96039. *Affiliations:* Lecturer on American Indian religions, University of South Dakota, University of Northern Michigan, Myrin Institute, Haskell Institute; field collector in natural history; lecturer. *Travels:* Visits to many Indian tribes in the U.S., Canada, and Alaska, 1960-1972. *Published works: Exploring Ancient Life* (Science Materials Center, 1958); *Warriors of the Rainbow,* with William Willoya (Naturegraph, 1965); *Pomo Indians of California and Their Neighbors* (Naturegraph, 1969); *Great Upon the Mountain — Crazy Horse of America* (Naturegraph, 1971, cloth ed., Macmillan); *Voices of the Earth and Sky: The Vision-Search of the American Indians* (Stackpole, 1974); *Peoples of the Sea Wind—Native Americans of the Pacific Coast* (Macmillan, 1977); and others which pertain to nature.

BROWN, WILFRED
(B.I.A. superintendent)

Affiliation: Superintendent, Fort Defiance Agency, Bureau of Indian Affairs, P.O. Box 619, Fort Defiance, Ariz. 86504.

BROWNING, ZANE
(B.I.A. superintendent)

Affiliation: Superintendent, Ardmore Agency, Bureau of Indian Affairs, P.O. Box 997, Ardmore, Okla. 73401.

BRUCE, LOUIS R.
(consultant)

Affiliation: President, Native American Consultants, Inc., 725 2nd St., N.E., Washington, D.C. 20002. Branch: 1001 Highland St., Arlington, Va. 22201.

BRUGGE, DAVID M. 1927-
(anthropologist)

Born September 3, 1927, Jamestown, N.Y. *Education:* University of New Mexico, B.A., 1950. *Principal occupation:* Anthropologist.

Affiliations: Various positions, Gallup Community Indian Center, Gallup, N.M., 1953-1957; salvage archaeologist, Four Corners Pipeline Co., Houston, Texas, 1957-1958; anthropologist, The Navajo Tribe, Window Rock, Ariz., 1958-1968. *Other professional posts:* Artchaeologist, Museum of Northern Arizona, Flagstaff, Ariz., 1957; director, Navajo Curriculum Center, Rough Rock, Ariz., 1968; instructor, College of Ganado, Ariz., 1973. *Military service:* U.S. Army, 1945-1947. *Community activities:* Sage Memorial Hospital, Ganado, Ariz. (secretary, advisory board); Title I Committee, Ganado Public Schools. *Memberships:* American Anthropological Association; Society for American Archaeology; Archaeological Society of New Mexico (trustee); American Society for Ethnohistory (secretary-treasurer, 1966-1968); Arizona Archaeological and Historical Society; New Mexico Historical Society; Northern Arizona Society for Science and Art, Inc.; American Association for the Advancement of Science; Plateau Sciences Society. *Interests:* Mr. Brugge writes, "Navajo studies, especially in archaeology, ethnohistory and history, and more generally of the greater Southwest. In addition to my work with the Navajos, I have done field work in northwestern Mexico, principally among the Pima Bajo (Lower Pima) of Sonora. My work with the Navajo Tribe involved research for various land disputes such as the Land Claims Case, the Navajo-Hopi boundary dispute, the McCracken Mesa land exchange and Utah school section case and the Huerfano Mesa land exchange." *Biographical sources: Who's Who in the West; The Official Museum Directory. Published works: Navajo Pottery and Ethnohistory* (The Navajo Tribe, 1963); *Long Ago in Navajoland* (The Navajo Tribe, 1965); *Navajo Bibliography,* with J. Lee Correll and Edith Watson (The Navajo Tribe, 1967); *Navajos in the Catholic Church Records of New Mexico, 1694-1875* (The Navajo Tribe, 1968); *Zarcillos Largos, Courageous Advocate of Peace* (The Navajo Tribe, 1970); *The Story of the Navajo Treaties,* with J. Lee Correll (The Navajo Tribe, 1971); *Navajo and Western Pueblo History* (Tucson Corral of Westerners, 1972); *The Navajo Exodus* (Archaeological Society of New Mexico, 1972.)

BRUNER, EDWARD M. 1924-
(professor of anthropology)

Born September 28, 1924, New York, N.Y. *Education:* Ohio State University, B.A., 1948, M.A., 1950; University of Chicago, Ph.D., 1954. *Principal occuaption:* Professor of anthropology. *Home address:* 2022 Cureton Dr., Urbana, Ill. 61801. *Affiliations:* Assistant professor, Department of Anthropology, Yale University, 1954-1960; associate professor, 1961-1965, professor, 1965-, head of department, 1966-1970, Department of Anthropology, University of Illinois, Urbana, director, Doris Duke American Indian Oral History Project, 1967-1973. *Other professional posts:* Chairman, test committee, Educational Testing Service, Princeton, N.J., 1967-1969. *Memberships:* American Anthropological Association (Fellow); Society for Applied Anthropology; Royal Anthropological Society; American Ethnological Society (past-president, 1981-1982); Association for Asian Studies (member, Indonesian studies committee, 1973-; chairman, 1976-1978.) *Awards, honors:* Fellowship, Center for Advanced Study in the Behavioral Sciences; senior scholarship, East-West Center, University of Hawaii. *Interests:* Anthropological field studies among Navajo Indians, Fort Berthold Indians; among Batak of Sumatra, Indonesia; processes of cultural and social change; urbanization. *Published works: Perspectives in American Indian Culture Change,* with Edward H. Spicer (University of Chicago Press, 1962).

BRUNO, ROBERT LEON
(tribal chairman)

Affiliation: Chairman, Citizen Band Potawatomi Business Committee, Route 5, Box 151, Shawnee, Okla. 74801.

BRYAN, RICHARD P.
(environmental health services)

Affiliation: Chief, Environmental Health Services, U.S. Public Health Service, Indian Health Service, 5600 Fishers Lane, Rockville, Md. 20857.

BUFFALO, GEORGE, Jr.
(B.I.A. superintendent)

Affiliation: Superintendent, Sac and Fox Area Field Office, Bureau of Indian Affairs, Tama, Iowa 52339.

BUFFALOHEAD, W. ROGER
(communications)

Affiliation: Director, Migizi Communications, Inc., 2300 Cedar Ave. South, Minneapolis, Minn. 55404.

BUFORD, BETTIE (LITTLE DOVE)
(Creek and Cherokee) 1935-
(shop owner)

Born February 20, 1935, Ocoee, Fla. *Principal occupation:* Shop owner. *Home address:* P.O. Box 521, Cox Osceola Indian Reservation, Orange Springs, Fla. 32682. *Affiliation:* Owner, Betties Antiques and Osceola Trading Post (furniture store; upholster shop owner, Ocala, Fla. (20 years). *Other professional posts:* Teacher, Indian culture, Osceola Christian Indian School. *Military service:* American Red Cross Military Hospital, Korean conflict. *Memberships:* Southeastern Cherokee Confederation (principal vice-chief); The Concerned Citizens League of America (president); Cox Osceola Cherokee & Creek Indian Reservation (vice chief.) *Awards, honors:* Indian Princess by blood; Marion Education Awards; several awards for teaching Indian culture an crafts. *Interests:* "My major interest is to help improve the lifestyles of my Indian people and to stop some of the prejudice against them. To let all people know what real Indians are, not the stereotypes that they see in the movies and on television. I would like to travel to all tribes." *Work in progress: Indians of the Oklawaka River in Florida.*

BURCH, LEONARD
(tribal council chairman)

Affiliation: Chairman, Southern Ute Tribal Council, P.O. Box 373, Ignacio, Colo. 81137.

BURNS, ROBERT I., S.J. 1921-
(clergyman, historian, educator)

Born August 16, 1921, San Francisco, Calif. *Education:* Gonzaga University, B.A., 1945, M.A., 1947 (D. Litt.), 1968; Fordham University, M.A., 1949; Jesuit Pontifical Faculty (Spokane, Wash., Phil.B., 1946, Phil.Lic., 1947) (Alma, Calif., S.Th.B., 1951, S.Th.Lic., 1953; Postgraduate, Columbia University, 1949, Oxford University, 1956-1957; Johns Hopkins University, Ph.D. (summa cum laude)(History), 1958; University of Fribourg, Switzerland, Doc. es Sc.Hist. (double summa cum laude)(History, Ethnohistory), 1961. *Principal occupation:* Clergyman, historian, educator. *Address:* History Department, Graduate School, University of California, Los Angeles, Calif. 90024. *Affiliations: Assistant archivist, Jesuit and Indian Archives of Pacific Northwest Province, Spokane, 1945-1947; instructor, History Department, University of San Francisco, (instructor, 1947-1948; assistant professor, 1958-1962; associate professor, 1963-1966; professor, 1967-1976); senior professor, History Department, U.C.L.A., 1976-. Other professional posts:* Director, Institute of Medieval Mediterranean, Spain, 1976-; staff, UCLA Center for Medieval-Renaissance Studies, 1977-; staff, UCLA Near Eastern Center, 1979-. *Editorial work:* Board editor, *Trend in History,* 1980; co-editor, Viator (UCLA), 1980; editorial committee, U.C. Press, 1985. *Memberships:* American Historical Association, Pacific Coast Branch (vice president, 1978; president, 1978-1980; presiding-delegate, International Congress of Historical Sciences, 1975, and U.S. Representative, 1980); American Catholic Historical Association (president, 1976); Medieval Association of the Pacific; Society for Spanish and Portuguese Historical Studies; Hill Monastic Library; North American Catalan Society; American Bibliographical Center (board, 1982-1989). *Awards, honors:* Guggenheim Fellow, 1964; ACLS Fellow, 1977; National Endowment for the Humanities grants, 1971-1983; many other grants; Medieval Academy of America (trustee, 1975-1977; executive, 1977-1978); Haskins Gold Medal, 1976 (Life Fellow, 1978); His-

panic Society of America (elected, 1985); five book awards from national historical associations, including American Historical (Pacific Coast Award), American Catholic Historical, and American Association for State and Local History, for *Jesuits and Indian Wars,* 1965; Dr. Burns gave the keynote address at the National Park Service's Sesquicentennial of the sustained Indian-white contact by Americans in the Pacific Northwest states, the (Protestant) Whitman Mission, July 1986 at Whitman College. *Interests:* "I have two fields, allied but distinct, in which I publish regularly. The medieval field is the moving frontier of the 13th-century Catalonia, particularly the absorption by the Catalan peoples of the Valencian kingdom of the Moslems. The American field is the Pacific Northwest, particularly, Indian-white relations and troubles, 1840-1880, as illumined especially by Jesuit documentation here and in Europe. Ethnohistory and the Pacific Northwest frontier is thus seen not in isolation but as illumined by other frontier experiences." *Biographical sources: Who's Who in America; Contemporary Authors;* among others. *Published works:* Co-author, *I lift My Lamp: Jesuits in America,* 1955; *Indians and Whites in the Pacific Northwest: Jesuit Contributions to Peace 1850-1880* (University of San Francisco Press, 1961); *The Jesuits and the Indian Wars* (Yale University Press, 1966); *The Jesuits and the Indian Wars of the Northwest,* reissue of 1966 edition (University of Idaho Press, 1985); articles include, "Northwest Indian Missions," position essay, *Handbook of North American Indians* (U.S. Government Printing Office, 1978; 1986 forthcoming); "Suore Indiane," *Dizionario degli istituti di perfezione,* ed. G. Rocca, 6 vols. (Rome: Edizioni Paoline, 1974); "Jesuit Missions," (North American Indians) *Dictionary of American History* (Charles Scribner's Sons, 1977); "Roman Catholic Missionaries," (to U.S. Indians) *The Reader's Encyclopedia of the Amerian West* (Thomas Y. Crowell Co., 1977); "The Opening of the West," (impact on Pacific Northwest Indians) *The Indian: Assimilation, Integration or Separation* (Prentice-Hall, Canada, 1972); numerous other articles.

BURTT, J. FREDERIC (Abenaki) 1908-
(professor)

Born April 4, 1908, Lowell, Mass. *Education:* Lowell Technological Institute, B.S., 1931; Boston University, A.B.A., 1942; Massachusetts Institute of Technology, M.S., 1958. *Principal occupation:* Professor of mechanical and textile engineering. *Home address:* 97 Hoyt Ave., Lowell, mass. 01852. *Affiliations:* Textile engineering, Eaton Rapids, Mich.; supt., assistant general manager, Newmarket Co., Lowell, Mass. (15 years); senior textile technologist, U.S. Research and Engineering Command (QM), Natick, Mass. (two years); professor, Lowell Technological Institute; professor emeritus, visiting lecturer, University of Lowell, 1978-1982. *Community activities:* City of Lowell Conservation Commission (vice chairman); Water Pollution Advisory Board, Northern Middlesex Area. *Memberships:* Society of the Sigma Xi; Massachusetts Archaeological Society (past vice president); New Hampshire Archaeological Society (past president); American Association for the Advancement of Science; AATT; Pennsylvania Institute of Anthropology; Societe Archeologique d'Alexandrie, Egypt; Greater Lowell Indian Cultural Association; Native American Rights Commission; Indian Institute, U.S. Dept. of Education. *Awards, honors:* Medallion of Merit, Alexandria University, Egypt; Chester B. Price Memorial Archaeological Award, New Hampshire Archaeological Society, 1965; Demolay Cross of Honor and Legion of Honor, 1936; honorable member, St. Francis Abenaki Tribe, 1977; Sigma Xi, Omicron Pi, Human Relations Award, 1980. *Interests:* Archaeological work in North and South America; consultant in the textile industry; Fullbright lecturer, Alexandria University, Egypt (two years); worked with Polish archaeologists on Greco-Roman excavations in Egypt; travels to Middle East countries under National Academy of Science's grant. *Biographical sources: Who's Who in American Education; Who's Who in the East; American Men of Science. Published works:* Co-author, *History of the City of Lowell,* 1976; co-editor and publisher, *Colby's Indian History,* 1975; numerous articles to professional journals.

BUSH, MICHAEL A. (Mohawk Caughnawaga) 1948-
(administrator)

Born August 10, 1948, Brooklyn, N.Y. *Education:* Brooklyn College, A.A., 1967; Dartmouth College, A.B., 1975. *Principal occupation:* Administrator. *Home address:* 1271 38th St., Brooklyn, N.Y. 11218. *Affiliation:* Executive director, American Indian Community House, Inc., New York, N.Y., 1976-. *Othjer professional post:* Co-director, Community Council of Greater N.Y., Native American Educational Research Program, 1975. *Military service:* U.S. Army, 1967-1970 (Sargeant E-5; five Commendations, 3rd Place Inter Service Annual Leap Fest, 1970). *Community activities:* Governor's Minority Task Force on Mental Health, N.Y. State, 1977; National Low Income Housing Board (executive committee); Minority Task Force, New York State Developmental Disabilities, 1985. *Memberships:* National Congress of American Indians; National Indian Education Association; American Indian Health Care Association (board member, 1984); National Urban Indian Council (former vice-president). *Awards, honors:* Ethnic New York Award, 1984 (Mayor Ed Koch, New York City). *Interests:* American Indian law; reservation economics; carpentry, auto mechanics, iron work; writing; extensive American and Canadian lecture circuit on American Indian Affairs. *Published works:* "Detecting Structural Heat Losses with Mobil Infra Red Thermography," (U.S. Army Corps, 1974); "An Overview of the Socio-Economic Forces Pertaining to Indian Education," (Community Council of Greater N.Y., 1975.)

BUSH, MITCHELL LESTER, Jr. (Onondaga) 1936-
(chief-tribal enrollment, B.I.A.)

Born February 1, 1936, Syracuse, N.Y. *Education:* Haskell Institute, 1951-1956. *Principal occupation:* Chief, tribal enrollmen, B.I.A. *Home address:* 519 5th St., S.E., Washington, D.C. 20003. *Affiliation:* Chief, Branch of Tribal Enrollment Services, Bureau of Indian Affairs, Washington,

D.C., 1956-. *Military service:* U.S. Army, 1958-1961 (Specialist 4th Class). *Community activities:* Northern Virginia Folk Festival (board of directors); Haskell Alumni Association of the Nation's Capitol (board of directors); American Indian Inaugural Ball (committee member, 1969, 1973, 1977, 1981, and 1985); American Indian Society, Washington, D.C. (president, 1966-). *Awards, honors:* American Indian Society Distingished Service Award; Maharishi Award conferred by the Maharishi University. *Interests:* Lecturer and Indian dancer for American Indian Society; participant, 1990 Census Planning Conference on Race and Ethnic Items sponsored by the Census Bureau; tour leader to Virginia Indian reservations for Resident Associate Program, Smithsonian Institution; honored at the 1982 Nanticoke (Delaware) Pow wow; judge at the 1978, 1980, 1982, 1984 and 1985 Miss Indian American Pageants held in Sheridan, Wyoming, and Bismarck, North Dakota; photo and bio included in "Shadows Caught: Images of Native Americans," by Stephen Bambaro at Gilcrease Institute, Tulsa, Oklahoma. *Biographical sources: To Live in Two Worlds,* by Brent Ashabranner; *American Indian Wars,* by John Tebbel, 1960; *Successful Indian Career Profiles,* to be published by North American Indian Club, Syracuse, N.Y. *Published works:* Editor, *American Indian Society Cookbook* (American Indian Society, 1975 and 1984 editions); editor, *American Indian Society Newsletter,* 1966-1986; Movies & Television shows: "Lives of the Rich and Famous," segment featuring Connie Stevens, MGM, "George Washington TV Mini-Series"; "Indians," Walt Disney Productions; numerous television programs.

C

CAIN, H. THOMAS 1913-
(museum curator, anthropologist)

Born May 18, 1913, Seattle, Wash. *Education:* University of Washington, B.A., 1938; University of Arizona, M.A. (Anthropology), 1946. *Principal occupation:* Museum curator, anthropologist. *Home Address:* 1824 E. Ocotillo Rd., Phoenix, Ariz. 85016.

Affiliations: Curator of anthropology, San Diego Museum of Man, 1946-1950; director, curator, Heard Museum, Phoenix, Ariz., 1952-. *Other professional posts:* Instructor of museum methods course, Arizona State University. *Military service:* U.S. Marine Corp, 1944. *Memberships:* American Anthropological Association (Fellow); American Association of Museums. *Awards, honors:* Thaw Fellow, Harvard University, 1950; University Fellow, University of Arizona, 1945-1946. *Expeditions:* Field work in Canadian Arctic, Alaska, Georgia, New Mexico, North Dakota. *Published works: Petroglyphs of Central Washington* (University of Washington Press); *Pima Indian Basketry* (Heard Museum Publications in Anthropology.)

CALKIN, LAURIE ARCHER
(Cherokee) 1935-
(designer)

Born February 17, 1935, Corbin, Ky. *Education: Colorado College, B.A., 1959; City College. Principal occupation:* Designer. *Home address:* Route 1, Box 267, Santa Fe, N.M. 87501. *Other professional post:* Former professional dancer, New York City. *Memberships:* Don Juan Little Theatre; Los Alamos Light Opera Association. *Awards, honors:* John Hay Whitney Fellow in theatre; Fulbright Scholar to Peru in dance and the arts.

CALLENDER, CHARLES 1928-
(anthropologist)

Born October 30, 1928, Union Grove, Wisc. *Education:* University of Chicago, Ph.B., 1949, M.A., 1954, Ph.D., 1958. *Principal occupation:* Anthropologist. *Home address:* 2512 Edgehill Rd., Cleveland Heights, Ohio 44106. *Affiliations:* Assistant editor, *Current Anthropology,* 1959-1961; research associate, American University at Cairo, Egypt, 1961-1963; professor, Case Western Reserve University, 1966-. *Memberships:* American Anthropological Association; Middle East Studies Association of North America. *Interests:* "Major professional interests are American Indians and the Middle East. Field work among the Mesquakie

(1954), Sauk (1954), and Prairie Potawato-
mie (1955); in Cairo and Alexandria (1961-
1962), and in Egyptian Nubia (1962-1963).
Published works: Editor, with Sol Tax,
Issues in Evolution (University of Chicago
Prss, 1960); *Central Algonkian Social
Organization* (Milwaukee Public Museum,
1962); *Life-Crisis Rituals Among the Kenuz,*
with Fadwa el Guindi (Case Western
Reserve University Press, 1971).

CANADAY, DAYTON W. 1923-
(historical society director)

Born October 30, 1923, Litchfield, Ill. *Education:* Illinois College, A.B., 1948; Miami
University, 1942, 1946-1947; University of
Illinois, M.S., 1950. *Principal occupation:*
Historical society director. *Home address:*
1906 E. Erskine, Pierre, S.D. 57501. *Affilia-
tions:* Superintendent, South Dakota
Department of History, 1968-1973; director,
South Dakota State Historical Society,
1968-. *Military service:* U.S. Marine Corps
(First Lieutenant; Pacific Medal, Japanese
occupation; American Defense; Good Con-
duct; Korean Service Medal). *Community
activities:* Federal Lewis and Clark Trail
Commission (board member); South
Dakota American Revolution Bicentennial
Commission (board member); South
Dakota Historical Publications Advisory
Committee (member); State Library Advi-
sory Committee (member); South Dakota
Historic Preservation (member); Presbyterian Church (elder); Boy's Club of America
(board); Chamber of Commerce (board).
Memberships: American Association for
State and Local History; State Historical
Administrators Committee; Western His-
torical Association. *Awards, honors:* Key-
man. St. Louis Jr. Chamber of Commerce;
naming of Canaday Room in St. Charles
County Historical Society Museum. *Interests:* Local history; writing; rare books;
travel. *Published works: Collections—
South Dakota History* (South Dakota Historical Society, 1968, 1970, 1971).

CANARD, CURTIS LEE (Muskogee-
Creek) 1932-
(petroleum geologist)

Born February 9, 1932, Wetumka, Okla.

Education: Oklahoma State University,
B.S., 1956. *Principal occupation:* Petroleum
geologist. *Home address:* P.O. Box 35112,
Tulsa, Okla. 74135. *Affiliations:* Senior petroleum geologist (petroleum exploration)
Exxon Corp., Houston, Texas (16 years);
project manager (resource exploration and
evaluations), William Brothers Engineering
Co., Tulsa, Okla. (3 years). *Other professional posts:* Mineral consultant. *Community activities:* Thlopthlocco Tribal Town
(chairman); Oklahomans for Indian Opportunity (board of directors); Oklahoma State
University for Indian Students (geologic
advisor). *Memberships:* American Association for Petroleum Geologists, 1956-; Tulsa
Geologic Scoiety, 1974-. *Awards, honors:*
Scholarship from Congregational Christian
Churches; educational grant, B.I.A. *Interests:* Principal stockholder of minority
owned Deer Stalker Gallery financed
through the Indian Finance Act and deals in
fine Indian art, Tulsa, Okla. *Published
works: Thlophlocco Development Plan*
(Dept. of Housing and Urban Development,
1976), distributed by Oklahoma Indian
Affairs Commission, Oklahoma City, Okla.

CANNON, T.C. *(Pai Doung-U-Day)*
(Kiowa-Caddo) 1946-
(painter, printmaker)

Born September 27, 1946, Lawton, Okla.
Education: Institute of American Indian
Arts, Santa Fe, N.M.; Central State Univer-
sity, Edmond, Okla. *Principal occupation:*
Painter, printmaker. *Home address:* 400 E.
Danforth, #134, Edmond, Okla. 73034. *Mil-
itary service:* U.S. Army (Airbourne
Division-Vietnam, 1968; two Bronze Stars).
Memberships: Council of Regents, Institute
of American Indian Arts: Pacific Northwest
Indian Center. *Exhibitions:* Edinburgh Art
Festival, Scotland; Berlin Festival, Amerika
Haus; National Collection of Fine Arts,
Smithsonian Institution; Bureau of Indian
Affairs, Washington, D.C.; Oklahoma Art
Center, Oklahoma City, Okla.; Museum of
New Mexico, Santa Fe; two-man touring
exhibition, "Two American Painters," with
Fritz Scholder — Madrid, Berlin, Buchar-
est, Warsaw, Ankara, Athens, and London,
1972-1973. *Awards, honors:* Second Prize
and Grand Award, American Indian Expo-

sition; First Prize, Southwestern Scholastic Exhibit, 1962-1964; Governor's Trophy, Scottsdale National Exhibit, 1966. *Biographical sources: Who's Who in American Art; American Indian Painters; Art in America,* summer, 1972.

CARGILE, ELLEN YEAGER 1931-
(educator, artist)

Born January 28, 1931, Dallas, Texas. *Education:* University of Texas, B.S., 1953; University of Arkansas, M.Ed., 1965. *Principal occupation:* Educator, artist. *Home address:* 3059 County Rd. 203, Durango, Colo. 81301. *Affiliation:* Instructor, Division of Cultural Studies, Fort Lewis College, Durango, Colo., 1972-. *Memberships:* Delta Kappa Gamma; AAUW. *Interests:* "(I) teach arts and crafts of the Southwest Indians, and art history of the Southwest; jewelry design; travel; lecture on Indian art forms (International Symposium of Anthropology, Santa Fe, N.M., 1975); consultant/lecturer (Multi-Cultural Education Conference, University of Utah, 1975); has exhibited paintings and sculpture in Texas, New Mexico, Louisiana, Arkansas, Colorado; national travelling exhibitions—one person show in Farmington Civic Center, 1977." *Published works: Understanding and Executing Arts of the Southwest,* 1976; *Walk in Beauty,* Vols. I and II (editor, 1975-1976); *Alecia in Flowerland,* with John R. Tapia, 1976. All published by Basin Reproduction Co.

CARPIO, JOSE
(B.I.A. agency superintendent)

Affiliation: Superintendent, Northern Pueblos Agency, Bureau of Indian Affairs, Box 849, Federal Office Bldg., Santa Fe, N.M. 87501.

CARR, PATRICK J. 1941-
(education specialist)

Born December 16, 1941, New York, N.Y. *Education:* Hunter College, CUNY, B.A., 1966; Northern Arizona University, Flagstaff, M.A., 1974. *Principal occupation:* Education specialist (audio visual services.)

Home address: P.O. Box 2032, Tuba City, Ariz. 86045. *Affiliation:* Tuba City High School, Bureau of Indian Affairs, P.O. Box 160, Tuba City, Ariz. 86045. *Military service:* U.S. Marine Corps, 1966-1968. *Memberships:* Arizona Educational Media Association (past president); National Council of Bureau of Indian Affairs Educators (president); Association for Educational Communication and Technology; Arizona Educational Media Association. *Interests:* "Traveled extensively in Western Europe, Mexico and the U.S. Active in professional educational associations; enjoy writing human interest articles and photography; enjoy balley and visiting art museums."

CARTER, EDWARD RUSSELL, 1910-
(minister)

Born December 8, 1910, Bloomingdale, Ind. *Education:* Earlham College, B.A., 1932; Kansas State University, M.A., 1947. *Principal occupation:* Minister. *Home address:* 66 Linwood St., Bergenfield, N.J. 07621. *Affiliation:* Director, Special Ministries, Division of Christian Life and Mission, National Council of Churches, 1937-. *Memberships:* National Social Welfare Assembly; Council on Indian Affairs; National Fellowship of Indian Workers. *Interests:* "Extensive involvement in Indian life and affairs as well as with seasonal farm workers, Spanish Americans, and natives of Alaska. (I) frequently travel to Alaska and Mexico as well as (to) Indian reservation areas in the U.S." *Published work: The Gift is Rich* (Friendship Prss, 1954).

CASEBOLT, JACK V.
(Indian health service)

Affiliation: Director, Office of Program Planning, Indian Health Service, 5600 Fishers Lane, Rockville, Md. 20857.

CASIUS, EVERLYN
(museum curator)

Affiliation: Curator, Ute Indian Museum, 17253 Chipeta Dr., P.O. Box 1736, Montrose, Colo. 81402.

CASTOR, DELIA FRANKLIN 1913-
(museum curator)

Born July 12, 1913, Cordell, Okla. *Education:* University of Oklahoma, B.F.A., 1936; Oklahoma State University, Library Science, 1965. *Principal occupation:* Museum curator. *Home address:* 408 N. 5th, Ponca City, Okla. 74601. *Affiliation:* Curator, Indian Museum and Cultural Center, Ponca City, Okla. *Community activities:* Teacher and lecturer, Flower Show Schools Organization, National Council of Garden Clubs, 1938-. *Memberships:* Special Libraries Association, 1967-; Oklahoma Historical Society; American Association for State and Local History; American Association of Museums. *Interests:* Fingerweaving or Indian braiding. *Biographical source: American Museums Director.*

CHANA, ANTHONY M. (Papago) 1939-
(teacher-elementary education)

Born August 4, 1939, Santa Rosa Village (Ge Aji), Ariz. *Education:* Phoenix College, A.A., 1967; Arizona State Unviersity, B.A., 1970. *Principal occupation:* Teacher-elementary education. *Home address:* 5544 S. Hildreth Ave., Tucson, Ariz. 85706. *Affiliation:* Counselor, Pima Community College, Tucson, Ariz., 1971-. *Memberships:* Arizona State University Alumni Association; Kiwanis Club, 1971-1972; National Indian Education Association, 1973-; American Indian Association (board of directors, 1974-; vice-chairman, 1975-1977; chairman, 1976); Information and Referral Service Board (member, 1975-1976); Committee for Economic Opportunity (board member, 1976-1977); *Interests:* "I am interested in the studies which research the success and failure of students among the urban and reservation Indians. I think the study will demonstrate the phenomenon of success and failure that can be utilized to counsel students effectively. I am also interested in the study of the Papago language and the development of instructional material for the elementary, high school, and college classes. The area that intrigues me most is the Papago that pre-date Spanish influence, which is all but lost."

CHAPMAN, JANE (Mrs. G. Courtney) 1938-
(dealer-Indian arts and crafts)

Born April 11, 1938, Columbus, Ohio. *Education:* University of Chicago, 1953-1955; Ohio Wesleyan University, 1955-1956; University of Illinois, B.A., 1958. *Principal occupation:* Dealer, American Indian arts and crafts—Kiva Indian art. *Home address:* 488 Greenglade Ave., Worthington, Ohio 43085. *Professional post:* Indian Arts and Crafts Association (member, secretary, board of directors). *Community activities:* PTA (president, 1976-1977); Civic Association.

CHAPMAN, ROBERT L.
(tribal official)

Affiliation: President, Pawnee Business Council, P.O. Box 470, Pawnee, Okla. 74058.

CHARLES, ALAN
(tribal chairman)

Affiliation: Chairman, Lower Elwha Community Council, P.O. Box 1370, Port Angeles, Wash. 98362.

CHARLES, RONALD G.
(tribal chairman)

Affiliation: Chairman, Port Gamble Community Council, P.O. Box 280, Kingston, Wash. 98346.

CHASE THE BEAR, LIONEL
(B.I.A. agency superintendent)

Affiliation: Superintendent, Standing Rock Agency, Bureau of Indian Affairs, Fort Yates, N.D. 58538.

CHAVERS, DEAN (Lumbee) 1941-
(president, MANAGE, Inc.)

Born February 4, 1941, Pembroke, N.C. *Education:* University of Richmond, 1960-1962; University of California, Berkeley, B.A. (Journalistic Studies), 1970; Stanford University, M.A. (Anthropology), 1973,

M.A. (Communications), 1975, Ph.D. (Communications Research), 1976. *Principal occupation:* President, MANAGE, Inc. *Home address:* 6709 Esther Ave., N.E., Albuquerque, N.M. 87109. *Affiliations:* President, Native American Scholarship Fund, 1970-1978; president, Bacone College, Muskogee, Okla., 1978-1981; president, Dean Chavers & Associates, 1981-1985; president, MANAGE, Inc., 1985-. *Other professional posts:* Assistant professor, California State University, Hayward, 1972-1974; member, Advisory Panel for Minority Concerns, The College Board, 1980-1985; member, Minority Achievement Program, Association of American Colleges, 1980-1984; board member, National Indian Education Association, 1983-1986. *Military service:* U.S. Air Force, 1963-1968 (Navigator, Captain; Distinguished Flying Cross, Air Medal). *Community activities:* Democratic Party of Wagoner County, Oklahoma (former secretary-treasurer). *Memberships:* National Indian Education Association (board member); National Congress of American Indians; International Communication Association; National Society of Fund Raising Executives; Association for Educational Data Systems. *Awards, honors:* Ford Foundation Graduate Fellow; National Honor Society; Virginia State Spelling Champion, 1959. *Interests:* "Main interest is Indian education, secondary interest is Indian economic development. Have published five books and technical manuals in these areas, as well as some 30 journal articles. Main occupation is providing technical assistance in fund raising, financial management, computer software development, and training for Indian tribes, contract schools, and Indian health clinics." *Published works: How to Write Winning Proposals* (DCA Publications, 1983); *Funding Guide for Native Americans* (DCA Publications, 1983; 2nd ed., 1985); *Grants to Indians* (DCA Publications, 1984); *Tribal Economic Development Directory* (DCA Publications, 1985); *Basic Fund Raising* (Taft Publications, 1986).

CHAVES, ESQUIPULA
(governor-Pueblo)

Affiliation: Governor, Sandia Pueblo, P.O. Box 6008, Bernalillo, N.M. 87004.

CHAVIS, ANGELA YELVERTON (Lumbee) 1950-
(dentist)

Born May 11, 1950, Pembroke, N.C. *Education:* Pembroke State University, B.S., 1971; University of North Carolina, Chapel Hill, School of Dentistry, D.D.S., 1980. *Principal occupation:* Dentist. *Home address:* Route 2, Box 232, Pembroke, N.C. 28372. *Community activities:* Student Health Action Committee; Voter Registration. *Memberships:* North Carolina Association for Preventive Dentistry, 1976-; American Dental Association. *Awards, honors:* Graduated "Cum Laude," Pembroke State University, 1971; scholarship from the American Fund for Dental Health, 1976-1980. *Interests:* "My vocational interest is dentistry. I plan to return to my home town and work to better the dental health of the Indian people in my town and surrounding community." *Biographical source: Who's Who Among Students in American Universities & Colleges, 1971.*

CHIAGO, ROBERT KEAMS (Navajo-Pima) 1942-
(educator and businessman)

Born June 22, 1942, Los Angeles, Calif. *Education:* Arizona State University, B.A., 1965; Northern Illinois University, Dekalb, M.S., 1970; University of Utah, 1974-1976 (61 hours towards Ph.D.). *Principal occupation:* Educator and businessman. *Home address:* 3609 East 3800 South, Salt Lake City, Utah 84109. *Affiliations:* Associate director, American Indian Culture Center, UCLA, 1970; director, Ramah Navajo School Board, Inc., Ramah, N.M., 1970-1971; director, Navajo Division of Education, Navajo Nation, Window Rock, Ariz., 1971-1973; consultant, Mesa Consultants, Albuquerque, N.M., 1973; visiting assistant professor of humanities, University of Utah, Salt Lake City, 1976-1979; director, Native Amerian Studies, University of Utah, 1973-1981; director of Indian Teacher/Counselor Education Programs, University of Utah, 1980-1984; president, Western Indian Technologies, Salt Lake City, Utah, 1984-. *Other professional posts:* Editor and founder, *Utah Indian Journal,* which was a statewide Indian newspaper in 1976 & 1977; founder and coordinator, Western Indian Education

Conference; consulting; proposal writing and evaluation. *Military service:* U.S. Marine Corps, 1965-1968 (Captain, infantry officer; Presidential Unit Citation, Navy Unit Citation, National Defense Service Medal, Vietnam Service Medal and Campaign Medal). *Community activities:* Presidential appointee, National Advisory Council on Indian Education; gubanatorial appointee to the Utah State Board of Indian Affairs; National Congress of American Indians (resolutions committee chairman, 1976-1980); advisory committee for the creation of the Native American Rights Fund, 1971-1972; member, State of Utah ESEA Title IV Advisory Council, 1977-1979; Community Services Council of Utah (board member, 1974-1975; director, Minority Economic Development Council. *Memberships:* National Congress of American Indians; Western Indian Education Conference (coordinator, 1983, 1984, 1986); National Advisory Council on Indian Education, 1983-1986. *Interests:* "Major areas of interest include education, economic development, and employment."

CHIAO, CHIEN 1935-
(professor, researcher)

Born February 6, 1935, China. *Education:* National Taiwan University, B.A., 1958, M.A., 1961; Cornell University, Ph.D., 1969. *Principal occupation:* Professor, researcher. *Home address:* Department of Anthropology, New Asia College, The Chinese University of Hong Kong, Shatin, N.T., Hong Kong. *Affiliations:* Assistant, associate professor, Indiana University, 1966-1976; senior lecturer, chairman, Department of Anthropology, The Chinese University of Hong Kong, 1976-. *Other professional posts:* Adjunct Research Fellow, Institute of Ethnology, Academia Sinica, 1978-; honorary professor, Honan Institute of Museology, 1985-. *Memberships:* Hong Kong Anthropological Society (founder and founding chairman, 1978-1981); American Anthropological Association (Fellow); Royal Asiatic Society - Hong Kong Branch. *Interests:* Cultural anthropology, political anthropology, social structure, religion, culture change; North American with emphasis on the Navajo, with specific focus on Navajo ceremonialism; and East Asia with emphasis on China. *Biographical sources:* "Dr. Chiao Chien Talks About Anthropology," by Bin Xiao *(Readers,* No. 5 1985, Hauiyin, China); "Professor Chiao Chien Returns Home," by Yunho Li *(Unity Weekly,* No. 726, Aug. 24, 1985, Beijing, China). *Published works: Continuation of Tradition in Navajo Society* (Institute of Ethnology, Academia Sinica, 1971).

CHICKS, SHELDON A. (Stockbridge-Munsee) 1928-
(physician)

Born December 20, 1928, Shawano County, Wisc. *Education:* Marquette University, School of Medicine, M.D., 1963. *Principal occupation:* Physician (private practice). *Home address:* 6324 Upper Parkway North, Wauwatosa, Wisc. 53213. *Community activities:* Milwaukee Indian Health Board, Inc. (vice-chairman, board of directors); Milwaukee Indian Community School (board of directors, 1973-1975). *Memberships:* American Psychiatric Association; Association of American Indian Physicians (president, 1974-1975, 1977-1978).

CHIEF, LEROY
(principal)

Affiliation: Principal, Wahpeton Schoo, Bureau of Indian Affairs, Wahpeton, N.D. 58075.

CHILTOSKEY, GOINGBACK (Cherokee) 1907-
(arts and crafts specialist)

Born April 20, 1907, Cherokee, N.C. *Education:* Chicago Art Institute; Purdue University. *Principal occupation:* Arts and crafts specialist. *Home address:* Cherokee, N.C. 28719. *Affiliations:* Instructor, Cherokee Indian School, Cherokee, N.C., 1937-1942, 1947-1953; modelmaker, Engineer Board, Fort Belvior, Va., 1942-1946; partner, Imagineering Associates, Hollywood, Calif., 1946-1947; modelmaker, E.R.D.L., Fort Belvior, Va., 1954-1966; self-employed as craftsmen, Cherokee, N.C., 1966-. *Memberships:* Southern Highlands Handicraft Guild, 1948-; Qualla Arts and Crafts Mutual, 1947-; Washington Society of Artists, 1960-1963; Federal Artists and Designers, 1962-1964. *Awards, honors:* Purchase Award, North Carolina Art Society, 1953; First Prize, Blowing Rock, N.C., Exhibit; Second Prize, Philbrook Art Center, Tulsa, Okla.; prizes at North Carolina State Fair and Cherokee Indian Fair. Work chosen for exhibit at Smithsonian Institution. *Interests:* Mr. Chiltoskey writes, "(My) instructional career included teaching high school students and adults to do wood carving, sculpture, and furniture-making. During spare time and since retirement, (I) design and make wood carvings and sculpture. Lapidary and jewelry making are other interests. Summer camp counseling and personal interests have taken me into most states in the U.S." *Published works: To Make My Bread: Cherokee Cooklore* (Stephens Press, 1951).

CHINO, WENDELL (Mescalero Apache) (tribal council president)

Affiliation: President, Mescalero Apache Tribal Council, P.O. Box 176, Mescalero, N.M. 88340.

CHOUTEAU, M.M. (Kaw) (tribal chairman)

Affiliation: Chairman, Kaw Business Committee, Drawer 50, Kaw City, Okla. 74641.

CHRISTIE, JOE C. (B.I.A. agency superintendent)

Affiliation: Superintendent, Winnebago Agency, Bureau of Indian Affairs, Winnebago, Neb. 68071

CHRISTMAN, RICHARD T, 1937- (B.I.A. agency superintendent)

Born July 5, 1937, Library, Penna. *Education:* Colorado School of Mines, 1954-1955; California State Teachers College, B.S., 1963; Arizona State University, M.S. (Indian Education), 1967. *Principal occupation:* B.I.A. agency superintendent. *Home address:* 2552 West Capsitrano Rd., Tucson, Ariz. 85706. *Affiliation:* Superintendent,

B.I.A., Papago Agency, Sells, Ariz., 1976-. *Other professional posts:* Education program administrator (supt. of schools, Papago Agency), six years. *Community activities:* American Indian Committee, The Church of Jesus Christ (board member); Quorom of Seventy (vice-chairman). *Awards, honors:* Special Achievement Award for Education Improvement, Bureau of Indian Affairs; Field Management Training Award. *Interests:* "Extensive travel to reservations in the Southwest, Northwest Plains, Canada and Eastern seaboard."

CLAH, HERBERT, Jr. (Navajo) 1949- (administrator)

Born June 1, 1949, Farmington, N.M. *Education:* Brigham Young University, B.S., 1975, MPA, 1981. *Principal occupation:* Executive director, administrator. *Home address:* 484 West Center St. (46-15), Blanding, Utah 84511. *Affiliation:* Executive director, Utah Navajo Development Council, 1981-. *Community activities:* Rural Commuity Assistance Corporation (board of directors). *Memberships:* Indian Education Advisory Committee; Utah State Board of Education. *Awards, honors:* Exxon Fellowship; Deans Leadership Award, BYU; Janie Thompson Award; Outstanding Young Men of America; Defense Department Recognition, USO Tours, Military Bases in Germany, 1974. *Biographical source: Outstanding Young Men of America,* publication.

CLARK, DONALD E. (Chippewa) 1922- (teacher)

Born May 16, 1922, Frazee, Minn. *Education:* El Camino College, A.A., 1950; Michigan State University, B.S. (Wildlife Biology), 1954. *Principal occupation:* High school biology teacher. *Home address:* 1220 Furlong Rd., Sebastopol, Calif. 95472. *Military service:* U.S. Navy, 1942-1945. *Community activities:* Native American Club (sponsor). *Memberships:* California Teachers Association; National Educational Association. *Interests:* "Native studies, especially religion and art, and "traditional" photography."

CLARK-PRICE, MARGARET A.
(Wyandotte-Shawnee-Chippewa) 1944-
(publisher, artist)

Born August 2, 1944, Colville Indian Reservation, Nespelem, Wash. *Education:* St. Michael's High School, St. Michael's, Ariz., 1962; Sierra Nevada College, Incline Village, Nev. (2½ years). *Principal occupation:* Publisher and artist. *Home address:* P.O. Box 6338, Incline Village, Nev. 89450. *Affiliation:* Publisher, *Native American* (magazine to develop an information non-political, bridge between the many tribes, extending to the reaches of the general public). *Exhibits:* Her pastels, oils, acrylics, watercolors and pencil works hang in galleries in Arizona, California, and Nevada as well as in many private collections throughout the U.S. *Awards, honors:* Six awards and a Grand prize for a large pastel entitled "Caught in the Middle," at the 1982 annual Navajo Nation Fair, Window Rock, Ariz. *Interests:* "My main interests, obviously, surround the Indian world. I have spect years on my own family genealogy, necessitating journeying across the U.S. and into Canada. I hope to instill such an interest in others through the journey among the pages of the *Native American* annual and its subsequent issues."

CLARKE, FRANK, M.D. (Hualapai)
1921-
(physician/administrator)

Born November 11, 1921, Blythe, Calif. *Education:* Sherman Institute, Riverside, Calif. (seven years); Los Angeles City College (two years); University of California at Los Angeles, B.S., 1946; St. Louis University, School of Medicine, M.D., 1950. *Principal occupation:* Physician/administrator. *Home address:* 7909 Rio Grande Blvd., N.W., Albuquerque, N.M. 87114. *Affiliation:* Clinical director, Albuquerque Service Unit, Public Health Service, Indian Health Service, Albuquerque, N.M., 1975-. *Other profesional post:* Secretary, National Council of Clinical Directors. *Military service:* U.S. Navy, 1942-1946 (Presidential Unit Citation), 1950-1953 (Lt. (MC) USNR). *Memberships:* USPHS Commissioned Officers Association; American Academy of Family Physicians (Charter Fellow); New

Mexico Academy of Family Physicians; Association of American Indian Physicians (president, 1973-1974). *Awards, honors:* Fellow, John Hay Whitney Foundation, 1950; Indian Achievement Award, Indian Council Fire, Chicago, 1961; Man of the Year, City of Woodlake, 1962; Layman of the Year in Education, Tulane County Chapter of California Teacher's Association. *Interests:* Recruitment of Indian students into health professions; lecturer on alcoholism. *Biographical sources: Indians of Today; Who's Who in the West; Community Leaders & Noteworthy Americans.*

CLARY, THOMAS C. (Miami
of Oklahoma) 1927-
(corporate president)

Born March 3, 1927, Joplin, Mo. *Education:* Pace University, New York City, B.B.A. (Marketing); University of Oklahoma, Norman, M.A. (Public Administration); California Western University, Santa Ana, Ph.D. (Psychology). *Principal occupation:* Corporate president. *Home address:* 3410 Garfield St., N.W., Washington, D.C. 20007. *Affiliations:* Director, Light, Inc., Columbus, Ohio (four years); director, Science of Mind Church Counseling and Healing Center, Washington, D.C. (two years); director, Alternative Health Therapies, Washington, D.C. (three years); president, TCI, Inc., Washington, D.C. (ten years). *Other professional posts:* Minister, Science of Mind Church. *Military service:* U.S. Army, 1945-1968 (Lt. Colonel) (Legion of Merit, Army Commendation Medal). *Memberships:* International Transactional Analysis Association (teaching member); American Association of Profesional Hypnotherapists. *Awards, honors:* Silver Anvil Award for International Community Relations by Public Relations Society of America, 1968; Master Hypnotist by Ameriacn Council of Hypnotist Examiners, 1983; Urban Mass Transportation Administration Minority Business Enterprise Award, 1985. *Interests:* Teach courses in "psychic potential," "spiritual healing" and "stress management." *Published works:* "Script Analysis is a New Approach to OD," chapter 12 of *Everybody Wins: Transactional Analysis Applied to Organizations* (Addison-

Wesley, 1974); *How to Live with Stress* (NTDS Press, 1977); *At the Organizational Precipice* (NTDS Press, 1977).

CLAUS, TOM (Mohawk) 1929-
(ordained clergyman, administrator)

Born December 26, 1929, Niagara Falls, N.Y. *Education:* High school; private tutoring in theology. *Principal occupation:* Ordained clergyman, administrator. *Home address:* 2302 W. Port au Prince Lane, Phoenix, Ariz. 85023. *Affiliations:* Director, American Indian Crusade, Inc., Glendale, Ariz., 1952-; president, Christian Hope Indian Eskimo Fellowship, Orange, Calif., 1975-. *Other professional posts:* American Indian delegate to World Congress on Evangelism, Berlin, Germany, 1966; delegate to International Congress on World Evangelization, Lausanne, Switzerland, 1974. *Community activities:* Billy Graham Evangelistic Association Crusades (Indian coordinator). *Interests:* "Extensive travels to Indians, Eskimos, Aleuts in Alaska, Canada, U.S., Mexico, Guatamala, Panama, Suriname." *Published works: On Eagles Wings* (Thunderbird Press, 1976); *Christian Leadership in Indian America* (Moody Press, 1977).

CLEGHORN, MILDRED (Fort Sill Apache)
(tribal chairwoman)

Affiliation: Chairwoman, Fort Sill Apache Business Committee, Route 2, Box 121, Apache, Okla. 73006.

CLEMMER, JANICE WHITE
(Wasco-Shawnee-Delaware) 1941-
(professor)

Born February 17, 1941, Warm Springs Reservation, Oregon. *Education:* Brigham Young University, Provo, Utah, B.S. (Archaeology/history), 1964; Dominican College of San Rafael, Calif., M.A. (History), 1975; University of San Francisco, M.A. (Education), 1976; University of Utah, Salt Lake City, (Ph.D., Cultural Foundation of Education, 1979; Ph.D. History, 1980). *Principal occupation:* Professor.

Home address: 1445 E. Princeton Ave., Salt Lake City, Utah 84105. *Affiliations:* Professor, College of Education, Brigham Young University, Provo, Utah, 1980-. *Other professional posts:* Editorial board, *American Indian Culture and Research Journal;* reviewer. *American Indian Quarterly,* University of California at Berkeley. *Community activities:* Boy Scouts-Cub Scouts (merit badge counselor/den mother); leader, Girl Scouts-Brownies; board chairman, Native American Advisory Board, State of Utah Board of Education; committee member, Utah Endowment for the Humanities; board member, American Indian Services; volunteer, Utah State Heart and Lung Association. *Memberships:* SIETAR (Society for Intercultural Education, Training and Research, International Organization); Native American Historians' Association (founding member); American Studies Association; OHOYO - National Native American Women's Program; Association for Supervision and Curriculum Development; State of Utah Bilingual Association; American Historians Western History Association; Utah State Historical Society; Oregon Historical Society; California Historical Society; National Archives (associate); Jefferson Forum; American Association for State and Local History. *Awards, honors:* University of Utah Danforth Foundation Fellowship Candidate; Distinguished Teaching Award Candidate, University of Utah; Tribal Archives Conference Award Recipient; Consortium for Native American Archives; OHOYO One Thousand, Native American Women Award Listing; American Indian Alumni Award, Brigham Young University; Lamanite Award, American Indian Services, BYU; D'Arcy McNickle, Newberry Library Fellowship Research Award, Chicago, Ill.; Spencer W. Kimball Memorial Award, Private Corporation Endowment & AIS, BYU; Phi Alpha Theta; Phi Delta Kappa; Phi Kappa Phi; first Native American woman in U.S. history to earn two Ph.D.s; 1982 Women's Conference "Spotlight", outstanding woman faculty member from the College of Student Life, BYU; Multicultural Week Advisor Awards, BYU; Multicultural Programs Awards, BYU. *Biographical sources:* University of Utah Public Relations Office,

Salt Lake City, Utah rgarding the earning of two Ph.D.s; stories in *Deseret News,* Church News Section, 1980; and in Lifestyle section of the *Salt Lake Tribune,* Salt Lake City, Spring, 1980; hometown newspapers, *Bend Bulletin, Bend, Oregon, Spilya Tymoo,* Warm Springs, Oregon, and *Madras Pioneer,* Madras, Oregon. *Published works:* "The Good Guys and the Bad Guys," *The Utah Indian,* Journal, Spring, 1979; "Ethnic Traditions and the Family--The Native Americans," *Ethnic Traditions and the Family* series, Salt lake City Board of Education, Fall, 1980; editor, *Minority Women Speak Out* (in progress); various book reviews pertaining to Native American topics; printed works primarily in-house curriculum development material, Brigham Young University.

CLIFTON, JAMES A. 1927-
(professor)

Born January 6, 1927, St. Louis, Mo. *Education:* University of Chicago, Ph.B., 1950; University of Orgon, Ph.D., 1960. *Principal occupation:* Professor. *Home address:* 332 Bretcoe Dr., Green Bay, Wisc. 54302. *Affiliation:* Professor, University of Wisconsin, Green Bay, 1970-. *Military service:* U.S. Marine Corps, 1951-1955 (Captain; Purple Heart). *Memberships:* American Anthropological Association; American Society for Ethnohistory; American Historical Association. *Awards, honors:* Frankenthal Professor of Anthropology and History, University of Wisconsin, Green Bay. *Interests:* "Research among Klamath of Oregon, Ute of Colorado, Potawatomi of Kansas, Wisconsin, Michigan, and Canada. Historical research on Wyandot and Indians of the Old Northwest Territory generally; research in Chile. Expert witness, Indian Claims Commission and Great Lakes Indians Treaty Rights." *Published works: Klamath Personalities* (University of Oregon, 1962); *Cultural Anthropology* (Houghton Mifflin, 1967); *A Place of Refuge for All Time* (Museum of Man, 1974); *The Prairie People* (Kansas University Press, 1977); *Star Woman and Other Shawnee Tales* (University Press of America, 1983); *The Pokagons* (University Press of America, 1985).

CLINCHER, BONNIE MARIE (Sioux)
1952-
(editor-tribal newspaper)

Born July 6, 1952, Poplar, Mont. *Education:* Haskell Indian Junior College, 1973-1975. *Principal occupation:* Editor of tribal newspaper. *Home address:* Box 631, Poplar, Mont. 59255. *Memberships:* Survival of American Indians Association, 1976-. *Interests:* "I am most interested in the media, especially when I can assist in informing and making concerned the Indian people. My travels only go as far as celebrations across the northern Plains, on weekends, to just be among the Indian people and refresh my spirit in the old ways before returning to the new ways"; photography.

COCHRAN, GEORGE McKEE
(Cherokee— 1908-
(artist, barber)

Born October 5, 1908, Stilwell, Okla. *Education:* Haskell Institute, 1927. *Principal occupation:* Artist, barber. *Home address:* 681 Chase St., Eugene, Oregon 97402. *Community activities:* Kiwanis Club. *Memberships:* Cherokee Foundation, Inc.; Indian Festival of Arts, Inc. (board member); Maude I. Kerns Art Center; National Congress of American Indians; Oregon Archaeological Society (life member), 1964- Red Dirt or War Paint Clan of the North American Indian; Mormon Church. *Awards, honors:* American Eagle Feather Award for outstanding work among the Indian people, American Indian Festival of Arts, Inc., 1960-1961; Grand Award, All American Indian Art Exhibit, 1961-1962; several others. Mr. Cochran's work has been exhibited in many one-man shows over the country, including the Seattle Public Library, Haskell Institute, Philbrook Art Center, Barnsdall Art Gallery, Truman Library, University of Oregon, Hotel Utah Art Gallery, Lloyd's Center Art Gallery, Wilshire Federal and Loan Art Gallery. *Published works: Indian Portraits of the Pacific Northwest* (Binfords and Mort, 1959).

COLLIER, L.W.
(B.I.A. agency superintendent)

Affiliation: Superintendent, Wind River Agency, Bureau of Indian Affairs, Fort Washakie, Wyo. 82514.

COLLIER, LAVERN
(B.I.A. agency superintendent)

Affiliation: Superintendent, Uintah and Ouray Agency, Bureau of Indian Affairs, Fort Duchesne, Utah 84026.

COLLINS, ADELE VICTOR (Chickasaw)
1908-
(painter)

Born January 24, 1908, Blanchard, Okla. *Education:* St. Elizabeth's Academy Indian School, Purcell, Okla.; various art courses at Art League; studied with Emalita Newton Terry. *Principal occupation:* Painter. *Home address:* 1631 Curtis Dr., Las Vegas, Nevada 89104. *Exhibitions:* Oklahoma State Show, Oklahoma City; Oklahoma Indian Show, Philbrook Museum, Tulsa; Arts and Crafts Board, U.S. Dept. of the Interior, Washington, D.C.; Contemporary Indian Art Show, Santa Fe, N.M.; Inter-Tribal Indian Ceremonials, Gallup, N.M.; Scottsdale Contemporary Indian Show, Ariz.; University of South Dakota, Vermillion; La Grande, Oreg. Indian Annual; Smithsonian Institution; Five Civilized Tribes Museum, Muskogee, Okla.; All American Indian Days, Sheridan, Wyoming; Miss Collin's work is in the following permanent collections: U.S. Dept. of the Interior, Washington, D.C.; Vincent Price Collection, Hollywood, Calif.; Heard Museum, Phoenix, Ariz.; Gonzaga University Indian Center, Spokane, Wash.; Southern Nevada University, Las Vegas, Nev. *Awards, honors:* Mis Collins has received many awards and prizes for her art, too numerous to mention.

COLLINS, CARL
(president-Bible Institute)

Affiliation: President, Amerian Indian Bible Institute, 100020 N. 15th Ave., Phoenix, Ariz. 85021.

COLLINS, REBA NEIGHBORS 1925-
(director-Will Rogers Memorial)

Born August 26, 1925. *Education:* Central State University, Edmond, B.A., 1958; Oklahoma State University, M.S. (Journalism), 1959, Ed.D. (Higher Education in Journalism), 1968. *Principal occupation:* Director, Will Rogers Memorial, Claremore, Okla., 1975-. *Address:* c/o Will Rogers Memorial, Box 157, Claremore, Okla. 74018. *Affiliations:* Instructor, professor of journalism, Central State University, 1958-1975; director of public relations, sponsor of alumni publications, school newspaper and college yearbook, Central State University, 1958-1975. *Community activities:* Edmond Guidance Center (board of directors); Claremore Chamber of Commerce (board of directors); member, Claremore Ambassadors; Claremore Pilot Club (charter president); member, Governor's mini-cabinet for tourism and recreation. *Memberships:* Delta Kappa Gamma; Sigma Delta Chi; American Association of Unviersity Women; Oklahoma Public Relations Association for Higher Education (charter president); Oklahoma Education Association (public relations board); CSU Alumni Association; Oklahoma Museum Association (board of directors, treasurer). *Awards, honors:* Outstanding Senior Woman, and Outstanding Future Teacher, Central State University, 1958; (2) First Place Awards, Oklahoma Press Association for Best Feature on Education; Outstanding Communicator Award from Oklahoma Women in Journalism, 1975; Service Award from VFW, 1971; Okie Award from Governor Dewey Bartlet, 1974; Service Award for Helping Organize First Fourth of July Celebration in Edmond, Okla., 1973; Distinguished Former Stduent Award, Central State University, 1979. *Interests:* Genealogy, travel and travel writing. *Published works:* In the Shadows of Old North, 1974; History of the Janes, Peek Family, 1975, plus three follow up books; Will Rogers Memorial Booklet, 1979; Roping Will Rogers' Family Tree, 1982; Will Rogers and Wiley Post in Alaska, 1983; editorial staff, Photolith magazine (seven years); hundreds of featurer articles for state and national magazines.

COLOMBEL, PIERRE
(Indian health service)

Affiliation: Chief, Human Resource Management, Indian Health Service, 5600 Fishers Lane, Rockville, Md. 20857.

COLOSIMO, THOMAS
(executive secretary-Indian association)

Affiliations: Executive director, Arrow, Inc., 1000 Connecticut Ave., N.W., Washington, D.C. 20036; executive secretary, National American Indian Court Judges Association, 1000 Connecticut Ave., N.W., Suite 401, Washington, D.C. 20036.

COLTON, ALFRED *(Qoyawayma)*
(Hopi) 1938-
(professional engineer)

Born 1938, Los Angeles, Calif. *Education:* California State Polytechnic University, B.S., 1961; University of Southern California, M.S. (Mechanical Engineer), 1966, graduate program in water resources and environmental engineering, 1970; Westinghouse International School of Environmental Management, graduate. *Principal occupation:* Professional engineer. *Home address:* 8738 E. Clarendon Ave., Scottsdale, Ariz. 85251. *Affiliations:* Project engineer, Litton Systems, Inc., 1961-1970; supervisor of the Environmental Dept., Salt River Project, Phoenix, Ariz., 1971-. *Other professional posts:* Advisor, University of New Mexico, Native American Program, College of Engineering (NAPCOE); National Representative, Electric Power Research Institute's (EPRI) Environmental Task Force (1974-1977); Bureau of Land Management's (BLM) Arizona Multi-Use Advisory Board (one term). *Community activities:* Western Systems Coordinating Council (WSCC) Environmental Committee (member, past vice-chairman); American Indian Science and Engineering Society (chairman); American Indian Engineering Council (past associate chairman); Heard Museum Men's Council (board of directors); Museum of Northern Arizona (member); Registered Arizona Lobbyist. *Memberships:* Arizona Society of Professional Engineers; Institute of Electrical and Electronic Engineers; American Association for the Advancement of Science; American Public Power Association; Edison Electric Institute Environemntal Committees. *Awards, honors:* First Place Popovi Da Memorial Award for pottery, 1976, Scottsdale National Indian Arts Exhibition,; two blue ribbon awards, 1976, one blue ribbon, 1977, Heard Museum Indian Arts Exhibition, Phoenix, Ariz.; pottery work featured at 1977 Arizona Kidney Foundation Auction, Numkena Studio of Indian Art, Phoenix; individual showing at Santa East, Austin, Texas; first place and special award at the Museum of Northern Arizona's 1977 Hopi Show; second and third place at Gallup Ceremonial, N.M.; holds patents in engineering work in the U.S. and several foreign countries. *Interests:* Pottery and weaving in the Hopi tradition.

CONLEY, ROBERT J. (Cherokee) 1940-
(director of Indian studies)

Born December 29, 1940, Cushing, Okla. *Education:* Midwestern University, Wichita Falls, Texas, B.A., 1966, M.A., 1968. *Principal occupation:* Director of Indian Studies. *Home address:* 3830 Garretson Ave., Sioux City, Iowa 51106. *Affiliations:* Coordinator of Indian culture, Eastern Montana College, 1975-1976; assistant program director, The Cherokee Nation of Oklahoma, 1976-1977; director of Indian studies, Bacone College, 1978-1979; director of Indian studies, Morningside College, Sioux City, Iowa, 1979-. *Military service:* U.S. Marine Corps Reserve, 1957-1962. *Membership:* Western Writers of America. *Interests:* Writing—Mr. Conley writes, "my first novel, *Back to Malachi* (working title) has just been contracted to Doubleday for Fall, 1986 publication;" and acting. *Published works:* Poetry in various magazine and anthologies, including: *Indian Voice* (Feb. and July, 1972), *The Blue Cloud Quarterly* (Vol. 18, #3, 1973), *The Beloit Poetry Journal* (Vol. 30, #2, Winter 1979-1980), *Compages* (Winter and May, 1982); poems such as: *The Rattlesnake Band and Other Poems* (Indian University Press, 1984), "The Hills of Tsa-la-gi," "Morning and Night," and "The Rattlesnake Band," in *The Clouds Threw This Light: Contemporary Native American Poe-*

try, Phillip Foss, editor (Institute of American Indian Arts Press, 1983); "Cherokees 'On the Scout'" in *The Roundup* (Nov.-Dec. 1984); among others. Short Stories in the following periodicals and anthologies: *Indian Voice,* 1972, *Sun Tracks,* Fall 1976; *The Remembered Earth* (Red Earth Press, 1979); and short stories, "Wesley's Story," in *The Greenfield Review* (summer/fall, 1984), and "The Immortals," in *Iowa Archaeological Newsletter* (summer, 1984).

CONN, RICHARD
(curator)

Education: University of Washington, B.A., 1950, M.A., 1955. *Affiliation:* Curator, Denver Art Museum, Denver, Colo. *Military service:* U.S. Army, 1951-1953. *Memberships:* American Association of Museums. *Awards, honors:* McCloy Fellowship in Art, 1979. *Interests:* Native American art in general; fieldwork in eastern Washington, Montana, and Central Canada. *Published works: Robes of White Shell and Sunrise* (Denver Art Museum); *Native American Art in the Denver Art Museum* (Denver Art Museum, 1978); *Circles of the World* (Denver Art Museum, 1982).

CONNER, ROSEMARY
(coordinator-Indian association)

Affiliation: Coordinator, North American Indian Women's Association, National Office, 1411 K St., Suite 200, Washington, D.C. 20005.

COOK, JOHN A. (St. Regis Mohawk) 1922-
(tribal chief)

Born April 22, 1922, Syracuse, N.Y. *Education:* University of Idaho; Loyola University; National Radio Institute; Franklyn Tech. *Principal occupation:* Tribal chief, iron welder. *Home address:* R.F.D., Hogansburg, N.Y. *Affiliation:* Chief, St. Regis Mohawk Tribe. *Military service:* U.S. Air Force, 1942-1945 (Air Medal). *Community activities:* Economic Opportunity Council of Franklyn County (director); Masons; American Legion.

COOK-LYNN, ELIZABETH
(Crow Creek Sioux) 1930-
(associate professor of Indian studies)

Born November 17, 1930, Fort Thompson, S.D. *Education:* South Dakota State College, B.S. (Journalism/English, 1952; University of South Dakota, M.S. (Education/Psychology & Counseling), 1970; University of Nebraska, Lincoln, ABD (all but dissertation) status for Ph.D.; additional graduate work: Stanford University(literary criticism seminar); For teaching credentials - Black Hills State Teachers College and New Mexico State University. *Principal occupation:* Associate professor of Indian studies. *Home address:* Route 12, Box 59, Davenport, Wash. 99122. *Affiliations:* Newspaper work, editing and writing in S.D., 1952-1957; part-time teaching, Carlsbad, N.M., 1958-1964; secondary teaching, Carlsbad, N.M., 1965-1968, Rapid City, S.D., 1968-1969; assistant professor of English, 1970-1980, associate professor of English and Indian Studies, 1980-, Monroe Hall #113, Eastern Washington University, Cheney, Wash. *Other professional posts:* Editor of *The Wicazo SA Review,* a journal of Native Studies, Eastern Washington University. *Professional activities:* Consultant and participant in the curriculum development seminar RMMLA, Flagstaff, Ariz., 1978; project director (planning grant) NEH Media Project: *Indian Scholar's Journal. Published works:* Short stories, poems, and papers: "Problems in Indian Education," *(South Dakota Review),* "A Severe Indictment of Our School Systems," and "Authentic Pictures of the Sioux?" *(Great Plains Observer),* 1970; "Propulsives in Native American Literatures," paper read at National meeting of Conference of College Composition, and Communications, New Orleans, 1973; "The Teaching of Indian Literatures," NCTE, Minneapolis, Minn., 1974; "The Image of the American Indian in Historical Fiction," RMMLA, Laramie, Wyoming; "Delusion: The American Indian in White Man's Fiction," RMMLA, El Paso, Texas; "Three," prose and poetry in *Prairie Schooner,* Fall, 1976; "A Child's Story," short story in *Pembroke Magazine,* 1976; poems published in *Sun Tracks* (University of Arizona, 1977), and *The Ethnic Studies Journal; Then Badger Said This,* collection of poems (Vantage Press, 1978); "The Indian Short Story," and bibliography for *Encyclopedia of Short Fiction,* edited by Walton Beacham (Salem Press, 1980); "The Cure," short story accepted for *Anthology of Native American Literature,* edited by Berud Pryor, UCLA, Davis, 1980; two short stories, "The Power of Horses," and "A Good Chance," accepted by Simon J. Ortiz (Pueblo writer and poet)for inclusion in anthology *The Short Story in Native American Literatures* (Navajo College Press, 1983); 12 poems entitled *Seek the House of Relatives* (Blue Cloud Press, 1983); "Within Walking Distance," Spring issue, 1984, of *Bearing Witness, Sobreviviendo,* an anthology of writing and art by Native American-/Latina women; three poems, *Harper's Book of Twentieth Century Native American Poetry,* 1986, edited by Duane Niatum; among other short stories, articles, and essays.

COOKE, DAVID C. 1917-
(writer)

Born June 7, 1917, Wilmington, Delaware. *Education:* New York University, 1946-1947. *Principal occupation:* Writer. *Home address:* 57 E. Carpenter St., Valley Stream, N.Y. *Awards, honors:* Edgar Award, for *Best Detective Stories of the Year,* 1960: *Interests:* Writing; aviation; the American Indian; travel. *Published works: Famous Indian Tribes* (Random House, 1953); *Fighting Indians of the West* (Dodd, Mead, 1954); *Indians on the Warpath* (Dodd, Meade, 1957); *Tecumseh: Destiny's Warrior* (Julian Messner, 1959); *Indian Wars and Warriors* (Dodd, Mead, 1966).

COOPER, HARRY E. (Nooksack)
(tribal chairman)

Affiliation: Chairman, Nooksack Tribal Council, P.O. Box 157, Deming, Wash. 98244.

COOPER, KAREN COODY (Cherokee) 1946-
(educator, administrator)

Born November 10, 1946, Tulsa, Okla. *Edu-*

cation: Oklahoma College of Liberal Arts, Chickasha, Okla., 1965-1966; Western Connecticut State University, Danbury, B.A. (Anthropology), 1981. *Princopal occupation:* Educator/administrator. *Home address:* 2192 Litchfield Rd., Watertown, Conn. 06795. *Affiliation:* American Indian Archaeological Institute, Curtis Rd., Washington, Conn. 06793. *Other professional post:* Adjunct instructor, Western State Connecticut State University. *Community activities:* Board member, *Eagle Wing Press,* an American Indian newspaper. *Memberships:* Connecticut Indian Education Council; National Organization for Women; Connecticut Council for Social Studies. *Interests:* Ms. Cooper writes, "I am studying fingerweaving, an ancient craft of American Indians in the Woodlands, and have won prizes and written articles; I am also studying the historic events affecting Connecticut's Indian population; I am a published poet; I enjoy black and white photography."

CORBINE JOSEPH
(tribal chairman)

Affiliation: Chairman, Bad River Tribal Council, Route 39, Ashland, Wis. 54806.

CORNELIUS-FENTON, KAREN
(president-Indian association)

Affiliation: President, National Indian Education Association, 1115 Second Ave. South, Minneapolis, Minn. 55403.

CORNETT, JAMES D. 1923-
(B.I.A. agency superintendent)

Born January 1, 1923, Moorewood, Okla. *Education:* Sayre Jr. College, 1949-1950; Oklahoma State University, B.A., 1952. *Principal occupation:* B.I.A. agency superintendent. *Home address:* Box 425, Warm Springs, Oreg. 97761. *Affiliations:* Soil scientist, Fort Peck Agency, B.I.A., 1952-1956; soil conservationist, Blackfeet Agency, B.I.A., 1956-1962; land operations officer, Zuni Agency, B.I.A.; superintendent, Fort Totten Agency, Zuni Agency; area natural resource officer, Albuquerque Area Office; superintendent, Warm Springs

Agency, Warm Springs, Oreg. *Military service:* U.S. Navy, 1942-1948 (Campaign Medal, Good Conduct Medal). *Community activities:* 4-H; Boy Scouts of America; Lions Club (president, secretary, director).

CORTEZ, RONALD D.
(business committee chairman)

Affiliation: Chairman, Torres-Martinez Business Committee, 1866 E. George, Banning, Calif. 92220.

COSGROVE, STEPHEN FRANCIS (Sioux) 1943-
(ex-professional baseball player)

Born March 8, 1943, Marysville, Kansas. *Education:* Haskell Institute. *Principal occupation:* Ex-professional baseball player, Baltimore Orioles (baseball team).

COTTER, LEONARD N. (Wyandotte) 1906-
(ex-chief, Wyandotte Tribe)

Born July 3, 1906, Wyandotte, Indian Territory, Okla. *Education:* High school. *Principal occupation:* Ex-chief, Wyandotte Tribe; diesel mechanic. *Home address:* Box 15, Wyandotte, Okla. 74370. *Affiliations:* Garage and service station attendant and owner, 1926-1937; staff member, Indian Roads Dept., Okla., 1938-1940; Dunning, James & Patterson Construction Co., Oklahoma City, Okla., 1942-1943; E.A. Martin Machinery Co., Joplin, Mo., 1943-1944; S.E. Evans Construction Co., Ft. Smith, Ark., 1944-1945; diesel mechanic, Oklahoma State Highway Dept., 1946-retirement. *Other professional posts:* Second chief, Wyandotte Tribe, 1932-1936; chief, 1936-1942, 1948-1954, 1963-retirement. *Military service:* U.S. Marines, 1943. *Community activities:* Wyandotte Lions Club (past president); Wyandotte Methodist Church (past lay leader); American Legion. *Published works: Constitutions and By-Laws of the Wyandotte Tribe of Oklahoma* (Dept. of the Interior, 1937); *Corporate Charter of the Wyandotte Tribe of Oklahoma* (Dept. of the Interior, 1937).

COULTER, ROBERT T.
(director-Indian center)

Affiliation: Director, Indian Law Resource Center, 601 E St., S.E., Washington, D.C. 20003.

COURNOYER, FRANK (Yankton Sioux) 1952-
(visual artist)

Born December 26, 1952, Wagner, S.D. *Principal occupation:* Visual artist. *Home address:* Box 551, Wagner, S.D. 57380. *Affiliations:* Member, board of directors, Dakota Plains Institute of Learning, Marty, S.D. 57361, 1984-; chairman, board of directors, Oyate Kin Cultural Society, Marty, S.D., 1984-. *Military service:* U.S. Army, 1971-1974 (Specialist E-4, 82nd Airborne Division) (National Defense Ribbon, Expert Rifleman Badge, Jump Wings). *Community activities:* "Dakota Plains Institute of Learning" is the higher adult education branch of the Yankton Sioux Tribe; "Oyate Kin Cultural Society" is a newly formed organization intent on reviving, preserving and promoting Sioux arts and crafts. *Interests:* Mr, Cournoyer writes, "My major goals include the revival of Sioux arts and crafts to help promote the working artist and teach the future artists/craftspeople the art of marketing, quality, and culture, aiming at a more productive and self-reliant people." *Published works:* "I have an illustration in the book *Remember Your Realtives,* by Renee Sansome-Flood and Shirley A. Bernie, and I'm being considered for some illustrations in an upcoming biography of southeast South Dakota and have been selected to submit an illustration for another upcoming historical biography."

COX, BRUCE 1934-
(professor)

Born June 29, 1934, Santa Rosa, Calif. *Education:* Reed College, B.A., 1956; University of Oregon, M.A., 1959; University of California at Berkeley, Ph.D., 1968. *Principal occupation:* Professor of anthropology. *Home address:* 140 Kenilworth, Ottawa, Ontario, Canada. *Affiliations:* Instructor, Lewis and Clark College, 1964-1965; visiting professor, University of Florida, 1966; assistant professor, University of Alberta, 1967-1969; assistant professor, professor, Carleton University, 1969-. *Memberships:* American Anthropological Association; Law and Society Association. *Interests:* Dr. Cox writes, "I am interested in the cultural ecology of indigenous North American peoples...particularly the disrupted effects of large-scale energy development projects on such peoples' environments. Here, I have in mind the James Bay hydroelectric project in Quebec, the proposed Mackenzie Valley petroleum pipeline corridor in the N.W.T., and coal strip-mining on Black Mesa, and I am collecting information on all these areas." *Published works: Cultural Ecology of Canadian Native Peoples* (Carleton Library, 1973).

COX, CLAUDE (Creek)
(tribal chief)

Affiliation: Chief, Creek Nation, P.O. Box 580, Okmulgee, Okla. 74447.

CRAMPTON, C. GREGORY 1911-
(professor of history)

Born March 22, 1911, Kankakee, Ill. *Education:* Modesto Junior College, 1933; University of California, Berkeley, B.A., 1935, M.A., 1936, Ph.D., 1941. *Principal occupation:* Professor of history. *Home address:* 327 S. 12th E., Salt Lake City, Utah 84102. *Affiliations:* Teaching assistant in history, University of California, Berkeley, 1937-1940; special agent, F.B.I., U.S. Department of Justice, 1943-1945; depot historian, California Quartermaster Depot, U.S. War Department, 1944-1945; professor of history, University of Utah, 1945-; director, Duke Indian Oral History Project, University of Utah, 1967-. *Awards, honors:* Rockefeller Foundation, traveling Fellowship, 1941-1942; postwar Fellowship, Humanities, 1948-1949. *Memberships:* Phi Alpha Theta (vice-president, 1941-1948; president, 1949-1950). *Published works: Outline History of the Glen Canyon Region, 1776-1922* (University of Utah Press, 1959); *Historical Sites in Glen Canyon, Mouth of the San Juan River to Lee's Ferry* (Univerity of Utah Press, 1960); editor with Dwight L. Smight,

The Hoskaninni Papers of Robert B. Stanton, Mining in Glen Canyon, 1897-1902 (Univerity of Utah Press, 1961); *Historical Sites in Glen Canyon, Mouth of Hansen Creek to Mouth of San Juan River* (University of Utah Press, 1962); *The San Juan Canyon Historical Sites* (University of Utah Press, 1964); *Historical Sites in Cataract and Narrow Canyons, and in Glen Canyon to California Bar* (University of Utah Press, 1964); *Standing Up Country, the Canyon Lands of Utah and Arizona* (Alfred A. Knopf; University of Utah Press in association with the Amon Carter Museum of Western Art); *Land of Living Rock, The Grand Canyon and the High Plateaus: Arizona, Utah, Nevada* (Alfred A. Knopf, 1972); *The Zunis of Cibola* (University of Utah Press, 1977); numerous articles in journals.

CRAWFORD, EUGENE
(executive director)

Affiliation: Executive director, National Indian Lutheran Board, 35 E. Hacker Dr., Suite 1847, Chicago, Ill. 60641.

CRAWFORD, MAURICE
(tribal official)

Affiliation: Chairman, Bridgeport General Council, P.O. Box 37, Bridgeport, Calif. 93517.

CRAWFORD, MICHAEL ROBERT
(Penobscot) 1943-
(Indian education administrator)

Born December 5, 1943, Penobscot Indian Reservation, Old Town, Maine. *Education:* Washington State College; University of Maine. *Principal occupation:* Indian education administrator. *Affiliations:* Announcer, WMCS Radio, 1967; teacher of the physically handicapped, Bangor Public Schools, 1967-1968; teacher of Junior high level math and science, Bangor Public Schools, 1968-1969; deputy commissioner, Department of Indian Affairs, State of Maine, 1969-1970;

director, T.R.I.B.E., Inc. (Indian learning center), 1970-. *Interests:* Mr Crawford writes, "I am channeling my career to areas where I can work with other Indians and help find solutions to some of the problems we face. My major interest is in education, and my present position as director of an all-Indian educational center is very challenging. It will give us a chance to show non-Indians what we can do. I expect that T.R.I.B.E., Inc. and its programs will set an example for non-Indian schools."

CROOKS, NORMAN (Mdewakanton Sioux)
(tribal chairman)

Affiliation: Chairman, Shakopee Business Council, Box 150, Sioux Trail, Prior Lake, Minn. 55372.

CROW, JOHN O. (Cherokee) 1912-
(B.I.A. official-retired)

Born September 7, 1912, Salem, Mo. *Education:* Haskell Institute. *Principal occupation:* B.I.A. Official-retired. *Home address:* 9301 Lona Lane, N.E., Albuquerque, N.M. 87111. *Affiliations:* B.I.A. superintendent at Truxton Canyon Agency, Mescalero Agency, Fort Apache Agency, Uintah and Ouray Agency; chief of realty, 1960-1961; acting commissioner, 1961; deputy commissioner, 1961-1965; associate director, Bureau of Land Management, B.I.A., 1965-1971; deputy commissioner of Indian Affairs, B.I.A., 1971-1973. *Awards, honors:* Career Service Award, National Civil Service League, 1964.

CROW, PERCE B. (Lower Brule Sioux) 1925-
(administrative law hearing officer)

Born July 13, 1925, Pierre, S.D. *Education:* Morningside College, Sioux City, Iowa, B.S., 1950, B.S.L., 1972; California College of Law, J.D., 1974. *Principal occupation:* Administrative law hearing officer. *Home address:* 844 Catania Pl., Claremont, Calif. 91711. *Affiliations:* State of California Community Release Board, Sacramento, Calif., 1974-. *Other profesional posts:*

Member, board of directors, American Indian Volunteers; college instructor, Police Science. *Military service:* P.F.C., U.S. Marines, 1943-1946. *Community activities:* Los Angeles County Department of Mental Health Services (member, Citizens Advisory Board).

CROWE, AMANDA (Cherokee) 1928-
(teacher, sculpture)

Born July 16, 1928, Murphy, N.C. *Education:* School of Art, Institute of Chicago, B.F.A., 1950, M.F.A., 1952. *Principal occupation:* Teacher, sculpture. *Home address:* Cherokee, N.C. 28719. *Affiliations:* Teacher of wood-carving and sculptures, Cherokee High School, Cherokee, N.C., 1953-. *Memberships:* Southern Highland Handicraft Guild, 1953- (board of directors, 1958-1961; education committee, 1953-1959; standards committee, 1959-1961); Qualla Arts and Crafts Mutual, 1953- (executive and standards committee, 1954-). *Awards, honors:* Faculty Honorable Mentions in sculpture, anatomy, ceramics, and architectural scupture. *Published work:* Illustrator, *Cherokee Legends* (Tom B. Underwood, 1956).

CROWFEATHER, ISABELLE (Standing RockSioux)
(arts and crafts manager)

Affiliation: Manager, Standing Rock Sioux Arts and Crafts, Fort Yates, N.D. 58538.

CUMMING, KENDALL 1925-
(B.I.A. agency superintendent)

Born August 14, 1925, Nogales, Ariz. *Education:* University of Arizona, B.S., 1949, M.S., 1951. *Principal occupation:* B.I.A. agency superintendent. *Home address:* 549 W. Dublin, Chandler, Ariz. 85224. *Affiliations:* Bureau of Indian Affairs, 1950- (served on Navajo, Hopi, Jicarilla and Pima Reservations; superintendent, Pima Agency, B.I.A., Sacaton, Ariz. *Military service:* 101st Airborne Division in Europe, 1943-1945. *Awards, honors:* Meritorious Service Award, U.S. Department of the Interior. *Interests:* Indian affairs, range management.

CUMMINGS, VICKI
(museum director)

Affiliation: Director, Museum of Indian Heritage, 6040 De Long Rd., Indianapolis, Ind. 46254.

D

DAILEY, CHARLES 1935-
(Native American museum director)

Born May 25, 1935, Golden, Colo. *Education:* University of Colorado, B.F.A.-Fine Arts, 1961. *Principal occupation:* Native American museum director. *Home address:* 412 Sosoya Lane, Santa Fe, N.M. 87501. *Affiliations:* Museum director and museum training coordinator, Institute of American Indian Arts (national junior college, Native American museum), Santa Fe, N.M., 1972-. *Military service:* U.S. Marine Corps, Sergeant, 1953-1956. *Community activities:* National Ski Patrol Member, 1960-1983; Professional Ski Patrolman, 1962-1970. *Memberships:* American Association for State and Local History, 1956-; MPMA, 1960-1980; American Association of Museums, 1964-; New Mexico Association of Museums, 1972-; Native American Museum Association (charter member). *Awards, honors:* Minor painting awards since 1970; numerous awards state and local competitions, 1960-1970; kayacking - invited to participate in World Championships, Italy, 1961; various whitewater championships, 1958-1962. *Interests:* Native American museums survey, 1965-; research, 8,000 slides inventory; museum training interests, 1956-; various sports activities: kayacking, skiing, mountaineering, camping. *Biographical sources: Artists in America,* 1971, 1972; *Santa Fe Artists,* 1968; International Men of Achievement; Who's Who in the West; Contemporary Personage in the Arts. Published works: Creating a Crowd: Mannikens for Small Museums," El Pacio, MNM Press, 1969; "Museum Training Workbooks," IAIA, DOI, BIA, Bureau of Publications, 1973; "Art History; Vol. I/II," IAIA, DOI, BIA BOP, 1974; "Major Influences, Contemporary Indian Art," IAIA, DOI, BOP, 1982.

DALRYMPLE, KATHRINE C.
(Western Cherokee) 1940-
(fashion designer)

Born January 30, 1940, Pryor, Oklahoma. *Education:* Oklahoma State University, B.A. (Education), 1961. *Principal occupation: Fashion designer (self-employed). Home address:* 917 N. Lexington, Arlington, Va. 22205. *Affiliations:* Associate Home Extension agent for the North Dakota State Extension Service and Standing Rock Sioux Tribe, and taught extension courses at graduate level for University of North Dakota, Grand Forks, 1961-1973; selected representative art objects from Native American artisans from all sections of the U.S., 1961-1973; co-owner, president, Friendship House, Inc. (gift shop specializing in Native American and American-made crafts), 1975-1977; design clothing for specialty shops, catered Native American food, 1977-1978; part-time volunteer coordinator, fashion consultant to executive director, American Indian Heritage Foundation, 1978-1980; owner, American Naturals (design and execute men and women's clothing, jewelry, and accessories based on traditional and contemporary Native American fashions. *Other professional posts:* Ran own catering and fashion design services, Navajo Reservation, 1961-1973; coordianted exhibits featuring her own fashions and jewelry, 1975-1977, Arlington, Va. *Community activities:* Taught crafts classes at various schools and youth clubs in the Washington D.C. area, as well as at the Smithsonian Institution, the Capitol Hill Club, and at a number of Embassies. *Memberships:* American Indian Society of Washington, D.C. *Awards, honors:* Epsilon Sigma Alpha's Outstanding Woman of the Year for Arizona in 1971; her fashions have received three First Prizes at the Gaithersburg, Maryland Exposition, 1973-1978; her fashions have been shown at the Congrssional Club, Capitol Hill Club, and the International Club of Washington, D.C.; her fashions have recently been worn at the Cherry Blossom Parade, Presidntial Inaugural Ball and Parade for Ronald Reagan, several White House teas, and Oklahoma Society Gala; In March, 1982, thirty-one of Mrs. Dalrymple's fashions were worn at the

John F. Kennedy Center for the Performing Arts during the "Night of the First Americans," an event held in celebration of the contributions of the American Indian people; special exhibition, organized by the Indian Arts and Crafts Board's Southern Plains Indian Museum and Crafts Center, the first comprehensive showing of Mrs. Dalrymple's fashions to be presented in the State of Oklahoma; she made the dress worn by the 1983 American Indian Society Princess; in 1976 and 1983, Kathy's work was featured in the *American Indian Society Cookbook*. *Interests:* Mrs. Dalrymple writes, "I feel so fortunate to have grown up among the many Native American cultures in Oklahoma, and especially to have known not only my grandparents, but four of my great grandparents and many of their friends as well. Seeing them create, from necessity, beautiful and useful articles for everyday use from whatever was available was the origin of my interest in the arts of the American Indian. As we have lived and worked in many areas of this great land, I've marveled at the resourcefulness and creativity of the people, and of the women, in particular. No matter how busy and difficult their lives have been, they have always managed to provide many and varied forms of useful, beautiful articles to enrich the lives of the people around them. Trading of ideas, supplies, and patterns as tribes came into contact with each other is greatly apparent. How each group adapted the trade goods brought by the Europeans is a unique and fascinating study of American history. I especially enjoy creating traditional clothing for pow-wow wear." *Works in Progress:* Currently writing a book detailing her family's experiences living on Indian reservations around the country.

DAMAS, DAVID 1926-
(anthropologist)

Born December 27, 1926, Algoma, Wis. *Education:* University of Toledo, B.A., 1950; University of Chicago, M.A., 1960, Ph.D., 1962. *Principal occupation:* Anthropologist. *Home address:* 2160 Lakeshore Rd., Apt. 1202, Burlington, Ontario, Can. *Affiliations:* Arctic ethnologist, National Museum of Canada, Ottawa, Ont., Canada; associate professor of anthropology, McMaster University, Hamilton, Ont., Canada. *Military service:* U.S. Marine Corps, 1945-1946. *Memberships:* American Anthropological Association; American Ethnological Society; Canadian Sociology and Anthropology Association; Northeastern Anthropological Association. *Interests:* Eskimo ethnology; social structure; cultural ecology. *Fieldwork:* Among the Igulik Eskimos, 1960-1961; Copper Eskimos, 1962-1963; Netsilik Eskimos, 1965; Netsilik and Ingulik Eskimos, 1967, 1968. *Published works: Igluligmiut Kinship and Local Grouping* (National Museum of Canada, 1963); *Band Societies* (National Museum of Canada, 1969); *Ecological Essays* (National Museum of Canada, 1969).

DANA, RALPH F. (Passamaquoddy)
(reservation governor)

Affiliation: Governor, Pleasant Point Passamaquoddy Reservation, P.O. Box 343, Perry, Maine 04667.

DARDEN, STEVEN
(executive director-Indian center)

Affiliation: Executive director, Flagstaff Indian Center, 15 N. San Francisco, P.O. Box 572, Flagstaff, Ariz. 86001.

DAUGHERTY, JOHN, Jr. (Shawnee-Delaware) 1948-
(health systems administrator)

Born August 9, 1948, Claremore, Okla. *Education:* Northeastern State University, Tahlequah, Okla., B.A. (Social Sciences), B.S. (Business), 1976; University of Minnesota, Minneapolis, 1984- (working toward advanced certificate in health administration). *Principal occupation:* Health systems administrator. *Home address:* 2237 Elmwood Lane, Miami, Okla. 74354. *Affiliation:* Executive director, Native American Coalition of Tulsa, 1978-1979; administrator, USPHS Miami Indian Health Center, Miami, Okla., 1979-. *Military service:* U.S. Air Force, 1969-1972 (in Madrid, Spain) (U.S.A.F. Commendation Medal for Meritorious Service). *Community activities:* Member, Rotary International; chairman, Title IV, Indian Education Parent Committee; officer, Native American Student Association at Northeast Oklahoma A&M Junior College and Northeastern Oklahoma State University, Tahlequah, 1973-1976. *Awards, honors:* Who's Who Among Students in American Universities and Colleges, 1976-1977; golf team; deans honor roll, 1976, NEOSU, Tahlequah; chosen by University of Minnesota Independent Study Program to give presentation on Indian Health in U.S. during International Health Night, July 17, 1985. *Interests:* "My educational and vocational interest is in health care administration. My goals are to better myself in these areas. Indian cultures and the presentation of my tribal ceremonies are of great concern to me. Participating in tribal activities of other tribes, as well as my tribe and encouraging others to participate are very important to me."

DAVIS, GEORGE
(B.I.A. agency superintendent)

Affiliation: Superintendent, Colville Agency, Bureau of Indian Affairs, P.O. Box 111-011, Nespelem, Wash. 99155.

DAVIS, ROBERT C. 1922-
(film producer, lecturer)

Born May 7, 1922, Kansas City, Mo. *Education:* High school. *Principal occupation:* Film producer, lecturer. *Home address:* P.O. Box 12, Cary, Ill. 60013. *Affiliations:* Self-employed. *Military service:* U.S. Signal Corps, 1942-1945. *Memberships:* Film Lecturer's Association, 1970-. *Awards, honors:* Amerian Film Festival Awards for *Arizona Revealed;* Columbus Film Festival Awards for seven other films. *Films produced: Land of the Crimsoned Cliffs,* 1955; *Arizona Utopia,* 1961; *Arizona Revealed,* 1964; *Arizona Adventure,* 1975; many 35mm and 2¼ x 2¼ color transparencies of Navajo, Pima and Hopi Indians.

DAVIS, ROSE-MARIE
(president-Indian community college)

Affiliation: President, Little Hoop Community College, P.O. Box 147, Fort Totten, N.D. 58335.

DAYLEY, JON P. 1944-
(professor of linguistics)

Born October 8, 1944, Salt Lake City, Utah. *Education:* Idaho State University, B.A., 1968, M.A., 1970; University of California, Berkeley, M.A., 1973, Ph.D., 1981. *Principal occupation:* Professor of linguistics. *Home address:* 5953 Eastwood Place, Boise, Idaho 83712. *Affiliations:* Visiting lecturer in linguistics, University of California, Berkeley, 1982; assistant professor of linguistics, Boise State University, 1982-. *Other professional posts:* Linguista - Projecto Linguistico Francisco Marroquin, Guatemala, 1973-1978; writer, resercher, Experiment in International Living, Brattleboro, Vt., 1978-1979. *Memberships:* Linguistic Society of Amcrica; Society of Mayanists; Berkeley Linguistics Society; National Association for Foreign Student Affairs; Guatemalan Scholars Network. *Interests:* American Indian languages: Mayan language—Tzutujil Maya, Uto-Aztecon languages—Shoshone; Creole languages; general linguistics. *Published works: Tzutujil Grammar* (University of California Prss, 1985); *Belizean Creaole Handbook,* Vols. I-IV (Experiment in International Living, U.S. Peace Corps, 1979); and many articles on Mayan languages, shoshone and general linguistics.

DeBOER, ROY J. (Lummi) 1936-
(school principal)

Born July 23, 1936, Bellingham, Wash. *Education:* Olympic Junior College, Bremerton, Wash., A.A., 1960; Western Washington State University, Bellingham, B.A., 1962; University of Puget Sound, Tacoma, Wash., M.Ed., 1981. *Principal occupation:* School principal. *Home address:* 3528 S.E. Pine Tree Dr., Port Orchard, Wash. 98366. *Affiliations:* Director of Indian Education, South Kitsap School District, Port Orchard, Wash., 1973-1980; principal, Wolfe Elementary School, Kingston, Wash., 1981-. *Other professional posts:* Seven years on Washington State Advisory Committee, Indian Education to Washington State Supervisor of Schools. *Military service:* U.S. Air Force, 1954-1958 (A 1/C). *Community activities:* Pacific Lutheran Theological Seminary (board of directors); Division of Service and Mission in America, American Lutheran Church (board of dirctors); Chamber of Comerce, Kingston, Wash.; Sons of Norway, Poulsbo, Wash.. *Memberships:* National Education Association; Washington Education Asscoiation; ASCD; ESPA. *Awards, honors:* Outstanding Secondary Teacher of America, 1973; Quill and Scroll Adult Leadership Award, 1969. *Interests:* Reading, travel, photography; singing with Twana Dancers, Skokomish traditional dance group.

DEER, ADA E. (Menominee) 1935-
(social worker)

Born August 7, 1935, Keshena, Wis. *Education:* University of Wisconsin, Madison, B.A., 1957; Columbia University, School of Social Work, M.S.W., 1961. *Principal occupation:* Social worker. *Home address:* 5689 Lincoln Rd., Oregon, Wisc. *Business address:* Native Americn Studies Program, University of Wisconsin, 1188 Educational Sciences Bldg., 1025 W. Johnson St., Madison, Wis. 53706. *Affiliations:* Lecturer, School of Social Work and Native American Studies Program, University of Wisconsin, 1977-. *Other profesional posts:* Chairperson, Menominee Restoration Committee, 1973-1976; vice president and Washington lobbyist, National Committee to Save the Menominee People and Forest, Inc., 1972-1973; chairperson, Menominee Common Stock and Voting Trust, 1971-1973. *Community activities:* American Indian Policy Review Commission (member, 1975-1977). *Memberships:* National Association of Social Workers; National Organization of Women; Common Cause; Girl Scouts of America; Democratic Party of Wisconsin; National Congress of American Indians. *Awards, honors:* Doctor of Humane Letters, University of Wisconsin, 1974; Doctor of Public

Service, Northland College, Ashland, Wisc., 1974; White Buffalo Council Achievement Award, Denver, Colo., 1974; Pollitzer Award, Ethical Cultural Society, N.Y., 1975; Fellow, Harvard Institute of Politics, 1977. *Interests:* Social work; community organization and social action; minority rights. *Biographical sources: I Am the Fire of Time,* Jane B. Katz, editor (E.P. Dutton, 1977); *Ms Magazine,* April, 1973; *Indians of Today,* 4th Edition; *The Circle,* Dec. 1977.

DeGROAT, ELLOUISE (Navajo) 1939-
(social worker)

Born May 12, 1939, Tuba City, Ariz. *Education:* Arizona State University, B.S., 1962, M.S.W., 1966. *Principal occupation:* Social worker. *Home address:* P.O. Box 521, Fort Defiance (Navajo Nation), Ariz. 86504. *Affiliation:* Social worker, Tribal Affairs Officer, Window Rock, Ariz., 1976-. *Other professional posts:* Consultant, American Child Psychiatry (Committee on Indian Affairs) and the Indian Task Force on Mental Health. *Community activities:* St. Michaels Special Education Association (member); instrumental in staging the First Annual Navajo Health Symposium; involvement with education of Indian children and special concern for the handicapped. *Memberships:* American Indian Health Association; National Association of Social Workers; National Conference of Social Workers (national board member, 1972-1974). *Awards, honors:* DFisquisition Service Award, The Navajo Tribe, 2nd Annual Navajo Helth Symposium. *Interests:* Tribal government; national legislation for Indian tribes; advocate for Indian causes, especially health; American Indian woman; served on the Policy Committee on the Indian Policy Statement on national health insurance. *Published work: Navajo Medicine Man* (Psychiatric Annuals, 1974).

DeHOSE, JUDY
(chairperson-Indian school)

Affiliation: Chairperson, Cibecue Community School, Cibecue, Ariz. 85911.

DELACRUZ, JOSEPH (Quinault)
(president-tribal committee)

Afiliation: President, Quinault Business Committee, P.O. Box 189, Taholah, Wash. 98587.

DeLAGUNA, FREDERICA 1906-
(anthropologist, professor emeritus)

Born October 3, 1906, Ann Arbor, Mich. *Education:* Bryn Mawr College, B.A., 1927; Columbia University, Ph.D., 1933. *Principal occupation:* Anthropologist. *Home address:* 221 Roberts Rd., Bryn Mawr, Penna. 19010. *Affiliation:* Professor of anthropology, Brun Mawr College, 1938-1975. *Other professional posts: Visiting professor, University of Pennsylvania; visiting profesor, Univerity of California, Berkeley. Military service:* U.S. Naval Reserve, 1942-1945 (Lt. Commander). *Memberships.* American Anthropological Association (past president); American Ethnological Society; Society for American Archaeology; Society for Pennsylvania Archaeology; Philadelphia Anthropological Society; Arctic Institute of North America; National Academy of Sciences. *Awards, honors:* Postdoctoral fellowships: National Research Council, Viking Fund (Wenner-Gren Foundation), Rockefeller Post-War Fellowship. *Interests:* "Archaeological and ethnological field work among Eskimos (Greenland and Alaska), Indians (Tlingit, Alaskam Athabascans); archaeological work in northern Arizona. Expeditions to Alaska, 1930-1968, Greenland, 1929; to Arizona, 1941. Have tape-recorded and enjoy Indian music." *Biographical sources: American Men of Science; Who's Who in America; International Biography: World Who's Who. Published works: The Archaeology of Cook Inlet, Alaska* (University of Pennsylvania Press, 1934); *The Prehistory of Northern North America* (Society for American Archaeology, 1947); *The Eyak Indians of the Copper River Delta, Alaska,* with Kaj Birket-Smith; *Chugach Prehistory: The Archaeology of Prince William Sound* (University of Washington Press, 1956, 1960); *The Story of a Tlingit Community* (Bureau of American Ethnology, 1960); *Archaelogy of the Yakutat Bay Area, Alaska,* with Riddell, McGeein, Lane,

Freed, Osborne (Bureau of Amerian Ethnology, 1964); *Under Mount St. Elias: The History and Culture of the Yakutat Tlingit* (Smithsonian, 1972); *Voyage to Greenland: A Personal Initiation Into Anthropology* (W.W. Norton, 1977).

DELAWARE, ROBERT
(B.I.A. job placement)

Affiliation: Job Placement, Bureau of Indian Affairs, 1951 Constitution Ave., N.W., Washington, D.C. 20245.

DELORIA, P.S.
(director-Indian law center)

Affiliation: Director, American Indian Law Center, Univerity of New Mexico, School of Law, P.O. Box 4456, Station A, 1117 Stanford, N.E., Albuquerque, N.M. 87196.

DELORIA, VINE, Jr. (Standing Rock Sioux) 1933-
(writer, professor)

Born March 26, 1933, Martin, S.D. *Education:* Iowa State University, B.S., 1958; Lutheran School of Theology, M. Sac. Theo., 1963; University of Colorado, School of Law, J.D., 1970. *Principal occupation: Writer, professor. Address:* Department of Political Science, University of Arizona, Tucson, Arizona 85721. *Affiliation:* Welder, McLaughlin Body Company, Moline, Illinois, 1959-1963; staff associate, United Scholarship Service, Denver, Colorado, 1963-1964; executive director, National Congress of American Indians, Washington, D.C., 1964-1967; consultant on programs, National Congress of American Indians, FUND, Denver, Colorado, 1968; lecturer, College of Ethnic Studies, Western Washington State College, Bellingham, Washington, 1970-1972; lecturer, American Indian Cultural and Research Center, UCLA, Los Angeles, California, 1972-1973; executive director, Southwest Intergroup Council, Denver, Colorado, 1972; special counsel, Native American Rights Fund, Boulder, Colorado, summer-1972; script writer (Indian series), KRMA-TV, Denver, Colorado, 1972-1973; American Indian

Resource Associates, Oglala, South Dakota, 1973-1974; American Indian Resource Consultants, Denver, Colorado, 1974-1975. visiting lecturer, Pacific School of Religion, Berkeley, California, summer, 1975; visiting lecturer, New School of Religion, Pontiac, Michigan, summer, 1976; visiting lecturer, Colorado College, Colorado Springs, Colorado, 1977-1978; professor, University of Arizona, Tucson, Arizona, 1978-. *Military Service:* U.S. Marine Corps Reserve, San Diego, Calif. and Quantico, Va., 1954-1956. *Organizational Memberships:* White Buffalo Council, Denver, Colo. (board of directors, 1964-1966); Citizens Crusade Against Poverty, Washington, D.C. (board of directors, 1965-1966); Council on Indian Affairs, Washington, D.C. (vice-chairman, 1965-1968); Board of Inquiry Into Hunger and Malnutrition in the U.S.A., New York, N.Y., 1967-1968; National Office for the Rights of the Indigent, New York, N.Y. (board of directors, 1967-1968); Ad-Hoc Committee on Indian Work, Episcopal Church, New York, N.Y. (chairman, 1968-1969); Executive Council of the Protestant Episcopal Church, New York, N.Y., 1968-1969; Southwest Intergroup Council, Austin, Texas (board of directors, 1969-1971); Institute for the Development of Indian Law, Washington, D.C. (chairman and founder, 1971-1976); Model Urban Indian Centers Project, San Francisco, Calif. (board of directors, 1971-1973); Oglala Sioux Legal Rights Foundation, Pine Ridge, S.D. (board of directors, 1971); National Friends of Public Broadcasting, New York, N.Y., 1971-1976; Colorado Humanities Program, Boulder, Colo., 1975-1977; National Indian Youth Council, Albuquerque, N.M. (advisory council, 1976); American Civil Liberties Union, Denver, Colo. (Indian committee, 1976-1978); The Center for Land Grant Studies, Santa Fe, N.M., 1976; American Lutheran Church, Minneapolis, Minnesota (consultant, 1976-1978); Nebraska Educational Television Network, Lincoln, Neb. (advisory council, American Indian Series, 1976-1978); Denver Public Library Foundation, Denver, Colo. (board of directors, 1977-1978); Museum of the American Indian, New York, N.Y. (board of trustees, 1977-1982); American Indian Development, Inc., Bellingham, Washington, 1978-1981; Day-

break Films, Denver, Colo. (board of directors, 1979-1981); Field Foundation, New York, N.Y. (board of directors, 1980); Indian Rights Association, Philadelphia, Pa. (board of directors, 1980); Institute of the American West, Sun Valley, Idaho (national advisory council, 1981-1983); Disability Rights & Education Defense Fund, Berkeley, Calif. (advisory council, 1981); Save the Children Federation, Westport, Conn. (national advisory council, 1983). *Professional Memberships:* American Judicature Society, 1970-; Colorado Authors League, 1970-. *Editorial Boards and Contributing Editorships:* American Indian Historical Society, San Francisco, Calif. (editorial board, 1971-1972); *Handbook of North American Indians, Smithsonian Institution, Washington, D.C. (planning committee, 1971-1972); The World of the American Indian,* (National Geographic Society, 1972-1976); Clearwater Press (consultant, advisory board, 1972-1978); *American Indian Cultural and Research Center Journal,* UCLA (editorial board, 1972); Race Relations Information Center (contributing editor, 1974-1975); *Integrateducation,* University of Massachusetts, Amherst, Mass. (editorial advisory board, 1975); *American Heritage Dictionary of the English Language,* Houghton-Mifflin (usage panel, 1976-1983); *Explorations in Ethnic Studies,* (LaCrosse, Wis., 1977-); *Katallagete,* Berea, Ky. (editorial board, 1977); *The Historical Magazine of the Episcopal Church,* Austin, Texas (editorial board, 1977); *The Colorado Magazine,* Colorado Historical Society, Denver, Colo. (editorial review board, 1979); *National Forum,* Phi Kappa Phi, Johnson City, Tenn. (contributing editor, 1979); *Studies in American Indian Literature,* Columbia University, New York, N.Y. (advisory board, 1981); *Adherent Forum,* New York, N.Y. (contributing editor, 1981). *Special Activities:* White House Conference on Youth (delegate, 1970); Avco-Embassy Pictures on movie *Soldier Blue* (consultant, 1970); Educational Challenges, Inc., Washington, D.C. (consultant, 1971-1972); Senate Committee on Aging, Washington, D.C. (consultant, 1971-1972); Served as expert witness in four trials involving the occupation of Wounded Knee and aftermath as expert on 1868 Fort Laramie treaty and Sioux history (1974); Project 76, National Council of Churches (sponsor, 1974-1976); Served as appointed counsel in "Consolidated Wounded Knee Cases," treaty hearing in federal court (1975); Colorado Centennial-Bicentennial Commission (commissioner, 1975-1977); EVIST, National Science Foundation (advisory board, 1975-1978); Robert F. Kennedy Journalsim Awards (judge, 1975); Sun Valley Center for the Arts and Humanities, Sun Valley, Idaho (advisory council, 1976-1978, 1980-1983); *Handbook of North American Indians,* Volume Two, "Indians in Contemporary Society," Smithsonian Institution (editor, 1978-); American Indian Studies Program, University of Arizona (chairman, 1978-1981). *Special Honors and Awards:* Anisfield Wolf Award, 1970, for *Custer Died for Your Sins;* Special Citation, 1971, National Conference of Christians and Jews, for *We Talk, You Listen;* Honorary Doctor of Humane Letters, 1972, Augustana College; Indian Achievement Award, 1972, Indian Council Fire, Chicago; Named one of eleven "Theological Superstars of the Future," 1974, by Interchurch Features, New York, N.Y.; Honorary Doctor of Letters, 1976, Scholastica College, Duluth, Minn.; Distinguished Alumni Award, 1977, Iowa State University; Honorary Professor, 1977, Athabasca University, Edmonton, Can.; Honorary Doctor of Human Letters, 1979, Hamline University, St. Paul, Minn. *Published works:* Books: *Custer Died For Your Sins* (Macmillan, 1969); *We Talk, You Listen* (Macmillan, 1970); *Of Utmost Good Faith* (Straight Arrow, 1971); *Red Man in the New World Drama,* edited and revised (Macmillan, 1972); *God Is Red* (Grosset and Dunlap, 1973); *Behind the Trail of Broken Treaties* (Delacourte, 1974); *The Indian Affair* (Friendship Press, 1974); *Indians of the Pacific Northwest* (Doubleday, 1977); *The Metaphysics of Modern Existence* (Harper & Row, 1979); *American Indians, American Justice,* with Clifford Lytle (University of Texas Press, 1983); *A Sender of Words,* editor-The Neihardt Centenial Essays (Howe Brothers, 1984); *The Nations Within,* with Clifford Lytle (Pantheon Books, 1984); *The Aggressions of Civilization,* edited with Sandra Cadwalader (Temple University Press, 1984); *American Indian Policy in the Twentieth Century,* edi-

tor (University of Oklahoma Press, 1985). *Special Reports:* "The Lummi Indians," — Center for the Study of Man, Smithsonian Institution, 1972; "Legal Problems and Considerations Involved in the Treaty of 1868," prepared for the John Hay Whitney Foundation, 1974; "Indian Education Confronts the Seventies," editor and contributor, five volumes, Ofice of Indian Education, 1974; "Contemporary Issues of American Indians, A Model Course," prepared for the National Indian Education Association, 1975; "Legislative Analysis of the Federal Role in Indian Education," Office of Indian Education, 1975; "A Better Day for Indians," issued by the Field Foundation, 1977. Also, articles as contributing editor, editorials, and introductions to books—too numerous to mention.

De MAIN, PAUL (White Earth Chippewa) 1955-
(advisor on Indian affairs policy)

Born October 8, 1955, Hayward, Wis. *Education:* University of Wisconsin, Eau Claire, 1975-1977. *Principal occupation:* Advisor on Indian affairs policy. *Home address:* Route 5, Box 5346, Hayward, Wis. 54843. *Affiliations:* Assistant manager and manager, Lac Courte Oreilles Graphic Arts, Inc., 1979-1980; acting director, Great Lakes Indian News Association, 1980-1982; self determination information officer, Lac Courte Oreilles Tribal Government, 1981-1982; managing editor, *Lac Courte Oreilles Journal,* Hayward, Wisc., 1977-1982; owner/manager, Great Lakes Indian News Bureau, Hayward, Wisc., 1981-1982; sectretary, Native Horizons, Inc., 1983-; advisor on Indian affairs policy to Governor Anthony S. Earl, State of Wiscosnin, 1983-. *Community activities:* Governor's representative, State Council on Alcohol and Other Drug Abuse; lay counselor, Lac Courte Oreilles Tribal Court; board member, Lac Courte Oreilles Honor the Earth Education Foundation; faculty, Lac Courte Oreilles Community College; board of directors, Wisconsin Rural Leadership Conference; representative, Governor's Council on Minority Business Development; planning committee, National Indian Media Conference; chairman, Sawyer County Democratic

Party, 1982; advisory board, Center for Mining Alternatives; member, Northwestern Wisconsin Mining Impact Committee; member, Governor's Study Committee on Equal Rights, 1977. *Memberships:* National Congress of American Indians (conference planning committee, 1983). *Interests:* "As advisor on Indian affairs, I currently have the prime responsibility of liaison between the Governor's Office, 11 federally recognized tribes and urban Indian communities. In addition, development of policy, recommendations on state services, legislation, communications outreach and advisory services to Indian and non-Indian organizations is provided. In this capacity, I am consistently in contact with lobbyists, legislators and state agency program directors as well as making presentations to state personnel and public audiences."

DEMPSEY, HUGH A. 1929-
(historian)

Born November 7, 1929, Edgerton, Alberta, Can. *Principal occupation:* Historian. *Home address:* 95 Holmwood Ave., N.W., Calgary, Alberta, Can. *Affiliations:* Reporter, Edmonton *Bulletin;* Publicity Bureau, Province of Alberta, Canada; Glenbow Alberta Institute, Calgary, Alberta (archivist, 1956-1967; technical director, 1967-1970; director of history, 1970-1978; chief curator, 1978-). *Other professional posts:* Editor, *Alberta History,* 1958-; editor, *Canadian Archivist,* 1963-1966; editor, *Glenbow,* 1968-1974; Canadian editor, *Montana Magazine of History;* editorial board, Royal Canadian Geographical Society; contributing editor, *American West. Community activities:* Alberta Indian Treaties Comemeorative Program, 1976-1978; Alberta Heritage Learning Resources Advisory Committee, 1978-. *Memberships:* Historical Society of Alberta (executive committee, 1953; vice president, 1955-1956; president, 1956-1957); Canadian Historical Association (chairman, archives section, 1961-1962); Indian Association of Alberta (secretary, 1959-1964; advisory board, 1959-1968); Canadian Museums Association (executive committee, 1968-1970); Indian - Eskimo Association of Canada (executive committee, 1960-1965); International Coun-

cil of Museums (Canadian committee, 1968-1971). *Awards, honors:* Alberta Historian of the Year, 1962; honorary doctorate, University of Calgary, 1974; Order of Canada, 1975; Alberta Achievement Award, 1974-1975; honorary chief, Blood Tribe, 1967; winner of Alberta Non-Fiction Award, 1975. *Published works: Crowfoot, Chief of the Blackfeet* (University of Oklahoma Press, 1972). Monographs: *A Blackfoot Winter Count,* 1966; *Tailfeathers, Indian Artist,* 1970; *Blackfoot Ghost Dance,* 1968; *Indian Names for Alberta Communities, 1969.*

DENTON, COYE ELIZABETH
(Cherokee) 1914-
(artist)

Born October 14, 1914, Romulus, Okla. *Education:* East Central State College, B.S., M.A., 1969. *Principal occupation:* Artist. *Home address:* Box 444, Ada, Okla. 74820. *Community activities:* Fornightly Tamti (past president); Tanlettes; Wednesday morning music, Salvation Army Auxiliary; Great Books Organization; Salvation Army (advisory board). *Memberships:* Ada Artists Association, 1958- (vice president); Salvation Army (advisory board, 1955-); League of Women Voters; First United Methodist Church. *Interests:* "Human, ecological and environmental resources — esthetic and active;" travel. *Biographical sources: Who's Who of American Women; American Indian Painters.*

DESJARLAIT, PATRICK ROBERT
(Chippewa) 1921-
(commercial artist)

Born March 1, 1921, Red Lake, Minn. *Principal occupation:* Commercial artist. *Home address:* 7641 62nd Ave., N., New Hope, Minn. 55428. *Military service:* U.S. Navy, 1941-1945 — visual education training, slide films, animation, training films. *Memberships:* Minneapolis Art Directors Club. *Awards, honors:* First Prize, Philbrook Art Center, Tulsa, Okla., 1946; First Prize, Elkus Memorial Award, Inter-Tribal Indian Ceremonial, Gallup, N.M., 1964; Second Award, Scottsdale National Indian Arts

Exhibition, 1964. *One-man shows and exhibitions:* Fine Arts Gallery, San Diego, Calif., 1945; St. Paul Art Gallery, 1946; Gallery of American Indian Art, U.S. Dept. of the Interior, Washington, D.C.

DI MAIO, SUE (Pocahantus) 1920-
(owner-trading post)

Born July 6, 1920, Houston, Tex. *Education:* University of Redlands, A.B., Scripps College, Pomona, Calif. (one year-Arts); University of Southern California, M.A., 1977. *Principal occupation:* Owner, Capistrano Trading Post, 31741 Camino Capistrano, San Juan Capistrano, Calif., 1943-. *Home address:* P.O. Box 2142, Capistrano Beach, Calif. 92672. *Memberships:* Indian Arts & Crafts Association (charter member); Southwest Association on Indian Affairs; Hear Museum; Museum of Natural History, Los Angeles. *Awards, honors:* Bronze plaque erected bearing Ms. Di Maio's name for meritorious fund raising for the Navajo Tribal Museum, Window Rock, N.M. *Biographical sources:* Articles in 1973, 1974, *Western Financial Journal* (success story about Indian crafts and follow up story); nine articles published in series by *Indian Trader Paper,* 1974. *Published works:* 1975 Orange County illustrative article about the Hopi; *Blue Gold,* series of nine articles related to Indian crafts (Main St. Press, 1976).

DI PESO, CHARLES C. 1920-
(archaeologist, foundation
and museum director)

Born October 20 1920, St. Louis, Mo. *Education:* Beloit College, B.S. (Anthropology and Geology, 1942); American Institute of Foreign Trade, B.F.T., 1947; University of Arizona, M.A., 1950, Ph.D., 1952. *Principal occupation:* Archaeologist, foundation and museum director. *Address:* The Amerind Foundation, Inc., P.O. Box 248, Dragoon, Ariz. 85609. *Affiliations:* Director, The Amerind Foundation, Inc. *Other professional posts:* Arizona Historical Advisory Commission, 1967-; consultant, Texas Tech University, 1968-; Arizona Landmarks Commission, 1971- (chairman, 1971-1975);

Arizona Commission for State Parks, 1966-; *American Indian Quarterly* (editor, advisory board, 1974-); consultant Educational Expeditions International, television series, 1974-; advisory council, Cochise Chapter, National Society of Arts and Letters, 1972-; board of directors, Sulphur Springs Valley Historical Society, 1974-; editor and advisory board, *American Indian Art Magazine,* 1975-; advisory board, Arizona Historical Records, 1976-1979 (Governor appointed term); board of directors, Arizona Historical Society, 1976-. *Community activities:* Cochise College (board of governors, 1962-; chairman, 1966-1968, 1975-1976; secretary, 1965-1966, 1974-1975); Tucson Art Center (board of directors, 1972-1976); The Explorers Club (Fellow, 1969-). *Memberships:* Society for American Archaeology (Fellow, 1960-; executive committee, 1970-1971; president-elect, 1971-1972; president, 1972-1973); American Anthropological Association (Fellow, 1962-; nominating committee, 1976-1977); American Association for the Advancement of Science (Fellow, 1960-); Society for Historical Archaeology, 1967-; Arizona Academy of Sciences, 1972-; Southwestern Anthropological Association; Amerian Society for Ethnohistory; The American Association pf Museums; Western History Association, 1964-; Association of Borderline Scholars, 1976-; Southwestern Archaeological Research Group; Latin American Studies Association, 1966-; Institue of Andean Research, 1965-; International Congress of Americanists; Pimeria Alta Historical Society; Cochise County Historical and Archaeological Society (Honorary). *Military service:* U.S. Air Force, 1942-1946 (1st Lt., Pilot). *Awards, honors:* Alfred Vincent Kidder Award, for achievement in American archaeology, American Anthropological Association, 1959; Beloit College, Dr.S., 1970. *Interests:* "Anthropology, archaeology, and ethnohistory of the American Southwest and northern Mexico. Excavation of prehistoric ruins and study of prehistoric man in the New World in an attempt to recreate the history of this area as lived by the Chichimecans. The study of frontier urban areas in regard to donor and recipient cultures and the mechanisms of urbanization in arid lands. *Expeditions:* Principal director, Joint Casas Grandes Expedition, northwestern Chihuahua, Mexico. *Biographical sources: Who's Who in the U.S.; Who's Who Honorary Society of America; Who's Who in the West; American Men and Women of Science; Dictionary of International Biography.* Published works: *The Babaocomari Village Site on the Babocomari River, Southeastern Arizona,* 1951; *The Sobaipuri Indians of the Upper San Pedro Valley, Southeastern Arizona,* 1953; *The Upper Pima of San Cayetano del Tumacacori,* 1956; The Reeve Ruin of Southeastern Arizona, 1958; *Casas Grandes: A Fallen Trading Center of the Gran Chichimeca,* 1974. All published by Amerind Foundation, Inc. Publications.

DIXON, LAWRENCE DWYER (Sioux) 1916-
(director of Indian center)

Born April 14, 1916, Pine Ridge, S.D. *Education:* Pine Ridge Indian School, 1936-1939. *Principal occupation:* Director of Indian center. *Home address:* 6312 Linden Lane, Bremerton, Wash. 98310. *Affiliations:* Director, Kitsap County Indian Center, NW Byron St., Silverdale, Wash., 1975-. *Other professional posts:* Publicity chairman, Off-Reservation Indians Board, 1974-1975; CETA Consortium Board of Small Indian Tribes of Western Washington. *Community activities:* Executive committee, Kitsap County Overall Economic Development Program; Indian child welfare advisory committee, Department of Social/Health Services, State Level, 1977-1979. *Awards, honors:* Washington Central Kitsap School District Recognition Award, 1983; Washington State DSHS Certificate of Appreciation, 1982; CKHS and Bremerton Kiwanis Air Fair Society; Meritorious Performance, 1976; Superior Achievement from Commanding Officer, USS Pueblo, 1967; National Indian Management, 1980; outside Volunteer Award, 1984; Washington State Jefferson Award, 1984. *Interests:* Indian self-determination; Indian program administration, fundraising; Indian program development, publicity; public relations, recruitment, training and supervision; policy making. *Published works: Are You Listening Neighbor? and the People Speak, Will You Listen?* (State of Washington, 1978).

DIXON, PATRICIA A. (Pauma)
(tribal council chairwoman)

Affiliation: Chairwoman, Pauma Tribal Council, P.O. Box 86, Pauma Valley, Calif. 92061.

DOBYNS, HENRY F. 1925-
(consultant, director-Indian project)

Born July 3, 1925, Tucson, Ariz. *Education:* University of Arizona, B.A., 1949, M.A., 1956; Cornell University, Ph.D., 1960. *Principal occupation:* Consultant, director Indian project. *Home address:* 1943 West North Lane No. 9, Phoenix, Ariz. 85021. *Affiliations:* Research associate, Cornell University, 1960-1966; professor, University of Kentucky, 1966-1970; professor, Prescott College, Ariz., 1970-1973; visiting professor, University of Wisconsin, Parkside, 1974-1975; visiting professor, University of Florida, 1977-1979; director, Native American Historical Demography Project, D'Arcy McNickle Center for the History of the American Indian, The Newberry Library, Chicago, Ill., 1979-. *Military service:* U.S. Army, 1943. *Memberships:* American Association for the Advancement of Science (Fellow); American Anthropological Association; American Society for Ethnohistory (former president). *Awards, honors:* Shared Anisfield-Wolff Award, 1968; Malinowski Award, Society for Applied Anthropology, 1952. *Published works: The Apache People (Coyotero)* (Indian Tribal Series, 1971); *The Papago People* (Indian Tribal Series, 1972); *The Mescalero Apache People* (Indian Tribal Series, 1973); *Prehistoric Indian Occupation Within the Eastern Area of the Yuman Complex: A Study in Applied Archaeology* (Garland, 1974); *Spanish Colonial Tucson* (University of Arizona Press, 1976); *Native American Historical Demography* (Indiana University Press, 1976); *From Fire to Flood* (Ballena Press, 1981); *"Their Number Become Thinned"* (University of Tennessee Press, 1983).

DOCKSTADER, FREDERICK J. 1919-
(museum consultant)

Born February 3, 1919, Los Angeles, Calif. *Education:* Arizona State College, B.A.,

M.A.: Western Reserve University, Ph.D., 1951. *Principal occupation:* Museum consultant. *Home address:* 165 West 66 St., New York, N.Y. 10023. *Affiliations:* Teacher, Flagstaff, Arizona schools, 1942-1950; staff ethnologist, Cranbrook Institute of Sciences, 1950-1952; faculty member and curator of anthropology, Dartmouth College, 1952-1955; assistant director, director, Museum of the American Indian, Heye Foundation, 1955-1975. *Other professional posts:* Advisory editor, *Encyclopedia Americana,* 1957-

Indian Arts and Crafts Board (commissioner, 1955-1964; chairman, 1964-1967); visiting professor of art and archaeology, Columbia University, 1961-; member, New York State Museum Advisory Council; trustee, Huntington Free Library, Futures for Children Foundation. *Memberships:* American Association for the Advancement of Science (Fellow); Cranbrook Institute of Sciences (Fellow); American Anthropological Association (Fellow); Society for American Archaeology; New York Academy of Sciences; Cosmos Club; Century Club. *Awards, honors:* First Prize (silversmithing), Cleveland Museum of Art, 1950; Fellow, Rochester Museum of Arts and Sciences. *Biographical sources: Who's Who in America; Who's Who in Art; American Men of Science; Who's Who in the East; American Indian Authors; Who's Who in the World. Published works: The Kachina and the White Man* (Cranbrook Institute of Sciences, 1954); *The American Indian in Graduate Studies* (Museum of the American Indian, 1957, revised in two volumes, 1974); *Indian Art in America* (New York Graphic Society, 1960); *Indian Art in Middle America* (New York Graphic Society, 1964); *Indian Art in South America* (Ne York Graphic Society, 1966); *Pre-Columbian and Later Tribal Arts* (Abrams, 1968); *Indian Art of the Americas* (New York, 1973); *Great North American Indians: Profiles of Life & Leadership* (New York, 1977); *Weaving Arts of the North American Indian,* 1978.

DODGE, DONALD (Navajo 1929-
(B.I.A. area director)

Born July 15, 1929, Crystal, N.M. *Education:* Albuquerque Indian School (high school); University of New Mexico. *Principal occupation:* B.I.A. area director. *Home address:* P.O. Box 114, Window Rock, Ariz. 86515. *Affiliation:* Director, Navajo Tribe's Public Service Division, 1969-1970; superintendent, B.I.A., Fort Defiance Agency, Ariz., 1972-1976; director, B.I.A., Navajo Area Office, Window Rock, Ariz., 1977-. *Military service:* U.S. Army - Korean War. *Awards, honors:* Grandson of famous Navajo leader, Chee Dodge, first chairman of Navajo Tribal Council. *Interests:* Mr. Dodge sees the Bureau's relationship to the Tribe as "government-to-government." "We have our government structure and the Tribe has its structure. We need to get together and compare the two and see where the relationship can be improved. Most of our programs are contractable except those involving areas of trust responsibility." Mr. Dodge concludes, "My main objective is to get a good organization going, one that can coordinate and communicate with the Tribe, so that the best interests of the individual will be served."

DODGE, GARY
(public information officer)

Affiliation: Public Information Officer, Lac du Flambeau Tribe, Lac du Flambeau, Wis. 54843.

DODGE, HENRY
(B.I.A. agency superintendent)

Affiliation: Superintendent, Fort Apache Agency, Bureau of Indian Affairs, Whiteriver, Ariz. 85941.

DODGE, MARJORIE T. (Navajo) 1941-
(school administrator)

Born June 5, 1941, Crownpoint, N.M. *Education:* Western New Mexico University, B.A., 1964; Northern Arizona University, M.A., 1970; University of Montana, Certificate for E.S.O.L., summer, 1967; University of Southern California, Certficate for Adult Leadership, summer, 1969; New Mexico State University, Education Specialist - School Administration, 1971-1972. *Principal occupation:* School administrator.

Home address: P.O. Box 717, Shiprock, N.M. 87420. *Affiliations:* Teacher, Crystal Boarding School, Navajo, N.M. (five years); student teacher supervisor, Chuska/Tohatchie Schools, N.A.U. 4th Cycle National Teacher Corps Program, Navajo Reservation (two years); teacher, first grade, Hunter's Point School, St. Michaels, Ariz., (one year); vice principal, Mesa Elementary School, Independent School District #22 (three years); administrative education specialist, B.I.A., Shiprock Agency, Crownpoint, N.M., 1977-. *Other professional post:* Represent San Juan and McKinley County on Governor's Council on Manpower. *Community activity:* Council of Citizens for San Juan County, N.M. (member). *Memberships:* Ding Be Olta Association; Navajo Education Association; National Indian Education Association; American Association for the Advancement of Science; San Juan Business & Professional Women Association. *Awards, honors;* Ten years B.I.A. Service Award & Letter of Commendation for Superior Performance. *Interests:* "My interest is in the education of the Indian children." *Biographical source:* Biography published in 1973 in the "Arizona Historical Society," Western Publishing Co. *Published work:* "Value Teachings in the Classroom," *Journal of American Indian Education,* Jan. 1972.

DOERFORT, HANS M. 1923-
(Indian education)

Born January 9, 1923, Germany. *Education:* University of Rochester, 1947-1949; University of Washington, A.B., 1951; Boston University, Ed.M., 1956. *Principal occupation:* Indian education. *Home address:* 1104 Rio Brazos Rd., Aztec, N.M. 87410. *Affiliation:* Principal, B.I.A., Aztec Dormitory, Aztec, N.M., 1954-. *Military service:* U.S. Air Force, 1943-1946 (Sergeant). *Community activities:* Kiwanis Club of Aztec (president, 1960); Aztec Chamber of Commerce (president, 1971-1973); San Juan Symphony League (president, 1972-1974); Aztec Museum Association (president, 1975-1976).

DOERING, MAVIS (Cherokee) 1929-
(basketweaving artist)

Born August 31, 1929, Hominy, Okla. *Education:* San Jose State University, 1946; Sacramento City College, 1968. *Principal occupation:* Basketweaving artist. *Home address:* 5918 N.W. 58th St., Oklahoma City, Okla. 73122. *Affiliations:* Consultant (Title IV, Indian pupil education), Putnam City School District, Warr Acres, Okla., 1977-1981; cultural consultant, Indian Student Association, University of Oklahoma, Norman, 1981-; consultant, United National Indian Tribal Youth Organization, 1979-. *Other professional posts:* Basketweaving instructor, Lone Grove School District, Western Heights School District, Deer Creek School District, Oklahoma Baptist University for Upward Bound students, Oklahoma Museum of Art, Willard Art Center, St. John's Methodist Church, the Native American Center of Oklahoma City (elderly program), American Indian Institute of the University of Oklahoma, and Cowboy Hall of Fame, 1977-1984. *Community activities:* Advisory board, Oklahoma Indian Artists and Craftsmen Guild; member, Advisory Arts Council, Native American Center of Oklahoma City; member, National Advisory Council, Wheelwright Museum of the American Indian, Santa Fe, N.M.; newsletter editor, Oklahoma Cherokee Organization; member, Arts Advisory Committee, Crosswinds Gallery; precinct chairman for Democratic Party; Arts Advisory Committee, Diamond Jubilee of the State of Oklahoma (selected by the State of Oklahoma to complete a TV public service announcement for the Diamond Jubilee Celebration. *Memberships:* Oklahoma Museum of Art, 1980-; Cherokee Historical Society, 1980-; Oklahoma Cherokee Organization (secretary, newsletter editor, 1978-); Oklahoma Indian Artists and Craftsmens Guild (2nd vice president and board of directors, 1976-); Wheelwright Museum of the American Indian (advisory board, 1981-); Southwestern Associaton on Indian Affairs, Inc.; Goingsnake Historical Society, 1981-; Five Civilized Tribes Museum, 1978-; Oklahoma Anthropological Society, 1985-; Museum of the American Indian, 1985-. *Awards, honors:* Awards for artwork received from:

Oklahoma Indian Artists and Craftsmens Guild, Oklahoma Museum of Art, Five Civilized Tribes Museum, Galleria American Indian Exposition, Rose State College, Oklahoma Indian Women's Federation, Indian Arts and Crafts Association, Southwestern Association on Indian Affairs, "Four Directions Arts Festival"; "Oklahoma Artist of Month," October 1978; featured artist on three "Creative Crafts" television shows, 1978, 1979, 1982; appearances and interviews on "Voices from the Land," "Unity" and "Danny's Day" television shows; selected as a participant in the Smithsonian Folklife Festival in Washington, D.C. in 1982; commissioned to complete baskets for the 50 Governors at the National Governors' Conference in 1982 by the Oklahoma State Arts Council; selected as ambassador of goodwill for the State of Oklahoma by Governor George Nigh in October 1982; made honorary member of Oklahoma State Anthropoogical Society in October 1982; recipient of the Governor's Arts Award, 1984; received "Women in Communications" Arts Award in 1984; selected for one person exhibits at Southern Plains Indian Museum and the Coulter Bay Indian Museum; work selected for permanent collections at Southern Plains Indian Museum, Windstar Foundation, Oklahoma State Arts Collection, Cultural Center for the American Indian in Houston, National Building of Future Homemakers of America in Washington, D.C., and Mabee-Gerrer Museum. *Interests:* "I am interested in all phases of the arts. I am interested in the promotion of young Indian artists, in the promotion of the American Indian culture to the general populace and I am especially interested in the education of American Indian youth in all fields." *Biographical sources: Oklahoma Today,* Fall 1981; *American Craft,* May 1982; *American Indian-Alaskan Native Resource Guide; Daily Oklahoman,* October 1984, August, 1985; *Crafts in America,* 1984.

DONALD, GARY (Chippewa)
(tribal chairman)

Affiliation: Chairman, Fond du Lac Reservation Business Committee, 105 University Rd., Cloquet, Minn. 55720; Nett Lake Reservation Business (Bois Fort) Committee, Nett Lake, Minn. 55772.

DOONKEEN, EULA NARCOMEY (Seminole) 1931-
(artist)

Born December 12, 1931, Oklahoma City, Okla. *Education:* Central State College, B.A. (Eduction), 1965. *Principal occupation:* Artist; co-owner, Alco Printing Co., Oklahoma City, Okla. *Home address:* 1608 N.W. 35th, Oklahoma City, Okla. 73118. *Military service:* U.S.A.F. Women's Reserve, 1951-1955. *Community activities:* Shawnee Area Health Advisory Board; Neighborhood Services Organization, Oklahoma City (secretary, 1972); Oklahoma City Community Council; Oklahoma City Area Health Advisory Board; West Central Neighborhood All Sports Association (vice president). *Memberships:* Seminole General Tribal Council (member; assistant chief); Five Civilized Tribes Inter-Tribal Council (seregeant-at-arms); National Congress of American Indians (area vice president, 1967-1968); Kappa Pi; Bacone Alumni Association; Oklahoma Feeration of Indian Women; American Indian Center (secretary, 1968); Feathers and Buckskin Society; American Indian Press Association; Indian Development Center, Inc.; Universal Link, Plains Center, Oklahoma City (vice president). *Awards, honors:* Several awards for painting in acrylics. *Exhibits:* Mrs. Doonkeen writes, "I have exhibited at the Smithsonian Institution (but) I paint mainly on commission and rarely enter competitions because I feel most competitions are based on bias and inherent traditional favoritism, and not on realistic approaches." *Interests:* "I am very interested in athletic events, both as a participant and (an) observer. In 1965, I captured the women's collegiate fencing championship of Oklahoma in the novice division. I have traveled extensively over the U.S. on business for Indian organizations and my own Seminole Nation's business. I also travel extensively for my own business, the Alco Printing Co. I am well known all over the country for my greeting card and stationery designs."

DORRIS, MICHAEL A. (Modoc) 1945-
(chairman-Native American studies)

Born January 30, 1945, Dayton, Wash. *Education:* Georgetown University, B.A. (magna cum laude), 1967; Yale University, M. Phil (Anthropology), 1970. *Principal occupation:* Chairman, Native Studies Department, Dartmouth College, Hanover, N.H., 1972-. *Address:* Hinman Box 6152, Dartmouth College, Hanover, N.H. 03755. *Affiliations:* Assistant professor of anthropology, Johnston College, University of the Redlands, 1970-1971; assistant professor, Franconia College, N.H., 1971-1972; professor, chairman, Department of Native American Studies, Dartmouth College, 1972-. *Community activities:* Explorers Club (Fellow); Society for Values in Higher Education (Fellow). *Memberships:* Society for Applied Anthropology (Fellow); Society for Values in Higher Education; American Anthropological Association; National Congress of American Indians; National Indian Education Association; National Indian Youth Council; Alpha Sigma Nu; *American Indian Culture Center Journal,* UCLA, 1974- (editorial board); *Viewpoint Magazine* (editor); Panel of Native American Scientists, AAAS (member); Minority Commission, MLA (member); Museum of the Ameriacn Indian (trustee). *Awards, honors:* National Endowment for the Humanities, 1976-; Guggenheim Fellow, 1978; Phil Beta Kappa; Danforth Graduate Fellow; Woodrow Wilson Faculty Fellow, 1980; National Institute of Mental Health Fellow. *Interests:* Contemporary Alaska; culture change; politics of energy resource development; sovereignty and international law; curriculum reform. *Biographical sources: Who's Who in America. Published works: Native Americans Today,* 1975; *Grandmother's Watch,* 1975; *Native Americans: 500 Years After,* (T.Y. Crowell, 1975); *Man in the Northeast,* 1976; *A Sourcebook for Native American Studies,* (American Library Association, 1977); chapter: "Native American Curriculum," *Racism in the Textbook* (Council on Interracial Books for Children, 1976); chapter in "Modoc Bibliographies," in *Encyclopedia of Indians of the Americas,* 1975.; *Pre-Contact North America,* textbook (Harper & Row, 1979); *Introduction to Native American Studies,* textbook (Harper & Row, 1980); editor, *Suntracks,* Arizona State University, 1978-.

DOSS, MICHAEL
(company president)

Affiliation: President, Arrow Creek Associates, 2450 Virginia Ave., N.W. #E106, Washington, D.C. 20037

DOWNING, ERNEST V. (Cherokee-Caddo) 1910-
(government official)

Born November 26, 1910, Verden, Okla. *Education:* Oklahoma City University, 1929-1930; University of Kansas, 1931-1932. *Principal occupation:* Government official. *Home address:* 4713 N.W. 29th, Oklahoma City, Okla. 73127. *Affiliations:* Employed in various capacities by the Bureau of Indian Affairs in Arizona, Illinois, New Mexico and Oklahoma, 1933-1935; executive officer, U.S. Public Health Service, Oklahoma City, Okla., 1955-retirement. *Community activities:* Interstate Council on Indian Affairs (governor's representative, 1952-1954). *Interests:* Mr. Downing writes, "I am interested in fine arts. Presently and for the past six years, I have participated in Oklahoma county libraries sponsoring of adult discussion groups in the liberal arts and great books program. I moderated a television series of eight programs on public-interest subjects sponsored by the Oklahoma Better Business Bureau, 1965."

DOYEL, DAVID E.
(museum director)

Affiliation: Director, Pueblo Grande Museum, 4619 E. Washington St., Phoenix, Ariz. 85034.

DRAKE, ELROY (Navajo) 1942-
(financial manager)

Born March 20, 1942, Tuba City, Ariz. *Education:* Northern Arizona University, B.S. (Business Administration), 1972. *Principal occupation:* Financial manager. *Home address:* P.O. Box 805, Window Rock, Ariz. 86045. *Affiliation: Manager, Navajo Sav-*

ings Branch of First Federal Savings, Phoenix, Ariz., 1975-. Other professional post: Industrial developer. *Military service:* U.S. Army, 1964-1966 (Vietnam Service Medal; SP/4 Class-Military Police). *Community activities:* VFW. *Memberships:* Northern Aruzona University Indian Club (social manager). *Awards, honors:* "1977 Young Navajo of Year," The Navajo Tribe. *Interests:* "Established first Savings & Loan Association on Indian Reservation to promote housing."

DRENNAN, ANTHONY, Sr.
(tribal chairman)

Affiliation: Chairman, Colorado River Tribal Council, Tribal Administration Center, Route 1, Box 23-B, Parker, Ariz. 85344/

DREW, ROBERT (Creek) 1922-
(government official)

Born June 12, 1922, Eufala, Okla. *Education:* Bacone Junior College, Certificate, 1947, B.S. (Education), 1949; Southeastern State College, M.S. (Education), 1957; University of Minnesota, graduate work, 1962-1963. *Principal occupation:* Government official. *Affiliations:* Teacher, coach, B.I.A., Parmelee, S.D., 1949-1950; principal, teacher, B.I.A., Mission, S.D., 1950-1952; principal, teacher, B.I.A., Cherry Creek, S.D., 1952-1955; principal, teacher, B.I.A., Eagle Butte, S.D., 1955-1957; community health worker, Public Health Service, Division of Indian Health, Pine Ridge, S.D., 1957-1959; education specialist (health), Public Health Service, Division of Indian Health, Bemidji, Minn., 1959-1962; area tribal affairs officer, Public Health Service, Division of Indian Health, Oklahoma City, Okla., 1963-1965; acting chief, Office of Tribal Affairs, Public Health Service, Division of Indian Health, Silver Spring, Md., 1966-. *Military service:* U.S. Army, 45th Infantry Division, 1940-1941, 1942-1945 (Purple Heart and Silver Star). *Community activities:* American Legion. *Memberships:* National Congress of American Indians, 1965-; Oklahoma Health and Welfare Associaton, 1965-. *Interests:* Mr. Drew writes, "I was an athletic official in high school foot-

ball and basketball, 1951-1958, and organized and managed independent football teams in Indian communities, 1949-1957, in South Dakota."

DU BRAY, ALFRED WILLIAM
(Rosebud Sioux) 1913-
(B.I.A. official)

Born April 1, 1913, Tripp County, S.D. *Education:* Mitchell Business College, 1937. *Principal occupation:* B.I.A. official. *Address:* c/o Bureau of Indian Affairs, Winnebago Agency, Winnebago, Neb. 68071. *Affiliations:* Mr. DuBray has held various positions with the B.I.A. since 1938; ex-superintendent, Winnebago Agency, 1963-retired. *Military service:* U.S. Army, 1945-1946. *Interests:* Mr. DuBray writes, "My entire career in the federal service has been with the B.I.A. I am keenly interested in the affairs of the American Indians and the policies and programs that have been developed for the improvement of conditions on the Indian reservations. My position as superintendent of an Indian agency has provided the opportunity to be associated with various tribal groups and with individual members of the tribes involved. Such experience provides a real opportunity to observe first hand the problems faced by the American Indian people in their struggle to advance socially and economically and to become part of the mainstream of American life."

DUCHENEAUX, FRANKLIN D.
(Cheyenne River Sioux) 1940-
(attorney)

Born January 30, 1940, Cheyenne Agency, S.D. *Education:* University of South Dakota, B.S. (Business), 1963; University of South Dakota Law School, J.D., 1965. *Principal occupation:* Attorney. *Home address:* 11539 Hickory Cluster, Reston, Va. 22090. *Affiliation:* Special Counsel on Indian Affairs, Committee on Interior & Insular Affairs, U.S. House of Representatives, Washington, 1973-.

**DUFFIELD, LATHEL F. (Cherokee)
1931-
(professor, curator)**

Born December 1, 1931, Collinsville, Okla. *Education:* University of Oklahoma, B.A., 1953, M.A., 1963; University of Wisconsin, Ph.D., 1970. *Principal occupation:* Professor, curator. *Home address:* 347 Sheridan Dr., Lexington, Ky. 40503. *Affiliations:* Executive director, Texas Archaeological Research Center, University of Texas, Austin, 1963-1964; assistant professor of anthropology, Eastern Kentucky University, 1964-1966; associate professor and profesor of anthropology, University of Kentucky, 1969-. *Other professional posts:* Curator, Gilcrease Institute of American History and Art; director, Arkansas Museum of Natural History and Antiquities; director, Museum of Anthropology, University of Kentucky. *Memberships:* American Association of University Professors; American Anthropological Associaton (Fellow); Society for American Archaeology; Kentucky Archaeological Association (editor); Texas Archaeological Society; Oklahoma Anthropological Society; Plains Anthropological Association. *Awards, honors:* Will Rogers Fellowship, University of Oklahoma; traineeship, National Science Foundation. *Interests:* "Interested in Southeastern, Southern Plains and Midwestern archaeology, ethnology, and paleontology. Have conducted archaeological investigations in Texas, Kentucky and Arkansas, and have worked on crews in Arizona, North Dakota, Oklahoma, and Guatemala." *Published works: Engraved Shells from the Craig Mound* (Oklahoma Anthropoogical Society, 1964); *co-author, The Pearson Site: A Historic Indian Site at Iron Bridge Reservoir (Dept. of Anthropology, University of Texas, 1964).*

**DUNCAN, CLIFFORD
(museum director)**

Affiliation: Director, Ute Tribal Museum, P.O. Box 190, Ft. Duchesne, Utah 84026.

**DUSHANE, HOWARD S. (Eastern
Shawnee) 1911-
(B.I.A. officer)**

Born July 10, 1911, Seneca, Mo. *Education:* Oklahoma Baptist University, 1931-1932. *Principal occupation:* B.I.A. officer. *Affiliations:* Truxton Canyon Agency, B.I.A., 1934-1950; district agent, Hoopa, Calif., 1950-1952; program officer, Hooper, Calif., 1952-1955; area program officer, Portland, Oreg., 1955-1957; superintendent, Fort Belknap Agency, B.I.A., MOnt., 1957-1960; superintendent, Cheyenne Agency, B.I.A., S.D., 1960-1966; area credit officer, Albuquerque Area Office, B.I.A., 1966-retirement). *Military service:* U.S. Army, 1945-1946. *Interests:* "Vocational interests have, of course, been in the development and progress of the Indian people with whom assigned in both cultural and economic fields. Being of Indian extraction, I have been involved and intensely interested in the progress of the American Indian, and my entire adult life has been devoted to this cause." *Biographical source: Indians of Today* (Indian Council Fire).

**DYC, GLORIA 1950-
(instructor)**

Born April 15, 1950, Detroit, Mich. *Education:* Wayne State University, B.Ph., 1973, M.A. (Speech, Theatre), 1976; Univerity of Michigan, D.A. (ABD-English), 1982. *Principal occupation:* Instructor. *Home address:* Box 66, Mission, S.D. 57555. *Affiliation:* Chair, General Studies Department, Sinte Gleska College, Rosebud, S.D., 1982-. *Other profesional post:* Instructor, Wayne County Community College, Detroit; artist in the schools, Michigan and South Dakota. *Membership:* Phi Beta Kappa. *Awards, honors:* Hopwood Award for Fiction, The University of Michigan, 1982; Wayne State University Playwriting Contest, 1973. *Interests:* "I'm doing community-based sociolinguistic research on Indian English, the ethnography of speaking, bilingual, bicultural education." *Published works:* Fiction and poetry in numerous small press journals.

E

EAGER, GEORGE B.
(assistant director-museum)

Affiliation: Assistant director, Museum of the American Indian, Heye Foundation, Broadway at 155th St., New York, N.Y. 10032.

EBERHART, CHARLES M. 1919-
(shop owner)

Born March 30, 1919, Boulder, Colo. *Education:* High school. *Principal occupation:* President, Western Trading Post, Inc., Denver, Colo., 1953-. *Military service:* Army Air Corps, 1941-1946 (Staff Sergeant). *Community activities:* South Denver, Chamber of Commerce (member); Chief Iron Shell Museum (director, curator, 1968-1975); White Buffalo Council of American Indians (advisor). *Memberships:* Denver Art Museum; Denver Museum of Natural History; Colorado Historical Society; Museum of the American Indian; Indian Arts and Crafts Association. *Awards, honors:* 1969 Friendship Award, White Buffalo Council of American Indians. *Interests:* "While I have made a study of most facets of the material culture of the American Indian, my main interest is in the use of glass beads and other ornamentation. My studies include not only the effect of the use of trade goods on the Indian historically, but also the preference for different items by various groups today. My interest in this material lead to repeated travel to all the Plains Indian reservations and the starting of a business dealing in these items in order to obtain close first hand information. We sell an extensive line of beads of all kinds, especially glass. Also, being in business, we have many Indians of all tribes request materials and in this way can keep up with the current trends of the various groups. We also have a good line of books on Indian topics and current newspapers."

ECHOHAWK, BRUMMETT (Pawnee) 1922-
(artist, writer, actor)

Born March 3, 1922, Pawnee, Okla. *Educa-*

tion: Detroit School of Arts and Crafts, 1945; Art Institute of Chicago, 1945-1948; studied creative writing at the University of Tulsa. *Principal occupation:* Artist, writer, actor. *Home address:* P.O. Box 1922, Tulsa, Okla. 74101. *Affiliations:* Staff artist, Chicago *Daily Times* and Chicago *Sun Times;* artist, *Bluebook,* McCall's Magazine Corp., New York. *Military service:* U.S. Army, 1940-1945 (Purple Heart with oak-leaf cluster; did Combat sketches published in the Army's *Yank Magazine,* and 88 newspapers by N.E.A. News Syndicate). *Community activities:* Gilcrease Museum, Tulsa, Okla. (board member). *Exhibitions:* Paintings shown in Pakistan, India through the Art in the Embassies Program, State Department; other works shown at the De Young Museum, San Francisco; Amon Carter Museum, Fort Worth, Texas; Gilcrease Museum; Imperial War Museum, London; Bad Segeberg, Hamburg, West Germany. *Acting:* As stage actor, Mr. Echohawk has appeared in the role of Sitting Bull in Kopit's play *Indians* in Tulsa, Fort Worth, and Lincoln, Neb. Also played at the Virginia Museum Theater, Richmond, Questor's Theater, London, and Karl May Theater, Bad Segeberg, West Germany; he did a TV film in Hamburg, W. Germany. *Awards, honors:* Assisted Thomas Hart Benton with one of the "greatest" mural in America: The Truman Memorial Library mural called "Independence and the Opening of the West," at Independence, Mo.; commissioned by the Aluminum Co. of America for a painting depicting early American history of the Tennessee Valley; commissioned by Leaning Tree Publishing Co., Boulder, Colo. for paintings to be reproduced as Christmas cards; Mr. Echohawk's paintings are of a classic and representational style, which cover the subjects of the Indian and the American West. *Biographical sources: Encyclopedia of the American Indian; Indians of Today; Dictionary of International Biography;* National Geographic's *American Indians. Published works:* Writings, with illustrations, have appeared in the Tulsa *Sunday World, Oklahoma Today* Magazine, *The Western Horseman* Magazine, and others.

**ECHOHAWK, JOHN E. (Pawnee) 1945-
(attorney)**

Born August 11, 1945, Albuquerque, N.M. *Education:* University of New Mexico, B.A., 1967; University of New Mexico, School of Law, J.D., 1970. *Principal Occupation:* Attorney. *Home Address:* 2350 Panorama, Boulder, Colo. 80302. *Affiliations:* Native American Rights Fund, Boulder, Colo. (research associate, 1970-1972; deputy director, 1972-1973, 1975-1977; executive director, 1973-1975, 1977-). *Community Activities:* Association on American Indian Affairs (board of directors); American Indian Lawyer Training Program (board of directors); National Committee on Responsive Philanthropy (board of directors). *Memberships:* American Indian Bar Association; American Bar Association. *Awards, Honors:* Americans for Indian Opportunity, Distinguished Service Award; White Buffalo Council, Friendship Award; National Congress of American Indians, President's Indian Service Award. *Interests:* Indian law.

**EDDY, FRANK W. 1930-
(archaeologist-anthropologist)**

Born May 7 1930, Roanoke, Va. *Education:* University of New Mexico, B.A., 1952; University of Arizona, M.A., 1958; University of Colorado, Ph.D., 1968. *Principal occupation:* Archaeologist-anthropologist. *Addresses:* 2228 Bluff St., Boulder, Colo. 80302 (home); Department of Anthropology, University of Colorado, Boulder, Colo. (professional). *Affiliations:* Curator, Museum of New Mexico, researcher and director of the Navajo Reservoir Salvage Archaeological Project, 1959-1965; research assistant at the University of Colorado Museum—dig foreman at Yellow Jacket and Jurgens Site excavations, 1965-1968; executive director, Texas, Archaeological Salvage Project, University of Texas, Austin, 1968-1970; director, Chimney Rock Archaeological Project, University of Colorado, 1970-1973; associate professor, professor of anthropology, University of Colorado, 1970-. *Other professional posts:* Director and prinicpal investigator, Two Forks Archaeological Project, University of Colorado, 1974-1975; intern, Interagency

Archaeological Services, Denver, National Park Service, 1975-1976; co-director and principal investigator of the Bisti-Star Lake Cultural Resource Inventory, Archaeological Associates, Inc., summer, 1977. *Military service:* U.S. Army, 1952-1954. *Memberships:* Society for American Archaeology, 1953-; Society for the Sigma Xi, 1965--1973; American Quaternary Associaton, 1970-; Colorado Archaeological Society, 1970-; Society of Professional Archaeologists, 1976- (counselor, standards board); Association of Field Archaeologists, 1977-. *Interests:* Cultural ecology; prehistoric settlement studies; cultural change as revealed by archaeology; technology of primitive societies. *Published works: An Archaeological Survey of the Navajo Reservoir District, Northwestern New Mexico,* with Alfred E. Dittert, Jr., and James J. Hester (Monograph, School of American Research, Museum of New Mexico, 1961); *Excavations at Los Pinos Phase Sites in the Navajo Reservoir District* (Museum of New Mexico, 1961); "Excavations at the Candelaria Site, LA 4406," chapter II in *Pueblo Period Sites in the Piedra River Section, Navajo Reservoir District,* assembled with A.E. Dittert, Jr. (Museum of New Mexico, 1963); *Prehistory in the Navajo Reservoir District, Northwestern New Mexico* (Museum of New Mexico, 1966); *Archaeological Investigations at Chimney Rock Mesa: 1970-1972* (Memoirs of the Colorado Archaeological Society, 1977); *An Archaeoogical Study of Indian Settlements and Land Use in the Colorado Foothills,* with Ric Windmiller (Memoirs of Southwestern Lore, Colorado Archaeological Society). Several articles in journals, and papers delivered at regional meetings and national conferences.

**EDEN, RONALD D.
(B.I.A.-director of administration)**

Affiliation: Director of administration, Bureau of Indian Affairs, 1951 Constitution Ave., N.W., Washington, D.C. 20245.

**EDER, EARL A (Sioux) 1944-
(painter)**

Born November 17, 1944, Poplar, Mont.

Education: Institute of American Indian Arts, Santa Fe, N.M.: San Francisco Art Institute, B.F.A.: University of Montana, M.A., 1971. *Principal occupation:* Painter. *Exhibits:* De-Mo-Lay Gallery, Great Falls, Mont., 1965; Alaska Centennial, 1966; American Indian Historical Society, 1968; Philbrook Art Center, 1969; University of San Francisco, 1969; Scottsdale National Indian Arts Exhibit, 1968, 1970. *Awards, honors:* Second Place, Scottsdale National Indian Arts Exhibit, 1970; First Place (sculpture), Heard Museum, 1970; Second Place (sculpture), Heard Museum, 1972. *Interests:* Mr. Eder writes, "I am a painter, and (painting) is what I would eventually like to teach, and keep moving in that direction." *Biographical sources: House Beautiful,* June, 1972; *Art in America,* July, 1972.

EDMO, KESLEY
(tribal chairman)

Affiliation: Chairman, Fort Hall Business Council, Fort Hall Tribal Office, Fort Hall, Idaho 83203

EDMO, LORRAINE P.
(director-Indian organization)

Affiliation: Director, American Indian Scholarships, 5106 Grand Ave., N.E., Albuquerque, N.M. 87108.

EDMONDSON, ED 1919-
(congressman)

Born April 7, 1919, Muskogee, Okla. *Education:* University of Oklahoma, B.A., 1940; Georgetown University, LL.B., 1947. *Principal occupation:* Congressman (member of Congress, 2nd District, Oklahoma). *Home address:* 219 N. 14th St., Muskogee, Okla. *Military service:* U.S. Navy Reserve. *Memberships:* American Bar Association; Oklahoma Bar Association. *Awards, honors:* Honorary memberships in several Oklahoma tribes. *Interests:* Committee on Interior and Insular Affairs (member); Subcommittee on Indian Affairs (second-ranking Democrat); Committee on Public Works, U.S. House of Representatives (member).

EDMUNDS, JUDITH A. 1943-
(dealer-American Indian jewelry)

Born September 8, 1943, Waltham, Mass. *Education:* Massachusetts College of Pharmacy. *Principal occupation:* Dealer of fine American Indian jewelry and related items. *Home address:* Box 788, West Yarmouth, Mass. 02673. *Affiliation:* President-treasurer, Edmonds of Yarmouth, Inc., 1973-. *Other professional posts:* State chairperson, Indian Arts & Crafts Association (served on Education & Public Relations Committee; currently chairperson for Massachusetts). *Interests:* Ms. Edmunds writes, "My business is a retail outlet, but my greatest pleasure is educating the general public on the different Indian tribes and their style of work and their living conditions, and to create collectors of fine Indian art. By educating these people - those dealers that are selling fakes and misrepresenting their wares will soon be out of business, I travel to reservations a couple of times a year and spend time in the Hopi Mesas and San Domingo Pueblos, as well as on the Navajo Reservation, as we have Indian friends spread out through the various reservations, as well as Anglo friends. My interests outside of the Indian field is fine American antiques."

EDWARDS, JOHN
(Indian school principal)

Affiliation: Principal, Concho Indian School, P.O. Box 8, Concho, Okla. 73022.

EID, LEROY V. 1932-
(professor of history)

Born December 22, 1932, Cincinnati, Ohio. *Education:* University of Dayton, B.S. (Education), 1953; St. John's University, M.S. (History), 1958, Ph.D. (History), 1961; University of Toronto, M.A. (Philosophy), 1968. *Principal occupation:* Professor of history. *Home address:* 1181 Kentshire Dr., Centerville, Ohio 45459. *Affiliation:* Professor, Department of History, University of Dayton, Dayton, Ohio, 1961- (chairman of dept. 1969-1983). *Awards, honors:* Ontario Graduate Fellowship, 1967. *Interests:* "Teacher of history of American Indians. Research interest is in American Indian military expertise (Northeast Woodland of the Colonial period. My writing tries to present this military world from the Indian viewpoint, weaknesses as well as strengths. The overall thesis is that Northeast Woodland Indians showed on important occasions (e.g. Braddock's defeat in Pennsylvania and St. Clair's defeat in Ohio) an army with disciplined soldiers who followed skilled leaders who had excellent tactics." *Published works:* Articles: "National War Among Indians of Northeastern North America: Ethnohistorical Insight or Anthropological Nonsense?" *(Canadian Review of American Studies,* Summer, 1985); "The Cardinel Principle of Northeast Woodland Indian War," *(Papers of the Thirteenth Algonquian Conference,* Toronto, 1982); "I Am An Indian," *(Illinois Quarterly,* 1982); "Liberty and the Indian," *(Midwest Quarterly,* 1982); "The Neglected Side of American Indian War in the Northeast," *(Military Review,* Feb. 1981); "The War of the Iroquois Lost," *(Journal of the Order of the Indian Wars,* Spring 1980); "The Ojibwa-Iroquois War," *(Ethnohistory,* 1979). Papers: "Surprise: The Central Indian Military Tactic," Great Lakes Historical Conference, April, 1984; "Two Types of Indian War: Private and National," paper at Joint Conference of CAAS and ASCUS, October, 1982; "The Cardinal Principle of Northeast Indian War," paper at the Algonquian Conference, October, 1981; "I Am An Indian," paper at American Association for Eighteenth Century Studies, October, 1981; "That Unconquered Nation," paper at Great Lakes History Conference, April, 1980; "Teaching American Indian History, Literature, and Values," paper at the Great Lakes Regional Conference of the National Council for the Social Studies, March, 1980; "Liberty and the Indian," paper at Popular Culture Association, April, 1978. Book reviews: Leonard Carlson's *Indians, Bureacrats, and Land,* in *Journal of the West,* Oct., 1982; Francis P. Prucha's *Indian Policy in the United States* in *Journal of the West, Jan. 1983; Vine Deloria Jr. and Clifford M. Lytle's American Indians, American Justice* in *Journal of the West; among others.*

ELAM, EARL H. 1934-
(professor of history, vice president for academic affairs)

Born December 7, 1934, Wichita Falls, Tex. *Education:* Midwestern University, Wichita Falls, Texas, B.A., 1961; Texas Tech University, Lubbock, M.A., 1967, Ph.D., 1971. *Principal occuaption: Professor of history, vice president for academic affairs. Home address:* 407 N. Cockrell, Alpine, Texas 79830. *Affiliations:* Instructor, Texas Tech University, 1967-1971; professor of history, and vice president for academic affairs, Sul Ross State University, Alpine, Texas, 1972-. Military service: U.S. Navy, 1953-1957 (Radioman). *Memberships:* Western History Association; West Texas Historical Association; Texas State Historical Association. *Interests:* American Indian history; Indian land claims; American Indian ethnology and archaeology; Texas history, Southwestern American history, Spanish borderland history. *Published works:* Several articles and reports; thesis, dissertation, and reports on Wichita Indian history and ethnology.

ELGIN, ALFRED G., Jr.
(executive director-Indian council)

Affiliation: Executive director, National Indian Council on Aging, P.O. Box 2088, Albuquerque, N.M. 87103

ELLISON, THOMAS J. (Oklahoma Choctaw) 1924-
(B.I.A. official)

Born June 17, 1924, Choctaw County, Okla. *Education:* Haskell Indian Junior College; Colorado A & M College, B.S. (Agriculture), 1950. *Principal occupation:* B.I.A. official. *Home address:* Route 4, Box 654, Muskogee, Okla. 74401. *Affiliations:* Extension & Soil Conservation, B.I.A., Anadarko, Okla, 1950-1952, Albuquerque, N.M., 1952-1954, Ardmore, Okla., 1954-1957; credit and financing officer, B.I.A., Winnebago, Neb., 1957-1960, Rosebud, S.D., 1960-1962, Muskogee Area Office, 1963-1967; tribal operations and industrial development, B.I.A., Crow Agency, Mont., 1962; superintendents, Stabding Rock

Agency, B.I.A., 1967-1968; B.I.A., Muskogee Area Office (tribal operations officer, 1969-1972; deputy area director, 1972; acting area director, 1973-1974; area director, 1974-). *Military service:* U.S. Army, 1943-1946. *Community activities:* The Native American Legal Defense and Education Fund (advisory committee, Oklahoma Research Project); Muskogee State Fair Board (chairman, Specialty Day Committee); Bacone College (Academic Committee, Board of Trustees, 1975-1978); Fun Country R C & D steering committee, Ardmore, Okla. (technical assistant).

ELROD, SAM
(deputy administrative director,
Indian Health Service)

Affiliation: Deputy administrative director, Indain Health Service, 5600 Fishers Lane, Rockville, Md. 20857.

EMELIO, JOHN
(EMS program director)

Affiliation: EMS program director, Indian Health Service, 5600 Fishers Lane, Rockville, Md. 20857.

EMGEE, Sr. JUDITH
(executive director-Indian school)

Affiliation: Executive director, Ojibwa Indian School, Box A-3, Belcourt, N.D. 58316.

ENGELSTAD, KURT (Eskimo) 1937-
(business executive, attorney)

Born October 3, 1937, Corvallis, Ore. *Education:* Oregon State University, Corvallis, B.S. (Education), 1960; Northwest School of Law, Lewis & Clark College, Portland, Ore., J.D., 1972. *Principal occupation:* Business excutive, attorney. *Home address:* 2125 S.E. Sherman St., Portland, Ore., 97214. *Affiliations:* President and chairman of board, The 13th Regional Corporation, Seattle, Wash., 1983-. *Other professional posts:* President and executive producer, Alaska Native Film Productions, Inc.;

member, board of directors, Alaska Federation of Natives; principal, Engelstad & Associates, a private Oregon-based consulting firm. *Military service:* U.S. Air Force (active duty), 1960-1961; active Air Force reserve, 1961-; (Lt. Colonel; Air Force Longevity Service Ribbon with hour glass device; Air Force Reserve Medal with 4 oak leaves; Small Arms Marksmanship Medal). *Community activities:* Former Boy Scout troop leader; former director and board chairman, Multnomah County, Oregon legal services. *Memberships:* Oregon State Bar, 1972-; Multnomah Bar, 1972-; District Court Bar, 1972-; joint committee of Oregon Bar with Press and Broadcasters (1974-1977 member and chairman). *Awards, honors:* Chief Frank White Buffaloman award for Outstanding Service to the Native American community of Portland, Oregon by Portland Urban Indian Council; Outstanding Journalism graduate for 1960 bestowed by Sigma Delta Chi honorary, Oregon State University chapter. *Interests:* Vocational: Indian law, business management and finance; Avocational: Writing, photography, philately. *Biographical source:* "Natives Without a Land Base," by Elizabeth Roderick, October, 1983 edition *Alaska Native News Magazine. Published works: Editorial staff, Environmental Law Review of Northwest School of Law of Lewis & Clark College, 1972.*

ENGLES, WILLIAM LYNN (Oneida)
1935-
(commissioner-administration
for Native Americans)

Born September 29, 1935, Poplar, Mont. *Education:* The Evergreen State College, Olympia, Wash., B.A., 1974. *Principal occupation:* Commissioner, Administration for Native Americans. *Home address:* 3751 Gunston Rd., Alexandria, Va. 22302. *Affiliations:* Public information officer, Bureau of Indian Affairs, Washington, D.C., 1974-1984; commissioner, Administration for Native Americans, Department of Health & Human Services, Washington, D.C., 1984-. *Other professinal posts:* Reporter and Bureau Chief, Unite Press International. *Military service:* U.S. Army, 1955-1957 (Corporal).

ENGLISH, SAMUEL F. (Turtle Mountain Band and Redlake Band Chippewa) 1942-
(artist)

Born June 2, 1942, Phoenix, Ariz. *Education:* Bacone College, Bacone, Okla., 1960-1962; University of San Francisco, 1967-1968. *Principal occuaption:* Artist. *Home address:* 400 San Felipe N.W., Albuquerque, N.M. 87104. *Affiliation: Owner, Native American Art Gallery, Albuquerque, N.M., 1982-.*

ERASMUS, GEORGES HENRY (Dene) 1948-
(Dene politician)

Born August 8, 1948, Fort Rae, N.W.T., Can. *Education:* High school, Yellowknife, N.W.T. *Principal occupation:* Dene politician. *Home address:* P.O. Box 222, Yellowknife, N.W.T., Canada. *Affiliations:* Secretary, Indian Band Council, Yellowknife, N.W.T., Can., 1969-1971; Organizer and chairman, Community Housing Association, Yellowknife, 1969-1972; advisor to president, Indian Brotherhood of N.W.T., 1970-1971; fieldworker and regional staff director, Company of Young Canadians, 1970-1973; chairman, University Canada North, 1971-1975; director, Community Development Program, Indian Brotherhood of Northwest Territories (later the Dene Nation) (director, Community Development Program, 1973-1976; president, 1976-1983); president, Denedeh Development Corporation, 1976-1983; elected Northern vice-chief, Assembly of First Nations, 1983; elected National Chief, Assembly of First Nations, Ottawa, Canada. *Awards, honors:* Representative for Canada on Indigenous Survival International, 1983; Canadian delegate to World Council of Indigenous Peoples International Conferences, 1984-1985; art, school, athletic awards. *Interests:* Reading, travel, outdoors, canoeing and art. "Presently working on a book, due for publication in August, 1987." *Biographical sources: New Canadian Encyclopedia; Who's Who in Canada.*

ERICKSON, JOHN
(chief-Smoki People)

Affiliation: Chief, Smoki People, P.O. Box 123, Prescott, Ariz. 86302.

ERICKSON, VINCENT O. 1936-
(professor of anthropology)

Born January 17, 1936, Mount Vernon, Wash. *Education:* University of Washington, B.A., 1958, M.A., 1961, Ph.D., 1968. *Principal occupation:* Professor of anthropology. *Home address:* 175 Southampton Dr., Fredericton, New Brunswick, Can. E3B 4T5. *Affiliation:* University of New Brunswick, Fredericton, Can., 1966-. *Memberships:* American Anthropological Association; American Ethnological Society; Canadian Ethnology Society; American Folklore Society; Canadian Folklore Society. *Interests:* Ethnohistory, ethnolinguistics, ethnography and folklore of the Eastern Algonkians, especially of the Indians of New Brunswick. Indian agent to the Passamaquoddy, 1965-; fieldwork among Passamaquoddy, 1967-, and among the Coast Salish Indians of Washington and British Columbia, 1960-1962.

ESTEVES, PAULINE
(tribal chairwoman)

Affiliation: Chairwoman, Death Valley Indian Community, P.O. Box 108, Death Valley, Calif.92325.

EULER, ROBERT C. 1924-
(professor of anthropology)

Born August 8, 1924, New York, N.Y. *Education:* Arizona State College, B.A., 1947, M.A. (Economics), 1948; University of New Mexico, Ph.D. (Anthropology), 1958. *Principal occupation:* Professor of anthropology. *Affiliations:* Ranger, National Park Service, Wupatka National Monument, 1948-1949; anthropological consultant, Albuquerque Area Office, B.I.A., 1950-1951; instructor, associate professor, Arizona State College, 1952-1964; curator of anthropology, Museum of Northern Arizona, 1952-1956; research associate, Museum of Northern Arizona, 1956-; associate professor, professor and chairman, Department of Anthropology, University of Utah, 1964-? *Other professional posts:* Anthropological consultant, Hualapai Tribe, land claim litigation, 1953-1957; member, board of trustees, Museum of Navajo Ceremonial Art, 1954-1964; anthropological consultant, U.S. Department of Justice, Southern Paiute land claim litigation, 1956; consultant in cross-cultural education, Phoenix, Ariz., public school system, 1961, 1964; ethnohistorian, Upper Colorado River Basin Archaeological Salvage Project, University of Utah, 1962; Arizona Governor's Historical Advisory Committee, 1961-1964; ethnohistorical consultant, Arizona Commission on Indian Affairs, 1962-1964; anthropological consultant, Operation Headstart, U.S. Office of Economic Opportunity, involving Navajo, Paiute, Mojave, and Chemehuevi participation, 1965. *Memberships:* Amerian Anthropological Association (Fellow); American Ethnological Society; Society for Applied Anthropology (Fellow); Society for American Archaeology; Current Anthropology (associate); American Association for the Advancement of Science (Fellow); American Indian Ethnohistoric Conference; The Society for Sigma Xi; The Western History Association (member, editorial board, *The American West);* Arizona Academy of Science (charter member; president, 1962-1963); Arizona Archaeological and Historical Society; New Mexico Historical Society; Ne Mexico Archaeological Society; Utah Historical Society. *Interests:* Ethnographic fieldwork involving historical ethnography, ethnohistory and applied anthropology among the Navajo, Hopi, Walapai, Havasupai, Yavapai, Chemehuevi, Southern Paiute, Southern Ute, Isleta Pueblo, and Zia Pueblo; historica archaeological research in Walapai, Havasupai, Yavapai, and Southern Paiute sites. *Published works:* Editor, *Woodchuck Cave, A Basketmaker II Site in Tsegi Canyon, Arizona,* with H.S. Colton (Museum of Northern Arizona, 1953); *Walapai Culture History* (University of New Mexico, doctoral disserttion, University Microfilms, 1958); *Southern Paiute Archaeology in the Glen Canyon Drainage: A Preliminary Report* (Nevada State Museum, 1963); *Havasupai Religion and Mythology* (Anthropolgoical Papers, University of Utah, 1964); numerous articles, reviews and monographs.

EVANS, REX
(executive director-Indian organization)

Affiliation: Executive director, United South and Eastern Tribes, 1101 Kermit Dr., Suite 800, Nashville, Tenn. 37217.

EVANS, WAYNE H. (Rosebud Sioux) 1938-
(Indian academic/student affairs)

Born April 19, 1938, Rosebud, S.D. *Education:* Black Hills State College, B.S., 1962; University of South Dakota, Ed.D., 1976. *Principal occupation:* Indian academic/student affairs. *Home address:* Vermillion, S.D., 57069. *Affiliation:* University of South Dakota, Vermillion, S.D., 1969-. *Memberships:* South Dakota Indian Education Association (president); South Dakota Indian Counselor's Association (board member). *Awards, honors:* Outstanding Young Man of America. *Interests:* Counseling, guidance; family therapy; values - value orientation. *Published work: Indian Student Counseling Handbook* (Black Hills State College, 1977).

EWAN, ROY S. (Athabascan) 1935-
(corporate president)

Born February 2, 1935, Copper Center, Alaska. *Education:* Mt. Edgecumbe High School. *Principal occupation:* Corporate president. *Home address:* P.O. Box 215, Gakona, Alaska 99586. *Affiliations:* President, Ahtna, Inc.; board member, Grandmet/Ahtna; board member, Ahtna Development Corporation. *Other professional posts:* Serves as ex-officio member on all corporate committees, and shareholder committees and subsidiary boards. *Military service:* U.S. Army, 1953-1955 (Corporal). *Community activities:* Gulkana Vilage Council (Indian education, past president). *Memberships:* Alaska Feeration of Natives (board member); Alaska Native Federation; The Alliance. *Awards, honors:* 1985 AFN Citizen of the Year, Alaska Federation of Natives.

EWERS, JOHN CANFIELD 1909-
(ethnologist emeritus, Smithsonian)

Born July 21, 1909, Cleveland, Ohio. *Education:* Dartmouth College, B.A., 1931, D.Sc., 1968; Yale University, M.A. (Anthropology), 1934; University of Montana, LL.D., 1966. *Principal occupation:* Ethnologist emeritus, Smithsonian. *Home address:* 4432 N. 26th Rd., Arlington, Va. 22207. *Affiliations:* Field curator, Museum Division, National Park Service, 1935-1940; curator, Museum of the Plains Indian, 1941-1944; associate curator of ethnology, planning officer, U.S. National Museum, Smithsonian Institution, 1946-1959; assistant director, director, Museum of History and Technology, Smithsonian, 1959-1965; senior scientist, Office of Anthropology, now ethnologist emeritus, Department of Anthropology, Smithsonian Institution, Washington, D.C. *Other professional posts:* Museum planning consultant, Bureau of Indian Affairs, 1948-1949; Montana Historical Society, 1950-1954; editor, *Journal of the Washington Academy of Sciences,* 1955; member, editorial board, *The American West, Western Historical Quarterly,* and *Great Plains Quarterly,* 1979-; consultant, American Heritage, 1959; research associate, Museum of the American Indian, Heye Foundation, 1979-. *Military service:* U.S. Naval Reserve, 1944-1946. *Memberships:* American Indian Ethnohistoric Conference (president, 1961); American Anthropological Association (Fellow); Washington Academy of Sciences (Fellow); Rochester Museum of Arts and Science (Fellow); Sigma Xi (president, D.C., chapter); Western History Association (honorary life member). *Awards, honors:* Recipient First Exceptional Service Award for contributions to American history and ethnology, Smithsonian Institution, 1965; Oscar O. Winthor Award, Western History Association, 1976; "Distinguished Published Writings in the Field of American Western History," 1985, Western History Association. *Interests:* "Field research in ethnology and ethnohistory conducted among the Blackfeet tribes of Montana and Alberta (Canada), the Assiniboine of Montana, the Flathead of Montana, the Sioux of South Dakota, and the Kiowa of Oklahoma; studies of Indian art since 1932." *Biographical sources: Who's Who in America; The Read-*er's *Encyclopedia of the American West,* 1977, by Howard Lamar, editor; *Plains Indian Studies,* Douglas H. Ubelaker and Herman J. Viola, editors (Smithsonian Contribution to Anthropology) - a collection of essays in honor of John C. Ewers and Waldo R. Wedel (includes a complete list of John C. Ewer's approximately 163 publications through 1981; *Fifth Annual Plains Indian Seminar in Honor of Dr. John C. Ewers,* George Horse Capture and Gene Ball, editors *(Buffalo Bill Historical Center, 1984); Western Historical Quarterly* (April, 1986). *Published works:* Mr. Ewers writes, "I have published more than 20 books and monographs, and over 100 articles on the American Indian, the fur trade of the American West, artists who interpreted Indians, etc. Among the books — *Plains Indian Painting* (Stanford University Press, 1940); *The Horse in Blackfeet Indian Culture* (Smithsonian Institution, 1955); *The Blackfeet: Raiders on the Northwestern Plains* (University of Oklahoma Press, 1958); *Artists of the Old West* (Doubleday, 1965); *Indian Life on the Upper Missouri* (University of Oklahoma Press, 1968); *Murals in the Round: Painted Tipis of the Kiowa and Kiowa-Apache Indians,* 1978; Editor: *Adventures of Zenas Leonard, Fur Trader,* 1959; *Crow Indian Medicine Bundles,* 1960; *Five Indian Tribes of the Upper Missouri,* 1961; *O-Keepa: A Religious Ceremony and Other Customs of the Mandans,* (George Catlin), 1967; *Indians of Texas in 1830* (Smithsonian Institution, 1969); *Indian Art in Pipestone, George Catlin's Portfolio in the British Museum,* 1979; *Plains Indian Sculpture, Traditional Art from America's Heartland* (Smithsonian Institution, 1986).

EXENDINE, LEAH
(director-Indian resource liaison)

Affiliation: Director, Indian Resource Liaison Staff, Indian Health Service, 5600 Fishers Lane, Rockville, Md. 20857.

EXENDINE, Dr. JOSEPH N.
(deputy director-Indian Health Service)

Affiliation: Deputy director, Indian Health Service, 5600 Fishers Lane, Rockville, Md. 20857

F

FADDEN, JOHN KAHIONHES
(Mohawk-Turtle Clan) 1938-
(artist, illustrator)

Born December 26, 1938, Massena, N.Y. (near Akwesasne, St. Regis Indian Reservation). *Education: Rochester Institute of Technology, B.F.A., 1961; St. Lawrence University and SUNY at Plattsburgh, graduate courses. Principal occupation:* Artist, illustrator. *Address:* Six Nations Indian Museum, Onchiota, N.Y. 12968. *Exhibitions:* Six Nationa Indian Museum, 1954-; Pennsylvania State Museum, Harrisburg, 1962; "Art of the Iroquois," Erie County Savings Bank, Buffalo, N.Y., 1974; Ne York State Fair, Syracuse, 1977; The Woodland Indian Cultural - Educational Centre, Brantford, Ontarlo, 1977, 1980, 1984, American Indian Community Hosue Gallery, New York City, 1977, 1980, 1982, 1984; Akwesasne Museum, Hogansburg, N.Y., 1980; Schoharie Museum of the Iroquois Indian, 1981-1985; Iroquois Indian Festival II, feature artist, Cobleskill, N.Y., 1983; "Akwesasne: Our Strength, Our Spirit," World Trade Center, Ne York City, 1984; among others. *Interests:* As John looks back over the years, he sees the 1961-1968 period as one of experimentation in which he worked with pen and ink and painted in tempera, selling a few of his works at the family museum (Six Nations Indian Museum), and giving away others. As became more aware of the political changes taking place at Akwesasne, and throughout Native America, he began to make more political statements through his art, mainly through drawings and cover illustrations for *Akwesasne Notes,* a nespaper published by the Mohawk Nation at Akwesasne. The details of his work typically show native nationalism and political ascertiveness based on the traditions of the native peoples. He has illustrated many books and periodicals, and has done cover art for many books; also, calendar art for *Akwesasne Notes Calendar,* 1972-. He has taken part in three films: *Who Were the Ones* (National Film Board of Canada, 1970); *Hodenosaunee: People of the Longhouse* (Stiles-Akin Films, 1981); *The Iroquois Creation Myth* (video tape, Image Film, 1982).

FADDEN, RAY
(museum owner)

Affiliation: Owner, Six Nations Indian Museum, Ochiota, N.Y. 12968.

FAIRBANKS, MICHAEL
(B.I.A. agency superintendent)

Affiliation: Superintendent, Blackfeet Agency, Bureau of Indian Affairs, Browning, Mont. 59417.

FALLEY, NANCI
(president-Indian organization)

Affiliation: President, American Indian Horse Registry, Route 1, Box 64, Lockhart, Tex. 78644.

FALLING, LEROY (Cherokee) 1926-
(administrator)

Born June 15, 1926, Estella, Okla. *Education:* Warner Pacific College, Diploma, 1948; Anderson College, B.S., 1950; Oregon College of Education, Diploma, 1951; Arizona State University, M.S., 1966. *Principal occupation:* Administrator. *Address:* c/o Kinlichee Boarding School, Ganado, Ariz. 86505. *Affiliations:* Teacher, Lapwai Public School, York Public School; educational specialist, Window Rock, Ariz. *Military service:* U.S. Navy, 1944-1946 (World War II Victory Medal). *Community activities:* Window Rock, Fort Defiance Lions Club; Kit Carson Council (vice-chairman, Leadership Training); Boy Scouts of America; Indian Workers Conference (president, 1965-1966); National, International Social Concerns Committee, 1964-1966.

FALLS, ALVIN (Sac and Fox)
(tribal chief)

Affiliation: Principal chief, Sac and Fox Business Committee, Route 2, Box 246, Stroud, Okla. 74079.

FAWCETT, JAYNE GRANDCHAMP
(Mohegan of Connecticut) 1936-
(teacher, assistant curator)

Born January 6, 1936, New London, Conn. *Education:* University of Connecticut, B.A., 1957; Eastern Connecticut State College. *Principal occupation:* Teacher, assistant curator. *Affiliations:* Teacher, Ledyard Junior High School, Gales Gerry, Conn., 1972-; assistant curator, Tantaquidgeon Indian Museum. *Other professional posts:* Lecturer, American Field Studies. *Interests:* "Inspired by the travels of my Aunt, Gladys Tantaquidgeon, my family and I have traveled extesnively throughout the western part of America, visiting as many groups of native American as we were able."

FELSEN, DR. JAMES D.
(chief medical officer, Indian Health Service)

Affiliation: Chief medical officer, Indian Health Service, 5600 Fishers Lane, Rockville, Md. 20857.

FELSMAN, JOSEPH
(tribal chairman)

Affiliation: Chairman, Confederated Salish & Kootenai Tribal Council, P.O. Box 278, Pablo, Mont. 59855.

FELTS, JACK LEON (Choctaw) 1921-
(publisher, writer)

Born January 7, 1921, Blanchard, Okla. *Principal occupation:* Publisher, writer. *Affiliations:* Founder, Pan Press, Hollywood, Calif.; associate, Beth Kramer Literary Agency, 1953-; scenarist, 1953-1956. *Military service:* U.S. Coast Guard, 1943-1946. *Memberships:* International director, Individualist Society (editor, I.S. *Tablet*); Descendants of the Choctaws. *Interests:* Established Tahlequah Writers' Conference, 1961-1965; exploration and excavation in Mexico and Central America, 1963-1965; directing historical acquisition and study.

FENTON, WILLIAM NELSON 1908
(anthropologist, professor)

Born December 15, 1908, New Rochelle, N.Y. *Education:* Dartmouth College, B.A., 1931; Yale University, Ph.D., 1937; Hartwick College, LL.D., 1968. *Principal occupation:* Anthropologist, professor. *Home address:* 7 N. Helderberg Parkway, Slingerlands, N.Y. 12159. *Affiliations:* Community worker, U.S. Indian Setvice, in charge of Tuscarora and Tonawanda Reservations, 1935-1937; instructor, assistant professor, St. Lawrence University, 1937-1939; ethnologist, Smithsonian Institution, Bureau of American Ethnology, 1939-1951; lecturer, Johns Hopkins University, 1949-1950, Catholic University of America, 1950-1951; executive secretary for anthropology and psychology, National Academy of Sciences, National Research Council, 1952-1954; assistant commissioner, State Museum and Science Service, New York State Education Department, 1954-1968; research professor of anthropology, S.U.N.Y. at Albany, 1968-1974, distinguished professor, 1974-1979. *Military service:* Research associate, Ethnogeographic Board, 1942-1945. *Memberships:* American Anthropological Association (executive board); American Folklore Society (Fellow; past president); American Indian Ethnohistorical Society; American Ethnological Society (past president); American Association for the Advancement of Science (Fellow); Museum of the American Indian (trustee, 1976-1980). *Awards, honors:* Adopted Seneca (Iroquois); Peter Doctor Award, Seneca Nation of Indians, 1958, for outstanding service to Iroquoian peoples; Cornplanter Medal for Iroquois Research, Cayuga County Historical Society, 1965; Hon. LL.D., Hartwick College, 1968; Dartmouth College Class of 1930 Award, 1979; named Dean in Perpetuum of Iroquoian Studies, 30th Conference on Iroquois Research, 1979; Fulbright-Hays research fellow to New Zealand, 1975; National Endowment for the Humanities fellow, Huntington Library, 1977-1979; member, Iroquois Documentary History Project, Newberry Library, 1979-1981. *Published works: The Iroquois Eagle Dance* (Bureau of American Ethnology, 1953); editor, *Symposium on Local Diversity in Iroquois Culture* (Bureau of American

Ethnology, 1955); editor, *Symposium on Cherokee and Iroquois Culture* (Bureau of American Ethnology, 1961); *American Indian and White Relations to 1830* (Institute of Early American History and Culture, University of North Carolina, 1957); *Parker on the Iroquois* (Syracuse University Press, 1968); editor and translated with E.L. Moore, Lafitan's *Customs of the American Indian (1724)* (The Champlain Society, 1974, 1977).

FERGUSON, ROBERT B. 1927-
(writer, producer)

Born December 30, 1927, Willow Springs, Mo. *Education:* Washington State University, B.A., 1954; Vanderbilt University, M.A., 1973. *Principal occupation:* Writer, producer. *Home address:* Box 12392, Nashville, Tenn. 37212. *Affiliations: Conservation film prodcuer, Tennessee Game and Fish Commission, Nashville, Tenn., 1956-1961; senior record producer, RCA Records, Nashville, Tenn., 1963-.* Military service: Field Artillery, 1946-1947; corporal, U.S. Marine Corps, 1950-1951. *Community activities:* Southeastern Institute of Anthropoogy (director of operations, 1966-); Tennessee Council on Archaeology. *Memberships:* Americn Philosophical Society, 1966-; MENSA, 1971-; Choctaw Nation Historical Society, 1971-. *Interests:* Writings on Southeastern Indian ethnohistory and contemporary affairs (editor, *Chahta Anumpa - The Choctaw Times,* 1968-1972); ethnography of the Mississippi Choctaws; related expeditions. *Published works:* Editor, *The Middle Cumberland Culture* (Vanderbilt Unviersity Press, 1972); *Indians of the Southeast, Then and Now,* with Jesse Burt (Abingdon Press, 1973).

FIELD, RAYMOND C.
(executive director-Indian association)

Affiliation: Executive director, National Tribal Chairmen's Association, 818 18th St., N.W., Suite 420, Washington, D.C. 20006.

FIELDS, AUDREY
(museum coordinator)

Affiliation: Coordinator, Dinjii Zhuu Enjit Museum, P.O. Box 42, Fort Yukon, Alaska 99740.

FISHER, DOROTHY D. (½ Coushatta) 1930-
(merchant-Indian arts and crafts)

Born July 7, 1930, Campti, La. *Principal occupation:* Owner, The Indian Maid, 153 Redlands Mall, Redlands, Calif. 92373. *Home address:* 210 E. Sunset Dr., N., Redlands, Calif. 92373. *Membership:* Indian Arts and Crafts Association. *Interests:* Collector and vendor of all types of Indian arts and crafts.

FISHER, JOE (Blackfeet) 1943-
(tribal administrator, photographer)

November 19, 1943, Santa Monica, Calif. *Education:* Haskell Indian Junior College, Lawrence, Kan., A.A., 1964; Northern Montana College, Havre, 1964-1966; University of Montana, Missoula, 1973-1974. *Principal occupation:* Tribal administrator, photographer. *Home address:* P.O. Box 944, Browning, Mont. 59417. *Affiliation:* Blackfeet Tribe, Box 850, Browning, Mont.; historical documentor, photographer. *Community activities:* American Legion; Blackfeet Societies: Rough Rides, Slickfoot, and Crazy Dog. *Military service:* U.S. Army (Sp-5 Engs.) (Vietnam Service Unit Commendation). *Membership:* VFW. *Interests:* Photographic showing, "Indian Pride on the Move," in Browning, Missoula, Helena; Blackfeet art slide presentation. *Published work: Blackfeet Nation,* 1977.

FLEMING, DARRELL (Cherokee) 1911-
(government administrator)

Born June 22, 1911, Bernice, Okla. *Education:* Haskell Institute, 1927-1933. *Principal occupation:* Government administrator. *Home address:* 8906 Knox Ave., S., Minneapolis, Minn. 55431. *Affiliation:* Assistant area director, B.I.A., Minneapolis, Minn. *Military service:* U.S. Navy, 1944-1946. *Awards, honors:* Presidntial Citation in recognition of outstanding contribution to greater economy and improvement in governmental operations, 1964.

FLORES, WILLIAM VANN (Cherokee-Papago) 1927-
(medical illustrator)

Born October 2, 1927, Appleton, Wis. *Education:* Chilocco Indian School, 1947; Kansas City Art Institute, 1949-1951; Art Center School, Los Angeles, 1955-1957; Oklahoma City University, 1958-1959; El Reno Junior College, 1965-1967. *Principal occupation:* Medical illustrator. *Home address:* P.O. Box 84, Concho, Okla. 73022. *Affiliation:* Medical illustrator, Federal Aviation Agency, Will Rogers Field, Oklahoam City, Okla., 1961-. *Military service:* U.S. Army, 1952-1954 (Korean Service Medal with two Bronze Stars; Presidential Unit Citation; Meritorious Unit Commendation; Good Conduct Medal; national Defense Service Medal; United Nations Service Medal). *Memberships:* Association of Medical Illustrators (first American Indian member); Kansas City Art Institute, Alumni; Society of Art Center Alumni, Los Angeles, Calif.

FOGELMAN, GARY L. 1950-
(editor/publisher)

Born January 1, 1950, Muncy, Pa. *Education:* Lock Haven State University, B.S., 1972; West Chester State University (two years; 18 credits for Masters). *Principal occupation:* Editor/publisher. *Home address:* RD# 1, Box 240, Turbotville, Pa. 17772. *Affiliation:* Editor/publisher, *Indian-Artifact Magazine. Memberships:* Local, state and northeastern archaeological societies; SPA (Chapter No. 8, vice president); IACAP (vice president). *Awards, honors:* Catlin Peace Pipe Award. *Interests:* Colecting Indian artifacts; hunting and fishing. *Published works: The Muncy Indians* (Grit Publishing, 1976); *The Pennsylvania Artifact Series (in progress).*

FOGLEMAN, BILLYE Y.S. 1927-
(anthropologist)

Born December 6, 1927, Plainview, Tex. *Education:* Hockaday Junior College, A.A., 1947; University of Texas, Austin, B.A., 1949; Southern Methodist University, M.A., 1971, Ph.D., 1972. *Principal occupation:* Anthropologist. *Home address:* Quail Call, Route 3, Box 44, Moscow, Tenn. 38057. *Affiliations:* Associate professor, Department of Psychiatry, Health Science Center, University of Tennessee, Memphis, 1976-. *Other professional posts:* Instructor, Texas Women's University, Eastfield Community College, Texas Christian University; consultant, Alcohol Abuse Training Project Related to Minority Populations, Memphis State University, 1976-1979; project administrator, Health Careers Opportunity Program, University of Tennessee, Memphis, 1981-1985. *Memberships:* American Anthropological Association (Fellow), 1972-; Society for Applied Anthropology (Sustaining Fellow), 1972-; Southern Anthropological Society, 1972-. *Awards, honors:* Graduated with honors, University of Texas, Austin; National Defense Education Scholarships, 1970-1972; Outstanding Women of Memphis, Chamber of COmmerce, 1975; Sigma Xi Honorary; Delta Kappa Gamma Hnorary; honored for contribution to Family Medicine Student Association, 1985. *Interests:* "Doctoral research on Native Americans in a southern metropolitan area; research on Vietnamese Refugees in a southern metropolitan area; medical student education; cultural considerations in patient care; avocational interests include travel, camping, fishing, theatre, visiting art museums, and family. *Published works:* "The Appropriation Hypothesis: Primary Interaction Among Urban Indians, II," (*International Migration Review,* Fall, 1973); "Abstract, "Will One Intertribal Center Clinic Survive?" (*In* Abstracts, 1974); "The Housewife Syndrome Among Native American Women," (*Tennessee Anthropologist,* 1977).

FOLLIS, WILLIAM (Modoc)
(tribal chief)

Affiliation: Chief, Modoc Tribal Council, P.O. Box 939, Miami, Okla. 74355.

FORBES, JACK D. (Powhatan (Renape) and Lenape) 1934-
(professor-Native American studies)

Born January 7, 1934, Long Beach, Calif. *Education:* University of Southern California, B.A., 1953; M.A., 1955, Ph.D., 1959. *Principal occupation:* Professor, Native American studies. *Home address:* Route 1, Box 23, Yosemite Ave., Davis, Calif. 95616. *Affiliations:* Research program director, Far West Laboratory, Berkeley, Calif., 1967-1969; professor, Native American Studies, University of California, Davis, 1969-. *Other professional post:* Co-editor, *Attan-Akamik. Community activities:* Powhatan Confederation (Chief's Council); California Indian Legal Services, Inc. (board of directors). *Membership:* California Indian Education Association. *Interests:* "Founder, Native American Movement (chairman, 1961-1962); founder of Coalition of Eastern Native Americans; co-founder of the United Native Americans, 1968; co-founder, D-Q University (volunteer instructor); working with Renape, Lenape, and other related languages." *Biographical sources: Who's Who in the West; Contemporary Authors. Published works: Apache, Navajo and Spaniard* (University of Oklahoma Press, 1961); *Warriors of the Colorado* (University of Oklahoma Press, 1965); *The Indian in America's Past* (Prentice-Hall, 1965); *Native Americans of California and Nevada* (Naturegraph, 1969); *Nevada Indians Speak* (University of Nevada Press, 1967); *Handbook of Native American Studies* (Tecumseh Center, 1971); *Aztecas del Norte* (Fawcett, 1973).

FORCE, ROLAND W. 1924-
(anthropologist, museum director)

Born December 30, 1924, Omaha, Neb. *Education:* Stanford University, B.A. (Psychology), 1950, M.A. (Education), 1951, M.A. (Anthropology), 1952, Ph.D. (Anthropology), 1958. *Principal occupation:* Anthropologist, museum director. *Home address:* 21 Rockleigh Rd., Rockleigh, N.J. 07647. *Affiliations:* Assistant curator, Leland Stanford Jr. Museum, Stanford, Calif., 1952-1953; acting instructor in anthropology, Stanford University, 1954; associate in ethnology, B.P. Bishop

Museum, Honolulu, 1954-1956; lecturer, Det. of Anthropology, University of Chicago, 1956-1961; curator of Oceanic Archaeology and Ethnology, Chicago Natural History Museum (Field Museum of Natural History), Chicago, 1956-1961; member, Graduate Affiliate Faculty, University of Hawaii, 1962-1977; director, B.P. Bishop Museum, 1962-1976; holder, Charles Reed Bishop Distinguished Chair in Pacific Studies (1976-1977), director emeritus, B.P. Bishop Museum, 1976-; director and secretary, board of trustees, Museum of the American Indian, Heye Foundation, New York City, 1977-. *Other professional posts:* Chairman of the executive committee and member representing Hawaii, Pacific Science Council, Pacific Science Association, 1966-1978; Bishop Trust Company, Honolulu, (director, member, board of directors), 1969-1977; honorary consultant, B.P. Bishop Museum, 1977-; trustee, W.T. Yoshimoto Foundation, Hawaii, 1979-. *Military service:* U.S. Army, 1943-1946 (sergeant; Corps of Engineers; combat duty, European Theatre of Operations). *Community services:* Member, advisory board, State-based Humanities Program, Hawaii, 1972-1975; member, Distribution Committees, Sophie Russell Testamentary Trust and Jessie Ann Chalmers Charitable Trust, Honolulu, 1972-1977; member, Barstow Foundation Committee (Samoan Eduction), Hawaii, 1963-. *Memberships:* Pacific Club, Honolulu, 1962-; Social Science Association, Honolulu, 1962-; American Anthropological Association; American Association for the Advancement of Science; American Association of Museums; International Council of Museums; National Trust for Historic Preservation; Pacific Science Association. *Awards, honors:* Selected by Chicago Junior Chamber of Commerce as one of Chicago's ten outstanding young men, 1958; Honorary Member, Association of Hawaiian Civic Clubs, 1967; Honorary Doctor of Science, Hawaii Loa College, 1973; Honorary Life Member, Bishop Museum Association, 1976; comendation, Senate Concurrent Resolution, Hawaii, 1976; Honoray Life Fellow, Pacific Science Association. *Biographical sources: Who's Who in America; American Men of Science. Published works:* Many articles in the *Museum of the Ameri-*

can Indian Newsletter, and other periodicals, including: "Arctic Art: Eskimo Ivory," *American Indian Art Magazine,* 1981); "A Common Misperception," *(MAI Newsletter,* 1984); "That Without Which Nothing," *(MAI Nesletter,* 1984); "Becons in the Night," *(MAI Newsletter,* 1984); "The Owls' Eyes Obsession," *(MAI Newsletter,* 1984); "Solving the Puzzle of the Past," *(MAI Newsletter,* 1985); among others.

FORD, RICHARD IRVING 1941-
(curator of ethnology)

Born June 27, 1941, Harrisburg, Pa. *Education:* Oberlin College, Ohio, M.A., 1963; University of Michigan, M.A., 1965, Ph.D., 1968. *Principal occupation:* Curator of ethnology. *Home address:* 2825 Provincial, Ann Arbor, Mich. 48104. *Affiliation:* Assistant professor of anthropology, University of Cincinnati, 1967-1969; Curator of ethnology and director, Museum of Anthropology, University of Michigan, Ann Arbor, Mich., 1970-. *Other professional post:* Professor of anthropology and botany, University of Michigan. *Memberships:* Conference of Native American Studies (national advisory committee); American Anthropological Association; Society for American Archaeology (executive committee); Society for Economic Botany (editorial board); The Archaeological Conservancy (secretary); American Association for Advancement of Science (section H, chairperson). *Interests:* Expert witness, Zuni Pueblo, N.M.; consultant to San Juan Pueblo, N.M.; North American ethnobotany; origins of American Indian agriculture; excavations, Jemez Cave and Bat Cove, N.M., and Cloudspitter, Ky. *Awards, honors:* Distinguished Service Award, University of Michigan, 1971; National Science Foundation grantee, 1970-1973, 1975-1976, 1978-1979; Weatherhead scholar, School of American Research, 1978-1979; *Biographical source: Who's Who in America.* Published works: co-author, *Paleoethnobotany of the Koster Site* (Illinois State Museum, 1972); editor, *The Nature and Status of Ethnobotany* (University of Michigan, 1978); editor, *Prehistoric Food Production in North America* (University of Michigan, 1985).

FORREST, ERIN (Modoc-Pit River)
1920-
(rancher, health programs administrator)

Born January 12, 1920, Alturas, Calif. *Education:* Riverside Junior College. *Principal occupation:* Rancher, health programs administrator. *Home address:* P.O. Box 763, Alturas, Calif. 96101. *Affiliations:* State Inheritance Tax Appraiser, 1964-1968; administrative assistant, State Assemblywoman Pauline Davis, 1969-1975; president, XL Indian Reservation Board of Directors, 1946-. *Other professional posts:* Chairman, PL 94-437 Policy Council; chairman, NTCA Health Committee; chairman, NCAI Health Committee; national Indian Health Liaison Officer, NTCA. *Community activities:* Modoc County Democratic Central Committee (chairman, 1968-). *Military service:* U.S. Army, ETO, World War II. *Memberships:* National Tribal Chairmens Association; National Congress of American Indians; California Tribal Chairmens Association; National Health Insurance Health Team. *Awards, honors:* Rural Services Award, Sargeant Shriver, 1969; Outstanding Achievements in Indian Community Development, awarded by Division of Indian Community Development, Indian Health Service, 1975; honored by California Senate Resolution, 1970; honored by California Assembly Resolution, 1975. *Interests:* Indian health programs; Appaloosa horses; wild life conservation; Indian artifacts; National Indian health and social concerns.

FOX, DENNIS R. (Mandan-Hidatsa)
1943-
(assistant director-education, B.I.A.)

Born September 8, 1943, Elbowoods, N.D. *Education:* Dickinson State College, Pa., B.S., 1966; Penn State University, M.Ed., 1971, D.Ed., 1977. *Principal occupation:* Assistant director of education, B.I.A. *Home address:* 4133 Conrad Rd., Alexandria, Va. 22312. *Affiliations:* Education program administrator, Johnson O'Malley Program, Bureau of Indian Affairs, Cheyenne River Agency and Aberdeen Area Office, S.D., 1975-1983; assistant director of education, Bureau of Indian Affairs, Washington, D.C. 1983-. *Other professional post:* Teacher, worked in B.I.A. higher education grant program. *Memberships:* National Indian Education Association; Phi Delta Kappa. *Awards, honors:* Gave presentation at National School Administration Conference. *Interests:* Educational administration. *Biographical source: Indians of Today,* 1970 edition.

FOX, SANDRA J. (HARRELL (Oglala Cheyenne River Sioux) 1944-
(education specialist)

Born December 9, 1944, Kadoka, S.D. *Education:* Dickinson State College, N.D., B.S., 1966; Penn State University, M.Ed., 1971, D.Ed., 1976. *Principal occupation:* Education specialist. *Home address:* 4133 Conrad Rd., Alexandria, Va. 22312. *Affiliations:* Education specialist, Bureau of Indian Affairs, Aberdeen Area Ofice, S.D.; education specialist-curriculum, ORBIS, Inc., Washington, D.C., 1985-. *Other professional post:* Education specialist and consultant, B.I.A. *Memberships:* International Reading Association; National Indian Education Association; North American Indian Women's Association. *Awards, honors:* North Dakota Indian Scholarship; invited to join Pi Lambda Theta; given presentations at National Council of Teachers of English Convention, national Reading Conference, and International Reading Association Convention. *Interests:* "Elementary and secondary education reading improvement." *Published work: An Annotated Bibliography of Young People's Books on American Indians* (Bureau of Indian Affairs, 1973).

FRANCISCO, ELDON (Laguna Pueblo)
(elementary school principal)

Education: Brigham Young University, B.S., 1963; New Mexico State University, M.A., 1972. *Principal occupation:* Elementary school principal. *Home address:* Route 2, Box 236, Walnut GHrove, Miss 39189. *Affiliation:* Principal, Standing Pine Day School, B.I.A., Walnut Grove, Miss. *Other profesional posts:* Agriculture Extension Agent, 1963-1968; school counselor. *Awards, honors:* B.I.A. Ten-Year Pin; EPDA Fellowship. *Interests:* "Personal development of Indian poeple nased upon their own initiative, motivation and resources."

FRANK, EARL
(tribal chairman)

Affiliation: Chairman, Bishop Tribal Council, P.O. Box 548, Bishop, Calif. 93514.

FRANK, ROBERT L. (Washoe)
(tribal chairman)

Affiliation: Chairman, Washoe Tribal Council, Route 2, Box 68, Gardnerville, Nev. 89410.

FRAZIER, GREGORY W. (Crow-Santee Sioux) 1947-
(business executive)

Born September 5, 1947, Richmond, Ind. *Education:* Earlham College, Richmond, Ind., 1965-1967; Temple University, Philadelphia, Pa., B.A. (Business Administration), 1972; University of Puget Sound, Tacoma, Wash., M.B.A. (Finance), 1978. *Principal occupation:* Business executive. *Home address:* P.O. Box 427, Englewood, Colo. 80151. *Affiliations:* Member, National Indian Planning Council, U.S. DOL; instructor/consultant, American Indian Management Institute, Albuquerque, N.M., 1972-1974; executive director, Seattle Indian Center, Inc., 1974-1977; executive director, AL-IND-ESK-A (The 13th Regional Corp.), Seattle, Wash., 1977-1979; chairman, Absarokee Investments, Seattle, Wash., 1977-; chief executive, National Urban Indian Council, Denver, Colo., 1979-; president, national Council for Indian Business, Englewood, Colo., 1980-. *Other professional posts:* Preisidential appointec, National Advisory Council on Indian Education; appointee, Secretary's Advisory Group, Department of HUD; appointee, Department of Labor Ad Hoc Advisory Committee. *Community activities:* King County Housing Task Force (member); Billings-Yellowstone Housing Association (member); Indians for United Social Action (member); National Low Income Housing Coalition (member). *Memberships:* National Indian Education Association; Indian Motorcycle Owners Association (vice president); National Indian Business Council (chairman, 1983-); Registered Lobbyist, U.S. House and Senate, Colorado General Assembly; American Management Association, 1980-. *Awards, honors:* Outstanding Contribution Award, CETA Coalition; Individual Personal Achievement Award, IHRC, Inc.; Outstanding Minority Writer, 1985, U.S. Writers Association; Best Business Efforts, Community Chamber of Commerce, 1985. *Interests:* "Business and economic development; developing countries; writing; international travel; collecting motorcycles; motorcycle road racing; fund raising consultant; owns several businesses, including Mountain Area Leasing, Intra City Properties, First Preferred Properties; manages own Montana ranch, commutes between offices in Colorado, Utah and Washington. *Published works: While We're At It, Why Don't We Find You a Job* (NCIB Press, 1984); *American Indian Index* (Arrowstar Publishing, 1985).

FREDERICKS, OSWALD WHITE BEAR (Hopi) 1905-
(artist)

Born February 6, 1905, Old Oraibi, Ariz. (Hopi Reservation). *Education:* Phoenix Indian School; Haskell Institute, Lawrence, Kan.; Bacone College, Bacone, Okla., B.S. *Principal occupation:* Artist (Hopi traditional arts and crafts). *Home address:* Box 8, Sedona, Ariz. 86336. *Affiliations:* Artist, Art Studio, Oraibi and Sedona, Ariz. *Other professional posts:* Lecturing, publication, teaching, Hopi history and religion. *Community activities:* Art instructor, Boys Club of America, Phoeniz, Ariz.; art instructor, YMCA; judge of Hopi Court, Oraibi, Ariz. *Memberships:* Ancient Astronaut (honorary member); Boy's Club of America; President Club, Univerity of Northern Arizona, Flagstaff. *Awards, honors:* Judge of the Hopi Tribal Court, Oraibi, Ariz.; awards for Hopi arts and crafts, and sports; technical advisor and coordinator, Hopi legend made to movie *Boy and Eagle* (Disney Productions). *Interests:* Ancient Hopi culture and history; relation to ancient ruins and history in Mexico, Yucatan; rock writing; travel;

ancient cultures and their relationship to Hopi culture and religion. *Biographical sources: Community Leaders and Noteworthy Americans* (Bicentennial Edition, 1976-1977). *Published works: Book of Hopi,* with Frank Waters (Viking Press, 1963); *Kasskara,* in German (Dusseldorf, Munich, 1979).

FREEMAN, KING (Pala)
(tribal chairman)

Affiliation: Chairman, Pala Executive Committee, P.O. Box 43, Pala, Calif. 92059.

FREEMAN, ROBERT LEE (Dakota-Luiseno) 1939-
(artist, cartoonist, muralist, printmaker)

Born January 14, 1939, Rincon Indian Reservation, Calif. Education: Palomar College, San Marcos, Calif., A.A., 1976, 1974-. *Principal occupation:* Artist, cartoonist, muralist, printmaker. *Home address:* 1697 Curry Comb Dr., San Marcos, Calif. 92069. *Affiliation:* Art instructor, Palomar College. *Military service:* U.S. Army, 1957-1960 (E-2 Korea, 1959). *Exhibitions:* One-man shows: Schiver Gallery, St. Louis, Mo.; Sioux Museum, Rapid City, S.D.; Turtle Mountain Gallery, Phildelphia, Pa.; Gallery of the American Indian, Sedona, Ariz; among others. Group shows: U.S. Department of the Interior, Washington, D.C.; Heard Museum, Phoenix, Ariz.; Scottsdale National Indian Art Exhibit, Ariz.; among others. Murals: Los Angeles Public Library (45 ft.) and five private murals in homes. Numerous selected public and private collections. *Awards, honors:* 150 national Indian art awards from the following: Scottsdale National Indian Art Exhibit, Heard Museum, Red Cloud Art Show, Southern California Exposition, Gallup Ceremonial, and California State Fair. *Interests:* Mr. Freeman works in several media and has won awards in oil, watercolor, woodcarving, etching, pen and ink, bronze, airbrush and drawing, acrylic and lithography. He has instructed the course Native American Art at Grossmont College, San Diego, and Palomar College, San Marcos, Calif. Travel. *Biographical sources: Who's Who in Indian Art; International*

Artists and Writers (Cambridge, England). *Published works:* Mr. Freeman's work has appeared in such periodicals as *Ford Times, Western Horseman, Southwest Art Scene, Indian Voices, Genie, North County Living, Westerner,* and "Artist of the Rockies." Paintings included in two books, *I Am These People,* and *Contemporary Sioux Paintings. Mr. Freeman has illustrated two books: The Layman's Typology Handbook,* and *The Luiseno People.* He is author and publisher of two cartoon books, *For Indians Only,* 1971, and *War Whoops and All That Jazz,* 1973; *Robert Freeman Drawings,* 1985.

FRENCH, EDGAR L., Jr. (Delaware)
(tribal chairman)

Affiliation: Chairman, Delaware Executive Committee, P.O. Box 825, Anadarko, Okla. 73005.

FRIEND, DAVID NATHAN
(executive director-Indian organization)

Affiliation: Executive director, National Center for American Indian Alternative Education, P.O. Box 18329, Capitol Hill Station, Denver, Colo. 80218.

FRISCH, JACK A. 1940-
(anthropologist)

Born May 26, 1940, Glen Cove, N.Y. *Education:* Northeastern University, B.A., 1962; Indiana University, M.A., 1964, Ph.D., 1970. *Principal occupation:* Anthropologist. *Affiliations:* Instructor, State University of New York at Plattsburgh, 1965-1967; assistant professor, Wayne State University, 1968-1972; associate professor, Washington State University, 1972-. *Memberships:* American Anthropological Association; American Folklore Society; American Society for Ethnohistory; Society of Sigma Xi; Central States Anthropological Society; American Association of University Professors; Council on Anthropology and Education; Society for Applied Anthropology. *Awards, honors:* Indiana University Graduate School grant-in-aid for summer research among the Maricopa Indians, Salt River Reservation, Scottsdale, Ariz., 1965; National Museum of Canada Research Contracts for ethnographic research among the St. Regis Mohawks, St. Regis Reserve, N.Y., Quebec, and Ontario, 1967-1971; Wayne State University Faculty grant-in-aid to continue research on St. Regis Mohawk religious ceremonies, 1969. *Interests:* North American Indian ethnology and ethnohistory; cultural anthropology; folklore and culture; linguistic anthropology; cultural dynamics. *Published works:* Numerous papers published in scholarly journals.

FRITZ, LINDA
(native law librarian)

Afiliation: Librarian, Native Law Centre, University of Saskatchewan, 150 Diefenbaker Centre, Saskatoon, Saskatchewan, Can.

FRYE, BILLY J.
(tribal chairman)

Affiliation: Chairman, Las Vegas Colony Council, 1 Paiute Dr., Las Vegas, Nev. 89106.

FULLER, NANCY J.
(coordinator-Native American museums program)

Affiliation: Coordinator, Native American Museums Program, Office of Museum Programs, Smithsonian Institution, Washington, D.C. 20560. *Published works:* Editor, *Native American Museum Program Newsletter,* 1982-1985; *Tribal Archives: An Introduction Slide/Tape Program,* 1983; Native American Museums: Development and Related Issues, A Bibliography, 1984; *Some Sources of Information for Native American Museums and Cultural Organizations,* 1985; *A Brief Reference Guide for Materials Concerning Native American Culture and History,* 1986. All published by the Office of Museums Program, Smithsonian Institution.

FULTON, WILLIAM DINCAN
(president-Amerind Foundation)

Affiliation: President, Amerind Foundation, Inc., Dragoon Rd., Box 248, Dragoon, Ariz. 85609.

FUNMAKER, KENNETH, Sr.
(Wisconsin Winnebago)
(tribal chairman)

Affiliation: Chairman, Wisconsin Winnebago Business Council, P.O. Box 311, Tomah, Wis. 54660.

G

GAHBOW, ARTHUR (Chippewa)
(tribal chairman)

Affiliation: Chairman, Mille Lacs Reservation Business Committee, Star Route, Onamia, Minn. 56359.

GARCIA, ALEX (Pueblo)
(Pueblo governor)

Affiliation: Governor, Santo Domingo Pueblo, P.O. Box 99, Santo Domingo Pueblo, N.M. 87052.

GARCIA, MARCELINO (Tewa Pueblo)
1932-
(instructional aid worker)

Born June 2, 1932, San Juan Pueblo, N.M. *Education:* U.S. Indian School, Santa Fe, N.M. *Principal occupation:* Instructional aid worker, B.I.A. *Home address:* P.O. Box 854, San Juan Pueblo, N.M. *Community Activities:* San Juan Pueblo Church (chairman). *Awards, honors:* Prize for Indian ceremonial sash belt, New Mexico State Fair.

GARCIA, NORMA JEAN
(Indian council chairwoman)

Affiliation: Chairwoman, Alturas General Council, P.O. Box 1035, Alturas, Calif. 96101.

GARREAUX, HAZEL (Cheyenne River Sioux) 1916-
(tribal official)

Born June 23, 1916, LaPlant, S.D. *Education:* Normal Training School; commercial diploma, Haskell Institute, 1940. *Principal occupation:* Tribal official. *Home address:* Box 44, Eagle Butte, S.D. 57625. *Affiliation:* Secretary, Cheyenne River Sioux Tribal Council, Eagle Butte, S.D., 1946-1949, 1959-.

GARROW, LEONARD (Mohawk)
(tribal chief)

Affiliation: Head chief, St. Regis Mohawk Council, St. Regis Reservation, Hogansburg, N.Y. 13655.

GASHLER, DAN
(public affairs-Indian Health Service)

Affiliation: Public affairs officer, Indain Health Service, 5600 Fishers Lane, Rockville, Md. 20857.

GENTIS, THIERRY 1958-
(assistant curator)

Born March 3, 1958, Bordeaux, France. *Education:* Roger Williams College, Bristol, R.I., B.A., 1981. *Principal occupation:* Assistant curator. *Home address:* Mount Hope Grant, Bristol, R.I. 02809. *Affiliation:* Assistant curator, Haffenreffer Museum of Anthropology, Brown University, Providence, R.I., 1983-. *Awards, honors:* Magna Cum Laude, Roger Williams College, 1981. *Interests:* African ethnographic art; arctic ethnographic arts and culture; familiar with textile and basketry arts; North American Indian ethnography; Oceanic ethnography; Andean culture. *Published work:* Traditional Art of Africa (Haffenreffer Museum of Anthropology), 1984.

GENTRY, BEATRICE (Wampanoag)
1910-
(teacher)

Born August 31, 1910, Gay Head, Mass.

Education: Framingham State College, Mass., B.S. (Education), 1932; Bureau of Indian Affairs Summer Institute, Pine Ridge, S.D., summer, 1935; Tulsa University, Teacher Certificate, 1962; Bridgewater State College, Hyannis, Mass., 1967-1968. *Principal occupation:* Teacher. *Home address:* State Road, R.F.D. #159, Gay Head, Mass. 02535. *Affiliations:* Teacher, Fort Sill Indian School, Lawton, Okla., 1934-1941; teacher, Wagoner Elementary School, Okla., 1960-1964; teacher, Chilmark Elementary School, Mass., 1964-1974. *Other professional posts:* President, Wampanoag Tribal Council of Gay Head, 1972-1976 (helped establish modern organizational structure of tribal government, first governing officer); member, Massachusetts Commission on Indian Affairs, 1974-1976 (helped establish and organize the first Massachusetts Indian Commission in the 20th century, and whose membership was all Native Americans of Massachusetts) *Community activities:* Town of Gay Head (zoning committee; Gay head Public Library (trustee); Gay Head Community Council (charter member); Wagoner School Band (president); Officers' Wives' Club (member, 1943-1958; secretary, 1947-1948; Griffith Air Force Base, Rome, N.Y.). *Memberships:* Oklahoma Education Association, 1934-1942, 1961-1964; Massachusetts Teachers Association, 1964-1975; National Indian Education Association, 1972-1975; National Retired Teachers' Association, 1975-. *Awards, honors:* Alumni Achievement Award, 1982, from Framingham State College Alumni Association at 50th anniversary of graduating class; Ancient Aquinnah (Gay Head) Indian Cemetary on behalf of the Wampanoag Tribal Council of Gay Head; speaker at dedication ceremonies of Gay Head Cliffs as National Landmark, centennial celebration of Town of Gay Head, Oklahoma Education Association Conference, and J.F. Kennedy Bicentennial Memorial Dinner, Natick Democratic Town Committee. *Interests:* "As an Air Force officer's wife, I have had the opportunity to live and travel to all parts of the continental U.S. and Europe. As a Native American educator with experience providing direct services to Native American children from different tribes, and experience working within the public school system in different parts of the country, I have learned that the only way for Native American people to determine their own destiny economically and politically among the dominant white society is to make the necessary demands upon the educational system of Indians and non-Indians alike: to provide an avenue to attain the goals that each society deems essential and demand respect for those values and cultures. The educational system's complete disregard and disrespect for Native American values and culture along with lack of Native American input in education programs, communication, counselling and advisement, and lack of role models result in not only inadequate preparation for college, but inadequate for life. I feel it is only through those demands on the educational system for all Americans (including Native Americans) that Native American people will be able to realize our basic needs: the preservation of our lands, the preservation of our religion, culture, and history, and the preservation of our families; that is the sacred rights of our people."

GEORGE, EVANS McCLURE, Jr. Catawba) 1932-
(textile worker)

Born January 26, 1932, Rock Hill, S.C. *Education:* Clemson University, 1952-1956. *Principal occupation:* Textile worker. *Home address:* 1119 McDow Dr., Rock Hill, S.C. 29730. *Affiliation:* Celanese Corporation, Celriver Plant, Rock Hill, S.C., 1958-. *Community activities:* Member, Rock Hill Parks & Recreation Commission; member, Catawba Indian Tribe; York County IPTAY Club (past president); Church Youth leader, 1968-. *Awards, honors:* Captain of 1950 South Carolina Shrine Bowl team; Clemson University Footbal team (captain, 1955); drafted by Washington Redskins, 1955; outstanding volunteer, American Cancer Society. *Interests:* Lifelong vocational interest in the American textile industry; coaching football; carpentry; fishing. *Biographical source:* "Red Carolinian - Where Are They Now?" and "People of the River," Evening Herald articles.

**GEORGE, OSWALD C. (Coeur D'Alene)
1917-**
(tribal official)

Born May 22, 1917, De Smet, Idaho. *Education:* Gonzaga University, 1936-1937. *Principal occupation:* Tribal official. *Home address:* Route 1, Plummer, Idaho 83851. *Affiliation:* Coeur D'Alene Tribal Council. *Military service:* U.S. Army Infantry, 1940-1945. *Community activities:* Boy Scouts of America (institutional representative); Veterans of Foreign Wars. *Memberships:* Affiliated Tribes of Northwest Indians (past president); National Congrss of American Indians (vice president, Portland area); Pacific Northwest Indian Center, Inc., Spokane, Wash. (board of trustees). *Interests:* "My interest lies in the youth of our nation; promoting citizenship, and training the future leaders of our country. I'm also very much interested in the preservation of our Indian culture and heritage; preservation of our treaty rights and the perpetual retention of our land base — these to me are sacred rights and should be respected."

GERARD, PAT
(executive director-Indian bank
and foundation)

Affiliations: Executive director, American Indian National Bank and American Indian Economic Development Foundation, 1700 K St., N.W., 2nd Floor, Washington, D.C. 20006.

GIAGO, MILLIE
(director-Indian center)

Affiliation: Director, Native American Center, 2900 S. Harvey, Oklahoma City, Okla. 73109.

GIAGO, ROBERT
(director-Indian program)

Affiliation: Director, American Indian Training and Employment Program, 2900 S. Harvey, Oklahoma City, Okla. 73109.

**GIBSON, CLAY (Mississippi Choctaw)
1927-**
(employment assistance program director)

Born November 1, 1927, Leake County, Miss. *Education:* Clarke M. College, A.A., 1955; Mississippi College, B.A., 1957; Southwestern Baptist Theological Seminary, S.D., 1962; East Central Junior College. *Principal occupation:* Employment assistance program director. *Home address:* Route 7, Box 253, Philadelphia, Miss. 39350. *Affiliation:* Mississippi Band of Choctaw Indians, Philadelphia, Miss., 1967-. *Other professional posts:* Ordained Baptist Minister for thirty years; missionary tribal council member for two terms; tribal chairman, 1965-1967. *Community activities:* Community Development Club; church and religious activities. *Membership:* Baptist Association, 1945- (moderator, six years; clerk, five years). *Interests:* Ministry; business administration; social services; tribal programs, B.I.A.; travel.

**GIDDINGS, RUTH ELIZABETH
WARNER 1919-**
(anthropologist)

Born June 17, 1919, Yonkers, N.Y. *Education:* University of Arizona, B.A., 1941, M.A., 1945. *Principal occupation:* Anthropologist. *Home address:* Mount Hope Grant, Bristol, R.I. 02809. *Affiliations:* Research assistant, museum assistant, University of Arizona, Arizona State Museum, 1941-1942; excavations on expeditions to Alaska, 1960, 1964-1967; curator, dirctor of public education, Brown Unviersity, Haffenreffer Museum of Anthropology, 1965-. *Memberships:* Amerian Anthropological Association (Fellow); Society for American Archeaology; American Association for the Advancement of Science; Arctic Institute of North America; Archaeological Institute of North America, 1969-1971; Bristol Historical Society. *Awards, honors:* Honorary M.A., Brown University; Sigma Xi. *Interests:* "Anthropological and archaeological study in Alaska; expeditions to Canada, Alaska, Mexico, and Denmark. Special interests — Eskimo and their pottery, origins, earliest men to people of the new world; Indians of the Americas; how to teach school children in a museum setting about non-literate peoples, by using the collections, experiential techniques, and role-playing participation in the lifeways of the cultures being studied." *Published works: Yaqui Folk Literature* (University of Arizona Press, 1942; revised 1967); *Yaqui Myths and Legends* (Univerity of Arizona Press, 1967).

GILL, JOSEPH C. 1926-
(educator)

Born July 15, 1926, Madison, Wis. *Education:* Marquette University, 1944-1946; St. Louis University, B.A., 1950, M.A., 1953, S.T.L., 1961; University of South Dakota, Ed.D., 1971. *Principal occupation:* Station manager of "Kini," a public service FM radio station serving the Rosebud Reservation, St. Francis, S.D. *Home address:* St. Francis Mission, S.D. 57572. *Affiliations:* Kini Radio Station; instructor (part-time), St. Francis Indian School.

GILLILAND, HAP 1918-
(professor of education and Native American culture)

Born August 26, 1918, Willard, Colo. *Education:* Western State College, Gunnison, Colo., B.A., 1949, M.A., 1950; University of Northern Colorado, Greeley, Ed.D., 1958. *Principal occupation:* Professor of eucation and Native Americn culture. *Home address:* 517 Rimrock Rd., Billings, Mont. 59102. *Affiliations:* Director, Northern Cheyenne Campus Experience Project, 1965; director, Crow Indian Reservation Educational Survey, 1966-1967; director, Remedial Reading, Northern Cheyenne Reservation, 1965-1968; director, Indian Upward Bound Project, 1966-1969; director, EPDA and NDEA in Remedial Reading for Indian students, 1967, 1969-1970; reading specialist, Lake Penn Schools, Alaska (14 Indian and Eskimo villages), Fall 1980, 1981, 1983; professor of education and Native American culture, Eastern Montana College, Billings, 1960-. *Community activities:* Chairman, Northern Cheyenne Tribal Scholarship Committee, 1966-1969; Northern Cheyenne Education Planning Committee, 1965-1972;

Indian Education Committee, Eastern Montana College, 1967-1977. *Memberships:* Montana Council for Indian Education (president, 1976-); Committee on Native Americans and Reading, International Reading Association (chairman, 1979-1980); National Indian Edcution Committee; Association on American Indian Affairs, 1965-. *Interests:* "Three extended trips to South America to live with newly contacted Indian tribes; two trips to New Zealand to conduct teacher training for teachers of Maori students." *Published works: Practical Guide to Remedial Reading* (Chas. E. Merrill Publishing, 1974, 1978); *Chant of the Red Man* (Council for Indian Education, 1976); ten children's books books in 1976 for Council for Indian Education.

GIPP, GERALD
(superintendent-Indian college)

Affiliation: Superintendent, Haskell Indian Junior College, Bureau of Indian Affairs, Lawrence, Kan. 66044.

GIPP, WILLIAM C. (Standing Rock Sioux) 1940-
(B.I.A. agency superintendent)

Born November 11, 1940, Fort Yates, N.D. (Standing Rock Reservation). *Education:* Black Hills State College, Spearfish, S.D., B.S., 1968; South Dakota State University, Brookings, M.A., 1973. *Home address:* Box 408, Rosebud, S.D. 57570. *Affiliation:* Superintendent, Rosebud Sioux Agency, Rosebud, S.D., 1984-. *Other professionsal posts:* Board of directors, Boy Scouts of America, Minnesota. *Military service:* U.S. Army, 1963-1967 (Sergeant E-5, Special Forces, Vietnam Vet). *Memberships:* American Legion; Veterans of Foreign Wars; National Congress of American Indians; South Dakota Teachers Association.

GLAZER, SUZY
(editor)

Affiliation: Editor, *Indian Truth,* Indian Rights Association, 1505 Race St., Philadelphia, Pa. 19102.

GLUBOK, SHIRLEY
(writer, lecturer)

Born in St. Louis, Mo. *Education:* Washington University, B.A. (Art and Archaeology); Columbia University, M.A. (Childhood Education). *Principal occupation:* Writer, lecturer. *Affiliation:* Lecturer on art for children, Metropolitan Museum of Art, New York, N.Y., 1958-. *Memberships:* American Archaeological Society; American Association of Museums; Authors League of America. *Published works: The Art of the North American Indian* (Harper and Row, 1964); *The Art of the Eskimo* (Harper and Row, 1964); *The Fall of the Aztecs* (St. Martin's Press, 1965); among others.

GOFF, DAVID J. 1925-
(historical society director)

Born May 3, 1925, Canastoga, N.Y. *Principal occupation:* Historical society director. *Home address:* 6464 Burleson Rd., Oneida, N.Y. 13421. *Affiliation:* Director, Madison County Historical Society, Oneida, N.Y. *Other professional post:* Traditional crafts consultant, New York State Council on the Arts. *Memberships:* New York State Historical Society; American Association for State and Local History. *Awards, honors:* Adopted Blood Brother, Oneida Nation; Certificate of Commendation, American Association for State and Local History. *Interests:* "Traditional crafts of the Oneida Indians; Oneida language, customs, and history; traditional pioneer New York State crafts; conservation; education - taking history from the museum to the school."

GOGOL, JOHN M. 1938-
(university professor, publisher)

Born August 15, 1938, Westfield, Mass. *Education:* Clark University, B.A., 1960; University of Washington, M.A., 1965, ABD Doctoral Candidacy, 1969. *Principal occupation:* University professor, publisher. *Home address:* P.O. Box 66124, Portland, Oreg. 97266. *Affiliations:* Instructor, Colorado State University, 1965-1968; assistant professor of humanities, Pacific University, Forest Grove, Oreg., 1970-1974; publisher,

Mr. Cogito Press, Pacific University, 1973-; publisher, *American Indian Basketry and Other Native Arts,* 1979-; director, Institute for the Study of Traditional American Indian Arts, 1979-. *Memberships:* Oregon Archaeological Society; Oregon Historical Society; Central States Archaeological Society; Coordinating Council of Literary Magazines; COSMEP. *Awards, honors:* Graves Prize Award in the Humanities, 1971. *Interests:* "In a long teaching career (I) taught German, Russian, comparative literature, American Indian studies, American history, European history, mathematics, physics, and humanities; poet and translator of German, Russian and Polish poetry." *Biographical sources:* "Poetic Justice," by Walt Curtis (*Willamette Week,* Oct.-Nov., 1985); "Basketry and Reservation of Culture," by Paul Pintarich (*Northwest Magazine, The Oregonian,* June, 1983); among others. *Published works: Native American Words* (Tahmahnawi's Publishers, 1973); *Columbus Names the Flowers* (Mr. Cogito Press, 1984); articles and other publications in numerous periodicals.

GOLLNICK, WILLIAM
(school administrator)

Affiliation: Administrator, Oneida Tribal School, Box 365, c/o Oneida Tribe, Oneida, Wis. 54155-0365

GOODBEAR, PEARL ROSE GOODSON
(Choctaw) 1915-
(teacher, education specialist)

Born November 30, 1915, Tuskahoma, Okla. *Education:* University of New Mexico, 1936-1938; Southeastern State College, B.S., 1939; Southwestern State College, M.T., 1961; Oklahoma State University, graduate assistant in English, 1971-1972; Bureau of Indian Affairs, workshops (education, alcoholism, administration; attended summer courses at the following schools: University of Mexico, Spanish, 1941; U.C.L.A., elementary work, 1954; University of Arizona, management supervision, 1964, 1966, 1970; University of Brockport, N.Y., English, 1968. *Principal occupation:* Teacher, education specialist.

Home address: Route 2, Box 142, Stillwater, Okla. 74074. *Affiliations:* Teacher, Albuquerque Indian School, 1939-1940; teacher, Standing Rock Day School, Crownpoint, N.M., 1941-1942; head teacher, Crownpoint Boarding School, 1942; teacher, supervisor of dorms, Thoreau Boarding School, N.M., 1953, 1957-1958; teacher, Special Navajo Program, Chemawa Indian School, Oreg., 1955-1957; education specialist, Crownpoint, N.M., 1958-1961; department head, Chilocco Indian School, Okla., 1961-1970; graduate assistant, Department of English, Oklahoma State University, 1971-1972; administrator, Indian Recovery (alcoholism program), North Central Oklahoma Intertribal Helth Council, Pawnee, Okla., 1972-1974; director, Native American Alcoholism Program (formerly Indian Recovery), 1974-1977. *Military service:* U.S. Navy (WAVES), 1944-1945 *Awards, honors:* Husband was Paul Flying Eagle Goodbear, Cheyenne artist, deceased, 1954.

GOODMAN, LINDA J.
(professor)

Born in Denver, Colo. *Education:* University of Colorado, Boulder, B.A., 1966; Wesleyan University, Middleton, Conn., M.A., 1968; Washington State University, Pullman, Ph.D., 1978. *Principal occupation:* Professor. *Home address:* 4135 Dover St., Wheat Ridge, Colo. 80033. *Affiliation:* Assistant professor, Department of Music, Colorado College, Colorado Springs, Colo., 1979-. *Other professional posts:* Advisor of Native American students at Colorado College; director of tribes program for pre-college Native American students. *Community activities:* Talks on Native American music and culture to various museum groups, tour groups, and Native American groups; have organizaed various Native American music and dance performances for non-Indian audiences; consultant for Native American music education programs, District II public schools, Colorado Springs, Colo.; member, Colorado Springs Native Americans Women's Association; organized Native American symposia, art shows, and guest speakers at Colorado College. *Memberships:* American Anthropological Association, 1975-; American Folklore Society, 1975-; American Eth-

nological Society, 1975-; Society for Ethnomusicology, 1975-; Native American Women's Association, Colorado College, 1977-. *Awards, honors:* American Philosophical Society grant, 1967, to work on Pueblo Indian music; 1979 Humanities Division Research Grant from Colorado College, to work on life history of Makah Indian singer; 1980 Mellon Grant, to work on Southwest Indian music, to teach as a new course; 1983 American Council of Learned Societies Fellowship for work on life history of a Northwest Coast musician. *Interests:* "Native American music and culture, especially Northwest Coast and American Southwest. (I) have spent much time traveling and living on reservations in both areas, studying music and culture, attending ceremonies, learning from the people in those areas. Have lead many field trips of college students to various reservations in the Southwest so that they could see and talk to the people living there and learn from them first-hand. Have lead a tour group of older people to the Makah Reservation for the same purpose. I am writing books and articles on Native American music and culture. I am very interested in teaching, counseling, and advising Native American young people, helping them find a way to fit into two worlds. Have worked with a number of Native American students over the years, and I'm interested in Indian singing and dancing, and participate on the few occasions when it is appropriate." *Published works: Music and Dance in Northwest Coast Indian Life* (Navajo Community College Press, 1977); "A Makah Biography," in *Dalmoma: Digging for Roots* (Empty Bowl Press, 1985); "Nootka Indian Music," in *New Grove Dictionary of Music in the U.S.* (Macmillan, 1986).

GORANSON, FREDERICK ARNOLD 1926-
(educator)

Born January 11, 1926, Waltham, Mass. *Education:* University of Wyoming, B.S., 1951; University of Oregon, M.S., 1958. *Principal occupation:* Educator. *Home address:* RFD Poudre Canyon Route, Bellevue, Colo. 80512. *Affiliations:* Head the now well known 'Navajo Gourd Rattle Dance' for the Youth Group, Navajo Club of Los Angeles in 1962, adapted to Hopi version of Navajo Yei-bi-chei song of 1917. Hope to put photos, Navajo historical and cultural material I've gathered into book form."

GORMAN, CLARENCE N. (Navajo)
1931-
(monument superintendent)

Born May 28, 1931, Chinle, Ariz. *Education:* Northern Arizona University. *Principal occupation:* Monument superintendent. *Address:* Aztec National Monument, Route 1, Box U, Aztec, N.M. 87410. *Affiliations:* Maintenance foreman, park ranger, Canyon de Chelly National Monument, Chinle, Ariz.; park ranger, Mesa Verde National Park, Colo.; park ranger, White Sands National Monument, Alamagordo, N.M.; superintendent, Wupatki-Sunset Crater National Monument, Flagstaff, Ariz.; superintendent, Pipestone National Monument, Pipestone, Minn.; superintendent, Aztec National Monument, Aztec, N.M. *Other professional posts:* Navajo Tribal Ranger, 1958; teacher, Bureau of Indian Affairs, 1959. *Military service:* U.S. Marine Corps, 1951-1954 (Good Conduct Medal, U.S. Service Medal, National Defense Medal, Presidential Unit Citation, Korean Presidential Unit Citation, Korean Service Medal with three Battle Stars). *Memberships:* National Riflemen's Association; Southwest Parks and Monuments Association, Inc.; Parks & Recreation Association; Pipestone Shrine Association.

GORMAN, FREDERICK JOHN ELIOT
1943-
(professor)

Born August 16, 1943, Maine. *Education:* Northeastern University, B.A., 1966; University of Arizona, M.A., 1972, Ph.D., 1976. *Principal occupation:* Professor of anthropology and archaeology of prehistoric American Indians. *Home address:* 189 Bay State Rd., Boston, Mass. 02215. *Affiliation:* Assistant professor and professor of anthropology, Department of Anthropology, Boston University, Boston, Mass., 1974-. *Other*

professional posts: Director, Boston University Archaeological Field School. *Memberships:* Sigma Xi, 972-; American Anthropological Association, 1974-; Society for American Archaeology, 1974-; Society of Professional Archaeologists, 1976-; Society for Historical Archaeology, 1976-; Society for the Preservation of New England Antiquities, 1975-. *Awards, honors:* National Science Foundation Research Grants awarded to the Southwest Archaeological Expedition, Field Museum of Natural History, 1970-1972; National Park Service, Dept. of the Interior Grants fpr archaeological site development of the New England glass works, 1975-1978. *Interests:* Southwest Archaeological Field Expeditions; early American Indian hunters; rise and fall of ancient American Civilizations; prehistory of Southwestern Indians; Mohave Indian Tribe. *Biographical sources:* Who's Who in the West; Dictionary of International Biography; The Archaeologist's Yearbook, 1975; Who's Who in the U.S., 1975; American Men of Achievement (3rd Edition). *Published works:* Numerous articles in journals.

GORMAN, R.C. (Navajo) 1934-
(artist)

Born July 26, 1934, Chinle, Ariz. *Education:* Northern Arizona University; Mexico City College. *Principal occupation:* Artist. *Address:* Navajo Gallery, P.O. Box 1756, Taos, N.M. 87571. Military service: U.S. Navy, 1952-1956. *Memberships:* Pacific Northwest Indian Center, Gonzaga University (board member); Wheelwright Museum, Santa Fe, N.M. (board member); Kellogg Fellowship Screening Committee, Navajo Health Authority, Window Rock, Ariz. (Fellow); Four Corner State Art Conference; New Mexico Arts and Crafts Fair (standards committee, juror). *Exhibitions:* Mr. Gorman's work has appeared in numerous one-man and group shows and is part of public and private collections. *Awards, honors:* Numerous awards and prizes for art from the following exhibitions and shows: All American Indian Days Art Exhibition; American Indian Artists Exhibitions; Center for Arts for Indian America; Heard Museum; National Cowboy Hall of Fame;

teacher, Alaskam Territorial Schools, 1954-1960; adult, elementary, secondary education, and Job Corps, Bureau of Indian Affairs, in Alaska, Navajo, Mescalero Apache, and Cheyenne River Sioux Reservations, 1960-. *Military service:* U.S. Army, 1943-1945 (Europe with 66th Infantry Division). *Interests:* Community schools; continuing education for adults; the role of the federal government in local education.

GORDON, PATRICIA TRUDELL
(Santee Sioux-Mdewakantonwan Band) 1943-
(director, Indian organization)

Born August 24, 1943, Woodbury County, Iowa. *Education:* Morningside College, B.A., 1977. *Principal Occupation:* Executive Director, Indian Youth of America, Inc. *Home Address:* 2600 South Steele, Sioux City, Iowa 51106. *Affiliations:* Camp Director, Indian Youth Camps in Oregon, Arizona, Idaho, and South Dakota, summer of 1976-; Executive Director, Indian Youth of America, Sioux City, Iowa 51106, 1978-. *Other Professional Posts:* Assistant director/counselor, Indian Studies Program, Morningside College, 1977-1984. *Community Activities:* Iowa Supreme Court Commission on Continuing Legal Education (commissioner); Sioux City Human Rights Commission (chairperson); United Way of Siouxland Agency Relations Committee (member); Native American Child Care Center (panel chair, board of directors). *Awards, Honors:* Sertoma Service to Mankind Award, 1983; participant for the Community International Fellows, a program of the International Leadership Development Institute; Robert F. Kennedy Memorial Fellow. *Interests:* "My main concern and interest at this time is working with Indian young people and improving there lives. I am also very interested in the law especially pertaining to American Indians. Women's issues will always be one of my concerns. My work has taken me throughout the U.S. giving lectures and presentations. I have very little time for hobbies, however, I make time for racquetball, bicycling and reading."

GORMAN, CARL NELSON *(Kin-ya-onny beyeh)* (Navajo) 1907-
(artist, lecturer)

Born October 5, 1907, Chinle, Ariz. *Education:* Otis Art Institute, Los Angeles, Calif., Graduate, 1951, extension courses, 1952, 1953. *Principal occupation:* Artist, lecturer—Navajo culture. *Address:* P.O. Box 431, Window Rock, Ariz. 86515., or c/o Navajo Gallery, P.O. Box 1756, Taos, N.M. 87571. *Affiliations:* Illustrator and technical illustrator, Douglas Aircraft Co., Santa Monica, Lawndale, Torrance, Calif., 1951-1963; manager, Navajo Arts & Crafts Guild, 1964-1966; director, Navajo Culture Center, ONEO, Fort Defiance, Ariz., 1966-1969; lecturer, Navajo history and culture, and American Indian art in cultural perspective with workshop, and Navajo language, Native American studies, applied behavioral sciences, University of California, Davis, 1970-1973, retired; director, Office of Native Healing Sciences, Navajo Health Authority, Window Rock, Ariz., 1973-1976, retired; coordinator, Navajo Resources/Curriculum Development, Navajo Community College, Tsaile, Ariz., 1977-. *Other professional posts:* Kin-ya-onny beyeh Originals, professional arts and crafts, 1951-; lecturer-consultant, Navajo arts, history, culture, 1964-. *Military service:* U.S. Marine Corps, 1942-1945, "with group that developed Navajo Code." *Community activities:* Inter-Tribal Indian Ceremonial (executive committee, 1964-1965); Navajo Tribal Fair (arts and crafts exhibit chairman, 1964-1965; evening performance chairman, 1968); Navajoland Festival of the Arts (board member, 1976-). *Memberships:* Navajo Club of Los Angeles (board of directors, several offices, 1955-1964); Otis Art Institute Alumni Association, 1952-; 2nd Marine Division Association; Veterans of Foreign Wars (life member); Navajo Code Talkers Association; Kiwanis, 1978. *Exhibitions:* Mr. Gorman's work has appeared in numerous one-man and group shows and is part of public and private collections. *Interests:* "All phases of art, subjects chiefly Navajo, horses, rock art, but including non-Indian subjects, in a variety of styles and media. Interested in improving quality, expanding markets, and promoting new and adaptive Navajo arts and crafts. In dance, I originated

Philbrook Indian Art Exhibitions; Scottsdale National Indian Arts Exhibition. In the Fall of 1973, Mr. Gorman was the only living artist to be included in the show, "Masterworks of the Museum of the American Indian," held at the Metropolitan Museum in New York City. Two of his drawings were selected for the cover of the show's catalog. In 1975, he was honored by being the first artist chosen for a series of one-man exhibitions of contemporary Indian artists held at the Museum of the American Indian. *Interests:* Mexican art and artists; lithography; cave painting and petroglyphs. *Biographical sources: A Taos Mosaic* (University of New Mexico Press); *American Indian Painter; Arrow III* (Pacific Grove Press); *Art and Indian Individuals* (Northland Press); *Dictionary of International Biography; Indian Painter and White Patrons,* J.J. Brody; *Indians of Today; Masterworks from the Museum of the American Indian* (Metropolitan Museum of Art); *Register of U.S. Living Artists; Who's Who in America; Who's Who in the West; Who's Who in American Art. Published works:* Mr. Gorman's works appear inthe following books: *American Indian Painters* (Museum of the American Indian); *Great American Deserts* (National Geographic Society, 1972); *Southwest Indian Painting* (University of Arizona Press, 1973); *The Man Who Sent the Rain Clouds* (Viking Pres, 1974); *Gorman Goes Gourmet; The Lithographs of R.C. Gorman* (Northland Press); *Graphics: A Self Portrait of America.*

GOSS, JAMES ARTHUR 1934-
(professor of anthropology)

Born September 14, 1934, Marion County, Ohio. *Education:* University of Oregon, B.A., 1960; University of Chicago, M.A., 1962, Ph.D., 1972. *Principal occupation:* Professor of anthropology. *Address:* Department of Anthropology, Washington State University, Pullman, Wash. 99163. *Affiliations:* Visiting lecturer in anthropology and linguistics, University of California, Los Angeles, 1964-1966; assistant-associate professor of anthropology, Washington State University, 1966-. *Other professional posts:* Co-editor, *Northwest Anthropologi-*

cal Research Notes, 1967-1970. *Military service:* U.S. Air Force, 1954. *Community activities:* Consultant on problems of Nez Perce children learning English, Nez Perce Headstart Program. *Memberships:* American Anthropological Association; Linguistic Society of America; Society for American Archaeology; Society of Sigma Xi; Northwest Anthropological Conference; Great Basin Anthropological Conference; International Salish Conference. *Awards, honors:* NDEA Title IV Fellowship in Anthropology, University of Chicago, 1960-1963; research assistanship and linguistic research grant, Tri-Ethnic Project, University of Colorado, 1961, 1962; Department of the Interior, National Geographic Society Research Grant, Wetherill Mesa Verde National Park, Colo., 1961-1963; UCLA Academic Senate Grant for *A Pilot Demographic Study of the American Indian Community of the Greater Los Angeles Area,* 1965; WSU Grant-in-Aid for *A Survey of Interior Salish Languages,* 1967; consultant grant, Nez Perce Headstart Program, 1971; NEH Postdoctoral Fellowship in American Indian Studies, Indiana University, 1972-1973. *Interests:* Linguistic anthropology; ethnosemantics; culture-historical reconstruction. *Published works:* Various technical articles in professional journals.

GRANT, MORRIS (Sauk-Suiattle)
(tribal business manager)

Affiliation: Business manager, Sauk-Suiattle Tribal Council, 5318 Chief Brown Lane, Darrington, Wash. 98241.

GRAY, GERALD J.
(Indian school principal)

Affiliation: Principal, Chemawa Indian School, 3700 Chemawa Rd., NE, Salem, Ore. 97303.

GRAY, SHORTY "LITTLE SCOUT"
(United Lumbee-Cherokee) 1934-
(log scaler)

Born November 2, 1934, Los Angeles, Calif. *Education:* Modesto City Schools, Calif. *Principal occupation:* Log scaler. *Home address:* Star Route, McArthur, Calif. 96056. *Affiliation:* United Lumbee Nation of N.C. and the America's (Deer Clan chief). *Community activities:* Inter Mountain Horseman's Association (vice president, 1984; president, 1985). *Memberships:* United Lumbee Nation (vice-chief, 1984; chief, 1985-); United Lumbee Nation Mantoca Medicine Society; High Eagle Warrior Society (vice-chief, 1985-). *Awards, honors:* California State Horseman's Association (Region 18 High Point Champion Gymkhana Rider, 1983 and 1984; 1983 and 1985 High Point Rider, Inter Mountain Horseman's Association. *Interests:* "Traditional skills: hunting, fishing, scouting; fur training, bow hunting, horse-raising; shelter building, survival living."

GRAYSON, NOLEY (Choctaw) 1943-
(professor, educational administrator)

Born September 4, 1943, Talihina, Okla. *Education:* Southeastern Oklahoma State University, Durant, B.A., 1969; The Pennsylvania State University, M.Ed., 1975, Ph.D., 1979. *Home address:* 1443 N. Allen St., State College, Penn. 16803. *Affiliation:* Assistant professor, educational administration, director of American Indian Leadership Program, The Pennsylvania State University, University Park, Pa. 16802. *Military service:* U.S. Army, 1961-1964. *Memberships:* National Indian Education Association; Amerian Educational Research Association; Phi Delta Kappa. *Awards, honors:* Kellogg Fellowship, 1984-1987, W.W. Kellogg Foundation; Graduate Fellowship, American Indian Leadership Program, 1974.

GREEN, ELWOOD
(museum curator)

Affiliation: Curator, Native American Centre for the Living Arts, Inc., 25 Rainbow Mall, Niagara Falls, N.Y. 14303.

GREEN, RAYNA (Cherokee) 1942-
(program developer)

Born July 18, 1942, Dallas, Tex. *Education:* Southern Methodist University, Dallas, B.A., 1963, M.A., 1966; Indiana University, Bloomington, Ph.D. (Folklore, American Studies), 1974. *Principal occupation:* Program developer. *Home address:* 1369 F St., N.E., Washington, D.C. 20002. *Affiliations:* Program director, American Association for the Advancement of Science, 1975-1980; program director, Dartmouth College, Hanover, N.H., 1980-1983; planner, Smithsonian Institution, 1983-. *Other professional posts:* Visiting professor, University of Massachusetts, and Yale University; consultant to numerous federal agencies, tribes, tribal/Indian organizations, institutions, museums, and universities. *Community activities:* Ms. Foundation for Women (board member); Indian Law Resource Center, Fund for the Improvement of Post-Secondary Education (board member); Phelps-Stokes Fund (Indian advisory board). *Memberships:* American Folklore Society (president); American Engineering Society, Society for the Advancement of Native Americans and Chicano Scientists; Amerian Anthropological Association. *Awards, honors:* Smithsonian Fellow, 1970; Ford Foundation, National Research Council Fellow, 1983. *Interests:* Ameriacn folklorist; research on Native American women; Southern women; American material culture; Indian traditional science, technology, and medicine; Indian energy/minerals development; poetry/short fiction; film/TV script writing; exhibit production. *Published works: Native American Women: A Contextual Bibliography* (Indiana University Press, 1982); *That's What She Said: Contemporary Poetry and Fiction by Native American Women* (Indiana University Press, 1984); Introduction to Pissing in the Snow: Other Ozark Folktales; Handicrafts in the Southern Highlands; articles and essays in *Ms. Magazine, Southern Exposure, Science, Handbook of American Folklore, Handbook of North American Indians,* and *Signs.*

GREGORY, JACK DWAIN (Cherokee) 1930-
(professor, writer)

Born June 25, 1930, Muskogee, Okla. *Education:* University of Oklahoma, 1951-1952; Northeastern State University, Tahlequah, Okla., B.A., 1951, M.A., 1953; Arizona State University, doctoral work, 1971-1972.

Principal occupation: Professor, writer. *Affiliations:* Teacher, Muskogee Public Schools, Okla., 1953-1963; professor, University of Arkansas, 1964-1968; professor, University of West Florida, 1969-? *Other professional posts:* Director, forensics workshop, University of Arkansas, 1965-1968; director of forensics, University of West Florida. *Awards, honors:* Youth Work Awards, Elks, American Legion, Toastmasters; Chief's Sash Creek Tribal Award, Interfraternity Council Award. *Interests:* Speech communication and debate; forensics; frontier history; Indian history; Five Civilized Tribes; Indian mythology and folklore; archaeology and ethnohistory; oral communication history of tribes; Cherokee-Mexican Sequoyah Expedition; Indian herbs, cures, medicine men and witch doctors. *Published works: Sam Houston With the Cherokees* (University of Texas, 1965); *Cherokee Spirit Tales* (Indian Heritage, 1969); *Creek-Seminole Spirit Tales* (Indian Heritage, 1970); *Hell on the Border* (Indian Heritage, 1971); *Choctaw Spirit Tales* (Indian Heritage, 1972).

GRIFFITH, GLADYS GIBSON 1925-
(artist)

Born March 15, 1925, Piqua, Ohio. *Education:* High School. *Principal occupation:* Artist. *Home address:* 263 E. Main St., Piqua, Ohio 45356. *Other professional post:* Lecturer on Indian affairs. *Memberships:* Museum of Natural History, 1970-; Ohio Archaeological Society, 1970-; Miami County Historical Society, 1970-; Miami County Archaeological Society; Archaeological Society of Ohio (secretary-treasurer, Miami River Valley Chapter). *Awards, honors:* Ms. Griffith's work is displayed at the Indian Museum, Salamanca, N.Y.: Indian Museum, Oberlin, Kan.;; the Satte House, Boston, Mass.; Pacific Northwest Indian Center, Gonzaga University, Spokane, Wash. *Biographical source: Who's Who in the Arts.*

GRINDE, DONALD ANDREW, Jr.
(Yamasee) 1946-
(professor)

Born August 23, 1946, Savannah, Ga. *Education:* Georgia Southern College, Statesboro, B.A. (History), 1966; University of Delaware, M.A. (History), 1968, Ph.D. (History), 1974. *Principal occupation:* Professor. *Home address:* 1274 Reba St., San Luis Obispo, Calif. 93401. *Affiliations:* Assistant professor, Mercyhurst College, Erie, Pa., 1971-1973; assistant professor, SUNY, College at Buffalo, 1973-1977; associate professor, California Polytechnic State University, San Luis Obispo, 1977-1978; visiting associate professor, UCLA, 1978-1979; associate professor, California Polytechnic State University, 1979-1981; director, Native American Studies, University of Utah, Salt Lake City, 1981-1984; associate professor of history, California Polytechnic State University, 1984-. *Other professional posts:* Instructor in Native American history, United Southeastern Tribes, Inc., and SUNY, College at Buffalo, Program for Indian Teacher Education at Allegany and Cattaraugus (Seneca) Reservations, 1974-1975; Native American consultant, Buffalo City Schools, 1974-1975; consultant, Smithsonian Institution, 1977; Native American Consultant, Salt Lake City Schools, 1982-1983; editor, *Journal of Erie Studies,* 1971-1973; editorial board, *Indian Historian,* 1976-. *Community activities:* Buffalo North American Indian Culture Center (corresponding secretary and board member, 1974-1977); American Indian Historical Society (board member, 1976-); Central Coast Indian Council, Calif. (vice chairman, 1979-1980); Salt Lake Indian Center (chairman of board, 1983-1984). *Memberships:* National Indian Education Association (member of Resolutions Committee, 1981-1983); American Indian Historian's Association (charter member); American Indian Historical Society; Phi Alpha Theta; Smithsonian Institution. *Awards, honors:* Hagley Fellow, University of Delaware, 1966-1970; Grant-in-Aid Scholar, Eleutherian Mills Historical Library, 1970-1971; project historian and conservation consultant, Southern Railroad Restoration Project, National Park Service; Faculty Seed Grant, UCLA, American Indian Studies Center, 1978-1979; Outstanding Professional Award (Education), 1984, from *Wasatch Regional Minority Business and Professional Directory* (Salt Lake City, Utah). *Interests:* American Indian history including: 20th century Indian policy,

Native American science, American Indian political theory, history of American technology, museum administration. *Biographical sources: Wasatch Regional Minority Business and Professional Directory* (Salt Lake City, Utah, 1984). *Published works:* Contributing editor, *Readings in American History: Bicentennial Edition, II (Guilford, Conn., Dushkin Publishing, 1975); The Iroquois and the Founding of the American Indian* (Indian Historian Press, 1977).

GROBSMITH, ELIZABETH S. 1946-
(professor of anthropology)

Born May 27, 1946, Brooklyn, N.Y. *Education:* Ohio State University, Bachelor of Music, 1967; University of Arizona, M.A. (Anthropology), 1970, Ph.D. (Anthropology), 1976. *Principal occupation:* Associate professor of anthropology. *Home address:* 1901 South 23rd St., Lincoln, Neb. 68502. *Affiliation:* Associate professor of anthropology, University of Nebraska, Lincoln, Neb., 1976-. *Other professional posts:* Consultant, Association on American Indian Affairs, 1984-1985; consultant, Indian Club, Nebraska State Penitentiary, and American Anthropological Association lecture series. *Memberships:* Plains Anthropological Society (board of directors, 1979-1981); Plains Anthropological Society (vice president, 1980-1981); American Anthropological Association; University of Nebraska Graduate Faculty; Sigma Delta Epsilon, Iota Chapter (Graduate Women's Scientific Fraternity). *Interests:* "My major professional interests are in studying and working with American Indian communities, with specific interests in helping them to design strategies and programs which alleviate reservation problems, be they juvenile justice concerns, alcoholism, curriculum development, legal or economic. When possible, I enjoy traveling to observe indigenous peoples to achieve a better understanding of native cultures (e.g. Alaska, Guatemala). *Published work: Lakota of the Rosebud, A Contemporary Ethnography* (Holt, Rinehart and Winston, 1981).

GRISPE, LARRY
(executive director-Indian center)

Affiliation: Executive director, American Indian Center of Dallas, Inc., 1314 Munger Blvd., Dallas, Tex. 75206.

GROSS, MIKE
(school administrator)

Affiliation: Administrator, Lac Courte Oreilles Ojibwa School, Route #2, Hayward, Wis. 54843.

GRUNDE, RICHARD (Chippewa)
(tribal chairman)

Affiliation: Chairman, Red Cliff Tribal Council, P.O. Box 529, Bayfield, Wis. 54814.

H

HABERLAND, WOLFGANG 1922-
(museum vice-director)

Born August 29, 1922, Hamburg, Germany. *Education:* University of Hamburg, Ph.D., 1951. *Principal occupation:* Chief, American Department and vice-director, Hamburgisches Museum fur Volkerkunde, Hamburg, Germany, 1955-. *Memberships:* Society for American Archaeology, 1955-; Royal Anthropological Institute of Great Britain and Ireland, 1952-; other. *Interests:* Archaeology of Central America; Amerindian art, especially of North America; four expeditions to Central America; travel. *Published work: American Indian Art* (Atlantis-Verlag/Zurich, 1971); many others.

HAIL, BARBARA A. 1931-
(museum director/curator)

Born November 2, 1931. *Education:* Brown University, 1948-1951; Cornell University, B.A., 1952, M.A., 1953. *Principal occupation:* Associate director/curator. *Home address:* 220 Rumstick Rd., Barrington, R.I. 02809. *Affiliations:* Associate director/curator, Haffenreffer Museum of Anthropology, Brown University, Providence, R.I., 1973-. *Other professional posts:* American and world history teacher, Ithaca High School, Ithaca, N.Y., and White Plains High School, White Plains, N.Y. *Memberships:* American Association of Museums (curator's committee); New England Museum Association; Association of College and University Museums and Galleries; Amerian Anthropological Association; Native American Art Studies Association. *Awards, honors:* Elisha Benjamin Andrews Scholar, Pembroke College; Phi Beta Kappa, Brown University, 1950; National Endowment of the Arts Fellowship for Museum Professionals, 1976, 1985. *Interests:* History, ethnohistory, ethnology; museology, stylistica and technical aspects of material culture of North America; Peru; Africa; Nepal; current research is in the art and material culture of the Subarctic. *Published work: Hau, Kola! The Plains Indian Collection of the Haffenreffer Museum of Anthropology* (Haffenreffer Museum of Anthropology, 1983).

HAIL, RAVEN (Oklahoma Cherokee) (lecturer, writer)

Born in Dewey, Okla. *Education:* Oklahoma State University; Southern Methodist University. *Principal occupation:* Lecturer, writer. *Home address:* 3061 Cridelle, Dallas, Texas 75220. Membership: North Texas Herb Club (president). *Interests:* Lecture and write on Cherokee Indian culture, particularly wild edible and medicinal plants; wrote 3-act play *The Raven and the Redbird* (Cherokee Life of Sam Houston and his Cherokee wife). *Published works:* Numerous articles in various publications.

HAIR, JOHN (Oklahoma Cherokee) (tribal chief)

Affiliation: Chief, United Keetoowah Cherokee Council, P.O. Box 1329, Tahlequah, Okla. 74465.

HAIRE, WENONAH GEORGE (Catawba) 1953- (dentist)

Born November 27, 1953, York County, Rock Hill, S.C. *Education:* Clemson University, S.C., B.S., 1976; Medical University of S.C., Charleston, D.MD, 1979. *Principal occupation:* Dentist. *Home address:* 191 Country Club Dr., Rock Hill, S.C. 29730. *Community activities:* Education commit-

tee, Career Development Center; chairman, Dental Health Month, 1985; Girl Scout Aid. *Memberships:* Tri County Dental Society, Rock Hill, S.C. (secretary, 1985); U.S. Public Health Service (Lieutenant, inactive reserve); Medical University Alumni Association; First Baptist Church. *Interests:* "Enjoys "travel" vacations (Mexico and U.S.); collects Indian jewelry, paintings and pottery; enjoys pottery making (Catawba traditional coil method); enjoys canning. Only female dentist in Rock Hill, S.C.; just had her first child." *Biographical source: Charlotte Observer* article entitled "Rock Hill Dentist Drills by Day, Fills by Night."

HAKKINEN, ELISABETH S. 1914- (museum curator)

Born January 11, 1914, Skagway, Alaska. *Education:* San Bernardino Junior College, 1930-1932; Western College, Oxford, Ohio, B.A., 1935. *Principal occupation:* Museum curator. *Home address:* Box 236, Haines, Alaska 99827. *Affiliation:* Museum curator, The Sheldon Museum and Culture Center, Haines, Alaska, 1960-. *Awards, honors:* Adopted Kag-wan-tan, Eagle Clan, Grizzly Bear House. *Biographical source: Who's Who of American Women.*

HALL, C.R. (CLIFF) 1933- (owner-Indian arts and crafts shop)

Born October 19, 1933, Las Vegas, N.M. *Education:* McMurry College, Abilene, Texas (four years). *Principal occupation:* Owner, Squash Blossom, 304 10th, Alamagordo, N.M., 1973-. *Military service:* U.S. Navy, 1955-1957. *Community activities:* Downtown Merchants Association (president). *Memberships:* Indian Arts and Crafts Association (charter member). *Interests:* "All Indian arts and crafts; extensive travels to all parts of Navaho, Zuni and Hopi Reservations; Hopi kachina dolls."

HAMMACK, LAURENS CARY 1936- (archaeologist)

Born July 11, 1936, Chicago, Ill. *Education:* University of New Mexico, B.A., 1959, M.A., 1964. *Principal occupation:* Archaeologist. *Affiliation:* Curator,

Research Division, Museum of New Mexico, Santa Fe, N.M., 1964-. *Military service:* U.S. Army, 1959-1961. *Membership:* Society for American Archaeology, 1964-. *Interests:* Southwest and northern Mexico archaeology and ethnology; collecting of antique guns and Southwest Indian materials; archaeological excavations throughout New Mexico. *Published work:* Archaeology of the Ute Dam and Reservoir (Museum of New Mexico, 1965).

HAMILTON, RUBY
(resource coordinator)

Affiliation: Resource coordinator, The Seventh Generation Fund, P.O. Box 10, Forestville, Calif. 95436

HAMP, ERIC P. 1920-
(professor of linguistics and behavioral science)

Born November 16, 1920, London, England. *Education:* Amherst College, B.A., 1942; Harvard University, M.A., 1948, Ph.D., 1954. *Principal occupation:* Professor of linguistics and behavioral science, University of Chicago, 1950-. *Military service:* U.S. Army, 1946-1947 (Sergeant). *Community service:* Illinois Place-Name Survey (chairman, 1966-); consultant U.S. Office of Education, NEH, NSF. *Memberships:* Council on International Exchange of Scholars (advisory committee, 1966-); UNESCO (U.S. National Commission, 1972-); American Philosophical Society (Phillips Fund Committee, 1977-); Linguistic Society of America (president, 1971). *Awards, honors:* Collitz Professor, 1960, Linguistic Society of America; hon. LHD, Amherst College, 1972; Guggenheim Fellow, 1973-1974; Fellow, American Academy of Arts and Sciences, 1976-; Robert Maynard Hutchins Distinguished Service Professor, University of Chicago; various guest professorships. *Interests:* Languages and cultures pf the American Indian, the Balkins, and the Celts; travel and fieldwork: Ojibwa, Cheyenne, Quileute, several Salishan, Eskimo, Otomanguean of Oazaca. *Biographical sources:* Who's Who in America; Who's Who in the World; Directory of American Scholars; Dictionary of International Biography;

American Men & Women of Science; Men of Achievement; The Blue Book. Published works: Associate editor, *International Journal of American Linguistics* (University of Chciago Press, 1966-); editor, *Native American Text Series* (University of Chicago Press, 1974-); author of publications on Ojibwa, Narragansett, Algonquian, Wiyot, Yurok, Quileute, Upper Chehalis, Comox, Kwakwala, Karok, Miwok, Zuni, Crow, Eskimo, etc.

HAMPTON, CAROL CUSSEN McDONALD (Caddo) 1935-
(historian)

Born September 18, 1935, Oklahoma City, Okla. *Education:* H. Sophie Newcomb College, New Orleans, La., 1953-1954; University of Oklahoma, B.A., 1957, M.A., 1973, Ph.D., 1984. *Principal occupation:* Historian. *Home address:* 1414 N. Hudson, Oklahoma City, Okla. 73103. *Affiliations:* Teaching assistant, University of Oklahoma, Norman, 1973-1984; associate director and coordinator, Consortium for Graduate Opportunities for American Indians, University of California, Berkeley. *Community activities:* Caddo Indian Tribe of Oklahoma (tribal council, 1976-); Caddo Tribal Constitution Committee, 1975-1976; Oklahoma City Area Indian Health Service (advisory board); Junior League of Oklahoma City, 1965-; National Committee on Indian Work, Episcopal Church (Co-chair, 1986-); World Council of Churches (commissioner, Program to Combat Racism, 1985); Oklahoma State Regents for Higher Education on Social Justice (member, advisory board, 1984-). *Memberships:* National Indian Education Association; National Historical Society; Oklahoma Historical Society; Western Historical Association; Organization of American Historians; American Historical Association. *Awards, honors:* Francis C. Allen Fellowship, D'Arcy McNickle Center for the History of the American Indian, Newberry Library, 1983. *Interests:* "My interests are in history, philosophy and religion of Ameriacn Indians as well as social and racial justice. *Biographical sources:* Who's Who Among American Women; Who's Who in the

World; etc. Published.work: "Indian Colonization in the Cherokee Outlet and Western Indian Territory" *(Chronicles of Oklahoma,* 1976).

HAMPTON, EBER (Chickasaw) 1942-
(director-neighborhood center)

Born August 13, 1942, Talihini, Okla. *Education:* Westmont College, Santa Barbara, Calif., B.A., 1964; University of California at Santa Barbara, A.B.D., 1968; Harvard Graduate School of Education, 1978-. *Principal occupation:* Director, the Neighborhood Center, Minneapolis, Minn., 1975-. *Home address:* Route 3, Box 167-A, Matawan, Minn. 56072. *Other professional post:* Assistant professor of psychology, Mankata State University, Mankato, Minn. *Membership:* National Indian Education Association. *Awards, honors:* Regents Fellow, 1964-1965; Bush Fellow, 1978-1979.

HAMPTON, JAMES MILBURN, M.D.
(Chickasaw-Choctaw) 1931-
(physician, professor)

Born September 15, 1931, Durant, Okla. *Education:* University of Oklahoma, B.A., 1952; University of Oklahoma, School of Medicine, M.D., 1956. *Principal occupation:* Physician, professor. *Home address:* 1414 N. Hudson, Oklahoma City, Okla. 73103. *Affiliations:* Director of Medical Oncology, Baptist Medical Center, Oklahoma City, Okla.; Clincial Professor of Medicine, University of Oklahoma Medical School, 1956-. *Other professional posts:* Professor and head, Hematology-Oncology, University of Oklahoma Medical School, 1971-1977; head hematology research, Oklahoma Medical Research Foundation, 1971-1977. *Community activities:* Oklahoma County Medical Society (community legal service, 1970, 1972; editorial committee, 1976-; planned parenthood committee, 1974-1975); Heritage Hills, Inc. (member, board of dirtors, 1973-); Central Oklahoma American Indian Health Council (member of board, 1974-1975); Faculty House

(member of board, 1974-1975); Frontiers of Science Foundation of Oklahoma, Inc. (member of board, 1974-). *Memberships:* American Association for the Advancement of Science; American Association for Cancer Research, Southwest Section; American Association of Pathologists and Bacteriologist; American Association of University Professors; American Federation for Clinical Research; American Genetic Association; Amerian Meical Association; American Physiological Society; American Psychosomatic Society; American Society for Clinical Pharmacology and Therapeutics; American Society for Clinical Oncology; American Society of Angiology; American Society of Hematology; Central Society for Clinical Research; International Society on Thrombosis and Haemostasis; New York Academy of Sciences; Oklahoma County Medical Society; Oklahoma State Medical Association; Sigma Xi; Southern Society for Clinical Investigation; Southwest Cancer Chemotherapy Study Group; Association of American Indian Physicians; National Hemophilia Foundation; National Institutes of Health; American Heart Association. *Consultations:* Consultant in Medicine, Tinker Air Force Base Hospital, Oklahoma City, Okla., 1965-; consultant for National Institutes of Health, national Cancer Institute, 1973-1976; National Heart and Lung Institute, 1971-1976; consultant for Navajo Health Authority, 1974-1976; consultant for Regional Breast Cancer Detection and Treatment Center, 1974-. *Awards, honors:* NIH Career Development Award (Heart and Lung), 1965-1975; Angiology Research Foundation Honors Achievement Award, 1967-1968; Preservation and Restortion Award, Heritage Hills Association, 1973; member, Meical School Planning Committee for Native American Medical School, sponsored by the Navajo Health Authority, 1974-1976; associate editor, *Journal of Laboratory and Clinical Medicine,* 1974-1976; member, Blue Cord, 1974. *Biographical sources: Who's Who in the South and Southwest; American Men of Science; The International Registry of Who's Who. Publishe works:* Experimental articles, non-experimental articles, books, pamphlets, editorials in various journals; abstracts presented at national or international meetings; lectures.

HANSEN, JOAN LOUISE (Cherokee)
1945-
(reporter, photographer)

Born February 2, 1945, New Orleans, La. *Education:* Bacone College. *Principal occupation:* Reporter, photographer. *Home address:* 2310 E. Broadway, Muskogee, Okla. *Affiliation:* Reporter, photographer, Muskogee *Daily Phoenix* and *Times Democrat. Awards, honors:* Paintings shown at Philbrook Indian Annual, Tulsa, Okla.; paintings shown at Department of the Interior, Washington, D.C.; numerous awards at local fairs. *Interests:* Reading of Plains Indian traditions and legends; art.

HAOZOUS, BOB (Chiricahua Apache-Navajo) 1943-
(artist)

Born April 1, 1943, Los Angeles, Calif. *Education:* Utah State University; California College of Arts and Crafts. *Principal occupation:* Artist. *Home address:* Santa Fe, N.M. 87501. *Exhibitions:* Scottsdale National Indian Arts Exhibition; Philbrook Art Center Amerian Indian Artists Exhibitions; Oakland Museum Indian Show; Southwest Fine Arts Biennial-Museum of New Mexico. *Permanent collections:* Heard Museum; Southern Plains Indian Museum; Crafts Center, Anadarko, Okla. *Awards:* First Prize, Sante Fe Indian Market, 1971; Gold Medal, Wood Sculpture I and II, Heard Museum, 1973, 1974; Grand Prize, Heard Museum National Sculpture Competition, 1975; among others.

HARANAKA, NANCIE
(Indian services)

Affiliation: Indian/Family Services, Phoenix Indian Center, Inc., 1337 North 1st St., Phoenix, Ariz. 85004.

HARDY, DEE
(museum curator)

Affiliation: Curator, Anasazi Indian Village Museum, P.O. Box 393, Boulder, Utah 84716.

HARDY, JOSEPH (Navajo)
(corporate executive director)

Affiliation: Executive director, Navajo Small Business Development Corporation, P.O. Drawer L., Fort Defiance, Ariz. 86504.

HARE, HERBERT
(B.I.A. agency superintendent)

Affiliation: Superintendent, Yankton Agency, Bureau of Indian Affairs, Wagner, S.D. 57380.

HARJO, SUSAN SHOWN
(executive director-Indian organization)

Affiliation: Executive director, National Congress of American Indians, 804 D St., N.E., Washington, D.C. 20002.

HARLOW, FRANCIS H. 1928-
(physicist)

Born January 22, 1928, Seattle, Wash. *Education:* University of Washington, B.S., 1949, Ph.D., 1953. *Principal occupation:* Theoretical physicist. *Home address:* 1407 11th St., Los Alamos, N.M. 87544. *Affiliations:* Staff member, Los Alamos Scientific Laboratory, 1953-; research associate, Museum of New Mexico, 1965-. *Military service:* U.S. Army, 1946-1947. *Interests:* Theoretical fluid dynamics and numerical analysis; Pueblo Indian pottery, history, technology, and artistry. *Published works:* Contemporry Pueblo Indian Pottery (Museum of New Mexico, 1965); *Historic Pueblo Indian Pottery* (Museum of New Mexico, 1967; reprinted 1968, 1970); *The Pottery of San Ildefonso,* with Kenneth Chapman (School of American Research, 1970); *Mattepaint Pottery of the Tewa, Keres and Zuni Pueblos* (Museum of New Mexico Press, 1973); *Historic Pottery of the Pueblo Indians, 1600-1880,* with Larry Frank (New York Graphic Society, 1974); *Modern Pueblo Pottery, 1880-1960* (Northland Pres, 1977); *Glazed Pottery of the Southwest Indians (American Indian Art* Magazine, Nov. 1976); *Pueblo Indian Pottery Traditions* (VILTIS, 1978).

HARNEY, ROBERT
(tribal chairman)

Affiliation: Chairman, Winnemucca Colony Council, P.O. Box 1075, Winnemucca, Nev. 89445.

HARRINGTON, VIRGIL N. (Choctaw) 1919-
(former B.I.A. official)

Born 1919, Kiowa, Okla. *Education:* Oklahoma A & M College, B.A. (Agriculture), 1942. *Principal occupation:* B.I.A. Official. *Address:* 221 S. 12th, Muskogee, Okla. 74401. *Affiliations:* Civilian supervisor, U.S. Navy Department, 1943-1948; soil conservationist, Pawnee Indian Agency, 1948-1955; land operations officer, Consolidated Ute Agency, 1955-1958; superintendent, Seminole Indian Agency, 1958-1963; area director, Muskogee Area Office, B.I.A., 1963-? *Military service:* U.S. Army Signal Corps, 1942-1943. *Community activities:* Lions Club (past president); Rotary Club (past president); American Legion; Elk Club; Masons; Oklahoma State Fair (board of directors); Five Civilized Tribes (board of directors, child welfare advisory board). *Interests:* "Improvement and development of human resources from educational, sociological and economic viewpoints."

HARRIS, LaDONNA (Mrs. Fred Harris)(Comanche) 1931-
(president-Indian organization)

Born February 15, 1931, Temple, Okla. *Education:* High school. *Principal occupation:* President, Americans for Indian Opportunity, 1010 Massachusetts Ave., N.W., Suite 200, Washington, D.C. 20001. *Community activities:* Oklahomans for Indian Opportunity, Inc. (past president); Oklahoma Mental Health and Welfare Association (board member). *Awards, honors:* "Outstanding American Citizen of 1965," Anadarko (Okla.) American Indian Exposition and the Tulsa Indian Council, 1965. *Interests:* "Traveled through Argentina, Brazil, Childe, Peru in November, 1965, with (my) husband, Senator Fred Harris, and Senator and Mrs. Birch Bayh of Indiana."

HARRIS, ROBERT N., Sr. (Shoshone)
(tribal chairman)

Affiliation: Chairman, Shoshone Business Council, Fort Washakie, Wyo. 82514.

HARRISON, DAVID C. (Osage-Cherokee) 1945-
(federal Indian service)

Born July 28, 1945, Pawhuska, Okla. *Education:* Grinnell College, B.A., 1967; Harvard Law School, J.D., 1975. *Principal occupation:* Federal Indian service. *Home address:* 5535 Columbia Pike, Arlington, Va. 22204. *Affiliations:* Rights Protection Officer, Bureau of Indian Affairs, Washington, D.C. 1975-. *Military service:* U.S. Marine Corps, 1967-1971 (Captain, Vietnamese Cross of Gallentry, Bronz Star, Purple Heart). *Memberships:* Osage Heloshka Society; Harvard Law School Association. *Awards, honors:* "I served as senior investigator and authored several chapters of report called by *New York Times* editorial, "a magnificent document, sweeping in scope, meticulous in detail, unsparing in assessing blame." *Published work: Attica, Official Report of the New York State Special Commission on Attica* (Bantam, paper, Praeger, hardcover, 1972).

HARRISON, KATHERINE
(tribal chairwoman)

Affiliation: Chairwoman, Confederated Tribes of the Grande Ronde Indian Community, P.O. Box 94, Grande Ronde, Ore. 97347.

HART, ROBERT G. 1921-
(government official)

Born December 28, 1921, San Francisco, Calif. *Education:* American Institute for Banking, 1939-1941. *Principal occupation:* Governmental official. *Home address:* 916 25th St., N.W., Washington, D.C. 20037. *Affiliations:* Manager, Southern Highlanders, Inc., New York, N.Y., 1946-1952; Southwestern representative, Indian Arts and Crafts Board, Santa Fe, N.M., 1954-1957; treasurer, Westbury Music Fair, Inc.,

1957; director, public relations, Constructive Research Foundation, New York, N.Y., 1958-1959; editor, director of publications, Brooklyn Museum, 1959-1961; general manager, Indian Arts and Crafts Board, Department of the Interior, Washington, D.C. 20240, 1961-. *Other professional posts:* Chairman, Federal Inter-Departmental Agency for Arts and Crafts, 1963-; member, national advisory board, Foxfire Fund, Inc., 1981-. *Military service:* U.S. Army, 1943-1945. *Memberships:* Conseil Internationale des Musees; American Association of Museums; American Craftsmen's Council; World Crafts Council; American Political Science Association. *Awards, honors:* N.Y. State Governor's Award for Outstanding Service, 1951. *Interests:* Folk art. *Published works: How to Sell Your Handicrafts* (David McKay, 1953); *Guide to Alaska* (David McKay, 1959); editor, *Masters of Contemporary American Crafts* (Brooklyn Museum Press, 1960); among others.

HARTMAN, RUSSELL P.
(museum director)

Affiliation: Director, Navajo Tribal Museum, P.O. Box 308, Window Rock, Ariz. 86515.

HATATHLI, NED A. (Navajo) 1923-
(administrator)

Born October 11, 1923, Coalmine Canyon, Ariz. *Education:* Northern Arizona University, B.S., 1951. *Principal occupation:* Former president, Navajo Community College; chairman, board of directors, *American Indian Review. Military service:* U.S. Navy, 1943-1945. *Community activities:* Kit Carson Council; Boy Scouts of America. *Memberships:* Task Force on Minority Business Enterprise, Office of Economic Opportunity, Department of HEW; National Indian Education Association (board of directors); N.C.I.O. Special Indian Education Subcommittee; Regional Manpower Development Advisory Committee. *Awards, honors:* Phi Kappa Phi, Northern Arizona University, 1961; L.L.D. (hon.), Eastern Michigan University, 1971. *Biographical source: Indians of Today.*

HAURY, EMIL W. 1904-
(educator, archaeologist)

Born May 2, 1904, Newton, Kan. *Education:* Bethel College, 1923-1925; Univerity of Arizona, B.A., 1927, M.A., 1928; Harvard University, Ph.D., 1934; LL.D., University of New Mexico, 1959. *Principal occupation:* Educator, archaeologist. *Home address:* 2749 E. 4th St., Box 40543, Tucson, Ariz. 85717. *Affiliations:* Assistant director, Gila Pueblo, Globe, Ariz., 1930-1937; Department of Anthropology, University of Arizona (professor, 1937-1970; head of department, 1937-1964; Fred A. Riecker Distinguished professor, 1970-1980; emeritus, 1980-); director, Arizona State Museum, 1938-1964 (advisor, 1964-). *Memberships:* National Historic Parks, Historic Sites, Buildings and Monuments (advisory board); National Academy of Sciences (chairman, Division of Anthropology and Psychology, National Research Council, 1960-1962); National Council for the Humanities; Americn Philosophical Society; American Academy of Arts and Sciences; National Speleological Society (honorary life member); Society for American Archaeology; American Anthropological Association; American Association for the Advancement of Science; Phi Kappa Phi; Sigma Xi. *Awards, honors:* Guggenheim Fellow, 1949-1950; Viking Fund Medalist for Anthropology, 1950; University of Arizona, Alumni Achievement Award, 1957, Faculty Achievement Award, 1962; U.S. Department of the Interior Conservation Service Award, 1976; Alfred Vincent Kidder Award, 1977; Distinguished Citizen Award, University of Arizona Alumni Association, 1980. *Interests:* "Archaeological theory and method; early man in western America; the later Southwestern prehistoric societies." *Travels, expeditions:* National Geographic Society Arcaheological Expedition, Mexico City, Mexico, 1925; archaeological excavations, Bogota, Colombia, 1949-1950; International Congress of Americanists, Vienna, Austria, 1956, 1960; Intrnational Congress of Anthropological and Ethnological Sciences, paris, France. *Published works: The Excavations of Los Muertos and Neighboring Ruins in the Salt River Valley, Southern Arizona* (Peabody Museum Papers, 1945);

The Staratigraphy and Archaeology of Ventana Cave, Arizona (University of Arizona Press, 1950; University of New Mexico Press); *The Hohokam, Desert Farmers and Craftsmen: Excavations at Snaketown, 1964-1965* (University of Arizona Press, 1976); several articles in professional journals.

HAWKINS, RUSSELL (Sisseton-Wahpeton Sioux)
(tribal chairman)

Affiliation: Chairman, Sisseton-Wahpeton Sioux Tribal Council, Route 2, Agency Village, S.D. 57262.

HAYES, CHARLES F., III 1932-
(museum research director)

Born March 6, 1932, Boston, Mass. *Education:* Harvard University, A.B. (Anthropology), 1954; University of Colorado, M.A. (Anthropology), 1958. *Principal occupation:* Museum research director. *Home address:* 246 Commodore Parkway, Rochester, N.Y. 14625. *Affiliations:* Junior anthropologist, 1959-1961, associate curator of anthropology, 1961-1966, curator of anthropology, Rochester Museum; director, curator of anthropology, 1970-1979, research director, 1979-,Rochester Museum & Science Center, 657 East Ave., Rochester, N.Y. 14603. *Other professional posts:* Associate lecturer in anthropology, University of Rochester, 1970-1973; consultant, New York State Museum in salvage archaeology; trustee, Seneca Iroquois National Museum, 1977-. *Military service:* U.S. Air Force, 1954-1956 (Captain, Military Air Transport Service and Strategic Air Command, Personnel Officer, 1955-1956). *Memberships:* New York Archaeological Association (president, 1967-1969); New York Archaeological Council (president, 1983-); New York Academy of Sciences; Society of Professional Archaeologists; American Association of Museums. *Awards, honors:* One of fifteen U.S. representatives to the American Association of Museums, International Council of Museums, 1974-1977; New York State Representative of the Society for American Archaeology on the Committee

for Public Understanding of Archaeology, 1971. *Interests:* Anthropology, archaeology, ethnology, museology, travel. *Published works:* Books: Editor, *The Iroquois in the American Revolution, 1976 Conference Proceedings,* 1981; *Aspects of Change in Seneca Iroquois Ladles A.D. 1600-1900,* 1982; *Proceedings of the 1982 Glass Trade Bead Conference,* 1983; *The Origin and Development of the Seneca and Cayuga Tribes of N.Y. State,* 1984. All published by Rochester Museum and Science Center. Articles: "The Canoe Builder - Iroquois Artists Conception of an Old Technology," 1959; "New Archaeological Exhibits Illustrate Iroquois Culture Change," 1960; "An Approach to Iroquois - White Acculturation Through Archaeology," 1961; "Prehistoric Iroquois Studies in the Bristol Hills, New York: A Summary," 1963; "Excavating an Early Seneca Longhouse," 1966; "Indian Life During the Archaic - A New Alcove in the Hall of Man," 1967; among other articles published by Museum Service, *Bulletin,* of the Rochester Museum. Numerous archaeological and historical impact studies conducted by Rochester Museum and Science Center.

HAYWARD, RICHARD (Pequot)
(tribal chairman)

Affiliation: Chairman, Mashantucket Pequot Council, P.O. Box 160, Ledyard, Conn. 06339.

HEADLEY, LOUIS R. (Arapahoe) 1948-
(superintendent)

Born February 25, 1948, Fort Washakie, Wyo. *Education:* University of Montana, Missoula, B.A., 1974; University of South Dakota, Vermillion, M.A., 1977; University of Wyoming, Laramie, Ed.S., 1986. *Princi-*

pal occupation: Superintendent. *Home address:* Box 344, St. Stephens, Wyo. 82524. *Affiliations:* Teacher, principal, St. Stephens Indian School, 1977-; minority counselor, special services, University of Wyoming, Laramie, 1984-. *Other professional posts:* Home-school coordinator, Lander Valley High School, Lander, Wyo.; field coordinator, Tri-State Tribes, Inc., Billings, Mont. *Community activities:* Wind River Indian Education Association, Wind River, Wyo. (past chairman); Keepers of the Fire Indian Club, University of Wyoming (advisor); Cub Scout volunteer, St. Stephens, Wyo.; Head Start Policy Council, Ethete, Wyo. (vice chairman). *Memberships:* Phi Delta Kappa; National Association of Elementary School Principals; National Indian Education Association (treasurer); Wyoming Association for Bilingual Bicultural Education (treasurer). *Awards, honors:* Wyoming Golden Gloves Championship Scholarship Award; Korean Temple Band, Casper, Wyo; Outstanding Young Men of America, U.S. Jaycees, 1978. *Interests:* "I was a member of the Arapahoe and Shoshone Idian Dance Troupe that danced in Switzerland. I was also selected to dance in Washington, D.C. during the 1976 Bicentennial. I have been chosen to be the head dancer in Denver, Steamboat Spring, Colorado and Rocky Boy Reservation."

HEDRICK, HENRY E.
(director-Indian organization)

Affiliation: Director, American Indian Liberation Crusade, Inc., 4009 S. Halldale Ave., Los Angeles, Calif. 90062-1851.

HEELEY, STEVEN J.W.
(vice president-Indian organization)

Affiliation: Vice president, National Indian Education Association, 1115 Second Ave. So., Minneapolis, Minn. 55403.

HEINMILLER, CARL W
(museum director)

Affiliation: Executive director, Alaska Indian Arts, Inc., 23 Fort Seward Dr., P.O. Box 271, Haines, Alaska 99827.

HEINRICH, ALBERT C. 1922-
(professor of anthropology)

Born February 2, 1922, Ill. *Education:* New School for Social Research, B.A.; University of Alaska, M.Ed.; University of Washington, Ph.D., 1960. *Principal occupation:* Professor of anthropology. *Home address:* 56 Capri Ave., N.W., Calgary, Alberta, Canada. *Affilaition:* Professor of anthropology, University of Calgary, Alberta, Canada. *Memberships:* American Anthropological Association; American Association for the Advancement of Science. *Awards, honors:* Seattle Anthropologicl Society Prize, 1962. *Interests:* Linguistics; social structure; arctic; Indians of North America; South Asia; "Have spent extended periods of time in Alaska, Arctic Canada, The Labrador, South America, India, Europe. Have written numerous articles on Athabasoann, Eskimos."

HEIZER, ROBERT F. 1915-
(professor of anthropology)

Born July 13, 1915, Denver, Colo. *Education:* Univesity of California, Ph.D., 1940. *Principal occupation:* Professor of anthropology, Department of Anthropology, University of California, Berkeley. *Home address:* 85 Menlo Place, Berkeley, Calif. 94707. *Memberships:* Society for American Archaeology; American Anthropological Association; Societe des Americanistes des Paris; Institute for Andean Research. *Interests:* Archaeology and ethnology of the American Indians. *Published works:* Francis Drake and the California Indians, 1579 (University of California Press, 1947); editor, The California Indians, with M.A. Whipple (University of California Press, 1951); The Four Ages of Tsurai, with John E. Mills (University of California Press, 1952); Prehistoric Rock Art of Nevada and Eastern California, with M.A. Baumhoff (University of California Press, 1962); Man's Discovery of His Past (Spectrum Books, Prentice-Hall, Inc., 1962); Anza and the Northwest Frontier of New Spain (Southwest Museum, 1967); Hugo Reid's Letters on the Indians of Los Angeles County, 1852 (Southwest Museum, 1968); Almost Ancestors: The First Californians, with Theodora Kroeber (Sierra Club, 1968);

HENDRICKSON, JAMES (Chippewa)
(tribal chairman)

Affiliation: Chairman, Grand Portage Reservation Business Committee, P.O. Box 428, Grand Portage, Minn. 55605.

HENDRICKX, LEONARD 1953-
(director of Indian center)

Born July 10, 1953, Kellogg, Idaho. *Education:* State University of New York at Albany, B.A. (Philosophy). *Principal occupation:* Dirctor of Indian center. *Home address:* 2225 First St., Lot 79, Cheney, Wash. 99004. *Affiliations:* Administrative analyst, City of Redondo Beach, Calif., 1979-1982; executive director, Ameican Indian Community Center, Spokane, Wash., 1982-. *Community activities:* Spokane Urban Indian Health Service Board (chairman); Community Housing Resources Board (chairman); The Native American Alliance for Political Action (treasurer); Spokane Planning Affiliates Network (member); Vocational Advisory Council, Community Colleges (member). *Memberships:* Eastern Washington/Northern Idaho MENSA (treasurer). *Awards, honors:* Outstanding Young Man of America, 1985; Mayor's Proclamation/Community Services, City Council and Indian Community; frequent presenter at national and regional Indian employment and training and education conferences. *Interests:* "Extensive travels throughout the U.S. Outdoors enthusiast, particularly interested in the conceptualization and articulation of innovative program development ideas for Indian comunities, with expertise in successful grant and contract preparation, presentation, and negotiation." *Biographical source: Outstanding Young Men of America, 1985.*

HENSLEY, WILLIAM L. (Eskimo)
1941-
(state senator)

Born 1941, Kotzebue, Alaska. *Education:* University of Alaska, 1960-1961; George Washington University, B.A., 1966; Univerity of Alaska, 1966; University of New Mexico Law School, 1967; U.C.L.A. Law School, 1968. *Principal occupation:* State senator. *Home address:* Kotxebue, Alaska.

Affiliations: Alaska House of Representatives, 1966-1970; Alaska State Senate, 1970-. *Community activities:* Rural Affairs Commission, 1968-1972 (chairman, 1972); Land Claims Task Force (chairman, 1968); Northwest Regional Educational Laboratory (board of directors, 1968-1969); Northwest Alaska Native Association Regional Corporation (board of directors). *Memberships:* Alaska Federation of Natives, 1966- (organizer, 1966; president, 1972); Northwest Alaska Native Association (organizer, 1966); National Council on Indian Opportunity, 1968-1970. *Interests:* "Land claims implementation; rural economic development; education facilities in the bush; old-age centers; bilingual programs."

HENSON, C.L.
(B.I.A. agency superintendent)

Affiliation: Superintendent, Truxton Canon Agency, Bureau of Indian Affairs, P.O. Box 37, Valentine, Ariz. 86437.

HENSON, RICHARD ALLEN
(Comanche) 1942-
(B.I.A. employment assistance officer)

Born January 26, 1942, Pawnee, Okla. *Education:* Oklahoma State Tech, 1960-1962; Minot State College, B.A. (Business Administration), 1976. *Principal occupation:* B.I.A. employment assistance director. *Home address:* 13806 Congress Dr., Rockville, Md. 10853. *Affiliations:* Metropolitan Life Insurance Co., Ardmore, Okla., 1967-1971; guidance counselor, United Tribes Employment Training Center, Bismarck, N.D., equal employment opportunity counselor, job developer and employment assistance officer, United Tribes Employment Training Center, Minot, N.D., 1971-1974; employment assistance officer, Fort Berthold Agency, B.I.A., New Town, N.D., 1974-1976; area equal employment opportunity officer, B.I.A., Albuquerque, N.M., 1976-1977; director, equal employment opportunity, Indian Health Service, Rockville, Md. *Military service:* U.S. Air Force, 1963-1967. *Community activities:* Minot Indian Club (president, 1974); Minot Mayor's Human Rights Committee (member);

Minot's Mental Health & Retardation Board (member). *Interests:* "To continue to work with Indian people in Indian affairs and to return to school to earn my master's degree in public health."

HERON, GEORGE DAVID (Seneca) 1919-
(tribal officer)

Born February 22, 1919, Red House, N.Y. *Education:* High school. *Principal occupation:* Tribal officer. *Home address:* R.F.D. J-57, Salamanca, N.Y. 14779. *Affiliations:* Administrator, Seneca Nation; stockholder, Cattaraugus County Builder's, Inc., Fentier Village, Salamanca, N.Y. *Military service:* U.S. Naval Reserve, 1941-1945 (European-African Service Medal with three battle stars; Asiatic-Pacific; Philippine Liberation Medal; Navy Good Conduct Medal; Americn Caribbean Service Medal). *Community activities:* Veterans of Foreign Wars; American Legion; Governor's Interstate Indian Council (director). *Membership:* National Congress of American Indians. *Awards, honors:* Citizen of the Year Award, Junior Chamber of Commerce. *Interests:* "Lecturing on Indian culture and tradition."

HESSING, VALJEAN McCARTY (Choctaw) 1934-
(artist)

Born August 30, 1934, Tulsa, Okla. *Education:* Mary Hardin-Baylor College, 1952-1954; Tulsa University, 1954-1955. *Principal occupation:* Artist. *Awards, honors:* Numerous awards and prizes at various art exhibitions. *Interests:* Mrs. Hessing writes, "I am interested in illustrating books; I'm also interested in aiding children and adults in art, especially those who have little or no opportunity to have instruction of any kind."

HESTER, JAMES J. 1931-
(anthropologist)

Born September 21, 1931, Anthony, Kan. *Education:* University of New Mexico, B.A., 1953; Univerity of Arizona, Ph.D., 1961. *Principal occupation:* Anthropologist. *Affiliations:* Assistant curator, Museum of New Mexico, 1959-1964; adjunct professor, Southern Methodist University, 1964-1965; scientist administrator, National Institute of Health, 1965-. *Military service:* U.S. Air Force, 1954-1956. *Memberships:* American Anthropological Association (Fellow); Society for American Archaeology; Sigma Xi; American Society of Naturalists; Current Anthropology. *Interests:* Archaeology of Navajo Indians; prehistory of Sahara desert; directed culture change; relationship of man to his environment. *Published works: An Archaeological Survey of the Navajo Reservoir District, Northwestern New Mexico,* with A.E. Dittert, Jr. and Frank W. Eddy (Museum of New Mexico, 1961); *Early Navajo Migrations and Acculturation in the Southwest* (Museum of New Mexico, 1962); *Studies at Navajo Period Sites in the Navajo Reservoir District,* with Joel Shiner (Museum of New Mexico, 1963); among others.

HETH, CHARLOTTE WILSON (Oklahoma Cherokee) 1937-
(professor, director-Indian center)

Born October 29, 1937, Muskogee, Okla. *Education:* Oklahoma Baptist University, 1955-1956; University of Tulsa, B.A., 1959, M.M., 1960; University of California, Los Angeles, Ph.D., 1975. *Principal occupation:* Professor, director-Indian center. *Home address:* 4040 Grand View #20, Los Angeles, Calif. 90066. *Affiliations:* Associate professor of music, director, American Indian Studies Center, University of California, Los Angeles, Calif., 1974-. *Community activities:* Panel chair, Folk Arts Program, National Endowment for the Arts, 1981-1983; Indian Centers, Inc., Los Angeles (board member). *Memberships:* Society for Ethnomusicology (council chair, 1981-1982); National Indian Education Association; American Indian Historians' Association. *Awards, honors:* Senior Postdoctoral Fellowship, Center for the History of the American Indian, The Newberry Library, 1978-1979; Southern Fellowships Fund, Post-doctoral Fellowship, 1978-1979; National Research Council senior postdoctoral fellowship, 1984-1985 (Ford Foundation Minority Fellowship). *Interests:*

"American Indian music and dance; Cherokee language and culture; previously I was a Peace Corps volunteer in Ethiopia (1962-1964) teaching English as a second language. I also was a high school teacher in Oklahoma, New Mexico, and California from 1960-1972. I have traveled to Europe, the Middle East, East Africa, Mexico, and Canada. *Published works:* General editor, "The Music of the American Indians," (*Selected Reports in Ethnomusicology,* 1982); general editor, "Music and the Expressive Arts," (*American Indian Culture and Research Journal,* 1982); *Issues for the Future of American Indian Studies: A Needs Assessment and Program Guide,* co-authored with Susan Guyette (American Indian Studies Center, UCLA, 1985); general editor, organizer, and contributor, *Sharing a Heritage: American Indian Arts Conference,* No. 3 in the Contemporary American Indian Issues Series (American Indian Studies Center, UCLA, 1984).

HEWITT, ARNOLD (Tuscarora)
(tribal chief)

Affiliation: Chief, Tuscarora Nation, 5616 Walmore Rd., Lewiston, N.Y. 14092.

HIGHWATER, JAMAKE (Blackfeet-Eastern Band Cherokee) 1942-
(author, lecturer)

Born February 14, 1942, Glacier County, Mt. *Education:* Holds degrees in music, comparative literature, and cultural anthropology. *Principal occupation:* Author, lecturer. *Address:* c/o Alfred Hart, agent, 419 East 57th St., New York, N.Y. 10022. *Affiliations:* Lecturer, Indian culture, various Universities in U.S. and Canada; graduate lecturer, New York University, New York, N.Y., Continuing Education, 1979-; founder, host narrator and writer of TV series Songs of the Thunderbird, PBS Network, Miami, Fla., 1977-; consultant, N.Y. State Council on the Arts, 1975-; founding member, Indian Art Foundation, Santa Fe, N.M., 1980-. *Community activities:* Cultural Council of American Indian Community House, New York, N.Y. (past president and founding member); President's Commission on Mental Health (Art Task Panel, 1977);

N.Y. State Council on the Arts (member, task force on individual artist). *Memberships:* National Congress of American Indians; White Buffalo Society of Amerian Indians, Denver, Colo.; Dramatists Guild; Authors Guild; American Federation of Radio and Television Artists (AFTRA); BMI; League of American Authors. *Awards, honors:* Appointed Honorary Citizen by Governor of Oklahoma; appointed Colonel aid-de-camp on the Staff of the Governor of New Mexico; 1978 Newberry Honor Award for novel *Anpao* by the American Library Association; Jane Addams Peace Book Award, 1978, for *Many Smokes, Many Moons;* Anisfield-Wolf Award in race relations, 1980, for *Song From the Earth: American Indian Painting;* featured speaker, along with Ralph Coe, the Lord Mayor of London, the Governor of Missouri and Mrs. Joan Mondale at the opening night diner of "Sacred Circles, 2000 Years of American Indian Art" at the Nelson Gallery in Kansas City; featured speaker, along with Gov. Lamm of Colorado, at the opening night dinner of the Colorado Historical Society Museum in Denver; interviews with Mr. Highwater have appeared in most major American, European, Latin American and Near Eastern newspapers and magazines. *Interests:* Travels extensively and does fieldwork in North and Central Africa, most American Indian communities and resevations in the U.S.; travels to Central America and Mexico, Europe and the Near East; lectures extensively for E. Colston Leigh Bureau; contributing editor, *Stereo Review, 1972-1979;* classical music editor, New York *Soho Weekly News, 1975-1979; contributing editor, N.Y. Arts Journals, 1978-; contributing editor, Indian Trader,* 1977-1980; Senior editor, Fodor Travel Guides, 1970-1975; columnist, *Lone Star Revue,* 1981-; written and presented talks about American Indian studies for th BBC, Radio Three in London, Radio Pacifica, CBS-Radio, WMCA-Radio, and numerous other radio and television networks and stations. *Biographical sources: Who's Who in America; Directory of American Poetry; Directory of American Fiction Writers; International Who's Who; Dance World; Theatre World; Pop Bibliography; Who's Who in the East. Published works: Rock & Other Four Letter Words* (Bantam

Books, 1968); *Mick Jagger: The Singer Not the Song* (Popular Library, 1970); *Fodor's Europe Under 25,* (David McKay, 1971-1974); *Fodor's Indian American* (David McKay, 1975); *Song From the Earth: American Indian Painting* (New York Graphic Society, Little Brown, 1976); *Ritual of the Wind: American Indian Ceremonies, Music and Dances* (Viking Press, 1977); Anpao: An American Indian Odyssey (J.B. Lippincott, 1977); *Dance: Rituals of Experience* (A & W Visual Library, 1978); *Many Smokes, Many Moons: American Indian History Thru Indian Arts* (J.B. Lippincott, 1978); *Journey to the Sky: In Search of the Lost World of the Maya* (T.Y. Crowell, 1979); *The Sweet Grass Lives On: 50 Contemporary North American Indian Artists* (Viking Press, 1980); *Masterpieces of American Indian Painting,* 8 Vols., 1978-1980; *The Sun, He Dies: The End of the Aztec World,* 1980; *The Primal Mind: Vision and Reality in Indian America,* 1981. Mr. Highwater wrote introductions for: *Indian Boyhood,* by Charles Eastman (Rio Grande Press, 1976); and *Bears Heart: Scenes from the Life of a Cheyenne,* by Burton Supree (J.B. Lippincott, 1977). Also many articles in various journals and magazines.

HILL, ARLEIGH (Seneca) 1909-
(Indian arts and crafts)

Born June 5, 1909, Grand River Reservation, Ontario, Can. *Principal occupation:* Indian arts and crafts. *Home address:* 463 Mt. Read Blvd., Rochester, N.Y. 14606. *Affiliations:* Associate, Education Division, 1933-1944, associate in Indian Arts and Crafts, 1944-, Rochester Museum of Arts and Sciences; consultant on Indian programs for radio and television. *Community activities:* National Youth Administration (Indian camp counselor); Civilian Defense (educational instructor); Neighborhood Indian Society of Rochester (president); Indian Day Programs (chairman). *Memberships:* Imperial Order of Red Men, 1934-1963; Stadium Club of Rochester. *Awards, honors:* Honorary name bestowed by Turtle Clan of the Seneca Indians, 1951; Civil Defense Citation, 1945; Citation of Merit, Rochester Museum, 1959. *Interests:* Local

and national Indian affairs; reserch and writing on the American Indian. *Published works:* Articles for various sports magazines and for the Rochester Museum of Arts and Sciences *Bulletin.*

HILL, JAMES W. (Spokane)
(tribal chairman)

Affiliation: Chairman, Spokane Business Committee, P.O. Box 385, Wellpinit, Wash. 99040.

HILL, JOAN (Cherokee-Creek)
(artist)

Born in Muskogee, Okla. *Education:* Muskogee Junior College, A.A., 1950; Northeastern State College, B.A. (Education), 1952. *Principal occupation:* Artist. *Home address:* Route 6, Box 151, Muskogee, Okla. 74401. *Affiliations:* Art instructor, Tulsa Public Schools, 1952-1956; self-employed artist, 1956-. *Other professional posts:* Consultant, American Association of University Women; teacher, adult education. *Community activities:* Muskogee Art Guild (art director; publicity director; co-chairman). *Memberships:* National League of Amerian Penwomen, Inc., 1968-; Phi Theta Kappa; Northeastern State College Alumni Association (board of directors). *Awards, honors:* Of Ms. Hill's more than 250 awards, more than 100 are from national competitions. She has about 75 works in permanent collections; has had approximately 20 one-woman shows; has had over 450 juried and non-juried exhibitions throughout the U.S. and abroad; has participated in many traveling shows and has received numerous commissions. *Interests:* Ms. Hill works in oil, gouache, collage, acrylics, transparent wtercolor, tempera, ink, pastel, conte, pencil, and mixed media. Her preferred styles are representational realism, subjective expressionism, abstract symbolism, and nonobjective. *Biographical sources: Outstanding Young Women of America,* 1965; *Leadership Index, A Who's Who in Oklahoma,* 1964; *A Dictionary of American Indian Painters,* 1968; *American Indian Painting of the Southwest & Plains Areas,* 1968; *Indians of Today,* 1970; *Who's Who in American Art; The World Who's Who of*

Women (London, England); *Who's Who of American Women. Publishe works:* Ms. Hill's work has appeared in more than 30 publications.

HILL, NORBERT S., Jr.
(executive director-Indian society)

Affiliation: Executive director, American Indian Science and Engineering Society, 1310 College Ave., Suite 1220, Boulder, Colo. 80302.

HILLABRANT, WALTER JOHN
(Citizen Band Potawatomi) 1942-
(psychologist)

Born December 17, 1942, Corsicana, Tex. *Education:* University of California, Berkeley, A.B., 1965; University of California, Riverside, Ph.D., 1972. *Principal occupation:* Psychologist. *Home address:* 1927 38th St., N.W., Washington, D.C. 20007. *Affiliations:* Assistant professor, Howard University, Washington, D.C., 1971-1980; psychologist, Support Services, Washington, D.C., 1980-. *Memberships:* American Psychological Association; Washingon Academy of Sciences; National Indian Education Association. *Interests:* "Indian education; cross-cultural psychology; application of computer and telecommunication technology to social problems." *Published work: The Future Is Now* (Peacock Press, 1974).

HILLMAN, JAMES
(director-Indian center)

Affiliation: Director, Detroit American Indian Center, 360 John R, Detroit, Mich. 48226.

HINES, MIFAUNWY SHUNTONA
(director-Indian center)

Affiliation: Director, American Indian Information Center, 139-11 87th Ave., Briarwood, N.Y. 11435.

HINKLEY, EDWARD C. 1934-
(educator)

Born December 16, 1934, Bridgewater, Mass. *Education:* Harvard University, B.A., 1955, M.Ed., 1959. *Principal occupation:* Educator. *Home address:* RFD 1, 2d-1, Mt. Vernon, Maine 04352. *Affiliations:* Elementary school teacher, Bureau of Indian Affairs, Utah and Arizona, 1959-1961; educational specialist, U.S. Public Health Service, Division of Indian Health, Arizona and Nevada, 1961-1965; Commissioner of Indian Affairs, State of Maine, 1965-1969; eduction and management consultant, T.R.I.B.E., Inc. (Teaching and Research in Bicultural Education), Maine and Canada, 1969-. *Interests:* Indian affairs of Canada and the U.S. on a contemporary level; bicultural education; community development; leadership training and counseling.

HINDS, PATRICK SWAZO
(Tewa Pueblo) 1929-
(artist)

Born March 25, 1929, Tesuque Pueblo, N.M. *Education:* Hill and Canyon School of Art (summers, 1947-1948); California College of Arts and Crafts, B.A., 1952; Mexico City College, 1952-1953; Chicago Art Institute, 1953, 1955. *Principal occupation:* Artist. *Home address:* 224 Sena St., Santa Fe, N.M. 87501. *Military service:* U.S. Marine Corps, 1945-1946, 1950-1951 (two Purple Hearts). *Awards, honors:* Many awards for work entered in shows throughout the Southwest, 1964-. About 20 one-man shows in California; work represented in many permanent collection. *Biographical sources: Who's Who of American Indian Artists; The Indian Historian; The Bialac Collection of Southwest Indian Painting; American Indian Painting; American Indian Painters.*

HIRST, STEPHEN MICHAEL 1939-
(writer)

Born December 20, 1939, Dayton, Ohio. *Education:* Miami University, Oxford, Ohio, B.A., 1962; Johns Hopkins School of Advanced International Studies, Washington, D.C., M.A., 1966. *Principal occupation:* Writer. *Home address:* P.O. Box 321, Marquette, Mich. 49855. *Affiliations:* Preschool director, Havasupai Tribe, 1967-1968, 1970-1973; planner, Havasupai Tribe,

1975-1976. *Memberships:* The Authors Guild, 1976-. *Awards, honors:* 1961 Best Columnist Award of Ohio Collegiate Newspaper Association; 1962 Greer-Hepburn Fiction Award; 1966 U.S. Commerce Deartment Service Award; 1976 Havasupai Tribe Service Award; 1979 Cincinnati Arts Consortium Writing Award; 1981 Ohio Arts Council Fiction Award; finalist for 1982 Arizona Commission on the Arts fiction award. *Published works: Life In a Narrow Place: The Havasupai of the Grand Canyon* (David mcKay Co., 1976); *Havsuw'Baaja* (Havasupai Tribe, 1985).

HISER, DONALD H. 1923-
(archaeologist, museum director)

Born November 20, 1923, Columbiana, Ohio. *Education:* University of Arizona, B.A., 1953; Arizona State University, 1957-1958. *Principal occupation:* Archaeologist, museum director, Pueblo Grande Museum, 4619 E. Washington St., Phoenix, Ariz. 85034, 1953-. *Other professional posts:* Lecturer in anthropology, Phoenix Evening College; lecturer, Traveling Science Institute of Arizona Academy of Science (sponsored by the National Science Foundation). *Military service:* U.S. Naval Reserve, 1943-1945, 1946-1950. *Community activities:* Balsz School Parent-Teachers' Association (president, Indian affairs committee, 1960-1961). *Memberships:* Arizona Academy of Science (past secretary, anthropology section); American Anthropological Association (institutional member); Society for American Archaeology; Archaeological Institute of America. *Interests:* Southwestern U.S. archaeology — Hohokam; avophysical anthropology, ceramic rsearch, teaching and lecturing on Southwestern archacology. *Published works: Pueblo Grande Museum Popular Series* (Pueblo Grande Museum).

HISER, JOHNNY R. (Ysleta Pueblo)
(tribal governor)

Affiliation: Governor, Ysleta Del Sur Pueblo Museum, P.O. Box 17579, El Paso, Tex. 79917.

HOBSON, DOTTIE F. (Navaho) 1945-
(B.I.A. Indian school principal)

Born March 9, 1945, Tohatchi, N.M. *Education:* University of Arizona, B.A., 1972; University of New Mexico, M.A., 1977; Northern Arizona University, M.A., 1977. *Principal occupation:* Principal, Lukachukai School, B.I.A., Lukachukai, Ariz., 1976-. *Home address:* Box 6, Lukachukaim Ariz. 86507. *Affliation:* Chinle Agency, Bureau of Indian Affairs, Chinle, Ariz. *Other professional posts:* Assistant education program administrator, assistant school superintendent, Chinle Agency, 1978-. *Community activities:* Boy Scouts of America (institutional representative); Gir Scouts; Federal Women's Program Coordinator, Chinle Agency. *Memberships:* Navaho School Administratos Association; National Indian Education Association. *Published works: Kee's Grandfather* (Rough Rook Demonstration School, Chinle, Ariz., 1970).

HOEBEL, E. ADAMSON 1906-
(professor emeritus)

Born November 16, 1906, Madison, Wis. *Education:* University of Wisconsin, Madison, B.A., 1928; University of Cologne, Germany, 1928-1929; New York University, M.A., 1931; Columbia University, Ph.D., 1934. *Principal occupation:* Professor emeritus. *Home address:* 48 Groveland Terrace #30, Minneapolis, Minn. 55403. *Affiliations:* Professor of anthropology, New York University, 1929-1948, University of Utah, 1948-1954, University of Minnesota, 1954-1972 (chairman, Department of Anthropology, 1954-1968; Regent's professor, 1966-1972; professor emeritus, 1972-; adjunct professor of law, 1972-1981). *Other professional posts:* Special officer, U.S. Department of State, U.S. Arms Control, Disarmament Agency; Fellow, Center for Advanced Study in the Behavioral Sciences. *Community activities:* Governor's Council on Human Relations, Minnesota, 1955-1960; Association on American Indian Affairs (director, 1936-1955); Science Museum of Minnesota (trustee, 1978-). *Memberships: American Anthropological Association, 1932- (president, 1956-1957); American Ethnological Association, 1932-*

(president, 1947); American Association for the Advancement of Science, 1934-; American Philosophical Society, 1956-. Awards, honors: Fulbright Professor, Oxford University (England), 1956-1957, Catholic University (The Netherlands), 1970; Research Fellow, Laboratory of Anthropology, Santa Fe, N.M.; member, Governor's Commission on Human Relations, 1955-1964. *Expeditions:* Field research trips: Comanche Indians, Oklahoma, 1933; Northern Shoshone, Idaho, 1934; Northern Cheyenne, 1935-1936; Keresan Pueblos, New Mexico, 1945-1950; West Pakistan, 1961; New Guineau, 1967. *Biographical sources: Who's Who in America; Who's Who in the World; International Dictionary of Biography; International Encyclopedia of the Social Sciences; Law and Society Review* (Spring, 1972). *Published works: Political Organization and Law-Ways of the Comanche Indians* (American Anthropological Association, 1941); *The Cheyenne Way,* with K.N. Llewellyn (Univerity of Oklahoma Press, 1941); *Man in the Primitive World* (McGraw-Hill, 1948, 1949); *The Comanches: Lords of the South Plains,* with E. Wallace (University of Oklahoma Press, 1953); *The Law of Primitive Man* (Harvard University Press, 1954); *The Cheyennes: Indians of the Great Plains* (Holt, Rinehart & Winston, 1961); editor, *A Cheyenne Sketchbook* (University of Oklahoma Press); *Anthropology: The Study of Man* (McGraw-Hill, 1965); *The Plains Indians: A Critical Bibliography* (Indiana Univrsity Press, 1977); editor, *Law and Society Review,* 1969-1973; *Journal of Natural Law,* 1960-1965; *American Indian Quarterly,* 1972-; also articles and reviews in legal, historical and anthropological journals.

HOFFMAN, MICHAEL P. 1937-
(anthropologist, professor, museum curator)

Born September 15, 1937, Council Bluffs, Iowa. *Education:* University of Illinois, Urbana, B.A., 1959; Harvard University, Ph.D., 1971. *Principal occupation:* Anthropologist, professor, museum curator. *Home address:* 409 N. Washington, Fayetteville, Ark. 72701. *Affiliations:* Professor of anthropology, museum curator, University of Arkansas, Fayetteville, 1964-. *Commun-*

ity activities: Arkansas Folklore Society (board of directors); ANL Research Laboratory (board of directors); Arkansas Preservation Program (past member, State Review Committee). *Memberships:* Society for American Archaeology, 1960-; American Anthropological Association (Fellow) 1961- Caddo Conference, 1964-; Southeastern Archaeological Conference, 1975-; Current Anthropology (Associate); American Indian Historical Society; Association for American Indian Affairs; Arkansas Archaeological Society. *Awards, honors:* Phi Beta Kappa. *Interests:* Southeastern Indians, past and present; Caddo, Quapaw, and Cherokee ethnology and contemporary life; avocational interests—running, fishing; expeditions: archaeological fieldwork in Arkansas, Missouri, Illinois, Arizona, Massachusetts, and Guatemala. *Published works: Three Sites in Millwood Reservoir* (Arkansas Archaeological Survey, 1970); "The Kinkaid-Mainard Site," 3PU2 *(Arkansas Archaeologist,* 1977); *Ozark Reservoir Papers* (Arkansas Archaeological Survey, 1978); *Prehistoric Ecological Crises* (Kennikat Press, 1980); "Arkansas Indians," *(Arkansas Naturalist,* 1984).

HOHNANI, DANIEL
(college president)

Affiliation: President, College of Ganado, Ganado, Ariz. 86505.

HOKANSEN, SHERRY
(librarian)

Affiliation: Librarian, Yakima Nation Museum-Library, P.O. Box 151, Toppenish, Wash. 98948.

HOLLOW, A.E. (TONY) (Assiniboine Sioux) 1918-
(business management, administration)

Born March 8, 1918, Brockton, Mt. *Education:* Central Washington University, B.A. (Business Administration), 1975, M.A. (Occ. Ed.), 1978. *Principal occupation:* Business management and administration. *Home address:* 301 Hilltop Place, Wenatchee, Wash. 98801. *Affiliations:* President,

Dull Knife Memorial College, Lame Deer, Mt., 1977-. *Other professional posts:* National and State EPDA Research Coordinator, Central Washington State College, Ellensburg, 1973-1975; Higher Education Consultant, Miles Commuity College, Miles City, Mont., 1976-1977. *Military service:* U.S. Army, 1940-1945 (Administrative Assistant, Chief Warrant Officer). *Community activities:* Northwest Indian Economic Development Association (treasurer, 1966-1970); Indian Center, Wenatchee, Wash. (president, 1970-1973); Ethnic Advisory Council, Central Washington State College (chairman, 1973-1975); Washington State Vocational Education Advisory Board (member, 1975-). *Membership:* American Vocational Association. *Interests:* American Indian arts and crafts; business and administration. *Published works: Guidelines for Business Management Training for Native Americans* (Central Washington University, 1976); *Native American Vocational Education: State of the Art (Washington State)* (Central Washington University, 1976).

HOLLOW, MAUDE C. (Assiniboine Sioux) 1921-
(librarian, media specialist)

Born December 11, 1921, Poplar, Mt. *Education:* Central Washington State College, B.A. (Education), 1967, M.A. (Education), 1973. *Principal occupation:* Librarian, media specialist. *Home address:* 301 Hilltop Place, Wenatchee, Wash. 98801. *Affiliation:* Librarian and media specialist, Wenatchee School District #246, Wenatchee, Wash., 1967-. *Memberships:* National Education Association; Washington State Education Association; Wenatchee Education Asociation; Washington Association for Educational Communication and Technology; Washington State Association of School Librarians (secretary, Region 11).

HOLLOW, NORMAN (Assiniboine Sioux)
(tribal chairman)

Affiliation: Chairman, Fort Peck Tribal Executive Board, Poplar, Mont. 59255.

HOLLOWBREAST, DONALD (Northern Cheyenne) 1917-
(artist, newspaper contributor)

Born May 17, 1917, Birney, Mt. *Education:* Chemawa Indian School, Chemawa, Oreg., 1934-1936. *Principal ocupation:* Artist, newspaper contributor. *Home address:* Senior Citizens Center #28, Lame Deer, Mt. 59043. *Affiliations:* Editor, The Birney Arrow (Indian Newspaper), Lame Deer, Mont., 1977-. *Memberships:* National Mustang Association; Montana Institute of the Arts; Northern Cheyenne Landowners Association; *Awards, honors:* First Prize for water-color painting, Rosebud County Fair, Forsyth, Mt. *Interests:* Western art and writing; Indian newspapers; travel. *Biographical source: Montana,* the Magazine of Western History (Fall, 1964); *Great Falls Tribune; The Billings Gazzette; Sheridan Press; Wassaja. Published work:* Editor, The Birney Arrow, 1960-1971.

HOLMES, BEVERLY C. (Cherokee) 1936-
(research program analyst)

Born September 8, 1936, Tulsa, Okla. *Education:* Henager's Business College; Brigham Young University; Utah State University. *Principal occupation:* Research program analyst. *Home address:* 7155 Game Lord Dr., Springfield, Va. 22153. *Affiliations:* Chairperson, Federal Equal Opportunity Council of Utah; instructor, Weber State College's Division of Continuing Education conducting classes in Indian culture and women's programs; research program analyst for the Deputy Chief of the Forest Service. *Memberships:* Intermountain Indian Education Council (board of directors); National Congress of American Indians; Native American Indian Women's Association; Indian Leadership Training Center; American Indian Historical Society; Federal Employed Women. *Awards, honors:* Federal Woman of the Year, Bureau of Indian Affairs, 1973; Sustained Superior Performance Award, 1973; Special Achievement Award, 1975; nominated to receive a special award sponsored by the American Society for Public Administrators, 1976; Mrs. Holmes was a delegate nominee for the State of Utah to the National Women's Year

Conference, 1977, and has received the Outstanding Alumni Award from Henager's Business College. *Biographical sources: Who's Who of American Women; The World Who's Who of Women* (International Bibliographical Centre).

HOMERATHA, PHIL (Otoe-Missouri)
1943-
(education)

Born March 22, 1943, Pawnee, Okla. *Education:* Tarkio College, Mo., B.S., 1968; Northest Missouri State University, M.S., 1972. *Principal occupation:* Education. *Home address:* 901 W. 22nd, Lawrence, Kan. 66044. *Affiliations:* Head football coach, head wrestling coach, instructor of physical education, Haskell Indian Junior College, Lawrence, Kan., 1973-. *Other professional posts:* Teacher/coach. Dexfield Community Schools, Redfield, Iowa; head track, assistant football coach, Huron College, Huron, S.D. *Community activities:* Haskell Alumni Association (board of directors). *Memberships:* National Federal Government Employees; National Football Coaches Association; National WR Coaches Assocaition. *Awards, honors:* Outstanding Young Men of America, 1972; Tarkio College Outstanding Alumni, 1978. *Interests:* Football; "have served as coordinator for division of Indian studies here at Haskell. Have served as consultant to HEW-Westinghouse Learning on Indian Education; major interest at present job is in area of Indian education."

HONANIE, GILBERT, Jr. (Hopi)
1941-
(architect, planning)

Born April 11, 1941, Tuba City, Ariz. *Education:* Pasadena City College, Calif., A.A., 1969; Arizona State University, Bachelor of Architecture, 1972. *Principal occupation:* Architect, planning. *Home address:* 1711 East Missouri, Suite #5, Phoenix, Ariz. 85016. *Affiliation: President, owner, architect, Gilbert Honanie, Jr., Inc., Phoenix, Ariz., 1975-. Other professional posts:* National Council of Architectural Registration Board; American Indian Council of Architects & Engineers; Western & Arizona Society of Architects. *Community activities:* Member of Hopi Tribe; member, Arizona Indian Chamber of Commerce; member. Central Arizona Chapter of Architects. *Biographical sources:* Articles in the *Arizona Republic & Gazette, Arizona Builder, Progressive Architecture,* and *Architectural Journal.*

HONER, JANELLE A. (Seminole)
1954-
(artist, gardner)

Born February 28, 1954, Hayward, Calif. *Education:* Humboldt State University, Arcata, Calif., B.A. (Art, Native American Studies), 1976; Anderson Ranch, Snowmass Village, Colo. (seminars and workshops), 1978-1982. *Principal occupation:* Artist, gardner. *Home address:* P.O. Box 1302, Basalt, Colo. 81621. *Affiliations:* Owner operator, Doug and Janella's Garden, El Jebel, Colo., 1981-; gallery artist, Janie Beggs Fine Arts Ltd., Aspen, Colo., 1986-. *Community activities:* Advisor, Aspen Dance Connection. *Memberships:* National Gardening Association; American Crafts Council; Aspen Art Museum; Colorado Council on the Arts; Carbondale Council on the Arts & Humanities. *Art exhibitions and shows:* Featured artist, Cohen Gallery, Denver, Colo., 1985; "Roaring Fork Annual," Aspen Art Museum, 1985; Colorado Artists-Craftsmen Exhibit, Boulder, Colo., 1984; one-person show, Sioux National Museum, 1981; Roaring Fork Valley Art Show, Aspen Center for the Visual Arts, 1981; "Objects 81," Western Colorado Center for the Arts, Grand Junction, Colo., 1981; group show, Applequist Gallery, Aspen, Colo., 1980; Colorado Artists-Craftsmen Exhibit, Arvada Center for the Arts, 1980; Heard Museum Annual Art Show, 1979; "Spree 78," Colorado Council on the Arts Invitational, Denver, Colo., 1978; three-person show, Western Colorado Center for the Arts, Grand Junction, Colo., 1978; among others. *Awards, honors:* Magna Cum Laude, Humbodt State University, Arcata, Calif., 1976; 1983 Colorado Biennial (show toured Colorado in 1984), Denver, Colo.; first and second place prizes, Women Art West, Grand Junction, Colo., 1982-1983; *Craft Range* Magazine award for "Buy the Heartland," 1982; first place sculpture, Woman Art West, 1980; third place sculpture, Red Cloud Indian Art Show, 1980; inclusion in Northern Plains, Southern Plains Indian Museum art collections; among others. *Interests:* Vocational: "We are organic farmers with a gourmet produce market garden. We teach people basic skills and give garden tours, sell produce. We educate abou wild edibles, food storage; we both are chefs. I also do mixed media sculpture and ceramic sculpture, that is the art I show. We traveled extensively in 1985. My goal is to help feed the hungry in 1986."

HOOVER, HERBERT T. 1930-
(professor of history)

Born March 9, 1930, Oakwood Township, Wabasha County, Minn. *Education:* New Mexico State University, Las Cruces, B.A., 1960, M.A., 1961; University of Oklahoma, Norman, Ph.D., 1966. *Principal occupation:* Professor of history. *Home address:* Route 2, Box 25, Vermillion, S.D. 57069. *Affiliations:* Assistant professor of history, East Texas State University, Commerce, 1965-1967; professor of history, University of South Dakota, Vermillion, 1967-. *Other professional posts:* Director, Newberry Library Center for the History of the American Indian, Chicago, Ill., 1981-1983; director, South Dakota Oral History Center, 1967-. *Military service:* U.S. Navy, 1951-1955 (Fleet Marine Corpsman with First Marine Division in Korean War). *Community activities:* South Dakota Council of Humanists; South Dakota Committee on the Humanities; National Endowment for the Humanities (review panels); South Dakota Historical Society (board of trustees); South Dakota Fairview Township Bpard of Control; South Dakota Historical Publications and Records Commission. *Memberships:* Western History Association, 1962- (chair, nominating board; local arrangements committee; program committee; membership committee; board of editors); Organization of American Historians, 1970- (nominating board; membership committee); Phi Alpha Theta, 1960- (international councillor; international board of advisors); South Dakota Historical Society; Missouri Historical Society; Minnesota Wabasha County Historical Society.

Awards, honors: Augustana College Center for Western Studies, 1985 Achievement Award, National Board of Advisors; National Endowment for the Humanities, Research Grant Award, 1978-1981; National Teacher of the Year Award, 1985. *Interests:* "Travel and recreation is tied to principal occupational interests: the history of Indian-white relations, and the preservation of natural life." *Published works: To Be An Indian* (Holt, Rinehart & Winston, 1971); *The Practice of Oral History* (Microfilming Corp. of America, 1975); *The Chitimacha People* (Indian Tribal Series, 1975); *The Sioux: A Critical Bibliography* (Indiana University, 1979); *Bibliography of the Sioux* (Scarecrow Press, 1980).

HORSE, BILLY EVANS (Kiowa)
(tribal chairman)

Affiliation: Chairman, Kiowa Business Committee, P.O. Box 369, Carnegie, Okla. 73015.

HORSE CAPTURE, GEORGE P.
(museum curator)

Affiliation: Curator, Plains Indian Museum, Buffalo Bill Historical Center, P.O. Box 1000, Cody, Wyo. 82414.

HORSECHIEF, MARY ADAIR
(Cherokee) 1936-
(executive director-Murrow Indian Children's Home)

Born July 2, 1936, Sequoyah County, Okla. *Education:* Bacone Indian Junior College, A.A., 1955; Northeastern Oklahoma State University, B.A. (Education), 1957; Tulsa University (Art Couses), 1966. *Principal occupation:* Executive director, Murrow Indian Children's Home, Muskogee, Okla. (child care-residence care institution). *Home address:* 224 N. 15, Muskogee, Okla. 74401. *Other professional posts:* Teacher, B.I.A. school, public school, head start program-management at Tinker Air Force Base. *Community activities:* Community Council (board member); Indian Parent Committee; Soroptimist Club; American Baptist Indian Caucus; Oklahoma Association of Children's Institutions and Agencies (secretary-treasurer). *Memberships:* National Indian Education Association (past secretary); American Baptist Homes & Hospitals. *Awards, honors:* Painting awards and entries in the following shows: Philbrook Indian Annual Art Show; Five Tribes Annual Art Show; Cherokee Historical Museum Competition; American Indian Exposition Competition; Red Cloud Indian Art Show; Heard Museum and others. *Interests:* "I have interest in contemporary American Indian affairs, education and art. Have traveled to a number of traditional Indian communities and reservation areas for business and fellowship."

HORSMAN, REGINALD 1931-
(distinguished professor of history)

Born October 24, 1931, Leeds (Yorkshire) England. *Education:* University of Birmingham, England, B.A., 1952, M.A., 1955; Indiana University, Bloomington, Ph.D., 1958. *Principal occupation:* Distinguished professor of history. *Home address:* 3548 North Hackett Ave., Milwaukee, Wisc. 53211. *Affiliations:* Instructor, 1958-1959, assistant professor, 1959-1962, associate professor, 1962-1964, professor, 1964-1973, and distinguished professor of history, 1973-, University of Wisconsin, Milwaukee. *Memberships:* American Historical Association; Organization of American Historians; Society of American Historians; Society for Historians of the Early Republic (advisory council); Phi Beta Kappa (honorary member); Phi Kappa Phi (honorary member); Phi Eta Sigma (honorary member); Phi Alpha Theta. *Awards, honors:* University of Wisconsin Kiehofer Award for Excellence in Teaching, 1961; Guggenheim Fellowship, 1965. *Interests:* Research on race and expansion in American history; shaping of American Indian policy; early American foreign policy; Wisconsin Oneida. *Biographical source: Who's Who in America.* *Published works: The Causes of the War of 1812* (University of Pennsylvania Press, 1962); *Matthew Elliott: British Indian Agent* (Wayne State University Press, 1964); *Expansion and American Indian Policy, 1783-1812* (Michigan State University Press, 1967); *Napolean's Europe;*

The New America (Paul Hamlyn, London, 1970) *The Frontier in the Formative Years, 1783-1815* (Holt, Rinehart, 1970) *Race and Manifest Destiny: The Origins of American Racial Anglo-Saxonism* (Harvard University Press, 1981); *The Diplomacy of the New Republic, 1776-1815* (Harlan Davidson, 1985); *Dr. Nott of Mobile: Southerner, Physician, and Racial Theorist* (LSU press, forthcoming).

HORTON, DAVID A., Jr.
(B.I.A. agency superintendent)

Affiliation: Superintendent, Southeast Agency, Bureau of Indian Affairs, P.O. Box 3-8000, Juneau, Alaska 99802.

HOULIHAN, PATRICK T. 1942-
(anthropologist, museum director)

Born June 22, 1942, New Haven, Conn. *Education:* Georgetown University, B.S., 1964; University of Minnesota, M.A., 1969; University of Wisconsin, Ph.D., 1972. *Principal occupation:* Anthropologist, museum director. *Home address:* 1220 Wentworth Ave., Pasadena, Calif. 91106. *Affiliations:* Instructor, University of Wisconsin, Oshkosh, 1969-1971; director, Anthropology Museum, University of Wisconsin, Oshkosh, 1969-1971; museum intern, Milwaukee Public Museum, 1971-1972; adjunct professor, Arizona State University, Tempe, Ariz., 1972-1980; director, The Heard Museum, Phoenix, Ariz., 1972-1980; director, New York State Museum, Albany, 1980-1981; instructor, American Indian art, UCLA, Extension Division. 1981-; director, Southwest Museum, Los Angeles, Calif., 1981-. *Memberships:* American Association of Museums (first vice president, Western Regional Conference; American Anthropological Association (council on museum education); California Association of Museums (board of directors, 1985-1986). *Field work:* Urban Indian research for the Indian employment service (BIA sponsored), Minneapolis, Minn., 1967. *Interests:* American Indian art. *Published works:* "Museums and Indian Education," (*Journal of Indian Education,* Oct., 1973) "Southwest Pottery Today," (*Arizona Highways,* May, 1974);

"The Hopi Kachinas," (*Image Roche* Magazine, No. 63, 1974); "Indian Art: Fads and Paradoxes," (*Phoenix* Magazine, Feb., 1975); "Basketry Designs in the Greater Southwest," (Exhibit Catalog, Utah Fine Arts Museum, Salt lake City, April, 1976); "Contemporary Indian Art," (Exhibit Catalog, Mid-America Arts Association, Spring, 1979); "Prints and the American Indian Artist," (*American Indian Arts Magazine*, Spring, 1979); "Indians of the Northwest Coast," (*Reader's Digest*, 1980); various articles in *Masterkey*, a quarterly publication of the Southwest Museum, 1981-. Editorial director for the following Heard Museum publications: *Kachinas: A Hopi Artist's Documentary*, 1973; *Pueblo Shields*, April, 1976; *The Other Southwest: Indian Arts and Crafts of Northeastern Mexico*, April, 1977. Editorial director for the following Southwest Museum publications: *Native Faces: Indian Cultures in American Art*, co-author with Patricia Trenton, Ph.D., 1984; *Kachinas of the Zuni* (Northland Press, 1985); work in progress: *Lummis in the Pueblos* (Northland Press, Fall, 1986); *The American Indian in American Art* (Harry Abrams, Fall, 1987). Television programs: Script author for six one-half hour television programs, "Indian Art at the Heard," produced by KAET, 1975; script researcher/writer for five one-half hour television programs titles, "American Indian Artists," produced by KAET, 1976; script author for a one-half hour television program on "The Craft Arts of Northwestern Mexico," produced by KAET, 1977; guest curator, "Generation in Clay," traveling exhibit of Pueblo Pottery, the American Federation of Art, New York, 1980-1983; principal investigator (1977-1980), Navajo Film Project, KAET, Tempe, Ariz.

HOUSE, ERNEST (Ute Mountain Ute)
  (tribal chairman)

Affiliation: Chairman, Ute Mountain Tribal Council, Tribal Office Bldg., Towaoc, Colo. 81334.

HOUSER, ALLAN (Chiricahua Apache) 1914-
  (artist, art instructor)

Born June 30, 1914, Apache, Okla. *Education:* Santa Fe Indian School; Utah State University; private study. *Principal occupation:* Artist, art instructor. *Home address:* 1020 Camino Carlos Rey, Santa Fe, N.M. 87501. *Affiliation:* Instructor in sculpture and advanced painting, Institute of American Indian Arts, Santa Fe, N.M. (retired). *Membership:* Southwestern Association on Indian Affairs (board of directors). *Exhibitions:* One-man shows: Museum of New Mexico, Santa Fe., 1936; Heard Museum, Phoenix, Ariz., 1970; Southern Plains Museum, Anadarko, Okla., 1971; Philbrook Art Center, Tulsa, Okla., 1972; The Gallery Wall, Phoenix, Ariz., 1976, 1977. *Awards, honors:* Mural commissions: Washington, D.C., San Francisco Exposition and New York World's Fair, 1939; Guggenheim Scholarship for sculpture and painting, 1948; created seven and one-half feet tall marble statue, *Comrade in Mourning*, for Haskell Institute, Lawrence, Kan., 1949; 1954 recipient of *Palmes d3 Academique* from French Government for painting; awarded Waite Phillips Trophy for outstanding contributions to field of Indian art, Philbrook Art Center, 1969; appeared in a documentary film produced by National Educational Television, aired 1976. *Interests:* Sculpture, painting, book illustration, lecturing; writing; recording stories; travels to Navajo Reservtion, New York City, Mexico City. *Biographical sources: Indians of Today*, 1960; *Art and Indian Individualists*, by Guy and Doris Monthan, 1975; *Southwest Indian Painting*, by Clara Lee Tanner (University of Arizona Prss, 1973). *Published works:* Mr. Houser's illustrations have appeared in many books.

HOUSER, SCHUYLER
  (college president)

Affiliation: President, Sisseton-Wahpeton College, P.O. Box 262, Sisseton, S.D. 57262.

HOUSH, RAYMOND E. 1921-
(agricultural education)

Born July 26, 1921, Hay Springs, Neb. *Education:* Colorado State University, CTD, 1942-1943; University of Nebraska, 1946-1948; Chadron State College, Neb., B.A., 1959, B.S., 1965; Northern Arizona State University, M.S., 1968; International University, M.S. (Education Specialist), 1977; California Western University, Ph.D., 1978. *Principal occupation:* Agricultural education. *Home address:* 2200 Hidden Glenn, Farmington, N.M. 87401. *Affiliations:* Extension horticulture, Colorado State University, 1969-1974; director, Navajo Community College, Agriculture Program, 1975-. Military service: U.S. Army, 1942-1946 (pilot, radar, engineering corps). *Memberships:* American Horticultural Society; American Society of Animal Breeders; American Agronomy Society; American Dairy Association (state director, 1970-); National Pilots Association. *Awards, honors:* Spokesman of the Year, American Agriculture, 1975; Top Pilot Award, National Pilots Association. *Interests:* "I organized and developed Navajo Community College, Agriculture Program, to train Navajos to operate the Navajo Indian Irrigation Project." *Biographical sources:* Numerous articles: *Daily Times* (Farmington, N.M.); *Navajo Times* (Window Rock, Ariz.); Navajo Community College, *Annual Report, 1975* (Tsaile, Ariz.); *Published work: Developmental Agriculture* (Ph.D. diisertation, 1978).

HOVI, DOROTHY 1933-
(Indian jewelry sales)

Born April 17, 1933, Trenton, N.J. *Education:* Ursinus College, B.S., 1955. *Principal occupation:* Indian jewelry sales; owner, Way of the Arrow, 72 South St., New Providence, N.J. 07974, 1976-. *Membership:* Indian Arts and Crafts Association.

HOWARD, HELEN ADDISON 1904-
(author, historian)

Born August 4, 1904, Missoula, Mt. *Education:* University of Montana, B.A., 1927; University of Southern California, M.A., 1933. *Principal occupation:* Author, histo-

rian. *Home address:* 410 S. Lamer St., Burbank, Calif. 91506. *Affiliations:* Reporter and feature writer, *Daily Missoulian,* Missoula, Mont., 1923-1929; radio-TV monitor-editor, Radio Reports, Inc., 1943-1956; reviewer of scholarly books on American Indians, 1969-1986, editorial advisory board, 1978-, *Journal of the West,* Kansas State University, Manhattan, Kan. Memberships: Montana Historical Society, 1955-; California Writers Guild, 1973-1978. *Awards, honors: War Chief Joseph* dramatized for radio in commemoration of American Indian Day, over KFI-NBC network, 1949; lecturer on American Indian poetry, 1966-1967; *Saga of Chief Joseph,* transcribed in braille and taped, Library of Congress, 1967, microfilmed for college and library use, 1975; *Northwest Trail Blazers,* also microfilmed, 1975; appointed to editorial advisory board, 1978-, *Journal of the West,* scholarly historical quarterly. *Interests:* American Indians; Western history; ride own Arabian horses. *Biographical sources:* Subject biography, KLAC, Los Angeles, 1970, "Our American Heritage," on Indian radio program; *Contemporary Authors; Who's Who of American Women,* 1983-1984; *The Writers Directory,* 1981-1982; *Two Thousand Women of Achievement,* 1971-1972; *Dictionary of International Biography,* 1985-1986; World Who's Who of Women, 5th Edition; *International Authors & Writers Who's Who; Community Leaders & Noteworthy Americans; Personalities of the West and Midwest. Published works: War Chief Joseph* (Caxton, 1941-1978; *Northwest Trail Blazers* (Caxton, 1963-1968); *American Indian Poetry-Tusas 334* (G.K. Hall & Co., 1979-1985); *American Frontier Tales* (Mountain Press, 1982-); contributed three essays to *Dictionary of Indian Tribes of the Americas,* 4 Vols. (Scholarly Press, 1980); many articles in scholarly and popular history magazines, also in seven horse speciality magazines.

HOWE, OSCAR (Sioux) 1915-
(artist, professor emeritus)

Born May 13, 1915, Joe Creek, S.D. *Education:* Dakota Wesleyan University, B.A., 1952; University of Oklahoma, M.F.A.,

1954. *Principal occupation:* Artist, professor emeritus. *Home address:* 128 Walker St., Vermillion, S.D. 57069. *Affiliations:* Artist in residence, Dakota Wesleyan University, 1948-1952; director of art, Pierre High School, Pierre, S.D., 1953-1957; artist in residence, assistant professor of creative arts, professor emeritus, University of South Dakota, Vermillion, 1957-. *Military service:* U.S. Army, 1942-1945. *Memberships:* Delta Phi Delta; International Institute of Arts and Letters (Fellow). *Awards, honors:* Subject, *This Is Your Life* television program, 1960; Grand Purchase Award, Philbrook Art Center, 1947; named S.D. Artist Laureate, 1960; Certificate of Appreciation, Indian Arts and Crafts Board, 1962; Recognition Award, Foundation of North American Indian Culture, 1964; numerous awards in the following art shows from 1949-: Denver Art Museum, Museum of New Mexico, Philbrook Art Center, numerous one-man shows in the U.S.; paintings on permanent exhibit in several U.S. museums. *Books illustrated: Legends of the Mighty Sioux,* 1941; *The Little Lost Sioux,* 1942; *Bringer of the Mystery Dog,* 1943; *North American Indian Costumes,* 1952; among others.

HOWELL, GEORGE E. (Pawnee-Cheyenne) 1935-
(health systems administrator)

Born December 30, 1935, Pawnee, Okla. *Education:* Westminster College, Salt Lake City, Utah, B.S., 1978; University of Utah, Salt Lake City, M.S.W., 1980. *Principal occupation:* Health systems administrator. *Home address:* P.O. Box 712, Wagner, S.D. 57380. *Affiliations:* Health systems administrator, PHS Indian Health Center, Fort Thompson, S.D., 1983-1985; health systems administrator, PHS Indian Health Hospital, Wagner, S.D., 1985-. *Other professional posts:* Director, Mental Health/Social Services, social worker, clinical instructor, University of Utah. *Military service:* U.S. Air Force, 1954-1959 (A/1c). *Community activities:* Four Corners Gourd Dance Society (president); Alcohol Treatment Program (chairman, board of directors); UNAC (chairman, board of directors). *Memberships:* National Association of Social Workers; Native American-Alaska Native Social Workers Association. *Awards, honors:* CSWE Scholarship Grant.

HOWELL, IRENE (Santee Sioux)
(tribal chairwoman)

Affiliation: Chairwoman, Upper Sioux Board of Trustees, P.O. Box 147, Granite Falls, Minn. 56241.

HOXIE, FREDERICK E. 1947-
(director-Indian center)

Born April 22, 1947, Hoolehua, Molokai. *Education:* Amherst College, Mass., B.A., 1969; Brandeis University, Waltham, Mass., Ph.D., 1977. *Principal occupation:* Director-Indian center. *Home address:* 2717 Lincolnwood Ave., Evanston, Ill. 60201. *Affiliation:* Director, D'Arcy McNickle Center for the History of the Amerian Indian, Newberry Library, 60 W. Walton, Chicago, Ill., 1983-. *Other professional post:* Adjunct professor of history, Univerity of Illinois, Chicago. *Memberships:* American Historical Association; Organization of American Historians; American Society of Ethnohistory. *Awards, honors:* Rockefeller Foundation Humanities Fellowship, 1983-1984. *Published works:* Editor, With the Nez Perces (University of Nebraska Press, 1981); *A Final Promise* (University of Nebraska Press, 1984).

HUDSON, MELVIN, Jr. 1932-
(anthropologist)

Born December 24, 1932, Monterey, Ky. *Education:* University of Kentucky, B.A., 1959; University of North Carolina, Ph.D., 1965. *Principal occupation:* Anthropologist. *Home address:* Route 2, Danielsville, Ga. 30633. *Affiliation:* Professor of anthropology, University of Georgia, Athens, Ga., 1964-. *Memberships:* American Anthropological Association; Southern Anthropological Society (president, 1973-1974). *Awards, honors:* Woodrow Wilson Fellow, 1959-1960; senior fellow, Newberry Library, 1977-1978. *Interests:* "My primary interest is in the historical anthropology of the Indians of the Soutestern U.S." *Published works:*

The Catawba Nation (University of Georgia Press, 1970); editor, *Four Centuries of Southern Indians* (University of Georgia Press, 1975); *The Southeastern Indians* (University of Tennessee Press, 1976; editor, *Black Drink: A Native American Tea* (University of Georgia Press, 1978).

HUERTA, C. LAWRENCE (Yaqui Pasqua Pueblo) 1924-
(chancellor emeritus)

Born August 16, 1924, Nogales, Ariz. *Education:* University of Arizona, LLB & J.D., 1953. *Principal occupation:* Chancellor emeritus. *Home address:* P.O. Box 235, Tsaile (Navajo Reservation), Ariz. 86556. *Affiliations:* President, United Services of America, Inc., Washington, D.C., 1962-1974; holder of the Chair of Economic Development, Navajo Community College, Tsaile, Ariz., 1974-; Chancellor Chancellor Emeritus, Navajo Community College, 1975-. *Other professional posts:* Associate (Navajo) Tribal attorney; special assistant, Attorney General (Arizona); Commissioner, Arizona Industrial Commissione; Judge, Maricopa Superior Court, Phoenix, Ariz.; contract management specialist, U.S. Dept. of Commerce, Washington, D.C. *Community activities:* Founder, Navajo Judicial Systems; founder, American Indian School of Medicine; U.S. Dept. of State, Washington, D.C. (Foreign Service Evaluation/Selection Board). *Memberships:* American Indian Society, Washington, D.C.; Phi Delta Pji; International Legal Fraternity; Arizona State Bar; New Mexico State Bar; Bar of the District of Columbia; United States Supreme Court; Pasqua Yaqui Association; Tsaile Kiwanis Navajo Reservation. *Awards, honors:* Founder, American Coordinating Council on Political Education; Casey Club (businessmen) Vesta Club; 3rd Degree Knights of Columbus. *Interests:* "Copyrights, trademarks; student of Panama and U.S. Canal Zone; lecturer on American Indians (North and South America); Indian law, religion, government; student of Latin American affairs." *Published works: Enriquezca Su Vida* (self, 1968); *Arizona Law & Order* (self, 1968).

HUFF, DELORES (Western Cherokee) 1934-
(principal)

Born May 27, 1934, New York, N.Y. *Education:* Tufts University, B.A., 1972, M.A., 1973; Harvard University, Ed.D., 1978. *Principal occupation:* Principal. *Address:* Pierre Indian Learning Center, Pierre, S.D. 57501. *Affiliation:* Principal, Pierre Indian Learning Center, 1976-. *Other professional posts:* Harvard University, American Indian Program—research in planning for economic development in American Indian communities; planner, Boston Indian Council; director of education, Boston Indian Council; evaluator, Native American Committee Education Program; evaluator, O.E.O. Rural Health Programs. *Community activities:* Advisory council for the State of Massachusetts, Vocational and Technical Education (board member); WINNERS, Inc. (board member, co-founder). *Memberships:* National Indian Education Association; Phi Delta Kappa. *Interests:* "I plan on writing a book on planning education for economic development in American Indian comunities. I enjoy research and planning. I have been co-host of two Indian radio programs: the first, *Red Power,* ran for one year and won the national award for radio; the second, *Pow Wow,* ran for three years. I have visited most all of the reservations in this country. I have also been an evaluator for education and health programs for O.E.O. Health planning is another field that interests me. I was a member of the Institute for the Study of Health and Society. *Published works:* "Planning Indian Education," (*Current* Magazine, Dec., 1976); "Colonialism and Education: The Native American Experience," (*Harvard* Magazine, May, 1976).

HUGHES, J. DONALD 1932-
(professor)

Born June 5, 1932, Santa Monica, Calif. *Education:* Oregon State University, Corvallis, 1950-1952; UCLA, A.B., 1954; Boston University, Ph.D., 1960. *Principal occupation:* Professor. *Home address:* 2568 S. Columbine St., Denver, Colo. 80210. *Affiliation:* Professor of history, University of Denver, Denver, Colo., 1967-. *Other pro-*

fessional post: Visitng professor, University of Colorado, Boulder. *Memberships:* American Historical Society, 1961-; Forest History Society. *Awards, honors:* Burlington Northern Research Prize, 1985; Alumni Fellow, Boston University, 1957-1958; Phi Beta Kappa, 1954-. *Interests:* Teaching, writing; the environment; travel. *Published works: Ecology in Ancient Civilizations* (University of New Mexico Press, 1975); *In the House of Stone and Light* (Grand Canyon N.H.A., 1977); *American Indians in Colorado* (Pruett Press, 1978); *American Indian Ecology* (Texas Western Press, 1983); contributing editor (editor-in-chief, 1983-1985), *Environmental Review; member editorial board, Environmental Ethics.*

HUGHES, JUANITA (Eastern Cherokee) (museum curator)

Affiliation: Curator, Museum of the Cherokee Indian, P.O. Box 770-A, Cherokee, N.C. 28719.

HUNTER, ROBERT L. (B.I.A. agency superintendent)

Affiliation: Superintendent, Western Nevada Agency, Bureau of Indian Affairs, Stewart, Nev. 89437.

HUNTER, TERRY (executive director-Indian association)

Affiliation: Executive director, Association of American Indian Physicians, 6805 S. Western, Suite 504, Oklahoma City, Okla. 73139.

HURT, WESLEY R. 1917- (museum director)

Born September 20, 1917, Albuquerque, N.M. *Education:* University of New Mexico, B.A. (Anthropology), 1938, M.A. (Sociology), 1941; University of Michigan, Ph.D. (Anthropology), 1952. *Principal occupation:* Museum director. *Home address:* 120 Concord Rd., Bloomington, Ind. 47401.

Affiliation: Director, Indiana University Museum, Bloomington, Ind., 1964-. *Other professional post:* Professor of anthropology, Indiana University. *Military service:* U.S. Army, Counter Intelligence Corps, 1942-1945. *Memberships:* American Association of Museums; American Anthropological Association; Society for American Archaeology; Association of Science Museum Directors; Americn Quaternary Association. *Interests:* Arcaheology of the New World; directed archaeological project in Missouri Valley of South Dakota, 1949-1960; archaeological expeditions to South America, 1955, 1958, 1968, 1969. *Published works:* Approximately 100 articles and monographs on American Indian archaeology and ethnology.

HURTADO, ALBERT L. 1946- (assistant professor of history)

Born October 19, 1946, Sacramento, Calif. *Education:* Sacramento City College, Calif., 1964-1966; California State University, Sacramento, B.A., 1969, M.A., 1975; University of California, Santa Barbara, Ph.D., 1981. *Principal occupation:* Assistant professor of history, Arizona State University, Tempe, Ariz., 1986-. *Affiliations:* Assistant professor of history, Indiana University-Purdue University, Indianapolis, 1983-1986, Arizona State University, 1986-. *Other professional posts:* Lecturer, University of Maryland; instructor, Sierra College, Rocklin, Calif. *Military service:* U.S. Army, 1969-1971, Counter Intelligence Agent. *Community activities:* California Committee for the Promotion of History (chair, 1981-1983). *Memberships:* National Council on Public History (treasurer, 1985-1986; board of directors, 1982-1986); American Historical Association; Organization of American Historians; Western History Association; American Society for Ethnohistory; California Historical Society; Indiana Historical Society. *Awards, honors:* Bolton Prize for Spanish Borderlands History for the best article in the field, awarded biennially by the Western Historical Association for, "'Hardly a Farm House--a Kitchen Without Them': Indian and White Households on the California Borderland Frontier in 1860," (*Western Historical Quarterly,* July, 1982). *Interests:* Western history,

Indian history, public history; backpacking, photography. *Published works:* Articles and book reviews in various scholarly journals. "Indian Survival in Frontier California, 1820-1860," in progress.

HUTCHINGS, EVELYN K. (Choctaw-Chickasaw) 1946-
(director of special services)

Born September 19, 1946, Talihina, Okla. *Education:* Southeastern State University, Durant, Okla., B.S. (Business Administration), 1972, M.B.S. (Elementary Education), 1975, M.B.S. (Guidance and Counseling), 1976. *Principal occupation:* Director of special services, Murray State College, Tishomingo, Okla. *Home address:* 101 Faculty Dr., Apt. 10, Tishomingo, Okla. 73460. *Community activities:* Oklahoma Health Systems Agency (Sub-area Council IV - council member). *Memberships:* Southwest Association of Student Assistance Programs; Oklahoma Division of Student Assistance Programs; Oklahoma Personnel & Guidance Association; Indian Adult Advisory Committee, Athletic Committee, Murray State College; Emergency School Aid Assistance, Fillmore Schools (consultant); National Indian Education Association.

HYDE, DOUGLAS (Nez Perce) 1946-
(artist)

Born July 28, 1946, in "Nez Pece country," Idaho. *Education:* Institute of American Indian Arts. *Principal occupation: Artist. Awards, honors:* Numerous awards since 1965.

I

IDE, JOHN H. (Klamath) 1932-
(U.S. Air Force, retired)

Born November 30, 1932, Klamath Agency, Ore. *Education:* University of Tampa, Fla., B.A. (History), 1971; University of Hawaii, Honolulu, M.A. (TESL), 1975. *Principal occupation:* U.S. Air Force, retired. *Home address:* 85-175 Farrington Highway #B424, Waianae, Hawaii 96792. *Affiliation:* Professor of English, Hankuk University of Foreign Studies, Seoul, Korea, 1977-1983; JTPA director, Hawaii Council of American Indian Nations, Honolulu, 1984-. *Military service:* U.S. Army, 1952-1955 (radio operator); U.S. Air Force, 1956-1973 (munitions specialist, retired with rank of technical sergeant E-6). *Community activities:* American Indian Services Corp. (president); American Indian Powwow Association (vice president); Hawaiian Heritage Cultural Center of Waianae, Hawaii (member, board of directors). *Memberships:* Non-Commissioned Officer's Association; Retired Enlistee Association; National Association of Uniformed Services. *Interests:* "Served in Germany, 1949-1955, 1962-1966; Japan, 1957-1960; Taiwan, 1968-1970; Korea, 1972, 1977-1983. Interested in linguistics and history; was judo player and instructor, 1957-1971. Present interest is in educational and vocational counseling. I'm completing studies in counseling and guidance. Pursuing interests in Indian affairs and Klamath restoration." *Published works:* "Multi-Level Reinforcement in Language Teaching (*College English Teacher's Journal,* Korea, 1979); co-author, "North American Culture," (Hankuk University, 1980); "Easy Come, Easy Go," (*The Current English Magazine,* Korea, 1982); "Some Problems Encountered by Korean Students Studying Abroad," with David Cottrell, (*Journal of East-West Education,* Korea, 1981); "Teaching Culturally Appropriate English," (*College English Teacher's Journal,* Korea, 1982).

ISAAC, CALVIN JAMES (Choctaw) 1933-
(education)

Born December 5, 1933, Philadelphia, Miss. *Education:* Delta State University, B.A. (Music Education), 1954. *Principal occupation: Education. Home address:* Route 7, Box 21, Philadelphia, Miss. 39350. *Affiliations:* Education specialist, Title I, B.I.A., Philadelphia, Miss, 1972-1975; former tribal chief, Mississippi Band of Choctaw Indians, Philadelphia, Miss., 1975-1980. *Other professional posts:* Director, Choctaw Head Start Program, Service Unit director; teacher supervisor (elementary), B.I.A.; education specialist (fine arts). *Military ser-*

vice: U.S. Dept. of Defense, Army. *Community activities:* Choctaw Housing Authority (chairman); Choctaw Advisory School Board (chairman); Policy Advisory Council (tribal representative). *Memberships:* Mississippi State Advisory Committee, 1975-; United Southeastern Tribes, Inc., 1975-; National Tribal Chairman's Association, 1975-; Governor's Colonel Staff, 1976-; Goveror's Multicultural Advisory Council, 1976-. *Awards, honors:* John Hay Whitney Fellowship Scholar, 1967-1968; Phi Delta Kappa, Mississippi State University, 1976; Omicron Delta Kappa, Delta State University, 1975.

**ISAACS, IDA LUJAN (Taos-
San Juan Pueblo)
(owner/manager-Indian
House Recordings)**

Born Taos Pueblo, N.M. *Principal occupation:* Owner/manager, Indian House Recordings, P.O. Box 472, Taos, N.M. 87571. *Other professional post:* Guest assistant curator, Whitney Museum of American Art, "Two Hundred Years of American Indian Art" show. *Community activities:* Headstart Parents Group; Taos Pueblo School Board; B.I.A. Credit Committee. *Awards, honors:* Minority Business Award, Small Business Administration, 1976; announcer, Indian program, KXRT-FM, Taos.

J

**JABBOUR, ALAN ALBERT 1942-
(archivist)**

Born June 21, 1942, Jacksonville, Fla. *Education:* Univerity of Miami, B.A. (magna cum laude), 1963; Duke University, M.A., 1966, Ph.D., 1968. *Principal occupation:* Archivist. *Home address:* 3107 Cathedral Ave., N.W., Washington, D.C. 20008. *Affiliations:* Head, Archive of Folk Song, Library of Congress, 1969-1974; head, Folk Arts Program, national Endowment for the Arts, Washington, D.C., 1974-1976; director, The American Folklife Center, Library of Congress, Washington, D.C., 1976- (the Center engages in the preservation, presentation, and dissemination of American folk cultural traditions, and contributes to the cultural planning and prgramming of the Library, federal government and the nation). *Memberships:* American Folklore Society; Society for Ethnomusicology; Modern Language Association; California Folklore Society; John Edwards Memorial Foundation (advisor); American Folklife Center (member, board of trustees). *Awards, honors:* Phi Beta Kappa; University of Miami Music Scholarship, 1959-1962; Woodrow Wilson Fellowship, 1963; Duke Univerity Scholarship, 1964-1966; Dabforth Teaching Fellowship, 1966-1968; responsible for the initiation of one of the Library's American Revolution Bicentennial projects, an anthology of 15 long-playing records containing examples of major folk music traditions of the U.S. -- Anglo-American, Afro-American, American Indian, and other rural and urban ethnic groups. The series is called, *Folk Music in America. Interests:* Folk music and song; folklore; medieval English literature; musicology; American studies. *Published works:* Numerous papers presented and published.

**JACKSON, CHARLES (Cow Creek
Band Umpqua)
(tribal chairman)**

Affiliation: Chairman, Cow Creek Band of Upqua Indians, 283 S.E. Fowley, Rosebug, Ore. 97470.

**JACKSON, DEAN
(college president)**

Affiliation: President, Navajo Community College, Tsaile Rural Post Office, Tsaile, Ariz. 86556.

**JACKSON, WALTER (Quileute)
(tribal chairman)**

Affiliation: Chairman, Quileute Tribal Council, P.O. Box 279, La Push, Wash. 98350.

JACKSON, WILLIAM
"RATTLESNAKE"(Cherokee) 1928-
(civil service; principal chief-
Southeastern Cherokee Confederacy)

Born December 23, 1928, Norman Park, Colquitt County, Ga. *Principal occupation:* Civil service; principal chief, Southeastern Cherokee Confederacy. *Home address:* Route 1, Box 111, Leesburg, Ga. 31763. *Affiliations:* Civil service, Albany, Ga., 1964-; principal chief, Southeastern Cherokee Confederacy, Leesburg, Ga., 1978-. *Military service:* U.S. Army (Korean War Medal). *Memberships:* American Legion; VFW. *Awards, honors:* Letter of Appreciation, 20-Year Service Awards with Civil Service; safety awards. "I have received a Proclamation in person from ex-Governor, George Busbee." *Interests:* "I visit different clans and band meetings; attend chiefs of council meetings, annual meetings, and pow wows. I have posed for an artist to paint my portrait for Albany Junior College. I am also the publisher of newsletter for the Southeastern Cherokee Confederacy. We have members all over the United State, and I'm recognized as pricnipal chief of this tribe. We are a nation within a nation."

JACKSON, ZANE, Sr. (Cayuga)
(tribal chairman)

Affiliation: Chairman, Warm Springs Tribal Council, Warm Springs, Ore. 97761.

JACOBS, ALEX A. *(Karoniaktatie)*
(Mohawk) 1953-
(writer, artist, editor)

Born February 28, 1953, Akwesasne Reservation, via Rooseveltown, N.Y. *Education:* Institute of American Indian Arts, Santa Fe, N.M., AFA (sculpture, creative writing), 1977; Kansas City Art Institute, BFA (sculpture, creative writing), 1979. *Home address:* P.O. Box 223, Hogansburg, N.Y. 13655. *Affiliations:* Editor, *Akewesasne Notes,* via Rooseveltown, N.Y., 1979-1985; editor, *Akwekon Literary Journal, Akwesasne Notes, Hogansburg, N.Y., 1985. Other professional posts:* Board of directors, CKON-F, Radio Station, Mohawk Nation. *Awards, honors:* 1975 poetry award, Scottsdale

National Indian Art Exhibit; 1979 honorable mention, Society of Western Art, Kansas City, Mo. *Interests:* "Poetry, prose, short stories; graphic arts; sculpture; painting, printmaking; ceramics; video/audio/performance art; editor of Native American literature and journalism; networking national and international native peoples; poetry readings and workshops; travel U.S.A. with White Roots of Peace, 1973-1974 (native touring group/communications). *Published works:* "Native Colours" (*Akwesasne Notes,* 1974); "Landscape: Old & New Poems" (*Blue Cloud Quarterly,* 1984); Anthologies: "Come to Power," "The Remembered Earth," "The Next World, 3rd World Writers, and "Songs From the Earth on Turtle's Back," in various literary magazines, 1972-1985; editor, *Akwekon Literary Journal,* 1985-.

JACOBS, HARVEY
(Indian education)

Affiliation: Indian education, Bureau of Indian Affairs, 1951 Constitution Ave., N.W., Washington, D.C. 20245.

JACOBS, WILBUR R.
(professor of history)

Born in Chicago, Ill. *Education:* University of California, Los Angeles, Ph.D. *Principal occupation:* Professor of history, University of California, Santa Barbara, Calif. *Home address:* 199 Edgemound Dr., Santa Barbara, Calif. 93105. *Military service:* U.S. Air Force (World War II). *Memberships:* American Historical Association (former president, Pacific Coast Branch); American Society for Ethnohistory (former president); American Society for Environmental History (former president); Organization of American Historians. *Awards, honors:* Staford Prize for book, *Wilderness Politics and Indian Gifts,* American Historical Association University Press, Pacific Coast Branch. "Began the first class in American Indian history taught in any branch of the University of California. Class is still offered and graduates from it have gone on to teach Indian history at a number of leading universities and colleges in America." *Interests:* "American Indian environmental studies;

the achievements of American Indian women; the role and place of the Indian in American frontier history and in early American history. (I am) contributor to many historical journals, encyclopedias and to the *Handbook of the American Indians."* *Biographical sources: Encyclopedia of the American West,* edited by Howard Lamar; *Who's Who in America; Who's Who on the Pacific Coast; Who's Who in the World. Published works: The Southern Colonial Indian Frontier* (University of Nebraska Press, 1967); *Wilderness Politics and Indian Gifts* (University of Nebraska Press, 1972); *Dispossessing the American Indians,* Second Edition (University of Oklahoma Press, 1985).

JAEGAR, RONALD
(B.I.A. agency superintendent)

Affiliation: Superintendent, Central California Agency, Bureau of Indian Affairs, 1800 Tribute Rd., P.O. Box 15740, Sacramento, Calif. 95813-0740.

JACOBSEN, WILLIAM H., Jr. 1931-
(professor of English)

Born November 15, 1931, San Diego, Calif. *Education:* Harvard University, A.B., 1953; University of California, Berkeley, Ph.D., 1964. *Principal occupation:* Professor of English, University of Nevada, 1967-. *Home address:* 1411 Samuel Way, Reno, Nev. 89509. *Memberships:* Linguistic Society of America; International Linguistic Association; Society for the Study of the Indigenous Languages of the Americas; American Anthropological Association; Society for Linguistic Anthropology; Great Basin Anthropological Conference. *Awards, honors:* Outstanding Researcher Award, University of Nevada, Reno, 1983. *Interests:* "American Indian languages, primarily Washo and Makah, and the Hokan and Wakashan families; also, fieldwork or publication on Salinan, Yana, Nootka, Nez Perce, Numic, and Chimakuan. *Published work: First Lessons in Makah* (Makah Cultural and Research Center, 1979).

JAEGER, ROBERT
(B.I.A. area director)

Affiliation: Director, Minnesota Sioux Area Field Office, 1330 Sioux Trail, N.W., Prior Lake, Minn. 55372.

JAENEN, CORNELIUS J. 1927-
(professor of history)

Born February 2, 1927, Cannington Manor, Saskatchewan, Canada. *Education:* University of Manitoba, Winnipeg, M.A., 1950; Univerity of Ottawa, Ontario, Ph.D., 1963. *Principal occupation:* Professor of history, University of Ottawa. *Memberships:* American Society for Ethnohistory; Canadian Historical Association; French Colonial Historical Society (vice president); Canadian Ethnic Studies Association (vice president). *Awards, honors:* Ste. Marie Prize, 1973, for *Friend and Foe. Published works: Friend and Foe: Aspects of French-Amerindian Cultural Contact in the Sixteenth and Seventeenth Centuries* (Columbia University, 1976); *The Role of the Church in New France* (McGraw-Hill - Ryerson, Ltd., 1976); *The French Relationship With the Native Peoples of New France* (Indian and Northern Affairs, Canada, 1984); *Identites, Selected Problems and Interpretations in Canadian History* (Prentice-Hall, Canada, 1986); booklets, and numerous chapters of books on the American Indian.

JAFFE, A.J. 1912-
(statistician)

Born in 1912, Mass. *Education:* University of Chicago, Ph.D., 1941. *Principal occupation:* Statistician. *Home address:* 314 Allaire Ave., Leonia, N.J. 07605. *Affiliations:* Special research scholar, Department of Anthropology, Columbia University, New York, N.Y. *Other professional posts:* Research associate, Museum of the American Indian, New York, N.Y. *Memberships:* American Statistical Association; Population Association of America; American Association for the Advancement of Science; International Population Union. *Interests:* "Changing demography of the Native Americans." *Published works: Peo-*

ple, Jobs, and Economic Development (Free Press, 1959); *Changing Demography of Spanish Americans* (Academic Press, 1980); *Misuse of Statistics* (Marcel Dekker, Inc., 1986).

JAMES, OVERTON (Chickasaw) 1925-
(educator)

Born July 21, 1925, Bromide, Okla. *Education:* Southeastern State College, B.A., 1949, M.A., 1955. *Principal occupation:* Educator. *Home address:* 6033 Glencove Pl., Oklahoma City, Okla. 73132. *Affiliations:* Teacher and athletic coach, public schools of Ravia, Caddo and Shattuck, Okla.; sales manager, *Compton's Pictured Encyclopedia,* 1960-1965; governor, Chickasaw Nation of Oklahoma, 1963-; field representative, assistant director, State Department of Education Division, Oklahoma City, Okla., 1965-. *Military service:* U.S. Navy, 1943-1946. *Community activities:* Choctaw-Chickasaw Confederation (president); Women's Gridiron Club of Oklahoma (board of directors); Oklahoma State Indian Affairs (past chairman); Inter-Tribal Council of Five Civilized Tribes (past president); Five Civilized Tribes Museum (board of directors); Masons; VFW; American Legion. *Memberships:* National Education Association; Oklahoma Education Association; National Congress of American Indians. *Awards, honors;* In October, 1963, Mr. James became the 27th governor of the Chickasaw Nation, and the youngest ever to serve as governor. *Interests:* Sports, hunting and fishing.

JAMES, WABUN 1945-
(writer, lecturer, teacher)

Born April 5, 1945, Newark, N.J. *Education:* George Washington University, B.A., 1967; Columbia University, M.A. (Journalism), 1968. *Principal occupation:* Writer, lecturer, teacher. *Home address:* P.O. Box 9167, Spokane, Wash. 99209. *Affiliation:* Executive director, The Bear Tribe Medicine Society, Spokane, Wash., 1972-. *Published works: The People's Lawyers* (Holt, Rinehart & Winston, 1973); *The Bear Tribe's Self-Reliance Book* (Bear Tribe Publishing, 1977); *The Medicine Wheel Book* (Prentice-Hall, 1980); *Sun Bear: The Path to Power* (Bear Tribe Publishing, 1983).

JAMES, WALTER S., Jr.
(executive director-Indian organization)

Affiliation: Executive director, Council for Native American Indian Progress, 280 Broadway, Suite 316, New York, N.Y. 10007.

JAMES, WILLIE
(B.I.A. agency superintendent)

Affiliation: Superintendent, Chilocco Maintenance and Security Detachment, Bureau of Indian Affairs, P.O. Box 465, Newkirk, Okla. 74647.

JILEK, WOLFGANG GEORGE, M.D. 1930-
(psychiatrist, anthropologist)

Born November 25, 1930, Tetschen, Bohemia. *Education:* Medical schools of the universities of Munich, W. Germany, Innsbruck, Austria, and Vienna, Austria, M.D., 1956; McGill University, Montreal, Quebec, Canada, M.Sc., 1966; University of British Columbia, Vancouver, Canada, M.A. (Anthropology), 1972. *Principal occupation:* Clinical professor of psychiatry. *Home address:* 571 English Bluff Rd., Delta, British Columbia, Canada V4M 2M9. *Affiliations:* Department of Anthropology & Sociology, 1974-; clinical professor of psychiatry, Department of Psychiatry, 1980-, University of British Columbia, Vancouver, Canada. *Other professional posts:* Consultant psychiatrist, Greater Vancouver Mental Health Service; consultant in mental health, World Health Organization, 1984-1985. *Community activities;* American Psychiatric Association (member, Task Force on American Indians, 1971-1977). *Memberships:* Canadian Psychiatric Association (organizer and chairman of the Task Force, later Section, on Native People's Mental Health, 1970-1980); World Psychiatric Association (secretary, Transcultural Psychiatry section, 1983-); Canadian Medical Association; Fellow, Royal College of Physicians and Surgeons of Canada; editorial advisor, *Transcultural Psychiatric Research Review,* Montreal, Canada; editorial advisor, *Curare-Journal of Ethnomedicine and Transcultural Psychiatry,* Heidelberg, W. Germany. *Interests:* "Transcultural psychiatry; traditional medicine and ceremonialism, especially of aboriginal North and South American peoples; ethnomedical and ethnopsychiatric research among aboriginal people of Canada, U.S. (especially Northwest Pacific culture area), and South America; Haiti; East Africa; Southeast Asia; Papua, New Guinea, 1963-)." *Published works:* Salish Indian Mental Health and Culture Change (Holt, Rinehart & Winston, Toronto, 1974); *Indian Healing-Shamanic Ceremonialism in the Pacific Northwest Today* (Hancock House, 1982); *Traditional Medicine and Primary Health Care in Papua, New Guinea* (WHO & Papua, New Guinea University Press, 1985); numerous articles which deal with North American Indians.

JILEK-AALL, LOUISE M., M.D.
1931-
(psychiatrist, anthropologist)

Born April 25, 1931, Oslo, Norway. *Education:* University of Oslo, Norway, 1949-1950; University of Tuebingen, W. Germany, 1951-1955; University of Zurich, Switzerland, M.D., 1958, Dipl. of Trop. Med., 1959; University of Basal, Switzerland, 1959; McGill University, Montreal, Canada, Dipl. of Psychiatry, 1965; University of British Columbia, Vancouver, Canada, M.A. (Social Anthropology), 1972. *Principal occupation:* Psychiatrist, anthropologist. *Home address:* 571 English Bluff Rd., Delta, British Columbia, Can. V4M 2M9. *Affiliations:* Clinical professor of psychiatry, University of British Columbia, Vancouver, B.C., Canada (member, faculty of medicine, 1975-). *Other professional posts:* Consultant psychiatrist, Greater Vancouver Mental Health Service; consultant psychiatrist, Shaughnessy Hospital, Vancouver, B.C. *Military service:* Medical officer, U.N. Congo Mission, 1960-1961 (Citation and Congo Medal of the League of Red Cross Societies, 1961). *Memberships:* Canadian Psychiatric Association (vice chairperson, Section on Native Mental Health); Canadian Psychiatric Association (member, Task Force/Section on Native Mental Health, 1970-); Royal College of Physicians and Surgeons of Canada, 1966-(Fellow); World Psychiatric Association, 1974- (member, Transcultural Section). *Interests:* "Transcultural psychiatry; ethnomedicine; Canadian, American and Alaskan Native mental health; Native therapeutic resources; alcohol abuse prevention and rehabilitation. Fieldwork and research in transcultural psychiatry and ethnomedicine in North and South America, the Caribbean, Asia, Africa, Oceania; neurological research in epilepsy." *Published works:* Articles in various scientific and professional journals.

JIM, ROGER R., Sr. (Yakima)
(tribal chairman)

Affiliation: Chairman, Yakima Tribal Council, P.O. Box 151, Toppenish, Wash, 98948.

JIMMIE, LUKE, (Mississippi
Choctaw)
(chairman-tribal education)

Affiliation: Chairman, Education Committee, Mississippi Band of Choctaw Indians, Route 7, Box 21, Philadelphia, Miss. 39350.

JOHANNSEN, CHRISTINA BARBARA
1950-
(museum director)

Born October 29, 1950, Rahway, N.J. *Education:* Beloit College, Wis., B.A., 1972; Brown University, Ph.D., 1984. *Principal occupation:* Museum director. *Home address:* Star Route 1, Box 144, Warnerville, N.Y. 12187. *Affiliation: Director, Schoharie Museum of the Iroquois Indian, Box 158, Schoharie, N.Y. 12157, 1980-. Other professional post:* Trustee, Mohawk Caughnawaga Museum. *Community activities:* Schoharie County Tourism Development Corp. (secretary, board of directors). *Memberships:* American Association of Museums; Mid-Atlantic Association of Museums. *Interests:* "Research and promotion of contemporary Iroquois art. Actively involved in educating the public about the contributions of Iroquois peoples today and to an understanding of their past. Concern in maintaining professional museological standards in small museums and delineating a museum's purposes and goals. Continued field research in Iroquois communities throughout the U.S. and Canada. Special interest in creatively photographing museum objects." *Published works:* "European Trade Goods and Wampanoag Culture in the Seventeenth Century" in *Burr's Hill: A 17th Century Wampanoag Burial Ground in Warren, Rhode Island* (Haffenreffer Museum of Anthropology, Brown University, 1980); *Iroquois Arts: A Directory of a People and Their Work,* co-edited with Dr. John P. Ferguson (Association for the Advancement of Native North American Arts and Crafts, 1984); *Efflorescence and Identity in Iroquois Art,* Ph.D. Dissertation, Brown Univerity, 1984.

JOHN, ANGELO MARVIN (Navajo)
1946-
   (artist)

Born February 5, 1946, Holbrook, Ariz. *Education:* Institute of American Indian Arts, 1962-1965; Arizona State University. *Principal occupation:* Artist. *Home address:* 29 Clark Homes, Flagstaff, Ariz. 86001. *Community activities:* Navajo Youth Conference (president, 1965); Institute of American Indian Arts (student body president, 1965). *Awards, honors:* Awards received from Institute of American Indian Arts, Scottsdale Exhibition, Philbrook Art Center. *Interests:* Mr. John writes, "I am interested in track; Indian art; reading (recent history)."

JOHN, CALVIN (Seneca) 1920-
   (project director)

Born June 15, 1920, Coldspring, N.Y. *Principal occupation:* Project director, Iroquoia, a cultural/recreational/tourism project of the Seneca Nation. *Home address:* P.O. Box 343, Salamanca, N.Y. 14779. *Military service:* U.S. Army, 1942-1945 (Staff Sergeant, 31st Infantry Division). *Community activities:* Kiwanis Club; Congregational Reservation Temperance group; Cattaraugus County Planning Board; Jimersontown Presbyterian Church.

JOHNNY, RONALD EAGLEYE
   (president-Indian organization)

Affiliation: President, American Indian Law Students, American Indian Law Center, University of New Mexico School of Law, 1117 Stanford N.E., Albuquerque, N.M. 87196.

JOHNS, GLENN DAVID (Skokomish)
1947-
   (artist)

Born December 15, 1947, Shelton, Wash. *Education:* Stewart Indian School; Institute of American Indian Arts. *Awards, honors:* Second Place, 1965 Scottsdale National Indian Arts Exhibition. *Exhibits:* Second Annual Exhibition of American Indian Painting (U.S. Dept. of the Interior Art Gallery); Young American Indian Artist (Riverside Museum).

JOHNS, JOSEPH F. *(Cayoni)*
(Creek) 1928-
   (museum manager, artist)

Born January 31, 1928, Okefenokee Swamp, Ga. *Education:* High school (U.S. Armed Forces Institute). *Principal occupation:* Museum manager, artist. *Home address:* 7 Russell St., West Peabody, Mass. 01960. *Affiliation:* Building manager, Peabody Museum, Harvard University, Cambridge, Mass., 1974-. "I am also Indian artist in residence at the Peabody Museum (sculpture and carving in any medium). I maintain a small studio, at my home, for carving the eight traditional masks of the Creek people." *Military service:* U.S. Naval Amphibious Forces (Sniper), 1944-1946 (U.S. Navy P.O. 3; Asiatic Pacific Medal, Silver Star Medal); U.S. Coast Guard (reitired), 1947-1965 (U.S.C.G. P.O. 1; Silver Life Saving Medal presented by President Harry S. Truman in Washington, D.C., 1947). *Community activities:* Masonic Shriner at Aleppo Temple, Wilmington, Mass. *Membership:* Boston Indian Council. *Awards, honors:* "I was a crew member of the Coast Guard Cutter Westwind Expedition to the North Pole (Dew Line), 1953-1954; and a cre member of the Coast Guard's Cutter, Eastwind expedition to the South Pole (Operation Deep Freeze, 1961-1962); (I am) holder of Antarctica Service Medal. A book about my life is now being written by Mitchell Wade."

JOHNSON, PATRICIA LUCILLE PADDLETY (Kiowa) 1938-
(attorney)

Born October 22, 1938, Mountain View, Okla. *Education:* Oklahoma College of Liberal Arts, Chickasaw, B.S. (Economics), 1971; University of Oklahoma, Norman, J.D., 1975. *Principal occupation:* Attorney. *Home address:* Route 3, Anadarko, Okla. 73005. *Affiliation:* Associate Magistrate, Bureau of Indian Affairs, Code of Indian Offenses, Court, Anadarko, Okla. *Community activities:* Indian Capital Baptist Church (member and teacher); Oklahoma Indian Rights Association; Oklahoma Indian Women Association. *Memberships:* Oklahoma Bar Association, 1975- (Minorities Law Committee, 1976); Federal Bar for the Western District of Oklahoma, 1975-. *Interests:* "I am interested in assisting young Indian people to achieve their life's goals, whether in Law or in any other field of training. I work extensively with our church in attempting to inspire and inform Indians in this area of the opportunities available to them. Alcoholism and drug related offenders make up the majority of my clients, and when I have the time, I counsel and encourage them."

JOHNSON, ROBERT
(executive director-Indian association)

Affiliation: Executive director, American Indian Development Association, 1015 Indian School Rd. N.W., Albuquerque, N.M. 87102.

JOHNSON, ROY S. *(Crazy Horse)* (Rappahannock) 1928-
(research writer, lecturer, educator)

Born December 7, 1928, Caroline County, Va. *Education:* Temple University, 1947-1949; University of Pennsylvania, B.A., 1951; College of Metaphysics, Ps.D., 1972. *Principal occupation:* Research writer, lecturer on Indian affairs, educator. *Military service:* U.S. Army, 1943-1946 (1st Lieutenant; six major campaigns—Pacific Theatre

Medal, Silver Star, Bronze Star, Purple Heart, Presidential Unit Citation, Good Conduct Medal). *Community activities:* Coalition of Native Americans. *Memberships:* Rappahannock Tribe, State of Virginia (field chief); Powhatan Indians of Delaware Valley (chairman). *Interests:* Mr. Johnson teaches basic adult education to Native Americans; teaches self-defense and the Powhatan language. *Published work:* East Coast Indian Tribes, with Jack D. Forbes.

JOHNSON, SAM 1938-
(president-Indian village)

Born August 14, 1938, Ashdown, Ark. *Education:* University of Arkansas, Fayetteville, B.A. *Principal occupation:* President, Kado-ha Indian Village, Murfressboro, Ark., 1978-. *Military service:* U.S. Army (four years).

JOHNSON, SAMUEL
(B.I.A. Indian education)

Affiliation: Indian education, Bureau of Indian Affairs, 1951 Constitution Ave., N.W., Washington, D.C. 20245.

JOHNSTON, BASIL H. (Ojibway) 1929-
(teacher)

Born July 13, 1929, Parry Island Reserve, Ontario, Can. *Education:* Loyola College, Montreal (graduate cum laude, 1954); Ontario College of Education, Secondary School Teaching Certificate, 1962. *Principal occupation:* Teacher. *Home address:* 253 Ashlar Rd., Richmond Hill, Ontario, Can. L4C 2W7. *Affiliations:* Assistant manager, 1957-1959, manager, 1959-1961, Toronto Board of Trade; teacher, Earl Haig Secondary School, 1962-1969; lecturer, Royal Ontario Museum, Toronto, 1969-1972; teacher, private English teacher of Ojibway Indians, Toronto, 1974-. *Community activities:* Toronto Indian Club; Canadian Indian Centre of Toronto (executive and vice president, 1963-1969); Indian Eskimo Association (executive, legal committee, speakers committee, 1965-1968); Union of Ontario Indians; Feeral Indian Consultations,

Toronto; Indian Hall of Fame (committee member, 1968-1970); Wigwamen Inc., 1974-1975; Ontario Geographic Names Board, 1977-. *Awards, honors:* 1976 Fels Award for *Many Smokes,* Klamath Falls, Oreg. *Published works:* Numerous stories, essays, articles and poems in various publications.

JOHNSTON, ROBERT (Comanche)
1953-
(lawyer)

Born January 28, 1953, Little Rock, Ark. *Education:* Wichita State University, B.A., 1975; University of Oklahoma, College of Law, J.D., 1978. *Principal occupation:* Lawyer. *Home address:* 1330 Dorchester Dr., Norman, Okla. 73069. *Interests:* Indian law; oil and gas law; natural resources law. *Published work:* "Whitehorn v. State: Peyote and Religious Freedom in Oklahoma" *(American Indian Law Review,* Vol. V, No. 1, winter, 1977).

JOJOLA, TED (Isleta Pueblo)
1951-
(educator, administrator)

Born November 19, 1951, Isleta Pueblo, N.M. *Education:* University of New Mexico, B.A. (Archaeology); Massachusetts Institute of Technology, M.A. (City Planning); University of Hawaii-Manoa, Ph.D. (Political Science), 1982; University of Strasbourg, France, Certificate of International Human Rights Law, 1985. *Principal occupation:* Educator, administrator. *Home address:* Route 6, Box 578, Albuquerque, N.M. 87105. *Affiliations:* Internal planner, National Capital Planning Commission, Washington, D.C., 1973; legal/historical researcher, Institute for the Development of Indian Law, Washington, D.C., 1976; visiting research associate, Institute of Philippine Culture, Manila, 1977-1978; visiting professor of urban planning, UCLA, 1984; assistant professor of planning, University of New Mexico, Albuquerque, 1982-; director, Native American Studies Department, University of New Mexico, 1980-. *Other professional posts:* Consultant, Thurshun Consultants, Albuquerque, N.M., 1980-; coordinator, Ethnic/Minority Directors' Coalition, 1983-. *Community activities:* 9th

Inter-American Indian Congress, Santa Fe, N.M. (U.S. organizing committee, 1985-); Zuni Tribal Museum, Zuni, N.M. (advisory board, 1985-); JOM/Indian Education Parent's Committee, Isleta Pueblo, N.M. (chair). *Memberships:* Native American Studies Association. *Awards, honors:* Postdoctoral Fellow, American Indian Studies, UCLA, 1984; public grantee, Atherton Trust, Honolulu, 1976; recipient of Participant Award, East-West Center, Honolulu. *Interests:* "My main interest lay in the notion of continued tribal "survival," and the various and varying strategies that have ensued in the course of this struggle. Currently, I have been doing research in the notion of tribal (traditional) consensus making and its theoretical modeling toward the idea of using this mechanism for the integration of tribal policy in the regional development process." *Biographical source: Who's Who in the West. Published works: Memoirs of an American Indian House,* 1976; contributing articles to various publications.

JONES, BUDDY CALVIN
(Creek-Cherokee)

Born in Gladewater, Tex. *Education:* University of Oklahoma, M.A., 1968. *Principal occupation:* Archaeologist. *Home address:* Route 3, Box RPGA, Crawfordville, Fla. 32327. *Affiliations:* Curator, Caddo Indian Museum, Longview, Texas (27 years); archaeologist, Bureau of Arcaheological Research, Division of Archives, History and Records Management, Florida Department of State, R.A. Gray Bldg., Tallahasssee, Fla. (18 years). *Military service:* U.S. Army, 1963. *Memberships:* Society of American Archaeology; Southeastern Archaeological Society. *Awards, honors:* Ripley R. Bullon Award, 1983, for lifetime service award, presented by the Florida Anthropological Society. *Biographical sources: Who's Who in the South and Southeast; Men of Achievement,* Cambridge, England, 1976; "Interview with B. Calvin Jones" *(Florida Anthropologist,* 1982-1983 (two part interview). *Published work:* Article: "Southeastern Ceremonial Complex Manifestations at Mound 3, Lake Jackson Site, Leon County, Florida" *(Mid-Continental Journal of Archaeology,* Kent State University); among others.

JONES, DAVID S. (Choctaw) 1928-
(elementary school principal)

Born July 24, 1928, Boswell, Okla. *Education:* Eastern A & M College, Wilburton, Okla., 1950-1951; East Central State College, Ada, Okla., 1951-1952; Central State University, Edmonds, Okla., 1955-1963, B.A., M.A. *Principal occupation:* Elementary school principal. *Home address:* P.O. Box 1223, Navajo, N.M. 87328. *Affiliations:* Principal, Crystal Boarding School, Navajo, N.M., 1983-. *Other professional post:* Council for Exceptional Children, Navajo Area (vice president). *Military service:* U.S. Navy, 1945-1947; U.S. Naval Reserve (18 years); U.S. Army Reserve (Staff Sergeant, 12 years); (Meritorious Service Medal, World War II Victory Medal, Asiatic Pacific Medal, Armed Forces Reserve Medal, Marksman. *Community activities:* El Reno Lions Club, Okla. (past president); Methodist Church (chairman, official board); Methodist Mens Club; Church School (superintendent). *Memberships:* National Indian Education Association (life member); Elementary School Principals Association; Oklahoma Governor's Council for Vocational Education; National Indian Scouting Association. *Awards, honors:* Masonic Teacher of Today Award; American Legions Award for Achievement; Gray-Wolf Award for Outstanding Indian Scouter, Boy Scouts of America. *Interests:* Travels with Naval and Army Reserve trainings. *Published work:* Co-author, *A Guide for Teachers of Indian Students* (Oklahoma Department of Education, 1972).

JONES, JOAN MEGAN 1933-
(socio-cultural anthropologist)

Born September 7, 1933, Laramie, Wyo. *Education:* University of Washington, Seattle, B.A., 1956, M.A., 1968, Ph.D., 1976. *Principal occupation:* Socio-cultural anthropologist. *Home address:* 392 Yokeko Dr., Anacortes, Wash. 98221. *Affiliations:* Educator, Burke Museum, Seattle, 1969-1972; visiting lecturer, Primitive Art, University of British Columbia, 1978; visiting instructor, course: "Indians of the Northwest Coast," Anthropology Department, Western Washington University, Bellingham (Summer), 1981; research associate, Department of Anthropolgy, University of Washington, Seattle, 1982-. *Community activities:* Anacortes Arts and Crafts Festival Foundation, (board member, 1981-1983); Anacortes Branch, American Association of University Women (board member, 1982-1984); Skagit Valley Weavers Guild, (board member, 1985-1986). *Memberships:* American Anthropological Association (member, 1968-; Fellow, 1976-); Society for Applied Anthropology (Fellow, 1983-); American Association of Museums, 1969-; National Association for the Practice of Anthropology (charter member); Association for Women in Science, 1983-. *Awards, honors:* Wenner-Gren Foundation for Anthropological Research, Museum Research Fellow, 1967-1968; Ford Foundation, Dissertation Fellowship in Ethnic Studies, 1972-1973. *Interests:* "Professional specialization in Native American art and material culture studies and research with museum collections. Field work: Native basketmakers in southern British Columbia, for National Museum of Man, National Museums of Canada, Urgent Ethnology Research Contract, 1973-1974; anthropologist for basketry research, Quinault Indian Nation, 1976-1977; consultant, fiber arts, Samish Indian Tribe, 1985-. As a handweaver, handspinner, and knitter, I am active in local spinners and weavers groups. Travel." *Published works: Northwest Basketry and Culture Change* (Burke Museum, 1968); *Native Basketry of Western North America* (Illinois State Museum, 1978); *The Art and Style of Western Indian Basketry* (Hancock House, 1982); *Northwest Coast Indian Basketry Styles* (University of Washington Press and Burke Museum) (in press).

JONES, LEO (Pit River)
(tribal chairman)

Affiliation: Chairman, Pit River Tribal Council, P.O. Box 763, Alturas, Calif. 96101.

JONES, STANLEY, Sr. (Tulalip)
(tribal chairman)

Affiliation: Chairman, The Tulalip Board of Directors, 6700 Totem Beach Rd., Marysville, Wash. 98270.

JONES, STEPHEN S. *(Red Dawn)*
(Santee Sioux) 1921-
(lecturer, educator, folklorist, anthropologist)

Born June 1, 1921, Flandreau, S.D. *Education:* Sioux Falls College, S.D., B.A., 1948; California State University, Fullerton, M.A., 1978. *Principal occupation:* Lecturer, educator, folklorist, anthropologist, American Indian Programs, Anaheim, Calif. *Home address:* P.O. Box 9698, Anaheim, Calif. 92802. *Affiliations:* Curator of anthropology, Science Museum of Natural History, Gastonia, N.C. (six years); American Indian programs, Anaheim, Calif. *Other professional post:* Registered medical technologist. *Military service:* U.S. Army, 1942-1945 (Staff Sergeant). *Memberships:* American Indian Lore Association (director); Continental Confederation of Adopted Indians (director); American Anthropological Association; Southwest Museum; Minnesota Historical Society. *Awards, honors:* 1973 Catlin Peace Pipe Award, American Indian Lore Association. *Interests:* "Field of American Indian dance, ethnology, history and folklore. Lifelong avocation in interpreting Indian lifeways (traveling extensively throughout the nation presenting Indian programs for schools and civil groups). Tour master for college groups into the Southwest; major field of interest—customs and traditions of Southwest Indians. Traveled nationally lecturing and researching, 1976-." *Published work:* Editor, *Great on the Mountain: The Spiritual Life of Crazy Horse* (Naturegraph, 1971); editor, *Master Key* (Southwest Museum, 1972-1982).

JONES, VELMA
(tribal chairwoman)

Affiliation: Chairwoman, Big Pine General Council, P.O. Box 384, Big Pine, Calif. 93513.

JONES, WILLIAM M.
(director-Indian center)

Affiliation: Director, Mid-American All-Indian Center, 650 N. Seneca, Wichita, Kan. 67203.

JORDAN, JANET ETHRIDGE 1947-
(professor of anthropology)

Born February 2, 1947, Denver, Colo. *Education:* Colorado College, 1965-1967; Columbia University, B.A. (magna cum laude), 1969; Yale University, 1969-1971; University of Connecticut, Ph.D., 1974. *Principal occupation:* Professor of anthropology. *Affiliation:* Colorado State University, Fort Collins, Colo., 1974-? *Memberships:* American Anthropological Association; American Society for Ethnohistory; Association for Political and Legal Anthropology (vice president, 1977-1978; chairperson, 1976-1977; editor of newsletter, 1976-. *Awards, honors:* Phi Beta Kappa, Columbia University; Phi Kappa Phi, University of Connecticut. *Interests:* Fieldwork on politics and law of Miccosukees, 1975-1976; "Politics and Religion in a Western Cherokee Community: A Century of Struggle in a White Man's World," unpublished Ph.D. dissertation. *Published works:* "Social Aspects of Illness in a Western Cherokee," paper at Southern Anthropological Society Meetings, April, 1974, Blacksburg, Va.; "Self-Determination Implications of Federal and Local Networks," paper at American Anthropological Association meetings, December, 1977.

JORDAN, SUE ZANN (Mescalero Apache) 1959-
(teacher)

Born December 17, 1959. *Education:* University of Illinois, Urbana, B.A., 1979; Sangamon State University, M.A., 1983. *Principal occupation:* Teacher, Cibecue Community School, Cibecue, Ariz. 85911, 1984-. *Other professional post:* Part-time teacher, Northern Pioneer College. *Membership:* Arizona Media Association. *Awards, honors:* State of South Dakota Poetry Award and money certificate; Golden Poet Award, World of Poetry. *Interests:* General: Poetry, art, music, education, earth science, and literature. Vocational: Woodworking, graphic arts, ceramics, weaving, and horticulture. Travels: "(I) traveled extensively in North and South America and less extensively overseas." *Published works:* Poetry, too numerous to list.

JORGENSEN, JOSEPH GILBERT 1934-
(professor of anthropology)

Born April 15, 1934, Salt Lake City, Utah.
Education: University of Utah, Salt Lake
City, B.S., 1956; Indiana University, Bloomington, Ph.D., 1964. *Principal occupation:* Professor of anthropology. *Home
address:* 1517 Highland Dr., Newport
Beach, Calif. 92660. *Affiliations:* Assistant
professor, Antioch College, 1964-1965, Uni-
versity of Oregon, 1965-1968; professor of
anthropology, Univesity of Michigan, Ann
Arbor, 1968-1974, University of California,
Irvine, Calif., 1974-. *Other professional
post:* Coordinator, Northern Ute Tribe
(Unitah and Ouray Ute Indian Reservation,
Fort Duchesne, Utah), 1960, 1962; research
associate, John Muir Institute, 1970-. *Community activities:* Mariners Community
Association (president); Society to Preserve
Our Newport (board member); Newport
Bech Aquatics Support Group (president).
Memberships: Human Relations Area Files
(board of directors); Native Struggles Sup-
port Group (board of directors and co-
chair); Anthropology Resource Center
(board of directors); American Association
for the Advancement of Science (Fellow);
Sigma Xi. *Awards, honors:* John Simon
Guggenheim Fellow, 1974-1975; C. Wright
Mills Book Award for *Sun Dance Religion,*
1972; F.O. Butler Lecturer at South akota
State University, 1976; M. Crawford Lectures at the University of Kansas, 1980;
Rufus Wood Leigh Lecture at the University
of Utah, 1982. *Interests:* "Employed by
Northern Ute Tribe in several capacities,
1960-1962. Research among Northern Utes,
Southern Utes, Ute Mountain Utes, Fort
Hall Shoshone, Wind River Shoshone,
Crow, Soboba, and several Eskimo villages,
particularly Malakleet. Expert witness for
Indian and Eskimo plaintiffs in several fed-
eral cases." *Published works: Salish Lan-
guage and Culture* (Indiana University,
1969); *Sun Dance Religion* (University of
Chicago Press, 1972); *Native Americans and
Energy Development, I and II* (Anthropol-
ogy Resource Center, 1978, 1984); *Western
Indians* (W.H. Freeman, 1980); *Oil Age
Eskimos* (Human Relations Area Files
Press, 1987). Editorial board: *Behavioral
Science Research,* 1973-; *The Indian Histo-
rian,* 1974-; *Southwest Economy and*

Society, 1976-; *Social Science Journal,*
1978-; Environmental Ethics, 1978-; *Social
Policy Revue,* 1981-; contributing articles to
New York Review of Books, and to
professional journals

JOSEPHY, ALVIN M., Jr. 1915-
(author, historian)

Born May 18, 1915, Woodmere, N.Y. *Education:* Harvard College, 1932-1934. *Principal occupation:* Author, historian. *Home
address:* 4 Kinsman Lane, Greenwich,
Conn. 06830. *Affiliations:* Associate editor,
Time Magazine, 1951-1960; editor-in-chief,
American Heritage Publishing Co., Inc.,
New York, N.Y., 1960-1979. *Other professional posts:* Consultant, Secretary of the
Interior, 1963; commissioner and vice chair-
man, Indian Arts and Crafts Board, Dept. of
the Interior, Washington, D.C., 1966-1970;
president, National Council, Institute of the
American West, Sun Valley, Idaho, 1976-;
contributing editor, *American West* Maga-
zine, Tucson, Ariz., 1983-. *Military service:*
U.S. Marine Corps, 1943-1945 (Master
Technical Sergeant; Bronze Star). *Member-
ships:* Association on American Indian
Affairs (director, 1961-); Museum of the
American Indian (trustee, 1976-; president,
National Council, 1978-); Western History
Association; Society of American Histori-
ans; American Antiquarian Society.
Awards, honors: Western Heritage Award,
National Cowboy Hall of Fame, 1962, 1965;
Eagle Feather Award, National Congress of
American Indians, 1964; Award for Merit,
American Association on State and Local
History, 1965; Golden Spur, Golden Saddle-
man and Buffalo Awards, Western Writers
of America, 1965; National Book Award
nominee, 1968; Guggenheim Fellowship,
1966-1967. *Interests:* History, culture and
concerns of the American Indians; western
American history; conservation; extensive
western travel. *Biographical source: Who's
Who in America. Published works: American Heritage Book of the Pioneer Spirit,*
co-author (Simon & Schuster, 1959); *The
American Heritage Book of Indians* (Simon
& Schuster, 1961); *The Patriot Chiefs* (Viking Press, 1961); *The Nez Perce Indians and
the Opening of the Northwest* (Yale University Press, 1965); editor, *The American Her-*

itage History of the Great West (Simon & Schuster, 1965); The Indian Heritage of America (Knopf, 1968); Red Power (McGraw-Hill, 1971); Now That the Buffalo's Gone (Knopf, 1982); among others.

JOURDAIN, ROGER (Chippewa)
(tribal chairman)

Affiliation: Chairman, Red Lake Tribal Council, Red Lake, Minn. 56671.

JUANCITO, CHARLES H.
(Rappahannock)
(teacher)

Born in Philadelphia, Pa. Education: University of Pennyslvania, 1955-1958; Temple University, 1969-1972. Principal occupation: Teacher. Home address: 927 N. Sixth St., Philadelphia, Pa. 19123. Affiliations: Teacher, Chester-Upland School District, Chester, Pa.; director, Native American Cultural Center. Other professional posts: Engineering technician, draftsman. Memberships: National Education Association (secretary, First American Task Force); Pennsylvania Education Association; American Vocational Education Association; Pennsylvania Industrial Arts Association; Coalition of Eastern Native Americans. Awards, honors; Commendation for work as a teacher of adult basic education and English as a second language, State of Pennsylvania Adult Education Department, Harrisburg, Pa. Interests: Education; ethnology and anthropology; geology.

JUANICO, JUAN (Acoma Pueblo)
(museum director)

Affiliation: Director, Acoma Museum, P.O. Box 309, Acoma Pueblo, N.M. 87032.

JUDKINS, RUSSELL ALAN 1944-
(anthropologist)

Born August 8, 1944, Salt Lake City, Utah. Education: Brigham Young University, B.S., 1966; Cornell University, Ph.D., 1973. Principal occupation: Anthropologist. Home address: Homestead Gatehouse, Geneseo, N.Y. 14454. Affiliation: Assistant professor, and professor, State University of New York, College at Geneseo, N.Y., 1972-. Memberships: American Anthropological Association (Fellow); Northeastern Anthropological Association; Society for Medical Anthropology. Interests: "Contemporary American Indian society and culture, including medical research; growth and change in community and religious life; nutrition; Iroquoian, especially Seneca; Indians of Intermountain West, including Mormon Indians. Biographical source: American Men and Women of Science.

JUMPER, BETTY MAE (Seminole)
1927-
(director-Seminole communications)

Born April 27, 1927, Indiantown, Fla. Education: Cherokee Indian School, Cherokee, N.C., 1949 (first Seminole Indian to receive a high school diploma). Principal occupation: Director-Seminole communications. Home address: Hollywood, Fla. 33024. Affiliation: Chairperson, Seminole Tribe, 1967-1971; director of communications and editor-in-chief of the Seminole Tribune (the newspaper of the Seminole Tribe), Seminole Tribe of Florida, 6333 Forrest (N.W. 30th) St., Hollywood, Fla. 33024. Community activities: Speaker at schools throughout Florida about Seminole Tribe; advisor, Manpower Development and Training Committee for the State of Florida; member, Independent Bible Baptist Church. Memberships: Native American Press Association; Florida Press Association. Awards, honors: Served on first tribal council as secretary-treasurer, and later resigned to serve as vice chairperson. In 1967, Betty Mae was the first woman elected as chairperson of the Seminole Tribe, serving four years. In 1968, Betty joined three Southeastern Tribes in signing a Declaration of Unity in Cherokee, N.C. The declaration implemented the Inter-Tribal Council, United Southeastern Tribes. While serving as chairperson of the Seminole Tribe, she was appointed by the President of the U.S. to become one of eight Indian members to work with Vice President Agnew. Only two women were chosen to serve on the committee, the National Congress on Indian Opportunity under President Nixon. She was chosen "Woman of the Year" by the Department of Florida Ladies Auxiliary of Jewish War Veterans of the U.S. for her outstanding contributions in the field of humanities. Betty Mae received a medicine peace pipe and a gold pin from the United Southeastern Tribes. *Interests:* "Betty did much to improve the health, education and social conditions of the Seminole people. Through her efforts, the Tribe was one of the first tribes to obtain the CHR (Community Health Representative) Program. She was also effective in her concerns for Indian people on regional, national and state levels." *Published work: ...And With the Wagon - Came God's Word* (Seminole Print Shop, 1984).

JUNALUSKA, ARTHUR SMITH (Cherokee) 1918-
(writer, director, producer, lecturer, choreographer)

Born November 30, 1918, Cherokee Nation, Cherokee, N.C. *Education:* Cherokee Indian School; Haskell Institute; Okmulgee Junior College; Eckels College of Embalming; Lister Institute of Medical Research; London School of Medicine. *Principal occupation:* Executive and artistic director, American Indian Society of Creative Arts, Inc., New York, N.Y. *Other professional posts:* Writer of plays for radio, television and stage; performer; founder, American Indian Drama Company; director of drama, South Dakota Wesleyan University, 1958; creator, writer and producer of "Dance of the Twelve Moons," an American Indian Dance Company production; director and coordinator, Indian Village, Freedomland (New York City Amusement Park), 1960-1961; consultant and technical advisor for motion pictures and plays; director of performing arts, Indian Festival of Arts, LaGrande, Oreg. *Military service:* U.S. Army (World War II0.

JUNEAU, ALFRED LeROY (Blackfeet) 1919-
(public accounting)

Born August 21, 1919, Browning, Mt. *Education:* Southwestern University, Los Angeles, Calif., B.S., 1951. *Principal occu-*pation: Public accounting. *Home address:* 539 Crane Blvd., Los Angeles, Calif. 90065. *Affiliations:* Comptroller, Los Angeles Indian Center, Inc. (four years); Associate consultant, United Indian Development Association (Indian business development), 1976-; United American Indian Council (Indian socio-economic concerns), 1976-; commissioner (appointed by Mayor Bradley), Los Angeles City-County Native American Indian Commission, 1977-. *Other professional posts:* Secretary-treasurer, U.S. Steel Buildings Co., Los Angeles, Calif. *Military service:* U.S. Army Signal Corps, 1941-1945 (Sergeant; two Bronze Stars, Good Conduct Medal, Europe-Africa-Middle Eastern Theatre Servie Medal, Meritorious Unit Award). *Memberships:* California Public Accountants, 1951-; Loyal Order of Moose, 1973-; National Congress of American Indians, 1944-; Parent Teachers Association, Los Angeles, 1955-; Smithsonian Institution, 1975-; Blackfeet Indian Tribe, Browning, Mt. (enrolled member). *Interests:* "General accounting and related financial matters; continuing interest in socio-economic betterment of American Indians in urban areas and on reservations; invited and attended, February 2, 1978, President and Mrs. Carter's prayer breakfast in Washingtn, D.C.; invited on February 3, 1978 to attend an All-Indian prayer breakfast at the U.S. Capitol in Washington, D.C.; have played profesionally a trumpet in the U.S. and Europe." *Biographical source: Vida Reporter* (Los Angeles, April, 1977), a short biographical article with photo.

K

KAHN, FRANKLIN (Navajo) 1934-
(artist)

Born May 25, 1934, Pine Springs, Ariz. *Education:* Stewart Indian School. *Principal occupation:* Artist. *Home address:* 3315 N. Steues Blvd., Flagstaff, Ariz. 86001. *Affiliation:* Sketch artist and sign painter, Federal Sign and Signal Corp., Flagstaff, Ariz.. *Membership:* American Indian Service Committee. *Awards, honors:* Second Prize,

Scottsdale National Indian Art Show. *Interests:* Watercolor and oil painting; Indian designs and symbols. *Published work:* Illustrator, *Going Away to School* (Bureau of Indian Affairs, 1951).

KAHRAHRAH, BERNARD (Comanche)
(tribal chairman)

Affiliation: Chairman, Comanche Business Committee, P.O. Box 908, Lawton, Okla. 73502.

KANNON, CLYDE DAVID 1938-
(teacher, special education)

Born November 3, 1938, Maury County, Tenn. *Education:* Emory & Henry College, Emory, Va., B.A. (Psychology and English), 1960; Florida Atlantic University, 1968-1970; University of South Dakota, M.A. (Special Education), 1976. *Principal occupation:* Teacher, special education. *Address:* Community School, Crow Creek Reservation, Fort Thompson, S.D. 57339. *Affiliations:* Teacher, Tulare County School System, Earlimart, Calif., 1962-1963; teacher, Williamson County School System, Tenn., 1963-1968; teacher, South Florida Schools, principal/teacher K-6, Bureau of Indian Affairs (Big Cypress Reservation), Seminole Agency, Hollywood, Fla., 1968-1971; elementary teacher, special education teacher, teacher supervisor, principal, Fort Thompson Community School, B.I.A., Crow Creek Agency, Fort Thompson, S.D., 1971-. *Awards, honors:* Special Education Achievement Award, National Blue Key Honor Society, 1960.

KASCHUBE, DOROTHEA VEDRAL 1927-
(professor of anthropology)

Born November 6, 1927, Chicago, Ill. *Education:* Indiana University, B.A., 1951, M.A., 1953, Ph.D., 1960. *Principal occupation:* Professor of anthropology, Department of Anthropology, University of Colorado, Boulder, Colo., 1955-. *Home address:* 370 S. 36th St., Boulder, Colo. 80303. *Other professional posts:* Research associate, Stanford University (summers). *Memberships:* American Anthropological

Association; Linguistic Society of America; Sigma Xi. *Interests:* "Language of the Crow Indians and of the Siouan language family. Language as both biological and cultural behavior." *Published works: Structural Elements of the Language of the Crow Indians of Montana* (University of Colorado Press, 1967); co-author with Joseph H. Greenberg, *Word Prosodic Systems: A Preliminary Report* (Working Papers on Language Universals, Stanford University, 1976).

KAUFMAN, STEVEN, M.D.
(Indian health service)

Affiliation: Chief, Inpatient Services, Indian Health Service, 5600 Fishers Lane, Rockville, Md. 20857.

KEALIINOHOMOKU, JOANN WHEELE 1930-
(anthropologist)

Born May 20, 1930, Kansas City, Mo. *Education:* Northwestern University, B.S., 1955, M.A., 1958; Indiana University, Ph.D., 1976. *Princpal occupation:* Anthropologist. *Home address:* 518 South Agassiz St., Flagstaff, Ariz. 86001. *Affiliation:* Professor, Department of Anthropology, Northern Arizona State University, Flagstaff, Ariz. *Other professional posts:* Visiting professor for University of Hawaii, Manoa Campus; University of Hawaii, Hilo Campus; New York University; World Campus Afloat. *Community activities:* Native American for Community Action (board of directors, 1977-1982; secretary of board, 1979-1982); Cross-Cultural Dance Resources, Inc. (a non-profit organization - a "living museum" for scholars and performers to talk, study, consult) (president, board of directors). *Memberships:* American Anthropological Association (Fellow); American Ethnological Society; American Folklore Society; Association for the Anthropological Study of Play; Bishop Museum Association, CORD (Congress on Research in Dance) (board of directors, 1974-1977); Cross-Cultural Dance Resources, Inc. (founder and director); Society for Ethnomusicology (council member, 1967-1970, 1980-1983). *Awards, honors:* Weatherhead Resident Scholar, School of American Research,

Santa Fe, N.M. 1974-1975; Research Fellow, East-West Center, Honolulu, Hawaii, 1981; Dedicatee for Tenth Annual Flagstaff Indian Center's Basketball Tournament, 1983. *Interests:* "Cultural anthropology with strong interface to physical anthropology and linguistics; area studies: Southwestern American Indians, Midwestern American Blacks, Pacific peoples, especially Polynesians; focus: performance arts, affective culture, culture dynamics; field work in Southwest U.S., especially with Hopi and other Pueblos. *Biographical sources: Dictionary of International Biography; The World Who's Who of Women; Who's Who in Oceania; Who's Who of American Women. Published works:* "Hopi and Polynesian Dance: A Study in Cross-Cultural Comparison" (*Ethnomusicology,* 1967); with Frank Gillis, "Special Bibliography: Gertrude Prokosch Kurath" (*Ethnomusicology,* 1970); "Dance Culture as a Microcosm of Holistic Culture" (*New Dimensions in Dance Research: Anthropology and Dance—The American Indian,* 1974); *Theory and Methods for an Anthropological Study of Dance,* Ph.D. dissertation, anthropology (University Microfilms, 1976); "The Drama of the Hopi Ogres," chapter in *Southwestern Indian Ritual Drama,* edited by Charlotte Frisbie, (University of New Mexico Press, 1980); "Music and Dance of the Hawaiian and Hopi Peoples," chapter in *Becoming Human Through Music* (Music Educators National Conference, 1985); "The Would-Be Indian," chapter in *Anthropology and Music: Essays in Honor of David P. McAllester,* edited by Charlotte Frisbie (University of Michigan Press, 1985); among other articles, reviews and chapters in various publications.

KEEGAN, MARCIA (Cherokee) 1943-
(free-lance photographer, author)

Born May 23, 1943, Tulsa, Okla. *Education:* University of New Mexico, B.A., 1964. *Memberships:* American Society of Magazine Photographers; American Society of Picture Professionals; Southwestern American Indian Association; Wheelwright Museum; Museum of the American Indian, Heye Foundation; New York Women in Communications, Inc.; North American Indian Women's Association. *Awards,*

honors: Recipient of Creative Artists Program Grant, 1972. *Interests:* Ms. Keegan writes, "I am a writer/photographer specializing in documentation of the Southwest tribes, mainly Pueblo and Navajo. I am interested in presenting to non-Native Americans the traditional life-styles and ceremonies of the Southwest tribes. To this end I have also worked on educational filmstrips, one of which was, *We Are American Indians,* published by Guidance Associates of Harcourt Brace & Jovanovich, 1973. *Published works: The Taos Indians & Their Sacred Blue Lake* (Julian Messner, 1972); *Mother Earth, Father Sky* (Grossman Publishing, 1974); *We Can Still Hear Them Clapping* (Avon Books, 1975); *Pueblo & Navajo Cookery* (Morgan & Morgan, Inc., 1977).

KEELY, KAY
(B.I.A. Indian education)

Affiliation: Indian education, Bureau of Indian Affairs, 1951 Constitution Ave., N.W., Washington, D.C. 20245.

KEEN, RALPH F. (Cherokee) 1934-
(educator)

Born August 31, 1934, Hominy, Okla. *Education:* Northeastern State College, Okla., B.A. (Education), 1951; Kansas State College of Pittsburgh; Kansas State University. *Principal occupation:* Educator. *Affiliation:* Training instructor in painting, Haskell Indian Junior College, Lawrence, Kan. *Military service:* U.S. Air Force, 1958-1961. *Memberships:* Kansas Education Association; National Education Association; American Congress of Parents and Teachers.

KEGG, MATTHEW M. (Chippewa) 1953-
(teacher)

Born October 5, 1953, Brainerd, Minn. *Education:* Bemidji State University, Minn., B.A., 1976. *Principal occupation:* Teacher. *Home address:* Star Route P.O. Box 105, Onamia, Minn. 56359. *Affiliations:* Graduate assistant, Indian Studies Program, Bemidji State University, 1980-1981;

teacher, Mille Lacs Indian Reservation, Onamia, Minn., 1981-. *Awards, honors:* Recipient of Certificate of Appreciation from State Department of Education of Minnesota, 1980, for contributions to Indian education; Most Valuable Player award from hockey team, Bemidji Northland Icers, 1980. *Interests:* "Hockey; published several articles in magazines; poetry; outdoor activities: camping, backpacking, canoeing, biking."

KEHOE, ALICE BECK 1934-
(professor of anthropology)

Born September 18, 1934, New York, N.Y. *Education:* Barnard College, B.A., 1956; Harvard University, Ph.D., 1964. *Principal occupation:* Professor of anthropology. *Home address:* 3014 N. Shepard Ave., Milwaukee, Wis. 53211. *Affiliations:* Assistant professor of anthropology, University of Nebraska, 1965-1968; associate professor, professor of anthropology, Marquette University, Milwaukee, Wis., 1968-. *Memberships:* American Anthropological Association (Fellow); Society for American Archaeology; American Ethnological Society. *Interests:* Cultural anthropology and archaeology; field work among Blackfoot, Cree and Dakota tribes in the U.S. and Canada; archaeological field work in Montana and Saskatchewan. *Published works:* Hunters of the Buried Years (Regina, Sask. School Aids & Text Book Co., 1962); *North American Indians* (Prentice-Hall, 1981).

KEITH, C. HOBART *(Blue Horse)*
(Oglala Sioux) 1922-
(artist, sculptor)

Born March 8, 1922, Pine Ridge, S.D. *Education:* Colorado Springs Fine Arts Center, 1938-1941. *Principal occupation:* Artist, sculptor. *Home address:* P.O. Box 444, Pine Ridge, S.D. 57770. *Affiliations:* Chief judge, Oglala Sioux Tribal Court, 1967-; representative, Oglala Sioux Tribal Council. *Military service:* U.S. Navy, 1942-1946. *Community activities:* Veterans of Foreign Wars; American Legion; Tribal Land Owners Association. *Awards, honors:* Certificate of Appreciation, National Police Officers Association of America, Police Hall of Fame, Inc.

KELLER, GEORGE
(B.I.A. agency superintendent)

Affiliation: Superintendent, San Carlos Agency, Bureau of Indian Affairs, San Carlos, Ariz. 85550.

KELLER, NANCY (Sac and Fox)
(tribal chairwoman)

Affiliation: Chairwoman, Sac and Fox Tribal Council, P.O. Box 38, Reserve, Kan. 66434.

KELLY, ALVIN (Quechan)
(tribal president)

Affiliation: President, Quechan Tribal Council, P.O. Box 1352, Yuma, Ariz. 85364.

KENNEDY, JAMES H.
(school superintendent)

Affiliation: Superintendent, Kickapoo Nation School, P.O. Box 106, Powhattan, Kan. 66527.

KEPLIN, DEBBIE L. (Turtle Mountain Chippewa) 1956-
(general manager-radio station)

Born February 28, 1956, Belcourt, N.D. *Education:* Flandreau Indian School, 1974; University of North Dakota, Grand Forks (two years liberal arts instruction). *Principal occupation:* Public radio station general manager. *Home address:* P.O. Box 236, Belcourt, N.D. 58316. *Affiliation: General manager, KEYA Radio Station, Belcourt, N.D. Other professional posts:* Occupied positions at KEYA radio of program director, news director, music director, and executive secretary. *Community activities:* Member, St. Ann's Society, Belcourt, N.D.; assistant-religious education, St. Anthony's Catholic Church, Belcourt; member, Turtle Mountain Musicians; member, Turtle Mountain Historical Society. *Memberships:* National Association of Female Executives, 1985-; Corporation for Public Broadcasting/National Public Radio (authorized representative). *Awards, honors:* Certificate of Native American Leadership Training by the Community Council of the Northern

Plains Teacher Corps, Nov. 1979 & Feb. and April, 1980; Certificate of Training-Explosive Devices Training by the U.S. Department of the Interior, Sept., 1984; dedicated service to the KEYA Radio Station and the Belcourt community by Turtle Mountain Community School, Nov., 1985; for community service by Turtle Mountain Band of Chippewa Indians, Feb., 1985. *Interests:* "To promote and educate the local community and surrounding communities on the history and culture of the Turtle Mountain Band of Chippewa through the use of radio. To develop programs focusing on problems affecting the local community, such as alcoholism, unemployment, housing, recreation, etc...To encourage the training of high school students in the operation of broadcast facilities-radio. *Programs produced:* "All Nations Music," 1980- (features traditional and contemporary Native American music, legends and stories); "Memorial to James Henry," former chairman of Turtle Mountain Band of Chippewa, 5-minute piece aired nationally on radio series "First Person Radio" of Minn. in Sept., 1983; "Music of the Turtle Mountains," 1985- (program features the talents and biographies of local artists, musicians and poets); the music of Floyd Westerman, Sr. Mary Anthony Rogers, many local fiddlers, Adella and Gilbert Kills Pretty Enemy, 1985- (program features biographical sketches of artists through interview and music selections).

KICKINGBIRD, K. KIRKE
(executive director, Indian organization)

Affiliation: Executive director, Institute for the Development of Indian Law, 1104 Glyndon St., S.E., Vienna, Va. 22180.

KILPATRICK, ANNA GRITTS
(Oklahoma Cherokee) 1917-
(teacher, writer)

Born March 7, 1917, Echota, Okla. *Education:* Southern Methodist University, B.S., 1958. *Principal occupation:* Teacher, writer. *Affiliation:* Teacher, Dallas, Tex. public schools. *Published works: Friends of Thunder* (SMU Press); *Walk In Your Soul* (SMU Press); *The Shadow of Sequoyah* (University of Oklahoma Press), all with Jack Frederick Kilpatrick.

KILPATRICK, JACK FREDERICK
(Oklahoma Cherokee) 1915-
(professor of music)

Born September 23, 1915, Stilwell, Okla. *Education:* Bacone College, 1933-1935; Northeastern State College of Okla., 1935; University of Redlands, Mus.B., 1938; Catholic University, Mus.M., 1946; University of Redlands, Mus.D., 1950. *Principal occupation:* Professor of music, School of Arts, Southern Methodist University, Dallas, Texas. *Military service:* U.S. Naval School of Music, 1943-1945 (instructor). *Memberships:* Phi Beta Kappa; American Anthropological Association; Society for Ethnomusicology; American Composers Alliance; Pi Kappa Lambda. *Awards, honors:* National Science Foundation Grant; Danforth Foundation Fellowship; American Philosophical Society Grant; Carnegie Foundation Grant; Tobin Foundation Grant; achievement awards, Cherokee Nation, National Federation of Music Clubs. *Published works: Friends of Thunder* (SMU Press, 1964); *Walk In Your Soul* (SMU Press, 1965); *The Shadow of Sequoyah* (University of Oklahoma Press, 1965); all co-authored with Anna Gritts Kilpatrick; *Sequoyah: Of Earth and Intellect* (Encino Press, 1965).

KING, CLARENCE E., Sr.
(Ottawa) 1909-
(former chief-Ottawa Tribe of Oklahoma)

Born January 1, 1909, Miami, Okla. *Affiliations:* Former Principal Chief, Ottawa Tribe of Oklahoma; self-employed electrician. *Military service:* U.S. Navy, 1944-1946 (Asiatic and Pacific Medals, World War II Medal).

KING, MARY ELIZABETH 1929-
(anthropologist)

Born September 7, 1929, Williamsport, Pa. *Education:* Columbia University, A.B., 1951, M.A., 1958; University of Arizona, Ph.D., 1965. *Principal occupation:* Anthropologist. *Home address:* 515 Askin Rd., St. Davids, Pa. 19087. *Affiliations:* Museum assistant, librarian, and curator of Western Hemisphere textiles, The Textile Museum, Washington, D.C., 1953-1967; lecturer, assistant professor, associate professor of anthropology, Howard University, Washington, D.C., 1963-1971; professor of anthropology and curator of anthropology, The Museum of Texas Tech University, Lubbock, Texas, 1971-1977; keeper of collections, The University Museum, University of Pennsylvania, 1978-. *Memberships:* American Anthropological Association Fellow); Royal Anthropological Institute (Fellow); Society for American Archaeology; Current Anthropology (Associate); American Association for the Advancement of Science (Fellow); Sigma Xi; International Congress of Americanists; American Association of Museums (council member, 1978-). *Interests:* Archaeology and ethnography of North and South America; primitive art; material culture, especially textiles and basketry; human ecology; museology; fieldwork in South Dakota, Peru, Mexico; project director, The Lubbock Lake Site (fieldwork), 1975, 1976. *Published works:* Numerous articles, monographs, and reviews in various publications.

KINGMAN, A. GAY
(superintendent-Indian center)

Affiliation: Superintendent, Pierre Indian Learning Center, Star Route 3, Pierre, S.D. 57501.

KINLEY, LARRY (Lummi)
(tribal chairman)

Affiliation: Chairman, Lummi Business Council, 2616 Kwina Rd., Bellingham, Wash. 98225-9298.

KINNEY, RODNEY P. (Eskimo)
(consultant-engineering)

Education: University of California, San Jose, B.S. (Civil Engineering), 1960; graduate studies at Univerity of California, Berkeley and San Jose, and University of Alaska, Anchorage. *Principal occupation:* Consultant engineering. *Address:* P.O. Box 771102,

Eagle River, Alaska 99577. *Affiliations:* Geotechnical consultant, Woodward Clyde Consultants, Anchorage, Alaska, 1961-1975; engineering coordinator, Alyeska Pipeline Service Co., 1975-1979; manager of Engineering & Planning Division, Anchorage Water & Wastewater Utility, 1979-1980; principal engineer, Rodney P. Kinney Associates, Eagle River, Alaska, 1980-. *Military service:* U.S. Navy, 1951-1959. *Community activities:* Local Chamber of Commerce. *Memberships:* American Society of Civil Engineers; Bering Straits Native Association; American Indian Science and Engineering Society; American Water Works Association; American Public Works Association. *Interests:* "Rodney P. Kinney Associates, a qualified Eskimo firm, was established October 2, 1980. The firm emphasizes consultation and services in general civil engineering, including roads and drainage, water and sewer, as well as soil testing and data collection. We also offer geophysical (seismic refraction and resistivity) and slope inclinometer services, water resource development services, and consultation for private and public systems." *Biographical sources: Who's Who in the West; Who's Who in Technology Today; International Men of Distinction.*

KITTO, RICHARD (Santee Sioux)
(tribal chairman)

Affiliation: Chairman, Santee Sioux Tribal Council, Route 2, Niobrara, Neb. 68760.

KNIGHT, PHILIP (Wintun)
(tribal chairman)

Affiliation: Chairman, Rumsey Community Council, P.O. Box 18, Brooks, Calif. 95606.

KOOMSA, MARLAND
(chief-Indian health education)

Affiliation: Chief, Health Education, Indian Health Services, 5600 Fishers Lane, Rockville, Md. 20857.

KRAFT, HERBERT C. 1927-
(professor of anthropology,
archaeologist)

Born June 1, 1927, Elizabeth, N.J. *Education:* Seton Hall University, 1947-1950, M.A., (History), 1961; Hunter College, C.U.N.Y., M.A. (Anthropology), 1969. *Principal occupation:* Professor of anthropology and director of Archaeological Research Center, Seton Hall University, South Orange, N.J., 1960-. *Home address:* 15 Raymond Terrace, Elizabeth, N.J. 07208. *Other professional posts:* Archaeological consultant for cultural resources surveys. *Military service:* Merchant Marines, 1945-1947. *Community activities:* New Jersey Historic Sites (member, State Review Board). *Memberships:* Society of Professional Archaeologists; Archaeological Society of New Jersey (president, editor of *Bulletin*); Eastern States Archaeological Federation; New York State Archaeological Association (Fellow); New Jersey Academy of Sciences (Fellow); Society for Pennsylvania Archaeology. *Awards, honors:* Archie Award, Society for Pennsylvania Archaeology; recipient of two grants from the New Jersey Historical Commission; ten grants from the National Park Service, for excavations of prehistoric sites in New Jersey. *Interests:* "(My) primary interest is the prehistoric and contact period archaeology of New Jersey, and the Northeast and Middle Atlantic States generally. Since 1964, I have conducted archaeological excavations for the National Park Service, and for Seton Hall University sponsored research in the Upper Delaware Valley, N.J., and on several sites in northeastern New Jersey and Staten Island, N.Y. These excavations have encompassed the entire span from Paleo-Indian to the Historic Contact Period. I have traveled extensively in Meso-America and Europe especially to archaeologically oriented areas." *Biographical sources: Dictionary of International Biography; American Men and Women of Science; Current Biographies of Leading Archaeologists; Outstanding Educators of America, 1971. Published works: The Miller Field Site* (Seton Hall University Press, 1970); *Archaeology in the Upper Delaware Valley* (Pensylvania Historic and Museum Commission, 1972); *A Delaware Indian Symposium* (Pennsylvania

Historic and Museum Commission, 1974); *The Archaeology of the Tocks Island Area* (Archaeological Research Center, Seton Hall University, 1975); numerous articles in *Archaeology of Eastern North Ameica, Annals* of the New York Academy of Sciences, *Researches and Transactions* of the New York State Arcaeological Association, etc.

KREIPE, MARTHA (Prairie Band Potawatomi) 1944-
(museum professional)

Born November 9, 1944, Topeka, Kan. *Education:* Haskell Indian Junior College, Lawrence, Kan., (Certificate, Welding), 1975; University of Kansas, Lawrence, Kan., B.F.A. (Painting), 1978, M.A. (Special Studies-pending). *Principal occupation:* Museum professional. *Home address:* 900 West 190th St. #11-0, New York, N.Y. 10040. *Affiliation:* Manager, Indian Information Center, Museum of the American Indian, New York, N.Y., 1984-. *Community activities:* Indian Center, Lawrence, Kan. (board of directors); Circle of Red Nations, New York, N.Y. (president, board of directors); Native American Education Program, New York, N.Y. (parent's committee); Grupo Aymara Productions (board of directors). *Awards, honors:* HUD Minority Fellowship, University of Kansas. *Interests:* "Vocational interests: Contemporary North American Indian activities—cultural, social, artistic; Andean Indian life and music." *Published works: 49's, A Pan Indian Mechanism for Boundary Maintenance and Social Cohesion* (AAAmeeting, 1980); *Native American Conceptions of Time* (Manhattan Laboratory Museum Symposium, 1983); Teacher's Kit: "The Parfleche," Museum of the American Indian, Heye Foundation, 1985.

KRENZKE, THEODORE
(B.I.A. director-Indian services)

Affiliation: Director, Indian Services, Bureau of Indian Affairs, 1951 Constitution Ave., N.W., Washington, D.C. 20245.

KREPPS, ETHEL CONSTANCE (Kiowa/Miami) 1941-
(attorney)

Born October 31, 1941, Mt. View, Okla. *Education:* St. John's Medical Center, Tulsa, Okla., R.N., 1971; University of Tulsa, B.S., 1974; Univerity of Tulsa, College of Law, J.D., 1979. *Principal occupation:* Attorney. *Home address:* 3326 South 93rd East Ave., Tulsa, Okla. 74145. *Affiliation:* Lawyer, Native American Coalition of Tulsa, Inc., 1740 West 41st St., Tulsa, Okla. 74107, 1981-. *Other professional posts:* President, National Indian Social Workers Association; president, Oklahoma Indian Child Welfare Association; national vice president, Amerian Indian Nurses Association; secretary, Native American Chamber of Commerce. *Community activities:* Kiowa Tribe of Oklahoma (elected secretary); Native American Chamber of Commerce (secretary); Tulsa Indian Affairs Commission; American Indian Toastmasters. *Memberships:* National Trial Lawyers Association; American Bar Association; Federal Bar Association; Oklahoma Bar Association; Tulsa County Bar Association; Tulsa Women Lawyers Association; Women Lawyers Association of Oklahoma; Phi Alpha Delta Legal Fraternity. *Awards, honors:* Indian Business Person of the Year Award, 1984; Outstanding Leadership Award, 1985, from International Indian Child Conference; Trial Lawyers Association National Award. *Interests:* Writer, painting, collections, travel, photography. *Biographical sources: Who's Who in Finance and Industry; Who's Who in the South and Southwest; Who's Who of American Women; Who's Who in the World; Who's Who in Society; Personalities of the World. Published works: A Strong Medicine Wind* (Western Publications, 1981); *Oklahoma Memories,* chapter (University of Oklahoma Press, 1982); *Oklahoma Images,* chapter (University of Oklahoma Press, 1983).

KUHKLEN, ALBERT
(B.I.A. agency superintendent)

Affiliation: Superintendent, Anchorage Agency, Bureau of Indian Affairs, P.O. Box 100120, Anchorage, Alaska 99510.

KUKA, KING D. (Blackfeet) 1946-
(artist, art instructor)

Born August 13, 1946, Browning, Mt. *Education:* Institute of American Indian Arts, Diploma, 1965; University of Montana, BFA, 1973; Montana State University, M.A. *Principal occupation:* Artist (sculpture and painting), high school art teacher on Blackfeet Reservation; owner-operator, Blackwolf Gallery. *Home address:* Box 182, East Glacier Park, Mt. 59434. *Military service:* U.S. Army, 1965-1967. *Exhibits:* One-man shows: Reeder's Alley, Helena; University of Montana Center, Missoula; Museum of the Plains Indian, Browning; Rainbow Gallery, Great Falls; Flathead Lake Lookout, Lakeside. Painting and sculpture exhibits at Riverside Museum, New York, N.Y.; San Francisco; Philbrook Art Center, Tulsa, Okla.; Gallery of Indian Arts, Washington, D.C. *Awards, honors:* Numerous awards for art and creative writing. *Interests:* Mr. Kuka's main interest is in the arts, Indian culture and outdoor life. *Published works:* Poetry: *The Whispering Wind* (Doubleday); *Voices of the Rainbow* (Viking Press); Anthologies: *The First Skin Around Me* (Terrritorial Press); *The Remembered Earth* (Red Earth Press); among others.

KURATH, GERTRUDE PROKOSCH 1903-
(dance ethnologist, musicologist)

Born August 19, 1903, Chicago, Ill. *Education:* Bryn Mawr College, B.A., 1922, M.A., 1928; Yale School of Drama, 1929-1930. *Principal occupation:* Dance ethnologist, musicologist. *Home address:* 1125 Spring St., Ann Arbor, Mich. 48103. *Affiliations:* Pageant director, Rhode Island School of Design, 1932-1945; teacher of dance, Brown University Extension, 1936-1945; director, Creative Dance Guild, 1937-1946; dance critic, Ann Arbor *News,* 1961-1972. *Other professional posts:* Field employee, New York State Museum, 1952; dance consultant, *Webster's International Dictionary,* third edition; field employee, National Museum of Canada, 1962-1969. *Community activities:* Community Music School, Providence, R.I., (dance director, 1932-1940); Washtenong Youth Groups, Ann

Arbor, Mich., 1954-1959. *Memberships:* Michigan Folklore Society, 1947- (treasurer, editor, president); Dance Research Center, 1963-; Society for Ethnomusicology, 1953-(dance editor, 2nd vice president); Congress on Research in Dance (CORD), 1967-. *Awards, honors:* Adopted Chippewa and Onondaga; research grants: American Philosophical Society, 1949-1968; Indiana University Archives of Traditional Music; Michigan Academy of Science, Arts and Letters; Museum of New Mexico; National Museum of Canada; Wenner-Gren Foundation, 1949-1972; Chicago Folklore Prize for *Music and Dance of the Tewa Pueblos,* Department of Germanic Languages, University of Chicago; Steloff Research Award, CORD, 1983. *Interests:* Field trips: Mexico, 1946; Iroquois (New York and Ontario), 1948-1964; Cherokee (North Carolina), 1949-1952; Algonquians (Iowa, Wisconsin), 1952, 1956, (Michigan), 1953-1967, (Manitoba), 1968; Rio Grande Pueblos (New Mexico), 1957-1969. *Biographical sources: Who's Who of American Women; Who's Who of Music International; Dictionary of American Scholars;* special bibliography of Gertrtude P. Kurath, *Ethnomusicology,* 1970; *Research Method and Background of G.P.K.,* CORD Annual VI, 1972; *Dance Memoirs* (Chimera Press, Cambridge, 1983). *Published works: The Iroquois Eagle Dance,* with William Fenton (Bureau of American Ethnology, 1953); *Songs of the Wigwam* (Cooperative Recreation Service, 1955); *Songs and Dances of the Great Lakes Indians,* recording (Ethnic Folkways Library, 1956); *Algonquian Ceremonialism and Natural Resources of the Great Lakes* (Indian Institute of World Culture, 1957); *Dances of Anahuac: The Choreography and Music of Pre-Cortesian Dances* (Aldine, 1964); *Iroquois Music and Dance: Ceremonial Arts of Two Seneca Longhouses* (Bureau of American Ethnology, 1964); *Michigan Indian Festivals* (Ann Arbor Publishers, 1966); *Dance and Song Rituals of Six Nations Reserve, Ontario* (National Museum of Canada, 1968); *Music and Dance of the Tewa Pueblos, New Mexico* (Museum of New Mexico Press, 1970); "Tutelo Rituals on Six Nations Reserve" (*Ethnomusicology,* 1981); numerous other articles in *Encyclopaedia Britannica* and *Encyclopaedia Americana;* numerous articles and reviews in scholarly journals.

KURTH, REV. E.J.,
(school superintendent)

Affiliation: Superintendent, Red Cloud Indian School, Holy Rosary Mission, Pine Ridge, S.D. 57770.

KUTSCHE, PAUL 1927-
(social anthropologist)

Born January 3, 1927, Grand Rapids, Mich. *Education:* Harvard College, B.A. (cum laude), 1949; University of Michigan, M.A., 1955; University of Pennsylvania, Ph.D., 1961. *Principal occupation:* Social anthropologist. *Address:* Department of Anthropology, Colorado College, Colorado Springs, Colo. 80903. *Affiliations:* Professor, Colorado College, 1959-. *Community activities:* Pikes Peak Gay Community Center (newsletter editor, 1983-1985). *Memberships:* American Anthropological Association (Fellow), 1954-; Western Social Science Association, 1969- (executive council, 1969-1972); Association of Borderland Scholars, 1976- (executive council, 1977-1983); American Ethnological Society, 1975-; Anthropology Research Group on Homosexuality, 1983- (co-chair, 1984-). *Interests:* "Cherokee Indians, especially ethnohistory; New Mexico Hispanic village structure; rural-urban migration; Costa Rica; gender. *Published works: Survival of Spanish American Villages* (Colorado College Studies, 1979); *Canones: Values, Crisis and Survival* (University of New Mexico Press, 1981); *Bibliography of Unpublished Material on the Cherokee* (Scarecrow Press, 1986).

L

LA BARRE, WESTON 1911-
(professor of anthropology)

Born December 13, 1911, Uniontown, Penn. *Education:* Princeton University, A.B. (summa cum laude), 1933; Yale Graduate School, Ph.D. (with honors), 1937. *Principal occupation:* Professor of anthropology. *Home address:* Mt. Sinai Rd., Route 1, Box 171-B, Durham, N.C. 27705. *Affiliations:* Instructor, Rutgers University, 1939-1943; assistant professor, associate professor, James B. Duke Professor of Anthropology, professor emeritus, Duke University, Durham, N.C., 1946-. *Other professional posts:* Instructor, 1955-1959, visiting clinical professor, University of North Carolina Medical School, 1959-. *Military service:* U.S. Naval Reserve (World War II). *Memberships:* American Anthropological Association (Fellow); Current Anthropology (Fellow). *Awards, honors:* Roheim Memorial Award. *Interests:* "Primitive religion and art; culture and personality; psychological anthropology." *Biographical sources: American Men of Science; Who's Who in America; Who's Who in Latin America; International Dirctory of Anthropologists; Directory of American Scholars; Who's Who in the South and Southwest. Published works: The Peyote Cult* (Yale University Publications in Anthropology, 1939; Schocken Books, 1970); *The Aymara Indians of Lake Titicaca Plateau* (Memoir No. 68, American Anthropological Association, 1948); *They Shall Take Up Serpents* (Schocken Books, 1962, 1969); *Normal Adolescence,* with others (Scribners, 1968); *The Ghost Dance: Origins of Religion* (Doubleday, 1970); numerous articles, reviews and notes in scholarly publications, 1939-.

LA CLAIR, LEO JOHN (Muckleshoot) 1941-
(teacher)

Born February 15, 1941, Auburn, Wash. *Education:* Central Washington State College, B.A., 1964; University of Colorado; University of Utah. *Principal occupation:* Teacher. *Affiliation:* Program assistant, Indian Program, American Friends Service Committee, Seattle, Wash. *Community activities:* Committee on Educational Opportunities for American Indians and Alaska Natives (Council on Indian Affairs). *Memberships:* National Association of Intergroup Relations Officials; National Indian Youth Council. *Awards:* United Scholarship Service and American Indian Development, Inc. Scholarships; Eleanor Roosevelt Foundation Grant.

LA COURSE, RICHARD VANCE (Yakima) 1938-
(journalist, editor-in-chief)

Born September 23, 1938, Toppenish, Wash. *Education:* San Luis Rey College, Calif. (philosophical studies), 1957-1961; Old Mission Santa Barbara, Calif. (theological studies), 1961-1963; Portland State University, Wash. (English master's preparation), 1963; University of Washington, Seattle (non-thesis master's study), 1964-1968. Principal occupation: Journalist, editor-in-chief. *Address:* 1228 M St., N.W., Washington, D.C. 20005. *Affiliations:* Copy news editor, photo news editor, correspondent, *Seattle Post-Intelligencer,* Seattle, Wash., 1969-1971; news director, Washington News Bureau, American Indian Press Association, Washington, D.C., and AIPA Southwest News Bureau, Albuquerque, N.M., 1971-1975; managing editor, *Confederated Umatilla Journal,* Pendleton, Oreg., 1975-1976; managing editor, *Yakima Nation Review,* Toppenish, Wash., 1977-1978; founder/managing editor, *Manataba Messenger,* Colorado River Indian Tribes, Parker, Ariz., 1980-1981; managing editor, *CERT Report,* Council of Energy Resource Tribes, Washington, D.C., 1981-1983; president, managing editor, La Course Communications Corp., Washington, D.C., 1983-. *Military service:* U.S. Army Reserve, 1964-1970. *Memberships:* Native American Press Association (cofounder, board of directors); Northwest Indian News Association (co-founder); ASNE-ANPA Foundation (adjunct member, Minorities Committee); National Congress of American Indians; Americans for Indian Opportunity, Norman, Okla. (honorary lifetime member); *Race Relations Reporter,* Nashville, Tenn. (associate editor). *Awards, honors:* Presentor, "The Role of Communications in Indian Life," Native American Teacher Corps. Conference, Denver, Colo., 1973; presenter/panelist, annual conference, Association for Education in Journalism, Fort Collins, Colo./Seattle, Wash., 1974/1978; U.S. representative, work and planning sessions of Canadian Indian journalists of Alberta Native Communications Society, Edmonton, Alberta, Canada, 1972-1975; presenter, History of American Indian Journalism;

Techniques and Strategies of Investigative Journalism, Indian Investigative Journalism Project, National Indian Youth Council, Albuquerque, N.M., 1975; co-author, videoscript on tribal jurisdiction issues, National Congress of American Indians, Washington, D.C., 1975; presenter, Workshop on Investigative Journalism, Freedom of the Press in Indian Country, Minnesota Chippewa Tribes, Bemidji, Minn., 1977; keynote speaker and honoree, Second Annual Indian Media Conference and American Indian Film Festival, San Francisco, Calif., 1978; co-founder, Northwest Indian News Association (author of news network charter for association), 1978; recipient, Indian Media Man of the Year Award, National Indian Media Conference, Anaheim, Calif., 1980; recipient, National Recognition Award for Accomplishment, Americans for Indian Opportunity, Washington, D.C., 1984; co-founder, Native American Press Association, University Park, Pa. (author of news network charter, code of ethics, business plan of operation. *Interests:* "La Course Communications Corp., an Indian-owned media firm organized in October 1983, provides services in publication research and development, graphic design, publication of directories, market analysis and specialized mailing lists related to American Indian concerns. Plans to publish a full-size weekly newspaper, *Native America,* with syndication of its news copy nationally. The corporation will also launch computer programming and software services in the field of American Indian interests." *Published works: American Indian Media Directory* (American Indian Press Association, 1974 edition); editor, "1855 Yakima Treaty Chronicles: May 28, 1855 - June 11, 1855," special collector's edition, *Yakima Nation Review,* June 23, 1978; editor, *The Schooling of Native America,* Native American Teachers Corps, 1978; author-editor, *Northwest Tribal Profiles,* Portland Area Office, B.I.A., 1980); author-editor, *Red Pages: Business Across Indian America* (La Course Communications, 1984); *Native Hemisphere: The Emerging Social Continent* (in progress); *The Sandinista-Meskito War* (working title) (in progress).

LADD, EDMUND JAMES (Zuni) 1926-
(Pacific archaeologist-retired;
museum curator)

Born January 4, 1926, Fort Yuma, Calif. *Education:* University of New Mexico, Albuquerque, B.S., 1955, M.A., 1964. *Principal occupation:* Pacific archaeologist-retired; museum curator. *Home address:* 686 Calle Espejo, Santa Fe, N.M. 87505. *Affiliations:* Pacific archaeologist, USDI, National Park Service, Honaunar, Kona, Hawaii, (23 years); curator of ethnology, New Museum of Indian Arts and Culture, Santa Fe, N.M. *Military service:* U.S. Army, 1944-1946. *Memberships:* American Anthropological Association; Society for American Archaeology.

LAFROMBOISE, RICHARD (Chippewa)
(tribal chairman)

Affiliation: Chairman, Turtle Mountain Tribal Council, Belcourt, N.D. 58316.

LAMAR, NEWTON (Wichita)
(tribal president)

Affiliation: President, Wichita Executive Committee, Wichita Tribal Affairs Office, P.O. Box 729, Anadarko, Okla. 73005.

LAMB, CHARLES A. 1944-
(museum director)

Born September 25, 1944, Farragut, Idaho. *Education:* California Western University, B.A. (History), 1966; San Diego State University, Graduate School, 1970-1973. *Principal occupation:* Museum director. *Home address:* 1509 Mohave, Parker, Ariz. 85344. *Affiliations:* National Park Ranger, Crater Lake, Ore., and Yellowstone National Park, Wyo. (eight years); California State Park Ranger and Archaeologic Aid, 1971-1972; Museum director, Colorado River Indian Tribes Museum, Parker, Ariz., 1973-. *Community activities:* Parker Area Historical Society (president); Museums Association of Arizona (Western Regional Representative); Tribal Tourism Committee (chairman); Irataba Society (board member); Tribal Safety Committee (former chairman). *Memberships:* American Association of Museums (education committee); American Association for State and Local History; Society for California Archaeology; National Trust for Historic Preservation. *Awards, honors:* Copely Press Scholarship; graduate of Horace M. Albright Training Center for National Park Service; graduate of Montana State University, Law Enforcement Academy. *Interests:* History, archaeology, anthropology, biology; historic preservation; hunting, fishing, photography, painting. *Biographical sources:* Articles in the following: *Arizona Republic* newspaper; *Parker Pioneer* newspaper; *Yuma Daily Sun* newspaper; among others. *Published works: San Simeon: A Brief History,* illustrations by C. Lamb (Santana Press, 1971).

LAME BULL, LUCINDA (Paiute)
(tribal chairwoman)

Affiliation: Chairwoman, Fort Bidwell Community Council, P.O. Box 127, Fort Bidwell, Calif. 96112.

LAMPMAN, EVELYN SIBLEY 1907-
(writer)

Born April 18, 1907, Dallas, Ore. *Education:* Oregon State University, B.S., 1929. *Principal occupation:* Writer. *Home address:* 3410 W. Rosemont Dr., West Linn, Ore. 97086. *Interests:* Mr. Lampman writes, "History, particularly the Western U.S. I grew up close to a reservation, so I have known and liked Indians all my life. Many visited in our home as guests of my father when I was a child. I have traveled in Mexico." *Published works: Witch Doctor's Son* (Doubleday, 1954); *Navajo Sister* (Doubleday, 1956); *Shy Stegosaurus of Indian Springs* (Doubleday, 1962); *Temple of the Sun* (Doubleday, 1964); *The Tilted Sombrero* (Doubleday, 1966); *Half Breed* (Doubleday, 1967); *Cayuse Courage* (Harcourt Brace, 1970); *Year of Small Shadow* (Harcourt Brace, 1971); *Once Upon a Little Big Horn* (Thomas Y. Crowell, 1971); *Go Up the Road* (Atheneum, 1972).

LANDES, RUTH 1908-
(cultural anthropologist)

Born October 8, 1908, New York, N.Y. *Education:* New York University, B.S., 1928; NYU School of Social Work, MSW, 1929; Columbia University, Ph.D., 1935. *Principal occupation:* Cultural anthropologist. *Affiliations:* Professor of anthropology, McMaster University, Hamilton, Ontario, Can., 1965-? *Other professional posts:* Consultant to national agencies and educational systems, California Social Work Department, and agencies, California Bureau of Mental Hygiene, California Department of Education, California Public Health medicine and nursing, San Francisco Police Department, 1957-? *Membership:* Author's Guild. *Interests:* Cultural anthropology of the Santee Dakota and Prairie Potawatomi Indians; Spanish-speaking peoples of the Southwest; education and minoirty cultures; civil rights; status of women; bi- and multilingualism; culture and personality. *Published works: Ojibwa Sociology* (Columbia University Press, 1937, 1968); *The Ojibwa Woman* (Columbia University Press, 1938, 1968, 1970); *Ojibwa Religion and the Midewiwin* (University of Wisconsin Press, 1968); *Santee Sociology* (University of Wisconsin Press, 1969); *Potawatomi Culture* (University of Wisconsin Press, 1970).

LANG, RICHARD W.
(museum director)

Affiliation: Director, The Wheelwright Museum of the American Indian, P.O. Box 5153, Santa Fe, N.M. 87502.

LaROCHE, HAROLD L. (Lower Brule Sioux) 1931-
(B.I.A. agency superintendent)

Born January 16, 1931, Lower Brule, S.D. *Education:* University of South Dakota, B.S., 1956; University of Minnesota, M.A., 1971. *Principal occupation:* B.I.A. agency superintendent. *Address:* Seminole Agency, Bureau of Indian Affairs, 6075 Stirling Rd.,

Hollywood, Fla. 33024. *Affiliations:* Director of Home Living, Guidance and Counseling, Social and Psychoogical Services, and Student Activities, Flandreau Indian School, Flandreau, S.D., 1972-?; superintendent, Seminole Agency, Bureau of Indian Affairs, Hollywood, Fla. *Military service:* U.S. Marine Corps, 1951-1954 (Sergeant). *Memberships:* American Legion; University of Minnesota Alumni Association. *Biographical source: Who's Who in American Colleges and Universities* (1955-1956).

LASARTE, BERNARD J.
(Coeur D'Alene)
(tribal chairman)

Affiliation: Chairman, Coeur D'Alene Tribal Council, Plummer, Idaho 83851.

LAUBIN, GLADYS W.
(lecturer, entertainer)

Home address: Grand Teton National Park, Moose, Wyo. 83012. *Principal occupation:* Lecturer and entertainer (presentation of Indian dances on the concert stage). *Memberships:* Association on American Indian Affairs; National Congress of American Indians; Chicago Indian Center; Jackson Hole Fine Arts Foundation. *Awards, honors:* Adopted member of Sioux Tribe; dance prizes, Standing Rock and Crow Reservations; Capezio Dance Award, 1972; Catlin Peace Pipe Award, Special Literary Award, American Indian Lore Association, 1976. *Interests:* Research among Sioux, Crow, Blackfeet, Cherokee, Kiowa, and other American Indian tribes related to dance, customs, Indian lore, music; photography; painting; costume making; woodcraft. *Published works:* Co-author, *The Indian Tipi* (University of Oklahoma Press, 1957); documentary art films, produced with Reginald Laubin: *Old Chiefs Dance, Talking Hands, War Dance, Indian Musical Instruments, Ceremonial Pipes and Tipi How* (University of Oklahoma Press, 1951-1958); *Indian Dances of North America and Their Importance to Indian Life* (University of Oklahoma Press, 1977); *The Indian Tipi*, 2nd Edition (University of Oklahoma Press, 1977); *American Indian Archery* (University of Oklahoma Press, 1978).

LAUBIN, REGINALD K.
(lecturer, entertainer)

Home address: Grand Teton National Park, Moose, Wyo. 83012. *Education:* Hartford Art School; Norwich Art School. *Principal occupation:* Lecturer and entertainer (presentation of American Indian dances and lore on the concert stage). *Memberships:* Association on American Indian Affairs; National Congress of American Indians; Chicago Indian Center; Jackson Hole Fine Arts Foundation. *Awards, honors:* Guggenheim Fellowship, 1951; adopted son of Chief One Bull, nephew of Sitting Bull; dance prizes, Standing Rock and Crow Reservations; Capezio Dance Award, 1972; Catlin Peace Pipe Award, Special Literary Award, American Indian Lore Association, 1976. *Interests:* Research among Sioux, Crow, Blackfeet, Cherokee, Kiowa and other tribes on dance, custom, lore, music and general anthropology; archery; photography; duplication of Indian craft techniques; primitive camping and cooking; woodcraft. *Published works: The Indian Tipi* (University of Oklahoma Press, 1957); series in *Boy's Life* on Indian crafts; six documentary films on Indian dance and culture, produced with Gladys Laubin; *Indian Dances of North America, and Their Importance to Indian Life* (University of Oklahoma Press, 1978).

LAVIOLETTE, REV. G., OMI 1911-
(editor and manager-*Indian Journal*)

Born April 7, 1911, Clarence, Ontario, Can. *Education:* University of Ottawa, Ontario, B.A., 1929; Oblate Fathers Seminary, Lebret, Saskatchewan, B.Th, 1934. *Principal occupation:* Editor and manager, *Indian Record,* Winnipeg, 1934-. *Home address:* 480 Aulneau St. #503, Winnipeg, Manitoba, Canada R2H 2V2. *Affiliations:* Founder, editor-manager, *Indian Record,* 1934-; editor of various periodicals, 1938-. *Other professional posts:* Missionary to the Dakota-Sioux Indians in Canada. *Community activities:* Religious Order of the Oblate of M.I. Winnipeg; Latin American Association of Winnipeg (president). *Memberships:* Manitoba Historical Society; St. Boniface Historical Society (advisory board). *Interests:* "Publishing on extensive history of the Dakota-Sioux Indians in Canada, to be published in 1986. Specialized in the Dakota Indian language. Since 1965, worked with Spanish-speaking people in metropolitan Winnipeg. Travels to Europe, Israel, Egypt, Mexico, South American, Japan, Taiwan, Hong Kong, etc." *Biographical source: International Biographical Centre* (Cambridge, England). *Published work: The Sioux Indians in Canada* (Martin Press, Regina, Sask., 1944).

LAWRENCE, ERMA G. (Haida) 1912-
(native language instructor)

Born August 2, 1912, Hydaburg, Alaska. *Education:* Sheldon Jackson College, A.A. *Principal occupation:* Native language instructor. *Home address:* 320 Baldwin St. #415, Ketchikan, Alaska 99901. *Affiliation:* Ketchikan Gateway Borough School District, Ketchikan, Alaska. *Other professional posts:* Writer and consultant, Haida Society for the Preservation of Language and Literature, 1972-. *Community activities:* Curriculum Review Board (member). *Memberships:* Ketchikan Haida Society (secretary, 1973-); *Alaska Native Sisterhood, 1938-. Interests:* Bilingual education; linguistics; curriculum development; bilingual conferences and workshops. *Biographical sources: Ketchikan Daily News; Tundra Times,* Fairbanks; *Southeastern Log,* Ketchikan. *Published works: Haida Reader,* 1973; *Short Haida Stories,* 1974; compiler, editor, *Haida Noun Dictionary,* 1975, *Haida Verb Dictionary,* 1977; *Haida Teacher's Handbook,* 1976); and others.

LEAP, WILLIAM L. 1946-
(anthropologist)

Born November 28, 1946, Philadelphia, Pa. *Education:* Florida State University, B.A. (Anthropology and Linguistics), 1967; Southern Merhodist University, Ph.D. (Anthropology), 1970. *Principal occupation:* Anthropologist. *Home address:* 206 G St., N.W., Washington, D.C. 20024. *Affiliations:* Associate professor, professor of anthropology, American University, Washington, D.C., 1970-. *Other professional post:* Director, Indian Education Program, Center for Applied Linguistics,

Arlington, Va., 1974-. *Interests:* "My vocational interests center on Indian self-determination through education. A major component of such a strategy is relevant education, and that means addressing the Indian (e.g. tribal or traditional) as well as the mainstream cultural components of the students interests, lifestyle, and life-options. My work in the field has centered on assisting Tribal governments and Tribal agencies develop programs to provide Tribal members to take charge of and manage such programs without reliance on outside sources of support." *Published works: Language Policies in Indian Education: Recommendations,* 1973, and *Handbook for Staff Development in Indian Education,* 1976 (Center for Applied Linguistics); *Studies in Southwestern Indian English* (Trinity University Press, 1977); *American Indian Language Education* (National Bilingual Research Center, 1980); "American Indian Language Renewal" in *Annual Review of Anthropology,* 1981; and published as book by National Clearinghouse for Bilingual Education, 1982.

LEASK, JANIE (Haida-Tsimshean) 1948-
(president-Alaskan Native organization)

Born September 17, 1948, Seattle, Wash. *Education:* East Anchorage High School, 1966. *Principal occupation:* Alaska Federation of Natives, 411 W. 4th Ave., Suite 301, Anchorage, 1974- (vice president, 1977-1982; president, 1982-). *Address:* P.O. Box 104836, Anchorage, Alaska 99510. *Community activities:* Enrolled in Cook Inlet Region, Inc. (one of the 12 in-state Alaska Native Regional corporations; The State Board of Education; the Anchorage Organizing Committee for the 1992 Olympics; the Alaska Land Use Council; the ARCO Scholarship Committee. *Awards, honors:* Governor's Award in 1983 for work on behalf of Alaska Native people.

LEE, ROBERT H. 1920-
(newspaper editor)

Born May 28, 1920, Minneapolis, Minn. *Home address:* Boulder Canyon Route, Sturgis, S.D. 57785. *Affiliations:* Wire, state and Sunday editor, Rapid City *Daily Journal* (nine years); reporter, Minneapolis *Tribune, Rocky Mountain News,* Denver, Colo.; political columnist, *Daily Plainsman,* Huron, S.D., *Public Opinion,* Watertown, S.D., *American News,* Aberdeen, S.D.; vice president, editor, Black Hills Publishers, Sturgis, S.D. *Military service:* U.S. Army, 1940-1945, 1947-1964 (Bronze Star). *Memberships:* South Dakota Historical Society, 1947- (director, 1964-); Crazy Horse Memorial Commission (director); Western Writers of America. *Awards, honors:* Award for coverage of theft of Chief Sitting Bull's body from North Dakota grave and reburial in South Dakota, Associated Press. *Published works: Dakota Panorama* (Mid-West-Bear Printing Co., 1961); *Last Grass Frontier* (Black Hills Publishers, 1964); editor, *Gold, Gals, Guns, Guts, Centennial History of Deadwood, S.D.* (Black Hills Publishers, 1976).

LEE, THOMAS E. 1914-
(archaeologist)

Born April 6, 1914, Port Bruce, Ontario, Can. *Education:* Wayne State University, B.A., 1944; University of Toronto, 1942-1943; University of Chicago, 1947-1948; University of Michigan, M.A., 1949. *Principal occupation:* Archaeologist. *Home address:* 1575 Forlan Dr., Ottawa, Ontario Can. K2C 0R8. *Affiliations:* Biologist, National Museum of Canada, 1950-1959; professor invite, Centre d'Etudes Nordiques, Universite Laval, Quebec, 1966-. *Military service:* Royal Canadian Air Force, 1942-1946 (Corporal; CVSM & CLASP: Defense of Britain; 1939-1945 Star; Burma Star; War Medal). *Other professional posts:* Editor, *Anthropological Journal of Canada,* Ottawa; associate editor, *New World Antiquity,* London; associate editor, *The Chesopian,* Norfolk, Va. *Memberships:* Ontario Archaeological Society, 1953- (Life); Instituto Interamerican, 1958- (Fellow, Life); Anthropological Association of Canada, 1963- (Fellow, Life); Guild of American Prehistorians, 1964- (Co-founder; Life); The Chesopian Archaeological Association. *Awards, honors:* Title of Kitchi Donegachin, conferred by Wykwemikong Band of the Ojibways; Master Archaeologist Award,

Guild of American Prehistorians. *Interests:* Archaeology of the American Indian; historical archaeology; wild life; travel. *Published works: Archaeological Investigation, Lake Abitibi,* 1965; *Arcaheological Discovery Discovery, Payne Bay Region, Ungava 1966,* 1968; *Archaeological Investigation of a Longhouse, Pamiok, Ungava,* 1972; *Archaeological Investigation of a Longhouse Ruin, Pamiok Island,* 1974; *The Fort Abitibi Mystery,* 1974; among others, all published by Laval University. Plus more than 200 papers and book reviews.

LENZ, MONSIGNOR PAUL A. 1925-
(Roman Catholic Priest)

Born December 15, 1925, Gallitzin, Pa. *Education:* St. Vincent College, Latrobe, Pa.; St. Vincent Seminary, Latrobe, Pa.; Penn State University. *Principal occupation:* Executive director, The Bureau of Catholic Indian Missions, Washington, D.C. *Home address:* 2021 H St., N.W., Washington, D.C. 20006. *Other professional posts:* Board of trustees: The Catholic University of America, Washington, D.C.; Xavier University, New Orleans; St. Vincent Seminary, Latrobe; National Catholic Indian Tekakwitha Conference, and The National Catholic Development Conference, Washington, D.C. *Memberships:* Rotary Club of Washington, D.C.; George Washington University Faculty Club.

LERNER, ALBERT L. 1931-
(B.I.A. employment assistance officer)

Born December 6, 1931, New York, N.Y. *Education:* S.U.N.Y., Oswego, B.S., 1956; Oregon State University, M.Ed., 1961. *Principal occupation:* B.I.A. employment assistance officer. *Home address:* 2090 McCormack Lane, Placentia, Calif. 92670. *Affiliations:* Vocational teacher, Stewart Indian School, Nev., 1956-1961; head, Vocational Training Department, Flandreau Indian School, S.D., 1961-1965; adult vocational training officer, Cleveland, Ohio, Chicago, Ill., 1965-1967; employment assistance officer, B.I.A., Chicago, Ill., 1969-1971, Los Angeles, Calif. (director), 1971-. *Military service:* U.S. Navy (Aviation machinist, mate 3).

LESTENKOF, JACOB
(B.I.A. area director)

Affiliation: Director, Juneau Area Office, Bureau of Indian Affairs, P.O. Box 3-8000, Juneau, Alaska 99802.

LESTER, A. DAVID (Creek) 1941-
(executive director-Indian organization)

Born September 25, 1941, Claremore, Okla. *Education:* Brigham Young University, Provo, Utah, B.A. (Political Science and Public Administration), 1967. *Principal occupation:* Executive director, Council of Energy Resource Tribes (CERT), 1580 Logan St., Denver, Colo. 80203. *Home address:* 8688 East Otero Circle, Englewood, Colo. 80112. *Affiliations:* Vice-chairman, American Indian Scholarships, Inc., Taos, N.M. (two years); president, United Indian Development Association, Los Angeles, Calif. (seven years); economic development specialist, National Congress of American Indians, Washington, D.C. *Other professional posts:* Commissioner, Administration for Native Americans, U.S. Department of Health and Human Services, Washington, D.C.; Boards of Directors: American Indian National Bank , Washington, D.C.; Americans for Indian Opportunity, Albuquerque, N.M.; American Indian Scholarships, Inc., Taos, N.M.; National Area Development Institute, and Los Angeles Indian Center, Los Angeles, Calif.. *Community activities:* Served as a Presidential appointee to the National Advisory Council on Minority Enterprise, which advised cabinet-level officials on strategies to stimulate minority business ownership, and to the National Council on Indian Opportunity, devoted to improving social and economic opportunities for American Indians; served as Human Relations Commissioner for the City of Los Angeles and as Chairman of the Los Angeles County American Indian Commission. *Awards, honors:* Received the Indian Council First Indian Achievement Award, the Americans for Indian Opportunity's Distinguished Services "Peace Pipe" Award, a proclamation of "David Lester Day" by the Governor of Oklahoma, recognition by the California State Assembly for contributions to Indian-State relations, the United Indian Development Association's Jay Silverheels

Achievement Award, the White Buffalo Council of American Indians' National-Level Award for Outstanding Service to American Indians; created a self-supporting management institute which trained 2,000 Indian businessmen and women; presented a wide variety of Indian and Native American issues before conferences, coventions, and other meetings and on radio and television. *Interests:* Indian affairs; pow-wows; Indian cultures; "Indian economic progress is my vocational goal."

LESTER, JOAN 1937-
(museum curator)

Born July 4, 1937, New York, N.Y. *Education:* Brown University, B.A. (Art History), 1959; Sorbonne, Paris, France (Certificate of Studies, 1958; University of California, Los Angeles, M.A. (Primitive Art/American Indian Art), 1963. *Principal occupation:* Museum curator. *Home address:* 2 Muster Ct., Lexington, Mass. 02173. *Affiliations:* Museum assistant, 1963-1970, museum coordinator-Native American Advisory Board, 1973-, developer/curator, American Indian Collections and Programs, 1976-, associate curator, 1975-1978, curator of collections, 1978-, Boston Children's Museum, Mass.; coordinator of North American Indian resources and workshop (courses and workshops presenting Indian people in southern New England), co-developer of American Indian people in Greater Boston area, 1971-1974. *Other professional posts:* Chair, National Curator's Committee, 1982-member-at-large, Council for Museum Anthropology, 1983-; principal investigator, American Indian Games, National Endowment for the Humanities Planning Grant, 1983-. *Community activities:* Member, advisory boards: Phoenix School, Cambridge, Mass.; MIT Museum; Native American Studies Department of Plimoth Plantation, Mass.; Tomaquag Indian Memorial Museum, Exeter, R.I. MAP assessor, Museum Assessment Program. *Memberships:* American Association of Museums (curator's committee); International Council of Museums; New England Museum Association; Native American Art Studies Association; Council for Museum Anthropology; Peabody Museum Assocaition (member-at-large). *Awards, honors:* Boston Indian Council Certificate of Merit, 1975; Bay State Historical League Award of Excellence, for "Indians Who Met the Pilgrims," June, 1975. *Interests:* "American Indian art; American Indian arts in New England as they continue today; cooking, bicycling, cross country skiing, theater, classical music, folk dancing, reading." Published works: "The American Indian, A Museum's Eye View," in *Indian Historian, summer, 1972; "Indians Who Met the Pilgrims,"* the Match Program, *American Science and Enginnering, Boston, 1974;* "A Code of Ethics for Curator's," in *Museum News,* Jan./Feb., 1983; chapter I - *The Prodcuction of Fancy Bakets in Maine* (American Indian Archaeological Institute, 1986); *American Indian Art in New England* (Boston Chilren's Museum, 1986); *The Art of Tomah Joseph, Passamaquoddy Artist* (manuscript submitted). Reports: American Indian Art Association, "Tomah Joseph, Passamaquoddy Artist," Sept., 1983; Metropolitan Museum of Art, "The Northeast Native American Program at the Children's Museum," April, 1983; York Institute, Saco, Maine, "Northeast Native American Baskets: A Continuing Tradition," Oct., 1982); Massachusetts Indian Association, "The Significance of the Katherine Hall Newall Collection," Oct., 1982; American Indian Art Association, "They're Still Here, Native American Art in New England," March, 1982; Institute for Contemporary Art, "Native American Ash Splint Basketry in New England," Feb., 1982.

LEVI, JERRY R. (Cheyenne-Arapaho) 1946-
(Indian program administrator)

Born June 27, 1946, Concho, Okla. *Education:* Southeastern Oklahoma State University, B.S., 1971; Oklahoma City University, M.B.A., 1986. *Principal occupation:* Administrator, Potawatomi WIC & Food Distributor Programs. *Home address:* 419 S. Ardalotte, Shawnee, Okla. 74801. *Affiliations:* Chairman, Oklahoma, New Mexico Food Action Committee for Tribes (ON-FACT); member, National Association of WIC Directors. *Military service:* U.S. Army, 1968-1970 (SP5-E-5; Soldier of the Month, Feb., 1970; selected for All-Army

Trials). *Community activites:* Tribal chairman, Cheyenne-Arapaho Tribes, 1981; Concho School Board (chairman, 1981); El Reno Title IV Committee vice chairman, 1980-1981; El Reno YMCA wrestling coach; Yukon Jays football coach.

LEVIER, FRANCES ANDREW
(Citizen Band Potawatomi) 1950-
(tribal administrator, business committeeman)

Born November 13, 1950, Topeka, Kan. *Education:* Hofstra University, B.A. (Social Science and Secondary Education), 1973; University of Kansas, M.S.Ed. (Ecdutional Administration), 1975, Ed.D. (Administration and Higher Education), 1979. *Principal occupation:* Tribal administrator and business committeeman. *Home address:* 13 Lorie Lane, Shawnee, Okla. 74801. *Affiliations:* Acting director, Supportive Educational Services, 1975-1976, instructor, School of Social Welfare, 1977-1979, assistant director of Minority Affairs, 1974-1980, University of Kansas, Lawrence, Kan.; director, Health Programs, Prairie Band Potawatomi Tribe, 1980-1981; acting executive director, Prairie Band Potawatomi Tribe of Kansas, 1980-1981; executive director, Region VI Indian Alcoholism Training Program, 1982-1983; executive director, A proposal, Evaluation, Research, and Training consulting firm (P.E.R.T., Inc.), 1982-; director of economic development, Citizen Band Potawatomi Tribe, 1983-1985; tribal administrator and business committeeman, Citizen Band Potawatomi Tribe, Shawnee, Okla., 1983-. *Other professional post:* Member of the Board of Regents, Haskell Indian Junior College, Lawrence, Kan., 1979-1983; consultant, Rockefeller Foundation, 1979; consultant, instructor, Leavenworth Federal Penitentiary, Kan., 1978-1980; consultant, Kickapoo Tribe of Kansas, 1978; consultant, Powhatten School District, Kan., 1978; assistant director, Topeka Indian Center, Kan., 1977-1978. *Community activities:* Affirmative Action, University of Kansas (board member, 1976-1980); United Indian Recovery Association (board member, 1980-1981); Emergency Services Council, City of Lawrence, Kan. (chairman, 1977-1980). *Awards, honors:* Recipient of Ford Foundation Fellowship for American Indians, 1973-1976; "Elected to five-member Business Committee (governing body) of the Citizen Band Potawatomi Tribe in June, 1985. Was first business committee member ever named to the position of tribal administrator in the history of the 12,000 member tribe." *Published works:* "A Brief History of the Pedigree Papers," 1983; editor, "Using Indian Culture to Develop Alcohol & Drug Materials for Indian Adults and Youth," 1983; "Overview of Inhalent Abuse Among American Indian Youth," 1981; "An Attitude Survey of Urban Indians in N.E. Kansas Toward Higher Education," 1979; all published by the American Indian Institute, University of Oklahoma, 1983. "The Need for Indian Student Organizations in Large Institutions of Higher Edcuation," N.E.C.C.A. Conference Article, K.C., Mo., 1979.

LEWIS, DAVE
(director-Indian association)

Affiliation: Director, Indian Arts and Crafts Association, 4215 Lead SE, Albuquerque, N.M. 87108.

LEWIS, ROBERT E. (Zuni) 1914-
(former tribal official)

Born August 24, 1914, Zuni, N.M. *Education:* High school; U.S. Navy Torpedo School. *Principal occupation:* Former tribal official. *Home address:* Zuni, N.M. 87327. *Affiliation:* Governor, Pueblo of Zuni, N.M (elected Jan., 1965). *Military service:* U.S. Navy, 1942-1945 (Torpedoman; Pacific Theatre Award; Presidential Award. *Community activities:* All-Pueblo Indian Council; New Mexico Governor's Committee of 100 on Economic Development, State Constitutional Convention; Lions Club; American Legion; Committee on Indian Awareness; Dir Rama, Inc. (board of directors). *Awards, honors:* Outstanding Citizen of McKinley County, 1970; Conservation Award, New Mexico Bankers Association; Indian Leadership Award, B.I.A., U.S. Dept. of the Interior. *Interests:* "Traveling; speaking engagements throughout the U.S. on behalf of the genernal Indian movement." *Published work: Zuni Tales* (University of Utah Press, 1972).

LIBHART, MYLES
(director-Indian Arts
and Crafts Board)

Affiliation: Director, Indian Arts and Crafts Board, U.S. Department of the Interior, 18th & C Sts., N.W., Room 4004, Washington, D.C. 20240.

LIEB, BERTHA K.
(executive director-Indian center)

Affiliation: Executive director, The Indian Center of Lawrence, 2326 Louisiana St., P.O. Box 1016, Lawrence, Kan. 66044.

LINCOLN, DARAN
(tribal president)

Affiliation: President, Covelo Community Council, Round Valley Reservation, P.O. Box 448, Covelo, Calif. 95428.

LINFORD, LAURENCE D.
(executive director—Indian association)

Affiliation: Executive director, Inter-Tribal Indian Ceremonial Association, P.O. Box 1, Church Rock, N.M. 87311.

LINK, MARTIN ANDREW 1934-
(former museum director)

Born September 26, 1934, Madison, Wis. *Education:* University of Arizona, B.A., 1957. *Principal occupation:* Former director, Navajo Tribal Museum, Window Rock, Ariz. *Affiliation:* Treasurer, Gallup Museum of Arts and Crafts. *Military service:* U.S. Army Reserve, 1961. *Community activities:* Inter-Tribal Indian Ceremonial Association (board of directors, 1971-); Navajo Centennial Commission (chairman, 1968); Annual Navajo Science Fair (chairman); Knights of Columbus; Lions Club; Gallup Archaeological Society; Plateau Sciences Society (board of directors, 1965-). *Memberships:* Arizona Academy of Sciences; American Association of Museums; New Mexico Association of Museums; Western Museums League; New Mexico Archaeological Society (board of regents, 1971-). *Award:* Annual Award for improvement of the environment from Keep New Mexico Beautiful, Inc., 1970. *Interests:* Photography; western exploration. *Published works: Navajo—A Century of Progress* (KC Publications, 1968); *Navajo Treaty Negotiations of 1868* (KC Publications, 1968); *The Second Long Walk* (St. Michaels Press, 1968); *A Guide to the Navajo Museum* (Navajo Printing Dept., 1971).

LITTLE, HARLEY
(B.I.A. agency superintendent)

Affiliation: Superintendent, Okmulgee Agency, Bureau of Indian Affairs, P.O. Box 370, Okmulgee, Okla. 74447.

LITTLE, STEWART
(B.I.A. executive assistant)

Affiliation: Executive assistant, Bureau of Indian Affairs, 1951 Constitution Ave., N.W., Washington, D.C. 20245.

LITTLE, VINCENT
(B.I.A. area director)

Affiliation: Director, Albuquerque Area Office, Bureau of Indian Affairs, P.O. Box 8327, 5301 Central East, Albuquerque, N.M. 87198.

LITTLE AXE, DANNY (Absentee-Shawnee)
(tribal chairman)

Affiliation: Chairman, Absentee-Shawnee Executive Committee, P.O. Box 1747, Shawnee, Okla. 74801.

LITTLECHIEF, BARTHELL (Kiowa-Comanche) 1941-
(artist-sculptor/painter)

Born October 14, 1941, Kiowa Indian Hospital, Lawton, Okla. *Education:* Cameron University, Lawton, Okla., 1964-1965; University of Oklahoma, Norman, 1966-1967. *Principal occupation:* Artist-sculptor/ painter. *Home address:* Route 3, Box 109A, Anadarko, Okla. 73005. *Military service:* U.S. Army National Guard, 1966-1971

(SP/4). *Memberships:* Kiowa TIA-PAIH Society of Oklahoma; Native American Church. *Biographical sources: Who's Who in North American Indian Art; Who's Who in American Art; American Artists; Kiowa Voices;* articles in *Southern Living* magazine, and *Texhoma Monthly* magazine.

LITTLECOOK, OLIVER (Ponca)
(tribal chairman)

Affiliation: Chairman, Ponca Business Committee, P.O. Box 2, White Eagle, Ponca City, Okla. 74601.

LIVERMORE, EARL R. (Blackfeet)
1932-
(artist)

Born November 29, 1932, Browning, Mt. *Education:* Haskell Institute; University of Washington; Burnley Professional School of Art, Seattle, Wash.; Academy of Art, San Francisco, Calif. *Principal occupation:* Artist. *Home address:* 2149 Otis Dr., Apt. 236, Alameda, Calif. 94501. *Affiliations:* Mechanic, Boeing Airplane Co., Seattle, Wash., 1957-1959; operating engineer, Group Health Hospital, Seattle, 1959-1960; treating engineer, J.H. Baxter Co., Kenydale, Wash., 1960-1964; stationary engineer, Children's Hospital, San Francisco, Calif., 1964-1968; director, American Indian Center, San Francisco, 1968-1970; Indian desk director-consultant for American Indian Community Action Programs, Scientific Analysis Corp., San Francisco, 1970; director, Bay Area Alcoholism Program, Oakland, Calif., 1970-1972; consultant, National Institute on Alcohol Abuse and Alcoholism (National Indian Review Panel), Rockville, Md., 1973-1975; director, Native American Alcohoism and Drug Abuse Program/ Indian Womens Alcoholism Crisis Center, Oakland, Calif., 1972-? *Military service:* U.S. Coast Guard, 1952-1956. *Community activities:* Lone Mountain College, San Francisco (board member, 1973-1974); Human Rights Commission of the City and County of San Francisco (commissioner, 1968-1975; Native American Advisory Committee to the San Francisco Human Rights Commission (chairman); Youth and Education Committee of the Human Rights

Commission; State Acoholism Advisory Board, 1974-1977); National Indian Alcoholism Board, 1975-1977; San Francisco American Indian Center (president, 1970); California League for American Indians (board member, 1973). *Memberships:* American Indian Historical Society (board member); National Association of Blackfeet Indians, Seattle, Wash. *Exhibitions:* University of California, Berkeley; Philbrook Art Center, Tulsa, Okla.; Heard Museum, Phoenix, Ariz.; Scottsdale National Indian Arts Exhibition; Indian Festival of Arts, LaGrande, Ore.; American Indian Historical Society (one-man show), San Francisco; Oakland Museum; palace of Fine Arts, San Francisco; two paintings in the permanent collection of the Plains Indian Museum, Browning, Mont.; among others. *Interests:* Fine arts; sports.

LOCKLEAR, JUANITA O.
(director-Indian center)

Affiliation: Director, Native American Resource Center, Pembroke State University, Pembroke, N.C. 28372.

LOFTON, GENE TRAVIS (Chickasaw-Choctaw-Creek) 1934-
(museum curator)

Born March 8, 1934, Healdton, Okla. *Education:* Oklahoma A & M (three years). *Principal occuaption:* Curator, Tucker Tower Museum, Lake Murray, Okla., 1971-. *Home address:* P.O. Box 1649, Ardmore, Okla. 73401.

LOLOMA, CHARLES (Hopi) 1921-
(jeweler)

Born 1921, Hotevilla, Ariz. *Education:* School for American Craftsmen, S.U.N.Y. at Albany, Journeyman's Certificate. *Principal occupation:* Jeweler. *Memberships:* Arizona Commission on the Arts and Humanities (member); American Crafts Council (Fellow); Wheelwright Museum (board member); Native American Center for the Living Arts, Inc. (board member). *Interests:* "(I am) extremely active in Hopi ceremonies, ways of life, and farming;"

travel. *Biographical sources:* Numerous articles in *Arizona Highways, New Mexico Magazine,* and *American Indian Art.* PBS special film, *Loloma.*

LOMAHAFTEWA, LINDA (Hopi) 1947-
(teacher, artist)

Born July 3, 1947, Phoenix, Ariz. *Education:* San Francisco Art Institute, BFA, 1970, MFA, 1971. *Principal occupation:* Teacher, artist. *Home address:* Route 11, Box 20 SP 59, Santa Fe, N.M. 87501. *Affiliation:* Assistant professor of Native American Art, California State College, Rohnert Park, Calif., 1971-1973; teacher, painting and drawing, Native American Studies, University of California, Berkeley, 1974-1976; drawing and painting instructor, Institute of American Indian Arts, Santa Fe, N.M.. 1976-. *Exhibitions:* "Festival of Native American Art," Aspen Institute at Baca, 1982; "Contemporary Native American Art," Gardiner Art Gallery, Oklahoma State University, Stillwater, Okla., 1983; "Contemporary Native American Photography," Southern Plains Indian Museum, Anadarko, Okla., 1984; "Shadows Caught Images of Native Americans," Gilcrease Museum, Tulsa, Okla., 1984; "2nd Annual Heard Invitational," Heard Museum, Phoenix, Ariz., 1985; "One Woman Exhibit," American Indian Contemporary Arts, San Francisco, Calif., 1985; "Women of Sweetgrass, Cedar and Sage," Gallery of the American Indian Community House, New York, N.Y., 1985; "The Art of the Native American," Owensboro Museum of Fine Arts, Ky., 1985; "Native to Native," Alchemie Gallery, Boston, Mass., 1986. *Community activities:* City of Santa Fe Arts Board. *Memberships:* San Francisco Art Institute Alumni Association; Institute of American Indian Arts Alumni Association. *Awards, honors:* Indian Festival of Arts - First Place Painting, La Grande, Oreg., 1974; 61st Annual Indian Market - Third Place Painting, Santa Fe, N.M., 1982. *Interests:* Art—displayed at the following permanent collections: Southern Plains Indian Museum, Anadarko, Okla.; Millicent Rogers Museum, Taos, N.M.; University of Lethbridge, Native American Studies Department, Alberta, Canada; Native

American Center for the Living Arts, Inc., Niagara Falls, N.Y.; American Indian Historical Society, San Francisco, Calif.; Center for the Arts of Indian America, Washington, D.C. *Biographical sources: Who's Who in American Art,* 1976; *The Sweet Grass Lives on 50 Contemporary Native American Indian Artists,* by Jamake Highwater (Lippincott, 1980); *American Women Artists,* by Charlotte Streifer Rubinstein (Avon, 1982); *The World Who's Who of Women,* Eighth Edition, 1984; *Bearing Witness Sobreviviendo,* An Anthology of Writing and Art by Native American-/Latina Women (*Calyx:* A Journal of Art and Literature by Women, Corvallis, Ore., 1984); *The American West, The Modern Vision,* by Patricia Janis Broder (Little, Brown, 1984).

LONEFIGHT, EDWARD (Mandan-Hidatsa) 1939-
(B.I.A. Indian education)

Born May 28, 1939, Elbowoods, N.D. *Education:* Dickinson State College, N.D., B.S., 1964; Arizona State University, M.A., 1970. *Principal occupation:* B.I.A. Indian education. *Address:* Bureau of Indian Affairs, Roomm 4871, 1951 Constitution Ave., N.W., Washington, D.C. 20245. *Affiliation:* Superintendent, Riverside Indian School, Anadarko, Okla.; Indian education, B.I.A., Washington, D.C. *Community activities:* Jaycees; Kiwanis Club. *Membership:* National Education Association.

LOOKOUT, CHARLES E. (Osage-Delaware) 1922-
(reference/periodicals librarian)

Born December 29, 1922, Pawhuska, Okla. *Education:* Oklahoma State University, B.A., 1952; University of Oklahoma, Master of Library Science, 1968. *Principal occupation:* Reference/periodical librarian, Tulsa City-County Library System, Tulsa, Okla., 1964-. *Military service:* U.S. Navy, 1942-1946 (Machinist mate 3/C; served aboard aircraft carrier U.S.S. Saratoga; received Asiatic-Pacific American Theatre, Victory Medal, Good Conduct Medal, and six Battle Stars). *Community activities:* V.F.W.: American Legion; Osage War Dance Com-

mittee, Pawhuska, Okla. (member). *Memberships:* American Library Association; Oklahoma Library Association (recruitment committee-two years); Tulsa Library Staff Association (membership chairman-two years); O.U. and O.S.U. Alumni Associations. *Awards, honors:* National Poppy Director Award, 1962, by V.F.W. National Convention, Minneapolis, Minn.; Third Place, Strait War Dancing Contest, 1976, by Kihekah Steh Indian Club. *Interests:* Indian war dancing; theater; travel. "I have initiated a program to list the entire holdings of Tulsa City-County Library System on North American Indians in computer print-out."

LOUDNER, GODFREY, Jr. (Crow Creek Sioux) 1946-
(mathematics instructor)

Born September 30, 1946, Fort Thompson, S.D. *Education:* Black Hills State College, B.S.; South Dakota School of Mines and Technology, M.S.; University of Notre Dame, Ph.D. (Mathematics), 1974. *Principal occupation:* Mathematics instructor, Sinte Gleska College, Rosebud, S.D. *Home address:* Box 432, Mission, S.D. 57555. *Memberships:* American Mathematics Society. *Interests:* Professional: lie groups, differential geometry, harmonic analysis; mountain climbing, cave exploration. "Working on monograph about "Automonophic Forms With Applications."

LOUNSBERRY, GARY RICHARD 1944-
(social worker)

Born May 22, 1944, Wellsville, N.Y. *Education:* University of Rochester, N.Y., A.B., 1966; University of Michigan, M.S.W., 1968; University of Pittsburgh, M.P.H., 1981, Ph.D., 1985. *Principal occupation:* Social worker. *Home address:* R.R. 6, Box 281, Lawrence, Kan. 66046. *Affiliation:* Commissioned officer in the Commissioned Corps of the U.S. Public Health Service, Indian Health Service, 1970-; clinical social worker and service unit director, Sisseton Service Unit, Indian Health Service, Sisseton, S,D., 1970-1974; mental health consultant, Claremore Service Unit, Indian Health Service, Claremore, Okla., 1974-

1979; human service consultant, Haskell Health Center, Lawrence, Kan., 1981-. *Other professional posts:* Guest lecturer at Claremore Junior College (now Rogers State College), 1974-1979; Adjunct faculty, Haskell Indian Junior College, Lawrence, Kan., 1981-; adjunct faculty—field instruction, School of Social Welfare, University of Kansas, Lawrence, 1984-. *Community activities:* Trinity Episcopal Church — various offices and committees in South Dakota, Oklahoma, and Kansas; Douglas County Children's Advisory Committee. *Memberships:* Academy of Certified Social Workers, National Association of Social Workers, 1968-; Public Health Association; American Orthopsychiatric Association; Biofeedback Society of America. *Awards, honors:* U.S. Public Health Service, Career Development Training Award, 1979-1981, Isolated Hardship Service Ribbon, 1984; Employee of the Quarter, Haskell Health Center, 1984; George Abbott Scholarship, New York State Regent's Scholarship; Golden R Award (Rochester); National Merit Scholarship Finalist; Bausch and Lomb Science Award (Scio). *Interests:* "Vocational interests: Cross-cultural mental health and social services; family therapy with alcoholic families; computer applications to human services; human services in rural areas; human sexuality; psychosocial aspects of chronic illness. Avocational: Native American arts and crafts; Indian history during the colonial period; genealogy; regional American food, gardining, traveling, sailing, fishing." "Introduction of Biofeedback Training Into an IHS Mental Health Program," 1977, and "Social Networks and Utilization of Health Services by Urban Indians," 1982 (*Proceedings of the U.S.P.H.S. Professional Association,* April 1977); *Contemporary American Indians and Access to Health Services: Urban and Reservation Differences in Use of Social Networks to Access Health Services* (Dissertation, University Microfilms, 1985).

LOVE, TIMOTHY (Penobscot)
(tribal governor)

Affiliation: Governor, Penobscot Tribe, Six River Rd., Indian Island, Old Town, Maine 04468.

LOVELY, DEBORAH
(executive director, Indian center)

Affiliation: Executive director, United American Indian Education Center, 2100 28th St., Sacramento, Calif. 95818.

LOWRY, IRENE
(executive director-Indian association)

Affiliation: Executive director, North American Indian Association, 360 John R, Detroit, Mich. 48226.

LUCAS, MERLE R. (Sioux) 1944-
(administrator)

Born June 9, 1944, Vanport City, Ore. *Education:* Northern Montana College, Havre, 1963-1964. *Principal occupation:* Administrator. *Home address:* 3305 5th Ave. South, Billings, Mont. 59101. *Affiliations:* Director, Native American Studies, Carroll College, Helena, Mt. (one year); associate professor, Native American Studies, Blackfeet Community College, Browning, Mt. (two years); coordinator of Indian affairs, State of Montana, State Capitol, Helena, Mt. (nine years); associate planner, Department of Planning and Economic Development, State of Montana (three years); executive director, Montana Inter-Tribal Policy Board, 1983-. *Military service:* U.S. Army Airborne, 1965-1968 (E-5; Bronze Star; Army Commendation Medal with one Oak Leaf; Purple Heart; National Defense Service Medal; Vietnam Service Medal with 3 Bronz Service Stars; Republic of Vietnam Campaign Medal). *Community activities:* Helena Indian Center, Mont. (president, three years); Montana United Indian Association, Helena, Mt. (treasurer, two years). *Memberships:* Governors Inter-State Indian Council, 1973-1982; Montana Indian Edcuation Association, 1980-; Montana Indian Education Advisory Board, 1985-. *Awards, honors:* Outstanding Vietnam Era Veteran (1977) of the Nation for outstanding contributions shown to the community, state, and nation since returning to civilian life, No Greater Love Organization, Washington, D.C. *Biographical sources: Western Business Magazine* article concerning economic development for Montana reservations; periodic news articles concerning Indian issues relating to Native Americans in Montana. *Published works: Profile of Montana Native American* (State of Montana, 1974); "Annual Report of the Governors' Interstate Indian Council Conference," 1979.

LUCERO, ALVINO (Isleta Pueblo) (tribal governor)

Affiliation: Governor, Isleta Pueblo, P.O. Box 317, Isleta, N.M. 87022.

LUCERO, RICHARD, Jr. (Mescalero Apache-Seminole) 1944- (administrator)

Born September 24, 1944, Billings, Mt. *Education:* University of Wyoming, Laramie, 1964-1966; Eastern Montana College, Billings, 1966-1967; Rocky Mountain College, Billings, Mont., B.A. (Psychology), 1968. *Principal occupation:* Administrator. *Home address:* 3733 Magnolia, Grand Prairie, Tex. 75051. *Affiliations:* Psychology technician, Veterans Administration, Psychiatric Hospital, Sheridan, Wyo., 1971-1972; director, Alcoholism Treatment and Recovery Program, San Acadio, Colo., 1972-1974; director, Alcoholism Family Services Division, Weld Mental Health Center, Inc., Greeley, Colo., 1974-1977; director, Drug Abuse Services Project, Mental Health Center of Boulder County, Inc., Boulder, Colo., 1977-1978; associate professor, University of Northern Colorado, 1977-1978; director, Montana United Indian Association, Health Department, Helena, Mt., 1978-1980; executive director, Dallas Inter-Tribal Center, Tex., 1980-. *Other professional posts:* President, board of directors, American Indian Health Care Association, 1984-; certified management consultant with Performax Systems International, Inc., 1983-. *Community activities:* Colorado Alcohol and Drug Treatment Committee (member, 1976-1978); Indian Health Planners Task Force, (advisory committee, 1978-1979; chairman, 1979-1980; compiled, edited and wrote the National Urban Specific Health Plan submitted to the Secretary of Health and Human Services); Youth Advisory Committee, Fort McKenzie Veterans Administration Psychiatric Hospital (chairman, 1970-1972). *Memberships:* Colorado Association of Professional Alcoholism Counselors, Inc. (member of committee that developed state certification standards); American Indian Health Care Association (chairman, Region VII, Health Directors Board, 1982-1984; treasurer, 1983-1984; president, 1984-); Awards, honors: Recipient of Superior Performance Award, 1970, Public Relations Award, 1972, Fort McKenzie V.A. Psychiatric Hospital, Sheridan, Wyo.; guest speaker, National Council on Alcoholism Annual Conference, 1974; appointed by President Gerald Ford to serve on National Drug Abuse and Adolescents Task Force, 1977; developed special proposal to provide therapeutic community treatment center for Eastern Colorado. *Interests:* Music, tennis, coaching baseball, basketball.

LUMSDEN, JOSEPH K. (Chippewa) 1934- (educational administration, tribal chairman)

Born October 10, 1934, Sault Ste. Marie, Mich. *Education:* Michigan Technological University, B.S., 1967; Northern Michigan University, Teaching Certificate, 1969. *Principal occupation:* Educational administration, tribal chairman. *Home address:* 1101 Johnston St., Sault Ste. Marie, Mich. 49783. *Affiliation:* Tribal chairman, Sault Ste Marie Tribe of Chippewa Indians, 1973-. *Military service:* U.S. Marine Corps, 1953-1956 (Corporal). *Community activities:* Michigan Fishery Advisory Committee (chairman); Chippewa-Ottawa Fishery Management Authority. *Memberships:* National Congress of American Indians; National Tribal Chairman's Association. *Awards, honors:* Recognition of Leadership and Achievement, Bureau of Indian Affairs, 1984.

LUPE, RONNIE (White Mountain Apache (tribal chairman)

Affiliation: Chairman, White Mountain Apache Tribal Council, P.O. Box 700, Whiteriver, Ariz. 85941.

LURIE, NANCY OESTREICH 1924-
(museum curator)

Born January 24, 1924, Milwaukee, Wis. *Education:* University of Wisconsin, Madison, B.A., 1945; University of Chicago, M.A., 1947; Northwestern University, Ph.D., 1952. *Principal occupation:* Curator and head, Anthropology Section, Milwaukee Public Museum. *Home address:* 3342 N. Gordon Place, Milwaukee, Wis. 53212. *Affiliations:* Instructor, anthropology and sociology, University of Wisconsin, Milwaukee, 1947-1949, 1951-1953; research associate, North American ethnology, Peabody Museum, Harvard University, 1954-1956; consultant and expert witness for law firms representing tribal clients before the U.S. Indian Claims Commission, 1954-; lecturer in anthropology, Rackham School of Graduate Studies Extension Service, University of Michigan, 1956-1961; lecturer in anthopology, School of Public Health, University of Michigan, 1959-1961; assistant coordinator, American Indian Chicago Conference, University of Chicago, 1960-1961; associate professor of anthropology, University of Wisconsin, Milwaukee, 1963; Fulbright appointment (lectureship, University of Aarhus, Denmark) involved teaching a course on the American Indian and a course on applied anthropology, 1964-1965; professor, 1965-, department chairman, 1967-1970, adjunct professor, 1973-, Department of Anthropology, University of Wisconsin, Milwaukee; curator and head, Anthropology Section, Milwaukee Public Museum, 800 W. Wells St., Milwaukee, Wis. 53233. *Community activities:* Wisconsin Historic Sites Preservation Board, 1972-1979; Wisconsin Humanities Committee, NEH, 1981-1983. *Memberships:* American Anthropological Association (president, 1983-1985); American Ethnological Society; American Society for Ethnohistory; Wisconsin Archaeological Society; Central States Anthropological Society (president, 1967); Council for Museum Anthropology; American Association of Museums; Sigma Xi; Society for Aplied Anthropology; member of editorial board of Northeast Vol. 15 of *Handbook of North American Indians.* *Awards, honors:* Award of Merit for *Mountain Wolf Woman,* American Society for State and Local History, 1962; Saturday Review Anisfield Wolf Award with co-editor for *The American Indian Today, 1968;* Woman of the Year, Milwaukee Municipal Women's Club, 1975; Honorary Doctorate of Letters, Northland College, Ashland, Wis., 1976; Increase Lapham Medal, Wisconsin Archaeologicl Society, 1977; Merit Award, Northwestern University Alumni Association, 1982; several awards for publications, including *A Special Style,* from Wisconsin State Historical Society, 1985, and from Milwaukee County Historical Society, 1984; with Stuart Levine for *American Indian Today,* from *Saturday Review; Award of Merit, Wisconsin Academy of Sciences, Arts, & Letters, 1984.* *Interests:* "Major field research, Winnebago Indian communities in Wisconsin and Nebraska; Dogrib Indians, Northwest Territories, Canada; researcher and expert witness in six cases before the U.S. Indin Claims Commission; other Indian-related testimony in U.S. Court of Claims and district courts." *Biographical sources:* Who's Who in America; Who's Who of American Women. *Published works:* Editor, *Mountain Wolf Woman, Sister of Crashing Thunder* (University of Michigan Press, 1961); *The Substance Economy of the Dogrib Indians of Lac La Marte, Canadian Northwest Territories,* with June Helm (Northern Research and Coordination Centre, Ottawa, 1961); editor, with Stuary Levine, *The American Indian Today* (Everett/Edwards Press, 1968; Penguin, 1970); editor, with Eleanor B. Leacock, *The North American Indian in Historical Perspective* (Random House, 1971); *Wisconsin Indians* (State Historical Society of Wisconsin, 1980); *A Special Style: The Milwaukee Public Museum, 1882-1982* (Milwaukee Public Museum, 1982); *North Amerian Indian Lives* (Milwaukee Public Museum, 1985).

LYNN, SHARON
(B.I.A. Indian education)

Affiliation: Indian Education, Bureau of Indian Affairs, 1951 Constitution Ave., N.W., Washington, D.C. 20245.

Mc

McALLESTER, DAVID P.
(Narragansett) 1916-
(professor-retired)

Born August 6, 1916, Everett, Mass. *Education:* Harvard University, B.A., 1938; Columbia University, Ph.D., 1949. *Principal occupation: Professor-retired. Home address:* Star Route 62, Box 40, Monterey, Mass. 01245. *Affiliations:* Professor of anthropology and music, Wesleyan University, Middletown, Conn., 1947-1986 (retired). *Other professional posts:* Visiting professor, Yale University, University of Hawaii; University of Sydney and University of Queensland, Australia; consultant, American Folklife Festival, Smithsonian Institution, Washington, D.C., 1975-1976; one of the founders and secretary-treasurer, editor, and president of Society for Ethnomusicology. *Community activities:* Valley View Hospital (advisory board); a founder of Middletown Friends Meeting and South Berkshire Friends Meeting. *Memberships:* Society for Ethnomusicology (secretary-treasurer, editor, president, 1953-); American Anthropological Association (Fellow), 1949-1976; American Academy of Arts and Sciences, 1968-; Institute of American Indian Arcaheology, Washington, Conn. (trustee, 1976-). *Awards, honors:* Social Science Research Council Grant, 1950; Guggenheim Foundation Fellowship, 1957-1958 (study Navajo religion); National Science Foundation Grants, 1963-1965 (study Nanavjo religion); J.D.R. III Foundation Grant, 1971; National Endowment for the Humanities Grant, 1976; Fulbright Foundation (senior lecturer in Australia), 1978; Tokyo National Research Institute of Cultural Properties (lecture), 1980. *Interests:* "Studies of American Indian ceremonialism, music, folklore, mythology, religious literature. Field work with Navajos, Apaches, Zunis, Passamaquoddies, Penobscots, Comanches, Hopis. Canoeing, hiking, mountain-climbing, camping. Musical performance of Native American songs. *Biographical source:* Autobiographical sketch in a Festschrift due to be published in 1986, edited by Charlotte Frisbie, Department of Anthropology, Southern Illinois University, Edwardsville, Ill. *Published works: Peyote Music* (Viking Fund, 1949); *Enemy Way Music* (Peabody Museum, 1954); *Myth and Prayers of the Great Star Chant* (Wheelwright Museum, 1956); *Indian Music of the Southwest* (Taylor Museum, 1961); *Reader in Ethnomusicology* (Johnson Reprint, 1971); *Navajo Blessigway Singer,* with Charlotte Frisbie (University of Arizona, 1978); *Hogans: Navajo Houses and House Songs,* with Susan McAllester, (Wesleyan University, 1980); other monographs and pamphlets; about sixty articles and other contributions. *Recordings: Music of the American Indian,* 12" LP with pamphlet (Litton Educational Publishing, 1978; *Music of the Pueblos, Apache, and Navajo,* with Don N. Brown, 12" LP with 7-page pamphlet, texts, photographs (Taylor Museum, 1962); *Navajo Creation Chants,* five 10" 78 rpm records, with pamphlet (Peabody Museum, 1952.

McBRIDE, MARY (San Felipe Pueblo) 1948-
(elementary school principal)

Born June 3, 1948, Albuquerque, N.M. *Education:* Eastern New Mexico University, Portales, B.S., 1971; New Mexico Highlands University, Las Vegas, M.A., 1982. *Principal occupation:* Elementary school principal, B.I.A., Isleta Pueblo, N.M., 1984-. *Home address:* P.O. Box 751, Algodones, N.M. 87001. *Other professional post:* Elementary teacher, Isleta Pueblo. *Community activities:* Bernalillo Public School (parent advisory committee); Five Pueblo Indian Education Section; Save the Children Federation Committee; Parent-Teacher Organization, public and B.I.A. schools. *Awards, honors:* Graduate Professional Opportunity Program. *Interests:* "(My) vocational interest is to return to the university to work on a degree in gifted education and to hopefully have my own school addressing the needs and serving the Indian gifted children."

McCABE, EDWARD, Jr.
(B.I.A. agency superintendent)

Affiliation: Superintendent, Shiprock Agency, Bureau of Indian Affairs, Shiprock, N.M. 87420.

McCARTHY, JOAN DOLORES
(Blackfoot) 1935-
(reservation trader-wholesale/retail)

Born January 14, 1935, Easton, Pa. *Education:* Churchman's Business College, Easton, Pa. (one year). *Principal occupation:* Reservation trader. *Home address:* 1500 Eddy St., Merritt Island, Fla. 32952. *Affiliation:* Owner-two shops: Cocoa Village, Fla.—authentic Native American jewelry and crafts; and Merritt Square Mall—unique gifts and art deco/nouveau access. "I'm known as "Sun Dancer" woman who keeps spirits together and bright, and "Bear Clan" bringer of light (lightening the soul or spiritual healing). (I) started business on my own as a single parent with three children to raise—no outside help or child support." *Community activities:* "Counsel Native Americans on their rights, on or off the reservation, the business or schooling open to them, water rights, etc.; give speeches to youth groups, all sorts of organizations; display in libraries, schools, and banks. *Awards, honors:* Art awards in silversmithing, pen and ink, watercolors, copper and enamel work, and sketching. *Interests:* "My desire is to give back the pride to the Native American encouraging them to protect their culture. It may save the world for all! I travel to all the Southwestern reservations; encourage artists in their work, get publicity for them, set up shows, etc. to show their work or talents. Sell to rock stars and movie stars—promote the beauty of their craftmanship—to people that can help the cause. I worked to keep the water on the Apache Reservation at Fort McDowell several years ago. I'm currently involved in trying to help in the Hopi/Navajo problem and the Taos water supply. Also trying to reinstate the rights of Native Americans to sell in Old Town Albuquerque—they're being displaced by greedy whites." *Biographical source:* The Department of Interior *Source Book.*

McCLELLAND, JOHN
(chairman-Indian organization)

Affiliation: Chairman, Native American Coalition of Tulsa, Inc., 1740 West 41st St., Tulsa, Okla. 74107.

McCLOSKEY, RICHARD J.
(Indian health service)

Affiliation: Director, Office of Legislation and Regulations, Indian Health Service, 5600 Fishers Lane, Rockville, Md. 20857.

McCOMBS, SOLOMON (Creek) 1913-
(artist, former vice chief-Creek Nation of Oklahoma)

Born May 17, 1913, Eufaula, Okla. *Education:* Bacone College, 1931-1937; Tulsa University (downtown college), 1943. *Principal occupation:* Artist, former vice-chief, Creek Nation of Oklahoma. *Home address:* 3238 East 3rd St., Tulsa, Okla. 74104. *Affiliation:* Foreign service reserve officer, U.S. Department of State, Washington, D.C., 1966-1973. *Other professional posts:* Board of directors, American Indian National Bank, Washington, D.C., 1973-1975; lifetime member of board of directors, designed bank logo. "Served as a member of th Subcommittee on Indian participation during President Johnson's and President Nixon's Inaugural parades--supervised the construction of four American Indian floats." *Memberships:* National Congress of American Indians, 1965-; Five Civilized Tribes (council member, Inter-Tribal Council; chaplain, 1976-); National Council of the Creek Nation (speaker, 1976-); CWYW Club of Tulsa (lifetime member, 1977-). *Awards, honors:* Five Civilized Tribes Museum Seal, 1955; Waite Phillips Special Indian Artists Award for contributions in Indian Art over a period of five years, Philbrook Art Center, Tulsa, Okla., 1965; Grand Award, Philbrook Art Center, 1965; Grand and Gran Masters Award, 1965, 1970, 1973, 1977; Army Award (commissioned to paint depicting one of the American Indian Congressional Medal of Honor recipients of World War II in battle), Washington, D.C., 1976; First Prize Awards, All American Indian Days, Sheridan, Wyo., and Pawnee Bill Museum, Pawnee, Okla., 1970; Bacone College Distinguished Service Award, 1972; Heritage Award, Five Civilized Tribes Museum, Muskogee, Okla., 1977; Grand Prize of $1,000 at Central Washington State College; among others. *Interests:* Graphics, architectural design; lecturing on American

Indian art; Indian painting (traditional); tours of paintings; exhibits and lectures throughout the Middle East, Africa, India, and Burma, sponsored by the U.S. Department of State, Washington, D.C. *Biographical sources: Indians of Today,* 1960-1970; *Who's Who in the South and Southwest; Register of U.S. Living Artists,* 1968; *Personalities of the South; Dictionary of International Biography; Notable Americans,* 1976-1977. *Published works: McCombs Indian Art Calendar,* 1978; *White Eagle-Green Corn,* 1979.

McCONE, ROBERT CLYDE 1915-
(professor of anthropology)

Born September 30, 1915, Redfield, S.D. *Education:* Wessington Springs College, S.D., B.A., 1946; South Dakota State University, Brookings, M.S., 1956; Michigan State University, Ph.D., 1961. *Principal occupation:* Professor of anthropology. *Home address:* 1901 Snowden Ave., Long Beach, Calif. 90805. *Affiliations:* Professor of anthropology, California State University, Long Beach, Calif., 1961-1986; ordained elder, Dakota District of the Wesleyan Church, Rapid City, S.D., 1952-. *Memberships:* American Anthropological Association (Fellow); Royal Anthropological Institute of Great Britain & Ireland (Fellow); American Scientific Affiliation (Fellow); Phi Kappa Phi. *Interests:* Cultural sources of belief conflict in Christianity; cultural problems of contact of American Indian culture with Christianity. *Biographical sources: International Scholar's Directory; Contemporary Authors. Published works:* "Time and the Dakota's Way of Life," Agricultural Experiment Station, South Dakota State College, 1956; "The Time Concept Perspective and Premise in the Socio-cultural Order of the Dakota Indians," (*Plains Anthropologist,* 1960); "Cultural Factors in Crime Among the Dakota Indian," (*Plains Anthropologist,* 1966); "Death and the Persistance of Basic Personality Structure Among the Lakota," (*Plains Anthropologist,* 1968); *Man and His World* (Creation Science Research Center, 1971); *Culture and Controversy: An Investigation of the Tongues of Pentecost* (Dorrance, 1978).

McCORD, DAVID
(executive director-Indian organization)

Affiliation: Executive director, Confederation of American Indians, P.O. Box 5474, New York, N.Y. 10163.

McDERMOTT, RICHARD S.
(B.I.A. area director)

Affiliation: Director, Palm Springs Area Field Office, Bureau of Indian Affairs, Box 2245, 441 S. Calle Encilia, Palm Springs, Calif. 92262.

McDONALD, ARTHUR LEROY (Sioux) 1934-
(research consultant)

Born December 26, 1934, Martin, S.D. *Education:* University of South Dakota, A.B., 1962, M.A., 1963, Ph.D., 1966. *Principal occupation:* Research consultant. *Home address:* Box 326, Lame Deer, Mt., 59043. *Affiliation:* Owner, Cheyenne Consulting Service. *Other professional posts:* Acting head, Psychology Department, Central College, 1963-1964; head, Psychology Department, Montana State University, 1968-1971. *Military service:* U.S. Marine Corps, 1953-1956 (Sergeant). *Memberships:* Pine Ridge Sioux Tribe; Sigma Xi; American Association for the Advancement of Science; American Quarter Horse Association. *Interests:* "Indian research in mental health, education, alcohol, and evaluation; raising quality American quarter horses. *Published works: Psychology and Contemporary Problems* (Brooks-Cole, 1974) numerous articles in scientific journals.

McDONALD, JOSEPH
(college president)

Affiliation: President, Salish-Kootenai Community College, P.O. Box 278, Pablo, Mt. 59855.

McDONALD, MIKI 1946-
(museum director)

Born December 10, 1946, Orange, Calif. *Education:* University of Washington, B.A.,

1974, M.A., 1976. *Principal occupation:* Museum director. *Home address:* 343 SW Alfred St., Chehalis, Wash. 98532. *Affiliation:* Director, Lewis County Historical Museum, Chehalis, Wash., 1976-. *Membership:* American Association for State and Local History. *Interests:* "My major fields of interest have been with the cultures of the Native American people of the Northwest region. I have a strong background in genealogical research for Native Americans, physical anthropology of the region, and Native American education."

McDONALD, WALTER (Salish-Nez Perce) 1910-
(rancher)

Born February 16, 1910, St. Ignatius (Flathead Indian Reservation), Mt. *Education:* Haskell Institute. *Principal occupation:* Rancher. *Home address:* St. Ignatius, Mt. *Affiliation:* Liaison officer, State of Montana, working with Indian youth and their parole/probation officers. *Other professional post:* Montana Council on Corrections. *Community activities:* Lake County Rural Development Council; Western Montana Cattle Marketing Association. *Memberships:* Confederated Salish-Kootenai Tribal Council, 1941-1965 (chairman, 14 years). *Awards, honors:* Bronze Buffalo Plaque presented by the Confederated Salish-Kootenai Tribal Council. *Interests:* Congressional lobbying to further tribal interests.

McELVAIN, W. LEE 1939-
(attorney)

Born January 6, 1939, Grand Junction, Colo. *Education:* University of Colorado, B.A., 1961; George Washington University Law School, LL.B., 1964. *Principal occupation:* Attorney. *Home address:* 2123 Natahoa Ct., Falls Church, Va. 22043. *Affiliation:* General Counsel, Committee on Interior & Insular Affairs, U.S. House of Representatives, Washington, D.C., 1967-. *Memberships:* Congressional Staff Club; Federal Bar Association; Virginia Bar Association; National Trust for Historic Preservation; American Forestry Association; U.S. Supreme Court.

McGEE, HAROLD FRANKLIN, Jr. 1945-
(professor of anthropology)

Born June 5, 1945, Miami, Fla. *Education:* Florida State University, B.A., 1966, M.A., 1967; Southern Illinois University, Ph.D., 1974. *Principal occupation:* Professor of anthropology. *Home address:* 3608 Leaman St., Halifax, Nova Scotia, Can. B3K 3Z9. *Affiliations:* Associate professor, Department of Anthropology, Saint Mary's University, Halifax, Nova Scotia, Can. *Other professional post:* Consultant to museums and other institutions. *Memberships:* Canadian Ethnology Society; Royal Anthropological Institute of Great Britain and Ireland (Fellow). *Interests:* Mr. McGee writes, "(My) major area of interest and expertise is with contemporary and historic Micmac and Malecite peoples of Atlantic Canada. In addition to standard ethnological concerns as an academic, I am interested in getting the non-native population to understand the reasons for similarity and difference of the native peoples' life ways to their own so that they will encourage governments to allow for greater local autonomy by the native people. Academically, I am particularly interested in native "world view," politics, aesthetics, and reconstruction of aboriginal society and culture," *Published works:* Native Peoples of Atlantic Canada (McClelland and Stewart, 1974); *The Micmac IndiansL The First Migrants in Banked Fires-The Ethnics of Nova Scotia,* edited by D. Campbell (Scribbler's Prss, 1978); journal articles and papers.

McGEE, PATRICIA (Yavapai Apache)
(tribal chairwoman)

Affiliation: Chairwoman, Yavapai-Prescott Board of Directors, P.O. Box 348, Prescott, Ariz. 86301.

McGILBARY, RAY (Creek) 1927-
(educational administrator)

Born January 10, 1927, Haskell, Okla. *Education:* University of Oklahoma, B.S., 1953, M.A., 1957. *Principal occupation:* Educational administrator. *Affiliations:* Principal/teacher, Standing Rock Community School, Crownpoint, N.M.; principal, Thoreau Boarding School, Thoreau, N.M.; principal, Many Farms Jr. High School, Many Frams, Ariz. *Military service:* U.S. Army, 1945-1949 (Sergeant). *Community activities:* Booster Club of Chinle; Chinle Navajo Committee. *Memberships:* Association of School Administrators; Common Cause. *Awards, honors:* Distinguished Service Award, Bacone Junior College, Bacone, Okla.

McGRATH, JAMES A. 1928-
(specialist in intercultural education)

Born September 2, 1928, Tacoma, Wash. *Education:* Central Washington State College, 1946-1948; University of Oregon, B.S., 1950; University of Montana, 1951; University of Washington, 1952; University of New Mexico, M.A., 1952. *Principal occupation:* Specialist in intercultural education. *Home address:* 948 Acequia Madre, Santa Fe, N.M. 87501. *Affiliations:* Teacher-director of arts and crafts, U.S. Dependents Education Group Schools, Europe-Germany, France, Italy, Eritrea, 1955-1962; teacher, assistant art director, director of arts, director of special services, Institute of American Indian Arts, Santa Fe, N.M. 1962-. *Other professional posts:* Exhibiting artist and sculptor, 1948-; specialist in American Indian culture, U.S. State Department, 1966-1968; director of first White House Indian Dance Program, 1965. *Community activities:* Community Arts Council (president); New Mexico Arts Commission (consultant). *Memberships:* International Society for Edcuation Through Art. *Awards, honors:* J.K. Gill Arts Media Fellowship, University of Oregon; First Prize in Sculpture, Bellevue, Wash. Fair; First Prize in Painting, Museum of New Mexico; Honorable Mention in Sculpture and Drawing, Museum of New Mexico. *Interests:* Mr. McGrath writes, "Chicf interest is art and nature—the use of art as an intercultural education tool; Indian art in the Western Hemisphere; cross-cultural education through the arts; all phases of art education, especially those relating to Native American (Indian) arts and crafts;" travel. *Published works: Quilaut: The Art of Getting in Touch With the Spirits* (Center for the Arts of Indian America, 1967); *Powhoge: The Mar-*

tinez Family of San Ildefonso (Center for the Arts of Indian America, 1968); Art and Indian Children (Bureau of Indian Affairs, 1970); *My Music Reaches to the Sky: Native American Musical Instruments* (Vergara, 1972); *Sound, The Flute Voice: Dance With Indian Children* (Vergara, 1972).

McGREEVY, SUSAN BROWN 1934-
(museum director)

Born January 28, 1934, Chicago, Ill. *Education:* Mt. Holyoke College (two years); Roosevelt University, B.A., 1969; Northwestern University, M.A., 1971. *Principal occupation:* Director, The Wheelwright Museum, Santa Fe, N.M., 1977-. *Home address:* 704 Camino Lejo Box 5153, Santa Fe, N.M. 87502. *Other professional posts:* Curator of North American Ethnology, Kansas City Museum, Mo., 1975-1977. *Memberships:* American Anthropological Association; Society for American Archaeology; American Society for Ethnohistory; Society for Applied Anthropology; American Ethnological Society; Council for Museum Anthropology; American Association of Museums. *Interests:* North American ethnology, specifically southern and central Plains and the Southwest; field work with the Navajos. *Published work:* "The Dyer Collection," (*American Indian Art Magazine,* 1978); *Lullabies From the Earth: Cradles of Native North America,* 1980; contributing articles to professional publications.

McKIBBEN, JESSE (Quapaw)
(tribal chairman)

Affiliation: Chairman, Quapaw Tribal Business Committee, P.O. Box 765, Quapaw, Okla. 74363.

McKINNEY, WHITNEY (Shoshone-Paiute)
(tribal chairman)

Affiliation: Chairman, Shoshone-Paiute Business Council, P.O. Box 219, Owyhee, Nev. 89832.

McLEAN, ROBERT ELDON 1930-
(teacher)

Born August 5, 1930, Salt Lake City, Utah. *Education:* University of Utah, B.S., 1960, M.S., 1961. *Principal occupation:* Teacher. *Home address:* 1105 First Ave., Salt Lake City, Utah 84103. *Affiliation: Teacher, physical education specialist, Salt Lake City Board of Education, 1961-. Military service:* U.S. Navy, 1947-1951. *Memberships:* Utah State Archaeological Society, 1964-1965; Inter-Tribal Indian Ceremonial Group, Utah, 1961. *Awards, honors:* Indian Service Award, Inter-Tribal Pow-Wow, Salt Lake City, Utah; Sweepstake Awards for Indian outfits, Utah State Fair; others. *Interests:* Indian culture—dancing, lore, crafts and history; lectured for sociology/anthropology departments of universities throughout the country. *Published works: American Indian Dances,* with John Squires (Ronald Press); *Recreational Program of the Hopi Indians,* thesis (University of Utah).

M

MacDONALD, GEORGE F. 1938-
(archaeologist)

Born July 4, 1938, Galt, Ontario, Can. *Education:* University of Toronto, B.A., 1961; Yale University, Ph.D., 1966. *Principal occupation:* Archaeologist. *Home address:* RR #1, Cantley, Quebec, Can. J0X 1L0. *Affiliations:* Atlantic Provinces Archaeologist, 1964-1966, head-Western Canada Section, 1966-1969, National Museums of Canada; chief, Archaeology Division, 1969-1971; chief, Archaeological Survey of Canada, 1971-1977, senior archaeologist, Office of the Director, 1977-, National Museum of Man. *Other professional post:* Conjunct professor, Department of Anthropology, Trent University, 1974-. *Memberships:* Canadian Archaeological Association (president, 1969-1970); American Association for the Advancement of Science (Fellow); American Anthrological Association (Fellow); Archaeological Institute of America, Ottawa Chapter (vice president, 1976-1977); Society for American Archaeology (first positions, executive committee, 1977-1978); International Quarternary Association

(head, working group for Eastern North America-Commission for the Paleo-Ecology of Early Man, 1976-1977); Council for Canadian Archaeology; International Union of Prehistoric and Protohistoric Sciences. *Awards, honors:* Numerous awards and research grants. *Interests:* Native peoples of North and South America; prehistory, field research, Atlantic and Pacific Coast of Canada, Ontario and Yukon Territories; traditional Native American arts and crafts; Northwest Coast Indian print-making, scultpure, Ojibwa print-making; "assembled and wrote catalogues for numerous exhibitions of contemporary and traditional Native American art that traveled in Europe, North America, Asia, New Zealand;" study travel. *Published works:* Numerous articles, papers, reports, and reviews, 1965-; directed the prodcution of 45 short study 16mm, color films on West Coast art and technology; production of gallery films and study video tapes and public release films such as *To Know the Hurons,* 1977.

MacDONALD, PETER, Sr. (Navajo) 1928-
(former chairman, Navajo Tribal Council)

Born December 16, 1928, Teec Nos Pos, Ariz. *Education:* Bacone Junior College, A.A., 1951; University of Oklahoma, B.S. (Electrical Engineering), 1957; U.C.L.A., graduate studies, 1958-1962. *Home address:* 9 Chee Dodge Dr., Drawer 685, Window Rock, Ariz. 86515. *Affiliations:* Project engineer, member of technical staff, Hughes Aircrafts Co., El Segundo, Calif., 1957-1963; director, Management, Methods & Procedures, 1963-1965; Office of Navajo Economic Opportunity, 1965-1970, The Navajo Tribe, Window Rock, Ariz.; chairman, Navajo Tribal Council, 1970-? *Military service:* U.S. Marine Corps, 1944-1946 (Corporal; member, "Navajo Code Talkers" in the South Pacific). *Community activities:* New Mexico Governor's Economic Development Advisory Group, 1963-1967; New Mexico State Planning Commission, 1963-1967; Navajo Community College, Tsaile, Ariz. (board of regents, 1971-); Antioch School of Law, Washington, D.C. (board of visitors, 1972-); Patagonia Corporation, Tucson, Ariz. (board of directors, 1972-); Navajo Agricultural Products Industry, Farmington, N.M. (board of directors, 1972-); New Mexico Governor's Energy Task Force, Santa Fe, N.M., 1972-; New Mexico Commission, Regional Housing Authority, Santa Fe, N.M., 1973-; Non-Profit Housing/Community Development Corp., Shiprock, N.M., 1972; Arizona State Justice Planning Agency Governing Board, 1975-; Arizona Advisory Committee of U.S. Commission on Civil Rights, Washington, D.C., 1970-1974. Memberships: University of Oklahoa Alumni Association; National Association of Community Development (board of directors, 1968-1970; National Tribal Chairman's Association; American Indian National Bank, Washington, D.C. (board of directors, 1974-). *Awards, honors:* Appointed by President Nixon to the National Center for Voluntary Action, 1970-1974; Presidential Commendation for exceptional services to others, 1970; Citation, Distinguished American, National Institute for Economic Development, 1970; Citation, Distinguished Baconian, Bacone Junior College, Okla., 1971; Arizona Indian of the Year, 1971; Good Citizenship Medal, National Society of Sons of the American Revolution, 1972; Silver Beaver Award, Boy Scouts Of America, Kit Carson Council, 19731 member (appointed by Secretary of Commerce), National Public Advisory Committee on Regional Economic Development, U.S. Department of Comerce, Washington, D.C., 1973-1977; Citation, One of the 200 Rising American Leaders by *Time* Magazine, 1974; inducted into Engineering Hall of Fame, University of Oklahoma, 1975. *Biographical sources: Who's Who in America; Who's Who in the West;* Mr. MacDonald has been written about in magazines and newspapers, such as: *Newsweek; Time; U.S. News & World Report; Signature; People; Washington Post; New York Times; Chicago Times; Los Angeles Times,* etc.

MacLACHLAN, BRUCE B. 1935-
(anthropologist, educator)

Born May 26, 1935, Cambridge, Mass. *Education:* University of Chicago, A.B., 1954, M.A., 1955, Ph.D., 1962. *Principal occupa-*

tion: Anthropologist and educator. *Home address:* 12 Hillcrest, Carbondale, Ill. 62901. *Affiliations:* Associate professor of anthropology, Southern Illinois University, Carbondale, 1964-. *Military service:* U.S. Army Reserve, 1958-? (Major; Army Commendation Medal; Army Reserve Components Achievement Medal). *Memberships:* Royal Anthropological Institute (Fellow); American Anthropological Association (Fellow); American Association for the Advancement of Science (Fellow); American Ethnological Society; Law and Society Association; Reserve Officers Association; Civil Affairs Association. *Interests:* Mr. MacLachlan writes, "Have worked with Indian comunities: Tahltan Indians, British Columbia; Klallam, Washington; Mescalero Apache, New Mexico; Shoshoni and Arapaho, Wind River, Wyo.; with special interest in tribal moral values and tribal law."

MacNABB, ALEXANDER S. (Micmac) 1929-
(government official)

Born August 24, 1929, Bay Shore, N.Y. *Education:* Colgate University, A.B., 1956; Washington and Lee University Law School, J.D., 1959; New York University Law School, postgraduate, 1960-1961. *Principal occupation:* Government official. *Home address:* 10600 Sunlit Rd., P.O. Box 86, Oakton, Va. 22124. *Affiliations:* President, Alexander MacNabb Associates, Bay Shore, N.Y., 1960-1967; president, Town Almanac Publishing Co., Bay Shore, N.Y., 1960-1967; member, President's Committee on Manpower, U.S. Office of Economic Opportunity, 1966-1967, special assistant to director, Community Action Program, 1967-1969; OEO representative to Presidentially established National Program for Voluntary Action, Washington, D.C., 1969-1970; director, Office of Operating Services, U.S. Department of the Interior, B.I.A., Washington, D.C., 1970-1972, director, Office of Engineering, 1972-1973; director, Office of Indian and Territorial Development, U.S. Dept. of the Interior, 1973-1974; deputy director, Office of Feeral Contract Compliance, Empoyment Standards Administration, Dept. of Labor, 1974-1975; director, Indian and Native American Programs, Employment and Training Administration, Washington, D.C., 1975-. *Military service:* U.S. Naval Reserve, 1952-1954. *Memberships:* American Political Science Association; American Academy of Political and Social Sciences; National Congress of American Indian (Micmac Tribe); National Indian Youth Council.

MADSEN, BRIGHAM D. 1914-
(professor emeritus of history)

Born October 21, 1914, Magna, Utah. *Education:* Idaho State University, Certificate, 1934; University of Utah, B.A., 1938; University of California, Berkeley, M.A., 1940, Ph.D., 1948. *Principal occupation:* Professor emeritus of history. *Home address:* 2181 Lincoln Lane, Salt Lake City, Utah 84124. *Affiliation: University of Utah, Salt Lake City, 1965-. Other professional posts:* Dean of Continuing Education, 1965-1966; deputy academic vice president, 1966-1967; administrative V.P., 1967-1971; director of libraries, 1971-1973; chairman of History Department, 1974-1975; professor of history, University of Utah. *Military service:* U.S. Army Infantry, 1943-1946. *Community activities:* Peace Corps, Washington, D.C. (assistant director of training, 1964); Vista Program, Office of Economic Opportunity, Washington, D.C. (first director of training, 1965. *Memberships:* Western History Association; Utah State Historical Society (Fellow); Montana State Historical Society; Western Writers of America; Idaho State Historical Society; Utah Westerners (board member). *Awards, honors:* Distinguished Teaching Award, 1977, University of Utah; Utah Academy, Charles Reed Award, 1983; Westerners Interantional Best Non-Fiction Book for 1980, and 2nd Place - Western Writers of America, Spur Awards, *North to Montana. Interests:* Northern Rocky Mountain region—Utah, Nevada, Wyoming, Idaho and Montana. Major interest in Shsohone-Bannock Tribes of Fort Hall, Idaho, having served as consultant-historical rsearcher for tribes in two claims cases against the U.S. Government. Operated building company for ten years and still hold a Utah contractors license. *Biographical source:* Who's Who of America. Published works: The Bannock of Idaho, 1958; *The Lemhi: Sacajawea's People,* 1979; *The Northern Shoshoni,* 1980; co-author, *North to Montana,* 1980; *Gold Rush Sojourners in Salt Lake City, 1849-1850,* 1983; *The Shoshoni Frontier and the Bear River Massacre,* 1985; *Chief Pocatello: The White Plume,* 1986.

MAHAN, HAROLD D. (½ Cherokee) 1931-
(biologist, museum administrator)

Born June 11, 1931, Ferndale, Mich. *Education:* Wayne State University, B.A., 1954; University of Michigan, M.S., 1957; Michigan State University, Ph.D., 1964. *Principal occupation:* Biologist, museum administrator. *Home address:* 28050 Gates Mill Blvd., Pepper Pike, Ohio 44124. *Affiliations:* Professor, Central Michigan University, Mt. Pleasant, Mich., 1957-1972; director, Central Michigan University Museum, 1969-1972; director, Cleveland Museum of Natural History, 1973-. *Military service:* U.S. Air Force (Special Services, 1950-1953). *Community activities:* Michigan Audubon Society (president); Mid-West Museums Conference (ex-vice president); Ohio Museums Association (president). *Memberships:* Phi Kappa Phi, 1968-; Sigma Xi, 1968-; Animal Behavior Society; Association of Science Museums Directors (president, 1980-); Association of Systematic Collection (vice president, 1980-). *Awards, honors:* Recipient, Louis Agassiz Research Fuertes Award, 1957, Wilson Ornithological Society. *Interests:* Ornithology; wildlife photography; bird distribution research; travel. *Biographical sources: Who's Who in America; Who's Who in the Midwest; Who's Who in Ecology.* Published works: An *Introduction to Ornithology,* co-author (Macmillan, 1975); *The Jack Pine Warbler* (Michigan Audubon Society, 1967-1972).

MAIN, ELMER
(B.I.A. agency superintendent)

Affiliation: Superintendent, Fort Belknap Agency, Bureau of Indian Affairs, P.O. Box 80, Harlem, Mt. 59526.

MALLOTT, BYRON (Tlingit) 1943-
(chief executive officer)

Born April 6, 1943, Yakutat, Alaska. *Education:* Western Washington State College, Bellingham, (completed major in political science-no degree), 1961-1964. *Principal occupation:* Chief executive officer, Sealaska Corporation, Juneau, Alaska. *Home address:* P.O. Box 322, Yakutat, Alaska 99689. *Affiliations:* Mayor, City of Yakutat, 1965; elected to City Council, City of Yakutat, 1968; local government specialist, Office of the Governor, Juneau, 1966-1967; special assistant to U.S. Senator Mike Gravel, Washington, D.C., 1969; executive director, Rural Alaska Community Action Program, Inc., Anchorage, 1970; director, Local Affairs Agency, Office of the Governor, 1971-1972; commissioner, Department of Community and Regional Affairs, State of Alaska, 1972-1974; consultant, Alaska Natives Resources, Inc., 1974-1978; president, Alaska Federation of Natives, Inc., 1977-1978; chairman of the board, Sealaska Corporation, Juneau, 1976-1984; chief executive officer, Sealaska Corporation, Juneau, 1982-. *Other professional post:* Owner Yakutat Bay Adventures (commercial fishing), 1974-; director, Alaska Airlines, 1982-; chairman of the board of trustees, Permanent Fund Corp., Seattle, Wash., 1982; board member, Alaska United Drilling, Inc., 1982- director, Federal Reserve Bank, Seattle Branch, 1982-; board member, United Bank of Alaska, 1984-; board member, Colville Tribal Enterprise Corp., 1985-; board member, The Mediation Institute, 1985-. *Community activities:* Rural Affairs Commission, State of Alaska, 1972-1976; Alaska Native Foundation (vice chairman, 1975-1979); Yak-Tat Kwaan, Inc. (Yakutat Village Corp.) (board of directors, 1974-1978; chairman, 1976-1977); B.M. Behrends Bank (director, 1975-1984); Capital Site Planning Commission, State of Alaska, 1977-1979; Governor's Rapportionment Board, State of Alaska (chairman, 1979-1980); White House Fellowship Selection Commission-Western Region, 1978-1983; Commercial Fisheries & Agricultural Bank, State of Alaska (director, 1979); University of Alaska Foundation (director, 1980-1985). *Awards, honors:* Governor's Award for Service to Alaska, 1982; recipient of the "Alaska Native Citizen of the Year Award" from the Alaska Federation of Natives, 1982; Honorary Doctorate Degree in the Humanities by the University of Alaska, 1984. *Published works:* Several recent articles are "One Day in the Life of a Native Chief Executive," in two parts, *Alaska Native Magazine,* Sept. and Oct., 1985; "Byron's Brew," *Alaska Business Monthly,* Oct., 1985; "Sealaska: Soon to Rival Oil Companies in Power?" an interview with Byron Mallott, *Alaska Industry,* Sept., 1981.

MANKILLER, WILMA P. (Oklahoma Cherokee)
(tribal chief)

Affiliation: Principal Chief, Cherokee Nation of Oklahoma, P.O. Box 948, Tahlequah, Okla. 74465.

MANN, ROBERT C.
(B.I.A. agency superintendent)

Affiliation: Superintendent, Choctaw Agency, Bureau of Indian Affairs, 421 Powell, Philadelphia, Miss. 39350.

MANNERS, ROBERT A. 1913-
(professor emeritus)

Born August 21, 1913, Ne York, N.Y. *Education:* Columbia University, B.S., 1935, M.A., 1939, Ph.D., 1950. *Principal occupation:* Ralph Levits professor emeritus. *Home address:* 134 Sumner St., Newton Centre, Mass. 02159. *Affiliation:* Professor of anthropology, Brandeis University, Waltham, Mass., 1952-1979; Ralph Levitz Professor Emeritus, Brandeis University, 1980-. *Other professional post:* Editor-in-chief, *American Anthropologist,* 1974-1976; president, Northeastern Anthropological Association, 1978. *Military service:* AUS, 1942-1946 (Captain). *Memberships:* American Anthropological Association (Fellow), 1946-; American Ethnological Society; Northeast Anthropological Association. *Awards, honors:* Fellowships and grants. *Interests:* Field work in Caribbean area; ethnohistorical research, North American Indians, 1952-1953; anthropological field work in Kenya, 1957-1959, 1961-1962. *Biographi-*

cal source: Who's Who in America. Published works: Culture Theory (Prentice-Hall, 1972); Ethnohistory of Southern Paiute (Garland, 1974); Ethnohistory of Walapai (Garland, 1974); Ethnohistory of Havasupai (Garland, 1974); Southern Paiute and Chemehuevi, An Ethnohistorical Report (Garland, 1974); An Ethnological Report on the Hualapai Indians of Arizona (Garland, 1975); numerous articles in professional journals.

MANSON, SPERO M. (Pembina Chippewa) 1950-
(mental health researcher)

Born May 2, 1950, Everett, Wash. Education: University of Washington, B.A., 1972; University of Minnesota, M.A., 1975, Ph.D. (Anthropology), 1978. Principal occupation: Mental health researcher. Affiliations: Director, National Center for American Indian and Alaska Native Mental Health Research, Denver, Colo., 1986-; professor, Department of Psychiatry, Univerity of Colorado Health Sciences Center, Denver, Colo., 1986-. Other professional posts: Professor and director, Institute on Aging, School of Urban and Public Affairs, Portland State University, Ore., 1982-1986; associate professor and director, Social Psychiatric Research, Department of Psychiatry, School of Medicine, Oregon Health Sciences University, Portland, 1982-1986; adjunct associate professor of anthropology, Portland State University, 1982-1986. Consultantships: Billings Area Office, Indian Health Service, Mt., 1984-; Northwest Portland Area Indian Health Board, 1985-; Alaska Native Health Board, 1985-. Community activities: National Institute of Mental Health Epidemiology and Services Research Review Committee, 1983-1987; NIDA Advisory Committee on Prevention, 1983-1985; Oregon State Governor's Task Force on Alcohol and Drug Abuse, 1984-1986. Memberships: American Anthropological Association; Gerontological Society of America; Society for Applied Anthropology. Awards, honors: 1984 Oregon State System of Higher Education, Faculty Excellence Award; Fulbright-Hays Scholar; CIC Traveling Scholar; National Science Foundation Scholarship. Interests: Professional: psychiatric epidemiology; diagnostic instru-

ment construction; preventive intervention research. Avocational: Photography, writing, upland game bird hunting; travel. Published works: Co-editor, books in preparation: American Indian Youth: Seventy-five Years of Psychosocial Research (Greenwood Press); Health and Behavior: A Research Agenda for American Indians (Oregon Health Sciences University); editor, Medical Anthropology: Implications for Stress Prevention Across Cultures (National Institute of Mental Health, Government Printing Office). Numerous articles in professional journals.

MARACLE, BRIAN (Cayuga-Mohawk) 1947-
(editor, reporter, writer)

Born March 18, 1947, Six Nations, Ontario, Can. Education: Dartmouth College, B.A., 1969. Principal occupation: Editor, reporter, writer. Home address: 86-1947 Pendrell, Vancouver, British Columbia, Can. Affiliation: Editor, Nesika newspaper, Vancouver, B.C., 1975-. Community activities: British Columbia Native People's Credit Union (charter member, 1972; president, 1974-).

MARCHAND, THELMA (Colville) 1932-
(tribal officer)

Born April 17, 1932, Okanogan County, Wash. Education: Wenatchee Junior College. Principal occupation: Secretary, Colville Business (Tribal) Council. Home address: 320 Columbia St., Omak, Wash. 98841.

MARKEN, JACK W. 1922-
(professor, writer)

Born February 11, 1922, Akron, Ohio. Education: University of Akron, B.A., 1947; Indian University, M.A., 1950, Ph.D., 1953. Principal occupation: Professor of English, South Dakota State University, Brookings, S.D., 1967-. Military service: U.S. Army Air Force, 1946. Community activities: South Dakota Committee on the Humanities (chairman). Memberships: Midwest Modern Language Association (chairman, seminar on the American Indian); National

Indian Education Association; American Association of University Professors. *Awards, honors:* Fulbright lecturer, University of Jordan, 1965-1966; lecturer on the American Indian, U.S.I.S. and Finnish-American Society, Sept., 1970. *Interests:* "Literature of the American Indian (paper on it a CCCC in Ne Orleans, April, 1973; lectured on it at Miami University, Ohio, May, 1973). Interested in Indian stories and photographs; also in English literature, especially William Godwin. Director of two major programs on the American Indian in the summers of 1969 and 1970 funded by the National Endowment for the Humanities." *Biographical sources: Who's Who in American Education; Directory of American Scholars; Personalities of the West and Midwest; Dictionary of International Biography. Published work: Bibliography of Books By and About the American Indian in Print, 1972* (Dakota Press, 1970).

MARKS, PATRICIA ANN 1954-
(lobbyist, consultant)

Born March 2, 1954, Brockport, N.Y. *Education:* S.U.N.Y. at Brockport, B.S. (Political Science), 1976; Georgetown University Law Center (J.D. expected May, 1987). *Principal occupation:* Lobbyist, consultant. *Home address:* 4226 34th St., Mt. Ranier, Md. 20712. *Affiliations:* Personal staff member, U.S. Senator James Abourezk, Washington, D.C., 1975-1976 (during this period, Sen. Abourezk was chairman of the Senate Indian Affairs Subcommittee of the Senate Interior and Insular Affairs Committee); professional staff member, Amerian Indian Policy Review Commission, Washington, D.C., 1976-1977; legislative assistant, U.S. Senate Select Committee on Indian Affairs, Washington, D.C., 1977-1979; vice president and co-founder, Karl A. Funke & Associates, Inc., Washington, D.C., 1979- (a lobbying and consulting firm which represents Indian tribes, national Indian organizations, business and local governments). *Other professional post:* Co-founder and officer, AAA Roofing Co., Inc. *Memberships:* National Congress of American Indians; ABA Student Bar Association. *Awards, honors:* National Indian Health Board Award for Service, 1983. *Interests:*

Indian health; Indian legislative specialist; Indian Child Welfare Act; national Indian budget issues; Indian economic development. *Published work:* American Indian Policy Review Commission "Final Report," U.S. Congress.

MARTIN, JAMES
(B.I.A. Indian education)

Affiliation: Indian Education, Bureau of Indian Affairs, 1951 Constitution Ave., N.W., Washington, D.C. 20245.

MARTIN, JOY
(B.I.A. Indian education)

Affiliation: Indian Education, Bureau of Indian Affairs, 1951 Constitution Ave., N.W., Washington, D.C. 20245.

MARTIN, PETER J. (White Earth Chippewa) 1937-
(federal government administrator-Indian affairs)

Born July 21, 1937, White Earth Indian Reservation, White Earth, Minn. *Education:* North Dakota State School of Science, 2-year drafting/trade course), 1958; University of New Mexico, B.A. (Public Administration), 1967. *Principal occupation:* Federal government administrator-Indian affairs. *Home address:* P.O. Box 363, White Earth, Minn. 56591. *Affiliations:* Administrative manager, Albuquerque Indian School, 1966-1969; administrative director, Institute of American Indian Arts, Santa Fe, N.M., 1969-1970; executive assistant, 1970, chief, 1970-1972, Plant Management Engineering Center, B.I.A., Denver, Colo.; chief, Indian Technical Assistance Center, Denver, Colo., 1972-1977; program specialist, Muskogee Area Office, B.I.A., 1977-1980; owner, Indian consultant business, American Indian Programs, White Earth, Minn., 1980-. *Memberships:* Anishnabe Akeeng (The People's Land); National Congress of American Indians; Minnesota Indian Contactor's Association; Minnesota Democratic Farm Labor Party - National Roster of Buy Indian Contractor's. *Awards, honors: Certificate of Superior Perfor-*

mance, Department of the Interior, Bureau of Indian Affairs (For service in connection with the placement of 220 Job Corps employees, July 1969); Department of the Interior, Bureau of Indian Affairs, 20-year Service Pin, April, 1978. *Interests:* "Interested in and work for betterment of all American Indians; presently engaged as nationwide consultant in American Indian Programs (sole proprietorship enterprise); have visited over 200 Indian reservations and worked with respective tribal councils and program heads; research, writing articles and books, and study of American Indian tribes and involvement with Indian-Federal-State-Municipal programs and relationships."

MARTIN, PHILLIP (Mississippi Choctaw) 1926-
(chief, Mississippi Band of Choctaw Indians)

Born March 13, 1926, Philadelphia, Miss. *Education:* Cherokee High School, Cherokee, N.C., 1945; Meridian Junior College, Meridian, Miss., 1955-1957. *Principal Occupation:* Chief, Mississippi Band of Choctaw Indians. *Address:* Route 7, Box 256, Philadelphia, Miss. 39350. *Affiliations:* Tribal Chairman, Mississippi Band of Choctaw Indians, 1959-1965, 1971-1975; President, National Indian Management Service, Philadelphia, Miss., 1975-; Chief, Mississippi Band of Choctaw Indians, 1979-. *Other Professional Posts:* President, United South and Eastern Tribes, 1968-1969, 1971-1972; President, National Tribal Chairmen's Association, 1981-1983. *Military Service:* U.S. Air Force, 1945-1955. *Community Activities:* Mississippi Band of Choctaw Indians (councilman, 1957-1966, 1971-1975, 1977-1979); Choctaw Housing Authority (chairman of board, 1964-1971); Choctaw Community Action Agency (executive director, 1966-1971); Chata Development Company (president-board of directors, 1969-1975); Haskell Indian Junior College (president-board of regents, and board member, 1970-; Chahta Enterprise, Choctaw Greetings Enterprise, and Choctaw Electronics Enterprise (chairman). *Memberships:* National Tribal Chairmen's Association; National Congress of American Indians; United

South and Eastern Tribes; Americans for Indian Opportunity; American Indian Policy Review Commission (member, Task Force #7); Master's in Public Health for Native Americans Program, University of California at Berkeley (advisory committee); Neshoba County Chamber of Commerce. *Awards, Honors:* Indian Council Fire, Indian Achievement Award; United South and Eastern Tribes Leadership Award, 1984. *Interests:* Indian tribal government development and economic development.

MARTIN, ROBERT (Serrano)
(tribal spokesman)

Affiliation: Spokesman, Morongo General Council, 11581 Potrero Rd., Banning, Calif. 92220.

MASON, K. GOYLE
(executive director-Indian organization)

Affiliation: Executive director, Union of Ontario Indians, 27 Queen St. East, Toronto, Ontario, Can. M5C 2M6.

MASSEY, EDNA H. (Mrs. Fred H.) (Oklahoma Cherokee) 1913-
(artist, designer, teacher)

Born July 11, 1913, Stilwell, Okla. *Education:* Haskell Institute; George Washington University. *Affiliation:* Artist, art teacher, textile designer; interior designer, arts and crafts specialist, Bureau of Indian Affairs, U.S. Dept. of the Interior, Washington, D.C. *Memberships:* Creative Crafts Council, Smithsonian Institution; American Craftsmans Council. *Awards, honors:* First Prize, Textile Design, 1960, Second Prize, 1962, Creative Crafts Biennial.

MATSON, DANIEL SHAW 1908-
(teacher)

Born May 17, 1908, Mediapolis, Iowa. *Education:* University of Arizona, A.B., 1930; San Luis Rey Seminary, San Luis Rey and Santa Barbara, Calif., M.A., 1944. *Principal occupation:* Teacher of Papago language, culture, and linguistics; and German, Univerity of Arizona, 1950-1954, 1969-. *Awards, honors:* Honorary Spanish Fraternity. *Interests:* "Study and analysis of Papago and Pima language—structure, vocabulary, tradition; transcription, translation and analysis of historical documents relating to the history of Mexico and Southwest U.S." *Published works: A Colony on the Move* (School of American Research, 1965); *Friar Brings Reports to the King* (University of Arizona Press, 1977).

MATTE, SARA J. (Gros Ventre-Flathead) 1952-
(personnel officer)

Born March 14, 1952, St. Ignatius, Mt. *Education:* Montana State University, Bozeman, B.S., 1974. *Principal occupation:* Personnel officer, Bureau of Indian Affairs, Washington, D.C., 1984-. *Home address:* 3372 Gunston Rd., Alexandria, Va. 22302. *Other professional post:* Personnel management specialist, Bureau of Reclamation, Sacramento, Calif., 1980-1984.

MATTHEWS, ANN M. 1942-
(museum curator)

Born July 25, 1942, Carmel, Calif. *Education:* Tallahassee State University, B.A., 1971. *Principal occupation:* Curator, Tallahassee Junior Museum, 1970-. *Home address:* Box 474, Havana, Fla. 32333. *Memberships:* American Association of Museums; American Association for State and Local History. *Interests:* 19th century history, architecture, and decorative arts, historic farms and farming; Florida Indians (pre-Columbian); native wildlife. *Published work: Apalachee Indian Farm Guide Book* (Tallahassee Junior Museum, 1976).

MAUDLIN, STANISLAUS IRVIN 1916-
(founder/executive director-American Indian Cultural Research Center)

Born December 16, 1916, Greensburg, Ind.

Education: St. Meinrad College, Ind., B.A., 1936; Collegio di St. Anselmo, Rome, 1939; Institute of Alcoholism, N.D., 1966. *Principal occupation:* Founder and director of American Indian Culture Research Center, Marvin, S.D. 57251. *Professional posts:* Associate pastor, work in adolescent and adult eduction, Liaison with Turtle Mountain Chippewa Tribe, Belcourt, N.D., 1941-1950; superintendent of schools, St. Michael, N.D., 1950-1956; member of Industrial Development Committee, Devils Lake, N.D., 1954-1956; president of five state Tekakwitha Indian Missionar Conference, 1955-1956; fundraising on Fort Totten Indian Reservation; founder and pastor of St. John Indian Mission, Pierre, S.D., 1955-1966; counselor, Pierre Indian School, Belcourt, N.D., 1966-1968; founder and executive director, American Indian Culture Research Center, 1968-. *Community activities:* South Dakota Committee for the Humanities (executive committee, 1972-), *Awards, honors:* Adopted into the Yankton Band of Dakota Tribe, 1941 (*Wambdi Wicasa*); adopted into Fort Totten Band, Dakota Tribe, 1954 (*Tikdisni*); adopted into Crow Creek Band, Dakota Tribe, 1961 (*Nasdad Mani*); adopted into Turtle Mountain Chippewa Tribe, 1966 (*Mahcheekwaneeyash*); Citation from South Dakota Association of Counselors and Student Personnel Service Directors for Outstanding Service to Youth, 1971; Citation from South Dakota Social Welfare Conference for services to the social, cultural and humanitarian development of individuals in our State, 1972. *Service activities:* Invited to Washington, D.C., as advisor to Senator McGovern and the late Senator Humphrey, in first anti-poverty legislation, 1964; wrote first Teacher and Student *Handbook,* Stephen High School, Stephan, S.D., 1964; requested by Governor's Commission on Youth (North Dakota) to write position paper on "Juvenile Delinquincy Among Indian Youth: Causes, Forms, Possible Means of Solution," 1967; lecturer to numerous groups, especially to college and university audiences, as well as state and national Church conferences; director of workshops on Indian culture, religion and education; member of evaluation board for Methodist Fund for Reconciliation (South Dakota region).

MAY, CHERYL (Oklahoma Cherokee)
1949-
(journalist)

Born February 22, 1949, Kansas City, Mo. *Education:* University of Missouri, K.C., B.A. (English), 1974; Kansas State Univerity, Manhattan, M.S. (Journalism), 1985. *Principal occupation:* Journalism. *Home address:* 1301 Overlook Dr., Manhattan, Kan. 66502. *Affiliations:* Communications director, American Maine-Anjou Association, Kansas City, Mo., 1975-1979; deputy managing editor/research editor, University Relations, Kansas State University, Manhattan, Kan., 1979-. *Community activities:* United Way, KSU publicity chair, 1985; Riley County Historical Society volunteer (organized "Celebrate American Indian Heritage"); 4-H project leader. *Memberships:* National Association of Science Writers; Council for Advancement and Support of Education (CASE). *Awards, honors:* Special Merit Award for "Cattle Research in Kansas," Council for Advancement and Support of Education CASE, writer, 1984; scholarship winner, "Communicating University Research," CASE, 1983; selected for listing in *Ohoyo 1000,* 1982, and for the *Resource Directory of Alaskan and Native American Indian Women,* 1980; Award for Merit for "Artificial Insemination of Beef and Dairy Cattle, " slide script, Society for Technical Communication, 1980; Award for Achievement for "Safety in Handling Livestock," slide script, Society for Technical Communication, 1980; Award for Outstanding News Reporting, Carlsbad, Calif. Chamber of Commerce, 1969. *Interests:* "I'm a journalist specializing in science writing. I developed and edit a research magazine, *Perspectives,* which provides a view of all types of research at Kansas State University. I'm also interested in photography and have won several awards for both writing and photography. In my current position I supervise several units in the KSU University Relations office including photo services, public affairs, news, publications, and support staff." *Published works: Cattle Management* (Reston-Prentice-Hall, 1981); *Legacy, Engineering at Kansas State University* (KSU Press, 1983).

MAYOTTA, RAYMOND
(B.I.A. agency superintendent)

Affiliation: Superintendent, Minnesota Agency, Bureau of Indian Affairs, RR #2, FC 200, Cass lake, Minn. 56633.

MEANS, RUSSELL (Oglala Sioux)
(co-founder-American Indian Movement)

Affiliation: Co-founder, American Indian Movement (AIM), 1209 Fourth St., S.E., Minneapolis, Minn. 55414.

MEANS, WARREN W. (Oglala Sioux)
1937-
(organization executive)

Born November 17, 1937, Pine Ridge, S.D. *Education:* University of Montana, B.A., 1971; University of Montana School of Law, 1971-1972. *Principal occupation:* President-owner, Means Development Corporation. *Other profesional post:* Executive director, United Tribes Educational Technical Center, 1972-1976; "liaison between North American Indian Alliance of Butte, Mt. with federal and state agencies involved in the delivery of services to Indian people." *Memberships:* Montana Adult Education Association; National Advisory Council on Vocational Education (Presidential appointee, 1977-1978); South Dakota Indian Contractors Association.

MEANS, WILLIAM A.
(executive director-Indian organization)

Affiliation: Executive director, International Indian Treaty Council, 777 U.N. Plaza, Room 10F, New York, N.Y. 10017.

MECKLENBURG, ROBERT,
(Indian health service)

Affiliation: Chief, Dental Services Branch, Indian Health Service, 5600 Fishers Lane, Rockville, Md. 20857.

MEDFORD, CLAUDE, Jr. (Choctaw)
1941-
(artist)

Born April 14, 1941, Lufkin, Tex. *Education:* University of New Mexico, B.A., 1964; Oklahoma State University, 1969. *Principal occupation: Artist. Home address:* Natchitoches, La. 71457. *Affiliations:* Museum director, Alabama-Coushatta Indian Reservation; manager of the Coushatta Cultural Center, La.; taught classes and workshops at the American Indian Archaeological Institute in Washington, Conn. in 1979, and the Clifton Choctaw Indian Community west of Alexandria, La. in 1981; received a folk arts apprenticeship fellowship from the Louisiana State Arts Council, Division of the Arts, and now teachers basketry to any interested Indian among the five surviving tribes of Louisiana. Mr. Medford is a gifted craftsman and practitioner of Southeast Indian arts, including basketry, pottery, wood working, shell working, metalworking, fingerweaving, beadwork, featherwork, horn and hoofwork, brain tanning of deer hides, leatherworking and gourd work. His baskets are in numerous private collections as well as several public collections, that of the Southern Plains Indian Museum, the Museum of the Red River in Idabel, Okla., Tantaquidgeon Mohegan Museum in Uncasville, Conn. and a traveling exhibit to be circulated by the Smithsonian Institution Traveling Exhibition Service. Since 1972, he has show his work each year at the New Orleans Jazz and Heritage Festival. *Interests:* To perpetuate the arts and culture of the Southeastern Indian tribes. *Published works: numerous articles for various publications.*

MEDICINE BULL, BERTHA (Northern Cheyenne) 1950-
(newspaper editor)

Born June 1, 1950, Crow Agency, Mt. *Education:* University of Montana, 1974-1976. *Principal occupation:* Newspaper editor, 1976-. *Other professional posts:* Artist and photographer, *Award:* Best Write-Up Award, *Wassaja,* San Francisco, Calif. *Interests:* Art; radio/TV.

MEINHOLTZ, ROLLAND R. (Cherokee)
1937-
(drama instructor)

Born August 20, 1937, Oklahoma City, Okla. *Education:* Northwestern University, B.S., 1959; University of Washington, M.A. (Drama), 1964. *Principal occupation:* Drama instructor. *Affiliations:* Teacher, public schools of Washington and California; instructor in drama, Institute of American Indian Arts, Santa Fe, N.M. *Interests:* Acting; direction and adaptation of plays; travels throughout the U.S. in connection with the Festival of Indian Performing Arts, Washington, D.C.

MENARD, NELLIE (STAR BOY)
(Rosebud Sioux) 1910-
(arts and crafts specialist)

Born June 3, 1910, Rosebud, S.D. *Affiliations:* Manager, Rosebud Arts and Crafts, 1937-1942; manager, Northern Plains Arts and Crafts, 1943-1946; arts and crafts specialist, Sioux City Museum and Crafts Center, Rapid City, S.D., 1953-. *Community activities:* Rosebud Reservation delegate to Museum of Modern Art and Museum of the American Indian; attended Indian Arts and Crafts Conference, Central Office, B.I.A., Washington, D.C. *Awards, honors:* Pendleton Robe, for submitted blanket design, Pendleton Mills, 1929; Superior Performance Award, Indian Arts and Crafts Board, U.S. Dept. of the Interior; numerous awards bestowed by the Sioux people. *Interests:* Sioux culture.

MEREDITH, HOWARD L. (Cherokee)
1938-
(historian)

Born May 25, 1938, Galveston, Tex. *Education:* University of Texas, B.S., 1961; S.F. Austin State University, M.A., 1963; University of Oklahoma, Ph.D., 1970. *Principal occupation:* Historian. *Home address:* 623 Lulbertson Dr., Oklahoma City, Okla. 73105. *Affiliations:* Chairman, Cookson Institute, Oklahoma City, Okla., 1974-. *Memberships:* Oklahoma Historical Society (director, 1975-?); Cherokee National Historical Society; Oklahoma Heritage Association; Western Historical Association. *Interests:* "History of American Indian thought; cross cultural education—late maturing youth." *Biographical source: Oklahoma Monthly* (June, 1977). *Published works: The Native American Factor* (Seabury Press, 1973); *Native Response...Rural Oklahoma* (Oklahoma Historical Society, 1977).

MERRELL, JAMES H. 1953-
(professor of history)

Born October 19, 1953, Minneapolis, Minn. *Education:* Lawrence University, Appleton, Wis., B.A., 1975; Oxford University, England, B.A., 1977; Johns Hopkins University, M.A., 1979, Ph.D., 1982. *Home address:* Vassar College, Box 527, Poughkeepsie, N.Y. 12601. *Affiliation:* Assistant professor of history, Vassar College, Poughkeepsie, N.Y., 1984-. *Memberships:* American Historical Association, 1977-; Organization of American Historians, 1977-; American Society for Ethnohistory, 1983-. *Awards, honors:* Rhodes Scholarship; Danforth Fellowship; Predoctoral Fellowship, Newberry Library; Postdoctoral Fellowship, Institute of Early American History and Culture; American History and Life Award, and Robert F. Heizer Award for article, "The Indians New World: The Catawba Experience."

MESSINGER, CARLA J.S. (Lenni Lenape Delaware) 1949-
(founder and president, Lenni Lenape Historical Society)

Born May 20, 1949, Allentown, Pa. *Education:* Kutstown University, Pa., B.S., 1971; Lehigh University, Bethlehem, Pa., M.Ed., 1973. *Principal occupation:* Founder and president, Lenni Lenape Historical Society, Fish Hathcery Rd., Allentown, Pa. 18103. *Home address:* 1819½ Linden St., Allentown, Pa. 18104. *Other professional post:* Former substitute teacher of elementary education and special education (12 years); special consultant on Lenape culture to other organizations, such as Philadelphia school district. *Awards, honors:* 1985 President's Volunteer Action Award, Citation by the House of Representatives, Pa.; Keystone

Award of Merit, Governor's Private Sector Initiatives Task Force for Lenni Lenape Historical Society. *Interests:* Multi-media, cultural programs for all ages given at the Lenni Lenape Historical Society. *Biographical sources: Allentown Neighbors,* "Call/Chronicle, July 8, 1982; *Daily Record,* N.J. You Magazine feature, July 21, 1985; *Easton Express,* Discover-Travel/Leisure, Sept. 15, 1985.

MIKE, LORNA J. (Lower Elwha Klallam) 1955-
(fisheries manager)

Born May 16, 1955, Tacoma, Wash. *Education:* Peninsula College, Port Angeles, Wash. (one year-working on degree). *Principal occupation:* Fisheries manager. *Home address:* 1123 East Columbia St., Port Angeles, Wash. 98362. *Affiliations:* Fisheries manager, Lower Elwha Fisheries, Point No Point Treaty Council, Kingston, Wash., 1985- (fisheries secretary, 1979-1985). *Other professional posts:* Chairman of Tribal Fisheries Committee; vice chairman of the Lower Elwha Tribal Business Committee; board member of the Lower Elwha Indian Child Welfare Consortium.

MILAM, JAMES (Oklahoma Seminole)
(tribal chief)

Affiliation: Chief, Seminole General Council, P.O. Box 745, Wewoka, Okla. 74884.

MILITAIRE, DELBERT
(executive director-Indian organization)

Affiliation: Executive director, National Indian Business Council, 3575 S. Fox, Box 1263, Englewood, Colo. 80150-1263.

MILLER, FRED (Cocopah)
(tribal chairman)

Affiliation: Chairman, Cocopah Tribal Council, P.O. Box Bin G, Somerton, Ariz. 85350.

MILLER, HURON
(president-Indian centre)

Affiliation: President, Native American Centre for the Living Arts, Inc., 25 Rainbow Mall, Niagara Falls, N.Y. 14303.

MILLER, JAY (Delaware) 1947-
(professor of anthropology)

Born April 7, 1947. *Education:* University of New Mexico, B.A., 1969; Rutgers University, Ph.D., 1972. *Principal occupation:* Professor of anthropology, University of Washington, Seattle, Wash. 98195. *Affiliations:* Teaching assistant, lecturer, instructor of anthropology, Rutgers University at Livingston and Newark, 1969-1972; assistant professor of anthropology, Montclair State College. *Other professional posts:* Adjunct curator, North American Ethnology, Washington State Memorial Thomas Burke Museum; executive committee, Indian Studies Program, University of Washington, 1975-; consultant, San Juan County Archaeological Research Project, 1973-; reviewer, National Science Foundation, 1977; contributor, *Smithsonian Handbook of North American Indians.* *Memberships:* American Anthropological Association (Fellow); Society fpr American Archaeology. *Awards, honors:* National Science Foundation Predoctoral Fellowship, 1969; grant-in-aid for research in New Jersey history from the New Jersey Historical Commission, 1973; Summer Salary Award, University of Washington Graduate Research Fund, 1974; research grant from the Alcoholism and Drug Abuse Institute, University of Washington, 1974; "Delaware Indian Music," University of Washington Graduate Research Fund, Interdisciplinary Grant, 1975-1976; "Social Context of Southern Tsimshian," Jacobs Research Fund, Whatcom County Museum, 1977; among others. *Field research:* Archaeology, Anasazi Origins Project (summers, 1966-1967); ethnography, Southwestern Pueblos, 1966-1969; ethnography, Unami Delaware, 1972-; Southern Tsimshian: new language and ethnography at Hartley Bay, 1976 and Kelmtu, 1977, British Columbia; Colville Reservation: conceptual landscape, 1977-. *Dissertation: The Anthropology of Keres Identity* (A Structural Study of the Ethnographic and Archaeological Record of the Keres Pueblos). *Published works:* Numerous papers and articles; books in review and preparation.

MILLER, LEON, Jr. (Mohican)
(tribal chairman)

Affiliation: Chairman, Stockbridge-Munsee Tribal Council, RR 1, Bowler, Wis. 54416.

MILLER, MICHAEL R. (Chippewa-Stockbridge Munsee) 1946-
(director-Native American programs)

Born April 26, 1946, Minneapolis, Minn. *Education:* Appalachian State University, Boone, N.C., B.S. (Business), 1968; University of Minnesota, Duluth, M.S.W., 1984. *Principal occupation:* Director of Native American programs. *Home address:* 113 Emory Dr., River Falls, Wis. 54022. *Affiliations:* Indian education coordinator-supervisor, Title IV-A, Superior Public Schools, Wis., 1974-1981; Native American Outreach Coordinator, Northland College, 1981-1984; director of Native American programs, international student advisor, University of Wisconsin, River Falls, Wis., 1984-. *Memberships:* Wisconsin Indian Education Association, 1985-; National Association for Foreign Student Affairs, 1985-. *Interests:* "My main areas of interest include Indian education, the social aspects of education, improving the image of Native Americans as this image relates to alcoholism, and learning more about international problems and how they relate to the U.S. and Native American experience."

MILLER, ROLAND E. (Stockbridge-Munsee) 1918-
(B.I.A. officer)

Born April 21, 1918, Gresham, Wis. *Education:* Haskell Institute, 1932-1937. *Principal occupation:* B.I.A. officer. *Affiliations:* Various administrative positions with the Bureau of Indian Affairs, 1937-. *Military service:* U.S. Army, 1940-1945, 1950-1952. *Community activities:* Lutheran Church.

MILLER, STEPHEN
(monument superintendent)

Affiliation: Superintendent, Navajo National Monument, Tonalea, Ariz. 86044.

MILLER, THOMAS G.
(school administrator)

Affiliation: Administrator, Hannahville Indian School, Route #1, Wilson, Mich. 49896.

MILLER, VIRGINIA P. 1940-
(professor of anthropology)

Born October 28, 1940, Patterson, N.J. *Education:* Smith College, 1958-1960; University of California, Berkeley, B.A., 1962; University of California, Davis, M.A., 1970, Ph.D., 1973. *Principal occupation:* Assistant professor of anthropology, Dalhousie University, Halifax, Nova Scotia, Can., 1974-. *Memberships:* American Anthropological Association; American Society for Ethnohistory; Canadian Ethnological Society. *Interests:* "Ethnohistory of North America, especially California and Eastern Canada; historical demography." *Published work: Ukomno'm: The Yuki Indians of Northern California* (Ballena Press, 1978).

MILLER, WALLACE W. (Omaha)
(tribal chairman)

Affiliation: Chairman, Omaha Tribal Council, Macy, Neb. 68039.

MILLETT, JERRY (Shoshone)
(tribal chairman)

Affiliation: Chairman, Duckwater Shoshone Tribal Council, P.O. Box 68, Duckwater, Nev. 89314.

MILLIGAN, HARRIET
(museum curator)

Affiliation: Curator, Kaw Indian Mission, 500 N. Kission, Council Grove, Kan. 66846.

MILLS, EARL H. (Mashpee Wampanoag) 1929-
(teacher, tribal officer)

Born March 30, 1929, Mashpee, Mass. *Education:* Arnold College, B.S., 1952; Bridgewater State College, M.A., 1959. *Principal occupation:* Teacher, tribal officer. *Address:* Box 22, Falmouth, Mass. 02541. *Affiliation:* Director of physical education and athletics, Falmouth High School. *Military service:* U.S. Army, 1946-1948. *Community activities:* Old Indian Meeting House Authority, Inc. (president); Mashpee Wampanoag Tribe (tribal executive). *Memberships:* Massachusetts Coaches Association; Athletic Directors Association; Massachusetts Teachers Organization.

MILLS, WALTER R.
(B.I.A. agency superintendent)

Affiliation: Superintendent, Colorado River Agency, Bureau of Indian Affairs, Route 1, Box 9-C, Parker, Ariz. 85344.

MINER, MARCELLA HIGH BEAR
(Cheyenne River Sioux) 1935-
(tribal official)

Born July 31, 1935, Cheyenne Agency, S.D. *Education:* Cheyenne River Boarding School; Aberdeen School of Commerce. *Principal occupation:* Tribal official. *Home address:* Eagle Butte, S.D. 57625. *Affiliations:* Tribal treasurer, 1962-1966, assistant finance officer, 1968-1969, bookkeeper, 1969-, Cheyenne River Sioux Tribal Council. *Community activities:* Cheyenne River Mission, Episcopal Church (treasurer, 1963-1966).

MITCHELL, JIMMY
(contract health services)

Affiliation: Chief, Contract Health Services, Indian Health Services, 5600 Fishers Lane, Rockville, Md. 20857.

MITCHELL, LOUIS (Sac and Fox)
(tribal chairman)

Affiliation: Chairman, Sac and Fox Tribal Council, Route 2, Box 52C, Tama, Iowa 52339.

MITCHELL, WAYNE LEE
(Santee Sioux-Mandan) 1937-
(educator, social worker)

Born March 25, 1937, Rapid City, S.D. *Education:* Bacone College, A.A., 1957; University of Redlands, Calif., B.A., 1959; Arizona State University, M.S.W., 1970, Ed.D., 1979. *Principal occupation:* Educator, social worker. *Home address:* P.O. Box 61, Phoenix, Ariz. 85001. *Affiliations:* Professional social worker, various county, state and federal agencies, 1962-1970; social worker, B.I.A., Phoenix, Ariz., 1970-1977; social worker, 1977-1984, supervisor, 1984-, U.S. Public Health Service, Phoenix, Ariz. *Other professional post:* Assistant professor, Arizona State University. *Military service:* U.S. Coast Guard, 1960-1966. *Community activities:* Phoenix Indian Community School (board of directors); Phoenix Indian Center (board of directors); Phoenix Area Health Advisory Board, 1975; Community Behavioral Mental Health Board, 1976. *Memberships:* National Congress of American Indians; National Association of Social Workers; Association of American Indian Social Workers; American Orthopsychiatric Association; Phi Delta Kappa; Kappa Delta Pi; Chi Sigma Chi. *Awards, honors:* Delegate to White House Conference on Poverty, 1964; nominated, Outstanding Young Men of America, 1977; Phoenix Indian Center Community Service Award, 1977; Temple of Islam Community Service Award, 1980. *Interests:* World traveler—China (twice), Russia, India, Nepal, Thailand, Egypt, Israel, Mexico, Central American countries, Colombia, Peru, Equador, European countries, etc. *Biographical sources:* Who's Who in the West; Who's Who in the World; Men of Achievement. *Published works: A Study of Cultural Identification on the Educational Objectives of Hopi Indian High School Seniors* (master's thesis), (Arizona State University, 1970); *Native American Substance Abuse* (Arizona State University Press, 1983); *American Indian Families: Developmental Strategies and Community Health* (Arizona State University Press, 1983).

MITHUN, MARIANNE 1946-
(linguist, professor of linguistics)

Born April 8, 1946, Bremerton, Wash. *Education:* Pomona College (Calif.), B.A., 1969; Yale University, M.A., M.Phil., Ph.D., 1969-1974. *Principal occupation:* Linguist, professor of linguistics. *Address: Department of Linguistics, University of California, Santa Barbara, Calif. 93106. Affiliations:* Assistant professor of linguistics, S.U.N.Y. at Albany, 1973-1981; professor of linguistics, University of California, Berkeley, 1981-1986; professor of linguistics, University of California, Santa Barbara, Calif., 1986-. *Community activities:* Organizer, Iroquois Conference, 1973-1985. *Memberships:* Society for Linguistic Anthropology (president); American Anthropological Association (executive committee, board of directors, administrative advisory committee); Society for the Study of the Indigenous Languages of the Americas (executive board); *Interests:* "American Indian languages and linguistics, especially Iroquoian (Mohawk, Oneida, Onondaga, Cayuga, Seneca, Tuscarora, Huron), Pomo (Central Pomo), Siouan (Dakota, Lakota, Tutelo), Algonquian (Cree)." *Published works: A Grammar of Tusarora* (Garland Press, 1976); *Kanien'keha'Okara'shon:'a (Mohawk Stories)* and *Iontenwennaweienstahkhwa' (Mohawk Spelling Dictionary)* (New York State Museum *Bulletin, 1976,1977); The Languages of Native America* (University of Texas Press, 1979); *Watewayestanih: A Grammar of Cayuga* (Woodland Indian Culture & Education Centre, 1982); *Extending the Rafters: An Interdisciplinary Approach to the Iroquois* (SUNY Press, 1984).

MODUGNO, REV. THOMAS A.
(director-Indian organization)

Affiliation: Director, Marquette League for Catholic Indian Missions, 1011 First Ave., New York, N.Y. 10022.

MOFFETT, WALTER L. (Nez Perce)
1927-
(pastor)

Born June 23, 1927, Kamiah, Idaho. *Education:* College of Idaho, B.A., 1955. *Principal occupation:* Pastor. *Home address:* P.O. Box 668, Kamiah, Idaho 83536. *Affiliations:* Clerk-stenographer, U.S. Department of the Interior, Standing Rock Reservation, N.D., 1949-1950; intern pastor, Brigham City, Utah, 1955-1958; clerk and sanitarian, U.S. Public Health service, Indian Health Service, Idaho and Washington, 1958-1962; pastor, Kamiah-Kooshia United Presbyterian Churches, Kamiah, Idaho, 1964-; council member, Nez Perce Tribal Executive Committee, 1970-. *Other professional posts:* Guidance counselor, Kamiah Public Schools (two years). *Military service:* 945-1947 (Corporal). *Community activities:* Northwest Regional Eductional Laboratory (past member, board of directors); Small Business Administration (advisory council); State Advisory Council, Title III ESEA, Idaho; Idaho Historic Sites Review Board; Community Relations Council, Cedar Flats Job Corps Center, Kooshia, Idaho (past chairman). *Memberships:* Affiliated Tribes of Northwest Indians (president); National Congress of American Indians (area vice president); National Indian Council on Aging. *Interests:* Politics—1974 Republican candidate for State Senator; held pastorate fourteen years. *Biographical source: Personalities of the West and Midwest,* 1971.

MOFSIE, LOUIS (Hopi-Winnebago)
1936-
(art instructor)

Born May 3, 1936, Brooklyn, N.Y. *Education:* S.U.N.Y. at Buffalo, B.S., 1958; Pratt Institute; Hofstra University, M.S. *Principal occupation:* Art instructor, East Meadow, N.Y. *Community activities:* Thunderbird American Indian Dancers of New York (director); Indian League of the Americas of New York (president, 1961-1963); *Memberships:* New York State Art Teachers Association; Classroom Teachers Association. *Awards, honors:* Association of Southwestern Indians Award for painting submitted to the Annual Indian Artists Exhibition, Santa Fe Art Museum. *Interests:* Art instruction; Indian dance; travel. *Published work: The Hopi Way* (M. Evans & Co., 1970).

MOHAWK, JOHN (Seneca) 1945-
(journalist)

Born August 30, 1945, Buffalo, N.Y. *Education:* Hartwick College, B.A., 1968; State University of New York at Buffalo, Ph.D., 1975. *Principal Occupation:* Journalist. *Home Address:* Route 438, Gowanda, N.Y. 14070. *Affiliations:* Editor, *Akwesasne Notes,* 1976-1983; President, Associated Indigenous Communications, 1985. *Other Professional Post:* Lecturer, State University of New York at Buffalo, American Studies Program. *Community Activities:* Seventh Generation Fund (chairman of board); Indian Law Resource Center (board member). *Published Work: A Basic Call to Consciousness* (Akwesasne Notes, 1978).

MOLLENHOFF, LORI
(president-Indian organization)

Affiliation: President, Migizi Communications, Inc., 2300 Cedar Ave. South, Minneapolis, Minn. 55404.

MOMADAY, AL (Kiowa) 1913-
(artist, educator)

Born July 2, 1913, Mountain View, Okla. *Education:* University of New Mexico; U.C.L.A.: Famous Artists Schools. *Principal occupation:* Artist, educator. *Home address:* Jemez Pueblo, N.M. 87024. *Affiliation:* Principal, Jemez Day School, N.M. *Memberships:* National Congress of American Indians; Artists' Equity Association; National Education Association; New Mexico Indian Arts Committee. *Awards, honors:* Grand Award, Indian Painting, All American Indian Days, Sheridan, Wyo., 1955; Grand Award, Indian Painting, American Indian Exposition; Outstanding Southwestern Indian Artists Award, Dallas Exchange Club, 1956; First Prize, Indian Painting, Philbrook Art Center, Tulsa, Okla., 1956; First Prize, Indian Painting, Scottsdale National Indian Arts Exhibition, 1964; among others.

MOMADAY, NATACHEE SCOTT
(Eastern Cherokee) 1913-
(artist, writer, teacher)

Born February 13, 1913, Fairview, Ky. *Education:* Haskell Institute; Crescent College, B.A., 1933. *Principal occupation:* Artist, teacher, writer. *Home address:* Jemez Pueblo, N.M. 87024. *Affiliations:* Civil service teacher, Albuquerque, Shiprock, Chinle, Navajo Service, Ariz. *Other professional posts:* Personnel director, H.A.A.F., Hobbs, N.M.; former newspaper reporter. *Memberships:* Delta Kappa Gamma; National League of American Pen Women; United Daughters of the Confederacy; Daughters of the American Revolution. *Awards, honors:* Arts and Crafts Fair, Albuquerque, N.M.; Inter-Tribal Indian Ceremonial Association. *Published works:* Woodland Princess, a book of 24 poems (McHughes Co., 1931); co-author, *Velvet Ribbons,* 1942; *Owl in the Cedar Tree* (Ginn & Co., 1965).

MOMADAY, NAVARRE SCOTT
(Kiowa-Cherokee) 1934-
(author, educator)

Born February 27, 1934, Lawton, Okla. *Education:* University of New Mexico, B.A., 1958; Stanford University, M.A., 1960, Ph.D., 1963. *Principal occupation:* Author, educator. *Address:* Department of English, Stanford University, Stanford, Calif. 94305. *Affiliations:* Assistant professor, associate professor of English, University of California, Santa Barbara, 1962-1969; professor of English and Comparative Literature, University of California, Berkeley, 1969-1972; professor of English, Stanford University, 1972-. *Other professional posts:* Consultant, National Endowment for the Humanities, 1970-; trustee, Museum of the American Indian, 1978-. *Memberships:* American Studies Association; MLA. *Awards, honors:* Guggenheim Fellowship, 1966; Recipient Pulitzer Prize for fiction, 1969; Premio Letterario Internazionale Mondello, Italy, 1979. *Biographical source: Who's Who in America. Published works:* The Complete Poems of Frederick Goddard Tuckerman, 1965; *House Made of Dawn,* 1968; *The Way to Rainy Mountain,* 1969; *Angle of Geese*

and Other Poems, 1973; *The Gourd Dancer,* 1976; *The Names,*1976.

MONETTE, GERALD
(college president)

Affiliation: President, Turtle Mountain Community College, P.O. Box 340, Belcourt, N.D. 58316.

MONSEN, MARIE A. 1939-
(federal government program analyst)

Born October 18, 1939, New York, N.Y. *Education:* Bucknell University, Lewisburg, Pa., B.A. (Sociology), 1961; East-West Center, Honolulu, Hi., M.A. (Sociology), 1963. *Principal occupation:* Federal government program analyst. *Home address:* 6807 Hopewell Ave., Springfield, Va. 22151. *Affiliations:* Training officer, Peace Corps, Thailand Program, 1964-1970; evaluation specialist, Department of the Interior, Washington, D.C., 1971-1979; chief, Local and Indian Affairs, Department of Energy, Washington, D.C., 1979-. *Community activities:* Annandale Christian Community for Action (vice president); Shelter House, Fairfax County (board of directors); elder in Presbyterian Church. *Membership:* Women's Council on Energy and the Environment, 1983-. *Awards, honors:* Certificate of Special Achievement, Bureau of Indian Affairs, 1979; Outstanding Achievement Award, 1984, Americans for Indian Opportunity; Superior Job Performance Awards, 1984-1985, Department of Energy. *Interests:* Indian energy; tribal government.

MONTAGUE, FELIX J.
(B.I.A. agency superintendent)

Affiliation: Superintendent, Fort Yuma Agency, Bureau of Indian Affairs, P.O. Box 1591, Yuma, Ariz. 85364.

MONTGOMERY, JOHN
(B.I.A. agency superintendent)

Affiliation: Superintendent, Zuni Agency, Bureau of Indian Affairs, P.O. Box 338, Zuni, N.M. 87327.

MONTOYA, GERONIMA CRUZ
(Pueblo) 1915-
(artist, teacher)

Born September 22, 1915, San Juan Pueblo, N.M. *Education:* St. Joseph's College, B.S., 1958; University of New Mexico; Claremont College. *Principal occupation:* Art teacher, Santa Fe, N.M. *Home address:* 1008 Calle de Suenos, Santa Fe, N.M. *Community activities:* Community Concert Association (captain); San Juan Pueblo Choir (secretary-treasurer). *Awards, honors:* School of American Research Purchase Award; Museum of New Mexico Special Category Prize, Inter-Tribal Indian Ceremonial, Gallup, N.M.; Special Prize, Philbrook Art Center, Tulsa, Okla.; DeYoung Museum Purchase Prize; among others.

MONTOYA, SAMUEL
(B.I.A. agency superintendent)

Affiliation: Superintendent, Southern Pueblos Agency, Bureau of Indian Affairs, P.O. Box 1667, Albuquerque, N.M. 87103.

MOORE, DAISY POCAHONTAS
(Wampanoag) 1931-
(director-Wampanoag Indian program)

Born July 6, 1931, Mashpee, Mass. *Education:* Boston University, B.A., 1958. *Principal occupation:* Director, Wampanoag Indian Program, Living History Museum, Plimoth Plantation, Plymouth, Mass., 1983-. *Home address:* 400 Plymouth St., Middleboro, Mass. 02346. *Other professional post:* Member, Mashpee Tribal Council (Wampanoag). *Membership:* American Museum Association. *Interest:* "Primary area of interest—museum; have traveled throughout Africa; taught school in Africa for three years under the auspices of the Methodist Church; limited travel to Europe; attended the University of Grenoble, France for one year." *Biographical sources:* Articles in local newspapers: "In Harmony With Nature," *Cape Cod Times,* June 13, 1985; "Collection at Mashpee Wampanoag Museum Enhanced by Plimoth Plantation Loan," *The Enterprise* (Falmouth, Mass., May 24, 1985).

MOORE, JOHN H. 1939-
(anthropologist)

Born February 27, 1939, Williston, N.D. *Education:* New York University, Ph.D., 1974. *Principal occupation:* Associate professor of anthropology, University of Oklahoma, Norman, Okla. *Home address:* 1311 Spruce Dr., Norman, Okla. 73072. *Other professional posts:* Consultant, Sand Creek Descendents Association, Muskogee Creek Tribal Towns, Inc. *Military service:* U.S. Army, 1962-1964 (lieutenant). *Memberships:* American Anthropological Association; American Ethnological Society; American Association for the Advancement of Science. *Interests:* Treaty rights; health; demography. *Biographical source:* "Search for the Sand Creek Descendents," *Sooner Magazine,* Spring, 1983. *Published works: Ethnology in Oklahoma* (Papers in Anthropology, 1980); *The Cheyennes in Moxtavhohona* (Northern Cheyenne Tribe, Inc., 1981); *The Cheyenne Nation* (University of Nebraska Press, 1986).

MOORE, JOSIAH N. (Papago)
(tribal chairman)

Affiliation: Chairman, Papago Tribal Council, P.O. Box 837, Sells, Ariz. 85634.

MOORE, LOUIS (Miami)
(tribal chief)

Affiliation: Chief, Miami Business Committee, P.O. Box 636, Miami, Okla. 74355.

MOORE, PAUL V.
(college president)

Affiliation: President, Bacone College, East Shawnee, Muskogee, Okla. 74402.

MOORE, RAMONA
(president-Indian association)

Affiliation: President, North American Indian Women's Association, 1411 K St., N.W., Suite 200, Washington, D.C. 20005.

MOORE, TRACEY ANN *(E-ne-opp-e)*
(Pawnee-Otoe-Osage-Sac and Fox)
1964-
(student)

Born August 14, 1964, Fairfax, Okla. *Education:* Northern Oklahoma College, Tonkawa, 1982-1984; University of Oklahoma, 1984-. *Principal occupation:* Student, University of Oklahoma, Norman. *Home address:* 401 Tallchief Dr., Fairfax, Okla. 74637. *Affiliations:* Vice president, American Indian Student Association, University of Oklahoma, 1985-1986; Intramurals Committee for Minority Students, University of Oklahoma Student Association, 1985-1986; American Indian Student Service, University of Oklahoma, Norman, 1986-. *Other professional posts:* CETA Summer Youth Progam, The Osage Nation, 1981-. *Awards, honors:* Nominated twice for Outstanding Young Women of America, 1985; Osage Nation representative for Miss National Congress of American Indians Pageant, 1985; University of Oklahoma, American Indian Student Association Princess, 1985-1986; Tulsa Powwow Princess, 1984; Miss Indian Oklahoma, 1st runner-up-most talented; National Viet Nam Veterans Powwow Princess & Association Princess, 1982-1984; Osage Tribal Princess, 1980 and 1983; recommended to submit autobiography for International Youth in Achievement, Cambridge, England. *Interests:* "My major is physical education. I hope to teach or be a women's basketball coach, I feel education is the key to life and I stress it to the Native American youth that it is important, and that they can also compete in sports as well. I enjoy traveling across the U.S. to Native American celebrations of every kind. I have represented my tribe at powwows, state and national organizations which involved me traveling to all 4 directions. My parents are Ted Moore, Sr., a former world champion fancy dancer for a number of consecutive years at the American Indian Exposition in Anadarko, Okla., and Thomasine Moore, a former Osage princess and current Osage Tribal Director at the American Indian Exposition. My great-grandfather was See-Haw, a great leader of the Osage Nation."

MORAN, ERNEST T. (BUD)
(Confederated Salish & Kootenai
-Chippewa Cree) 1939-
(B.I.A. agency superintendent)

Born August 27, 1939, Harlem, Mt. *Education:* Oceanside Junior College, 1960; Santa Ana Junior College, 1962-1963; received numerous training courses in administration and management while in the U.S. Marines. *Principal occupation:* B.I.A. agency superintendent. *Home address:* #14 Phinney Dr., Lapwai, Idaho 83540. *Affiliations:* Credit and business development officer, director of economic development program, Confederated Salish & Kootenai Tribes; Indian Community Action Program, University of Montana, Missoula; Bureau of Indian Affairs: housing officer, Rocky Boy, Mt.; reservation programs officer, Lame Deer, Mt.; credit and business development, Jicarilla Agency, Dulce, N.M.; tribal operations officer, Western Nevada Agency, Stewart, Nev.; field representative in Klamath, Calif.; superintendent, Northern Cheyenne Agency, Lame Deer, Mont., 1980-1985; superintendent, Northern Idaho Agency, Lapwai, Idaho, 1985-. *Other professional posts:* President, Indian American Foundation; past president, NFFE Union, Jicarilla Apache Agency Post, N.M. *Military service:* U.S. Marine Corps, 1958-1967 (Navy Unit Citation; Vietnam Unit Citation with Star; Vietnam Service Medal with Star; National Defense Service Medal with Star; Armed Forces Expeditionary Medal with 2 Stars). *Community activities:* Active Corps of Executives (member); Aide de Camp to Governor of New Mexico; Toastmasters Club, Lame Deer, Mt. (past president); coached four years of Little League, Lame Deer. Mt. *Memberships:* Confederated Salish & Kootenai Tribe; tribal affiliations with Chippewa Cree Tribe and Rocky Boy Tribe. *Awards, honors:* Special Achievement Award from Bureau of Indian Affairs; Letter of Appreciation from Jicarilla Apache Tribe and Northern Cheyenne Tribe; guest speaker (at Dull Knife Memorial College on numerous occasions) on government and their relations with tribes.

MORGAN, DONALD I. (Blackfeet) 1934-
(B.I.A. official)

Born June 12, 1934, Browning, Mt. *Education:* College of Great Falls, Mt.; University of New Mexico; Central Washington University. *Principal occupation:* B.I.A. official. *Home address:* P.O. Box 654, Fort Thompson, S.D. 57339. *Affiliations:* Administrator, Wind River Agency, B.I.A., Fort Washakie, Wyo.; administrator, vocational training and job placement worker, Los Angeles Field Employment Office, Los Angeles, Calif.; vocational counselor, Blackfeet Agency, Browning, Mt., Northern Cheyenne Agency, Lame Deer, Mt., Yakima Agency, Toppenish, Wash.; administrator, Crow Creek Agency, B.I.A., Fort Thompson, S.D. *Military service:* U.S. Army, 1957-1959.

MORGAN, GUY (Navajo) 1921-
(tribal official)

Born September 15, 1921, Woodspring (Kinlichee), Ariz. *Education:* Various B.I.A.-operated schools, 1930-1940. *Principal occupation:* Tribal official. *Home address:* Woodspring Trading Post, Ganado, Ariz. 86505. *Affiliations:* Owner, Woodspring Trading Posts #1 & 2, Ariz. *Other professional posts:* Delegate, Navajo Tribal Council, Window Rock, Ariz.; Navajo Tribal Welfare Committee, 1963-1966; Navajo Tribe Commission on Alcoholism, 1967-1971; Navajo Tribe Transportation and Roads Committee, 1971-. *Awards, honors:* Ten-year pin, B.I.A. *Interests:* As chairman of the Navajo Tribe Transportation and Roads Committee, Mr. Morgan is concerned that taxes paid by his tribe to four different states result in better facilities for his people.

MORGAN, MARILYN ELIZABETH 1944-
(technical editor)

Born June 30, 1944, Bremerton, Wash. *Education:* California State University, San Francisco, B.A., 1972. *Principal occupation:* Technical editor. *Home address:* 2858 North Highview Ave., Altadena, Calif. 91001. *Affiliations:* Technical editor, Jet Propulsion Laboratory, California Institute of Technology, Pasadena, Calif. *Other professional post:* Editor, *Native American Annual. Memberships:* Society for Technical Communication (audio-visual committee); Astronomical Society of the Pacific. *Interests:* Technical communiction; astronomy and science in general; Native American progress and cultural integrity. *Published work:* Editor, *Native American Annual* (Native American Publishing Co., Margaret Clark-Price, Publisher, 1985).

MORGAN, RONALD JOSEPH WHITEWOLF (¼ Blackfeet) 1940-
(writer, photographer, jeweler)

Born October 4, 1940, Seattle, Wash. *Education:* Bachelor degree in history from Universal Life Church, Modesto, Calif., 1974. *Principal occupation:* Writer, photographer, jeweler. *Home address:* P.O. Box 297, Redwater, Tex. 75573. *Occupational activities:* "I'm a public speaker, lecturer and dancer. I give talks on the Old West and Indians, also have slide shows and relic displays using artifacts from my collections. As a dancer, I've demonstrated Indian dances for tourists, school and youth groups. I have appeared in three video movies, filmed on the Alabama-Coushatta Reservation, Livingston, Texas. I speak the Dakota Sioux language, sign language and Spanish." *Memberships:* Smithsonian Institution; National Archives. *Awards, honors:* Awarded honorary title, "Special Consultant-American Indian Affairs," 1969; "I have been consulted by writers, U.S. Senators and many Indian organizations over the years." *Interests:* "Research is one of my main interests. I'm an Indian historian and always try to learn the old ways. My interests are many: archaeology, linguistics, publishing and law. I'm especially interested in state and federal law books relating Indian court cases. Collecting Indian artifacts; documents, photographs and original historical newspapers are just some of my interests, As a professional photographer, I'm busy recording western and Indian historical sites, graves of famous Indians and Indian powwows. I'm a part-time jeweler, casting in both gold and silver. My future plans are to produce video movie documentaries pertaining to Indian ceremonies and wild life. I'm currently working on fictional book about intertribal wars. The University of South Dakota, Institute of Indian Studies, has expressed an interest in using my photographs in a future publication, *Who's Who Among the Sioux.*" *Biographical sources: Source Directory* (U.S. Dept. of the Interior, B.I.A., 1985-1987); *The American Indian Index: A Directory of Indian Country* (Arrowstar Publishing, 1986-1987). *Published works:* Articles: "I Fought With Geronimo" by Jason Betzinez as told to Ronald Morgan (*The Westerner,* Stagecoach Publishing, 1971); series, "The Indian Side," in *The Frontier, Real West, True West,* and *American West* Magazines; among others.

MORRIS, ELIZABETH (Athabascan) 1933
(director-Indian organization)

Born February 16, 1933, Holikachuk, Alaska. *Education:* Seattle Community College, 1969-1970. *Principal occupation:* Former executive director, Seattle Indian Center, 1971-? *Home address:* 946 16th Ave., E., Seattle, Wash. 98112. *Community activities:* Candidate for Washington State Legislature, 1970; Seattle Community Council (advertising screening committee). *Interests:* Ms. Morris writes, "(I am) interested in the welfare of my people, and devote most of my time toward improving the quality of (their) lives. Because of my own experiences and difficulties, I am interested in helping (my people) maintain their identity and unique culture, (while) at the same time adapt(ing) to the urban scene."

MORRIS, C. PATRICK 1938-
(professor of Native American studies)

Born December 5, 1938, Watsonville, Calif. *Education:* Arizona State University, B.A. (History), 1964, M.A., 1970, Ph.D. (Anthropology), 1974. *Principal occupation:* Professor of Native American Studies, Center for Native American Studies, Montana State University, Bozeman, Mt. *Home address:* 8210 Balsam Dr., Bozeman, Mt. 59715. *Community activities:* Assist tribal colleges organize International Exchange Program

for 23 Indian tribes with Norway and France. *Memberships:* National Indian Education Association; Montana Indian Education Association. *Awards, honors:* Marshall Fellowship, Norway; Fulbright Award, Norway, University of Oslo; Goodwill Award for International Understanding, Norway. *Interests:* "Indian law and policy; international human rights and indigenous people; Indian reservation economies; tribally controlled colleges; American Indian religious thought; Indian literature—oral and written. *Published works:*" As Long As the Water Flows: Indian Water Rights, A Growing National Conflict in the U.S.," in *Native Power,* edited by J. Brosted, et al. (University of Oslo, 1985); *The Hill of Sorrow: Ethnohistory of the Little Shell Chippewa (in press).*

MORRISON, GEORGE (Chippewa) 1919-
(artist, art teacher)

Born September 30, 1919, Grand Marais, Minn. *Education:* Minneapolis School of Art, Certificate, 1943; Art Students League, New York, N.Y., 1943-1946; University of Aix-Marseilles, France, 1952-1953; M.F.A. (hon.), Minneapolis College of Art and Design, 1969. *Principal occupation:* Artist, art teacher. *Home address:* 2050 Stanford Ave., St. Paul, Minn. 55105. *Affiliations:* Assistant professor, associate professor, Rhode Island School of Design, 1963-1970; visiting professor of art and American Indian Studies, University of Minnesota, 1970-1973, professor, 1973-. *Memberships:* Audubon Artists, New York, 1955-; Federation of Modern Painters and Sculptors, New York, 1955-. *Exhibitions:* Numerous one-, two-, and three-man shows, invitational exhibitions and group shows in the U.S., France, The Netherlands, South America and Japan. Mr. Morrison's work is in the permanent collections of the Whitney Museum, New York City, New York University, Rochester Memorial Museum, St. Lawrence University, Canton, N.Y., Penn State University, Altoona, Pa., The Philadelphia Museum, University of Massachusetts, Virginia Museum of Fine Arts, Minneapolis Institute of Art, University of Minesota, Duluth, Amon Carter Museum of Western Art, Pacific Northwest Indian Center, Spokane, Wash. and many others. *Awards, honors:* Scholarship grants, Consolidated Chippewa Agency, 1941-1943; Fulbright Scholarship (FRance), 1952-1953; John Hay Whitney Fellowship, 1953-1954; numerous prizes and awards for paintings. *Biographical source: George Morrison: The Story of an American Indian,* by Dragos Kostich (Dillon Press, 1976).

MOSE, E.
(executive director-Nevada Indian Commission)

Affiliation: Executive director, Nevada Indian Commission, 472 Galleti Way, Reno, Nev. 89431.

MOSES, DAVID (Sauk-Suiattle)
(tribal chairman)

Affiliation: Chairman, Sauk-Suiattle Tribal Council, 5318 Chief Brown Lane, Darrington, Wash. 98241.

MOSES, LILLY L. (Nez Perce) 1949-
(economic development planner)

Born November 8, 1949, Seattle, Wash. *Education:* Oregon State University, B.S. (Education), 1976; University of Idaho, College of Law, 1979-1980. *Principal occupation:* Economic development planner. *Home address:* Route 1, Box 24, Kamiah, Idaho 83536. *Affiliations:* Cooperative education coordinator, American Indian Higher Education Consortium, Denver, Colo., 1973-1974; teacher intern, Madras Public Schools, Madras, Oreg., 1975-1976; grants/contracts specialist, Planning Department, Warm Springs Confederated Tribes, Warm Springs, Oreg., 1976-1977; community service manager, Nez Perce Tribe, Lapwai, Idaho, 1977-1979; researcher, Cobe Consultants, Portland, Ore., 1980-1981; economic development planner/manager, Limestone Enterprise, Nez Perce Tribe, P.O. Box 365, Lapwai, Idaho 83540. *Community activities:* Kamiah Revitalization Committee, Kamiah, Idaho (member, 1983-); elected to Housing Board of Commissioners, Nez Perce Tribal Hous-

ing Authority, 1985-1989). *Memberships:* Association for the Humanities in Idaho , 1978-1981. *Awards, honors:* 1971 After Dinner Speech Award; All-Indian Debate Tournament, Dartmouth College. *Interests:* "To gain a professionally gratifying position in the federal government that assists American Indian tribes in achieving self-sufficiency;" camping, hunting, fishing, beadwork, dancing.

MOYLE, ALVIN (Paiute-Shoshoni)
(tribal chairman)

Affiliation: Chairman, Fallon Paiute-Shoshini Business Council, 8955 Mission Rd., Box 232A, Fallon, Nev. 89406.

MUNGER, LYNN 1918-
(museum curator)

Born May 24, 1918, Steuben County, Ind. *Education:* Manchester College, Ind. *Principal occupation:* Museum curator. *Home address:* Box 486, Fremont, Ind. 46737. *Affiliations:* Teacher, Steuben County School System (15 years); Curator, Potawatomi Museum, Fremont, Ind. *Military service:* U.S. Navy, 1939-1945 (Presidential Unit Citation; Pearl Harbor Survivor; European Theatre Decoration). *Memberships:* Central States Archaeological Society (consultant); Ohio Primitive Art Society (consultant); Smithsonian Institution. *Interests:* "Although my interests are many and diversified, I retain the major focus of interest on the American Indian, working with school groups, service clubs and archaeological societies to dispel some of the common misconceptions concerning the heritage of the American Indian. Other fields of interest are ecology and entomology."

MURPHY, CHARLES W. (Standing Rock Sioux) 1948-
(tribal chairman)

Born December 27, 1948, Fort Yates, N.D. *Education:* Saint Benedict College, Atchison, Kan., 1968-1969. *Principal occupation:* Tribal chairman. *Home address:* P.O. Box D, Fort Yates, N.D. 58538. *Affiliations:* Police officer, B.I.A., Fort Yates, N.D., 1970-1972; range technician, B.I.A., Standing Rock Sioux Tribe, 1972-1976; agricultural director, 1976-1979, economic development planner, 1979-1981, vice chairman and councilman, 1981-1983, chairman, 1983-, Standing Rock Sioux Tribe, Fort Yates, N.D. *Military service:* U.S. Army, 1969-1970 (Vietnam Veteran; Army Commendation Medal; Bronze Star). *Community activities:* Standing Rock Irrigation Board, Standing Rock Sioux Tribe (chairman, 1981-); United Tribes Educational Technical Center, Bismarck, N.D. (board of directors, 1983-); Aberdeen Area Roads Commission (chairman, 1985-); Aberdeen Tribal Chairman's Association (chairman, 1986-); Theodore Jamerson Elementary School, Bismarck, N.D. (school board, 1984-); Saint Alexius Medical Center, Bismarck, N.D. (board of directors, 1985-). *Memberships:* National Tribal Chairman's Association, 1983-; United Sioux Tribes, Pierre, S.D. (chairman, 1985-. *Awards, honors:* Certificate of Special Achievement, Department of the Interior, 1980. *Interests:* "Elected by the enrolled members of the Tribe (Standing Rock Sioux), (I) serve as the chair of the Tribal Council and the chief executive officer of the tribal government. Specialized experience or other related background in personnel management, administration, planning and budgeting, and land and resource management. Responsible for implementation of tribal law; and represent the Tribe before Congress and government agencies."

MURRAY, DONALD CLYDE
(Micmac-Algonquian) 1932-
(engineering manager)

Born April 11, 1932, Bayside, N.Y. *Education:* University of Louisville, B.A. (Physics), 1952; University of Southern California, M.A. (Psychology), 1965; U.C.L.A., Ph.D. (Psychology), 1973. *Principal occupation:* Engineering manager, Hughes Aircrafts Co., Los Angeles, Calif., 1953-. *Home address:* 2106 West Willow Ave., Anaheim, Calif. 92804. *Other professional posts:* Licensed psychologist, State of California; senior associate, Al. J. Murray & Associates (mechanical consultants). *Military service:* U.S. Marine Corps, 1952-1954 (Captain; Reserves-retired). *Memberships:* American Association for the Advancement of Science; Amerin Physical Society. *Awards, honors:* Howard Hughes Doctoral Fellowships, 1968-1973; Order of the Chevalier, Cross of Honor, and Legion of Honor recipient, International Order of DeMolay. *Interests:* Consultant and lecturer; management psychology; executive counseling. *Biographcial source:* Registry of Native American Professionals.

MURRAY, WALLACE C. (Ioway)
(tribal chairman)

Affiliation: Chairman, Iowa Business Committee, Iowa Veterans Hall, P.O. Box 190, Perkins, Okla. 74059.

MUSKRAT, JEFF W. (Oklahoma
Cherokee) 1922-
(former B.I.A. official)

Born June 17, 1922, Grove, Okla. *Education:* Northeast Oklahoma Junior College, 1941-1942; Tulsa University, 1946-1947. *Principal occupation:* Former superintendent, Cherokee Agency, B.I.A., Cherokee, N.C., 1974-? *Home address:* P.O. Box 245, Cherokee, N.C. 28719. *Military service:* U.S. Army, 1942-1967 (Lt. Col.-retired; Silver Star; Bronze Star with Oak Leaf Cluster; Army Commendation Medal with two Oak Leaf Clusters; Presidential Citation). *Community activities:* Cherokee Boys Club (board of directors); Museum of the Cherokee Indian (board of directors). *Memberships:* Retired Officer's Association; Veterans of Foreign Wars; American Legion; Quarter Horse Association; American Indian Cattleman's Association.

N

NARANJO, TITO E. (Santa Clara
Pueblo) 1937-
(professor of social work)

Born August 8, 1937, Santa Clara Pueblo, N.M. *Education:* Baylor University, Waco, Tex., 1956-1958; Hardin-Simmons University, Abilene, Texas, 1958-1959; New Mexico Highlands University, Las Vegas, B.A., 1962, M.A., 1963; University of Utah, M.S.W., 1967. *Principal occupation:* Associate professor of social work. *Home address:* P.O. Box 516, Mora, N.M. 87732. *Affiliations:* Director of social services, Mora County, N.M., 1970-1971; assistant professor, College of Santa Fe, N.M, 1972-1975; associate professor of social work, New Mexico Highlands, University, Las Vegas, N.M., 1976-. *Other professional post:* Mora Valley Health Services, Inc. (board of directors). *Community activities:* Intermountain Centers for Human Development (board member); tribal secretary for Santa Clara Pue, 1976. *Memberships:* American Indian Higher Education (board of directors). *Interests:* "I am a part time rancher, part-time artist and writer. I enjoy hunting, fishing and photography. I am a distance runner in the mastes category and I also love to canoe, hike and adventure in Alaska and Mexico. *Biographical source:* "A Conversation With Tito Naranjo," in (*Confluencia, summer, 1980*).

NARCIA, LEROY (Papago)
(tribal chairman)

Affiliation: Chairman, Ak Chin Community Council, Route 2, Box 27, Maricopa, Ariz. 85239.

NASH, GARY B. 1933-
(historian)

Born July 27, 1933, Philadelphia, Pa. *Education:* Princeton University, B.A., 1955, Ph.D., 1964. *Principal occupation:* Historian. *Home address:* 16174 Alcima Ave., Pacific Palisades, Calif. 90272. *Affiliations:* Assistant to the Dean of the Graduate School, 1959-1961, assistant professor, Department of History, 1964-1966, Princeton University; assistant professor, 1966-1968, associate professor, 1969-1972, professor, 1972-, Department of History, University of California at Los Angeles. *Other professional posts:* Dean, Council on Educational Development, U.C.L.A., 1980-1984; dean of Undergraduate and Intercollege Curricula Development, U.C.L.A., 1984-; faculty advisory committee, American Indian Studies Center, U.C.L.A., 1973-1982; editorial board, *American Indian Culture and Research Journal*, 1980-. Mem-

berships: American Historical Association; Institute of Early American History and Culture; Organization of American Historians (nominating committee, 1980-1983; American Antiquarian Society. *Awards, honors:* Research grants from University of California Institute of Humanities and Research Committee, UCLA, 1966-1983; Guggenheim Fellowship, 1970-1971; Prize from the American Historical Association, Pacific Coast Branch, 1970, for best book, *Quakers and Politics: Pennsylvania, 1681-1726;* American Council for Learned Society Fellow, 1973-1974; American Philosophical Society grants, 1977, 1981, 1984; runner-up Pulitzer Prize in History for *The Urban Crucible,* 1979; 1980 Commonwealth Club of California, Silver Prize in Literature for *The Urban Crucible. Published works:* Co-edited, *Struggle and Survival in Colonial America* (University of California Press, 1981); *Red, White and Black: The Peoples of Early America* (Prentice-Hall, 1974; 2nd Ed., 1982); The American People: Creating a Nation and a Society (Harper and Row, 1986); *Retracing the Past: Readings in the History of the American People* 2 volumes (Harper and Row, 19860; among others. Numerous articles in various professional journals.

NASON, JAMES D. (Comanche) 1942-
(museum curator, social
anthropologist)

Born July, 1942, Los Angeles, Calif. *Education:* University of California, Riverside, B.A., 1964; University of Washington, M.A., 1967, Ph.D., 1970. *Principal occupation:* Museum curator, social anthropologist, Thomas Burke Memorial Washington State Museum, University of Washington, Seattle, Wash. *Affiliations:* Chairman, Anthropology Division and Curator of Ethnology, Thomas Burke Memorial Museum; professor, Department of Anthropology, University of Washington. *Other professional posts:* Commissioner, Kings County Arts Commission, Wash. *Memberships:* American Anthropological Association, 1970 (Fellow); American Association for the Advancement of Science, 1970- (Fellow); American Ethnological Society, 1970- (Fellow); American Association of Museums; International Council of Museums; Association for Social Anthropology in Oceana, 1971- (Fellow). *Interests:* Social anthropology and museology; culture change and modernization; Oceana (Micronesia) and North America; ethnohistory research. Field research. *Published works:* Edited with Mac Marshall, *Micronesia, 1944-1974* (Human Relations Area Files Press, 1976).

NAUMAN, CHARLES W. 1925-
(motion picture production)

Born December 14, 1925, Gettysburg, S.D. *Education:* University of Iowa, M.A., 1950. *Principal occupation:* Motion picture production. *Home address:* Box 232, Custer, S.D. 47730. *Affiliation: Nauman Films, Inc., Custer, S.D., 1955-. Military service:* U.S. Air Force, 1944-1946 (Sergeant; Presidential Unit Citation; Battle Star, Central Europe). *Awards, honors:* Cine "Golden EagleE Award (twice); New York Film Festival; American Film Festival; among others. *Interests:* Native American Indian Culture; travel; "interested in any world travel involving filmmaking or other positive involvement with cultures; expedition into canyons of Sierra Madre Occidental of Mexico to film Tarahumara Indian culture and Easter festival. *Films produced: The Grass That Never Breaks; Tahtonka,* 16mm documentary of Plains Indians from prehorse era to Wounded Knee Massacre—1967, voted best film of the week on B.B.C.—voted among 100 best educational films in the U.S.—awarded top honors at most major international film festivals in U.S. and abroad; *The Child Is A Piper,* best cable film of the year for television, 1970; *Johnny Vik,* 35mm full length feature film, 1971; *Sioux Legends,* 16mm documentary of Plains Indians culture, 1972 (Cine "Golden Eagle Award; Martin Luther King, Jr. Award).

NAUMAN, H. JANE 1929-
(motion picture production)

Born May 4, 1929, Grinnell, Iowa. *Education:* University of Iowa, B.A., 1950. *Principal occupation:* Motion picture production. *Home address:* Box 232, Custer, S.D. 57730. *Affiliaitons:* Nauman Films, Custer, S.D., 1955-; president, Sun Dog Distributing

(motion pictures), 1976-. *Awards, honors:* Fulbright Scholarship Award. See previous listing of husband, Charles W. Nauman for more information.

NAYLOR, JACK
(B.I.A. agency superintendent)

Affiliation: Superintendent, Miami Agency, Bureau of Indian Affairs, P.O. Box 391, Miami, Okla. 74354.

NEAMAN, KENNETH L. (Shoshoni)
(tribal chairman)

Affiliation: Chairman, Northwestern Band of Shoshoni Nation, Star Route 2 W, Rock Springs, Wyo. 82901.

NEELY, SHARLOTTE 1948-
(anthropologist)

Born August 13, 1948, Savannah, Ga. *Education:* Georgia State University, B.A., 1970; University of North Carolina, M.A., 1971, Ph.D., 1976. *Principal occupation:* Anthropologist. *Home address:* 3010 Marshall Ave., Cincinnati, Ohio 45220. *Affiliation:* Assistant professor, associate professor of anthropology, Northern Kentucky University, Highland Heights, Ky., 1974-. *Memberships:* American Anthropological Association, 1970- (Fellow); Southern Anthropological Association, 1974-; Central States Anthropological Society, 1975-; American Society for Ethnohistory, 1976-. *Awards, honors:* Predoctoral Research Fellowship, National Institutes of Mental Health, 1974; Alternate for Postdoctoral Fellowship, (D'Arcy McNickle) Center for the History of the American Indian, Newberry Library, Chicago, Ill., 1974. *Interests:* "Major research with Southeastern Indians, especially the Eastern Band of Cherokee Indians of North Carolina -- on-going research, including fieldwork, since 1971; also travel experience in the Indian areas of the Southwest, Plains, and Mexico. Major topical interests relating to Indians: ethnohistory, politics, ethnic relations, education, and the role women." Unpublished Ph.D. dissertation *Ethnicity in a Native American Community, and unpub-*

lished M.A. thesis, The Role of Formal Education Among the Eastern Cherokee Indians, 1880-1971, University of North Carolina, Chapel Hill. *Published works:* Numerous articles and papers.

NELSON, MICHAEL (Navajo) 1941-
(corporate president)

Born February 2, 1941, Whitecone (Navajo Nation), Ariz. *Education:* Fort Lewis College, Durango, Colo., B.A. (Business Administration), 1966. *Principal occupation:* President, Michael Nelson & Associates, Inc., Window Rock, Ariz.. *Home address:* P.O. Box 614, Window Rock, Ariz. 86515. *Affiliation:* Michael Nelson & Associates, Inc. maintains retail outlets in Teesto, Tuba City and Kayenta, Ariz. *Memberships:* Navajo Business Association (president, 1974-1978). *Awards, honors:* National Indian Businessperson of the Year, 1983; Minority Retail Firm of the Year, 1985; other local awards. *Interests:* "Travels to other parts of the world; recent travels to Hawaii, Hong Kong, Bahamas, and all the small islands in the Caribbean, Mexico." *Biographical source: The Maazo Magazine,* Vol. 1, No. 3, entitled "Business on the Navajo Reservation, The Maazo Interview with Michael Nelson a Successful Navajo Businessman." *Published work:* Publisher and editor of 1979 and 1980, *Airca Rodeo Championship Edition* (All Indian Rodeo Cowboy Association).

NENEMA, GLEN (Kalispel)
(tribal chairman)

Affiliation: Chairman, Kalispel Business Committee, P.O. Box 38, Usk, Wash. 99180.

NESETH, EUNICE (Aleut) 1907-
(elementary teacher-retired)

Born January 6, 1907, Afognak, Alaska, *Eduction:* Western Washington College of Educatin, B.A., 1942. *Principal occupation:* Elementary teacher-retired, Grades 1-6, Kodiak, Alaska, 1943-1967. *Home address:* Box 456, Kodiak, Alaska 99615. *Other professional posts:* Acquisitions Committee, Alaska Museum; instructor of basket weaving. *Community activities:* Senior Citizens,

Afognak Native Association (board member); Koniag and Kodiak Islands Native Association (member); Memberships: Alaska Education Association; Kodiak Education Association; Alaska Historical Society; Kodiak Historical Society (curator, 1957-1975; life member, 1975-). *Interests:* Education; travel; languages: "grass basket weaving. having learned from Anfesia Shapsnikoff of Unalaska during ten sessions while she lived in with us."

NESPOR, ELSIE PASCHAL 1927-
(principal)

Born October 3, 1927, Marvell, Ark. *Education:* University of Tulsa, B.S., 1971, Graduate School, 1971-1973; Black Hills State College, M.S. (Education), 1976. *Principal occupation:* Principal, Loneman School (Oglala Sioux Tribe), Oglala, S.D. *Home address:* Oglala, S.D. 57764. *Affiliations:* Owner-manager, Nespor Ranch, Okemah, Okla., 1952-1959; curriculum specialist, Tulsa Public Schools, 1971-1973. *Memberships:* Kappa Delta Pi (membership chairman); South Dakota Educatin Association; South Dakota Indian Education Association. *Awards, honors:* Outstanding Educator, Elementary and Secondary Education, 1976. *Interests:* Early childhood; Indian educational research and curriculum development; "employed by Creek Nation of Oklahoma, Okmulgee, Okla., to do field research study preparatory to writing Early Childhood Family Development Program for Creek Nation, 1977, summer;" consulting; poetry (published in *Nimrod,* University of Tulsa, and *Obsidian*). *Biographical sources: Who' Who in American Education; Notable Americans,* 1977. *Published works: Environment for Early Learning* (Tulsa Public Schools, 1972); *Student Handbook (Loneman School)* (Bureau of Indian Affairs, 1974); *Young Creek Americans and Their Families: Possibilities for Change* (Creek Nation, 1977).

NEW, LLOYD H. (professional name-
Lloyd Kiva) (Cherokee) 1916-
(artist, craftsman)

Born February 18, 1916, Fairland, Okla. *Education:* Oklahoma State University,

1933-1934; Art Institute of Chicago, 1934-1935; University of New Mexico, 1937; University of Chicago, B.A.E., 1938; Laboratory of Anthropology, Santa Fe, N.M. , 1939. *Principal occupation:* Artist, craftsman. *Address:* Institute of American Indian Arts, Cerrillos Rd., Santa Fe, N.M. 87501. *Affiliations:* Director, Indian Exhibit, Arizona State Fair, 1939-1950; instructor in arts and crafts, U.S. Indian School, Phoenix, Ariz., 1939-1941; established Lloyd Kiva Studios, Scottsdale, Ariz., 1945; instructor in art education, U.S. Indian summer schools for teachers, 1949-1951; co-director, Southwest Indian Arts Project (sponsored by the Rockefeller Foundation), University of Ariozna, 1959-1961; art director, Institute of American Indian Arts, 1962-? *Awards, honors:* Mr. New writes, referring to the period during which he established the Lloyd Kiva Studios in Scottsdale, Ariz., "During this period (I) was devoted to the problem: Can Indian craftsmen produce contemporary craft items for general use, enabling the craftsmen to earn a living, pursuing their crafts in a general society? This implies some understanding of design inspiration from Indian tradition, careful craftsmanship, fashion, and marketing. (My) 'Kiva Bags' (a craft item Mr. New created) have been marketed by outstanding fashion stores throughout the country. Top fashion publications have featured these and other Kiva fashions from time to time." Mr. New has attended various conferences relating to indigenous arts and crafts forms in the U.S. and Mexico. *Published work: Using Cultural Differences as a Basis for Creative Expression* (Institute of American Indian Arts, 1964).

NEWCOMB, WILLIAM W., Jr. 1921-
(professor of anthropology)

Born October 30, 1921, Detroit, Mich. *Education:* University of Michigan, B.A., 1943, M.A., 1946, Ph.D., 1953. *Principal occupation:* Professor of anthropology, University of Texas, Austin, Texas, 1962-. *Home address:* 6206 Shoal Creek Blvd., Austin, Texas 78757. *Other professional post:* Director, Texas Memorial Museum, 1957-1978. *Military service:* U.S. Army Infantry, 1943-1946. *Memberships:* American Anthropological Association (Fellow);

Texas Archaeological Society. *Awards, honors:* Awards for *Indians of Texas,* Texas Institute of Letters, Dallas Public Library. *Interests:* American Indian ethnology, particularly Plains and Texas; culture change; primitive art; ethnographic field work with Delaware Indians; archaeological field work in Arkansas and Texas; rock art of the Texas Indians; ethnohistory of Wichita. *Published works: The Culture and Acculturation of the Delaware Indians* (University of Michigan Press, 1956); *The Indians of Texas* (University of Texas Press, 1961); *The Rock Art of Texas* (Univerity of Texas Press, 1967); *A Lipan Apache Mission, San Lorenzo de la Santa Cruz, 1762-1771,* with Curtis Tunnell (Texas Memorial Museum, 1969); *North American Indians: An Anthropological* (Texas Memorial Museum, 1974); *The People Called Wichita* (Texas Memorial Museum, 1976); *German Artist of the Texas Frontier, Richard Friedrich Petri* (Univerity of Texas Press, 1978).

NEWMAN, HARRISON 1912-
(writer)

Born April 17, 1912, Newark, Ohio. *Education:* Centre College, B.A., 1933. *Principal occupation:* Writer. *Home address:* 296 Pine St., Lockport, N.Y. 14094. *Awards, honors:* Honorary adoption into Turtle Clan, Tonawanda Band of Seneca Indians, 1933. *Interests:* American Indians; archaeology. *Published works: Primitive Peoples of Western New York,* and *The Iroquois,* both with Richard L. McCarthy (Buffalo and Erie County Historical Society).

NICKLASON, FRED 1931-
(historian)

Born May 5, 1931, Swatara, Minn. *Education:* Gustavus Adolphus College, St. Peter, Minn., B.S., 1953; University of Pennsylvania, M.A., 1955; Yale University, Ph.D., 1967. *Principal occupation:* Historian. *Home address:* 6323 Utah Ave., N.W., Washington, D.C. 20015. *Affiliations:* Assistant professor, University of Maryland, College Park, Md., 1967-; director, Nicklason Research Associates, Washington, D.C., 1971-. *Military service:* U.S. Army, 1955-1957 (Research Analyst). *Mem-

berships: American Historical Association; Western Historical Association; Southern Historical Association; American Studies Association; American Ethnohistorical Association. *Awards, honors:* American Philosophical Society Grant. *Interests:* American Indian policy; American Southwest travel.

NICHOLSON, MARY EILEEN
(Colville) 1924-
   (tribal official)

Born March 1, 1924, Okanogan County, Wash. *Education:* St. Mary's Mission. *Principal occupation:* Member, Colville Business (Tribal) Council, Nespelem, Wash. *Home adress:* Route 1, Box 90, Tonasket, Wash. 98855. *Community activities:* Western Farmers Association; Agricultural Stabilization Conservation Service (committee member).

NICHOLSON, NARCISSE, Jr.
(Colville) 1925-
   (tribal official)

Born February 5, 1925, Tonasket, Wash. *Education:* High school. *Principal occupation:* Tribal official. *Home address:* 618 S. Index, Omak, Wash. 98841. *Affiliation:* Former chairman, Colville Business (Tribal) Council, Nespelem, Wash. *Other professional post:* Recreation Development Committee, Grand Coulee and Coulee Dam Chambers of Commerce (executive committee). *Military service:* U.S. Army, 1943-1946 (European-African-Middle Eastern Service Medal; American Theatre Service Medal; Victory Medal; Good Conduct Medal).

NIELSEN, ANITA G. (Wampanoag)
1922-
   (educational program supervisor)

Born June 21, 1922, Mashpee, Mass. *Education:* Massasoit Community College (two years). *Principal occupation:* Wampanoag educational program supervisor (teacher), Plimoth Plantation, Living Museum, Plymouth, Mass., 1983-. *Membership:* Wampanoag Tribal Council (life membership). *Awards, Honors:* Honorable Mention, Heard Museum; National Competition,

Contemporary Craft - Finger-Twined Bag. *Interests:* "Native tribal peoples' uses of natural resources—for food, shelter, clothing, crafts (i.e. basketry, mats, twining bags); would like to pursue research in natural native plants for dye."

NIMOHOYAH, SEKON (JIM) (Kiowa)
   (Indian health service)

Education: University of Oklahoma, B.A., 1966, M.A. (Anthropology), 1972; University of Houston, B.S. (Optometry), 1976; University of Texas, School of Public Health, M.P.H., 1977. *Principal occupation:* Indian health service. *Home address:* P.O. Box 13, White Earth Ojibwa Nation, Ogema, Minn. 56569. *Affiliations:* Chief, Area Director of all Vision Care Programs in Minnesota, Michigan and Wisconsin for the Indian Health Service, White Earth, Minn. 56591. *Other professional post:* Consultant to Minnesota Chippewa Tribe on PL 94-437. *Military service:* U.S. Army, 1966-1968 (Sergeant E-5, Special Forces Group, Medic, Airborne Pathfinder, Jungle Expert; Bronze Star for Valor; two Purple Hearts, Vietnamese Service Ribbon, Presidential Unit Citation). *Memberships:* Association of American Indian Physicians, 1973-; American Optometric Association, 1972-; Beta Sigma Kappa Optemtric Honor Fraternity International, 1975-; Texas Optometric Society, 1973-; American Public Health Association, 1975-; U.S. Public Health Service Commissioned Officer Society, 1976-. *Awards, honors:* Better Vision Institute Scholarship, 1973-1975; Most Outstanding 2nd Year Vision Analysis Clincian, 1974; Public Health Teaching Fellowship, 1975-1976; Community Health Optometry Award, 1976; invited to lecture to Academy of Optometry and Physiological Optics, Public Health Section, December, 1975, on my grant and project, "Native American Vision Care Project to Navajo Nation." *Biographical source:* *Who's Who in American Health Care* (Hanover Publications). *Published articles:* "Vision Anomalies of Clinical Patients, Navajo Nation," 1975; "Vision Anomalies, A Demographic and Epidemiological Study of Cheyenne River Sioux Nation," 1977; "Anaphylactic Shock and Other Ocular Emergencies," with William R. Jones, 1975; among others.

NITSCH, TWYLAH HURD (Seneca) 1912-
(teacher, lecturer)

Born December 5, 1912, Irving, N.Y. *Education:* Empire State College, S.U.N.Y. at Buffalo. *Principal occupation:* Teacher, lecturer. *Home address:* 12199 Brant-Reservation Rd., Irving, N.Y. 14081. *Affiliation:* Founder and president, Seneca Indian Historical Society. *Interests:* "Lecturer devoted to the dissemination of the wisdom, prophecy and philosophy of the Seneca Nation; programs presented at home and away to this end. Showing through these programs and lectures how the ancient wisdom of the Senecas can enrich the lives and increase the awareness of other cultures in the present. Programs in Scotland, Ireland, England, Italy, Hawaii, Canada, Mexico, most of the U.S." *Biographical sources: Medicine Power,* and *Medicine Talk* by Brad Steiger, *Flight of the Seventh Moon* by Lynn Andrews (dedicated to Twylah Nitsch) (Human Dimension Institute, Columbus, N.C.). *Published works: Wisdom of the Senecas* (S.U.N.Y.-Dept. of Bilingual Education, 1979); *Entering Into the Silence—The Seneca Way,* 1976, *Language of the Stones,* 1980/1983, *Language of the Trees,* 1982, *Nature Chants and Dances,* 1984 (all published by The Seneca Indian Historical Society).

NOLEY, GRAYSON (Choctaw) 1943-
(director-Indian program)

Born September 4, 1943, Talihina, Okla. *Education:* Southeastern Oklahoma State University, Durant, B.A., 1969; The Pennsylvania State University, University Park, M.Ed., 1975, Ph.D., 1979. *Principal occupation:* Director, American Indian Leadership Program, Penn State University. *Home address:* 1443 North Allen St., State College, Pa. 16802. *Affiliations:* Director, American Indian Leadership Program, The Pennsylvania State University, Education Policy Studies, University Park, Pa., 1979-. *Other professional posts:* Assistant professor of education; assistant director, American Indian Special Education Teacher Training Program; director, American Indian Education Policy Center, Pennsylvania State University. *Military service:* U.S. Army,

1961-1964. *Community activities:* Partnership Coordinating Committee; Committee for Understanding Others (local school district); Minorities Committee (graduate record examination board), *Memberships:* American Educational Research Association; Comparative and International Education Society; National Indian Education Association. *Awards, honors:* Kellogg Foundation, National Fellowship Program, 1984-1987; participant, Phoenix Seminar, Penn State University, 1975; American Indian Ledership Program Fellowship, Penn State University, 1974-1979; Music Scholarship, Southeastern State University, Durant, Okla. *Interests:* "Federal policies on Native American education; drug and alcohol abuse in adolescent Native Americans; travel." *Published work:* Two chapters in *The Choctaw Before Removal* (Mississippi University Press, 1985); articles in various education journals and American Indian journals.

NORDWALL, CURTIS
(B.I.A. agency superintendent)

Affiliation: Superintendent, Papago Agency, Bureau of Indian Affairs, Sells, Ariz. 85634.

NORMAN, MARGARET JANE
(museum curator)

Affiliation: Curator, Seminole Nation Museum, P.O. Box 1532, Wewoka, Okla. 74884.

NORRIS, LEONARD
(director-Indian organization)

Affiliation: Director, Organization of the Forgotten American, 1020 Pine St., Klamath Falls, Ore. 97601.

NUVAYESTEWA, EVANGELINE (Tewa-Hopi) 1940-
(elementary teacher)

Born February 17, 1940, Keams Canyon, Ariz. *Education:* Phoenix College, A.A., 1961; Northern Arizona University. *Principal occupation:* First grade teacher,

Polacca, Ariz., 1971-. *Home address:* P.O. Box 637, Polacca, Ariz. 86042. *Community activities:* Save the Children Federation (advisor-secretary). *Award:* Outstanding Elementary Teachers of America, awarded by Gilbert Beers, Ph.D., director.

O

OANDASAN, WILLIAM (Yuki of the Covelo Indian Community) 1947-
(senior editor, poet)

Born January 17, 1947, Santa Rosa, Calif. *Education:* University of California, Santa Cruz, B.A., 1974; University of Illinois, Chicago, M.A., 1981; Vermont College, Montpelier, M.F.A., 1984. *Principal occupation:* Senior editor, poet. *Home address:* 2852 Sawtelle Blvd., #42, Los Angeles, Calif. 90064. *Affiliations:* Senior editor, *American Indian Culture and Research Journal,* American Indian Studies Center, U.C.L.A., Calif., 1980-; executive director, A Publications, Los Angeles, Calif., 1976-1984. *Other professional post:* Poet in residence at the Dorland Mountain Colony for writers, artists and composers. *Community activities:* California Arts Council (member of multicultural arts panel); A Writers Circle (member of board of directors); tutor for elementary and high school students for Indian centers of Los Angeles. *Memberships:* A Writers Circle; Native American Education Service; MLA; RMMLA; MELUS. *Awards, honors:* 1985 American Book Award from Before Columbus Foundation. *Interests:* "Traveled to Canada, Mexico and the Philippine Islands. Poet, writer, editor and publisher. (I) Compiled a bibliography of the tribes of the Round Valley Reservation in northern California for the D'Arcy McNickle Center for the History of the American Indian at the Newberry Library, and compiling a bibliography of the northern California Indian tribes for the American Indian Bibliography Series of Scarecrow Press. Consultant on American Indian affairs; poetry reading. *Published works: A branch of California Redwood* (UCLA-American Indian Studies Center, 1981); *Moving Island* (A Publications, 1984); *Round Valley Songs* (West End Press, 1984); editor, *American Indian Culture and Research Journal (UCLA-American Indian Studies Center, 1980-);* editor, *A,* a journal of contemporary literature, 1976-1984.

O'BRIEN, PATRICIA J. 1935-
(North American archaeologist)

Born April 1, 1935, Chicago, Ill. *Education:* University of Illinois, Urbana, B.A., 1962, Ph.D., 1969. *Principal occupation:* North American archaeologist. *Home address:* 1902 Blue Hills Rd., Manhattan, Kan. 66502. *Affiliation:* Professor of anthropology, Kansas State University, Manhattan, Kan., 1969-. *Community activities:* Kansas Antiquity Commission (member). *Memberships:* Society for American Archaeology; American Anthropological Association; Sigma Xi; American Association for the Advancement of Science. *Interests:* "Archaeological research in north-central Kansas, the Kansas City, Mo. area, the Quad City area in Illinois, and in the Yucatan, Mexico." *Published works: Formal Analysis of Cahokia Ceramics: Powell Tract* (Illinois Archaeological Survey Monograph No. 3, 1972); *Archaeology of Kansas* (Museum of Natural History, University of Kansas, 1984).

O'CONNOR, LEO
(B.I.A. agency superintendent)

Affiliation: Superintendent, Lower Brule Agency, Bureau of Indian Affairs, Lower Brule, S.D. 57548.

OESTREICHER, DAVID M. 1959-
(writer, salvage ethnographer, student, teacher)

Born December 5, 1959, New York, N.Y. *Education:* S.U.N.Y. at Purchase, B.A. (with honors), 1981; New York University, M.A., 1985; currently in graduate program at N.Y.U. *Principal occupation:* Writer, salvage ethnographer, student, teacher. *Home address:* 19 Forbes Blvd., Eastchester, N.Y. 10709. *Interests:* "Participated in government funded expedition lead by Nicholas A. Shoumatoff to visit the last remnants of the

Delaware (Lenape) Indians in Oklahoma, November, 1977. Thereafter, worked individually to record the culture and language of the Delaware. Much of the work is recorded on tapes, notes and video, and has been a major contribution to the Delaware Indian Resource Center at the Ward Pound Reservation in New York. His research comprises one of the main bodies of information on this vanishing tribe. Mr. Oestreicher has lectured widely on the subject of the Delaware Indians. He has taken part and helped arrange various symposiums and programs at Yale University, Tulsa University, Seton Hall, CUNY at Purchase, New York City Hall and elsewhere. He has appeared as a guest on WOR radio in New York with Ed and Pegeen Fitzgerald. David Oetreicher was a teacher for the Title IV American Indian Education Program in Mahwah, New Jersey for a period of two years. His students, members of the Ramapo Mountain Indian Tribe, studied Delaware language and culture with him. For seven years until her death in November of 1984, he worked intensely with Nora Thompson Dean, "Touching Leaves Woman," the last full-blooded traditionalist of the Unami Delaware. The results of the work are chronicled in a book that tells not only the tragic story of a tribe on the verge of extinction but also the human element involved in being the last of a people. The book is entitled *Conversations With Touching Leaves: Voices of the Lenape,* and will soon be published. Before her death in 1984, Touching Leaves blessed the manuscript and expressed the hope that "through this book my people will be remembered." Oestreicher has also been a consultant for films and book in connection with the Delaware Indians. Other interests include: ancient Near Eastern and Jewish history, poetry, classical and folk music, art, conservation, canoeing and the outdoors."

OFFICER, JAMES E. 1924-
(professor of anthropology)

Born July 28, 1924, Boulder, Colo. *Education:* University of Kansas, 1942-1943; University of Arizona, B.A., 1950, Ph.D., 1964. *Principal occupation:* Professor of anthropology, University of Arizona. *Home address:* 621 North Sawtelle Ave., Tucson,

Ariz. 85716. *Affiliations:* Information officer, Department of State, 1950-1953; instructor, University of Arizona, 1957-1960; associate commissioner, Bureau of Indian Affairs, 1961-1967; assistant to the Secretary of the Interior, 1967-1969; coordinator of international programs, University of Arizona, 1969-1976; professor of anthropoogy, University of Arizona, Tucson, Ariz., 1969-. *Community activities:* U.S. Representative, Interamerican Indian Institute (Mexico City), 1968-1978; Democratic Precinct Committeeman, 1970-1976. *Memberships:* Arizona Historical Society (board of directors); American Anthropological Association (Fellow), 1958-; Society for Applied Anthropology (Fellow), 1958-; Tucson Corral of the Westerners, 1969-(board of directors); Tucson Rotary Club, 1973-; Phi Beta Kappa, 1950-; Pacific Council on Latin American Studies, 1973-. *Awards honors:* Distinguished Service Award, Department of the Interior, 1968; Quill and Scroll National Journalism Scholarship, 1942; Tucson-Mexico Goodwill Award, Tucson Trade Bureau, 1982; Creative Teaching Award, University of Arizona Foundation, 1983. *Interests:* "Social history of the Indians of the Americas; land tenure among pre-Columbian and contemporary Indian groups in Mexico, Chile, and the U.S.; Indian servitude in Spanish colonial America. Have lived among and worked with Indian and mextizo groups in Mexico and Chile; and have been closely associated with various Indian groups in the U.S. *Published works: Indians in School* (University of Arizona Press, 1956); *Anthropology and the American Indian* (Indian Historian Press, 1974); *Arizona's Hispanic Perspective* (Arizona Academy, Phoenix, 1982); *Hispanic Arizona, 1536-1956* (forthcoming-University of Arizona Press, 1987).

OKLEASIK, M. LaVONNE 1936-
(clerk, teacher)

Born July 4, 1936, Iowa. *Education:* Luther College, Decorah, Iowa, B.A., 1960. *Principal occupation:* Clerk, teacher. *Home address:* Box 356, Nome, Alaska 99762. *Affiliations:* Clerk, City of Nome, Alaska; financial secretary, education chairman, bible study teacher, Our Savior's Lutheran Church, Nome. *Other professional post:*

Private piano teacher. *Community activities:* Community alcohol program in Nome since 1980. "These activities have been with the Eskimo people. My husband is an Eskimo from Teller, Alaska. My desire for the people in this area is for them to be confident, to be happy about themselves and able to look at problems realistically and try to solve them in a satisfying manner. This I have tried to do in a volunterr basis through the church and the community alcohol program, working with all ages—children and elderly."

OLD COYOTE, BARNEY (Crow) 1923-
(government official, professor)

Born April 10, 1923, St. Xavier, Mt. *Education:* Morningside College, 1945-1947, *Principal occupation:* Government official, professor. *Address:* Montana State University, Bozeman, Mt. *Affiliations:* National Park Service, Crow Agency, Mt.; Bureau of Indian Affairs: Fort Yates, N.D., Crow Agency, Mt., Aberdee, S.D., Rocky Boys, Mt., Rosebud, S.D.; special assistant to the secretary, U.S. Department of the Interior, 1964-1969; assistant area director, B.I.A., Sacramento, Calif., 1969-1970; professor and director, American Indian Studies, Montana State University, Bozeman, Mt., 1970-. *Military service:* U.S. Army Air Corps, 1941-1945. *Community activities:* American Legion (post commander); Knights of Columbus (grand knight). *Memberships:* National Federation of Federal Employees (president, credit union; chairman, board of directors). *Awards, honors:* Special Achievement Award and Management Training Intern, Bureau of Indian Affairs; Doctor of Humane Letters (honor), Montana State University, 1968; Distinguished Service Award, U.S. Department of the Interior, 1968. *Interests:* Mr. Coyote writes, "Genberal interest is in the welfare of Indians and youth of all races, particularly in the education and general participation in the American way of life of all citizens during formative years; conservation of natural and human resources and the general appreciation of the aesthetic values of the American way of life."

OLD PERSON, EARL (Blackfeet)
(tribal chairman)

Affiliation: Chairman, Blackfeet Tribal Business Council, Browning, Mt. 59417.

OLDS, FOREST D. (Miami) 1911-
(farmer, stockman)

Born March 5, 1911, Miami, Okla. *Principal occupation:* Farmer, stockman. *Home address:* Route 2, Miami, Okla. *Affiliations:* Former chief, Miami Tribe of OKlahoma; clerk, North Fairview School Board. *Community activities:* Ottawa County Farm Bureau; Ottawa County Soil and Water Conservation District. *Memberships:* Oklahomans for Indian Opportunity (board of directors); Miami Co-Op Association, Inc. (former vice president). *Awards, honors:* Goodyear Tire and Rubber Co. Award for soil conservation, 1964. *Interests:* "Conservation; research into history of Miami Tribe; travel to former homesites of the Miami Tribe in Indiana, Kansas and Ohio; trip to Washington, D.C. to testify before Congressional committees as a representative of the Miami Tribe.

OLIVIERO, MELANIE BETH
(executive director-Indian Rights Association)

Affiliation: Executive director, Indian Rights Association, 1505 Race St., Philadelphia, Pa. 19102.

OLNEY, HIRAM
(B.I.A. agency superintendent)

Affiliation: Superintendent, Yakima Agency, Bureau of Indian Affairs, P.O. Box 632, Toppenish, Wash. 98948.

OLSON, MARTIN L. (Eskimo) 1927-
(commercial pilot, merchant)

Born June 24, 1927, White Mountain, Alaska. *Education:* Spartan School of Aeronautics, Tulsa, Okla.(aircraft and engine mechanic license, commercial pilot license). *Principal occupation:* Commercial pilot, merchant. *Home address:* 5 Front St., Golovin, Alaska 99762. *Affiliations:* President, Olson Air Service, Golovin, Alaska. *Military service:* U.S. Navy. *Community activities:* Bering Straits Native Association, Nome, Alaska (first vice president); Golovin Village Council (past president).

OPLER, MORRIS EDWARD 1907-
(professor emeritus)

Born May 16, 1907, Buffalo, N.Y. *Education:* University of Buffalo, B.A. (Sociology), 1929, M.A. (Anthropology), 1930; University of Chicago, Ph.D. (Anthropology), 1933. *Principal occupation:* Professor emeritus. *Home address:* 4006 Brookhollow Rd., Norman, Okla. 73069. *Affiliations:* Research assistant and associate, Department of Anthropology, University of Chicago, 1933-1935; assistant anthropologist, Bureau of Indian Affairs, 1936-1937; assistant professor of anthropology, Claremont College, 1938-1942; visiting and assistant professor, Howard University, 1945-1948; professor of anthropology and Asian studies, Cornell University, Ithaca, N.Y., 1948-?; director, Cornell University Indian Program, 1948-?; professor emeritus, Department of Anthropology, Cornell University. *Other professional post:* Associate editor, *Journal of American Folklore,* 1959-? *Memberships:* Sigma Xi; Phi Delta Kappa; Phi Beta Kappa; Alpha Kappa Delta; American Association of University Professors; American Sociological Association; American Anthropological Association (Fellow; executive board, 1949-1952; president-elect, 1961-1962; president, 1962-1963); Society for Applied Anthropology; Association for Asian Studies; American Ethnological Society; American Folklore Society (Fellow; first vice president, 1946-1947; executive committee, 1950; council member, 1957-1960). *Published works: The Ethnobiology of the Chiricahua and Mescalero Apache,* with E.F. Castetter (*Bulletin,* University of New Mexico Press, 1936); *Dirty Boy: A Jicarilla Tale of Raid and War* (American Anthropological Association, Memoirs No. 52, 1938); *Myths and Tales of the Jicarilla Apache Indians* (Stechert, 1938); *Myths and Legends of the Lipan Apache Indians* (J.J. Augustin, 1940); *An Apache Life-Way: The Economic, Social,* *and Religious Institutions of the Chiricahua Indians* (University of Chicago Press, 1941; University Microfilms; Cooper Square Publishers, 1966); *Myths and Tales of the Chiricahua Apache Indians* (Banta, 1942); *The Character and Derivation of the Jicarilla Holiness Rite* (University of Ne Mexico, 1943); *Childhood and Youth in Jicarilla Apache Society* (The Southwest Museum, 1946); among others.

ORR, CAROL (Colville) 1943-
(artist)

Born August 21, 1943, Republic, Wash. *Education:* University of Washington, B.A., 1965. *Principal occupation:* Freelance artist (portraits, murals, Indian theme paintings). *Awards:* Four-year scholarship, Colville Tribe; Federal Scholarship for four years (art studies, University of Washington), award, Philbrook Art Exhibit; second prize, Indian Show, La Grande, Oreg., 1965. *Interests:* Portraits on commission, book jackets and illustrations, feature illustrations, mural commissions on any theme, etc. Ms. Orr's work appears in various museums and private collections.

ORR, HOWELL McCURDY (Chickasaw) 1929-
(artist)

Born May 20, 1929, Washington, Okla. *Education:* Bacone College; Northeastern Oklahoma State College, B.F.A.; University of Tulsa, graduate work; University of Gto San Miguel Allende, Mexico, M.F.A.; University of the Americas, Mexico City; Univerity of Nevada, Las Vegas. *Principal occupation:* Artist. *Address:* New Mexico Highlands University, Las Vegas, N.M. 87701. *Affiliations:* Indian studies coordinator and assistant professor of art, New Mexico Highlands University. Las Vegas, N.M. *Military service:* U.S. Army, 1952-1954. *Awards, honors:* Numerous awards and exhibitions in the U.S. and Mexico. *Biographical sources: Indians of Today,* 4th Edition; *American Indian Painters* (Museum of the American Indian, 1968).

ORTIZ, ALFONSO ALEX
(San Juan Pueblo) 1939-
(professor of anthropology)

Born April 30, 1939, San Juan Pueblo, N.M. *Education:* University of New Mexico, B.A., 1961; Arizona State University, postgraduate studies, 1961-1962; University of Chicago, M.A., 1963, Ph.D., 1967. *Principal occupation:* Professor of anthropology. *Home address:* 830 E. Zia Rd., Santa Fe, N.M. 87501. *Affiliations:* Assistant professor, Pitzer College, Claremont, Calif., 1966-1967; assistant professor, associate professor, Princeton University, 1967-1974; professor of anthropology, University of New Mexico, Albuquerque, N.M., 1974-. *Other professional posts:* Charles Charropin visiting scholar, lecturer, Rockhurst College, 1977; chairman, Native American advisory group, Division of Performing Arts, Smithsonian Institution, 1975-1976; chairman, selection committee, Doctoral Fellowships for American Indians, Ford Foundation, 1975-1978; member, advisory council, National Indian Youth Council; board of directors, Social Science Research Council, 1972-1974; board of directors, Institute for the Development of Indian Law; member, advisory council, D'Arcy McNickle Center for the History of the American Indian, Newberry Library, 1972-, chairman, 1978-; member, National Humanities Faculty, 1972-; member, national advisory council, Institute of the American West, Sun Valley Center for the Humanities, 1976-; member, minority advisory panel, Danforth Graduate Fellowship Program, 1976-1979. *Memberships:* Committee for the Education of Women and the Minorities in the Sciences, NRC, 1975-; National Commission for the Minorities in Higher Education, 1979-1981; American Anthropological Association (Fellow); Royal Anthropological Institute (Fellow); Association on American Indian Affairs (director, 1967-; president, 1973-). *Awards, honors:* Roy D. Albert Prize for outstanding master's thesis in anthropology, University of Chicago, 1962-1963; keynote speaker, Second National Indian Education Conference, August, 1970; distinguished lecturer, Department of Religion, University of Oregon, Jan., 1973; distinguished Bicentennial professor, University of Utah, 1976;

Guggenheim Fellow, 1975-1976; Fellow, Center for Advanced Study in the Behavioral Sciences, 1977-1978; Weatherhead scholar in residence, Navajo Community College, 1976; numerous other educational and civic panels. *Interests:* "Contemporary American Indian affairs; religion and society; space, time, color and number in world view; the oral tradition." *Biographical source: Who's Who in America.* Published works: *The Tewa World: Space, Time, Being, and Becoming in a Pueblo Society* (University of Chicago Press, 1969); editor, *New Perspectives on the Pueblos* (University of New Mexico Press, 1972); *To Carry Forth the Vine: An Anthology of Traditional Native American Poetry;* editor, southwest volumes, *Handbook of North American Indians,* Vol. 9 (Smithsonian Institution, 1980).

ORTIZ, ROXANNE DUNBAR
(Southern Cheyenne) 1938-
(professor-Native American studies)

Born September 10, 1938, Oklahoma. *Education:* San Francisco State University, B.A., 1963; U.C.L.A., M.A., 1965, Ph.D. (History), 1974. *Principal occupation:* Professor, Native American Studies, California State University, Hayward, Calif., 1974-. *Home address:* 275 Grand View Ave., San Francisco, Calif. 94114. *Community activities:* Staff member, International Indian Treaty Council (non-governmental organization in consultative status with U.N.). *Published work: The Great Sioux Nation* (Random House, 1977).

ORTIZ, SIMON J. (Acoma Pueblo) 1941-
(writer, poet, teacher)

Born May 27, 1941, Albuquerque, N.M. *Education:* Fort Lewis College, Durango, Colo., 1961-1962; University of New Mexico, Albuquerque, 1966-1968; University of Iowa, Iowa City, 1968-1969. *Principal occupation:* Writer, poet, teacher. *Home address:* P.O. Box 263, Mission, S.D. 57555. *Affiliation:* Instructor and co-director, Creative Writing Program, Sinte Gleska College, Mission, S.D. *Other professional posts:* Consulting editor to Pueblo of

Acoma, Institute of American Indian Arts Press, and Navajo Community College Press. *Military service:* U.S. Army, 1963-1966. *Community activities:* National Indian Youth Council (community organizer, 1970-1973); Adult Community Education, Acoma Pueblo, N.M. (director, 1975); AIM House, Oakland, Calif. (member of board, 1977-1979). *Memberships:* Americans Before Columbus Foundation (board of directors, 1978-); American PEN, 1980-. *Awards, honors:* Discovery Award (Creative Writing, 1970), Fellowship (Creative Writing, 1981), National Endowment for the Arts. *Interests:* "Avocational interests include listening to music, long distance running, travel. Places I've traveled include all of the areas of the U.S., including Alaska in 1979, 1981, and 1984; I traveled to Europe, including Holland, Belgium, and Germany. *Biographical sources:* "This Song Remembers" (article-interview)(Macmillan, 1980); "Coyote Said This" (biographical article)(University of Aarhus, Denmark, 1984); "I Tell You Now" (autobiographical article)(University of Nebraska Press, 1986). *Published works: Naked In The Wind* (Quetzal-Vihio Press, 1971); *Going For The Rain* (Harper & Row, 1976); *A Good Journey* (Turtle Island Press, 1977); *Howbah Indians* (Blue Moon Press, 1978); *The People Shall Continue* (Children's Press Books, 1978); *Fight Back* (INAD-University of New Mexico, 1980); *From Sand Creek* (Thunder's Mouth Press, 1981); *A Poem Is A Journey* (Pternandon Press, 1982); *Fightin'* (Thunder's Mouth Press, 1983); *Blue and Red* (Acoma Pueblo Press, 1983); *The Importance of Childhood* (Acoma Pueblo Press, 1983).

OTT, WILLIAM
(B.I.A. area director)

Affiliation: Eastern Area Director, Bureau of Indian Affairs, 1951 Constitution Ave., N.W., Washington, D.C. 20245.

OVERFIELD, THERESA 1935-
(professor of nursing; research professor of anthropology)

Born July 22, 1935, Buffalo, N.Y. *Education:* D'Youville College, Buffalo, N.Y., B.S.

(Nursing), 1958; Columbia University, M.P.H. (Public Health), 1962; University of Colorado, M.A. (Anthropology), 1972, Ph.D. (Physical Anthropology), 1975. *Principal occupation:* Professor of nursing, research professor of anthropology. *Home address:* 172 Braewick Rd., Salt Lake City, Utah 84103. *Affiliations:* Intinerant public health nurse, Alaska Department of Health, Bethel, Alaska, 1959-1961; nurse epidemiologist, Arctic Health Research Center, USPHS, Anchorage, Alaska, 1962-1965; nursing consultant, Colorado Department of Public Health, Denver, 1966-1969; research assistant professor, 1975-1976, assistant professor of nursing, 1976-1978, College of Nursing, University of Utah, Salt Lake City; associate professor, College of Nursing, Brigham Young University, Salt Lake City, 1978-1984; adjunct assistant and associate professor, 1976-1985, research professor, 1985-, Department of Anthropology, University of Utah, Salt Lake City; director of research, 1979-, professor, 1984-, College of Nursing, Brigham Young University, Salt Lake City. *Other professional posts:* Advisory board, 1978-1982, reviewer, 1979-, *Western Journal of Nursing;* reviewer, *Research in Nursing and Health. Community activities:* Western Commission on Higher Education in Nursing, Boulder, Colo. (research steering committee member, 1978-1982); Transcultural Nursing Conference Group, Utah Nurses Association, Salt Lake City (chairperson, 1978-1980); Salt Lake Indian Health Center, Inc. (advisory committee member and board of directors, 1981-1982); Veterans Administration Medical Center, Salt Lake City (nursing research committee member, 1982-; member, Health Services Research and Development Review Board, 1983-); Utah Nurses Association *Newsletter,* Salt Lake City, (committee on research, 1985-); various college and university committees. *Memberships:* American Nurses Association (Utah); Utah Public Health Association (board member, 1983-); American Association of Physical Anthropologists; Society for Medical Anthropologists; Human Biology Council; American Association for the Advancement of Science; Western Society for Research in Nursing; Council for Nursing and Anthropology; Society for the Study of Human Biology; American Public Health Association. *Awards, honors:* USPHS, Special Nurse Predoctoral Fellowships, 1969-1974; American Nurses Foundation, Inc. Grant for Pseudocholinesterase Silent Allele in Alaskan Eskimos, 1974; University of Utah, Demography Study Group, Grant for computer use on Eskimo data for fertility study, 1976-1977; *American Journal of Nursing,* Excellence in Writing Award, 1981; Brigham Young University, Womens Research Institute Grant and College of Nursing Research Grant, 1985. *Interests:* Racial variation; biomedical research; Eskimos—western Alaska; papers, lectures, workshops and conferences presented on the Alaskan Eskimo and the American Indian, too numerous to mention. *Published works:* Numerous articles in various professional journals.

OWENS, ROGER C. 1928-
(anthropologist, professor)

Born September 14, 1928, Port Arthur, Tex. *Education:* Michigan State University, B.A., 1953; University of Arizona, M.A., 1957; U.C.L.A., Ph.D. (Anthropology), 1962. *Principal occupation:* Anthropologist, professor. *Home address:* 54 Fort Hill Rd., Huntington, N.Y. 11743. *Affiliations:* Instructor, assistant and associate professor of anthropology, University of California, Santa Barbara, 1959-1967; professor of anthropology, Queens College, C.U.N.Y., Flushing, N.Y., 1967-. *Other professional post:* Curriculum development consultant, Holt, Rinehart and Winston, Inc., 1968-1977. *Military service:* U.S. Army, 1946-1947. *Memberships:* American Anthropological Association (Life Fellow); Current Anthropology (Associate); Sigma Xi (Fellow); numerous nonprofessional organizations devoted to topics in anthropology and Native American affairs. *Awards, honors:* National Science Foudnation Undergraduate Research Participation Award, 1961-1963; Research Grants, University of California, Santa Barbara, 1961-1966; Grant-in-aid, Holt, Rinehart and Winston, Inc., 1969-1971; Distinguished Teacher of the Year, Queens College, 1983-1984; Mellon Foundation Fellowship, Queens College, 1983-1984. *Interests:* American Indians; Latin America. *Biographical*

source: Who's Who in the East. Published works: Senior editor, *North American Indians: A Sourcebook* (Macmillan, 1967); "The Contemporary Ethnography of Baja, California, Mexico," chapter in *Handbook of Middle American Indians* (Tulane University Press, 1969); "American Indian Society and Culture: A Conspectus," in *Encyclopedia of Indians of the Americas,* Vol. 1 (Scholarly Press, 1974); *Native North Americans: The Anthropology of Americans Original Inhabitant* (Queens College Reprographics, 1977); "Indians, American," in *Academic American Encyclopedia* (Arete Publishing Co., 1980); *The Mountain Pai; An Ethnography of the Indians of Baja, California, Mexico* (typescript, 1984); among others; numerous papers on the American Indian read at meetings.

OWHI, HARRY (Colville) 1928-
(tribal officer)

Born November 14, 1928, Nespelem, Wash. *Education:* North Idaho Colege of Education; Kinman Business University; University of Ne Mexico. *Principal occupation:* Executive secretary, Colville Business (Tribal) Council, Nespelem, Wash. *Home address:* P.O. Box 324, Nespelem, Wash. *Military service:* U.S. Army, 1946-1947.

OXENDINE, THOMAS (Lumbee) 1921
(naval officer, government information officer)

Born December 23, 1921, Pembroke, N.C. *Education:* Pembroke State College, B.A., 1948; Armed Forces Information School, 1966. *Principal Occupation:* Naval Officer and Government Information Officer. *Home Address:* 1141 North Harrison St., Arlington, Va. 22205. *Affiliations:* U.S. Navy, Naval Aviator, 1942-1947, Commander, 1951-1970; Public Information Officer, Bureau of Indian Affairs, Washington, D.C., 1970-. *Military Service:* Naval Aviator-World War II, United States Navy, 1942-1947 (Distinguished Flying Cross-Air Medal); Navy Jet Fighter Pilot, 1951-1960; Commanding Officer, Training Squadron Two, Naval Air Basic Training Command,

Pensacola, Florida, 1960-1962; Deputy Fleet Information Officer, Staff of the Commander-in-Chief, U.S. Pacific Fleet, 1962-1965; Public Affairs Officer, Commander Task Force 77, Gulf of Tonkin, 1965; Aviation Plans Officer/ Director, Plans Division, Office of Information, Department of Navy, The Pentagon, Washington, D.C., 1965-1968; Public Affairs Officer, Naval Air Systems Command, Department of Navy, Washington, D.C., 1968-1970. *Memberships:* National Congress of American Indians; National Aviation Club; National Press Club. *Awards, Honors:* First Distinguished Alumnus Award, 1967, Pembroke State College; Athletic Hall of Fame, 1980, Pembroke State University; extensive press coverage as "First American Indian to complete Naval Aviation Cadet Flight Program." *Biographical Sources: Who's Who in Government; Who's Who in the East.*

P

PABLO, MATT
(museum director/curator)

Affiliation: Director/curator, Malki Museum, Inc., 11-795 Fields Rd., Morongo Indian Reservation, Banning, Calif. 92220.

PADILLA, JOE A. (Tesuque Pueblo)
(Pueblo governor)

Affiliation: Governor, Tesuque Pueblo, Route 11, Box 1, Santa Fe, N.M. 87501.

PADILLA, NICOLAS J.
(Rancheria chairman)

Affiliation: Chairman, Susanville Indian Rancheria Business Council, Drawer 'U', Susanville, Calif. 96130.

PALE MOON, PRINCESS
(president-Indian foundation)

Affiliation: President and executive director, American Indian Heritage Foundation, 6051 Arlington Blvd., Falls Church, Va. 22044.

PARASHONTS, TRAVIS N.
(Southern Paiute) 1953-
(director-Utah Indian affairs)

Born October 10, 1953, Cedar City, Utah. *Education:* Southern Utah State College, Ceadr City, B.A., 1979; University of Utah, Salt Lake City (Masters of Social Work candidate). *Principal occupation:* Director, Utah Division of Indian Affairs, 6220 State Office Bldg., Salt Lake City, Utah. *Home address:* 689 S. Pitford Dr., Centerville, Utah 84014. *Other professional posts:* Former tribal chairman, Paiute Tribe; American Indian Service, Brigham Young University, Provo, Utah (board member); American Indian Cultural Foundation, Page, Ariz. (board member); Indian Affiliates, Orem, Utah (board member). *Awards, honors:* Spencer W. Kimball Award for working with Indian people; Paiute Tribal Award for service as tribal chairman; Cedar City Chamber of Commerce Award. *Interests:* "I assisted the Paiute Tribe in getting federal recognition in 1980 and helped them get back 5,000 acres of land and established a 2.5 million dollar irrevocable trust fund for economic development." *Published work: Paiute Language— For Beginner* (Southern Utah State College, 1980).

PARENT, ELIZABETH ANNE
(Athabascan) 1941-
(associate professor)

Born January 12, 1941, Bethel, Alaska. *Education:* Harvard Graduate School of Education, M.Ed and CAS, 1972-1974; Stanford University, M.A. and Ph.D., 1974-1984. *Principal occupation:* Associate professor, American Indian Studies, San Francisco State University, 1600 Holloway Ave., San Francisco, Calif., 1980-. *Memberships:* Society for Values in Higher Education; American Association for Higher Education; National Indian Education Association. *Awards, honors:* Postdoctoral Fellow, American Indian Studies Center, U.C.L.A., 1985-1986; Ford Fellow; Danforth Fellow. *Interests:* American Indian education, history and politics; educational psychology; women's issues; child development and pedagogy. *Published work: The Educational Experiences of the Residents of Bethel, Alaska,* Ph.D. dissertation (Stanford University).

PARKER, ALAN
(president-American Indian
National Bank)

Affiliation: President, American Indian National Bank, 1700 K St., N.W., Suite 2000, Washington, D.C. 20006.

PARKER, E.M., Sr. 1902-
(museum curator)

Born April 19, 1902, Hopkins, Pa. *Education:* Detroit School of Lecturing; DuBois Business College. *Principal occupation:* Museum curator. *Home address:* 247 East Main St., Brookville, Pa. 15825. *Affiliations:* Sign writer, 1924-1967; curator, E.M. Parker Indian Museum, Brookville, Pa. *Memberships:* Genuine Indian Relics Society; American Association of Museums; Pennsylvania Archaeological Society; Ohio Archaeological Society. *Awards, honors:* Adopted into the Seneca Indian Wolf Clan, 1954; Cold Spring Longhouse; received 25 trophies for displaying Early Flint Locks from 1730-1847, plus displaying fine Indian artifacts from western Pennsylvania, Ohio, and western New York. *Interests:* "History of the American Indian, particularly the Iroquois; American military arms before 1900; interested in cultures of the Ohio Basin, Ohio and Pennsylvania, Adena and Hopewell, late B.C. and early A.D. *Biographical sources: Who's Who in Indian Relics,* Third Edition (Cameron Park, 1972); *Dictionary of International Biography; Men of Achievement; Community Leaders and Noteworthy Americans; Notable Americans of the Bi-Centennial Era,* 1976.

PARKER, JOE
(B.I.A. agency superintendent)

Affiliation: Superintendent, Tahlequah Agency, P.O. Box 828, Tahlequah, Okla. 74465.

PARKER, SHARON
(program coordinator)

Affiliations: Coordinator, American Indian Lawyer Training Program, and chairwoman, National Institute for Women of Color, 1712 N. St., N.W., Washington, D.C. 20036.

PARKER, WAYNE (Comanche) 1938-
(farmer and rancher)

Born September 23, 1938, Spur, Tex. *Education:* West Texas State University, B.S., 1961. *Principal occupation:* Farmer and rancher. *Home address:* HCR 2, Box 127, Ralls, Tex. 79357. *Affiliations:* Archaeological curator, Pioneer Memorial Museum, Crosbyton, Texas, and Ralls Historical Museum, Ralls, Texas; editorial staff for *Artifacts Society* of Ohio, and *La Tierra* archaeological journal. *Community activities:* Cotton Gin Board (member); Museum Board (member); Boy Scout Commission; Crosby County Historical Commission. *Memberships:* Texas Archaeological Society; Central States Archaeological Society; South Plains Archaeological Society; Artifacts Society; Southern Texas Archaeological Society (editorial board, *Journal*). *Awards, honors:* Life Saving Award signed by President Eisenhower; "Best Committee Member," Texas Historical Commission, 1971; guest speaker at "History Day at the Ranch," Matador Ranch, 1984 and 1985; 4th cousin to Chief Quanah Parker (Kwahadi Comanches). *Interests:* "I have written over 95 articles concerning Indian artifacts which have been published throughout the U.S. (I) hunted bull elk in Colorado for 20 years. *Biographical sources: Arrowheads and Projectile Points; North American Indian Artifacts; Selected Preforms, Points and Knives of the North American Indians. Published works: The Bridwell Site* and *The Roberson Site* (Crosby County Museum Association, 1982 and 1986.

PARKS, DOUGLAS R. 1942-
(linguist)

Born August 28, 1942, Long Beach, Calif. *Education:* University of California, Berkeley, B.A., 1964, Ph.D., 1972. *Principal occupation:* Linguist. *Home address:* 8275 East State Road 46, Bloomington, Ind. 47401. *Affiliations:* Director, Title VII Program, White Shield School District, Roseglen, N.D. (three years); research associate,

Department of Anthropology, Indiana University, Bloomington, 1983-. *Other professional post:* Associate director, American Indian Studies Research Institute, Indiana University. *Memberships:* Plains Anthropological Society (board of directors, 1980-1982; president, 1982); American Anthropological Association; American Society for Ethnohistory. *Awards, honors:* American Council of Learned Societies Fellow, 1982-1983; Smithsonian Fellow (Smithsonian Institution, 1973-1974). *Published works: A Grammar of Pawnee* (Garland Publishing, 1976); *An Introduction to the Arikara Language* (Title VII Materials Development Center, Anchorage, Alaska, 1979); *Ceremonies of the Pawnee,* 2 Vols. (Smithsonian Institution Press, 1981); *Arikara Coyote Tales: A Bilingual Reader* (White Shield School, 1984); *An English-Arikara Student Dictionary* (White Shield School, 1986).

PARMAN, DONALD L. 1932-
(historian)

Born October 10, 1932, New Point, Mo. *Education:* Central Missouri State College, B.S., 1958; Ohio University, M.A., 1963; University of Oklahoma, Ph.D., 1967. *Principal occupation: Historian. Home address:* 614 Rose St., West Lafayette, Ind. 47906. *Affiliation:* Department of History, Purdue University, West Lafayette, Ind., 1966-. *Military service:* U.S. Army, 1953-1955 (Corporal). *Memberships:* Organization of American Historians; Western History Association; Agricultural History Society; American Society for Ethnohistory; Indian Association of Historians. *Interests:* "Main research interests are Navajo Indian history and twentieth century Indian affairs; main travels are in the Southwest and elsewhere in 'Indian Country'." *Biographical sources:* Directory of American Scholars, Vol. 1; *Dictionary of International Biography; Contemporary Authors. Published works:* Co-editor, *American Search,* 2 Vols. (Forum Press, 1973); *Navajos and the New Deal* (Yale University Press, 1976).

PARRA, DONNA C. (Navajo) 1941-
(counseling services)

Born September 7, 1941, Rehoboth, N.M. *Education:* University of New Mexico, B.A., 1970, M.A., 1974. *Principal occupation:* Counseling services. *Home address:* 819 Gonzales Rd., Santa Fe, N.M. 87501. *Affiliations:* Medical secretary, USPHS Indian Hospital, Gallup, N.M., 1961-1963, 1965; research assistant, National Institutes of Mental Health (Alcoholism Project: "A Community Treatment Plan for Navajo Problem Drinkers"), Family Service Agency, 1966-1968; director of counseling services, Institute of American Indian Arts, Sante Fe, N.M., 1976-. *Other professional posts:* Instructor of English, counselor, Gallup High School, 1970-1975; consultant to teach workshops on ethnic literature, 1973-1975, consultant, Curriculum Development, Native American Literature, 1974-1975, Gallup-McKinley County Schools; consultant, University of New Mexico Cultural Awareness Center, Albuquerque, N.M., 1975. *Community activities:* Santa Fe Public Schools Title IV Indian Education Parent Committee (officer); New Mexico Human Rights Commission Film Project (scholar and advisor); Ford Canyon Youth Center, Gallup, N.M. (advisory board); Gallup Inter-Agency Alcoholism Coordinating Committee (member); New Mexico International Women's Year Convention, June, 1977 (workshop leader on "Indian Women"). *Memberships:* League of Women Voters; New Mexico Association of Women Deans and Counselors; National Indian Education Association. *Awards, honors:* Four-year Navajo Tribal Scholarship recipient; Charles S. Owens Future Teachers of America Scholarship (Gallup High School, 1959); Sequoyah Indian Fellowship, University of New Mexico, 1970. *Interests:* "Ms. Parra writes, "I have great interest in the field of human rights, specifically issues of Indian sovereignty, because I feel that this whole issue relates directly to the survival of the American Indian as a group. I also have great interest in Native American literature and have developed a curriculum on this which has been adopted by the Gallup-McKinley County School district. I have been involved in alcohol research among the American Indian in a National Institutes of

Mental Health Project in Gallup, "A Community Treatment Plan for Indian Problem Drinkers" (1966-1968), and am presently directing a program I designed with students and staff of our educational facility.

PARRISH, RAIN (Navajo) 1944-
(museum curator)

Born February 8, 1944, Tuba City, Ariz. *Education:* University of Arizona, B.A. (Anthropology), 1967. *Principal occupation:* Museum curator. *Home address:* 704 Kathryn Ave., Santa Fe, N.M. 87501. *Affiliation:* Curator of American Indian Collections, Wheelwright Museum of the American Indian, Santa Fe, N.M., 1979-. *Membership:* New Mexico Museum Association. *Awards, honors:* Navajo Woman of the Year in the Arts, 1985; "10 Who Made a Difference," 1985 *The New Mexican Newspaper). Interests:* "Travel, art history, anthropology, sports, skiing, hiking, reading, writing." *Published works: The Stylistic Development of Navajo Jewelry* (Minneapolis Institute of the Arts, 1982); *Woven Holy People* (Wheelwright Museum, 1983); *The Pottery of Margaret Tafoya* (Wheelwright Museum, 1984).

PARSONS, NEIL (Blackfoot) 1938-
(art instructor)

Born March 2, 1938, Browning, Mt. *Education:* Montana State University. B.A. (Art), 1961, M.S. (Applied Art), 1964. *Principal occupation:* Art instructor. *Home address:* 513 Salazar, Santa Fe, N.M. 87502. *Affiliations:* Graphic illustrator, Boeing Aircraft Co.; art instructor, Institute of American Indian Arts, Santa Fe, N.M. *Military service:* U.S. Air Force Reserve, 1961-1964. *Memberships:* Pi Kappa Alpha; Delta Phi Delta; Montana Insitute of Arts. *Award:* Joseph Kinsey Howard Memorial Fellowship, 1963. *Exhibitions:* Museum of New Mexico—Contemporary American Indian Artists, and New Mexico Biannual; Bureau of Indian Affairs—Indian Invitations; Montana Institute of Arts State Festival; Seattle Art Museum; Atkins Museum, Kansas City, Mo.; and others. Work featured in collections of Dr. Verne Dusenberry, Lloyd Kiva New, Museum of the Plains Indian.

PARTON, PETRY D.
(B.I.A. agency superintendent)

Affiliation: Superintendent, Jicarilla Agency, Bureau of Indian Affairs, Dulce, N.M. 87528.

PATAWA, ELWOOD (Umatilla)
(tribal chairman)

Affiliation: Chairman, Umatilla Board of Trustees, P.O. Box 638, Pendleton, Ore. 97801.

PATTERSON, ELMA (JONES)
(Tuscarora) 1926-
(social worker)

Born August 13, 1926, Lockport, N.Y. *Education:* Cornell University, B.S., 1949; S.U.N.Y. at Buffalo, School of Social Work, M.S.W., 1963. *Principal occupation:* Social worker. *Home address:* 1162 Ridge Rd., Lewiston, N.Y. 14092. *Affiliations:* Supervisor of Field Services for Indians...A State Agency. *Community activities:* New York Iroquois Conference, Inc. (founder; past chairman; board of directors); Seneca Nation Educational Foundation, Inc. (trustee); Americans for Indian Opportunity (AIO)(past vice chairman and secretary-treasurer); Governor's Interstate Indian Council (chairman); New York State Library Services for Indians (advisory committee); Leisuretimers of the Tonawanda Indian Reservation (advisory committee); Niagara County Department of Social Services (advisory committee). *Memberships:* American Indian Social Workers Association (charter member).

PATTERSON, PATRICK *(Kemoha)*
(Apache-Seneca) 1914-
(artist)

Born December 29, 1914, Centralia, Ill. *Education:* University of Oklahoma, B.F.A. *Principal occupation:* Artist. *Home address:* 201 Main St., Woodward, Okla. 73801. *Affiliation:* Director, Woolaroc Museum (32 years). *Art:* Glass design; marble design; church murals. *Community activities:* Girl Scout Board. *Interests:* Autropological trips to Panama, Guatemala, Mexico and Peru.

Helped excvate Spiro Mound in Oklahoma. *Published work: Woolaroc Museum* (Frank Phillips Foundation, Inc.).

PAUL, BLAIR F. (Tlingit) 1943-
(lawyer)

Born July 5, 1943, Juneau, Alaska. *Education:* Western Washington State College, B.A., 1966; University of Washington Law School, J.D., 1970. *Principal occupation:* Lawyer. *Home address:* 6810 31 N.E., Seattle, Wash. 98115. *Community activities:* Pioneer Square Historic Preservation Board, 1974-; Washington Trust for Historic Preservation (president, 1976-1977); United Indians of All Tribes (board member, 1969-1971): Seattle Indian Health Board, 1970-1973; Seattle Indian Services Commission, 1972-1973. *Memberships:* American Trial Lawyers; Washington Trial Lawyers; Seattle-Kings County Bar.

PAYNE, SUSAN F.
(president-Indian Institute)

Affiliation: President, American Indian Archaeological Institute, Route 199, Box 260, Washington, Conn. 06793.

PAYTON, KENNETH L. (Cherokee) 1926-
(former B.I.A. agency superintendent)

Born August 3, 1926, Picher, Okla. *Education:* Oklahoma State University, B.S., 1949. *Affiliation:* Former superintendent, Mescalero Agency, B.I.A., Mescalero, N.M. *Military service:* U.S. Navy, 1944-1946. *Membership:* Soil Conservation Society of America.

PEACOCK, KENNETH 1922-
(musicologist)

Born April 7, 1922, Toronto, Can. *Education:* University of Toronto, Mus.B., 1943. *Principal occupation:* Musicologist. *Home address:* 540 Brierwood Ave., Ottawa, Can. *Affiliation:* Musicologist, National Museums of Canada, Ottawa, Ontario, Can. *Memberships:* Canadian Folk Music Society; Canadian Authors Association.

Interests: Musicological research among Indian tribes of Ontario, Manitoba, Saskatchewan, Alberta and British Columbia. *Published works: The Native Songs of Newfoundland,* 1960; *Survey of Ethnic Folkmusic Across Western Canada,* 1963; *Twenty Ethnic Songs from Western Canada,* 1965; *Music of the Doukhobors,* 1966 (all published by Queen's Printer); among others.

PEARSON, BILLY
(environmental health)

Affiliation: Director, Environmental Health, Indian Health Service, 5600 Fishers Lane, Rockville, Md. 20857.

PEASE-WINDY BOY, JANINE
(college president)

Affiliation: President, Little Big Horn Community College, P.O. Box 370, Crow Center, Education Commission, Crow Agency, Mt. 59022.

PEASLEY, BOB D. (½ Oglala-Omaha) 1932-
(artist)

Born August 23, 1932, Sioux City, Iowa. *Education:* Portland Community College; Clark College, Vancouver, Wash., 1964-1968; University of Washington, 1968-1971; University of British Columbia (art and anthropology studies). *Principal occupation:* Artist. *Affiliation:* Artist-master carver, director, Indian Arts Studies Centre, Estacada, Ore. *Other professional post:* Retired police chief. *Military service:* U.S. Army, 1950-1951. *Membership:* Indian Arts & Crafts Association, Albuquerque, N.M., 1975- (board of directors; appointed, National Security Chief, Oct., 1977). *Awards, honors:* Numerous awards for art from the following: New Mexico State Fair; Heard Museum; among others. *Interests:* "Contemporary production, instruction, research of all seven major tribal areas of Northwest Coast Indian art; theatrical arts of Indian productions, music ethnographical studies; participant in "The American West Program," Colorado State University,

1977 (first artist in residence, Fort Collins City Museum, Colo.); selected by Department of State and The African-American Institute for a cultural exchange trip to several countries in West Africa in 1979; family documents and antique photographs; family heir-looms. *Biographical sources:* Featured in "Community Focus, *Coloradoan* Newspaper (July 10, 1977); *The Indian Trader,* news Magazine (Sept. 1977). *Published work:* "Masks & Meanings of the Northwest Coast Indians" *(The Indian Trader,* December, 1977).

PENA, GILBERT M. (Pueblo)
(chairman-All Indian Pueblo Council)

Affiliation: Chairman, All Indian Pueblo Council, 2401 12th St., N.W., Albuquerque, N.M. 87197.

PENCILLE, HERBERT W. (Chemehuevi)
1927-
(businessman)

Born January 29, 1927, Los Angeles, Calif. *Education:* Los Angeles Valley College (Business Law). *Principal occupation:* Businessman. *Home address:* 12243 Hartland St., N. Holywood, Calif. 91605. *Affiliations:* General manager, Hydrex Termite Control Co. of Southern California, 1969-?; chairman, Chemehuevi Indian Tribal Council, 1972-?; Owner, Hydrex Pest Control Co., East San Fernando Valley, 1975-. *Military service:* U.S. Army Air Corps, 1946-1947. *Memberships:* National Pest Control Association, 1949- (director, 1962); Pest Control Operators of California, Inc. (president, 1959; director, 1959, 1960). *Awards, honors:* Man of the Year Award, Pest Control Operators of California, Inc., 1968. *Interests:* Private pilot license.

PENISKA, JOSEPH N. (Northern
Ponca-Santee Sioux) 1932-
(junior college administrator)

Born April 27, 1932, Niobrar, Neb. *Education:* Deane College, Crete, Neb., B.A., 1956; University of South Dakota, M.Ed., 1961; College of Idaho; Arizona State University; Northeastern Oklahoma State University. *Principal occupation:* Director of

student affairs, The College of Ganada, Ganado, Ariz., 1974-. *Other professional posts:* College track coach, assistant professor and director of physical education; guidance director; director of Indian studies. *Military service:* U.S. Army, 1953-1955 (Corporal; Good Conduct Medal). *Memberships:* Arizona Native American Education Association; National Indian Education Association. *Awards, honors:* First American Indian Leadership Program Award, Arizona State University, 1970. *Published work:* Co-author, *American Indians in Higher Edcuation* (Region IV West, national Association of Student Personnel Administrators, 1977).

PENSONEAU, RALPH
(B.I.A. agency superintendent)

Affiliation: Superintendent, Southern Ute Agency, Bureau of Indian Affairs, P.O. Box 315, Ignacio, Colo. 81137.

PENTEWA, RICHARD SITKO (Hopi)
1927-
(artist)

Born April 12, 1927, Oraibi, Ariz. *Education:* Oklahoma A & M College, School of Technical Training, 1957. *Principal occupation:* Artist (painting and sculpture). *Home address:* P.O. Box 145, Oraibi, Ariz. *Military service:* U.S. Army (Koran Service Medal; Combat Infantry Badge; U.N. Service Medal; National defense Service Medal). *Membership:* Hopi Tribal Council. *Awards, honors:* Numerous awards for art. *Interests:* Art; travel.

PEPION, DONALD D. (Blackfeet)
(college president)

Born in Browning, Mt. *Education:* New Mexico State University, Las Cruces, B.S., 1974; Montana State University, Bozeman, M.Ed., 1979. *Principal occupation:* President, Blackfeet Community College. *Home address:* P.O. Box 812, Browning, Mt. 59417. *Affiliations:* Executive director, Blackfeet Housing Programs, Browning, Mt. (seven years); instructor, Native American studies, Blackfeet Community College, Browning, Mt. (four years). *Other professional posts:* Accountant; vocational education and training. *Community activities:* Blackfeet Developmental Disabilities (chairman); Blackfeet Indian Preference Committee (member). *Memberships:* American Indian Higher Education Consortium; National Indian Education Association.

PERATROVICH, ROY (Tlingit) 1910-
(former B.I.A. agency superintendent)

Born May 1, 1910, Klawock, Alaska. *Principal occupation:* Former superintendent, Anchorage Agency, Bureau of Indian Affairs, Anchorage, Alaska, 1968-? *Home address:* 1002 W. 30th #15, Anchorage, Alaska 99503. *Other professional posts:* Chief territorial tax collector, and director of land registration, Territory of Alaska. *Community activities:* Alaska Native Brotherhood (grand president, five terms; executive committee). *Memberships:* Federal Executive Committee, 1968-. *Awards, honors:* United Nations Fellowship; John Hay Whitney Fellowship; Boss of the Year, Anchorage Agency, 1976.

PEREAU, JOHN
(B.I.A. agency superintendent)

Affiliation: Superintendent, Rocky Boy's Agency, Bureau of Indian Affairs, Box Elder, Mt. 59521.

PEREZ, DAVID (Nambe Pueblo)
(Pueblo governor)

Affiliation: Governor, Nambe Pueblo, Route 1, Box 117-BB, Santa Fe, N.M. 87501.

PEREZ, FRANKLIN (RANDY)
(Assiniboine Sioux)
(tribal president)

Affiliation: President, Fort Belknap Community Council, Harlem, Mt. 59526.

PESHEWA, MACAKI (Shawnee) 1941-
(priest-Native American Church)

Born May 23, 1941, Spartanburg, S.C. *Education:* Spartanburg Junior College, S.C., A.A., 1966; Wofford College, Spartanburg, B.A., 1968; Furman University (postgraduate work, 1969); University of South Carolina (post-graduate work, 1971-1973); Univerity of Tennessee, Knoxville, M.S., 1974 (post graduate work, 1976-1977); Auburn University (post-graduate work, 1974-1975); Native Americas University (Doctorate-Human Development, 1975; Doctorate-System Theory of Life Science, 1976). *Principal occupation:* Priest-Native American Church, Knoxville, Tenn. *Home address:* P.O. Box 53, Strawberry Plains, Tenn. 37871. *Affiliations:* Chairman, Tennessee Indian Council, Knoxville, Tenn.; chairman and founder, Native American Indians In Media Corporation, Knoxville, Tenn.; chairman, Indian Historical Society of the Americas, Knoxville, Tenn. *Other professional post:* Chairman, Systems Theories and Human Development Corporation, P.O. Box 16115 U.T. Station, Knoxville, Tenn., 1977-. *Military service:* U.S. Air Force. *Commuity activities:* Work with off-reservation Indians; Tennesse Band of Cherokees (medicine man, business advisor); The American Indian Movement (urban Indian, Shawnee Nation); Native American Church of the Southeast (incorporator and head); National Lenape Band of Indians (medicine man); Consciousness Expansion Movement of Native Americans (president, chairman of the board); Tuskegee Alumni Foundation, Knoxville, Tenn. (advisory board); Knoxville Communications Cooperative (advisory board); Native Americas University (Southeast regional coordinator; board of regents; Indian Voters League. *Memberships:* Association of Humanistic Psychology; XAT-Amerian Indian Medicine Society; International Minority Business Council/Association; Phi Delta Kappa; Alpha Delta Omega. *Awards, honors:* Notary-at-Large, Tennessee; Key-to-City Certificate of Appreciation, Knoxville, Tenn.; Governor Recognitions: Appreciation Certificate, and Colonel-past and present administration. *Interests:* "Archives of living elders in America today; art collector for Native American Church collection. Parapsychology; existential philosophy; existential phenomenology; altered states of consciousness and metaphysics; herbal medicine; yoga; handball; travel. *Published work:* Film produced: *Amonita Sequoyah* (Native American Media, 1982); *Archives: Longest Walk for Survival,* 1981; *Archives: Black Elk, Sun Bear, AmyLee, Simon Brasquepe.*

PETERSON, FRANK R. (Aleut) 1940-
(former chief executive-
Alaska Native association)

Born July 9, 1940, Lazy Bay, Alaska. *Education:* Yale University; Sheldon Jackson Junior College, Sitka, Alaska, 1965-1966. *Home address:* Waldo Apartments, Kodaik, Alaska 99615. *Affiliation:* Former chief executive, Kodiak Area Native Association, Kodiak, Alaska, 1973-? *Other professional posts:* Ayakulik, Inc. (president, Regional Village Corporation); president, Association of Small Koniag Tribes; assemblyman, Kodiak Island Borough; advisory board member, Kodiak Baptist Mission; board of directors, Kodiak Public Broadcasting Corp. (KMXT); KANA Housing Authority; ex-officio, Kodiak Community College Advisory Board; ex-officio member, Board of Commissioners. *Military service:* U.S. Marine Corps, 1960-1965 (Corporal E-4).

PETERSON, GARY (Skokomish)
(tribal chairman)

Affiliation: Chairman, Skokomish Tribal Council, Route 5, Box 432, Shelton, Wash. 98584.

PETTIGREW, JACKSON D. (Chickasaw)
1942-
(artist, business manager)

Born July 2, 1942, Ada, Okla. *Education:* East Central University, Ada, Okla., B.A., 1973. *Principal occupation:* Artist, business manager. *Home address:* 3727 Governor Harris Dr., Ada, Okla. 74820. *Affiliations:* Owner, Native American Arts (retail-/wholesale), Ada, Okla., 1984-. *Other professional post:* Chairman of the board, First American Foundry Arts, Inc. (art bronze), Ada, Okla. *Community activities:* Teach art classes for young people, J.O.M. Indian pro-

gram. *Membership:* Southern Oklahoma Artist Association. *Interests:* "Artistic growth and sharing concepts with young people who are interested in art as a career. Also interested in civil rights. I was an equal opportunity specialist at the Dallas Regional Office of Civil Rights, Dallas, Tex., 1973-1979. I was also vice chairperson for the Regional Indian Affairs Council from 1974-1978. We served as an advocate for Native Americans in Region VI and the nation. Other interests include: silversmithing, painting and sculpturing. I have competed in various national juried art shows."

PHILEMON, HENRY, Sr. (Potawatomi)
(tribal chairman)

Affiliation: Chairman, Hannahville Indian Community Council, Route 1, Community Center, Wilson, Mich. 49896.

PHILLIPS, GEORGE HARWOOD 1934-
(professor of history)

Born January 27, 1934, San Diego, Calif. *Education:* San Diego State University, B.A. (English), 1959; University of California, Los Angeles, M.A. (African History), 1967, Ph.D. (American History), 1973. Ph.D. dissertation: *Indian Resistance and Cooperation in Southern California: The Garra Uprising and Its Aftermath. Principal occupation:* Professor of history. *Home address:* 1065 8th St., Boulder, Colo. 80302. *Affiliations:* Lecturer in history, University of West Indies, Jamaica, 1969-1971; lecturer in Afro-Ethnic Studies, Fullerton State University, Calif., 1972-1973; acting assistant professor of history, U.C.L.A., 1973-1975; visiting lecturer in history, 1977-1978, assistant professor of history, 1978-1981, associate professor of history, University of Colorado, Boulder, 1981-. *Other professional posts:* Contributing editor, *The Journal of California and Great Basin Anthropology;* board of editors, *Pacific Historical Review. Military service:* U.S. Marine Corps, 1954-1956. *Memberships:* American Historical Association (Pacific Coast Branch). *Published works: Chiefs and Challengers: Indian Resistance and Cooperation in Southern California* (University of California-Berkeley Press, 1975); *The*

Enduring Struggle: Indians in California History (Boyd & Fraser, 1981). Articles: "The Indian Paintings from Mission San Fernando: An Historicl Interpretation" *(The Journal of California Anthropoogy,* Summer, 1976); "Indians and the Breakdown of Spanish Mission System in California" *(Ethnohistory,* Fall, 1974); "Indians in Los Angeles, 1781-1875: Economic Integration, Social Disintegration" *(Pacific Historical Review,* August, 1980).

PHILP, KENNETH 1941-
(professor of history)

Born December 6, 1941, Pontiac, Mich. *Education:* Michigan State University, B.A., 1963, Ph.D., 1968; University of Michigan, M.A., 1964. *Principal occupation:* Professor of history, University of Texas, Arlington, 1968-. *Memberships:* American Historical Association; Western History Association; Organization of American Historians. *Interests:* American Indian history; federal Indian policy. *Published works: Co-editor, Essays on Walter Prescott Webb* (University of Texas Press, 1976); *John Collier's Crusade for Indian Reform* (University of Arizona Press, 1977); editor, *Indian Self-Rule: From Roosevelt to Reagan* (Howe Brothers, 1986).

PHOENIX, ANDREW (Paiute)
(tribal chairman)

Affiliation: Chairman, Cedarville Community Council, P.O. Box 142, Cedarville, Calif. 96104.

PICOTTA, ALVIN
(B.I.A. agency superintendent)

Affiliation: Superintendent, Michigan Agency, Bureau of Indian Affairs, Federal Square Office Plaza, P.O. Box 884, Sault Ste. Marie, Mich. 49783.

PICO, ANTHONY (Diegueno)
(tribal spokesman)

Affiliation: Spokesman, Viejas Tribal Committee, P.O. Box 908, Alpine, Calif. 92001.

PIERCE, LYMON
(director-Indian center)

Affiliation: Director, Los Angeles Indian Center, Inc., 1610 West Seventh St., 3rd Floor, Los Angeles, Calif. 90017.

PIETROFORTE, ALFRED 1925-
(speech instructor)

Born March 25, 1925, Philadelphia, Pa. Education: College of the Sequoias, A.A., 1952; Fresno State College, B.A., 1954, M.A., 1961. *Principal occupation:* Instructor in speech and general semantics, College of the Sequoias. *Home address:* 2113 S. Church St., Visalia, Calif. *Interests:* English; public speaking; general semanitcs; American folk music—especially the music of the California Indians. Mr. Pietroforte writes, "My publication, *Songs of the Yokuts and Paiutes,* took two years to complete. This meant extensive travel to a number of Indian reservations and rancherias as well as visiting informants who have left the reservations and have made their homes in the cities and towns of California."

PIGSLEY, DELORES (Siletz)
(tribal chairwoman)

Affiliation: Chairwoman, Confederated Tribes of Siletz Indians Tribal Council, P.O. Box 549, Siletz, Ore. 97380.

PINKHAM, ALLEN V. (Nez Perce)
(tribal chairman)

Affiliation: Nez Perce Tribal Executive Committee, P.O. Box 305, Lapwai, Idaho 83540.

PINO, AUGUSTIN (Zia Pueblo)
(Pueblo governor)

Affiliation: Governor, Zia Pueblo, General Delivery, San Ysidro, N.M. 87053.

PINTO, TONY J. (Diegueno)
(tribal chairman)

Affiliation: Cuyapaipe General Council, P.O. Box 187, Campo, Calif. 92006.

PLUMMER, EDWARD O.
(B.I.A. agency superintendent)

Affiliation: Superintendent, Eastern Navajo Agency, Bureau of Indian Affairs, P.O. Box 328, Crownpoint, N.M. 87313.

POLESE, RICHARD 1941-
(editor)

Born November 16, 1941, Berkeley, Calif. *Education:* San Jose State College, 1959-1961; Hanover College, Hanover, Ind., B.A., 1962. *Principal occupation:* Editor. *Home address:* P.O. Box 1295, Santa Fe, N.M. 87501. *Affiliations:* Editor, *El Palacio,* Southwestern Quarterly; book editor, Museum of New Mexico Press, 1969-. *Other professional posts:* Columnist for the Santa Fe *Reporter. Awards, honors:* Edited and designed the award-winning book, *Music and Dance of the Tewa Pueblos,* by Dr. Gertrude Kurath. *Interests:* Mr. Polese has written and edited publications on the Southwest and its people since 1962. These include several articles in *El Palacio* magazine, and editing and designing of several books and is recognized as an authority on the New Mexico Zia sun symbols, its origins and variations. *Published works: Original New Mexico Cookery,* 1965; editor, *Pueblo Pottery of New Mexico Indians,* 1977; editor, *Music and Dance of the Tewa Pueblos,* 1969; editor, *In Search of Maya Glyphs,* 1970; editor, *Navajo Weaving Handbook,* 1977. All published by Museum of New Mexico Press.

POOCHA, FRITZ T. (Hopi) 1933-
(school administrator)

Born February 26, 1933, Polacca, Ariz. *Education:* Arizona State University, B.A., 1961; Penn State University, M.A., 1971. *Principal occupation:* School administrator. *Home address:* P.O. Box 1247, Tuba City, Ariz. 86045. *Affiliations:* Teacher, Tuba City Boarding School, 1961-1971; principal, Polacca Day School, Polacca, Ariz., 1971-1975; principal, Moenkopi Day School, Tuba City, Ariz., 1975-. *Military service:* U.S. Army, 1953-1955 (Corporal-79th Army Engineer, Korean Conflict). *Community activities:* American Legion (special services officer, 1971-); V.F.W., 1974-. *Inter-*

ests: Mr. Poocha writes, "Bilingual and bicultural education; minorities have languages that are structured differently and consist of sounds not found in the English language. In teaching the English language, thought process must be changed. Cultural values are perceived differently."

POOLAW, LINDA S. (Delaware-Kiowa) 1942-
(tribal cultural consultant, writer-playwrite)

Born April 8, 1942, Lawton, Okla. *Education:* University of Sciences and Arts of Oklahoma, Chickasha, B.A. (Sociology), 1974; University of Oklahoma (two years Masters work in Communications). *Principal occupation:* Tribal cultural consultant, Delaware Tribe of Western Oklahoma, Anadarko, Okla. *Home address:* P.O. Box 986, Anadarko, Okla. 73005. *Other professional post:* Playwrite. *Community activities:* Salvation Army, Caddo County (chairperson); Delaware Tribe of Western Oklahoma (treasurer); Riverside Indian School Board (vice president); American Indian Exposition (vice president). *Memberships:* Indian and Western Arts Association (vice president). *Interests:* "Writing fiction and history about American Indians. (I) have traveled coast to coast to develop relationships with tribes. In 1986, I plan to research and write a book on my deceased father's work in photography, "50 Years of Life on the Southern Plains," (Horace Poolaw)." *Plays:* "Skins," 1974; "Happiness Is Being Married to a White Woman," and "Written, Spoken and Unspoken Word" (University of Oklahoma Press, 1982); "The Day the Tree Fell," children's play (American Indian Institute, Norman, Okla., 1983).

POPOVI DA (Tewa Pueblo) 1922-
(potter)

Born April 10, 1922, Santa Fe, N.M. *Education:* Canyon School of Art. *Principal occupation:* Potter. *Home address:* San Ildefonso Pueblo, Santa Fe, N.M. 87501. *Military service:* U.S. Army, 1943-1946 (Good Conduct Medal; special recognition for service under the Manhattan Engineers). *Community activities:* San Ildefonso Pueblo (governor); All-Pueblo Indian Council (chairman); New Mexico State Art Commission (board of directors). *Memberships:* New Mexico Assocaition on Indian Affairs (board of directors); Gallup Inter-Tribal Ceremonial Association (board of directors). *Awards, honors:* National Indian Arts Council, Scottsdale, Ariz.; Inter-Tribal Ceremonial; New Mexico Craft Fair; Philbrook Museum, Tulsa, Okla.; Museum Fur Volkerkunde, Germany; among others. *Interests:* "Preservation of traditional art and culture of the Pueblos."

POPE, JERRY L. (Shawnee) 1941-
(artist)

Born April 26, 1941, Greenfield, Ind. *Education:* John Heron School of Art; Indiana University, B.F.A., 1964. *Principal occupation.* Artist. *Affiliations.* Curator, American Indian People's Museum, Indianapolis, Ind.; editor, *Tosan,* American Indian People's News, Indianapolis, Ind.; principal chief, United Remnant Band, Shawnee nation of Indiana, Ohio, Kentucky and Pennsylvania; director, Three Feather Society (Native-professional-social organization). *Other professional post:* Assisted in the compilation of Smithsonian Institution's list of native publications. *Memberships:* League of Nations, Pan-American Indians; National Association of Metis Indians; Three Feather Society (director); Mide Widjig, Grand Medicine Lodge Brotherhood, Albuquerque, N.M. *Awards, honors:* First Prize, national Exhibition of Small Paintings; selected to preside over and organize dedication of world's largest collection of Cuna Indian art, Dennison University, Granville, Ohio, 1972; among others. *Interests:* Mr. Pope writes, "1. Professional Native artist, by voction; 2. editing and publishing of the Inter-Tribal Native publiction, *Tosan;* 3. rebuilding the United Remnant Band of the Shawnee Nation, beginning in 1970 with seven persons; we now have re-established all twelve clans; 4. re-education of my people in traditional ways, instilling due pride in knowledge of their birthright; 5. work with in-prison Native groups." *Published work: Native Publications in the United States and Canada* (Smithsonian Institution, 1972).

PORTER, FRANK WILLIAM, III 1947-
(ethnohistorian)

Born July 9, 1947, Charleston, W.V. *Education:* University of Maryland, M.A., 1973, Ph.D., 1978. *Principal occupation:* Ethnohistorian. *Home address:* 409 Ridge Rd., Gettysburg, Pa. 17325. *Affiliation:* Director, American Indian Research and Resource Institute, Gettysburg College, Gettysburg, Pa. 17325. *Military service:* U.S. Air Force, 1967-1971. *Memberships:* American Society of Ethnohistory; Maryland Historical Society. *Awards, honors:* Phi Alpha Theta Award, 1973. *Interests:* Photography, woodworking, oil painting, organic gardening, book collecting. *Published works: Indians in Maryland and Delaware* (Indiana University Press, 1979); *Maryland Indians* (Maryland Historical Society, 1983); *Strategies for Survival* (Greenwood Press, 1986); *In Pursuit of the Past* (Scarecrow Press, 1986).

POWELL, DICK & DONNA 1934-, 1939-
(Indian store owner/operators)

Born (Dick) February 13, 1934, Oakland, Calif.; (Donna) October 6, 1939, Sacramento, Calif. *Principal occupation:* Owner-/operator, Bear Track Trader, Ludington, Mich., 1976-. *Military service:* (Dick) U.S. Army, 1956-1958 (1st Sergeant). *Membership:* Indian Arts and Crafts Association, 1976-. *Interests:* "We have traveled throughout the Southwest extensively in the 1960-1970 period. Now that we have our own retail store we hand select all merchandise we sell, and usually are not able to go more than once a years to the reservation area."

POWERS, MARIA N. 1938-
(anthropologist)

Born January 8, 1938, Cranston, R.I. *Education:* Brooklyn College, C.U.N.Y., B.A. (Psychology; magna cum laude), 1973; Rutgers University, M.A. (Anthropology), 1979, Ph.D. (Anthropology; dissertation: *Oglala Women in Myth, Ritual, and Reality), 1982. *Principal occupation:* Anthropologist. *Home address:* 74 Stillwell Rd.,

Kendall Park, N.J. 08824. *Affiliation:* Visiting research associate, Institute for Research on Women, Rutgers University, New Brunswick, N.J., 1983-. *Other professional posts:* Associate editor, *Powwow Trails: American Indians, Past and Present,* Somerset, N.J., 1964-1966; consultant, Title IV Bilingual Health Program, Pine Ridge Indian Reservation, Pine Ridge, S.D., Summer, 1976; consultant, Psychiatric Nursing Program, University of South Dakota and U.S. Public Health Service satellite program, Oglala Sioux Community, Pine Ridge Reservation, Summer, 1976; consultant, Lakota Culture Camp (program evaluation for Dept. of Special Education, State of S.D.), Pine Ridge Indian Reservation, Summer, 1980; member of thesis committee in Psychiatric Nursing, Rutgers University—thesis title: *An Exploratory Study of Mentoring Relationships Among Indian Women in the Profession of Nursing,* 1982; also thesis committee in anthropology—Ph.D. thesis entitled: *Comanche Belief and Ritual,* 1985. *Memberships:* American Anthropological Association; Society for Medical Anthropology; Society for Visual Anthropology; American Folklore Society; American Ethnological Society; Philadelphia Anthropological Society; Society for Ethnomusicology; Nebraska State Historical Society; American Dance Therapist Association; American Craftsman's Council; Actor's Equity; American Federation of Television and Radio Artists. *Fieldwork:* Pine Ridge, South Dakota, Oglala ("Sioux"), also various tribes of New Mexico, Arizona, Oklahoma and Wyoming; urban U.S. "I have done extensive anthropological research among the Oglala Lakota on the Pine Ridge Indian Reservation in South Dakota. A major part of the research focused on native subsistence, food procurement, preparation, storage, distribution, and nutrition. I also studied native therapeutic techniques, particularly treatment of psychosomatic disorders." *Awards, honors:* Wenner-Gren Foundation Grant-in-aid, Summer, 1980 (field research on the relationship of Oglala traditional women's roles to social structure); National Endowment for the Humanities, Research Assistant on "Oglala Music and Dance," September, 1980 - August, 1982, January, 1983 - December, 1983; Douglass Fellows Grant for Research on photo-

graphs of American Indian women, Spring, 1983, 1984; National Endowment for the Humanities, Planning Grant: principal investigator, "Lakota Women: A Photographic Retrospective," January, 1985 - December, 1985; Minnesota Historical Society, grant for field research on Lakota medicine, Summer, 1985. *Interests:* "American Indians, particularly Northern Plains, urban U.S.; intercultural health care systems; anthropology of gender, medicine, art, and dance." Dance: "have appeared in numerous Broadway and off-Broadway shows; on major network television shows; taught dance." American Indian art: "have studied traditional crafts among the Sioux and Comanches and am proficient in various techniques of American Indian beadwork, quillwork, and ribbonwork." *Papers presented:* "Images of American Indian Women: Myth and Reality," Rome, Italy, 1984, tour in West Germany-1985; "Symbols in Contemporary Oglala Art," Vienna, Austria; "Workshop on American Indian Music and Dance" (with William K. Powers), Budapest, Hungary, 1985; "Stereotyping American Indians," Cologne, West Germany, 1985; "Native American Motherhood: A View From the Plains," Rutgers University, 1985; among others. *Published works:* Co-editor, *Lakota Wicozanni-Ehank'ehan na Lehanl (Lakota Health Traditional and Modern),* three volumes plus teacher's guide (Oglala Sioux Community College, 1977); "Metaphysical Aspects of an Oglala Food System," in *Food and the Social Order* (Russell Sage Foundation, 1984); *Oglala Women: Myth, Ritual, and Reality* (University of Chicago Press, 1986); "Puting on the Dog: Ceremoniousness in an Oglala Stew," with William K. Powers, in *Natural History* (American Museum of Natural History-in press); *Lakota Foods,* with William K. Powers (in preparation); *Lakota Medicine* (Minnesota Historical Society Press-in preparation).

POWERS, WILLIAM K. 1934-
(professor of anthropology, journalist)

Born July 31, 1934, St. Louis, Mo. *Education:* Brooklyn College, B.A. (summa cum laude, honors in anthropology), 1971; Wesleyan University, M.A. (Anthropology; thesis: *Yuwipi Music in Cultural Context*), 1972; University of Pennsylvania, Ph.D. (Anthropology; dissertation: *Continuity and Change in Oglala Religion*). *Principal occupation:* Professor of anthropology, journalist. *Home address:* 74 Stillwell Rd., Kendall Park, N.J. 08824. *Affiliations:* Associate editor, *American Indian Tradition, 1960-1962; editor and publisher, Powwow Trails,* 1964-1966; consulting editor, *American Indians Then and Now Series* (G.P. Putnam's Sons), 1968-; instructor, North American Indian music and dance, Wesleyan University, 1971-1972; teaching fellow, 1972-1973, lecturer, 1973-1977, (North American Indians),University of Pennsylvania; visiting lecturer, assistant professor and acting chairman, Department of Anthropology, Rutgers University, New Brunswick, N.J., 1974-. *Fieldwork:* Primarily among the Oglala Sioux, Pine Ridge, South Dakota, 1966-; also various tribes in New Mexico, Arizona, Oklahoma and Wyoming. *Grants and fellowships:* Research in American Indian religion, linguistics, and music, American Philosophical Society, 1966, 1967, 1977; among others. *Awards, honors:* Award of Excellence in Juvenile Literature, New Jersey State Teachers of Enblish, 1972, 1973; Faculty Merit Award, Rutgers University, 1977; among others. *Memberships:* American Anthropological Association; Society for Applied Anthropology; Washington Anthropological Society; Philadelphia Anthropological Society; Society for Ethnomusicology; Indian Rights Association (director, 1977-?). *Interests:* North American Indian studies—historical and contemporary Indian affairs; urban U.S.; social organization; comparative religion; history of anthropology; sociolinguistics; ethnomusicology; culture change. *Published works: Indian Dancing and Costumes* (G.P. Putnam's Sons, 1966); *Young Brave* (For Children, Inc., 1967); *Crazy Horse and Custer* (For Children, Inc., 1968); *Indians of the Northern Plains* (G.P. Putnam's Sons, 1969); *The Modern Sioux: Reservation Systems and Social Change* (University of Nebraska Press, 1970); *Indians of the Southern Plains* (G.P. Putnam's Sons, 1971); *Continuity and Change in the American Family,* with Marla N. Powers (Dept. of HEW); *Indians of the Great Lakes* (G.P. Putnam's

Sons, 1976); co-author, *Lakota Wicozani - Ehank'ehan na Lehanl* (Indian Health-Traditional and Modern), 1976; *Oglala Religion* (University of Nebraska Press, 1977); *Lakota Foods,* with Marla N. Powers (in preparation); numerous papers, articles in scholarly journals, notes, book reviews, abstracts, etc.

POWLESS, PURCELL (Oneida)
(tribal chairman)

Affiliation: Chairman, Oneida Executive Committee, P.O. Box 365, Oneida, Wis. 54155.

PRESCOTT, MICHAEL (Sioux)
(tribal president)

Affiliation: President, Lower Sioux Indian Community Council, RR 1, Box 308, Morton, Minn. 56270.

PRESS, DANIEL S.
(tribal employment)

Affiliation: General counsel, Council on Tribal Employment, 918 16th St., N.W., Suite 503, Washington, D.C. 20006.

PRICE, B. LEIGH 1939-
(attorney)

Born June 15, 1939, Waco, Tex. *Education:* University of California, Berkeley, B.A., 1961; Yale University Law School, J.D., 1972. *Principal occupation:* Attorney. *Home address:* 6705 Tomlinson Terrace, Cabin John, Md. 20818. *Affiliation:* American Indian coordinator, Environmental Protection Agency, Washington, D.C. *Other professional post:* Visiting professor, Arizona State College of Law, 1985-1986. *Military service:* U.S. Marine Corps, 1966-1969 (Captain; Vietnam Service Medal). *Memberships:* New Mexico State Bar Association. *Awards, honors:* A&O Distinguished Service Award, 1981. *Interests:* "Indian law and environmental law; design and development of pollution control programs for tribes and state governments; land use; land rcordation and registration."

PRICE, FRANK
(president-Alaskan Native organization

Affiliation: President, Thirteenth Regional Corporation, 4241 21st Ave. West, Suite 100, Seattle, Wash. 98199.

PRICE, JOHN A. 1933-
(professor of anthropology)

Born February 16, 1933, Merced, Calif. *Education:* University of Utah, B.A., 1959, M.A., 1962; University of Michigan, Ph.D., 1967. *Principal occupation:* Professor of anthropology, York University, Downsview, Ontario, Can. *Other professional posts:* Editor, *Canadian Journal of Native Studies;* editor, Canadian Society for Applied Anthropology. *Military service:* U.S. Army, 1952-1955 (Sergeant; Korean Battle Ribbon). *Interests:* Computer programming. *Published works: Native Studies: American & Canadian Indians* (McGraw-Hill-Ryerson, 1978); *Indians of Canada* (Prentice-Hall-Canada, 1979); *The Washo Indians* (Nevada State Museum, 1980).

PRINTUP, MARIBEL
(B.I.A. Indian education)

Affiliation: Indian Education, Bureau of Indian Affairs, 1951 Constitution Ave., N.W., Washington, D.C. 20245.

PRUCHA, FRANCIS PAUL 1921
(professor of history)

Born January 4, 1921, River Falls, Wis. *Education:* River Falls State College, B.S., 1941; University of Minnesota, M.A., 1947; Harvard University, Ph.D., 1950; St. Louis University, 1952-1954; St. Mary's College, s.t.l, 1958. *Principal occupation:* Professor of history. *Address:* Department of History, Marquette University, Milwaukee, Wis. 53233. *Affiliations:* Society of Jesus, 1950; ordained priest, 1957; professor of history, Marquette University, Milwaukee, Wis., 1960-. *Military service:* U.S. Army Air Force, 1942-1946. *Memberships:* American Historical Association, 1949-; Organization of American Historians, 1954-; State Historical Society of Wisconsin, 1960- (board of curators, 1972-1978, 1981, president, 1976-1978); Western History Association, 1962- (president, 1983); Milwaukee County Historical Society (board of directors, 1964- *Published works: Broadax and Bayonet* (State Historical Society of Wisconsin, 1953); *Army Life on the Western Frontier* (University of Oklahoma Press, 1958); *American Indian Policy in the Formative Years* (Harvard University Press, 1962); *Guide to Military Posts of the U.S., 1789-1895* (State Historical Society fo Wisconsin, 1964); *The Sword of the Republic* (Macmillan, 1969); *Indian Peace Medals in American History* (State Historical Society of Wisconsin, 1971); *The Indians in American History* (Holt, Rinehart & Winston, 1971); Americanizing the American Indians: Writings by the "Friends of the Indians" 1880-1900 (Harvard University Press, 1973); *Documents of the United States Indian Policy* (University of Nebraska Press, 1975); *American Indian Policy in Crisis: Christian Reformers and the Indian, 1865-1900* (University of Oklahoma Press, 1976); *A Bibliographical Guide to the History of Indian-White Relations in the U.S.* (University of Chicago Press, 1977); *United States Indian Policy: A Critical Bibliography* (Indiana University Pres, 1977); *The Churches and the Indian Schools, 1888-1912* (University of Nebraska Press, 1979); editor, *Cherokee Removal: The "William Penn" Essays and Other Writings,* by Jeremiah Evarts (Univrsity of Tennessee Press, 1981); *Indian Policy in the United States: Historical Essays* (University of Nebraska Press, 1981); *Indian-White Relations in the United States: A Bibliography of Works Published, 1975-1980* (University of Nebraska Pres, 1982); *The Great Father: The United States Government and the American Indians,* 2 vols. (University of Nebraska Press, 1984); *The Indians in American Society: From the Revolutionary War to the Present* (University of California Press, 1985).

PULLAR, GORDON L. (Koniag) 1944-
(president-Kodiak Area Native Association)

Born January 22, 1944, Bellingham, Wash. *Education:* Western Washington Univerity, Bellingham, B.A., 1973; University of

Washington, Seattle, M.P.A. (Tribal Administration Program - course of study designed to meet the contemporary management needs of Native American corporations, organizations, and tribal governments as well as federal and state agencies dealing with Native American issues and programs), 1983. *Principal occupation:* President/executive director, Kodiak Area Native Association, Kodiak, Alaska 99615. *Home address:* P.O. Box 4331, Kodiak, Alaska 99615. *Affiliations:* Rewind operator/supervisor, Georgia Pacific Corp., Bellingham, Wash., 1963-1979; business analyst/marketing specialist, Small Tribes Organization of Western Washington, Sumner, Wash., 1979-1981; associate editor, *Nations* magazine (National Communications, Inc., Seattle, Wash.), 1981; owner/publisher, *Kodiak Times,* Kodaik, Alaska, 1983-1985; president/executive director, Kodiak Area Native Association, Kodiak, Alaska, 1983-. *Other professional post:* Assistant editor, business editor, *The Indian Voice* (Small Tribes Organization of Western Wash.), 1979-1981. *Community activities:* Volunteer work in social programs involving Native Americans: Washington State Dept. of Social and Health Services, Whatcom County Detoxification Center, and Whatcom County Juvenile Probation Dept.; Northwest Indian News Association (board of directors, 1979-1981); Governor's Minority and Women's Business Development Advisory Council (appointed by Governor of State of Washington, 1980-1981); Native American Business Alliance (board of directors, vice president-publicity chairman, 1981-1983); Alaska Regional Energy Association (board of directors, 1984-1985); Kodiak Area State Parks Advisory Board, 1983; Alaska Federation of Natives, Inc. (board of directors, 1983-). *Memberships:* Koniag, Inc. (regional Native corporation); Leisnoi, Inc, Woody Island ANCSA Corp.; National Congress of American Indians; American Society for Public Administration (South Central Alaska Chapter).

PUNLEY, RANDOLPH J.
(director-Indian center)

Affiliation: Director, National Indian Employment Resource Center, 2258 South Broadway, Denver, Colo. 80210.

PURICH, DON
(director-Indian law center)

Affiliation: Director, Native Law Centre, Univerity of Saskatchewan, 150 Diefenbaker Centre, Saskatoon, Saskatchewan, Can.

Q

QUIMBY, GEORGE IRVING 1913-
(museum director; professor
of anthropology)

Born May 4, 1913, Grand Rapids, Mich. *Education:* University of Michigan, B.A., 1936, M.A., 1937, Graduate Fellow, 1937-1938; University of Chicago (Postgraduate work),1938-1939. *Principal occupation:* Museum director. *Home address:* 6001 52nd Ave., NE, Seattle, Wash. 98115. *Affiliations:* Director, Muskegon (Mich.) Museum, 1941-1942; Assistant curator, 1942-1943, curator, 1954-1965, research associate, 1965-, North American Archaeology and Ethnology (Field Museum), curator of exhibits, anthropology, 1943-1954, Field Museum of Natural History, Chicago, Ill.; curator of anthropology, 1965-1968, director, 1968-, Thomas Burke Memorial Museum, professor of anthropology, University of Washington, Seattle, Wash., 1965-

Other professional posts: Lecturer, University of Chicago, 1947-1965, Northwestern University, 1949-1953. *Archaeological expeditions and field work:* Michigan, 1935, 1937, 1942, 1956-1963; Wisconsin, 1936; Hudson's Bay, 1939; Louisiana, 1940-1941; New Mexico, 1947; Lake Superior, 1956-1961. *Memberships:* American Association for the Advancement of Science (Fellow); American Anthropological Association; Society for American Archaeology (president, 1958); American Society for Ethnohistory; Wisconsin Archaeological Society; Society for Historical Archaeology (council, 1971-1974, 1975-1978); Association of Science Museum Directors (president 1973-); Norwegian Totemic Society; Arctic Institute of North America; American Association of Museums (council, 1971-1974); Sigma Xi. *Published works: Aleutian Islanders, Eskimos of the North Pacific* (Chicago Natural History Museum, Anthropology Leaflet No. 35,

1944); *The Tehefuncte Culture, An Early Occupation of the Lower Mississippi Valley* (Memoirs-Society for American Archaeology, No. , 1945); *Indians Before Columbus,* with Paul Martin and Donald Collier (Chicago, 1947); *Indians of the Western Frontier, paintings of George Catlin* (Chicago Natural History Museum, 1954); *Indian Life in the Upper Great Lakes, 11,000 B.C. to A.D. 1800* (University of Chicago Press, 1960); *Indian Culture and European Grade Goods,* 1966; co-editor, documentary film, *In the Land of the War Canoes,* 1973; (with Bill Holm-two documentary films) *The Image Maker and the Indians,* 1979, and *Edward S. Curtis in the Land of the War Canoes: A Pioneer Cinematographer in the Pacific Northwest,* 1980; contributing articles to professional journals.

R

RAGAN, CONNIE SEABOURN
(Oklahoma Cherokee) 1951-
(artist-painter/printmaker)

Born September, 20, 1951, Purcell, Okla. *Education:* University of Oklahoma, B.F.A., 1980. *Principal occupation:* Artist-painter/printmaker (self-employed). *Home address:* 2605 SW 99 St., Oklahoma City, Okla. 73159. *Interests:* "My entire life is devoted to doing art and being a good wife and mother." *Biographical sources: Who's Who in American Art,* 1984; *Community Leaders of the World,* 1984; *Directory of Distinguished Americans,* Third Edition; *The International Who's Who of Contemporary Achievement,* 1984; *Personalities of the South,* 1985; *The World Who's Who of Women,* 1985; "The Emergence of an Artist," *Art Gallery International,* 1980; "The Rising Star of Connie Seabourn Ragan," *Indian Trader,* 1982.

RAGSDALE, WILLIAM P.
(B.I.A. area director)

Affiliation: Director, Anadrko Area Office, Bureau of Indian Affairs, WCD - Office Complex, P.O. Box 368, Anadarko, Okla. 73005.

RAMIREZ, DAVID (Yaqui)
(tribal chairman)

Affiliation: Chairman, Pascua Yaqui Tribal Council, 4821 West Calle Vicam, Tucson, Ariz. 85706.

RAMIRIZ, RAYMOND
(museum superintendent)

Affiliation: Superintendent, Ysleta Del Sur Pueblo Museum, P.O. Box 17579, El Paso, Tex. 79917.

RAPHAEL, JOSEPH (Chippewa)
(tribal chairman)

Affiliation: Chairman, Grand Traverse Band Tribal Council, Route 1, Box 118, Suttons Bay, Mich. 49682.

RATON, ELI SEO, Sr. (Santa Ana Pueblo)
(Pueblo governor)

Affiliation: Governor, Santa Ana Pueblo, P.O. Box 37, Bernalillo, N.M. 87004.

RAVE, AUSTIN JERALD
(Minneconjou Sioux) 1946-
(artist)

Born August 5, 1946, Cheyenne River Sioux Reservation, S.D. *Education:* Institute of American Indian Arts, Santa Fe, N.M., 1964-1966; San Francisco Art Institute, 1966-1967; Engineering Drafting School, Denver, Colo., 1970-1972. *Principal occupation:* Artist. *Home address:* Eagle Butte, S.D. 57625. *Other professional posts:* Draftsman, technical illustrator. *Awards, honor:* Numerous awards for art. *Biographical source: Dictionary of International Biography.*

REASON, JAMIE TAWODI
(Southeastern Cherokee) 1947-
(carver/painter)

Born March 11, 1947, Muncie, Ind. *Principal occupation:* Owner/manager, Sacred Earth Studio, Mastic Beach, N.Y., 1980- (Native American art studio). *Home address:* 197 Longfellow Dr., Mastic Beach, N.Y. 11951. *Military service:* U.S. Air Force, 1966 (A/3/C; Vietnam Veteran; National Defense Expert Marksman; Air Police). *Community activities:* Committee for Annual Paumanoke Inter-Tribal Pow-Wow (publicity director/head judge); member of "The Painted Fan Singers." *Memberships:* Indian Arts & Crafts Association; Vietnam Er Veterans Inter-Tribal Association; East End Arts & Humanities Council; Ani-Yvwiya Association of New York. *Interests:* "My art has been exhibited at the Museum of the American Indian, The Gallery of the American Indian Community House (New York City), Red Cloud Indian Art Show, Dartmouth College, Native American Symposium at Old Westbury College (N.Y.), Rhode Island Indian Council, and many galleries. My work is in over 100 private collections." Mr. Reason is probably best known for his solid carved cedar feather boxes, mirror boards, horse memorial sticks, and his traditional bone roach spreaders. *Biographical sources:* The Museum of the American Indian *News,* Sept. 24, 1983; *Suffolk Life,* 1983-1984; Southeastern Cherokee *News; American Indian Community House Newsletter,* 1984; *The Knoxville Journal,* April 7, 1984; *Daily News,* April 4, 1984; *New York Times,* August 18, 1985.

RED SHE BEAR (DEANNA BARNES) (Ute) 1938-
(teacher, craftswoman)

Born June 25, 1938, Boise, Idaho. *Education:* College of the Redwoods, Eureka, Calif.; Humboldt State University, Arcata, Calif.; Lela Center for Holistic Therapy, Arcata, Calif.; Indian Survival Society, Bandon, Ore. *Principal occupation:* Founder-/manager, Red Bear Creations, Bandon, Ore. *Home address:* 358 N. Lexington Ave., Bandon, Ore. 97411. *Affiliations:* Founder, Indian Survival Society; founder and president, Women's Center. *Community activities:* American Red Cross (provider and secretary); Coos and Curry Area Agency on Aging (provider); Intertribal Sweat Lodge Board (officer); District 7 Sub-Area Health Advisory Council (provider); Women's Crisis Service (advisory board). *Membership:* National Indian Health Care Association

(spokeswoman). *Interests:* "Making traditional quilts and blankets. Preserving our old culture and traditions is very important to me. I am an elder, pipecarrier, sweatleader, storyteller in the winter, tech survival skills in the woods, lecture on traditional uses of indigenous plants as food and medicine, and on Indian women's roles in society. I'm currently writing book, *Crystal Wind Warrior,* about a crystal who became a human to help the people (manuscript, 1986)."

REDCLOUD, MERLIN (Winnebago) (tribal chairman)

Affiliation: Chairman, Winnebago Business Committee, P.O. Box 311, Tomah, Wis. 54660.

REED, SILVER STAR (United Lumbee-Cherokee-Choctaw) 1929- (homemaker, national chieftain)

Born November 29, 1929, Vanita, Okla. *Home address:* P.O. Box 512, Fall River Mills, Calif. 96028. *Affiliation:* National chieftain, United Lumbee Nation of N.C. and America, 1983-. *Other professional posts:* Parent committee of Title IV and Johnson O'Malley Indian Education Program, Tulare-Kings Counties, Calif; National Secretary (four years), and Grand Council (member-board of directors)(six years), United Lumbee Nation of N.C. and America. *Memberships:* Native American Wolf Clan (secretary, 1977-); Chapel of Our Lord Jesus, 1974-. *Published works:* Compiler, *Over the Cooking Fires,* featuring traditional Lumbee recipes (United Lumbee Nation, 1982); *Lumbee Indian Ceremonies* (United Lumbee Nation, 1982).

REESER, RALPH R. 1932- (B.I.A. attorney)

Born November 26, 1932, Fairbanks, Alaska. *Education:* Seattle University, 1952-1955; Univerity of Washington, B.A., 1956; George Washington University Law School, J.D., 1960. *Principal occupation:* Attorney. *Home address:* 3702 Spruell Dr., Wheaton, Md. 20902. *Affiliations:* Attorney-advisor, Public Housing Administration, Washington, D.C., 1961-1966; director, Housing Development, Bureau of Indian Affairs, Washington, D.C., 1966-1970; deputy director, Publicly Financed Housing, Department of HUD, Washington, D.C., 1970-1972; director, Congressional & Legislative Affairs, Bureau of Indian Affairs, Washington, D.C., 1972-. *Military service:* U.S. Air Force, 1951-1952 (S/Sgt.).

REUTLINGER, BARBARA N. 1933-
(journalist-editor)

Born March 14, 1933, Scholls, Ore. *Education:* Central Oregon Community College (one year). *Principal occupation:* Editor, *Rawhide Press,* Times Publishing Co., Wellpinit, Wash., 1971-. *Home address:* P.O. Box 393, Wellpinit, Wash. 99040. *Other professional post:* Free-lance article writer. *Memberships:* Washington Press Women; National Federation of Press Women; Northwest Indian Press Association (board member, 1977-). *Awards, honors: Rawhide Press,* nominated as on of top ten Indian papers in the nation; numerous editorial awards. *Interests:* "Writing is my vocation and avocation, with spare time spent in painting and fine arts and crafts."

REYES, JOYCE (Yakima) 1937-
(organization executive)

Born May 21, 1937, Redmond, Ore. *Education:* University of Washington. *Affiliation:* President, American Indian Women's Service League, Seattle, Wash. *Community activities:* Seattle Human Rights Commission (social and health services advisory committee); United Indians of All Tribes Foundation (secretary). *Interests:* Ms. Reyes writes, "I am active now in the development of an Indian cultural/educational facility to be located on 17 acres in the City of Seattle."

REYES, LUANA L.
(Indian health service)

Affiliation: Director, Division of Program Formulation, Indian Health Service, 5600 Fishers Lane, Rockville, Md. 20857.

REYHNER, JON ALLAN 1944-
(school administrator)

Born April 29, 1944, Fountain Hill, Pa. *Education:* University of California, Davis, B.A., 1966, M.A., 1967; Northern Arizona University, Flagstaff, M.A., 1973, Ed.S., 1977; Montana State University, Bozeman, Ed.D., 1984. *Principal occupation:* School administrator. *Home address:* General Delivery, Cibecue, Ariz. 86435. *Affiliations:* Math/science teacher, Chinle Junior High School, Chinle, Ariz., 1971-1973; social studies teacher, Fort Defiance Junior High School, Fort Defiance, Ariz., 1973-1975; assistant principal, Navajo Public School, Navajo, N.M., 1975-1977; principal, Wallace Public School, Parker, Ariz., 1977-1978; principal, Rocky Boy Public School, Box Elder, Mt., 1978-1980; university supervisor of professional and student teachers, Department of Elementary Education, Montana State University, Bozeman, 1980-1981; principal/federal projects director, Heart Butte Public Schoos, Mt., 1982-1984; administrator/principal, Havasupai School, Supai, Ariz., 1984-1985; academic coordinator, Cibecue Community School, Ariz., 1985-. *Memberships:* International Reading Association, 1982-; American Association of School Administrators, 1984-; National Indian Education Association, 1984-; Council for Indian Education, 1984-; Phi Delta Kappa, 1973-; Phi Alpha Theta. *Interests:* Bilingual education; photography; historical research on Western America. *Published works: Heart Butte: A Blackfeet Indian Community,* 1984; editor, *Stories of Our Blackfeet Grandmothers,* 1984; editor, *The Story of Running Eagle,* by James Willard Schultz, 1984; editor, *Famine Winter,* by James Willard Schultz, 1984; editor, *The Loud Mouthed Gun,* by James Willard Schultz, 1984; all published by Council for Indian Education. Articles: "The Self Determined Curriculum: Indian Teachers as Cultural Translators" (*Journal of American Indian Education,* Nov., 1981).

RHOADES, EVERETT RONALD, M.D.
(Oklahoma Kiowa) 1931-
(physician, director-Indian
Health Service)

Born October 24, 1931, Lawton, Okla. *Education:* Lafayette College, 1949-1952; University of Oklahoma College of Medicine, M.D., 1956. *Principal occupation:* Physician, director-Indian Health Service, Rockville, Md. *Affiliations:* Chief, Infectious Diseases, Wilford Hall, U.S. Air Force Hospital, 1961-1966; professor of medicine, Chief, Infectious Diseases, University of Oklahoma College of Medicine, Oklahoma City, 1966-?; director, Indian Health Service, Room 5A-55, Parklawn Bldg., 5600 Fishers Lane, Rockville, Md. 20857. *Military service:* U.S. Air Force, 1957-1966 (Major; Certificate of Merit, 1967). *Community activities:* Association of American Indian Physicians (president, 1972, 1976); Oklahoma Lung Association (board of directors); Association on American Indian Affairs (vice president, 1977-); Task Force on Health of American Indian Policy Review Commission (chairman, 1975); National Advisory Allergy and Infectious Disease Council (NIH), 1971-1975; Central Oklahoma Indian Health Project (board of directors; chairman, 1976); Kiowa Tribal Business Committee (vice chairman, 1973-1975); founder and donor, Dorothy Rowell Rhoades Prize to outstanding graduating Indian student, Elgin High School, Okla. *Memberships:* American Thoracic Society, 1960-; American Federation for Clinical Research, 1960-; American College of Physicians, 1963- (Fellow); American Society for Microbiology, 1967-; National Congress of American Indians; Sigma Xi. *Awards, honors:* Markle Scholar, Academic Medicine, 1967-1972; John Hay Whitney Opportunity Fellow, 1952-1956; Student Research Achievement Award, 1956; Outstanding Achievement, Veterans Administration Hospital, 1960, 1961; Recognition Award, Association of American Indian Physicians, 1973, 1976; Breath of Life Award, Oklahoma Lung Association, 1977; Public Health Service Recognition Award, 1977; among others. *Interests:* Internal medicine; infectious diseases; Kiowa Gourd Clan; Kiowa Blacklegging Society; dancing and powwows; amateau archaeology; history of medicine and Indians; travel. *Biographical sources: Directory of Medical Specialists; Dictionary of International Biography; Who's Who in the South and Southwest; American Men & Women of Science; Indians of Today; Contemporary American Indian Leaders. Published works:* Numerous articles in scientific journals relating to infectious diseases, microbiology, and Indian life; author of "Kiowa Tribe" for *World Book Encyclopedia*; edited "Task Force Report" to American Indian Policy Review Commission (Health), U.S. Government Printing Office, 1975.

RICHARDSON, BARRY
(director-Indian center)

Affiliation: Baltimore American Indian Center, 113 South Broadway, Baltimore, Md. 21231.

RICHARDSON, KENNETH (Paiute)
(tribal chairman)

Affiliation: Chairman, Yerington Tribal Council, 171 Campbell Lane, Yerington, Nev. 89447.

RICHARDSON, PATRICIA ROSE
(BREWINGTON)(Coharie-Cherokee)
1933-
(crafts consultant)

Born July 21, 1933, Clinton, N.C. *Education:* East Carolina Indian School, 1952; Nash Technical College, Rocky Mt., N.C., A.A. (Education), 1986. *Principal occupation:* American Indian crafts consultant-/pottery and beadwork. *Home address:* P.O. Box 130, Hollister, N.C. 27844. *Affiliations:* Instructor, Title IV Indian Education, Halifax Board of Education, N.C. (six years); crafts instructor, Haliwa-Supai Indian Tribe, Hollister, N.C. (five years). *Memberships:* North Carolina Crafts Association (board member); American Indian Heritage Foundation. *Awards, honors:* First Place Awards—Excellence in Beadwork, Schiele Museum Indian Festival, 1978/1986; Good Medicine Crafts Award, 1980/1986. *Interests:* Exhibitions at major Indian festivals: Grand Prairie, Tex., Hunter Mountain, N.Y., Palm Beach, Fla., North Carolina Indian festivals, National Indian Festival, Washington, D.C.

RIDDLES, LEONARD *(Black Moon)* **(Comanche) 1919-**
(artist, farmer/rancher)

Born June 28, 1919, Walters, Okla. *Education:* High school. *Principal occupation:* Artist, farmer/rancher. *Hoe address:* Route 1, Walter, Okla. *Military service:* U.S. Army, 1941-1945 (Service Ribbon, American Defense Ribbon). *Community activities:* Comanche Tribal Council (former officer); Masons. *Membership:* American Indian Artists Association. *Awards, honors:* Numerous awards from 1963-. *Exhibitions:* Philbrook Art Center, Inter-Tribal Indian Ceremonial; Museum of New Mexico; U.S. Department of the Interior Gallery; among others. *Interests:* Mr. Riddles writes, "I am interested in the history of the American Indian and in any phase of archaeological study. We do research on the Comanche Tribe, so (I) find all expeditions of real interest. Museums are also of great interest to me." Mr. Riddles illustrated the jacket for *Buried Colts,* by Harley Smith.

RIDENHOWER, MARILYN
(college president)

Affiliation: President, Fort Peck Community College, P.O. Box 575, Poplar, Mt. 59255.

RIDINGTON, ROBIN 1939-
(professor of anthropology)

Born November 1, 1939, Camden, N.J. *Education:* Swarthmore, B.A., 1962; Harvard University, Ph.D., 1968. *Principal occupation:* Professor of anthropology. *Home address:* 3464 W. 27th Ave., Vancouver, British Columbia, Can. V6S 1P6. *Affiliation: Assistant and associate professor of anthropology, Univerity of British Columbia, Vancouver, B.C., 1967-. Memberships:* Society for Humanistic Anthropology (Canadian representative); Canadian Ethnology Society; American Anthropological Association. *Interests:* Field research among

Beaver Indians, 1964-; writing about Omaha ceremony, 1985-1986. *Published works:* Articles: "From Artifice to Artifact: Stages in the Industrialization of a Northern Native Community" (*Journal of Canadian Studies,* 1983); "Laurie Anderson: Shaman of the Post-Modern Era" (*The Vancouver Literary News,* May, 1983); "Stories of the Vision Quest Among Dunne-za Women" (*Atlantis,* 1983); "Beaver Indians" (*The Canadian Encyclopedia,* Hurtig, 1985); "Native People, Subarctic" (*The Canadian Encyclopedia,* Hurtig, 1985); "Fix and Chicadee: The Writing of Indian White History" in volume edited by Calvin Martin (in press); "Mottles As By Shadows: A Sacred Symbol of the Omaha Tribe" in *First Voices of the First America* (New Scholar, in press); among others.

RINER, REED D. 1941-
(anthropologist/futurist)

Born December 22, 1941, Mentone, Ind. *Education:* University of Colorado, Ph.D., 1977 (dissertation: *A Study of Attitudes Toward Formal Education Among Indian Parents and Students in Six Communities. Principal occupation:* Associate professor of anthropology, Northern Arizona State University, Flagstaff, 1975-. *Home address:* 506 Charles Rd., Flagstaff, Ariz. 86001. *Other professional post:* Advisor, Native American Indian Studies Program, Northern Arizona University; editor/publisher, *Cultural Futures Research. Military service:* U.S. Naval Reserve, 1963-1968. *Memberships:* American Anthropological Association; Society for Appplied Anthropology; High Plains Society for Applied Anthropology (past president); World Future Studies Federation; World Future Society; Contact Cultures of the Imagination (board of directors); Cross-Cultural Dance Resources (board of directors). *Interests:* "My primary professional interests are applied futures research; Native American Indian studies, especially Indian education; and the application of anthropology in the solution of— especially institutional—organizational problems such as the future of Native American Indians." *Published works:* Numerous articles in professional journals.

ROACH, MILBURN H.
(administrative director-
Indian Health Service)

Affiliation: Administrative director, Indian Health Service, 5600 Fishers Lane, Rockville, Md. 20857.

ROBERTS, HOLLIS (Choctaw)
(tribal chief)

Affiliation: Chief, Choctaw Tribal Council, Drawer 1210, 16th & Locust St., Durant, Okla. 74701.

ROBERTSON, ELLEN (Oklahoma
Cherokee) 1945-
(librarian)

Born March 7, 1945, Washington, D.C. *Education:* University of California, Berkeley, B.A., 1973, M.L.S., 1974. *Principal occupation:* Librarian, American Indian Law Center, University of New Mexico School of Law, Albuquerque, N.M., 1975-. *Home address:* 1125 Lafayette, N.E., Albuquerque, N.M. 87110. *Other professional post:* Editor, *American Indian Law Newsletter,* Univerity of New Mexico School of Law. *Interests:* Photography and literature; Pece Corps, 1966-1968 (Tunesia); travel.

ROBINSON, GARY (Cherokee-
Mississippi Choctaw) 1950-
(film/video producer)

Born January 12, 1950, Dallas, Tex. *Education:* University of Texas, Austin, B.S., 1973; M.A. (Radio, TV, Film), 1978. *Principal occupation:* Film/video producer. *Home address:* P.O. Box 781, Okmulgee, Okla. 74447. *Affiliations:* Production assistant, Instructional Media Department, Tulsa Public Schools, Tulsa, Okla., 1973-1974; media specialist, Texas Department of Mental Health/Mental Retardation, Austin, Tex., 1975-1978; branch sales manager, Magnetic Media Corp., Austin, Tex., 1978-1979; independent media producer/writier, 1980; communication specialist, Creek Nation, Okmulgee, Okla., 1981-; owner-producer, Pathfinder Communications (production and consultant company),

Okmulgee, Okla. *Membership:* Oklahoma Film & Tape Professionals Association. *Interests:* "Develop, produce and direct educational and promotional programs about Creek Indian Tribe. Regularly produce informational videotapes on Creek culture, history, art and current tribal activities. Currently developing a feature film for the tribe on Alexander Posey and the Creek Nation of Oklahoma. Avocational interests include: music, religion, movies, travel." *Video productions: The Green Corn Festival* (documentary of ancient Creek ceremony), 1982, 20 minutes; *1,000 Years of Muscogee (Creek) Art,* 1982, 26 minutes; Folklore of the Muscogee People (Creek Indian legends), 1983, 28 minutes; *Continuing Progress for the Muscogee People* (public relations on Creek Tribe), 1983, 13 minutes; *Nova-Make My People Live* (nationally broadcast documentary on the Indian health crisis), 1983, 58 minutes, *Strength of Life. Knokovitee Scott* (Creek/Cherokee artist), 1984, 28 minutes; *Stickball: The Little Brother of War* (documentary on ancient Creek game), 1984, 12 minutes; *Consider Your Future* (medicine employment recruitment), 1984, 10 minutes; *Bacone College: Headed for the Future* (promotional fundraiser program for Muskogee based private college), 1984, 11 mintues; *Estee Muskogee (The Muskogee People),* 1985, 24 minutes; *Indian Law/Theology Symposium Highlights* (project of the National Indian ministries task force), 1985, 90 minutes; *Bingo Is Our Business* (information about Creek Nation's business enterprise), 1985, 20 minutes; *Native American Producers Showcase* (film/video work of six Indian produers, for the Native American Public Broadcasting Consortium), 1985, 28 minutes.

ROBINSON, NATHAN WINFIELD
(Eastern Band Cherokee) 1938-
(motel/restaurant owner)

Born October 29, 1938, Ashland, Wis. *Education:* Southern Tech, Atlanta, Ga., 1957-1958. *Principal occupation:* Owner/operator, El Camino Motel, and El Camino Craft Gallery, 1960-. *Home address:* P.O. Box 482, Cherokee, N.C. 28719. *Military service:* U.S. Army, 1961-1962. *Community activities:* Cherokee (Tribal) Health Board (vice chairman and chairman, 1974-1976); Cherokee Sheltered Workshop (board of directors); Cherokee Baptist Church (youth committee). *Interests:* "Own and operate El Camino Motel; own restaurant, but have leased to another party; own and operate El Camino Craft Gallery, dealing in hand made crafts from all over the U.S. Hobbies: gardening, vintage cars, phhotography, racing karts."

ROBINSON, ROSE W. (Hopi) 1932- (director-American Indian programs, writer-editor)

Born March 27, 1932, Winslow, Ariz. *Education:* Haskell Institute, 1951; American University (Journalism Studies), 1970-1971. *Principal occupation:* Director-American Indian programs, writer-editor. *Home address:* 3805 Windom Pl, N.W., Washington, D.C. 20016. *Affiliations:* Writer-editor, Indian Arts and Crafts Board, U.S. Department of the Interior, Washington, D.C., 1963-1968; information officer, Office of Public Instruction, Bureau of Indian Affairs, Washington, D.C., 1968-1972; executive director, American Indian Press Association, Washington, D.C. 1972-1975; assistant director, Bicentennial Program, Bureau of Indian Affairs, 1975-1976; vice president and director, American Indian Program, Phelps-Stokes Fund, Washington, D.C., 1976-; editor, Native American Philanthropic News Service publications, Phelps-Stokes Fund, 1976-. *Other professional posts:* Chairman, Eastern Region, National Indian Lutheran Board, Lutheran Church in the U.S.A., 1976-; president, D.C. Chapter, North American Indian Women's Association, 1976-; board of directors, College of Ganado, Ganado, Ariz.; board of directors, American Indian Scholarships, Inc., Albuquerque, N.M. *Community activities:* American Indian Society of Washington, D.C., 1964- (vice president, 1967-1969; publicity chairman, 1969-1971); National Endowment for the Arts, 1977- (expansion arts advisory panel). *Memberships:* National Indian Education Association (board of directors, 1985-); Native American Science Education Association (board of directors, 1982-); National Congress of American Indians, 1969-1985; Women in Foundations, 1977-; North American Indian Women's Association, 1970-. *Biogra-*

phical source: Directory of Significant 20th Century American Minority Women, Vol. I, (Gaylord Professional Publications, Fisk University, Nashville, Tenn., 1978). Published works: Editor, *IDRA News* (Interior Dept. Recreation Association newsletter), 1957-1961; editor, *Smoke Signals* (Indian Arts and Crafts Board monthly publication), 1965-1968; editor, *Indian Record* (B.I.A. monthly publication), 1968-1972, 1975); *Indian Funding Programs* (Joint Strategy and Action Committee pamphlet on church funding sources for Indian programs, 1974); compiler and editor, *American Indian Directory* (National Congress of American Indians, 1972, 1974); co-editor, with Richard LaCourse, *American Indian Media Directory* (American Indian Press Association, 1974); editor, conference report, *Conference on Indian Higher Education for Private Philanthropists and Indian Educators* (Phelps-Stokes Fund, 1975); editor, *The Exchange, The Roundup,* and *Bulletins* (Native Philanthropic News Service, the Phelps-Stokes Fund, 1976-).

RODRIGUEZ-SELLAS, JOSE E. 1954- (outreach intake coordinator)

Born May 4, 1954, Ponce, Puerto Rico. *Education:* University of New Haven (Conn.), B.A. (History), 1978; University of Puerto Rico/Rio Piedras, Labor Relations Institute, 1979-1981; Labor Education Institute, Santurce, P.R., 1981. *Principal occupation:* Outreach Intake Coordinator for American Indians for Development. *Home address:* 1450 Ella T. Grasso Blvd., New Haven, Conn. 06511. *Other professional posts:* Editor of American Indians for Development *Newsletter;* Connecticut journalist for *Que Pasa* (the only Latin American newspaper in Connecticut). *Community activities:* President of Latin Student Organization (1978), University of New Haven, West Haven, Conn. *Memberships:* Brother-/Sisterhood of People of the Caribbean and Latin America (spokesperson and coordinator of "Hermandad Caribena y Latinoamericana"). *Awards, honors:* Certificate of Appreciation for services rendered to the members of Hermandad de Trabajadores de Servicios Sociales de Puerto Rico by the National Leadership of the Brotherhood of Social Services Workers of Puerto Rico,

1979-1981. *Interests:* "My main interests at present are : journalism, graphic arts, printing, photography and writing. I write in Spanish and English. I write about history, culture, politics and I also write poems. My main concerns are the daily struggles of the so-called "minorities" for civil rights and economic justice, and the struggle for self-determination of all the people of Latin America."

ROEHL, ROY F.
(Chairman-Alaskan Native corporation)

Affiliation: Chairman, Chugach Alaska Corporation, Chugach Alaska Bldg., 3000 A St., Suite 400, Anchorage, Alaska 99503.

ROESSEL, ROBERT A., Jr. 1926-
(teacher, administrator)

Born August 26, 1926, St. Louis, Mo. *Education:* Washington University, St. Louis, Mo., B.A., 1949, M.A., 1951; University of Chicago; Arizona State University, Ph.D., 1960. *Principal occupation:* Teacher, administrator. *Affiliation:* Teacher and administrator, Navajo Reservation, B.I.A.; director of Indian education, Arizona State University, Tempe, Ariz.; director, Rough Rock Demonstration School, Chinle, Ariz.; chancellor, Navajo Community College, Tsaile, Ariz.. *Military service:* U.S. Army, 1944-1946. *Awards, honors:* Distinguished Service Award in Navajo Education, 1967. *Interests:* "Indian control over Indian education is a major concern and interest. (I am) also interested in developing materials reflecting positive aspects of Navajo life and culture for various classrooms." *Published works: Arizona Cultures* (Arizona State University, 1960) *Success and Failure of Southwestern Indians in Higher Education,* (Arizona State University, 1961); *Indian Communities in Action* (Amerindian, 1961; Arizona State University, 1967); *Education of the Indian Adult,* (Arizona State University, 1962); *Cases and Concepts in Community Development (Arizona State University, 1963).*

ROESSEL, RUTH (Navajo) 1934-
(teacher)

Born April 14, 1934, Round Rock, Ariz. *Education:* Univerity of Northern Arizona, 1955; Arizona State University, B.A., 1969. *Principal occupation:* Teacher. *Affiliations:* Teacher, Low Mountain School, B.I.A., 1955-1958; director of dormitory services, Rough Rock Demonstration School, Rough Rock, Ariz., 1966-1968; director of Navajo and Indian studies, Navajo Community College, Tsaile, Ariz., 1968-? *Community activities:* Dine Bi Olta Association (board of directors). *Memberships:* American Association for Higher Education; National Indian Education Association; American Anthropological Association. *Awards, honors:* Navajo Woman of the Year, State Fair Commission, State of Arizona, 1960. *Interests:* "Interested in Indian and Navajo history and culture; arts and crafts, especially weaving. Involved in producing materials (publication) by Navajo, about Navajo, and for Navajo. Visiting on a continuing basis, major Indian groups in the U.S. and Canada." *Published works: Papers on Navajo Life and Culture,* 1971; *Navajo Studies at Navajo Community College,* 1972; *Stock Reduction: A National Disgrace,* 1973; all published by Navajo Community College Press.

ROESSLER, PAUL ALBERT (Navajo) 1920-
(economic consultant)

Born October 8, 1920, Buckman, N.M. *Education:* Georgetown University, B.S. (Foreign Service), 1949, postgraduate, 1949-1951; University of Maryland, postgraduate, 1965-. *Principal occupation:* Economic consultant. *Addresses:* P.O. Box 3045, Tucson, Ariz. 85701; P.O. Box 34137, Bethesda, Md. 20817. *Affiliations:* Field representative, War Claims Commission, Washington, D.C., 1949-1951; lesgislative analyst, Foreign Claims Settlement Commission, 1951-1952; Philippine Liaison officer, 1952-1953; foreign liaison officer, 1952-1956; staff assistant, Atomic Energy Commission (AEC), 1956-1957; assistant atomic energy attache, Japan, 1957-1961; senior foreign affairs officer, 1961-1963; associate program director, National

Science Foundation, Washington, D.C. 1963-1965; international economist, U.S. Department of the Army, 1965-1975; director, Office of Policy Planning, 1975-1975, chief, Division of Economic Development, 1976-1980, Bureau of Indian Affairs, Department of the Interior; president, American Economic Consultants, Inc., Tucson, Ariz., 1980-, Bethesda, Md., 1982- *Military service:* U.S. Army, 1941-1946, PTO; col., U.S. Army Reserve, 1956- (Purple Heart with cluster; Philippine Defense Medal; Philippine Liberation Medal; Philippine Presidential Unit Citation with two clusters; others). *Memberships:* National Economists Club; Society of Government Economists; American Political Science Association; DAV; VFW; American Legion; Delta Phi Epsilon. *Biographical sources: Who's Who in the East; Who's Who in the South and Southwest; Who's Who in the U.S.; American Men of Science; International Biographic Dictionary* (London); *Men of Distinction* (London); and others.

ROGERS, EDWARD S. 1923-
(ethnologist)

Born May 2, 1923, Lee, Mass. *Education:* Massachusetts Institute of Technology, 1942-1944; 1946-1947; Middlebury College, B.A., 1951; University of New Mexico, M.A., 1953, Ph.D., 1958. *Principal occupation:* Curator, Department of Ethnoogy, Royal Ontario Museum, 100 Queen's Park, Toronto, Ontario, Can. M5S 2C6. *Other professional post:* Part-time professor of anthropology, McMaster University, Hamilton, Ontario, Can. *Military service:* U.S. Army, 1943-1946 (Army Specialized Training Program, 1943-1944; Infantry, 1944-1945). *Community activities:* Archaeological and Historic Sites Board of Ontario, 1966-1972; Ministry of Natural Resources, 1962-1975; Northern Studies Committee, University of Toronto, 1971-1973. *Memberships:* Arctic Institute of North America; American Anthropological Association. *Interests:* Consultation on contemporary matters concerning North American Indians. *Publshed works: The Round Lake Ojibwa* (Royal Ontario Museum, 1962); *The Hunting Group-Hunting Territory Complex Among the Mistassini Indians* (National Museums of Canada, 1963); *Bibliography of Ontario Anthropology* (Royal Ontario Museum, 1964); *An Athapaskan Type of Knife* (National Museums of Canada, 1965); *Sibsistence Areas of the Cree-Ojibwa of the Eastern Subarctic: A Preliminary Study,* two parts (National Museums of Canada, 1963-1966); *North Pacific Coast Indians* (Canadian Antiques Collector, 1967); *The Material Culture of the Mistassini* (National Museums of Canada, 1967); *Indian Farmers of Parry Island* (Royal Ontario Museum, 1967); *Canadian Indians* (Swan Publishing, 1967); *Indians of Canada* (Clarke, Irwin, 1969); *Forgotten Peoples* (Royal Ontario Museum, 1969); *Band Organization Among the Indians of Eastern Subarctic Canada* (National Museums of Canada, 1969); *Natural Environment-Social Organization-Witchcraft: Cree Versus Ojibwa-A Test Case* (National Museums of Canada, 1969); *Indians of the North Pacific Coast* (Royal Ontario Museum, 1970); *Iroquoians of the Eastern Woodlands* (Royal Ontario Museums, 1970); *Indians of th Subarctic* (Royal Ontario Museum, 1970); *Indians of the Plains* (Royal Ontario Museum, 1970); *Algonkians of the Eastern Woodlands* (Royal Ontario Museum, 1970); *The Indians of Canada/A Survey* (Royal Ontario Museum, 1970); *The Quest Food and Furs-The Mistassini Cree, 1953-1954* (National Museums of Canada, 1973); *Parry Island Farmers: A Period of Change in the Way of Life of the Algonkians of Southern Ontario,* with Flora Tobobondung (National Museum of Man, 1975); and others; also numerous papers, reviews, and articles in scholarly journals.

ROGERS, JAMES BLAKE (Oklahoma Cherokee) 1915-
(cattle rancher and feeder)

Born July 25, 1915, New York, N.Y. *Education:* Pomona Colege, 1935-1937. *Principal occupation:* Cattle rancher and feeder. *Home address:* 1 Greenfair Court, Bakersfield, Calif. 93309. *Affiliations:* Actor, Hal Roach and Harry Sherman Studios, 1942-1943; associate publisher, *Beverly Hills Citizen,* newspaper., 1943-1953. *Military service:* U.S. Marine Corps, 1944-1945 (Staff Sergeant). *Community activites:* Cherokee Historical Society (director); Will

Rogers Memorial Commission, State of Oklahoma (member). *Memberships:* The Pacific Coast Hunter, Jumper and Stock Horse Association (past director); California Professional Horsemen's Association (past director).

ROGERS, WILL, Jr. (Cherokee) 1911-
(publisher, journalist)

Born October 20, 1911, New York, N.Y. *Eduction:* Stanford University, B.A., 1935. *Principal occupation:* Publisher, journalist. *Home address:* Santos Ranch, Tubac, Ariz. 85646. *Affiliations:* Publisher/journalist, *Beverly Hills Citizen,* newspaper, 1935-1953; U.S. Congressman, 16th District, California, 1942-1944; special assistant to the Commissioner of Indian Affairs, 1967-1969; creative coonsultant, George Spota Theatre Production of "Will Rogers, U.S.A." starring James Whitmore, 1968-. *Other professional posts:* Motion picture actor, television commentator, lecturer. *Military service:* U.S. Army, 1944-1945 (Bronze Star). *Community activities:* Beverly Hills Chamber of Commerce; chairman, Southern California Truman campaign committee, 1948; Will Rogers Memorial Commission, State of Oklahoma (member); California State Parks Commission (chairman). *Memberships:* Arrow, Inc. (founder and honorary president); National Congress of American Indians, 1946-; Oklahoma Cherokee Tribe. *Interests:* "In recent years he has divided his energies between his real estate business in Beverly Hills and his ranch in Tubac, Arizona. He continues to be active in Indian affairs, making occasional trips for the Bureau of Indian Affairs. A well known lecturer, he continues active in this field. He has worked with the Alaskan Federation of Natives. *Theatrical activities:* Movies: Star in *The Will Rogers Story,* (Warner Brothers, 1951); *The Boy From Oklahoma,* and *Wild Heritage.* Plays: *Ah, Wilderness,* and *Street Scene* (Pasadena Playhouse). Radio: *Rogers of the Gazette.* Television: *Good Morning Show,* CBS.

ROHN, ARTHUR HENRY 1929-
(professor of anthropology, archaeologist)

Born May 15, 1929, Elmhurst Ill. *Education:* Harvard College, B.A., 1951; University of Arizona, 1955-1956; Harvard University, Ph.D., 1966. *Principal occupation:* Professor of anthropology, Wichita State University, Wichita, Kan., 1970-. *Home address:* 320 North Parkwood, Wichta, Kan. 67208. *Military service:* U.S. Navy, 1951-1954 (Lieutenant; Korean Service Medal with one star K7; United Nations Service Medal; National Defense Service Medal). *Memberships:* Society for American Archaeology, 1953- (review editor, *American Antiquity, 1967-1970);* Current Anthropology, 1960-; American Anthropological Association *(Fellow),* 1966-; American Association for the Advancement of Science, 1966-1976; American Society for Conservation Archaeology, 1973-; Archaeological Institute of America; Tree Ring Society. *Awards, honors:* Outstanding Educators of America, 1973; City of Wichita, Distinguished Service Citation, 1976; Leadership Award, Wichita State University, 1978. *Interests:* "Pueblo Indian culture history, especially social organization and economics; archaeology of the Central Plains, especially Kansas; New England archaeology; Delaware culture history; research focused most heavily on archaeology of the Southwest and Plains—expeditions at Mesa Verde and Yellowjacket, Colo.; Wolf Creek, Marion, and Hillsdale, Kan.; and Marshfield, Mass. *Biographical sources: American Men and Women of Science; Who's Who in the Midwest; Contemporary Authors; Who's Who Among Authors and Journalists.* Published works: *Mug House, Mesa Verde National Park, Colorado* (National Park Service, 1971); *Prehistoric Ceramics of the Mesa Verde Region* (Museum of Northern Arizona, 1974); *Cultural Change and Continuity on Chapin Mesa* (Regents Press, of Kansas, 1977) among others; also numerous articles, chapters, and book reviews.

ROKWAHO (DAN THOMPSON)
(Mohawk) 1953-
(publications/graphic design consultant)

Born November 7, 1953, Akwesasne Territory. *Education:* High school. *Principal occupation:* Publications and graphic design consultant. *Home address:* P.O. Box 166, Rooseveltown, N.Y. 13683. *Affiliations:* Media specialist, St. Regis Mohawk Language Program, 1980-1982; co-founder (with John Fadden) and production manager, Pictographics, P.O. Box 166, Rooseveltown, N.Y., 1977-. *Other professional posts:* Literary editor, artist and photographer, *Akwesasne Notes,* 1982-1983; founding editor, *Indian Time,* an Akwesasne biweekly newspaper, 1983; art director for Indian Studies, Cornell University, Ithaca, N.Y., 1984; editor, *Akwesasne Notes* and *Indian Time,* 1984-1985; co-founder of *Akwekon,* a literary and arts quarterly published by Akwekon/Akwesasne Notes; cofounder of "Suntracks," a tracking and nature observation school in the Adirondack Mountains near Ochiota, N.Y. *Membership:* Association for the Advancement of Native North American Arts and Crafts (administrative executive; project, *Iroquois Arts: A Directory of a People and Their Work,* published, 1984). *Interests:* "Music, literature, theatre, computer science, electronic and mechanical gaggetry, the sciences, and archaic Mohawk words and semantics (compiling a dictionary of terms)." *Published works:* Editor and designer, *Trail of Broken Treaties. B.I.A. I'm Not Your Indian Anymore* (Akwesasne Notes, 1974); translator and illustrator, *Teiohakwente,* a Mohawk language textbook (Dept. of Indian Affairs, Ottawa, Can., 1977); author and artist, *Covers* (poetry, illustrations) (Strawberry Press, 1982); contributor of poetry to numerous anthologies; cover art and illustrations for many publications, as well as design production for *Akwesasne Notes Calendars.*

ROLATOR, FRED S. 1938-
(professor of history)

Born July 22, 1938, McKinney, Tex. *Education:* Wake Forest University, B.A., 1960; University of Southern California, M.A., Ph.D., 1960-1963. *Principal occupation:* Professor of history, Middle Tennessee State University, Murfreesboro, Tenn., 1967-. *Home address:* Route 8, Box 467, Murfressboro, Tenn. 37130. *Other professional post:* Associate professor of history and chairman of the History and Social Sciences Department, Grand Canyon College, Phoenix, Ariz., 1964-1967. *Community activities:* Frequent speaker on Indian matters for civic organizations and school in area; co-director, The American Indian and the Jacksonian Era: The Impact of Removal: A Sequi-centennial Symposium (The national symposium on the adoption of the Indian Removal Bill of 1830) held Feb., 1980; Rutherford County Heritage Commission (member, 1978-1980). *Memberships:* Tennessee Baptist Historical Society (vice president; former president); Southern Baptist Historical Commission (commissioner); *Baptist History and Heritage* (board of directors); Organization of American Historians; The Western Historical Association; The Southern Historical Society; The Society for Historians of the Early American Republic. *Awards, honors:* National Merit Scholar, Wake Forest, 1956-1960; national Defense and Haynes Fellow, USC, 1960-1963; Tennessee Baptist Convention, Heritage Award, 1984. *Interests:* "History of the American Indian, especially previous to 1492; American church history; director of Historic Preservation effort, Camp Palma, located near Tupa, Sao Paulo state, Brazil (1976). extensive travel to several states and Mexico." *Biographical sources: Directory of American Scholars; Dictionary of International Biography; Who's Who in the South and Southwest. Published works: The Continental Congress: A Study in the Origins of American Public Administration* (Xerox, 1971); *Charles Thompson* (Harrington Associates, 1977); *The Triumphant Indians: The History of North America to 1492* (in preparation).

ROSELEIGH, PATRICIA F.
(chief-nutrition & dietetics-Indian Health Service)

Affiliation: Chief, Nutrition & Dietetics Branch, Indian Health Service, 5600 Fishers Lane, Rockville, Md. 20857.

ROSEN, LAWRENCE 1941-
(professor of anthropology)

Born December 9, 1941, Cincinnati, Ohio. *Eduction:* Brandeis University, B.A., 1963; University of Chicago, M.A., 1965, Ph.D., 1968, J.D., 1974. *Principal occupation:* Professor of anthropology, Princeton University, Princeton, N.J., 1977-. *Home address:* 180 Prospect Ave., Princeton, N.J. 08540. *Other professional posts:* Former summer clerk, Native American Rights Fund, Boulder, Colo., 1972; visiting professor of law, Columbia University, Spring, 1979. *Memberships:* American Anthropological Association; North Carolina and Federal bars. *Interests:* American Indian legal problems. *Biographical source: American Men and Women of Science. Published work:* Editor, *The American Indian and the Law* (Transaction Books, 1978).

ROSS, AGNES ALLEN (Santee Sioux) 1910-
(educator)

Born October 27, 1910, Flandreau, S.D. *Education:* Haskell Institute, A.A., 1931; Northern Arizona University, Flagstaff, B.S., 1938; Nebraska State, Chadron, M.S., 1960. *Principal occupation:* Educator. *Home address:* Flandreau, S.D. 57028. *Affiliations:* Teacher, Day School, Rosebud, S.D., 1938-1941; teacher, teacher supervisor, education specialist, Pine Ridge, S.D., 1951-1970. *Other professional posts:* Instructor, Pine Ridge Community College, affiliated with Black Hills State College and University of Colordo, Boulder; Title I coordinator, Flandreau Indian School, 1970-1973. *Community activities:* State Cultural Preservation (board member); Tribal Health Board; National Advisory Board for Teacher Corp.; Santee Sioux Tribal Council (chairperson, 1972-1976). *Memberships:* Delta Kappa Gamma; North American Indian Women's Association; South Dakota Indian Education Association; Veteran's of Foreign Wars Aux (past president); American Legion Aux. (past president). *Awards, honors:* South Dakota's Teacher of the Year, 1958; B.I.A. Outstanding Performance, 1959, 1970; recognized as first woman chairperson in the United Sioux Tribes. *Interests:* Ms. Ross writes, "Now

retired—however—still involved in consultant services in Indian education and bilingual education; assists colleges and universities as an advisor in Indian education, and (I) enjoy speaking to school groups.

ROSS, DONALD
(school superintendent)

Affiliation: Superintendent, Crow Creek Reservation High School, Stephen, S.D. 57346.

ROSSE, WILLIAM, Sr. (Shoshone)
(tribal chairman)

Affiliation: Chairman, Yomba Tribal Council, Route 1, Box 24A, Austin, Nev. 89310.

ROUBIDEAUX, NANETTE S. (Ioway of Kansas/Nebraska) 1940-
(museum professional)

Born July 20, 1940, Porcupine, S.D. *Education:* Haskell Indian Junior College, A.A.S., 1975; Univerity of Kansas, B.A. (Honors), 1977, Ph.D. candidate, 1977-. *Principal occupation:* Museum professional. *Home address:* 900 West 190 St., Apt. 11-O, New York, N.Y. 10040. *Affiliations:* Teaching assistant, research assistant, assistant instructor, graduate assistant, University of Kansas, Lawrence, Kan., 1977-1983; co-director, Kansas Committee for the Humanities Project "Change, Continuities, and Challenges, Haskell Indian Junior College, 1884-1984," 1984-1985; intern fellowship, Museum of the American Indian, Ne York, N.Y., 1985-. *Other professional posts:* Consultant: KANU Radio, University of Kansas, 1981-; Women's Transitional Care, Lawrence, Kan., 1982-; Haskell Indian Junior College, 1984-; Museum of the American Indian, 1985-; chairperson, Grand Review Committee for Department of Health and Human Services, Office of Human Development Services, 1985-. *Memberships:* American Historical Association; American Anthropological Association; Phi Alpha Theta; Society for Values in Higher Education. *Awards, honors:* Danforth Foundation Fellowship, 1979-1982; Outstanding

Americans Program, listed in *Outstanding Young Women in America,* 1977; American Indian Scholarship Program, 1977-1980; Lawrence Professional and Business Women's Outstanding Haskel Indian Junior College Student, 1975; Merwlyn Foundation Research Grant, 1976; Commission of the Status for Women, Outstanding Student in Contributions to a Minority Culture, 1976; Minority Affairs Teaching Assistant Award, 1977; Graduate School, Dissertation Fellowship, 1984-1985. *Interests:* Contemporary Native American activities. *Biographical source: Outstanding Young Women in America,* 1977. *Published works: The Native American Woman: A Cross-Disciplinary Bibliography* (in preparation); "Up Before Dawn: A Study of the Family Farm," paper given at regional meeting of American Anthropological Association, Memphis, Tenn., 1979.

ROUFS, TIMOTHY G. 1943-
(professor)

Born August 30, 1943, Cokato, Minn. *Education:* University of Notre Dame, A.B., 1965; University of Minnesota, Ph.D., 1971. *Principal occupation:* Professor, Department of Sociology, Anthropology, Geography, University of Minnesota, Duluth, 1970-. *Community activities:* A.M. Chisholm Museum, Duluth, Minn. (board of directors). *Memberships:* American Ethnological Society; Society for Applied Anthropology (Fellow); American Anthropological Association (Fellow); The Royal Anthropological Association of Great Britain and Ireland (Fellow); Current Anthropology (Associate); Sigma Xi, 1980-. *Awards, honors:* 1973 Service Award from *Anishnabe,* University of Minnesota-Duluth, American Indian Student Association; 1976 City of Duluth Bicentennial Award; 1980 Outstanding Young Men of America. *Interests:* Anishnabe, Chippewa, and Ojibwa ethnohistory; culture and personality studies. *Biographical source: Who's Who in the Midwest. Published works: The Anishnabe of the Minnesota Chippewa Tribe* (Indian Tribal Series, Phoenix, 1975); *Working Bibliography of the Anishnabe and Selected Related Works* (Lake Superior Basin Studies Center, Duluth, 1981, 1984); editor, with Larry P. Atkins, *Information Relating*

to *Chippewa Peoples* (from the *Handbook of American Indians North of Mexico, 1907-1910*) (Lake Superior Basin Studies Center, Duluth, 1984).

ROUILLARD, JOHN C. (Santee Sioux)
1928-
(professor-American Indian studies)

Born December 31, 1928, Rapid City, S.D. *Education:* Northwestern Univerity, B.M.Ed., 1952, M.M., 1958. *Principal occupation:* Professor-American Indian studies. *Home address:* 6040 Manon St., La Mesa, Calif. 92041. *Affiliation:* Chairman, American Indian Studies, San Diego State University, San Diego, Calif., 1971-. *Military service:* U.S. Army, 1946-1948. *Memberships:* California Indian Education Association; National Indian Education Association, 1972-; National Congress of American Indians, 1972-; Santee Sioux Tribe (enrolled member); Pi Kappa Lambda. *Interests:* Educational program development--main interest in post secondary education, alternative school development; music—amateau and professional performance and research in American Indian music. *Published works:* "The Tale of Iktomi and the Sheeo," in *Spectrum of Music* (Macmillan, 1974); "Contemporary Indian Education," in *The People Cabrillo Met* (Third Annual Cabrilla Festival Historical Seminar, 1975).

ROUSE, IRVING 1913-
(professor and curator emeritus
of anthropology)

Born August 29, 1913, Rochester, N.Y. *Education:* Yale University, B.S., 1934, Ph.D., 1938. *Principal occupation:* Professor and curator emeritus of anthropology, Peabody Museum and Department of Anthropology, Yale University, New Haven, Conn., 1938-. *Other professional post:* Research associate, Museum of the American Indian, New York, N.Y. *Memberships:* American Anthropological Association, 1935-; Society for American Archaeology, 1935-; Association for Field Archaeology, 1974-. *Awards, honors:* A. Cressy Morrison Prize in Natural Science, New York Academy of Sciences, 1948; Viking Fund Medal and

Award in Anthropology, 1960; Distinguished Service Award, American Anthropological Association, 1984; Fiftieth Anniversary Award, Society for American Archaeology, 1985. *Interests:* Archaeological fieldwork. *Published works: A Survey of Indian River Archaeology, Florida* (Yale University Publications in Anthropology, 1951); *Introduction to Prehistory: A Systematic Approach* (McGraw-Hill, 1972); among others.

ROWLAND, ALLEN (Northern Cheyenne)
(tribal president)

Affiliation: President, Northern Cheyenne Tribal Council, Lame Deer, Mt. 59043.

ROWLAND, DARIUS
(college president)

Affiliation: President, Dull Knife Memorial College, P.O. Box 206, Lame Deer, Mt. 59043.

RUBY, ROBERT H., M.D., 1921-
(physician and surgeon)

Born April 23, 1921, Mabton, Wash. *Education:* Whitworth College, B.S., 1943; Washington University School of Medicine, M.D., 1945. *Principal occupation:* Physician and surgeon. *Home address:* 1022 Ivy, Moses Lake, Wash. 98837. *Affiliations:* Director, USPHS Hospital, Pine Ridge Indian Reservation, 1953-1955; private practice of medicine, Moses Lake, Wash., 1955-. *Other professional post:* Instructor (course on Native Americans), Department of Anthropology, Big Bend Community College, Moses Lake, Wash. *Military service:* U.S. Army Air Corps, 1946-1948. Schiffner Military Museum (board member); Washington State Library Association; Grant County Historical Society; Moses Lake Migrant Committee; Moses Lake Public Library. *Memberships:* Amerian Medical Association, 1945-; Washington State Medical Society, 1955-; American College of Surgeons, 1954-. *Awards, honors:* The Robert Gray Medal Award by the Washington State Historical Society;

The Distinguished Author of History Award of the Esatern Washington State Historical Society; Certificate of Recognition at the Governor's Writers Day in 1967, 1971, 1983; the Pacific Norhwest Booksellers Award, 1966; The Northwest Author's Award for nonfiction, 1966; a resolution of commendation by the Moses Lake City council, Dec., 1971. *Interests:* "Writing and traveling. My writing consists of many articles on the Native Americans for newspapers, and magazines, besides the numerous books (listed below). I have also written a portion of a text book for Native Americans used in some Spokane (Wash.) schools." *Biographical sources: Who's Who in the West. Published works: The Oglala Sioux* (Vantage Press, 1955); *Myron Eels and the Puget Sound Indians* (Superior Publishing, 1975); *Half-Sun on the Columbia,* 1963, *The Spokane Indians,* 1970, *The Cayuse Indians,* 1972, *The Chinook Indians,* 1975, *Indians of the Pacific Northwest: A History,* 1981, and *A Guide to the Indian Tribes of the Pacific Northwest,* 1986, all published by the University of Oklahoma Press.

RUDDELL, J. PRESTON, Jr. 1949-
(attorney)

Born December 20, 1949, Schenectady, N.Y. *Education:* University of North Carolina, B.A., 1971; UNC Law School, J.D., 1975. *Principal occupation:* Attorney. *Home address:* Box 985, Eagle Butte, S.D. 57625. *Affiliations:* Attorney, South Dakota Legal Services, Fort Thompson and Eagle Butte, S.D., 1976-1977; attorney general, Cheyenne River Sioux Tribe, Eagle Butte, S.D., 1977-. *Military service:* U.S. National Guard, SP-4, 1970-1976. *Community activities:* Crow Creek Commission on Alcoholism, Fort Thompson, S.D. *Membership:* South Dakota Bar Association. *Awards, honors:* Reginald Heber Smith Community Lawyer Fellowship Program, 1975-1977. *Interests:* Indian law; "have played professional baseball and am interested in all sports. I'm an eastern transplant who loves South Dakota and working with Native American people."

RUSSELL, JERRY
(chairman-Indian organization)

Affiliation: National chairman, Order of the Indian Wars, P.O. Box 7401, Little Rock, Ark. 72217.

RUSSELL, NED (Yavapai-Apache)
(tribal chairman)

Affiliation: Chairman, Yavapai-Apache Community Council, P.O. Box 1188, Camp Verde, Ariz. 86322.

S

SABATTIS, CLAIR (Maliseet)
(tribal chairwoman)

Affiliation: Chairwoman, Houlton Maliseet Band Council, P.O. Box 576, Houlton, Maine 04730.

SAINTE-MARIE, BUFFY (Cree) 1942-
(folksinger, poet)

Born February 20, 1942, Craven, Saskatchewan, Can. *Education:* University of Massachusetts, B.A. (Philosophy), 1963. *Principal occupation:* Folksinger, poet. *Affiliations:* Recording artist, Vanguard Recording Society. *Other occupation:* Free-lance writer on Indian culture and affairs; associate editor, *The Native Voice* (Vancouver, B.C., Can.). *Interests:* Lecturing on Indian affairs; composing, singing. Miss Sainte-Marie writes, "I am best known for songs and poems directly related to past and present American Indian affairs. (I have contributed) to *The Native Voice, Thunderbird, American Indian Horizons,* and *Boston Broadside* in the fields of North American Indian music and Indian affairs. Have lived on and visited reserves (reservations) in fifteen states and four provinces; have traveled, lectured and sung in England, France, Canada, Italy, and Mexico, and have given performances in concert and on television internationally and in all major American cities."

ST. CLAIR, ROBERT N.
(professor of linguistics; consultant-Indian affairs)

Education: Univerity of Hawaii, B.A., 1963; University of Kansas, Ph.D., 1974. *Principal occupation:* Professor of linguistics, University of Louisville, Louisville, Ky., 1973-; consultant in Indian affairs. *Military service:* U.S. Army, 1957-1960. *Professional activities:* Xth International Conference on Salish Languages (chairman); editor, *Lektos;* editor, *Language Today;* editorial board: language problems and language planning, invisible speech, Annuario (Santo Domingo); co-editor, *Philosophical Linguistics. Memberships:* National Council of Teachers of English; Modern Language Association; International Conference on Salishan Languages; Linguistics Society of America; American Association for the Advancement of Science. *Awards, honors:* Outstanding Educator Award, 1975; Distinguished Visiting Professor (New Mexico State University), 1977. *Field work:* Salishan languages: Skagit, Lummi; Sahaptian languages: Yakima, Wanapam; Eskimo: Yupik Eskimo. *Interests:* Bilingual education; sociolinguistics; political linguistics; travel. *Dissertation;* "Theoretical Aspects of Eskimo Phonology," University of Kansas, Department of Linguistics. *Biographical sources: Who's Who in the South and Southwest; Dictionary of International Biography. Published works:* Numerous articles, papers, monographs, and book reviews in scholarly journals.

SALABIYE, VELMA
(librarian)

Affiliation: Librarian, American Indian Studies Center Library, 3220 Campbell Hall, U.C.L.A., Los Angeles, Calif. 90024.

SALISBURY, NEAL 1940-
(historian, teacher)

Born May 7, 1940, Los Angeles, Calif. *Education:* University of California, Los Angeles, B.A., 1963, M.A., 1966, Ph.D., 1972. *Principal occupation:* Historian, teacher. *Address, Affiliation:* Associate professor, Department of History, Smith College, Northamtpon, Mass. 01063 (1973-). *Memberships:* American Historical Association; American Society for Ethnohistory; Organization of American Historians. *Awards, honors:* Fellow, Smithsonian Institution, 1972-1973; Fellow, Newberry Library Center for History of the American Indian, 1977-1978; Fellow, National Endowment for the Humanities, 1984-1985. *Published works: Manitou and Providence: Indians, Europeans, and the Beginnings of New England, 1500-1643* (Oxford University Press, 1982); *The Indians of New England: A Critical Bibliography* (Indiana University Press, 1982).

SALVADOR, LILLY (Acoma Pueblo) 1944-
  (potter)

Born April 6, 1944, McCartys Village, Acoma Pueblo, N.M. *Education:* New Mexico State, Grants, N.M. (one year). *Principal occupation:* Self-employed potter. *Home address:* P.O. Box 342, Acoma Pueblo, N.M. 87034. *Affiliations: Pottery is displayed at the following museums and galleries: Boston Museum of Fine Arts, Boston, Mass.; The Heard Museum, Phoenix, Ariz.; The Museum of Man, San Diego, Calif.; The Natural History Museum, Los Angeles, Calif.; The Whitehorse Gallery, Boulder, Colo. Other institutional affiliation:* National Indian Council on Aging Catalogue. *Community activities:* Native needle embroidery instructor, Acoma Adult Education Programs; secretary, Sky City Community School; member, parent-student association of Saint Joseph School, San Fidel, N.M. *Memberships:* Southwest American Indian Arts Association, 1964-; National Indian Arts & Crafts Association (Albuquerque, N.M.), 1985-1986; Smithsonian Institution, 1985. *Awards, honors:* 1st and 2nd Prize Awards for handcrafted pottery from Whitehorse Gallery, Boulder, Colo; 1st and 3rd Prize Award Ribbons from New Mexico State Fair; 1st, 2nd and 3rd Prize Awards for handcrafted/handpainted pottery from the Southwest American Indian Arts Association, 1st, Honorable Mention Awards from the Gallup Intertribal Indian Ceremonial; 1st, Special Award Ribbon from the Heard Museum, Phoenix, Ariz. *Interests:* "To develop and expand my present pottery gallery (the first at the Pueblo Acoma) into a major showcase for collectors, tourists (who visit annually the oldest inhabited village in the U.S.) and discriminating curators of various museums throughout the U.S. With the private invitations extended by the above mentioned museums and galleries, I have traversed the southwest and northwest region of the U.S. exhibiting my traditional handcrafted-handpainted Acoma Pueblo pottery and figurines." *Biographical sources: American Indian Pottery,* 2nd Edition; *Amerika* newsletter, Chicago, Ill.; National Indian Council on Aging *Catalogue.*

SALZMANN, ZDENEK 1925-
  (professor of anthropology)

Born October 18, 1925, Prague, Czechoslovakia. *Education:* Caroline University, Prague, 1945-1947 (Absolutorium, 1948); Indiana University, M.A., 1949, Ph.D., 1963. *Principal occupation:* Professor of anthropology, University of Massachusetts, Amherst, 1968-. *Home address:* 25 Chapel Rd., Amherst, Mass. 01002. *Other professional posts:* Visiting professor, Yale University; consultant to Wind River Reservation schools on Arapaho language and culture curriculum, 1979-. *Memberships:* Linguistic Society of America, 1949-; American Anthropological Association, 1954-; Current Anthropology, 1961-; Ameriacn Folklore Society, 1966-. *Awards, honors:* Research grants from the following: American Philosophical Society; National Endowment for the Humanities; Senior Fulbright-Hays Scholar, International Research and Exchange Board; American Council of Learned Societies. Given in a public ceremony and with the approval of Arapaho elders, the name *hinono'ei neecee* ("Arapaho Chief"). *Interests:* Fieldwork among Northern Arapaho Indians, 1949-; numerous trips to the Wind River Reservation under various auspices. *Biographical sources: American Men and Women of Science; Contemporary Authors; Directory of American Scholars. Published works: Dictionary of Contemporary Arapaho Usage* (Arapaho Language and Culture Commission, 1983); *Analytical Bibliography of Sources Concerning the Arapaho Indians* (Arapaho Language and Culture

236

Commission, 2nd revised edition); among others; numerous articles in various scholarly journals.

SAM, JIMMY L.
(executive director-Indian center)

Affiliation: Executive director, Boston Indian Council, Inc., 105 S. Huntington, Jamaica Plain, Mass. 02130.

SAMUELSON, LILLIEN THOMPSON
1926-
(owner/manager-Indian shop)

Born July 13, 1926, Mecklenburg County, Va. *Education:* Virginia Polytechnic Institute, 1945-1947; Illinois Institute of Technology, B.S., 1949. *Principal occupation:* Owner/manager, American Indian Treasures, Inc., 2558 Western Ave., Guilderland, N.Y. 12084., 1968-. *Home address:* P.O. Box 595, Guilderland,N.Y. 12084. *Community activities:* Sponsors Native American art show at Sienna College, Loudonville, N.Y. each Spring; co-sponsors celebration of American Indian Day each Fall at the Albany, N.Y. Library. *Memberships:* American Home Economic Association, 1949-; National Congress of American Indians; Association on American Indian Affairs, Inc.; Indian Arts and Crafts Association (board of directors, 1976; vice president, 1978). *Interests:* Ms. Samuelson writes, "My interest in the American Indian goes back to early childhood, with serious studies of the arts and crafts of living Indians having been pursued the last 20 years, Travel has been extensive during this time, and I've come to know the products of most reservations in the U.S. (I) worked as a consultant on Indian education for the New York State Education Department. I started American Indian Treasures in 1967, selling only jand-made Indian crafts from a broadrange of tribes and cultures. Items sold are personally collected to assure authenticity, with buying trips made regularly throughout the year." *Published works:* Articles published in monthlies, distributed nationally, about American Indian artists.

SANBORN, JAMES H. (Penobscot)
1931-
(Indian school principal)

Born January 2, 1931, Milford, Maine. *Education:* University of Alaska, Anchorage, B.S., 1971; University of Southern Maine, Gorham, M.S. (Education), 1973; University of Maine, Orono, C.A.S. (Administration), 1983. *Principal occupation:* Principal, Indian Township School, Princeton, Maine. *Home address:* Box 96, Princeton, Maine 04668. *Military service:* U.S. Air Force, 1948-1971 (retired-Msgt; Air Medal/6OLC; Combat Readiness Badge; Vietnam Service; Korean Service). *Memberships:* American Association of School Administrators; Council for Exceptional Children; Maine Reading Association; International Reading Association. *Interests:* Outdoor sports; travel.

SANCHEZ, GILBERT (San Ildefonso Pueblo)
(Pueblo governor)

Affiliation: Governor, San Ildefonso Pueblo, Route 5, Box 315A. Santa Fe, N.M. 87501.

SANDERS, E. FRED (Catawba) 1926-
(machinist, assistant chief)

Born April 9, 1926, Catawba Indian Reservation, York County, S.C. *Education:* Catawba Indian School; vocational and technical school—machinist courses. *Principal occupation:* Maintenance machinist, General Tire Corp, Charlotte, N.C., 1967-. *Home address:* Reservation Rd., Rural Box 327, Rock Hill, S.C. 29730. *Other professional post:* Master barber. *Military service:* U.S. Army, 1944-1950 (1st Sergeant; Infantry, World War II: Combat Infantry Badge; Bronze Star; 2 Campaign Battle Stars; V.E. Ribbon; Army Occupation Award-Austria). *Community activities:* Assistant chief, Catawba Nation, S.C., 1975-; Charlotte-Mecklenburg Public School System—Indian Education (chairperson-Title IV Program). *Memberships:* National Congress of American Indians; Veterans of Foreign Wars, Rock Hill, S.C.; American Legion, Rock Hill, S.C. *Interests:* "Travel as official tribal delegate to many National Congress of American Indians' conferences and conventions in various states. Support tribal leaders with positive attitude and assurance that Native Americans will continue to have a voice and input concerning the future destiny of tribal government and its people."

SANDO, JOE SIMON *(Paa Peh)*
(Jemez Pueblo) 1923-
   (teacher, writer)

Born August 1, 1923, Jemez Pueblo, N.M. *Education:* Eastern New Mexico State University, Portales, B.A., 1949; University of New Mexico, 1950-1951, 1973; Vanderbilt University, 1959-1960. *Principal occupation:* Instructor (ethnohistory), Institute of American Indian Arts, Sante Fe, N.M., 1982-. *Other professional posts:* Lecturer on history, Pueblo Indian Cultural Center; education specialist and teacher of Pueblo Indian history, University of New Mexico. *Military service:* U.S. Navy, 1943-1946 (Yeoman 2nd; World War II; Pacific Campaign Ribbon with four stars). *Community activities:* All Indian Pueblo Council (chairman of education, 1970); New Mexico State Judicial Council (chairman, 1970); American Indian Scholarships (secretary/treasurer - 14 years); Ancient City Toastmasters Club, Santa Fe, N.M. (president, 1968). *Awards, honors:* Alumnus of the Year, 1970, Eastern New Mexico University. *Interests:* "Gardening with numerous blue ribbons for garden crops from New Mexico State Fair; woodworking; writing for publication on Indian history and education; lecture tour of New Zealand Maori area in 1979; lecture tour of Switzerland and West Germany in 1981; lecturing to civic groups in State and other states on Indian history. *Biographical sources: Personalities of the West and Midwest,* 1971; *Indians of Today,* Fourth Edition, 1971. *Published works: The Pueblo Indians* (Indian Historian Press, 1976, 1982); *Pueblo Indian Biographies* (S.I.P.I. Press, Albuquerque, 1976); *Nee Hemish, The History of Jemez Pueblo* (University of New Mexico Press, 1982); *Pope* (World Book Encyclopedia, 1970); many articles in *New Mexico Magazine, The Indian Historian, HUD Magazine.*

SANDOVAL ANNA (Diegueno)
   (tribal spokeswoman)

Affiliation: Spokeswoman, Sycuan General Council, P.O. Box 2929, El Cajon, Calif. 92021.

SANDOVAL, JOSEPH C. (Taos Pueblo)
   (Pueblo governor)

Affiliation: Governor, Taos Pueblo, P.O. Box 1846, Taos, N.M. 87571.

SANDOVAL, WILLIAM
   (B.I.A. agency superintendent)

Affiliation: Superintendent, Umatilla Agency, Bureau of Indian Affairs, P.O. Box 520, Pendleton, Ore. 97801.

SATZ, RONALD N. 1944-
   (professor of history)

Born February 8, 1944, Chicago, Ill. *Education:* Illinois Institute of Technology, B.S., 1965; Illinois State University, M.A., 1967; University of Maryland, Ph.D., 1971 (Dissertation: *Federal Indian Policy, 1829-1849). Principal occupation:* Professor of history. *Home address:* 4015 White Pine Dr., East, Eau Claire, Wis. 54701-7465. *Affiliations:* Assistant professor, 1971-1975, associate professor with tenure, 1977-1980, dean of graduate studies, 1976-1983, dean of research, 1977-1893, professor with tenure, 1980-1983, University of Tennessee at Martin; dean, School of Graduate Studies, director, Office of University Research, and professor of history, The University of Wisconsin, Eau Claire, Wis., 1983-. *Other professional posts:* Proposal reviewer, National Endowment for the Humanities, 1978-; editorial committee, The Council of Graduate Schools in the U.S., 1983-; advisory committee on minority student affairs, and undergraduate teaching improvement council, University of Wisconsin, Madison, 1984-; camous liaison, University of Wisconsin System Committee on University/Industry Cooperation, 1985-; Publications Committee, Midwestern Association of Graduate Schools, 1985-1988. *Community activities:* Ad Hoc Commission on Racism of the Lac Courte Oreilles Lae Superior Ojibwa Tribal

Governing Board (member); Parent-Teacher Organization, Manz Elementary School and South Junior High School, Eau Claire, Wis. (member); The Heritage Club of the Chippewa Valley Museum, Eau Claire (member). *Memberships:* American Association for Higher Education; American Association of University Professors; American Historical Association; Organization of American Historians; Society for American Indian Studies and Research; Society for Historians of the Early American Republic; Western History Association; Sigma Xi; Pi Gamma Mu; Phi Alpha Theta; Phi Kappa Phi; Delta Tau Kappa; among others. *Award, honors:* University of Tennessee at Martin Liberal Arts Merit Award, 1974, and Phi Kappa Phi Scholar Award, 1983; National Defense Education Act Fellow, University of Maryland, 1970; Fellow in Ethnic Studies, Ford Foundation, 1971; Younger Humanist Research Fellow, National Endowment for the Humanities, 1974; Title III Grant, U.S. Office of Education, University of Tennessee at Martin, 1978, 1981, 1982; University of Wisconsin System Undergraduate Teaching Improvement Council Grant for Critical Thinking Across Disciplines Project, 1985. *Interests:* "Indian-white relations, especially the 19th century; American Indian policy; tribal history; Indian-black relations; Indian religious beliefs and the impact of Christian missionary efforts on Indian religions." *Biographical sources: Outstanding American Educators,* 1974-1975; *Directory of American Scholars,* 6th-8th Eds.; *Contemporary Authors,* 1982; *Dictionary of International Biography,* 1976-1977; *Who's Who in the South and Southwest,* 16th-18th Eds.; *Personalities of the South,* 1978-1979, 1979-1980 Eds.; *International Who's Who in Education,* 1980 Ed.; *Who's Who in the Midwest,* 20th Ed. *Published works: American Indian Policy in the Jacksonian Era* University of Nebraska Press, 1975); *Tennessee's Indian Peoples: From White Contact to Removal, 1540-1840* (University of Tennessee Press, 1979); co-author: *America: Changing Times,* textbook, 1979- (John Wiley & Sons, 1979-1984; Alfred A. Knopf, 1984-); contibutor: *Heroes of Tennessee* (Memphis State University Press, 1979); *The Commissioners of Indian Affairs, 1824-1977* (University of Nebraska Press, 1979);

American Vistas, 1607-1877, 3rd-4th Eds. (Oxford University Press, 1979, 1984); *After Removal: The Choctaw in Mississippi* (University Press of Mississippi, 1986); *Handbook of North American Indians,* 4th Ed. (Smithsonian Institution Press-in press).

SAUBEL, KATHERINE SIVA
(Cahuilla) 1920-
(museum trustee)

Born March 7, 1920, Los Coyotes Reservation, Calif. *Principal occupation:* Trustee and president, Malki Museum, Inc., Banning, Calif. *Home address:* Box 373, Banning, Calif. 92220. *Other professional posts:* Advisory representative, County of Riverside, Calif., Historical Commission; consultant-lecturer, California State College at Hayward, Calif., University of Colorado, and University of California. *Community activities:* Los Coyotes Tribal Council; Mothers Club, Morongo Indian Reservation. *Interests:* Ms. Saubel participated in the Indian Leadership Training Program at the University of California; other interests are Indian history and ethnography, and linguistics. She writes, "I have traveled extensively in the Southwest and California, visiting reservations and museums which display Indian history and culture." *Published works: Cahuilla Ethnobotanical Notes: Oak,* and *Mesquite and Screwbean,* both with Lowell J. Bean (University of California, Archaeological Survey Annual Report, 1962, 1968); *Temalpah: Economic Botany of the Cahuilla Indians,* with Lowell J. Bean (Malki Museum, 1969); *Kunvachmal, A Cahuilla Tale* (The Indian Historian, 1969).

SAUL, C. TERRY *(Tobaksi)*
(Choctaw-Chickasaw) 1921-
(artist)

Born April 2, 1921, Sardis, Okla. *Education:* Bacone Junior College, 1940; University of Oklahoma, B.F.A., 1949. *Principal occupation:* Commercial artist, Phillips Petroleum Co., Bartlesville, Okla., 1955-; "I have a studio in my home and paint for various Indian shows and exhibits and commissioned murals and paintings." *Military service:* U.S.

Army, 1940-1945 (Infantry; Purple Heart, Bronze Star, American Defense Service Ribbon). *Memberships:* Art Students' League (life member). *Awards, honors:* Numerous awards received at various national Indian art shows and exhibitions, such as: American Indian Exposition, Anadarko, Okla.; National Indian Art Show, Bismarck, N.D.; Denver Art Museum; Museum of New Mexico; and National Indian Art Exhibition, Scottsdale, Ariz. Numerous one-man and group shows, traveling exhibitions, etc. Represented in many private and public collections throughout the U.S. and elsewhere.

SAULQUE, JOSEPH C. (Paiute)
1942-
(tribal administrator)

Born October 20, 1942, Bishop, Calif. *Education:* West Valley Community College, Campbell, Calif., A.A., 1970; Brigham Young University, B.A., 1973. *Principal occupation:* Administrative officer, Indian reservation. *Home address:* P.O. Box 1212, Bishop, Calif. 93514. *Affiliation:* Chairman, Utu Utu Gwaitu Paiute Tribe, Benton Paiute Reservation, Benton, Calif. (six years). *Military service:* U.S. Army, 1961-1964 (E-4/Sp-4 Airborne Division). *Memberships:* National Congress of American Indians, 1974-; California Tribal Chairman's Association, Sacramento, Calif. (secretary-three years). *Interests:* Indian affairs.

SAUNOOKE, OSLEY BIRD, Jr.
(Eastern Cherokee) 1943-
(attorney, business consultant)

Born April 6, 1943, Jacksonville, Fla. *Education:* East Tennessee State University, 1962-1963; Brigham Young University, B.S., 1965; Univerity of New Mexico Law School, J.D., 1972. *Principal occupation:* Attorney, business consultant. *Home address:* 2435 Gulf Gate Dr., Sarasota, Fla. 33581. *Affiliations:* Teacher-guidance counselor, Cleveland, Ohio, Chicago, Ill., 1965-1969; executive director, United Southeastern Tribes, Inc., 1972-1973; executive director, Florida Governor's Council on Indian Affairs, 1973-1974. *Memberships:* National Congress of American Indians

(Southeast area vice president, 1972-1973; first vice president, 1973-1974; board member, American Indian Scholarships, 1974-).

SAVALA, DELORES (Paiute)
(tribal chairwoman)

Affiliation: Chairwoman, Kaibab Tribal Council, Tribal Affairs Bldg., Pipe Springs, Ariz. 86022.

SAVARD, REMI 1934-
(professeur)

Born March 27, 1934, Quebec, Can. *Education:* Universite Laval, Quebec, Maitrise (Sociologie); Sorbonne, Paris France, Doctorate (Ethnologie). *Principal occupation:* Associate professeur, Dept. D'Anthropologie, Universite de Montreal, Montreal, Quebec, Can. *Memberships:* Canadian Association in Support of the Native People; Canadian Sociology and Anthropology Association. *Interests:* Northeastern Indian mythology; Indian land claims; Indian-non-Indian relationships. *Published works:* Carcajou et le Sens Du Monde Recits Montagnais-Naskapi (Editeau Officiel du Quebec, 1971, 1972, 1974 - 3rd ed.); *Signes et Langages des Ameriques* (Recherches Amerindiennes au Quebec, 1973); *Lerire Precolumbien Dans le Quebec D'Aujourd Hui* (L'Hexagone/Parti Pris, 1977).

SAVILLA, ELMER
(executive director-Indian association)

Affiliation: Executive director, National Tribal Chairman's Association, 818 18th St., N.W., Suite 420, Washington, D.C. 20006.

SCHAAFSMA, POLLY DIX 1935-
(artist, archaeologist)

Born October 24, 1935, Springfield, Vt. *Education:* Mt. Holyoke Colege, B.A., 1957; University of Colorado, M.A., 1962. *Principal occupation:* Artist, archaeologist. *Home address:* Box 289, Arroyo Hondo, N.M. 87513. *Affiliation: Non-staff research archaeologist, Museum of New Mexico, 1963-1967; research assistant, Peabody*

Museum, Harvard University, 1968-1969; author, School of American Research. Memberships: American Rock Art Research Association; Society for American Archaeology; Taos Art Association (exhibiting artist, 1969-). *Interests:* Prehistoric Indian rock art, particularly of the Southwest; evolution and stylistic development of art forms; Indian religion; primitive art; travels to Mexico. *Published works: Rock Art of the Navajo Reservoir District,* (Museum of New Mexico, 1963); *Southwest Indian Pictographs and Petroglyphs,* (Museum of New Mexico, 1965); *Early Navaho Rock Paintings & Carvings* (Museum of Navaho Ceremonial Art, 1966); *Rio Grande Petroglyphs of the Cochiti Reservoir* (Museum of New Mexico, 1975); *The Rock Art of Utah* (Peabody Museum, 1971); *Indian Rock Art of the Southwest* (University of New Mexico, School of American Research).

SCHEIRBECK, HELEN MAYNOR (Lumbee) 1935-
(human resources administrator)

Born August 21, 1935, Lamberton, N.C. *Education:* Berea College, Berea, Ky., B.A., 1957; VPI - SU, Blacksburg, Va., Ed.D., 1980. *Principal occupation:* Human resources administrator. *Address, Affiliation:* Director, American Indian Programs, Save the Children Federation, 54 Wilton Rd., Westport, Conn. 06880 (1983-). *Other professional posts:* Chairwoman, Indian Education Task Force, American Indian Policy Review Commission, U.S. Congress; director, Office of Indian Affairs, U.S. Office of Education, Dept. of HEW; professional staff, U.S. Senate Subcommittee on Constitutional Rights. *Memberships:* United Indians of America (project advisor); National Indian Education Association (vice president). *Awards, honors:* John Hay Whitney Foundation, Opportunity Award; Outstanding Lumbee Award; Outstanding American Indian Award; Pepsi People Pour It On Award. *Interests:* "Dr. Scheirbeck has traveled and worked throughout the U.S. She has worked with the majority of Indian tribes in the U.S. She has served on Legislature and Executive Task Forces investigating various issues affecting Indian people. Her hobbies include photography, writing,

collecting legends, and swimming." *Biographical sources: Outstanding Indians in USA; Indians of the Southwest; Outstanding Minority Women; Biographies of Outstanding American Indian Women. Published works:* "Indian Education: Tool for Cultural Politics" (Harvard Center for Law & Education, Dec., 1970); "The First Americans" (American Red Cross Youth News, Nov., 1972); *The History of Federal Indian Education Policy* (American Indian Policy Review Commission, 1976); *A Study of Three Selected Laws & Their Impact on American Indian Education* (House of Interior & Insular Affairs, Oct., 1976); *Public Policy and Contemporary Education of the American Indian* (Ph.D. Dissertation, 1980).

SCHINDLER, DUANE E. (Turtle Mountain Chippewa) 1944-
(Indian high school principal)

Born April 22, 1944, Turtle Mountain Indian Reservation, Belcourt, N.D. *Education:* University of North Dakota; Valley City State College, N.D.; University of Wisconsin, Eau Claire; Arizona State University; University of South Dakota. *Principal ocupation:* Principal, Turtle Mountain Chippewa High School, Belcourt, N.D. *Home address:* Belcourt, N.D. 57318. *Affiliations:* Program development specialist, Eastern Montana State College, Billings, Mt. (two years); program specialist, University of New Mexico, Albuquerque, N.M. (one year); instructor, Adult Programs, Wenatchee Valley College, Omak, Wash. (two years); director, Adult Education, Colville Confederated Tribes, Nespelem, Wash. (one year); director, American Indian Student Division, University of Washington, Seattle, Wash. (one year). *Other professional posts:* Field reader, consultant: Logo language; computer applications, computer literacy, computer office systems; curriculum development; school board training; program evaluation management. *Community activities:* American Indian Center, Spokane, Wash. (chairman). *Memberships:* National Association of Secondary School Principals; National Indian Education Association; ASCD, NABE. *Awards, honors:* Outstanding Teacher, Oglala Community Schools, Pine Ridge, S.D. *Interests:*

Computers in the classroom; research in mathematics. *Biographical source: Outstanding Young Men of America*, 1973. *Published works: Concepts of American Indian Learners* (Education, Tempe, Ariz.); *Language, Culture and the Mathematics (Journal of the American Indian*, 1986).

SCHLENDER, JAMES
(Attorney)

Affiliation: Attorney, Lac Courte Oreilles, Route 2, Box 421, Hayward, Wis. 54843.

SCHOLDER, FRITZ (Mission) 1937-
(artist)

Born October 6, 1937, Breckenridge, Minn. *Education:* Sacramento State College, B.A., 1960; University of Arizona, M.F.A., 1964. *Principal occupation:* Artist. *Home address:* 1008 Canton Rd., Santa Fe, N.M. 87501. *Other professional posts:* Participant, Southwest Indian Art Project, Rockefeller Foundation, 1961-1963; chairman, Fine Arts Committee, First Convocation of Amerian Indian Scholars, Princeton University, 1970. *Awards, honors:* Numerous awards for painting at the following exhibitions: Southwestern Drawing and Print Exhibition, Dallas Museum of Fine Arts; Mid-America Exhibition, Nelson Gallery of Art, Kansas City, Mo.; National Indian Exhibition, Scottsdale, Ariz.; among others. *Biographical sources: Who's Who in the West; Who's Who in American Art; Dictionary of International Biography.*

SCHUSKY, ERNEST L. 1931-
(professor of anthropology)

Born October 13, 1931, Portsmouth, Ohio. *Education:* Miami University, Ohio, A.B., 1952; University of Chicago, M.A., 1957, Ph.D. (Anthropology), 1960. *Principal occupation:* Professor of anthropology, Southern Illinois University, Edwardsville, Ill., 1960-. *Home address:* 412 Willowbrook, Collinsville, Ill. 62234. *Other professional post:* Author. *Military service:* U.S. Army, 1953-1954 (Corporal; served in Korea).

Memberships: American Anthropological Association; Royal Anthropological Society of Great Britain. *Awards, honors:* Fulbright Professor, 1982 (taught a course on the American Indian at Seoul National University). *Interests:* Mr. Schusky writes, "My interest in American Indians started in 1953 with the Papagos. Later field trips were made among New England Indians. Fieldwork occured among the Lower Brule and Pine Ridge Sioux between 1958-1960. The political and economic problems of Native Americans has been a professional interest throughout." *Published works: Introducing Culture* (Prentice-Hall, Inc., (four editions) 1967, 1972, 1978, 1986); *The Right to Be Indian* (Institute of Indian Studies, Vermillion, S.D., 1965; Indian Historian Press, 1970); *The Forgotten Sioux* (Nelson Hall, 1975); editor, *Political Organization of Native North Americans* (University Press of America, 1980).

SCHWIND, MARIE N.
(president-Alaskan Native association)

Affiliation: President, Maniilaq Association, P.O. Box 256, Kotzebue, Alaska 99752.

SCOTT, JAMES ROBERT 1947-
(tribal education-measurement and evaluation specialist)

Born July 7, 1947, Norman, Okla. *Education:* Oklahoma State University, B.A., 1970; University of Texas, Ph.D., 1975. *Principal occupation:* Measurement and evaluation specialist. *Home address:* Route 3, Box 556, Philadelphia, Miss. 39350. *Affiliations:* Choctaw Department of Education, Philadelphia, Miss., 1975 ; Choctaw Bilingual Education Project, Route 7, Box 21, Philadelphia, Miss., 1975-. *Memberships:* National Indian Education Association; National Amerian Bilingual Education Committee; Phi Delta Kappa. *Interests:* Program development and evaluation; improving Indian education programs; legislative interaction with tribes; educational management; curriculum development.

PRINCESS ROSE SCRIBNER
(Penobscot) 1940-
(president/founder, White Cloud Cultural Center, Inc.)

Born April 3, 1940, Gardiner, Maine. *Education:* Mohegan Community College, Norwich, Conn., A.A., 1978. *Principal occupation:* President/founder, White Cloud Cultural Center, Inc., Norwich, Conn., 1975-. *Home address:* 89 Broad St., Norwich, Conn. 06361. *Memberships:* National Historic Preservation Society; National Indian Education Association; Indian Rights Association. *Awards, honors:* Outstanding Minority Award, Mohegan Community College; American Education Award, University of Connecticut. *Interests:* "My main goal in life (vocational) is to become a good Indian leader in serving our Native American people. I've traveled throughout the U.S. in observing model education programs much needed for Indian people. I hope to be appointed by the President of the U.S. in serving on the National Indian Education Advisory Board, Washington, D.C. I feel by this appointment, I can have the opportunity of getting more school books portraying Indian children properly, so that other children can read and learn what Indian people are all about. To wipe out the present stereotype Indian. Any expeditions I plan for the future will be one of taking a canoe trip down the "Allegash," this area is one in which my famous grandfather guided many famous authors, Lord's of England, Countess's of Canada, on many a trip or expedition." *Published work: Ethnic People of Connecticut* (University of Connecticut, 1979).

SEAMAN, P. DAVID 1932-
(professor of linguistics)

Born January 31, 1932, Connellsville, Pa. *Education:* Asbury College, A.B., 1957; University of Kentucky, M.A., 1958; Indiana University, Ph.D. (Linguistics), 1965. *Principal occupation:* Professor of Linguistics, Department of Anthropology, Northern Arizona University, Flagstaff, Ariz., 1967-. *Home address:* 3600 Moore Circle, Flagstaff, Ariz. 86001. *Other professional posts:* Bilingual/bicultural consulting for Zuni Tribal Council, 1970-1972; linguistic consulting for Bureau of Indian Affairs, 1968-1969, 1970-1976; cross-cultural management consulting for Hopi Tribal Council, 1974-1979; accounting and management consulting for Fort Mojave Tribal Council, 1977-1980. *Military service:* U.S. Army, 1951-1954 (Sergeant; U.S. Army Commendation Medal for efficient administration of U.S. Army field hospital in Korea, 1953). *Community activities:* University Heights Corporation, Flagstaff (director and corporate secretary, 1972-); Flagstaff Medical Center (finance committee, 1980-). *Memberships:* Linguistic Society of America; Society for Study of Indigenous Languages in America; Society for Linguistic Anthropology; Friends of Uto-Aztecan. *Awards, honors:* Distinguished Faculty Award, Northern Arizona University, 1980; among others. *Research:* Hopi dictionary project; traditional Havasupai culture; American Indian language/cultures; Alfred F. Whiting Indian archives. *Interests:* American Indian languages and culture; Greek language and culture. *Paper delivered:* "Hopi Dictionary and Computers," joint meeting, Arizona Humanities Association and Arizona Alliance for Arts Education, Scottsdale Community College, 1983 (article—Arizona Humanities Association *Journal,* Feb., 1984). *Published works: Modern Greek and American English in Contact* (Mouton & Co., The Hague, 1972); co-editor, *Havasupai Habitat: A.F. Whiting's Ethnography of a Traditional Indian Culture* (University of Arizona Press, 1985); *Hopi Dictionary: Hopi-English, English-Hopi* (Northern Arizona University Anthropoogical Paper No. 2, 1985); article: "Hopi Linguistics: An Annotated Bibliography (*Anthropological Linguistics,* 1977).

SECAKUKU, ALPH
(B.I.A. agency superintendent)

Affiliation: Superintendent, Hopi Agency, Bureau of Indian Affairs, Keams Canyon, Ariz. 86034.

SENECA, WILLIAM
(B.I.A. agency superintendent)

Affiliation: Superintendent, New York Liaison Office, Bureau of Indian Affairs, Federal Bldg., 100 S. Clinton St., Syracuse, N.Y. 13202.

SEVELLA, GWENDOLYN (Luiseno)
(tribal chairwoman)

Affiliation: Chairwoman, La Posta General Council, P.O. Box 894, Boulevard, Calif. 92005.

SHAKE SPEAR, VERNON (Paiute)
(tribal chairman)

Affiliation: Chairman, Burns-Paiute General Council, P.O. Box 71, Burns, Ore. 97720.

SHARLOW, JAMES
(chief-personnel operations,
Indian Health Service)

Affiliation: Chief, Personnel Operation Branch, Indian Health Service, 5600 Fishers Lane, Rockville, Md. 20857.

SHAW, CARL F.
(director of public affairs-B.I.A.)

Affiliation: Director of Public Affairs, Bureau of Indian Affairs, 1951 Constitution Ave., N.W., Washington, D.C. 20245.

SHAW, FRANCES (Diegueno)
(tribal chairman)

Affiliation: Chairman, Manzanita General Council, P.O. Box 1302, Boulevard, Calif. 92005; chairman, Southern Indian Health Council, P.O. Box 20889, El Cajon, Calif. 92021.

SHAW, WILFRED (Paiute)
(tribal chairman)

Affiliation: Chairman, Pyramid Lake Paiute Tribal Council, P.O. Box 256, Nixon, Nev. 89424.

SHEA, ESTHER S. (Mrs.)
(Tlingit-Haida) 1917-
(Tlingit language instructor)

Born April 21, 1917, Ketchikan, Alaska. *Principal occupation:* Tlingit language instructor, Ketchikan Indian Education, Ketchikan, Alaska, 1974-. *Community activities:* Alaska Native Sisterhood (Tlingit Naa president, 1976-1977; board); Ketchikan Indian Corporation (board of directors, 1978). *Interests:* Native language preservation; curriculum development; bilingual conferences; bicultural exchange. *Published works:* Three children's books in Tlingit, 1975; *Tlingit Conversation Book*, 1977; numerous Tlingit daily lesson plans and worksheets; Tlingit number and animal coloring books; song translations into Tlingit, like "Jingle Bells."

SHEA, JAMES
(chief-health services planning,
Indian Health Service)

Affiliation: Chief, Health Services Planning Branch, Indian Health Service, 5600 Fishers Lane, Rockville, Md. 20857.

SHEA, W. TIMOTHY 1936-
(public health analyst)

Born December 22, 1936, Columbus, Ohio. *Education:* Xavier University, B.S., 1961; University of Michigan, M.P.H., 1971. *Principal occupation:* Director, Division of Program Evaluation and Policy Analaysis, Indian Health Service, 5600 Fishers Lane, Washington, D.C., 20245, 1971-. *Home address:* 16205 Oak Meadow Dr., Rockville, Md. 20855. *Memberships:* Toastmasters International; American Management Association; Public Health Advisors Association; American Public Health Association. *Awards, honors:* Four recent awards from the Health Resources and Service Administration. *Interests:* Program evaluation; policy analysis; management sciences; contemporary political analysis; decision theory resource allocation; sports; military science; philosophy.

SHEMAYME, HENRY (Caddo)
(tribal chairman)

Affiliation: Chairman, Caddo Tribal Council, P.O. Box 487, Binger, Okla. 73009.

SHENANDOAH, LEON (Onondaga)
(tribal chief)

Affiliation: Chief, Onondaga Nation, P.O. Box 270A, Nedrow, N.Y. 13120.

SHEPPARD, LAVERNE (Shoshone-Bannock) 1960-
(editor)

Born April 17, 1960, Blackfoot, Idaho. *Education:* University of Arizona (one year); Washington State University (three years); Idaho State University, B.A. (Journalism), 1984. *Principal occupation:* Editor, *Sho-Ban News*, 1984-. *Home address:* S033 Hawthorne Rd. #23, Chubbuck, Idaho 83202. *Affiliations:* News editor, Idaho State University student newspaper (one year); reporter, American Microsystems, Inc. magazine (six months); reporter, *Indian Youth Magazine* (one year); reporter, *The Exchange*, Phelps-Stokes Fund, Washington, D.C. (one year—. *Community activities:* Fort Hall Voter Education Committee (chairperson); Tribal Safety Committee (training coordinator); Washington State University Indian Club (president). *Memberships:* Native American Indian Women's Association; Native American Press Association. *Awards, honors:* 1985 Native American Press Association Award: Best Advertisement; honorable mention, best news series and best editorial; commendation by Idaho Governor for contribution to state's grasshopper spraying effort; Ben Davis Scholarship. *Interests:* "Since entering college back in 1978, I have interned at the Idaho Human Rights Commission, Boise, the Phelps-Stokes Fund in Washington, D.C., and American Microsystems, Inc. in Pocatello, Idaho. I participated in the Indian Business Development Program at University of Arizona, Tucson (one year) and have attended many major Indian conferences." *Biographical source: Sho-Ban News*, Fall, 1984.

SHING, LE ROY NED (Hopi) 1942-
(Indian education)

Born August 4, 1942, Keams Canyon, Ariz. *Education:* Northern Arizona University, B.S. (Sociology), 1969; Pennsylvania State University, M.Ed. (Administration), 1972. *Principal occupation:* Indian education. *Home address:* 4532 N. 18th St., Apt. 17, Phoenix, Ariz. 85016. *Affiliations:* Education Committee, education coordinator, 1969-1971, Hopi Tribe; teacher, staff trainer, principal, Hopi Reservation, Ariz. (six years); Title IV Cooridnator, Philipsburg, Pa. (one year); teacher supervisor, secondary education, Phoenix, Ariz., 1976-. *Community activities:* Urban Advisory Indian Board, Phoenix, Ariz.; chairperson, Title IV-JOM, Madison School District, Phoenix, Ariz. *Memberships:* National Indian Education Association; American Indian Research Association; Phi Delta Kappa. *Interests:* Mr. Shing writes, "(My) major interest is to better the educational opportunities for Indian students and tribes. Develop materials and curriculum that will help to upgrade the education of Indian people in the world. Do research that will improve and help others improve education." *Biographical source: International Who's Who in Community Service. Published work: Teacher Training Handbook* (State of Pennsylvania, 1976).

SHIPEK, FLORENCE C. 1918-
(professor of anthropology)

Born December 11, 1918, North Adams, Mass. *Education:* University of Arizona, B.A., 1940, M.A., 1940; University of Washington (Geology), 1940-1941, 1944-1946; University of Hawaii, Ph.D. (Anthropology), 1977. *Principal occupation:* Professor of anthropology. *Address:* Department of Anthropology, University of Wisconsin-Parkside, Box N-2000, Kenosha, Wis. 53141. *Affiliation:* Director, Program for Community Development Education for Southern California Indian Reservation, Sociology Department, University of San Diego, Calif., 1970-1972; assistant professor, associate professor, University of Wisconsin-Parkside, 1977-. *Other professional posts:* Anthropologist for the enrollment committee of the San Pascual Band of

Mission Indians, 1956-1968; ethnohistorical researcher, Mission Indian Land Claims Case (land use and identity of Diegueno-Kamia-Kumeyaay), 1959-1964; ethnohistorical researcher, Water Claims Case of San Luis Rey Indian reservations, 1965-1985; consultant to Environmental Impact Firms such as Wirth Associates, Cultural Systems Research, Inc., 1976-; consultant to Indian Freedom Ranch, San Diego County (a rural alcoholic rehabilitation center for Indians), 1978-1982; consultant for Southern California Indian Law Seminar, 1979; consultant for San Pascual Band Education Project, 1981; consultant to Kumeyaay Elders Association, 1981-1983; consultant for Kumeyaay Elders and Cayapaipe Reservation, 1982-; consultant and seminar lecturer for Rincon Band of San Luiseno Indians, 1984; with Dr. Lowell Bean of Cultural Systems Research, Inc., expert witness for water claims case for six southern California Indian Bands (San Luis Rey, Cuyapaipe, Pechanga, Santa Rosa, Morongo, and La Posta), 1984-; with Dr. Lowell J. Bean, consultant to San Luis Rey Band of Mission Indians in its quest for Federal recognition, 1985; consultant to Santa Ynez Reservation on membership genealogies for enrollment, 1986. *Memberships:* American Anthropological Association (Fellow); Society for Applied Anthropology (Fellow); Royal Anthropological Institute (Fellow); American Ethnological Association; American Society for Ethnohistory; Council on Anthropology and Education; Malki Museum Association; Phi Kappa Phi. *Awards, honors:* Grant from Wenner-Gren Foundation for Anthropological Research (autobiography of the last traditional leader of the Kumeyaay), 1982; appointed by the Society for American Archaeology and Society of Professional Archaeology to the Subcommittee to consider revisions to the ethics code and procedures for handling excavation and reburial of American Indian human remains and suggest modifications for state laws concerning unmarked graves, 1985. *Interests:* North American Indians; California and Southwest Indians; Research and consulting: "From 1954 to the present, I have been working directly for and with the various Southern California Indian bands and individuals, doing research for them aimed at solving specific problems.

Research included the history of changing land use and tenure rights, economic and agriculture, socio-political changes, genealogies. I have been meeting with their various political bodies and providing information directly to them. I have appeared as a witness or submitted prepared testimonies to various governmental agencies, such as the Commissioner of Indian Affairs, Indian Claims Commission, Department of Public Welfare, etc. *Published works: Lower California Frontier 1870: Articles from the San Diego Union, 1870* (Dawson's Book Shop, 1965); *The Autobiography of a Diegueno Woman, Delfina Cuero* (as told to Florence C. Shipek) (Dawson's Book Shop, 1969; paperback edition, Malki Museum Press, 1970; available in Talking Books from Library of Congress, 1975); *Pushed Into the Rocks: Changes in Southern California Indian Land Tenure, 1769-1985* (in preparation); *A Strategy for Change: The Luiseno of Southern California* (in preparation); numerous chapters in books, journal articles, book reviews, limited circulation reports, social impact assessments, written legal testimonies, papers presented; Audio Visual Material: *The Indian Heritage—The Life of Delfina Cuero* (videotape prepared for "Heritage San Diego" Educational TV series, San Diego County Education Department.

SHOPTEESE, JOHN T. (Prairie Band Potawatomi) 1938-
(Indian health service)

Born February 28, 1938, Mayetta, Kan. *Education:* Haskell Indian Junior College, 1956-1958. *Principal occupation:* Indian health service. *Home address:* 724 Parkside Dr. N.E., Albuquerque, N.M. 87123. *Affiliation:* Real Property Officer, Office of Administrative Management, Indian Health Service, Albuquerque, N.M., 1958-. *Military service:* U.S. Army, 1962-1964. *Memberships:* Albuquerque Artist Association; Indian Arts and Crafts Association (board of directors; chairman, Native Arts Committee, 1982-1983); Eight Northern Pueblos Arts Guild, 1982-1984. *Awards, honors:* Several awards for achievement in the arts (I am a jeweler—gold/silver smith); sculpture in bronze, pewter, clay; received several juried art show awards throughout the Southwest. *Interests:* "Pursuing excellence in Native arts; to enhance cultural awareness and enact the trends of art through significant application of contemporary overtones. (I) have displayed my arts/crafts at major art shows of Native American artists."

SHIPP, CECIL
(B.I.A. agency superintendent) *Affiliation:*

Superintendent, Wewoka Agency, Bureau of Indian Affairs, P.O. Box 1060, Wewoka, Okla. 74884.

SHOEMATA, JACK
(B.I.A. agency superintendent)

Affiliation: Superintendent, Osage Agency, Bureau of Indian Affairs, Pawhuska, Okla. 74056.

SHOUMATOFF, NICHOLAS A. 1942-
(museum curator)

Born August 20, 1942, Glen Cove, N.Y. *Education:* Pembroke College, Oxford, England; Stanford University; Western Connecticut State College; Empire State College (N.Y.), B.A., 1972. *Principal occupation:* Museum curator. *Home address:* R.D. #2, Route 100, Katonah, N.Y. 10518. *Affiliations:* Instructor, Fairfield University, Fairfield, Conn.; curator, Trailside Nature Museum, Cross River, N.Y. *Memberships:* New York Archaeological Association; New Jersey Archaeological Society; Society for Pensylvania Archaeology; Connecticut Archaeological Society; American Indian Archaeological Institute. *Awards, honors:* Historic Tomahawk Award, Westchester County Historical Society, 1972. *Interests:* Delaware expeditions, 1976 and 1977; directed linguistic and ethnobotanical fieldwork among the Delaware Indians and related tribes of Oklahoma, Wisconsin, and Ontario, Can. *Published works:* Numerous articles in various journals.

SHUNATONA, GWEN
(president-Indian education organization)

Affiliation: President, ORBIS, Inc., 1411 K St., N.W., Suite 200, Washington, D.C. 20005.

SHUNK, HAROLD W. (Yankton Sioux) 1907-
(lecturer)

Born July 25, 1907, Philip, S.D. *Education:* Southern State College, B.S., 1931; South Dakota State University (graduate work). *Principal occupation:* Lecturer. *Home address:* Rimrock Hiway, R.R. 1, Box 115, Rapid City, S.D. 57701. *Affiliations:* Teacher, school administrator, superintendent of Indian agencies, Bureau of Indian Affairs, 1933-1968. *Military service:* U.S. Army, 1943-1946. *Memberships:* American Forestry Association; American Association for State and Local History; South Dakota State Historical Society (lifetime member; president, 1963-1969); The Cowboy and Western Heritage Hall of Fame, State of South Dakota, Fort Pierce, S.D. (vice chairman; chairman-Selection Comittee; chairman, 1977-). *Awards, honors:* Citation for Service Rendered, Rosebud Sioux Tribal Council; Meritorious Service Award, U.S. Department of the Interior, 1968; appointed by President Nixon to the National Council on Indian Opportunity, 1970. *Published works:* Written historical stories for *The Dakotan,* South Dakota State University, and Kansas State historical publications.

SIDNEY, IVAN (Hopi)
(tribal chairman)

Affiliation: Chairman, Hopi Tribal Council, P.O. Box 123, Oraibi, Ariz. 86039.

SIMLA, MARLENE R (Yakima) 1939-
(director-Indian center)

Born January 1, 1939, Toppenish, Wash. *Education:* Institute for American Indian Arts (four Certificates), 1963; Fort Lewis College, Durango, Colo., B.A., 1967; Fort Wright College of Holy Names, Spokane,

Wash., 1976-1979 (lack thesis for Masters degree in Education); Bank St. College (Child Development Associate), 1982. *Principal occupation:* Director, Toppenish Center, Yakima Tribal Preschool Program. *Community activities:* Toppenish Chamber of Commerce; Eagles Auxiliary #2229; Speelyi-me Arts & Crafts Club, 1975-. *Memberships:* Yakima Valley Museum; National Indian Education Association; Allied Arts Council of Yakima; Fort Lewis College Alumni Association. *Awards, honors:* Won Blue & Red ribbons at various art shows for painting (oil, water color, and acrylic); honorable mention at Southwest Indian Art Show, Santa Fe, N.M. *Interests:* "Coordinate and co-direct small traditional dance groups for local community events and celebrations; travel throughout Oregon, Washington and Canada and promote White Swan Rodeo, All-Indian Rodeo Association for 26 years." *Published work: Multi-Cultural Early Childhood Curriculum for the Yakima Indian Nation* (Yakima Indian Nation/ Fort Wright College, 1978).

SIMMS, RUSSELL
(executive director-Indian center)

Affiliation: Executive director, Council of Three Rivers American Indian Center, Inc., 200 Charles St., Pittsburgh, Pa. 15238.

SIMON, BRO. C.M.
(director-Indian center)

Affiliation: Director, The Heritage Center, Box 100, Pine Ridge, S.D. 57770.

SIMPLICO, CHAUNCEY (Zuni Pueblo)
(Pueblo governor)

Affiliation: Governor, Zuni Pueblo Tribal Council, P.O. Box 737, Zuni, N.M. 87327.

SIMPSON, DANA
(editor)

Affiliation: Editor, *American Indian Law Review,* Univerity of Oklahoma, College of Law, 300 Timberdell Rd., Norman, Okla. 73019.

SINGER, LAWRENCE (Santa Clara Pueblo)
(Pueblo governor)

Affiliation: Governor, Santa Clara Pueblo, P.O. Box 580, Espanola, N.M. 87532.

SINYELL, EDGAR (Hualapai)
(tribal chairman)

Affiliation: Chairman, Hualapai Tribal Council, P.O. Box 168, Peach Springs, Ariz. 86434.

SINYELLA, WAYNE (Havasupai)
(tribal chairman)

Affiliation: Chairman, Havasupai Tribal Council, P.O. Box 10, Supai, Ariz. 86435.

SIRIA, LARRY
(editor)

Affiliation: Editor, *American Indian Law Review,* University of Oklahoma, College of Law, 300 Timberdell Rd., Norman, Okla. 73019.

SISK, KENNETH (Pit River)
(tribal president)

Affiliation: President, Big Bend General Council, P.O. Box 255, Big Bend, Calif. 96001.

SKENANDORE, PAUL A. (Shenandoah)
***(Scan doa)* (Oneida) 1939-**
(lecturer, editor/publisher, owner/operator of bookstore)

Born January 21, 1939, Kaukauna, Wis. *Education:* High school. *Principal occupation:* Lecturer, editor/publisher, owner/operator of bookstore. *Home address:* 736 W. Oklahoma, Appleton, Wis. 54911. *Affiliations:* Editor/publisher of *Shenandoah* monthly Oneida newsletter begun in 1973; owner/operator, Shenandoah Books, 133 E. Wisconsin Ave., Appleton, Wis. *Other professional post:* Lecturer. *Military service:* U.S. Army, 1962-1964 (E-4 Sergeant). *Interests:* History; to see Native nations re-established with sovereign powers to include treaty-rights; taking the U.S. (Government) to World Court and charging them with trespass and genocide."

SKENADORE, FRANCIS
(attorney)

Affiliation: Attorney, Oneida Tribe, P.O. Box 129, Oneida, Wis. 54155.

SKENEDORE, LYNN (Menominee)
(tribal chairman)

Affiliation: Chairman, Menominee Tribal Legislature, P.O. Box 397, Keshena, Wis. 54135.

SKYE, CLARENCE
(executive director-Indian organization)

Affiliation: Executive director, United Sioux Tribes of South Dakota, P.O. Box 1193, Pierre, S.D. 57501.

SLICKPOO, ALLEN P., Sr.
(Nez Perce-Walla Walla-Cayuse) 1929-
(tribal historian, tribal councilman-administrator)

Born May 5, 1929, Slickpoo Mission, Culdesac, Idaho. *Education:* Chemawa Indian School, 1945-1948; University of Idaho, 1953-1955. *Principal occupation:* Tribal historian, councilman, administrator, Nez Perce Tribal Executive Committee, Lapwai, Idaho. *Home address:* P.O. Box 311, Kamiah, Idaho 83536. *Affiliation:* Nez Perce Tribal Executive Committee, Box 305, Lapwai, Idaho, 1955-. *Other professional post:* Consultant to the Northwest Regional Educational Laboratory on Indian education and curriculum; served on the Governor's Indian Advisory Council, Idaho. *Military service:* U.S. Army, 1948-1952 (Japanese Occupation/Korea/UN Service). *Community activities:* Veterans of Foreign Wars (Kamiah, Idaho); 2nd Presbyterian Church of Kamiah; Mat'alym'a (Upriver Nez Perce) Culture Club. *Awards, honors:* Outstanding Achievement Award, Indian Child Welfare, 1983; Governor of Idaho Award for "Promotor of the Week,"

1961. *Interests:* "Have traveled to Mexico City and Canada to participate and/or speak at conference relating to the Indian of North America; bilingual/bicultural activities; consultant on historical and cultural concerns (recognized as authority on the history and culture of the Nez Perce people; has lectured in public schools, colleges and universities, to students and organizations relative to American Indian history, culture, government, education, and economic status; has been a reader and/or panelist for the National Endowment for the Humanities." *Published works: NuMeePoom Tit-Wah-tit* (Pruitt Press, Colo., 1973); *Noon Nee MePoo* (Pruitt Press, 1974); wrote a paper for the *Northwest Quarterly on Anthropology,* relating to Indian fishing rights controversy; articles for *World Book Encyclopedia,* 1983-.

SLOBODIN, RICHARD 1915-
(professor emeritus)

Born March 6, 1915, New York, N.Y. *Education:* City College of New York, B.A., 1936, M.S., 1938; Columbia University, Ph.D., 1959. *Principal occupation:* Professor emeritus, Department of Anthropology, McMaster University, Hamilton, Ontario, Can., 1964-. *Military service:* U.S. Army Air Force; U.S. Navy, 1942-1946 (Lieutenant, U.S. Naval Reserve) (Soldier's Medal; Silver Star). *Memberships:* American Anthropological Association; Canadian Sociology & Anthropology Association; Northeastern Anthropological Association. *Interests:* Subarctic American people—Indian and Metis (fieldwork, 1938-). Areas of special interest are, social organization, ethnohistory, folklore, mythology, and religion. *Published work: Band Organization of the Peel River Kutchin* (National Museum of Canada, 1962); *Metis of the Mackenzie District* (Canadian Research Centre for Anthropology, 1966).

SMITH, DON LELOOSKA (Cherokee) 1933-
(woodcarver)

Born August 31, 1933, Sonora, Calif. *Principal occupation:* Woodcarver. *Home address:* Ariel, Wash. *Affiliation:* Lecturer, dance programmer, Oregon Museum of Science and Industry. *Award:* Inter-Tribal Indian Ceremonial, Gallup, N.M., 1966. *Interests:* Woodcarving, Northwest Coast styles; Indian dance and drama; Indian music; various forms of Indian arts and crafts.

SMITH, GERALD L. (Confederated Tribes of Warm Springs-Jemez Pueblo) 1949-
(justice services manager)

Born August 24, 1949, Albuquerque, N.M. *Education:* Univerity of Oregon, B.S. (Personnel and Industrial Management), 1972. *Principal occupation:* Justice Services Manager, The Confederated Tribes of Warm Springs, Warm Springs, Ore., 1984-. *Home address:* P.O. Box 937, Warm Springs, Ore. 97761. *Community activities:* Warm Springs Boxing Club (coach/president). *Memberships:* National Indian Traders Association (director); National Indian Business Council (director); International Association of Chiefs of Police (member-Tribal/State & Local Police Cooperation Committee); Oregon Association-USA Amateur Boxing Federation (vice president). *Awards, honors:* Selected as referee and judge to represent Region XII at the National Junior Olympic Boxing Championships. *Interests:* "Interesting in assisting Indian tribes and organizations In their business endeavors. *Published works: Economic Analysis of National Indian Cultural/Education Centers* (UIATF, 1974); *National Indian Planning Assessment* (UIPA, 1977); *The American Indian Index* (Arrowstar Publishing, 1985).

SMITH JAMES G.E.
(museum curator)

Affiliation: Curator of North American Ethnology, Museum of the American Indian, Heye Foundation, Broadway at 155th St., New York, N.Y. 10032.

SMITH, JAMES R.
(associate director-intergovernmental affairs-Indian Health Service)

Affiliation: Associate director for Intergo-

vernmental Affairs, Indian Health Service, 5600 Fishers Lane, Rockville, Md. 20857.

SMITH, LaMARR
(museum director)

Affiliation: Director, Memorial Indian Museum, P.O. Box 483, Broken Bow, Okla. 74728.

SMITH, LOUISE (Mescalero Apache) 1920-
(teacher)

Born September 9, 1920, Los Lunas, N.M. *Education:* University of New Mexico, B.A. (Music), 1940; Temple University, Harcum College, Fairfield University (graduate courses). *Principal occupation:* Teacher. *Home address:* 53-2 Revere Rd., Drexel Hill, Pa. 19026. *Affiliations:* Co-owner, Springfield Children's House—A Montessori School, 741 Beatty Rd., Springfield, Pa. *Other professional post:* Teacher, Ivy Leaf School, St. Barnabas School, Wyndmoor Montessori School, and Walden Montessori School, Drexel, Pa.; director of education, United American Indians of Delaware Valley, 225 Chestnut St., Philadelphia, Pa. 19106. *Interests:* Music; travel.

SMITH, MICHAEL H.
(B.I.A. agency superintendent)

Affiliation: Superintendent, Ute Mountain Ute Agency, Bureau of Indian Affairs, Towaoc, Colo. 81334.

SMITH, NOREEN
(director-Indian health board)

Affiliation: Director, Indian Health Board of Minnesota, 1315 E. 24th St., Minneapolis, Minn. 55404.

SMITH, ROBERT
(museum director)

Affiliation: Director, Oneida Nation Museum, P.O. Box 365, Oneida, Wis. 54155.

SMITH, SHEILA S. (Oneida of Wisconsin) 1962-
(artist)

Born September 19, 1962, Green Bay, Wis. *Education:* University of Wisconsin, La Crosse, Wis. *Principal occupation:* Artist. *Home address:* 1795 Poplar Lane, Seymour, Wis. 54165. *Affiliation:* Volunteer, Oneida Nation Museum, Oneida, Wis., 1980-. *Awards, honors:* 1st Place, University of Wisconsin, Stevens Point, 1985 Woodlands Indian Arts Festival; "proclaimed a master of my art by the U.S. Department of the Interior and the Wisconsin Arts Board." *Interests:* "I have brought back the last art of the Iroquois costume designs. I have sold four costumes to the U.S. Department of the Interior for their permanent colection of Indian artifacts. I had two costumes worn during President Reagan's Inaugural Festivities. I was also a selected artist from Wisconsin to be videotaped and exhibited by the National Endowment of the Arts and Wisconsin Arts Council as a national traveling exhibit. I have also had a cover of the Stevens Point *Magazine* published in Stevens Point, Wisconsin." *Biographical sources: Wisconsin Arts Board Source Directory,* 1986-1987; U.S. Department of the Interior—Indian Owned and Operated Businesses, 1985-1987.

SNAKE, REUBEN A., Jr. (Winnebago)
(tribal chairman)

Affiliation: Chairman, Winnebago Tribal Council, Winnebago, Neb. 68071.

SNEVE, VIRGINIA DRIVING HAWK (Rosebud Sioux) 1933-
(author, lecturer)

Born February 21, 1933, Rosebud, S.D. *Education:* South Dakota State University, B.S., 1954, M.Ed., 1969. *Principal occupation:* Author, lecturer. *Home address:* 723 Wright Court, Rapid City, S.D. 57701. *Affiliations:* Teacher-counselor, Flandreau Indian School, Flandreau, S.D., 1966-1970; editor, Brevet Press, Sioux Falls, S.D., 1970-1972; consultant, producer-writer, South Dakota Public TV, Brooking, S.D., 1973-1980; educational counselor, Flandreau Indian School, 1981-1985. *Community activities:* South Dakota State Library Association (Precentennial Project Advisory Advisory Board); St. Mary's School Board; Emanual Episcopal Church. *Memberships:* South Dakota Press Women (secretary, 1976-1978); National Federation Press Women; South Dakota Diocese of the Episcopal Church (historiographer, 1977-1985); Diocese Commission of the Dakota-/Lakota Culture; Enrolled member of Rosebud Sioux Tribe. *Awards, honors:* South Dakota Press Woman of the Year, 1974; National Federation Press Alumnus Women, Achievement, 1974; Distinguished Alumnus Award, South Dakota State University, 1974; Special Contribution to Education, South Dakota Indian Education Association, 1975; Honorary Doctorate of Letters, Dakota Wesleyan University, 1979; Distinguished Contribution to South Dakota History, Dakota History Conference, 1982; Council on Interracial Book Award for *Jimmy Yellow Hawk,* 1972; Western Writers of America Award for *Betrayed,* 1974. *Interests:* "Education; teacher and counselor at the Flandreau Indian School for ten years." *Biographical source: Who's Who of American Women. Published works: Jimmy Yellow Hawk* (Holiday House, 1972); *High Elk's Treasure* (Holiday House, 1972); editor, *South Dakota Geographic Names* (Brevet Press, 1973); *Betrayed* (Holiday House, 1974); *When Thunders Spoke* (Holiday House, 1974); *The Dakota's Heritage* (Brevet Press, 1974); *The Chichi Hoohoo Bogeyman,* Ms. Sneve wrote the script for the screen play of the same title for the "Vegetable Soup Children's TV series" (Holiday House, 1975); *They Led a Nation* (Brevet Press, 1975); That They May Have Life: The Episcopal Church in South Dakota, 1859-1976 (Seabury Press, 1981); short stories and nonfiction articles.

SNYDER, FRED (Chippewa-Colville) 1951-
(director-consultant, editor/publisher)

Born March 8, 1951, Pennsylvania. *Education:* Rutgers University, Camden, N.J. (two years). *Principal occupation:* Director-consultant, National Native American Co-Operative, San Carlos, Ariz. *Home address:* P.O. Box 301, San Carlos, Ariz. 85550.

Other professional posts: Editor/publisher, *Native American Directory—Alaska, Canada, U.S.;* educator. *Community activities: American Indian Market,* monthly, Phoenix, Ariz. (sponsor); Pow Wow Attender for North America. *Awards, honors:* Blue Ribbon (three years), Beadwork Competition, Heard Museum of Anthropology, Phoenix, Ariz.; numerous awards from Indian cultural programs, Title IV, Indian education, ethnic fairs. *Interests:* "Most of all my time is shared between directing the Co-Op (2,700 members), distribution of *Native American Directory* (40,000 copies), traveling extensively throughout North America to Indian powwows, rodeos, craft shows and conventions, and establishing the first Watts Line American Indian Information Center and Chamber of Commerce." *Biographical sources: Arizona Republic,* "Close Up" feature article (May, 1984); *Intertribal Enterprise,* "Close Up" feature article (April, 1985); *Navajo Times Today* (May, 1985). *Published work: Native American Directory—Alaska, Canada, U.S.* (National Native American Co-Op, 1982).

SOBOLEFF, SASHA (Puyallup)
(superintendent-tribal education system)

Affiliation: Superintendent, Puyallup Nation Education System, 2002 East 28th St., Tacoma, Wash. 98404.

SOBOLEFF, WALTER A. (Tlinget
of Southeast Alaska) 1908-
(clergy)

Born November 14, 1908, Killisnoo, Alaska. *Education:* University of Dubuque, Iowa, B.A., 1937, B.D., 1940. *Principal occupation:* Clergy, Presbyterian Church, 1940-1970. *Home address:* P.O. Box 535, Tenakee Springs, Alaska 99841. *Affiliations:* Clergy, 1940-1970, minister-at-large, 1962-1970, Presbyterian Church, Juneau, Alaska. *Other professional post:* Head, Department of Native Studies, University of Alaska, Juneau, 1970-1974. *Military service:* Army National Guard (Alaska Distinguished Service Medal). *Community service:* Lions Club (board of directors, secretary); Mason, Eastern Star, Scottish Rite 33rd; Knight Templar; American Legion; Alaska Native

Brotherhood (president); State Board of Education (chairman); Alaska Presbytery (state clerk; moderator; Synod-Washington-Alaska (moderator). *Memberships:* Southeast Alaska Adult Education Advisory Board, 1982-; Sealaska Heritage Foundation (trustee, 1986-); National Congress of American Indians (life member); Alaska Historical Society (life member); Commerce-Commission on Strategic Planning for the 1990's, 1985-1986; National Indian Education Association; American Indian, Athletic Hall of Fame (board of directors); Alaska Heritage Writers Association. *Awards, honors:* Christian Citizenship Award, Sheldon Jackson College Junior College, 1965; Alaska 49'er, 1973; Public Service Award by U.S. Department of the Interior, 1980; U.S. Forest Service 75th Anniversary Award, 1980; United Presbyterian Church, USA Board of National Missions, 25 Year Servie Award. *Biographicl sources: Who's Who in the West,* 1971; *Indians of Today,* 4th Edition; *Who's Who in Education,* 1970; *International Who's Who in Community, Service,* 1976-1977. *Publications:* "Historic Origin of the Cross," Bachelor of Divinity Thesis; *Grand Camp Alaska Native Brotherhood and Alaska Native Sisterhood, Manual of Ceremonies; Philosophy of Education for Alaska Natives;* numerous bulletins, brochures and articles.

SOCKYMA, MICHAEL C., Jr. (Hopi)
1942
(silver/gold smith, artist)

Born June 4, 1942, Hotevilla, Ariz. *Education:* Phoenix Indian High School. *Principal occupation:* Silver/gold smith, artist. *Home address:* P.O. Box 96, Kykotsmovi, Ariz. 86039. *Awards, honors:* "(I) have won ribbons for jewelry at Jemez Indian art shows, and Gallup Indian art shows." *Interests:* "21 years in making overlay jewelry in silver and gold; custom jewelry in precious stones; artist in oil and acrylic; council member for the Hopi Tribe; active in traditional cultural activities." *Biographical source: Government Directory of Indian Arts; Hopi Silver I & II,* by Margaret Wright.

**SOPIEL, SYLVIA (Passamaquoddy)
1929-
(editor)**

Born November 3, 1929, Peter Dana Point, Me. *Education:* Hasson College, Bangor, Me. *Principal occupation:* Editor, *Mawiw Kilun,* Princeton, Me., 1977-. *Home address:* Box 186, Princeton, Me. 04668. *Other professional post:* Ex-Justice of the Peace. *Community activities:* Vista volunteer. *Interests:* "(I) have flown all over the country— met a lot of "new" Indian tribes. Life sports, outdoors, serving and making clothes, basket weaving, braiding sweet grass, making necklaces of beads."

**SORENSEN, CAROLYN (Santee-Sioux)
(tribal president)**

Affiliation: President, Flandreau Santee-Sioux Executive Committee, P.O. Box 292, Flandreau, S.D. 57028.

**SORRELL, CHERYL
(executive director-Indian center)**

Affiliation: Executive director, Winslow Indian Center, 110 E. Second St., Winslow, Ariz. 86047.

**SOWMICK, ARNOLD (Saginaw-Chippewa)
(tribal chief)**

Affiliation: Chief, Saginaw-Chippewa Tribal Council, 7070 E. Broadway Rd., Mt. Pleasant, Mich. 48858.

**SPEAKS, STANLEY M. (Oklahoma Chickasaw) 1933-
(B.I.A. area director)**

Born November 2, 1933, Tishomingo, Okla. *Education:* Northeastern State College, Tahlequah, Okla., B.S., 1959, M.Ed., 1962. *Principal occupation:* B.I.A. area director. *Address:* Portland Area Office, B.I.A., 1425 N.E. Irving St., P.O. Box 3785, Portland, Ore. 97208. *Affiliations:* Acting supervisor, Intermountain School, Brigham City, Utah, 1974-1975; superintendent, Anadarko Agency, B.I.A., 1975-1977; area director,

Anadarko Area Office, B.I.A., Anadarko, Okla., 1976-1980; director, Portland Area Office, B.I.A., Portland, Ore. *Community activities:* Boy Scouts of America (member-American Indian Relations Committee); 16th American Indian Tribal Leader's Seminar on Scouting (chairman, 1972-1973); Rotary International (member); Oklahoma Governor's Committee on Small Business (member). *Interests:* Boating, fishing, hunting, golf; Boy Scouts of America.

**SPEARS, PATRICK (Lower Brule Sioux)
(tribal chairman)**

Affiliation: Chairman, Lower Brule Sioux Tribal Council, Lower Brule, S.D. 57548.

**SPENCER, HARGLE
(B.I.A. agency superintendent)**

Affiliation: Superintendent, Sisseton Agency, Bureau of Indian Affairs, Sisseton, S.D. 57262.

**SPENCER, ROBERT F. 1917-
(professor of anthropology)**

Born March 30, 1917, San Francisco, Calif. *Education:* University of California, Berkeley, B.A., 1937, Ph.D., 1946; University of New Mexico, M.A., 1940. *Principal occupation:* Professor of anthropology, University of Minnesota, Minneapolis, Minn. *Home address:* 1577 Vincent St., St. Paul, Minn. 55108. *Other professional post:* Editor, American Ethnological Society, 1968-. *Memberships:* American Ethnological Society; Arctic Institute of North America; Royal Anthropological Institute; American Folklore Society. *Interests:* "Anthropology and ethnology of North America—field research among American Indian groups: Keresan, 1938-1940; Klamath, 1947-1948; Eskimo, Point Barrow, Anaktuvuk Pass, etc., 1952-1953, 1968." *Published works:* *The North Alaskan Eskimo* (Smithsonian Institution, 1959, 1969); *The Native Americans,* with J.D. Jennings, et al (Harper & Row, 1965; revised, 1977).

SPICER, EDWARD HOLLAND 1906-
(professor emeritus)

Born November 29, 1906, Cheltenham, Pa. *Education:* University of Arizona, B.A., 1932, M.A., 1933; University of Chicago, Ph.D., 1939. *Principal occupation:* Professor emeritus, University of Arizona. *Home address:* 5344 E. Fort Lowell Rd., Tucson, Ariz. 85712. *Affiliation:* Instructor, 1939-1941, associate professor, 1946-1950, professor, 1950-1978, professor emeritus, 1978-, Department of Anthropology, University of Arizona, Tucson, Ariz. *Military service:* War Relocation Authority, Washington, D.C., 1943-1946. *Other professional posts:* Editor, *Journal* of the American Anthropological Association, 1960-1963; director, Pascua Yaqui Development Project, OEO, Tucson, Ariz., 1966-1969; consultant, U.S. Bureau of Indian Affairs, 1967-1969; member, Arizona Commission on Indian Affairs, 1964-1966. *Memberships:* American Anthropological Association (Fellow- (president, 1974; editor, executive board); Society for Applied Anthropology (vice president); American Association for the Advancement of Science; American Philosophical Society; National Academy of Sciences. *Awards, honors:* Southwestern Library Association for best book on the Southwest, 1964; Malinowski Award, 1976, Society for Applied Anthropology; Guggenheim Fellow, 1941-1942, 1955-1956; National Science Foundation, Senior Postdoctoral Fellowship, 1963-1964; Senior Fellow, National Endowment for the Humanities, 1970-1971. *Interests:* Acculturation; Southwestern U.S.; Northwestern Mexico; research in Mexico and Peru. *Published works: A Yaqui Village in Arizona* (University of Chicago Press, 1940); *Potam, A Yaqui Village of Sonora* (American Anthropological Association, 1954); editor, *Human Problems in Technological Change* (Russell Sage, 1952; John Wiley, 1965); editor, *Perspectives in American Indian Culture Change* (University of Chicago Press, 1962); *Cycles of Conquest: The Impact of Spain, Mexico, and the U.S. on the Indians of the Southwest, 1533-1960* (University of Arizona Press, 1963); *A Short History of the Indians of the U.S.* (Van Nostrand, 1969); *The Yaquis; A Cultural History,* 1980.

SPIVEY, TOWANA (Chickasaw) 1943-
(curator, archaeologist)

Born November 8, 1943, Madill, Okla. *Education:* Southeastern State University, Durant, Okla., B.A., 1968; University of Oklahoma, 1970-1971. *Principal occupation:* Curator, archaeologist. *Home address:* 2101 Oak St., Duncan, Okla. 73533. *Affiliation:* Curator of anthropology, Museum of the Great Plains, Lawton, Okla., 1974-. *Other professional posts:* Curator-archaeologist, Oklahoma Historical Society, 1974-; archaeologist, Oklahoma Archaeological Survey (two years). *Military service:* Army National Guard, 1960-1968. *Memberships:* Oklahoma Anthropological Society, 1963- (board member); Oklahoma Museums Association, 1973- (council member); Society for Historic Archaeology, 1973-; Council on Abandoned Military Posts (vice president of Oklahoma Department, 1975-). *Interests:* Historic sites-restoration, archaeology, etc.; 19th century military forts and camps; fur trade and exploration of the Trans-Mississippi West; conservation of cultural material or artifacts; wagon restoration. *Published works:* Co-author, *An Archaeological Reconnaissance of the Salt Plains Areas of Northwest Oklahoma* (Museum of the Great Plains, 1976); co-author, *Archaeological Investigations Along the Waurika Pipeline* (Museum of the Great Plains, 1977).

SPOTTED EAGLE, CHRIS
(president-Indian society)

Affiliation: President, American Indian Talent Society, 2225 Cavell Ave., North, Golden Valley, Minn. 55427.

SPOTTED BEAR, ALYCE (Mandan-Hidatsa)
(tribal chairman)

Affiliation: Chairman, Fort Berthold Tribal Business Council, P.O. Box 220, New Town, N.D. 58763.

STALLING, STEVEN L.A.
(San Luiseno Band of Mission Indians
at Rincon Reservation)
(president-Indian association)

Education: California State University, Long Beach, B.S.; University of Southern California, M.B.A. *Principal occupation:* President, United Indian Development Association, 1541 Wilshire Blvd., Suite 418, Los Angeles, Calif. 90017, 1976-. *Home address:* 28776 Charreadas, Laguna Niguel, Calif. 92677. *Affiliations:* Prior to joining the UIDA, Mr. Stalling was executive director of a consulting firm in San Francisco, Calif. and supervised a job creation program which trained 300 American Indians. *Other professional posts:* Session chairman, Fifth International Symposium on Small Business, 1978; delegate to the White House Conference on Small Business, 1978. *Community activities:* Coordinator for the National Congress of American Indians, a lobbying group; former member of the steering committee for the National Indian Education Association; member of Board of Directors for a beginning Development Band directed at solving the domestic financing needs of American Indians; member of Advisory Committee for 1984 Olympics; served on Los Angeles Bicentennial Commission and the Los Angeles Private Industry Council; appointed to the Los Angeles City/County Indian Commission by Republican Supervisor Dean Dana. *Awards, honors:* Cited and recognized by the State Assembly of California for his contributions and efforts in small business and economic development. *Interests:* UIDA assists over 600 businesses annually and has secured over $52 million in financing and contracts for its clients. Long interested in developing American Indian talent, an interest that has accelerated since the formation of UIDA's Management Institute which trains Indian managers, Mr. Stallings has conducted dozens of workshops and seminars. Two of his training books are used throughout America by Indians learning planning and management. *Biographical sources: Who's Who in Finance and Industry,* 1982-1983; *Who's Who in the West,* 1982-1983.

STANDING, NETTIE L. (Kiowa) 1916-
(manager-OKlahoma Indian
Arts & Crafts Cooperative)

Born August 15, 1916, Caddo County, OKla. *Education:* Riverside Indian School; Santa Fe Indian Boarding School, 1934-1935. *Principal occupation:* Founding member and manager, Oklahoma Indian Arts & Crafts Cooperative, Anadarko, Okla., 1962-. *Home address:* P.O. Box 114, Gracemont, Okla. 73042. *Membership:* Oklahoma Federation of Indian Women. *Awards, honors:* 1975 National Endowment Award, recipient of grant for $5,000, for outstanding crafts person and teacher, and to research Kiowa beadwork; Grand Award Winner, 1977, Great Western Shows, Los Angeles, Calif.; 1976 Award from the Department of the Interior, Indian Arts and Crafts Board, for outstanding service to promote, prserve and develop all Indian crafts; 1985 O.I.O—one of the finalists for Indian Business Person of the Year for Oklahoma. *Interests:* "Kiowa beadwork; travel to Smithsonian Institution, and to the Museum of the American Indian in New York City in 1975-1976, to view collection, and to visit the Indian Arts and Crafts Board in Washington, D.C.."

STANDING ELK, DONALD
(B.I.A. Indian Education)

Affiliation: Indian Education, Bureau of Indian Affairs, 1951 Constitution Ave., N.W., Washington, D.C. 20245.

STARBLANKET, NOEL V.
(Saskatchewan) 1946-
(president-National Indian Brotherhood)

Born September 27, 1946, Starblanket Indian Reserve, Balcarres, Saskatchewan, Can. *Principal occupation:* President, National Indian Brotherhood, Ottawa, Ontario, Can., 1976-. *Affiliations:* President-elect, Canadian Indian Youth Council, Ottawa, 1967-1968; employed as an Indian filmmaker by the National Film Board of Canada, Montreal, 1968-1969; liaison officer, National Indian Brotherhood of

Canada, Winnipeg, Manitoba, 1970; chief, Starblanket Indian Reserve, Baclarres, Saskatchewan, 1971-1973; vice president, 1973, 1975-1976, director, Indian Rights and Treaties Research Program, Provincial Indian Organization, Federation of Saskatchewan Indians. *Community activities:* Economic Development for Indian People, Department of Indian and Northern Affairs (numerous committees). *Honors:* Greatgreat grandson of Chief White Calf, who signed treaty No. 4, 1875; great grandfather Starblanket, inherited chieftainship, Reserve and band named after him; father Victor was chief for 16 years on Starblanket Resrve. *Films:* Developed documentary film, *Starblanket*, produced and telecasted on National TV by the National Film Board of Canada and the Canadian Broadcasting Corporation; consultant, and acted bit part in *Cold Journey*, commercial documentary feature developed by Indian film crew for National Film Board.

STARCHILD, ADAM ARISTOTLE 1946-
(business consultant, author)

Born September 20, 1946, Minneapolis, Minn. *Education:* Sussex College of Technology (England), M.B.A., 1978; Blackstone School of Law (England), J.D., 1982. *Principal occupation:* President, Minerva Consulting Group, New York, N.Y., 1978-. *Address:* P.O. Box 5474, New York, N.Y. 10163. *Community activities:* Council of American Indian Artists (chairman, 1981-); Confederation of American Indians (trustee, 1981). *Memberships:* World Future Society; International Tax Planning Association; Mensa; Associated Business Writers of America. *Awards, honors:* Presidential Sports Award, 1975, 1982; Financial Writers Award, 1981. *Interests:* Canoeing and horsemanship; travels to Europe, Hong Kong, Soviet Union, Caribean. *Published works:* Author of hundreds of articles and over a dozen books.

STEELE, CHESTER (Goshute)
(tribal chairman)

Affiliation: Chairman, Goshute Tribal Council, Ibapah, Utah 87034.

STEELE, WILLIAM OWEN 1917-
(author)

Born December 22, 1917, Franklin, Tenn. *Education:* Cumberland University, B.A., 1940; University of Chattanooga, 1951-1952, *Principal occupation:* Author. *Home address:* 808 Fairmount Ave., Signal Mt., Tenn. *Awards, honors:* Numerous awards for books written. *Published works: The Buffalo Knife* (1952); *Wilderness Journey* (1953); *Tomahawks and Trouble* (1955); *Flaming Arrows* (1957); *Perilous Road* (1958); *Westward Adventure: The True Stories of Six Pioneers* (1962); all published by Harcourt, Brace & World; *Wayah of the Real People* (1964) and *Tomahawk Border* (1966) published by Colonial Williamburg; *The Wilderness Tattoo: A Narrative of Juan Ortiz* (Harcourt, Brace, Jovanovich, 1972); *Surgeon, Trader, Indian Chief: Henry Woodward of Carolina* (Sandpiper Press, 1972); *The Cherokee Crown of Tannassy* (John F. Blair, Publisher, 1977); *Talking Bones: Secrets of Indian Burial Mounds* (Harper & Row, 1978); and others.

STEIN, WAYNE
(college president)

Affiliation: President, Standing Rock Community College, P.O. Box 450, Fort Yates, N.D. 48438.

STEPHENSON, BONNIE (Delaware)
(tribal administrator)

Affiliation: Administrator, Delaware Executive Committee, P.O. Box 825, Anadarko, Okla. 73005.

STEVENS, CONNIE (Iroquois-Cherokee) 1938-
(actress)

Born August 8, 1938, Brooklyn, N.Y. *Principal occupation:* Actress (25 years). *Address:* 243 Delfern Dr., Los Angeles, Calif. 90077. *Affiliation:* Founder, president, executive director, Windfeather Foundation. *Memberships:* Screen Actors Guild, AFTRA, Actors Equity.

STEVENS, JOHN W. (Passamaquoddy) 1933-
(tribal governor)

Born August 11, 1933, Washington County, Me. *Education:* High school. *Principal occupation:* Tribal governor, Indian Township—Passamaquoddy Tribal Council, P.O. Box 301, Indian Township, Me. 04668. *Home address:* Peter Dana Point, Indian Township Reservation, Washington County, Me. *Military service:* U.S. Marines, 1951-1954 (Presidential Unit Citation; Korean Presidential Unit Citation; United Nations Medal). *Interests:* Mr. Stevens writes, "Being the chief of an Indian tribe of about a thousand members who are struggling in court and on all fronts to overcome local discrimination and poverty and to have our reservation treaty rights respected by the State of Maine is enough of a task, and doesn't leave much time for anything else."

STEWART, DONALD, Sr. (Crow)
(tribal chairman)

Affiliation: Chairman, Crow Tribal Council, Crow Agency, Mt. 59022.

STEWART, OMER C. 1908-
(anthropologist, ethnogeographer, educator, professor emeritus)

Born August 17, 1908, Provo, Utah. *Education:* University of Utah, B.A., 1933; University of California, Berkeley, Ph.D., 1939. *Principal occupation:* Anthropologist, ethnogeographer, educator, professor emeritus. *Home address:* 921 5th St., Boulder, Colo. 80302. *Affiliations:* Professor of anthropology, 1945-1974, professor emeritus, 1974-, University of Colorado, Boulder, Colo. *Military service:* Liaison officer to Ethnographic Board, Office of Chief of Staff, War Department, Washington, D.C., 1942-1943. *Memberships:* American Anthropological Association (Fellow); Society for American Archaeology; Society for Applied Anthropology (Fellow); Colorado Archaeological Society; American Association for the Advancement of Science; American Ecological Association; Sigma Xi. *Interests:* Expeditions and field work—archaeology of Ute and northern

Arizona, 1931-1933; ethnography of Pomo Indians, northern California; culture element distribution of Northern Paiute and Washo Indians of Nevada, Oregon and California, and Ute and Southern Paiute of Utah, Arizona, and Colorado; study of peyote cult of Washo and Northern Paiute of Nevada and eastern California, University of California, 1935-1938; study of primitive child development, Zuni, N.M., and community study of Morman vilage of Alpine, Ariz., Social Science Research Council, 1940-1941; community analysis, Ignacio, Colo., University of Colorado, 1948-1950; ethnohistory of Pit River, Washo, Northern Paiute, Ute, Chippewa, and Ottawa, 1953-1958; values and behavior on the Ute Reservation, U.S. Department of H.E.W., 1959-1963. *Published works: Ute Peyotism* (Series in Anthropology, University of Colorado, 1948); *Navaho and Ute Peyotism: A Chronological and Distributional Study,* with David F. Aberle (University of Colorado, 1957); editor, *Southwestern Lore,* 1949-1953; contributor to Encyclopedia Americana and Britannica; numerous articles, papers, and chapters in books.

STONE, WILLARD (Cherokee) 1916-
(artist, wood sculptor)

Born February 26, 1916, Oktaha, Okla. *Education:* High school. *Principal occupation:* Artist, wood sculptor. *Home address:* Star Route East, Locust Grove, Okla. *Other professional occupations:* Die finisher, designer, patternmaker, inventor. *Memberships:* Five Civilized Tribes Museum, Muskogee, Okla.; National Cowboy Hall of Fame, Oklahoma City, Okla.; Philbrook Art Center, Tulsa, Okla.. *Awards, honors:* Numerous awards for art and sculptor; special award, Indian Arts and Crafts Board, Department of the Interior, 1966; Outstanding Indian Award, Council of American Indians, 1969; inducted into the Oklahoma Hall of Fame, 1970, Oklahoma Heritage Association; Special Service Award, Cherokee Nation, 1971; Distinguished Service Award, Bacone College, Muskogee, Okla., 1972; Distinguished American Citizen Award, Oklahoma Christian College, Oklahoma City, Okla., 1974; Doctor of Humanities Degree, Oklahoma Christian College, 1976; Citizen of the Year Award, Locust Grove, Okla., 1976. *Interests:* Sculpture, painting, sketching. Mr. Stone is an official representative of the Cherokee Tribe.

STOTT, MARGARET 1945-
(museum curator; honorary assistant professor)

Born September 25, 1945, Vancouver, Can. *Education:* University of British Columbia, B.A. (Honours), 1966; McGill University, M.A., 1969; University of London (England), Ph.D., 1982. *Principal occupation:* Museum curator of ethnology, honorary assistant professor, Department of Anthropology and Sociology, University of British Columbia, Vancouver, 1979-. *Memberships:* British Columbia Museums Association; Canadian Museums Association; American Association of Museums; Canadian Ethnology Society; Canadian Anthropology and Sociology Association; Mediterranean Institute; Modern Greek Studies Association; Council for Museum Anthropology. *Interests:* "Northwest Coast Indian material culture and art with particular emphasis on the Bella Coola Indians; material culture studies; museum studies; Mediterranean ethnography with particular emphasis on modern Greece; tourism studies, particularly in the Mediterranean." *Published works: Bella Coola Ceremony and Art* (National Museums of Canada, 1975); *Material Anthropology: Contemporary Approaches to Material Culture* (University Press of America, in press). *Exhibitions:* "Northwest Coast Indian Art," exhibition of contemporary Indian art (20 pieces), displayed in four cases at Air Canada Maple Leaf Lounge, Vancouver International Airport, 1980-; numerous other exhibitions in the past. *Audio-visual productions: The Raven and the First Man,* visuals of the sculpture carved by Haida artist Bill Reid, with the artist narrating the Haida origin myth depicted in the carvings; *Salish Art and Culture,* an interview with an anthropologist in the Museum exhibition "Visions of Power, Symbols and Wealth; among others.

STOUT, RICHARD ALAN
(executive director-Native American studies program)

Affiliation: Executive director, Southeastern Native American Studies Program, P.O. Box 953, Gastonia, N.C. 28053-0953.

STOUT, SADIE
(chief of nursing—Indian Health Service)

Affiliation: Chief of Nursing, Indian Health Service, 5600 Fishers Lane, Rockville, Md. 20857.

STRICKLAND, RENNARD JAMES
(Cherokee-Osage) 1940-
(professor of law)

Born September 26, 1940, St. Louis, Mo. *Education:* Northeastern State College, Tahlequah, Okla., B.A., 1962; University of Virginia, J.D., 1965, S.J.D., 1970; University of Arkansas, M.A., 1966. *Principal occupation:* Professor of law. *Affiliations:* Professor, University of Arkansas, 1965-1969; professor of law, University of Tulsa, 1972-. *Other professional posts:* Director, Indin Heritage Association, Muskogee, Okla., 1966-; director, Oral History Project, University of Florida, 1969-1971. *Memberships:* American Society of Legal History; Selden Society; Communications Association of America; Oklahoma Historical Society; American Ethnohistory Society. *Awards, honors:* Sacred Sash of the Creeks for Preservation Tribal History; Fellow in Legal History, American Bar Association, 1970-1971. *Interests:* Mr. Strickland writes, "Primary interest (is in) law and the American Indian, including programs to attract Indian students to the law as a profession, and programs to make the law responsive to the needs of Indian citizens; culture of the American Indian, with primary emphasis upon myths and legends and upon the arts and crafts of native tribes; contemporary American Indian paintings, and the evolution of Indian culture as reflected in evolving styles; ethnohistory of specific tribes—the Cherokee, Creek. Seminole, Choctaw and Chickasaw; development of traditional legal systems among the tribes." *Published works: Sam Houston With the Cherokees,* with Jack Gregory (University of Texas Press, 1967); *Starr's History of the Cherokees* (1968); *Cherokee Spirit Tales* (1969); *Cherokee Cook Book* (1969); *Creek-Seminole Spirit Tales* (1971); *Choctaw Spirit Tales* (1972); *Hell on the Border* (1971); *Adventures of an Indian Boy* (1973); *American Indian Spirit Tales* (1973); all with Jack Gregory, published by Indian Heritage Association; *Cherokee Law Ways* (University of Oklahoma Press, 1972).

STRUCHER, JIM
(general manager-Alaskan Native corporation)

Affiliation: General manager, Ahtna Development Corporation, 406 W. Fireweed Lane, Suite 101, Anchorage, Alaska 99503.

STUMP, ROCKY, Sr. (Chippewa Cree)
(tribal chairman)

Affiliation: Chairman, Chippewa Cree Business Comittee, P.O. Box 137, Box Elder, Mt. 59521.

SULCER, PATRICIA KAY 1951-
(editor, assistant administrator)

Born July 30, 1951, Charlotte, Mich. *Education:* Lansing Community College, Lansing, Mich. (two years); Thomas Jefferson College, Allendale, Mich., B.A. (Philosophy). *Principal occupation:* Editor, *HowNiKan,* Potawatomi newspaper, 1983-; assistant administrator, Citizen Band Potawatomi Tribe, Shawnee, Okla., 1983-. *Home address:* 22 E. Severn St., Shawnee, Okla. 74801. *Other professional post:* Board of directors, Native American Publishing Co. *Memberships:* Smithsonian Institution; National Press Photographers Association; Oklahoma Press Association; Native American Press Association (charter member-board of directors); American Association of University Women. *Awards, honors:* 1985 Native American Press Association, Honorable Mention for General Excellence, First Place News or Photo Series. *Interests:* "Cultural reclamation work, organizing council meetings for tribal members across the country, currently writing a Potawatomi dictionary." *Published work:* Editor, *Grandfather, Tell Me a Story* (Citizen Band Potawatomi Tribe, 1984).

SUMMERS-FITZGERALD, DIOSA
(Mississippi Choctaw) 1945-
(director of education, artist)

Born December 23, 1945, New York, N.Y. *Education:* State University College at Buffalo, B.A., 1977; Northwestern University Arcaheological Center, Kampsville, Ill. (Certificate), 1981; Harvard University Graduate School of Education, Ed.M., 1983. *Principal occupation:* Director of education, artist. *Home address:* 226 Ward Ave., Staten Island, N.Y. 10304. *Affiliations:* Instructor, History Department and Continuing Education Department, State University College at Buffalo, N.Y., 1975-1977; instructor, Haffenreffer Museum of Anthropology, Bristol, R.I., 1979-1980; acting tribal coordinator, Narragansett Tribal Education Project, Inc., 1980; administration, instructor, proposal writer, program coordinator, 1980-1981, education director, instructor, 1982-1985, Tomaquag Indian Memorial Museum, Exeter, R.I.; Native American historical and educational consultant, Plimoth Plantation, Plymouth, Mass., 1981-1982; artist in residence, Folk Arts Program, Rhode Island State Council on the Arts, Providence, 1982-1985; artist, Native American Art Forms Nishnabeykwa Productions, Charlestown, R.I., 1982-1985; education director, Jamaica Arts Center, Jamaica, N.Y., 1985-. *Other professional post:* Owner, artist, consultant, Nishnabeykwa Productions, Staten Island, N.Y., 1982-. *Memberships:* Harvard Club of Rhode Island. *Awards, honors:* 1st Prize, Photography, Thomas Indian School Exhibit; Kappa Delta Pi, national Undergraduate Honor Society; Phi Alpha Theta, International History Honor Society. *Interests:* "Over the years, I have devoted most of life to Native American art, and a clear understanding of the roots of Native American tradition through art. I have also sought to develop a better understanding of the Native American through art as well as in the classroom initially as a teacher, and more recently a curriculum developer, and program developer." *Other expertise:* Cultural consultant and educational consultant; craft demonstrations; curator of exhibitions. *Published works: Native American Foods; Fingerweaving,* narrative and instruction; *Ash Splint Basketry;* Tomaquag Indian Museum brochures.

SUMNER, DELORES T. (Comanche) 1931-
(special collections librarian)

Born May 11, 1931, Lawton, Okla. *Education:* Northeastern State University, Okla., B.S., 1964, Masters in Teaching, 1967; University of Oklahoma, Masters in Library Science, 1981. *Special collections librarian. Home address:* Route 3, Box 264C, Tahlequah, Okla. 74464 *Affiliations:* Coordinator/director, Comanche Cultural Center, Comanche Complex, Lawton, Okla. (2½ years); SPC librarian, John Vaughn Library, Northeastern State University, Tahlequak, Okla., 1982-. *Other professional post:* Public school teacher (five years). *Community activites:* Northeastern State University Symposium on the American Indian (appointed member-four years). *Memberships:* American Indian Library Association, 1980-; Tahlequah Arts and Humanities Council, 1980-; Oklahoma Library Association, 1981-; American Library Association, 1981-; Western History Collection Association (Oklahoma University), 1981-; Philbrook Friends of American Art, 1983-; Delta Kappa Gamma Society International (Alpha Eta Chapter), 1984-; Gilcrease Museum Association, 1985-. *Awards, honors:* Certificate of Appreciation, Oklahoma Library Association . *Intersts:* "Supporting the traditional artists in Native American art by traveling to exhibits, showings, and galleries is one of my main interests. I am very much interested in the preservation of Native American culture and tradition through oral history, art work, and the retention of the native language, of which I have accomplished only a small portion while working for my tribe as their cultural director. Today, I am still working toward this goal by personally contacting elders to record their songs, stories, and memories. I also record Comanche hymns whenever possible." *Published work:* Numa-Nu: The Fort Sill Indian School Experience (Oklahoma Humanities Committee, 1980).

SUN BEAR (Chippewa) 1929-
(author, lecturer, teacher, founder of the Bear Tribe)

Born August 31, 1929, White Earth Reservation, Minn. *Principal occupation:* President, The Bear Tribe Medicine Society, Spokane, Wash., 1970-. *Home address:* P.O. Box 9167, Spokane, Wash. 99209. *Other professional posts:* Editor/publisher, *Many Smokes* magazine; motion picture actor and extra, 1955-1965; technical director, "Wagon Train," "Bonanza," and "Wild, Wild West," television series. *Membership:* National Congress of American Indians. *Interests:* "I have been involved in Indian affairs most of my life, and I've spent some time teaching survival living to Indian and non-Indian people. I'm concerned with our Indian people, and other people, becoming more self-sufficient on the land, and learning a better balance with each other, and the Earth Mother." Sun Bear is a world traveler and lecturer, his travels having taken him to Europe, Australia, and India. *Published works: At Home in the Wilderness* (Naturegraph, 1968); *Buffalo Hearts* (Bear Tribe Publishing, 1970); *The Bear Tribe's Self-Reliance Book* (Bear Tribe Publishing, 1977); *The Medicine Wheel Book* (Prentice-Hall, 1980); *Sun Bear: The Path of Power* (Bear Tribe Publishing, 1983).

SUNDOWN, CHIEF CORBETT (Tonawanda Seneca) 1909-
(retired chief)

Born February 21, 1909, Tonawanda Indian Reservation, Basom, N.Y. *Education:* Reservation school, Basom, N.Y. *Professional post:* Chairman, Tonawanda Band of Senecas Chief's Council. *Home address:* 299 Lone Rd., Basom, N.Y. 14013. *Military service:* U.S. Air Force, 1941-1942. *Honor:* Cited by the Iroquois Conference for his role as a leader and educator among Indian people. *Interests:* "Traveled to Geneva, Switzeralnd to attend an International Non-Governmental Organizations Conference on Discrimination Against Indigenous Populations."

SURRETT, CLIFTON R. (Moapa)
(tribal chairman)

Affiliation: Chairman, Moapa Business Council, P.O. Box 56, Las Vegas, Nev. 89025.

SURVEYOR, VIRGIL R. (Cheyenne) 1937-
(school superintendent)

Born November 28, 1937, Canton, Okla. *Education:* Oklahoma City University, B.A., 1969, M.A.T., 1978. *Principal occupation:* Superintendent, Kickapoo Nation School, Powhattan, Kan. *Home address:* P.O. Box 53, Powhattan, Kan. 66527. *Affiliations:* Physical education teacher and coach, Concho School (eleven years); social studies teacher, Crescent Public School, Crescent, Okla. (two years); principal, Canton Public School, Canton, Okla. (one year); principal, Winnebago Public School, 1984-1985. *Other professional post:* Athletic director, Kickapoo Nation School. *Military service:* U.S. Army, 1959-1960. *Community activities:* Lions Club, Canton, Okla.; Cub Scouts Den Father, Canton, Okla.; Canton Indian High School Club, 1982-1984. *Memberships:* Kansas Athletic High School Coaches Association, 1985-; Oklahoma Indian Education Association; Oklahoma Middle School Association, 1984-; Kansas Education Association, 1986-.

SWAMP, CHIEF JAKE (Mohawk)
(tribal chief)

Affiliation: Chief, Mohawk Nation, via 188C Cook Rd., Hogansburg, N.Y. 13655.

SWETTER, DONALD A.
(resource coordinator-Indian Health Service)

Affiliation: Director, Division of Resource Coordination, Indian Health Service, 5600 Fishers Lane, Rockville, Md. 20857.

SWIMMER, ROSS O. (Oklahoma Cherokee) 1943-
(Assistant Secretary-Indian Affairs-U.S. Department of the Interior)

Born October 26, 1943, Oklahoma. *Education:* University of Oklahoma, B.S. (Political Science), 1965; University of Oklahoma School of Law, J.D., 1967. *Principal occupation:* Assistant Secretary-Indian Affairs, U.S. Department of the Interior. *Address: Bureau of Indian Affairs, Room 4160 N, 1951 Constitution Ave., N.W., Washington, D.C. 20245. Affiliations:* Law partner, Hansen, Peterson and Thompkins, Oklahoma City, Okla., 1967-1972; general counsel, 1972-1975, principal chief, 1975-1985, Cherokee Nation of Oklahoma, Tahlequah, Okla.; executive vice president, 1974-1975, president, 1975-1985, First National Bank in Tahlequah, Okla.; assistant secretary-Indian Affairs, 1985-. *Other professional post:* Co-chairman, Presidential Commission on Indian Reservation Economies (a panel of tribal leaders appointed to seek ways to help tribes improve economic conditions), 1983-1984. *Community activities:* Boy Scouts of America in Eastern Oklahoma (executive committee); Cherokee National Historical Society (past president); Tahlequah Planning and Zoning Commission (former chairman); Eastern Oklahoma Indian Health Advisory Board (secretary-treasurer); Inter-Tribal Council of the Five Civilized Tribes (advisory board, director). *Memberships:* Oklahoma and American Bar Association; Oklahoma Historical Society; Oklahoma Industrial Development Commission. *Interests:* Interior Secretary Donald Hodel said of Swimmer, "He combines a solid knowledge of tribal and Indian affairs with understanding and skill in modern business management." Swimmer has frequently expressed his views that Indian tribes should be less dependent on the federal government. When nominated for the position of Assistant Secretary, Swimmer said of President Reagan: "I know he is committed to an Indian policy that supports tribal self-determination, which is something I have worked for during my ten years at the Cherokee Nation."

T

TALL CHIEF, GEORGE EVES
(Osage) 1916-
(tribal chief, coach, teacher)

Born November 16, 1916, Arkansas City, Kan. *Education:* Central State College, Edmond, Okla., B.A., 1952; Pacific University, Forest Grove, Ore., M.A., 1957. *Principal occupation:* Principal Chief, Osage Tribe of Oklahoma. *Home address:* P.O. Box 14, Fairfax, Okla. 74637. *Other professional posts:* Coach and teacher. *Community activities:* Rotary Club; Chamber of Commerce; Quarterback Club. *Membership.* National Tribal Chairman's Association (vice president). *Awards, honors:* Iron Eyes Cody Peace Medal; Golden Glove Champion of Oklahoma (in college); Little All-American Coach of the Year in Pacific Coast Wrestling Conference. *Interests:* "My interests at the present time is to better the lot of the American Indian; sports; raise Appaloosa Show horses."

TANNER, CLARA LEE 1905-
(professor emerita)

Born May 28, 1905, Biscoe, N.C. *Education:* University of Arizona, B.A., 1927, M.A. (Archaeology), 1928. *Principal occupation:* Professor emerita. *Home address:* P.O. Box 40904, Tucson, Ariz. 85717. *Affiliation:* Instructor, 1928-1935, assistant professor, 1935-1957, associate professor, 1957-1968, professor, 1968-1978, professor emerita, 1978-, Department of Anthropology, University of Arizona, Tucson, Ariz. *Other professional posts:* Editor, *The Kiva,* 1938, 1948; editorial advisory board, *American Indian Art,* and *Indian America;* numerous University of Arizona committees. *Community activities:* Cummings Publication Council; Southwest Indian Arts and Crafts Committee; Tucson Fine Arts Association; judging of grant applications for the National Endowment for the Humanities, National Science Foundation, and Wenner-Gren Foundation for Anthropological Research. *Memberships:* Southwest Association of Indian Affairs, Sante Fe, N.M. (life member); Arizona Archaeological and Historical Society, Tucson, Ariz. (life member); American Anthropological Association; American Ethnological Society; Society of American Archaeology; National Federation of Press Women; Phi Beta Kappa; Society of Sigma Xi; Delta Kappa Gamma (educational honorary); Arizona Academy of Science; Arizona Historical Society; Arizona Press Women; Society of Southwest Authors; Archaeological Society of New Mexico. *Awards, honors:* Sharlot Hall Award, 1985; LLD Honorary Doctor of Letters, University of Arizona, 1983; Tucson Panhellenic Athena Award for Professional Achievement, 1983; Mortar Board Hall of Fame, University of Arizona, 1977; University of Arizona Alumni Association Faculty Achievement Award, 1974; Faculty Recognition Award, Tucson Trade Bureau, 1972-1973; Woman of the Year, Arizona Press Women, 1971-1972; 50th Anniversary Award of the Gallup Inter-Tribal Indian Ceremonial Association, 1971; Univerity of Arizona, 75th Anniversary Award, 1960; One of Outstanding Tucson Women of 1957; Arizona Press Women First Awards for books written, 1960- (the latest for *Apache Indian Baskets,* 1984); National Federation of Press Women awards, 1969- (the latest for *Apache Indian Baskets,* 1984); Society of Southwestern Authors awards; Border Regional Library Award, 1984 for *Apache Indian Baskets. Interests:* "Public lectures, 1928 to present, predominantly on the subject of Indians of the Southwest and their arts and crafts, to organizations throughout Arizona and in New Mexico, Colorado, California, Texas and Florida; lectures to school classes throughout southern Arizona; craft judging; travel." *Biographical sources: Who's Who in America, Who's Who of American Women; Who's Who in the West; American Men and Women of Science; Contemporary Authors. Published works: Southwest Indian Painting* (1957); *Southwest Indian Craft Arts* (1968); *Southwest Indian Painting, A Changing Art* (1973); *Prehistoric Southwest Craft Arts* (1978); *Apache Indian Baskets* (1982); *Indian Baskets of the Southwest* (1983).

TANNER HELEN HORNBECK 1916-
(consultant historian, expert witness)

Born July 5, 1916, Northfield, Minn. *Education:* Swarthmore College, B.A., 1937; University of Florida, M.A., 1949; University of Michigan, Ph.D., 1961. *Principal occupation:* Consultant historian, expert witness. *Home address:* 1319 Brooklyn Ave., Ann Arbor, Mich. 48104. *Affiliation:* Project director, 1976-1981, research associate, 1982-, The Newberry Library, Chicago, Ill. *Other professional post:* Expert witness in cases before the Indian Claims Commission, and Court of Claims, as well as state and circuit courts, 1962-1982. *Community activities:* Commission on Indian Affairs, State of Michigan, (member, 1965-1969). *Memberships:* American Historical Association; Conference on Latin American History; American Society for Ethnohistory (president, 1983-1984); Historical Society of Michigan. *Awards, honors:* Grantee, 1976, National Endowment for the Humanities (for Atlas of Great Lakes Indian History project). *Interests:* "Special interest in mapping and geographic background of Indian history-location of towns, hunting camps, fishing stations, and trails over land as well as canoe routes." *Biographical sources: Directory of American Scholars; Who's Who of American Women; Who's Who of the Midwest; Historians of Latin America in the U.S. Published works: Zespedes in East Florida, 1784-1790* (University of Miami Press, 1963); *Territory of the Caddo* (Garland, 1974); *Bibliography of the Ojibwa* (Indiana University Press, 1975); editor, *Atlas of Great Lakes Indian History* (University of Oklahoma Press, 1986).

TANTAQUIDGEON, GLADYS
(Mohegan1899-
(museum curator)

Born June 15, 1899, New London, Conn. *Education:* University of Pennsylvania. *Principal occupation:* Co-owner, curator, Tantaquidgeon Indian Museum, Uncasville, Conn. (40 years). *Home address: 1819 Norwich-New London Tpke., Uncasville, Conn. 06382. Other professional posts:* Surveyor of New England tribes for the Bureau of Indian Affairs; field specialist in Indian arts and crafts (area served-Northern Plains), U.S. Department of the Interior, Washington, D.C. *Memberships:* Archaeological Society of Connecticut; American Indian Archaeological Institute. *Awards, honors:* Honorary member, Alpha Kappa Gamma; Deconess Emeritus, Mohegan Congregational Church, Uncasville, Conn. *Published works: Mohegan Medicine Practices and Folk Beliefs,* 1928; *Notes on the Gay Head Indians of Massachusetts,* 1930; *Newly Discovered Basketry of the Wampanoag Indians of Masachusetts,* 1930; *Lake St. John Medicine Lore,* 1932; *Delaware Indian Designs,* 1933; *Uses of Plants Among the Indians of Southern New England,* 1940; *Delaware Indian Art Designs,* 1950); *Mohegan,* 1947); *Folk Medicine in the Delaware and Realted Algonkian Indians,* 1972).

TAPAHE, LOREN (Navajo) 1953-
(publishing)

Born September 17, 1953, Fort Defiance, Ariz. *Education:* Brigham Young University, A.A., 1974. *Principal occupation:* General manager, Navajo Time Publishing, Window Rock, Ariz., 1977- *Home address:* P.O. Box 481, Window Rock, Ariz. 86515. *Other professional post:* Assistant director, Office of Business Management, The Navajo Tribe, Window Rock, Ariz. *Interests:* Journalism; advertising; photography; river expeditions; personal journal composition; travel—Northwestern tribes of North America, Southwestern tribes, Europe.

TAULBEE, DANIEL J. (Comanche) 1924-
(artist)

Born April 7, 1924, Montana. *Education:* Famous Artists School, Westport, Conn. *Principal occupation:* Artist. *Home address:* 2712 Nettie, Butte, Mt. *Affiliations:* Illustrator, Anaconda Co.; proprietor, Heritage American Award Gallery. *Military service:* U.S. Army. *Awards, honors:* Gold Medal, Burr Gallery, New York, N.Y. *Interests:* One-man exhibits of oil paintings, watercolors, pen and ink drawings throughout the U.S.; depicts "authentic Indian and Western life as I saw and lived them." *Permanent collections:* Farnsworth Museum, Maine; Peabody Museum, Harvard University,

Cambridge, Mass.; Philbrook Art Center, Tulsa, Okla.; Russell Museum, Mt.; Statesville Museum, N.C.; Whitney Museum, Cody, Wyo.

TAX, SOL 1907-
(professor emeritus)

Born October 30, 1907, Chicago, Ill. *Education:* University of Wisconsin, Ph.B., 1931; University of Chicago, Ph.D., 1935. *Principal occupation:* Professor emeritus. *Home address:* 1700 E. 56th St., Chicago, Ill 60637. *Affiliation:* Professor, professor emeritus of anthropology, University of Chicago, 1948- (dean, University Extension, 1963-1968). *Other professional posts:* Director, Fox Indian Project, 1948-1962; research associate, Wenner-Gren Foundation for Anthropological Research, 1958-; editor, *Current Anthropology,* 1959-1974; consultant, U.S. Office of Education, 1955-; founding director, Center for the Study of Man, Smithsonian Institution, 1968-1976. *Community activities:* American Indian Development (board of directors, 1965-1972); Center for the History of the American Indian, Newberry Library, Chicago, Ill. (board of directors, 1975-); Native American Education Services (board of directors, 1976-). *Memberships:* American Anthropological Association (Fellow); president, 1958-1959); National Research Council; American Association for the Advancement of Science; Society for Applied Anthropology; American Folklore Society. *Awards, honors:* Distinguished Service Award, American Anthropological Association, 1977. *Interests:* Social anthropology of North and Middle American Indians; originator of concept of "action" anthropology. *Published works: Heritage of Conquest* (Free Press, 1952); editor, *Indian Tribes of Aboriginal America* (University of Chicago Press, 1952); editor, *Acculturation in the Americas,* (University of Chicago Press, 1952; *Penny Capitalism: A Guatemalan Indian Economy,* (Smithsonian Institution Press, 1953); editor, *Appraisal of Anthropology Today* University of Chicago Press, 1953); among others; general editor, *World Anthropology,* 92 volumes; associate editor, 1948-1953, editor, 1953-1956, *American Anthropologist.*

TAYLOR, GENE (St. Croix Chippewa)
(tribal chairman)

Affiliation: Chairman, St. Croix Council, Star Route, Webster, Wis. 54893.

TAYLOR, GERALD W.
(B.I.A. agency superintendent)

Affiliation: Superintendent, Seattle Support Center, Bureau of Indian Affairs, P.O. Box 80947, Seattle, Wash. 98108.

TAYLOR, PETER S. 1937-
(lawyer)

Born June 9, 1937, St. Paul, Minn. *Education:* Washburn University, Topeka, Kan., B.A., 1959; George Washington University, School of Law, LLB, 1963. *Principal occupation:* Lawyer. *Home address:* 1819 North Lincoln St., Arlington, Va. 22207. *Affiliations:* Co-director, Indian Civil Rights Task Force, Office of the Solicitor, Department of the Interior, 1971-1975 (projects were the compilation of the Opinions of the Solicitor on Indian affairs; updating Kappler's, *Indian Affairs, Laws and Treaties;* development of a Model Procedural Code for use in courts of Indian offenses; and revision of Felix Cohen's, *Handbook of Federal Indian Law);* chairman, Task Force on Revision and Codification of Federal Indian Law, with the American Indian Policy Review Commission, 1975-1977 (upon completion of the Task Force report, served on the editorial board of the Commission in preparation of the AIPRC report; special counsel, 1977-1980, general counsel, 1981-1985, staff director, 1985-, Senate Select Committee on Indian Affairs. *Memberships:* District of Columbia Bar Association; Virginia State Bar Association. *Published works: Opinions of the Solicitor, Department of the Interior, Indian Affairs* (U.S. Government, 1976); editor, *Kappler's, Indian Affairs, Laws and Treaties* (revision, U.S. Government, 1976); *Development of Tripartite Jurisdiction in Indian Country* (Kansas Law Review, 1974).

TAYLOR, RHONDA HARRIS
(president-Indian association)

Affiliation: President, American Indian Library Association, American Library Association, Office of Outreach Services, 50 East Huron St., Chicago, Ill. 60611.

TAYLOR, VIRGINIA (Cherokee) 1922-
(graphic and commercial artist)

Born September 15, 1922, Los Angeles, Calif. *Education:* Art Center School, Los Angeles, Calif. *Principal occupation:* Graphic and commercial artist. *Home address:* 4754 Hwy. 20 NW, Albany, Ore. 97321. *Affiliation:* Staff artist, Office of Publications, Oregon State University, art coordinator and designer, Oregon State University Press, 1963-1967; assistant professor of art, Oregon State University, 1966, 1976; graphic designer and assistant to museum coordinator, Marine Science Laboratory, Department of Oceanography, Oregon State University, Corvallis, Ore., 1969-. *Other professional posts:* Taught Indian history and crafts, Linn Benton Community College; taught basic design, Oregon State University, 1975. *Interests:* Jury Indian art exhibitions; "(I) frequently speak to civic, school and other organizations on Indian art. Numerous awards, joint and one-man exhibitions; work in private and public collections."

TAYLOR-GOINS, ELISE
(director-Indian organization)

Affiliation: Director, Bird Clan Associates, 102 Longfellow St., N.W., Washington, D.C. 20011.

TEBBEL, JOHN (Ojibwa) 1912-
(teacher, writer)

Born November 16, 1912, Boyne City, Mich. *Education:* Central Michigan University, B.A., 1935, Litt.D., 1948; Columbia University, School of Journalism, M.S., 1937. *Principal occupation:* Teacher, writer. *Affiliations:* Writer, *Newsweek* Magazine, 1937; reporter, *Detroit Free Press,* 1937-1939; feature writer, roto news editor, *Providence Journal,* 1939-1941; managing editor,

American Mercury, 1041-1943; Sunday staff writer, *New York Times,* 1943; associate editor, E.P. Dutton, 1943-1947; assistant in journalism, School of Journalism, Columbia University, 1943-1945; chairman, Department of Journalism, N.Y.U., 1954-1965, professor of journalism, N.Y.U., 1965- *Other professional post:* Consultant, Ford Foundation, 1966-. *Biographical source: Who's Who in America.* Published works: *George Washington's America* (1954); *The Magic of Balanced Living* (1956); *The American Indian Wars* (Harper & Row, 1960); *The Inheritors* (Putnam, 1962); *Compact History of the Indian Wars* (1966); among other books; contibutor to *Saturday Review* and other magazines.

TEEPLE, WADE (Chippewa)
(tribal president)

Affiliation: President, Bay Mills Executive Council, Route 1, Box 313, Brimley, Mich. 49715.

TENORIO, FRANK (San Felipe Pueblo)
(Pueblo governor)

Affiliation: Governor, San Felipe Pueblo, P.O. Box A, San Felipe Pueblo, N.M. 87001.

THEISZ, R.D. 1941-
(professor)

Born May 4, 1941. *Education:* Middlebury College, Vt., M.A., 1965; New York University, Ph.D., 1972. *Principal occupation:* Professor. *Home address:* 14 W. Pine, Spearfish, S.D. 57783. *Affiliations:* Professor, Sinte Gleska College, Rose Bud, S.D., 1972-1977; professor, Center on Indian Studies, Black Hills State College, Spearfish, S.D., 1977-. *Memberships:* Modern Language Association; South Dakota Indian Education Association; National Council of Teachers of English; Porcupine Singers (traditional Lakota singing group). *Awards, honors:* 1972 Excellence in Scholarship Award, N.Y.U.; 1981 Special Contribution to Education, South Dakota Indian Education Association. *Interests:* "Native American cultural history, especially literature, music, dance, and art; cross cultural education." Published works: Buckskin Tokens (Sinte Gleska College, 1974); *Songs and Dances of the Lakota* (Sinte Gleska College, 1976); *Perspectives on Teaching Indian Literature* (Black Hills State College, 1977); *Lakota Art Is An American Art* (Black Hills State College, 1981); Readings in Traditional and Contemporary Sioux Art (Black Hills State College, 1985).

THOMAS, ARTHUR
(director-tribal affairs-
Indian Health Service)

Affiliation: Director, Office of Tribal Affairs, Indian Health Service, 5600 Fishers Lane, Rockville, Md. 20857.

THOMAS, DAVID HURST 1945-
(archaeologist, museum curator)

Born May 27, 1945, Oakland, Calif. *Education:* University of California, Davis, B.A., 1967, M.A., 1968, Ph.D., 1971. *Principal occupation:* Museum curator. *Home address:* 210 Myrtle Ave., New Milford, N.J. 07646. *Affiliations:* Assistant curator, 1972-1977, associate curator, 1977-, chairman, Department of Anthropology, 1976-, American Museum of Natural History, New York, N.Y. *Memberships:* Society for American Archaeology; American Anthropological Association; American Association for the Advancement of Science; Sigma Xi. *Interests:* Mr. Thomas writes, "I am primarily involved in archaeological investigations in North America. These include ten years of directing excavations in the Great Basin, primarily in central Nevada. I also have directed a project on the prehistory of St. Catherine's Island, Georgia. I am interested in general archaeological theory, and have written two textbooks on this topic." *Biographical source: Who's Who in America;* 30 minute educational film on Mr. Thomas' Nevada excavations: *Gatecliff, An American Indian Rock Shelter.* Published works: "A Test of Shoshonean Settlement Patterns" (*American Antiquity,* 1973); *Predicting the Past* (Holt, Rinehart & Winston, 1974); *Figuring Anthropology* (Holt, Rinehart, 1976); "Shoshonean Bands" (*American*

Anthropologist, 1976); "Western Shoshoni" (*Handbook of the American Indians,* Smithsonian Institution Press); *Archaeology,* (1979).

THOMAS, FREDERICK R. (Kickapoo) 1946-
(tribal chairman)

Born February 21, 1946, Horton, Kan. *Education:* Haskell Indian Junior College, A.A., 1966. *Principal occupation:* Tribal chairman, manager, Kickapoo Tribal Council, Horton, Kan. *Home address:* Route 1, Horton, Kan. 66439. *Other professional posts:* Chairman, Kansas Service Unit, Health Advisory Board. *Military service:* U.S. Army, 1966-1968. *Community activities:* Powhattan Precinct (past board member); Kickapoo Housing Authority (past president); community fundraising projects; community food and clothing bank (founding member); Horton Chamber of Commerce; Horton City Commissioner for Economic Development. *Memberships:* National Tribal Chairman's Association; American Legion; Kickapoo Chapter, Lions International; National Indian Gaming Association (treasurer). *Awards, honors:* Goodyear—Tire Builder of the Year. *Interests:* Member of Delaware Singers; enjoys hunting and fishing, farming, traveling.

THOMPSON, DUANE F.
(B.I.A. agency superintendent)

Affiliation: Superintendent, Fort Hall Agency, Bureau of Indian Affairs, Fort Hall, Idaho 83203.

THOMPSON, EDMOND
(B.I.A. agency superintendent)

Affiliation: Superintendent, Pima Agency, Bureau of Indian Affairs, Sacaton, Ariz. 85247.

THOMPSON, RUPERT
(B.I.A. agency superintendent)

Affiliation: Superintendent, Anadarko Agency, Bureau of Indian Affairs, P.O. Box 309, Anadarko, Okla. 73005.

THUNDER, FAYE ESTHER
(Winnebago) (social worker)

Education: University of Wisconsin, Eau Claire (Sociology), 1976-1980; University of Wisconsin, La Crosse, 1986-. *Principal occupation:* Social worker. *Home address:* Route 1, Fairchild, Wis. 54741. *Affiliations:* Indian child welfare consultant and casefinder, case management for women, Department of Health and Social Services, Wisconsin Winnebago Business Committee, Tomah, Wis. (three years); secretary, Department of Natural Resources. *Military service:* Wisconsin Army National Guard, 1985-1993 (food service specialist). *Community activities:* American Indian Student Council (treasurer, 1976-1980); American Indian Studies Committee, 1976-1980, 1982); Black River Falls Health Commission (chairperson, 1981); Native American Church (secretary, 1979-1980); West Central Native American Community (health committee, 1975). *Memberships:* Mental Health Association, Jackson County (board of directors, 1982-1986); Wisconsin Women's Network, 1983; National Congress of American Indians. *Awards, honors:* State Advisory Council for Legal Services, 1984-1986 (appointed by the Governor); Certificate of Appreciation, Board of Directors, Advisory Council, Eau Claire County Human Services, 1984. *Interests:* "Complete my degree in Sociology; hopefully attend law school or graduate school. I do plan on running for public office (tribal/local).

THUNDER HAWK, MADONNA
(Cheyenne River Sioux) 1940-
(community organizer)

Born June 18, 1940, South Dakota. *Education:* University of San Francisco, 1967-1969; Black Hills State College, Spearfish, S.D., 1980-1982. *Principal occupation:* Community organizer. *Home address:* Eagle Butte, S.D. 57625. *Affiliations:* Dakota Women of All Red Nations; Dakota American Indian Movement. *Community activities:* Musicians for Safe Energy (board member); Nationwide Womens Program— American Friends Service Committee (board member); Black Hills Alliance (board member). *Memberships:* South

Dakota Women's Advocacy Network; Native American Task Force (Rural Coalition). *Interests:* "International advocate for Native American treaty rights; travels: Europe, Japan, Mexico, Honduras, Nicaragua, Costa Rica; attended U.N. Sub-Committee on Racism, Apartheid and Decolonialization, Geneva, Switzerland.

THURMAN, ROBERT
(health care administrator)

Affiliation: Chief, Health Care Administration Branch, Indian Health Service, 5600 Fishers Lane, Rockville, Md. 20857.

TIGER, BUFFALO (Miccosukee-Creek)
(tribal chairman)

Affiliation: Chairman, Miccosukee Business Committee, Box 44021, Tamiami Station, Miami, Fla. 33144.

TIGER, GEORGIANA
(Indian education)

Affiliation: Staff Associate, Indian Education Information Service, Com Tec, Inc., 1228 M St., N.W., Washington, D.C. 20005.

TIPPECONNIC, THOMAS
(B.I.A. area director)

Affiliation: Director, Navajo Area Office, Bureau of Indian Affairs, P.O. Box M, Window Rock, Ariz. 86515.

TITLA, PHILLIP, Sr. (San Carlos
Apache) 1943-
(artist)

Born September 17, 1943, Miami, Ariz. *Education:* Eastern Arizona College, Thatcher, Ariz., A.A., 1979. *Principal occupation:* Artist. *Home address:* P.O. Box 497, San Carlos, Ariz. 85550. *Affiliations:* Director of development, San Carlos Apache Tribe, San Carlos, Ariz., 1967-1981; director, Phillip Titla Apache Galleria, San Carlos, Ariz., 1981-. *Other professional post:* Board member, San Carlos Arts and Crafts Association, 1981-. *Community activities:*

Bylas Recreation Program (chairman); San Carlos Powwow Association, 1980-; San Carlos Pageant Committee, 1978-; Cobke Valley Fine Arts Guild, Inc., 1985-1986. *Awards, honors:* Sculpture Award, Best of Show, Pasadena, Calif. Art Show. *Interests:* "My interest is to continue to grow in the art field; prsently doing some gallery shows and lecture at various clubs on Apache culture; also sing Apache songs; shows at colleges, high schools and elementary schools of my work—for education." *Biographical source: Art West,* Sept./Oct., 1984.

TODD, JOHN G., M.D.
(Chief of staff-Indian Health Service)

Affiliation: Chief of Staff, Indian Health Service, 5600 Fishers Lane, Rockville, Md. 20857.

TOLONEN, MYRTLE (Chippewa)
(tribal president)

Affiliation: President, Keweenaw Bay Tribal Council, Tribal Center Bldg., Route 1, Baroga, Mich. 49908.

TOMHAVE, JEROME
(B.I.A. agency superintedent)

Affiliation: Superintendent, Southern California Agency, Bureau of Indian Affairs, 5750 Division St., Suite 201, Riverside, Calif. 92506.

TOPASH, BERNARD
(B.I.A. agency superintendent)

Affiliation: Superintendent, Siletz Agency, Bureau of Indian Affairs, P.O. Box 539, Siletz, Ore. 97380.

TOWNSEND, JOAN B. 1933-
(anthropologist, professor)

Born July 9, 1933, Dallas, Tex. *Education:* University of California, Los Angeles, B.A., 1959, Ph.D., 1965 (Dissertation: *Ethnohistory and Culture Change of the Iliamna Tanaina*). *Principal occupation:* Anthropologist, professor. *Home address:* 85 Tunis Bay, Winnipeg, Manitoba, Can. R3T 2X2.

Affiliation: Lecturer, assistant professor, associate professor, professor of anthropology, University of Manitoba, Winnipeg, Manitoba, Can., 1964-. *Other professional posts:* Consultation and assistance in gathering data on Tanaina society and archaeological sites; for Cook Inlet Region, Inc. (Alaskan Native organization). *Field research:* Archival and ethnohistoric research of the 18th-20th centuries of southern Alaska with special emphasis on social, political, and economic conditions of Indians, Eskimos and Aleuts. *Memberships:* American Anthropological Association (Fellow); Arctic Institute of North America (Fellow); Society for Applied Anthropology (Fellow); Current Anthropology; Canadian Ethnology Society (editorial board, *Culture,* 1980). *Interests:* Ethnohistory and sociocultural change: North American Indians—Athapaskan Indians; primary focus on Tanaina; Alaskan Pacific Rim ranked societies (Aleuts, Koniag and Chugach Eskimo; Tanaina, Ahtna, Eyak, and Tlingit Indians; traditional trading systems and alliances; mercantile and the fur trade in Alaska; political evolution; new religions and revitalization movements. *Published works:* Monographs: *Kijik: An Historic Tanaina Settlement* (Field Museum of Natural History, 1970); *Russian Mercantilism and Alaskan Native Social Change* (in preparation); *Tanaina Ethnohistory, Social and Economic Change* (in preparation); *The Archaeology of Pedro Bay, Alaska* (in preparation); numerous papers and book reviews.

TOYA, RONALD GEORGE
(Jemez Pueblo) 1948-
(B.I.A. assistant area director)

Born March 8, 1948, Albuquerque, N.M. *Education:* Westmont College, Santa Barbara, Calif., B.A. (Economics and Business Administration), 1970, B.A. (Psychology), 1971; A.A. (Political Science), 1971. *Principal occupation:* B.I.A. assistant area director. *Home address:* 5017 La Fiesta, Albuquerque, N.M. 87109. *Affiliations:* Chief, Branch of Reservation Programs, Southern Pueblos Agency, B.I.A., Albuquerque, N.M.; chief, Branch of Self-Determination Services, assistant area director, B.I.A., Albuquerque Area Office;

superintendent, Mescalero Agency, B.I.A., Mescalero, N.M.; superintendent, Southern Ute Agency, B.I.A., Ignacio, Colo.; special assistant to the Assistant Secretary of the Interior for Indian Affairs, Washington, D.C.; special assistant to the Commissioner of Indian Affairs; chief, Branch of Tribal Government Services, U.S. Department of Interior, B.I.A., Albuquerque Area Office. *Other professional post:* Executive director and chairman of the board, Tribal Government Institute. *Community activites:* Conduct radio show on Indian affairs entitled "Native American Perspective"; involved in youth activities, including baseball and special olympics. *Memberships:* New Mexico Industrial Development (board of directors, 1975-1981; CEDAM - international scuba and archaeological association; Society for American Baseball Research. *Awards, honors: Special and Superior Achievement Awards, B.I.A., 1972, 1979, 1981, 1982; various letters and citations. Interests:* Interested in the management of tribal governments; economic development and preservation of Indian culture; travel; baseball; scuba diving; car racing; hang gliding; dancing. *Published work: Pueblo Management Development* (Southwest Indian Polytechnic Institute, 1976).

TRAHANT, MARK N. (Shoshone-Bannock) 1957-
(editor-in-chief)

Born August 13, 1957, Fort Hall, Idaho. *Education:* Pasadena City College; Idaho State University. *Principal occupation:* Editor-in-chief, *The Sho-Ban News,* Fort Hall, Idaho, 1976-. *Home address:* P.O. Box 488, Fort Hall, Idaho 83203. *Membership:* Northwest Indian Press Association. *Interests:* "Also make films on available topics (16mm).

TREADWELL, ERWIN *(Red Fox)*
(Unkechaug) 1918-
(tribal chief)

Born January 17, 1918, Roslyn Heights, N.Y. *Principal occupation:* Tribal chief, Unkechaug Indian Tribe. *Community activities:* AFL-CIO (committeeman); Boy

Scouts of America. *Awards, Honors:* Award for aircraft work, Grumman Aircraft Co. *Interests:* Lecturing on Long Island Indian tribes; Indian dance group. Mr. Treadwell is working on a history of the Long Island tribes.

TRIBBETT, NORMAN HENRY
(Wisconsin Potawatomi) 1948-
(tribal librarian)

Born November 5, 1948, Hayward, Wis. *Education:* University of Wisconsin, Oshkosh, B.S., 1981; University of Wisconsin, Madison, M.A., 1983. *Principal occupation:* Librarian, Seminole Tribe, Hollywood, Fla. *Address:* 6073 Stirling Rd., Hollywood, Fla. 33204.

TRUJILLO, JOSE EMELIO
(San Juan Pueblo)
(Pueblo governor)

Affiliation: Governor, San Juan Pueblo, P.O. Box 1099, San Juan Pueblo, N.M. 87566.

TRUSSELL, LARRY (Tigua Pueblo)
(tribal chairman)

Affiliation: Chairman, Tigua Indian Tribal Enterprise, P.O. Box 17579, Ysleta Station, El Paso, Tex. 79917.

TSABETSAYE, ROGER JOHN (Zuni)
1941-
(artist, craftsman)

Born October 29, 1941, Zuni, N.M. *Education:* Institute of American Indian Arts; School for American Craftsmen, Rochester Institute of Technology. *Principal occupation:* Artist, craftsman. *Home address:* Box 254, Zuni, N.M. 87327. *Affiliation:* Owner-founder, Tsabetsaye Enterprises, Box 254, Zuni, N.M. (Zuni jewelry—wholesale/retail). *Membership:* Zuni Craftsmen's Coop Association. *Awards, honors:* Numerous awards from various exhibitions and shows, 1968-.

TSINAJINNIE, ANDY (Navajo) 1919-
(artist)

Born November 16, 1919, Chinle, Ariz. *Education:* College of Arts and Crafts, Oakland, Calif. *Principal occupation:* Artist. *Home address:* Box 542, Scottsdale, Ariz. *Military service:* U.S. Army Air Force, 1940-1945. *Awards, honors:* Numerous awards from various exhibitions and shows. *Published works:* As illustrator, *Spirit Rocks and Silver Magic,* and *Peetie the Pack Rat and Other Desert Stories* (Caxton Printers, Ltd.); Who Wants to Be a Prairie Dog? (Haskell Institute); and others.

TSOSIE, LORETTA A.W. (Navajo) 1943-
(teacher)

Born March 13, 1943, Morenci, Ariz. *Education:* University of New Mexico, B.S., 1971, M.A., 1976. *Principal occupation:* Home economics instructor, Navajo Community College, Tsaile, Ariz., 1972-. *Home address:* P.O. Box 112, Window Rock, Ariz. 86515. *Other professional post:* Chairperson, Career Education Division, Navajo Community College.

TWO HAWK, WEBSTER (Rosebud Sioux)
(tribal president)

Affiliation: President, Rosebud Sioux Tribal Council, Rosebud, S.D. 57570.

TYNDELL, WAYNE
(executive director-Indian center)

Affiliation: Executive director, American Indian Center of Omaha, Inc., 613 South 16th St., Omaha, Neb. 68102.

TYNER, JAMES W. (Cherokee) 1911-
(historian)

Born September 13, 1911, Tahlequah, Okla. *Education:* Haskell Institute. *Principal occupation:* Historian. *Home address:* 112 Cowley Ave., Chouteau, Okla. 74337. *Affiliation:* Historian for Indian history project, American Indian Institute, University of

Oklahoma, Norman, Okla. *Military service:* U.S. Navy, 1942-1945 (Chief Petty Officer, World War II). *Awards, honors:* National Certificate of Commendation for published work, *Our People and Where They Rest* (Hooper Publishing, 1969-1972), American Association for State and Local History. *Interests:* Indian history, including research and recording old cemetaries; woodcarving; cartridge collecting.

U

UNGER, STEVEN
(executive director-Indian association)

Affiliation: Executive director, Association of American Indian Affairs, 95 Madison Ave., New York, N.Y. 10016

V

VANATTA, SHIRLEY PRINTUP (Seneca) 1922-
(writer, artist)

Born October 29, 1922, Red House, N.Y. *Education:* Bacone College. *Principal occupation:* Writer, artist. *Home address:* 116 Jimersontown, Salamanca, N.Y. 14779. *Affiliation:* Editor, *O He Yoh Noh, newsletter of the Seneca Nation. Community activities:* Iroquois Indian Conference of New York (artist; publicist); Everson Museum (board of directors). *Memberships:* Society for Pennsylvania Archaeology. *Awards, honors:* New York State Indian of the Year, Iroquois Temperance League, given by Governor Nelson Rockefeller, 1972; numerous others. *Interests:* Ms. Vanatta writes, "(I was) instrumental in bringing about archaeological research on the Allegany Reservation through the Carnegie Museum—work on 'Vanatta Archaeological Site,' 900-1,000 A.D. Iroquois village, where ceremonial masks (were) uncovered. I instituted the annual Inter-Community Christmas Party, where all children of Indian descent receive gifts; also the elderly, the infirm and the imprisoned. I am an oil and wastercolor artist."

VASKA, ANTHONY (Yup'ik Eskimo) 1948-
(B.I.A. agency superintendent)

Born August 25, 1948, Kalskag, Alaska. *Education:* University of Alaska, Fairbanks, B.A.; Stanford University, M.A. *Principal occupation:* Superintendent, Bethel Agency, Bureau of Indian Affairs, Bethel, Alaska. *Home address:* P.O. Box 1495, Salmon Berry St., Bethel, Alaska 99559. *Other professional post:* Alaska State Legislature, 1980-1984. *Awards, honors:* Ford Foundation Fellow. *Interests:* Arctic anthropology; U.S. American Indian policy.

VASQUEZ, JOSEPH C. *(Lone Eagle)*
(Sioux-Apache) 1917-
(Indian programs administrator)

Born February 21, 1917, Primero, Colo. *Education:* U.S. Armed Forces Institute; Los Angeles City College Extension; U.C.L.A. Extension. *Principal occupation:* Indian programs administrator. *Home address:* 5208 11th St., South, Arlington, Va. 22204. *Affiliations:* Small business coordinator/minority representative, Hughes Aircraft Co., El Segundo, Calif., 1947-1968; appointed Los Angeles City Commissioner, Los Angeles, Calif., 1968-1970; National Council on Indian Opportunity, Washington, D.C., 1970-1972; director, Indian Office, U.S. Department of Commerce, Office of Minority Business Enterprise, Washington, D.C., 1972-. *Other professional posts:* President and council chairman, Los Angeles Indian Center, 1958-1970; founded and promoted the National Business Development Organization (Indian), Los Angeles, 1968-1970. *Military service:* U.S. Army Air Corps, 1943-1945 (Pilot-Flight Engineer). *Community activities:* UCLA Cultural Center (chairman); Los Angeles Mayor's Advisory Committee (board member); California Attorney General's Advisory Committee (board member). *Memberships:* National Indian Education Association (board member); United Indian Development Association (founder). *Awards, honors:* Family of the Year, Hughes Aircraft Co., 1956; Resolution by Governor Pat Brown, California, 1956; plaque for being first Indian to drive car in parade for a President of the U.S., 1964;

Resolution, Indians of Los Angeles, 1967; Resolution, Indian Leader of the Year, National Congress of American Indians, 1968; appointment by President Nixon, 1970. *Biographical sources: Who's Who in Government,* 1972, 1973; *Contemporary Indian Leaders of America,* 1973; *Community Leaders and Noteworthy Americans,* 1975-1976; *Who's Who Honorary Society,* 1976.

VIARRIAL, JACOB (Pojoaque Pueblo)
(Pueblo governor)

Affiliation: Governor, Pojoaque Pueblo Tribal Council, Route 11, Box 71, Santa Fe, N.M. 87501.

VIOLA, HERMAN J. 1938-
(historian)

Born February 24, 1938, Chicago, Ill. *Education:* Marquette University, B.A., 1962, M.A., 1964; Indiana University, Ph.D., 1970. *Principal occupation:* Historian. *Home address:* 7307 Pinewood St., Falls Church, Va. 22046. *Affiliation:* Director, National Anthropological Archives, Smithsonian Institution, Washington, D.C., 1972-. *Other professional post:* Founder and first editor of *Prologue,* The Journal of the National Archives, 1968-1972. *Military service:* U.S. Navy, 1960-1962. *Memberships:* Society of American Archivists; Western History Association; Organization of American Historians. *Biographical source: Who's Who in America. Published works: Thomas L. McKinney, Architect of America's Early Indian Policy, 1816-1830* (Swallow Press, 1974); *The Indian Legacy of Charles Bird King* (Smithsonian Institution Press, 1976); *Diplomats in Buckskin* (Smithsonian Institution Press, 1981); *The National Archives* (Harry N. Abrams, 1984).

VOZNIAK, DEBBIE
(administrative officer-
Indian education)

Affiliation: Administrative Officer, National Advisory Council on Indian Education, 2000 L St., N.W., Suite 574, Washington, D.C. 20002.

VIZENOR, GERALD ROBERT
(Chippewa) 1934-
(teacher, poet)

Born October 22, 1934, Mineapolis, Minn. *Education:* New York University; University of Minnesota, B.A., 1960. *Principal occupation:* Teacher, poet. *Affiliations:* Executive director, American Indian Employment Center, Minneapolis, Minn.; staff writer, Minneapolis *Tribune,* 1968-1969; lecturer, Department of Anthropology, Lake Forest College, Lake Forest, Ill., 1970-? *Military service:* U.S. Army, 1952-1955. *Published works: Raising the Moon Vines* (The Nodin Press, 1964); *Seventeen Chirps* (The Nodin Press, 1964); *Summer in the Spring: Ojibway Lyric Poems* (The Nodin Press, 1965); *Empty Swings* (The Nodin Press, 1967); *Escorts to White Earth* (The Four Winds, 1968); *Anishnabe Adisokan,* tales (The Nodin Press, 1970); *Anishnabe Nagamon,* song poems (The Nodin Press, 1970); *New Voices fromthe People Named the Chippewa* (Crowell-Collier, 1971).

VOGET, FRED W. 1913-
(professor emeritus)

Born February 12, 1913, Salem, Ore. *Education:* University of Oregon, B.A., 1936; Yale University, Ph.D., 1948. *Principal occupation:* Professor emeritus. *Home address:* 4020 SW 75th, Portland, Ore. 97225. *Affiliation:* Professor of anthropology, 1965-1981 (chairman, 1969-1971), professor emeritus, 1981-, Southern Illinois University at Edwardsville. *Military service:* U.S. Army, 1942-1946 (Sergeant Major; European Theatre). *Memberships:* American Anthropological Association (Fellow); Society for Applied Anthropology (Fellow; executive committee, 1974-1976; Malinowski Award Committee, 1976-1977); American Ethnological Society; Central States Anthropological Society; American Association of University Professors; Sigma Xi; Lambda Alpha; Alpha Kappa Delta; Current Anthropology (Associate). *Awards, honors:* Canada Council Grant, 1964-1965; Senior Fulbright-Hay Award, Germany, 1971. *Interests:* Ethnological theory; culture change and acculturation; ethnoogy of North America and Africa; ethnology of the Plains, North America; religious movements and culture change; institutional and value analysis of culture as systems; social organization. *Published works: Osage Indians I. Osage Research Report* (Garland, 1974); *A History of Ethnology* (Holt, Rinehart & Winston, 1975); *The Shoshoni-Crow Sun Dance* (University of Oklahoma Press, 1984); *Storia dell'etnologia contemporanea* (Laterza & Figli, 1984).

VOIGHT, VIRGINIA FRANCES 1909-
(writer)

Born March 30, 1909, New Britain, Conn. *Education:* Yale School of Fine Arts; Austin School of Commercial Art. *Principal occupation:* Writer. *Home addres:* 1732 Dixwell Ave., Apt. 1 H, Hamden, Conn. 06514. *Awards, honors: New York Times,* 100 best books of the year, *Uncas, Sachem of the Wolf People. Interests:* Historical research, book and field research on wildlife and natural history in general. *Biographical sources: More Junior Authors* (H.W. Wilson Co.); *Contemporary Authors; The Directory of British and American Authors (St. James Press). Published works: Uncas, Sachem of the Wolf People* (Funk & Wagnalls, 1963); *Mohegan Chief: The Story of Harold Tantaquidgeon* (Funk & Wagnalls, 1965); *Sacajawea, Guide to Lewis and Clark* (Putnam, 1966); *The Adventures of Hiawatha* (Garrard, 1969); *Massasoit, Friend of the Pilgrims* (Garrard, 1971); *Close to the Rising Sun, Algonquian Indian Legends* (Garrard, 1972); *Red Blade and the Black Bear* (fiction (Dodd, Mead, 1973); *Red Cloud, Sioux War Chief* (Garrard, 1975); *Indian Patriots East of the Mississippi* (Anthology) (Garrard, 1976); *Pontiac, Mighty Ottawa Chief* (Garrard, 1977); *Bobcat* (Dodd, Mead, 1978).

W

WADE, JON C.
(college president)

Affiliation: President, Institute of American Indian Arts, College of Santa Fe Campus, Alexis Hall, St. Michaels Dr., Santa Fe, N.M. 87501.

WADENA, DARRELL (Minnesota Chippewa)
(tribal chairman)

Affiliations: Chairman, White Earth Reservation Business Committee, P.O. Box 418, White Earth, Minn. 56591; presdident, Minnesota Chippewa Tribal Executive Committee, P.O. Box 217, Cass Lake, Minn. 56633.

WAHPEHAH, JAMES (Kickapoo)
(tribal chairman)

Affiliation: Chairman, Kickapoo Business Committee, P.O. Box 58, McCloud, Okla. 74851.

WAKEMAN, RICHARD K. (Flandreau Santee Sioux) 1923-
(tribal officer)

Born February 9, 1923, Flandreau, S.D. *Education:* Haskell Institute. *Principal occupation:* Tribal officer. *Home address:* R.R. 1, Flandreau, S.D. 57028. *Affiliation:* Former president, Flandreau Santee Sioux Business Council. *Military service:* U.S. Marine Corps, 1942-1945; U.S. Army, 1951-1953 (Presidential Unit Citation; Commendation; Asiatic Pacific Award). *Community activities:* South Dakota Indian Commission; South Dakota Letter Carriers (president); Dakota Prebytery (moderator); Masonic Lodge. *Interests:* Tribal history.

WALDRAM, JAMES B. 1955-
(professor)

Born August 20, 1955, Oshawa, Ontario, Can. *Education:* University of Waterloo, Ontario, B.A. (Honors), 1978; University of Manitoba, Winnipeg, M.A., 1980; University of Connecticut, Ph.D. (Anthropology), 1983. *Principal occupation:* Professor. *Home address:* 247 Sylvian Way, Saskatoon, Saskatchewan, Can. *Affiliation:* Assistant professor, Department of Native American Studies, University of Saskatchewan, Saskatoon, Saskatchewan, Can., 1983- *Other professional post:* Associate editor, *Native Studies Review.* *Memberships:* Canadian Ethnology Society; Canadian Indian-Native Studies Association; Canadian Association for Medical Anthropology;

American Anthropological Association; Society for Applied Anthropology. *Awards, honors:* Social Sciences and Humanities Research Council of Canada Doctoral Fellowship. *Interests:* "The impact of hydroelectric development of northern Canadian Native communities. Dietary change in the Canadian north; education needs assessment of urban Native people; health and health care delivery of urban Native people." *Published work: 1885 and After: Native Society in Transition* (Canadian Plains Research Center, Regina, Can., 1986).

WALKER, JERRY CLAYTON 1937-
(school principal, educator)

Born February 2, 1937, Fort Sumner, N.M. *Education:* Eastern New Mexico University, Portales, B.S., 1964, EDSp., 1981; Northern Arizona University, Flagstaff, M.A. (Education), 1971. *Principal occupation:* School principal, educator. *Home address:* P.O. Box 906, Teecnospos, Ariz. 86514. *Affiliations:* Teacher-Special Education,Tuba City Boarding School, Tuba City, Ariz. (nine years); education specialist, Western Navajo Agency, B.I.A., Tuba City, Ariz. (eight years); principal, Teecnospos Boarding School, Teecnospos, Ariz., 1982-. *Memberships:* National Council of Bureau of Indian Affairs Educators (charter member); Council for Exceptional Children, 1967-1982.

WALKER, JOE B.
(B.I.A. agency superintendent)

Affiliation: Superintendent, Shawnee Agency, Bureau of Indian Affairs, Federal Bldg., Shawnee, Okla. 74801.

WALKER, WILLARD 1926-
(professor of anthropology)

Born July 29, 1926, Boston, Mass. *Education:* Harvard College, B.A., 1950; University of Arizona, M.A., 1953; Cornell University, Ph.D., 1964. *Principal occupation:* Professor of anthropology, Wesleyan University, Middletown, Conn., 1967-. *Home address:* Culver Lane, Portland, Conn. 06480. *Memberships:* American Anthropological Association (Fellow);

Society for Applied Anthropology (Fellow); Linguistics Society of America; American Ethnological Society; American Society for Ethnohistory; Southern Anthropological Association; Northeast Anthropological Association ; Museum of the Cherokee Indian Association. *Interests:* "Indian American languages, cultures, ethnohistory. Particular interest in Creeks and Cherokees in the Southeast, the Zuni, Hopi and Yaqui pueblos in the Southwest, and the Algonquian peoples of the Maine-Maritime area. *Published works: Cherokee Primer* (Carnegie Corp. Cross-Cultural Project of the University of Chicago, 1965); co-author, *Cherokee Stories* (Laboratory of Anthropology, Wesleyan University, 1966); co-editor, *Hopis, Tewas, and the American Road* (Wesleyan University, 1983).

WALKING BULL, CHARLES GILBERT, Jr. (Oglala Sioux) 1930-
(artist, singer, writer)

Born June 18, 1930, Hot Springs, S.D. *Education:* Oregon College of Education (two years). *Principal occupation:* Self-employed artist, singer, writer. *Home address:* 11750 Mistletoe Rd., Monmouth, Ore. 97361. *Community activities:* Oregon College of Education, Native American Student Association (president, 1976-1977); singer at Cross-Cultural Dialogue, Sun Valley. *Memberships:* Inter-Tribal Council, Portland, Ore.; National Indian Education Association (Project Media evaluation team); Independent Indian Arts and Crafts Persons Association (helped to organize). *Awards, honors:* Award for Distinction for Art, La Grande Indian Arts Festival, 1974; First Prize Award for Traditional Sioux Fancy Dance, Siletz, Ore., 1973; First Prize Award for Traditional Sioux painting, 1976, 1977, La Grande Indian Arts Festival. *Interests:* "Do traditional Sioux geometrical designs on canvas in oil and acrylics; do Sioux crafts in beadwork and leather. (I am a) soloist, singing in the Lakota language with guitar and drum in public performance. Fancy dancer and participator in Indian gatherings since youth, winning many awards. At present, I am concentrating on traditional Sioux art, translating the legends of my people. I am traditional and bilingual. In my books, I am recording tales from the reservation, writing original poetry, transalting songs and scoring songs." *Published works: O-hu-kah-kan (Poetry, Songs, Legends, Stories),* 1975; *Wo ya-ka-pi (Telling Stories of the Past and Present),* 1976; *Mi ta-ku-ye (About Our People),* 1977; all books co-authored with Montana Walking Bull, printed by the *Itemizer Observer,* Dallas, Ore., and may be purchased from the Walking Bulls at their home address.

WALKING BULL, MONTANA HOPKINS RICKARDS (Oklahoma Cherokee) 1913-
(professor)

Born January 22, 1913, Butte, Mt. *Education:* University of Oklahoma, B.F.A., 1935, M.A. (Education), 1942; University of Oregon, Ed.D., 1967. *Principal occupation:* Professor of humanities/education, Oregon College of Education, Monmouth, Ore., 1963-. *Home address:* 11750 Mistletoe Rd., Monmouth, Ore. 97361. *Community activities:* Independent Indian Arts and Crafts Persons Association of the Northwest (coordinator); Sun Valley Cross-Cultural Dialogue (participant); book reviewer, *Daily Oklahoman;* speaker for "A Look at Native American Treaty Rights," Glenedon Beach, Ore. *Memberships:* National Indian Education Association (Project Media); National Council of Teachers of English; National School Public Relations Association (NEA); Oregon Education Association (chairman). *Interests:* Reading, writing, music and art; travel; speaker at meetings; attended the first and second Convocations of American Indian Scholars at Princeton University and at Aspen, Colo. *Biographical sources: Directory of American Scholars; Who's Who of American Women, 1972-1973; Who's Who in the West; Dictionary of International Biography; Two Thousand Women of Achievement,* 1970. *Published works:* Co-author, *Two by Two,* in Eugene, Ore. (late 1950's); co-author, *Duo,* with sister, Rosemary Bogart, Euegen, Ore. (late 1950's); co-editor, *Calapooya Collage of Poetry* for Oregon College of Education, Humanities poets, 1970-1976; co-author, with Gilbert Walking Bull, *O-hu-kah-kan,* 1975; *Wo ya-ka-pi,* 1976; and *Mi ta-ku-ye,* 1977; writer for "Search for America," 1970, for NCTE Task Force on Racism and Bias in the Teaching of English.

WALKING ELK, MITCH *(Mo-o-da-me-yotz)* **(Cheyenne-Arapaho-Hopi) 1950-**
(Native American drug/alcohol/ cultural counselor)

Born December 28, 1950, Claremore, Okla. *Education:* Augustana College (Social Work major), 1984-. *Principal occupation:* Native American drug/alcohol/cultural counselor. *Home address:* P.O. Box 264, Hatfield, Minn. 56135. *Community activities:* Indian youth worker, Marty and Sioux Falls, S.D., 1979-1982. *Awards, honors:* 2nd Place music competition, Pipestone Vocational "Snow Week" competition, Community Event, Pipestone, Minn. *Interests:* "I auditioned for "You Can Be A Star" competition, Opryland USA, Nashville, Tenn.—results not yet in; currently working on first album of original composition. One song published by George B. German, Music Archives, Sioux Falls, S.D.—title, *Washita River,* a contemporary Indian tune."

WALLACE, ANTHONY F.C. 1923-
(professor of anthropology)

Born April 15, 1923, Toronto, Can. *Education:* University of Pennsylvania, B.A., 1947, M.A., 1949, Ph.D., 1950. *Principal occupation:* Professor of anthropology. *Home address:* 614 Convent Rd., Chester, Pa. *Affiliations:* Professor of anthropology, University of Pennsylvania, 1961-; medical research scientist, Eastern Pennsylvania Psychiatric Institute, 1961-. *Other professional posts:* Member, National Research Council, Division of Behavioral Sciences; U.S. Office of Education, Research Advisory Committee; member, Behavioral Science Study Section, National Institute of Mental Health. *Military service:* U.S. Army, 1942-1945. *Memberships:* American Anthropological Association (Fellow); American Association for the Advancement of Science (Fellow; chairman, Section H); American Sociological Association (Fellow); Sigma Xi; Philadelphia Anthropological Society. *Published works:* The Modal Personality Structure of the Tuscarora Indians, as Revealed by the Rorschach 952); editor and author of introduction, *The Ghost-Dance Religion and the Sioux Outbreak of 1890* (Univerity of Chicago Press, 1965); *The Death and Rebirth of the Seneca* (Knopf, 1970); other books and numerous articles in professional journals.

WALTERS, GEORGE A.
(B.I.A. agency superintendent)

Affiliation: Superintendent, Nome Agency, Bureau of Indian Affairs, P.O. Box 1108, Nome, Alaska 99762.

WARE, KENT C., II (Kiowa) 1941-
(Indian affairs director)

Born October 5, 1941, Lawton, Okla. *Education:* Arizona State University, B.S., 1966, Law School, J.D., 1970. *Principal occupation:* Director of Indian Affairs, Gulf Oil Corp., Denver, Colo., 1975-. *Home address:* 3724 S. Fairplay Way, Aurora, Colo. 80014.

WARREN, DAVE (Chippewa-Tewa Pueblo) 1932-
(educator)

Born April 12, 1932, Santa Fe, N.M. *Education:* University of New Mexico, B.A., 1955, M.A., 1961, Ph.D. *Principal occupation:* Educator. *Affiliations:* Instructor, Department to History, Oklahoma State University, 1964-1966; assistant professor, Department of History, University of Nebraska, 1966-1968; director of curriculum and instruction, 1968-1970, director, research and cultural studies materials development, 1970-, Institute of American Indian Arts, Santa Fe, N.M. *Other professional posts:* Member, advisory board, Center for Studies of the American West, University of Utah; member, advisory committee, University of New Mexico Indian Studies Program; chairman, selection committee, National Graduate Indian Scholarship Program (Donner Foundation); member, editorial board, *Indian Historian,* American Indian Historical Society, *Military service:* U.S. Air Force, 1955-1957 (Captain). *Memberships:* Latin American Studies Association; National Congress of American Indians. *Interests:* Mr. Warren writes, "Basic area of professional training has been with studies of the advanced Indian cultures of Mexico, prconquest and at the time of Spanish contact. Investigation of the Indian pictorial documents (codices) has been part of this professional study and interest. Currently, my work concerns the organization of cultural studies material into the instructional programs of the Bureau of Indian Affairs and other systems requiring information and resources about the American Indian—materials which reflect the history and current development of American Indians in the U.S., Canada, and Latin America. Of particular concern is finding programs and materials initiated by the Indian people, therefore reflecting their ideas and interpretations of issues, events or other concerns affecting Indian life and history, and utilizing such information in educational programs. Other areas of interest and activity; curriculum development, historical/ethnological writing and research," *Published works:* Articles in scholarly publications.

WARREN, WANDA EVANS GEORGE (Catawba) 1960-
(consultant, student) Born November 16, 1960, Rock Hill, S.C. *Education:* Georgetown University, B.S., 1983; Clemson University, M.A. (Economics), 1986; Georgia State University, 1986- (J.D. expected in 1989). *Principal occupation:* Consultant. Home address: 2986 Whispering Hills Dr., Chamblee, Ga. 30341. *Affiliations:* W.E., Desk Officer (NMFS), U.S. Department of Commerce, Washington, D.C. (three years); International Internship Planning Committee, Clemson University (two years); private consultant, Atlanta, Ga., 1986-. *Community activities:* Governor's Youth Advisory Council, 1979-1980; Governor's Council on Education, 1980-1981. *Memberships:* International Law Society, 1985; Student Bar Association, 1985; Lawyer's Guild Society, 1985; Georgetown Alumni Association; Atlanta Club. *Awards, honors:* Delegate to National Junior Achievements Convention, 1976; Junior Achievement President of the Year; American Indian Scholar, 1984-1985. *Interests:* "Interested in international trade and development as well as international law. (I) speak German and French. Recreational interests include international travel, and downhill skiing."

WASHBURN, WILCOMB E. 1925- (historian)
Born Januaery 13, 1925, Ottawa, Kan. *Education:* Dartmouth College, A.B. (summa cum laude), 1948; Harvard University, M.A., 1951, Ph.D., 1955. *Principal occupation:* Historian. *Home address:* 2122 California St., N.W., #157, Washington, D.C. 20560. *Affiliations:* Curator, Division of Political History, U.S. National Museum, Smithsonian Institution, 1958-1965; chairman, Department of American Studies, National Museum of History and Technology, Smithsonian Institution, 1965-1968; director, American Studies Program, Smithsonian Institution, Washington, D.C., 1968-. *Other professional posts:* Adjunct professor, American University, Washington, D.C., 1976-; consultant in research, Graduate School of Arts and Sciences, The George Washington University, Washington, D.C., 1966-. *Military service:* U.S. Marine Corps, 1943-1946, 1951-1952; presently Colonel, U.S. Marine Corps Reserves (retired). *Memberships:* American Anthropological Association (Fellow); American Antiquarian Society; American Association for the Advancement of Science; American Association of Museums; American Historical Association; American Society for Ethnohistory (president, 1957-1958); American Studies Association (president, 1978-1979); Anthropological Society of Washington; Indian Rights Association; Institute for Early Amerian History and Culture; Organization of American Historians; Society for the History of Discoveries (president, 1963-1965); Society for American Historians; among others. *Awards, honors:* Honorary Doctor of Letters, St. Mary's College of Maryland, 1970; Honorary Doctor of Humanities, Assumption College, Worcester, Mass., 1983; Phi Beta Kappa Lecturer, Spring, 1980. *Published works: Editor, The Indian and the White Man* (Doubleday, 1964); *Red Man's Land/White Man's Law: A Study of the Past and Present Status of the American Indian* (Scribner's, 1971); editor, *The American Indian and the U.S.: A Documentary History,* 4 volumes (Random House, 1973); *The Indian in America* (Harper & Row, 1975); *The Assault on Indian Tribalism: The General Allotment Law (Dawes Act) of 1887* (Lippincott, 1975;

reprint, Robert E. Krieger Publishing, 1986); *The American Heritage History of the Indian Wars,* with Robert M. Utley (American Heritage Publishing, 1977); numerous chapters in books, and articles in professional and scholarly journals.

WASILE, JEANNE
(executive director-Indian corporation)

Affiliation: Executive Director, International Vice President, American Indian International Development Corporation, Woodward Bldg., Suite 438, 733 15th St., N.W., Washington, D.C. 20005.

WATERS, DEANA J. HARRAGARRA
(library director)

Affiliation: Dirctor, National Indian Law Library, Native American Rights Fund, 1506 Broadway, Boulder, Colo. 80302-6296.

WATKINS, MARY BETH OZMUN
(Creek)
(library director)

Education: University of Oklahoma, B.S., 1959, M.L.S., 1968, post-graduate, 1968-1971. *Principal occupation:* Library director. *Home address:* 2503 Margaret Lynn Lane, Muskogee, Okla. 74401. *Affiliations:* Elementary field librarian, 1968-1970, media consultant, 1970-1971, Oklahoma City Public Schools; associate director, Eastern Oklahoma District Library, Muskogee, Okla., 1971-1977; director of libraries, Bacone College, Muskogee, Okla. 1977-. *Memberships:* Oklahoma Library Association, 1968- (secretary, 1972-1973; chairperson, membership committee, 1972-1976; chairperson, publicity committee, 1972-1973; chairperson, Sequoyah Children's Book Award, 1971-1972; chairperson, intellectual freedom committee, 1976-1977; co-chairperson, ad hoc committee serving as Humanities Council Project liaison, 1976-1977, chairperson, 1977-1978); Southwest Library Association, 1968- (SWLA membership chairperson for OLA, 1975-1976, 1977-1978); Oklahoma Education Association; National Education Association; Oklahoma Association of School Librarians

(district chairperson, 1969-1971); American Library Association, 1971- (member, Membership Task Force; chairperson, Southwest Region, 1976-1978); Oklahoma Association for Educational Communication and Technology, 1975-; Bacone Professional Association, 1977- (program committee; by-laws committee; vice president); Oklahoma Humanities Committee, 1977-1980; American Association of University Women (treasurer, 1976-1978; first vice president, program chairperson, 1978-1980). *Awards, honors:* Outstanding Young Women of America, 1970. *Published works:* Articles in *Oklahoma Librarian.*

WATSON, GEORGE (Narragansett)
(tribal chief)

Affiliation: Chief, Narragansett Indian Tribe, RFD #1, Kenyon, R.I. 02836.

WATTS, STEVEN M. 1947-
(Native American studies)

Born July 25, 1947, Lincoln County, N.C. *Education:* Appalachian State University, Boone, N.C., B.A., 1969; Duke University, M.Div., 1972. *Principal occupation:* Native American studies program specialist, Schiele Museum, Gastonia, N.C., 1984-. *Home address:* 622 Caroline Ave., Gastonia, N.C. 28052. *Other professional posts:* Workshop leader and consultant to museums and Native American organizations and groups in the field of aboriginal technologies. *Past work experience:* Minister, school counselor, classroom teacher, camp director, and substance abuse educator. *Community activities:* Commission on the Status of Women; Southeastern Indian Culture Study Group (director); American Indian Cultural Association (past director); Mental Health Association; volunteer work with schools, churches, scout groups, etc. *Memberships:* Center for the Study of Early Man; The Archaeological Society of N.C.; Continental Confederacy of Adopted Indians; Southeastern Cherokee Confederacy, 1980-1981. *Awards, honors:* Statewide speaker for N.C. Mental Health Association (1984); Master of ceremonies, N.C. Comission of Indian Affairs—"Unity Conference"

Intertribal Dance (1981); Outstanding Service Award, Mental Health Association, 1985. *Interests:* "Major interests is replication and experimental use of Native American tools, weapons, utensils, etc.—with the goal of (through educational programs) increasing the appreciation of native skills and lifestyles among participants—helping to rediscover and preserve native technologies for generations to come. Most "spare" time is spent visiting native communities in the Southeast and historic and prehistoric native sites to increase the understanding and collection of knowledge." *Biographical sources:* Approximately a dozen newspaper articles in local and statewide newspapers (copies available upon request). *Published works:* "The Old Bearskin Report," journal (Schiele Museum, 1985); "Southeastern Craft Articles," series (*The Backwoodsman*, Tex., 1984 & 1985).

WAUNEKA, ANNIE DODGE (Navajo) 1910-
(tribal council member)

Born April 10, 1910, Sawmill, Ariz. *Principal occupation:* Tribal council member, Navajo Tribal Government, Window Rock, Ariz., 1951-. *Other professional post:* Lecturer. *Home address:* Box 629, Ganado, Ariz. *Community activities:* President, "School For Me," Navajo Project Concern, Project Hope; Navajo Nation School Board Association (board member); Navajo Tribal Utility Authority (board member); Navajo Health Authority (board member). *Memberships:* National Public Health Education; American Public Health Association; National TB Association; Society for Public Health (honorary lifetime member). *Awards, honors:* President's Freedom Medal Award, 1963; Woman of the Year in Arizona; Honorary Doctor of Humanities Degree, University of Albuquerque, N.M., 1972; Woman of the Year, 1976, *Ladies Home Journal. Interests:* "Main interest is in health of American Indians; education and tribal government." *Biographical sources: Indian Women of Today; Navajo Biography.*

WAX, MURRAY L. 1922-
(professor)

Born November 23, 1922, St. Louis, Mo. *Education:* University of Chicago, B.S., 1942, Ph.D., 1959; University of Pennsylvania, 1947. *Principal occupation:* Professor. *Home address:* 7030 Dartmouth Ave., #2, University City, Mo. 63130. *Affiliations:* Professor of Sociology & Anthropology, University of Kansas, Lawrence, Kan., 1964-1973, Washington University, St. Louis, Mo., 1973-. *Other professional posts:* Executive associate, Workshop on American Indian Affairs, University of Colorado, Boulder, 1959-1960; director, Oglala Sioux Education Research Project (Emory University), 1962-1963; director, Indian Education Research Project (University of Kansas), 1965-1968. *Memberships:* American Anthropological Association (Fellow); American Association for the Advancement of Science (Fellow); American Sociological Association (Fellow); Current Anthropology (Associate); Royal Anthropological Institute of Great Britain and Ireland (Fellow); Society for Applied Anthropology (Fellow); Society for the Study of Religion; Society for the Study of Social Problems; American Educational Research Association; Midwest Sociological Society; Council on Anthropology and Education. *Awards, honors:* Adopted by Oglala Sioux Tribe; Phi Beta Kappa; Sigma Xi; National Institute of Education Grants, 1973-1974, 1978-1979; National Science Foundation Grant, 1978-1981; grants from: U.S. Office of Economic Opportunity, U.S. Office of Education, Wenner-Gren Foundation. *Editorial boards, advisory editor: Human Organization* (editorial board, 1966-); *Journal of Cultural & Educational Futures* (1979-); *Phylon* (1973-); *Qualitative Sociology* (1982-); *Symbolic Interaction* (1983-). *Published works: Formal Education in an American Indian Community* (Monograph #1, Society for the Study of Social Problems, 1964); co-editor, *Indian Education in Eastern Oklahoma: A Report of Fieldwork Among the Cherokee* (U.S. Office of Education, 1969); *Indian Americans: Unity and Diversity* (Prentice-Hall, 1971); *Solving "The Indian Problem"* (New Viewpoints/Franklin Watts, 1975); numerous articles and essays in professional journals.

WEATHERFORD, ELIZABETH 1945-
(museum curator-film and video)

Born July 30, 1945, Anson County, N.C. *Education:* Duke University, B.A., 1966; The New School for Social Research, New York, N.Y., M.A., 1970. *Principal occupation:* Museum curator-film and video. *Address:* Museum of the American Indian, Heye Foundation, Broadway at 155th St., New York, N.Y. 10032. *Affiliations:* Assistant professor, School of Visual Arts, New York, N.Y., 1970-1981; adjunct curator, Museum of the American Indian, New York, N.Y., 1981-. *Memberships:* Educational Film Library Association; American Anthropological Association; Association for Independent Video and Film Makers; Media Alliance; National Alliance of Media Arts Centers, New York Women's Anthropological Caucus; Society on Visual Anthropology; Cultural Survival. *Interests:* "Recent and archival documentary films and videotapes about Native Americans." *Published works: Native Americans on Film and Video (Museum of the American Indian, 1981); Native Americans on Film and Video II* (Museum of the American Indians, 1986); "Anthropology" and "Native Americans" in *Good Reading* (R.R. Bowker, 1985).

WEATHERLY, JOHN
(college president)

Affiliation: President, Nebraska Indian Community College, P.O. Box 752, Winnebago, Neb. 68071.

WEBSTER, EMERSON C. (Seneca)
(tribal chief)

Affiliation: Chief, Tonawanda Band of Senecas, Council of Chiefs, 7027 Meadville Rd., Basom, N.Y. 14013.

WELCH, KAY
(B.I.A. agency superintendent)

Affiliation: Superintendent, Warm Springs Agency, Bureau of Indian Affairs, Warm Springs, Ore. 97761.

WELLS, RICHARD (Nisqually)
(tribal chairman)

Affiliation: Chairman, Nisqually Indian Community Council, 4820 She-Na-Num Dr., S.E., Olympia, Wash. 98503.

WELLS, VINE (Mdewakanton Sioux)
(tribal president)

Affiliation: President, Prairie Island Community Council, Route 2, Welch, Minn. 55089.

WELLS, WALLACE (Crow Creek Sioux)
(tribal chairman)

Affiliation: Chairman, Crow Creek Sioux Tribal Council, P.O. Box 658, Fort Thompson, S.D. 57339.

WERITO, CECILIA
(coordinator-Indian women's program)

Affiliation: Coordinator, Federal Women's Program, Indian Health Service, 5600 Fishers Lane, Rockville, Md. 20857.

WESLAGER, CLINTON ALFRED 1909-
(professor emeritus)

Born April 30, 1909, Pittsburgh, Pa. *Education:* University of Pittsburgh, B.A., 1933. *Principal occupation:* Professor emeritus, Widener University. *Home address:* RD 2, Box 104, Old Public Rd., Hockessin, Dela. 19707. *Memberships:* Archaeological Society of Delaware (past president); Eastern States Archaeological Federation (past president). *Awards, honors:* Christian Lineback Award for excellence in teaching; Archibold Crozier Award; two awards for outstanding books, Association for State and Local History; Fellow, Archaeological Society of New Jersey; Fellow, Holland Society of New York. *Interests:* "Ethnohistorical research among survivors of Eastern Woodland tribes, especially Nanticoke, Delaware, Conoy, Minquas, Mahican, and Munsee." *Published works: Delawares Forgotten Folk,* (1943); *Delaware's Buried Past* (1944); *The Nanticoke Indians* (1948);

Indian Place-Names in Delaware (1950); Red Men on the Brandywine (1953); *Magic Medicines of the Indians* (1973); *The Delaware Indians, A History* (Rutgers University, 1973); *The Delawares: A Critical Bibliography* (1978); *The Delaware Indian Westward Migration;* (Middle Atlantic Press, 1979); *Magic Medicine of the Iroquois* (Middle Atlantic Press, 1980); *The Nanticoke Indians, Past and Present* (University of Delaware, 1983); among others.

WEST, W. RICHARD (DICK)
(Wah-pah-nah-yah) **(Southern Cheyenne) 1912-**
    (teacher, artist, consultant, lecturer, sculptor)

Born September 8, 1912, Darlington, Okla. *Education:* Concho Indian School; Haskell Institute; Bacone Junior Colege, A.A., 1938; University of Oklahoma, B.F.A., 1941, M.F.A., 1950. *Principal occupation:* Teacher, artist, consultant, lecturer, sculptor. *Home address:* RR #1, Box 447, Fort Gibson, Okla. 74434. *Affiliations:* Director, Art Department, Bacone College, Muskogee, Okla., 1947-1970; chairman, Division of Humanities, Haskell Indian Junior College, Lawrence, Kan., 1970-. *Military service:* U.S. Navy, 1942-1946. *Community activities:* Muskogee Art Guild; Bacone College Education Association (president); Indin Club sponsor. *Memberships:* Delti Phi Delta; Southwestern Art Association; Oklahoma Education Association (chairman of art section, district). *Awards, honors:* Outstanding Cheyenne of the Year, 1968, by Cheyennes of Oklahoma; Teacher of the Year, 1969, Bacone College; Outstanding Alumnus, 1973, Haskell Alumni Association; contract artist, Franklin Mint, Franklin Center, Pa., 1974, 1975, to create subject drawings for a series of fifty medallions to be struck or cast on the history of the American Indians; Outstanding Professor, 1976-1977, Haskell Indian Junior College. *Exhibitions:* Numerous one-man shows and art awards throughout the U.S., 1949-. *Interests:* "Mr. West speaks and lectures on his art in general, often on Indian art, and very often on his series of oils portraying Christ as a Plains Indian. He has juried numerous Indian art shows, non-Indian art competitions, and more recently has served as a aconsultant to

colleges and universities on Indian studies programs and education of Indian youths. Dick West has been the inspiration of many artists all over America. Dick's prime aim in his art is to show that the Indian, with his priceless heritage of history, legend and color could make himself an important place in contemporary American art. Possibly the best known of his paintings is the "Indian Christ in Gethsemane" at the alter of Bacone's beautiful chapel. Included in his religious series are "The Madonna and Child," The Annunciations," "The Last Supper," "The Crucifixion," and "The Ascension." *Biographical sources: Who's Who in American Art; Who's Who in the South and Southwest; Who's Who in Oklahoma; Personalities of the South; Community Leaders and Noteworthy Americans; International Who's Who in Art and Antiques.* A filmstrip of the life and works of Dick West was made and produced by the American Baptist Films, Valley Forge, Pa., in 1969. Also in 1969 a biography of the artist was written by Charles Waugamen and published by Friendship Press, New York.

WESTERMEYER, JOSEPH, M.D. 1937-
    (psychiatrist)

Born April 8, 1937, U.S.A. *Education:* University of Minnesota, M.D., 1961, M.A., M.P.H., Ph.D., 1969-1970, *Principal occupation:* Psychiatrist. *Home addres:* 1935 Summit Ave., St. Paul, Minn. 55105. *Affiliation:* Professor of psychiatry, Department of Psychiatry, University of Minnesota Hospitals and Clincis (UMHC), Minneapolis, Minn., 1970-. *Other professional posts:* Director, Alcohol-Drug Dependence Program, (UMHC), 1982-; director, International Clinic (UMHC), 1984-. *Community activities:* Indian Guest House (halfway house for Indian alcoholics), Minneapolis, Minn. (board member, 1969-1972); Juel Fairbanks House (halfway house for Indian alcoholics, St. Paul, Minn. (board member, 1970-1973); South Side Receiving Center (a detoxification unit for American Indian alcoholics), Minneapolis, Minn. (consultant, 1974-1975); Association of American Indian Affairs, including Senate subcomittee hearing on American Indian child welfare, 1973-1976. *Memberships:* American

Anthropological Association (Fellow); American Association for the Advancement of Science; American Medical Society on Alcoholism; American Psychiatric Association (Fellow); American Public Health Association; American Association of Family Practice (Fellow); Association of Academic Psychiatrists; Minnesota Psychiatric Association; Society on Medical Anthropology; World Psychiatric Association, Transcultural Section ; among others. *Awards, honors:* Meritorious Service Award, U.S. Agency for International Development, 1967; Ginzburg Fellow, Group for the Advancement of Psychiatry, 1969-1970; numerous research grants. *Published works:* Chapters in books and monographs: "The Ravage of Indian Families in Crisis," in *The Destruction of Indian Fanily Life,* ed., S. Unger (Association of American Indian Affairs, 1976); "Alcoholism and American Indian Alcoholism," in *Alcoholism Development, Intervention and Consequences,"* with *J. Baker, ed., E. Heinman (1986).*

WETMORE, RUTH L. (Mrs.) 1934-
(Indian museum curator)

Born 1934 in Nebraska. *Education:* Park College, B.A., 1956; University of Kansas, M.A., 1959. *Principal occupation:* Curator, Indian Museum of the Carolinas, Laurinburg, N.C., 1974-. *Home address:* 811 S. Main St., Laurinburg, N.C. 28352. *Memberships:* Archaeological Society of North Carolina; Oklahoma Anthropological Society; North Carolina Museums Council; Phi Beta Kappa; Pi Sigma Alpha. *Interests:* Philatelic writing and exhibiting. *Published work: First on the Land: The North Carolina Indians* (John F. Blair, Publisher, 1975).

WHITE, ELMER, Sr. (Devil's Lake Sioux)
(tribal chief)

Affiliation: Chief, Devil's Lake Sioux Tribal Council, Sioux Community Center, Fort Totten, N.D. 58335.

WHITE, HARTLEY (Chippewa)
(tribal chairman)

Affiliation: Leech Lake Reservation Business Committee, Box 308, Cass Lake, Minn. 56633.

WHITE,LINCOLN C.
(executive director-Indian education)

Affiliation: Executive director, National Advisory Council on Indian Education, 2000 L St., N.W., Suite 574, Washington, D.C. 20036

WHITE, LONNIE J. 1931-
(professor of history)

Born February 12, 1931, Haskell County, Tex. *Education:* West Texas State College, B.A., 1950; Texas Tech University, M.A., 1955, University of Texas, Ph.D., 1961. *Principal occupation:* Professor of history, Memphis State University, Memphis, Tenn., 1961-. *Home address:* 4272 Rhodes Ave., Memphis, Tenn. 38111. *Military service:* U.S. Army, 1951-1953 (Sergeant). *Memberships:* Western History Association; Southern Historical Association; American Military Institute; American Historical Association; *Journal of the West* (editorial advisory board). *Interests:* Teacher of course on history of American Indians at Memphis State University from 1968 to the present. *Biographical source: Who's Who in the South and Southwest. Published works:* Editor, co-author, *Hostiles and Horse Soldiers: Indian Battles and Campaigns in the West* (Pruett Press, 1972); editor, *The Miles Expedition of 1874-1875: An Eyewitness Account of the Red River War, by Scout J.T. Marshall (Encino Press, 1971); editor, Chronicle of a Congressional Journey: The Doolittle Committee in the Southwest, 1865* (Pruett Press, 1975); *Panthers to Arrowheads: The 36th (Texas-Oklahoma) Division in World War I* (Presidial Press, 1984); *Politics on the Southwestern Frontier: Arkansas Territory, 1819-1836* (Memphis State University Press, 1964); numerous articles in professional journals.

WHITE HAT, ALBERT H. (Rosebud Sioux) 1938-
(bilingual teacher)

Born November 18, 1938, St. Francis, S.D. *Education:* Sinte Gleska College, A.A. (Lakota Studies), 1986. *Principal occupation:* Bilingual teacher. *Home address:* Box 168, St. Francis, S.D. 57572. *Affiliations:* Indian studies program teacher, St. Francis Indian School, 1974-1980; part-time teacher, Lakota Medicine, 1979-1985, director of Title VII, Bilingual Teacher Training Program, Sinte Gleska College, Rosebud, S.D., 1983-. *Other professional posts:* Tribal council (Rosebud Sioux) representative and committee work, 1979-1981; president, board of directors, Sinte Gleska College, 1981-1983. *Community activities:* Rosebud Community Action Program, 1967-1970; Rosebud Ambulance Service, 1970-1972; St. Francis Indian School (chairman of the board). *Memberships:* National Association for Bilingual Education; South Dakota Association for Bilingual Education; South Dakota Indian Education Association. *Awards, honors:* Fellowship award in 1978 to research Native American History for high school history course at Newberry Library, Chicago, Ill. *Interests:* Carpentry, woodwork and construction; horse training; cultural and traditional activities. "Presently, I am coordinating three instructional pamphlets in the areas of Lakota kinship— early childhood development, bilingual science, and bilingual language arts." *Published work:* Co-editor, *Lakota Ceremonial Songs* (song book with cassette tape) (Sinte Gleska College).

WHITEBEAR, BERNIE
(executive director-Indian center)

Affiliation: Executive director, Daybreak Star Arts Center, P.O. Box 99253, Seattle, Wash. 98199.

WHITECROW, JAKE L. (Quapaw-Seneca-Cayuga of Oklahoma) 1928-
(health administrator)

Born July 2, 1928, Miami, Okla. Education: Oklahoma State University, Stillwater, B.S. (Agriculture), 1951. *Principal occupation:*

Health administrator, National Indian Health Board, Denver, Colo. *Home address:* 5100 Leetsdale Dr., #241, Denver, Colo. 80222. *Affiliations:* Americans for Indian Opportunity, Washington, D.C. (board member, seven years); American Indian Heritage Foundation, Washington, D.C. (board member, advisory council, two years). *Other professional posts:* Health committee chairman, National Congress of American Indians; founder, Native American Free Loan Society, Denver, Colo. *Military service:* U.S. Army, 1951-1978 (Major-U.S. Army Reserve-retired; U.N. Medal; Korean War Medal with two Battle Stars; National Defense Medal; Army Reserve Medal). *Community activities:* Quapaw Tribe (chairman); American Legion (precinct co-chairman, post commander); Native American Cattle Co. of Oklahoma (president) *Memberships:* Oklahoma State Historical Society (listed speaker); Thomas Jefferson Forum of Washington, D.C. (listed speaker). *Awards, honors:* Honorary member of 4-H Clubs of Oklahoma; "I was the only Oklahoma Indian to serve as a commissioner with the American Policy Review Commission (U.S. Congress, 1975-1977)." *Interests:* "My avocational interests are: sport of rodeo, Indian customs and history, football, basketball, Indian dice, horse training, dog training. *Biographical source: Indians of Oklahoma* (University of Oklahoma Press). *Published work: American Indian Policy Review Commission Final Report* (U.S. Government Printing Office, 1977).

WHITEHEAD, RUTH HOLMES EVERETT (Sioux) 1947-
(ethnologist, assistant curator)

Born October 10, 1947, Charleston, S.C. *Education:* College of Charleston, B.A., 1971. *Principal occupation:* Ethnologist, assistant curator, Nova Scotia Museum, Halifax, Nova Scotia, Can., 1972-. *Home address:* Box 2, Site 24, R.R. One, Tantallon, Nova Scotia, Can. B0J 3J0. *Interests:* Porcupine quillwork as practiced by the Micmac Indians from 1500-9150; Micmac art in general. *Published works: The Micmac Ethnology Collection of the Nova Scotia Museum* (The Nova Scotia Museum, 1974); *Christina Morris: Micmac Artist and Artist's Model* (National Museums of Canada, 1977); "Decorating Bark With Porcupine Quills (*Ahoy,* children's magazine, 1977); *Micmac Quillwork* (Nova Scotia Museum, 1978); *Inventory of Micmac Material Culture Outside Canada,* with Dr. Harold McGee (Nova Scotia Museum, 1978); "Micmac Quillwork in the Nineteenth Century" (National Museums of Canada, 1978).

WHITELY, PETER M. 1953-
(anthropologist)

Born March 13, 1953, Leicester, England. *Education:* Cambridge University (England), B.A., 1975, M.A., 1980; University of New Mexico, Ph.D., 1982. *Principal occupation:* Assistant professor of anthropology, Sarah Lawrence College, Bronxville, N.Y., 1985-. *Memberships:* American Anthropological Association; American Ethnological Society; Royal Anthropological Institute; Sigma Xi. *Interests:* Hopi ethnology. *Published works: Deliberate Arts: Changing Culture in a Hopi Community* (University of Arizona Press, 1987); *Journey to Reed Springs: A History of the Hopi Village of Bacari* (Northland Press, 1987).

WHITEMAN, DENNIS
(B.I.A. agency superintendent)

Affiliation: Superintendent, Red Lake Agency, Bureau of Indian Affairs, Red Lake, Minn. 56671.

WHITENER, DONALD E.
(B.I.A. agency superintendent)

Affiliation: Superintendent, Crow Creek Agency, Bureau of Indian Affairs, P.O. Box 616, Fort Thompson, S.D. 57339.

WHITESIDE, DON *(Sin-a-paw)*
(Creek) 1931-
(research analyst)

Born May 9, 1931, Brooklyn, N.Y. *Educa-* tion: Wisconsin State University, B.S., 1958; University of Wisconsin, M.S., 1960; Stanford University, Ph.D., 1967. *Principal occupation:* Research analyst. *Home address:* 4 Newgale St., Nepean, Ontario, Can K2H 5R2. *Affiliations:* Assistant professor, University of Alberta, Edmonton, Can., 1967-1970; consultant, Government of Canada, Ottawa, 1970-1972; research director, National Indian Brotherhood, Ottawa, 1972-1973; professor, Manitou College, LaMacaza, Quebec, 1973-1975; INA, 1976-1979; owner, Whiteside and Associates, 1979-1982; research analyst, Government of Canada (NHW), 1982-. *Military service:* Merchant Marine, 1947-1948; U.S. Army, 1948-1954. *Community activities:* Alberta Human Rights Association (president, 1969-1970); Civil Liberties Association, National Capital Region (president, 1970-1971, 1973, 1974, 1977-); Canadian Rights and Liberties Federation (secretary/treasurer, 1972-1974; president, 1974-1977, 1983- Aboriginal Institute of Canada (president, 1973-). *Memberships:* United Native Americans. *Awards:* National Science Foundation Fellowship, 1963; Stanford University Fellow, 1963-1964. *Interests:* Genealogy. *Published works: Aboriginal People: A Selected Bibliography* (National Indian Brotherhood, 1973); *Aboriginal People: A Selected Bibliography,* Vol. II (Canadian Association in Support of Native peoples, 1977); *A Look Into Indian History* (Aboriginal Institute of Canada, 1983); *Indians, Indians, Indians* (National Library of Canada, forthcoming).

WHITFORD, THOMAS
(B.I.A. agency superintendent)

Affiliation: Superintendent, Eastern Nevada Agency, Bureau of Indian Affairs, P.O. Box 28, Elko, Nev. 89832.

WHITISH, RACHEL (Shoalwater)
(tribal chairwoman)

Affiliations: Chairwoman, Shoalwater Bay Tribal Council, P.O. Box 579, Tokeland, Wash. 98590.

WHITMAN, KATHY (ELK WOMAN) (Manadan-Hidatsa-Arikara) 1952- (designer, sculptor, painter)

Born August 12, 1952, Bismarck, N.D. *Education:* University of South Dakota; Sinte Gleska College, Rosebud, S.D.; Standing Rock Community College, Ft. Yates, N.D. *Principal occupation:* Professional artist—designer, sculptor, painter. *Home address:* 111 San Salvador, Santa Fe, N.M. 87501. *Affiliations:* Owner, Nux-Baga Lodge, New Town, N.D., 1981-1985; owner, Recreation Center, New Town, N.D., 1985. *Other professional post:* Art instructor, Standing Rock Community College and Sinte Gleska College. *Community activities:* Parent representative-Headstart, Ft. Yates, N.D.; Ft. Berthold Community College, New Town, N.D. (board of directors); Pow-Wow, Canonball, N.D. (president, committee member). *Memberships:* Indian Arts and Crafts Association; North Dakota Council on the Arts (artist-in-residence; board member). *Awards, honors:* Governors Award, Directors and Choice Merit Award, United Tribes Educational Training Center, Bismarck, N.D. *Interests:* "Demonstrated and exhibited paintings in New York City at Museum of the American Indian; danced and exhibited artwork in Charleroi, Belgium and Dijon, France; started a recreation center on Ft. Berthold Reservation for the youth and sponsored an alternative camp for youth. Presently, moved south to Santa Fe, N.M. and promoting own work in stone sculptor with the help of art agents at the Flute Player Gallery, Colorado Springs, Colo." *Biographical sources: Wanbli Ho* (Sinet Gleska College, 1976); *Minot Daily News* (Minot, N.D., 1982); *Denver Post* (Denver, Colo., 1982); *Beulah Beacon* (Beulah, N.D., 1983); *Draw* Magazine (Brookville, Ohio, 1984).

WHITTENER, DAVID (Squaxin Island) (tribal chairman)

Affiliation: Chairman, Squaxin Island Tribal Council, W. 81 Hwy. 108, Shelton, Wash. 98584.

WICKCLIFFE, DENNIS L. (Oklahoma Cherokee) 1944- (B.I.A. public information officer)

Born April 18, 1944, Claremore, Okla. *Education:* Northeastern State University, Tahlequah, Okla., B.A, 1966; University of Oklahoma, M.Ed., 1973. *Principal occupation:* Area public information officer, Bureau of Indian Affairs, Anadarko, Okla., 1976-. *Home address:* P.O. Box 1195, Anadarko, Okla. 73005. *Military service:* U.S. Air Force, 1968-1972 (E-5 highest rank; Air Force Commendation Medal for service in Southeast Asia). *Other professional posts:* English teacher/journalism teacher/Title I coordinator, Riverside Indian School, Anadarko, Okla., 1972-1976; acting principal, Riverside Indian School, 1976. *Memberships:* University of Oklahoma Alumni Association, 1973-; Cherokee Tribe of Oklahoma. *Interests:* Travel; sports; working with and for Indian people through the Bureau of Indian Affairs.

WILCOX, U. VINCENT, III, 1945- (museum anthropologist and curator)

Born September 26, 1945, Washington, D.C. *Education:* Yale University, B.A., 1967; Harvard University, M.A., 1968; Columbia University, M.Phil., 1974. *Principal occupation:* Museum anthropologist and curator. *Home address:* 7434 Colshire Dr. #3, McLean, Va. 22101. *Affiliations:* Curator of North American Archaeology and Ethnology, and head of the Research Branch, Museum of the American Indian, Heye Foundation, New York, N.Y. , 1968-1977; collections manager, Department of Anthropology, National Museum of Natural History, Smithsonian Institution, Washington, D.C., 1977-? *Memberships:* American Anthropological Association; Society for American Archaeology; American Association of Museums; International Council for Museums; Council for Museum Anthropology; The Explorers Club. *Interests:* Material culture of the North American Indian—the curation and conservation of anthropological collections, general museology; archaeological fieldwork. *Published works:* Numerous articles in scientific and popular journals.

WILDCAT, WILLIAM (Chippewa)
(tribal president)

Affiliation: President, Lac du Flambeau Tribal Council, P.O. Box 67, Lac du Flambeau, Wis. 54538.

WILKINSON, GERALD
(executive director-Indian organization)

Affiliation: Executive director, national Indian Youth Council, 201 Hermosa, N.E., Albuquerque, N.M., 87108.

WILLIAMS, DAVID EMMETT *(Tosque)*
(Kiowa-Apache-Tonkawa) 1933-
(artist)

Born August 20, 1933, Redstone, Okla. *Education:* Bacone College. *Principal occupation:* Artist. *Membership:* American Tribal Dancers and Singers Club, 1963- (head drummer and singer). *Awards, honors, exhibits:* Numerous art awards and one-man shows; work represented in permanent collections of several museums.

WILLIAMS, DEAN V (Seneca) 1925-
(tribal official)

Born April 30, 1925, Cattaraugus Reservation, N.Y. *Home address:* Route 438, Gowanda—Irving Rd., Irving, N.Y. 14081. *Affiliation:* Former president, Seneca Nation of Indians, Cattaraugus Reservation, N.Y. *Military service: U.S. Navy Submarine Service, 1943-1946.*

WILLIAMS, DELLA R. (SAM)
(Papago) 1936-
(school principal)

Born February 13, 1936, Ventana Village, Papago Reservation, Ariz. *Education:* Phoenix Junior College, A.A., 1958; Arizona State University, B.A., 1962. *Principal occupation:* School principal. *Home address;* Star Route, Box 92, San Simeon School, Sells, Ariz. 85634. *Affiliations:* Teacher, Santa Rosa Boarding School, B.I.A., 1962-1975; principal, San Simeon School, B.I.A., Papago Indian Agency, 1977-. *Community activities:* Papago Tribal Education Com-

mittee (chairperson, 1965-1970); OEO's Community Action Program; tribal representative at various state and national conferences and workshops, as well as at congressional hearings. *Honor:* Inducted into the Phoenix Indian High School Hall of Fame as a charter member, 1977. *Interests:* Consulting with students, teachers and administrators concerning grades and adjustment; higher education students, consultant and advisor; directed Tribal Education Grants and assisted with other financial needs of higher education; monthly reports to the General Council; participated and assisted in the introduction, planning and development of the first poverty program on the Papago Reservation; participated in supervising and hiring the first Head-Start school teachers, evaluated and made recommendations; participated as guest speaker in Indian education conferences in Tempe, Indian Clubs, The Papago Council, Phoenix Indian High School, Tucson Indian Center, and Papago District Councils.

WILLIAMS, FLOYD (Skagit)
(tribal chairman)

Affiliation: Chairman, Upper Skagit Tribal Council, 2284 Community Plaza, Sedro Woolley, Wash. 98284.

WILLIAMS, ROBERT A., Jr. (Lumbee)
1955-
(law professor)

Born March 11, 1955, Baltimore, Md. *Education:* Loyola College, Baltimore, Md., B.A., 1977; Harvard Law School, J.D., 1980. *Principal occupation:* Assistant professor of law, University of Wisconsin, Madison, 1980-. *Home address:* 1621 Adams St., Madison, Wis. 53711. *Other professional post:* Legal consultant. *Community activities:* Indian Rights Association, Philadelphia, Pa. (vice president, 1984; board of directors, 1980-1985). *Awards, honors:* American Council of Learned Societies-/Ford Foundation Fellowship recipient, 1985-1986; National Endowment for the Humanities Fellowship recipient, Summer, 1982. *Interests:* American Indian legal history, and economic development.

WILLIAMS, WALTER L. 1948-
(professor)

Born November 3, 1948, Durham, N.C. *Education:* Georgia State University, B.A., 1970; University of North Carolina, Chapel Hill, M.A., 1972, Ph.D., 1974. *Principal occupation:* Associate professor, Anthropology Department, University of Southern California, Los Angeles, Calif. *Home address:* 3400 Ben Lomond Place #130, Los Angeles, Calif. 90027. *Other professional post:* Consultant, American Indian Studies Center, UCLA. *Community activities:* Gay American Indians, Inc. (consultant); Museum of the Cherokee Indians (consultant); International Gay and Lesbian Archives (president, board of directors). *Memberships:* American Anthropological Association; Organization of American Historians, *Awards, honors:* Woodrow Wilson Fellow, 1970; American Council of Learned Societies grant awards, 1977, 1983; UCLA American Indian Studies Center Fellow, 1980, 1982; Newbery Library Fellow, 1978. *Interests:* Fieldwork: Eastern Cherokees, Lakotas, Mayas. *Published works:* Editor, *Southeastern Indians Since the Removal Era* (University of Georgia Press, 1979); editor, *Indian Leadership* (Sunflower University Press, Manhattan, Kan., 1984); *The Spirit and the Flesh: American Indian Androgyny and Male Sexuality* (Beacon Press, 1986. Articles: "Detour Down the Trail of Tears: Southern Indians and the Land" (*Southern Exposure*, Fall, 1974); "The Proposed Merger of Apaches with Eastern Cherokees in 1893" (*Journal of Cherokee Studies*, Spring, 1977); book reviews on Southeastern Indians in: *Ethnohistory, North Carolina Historical Review, American Indian Journal,* and *Journal of Southern History.*

WILLIE, ELVIN, Jr. (Paiute)
(tribal chairman)

Affiliation: Chairman, Walker River Paiute Tribal Council, P.O. Box 220, Schurz, Nev. 89427.

WILNOTY, JOHN JULIUS (Cherokee) 1940-
(stone carver)

Born April 10, 1940, Cherokee, N.C. *Principal occupation:* Stone carver. *Home address:* Cherokee, N.C. 28719. *Membership:* The Qualla Indian Arts and Crafts Cooperative. *Interests:* Building toys for children; rebuilding and designing machinery. Mr. Wilnoty's work is displayed at the Smithsonian Institution and the Museum of the American Indian.

WILSON, DUFFY
(museum director)

Affiliation: Executive director, Native American Centre for the Living Arts, Inc., 25 Rainbow Mall, Niagara Falls, N.Y. 14303.

WILSON, RAYMOND 1945-
(professor of history)

Born April 11, 1945, New Kensington, Pa. *Education:* Fort Lewis College, Durango, Colo., B.A., 1967; University of Nebraska, Omaha, M.A., 1972; University of New Mexico, Ph.D., 1977. *Principal occupation:* Assistant-associate professor of history, Fort Hays State University, Hays, Kan., 1979-. *Home address:* 1721 Haney, Hays, Kan. 67601. *Other professional post:* History instructor, Sam Houston State University, 1977-1979. *Memberships:* Western History Association; Indian Rights Association; Kansas Council for the Social Studies; Kansas Corral of the Westerners; Phi Alpha Theta; Pi Gamma Mu; Phi Delta Kappa; Phi Kappa Phi. *Interests:* "My major area of study is the American West with an emphasis on 19th and 20th century American Indian history. I enjoy traveling throughout western America." *Published works: Administrative History, Canyon de Chelly National Monument, Arizona* (U.S. Dept. of the Interior/National Park Service, 1976); co-author, David M. Brugge, *Ohiyesa: Charles A. Eastman, Santee Sioux* (University of Illinois Press, 1983); *Native Americans in the Twentieth Century* (Brigham Young University Pres, 1984); co-author, James S. Olson, *Indian Lives:*

Essays on 19th and 20th Century Native American Leaders (University of New Mexico Press, 1985).

WILSON, WILLIAM
(assistant director-Indian Health Service)

Affiliation: Assistant director, Indian Health Service, 5600 Fishers Lane, Rockville, Md. 20857.

WINDER, NATHAN W. (STRONG ELK) (Ute-Navajo-Paiute) 1960-
(counselor-grants/contracts administrator)

Born October 2, 1960, Albuquerque, N.M. *Education:* Stanford University, B.A., 1983; University of Oregon, School of Law, 1984-1985. *Principal occupation:* Counselor, grants/contracts administrator, Pyramid Lake Paiute Tribal Council, Nixon, Nev., 1985-. *Home address:* P.O. Box 242, Nixon, Nev. 89424. *Other professional post:* Director, Wambli Gleska Indian Program. *Community activities:* Native American Church (vice president, Pyramid Lake chapter); Save the Children Committee (chairman). *Interests:* "I am interested in returning back to law school or applying to medical school. I am interested in some day becoming a spiritual leader or a medicine man. I am also interested in sponsoring a sun dance for the four colors of humanity."

CHARITY WING (Sioux) 1902-
(nursing, homemaking)

Born March 9, 1902, Montana Territory. *Education:* Haskell Institute, Lawrence, Kan., A.A., 1926. *Principal occupation:* Nursing, homemaking. *Home address:* P.O. Box 64, Poplar, Mt. 59255. *Affiliation:* Member, Indian Tribal Affairs, Citizens Committee, Fort Peck Sioux Tribe, Poplar, Mt. (20 years); advocate, Fort Peck Sioux Claims Committee for Black Hills (ten years). *Other professional post:* Presbyterian Church Elder; Ladies Aid Healer (70 years; president, three terms). *Awards, honors:* Woman of the Day, Presbyterian Church, Special Recognition, 1981. *Interests:* "Sewing—starquilt construction; travel; guest lecturer for Indian history, lore, crafts, life styles, method of rearing Indian children; Grandfather Basil Reddoor was first ordained minister of Presbyterian Church on the Fort Peck Reservation in Montana."

CHIEF WISE OWL (Tuscarora) 1939-
(chief and medicine man)

Born February 16, 1939, Robeson County, N.C. *Principal occupation:* Chief and medicine man, Tuscarora Indian Tribe, Drowning Creek Reservation. *Home address:* Route 2, Box 108, Maxton, N.C. 28364. *Other professional posts:* Businessman; teacher of herbs to next medicine man. *Community activities:* Built tribal community center. *Membership:* National Congress of American Indians.

WITTSTOCK, LAURA WATERMAN (Seneca) 1937-
(administrator)

Born September 11, 1937, Cattaraugus Indian Reservation, N.Y. *Education:* University of Minnesota, B.S. candidate. *Principal occupation:* Non-profit administrator. *Home address:* 3031 Dakota Avenue South, St. Louis Park, Minn. 55416. *Affiliations:* Editor, *Legislative Review,* 1971-1973; executive director, American Indian Press Association, Washington, D.C., 1975; associate director, Red School House, St. Paul, Minn., 1975-1977; director, Project Media, National Indian Education, Minneapolis, Minn., 1973-1975; office manager, Native American Research Institute, Minneapolis, Minn., 1981; administrator, Heart of the Earth Survival School, Minneapolis, Minn., 1982-1985; independent education consultant, 1976-; director, curriculum project, Migizi Comunications, Inc., Minneapolis, Minn., 1985-. *Community activities:* Minnesota Governor's Job Training Council (vice chair, 1983-); Minneapolis Community Business Employment Alliance (vice chair, 1983-); Migizi Communications, Inc. (president-on leave); United Way Planning and Priorities Committee (member); Christian Sharing Fund, Minneapolis-St. Paul Archdiocese (chair, 1981-1986); Minnesota Women's Fund (executive committee, 1983-);

Children's Theatre and School, Minneapolis (board member, 1984-). *Interests:* Journalism, writing; American Indian education—program designer, evaluator, administrator; American Indian alcoholism and related problems; employment-program designer, board member, policy-maker; American Indian urban studies. *Biographical sources: Let My People Know: American Indian Journalism,* James E. and Sharon M. Murphy (University of Oklahoma Press, 1981); *I Am the Fire of Time: The Voices of Native American Women,* Jane Katz, editor (E.P. Dutton, 1977); *Minnesota Women's Yearbook,* 1978, 1984; *Who's Who in the Midwest; Who's Who of American Women; Contemporary Native American Address* (Brigham Young University, 1977; *Women of Color poster series* (St, Paul Public Schools, 1980). *Published works: Indian Alcoholism in St. Paul,* study with Michael Miller (University of Minnesota, 1981); "Native American Women: Twilight of a Long Maidenhood," *Comparative Perspectives of Third World Women,* Beverly Lindsay, editor (Praeger, 1980); "On Women's Rights for Native Peoples" (Akwesasne Notes, 1975); editor, *Indian Education,* National Indian Education Association, 1973-1974; "The Federal Indian Relationship," *Civil Rights Digest,* Oct., 1973; editor, *Legislative Review,* 1971-1973.

WOODARD, DON 1935-
(Indian arts dealer)

Born May 12, 1935, Gallup, N.M. *Education:* University of New Mexico, B.A., 1957; North Arizona University, M.A., 1972. *Principal occupation:* Indian arts dealer. *Home address:* Box BBB, Cortez, Colo. 81321. *Affiliation:* Owner, Woodard's Indian Arts, Gallup, N.M., 1952-1972; owner, Don Woodard's Indian Trading Post, Cortez, Colo., 1972-. *Other professional posts:* Land claims archaeologist for the Pueblos of Zia, Santa Anna, Jemez, Acoma and Laguna; group leader for Navajo Long Walk Re-enactment. *Memberships:* Inter-Tribal Indian Ceremonial, Gallup, N.M. (board member; program director; exhibition hall chairman); American Society of Appraisers; Indians Arts and Crafts Association (board member; ethics committee chairman). *Interests:* Indian arts and crafts; anthropology .

WOODARD, TOM 1936-
(Indian arts and crafts dealer)

Born August 15, 1936, Gallup, N.M. *Education:* University of Arizona, 1958-1964. *Principal occupation:* Indian arts and crafts dealer, Gallup, N.M., 1960-. *Home address:* 1100 S. Grandview, Gallup, N.M. 87301. *Other professional post:* Collector f Indian art. Memberships: Indian Arts and Crafts Association (president); New Mexico Retail Association (president-elect). *Interests:* Judge at Indian arts and crafts shows.

WOOSLEY, ANNE I.
(director-Amerind Foundation)

Affiliation: Director, The Amerind Foundation, Inc., Dragoon, Ariz. 85609.

WOPSOCK, FRANK (Ute)
(tribal chairman)

Affiliation: Chairman, Uintah and Ouray Tribal Business Council, Fort Duchesne, Utah 84026.

WRIGHT, BARTON A. 1920-
(B.I.A. chief administrator)

Born December 21, 1920, Bisbee, Ariz. *Education:* University of Arizona, B.A., 1952, M.A., 1954. *Principal occupation:* B.I.A. chief administrator. *Address:* Bureau of Indian Affairs, Room 3519N, 1951 Constitution Ave., N.W., Washington, D.C. 20245. *Affiliations:* Archaeologist, Amerind Foundation, Dragoon, Ariz., 1952-1955; curator, Museum of Nothern Arizona, Flagstaff, Ariz., 1955-1957; scientific director, Museum of Man, San Diego, Calif., 1977-1982; chief, Administration, Bureau of Indian Affairs, Washington, D.C., 1982-. *Military service:* U.S. Army, 1943-1946. *Memberships:* American Association of Museums, 1971-; Western Museums League (vice president, 1964-); Society for American Archaeology, 1950-; Arizona-Nevada Academy of Science, 1958-; Indian Arts and Crafts Association (board member); Societe des Amerinistes de Paris, 1978-. *Interests:* Mr. Wright writes, "Museology, especially in the fields of anthropology and geology; ethnology of Hopi Indians; arts and crafts of

Southwestern Indians; painting and drawing the U.S. Southwest; history of the U.S. Southwest; judging arts and crafts shows; advising on the establishment and care of cultural centers." *Biographical sources: Who's Who in the West; Who's Who in American Art. Published works: Kachinas: A Hopi Artist's Documentary* (Northland Press-Heard Museum, 1973); *Kachinas: The Goldwater Collection* (Heard Museum, 1975); *The Unchanging Hopi* (Northland Press, 1975); *Pueblo Shields* (Northland Press, 1976); *Hopi Kachinas, Guide to Collecting Dolls* (Northland Press, 1977).

WRIGHT, FRANK, Jr. (Puyallup)
(tribal chairman)

Affiliation: Chairman, Puyallup Tribal Council, 2002 E. 28th St., Tacoma, Wash. 98404.

WYNECOOP, JOSEPH A. (Spokane) 1919-
(manager, aerospace-information support)

Born March 22, 1919, Reardan, Wash. *Education:* Eastern Washington University, B.A., 1946; Glendale University College of Law, B.S.L., 1971. *Principal occupation:* Manager, aerospace-information support. *Home address:* 3832 Hillway Dr., Glendale, Calif. 91208. *Affiliations:* Training director, 1968-1971, administrative specialist, 1971-1974, advisory committee for minority affairs, 1970-1976, Affirmative Action Program representative, 1970-, Jet Propulsion Laboratory, California Institute of Technology, Pasadena, Calif. *Military service:* U.S. Air Force, 1942-1968 (Lt. Colonel, retired; Air Force Outstanding Unit Award; Medal for Humane Action; Joint Chiefs of Staff Commendation Medal; Air Force Commendation Medal; Alexander the Great Medal (Greece); Greek Joint Chiefs Letter of Commendation). *Community activities:* All American Indian Celebration Corporation (vice president and director, 1969-1970); Governor's "California Indian Assistance Project" (representative, 1969-1974); American Indian Enterprise (vice president, 1969-1975); Pacific Northwest Indian Center (financial commissioner, 1971-1973). *Memberships:* Indian Scholarship Fund Associa-

tion (director and vice president, 1969-1975); Urban Indian Development Association (vice president, 1969-1975); Retired Officers Association, 1968-; Air Force Association, 1976-; National Congress of American Indians (member of board, Indian Scholarship Committee, 1977-).

Y

YELLOWHAMMER, JOYCE
(office manager-Indian association)

Affiliation: Office manager, National Indian Education Association, 1115 Second Ave. South, Minneapolis, Minn. 55403.

YORK, KENNETH HAROLD
(Mississippi Choctaw) 1948-
(educational consultant)

Born May 15, 1948, Neshoba County, Miss. *Education:* Northeastern Oklahoma State University, Tahlequah, B.A., 1971; University of Minnesota, M.A. (Educational Administration), 1975. *Principal occupation:* Educational consultant. *Home address:* 807 Black Jack Rd., Philadelphia, Miss. 39350. *Affiliations:* President, Tisho and Associates, Philadelphia, Miss. (ten years); president, Choctaw Associated Members for Progress, Philadelphia, Miss. (three years). *Other professional post:* Adjunct professor, Mississippi State University. *Community activities:* Choctaw Federal Credit Union (president, 1976-1983); Pearl River Choctaw Commuity Development Club (president, 1985-1986); St. Theresa Catholic Church Council, 1985-. *Memberships:* National Indian Education Association; National Association of Bilingual Education; International Reading Association. *Awards, honors:* American Legion's Boys State, 1966; Pearl Service Award, 1982; Outstanding Young Men of America, 1976. *Interests:* Bilingual bicultural education; literacy among Native Americans; farming and agribusiness; business and management development among Native Americans; sovereignty and human rights.

Biographical sources: Meridian Star, 1983; "Faces," video program on Mississippi ETV; "Mississippi Roads," video documentary on Mississippi ETV. *Published works: Recommended Teacher Training Curriculum for Native American Bilingual Education Programs* (Mississippi State University, 1977); *Working with the Bilingual Commuity* (National Clearinghouse for Bilingual Education, 1979) *Made By Hand: Mississippi Folk Art* (Mississippi History and Archives, 1980); *LaSalle and His Legacy: Frenchmen and Indians in the Lower Mississippi Valley* (University of Mississippi Press, 1982).

YOUCKTON, PERCY (Chehalis)
(tribal chairman)

Affiliation: Chehalis Community Council, P.O. Box 536, Oakville, Wash. 98568.

YOUNGDEER, ROBERT (Eastern Band Cherokee)
(tribal chief)

Affiliation: Chief, Eastern Band of Cherokee Indians, P.O. Box 455, Cherokee, N.C. 28719.

Z

ZAH, PETERSON (Navajo) 1937-
(tribal chairman)

Born December 2, 1937, Low Mountain, Ariz. *Education:* Phoenix College, A.A., 1960; Arizona State University, B.A. (Education), 1963. *Principal occupation:* Chairman, Navajo Nation, Window Rock, Ariz., 1983-. *Home address:* P.O. Box 308, Window Rock, Ariz. 86515. *Other professional posts:* Education-secondary education techer; executive director of DNA—People's Legal Services. *Community activities:* Wide Public School Association; Window Rock School Board (past president); National Association of the Indian Legal Services (founder); Arizona State Advisory Committee to the U.S. Civil Rights Commission (member). *Memberships:* Navajo Education & Scholarship Foundation; National Tribal Chairmen's Association; Council of Energy Resource Tribes. *Awards, honors:* Humanitarian Award, City of Albuquerque, N.M.— Mayor Harry Kinney; Honorary Doctorate (Humanitarium), Santa Fe College.

ZAHARLICK, ANN MARIE, 1947-
(professor of anthropology)

Born March 24, 1947, Scranton, Pa. *Education:* Cedar Crest College, B.A., 1969; Lehigh University, M.A., 1973; The American University, Ph.D., 1977 (Dissertation: *Picuris Syntax). Principal occupation:* Professor of anthropology. *Home address:* 4071 Garrett Dr. West, Columbus, Ohio 43214. *Affiliations:* Instructor and curriculum development specialist, Bilingual/Multicultural Teacher Training Program for Native Americans, The University of Albuquerque, N.M., 1975-1977; assistant professor and language development specialist, Native American Bilingual Teacher Education Program, The University of Albuquerque, 1977-1979; assistant professor, Department of Anthropology, The Ohio State University, Columbus, Ohio, 1979-. *Other professional posts:* Instructor, Acoma Pueblo Bilingual Education Program, 1978; instructor, Sandia Pueblo Language Program. *Research/fieldwork:* Research on the Picuris language, Picuris Pueblo, N.M., 1973; research on Picuris syntax, Picuris and Taos, N.M., 1974-1976; development of Keresan language spoken by the pueblos of Acoma, Cochiti, Santo Domingo, Laguna, Zia, Santa Ana, and San Felipe, and development of curriculum guides and bilingual education materials in Keres and Picuris; analysis of Picuris syntax and semology—updating of John P. Harrington's *Picuris Children's Stories* and preparation of a dictionary and grammar for use in the Picuris bilingual education program, 1976-; linguistic research on passive construction and tone in Picuris, Picuris, N.M., 1980-1981. *Community activities:* Assisted in the establishment of bilingual education programs at Acoma, Laguna, Cochiti, Santa Ana, and Picuris Pueblos, 1975-1979; produced teaching guides and materials for the Picuris Bilingual Education Programs (10 stories and booklets in Picuris, 1975-); presentations on

American Indians to 4th and 5th grade students in the Albuquerque and Columbus Public Schools, 1978-1982. *Memberships:* American Anthropological Association (Fellow); American Association for the Advancement of Science; American Ethnological Society; Linguistic Association of the Southwest; Linguistic Society of America; New Mexico Association for Bilingual Education; New York Academy of Sciences; Society for Applied Anthropology (Fellow), Society for the Study of the Indigenous Languages of the Americas; Southwestern Anthropological Association; The Southwest Circle; *Southwest Journal of Linguistics* (editorial board, 1985-1987); among others. *Awards, honors:* Distinction awarded for Ph.D. comprehensive examination: Language Acculturation, 1974; The American University Dissertation Fellowship, 1974-1975; The Honor Society pf Phi Kappa Phi; Edward Sapir Award in Linguistics (for *Picuris Syntax*), The New York Academy of Sciences, 1978; nominated for Outstanding Teaching Award, College of Arts and Sciences, The Ohio State University; Certificate of Award, Ohio Coalition of Refugee Mutual Assistance Association, for volunteer service with the Laotian refugee community. *Interests:* Cultural and linguistic anthropology. *Biographical sources: Outstanding Young Women of America; Who's Who in the Midwest; The International Directory of Distinguished Leadership; Personalities of America; The World Who's Who of Women.* Published works: *Picuris Syntax* (University Microfilms, 1977); A Picuris/English Dictionary (in progress); *Picuris Grammar* (in progress); editor, *Native Languages of the Americas* (special issue of the *Journal of the Linguistic Association of the Southwest,* 1981); numerous book chapters, articles, book reviews, papers and presentation.

ZEPHIER, ALVIN (Yankton Sioux)
(tribal chairman)

Affiliation: Chairman, Yankton Sioux Tribal Business and Claims Committee, Route 3, Box 248, Marty, S.D. 57361.

ZILKA, CAROL L. (Cheyenne River Sioux) 1949-
(B.I.A. special educator)

Born December 24, 1949, Sioux Falls, S.D. *Education:* Mankato State University, Mankato, Minn., B.S., 1972; Pennsylvania State University, M.Ed., 1984. *Principal occupation:* Special educator. *Home address:* 9063 Giltinan Ct., Springfield, Va. 22153. *Affiliations:* Special education teacher, Hennepin Technical Centers, Hennepin, Minn. (two years); educational case manager (seven years), special education coordinator, 1984-, Office of Indian Education Programs, Eastern Area Office, Bureau of Indian Affairs, 1951 Constitution Ave., N.W., Washington, D.C. 20245. *Memberships:* Council for Exceptional Children, 1977- (Minnesota board of directors, 1979-1981; 1980 local arrangements chairperson for National Topical Conferences on seriously emotionally disturbed; 1978-1981 Minnesota convention director; 1978 Minnesota chapter #32, president; 1977 Minnesota chapter #32 publicity and membership chairperson. *Awards, honors:* 1985 Certificate of Special Achievement, Department of the Interior, Bureau of Indian Affairs; 1983 Graduate Fellowship, Pennsylvania State University, American Indian Special Education Teacher Training Program (member of first graduating class); 1980 National Council for Exceptional Children, Certificate of Appreciation (served as local arrangements chairperson for national conference on seriously emotionally disturbed; 1980 Minnesota Council for Exceptional Children, President's Award for Personal Contribution, dedicated effort and planning of Minnesota's first CEC Topical Conference; 1980 Hennepin Technical Center, Superintendent's Award for advancing professional development.

ZIOLKOWSKI, RUTH
(foundation chairperson)

Affiliation: Chairperson, Crazy Horse Memorial Foundation, Ave. of the Chiefs, Black Hills, Crazy Horse, S.D. 57730.

GEOGRAPHICAL INDEX

ARKANSAS

Fayetteville
Hoffman, Michael P.

Little Rock
Brown, Dee Alexander
Russell, Jerry

ALASKA

Anchorage
Kuhklen, Albert
Leask, Janie
Peratrovich, Roy
Roehl, Roy F.
Strucher, Jim

Bethel
Vaska, Anthony

Delta Junction
Alfonsi, John

Eagle River
Kinney, Rodney P.

Fort Yukon
Fields, Audrey

Gakona
Ewan, Roy S.

Golovin
Olson, Martin L.

Haines
Hakkinen, Elisabeth S.
Heinmiller, Carl W.

Juneau
Antiqua, Clarence
Horton, David A., Jr.
Lestenkof, Jacob

Ketchikan
Lawrence, Erma G.

Kodiak
Peterson, Frank R.
Neseth, Eunice
Pullar, Gordon L.

Kotzebue
Hensley, William L.
Schwind, Marie N.

Murfreesboro
Johnson, Sam

Ninilichik
Bouwens, William

Nome
Okleasik, M. LaVonne
Walters, George A.

Tenakee Springs
Soboleff, Walter A.

Yakutat
Mallott, Byron

ARIZONA

Camp Verde
Russell, Ned

Chandler
Cummings, Kendall

Cibecue
DeHose, Judy
Reyhner, Jon Allen

Dragoon
Di Peso, Charles C.
Fulton, William Dincan
Woosley, Anne I.

Flagstaff
Ambler, J. Richard
Darden, Steven
John, Angelo Marvin
Kahn, Franklin
Kealiinohomoku, Joann
Riner, Reed D.
Seaman, P. David

Fort Defiance
Brown, Wilfred
DeGroat, Ellouise
Hardy, Joseph

Ganado
Falling, LeRoy
Hohnani, Daniel
Morgan, Guy
Wauneka, Annie Dodge

Glendale
Artichoker, John Hobart

Keams Canyon
Secakuku, Alph

Kykotsmovi
Sockyma, Michael C., Jr.

Lukachukaim
Hobson, Dottie F.

Maricopa
Narcia, Leroy

Oraibi
Pentewa, Richard Sitko
Sidney, Ivan

Parker
Drennan, Anthony, Sr.
Lamb, Chalres A.
Mills, Walter R.

Peach Springs
Sinyell, Edgar

Phoenix
Blue Spruce, George, Jr.
Cain, H. Thomas
Claus, Tom
Collins, Carl
Dobyns, Henry F.
Doyel, David E.
Haranaka, Nancie
Honanie, Gilbert, Jr.
Mitchell, Wayne Lee
Shing, Le Roy Ned

Pipe Springs
Savala, Delores

Polacca
Nuvayestewa, Evangeline

Prescott
Erickson, John
McGee, Patricia

Rough Rock
Begay, Jimmie C.

Sacaton
Thompson, Edmond

San Carlos
Keller, George
Snyder, Fred
Titla, Phillip, Sr.

Scottsdale
Colton, Alfred
Tsinajinnie, Andy

Sedona
Fredericks, Oswald

Sells
Christman, Richard T.
Moore, Josiah N.
Nordwall, Curtis
Wiliams, Della R.

Somerton
Miller, Fred

Supai
Sinyella, Wayne

Teecnospos
Walker, Jerry Clayton

Tonalea
Miller, Stephen

Tsaile
Begay, Ruth Tracy
Huerta, C. Lawrence
Jackson, Dean

Tuba City
Carr, Patrick J.

Poocha, Fritz T.
Tubac
Rogers, Will, Jr.
Tucson
Bahti, Mark
Chana, Anthony M.
Deloria, Vine, Jr.
Haury, Emil W.
Officer, James E.
Ramiriz, David
Roessler, Paul Albert
Spicer, Edward Holland
Tanner, Clara Lee
Valentine
Henson, C.L.
Whiteriver
Bradley, Russell
Dodge, Henry
Lupe, Ronnie
Window Rock
Atkinson, La Verne D.
Dodge, Donald
Drake, Elroy
Gorman, Carl Nelson
Hartman, Russell P.
MacDonald, Peter, Sr.
Nelson, Michael
Tapahe, Loren
Tippeconnic, Thomas
Tsosie, Loretta A.W.
Zah, Peterson
Winslow
Sorrell, Cheryl
Yuma
Kelly, Alvin
Montague, Felix J.

CALIFORNIA

Alameda
Livermore, Earl R.
Alpine
Pico, Anthony
Altadena
Morgan, Marilyn Elizabeth
Alturas
Forrest, Erin
Garcia, Norma Jean
Jones, Leo
Anaheim
Jones, Stephen S.
Murray, Donald Cylde

Bakersfield
Rogers, James Blake
Banning
Cortez, Ronald D.
Martin, Robert
Pablo, Matt
Saubel, Katherine Siva
Berkeley
Heizer, Robert F.
Big Bend
Sisk, Kenneth
Big Pine
Jones, Velma
Bishop
Frank, Earl
Saulque, Joseph C.

Bridgeport
Crawford, Maurice
Brooks
Knight, Philip
Buena Park
Aguilar, Jose V.
Burbank
Howard, Helen Addison
Campo
Pinto, Tony J.
Capistrano Beach
Di Maio, Sue
Cedarville
Phoenix, Andrew
Claremont
Batalille, Gretchan M.
Crow, Perce B.
Covelo
Lincoln, Daran
Davis
Forbes, Jack D.
Death Valley
Esteves, Pauline
El Cajon
Sandoval, Anna
Fall River Mills
Boyer, Momma Quail
Reed, Silver Star
Forestville
Hamilton, Ruby
Bidwell
Lame Bull, Lucinda
Glendale
Wynecoop, Joseph A.

Happy Camp
Brown, Vinson
Hollywood
Pencille, Herbert W.
Hoopa
Bennett, Ruth
Laguna Niguel
Stalling, Steven L.A.
Long Beach
McCone, Robert Clyde
Los Angeles
Burns, Robert I.
Hedrick, Henry E.
Heth, Charlotte Wilson
Juneau, Alfred LeRoy
Oandasan, William
Pierce, Lymon
Salabiye, Velma
Stevens, Connie
Williams, Walter L.

McArthur
Gray, Shorty
Newport Beach
Jorgennsen, Joseph G.
Oakland
Bean, Lowell John
Pacific Grove
Adams, Margaret B.
Pacific Palisades
Nash, Gary B.
Pala
Freeman, King
Palm Springs
McDermott, Richard S.
Pasadena
Houlihan, Patrick T.
Pauma Valley
Dixon, Patricia A.
Placentia
Lerner, Albert L.
Redlands
Fisher, Dorothy D.
Riverside
Beatty, Patricia
Tomhave, Jerome
Sacramento
Jaegar, Ronad
Lovely, Deborah
San Francisco
Ortiz, Roxanne D.

San Luis Obispo
Grinde, Donald A., Jr.
San Marcos
Freeman, Robert Lee
Santa Barbara
Jacobs, Wilbur R.
Sebastopol
Clark, Donald E.
Stanford
Momaday, Navarre S.
Susanville
Padilla, Nicolas J.
Visalia
Pietroforte, Alfred

COLORADO

Aurora
Ware, Kent C., II
Basalt
Honer, Janelle A.
Bellevue
Goranson, Frederick A.
Boulder
Echohawk, John E.
Eddy, Frank W.
Hill, Norbert S., Jr.
Kaschube, Dorothea V.
Phillips, George H.
Stewart, Omer C.
Waters, Deana J. H.
Cortez
Austin, Frank
Woodard, Don
Denver
Friend, David N.
Hughes, J. Donald
Punley, Randolph J.
Whitecrow, Jake L.
Durango
Cargile, Ellen Y.
Englewood
Frazier, Gregory W.
Lester, A. David
Militaire, Delbert
Fort Collins
Becenti, Francis D.
Ignacio
Burch, Leonard
Pensoneau, Ralph

Montrose
Casius, Everlyn
Towaoc
House, Ernest
Smith, Michael H.
Wheat Ridge
Goodman, Linda J.

CONNECTICUT

Greenwich
Josephy, Alvin M., Jr.
Hamden
Voight, Virginia F.
Ledyard
Hayward, Richard
New Haven
Rodriguez-Sellas, Jose E.
Norwich
Princess Rose Scribner
Portland
Walker, Willard
Uncasville
Tantaquidgeon, Gladys
Washington
Payne, Susan F.
Waterbury
Benedict, Patricia
Watertown
Cooper, Karen Coody
Westport
Scheirbeck, Helen M.

DELAWARE

Hockessin
Weslager, Clinton A.

DISTRICT OF COLUMBIA

Blumer, Thomas J.
Bush, Mitchell L., Jr.
Clary, Thomas C.
Colosimo, Thomas
Conner, Rosemary
Coulter, Robert T.
Delaware, Robert
Doss, Michael
Eden, Ronad D.

Field, Raymond
Gerard, Pat
Green, Rayna
Harjo, Susan Shown
Hart, Robert G.
Hillabrant, Walter J.
Jabbour, Alan A.
Jacobs, Harvey
Johnson, Samuel
Keely, Kay
Krenzke, Theodore
La Course, Richard V.
Leap, William L.
Lenz, Msr. Paul A.
Libhart, Myles
Little, Stewart
Lonefight, Edward
Lynn, Sharon
Martin, James
Martin, Joy
Moore, Ramona
Nicklason, Fred
Ott, William
Parker, Alan
Parker, Sharon
Press, Daniel S.
Printup, Maribel
Robinson, Rose W.
Savilla, Elmer
Shaw, Carl F.
Shunatona, Gwen
Standing Elk, Donald
Swimmer, Ross O.
Taylor-Goins, Elise
Tiger, Georgiana
Vozniak, Debbie
Washburb, Wilcomb E.
Wasile, Jeanne
White, Lincoln C.
Wright, Barton A.

FLORIDA

Crawfordville
Jones Buddy C.
Havana
Matthews, Ann M.
Hollywood
Jumper, Betty Mae
LaRoche, Harold L.
Tribbett, Norman H.
Merritt Island
McCarthy, Joan D.

Miami
Tiger, Buffalo
Orange Springs
Buford, Bettie
Sarasota
Saunooke, Osley B., Jr.

GEORGIA

Atlanta
Bealer, Alex W., III
Chamblee
Warren, Wanda E.G.
Danielsville
Hudson, Melvin, Jr.
Leesburg
Jackon, William

HAWAII

Waianae
Ide, John H.

IDAHO

Boise
Dayley, Jon P.
Chubbuck
Sheppard, Laverne
Fort Hall
Edmo, Kesley
Thompson, Duane F.
Trahant, Mark N.
Kamiah
Moffett, Walter L.
Moses, Lily L.
Slickpoo, Allen P., Sr.
Lapwai
Moran, Ernest T.
Pinkham, Allen V.
Plummer
George, Osald C.
Lasarte, Bernard J.

ILLINOIS

Carbondale
MacLachlan, Bruce B.
Cary
David, Robert C.

Chicago
Crawford, Eugene
Tax, Sol
Taylor, Rhonda Harris
Collinsville
Schusky, Ernest L.
Evansville
Borman, Leonard D.
Hoxie, Frederick E.
Urbana
Bruner, Edward M.

INDIANA

Bloomington
Hurt, Wesley R.
Parks, Douglas R.
Fremont
Munger, Lynn
Indianapolis
Cummings, Vicki
Lafayette
Berthrong, Donald J.
West Lafayette
Parman, Donald L.

IOWA

Sioux City
Conley, Robert J.
Gordon, Patricia T.
Tama
Buffalo, George, Jr.
Mitchell, Louis

KANSAS

Council Grove
Milligan, Hariet
Hays
Wilson, Raymond
Horton
Thomas, Frederick R.
Lawrence
Ahshapanek Don C.
Gipp, Gerald
Homeratha, Phil
Lieb, Bertha K.
Lounsberry, Gary R.

Manhattan
May, Cheryl
O'Brien, Patricia J.
Powhattan
Kennedy, James H.
Surveyor, Virgil R.
Reserve
Keller, Nancy
Wichita
Jones, William M.
Rohn, Arthur H.

KENTUCKY

Lexington
Duffield, Lathel F.

LOUISIANA

Natchitoches
Medford, Claude, Jr.

MAINE

Houlton
Sabattis, Clair
Mt. Vernon
Hinkley, Edward C.
Old Town
Love, Timothy
Perry
Dana, Ralpha F.
Princeton
Sanborn, James H.
Sopiel, Sylvia
Washington County
Stevens, John W.

MARYLAND

Baltimore
Richardson, Barry
Cabin John
Price, B. Leigh
Mt. Ranier
Marks, Patricia Ann
Rockville
Bryan, Richard P.
Casebolt, Jack V.
Colombel, Pierce

Elrod, Sam
Emelio, John
Exendine, Joseph, M.D.
Exendine, Leah
Felsen, James, M.D.
Gashler, Dan
Henson, Richard A.
Kaufman, Steven, M.D.
McCloskey, Richard J.
Mecklenburg, Robert
Mitchell, Jimmy
Pearson, Billy
Reyes, Launa L.
Roach, Milburn H.
Roseleigh, Patricia F.
Sharlow, James
Shea, James
Shea, W. Timothy
Smith, James R.
Stout, Sadie
Swetter, Donald A.
Thomas, Arthur
Thurman, Robert
Todd, John, M.D.
Werito, Cecilia
Wilson, William
Wheaton
Reeser, Ralph R.

MASSACHUSETTS

Amherst
Salzmann, Zdenek
Boston
Gorman, Frederick J.E.
Falmouth
Mills, Earl H.
Gay Head
Gentry, Beatrice
Jamaica Plain
Sam, Jimmy L.
Lexington
Lester, Joan
Lowell
Burtt, J. Frederic
Middleboro
Moore, Daisy P.
Monterey
McAllester, David P.
Newton Centre
Manners, Robert A.

Northampton
Salisbury, Neal
West Peabody
Johns, Joseph F.
West Yarmouth
Edmunds, Judith A.

MICHIGAN

Ann Arbor
Ford, Richard I.
Kurath, Gertrude P.
Tanner, Helen H.
Baroga
Tolonen, Myrtle
Brimley
Teeple, Wade
Coldwater
Brauker, Shirley M.
Detroit
Boyd, Rose Marie
Hillman, James
Lowry, Irene
Kalamazoo
Bank, Theodore P., III
Ludington
Powell, Dick & Donna
Marquette
Hirst, Stephen M.
Pleasant
Sowmick, Arnold
Saulte Ste. Marie
Lumsden, Joseph K.
Picotta, Alvin
Suttons Bay
Raphael, Joseph
Wilson
Miller, Thomas G.
Philemon, Henry, Sr.

MINNESOTA

Cass Lake
Mayotta, Raymond
Wadena, Darrell
White, Hartley
Golden Valley
Spotted Eagle, Chris
Grand Portage
Hendrickson, James

Granite Falls
Howell, Irene
Hatfield
Walking Elk, Mitch
Matawan
Hampton, Eber
Minneapolis
Buffalohead, W. Roger
Cornelius-Fenton, Karen
Fleming, Darrell
Heeley, Steven, J.W.
Hoebel, E. Adamson
Means, Russell
Mollenhoff, Lori
Smith, Noreen
Yellowhammer, Joyce
Morton
Prescott, Michael
Nett Lake
Donald, Gary
Ogema
Nimohoyah, Sekon
Onamia
Gahbow, Arthur
Kegg, Matthews M.
Prior Lake
Crooks, Norman
Jaeger, Robert
Red Lake
Jourdain, Roger
Whiteman, Dennis
St. Louis Park
Wittstock, Laura W.
St. Paul
Morrison, George
Spencer, Robert F.
Westermeyer, Joseph, M.D.
Welch
Wells, Vine
White Earth
Martin, Peter J.

MISSISSIPPI

Carthage
Bell, William F.
Benn, Robert C.
Philadelphia
Gibson, Clay
Isaac, Calvin J.
Mann, Robert C.
Martin, Phillip

Scott, James R.
York, Kenneth H.
Union
Brescia, William, Jr.
Walnut Grove
Francisco, Eldon

MISSOURI

St. Louis
Browman, David L.
University City
Wax, Murray L.

MONTANA

Billings
Gilliland, Hap
Lucas, Merle R.
Box Elder
Stump, Rocky, Sr.
Bozeman
Morris, C. Patrick
Old Coyote, Barney
Browning
Baker, Anson A.
Boy, Calvin J.
Fairbanks, Michael
Fisher, Joe
Old Person, Earl
Pepion, Donald D.
Butte
Taulbee, Daniel J.
Crow Agency
Pease-Windy Boy, Janine
Stewart, Donald, Sr.
East Glacier Park
Bigspring, William F., Sr.
Kuka, King D.
Elder
Pereau, John
Harlem
Main, Elmer
Perez, Franklin
Lame Deer
Beartusk, Keith L.
Hollowbreast, Donald
McDonald, Arthur L.
Rowland, Allen
Rowland, Darius

Pablo
Felsman, Joseph
McDonald, Joseph
Poplar
Charity Wing
Clincher, Bonnie M.
Hollow, Norman
Ridenhower, Marilyn
St. Ignatius
Allard, L. Doug
McDonald, Walter
Stevensville
Brown, Joseph Epes

NEBRASKA

Lincoln
Grobsmith, Elizabeth
Macy
Miller, Wallace W.
Niobrara
Kitto, Richard
Omaha
Tyndell, Wayne
Winnebago
Christie, Joe C.
Du Bray, Alfred W.
Snake, Reuben A., Jr.
Weatherly, John

NEVADA

Austin
Rosse, William, Sr.
Carson City
Belgrade, Harold
Duckwater
Millett, Jerry
Elko
Whitford, Thomas
Fallon
Moyle, Alvin
Gardnerville
Frank, Robert L.
Incline Village
Clark-Price, Margaret
Las Vegas
Collins, Adele V.
Frye, Billy J.
Surrett, Clifton R.

Nixon
Shaw, Wilfred
Winder, Nathan W.
Owyhee
McKiney, Whitney
Reno
Jacobsen, William H., Jr.
Mose, E.
Schurz
Aragon, Arnold
Willie, Elvin, Jr.
Stewart
Hunter, Robert L.
Winnemucca
Harney, Robert
Yerington
Richardson, Kenneth

NEW HAMPSHIRE

Hanover
Dorris, Michael A.

NEW JERSEY

Bergenfield
Carter, Edward R.
Elizabeth
Kraft, Herbert C.
Fort Lee
Boissevain, Ethel

Leonia
Jaffe, A.J.
New Milford
Thomas, David H.
Princeton
Rosen, Lawrence
Rockleigh
Force, Roland W.
Teaneck
Begay, Eugene A., Sr.
Woodcliff
Begay, D.Y.

NEW MEXICO

Acoma Pueblo
Juanico, Juan
Salvador, Lilly

Alamagordo
Hall, C.R.

Albuquerque
Benham, William J., Jr.
Bennett, Robert L.
Brody, J.J.
Chavers, Dean
Clarke, Frank, M.D.
Crow, John O.
Deloria, P.S.
Edmo, Lorraine P.
Elgin, Alfred G., Jr.
English, Samuel F.
Johnny, Ronald E.
Johnson, Robert
Jojola, Ted
Lewis, Dave
Little, Vincent
Montoya, Samuel
Pena, Gilbert M.
Robertson, Ellen
Shopteese, John T.
Toya, Ronald G.
Wilkinson, Gerald

Algodones
McBride, Mary

Aztec
Doerfort, Hans M.
Gorman, Clarence N.

Arroyo Hondo
Schaafsma, Polly Dix

Bernalillo
Chaves, Esquipula
Raton, Eli Seo, Sr.

Church Rock
Linford, Laurence D.

Corrales
Bennett, Noel K.

Crownpoint
Plummer, Edward O.

Dulce
Parton, Petry D.

Espanola
Singer, Lawrence

Farmington
Housh, Raymond E.

Gallup
Bennet, Kay C.
Woodard, Tom

Isleta
Lucerno, Alvino

Jemez Pueblo
Momaday, Al
Momaday, Natachee S.

Las Vegas
Orr, Howell M.

Los Alamos
Harlow, Francis, H.

Mescalero
Chino, Wendell

Mora
Naranjo, Tito E.

Navajo
Jones, David S.

Portales
Agogino, George A.

Ruidoso
Ball, Eve

San Felipe Pueblo
Tenorio, Frank

San Juan Pueblo
Garcia, Marcelino
Trujillo, Jose E.

San Ysidro
Pino, Augustin

Santa Fe
Aguilar, Alfred
Ballard, Louis W.
Boissiere, Robert
Bovis, Pierre G.
Calkin, Laurie A.
Carpio, Jose
Dailey, Charles
Haozous, Bob
Hinds, Patrick S.
Houser, Allan
Ladd, Edmund J.
Lang, Richard W.
Lomahaftewa, Linda
McGrath, James A.
McGreevy, Susan B.
Montoya, Geronima C.
New, Lloyd H.
Ortiz, Alfonso A.
Padilla, Joe A.
Parra, Donna C.
Parrish, Rain
Parsons, Neil
Perez, David
Polese, Richard
Popovi Da
Sanchez, Gilbert
Scholder, Fritz
Viarrial, Jacob

Wade, Jon C.
Whitman, Kathy

Santo Domingo Pueblo
Garcia, Alex

Shiprock
Dodge, Marjorie T.
McCabe, Edward, Jr.

Taos
Gorman, R.C.
Sandoval, Joseph C.

Tohatchi
Bitsie, Oscar

Zuni
Lewis, Robert E.
Montgomery, John
Simplico, Chauncey
Tsabetsaye, Roger J.

NEW YORK

Basom
Sundown, Chief Corbett
Webster, Emerson C.

Briarwood
Hines, Mifauney S.

Brooklyn
Beatty, John J.
Bush, Michael A.

Eastchester
Oestreicher, David M.

Geneseo
Judkins, Russell A.

Gowanda
Mohawk, John

Guilderland
Samuelson, Lillien T.

Hogansburg
Cook, John A.
Garrow, Leonard
Jacobs, Alex A.
Swamp, Chief Jake

Huntington
Owens, Roger C.

Irving
Nitsch, Twylah H.
Williams, Dean V.

Katonah
Shoumatoff, Nicholas A.

Lewiston
Hewitt, Arnold
Patterson, Elma
Lockport
Newman, Harrison
Mastic
Beller, Samuel W., Jr.
Mastic Beach
Reason, Jamie T.

New York
Barz, Sandra
Dockstader, Frederick J.
Eager, George B.
Highwater, Jamake
James, Walter S., Jr.
Kreipe, Matha
McCord, David
Means, William A.
Roubideaux, Nanette S.
Smith, James G.E.
Starchild, Adam A.
Unger, Steven
Weatherford, Elizabeth
Nedrow
Shenandoah, Leon
Niagara Falls
Green, Elwood
Miller, Huron
Wilson, Duffy
Onchiota
Fadden, John K.
Fadden, Ray
Oneida
Goff, David J.
Ossining
Brennan, Louis A.
Poughkeepsie
Merrell, James H.
Rochester
Bell, Amelia R.
Hayes, Charles F., III
Hill, Arleigh
Rooseveltown
Rokwaho (Dan Thompson)
Salamanca
Abrams, George H.J.
Heron, George D.
John, Calvin
Vanatta, Shirley P.
Slingerlands
Fenton, William N.

Staten Island
Summers-Fitzgerald, Diosa
Syracuse
Seneca, William
Valley Stream
Cooke, David C.
Warnerville
Jimmie, Luke
Johannsen, Christina B.

NORTH CAROLINA

Cherokee
Chiltoskey, Goingback
Crowe, Amanda
Hughes, Juanita
Muskrat, Jeff W.
Robinson, Nathan W.
Wilnotu, John J.
Youngdeer, Robert
Durham
La Barre, Weston
Gastonia
Stout, Richard A.
Watts, Steven M.
Hollister
Richardson, Patricia R.
Laurinburg
Wetmore, Ruth L.
Maxton
Chief Wise Owl
Mooresville
Bonney, Rachel A.
Pembroke
Chavis, Angela Y.
Locklear, Juanita O.

NORTH DAKOTA

Belcourt
Emgee, Sr. Judith
Kepkin, Debbie L.
Lafromboise, Richard
Monette, Gerald
Schindler, Duane E.
Fort Totten
Davis, Rose-Marie
White, Elmer, Sr.
Fort Yates
Chase the Bear, Lionel
Crowfeather, Isabelle

Murphy, Charles W.
Stein, Wayne
New Town
Spotted Bear, Alyce
Wahpeton
LeRoy Chief

OHIO

Centerville
Eid, Leroy V.
Cincinnati
Neely, Sharlotte
Cleveland Heights
Callender, Charles
Columbus
Zaharlick, Ann Marie
Pepper Pike
Mahan, Harold D.
Piqua
Griffith, Gladys G.
Portsmouth
Brown, Charles Asa
Tippecanoe
AmyLee
Worthington
Chapman, Jane

OKLAHOMA

Ada
Denton, Coye E.
Pettigrew. Jackson D.
Anadarko
French, Edgar L., Jr.
Johnson, Patricia L.
Lamar, Newton
Littlechief, Barthell
Poolaw, Linda S.
Ragsdale, William P.
Stephenson, Bonnie
Thompson, Rupert
Wickcliffe, Dennis L.
Apache
Cleghorn, Mildred
Ardmore
Beaver, Fred
Browning, Zane
Lofton, Gene T.
Binger
Shemayne, Henry

Broken Bow
Smith, LaMarr

Chouteau
Tyner, James W.

Claremore
Collins, Reba N.

Concho
Edwards, John
Flores, William V.

Duncan
Spivey, Towana

Durant
Roberts, Hollis

Edmond
Cannon, T.C.

Fairland
Baker, Arlene R.

Fairfax
Moore, Tracey Ann
Tall Chief, George Eves

Fort Gibson
West, W. Richard

Gracemont
Standing, Nettie L.

Kaw City
Chouteau, M.M.

Lawton
Kahrahrah, Bernard

Locust Valley
Stone, Willard

McCloud
Wahpehah, James

Miami
Daugherty, John, Jr.
Follis, William
Moore, Louis
Naylor, Jack
Olds, Forest D.

Muskogee
Edmondson, Ed.
Ellison, Thomas J.
Hansen, Joan L.
Harrington, Virgil N.
Horsechief, Mary A.
Moore, Paul V.
Watkins, Mary Beth

Newkirk
James, Willie

Norman
Barse, Harold G.
Johnston, Robert
Moore, John H.

Opler, Moris E.
Simpson, Dana
Siria, Larry

Okmulgee
Cox, Claude

Oklahoma City
Doering, Mavis
Doonkeen, Eula N.
Downing, Ernest V.
Giago, Millie
Giago, Robert
Hampton, Carol C.M.
Hampton, James W., M.D.
Hunter, Terry
James, Overton
Meredith, Howard L.
Ragan, Connie S.

Okmulgee
Little, Harley
Robinson, Gary

Pawhuska
Shoemata, Jack

Pawnee
Chapman, Robert L.

Perkins
Murray, Wallace C.

Ponca City
Castor, Delia F.
Littlecook, Oliver

Quapaw
McKibben, Jesse

Sasakwa
Brown, John

Shawnee
Barrett, John A.
Bruno, Robert L.
Levi, Jerry R.
Levier, Francis A.
Little Axe, Danny
Sulcer, Patrick K.
Walker, Joe B.

Stillwater
Goodbear, Pearl R.G.

Stroud
Falls, Alvin

Tahlequah
Hair, John
Mankiller, Wilma P.
Parker, Joe
Sumner, Delores T.

Tecumseh
Bowlan, Lori A.

Tishomingo
Hutchings, Evelyn K.

Tulsa
Canard, Curtis Lee
Echohawk, Brummet
Krepps, Ethel C.
McClelland, John
McCombs, Solomon

Walter
Riddles, Leonard

Washita
Bales, Jean E.M.

Wewoka
Milan, James
Norman, Margaret J.
Shipp, Cecil

Woodward
Patterson, Patrick

Wyandotte
Cotter, Leonard N.

OREGON

Albany
Taylor, Virginia

Bandon
Red She Bear

Burns
Shake Spear, Vernon

Eugene
Cochran, George M.

Grande Ronde
Harrison, Katherine

Klamath Falls
Norris, Leonard

Monmouth
Walking Bull, Charles
Walking Bull, Montana

Pendleton
Patawa, Elwood
Sandoval, William

Portland
Engelstad, Kurt
Gogol, John M.
Speaks, Stanley M.
Voget, Fred W.

Roseburg
Jackson, Charles

Salem
Gray, Gerald J.

Siletz
Pigsley, Delores
Topash, Bernard
Warm Springs
Cornett, James D.
Jackson, Zane, Sr.
Smith, Gerald L.
Welch, Kay
West Linn
Lampman, Evelyn S.

PENNSYLVANIA

Allentown
Messinger, Carla J.S.
Brookville
Parker, E.M.
Bryn Mawr
DeLaguna, Frederica
Chester
Wallace, Anthony F.C.
Davids
King, Mary E.
Drexel Hill
Smith, Louise
Gettysburg
Porter, Frank W., III
Philadelphia
Glazer, Suzy
Juancito, Charles H.
Oliviero, Melanie Beth
Pittsburgh
Simms, Russell
State College
Noley, Grayson
Turbotville
Fogelman, Gary L.

RHODE ISLAND

Barrington
Hail, Barbara A.
Bristol
Gentis, Thierry
Giddings, Ruth E.
Kenyon
Watson, George

SOUTH CAROLINA

Rock Hill
Beck, Samuel
George, Evans M., Jr.
Haire, Wenonah G.
Sanders, E. Fred

SOUTH DAKOTA

Agency Village
Hawkins, Russell
Crazy Horse
Ziolkowsky, Ruth
Custer
Nauman, Chalres W.
Nauman, H. Jane
Eagle Butte
Garreaux, Hazel
Miner, Marcella
Rave, Austin J.
Rudell, J. Preston, Jr.
Thunder Hawk, Madonna
Flandreau
Ross, Agnes Allen
Sorensen, Carolyn
Wakeman, Richard K.
Fort Thompson
Kannon, Clyde D.
Morgan, Donald I
Wells, Wallace
Whitener, Donald E.
Lower Brule
O'Connor, Leo
Spears, Patrick
Marty
Zephier, Alvin
Mission
Beauvais, Archie B.
Dyc, Gloria
Loudner, Godfrey, Jr.
Ortiz, Simon J.
Oglala
Nespor, Elsie P.
Pierre
Canaday, Dayton W.
Kingman, A. Gay
Skye, Clarence
Pine Ridge
Bettleyoun, Lulu F.
Keith, C. Hobart
Kurth, Rev. E.J.

Simon, Bro. C.M.
Rapid City
Shunk, Harold W.
Sneve, Virgina D.H.
Rosebud
Gipp, William C.
Two Hawk, Webster
St. Francis
Gill, Joseph C.
White Hat, Albert H.
Sisseton
Houser, Schuyler
Spencer, Hargle
Spearfish
Theisc, R.D.
Stephen
Ross, Donald
Sturgis
Lee, Robert H.
Vermillion
Evans, Wayne H.
Hoover, Herbert T.
Howe, Oscar
Wagner
Cournoyer, Frank
Hare, Herbert
Howell, George E.

TENNESSEE

Memphis
White, Lonnie J.
Moscow
Fogelman, Billye Y.S.
Murfreesboro
Rolator, Fred S.
Nashville
Evans, Rex
Ferguson, Robert B.
Signal Mountain
Steele, William O.
Strawberry Plains
Peshewa, Macaki

TEXAS

Alpine
Elam, Earl H.
Austin
Apodaca, Raymond D.
Newcomb, William W., Jr.

Dallas
Grispe, Larry
Hail, Raven

El Paso
Hiser, Johny R.
Ramiriz, Raymond
Trussell, Larry

Grand Prairie
Lucero, Richard, Jr.

Lockhart
Falley, Nanci

Ralls
Parker, Wayne

Redwater
Morgan, Ronald J.

San Antonio
Adams, Richard E.W.

UTAH

Blanding
Clah, Herbert, Jr.

Boulder
Hardy, Dee

Centerville
Parashonts, Travis N.

Fort Duchesne
Collier, Lavern
Dincan, Clifford
Wopsock, Frank

Ibapah
Steele, Chester

Salt Lake City
Chiago, Robert K.
Clemmer, Janice W.
Crampton, C. Gregory
Madsen, Brigham D.
McLean, Robert E.
Overfield, Theresa

VIRGINIA

Alexandria
Engles, William L.
Fox, Dennis R.
Fox, Sandra J.H.
Matte, Sara J.

Arlington
Bruce, Louis R.
Dalrymple, Katherine C.
Harrison, David C.
Oxendine. Thomas

Taylor, Peter S.
Vasquez, Joseph C.

Falls Church
McElvain, W. Lee
Pale Moon, Princess
Viola, Herman J.

McLean
Wilcox, U. Vincent

Oakton
Armagost, James G.
MacNabb, Alexander S.

Reston
Ducheneaux, Franklin D.

Springfield
Holmes, Beverly C.
Monsen, Marie A.
Zilka, Carol L.

Vienna
Kickingbird, K. Kirke

WASHINGTON

Anacortes
Jones, Joan M.

Ariel
Smith, Don Lelooska

Bellingham
Kinley, Larry

Bremerton
Dixon, Lawrence D.

Chehalis
McDonald, Miki

Cheney
Hendrickx, Leonard

Darrington
Grant, Morris
Moses, David

Davenport
Cook-Lynn, Elizabeth

Deming
Cooper, harry E.

Inchelium
Bourgeau, Dean

Kingston
Charles, Ronald G.

La Push
Jackson, Walter

Marysville
Jones, Stanley, Sr.

Moses Lake
Ruby, Robert, M.D.

Nespelem
Davis, George
Owhi, Harry

Oakville
Youckton, Percy

Olympia
Wells, Richard

Omak
Marchand, Thelma
Nicholson, Narcisse, Jr.

Port Angeles
Charles, Alan
Mike, Lorna J.

Port Orchard
DeBoer, Roy J.

Pullman
Ackerman, Lillian A.
Ackerman, Robert E.
Goss, James A.

Seattle
Morris, Elizabeth
Paul, Blair F.
Price, Frank
Quimby, George I.
Taylor, Gerald W.
Whitebear, Bernie

Shelton
Peterson, Gary
Whittener, David

Spokane
Brown, Joseph
James, Wabun
Sun Bear

Tacoma
Soboleff, Sasha
Wright, Frank, Jr.

Taholah
Delacruz, Joseph

Tokeland
Whitish, Rachel

Tonasket
Nicholson, Mary E.

Toppenish
Hokansen, Sherry
Jim, Roger R., Sr.
Olney, Hiram

Usk
Nenema, Glen

Wellpinit
Hill, James W.
Reutlinger, Barbara N.

Wenatchee
Hollow, A.E.
Hollow, Maude C.

WISCONSIN

Appleton
Skenandore, Paul A.
Ashland
Corbine, Joseph
Bayfield
Grunde, Richard
Eau Claire
Satz, Ronald N.
Fairchild
Thunder, Faye E.
Green Bay
Clifton, James A.
Hayward
Baker, Odric
DeMain, Paul
Gross, Mike
Schlender, James
Kenosha
Shipek, Florence C.
Keshena
Skenedore, Lynn
Lac du Flambeau
Dodge, Gary
Wildcat, William
Madison
Baerreis, David A.
Beaudin, John A.
Williams, Floyd
Williams, Robert A., Jr.
Milwaukee
Horsman, Reginald
Kehoe, Alice Beck
Lurie, Nancy O.
Prucha, Francis P.
Oneida
Gollnick, William
Powless, Purcell
Skenadore, Frances
Smith, Robert
Oregon
Deer, Ada E.
Seymour
Smith, Sheila S.
Tomah
Funmaker, Kenneth, Sr.
Redcloud, Merlin

Wauwatosa
Chicks, Sheldon A.
Webster
Taylor, Gene

WYOMING

Cody
Horse, Billy Evans
Horse Capture, George P.
Fort Washakie
Harris, Robert N., Sr.
Moose
Laubin, Gladys W.
Laubin, Reginald K.
Rock Springs
Neaman, Kenneth L.
St, Stephens
Headley, Louis R.

CANADA

ALBERTA
Calgary
Dempsey, Hugh A.
Heinrich, Albert C.

BRITISH COLUMBIA
Delta
Jilek, Wolfgang, M.D.
Jilek-Aall, Louise, M.D.
Vancouver
Ames, Michael M.
Maracle, Brian
Ridington, Robin

MANITOBA
Winnipeg
Laviolette, Rev. G. Omi
Townsend, Joan B.

NEW BRUNSWICK
Fredericton
Erickson, Vincent O.

N.W.T.
Yellowknife
Erasmus, Georges H.

NOVA SCOTIA
Halifax
McGee, Harold F., Jr.
Tantallon
Whitehead, Ruth H.

ONTARIO
Burlington
Damas, David
Nepean
Whiteside, Don
Ottawa
Cox, Bruce
Lee, Thomas E.
Peacock, Kenneth
Richmond Hill
Johnston, Basil H.
Toronto
Mason, K. Goyle

QUEBEC
Cantley
MacDonald, George F.

SASKATCHEWAN
Saskatoon
Fritz, Linda
Purich, Don
Waldram, James B.

HONG KONG

Shatin
Chiao, Chien

JAPAN

Ehime
Ballard, W.L.

7849